About the Authors

NICHOLAS DELBANCO

is the Robert Frost Distinguished University Professor of English Language and Literature at the University of Michigan, where he directs the prestigious Hopwood Awards Program. He was for fifteen years the director of the MFA in Writing Program at the University of Michigan, and is also a co-founder (together with the late John Gardner) of the Bennington Writing Workshops. As a teacher, his students have praised his enormous frame of literary reference, his eagerness to devour a new work, his sociability (he loves a good story, to tell it and to hear it), his honesty, and his devotion to craft. One student said, "He gave me confidence when I had no confidence." He has written twenty-five books of fiction and non-fiction, including *Sherbrookes*, *What Remains*, and *Lastingness: The Art of Old Age*. Among the volumes he has edited is *The Sincerest Form: Writing Fiction by Imitation*. His recent work of historical fiction tells the tale of Count Rumford, inventor, philosopher, and spy; of it, the *Chicago Tribune* writes, "In *The Count of Concord*, we see a veteran novelist working at the height of his powers." Among his many awards, Nicholas Delbanco has been awarded a Guggenheim Fellowship and two Writer's Fellowships from the National Endowment for the Arts. He has served as judge for, among others, The National Book Award in Fiction, the Pen/Faulkner Award, and the Pulitzer Prize.

ALAN CHEUSE

"The Voice of Books on National Public Radio"—that's how novelist, essayist, story writer, and teacher Alan Cheuse has been described. For nearly thirty years, Cheuse has been "reading for America" every week on National Public Radio's evening news-magazine *All Things Considered* and writing books, and for nearly twenty-five years, he has been teaching literature and writing at George Mason University. Cheuse earned a Ph.D. in Comparative Literature from Rutgers University and has also taught at the University of the South, the University of Michigan, the University of Virginia, and Bennington College. He splits his time between the two coasts, spending nine months of the year in Washington, D.C., and summers in California, where he teaches writing at the Squaw Valley Community of Writers. His essay collection, *Listening to the Page*, appeared in 2001. His travel essays were published in the summer of 2009 as *A Trance After Breakfast*. Cheuse's 2008 novel, *To Catch the Lightning*, follows the career of turn-of-the-century photographer Edward S. Curtis and his quest to photograph the western tribes of North America. Writing in *The Jewish Journal*, critic Jonathan Kirsch described Cheuse's latest novel, *Song of Slaves in the Desert* (2011), as "a Great American Novel in the most profound and important sense—a novel about the human experience of slavery in the American South." He is the co-editor with Nicholas Delbanco of *Talking Horse: Bernard Malamud on Life and Art*.

Conversations on Writing

Videos available online at connect.mcgraw-hill.com

LITERATURE

Craft & Voice

SECOND EDITION

NICHOLAS DELBANCO

University of Michigan

ALAN CHEUSE

George Mason University

To Our Students

Connect
Learn
Succeed™

Published by McGraw-Hill, an imprint of The McGraw-Hill Companies, Inc., 1221 Avenue of the Americas, New York, NY 10020. Copyright © 2012, 2010. All rights reserved. Printed in the United States of America. No part of this publication may be reproduced or distributed in any form or by any means, or stored in a database or retrieval system, without the prior written consent of The McGraw-Hill Companies, Inc., including, but not limited to, in any network or other electronic storage or transmission, or broadcast for distance learning.

This book is printed on acid-free paper.

1 2 3 4 5 6 7 8 9 0 DOC/DOC 1 0 9 8 7 6 5 4 3 2

ISBN: 978-0-07-338492-4
MHID: 0-07-338492-5

Sponsoring Editor: *Christopher Bennem*
Marketing Manager: *Kevin Colleary*
Developmental Editor: *Lisa Colleen Moore/Linda Stern*
Production Editor: *Mel Valentín*
Manuscript Editor: *Stacey Sawyer*
Design Manager: *Allister Fein*
Text Designer: *Linda Robertson*
Cover Designer: *Kirk DouPonce, DogEared Design*
Photo Research Coordinator: *Nora Agbayani*
Photo Research: *PhotoFind, LLC*
Permissions Editor: *Marty Moga*
Buyer: *Susan K. Culbertson*
Media Project Manager: *Mathew Sletten*
Digital Product Manager: *Janet Smith*
Composition: *9.25/11.25 Miller Text by Thompson Type*
Printing: *40# Education Matte, R. R. Donnelley & Sons/Crawfordsville, IN*

Vice President Editorial: *Michael Ryan*
Publisher: *David S. Patterson*
Director of Development: *Dawn Groundwater*
Editorial Coordinator: *Dana Wan*

Cover: ©*Sarolta Ban/Trigger Image*

Credits: The credits section for this book begins on page C-1 and is considered an extension of the copyright page.

Library of Congress Cataloging-in-Publication Data
Delbanco, Nicholas.
   Literature : craft & voice / Nicholas Delbanco, Alan Cheuse. — 2nd ed.
      p. cm.
   Includes bibliographical references and index.
   ISBN 978-0-07-338492-4 (acid-free paper) — ISBN 0-07-338492-5 (acid-free paper)
1. Literature.   I. Cheuse, Alan.   II. Title.
   PN45.D457 2012
   800—dc23

                          2011046967

The Internet addresses listed in the text were accurate at the time of publication. The inclusion of a website does not indicate an endorsement by the authors or McGraw-Hill, and McGraw-Hill does not guarantee the accuracy of the information presented at these sites.

www.mhhe.com

Contents

4 Writing across the Curriculum   64

5 Writing the Research Paper, Avoiding Plagiarism, and Documenting Sources   96

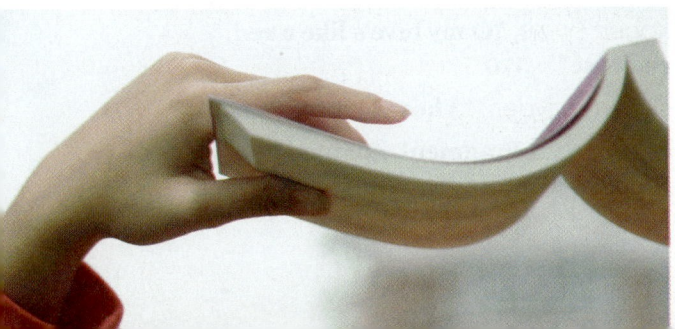

PART 3
POETRY

17 Reading a Poem in Its Elements   560

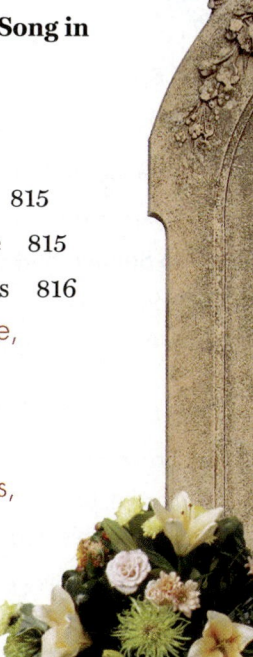

25 Fixed Poetic Forms 830

A Conversation on Writing with Edward Hirsch, video interview available online at connect.mcgraw-hill.com 832

26 Open Form   880

27 Langston Hughes: A Case Study on Langston Hughes and His Contemporaries 922

28 American Plain Style: A Case Study on Emily Dickinson and Robert Frost 948

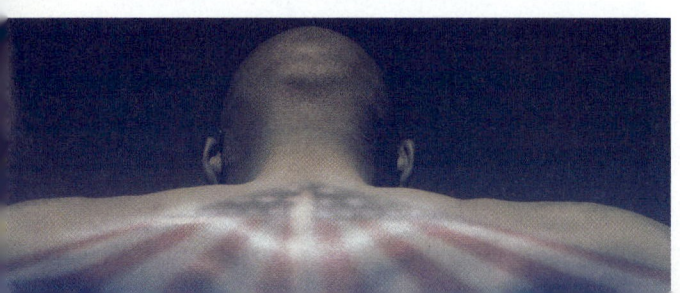

29 An Anthology of Poetry for Further Reading 973

PART 4
DRAMA

30 Reading and Viewing a Play in its Elements   1002

31 Writing about Drama   1024

Preface

Engaging Students by Bringing Writers to Readers

When setting out to create *Literature: Craft & Voice*, we believed that it was incumbent on us as authors and educators to design a new kind of literature project, one that would utilize a variety of strategies to reach today's students and help them to achieve an immersive experience as readers; this would, in turn, help to stimulate them as writers. We subtitled this work "Craft & Voice," because as writers we believe firmly two things: first, that an understanding of the writer's craft requires critical and engaged readers. And, second, that close reading helps students to establish their own voice as confident and authoritative writers. Therefore, leveraging students' natural desire for critical and substantive engagement became central to this project's design.

The strategies we developed for *Literature: Craft & Voice* were designed to help students become more practiced at sustained reading, confident at thinking critically, and skilled at writing analytically—all challenges that students must meet to succeed in this course and in their college careers. As has been often observed, the writing process is not linear, it is recursive. Similarly, the skills that students develop throughout this course are not developed in linear fashion. They are honed through repeated—and recursive—practice and are mutually reinforcing. Not only do better readers become better thinkers and better writers, but better writers naturally become better readers and thinkers.

This project was designed to work in the same way by keeping students critically and substantively engaged at every step—and at every turn—in the process of developing, honing, and practicing these skills. Ultimately, this text brings writers in closer proximity to its readers than any other, and by doing so systematically removes the barriers that inhibit student engagement. This highly intentional and mutually reinforcing design relies on three key strategies:

- A **visual design** developed to draw readers in and help them to gain more practice at sustained reading
- A **digital design** created with the authors featured in this text, specifically *for* this text, to encourage students to think critically about the selections they read
- An **instructional design** that will help students to develop the analytic skills needed to write substantive arguments

The Visual Design of *Literature: Craft & Voice*

A TEXT DESIGNED FOR READING: Enormous thought and care and research have gone into this design, which students tell us makes them want to read further. By beginning with a compelling chapter opener and a quotation from literature, students find themselves reading before they've thought about whether they will or want to read this work. This text's design functions as an invitation to explore further, think harder, and write better. Our student responses have been unanimous and gratifying.

"Well chosen . . . I'm delighted with the inclusion of . . . a number of stories that could be used to introduce students to multicultural literature."

—Richard C. Taylor, East Carolina University

"I love the chapter openings! They're not just random pictures—they relate to the text. The spread also includes more than just a plot summary . . . it has a snippet of the text for every kind of reader and personality: a summary, a quote from the text, and a quote from the author."

—Alexandra V. Loizzo, student, Barnard College

The Digital Design of *Literature: Craft & Voice*

EXCLUSIVE INTERVIEWS: Powered by McGraw-Hill's Connect, nearly every chapter is accompanied by a video interview of a featured writer. These interviews were created exclusively for this project and include the writer's thoughts on what a new reader might find interesting about that work. Quotations from these interviews and excerpted "Conversations on Writing" are included in each chapter, creating a human connection to each subject, sustaining these writers' voices in the pages, making a complex text more personally inviting to students and helping them to think critically about it.

Amy Tan ... *The interesting thing that happens is that fiction, as you write it, becomes subversive.*

A Conversation on Writing

Becoming a Reader

I was a very lonely child much of my childhood. Books were a place where I could find someone who understood me. That someone could have lived 200 years ago. Jane Eyre had nothing to do with my life. And yet she did. She was that lonely girl nobody understood . . . and I imagined myself living that life. . . . That made me not feel so lonely.

The Meaning of Your Life

If you . . . walk up to somebody on the street or somebody comes up to you and says, "What's your meaning of life? What is the meaning of your life?" You might come up with an idea right on the spot: I want to be happy or I want to be in love, I want to be loved. But what you get out of writing is thinking about that question for a very long time. . . . You take a situation from your life . . . a time that you thought you'd get a new bicycle, and then you didn't think you would, and then you got it, and then you got it stolen. What's in that? . . . Suddenly there's a glimpse of the meaning of your life.

On Voice and the Writing Process

When I started to write, I had this basic question that was posed to me by a woman named Molly Giles, a wonderful writer. She had read my work. And she said, "You know, what you've written here is not a story. It is the beginnings of a dozen stories." And she pointed out these sentences. She said, "This is the beginning of a story, this is the beginning of a story, this is the beginning. This is a voice, this is a voice, this is a voice." And I thought, Well, what is a voice? . . . The questions are still there, and there's no absolute answer. . . . You discover it each time you sit down and write.

To watch this entire interview online and hear the author read from "Two Kinds," go to **connect.mcgraw-hill.com.**

Amy Tan was born (1952) in Oakland, California, to Chinese immigrants. After college she became successful as a business writer and took up jazz piano as a hobby, a young Chinese American woman who had not yet clearly faced the matter of her cultural origins. It wasn't until after her marriage to a Bay Area tax attorney that she eventually began to try to write fiction based on her cultural heritage.

Like many first generation Americans, Tan had not fully explored her relationship to her parents' culture until she had established herself as a successful working adult. After her father and brother died within a year from brain tumors, she and her mother were left to work out their own difficulties. Her troubled relations with her mother eventually smoothed out, and after her mother recovered from a serious illness, the two of them traveled to China. There Tan got a firsthand look at the country of her parents' birth, beginning to explore her origins as possible material for fiction. This led to the composition of a series of stories, which Tan revised and made into the novel *The Joy Luck Club*. That book became a national best seller in 1989, and Tan has since published the novels *The Kitchen God's Wife*, *The Hundred Secret Senses*, *The Bonesetter's Daughter*, *Saving Fish from Drowning*, and two children's books, *The Moon Lady* and *Sagwa*.

RESEARCH ASSIGNMENT Amy Tan says in her interview that reading and writing fiction are subversive. Watch the interview and explain what she means. Do you agree with her?

BLACKBOARD: Some 30 different conversations are broken up into over 100 topical video segments, all accessible in Blackboard through the use of McGraw-Hill's Connect digital platform. Single sign-on provides seamless integration between Connect and Blackboard. Autogradable quizzes and activities for both the videos and the selections provide optional tools for assessment that are easy to assign and track.

Mc Graw Hill

Bb
Blackboard

Do More

The **Best** of **Both Worlds**

ONLINE CASEBOOKS: Powered by McGraw-Hill's Connect, 10 online collections provide a diverse range of materials to engage with, including three Multimedia Casebooks featuring video clips, screenplay excerpts, critical essays, and film adaptations as well as original selections of fiction, poetry, and drama. "Masters of Craft" and "Contemporary Voices" casebooks present even greater variety with additional classics and emerging talents never before anthologized selected by an author team whose combined eye for talent has helped to award the Pulitzer and National Book Awards.

"The anthology's treatment of authors and the depth with which the anthology invites students to engage with authors as writers (not unlike themselves) make it a terrifically enabling experience for students."

—Elizabeth Rich, Saginaw Valley State University

"The use of author interviews not only provides a sense of cohesion but also creates interest as students see and hear professional authors discussing their own writing processes and problems. I also like the emphasis and instruction on sustained reading skills needed for both analyzing and writing about literature."

—Linda Smith, Midlands Technical Community College

"The 'Interactive Reading' sections are incredibly useful. . . . While these models are presented as reading tools, the active reading, deciphering, interpreting, and wordsmithing teach students not only to read but how to write. . . . They see firsthand how to break down and comment on various aspects of the work, obviously an integral part of research or explication."

—Kristin Le Veness, Nassau Community College

The Instructional Design of *Literature: Craft & Voice*

A FOCUS ON WRITING: A completely new Part I, Writing from Reading, introduces students to core concepts of the writing process and writing with sources, emphasizing critical reading and writing skills for composing in a variety of genres in college. Additional chapters on reading and writing in each part walk students through how reading a text interactively is the basis of writing their own interpretation of a text.

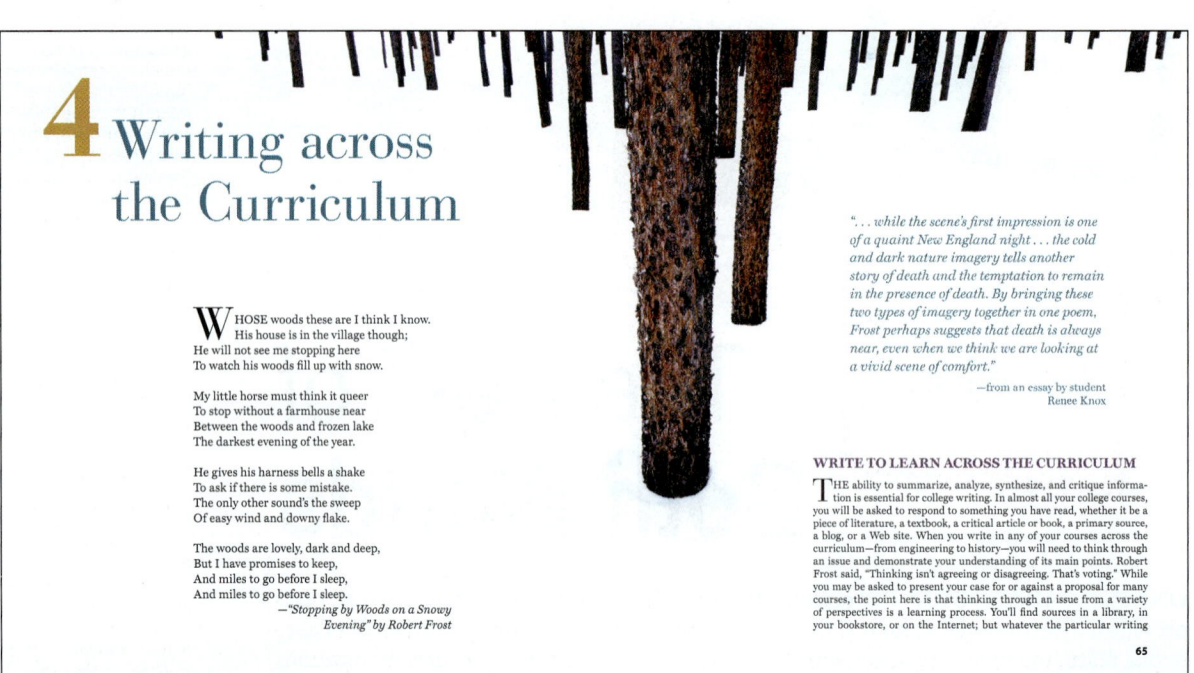

4 Writing across the Curriculum

W HOSE woods these are I think I know.
His house is in the village though;
He will not see me stopping here
To watch his woods fill up with snow.

My little horse must think it queer
To stop without a farmhouse near
Between the woods and frozen lake
The darkest evening of the year.

He gives his harness bells a shake
To ask if there is some mistake.
The only other sound's the sweep
Of easy wind and downy flake.

The woods are lovely, dark and deep,
But I have promises to keep,
And miles to go before I sleep,
And miles to go before I sleep.
—*"Stopping by Woods on a Snowy Evening" by Robert Frost*

"...while the scene's first impression is one of a quaint New England night...the cold and dark nature imagery tells another story of death and the temptation to remain in the presence of death. By bringing these two types of imagery together in one poem, Frost perhaps suggests that death is always near, even when we think we are looking at a vivid scene of comfort."
—from an essay by student Renee Knox

WRITE TO LEARN ACROSS THE CURRICULUM

T HE ability to summarize, analyze, synthesize, and critique information is essential for college writing. In almost all your college courses, you will be asked to respond to something you have read, whether it be a piece of literature, a textbook, a critical article or book, a primary source, a blog, or a Web site. When you write in any of your courses across the curriculum—from engineering to history—you will need to think through an issue and demonstrate your understanding of its main points. Robert Frost said, "Thinking isn't agreeing or disagreeing. That's voting." While you may be asked to present your case for or against a proposal for many courses, the point here is that thinking through an issue from a variety of perspectives is a learning process. You'll find sources in a library, in your bookstore, or on the Internet; but whatever the particular writing

65

INTEGRATING SOURCES: A new feature on "Crafting your Own Voice" appears in chapters 7, 18, and 31, showing students clear examples of incorporating summary, quotation, and paraphrase into their academic prose. Along with numerous other examples throughout part 1, this coverage of the critical skill of incorporating sources helps students develop their own confidence and authority as writers.

WRITING ARGUMENTS: The focus on writing analytically is reinforced in question sets that follow the readings, providing a building-block approach to critical thinking from summarizing (for comprehension), to analyzing craft and voice, synthesizing summary and analysis, and using that synthesis to interpret a text and construct an argument about it. Tips for interactive reading, "As You Read" suggestions for most selections, and "If you like this, you might like this" suggestions draw students into other selections in the text.

W. H. Auden **FUNERAL BLUES** | **637**

Funeral Blues (1940)

Stop all the clocks, cut off the telephone,
Prevent the dog from barking with a juicy bone,
Silence the pianos and with muffled drum
Bring out the coffin, let the mourners come.

5 Let aeroplanes circle moaning overhead
Scribbling on the sky the message He is Dead.
Put crêpe bows round the white necks of the public doves,
Let the traffic policemen wear black cotton gloves.

He was my North, my South, my East and West,
10 My working week and my Sunday rest,
My noon, my midnight, my talk, my song;
I thought that love would last forever: I was wrong.

The stars are not wanted now; put out every one,
Pack up the moon and dismantle the sun,
15 Pour away the ocean and sweep up the wood;
For nothing now can ever come to any good.

Writing from Reading

Summarize

1 What is the speaker responding to in this poem, and what does the title convey?

2 How does the speaker feel about the subject of the poem?

3 How do such phrases as "muffled drum," "mourners," and "crêpe bows," which refer to the traditional trappings of a funeral, contrast with the actual occasion of the poem?

Analyze Craft

4 Describe the diction in this poem. When does it seem formal or informal?

5 What emotions or meaning come to mind when you read "the white necks of the public doves"? What comes to mind when you read other images?

Analyze Voice

6 Describe tone in the poem. Is it uniformly mournful? If not, where does the tone shift, and where does it remind you of the blues?

7 There's wild exaggeration in the last stanza's set of instructions: "Pack up the moon and dismantle the sun"—as if we could indeed "Pour away the ocean" and "put out" the stars. What does this tell us about the emotion of the speaker?

Synthesize Summary and Analysis

8 How many sentences make up this poem? Discuss the consistency of the arrangement of sentences—how do they affect or reflect the poem's subject?

Interpret the Poem

9 Compare the last lines of this poem to "What the Living Do." What does Auden's poem say about death? Explain how it is the same as, or different from, Howe's "What the Living Do."

10 Look at John Donne's "A Valediction: Forbidding Mourning" in the "For Review and Further Study" section of this chapter. Compare Auden's use of the compass with that of Donne's.

INSTRUCTOR RESOURCES

Instructor resources for teaching *Literature: Craft & Voice* are available online and include an alternate thematic table of contents, sample syllabi, PowerPoints, quizzes (that students can take online), and support for teaching every selection and author conversation associated with *Literature: Craft & Voice*. For students, we put our casebook sources online, to keep our book easy to carry and inviting (which both students and instructors asked for) and to provide a reliable place for students to get started on their research. Additional student resources include an interactive tutorial for avoiding plagiarism and evaluating sources plus information on conducting research and formatting works cited pages. Our online learning solutions support team can work with qualified adopters to adapt any of these materials to the learning management system at your institution.

Select trade titles and reference sources can be packaged at a discount with *Literature: Craft & Voice*. If you are interested in a dictionary, thesaurus, or other trade title, please contact your local McGraw-Hill representative or our Marketing Coordinator for English at English@McGraw-Hill.com.

LITERATURE
Craft & Voice
SECOND EDITION
NICHOLAS DELBANCO
ALAN CHEUSE

Acknowledgments

This book is, truly, a collective effort: no single person or pair of authors could have produced it alone. From the first to the final chapter, we have relied on the work of others; our Table of Contents represents the essence of shared enterprise. The individual voices here became a kind of chorus, and our first debt of gratitude goes to the splendid writers (some of them anonymous) who produced the fiction and poetry and plays that *Literature: Craft & Voice* contains.

We have dedicated this book to our students. In addition to our own students, there were more than 4,000 others at 132 institutions across the country who participated in ethnographic research by letting us into their daily lives and discussing how they live and learn. We thank them for allowing us to observe them at work, at leisure, and in their place of study. To the thousands of young people across the country who participated in this ethnographic research, we thank you, and we extend a special thanks to the several students who gave up their time to provide detailed information and in some cases meet with us personally:

Danielle Crochiere, Colby College; Brittany Davis, University of Southern Mississippi; Alvin Flete, SUNY Stony Brook; Rosellen Flete, SUNY New Paltz; Jane Fountain, Central Piedmont Community College; Drew Henry, New York University; Nancy Kurien, Hunter College; Alex Limanowski, Roosevelt University; Alexandra Loizzo, Barnard College; Selena Poznak, Tulane University; Emily Rejouis, Cornell University; Josie Sayegh, University of California, Santa Cruz; Kaitlyn Taylor, University of Delaware; Liz Wechter, University of Illinois; Brian Yu, University of Michigan.

We also wish to express our gratitude to the professors, colleagues, and students who have contributed to *Literature: Craft & Voice*. Many professors took the time to let some book people from McGraw-Hill into their offices to discuss their challenges with this course. The surveys that emerged from these interviews helped us create a new pedagogical program that we hope these friends recognize as emerging from their thoughtful comments about teaching today.

Heidi Ajrami, Victoria College
Norma Akins, Heart of Georgia Technical College
Frank Albert, Community College of Beaver County
Deborah Albritton, Jefferson Davis Community College–Brewton
Michael Alleman, Louisiana State University–Eunice
Michael Allen, North Central State College
Stephanie Almagno, Piedmont College
Maribeth Anderson, Ivy Tech Community College of Indiana
Helane Androne, Miami University–Middletown
Judith Angona, Ocean County College
Sonia Apgar Begert, Olympic College

Sue Apshaga, Community College of Rhode Island
Saye Atkinson, Georgia Military College
Les Bailey, Saint Martin's University
Ronda Bailey, Fort Scott Community College
Eileen Baland, East Texas Baptist University
John Balcer, Shenandoah University
Allison Bartlett, Wor-Wic Community College
Kathleen Bartlett, Florida Institute of Technology
Jonathan Barz, University of Dubuque
Janice Baskin, Azusa Pacific University
Lynne Belcher, Southern Arkansas University
John Bennett, Lake Land College

Bill Berry, Cape Cod Community College
Ken Bishop, Itawamba Community College
Mark Blaauw-hara, North Central Michigan College
Lawrence Blasco, Wor-Wic Community College
Laura Bloxham, Whitworth University
Paula Bolduc, Salve Regina University
Laurel Bollinger, University of Alabama–Huntsville
Ellen Boose, Bossier Parish Community College
Troy Boucher, Southwestern College
Michelle Bowie, Southern Nazarene University
David Breith, University of the Southwest
Jason Brown, Herkimer County Community College
Kristin Brunnemer, Pierce College
Mitzi Brunsdale, Mayville State University
Laurie Buchanan, Clark State Community College
Dawn Buckey, Charleston Southern University
Suzanne Bufamanti, Niagara County Community College
Dottie Burkhart, Davidson County Community College
Kelly Ann Butterbaugh, Lehigh Carbon Community College
Dona Cady, Middlesex Community College
Mechel Camp, Jackson State Community College
Sarah Canfield-Fuller, Shenandoah University
Robert Canipe, Catawba Valley Community College
Joan Canty, Columbia College
Judith Cavanaugh, Clinton Community College
Sean Cavanaugh, Assumption College
Marlys Cervantes, Cowley County Community College
Diane Chambers, Malone University
Windy Charles, Piedmont College
Maria Chiancola, Salve Regina University
Bill Church, Missouri Western State University
Lori Cinotte, Illinois Valley Community College
Stacy Clanton, Southern Arkansas University
Pam Clark, Frederick Community College
Jessica Cobbs, Bossier Parish Community College
Stanly Coberly, West Virginia University–Parkersburg
Michael Cocchiarale, Widener University
Rose Collins, Dallas Baptist University
Jim Compton, Muscatine Community College
Nancy Corbett, Maysville Community and Technical College
Jean Crockett, Cleveland State Community College
Sarah Dangelantonio, Franklin Pierce University
Judy Daniel, McMurry University
Cherie Dargan, Hawkeye Community College
Rebecca Dark, Dallas Baptist University
Bonita Dattner-Garza, St. Mary's University
Daniel de Roulet, Vanguard University
Laurie Delaney, Kent State University–Stark Campus
Mikee Delony, Abilene Christian University
Louise DeSantis Deutsch, Cape Cod Community College
Anna Crowe Dewart, College of Coastal Georgia
Betty Dobry, Redlands Community College
Scott Douglass, Chattanooga State Technical Community College

Lisa Dresdner, Norwalk Community College
Marilyn Durham, University of Wisconsin–Whitewater
Linda Eicken, Cape Fear Community College
Margaret Ellington, Georgia Southwestern State University
Scott Emmert, University of Wisconsin–Fox Valley
Joseph Ervin, Rend Lake College
Cassandra Falke, East Texas Baptist University
Tyler Farrell, University of Dubuque
William Feeler, Midland College
Sandy Feinstein, Penn State Berks
Maribeth Fell, College of Coastal
Georgia Robin Field, King's College
Jim Fisher, Peninsula College
Michael Flaherty, Triton College
Joey Flamm-Costello, Reading Area Community College
Juliene Forrestal, Olivet Nazarene University
Chriss Foster, San Francisco State University
Deborah Fox, Matanuska-Susitna College
Holly French, Bossier Parish Community College
Julie Fulbright, Cleveland State Community College
Robert Furstoss, Ocean County College
Joanne Gabel, Reading Area Community College
Naomi Gal, Moravian College
Xiongya Gao, Southern University at New Orleans
Maryanne Garbowsky, County College of Morris
Jennifer Garlen, University of Alabama in Huntsville
Vicki Garton, Crowder Community College–Nevada
Tony Giffone, Farmingdale State College
Wayne Gilbert, Community College of Aurora
Michelle Gompf, Concord University
Ron Goulet, Northland Pioneer College
Judith Griffith, Wartburg College
Brian Hale, Chattanooga State Technical Community College
Gary Hall, Victoria College
Carol Harding, Western Oregon University
Simon Hay, Connecticut College
Hunter Hayes, Texas A&M University–Commerce
Catherine Heath, Victoria College
Michael Helfin, Cape Cod University
Sue Henderson, East Central College
Marylou Horn, Middlesex Community College
Dianne Hunter, Trinity College
Deborah Hysell, North Central State College
Adriane Ivey, Oxford College of Emory University
Joanne Jacobs, Shenandoah University
John Jacobs, Shenandoah University
Kathleen Jacquette, Farmingdale State College
Kelli Johnson, Miami University–Hamilton
Dean Karpowicz, University of Wisconsin–Parkside
Robert Kellerman, University of Maine at Augusta
Tim Kelley, Northwest-Shoals Community College
Nora Kindley, Ulster Community College
Mark King, Gordon College

Bette Kirschstein, Pace University
Deborah Klein, Truman State University
John Krafft, Miami University–Hamilton
Theresa Kulbaga, Miami University–Hamilton
Celena Kusch, University of South Carolina Upstate
James Lake, Louisiana State University in Shreveport
Dana Lauro, Ocean County College
David Leigh, Seattle University
Bruce Litte, Northwest Missouri State University
Keming Liu, Medgar Evers College
Megan Lloyd, King's College
Deborah Luoma, Gavilan Community College
Brent Lynn, Wayland Baptist University
Robert Mahon, East Central University
Kathleen Maloney, St. Mary's University
Kelli Maloy, University of Pittsburgh at Greensburg
Beulah Manuel, Columbia Union College
Michael Martin, University of Wisconsin
Cindy McClenagan, Wayland Baptist University
Jeannine McDevitt, Pennsylvania Highlands Community
    College
Kathleen McDonald, Norwich University
Amy Minervini-Dodson, Arizona Western College
Brooke Mitchell, Wingate University
Kelly Moffett, Kentucky Wesleyan College
D'Juana Montgomery, Southwestern Assemblies of God
    University
Margaret Morlier, Reinhardt College
David Murdoch, Gadsden State Community College
Josephine Neill-Browning, Holmes Community College
Jeff Nelson, University of Alabama in Huntsville
Ode Ogede, North Carolina Central University
Michael Olendzenski, Cape Cod Community College
Salisa Olmstead, Lake Land College
Kim Overcash, Central Carolina Community College
Renelda Owen, Delta State University
Allison Palumbo, Elizabethtown Community and Technical
    College
Jeff Patridge, Capital Community College
Michelle Paulsen, Victoria College
Jared Pearce, William Penn University
Shannon Phillips, Lake Land College
Meenakshi Ponnoswami, Bucknell University
Nancy Popkin, Harris-Stowe State University
David Pulling, Louisiana State University–Eunice
Ken Raines, Eastern Arizona College
Wilbur Reames, Erskine College

Shirley Rehberg, Lake City Community College
Margaret Reimer, University of Southern Maine
Chauncey Ridley, Sacramento State University
Nancy Risch, Florence Darlington Technical College
Jason Roberts, Sierra College
Mary Rogerson, West Liberty State College
Patricia Roy, Mount Ida College
Jill Rubinson, University of Maine at Augusta
Wolfgang Runzi, Rogue Community College
Christine Ryan, Middlesex Community College
Elizabeth Sachs, Niagara County Community College
Joe Sarnowski, San Diego Christian College
Jane Schreck, Bismarck State College
Tracy Schrems, St. Bonaventure University
Jolly Sharp, University of the Cumberlands
Maggie Shear, South Suburban College
Deepa Sitaraman, Shawnee State University
Amy Smith, Hilbert College
Matt Smith, University of St. Francis
Amos St. Germain, Wentworth Institute of Technology
Gabriele Stauf, Georgia Southwestern State University
Michael Steven, Wayland Baptist University
Bill Stifler, Chattanooga State Technical Community College
Ron Stormer, Culver-Stockton College
Monnette Sturgill, Big Sandy Community and Technical College
Richard Swanson, University of Wisconsin–Stout
Nannette Tamer, Stevenson University
Richard Terdiman, University of California–Santa Cruz
Jennifer Thompson, Saint Xavier University
Alan Trusky, Florence-Darlington Technical College
Randal Urwiller, Texas College
Scott Vander Ploeg, Madisonville Community College
Leila Wells, Griffin Technical College
Eleanor Welsh, Chesapeake College
Cynthia Wesson, Cowley County Community College
Jeana West, Murray State College
Patricia White, Norwich University
Edward Whitelock, Gordon College
Brenda Williams, University of New Haven
Mary Williams, Midland College
Daniel Wolkow, Eastern New Mexico University–Roswell
Whitney Womack Smith, Miami University–Hamilton
Jane Wood, Park University
P. J. Yongbloed, Springfield Technical Community College
Adam Young, Middle Georgia College
Sarah Young, Baker University
J. B. Zwilling, Allen Community College

In addition, over 175 professors from 113 institutions provided their responses about design, selections, and content by way of WebEx, symposia, focus groups, phone interviews, design surveys, and detailed manuscript reviews. A special thanks to our students Margaret Dean and Valerie Laken, and especially Elizabeth Eshelman,

Nicholas Harp, and Anne Stameshkin, who, with Professors Santi Buscemi (Middlesex County College) and Chris Thaiss (University of California–Davis), contributed importantly to the shape and sense of our writing coverage as well as to the other sections on fiction, poetry, and drama in this book. Elizabeth Eshleman stayed with us throughout the work on the Second Edition, and we are doubly grateful. Tom Kitts (St. John's University) not only reviewed our text but also deserves special recognition here for his herculean service to our resources for teaching. We can safely say that every page of this volume has been guided by at least a dozen people dedicated to education and to literature. And for that, to all of you, we offer our sincerest thanks.

Emory Reginald Abbott, Georgia Perimeter College
Kirk Adams, Tarrant Community College
Donna Allego, Gwynedd–Mercy College
Francesco Ancona, Sussex County Community College
Brian Anderson, Central Piedmont Community College
Peter Auski, University of Western Ontario
Beverly Bailey, Seminole Community College
Cynthia Baker-Schverak, Brevard Community College
Elizabeth Barnes, Daytona Beach Community College
Jim Baskin, Joliet Junior College
Amy Beaudry, Quinsigamond Community College
Valerie Belew, Nashville State Community College
Cole Bennett, Abilene Christian University
Randy Blankenship, Valencia Community College
Ethel Bonds, Virginia Western Community College
Debbie Borchers, Pueblo Community College
Patricia Bostian, Central Piedmont Community College
Linda Bow, Blinn College
Steve Brahlek, Palm Beach Community College–Lake Worth
Tamara Brattoli, Joliet Junior College
Joe Bryan, El Paso Community College
JoAnne Bryant, Troy University–Montgomery Campus
Donna Campbell, Washington State University
Patricia Campbell, Lake Sumter Community College
Carlos Campo, College of Southern Nevada
Kathy Carlson, Brevard Community College
Rosa Maria Chacon, California State University, Northridge
Lisbeth Chapin, Gwynedd–Mercy College
April Childress, Greenville Technical College
Kathleen Chrismon, Northeastern Oklahoma A&M University
John Cole, Community College of Rhode Island–Flanagan
Susan Constantine, Keystone College
Linda Cook, Sam Houston State University
Susan Dauer, Valencia Community College
Curtis Derrick, Midlands Technical College
Jason Dew, Georgia Perimeter College
Jennifer Diamond, Bucks County College
Joshua Dickinson, Jefferson Community College
Charles Dielman, Erie Community College
Regina Dilgen, Palm Beach Community College–Lake Worth

Scott Douglass, Chattanooga State Technical Community College
Caroline Dreyer, Pensacola Junior College
Leigh Anne Duck, University of Memphis
Jennifer Duncan, Chattanooga State Community College
Mildred Duprey-Smith, College of Southern Nevada
Heather Elko, Brevard Community College
John Esperian, College of Southern Nevada
Renee Field, Moberly Area Community College
John Freeman, El Paso Community College
Muriel Fuqua, Daytona Beach Community College
Fernando Ganivet, Florida International University
Stephen Gardner, University of South Carolina–Aiken
Richard Gaspar, Hillsboro Community College
Michael Gavin, Prince George's Community College
Joanna Gibson, Texas A&M University
Janine Gilbert, Brigham Young University–Idaho
Kimberly Greenfield, Lorain County Community College
Ross Gresham, U.S. Air Force Academy
Loren Gruber, Missouri Valley College
Frank Gunshanan, Daytona Beach Community College
Grace Haddox, El Paso Community College
Jill Hampton, University of South Carolina–Aiken
Holly Hassel, University of Wisconsin–Marathon County
Levia Hayes, College of Southern Nevada
Joel Henderson, Chattanooga State Community College
Deana Holifield, Pearl River Community College
Matthew Horton, Gainesville State College
Christine Hubbard, Tarrant County Community College
Mary Huffer, Lake Sumter Community College
Rob Hurd, Anne Arundel Community College
Heidi Johnsen, La Guardia Community College
Ken Johnson, Georgia Perimeter College
Theodore Johnston, El Paso Community College
Pamela Kannady, Tulsa Community College–Metro Campus
Barbara Kenney, Texas State Technical College
Nancy Kersell, Northern Kentucky University
Elizabeth Kessler, University of Houston
Rachel Key, East Central University
James Kirkpatrick, Central Piedmont Community College
Tom Kitts, St. John's University

Elaine Kromhout, Indian River Community College
Joseph Kronick, Louisiana State University
Kris Kurrus, Spokane Falls Community College
Angela Laflen, Marist College
James Lake, Louisiana State University
Ilona Law, University of South Carolina–Aiken
Kristin Le Veness, Nassau Community College
Sandy Longhorn, Pulaski Technical College
Joe Lostracco, Austin Community College
Cecilia Macheski, La Guardia Community College
Angela Macri, Pulaski Technical College
Al Maginnes, Wake Technical Community College
Tammy Mata, Tarrant County College
Virgin Mathes, University of New Mexico
Michael Matthews, Central Texas College
Beth Maxfield, Henderson State University
Laura McBride, College of Southern Nevada
Nicole McDaniel, Texas A&M University
Denise McNelly, Old Dominion University
Agnetta Mendoza, Nashville State Community College
Shellie Michael, Volunteer State Community College
Lawrence Milbourn, El Paso Community College
Dorothy Minor, Tulsa Community College–Metro Campus
David Mirchman, Moorpark College
Deborah Montuori, Shippensburg University
Cleatta Morris, Louisiana State University
Jake Morris, Louisiana State University, Shreveport
Kevin Morris, Greenville Technical College
Paul Munn, Saginaw Valley State University
William Myers, University of Colorado
Michelle Navarro, Dallas County Community College
Louise Nayer, City College of San Francisco
Jennifer Nelson, College of Southern Nevada
Shirley Nelson, Chattanooga State Community College
Andrea Neptune, Sierra College
Sally Nielsen, Florida Community College–Jacksonville
Cheryl Nixon, University of Massachusetts
Troy Nordman, Butler Community College
Claire O'Donoghue, St. John's University
Jay O'Leary, Santa Fe Community College
Ben Olguin, University of Texas at San Antonio
Danel Olsen, North Harris College
Thomas O'Neal, St. Johns River Community College
John Padgett, Brevard Community College
Neil Placky, Broward Community College
H. F. Poehlmann, Blinn College
Doranne Polcrack, Kutztown University
Tony Procell, El Paso Community College

Roberta Proctor, Palm Beach Community College–Lake Worth
Jessica Rabin, Anne Arundel Community College
Mary Anne Reiss, Elizabethtown Community and Technical College
Dana Resente, Montgomery County Community College
Elizabeth Rich, Saginaw Valley State University
Nandi Riley, Florida A&M University
Lou Ethel Roliston, Bergen Community College
Valerie Russell, Valencia Community College
Robert Saba, Florida International University
Mark Sanders, Lewis and Clark State College
John Schaffer, Blinn College
Ann Shillinglaw, Moraine Valley Community College
Ronald Shumaker, University of New Mexico
Gerald Siegel, York College
Mary Simpson, Dominican University
Donald Skinner, Indian River Community College
Patrick Slattery, University of Arkansas–Fayetteville
Beverly Slaughter, Brevard Community College
Derek Soles, Drexel University
Jean Sorensen, Grayson Community College
Anne Spurlock, Mississippi State University
Joyce Steelman, Catawba Valley Community College
Greg Stone, Tulsa Community College–Metro Campus
Victor Strandberg, Duke University
Beverly Stroud, Greenville Technical College
Richard Taylor, East Carolina University
Patricia Teel, Victor Valley College
Tracy Teel, California State University–Northridge
Matthew Teutsch, University of Louisiana, Monroe
Amber Flora Thomas, University of Alaska, Fairbanks
Anne-Marie Thomas, Austin Community College
Andrew Tomko, Bergen Community College
Pauline Uchmanowicz, SUNY–New Paltz
Carla Walker, St. Louis Community College
Brad Waltman, College of Southern Nevada
Carol Warren, Georgia Perimeter College
Linda Weeks, Dyersburg State Community College
Bridgette Weir, Nashville State Community College
Bart Welling, University of North Florida
Eleanor Welsh, Chesapeake College
Marian Wernicke, Pensacola Junior College
Sharon Wilson, University of Northern Colorado
Julie Wishart, Butler Community College
Jane Wood, Park University
Daphne Young, College of Southern Nevada
Robyn Younkin, Community College of Rhode Island
John Ziebell, College of Southern Nevada

The second edition began with a comprehensive assessment of existing selections currently used by instructors in this course. We are grateful to the following people, whose input gave us enormous insight to the complex landscape that constitutes this area:

Kirk Adams, Tarrant County College
Jacob Agatucci, Central Oregon Community College
Liz ann Baez Aguilar, San Antonio College
Carmen Amavizca, Pima Community College
Ellen Arnold, Coastal Carolina University
Abigail Bardi, Prince George's Community College
Patricia A. Barker, Ph.D. Lonestar College Kingwood
Melissa Batai, Triton College
Norman W. Bates, Cochise College
Alex Blazer, Georgia College & State University
Bonnie Bonincontri, Palm Beach State College
Kimberly Britt, Horry Georgetown Technical College
Ken Claney, Tulsa Community College
Jackie Corbit, Cochise College
Darin Cozzens, Surry Community College
Meri Culp, Tallahassee Community College
Jennifer Daniels, Northern Virginia Community College
Emma W. Dawson, Florida A&M University
Alexandra Dragin, Triton College
Thomas B. Frazier, University of the Cumberlands
Chloe Warner Gamble, Polk State College
Robert Goldberg, Prince George's Community College
Barbara Goldstein, Hillsborough Community College
Jeff Grieneisen, State College of Florida
Marlene Groner, Farmingdale State SUNY
Lynn M. Grow, Broward College
Susan Guzman-Trevino, Temple College
Kristin Hahn, Rose State College
Michael Hedges, Horry-Georgetown Technical College
Rebecca M. Heintz, Polk State College
Vicki Hendricks, Broward College
Brenda S. Hines, Highland Community College
Deana Holifield, Pearl River Community College
Naana Banyiwa Horne, Santa Fe College
Rebecca Hubbard, Horry-Georgetown Technical College
Joseph Jackson, Buena High School Cochise College
Heidi Johnsen, LaGuardia Community College, CUNY
Leela Kapai, Prince George's Community College
Amelia Keel, Lone Star College–Kingwood
Sandra K. Keneda, Rose State College
Saiyeda Khatun, Johnson & Wales University
Dr. Alisha Knight, Washington College
Odeana Kramer, Prince George's Community College
Diana Krisciunas, North Platte CC, a division of Mid-Plains CC
Dianne Krob, Rose State College
Gordon Lee, Lee College

Kimmarie Lewis, Lord Fairfax Community College
Eric Carl Link, University of Memphis
Robin Lyons, Mississippi Gulf Coast Community College
Paul Madachy, Prince George's Community College
L. Adam Mekler, Morgan State University
Joan Menefee, University of Wisconsin–Stout
Dorothy Minor, Tulsa Community College
Adelaide Mitchell, Tallahassee Community College
Lyle W. Morgan, Pittsburg State University
Rhonda Morris, Santa Fe College
Lori R. Morrow, Rose State College
Barbara M Murray, Dalton State College
Mary Nielsen, Dalton State College
Marjorie Paoletti, Anne Arundel Community College
Joan Perillo, Hillsborough Community College
Neil Plakcy, Broward College
Jessica Powers, El Paso Community College
Joan Reeves, Northeast Alabama Community College
Courtney Ruffner, State College of Florida
Vicki J. Sapp, Tarrant County College
Jennifer Schaefer, Lord Fairfax Community College
Andrew Scheiber, University of St. Thomas
Jim Schrantz, Tarrant County College–Trinity River Campus
Dr. Arthur L. Schuhart, Northern Virginia Community College
Shannon C. Stewart, Coastal Carolina University
Hilary Stillwell, Tallahassee Community College
Kara Strebeck, Pearl River Community College
John Stevens, Temple College
Adam Tavel, Wor-Wic Community College
Gina Thompson, East Mississippi Community College
Donna Thomsen, Johnson & Wales University
Marjory Thrash, Pearl River Community College
Andrew Tomko, Bergen Community College
Dr. William Tomory, Southwestern Michigan College
Susan M Topping, Three Rivers Community College
Tom Treffinger, Greenville Technical College
Gregory J. Underwood, Pearl River Community College
Geraldine Wagner, Johnson & Wales University
Theresa Walther, Rose State College
Gail Watson, County College of Morris
Roger West, Trident Technical College
Justin Williamson, Pearl River College
Martha Willoughby, Pearl River Community College
Kelli Wood, El Paso Community College
Earl Yarington, Prince George's Community College

We are further indebted to our reviewers of the second edition, who include:

Kirk Adams, Tarrant County College–Southeast Campus
Jacob Agatucci, Central Oregon Community College
Paul Robert Andrews, St. Johns River State College
Abby Bardi, Prince George's Community College

Cedric Bradley, Meridian Community College
Kenneth Claney, Tulsa Community College
Meri Lynn Culp, Tallahassee Community College
Rebecca Dark, Dallas Baptist University

Eric W. Devlin, Tarrant County College–Northeast Campus
Robert Goldberg, Prince George's Community College
Carey L. Goyette, Clinton Community College
Sinceree Renee Gunn, The University of Alabama in Huntsville
Chad Hammett, Texas State University–San Marcos
Kevin Hayes, Essex County College
Michael Nelson Hedges, Horry-Georgetown Technical College
Rebecca M. Heintz, Polk State College
Dr. Randall E. Jedele, Des Moines Area Community College
James P. Kain, Neumann University
Kendall Kelly, Texas State University–San Marcos
Saiyeda Khatun, Johnson & Wales University
Thomas M. Kitts, St. John's University
Robin Lyons, Mississippi Gulf Coast Community College
Christopher Scott "Twister" Marquiss, Texas State University–San Marcos
Ruth McAdams, Tarrant County College
Gary S. Montano, Tarrant County College
Lori Renae Morrow, Rose State College
Robin P. Nealy, Wharton County Junior College

Andrew J. Pegman, Cuyahoga Community College
Joan Liguori Perillo, Hillsborough Community College
Joshua Phillips, University of Memphis
Neil Plakcy, Broward College
Deborah Prickett, Jacksonville State University
Vicki J. Sapp, Tarrant County College
Arthur L. Schuhart, Northern Virginia CC–Annandale
Sandra Shattuck, University of Alabama in Huntsville
Connie St. Clair-Andrews, Flagler College
Linda Suddeth Smith, Midlands Technical College
Adam Tavel, Wor-Wic Community College
Donna Thomsen, Johnson & Wales University
Gregory J. Underwood, Pearl River Community College
Roger Vaccaro, St Johns River State College
Theresa Walther, Rose State College
Chloe Warner, Polk State College
Gail Watson, County College of Morris
Roger West, Trident Technical College
Rita Wisdom, Tarrant County College–Northeast Campus
Kelli Wood, El Paso Community College
Earl Frank Yarington III, Prince George's Community College

The video interviews were a labor of love for all who participated—those interviewed were brought on board by their own deep love of students, writing, and literature. These conversations are as lively and varied and richly engaging as the work of the writers that we've included to represent them in *Literature: Craft & Voice*. Here we want to also add our sincerest thanks for the advice of our board of video advisors, many of whom provided their insight on other aspects of the project as well. These professors from across the country worked with our project for several months to guide the way for its use as part of an effective learning experience.

Paul Andrews, St. Johns River Community College
Christian Clark, College of Southern Nevada–Las Vegas
Chad Hammett, Texas State University
Ruth McAdams, Tarrant County College
Louise McKinney, Georgia Perimeter College–Dunwoody

Roxanne Munch, Joliet Junior College
Deborah Prickett, Jacksonville State University
Linda Smith, Midlands Technical College
Kathy Sanchez, Lone Star College–Tomball
Donna Thomsen, Johnson & Wales University

We are deeply grateful to McGraw-Hill for its many contributions to the development of this new learning program. In particular, the remarkable upgrade of Connect Literature could not have happened without the singular efforts and talents of Amy Flauaus, Janet Smith, Paul Banks, Elena Mackagy, and Mathew Sletten. Jay Chakrapani, President, and Aoife Dempsey, Vice President, of Digital, also brought information to the table for delivering media to students. Thanks also to Patrick Murphy of the University of Michigan for a pair of video interviews and to Laurence Goldstein of MQR and John Darnton of *The New York Times* for assistance with procuring the interviews of Arthur Miller and Edward Albee, respectively. Special thanks go out to Jane Hirshfield (and her colleague Mariko Aratani) for the gift of her beautiful haiku translations.

We've had a special opportunity to spend time with many in the marketing and sales group, including the driving force of Suzanne Guinn, Director of Market Development; Kevin Colleary, Marketing Manager; and Julie Bickar, Director of Marketing.

Some of our field publishers have seen this project through from beginning to end. Byron Hopkins was there at our initial lunch, quoting poetry and wondering if this project would ever come to fruition. Our Senior Field Publisher, Ray Kelley, came to our speeches and sat in on several of our interviews. We met others along the way such as Dawn Groundwater, Director of Development, and Linda Stern, Development Editor, who kept us on track and on schedule, David Patterson, Publisher of English, and Dana Wan, Editorial Coordinator, whose many efforts, but particularly her excellent work on the Online Casebooks, are enormously appreciated. Thank you all.

We've saved for our penultimate note of thanks to McGraw-Hill a special acknowledgment of those who've designed our book. Jeanne Schreiber, Creative Director, brought her tremendous design talent to the look of a new generation of textbooks—along with the tireless efforts of many others in the editorial, design, and production group, especially Terri Schiesl, Vice President, Editing, Design, and Production; Mel Valentin, Senior Production Editor; Nora Agbayani, Photo Research Coordinator; Allister Fein, Design Manager; Christina Gimlin, Senior Managing Editor; and Stacey Sawyer, Copy Editor.

This book would not have come into existence had it not been for Steve Debow, President of Humanities and Social Sciences for McGraw-Hill Higher Education, and Michael Ryan, Editor-in-Chief for the Humanities and Social Sciences. Both lent their ears and time and drive to *Literature: Craft & Voice,* bringing McGraw-Hill's extensive resources to bear on innovation and learning in the twenty-first century.

And finally, our great gratitude to Lisa Moore, from whom we learned that writing a textbook is at least as difficult—and as rewarding—as writing novels. Lisa was the first to suggest this project, its tireless supervisor, enthusiastic sponsor, and pitch-perfect voice of experience; without her devotion to detail and eye for quality control we could neither be as proud of nor as pleased with the result. And to Christopher Bennem, captain of this ship of literature, always at the helm, by day and by night, steering us through fog and cheering us on through clear skies, avoiding the icebergs (*see chapter etc. on Metaphor, etc.*) and bringing us all home at last, our deep and constant thanks and thanks.

The authors would like to register their gratitude to their respective agents, Gail Hochman, of Hochman and Brandt, and Timothy Seldes, of Russell & Volkening; they have been careful stewards from the first. Nicholas Delbanco would like to thank the Institute for the Humanities at the University of Michigan (and its director, Daniel Herwitz) for safe haven at this project's start, and Alan Cheuse is grateful to George Mason University for a leave of absence that helped bring it to completion. From the very beginning of this shared enterprise, through the many years of composition and labor, we have had the great good luck of being married to two close critics indeed. Elena Delbanco and Kristin O'Shee were indispensable to this endeavor, as they have long been to our lives; all thanks to each and both of them for everything they do and everything they are.

Part 1

Writing from Reading

1 Reading and Writing Today

DO you know what I think?

I think it was the tremors. That's what must have done it. The way the floor rolled like bongo boards under our feet? Remember it was you and Daddy and me having lunch? "I guess that's not an earthquake," you said. "I guess you're shaking the table?"

That's when it must have happened. A watch on a dresser, a small thing like that—it must have been shaken right off, onto the floor.

—*from "San Francisco" by Amy Hempel*

"The good news is that everybody can [write]. . . . Anybody on a given day can single out half a dozen moments when something changed. . . . It's just the way you experience your life."

Conversation with Amy Hempel, available on video at connect .mcgraw-hill.com

HUMAN beings delight in telling and listening to stories. This basic urge has lasted from the Greek and Roman epics to the present day of TV, movies, email, text messages, and the Internet. As does the speaker in Amy Hempel's short-short story "San Francisco," we often tell—and retell—stories that we sort through to find meaning in the events, people, and places that populate our lives. So it should come as no surprise that, although the means by which we tell them change, the impulse to tell stories—and to find meaning in them—remains.

Literature can serve a student as a bridge between reading closely and writing analytically. Learning how to read stories can entertain and, at times, move you. Learning how to write about them can create an argument that, if well done, helps to persuade the reader of the truth of your ideas. In short, understanding the writer's craft can help you establish your own voice.

THE ROLE OF LITERATURE IN A VISUAL AGE

Stories, poems, and plays are explorations and, often as not, *adaptations:* old tales refashioned into contemporary formats. Stories remain so important to the vitality of a culture—to life and all we do in life—that writers tell them over and over again. Think

> "The pictorial and the literary . . . after all, handwriting is itself a kind of drawing and letters are in a way visual objects. . . . So it's a very short hop from one to the other." Conversation with John Updike

of how many times the Cinderella story has been told and told anew in different **genres** (from **fairy tales** to poems to film) or how different media reveal the home truths of a **fable** such as "The Tortoise and the Hare" from ancient Greece. (**Aesop's "The Tortoise and the Hare" is available online at connect.mcgraw-hill.com.**) With new technologies, our culture has become increasingly based on visual media. As in some earlier peri-

This window in the Cathedral of our Lady of Chartres illustrates the **parable** of the Good Samaritan from the Gospel of Luke. Windows like these were endowed by the Church, which, until the birth of movable type in the fifteenth century and the consequent widespread printing of Bibles, allowed few of its communicants to read Holy Scripture. (**The parable of the Good Samaritan is available online at connect.mcgraw-hill.com.**)

ods, visual elements assist in transmitting knowledge from one realm to another. Generally, the new media rapidly transmit information from one person to another and from one generation to another, and they serve as a bridge between different perspectives and different ways of thinking about problems. After all, putting images together with text is not a recent invention. As long ago as 1300 B.C.E., Egyptians were using a series of pictures to depict an action or a story. The visual and the verbal modes were linked; they have always been hand-in-glove. The statues on the Parthenon in Athens celebrated tales of ancient Greece. In drawings on their surfaces, Greek vases showed illustrations from myth and religion.

With the rise of Christianity, an art form developed in Europe that offered a middle ground between oral recitation of epic (which required an audience of listeners) and the inscription of narrative poetry—and, subsequently, prose fiction—on papyrus and in books. That art form was the Christian tableau, or church window.

The scenes in stained glass church windows served as memorable pictures "illuminating" the stories of their faith. In non-Western traditions, elaborately carved panels of sculpture served a similar narrative role in many Hindu and Buddhist temples. A worshipper could "read" a story without the gift of literacy; pictures played the role of words. For many American students of the post-World War II generation, comic books would serve as a bridge from childhood stories to printed books. (Go to connect.mcgraw-hill.com to see the interview with John Updike on how he came to literature through comics and aspired to be an illustrator at the beginning of his career.)

Many of the selections in this anthology originally appeared in a format that included accompanying images, whether published in magazines or as broadsides, books, or bound pamphlets.

Motion pictures—perhaps the greatest technological gift to culture since the invention of movable type—together with radio and television fill our current leisure time. So, too, do various Internet permutations of visualized stories, often with music, and the currently popular graphic novel. At their best, movies rise to the

One of the most famous instances of images accompanying texts is in William Blake's collection *Songs of Innocence and Experience* (1789). *Songs of Innocence* was first published as a privately printed and bound pamphlet of seventeen poems, each accompanied by an engraving illustrated by Blake. (For more on *Songs of Innocence and Experience*, see Chapter 22.)

The dragon Smaug as he appears in Tolkien's original illustration for his 1937 edition of *The Hobbit* (at left) and in the motion picture adaptation. Smaug and many other elements found in Tolkien's work can be traced back to *Beowulf*.

level of great entertainment, and they do so by presenting us with a pictorial version of a traditional story. These contemporary art forms teach us something about how our ancestors used to live and what they used to believe.

Beowulf, for example, one of the earliest myths of Anglo-Saxon literature, concerns a hero (named Beowulf, meaning Bear Wolf or Bear Hunter) who comes to help a king save his kingdom from the ravages of a powerfully murderous demon. He returns years later to rid the kingdom of the dead demon's mother, now revenging the death of her son. First an epic poem, this tale has since been reinvented in prose translations, novels (such as *Grendel* by John Gardner, in 1971, and *Eaters of the Dead* by Michael Crichton, in 1976), and major motion pictures. Perhaps its most famous influence, however, was on a linguist and translator from Oxford who published an academic article on *Beowulf* that transformed the scholarship around this poem. Although his work "Beowulf: The Monsters and the Critics" is well known among *Beowulf* scholars, J.R.R. Tolkien would become world famous for his books *The Hobbit* and *The Lord of the Rings*—both heavily influenced by *Beowulf*. (Find *Beowulf*, the epic, online at connect.mcgraw-hill.com.)

TWO FILM ADAPTATIONS OF *BEOWULF*

The ancient epic has been reinterpreted in several films, two of which are *The 13th Warrior* and *Beowulf, The Movie*. Although those who study film adaptation lament the criticism that a movie "wasn't like the book," the truth is that reading a book and watching a movie remain completely different experiences. Though we may profit from comparing the two, we cannot precisely replicate one experience in another medium. This holds true whether the experience is of film or prose or poetry or drama: the ancient urge for "story" reinvents itself with the technology of each age. For an example of a student paper comparing two versions of *Beowulf,* see Chapter 4.

The 13th Warrior (1999)

Adapted from the novel Eaters of the Dead *by Michael Crichton*
Screenplay by: William Wisher Jr. and Warren Lewis
Director: John McTiernan
Starring: Antonio Banderas (Ibn Fadlan), Vladimir Kulich (Buliwyf)

In *The 13th Warrior* Ahmed Ibn Fadlan, an Arab devoted to Allah, is conscripted by a band of Vikings, led by Buliwyf, to fight the demons (called "the wendol") in a faraway land. At first he is disgusted by the Vikings and does not want to participate in the quest, but after seeing the remains of human victims who have been eaten by the demons, he has a change of heart. He fights alongside Bulywif as Bulywif is pursued by the demons and ultimately killed. By the end of the movie, Ahmed sets sail for home, having become a brave warrior and friend of the Vikings.

Beowulf: The Movie (2007)

Written by: Roger Avary and Neil Gaiman
Director: Robert Zemeckis
Starring: Anthony Hopkins (King Hrothgar), Ray Winstone (Beowulf),
Crispin Glover (Grendel), Angelina Jolie (Grendel's mother)

Originally released in a 3D format, the movie uses motion capture animation—a technique in which infrared light captures the movements of real actors, which are then put into computer animation to create the look and color desired by the animators. The major change to the plot of the original epic is that Beowulf is seduced by Grendel's mother, and their offspring is the dragon that Beowulf must kill.

MOVIE STILLS FROM *THE 13TH WARRIOR*

Buliwyf, his sword bloody from battling his way into the subterranean lair of the wendol, prepares to do battle with the wendol queen. Contrast his weary expression and dirty clothes with the naked, glistening bravura of Beowulf from *Beowulf: The Movie* (facing page, bottom).

The wendol queen, adorned in snakes and human bones, casts a baleful look at Buliwyf. How does the outward appearance of her warped humanity compare to the twisted, gigantic form of Grendel from *Beowulf: The Movie* (facing page, center)?

Buliwyf wields the mighty sword Hrunting in a fatal blow to the wendol leader. By using weapons and fighting foes his own size, does Buliwyf appear to be more or less heroic? Does he or the Beowulf of *Beowulf: The Movie* (facing page, center and bottom) seem more believable?

MOVIE STILLS FROM *BEOWULF: THE MOVIE*

The hulking, twisted Grendel bursts into King Hrothgar's mead hall, intent on a feast of human flesh. Compare his bent posture to the coiled crouch of the wendol queen (facing page, center). Which monster seems more threatening?

Beowulf gains the advantage over the giant Grendel and pummels him with his bare fists. Which version of the epic presented in this chapter does this representation call to mind? Is this how you might imagine the fight?

Beowulf, naked and unarmed, steps forward to challenge Grendel in combat. In what ways is he "larger than life" compared with Buliwyf from *The 13th Warrior* (facing page, top)? What effect does computer rendering of a real actor have on your perception of the Beowulf character?

Gareth Hinds (b. 1971)
Beowulf: A Graphic Novel
[Grendel's Attack] (2007)

In 2007 Gareth Hinds created *Beowulf: A Graphic Novel*, featuring full-color illustrations of the classic epic. The graphic novel relies on panels to show emphasis or changes in time, whereas narrative prose unfolds over time much like a movie.

THE REWARDS OF CLOSE READING

Given the technologies that define our own Information Age, you might ask why anyone would take the time to read a story or a poem or a play. You might ask the same question with respect to good food. Should we eat well but just gulp it down? If you want to savor a cup of coffee or a delicious meal, you have to linger over it. And do we want to rush through the time we spend with people we love, with family, friends, children? In this supercharged world of instant access and the Internet, reading literature helps you slow down long enough to feel, almost firsthand, the experience of characters from nations, cultures, religions, genders, social classes, and temperaments that differ from your own.

"It's a different experience to be alone with a book, and you're kind of in it—you're there with Huck on the raft. You're decoding the language. It's not just being presented to you. You're making up the scenes in your head. It's not on a screen. . . . You feel that you're part of something mysterious and universal . . . something that's grand and scary and beautiful." Conversation with Tim O'Brien

Yet there's an important difference between life and art. You live only once. But you can turn and return to the best stories, poems, and plays; the great ones continue to live. So whether a work was created in the sixth or the sixteenth century, you learn from the mistakes of characters you read about, revel in their pleasures, and grieve at their dismay. And as you spend time with them, you may discover explanations for your own behavior as well, establishing a kind of kinship with characters who came before our time. Juliet and Queen Guenevere, King Priam and Captain Ahab, little Nell and Willy Loman—all "invented" people—continue their existence on the page and stage. They stay with us as part of our imagination's family. Sometimes we understand them better than we understand our close relatives. Sometimes we understand them better than we seem to understand ourselves, which is one of the reasons we

"We have a tendency, I think, to forget who we want to be, we forget what it is we want to mean in the world. . . . And if I can come into your story and imagine myself . . . [t]hen . . . that's what we need. We need the story to take care of us." Conversation with Barry Lopez

should pay close attention to the stories about their loves and losses, their striving, and their victories and defeats.

There are other advantages to making literature a jumping-off point for the college experience. Any work of literature is a complex text. Reading it closely—within its own context and tradition—may seem strange at first. Yet it's like learning how to break down and rebuild an automobile engine or construct a defense in football or dance the tango or prepare a meal; you need to study the turns and twists of these various activities. Repeated application—practice—is the key to success. In sports you know how important it is to practice. If you play a musical instrument, you know you have to practice. If you perform as a singer or an actor, or work as a salesman or an auto mechanic, you know how critical it is to have been taught and, month after month, to rehearse what you do. All these activities require the use of certain techniques and depend on instruction.

But there's a difference here, too. Unlike taking the controls of an airplane, or performing surgery before you're fully trained, you can read a story and take control of it without doing damage to yourself or someone else in the process. There's reason to hope that you will understand a great work of fiction, poetry, or drama in a better and deeper way each time you read it again. By *understanding* we mean *learning* about how works are made up out of language that the writer has carefully crafted and shaped. We learn about the way the characters think and feel, and we learn about the world in which they find themselves. In other words, you can acquire all those things that lend depth and breadth to your own sense of life.

In an era when the global economy makes the world smaller every day, this experience can enhance your ability to understand complex situations and work with diverse groups of people, both in college and in your career, by helping you see clearly other points of view. Reading closely—carefully, analytically—will help to prepare you for most of the writing you will do in college as well, where understanding a variety of viewpoints is fundamental to academic thinking.

READING PREPARES YOU FOR WRITING

So our first article of faith is that *literature rewards close reading*. And as professional writers of many years' experience, we can testify to this book's second article of faith: *Reading prepares you for writing*. The ability to read closely and to write clearly about what you've read has practical value; these skills will help you in your other courses as well.

"Books teach you without your realizing that they're teaching you. So you're having fun, but you don't know how much you're learning, and it opens your world." Conversation with Chimamanda Ngozi Adichie

Reading literature helps you to think in new and powerful ways; writing about it helps you to express what you think. Both reading and writing helps you to know yourself better and make yourself better known to others. Your success in college depends on your ability to write well, and the better a reader you train yourself to be, the better you prepare yourself to become a better writer. (Note, for example, how the previous sentence uses the same word three times; does repeating "better" seem like a good idea?) It is not easy to read well. It is not easy to write well. (Does the one-word substitution—"write" for "read"—in the two previous sentences seem overly obvious, or does it make a point?) The skills of analysis and composition grow simpler to acquire when your instructor has selected works for you that provide a rich introduction to these critical components of your college life.

"Look for the things that speak to you. . . . And in that connection opens up the space for other connections." Conversation with Aimee Bender

Most of your college courses will require reading and in many cases, you will be required to write about what you read. Your success will depend on how well you can turn your reading into writing. In a recent survey among college instructors and department chairs across the curriculum, 85% of respondents characterized writing as "important" or "critical" to success in their major. College writing assignments have a variety of specific purposes, but one of their main benefits is that when you write about what you read, you become a better reader as well. Your personal reaction causes you to be more attentive to the text, and this focused response contributes to your ability to remember what you've read, clarify your observations, and explore complex relationships. Complexity requires consciously sensing multiple aspects of an experience at one time, and reading literature is a training ground for understanding complex situations. In this book you will find a step-by-step approach to any text-based writing assignment, from a short response to a research paper, and several sample papers for a variety of common writing assignments.

WRITING PREPARES YOU FOR SUCCESS

Although it is unlikely that someone will ask you to write an essay on Coleridge's "Kubla Khan" or Shakespeare's *Hamlet* after graduation, quite probably someone will ask you to articulate an argument that reveals a clear understanding of a complex situation and a complex text or set of texts. In our digital age, we actually write more than ever, and our writing is quite public—on Facebook pages, blogs, and email, as well as in business memos and position papers. Successful writing, especially in the business world, must be succinct, logical, and persuasive. Most professions demand excellent language skills, even if the job does not seem to depend on writing. More than half of major corporations indicate they take writing skills into consideration when hiring

Every writer comes to writing—and every reader to reading—by his or her own path. Fiction writers Tim O'Brien and Jamaica Kincaid and poet Lee Young-Li all had distinctly different inspirations for writing. (To hear them read their work and tell the "stories behind their stories," go to connect.mcgraw-hill.com.)

salaried employees—and exceptional writing skills are required for advancement. If reading literature is a training ground in dealing with complexity, writing about literature is a training ground for expressing yourself with clarity and success in the world beyond college.

WAYS INTO WRITING

Writing is important for success in college and beyond, but everyone has a unique way of coming to reading and writing. Some who eventually became successful writers knew writing was what they wanted to do early on. But even more of the many accomplished writers included and interviewed here were slow or, rather, roundabout starters. Sometimes, as in the case of Stephen Dunn, an intense dedication to a sport provided a foundation for working diligently at a craft while sitting still. Sometimes it was regional pride and a love of place, as proved true for William Kittredge. Sometimes a writer started his artistic career in music (trying to be a punk rocker), as did T. C. Boyle. Sometimes, as Jamaica Kincaid informs us, the desire to excel in language came from struggling with a parent. Sometimes it was just the desire to win a radio in a local library contest, as in the case of Amy Tan. Sometimes dyslexia led a writer to write *before* he could read, as for the young Richard Ford. Reading and writing might have been a solitary defiance of persecution and a spiritual renewal, as was the case for the Indonesian-born Chinese refugee Lee Young-Li. Or maybe a writer just wanted to leave a message about his life as a soldier when he didn't know if he'd come back from war alive, as in the example of Tim O'Brien. Each case is different.

"I struggled. I was not a good natural writer. I think I was smart enough. But writing was a major struggle for me. I didn't really know about periods, why they went where they went. . . . [But] in that class she would tell me, 'You should write down your stories.'" Conversation with Dagoberto Gilb

We've had many conversations with writers, including those just mentioned, about how they came to reading and writing, and their stories might surprise you. Those conversations are on the Web site that accompanies this book. Watch and listen—most are around only 15 minutes long—to learn how these artists first encountered reading and first began to write. You'll find that there is no single "approved" way to write; each writer's process is an individual one. In these conversations, short-story writers, poets, and playwrights also talk about the craft involved in the specific work of literature included by them in this text. Take a moment to think about your earliest experience with reading. Maybe it was with a picture book, or maybe you loved comics, as John Updike did. Was your house full of bookshelves, or did it contain few bound books? Whereas some writers, such as Jamaica Kincaid, were in love with the dictionary before they went to school, others, such as Dagoberto Gilb, didn't even believe they were smart. Maybe reading was your refuge, as it was for Amy Hempel, whose short-short story follows. See the Conversation with Amy Hempel to find out more about how she began and why she writes short-short stories. For the entire interview, go to connect.mcgraw-hill.com.

> "My strategy writing any story is the same as it is here in this short-short. And that is to take on a large subject—the largest ideas and concerns—and find a very small personal way in."
>
> Conversation with Amy Hempel

After you have read "San Francisco," move beyond the reading of this story and relate the experience of reading this story to the close reading you do in your other courses. As with all your college reading, try to find "your personal way in." In the case of this story, for example, how might you link her troubles to a troubling situation of your own? Close attention to the story and to the techniques the writer employs, for example, will help you thread your way through a series of cases in a psychology course, understand the process in a science problem, or analyze primary documents in a history seminar.

Language is with us from morning to night, from infancy to great old age, in times of pleasure, happiness, even joy, and sometimes in sorrow, grief, misery, distress; the better use we make of it, the better lives we live. Whatever your early experiences with reading may have been, we hope that you will see that there is no one way that someone becomes a writer. Similarly, the role that writing plays in our lives is as various as the paths we take to becoming writers. Make no mistake—from text messages to your friends to emails to your instructors, you are already a writer. Being a successful writer is not limited to being a published fiction writer, poet, or playwright. It means being successful at writing in those ways you need to be successful in your life moving forward. As you move forward through this text, pay attention to what the many writers here have to teach us, and listen for the stories that will mean the most to you as you find your way to becoming the writer you want to be.

Amy Hempel ... *I want to write shorter, even shorter—not longer.*

A Conversation on Writing

Learning to Write

I was not a good student. I was not particularly good in English. I was not particularly good in composition. Yet I'm a writer. And this, I think, points to something relevant, which is that it's not about talent, necessarily. . . . You would not have picked me out of the lineup of most likely to succeed at writing at all. But I wanted to do it more than a lot of other people, and so I toughed it out. It is important, I think, to know this. No one ever told me when I was growing up or in school, "Gee, you're really good at this." Quite the contrary. So it's nice to know that actually it didn't make any difference at all.

"Anybody Can Do That"

I think the way people write stories or a novel comes in part from the way they experience their lives or a given day. I see things in moments. I don't see big stretches of time with cause and effect. I see a moment when something shifts or something changes. And I think, again, the good news is that everybody can do that. Anybody can do that. Anybody on a given day can single out half a dozen moments when something changed. . . . The cumulative effect of these moments can often yield a story.

Why the Short-Short Story

So it's just the way you experience your life. Some people take their time. And some people feel that there will be people wanting to listen to them as long as they can keep talking. And I don't. . . . I don't

assume that someone will listen to me indefinitely. I feel I have to get their attention with a really sharp opening sentence and work to keep it. And so that's why I think my stories are as compressed, as short, as they are. And, if anything, I want to write shorter, even shorter—not longer. . . .

Born in Chicago (1951), Amy Hempel lived for a time in California. Known as a so-called minimalist in her writing—she prefers Raymond Carver's term, "precisionist"—Hempel made her reputation solely on short fiction. She has published four short story collections: *Reasons to Live* (1985), *At the Gates of the Animal Kingdom* (1990), *Tumble Home* (1997), and *The Dog of the Marriage* (2005). As the last title suggests, Hempel has an interest in dogs; she even co-edited an anthology of poems written in dogs' voices, *Unleashed: Poems by Writers' Dogs* (1995). A well-respected and much anthologized writer, Hempel has been published in such venues as *Harper's, Vanity Fair, The Quarterly,* and *Playboy.* She has received many honors, including a Guggenheim Fellowship and, in 2008, the REA Award for the Short Story. *The Collected Stories,* published in 2006, won the Ambassador Book Award for best fiction of the year, was a finalist for the PEN/Faulkner Award, and became one of *The New York Times'* Ten Best Books of the Year. She teaches at Harvard University.

To watch this entire interview and hear the author read "San Francisco," go to connect.mcgraw-hill.com.

RESEARCH ASSIGNMENT What is the "big issue" Hempel is dealing with in this short-short story? What is her "personal way in" to this topic?

AS YOU READ   Amy Hempel has said in her interview that this story "relies on a kind of punch line, like a joke or like a parable. . . . You have to compress all your thoughts into the most succinct kind of line of thinking and form." See if you can follow the multiple meanings of the series of puns—words used in such a way as to suggest two or more meanings or different associations—employed by the speaker of this story.

San Francisco (1985)

1   DO you know what I think?
     I think it was the tremors. That's what must have done it. The way the floor rolled like bongo boards under our feet? Remember it was you and Daddy and me having lunch? "I guess that's not an earthquake," you said. "I guess you're shaking the table?"

That's when it must have happened. A watch on a dresser, a small thing like that—it must have been shaken right off, onto the floor.

And how would Maidy know? Maidy at the doctor's office? All those years on a psychiatrist's couch and suddenly the couch is *moving*.

5   Good God, she is on that couch when the big one hits.

Maidy didn't tell you, but you know what her doctor said? When she sprang from the couch and said, "My God, was that an earthquake?"

The doctor said this: "Did it *feel* like an earthquake to you?"

I think we are agreed, you have to look on the light side.

SO that's when I think it must have happened. Not that it matters to me. Maidy is the one who wants to know. She thinks she has it coming, being the older daughter. Although where was the older daughter when it happened? Which daughter was it that found you?

When Maidy started asking about your watch, I felt I 10 had to say it. I said, "With the body barely cold?"

Maidy said the body is not the person, that the *essence* is the person, and that the essence leaves the body behind it, along with the body's possessions—for example, its watch?

"Time flies," I said. "Like an arrow."

"*Fruit flies*," I said, and Maidy said, "What?"

"Fruit flies," I said again. "Fruit flies like a banana."

That's how easy it is to play a joke on Maidy. 15

Remember how easy?

Now Maidy thinks I took your watch. She thinks because I got there first, my first thought was to take it. Maidy keeps asking, "Who took Mama's watch?" She says, "Did *you* take Mama's watch?"

IF YOU LIKED "SAN FRANCISCO," YOU MIGHT ALSO LIKE . . .

. . . another spare, trim story, found in the fiction anthology section of this book—"Cathedral" by Raymond Carver. Amy Hempel talks about Raymond Carver in her interview; his work, like hers, is thought of as "minimalist" by some contemporary critics.

GOING FURTHER   You might also enjoy a stripped down, spare novel of varied voices, such as Peter Matthiessen's *Far Tortuga*, and the "less is more" school of writing, such as *Play It As It Lays* by novelist Joan Didion.

Writing from Reading

Summarize

1 Who is speaking, and what is the occasion she is recounting?

2 How would you describe the speaker? Where does she live? Describe her family.

3 Describe the literal situation in which she finds herself. What emotions does she express as she speaks?

Analyze Craft

4 What effect does the first-person point of view create? How would the story sound if Hempel had written it in the third person? What difference does point of view make?

5 How does the word play ("Time flies. *Fruit flies*," and so on) add to the story?

6 What does the setting contribute to the story? What if the story took place in Miami or New York? How might that change it?

Analyze Voice

7 How does the way the speaker chooses her words give you a sense of how she feels?

Synthesize Summary and Analysis

8 How do the literal events of the story come together to make something more than an anecdote or personal lament?

Interpret the Story

9 In her interview, Hempel says that when she wrote this story, she "felt in sync with a place that was literally on shaky ground." How might the speaker have been in sync with the earthquake as well?

10 Does the speaker lose the watch or keep it in the end?

"In order to craft [your writing] you need . . . a writer's tool box— and all of that has to do with sentence structure and grammar, and what you learned about dialog, and what you learn about all sorts of things, point of view and that sort of thing. And then voice sometimes seems to draw from this other set of tools, mainly kind of intuitive tools and observational tools, just the way in which you see the world, the way in which you notice certain ticks about a person. And so they may seem to counter each other, voice and craft, but I think that in the end voice and craft together make for an incredibly powerful story." Conversation with ZZ Packer

Suggestions for Writing

Some of you have been avid readers since childhood, some since you began school, and others since high school. Some of you may not yet be interested in reading, preferring to devote your leisure time to video games and movies and the various fare of the Internet. So as you focus on the story you have just read—a story you now need to read again (it's certainly short enough) in order to answer a few questions about what to make of this brief piece of fiction—you may discover you are answering in a different way than other people in the group. Some of you no doubt will read less carefully than others; some will read with wildly different results. We hope all of you discover (before you complete the reading of this textbook, and the writing it will inspire, and the course itself) that you've moved beyond the level where you just began.

Create Your Own Literacy Narrative

1. Imagine your personal history of "bookishness," however full or limited it may be.

2. Compare it with Amy Hempel's.

3. Comment on whether you feel the way she does when she says, "You would not have picked me out of the lineup of most likely to succeed at writing at all"?

2 Writing from Reading

YOU can best develop your reading skills by closely examining a piece of literature—whether a short story, novel, poem, or any other form—and the craft that made it possible for the writer to create the work. In this kind of an examination you will use examples from the work itself as **evidence** to support your analysis. For instance, you might argue that a story's theme is a comment on current-day celebrity culture, using quotations from the work itself as evidence. Or you might argue that the ending of a story is particularly effective or ineffective due to the lack of any kind of real change in the characters. Examining the language, characters, and structure of a story helps you write meaningfully about a work. Reading a work critically allows you to make supportable associations that are important to you. It can also help you to begin to develop your own writing powers and your own voice. Take a moment to look at one student's reading of Anton Chekhov's "Rapture."

An Interactive Reading of Anton Chekhov's "Rapture"

Rapture

Setting: The story takes place in the middle of the night in his parents' apartment. Looks like the stage is set for trouble.

Character: Mitya and his parents are the main characters. Is this a story about their relationship?

Mitya is "wild." Mitya's oblivious to everyone around him. Has he done this before? He is behaving so strangely.

Tone, Language, Style: "burst"— same word, twice.

Tone, Language, Style: Second time Mitya has used word "incredible."

Theme: fame?

Tone, Language, Style: Mitya keeps saying "happy."

Plot: Is this the turning point in the plot?

His parents are worried as if to say "nothing good can come of this." It feels as if this isn't the first time they've had to worry about Mitya.

"Rapture" means "ecstasy," "transported to Heaven"—this title tells me the story is about this emotion.

Plot: As the parents see it, there's something "wrong," but the title suggests something else.

Plot: Why is Mitya so happy (when nobody else is)? More uneasy suspense.

Plot: The whole house is in an uproar now.

Plot: Mitya's constant motion contributes to the tension.

Theme: Mitya believes he is famous now. His name is in the paper. This is what has made him rapturous.

Midnight.

Wild-eyed and disheveled, Mitya Kuldarov burst into his parents' flat and dashed into every room. His parents were about to go to bed. His sister was in bed already and had just got on to the last page of her novel. His schoolboy brothers were asleep.

"Where've you come from?" his parents exclaimed in astonishment. "Is something wrong?"

"Oh, I don't know how to tell you! I'm staggered, absolutely staggered. It's . . . it's quite incredible!"

Mitya burst out laughing and collapsed into an armchair, overcome with happiness.

"It's incredible! You'll never believe it! Take a look at this!"

His sister jumped out of bed and came over to him, wrapping a blanket around her. The schoolboys woke up.

"Is something wrong? You look awful."

"I'm so happy, Mum, that's why! Now everyone in Russia knows about me! Everyone! Till now only you knew of the existence of clerical officer of the fourteenth grade, Dimitry Kuldarov, but now everyone in Russia knows! O Lord, Mum!"

Mitya jumped up, ran round every room and sat down again.

"But tell us what's happened, for goodness sake."

"Oh, you lie here like savages, you don't read the papers, you've no ideas what's going on, and the papers are full of such remarkable things! As soon as anything happens, they make it all public, it's down there in black and white! O Lord, I'm so happy! Only famous people get their names in the paper, then all of a sudden—they go and print a story about me!"

"What? Where?"

Dad turned pale. Mum looked up at the icon and crossed herself. The schoolboys jumped out of bed and ran over to their elder brother, wearing nothing but their short little nightshirts.

"They have! About me! Now I'm known all over Russia! You'd better keep this copy, Mum, and we can take it out now and then and read it. Look!"

Mitya pulled the newspaper out of this pocket and handed it to his father, jabbing his finger at a passage ringed with blue pencil. "Read it out!"

Father put on his glasses.

"Go on, read it!"

Mum looked up at the icon and crossed herself. Dad cleared his throat and began: "On December 29th at 11 P.M. clerical officer of the fourteenth grade, Dimitry Kuldarov—"

"See? See? Go on, Dad!"

". . . clerical officer of the fourteenth grade, Dimitry Kuldarov, emerging from the public ale-house situated on the ground floor of Kozikhin's Buildings in Little Bronnaya Street and being in a state of intoxication—"

"It was me and Semyon Petrovich . . . They've got all the details! Go on! Now listen, listen to this bit!"

". . . and being in a state of intoxication, slipped and fell in front of a cab-horse belonging to Ivan Knoutoff, peasant, from the village of Bumpkino in Pnoff district, which was standing at that spot. The frightened horse, stepping across Kuldarov, dragged over him the sledge in which was seated Ivan Lukov, merchant of the Second Guild in Moscow, bolted down the street and was arrested in its flight by some yard-porters. Kuldarov, being at first in a state of unconsciousness, was taken to the police-station and examined by a doctor. The blow which he had received on the back of the head—"

"I did it on the shaft, Dad. Go on and read the rest of the story."

". . . which he had received on the back of his head, was classified as superficial. A police report was drawn up concerning the incident. Medical assistance was rendered to the victim."

"They dabbed the back of my head with cold water. Finished? So what do you say to that, eh? It'll be all over Russia by now! Give it here!"

Mitya grabbed the newspaper, folded it and stuffed it into his pocket.

"Must run now and show the Makarovs . . . Then on to the Ivanitskys, Nataliya Ivanova and Anisim Vasilich . . . Can't stop! Bye."

Mitya put on his official cap with the cockade and radiant, triumphant, ran out into the street.

Marginal annotations:

Tone, Language, Style: Second time she has done this, as if to imply, My God, what has he gotten himself into this time?

Theme: So he's famous for being intoxicated. Why isn't he embarrassed? Why is he so happy about this? What is the point here?

Point of View: The author really doesn't think much of Mitya.

Character: Mitya is impatient again. Why is it so important to him that he is now "known"? He might have been intoxicated throughout the whole story, which would account for his sloppy collapsing in a chair and wild outbursts.

I don't know if I like this ending. Mitya never grows up. His parents just let him go on like this.

Character: Mitya's impatient. If it's not about him, he doesn't care. He's already played superior to his parents by calling them "savages."

Plot: The story is now winding down.

Character: Mitya is a joke. His "rapture" about his fame shows how comical a character he is.

Plot: His parents read the story instead of telling him off. They play along with his delusion. They let him go on thinking this is a great thing. Why? It looks as if the parents didn't really expect much more from him.

Theme: Kind of a sad statement about people. Mitya is a fool. He is proud to be famous for being drunk. He's so deluded that he even wants his parents to know, and his parents do nothing to stop him. He seems ridiculous to me, but he's not acting all that different from how some celebrities act these days.

IF YOU LIKED "RAPTURE," YOU MIGHT ALSO LIKE . . .

. . . Chekhov's masterwork "The Lady with the Pet Dog" (in Chapter 16, An Anthology of Stories for Further Reading), composed when he had more fully developed both his craft and his voice.

A STUDENT'S INITIAL REACTION TO "RAPTURE"

When I first read this, I thought it was amazing how short it is—and how funny it is!
Mitya, the main character, doesn't have a clue. He sounds like some of the people I know
on campus who like to tell stories about what happened when they were drunk. I had
to look up what "rapture" meant, and I'm still thinking about what it means. This is a
translation, so I wonder if there are other ways to translate the title and how another
title might change how I feel about this story. When I read this a second time, I plan to
make some notes in the margin.

USING CRITICAL READING STRATEGIES THAT SUPPORT WRITING

What you have seen at work here is a student applying the techniques of **critical reading** to a story that on the surface seems self-explanatory. A young man gets drunk and makes a fool of himself, yes. But his actions come at some cost to his family, and what *he* feels about his fame is not what we readers feel. The way Chekhov makes "Rapture" unfold underscores the links between, on the one hand, the ordinary experience of one young man and, on the other hand, a larger understanding of the way young people may act, the way family members may respond, and how all this fits into the social scheme of things. So to expand the meaning of what you read beyond the merely literal, you'll find it useful to sharpen your understanding of how various literary techniques—the verbal tactics and strategies of an artist who works with language— make something such as an anecdote into a memorable work of short fiction.

Critical reading is the process of digesting and understanding a text so you can appreciate not just the story it tells or the ideas it contains but *how* it presents those ideas, *why* it presents them, and the way those ideas exist in a certain context. However you approach the text, you will of necessity go from the outside in. As you grow more comfortable, what was strange becomes familiar, and what was a puzzle gets solved.

Reading literature is like passing through a door and entering a world not precisely your own. We meet people in the throes of private trouble or pleasure, and we may see in them, however briefly, our own family or loved ones or close friends—and, finally, ourselves. Reading from the "inside out" also means temporarily ignoring the fact that we're dealing with a "cab-horse," not a car, and that the action takes place in Moscow, not Chicago or Los Angeles or Atlanta. Despite the distance, Anton Chekhov's "Rapture" comes alive today as an example of the way we may be dazzled by fame.

Strategies for Exploring Ideas

Writing about a text begins with your interactions with the text. To find ideas, you can also use the steps of summary through interpretation for exploring a text discussed later in this chapter. In addition, walkthroughs of the entire writing process for each genre, from exploring ideas to writing the final draft, can be found in Chapter 7 (Writing about Fiction), Chapter 18 (Writing about Poetry), and Chapter 31 (Writing about Drama). If you get stuck, the following strategies might help you get going again.

1. **Freewriting or Expanding on Your Notes:** It is all right to start with obvious impressions. Try to answer some of the questions that you asked yourself while annotating the text. Don't worry about finding the "right" answer, and don't limit yourself to just one: there are probably many possible interpretations. *Freewriting* is private writing, just for you.

2. **Talking about the Work:** Try explaining a story, poem, or play to someone who has never read it before, and encourage that person to ask you questions. If this technique sounds odd to you, consider what you do after seeing a new movie you had looked forward to seeing.

3. **Brainstorming:** If you find it simpler to think in diagrams, your freewriting might take the shape of a web or cluster of related or unrelated impressions. Start with a central idea, literary device, or character that you wish to explore, and place that in the center. Then, write down elements or characteristics associated with your central term and draw connecting lines.

4. **Charting:** Another way to draw connections between your observations is by charting them. This is an especially helpful method if you have identified opposites of some sort in the text, whether they are a hero and a villain, rainy weather and fair weather, or light images and dark images. You can create a chart with two columns. In one column you would write, say, "Rainy weather" together with all the occurrences of the pattern. In the adjoining column you would do the same for "Fair weather."

READING IN CONTEXT

Sometimes while working closely with a story and its meanings, it is easy to lose sight of the bigger picture, the **context.** It's important to return to the fact that "Rapture" is set in another country and in another century, and was written in another language. (For more on translation, go to connect.mcgraw-hill.com to watch an interview with the distinguished Stephen Mitchell.) Understanding the tradition and context—the situation of, or reason for, the writing—also makes the reading experience richer. Robert Frost once wrote, "The way to read a poem is in the light of all the other po-

"I like the sounds of a sentence, the acoustics of a sentence, not just what it's saying or the information in it." Conversation with Amy Hempel

ems ever written." Though none of us will ever know all the other poems—or stories or plays—ever written, we can know that no piece of writing exists in a vacuum. Nineteenth-century Russia—with its detailed newspaper stories and "official cap with the cockade"—is a certain time and place, and works from this era belong to a particular tradition; taking these aspects into consideration is called **contextual reading.** The most complete analyses of craft and voice push us in the direction of contextual reading, just as the right kind of contextual reading pushes us, throughout the process, to turn back to the text itself.

Below are three steps that will help you read contextually and critically.

1. **Preview the text.** The process of gathering information about a piece of literature before you read it is called *previewing*. When you **preview,** look for information that will help you know how to approach the text. Note the *date of publication*. This will help you to determine whether the author was writing about his or her own time, or about a historical period. Note the *genre*. Is it a poem, a story, or a play? A piece of nonfiction? Knowing whether what you are about to read is fiction or nonfiction (and if it is, say, science fiction, crime writing, or literary fiction) will help you focus your expectations of your reading experience. Note any *introductory material*. In a book, you'll often find a foreword or a preface. Read the introductory notices to help prepare for your study. If the selection is part of an anthology or a textbook, the surrounding text and questions will be especially helpful in giving your reading direction.

2. **Interact with the text: Annotate, keep a journal, take notes.** Annotation is a skill that, like any other, improves with practice. Annotating a text is a very basic process of noting impressions as they occur throughout a reading. The skill of annotation is best described as learning to notice what you notice. Everyone has had the experience of reading a story, poem, or play for the first time and coming across something odd or jarring. Students new to reading literature are often tempted to ignore that feeling of surprise, blaming themselves for the disruption. "I must not get what the author is trying to do," they think, or, "I just don't understand literature." In fact, that feeling is useful, the beginning of your ideas. Don't ignore it. Even feeling bored by what you read is worth noticing. Annotation should be as simple as circling repeated words, underlining interesting phrases, and jotting down brief sets of words. Remember that annotating is a process of observation; deeper analysis and interpretation will come later.

   Keeping a reading journal is a great way to develop all kinds of skills—your observational skills, your writing skills, and your ability to appreciate literature. Often, instructors will ask you to keep a journal and give you prompts to which you will respond. But whether or not you have that kind of guidance, you can keep your own journal in which you record what you have read and what you thought and felt about it. There is no one right way to keep a journal; you may choose to fill it with personal reactions to literature, with ideas for paper topics, or with quotes that you liked and a description of what each quote means to you.

3. **Read the text again for craft and context.** Reading a good piece of literature is like getting to know somebody new: your first impression is meaningful, but your second and third impressions can reveal to you entirely different aspects of the work. For a second reading, take into account how the elements of craft work together to create the selection you are reading, and for a third reading, put the selection into context. When was it written? What does its theme say about the perspective of the author on the issues or circumstances of the day? Note these impressions as well, because they will become the body of information you draw from when you write your responses. The practices of annotation and note taking will not only produce a fuller, more informed response but will also save you time.

MOVING FROM SUMMARY TO INTERPRETATION

There is no secret to learning the route from reading to writing. You start with your annotations—your first impressions—and you build from there. When you start to write down your thoughts about a piece of literature, first make sure you understand the basics: what has happened in the selection, who is the main character or speaker, and whose point of view do we see? Does the action occur in the present or past tense? This is a summary.

Building on your summary, you will want to think about the tone and style of the work, analyzing how the story, poem, or play is told. As you analyze, look for the role of the setting (particularly if you're reading a story), important symbols, repeated words and sounds (crucial when reading a poem), and the way dialogue pushes the plot forward (a central element in analyzing a play). Your analysis should take special note of who is telling the story; in a poem, identifying the speaker allows you to get underneath the hood of the "machine of words."

When you look at what was said (summary) and how it was said (analysis), you can put these together, bring in the context in which a work was written, and synthesize the work of literature to find themes and subthemes that the substance and style mutually support. You are now prepared to interpret the selection and support your interpretation with points taken from the selection. You may take a particular critical approach (see Critical Approaches to Literature at the end of this text) or a more personal point of view, and this framework can be useful as you interpret anything you read. Whatever your method, the process of reading critically—summary, analysis, synthesis, and interpretation—will set you up to express your thoughts on what is important and meaningful to you in any literary work. And note that you can also use this process with any nonliterary texts you read.

1. **Summarize.** After a first reading, solidify your understanding of the text by *summarizing* what you have read. **Summary** involves condensing a story, poem, or play into your own words, making sure to capture the text's main points. In the case of prose, an overview is much shorter than the original source and is often no more than a paragraph or two. For poetry, you may need to make a line-by-line paraphrase to get the information you need to condense into the summary of a poem. Before summarizing,

you might reread your annotations and notes with an eye toward picking out important points to include.

Remember that a summary should be *objective*—focused more on what you saw happen in the work than on how you reacted to it. It should also not get bogged down with details and examples but should focus on capturing the main events of the story or the main idea if the work is a poem or an article.

- *Pinpoint the main idea and write it in a sentence.* For a scholarly article, a main idea usually emerges in the thesis or is stated concisely in the conclusion. For a story, the main idea is often contained in the broad trajectory of the main character.

- *Break the text into parts.* In a story or poem, identify the places where shifts occur—scene changes, a change in tone, or other points where the work takes a new direction. Some scholarly sources might already have headings that divide the text for you.

- *Summarize each section's main idea.* Write a sentence describing the key point the author makes in each section or, for a piece of literature, the key action or idea of the section. Think of this step as writing a topic sentence for each section.

2. **Analyze craft and voice.**   Summary helps you understand *what* happened in the text, and you will probably use your summary to support a point. The next step is to **analyze** the text by determining *how* the author created the work. When you analyze, you take the text apart and examine its elements: the different writing devices the author uses (such as point of view, plot, and imagery) and the voice the author brings to the piece (tone, word choice).

3. **Synthesize summary and analysis.**   The goal of **synthesis** is to bring together the ideas and observations you've generated in your reading and analysis in order to make a concrete statement about the work you've read. The secret ingredients to synthesis are your own personal opinions and perspectives. (In a research paper, you should include the opinions and perspectives from academic sources as well.) Thus, synthesis takes the *what happened* from summary and the *how the work was accomplished* from analysis and shapes them into an argument or a statement.

4. **Interpret the text.**   After *analyzing* a text and *synthesizing* your thoughts into a statement on the text, you will be able to interpret a particular element of a work by suggesting what that element means. **Interpretation** strives to increase our understanding of some aspect of a work as a way to illuminate the work's meaning. Interpretation does not mean identifying one correct answer, one key to unlock a text. Rather, it means taking an argument or a statement you've generated through synthesis and using that as an angle from which to enter a work and explore some new, insightful aspect. Interpretations can certainly vary, but note that an interpretation must have a strong foundation of evidence from the text itself. (See also Critical Approaches to Literature at the end of the book.)

We explore further how to develop a text-based **argument** later in this section, but whether you care more for the factual than the fictional, or ever paid much attention to stories other people made up, or found your way to the library, you can take on the job of forming a text-based argument. You will need to understand what to make of twenty-six separate things (the English alphabet), crack the code of sentences and paragraphs, and solve the mysteries of punctuation. Are the author's sentences mostly

"I remember reading books about people in Russia, people in India, and people in England, and understanding them—and how surprising this was. Because on the one hand, you realize they're so different from me. But on the other hand, what literature does [is] remind you of how there is that human bond that we all have in common." Conversation with Chimamanda Ngozi Adichie

long or short? Is the text dominated by descriptive prose or lots of dialogue? In every work of fiction, in every poem and play, a *voice* inhabits the page. Try to hear the writers' voices in this book. Each writer will have a special way of using language that sets his or her work apart.

A STUDENT PAPER: A RESPONSE TO ANTON CHEKHOV'S "RAPTURE"

Now let's look at the critical response paper that is based on the previous reading of "Rapture." Remember that reading closely is the first step to writing about literature. A careful reading and simple markup leads to observations that can form the basis of a written response. Look back at the student's annotation of "Rapture," and note that this student does not come up with any actual *ideas* in her annotation. Instead, she makes *observations* about what she noticed as she read the story. This is an important distinction. For example, our student, Liane, noticed that the narrator repeats certain phrases in the story, but she doesn't yet ask why. She first had to notice many details about the story's tone, patterns, and words, and note her own reactions, before she could start narrowing down the details that would be helpful in firming up her interpretation.

In the Chekhov paper, our student argues that the story is incomplete and unsatisfying. Take the Chekhov paper to heart; the validity of an evaluation rests not on how highly you rank a noted author but on how your analysis of the story supports your argument. In this case, our student has analyzed the structure of the story and found that, in a story set up for a three-part movement, the third part is missing. Therefore, when she claims that the story is incomplete and unsatisfying, we see her point. (Note—and here is one of the reasons we begin with this example—that not every selection in *Craft and Voice* will earn your admiration; as long as you support your response with a coherent argument, your assessment can well be negative or "critical.") In a single-source paper such as this **critique** of Chekhov's "Rapture," the evidence will be examples and quotations from the text itself. Our student develops her position by citing Chekhov's text directly. For an argument using multiple sources, see the research paper in Chapter 5. Nearly every sample paper in the next chapter is also an argument paper in some sense—because each posits an opinion that the writer must then support.

Lau 1

Liane Lau

Professor Cheuse

Composition 120

23 April 2011

Mitya's False Finale: A Critical Response to Chekhov's "Rapture"

Although it is difficult to talk about language as such in Anton Chekhov's "Rapture," written in Russian in nineteenth-century Moscow, the structure of the story transcends language barriers. Chekhov's setting is domestic: an apartment serves as the location for the entire action, a stage of sorts. The young clerk runs in, stirs up his family, and makes them read a newspaper article in which he has been named. Then, still raving about his new-found fame, he runs out again. He is "wild-eyed and disheveled" (21). He runs from room to room. He has laughing outbursts and collapses in a chair. Chekhov paints the portrait of a man out of control, one in an unvoiced conflict with his parents who are "pale" with worry, asking Mitya "Is something wrong? You look awful" (21). Mitya appears to want everyone, beginning with his family, to know his name; he wants to establish himself in the minds of others as someone *important*. However, the young "clerical officer of the fourteenth grade" does not come to any new realization or perception, and therefore, the resolution of the story is not ultimately satisfying (22).

The setting of the story looks like a scene from a play (and it's worth mentioning here that Anton Chekhov would also become a great Russian playwright). The story breaks into three distinct parts. First, the clerk runs in, announcing himself, disrupting the household, waking his brothers. Second, Mitya takes out the newspaper and urges his father to read it aloud. He adds

Introduction provides story elements: setting, characters, plot.

Introductory sentence focuses the reader immediately: Essay will center on story elements.

Quotes support statements, lend credibility, bring Chekhov's voice to the paper as an ally.

Thesis statement, presents paper's argument: Story elements (listed in paragraph's body) do not add up to a satisfying resolution.

"Three distinct parts": As stated in lead sentence, this argument is based on story structure.

Lau 2

Paragraph two critically analyzes elements detailed in intro paragraph.

his own enthusiastic comments to propel the action forward, and we discover that he was drunk the night before; quite plausibly, he remains under the influence now. In the third sequence, a reader may expect something to happen as a result of Mitya's *rapture,* that he has become famous because his name is in the paper and on the police record. The use of the word *rapture* in itself ironically underscores how far the distance is between Mitya's experience of the truth and the actual truth of his situation. There is nothing elevated about his actions, and to some extent the whole story turns comically on this divide.

Critical evidence builds up to the initial debate: Does the story have a clear, satisfying ending?

However, as the ancient philosopher and critic Aristotle might put it, what is the dramatic purpose here? It looks like Mitya's parents are used to his antics, as his mother crosses herself twice in anticipation of Mitya's supposedly "incredible" news (20). His parents and his siblings humor him instead of contradicting or berating him, thus making change less likely for Mitya. Mitya is completely happy with his newfound notoriety, even though it announces to the world that he is a drunkard. As we readers come to understand the nature of Mitya's delusion, we are entitled to wonder what Chekhov is after: what point is he attempting to make? Is "Rapture" a story about the folly of ambition? Is it, perhaps, a presage of our publicity-hungry world and the press agent's promise that any mention in the newspaper is more important than none? Or is it simply poking fun at a simple soul? The reader is left to wonder what the point is, and without that concluding action, the dramatic purpose is unclear, so the story is incomplete, and ultimately unsatisfying.

Topic sentence states the question posed by preceding paragraphs: Do the story elements allow us to determine whether this is a tragedy or a comedy?

Conclusion restates the thesis, including logic established by body of the paper.

Questions reflect the argument that Chekhov has offered no clear resolution.

Quick, challenging question statements build tension that the conclusion sentence relieves.

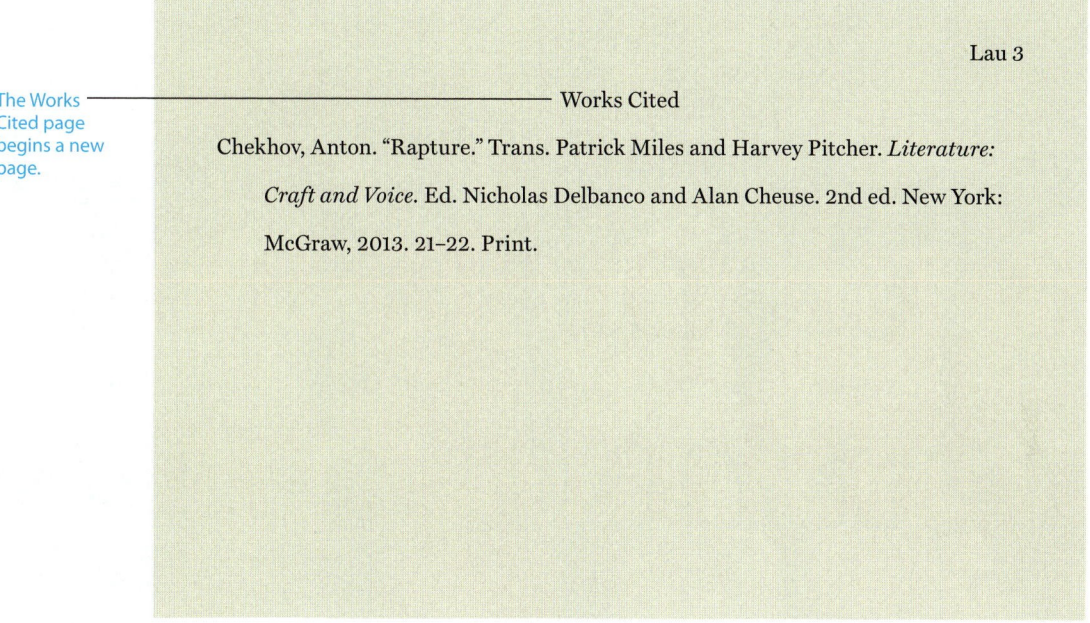

The Works Cited page begins a new page.

Lau 3

Works Cited

Chekhov, Anton. "Rapture." Trans. Patrick Miles and Harvey Pitcher. *Literature: Craft and Voice.* Ed. Nicholas Delbanco and Alan Cheuse. 2nd ed. New York: McGraw, 2013. 21–22. Print.

For samples of journal entries as part of the entire writing process, see Chapter 7 (Writing about Fiction), Chapter 18 (Writing about Poetry), and Chapter 31 (Writing about Drama). The students whose papers appear in Chapters 7 and 18 used their journals as a place to write a slightly more formal and focused response. Their strategy is worth emulating: because they focused their ideas in their journals, the students will be able to look back later in the semester to study for exams—or later in their college careers when they want to revisit literature that they enjoyed—and have an immediate springboard into remembering the story or the poem and what makes it effective.

Interactive Readings

- Anton Chekhov's story "Rapture" (this chapter)
- Jamaica Kincaid's story "Girl" (Chapter 7)
- Carolyn Forché's poem "The Museum of Stones" (Chapter 17)
- William Shakespeare's poem "My mistress' eyes are nothing like the sun" (Chapter 17)
- Li-Young Lee's poem "Eating Alone" (Chapter 18)
- Edward Albee's play *The Zoo Story* (Chapter 31)

3

Developing an Argument

THE back, the yoke, the yardage. Lapped seams,
The nearly invisible stitches along the collar
Turned in a sweatshop by Koreans or Malaysians

Gossiping over tea and noodles on their break
Or talking money or politics while one fitted
This armpiece with its overseam to the band

Of cuff I button at my wrist. The presser, the cutter,
The wringer, the mangle. The needle, the union,
The treadle, the bobbin. The code. The infamous blaze

At the Triangle Factory in nineteen-eleven.
One hundred and forty-six died in the flames

—*from "Shirt" by Robert Pinsky*

A LITERARY analysis builds a complex argument around a particular aspect of a work of literature. Summarizing, analyzing, and synthesizing might help you to come up with an interpretation that could be your paper's topic, but when you're looking for a topic for a paper, you probably wonder: where do ideas come from? For all of us, coming up with ideas—and developing those ideas into claims worth writing about—is a challenge. The logic of your argument and the evidence you provide determine whether you have effectively proven your claim. Your claim, logic, and evidence are the core components of any argument.

- **Claim:** A paper's purpose and argument is defined by its thesis statement. Your thesis should be arguable, supportable, complex yet focused, and purpose-driven. An arguable thesis is one that reasonable people might disagree about. An arguable thesis isn't an opinion ("I liked the characters in this story"), and it isn't a generally recognized truth ("Langston Hughes is one of the most important American poets"), but rather it is based on claims—logical statements supported by the evidence you present in your paper. For guidance on creating a thesis that makes strong claims, see Making Claims: Supporting a Defensible Thesis later in this chapter.

- **Logic:** Aristotle, the same great philosopher who defined tragedy in ancient Greek theater (Chapter 32), also defined logic and the art of persuasion. What we call *logic* today Aristotle would have called *analytics*, as in *to analyze*. When we refer to an academic argument, we are not referring to a fight but rather to a well-reasoned, logical analysis that is based on evidence.

CONTINUED ON PAGE 36

Robert Pinsky

...I'm as likely to refer to the Captain Easy comic strip as I am to the Aeneid.

A Conversation on Writing

The Presence of the Past in Everything

That the past is present in everything is just a deep conviction for me. . . . I grew up in a town where my mother and father went to the same high school as me. My father and I both had Miss Scott for homeroom. . . . Long Branch is a very historical town. . . . Grant, Lincoln, and Mrs. Lincoln visited Long Branch. Diamond Jim Brady went to stay there with Lillian Russell. . . . I grew up with a sense . . . that there's always lore and information behind everything. . . . I want the reader [of my poems] to know that the presence of information is there. . . . I do like that feeling of information accumulating.

A Tradition of Makers

The poem is very much about making, traditions of making, and making up. The associations aren't random; they're historical. So the extension of the poem that goes on and goes on and thinks of another thing is a reflection of how deep the history of everything is. The history of the language I am speaking now, the history of the metal and plastic in the chair that I am sitting [in], to now, the history of video technology. It doesn't . . . it doesn't end when the encyclopedia entry ends. It goes right back to the first smelting of any metal at all. It goes back to the primate's ingenuity.

Writing as an Amateur Collector of Information

I've never mastered a subject. I've never become a scholarly expert in anything at all. I always make mistakes about dates. Most of the information in my poems is slightly wrong, and frequently made up altogether. . . . I was not a successful student in high school. I was a real failure, a literal failure, in junior high school. In the eighth grade I was in the "dumb class," also called the "bad class." . . . So I'm more like one of those birds or apes that collects things than I am like a seriously scholarly person.

A New Jersey boy from birth (1940) through his undergraduate years at Rutgers University, Robert Pinsky originally hoped to be a musician. When he changed his focus to poetry in college, however, the change was not wholly unexpected; as a child, he loved the sounds of words, even if he was too young to understand them. This love of language combined with his compelling intellect has made his poetry in collections such as *Sadness and Happiness* (1975), *The Figured Wheel: New and Collected Poems 1966–1996* (1996), and *Jersey Rain* (2000) so striking.

His translation of the first volume of Dante's *Divine Comedy* (1995) became a best-seller; his work on *The Life of David* (2005) was a close examination of that biblical hero's consequence. Pinsky's recent collections of verse include *First Things to Hand* (2006), *Gulf Music* (2007), and *Selected Poems* (2011). In addition to being a Stegner Fellow at Stanford University, Pinsky counts among his honors a Pulitzer Prize nomination, an American Academy of Arts and Letters award, and the position of Poet Laureate of the United States. Pinsky currently teaches in the graduate program at Boston University and edits the poetry for the online journal *Slate*.

RESEARCH ASSIGNMENT View the interview with Robert Pinsky and explain why history is so important to him. List some of the historical references related to "Shirt" that he mentions in his interview. How does knowing the history of the shirt affect your understanding of the poem?

AS YOU READ   Consider the variety of historical connections Pinsky makes. The poem seeks to bridge subjects and elements as diverse as the famous fire at the Triangle Shirtwaist Factory, sweatshops, American slavery, the twentieth-century immigrant experience, and the seventeenth-century British poet George Herbert. Alongside these references are words from the world of sewing and tailoring, such as "yoke," "mangle," and "bobbin." Pinsky uses this jargon—technical language specific to a trade, craft, or profession—to further connect the centuries-old history of garment-making to the culture and events of the poem.

Shirt (1990)
Robert Pinsky

The back, the yoke, the yardage. Lapped seams,
The nearly invisible stitches along the collar
Turned in a sweatshop by Koreans or Malaysians

Gossiping over tea and noodles on their break
5   Or talking money or politics while one fitted
This armpiece with its overseam to the band

Of cuff I button at my wrist. The presser, the cutter,
The wringer, the mangle. The needle, the union,
The treadle, the bobbin. The code. The infamous blaze

10 At the Triangle Factory in nineteen-eleven.
One hundred and forty-six died in the flames
On the ninth floor, no hydrants, no fire escapes—

The witness in a building across the street
Who watched how a young man helped a girl to step
15 Up to the windowsill, then held her out

Away from the masonry wall and let her drop.
And then another. As if he were helping them up
To enter a streetcar, and not eternity.

A third before he dropped her put her arms
20 Around his neck and kissed him. Then he held
Her into space, and dropped her. Almost at once

He stepped up to the sill himself, his jacket flared
And fluttered up from his shirt as he came down,
Air filling up the legs of his gray trousers—

Like Hart Crane's Bedlamite, "shrill shirt ballooning."   25
Wonderful how the pattern matches perfectly
Across the placket and over the twin bar-tacked

Corners of both pockets, like a strict rhyme
Or a major chord. Prints, plaids, checks,
Houndstooth, Tattersall, Madras. The clan tartans   30

Invented by mill-owners inspired by the hoax of Ossian,
To control their savage Scottish workers, tamed
By a fabricated heraldry: MacGregor,

Bailey, MacMartin. The kilt, devised for workers
To wear among the dusty clattering looms.   35
Weavers, carders, spinners. The loader,

The docker, the navvy. The planter, the picker, the sorter
Sweating at her machine in a litter of cotton
As slaves in calico headrags sweated in fields:

George Herbert, your descendant is a Black   40
Lady in South Carolina, her name is Irma
And she inspected my shirt. Its color and fit

And feel and its clean smell have satisfied
Both her and me. We have culled its cost and quality
Down to the buttons of simulated bone,   45

The buttonholes, the sizing, the facing, the characters
Printed in black on neckband and tail. The shape,
The label, the labor, the color, the shade. The shirt.

Writing from Reading

Summarize

1 What connections does the poet make between the people, objects, and events in the poem?

Analyze Craft

2 Why do you think this poem is so full of people and objects?

3 How does the recurring pattern of clothing help link historical periods throughout the poem?

Analyze Voice

4 What attitude does the poet express toward the events described here?

5 Would you call this poem a political statement, a social statement, a moral statement—or all of these? Why?

Synthesize Summary and Analysis

6 As Pinsky says, "The associations [in the poem] aren't random. They're his-torical." How does the historical material help to broaden the impact of the poem?

Interpret the Poem

7 Link the details of shirt-making to the larger story here. How might the shirt factory workers be viewed as artists? Why does Pinsky compare these "crafts"? What is the significance of Pinsky's com-parisons of Irma and George Herbert?

Source-Based Evidence: Quotations vs. Paraphrase vs. Summary

Quotation: When the meaning of what was said would be distorted or changed in any other words, a quotation needs to be used to make your point. Do not avoid making a point by overusing quotations. Build your point by using a quotation as your evidence, as a springboard for your own ideas.

Paraphrase: Using your own words, a paraphrase is a restatement ("in other words") of someone else's language that makes a point more clearly than could be made by using the quotation itself. A paraphrase, therefore, may blend your own view with the words of the source. A paraphrase can help you to understand a passage, particu-larly in poetry. Make sure you mention the source when you paraphrase. Use such phrases as "According to," "As said in," "We know from."

Summary: A boiled-down analysis of the line of action or thought in a passage or full text, a summary is used not only to represent your understanding of a text but also as a point of reference that provides context for your argument. See the summary paper in the next chapter.

Note: The accurate citation of sources is critical for avoiding plagiarism. For more guidance on avoiding plagiarism, see the section on avoiding plagiarism in source-based evidence and the Tips boxes later in this chapter.

CONTINUED FROM PAGE 33

- **Evidence:** For literature, the text itself is your most convincing evidence; other kinds of evidence might be statistics, expert opinions, and anecdotes. You will need to show details, patterns, and ideas from the text when you present your evidence.

Whenever possible, relate your argument to something that genuinely interests you. You might, for example, explore the subject online and relate the historical considerations to your reading of the poem. For a paper on Pinsky's "Shirt," for example, you could do research about The Triangle Factory fire or the hoax of Ossian.

LINKS RELATED TO ROBERT PINSKY'S "SHIRT"

From Cornell University, The Kheel Center
www.ilr.cornell.edu/trianglefire/
The site includes an account of what happened, interviews with survivors, pictures and illustrations, and bibliographic information. Much of the site is taken from primary and secondary documents housed at Cornell.

From *The New York Times*
www.nytimes.com/2011/02/21/nyregion/21triangle.html
The article "100 Years Later, the Roll of the Dead in a Factory Fire Is Complete," by Joseph Berger, published on March 20, 2011, is about identifying the six unknown victims of the Triangle fire.

From *The New York Times*
www.nytimes.com/2010/03/26/nyregion/26nyc.html
Clyde Haberman's article "Choosing Not to Forget What Is Painful to Recall," published on March 25, 2011, is about how New York City commemorates the Triangle Shirtwaist Factory disaster.

From Remember the Triangle Fire Coalition
http://rememberthetrianglefire.org/
This Web site is sponsored by the active coalition for commemorating the Triangle fire. In addition to the organization's calendar and the opportunity to donate, the site includes names and ages of victims, as well as an open archive with individual stories about the fire. It also provides information and updates on the permanent memorial the coalition plans to build.

From NPR (National Public Radio)
www.npr.org/templates/story/story.php?storyId=1416870
In this interview with David Von Drehle, author of *Triangle: The Fire That Changed America,* Von Drehle tells the story of what happened. Listeners can also hear a 1984 report on the women of the Triangle Shirtwaist Factory.

continued

From PBS (Public Broadcasting Service)
www.pbs.org/wgbh/americanexperience/films/triangle/
This Web site for a PBS documentary that aired February 28, 2011 includes the original *New York Times* article from March 26, 1911, as well as a biography of a victim, information on the aftermath, and links to other resources.

From the English Department, University of Illinois at Urbana-Champaign
www.english.illinois.edu/maps/poets/m_r/pinsky/triangle.htm
Robert Pinsky's page on the *Modern American Poetry* site, put together by the University of Illinois at Urbana-Champaign, includes a photo-essay of the fire.

From a faculty project at the University of Missouri-Kansas City
http://law2.umkc.edu/faculty/projects/ftrials/triangle/trianglefire.html
Extensive information on the trial that followed the Triangle Shirtwaist Factory fire appears on this Web site.

From HBO (Home Box Office)
www.hbo.com/#/documentaries/triangle-remembering-the-fire
The HBO website contains information, including photographs, from the documentary "Triangle: Remembering the Fire," which aired on March 21, 2011, as well as other resources.

"I would hope that a student would feel a sense of permission . . . in terms of thinking about what reading could be."

Conversation with Aimee Bender

Use the tips that follow as possible ways to develop your ideas and find the evidence to support them. They will help you arrive at an effective argument.

TEN WAYS TO REFINE YOUR IDEAS

1. **Follow your interests and expertise whenever possible.**
   If you are a psychology major and the various family members' relations with each other in Arthur Miller's *Death of a Salesman* (Chapter 34) remind you of a theory you have just studied in a psychology seminar, don't be afraid to use that knowledge to aid in your interpretation. If you are an avid sailor, and that makes you especially interested in analyzing the "open boat" scenes in Stephen Crane's short story "The Open Boat" (Chapter 13), take advantage of your knowledge in creating your argument.

2. **Acknowledge your gut reactions, but then analyze them.**
   If you found a given text or page extremely frustrating to read, it is absolutely legitimate to admit this to yourself and others. But don't stop there. Ask yourself,

- What was it that frustrated me so much about this passage?
- Was it the slow pace of the action?
- Was it my own lack of familiarity with the language used at the time the piece was written?
- Was it the fact that the character I most identified with died in the previous scene?
- Was it the wordy prose style?
- What might have motivated the author to use such convoluted language?
- Are there any benefits to it?

Certainly some works of art will appeal to you more than others; elements of taste and personal preference affect every reading. It is legitimate to say, "I hated that story," and intelligent analysis can come from that reaction if you analyze the ways in which the text creates specific impressions on readers.

Similarly, if you enjoy a text and feel a deep personal connection with it, keep in mind that you will have to ask yourself questions like those above to make sure you are being specific in examining the attributes you admire. You need not try to develop negative observations, but make certain that your affection isn't clouding your ability to see all aspects of the work clearly.

3. **Choose a single aspect of the genre to examine.**

For instance, look at meter in poetry, voice in fiction, or stage directions in drama. Reread the text closely, looking only at that one aspect. It can be especially useful to choose an aspect of the genre that is *not* the most noticeable in the particular text even though doing so might seem counterintuitive. For instance, most readers notice right away that Elizabeth Bishop's poem "One Art" (Chapter 25) is a villanelle, a tricky form that requires repetition and a complex rhyme scheme. The predictable choice would be to comment on her use of the form, but it might be more fruitful, and certainly more original, to think about something less obvious, such as the poem's use of images or its rhythm.

4. **Pay attention to detail.**

One convention of literary criticism is to assume that *every* element of a text is potentially significant, no matter how small it seems. Whether or not the author specifically intended everything we notice, once it is written down, everything is fair game for interpretation. When a literary argument does go too far, this is generally *not* because the argument depended on minor details for its support but because it failed to present sufficient evidence or to form a coherent, logical argument. Some of the most insightful interpretations sound as though they are "reading too deeply" into the text until we hear all the supporting evidence and analysis.

Of course, this does not mean that we can arbitrarily assign meaning to any single detail in a text. It is not convincing, for instance, to argue that "Bartleby, the Scrivener" (available at connect.mcgraw-hill.com) is Herman Melville's rallying cry for Marxism, since there is little evidence for that interpretation in Melville's biography or his other works. The details, however, that might lead to this conclusion—Bartleby's escalating refusal to make copies, his boss's obliviousness to his condition, and the depressing metaphor of Bartleby staring at the brick wall—*could* work together to support a more subtle, complex claim about work and social class in the story. Each of these details on its own does not necessarily carry meaning, but a good paper will *note* them *and put them together* to form a meaningful interpretation.

So, do not be nervous about "reading too deeply" into a text. No claim is too outlandish, no detail too random or seemingly insignificant, no conclusion too far-fetched or implausibly small if your literary argument provides sufficient evidence. "Did Herman Melville *really* mean to use the brick wall as a symbol of class struggle?" you might ask. "Is every tiny detail really so important?" Keep in mind that some interpretations that seemed to be reading too much into the text when they first appeared later became widely accepted. Today's audacious argument might be tomorrow's commonplace one, so don't be afraid to add to the conversation.

5. **Compare the text with other works you have read.**
    Even if your assignment does not require or allow you to discuss more than one work of art, you may still find it helpful to compare your text with others while in the process of developing your topic. Comparing the spare, straightforward prose of Ernest Hemingway (Chapter 11) with the more elaborate prose style of James Joyce (Chapter 8), for example, may lead you to useful conclusions about the ways each of these authors uses language. It often helps to look at texts in juxtaposition or opposition; the differences are as important as the similarities.

6. **Pay attention to the things a text does *not* contain.**
    Thinking about what an author decides to leave out of a text is as revealing as considering what he or she includes. Painters talk about the blank space surrounding an object in a composition, and literary critics often do the same. Looking at the blank space, or what *isn't there*, casts the subject in relief, enabling you to see it more clearly. Consider which events a play summarizes through dialogue rather than staging; consider whose points of view are left out of a short story; consider why a poet writes without using rhyme. What are the possible motivations for and consequences of those decisions?

7. **Try lumping ideas together.**
    Sometimes two (or more) minor ideas can combine into one strong one. You might find linking a poem from Seamus Heaney on "Digging" (Chapter 22)—another form of manual labor that is used in this poem to discuss poetry—and this poem from Pinsky on sewing. You find it interesting that the two occupations seem so different, and they might represent two different responses to male "nature," one American and one Irish. By *lumping* your two separate observations together, you stumble on a complex and specific idea for an essay.

8. **Or try splitting ideas apart.**
    You might *split* an unwieldy idea into two or more by narrowing or qualifying it. Narrow a broad observation to just one character, scene, or metaphor. For example, in Flannery O'Connor's "A Good Man Is Hard to Find" (Chapter 15) you might notice that every scene in the story contains a moment of foreshadowing that the family will encounter the Misfit. This is a useful observation, but too broad for a short essay. If you instead concentrate on how descriptions of objects foreshadow the end (the car that looks like a hearse, for example), you will find it more manageable to gather evidence and make a clear argument.

9. **Look for patterns.**
   If an author repeats an image, word, metaphor, gesture, or setting, make note of it. A poem might use words with "sh" sounds in many lines, a story might include images of animals repeatedly, or a play might have two important scenes set in kitchens. Note these patterns and ask yourself how they are working: is the pattern emphasizing something, providing a sense of comfort, showing the ineffectuality of characters' attempts to change things? Repetition often works together with other aspects of the work and can serve as evidence that the author wanted to emphasize a point.

10. **Look for breaks in the pattern.**
    Once an author establishes a given pattern, he or she may also disrupt that pattern in a way that compels a reader's attention. If there is a part that seems quite different from the rest of the text, don't ignore it! You can safely assume that such a passage merits special consideration. If a poem is in perfect sonnet form, conforming exactly to the traditional meter and rhyme scheme *except for one line*, it is likely the author wanted this line to disrupt the pattern and create a sense of surprise. If two characters seem alike in almost every regard, look more closely to discover what *distinguishes* them. If a play contains two scenes in the same setting, with nearly the same action, pay attention to the *differences* in these scenes.

Developing an Argument for Robert Pinsky's "Shirt"

Follow your interests and expertise whenever possible.	Maybe your gender studies course has been discussing the treatment of women who work in sweatshops; a research paper could combine information about how clothes are made now with Pinsky's description of garment workers in the twentieth century. Or: Let's say your journalism course has been studying newspaper stories from the turn of the twentieth century. You could use your new knowledge about how stories were written to compare and contrast *The New York Times* coverage of the Triangle Shirtwaist Factory fire with the description of the fire in Pinsky's poem.
Acknowledge your gut reactions, but then analyze them.	This poem at first seems like a mishmash of depressing situations: the sweatshop workers, the girls jumping to their deaths in the Triangle fire, Scottish workers tricked into believing in a fake heritage, slaves growing cotton. All of this is disturbing when combined with the speaker's satisfaction with his new shirt—in the face of the workers' suffering, that satisfaction seems shallow. But these histories are not just tragic, because many of the people in the stories are behaving nobly (for example, the man who helped girls jump out of the burning building). Maybe Pinsky is saying that every object we own has this kind of tragic history or that our belongings' histories are also positive, because people like Irma are proud of doing good work even if they are exploited.
Choose a single aspect of the genre to examine.	Some of the more obvious aspects of this poem to write about are Pinsky's use of lists and his inclusion of stories and images from history. Those might lead to good essay topics, but it might be more interesting to look at a less obvious aspect of the poem, such as Pinsky's use of sound. For example, compare the hard, **iambic** words in the lists of objects with the longer, softer sounds of words in the stories.

continued

Pay attention to detail.	The speaker's comparison of the matching pattern to "a strict rhyme" seems to say that the speaker finds rhyme pleasing. But this poem does not rhyme. What might that seem to suggest? It would be going too far to argue that the speaker of "Shirt" dislikes the poem and is presenting it ironically, based on this one word. However, the observation of the word "rhyme" in an unrhymed poem is intriguing—maybe it could lead to looking for other kinds of rhyme, for instance combinations such as "the back, the yoke" and "sizing and facing."
Compare the text with other works you have read.	It might be useful to compare this poem with other poems by Robert Pinsky (see "Sonnet" in Chapter 23), other poems about work (see Seamus Heaney's "Digging," in Chapter 22), or other poems that closely examine a single object (William Carlos Williams's "The Red Wheelbarrow," Chapter 20, Wallace Stevens's "The Emperor of Ice-Cream," Chapter 20, or Jane Hirschfield's "Button," Chapter 20).
Pay attention to the things a text does not contain.	You might notice that the poem doesn't contain any information about the speaker except that the speaker has a new shirt. The poem offers no name, no history of the speaker, and no other people in the poem except those the speaker imagines sewing shirts. You might come up with some ideas about what effect this anonymity has on the poem: how would the poem be different if we knew the speaker's name, occupation, tastes and preferences, or other information?
Try lumping or splitting your ideas.	Let's say you noticed the repeated use of **jargon** (vocabulary specialized to a specific profession)— terms such as *yoke* and *navvy*—that most readers will not be familiar with. You are also struck by the detail about Scottish workers being tricked into believing a false story about their heritage. Neither of these observations on its own is very useful, so you try lumping them: both the jargon and the lies about heritage are instances of people being left out of some important knowledge because of language. Or you noticed that all the workers in the poem seem to be somehow exploited. Your first idea is to write a research paper exploring the situations of garment workers Pinsky mentions— Koreans and Malaysians, labor unions, the Triangle Factory, Scottish workers, and slaves in the American South. Then you realize this is too much even for a long essay. Instead, you decide to split these possibilities and focus on only one, the Triangle Factory workers' union.
Look for patterns.	You might notice that most of the poem is made up of sentences that are not gramatically complete but are just noun phrases. Even some long sentences, such as the second one (48 words), are just noun phrases, though they span multiple stanzas.
Look for breaks in the pattern.	The pattern of noun phrases breaks in the fourth stanza with "One hundred and forty-six died in the flames. . . ." The verb "died" jumps out and seems even more disturbing because it's the first verb in the poem.

MAKING CLAIMS: SUPPORTING A DEFENSIBLE THESIS

Once you have an idea for your paper, you will need to create a working thesis. A thesis is not the topic of the paper or the topic sentence to the entire paper. A **thesis** is your paper's controlling idea that you will support with claims and evidence throughout the body of the essay. Your interpretation needs to be set forth in a strong, arguable thesis. Two strategies may be useful in developing your thesis:

- **Do a focused freewrite.** For example, if you are interested in how Shakespeare uses the seasons symbolically, you might want to highlight all the lines in the sonnets you are addressing that have to do with spring, summer, fall, or winter. Then write a few sentences about your initial impressions of his handling of the seasons: Does he mention more than one season in a given poem, or does he limit each poem to one season? What details of the season does he incorporate? Is the season mentioned a principal subject of the poem or a subpoint?

- **Write an observation as a sentence.** Then ask yourself which part of the observation you wrote about is arguable. Try to imagine the opposite of your statement. If there is an opposite, you are well on your way to having a thesis. If not, you might try writing another of your impressions as a statement, and then see if there is an opposite or argument in your new sentence.

Often, you may find it difficult to know exactly what your argument is until you have made it in the course of writing the paper. That's perfectly fine. Although you want to give yourself the best start possible with a well-planned thesis, don't worry too

> ## "The muscle that makes the brain the strongest is reading. . . . When people talk, you'll catch when they're not telling the truth, because your muscles are ready to hear and you're listening."
>
> Conversation with Dagoberto Gilb

much about getting your thesis right the first time. Instead, look at the thesis in your first draft as a *working thesis,* one that serves as a diving board to launch you into a draft of your paper. At the end of the paper, chances are you'll have come to a more nuanced understanding of your topic. At that point, you'll want to revise your thesis so that it accurately reflects what you ended up saying in the paper itself. The defensible thesis that follows is taken from the paper at the end of this chapter. A thesis statement should be arguable, supportable, complex, and purpose-driven. The analysis of the thesis statement that follows shows how it meets these criteria. (For another example of how to create an arguable thesis, see the research paper on Langston Hughes in Chapter 5.)

1. **A thesis must be arguable.** A thesis is not just a statement of fact. Rather, a thesis is your argument, or to put it another way, your thesis presents a meaning you see in the story that not every other reader will necessarily see. Since your idea is not readily apparent to every reader, it is your job, over the course of the paper, to present claims that show why and how you have formed your interpretation. A good way to test whether you have a thesis statement rather than simply a statement of fact is to ask, "What is the opposite side of this statement? Is that opposite equally arguable?" If your statement has an arguable opposite, you have a good thesis. If not, you have either a statement of fact or a weak argument, one that is widely accepted as true without needing to be explored in a paper.

INEFFECTIVE THESIS

"Shirt" presents several historical examples of worker exploitation.

➡ *The statement is a fact. Although this particular sentence may function as a good topic sentence or a sentence in the introduction to the paper, it is not an effective thesis statement, because there is nothing about it that the writer has to defend.*

ARGUABLE THESIS

Despite the speaker's satisfaction with his shirt, the historical examples of worker exploitation and the way they are presented make "Shirt" more a lamentation than a celebration.

➡ *This statement takes a fact—that the poem uses historical examples—and offers a particular and original interpretation of those examples' significance. Note that the sentence is arguable: one could say that the speaker's admiration of the shirt and the way it commemorates diverse people makes the poem positive and celebratory.*

2. **A thesis must be supported by the text.**   In a good thesis, the writer puts forth a statement that is arguable. It may seem that the writer can say whatever he or she wants in a thesis, but, on the contrary, a thesis must be supportable. This support will come primarily from evidence you find in the text itself. You don't want to quote the text in a way that misrepresents it, simply to make your idea work. Instead, your thesis should be a reflection of your broad and open reading of the text. Although you must ultimately settle on a point of view in your thesis, you must reach that perspective through observation, not through fabrication.

INEFFECTIVE THESIS

The historical examples of worker exploitation in "Shirt" are Pinsky's call for reform in wages, building codes, and fair trade practices.

➡ *While the poem's historical examples may show instances of hazardous working conditions and unfair compensation, the poem neither focuses on these issues nor gives a call for reform. Therefore the text itself does not support this thesis statement. You would have to quote selectively and distort the emphasis of the poem—both practices to avoid—in order to make this thesis work.*

> "Writing is subversive. . . . It goes hand in hand with reading being the same way. . . . I don't mean subversive in that you would read something and then want to go out and cause a riot. I think of subversive in thinking about things you have never wanted to think about before." Conversation with Amy Tan

This thesis is also problematic because it claims that elements in the poem are "Pinsky's call for reform." The poem alone is not evidence enough for us to draw conclusions about Pinsky's personal views. And although a long research paper might provide an opportunity to examine a poet's worldview as expressed in several of his or her writings, an argument based on a single poem should say something about the poem itself.

SUPPORTABLE THESIS

> Despite the speaker's satisfaction with his shirt, the historical examples of worker exploitation and the way they are presented make "Shirt" more a lamentation than a celebration.

➡ *This statement points to two major areas of support: a close reading of the historical examples and the devices Pinsky uses to present them. Notice that the promise to examine "the way they are presented" sets up an argument that will be faithful to the poem.*

3. **A thesis must be complex, yet focused.** You may not perfect this aspect of your thesis until a later draft, but your goal is to write a thesis that points you toward a topic with enough material to fill a paper. However, the thesis should also be refined enough that the scope of your topic is manageable; that is, in a paper about Shakespeare's sonnets, you need not address the entire evolution of the sonnet form, just one aspect that interests you, such as Shakespeare's symbolic use of the seasons.

INEFFECTIVE THESIS

> The many workplace malpractices that contributed to the Triangle Shirtwaist Factory fire cannot be boiled down to a few lines of poetry, as Robert Pinsky attempts to do in "Shirt."

➡ *The focus of this argument is unclear. Is the main focus here the many historical details of the Triangle fire, which would require outside research on the writer's part? Or is it to look at Pinsky's handling of the fire in "Shirt"? A second problem is scope: if you have been assigned to write an argument about a poem without using outside research, then a thesis statement such as this one leads you in the wrong direction. Here, the writer would need to provide examples of "the many workplace malpractices," which would require research beyond the scope of the assignment.*

COMPLEX, YET FOCUSED THESIS

Despite the speaker's satisfaction with his shirt, the historical examples of worker exploitation and the way they are presented make "Shirt" more a lamentation than a celebration.

➡ *This thesis suggests that the writer will focus not only on the presentation of historical examples but also on ways in which a shallow reading of the poem might lead the reader to believe the shirt is an object of contentment.*

4. **A thesis must be purpose-driven and significant.**   If your thesis is doing its job well, it should lead the reader to answer the question "So what?" As the writer of the paper, you must answer this question over the course of your paper and perhaps more explicitly in its conclusion. But the seed of the answer to "So what?" or "Why is this significant?" lies in the thesis. A good thesis leads the writer (and the reader) to a particular perspective of an aspect of the text, or the writer's *oeuvre* (body of work), or literature in general.

INEFFECTIVE THESIS

The speaker of "Shirt" is so satisfied with his shirt, he celebrates it throughout the poem.

➡ *This thesis will simply reiterate an aspect of the poem that is apparent on a first read; therefore, it lacks a larger purpose.*

PURPOSE-DRIVEN THESIS

Despite the speaker's satisfaction with his shirt, the historical examples of worker exploitation and the way they are presented make "Shirt" more a lamentation than a celebration.

➡ *The purpose of this thesis is to arrive at a deeper understanding of the poem than what initially meets the eye. Further, illuminating the nuances of the poem may lead you to larger conclusions of meaning: that a material item is not worth the sacrifice of human life, for example, or that consumers blindly accept material goods without realizing the troubling backstory of how those goods came into being.*

USING LOGIC TO ORGANIZE YOUR ARGUMENT

While your thesis is the controlling idea of your paper, whether your analysis is persuasive or not depends on the logic you use to organize your argument. With an **inductive** approach, you present your claims, support them with evidence, and then draw your conclusion. The **deductive** approach begins by stating your thesis and then produces the reasons for taking that position, supported by evidence. Aristotle, in his study of rhetoric (the art of persuasion), claimed that effective arguments are based on three rhetorical appeals: *logos, pathos,* and *ethos.* You are likely to use all three appeals as you develop your argument.

- **Logos,** the logical appeal, makes your case through claims that are animated by the accumulation of hard facts such as statistics (for instance, the number of times a word is used in a poem), examples from the text itself, or the testimony of experts (scholars, if you are doing a researched argument).
- **Pathos,** the emotional appeal, finds common ground through shared emotion, negative or positive (for example, grief at the tragic death of innocent victims).
- **Ethos,** the ethical appeal, establishes a foundation of credibility on which to present your support for your claim, usually through your reasonable tone and your unbiased use of evidence.

To make your case, you need to understand your own assumptions so that you aren't tripped up by something that will derail your case. A persuasive argument is about what is *probable* as well as what is *true.* It is true that Pinsky uses historical references throughout his poem. It is probable that these references create a sense of historical injustice toward workers. But while Pinsky makes the case that the "shirt"

"Imagination to me is the closest thing we have to compassion."

Conversation with Amy Tan

the speaker is so proud of wearing has a bloody history, there are other more hidden assumptions that make the meaning of his text more complex, such as Pinsky's *probable* association of the craft of writing with the craft of shirt-making, his *probable* identification with the workers but his ambivalent affinity for the aristocratic poet George Herbert and the pride of craft the speaker claims Irma shares with him. Making an argument means turning over rocks, looking between the cracks, and making sure all the while that the reasons for your interpretation—and the claims you wish to make about the text—are explicitly clear and supported by evidence.

A typical approach to argument follows a basic deductive approach which might look something like this:

- **Introduction and thesis:** Present your thesis and show how it is significant; outline what you will present in your argument.
- **Body with evidence supporting claims:** Present your claims and connect your experiences, observations, and feelings to your claims; provide a point-by-point account for your position; include supporting evidence for each major claim. Each paragraph should stick to one topic that links to the preceding paragraph's point. It should include a topic sentence that describes the point of the evidence in that paragraph. This is the logic of your argument. (You may bring in counter arguments to show how your view is different and build credibility through a thoughtful, respectful, and open-minded tone. Your paper should be an invitation to the reader to think through the topic together.)
- **Conclusion:** Restate your thesis and place it in a larger context to show why you find it meaningful.

If you wish to try an approach that is more nuanced, you may wish to experiment with an inductive structure to your paper. You might also try returning to your thesis in an original way, using language that evokes and provides closure for your thesis without explicitly restating it, such as can be seen in the sample paper on "Shirt," the conclusion of which can be seen on page 62.

Logical Fallacies

In addition to helping you to avoid these errors in logic as you create your argument, knowing the way fallacies work will help you to read with a more critical eye.

Ad hominem **attack:** An attack on the character of a person rather than on the argument that person is making.

Bandwagon appeal: The assumption that an idea must be true if others think it is true.

Begging the question: The acceptance of an opinion as true simply because it has been stated.

Circular reasoning: The restatement of the claim or reasons as though they were evidence.

Either/or fallacy (false dichotomy): The false assumption that two ideas are mutually exclusive.

False cause (*post hoc* fallacy): The assertion that an action caused a particular situation simply because the action preceded the situation..

Hasty generalization: A conclusion that isn't justified by sufficient evidence.

Non sequitur: An example, reason, or conclusion that the evidence doesn't logically support.

Red herring: An argument that is irrelevant to the main critique and therefore merely a distraction.

Sweeping generalization: A statement that is too broad to be useful

SOURCE-BASED EVIDENCE: QUOTING, PARAPHRASING, SUMMARIZING, AND AVOIDING PLAGIARISM

Quotation, paraphrase, and summary are the evidence you use for your interpretation of a work, and learning how to use them correctly is a critical element to your establishing credibility and developing your own voice in your writing (for more coverage of quotation, paraphrase, and summary see the "Crafting Your Voice" features on pages 178, 604, and 1068, and the box on Source-Based Evidence earlier in this chapter).

> "Watch out for the word truth, especially if it's capitalized. It's an ambiguous and blurry and swirly thing, and as mature human beings moving into college I think you ought to watch out for the word. It doesn't mean don't use it, but watch out for it."
>
> Conversation with Tim O'Brien

It is common for all three to be employed in the same paper. You can expand on a quotation, paraphrase, or summary. You can interpret it. You can indicate what you believe the work implies. You can refer to a quotation, paraphrase, or summary. You can even disagree. Don't apologize by suggesting this is only your opinion ("it seems to me" or "in my opinion"). Make your case. Be confident that, if you have discovered something that is interesting to you, it will also be interesting to your reader.

- A paper with too few references to sources does not provide the evidence you need to support your case.
- A paper with too many references to sources prevents you from making your case, because it is overshadowed by the ideas of others.

Use Quotation, Summary, Paraphrase

- To support a point
- To present your source's point of view
- To disagree with your source
- To generalize from examples
- To reason through examples
- To make comparisons
- To distinguish fact from opinion
- To provide context

Formatting your quotations, paraphrases, or summaries properly makes the difference between being a credible writer and committing unintentional **plagiarism.** Here are guidelines that should help you avoid plagiarizing unintentionally. And note: Professors are adept at recognizing papers obtained via the Web—they've probably seen them before! However unintentional plagiarism may be, it carries the same penalties as deliberate plagiarism, and you will soon be found out if your plagiarism is of the deliberate kind. (For more on the perils of plagiarism in the Internet age see: www.nytimes.com/2010/08/02/education/02cheat.html.)

Two Kinds of Plagiarism

Intentional plagiarism	Intentional plagiarism occurs when you buy someone else's work or copy something from a source, usually word for word, and use it without quotation marks or acknowledgment of the source, as if it were your own words.
Unintentional plagiarism	Unintentional plagiarism can result from careless note taking, such as forgetting to put quotation marks around material you copy, cutting and pasting from the Web, and using material you have summarized or paraphrased but forgetting to tell readers the source of that material.

1. **Quotation:** *A word-for-word copy from an original source.* Direct quotation is especially useful when you are writing about literature, because the way a writer uses words is central to an understanding of the text. You will use quotations from the work you are analyzing as examples of the way a writer uses language. However, you can also use a quotation from another source. For example, you may wish to use quotation for a technical term that is not easily rephrased. Or you may want to use a quotation when the ideas are so vividly and beautifully expressed that you prefer to avoid paraphrase. However, a direct quotation doesn't stand on its own. You must expand on any quotation—or paraphrase or summary—that you include in your paper.

Avoiding Plagiarism in a Quotation

- Changing or omitting information from a direct quotation is a serious error. Use brackets [ ] around a word or words you insert in a quotation. Use three periods in succession (ellipses) to show that you have omitted something that was in the original quotation: "He turned green . . . but he went on [to steer the ship]."

2. **Paraphrase:** *Someone else's ideas in your own words.* When writing about literature, you may paraphrase some of the story line in order to get to the point you want to make. In research, paraphrase is most often used when you are referring to the work of critics and scholars. If you find that the language you are trying to put into your words is already broken down to its most simple form, or that the language is too perfectly worded

to change, you may want to use a quotation instead of a paraphrase. Don't paraphrase if you are not entirely sure you understand the original, or you risk misrepresenting its original meaning. One test of a good paraphrase is if you can restate what you are trying to paraphrase without looking at the source.

TIP

Avoiding Plagiarism in a Paraphrase

• A true paraphrase is not just a few different words, even if you feel the scholar has said something better than you could have said it yourself. *Your words* are the words that matter to your instructor. Just changing a few words—*even when you indicate the source of the paraphrase*—is still plagiarism. In a true paraphrase, the sentence structure is your own. The sentence doesn't sound like the author's writing; it sounds like yours.

3. **Summary:** *A condensation of the main idea or action that includes only the supporting details related directly to that main idea.* Unlike a paraphrase, where a concept or an action from a brief passage is explained in your own words, a summary lays out a long passage (such as an act in a play or a whole poem, story, play, or other work). A paper about a work of literature is not a plot summary. But a summary can set the stage for an analysis, providing your readers with enough information for them to understand your commentary. In a research paper, summary can also be used to provide examples of a variety of points of view on your topic. Make comparisons between two points of view; then summarize several sources to build on for your conclusion. (See Chapter 4 for a discussion of the summary paper.)

TIP

Avoiding Plagiarism in a Summary

• When you summarize material, you must include information on the source, or it will appear as if you are using someone else's ideas as your own. Omitting information in a summary that alters the source's meaning is also unacceptable. Offering an inaccurate interpretation of your source in a summary is not satisfactory either. If the source's words or meaning do not support your argument as fully as you might like, find another source that does.

USING QUOTATIONS AND AVOIDING PLAGIARISM

When you integrate your ideas with those of your sources, you will want to format your quotations so that they flow naturally into your sentences and build toward your conclusion. Where possible, keep your quotation brief—four or fewer lines for prose and no more than three for poetry or drama—since you will comment on the entire quotation in your paper. If you include a long quotation, make sure you deal with the entire quotation for your interpretation or analysis. Otherwise, the quotation overshadows your argument instead of supporting it. Introducing a direct quotation into a text can happen in two ways depending on whether it is short or long; each is formatted differently.

"I walked into a store once in San Francisco and the clerk said, 'Are you here for all the things that I don't have?' And I thought, Well, that's my whole relationship with my mother. . . . What a gorgeous line. I was thrilled to have it, to recognize that it was gold." Conversation with Amy Hempel

- A short quotation within a sentence is identified by quotation marks.
- A long quotation is formatted as an indented block of text separated from a sentence and does not use quotation marks.

1. **Refer to your source in an introductory phrase.**   Whether your quotation is short or long, however, you will need to introduce it with an introductory (*signal*) phrase. You need to identify the source and the author *before* the quotation. Include the author's full name (without *Mr., Miss, Mrs.,* or *Ms.*) the first time you quote from the source. Unless there is a long lapse between references to the source, the second time you quote from the same source you should use only the author's last name. Treat women and men equally when you cite them as authors, using the last name only for the second citation and no *Miss, Mrs.,* or *Ms.* Avoid the repetition of "the author says."

Example: As John Smith points out, "Your reader might want to see the source for his or her own research" (42).

Words to Use in an Introductory Phrase

according to	compares	establishes	proposes
acknowledges	complains	explains	proves
adds	concedes	expresses	refutes
admits	concludes	finds	rejects
agrees	considers	holds	remarks
argues	contends	implies	reports
asks	continues	insists	responds
asserts	declares	interprets	shows
believes	denies	maintains	speculates
charges	describes	notes	states
claims	disagrees	observes	suggests
comments	emphasizes	points out	warns

2. **Integrate a short quotation in a sentence and always use quotation marks.** Always put a short quotation into quotation marks. Failing to do so constitutes plagiarism. Keep your quotations to the point. The source material you quote as a reference should provide backup for the argument you have made. Avoid the temptation to use sources to make your arguments for you, however well the source is worded. References from outside sources, whether they are paraphrased or quoted, are *evidence* or *support* for your own arguments.

> **Example:** This new form of jazz became known as be-bop, a form of music that many critics see as "the revolt of young black musicians of the ghetto against the commercialization of 'swing music' of the time" (Lenz 274).

The following guidelines can help you cite the outside sources you use to support your argument.

- Use an introductory phrase to identify the source.
- If the quotation flows into the natural wording of the sentence, begin the quotation with a lowercase letter, whether or not the original is capitalized.
- If your introductory phrase ends with a comma, use a capital letter.
- Use quotation marks.
- When quoting poetry in a sentence, use the format of the lines in the poem and break the lines exactly as they appear in the poem with a slash (/) mark. Put a space before and after the slash.
- Place periods and commas inside the quotation marks.
- Semicolons, colons, and dashes are placed outside the quotation marks.
- Question marks and exclamation points are sometimes placed inside the quotation marks and sometimes placed outside. If the quotation is itself a question or exclamation, the question mark/exclamation point goes inside the quotation marks.
- If a quotation that ends with an exclamation point or a question mark is followed by a parenthetical page reference, retain the punctuation mark inside the quotation marks. If a quotation that ends with a period is followed by a parenthetical page reference, move the period to after the parentheses: ". . . !" (234)." or ". . . ?" (235). or ". . ." (236).
- Include page numbers for prose; line numbers for poems; act, scene, and line numbers for plays written in verse; and page numbers for plays written in prose.

A Short Quotation from a Poem

In the opening stanzas, the "Koreans or Malaysians / Gossip . . . over tea and noodles" (3–4), which affords a comforting view of community.

A Quotation Integrated with a Lowercase Letter

Similarly, before we read about the Scottish workers, the speaker describes the corners of the shirt pockets as "bar-tacked, . . . like a strict rhyme / Or a major chord" (28–29).

Period Inside Quotation Mark

First of all, "cull" means not just to select, but also, as *Merriam-Webster* defines it, "to reduce or control the size of (as a herd) by removal (as by hunting) of especially weaker animals; *also:* to hunt or kill (animals) as a means of population control."

3. **Set off a long quotation in a block, and don't use quotation marks.** Quotations in block format should be used sparingly, because they break up your discussion and can be distracting. If you find that you do not need to refer back to a long quote in several instances, consider using a paraphrase or more precise direct quotation to present the information. If you use a long quotation—one that is four lines or longer in poetry or five lines or longer in prose—to support your point, you must set the quote apart:

   - Use an introductory sentence to identify the source. Punctuate the end of the introductory sentence with a colon.
   - Do not use quotation marks.

- Indent each line of the quotation by one inch from the left margin (right margin is not indented).
- Capitalize the first word whether or not it is capitalized in the original when you are quoting prose.
- When quoting poetry, follow the line format and capitalization exactly as they appear in the poem.
- Double-space.
- Include a page number (or line numbers for a poem) in parentheses after the final punctuation in the quotation.

Block Quotation

As her spirit wanes, our heroine in Charlotte Perkins Gilman's "Yellow Wallpaper" gives her soliloquy:

> I lie down ever so much now. John says it is good for me, and to sleep all
> I can. Indeed he started the habit by making me lie down for an hour after
> each meal. It is a very bad habit, I am convinced, for you see, I don't sleep.
> And that cultivates deceit, for I don't tell them I'm awake—oh, no! The fact is
> I'm getting a little afraid of John. (226)

See Chapter 7, Writing about Fiction, Chapter 18, Writing about Poetry, and Chapter 31, Writing about Drama, for more examples of quoting from fiction, poetry, and drama.

USING PARAPHRASE AND AVOIDING PLAGIARISM

Using paraphrase in your paper is similar to using quotation, but there are some areas that require extra care. Make sure you have understood the text you are paraphrasing; your paraphrase must be true to the original meaning of the text. Don't guess at the meaning of a text by changing a few words and letting that stand as your own ideas. This is plagiarism. Even if one part of the text can be construed to support your argument, don't use it if that part doesn't represent the whole source accurately. Make it clear where your ideas end and the ideas of others begin. In addition to giving credit to others for their ideas, a clear transition from your own work to your source materials gives your writing credibility.

- Keep your paraphrase brief.
- Refer to the source in an introductory phrase.
- Include the page number in parentheses after the paraphrase.

In the examples that follow, note how student author Christine Keenan refers to her source by using paraphrase (and summary) and revising to avoid plagiarism. For the complete paper and the process she used to research and write it, see Chapter 5.

Original Source

In the guise of swing, jazz became domesticated in the 1930s. Earlier, jazz had been associated with gin mills and smoky cabarets, illegal substances (alcohol and drugs) and illicit sex.

Tucker, Mark, and Travis A. Jackson. "Jazz." *Grove Music Online*. Oxford UP, 2011. Web. 11 May 2011.

What's wrong? As seen in the highlighted sections, words have been changed, but essentially these are just synonyms arranged in sentences with identical structures. Underlined phrases are exact duplicates of the original source.

Unacceptable Paraphrase

As swing, jazz became more acceptable in the 1930s. Before that time, jazz had been associated with bars, clubs, drugs, and sex.

An even bigger problem is the lack of an in-text citation at the conclusion of the passage. No indication is made that this information came from an outside source. This is plagiarism.

What works? Notice how the author shifts the language to frame a reference to *behaviors* of the time: "drug use, drinking" instead of "alcohol and drugs." She stays true to the source, but must use her own sentence structure.

Paraphrase That Doesn't Plagiarize

Jazz itself was popular but connoted rebellion as it was typically associated with the hallmarks of dangerous behavior including drug use, drinking, and sex (Tucker).

USING SUMMARY AND AVOIDING PLAGIARISM

Summary and paraphrase are certainly related, but they are not the same thing. In general, paraphrase is used for a smaller portion of the original source, and your goal is to capture the spirit of the passage you are paraphrasing, without exactly copying the sentence structure or word choice. Summary is useful for relating a larger idea that you gained from a longer passage of text.

When you write a summary, introduce your source and identify the main ideas of the text. Break the discussion of those ideas into sections, and then write a sentence or two in your own words that captures each section.

Original Source

A figure who played a major role in popularizing swing in the mid-1930s was Benny

Goodman. Like Whiteman earlier and Elvis Presley a few decades later, Goodman was

a white musician who could successfully mediate between a black American musical

tradition and the large base of white listeners making up the majority population in the

USA. Wearing glasses and conservative suits—"looking like a high school science teacher,"   5

according to one observer (Stowe 45)—Goodman appeared to be an ordinary, respectable

white American. Musically he was anything but ordinary: a virtuoso clarinetist, a skilled

improviser who could solo "hot" on up temp numbers and "sweet" on ballads, and a

bandleader who demanded excellence from his players. . . . In the guise of swing, jazz

became domesticated in the 1930s. Earlier, jazz had been associated with gin mills and   10

smoky cabarets, illegal substances (alcohol and drugs) and illicit sex. Swing generally

enjoyed a more wholesome reputation, although some preached of the dangers it posed

to the morals of young people. This exuberant, extroverted music performed by well-dressed

ensembles and their clean-cut leaders entered middleclass households through everyday

appliances like the living-room Victrola and the kitchen radio. It reached a wider populace   15

as musicians transported it from the large urban centers into small towns and rural areas.

Criss-crossing North America by bus, car, and train, big bands played single night engagements in dance halls, ballrooms, theatres, hotels, night clubs, country, clubs,

military bases, and outdoor pavilions. They attracted hordes of teenagers who came to hear

20   the popular songs of the day and dance the jitterbug, lindy hop and Susie Q.

Tucker, Mark, and Travis A. Jackson. "Jazz." *Grove Music Online*. Oxford UP, 2011. Web.

     11 May 2011.

Unacceptable Summary

What's wrong?
In this summary you can see that the author tried (in some places) to create her own sentence structure, but did so by simply rearranging words (those which are underlined) found throughout the source (see lines 1, 6, 12, 13, and 15.) Even though it includes an in-text citation this would be considered plagiarism.

Someone who played a key role in popularizing swing was Benny Goodman. Anything but ordinary, this clean-cut bandleader and his well-dressed ensemble criss-crossed North America, attracting hordes of teenagers everywhere they went, ultimately entering the households of the middleclass by way of their Victrolas and kitchen radios (Tucker).

Summary without Plagiarizing

What works?
Here the author retains the over-all sense of the source by using her own phrasing. Use of the same words is limited to key terms—"swing"; "jazz"; "Benny Good-man"; "middle class"—which *should* appear in the summary.

Swing, which became the popular dance music in more reputable venues than just bars and clubs, was usually performed by big bands under the direction of white leaders like Benny Goodman and Glenn Miller. Thus, jazz became mainstream and middle class, unlike the "hot jazz" of the 20s (Tucker).

Paraphrase	Summary
A relatively short passage	*A passage of any length*
Covers every point in the passage	*Condenses main idea and support*
Takes up points consecutively	*Changes order when necessary*
Includes no interpretation	*Explains point of passage*

A STUDENT PAPER: A RESPONSE TO ROBERT PINSKY'S "SHIRT"

The following student paper develops an argument about Robert Pinsky's "Shirt." Note how the student uses supporting examples from the text and formats them to avoid plagiarism.

Garcia 1

Robert Garcia

Professor Anderson

English 180

15 February 2011

Lamentation, Not Celebration: Tracing the Dark Side of Robert Pinsky's "Shirt"

At first read, Robert Pinsky's poem "Shirt" seems like a democratic celebration of how diverse people from diverse time periods are linked together. The poem accordingly ends on what seems to be a positive note, assuring the reader that the shirt has "satisfied" the speaker (line 43). However, the moments of connection and positive feeling belie the sinister elements that have worked together to create this material product. Despite the speaker's satisfaction with his shirt, the historical examples of worker exploitation and the way they are presented make "Shirt" more a lamentation than a celebration.

Perhaps the clearest way "Shirt" establishes itself as a lamentation is in the subject matter: Pinsky consistently selects historical instances that exemplify class exploitation and oppression. In the opening stanzas, the "Koreans or Malaysians / Gossip . . . over tea and noodles" (3-4), which affords a comforting view of community. But even this romanticized image does not stop the speaker from explicitly stating that the workers are in a sweatshop. Indeed, their gossip turns

Include a line number for every quotation from a poem; a work of fiction would use a page number; a work of drama would include act and scene numbers as well as line numbers if the play is written in verse. Note the word "line" is used at the first quotation from a poem; numbers alone are used thereafter. Note also that the line reference comes before the period.

Thesis

Topic 1: subject matter

The slash mark with a space on either side identifies the line break. Ellipses indicate words left out of the quotation.

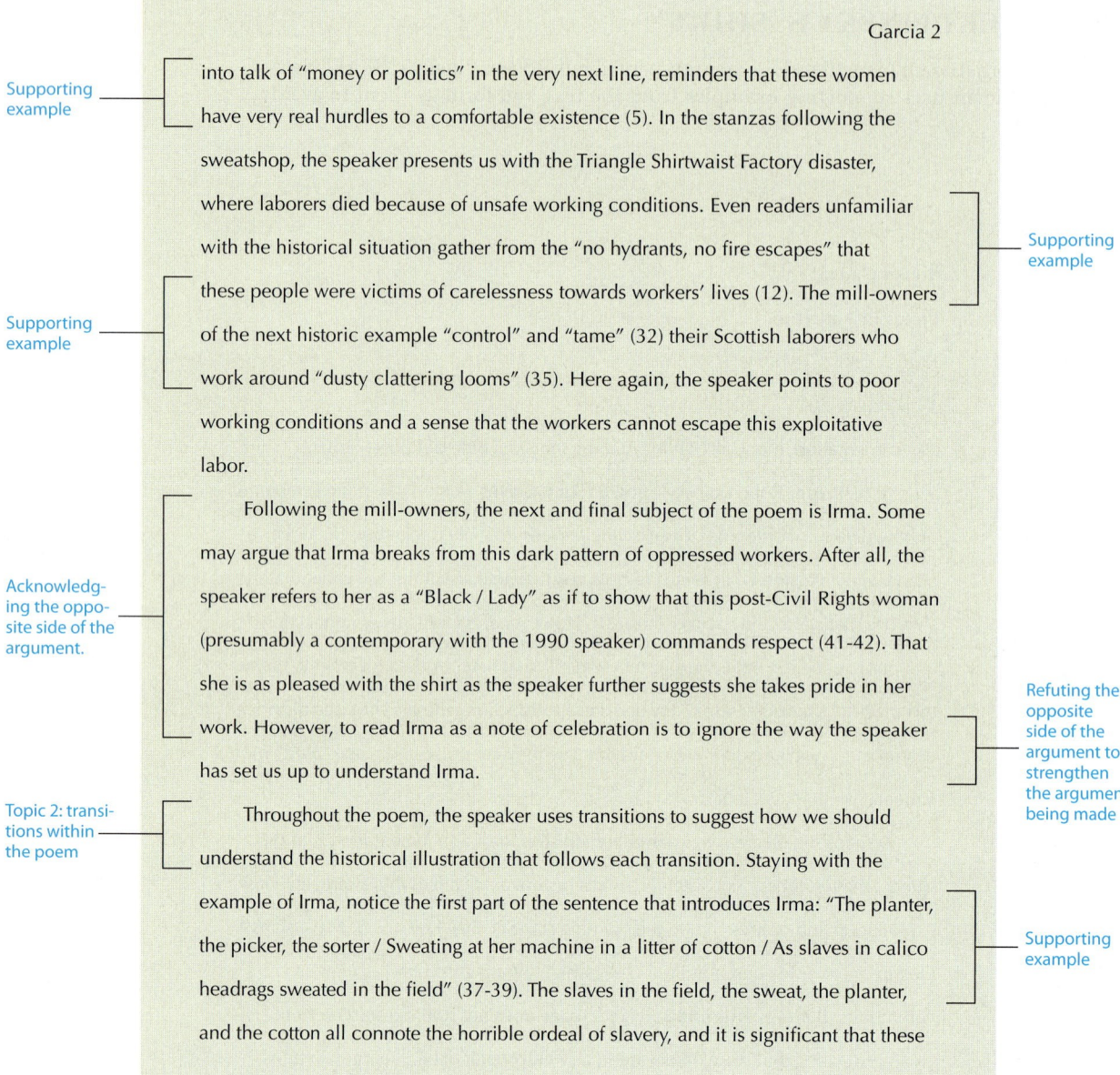

Garcia 2

Supporting example

into talk of "money or politics" in the very next line, reminders that these women have very real hurdles to a comfortable existence (5). In the stanzas following the sweatshop, the speaker presents us with the Triangle Shirtwaist Factory disaster, where laborers died because of unsafe working conditions. Even readers unfamiliar with the historical situation gather from the "no hydrants, no fire escapes" that

Supporting example

these people were victims of carelessness towards workers' lives (12). The mill-owners of the next historic example "control" and "tame" (32) their Scottish laborers who work around "dusty clattering looms" (35). Here again, the speaker points to poor working conditions and a sense that the workers cannot escape this exploitative labor.

Supporting example

Acknowledging the opposite side of the argument.

Following the mill-owners, the next and final subject of the poem is Irma. Some may argue that Irma breaks from this dark pattern of oppressed workers. After all, the speaker refers to her as a "Black / Lady" as if to show that this post-Civil Rights woman (presumably a contemporary with the 1990 speaker) commands respect (41-42). That she is as pleased with the shirt as the speaker further suggests she takes pride in her work. However, to read Irma as a note of celebration is to ignore the way the speaker has set us up to understand Irma.

Refuting the opposite side of the argument to strengthen the argument being made

Topic 2: transitions within the poem

Throughout the poem, the speaker uses transitions to suggest how we should understand the historical illustration that follows each transition. Staying with the example of Irma, notice the first part of the sentence that introduces Irma: "The planter, the picker, the sorter / Sweating at her machine in a litter of cotton / As slaves in calico headrags sweated in the field" (37-39). The slaves in the field, the sweat, the planter, and the cotton all connote the horrible ordeal of slavery, and it is significant that these

Supporting example

images are connected to Irma by a colon. Pinsky could have used a period at the end of line 39, but the choice of a colon signals that what came before it—the slavery images—is linked to what comes after it: Irma. In other words, the reader is set up to understand Irma as one in a long line of exploited workers, and although her more recent historical context may suggest her conditions are better than her ancestors', she is nonetheless part of something lamentable.

Transitions highlight lamentable circumstances elsewhere in the poem. Moving from the sweatshop to the Triangle Factory, the speaker presents a list that includes "the presser, the cutter, / The wringer, the mangle," words that, besides denoting equipment used in producing clothing, make the reader cringe at the brutal and violent connotations (7-8). "Mangle" especially seems to foreshadow the man dropping girls down from the "masonry wall" to the street below, so that even the romance of one of the girls stopping to kiss the helping man doesn't blind us to the brutality of the moment (16). Similarly, before we read about the Scottish workers, the speaker describes the corners of the shirt pockets as "bar-tacked, . . . like a strict rhyme / Or a major chord" (28-29). The speaker notes these details in praise of his shirt, but when we think about how these images suggest something held firmly in place—or held in check, a play on the idea of "checks" in line 30—directly before a story of Scottish workers being controlled and tamed, they suddenly underscore how oppressed these workers are. Even the major chord is restricted to one definition of the exact notes in the exact chord, forced into harmony by its player.

The final stanzas, however, seem to depart from this pattern of horrific oppression and arrive at a sense of satisfaction. Yet no sooner has the speaker assured us

Supporting example

Supporting example

Supporting example

Garcia 4

that the shirt's "color and fit / And feel and its clean smell have satisfied / Both [Irma] and me" than he adds, "We have culled its cost and quality / Down to the buttons of simulated bone" (42-45). The diction here is especially significant. First of all, "cull" means not just to select but also, as *Merriam-Webster* defines it, "to reduce or control the size of (as a herd) by removal (as by hunting) of especially weaker animals; *also* : to hunt or kill (animals) as a means of population control." Sweatshops, the Triangle Factory, Scottish workers, American slaves—each historic example comes to mind as a group of people whose individuals counted little to those overseeing them, their lives valuable to those masters only in the goods they produced. Thus, although it is cost and quality that are "culled" in line 44, the word itself seems to refer back to the horrors of the poem. Further, "cull" is in close proximity to "cost" as well as "bone." Literally, the speaker is referring to the shirt. But reading with a sensitivity to the connotations of these words, we see the simulated bone of the buttons not merely as a description but as a reminder of the human bones that have been sacrificed to labor; the "cost" of the shirt is not monetary, but the cost of human life itself.

Under the speaker's admiration of his shirt, then, a cold current flows. Through subject matter, transitions, and diction, Pinsky creates a sort of second speaker, this one quietly, though decidedly, lamenting the brutalities of history that continue up through Irma and even to the present-day sweatshop laborers. And though the connection is never explicitly made, perhaps the greatest lament of the poem is that these instances of human suffering and death have occurred in service of a material object whose qualities dazzle us from start to finish: the shirt.

Marginal annotations:

Topic 3: Diction

Supporting example

Recap of three main points

Conclusion Restatement of thesis

Taking the interpretation one step farther to leave the reader with something to ponder

Garcia 5

Works Cited

"Cull." *Merriam-Webster Online Dictionary*. Merriam-Webster, 2011. Web.

12 February 2011.

Pinsky, Robert. "Shirt." *Literature: Craft and Voice*. Ed. Nicholas Delbanco and Alan

Cheuse. 2nd ed. New York: McGraw, 2013. 35. Print.

The Works Cited begins a new page

4 Writing across the Curriculum

WHOSE woods these are I think I know.
His house is in the village though;
He will not see me stopping here
To watch his woods fill up with snow.

My little horse must think it queer
To stop without a farmhouse near
Between the woods and frozen lake
The darkest evening of the year.

He gives his harness bells a shake
To ask if there is some mistake.
The only other sound's the sweep
Of easy wind and downy flake.

The woods are lovely, dark and deep,
But I have promises to keep,
And miles to go before I sleep,
And miles to go before I sleep.

—*"Stopping by Woods on a Snowy
Evening" by Robert Frost*

". . . while the scene's first impression is one of a quaint New England night . . . the cold and dark nature imagery tells another story of death and the temptation to remain in the presence of death. By bringing these two types of imagery together in one poem, Frost perhaps suggests that death is always near, even when we think we are looking at a vivid scene of comfort."

—from an essay by student
Renee Knox

WRITE TO LEARN ACROSS THE CURRICULUM

THE ability to summarize, analyze, synthesize, and critique information is essential for college writing. In almost all your college courses, you will be asked to respond to something you have read, whether it be a piece of literature, a textbook, a critical article or book, a primary source, a blog, or a Web site. When you write in any of your courses across the curriculum—from engineering to history—you will need to think through an issue and demonstrate your understanding of its main points. Robert Frost said, "Thinking isn't agreeing or disagreeing. That's voting." While you may be asked to present your case for or against a proposal for many courses, the point here is that thinking through an issue from a variety of perspectives is a learning process. You'll find sources in a library, in your bookstore, or on the Internet; but whatever the particular writing assignment, you will use writing to *show that you understand* the text and *explain* it clearly, and you will have to *develop your own ideas* about how it works and *persuade* your reader that your interpretation is correct. The distillation of your thoughts in the writing process is what it means to "write to learn." And you will do this whether you are writing an essay exam (see the quotation on p. 65 and the essay on p. 93) or an analysis, and whether you are writing for college or in any area of your life.

As you interpret a work of literature, you will use critical thinking skills—from summary to analysis, synthesis, and critique—that require you to look more carefully at how the text has been put together and whether the text effectively accomplishes its purpose. These skills prepare you for writing across the curriculum. You will use your critical thinking skills in a summary to determine which details to leave out and which ones to keep, or in a research paper when you synthesize your research into your presentation. The interpretations that you create in writing about literature employ a number of strategic skills that will prepare you to write throughout your college career:

- Summary
- Analysis
- Synthesis
- Critique

USE SUMMARY TO DISTILL A TEXT

You use summary across the curriculum. It allows you to condense an entire passage or text, and a summary may be a specific part of another paper (where it is a necessary reference point for your readers to understand your analysis) or the purpose of your paper as a whole (as when you are asked to write a summary of a particular article). You will use a summary whenever you need to communicate the content of a text and represent the ideas behind any article or complex essay accurately. Summary is a mainstay of academic writing, and you will find yourself using it in a variety of ways in all your courses, including some of these:

- To summarize a source in order to critique it (as you would in a book review)
- To summarize several sources to reveal the body of knowledge on a particular topic (as in a report)
- To summarize the evidence you have compiled in an argument
- To summarize a critical perspective you are using to analyze a work

The goal of a summary paper (or **précis** or **abstract**) is to boil down into a few of your own words a whole text, without using your opinion or commentary. Although you do have to decide what to include and what to leave out, your presentation should strive to be fair-minded and neutral. The **summary paper** demonstrates to your instructor that you understand the main trajectory of action or thought in a reading.

Throughout this text, we employ summary to enhance learning, to help you to make sure you have understood what has happened in a reading. The summary, therefore, needs to show that you have understood the overarching idea of what you've read.

> ## "The world exists in a condition of a saturated presence and meaning and being. . . . And sometimes it's difficult just to rescue . . . a little moment's clarity out of that." Conversation with Li-Young Lee

Begin by distilling the text to its single most compelling issue. Unlike a paraphrase, which is something said in another way, a summary begins with a sentence that is a general condensation of all the various things that were said and done in a text. (See also the box on Source-Based Evidence: Quotation vs. Paraphrase vs. Summary on page 36 in Chapter 3.)

Your interaction with the text—the notes and annotations you have made while reading—will guide you as you identify how the story, play, or poem unfolds. You may find it useful to break the text into parts and write down each part's main idea. Use your notes or annotations to help you to understand the text's twists and turns, its patterns and its allusions, and to explain comprehensively, concisely, and coherently how the main idea is supported by the entire reading. The following précis is of Herman Melville's "Bartleby, the Scrivener." **You can read "Bartleby" at connect.mcgraw-hill.com.**

TIP

Writing a Summary: Just the Facts

- Be neutral; don't include your opinion.
- Begin with a summary sentence of the whole text.
- Be concise; do not paraphrase the whole text.
- Explain how the elements in the reading work with the main idea.
- Look for repetitions and variations that provide insight into the main idea of the text.
- Check the text's context: When was it written? What form does it use?

A STUDENT PAPER: A SUMMARY OF HERMAN MELVILLE'S "BARTLEBY, THE SCRIVENER"

Solis 1

Lily Solis

Professor Bennett

Composition 102

30 September 2011

Précis of "Bartleby, the Scrivener"

Herman Melville's short story "Bartleby, the Scrivener" presents a businessman narrator who hires an unusual employee named Bartleby, and who consequently struggles with what to do about Bartleby's behavior. The first-person narrator introduces himself as an elderly gentleman who owns a law office. His three employees—Turkey, Nippers, and Ginger Nut—are so temperamental that the narrator is forced to hire a fourth man to fill in the gaps of their work. He hires Bartleby, who at first works industriously. However, when the narrator asks him to fulfill tasks beyond copying, Bartleby consistently replies, "I would prefer not to." This pattern continues, with the narrator becoming more annoyed at Bartleby's refusals and yet feeling unwilling to turn him out. When the narrator discovers that Bartleby is living at the office, he makes an attempt at befriending Bartleby, which Bartleby evades with his usual "prefer not to" responses. Soon Bartleby stops working entirely, because of his damaged eyesight, but even when his eyes improve, Bartleby does nothing but stand all day in the office. The narrator gives Bartleby a friendly ultimatum that he must leave in six days. However, at the end of six days, Bartleby is still there, and the narrator—out of Christian charity—decides to let him remain. Still, Bartleby's

[Marginal annotations:]

Begins with a neutral statement that presents the basis for all plot elements in the story.

Important element identified specifically.

Concise statements introduce major characters and define their roles in the story.

Concise, neutral statements explain the sequence of action.

Solis 3

presence is a nuisance, and the narrator at last decides to move his offices to another building. He receives complaints from the new tenants, asking him to remove the man he left behind. The narrator returns to the old building and invites Bartleby to come to the narrator's private home and live there, but Bartleby refuses. A short time later, the narrator learns that Bartleby has been taken to prison as a vagrant. Although the narrator makes provisions for Bartleby to be well fed in prison, Bartleby refuses to eat, and the narrator visits one day to find him dead. The narrator concludes the story by offering a rumor that Bartleby previously worked in a Dead Letter Office.

Gives story's resolution without offering reader's interpretation.

Solis 3

Work Cited

Melville, Herman. "Bartleby, the Scrivener." *Literature: Craft and Voice*. Ed. Nicholas Delbanco and Alan Cheuse. 2nd ed. New York: McGraw, 2013. Web. 22 Sept. 2011.

USE ANALYSIS TO EXAMINE HOW THE PARTS CONTRIBUTE TO THE WHOLE

Like summary, analysis is critical to college writing. In an analysis, you break the selection down into its parts and examine how the parts of a work contribute to the whole. Whether you are writing about irony in Flannery O'Connor or the impact of gunpowder on warfare, your analysis will look at how your source has put together its case, and you will use the source as evidence for your analysis. Your thesis will point specifically to the scope of your analysis. Possible analyses include:

- An explication of several aspects of how language is used—most often line by line—to point out the connotations and denotations of words as well as the reinforcing images that are used (see the following paper on William Blake's "The Garden of Love").
- An analysis of one aspect of a specific text, such as dialect in Gish Jen's "Who's Irish?" (Chapter 9) or parallelism in "The Museum of Stones" by Carolyn Forché (Chapter 17).
- A card report on the various elements of a story, generally only what you can fit on a 5-by 8-inch index card (see the sample card report on pages 76–79).

Explication

An **explication** is a kind of analysis that shows how words, images, or other textual elements relate to one another and how these relationships make the meaning of the text clearer. Beyond literary study, an explication is a close reading of any text whereby the goal is to logically analyze details within the text to uncover deeper meanings or contradictions. According to *Merriam-Webster,* the definition of *explicate* is "to give a detailed explanation of" or "to develop the implications of; analyze logically." An

> ### "Life comes down to some small object and looks at it and knows itself differently through looking at the object, whether it's a button or a cup or a door knob . . . and transform[s] itself and transform[s] the world and give[s] you a way to talk about things."
>
> Conversation with Jane Hirshfield

explication paper does both of these things, because it *gives a detailed explanation of* the devices present in order to *analyze logically* the work in question. In other words, the goal of an explication is to unpack the elements of a poem, short passage of fiction or drama, or other text. The thesis statement in an explication is usually a summary of the central idea that all the devices combine to create.

Many explications take a line-by-line or sentence-by-sentence approach. Others organize the paper according to a few elements of craft that seem most meaningful to the work. However you decide to tailor your paper, remember that an explication should touch on more than one element. When explicating fiction or drama, pay attention to character, diction, and tone, and how those connect with larger thematic concerns. In the following paper on a poem, you will see an explanation of the significance of such elements as rhyme, meter, diction, simile, metaphor, symbol, imagery, tone, and allusion. Although the author doesn't exactly move line by line through the poem, she does start where the poem starts and walks through it to the end. She organizes her paper in light of the shift (the dramatic turn that signals a change in the way the speaker sees and feels about the situation), which she identifies in the poem and addresses in the introduction. Notice, too, that her thesis states the sum total of the devices explicated: an overall shift from an innocent state to a repressed state.

The Garden of Love (1794)
William Blake (1757–1827)

I went to the Garden of Love,
And saw what I never had seen:
A Chapel was built in the midst,
Where I used to play on the green.

5   And the gates of this Chapel were shut,
And "Thou shalt not" writ over the door;
So I turn'd to the Garden of Love
That so many sweet flowers bore;

And I saw it was filled with graves
10 And tomb-stones where flowers should be;
And Priests in black gowns were walking
    their rounds,
And binding with briars my joys & desires.

For a brief biography of William Blake, see Chapter 22.

A STUDENT PAPER: AN EXPLICATION
OF WILLIAM BLAKE'S "THE GARDEN OF LOVE"

Brown 1

Deborah Brown

Dr. Cranford

English 200

16 September 2011

Repression and the Church: Understanding Blake's "The Garden of Love"

William Blake's "The Garden of Love" is seemingly appropriate for either *Songs of Innocence* or *Songs of Experience,* because it contains elements of both states. In publishing the poem in the latter, however, Blake suggests that beneath the singsong, child-like quality is a serious message. Although the poem begins with colorful imagery and nursery-rhyme rhythm, there is a marked shift as it progresses with an increasingly dark setting and disrupted meter. This shift is triggered by the appearance of a chapel. It is only when considering how this shift occurs that we can fully appreciate how "The Garden of Love" inverts the idea of the church as good, aligning it instead with oppression.

At the beginning of the poem, several poetic factors work together to create the impression of youthfulness, and therefore a sense of innocence. The meter consists of an iamb followed by two anapestic feet, which makes a beat reminiscent of a nursery rhyme recitation. This nursery rhyme quality is supported by the rhyme scheme which, until the last stanza, follows a regular pattern of abcb. In addition to the structure of the poem, Blake's diction contributes to the child-like voice of the speaker, since he selects simple words that are, for the most part, monosyllabic. At the most, the words

Title introduces the poem and poet.

Thesis statement that gives the central idea conveyed by the elements to be explicated.

Brown 2

Discusses how each poetic device—meter, rhyme, diction, simile, and imagery—contributes to theme of innocence.

First line reference includes the word *lines*; numbers only after.

Specific support from the poem.

contain two syllables, the longest being "garden" (lines 1, 7), "chapel" (3, 5), and "tombstones" (10). Furthermore, the syntax follows in accord with the simplicity of the diction, as the words are organized in a straightforward, sentence-like manner. The tone comes across as particularly child-like when we consider that seven of the twelve lines in this poem begin with "And," which creates the effect of a child who is incapable of forming complex sentences and so advances his story by adding onto the same sentence time and again. The absence of simile and metaphor also lends a lack of complexity to the speaker (although this is certainly not to say that there is a lack of complexity in the poem). In fact, the seeming simplicity of the poem is furthered by the way in which the speaker offers observations rather than reflections. This is set up in the second line when the speaker says, "And saw what I never had seen." The rest of the poem, then, is merely a description of the scene without offering any interpretation. The innocence of the speaker is also established through the imagery at the beginning of the poem. Blake describes the Garden of Love as full of "so many sweet flowers" (8), and he also mentions "the green" (4). These images suggest growth and spring, both of which connote youth. Green especially holds connotations of innocence or a lack of maturity, since both wood that is not yet mature and unripened fruit are green.

Topic sentences Identify the shift in the poem.

All these elements that are associated with childhood and innocence are found at the beginning of the poem. In the second stanza, there is a change in meter with the line "And the gates of the Chapel were shut" (5). Here, just before the first hint of repression found in the word "shut," Blake has omitted the iamb and included three anapests instead of two. Although the meter is still predominantly anapestic, Blake

Brown 3

continues to vary it, as in lines 11 and 12 in which he alternates an iamb with an

anapest and further deviates from his original form by changing from the abcb

end rhyme scheme to internal rhyme: "And binding with *briars* my joys & *desires*"

emphasis added (12). This altered structure is significant, because it indicates that

something has changed from the beginning of the poem. To understand this shift, we

must first note where the disruptions occur.

> Discusses how meter contributes to shift identified in topic sentence.

The first major disruption of meter comes when Blake writes, "And 'Thou shalt

not' writ over the door" (6). Because there are so many monosyllabic words, it is

ambiguous where the stresses should lie, yet it is clearly impossible to read this as

strictly anapestic. The result is that "Thou shalt not" is emphasized, a message that

contrasts the carefree state of "play" (4) in the first stanza. Blake again disrupts the

meter when he writes, "And I saw it was filled with graves" (9), which draws attention

to the word "graves." Here, too, Blake creates a stark contrast between the image of

a garden full of life and the image of a garden filled with graves. Furthermore, the

change in the color of Blake's imagery from the first stanza to the last represents a loss

of the vibrant nature of youth. What began as a green is now filled with the bleak,

monochromatic image of "tombstones where flowers should be" (10) while the priests

add to the gloom of the scene by wearing "black gowns" (11). Although all these

changes are important to note, the key to understanding this poem can be found in

the source that sparked this change of setting: a Chapel.

> Specific support from the poem.

The Chapel in the poem acts as a symbol, a metonymical device that can be

taken as a representative of the church as an institution. The shut doors and the phrase

"Thou shalt not" written over them suggest that the Chapel represents repression.

> Discusses symbol.

Brown 4

Blake writes, "A Chapel was built in the [garden's] midst, / Where I used to play on the green" (3-4), furthering the Chapel—a symbol of religion—as a repressive force by implying that it impedes playing and all the carefree ways that accompany playing. The Priests, who enter the scene with the Chapel, enforce the repression dictated by the church, because they are the ones who end up "binding with briars [the speaker's] joys & desires" (12). Blake's choice of the word "binding" is significant, because it implies passivity and restraint; the same qualities are evoked in the idea of routine found in the image of the priests "walking their rounds" (11).

Topic sentence moves discussion towards the thesis. — In addition to the Chapel and the Priests, there are several religious elements that suggest that this poem is making a statement about the church. To begin with, the Garden of Love is in many ways reminiscent of the Garden of Eden. Both house abundant growth and are originally places of innocence. However, each contains something forbidden that brings a loss of innocence and death. In Eden, it was the forbidden fruit from the Tree of Knowledge that led to sin and ultimately death. The forbidden part in the Garden of Love is the implication of "Thou shalt not." The *Further explication of symbol.*

Identifies allusion. — appearance of this forbidding message—a statement of repression—is accompanied by an appearance of graves (representative of death) instead of flowers (representative of growth and life). A second religious element in the poem is the phrase "Thou shalt not," which alludes to the Bible and, more specifically, the Ten Commandments. These commandments are statements of what people should not do; thus, the phrase automatically echoes with connotations of restraint and repression. Another element reminiscent of religion is Blake's use of capitalization. Just as "He" is capitalized as a sign of respect when used in reference to God, so, too, does Blake capitalize only

Explains significance of Biblical allusions; ties elements previously discussed to thesis.

Brown 5

those words that are related to religion: Garden of Love, Chapel, and Priests. The poem becomes ironic when one considers that it is the Chapel and the Priests, the very objects that the capitalization suggests we should revere, that bring about the change from a place of life and play to a place of restraint and death. It is through these religious allusions that Blake allows the reader to connect the repressive, restrictive setting wrought by the appearance of a Chapel to the church at large as an institution.

The diction, imagery, symbols, and allusions used in "The Garden of Love" work together to create a contrast between the energy and youthfulness of innocence found in the first stanza and the repression and death that is increasingly present after the chapel's appearance. In this way, Blake shows that the church turns happy innocence into dark forbidding, creating in a mere twelve lines of poetry a statement against the repressive nature of the church in his time.

Reviews key points of the discussion; restatement and refinement of thesis.

Brown 6

Work Cited

Blake, William. "The Garden of Love." *Literature: Craft and Voice.* Ed. Nicholas Delbanco and Alan Cheuse. 2nd ed. New York: McGraw, 2013. 71. Print.

Card Report

A card report asks you to represent in a condensed space the various elements of a story. Most instructors require that your report not exceed the amount of information you can fit on a 5- by 8- inch note card, and therefore you must make every word count. As you closely examine the pieces of the story, you will naturally forge a deeper understanding of it, and very likely a new opinion of the work as a whole. Card reports help you to keep track of what you have read and can be an invaluable tool in preparing for exams.

In the following card report, our student, Tessa Harville, was instructed to include the list of information that appears below:

1. Title of the story and date of publication
2. Author's name, dates of birth and death, and the nationality or region (if applicable) with which he or she is associated.
3. The name and a brief description of the main character, especially important personality traits
4. Additional characters who play important roles and their major traits
5. The setting, including time and place
6. The type of narration (point of view)
7. A summary of the story's major events in the order in which they occur
8. The tone or voice in which the author relates the story
9. The overall style of the work, including (if space allows) short quotes that exemplify the style
10. A brief analysis of irony in the story
11. The theme of the story
12. The major symbols in the story and a brief explanation of what you think each means
13. A critique of the story in which you give your evaluation or opinion of the story

As you look at the following model, note the amount of thought and effort that the student put into refining the language in the "Critique" portion. Although it is brief, your critique should reflect the amount of thought you might put into a three-page paper.

A STUDENT CARD REPORT ON FLANNERY O'CONNOR'S "A GOOD MAN IS HARD TO FIND"

Front of Card

Tessa Harville

English 101, Section 2

Title: "A Good Man Is Hard to Find" (1955)

Author: Flannery O'Connor, 1925–1964, American, Southern writer

Main Character: The grandmother, who lives with her son's family and refuses to be ignored. She considers herself a lady but is stubborn, talkative, and insists on her own way.

Other Characters: Bailey, the father of the family, who is grumpy and sullen; Bailey's unnamed wife, who quietly tends the children and is ineffectual; John Wesley and June Star, Bailey's son and daughter, who are typical children that bluntly speak their minds and are excited by adventure; and The Misfit, an escaped murderer who philosophizes with the grandmother.

Setting: Georgia, presumably around the 1950s, when the story was written. Much of the story recounts a car trip, so the scenery changes.

Narration: Third-person omniscient; primarily follows grandmother.

Summary: 1. The grandmother tries to convince Bailey to take the family to Tennessee for vacation, rather than Florida, and uses the newspaper article she reads about The Misfit as a reason not to travel toward Florida. 2. The family leaves for Florida. The car trip is full of bickering; a restaurant stop, where the grandmother talks with the owners about how bad people have become. 3. Back on the road, the grandmother convinces Bailey to take a detour so she can see a plantation she visited years ago. 4. The grandmother's cat, which she snuck into the car, causes an accident while they are on a deserted road looking for the plantation. 5. Three men arrive to help the family. The grandmother recognizes one as The Misfit, and as a result, he has his men shoot the family, one by one. The grandmother is shot last, after a moment of connection with The Misfit in which she sees him as "one of [her] own children" (501).

Tone/Voice: The tone is deadpan, with no comments from the narrator. This makes for a reportorial voice with the precision of an acute observer.

Back of Card

Style: The sentences are straightforward and often declarative: "The grandmother didn't want to go to Florida" (493). The description is vivid but concise: "The car raced roughly along in a swirl of pink dust" (497).

Irony: Becomes most apparent after reading the story and looking back, making it dramatic irony. The family does not know to heed the grandmother's preposterous warning about The Misfit before taking the vacation, but the reader knows she is right. The dramatic irony is aided by the large amount of foreshadowing, such as the grandma's remembering the plantation outside of "Toombsboro" (496). The grandmother's behavior is at times ironic—she is concerned with being a lady but talks too much; she says people should be more respectful but then uses biased language as she ogles a "pickaninny" (494). The way she causes her own trouble is ironic.

Theme: A feeling of connection can transcend the shocking reality of life's brutality.

Symbols: The grandmother could symbolize the South: her vanity and pretense to being a lady cause a violent downfall. The family burial ground with "five or six graves" seen from the car is both a foreshadowing tool and symbolic of the family's impending death (495).

Critique: Although the story relies on wild coincidence, elements including highly believable characters, perfectly placed description, and economic movement of the plot make this story gripping and a representation of life with all its vanity, surprises, and connections.

USE SYNTHESIS TO SHOW RELATIONSHIPS

Synthesis requires two or more sources and shows significant relationships among those sources. The classic synthesis in college writing is the research project, which asks you to look at a topic in depth and from multiple perspectives. The next chapter closely follows a research paper on the poetry of Langston Hughes, from finding a topic to selecting sources. Here we look at how that research project is an argument. Another synthesis across the curriculum could be a report on a body of information (on, for example, the effect of AIDS on Africa). The comparison-contrast paper, like the research project, is found in almost every area of college study.

Argument

The primary goal of an argument paper is to take a position on an issue or form an opinion about a piece of literature and defend that position or opinion using evidence. In a single-source paper (such as the critique of Chekhov's "Rapture" in Chapter 2 and the argument paper on Pinsky's "Shirt" in Chapter 3), your evidence will be examples and quotations from the text. Most of the time, however, an argument paper is an assignment that involves outside or secondary sources. Secondary sources, such as literary criticism, report on, describe, comment on, or analyze a written work. You can use secondary sources to see what people have learned and written about a topic or an existing work of literature. (For more on argument, see also Chapter 3, Developing an Argument.)

Nearly every sample paper cited in this chapter is an argument in some sense; a thesis statement in most papers is a type of argument, because it posits an opinion that the writer must then support. The best examples of argument papers are the Chekhov student paper, which appears in Chapter 2, the Pinsky student paper in Chapter 3, and

"The world exists in a condition of a saturated presence and meaning and being. . . . And sometimes it's difficult just to rescue . . . a little moment's clarity out of that." "Conversation with Li-Young Lee

the student research project, which appears in the next chapter. In the Chekhov and Pinsky papers, the student responds to a single source, so these papers cite the Chekhov and Pinsky text directly.

In the research paper on Langston Hughes in the next chapter, the student argues that Langston Hughes uses only those aspects of jazz that reflect the African-American experience. In that paper, the student uses multiple sources to make her argument. To support her points about jazz, she uses secondary sources that provide historical context. To support her reading of jazz devices in Hughes's poems, she relies on quotes taken directly from two of the poems.

Comparison and Contrast

A **comparison-contrast** paper asks you to consider two works side by side and highlight the similarities and differences between them in order to make a point about one or both texts. When you are selecting texts to compare, you must make sure that there is some basis for the comparison—perhaps the works share a common theme; or they may be vastly different but both products of the same region.

Let's break that definition down a little bit, by comparing *Beowulf* the epic poem with *Beowulf* the 2007 movie version (see Chapter 1 for information on these two works; **read selections from** *Beowulf,* **the epic, at connect.mcgraw-hill.com**). The basis for comparison of these sources is that they are two versions of the same story. After reading the epic and watching the movie, you would decide what the major similarities are

> "When you try to make something, then you are participating. . . . When you're just expressing yourself, you're not. . . . It's not just writing down what you feel. It's trying to take what you feel and make something out of it." Conversation with Edward Hirsch

and list them. In this case, you might make a list of the characters that the two have in common or the scenes that are common to both text and movie. Then, you should do the same for differences. In the *Beowulf* example, you might note the major plot change in the movie is that Grendel's mother seduces King Hrothgar and Beowulf, so that they are the fathers of monsters. Does this have something to do, you might ask, with the fact that a major movie star—Angelina Jolie—has been cast in the role of Grendel's mother? Does this radical shift in the story line feel sensible or silly to you? Why?

As you make your lists, you might also think about whether some of the items you listed as similarities might in fact hold small differences when examined closely. Continuing with the *Beowulf* example, you might first have noted that Grendel appears in both versions and is a monster in both versions. But as you think about the movie, you might see that, in fact, he seems more distressed than evil.

The following student paper grew out of just such a comparison. Our author, Anthony Melmott, used the similarities and particularly the differences he saw in the two versions of Grendel to make a point about the role of the villain in today's world. Note how he moves through the paper: after an introduction and an overview of the characters' similarities, Anthony delves into a detailed analysis of how the two differ. He then ties his entire discussion together in the concluding paragraph and impressively broadens it to make a statement about contemporary society.

> "Look for the things that speak to you. . . . And in that connection opens up the space for other connections." Conversation with Aimee Bender

A STUDENT COMPARISON-CONTRAST PAPER ON *BEOWULF*

Melmott 1

Anthony Melmott

Professor Wallace

English 150

30 November 2011

Visions of the Villain:

The Role of Grendel in *Beowulf* the Epic and the Movie

In the movie version of *Beowulf,* directed by Robert Zemeckis and released in 2007, there are obvious deviations from the plot of the original epic. Most viewers who are familiar with the epic will readily recognize a major change: Beowulf does not kill Grendel's mother but is instead seduced by her. Clearly, Beowulf in the movie version is no longer the hero that he was in the original epic. But what many viewers might miss is that the movie changes more than the hero. Grendel, too, is no longer the evil villain he was in the original epic. Whereas the poem leaves no question that Grendel is a demon with evil intent, the movie portrays him as a tortured, childish soul through differences in his motivation, his power status, and his lineage.

The reason that many *Beowulf* movie viewers might miss the change to Grendel's character is that in many respects, he is similar to the original Grendel. In both versions, Grendel is a monster who eats and kills men. His overall trajectory does not change from the epic to the movie: in each, he attacks Heorot's hall and gets away with it until Beo-wulf comes and tears off his arm, thereby killing him. Even certain details of Grendel's

---

Opening sentence establishes the works that will be compared.

Thesis statement. Also, the mention of three points sets up the organization of the paper.

Discussion of similarities.

Melmott 2

portrayal in the movie echo the original epic. For example, the epic as it is translated by Chauncey Brewster Tinker introduces Grendel by calling him an inhabitant of "the abode of monster kind" (14). The movie visually represents him as a monster by making him tall and hideous: his body—which drips with slime—looks as if it is turned inside out. As in the original epic, Grendel appears at night; thus, he is aligned with darkness in both versions. In these ways, he is meant to be seen as a terrible being in each.

But a little digging suggests otherwise. A major difference between the epic and the movie is that Grendel does not speak in the epic but does speak in the movie. Since Grendel does not speak, and since he is portrayed through narrative rather than visual effect, the epic uses a variety of language to describe Grendel. He is called a "fiend of hell"; "wrathful spirit"; "mighty stalker of the marches" (14); "creature of destruction, fierce and greedy, wild and furious" (15); and a "terrible monster, like a dark shadow of death" (17). All of this language reinforces Grendel's evilness and angry mode of existence. Grendel's fearsome appearance in the movie might lead a viewer to imagine him as the above list describes. However, the movie version allows Grendel to speak, and when he does, we hear a different story. Grendel speaks in Old English, even though the other characters speak in contemporary English, so his lines are difficult to understand. But listening closely reveals that when Beowulf says to Grendel, whose arm is caught in the door, "Your bloodletting days are finished, demon," Grendel replies, "I am not a demon."

On its own, this example could be explained as Grendel lacking the self-awareness that he is a demon. But other details corroborate Grendel's statement. Both of Grendel's attacks are triggered by the loud rollicking of the men in Heorot. As the

Transition into discussion of differences.

Textual support.

Support from the movie.

Fig. 1. In the movie *Beowulf,* Grendel is pictured as the "terrible monster" described in the epic, but by giving him dialogue the movie portrays him in a more sympathetic light than the epic does (*Beowulf,* Paramount Pictures, 2007).

scene pans from the mead hall to Grendel's underground lair, the noise of the chanting sounds as if it has been submerged. The effect is that we are hearing the men as Grendel hears them—a constant, throbbing, bass line that makes Grendel's membranous ears quiver. When Grendel bursts into full view, his screams are more like cries of anguish than roars meant to frighten. The attention given to Grendel's sensitive ears, his clutching at his head as he screams, and his posture all suggest that he is in physical agony from the parties at Heorot, and thus he bursts in to put a stop to the noise. This is a far less demonic motivation than that cited in the epic.

In the original, Grendel's first attack reads, "The creature of destruction, fierce and greedy, wild and furious, was ready straight. He seized thirty thanes upon their bed" (15). Nothing in this suggests any sort of pain or anguish that Grendel experiences, as he appears to in the movie. Further, while the movie shows him as provoked, the

Melmott 4

epic clearly states after that first attack, "It was no longer than a single night ere he wrought more deeds of murder; he recked not of the feud and the crime—he was too fixed in them!" (16). According to the *Oxford English Dictionary,* "reck" means "To take heed or have a care of some thing (or person), so as to be alarmed or troubled thereby, or to modify one's conduct or purpose on that account." In other words, this quote shows that Grendel's killings do not bother him or give him pause, because he is so set in his evil ways. Hence, even if Grendel could speak in the original epic, he certainly wouldn't say "I am no demon," and even if he did, we would know by his actions that this was not true. On the contrary, when Grendel utters that line in the movie, we have seen that, indeed, his motivation is not naturally demonic but provocation.

> Defines unknown word to add textual support.

Consistent with the change in motivation is the change in Grendel's power status from the epic to the movie. In the epic, Grendel holds a reign of terror. Although it is difficult to analyze language in a translation, it is safe to say that the text refers to Grendel in several places as a ruling authority of sorts. One translation of a line on Grendel's first series of attacks uses "tyrannized": "Thus he tyrannized over them" (16). In another translation, that of Seamus Heaney, the same line is translated as, "So Grendel ruled" (35). Both "rule" and "tyranny" are ways of describing an all-powerful governing body. Later, when he fights Beowulf, Grendel is described as the "master of evils" (43), and in the Heaney translation as "the captain of evil" (47). "Master" and "captain" both refer to someone in charge, someone with power, and both are applied to Grendel in the original epic.

> Transition sentence that leads into the second point of the thesis.

> Textual support.

Yet for all the power the epic accords to Grendel, the movie portrays Grendel as child-like. Although Grendel has a mother in both versions, only the movie shows Grendel interact with her like a child. After his first attack in the movie, he returns to

Melmott 5

his lair and speaks with his mother. Throughout their dialogue, he lies on the floor of the cave in a position reminiscent of a fetus. The words he speaks are likewise childish; at one point, he cries out, "The men screamed! The men bellowed and screamed! The men hurt me, hurt my ear." Not only do his simple, repetitive sentences suggest a child's voice, but his fear of and dismay at the men show him to be the opposite of their tyrant, ruler, master, or captain.

Support from the movie.

The reduction of Grendel's evilness and power can perhaps be traced to the biggest difference between the epic's Grendel and the movie's: that of Grendel's lineage. As mentioned in the introduction, the movie portrays Grendel's mother as a seductress, with the premise that she once seduced King Hrothgar, making Grendel the offspring of Hrothgar and the mother. On the other hand, the original epic is very clear—and frequently emphasizes—that Grendel is a descendent of Cain, who committed the first murder. Referring to Cain, the epic reads, "From him there woke to life all the evil broods, monsters and elves and sea-beasts, and giants too, who long time strove with God" (14-15). There is no room for a human in this description, and certainly not Hrothgar, whom the epic praises as being a "good king." By changing Grendel's parentage, the movie shifts the root of evil from Grendel to Hrothgar. It is because of Hrothgar's past weakness that his kingdom is plagued by the fruit of that very weakness. Grendel, then, is a by-product, a mere pawn in the struggle between Hrothgar's kingdom and the mother's corrupting ways. The mother uses Grendel's death as a way to further corrupt the kingdom through her seduction of Beowulf—and Beowulf succumbs.

Transition sentence that leads into the third point of the thesis.

In the retelling of an existing story—whether that retelling be in the form of a story, a poem, or a movie—there will always be similarities and differences. But the

Melmott 6

Fig. 2. Another key difference between the motion picture and the epic: Grendel's mother as temptress. Her seduction of both Hrothgar and Beowulf shifts the origin of evil from biblical Cain in the epic, to the fallibility of the story's all-too-human heroes in the film (*Beowulf,* Paramount Pictures, 2007).

difference in the role of the villain between an epic written in the year 1000 and a movie filmed in 2007 tells us something about our contemporary society. As we noted briefly in the introduction, Beowulf's seduction makes him less heroic; likewise, we have seen that the movie makes Grendel less villainous in motivation, in power, and in lineage. We might ask: what does it mean to live in an age when we see heroes as fallible and villains as innocent? The difference between the epic Grendel and the movie Grendel offers an answer: the original villain has been turned into a product of human vice, which suggests that true villainy lies in human behavior. Or, to put it another way, in a world where human deeds are monstrous, there isn't much room for a monster.

Brief reiteration of the three points made in the paper.

Conclusion broadens significance to our own society.

Conclusion explains the implication of the thesis; answers the "so what?" question.

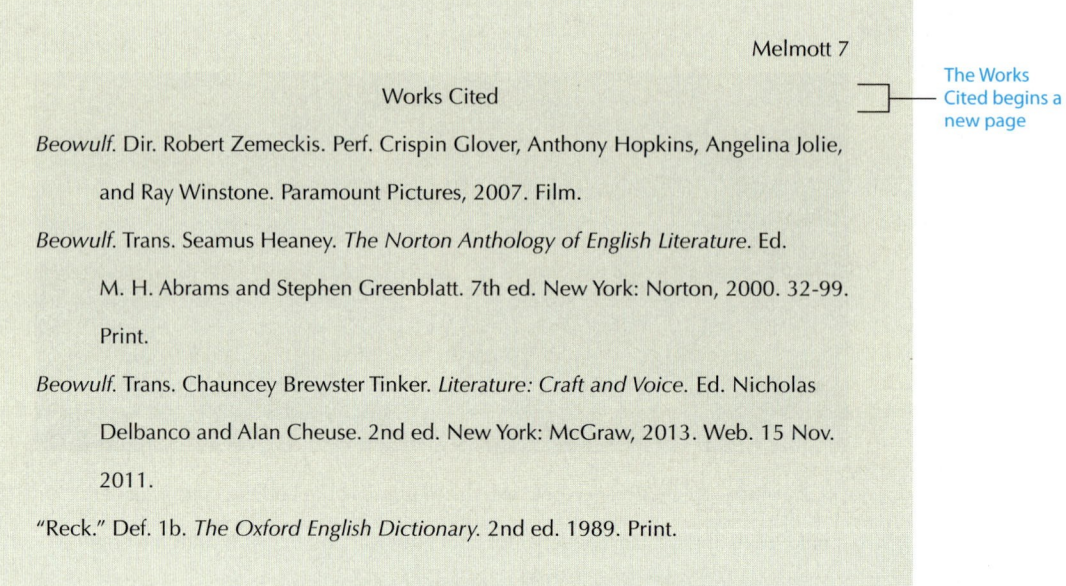

Melmott 7

Works Cited

Beowulf. Dir. Robert Zemeckis. Perf. Crispin Glover, Anthony Hopkins, Angelina Jolie,

and Ray Winstone. Paramount Pictures, 2007. Film.

Beowulf. Trans. Seamus Heaney. *The Norton Anthology of English Literature.* Ed.

M. H. Abrams and Stephen Greenblatt. 7th ed. New York: Norton, 2000. 32-99.

Print.

Beowulf. Trans. Chauncey Brewster Tinker. *Literature: Craft and Voice.* Ed. Nicholas

Delbanco and Alan Cheuse. 2nd ed. New York: McGraw, 2013. Web. 15 Nov.

2011.

"Reck." Def. 1b. *The Oxford English Dictionary.* 2nd ed. 1989. Print.

The Works Cited begins a new page

USE CRITIQUE TO BRING IN YOUR OWN EVALUATION

We define a critique as a summary that leads to the statement of your own reasonable opinion. Whether you are asked to critique a reading for an essay exam, to assess the accuracy of a Web site as a source, or to respond to an argument, in most of your courses, you will be required to evaluate the presentation of information.

- What is the work (or performance) trying to accomplish?
- Does it achieve its purpose?
- Do you agree or disagree with the piece, like or dislike it?
- How has the piece created this reaction in you?

Review

A critique is a formal evaluation of a text, and one of the most common forms of critique in literature is the review. In a review, you—as the reviewer—get to evaluate the text or, in the case of live theater, a performance. For an example of a review, see the response to Anton Chekhov's early story "Rapture" in Chapter 2. After a few general, opening sentences, the discussion becomes more specific as the student asserts that the main character's lack of change makes the story unsatisfying. The student continues by analyzing the various parts of the story. As your review progresses and you begin to make evaluative statements—such as *The story begins on a strong note but deteriorates; The casting was so well done that it carries the play from start to finish; The poem's sonnet form is perfect for its content*—you will also need to analyze why you are reacting to the text in that particular way. Particularly strong is the student reviewer's division of the story into three parts. Notice here that she is not afraid to make bold claims: that the story is incomplete and unsatisfying.

> Part one: the clerk runs in, announcing himself, disrupting the household, waking his brothers. Part two: Mitya takes out the newspaper and urges his father to read it aloud. In the closing sequence, a reader may expect something to happen as a result of Mitya's "rapture" that he has become famous, because his name is in the paper and on the police record. However, as the ancient philosopher and critic Aristotle might put it, what is the dramatic purpose here? . . . His parents and his siblings humor him instead of contradicting or berating him; thus making change less likely for Mitya. The reader is left to wonder what the point is, and without that concluding action, the dramatic purpose is unclear, and the story is incomplete and ultimately unsatisfying.

You may feel a little intimidated the first time you write a review, especially if the author is well known. Take the Chekhov paper to heart; the validity of an evaluation rests not on how highly you are ranking a noted author but on how your analysis of the story supports your evaluation. In this case, the student has analyzed the structure of the story, and found that in a story set up for a three-part movement, the third part is missing. Therefore, when the reviewer claims the story is incomplete and unsatisfying, we see her point. For an additional example, see the review of Edward Albee's *The Zoo Story* in Chapter 31.

Guidelines for Writing Reviews

1. Introduce What You Are Evaluating

Include the title and author.

For a live performance, include who performed, when, and under what circumstances (a full or empty house? an outdoor amphitheater?).

Be clear about what you are evaluating.

2. Set Up Your Review with a Summary

Your summary is to be used as a reference point for your discussion; you may not want to give the ending away, however.

continued

3. **Put the Piece into Context**

   What type of work is it? A comedy? A tragedy?

   When was it written?

   If it is a well-known and much-produced play, include any unusual information on the "take" of the director (what's the director's purpose in staging Shakespeare's *Hamlet* in contemporary Belfast, for example).

4. **Analyze the Text**

   For a play, note the staging, lighting, and costuming as well as the acting.

   Note how the work is structured.

   Look at the individual elements: plot, character, dialogue.

   Determine the purpose of the work.

5. **Include Your Reasoned Opinion: This Is Your Evaluation**

   Did the work achieve its purpose?

   What is your response to the selection and why?

   Agree or disagree with the presentation of information (whether or not it achieved its purpose).

   Base your agreement or disagreement on evidence.

6. **End with a Balanced Conclusion**

   Recap the pros and cons of the piece.

   Give your overall reaction.

FIND AN EFFECTIVE APPROACH TO THE ESSAY EXAM

Timed writing on an exam may seem to be an intimidating prospect. Reviewing the tips below will help you learn an effective approach to essay exams, whether you are taking one for a class in English, political science, or psychology.

1. **Prepare.** If you have been diligent in annotating the texts you read and keeping a journal, be sure to review these materials before the day of your exam. Jog your memory about each story, poem, novel, or play you have read for the class by reviewing major characters and events of the work, as well as any important information about the authors.

2. **Pace yourself.** When you receive the exam, glance through it to see approximately how much time you should spend on each section. Remember that if an essay is worth, say, 70 percent of the grade, you want to make it a priority to spend sufficient time on it.

3. **Read the assignment carefully.** When you arrive at the essay question, circle key words as you read the assignment. Pay particular attention to the verbs your instructor uses: common choices are *explain, discuss, analyze, compare, contrast, interpret,* and *argue.* Your understanding of the different types of assignments addressed in this chapter can help you here.

Understanding Essay Exam Assignments

- The words *explain* and *discuss* ask you to engage in a detailed way, much as you would in an explication or a close reading.
- *Analyze* should remind you of what you know about an analysis paper—that your job is to explore one element of the text and show how it contributes to the overall work.
- *Compare* and *contrast* ask you to find similarities and differences between two items and to suggest what those similarities or differences emphasize or illuminate.
- *Argue* is a way of asking you to take a position about an issue or, in the case of a literary text, to defend what you see in the work that may not be readily apparent to others.

4. **Form a thesis.**   In an essay exam, your thesis will probably be a simpler statement than the type of complex argument you would form in a longer research paper or analysis. Look at the phrasing of the question itself for help in shaping your thesis.

EXAMPLE OF AN ESSAY EXAM ASSIGNMENT

➡ *Analyze Frost's use of imagery in "Stopping by Woods on a Snowy Evening."*

EXAMPLE OF A THESIS THAT RESPONDS TO THE ASSIGNMENT

Frost uses idyllic, New England imagery to disguise a more serious statement about death.

5. **Outline briefly.**   Even if you don't typically work from an outline when writing a paper, take a few moments to jot down a brief outline. In an essay exam, even a brief outline will keep you from freezing up entirely. And, if you find you are spending too much time on the first paragraph, you can quickly wrap it up to move on to the next point in your outline. In short, an outline can help you budget time and allocate space in your essay while eliminating the stressful feeling of not knowing where to go next.
6. **Check your work.**   Try your best to allow a little extra time in which to read over what you have written. Time constraints often make even the best students leave out words or write sentences that make no sense. Rereading your work will allow you to fix these problems.

Follow our model student, Renee Knox, as she completes the following essay assignment on a timed exam.

Sample Notes for a Student Essay Exam

Renee identifies key words in the prompt. Already, she knows her paper must focus on the significance of the imagery.

Renee underlines the imagery in the poem and highlights phrases she finds significant.

Assignment: Analyze Frost's use of imagery in "Stopping by Woods on a Snowy Evening," reproduced below.

Stopping by Woods on a Snowy Evening

1   Whose woods these are I think I know.
2   His house is in the village though;
3   He will not see me stopping here
4   To watch his woods fill up with snow.
5   My little horse must think it queer
6   To stop without a farmhouse near
7   Between the woods and frozen lake
8   The darkest evening of the year.
9   He gives his harness bells a shake
10 To ask if there is some mistake.
11 The only other sound's the sweep
12 Of easy wind and downy flake.
13 The woods are lovely, dark and deep.
14 But I have promises to keep,
15 And miles to go before I sleep,
16 And miles to go before I sleep.

Renee numbers the lines for easy reference when she quotes in the essay.

Renee notes that many of her underlined phrases bring to mind a farmlike, New England setting. Then she separates out the other images and names their connotations.

Important images: woods, snow, horse, house, village, dark, wind, snowflakes, dark

—woods, snow, horse, farmhouse, village = New England; ideal Christmas scene
—no farmhouse near, dark, deep, winter = cold, alone, death??
—sleep = death?

Thesis: Frost uses pretty New England imagery to disguise a more serious statement about death.

Renee formulates a thesis based on her observations.

Renee generates a brief outline to follow. In constructing her essay, she will use a 5-paragraph structure.

I.   Introduction and thesis
II.   Set up "pretty" imagery
      A.   Mention horse
      B.   Mention farmhouse
      C.   Mention woods
      D.   Mention snow
      E.   Adds up to ideal Christmas village scene

III. Set up dark imagery and cold effect
   A. Snow
   B. Woods
   C. Wind
   D. Solitary
IV. Discuss symbolic significance of images
   A. Snow = winter = death
   B. Woods = wild, easily lose your way
   C. Sleep = form of death
V. Conclusion—why would Frost do this?

A STUDENT ESSAY EXAM ON ROBERT FROST'S "STOPPING BY WOODS ON A SNOWY EVENING"

Renee Knox

Imagery in Frost's "Stopping by Woods on a Snowy Evening"

Many times in literature, as in life, something appears to be one thing but is actually another. One need only think of tales such as "Little Red Riding Hood" in which the woman who appears to be her grandmother turns out to be a wolf. In a similar way, Robert Frost's "Stopping by Woods on a Snowy Evening" appears to be a simple and charming experience. Instead, Frost uses idyllic New England imagery to disguise a more serious statement about death.

Even in the poem's title, Frost is already using imagery: woods, snow, and evening. We can picture an evening scene in which snow is softly falling on woods. And indeed, the speaker is there with his "little horse" (line 5) that wears "harness bells" (9). The mention of a village (2) and a farmhouse (6), even though the speaker is not near them,

Renee uses a simple but complete title, in order not to spend too much time on it.

Renee stays on topic by following her outline.

Thesis statement. When Renee reread her essay, she changed "pretty" to "idyllic" for more sophisticated diction.

suggests that villages and farmhouses dot the landscape in which the speaker moves. Put all together—snow, a horse with harness bells, a village, and a farmhouse—Frost's imagery conjures a New England scene that is so quaint, it is exactly the type of scene many people replicate with porcelain villages at Christmas time: it is that perfect.

However, if we look at the nature imagery, we get a much darker picture. While evening might connote a soothing time of leisure after the day's work is done, it is also the time of oncoming dark, as Frost's imagery indicates when he describes it as the "darkest evening of the year" (8). In fact, Frost calls attention to the fact that it is the darkest evening by placing that description in line 8, the exact center of the 16-line poem. Furthermore, he repeats "dark" again when he describes the woods as "dark and deep" (13), adding emphasis to the imagery of darkness through repetition. We also know that the evening is cold, and although snow is a part of an idyllic New England Christmas scene, it is equally an unpleasant feeling with bleak connotations. If the world is cold, it means that it is not treating you well. Beyond this kind of cold, there is the sensory imagery of the only sound being "the sweep / of easy wind and downy flake" (11-12). In other words, not only is the narrator out in the cold, but he is so alone that he actually hears the snowflakes falling in the wind. When put together with the dark, this is a bleak and lonely scene.

Beyond the sensory unpleasantness of dark and cold, these images have symbolic meaning when placed in the context of other literature. Frost's imagery clearly places this moment in winter, which traditionally symbolizes death, much as spring symbolizes rebirth. Moreover, even though the woods are "lovely," they are also "dark and deep," a place where in much of literature, as in Shakespeare's "A Midsummer Night's Dream," characters easily lose themselves or succumb to supernatural forces.

Renee helps her paper flow by using "however" to signal her transition to her next point.

Renee supports her point with specific examples from the text.

Renee further analyzes the imagery she set up in the previous paragraph to ensure she sufficiently answers the prompt.

Perhaps the woods are "lovely" because their darkness tantalizes the narrator to lose himself, but if you followed such an idea through, the speaker would end up lost and frozen in the dark woods. The last lines reinforce the idea that he is being tempted by death. When recalling himself from gazing into the cold, dark woods, the speaker gives his reason as having "miles to go before I sleep" (15). Sleep, like winter, is another way of suggesting death, for much of literature speaks of death as a type of eternal sleep.

Thus, while the scene's first impression is one of a quaint New England night—an impression built through imagery of horse, village, farmhouse, and snow—the cold and dark nature imagery tells another story of death and the temptation to remain in the presence of death. By bringing these two types of imagery together in one poem, Frost perhaps suggests that death is always near, even when we think we are looking at a vivid scene of comfort. Or, to put a more optimistic spin on things, since some of the images overlap (snowy woods are both beautiful and dangerous), Frost might be trying to tell us that death is nothing to fear, that even on the darkest evening, there is still loveliness in the dark of the woods and the sweep of the flake.

Renee moves to a brief but insightful conclusion.

In reading Renee's essay, you may have noticed that there were places that sounded a little rough or colloquial and other spots that weren't perfectly explained, such as the end of the fourth paragraph. However, her main ideas are clear and her conclusion compelling. She also used specific support and stayed exactly on topic with what the assignment asked her to do. For these reasons, Renee's essay is well done, because the constraints of a timed setting often force the writer to leave a few rough spots.

5 Writing the Research Paper, Avoiding Plagiarism, and Documenting Sources

BRING me all of your dreams,
You dreamers,
Bring me all of your
Heart melodies
That I may wrap them
In a blue cloud-cloth
Away from the too-rough fingers
Of the world.

—"The Dream Keeper" by Langston Hughes

. . . Hughes effectively incorporated new forms of jazz as they arose. While he does successfully use formal elements of jazz music, to end a reading there would be to miss Hughes's larger achievement. Hughes did not simply adopt jazz technique; he selected only those trends in jazz that reflected the African-American experience of the time in which he wrote.

—from an essay by student Christine Keenan

A RESEARCH project is as much about you as it is about your sources. Your instructor wants to know what *you* think, not just what your sources say. So when you receive your research paper assignment, think about how to make it your own. How is the topic relevant to you personally? What interests you about it? Research is about asking questions as much or more than it is about finding answers. Don't be afraid not to have an opinion immediately. If you follow your own native interests, you'll find the process more interesting, and you'll be able to keep your paper sounding like you even as you quote, paraphrase, and summarize your sources. Preparing yourself now will help you avoid some of the mistakes—such as trying to start work on your paper late on the night before it is due—which can happen early in your college career. This chapter will not only provide you with a step-by-step walkthrough of the research process, it will also help you address a range of critical skills for one of the most common assignments across the curriculum.

RESEARCH TODAY

The Web has been a huge boon to researchers: information is more accessible now than it has ever been at any time in human history. Although the Web makes it more convenient to do your research at three o'clock in the morning if you like, it also brings with it a variety of challenges. Today you don't just find sources, you have to manage the thousands (and often millions) of hits you might get when you do a Google search for a topic. This avalanche of information can make it difficult to see what is credible and valid when every site looks largely the same on the computer screen. The Web also makes it easy to create a cut-and-paste patchwork of sources that can lead to unintentional plagiarism. **Plagiarism** occurs when a source is not properly acknowledged, and whenever you conduct research from outside sources, you run the risk of taking credit for another person's ideas.

> **"[I gather] my research, and then I start dealing with relationships. Change comes from what you absorbed from your relationships."**
>
> Conversation with Ruben Santiago-Hudson

Always remember that the objective here is to help you craft your own voice as a writer: to help you to learn the process of generating ideas—of developing what you want to say—and putting those ideas into words. In this respect, your task as a writer is not much different from that of the many authors whose works are featured in this text. But academic writing is different from writing literature in important ways. Although literature frequently is shaped by the ideas of others (the influence of *Beowulf* on Tolkien mentioned in Chapter 1 is but one example among many), creative writers are under no obligation to reveal their sources. In fact, it is often the objective of literary scholars to discover these influences, or at least speculate about them.

This scholarly role is seen in other disciplines as well; whether in history or sociology, business or economics, chemistry or physics, you may be asked to inquire into the root causes of events or phenomena. Where something came from, why something happened, or how something came to be the way it is are central questions in academic writing. Your purpose is to make these processes, causes, and influences transparent to others. When conducting research, you are actively seeking information and ideas about a topic from other writers. Your objective is to find sources that you can learn from. But one of the most difficult aspects of this process is learning how to use these sources to enhance and support your own ideas, and to incorporate them into your writing, without accidentally appropriating the language or ideas from other writers as your own. You must reveal rather than conceal these relationships. Otherwise, you may inadvertently plagiarize. You must make your influences as transparent as possible to your readers so that they may retrace your steps. Therefore, how you take notes is more important than ever if you are to distinguish your work from the work you have found online (or in print).

In college, your instructors are likely to want a variety of sources, with an eye focused on their credibility. Thus although you may obtain many sources online, many others remain available only in print. In addition, it is important to utilize the unique advantages of the online sources available to you in college: most colleges allow you to access their library collections online, and many also provide access to a variety of academic databases that have been editorially vetted for credibility. This chapter gets you started navigating the research process and also provides guidelines for finding, evaluating, and documenting sources that will keep you from unintentionally plagiarizing someone else's work.

The type of source you want to use depends on the type of project you are working on. If you are approaching a piece of literature from a particular critical perspective—such as the feminist, Marxist, or psychoanalytical schools of thought discussed in the chapter on Critical Approaches to Literature at the end of the book—your research will probably involve reading literary criticism. If you are embarking on historical criticism or biographical criticism, you will need to gear your research to sources that inform you about a time period or your author's life. Even before you choose your topic, you are likely to do some research to determine what you might be interested in doing your research on.

> **"If you're going to write about the 19th century, you don't just make it up. You try to do a little research. And you try to concentrate. You try to be aware that you are not writing about your own century and that therefore you have to pay a little more attention."** Conversation with Gish Jen

There are three basic kinds of text sources with which you will be working: books; print periodicals (magazines, newspapers, and scholarly journals); and online sources. The examples on pages 100–102 identify the information you need to keep track of throughout the research process. (See the MLA Documentation Style Guide at the end of the book for examples of how to incorporate the information into a Works Cited page.) Read the student research paper on Langston Hughes at the end of this chapter to see how the steps outlined in this chapter look in action.

ELEMENTS IN A WORKS CITED ENTRY: BOOKS

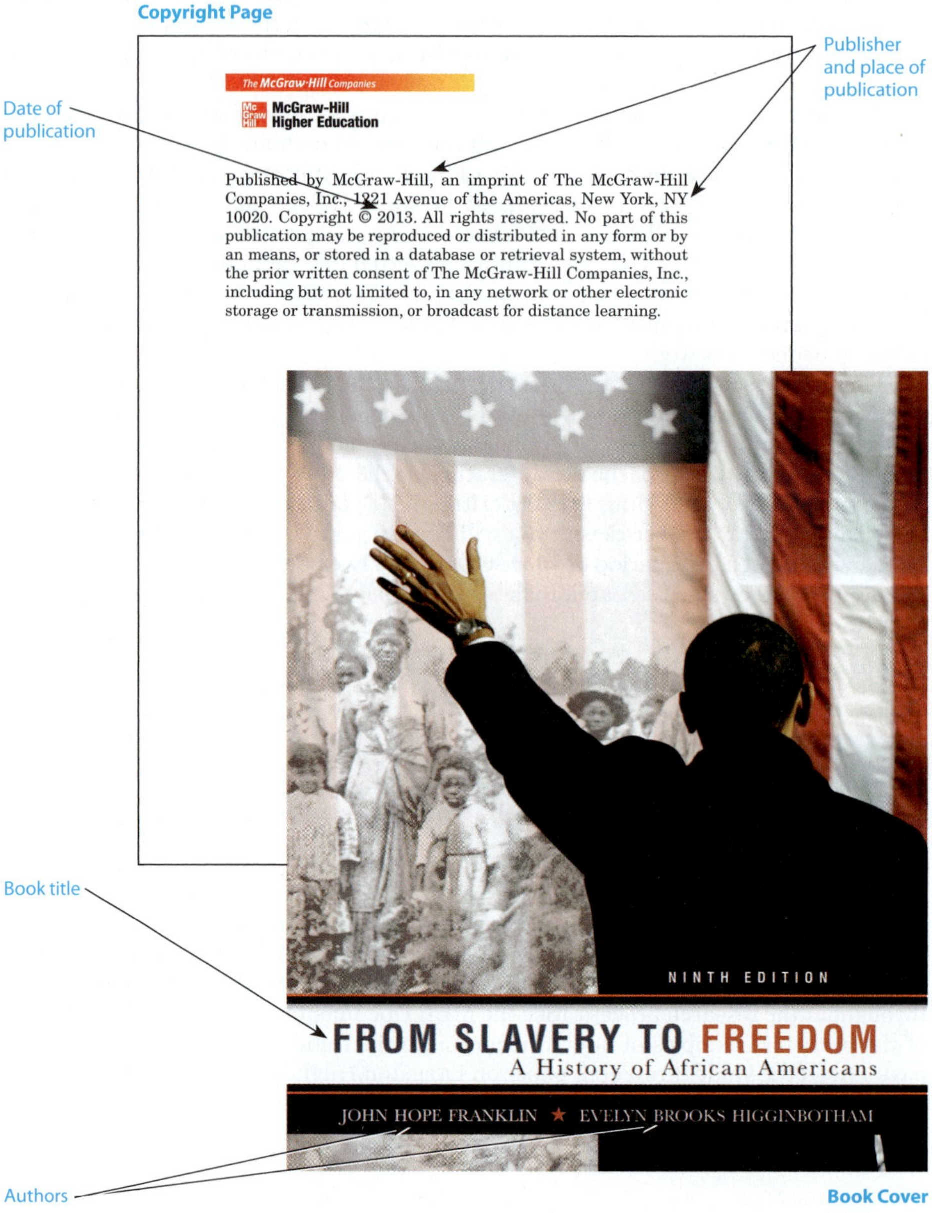
Copyright Page
The McGraw-Hill Companies
McGraw-Hill Higher Education
Published by McGraw-Hill, an imprint of The McGraw-Hill Companies, Inc., 1221 Avenue of the Americas, New York, NY 10020. Copyright © 2013. All rights reserved. No part of this publication may be reproduced or distributed in any form or by an means, or stored in a database or retrieval system, without the prior written consent of The McGraw-Hill Companies, Inc., including but not limited to, in any network or other electronic storage or transmission, or broadcast for distance learning.
Date of publication
Publisher and place of publication
NINTH EDITION
FROM SLAVERY TO FREEDOM
A History of African Americans
JOHN HOPE FRANKLIN ★ EVELYN BROOKS HIGGINBOTHAM
Book title
Authors
Book Cover

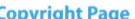

ELEMENTS IN A WORKS CITED ENTRY: PERIODICALS

Journal title ·····→

Volume ·····→

Page numbers ←·····

Date of publication ←·····

Starting page number ←·····

Article title ·····→

Author ·····→

Author affiliation ·····→

Dialectical Anthropology **26:** 267–272, 2001.
© 2001 *Kluwer Academic Publishers. Printed in the Netherlands.*

267

"I, Too, Sing America": Jazz and Blues Techniques and Effects in Some of Langston Hughes's Selected Poems

LIONEL DAVIDAS
Université des Antilles et de la Guyane, Martinique, West Indies

It is commonly accepted that oral poetry has been greatly influenced by jazz and blues, a phenomenon that developed mainly in the USA. In light of this, we may infer that such poems should logically be considered as mere scores to be deciphered and performed, or records that should be heard rather than read, and that have many of the dynamics of "the music" about them.[1] In point of fact, a significant number of jazz techniques are to be found within the framework of poetry and combine with it to produce a highly personalized mode of free expression, which is the essence and spirit of of jazz creation. As it appears, Langston Hughes's outstanding collection of poems exemplifies the greatest of those qualities of jazz and blues, and his talent truly makes these poems come alive in the same way that jazz and blues music comes alive for the audience as well as for the musicians.

To those who are familiar with such music, it is quite clear that *Selected Poems of Langston Hughes*, a book which reveals the author's personal choice, unquestionably includes blues poetry, as evidenced by the many characteristics of blues music that pervade most of the selected pieces. To start with, it is significant to note that Hughes's poems are not at all static. They are pervaded with lively and active repetitions, and we notice a series of variations within each poem which closely resemble the variations present in a blues song. Many of Hughes's poems exhibit a slow tempo and rhythm which is a common trait to most styles of blues. What is more, there exists some degree of internal variation in breath rhythm that contributes to the blues effect. In addition, those poems definitely seek the interaction of call-and-response, making the reader feel an active participant in the "concert" provided by the poet as musician, as performer.

ELEMENTS IN A WORKS CITED ENTRY: ONLINE RESOURCES

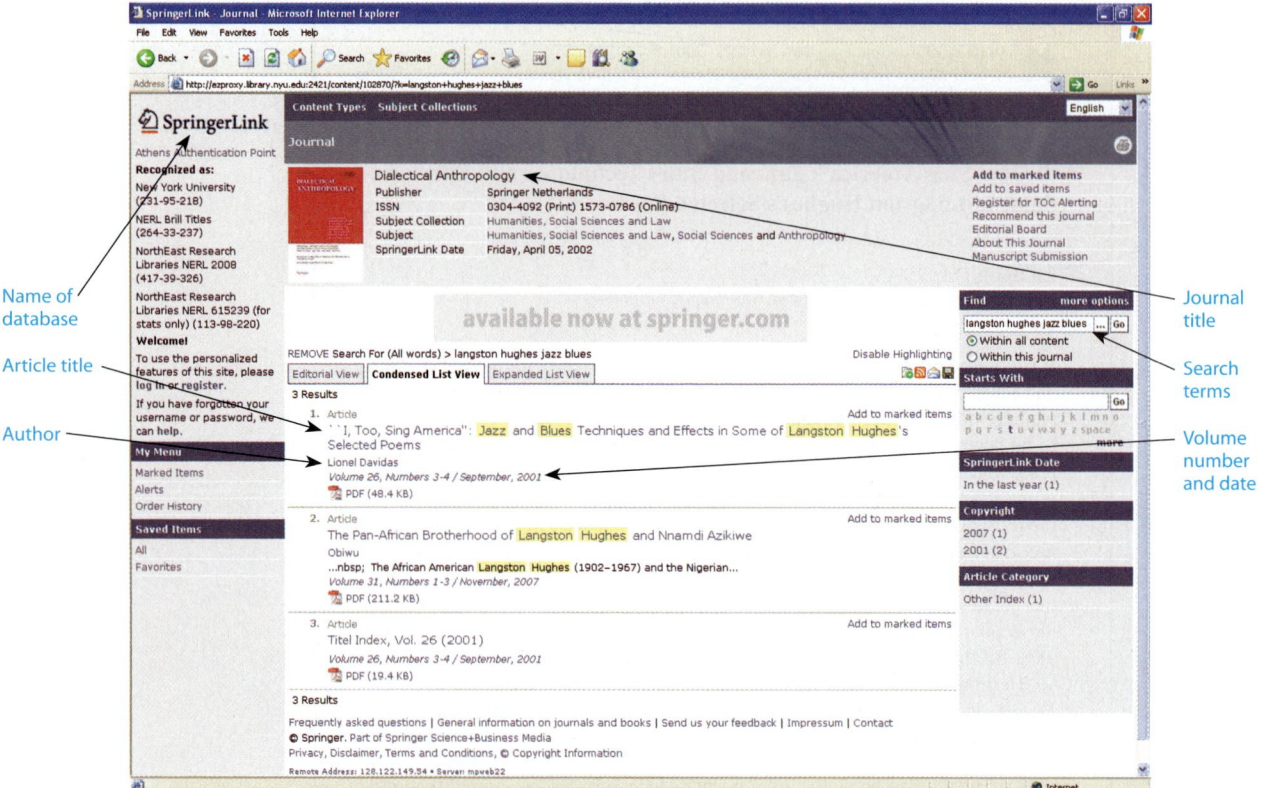

WHAT INFORMATION REQUIRES DOCUMENTATION?

When writing from sources—whether a single source, as when you respond to a story, poem, or play you have just read, or multiple sources, as when you include research—you will need to effectively use quotation, paraphrase, and summary in your paper. Quotation, paraphrase, and summary are the evidence you use for your interpretation of a work, and it is common for all three to be employed in the same paper. You commit plagiarism when you don't acknowledge a source. You commit plagiarism when you don't accurately present your material. Keeping track of sources is critical, because how you present your evidence determines more than just how convincing your paper is; it keeps your paper honest by giving your readers the following information:

- A framework (who, what, when, where, and how) for your response.
- The specifics in the source that led you to your observations, thoughts, and connections.

Marginal annotations, underlined and highlighted passages, or notes in a reading journal help you trace your response back to specific source material. Your interaction with one text or many texts provides the basis of your interpretation and of your paper's thesis. Whether you base your paper on a single source or you work with multiple sources, you will probably need to summarize a work to provide your reader with a framework for your analysis. When working with multiple sources, you may also need to summarize a number of critical opinions. It is likely you will paraphrase a short passage to give your reader context for your assessment or the point of view of a scholarly work. Should you be writing about drama, you'll probably quote from the play; should you be discussing a poem, it's almost inevitable that you will include several lines of poetry in your discussion. The guidelines provided here will keep you from plagiarizing when you have summarized, paraphrased, or quoted sources. You will always want to document in your paper where you found the kinds of information listed in the following box.

Information Requiring Documentation

- Lines from a story, poem, or play
- Opinions, observations, and interpretations by writers, critics, and scholars
- Information from expert and/or sponsored sites
- Visual materials, including tables, charts, and graphs
- Footnotes from printed sources
- Statements that are open to debate
- Historical information that is not commonly known
- Statistics, material from surveys, and census or poll results if you use them

SAMPLES OF TYPES OF INFORMATION REQUIRING DOCUMENTATION

The whaling industry in nineteenth-century America collapsed when flexible steel hoops replaced whalebone in women's corsets.

A twenty-year Swiss study of organic farming found that organic farms yielded more produce per unit of energy consumed than farms that did not use organic farming methods.

Smoking kills more than 418,000 people every year in the United States.

The easiest way to avoid plagiarism is to remember that you must tell your reader the sources of all facts, ideas, and opinions that are taken from others and that are not considered common knowledge. *Common knowledge* is information that is contained in a number of sources and is widely considered to be true. For example, in biology, the structure of DNA and the processes of cell division and photosynthesis are considered common knowledge. A recent scientific discovery about genetics, however, would not be common knowledge, so you would need to cite the source of this information. When in doubt, cite your source; citing is never incorrect.

COMMON KNOWLEDGE (DOCUMENTATION NOT REQUIRED)

Millions of soldiers died in the trenches of the Western front in World War I.

Mohandas K. Gandhi was assassinated in 1948.

The cheetah is the fastest-moving land animal.

WORKING WITH SOURCES TO AVOID PLAGIARISM

There are two main approaches to documenting outside information in your own research paper: MLA (Modern Language Association) style and APA (American Psychological Association) style. Both require **in-text parenthetical citation** (to be used with quotation, paraphrase, and summary) and documentation in a **Works Cited** list (MLA) or a References list (APA) at the end of your paper. All the texts you have cited in your paper will need to appear in a list at the end of your paper (sometimes called a bibliography). See the research paper in this chapter for an example of a Works Cited page in MLA Style. Any formal paper—even those that only cite one source, as many do in this book—requires a Works Cited pages (see the papers in Chapter 4, Writing across the Curriculum, as well as Chapter 7, Writing about Fiction, and Chapter 18, Writing about Poetry, for additional papers with examples of Works Cited pages). For guidelines on how to create a Works Cited page, see the MLA Documentation Style Guide at the end of the book. Anything you have cited in your paper must be included in the final Works Cited page for that paper.

As you collect your sources for your papers, your source notes will protect you from plagiarism. The three samples on pages 100–102 show you what kind of information you need to cite in a research paper. You may want to use sticky notes to flag specific quotations or passages that you find interesting or of particular relevance to your topic.

Always be sure to copy the bibliographical information (the information that is required in your Works Cited page) of the source so you can easily return to it when writing your paper and properly cite it. Ineffective citation is one cause of plagiarism, and the following guidelines will help you avoid plagiarism and cite your sources effectively.

- Take notes on your sources
- Do not copy and paste directly into your paper
- Keep a *working bibliography,* a running list of works with source information that you will need for your Works Cited page

Take Notes on Your Sources

First, when taking notes, make sure to underline or put into quotation marks all direct quotations you copy from books or journals. Record the page numbers and other source information that you'll need for your in-text parenthetical citation. By underlining and putting quotation marks on direct quotations (and recording the page number and source information), you will help distinguish your own impressions and conclusions from those that you copied directly and avoid plagiarism by correctly citing your sources.

Do Not Copy and Paste Directly into Your Paper

Next, when working with Web sources, try not to copy and paste directly into the body of your work; consider instead pasting into a separate document and printing that document to consult alongside your other notes. It's much easier to catch yourself retyping whole passages from another source.

Keep a Working Bibliography

The best way to prevent plagiarism is to make sure you keep precise records of the sources you consult while preparing your paper in a working bibliography—a list of all the sources you've used, as well as all the information you'll use to cite them later. The more accurate and complete the information on your sources, the easier it will be to present that source accurately and completely in your paper. Choose an appropriate documentation style (usually MLA or APA) early and stick to it as you create the body of your work. Usually, your instructor will have assigned you a style. If you cannot cite as you write, make sure to note "citation needed" in appropriate places, such as after paraphrases, figures, or direct quotations. For your working bibliography, make sure to include this information:

- The names of all the authors, editors, and/or translators of the piece.
- The complete title of the work and relevant chapter title or heading; for Web pages, the name of the site and the page on which the information appears.

- The publisher, copyright date, edition, and place of publication for sources from books.
- The date, volume, issue, and page number for all sources from periodicals or journals (including those you have pulled from an online database).
- The date you viewed the page for all sources from the Internet.
- The medium of the work, for example, *Print, Web, Film, Performance, DVD, Radio, Podcast, Television.*

The Web and Avoiding Plagiarism

With Web resources, you need to take extra precautions to make sure you document correctly where you got your information. Do not assume that what you find on the Web is common knowledge. Write in your notes the URL as well as the date that you accessed the site. Web sites are notoriously prone to change, so this helps you keep your source clear. In your notes, put quotation marks around anything that is a direct quotation (wherever you found the information, print or online) so that you can easily see when you are using another's words. It is easy to cut whole passages from the Internet and paste them into your paper, or to think you have paraphrased when you have quoted, if your notes aren't effective. This is plagiarism.

CHOOSING A TOPIC

Often, your instructor will assign a topic or provide some guidance. Or, you may have found something on the Web that you want to pursue. You can also find several research topics in this textbook, especially at the end of each case study. We have provided not only the topics but also a list of good sources to get you started. In Chapter 2,

> **"You can't pack in every thought by every human being who lived during whatever period you are writing about. We're automatically excluding . . . when we begin writing. . . . That principle applies to every newspaper article you'll ever read, every magazine article. . . . Pick out portions . . . and then to try and make some sense of it and order it."** Conversation with Tim O'Brien

we provide guidelines that will help you to annotate a text. In Chapter 3, we give more details on how you can refine those initial reactions to develop ideas to write about. Chapter 4 shows how you can use the process of summary, analysis, synthesis, and interpretation or critique as a key to unlock the writing process. The first step in finding a topic for your research paper is to explore a topic that interests you and discover new ideas that will help to inform your own idea. Break the topic down so that you can manage your research and create a project that teaches you about a subject you enjoy.

Let your research help you find out more about a variety of potential topics, so you can discover what interests you.

1. **Identify what interests you.** Choose your topic, or choose how you want to address your assigned topic, by considering what strikes you as important or interesting in the work of literature you are researching.

> **Example:** Our student author, Christine Keenan, was assigned to write a research paper on Langston Hughes. To find a topic, she thought of what she knew about Hughes that interested her. Since Christine loves music, she decided she would like to know more about how jazz influenced Langston Hughes.

2. **Form a question.** Once you have a topic in mind, explore how that aspect of the work is meaningful to you. Do some of the brainstorming exercises that students used to get started in Chapter 7, Writing about Fiction, Chapter 18, Writing about Poetry, and Chapter 31, Writing about Drama. Turn this aspect into a question. Christine made a list of words that she associated with jazz.

> *improvisation, be-bop, Duke Ellington,* and *nightclubs*

She also considered that jazz has several forms, including blues, swing, be-bop, and cool jazz. Using this material as a basis, she formed a question.

> **Example:** "What elements of jazz influenced Langston Hughes when he wrote his poems?"

3. **Narrow your topic.** Christine then decided to narrow her question further by picking two poems influenced by jazz—an early poem, "The Dream Keeper," and a later poem, identified as "Harlem (Dream Deferred)" in this text, although "Dream Deferred" is an alternative title sometimes used by Hughes.

> "I think if a reader is struggling with the experience of entering a story that someone should be there to help that person. . . . Thank God there are libraries. There's a whole range of people writing . . . [and] they want you to make it." Conversation with Barry Lopez

Langston Hughes (1902–1967)

For a biography of Langston Hughes, see Chapter 27, A Case Study on Langston Hughes and His Contemporaries .

The Dream Keeper (1932)

Bring me all of your dreams,
You dreamers,
Bring me all of your
Heart melodies
5   That I may wrap them
In a blue cloud-cloth
Away from the too-rough fingers
Of the world.

Harlem (Dream Deferred) (1951)

What happens to a dream deferred?

Does it dry up
like a raisin in the sun?
Or fester like a sore—
5   And then run?
Does it stink like rotten meat?
Or crust and sugar over—
like a syrupy sweet?

Maybe it just sags
10   like a heavy load.

Or does it explode?

FINDING RELIABLE AND RELEVANT SOURCES

When you go online for help, you may think that all the information is the same. It only looks that way. The sources you cite in your research should be reliable and relevant—significant in the context of your current discussion. The Internet serves up information in a couple of ways that must be differentiated.

- A general search from the entire World Wide Web includes everything that anyone has posted on your topic, from very personal blogs to news groups. You will need to carefully evaluate anything you find in a general search to determine the information's reliability.

- An online database available at your library where you can search through a collection of reliable published articles and electronic journals. The results of a database search will include only publications and will connect you to abstracts, summaries, or full text (that is, the entire article).

The Web does not offer any guarantees about the accuracy of its content. However, some Web sites and search engines are better than others for trustworthiness. If a Web site's URL ends in *.org, .edu,* or *.gov,* that's like having a good character reference for the content on the site. If your search engine has preselected source material (such as GoogleScholar) or if you have accessed a library database, you will have saved yourself the painful weeding through of hits that cannot help you. Library searches can help you find the kinds of sources your professor wants to see on your topic.

> **Example:** Christine used a database through her university's library to do
>
> keyword searches using the terms "Langston Hughes" and "jazz." She skimmed
>
> the results and picked a few that seemed most related to her topic.

Your instructor may also have some recommendations for good sources on a topic, and there are also sources listed in this textbook as good starting places. Here are some additional tips for finding reliable and relevant sources:

1. **Refine your keyword search.**   Whether you are searching one of your library's databases or the Web, refine your keywords by grouping words together, for example, "Harlem Renaissance." Use *and* or a plus sign (+) to bring up sites that have both topics together. Use *or* when you want results that are for either topic. Two words are better than one to help you narrow the number of sites that come up; use quotation marks around titles or parentheses around key phrases to manage the number of hits as well. To find information on Web pages and avoid the information flood, a good keyword search is essential. Experiment with the phrasing of your keyword.

2. **Use more than one search engine.**   The Internet brings the world to your door, but don't use just Google. Use at least three general search engines to locate the sources you need. In addition to Google, you may want to try Yahoo! (yahoo.com) or WebCrawler (webcrawler.com). Some sites search several different search engines at once: Library of

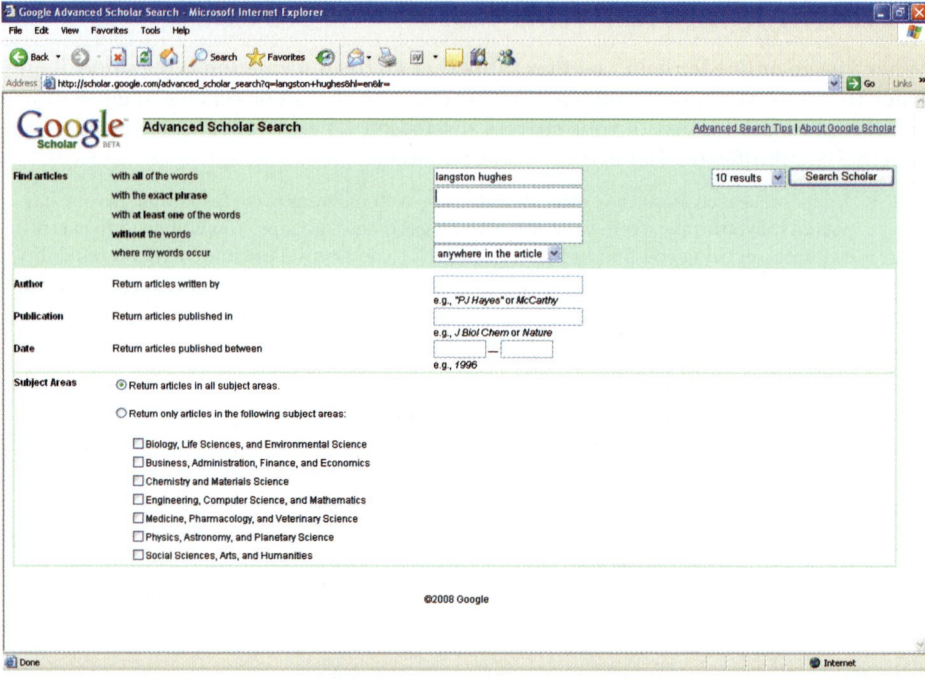

Google Scholar's Advanced Scholar Search page

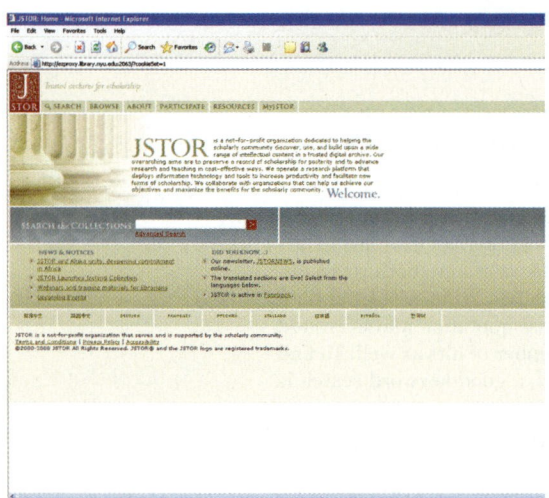

JSTOR online database

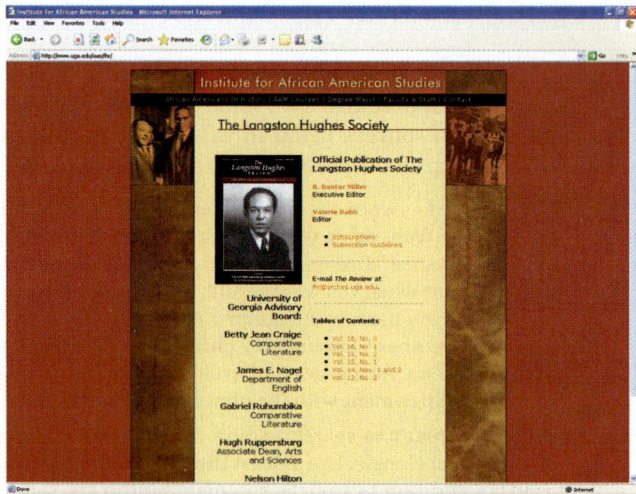

Langston Hughes Society online periodical

Congress (loc.gov) or the Librarian's Index to the Internet (lii.org). You even have search sites that have already been vetted by experts, such as Google Scholar (scholar.google.com) and About.com (about.com).

3. **Use the library, on campus and online.** Check out your library's Web site. Talk to your librarian. The library is not just a collection of printed texts anymore. Your librarian can help you find the library's computerized catalog of books and discipline-specific encyclopedias, bibliographies, and almanacs, such as the *MLA International Bibliography of Books and Articles on Modern Language and Literature* (also available online) or the *Oxford History of English Literature*. In addition, the librarian can help you locate the library's database of scholarly journals and other electronic resources.

RECOGNIZING SIGNS OF UNRELIABLE WEB SITES

The following example shows two Web sites—one unreliable and one reliable—containing the text of Langston Hughes's poem "Harlem." Note the striking differences between the two. It's likely that your eye will go first to the unreliable site;

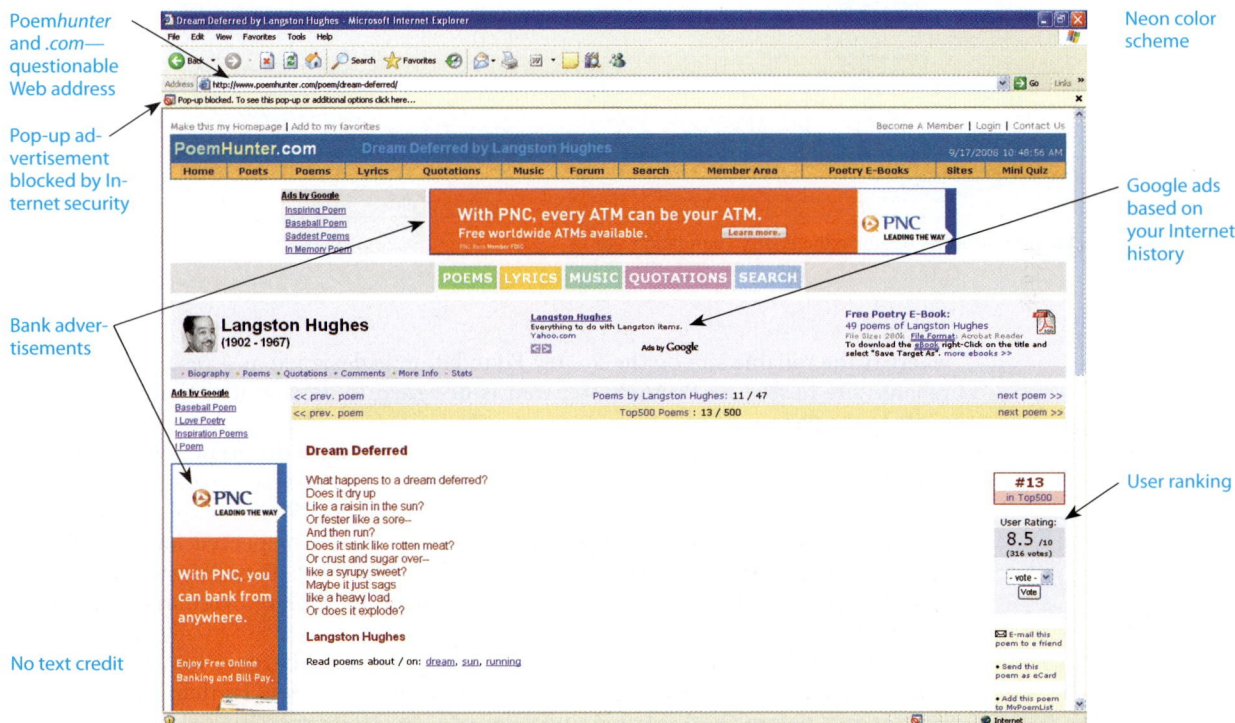

Poem*hunter* and *.com*—questionable Web address

Pop-up advertisement blocked by Internet security

Bank advertisements

No text credit

Neon color scheme

Google ads based on your Internet history

User ranking

A Langston Hughes poem on PoemHunter.com

Poetry Foundation and .org: trustworthy publisher and domain

Subdued color scheme

Functional, professional search tool

Uncluttered, no advertisements

Text credit and citation

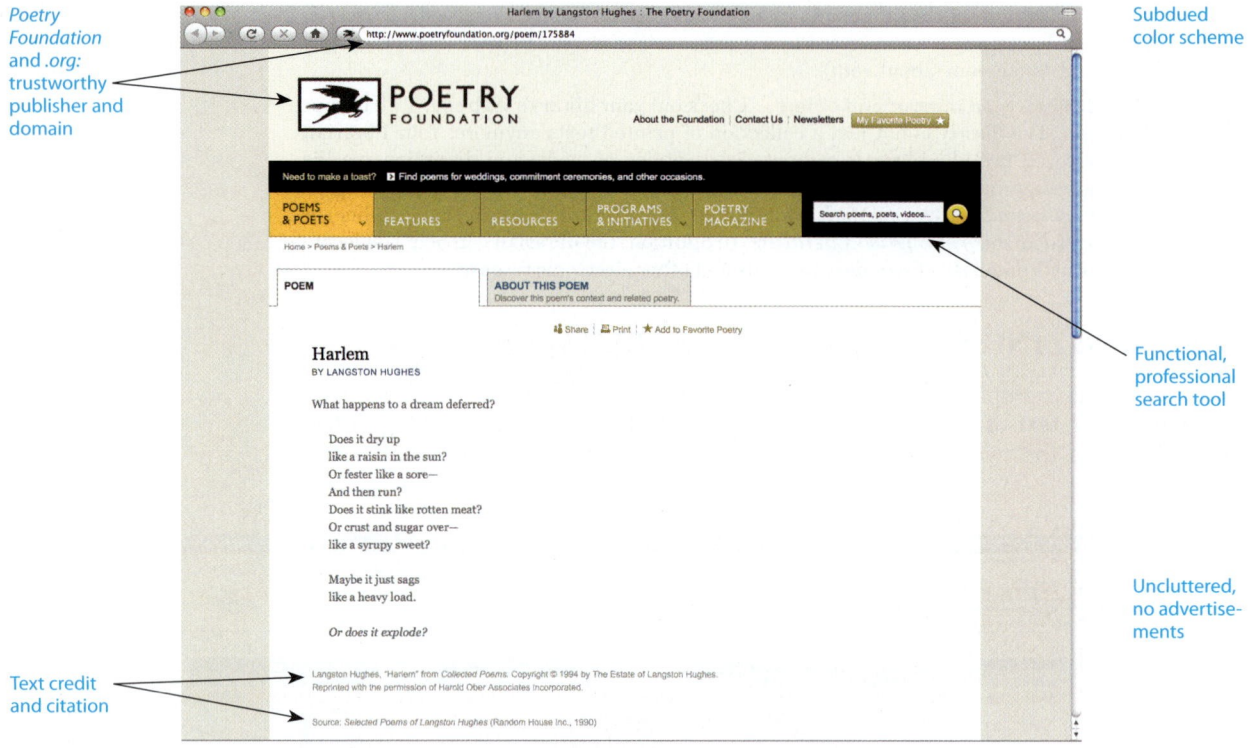

Langston Hughes poem on the Poetry Foundation site

whereas the reliable site by the Poetry Foundation is designed as a resource, the unreliable site hosted by PoemHunter.com is designed to attract attention and amass visits to the page.

Besides flashy colors and design, there are other major differences between the two. Whereas PoemHunter.com has bank ads (don't ignore that blocked pop-up ad, it's a major clue to unreliability), the Poetry Foundation Web site advertises only its own publication, *Poetry* magazine, a well-known and respected journal of poetry. Notice also the references that follow the poem text: PoemHunter.com does give the author of the poem but does not cite any permission or original publication information.

It will save you time if you can quickly recognize the difference between reliable and unreliable sites. A Google search for Langston Hughes's "Harlem" lists PoemHunter.com before the Poetry Foundation site, so strong searching skills and judgment are your keys to efficient, effective Web research.

Evaluating Web Sources

You may find it difficult when using the Web to tell the difference not only between a popular and a scholarly site but also between a reliable site and one that is biased. Whenever you are conducting research, if an opinion or piece of information seems fishy or flimsy, you should double-check it. If you find that information or point of view in only one place, there's a good chance it is unsupported or not widely agreed on by the academic community. When considering whether a publication is reliable and relevant, make note of the following elements.

1. **The Tone of the Information**

   Tone is a major indicator of scholarliness and bias. Avoid Web pages that use poor grammar and punctuation or employ colloquial Internet shorthand. Scholarly information is seldom presented so informally. Also take note of an aggravated tone of voice, or hyperbolic claims, or a failure to consider more than one point of view. These are indicators of bias—which might support your point of view but will detract from the legitimacy of your work.

2. **The Visual Presentation**

   Is the site flashy and full of ads and cartoons? Or is it mostly text-based, with fewer, but higher quality, captioned images? As with print sources, you can tell a lot about a Web page's content and intended audience just by looking at how it is presented. Flashy ads, pop-up windows, intricate backgrounds, complex layouts, and funky colors are all indications that a Web site might not contain reliable content.

3. **The Credentials of the Author**

   Consider how the authors' names and their affiliations (generally universities for scholarly articles) match up with the topic of their article. For instance, Alton Brown might be a name you recognize as an authority from The Food Network, but he would not be a trustworthy expert to cite in a paper on comparative politics. Many databases now provide information on where an article or book has been cited by other academics in their research; this can be a valuable resource in confirming the reliability of a research source.

4. **The Source**

   Sources can be popular or scholarly. A popular source is something you could buy easily at a store, such as *Time* magazine. It is likely to have advertisements in it or be advertised to the general public (for example, a self-help book such as *Rich Dad, Poor Dad*). A scholarly source is generally found through a library rather than a store. Ask whether the source is refereed or peer-reviewed. A publication may or may not specify this, but most trustworthy scholarly publications accept articles only after they have been reviewed, debated, and accepted by a body of experts in the field. Some research databases will allow you to filter for peer-reviewed publications; or, when in doubt, you can ask your librarian whether a publication has been refereed.

5. **The Publisher**

   A commercial publisher will probably suggest a popular aim, whereas an academic publisher such as a university press will suggest a scholarly aim. Is the Web page hosted by a university or academic association? Is it an article of an online encyclopedia? Wikipedia is often a first stop for research. It is updated by readers themselves. While it is a good starting point, it is unlikely your instructor will accept Wikipedia in a college paper. It is better to verify the content you find on Wikipedia through another source that has been vetted by a reliable authority. If it is common knowledge (a birth date, for example), it won't need a citation.

(continued)

> **6. The Articles Themselves**
> Academic articles are often preceded by abstracts that summarize their findings and followed by bibliographies or listings of works cited. Popular articles, however, may lead in with a catchy line that leaves an unanswered question and will seldom list references.

USING VISUAL SOURCES

A picture is worth a thousand words, or so the old proverb goes. We live in a visual world, and visual data are now as easy to acquire as a cut-and-paste job off Google Images. Like all source information, however, the data must be relevant and reliable. Visuals must serve a specific purpose in your paper. A graph or chart can be a useful snapshot of quantitative data. A diagram or flowchart is useful for explaining a process. A picture is qualitative evidence that is used to strengthen or amplify your point. Remember that any visuals, whether from the Web or another source, must be documented in your Works Cited or References list and identified in your paper with a caption. The example here is evidence for a paper on adapting the *Beowulf* epic.

These film shots illustrate portrayals of the Grendel monster and the Beowulf hero in the movie *Beowulf* (top) and the movie *The 13th Warrior* (bottom).

DEVELOPING A THESIS

1. **Connect your interpretation of a text to various sources.** Consider what each source tells you about your topic. Particularly if you are reading literary criticism, decide whether you agree with the critic. If you agree, you may want to use what that critic says to corroborate your reading. If you disagree, use that critic's perspective as a springboard into talking about your own perspective.

   Example: Christine read the following quote in one of her sources:

   > Langston Hughes, in his collection of poems, lavishly uses such characteristics of jazz as repetitions, choruses, riffs, scats, and nonsensical onomatopoeia, to achieve musical success as well as audience participation. It is also significant to note that Hughes's poems are often marked by dissonance, discordance, and line irregularity, which all contribute to the representation of the jazz spirit in verse forms.

   Although this quote directly related to her topic, Christine found that she was dissatisfied with the vague way in which most sources—as this one does—talked about the jazz elements in Hughes's poems. She began to consider the historical reasons why Hughes might have chosen these specific elements.

2. **Form a working thesis.** Once you have gathered your own ideas and taken notes on your sources, try to state your overall idea in a sentence or two. Most likely, your thesis will have the kernel of the idea that you started with, but it will have become more nuanced by your research.

   Example: Christine's original idea was to talk about jazz elements in Hughes's poems. Her research showed her that most critics approach his jazz poetry from a general angle. As a result, she formed the following thesis, which shows a very specific interpretation of why Hughes chose certain jazz elements.

   > *Working thesis:* Hughes used jazz in a significant way. More than simply feeling jazz's influence generally, Hughes felt the influence of African-American jazz specifically.

3. **Refine your thesis.** Rework your thesis to make sure it is arguable; supportable; focused yet complex; and purpose-driven and significant. (See Chapter 3, Developing an Argument, for more on refining your thesis.) Analyze the possible thesis statements that appear below. The first, for example, is a widely accepted fact. Although this particular sentence may function as a good topic sentence or a sentence in the introduction to the paper, it is not an effective thesis statement, because there is nothing about it that the writer has to defend.

INEFFECTIVE THESIS, NOT ARGUABLE

Some of Langston Hughes's poetry was inspired by jazz.

INEFFECTIVE THESIS, NOT SUPPORTABLE

Beyond being a jazz poet, Hughes understood the significance of jazz—even as it was being created—and deliberately used very specific elements of jazz to exclude nonmusical audiences.

INEFFECTIVE THESIS, NOT FOCUSED

Beyond being a jazz poet, Hughes understood the significance of jazz—even as it was being created—and aspects of the jazz form can be found in every one of his poems.

INEFFECTIVE THESIS, NOT PURPOSE-DRIVEN

Beyond being a jazz poet, Langston Hughes was also a big fan of listening to jazz music.

The thesis that Christine ultimately developed is arguable; supportable; complex yet focused; and purpose-driven and significant. This statement takes a widely accepted fact—that Hughes is a jazz poet—and offers a particular and original interpretation of the significance of jazz in Hughes's poetry.

EFFECTIVE THESIS: ARGUABLE, SUPPORTABLE, FOCUSED, AND PURPOSE-DRIVEN

> Beyond being a jazz poet, Hughes understood the significance of jazz—even as it was being created—and used only those aspects of jazz that express the African-American experience.

ARGUABLE: Note that the sentence is arguable: one could say that Hughes's interest in jazz was for another reason altogether—perhaps that it served the type of free verse he wanted to write or that it gave a popular appeal to his poetry. With this thesis, Christine promises to show how race is the prominent factor in determining Hughes's use of jazz, and in so doing, she also promises a nuanced discussion of the elements of jazz present in Hughes's poetry.

SUPPORTABLE: Christine may choose to support this thesis with poems from Hughes's *Montage of a Dream Deferred* collection, which Hughes identified as being "like bebop." Also, since the thesis has to do with all of Hughes's jazz poetry, she would want to choose support from poems written at different times in Hughes's career. Whichever poems Christine chooses, she will need to explicate sections of those poems to show how their elements are primarily influenced by race.

COMPLEX YET FOCUSED: This thesis has plenty of potential for a long paper. Christine can easily limit the scope, however, by choosing a few key poems to use in her discussion.

PURPOSE-DRIVEN AND SIGNIFICANT: The purpose of this thesis is to better understand the role of race and jazz in Hughes's poems—an endeavor that may lead to a greater appreciation of Hughes's achievement and a deeper understanding of how to read his poems.

CREATING A PLAN

If you have ever printed road directions from such Web sites as MapQuest and Google Maps, you know that they provide step-by-step instructions for how to get from point A to point B. Some students may have such a finely tuned sense of direction that they are able to dive directly into writing a first draft. Or maybe a lucky few simply prefer to see where their writing takes them. Most, however, need some kind of a road map for their paper.

> "I trust in my instinct. . . . I don't start with a structure and then go someplace and impose the structure. . . . I'm taking notes all of the time. . . . And then when I get all of that material assembled, often what I do is go back and think about that instinct . . . trusting that where you reacted deeply, emotionally to something, that's the framework." Conversation with Barry Lopez

Choose your best support. Review the notes you took on your sources and on the primary text. Select a few quotes that best illustrate a point you want to make. Note ideas that you will want to paraphrase or summarize in your paper, and remember that these are important forms of support as well. An outline provides you with step-by-step instructions on how to get from your introduction (Point A) to your conclusion (Point B). It might also help to sketch out an informal plan like this one.

- **Introduction:** Includes your thesis, why the thesis is important, and why you want to explore it in your paper
- **Body:** Indicates the points you will use to support your thesis in a series of paragraphs
- **Conclusion:** Adds a final comment that connects your thesis to a larger issue, or places your thesis in a larger context, which will make it more meaningful to your audience

Outlines can be very brief and simple, or longer and in-depth. You might just write a *scratch outline*—a list of topics you want to cover. If you're writing a shorter paper that analyzes one work, such a topic outline might be enough. Topic outlines simply provide the order in which you plan to talk about your broad topics. Alternatively, instead of single words or phrases, you might find it more helpful to state every idea in a complete sentence, which would give you a *sentence outline* to work from.

Until you have written many papers and learned more about the way your own writing process works best for you, an outline can help you to organize your thoughts and to understand where your paper is headed. Generally, the longer or more complex your paper, the more useful a detailed outline will be. For example, before writing a research paper, you may want to make an outline so detailed that it includes the quotes you plan to integrate. In fact, you may find a full formal outline absolutely necessary.

Part of Christine's detailed outline for her research paper on Langston Hughes and jazz is given here. Compare this slice of outline with the third and fourth paragraphs of the paper (pages 122–123). Note how the outline is so detailed that Christine had only to flesh out the outline points into complete sentences when writing the actual paper.

II. Blues in the Jazz Age
    A. "The Dream Keeper" and the Jazz Age
        1. Hughes's *The Weary Blues* published in 1925
        2. 1925 was middle of Jazz Age
           a. Marked by energy and optimism
           b. Jazz connoted rebellion
        3. "The Dream Keeper" influenced by blues, not jazz
           a. Reads like abbreviated blues lyrics
           b. Compound words "cloud-cloth" and "too-rough" create slow blues pace
    B. The Jazz Age and African-American experience
        1. Jazz Age and the blues have contrasting relationship
           a. Blues related to jazz; jazz grew out of blues roots
           b. Jazz exuberant; blues melancholy
        2. Historical context is key
           a. Jazz Age "unprecedented prosperity" ("Roaring Twenties" article) for whites
           b. Great Migration—10% of blacks moved from South to North
               (1) Low wages, poor housing conditions
               (2) Disease

Once you have conducted your research, developed a thesis, and created a plan, you are ready to draft your paper. This is just a first draft, so leave yourself time to revise.

DRAFTING YOUR PAPER

The word *draft* is used here to help keep the pressure down. *Draft* connotes that what you are writing is not final, that it is a work-in-progress. Get your thoughts out on paper. You will probably revise your first draft, so you will want to save your drafts early and often. Label your drafts so that you can retrace your steps (put "draft l," "draft 2," and so on in the filename or use specific dates to show what the most current draft is). Print the original. Having a hard copy may free you to tinker and explore.

Introductions, Conclusions, and Body Paragraphs

You may find you want to write your introduction last, or right before you write your conclusion but after you've developed the supporting points of the paper. If you do, these two framing paragraphs can speak to each other more obviously, with the introduction stating your thesis and why it matters to you and the conclusion bringing in your thesis and why it might matter to your reader.

Drafting Body Paragraphs

- Focus each paragraph on one idea.
- State the main idea of each paragraph in a topic sentence.
- Connect the information clearly in each paragraph to support the topic.
- Make sure the paragraph clearly supports your thesis.

REVISING YOUR DRAFT

When you've finished a draft you feel is complete, take a break from your paper—distance can sometimes help you see if your ideas flow as naturally as you thought when you first wrote them. Distance can also help you catch editing mistakes you miss in the heat of developing your ideas. It is also good to get some feedback from a fellow student or a friend. When you come back to your paper, annotate the issues you find. (It is great if you can get your peer to annotate your paper as well.) As you write and revise your paper, you have a chance to re-envision how to make your argument clearer and to support it more effectively.

DRAFT INTRODUCTORY PARAGRAPH

Jazz poetry, according to the American Academy of Poets Web site, is "a literary genre defined as poetry necessarily informed by jazz music—that is, poetry in which the poet responds to and writes about jazz." By this definition, Langston Hughes was a jazz poet. Many critics point to specific techniques that Hughes employs to create the effect of jazz. Although the observations are true, such technical readings fail to show the full extent of Hughes's achievement in jazz poetry. More than just a jazz poet, Hughes understood the significance of jazz as it was being created, and he used only the aspects of jazz that expressed the African-American experience.

In what way? Back up this assertion.

Which critics? What techniques? May be a good place for an outside source.

Used how? Maybe back this up. Is there an existing critical argument my claim could respond to in order to create a stronger thesis?

REVISED INTRODUCTORY PARAGRAPH

Jazz poetry, according to the American Academy of Poets Web site, is "a literary genre defined as poetry necessarily informed by jazz music—that is, poetry in which the poet responds to and writes about jazz." Langston Hughes was a jazz poet in that his poetry often captured jazz in a literary form. Many critics point to specific techniques that Hughes employs to create the effect of jazz. One such critic is Lionel Davidas. Davidas observes how Hughes creates jazz rhythms in his poetry through the use of repetitions, line irregularity, nonsensical sounds, and other elements associated with jazz music:

> Langston Hughes, in his collection of poems, lavishly uses such characteristics of jazz as repetitions, choruses, riffs, scats, and nonsensical onomatopoeia, to achieve musical success as well as audience participation. It is also significant to note that Hughes's poems are often marked by dissonance, discordance, and line irregularity, which all contribute to the representation of the jazz spirit in verse forms. (268)

Although these observations are true, readings like Davidas's fail to show the full extent of Hughes's achievement in jazz poetry. Beyond being a jazz poet, Hughes understood the significance of jazz—even as it was being created—and used only those aspects of jazz that express the African-American experience.

DRAFT SUPPORTING PARAGRAPH (BODY)

The discussion here is a little unfounded . . . maybe I need a researched source.

This is too informal! Need to keep an eye out for these.

Are these common knowledge? Maybe include a brief description.

Didn't I see a good image for this when I was researching online? That might help engage the reader here and enrich the discussion of historical context.

"The Dream Keeper" was published in 1925. At that time, America was in the midst of the "Jazz Age," the period from 1920 to 1930 marked by energy and optimism. Jazz itself was popular and connoted rebellion. However, Hughes's collection *The Weary Blues* was influenced more by (obviously) the blues than by this new form of jazz. While "The Dream Keeper" doesn't have as obvious a connection to the blues as Hughes's poems that copy blues lyrics directly—such as "Po' Boy Blues"—the repetition early in the poem bears echoes of the repetition characteristic of the blues. Consider the repetition of "Bring me all of your" in the first three lines; typical blues lyrics follow a pattern where the first couplet repeats before a third couplet ends the lyric Here, half the couplet is repeated and half resolved in both instances. Since Hughes was writing in the "Jazz Age," it may seem surprising that so many of his poems in *The Weary Blues* reflect the blues (lines 1, 3). His decision may in part have been informed by the fact that jazz grew out of the blues, and they were closely related enough that Hughes could use blues and be safe in the jazz realm. But whereas blues are "blue" and melancholy, jazz is "jazzy." The solution to this puzzle is in the historical context. The Roaring Twenties brought "unprecedented prosperity" to the United States ("Roaring Twenties") but it was also the era of the Great Migration, when many African Americans left the south and moved north. Times were difficult for blacks, who faced low wages and poor housing conditions (Marks). So, at the time that Hughes was writing these poems, jazz had two forms: the exuberant, new jazz, and the blues roots it came from. Hughes chose the form—the blues—that best reflected the state of the common black man at the time.

Maybe need some more here—how did jazz, just a music form, connote rebellion?

This explanation is cluttered and a bit confusing; illustrate or clarify.

Reads like a topic sentence. Break the paragraph here?

Cute, but is it meaningful?

Maybe I need more research here, since understanding historical context is so important to my argument.

Could this point have its own paragraph?

REVISED SUPPORTING PARAGRAPH (BODY)

Hughes first published "The Dream Keeper" in 1925 and included it in his collection *The Weary Blues* the following year ("Chronology" 9). At that time, America was in the midst of the "Jazz Age," the period from 1920 to 1930 marked by energy and optimism. Jazz itself was popular and connoted rebellion, as it was associated with nightclubs, sex, and drinking (Tucker). But Hughes's collection was clearly influenced more by the blues than by this new form of jazz. The title of the collection suggests the blues idiom takes center stage in these poems, and indeed, "The Dream Keeper" is no exception. Although it does not have as overt a connection to the blues as Hughes's poems that replicate blues lyrics directly—such as "Po' Boy Blues"—the repetition early in the poem bears echoes of the repetition characteristic of the blues. "Bring me all of your" is repeated twice within the first three lines; the object the addressee is told to bring, however, varies (lines 1, 3). In a way, lines 1 through 3 are a compounded version of blues lyrics. Typical blues lyrics follow a pattern where the first couplet repeats before a third couplet. Here, half the couplet is repeated and half resolved in both instances. Blues also has a hand in the pace of the poem. Compound phrases like "cloud-cloth" and "too- rough" slow the pace of reading, as does the high number of line breaks compared with the small number of words (6, 7).

DRAFT CONCLUDING PARAGRAPH

Too familiar, not the right tone for a research paper.

Elaborate or change wording; doesn't sound right.

Embellish conclusion to include new arguments based on content. Remember to restate the argument.

Tie in history and time period with this, since it's the basis for the argument.

As you can see, "The Dream Keeper" and "Harlem (Dream Deferred)" demonstrate how Hughes effectively incorporated new forms of jazz as they arose. Although he does successfully use technical elements of jazz music, to end a reading there would be to miss Hughes's larger achievement. He did not simply adopt jazz technique; he selected only the trends that reflected the African-American experience. He leaves out the "white" sounds of swing and opts instead for the forms of blues and be-bop. In so doing, Hughes's poetry captures both the music, as it evolved from blues to be-bop, and the African-American experience.

REVISED CONCLUDING PARAGRAPH

As "The Dream Keeper" and "Harlem (Dream Deferred)" demonstrate, Hughes effectively incorporated new forms of jazz as they arose. Although he does successfully use formal elements of jazz music, to end a reading there would be to miss Hughes's larger achievement. Hughes did not simply adopt jazz technique; he selected only those trends in jazz that reflected the African-American experience of the time in which he wrote. There is no room in his poetry for the smooth sounds of swing at the hands of whites; instead, he used the true African-American forms of blues and be-bop. In so doing, Hughes's poetry captures both the music, as it evolved from blues to be-bop, and the African-American experience, as it moved from the blues of the Great Migration to the bitter conflict of continued discrimination.

EDITING AND FORMATTING YOUR PAPER

After you have looked at your paper as a whole, take one more look at its sentence structure, spelling, and formatting. These simple matters, if not done correctly, can interfere with your instructor's good opinion of a well thought-out paper. You may have been making small corrections all along, but consider this last edit your dress rehearsal for making your paper public.

Questions to Guide Editing

1. Are my sentences wordy?
2. Have I dropped a word out of a sentence?
3. Is my point of view consistent?
4. Does each sentence make sense?
5. Do I have any sentence fragments?
6. Are my commas in the right places?
7. Do my subjects and verbs agree—single to single and plural to plural?
8. Are my apostrophes used correctly—**'s** for singular possession (this *critic's* opinion; *Hughes's* work); **s'** for plural possession when the word ends in s (the *singers'* music)?
9. Do my quotation marks represent the exact words of the writer?
10. Have I paraphrased without giving credit to the source?

In addition to formatting your paper with a heading and a title, you will need to follow the formatting guidelines your professor prefers, particularly as you cite sources in your papers:

- The *Modern Language Association Handbook for Writers of Research Papers* (MLA) provides guidelines for formatting papers and citing sources for courses in the humanities (see the MLA Documentation Style Guide at the end of this book).
- *The Chicago Manual of Style* (University of Chicago Press) or *A Manual for Writers of Term Papers, Theses, and Dissertations* (Turabian) is sometimes required for humanities courses in which an instructor requires that footnotes be used.
- *The Publication Manual of the American Psychological Association* (APA) has a different set of formatting guidelines for citing sources in the social sciences.
- The Council of Science Editors (CSE) has put together *Scientific Style and Format*, guidelines for papers in mathematics, engineering, computer sciences, and the natural sciences.

Whatever form your instructor wishes you to follow, pay close attention to the conventions for quoting and citing sources that are provided. Mistakes can be misconstrued as plagiarism, and following the correct form will have the added benefit of making your paper consistent and clear. This is the effect you want your paper's design to convey.

"I want the reader to know that the presence of information is there." Conversation with Robert Pinsky

Variety is the spice of life, but not the spice you need for your paper. Be consistent with the features of your design, and make your paper look clean, clear, and serious.

You can see in-text references and a properly formatted Works Cited page by looking at the student research paper that follows. Other student papers, such as the explication of William Blake's "The Garden of Love," which appears in Chapter 4, Writing across the Curriculum, and the argument paper on Robert Pinsky's "Shirt" in Chapter 3, Developing an Argument, can also serve as models for in-text references. In the latter paper, note the proper parenthetical citation of lines of poetry rather than page numbers.

Remember, too, that even if you respond to a single source, you should still cite that work. This is especially important when many versions of the same text exist. For example, if you are reading Charlotte Brönte's classic *Jane Eyre* from a Penguin Classics edition, the pagination will be different from the edition of *Jane Eyre* published in the Oxford World's Classics series. Only a full citation in a Works Cited list will tell your reader from which version you are reading. For an example of a single source, see the final draft of the student paper in Chapter 7 on Jamaica Kincaid's "Girl."

A STUDENT PAPER: A RESEARCH PAPER ON LANGSTON HUGHES

Keenan 1

Christine Keenan

Professor Jackson

English 200

15 May 2011

From "Dream Keeper" to "Dream Deferred":

Langston Hughes and Jazz Poetry

Jazz poetry, according to the American Academy of Poets Web site, is "a literary genre defined as poetry necessarily informed by jazz music—that is, poetry in which the poet responds to and writes about jazz" ("A Brief Guide to Jazz Poetry"). Langston Hughes was a jazz poet in that his poetry often captured jazz in a literary form. Many critics point to specific techniques that Hughes employs to create the effect of jazz. One such critic is Lionel Davidas. Davidas observes how Hughes creates jazz rhythms in his poetry through the use of repetitions, line irregularity, nonsensical sounds, and other elements associated with jazz music:

> Langston Hughes, in his collection of poems, lavishly uses such characteristics of jazz as repetitions, choruses, riffs, scats, and nonsensical onomatopoeia, to achieve musical success as well as audience participation. It is also significant to note that Hughes's poems are often marked by dissonance, discordance, and line irregularity, which all contribute to the representation of the jazz spirit in verse forms. (268)

Title centered; no underline.

Quote from Web site source.

Block quote (more than four lines long) from a periodical source.

Establishes a critical reading to which the student responds.

Keenan 2

Although these observations are true, readings like Davidas's fail to show the full extent of Hughes's achievement in jazz poetry. Beyond being a jazz poet, Hughes understood the significance of jazz—even as it was being created—and used only those aspects of jazz that express the African-American experience.

Thesis statement

Two of Hughes's collections that have an overt connection to music are *The Weary Blues,* published in 1926, and *Montage of a Dream Deferred,* published in 1951. In the twenty-five years between their publications, jazz music changed dramatically. Two poems, "The Dream Keeper" from *The Weary Blues* and "Harlem (Dream Deferred)" from *Montage of a Dream Deferred,* show how Hughes effectively responded to the current trends in jazz from an African-American perspective.

Author maps out how she will support her thesis.

Hughes first published "The Dream Keeper" in 1925 and included it in his collection *The Weary Blues* the following year ("Chronology" 9). At that time, America was in the midst of the "Jazz Age," the period from 1920 to 1930 marked by energy and optimism. Jazz itself was popular but connoted rebellion, as it was typically associated with the hallmarks of dangerous behavior, including drug use, drinking, and sex (Tucker). But Hughes's collection was clearly influenced more by the blues than by this new form of jazz. The title of the collection suggests the blues idiom takes center stage in these poems, and indeed, "The Dream Keeper" is no exception. Although it does not have as overt a connection to the blues as Hughes's poems that replicate blues lyrics directly—such as "Po' Boy Blues"—the repetition early in the poem bears echoes of the repetition characteristic of the blues. "Bring me all of your" is repeated twice within the first three lines; the object the addressee is told to bring, however, varies (lines 1, 3). In a way, lines 1 through 3 are a condensed version of blues lyrics.

Topic sentence introduces first poem to be analyzed.

Example of paraphrase.

Student's own analysis.

Keenan 3

Typical blues lyrics follow a pattern where the first couplet repeats before a third couplet ends the lyric. Here, half the couplet is repeated and half resolved in both instances. Blues also has a hand in the pace of the poem. Compound phrases like "cloud-cloth" and "too-rough" slow the pace of reading, as does the high number of line breaks compared with the small number of words (6, 7).

Since Hughes was writing in the Jazz Age, it may seem surprising that so many of his poems in *The Weary Blues* reflect the blues. In part, his decision may have been informed by the fact that jazz grew out of the blues, and the close relationship of the two forms of music allowed Hughes to use blues and still be in the realm of jazz. But blues is marked by a "blue" or melancholy frame of mind (Oliver), not the exuberance of the Jazz Age. Examining the historical context offers an answer for why Hughes chose blues over jazz. Although the Roaring Twenties brought "unprecedented prosperity" to the United States ("Roaring Twenties"), it was also the era of the Great Migration, the movement in which ten percent of African-Americans left the South and moved North. These were difficult times for blacks, as they faced low wages, poor housing conditions, and disease in the northern cities to which they relocated (Marks). Although positive advances did occur in the African-American community, such as the Harlem Renaissance, Emily Bernard has noted that most blacks were not affected by the Renaissance—only a so-called talented tenth participated, leaving most blacks to face everyday problems (xvi-xvii).

To put it simply, jazz at the time that Hughes was writing poems for *The Weary Blues* had two forms: the exuberant new jazz and the blues roots from which it came. Hughes chose the form of music—the blues—that best reflected the state of

Topic sentence that introduces a new thread of discussion.

Example of summary.

Transition paragraph. The first two sentences conclude the blues discussion. The last sentence segues into discussion of the second poem.

Student's analysis.

Keenan 3

the common black man. By the time Hughes was writing the poems for *Montage of a Dream Deferred,* however, jazz had changed and once again offered two new forms.

The 1930s and 1940s brought a change to jazz: ensembles of about twelve players began to change the rhythms of jazz into swing. Swing, which became the popular dance music in more reputable venues than just bars and clubs, was usually performed by big bands under the direction of white leaders like Benny Goodman and Glenn Miller (see fig. 1). Thus, jazz became mainstream and middle class, unlike the "hot jazz" of the 1920s (Tucker). Also, the traditionally African-American art form had now been taken over and turned into a commercial success largely by whites, with a few exceptions like Duke Ellington and Count Basie (Borshuk 61–62).

Jazz underwent another major change in the 1940s. Young African-American musicians in Harlem met in informal jam sessions where they began to experiment with nearly every aspect of the music—melody, harmony, and rhythm. Musicians such as Dizzy Gillespie, Thelonious Monk, and Charlie Parker increasingly championed improvisation and creativity over the organized big band aesthetic (see fig. 2). Their innovations included "rapid tempo, irregular phrase groups . . . sudden, sharp drum accents, [and] chromatically altered notes" (Tucker). This new form of jazz became known as be-bop, a form of music that many critics see as "the revolt of young black musicians of the ghetto against the commercialization of 'swing music' of the time" (Lenz 274). In other words, be-bop made jazz into a predominantly African-American art once more.

When Langston Hughes penned "Harlem (Dream Deferred)," two types of jazz existed: the mellow, organized sound of swing and the creative, frantic sound of be-bop. For *Montage of a Dream Deferred,* Hughes chose to use the latter

Marginal annotations:

Example of summary.

Example of paraphrase.

Reference figures in the body of the paper.

Citation of both paraphrase and direct quote.

Topic sentence introduces the second poem to be analyzed.

Keenan 4

Fig. 1. The Glenn Miller Orchestra. From *Glenn Miller Orchestra Online;* Glenn Miller Productions, n.d.; Web; 12 May 2011.

Figures are cited when they appear, so do not need to appear on the Works Cited page.

type. We know this was a conscious choice, as Hughes's own note to the collection explains:

> In terms of current Afro-American popular music and the sources from
> which it has progressed—jazz, ragtime, swing, blues, boogie-woogie, and
> be-bop—this poem on contemporary Harlem, like be-bop, is marked by
> conflicting changes, sudden nuances, sharp and impudent interjections,
> broken rhythms, and passages sometimes in the manner of the jam session,
> sometimes the popular song,

Keenan 5

Fig. 2. Tommy Potter, Charlie Parker, Dizzy Gillespie, and John Coltrane—leaders of the be-bop movement—at the famous jazz club Birdland, c. 1951. From Nate Chinen; "Charlie Parker, Uptown and Down"; *The New York Times;* The New York Times, 24 Aug. 2007; Web; 12 May 2011.

punctuated by the riffs, runs, breaks, and disc-tortions [*sic*] of the music of a

community in transition. (387)

Indeed, these be-bop-like traits are present in "Harlem (Dream Deferred)":

"conflicting changes" and "sudden nuance" can be seen in the series of images

Conclusion that shows significance of student's preceding analysis.

Keenan 6

Hughes selects; "sharp and impudent interjections" occur in the form of the last line,

"Or does it explode?" (line 11); and "broken rhythms" are created by the space after

the first line and the space before the last line. Hughes, then, successfully reflects

be-bop technique in his poetry and, in so doing, uses the form of jazz aligned with

African Americans, rather than the form associated with mainstream, middle-class

whites.

More significant than the blues and be-bop form, however, is Hughes's use of

blues and be-bop content. "The Dream Keeper" and "Harlem (Dream Deferred)"

share the theme of dreams, yet each reflects the mindset of the music that influenced

it—music that in turn was influenced by the historical events of its day. "The Dream

Keeper" is itself dreamy in its imagery of "blue cloud-cloth" and the diction of phrases

like "heart melodies" (6, 7). Despite these whimsical elements, the act of tucking

away one's dreams so the world will not harm them is a sad one. In fact, the tone

of the poem is melancholy, or "blue." Even the one color mentioned in the poem is

"blue," which guides the reader toward blue (i.e., sad) feelings (6). This laying aside

of dreams is more than the material of blues music; it was also, for many blacks,

the reality of the Great Migration. Reading "The Dream Keeper" with the Great

Migration in mind makes the poem seem as if it is directly about the blues created by

the migration. Blacks were motivated to migrate by the promise of opportunity and

freedom from the South's discrimination; once in the North, however, blacks often

found limited advancement possibilities in their jobs and continued to suffer from

segregation (Marks). In a sense, then, African Americans of the Great Migration often

had to lay aside their dreams from the "too-rough fingers" of reality (7).

Margin annotations:

Reiteration that citation is to poetic line. Avoids confusion with source page numbers found in other citations.

Citation of line in poem.

Topic sentence that introduces a new thread of discussion and analysis.

Student's analysis.

Student's synthesis of poem and historical context.

Example of summary.

Keenan 7

Similarly, "Harlem (Dream Deferred)" captures the mindset and historical context that gave rise to be-bop. Although the dream theme is the same as in "The Dream Keeper," its imagery of "fester[ing] like a sore" and "stink[ing] like rotten meat" suggests an uglier, bitterer side of dreams than anything that appears in "The Dream Keeper" (4, 6). John Lowney's characterization of Harlem is helpful in understanding this shift; he writes, "By the 1940s, Harlem was of course no longer the center of refuge and hope associated with the New Negro Renaissance. Although still a major destination for poor migrant blacks during the Great Depression, Harlem had become better known nationally as an explosive site of urban racial conflict, first in 1935 and then in 1943" (362). Those years saw race riots in Harlem, and racial tension continued to grow as blacks faced discrimination even in the World War II era (362). Lowney notes that "the agitated sound of *Montage* struck many of [Hughes's] contemporaries as a radical departure from the more straightforward 'populist' rhetoric of his best-known work" (369). Indeed, in reflecting be-bop's dramatic change from swing, Hughes's poetry also takes a dramatic shift from earlier modes. This shift shows the rising frustration of African Americans whose dreams were no longer rooted in melancholy from being tucked away, but were now the product of dreams that continued to be deferred, nearly halfway into the twentieth century.

As "The Dream Keeper" and "Harlem (Dream Deferred)" demonstrate, Hughes effectively incorporated new forms of jazz as they arose. Although he does successfully use formal elements of jazz music, to end a reading there would be to miss Hughes's larger achievement. Hughes did not simply adopt jazz technique; he selected only those trends in jazz that reflected the African-American experience of

Student's analysis.

Example of direct quotation.

Student's synthesis of poem and historical context.

Reiteration of thesis and broadening to encompass Hughes's overall achievement.

Reiteration of thesis and broadening to encompass Hughes's overall achievement.

Topic sentence that signals conclusion.

Keenan 8

the time in which he wrote. There is no room in his poetry for the smooth sounds of swing at the hands of whites; instead, he used the true African-American forms of blues and be-bop. In so doing, Hughes's poetry captures both the music, as it evolved from blues to be-bop, and the African-American experience, as it moved from the blues of the Great Migration to the bitter conflict of continued discrimination.

> Broadens thesis to include historical discussion presented in the body of the paper.

Keenan 9

Works Cited

Introduction to a book.
> Bernard, Emily. Introduction. *Remember Me to Harlem: The Letters of Langston Hughes and Carl Van Vechten, 1925–1964*. Ed. Bernard. New York: Knopf, 2001. xiii–xxviii. Print.

Book.
> Borshuk, Michael. *Swinging the Vernacular*. New York: Routledge, 2006. Print.

> "A Brief Guide to Jazz Poetry." *Poets.org*. Academy of American Poets, 2011. Web. 8 May 2011.

Article on a Web site.

Selection from a collection, cross-referenced.
> "A Chronology of Langston Hughes." Rampersad and Roessel 8–20.

> Davidas, Lionel. " 'I, Too, Sing America': Jazz and Blues Techniques and Effects in Some of Langston Hughes's Selected Poems." *Dialectical Anthropology* 26 (2001): 267–272. Print.

Print periodical.

Anthology.
> Delbanco, Nicholas, and Alan Cheuse, eds. *Literature: Craft and Voice*. 2nd ed. New York: McGraw, 2013. Print.

Keenan 10

Hughes, Langston. "The Dream Keeper." Delbanco and Cheuse 161.

——. "Harlem (Dream Deferred)." Delbanco and Cheuse 161.

——. *Montage of a Dream Deferred*. Rampersad and Roessel 387–429.

——. "The Weary Blues." Delbanco and Cheuse 929.

Lenz, Gunter. "The Riffs, Runs, Breaks, and Distortions of the Music of a Community

in Transition." *Massachusetts Review* 44.1–2 (2003): 269–282. *ProQuest*. Web.

11 May 2011.

Lowney, John. "Langston Hughes and the 'Nonsense' of Bebop." *American Literature*

72.2 (2000): 357–385. Web. 11 May 2011.

Marks, Carole. "The Great Migration: African Americans Searching for the Promised

Land, 1916–1930." *In Motion: The African-American Migration Experience*.

Ed. Howard Dodson and Sylviane A. Diouf. Schomburg Center for Research in

Black Culture, n.d. Web. 11 May 2011.

Oliver, Paul. "Blues." *Grove Music Online*. Web. 11 May 2011.

Rampersad, Arnold, and David Roessel, eds. *The Collected Poems of Langston*

Hughes. New York: Vintage, 1995. Print.

Tucker, Mark, and Travis A. Jackson. "Jazz." *Grove Music Online*. Web. 11 May 2011.

Ward, Geoffrey C., and Ken Burns. "Roaring Twenties." *Jazz: A Film by Ken Burns*.

PBS, n.d. Web. 11 May 2011.

Margin annotations:

Selection from an antholgy, cross-referenced.

Selection from a collection, cross-referenced.

Article from a database.

Online periodical.

Article on a scholarly Web site.

Entry in a database.

Collection.

Entry in a database.

Article on a Web site.

Part 2 Fiction

6 Reading a Story for Its Elements

THE store's pretty empty, it being Thursday afternoon, so there was nothing much to do except lean on the register and wait for the girls to show up again. The whole store was like a pinball machine and I didn't know which tunnel they'd come out of. After a while they come around out of the far aisle, around the lightbulbs, records at discount of the Caribbean Six or Tony Martin Sings or some such gunk you wonder they waste the wax on, six-packs of candy bars, and plastic toys done up in cellophane that fall apart when a kid looks at them anyway. Around they come, Queenie still leading the way, and holding a little gray jar in her hand. Slots Three through Seven are unmanned and I could see her wondering between Stokes and me, but Stokesie with his usual luck draws an old party in baggy gray pants who stumbles up with four giant cans of pineapple juice (what do these bums do with all that pineapple juice? I've often asked myself) so the girls come to me. Queenie puts down the jar and I take it into my fingers icy cold.

—from "A&P" by John Updike

A FIRST READING

Most of us read *casually* most of the time, not worrying too much about the way the piece—whether fiction or nonfiction—is put together. The first time we read something is one of the most fruitful times. When you first are exposed to a good story, you experience the pleasure of surprise, because the fiction writer has used a sophisticated grasp of technique to create a fresh impression—permitting you to see and feel and recognize something new. Sometimes that first experience will be a physical sensation like those "icy cold" fingers on the jar in the last sentence of the excerpt from "A&P." Sometimes that experience will be something more complex, like the jaded anticipation of the narrator at the cash register as he or she (we don't yet know which) follows the movements of customers at the A&P. You will probably have a gut feeling about the characters and what happens to them. You may feel sympathy with or confusion at the characters' thoughts or actions. You may enjoy the tale's beautiful language or find the dialogue between characters amusing. But *why* do you have these responses?

A CRITICAL READING

A writer creates a story out of material he or she has observed in the world and from incidents or feelings in his or her own life. But the result will not hold up well if the writer lacks a firm grasp of the **craft,** or conscious artistry, of fiction. As a noun, *craft* refers to the elements that constitute a story; as a verb, *craft* refers to the process of making or fashioning a story out of those elements. When authors write fiction, what they think they know—or believe or dream about or feel—needs to be made clear to others, and that process of transmission requires skill. Among the major elements of the craft of fiction are these:

> **plot**—the sequence of events in a story (see Chapter 8).
>
> **character**—the depiction of human beings (and nonhumans) within the story (see Chapter 9).
>
> **setting**—when and where a story takes place (see Chapter 10)
>
> **point of view**—who tells the story (see Chapter 11).
>
> **language, tone, and style**—the elements that conjure a story's particular flavor and voice, as achieved because of the words the author chooses and the rhythm with which he or she puts the words together (see Chapter 12).
>
> **theme**—the large meanings and connections explored in a piece of writing. Theme is what a story is "about" beyond the specific characters and events of the story (see Chapter 13).
>
> **symbol**—an object or an event that transcends literal interpretation. A symbol works by using a particular object or event to represent something larger than the object or event itself (see Chapter 14).

CONTINUED ON PAGE 145

"The reading habit and the love of books physically, this particular package of words, the smell of the glue, the look of the print, was all that mattered to me to the point that I thought it would be wonderful to create such objects."

Conversation with John Updike, available on connect.mcgraw-hill.com

John Updike *...you...draw with words when you write.*

A Conversation on Writing

Writing and the Visual Arts

The pictorial and the verbal are similar in that they both take place in two dimensions on paper or canvas. . . . Drawing was a part of the gentleman's equipment, in fact, in the nineteenth century, just like operating a camera is for a twentieth-century person. . . . Handwriting is itself a kind of drawing and the letters are in a way visual objects. . . . I wanted to be a cartoonist but I fairly slowly saw that there were others more gifted than I at drawing [, so] I contented myself with being a writer in the theory that in a way you . . . draw with words when you write.

Reading "A&P"

As I read those two paragraphs things come back to me that I'm tempted to share. One was the line "with a good tan and a sweet, soft, broad looking can." Some of the publishers who had to deal with this story in an anthology had great trouble with that *can*. . . . If they wanted to put it in there they should put it all in and let the kids get the shock of the word *can* in print. . . . The parenthetical thought, "Do you really think it's a mind in there or just a little buzz like a bee in a glass jar?" I think has served as the start of a lot of classroom discussions. But to me it seemed true of Sammy's worldview. Your job as a writer of fiction is not to present an ideal world but to try to present the world that you see and hear around you.

To watch this entire interview and hear the author read from "A&P," go to connect.mcgraw-hill.com.

RESEARCH ASSIGNMENT   In his interview, Updike talks about how he originally wrote several more scenes in this story but his editor at *The New Yorker* convinced him that the story should end where it does. Which would you prefer? Explain your answer.

Born in Reading, Pennsylvania, John Updike (1932–2009) began writing at a young age; his mother suggested it might cure him of a stammer. He became one of America's most celebrated authors, with abundant honors and a widespread readership and published over fifty titles of fiction, nonfiction, and poetry—including two volumes of art criticism and several children's books. Updike began his career writing "Talk of the Town" pieces for *The New Yorker,* the magazine where his first published story appeared. Much (but not all) of Updike's fiction concerns the conflicts—internal and external—among middle-class Protestants in the American Northeast. He is most famous for his "Rabbit" quartet; these four novels follow an ex–basketball player named Harry "Rabbit" Angstrom, who struggles with the lack of fulfillment he feels in the presence of—and when deprived of—his family. (Those novels are, in order of publication, *Rabbit, Run; Rabbit Redux; Rabbit Is Rich;* and *Rabbit at Rest*—notice the pattern of repeated "R"s.) While some of Updike's characters do reprehensible or embarrassing things, the author manages to elicit our sympathy for them. He convinces us, even in the short space of a story, that his characters live and breathe in the American landscape—and that their problems are similar to ours. A number of Updike's short stories, including "A&P" (1961), are considered classic examples of the form. He died in January 2009, at the age of seventy-six, leaving behind what many consider the finest legacy of realistic fiction in modern American life.

AS YOU READ   Consider who is telling the story and how you feel about this storyteller. Would you want this person for a friend? Why or why not? Does the outcome of this story surprise you? What outcome might you have predicted?

A&P (1961)

1   IN walks these three girls in nothing but bathing suits. I'm in the second checkout slot, with my back to the door, so I don't see them until they're over by the bread. The one that caught my eye first was the one in the plaid green two-piece. She was a chunky kid, with a good tan and a sweet broad soft-looking can with those two crescents of white just under it, where the sun never seems to hit, at the top of the backs of her legs. I stood there with my hand on a box of Hi Ho crackers trying to remember if I rang it up or not. I ring it up again and the customer starts giving me hell. She's one of these cash-register-watchers, a witch about fifty with rouge on her cheekbones and no eyebrows, and I know it made her day to trip me up. She'd been watching cash registers for fifty years and probably never seen a mistake before.

By the time I got her feathers smoothed and her goodies into a bag—she gives me a little snort in passing, if she'd been born at the right time they would have burned her over in Salem—by the time I get her on her way the girls had circled around the bread and were coming back, without a pushcart, back my way along the counters, in the aisle between the check-outs and the Special bins. They didn't even have shoes on. There was this chunky one, with the two-piece—it was bright green and the seams on the bra were still sharp and her belly was still pretty pale so I guessed she just got it (the suit)—there was this one, with one of those chubby berry-faces, the lips all bunched together under her nose, this one, and a tall one, with black hair that hadn't quite frizzed right, and one of these sun-burns right across under the eyes, and a chin that was too long—you know, the kind of girl other girls think is very "striking" and "attractive" but never quite makes it, as they very well know, which is why they like her so much—and then the third one, who wasn't quite so tall. She was the queen. She kind of led them, the other two peeking around and hunching over a little. She didn't look around, not this queen, she just walked straight on slowly, on these long white prima-donna legs. She came down a little hard on her heels, as if she didn't walk in her bare feet that much, putting down her heels and then letting the weight move along to her toes as if she was testing the floor with every step, putting a little deliberate extra action into it. You never know for sure how girls' minds work (do you really think it's a mind in there or just a little buzz like a bee in a glass jar?) but you got the idea she had talked the other two into coming in here with her, and now she was showing them how to do it, walk slow and hold yourself straight.

She had on a kind of dirty-pink—beige maybe, I don't know—bathing suit with a little nubble all over it and, what got me, the straps were down. They were off her shoulders looped loose around the cool tops of her arms, and I guess as a result the suit had slipped a little on her, so all around the top of the cloth there was this shining rim. If it hadn't been there you wouldn't have known there could have been anything whiter than those shoulders. With the straps pushed off, there was nothing between the top of the suit and the top of her head except just *her,* this clean bare plane of the top of her chest down from the shoulder bones like a dented sheet of metal tilted in the light. I mean, it was more than pretty.

She had sort of oaky hair that the sun and salt had bleached, done up in a bun that was unravelling, and a kind of prim face. Walking into the A&P with your straps down, I suppose it's the only kind of face you *can* have. She held her head so high her neck, coming up out of those white shoulders, looked kind of stretched, but I didn't mind. The longer her neck was, the more of her there was.

5 She must have felt in the corner of her eye me and over my shoulder Stokesie in the first slot watching, but she didn't tip. Not this queen. She kept her eyes moving across the racks, and stopped, and turned so slow it made my stomach rub the inside of my apron, and buzzed to the other two, who kind of huddled against her for relief, and then they all three of them went up the cat-and-dog-food-breakfast-cereal-macaroni-rice-raisins-seasonings-spreads-spaghetti-soft-drinks-crackers-and-cookies aisle. From my slot I can look straight up this aisle to the meat counter, and I watched them all the way. The fat one with the tan sort of fumbled with the cookies, but on second thought she put the package back. The sheep pushing their carts down the aisle—the girls were walking against the usual traffic (not that we have one-way signs or anything)—were pretty hilarious. You could see them, when Queenie's white shoulders dawned on them, kind of jerk, or hop, or hiccup, but their eyes snapped back to their own baskets and on they pushed. I bet you could set off dynamite in an A&P and the people would by and large keep reaching and checking oatmeal off their lists and muttering "Let

me see, there was a third thing, began with *A*, asparagus, no, ah, yes, applesauce!" or whatever it is they do mutter. But there was no doubt, this jiggled them. A few houseslaves in pin curlers even looked around after pushing their carts past to make sure what they had seen was correct.

You know, it's one thing to have a girl in a bathing suit down on the beach, where what with the glare nobody can look at each other much anyway, and another thing in the cool of the A&P, under the fluorescent lights, against all those stacked packages, with her feet paddling along naked over our checkerboard green-and-cream rubber-tile floor.

"Oh Daddy," Stokesie said beside me. "I feel so faint."

"Darling," I said. "Hold me tight." Stokesie's married, with two babies chalked up on his fuselage already, but as far as I can tell that's the only difference. He's twenty-two, and I was nineteen this April.

"Is it done?" he asks, the responsible married man finding his voice. I forgot to say he thinks he's going to be manager some sunny day, maybe in 1990 when it's called the Great Alexandrov and Petrooshki Tea Company or something.

10 What he meant was, our town is five miles from a beach, with a big summer colony out on the Point, but we're right in the middle of town, and the women generally put on a shirt or shorts or something before they get out of the car into the street. And anyway these are usually women with six children and varicose veins mapping their legs and nobody, including them, could care less. As I say, we're right in the middle of town, and if you stand at our front doors you can see two banks and the Congregational church and the newspaper store and three real-estate offices and about twenty-seven old freeloaders tearing up Central Street because the sewer broke again. It's not as if we're on the Cape; we're north of Boston and there's people in this town haven't seen the ocean for twenty years.

> ## The whole store was like a pinball machine . . .

The girls had reached the meat counter and were asking McMahon something. He pointed, they pointed, and they shuffled out of sight behind a pyramid of Diet Delight peaches. All that was left for us to see was old McMahon patting his mouth and looking after them sizing up their joints. Poor kids, I began to feel sorry for them, they couldn't help it.

NOW here comes the sad part of the story, at least my family says it's sad, but I don't think it's so sad myself. The store's pretty empty, it being Thursday afternoon, so there was nothing much to do except lean on the register and wait for the girls to show up again. The whole store was like a pinball machine and I didn't know which tunnel they'd come out of. After a while they come around out of the far aisle, around the lightbulbs, records at discount of the Caribbean Six or Tony Martin Sings or some such gunk you wonder they waste the wax on, six-packs of candy bars, and plastic toys done up in cellophane that fall apart when a kid looks at them anyway. Around they come, Queenie still leading the way, and holding a little gray jar in her hand. Slots Three through Seven are unmanned and I could see her wondering between Stokes and me, but Stokesie with his usual luck draws an old party in baggy gray pants who stumbles up with four giant cans of pineapple juice (what do these bums *do* with all that pineapple juice? I've often asked myself) so the girls come to me. Queenie puts down the jar and I take it into my fingers icy cold. Kingfish Fancy Herring Snacks in Pure Sour Cream: 49¢. Now her hands are empty, not a ring or a bracelet, bare as God made them, and I wonder where the money's coming from. Still with that prim look she lifts a folded dollar bill out of the hollow at the center of her nubbled pink top. The jar went heavy in my hand. Really, I thought that was so cute.

Then everybody's luck begins to run out. Lengel comes in from haggling with a truck full of cabbages on the lot and is about to scuttle into that door marked MANAGER behind which he hides all day when the girls touch his eye. Lengel's pretty dreary, teaches Sunday school and the rest, but he doesn't miss that much. He comes over and says,"Girls, this isn't the beach."

Queenie blushes, though maybe it's just a brush of sunburn I was noticing for the first time, now that she was so close. "My mother asked me to pick up a jar of herring snacks." Her voice kind of startled me, the way voices do when you see the people first, coming out so flat and dumb yet kind of tony, too, the way it ticked over "pick up" and "snacks." All of a sudden I slid right down her voice into her living room. Her father and the other men were standing around in ice-cream coats and bow ties and the women were in sandals picking up herring snacks on toothpicks off a big glass plate and they were all holding drinks the color of water with olives and sprigs of mint in them. When my parents have somebody over they get lemonade and if it's a real racy affair Schlitz in tall glasses with "They'll Do It Every Time" cartoons stencilled on.

"That's all right," Lengel said. "But this isn't the beach." His repeating this struck me as funny, as if it had just occurred to him, and he had been thinking all these years the A&P was a great big dune and he was the head lifeguard. He didn't like my smiling—as I say, he doesn't miss much—but he concentrates on giving the girls that sad Sunday-school-superintendent stare.

Queenie's blush is no sunburn now, and the plump one in plaid, that I liked better from the back—a really sweet can—pipes up, "We weren't doing any shopping. We just came in for the one thing."

"That makes no difference," Lengel tells her, and I could see from the way his eyes went that he hadn't noticed she was wearing a two-piece before. "We want you decently dressed when you come in here."

15

"We *are* decent," Queenie says suddenly, her lower lip pushing, getting sore now that she remembers her place, a place from which the crowd that runs the A&P must look pretty crummy. Fancy Herring Snacks flashed in her very blue eyes.

"Girls, I don't want to argue with you. After this come in here with your shoulders covered. It's our policy." He turns his back. That's policy for you. Policy is what the kingpins want. What the others want is juvenile delinquency.

20   All this while, the customers had been showing up with their carts but, you know, sheep, seeing a scene, they had all bunched up on Stokesie, who shook open a paper bag as gently as peeling a peach, not wanting to miss a word. I could feel in the silence everybody getting nervous, most of all Lengel, who asks me, "Sammy, have you rung up their purchase?"

I thought and said "No" but it wasn't about that I was thinking. I go through the punches, 4, 9, GROC, TOT—it's more complicated than you think, and after you do it often enough, it begins to make a little song, that you hear words to, in my case "Hello (*bing*) there, you (*gung*) hap-py *pee*-pul (*splat*)!"—the *splat* being the drawer flying out. I uncrease the bill, tenderly as you may imagine, it just having come from between the two smoothest scoops of vanilla I had ever known were there, and pass a half and a penny into her narrow pink palm, and nestle the herrings in a bag and twist its neck and hand it over, all the time thinking.

The girls, and who'd blame them, are in a hurry to get out, so I say "I quit" to Lengel quick enough for them to hear, hoping they'll stop and watch me, their unsuspected hero. They keep right on going, into the electric eye; the door flies open and they flicker across the lot to their car, Queenie and Plaid and Big Tall Goony-Goony (not that as raw material she was so bad), leaving me with Lengel and a kink in his eyebrow.

"Did you say something, Sammy?"

"I said I quit."

"I thought you did."

"You didn't have to embarrass them."

"It was they who were embarrassing us."

I started to say something that came out "Fiddle-de-doo." It's a saying of my grandmother's, and I know she would have been pleased.

"I don't think you know what you're saying," Lengel said.

"I know you don't," I said. "But I do." I pull the bow 30 at the back of my apron and start shrugging it off my shoulders. A couple customers that had been heading for my slot begin to knock against each other, like scared pigs in a chute.

Lengel sighs and begins to look very patient and old and gray. He's been a friend of my parents for years. "Sammy, you don't want to do this to your mom and dad," he tells me. It's true, I don't. But it seems to me that once you begin a gesture it's fatal not to go through with it. I fold the apron, "Sammy" stitched in red on the pocket, and put it on the counter, and drop the bow tie on top of it. The bow tie is theirs, if you've ever wondered. "You'll feel this for the rest of your life," Lengel says, and I know that's true, too, but remembering how he made that pretty girl blush makes me so scrunchy inside I punch the No Sale tab and the machine whirs "*pee*-pul" and the drawer splats out. One advantage to this scene taking place in summer, I can follow it up with a clean exit, there's no fumbling around getting your coat and galoshes, I just saunter into the electric eye in my white shirt that my mother ironed the night before, and the door heaves itself open, and outside the sunshine is skating around on the asphalt.

I look around for my girls, but they're gone, of course. There wasn't anybody but some young married screaming with her children about some candy they didn't get by the door of a powder-blue Falcon station wagon. Looking back in the big windows, over the bags of peat moss and aluminum lawn furniture stacked on the 25 pavement, I could see Lengel in my place in the slot, checking the sheep through. His

face was dark gray and his back stiff, as if he'd just had an injection of iron, and my stomach kind of fell as I felt how hard the world was going to be to me from here on in.

IF YOU LIKED "A&P," YOU MIGHT ALSO LIKE . . .

. . . other initiation stories—stories about growing up and acquiring increased awareness of our relation to the world—James Joyce's "Araby," for example, in Chapter 8. You might also want to compare what the future holds for the narrator in "A&P" with the remembrances of the narrator in Alice Munro's "An Ounce of Cure" at the end of this chapter.

GOING FURTHER   John Updike's novels, several of which are listed in the note about the author, may also interest you. In the eyes of many readers and critics, no one surpasses Updike when it comes to describing the manners and way of life of Americans during the last four decades.

Writing from Reading

Summarize

1 What are the literal events—the incidents—of this narrative? How do these events add up to Sammy's decision at the end of the story?

Analyze Craft

2 "A&P" is confined to one setting (the inside of a supermarket) and a brief period of time. How would the *plot* change if it began with Sammy waking up at his house on the morning of the same day?

Analyze Voice

3 Discuss the impact of Sammy's attitude on the narrative. Point to places in the text where Sammy interprets events rather than reports them objectively. What events might be reported differently (or left out altogether) if the story were told by Stokesie, or Queenie?

Synthesize Summary and Analysis

4 In the interview, Updike talks about the importance of making the reader "see." Did he succeed in making you see the scene he was describing? Choose two images that you were able to see very clearly and analyze what Updike did to help you see them.

Interpret the Story

5 Discuss why Sammy quits his job. What does he mean when he recognizes "how hard the world was going to be to me from here on in"?

6 Imagine an alternative ending to "A&P." What ideas in the story lead you to your version of the ending?

CONTINUED FROM PAGE 139

None of these elements operates in isolation, of course, but focusing on one in each chapter will allow us—as readers and writers—a particular "way in," or way of seeing how the story functions as a whole. By reading deeply and examining not just the obvious content of a story but also its context and form, its craft and voice, you can see beyond the story's surface, beyond merely "what" is happening.

This kind of critical reading begins when you actively engage with the story. As you read a story, mark it up with questions, ideas, and comments. Underline phrases and sentences you admire. Does the main character in a story seem to contradict himself? Does the author suddenly flash forward twenty years on page 2? Ask yourself why. If an author uses the word "idled" instead of "paused," circle the word and ask yourself why she made that choice. If an author titles a story "Would You Please Be Quiet, Please?" ask why he chooses to repeat the word "please." In other words, by formulating questions when you read, you can begin to grasp the techniques that make powerful expression possible.

> **"I discovered a world that opened out to me in all kinds of directions. I began to understand things I hadn't understood before. And I began to find other things that I didn't understand yet that I wanted to understand. The world became more interesting to me. Fuller and richer. And I got all of that from reading."** Conversation with William Kittredge

The word *fiction* derives from a Latin word, *fingere*, meaning "to fashion or form." Thus, fiction has to do with shaping, the way a sculptor fashions form. It has to do with making a narrative where nothing existed before. Each work of fiction, as the late Bernard Malamud once wrote, "predicates," or brings to life, an entire world.

Some of the earliest fiction consisted of **fables** and **parables,** short tales designed to impart a moral lesson. In one famous ancient Greek fable, for example, a shepherd boy, tending his family's flock, grows lonely and, to attract company, cries out the alarm signal "Wolf!" Villagers come running to the boy's aid, but when they see no wolves, they leave. Again the boy cries "Wolf!" and once more the neighbors come running but can find no wolves. Eventually, the villagers ignore the boy's cries, and one day, when wolves really do appear, nobody comes to his aid. The moral? No one believes a liar, even when he's telling the truth. This story about seeking attention by deliberately raising a false alarm is the source of the expression "to cry wolf." (See Chapter 1 for a discussion of how fairy tales, fables, and parables have been refashioned over time and in different media, and to find a picture of the beautiful window from Chartres Cathedral depicting the parable of the Good Samaritan.)

> **"I came to reading, in a way, by way of drawing. I certainly could appreciate cartooning. . . . And I think it was those books that I first read."** Conversation with John Updike

Today, much fiction is referred to according to its contemporary category: horror, spy, romance, and so on. Categories such as these have stricter conventions of form

STORY AND HISTORY

The words *story* and *history* share a common root, the Latin word *historia,* which means a presumably true account of events and persons from a more or less remote past. In their earliest forms, stories were about purportedly real figures—sometimes gods and goddesses, sometimes human beings. The Latin words in turn go back to the Greek *historia,* meaning "narrative or history," from *histor* or "learned, wise man."

than most contemporary fiction. Horror stories, for example, evoke a world of supernatural or psychological terror:

> From a private hospital for the insane near Providence, Rhode Island, there recently disappeared an exceedingly singular person. He bore the name of Charles Dexter Ward, and was placed under restraint most reluctantly by the grieving father who had watched his aberration grow from a mere eccentricity to a dark mania involving both a possibility of murderous tendencies and a profound and peculiar change in the apparent contents of his mind. Doctors confess themselves quite baffled by his case, since it presented oddities of a general physiological as well as psychological character.
>
> In the first place, the patient seemed oddly older than his twenty-six years would warrant. . . .

—from "The Case of Charles Dexter Ward,"
by H. P. Lovecraft

Spy thrillers create a sense of suspense, often involving an international crisis:

> It took only two minutes from the time Willy's car arrived at the White House grounds to the time he was knocking on Nelson Cummin's door. Willy had done the trip many times. He reckoned that between security checks, registration, elevators, and a little wait in the outer office of the national security advisor, the average entry time to see Nelson—from entering the White House grounds to shaking his hand—was fifteen to twenty minutes. This time his car was waved through and a secretary waited for him at the side door of the building. . . .

—from *Point of Entry*, by Peter Schechter

Science fiction is set in an imagined future, often on other planets:

> Got a job for you. Pays a billion.
>
> The message blinked at the top of the screen three times, then disappeared. Rod Morgan smiled. He had been hearing rumors about a quasi-multigovernment, quasi-commercial consortium that was raising capital to sponsor a risky trip to Saturn. He closed down his game of WARPWORLD,

and switched to net-mail to read the rest of the message. He'd guessed right, it was from the consortium. The job must really be risky for them to be offering a billion dollars. Although the penny was no longer legal tender, a billion dollars was still a large fortune. . . .

—from *Saturn Rukh*, by Robert L. Forward

Genres such as romance, crime, and fantasy help you know what to expect when you read particular texts. Suppose you picked up *Saturn Rukh,* the novel from which we took the preceding example, and you knew it was science fiction. It would not surprise you to see a reference to a trip to Saturn. But if you were unaware of the science fiction genre, you might have a hard time deciding how to approach the information about a trip to Saturn—whether to take it seriously or to laugh at it. Genre fiction is powerful because of the way in which it manipulates your response: What might seem utterly ridiculous or out of place in the real world becomes something we understand if we know to approach it with the set of expectations created by genre.

"There's a whole range of people writing, and somewhere in there is somebody who respects you, and when you read their stories, you're thinking, 'I'm in here, and I can feel myself coming to life.'"

Conversation with Barry Lopez

Many works of fiction do not fall into a category such as crime, horror, or romance; texts that defy this type of classification are generally referred to as mainstream or literary fiction. Most of the stories you will encounter in this book are examples of literary fiction. As with any fashioned form, the art of fiction comes in many sizes, from the briefest story (for an example, see Amy Hempel's couldn't-be-shorter "San Francisco" in Chapter 1) to novels of a thousand pages or more, such as Leo Tolstoy's *War and Peace.* Novels almost by definition need to tell more than one story, but short stories are dense and intense. Simply put, a **short story** is a brief fictional narrative. It attempts to dramatize or illustrate the effect or meaning of a single incident or small group of incidents in the life of a single character or small group of characters. Even in these compressed lengths, however, you'll find elements of horror (see Edgar Allan Poe's "The Cask of Amontillado" in Chapter 10), science fiction (see Ursula LeGuin's "Kerastion" in An Anthology of Stories for Further Reading), and detective romance (see William Faulkner's "A Rose for Emily" in Chapter 11).

Whatever the category, reading can expand our emotional range, as Heather King suggests in her memoir, *Parched:*

I loved the way books looked, loved the way books smelled, loved that books made me forget. My favorites were The Diary of Anne Frank, The Yearling, Uncle Tom's Cabin: *tales of grotesque cruelty and unbearable loss. That was precisely why I liked them. Even back then I understood the real purpose of literature. I didn't want to hear that people lived happily ever after. I wanted to know that other people suffered, too.*

You may prefer something with a lighter touch, but reading can give you a view into another world, and the analytical ability you develop from reading critically will stand you in good stead whether you're reading fiction or sociology or a political pamphlet.

WHAT READING FICTION GIVES US

As the early-twentieth-century Austrian writer Robert Musil once put it, when troubled, we like to imagine that there is only one law of life, the law of narrative order. What he meant is that we tend to view our lives as meaningful, and endowed with the same kind of narrative coherence found in good fiction. Fiction allows us a close look at charac-

> **"Stories console me. If I'm lying in bed at night I'm a little less alone in a lonely universe. Stories connect me not to just other people, but to myself."** Conversation with Tim O'Brien

ters as it explicitly or implicitly tells the stories of their lives in an effort to make sense of them. Reading fiction gives us the opportunity to investigate our own lives by comparison, to notice how we put together the elements of our own stories—our family or friends, our emotions, our decisions, and our hopes—in order to try to understand who we are, where we have come from, and where we might be going. As we delve into good stories in order to understand them better, we come to better understand ourselves.

Kate Chopin (1851–1904)

The daughter of an Irish father and a French Creole mother, Kate Chopin grew up in St. Louis, where she studied French and English literature at a Catholic school. Her father died in a work-related accident when she was very young, an event that may have inspired this story. By the time she was married to the wealthy businessman Oscar Chopin and living in Louisiana, she was known as an unconventional woman. She drank, smoked, held her own opinions, and even ran her late husband's business for a year—all the while raising six children. Like many stories in this book, this story follows what some call the "unities" of time, place, and action that are found in classical drama and in a great deal of short fiction. The title suggests that this story will be brief. But when you read to write, remember that a short story, however brief, is not merely a joke or an anecdote—a funny thing that happened on the way to the parking lot or how your sister's cat got stuck in a tree. The fiction writer must take it further—selecting and arranging events in an artful way to show, for example, how a girl whose cat gets stuck in a tree comes to understand what really matters to her and why she calls for help.

AS YOU READ   Notice the pace of the story. Where does it speed up and slow down? How are you feeling as the pace slows and quickens? Where are the surprises in the story? How do they make you feel?

FOR INTERACTIVE READING . . .

"The Story of an Hour" is not written in Louise's voice, but the narrator does seem to know Louise's thoughts. Annotate in the margins instances where the narrator offers insights into Louise's personal thoughts or past. Review your notes. Do you think the narrator tells the story objectively or with a bias?

The Story of an Hour (1894)

KNOWING that Mrs. Mallard was afflicted with a heart trouble, great care was taken to break to her as gently as possible the news of her husband's death.

It was her sister Josephine who told her, in broken sentences; veiled hints that revealed in half concealing. Her husband's friend Richards was there, too, near her. It was he who had been in the newspaper office when intelligence of the railroad disaster was received, with Brently Mallard's name leading the list of "killed." He had only taken the time to assure himself of its truth by a second telegram, and had hastened to forestall any less careful, less tender friend in bearing the sad message.

She did not hear the story as many women have heard the same, with a paralyzed inability to accept its significance. She wept at once, with sudden, wild abandonment, in her sister's arms. When the storm of grief had spent itself she went away to her room alone. She would have no one follow her.

There stood, facing the open window, a comfortable, roomy armchair. Into this she sank, pressed down by a phys-ical exhaustion that haunted her body and seemed to reach into her soul.

She could see in the open square before her house the 5 tops of trees that were all aquiver with the new spring life. The delicious breath of rain was in the air. In the street below a peddler was crying his wares. The notes of a distant song which some one was singing reached her faintly, and countless sparrows were twittering in the eaves.

There were patches of blue sky showing here and there through the clouds that had met and piled one above the other in the west facing her window.

She sat with her head thrown back upon the cushion of the chair, quite motionless, except when a sob came up into her throat and shook her, as a child who has cried itself to sleep continues to sob in its dreams.

She was young, with a fair, calm face, whose lines bespoke repression and even a certain strength. But now there was a dull stare in her eyes, whose gaze was fixed away off yonder on one of those patches of blue sky. It was not a glance of reflection, but rather indicated a suspension of intelligent thought.

There was something coming to her and she was waiting for it, fearfully. What was it? She did not know; it was too subtle and elusive to name. But she felt it, creeping out of the sky, reaching toward her through the sounds, the scents, the color that filled the air.

10 Now her bosom rose and fell tumultuously. She was beginning to recognize this thing that was approaching to possess her, and she was striving to beat it back with her will—as powerless as her two white slender hands would have been.

When she abandoned herself a little whispered word escaped her slightly parted lips. She said it over and over under her breath: "free, free, free!" The vacant stare and the look of terror that had followed it went from her eyes. They stayed keen and bright. Her pulses beat fast, and the coursing blood warmed and relaxed every inch of her body.

She did not stop to ask if it were or were not a monstrous joy that held her. A clear and exalted perception enabled her to dismiss the suggestion as trivial.

She knew that she would weep again when she saw the kind, tender hands folded in death; the face that had never looked save with love upon her, fixed and gray and dead. But she saw beyond that bitter moment a long procession of years to come that would belong to her absolutely. And she opened and spread her arms out to them in welcome.

There would be no one to live for her during those coming years; she would live for herself. There would be no powerful will bending hers in that blind persistence with which men and women believe they have a right to impose a private will upon a fellow-creature. A kind intention or a cruel intention made the act seem no less a crime as she looked upon it in that brief moment of illumination.

15 And yet she had loved him—sometimes. Often she had not. What did it matter! What could love, the unsolved mystery, count for in face of this possession of self-assertion which she suddenly recognized as the strongest impulse of her being!

"Free! Body and soul free!" she kept whispering.

Josephine was kneeling before the closed door with her lips to the keyhole, imploring for admission. "Louise, open the door! I beg; open the door—you will make yourself ill. What are you doing, Louise? For heaven's sake open the door."

"Go away. I am not making myself ill." No; she was drinking in a very elixir of life through that open window.

Her fancy was running riot along those days ahead of her. Spring days, and summer days, and all sorts of days that would be her own. She breathed a quick prayer that life might be long. It was only yesterday she had thought with a shudder that life might be long.

She arose at length and opened the door to her sister's 20 importunities. There was a feverish triumph in her eyes, and she carried herself unwittingly like a goddess of Victory. She clasped her sister's waist, and together they descended the stairs. Richards stood waiting for them at the bottom.

Some one was opening the front door with a latchkey. It was Brently Mallard who entered, a little travel-stained, composedly carrying his grip-sack and umbrella. He had been far from the scene of accident, and did not even know there had been one. He stood amazed at Josephine's piercing cry; at Richards' quick motion to screen him from the view of his wife.

But Richards was too late.

When the doctors came they said she had died of heart disease—of joy that kills.

> She breathed a quick prayer that life might be long.

IF YOU LIKED "THE STORY OF AN HOUR," YOU MIGHT ALSO LIKE . . .

. . . other stories with strong heroines who desire more from life than being a wife or mother, such as "The Yellow Wallpaper" by Charlotte Perkins Gilman (in Chapter 12), another classic feminist work.

GOING FURTHER Although the public responded well to Chopin's less controversial fiction about French Creole life, you may be interested in reading the book that lost her work its critical favor, *The Awakening* (1899), which critics called immoral. It is quite well regarded today.

Writing from Reading

Summarize

1 Summarize the development of Louise's emotions over the course of the story. Is it ultimately joy or despair that causes her death?

Analyze Craft

2 How well has Chopin succeeded in making you *see* the details of this story? Which images are particularly vivid, and how does Chopin make them so?

Analyze Voice

3 How would you describe Chopin's attitude toward her character: does she admire or disdain the way Louise behaves? A "mallard" is a male duck; what does the name "Mrs. Mallard" suggest? What specific language from the story suggests how Chopin wanted the reader to respond to Louise?

Synthesize Summary and Analysis

4 Though "The Story of an Hour" describes only one hour's time, its events are predicated on the emotions Louise has developed over the course of her entire marriage. Summarize what we know about Louise's relationship with her husband, and discuss whether Chopin provides enough detail to justify Louise's death by the end.

Interpret the Story

5 The first line of the story says that "Mrs. Mallard was afflicted with a heart trouble." Discuss whether Chopin undermines or reinforces the emotional significance of Louise's death by announcing her heart condition so early in the story.

Alice Munro (b. 1931)

Alice Munro (née Laidlaw) was born on a farm in Wingham, Ontario, to a family of fox and potato farmers. She published her first short story at the age of nineteen while attending college and working as a waitress, library clerk, and tobacco picker. After leaving school to marry James Munro, she moved with her husband to British Columbia, where the couple ran a bookstore. In 1968 she published her first collection of stories, *Dance of the Happy Shades,* and in 1971 her first and only novel, *Lives of Girls and Women.* When her marriage ended in 1972, Munro returned to Ontario, remarried (to Gerald Fremlin, a geographer), and went on to publish eleven more collections of short stories (including *The Beggar Maid, The Moons of Jupiter, Friend of My Youth, Open Secrets, Runaway, The View from Castle Rock,* and, in 2009, *Too Much Happiness*). Her work has won many literary awards, including three of Canada's Governor General's Literary Awards and its Giller Prize; the Rea Award for Short Fiction; and the U.S. National Book Critics Circle Award. Her stories continue to appear in magazines such as *The New Yorker, The Atlantic Monthly,* and *The Paris Review.* Because of her ability to portray everyday human relationships—particularly, though not only, in Ontario—and her clean prose, Munro is widely considered to be one of the most accomplished short story writers alive today. She finds the extraordinary in the ordinary, the strange in the familiar; her influence is large.

AS YOU READ   Imagine yourself face-to-face with this narrator as she tells her story. What does she say that makes you laugh? What makes you gasp? What makes you shake your head in disbelief or amazement? Does she seem real to you?

TIP

FOR INTERACTIVE READING . . .

Annotate the text using two systems of notation. Mark all the places in the text where the narrator says "I remember." Now mark the places where she says "I don't remember."

An Ounce of Cure (1968)

1   MY parents didn't drink. They weren't rabid about it, and in fact I remember that when I signed the pledge in grade seven, with the rest of that superbly if impermanently indoctrinated class, my mother said, "It's just nonsense and fanaticism, children of that age." My father would drink a beer on a hot day, but my mother did not join him, and—whether accidentally or symbolically—this drink was always consumed *outside* the house. Most of the people we knew were the same way, in the small town where we lived. I ought not to say that it was this which got me into difficulties, because the difficulties I got into were a faithful expression of my own incommodious nature—the same nature that caused my mother to look at me, on any occasion which traditionally calls for feelings of pride and maternal accomplishment (my departure for my first formal dance, I mean, or my hellbent preparations for a descent on college) with an expression of brooding and fascinated despair, as if she could not possibly expect, did not ask, that it should go with me as it did with other girls; the dreamed-of spoils of daughters— orchids, nice boys, diamond rings—would be borne home in due course by the daughters of her friends, but not by me; all she could do was hope for a lesser rather than a greater disaster—an elopement, say, with a boy who could never earn his living, rather than an abduction into the White Slave trade.

But ignorance, my mother said, ignorance, or innocence if you like, is not always such a fine thing as people think and I am not sure it may not be dangerous for a girl like you; then she emphasized her point, as she had a habit of doing, with some quotation which had an innocent promposity and odour of mothballs. I didn't even wince at it, knowing full well how it must have worked wonders with Mr. Berryman.

The evening I baby-sat for the Berrymans must have been in April. I had been in love all year, or at least since the first week in September, when a boy named Martin Collingwood had given me a surprised, appreciative, and rather ominously complacent smile in the school assembly. I never knew what surprised him; I was not looking like anybody but me; I had an old blouse on and my home-permanent had turned out badly. A few weeks after that he took me out for the first time, and kissed me on the dark side of the porch—also, I ought to say, on the mouth; I am sure it was the first time anybody had ever kissed me effectively, and I know that I did not wash my face that night or the next morning, in order to keep the imprint of those kisses intact. (I showed the most painful banality in the conduct of this whole affair, as you will see.) Two months, and a few amatory stages later, he dropped me. He had fallen for the girl who played opposite him in the Christmas production of *Pride and Prejudice*.

I said I was not going to have anything to do with that play, and I got another girl to work on Makeup in my place, but of course I went to it after all, and sat down in front with my girl friend Joyce, who pressed my hand when I was overcome with pain and delight at the sight of Mr. Darcy in white breeches, silk waistcoat, and sideburns. It was surely seeing Martin as Darcy that did it for me; every girl is in love with Darcy anyway, and the part gave Martin an arrogance and male splendour in my eyes which made it impossible to remember that he was simply a high-school senior, passably good-looking and of medium intelligence (and with a reputation slightly tainted, at that, by such preferences as the Drama Club and the Cadet *Band*) who happened to be the first boy, the first really presentable boy, to take an interest in me. In the last act they gave him a chance to embrace Elizabeth (Mary Bishop, with a sallow complexion and no figure, but big vivacious eyes) and during this realistic encounter I dug my nails bitterly into Joyce's sympathetic palm.

5   That night was the beginning of months of real, if more or less self-inflicted, misery for me. Why is it a temptation to refer to this sort of thing lightly, with irony, with amazement even, at finding oneself involved with such preposterous emotions in the unaccountable past? That is what we are apt to do, speaking of love; with adolescent love, of course, it's practically obligatory; you would think we sat around, dull afternoons, amusing ourselves with these tidbit recollections of pain. But it really doesn't make me feel very gay—worse still, it doesn't really surprise me—to remember all the stupid, sad, half-ashamed things I did, that people in love always do. I hung around the places where he might be seen, and then pretended not to see him; I made absurdly roundabout approaches, in conversation, to the bitter pleasure of casually mentioning his name. I daydreamed endlessly; in fact if you want to put it mathematically, I spent perhaps ten times as many hours thinking about Martin Collingwood—yes, pining and weeping for him—as I ever spent with him; the idea of him dominated my mind relentlessly and, after a while, against my will. For if at first I had dramatized my feelings, the time came when I would have been glad to escape them; my well-worn daydreams had

become depressing and not even temporarily consoling. As I worked my math problems I would torture myself, quite mechanically and helplessly, with an exact recollection of Martin kissing my throat. I had an exact recollection of *everything*. One night I had an impulse to swallow all the aspirins in the bathroom cabinet, but stopped after I had taken six.

> I am sure it was the first time anybody had ever kissed me effectively . . .

MY mother noticed that something was wrong and got me some iron pills. She said, "Are you sure everything is going all right at school?" *School!* When I told her that Martin and I had broken up all she said was, "Well so much the better for that. I never saw a boy so stuck on himself." "Martin has enough conceit to sink a battleship," I said morosely and went upstairs and cried.

The night I went to the Berrymans was a Saturday night. I baby-sat for them quite often on Saturday nights because they liked to drive over to Baileyville, a much bigger, livelier town about twenty miles away, and perhaps have supper and go to a show. They had been living in our town only two or three years—Mr. Berryman had been brought in as plant manager of the new door-factory—and they remained, I suppose by choice, on the fringes of its society; most of their friends were youngish couples like themselves, born in other places, who lived in new ranch-style houses on a hill outside town where we used to go tobogganing. This Saturday night they had two other couples in for drinks before they all drove over to Baileyville for the opening of a new supper-club; they were all rather festive. I sat in the kitchen and pretended to do Latin. Last night had been the Spring Dance at the High School. I had not gone, since the only boy who had asked me was Millerd Crompton, who asked so many girls that he was suspected of working his way through the whole class alphabetically. But the dance was held in the Armouries, which was only half a block away from our house; I had been able to see the boys in dark suits, the girls in long pale formals under their coats, passing gravely under the street-lights, stepping around the last patches of snow. I could even hear the music and I have not forgotten to this day that they played "Ballerina," and—oh, song of my aching heart—"Slow Boat to China." Joyce had phoned me up this morning and told me in her hushed way (we might have been discussing an incurable disease I had) that yes, M.C. *had* been there with M.B., and she had on a formal that must have been made out of somebody's old lace tablecloth, it just *hung*.

When the Berrymans and their friends had gone I went into the living room and read a magazine. I was mortally depressed. The big softly lit room, with its green and leaf-brown colours, made an uncluttered setting for the development of the emotions, such as you would get on a stage. At home the life of the emotions went on all right, but it always seemed to get buried under the piles of mending to be done, the ironing, the children's jigsaw puzzles and rock collections. It was the sort of house where people were always colliding with one another on the stairs and listening to hockey games and Superman on the radio.

I got up and found the Berrymans' "Danse Macabre" and put it on the record player and turned out the living-room lights. The curtains were only partly drawn. A street light shone obliquely on the windowpane, making a rectangle of thin dusty gold, in which the shadows of bare branches moved, caught in the huge sweet winds of spring. It was a mild black night when the last snow was melting. A year ago all this—the music, the wind and darkness, the shadows of the branches—would have given me tremendous happiness; when they did not do so now, but only called up tediously familiar, somehow humiliatingly personal thoughts, I gave up my soul for dead and walked into the kitchen and decided to get drunk.

10   No, it was not like that. I walked into the kitchen to look for a coke or something in the refrigerator, and there on the front of the counter were three tall beautiful bottles, all about half full of gold. But even after I had looked at them and lifted them to feel their weight I had not decided to get drunk; I had decided to have a drink.

Now here is where my ignorance, my disastrous innocence, comes in. It is true that I had seen the Berrymans and their friends drinking their highballs as casually as I would drink a coke, but I did not apply this attitude to myself. No; I thought of hard liquor as something as to be taken in extremities, and relied upon for extravagant results, one way or another. My approach could not have been less casual if I had been the Little Mermaid drinking the witch's crystal potion. Gravely, with a glance at my set face in the black window above the sink, I poured a little whisky from each of the bottles (I think now there were two brands of rye and an expensive Scotch) until I had my glass full. For I had never in my life seen anyone pour a drink and I had no idea that people frequently diluted their liquor with water, soda, et cetera, and I had seen that the glasses the Berrymans' guests were holding when I came through the living room were nearly full.

I drank it off as quickly as possible. I set the glass down and stood looking at my face in the window, half expecting to see it altered. My throat was burning, but I felt nothing else. It was very disappointing, when I had worked myself up to it. But I was not going to let it go at that. I poured another full glass, then filled each of the bottles with water to approximately the level I had seen when I came in. I drank the second glass only a little more slowly than the first. I put the empty glass down on the counter with care, perhaps feeling in my head a rustle of things to come, and went and sat down on a chair in the living room. I reached up and turned on a floor lamp beside the chair, and the room jumped on me.

WHEN I say that I was expecting extravagant results I do not mean that I was expecting this. I had thought of some sweeping emotional change, an upsurge of gaiety and irresponsibility, a feeling of lawlessness and escape, accompanied by a little dizziness and perhaps a tendency to giggle out loud. I did not have in mind the ceiling spinning like a great plate somebody had thrown at me, nor the pale green blobs of the chairs swelling, converging, disintegrating, playing with me a game full of enormous senseless inanimate malice. My head sank back; I closed my eyes. And at once opened them, opened them wide, threw myself out of the chair and down the hall and reached—thank God, thank God!—the Berrymans' bathroom, where I was sick everywhere, everywhere, and dropped like a stone.

From this point on I have no continuous picture of what happened; my memories of the next hour or two are split into vivid and improbable segments, with nothing but murk and uncertainty between. I do remember lying on the bathroom floor looking sideways at the little six-sided white tiles, which lay together in such an admirable and logical pattern, seeing them with the brief broken gratitude and sanity of one who has just been torn to pieces with vomiting. Then I remember sitting on the stool in front of the hall phone, asking weakly for Joyce's number. Joyce was not home. I was told by her mother (a rather rattlebrained woman, who didn't seem to notice a thing the matter—for which I felt weakly, mechanically grateful) that she was at Kay Stringer's house. I didn't know Kay's number so I just asked the operator; I felt I couldn't risk looking down at the telephone book.

15   Kay Stringer was not a friend of mine but a new friend of Joyce's. She had a vague reputation for wildness and a long switch of hair, very oddly, though naturally, coloured—from soap-yellow to caramel-brown. She knew a lot of boys more exciting than Martin Collingwood, boys who had quit school or been imported into town to play on the hockey team. She and Joyce rode around in these boys' cars, and sometimes went with them—having lied of course to their mothers—to the Gay-la dance hall on the highway north of town.

    I got Joyce on the phone. She was very keyed-up, as she always was with boys around, and she hardly seemed to hear what I was saying.

    "Oh, I can't tonight," she said. "Some kids are here. We're going to play cards. You know Bill Kline? He's here. Ross Armour—"

    "I'm *sick*," I said trying to speak distinctly; it came out an inhuman croak. "I'm *drunk*. Joyce!" Then I fell off the stool and the receiver dropped out of my hand and banged for a while dismally against the wall.

    I had not told Joyce where I was, so after thinking about it for a moment she phoned my mother, and using the elaborate and unnecessary subterfuge that young girls delight in, she found out. She and Kay and the boys—there were three of them—told some story about where they were going to Kay's mother, and got into the car and drove out. They found me still lying on the broadloom carpet in the hall; I had been sick again, and this time I had not made it to the bathroom.

20   It turned out that Kay Stringer, who arrived on this scene only by accident, was exactly the person I needed. She loved a crisis, particularly one like this, which had a shady and scandalous aspect and which must be kept secret from the adult world. She became excited, aggressive, efficient; that energy which was termed wildness was simply the overflow of a great female instinct to manage, comfort and control. I could hear her voice coming at me from all directions, telling me not to worry, telling Joyce to find the biggest coffeepot they had and make it full of coffee (*strong* coffee, she said), telling the boys to pick me up and carry me

> She loved a crisis, particularly one like this, which had a shady and scandalous aspect and which must be kept secret from the adult world.

to the sofa. Later, in the fog beyond my reach, she was calling for a scrub-brush.

    Then I was lying on the sofa, covered with some kind of crocheted throw they had found in the bedroom. I didn't want to lift my head. The house was full of the smell of coffee. Joyce came in, looking very pale; she said that the Berryman kids had wakened up but she had given them a cookie and told them to go back to bed, it was all right; she hadn't let them out of their room and she didn't believe they'd remember. She said that she and Kay had cleaned up the bathroom and the hall though she was afraid there was still a spot on the rug. The coffee was ready. I didn't understand anything very well. The boys had turned on the radio and were going through the Berrymans' record collection; they had it out on the floor. I felt there was something odd about this but I could not think what it was.

    Kay brought me a huge breakfast mug full of coffee.

    "I don't know if I can," I said. "Thanks."

    "Sit up," she said briskly, as if dealing with drunks was an everyday business for her, I had no need to feel myself important. (I met, and recognized, that tone of voice years later, in the maternity ward.) "Now drink," she said. I drank, and at the same time realized that I was wearing only my slip. Joyce and Kay had taken off my blouse and skirt. They had brushed off the skirt and washed out the blouse, since it was nylon; it was hanging in the bathroom. I pulled the throw up under my arms and Kay laughed. She got everybody coffee. Joyce brought in the coffeepot and on Kay's instructions she kept filling my cup whenever I drank from it. Somebody said to me with interest. "You must have really wanted to tie one on."

    "No," I said rather sulkily, obediently drinking my cof- 25 fee. "I only had two drinks."

    Kay laughed, "Well it certainly gets to you, I'll say that. What time do you expect *they*'ll be back?" she said.

    "Late, after one I think."

    "You should be all right by that time. Have some more coffee."

    Kay and one of the boys began dancing to the radio. Kay danced very sexily,

but her face had the gently superior and indulgent, rather cold look it had when she was lifting me up to drink the coffee. The boy was whispering to her and she was smiling, shaking her head. Joyce said she was hungry, and she went out to the kitchen to see what there was—potato chips or crackers, or something like that, that you could eat without making too noticeable a dint. Bill Kline came over and sat on the sofa beside me and patted my legs through the crocheted throw. He didn't say anything to me, just patted my legs and looked at me with what seemed to me a very stupid, half-sick, absurd and alarming expression. I felt very uncomfortable; I wondered how it had ever got around that Bill Kline was so good looking, with an expression like that. I moved my legs nervously and he gave me a look of contempt, not ceasing to pat me. Then I scrambled off the sofa, pulling the throw around me, with the idea of going to the bathroom to see if my blouse was dry. I lurched a little when I started to walk, and for some reason—probably to show Bill Kline that he had not panicked me—I immediately exaggerated this, and calling out, "Watch me walk a straight line!" I lurched and stumbled, to the accompaniment of everyone's laughter, towards the hall. I was standing in the archway between the hall and the living room when the knob of the front door turned with a small matter-of-fact click and everything became silent behind me except the radio of course and the crocheted throw inspired by some delicate malice of its own slithered down around my feet and there—oh, delicious moment in a well-organized farce!—there stood the Berrymans, Mr. and Mrs., with expressions on their faces as appropriate to the occasion as any old-fashioned director of farces could wish. They must have been preparing those expressions, of course; they could not have produced them in the first moment of shock; with the noise we were making, they had no doubt heard us as soon as they got out of the car; for the same reason, we had not heard them. I don't think I ever knew what brought them home so early—a headache, an argument—and I was not really in a position to ask.

30   MR. Berryman drove me home. I don't remember how I got into that car, or how I found my clothes and put them on, or what kind of a good-night, if any, I said to Mrs. Berryman. I don't remember what happened to my friends, though I imagine they gathered up their coats and fled, covering up the ignominy of their departure with a mechanical roar of defiance. I remember Joyce with a box of crackers in her hand, saying that I had become terribly sick from eating—I think she said *sauerkraut*—for supper, and that I had called them for help. (When I asked her later what they made of this she said, "It wasn't any use. You *reeked*.") I remember also her saying, "Oh, no, Mr. Berryman I beg of you, my mother is a terribly nervous person I don't know what the shock might do to her. I will go down on my knees to you if you like but *you must not phone my mother*." I have no picture of her down on her knees—and she would have done it in a minute—so it seems this threat was not carried out.

"...I will go down on my knees to you if you like but *you must not phone my mother*."

Mr. Berryman said to me, "Well I guess you know your behaviour tonight is a pretty serious thing." He made it sound as if I might be charged with criminal negligence or something worse. "It would be very wrong of me to overlook it," he said. I suppose that besides being angry and disgusted with *me*, he was worried about taking me home in this condition to my strait-laced parents, who could always say I got the liquor in his house. Plenty of Temperance people would think that enough to hold him responsible, and the town was full of Temperance people. Good relations with the town were very important to him from a business point of view.

"I have an idea it wasn't the first time," he said. "If it was the first time, would a girl be smart enough to fill three bottles up with water? No. Well in this case, she *was* smart enough, but not smart enough to know I could spot it. What do you say to that?" I opened my mouth to answer and although I was feeling quite sober the only sound that came out was a loud, desolate-sounding giggle. He stopped in front of our house. "Light's on," he said. "Now go in and tell your parents the straight truth. And if you don't, remember I will." He did not mention paying me for my baby-sitting services of the evening and the subject did not occur to me either.

I went into the house and tried to go straight upstairs but my mother called to me. She came into the front hall, where I had not turned on the light, and she must have smelled me at once for she ran forward with a cry of pure amazement, as if she had seen somebody falling, and caught me by the shoulders as I did indeed fall down against the bannister, overwhelmed by my fantastic lucklessness, and I told everything from the start, not omitting even the name of Martin Collingwood and my flirtation with the aspirin bottle, which was a mistake.

On Monday morning my mother took the bus over to Baileyville and found the liquor store and bought a bottle of Scotch whisky. Then she had to wait for a bus back, and she met some people she knew and she was not quite able to hide the bottle in her bag; she was furious with herself for not bringing a proper shopping-bag. As soon as she got back she walked out to the Berrymans'; she had not even had lunch. Mr. Berryman had not gone back to the factory. My mother went in and had a talk with both of them and made an excellent impression and then Mr. Berryman drove her home. She talked to them in the forthright and unemotional way she had, which was always agreeably surprising to people prepared to deal with a mother, and she told them that although I seemed to do well enough at school I was extremely backward—or perhaps eccentric—in my emotional development. I imagine that this analysis of my behaviour was especially effective with Mrs. Berryman, a great reader of Child Guidance books. Relations between them warmed to the point where my mother brought up a specific instance of my difficulties, and disarmingly related the whole story of Martin Collingwood.

35 Within a few days it was all over town and the school that I had tried to commit suicide over Martin Collingwood. But it was already all over school and the town that the Berrymans had come home on Saturday night to find me drunk, staggering, wearing nothing but my slip, in a room with three boys, one of whom was Bill Kline. My mother had said that I was to pay for the bottle she had taken the Berrymans out of my baby-sitting earnings, but my clients melted away like the last April snow, and it would not be paid for yet if newcomers to town had not moved in across the street in July, and needed a baby sitter before they talked to any of their neighbours.

My mother also said that it had been a great mistake to let me go out with boys and that I would not be going out again until well after my sixteenth birthday, if then. This did not prove to be a concrete hardship at all, because it was at least that long before anybody asked me. If you think that news of the Berrymans' adventure would put me in demand for whatever gambols and orgies were going on in and around that town, you could not be more mistaken. The extraordinary publicity which attended my first debauch may have made me seemed marked for a special kind of ill luck, like the girl whose illegitimate baby turns out to be triplets: nobody wants to have anything to do with her. At any rate I had at the same time one of the most silent telephones and positively the most sinful reputation in the whole High School. I had to put up with this until the next fall, when a fat blonde girl in Grade Ten ran away with a married man and was picked up two months later, living in sin—though not with the same man—in the city of Sault Ste. Marie. Then everybody forgot about me.

But there was a positive, a splendidly unexpected, result of this affair: I got completely over Martin Collingwood. It was not only that he at once said, publicly, that he had always thought I was a nut; where he was concerned I had no pride, and my tender fancy could have found a way around that, a month, a week, before. What was it that brought me back into the world again? It was the terrible and fascinating reality of my disaster; it was *the way things happened.* Not that I enjoyed it; I was a self-conscious girl and I suffered a good deal from all this exposure. But the development of events on that Saturday night—that fascinated me; I felt that I had had a glimpse of the shameless, marvellous, shattering absurdity with which the plots of life, though not of fiction, are improvised. I could not take my eyes off it.

And of course Martin Collingwood wrote his Senior Matric that June, and went away to the city to take a course at a school for Morticians, as I think it is called, and when he came back he went into his uncle's undertaking business. We lived in the same town and we would hear most things that happened to each other but I do not think we met face to face or saw one another, except at a distance, for years. I went to a shower for the girl he married, but then everybody went to everybody else's showers. No, I do not think I really saw him again until I came home after I had been married several years, to attend a relative's funeral. Then I saw him; not quite Mr. Darcy but still very nice-looking in those black clothes. And I saw him looking over at me with an expression as close to a reminiscent smile as the occasion would permit, and I knew that he had been surprised by a memory either of my devotion or my little buried catastrophe. I gave him a gentle uncomprehending look in return. I am a grown-up woman now; let him unbury his own catastrophes.

IF YOU LIKED "AN OUNCE OF CURE," YOU MIGHT ALSO LIKE . . .

. . . T. C. Boyle's "Greasy Lake" in Chapter 8, which features another narrator looking back on a youthful experience, with surprising conclusions.

GOING FURTHER   Alice Munro is one of many in the group of contemporary Canadian writers with international acclaim. You may also want to look at her work in the context of books by her fellow Canadians, like Michael Ondaatje's *The English Patient* or Margaret Atwood's *The Handmaid's Tale*. Both of these authors are also poets, and samples of their poetry have been included in this book.

Writing from Reading

Summarize

1 The narrator and her mother have very defined views of each other. Summarize their respective opinions, and discuss how they shape (or are shaped by) the events of the story.

Analyze Craft

2 Munro describes the narrator's drunken experience using the same language she uses throughout the story. What words and techniques does she use to convey "drunkenness"?

Analyze Voice

3 Is the description of the narrator's drunken escapade meant to be humorous or tragic? Which aspects of Munro's language create this tone?

Synthesize Summary and Analysis

4 The narrator tells the story as an adult, looking back on an awkward, confusing, and sometimes painful phase in her life. Discuss how the narrator's distance from the story affects the details she presents, and the plot overall.

Interpret the Story

5 "An Ounce of Cure" opens with a description of the narrator's relationship with her parents and closes with a description of her relationship with Martin Collingwood. Compare and contrast these two relationships, and discuss how both affect and are affected by the narrator's first drinking experience.

Further Suggestions for Writing

1. The narrator of "A&P" is young and facing forward; the narrator of "An Ounce of Cure" is older, looking back. What might happen if "A&P" were told from the vantage point of the store manager or "An Ounce of Cure" as a conversation between the Berrymans?

2. Nothing in "A&P" and "An Ounce of Cure" is *important* in the traditional sense; nobody falls in love eternally or fights to the finish or dies. What *does* seem to matter in each of these modest-seeming tales?

3. In the case of "The Story of an Hour," note that the narration here comes from "outside" the character and not as a first-person memory. Do you find you know more about the feelings of the first-person narrators in "A&P" and "An Ounce of Cure" than you do about Mrs. Mallard's feelings in "The Story of an Hour"? Or is the outside narrator in "The Story of an Hour" able to convey all that you need to know?

7

Writing about Fiction

WASH the white clothes on Monday and put them on the stone heap; wash the color clothes on Tuesday and put them on the clothesline to dry; don't walk barehead in the hot sun; cook pumpkin fritters in very hot sweet oil; soak your little cloths right after you take them off . . .

—from "Girl" by Jamaica Kincaid

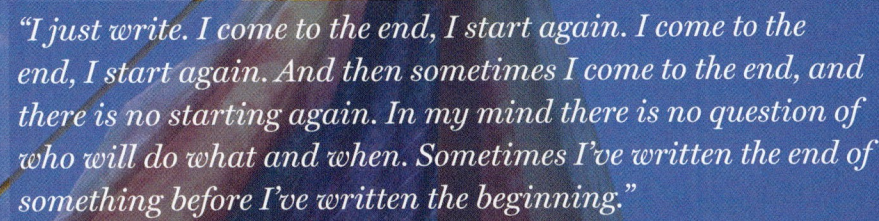

"I just write. I come to the end, I start again. I come to the end, I start again. And then sometimes I come to the end, and there is no starting again. In my mind there is no question of who will do what and when. Sometimes I've written the end of something before I've written the beginning."

Conversation with Jamaica Kincaid, available on video at connect.mcgraw-hill.com

SOME writers, like John Updike in the previous chapter, respond to material from the world around them and present it in a straightforward fashion. Other writers, like Jamaica Kincaid in "Girl," combine realistic and fantastic elements, such as dreams, myths, convoluted plots, and non-naturalistic description. Her "Girl" is an extended monologue, a compilation of lines strung together and remembered but not transcribed as overheard speech. Here the author hopes to highlight aspects of reality that don't mimic everyday life. Kincaid's "Girl" may seem like an unconventional short story. It's quite brief. Also, it is written entirely in the back-and-forth of dialogue, without "objective" descriptive prose or so-called tag lines to alert you to the identity of the speaker. Much of it reads like a repeated instruction; the "girl" has been told all this often. By comparison with such stories as Updike's "A&P," this brief, dense summary of a relationship seems less "realistic." However, "Girl" does contain all the components of successful short fiction—from plot and character to theme and symbol.

CONTINUED ON PAGE 164

Jamaica Kincaid
It's more important to read than to write.

A Conversation on Writing

On Reading and Writing

The advice I always give to people who are going to write is, it's more important to read than to write. I sometimes think I became a writer really to have the opportunity to read some more, because it's the only excuse. It's the only way you are really allowed to read and say, "Well, I'm writing. You think I'm reading but really it's part of writing." . . . So, no, reading is the most important thing, and not your own work, reading other things.

On Form, the Voice in "Girl," and Her Mother

Whatever a novel is, I'm not it, and whatever a short story is, I'm not it. If I had to follow these forms, I couldn't write. I'm really interested in breaking the form. . . . With "Girl," I wanted to write something new. . . . Certainly at the time I wrote ["Girl"], I didn't know how to interpret my own experience. I had only the voice . . . of my mother . . . firmly embedded in and interwoven into the way I express myself. . . . I was taught all those instructions. Yes, everything was by her.

On the Writing Process

I generally only have one draft. The first draft is the last draft, but that's because I tend not to commit things to paper before I've fully worked them out in my head. I'm really writing all the time; it sometimes will take me a week to complete a sentence. But that's because it's not right. It doesn't sound right the way I see it in my head. And then when it's completed, and I can judge it, I can see how it works inside my head, I put it to paper and there it is.

To watch this entire interview and hear the author read from "Girl," go to connect.mcgraw-hill.com.

RESEARCH ASSIGNMENT   In her interview, Kincaid talks about her relationship with her mother. Listen to the interview and comment on how you think this influences the writing of "Girl."

Jamaica Kincaid was born (1949) Elaine Potter Richardson in St. Johns, Antigua, a small Caribbean island in the British West Indies. Images of Kincaid's mother and the close bond they shared run through much of her writing. Kincaid was a precocious child educated in the government school system, which was largely shaped by British influence and which fostered in this particular student a growing disdain for England. Indeed, the British use the expression "don't tell stories" when they reprimand their children for lying—but Jamaica Kincaid has been telling stories ever since.

At the age of seventeen, Kincaid traveled to the United States to work as a nanny for the children of affluent families—an experience reported in her novel *Lucy.* Before long she found her way to New York City, changed her name, and began writing for magazines such as *Ms., Ingenue,* and the *Village Voice.* She became a regular writer for *The New Yorker,* which published her first short stories as well as brief prose pieces in its "Talk of the Town" page; these have been collected in *Talk Stories* (2001).

Kincaid is perhaps best known for turning the facts of her personal history into fictions that blend fantasy and reality, the imagined and the actual. Her first published collection of stories, *At the Bottom of the River* (1983), and novels such as *Annie John* (1985), *Lucy* (1991), *The Autobiography of My Mother* (1996), and *Mr. Potter* (2002), all explore the boundaries of actual and imagined life, or memoir and dream. Her books defy easy classification, falling into the gray area between autobiography and fiction: the incantatory rhythms of her first-person narrator have the quality of song.

Girl (1983)

1 WASH the white clothes on Monday and put them on the stone heap; wash the color clothes on Tuesday and put them on the clothesline to dry; don't walk barehead in the hot sun; cook pumpkin fritters in very hot sweet oil; soak your little cloths right after you take them off; when buying cotton to make yourself a nice blouse, be sure that it doesn't have gum on it, because that way it won't hold up well after a wash; soak salt fish overnight before you cook it; is it true that you sing benna[1] in Sunday school?; always eat your food in such a way that it won't turn someone else's stomach; on Sundays try to walk like a lady and not like the slut you are so bent on becoming; don't sing benna in Sunday school; you mustn't speak to wharf-rat boys, not even to give directions; don't eat fruits on the street—flies will follow you, *but I don't sing benna on Sundays at all and never in Sunday school;* this is how to sew a button; this is how to make a buttonhole for the button you have just sewed on; this is how to hem a dress when you see the hem coming down and so to prevent yourself from looking like the slut I know you are so bent on becoming; this is how you iron your father's khaki shirt so that it doesn't have a crease; this is how you iron your father's khaki pants so that they don't have a crease; this is how you grow okra—far from the house, because okra tree harbors red ants; when you are growing dasheen,[2] make sure it gets plenty of water or else it makes your throat itch when you are eating it; this is how you sweep a corner; this is how you sweep a whole house; this is how you sweep a yard; this is how you smile to someone you don't like too much; this is how you smile to someone you don't like at all; this is how you smile to someone you like completely; this is how you set a table for tea; this is how you set a table for dinner; this is how you set a table for dinner with an important guest; this is how you set a table for lunch; this is how you set a table for breakfast; this is how to behave in the presence of men who don't know you very well, and this way they won't recognize immediately the slut I have warned you against becoming; be sure to wash every day, even if it is with your own spit; don't squat down to play marbles—you are not a boy, you know; don't pick people's flowers—you might catch something; don't throw stones at blackbirds, because it might not be a blackbird at all; this is how to make a bread pudding; this is how to make doukona;[3] this is how to make pepper pot;[4] this is how to make a good medicine for a cold; this is how to make a good medicine to throw away a child before it even becomes a child; this is how to catch a fish; this is how to throw back a fish you don't like, and that way something bad won't fall on you; this is how to bully a man; this is how a man bullies you; this is how to love a man, and if this doesn't work there are other ways, and if they don't work don't feel too bad about giving up; this is how to spit up in the air if you feel like it, and this is how to move quick so that it doesn't fall on you; this is how to make ends meet; always squeeze bread to make sure it's fresh; *but what if the baker won't let me feel the bread?;* you mean to say that after all you are really going to be the kind of woman who the baker won't let near the bread?

> ...this is how you smile to someone you don't like too much...

---

[1] A form of folk music that originated in the Caribbean islands of Antigua and Barbuda and is usually about lewd or scandalous subjects.

[2] A tropical plant, similar in appearance to elephant ear plants, that grows up to seven feet tall and has edible roots.

---

[3] A spicy pudding.

[4] A Caribbean stew made of meat, vegetables, and spices.

IF YOU LIKED "GIRL," YOU MIGHT ALSO LIKE . . .

. . . magical realism—a style that emerged in the literature of the Caribbean region during the mid-twentieth century and gained practitioners throughout South America—and would enjoy reading the work of Gabriel García Márquez, whose story "A Very Old Man with Enormous Wings" appears in An Anthology of Stories for Further Reading.

GOING FURTHER   In her interview, Kincaid says "Girl" is in a way a condensed version of her novel *Annie John*, which you might like to read in relation to this short work.

Writing from Reading

Summarize

1 Who are the story's characters, and what do you know about them?

Analyze Craft

2 Consider the structure of the story, the order in which the author presents the pieces of advice. How important is the organization of information, and what meaning does the organization convey?

3 What do you know about the setting of the story? Give examples that reveal and describe it.

4 Is there dialogue in the story? If so, what form does it take and what function does it serve?

Analyze Voice

5 How does the way the girl receives and responds to advice serve to characterize her? Is she a passive character? Why or why not?

Synthesize Summary and Analysis

6 What are the distinct characteristics of the two voices in the story? Dis-

cuss how these two voices help generate the implied setting and motion of the story. How would your mental image of the story change if Kincaid had not included the girl's responses?

Interpret the Story

7 In her interview, Kincaid says that the voice in "Girl" is the voice of her mother, but she also says that there is no difference between her voice and the voice in which she writes. Discuss whether Kincaid has captured her mother's voice, or whether she has filtered that voice through her own.

CONTINUED FROM PAGE 161

FROM READING TO WRITING

In Part 1, we discussed how reading critically is the way to get your writing started. You look at the title of the work, find out about the author and the context within which a piece was written, and record your impressions by annotating a text or keeping a reading journal about how the elements of craft and the writer's voice work in a particular story. Whatever your assignment—a summary of the work, a short critical response, or a full-fledged research paper requiring multiple sources—one crucial

Checklist for Writing

✓ **EXPLORE YOUR IDEAS.**

Journal, annotate, brainstorm, freewrite, surf the Web, browse the library, and recognize this: Finding meaning is a complex issue that involves multiple perspectives. Toward what aspect of a story do you find yourself turning in thought? What aspect of the story stirs your emotions the most? These turns of mind and feeling will often alert you to your special interest in a story.

✓ **DEVELOP A WORKING THESIS.**

Make a strong claim that is specific and significant. To maintain a thoughtful tone, you may want to frame your claim as a question you will explore throughout your paper.

✓ **CREATE A PLAN.**

Outlines (formal and informal) can help you support and develop your claim with evidence.

✓ **GENERATE A FIRST DRAFT.**

Avoid straight summary (unless this is the assignment), and, unless you revise in your head like Jamaica Kincaid, give yourself time to go back to revise, edit, and format your paper. At this point you may want to get comments from other readers; their comments may help you improve your paper.

✓ **REVISE YOUR DRAFT.**

Focus on the purpose of your writing and rethink to revise: test your thesis (an exploration of any topic might lead you somewhere you didn't originally set out to go); check that your introduction states your claim; make sure the organization of your paper is clear; note whether your paragraphs are unified and cohesive; check the effectiveness of your transitions; check and double-check your use of quotation and paraphrase; make sure your conclusion answers the question of why your topic (as expressed in your thesis) is important. Save your drafts, label revised drafts with different names, and print hard copies frequently.

✓ **EDIT YOUR SENTENCES.**

Grammar-checkers are unreliable, and editing is more than a spell-check. A spell-check can't tell you if your sentences are correct and clear.

✓ **PROOFREAD AND FORMAT YOUR PAPER.**

Spell-checkers don't always catch your typos. Read over your paper carefully and format it according to the instructions of your instructor, or follow the guidelines outlined by the Modern Language Association. Some tips: Use a 12-point font, ragged right margin, one-inch margins on all four sides of your paper, double-space, and assign page numbers. Usually a paper will need your name, the professor's name, and the course and section number at the top of the page.

"I think that you really can't be a writer without being a reader."

Conversation with ZZ Packer

component of writing effectively emerges when you discover something in the subject that is meaningful to *you*. Review the checklist on the previous page for writing a paper that may help you get started.

A SAMPLE STUDENT ESSAY IN PROGRESS

When Andrew Papadopoulis read "Girl," he annotated the story and took notes on his initial responses. Both his annotations and his notes, reproduced here, show him engaged with the text. He reads *actively* to scrutinize the story's language, asks questions about possible meanings, records thoughts and reactions, and notes important insights. By highlighting and annotating the story, this student interacts, or converses, with it, moving back and forth between the story's details and his developing understanding of those details. As he notes in his commentary, "Girl" condenses the elements of fiction into a single paragraph.

"My writing process, I don't really have one. I read. I find that both walk hand in hand, that when I'm writing, I have to read. Somehow I find that it feeds my own work, and not in a direct way." Conversation with Chimamanda Ngozi Adichie

Andrew focuses on the relationship between the story's two main characters—the second-person narrator, who uses *you* and commands ("Wash the white clothes on Monday"), and the listener, the girl of the story's title. He uncovers meaning from the details contained within this brief narrative to understand who the main characters are and where the story takes place. He notes those clues that point to the nature of the relationship between the speaker and the listener—the speaker's repeated use of the word *slut;* her admonitory, accusatory, and sometimes humorous tone; her reference to "your father"; and her advice on how to behave like a proper woman who tends to home and husband. Andrew interprets the story as an interaction between mother and daughter and isolates the details that reveal the story's domestic setting: okra, dasheen, doukona, and a host of household chores. He makes connections between the story's portrayal of domesticity and its broader implications of gender roles, identity, and society.

Next Andrew develops this initial exploration into a full-length essay that examines how Kincaid's distinctive use of literary techniques—especially the way her narrator addresses the readers directly with *you* (second-person point of view, see

Chapter 11)—allows the reader to feel like a participant in the story, an eavesdropper on a series of telling exchanges between mother and daughter. As this student demonstrates, fiction can be a lens through which we better visualize our relationship to the world. It can help us to see aspects of our own lives in new ways, or to catch a glimpse of imaginative worlds we find strange and interesting.

"There is a kind of magic to writing. . . . Anybody here who has written a term paper knows that there is a kind of magic to it. You don't know what it will be. You take notes, but the final product is utterly different from your initial conception of it. That's the joy of writing something." Conversation with T. Coraghessan Boyle

We emphasize throughout this text that literary works don't possess a *single* meaning, but rather *multiple* meanings; these are in turn revealed by reading and writing about a story with a close critical eye. We offer this not as a "finished" critique of "Girl" but as a way of demonstrating the process of responding to a text.

The rest of the chapter charts Andrew's progress as he works through his response to this writing assignment:

Assignment: Expand the close reading you completed of Jamaica Kincaid's "Girl" into a 4- to 5-page essay in which you analyze one or both of the story's main characters. Your analysis should take into account Kincaid's distinctive voice and use of literary techniques.

An Interactive Reading

Written in second person: directed at whom?

Wash the white clothes on Monday and put them on the stone heap; wash the color clothes on Tuesday and put them on the clothesline to dry; don't walk barehead in the hot sun; cook pumpkin fritters in very hot sweet oil; soak your little cloths right after you take them off; when buying cotton to make yourself a nice blouse, be sure that it doesn't have gum on it, because that way it won't hold up well after a wash; soak salt fish overnight before you cook it; is it true that you sing benna in Sunday school?; always eat your food in such a way that it won't turn someone else's stomach; on Sundays try

Advice for a variety of situations

Narrator asks a question

Now it's a command: "Don't sing…"

Voice change: Listener responds…

But completely ignored…

Now "outdoor" directions

No periods anywhere; very tense, intense

What else would a blackbird be? A soul?

Attitude toward love is same as attitude toward work, etc.

Loaded term—gender implications?

Why the repetition?

Suggest mother-daughter conversation

Unwanted fish and child treated the same.

Finally acknowledged at the end…

to walk like a lady and not like the slut you are so bent on becoming; don't sing benna in Sunday school; you mustn't speak to wharf-rat boys, not even to give directions; don't eat fruits on the street—flies will follow you; *but I don't sing benna on Sundays at all and never in Sunday school;* this is how to sew a button; this is how to make a buttonhole for the button you have just sewed on; this is how to hem a dress when you see the hem coming down and so to prevent yourself from looking like the slut I know you are so bent on becoming; this is how you iron your father's khaki shirt so that it doesn't have a crease; this is how you iron your father's khaki pants so that they don't have a crease; this is how you grow okra—far from the house, because okra tree harbors red ants; when you are growing dasheen, make sure it gets plenty of water or else it makes your throat itch when you are eating it; this is how you sweep a corner; this is how you sweep a whole house; this is how you sweep a yard; this is how you smile to someone you don't like too much; this is how you smile to someone you don't like at all; this is how you smile to someone you like completely; this is how you set a table for tea; this is how you set a table for dinner; this is how you set a table for dinner with an important guest; this is how you set a table for lunch; this is how you set a table for breakfast; this is how to behave in the presence of men who don't know you very well, and this way they won't recognize immediately the slut I have warned you against becoming; be sure to wash every day, even if it is with your own spit; don't squat down to play marbles—you are not a boy, you know, don't pick people's flowers—you might catch something; don't throw stones at blackbirds, because it might not be a blackbird at all; this is how to make a bread pudding; this is how to make doukona, this is how to make pepper pot; this is how to make a good medicine for a cold; this is how to make a good medicine to throw away a child before it becomes a child; this is how to catch a fish; this is how to throw back a fish you don't like, and that way something bad won't fall on you; this is how to bully a man; this is how a man bullies you; this is how to love a man, and if this doesn't work there are other ways, and if they don't work don't feel too bad about giving up; this is how to spit up in the air if you feel like it, and this is how to move quick so that it doesn't fall on you; this is how to make ends meet; always squeeze bread to make sure it's fresh; *but what if the baker won't let me feel the bread?;* you mean to say that after all you are really going to be the kind of woman who the baker won't let near the bread?

Initial Response

Write an initial response to the text without concern for how formal it sounds or even how logically it flows. In other words, this response is simply your first impressions of the story. Did something stand out to you as important? Were there confusing elements? Don't worry at this point if you don't understand major parts of the story; the more you review the notes you've made and the text itself, the more you will begin to understand. Here's Andrew's initial response.

> The first time I read "Girl," I thought it might be difficult to find a lot to say about such a short piece. But after a second and third reading, I realized the story is packed with layers of detail that make it a rich fictional work. I tried to highlight revealing words and phrases and draw connections among sections to show how Kincaid develops elements of craft—like character and setting—and how Kincaid's voice affected my understanding of the story. I found the relationship between the speaker and listener especially interesting; the mother's (I think she's her mother) warnings and advice, and the daughter's sparse, interspersed retorts, define what it means (and doesn't mean) to be a "girl." Being a good "girl," of course, has all sorts of implications about being a good woman, wife, and mother. I'd like to explore these ideas further.

Explore Your Ideas

Freewriting is similar to the initial response—once again, do not worry about the flow of ideas or the language you are using. The difference is that freewriting comes after you have had some time to think about the story and reread it. In a sense, it's your "second response," rather than your initial one, and as such, you may find that you have more ideas and that your freewriting runs longer.

"There's nothing worse than a sheet of blank paper in front of you."

Conversation with William Kittredge

After carefully considering his assignment, Andrew reread his close reading of "Girl" and the notes he took during his initial readings of the story. Andrew then moved on to freewrite about the story, writing continuously to get his ideas down on paper, without worrying about making mistakes or whether his initial ideas could be developed into a suitable paper topic. The following excerpt comes from Andrew's freewriting exercise.

> This was a very strange but a very beautiful story. For the first few lines I was def. confused, but the more I read the more I got it. It's a mother talking to her daughter, telling her everything she needs to know. I wonder where this story is set? Need to do some research to find out—need to look up a lot of the terms in the dictionary. But even w/o knowing where the story is set, I liked it. My mother always gives me tons & tons of advice. My mother and this mother are actually pretty similar in a lot of ways, even though my mother doesn't like to cook or garden or anything. It's different, too, that I'm a son not a daughter; must keep the diff. in mind. That's prob. the mark of a good piece of writing, that you can get into it even if it doesn't directly relate to you.

Journaling is a writing exercise that helps you focus the ideas you generated in your notes and freewriting. This is the first step in which you should begin to feel your ideas coming together to form something that will eventually become a paper. The idea you found the most interesting from your reading and notes is a good starting place for a journal entry.

Andrew put aside his freewriting for several hours and returned to the story with a fresh perspective. In the following journal entry, he expands his initial freewriting into a more focused discussion of his growing understanding of the story. He considers how the story's characterizations and point of view create interesting effects.

> My initial reaction to the first few lines of "Girl" was confusion. But the further I read, the more I warmed up to the character of the narrator. I realized that she is not totally different from my mother, even though it seems clear that this mother and my mother are from very different worlds. But my mother, like the narrator, is constantly emphasizing the right way (or maybe I should say her way) of doing things. And, like

the narrator, although my mother can come across as harsh, I know she cares deeply about my success in life.

What's interesting to me, also, is how or why I assume I know that this story is about a mother talking to her daughter. Maybe it's because of the word "slut"—something my mother wd obviously never say to me! And Kincaid never states this directly. In fact, in "Girl," almost nothing about character is stated directly. And yet, after reading this story, I feel like I have a good idea of who the narrator is, and, just as importantly, who the person being talked to is. It would be interesting to go back and see just where and how Kincaid reveals personality and other character details in this story.

All in all, I really enjoyed "Girl." You don't read many stories written from this perspective (the "you" perspective), and it's an interesting way to experience a narrative. Once I pushed through some initial confusion, I found "Girl" was definitely an engaging piece of writing.

Brainstorming may take the form of a list or a web connecting your thoughts. Once you have used a journal entry to narrow down your interests, use your brainstorming session to generate ideas on how to turn the topics that interest you most into a paper.

Andrew's freewriting and journal entry sparked more and more ideas about how he might develop his character analysis. In the following brainstorming excerpt, Andrew lists possible topics for his paper, charts details about the story's characterizations, and works toward a **thesis statement.**

Most interesting topics:

—narrator's personality (funny)

—daughter's personality

—setting (Caribbean)

—WHY does the mother say all this . . .

WHO is the narrator and WHO is the daughter—

Learning WHO the characters are and WHY they do things.

CHARACTERS' ACTION	MOTIVATION
Mother telling about cooking	Teaching girl how to run a household
Mother telling her not to talk to wharf-rat boys	Teaching girl how to behave like a girl. My sister Eleni?
Girl arguing with mother	Being independent, tough

Reading "Girl" = much interesting info

Reading the story "Girl," you can learn a lot about who the characters are and why they do what they do.

Develop a Working Thesis

A thesis is a sentence that states the topic of the paper. More than that, a thesis is the writer's argument, the controlling idea that he or she will show and develop in the body of the essay. For more details on how to write a good thesis, see Chapter 3, Developing an Argument, and pages 113–115 in Chapter 5 on research in Part 1, Writing from Reading.

Andrew used his brainstorming notes to sharpen his topic and refine his thesis. The following drafted and revised thesis statements show Andrew's progress as he focused his claim and pruned his language.

FIRST-DRAFT THESIS:

In "Girl," you can actually learn a lot about the characters.

SECOND-DRAFT THESIS:

A close reading of "Girl" reveals much about the characters of the story.

THIRD-DRAFT THESIS:

> A close reading of "Girl" reveals a lot of information about the narrator and her daughter.

FINAL-DRAFT THESIS:

> A close reading of "Girl" reveals that Kincaid provides a lot of information about the narrator and the "you" of the story.

REVISED FINAL-DRAFT THESIS:

> A careful, close reading of "Girl" reveals that Kincaid has painted a portrait of both the narrator and the "you" to whom the story is directed.

Create a Plan

With his thesis in mind, Andrew next considered how he would organize his paper to best support his points. He drafted a **topic outline** to guide him through the writing and revising process.

> I. Introduction
>   A. "Girl" initially confusing
>   B. Thesis: A careful, close reading of "Girl" reveals that Kincaid provides a great deal of information about the narrator and the "you" to whom the story is directed.
> II. Identity of characters
>   A. Discussion of tone
>   B. Analysis of clues about gender and relationship of characters
>   1. Specific lines directly related to gender
>   2. Nature of narrator's advice

III. Analysis of the narrator
    A.   Humorous setting
    B.   Demonstrates warmth
IV. Analysis of the listener
    A.   Independent and uninterested in mother's advice
    B.   Actually similar to her mother
 V. Narrator's motives
    A.   Discussion of story's final line
    B.   Mother's advice meant to make daughter a respectable woman
VI. Conclusion
    A.   Analysis of setting of "Girl"
    B.   Transcends specific setting

Generate a First Draft

After completing his topic outline, Andrew was now ready to write his first draft. He tried to follow the organization of his outline, making each of the important points he planned to elaborate on and support with examples in subsequent drafts.

FIRST DRAFT

Andrew Papadopoulis

Professor Delbanco

Composition 102

A Mother's Advice

Jamaica Kincaid's short-short story "Girl" can seem weird, if not totally bizarre. But careful, repeated reading reveals that Kincaid provides a great deal of information about the narrator and the person the narrator talks to. In other words, "Girl" hides much beneath its mysterious surface.

The first clues as to the identity of the narrator of "Girl" can be found in the story's tone. The narrator's speech is mean and tough. From the language, it is clear that the speaker is someone who is used to being in charge, believes they know the right way to do things, and believes that the person listening must obey. For these reasons, it is likely that the narrator is a parent, speaking to his or her child.

Further, the narrator is probably a woman talking to her daughter. The narrator even says, at one point, "You are not a boy." The narrator's identity as the girl's mother is suggested by the line: "This is how you iron your father's khaki pants so that they don't have a crease." This instruction suggests a relationship among the narrator, the girl, and the girl's father. The most obvious characterization of this relationship is that the speaker is the girl's mother. The nature of the advice the narrator gives only reinforces this idea, that "Girl" consists of mother-to-daughter counsel.

Parenthetical citation of page number is not necessary for a story printed on one page. The page reference should appear in the Works Cited only.

Kincaid offers other insight into the characters of the story. As mentioned previously, the tone suggests that the narrator is strict and authoritarian. At times, though, she can be humorous. At other times, the narrator shows affection for her daughter.

What we learn about the listener is of course filtered through the view of the narrator. From the more direct statements her mother makes, one could conclude that the girl is in grave danger of becoming a slut. But beyond this, it is possible to learn something of her personality. The sheer amount of advice she is given suggests that she has a lot to learn, at least about cooking and all of that stuff. Thus, she could very well be independent, uninterested in the traditional activities about which her mother instructs her. Even more interestingly, she is probably very similar to her mother: stubborn and strong-willed.

Why is the narrator giving so much advice? We need to look at the final line to answer that question. After the daughter, in another moment of italicized response, questions whether the baker will let her squeeze the bread to see if it's fresh, the narrator says: "You mean to say that after all you are really going to be the kind of woman who the baker won't let near the bread?" This seems to get at what the mother is trying to teach her daughter: what *kind* of woman she should turn out to be.

All the counsel the mother gives the daughter in "Girl" is specific to the setting, the Caribbean. Nonetheless, in the mother's resolve to make her daughter into the kind of woman she envisions, there is something that transcends the specifics. Every parent wants his or her child to grow up to be a respectable adult, and whether the parent goes about it by saving money for college, exposing the child to different languages and cultures, or, as in the story, giving instructions on how to behave, this drive seems as innate as eating or sleeping. Hence, nearly any mother or father can identify with what the narrator is trying to accomplish.

WRITER'S BLOCK

Sometimes called *the midnight disease,* writer's block can be avoided, especially with freewriting, brainstorming, and other exploratory techniques to get you started. Additional strategies to avoid writer's block include:

Resist the temptation to be a perfectionist. Save getting the right word, the stylish phrase, or even the correct spelling for your revising and editing stages.

Take it "bird by bird." Writer Anne Lamott passes along her father's advice to her brother, who had procrastinated on a report about birds—"Bird by bird, buddy, just take it bird by bird"—when she counsels students to break down writing assignments into manageable units.

Start anywhere. If you're stuck on the beginning, pick another section. Go back later and work out the introduction.

Generate more ideas. If you are drawing a blank, you may need to do some more reading or brainstorming. But don't let yourself use "reading some more" as a stalling tactic.

—from Maimon et al., *A Writer's Resource,* 4th ed. (New York: McGraw-Hill, 2012).

Revise Your Draft

Andrew's second draft includes his changes and annotations to remind himself to clarify and refine his language, provide more textual evidence to bolster his claims, and format his paper according to MLA guidelines (see Chapter 5 and Chapter 37).

"You're asking [for] a reader's time, so to my way of thinking, you owe them. You owe them clarity." Conversation with Barry Lopez

SECOND DRAFT

Andrew Papadopoulis

Professor Delbanco

Composition 102

A Mother's Advice

Jamaica Kincaid's short-short story "Girl" can seem weird, if not totally bizarre. A full appreciation of "Girl" requires careful, and even repeated, reading. Such an approach, though, reveals that Kincaid provides a great deal of information about the narrator and the "you" to whom the story is directed. In other words, "Girl" hides much beneath its initially mysterious surface.

The first clues as to the identity of the narrator of "Girl" can be found in the story's tone. The narrator's speech is admonitory, domineering, and tough. From this blunt language, it is clear that the speaker is someone who is used to being in charge, believes he or she knows the right way to do things, and believes that the person listening must obey. For these reasons, it is likely that the narrator is a parent, speaking to his or her child.

Further, it is not difficult to conclude that the narrator is a woman, talking to her daughter. The narrator even says, at one point, "You are not a boy." The narrator's identity as the girl's mother is suggested by a different line. The narrator says: "This

[Margin annotations:]

Why? Explain what's so weird, why you need to be careful.

Be more specific. More formal language?

Much what? Characterization? Details?

Quote example from the story.

is how you iron your father's khaki pants so that they don't have a crease." This instruction, with its casual reference to "your father," suggests a relationship among the narrator, the girl, and the girl's father. The most obvious characterization of this relationship is that the speaker is the girl's mother, and she is telling her daughter how to iron her father's pants. The nature of the advice the narrator gives only re-inforces the idea that "Girl" consists of mother-to-daughter counsel.

More specific.

Explain "so what"?

Kincaid offers other insight into the characters of the story. As mentioned previously, the tone suggests that the narrator is strict and authoritarian. At times, though, she can be humorous. At other times, the narrator shows affection for her daughter.

Paragraph's too short. Fill out with text examples.

Other ways this shows up?

What we learn about the listener is of course mainly filtered through the view of the narrator. From the more direct statements her mother makes, one could conclude that the girl is in grave danger of becoming a "slut." But beyond this, it is possible to learn something of her personality. The sheer amount of advice she is given suggests that she has a lot to learn, at least about cooking and all of that stuff. Thus, she could very well be independent, disinterested in the traditional activities about which her mother instructs her. This idea is supported by the brief moments of interaction in the story (the daughter's responses to her mother's words are set off in italics). These show her questioning her mother and arguing with her assertions. For instance, she insists, *"But I don't sing benna on Sundays at all and never in Sunday school."* From this sort of headstrong defense one can conclude that this girl is very much her mother's daughter, strong-willed and determined.

Too informal—clean up.

Need to show how mom's strong willed?

The larger motives of the narrator can be detected in the story's final line. After her daughter, in another moment of italicized response, questions whether the baker will let her squeeze the bread to see if it's fresh, the narrator says: "You mean to say that after all you are really going to be the kind of woman who the baker won't let near the bread?" This seems to get at what the mother is trying to teach her daughter. Ultimately, it is not important *what* the girl knows, but the "kind of woman" the girl becomes.

> Too deep. Need to relate to the thesis—what's hidden?

All the counsel the mother gives the daughter in "Girl" is specific to the setting, the Caribbean. Nonetheless, in the mother's resolve to make her daughter into the kind of woman she envisions, there is something that transcends the specifics. Every parent wants his or her child to grow up to be a respectable adult, and whether the parent goes about it by saving money for college, exposing them to different languages and cultures, or, as in the story, giving instructions on how to behave, this drive seems as innate as eating or sleeping. Hence, nearly any mother or father can identify with what the narrator is trying to accomplish.

> Need text proof?

> Sentence too long—break up or rewrite.

Edit Your Sentences; Proofread and Format Your Paper

Andrew uses these notes to develop his final draft, in which he fleshes out his character analysis and discusses the significance of the story's point of view, tone, and setting. For the final draft, he also checks his spelling, word choice, transitions, and sentences for clarity and grammatical correctness. He also makes sure he has provided ample evidence from the story itself with quotations, and he checks to make sure these quotations are correctly formatted in-text references, which correspond to a Works Cited page at the end of his paper (see Chapter 5 and Chapter 37 for MLA formatting guidelines). He also incorporates paraphrase and summary where context is needed but quotations are not necessary. Andrew's progress shows his easeful back and forth with the story as he continually revises his interpretation of it.

> **"I was not a good student. I was not particularly good in English. Yet I am a writer. And this, I think, points to something relevant which is that it's not about talent, necessarily. You [just need to] do whatever is required, because you want it more. That was my experience."** Conversation with Amy Hempel

Crafting Your Own Voice: Summary

When writing and responding to literature, you will find it enormously helpful to learn how to represent other writers' ideas in your own language. This skill is essential for any kind of academic writing where you will be referring to outside sources, and, depending on your situation, you will need to choose whether it is appropriate to integrate the source material into your work as a summary, a quotation, or a paraphrase.

- For more on summary, quotation and paraphrase see pages 36, 49–58.
- For **Crafting Your Own Voice: Quotation,** see page 599.
- For **Crafting Your Own Voice: Paraphrase,** see page 1059.

For example, in his paper on Jamaica Kincaid's short story "Girl," student writer Andrew Papadopoulis varies the way in which he refers to the source depending on his purpose (his essay is reproduced in full on pages 181–185; Kincaid's story on page 163). In the paragraph below, he includes a brief summary as part of his textual analysis of the narrator's relationship to the "girl" being addressed in the story. Notice how he quotes two words *within* his summary to create emphasis; both words are marked off by quotation marks.

Andrew's claim in this paragraph is that the narrator is, in fact, the mother of the "girl" being addressed.

The paragraph concludes with his characterization of the summary.

> The nature of the advice the narrator gives only reinforces the idea that "Girl" consists of mother-to-daughter counsel. The narrator has recommendations for cleaning, cooking, gardening, and washing—all domestic chores, traditionally considered women's work. Further, the narrator has plenty of ideas on how to behave like a "lady" and not a "slut." Obviously, this is the sort of gender etiquette one woman would pass on to another, particularly a mother to a daughter.

His claim is followed by an example: a brief summary of the advice in his own language.

Tips to Avoiding Plagiarism

Craft & Voice: Notice how the summary uses Andrew's own words and is situated between his own statements about the work, which are the first and last sentences of the paragraph. Using a summary to complete your own thought or idea is a good way of making sure you use your own words. If you use the language of your source without quoting it, you are presenting it as your own, and this means you are plagiarizing it.

Citing Sources: Typically, your paper will include two forms of citation—a parenthetical, in-text citation located at the conclusion of your reference to the outside source and an entry in your works cited page (see Chapter 5, especially pages 104–106). In this instance, the passage shown does *not* include a parenthetical citation, because the work cited is only one page long.

FINAL DRAFT

Papadopoulis 1

Student name, instructor name, course number, and date

Andrew Papadopoulis

Professor Delbanco

Composition 102

15 April 2011

A Mother's Advice   — *Essay title*

On first encounter, Jamaica Kincaid's short-short story "Girl" can seem enigmatic, if not simply baffling. While most works of fiction are written in either the first or the third person, "Girl" is written in the second person: the "you" voice. This makes the beginning of the story fairly disorienting, as the reader is likely unaccustomed to this narrative perspective. Additionally, because the story is so short, the reader may reach the end before the feeling of disorientation ever goes away. A full appreciation of "Girl" requires careful, and even repeated, reading. Such an approach, though, reveals that Kincaid provides a great deal of information about the narrator and the "you" to whom the story is directed. In other words, "Girl" hides much beneath its initially mysterious surface, mainly, details about the characters.

Introduction leading toward thesis

Thesis

The first clues as to the identity of the narrator of "Girl" can be found in the story's tone. From the first lines, the narrator's speech is admonitory, domineering, and tough. The story begins with "Wash the white clothes on Monday and put them on the stone heap; wash the color clothes on Tuesday and put them on the clothesline to dry; don't walk barehead in the hot sun." From this direct, blunt language, it is clear that the speaker is someone who is used to being in charge,

Discussion of tone illustrated with example

Papadopoulis 2

believes he or she knows the right way to do things, and, importantly, believes that the person listening must obey. For these reasons, it is likely that the narrator is a parent, speaking to his or her child. This interpretation certainly fits the relationship suggested by the story's commanding language.

Further, it is not difficult to conclude that the narrator is a woman, talking to her daughter. The narrator even says, at one point, "You are not a boy." This fairly well clears up any mystery as to the listener's gender! The narrator's identity as the girl's mother is suggested by a line earlier in the story. The narrator says, "This is how you iron your father's khaki pants so that they don't have a crease." This instruction, with its casual reference to "your father," suggests a relationship among the narrator, the girl, and the girl's father. The most obvious characterization of this relationship is that the speaker is the girl's mother, and she is telling her daughter how to iron her father's pants.

Textual analysis as part of a discussion of the characters' genders.

The nature of the advice the narrator gives only reinforces the idea that "Girl" consists of mother-to-daughter counsel. The narrator has recommendations for cleaning, cooking, gardening, and washing—all domestic chores, traditionally considered women's work. Further, the narrator has plenty of ideas on how to behave like a "lady" and not a "slut." Obviously, this is the sort of gender etiquette one woman would pass on to another, particularly a mother to a daughter.

Further textual analysis of characters' relationship

In addition to the familial relationship between the narrator and the listener, Kincaid offers other insight into the characters of the story. As mentioned previously, the tone suggests that the narrator is strict and authoritarian. At times, though, she can be humorous, as when she says, "Always eat your food in such a way that it won't turn someone else's stomach." Although the statement implies

Character analysis of the narrator

Papadopoulis 3

criticism (specifically, that the girl eats in a way that *does* turn people's stomachs), the advice cannot be taken as wholly serious. At other times, the narrator demonstrates affection for her daughter. For example, about men, she says, "This is how to love a man, and if this doesn't work there are other ways, and if they don't work don't feel too bad about giving up." There is a warmth to these lines that shows the narrator truly cares that her daughter avoids the deeper pitfalls of love.

Character analysis of the listener

What we learn about the listener, the "girl" of the story's title, is of course mainly filtered through the view of the narrator. From the more direct statements her mother makes, one could conclude that the girl is in grave danger of becoming a "slut." But beyond this, it is possible to learn something of her personality. The sheer amount of advice she is given suggests that she has a lot to learn, at least about cooking and such. Thus, she could very well be independent, uninterested in the traditional activities about which her mother instructs her. This idea is supported by the brief moments of interaction in the story (the daughter's responses to her mother's words are set off in italics). These show her questioning her mother and arguing with her assertions. For instance, she insists, *"But I don't sing benna on Sundays at all and never in Sunday school."* From this sort of headstrong defense one can conclude that this girl is very much her mother's daughter, strong willed and determined.

Given what can be learned about the two characters in the story—mother and daughter—it is interesting to consider *why* the narrator feels compelled to give the girl so much advice. It almost seems as if she wants to tell her daughter every single thing she will need to know, but this of course is impossible. Her larger motives can be detected in the story's final line. After her daughter, in another moment of

Larger discussion of the narrator's motives

Papadopoulis 4

italicized response, questions whether the baker will let her squeeze the bread to see if it's fresh, the narrator says, "You mean to say that after all you are really going to be the kind of woman who the baker won't let near the bread?" This seems to get at the heart of what the mother is trying to teach her daughter. Ultimately, it is not important *what* the girl knows, but the "kind of woman" the girl becomes. The many lessons of the story represent the accumulated knowledge of a particular type of woman—dignified, competent, capable, wise. These are the qualities the mother hopes to pass on, more than tips about planting okra.

All the counsel the mother gives the daughter in "Girl" is specific to a particular setting. From the details of food (okra, dasheen) and music (benna), one can conjecture that this setting is in the Caribbean, where Jamaica Kincaid grew up. Further, all the counsel deals with the rural, domestic realm the mother inhabits and controls. Nonetheless, in the mother's resolve to make her daughter into the kind of woman she envisions, there is certainly an element that transcends these specifics. Every parent wants his or her child to grow up to be a respectable adult. Whether the parent goes about it by saving money for the child's college, exposing him or her to different languages and cultures, or, as in "Girl," giving instructions on how to behave like a lady, this drive seems as innate as any fundamental parental instinct. Hence, nearly any mother or father, or even anyone who has mentored another in any capacity, can identify with what the narrator is trying to accomplish.

Conclusion broadening the essay's argument to a more general point

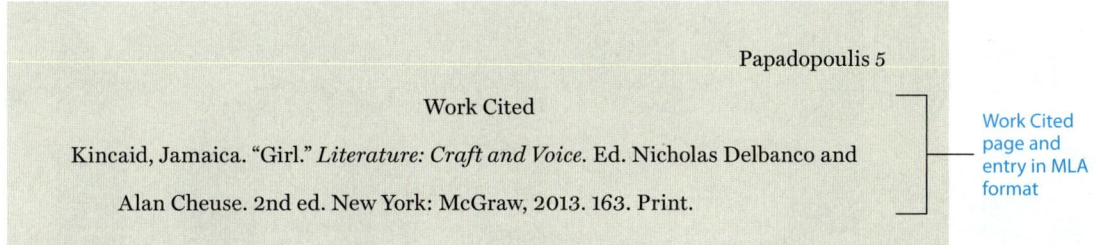

Papadopoulis 5

Work Cited

Kincaid, Jamaica. "Girl." *Literature: Craft and Voice.* Ed. Nicholas Delbanco and

Alan Cheuse. 2nd ed. New York: McGraw, 2013. 163. Print.

Work Cited page and entry in MLA format

Compiling a Writing Portfolio

If you are compiling a portfolio or just several drafts of a single paper for your instructor, here's some advice:

- Gather your writing.
- Review what you have gathered and make selections.
- Arrange selections in a deliberate order.
- Write a reflective essay or letter to explain what is in your portfolio.
- Suggest who you are as a writer—that is, highlight your strengths and tell how you envision your writing taking shape in future written work.

Your instructor may prefer you to submit your work as an e-portfolio.

- Use the opening screen to establish your purpose and appeal to your audience.
- Provide links to help readers navigate your portfolio.
- Consider using links to connect with related files external to the portfolio like audio or video clips.
- Reread and revise one final time to make sure it's conceptually and structurally right before releasing it.

8 Plot

THE first mistake, the one that opened the whole floodgate, was losing my grip on the keys. In the excitement, leaping from the car with the gin in one hand and a roach clip in the other, I spilled them in the grass—in the dark, rank, mysterious night-time grass of Greasy Lake. This was a tactical error, as damaging and irreversible in its way as Westmoreland's decision to dig in at Khe Sanh. I felt it like a jab of intuition, and I stopped there by the open door, peering vaguely into the night that puddled up round my feet.

The second mistake—and this was inextricably bound up with the first—was identifying the car as Tony Lovett's.

—from "Greasy Lake" by T. Coraghessan Boyle

"A story like 'Greasy Lake' develops through the opening . . . which is the setup: 'I went there one night.' . . . Each of the incidents of the story strings out from that in an escalating way, until we . . . find out what happened. . . . It's not the kind of plot in which they all went to jail . . . the end. No, it ends on a gesture, and that gesture brings you back into the story to rethink what it means. . . ."

Conversation with T. Coraghessan Boyle, video available at connect.mcgraw-hill.com

IN the excerpt that begins this chapter, the narrator, a nineteen-year-old and a self-described "dangerous character," identifies the moment when his night of random thrill seeking begins to take shape. He tells the tale in retrospect—so we as readers know "the first" and "the second mistake" won't be fatal, but we also know the "error" will prove "irreversible." He and his two buddies had been cruising their town on the third night of summer vacation, looking for "something we never found." (The reference to "Westmoreland's decision to dig in at Khe Sanh" evokes U.S. Army general William Westmoreland's tactical blunder in Vietnam, and there's a not-so-casual suggestion that "losing my grip on the keys" opens a "floodgate" of trouble in a kind of small-scale war.) Restless with longing, the boys drive up to Greasy Lake and pull in behind the car they think belongs to Tony Lovett. Honking and blinking their headlights, they stumble out of their own car, hoping to catch Tony in the act of whatever he's doing.

And what happens then? This is the moment when the plot of "Greasy Lake" starts in earnest and the real action begins.

CONTINUED ON PAGE 196

T. Coraghessan Boyle *I don't consciously make a plot beforehand . . .*

A Conversation on Writing

"It all just happens" . . .

I don't consciously make a plot beforehand, nor do I make a plot in revision. . . . I revise as I go along, so that the story that you see is exactly what it was. I don't ever write scenes and change them around or anything like that. . . . For me it just happens, and it happens slowly . . . , and I perfect each line. I couldn't go on if I didn't feel that what is behind me is good. And at some point the end arrives. There's no major revision after that, and there's no detailing for plot, or theme, or symbols, or anything else. They are organic—it all just happens as one whole. So I don't do any revision whatsoever, beyond daily revision of each line till I think it's right.

From Music to Writing

As a teenager . . . I wanted to be a serious musician, and I went to music college. I played a saxophone and clarinet. . . . As soon as I got there . . . I realized that I couldn't hack it. The others were so much more advanced and better than I at their instruments. . . . In the first English course I took, which was on the contemporary short story, I discovered Flannery O'Connor, her story "A Good Man Is Hard to Find" [in Chapter 15]. And it was a revelation for me, because here was a very funny story about a family going on vacation, and it's hilarious. And then the story turns on you and becomes utterly tragic and heartbreaking. And it just woke me up, and I thought, "This is an amazing thing."

To watch this entire interview and hear the author read from "Greasy Lake," go to connect.mcgraw-hill.com.

RESEARCH ASSIGNMENT   In the interview, Boyle says, "Plot is essential to all fiction." After watching the interview, explain why Boyle feels that way. Do you agree with him? What stories can you think of that either support or refute his claim?

T. Coraghessan (core-AG-issin) Boyle (also known as T. C. Boyle), born Thomas John Boyle in Peekskill, New York (1948), is a novelist and short story writer. Boyle earned a B.A. in English and history from the State University of New York at Potsdam in 1968, after which he taught for four years in his hometown high school where his mother worked as head secretary and his father as a janitor. In 1972 he was accepted into the Iowa Writer's Workshop and has since written over twenty books of fiction. His novels include *World's End* (1987, winner of the PEN/Faulkner Award for Fiction); *The Road to Wellville* (1993); and *The Tortilla Curtain* (1995, winner of France's Prix Médicis Étranger). Boyle is also one of America's most accomplished short story writers; his story collections include *Descent of Man* (1979), *Greasy Lake* (1985), *If the River Was Whiskey* (1989), and *Without a Hero* (1994).

Boyle is known for his imagination and humor as he writes on such subjects as hippies, the environment, illegal immigration, the nineteenth-century health food movement, and identity theft. He describes writing as an addiction and explains that in his own fiction "the themes and obsessions—the search for the father, racism, class and community, predetermination versus free will, cultural imperialism, sexual war and sexual truce—keep repeating." He adds, "I can see this, but only in retrospect. That's the beauty of this addiction—you have to move on, no retirement here, look out ahead, though you can't see where you're going." Boyle has taught at the University of Southern California since 1978.

AS YOU READ "Greasy Lake," consider these questions: Where does the tension mount? Why? As the plot unfolds, what does the main character worry about? What do you worry about?

Greasy Lake (1985)

It's about a mile down on the dark side of Route 88.
—Bruce Springsteen

1   THERE was a time when courtesy and winning ways went out of style, when it was good to be bad, when you cultivated decadence like a taste. We were all dangerous characters then. We wore torn-up leather jackets, slouched around with toothpicks in our months, sniffed glue and ether and what somebody claimed was cocaine. When we wheeled our parents' whining station wagons out onto the street we left a patch of rubber half a block long. We drank gin and grape juice, Tango, Thunderbird, and Bali Hai. We were nineteen. We were bad. We read André Gide and struck elaborate poses to show that we didn't give a shit about anything. At night, we went up to Greasy Lake.

Through the center of town, up the strip, past the housing developments and shopping malls, street lights giving way to the thin streaming illumination of the headlights, trees crowding the asphalt in a black unbroken wall: that was the way out to Greasy Lake. The Indians had called it Wakan, a reference to the clarity of its waters. Now it was fetid and murky, the mud banks glittering with broken glass and strewn with beer cans and the charred remains of bonfires. There was a single ravaged island a hundred yards from shore, so stripped of vegetation it looked as if the air force had strafed it. We went up to the lake because everyone went there, because we wanted to snuff the rich scent of possibility on the breeze, watch a girl take off her clothes and plunge into the festering murk, drink beer, smoke pot, howl at the stars, savor the incongruous full-throated roar of rock and roll against the primeval susurrus of frogs and crickets. This was nature.

I was there one night, late, in the company of two dangerous characters. Digby wore a gold star in his right ear and allowed his father to pay his tuition at Cornell; Jeff was thinking of quitting school to become a painter/musician/head-shop proprietor. They were both expert in the social graces, quick with a sneer, able to manage a Ford with lousy shocks over a rutted and gutted blacktop road at eighty-five while rolling a joint as compact as a Tootsie Roll Pop stick. They could lounge against a bank of booming speakers and trade "man"s with the best of them or roll out across the dance floor as if their joints worked on bearings. They were slick and quick and they wore their mirror shades at breakfast and dinner, in the shower, in closets and caves. In short, they were bad.

I drove. Digby pounded the dashboard and shouted along with Toots & the Maytals while Jeff hung his head out the window and streaked the side of my mother's Bel Air with vomit. It was early June, the air soft as a hand on your cheek, the third night of summer vacation. The first two nights we'd been out till dawn, looking for something we never found. On this, the third night, we'd cruised the strip sixty-seven times, been in and out of every bar and club we could think of in a twenty-mile radius, stopped twice for bucket chicken and forty-cent hamburgers, debated going to a party at the house of a girl Jeff's sister knew, and chucked two dozen raw eggs at mailboxes and hitchhikers. It was 2:00 A.M.; the bars were closing. There was nothing to do but take a bottle of lemon-flavored gin up to Greasy Lake.

5   The taillights of a single car winked at us as we swung into the dirt lot with its tufts of weed and washboard corrugations; '57 Chevy, mint, metallic blue. On the far side of the lot, like the exoskeleton of some gaunt chrome insect, a chopper leaned against its kickstand. And that was it for excitement: some junkie halfwit biker and a car freak pumping his girlfriend. Whatever it was we were looking for, we weren't about to find it at Greasy Lake. Not that night.

But then all of a sudden Digby was fighting for the wheel. "Hey, that's Tony Lovett's car! Hey!" he shouted, while I stabbed at the brake pedal and the Bel Air nosed up to the gleaming bumper of the parked Chevy. Digby leaned on the horn, laughing, and instructed me to put my brights on. I flicked on the brights. This was hilarious. A joke. Tony would experience premature withdrawal and expect to be confronted by grim-looking state troopers with flash-lights. We hit the horn, strobed the lights, and then jumped out of the car to press our witty faces to Tony's windows; for all we knew we might even catch a glimpse of some little fox's tit, and then we could slap backs with red-faced Tony, roughhouse a little, and go on to new heights of adventure and daring.

The first mistake, the one that opened the whole floodgate, was losing my grip on the keys. In the excitement, leaping from the car with the gin in one hand and a roach clip in the other, I spilled them in the grass—in the dark, rank, mysterious nighttime grass of Greasy Lake. This was a tactical error, as damaging and irreversible in its way as Westmore-land's decision to dig in at Khe Sanh.

I felt it like a jab of intuition, and I stopped there by the open door, peering vaguely into the night that puddled up round my feet.

The second mistake—and this was inextricably bound up with the first—was identifying the car as Tony Lovett's. Even before the very bad character in greasy jeans and engineer boots ripped out of the driver's door, I began to realize that this chrome blue was much lighter than the robin's-egg of Tony's car, and that Tony's car didn't have rear-mounted speakers. Judging from their expressions, Digby and Jeff were privately groping toward the same inevitable and unsettling conclusion as I was.

In any case, there was no reasoning with this bad greasy character—clearly he was a man of action. The first lusty Rockette kick of his steel-toed boot caught me under the chin, chipped my favorite tooth, and left me sprawled in the dirt. Like a fool, I'd gone down on one knee to comb the stiff hacked grass for the keys, my mind making connections in the most dragged-out, testudineous way, knowing that things had gone wrong, that I was in a lot of trouble, and that the lost ignition key was my grail and my salvation. The three or four succeeding blows were mainly absorbed by my right buttock and the tough piece of bone at the base of my spine.

Meanwhile, Digby vaulted the kissing bumpers 10 and delivered a savage kung-fu blow to the greasy character's collarbone. Digby had just finished a course in martial arts for phys-ed credit and had spent the better part of the past two nights telling us apocryphal tales of Bruce Lee types and of the raw power invested in lightning blows shot from coiled wrists, ankles, and elbows. The greasy character was unimpressed. He merely backed off a step, his face like a Toltec mask, and laid Digby out with a single whistling roundhouse blow . . . but by now Jeff had got into the act, and I was beginning to extricate myself from the dirt, a tinny compound of shock, rage, and impotence wadded in my throat.

Jeff was on the guy's back, biting at his ear. Digby was on the ground, cursing. I went for the tire iron I kept under the driver's seat. I kept it there because bad characters always keep tire irons under the driver's seat, for just such an occasion as this. Never mind that I hadn't been involved in a fight since sixth grade, when a kid with a sleepy eye and two streams of mucus depending from his nostrils hit me in the knee with a Louisville slugger, never mind that I'd touched the tire iron exactly twice before, to change tires: it was there. And I went for it.

> We were bad characters, and we were scared and hot and three steps over the line . . .

I was terrified. Blood was beating in my ears, my hands were shaking, my heart turning over like a dirt-bike in the wrong gear. My antagonist was shirtless, and a single cord of muscle flashed across his chest as he bent forward to peel Jeff from his back like a wet overcoat. "Mother-fucker," he spat, over and over, and I was aware in that instant that all four of us—Digby, Jeff, and myself included—were chanting "mother-fucker, mother-fucker," as if it were a battle cry. (What happened next? The detective asks the murderer from beneath the turned-down brim of his porkpie hat. I don't know, the murderer says, something came over me. Exactly.)

Digby poked the flat of his hand in the bad character's face and I came at him like a kamikaze, mindless, raging, stung with humiliation—the whole thing, from the initial boot in the chin to this murderous primal instant involving no more than sixty hyper-ventilating, gland-flooding seconds—I came at him and brought the tire iron down across his ear. The effect was instantaneous, astonishing. He was a stunt man and this was Hollywood, he was a big grimacing toothy balloon and I was a man with a straight pin. He collapsed. Wet his pants. Went loose in his boots.

A single second, big as a zeppelin, floated by. We were standing over him in a circle, gritting our teeth, jerking our necks, our limbs and hands and feet twitching with glandular discharges. No one said anything. We just stared down at the guy, the car freak, the lover, the bad greasy character laid low. Digby

looked at me; so did Jeff. I was still holding the tire iron, a tuft of hair clinging to the crook like dandelion fluff, like down. Rattled, I dropped it in the dirt, already envisioning the headlines, the pitted faces of the police inquisitors, the gleam of handcuffs, clank of bars, the big black shadows rising from the back of the cell . . . when suddenly a raw torn shriek cut through me like all the juice in all the electric chairs in the country.

It was the fox. She was short, 15 barefoot, dressed in panties and a man's shirt. "Animals!" she screamed, running at us with her fists clenched and wisps of blow-dried hair in her face. There was a silver chain round her ankle, and her toenails flashed in the glare of the headlights. I think it was the toenails that did it. Sure, the gin and the cannabis and even the Kentucky Fried may have had a hand in it, but it was the sight of those flaming toes that set us off—the toad emerging from the loaf in *Virgin Spring*, lipstick smeared on a child; she was already tainted. We were on her like Bergman's deranged brothers—see no evil, hear none, speak none—panting, wheezing, tearing at her clothes, grabbing for flesh. We were bad characters, and we were scared and hot and three steps over the line—anything could have happened.

It didn't.

Before we could pin her to the hood of the car, our eyes masked with lust and greed and the purest primal badness, a pair of headlights swung into the lot. There we were, dirty, bloody, guilty, dissociated from humanity and civilization, the first of the Ur-crimes behind us, the second in progress, shreds of nylon panty and spandex brassiere dangling from our fingers, our flies open, lips licked—there we were, caught in the spotlight. Nailed.

We bolted. First for the car, and then, realizing we had no way of starting it, for the woods. I thought nothing. I thought escape. The headlights came at me like accusing fingers. I was gone.

Ram-bam-bam, across the parking lot, past the chopper and into the feculent undergrowth at the lake's edge, insects flying up in my face, weeds whipping, frogs and snakes and red-eyed turtles splashing off into the night: I was already ankle-deep in muck and tepid water and still going strong. Behind me, the girl's screams rose in intensity, disconsolate, incriminating, the screams of the Sabine women, the Christian martyrs, Anne Frank dragged from the garret. I kept going, pursued by those cries, imagining cops and bloodhounds. The water was up to my knees when I realized what I was doing: I was going to swim for it. Swim the breadth of Greasy Lake and hide myself in the thick clot of woods on the far side. They'd never find me there.

20   I was breathing in sobs, in gasps. The water lapped at my waist as I looked out over the moon-burnished ripples, the mats of algae that clung to the surface like scabs. Digby and Jeff had vanished. I paused. Listened. The girl was quieter now, screams tapering to sobs, but there were male voices, angry, excited, and the high-pitched ticking of the second car's engine. I waded deeper, stealthy, hunted, the ooze sucking at my sneakers. As I was about to take the plunge—at the very instant I dropped my shoulder for the first slashing stroke—I blundered into something. Something unspeakable, obscene, something soft, wet, moss-grown. A patch of weed? A log? When I reached out to touch it, it gave like a rubber duck, it gave like flesh.

In one of those nasty little epiphanies for which we are prepared by films and TV and childhood visits to the funeral home to ponder the shrunken painted forms of dead grandparents, I understood what it was that bobbed there so inadmissibly in the dark. Understood, and stumbled back in horror and revulsion, my mind yanked in six different directions (I was nineteen, a mere child, an infant, and here in the space of five minutes I'd struck down one greasy character and blundered into the water-logged carcass of a second), thinking, The keys, the keys, why did I have to go and lose the keys? I stumbled back, but the muck took hold of my feet— a sneaker snagged, balance lost—and suddenly I was pitching face forward into the buoyant black mass, throwing out my hands in desperation while simultaneously conjuring the image of reeking frogs and muskrats revolving in slicks of their own deliquescing juices. AAAAArrrgh! I shot from the water like a torpedo, the dead man rotating to expose a mossy beard and eyes cold as the moon. I must have shouted out, thrashing around in the weeds, because the voices behind me suddenly became animated.

"What was that?"

"It's them, it's them: they tried to, tried to . . . *rape* me!" Sobs.

A man's voice, flat Midwestern accent. "You sons a bitches, we'll kill you!"

Frogs, crickets.   25

Then another voice, harsh, *r*-less, Lower East Side: "Motherfucker!" I recognized the verbal virtuosity of the bad greasy character in the engineer boots. Tooth chipped, sneakers gone, coated in mud and slime and worse, crouching breathless in the weeds waiting to have my ass thoroughly and definitively kicked and fresh from the hideous stinking embrace of a three-days-dead-corpse, I suddenly felt a rush of joy and vindication: the son of a bitch was alive! Just as quickly, my bowels turned to ice. "Come on out of there, you pansy mothers!" the bad greasy character was screaming. He shouted curses till he was out of breath.

The crickets started up again, then the frogs. I held my breath. All at once was a sound in the reeds, a swishing, a splash: thunk-a-thunk. They were throwing rocks. The frogs fell silent. I cradled my head. Swish, swish, thunk-a-thunk. A wedge of feldspar the size of a cue ball glanced off my knee. I bit my finger.

It was then that they turned to the car. I heard a door slam, a curse, and then the sound of the headlights shattering—almost a good-natured sound, celebratory, like corks popping from the necks of bottles. This was succeeded by the dull booming of the fenders, metal on metal, and then the icy crash of the windshield. I inched forward, elbows and knees, my belly pressed to the muck; thinking of guerrillas and commandos and *The Naked and the Dead*. I parted the weeds and squinted the length of the parking lot.

The second car—it was a Trans-Am—was still running, its high beams washing the scene in a lurid stagy light. Tire iron flailing, the greasy bad character was laying into the side of my mother's Bel Air like an avenging demon, his shadow riding up the trunks of the trees. Whomp. Whomp. Whomp-whomp. The other two guys—blond types, in fraternity jackets—were helping out with tree branches and skull-sized boulders. One of them was gathering up bottles, rocks, muck, candy wrappers, used condoms, pop-tops, and other refuse and pitching it through the window on the driver's side. I could see the fox, a white bulb behind the windshield of the '57 Chevy. "Bobbie," she whined over the thumping, "come on." The greasy character paused a moment, took one good swipe at the left taillight, and then heaved the tire iron halfway across the lake. Then he fired up the '57 and was gone.

Blond head nodded at blond head. One said something to the other, two low for me to catch. They were no doubt thinking that in helping to annihilate my mother's car they'd committed a fairly rash act, and thinking too that there were three bad characters connected with that very car watching them from the woods. Perhaps other possibilities occurred to them as well—police, jail cells, justices of the peace, reparations, lawyers, irate parents, fraternal censure. Whatever they were thinking, they suddenly dropped branches, bottles, and rocks and sprang for their car

in unison, as if they'd choreographed it. Five seconds. That's all it took. The engine shrieked, the tires squealed, a cloud of dust rose from the rutted lot and then settled back on darkness.

I don't know how long I lay there, the bad breath of decay all around me, my jacket heavy as a bear, the primordial ooze subtly reconstituting itself to accommodate my upper thighs and testicles. My jaws ached, my knee throbbed, my coccyx was on fire. I contemplated suicide, wondered if I'd need bridgework, scraped the recesses of my brain for some sort of excuse to give my parents—a tree had fallen on the car, I was blinded by a bread truck, hit and run, vandals had got to it while we were playing chess at Digby's. Then I thought of the dead man. He was probably the only person on the planet worse off than I was. I thought about him, fog on the lake, insects chirring eerily, and felt the tug of fear, felt the darkness opening up inside me like a set of jaws. Who was he, I wondered, this victim of time and circumstance bobbing sorrowfully in the lake at my back. The owner of the chopper, no doubt, a bad older character come to this. Shot during a murky drug deal, drowned while drunkenly frolicking in the lake. Another headline. My car was wrecked; he was dead.

When the eastern half of the sky went from black to cobalt and the trees began to separate themselves from the shadows, I pushed myself up from the mud and stepped out into the open. By now the birds had begun to take over for the crickets, and dew lay slick on the leaves. There was a smell in the air, raw and sweet at the same time, the smell of the sun firing buds and opening blossoms. I contemplated the car. It lay there like a wreck along the highway, like a steel sculpture left over from a vanished civilization. Everything was still. This was nature.

I was circling the car, as dazed and bedraggled as the sole survivor of an air blitz, when Digby and Jeff emerged from the trees behind me. Digby's face was

> Then I thought of the dead man. He was probably the only person on the planet worse off than I was.

30

cross-hatched with smears of dirt; Jeff's jacket was gone and his shirt was torn across the shoulder. They slouched across the lot, looking sheepish, and silently came up beside me to gape at the ravaged automobile. No one said a word. After a while Jeff swung open the driver's door and began to scoop the broken glass and garbage off the seat. I looked at Digby. He shrugged. "At least they didn't slash the tires," he said.

It was true: the tires were intact. There was no windshield, the headlights were staved in, and the body looked as if it had been sledge-hammered for a quarter a shot at the county fair, but the tires were inflated to regulation pressure. The car was drivable. In silence, all three of us bent to scrape the mud and shattered glass from the interior. I said nothing about the biker. When we were finished, I reached in my pocket for the keys, experienced a nasty stab of recollection, cursed myself, and turned to search the grass. I spotted them almost immediately, no more than five feet from the open door, glinting like jewels in the first tapering shaft of sunlight. There was no reason to get philosophical about it: I eased into the seat and turned the engine over.

35 It was at that precise moment that the silver Mustang with the flame decals rumbled into the lot. All three of us froze; then Digby and Jeff slid into the car and slammed the door. We watched as the Mustang rocked and bobbed across the ruts and finally jerked to a halt beside the forlorn chopper at the far end of the lot. "Let's go," Digby said. I hesitated, the Bel Air wheezing beneath me.

Two girls emerged from the Mustang. Tight jeans, stiletto heels, hair like frozen fur. They bent over the motorcycle, paced back and forth aimlessly, glanced once or twice at us, and then ambled over to where the reeds sprang up in a green fence round the perimeter of the lake. One of them cupped her hands to her mouth. "Al," she called. "Hey, Al!"

"Come on," Digby hissed. "Let's get out of here."

But it was too late. The second girl was picking her way across the lot, unsteady on her heels, looking up at us and then away. She was older—twenty-five or -six—and as she came closer we could see there was something wrong with her: she was stoned or drunk, lurching now and waving her arms for balance. I gripped the steering wheel as if it were the ejection lever of a flaming jet, and Digby spat out my name, twice, terse and impatient.

"Hi," the girl said.

We looked at her like zombies, like war veterans, 40 like deaf-and-dumb pencil peddlers.

She smiled, her lips cracked and dry. "Listen," she said, bending from the waist to look in the window, "you guys seen Al?" Her pupils were pinpoints, her eyes glass. She jerked her neck. "That's his bike over there—Al's. You seen him?"

Al. I didn't know what to say. I wanted to get out of the car and retch, I wanted to go home to my parents' house and crawl into bed. Digby poked me in the ribs. "We haven't seen anybody," I said.

The girl seemed to consider this, reaching out a slim veiny arm to brace herself against the car. "No matter," she said, slurring the *t*'s, "he'll turn up." And then, as if she'd just taken stock of the whole scene— the ravaged car and our battered faces, the desolation of the place—she said: "Hey, you guys look like some pretty bad characters—been fightin', huh?" We stared straight ahead, rigid as catatonics. She was fumbling in her pocket and muttering something. Finally she held out a handful of tablets in glassine wrappers: "Hey, you want to party, you want to do some of these with me and Sarah?"

I just looked at her. I thought I was going to cry. Digby broke the silence. "No, thanks," he said, leaning over me. "Some other time."

I put the car in gear and it inched forward with 45 a groan, shaking off pellets of glass like an old dog shedding water after a bath, heaving over the ruts on its worn springs, creeping toward the highway. There was a sheen of sun on the lake. I looked back. The girl was still standing there, watching us, her shoulders slumped, hand outstretched.

IF YOU LIKED "GREASY LAKE," YOU MIGHT ALSO LIKE . . .

. . . to compare the main character and his lessons learned in "Greasy Lake" with those learned by the young woman in Alice Munro's "An Ounce of Cure" (Chapter 6).

GOING FURTHER   You can find another comic antihero, like Boyle's, in *Garden State* by Rick Moody, and you may enjoy the comic sensibility in the essays of Steve Almond in *(Not That You Asked) Rants, Exploits, and Obsessions.*

"And everybody has been to Greasy Lake." Conversation with T. Coraghessan Boyle

Writing from Reading

Summarize

1 Consider all the plot complications the author introduces to keep the tension in the story mounting. At what point does the story reach its climax (point of greatest tension)? Discuss whether the events following the climax decline to a resolution for the story.

2 When the narrator wades into the lake, he "blundered into something. Something unspeakable, obscene." What does he blunder into, and what effect does it have on him? How does this plot complication differ from the others?

Analyze Craft

3 Describe how Boyle reveals the characters' context. What is the socio-economic status of the three main characters in "Greasy Lake"? What clues does Boyle give to reveal this? How is economic status a factor in the plot of this story?

Analyze Voice

4 In the first paragraph of the story, the narrator describes what it means to be "bad." Does his voice throughout the story suggest he thinks of himself as a "bad guy"? How does the narrator's description of events support or refute his idea of himself as a "bad guy"?

Synthesize Summary and Analysis

5 "Greasy Lake" is written in past tense, presumably some time after the events of the story. How does this distance affect the tone of the story? Discuss how the plot and the description of events might change if the story were told in present tense by the narrator at age nineteen.

Interpret the Story

6 Discuss the relationship between plot and character. When the girls arrive at the end of the story, the boys turn down the chance to party with them, because, as Boyle says in his interview, "these boys have their tails between their legs." Why do they now have their "tails between their legs"? Use examples from the text to support your answer.

CONTINUED FROM PAGE 187

AN ARTFUL ARRANGEMENT OF INCIDENTS

When we lose ourselves in fiction, are we caught up in the story or its plot? Do *plot* and *story* mean the same thing? In *Aspects of the Novel*, E. M. Forster distinguishes between story and plot with this illustration:

> *"The king died, and then the queen died" is a story. "The king died, and then the queen died of grief" is a plot.*

If an event takes place in a story, we say, "and then?" If it is in a plot we ask, "why?" A **plot** is the artful arrangement of incidents in a story, with each incident building on the next in a series of causes and effects. If the three restless teens in "Greasy Lake" had simply spent the night driving and drinking, stopping at friends' houses, and throwing eggs at mailboxes, the story would be a mere arrangement of chronological events. Once the narrator loses his car keys and taunts the wrong guy, however, the "plot thickens." Event piles on event, succeeding each other in causal but unpredictable ways. The reader becomes engaged, wondering "What next?"

This creates **suspense**—a sense of anticipation or excitement about what will happen and how the characters will deal with their newfound predicament. It's worth remembering that a secondary meaning of the word *plot* is "conspiracy." In this sense, the word has negative connotations and suggests something faintly illegal, as in: *there was a plot against the king.* What keeps readers enthralled is most often not the root sequence of story, the *and then and then and then* of events; it's the surprise, the *then and therefore* that introduces the idea of motive and permits us to question behavior. Since unexplained behavior lies at the root of mystery, *plot* in its sophisticated manifestations offers the promise of surprise and the excitement of suspense.

"Plot is the essential element of all stories." Conversation with T. Coraghessan Boyle

As T. C. Boyle says in his interview, "The rest of the story—that's where the plot evolves: what happened that night. Each of the incidents of the story strings out from that in an escalating way, until we try to wrap it up and find out what happened." Authors arrange the incidents of their stories in a variety of ways to show us as readers "what happened."

Crafting Plot

One way writers set up a story and try to draw a reader into the plot is by means of **exposition,** the presentation of necessary information about the character, setting, or characters' history provided to make the reader care what happens to the characters in the story. In Anton Chekhov's "The Lady with the Pet Dog" (in An Anthology of Stories for Further Reading), the story starts off with this technique. The opening paragraphs set up the situation: A man alone, on vacation, perhaps restless after two weeks, notices a woman alone and considers approaching her.

> *It was said that a new person had appeared on the sea-front: a lady with a little dog. Dmitri Dmitritch Gurov, who had by then been a fortnight at Yalta, and so was fairly at home there, had begun to take an interest in new arrivals. Sitting in Verney's pavilion, he saw, walking on the sea-front, a fair-haired young lady of medium height, wearing a* béret; *a white Pomeranian dog was running behind her.*
>
> *And afterwards he met her in the public gardens and in the square several times a day. She was walking alone, always wearing the same* béret, *and always with the same white dog; no one knew who she was, and every one called her simply "the lady with the dog."*
>
> *"If she is here alone without a husband or friends, it wouldn't be amiss to make her acquaintance," Gurov reflected.*

Some stories begin *in medias res,* or in the middle of things. In "The Story of an Hour" (Chapter 6), for example, we immediately learn what's at stake: Mr. Mallard has died, and someone has to inform the fragile Mrs. Mallard. This is a common technique in dramatic presentations—an almost standard strategy in plays and movies and on TV. The first episode of the popular television show *Lost* begins with a plane crash that leaves dozens of survivors stranded on a strange island. The story line is built on a series of **flashbacks,** the device of moving back in time to a point before the primary action of the story, to reveal how and why this particular group of people crashed in this particular place—but the "backstory" is only slowly revealed.

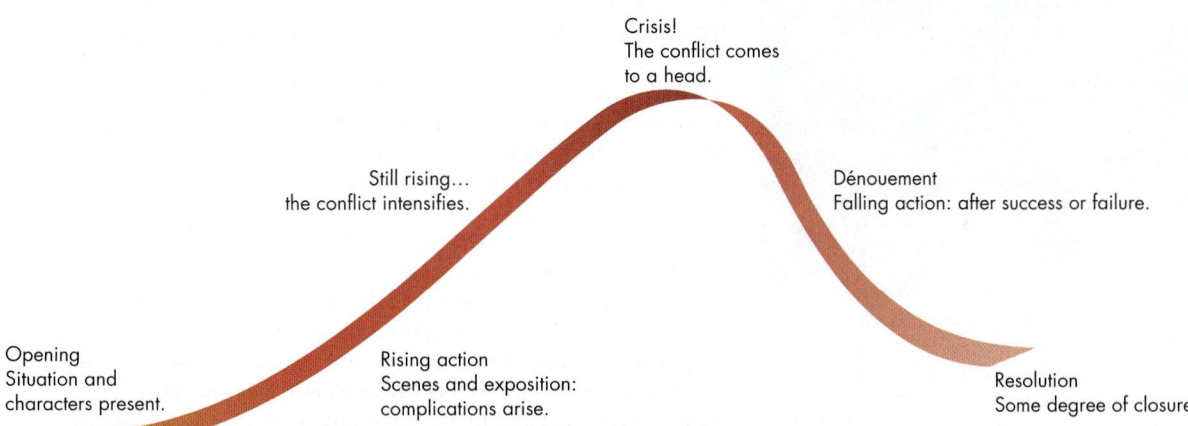

Crisis!
The conflict comes to a head.

Still rising…
the conflict intensifies.

Dénouement
Falling action: after success or failure.

Opening
Situation and characters present.

Rising action
Scenes and exposition: complications arise.

Resolution
Some degree of closure.

Authors also use **foreshadowing,** a hint about plot elements to come, to both advance the plot and build suspense. For example, in "Greasy Lake," Boyle "flashes forward" with this line, about his narrator's "mistakes": "This was a tactical error, as damaging and irreversible in its way as Westmoreland's decision to dig in at Khe Sanh." He's letting the reader know that trouble surely lies ahead, trouble as bad as a bad decision made by a military officer during the Vietnam War.

"Characters may not want to do what you want them to do in the story. They may want to do something that's just going to ruin the story. Guess what, they get to do it." Conversation with William Kittredge

All stories have a **protagonist,** the main figure (or principal actor) in a work of literature. Like any human being, a protagonist will have desires or objectives. A story's plot hinges equally on the protagonist's efforts to realize his or her desires and the protagonist's ability to cope with failure if and when plans are thwarted and desires left unfulfilled. Thus, the characters in a story often drive plot development.

The moment of greatest tension in a story is its **climax,** or crisis, the narrative's turning point in a struggle between opposing forces.

Conflict in a narrative can consist of struggles within the mind and soul of the protagonist, and it can also involve physical struggles. Complications that deepen the protagonist's predicament create the **rising action** of the story. Characters' emotional and psychological conflicts intensify their **conflict** with one or more **antagonists.** The internal and external worlds stand at odds; desires oppose each other; opposition mounts.

In J. R. R. Tolkien's classic story *The Lord of the Rings,* the main character, Frodo, faces a powerful inner struggle: He must resist the corrupting spell of the magic ring so that he can pursue his mission to destroy it and save Middle Earth. He also faces numerous external struggles on his journey, as a series of enemies seek to kill him and steal the ring. These confrontations with his enemies intensify his internal conflict—the desire to use the ring for his own benefit. The climax in *The Lord of the Rings* occurs when Frodo stands before the Lake of Fire in his mission to destroy the ring forever. Frequently, the climax causes the protagonist to change or at least to gain new understanding.

At this moment of internal conflict, Gollum attacks Frodo, and the climax resolves with both the ring and Gollum plunging into the fire toward everlasting destruction.

In the film version of *The Lord of the Rings,* Gollum (Andy Serkis) plummets into the Lake of Fire holding the magic ring, which resolves the overarching conflict of the story and advances the plot toward the dénouement.

The conclusion of the story, or the resolution that follows the climactic moment, is referred to as the **dénouement,** the **falling action** and **resolution.** Here conflicts are resolved and the story comes—at least provisionally—to an end. In the dénouement of *The Lord of the Rings,* peace is restored to Middle Earth, the new king marries his queen, and Frodo and his companions return home to the Shire.

Often, the internal transformation of the protagonist is the focal point of the story. The majority of modern and contemporary short fictions hinge on such moments, in which a significant truth or the essence of something is revealed to a character—and, by extension, the reader. Conflict, in other words, need not consist of a kick in the chin or a battle by a Lake of Fire; its resolution can be as simple as a character saying "Yes" or "No" or "Please stay" or "Go."

> **"Faulkner said, 'Fiction is the human heart in conflict with itself.' And it does seem to me that the human heart is always in conflict with itself, and that it is the fiction writer's job to understand the nature of that conflict and to make fiction out of it."** Conversation with Gish Jen

Remember that no writer sitting at the work desk (except perhaps a screenwriter) says, "Well, I've had my anticlimax, now I need a falling action and a dénouement," or "I've had my turning point and must write a resolution." The terminology we use to describe the craft of fiction is used to understand how the story makes its impact on us—long after the fact of it being written. The language is useful primarily as a tool for analytic discussion as we share our thoughts about how stories are put together, how they work, and which ones work best.

James Joyce (1882–1941)

Born in Ireland, James Joyce chose to live much of his life as an expatriate in Paris, Zurich, and Trieste. The country of his birth, however, is the subject of almost all his fiction.

The publication of Joyce's short story collection *Dubliners* (1914) was held up for years for fear of libel; the characters and places of his stories were based on real people and locations in Dublin, and publishers feared readers would recognize them as such. Joyce rendered the Dublin of his novel *Ulysses* so accurately that he once joked the city could be reconstructed solely by consulting the "map" of his book. Ezra Pound wrote of Joyce: "He presents his people swiftly and vividly, he does not sentimentalize over them, he does not weave convulsions. He is a realist. . . . He gives the thing as it is. He is not bound by the tiresome convention that any part of life, to be interesting, must be shaped into the conventional form of a 'story.'"

The story "Araby," like the others in *Dubliners,* reflects the influence of nineteenth-century realism, an artistic movement that advocated portraying the world as it is, without idealizing it. His later works—*A Portrait of the Artist as a Young Man, Ulysses,* and *Finnegans Wake*—become progressively more experimental in terms of language and form. Although it is longer than some nineteenth-century epic novels that span generations, the real-time action of *Ulysses* takes place entirely within the span of a single day.

AS YOU READ   "Araby," consider these questions: Who is telling the story? What does he want? What complications does he face in getting what he wants? How do these desires and confusions drive the story's plot?

Araby (1914)

1   NORTH Richmond Street, being blind, was a quiet street except at the hour when the Christian Brothers' School set the boys free. An uninhabited house of two storeys stood at the blind end, detached from its neighbours in a square ground. The other houses of the street, conscious of decent lives within them, gazed at one another with brown imperturbable faces.

The former tenant of our house, a priest, had died in the back drawing-room. Air, musty from having been long enclosed, hung in all the rooms, and the waste room behind the kitchen was littered with old useless papers. Among these I found a few paper-covered books, the pages of which were curled and damp: *The Abbot*, by Walter Scott, *The Devout Communicant* and *The Memoirs of Vidocq*. I liked the last best because its leaves were yellow. The wild garden behind the house contained a central apple-tree and a few straggling bushes under one of which I found the late tenant's rusty bicycle-pump. He had been a very charitable priest; in his will he had left all his money to institutions and the furniture of his house to his sister.

When the short days of winter came dusk fell before we had well eaten our dinners. When we met in the street the houses had grown sombre. The space of sky above us was the colour of ever-changing violet and towards it the lamps of the street lifted their feeble lanterns. The cold air stung us and we played till our bodies glowed. Our shouts echoed in the silent street. The career of our play brought us through the dark muddy lanes behind the houses where we ran the gantlet of the rough tribes from the cottages, to the back doors of the dark dripping gardens where odours arose from the ashpits, to the dark odorous stables where a coachman smoothed and combed the horse or shook music from the buckled harness. When we returned to the street light from the kitchen windows had filled the areas. If my uncle was seen turning the corner we hid in the shadow until we had seen him safely housed. Or if Mangan's sister came out on the doorstep to call her brother in to his tea we watched her from our shadow peer up and down the street. We waited to see whether she would remain or go in and, if she remained, we left our shadow and walked up to Mangan's steps resignedly. She was waiting for us, her figure defined by the light from the half-opened door. Her brother always teased her before he obeyed and I stood by the railings looking at her. Her dress swung as she moved her body and the soft rope of her hair tossed from side to side.

Every morning I lay on the floor in the front parlour watching her door. The blind was pulled down to within an inch of the sash so that I could not be seen. When she came out on the doorstep my heart leaped. I ran to the hall, seized my books and followed her. I kept her brown figure always in my eye and, when we came near the point at which our ways diverged, I quickened my pace and passed her. This happened morning after morning. I had never spoken to her, except for a few casual words, and yet her name was like a summons to all my foolish blood.

5   Her image accompanied me even in places the most hostile to romance. On Saturday evenings when my aunt went marketing I had to go to carry some of the parcels. We walked through the flaring streets, jostled by drunken men and bargaining women, amid the curses of labourers, the shrill litanies of shop-boys who stood on guard by the barrels of pigs' cheeks, the nasal chanting of street-singers, who sang a *come-all-you* about O'Donovan Rossa, or a ballad about the troubles in our native land. These noises con-

verged in a single sensation of life for me: I imagined that I bore my chalice safely through a throng of foes. Her name sprang to my lips at moments in strange prayers and praises which I myself did not understand. My eyes were often full of tears (I could not tell why) and at times a flood from my heart seemed to pour itself out into my bosom. I thought little of the future. I did not know whether I would ever speak to her or not or, if I spoke to her, how I could tell her of my confused adoration. But my body was like a harp and her words and gestures were like fingers running upon the wires.

One evening I went into the back drawing-room in which the priest had died. It was a dark rainy evening and there was no sound in the house. Through one of the broken panes I heard the rain impinge upon the earth, the fine incessant needles of water playing in the sodden beds. Some distant lamp or lighted window gleamed below me. I was thankful that I could see so little. All my senses seemed to desire to veil themselves and, feeling that I was about to slip from them, I pressed the palms of my hands together until they trembled, murmuring: *O love! O love!* many times.

At last she spoke to me. When she addressed the first words to me I was so confused that I did not know what to answer. She asked me was I going to *Araby*. I forget whether I answered yes or no. It would be a splendid bazaar, she said; she would love to go.

—And why can't you? I asked.

While she spoke she turned a silver bracelet round and round her wrist. She could not go, she said, because there would be a retreat that week in her convent. Her brother and two other boys were fighting for their caps and I was alone at the railings. She held one of the spikes, bowing her head towards me. The light from the lamp opposite our door caught the white curve of her neck, lit up her hair that rested there and, falling, lit up the hand upon the railing. It fell over one side of her dress and caught the white border of a petticoat, just visible as she stood at ease.

10 —It's well for you, she said.

—If I go, I said, I will bring you something.

What innumerable follies laid waste my waking and sleeping thoughts after that evening! I wished to annihilate the tedious intervening days. I chafed against the work of

> **I had never spoken to her,** except for a few casual words, and yet her name was like a summons to all my foolish blood.

school. At night in my bedroom and by day in the classroom her image came between me and the page I strove to read. The syllables of the word *Araby* were called to me through the silence in which my soul luxuriated and cast an Eastern enchantment over me. I asked for leave to go to the bazaar Saturday night. My aunt was surprised and hoped it was not some Freemason affair. I answered few questions in class. I watched my master's face pass from amiability to sternness; he hoped I was not beginning to idle. I could not call my wandering thoughts together. I had hardly any patience with the serious work of life which, now that it stood between me and my desire, seemed to me child's play, ugly monotonous child's play.

On Saturday morning I reminded my uncle that I wished to go to the bazaar in the evening. He was fussing at the hallstand, looking for the hat-brush, and answered me curtly:

—Yes, boy, I know.

As he was in the hall I could not go into the front parlour and lie at the window. I left the house in bad humour and walked slowly towards the school. The air was pitilessly raw and already my heart misgave me. 15

When I came home to dinner my uncle had not yet been home. Still it was early. I sat staring at the clock for some time and, when its ticking began to irritate me, I left the room. I mounted the staircase and gained the upper part of the house. The high cold empty gloomy rooms liberated me and I went from room to room singing. From the front window I saw my companions playing below in the street. Their cries reached me weakened and indistinct and, leaning my forehead against the cool glass, I looked over at the dark house where she lived. I may have stood there for an hour, seeing nothing but the brown-clad figure cast by my imagination, touched discreetly by the lamplight at the curved neck, at the hand upon the railings and at the border below the dress.

When I came downstairs again I found Mrs. Mercer sitting at the fire. She was an old garrulous woman, a pawnbroker's widow, who collected used stamps for some pious purpose. I had to endure the gossip of the tea-table. The meal was prolonged beyond an hour and still my uncle did not come. Mrs. Mercer stood up to go: she was sorry she couldn't wait any longer, but it was after eight o'clock and she did not like to be out late, as the night air was bad for her. When she had gone I began to walk up and down the room, clenching my fists. My aunt said:

—I'm afraid you may put off your bazaar for this night of Our Lord.

At nine o'clock I heard my uncle's latchkey in the halldoor. I heard him talking to himself and heard the hallstand rocking when it had received the weight of his overcoat. I could interpret these signs. When he was midway through his dinner I asked him to give me the money to go to the bazaar. He had forgotten.

20 —The people are in bed and after their first sleep now, he said.

I did not smile. My aunt said to him energetically:

—Can't you give him the money and let him go? You've kept him late enough as it is.

My uncle said he was very sorry he had forgotten. He said he believed in the old saying: *All work and no play makes Jack a dull boy*. He asked me where I was going and, when I had told him a second time he asked me did I know *The Arab's Farewell to his Steed*. When I left the kitchen he was about to recite the opening lines of the piece to my aunt.

I held a florin tightly in my hand as I strode down Buckingham Street towards the station. The sight of the streets thronged with buyers and glaring with gas recalled to me the purpose of my journey. I took my seat in a third-class carriage of a deserted train. After an intolerable delay the train moved out of the station slowly. It crept onward among ruinous houses and over the twinkling river. At Westland Row Station a crowd of people pressed to the carriage doors; but the porters moved them back, saying that it was a special train for the bazaar. I remained alone in the bare carriage. In a few minutes the train drew up beside an improvised wooden platform. I passed out on to the road and saw by the lighted dial of a clock that it was ten minutes to ten. In front of me was a large building which displayed the magical name.

25 I could not find any sixpenny entrance and, fearing that the bazaar would be closed, I passed in quickly

through a turnstile, handing a shilling to a weary-looking man. I found myself in a big hall girdled at half its height by a gallery. Nearly all the stalls were closed and the greater part of the hall was in darkness. I recognised a silence like that which pervades a church after a service. I walked into the centre of the bazaar timidly. A few people were gathered about the stalls which were still open. Before a curtain, over which the words *Café Chantant* were written in coloured lamps, two men were counting money on a salver. I listened to the fall of the coins.

Remembering with difficulty why I had come I went over to one of the stalls and examined porcelain vases and flowered tea-sets. At the door of the stall a young lady was talking and laughing with two young gentlemen. I remarked their English accents and listened vaguely to their conversation.

—O, I never said such a thing!

—O, but you did!

—O, but I didn't!

—Didn't she say that?   30

—Yes. I heard her.

—O, there's a . . . fib!

Observing me the young lady came over and asked me did I wish to buy anything. The tone of her voice was not encouraging; she seemed to have spoken to me out of a sense of duty. I looked humbly at the great jars that stood like eastern guards at either side of the dark entrance to the stall and murmured:

—No, thank you.

The young lady changed the position of one   35
of the vases and went back to the two young
men. They began to talk of the same
subject. Once or twice the young
lady glanced at me over her
shoulder.

I lingered before her stall, though I knew my stay was useless, to make my interest in her wares seem the more real. Then I turned away slowly and walked down the middle of the bazaar. I allowed the two pennies to fall against the sixpence in my pocket. I heard a voice call from one end of the gallery that the light was out. The upper part of the hall was now completely dark.

Gazing up into the darkness I saw myself as a creature driven and derided by vanity; and my eyes burned with anguish and anger.

IF YOU LIKED THIS STORY, YOU MIGHT ALSO LIKE . . .

. . . John Updike's "A&P" (Chapter 6) for another take on a young man's experience with women and class and self-realization.

GOING FURTHER   Joyce's stories can be found in his collection *Dubliners.* His novel *A Portrait of the Artist as a Young Man* takes the theme of growing up and enlarges it to include the main character's initiation into matters of family, love, religion, art, and politics.

Writing from Reading

Summarize

1 The story begins with a long expository section in which the narrator describes the setting and his state of mind. Mark the place in the story where it shifts into a scene and the plot is launched.

2 List all the causes and effects you can find in the plot. What role does cause/effect have in the development of the plot?

Analyze Craft

3 Does the terse, isolated dialogue serve to advance the plot of "Araby"? Describe how more detailed interactions would affect the pace of the story.

Analyze Voice

4 The narrator reports this story as he looks back on it from a future time. Based on the language and voice, how distant in time is the narrator from the events he recounts? Using textual evidence, can you piece together the age and social status of the narrator as the story unfolds?

Synthesize Summary and Analysis

5 Consider the role of the priest who died in the drawing room in relation to the events of the story. Note the two instances in which the narrator visits the room where the priest died, and discuss these scenes in relation to the rising tension of the story.

Interpret the Story

6 At the end of the story, the narrator recognizes himself as a "creature driven and derided by vanity." Consider whether he is becoming such a person at that moment—whether the events of the story have brought about a change in him—or whether he is having an epiphany about the person he has always been. Which of the narrator's actions in the story support your conclusion?

Joyce Carol Oates

I hope readers read without thinking it's a work of fiction.

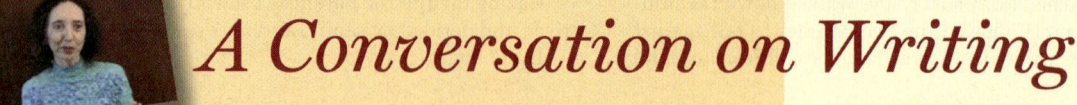

A Conversation on Writing

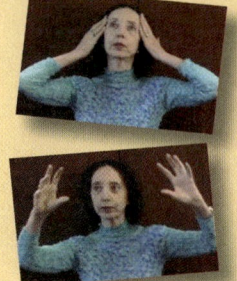

Falling in Love with Your Subject

You may see something happen and it lodges very deeply in you for a reason that you can't understand. I think it's almost like falling in love. . . . You might see something on television. It makes almost no impression. It just sort of glimmers and goes past you. But once in a while something will enter into you, and it imprints itself very deeply into you, because it struck a resonance with your own unconscious and your own personal life. I don't think that one can write or create any kind of art that doesn't have a deep resonance in the artist or writer's unconscious.

The Sport of Revision

Well, the process of revision I find so thrilling. And I encourage my students to deal with revision in a way that's competitive. They take a work of theirs that they've done several weeks ago, and you look through it quickly. And you say to yourself, "I can do better. I can do better than this." And it's true. You can always do better. Every sentence could be rewritten, paragraphs could be rewritten, the whole thing could be kind of restructured. You could have a different opening—more interesting—you could have a different ending, a different title. The whole thing belongs to you, and you say to yourself, "I can make this better." And the fact is that nobody else can touch that except you. You are the sole proprietor and owner of that material.

To watch this entire interview and hear the author read from her work, go to connect .mcgraw-hill.com.

RESEARCH ASSIGNMENT   In her interview, Oates talks about the original title of "Where Are You Going, Where Have You Been?" and how she originally thought about that story. What made her change her title and with it her story? Do you agree with her decision?

First educated in a one-room schoolhouse in rural western New York, Joyce Carol Oates, born in 1938, is now a professor of creative writing at Princeton University. For her fourteenth birthday, Oates received a typewriter, began writing, and went on to become one of America's most prominent contemporary authors. At age nineteen, Oates won *Mademoiselle* magazine's prestigious short story contest, continued to write steadily as an undergraduate at Syracuse University, published her first book at the age of twenty-eight, and established a rate of production of at least two books per year.

Although it is often the violence, or suggestion of violence, that draws attention to Oates' writing, Oates is offended when critics call attention to her sex and to the violence that her female protagonists often face. Oates's fiction is concerned with more than female suffering.

Rather, Oates is fascinated with human behavior and the way—even in the face of destructive outside forces—people create identity. Oates explains "I sometimes write about people who are ordinary people in extraordinary moments, because I think that people are much stronger and more interesting than they appear to be. Literature and art take people to places of conflict, where what is buried in them and perhaps even asleep in them is awakened suddenly. . . . And so with all of us I think we awaken from a kind of a sleep of ordinary life by some stressful thing that happens to us."

AS YOU READ   As a witness to society, Joyce Carol Oates has few if any equals; for more than forty years she has reported on America, its brightly lit arenas as well as its dark corners. Her tales are often fringed with menace, their resolutions violent. How does she build suspense in "Where Are You Going, Where Have You Been?" When does the story turn dark?

Where Are You Going, Where Have You Been? (1970)

For Bob Dylan

1   HER name was Connie. She was fifteen and she had a quick nervous giggling habit of craning her neck to glance into mirrors, or checking other people's faces to make sure her own was all right. Her mother, who noticed everything and knew everything and who hadn't much reason any longer to look at her own face, always scolded Connie about it. "Stop gawking at yourself, who are you? You think you're so pretty?" she would say. Connie would raise her eyebrows at these familiar complaints and look right through her mother, into a shadowy vision of herself as she was right at that moment: she knew she was pretty and that was everything. Her mother had been pretty once too, if you could believe those old snapshots in the album, but now her looks were gone and that was why she was always after Connie.

"Why don't you keep your room clean like your sister? How've you got your hair fixed—what the hell stinks? Hair spray? You don't see your sister using that junk."

Her sister June was twenty-four and still lived at home. She was a secretary in the high school Connie attended, and if that wasn't bad enough—with her in the same building— she was so plain and chunky and steady that Connie had to hear her praised all the time by her mother and her mother's sisters. June did this, June did that, she saved money and helped clean the house and cooked and Connie couldn't

do a thing, her mind was all filled with trashy daydreams. Their father was away at work most of the time and when he came home he wanted supper and he read the newspaper at supper and after supper he went to bed. He didn't bother talking much to them, but around his bent head Connie's mother kept picking at her until Connie wished her mother was dead and she herself was dead and it was all over. "She makes me want to throw up sometimes," she complained to her friends. She had a high, breathless, amused voice which made everything she said sound a little forced, whether it was sincere or not.

There was one good thing: June went places with girl friends of hers, girls who were just as plain and steady as she, and so when Connie wanted to do that her mother had no objections. The father of Connie's best girl friend drove the girls the three miles to town and left them off at a shopping plaza, so that they could walk through the stores or go to a movie, and when he came to pick them up again at eleven he never bothered to ask what they had done.

They must have been familiar sights, walking around   5 that shopping plaza in their shorts and flat ballerina slippers that always scuffed the sidewalk, with charm bracelets jingling on their thin wrists; they would lean together to whisper and laugh secretly if someone passed by who amused or interested them. Connie had long dark blond hair that drew anyone's eye to it, and she wore part of it pulled up on her head and puffed out and the rest of it she let fall down her back. She wore a pull-over jersey blouse that looked one way when she was at home and another way when she was away from home. Everything about her had two sides to it, one for home and one for anywhere that was not home: her walk that could be childlike and bobbing, or languid enough to make anyone think she was hearing music in her head, her mouth which was pale and smirking most of the time, but bright and pink on these evenings out, her laugh which was cynical and drawling at home—"Ha, ha, very funny"—but high-pitched and nervous anywhere else, like the jingling of the charms on her bracelet.

Sometimes they did go shopping or to a movie, but sometimes they went across the highway, ducking fast across the busy road, to a drive-in restaurant where older kids hung out. The restaurant was shaped like a big bottle, though squatter than a real bottle, and on its cap was a revolving figure of a grinning boy who held a hamburger aloft. One night in mid-summer they ran across, breathless with daring, and right away someone leaned out a car window and invited them over, but it was just a boy from high school they didn't like. It made them feel good to be able to ignore him. They went up through the maze of parked and cruising cars to the bright-lit, fly-infested restaurant, their faces pleased and expectant as if they were entering a sacred building that loomed out of the night to give them what haven and what blessing they yearned for. They sat at the counter and crossed their legs at the ankles, their thin shoulders rigid with excitement, and listened to the music that made everything so good: the music was always in the background like music at a church service, it was something to depend upon.

A boy named Eddie came in to talk with them. He sat backwards on his stool, turning himself jerkily around in semicircles and then stopping and turning again, and after a while he asked Connie if she would like something to eat. She said she did and so she tapped her friend's arm on her way out—her friend pulled her

He wagged a finger and laughed and said, "Gonna get you, baby."

face up into a brave droll look—and Connie said she would meet her at eleven, across the way. "I just hate to leave her like that," Connie said earnestly, but the boy said that she wouldn't be alone for long. So they went out to his car and on the way Connie couldn't help but let her eyes wander over the windshields and faces all around her, her face gleaming with a joy that had nothing to do with Eddie or even this place; it might have been the music. She drew her shoulders up and sucked in her breath with the pure pleasure of being alive, and just at that moment she happened to glance at a face just a few feet from hers. It was a boy with shaggy black hair, in a convertible jalopy painted gold. He stared at her and then his lips widened into a grin. Connie slit her eyes at him and turned away, but she couldn't help glancing back and there he was still watching her. He wagged a finger and laughed and said, "Gonna get you, baby," and Connie turned away again without Eddie noticing anything.

She spent three hours with him, at the restaurant where they ate hamburgers and drank Cokes in wax cups that were always sweating, and then down an alley a mile or so away, and when he left her off at five to eleven only the movie house was still open at the plaza. Her girl friend was there, talking with a boy. When Connie came up the two girls smiled at each other and Connie said, "How was the movie?" and the girl said, "*You* should know." They rode off with the girl's father, sleepy and pleased, and Connie couldn't help but look at the darkened shopping plaza with its big empty parking lot and its signs that were faded and ghostly now, and over at the drive-in restaurant where cars were still circling tirelessly. She couldn't hear the music at this distance.

Next morning June asked her how the movie was and Connie said, "So-so."

She and that girl and occasionally another girl went out several times a week that way, and the rest of the time Connie spent around the house—it was summer vacation—getting in her mother's way and thinking, dreaming, about the boys she met. But all the boys fell back and dissolved into a single face that was not even a face, but an idea, a feeling, mixed up with the urgent insistent pounding of the music and the humid night air of July. Connie's mother kept dragging her back to the daylight by finding things for her to do or saying, suddenly, "What's this about the Pettinger girl?"

10

And Connie would say nervously, "Oh, her. That dope." She always drew thick clear lines between herself and such girls, and her mother was simple and kindly enough to believe her. Her mother was so simple, Connie thought, that it was maybe cruel to fool her so much. Her mother went scuffling around the house in old bedroom slippers and complained over the telephone to one sister about the other, then the other called up and the two of them complained about the third one. If June's name was mentioned her mother's tone was approving, and if Connie's name was mentioned it was disapproving. This did not really mean she disliked Connie and actually Connie thought that her mother preferred her to June because she was prettier, but the two of them kept up a pretense of exasperation, a sense that they were tugging and struggling over something of little value to either of them. Sometimes, over coffee, they were almost friends, but something would come up—some vexation that was like a fly buzzing suddenly around their heads—and their faces went hard with contempt.

One Sunday Connie got up at eleven—none of them bothered with church—and washed her hair so that it could dry all day long, in the sun. Her parents and sister were going to a barbecue at an aunt's house and Connie said no, she wasn't interested, rolling her eyes to let her mother know just what she thought of it. "Stay home alone then," her mother said sharply. Connie sat out back in a lawn chair and watched them drive away, her father quiet and bald, hunched around so that he could back the car out, her mother with a look that was still angry and not at all softened through the windshield, and in the back seat poor old June all dressed up as if she didn't know what a barbecue was, with all the running yelling kids and the flies. Connie sat with her eyes closed in the sun, dreaming and dazed with the warmth about her as if this were a kind of love, the caresses of love, and her mind slipped over onto thoughts of the boy she had been with the night before and how nice he had been, how sweet it always was, not the way someone like June would suppose but sweet, gentle, the way it was in movies and promised in songs; and when she opened her eyes she hardly knew where she was, the back yard ran off into weeds and a fence-line of trees and behind it the sky was perfectly blue and still. The asbestos "ranch house" that was now three years old startled her—it looked small. She shook her head as if to get awake.

It was too hot. She went inside the house and turned on the radio to drown out the quiet. She sat on the edge of her bed, barefoot, and listened for an hour and a half to a program called XYZ Sunday Jamboree, record after record of hard, fast, shrieking songs she sang along with, interspersed by exclamations from "Bobby King": "An' look here you girls at Napoleon's—Son and Charley want you to pay real close attention to this song coming up!"

And Connie paid close attention herself, bathed in a glow of slow-pulsed joy that seemed to rise mysteriously out of the music itself and lay languidly about the airless little room, breathed in and breathed out with each gentle rise and fall of her chest.

After a while she heard a car coming up the drive. She sat up at once, startled, because it couldn't be her father so soon. The gravel kept crunching all the way in from the road—the driveway was long—and Connie ran to the window. It was a car she didn't know. It was an open jalopy, painted a bright gold that caught the sunlight opaquely. Her heart began to pound and her fingers snatched at her hair, checking it, and she whispered "Christ, Christ," wondering how bad she looked. The car came to a stop at the side door and the horn sounded four short taps as if this were a signal Connie knew.

She went into the kitchen and approached the door slowly, then hung out the screen door, her bare toes curling down off the step. There were two boys in the car and now she recognized the driver: he had shaggy, shabby black hair that looked crazy as a wig and he was grinning at her.

"I ain't late, am I?" he said.

"Who the hell do you think you are?" Connie said.

"Toldja I'd be out, didn't I?"

"I don't even know who you are."

She spoke sullenly, careful to show no interest or pleasure, and he spoke in a fast bright monotone. Connie looked past him to the other boy, taking her time. He had fair brown hair, with a lock that fell onto his forehead. His sideburns gave him a fierce, embarrassed look, but so far he hadn't even bothered to glance at her. Both boys wore sunglasses. The driver's glasses were metallic and mirrored everything in miniature.

15

20

"You wanta come for a ride?" he said.

Connie smirked and let her hair fall loose over one shoulder.

"Don'tcha like my car? New paint job," he said. "Hey."

25 "What?"

"You're cute."

She pretended to fidget, chasing flies away from the door.

"Don'tcha believe me, or what?" he said.

"Look, I don't even know who you are," Connie said in disgust.

30 "Hey, Ellie's got a radio, see. Mine's broke down." He lifted his friend's arm and showed her the little transistor the boy was holding, and now Connie began to hear the music. It was the same program that was playing inside the house.

"Bobby King?" she said.

"I listen to him all the time. I think he's great."

"He's kind of great," Connie said reluctantly.

"Listen, that guy's *great*. He knows where the action is."

35 Connie blushed a little, because the glasses made it impossible for her to see just what this boy was looking at. She couldn't decide if she liked him or if he was just a jerk, and so she dawdled in the doorway and wouldn't come down or go back inside. She said, "What's all that stuff painted on your car?"

"Can'tcha read it?" He opened the door very carefully, as if he was afraid it might fall off. He slid out just as carefully, planting his feet firmly on the ground, the tiny metallic world in his glasses slowing down like gelatine hardening and in the midst of it Connie's bright green blouse. "This here is my name, to begin with," he said. ARNOLD FRIEND was written in tarlike black letters on the side, with a drawing of a round grinning face that reminded Connie of a pumpkin, except it wore sunglasses. "I wanta introduce myself, I'm Arnold Friend and that's my real name and I'm gonna be your friend, honey, and inside the car's Ellie Oscar, he's kinda shy." Ellie brought his transistor radio up to his shoulder and balanced it there. "Now these numbers are a secret code, honey," Arnold Friend explained. He read off the numbers 33, 19, 17 and raised his eyebrows at her to see what she thought of that, but she didn't think much of it. The left rear fender had been smashed and around it was written, on the gleaming gold background: DONE BY CRAZY WOMAN DRIVER.

Connie had to laugh at that. Arnold Friend was pleased at her laughter and looked up at her. "Around the other side's a lot more—you wanta come and see them?"

"No."

"Why not?"

"Why should I?"

"Don'tcha wanta see what's on the car? Don'tcha wanta 40 go for a ride?"

"I don't know."

"Why not?"

"I got things to do."

"Like what?"

"Things." 45

He laughed as if she had said something funny. He slapped his thighs. He was standing in a strange way, leaning back against the car as if he were balancing himself. He wasn't tall, only an inch or so taller than she would be if she came down to him. Connie liked the way he was dressed, which was the way all of them dressed: tight faded jeans

> The way he straightened and recovered from his fit of laughing showed that it had been all fake.

stuffed into black, scuffed boots, a belt that pulled his waist in and showed how lean he was, and a white pullover shirt that was a little soiled and showed the hard small muscles of his arms and shoulders. He looked as if he probably did hard work, lifting and carrying things. Even his neck looked muscular. And his face was a familiar face, somehow: the jaw and chin and cheeks slightly darkened, because he hadn't shaved for a day or two, and the nose long and hawk-like, sniffing as if she were a treat he was going to gobble up and it was all a joke.

"Connie, you ain't telling the truth. This is your day set aside for a ride with me and you know it," he said, still laughing. The way he straightened and recovered from his fit of laughing showed that it had been all fake.

"How do you know what my name is?" she said suspiciously.

"It's Connie."

"Maybe and maybe not."

50 "I know my Connie," he said, wagging his finger. Now she remembered him even better, back at the restaurant, and her cheeks warmed at the thought of how she sucked in her breath just at the moment she passed him—how she must have looked to him. And he had remembered her. "El-

lie and I come out here especially for you," he said. "Ellie can sit in back. How about it?"

"Where?"

"Where what?"

"Where're we going?"

55   He looked at her. He took off the sunglasses and she saw how pale the skin around his eyes was, like holes that were not in shadow but instead in light. His eyes were chips of broken glass that catch the light in an amiable way. He smiled. It was as if the idea of going for a ride somewhere, to some place, was a new idea to him.

"Just for a ride, Connie sweetheart."

"I never said my name was Connie," she said.

"But I know what it is. I know your name and all about you, lots of things," Arnold Friend said. He had not moved yet but stood still leaning back against the side of his jalopy. "I took a special interest in you, such a pretty girl, and found out all about you like I know your parents and sister are gone somewheres and I know where and how long they're going to be gone, and I know who you were with last night, and your best girl friend's name is Betty. Right?"

He spoke in a simple lilting voice, exactly as if he were reciting the words to a song. His smile assured her that everything was fine. In the car Ellie turned up the volume on his radio and did not bother to look around at them.

60   "Ellie can sit in the back seat," Arnold Friend said. He indicated his friend with a casual jerk of his chin, as if Ellie did not count and she should not bother with him.

"How'd you find out all that stuff?" Connie said.

"Listen: Betty Schultz and Tony Fitch and Jimmy Pettinger and Nancy Pettinger," he said, in a chant. "Raymond Stanley and Bob Hutter—"

"Do you know all those kids?"

"I know everybody."

65   "Look, you're kidding. You're not from around here."

"Sure."

"But,—how come we never saw you before?"

"Sure you saw me before," he said. He looked down at his boots, as if he were a little offended. "You just don't remember."

"I guess I'd remember you," Connie said.

70   "Yeah?" He looked up at this, beaming. He was pleased. He began to mark time with the music from Ellie's radio, tapping his fists lightly together. Connie looked away from his smile to the car, which was painted so bright it almost hurt her eyes to look at it. She looked at that name, ARNOLD FRIEND. And up at the front fender was an expression that was familiar—MAN THE FLYING SAUCERS. It was an expression kids had used the year before, but didn't use this year. She looked at it for a while as if the words meant something to her that she did not yet know.

"What're you thinking about? Huh?" Arnold Friend demanded. "Not worried about your hair blowing around in the car, are you?"

"No."

"Think I maybe can't drive good?"

"How do I know?"

"You're a hard girl to handle. How come?" he said. 75 "Don't you know I'm your friend? Didn't you see me put my sign in the air when you walked by?"

"What sign?"

"My sign." And he drew an X in the air, leaning out toward her. They were maybe ten feet apart. After his hand fell back to his side the X was still in the air, almost visible. Connie let the screen door close and stood perfectly still inside it, listening to the music from her radio and the boy's blend together. She stared at Arnold Friend. He stood there so stiffly relaxed, pretending to be relaxed, with one hand idly on the door handle as if he were keeping himself up that way and had no intention of ever moving again. She recognized most things about him, the tight jeans that showed his thighs and buttocks and the greasy leather boots and the tight shirt, and even that slippery friendly smile of his, that sleepy dreamy smile that all the boys used to get across ideas they didn't want to put into words. She recognized all this and also the singsong way he talked, slightly mocking, kidding, but serious and a little melancholy, and she recognized the way he tapped one fist against the other in homage to the perpetual music behind him. But all these things did not come together.

She said suddenly, "Hey, how old are you?"

His smile faded. She could see then that he wasn't a kid, he was much older—thirty, maybe more. At this knowledge her heart began to pound faster.

"That's a crazy thing to ask. Can'tcha see I'm your own 80 age?"

"Like hell you are."

"Or maybe a coupla years older, I'm eighteen."

"Eighteen?" she said doubtfully.

He grinned to reassure her and lines appeared at the corners of his mouth. His teeth were big and white. He grinned so broadly his eyes became slits and she saw how thick the lashes were, thick and black as if painted with a black tar-like material. Then he seemed to become embarrassed, abruptly, and looked over his shoulder at Ellie. "*Him*, he's crazy," he said. "Ain't he a riot, he's a nut, a real character." Ellie was still listening to the music. His sunglasses told nothing about what he was thinking. He wore a bright orange shirt unbuttoned halfway to show his chest, which was a pale, bluish chest and not muscular like Arnold Friend's. His shirt collar was turned up all around and the very tips of the collar pointed out past his chin as if they were protecting him. He was pressing the transistor radio up against his ear and sat there in a kind of daze, right in the sun.

85 "He's kinda strange," Connie said.

"Hey, she says you're kinda strange! Kinda strange!" Arnold Friend cried. He pounded on the car to get Ellie's attention. Ellie turned for the first time and Connie saw with shock that he wasn't kid either—he had a fair, hairless face, cheeks reddened slightly as if the veins grew too close to the surface of his skin, the face of a forty-year-old baby. Connie felt a wave of dizziness rise in her at this sight and she stared at him as if waiting for something to change the shock of the moment, make it all right again. Ellie's lips kept shaping words, mumbling along, with the words blasting in his ear.

"Maybe you two better go away," Connie said faintly.

"What? How come?" Arnold Friend cried. "We come out here to take you for a ride. It's Sunday." He had the voice of the man on the radio now. It was the same voice, Connie thought. "Don'tcha know it's Sunday all day and honey, no matter who you were with last night today you're with Arnold Friend and don't you forget it!—Maybe you better step out here," he said, and this last was in a different voice. It was a little flatter, as if the heat was finally getting to him.

"No. I got things to do."

90 "Hey."

"You two better leave."

"We ain't leaving until you come with us."

"Like hell I am—"

"Connie, don't fool around with me. I mean, I mean, don't fool *around*," he said, shaking his head. He laughed incredulously. He placed his sunglasses on top of his head, carefully, as if he were indeed wearing a wig, and brought the stems down behind his ears. Connie stared at him, another wave of dizziness and fear rising in her so that for a moment he wasn't even in focus but was just a blur, standing there against his gold car, and she had the idea that he had driven up the driveway all right but had come from nowhere before that and belonged nowhere and that everything about him and even about the music that was so familiar to her was only half real.

> ## Connie stared at him, another wave of dizziness and fear rising in her . . .

"If my father comes and sees you—" 95

"He ain't coming. He's at the barbecue."

"How do you know that?"

"Aunt Tillie's. Right now they're—uh—they're drinking. Sitting around," he said vaguely, squinting as if he were staring all the way to town and over to Aunt Tillie's backyard. Then the vision seemed to get clear and he nodded energetically. "Yeah. Sitting around. There's your sister in a blue dress, huh? And high heels, the poor sad bitch—nothing like you, sweetheart! And your mother's helping some fat woman with the corn, they're cleaning the corn—husking the corn—"

"What fat woman?" Connie cried.

"How do I know what fat woman. I don't know every 100 goddam fat woman in the world!" Arnold Friend laughed.

"Oh, that's Mrs. Hornby. . . . Who invited her?" Connie said. She felt a little light-headed. Her breath was coming quickly.

"She's too fat. I don't like them fat. I like them the way you are, honey," he said, smiling sleepily at her. They stared at each other for a while, through the screen door. He said softly, "Now what you're going to do is this: you're going to come out that door. You're going to sit up front with me and Ellie's going to sit in the back, the hell with Ellie, right? This isn't Ellie's date. You're my date. I'm your lover, honey."

"What? You're crazy—"

"Yes, I'm your lover. You don't know what that is but you will," he said. "I know that too. I know all about you. But look: it's real nice and you couldn't ask for nobody better than me, or more polite. I always keep my word. I'll tell you how it is, I'm always nice at first, the first time. I'll hold you so tight you won't think you have to try to get away or pretend anything because you'll know you can't. And I'll come inside you where it's all secret and you'll give in to me and you'll love me—"

105 "Shut up! You're crazy!" Connie said. She backed away from the door. She put her hands against her ears as if she'd heard something terrible, something not meant for her. "People don't talk like that, you're crazy," she muttered. Her heart was almost too big now for her chest and its pumping made sweat break out all over her. She looked out to see Arnold Friend pause and then take a step toward the porch lurching. He almost fell. But, like a clever drunken man, he managed to catch his balance. He wobbled in his high boots and grabbed hold of one of the porch posts.

"Honey?" he said. "You still listening?"

"Get the hell out of here!"

"Be nice, honey. Listen."

"I'm going to call the police—"

110 He wobbled again and out of the side of his mouth came a fast spat curse, an aside not meant for her to hear. But even this "Christ!" sounded forced. Then he began to smile again. She watched this smile come, awkward as if he were smiling from inside a mask. His whole face was a mask, she thought wildly, tanned down onto his throat but then running out as if he had plastered makeup on his face but had forgotten about his throat.

"Honey—? Listen, here's how it is. I always tell the truth and I promise you this: I ain't coming in that house after you."

"You better not! I'm going to call the police if you—if you don't—"

"Honey," he said, talking right through her voice, "honey, I'm not coming in there but you are coming out here. You know why?"

She was panting. The kitchen looked like a place she had never seen before, some room she had run inside but which wasn't good enough, wasn't going to help her. The kitchen window had never had a curtain, after three years, and there were dishes in the sink for her to do—probably—and if you ran your hand across the table you'd probably feel something sticky there.

115 "You listening, honey? Hey?"

"—going to call the police—"

"Soon as you touch the phone I don't need to keep my promise and can come inside. You won't want that."

She rushed forward and tried to lock the door. Her fingers were shaking. "But why lock it," Arnold Friend said gently, talking right into her face. "It's just a screen door. It's

just nothing." One of his boots was at a strange angle, as if his foot wasn't in it. It pointed out to the left, bent at the ankle. "I mean, anybody can break through a screen door and glass and wood and iron or anything else if he needs to, anybody at all and specially Arnold Friend. If the place got lit up with a fire honey you'd come running out into my arms, right into my arms and safe at home—like you knew I was your lover and'd stopped fooling around. I don't mind a nice shy girl but I don't like no fooling around." Part of those words were spoken with a slight rhythmic lilt, and Connie somehow recognized them—the echo of a song from last year, about a girl rushing into her boyfriend's arms and coming home again—

Connie stood barefoot on the linoleum floor, staring at him. "What do you want?" she whispered.

"I want you," he said.   120

"What?"

"Seen you that night and thought, that's the one, yes sir. I never needed to look any more."

"But my father's coming back. He's coming to get me. I had to wash my hair first—" She spoke in a dry, rapid voice, hardly raising it for him to hear.

"No, your daddy is not coming and yes, you had to wash your hair and you washed it for me. It's nice and shining and all for me, I thank you, sweetheart," he said, with a mock bow, but again he almost lost his balance. He had to bend and adjust his boots. Evidently his feet did not go all the way down; the boots must have been stuffed with something so that he would seem taller. Connie stared out at him and behind him Ellie in the car, who seemed to be looking off toward Connie's right, into nothing. This Ellie said, pulling the words out of the air one after another as if he were just discovering them, "You want me to pull out the phone?"

"Shut your mouth and keep it shut," Arnold   125
Friend said, his face red from bending over or maybe from embarrassment because Connie had seen his boots. "This ain't none of your business."

"What—what are you doing? What do you want?" Connie said. "If I call the police they'll get you, they'll arrest you—"

"Promise was not to come in unless you touch that phone, and I'll keep that promise," he said. He resumed his erect position and tried to force his shoulders back. He sounded like a hero in a movie, declaring something important. He spoke too loudly and it was as if he were speaking to someone behind Connie. "I ain't made plans for coming in that house where I don't belong but just for you to come out to me, the way you should. Don't you know who I am?"

She thought, I'm not going to see my mother again.

"You're crazy," she whispered. She backed away from the door but did not want to go into another part of the house, as if this would give him permission to come through the door. "What do you . . . You're crazy, you . . ."

"Huh? What're you saying, honey?"

Her eyes darted everywhere in the kitchen. She could not remember what it was, this room.

"This is how it is, honey: you come out and we'll drive away, have a nice ride. But if you don't come out we're gonna wait till your people come home and then they're all going to get it."

"You want that telephone pulled out?" Ellie said. He held the radio away from his ear and grimaced, as if without the radio the air was too much for him.

"I toldja shut up, Ellie," Arnold Friend said, "you're deaf, get a hearing aid, right? Fix yourself up. This little girl's no trouble and's gonna be nice to me, so Ellie keep to yourself, this ain't your date—right? Don't hem in on me. Don't hog. Don't crush. Don't bird dog. Don't trail me," he said in a rapid meaningless voice, as if he were running through all the expressions he'd learned but was no longer sure which one of them was in style, then rushing on to new ones, making them up with his eyes closed, "Don't crawl under my fence, don't squeeze in my chipmunk hole, don't sniff my glue, suck my popsicle, keep your own greasy fingers on yourself!" He shaded his eyes and peered in at Connie, who was backed against the kitchen table. "Don't mind him honey he's just a creep. He's a dope. Right? I'm the boy for you and like I said you come out here nice like a lady and give me your hand, and nobody else gets hurt, I mean, your nice old bald-headed daddy and your mummy and your sister in her high heels. Because listen: why bring them in this?"

"Leave me alone," Connie whispered.

"Hey, you know that old woman down the road, the one with the chickens and stuff—you know her?"

"She's dead!"

"Dead? What? You know her?" Arnold Friend said.

"She's dead—"

"Don't you like her?"

"She's dead—she's—she isn't here any more—"

"But don't you like her, I mean, you got something against her? Some grudge or something?" Then his voice dipped as if he were conscious of a rudeness. He touched the sunglasses perched on top of his head as if to make sure they were still there. "Now you be a good girl."

"What are you going to do?"

"Just two things, or maybe three," Arnold Friend said. "But I promise it won't last long and you'll like me that way you get to like people you're close to. You will. It's all over for you here, so come on out. You don't want your people in any trouble, do you?"

She turned and bumped against a chair or something, hurting her leg, but she ran into the back room and picked up the telephone. Something roared in her ear, a tiny roaring, and she was so sick with fear that she could do nothing but listen to it—the telephone was clammy and very heavy and her fingers groped down to the dial but were too weak to touch it. She began to scream into the phone, into the roaring. She cried out, she cried for her mother, she felt her breath start jerking back and forth in her lungs as if it were something Arnold Friend were stabbing her with again and again with no tenderness. A noisy sorrowful wailing rose all about her and she was locked inside it the way she was locked inside the house.

After a while she could hear again. She was sitting on the floor with her wet back against the wall.

Arnold Friend was saying from the door, "That's a good girl. Put the phone back." She kicked the phone away from her.

"No, honey. Pick it up. Put it back right."

She picked it up and put it back. The dial tone stopped.

"That's a good girl. Now come outside."

She was hollow with what had been fear, but what was now just an emptiness. All that screaming had blasted it out of her. She sat, one leg cramped under her, and deep inside her brain was something like a pinpoint of light that kept going and would not let her relax. She thought, I'm not going to see my mother again. She thought, I'm not going to sleep in my bed again. Her bright green blouse was all wet.

Arnold Friend said, in a gentle-loud voice that was like a stage voice, "The place where you came from ain't there any more, and where you had in mind to go is cancelled out. This place you are now—inside your daddy's house—is nothing but a cardboard box I can knock down any time. You know that and always did know it. You hear me?"

She thought, I have got to think. I have to know what to do.

"We'll go out to a nice field, out in the country here where it smells so nice and it's sunny," Arnold Friend said. "I'll have my arms around you so you won't need to try to get away and I'll show you what love is like, what it does. The hell with this house! It looks solid all right," he said. He ran a fingernail down the screen and the noise did not make Connie shiver, as it would have the day before. "Now put your hand on your heart, honey. Feel that? That feels solid too but we know better, be nice to me, be sweet like you can because what else is there for a girl like you but to be sweet and pretty and give in?—and get away before her people come back?"

She felt her pounding heart. Her hand seemed to enclose it. She thought for the first time in her life that it was nothing that was hers, that belonged to her, but just a pounding, living thing inside this body that wasn't really hers either.

155 "You don't want them to get hurt," Arnold Friend went on. "Now get up, honey. Get up all by yourself."

She stood up.

"Now turn this way. That's right. Come over here to me—Ellie, put that away, didn't I tell you? You dope. You miserable creepy dope," Arnold Friend said. His words were not angry but only part of an incantation. The incantation was kindly. "Now come out through the kitchen to me honey and let's see a smile, try it, you're a brave sweet little girl and now they're eating corn and hotdogs cooked to bursting over an outdoor fire, and they don't know one thing about you and never did and honey you're better than them because not a one of them would have done this for you."

Connie felt the linoleum under her feet; it was cool. She brushed her hair back out of her eyes. Arnold Friend let go of the post tentatively and opened his arms for her, his elbows pointing in toward each other and his wrists limp, to show that this was an embarrassed embrace and a little mocking, he didn't want to make her self-conscious.

She put out her hand against the screen. She watched herself push the door slowly open as if she were safe back somewhere in the other doorway, watching this body and this head of long hair moving out into the sunlight where Arnold Friend waited.

"My sweet little blue-eyed girl," he said, in a half-sung 160 sigh that had nothing to do with her brown eyes but was taken up just the same by the vast sunlit reaches of the land behind him and on all sides of him, so much land that Connie had never seen before and did not recognize except to know that she was going to it.

IF YOU LIKED "WHERE ARE YOU GOING . . .," YOU MIGHT ALSO LIKE . . .

. . . other haunting suspense stories such as Edgar Allan Poe's "The Cask of Amontillado" (Chapter 10), or other stories that reflect on society, such as James Baldwin's story, "Sonny's Blues" (Chapter 9).

GOING FURTHER   As a testament to the quality of Oates's prose, twenty-eight of her stories have won O. Henry Prizes for Short Fiction and eleven Pushcart Prizes, and for her work in the form she was awarded the PEN/Malamud Award for Excellence in Short Fiction. Thirty-nine of her books have been *New York Times* Notable Books of the Year. Among her better-known novels are *them* (1969), winner of the National Book Award, *Black Water* (1992), a finalist for the Pulitzer Prize, and *We Were the Mulvaneys* (2001), selected for Oprah's Book Club.

"**What was so interesting about the original event was not so much that a serial killer had been preying on young people, which is unfortunately all too common, but that the young people had known about it. They had known that some girls had been killed and buried in the desert, but they kept the secret, because their allegiance was to this man. And I wanted to write a story about that phenomenon.**" Conversation with Joyce Carol Oates

Writing from Reading

Summary

1 List the characters besides Connie and Arnold. How are they important to our understanding of Connie?

Analyze Craft

2 Describe what we know of Arnold Friend when he first appears at Connie's house. Then describe what we know of him by the end of the story. What effect does this change have on us as readers? In other words, how does Oates's pacing build suspense?

3 Describe the setting—both time and place—of the story. Is it a place where we might expect to find someone like Arnold Friend? Why or why not?

4 Oates builds Connie's character by means of a series of details about her age, her appearance, her habits, her clothes. Which details make Connie believable or familiar to you? Which details represent larger personality traits in Connie?

Analyze Voice

5 The story opens with a bit of background exposition by the narrator. Discuss how this exposition is distinguished from the description of the story's main events. What relationship, if any, does the narrator seem to have or have had with Connie? Cite evidence from the text.

6 Consider Oates's use of dialogue, particularly the exchange between Arnold and Connie when he comes to her house. What in Arnold's speech suggests who he is and what he is doing? What in Connie's speech contributes to our understanding of her as a teenage girl?

Synthesize Summary and Analysis

7 In her interview, Oates suggests Connie's act may be considered heroic in that she sacrifices herself to save her family. What details about Connie suggest her motivation for complying with Arnold Friend? In light of these details, make a case for whether Connie's act is or is not heroic.

Interpret the Story

8 Much of Oates's fiction deals with violence and the aftermath of such violence. Develop an argument about whether this is a violent story; consider the difference between including actual violence and simply suggesting it.

Richard Wright (1908–1960)

One of twentieth-century America's most powerful novelists and short story writers, Richard Wright was born on a plantation in Mississippi into a religious, but mostly uneducated, African-American family. He spent his childhood and adolescence in Tennessee and Mississippi, having to drop out of school in order to earn money; his was a constant struggle against the strict rules imposed by family members as to formal religion and social behavior. At the age of nineteen Wright moved to Chicago, worked at various jobs, studied on his own, completed a draft of his first novel, and for several years became a force in the Midwest American Communist Party. He moved to New York City in 1935, where he focused mainly on his apprenticeship as a fiction writer.

His collection of stories, *Uncle Tom's Children,* came out in 1938. These portraits of Southern black people struggling to find individual freedom in a world of racial bias and segregation marked him as the first major African-American fiction writer in U.S. literary history. In 1940, Wright followed with his first published novel, *Native Son.* The book received great praise but also some negative reaction to the frankness with which he portrayed the life of the main character, Bigger Thomas, a young Chicago black man who becomes a murderer twice-over.

Wright's fame increased when the Book of the Month Club, at that time a commercial mainstay for serious American readers, made his novel a main selection. Soon after the publication of *Black Boy* (1945), his best-selling autobiography, Wright moved with his family to Paris, where he became friends with various writers and intellectuals—including James Baldwin—and spent more than a decade involved in various political causes. His rejection of communism became the subject of his essay in an epoch-making collection by various hands called *The God That Failed* (1949). While traveling in Africa in the late 1950s, he contracted a case of amoebic dysentery, which apparently weakened his heart. Wright died of a heart attack in Paris in 1960. Though his subject matter remained constant, the influence of Existential philosophy became noticeable in his posthumously published collection of stories, *Eight Men* (1961).

AS YOU READ Consider whether it is important that people of both races are present. What does Dave's thought that a gun could "Kill anybody, black or white" mean? What role does the gun play in building the narrative of this story?

The Man Who Was Almost a Man (1940)

DAVE struck out across the fields, looking homeward through paling light. Whut's the use of talkin wid em niggers in the field? Anyhow, his mother was putting supper on the table. Them niggers can't understan nothing. One of these days he was going to get a gun and practice shooting, then they couldn't talk to him as though he were a little boy. He slowed, looking at the ground. Shucks, Ah ain scareda them even ef they are biggern me! Aw, Ah know whut Ahma do. Ahm going by ol Joe's sto n git that Sears Roebuck catlog n look at them guns. Mebbe Ma will lemme buy one when she gits mah pay from ol man Hawkins. Ahma beg her t gimme some money. Ahm ol ernough to hava gun. Ahm seventeen.

Almost a man. He strode, feeling his long loose-jointed limbs. Shucks, a man oughta hava little gun aftah he done worked hard all day.

He came in sight of Joe's store. A yellow lantern glowed on the front porch. He mounted the steps and went through the screen door, hearing it bang behind him. There was a strong smell of coal oil and mackerel fish. He felt very confident until he saw fat Joe walk in through the rear door, then his courage began to ooze.

"Howdy, Dave! Whutcha want?"

"How yuh, Mistah Joe? Aw, Ah don wanna buy nothing. Ah jus wanted t see ef yuhd lemme look at tha catlog erwhile."

5 "Sure! You wanna see it here?"

"Nawsuh. Ah wans t take it home wid me. Ah'll bring it back termorrow when Ah come in from the fiels."

"You plannin on buying something?"

"Yessuh."

10 "Your ma lettin you have your own money now?"

"Shucks. Mistah Joe, Ahm gittin t be a man like anybody else!"

Joe laughed and wiped his greasy white face with a red bandanna.

"Whut you plannin on buyin?"

Dave looked at the floor, scratched his head, scratched his thigh, and smiled. Then he looked up shyly.

"Ah'll tell yuh, Mistah Joe, ef yuh promise yuh won't tell."

15 "I promise."

"Waal, Ahma buy a gun."

"A gun? Whut you want with a gun?"

"Ah wanna keep it."

"You ain't nothing but a boy. You don't need a gun."

20 "Aw, lemme have the catlog, Mistah Joe. Ah'll bring it back."

Joe walked through the rear door. Dave was elated. He looked around at barrels of sugar and flour. He heard Joe coming back. He craned his neck to see if he were bringing the book. Yeah, he's got it. Gawddog, he's got it!

"Here, but be sure you bring it back. It's the only one I got."

"Sho, Mistah Joe."

"Say, if you wanna buy a gun, why don't you buy one from me? I gotta gun to sell."

"Will it shoot?" 25

"Sure it'll shoot."

"Whut kind is it?"

"Oh, it's kinda old . . . a left-hand Wheeler. A pistol. A big one."

"Is it got bullets in it?"

"It's loaded." 30

"Kin Ah see it?"

"Where's your money?"

"Whut yuh wan fer it?"

"I'll let you have it for two dollars."

"Just two dollahs? Shucks, Ah 35 could buy tha when Ah git mah pay."

"I'll have it here when you want it."

"Awright, suh. Ah be in fer it."

He went through the door, hearing it slam again behind him. Ahma git some money from Ma n buy me a gun! Only two dollahs! He tucked the thick catalogue under his arm and hurried.

"Where yuh been, boy?" His mother held a steaming dish of black-eyed peas.

"Aw, Ma, Ah jus stopped down the road t talk wid the 40 boys."

"Yuh know bettah t keep suppah waitin."

He sat down, resting the catalogue on the edge of the table.

"Yuh git up from there and git to the well n wash yoself! Ah ain feedin no hogs in mah house!"

She grabbed his shoulder and pushed him. He stumbled out of the room, then came back to get the catalogue.

"Whut this?" 45

"Aw, Ma, it's jusa catlog."

"Who yuh git it from?"

"From Joe, down at the sto."

"Waal, thas good. We kin use it in the outhouse."

"Naw, Ma." He grabbed for it. "Gimme ma catlog, Ma." 50 She held onto it and glared at him.

"Quit hollerin at me! Whut's wrong wid yuh? Yuh crazy?"

"But Ma, please. It ain mine! It's Joe's! He tol me t bring it back t im termorrow."

She gave up the book. He stumbled down the back steps, hugging the thick book under his arm. When he had splashed water on his face and hands, he groped back to the kitchen and fumbled in a corner for the towel. He bumped into a chair; it clattered to the floor. The catalogue sprawled at his feet. When he had dried his eyes he snatched up the

> ## One of these days
> he was going to get a gun, . . .
> then they couldn't talk to him as
> though he were a little boy.

book and held it again under his arm. His mother stood watching him.

55 "Now, ef yuh gonna act a fool over that ol book, Ah'll take it n burn it up."

"Naw, Ma, please."

"Waal, set down n be still!"

He sat down and drew the oil lamp close. He thumbed page after page, unaware of the food his mother set on the table. His father came in. Then his small brother.

"Whutcha got there, Dave?" his father asked.

60 "Jusa catlog," he answered, not looking up.

"Yeah, here they is!" His eyes glowed at blue-and-black revolvers. He glanced up, feeling sudden guilt. His father was watching him. He eased the book under the table and rested it on his knees. After the blessing was asked, he ate. He scooped up peas and swallowed fat meat without chewing. Buttermilk helped to wash it down. He did not want to mention money before his father. He would do much better by cornering his mother when she was alone. He looked at his father uneasily out of the edge of his eye.

"Boy, how come yuh don quit foolin wid tha book n eat yo suppah?"

"Yessuh."

"How you n ol man Hawkins gitten erlong?"

65 "Suh?"

"Can't yuh hear? Why don yuh lissen? Ah ast yu how wuz yuh n ol man Hawkins gittin erlong?"

"Oh, swell, Pa. Ah plows mo lan than anybody over there."

"Waal, yuh oughta keep yo mind on whut yuh doin."

"Yessuh."

70 He poured his plate full of molasses and sopped it up slowly with a chunk of cornbread. When his father and brother had left the kitchen, he still sat and looked again at the guns in the catalogue, longing to muster courage enough to present his case to his mother. Lawd, ef Ah only had tha pretty one! He could almost feel the slickness of the weapon with his fingers. If he had a gun like that he would polish it and keep it shining so it would never rust. N Ah'd keep it loaded, by Gawd!

"Ma?" His voice was hesitant.

"Hunh?"

"Ol man Hawkins give yuh mah money yit?"

> He could almost feel
> the slickness of the weapon
> with his fingers.

"Yeah, but ain no usa yuh thinking bout throwin nona it erway. Ahm keepin tha money sos yuh kin have cloes t go to school this winter."

75 He rose and went to her side with the open catalogue in his palms. She was washing dishes, her head bent low over a pan. Shyly he raised the book. When he spoke, his voice was husky, faint.

"Ma, Gawd knows Ah wans one of these."

"One of whut?" she asked, not raising her eyes.

"One of these," he said again, not daring even to point. She glanced up at the page, then at him with wide eyes.

"Nigger, is yuh gone plumb crazy?"

80 "Aw, Ma—"

"Git outta here! Don yuh talk t me bout no gun! Yuh a fool!"

"Ma, Ah kin buy one fer two dollahs."

"Not ef Ah knows it, yuh ain!"

"But yuh promised me one—"

85 "Ah don care whut Ah promised! Yuh ain nothing but a boy yit!"

"Ma, ef yuh lemme buy one Ah'll *never* ast yuh fer nothing no mo."

"Ah tol yuh t git outta here! Yuh ain gonna toucha penny of tha money fer no gun! Thas how come Ah has Mistah Hawkins t pay yo wages t me, cause Ah knows yuh ain got no sense."

"But, Ma, we needa gun. Pa ain got no gun. We needa gun in the house. Yuh kin never tell whut might happen."

"Now don yuh try to maka fool outta me, boy! Ef we did hava gun, yuh wouldn't have it!"

90 He laid the catalogue down and slipped his arm around her waist.

"Aw, Ma, Ah done worked hard alla summer n ain ast yuh fer nothin, is Ah, now?"

"Thas whut yuh spose t do!"

"But Ma, Ah wans a gun. Yuh kin lemme have two dollahs outta mah money. Please, Ma. I kin give it to Pa. . . . Please, Ma! Ah loves yuh, Ma."

When she spoke her voice came soft and low.

95 "What yu wan wida gun, Dave? Yuh don need no gun. Yuh'll git in trouble. N ef yo pa jus thought Ah let yuh have money t buy a gun he'd hava fit."

"Ah'll hide it, Ma. It ain but two dollahs."

"Lawd, chil, whut's wrong wid yuh?"

"Ain nothin wrong, Ma. Ahm almos a man now. Ah wans a gun."

"Who gonna sell yuh a gun?"

100 "Ol Joe at the sto."

"N it don cos but two dollahs?"

"Thas all, Ma. Jus two dollahs. Please, Ma."

She was stacking the plates away; her hands moved slowly, reflectively. Dave kept an anxious silence. Finally, she turned to him.

"Ah'll let yuh git tha gun ef yuh promise me one thing."

105 "What's tha, Ma?"

"Yuh bring it straight back t me, yuh hear? It be fer Pa."

"Yessum! Lemme go now, Ma."

She stopped, turned slightly to one side, raised the hem of her dress, rolled down the top of her stocking, and came up with a slender wad of bills.

"Here," she said. "Lawd knows yuh don need no gun. But yer pa does. Yuh bring it right back t me, yuh hear? Ahma put it up. Now ef yuh don, Ahma have yuh pa lick yuh so hard yuh won fergit it."

110 "Yessum."

He took the money, ran down the steps, and across the yard.

"Dave! Yuuuuuh Daaaaave!"

He heard, but he was not going to stop now. "Naw, Lawd!"

THE first movement he made the following morning was to reach under his pillow for the gun. In the gray light of dawn he held it loosely, feeling a sense of power. Could kill a man with a gun like this. Kill anybody, black or white. And if he were holding his gun in his hand, nobody could run over him; they would have to respect him. It was a big gun, with a long barrel and a heavy handle. He raised and lowered it in his hand, marveling at its weight.

115 He had not come straight home with it as his mother had asked; instead he had stayed out in the fields, holding the weapon in his hand, aiming it now and then at some imaginary foe. But he had not fired it; he had been afraid that his father might hear. Also he was not sure he knew how to fire it.

To avoid surrendering the pistol he had not come into the house until he knew that they were all asleep. When his mother had tiptoed to his bedside late that night and de-

manded the gun, he had first played possum; then he had told her that the gun was hidden outdoors, that he would bring it to her in the morning. Now he lay turning it slowly in his hands. He broke it, took out the cartridges, felt them, and then put them back.

He slid out of bed, got a long strip of old flannel from a trunk, wrapped the gun in it, and tied it to his naked thigh while it was still loaded. He did not go in to breakfast. Even though it was not yet daylight, he started for Jim Hawkins' plantation. Just as the sun was rising he reached the barns where the mules and plows were kept.

"Hey! That you, Dave?"

He turned. Jim Hawkins stood eying him suspiciously.

"What're yuh doing here so early?"

120 "Ah didn't know Ah wuz gittin up so early, Mistah Hawkins. Ah was fixin t hitch up ol Jenny n take her t the fiels."

"Good. Since you're so early, how about plowing that stretch down by the woods?"

"Suits me, Mistah Hawkins."

"O.K. Go to it!"

He hitched Jenny to a plow and started across the 125 fields. Hot dog! This was just what he wanted. If he could get down by the woods, he could shoot his gun and nobody would hear. He walked behind the plow, hearing the traces creaking, feeling the gun tied tight to his thigh.

When he reached the woods, he plowed two whole rows before he decided to take out the gun. Finally, he stopped, looked in all directions, then untied the gun and held it in his hand. He turned to the mule and smiled.

"Know whut this is, Jenny? Naw, yuh wouldn know! Yuhs jusa ol mule! Anyhow, this is a gun, n it kin shoot, by Gawd!"

He held the gun at arm's length. Whut t hell, Ahma shoot this thing! He looked at Jenny again.

"Lissen here, Jenny! When Ah pull this ol trigger, Ah don wan yuh t run n acka fool now!"

Jenny stood with head down, her short ears pricked 130 straight. Dave walked off about twenty feet, held the gun far out from him at arm's length, and turned his head. Hell, he told himself, Ah am afraid. The gun felt loose in his fingers; he waved it wildly for a moment. Then he shut his eyes and tightened his forefinger. Bloom! A report half deafened him and he thought his right hand was torn from his arm.

> "Ah'll let yuh git tha gun ef yuh promise me one thing."

He heard Jenny whinnying and galloping over the field, and he found himself on his knees, squeezing his fingers hard between his legs. His hand was numb; he jammed it into his mouth, trying to warm it, trying to stop the pain. The gun lay at his feet. He did not quite know what had happened. He stood up and stared at the gun as though it were a living thing. He gritted his teeth and kicked the gun. Yuh almos broke mah arm! He turned to look for Jenny; she was far over the fields, tossing her head and kicking wildly.

"Hol on there, ol mule!"

When he caught up with her she stood trembling, walling her big white eyes at him. The plow was far away; the traces had broken. Then Dave stopped short, looking, not believing. Jenny was bleeding. Her left side was red and wet with blood. He went closer. Lawd, have mercy! Wondah did Ah shoot this mule? He grabbed for Jenny's mane. She flinched, snorted, whirled, tossing her head.

"Hol on now! Hol on."

Then he saw the hole in Jenny's side, right between the ribs. It was round, wet, red. A crimson stream streaked down the front leg, flowing fast. Good Gawd! Ah wuzn't shootin at tha mule. He felt panic. He knew he had to stop that blood, or Jenny would bleed to death. He had never seen so much blood in all his life. He chased the mule for half a mile, trying to catch her. Finally she stopped, breathing hard, stumpy tail half arched. He caught her mane and led her back to where the plow and gun lay. Then he stopped and grabbed handfuls of damp black earth and tried to plug the bullet hole. Jenny shuddered, whinnied, and broke from him.

135　　"Hol on! Hol on now!"

He tried to plug it again, but blood came anyhow. His fingers were hot and sticky. He rubbed dirt into his palms, trying to dry them. Then again he attempted to plug the bullet hole, but Jenny shied away, kicking her heels high. He stood helpless. He had to do something. He ran at Jenny;

Dave walked off about twenty feet, held the gun far out from him at arm's length, and turned his head.

she dodged him. He watched a red stream of blood flow down Jenny's leg and form a bright pool at her feet.

"Jenny . . . Jenny," he called weakly.

His lips trembled. She's bleeding t death! He looked in the direction of home, wanting to go back, wanting to get help. But he saw the pistol lying in the damp black clay. He had a queer feeling that if he only did something, this would not be; Jenny would not be there bleeding to death.

When he went to her this time, she did not move. She stood with sleepy, dreamy eyes; and when he touched her she gave a low-pitched whinny and knelt to the ground, her front knees slopping in blood.

"Jenny . . . Jenny . . ." he whispered.　　140

For a long time she held her neck erect; then her head sank, slowly. Her ribs swelled with a mighty heave and she went over.

Dave's stomach felt empty, very empty. He picked up the gun and held it gingerly between his thumb and forefinger. He buried it at the foot of a tree. He took a stick to cover the pool of blood with dirt—but what was the use? There was Jenny lying with her mouth open and her eyes walled and glassy. He could not tell Jim Hawkins he had shot his mule. But he had to tell something. Yeah, Ah'll tell em Jenny started gittin wil n fell on the joint of the plow. . . . But that would hardly happen to a mule. He walked across the field slowly, head down.

IT was sunset. Two of Jim Hawkins' men were over near the edge of the woods digging a hole in which to bury Jenny. Dave was surrounded by a knot of people, all of whom were looking down at the dead mule.

"I don't see how in the world it happened," said Jim Hawkins for the tenth time.

The crowd parted and Dave's mother, father, and small　145 brother pushed into the center.

"Where Dave?" his mother called.

"There he is," said Jim Hawkins.

His mother grabbed him.

"Whut happened, Dave? Whut yuh done?"

"Nothin."　　150

"C mon, boy, talk," his father said.

Dave took a deep breath and told the story he knew nobody believed.

"Waal," he drawled. "Ah brung ol Jenny down here sos Ah could do mah plowin. Ah plowed bout two rows, just like yuh see." He stopped and pointed at the long rows of upturned earth. 'Then somethin musta been wrong wid ol Jenny. She wouldn ack right a-tall. She started snortin n kickin her heels. Ah tried t hol her, but she pulled erway, rearin n goin in. Then when the point of the plow was stickin up in the air, she swung erroun n twisted herself back on it. . . . She stuck herself n started t bleed. N fo Ah could do anything, she wuz dead."

"Did you ever hear of anything like that in all your life?" asked Jim Hawkins.

155 There were white and black standing in the crowd. They murmured. Dave's mother came close to him and looked hard into his face. "Tell the truth, Dave," she said.

"Looks like a bullet hole to me," said one man.

"Dave, whut yuh do wid tha gun?" his mother asked.

The crowd surged in, looking at him. He jammed his hands into his pockets, shook his head slowly from left to right, and backed away. His eyes were wide and painful.

160 "Did he hava gun?" asked Jim Hawkins.

"By Gawd, Ah tol yuh tha wuz a gun wound," said a man, slapping his thigh. His father caught his shoulders and shook him till his teeth rattled.

"Tell whut happened, yuh rascal! Tell whut . . ."

Dave looked at Jenny's stiff legs and began to cry.

"Whut yuh do wid tha gun?" his mother asked.

"What wuz he doin wida gun?" his father asked.

165 "Come on and tell the truth," said Hawkins. "Ain't nobody going to hurt you. . . ."

His mother crowded close to him.

"Did yuh shoot tha mule, Dave?"

Dave cried, seeing blurred white and black faces.

"Ahh ddinn gggo tt sshooot hher. . . . Ah ssswear ffo Gawd Ahh ddin. . . . Ah wuz a-tryin t sssee ef the old gggun would sshoot—"

170 "Where yuh git the gun from?" his father asked.

"Ah got it from Joe, at the sto."

"Where yuh git the money?"

"Ma give it t me."

"He kept worryin me, Bob. Ah had t. Ah tol im t bring the gun right back t me. . . . It was fer yuh, the gun."

175 "But how yuh happen to shoot that mule?" asked Jim Hawkins.

"Ah wuzn shootin at the mule, Mistah Hawkins. The gun jumped when Ah pulled the trigger. . . . N fo Ah knowed anythin Jenny was there a-bleedin."

Somebody in the crowd laughed. Jim Hawkins walked close to Dave and looked into his face.

"Well, looks like you have bought you a mule, Dave."

"Ah swear fo Gawd, Ah didn go t kill the mule, Mistah Hawkins!"

"But you killed her!" 180

All the crowd was laughing now. They stood on tiptoe and poked heads over one another's shoulders.

"Well, boy, looks like yuh done bought a dead mule! Hahaha!"

"Ain tha ershame."

"Hohohohoho."

Dave stood, head down, twisting his feet in the dirt. 185

"Well, you needn't worry about it, Bob," said Jim Hawkins to Dave's father. "Just let the boy keep on working and pay me two dollars a month."

"Whut yuh wan fer yo mule, Mistah Hawkins?"

Jim Hawkins screwed up his eyes.

"Fifty dollars."

"Whut yuh do wid tha gun?" Dave's father demanded. 190

Dave said nothing.

"Yuh wan me t take a tree n beat yuh till yuh talk!"

"Nawsuh!"

"Whut yuh do wid it?"

"Ah throwed it erway."

"Where?" 195

"Ah. . . Ah throwed it in the creek."

"Waal, c'mon home. N firs thing in the mawnin git to tha creek n fin tha gun."

"Yessuh."

"Whut yuh pay fer it?" 200

"Two dollahs."

'Take tha gun n git yo money back n carry it to Mistah Hawkins, yuh hear? N don fergit Ahma lam you black bottom good fer this! Now march yosef on home, suh!"

Dave turned and walked slowly. He heard people laughing. Dave glared, his eyes welling with tears. Hot anger bubbled in him. Then he swallowed and stumbled on.

That night Dave did not sleep. He was glad that he had gotten out of killing the mule so easily, but he was hurt. Something hot seemed to turn over inside him each time he remembered how they had laughed. He tossed on his

> Dave took a deep breath and told the story he knew nobody believed.

bed, feeling his hard pillow. N Pa says he's gonna beat me. . . . He remembered other beatings, and his back quivered. Naw, naw, Ah sho don wan im t beat me tha way no mo. Dam em all! Nobody ever gave him anything. All he did was work. They treat me like a mule, n then they beat me. He gritted his teeth. N Ma had t tell on me.

205 Well, if he had to, he would take old man Hawkins that two dollars. But that meant selling the gun. And he wanted to keep that gun. Fifty dollars for a dead mule.

He turned over, thinking how he had fired the gun. He had an itch to fire it again. Ef other men kin shoota gun, by Gawd, Ah kin! He was still, listening. Mebbe they all sleepin now. The house was still. He heard the soft breathing of his brother. Yes, now! He would go down and get that gun and see if he could fire it! He eased out of bed and slipped into overalls.

The moon was bright. He ran almost all the way to the edge of the woods. He stumbled over the ground, looking for the spot where he had buried the gun. Yeah, here it is. Like a hungry dog scratching for a bone, he pawed it up. He puffed his black cheeks and blew dirt from the trigger and barrel. He broke it and found four cartridges unshot. He looked around; the fields were filled with silence and moonlight. He clutched the gun stiff and hard in his fingers. But, as soon as he wanted to pull the trigger, he shut his eyes and turned his head. Naw, Ah can't shoot wid mah eyes closed n mah head turned. With effort he held his eyes open; then he squeezed. *Bloooom!* He was stiff, not breathing. The gun was still in his hands. Dammit, he'd done it! He fired again.

Blooooom! He smiled. *Bloooom! Blooooom! Click, click.* There! It was empty. If anybody could shoot a gun, he could. He put the gun into his hip pocket and started across the fields.

When he reached the top of a ridge he stood straight and proud in the moonlight, looking at Jim Hawkins' big white house, feeling the gun sagging in his pocket. Lawd, ef Ah had just one mo bullet Ah'd taka shot at tha house. Ah'd like t scare ol man Hawkins jusa little. . . . Jusa enough t let im know Dave Saunders is a man.

To his left the road curved, running to the tracks of the Illinois Central. He jerked his head, listening. From far off came a faint *hoooof-hoooof; hoooof-hoooof; hoooof-hoooof.* . . . He stood rigid. Two dollahs a mont. Les see now. . . . Tha means it'll take bout two years. Shucks! Ah'll be dam!

He started down the road, toward the tracks. Yeah, 210 here she comes! He stood beside the track and held himself stiffly. Here she comes, erroun the ben. . . . C mon, yuh slow poke! C mon! He had his hand on his gun; something quivered in his stomach. Then the train thundered past, the gray and brown box cars rumbling and clinking. He gripped the gun tightly; then he jerked his hand out of his pocket. Ah betcha Bill wouldn't do it! Ah betcha. . . . The cars slid past, steel grinding upon steel. Ahm ridin yuh ternight, so hep me Gawd! He was hot all over. He hesitated just a moment; then he grabbed, pulled atop of a car, and lay flat. He felt his pocket; the gun was still there. Ahead the long rails were glinting in the moonlight, stretching away, away to somewhere, somewhere where he could be a man. . . .

IF YOU LIKED "THE MAN WHO WAS ALMOST A MAN," YOU MIGHT ALSO LIKE . . .

. . . another psychological portrait of family, anger, and place in John Steinbeck's "The Chrysanthemums" (Chapter 15).

GOING FURTHER   Richard Wright's novel *Native Son* exploded with great force on the American literary scene in the early 1940s. It remains to this day one of our country's most powerful "protest" novels, as James Baldwin described Wright's work.

Writing from Reading

Summarize

1 Identify the key events of this story and arrange them into rising action, climax, falling action (dénouement), and resolution. How does the story conform to (or not conform to) the standard plot arc described earlier in this chapter?

Analyze Craft

2 List any specific details you know about the setting, citing references from the story. What is the significance of the details Wright chose to include? Why do you think he chose to omit certain specific details such as the year the story takes place?

Analyze Voice

3 Dave's interior monologue, written in Dave's spoken dialect, is interspersed throughout the narrative. How would your understanding of Joe change if his thoughts were instead related through the narrator's exposition? How would the story change if it were told entirely from Dave's first-person point of view?

Synthesize Summary and Analysis

4 During the sleepless night after shooting Jenny, Dave compares himself to the mule. What does he feel he has in common with Jenny? Is he correct?

Interpret the Story

5 Compare Dave's thoughts walking home at the beginning of the story to his state of mind when he jumps the train at the story's conclusion. Have Dave's experiences with the gun, as he expected, made him a "man," or does he remain just a child? Why do you think so?

Reading for Plot

When reading for plot, ask yourself how the author has arranged the incidents in the story for cause and effect leading to the climax and the resolution of the story. We'll use a familiar fairy-tale as an example.

| **How does the story begin?** | • Is exposition included in the story? | EXAMPLE   In those days, it wasn't so unusual for a little girl to walk in the forest by herself—especially since her grandmother's house was close by. |
| | • Does it begin *in medias res*? | EXAMPLE   The forest felt especially dark and creepy, she thought, as she set off in her red cloak with a basket of goodies for her grandmother. |

How does the plot unfold?	• Does it include flashbacks?	EXAMPLE There had been another time—last spring, when the animals were hungrier than usual, after the long deprivation of winter—that she had felt afraid. She'd seen a wolf, at the bend of the path, and then again, by the pond, drinking. Both times, she passed quickly, not making eye contact, telling herself that so close to grandmother's, nothing could harm her.
	• Does the story include foreshadowing?	EXAMPLE Little Red Riding Hood shivered as she walked, drawing her cloak around her, listening for cries of wild animals, wondering whether she really should have come alone, whether that quick movement was the wind . . . or something else.
Which elements of plot can you identify?	• Who is the protagonist?	EXAMPLE Little Red Riding Hood
	• Who/What is the antagonist?	EXAMPLE the wolf
	• What is the conflict?	EXAMPLE The big bad wolf is leading the poor, defenseless Little Red Riding Hood into a trap.
	• What is the climax?	EXAMPLE The wolf tore off its cap and leapt from the bed, teeth and claws bared.
	• What is the dénouement, resolution, or conclusion?	EXAMPLE The woodcutter dusted off the little girl, found the grandmother, and they all had a lovely little snack together.

Writing about Plot

1. Compare the settings of "Araby," "Greasy Lake," and "Where Are You Going, Where Have You Been?" How do the grim settings of these stories propel the plot?

2. Compare the way each story in this chapter employs plot to achieve its dramatic purpose. What similarities do you see in the writers' techniques? Choose two stories and discuss the elements of plot that are common to both.

3. Make a case for how the young narrators of the stories in this chapter respond to new situations or opportunities. Who takes action and who does not? Which characters reach new levels of perception? Does anyone fulfill his or her desire?

9

IN China, daughter take care of mother. Here it is the other way around. Mother help daughter, mother ask, Anything else I can do? Otherwise daughter complain mother is not supportive. I tell daughter, We do not have this word in Chinese, *supportive*. But my daughter too busy to listen, she has to go to meeting, she has to write memo while her husband go to the gym to be a man. My daughter say otherwise he will be depressed. Seems like all his life he has this trouble, depression.

—from "Who's Irish?" by Gish Jen

Chara

"All characters are individual, first and foremost. I don't think that any successful piece of fiction can start from any premise, such as 'I am trying to represent an American, an Asian-American, or an Irish-American,' or any kind of anything. I think that I have certain preoccupations and those things arise naturally; but, first and foremost, I am concerned with character, individuals as individuals, but also in their place in the world."

Conversation with Gish Jen, available on video at connect.mcgraw-hill.com

WHOSE voice is this, and what can you tell about her from this short excerpt? You can tell quite a bit, actually. It's likely that the first thing you notice is the way the person speaks—with the inaccurate spelling and grammar of a person not native to English. It's also clear from the context that the speaker is female, the mother of a married daughter whose husband is depressed. "Here"—the first word of the second sentence—suggests that the speaker's no longer at home but is instead an immigrant, a stranger in what seems to her a strange land. The character/narrator doesn't use articles or pronouns, and she fails to use appropriate verb forms; her nouns and verbs disagree. The grammatically correct first sentence would have been "In China, *a* daughter *takes* care of *her* mother."

Next, because she knows the ways of China and the Chinese, we can safely guess where the mother comes from and what her native language is. Even the single word "supportive" provides us with much evidence; the speaker tells her daughter that there's no such word in Chinese, and she's evidently repeating a term the daughter—a better English speaker—

has previously used. So there's a family disagreement going on; the daughter has complained her mother's not being supportive while she, the younger woman, is earning a living—going to meetings, writing memos "while her husband go to the gym." Jen replicates the sound, accent, and cadence of inflected speech, bringing the character vividly to life.

Even in this brief excerpt, we get a sense of the mother's nature. Her flood of words has an edge. This narrator is not just reporting facts about her life and family; she's *complaining*, even *ranting*. Her daughter's entire way of life is, to the speaker, a puzzle. The mother doesn't approve of a husband who has to "go to the gym to be a man." That phrase, more than any other in the passage, underlines her disapproval and confusion; the behavior of the younger generation is hard for her to swallow, and roles have been reversed. Her child fails to provide her with the respectful attention an elder in China expects. We know that we will read a story about the clash of values, about generations in conflict and cultures at odds with each other.

CONTINUED ON PAGE 234

Gish Jen ... *the character is absolutely the font of all fiction.*

A Conversation on Writing

Using Character to Drive Fiction

I think the character is absolutely the font of all fiction. I think that's where the conflict comes from, and I think it's where the plot comes from: that's where the story comes from. And so when I feel that something is not going well, that it doesn't have its own drive, I don't look at the incidents to try to understand what's going wrong. I look at the character, and in particular I look at the character's ambivalence.

Using Humor to Confront Loaded Topics

[Humor] does seem to have a particular use in my writing, because I am interested in so many questions of ethnicity and identity, which are pretty loaded. With humor, it's like everything is just floating on a sea where they can all move around. And things, which perhaps would be crashing into each other in a very unpleasant way, are suddenly able to float.

On the Pleasure of Reading

I at least feel much more alive reading than I do living sometimes. I mean, there is a way in which life itself can be kind of a disappointment, which literature never is.

To watch this entire interview and hear the author read from "Who's Irish?" go to connect .mcgraw-hill.com.

RESEARCH ASSIGNMENT   In Jen's interview, she reflects on this quotation about story writing: "If you don't surprise yourself, you will not surprise the reader." What does this mean to Jen?

"I *am* the kind of person who would make a joke on someone's deathbed, tacky as it may seem," Gish Jen once said in an interview. And while she may have been speaking lightheartedly, she captured one of the essential elements of her craft—her ability to blend tragedy and humor. Born (1955) as Lillian Jen to Chinese immigrant parents in Scarsdale, New York, she changed her first name to "Gish" in honor of the silent film actress Lillian Gish. After graduating from Harvard, Jen taught English to engineers in China, later returning to the United States and earning her M.F.A. from the Iowa Writers' Workshop. She is the author of four novels—*Typical American* (1991), its sequel, *Mona in the Promised Land* (1996), *The Love Wife* (2004), and *World and Town* (2010)—as well as a collection of short stories, *Who's Irish?* (2000). In her fiction, Jen explores ideas of ethnic and cultural identity, assimilation, and integration, and how these ideas change for her characters as they adapt to new surroundings or situations. She now lives in Cambridge, Massachusetts, with her husband and two children.

AS YOU READ   Imagine that you are sitting across the table from the narrator of this story. Imagine that she is speaking directly to you. How do you feel about what she is telling you? What would you like to say to her? Would you say everything you are thinking?

Who's Irish? (1999)

1   IN China, people say mixed children are supposed to be smart, and definitely my granddaughter Sophie is smart. But Sophie is wild, Sophie is not like my daughter Natalie, or like me. I am work hard my whole life, and fierce besides. My husband always used to say he is afraid of me, and in our restaurant, busboys and cooks all afraid of me too. Even the gang members come for protection money, they try to talk to my husband. When I am there, they stay away. If they come by mistake, they pretend they are come to eat. They hide behind the menu, they order a lot of food. They talk about their mothers. Oh, my mother have some arthritis, need to take herbal medicine, they say. Oh, my mother getting old, her hair all white now.

I say, Your mother's hair used to be white, but since she dye it, it become black again. Why don't you go home once in a while and take a look? I tell them, Confucius say a filial son knows what color his mother's hair is.

My daughter is fierce too, she is vice president in the bank now. Her new house is big enough for everybody to have their own room, including me. But Sophie take after Natalie's husband's family, their name is Shea. Irish. I always thought Irish people are like Chinese people, work so hard on the railroad, but now I know why the Chinese beat the Irish. Of course, not all Irish are like the Shea family, of course not. My daughter tell me I should not say Irish this, Irish that.

How do you like it when people say the Chinese this, the Chinese that, she say.

5   You know, the British call the Irish heathen, just like they call the Chinese, she say.

You think the Opium War was bad, how would you like to live right next door to the British, she say.

And that is that. My daughter have a funny habit when she win an argument, she take a sip of something and look away, so the other person is not embarrassed. So I am not embarrassed. I do not call anybody anything either. I just happen to mention about the Shea family, an interesting fact: four brothers in the family, and not one of them work. The mother, Bess, have a job before she got sick, she was executive secretary in a big company. She is handle everything for a big shot, you would be surprised how complicated her job is, not just type this, type that. Now she is a nice woman with a clean house. But her boys, every one of them is on welfare, or so-called severance pay, or so-called disability pay. Something. They say they cannot find work, this is not the economy of the fifties, but I say, Even the black people doing better these days, some of them live so fancy, you'd be surprised. Why the Shea family have so much trouble? They are white people, they speak English. When I come to this country, I have no money and do not speak English. But my husband and I own our restaurant before he die. Free and clear, no mortgage. Of course, I understand I am just lucky; come from a country where the food is popular all over the world. I understand it is not the Shea family's fault they come from a country where everything is boiled. Still, I say.

She's right, we should broaden our horizons, say one brother Jim, at Thanksgiving. Forget about the car business. Think about egg rolls.

Pad thai, say another brother, Mike. I'm going to make my fortune in pad thai. It's going to be the new pizza.

10 I say, You people too picky about what you sell. Selling egg rolls not good enough for you, but at least my husband and I can say, We made it. What can you say? Tell me. What can you say?

Everybody chew their tough turkey.

I especially cannot understand my daughter's husband John, who has no job but cannot take care of Sophie either. Because he is a man, he say, and that's the end of the sentence.

Plain boiled food, plain boiled thinking. Even his name is plain boiled: John. Maybe because I grew up with black bean sauce and hoisin sauce and garlic sauce, I always feel something is missing when my son-in-law talk.

But, okay: so my son-in-law can be man, I am baby-sitter. Six hours a day, same as the old sitter, crazy Amy, who quit. This is not so easy, now that I am sixty-eight, Chinese age almost seventy. Still, I try. In China, daughter take care of mother. Here it is the other way around. Mother help daughter, mother ask, Anything else I can do? Otherwise daughter complain mother is not supportive. I tell daughter, We do not have this word in Chinese, *supportive*. But my daughter too busy to listen, she has to go to meeting, she has to write memo while her husband go to the gym to be a man. My daughter say otherwise he will be depressed. Seems like all his life he has this trouble, depression.

15 No one wants to hire someone who is depressed, she say. It is important for him to keep his spirits up.

Beautiful wife, beautiful daughter, beautiful house, oven can clean itself automatically. No money left over, because only one income, but lucky enough, got the baby-sitter for free. If John lived in China, he would be very happy. But he is not happy. Even at the gym things go wrong. One day, he pull a muscle. Another day, weight room too crowded. Always something.

Until finally, hooray, he has a job. Then he feel pressure.

I need to concentrate, he say. I need to focus.

He is going to work for insurance company. Salesman job. A paycheck, he say, and at least he will wear clothes instead of gym shorts. My daughter buy him some special candy bars from the health-food store. They say THINK! on them, and are supposed to help John think.

20 John is a good-looking boy, you have to say that, especially now that he shave so you can see his face.

I am an old man in a young man's game, say John.

I will need a new suit, say John.

This time I am not going to shoot myself in the foot, say John.

Good, I say.

25 She means to be supportive, my daughter say. Don't start the send her back to China thing, because we can't.

SOPHIE is three years old American age, but already I see her nice Chinese side swallowed up by her wild Shea side. She looks like mostly Chinese. Beautiful black hair, beautiful black eyes. Nose perfect size, not so flat looks like something fell down, not so large looks like some big deal got stuck in wrong face. Everything just right, only her skin is a brown surprise to John's family. So brown, they say. Even John say it. She never goes in the sun, still she is that color, he say. Brown. They say, Nothing the matter with brown. They are just surprised. So brown. Nattie is not that brown, they say. They say, It seems like Sophie should be a color in between Nattie and John. Seems funny, a girl named Sophie Shea be brown. But she is brown, maybe her name should be Sophie Brown. She never go in the sun, still she is that color, they say. Nothing the matter with brown. They are just surprised.

The Shea family talk is like this sometimes, going around and around like a Christmas-tree train.

Maybe John is not her father, I say one day, to stop the train. And sure enough, train wreck. None of the brothers ever say the word *brown* to me again.

Instead, John's mother, Bess, say, I hope you are not offended.

30 She say, I did my best on those boys. But raising four boys with no father is no picnic.

You have a beautiful family, I say.

I'm getting old, she say.

You deserve a rest, I say. Too many boys make you old.

I never had a daughter, she say. You have a daughter.

35 I have a daughter, I say. Chinese people don't think a daughter is so great, but you're right. I have a daughter.

I was never against the marriage, you know, she say. I never thought John was marrying down. I always thought Nattie was just as good as white.

I was never against the marriage either, I say. I just wonder if they look at the whole problem.

Of course you pointed out the problem, you are a mother, she say. And now we both have a granddaughter. A little brown granddaughter, she is so precious to me.

I laugh. A little brown granddaughter, I say. To tell you the truth, I don't know how she came out so brown.

40 We laugh some more. These days Bess need a walker to walk. She take so many pills, she need two glasses of water to get them all down. Her favorite TV show is about bloopers, and she love her bird feeder. All day long, she can watch that bird feeder, like a cat.

I can't wait for her to grow up, Bess say. I could use some female company.

Too many boys, I say.

Boys are fine, she say. But they do surround you after a while.

You should take a break, come live with us, I say. Lots of girls at our house.

45 Be careful what you offer, say Bess with a wink. Where I come from, people mean for you to move in when they say a thing like that.

NOTHING the matter with Sophie's outside, that's the truth. It is inside that she is like not any Chinese girl I ever see. We go to the park, and this is what she does. She stand up in the stroller. She take off all her clothes and throw them in the fountain.

Sophie! I say. Stop!

But she just laugh like a crazy person. Before I take over as baby-sitter, Sophie has that crazy-person sitter, Amy the guitar player. My daughter thought this Amy very creative—another word we do not talk about in China. In China, we talk about whether we have difficulty or no difficulty. We talk about whether life is bitter or not bitter. In America, all day long, people talk about creative. Never mind that I cannot even look at this Amy, with her shirt so short that her belly button showing. This Amy think Sophie should love her body. So when Sophie take off her diaper, Amy laugh. When Sophie run around naked, Amy say she wouldn't want to wear a diaper either. When Sophie go *shu-shu* in her lap, Amy laugh and say there are no germs in pee. When Sophie take off her shoes, Amy say bare feet is best, even the pediatrician say so. That is why Sophie now walk around with no shoes like a beggar child. Also why Sophie love to take off her clothes.

Turn around! say the boys in the park. Let's see that ass!

Of course, Sophie does not understand. Sophie 50 clap her hands, I am the only one to say, No! This is not a game.

It has nothing to do with John's family, my daughter say. Amy was too permissive, that's all.

But I think if Sophie was not wild inside, she would not take off her shoes and clothes to begin with.

You never take off your clothes when you were little, I say. All my Chinese friends had babies, I never saw one of them act wild like that.

Look, my daughter say. I have a big presentation tomorrow.

John and my daughter agree Sophie is a problem, 55 but they don't know what to do.

You spank her, she'll stop, I say another day.

But they say, Oh no.

In America, parents not supposed to spank the child.

It gives them low self-esteem, my daughter say. And that leads to problems later, as I happen to know.

My daughter never have big presentation the next day when the subject of spanking come up.

I don't want you to touch Sophie, she say. No spanking, period.

Don't tell me what to do, I say.

I'm not telling you what to do, say my daughter. I'm telling you how I feel.

I am not your servant, I say. Don't you dare talk to me like that.

My daughter have another funny habit when she lose an argument. She spread out all her fingers and look at them, as if she like to make sure they are still there.

My daughter is fierce like me, but she and John think it is better to explain to Sophie that clothes are a good idea. This is not so hard in the cold weather. In the warm weather, it is very hard.

Use your words, my daughter say. That's what we tell Sophie. How about if you set a good example.

As if good example mean anything to Sophie. I am so fierce, the gang members who used to come to the restaurant all afraid of me, but Sophie is not afraid.

I say, Sophie, if you take off your clothes, no snack.

I say, Sophie, if you take off your clothes, no lunch.

I say, Sophie, if you take off your clothes, no park.

Pretty soon we are stay home all day, and by the end of six hours she still did not have one thing to eat. You never saw a child stubborn like that.

I'm hungry! she cry when my daughter come home.

What's the matter, doesn't your grandmother feed you? My daughter laugh.

No! Sophie say. She doesn't feed me anything!

My daughter laugh again. Here you go, she say.

She say to John, Sophie must be growing.

Growing like a weed, I say.

Still Sophie take off her clothes, until one day I spank her. Not too hard, but she cry and cry, and when I tell her if she doesn't put her clothes back on I'll spank her again, she put her clothes back on. Then I tell her she is good girl, and give her some food to eat. The next day we go to the park and, like a nice Chinese girl, she does not take off her clothes.

She stop taking off her clothes, I report. Finally!

How did you do it? my daughter ask.

After twenty-eight years' experience with you, I guess I learned something, I say.

It must have been a phase, John say, and his voice is suddenly like an expert.

His voice is like an expert about everything these days, now that he carry a leather briefcase, and wear shiny shoes, and can go shopping for a new car. On the company, he say. The company will pay for it, but he will be able to drive it whenever he want.

A free car, he say. How do you like that.

It's good to see you in the saddle again, my daughter say. Some of your family patterns are scary.

At least I don't drink, he say. He say, And I'm not the only one with scary family patterns.

That's for sure, say my daughter.

EVERYONE is happy. Even I am happy, because there is more trouble with Sophie, but now I think I can help her Chinese side fight against her wild side. I teach her to eat food with fork or spoon or chopsticks, she cannot just grab into the middle of a bowl of noodles. I teach her not to play with garbage cans. Sometimes I spank her, but not too often, and not too hard.

Still, there are problems. Sophie like to climb everything. If there is a railing, she is never next to it. Always she is on top of it. Also, Sophie like to hit the mommies of her friends. She learn this from her playground best friend, Sinbad, who is four. Sinbad wear army clothes every day and like to ambush his mommy. He is the one who dug a big hole under the play structure, a foxhole he call it, all by himself. Very hardworking. Now he wait in the foxhole with a shovel full of wet sand. When his mommy come, he throw it right at her.

Oh, it's all right, his mommy say. You can't get rid of war games, it's part of their imaginative play. All the boys go through it.

Also, he like to kick his mommy, and one day he tell Sophie to kick his mommy too.

I wish this story is not true.

Kick her, kick her! Sinbad say.

95 Sophie kick her. A little kick, as if she just so happened was swinging her little leg and didn't realize that big mommy leg was in the way. Still I spank Sophie and make Sophie say sorry, and what does the mommy say?

Really, it's all right, she say. It didn't hurt.

After that, Sophie learn she can attack mommies in the playground, and some will say, Stop, but others will say, Oh, she didn't mean it, especially if they realize Sophie will be punished.

THIS is how, one day, bigger trouble come. The bigger trouble start when Sophie hide in the foxhole with that shovel full of sand. She wait, and when I come look for her, she throw it at me. All over my nice clean clothes.

Did you ever see a Chinese girl act this way?

100 Sophie! I say. Come out of there, say you're sorry.

But she does not come out. Instead, she laugh. Naaah, naah-na, naaa-naaa, she say.

I am not exaggerate: millions of children in China, not one act like this.

Sophie! I say. Now! Come out now!

But she know she is in big trouble. She know if she come out, what will happen next. So she does not come out. I am sixty-eight, Chinese age almost seventy, how can I crawl under there to catch her? Impossible. So I yell, yell, yell, and what happen? Nothing. A Chinese mother would help, but American mothers, they look at you, they shake their head, they go home. And, of course, a Chinese child would give up, but not Sophie.

105 I hate you! she yell. I hate you, Meanie!

Meanie is my new name these days.

Long time this goes on, long long time. The foxhole is deep, you cannot see too much, you don't know where is the bottom. You cannot hear too much either. If she does not yell, you cannot even know she is still there or not. After a while, getting cold out, getting dark out. No one left in the playground, only us.

Sophie, I say. How did you become stubborn like this? I am go home without you now.

I try to use a stick, chase her out of there, and once or twice I hit her, but still she does not come out. So finally I leave. I go outside the gate.

Bye-bye! I say. I'm go home now. 110

But still she does not come out and does not come out. Now it is dinnertime, the sky is black. I think I should maybe go get help, but how can I leave a little girl by herself in the playground? A bad man could come. A rat could come. I go back in to see what is happen to Sophie. What if she have a shovel and is making a tunnel to escape?

Sophie! I say.

No answer.

Sophie!

I don't know if she is alive. I don't know if she 115 is fall asleep down there. If she is crying, I cannot hear her.

So I take the stick and poke.

Sophie! I say. I promise I no hit you. If you come out, I give you a lollipop.

No answer. By now I worried. What to do, what to do, what to do? I poke some more, even harder, so that I am poking and poking when my daughter and John suddenly appear.

What are you doing? What is going on? say my daughter.

Put down that stick! say my daughter. 120

You are crazy! say my daughter.

John wiggle under the structure, into the foxhole, to rescue Sophie.

She fell asleep, say John the expert. She's okay. That is one big hole.

Now Sophie is crying and crying.

Sophia, my daughter say, hugging her. Are you 125 okay, peanut? Are you okay?

She's just scared, say John.

Are you okay? I say too. I don't know what happen, I say.

She's okay, say John. He is not like my daughter, full of questions. He is full of answers until we get home and can see by the lamplight.

Will you look at her? he yell then. What the hell happened?

130 Bruises all over her brown skin, and a swollen-up eye.

You are crazy! say my daughter. Look at what you did! You are crazy!

I try very hard, I say.

How could you use a stick? I told you to use your words!

She is hard to handle, I say.

135 She's three years old! You cannot use a stick! say my daughter.

She is not like any Chinese girl I ever saw, I say.

I brush some sand off my clothes. Sophie's clothes are dirty too, but at least she has her clothes on.

Has she done this before? ask my daughter. Has she hit you before?

She hits me all the time, Sophie say, eating ice cream.

140 Your family, say John.

Believe me, say my daughter.

A DAUGHTER I have, a beautiful daughter. I took care of her when she could not hold her head up. I took care of her before she could argue with me, when she was a little girl with two pigtails, one of them always crooked. I took care of her when we have to escape from China, I took care of her when suddenly we live in a country with cars everywhere, if you are not careful your little girl get run over. When my husband die, I promise him I will keep the family together, even though it was just two of us, hardly a family at all.

But now my daughter take me around to look at apartments. After all, I can cook, I can clean, there's no reason I cannot live by myself, all I need is a telephone. Of course, she is sorry. Sometimes she cry, I am the one to say everything will be

okay. She say she have no choice, she doesn't want to end up divorced. I say divorce is terrible, I don't know who invented this terrible idea. Instead of live with a telephone, though, surprise, I come to live with Bess. Imagine that. Bess make an offer and, sure enough, where she come from, people mean for you to move in when they say things like that. A crazy idea, go to live with someone else's family, but she like to have some female company, not like my daughter, who does not believe in company. These days when my daughter visit, she does not bring Sophie. Bess say we should give Nattie time, we will see Sophie again soon. But seems like my daughter have more presentation than ever before, every time she come she have to leave.

I have a family to support, she say, and her voice is heavy, as if soaking wet. I have a young daughter and a depressed husband and no one to turn to.

When she say no one to turn to, she mean me. 145

These days my beautiful daughter is so tired she can just sit there in a chair and fall asleep. John lost his job again, already, but still they rather hire a baby-sitter than ask me to help, even they can't afford it. Of course, the new baby-sitter is much younger, can run around. I don't know if Sophie these days is wild or not wild. She call me Meanie, but she like to kiss me too, sometimes. I remember that every time I see a child on TV. Sophie like to grab my hair, a fistful in each hand, and then kiss me smack on the nose. I never see any other child kiss that way.

The satellite TV has so many channels, more channels than I can count, including a Chinese channel from the Mainland and a Chinese channel from Taiwan, but most of the time I watch bloopers with Bess. Also, I watch the bird feeder—so many, many kinds of birds come. The Shea sons hang around all the time, asking when will I go home, but Bess tell them, Get lost.

She's a permanent resident, say Bess. She isn't going anywhere.

Then she wink at me, and switch the channel with the remote control.

150   Of course, I shouldn't say Irish this, Irish that, especially now I am become honorary Irish myself, according to Bess. Me! Who's Irish? I say, and she laugh.

All the same, if I could mention one thing about some of the Irish, not all of them of course, I like to mention this: Their talk just stick. I don't know how Bess Shea learn to use her words, but sometimes I hear what she say a long time later. *Permanent resident. Not going anywhere.* Over and over I hear it, the voice of Bess.

IF YOU LIKED "WHO'S IRISH?", YOU MIGHT ALSO LIKE . . .

. . . other stories that take up the subject matter of the life of first-generation Americans, such as Junot Diaz's "How to Date a Browngirl, Blackgirl, Whitegirl, or Halfie" (Chapter 11), Amy Tan's "Two Kinds" (Chapter 13), and Jhumpa Lahiri's "Interpreter of Maladies" (Chapter 13).

GOING FURTHER   Timothy Mo's *Sour Sweet* and Fae Myenne Ng's *Bone* also explore Asian characters who have one foot in one cultural world and the other foot in another.

Writing from Reading

Summarize

1 Summarize the narrator's views of her Irish in-laws at the beginning of the story; then summarize her views at the end. Discuss how these views have changed, and how they've stayed the same.

Analyze Craft

2 Discuss how Jen uses the grandmother's dialect to create her character. What details about the grandmother does this dialect suggest that are never mentioned in the story? Explain how the story would change if it were written in Jen's standard English voice, with only the dialogue in dialect.

Analyze Voice

3 Consider the use of humor in "Who's Irish?" Find and list specific examples of misunderstandings and explore why these are (or are not) used for humorous purposes.

4 Discuss the narrator's view of the words *supportive* and *creative*. What does her view reveal about cultural differences?

Synthesize Summary and Analysis

5 Describe how Jen uses the topic of Sophie's skin color to reveal character.

6 Imagine "Who's Irish?" told by a neutral party. How would your impressions of the various characters change if viewed without the grandmother's direct opinions?

Interpret the Story

7 A central theme of "Who's Irish?" is the speaker's adjustment—as restaurant owner, wife, mother, and grandmother—to the values and systems of behavior in America. Considering her various reactions and interactions throughout the story, do you think she has adjusted?

CONTINUED FROM PAGE 225

THE CRAFT OF CHARACTERIZATION

Characters—the people who inhabit literary works—should capture and hold our attention as they suffer, rejoice, rebel, and sometimes perish within the world of the story. It's the sleeping passenger who makes us care whether her train runs off the tracks and plunges into a ravine; it's the child in the upstairs bedroom who makes us hope the firefighters reach his burning house in time. Theirs are the faces we see, the voices we hear, the decisions we sympathize with or marvel at, and the fates we come to share and care about while we read.

> **"I don't sit down in the morning and say, 'Well how am I going to enter this character?' For me it's something which comes naturally, so all I have to do is be quiet. I sit and I listen and the voices come."** Conversation with Gish Jen

Characterization, or the way a writer crafts and defines personality, gives us an insight into thoughts and actions that real life rarely permits. In "The Jilting of Granny Weatherall," in this chapter, Katherine Anne Porter allows readers to share Granny's thoughts as she lies on her deathbed, listening to her daughter Cornelia and the doctor discuss her condition:

> *Well, and what if she was? She still had ears. It was like Cornelia to whisper around doors. She always kept things secret in such a public way. She was always being tactful and kind. Cornelia was dutiful; that was the trouble with her. Dutiful and good: "So good and dutiful," said Granny, "that I'd like to spank her."*

Together, the few sentences of that paragraph, combined with Granny's one line of dialogue ("So good and dutiful . . . that I'd like to spank her") bring the character to life. She's cantankerous and quarrelsome, impatient with Cornelia, and surprising us as readers with that desire to spank her daughter for being, of all things, "good and dutiful."

In fiction, because we have access to unspoken thoughts, we can understand **motivation,** or what causes people to behave as they do. In Alice Munro's "An Ounce of Cure" (Chapter 6), a heartbroken, melancholy teenage girl tells readers one version of what motivated her to act as she did the night she babysat for the Berryman family:

> *I got up and found the Berrymans' "Danse Macabre" and put it on the record player and turned out the living-room lights. The curtains were only partly drawn. A street light shone obliquely on the windowpane, making a rectangle of thin dusty gold, in which the shadows of bare branches moved, caught in the huge sweet winds of spring. It was a mild black night when the last snow was*

*melting. A year ago all this—the music, the wind and the darkness, the shadows
of the branches—would have given me tremendous happiness; when they did
not do so now, but only called up tediously familiar, somehow humiliatingly
personal thoughts, I gave up my soul for dead and walked into the kitchen and
decided to get drunk.*

"[Characters] aren't invented for the purposes of function and a plot. . . . They appear as I write." Conversation with Tim O'Brien

In the next paragraph, she changes her story somewhat—*No, it was not like that.*
Motivation, she seems to say, is a complex matter but something people want and need
to understand. It becomes more complex, she might have added, when one is trying to
remember one's own motivation many years later— as does the speaker here.

What You See Is What You Get

Because we usually judge people first on their appearance, the writers of prose fiction
give great thought to sketching in and filling out a character's looks—the curve of a
nose, the crease between brows, the shape of a hulking or a slender frame. However, in
literature, physical appearance has meaning beyond a simple list of features. For example, one would make a character seven feet tall and 350 pounds only if the size and
heft of the person have some significance signaling the impact he has on those around
him, how he views himself, and what frustrations or powers he carries with him as a
result. The following portrait of Captain Ahab from *Moby-Dick* uses physical traits to
establish character and portend aspects of the plot.

> *His whole high, broad form, seemed made of solid bronze, and shaped in an
> unalterable mould. . . . Threading its way out from among his grey hairs, and
> continuing right down one side of his tawny scorched face and neck, till it dis-
> appeared in his clothing, you saw a slender rod-like mark, lividly whitish. It
> resembled that perpendicular seam sometimes made in the straight, lofty trunk
> of a great tree, when the upper lightning tearingly darts down it, and without
> wrenching a single twig, peels and grooves out the bark from top to bottom,
> ere running off into the soil, leaving the tree still greenly alive, but branded.
> Whether that mark was born with him, or whether it was the scar left by some
> desperate wound, no one could certainly say. . . .*

Everything about Ahab is striking and distinctive: his statue-like form, his gray
hair, his tanned face and neck, and especially the scar that seems to run the length
of his body, a scar that Melville compares to a lightning strike. But this passage goes
beyond describing his bodily attributes. It also suggests, in the concluding lines about
the mark, that his fate may be a product either of his inner nature or of some encounter at sea, which raises the question about the essence of his character.

What's in a Name?

Authors may reveal aspects of character by their choice of names, though the meaning of those names may often turn ironic. A character named Swift may be slow. A character named Rough may be gentle. A writer may choose a name to suggest a certain nature, as does Nathaniel Hawthorne in the case of Goodman Brown (Chapter 14), who enters into a profound struggle between good and evil, thereby earning the "good" part of his name. Katherine Anne Porter's Granny Weatherall is a person who has thus far "weathered all"—meaning she has overcome multiple hardships in her life. Since "clothes make the man," characters can also be known by what they wear. Does a woman wear designer ball gowns or denim overalls? Does she shop at K-Mart or Saks Fifth Avenue or at a showroom for haute couture in Paris? These details allow readers to learn about a character's social class, lifestyle, and in some cases, aspirations.

"I think that most of the people that turn up in my stories are somewhat lost. . . . If you have a character who finds herself less than adequate in any situation, that makes that character appealing. You would think that we would see this person as sort of pathetic, but often it doesn't work that way at all." Conversation with Amy Hempel

The Clothes Make the Man (or Woman)

In "Miss Brill," Katherine Mansfield begins the story with a description of the fur that Miss Brill wears. She does so because both the details of the garment and the attitude Miss Brill has towards it reveal important characteristics of Miss Brill herself:

> Miss Brill put up her hand and touched her fur. Dear little thing! It was nice to feel it again. She had taken it out of its box that afternoon, shaken out the moth-powder, given it a good brush, and rubbed the life back into the dim little eyes.

The moth-powder (used to preserve the fur in storage) and the fact that Miss Brill must "rub the life" into the eyes tell us that this fur—and by extension, its owner—is old. However, Miss Brill doesn't see the fur that way: instead, she is proud and fond of it. Notice how Mansfield uses it again at the end of the story: when the young couple laugh at the fur, we see how blind Miss Brill has been not just to the appearance of the garment, but to her own marginal position in the world.

We Are What We (Repeatedly) Do

What characters do can include a wide array of possibilities that represent who they are: what they eat (brown rice and tofu versus fast-food burgers), what attracts their attention (the bud or the thorns on a rosebush), and how they respond to others—for example, with puzzlement and exasperation, as the narrator does in "Who's Irish?" They also interact with others, being arrogant or meek or devious, spurring responses that help us as readers know them. For example, we learn about Miss Brill from the way the young couple responds.

Can You Hear Me Now?

Another significant means of understanding characters comes to us through dialogue. Consider how the essential conflict of Sonny's brother, the narrator in "Sonny's Blues," is encapsulated in a few spoken lines. When Sonny's friend hints at his difficult past, Sonny's brother says, "Look. Don't tell *me* your sad story, if it was up to me, I'd give you one.' Then I felt guilty—guilty, probably, for never having supposed that the poor bastard *had* a story of his own, much less a sad one, and I added quickly, 'What's going to happen to him now?'" Here, as in the rest of the story, Sonny's brother is unwilling to consider another person's inner life, an unwillingness that he later regrets.

Dialogue, then, can add dimension to a character. In the bittersweet, teasing voice of Mangan's sister in James Joyce's "Araby" (Chapter 8), you can hear the lilt of turn-of-the-century Dublin's middle-class English. You can as easily hear the rich dialect of southern African Americans that Zora Neale Hurston brings to life in "The Gilded Six-Bits" (Chapter 10). At its best—as with dialogue in a stage play—speech both reveals character and advances a story's action.

ROUND AND FLAT CHARACTERS

Reading fiction is a bit like eavesdropping or spying; it allows an intimate sense of how people think and live. What gives us that sense of life lived off (as well as on) the page? What makes a character real?

We usually talk about characters in literature in terms of their psychological makeup, the way we speak of family members and friends. *He is a talker. She's a brain. He worries a lot about money. She smokes incessantly and doesn't seem capable of standing up to her mother.* In a story, we come to know characters by way of the sum of their physical and mental attributes or **characteristics.** *He has dark hair, gestures while he speaks, and chews on his lower lip. She wears a silver comb in her hair and taps her right foot while she smokes, and her voice rises into the high upper register when she gets upset.*

If this sum of characteristics is complex and multifaceted, the characters seem real, or, in the terminology of twentieth-century British writer E. M. Forster (in his book *Aspects of the Novel),* they grow **round.** By contrast, in Forster's view, a **flat** character possesses a very narrow range of speech and action; these figures are predictable and do not develop over the course of the plot. In other words, they are **static,** meaning that they are unchanging. Roundness and flatness can be a matter of degree, with characters in a story falling along a spectrum.

A HISTORY OF CHARACTER

The word *character* comes from *kharakter*, the Greek word for a stamping tool. Thus, the ancient Greeks believed that an individual's character—those defining traits that inform behavior and action—was static. Character made up one's fate or destiny. Whether a person was generous, loving, calm, excitable, level-headed, jittery, easily embarrassed, fearful, or brave, human personalities were seen as stable.

More recent notions of character have grown less absolute. In the nineteenth century, the age of psychology revolutionized and complicated our understanding of the human mind and, consequently, of character. Most people no longer regard personality and behavior as fixed. Instead, a person's behavior could be mutable, contradictory, unpredictable.

Far from a fixed stamp or *kharakter*, characterization and the study of character are, at least in part, ways of exploring an individual's capacity for change within the pages of a story *and* in our own lives.

This distinction between round and flat characters is a crucial one. Forster suggests, in effect, that no one is either entirely good or entirely bad, completely brave or cowardly, wholly smart or stupid. Instead, we're all a compound or mixture of opposite qualities, and the combination or proportion of these qualities can change. A story's protagonist, or central actor, is almost always round. Such characters are **dynamic,** meaning that their personality and behavior alter over the course of the action in response to challenges and changing circumstances. A protagonist who initially behaves as a coward, for instance, may well become valiant at a crucial moment.

"I like characters who have agency, who make the choice to change—who act, rather than having life or having the world act on them." Conversation with Chimamanda Ngozi Adichie

In most fiction, the developing (or disintegrating) relationship between the protagonist and the antagonist (see Chapter 8) has a significant effect on both people. A particular kind of protagonist who often appears in contemporary fiction is referred to as an **antihero**—a main character who acts outside the usual lines of heroic behavior (brave, honest, true). In "Sonny's Blues," Baldwin plays with the notion of an antihero. At first, the narrator seems the more heroic of the two brothers, as he is a settled school teacher while Sonny is in prison because of drugs. But by the end, Sonny helps the narrator achieve new understanding. Listen to the narrator's impressions as Sonny plays jazz—the music the narrator once disdained:

> *I seemed to hear with what burning he had made it his, and what burning we had yet to make it ours, how we could cease lamenting. Freedom lurked around us and I understood, at last, that he could help us to be free if we would listen, that he would never be free until we did.*

Both brothers are affected by the heroic end that Sonny achieves through antiheroic means.

In contrast to round characters, flat or **stock characters** represent a concept or type of behavior, such as *mean teacher* or *mischievous student,* and offer readers the comforts of repetition and reliability. Often, such characters are comic and provide us with comic relief—overeating, taking pratfalls, losing their glasses, and bumping into doors. The difference here, as we suggested, is the distinction between characters who are dynamic and those who are static. And it's not always the case that round is desirable and flat is less so; most fictions require both kinds of portrayals to fully establish a plot. Flat characters often play a limited role in a story's plot. As such, they may serve as **foils,** or contrasts, to a central player. A devious friend, for example, might bring out a protagonist's trusting nature, or a happy-go-lucky uncle might make his niece's sadness all the more noticeable.

James Baldwin (1924–1987)

Born in New York City, James Baldwin grew up in Harlem, the mostly black section at the north end of Manhattan. Though his formal education ended in high school, he asserted his place in contemporary letters before the age of thirty with a powerful debut novel about childhood in a Pentecostal Harlem church, *Go Tell It on the Mountain* (1953). For the next three decades Baldwin made a place for himself in American letters as both a fiction writer and an essayist, gaining a place as well in the unfolding saga of the American Civil Rights movement. His novels *Giovanni's Room* (1956) and *Another Country* (1962) drew solid readerships, but his polemical essay *The Fire Next Time* (1955)—which first appeared in the pages of *The New Yorker* magazine and then as a book—brought him national attention.

He never relinquished it. Like his sometime mentor Richard Wright, Baldwin exiled himself in France—living first in Paris, then in the village of St. Paul de Vence—for a large part of his adult life. His focus was always on America, however, and while living abroad he continued to write about politics and race at home. The Civil War and the Civil Rights Movement were, to this writer, two chapters of the one story. Such nonfiction texts as *No Name in the Street* (1972) and *Evidence of Things Not Seen* (1985) focus on both race and politics; his final fiction and essays about black-and-white life in America attested equally to his sharp eye and a troubled dream of harmony.

A lifelong adept of jazz, Baldwin wrote that when he first moved to Paris he took along a phonograph record of the jazz singer Bessie Smith in order to remind himself of what he'd left behind. "Sonny's Blues" points up to this fascination with music, its sorrows and delights.

AS YOU READ Note every time the narrator or another character makes a reference to listening. To what are they listening or not listening? When you get to the end of the story, consider whether your understanding of listening has changed.

Sonny's Blues (1957)

1   I READ about it in the paper, in the subway, on my way to work. I read it, and I couldn't believe it, and I read it again. Then perhaps I just stared at it, at the newsprint spelling out his name, spelling out the story. I stared at it in the swinging lights of the subway car, and in the faces and bodies of the people, and in my own face, trapped in the darkness which roared outside.

It was not to be believed and I kept telling myself that, as I walked from the subway station to the high school. And at the same time I couldn't doubt it. I was scared, scared for Sonny. He became real to me again. A great block of ice got settled in my belly and kept melting there slowly all day long, while I taught my classes algebra. It was a special kind of ice. It kept melting, sending trickles of ice water all up and down my veins, but it never got less. Sometimes it hardened and seemed to expand until I felt my guts were going to come spilling out or that I was going to choke or scream. This would always be at a moment when I was remembering some specific thing Sonny had once said or done.

When he was about as old as the boys in my classes his face had been bright and open, there was a lot of copper in it; and he'd had wonderfully direct brown eyes, and great gentleness and privacy. I wondered what he looked like now. He had been picked up, the evening before, in a raid on an apartment downtown, for peddling and using heroin.

I couldn't believe it: but what I mean by that is that I couldn't find any room for it anywhere inside me. I had kept it outside me for a long time. I hadn't wanted to know. I had had suspicions, but I didn't name them, I kept putting them away. I told myself that Sonny was wild, but he wasn't crazy. And he'd always been a good boy, he hadn't ever turned hard or evil or disrespectful, the way kids can, so quick, so quick, especially in Harlem. I didn't want to believe that I'd ever see my brother going down, coming to nothing, all that light in his face gone out, in the condition I'd already seen so many others. Yet it had happened and here I was, talking about algebra to a lot of boys who might, every one of them

> He had been picked up, the evening before, in a raid on an apartment downtown, for peddling and using heroin.

for all I knew, be popping off needles every time they went to the head. Maybe it did more for them than algebra could.

5   I was sure that the first time Sonny had ever had horse, he couldn't have been much older than these boys were now. These boys, now, were living as we'd been living then, they were growing up with a rush and their heads bumped abruptly against the low ceiling of their actual possibilities. They were filled with rage. All they really knew were two darknesses, the darkness of their lives, which was now closing in on them, and the darkness of the movies, which had blinded them to that other darkness, and in which they now, vindictively, dreamed, at once more together than they were at any other time, and more alone.

When the last bell rang, the last class ended, I let out my breath. It seemed I'd been holding it for all that time. My clothes were wet—I may have looked as though I'd been sitting in a steam bath, all dressed up, all afternoon. I sat alone in the classroom a long time. I listened to the boys outside, downstairs, shouting and cursing and laughing. Their laughter struck me for perhaps the first time. It was not the joyous laughter which—God knows why—one associates with children. It was mocking and insular, its intent was to denigrate. It was disenchanted, and in this, also, lay the authority of their curses. Perhaps I was listening to them because I was thinking about my brother. And myself.

One boy was whistling a tune, at once very complicated and very simple, it seemed to be pouring out of him as though he were a bird, and it sounded very cool and moving through all that harsh, bright air, only just holding its own through all those other sounds.

I stood up and walked over to the window and looked down into the courtyard. It was the beginning of the spring and the sap was rising in the boys. A teacher passed through them every now and again, quickly, as though he or she couldn't wait to get out of that courtyard, to get those boys out of their sight and off their minds. I started collecting my stuff. I thought I'd better get home and talk to Isabel.

The courtyard was almost deserted by the time I got downstairs. I saw this boy standing in the shadow of a doorway, looking just like Sonny. I almost called his name. Then I saw that it wasn't Sonny, but somebody we used to know, a boy from around our block. He'd been Sonny's friend. He'd never been mine, having been too young for me, and, anyway, I'd never liked him. And now, even though he was a grown-up man, he still hung around that block, still spent hours on the street corners, was always high and raggy. I used to run into him from time to time and he'd often work around to asking me for a quarter or fifty cents. He always had some real good excuse, too, and I always gave it to him, I don't know why.

10   But now, abruptly, I hated him. I couldn't stand the way he looked at me, partly like a dog, partly like a cunning child. I wanted to ask him what the hell he was doing in the school courtyard.

He sort of shuffled over to me, and he said, "I see you got the papers. So you already know about it."

"You mean about Sonny? Yes, I already know about it. How come they didn't get you?"

He grinned. It made him repulsive and it also brought to mind what he'd looked like as a kid. "I wasn't there. I stay away from them people."

"Good for you." I offered him a cigarette and I watched him through the smoke. "You come all the way down here just to tell me about Sonny?"

15   "That's right." He was sort of shaking his head and his eyes looked strange, as though they were about to cross. The bright sun deadened his damp dark brown skin and it made his eyes look yellow and showed up the dirt in his kinked hair. He smelled funky. I moved a little away from him and I said, "Well, thanks. But I already know about it and I got to get home."

"I'll walk you a little ways," he said. We started walking. There were a couple of kids still loitering in the courtyard and one of them said goodnight to me and looked strangely at the boy beside me.

"What're you going to do?" he asked me. "I mean, about Sonny?"

"Look. I haven't seen Sonny for over a year, I'm not sure I'm going to do anything. Anyway, what the hell *can* I do?"

"That's right," he said quickly, "ain't nothing you can do. Can't much help old Sonny no more, I guess."

> I couldn't stand the way he looked at me, partly like a dog, partly like a cunning child.

It was what I was thinking and so it seemed to me he   20 had no right to say it.

"I'm surprised at Sonny, though," he went on—he had a funny way of talking, he looked straight ahead as though he were talking to himself—"I thought Sonny was a smart boy, I thought he was too smart to get hung."

"I guess he thought so too," I said sharply, "and that's how he got hung. And how about you? You're pretty goddamn smart, I bet."

Then he looked directly at me, just for a minute. "I ain't smart," he said. "If I was smart, I'd have reached for a pistol a long time ago."

"Look. Don't tell *me* your sad story, if it was up to me, I'd give you one." Then I felt guilty— guilty, probably, for never having supposed that the poor bastard *had* a story of his own, much less a sad one, and I asked, quickly, "What's going to happen to him now?"

He didn't answer this. He was off by himself some   25 place. "Funny thing," he said, and from his tone we might have been discussing the quickest way to get to Brooklyn, "when I saw the papers this morning, the first thing I asked myself was if I had anything to do with it. I felt sort of responsible."

I began to listen more carefully. The subway station was on the corner, just before us, and I stopped. He stopped, too. We were in front of a bar and he ducked slightly, peering in, but whoever he was looking for didn't seem to be there. The juke box was blasting away with something black and bouncy and I half watched the barmaid as she danced her way from the juke box to her place behind the bar. And I watched her face as she laughingly responded to something someone said to her, still keeping time to the music. When she smiled one saw the little girl, one sensed the doomed, still-struggling woman beneath the battered face of the semi-whore.

"I never *give* Sonny nothing," the boy said finally, "but a long time ago I come to school high and Sonny asked me how it felt." He paused, I couldn't bear to watch him, I watched the barmaid, and I listened to the music which seemed to be causing the pavement to shake. "I told him it felt great." The music stopped, the barmaid paused and watched the juke box until the music began again. "It did."

All this was carrying me some place I didn't want to go. I certainly didn't want to know how it felt. It filled everything, the people, the houses, the music, the dark, quicksilver barmaid, with menace; and this menace was their reality.

"What's going to happen to him now?" I asked again.

30 "They'll send him away some place and they'll try to cure him." He shook his head. "Maybe he'll even think he's kicked the habit. Then they'll let him loose"—he gestured, throwing his cigarette into the gutter. "That's all."

"What do you mean, that's *all*?"

But I knew what he meant.

"I *mean*, that's *all*." He turned his head and looked at me, pulling down the corners of his mouth. "Don't you know what I mean?" he asked, softly.

"How the hell *would* I know what you mean?" I almost whispered it, I don't know why.

35 "That's right," he said to the air, "how would *he* know what I mean?" He turned toward me again, patient and calm, and yet I somehow felt him shaking, shaking as though he were going to fall apart. I felt that ice in my guts again, the dread I'd felt all afternoon; and again I watched the barmaid, moving about the bar, washing glasses, and singing. "Listen. They'll let him out and then it'll just start all over again. That's what I mean."

"You mean—they'll let him out. And then he'll just start working his way back in again. You mean he'll never kick the habit. Is that what you mean?"

"That's right," he said, cheerfully. "*You* see what I mean."

"Tell me," I said at last, "why does he want to die? He must want to die, he's killing himself, why does he want to die?"

He looked at me in surprise. He licked his lips. "He don't want to die. He wants to live. Don't nobody want to die, ever."

40 Then I wanted to ask him—too many things. He could not have answered, or if he had, I could not have borne the answers. I started walking. "Well, I guess it's none of my business."

"It's going to be rough on old Sonny," he said. We reached the subway station. "This is your station?" he asked. I nodded. I took one step down. "Damn!" he said, suddenly. I looked up at him. He grinned again. "Damn it if I didn't leave all my money home. You ain't got a dollar on you, have you? Just for a couple of days, is all."

All at once something inside gave and threatened to come pouring out of me. I didn't hate him any more. I felt that in another moment I'd start crying like a child.

"Sure," I said. "Don't sweat." I looked in my wallet and didn't have a dollar, I only had a five. "Here," I said. "That hold you?"

He didn't look at it—he didn't want to look at it. A terrible, closed look came over his face, as though he were keeping the number on the bill a secret from him and me. "Thanks," he said, and now he was dying to see me go. "Don't worry about Sonny. Maybe I'll write him or something."

"Sure," I said. "You do that. So long."

45 "Be seeing you," he said. I went on down the steps.

AND I didn't write Sonny or send him anything for a long time. When I finally did, it was just after my little girl died, he wrote me back a letter which made me feel like a bastard.

Here's what he said:

Dear brother,

50 *You don't know how much I needed to hear from you. I wanted to write you many a time but I dug how much I must have hurt you and so I didn't write. But now I feel like a man who's been trying to climb up out of some deep, real deep and funky hole and just saw the sun up there, outside. I got to get outside.*

I can't tell you much about how I got here. I mean I don't know how to tell you. I guess I was afraid of something or I was trying to escape from something and you know I have never been very strong in the head (smile). I'm glad Mama and Daddy are dead and can't see what's happened to their son and I swear if I'd known what I was doing I would never have hurt you so, you and a lot of other fine people who were nice to me and who believed in me.

I don't want you to think it had anything to do with me being a musician. It's more than that. Or maybe less than that. I can't get anything straight in my head down here and I try not to think about what's going to happen to me when I get outside again. Sometime I think I'm going to flip and never get outside and sometime I think I'll come straight back. I tell you one thing, though, I'd rather blow my brains out than go through this again. But that's what they all say, so they tell me. If I tell you when I'm coming to New York and if you could meet me, I sure would appreciate it. Give my love to Isabel and the kids and I was sure sorry to hear about little Gracie. I wish I could be like Mama and say the Lord's will be done, but I don't know it seems to me that trouble is the one thing that never does get stopped and I don't know what good it does to blame it on the Lord. But maybe it does some good if you believe it.

Your brother,
Sonny

> This was because I had begun, finally, to wonder about Sonny, about the life that Sonny lived inside.

55 Then I kept in constant touch with him and I sent him whatever I could and I went to meet him when he came back to New York. When I saw him many things I thought I had forgotten came flooding back to me. This was because I had begun, finally, to wonder about Sonny, about the life that Sonny lived inside. This life, whatever it was, had made him older and thinner and it had deepened the distant stillness in which he had always moved. He looked very unlike my baby brother. Yet, when he smiled, when we shook hands, the baby brother I'd never known looked out from the depths of his private life, like an animal waiting to be coaxed into the light.

"How you been keeping?" he asked me.

"All right. And you?"

"Just fine." He was smiling all over his face. "It's good to see you again."

"It's good to see you."

60 The seven years' difference in our ages lay between us like a chasm: I wondered if these years would ever operate between us as a bridge. I was remembering, and it made it hard to catch my breath, that I had been there when he was born; and I had heard the first words he had ever spoken. When he started to walk, he walked from our mother straight to me. I caught him just before he fell when he took the first steps he ever took in this world.

"How's Isabel?"

"Just fine. She's dying to see you."

"And the boys?"

"They're fine, too. They're anxious to see their uncle."

"Oh, come on. You know they don't remember me." 65

"Are you kidding? Of course they remember you."

He grinned again. We got into a taxi. We had a lot to say to each other, far too much to know how to begin.

As the taxi began to move, I asked, "You still want to go to India?"

He laughed. "You still remember that. Hell, no. This place is Indian enough for me."

"It used to belong to them," I said. 70

And he laughed again. "They damn sure knew what they were doing when they got rid of it."

Years ago, when he was around fourteen, he'd been all hipped on the idea of going to India. He read books about people sitting on rocks, naked, in all kinds of weather, but mostly bad, naturally, and walking barefoot through hot coals and arriving at wisdom. I used to say that it sounded to me as though they were getting away from wisdom as fast as they could. I think he sort of looked down on me for that.

"Do you mind," he asked, "if we have the driver drive alongside the park? On the west side—I haven't seen the city in so long."

"Of course not," I said. I was afraid that I might sound as though I were humoring him, but I hoped he wouldn't take it that way.

So we drove along, between the green of the park and 75 the stony, lifeless elegance of hotels and apartment buildings, toward the vivid, killing streets of our childhood. These streets hadn't changed, though housing projects jutted up out of them now like rocks in the middle of a boiling sea. Most of the houses in which we had grown up had vanished, as had the stores from which we had stolen, the basements in which we had first tried sex, the rooftops from which we had hurled tin cans and bricks. But houses exactly like the houses of our past yet dominated the landscape, boys exactly like the boys we once had been found themselves smothering in these houses, came down into the streets for light and air and found themselves encircled by disaster. Some escaped the trap, most didn't. Those who got out always left something of themselves behind, as some animals amputate a leg and leave it in the trap. It might be said, perhaps, that I had escaped, after all, I was a school teacher; or that Sonny had, he hadn't lived in Harlem for years. Yet, as the cab moved uptown through streets which seemed, with a rush, to darken with dark people, and as I covertly studied Sonny's face, it came to me that what we both were seeking through our separate cab windows was that part of ourselves which had been left behind. It's always at the hour of trouble and confrontation that the missing member aches.

The moment Sonny and I started into the house I had the feeling that I was simply bringing him back into the danger he had almost died trying to escape.

We hit 110th Street and started rolling up Lenox Avenue. And I'd known this avenue all my life, but it seemed to me again, as it had seemed on the day I'd first heard about Sonny's trouble, filled with a hidden menace which was its very breath of life.

"We almost there," said Sonny.

"Almost." We were both too nervous to say anything more.

We live in a housing project. It hasn't been up long. A few days after it was up it seemed uninhabitably new, now, of course, it's already rundown. It looks like a parody of the good, clean, faceless life—God knows the people who live in it do their best to make it a parody. The beat-looking grass lying around isn't enough to make their lives green, the hedges will never hold out the streets, and they know it. The big windows fool no one, they aren't big enough to make space out of no space. They don't bother with the windows, they watch the TV screen instead. The playground is most popular with the children who don't play at jacks, or skip rope, or roller skate, or swing, and they can be found in it after dark. We moved in partly because it's not too far from where I teach, and partly for the kids; but it's really just like the houses in which Sonny and I grew up. The same things happen, they'll have the same things to remember. The moment Sonny and I started into the house I had the feeling that I was simply bringing him back into the danger he had almost died trying to escape.

80   Sonny has never been talkative. So I don't know why I was sure he'd be dying to talk to me when supper was over the first night. Everything went fine, the oldest boy remembered him, and the youngest boy liked him, and Sonny had

remembered to bring something for each of them; and Isabel, who is really much nicer than I am, more open and giving, had gone to a lot of trouble about dinner and was genuinely glad to see him. And she's always been able to tease Sonny in a way that I haven't. It was nice to see her face so vivid again and to hear her laugh and watch her make Sonny laugh. She wasn't, or, anyway, she didn't seem to be, at all uneasy or embarrassed. She chatted as though there were no subject which had to be avoided and she got Sonny past his first, faint stiffness. And thank God she was there, for I was filled with that icy dread again. Everything I did seemed awkward to me, and everything I said sounded freighted with hidden meaning. I was trying to remember everything I'd heard about dope addiction and I couldn't help watching Sonny for signs. I wasn't doing it out of malice. I was trying to find out something about my brother. I was dying to hear him tell me he was safe.

"Safe!" my father grunted, whenever Mama suggested trying to move to a neighborhood which might be safer for children. "Safe, hell! Ain't no place safe for kids, nor nobody."

He always went on like this, but he wasn't, ever, really as bad as he sounded, not even on weekends, when he got drunk. As a matter of fact, he was always on the lookout for "something a little better," but he died before he found it. He died suddenly, during a drunken weekend in the middle of the war, when Sonny was fifteen. He and Sonny hadn't ever got on too well. And this was partly because Sonny was the apple of his father's eye. It was because he loved Sonny so much and was frightened for him, that he was always fighting with him. It doesn't do any good to fight with Sonny. Sonny just moves back, inside himself, where he can't be reached. But the principal reason that they never hit it off is that they were so much alike. Daddy was big and rough and loud-talking, just the opposite of Sonny, but they both had—that same privacy.

Mama tried to tell me something about this, just after Daddy died. I was home on leave from the army.

This was the last time I ever saw my mother alive. Just the same, this picture gets all mixed up in my mind with pictures I had of her when she was younger. The way I always see her is the way she used to be on a Sunday afternoon, say, when the old folks were talking after the big Sunday dinner.

I always see her wearing pale blue. She'd be sitting on the sofa. And my father would be sitting in the easy chair, not far from her. And the living room would be full of church folks and relatives. There they sit, in chairs all around the living room, and the night is creeping up outside, but nobody knows it yet. You can see the darkness growing against the windowpanes and you hear the street noises every now and again, or maybe the jangling beat of a tambourine from one of the churches close by, but it's real quiet in the room. For a moment nobody's talking, but every face looks darkening, like the sky outside. And

> **The way I always see her** is the way she used to be on a Sunday afternoon, say, when the old folks were talking after the big Sunday dinner.

my mother rocks a little from the waist, and my father's eyes are closed. Everyone is looking at something a child can't see. For a minute they've forgotten the children. Maybe a kid is lying on the rug, half asleep. Maybe somebody's got a kid in his lap and is absent-mindedly stroking the kid's head. Maybe there's a kid, quiet and big-eyed, curled up in a big chair in the corner. The silence, the darkness coming, and the darkness in the faces frightens the child obscurely. He hopes that the hand which strokes his forehead will never stop—will never die. He hopes that there will never come a time when the old folks won't be sitting around the living room, talking about where they've come from, and what they've seen, and what's happened to them and their kinfolk.

But something deep and watchful in the child knows that this is bound to end, is already ending. In a moment someone will get up and turn on the light. Then the old folks will remember the children and they won't talk any more that day. And when light fills the room, the child is filled with darkness. He knows that every time this happens he's moved just a little closer to that darkness outside. The darkness outside is what the old folks have been talking about. It's what they've come from. It's what they endure. The child knows that they won't talk any more because if he knows too much about what's happened to *them*, he'll know too much too soon, about what's going to happen to *him*.

The last time I talked to my mother, I remember I was restless. I wanted to get out and see Isabel. We weren't married then and we had a lot to straighten out between us.

There Mama sat, in black, by the window. She was humming an old church song, *Lord, you brought me from a long ways off.* Sonny was out somewhere. Mama kept watching the streets.

"I don't know," she said, "if I'll ever see you again, after you go off from here. But I hope you'll remember the things I tried to teach you."

"Don't talk like that," I said, and smiled. "You'll be here a long time yet."

She smiled, too, but she said nothing. She was quiet for a long time. And I said, "Mama, don't you worry about nothing. I'll be writing all the time, and you be getting the checks. . . ."

"I want to talk to you about your brother," she said, suddenly. "If anything happens to me he ain't going to have nobody to look out for him."

"Mama," I said, "ain't nothing going to happen to you *or* Sonny. Sonny's all right. He's a good boy and he's got good sense."

"It ain't a question of his being a good boy," Mama said, "nor of his having good sense. It ain't only the bad ones, nor yet the dumb ones that gets sucked under." She stopped, looking at me. "Your Daddy once had a brother," she said, and she smiled in a way that made me feel she was in pain. "You didn't never know that, did you?"

"No," I said, "I never knew that," and I watched her face.

"Oh, yes," she said, "your Daddy had a brother." She looked out of the window again. "I know you never saw your Daddy cry. But *I* did—many a time, through all these years."

I asked her, "What happened to his brother? How come nobody's ever talked about him?"

This was the first time I ever saw my mother look old.

"His brother got killed," she said, "when he was just a little younger than you are now. I knew him. He was a fine boy. He was maybe a little full of the devil, but he didn't mean nobody no harm."

Then she stopped and the room was silent, exactly as it had sometimes been on those Sunday afternoons. Mama kept looking out into the streets.

"He used to have a job in the mill," she said, "and, like all young folks, he just liked to perform on Saturday nights. Saturday nights, him and your father would drift around to different places, go to dances and things like that, or just sit around with people they knew, and your father's brother would sing, he had a fine voice, and play along with himself on his guitar. Well, this particular Saturday night, him and your father was coming home from some place, and they were both a little drunk and there was a moon that night, it was bright like day. Your father's brother was feeling kind of good, and he was whistling to himself, and he had his guitar slung over his shoulder. They was coming down a hill and beneath them was a road that turned off from the highway. Well, your father's brother, being always kind of frisky, decided to run down this hill, and he did, with that guitar banging and clanging behind him, and he ran across the road, and he was making water behind a tree. And your father was sort of amused at him and he was still coming down the hill, kind of slow. Then he heard a car motor and that same minute his brother stepped from behind the tree, into the road, in the moonlight. And he started to cross the road. And your father started to run down the hill, he says he don't know why. This car was full of white men. They was all drunk, and when they seen your father's brother they let out a great whoop and holler and they aimed the car straight at him. They was having fun, they just wanted to scare him, the way they do sometimes, you know. But they was drunk. And I guess the boy, being drunk, too, and scared, kind of lost his head. By the time he jumped it was too late. Your father says he heard his brother scream when the car rolled over him, and he heard the wood of that guitar when it give, and he heard them strings go flying, and he heard them white men shouting, and the car kept on a-going and it ain't stopped till this day. And, time your father got down the hill, his brother weren't nothing but blood and pulp."

Tears were gleaming on my mother's face. There wasn't anything I could say.

"He never mentioned it," she said, "because I never let him mention it before you children. Your Daddy was like a crazy man that night and for many a night thereafter. He says he never in his life seen anything as dark as that road after the lights of that car had gone away. Weren't nothing, weren't nobody on that road, just your Daddy and his brother and that busted guitar. Oh, yes. Your Daddy never did really get right again. Till the day he died he weren't sure but that every white man he saw was the man that killed his brother."

She stopped and took out her handkerchief and dried her eyes and looked at me.

> "You got to hold on to your brother," she said, "and don't let him fall, no matter what it looks like is happening to him."

"I ain't telling you all this," she said, "to make you scared or bitter or to make you hate nobody. I'm telling you this because you got a brother. And the world ain't changed."

I guess I didn't want to believe this. I guess she saw this in my face. She turned away from me, toward the window again, searching those streets.

"But I praise my Redeemer," she said at last, "that He called your Daddy home before me. I ain't saying it to throw no flowers at myself, but, I declare, it keeps me from feeling too cast down to know I helped your father get safely through this world. Your father always acted like he was the roughest, strongest man on earth. And everybody took him to be like that. But if he hadn't had *me* there—to see his tears!"

She was crying again. Still, I couldn't move. I said, "Lord, Lord, Mama, I didn't know it was like that."

"Oh, honey," she said, "there's a lot that you don't know. But you are going to find it out." She stood up from the window and came over to me. "You got to hold on to your brother," she said, "and don't let him fall, no matter what it looks like is happening to him and no matter how evil you gets with him. You going to be evil with him many a time. But don't you forget what I told you, you hear?"

"I won't forget," I said. "Don't you worry, I won't forget. I won't let nothing happen to Sonny."

My mother smiled as though she were amused at something she saw in my face. Then, "You may not be able to stop nothing from happening. But you got to let him know you's *there.*"

TWO days later I was married, and then I was gone. And I had a lot of things on my mind and I pretty well forgot my promise to Mama until I got shipped home on a special furlough for her funeral.

And, after the funeral, with just Sonny and me alone in the empty kitchen, I tried to find out something about him.

"What do you want to do?" I asked him.

"I'm going to be a musician," he said.

For he had graduated, in the time I had been away, from dancing to the juke box to finding out who was playing what, and what they were doing with it, and he had bought himself a set of drums.

"You mean, you want to be a drummer?" I somehow had the feeling that being a drummer might be all right for other people but not for my brother Sonny.

"I don't think," he said, looking at me very gravely, "that I'll ever be a good drummer. But I think I can play a piano."

I frowned. I'd never played the role of the older brother quite so seriously before, had scarcely ever, in fact, *asked* Sonny a damn thing. I sensed myself in the presence of something I didn't really know how to handle, didn't understand. So I made my frown a little deeper as I asked: "What kind of musician do you want to be?"

He grinned. "How many kinds do you think there are?"

120 "Be *serious*," I said.

He laughed, throwing his head back, and then looked at me. "I *am* serious."

"Well, then, for Christ's sake, stop kidding around and answer a serious question. I mean, do you want to be a concert pianist, you want to play classical music and all that, or—or what?" Long before I finished he was laughing again. "For Christ's *sake*, Sonny!"

He sobered, but with difficulty. "I'm sorry. But you sound so—*scared!*" and he was off again.

"Well, you may think it's funny now, baby, but it's not going to be so funny when you have to make your living at it, let me tell you *that*." I was furious because I knew he was laughing at me and I didn't know why.

125 "No," he said, very sober now, and afraid, perhaps, that he'd hurt me, "I don't want to be a classical pianist. That isn't what interests me. I mean"—he paused, looking hard at me, as though his eyes would help me to understand, and then gestured helplessly, as though perhaps his hand would help—"I mean, I'll have a lot of studying to do, and I'll have to study *everything*, but, I mean, I want to play *with*—jazz musicians." He stopped. "I want to play jazz," he said.

Well, the word had never before sounded as heavy, as real, as it sounded that afternoon in Sonny's mouth. I just looked at him and I was probably frowning a real frown by this time. I simply couldn't see why on earth he'd want to spend his time hanging around nightclubs, clowning around on bandstands, while people pushed each other around a dance floor. It seemed—beneath him, somehow. I had never thought about it before, had never been forced to, but I suppose I had always put jazz musicians in a class with what Daddy called "good-time people."

"Are you *serious?*"

"Hell, *yes*, I'm serious."

He looked more helpless than ever, and annoyed, and deeply hurt.

I suggested, helpfully: "You mean— 130 like Louis Armstrong?"

His face closed as though I'd struck him. "No. I'm not talking about none of that old-time, down home crap."

"Well, look, Sonny, I'm sorry, don't get mad. I just don't altogether get it, that's all. Name somebody—you know, a jazz musician you admire."

"Bird."

"Who?"

"Bird! Charlie Parker! Don't they teach you nothing in 135 the goddamn army?"

I lit a cigarette. I was surprised and then a little amused to discover that I was trembling. "I've been out of touch," I said. "You'll have to be patient with me. Now. Who's this Parker character?"

"He's just one of the greatest jazz musicians alive," said Sonny, sullenly, his hands in his pockets, his back to me. "Maybe *the* greatest," he added, bitterly, "that's probably why *you* never heard of him."

"All right," I said, "I'm ignorant. I'm sorry. I'll go out and buy all the cat's records right away, all right?"

"It don't," said Sonny, with dignity, "make any difference to me. I don't care what you listen to. Don't do me no favors."

I was beginning to realize that I'd never seen him so 140 upset before. With another part of my mind I was thinking that this would probably turn out to be one of those things kids go through and that I shouldn't make it seem important by pushing it too hard. Still, I didn't think it would do any harm to ask: "Doesn't all this take a lot of time? Can you make a living at it?"

He turned back to me and half leaned, half sat, on the kitchen table. "Everything takes time," he said, "and—well, yes, sure, I can make a living at it. But what I don't seem to be able to make you understand is that it's the only thing I want to do."

"Well, Sonny," I said, gently, "you know people can't always do exactly what they *want* to do—"

"*No*, I don't know that," said Sonny, surprising me. "I think people *ought* to do what they want to do, what else are they alive for?"

"You getting to be a big boy," I said desperately, "it's time you started thinking about your future."

"I'm thinking about my future," said Sonny, grimly. "I think about it all the time."

I gave up. I decided, if he didn't change his mind, that we could always talk about it later. "In the meantime," I said, "you got to finish school." We had already decided that he'd have to move in with Isabel and her folks. I knew this wasn't the ideal arrangement because Isabel's folks are inclined to be dicty and they hadn't especially wanted Isabel to marry me. But I didn't know what else to do. "And we have to get you fixed up at Isabel's."

There was a long silence. He moved from the kitchen table to the window. "That's a terrible idea. You know it yourself."

"Do you have a *better* idea?"

He just walked up and down the kitchen for a minute. He was as tall as I was. He had started to shave. I suddenly had the feeling that I didn't know him at all.

He stopped at the kitchen table and picked up my cigarettes. Looking at me with a kind of mocking, amused defiance, he put one between his lips. "You mind?"

"You smoking already?"

He lit the cigarette and nodded, watching me through the smoke. "I just wanted to see if I'd have the courage to smoke in front of you." He grinned and blew a great cloud of smoke to the ceiling. "It was easy." He looked at my face. "Come on, now. I bet you was smoking at my age, tell the truth."

I didn't say anything but the truth was on my face, and he laughed. But now there was something very strained in his laugh. "Sure. And I bet that ain't all you was doing."

He was frightening me a little. "Cut the crap," I said. "We already decided that you was going to go and live at Isabel's. Now what's got into you all of a sudden?"

"*You* decided it," he pointed out. "*I* didn't decide nothing." He stopped in front of me, leaning against the stove, arms loosely folded. "Look, brother. I don't want to stay in Harlem no more, I really don't." He was very earnest. He looked at me, then over toward the kitchen window. There was something in his eyes I'd never seen before, some

thoughtfulness, some worry all his own. He rubbed the muscle of one arm. "It's time I was getting out of here."

"Where do you want to *go*, Sonny?"

"I want to join the army. Or the navy, I don't care. If I say I'm old enough, they'll believe me."

Then I got mad. It was because I was so scared.

"You must be crazy. You goddamn fool, what the hell do you want to go and join the *army* for?"

"I just told you. To get out of Harlem."

"Sonny, you haven't even finished *school*. And if you really want to be a musician, how do you expect to study if you're in the *army*?"

He looked at me, trapped, and in anguish. "There's ways. I might be able to work out some kind of deal. Anyway, I'll have the G.I. Bill when I come out."

"*If* you come out." We stared at each other. "Sonny, please. Be reasonable. I know the setup is far from perfect. But we got to do the best we can."

"I ain't learning nothing in school," he said. "Even when I go." He turned away from me and opened the window and threw his cigarette out into the narrow alley. I watched his back. "At least, I ain't learning nothing you'd want me to learn." He slammed the window so hard I thought the glass would fly out, and turned back to me. "And I'm sick of the stink of these garbage cans!"

"Sonny," I said, "I know how you feel. But if you don't finish school now, you're going to be sorry later that you didn't." I grabbed him by the shoulders. "And you only got another year. It ain't so bad. And I'll come back and I swear I'll help you do *whatever* you want to do. Just try to put up with it till I come back. Will you please do that? For me?"

He didn't answer and he wouldn't look at me.

"Sonny. You hear me?"

He pulled away. "I hear you. But you never hear anything *I* say."

I didn't know what to say to that. He looked out of the window and then back at me. "OK," he said, and sighed. "I'll try."

Then I said, trying to cheer him up a little, "They got a piano at Isabel's. You can practice on it."

And as a matter of fact, it did cheer him up for a minute. "That's right," he said to himself. "I forgot that." His face relaxed a little. But the worry, the thoughtfulness, played on it still, the way shadows play on a face which is staring into the fire.

> "I think people *ought* to do what they want to do, what else are they alive for?"

B UT I thought I'd never hear the end of that piano. At first, Isabel would write me, saying how nice it was that Sonny was so serious about his music and how, as soon as he came in from school, or wherever he had been when he was supposed to be at school, he went straight to that piano and stayed there until suppertime. And, after supper, he went back to that piano and stayed there until everybody went to bed. He was at the piano all day Saturday and all day Sunday. Then he bought a record player and started playing records. He'd play one record over and over again, all day long sometimes, and he'd improvise along with it on the piano. Or he'd play one section of the record, one chord, one change, one progression, then he'd do it on the piano. Then back to the record. Then back to the piano.

Well, I really don't know how they stood it. Isabel finally confessed that it wasn't like living with a person at all, it was like living with sound. And the sound didn't make any sense to her, didn't make any sense to any of them—naturally. They began, in a way, to be afflicted by this presence that was living in their home. It was as though Sonny were some sort of god, or monster. He moved in an atmosphere which wasn't like theirs at all. They fed him and he ate, he washed himself, he walked in and out of their door; he certainly wasn't nasty or unpleasant or rude, Sonny isn't any of those things; but it was as though he were all wrapped up in some cloud, some fire, some vision all his own; and there wasn't any way to reach him.

At the same time, he wasn't really a man yet, he was still a child, and they had to watch out for him in all kinds of ways. They certainly couldn't throw him out. Neither did they dare to make a great scene about that piano because even they dimly sensed, as I sensed, from so many thousands of miles away, that Sonny was at that piano playing for his life.

175   But he hadn't been going to school. One day a letter came from the school board and Isabel's mother got it—there had, apparently, been other letters but Sonny had torn them up. This day, when Sonny came in, Isabel's mother showed him the letter and asked where he'd been spending his time. And she finally got it out of him that he'd been down in Greenwich Village, with musicians and other characters, in a white girl's apartment. And this scared her and she started to scream at him and what came up, once she began—though she denies it to this day—was what sacrifices

> It was as though
> Sonny were some sort of
> god, or monster.

they were making to give Sonny a decent home and how little he appreciated it.

Sonny didn't play the piano that day. By evening, Isabel's mother had calmed down but then there was the old man to deal with, and Isabel herself. Isabel says she did her best to be calm but she broke down and started crying. She says she just watched Sonny's face. She could tell, by watching him, what was happening with him. And what was happening was that they penetrated his cloud, they had reached him. Even if their fingers had been a thousand times more gentle than human fingers ever are, he could hardly help feeling that they had stripped him naked and were spitting on that nakedness. For he also had to see that his presence, that music, which was life or death to him, had been torture for them and that they had endured it, not at all for his sake, but only for mine. And Sonny couldn't take that. He can take it a little better today than he could then but he's still not very good at it and, frankly, I don't know anybody who is.

The silence of the next few days must have been louder than the sound of all the music ever played since time began. One morning, before she went to work, Isabel was in his room for something and she suddenly realized that all of his records were gone. And she knew for certain that he was gone. And he was. He went as far as the navy would carry him. He finally sent me a postcard from some place in Greece and that was the first I knew that Sonny was still alive. I didn't see him any more until we were both back in New York and the war had long been over.

He was a man by then, of course, but I wasn't willing to see it. He came by the house from time to time, but we fought almost every time we met. I didn't like the way he carried himself, loose and dreamlike all the time, and I didn't like his friends, and his music seemed to be merely an excuse for the life he led. It sounded just that weird and disordered.

Then we had a fight, a pretty awful fight, and I didn't see him for months. By and by I looked him up, where he was living, in a furnished room in the Village, and I tried to make it up. But there were lots of other people in the room and Sonny just lay on his bed, and he wouldn't come downstairs with me, and he treated these other people as though they were his family and I weren't. So I got mad and then he got mad, and then I told him that he might just as well be dead as live the way he was living. Then he stood up and he told me not to worry about him any more in life, that he *was* dead as far as I was concerned. Then he pushed me to the door and the other people looked on as though nothing were happening, and he slammed the door behind me. I stood in the hallway, staring at the door. I heard somebody laugh in the room and then the tears came to my eyes. I started down the steps, whistling to keep from crying, I kept whistling to myself, *You going to need me, baby, one of these cold, rainy days.*

180   I READ about Sonny's trouble in the spring. Little Grace died in the fall. She was a beautiful little girl. But she only lived a little over two years. She died of polio and she suffered. She had a slight fever for a couple of days, but it didn't seem like anything and we just kept her in bed. And we would certainly have called the doctor, but the fever dropped, she seemed to be all right. So we thought it had just been a cold. Then, one day, she was up, playing, Isabel was in the kitchen fixing lunch for the two boys when they'd come in from school, and she heard Grace fall down in the living room. When you have a lot of children you don't always start running when one of them falls, unless they start screaming or something. And, this time, Grace was quiet. Yet, Isabel says that when she heard that *thump* and then that silence, something happened in her to make her afraid. And she ran to the living room and there was little Grace on the floor, all twisted up, and the reason she hadn't screamed was that she couldn't get her breath. And when she did scream, it was the worst sound, Isabel says, that she'd ever heard in all her life, and she still hears it sometimes in her dreams. Isabel will sometimes wake me up with a low, moaning, strangled sound and I have to be quick to awaken her and hold her to me and where Isabel is weeping against me seems a mortal wound.

I think I may have written Sonny the very day that little Grace was buried. I was sitting in the living room in the dark, by myself, and I suddenly thought of Sonny. My trouble made his real.

One Saturday afternoon, when Sonny had been living with us, or, anyway, been in our house, for nearly two weeks, I found myself wandering aimlessly about the living room, drinking from a can of beer, and trying to work up the courage to search Sonny's room. He was out, he was usually out

> ## I didn't like the way
> he carried himself, loose and dreamlike all the time.

whenever I was home, and Isabel had taken the children to see their grandparents. Suddenly I was standing still in front of the living room window, watching Seventh Avenue.

The idea of searching Sonny's room made me still. I scarcely dared to admit to myself what I'd be searching for. I didn't know what I'd do if I found it. Or if I didn't.

On the sidewalk across from me, near the entrance to a barbecue joint, some people were holding an old-fashioned revival meeting. The barbecue cook, wearing a dirty white apron, his conked hair reddish and metallic in the pale sun, and a cigarette between his lips, stood in the doorway, watching them. Kids and older people paused in their errands and stood there, along with some older men and a couple of very tough-looking women who watched everything that happened on the avenue, as though they owned it, or were maybe owned by it. Well, they were watching this, too. The revival was being carried on by three sisters in black, and a brother. All they had were their voices and their Bibles and a tambourine. The brother was testifying and while he testified two of the sisters stood together, seeming to say, amen, and the third sister walked around with the tambourine outstretched and a couple of people dropped coins into it. Then the brother's testimony ended and the sister who had been taking up the collection dumped the coins into her palm and transferred them to the pocket of her long black robe. Then she raised both hands, striking the tambourine against the air, and then against one hand, and she started to sing. And the two other sisters and the brother joined in.

It was strange, suddenly, to watch, though I had been seeing these street meetings all my life. So, of course, had everybody else down there. Yet, they paused and watched and listened and I stood still at the window. *"Tis the old ship of Zion,"* they sang, and the sister with the tambourine kept a steady, jangling beat, *"it has rescued many a thousand!"* Not a soul under the sound of their voices was hearing this song for the first time, not one of them had been rescued. Nor had they seen much in the way of rescue work being done

around them. Neither did they especially believe in the holiness of the three sisters and the brother, they knew too much about them, knew where they lived, and how. The woman with the tambourine, whose voice dominated the air, whose face was bright with joy, was divided by very little from the woman who stood watching her, a cigarette between her heavy, chapped lips, her hair a cuckoo's nest, her face scarred and swollen from many beatings, and her black eyes glittering like coal. Perhaps they both knew this, which was why, when, as rarely, they addressed each other, they addressed each other as Sister. As the singing filled the air the watching, listening faces underwent a change, the eyes focusing on something within; the music seemed to soothe a poison out of them; and time seemed, nearly, to fall away from the sullen, belligerent, battered faces, as though they were fleeing back to their first condition, while dreaming of their last. The barbecue cook half shook his head and smiled, and dropped his cigarette and disappeared into his joint. A man fumbled in his pockets for change and stood holding it in his hand impatiently, as though he had just remembered a pressing appointment further up the avenue. He looked furious. Then I saw Sonny, standing on the edge of the crowd. He was carrying a wide, flat notebook with a green cover, and it made him look, from where I was standing, almost like a schoolboy. The coppery sun brought out the copper in his skin, he was very faintly smiling, standing very still. Then the singing stopped, the tambourine turned into a collection plate again. The furious man dropped in his coins and vanished, so did a couple of the women, and Sonny dropped some change in the plate, looking directly at the woman with a little smile. He started across the avenue, toward the house. He has a slow, loping walk, something like the way Harlem hipsters walk, only he's imposed on this his own half-beat. I had never really noticed it before.

185   I stayed at the window, both relieved and apprehensive. As Sonny disappeared from my sight, they began singing again. And they were still singing when his key turned in the lock.

"Hey," he said.

"Hey, yourself. You want some beer?"

"No. Well, maybe." But he came up to the window and stood beside me, looking out. "What a warm voice," he said.

> ## The music seemed to soothe a poison out of them.

They were singing *If I could only hear my mother pray again!*

"Yes," I said, "and she can sure beat that tambourine."   190

"But what a terrible song," he said, and laughed. He dropped his notebook on the sofa and disappeared into the kitchen. "Where's Isabel and the kids?"

"I think they went to see their grandparents. You hungry?"

"No." He came back into the living room with his can of beer. "You want to come some place with me tonight?"

I sensed, I don't know how, that I couldn't possibly say no. "Sure. Where?"

He sat down on the sofa and   195 picked up his notebook and started leafing through it. "I'm going to sit in with some fellows in a joint in the Village."

"You mean, you're going to play, tonight?"

"That's right." He took a swallow of his beer and moved back to the window. He gave me a sidelong look. "If you can stand it."

"I'll try," I said.

He smiled to himself and we both watched as the meeting across the way broke up. The three sisters and the brother, heads bowed, were singing *God be with you till we meet again.* The faces around them were very quiet. Then the song ended. The small crowd dispersed. We watched the three women and the lone man walk slowly up the avenue.

"When she was singing before," said Sonny, abruptly,   200 "her voice reminded me for a minute of what heroin feels like sometimes—when it's in your veins. It makes you feel sort of warm and cool at the same time. And distant. And—and sure." He sipped his beer, very deliberately not looking at me. I watched his face. "It makes you feel—in control. Sometimes you've got to have that feeling."

"Do you?" I sat down slowly in the easy chair.

"Sometimes." He went to the sofa and picked up his notebook again. "Some people do."

"In order," I asked, "to play?" And my voice was very ugly, full of contempt and anger.

"Well"—he looked at me with great, troubled eyes, as though, in fact, he hoped his eyes would tell me things he could never otherwise say—"they *think* so. And *if* they think so—!"

"And what do *you* think?" I asked.   205

He sat on the sofa and put his can of beer on the floor. "I don't know," he said, and I couldn't be sure if he were answering my question or pursuing his thoughts. His face didn't tell me. "It's not so much to *play*. It's to *stand* it, to be able to make it at all. On any level." He frowned and smiled: "In order to keep from shaking to pieces."

"But these friends of yours," I said, "they seem to shake themselves to pieces pretty goddamn fast."

"Maybe." He played with the notebook. And something told me that I should curb my tongue, that Sonny was doing his best to talk, that I should listen. "But of course you only know the ones that've gone to pieces. Some don't—or at least they haven't *yet* and that's just about all *any* of us can say." He paused. "And then there are some who just live, really, in hell, and they know it and they see what's happening and they go right on. I don't know." He sighed, dropped the notebook, folded his arms. "Some guys, you can tell from the way they play, they on something *all* the time. And you can see that, well, it makes something real for them. But of course," he picked up his beer from the floor and sipped it and put the can down again, "they *want* to, too, you've got to see that. Even some of them that say they don't—*some*, not all."

"And what about you?" I asked—I couldn't help it. "What about you? Do *you* want to?"

210 He stood up and walked to the window and remained silent for a long time. Then he sighed. "Me," he said. Then: "While I was downstairs before, on my way here, listening to that woman sing, it struck me all of a sudden how much suffering she must have had to go through—to sing like that. It's *repulsive* to think you have to suffer that much."

I said: "But there's no way not to suffer—is there, Sonny?"

"I believe not," he said and smiled, "but that's never stopped anyone from trying." He looked at me. "Has it?" I realized, with this mocking look, that there stood between us, forever, beyond the power of time or forgiveness, the fact that I had held silence—so long!—when he had needed human speech to help him. He turned back to the window. "No, there's no way not to suffer. But you try all kinds of ways to keep from drowning in it, to keep on top of it, and to make it seem—well, like *you*. Like you did something, all right, and now you're suffering for it. You know?" I said nothing. "Well you know," he said, impatiently, "why *do* people suffer? Maybe it's better to do something to give it a reason, *any* reason."

"But we just agreed," I said, "that there's no way not to suffer. Isn't it better, then, just to—take it?"

"But nobody just takes it," Sonny cried, "that's what I'm telling you! *Everybody* tries not to. You're just hung up on the *way* some people try—it's not *your* way!"

The hair on my face began to itch, my face felt wet. 215 "That's not true," I said, "that's not true. I don't give a damn what other people do, I don't even care how they suffer. I just care how *you* suffer." And he looked at me. "Please believe me," I said, "I don't want to see you—die—trying not to suffer."

"I won't," he said, flatly, "die trying not to suffer. At least, not any faster than anybody else."

"But there's no need," I said, trying to laugh, "is there? in killing yourself."

I wanted to say more, but I couldn't. I wanted to talk about will power and how life could be—well, beautiful. I wanted to say that it was all within; but was it? or, rather, wasn't that exactly the trouble? And I wanted to promise that I would never fail him again. But it would all have sounded—empty words and lies. So I made the promise to myself and prayed that I would keep it.

"It's terrible sometimes, inside," he said, "that's what's the trouble. You walk these streets, black and funky and cold, and there's not really a living ass to talk to, and there's nothing shaking, and there's no way of getting it out—that storm inside. You can't talk it and you can't make love with it, and when you finally try to get with it and play it, you realize *nobody's* listening. So *you've* got to listen. You got to find a way to listen."

And then he walked away from the window and sat on 220 the sofa again, as though all the wind had suddenly been knocked out of him. "Sometimes you'll do *anything* to play, even cut your mother's throat." He laughed and looked at me. "Or your brother's." Then he sobered. "Or your own." Then: "Don't worry. I'm all right now and I think I'll *be* all right. But I can't forget—where I've been. I don't mean just the physical place I've been, I mean where I've *been*. And *what* I've been."

"What have you been, Sonny?" I asked.

He smiled—but sat sideways on the sofa, his elbow resting on the back, his fingers playing with his mouth and chin, not looking at me. "I've been something I didn't recognize, didn't know I could be. Didn't know anybody could be." He

> "Please believe me," I said, "I don't want to see you—die—trying not to suffer."

stopped, looking inward, looking helplessly young, looking old. "I'm not talking about it now because I feel *guilty* or anything like that—maybe it would be better if I did, I don't know. Anyway, I can't really talk about it. Not to you, not to anybody," and now he turned and faced me. "Sometimes, you know, and it was actually when I was most *out* of the world, I felt that I was in it, that I was *with* it, really, and I could play or I didn't really have to *play*, it just came out of me, it was there. And I don't know how I played, thinking about it now, but I know I did awful things, those times, sometimes, to people. Or it wasn't that I *did* anything to them—it was that they weren't real." He picked up the beer can; it was empty; he rolled it between his palms: "And other times—well, I needed a fix, I needed to find a place to lean, I needed to clear a space to *listen*—and I couldn't find it, and I—went crazy, I did terrible things to *me*, I was terrible *for* me." He began pressing the beer can between his hands, I watched the metal begin to give. It glittered, as he played with it, like a knife, and I was afraid he would cut himself, but I said nothing. "Oh well. I can never tell you. I was all by myself at the bottom of something, stinking and sweating and crying and shaking, and I smelled it, you know? *my* stink, and I thought I'd die if I couldn't get away from it and yet, all the same, I knew that everything I was doing was just locking me in with it. And I didn't know," he paused, still flattening the beer can, "I didn't know, I still *don't* know, something kept telling me that maybe it was good to smell your own stink, but I didn't think that *that* was what I'd been trying to do—and—who can stand it?" and he abruptly dropped the ruined beer can, looking at me with a small, still smile, and then rose, walking to the window as though it were the lodestone rock. I watched his face, he watched the avenue. "I couldn't tell you when Mama died—but the reason I wanted to leave Harlem so bad was to get away from drugs. And then, when I ran away, that's what I was running from—really. When I came back, nothing had changed, *I* hadn't changed, I was just—older." And he stopped, drumming with his fingers on the windowpane. The sun had vanished, soon darkness would fall. I watched his face. "It can come again," he said, almost as though speaking to himself. Then he turned to me. "It can come again," he repeated. "I just want you to know that."

"All right," I said, at last. "So it can come again. All right."

> "It can come again," he repeated. "I just want you to know that."

He smiled, but the smile was sorrowful. "I had to try to tell you," he said.

"Yes," I said. "I understand that." **225**

"You're my brother," he said, looking straight at me, and not smiling at all.

"Yes," I repeated, "yes. I understand that."

He turned back to the window, looking out. "All that hatred down there," he said, "all that hatred and misery and love. It's a wonder it doesn't blow the avenue apart."

WE went to the only nightclub on a short, dark street, downtown. We squeezed through the narrow, chattering, jam-packed bar to the entrance of the big room, where the bandstand was. And we stood there for a moment, for the lights were very dim in this room and we couldn't see. Then, "Hello, boy," said a voice and an enormous black man, much older than Sonny or myself, erupted out of all that atmospheric lighting and put an arm around Sonny's shoulder. "I been sitting right here," he said, "waiting for you."

He had a big voice, too, and heads in the darkness **230** turned toward us.

Sonny grinned and pulled a little away, and said, "Creole, this is my brother. I told you about him."

Creole shook my hand. "I'm glad to meet you, son," he said, and it was clear that he was glad to meet me *there*, for Sonny's sake. And he smiled, "You got a real musician in *your* family," and he took his arm from Sonny's shoulder and slapped him, lightly, affectionately, with the back of his hand.

"Well. Now I've heard it all," said a voice behind us. This was another musician, and a friend of Sonny's, a coal-black, cheerful-looking man, built close to the ground. He immediately began confiding to me, at the top of his lungs, the most terrible things about Sonny, his teeth gleaming like a lighthouse and his laugh coming up out of him like the beginning of an earthquake. And it turned out that everyone at the bar knew Sonny, or almost everyone; some were musicians, working there, or nearby, or not working, some were simply hangers-on, and some were there to hear Sonny play. I was introduced to all of them and they were all very polite to me. Yet, it was clear that, for them, I was only Sonny's brother. Here, I was in Sonny's world. Or, rather: his kingdom. Here, it was not even a question that his veins bore royal blood.

They were going to play soon and Creole installed me, by myself, at a table in a dark corner. Then I watched them, Creole, and the little black man, and Sonny, and the others, while they horsed around, standing just below the bandstand. The light from the bandstand spilled just a little short of them and, watching them laughing and gesturing and moving about, I had the feeling that they, nevertheless, were being most careful not to step into that circle of light too suddenly: that if they moved into the light too suddenly, without thinking, they would perish in flame. Then, while I watched, one of them, the small, black man, moved into the light and crossed the bandstand and started fooling around with his drums. Then—being funny and being, also, extremely ceremonious—Creole took Sonny by the arm and led him to the piano. A woman's voice called Sonny's name and a few hands started clapping. And Sonny, also being funny and being ceremonious, and so touched, I think, that he could have cried, but neither hiding it nor showing it, riding it like a man, grinned, and put both hands to his heart and bowed from the waist.

235 Creole then went to the bass fiddle and a lean, very bright-skinned brown man jumped up on the bandstand and picked up his horn. So there they were, and the atmosphere on the bandstand and in the room began to change and tighten. Someone stepped up to the microphone and announced them. Then there were all kinds of murmurs. Some people at the bar shushed others. The waitress ran around, frantically getting in the last orders, guys and chicks got closer to each other, and the lights on the bandstand, on the quartet, turned to a kind of indigo. Then they all looked different there. Creole looked about him for the last time, as though he were making certain that all his chickens were in the coop, and then he—jumped and struck the fiddle. And there they were.

All I know about music is that not many people ever really hear it. And even then, on the rare occasions when something opens within, and the music enters, what we mainly hear, or hear cor-

> ## Here, it was not even a question that his veins bore royal blood.

roborated, are personal, private, vanishing evocations. But the man who creates the music is hearing something else, is dealing with the roar rising from the void and imposing order on it as it hits the air. What is evoked in him, then, is of another order, more terrible because it has no words, and triumphant, too, for that same reason. And his triumph, when he triumphs, is ours. I just watched Sonny's face. His face was troubled, he was working hard, but he wasn't with it. And I had the feeling that, in a way, everyone on the bandstand was waiting for him, both waiting for him and pushing him along. But as I began to watch Creole, I realized that it was Creole who held them all back. He had them on a short rein. Up there, keeping the beat with his whole body, wailing on the fiddle, with his eyes half closed, he was listening to everything, but he was listening to Sonny. He was having a dialogue with Sonny. He wanted Sonny to leave the shoreline and strike out for the deep water. He was Sonny's witness that deep water and drowning were not the same thing—he had been there, and he knew. And he wanted Sonny to know. He was waiting for Sonny to do the things on the keys which would let Creole know that Sonny was in the water.

And, while Creole listened, Sonny moved, deep within, exactly like someone in torment. I had never before thought of how awful the relationship must be between the musician and his instrument. He has to fill it, this instrument, with the breath of life, his own. He has to make it do what he wants it to do. And a piano is just a piano. It's made out of so much wood and wires and little hammers and big ones, and ivory. While there's only so much you can do with it, the only way to find this out is to try; to try and make it do everything.

And Sonny hadn't been near a piano for over a year. And he wasn't on much better terms with his life, not the life that stretched before him now. He and the piano stammered, started one way, got scared, stopped; started another way, panicked, marked time, started again; then seemed to have found a direction, panicked again, got stuck. And the face I saw on Sonny I'd never seen before. Everything had been burned out of it, and, at the same time, things usually hidden were being burned in, by the fire and fury of the battle which was occurring in him up there.

Yet, watching Creole's face as they neared the end of the first set, I had the feeling that something had happened, something I hadn't heard. Then they finished, there was scattered applause, and then, without an instant's warning, Creole started into something else, it was almost sardonic, it was *Am I Blue*. And, as though he commanded, Sonny began to play. Something began to happen. And Creole let out the reins. The dry, low, black man said something awful on the drums, Creole answered, and the drums talked back. Then the horn insisted, sweet and high, slightly detached perhaps, and Creole listened, commenting now and then, dry, and driving, beautiful and calm and old. Then they all came together again, and Sonny was part of the family again. I could tell this from his face. He seemed to have found, right there beneath his fingers, a damn brand-new piano. It seemed that he couldn't get over it. Then, for awhile, just being happy with Sonny, they seemed to be agreeing with him that brand-new pianos certainly were a gas.

Then Creole stepped forward to remind them that what they were playing was the blues. He hit something in all of them, he hit something in me, myself, and the music tightened and deepened, apprehension began to beat the air. Creole began to tell us what the blues were all about. They were not about anything very new. He and his boys up there were keeping it new, at the risk of ruin, destruction, madness, and death, in order to find new ways to make us listen. For, while the tale of how we suffer, and how we are delighted, and how we may triumph is never new, it always must be heard. There isn't any other tale to tell, it's the only light we've got in all this darkness.

And this tale, according to that face, that body, those strong hands on those strings, has another aspect in every country, and a new depth in every generation. Listen, Creole seemed to be saying, listen. Now these are Sonny's blues. He made the little black man on the drums know it, and the bright, brown man on the horn. Creole wasn't trying any

> **He was Sonny's witness that deep** water and drowning were not the same thing—he had been there, and he knew.

longer to get Sonny in the water. He was wishing him Godspeed. Then he stepped back, very slowly, filling the air with the immense suggestion that Sonny speak for himself.

Then they all gathered around Sonny and Sonny played. Every now and again one of them seemed to say, amen. Sonny's fingers filled the air with life, his life. But that life contained so many others. And Sonny went all the way back, he really began with the spare, flat statement of the opening phrase of the song. Then he began to make it his. It was very beautiful because it wasn't hurried and it was no longer a lament. I seemed to hear with what burning he had made it his, with what burning we had yet to make it ours, how we could cease lamenting. Freedom lurked around us and I understood, at last, that he could help us to be free if we would listen, that he would never be free until we did. Yet, there was no battle in his face now. I heard what he had gone through, and would continue to go through until he came to rest in earth. He had made it his: that long line, of which we knew only Mama and Daddy. And he was giving it back, as everything must be given back, so that, passing through death, it can live forever. I saw my mother's face again, and felt, for the first time, how the stones of the road she had walked on must have bruised her feet. I saw the moonlit road where my father's brother died. And it brought something else back to me, and carried me past it. I saw my little girl again and felt Isabel's tears again, and I felt my own tears begin to rise. And I was yet aware that this was only a moment, that the world waited outside, as hungry as a tiger, and that trouble stretched above us, longer than the sky.

Then it was over. Creole and Sonny let out their breath, both soaking wet, and grinning. There was a lot of applause and some of it was real. In the dark, the girl came by and I asked her to take drinks to the bandstand. There was a long pause, while they talked up there in the indigo light and after awhile I saw the girl put a Scotch and milk on top of the piano for Sonny. He didn't seem to notice it, but just before they started playing again, he sipped from it and looked toward me, and nodded. Then he put it back on top of the piano. For me, then, as they began to play again, it glowed and shook above my brother's head like the very cup of trembling.

240

IF YOU LIKED "SONNY'S BLUES," YOU MIGHT ALSO LIKE . . .

. . . Richard Wright's "The Man Who Was Almost a Man" (Chapter 8) and Ralph Ellison's "Battle Royal" (Chapter 15). Baldwin's predecessor Richard Wright, the author of *Native Son, Uncle Tom's Children,* and *Eight Men,* is one of the most important writers of the twentieth century. Both Wright and Baldwin fled America and settled in France. Wright also nurtured Ralph Ellison and his work, and Ellison's "Battle Royal" is one of the opening scenes in his award-winning novel *Invisible Man.*

GOING FURTHER   Another major black novelist and story writer worth considering in relation to James Baldwin is John Edgar Wideman, particularly his novel *Sent for You Yesterday.*

Writing from Reading

Summarize

1 Make a timeline of the scenes and conversations in "Sonny's Blues." Identify details that are presented out of chronological order. Why do you think James Baldwin chose to tell the story in the order that he used?

2 Summarize the "conversation" between the instruments at the end of the story.

Analyze Craft

3 Roughly when is the story set? What details does the narrator provide to bring you into this particular time period? How would the story change if it took place today?

4 The narrator provides details about Sonny's character, but he tells readers little about himself. What do we know about the narrator based on his actions in the story? In what ways does he differ from Sonny? In what ways is he the same?

Analyze Voice

5 Compare and contrast the narrative voice with the narrator's actual speech in dialogue. Why do you think James Baldwin chose not to write the entire story in the narrator's spoken voice?

Synthesize Summary and Analysis

6 Describe the characteristics of the narrative voice.

7 The teller of this tale relates it after the events have occurred and he has reconciled with Sonny. How would the tone of the story change if the narrator were telling the story in present tense, as the events occur? What details would be left out? Which details might be expanded upon?

8 The narrator witnesses two musical events during the story: the revival and Sonny's performance. Compare the reaction of the crowd during the revival to the narrator's reaction to Sonny's music. What is the effect of including these two different musical experiences?

Interpret the Story

9 What understanding does the narrator reach at the end of the story? What does the narrator suggest by saying that only some of the applause was "real"?

Katherine Mansfield (1888–1923)

Katherine Mansfield, one of the finest practitioners of the modern short story in English, was born Kathleen Mansfield Beauchamp in Wellington, New Zealand. As an adolescent she traveled to England to study and eventually left New Zealand permanently to make a life in bohemian literary circles in London and Europe. Her short stories, influenced by Chekhov but glowing with a mastery all their own, won her both the praise and the envy of such modernist writers as Virginia Woolf. She died too young to leave behind a major body of work, but her eye for detail and sense of nuanced emotion have assured her a place in the circle of important writers of the twentieth century.

AS YOU READ   Underline the sentences that seem to be in Miss Brill's voice, even though they are part of the narration and not given in quotation marks. How would you describe the tone of these inner exclamations? What impression do you get of Miss Brill from the things she "says" to herself?

Miss Brill (1920)

1 ALTHOUGH it was so brilliantly fine—the blue sky powdered with gold and great spots of light like white wine splashed over the Jardins Publiques—Miss Brill was glad that she had decided on her fur. The air was motionless, but when you opened your mouth there was just a faint chill, like a chill from a glass of iced water before you sip, and now and again a leaf came drifting—from nowhere, from the sky. Miss Brill put up her hand and touched her fur. Dear little thing! It was nice to feel it again. She had taken it out of its box that afternoon, shaken out the moth powder, given it a good brush, and rubbed the life back into the dim little eyes. "What has been happening to me?" said the sad little eyes. Oh, how sweet it was to see them snap at her again from the red eiderdown! . . . But the nose, which was of some black composition, wasn't at all firm. It must have had a knock, somehow. Never mind—a little dab of black sealing-wax when the time came—when it was absolutely necessary . . . Little rogue! Yes, she really felt like that about it. Little rogue biting its tail just by her left ear. She could have taken it off and laid it on her lap and stroked it. She felt a tingling in her hands and arms, but that came from walking, she supposed. And when she breathed, something light and sad—no, not sad, exactly—something gentle seemed to move in her bosom.

There were a number of people out this afternoon, far more than last Sunday. And the band sounded louder and gayer. That was because the Season had begun. For although the band played all the year round on Sundays, out of season it was never the same. It was like some one playing with only the family to listen; it didn't care how it played if there weren't any strangers present. Wasn't the conductor wearing a new coat, too? She was sure it was new. He scraped with his foot and flapped his arms like a rooster about to crow, and the bandsmen sitting in the green rotunda blew out their cheeks and glared at the music. Now there came a little "flutey" bit—very pretty!—a little chain of bright drops. She was sure it would be repeated. It was; she lifted her head and smiled.

Only two people shared her "special" seat: a fine old man in a velvet coat, his hands clasped over a huge carved walking-stick, and a big old woman, sitting upright, with a roll of knitting on her embroidered apron. They did not speak. This was disappointing, for Miss Brill always looked forward to the conversation. She had become really quite expert, she thought, at listening as though she didn't listen, at sitting in other people's lives just for a minute while they talked round her.

> Never mind, there was always the crowd to watch.

She glanced, sideways, at the old couple. Perhaps they would go soon. Last Sunday, too, hadn't been as interesting as usual. An Englishman and his wife, he wearing a dreadful Panama hat and she button boots. And she'd gone on the whole time about how she ought to wear spectacles; she knew she needed them; but that it was no good getting any; they'd be sure to break and they'd never keep on. And he'd been so patient. He'd suggested everything—gold rims, the kind that curve round your ears, little pads inside the bridge. No, nothing would please her. "They'll always be sliding down my nose!" Miss Brill had wanted to shake her.

5 The old people sat on the bench, still as statues. Never mind, there was always the crowd to watch. To and fro, in front of the flower beds and the band rotunda, the couples and groups paraded, stopped to talk, to greet, to buy a handful of flowers from the old beggar who had his tray fixed to the railings. Little children ran among them, swooping and laughing; little boys with big white silk bows under their chins, little girls, little French dolls, dressed up in velvet and lace. And sometimes a tiny staggerer came suddenly rocking into the open from under the trees, stopped, stared, as suddenly sat down "flop," until its small high-stepping mother, like a young hen, rushed scolding to its rescue. Other people sat on the benches and green chairs, but they were nearly always the same, Sun-

day after Sunday, and—Miss Brill had often noticed—there was something funny about nearly all of them. They were odd, silent, nearly all old, and from the way they stared they looked as though they'd just come from dark little rooms or even—even cupboards!

Behind the rotunda the slender trees with yellow leaves down drooping, and through them just a line of sea, and beyond the blue sky with gold-veined clouds.

Tum-tum-tum tiddle-um! tiddle-um! tum tiddley-um tum ta! blew the band.

Two young girls in red came by and two young soldiers in blue met them, and they laughed and paired and went off arm-in-arm. Two peasant women with funny straw hats passed, gravely, leading beautiful smoke-colored donkeys. A cold, pale nun hurried by. A beautiful woman came along and dropped her bunch of violets, and a little boy ran after to hand them to her, and she took them and threw them away as if they'd been poisoned. Dear me! Miss Brill didn't know whether to admire that or not! And now an ermine toque and a gentleman in gray met just in front of her. He was tall, stiff, dignified, and she was wearing the ermine toque she'd bought when her hair was yellow. Now everything, her hair, her face, even her eyes, was the same color as the shabby ermine, and her hand, in its cleaned glove, lifted to dab her lips, was a tiny yellowish paw. Oh, she was so pleased to see him—delighted! She rather thought they were going to meet that afternoon. She described where she'd been—everywhere, here, there, along by the sea. The day was so charming—didn't he agree? And wouldn't he, perhaps? . . . But he shook his head, lighted a cigarette, slowly breathed a great deep puff into her face, and, even while she was still talking and laughing, flicked the match away and walked on. The ermine toque was alone; she smiled more brightly than ever. But even the band seemed to know what she was feeling and played more softly, played tenderly, and the drum beat, "The Brute! The Brute!" over and over. What would she do? What was going to happen now? But as Miss Brill wondered, the ermine toque turned, raised her hand as though she'd seen some one else, much nicer, just over there, and pattered away. And the band changed again and played more quickly, more gayly than ever, and the old couple on Miss Brill's seat got up and marched away, and such a funny old man with long whiskers hobbled along in time to the music and was nearly knocked over by four girls walking abreast.

Oh, how fascinating it was! How she enjoyed it! How she loved sitting here, watching it all! It was like a play. It was exactly like a play. Who could believe the sky at the back wasn't painted? But it wasn't till a little brown dog trotted on solemn and then slowly trotted off, like a little "theater" dog, a little dog that had been drugged, that Miss Brill discovered what it was that made it so exciting. They were all on stage. They weren't only the audience, not only looking on; they were acting. Even she had a part and came every Sunday. No doubt somebody would have noticed if she hadn't been there; she was part of the performance after all. How strange she'd never thought of it like that before! And yet it explained why she made such a point of starting from home at just the same time each week—so as not to be late for the performance—and it also explained why she had quite a queer, shy feeling at telling her English pupils how she spent her Sunday afternoons. No wonder! Miss Brill nearly laughed out loud. She was on the stage. She thought of the old invalid gentleman to whom she read the newspaper four afternoons a week while he slept in the garden. She had got quite used to the frail head on the cotton pillow, the hollowed eyes, the open mouth and the high pinched nose. If he'd been dead he mightn't have noticed for weeks; she wouldn't have minded. But suddenly he knew he was having the paper read to him by an actress! "An actress!" The old head lifted; two points of light quivered in the old eyes. "An actress—are ye?" And Miss Brill smoothed the newspaper as though it were the manuscript of her part and said gently: "Yes, I have been an actress for a long time."

10   The band had been having a rest. Now they started again. And what they played was warm, sunny, yet there was just a faint chill—a something, what was it?—not sadness—no, not sadness—a something that made you want to sing. The tune lifted, lifted, the light shone; and it seemed to Miss Brill that in another moment all of them, all the whole company, would begin singing. The young ones, the laughing ones who were moving together, they would begin, and the men's voices, very resolute and brave, would join them. And then she too, she too, and the others on the benches—they would come in with a kind of accompaniment—something low, that scarcely rose or fell, something so beautiful—moving . . . And Miss Brill's eyes filled with tears and she looked smiling at all the other members of the company. Yes, we understand, we understand, she thought—though what they understood she didn't know.

Just at that moment a boy and girl came and sat down where the old couple had been. They were beautifully dressed; they were in love. The hero and heroine, of course, just arrived from his father's yacht. And still soundlessly singing, still with that trembling smile, Miss Brill prepared to listen.

"No, not now," said the girl. "Not here, I can't."

"But why? Because of that stupid old thing at the end there?" asked the boy. "Why does she come here at all—who wants her? Why doesn't she keep her silly old mug at home?"

"It's her fu-fur which is so funny," giggled the girl. "It's exactly like a fried whiting."

"Ah, be off with you!" said the boy in an angry whisper.   15
Then: "Tell me, ma petite chère—"

"No, not here," said the girl. "Not yet."

On her way home she usually bought a slice of honeycake at the baker's. It was her Sunday treat. Sometimes there was an almond in her slice, sometimes not. It made a great difference. If there was an almond it was like carrying home a tiny present—a surprise—something that might very well not have been there. She hurried on the almond Sundays and struck the match for the kettle in quite a dashing way.

But today she passed the baker's by, climbed the stairs, went into the little dark room—her room like a cupboard—and sat down on the red eiderdown. She sat there for a long time. The box that the fur came out of was on the bed. She unclasped the necklet quickly; quickly, without looking, laid it inside. But when she put the lid on she thought she heard something crying.

> They were all on stage.
> They weren't only the audience;
> they were acting.

IF YOU LIKED "MISS BRILL," YOU MIGHT ALSO LIKE . . .

. . . the next story in this chapter, Katherine Anne Porter's "The Jilting of Granny Weatherall." You might ask yourself how Mansfield's drawing of character compares with Porter's.

GOING FURTHER   You may want to read Mansfield's work alongside the dark psychological portraits, in *Mrs. Dalloway* or *To the Lighthouse,* by her contemporary, Virginia Woolf.

Writing from Reading

Summarize

1 Describe what you know about Miss Brill: her age, occupation, etc. Which details, if any, are explicitly stated in the story and which must you infer?

2 Describe Miss Brill's Sunday routine. What, if anything, does she do differently on the day the story takes place?

Analyze Craft

3 How does the success of the story stand or fall on the depiction of this singular character?

4 Note descriptions of the band's performance, particularly when the instruments "speak." How does Mansfield use the sound of the music to influence the tone of the story?

Analyze Voice

5 From what point of view is the story written? How would the story differ if it were told in first person by Miss Brill? How would the story differ if told from the perspective of someone else observing Miss Brill?

Synthesize Summary and Analysis

6 Is Miss Brill a static or a dynamic character? Do you think she will return the following Sunday to play her "role"? Why or why not?

Interpret the Story

7 In her reverie, Miss Brill sees the entire company of observers rise to sing, and thinks to herself, "Yes, we understand"; but the narrator informs us, "what they understood she didn't know." What is it that the other observers understand? Has Miss Brill come to this same understanding at the end of the story?

Katherine Anne Porter (1890–1980)

Callie Porter, a girl who grew up motherless and in extreme poverty, was destined to become Katherine Anne Porter, a writer, traveler, and woman of expensive tastes who changed her name after divorcing her first of four husbands. An independent woman with an active interest in life and politics, Porter worked on and off as a journalist, essayist, and book reviewer in a range of places, including Colorado, New York, Washington, D.C., and Mexico. Her work, although not voluminous, is known for its intensity of emotion and its refined and meticulously crafted prose. In her fiction, the personal becomes universal, because her stories are based on her own experiences. Although she lived to age ninety, her zest for life and her perfectionist approach to completing a story hindered her output. She published four collections of short stories—including *Flowering Judas* (1935) and *Pale Horse, Pale Rider* (1939)—and one novel, *Ship of Fools* (1962). Her work was much celebrated in her lifetime, and she won the Pulitzer Prize and the National Book Award in 1966 for her collected stories.

AS YOU READ   Notice the way you're drawn into the thoughts of the main character. Notice how her thoughts move back and forth through time, in and out of the present. How well do you get to know her as a result of being allowed to enter the privacy of her mind?

TIP

FOR INTERACTIVE READING . . .

Note when Granny Weatherall is experiencing events from the past. Using your notes, describe Granny as a young woman. Do the events you've identified explain how she's become the woman in the story's present?

The Jilting of Granny Weatherall (1930)

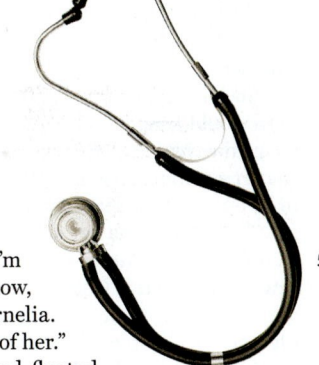

1   SHE flicked her wrist neatly out of Doctor Harry's pudgy careful fingers and pulled the sheet up to her chin. The brat ought to be in knee breeches. Doctoring around the country with spectacles on his nose! "Get along now, take your schoolbooks and go. There's nothing wrong with me."

Doctor Harry spread a warm paw like a cushion on her forehead where the forked green vein danced and made her eyelids twitch. "Now, now, be a good girl, and we'll have you up in no time."

"That's no way to speak to a woman nearly eighty years old just because she's down. I'd have you respect your elders, young man."

"Well, Missy, excuse me." Doctor Harry patted her cheek. "But I've got to warn you, haven't I? You're a marvel, but you must be careful or you're going to be good and sorry."

"Don't tell me what I'm going to be. I'm on my feet now, morally speaking. It's Cornelia. I had to go to bed to get rid of her."

Her bones felt loose, and floated around in her skin, and Doctor Harry floated like a balloon around the foot of the bed. He floated and pulled down his waistcoat and swung his glasses on a cord. "Well, stay where you are, it certainly can't hurt you."

"Get along and doctor your sick," said Granny Weatherall. "Leave a well woman alone. I'll call for you when I want you. . . . Where were you forty years ago when I pulled through milk- leg and double pneumonia? You weren't even born. Don't let Cornelia lead you on," she shouted, because Doctor Harry appeared to float up to the ceiling and out.

"I pay my own bills, and I don't throw my money away on nonsense!"

She meant to wave good-by, but it was too much trouble. Her eyes closed of themselves, it was like a dark curtain drawn around the bed. The pillow rose and floated under her, pleasant as a hammock in a light wind. She listened to the leaves rustling outside the window. No, somebody was swishing newspapers: no, Cornelia and Doctor Harry were whispering together. She leaped broad awake, thinking they whispered in her ear.

"She was never like this, *never* like this!" "Well, what can we expect?" "Yes, eighty years old. . . ."

10 Well, and what if she was? She still had ears. It was like Cornelia to whisper around doors. She always kept things secret in such a public way. She was always being tactful and kind. Cornelia was dutiful; that was the trouble with her. Dutiful and good: "So good and dutiful," said Granny, "that I'd like to spank her." She saw herself spanking Cornelia and making a fine job of it.

"What'd you say, Mother?"

Granny felt her face tying up in hard knots.

"Can't a body think, I'd like to know?"

"I thought you might want something."

15 "I do. I want a lot of things. First off, go away and don't whisper."

She lay and drowsed, hoping in her sleep that the children would keep out and let her rest a minute. It had been a long day. Not that she was tired. It was always pleasant to snatch a minute now and then. There was always so much to be done, let me see: tomorrow.

Tomorrow was far away and there was nothing to trouble about. Things were finished somehow when the time came; thank God there was always a little margin over for peace: then a person could spread out the plan of life and tuck in the edges orderly. It was good to have everything clean and folded away, with the hair brushes and tonic bottles sitting straight on the white, embroidered linen: the day started without fuss and the pantry shelves laid out with rows of jelly glasses and brown jugs and white stone-china jars with blue whirligigs and words painted on them: coffee, tea, sugar, ginger, cinnamon, allspice: and the bronze clock with the lion on top nicely dusted off. The dust that lion could collect in twenty-four hours! The box in the attic with all those letters tied up, well, she'd have to go through that tomorrow. All those letters—George's letters and John's letters and her letters to them both—lying around for the children to find afterwards made her un-

easy. Yes, that would be tomorrow's business. No use to let them know how silly she had been once.

While she was rummaging around she found death in her mind and it felt clammy and unfamiliar. She had spent so much time preparing for death there was no need for bringing it up again. Let it take care of itself now. When she was sixty she had felt very old, finished, and went around making farewell trips to see her children and grandchildren, with a secret in her mind: This is the very last of your mother, children! Then she made her will and came down with a long fever. That was all just a notion like a lot of other things, but it was lucky too, for she had once for all got over the idea of dying for a long time. Now she couldn't be worried. She hoped she had better sense now. Her father had lived to be one hundred and two years old and had drunk a noggin of strong hot toddy on his last birthday. He told the reporters it was his daily habit, and he owed his long life to that. He had made quite a scandal and was very pleased about it. She believed she'd just plague Cornelia a little.

"Cornelia! Cornelia!" No footsteps, but a sudden hand on her cheek. "Bless you, where have you been?"

"Here, Mother." 20

"Well, Cornelia, I want a noggin of hot toddy."

"Are you cold, darling?"

"I'm chilly, Cornelia. Lying in bed stops the circulation. I must have told you that a thousand times."

Well, she could just hear Cornelia telling her husband that Mother was getting a little childish and they'd have to humor her. The thing that most annoyed her was that Cornelia thought she was deaf, dumb, and blind. Little hasty glances and tiny gestures tossed around her and over her head saying, "Don't cross her, let her have her way, she's eighty years old," and she sitting there as if she lived in a thin glass cage. Sometimes Granny almost made up her mind to pack up and move back to her own house where nobody could remind her every minute that she was old. Wait, wait, Cornelia, till your own children whisper behind your back!

In her day she had kept a better house and had got 25 more work done. She wasn't too old yet for Lydia to be driving eighty miles for advice when one of the children jumped the track, and Jimmy still dropped in and talked things over: "Now, Mammy, you've a good business head, I want to know what you think of this? . . ." Old. Cornelia couldn't change the furniture around without asking. Little things, little things! They had been so sweet when they were little. Granny wished the old days were back again with the children young and everything to be done over. It had been a hard pull, but not too much for her. When she thought of all the food she had cooked, and all the clothes she had cut and sewed, and all the gardens she had made—well, the children showed it. There they were, made out of her, and they couldn't get away from that. Sometimes she wanted to see John again and point to them and say, Well, I didn't do so badly, did I? But that would have to wait. That was for tomorrow. She used to think of him as a man, but now all the children were older than their father, and he would be a child beside her if she saw him now. It seemed strange and there was something wrong in the idea. Why, he couldn't possibly recognize her. She had fenced in a hundred acres once, digging the post holes herself and clamping the wires with just a negro boy to help. That changed a woman. John would be looking for a young woman with the peaked Spanish comb in her hair and the painted fan. Digging post holes changed a woman. Riding country roads in the winter when women had their babies was another thing: sitting up nights with sick horses and sick negroes and sick children and hardly ever losing one. John, I hardly ever lost one of them! John would see that in a minute, that would be something he could understand, she wouldn't have to explain anything!

It made her feel like rolling up her sleeves and putting the whole place to rights again. No matter if Cornelia was determined to be everywhere at once, there were a great many things left undone on this place. She would start tomorrow and do them. It was good to be strong enough for everything, even if all you made melted and changed and slipped under your hands, so that by the time you finished you almost forgot what you were working for. What was it I set out to do? she asked herself intently, but she could not remember. A fog rose over the valley, she saw it marching across the creek swallowing the trees and moving up the hill like an army of ghosts. Soon it would be at the near edge of the orchard, and then it was time to go in and light the lamps. Come in, children, don't stay out in the night air.

Lighting the lamps had been beautiful. The children huddled up to her and breathed like little calves waiting at the bars in the twilight. Their eyes followed the match and watched the flame rise and settle in a blue curve, then they moved away from her. The lamp was lit, they didn't have to be scared and hang on to mother any more. Never, never, never more. God, for all my life, I thank Thee. Without Thee, my God, I could never have done it. Hail, Mary, full of grace.

I want you to pick all the fruit this year and see that nothing is wasted. There's always someone who can use it. Don't let good things rot for want of using. You waste life when you waste good food. Don't let things get lost. It's bitter to lose things. Now, don't let me get to thinking, not when I'm tired and taking a little nap before supper. . . .

The pillow rose about her shoulders and pressed against her heart and the memory was being squeezed out of it: oh, push down the pillow, somebody: it would smother her if she tried to hold it. Such a fresh breeze blowing and such a green day with no threats in it. But he had not come, just the same. What does a woman do when she has put on the white veil and set out the white cake for a man and he doesn't come? She tried to remember. No, I swear he never harmed me but in that. He never harmed me but in that . . . and what if he did? There was the day, the day, but a whirl of dark smoke rose and covered it, crept up and over into the bright field where everything was planted so carefully in orderly rows. That was hell, she knew hell when she saw it. For sixty years she had prayed against remembering him and against losing her soul in the deep pit of hell, and now the two things were mingled in one and the thought of him was a smoky cloud from hell that moved and crept in her head when she had just got rid of Doctor Harry and was trying to rest a minute. Wounded vanity, Ellen, said a sharp voice in the top of her mind. Don't let your wounded vanity get the upper hand of you. Plenty of girls get jilted. You were jilted, weren't you? Then stand up to it. Her eyelids wavered and let in streamers of blue-gray light like tissue paper over her eyes. She must get up and pull the shades down or she'd never sleep. She was in bed again and the shades were not down. How could that happen? Better turn over, hide from the light, sleeping in the light gave you nightmares. "Mother, how do you feel now?" and a stinging wetness on her forehead. But I don't like having my face washed in cold water!

30 Hapsy? George? Lydia? Jimmy? No, Cornelia, and her features were swollen and full of little puddles. "They're coming, darling, they'll all be here soon." Go wash your face, child, you look funny.

Instead of obeying, Cornelia knelt down and put her head on the pillow. She seemed to be talking but there was no sound. "Well, are you tongue-tied? Whose birthday is it? Are you going to give a party?"

Cornelia's mouth moved urgently in strange shapes. "Don't do that, you bother me, daughter."

"Oh, no, Mother. Oh, no . . ."

Nonsense. It was strange about children. They disputed your every word. "No what, Cornelia?"

35 "Here's Doctor Harry."

"I won't see that boy again. He just left five minutes ago."

"That was this morning, Mother. It's night now. Here's the nurse."

"This is Doctor Harry, Mrs. Weatherall. I never saw you look so young and happy!"

"Ah, I'll never be young again—but I'd be happy if they'd let me lie in peace and get rested."

40 She thought she spoke up loudly, but no one answered. A warm weight on her forehead, a warm bracelet on her wrist, and a breeze went on whispering, trying to tell her something. A shuffle of leaves in the everlasting hand of God, He blew on them and they danced and rattled. "Mother, don't mind, we're going to give you a little hypodermic." "Look here, daughter, how do ants get in this bed? I saw sugar ants yesterday." Did you send for Hapsy too?

It was Hapsy she really wanted. She had to go a long way back through a great many rooms to find Hapsy standing with a baby on her arm. She seemed to herself to be Hapsy also, and the baby on Hapsy's arm was Hapsy and himself and herself, all at once, and there was no surprise in the meeting. Then Hapsy melted from within and turned flimsy as gray gauze and the baby was a gauzy shadow, and Hapsy came up close and said, "I thought you'd never come," and looked at her very searchingly and said, "You haven't changed a bit!" They leaned forward to kiss, when Cornelia began whispering from a long way off, "Oh, is there anything you want to tell me? Is there anything I can do for you?"

Yes, she had changed her mind after sixty years and she would like to see George. I want you to find George. Find him and be sure to tell him I forgot him. I want him

to know I had my husband just the same and my children and my house like any other woman. A good house too and a good husband that I loved and fine children out of him. Better than I had hoped for even. Tell him I was given back everything he took away and more. Oh, no, oh, God, no, there was something else besides the house and the man and the children. Oh, surely they were not all? What was it? Something not given back. . . . Her breath crowded down under her ribs and grew into a monstrous frightening shape with cutting edges; it bored up into her head, and the agony was unbelievable: Yes, John, get the Doctor now, no more talk, my time has come.

When this one was born it should be the last. The last. It should have been born first, for it was the one she had truly wanted. Everything came in good time. Nothing left out, left over. She was strong, in three days she would be as well as ever. Better. A woman needed milk in her to have her full health.

"Mother, do you hear me?"

"I've been telling you—"

45 "Mother, Father Connolly's here."

"I went to Holy Communion only last week. Tell him I'm not so sinful as all that."

"Father just wants to speak to you."

He could speak as much as he pleased. It was like him to drop in and inquire about her soul as if it were a teething baby, and then stay on for a cup of tea and a round of cards and gossip. He always had a funny story of some sort, usually about an Irishman who made his little mistakes and confessed them, and the point lay in some absurd thing he would blurt out in the confessional showing his struggles between native piety and original sin. Granny felt easy about her soul. Cornelia, where are your manners? Give Father Connolly a chair. She had her secret comfortable understanding with a few favorite saints who cleared a straight road to God for her. All as surely signed and sealed as the papers for the new Forty Acres. Forever . . . heirs and assigns forever. Since the day the wedding cake was not cut, but thrown out and wasted. The whole bottom dropped out of the world, and there she was blind and sweating with nothing under her feet and the walls falling away. His hand had caught her under the breast, she had not fallen, there was the freshly polished floor with the green rug on it, just as before. He had cursed like a sailor's parrot and said, "I'll kill him for you." Don't lay a hand on him, for my sake leave something to God. "Now, Ellen, you must believe what I tell you. . . ."

Plenty of girls get jilted.

50 So there was nothing, nothing to worry about any more, except sometimes in the night one of the children screamed in a nightmare, and they both hustled out shaking and hunting for the matches and calling, "There, wait a minute, here we are!" John, get the doctor now, Hapsy's time has come. But there was Hapsy standing by the bed in a white cap. "Cornelia, tell Hapsy to take off her cap. I can't see her plain."

Her eyes opened very wide and the room stood out like a picture she had seen somewhere. Dark colors with the shadows rising toward the ceiling in long angles. The tall black dresser gleamed with nothing on it but John's picture, enlarged from a little one, with John's eyes very black when they should have been blue. You never saw him, so how do you know how he looked? But the man insisted the copy was perfect, it was very rich and handsome. For a picture, yes, but it's not my husband. The table by the bed had a linen cover and a candle and a crucifix. The light was blue from Cornelia's silk lamp-shades. No sort of light at all, just frippery. You had to live forty years with kerosene lamps to appreciate honest electricity. She felt very strong and she saw Doctor Harry with a rosy nimbus around him.

"You look like a saint, Doctor Harry, and I vow that's as near as you'll ever come to it."

"She's saying something."

"I heard you Cornelia. What's all this carrying on?"

55 "Father Connolly's saying—"

Cornelia's voice staggered and bumped like a cart in a bad road. It rounded corners and turned back again and arrived nowhere. Granny stepped up in the cart very lightly and reached for the reins, but a man sat beside her and she knew him by his hands, driving the cart. She did not look in his face, for she knew without seeing, but looked instead down the road where the trees leaned over and bowed to each other and a thousand birds were singing a Mass. She felt like singing too, but she put her hand in the bosom of her dress and pulled out a rosary, and Father Connolly murmured Latin in a very solemn voice and tickled her feet. My God, will you stop that nonsense? I'm a married woman. What if he did run away and leave me to face the priest by myself? I found another a whole world better. I wouldn't have exchanged my husband for anybody except St. Michael himself, and you may tell him that for me with a thank you in the bargain.

So, my dear Lord, this is my death and I wasn't even thinking about it.

Light flashed on her closed eyelids, and a deep roaring shook her. Cornelia, is that lightning? I hear thunder. There's going to be a storm. Close all the windows. Call the children in. . . . "Mother, here we are, all of us." "Is that you, Hapsy?" "Oh, no, I'm Lydia. We drove as fast as we could." Their faces drifted above her, drifted away. The rosary fell out of her hands and Lydia put it back. Jimmy tried to help, their hands fumbled together, and Granny closed two fingers around Jimmy's thumb. Beads wouldn't do, it must be something alive. She was so amazed her thoughts ran round and round. So, my dear Lord, this is my death and I wasn't even thinking about it. My children have come to see me die. But I can't, it's not time. Oh, I always hated surprises. I wanted to give Cornelia the amethyst set—Cornelia, you're to have the amethyst set, but Hapsy's to wear it when she wants, and, Doctor Harry, do shut up. Nobody sent for you. Oh, my dear Lord, do wait a minute. I meant to do something about the Forty Acres, Jimmy doesn't need it and Lydia will later on, with that worthless husband of hers. I meant to finish the altar cloth and send six bottles of wine to Sister Borgia for her dyspepsia. I want to send six bottles of wine to Sister Borgia, Father Connolly, now don't let me forget.

Cornelia's voice made short turns and tilted over and crashed. "Oh, Mother, oh, Mother, oh, Mother . . ."

"I'm not going, Cornelia. I'm taken by surprise. I can't go."

You'll see Hapsy again. What about her? "I thought you'd 60 never come." Granny made a long journey outward, looking for Hapsy. What if I don't find her? What then? Her heart sank down and down, there was no bottom to death, she couldn't come to the end of it. The blue light from Cornelia's lampshade drew into a tiny point in the center of her brain, it flickered and winked like an eye, quietly it fluttered and dwindled. Granny lay curled down within herself, amazed and watchful, staring at the point of light that was herself; her body was now only a deeper mass of shadow in an endless darkness and this darkness would curl around the light and swallow it up. God, give a sign!

For the second time there was no sign. Again no bridegroom and the priest in the house. She could not remember any other sorrow because this grief wiped them all away. Oh, no, there's nothing more cruel than this—I'll never forgive it. She stretched herself with a deep breath and blew out the light.

IF YOU LIKED "THE JILTING OF GRANNY WEATHERALL," YOU MIGHT ALSO LIKE . . .

. . . other stories about death—the darkest theme—such as "A Worn Path" by Eudora Welty (Chapter 14).

GOING FURTHER   Porter concentrates a single life into the briefest of times in the Granny Weatherall story, but she has produced a number of variations on the theme of time. In her quasi-allegorical novel *Ship of Fools,* Porter attempts to tell the story of an entire generation of Americans adrift.

Writing from Reading

Summarize

1 How many children did Granny have, and what are their names? Which of them are present in the room with her as she lies on her deathbed?

2 Although the author does not reveal a specific era or place for this story, she provides many details related to setting. Go through the text and find all the details you can that give you a feel for where and when these events occur. Write a paragraph summarizing your findings.

Analyze Craft

3 In revealing Granny's mental/emotional state, Porter sometimes layers past with present or mixes emotional pain with physical pain. Find two examples of this layering and mixing and discuss the effect.

4 How do the minor characters in this story—such as Doctor Harry and Cornelia—add dimension to Granny Weatherall's character? Are these minor characters flat? Support your reasoning with examples from the story.

Analyze Voice

5 How do Porter's use of dialogue and her description of the characters' gestures (particularly Granny's) make the characters seem real?

Synthesize Summary and Analysis

6 "The Jilting of Granny Weatherall" is written from Granny's limited point of view. How does this limited scope affect your understanding of the major and minor characters?

7 Because of Granny's increasing disorientation, you are able to get a snapshot of all the major moments in her life. Put these events in order and consider them as a story of their own. Is Granny a round or a flat character in this underlying plot? Discuss how her character in the past compares with her character in the present.

Interpret the Story

8 At the end of the story, Granny appears finally to become aware of her impending death. Do you believe she's been ignorant of her situation throughout the whole story? Search the story for evidence of Granny's recognition or ignorance, and discuss how her state of awareness affects your understanding of the story's conclusion.

Reading for Character

Does the name or physical appearance of the character reveal anything?

- How is the character dressed, and what does this reveal?
- What does the character look like and does this tell you anything?

What does the actions a character has taken or how the character expresses him or herself tell you about his or her motivation?	• How does the personality the author gives the character reveal what makes a character behave in a certain way? • How does the character's voice, by means of either internal thoughts or dialogue, "sound," and what does this tell you about the character?
Is the character complex—exhibiting both good and bad traits—and able to change?	• That character is a *round, dynamic* character.
Does the main character exhibit traits that are sympathetic but not heroic in the traditional sense?	• That character is likely to be an *antihero*.
Does the character represent primarily one characteristic, such as greed or vanity?	• That character is a *flat, stock* character.
What function do the flat characters play in the story?	• A flat character may function as a *foil* to reveal the hero more clearly.

Writing about Character

1. Write an argument for or against the usefulness of flat secondary characters in fiction; back up your main point with examples from at least two stories in this chapter.

2. "Who's Irish?" is told in first person, whereas "The Jilting of Granny Weatherall" is told in third person. (See Chapter 11 for a discussion of point of view.) How do the two narrators' biases and personalities affect your responses to the other characters and events in the stories?

3. Consider the role of motivation in a story's protagonist as well as in its antagonist. Choose two stories in this chapter and discuss the thoughts, feelings, beliefs, needs, and wants that drive the main characters.

4. Of the characters in the four stories from this chapter, which seems the most real and the roundest to you? Which seems the least real and the flattest? Compare and contrast these two characters, using examples to show what makes your round character round and your flat one flat.

IN late June 1844, after Foster had begun to despair of ever understanding either the fact or the meaning of the disappearance of the river, after a time of ritual cleansing and dreaming, perhaps agoraphobic or maddened by the inter-weaving of literalisms and metaphors and forms of proof, Foster began throwing his manuscripts into the river. According to a Pawnee called Wolf Finger, who spoke with the historian Henry Lake, Foster would go down naked in the afternoon, wade out into the Niobrara and hurl a fistful of pages into the water, or from the shore he would skip a journal across the surface like a stone. Eventually he threw everything he'd ever written down into the Niobrara River, turned the pack mules out with the Pawnee horses, and left. He went away to the north, "like a surprised grouse whirring off across the prairie."

—*from "The Location of the River" by Barry Lopez*

10 Setting

"I don't think of the setting for a story as window dressing, or of anecdotal value. I think setting is often part of what determines the nature of the story, and the nature of the characters. So it's very important for me to have characters involved in a place."

Conversation with Barry Lopez, available on video on connect.mcgraw-hill.com

THIS passage sets us down in a specific place on the earth: western Nebraska, on the banks of the Niobrara River. The year is 1844. In Barry Lopez's "The Location of the River," wandering historian Benjamin Foster has set out to solve a mystery. Had, as the Pawnee told him, the upper Niobrara truly disappeared the previous summer? As Foster attempts to understand how or whether such an occurrence was possible, he engages more and more deeply with the surrounding landscape and the people who inhabit it—the Pawnee, the Sioux, the Arapaho, the Arikara, and others. Increasingly preoccupied by what he does and does not know, what he can and cannot prove, he abandons the quest, perhaps half-mad, as portrayed in the excerpt at the beginning of the chapter.

SETTING AS PHYSICAL ENVIRONMENT

Consider the variety of settings you have encountered in the stories in this book: a grim view of Dublin in the early twentieth century in Joyce's "Araby," the 1800s in America in a well-appointed home in Chopin's "The Story of an Hour," the checkout counter of a grocery store in Updike's "A&P," and many more. Each setting—each particular time and place—comes with its own sights, sounds, and smells. Each creates a set of expectations among readers for the cast of characters they're likely to encounter and the range of events likely to occur.

In its basic sense, the term *setting* refers to the time and place in which a story unfolds. The conceptual meanings of time and place can be various in a work of fiction. Time, of course, can refer to the particular time of day and time of year. It can also refer to the era in which a story occurs—in Lopez's story, the mid-nineteenth century. Setting also includes weather. For example, the season dictates what characters will wear, what they will eat, see, smell, touch, and hear—what challenges of comfort or survival they will face. All these elements make up the physical environment of the story, and each decision the author makes in this regard shapes the story.

In his essay "A Writer's Sense of Place," the late California novelist James D. Houston describes the power of setting when "the place is profoundly felt, as a feature of the narrative that is working on the characters or through the characters or is somehow bearing upon their lives. . . . Our literature," he continues, "is rich with such works, stories wherein at least part of what's going on is some form of dialogue between a place—whether it be an island or a mountain or a city or a shoreline or a subregion of the continent—and the lives being lived. I look upon this as one more version of the endless dialogue we're all involved in, between the human imagination and the world we find ourselves inhabiting. . . ."

CONTINUED ON PAGE 276

Barry Lopez ... *I love the idea of making a place come alive like a person.*

A Conversation on Writing

The Role of Setting in a Story

I'm very comfortable writing a story in which a character just moves through a place, because I love the idea of making that place come alive like another person. . . . It's the thing that's outside the self. . . . And it's not until you get outside the self that you can come alive.

Setting in "The Location of the River"

In a story like "The Location of the River," I can go back and remember a time driving cross-country where I just pulled my truck off the road on the Niobrara River, and slept the night there. . . . So somewhere in my tissues is the sound of that river. . . . I can feel it in my mind, and I can pull it out, and it's attached to other things, and then it just unfolds in front of me. It's like the story is inside a little thing that happened when I was young and camping. . . . Years go by, and . . . it pulls all of the things out of my history of observation, and it's turned itself into a world. And then that world is where the story unfolds.

An Intimate Conversation with a *Place*

I feel that push in me all the time, when I'm in a place I've never been before, to have a conversation with it. "Who are you? Talk to me." If I can make myself vulnerable to a place, it senses that, and then it starts to talk to you. You have to trust, because trust is the only way to get to vulnerability, and vulnerability is the only way to get to intimacy. And that's what I want when I'm in a place, that intimate conversation with a place.

To watch this entire interview and hear the author read from "The Location of the River," go to connect.mcgraw-hill.com.

Among his many achievements, Barry Lopez (b. 1945) counts creating a university major—the B.A. in Natural Sciences and the Humanities at Texas Tech University. The major blends the very elements around which Lopez has built his career as he writes about the relationship between human beings and the physical environments they inhabit: how people are shaped, changed, or haunted by a landscape—and how they, in turn, shape the land. Lopez was born in New York and grew up both there and in California. After earning his bachelor's and graduate degrees from Notre Dame University, Lopez moved to Oregon, where he has lived ever since, devoting himself full-time to writing. His writing, which includes essay, memoir, and fiction, has earned awards such as the Pushcart Prize for both fiction and nonfiction, and his meditation on life in the northern latitudes, *Arctic Dreams,* received the National Book Award for nonfiction in 1986. Lopez also frequently collaborates with people engaged in other arts, such as the composers John Luther Adams and Arvo Pärt, and the illustrator Tom Pohrt. Above all else, Lopez loves the written word; as one of his characters in *Crow and Weasel* (1998), a children's story, says, "Sometimes a person needs a story more than food to stay alive. That is why we put these stories in each other's memory."

RESEARCH ASSIGNMENT Listen to the interview with Barry Lopez and explain what he means when he talks about a story "fighting" you off. Do you relate to this? Why or why not?

AS YOU READ   Picture the setting. In what ways is it hospitable and in what ways inhospitable? Does it seem like an inviting place, one you would like to see for yourself? Why or why not?

TIP

FOR INTERACTIVE READING . . .

Go through the story and mark all the details of physical setting, including names of towns or other landmarks, plant and animal life, and geographical features. Consult a map to get a feel for the region where the events in the story took place.

The Location of the River (1986)

1 ACCORDING to a journal kept by Benjamin Foster, a historian returning along the Platte River from the deserts of the Great Basin at the time, the spring of 1844 came early to western Nebraska. He recorded the first notes of a horned lark on the sixteenth of February. This unseasonable good weather induced him to stay a few weeks with a band of Pawnee camped just south of the Niobrara River. One morning he volunteered to go out with two men to look for stray horses. They found the horses grazing near an island of oak and ash trees on the prairie, along the edge of the river. When he saw the current and quicksand Foster was glad the horses had not crossed over.

On the way back, writes Foster—little of his last journal survives, but some fragments relevant to this incident are preserved—the Pawnee told him that the previous summer the upper Niobrara had disappeared.

At first Foster took this for a figurative statement about a severe drought, but the other Pawnee told him, no, the Niobrara had not run dry—in fact, the spring of 1843 had been very wet. It disappeared. That Foster took this information seriously, that he did not treat it with skepticism or derision, was characteristic of him.

The Pawnee, he goes to say, did not associate the disappearance of the river with any one particular phenomenon (Foster, I should say, was a confidant; he spoke fluent Pawnee and I'm sure they felt he was both knowledgeable and trustworthy); they attributed its disappearance to a sort of willful irritation, which they found amusing. They told Foster that the earth, the rivers, did not belong to men but were only to be used by them, and that the earth, though it was pleased with the Pawnee, was very disappointed in the white man. It suited the earth's purpose, they said, to suddenly abandon a river for a while, to confound men who were too dependent on such things always being there.

5   Foster thought this explanation narrow and self-serving and told the Pawnee so. But they were adamant. Foster writes that he himself was increasingly at a loss to understand what had happened, but he had been among Indians long enough to appreciate their sense of humor and to know their strength for allegory. He pointed out to them that if the river had shifted course or disappeared, the Pawnee would be as affected by it as the white men; but the Pawnee said, no, this was not so, because they saw things like this all the time and were not bothered by them.

   It is difficult to fathom what happened to the river or to Foster either, once he concluded, as he apparently did, that the Pawnee were literally correct, that sometime during the summer of 1843 the upper reaches of the Niobrara River, above the present town of Marshland and westward into Wyoming, did vanish for four or five months.

   An initial thought, he wrote, was that the people he was camped with were not Pawnee. He thought they might be a little too far north—in Sioux or possibly Arapaho country. Even though they spoke, ate, dressed, and even played at sleight-of-hand like Pawnee, they could be somebody else, with a cavalier regard for local truth. In others of his papers Foster writes about a rite of imitation in which a band of people from one tribe, Arikara, for example, would imitate a band from some other tribe for long periods of time, fifteen years or more. They began doing this on the northern plains in the 1820s, imitating each other in exacting detail, as a form of amusement. There was no way Foster could be certain he was not among Oglala Sioux pretending to be Pawnee and playing the Long Joke, fooling a white man and making at the same time a joke about their star-gazing neighbors the Pawnee who might not know what was going on at their very feet. But he had been intimate with the Pawnee; after extensive inquiry he believed he was among them, not someone else.

   It appears Foster tried systematically to establish a basis for belief in the river's disappearance, and pursued this course with increasing determination, as though he intuited the truth of the thing but didn't know how to demonstrate it. I don't know why, but I feel that, by that point, the man had begun to wonder at all he had seen in his life, and what of any of it would be believed.

   The possibility that the river had simply changed its channel seemed plausible to him, but after reconnoitering extensively through the hills he discounted it. And the river had not switched channels or run dry, it was repeatedly emphasized to him, it had vanished. There were no willows on the islands. There were no islands. There were no mud flats, no smooth places even in the sand, no abandoned channels, nothing. With the aid of survey maps made in 1840, and a theodolite, compass, artificial mercury horizon, and other instruments he borrowed from Fort Laramie some hundred miles to the southwest, Foster tried to compare the present location of the river with its location in November 1840, when the maps were made. The disagreements were too insignificant to have meaning, however, what one would have to expect given the crudeness of tools and methods in those days.

   Foster subsequently was unable to find any permanent resident to question, or to learn anything from men garrisoned at Fort Laramie or Fort Platte to the south. He rode as far north as the Sioux Agency in South Dakota looking for people to talk to. Exhausting all these traditional methods, he turned finally to something less conventional. It had long been his personal belief (and he was bolstered in this by some of those with whom he lived) that the history of the earth was revealed anew each spring in the shapes of the towering cumulus clouds that moved over the country from the north and west. If a man were blessed, were *wakan*, and had the patience and watched from the time of the first thunderstorm until the first prairie grass fire, he would see it. There 10 was no sequence; the events unfurled in an order of their own, so Foster prepared himself for a long vigil.

One April afternoon, seventeen days after he had begun, he saw on the horizon with the aid of an interpreter, as clear as the blades of blue grama grass and his moccasined feet before him, the fading and disappearance of the upper Niobrara River in the clouds. He judged the time of year to be late June.

> I imagine Foster, a **brilliant man** much troubled by the destruction of native cultures, simply fell prey to a final madness.

This must have been slightly disquieting for Foster, living in two worlds as he did, lying there on his back under the inexorable movement of clouds, feeling the earth turn under him, thinking what he did and did not know, could and could not prove. On the basis of what is a man to be believed?

There is something else here, too. In a letter to Foster dated July 7, 1831, the American explorer and painter George Catlin remarks on his terror of open space in Nebraska. While on foot in the tallgrass prairie, he and his party used a sextant and chronometer, as though at sea. I don't know whether having underlined this passage in Catlin's letter (it survives) means Foster's own perception of the prairie was oceanic—people later spoke of the "coasts of Nebraska"—or whether on his own he had always felt unsettled by the unbounded space, as he might particularly have been that spring.

THE disappearance of the upper Niobrara might never have come to light at all had it not been for Foster's breakdown at that point and, much later, the interest of a graduate student at Idaho State University called Anton Breverton. Breverton tried to document Foster's career in the west in his history thesis and he tried especially to clarify this one episode on the Niobrara. I lost touch with Breverton some years ago. He is either living today in obscurity, possibly in Europe, or he has passed on. His thesis, I am sorry to say, is also unavailable. The archival librarian at Pocatello believes his was among some twenty theses lost when the library transferred its collections to a new building in 1948. I read Breverton's thesis at his request when it came out, made a few notes, and returned it. Reconstructing Foster's life had been a preoccupation of mine, too, since coming into possession of the notes and journals he failed to destroy that spring.

Breverton read extensively in the literature of western Nebraska, in science and history, from both native and white sources, trying to find some hint of explanation for the disappearance of the river or what was meant by the Pawnee who told Foster this. He combed emigrants' journals, reports from Smithsonian, the Carnegie Institution—all fruitless. He even read regional novels, including those of Mari Sandoz, going so far as to go to New York and interview Miss Sandoz. An unusually sensitive woman who grew up in that country at the turn of the century, Sandoz had been particularly attentive to the stories of the region. But Breverton was unable to corroborate any part of it. He finally left it out of his thesis.

I understand a colleague of Breverton, irritated by the entire issue, nearly enraged in fact, secured some military funding to conduct a soil analysis throughout Dawes, Sioux, and Box Butte counties in Nebraska where the river flows, but I do not know what became of this information. I myself have communicated with the Pawnee Tribal Council, with friends among the Arapaho, and with faculty at the University of Nebraska who could be expected to add something, but to no avail.

FOR my part, I do not think the river ever disappeared. I imagine Foster, a brilliant man much troubled by the destruction of native cultures, simply fell prey to a final madness.

A catalytic event occurred in Foster's life in 1808 when he was living in a large Chippewa village near the present town of Bayfield, Wisconsin. Representatives of the Shawnee Prophet had come among them and instructed the people to extinguish all their fires, to rekindle fire in the old way with sticks, and to never let it go out. They said the old lifeways would return, that the prophet himself would bring back the dead. The psychologically depressed Chippewa enthusiastically adopted the beliefs of these impassioned young men. A demonstration of allegiance they required was that of throwing away one's personal possessions. As an eleven-year-old boy, Foster saw the shore of Lake Superior lined with the medicine bundles of a thousand men, all washed up by the waves. These small bundles, decorated with trade beads, strips of bright cloth, feathers, and quill work, must have been gathered up by someone (perhaps even Foster) and taken somewhere, for one morning the beaches were empty.

> Eventually he threw everything he'd
> **ever** written down into the
> Niobrara River . . .

From this time forward, I am sure Foster was possessed of the idea of recording the beliefs of native tribes before they fell victim to whites or to the panic of their own spiritual leaders. This much is clearly implied by a boyhood friend of Foster who wrote about the incident on the lake in *A Narrative of the Captivity and Adventures of John Tanner*. (It is further substantiated in the private papers of W. W. Warren in the manuscript collection of the Minnesota Historical Society. You can appreciate perhaps the difficulty of piecing together Foster's career, in the wake of the destruction of all his notes.)

Foster spent the next thirty years with six or seven different tribes. He is occasionally mentioned in the correspondence of Ogden, Sublette, and others as a translator and Indian expert of exceptional skill. He would apparently live for years with a tribe before moving on. Though loath to do it, he deposited this steady accumulation of field notes periodically at various American and British trading posts for safekeeping, intending one day to collect them all. This is what he was doing in 1844 when he was waylaid by the Pawnee and good weather. He had eleven pack mules with him at the time, all of them burdened with manuscripts. His writings were more detailed, complete, inclusive of fantastic incident, rigorous, and perceptive (to judge from the scraps) than anything Fontenelle, Maximilian, Ruxton, Stewart, or any of the rest ever wrote down. He was en route to Kansas City, where the great trading family of Chouteau had offered him money for publication. The collection would have equalled in scope and importance the collected volumes on the west edited by Reuben Thwaites some sixty years later. It is one of the great tragedies of American history that he did not arrive and that his manuscripts were ruined.

In late June 1844, after Foster had begun to despair of ever understanding either the fact or the meaning of the disappearance of the river, after a time of ritual cleansing and dreaming, perhaps agoraphobic or maddened by the interweaving of literalisms and metaphors and forms of proof, Foster began throwing his manuscripts into the river. According to a Pawnee called Wolf Finger, who spoke with the historian Henry Lake, Foster would go down naked in the afternoon, wade out into the Niobrara and hurl a fistful of pages into the water, or from the shore he would skip a journal across the surface like a stone. Eventually he threw everything he'd ever written down into the Niobrara River, turned the pack mules out with the Pawnee horses, and left. He went away to the north, "like a surprised grouse whirring off across the prairie."

WHAT was left of these documents came into my hands though my father, a tax assessor. He found them in a barn near Lusk, Wyoming, in 1901. Among them—there was about enough to fill one cardboard box—was the first page of an essay entitled "Studying the Indian." I have no idea of the date. In the first paragraph Foster says, "I have been among the Absarokee when they left the battlefield like sparrows. I have watched Navajo men run down antelope on foot and smother their last breath in a handful of corn pollen. One bad summer in the Desert of the Black Rocks I saw Shoshoni women go out at sunset and because they were starving call in the quail. I have heard the soft syllables of the Arapaho tongue and the choking sound of the Kiowa and the hissing Cheyenne sounds. A woman called Reaches Deep taught me how to dance, and once I danced until I entered the sun. But already in the fall of 1826, in Judith Basin, a Piegan called Coyote in the Camp had told me I was learning everything wrong. . . ." Foster goes on, a few words, the rest is washed out and sun bleached.

In an attempt to understand what little Foster had written down about the disappearance of the Niobrara (and with a sense of compassion for him), I visited that part of the state in 1963. I stayed in a small hotel, the Plainview, in the town of Box Butte. I had with me all of Foster's water-stained notes, which I had spread around the room and was examining again for perhaps the hundredth time. During the night a tremendous rainstorm broke over the prairie. The Niobrara threatened to flood and I was awakened by the motel operator. I drove across the river—in the cone of my headlights I could see the fast brown water surging against the bridge supports—and spent the rest of the night in my car on high ground, at some distance from the town, in some hills the name of which I do not remember. In the morning I became confused on farm roads and was unable to find my way back to the river. In desperation I stopped at a place I recognized having been at the day before and proceeded from there on foot toward the river, until I became lost in the fields themselves. I met a man on a tractor who told me the river had never come over in that direction. Ever. And to get away.

I have not been back in that country since.

IF YOU LIKED "THE LOCATION OF THE RIVER," YOU MIGHT ALSO LIKE . . .

. . . the many stories in this book in which landscape plays a significant role, including Leslie Marmon Silko's "The Man to Send Rain Clouds" (Chapter 15).

GOING FURTHER Barry Lopez has spent a large part of his career writing about the relationship between landscape—setting—and narrative or story making. His award-winning nonfiction work *Arctic Dreams* was a major step in this direction. *Home Ground,* an anthology he edited with his wife, Debra Gwartney, offers descriptive definitions by dozens of American writers on the various elements of landscape, such as arroyo, swale, muskeg, and so forth.

Writing from Reading

Summarize

1 Compare and contrast the various theories of the river's disappearance—the Native American views and the views of the white researchers: Foster, Breverton, and the narrator.

Analyze Craft

2 Most of this story is related almost as a report. How does this affect the information we receive about the setting? Do we see the place as a scientist would or as an artist or sightseeing traveler might view it?

Analyze Voice

3 Who is the narrator of this story? When and how does the narrator become an active participant? What is the role of this narrator?

4 Consider the narrator's descriptions of setting compared to Foster's. Discuss the fundamental differences and similarities between the narrator and Foster based on what they see.

Synthesize Summary and Analysis

5 Consider the comparison between open space in Nebraska and the open sea. How does George Catlin's use of a sextant and chronometer in the tall-grass prairie—and Foster's interest in this story—contribute to the story's setting, characterizations, and theme? What effect does this extended metaphor have on you as a reader?

6 List all the things in the story that are lost. Also note the people who get lost or lose their way. Referring to your findings, discuss how "loss" operates as a theme in "The Location of the River."

Interpret the Story

7 Consider the passage from the first page of Foster's essay "Studying the Indian," where he is told by an Indian that he has learned everything wrong. Compare this passage to the narrator's study of Foster in the preceding pages. By including the passage, what is Lopez suggesting about the narrator's conclusions?

CONTINUED FROM PAGE 269

SETTING AS SOCIAL ENVIRONMENT

Growing out of the physical environment of a story is something more various called the **social environment.** Elements such as the era and location combined with a character's living and working conditions make up the social environment. To understand

> **"I think one of the things that people read for is gossip, curiosity. They want to find out how things work. They want to understand what it's like to be somewhere."** Conversation with William Kittredge

social environment, consider the challenges and community being portrayed in any work of fiction. For example, in Lopez's story, Foster is a white man and an historian who is performing research among native peoples on the Great Plains of Wyoming and Nebraska in 1844. His physical environment consists of the great, uncharted outdoors, where he is often alone. When he is not alone, the Pawnee and Sioux, Arapaho and Arikara are his companions. Cultural differences, however, make it unclear how much trust exists in these relationships. Thus, Foster inhabits a social environment characterized by a particular kind of isolation.

SETTING AND MOOD

Writers approach setting the way designers use sets for plays or films. Each object is placed deliberately in order to create a particular effect. Consider the following excerpt from the 1957 short story "Wine" by British author Doris Lessing.

> *A man and woman walked toward the boulevard from a little hotel in a side street.*
>
> *The trees were still leafless, black, cold; but the fine twigs were swelling toward spring, so that looking upward it was with an expectation of the first glimmering greenness. Yet everything was calm, and the sky was a calm, classic blue.*
>
> *The couple drifted slowly along. Effort, after days of laziness, seemed impossible; and almost at once they turned into a café and sank down, as if exhausted, in the glass-walled space that was thrust forward into the street.*
>
> *The place was empty. People were seeking the midday meal in the restaurants. Not all: that morning crowds had been demonstrating, a procession had just passed, and its straggling end could still be seen. The sounds of violence, shouted slogans and singing, no longer absorbed the din of Paris traffic; but it was these sounds that had roused the couple from sleep.*

Lessing places the couple in Paris, conjuring up images of romance. We find them there in the spring, so we have the promise of new life and the possibility of a new beginning. It is midday, which gives us the impression they are people of leisure, at least at the moment. These details lend a flavor, and the setting establishes a mood. These details also hint at plot developments—the demonstrators in the background, the possibility that something is about to change.

SETTING AND CHARACTER

A setting, however, can play a bigger role than simply serving as backdrop and mood. A character's location often shapes his or her identity. A character who lives on a fifty-five-acre farm, for instance, will develop quite differently from a character who takes a crowded subway to work. In James Joyce's novel *A Portrait of the Artist as a Young Man* (1916), the protagonist, Stephen Dedalus, defines himself as a student, an Irish citizen, and a citizen of the world as he places himself at the top of the list he jots down in his geography book:

> *Stephen Dedalus*
> *Class of Elements*
> *Clongowes Wood College*
> *Sallins*
> *County Kildare*
> *Ireland*
> *Europe*
> *The World*
> *The Universe*

The setting can also explicitly reflect the inner lives of characters as well as foreshadow future events, as in this passage from Edgar Allan Poe's "The Cask of Amontillado."

> *At the most remote end of the crypt there appeared another less spacious. Its walls had been lined with human remains, piled to the vault overhead, in the fashion of the great catacombs of Paris. Three sides of this interior crypt were still ornamented in this manner. From the fourth the bones had been thrown down, and lay promiscuously upon the earth, forming at one point a mound of some size. Within the wall thus exposed by the displacing of the bones, we perceived a still interior recess, in depth about four feet, in width three, in height six or seven. It seemed to have been constructed for no especial use in itself, but formed merely the interval between two of the colossal supports of the roof of the catacombs, and was backed by one of their circumscribing walls of solid granite.*

In this passage, Poe describes the exhumed grave that will be Fortunato's—an oubliette within a crypt within a network of catacombs, far below the Montresor estate. As the story moves deeper into this deathly space, the claustrophobic setting adds to the

REGIONAL WRITERS

Critics sometimes refer to authors whose work tends to focus on a particular setting and its characters, customs, dialect, and topography as *regional writers,* a term historically used in a negative fashion. Texas writer Larry McMurtry, one of the most popular American writers of his generation, once joked in protest about the way in which Southern writers especially were defined as "regional" and thus put in a pigeonhole by reviewers. He had T-shirts made that said "Regional Writer" and passed them out to his friends. Today, we no longer object to writers merely because of their ties to a particular region. In fact, it's almost impossible *not* to have such ties or a sense of preferred location.

suspense of the narrative: What is foreshadowed by the "human remains," those bones that "lay promiscuously upon the earth"? At the same time that the narrator brings Fortunato to this hidden place, he leads him closer to the goal that he has cherished: his desire for revenge. The "still interior recess" is not only the setting for the climax of the story; it represents the central fact that drives the story, the narrator's intention and its fulfillment (for more on symbols and symbolism, see Chapter 14). Imagine how the story might read if it were set outdoors, in the daylight: Would you feel the same tension if the characters were walking through a flower garden or browsing at an open-air market on their way to the murder? How would the story be changed if it took place at Fortunato's estate instead of Montresor's—surely Fortunato could still be murdered in private at his own home?

Finally, the setting can itself be a character. Landscape can entwine with personality so that it expresses the soul of the narrator, as it does in Lopez's story. The Great Plains are a vast, unknowable presence baffling Foster and the others who follow him in trying to understand it. Together, the setting, characters, and plot express the writer's feeling about the impossibility of knowing anything with certainty in this vast world.

Kate Chopin (1851–1904)

For a brief biography of Kate Chopin, see Chapter 6.

AS YOU READ   The intensity of the storm seems to conjure the intensity of the sexual encounter between these old lovers. How does that seem persuasive or contrived to you?

The Storm (1898)

I

1   The leaves were so still that even Bibi thought it was going to rain. Bobinôt, who was accustomed to converse on terms of perfect equality with his little son, called the child's attention to certain sombre clouds that were rolling with sinister intention from the west, accompanied by a sullen, threatening roar. They were at Friedheimer's store and decided to remain there till the storm had passed. They sat

within the door on two empty kegs. Bibi was four years old and looked very wise.

"Mama'll be 'fraid, yes," he suggested with blinking eyes.

"She'll shut the house. Maybe she got Sylvie helpin' her this evenin'," Bobinôt responded reassuringly.

"No; she ent got Sylvie. Sylvie was helpin' her yistiday," piped Bibi.

5 Bobinôt arose and going across to the counter purchased a can of shrimps, of which Calixta was very fond. Then he returned to his perch on the keg and sat stolidly holding the can of shrimps while the storm burst. It shook the wooden store and seemed to be ripping great furrows in the distant field. Bibi laid his little hand on his father's knee and was not afraid.

II

Calixta, at home, felt no uneasiness for their safety. She sat at a side window sewing furiously on a sewing machine. She was greatly occupied and did not notice the approaching storm. But she felt very warm and often stopped to mop her face on which the perspiration gathered in beads. She unfastened her white sacque at the throat. It began to grow dark, and suddenly realizing the situation she got up hurriedly and went about closing windows and doors.

Out on the small front gallery she had hung Bobinôt's Sunday clothes to dry and she hastened out to gather them before the rain fell. As she stepped outside, Alcée Laballière rode in at the gate. She had not seen him very often since her marriage, and never alone. She stood there with Bobinôt's coat in her hands, and the big rain drops began to fall. Alcée rode his horse under the shelter of a side projection where the chickens had huddled and there were plows and a harrow piled up in the corner.

"May I come and wait on your gallery till the storm is over, Calixta?" he asked.

"Come 'long in, M'sieur Alcée."

> She was greatly occupied and did not notice the approaching storm.

His voice and her own startled her as if from a trance, 10 and she seized Bobinôt's vest. Alcée, mounting to the porch, grabbed the trousers and snatched Bibi's braided jacket that was about to be carried away by a sudden gust of wind.

He expressed an intention to remain outside, but it was soon apparent that he might as well have been out in the open: the water beat in upon the boards in driving sheets, and he went inside, closing the door after him. It was even necessary to put something beneath the door to keep the water out.

"My! what a rain! It's good two years sence it rain' like that," exclaimed Calixta as she rolled up a piece of bagging and Alcée helped her to thrust it beneath the crack.

She was a little fuller of figure than five years before when she married; but she had lost nothing of her vivacity. Her blue eyes still retained their melting quality; and her yellow hair, dishevelled by the wind and rain, kinked more stubbornly than ever about her ears and temples.

The rain beat upon the low, shingled roof with a force and clatter that threatened to break an entrance and deluge them there. They were in the dining room—the sitting room—the general utility room. Adjoining was her bedroom, with Bibi's couch along side her own. The door stood open, and the room with its white, monumental bed, its closed shutters, looked dim and mysterious.

Alcée flung himself into a rocker and Calixta nervously began to gather up from the floor the lengths of a cotton sheet which she had been sewing.

"If this keeps up, *Dieu sait* if the levees goin' to stan' it!" 15 she exclaimed.

"What have you got to do with the levees?"

"I got enough to do! An' there's Bobinôt with Bibi out in that storm—if he only didn't left Friedheimer's!"

"Let us hope, Calixta, that Bobinôt's got sense enough to come in out of a cyclone."

She went and stood at the window with a greatly disturbed look on her face. She wiped the frame that was clouded with moisture. It was stiflingly hot. Alcée got up and joined her at the window, looking over her shoulder. The rain was coming down in sheets obscuring the view of far-off cabins and enveloping the distant wood in a gray mist. The playing of the lightning was incessant. A bolt struck a tall chinaberry tree at the edge of the field. It filled all visible space with a blinding glare and the crash seemed to invade the very boards they stood upon.

20 Calixta put her hands to her eyes, and with a cry, staggered backward. Alcée's arm encircled her, and for an instant he drew her close and spasmodically to him.

"*Bonté!*" she cried, releasing herself from his encircling arm and retreating from the window, "the house'll go next! If I only knew w'ere Bibi was!" She would not compose herself; she would not be seated. Alcée clasped her shoulders and looked into her face. The contact of her warm, palpitating body when he had unthinkingly drawn her into his arms, had aroused all the old-time infatuation and desire for her flesh.

"Calixta," he said, "don't be frightened. Nothing can happen. The house is too low to be struck, with so many tall trees standing about. There! aren't you going to be quiet? say, aren't you?" He pushed her hair back from her face that was warm and steaming. Her lips were as red and moist as pomegranate seed. Her white neck and a glimpse of her full, firm bosom disturbed him powerfully. As she glanced up at him the fear in her liquid blue eyes had given place to a drowsy gleam that unconsciously betrayed a sensuous desire. He looked down into her eyes and there was nothing for him to do but to gather her lips in a kiss. It reminded him of Assumption.

"Do you remember—in Assumption, Calixta?" he asked in a low voice broken by passion. Oh! she remembered; for in Assumption he had kissed her and kissed and kissed her; until his senses would well nigh fail, and to save her he would resort to a desperate flight. If she was not an immaculate dove in those days, she was still inviolate; a passionate creature whose very defenselessness had made her defense, against which his honor forbade him to prevail. Now—well, now—her lips seemed in a manner free to be tasted, as well as her round, white throat and her whiter breasts.

They did not heed the crashing torrents, and the roar of the elements made her laugh as she lay in his arms. She was a revelation in that dim, mysterious chamber; as white as the couch she lay upon. Her firm, elastic flesh that was knowing for the first time its birthright, was like a creamy lily that the sun invites to contribute its breath and perfume to the undying life of the world.

25 The generous abundance of her passion, without guile or trickery, was like a white flame which penetrated and found response in depths of his own sensuous nature that had never yet been reached.

When he touched her breasts they gave themselves up in quivering ecstasy, inviting his lips. Her mouth was a fountain of delight. And when he possessed her, they seemed to swoon together at the very borderland of life's mystery.

He stayed cushioned upon her, breathless, dazed, enervated, with his heart beating like a hammer upon her. With one hand she clasped his head, her lips lightly touching his forehead. The other hand stroked with a soothing rhythm his muscular shoulders.

The growl of the thunder was distant and passing away. The rain beat softly upon the shingles, inviting them to drowsiness and sleep. But they dared not yield.

The rain was over; and the sun was turning the glistening green world into a palace of gems. Calixta, on the gallery, watched Alcée ride away. He turned and smiled at her with a beaming face; and she lifted her pretty chin in the air and laughed aloud.

> The fear in her liquid blue eyes had given place to a drowsy gleam that unconsciously betrayed a sensuous desire.

III

30 Bobinôt and Bibi, trudging home, stopped without at the cistern to make themselves presentable.

"My! Bibi, w'at will yo' mama say! You ought to be ashame'. You oughta' put on those good pants. Look at 'em! An' that mud on yo' collar! How you got that mud on yo' collar, Bibi? I never saw such a boy!" Bibi was the picture of pathetic resignation. Bobinôt was the embodiment of serious solicitude as he strove to remove from his own person and his son's the signs of their tramp over heavy roads and through wet fields. He scraped the mud off Bibi's bare legs and feet with a stick and carefully removed all traces from his heavy brogans. Then, prepared for the worst—the meeting with an over-scrupulous housewife, they entered cautiously at the back door.

Calixta was preparing supper. She had set the table and was dripping coffee at the hearth. She sprang up as they came in.

"Oh, Bobinôt! You back! My! but I was uneasy. W'ere you been during the rain? An' Bibi? he ain't wet? he ain't hurt?" She had clasped Bibi and was kissing him effusively. Bobinôt's explanations and apologies which he had been composing all along the way, died on his lips as Calixta felt him to see if he were dry, and seemed to express nothing but satisfaction at their safe return.

"I brought you some shrimps, Calixta," offered Bobinôt, hauling the can from his ample side pocket and laying it on the table.

35 "Shrimps! Oh, Bobinôt! you too good fo' anything!" and she gave him a smacking kiss on the cheek that resounded. "*J'vous réponds*, we'll have a feas' to-night! umph-umph!"

Bobinôt and Bibi began to relax and enjoy themselves, and when the three seated themselves at table they laughed much and so loud that anyone might have heard them as far away as Laballière's.

IV

Alcée Laballière wrote to his wife, Clarisse, that night. It was a loving letter, full of tender solicitude. He told her not to hurry back, but if she and the babies liked it at Biloxi, to stay a month longer. He was getting on nicely; and though he missed them, he was willing to bear the separation a while longer—realizing that their health and pleasure were the first things to be considered.

V

As for Clarisse, she was charmed upon receiving her husband's letter. She and the babies were doing well. The society was agreeable; many of her old friends and acquaintances were at the bay. And the first free breath since her marriage seemed to restore the pleasant liberty of her maiden days. Devoted as she was to her husband, their intimate conjugal life was something which she was more than willing to forego for a while.

So the storm passed and every one was happy.

IF YOU LIKED "THE STORM," YOU MIGHT ALSO LIKE ...

... reading later works by feminist writers—for example, Margaret Atwood's "Happy Endings" (in An Anthology of Stories for Further Reading)—or reading about the passionate mistakes made by the boys in T. C. Boyle's "Greasy Lake" (Chapter 8).

GOING FURTHER   Kate Chopin's heralded career came to an abrupt end amidst the scandal created by publication of her sexually explicit novel *The Awakening* (1899), and stories like "The Storm" would not be published in her lifetime. In addition to introducing topics picked up later by feminist writers, Chopin also introduced the themes of slavery and miscegenation in the old South, themes explored later by William Faulkner in *Absalom, Absalom!* and in Toni Morrison's *Beloved*.

Writing from Reading

Summarize

1 List the characters in the story and briefly describe how each reacts to the storm outside. Which character seems the most affected by the turbulent weather? Which character seems the least bothered?

Analyze Craft

2 Chopin never explicitly states where the story takes place, but the information can be gleaned from the details of the story. How does Chopin communicate the geographic setting of the story to readers?

3 Describe the social environment of the story. What is the significance of Calixta's affair in light of this particular social environment?

Analyze Voice

4 Calixta and Alcée reference time spent together in Assumption, where they shared a romance. Why do you think the two of them ended up married to different partners? Pay particular attention to the way each speaks.

Synthesize Summary and Analysis

5 Compare Calixta's mood before the storm to her mood when Babinôt and Bibi return home. How has the encounter with Alcée affected her? Why do you think she reacts this way?

Interpret the Story

6 If the story had included no actual weather phenomena, would the title "The Storm" still be appropriate? Why or why not?

Zora Neale Hurston (1891–1960)

Growing up in Eatonville, Florida—an all-black town—Zora Neale Hurston did not experience racial prejudice. Instead, she saw examples of black role models, such as her father, who served as the town mayor. She began her education at Howard University in Washington, D.C., and finished her B.A. in anthropology at Barnard College in New York City. Her love of folk culture and literature led her to write novels, short stories, and collections of folklore that captured the common black person; unlike her contemporaries, including Langston Hughes, Hurston cared more about authenticity than about how her depictions made blacks appear to white audiences. An important figure of the Harlem Renaissance, Hurston is famous for her charming, vibrant personality that made her the center of parties and social life in Harlem. Some of her early fiction was published in *Opportunity,* a black magazine of the Harlem Renaissance. Her best work appeared in the 1930s and 1940s with books such as *Mules and Men* (1935), which was the fruit of her ethnographic studies of blacks in Florida, and *Their Eyes Were Watching God* (1937), Hurston's classic novel about an African-American woman who forges her identity in relation to three different husbands. Although these works found an audience, Hurston sank into obscurity toward the end of her life. However, interest in her writing revived in the 1970s, thanks to Alice Walker's article "In Search of Zora Neale Hurston," which appeared in *Ms.* magazine. Today, Hurston is recognized as the most important African-American woman in early-twentieth-century literature.

AS YOU READ   Note that the writer studied her Southern subjects as an anthropologist. Do you detect any sense in the story of an objective observer studying her material—and, if so, where?

The Gilded Six-Bits (1933)

1   IT was a Negro yard around a Negro house in a Negro settlement that looked to the payroll of the G and G Fertilizer works for its support.

But there was something happy about the place. The front yard was parted in the middle by a sidewalk from gate to door-step, a sidewalk edged on either side by quart bottles driven neck down into the ground on a slant. A mess of homey flowers planted without a plan but blooming cheerily from their helter-skelter places. The fence and house were whitewashed. The porch and steps scrubbed white.

The front door stood open to the sunshine so that the floor of the front room could finish drying after its weekly scouring. It was Saturday. Everything clean from the front gate to the privy house. Yard raked so that the strokes of the rake would make a pattern. Fresh newspaper cut in fancy edge on the kitchen shelves.

Missie May was bathing herself in the galvanized washtub in the bedroom. Her dark-brown skin glistened under the soapsuds that skittered down from her wash rag. Her stiff young breasts thrust forward aggressively, like broad-based cones with the tips lacquered in black.

5   She heard men's voices in the distance and glanced at the dollar clock on the dresser.

"Humph! Ah'm way behind time t'day! Joe gointer be heah 'fore Ah git mah clothes on if Ah don't make haste."

She grabbed the clean meal sack at hand and dried herself hurriedly and began to dress. But before she could tie her slippers, there came the ring of singing metal on wood. Nine times.

Missie May grinned with delight. She had not seen the big tall man come stealing in the gate and creep up the walk grinning happily at the joyful mischief he was about to commit. But she knew that it was her husband throwing silver dollars in the door for her to pick up and pile beside her plate at dinner. It was this way every Saturday afternoon. The nine dollars hurled into the open door, he scurried to a hiding place behind the cape jasmine bush and waited.

Missie May promptly appeared at the door in mock alarm.

10   "Who dat chunkin' money in mah do'way?" she demanded. No answer from the yard. She leaped off the porch and began to search the shrubbery. She peeped under the porch and hung over the gate to look up and down the road. While she did this, the man behind the jasmine darted to the chinaberry tree. She spied him and gave chase.

"Nobody ain't gointer be chunkin' money at me and Ah not do 'em nothin'," she shouted in mock anger. He ran around the house with Missie May at his heels. She overtook him at the kitchen door. He ran inside but could not close it after him before she crowded in and locked with him in a rough and tumble. For several minutes the two were a furious mass of male and female energy. Shouting, laughing, twisting, turning, tussling, tickling each other in the ribs; Missie May clutching onto Joe and Joe trying, but not too hard, to get away.

"Missie May, take yo' hand out mah pocket!" Joe shouted out between laughs.

"Ah ain't, Joe, not lessen you gwine gimme whateve' it is good you got in yo' pocket. Turn it go, Joe, do Ah'll tear yo' clothes."

"Go on tear 'em. You de one dat pushes de needles round heah. Move yo' hand Missie May."

> "Who dat chunkin' money in mah do'way?" she demanded.

15 "Lemme git dat paper sack out yo' pocket. Ah bet it's candy kisses."

"Tain't. Move yo' hand. Woman ain't got no business in a man's clothes no how. Go way."

Missie May gouged way down and gave an upward jerk and triumphed.

"Unhhunh! Ah got it! It 'tis so candy kisses. Ah knowed you had somethin' for me in yo' clothes. Now Ah got to see whut's in every pocket you got."

Joe smiled indulgently and let his wife go through all of his pockets and take out the things that he had hidden there for her to find. She bore off the chewing gum, the cake of sweet soap, the pocket handkerchief as if she had wrested them from him, as if they had not been bought for the sake of this friendly battle.

20 "Whew! dat play-fight done got me all warmed up," Joe exclaimed. "Got me some water in de kittle?"

"Yo' water is on de fire and yo' clean things is cross de bed. Hurry up and wash yo'self and git changed so we kin eat. Ah'm hongry." As Missie said this, she bore the steaming kettle into the bedroom.

"You ain't hongry, sugar," Joe contradicted her. "Youse jes' a little empty. Ah'm de one whut's hongry. Ah could eat up camp meetin', back off 'ssociation, and drink Jurdan dry. Have it on de table when Ah git out de tub."

"Don't you mess wid mah business, man. You git in yo' clothes. Ah'm a real wife, not no dress and breath. Ah might not look lak one, but if you burn me, you won't git a thing but wife ashes."

Joe splashed in the bedroom and Missie May fanned around in the kitchen. A fresh red and white checked cloth on the table. Big pitcher of buttermilk beaded with pale drops of butter from the churn. Hot fried mullet, crackling bread, ham hock atop a mound of string beans and new potatoes, and perched on the window-sill a pone of spicy potato pudding.

25 Very little talk during the meal but that little consisted of banter that pretended to deny affection but in reality flaunted it. Like when Missie May reached for a second helping of the tater pone. Joe snatched it out of her reach.

After Missie May had made two or three unsuccessful grabs at the pan, she begged, "Aw, Joe gimme some mo' dat tater pone."

"Nope, sweetenin' is for us men-folks. Y'all pritty lil frail eels don't need nothin' lak dis. You too sweet already."

"Please, Joe."

"Naw, naw. Ah don't want you to git no sweeter than whut you is already. We goin' down de road a lil piece t'night so you go put on yo' Sunday-go-to-meetin' things."

30 Missie May looked at her husband to see if he was playing some prank. "Sho nuff, Joe?"

"Yeah. We goin' to de ice cream parlor."

"Where de ice cream parlor at, Joe?"

"A new man done come heah from Chicago and he done got a place and took and opened it up for a ice cream parlor, and bein' as it's real swell, Ah wants you to be one de first ladies to walk in dere and have some set down."

"Do Jesus, Ah ain't knowed nothin' 'bout it. Who de man done it?"

35 "Mister Otis D. Slemmons, of spots and places— Memphis, Chicago, Jacksonville, Philadelphia and so on."

"Dat heavy-set man wid his mouth full of gold teethes?"

"Yeah. Where did you see 'im at?"

"Ah went down to de sto' tuh git a box of lye and Ah seen 'im standin' on de corner talkin' to some of de mens, and Ah come on back and went to scrubbin' de floor, and he passed and tipped his hat whilst Ah was scourin' de steps. Ah thought Ah never seen *him* befo'."

Joe smiled pleasantly. "Yeah, he's up to date. He got de finest clothes Ah ever seen on a colored man's back."

40 "Aw, he don't look no better in his clothes than you do in yourn. He got a puzzlegut on 'im and he so chuckle-headed, he got a pone behind his neck."

Joe looked down at his own abdomen and said wistfully: "Wisht Ah had a build on me lak he got. He ain't puzzlegutted, honey. He jes' got a corperation. Dat make 'm look lak a rich white man. All rich mens is got some belly on 'em."

"Ah seen de pitchers of Henry Ford and he's a spare-built man and Rockefeller look lak he ain't got but one gut.

> "A new man done come heah from Chicago and he done got a place and took and opened it up for a ice cream parlor."

But Ford and Rockefeller and dis Slemmons and all de rest kin be as many-gutted as dey please, Ah'm satisfied wid you jes' lak you is, baby. God took pattern after a pine tree and built you noble. Youse a pritty man, and if Ah knowed any way to make you mo' pritty still Ah'd take and do it."

Joe reached over gently and toyed with Missie May's ear. "You jes' say dat cause you love me, but Ah know Ah can't hold no light to Otis D. Slemmons. Ah ain't never been nowhere and Ah ain't got nothin' but you."

Missie May got on his lap and kissed him and he kissed back in kind. Then he went on. "All de womens is crazy 'bout 'im everywhere he go."

45   "How you know dat, Joe?"

"He tole us so hisself."

"Dat don't make it so. His mouf is cut cross-ways, ain't it? Well, he kin lie jes' lak anybody else."

"Good Lawd, Missie! You womens sho is hard to sense into things. He's got a five-dollar gold piece for a stick-pin and he got a ten-dollar gold piece on his watch chain and his mouf is jes' crammed full of gold teethes. Sho wisht it wuz mine. And whut make it so cool, he got money 'cumulated. And womens give it all to 'im."

"Ah don't see whut de womens see on 'im. Ah wouldn't give 'im a wink if de sheriff wuz after 'im."

50   "Well, he tole us how de white womens in Chicago give 'im all dat gold money. So he don't 'low nobody to touch it at all. Not even put dey finger on it. Dey tole 'im not to. You kin make 'miration at it, but don't tetch it."

"Whyn't he stay up dere where dey so crazy 'bout 'im?"

"Ah reckon dey done made 'im vast-rich and he wants to travel some. He says dey wouldn't leave 'im hit a lick of work. He got mo' lady people crazy 'bout him than he kin shake a stick at."

"Joe, Ah hates to see you so dumb. Dat stray nigger jes' tell y'all anything and y'all b'lieve it."

"Go 'head on now, honey and put on yo' clothes. He talkin' 'bout his pritty womens—Ah want 'im to see *mine*."

55   Missie May went off to dress and Joe spent the time trying to make his stomach punch out like Slemmons' middle. He tried the rolling swagger of the stranger, but found that his tall bone-and-muscle stride fitted ill with it. He just had time to drop back into his seat before Missie May came in dressed to go.

On the way home that night Joe was exultant. "Didn't Ah say ole Otis was swell? Can't he talk Chicago talk? Wuzn't dat funny whut he said when great big fat ole Ida Armstrong come in? He asted me, 'Who is dat broad wid de forte shake?' Dat's a new word. Us always thought forty was a set of figgers but he showed us where it means a whole heap of things. Sometimes he don't say forty, he jes' say thirty-eight and two and dat mean de same thing. Know whut he tole me when Ah wuz payin' for our ice cream? He say, 'Ah have to hand it to you, Joe. Dat wife of yours is jes' thirty-eight and two. Yessuh, she's forte!' Ain't he killin'?"

"He'll do in case of a rush. But he sho is got uh heap uh gold on 'im. Dat's de first time Ah ever seed gold money. It lookted good on him sho nuff, but it'd look a whole heap better on you."

"Who, me? Missie May, youse crazy! Where would a po' man lak me git gold money from?"

Missie May was silent for a minute, then she said, "Us might find some goin' long de road some time. Us could."

"Who would be losin' gold money round heah? We ain't   60 even seen none dese white folks wearin' no gold money on dey watch chain. You must be figgerin' Mister Packard or Mister Cadillac goin' pass through heah."

"You don't know whut been lost 'round heah. Maybe somebody way back in memorial times lost they gold money and went on off and it ain't never been found. And then if we wuz to find it, you could wear some 'thout havin' no gang of womens lak dat Slemmons say he got."

Joe laughed and hugged her. "Don't be so wishful 'bout me. Ah'm satisfied de way Ah is. So long as Ah be yo' husband, Ah don't keer 'bout nothin' else. Ah'd ruther all de other womens in de world to be dead than for you to have de toothache. Less we go to bed and git our night rest."

It was Saturday night once more before Joe could parade his wife in Slemmons' ice cream parlor again. He worked the night shift and Saturday was his only night off. Every other evening around six o'clock he left home, and dying dawn saw him hustling home around the lake where the challenging sun flung a flaming sword from east to west across the trembling water.

That was the best part of life—going home to Missie May. Their whitewashed house, the mock battle on Satur-

> That was the best part of life—going home to Missie May.

day, the dinner and ice cream parlor afterwards, church on Sunday nights when Missie outdressed any woman in town—all, everything was right.

65   One night around eleven the acid ran out at the G and G. The foreman knocked off the crew and let the steam die down. As Joe rounded the lake on his way home, a lean moon rode the lake in a silver boat. If anybody had asked Joe about the moon on the lake, he would have said he hadn't paid it any attention. But he saw it with his feelings. It made him yearn painfully for Missie. Creation obsessed him. He thought about children. They had been married more than a year now. They had money put away. They ought to be making little feet for shoes. A little boy child would be about right.

He saw a dim light in the bedroom and decided to come in through the kitchen door. He could wash the fertilizer dust off himself before presenting himself to Missie May. It would be nice for her not to know that he was there until he slipped into his place in bed and hugged her back. She always liked that.

He eased the kitchen door open slowly and silently, but when he went to set his dinner bucket on the table he bumped it into a pile of dishes, and something crashed to the floor. He heard his wife gasp in fright and hurried to reassure her.

"Iss me, honey. Don't git skeered."

There was a quick, large movement in the bedroom. A rustle, a thud, and a stealthy silence. The light went out.

70   What? Robbers? Murderers? Some varmint attacking his helpless wife, perhaps. He struck a match, threw himself on guard and stepped over the door-sill into the bedroom

The great belt on the wheel of Time slipped and eternity stood still. By the match light he could see the man's legs fighting with his breeches in his frantic desire to get them on. He had both chance and time to kill the intruder in his helpless condition—half in and half out of his pants—but he was too weak to take action. The shapeless enemies of humanity that live in the hours of Time

There was a quick, large movement in the bedroom. A rustle, a thud, and a stealthy silence. The light went out.

had waylaid Joe. He was assaulted in his weakness. Like Samson awakening after his haircut. So he just opened his mouth and laughed.

The match went out and he struck another and lit the lamp. A howling wind raced across his heart, but underneath its fury he heard his wife sobbing and Slemmons pleading for his life. Offering to buy it with all that he had. "Please, suh, don't kill me. Sixty-two dollars at de sto'. Gold money."

Joe just stood. Slemmons looked at the window, but it was screened. Joe stood out like a rough-backed mountain between him and the door. Barring him from escape, from sunrise, from life.

He considered a surprise attack upon the big clown that stood there laughing like a chessy cat. But before his fist could travel an inch, Joe's own rushed out to crush him like a battering ram. Then Joe stood over him.

"Git into yo' damn rags, Slemmons, and dat quick."   75

Slemmons scrambled to his feet and into his vest and coat. As he grabbed his hat, Joe's fury overrode his intentions and he grabbed at Slemmons with his left hand and struck at him with his right. The right landed. The left grazed the front of his vest. Slemmons was knocked a somersault into the kitchen and fled through the open door. Joe found himself alone with Missie May, with the golden watch charm clutched in his left fist. A short bit of broken chain dangled between his fingers.

Missie May was sobbing. Wails of weeping without words. Joe stood, and after awhile he found out that he had something in his hand. And then he stood and felt without thinking and without seeing with his natural eyes. Missie May kept on crying and Joe kept on feeling so much and not knowing what to do with all his feelings, he put Slemmons' watch charm in his pants pocket and took a good laugh and went to bed.

"Missie May, whut you cryin' for?"

"Cause Ah love you so hard and Ah know you don't love *me* no mo'."

Joe sank his face into the pillow for a   80 spell then he said huskily, "You don't know de feelings of dat yet, Missie May."

"Oh Joe, honey, he said he wuz gointer give me dat gold money and he jes' kept on after me—"

Joe was very still and silent for a long time. Then he said, "Well, don't cry no mo', Missie May. Ah got yo' gold piece for you."

The hours went past on their rusty ankles. Joe still and quiet on one bed-rail and Missie May wrung dry of sobs on the other. Finally the sun's tide crept upon the shore of night and drowned all its hours. Missie May with her face stiff and streaked towards the window saw the dawn come into her yard. It was day. Nothing more. Joe wouldn't be coming home as usual. No need to fling open the front door and sweep off the porch, making it nice for Joe. Never no more breakfast to cook; no more washing and starching of Joe's jumper-jackets and pants. No more nothing. So why get up?

> **The yellow coin in his trousers** was like a monster hiding in the cave of his pockets to destroy her.

With this strange man in her bed, she felt embarrassed to get up and dress. She decided to wait till he had dressed and gone. Then she would get up, dress quickly and be gone forever beyond reach of Joe's looks and laughs. But he never moved. Red light turned to yellow, then white.

85   From beyond the no-man's land between them came a voice. A strange voice that yesterday had been Joe's.

"Missie May, ain't you gonna fix me no breakfus'?"

She sprang out of bed. "Yeah, Joe. Ah didn't reckon you wuz hongry."

No need to die today. Joe needed her for a few more minutes anyhow.

Soon there was a roaring fire in the cook stove. Water bucket full and two chickens killed. Joe loved fried chicken and rice. She didn't deserve a thing and good Joe was letting her cook him some breakfast. She rushed hot biscuits to the table as Joe took his seat.

90   He ate with his eyes in his plate. No laughter, no banter.

"Missie May, you ain't eatin' yo' breakfus'."

"Ah don't choose none, Ah thank yuh."

His coffee cup was empty. She sprang to refill it. When she turned from the stove and bent to set the cup beside Joe's plate, she saw the yellow coin on the table between them.

She slumped into her seat and wept into her arms.

95   Presently Joe said calmly, "Missie May, you cry too much. Don't look back lak Lot's wife and turn to salt."

The sun, the hero of every day, the impersonal old man that beams as brightly on death as on birth, came up every morning and raced across the blue dome and dipped into the sea of fire every evening. Water ran down hill and birds nested.

Missie knew why she didn't leave Joe. She couldn't. She loved him too much, but she could not understand why Joe didn't leave her. He was polite, even kind at times, but aloof.

There were no more Saturday romps. No ringing silver dollars to stack beside her plate. No pockets to rifle. In fact the yellow coin in his trousers was like a monster hiding in the cave of his pockets to destroy her.

She often wondered if he still had it, but nothing could have induced her to ask nor yet to explore his pockets to see for herself. Its shadow was in the house whether or no.

100   One night Joe came home around midnight and complained of pains in the back. He asked Missie to rub him down with liniment. It had been three months since Missie had touched his body and it all seemed strange. But she rubbed him. Grateful for the chance. Before morning, youth triumphed and Missie exulted. But the next day, as she joyfully made up their bed, beneath her pillow she found the piece of money with the bit of chain attached.

Alone to herself, she looked at the thing with loathing, but look she must. She took it into her hands with trembling and saw first thing that it was no gold piece. It was a gilded half dollar. Then she knew why Slemmons had forbidden anyone to touch his gold. He trusted village eyes at a distance not to recognize his stick-pin as a gilded quarter, and his watch charm as a four-bit piece.

She was glad at first that Joe had left it there. Perhaps he was through with her punishment. They were man and wife again. Then another thought came clawing at her. He had come home to buy from her as if she were any woman in the long house. Fifty cents for her love. As if to say that he could pay as well as Slemmons. She slid the coin into his Sunday pants pocket and dressed herself and left his house.

Halfway between her house and the quarters she met her husband's mother, and after a short talk she turned and went back home. Never would she admit defeat to that woman who prayed for it nightly. If she had not the substance of marriage she had the outside show. Joe must leave *her*. She let him see she didn't want his gold four-bits too.

She saw no more of the coin for some time though she knew that Joe could not help finding it in his pocket. But his health kept poor, and he came home at least every ten days to be rubbed.

105 The sun swept around the horizon, trailing its robes of weeks and days. One morning as Joe came in from work, he found Missie May chopping wood. Without a word he took the ax and chopped a huge pile before he stopped.

"You ain't got no business choppin' wood, and you know it."

"How come? Ah been choppin' it for de last longest."

"Ah ain't blind. You makin' feet for shoes."

"Won't you be glad to have a lil baby chile, Joe?"

110 "You know dat 'thout astin' me."

"Iss gointer be a boy chile and de very spit of you."

"You reckon, Missie May?"

"Who else could it look lak?"

Joe said nothing, but he thrust his hand deep into his pocket and fingered something there.

115 It was almost six months later Missie May took to bed and Joe went and got his mother to come wait on the house.

Missie May was delivered of a fine boy. Her travail was over when Joe came in from work one morning. His mother and the old women were drinking great bowls of coffee around the fire in the kitchen.

The minute Joe came into the room his mother called him aside.

"How did Missie May make out?" he asked quickly.

"Who, dat gal? She strong as a ox. She gointer have plenty mo'. We done fixed her wid de sugar and lard to sweeten her for de nex' one."

120 Joe stood silent awhile.

"You ain't ast 'bout de baby, Joe. You oughter be mighty proud cause he sho is de spittin' image of yuh, son. Dat's yourn all right, if you never git another one, dat un is yourn. And you know Ah'm mighty proud too, son, cause Ah never thought well of you marryin' Missie May cause her ma used tuh fan her foot round right smart and Ah been mighty skeered dat Missie May wuz gointer git misput on her road."

Joe said nothing. He fooled around the house till late in the day then just before he went to work, he went and stood at the foot of the bed and asked his wife how she felt. He did this every day during the week.

"Ah ain't blind. You makin' feet for shoes."

On Saturday he went to Orlando to make his market. It had been a long time since he had done that.

Meat and lard, meal and flour, soap and starch. Cans of corn and tomatoes. All the staples. He fooled around town for awhile and bought bananas and apples. Way after while he went around to the candy store.

125 "Hello, Joe," the clerk greeted him. "Ain't seen you in a long time."

"Nope, Ah ain't been heah. Been round in spots and places."

"Want some of them molasses kisses you always buy?"

"Yessuh." He threw the gilded half dollar on the counter. "Will dat spend?"

"What is it, Joe? Well, I'll be doggone! A gold-plated four-bit piece. Where'd you git it, Joe?"

130 "Offen a stray nigger dat come through Eatonville. He had it on his watch chain for a charm—goin' round making out iss gold money. Ha ha! He had a quarter on his tie pin and it wuz all golded up too. Tryin' to fool people. Makin' out he so rich and everything. Ha! Ha! Tryin' to tole off folkses wives from home."

"How did you git it, Joe? Did he fool you, too?"

"Who, me? Naw suh! He ain't fooled me none. Know whut Ah done? He come round me wid his smart talk. Ah hauled off and knocked 'im down and took his old four-bits way from 'im. Gointer buy my wife some good ole lasses kisses wid it. Gimme fifty cents worth of dem candy kisses."

"Fifty cents buys a mighty lot of candy kisses, Joe. Why don't you split it up and take some chocolate bars, too? They eat good, too."

"Yessuh, dey do, but Ah wants all dat in kisses. Ah got a lil boy chile home now. Tain't a week old yet, but he kin suck a sugar tit and maybe eat one them kisses hisself."

135 Joe got his candy and left the store. The clerk turned to the next customer. "Wisht I could be like these darkies. Laughin' all the time. Nothin' worries 'em."

Back in Eatonville, Joe reached his own front door. There was the ring of singing metal on wood. Fifteen times. Missie May couldn't run to the door, but she crept there as quickly as she could.

"Joe Banks, Ah hear you chunkin' money in mah do'way. You wait till Ah got mah strength back and Ah'm gointer fix you for dat."

IF YOU LIKED "THE GILDED SIX-BITS," YOU MIGHT ALSO LIKE . . .

. . . other stories by Southern writers, such as William Faulkner, Flannery O'Connor, and Ralph Ellison, all in the case study on the American South in Chapter 15; Faulkner can also be found in Chapter 11 , and Flannery O'Connor can also be found in Chapter 12.

GOING FURTHER   Hurston did primary anthropological research among black populations in Florida and hob-nobbed with the New York intellectual crowd in Manhattan during the period known as the Harlem Renaissance. Contemporary black American women writers such as Alice Walker and Toni Morrison point to her as an ancestor; the former's *The Color Purple* and the latter's *Song of Solomon* and *Beloved* owe much to the example of *Their Eyes Were Watching God*.

Writing from Reading

Summarize

1   This story is written as a single con-tinuous narrative, but the events take place over a long period of time. Estimate how much time actually passes between the beginning of the story and the end.

Analyze Craft

2   How does the narrator's use of figu-rative language, such as "The hours went past on their rusty ankles," affect the tone of the story?

3   Identify the key events of this story and arrange them into rising action, climax, falling action, and dénouement.

Does the story conform to the standard plot arc described earlier in Chapter 8?

Analyze Voice

4   In what ways does dialect suggest a sense of place; how do Joe and the candy shop clerk indicate location in and by their speech?

5   Compare the written voices of Joe and the candy shop clerk near the end of the story. How does the clerk's dialect differ? Why do you think Hurston chose to introduce this different voice into the story at the end?

Synthesize Summary and Analysis

6   Throughout the story, Joe gives coins to Missie May. What is the significance of the silver dollars at the beginning of the story? Contrast this with Joe's meaning when he leaves Missie May the gilded coin on the table. How has the significance of the silver dollars changed at the end of the story?

Interpret the Story

7   Why does Missie May sleep with Mr. Slemmons? In the end, why does Joe forgive his wife?

Edgar Allan Poe (1809–1849)

Edgar Allan Poe was born Edgar Arnold Poe in Boston. His parents were actors, and both died by 1811, leaving him orphaned. He spent much of his youth in Virginia under the care of John Allan, a tobacco merchant. Allan sent Poe to college at the University of Virginia, but when Poe turned to gambling, Allan withdrew his support, forcing Poe to drop out in 1826. That same year, Poe published his first book of poetry, *Tamerlane and Other Poems.* In the years that followed, Poe wore many hats. He briefly attended West Point Military Academy and served briefly in the U.S. Army. In 1836 he married his thirteen-year-old cousin, Virginia Clem. Editing and contributing to the *Southern Literary Messenger, Graham's Magazine,* and other publications, Poe also wrote book reviews for various periodicals. He published his own writing in popular magazines such as *The Broadway Journal,* and he dreamed of founding his own literary journal. Poe started out as a poet (his most famous poem is "The Raven"), and he did publish one short novel, *The Narrative of Arthur Gordon Pym* (1838), but he mostly devoted himself to short fiction. Today, he is best known for his horror stories (including "The Cask of Amontillado," "The Fall of the House of Usher," "The Masque of the Red Death," "The Black Cat," "The Tell-Tale Heart," and many others). Critics consider Poe to have invented the genre of the detective mystery with such stories as "The Purloined Letter" and "The Murders in the Rue Morgue."

In his horror stories, Poe uses lush language to render setting in great detail, creating an atmosphere of terror and, often, despair. His unsettling plots rely on suspense and the revelation of terrible secrets, but the settings, as perceived by troubled narrators who are drawn into the horror as actors or observers, are what give these stories their dark and bizarre flavor. In the tale that follows, "The Cask of Amontillado," a subterranean labyrinth takes on the literal and symbolic importance of a main character; in such fiction, setting both drives and embodies the plot. Poe died in Baltimore in 1849 when he was forty years old. The circumstances of his death were mysterious and have been the source of much speculation. His official obituary reported only "a congestion of the brain."

AS YOU READ   Consider the single-minded, and perhaps even simple-minded, goal of the main character, and ask yourself how a psychiatrist or therapist might describe his behavior. Does the setting in the end seem to correspond with the character's state of mind?

The Cask of Amontillado (1846)

1   THE thousand injuries of Fortunato I had borne as I best could, but when he ventured upon insult I vowed revenge. You, who so well know the nature of my soul, will not suppose, however, that gave utterance to a threat. At *length* I would be avenged; this was a point definitely settled—but the very definitiveness with which it was resolved precluded the idea of risk. I must not only punish but punish with impunity. A wrong is unredressed when

retribution overtakes its redresser. It is equally unredressed when the avenger fails to make himself felt as such to him who has done the wrong.

It must be understood that neither by word nor deed had I given Fortunato cause to doubt my good will. I continued, as was my wont, to smile in his face, and he did not perceive that my smile *now* was at the thought of his immolation.

He had a weak point—this Fortunato—although in other regards he was a man to be respected and even feared. He prided himself on his connoisseurship in wine. Few Italians have the true virtuoso spirit. For the most part their enthusiasm is adopted to suit the time and opportunity, to practise imposture upon the British and Austrian *millionaires*. In painting and gemmary, Fortunato, like his countrymen, was a quack, but in the matter of old wines he was sincere. In this respect I did not differ from him materially;—I was skillful in the Italian vintages myself, and bought largely whenever I could.

It was about dusk, one evening during the supreme madness of the carnival season, that I encountered my friend. He accosted me with excessive warmth, for he had been drinking much. The man wore motley. He had on a tight-fitting parti-striped dress, and his head was surmounted by the conical cap and bells. I was so pleased to see him that I thought I should never have done wringing his hand.

5   I said to him—"My dear Fortunato, you are luckily met. How remarkably well you are looking to-day. But I have received a pipe of what passes for Amontillado, and I have my doubts."

"How?" said he. "Amontillado, A pipe? Impossible! And in the middle of the carnival!"

"I have my doubts," I replied; "and I was silly enough to pay the full Amontillado price without consulting you in the matter. You were not to be found, and I was fearful of losing a bargain."

"Amontillado!"

"I have my doubts."

"Amontillado!"

10   "And I must satisfy them."

> **". . . I have received a pipe of what passes for Amontillado, and I have my doubts."**

"Amontillado!"

"As you are engaged, I am on my way to Luchresi. If any one has a critical turn it is he. He will tell me—"

"Luchresi cannot tell Amontillado from Sherry."

"And yet some fools will have it that his taste is a match   15
for your own."

"Come, let us go."

"Whither?"

"To your vaults."

"My friend, no; I will not impose upon your good nature. I perceive you have an engagement. Luchresi—"

"I have no engagement;—come."   20

"My friend, no. It is not the engagement, but the severe cold with which I perceive you are afflicted. The vaults are insufferably damp. They are encrusted with nitre."

"Let us go, nevertheless. The cold is merely nothing. Amontillado! You have been imposed upon. And as for Luchresi, he cannot distinguish Sherry from Amontillado."

Thus speaking, Fortunato possessed himself of my arm; and putting on a mask of black silk and drawing a *roquelaire* closely about my person, I suffered him to hurry me to my palazzo.

There were no attendants at home; they had absconded to make merry in honor of the time. I had told them that I should not return until the morning, and had given them explicit orders not to stir from the house. These orders were sufficient, I well knew, to insure their immediate disappearance, one and all, as soon as my back was turned.

I took from their sconces two flambeaux, and giving one   25
to Fortunato, bowed him through several suites of rooms to the archway that led into the vaults. I passed down a long and winding staircase, requesting him to be cautious as he followed. We came at length to the foot of the descent, and stood together upon the damp ground of the catacombs of the Montresors.

The gait of my friend was unsteady, and the bells upon his cap jingled as he strode.

"The pipe," he said.

"It is farther on," said I; "but observe the white web-work which gleams from these cavern walls."

He turned towards me, and looked into my eyes with two filmy orbs that distilled the rheum of intoxication.

"Nitre?" he asked, at length.   30

"Nitre," I replied. "How long have you had that cough?"

"Ugh! ugh! ugh!—ugh! ugh! ugh!—ugh! ugh! ugh!—ugh! ugh! ugh!—ugh! ugh! ugh!"

My poor friend found it impossible to reply for many minutes.

"It is nothing," he said, at last.

35　"Come," I said, with decision, "we will go back; your health is precious. You are rich, respected, admired, beloved; you are happy, as once I was. You are a man to be missed. For me it is no matter. We will go back; you will be ill, and I cannot be responsible. Besides, there is Luchresi—"

"Enough," he said; "the cough's a mere nothing; it will not kill me. I shall not die of a cough."

"True—true," I replied; "and, indeed, I had no intention of alarming you unnecessarily—but you should use all proper caution. A draught of this Médoc will defend us from the damps."

Here I knocked off the neck of a bottle which I drew from a long row of its fellows that lay upon the mould.

"Drink," I said, presenting him the wine.

40　He raised it to his lips with a leer. He paused and nodded to me familiarly, while his bells jingled.

"I drink," he said, "to the buried that repose around us."

"And I to your long life."

He again took my arm, and we proceeded.

"These vaults," he said, "are extensive."

45　"The Montresors," I replied, "were a great and numerous family."

"I forget your arms."

"A huge human foot d'or, in a field azure; the foot crushes a serpent rampant whose fangs are imbedded in the heel."

"And the motto?"

"*Nemo me impune lacessit.*"

50　"Good!" he said.

The wine sparkled in his eyes and the bells jingled. My own fancy grew warm with the Médoc. We had passed through long walls of piled skeletons, with casks and puncheons intermingling, into the inmost recesses of the catacombs. I paused again, and this time I made bold to seize Fortunato by an arm above the elbow.

"The nitre!" I said; "see, it increases. It hangs like moss upon the vaults. We are below the river's bed. The drops of moisture trickle among the bones. Come, we will go back ere it is too late. Your cough—"

> We had passed through long walls of piled skeletons, with casks and puncheons intermingling, into the inmost recesses of the catacombs.

"It is nothing," he said; "let us go on. But first, another draught of the Médoc."

I broke and reached him a flagon of De Grâve. He emptied it at a breath. His eyes flashed with a fierce light. He laughed and threw the bottle upwards with a gesticulation I did not understand.

I looked at him in surprise. He repeated the movement—a grotesque one.　55

"You do not comprehend?" he said.

"Not I," I replied.

"Then you are not of the brotherhood."

"How?"

"You are not of the masons."　60

"Yes, yes," I said; "yes, yes."

"You? Impossible! A mason?"

"A mason," I replied.

"A sign," he said, "a sign."

"It is this," I answered, producing from beneath the folds of my *roquelaire* a trowel.　65

"You jest," he exclaimed, recoiling a few paces. "But let us proceed to the Amontillado."

"Be it so," I said, replacing the tool beneath the cloak and again offering him my arm. He leaned upon it heavily. We continued our route in search of the Amontillado. We passed through a range of low arches, descended, passed on, and descending again, arrived at a deep crypt, in which the foulness of the air caused our flambeaux rather to glow than flame.

At the most remote end of the crypt there appeared another less spacious. Its walls had been lined with human remains, piled to the vault overhead, in the fashion of the great catacombs of Paris. Three sides of this interior crypt were still ornamented in this manner. From the fourth side the bones had been thrown down, and lay promiscuously upon the earth, forming at one point a mound of some size. Within the wall thus exposed by the displacing of the

bones, we perceived a still interior crypt or recess, in depth about four feet, in width three, in height six or seven. It seemed to have been constructed for no especial use within itself, but formed merely the interval between two of the colossal supports of the roof of the catacombs, and was backed by one of their circumscribing walls of solid granite.

It was in vain that Fortunato, uplifting his dull torch, endeavoured to pry into the depth of the recess. Its termination the feeble light did not enable us to see.

70 "Proceed," I said; "herein is the Amontillado. As for Luchresi—"

"He is an ignoramus," interrupted my friend, as he stepped unsteadily forward, while I followed immediately at his heels. In an instant he had reached the extremity of the niche, and finding his progress arrested by the rock, stood stupidly bewildered. A moment more and I had fettered him to the granite. In its surface were two iron sta-

A moment more and I had fettered him to the granite.

ples, distant from each other about two feet, horizontally. From one of these depended a short chain, from the other a padlock. Throwing the links about his waist, it was but the work of a few seconds to secure it. He was too much astounded to resist. Withdrawing the key I stepped back from the recess.

"Pass your hand," I said, "over the wall; you cannot help feeling the nitre. Indeed, it is *very* damp. Once more let me *implore* you to return. No? Then I must positively leave you. But I must first render you all the little attentions in my power."

"The Amontillado!" ejaculated my friend, not yet recovered from his astonishment.

"True," I replied; "the Amontillado."

As I said these words I busied myself among the pile of 75 bones of which I have before spoken. Throwing them aside, I soon uncovered a quantity of building stone and mortar. With these materials and with the aid of my trowel, I began vigorously to wall up the entrance of the niche.

I had scarcely laid the first tier of the masonry when I discovered that the intoxication of Fortunato had in a great measure worn off. The earliest indication I had of this was a low moaning cry from the depth of the recess. It was *not* the cry of a drunken man. There was a long and obstinate silence. I laid the second tier, and the third, and the fourth; and then I heard the furious vibrations of the chain. The noise lasted for several minutes, during which, that I might hearken to it with the more satisfaction, I ceased my labors and sat down upon the bones. When at last the clanking subsided, I resumed the trowel, and finished without interruption the fifth, the sixth, and the seventh tier. The wall was now nearly upon a level with my breast. I again paused, and holding the flambeaux over the mason-work, threw a few feeble rays upon the figure within.

A succession of loud and shrill screams, bursting suddenly from the throat of the chained form, seemed to thrust me violently back. For a brief moment I hesitated, I trembled. Unsheathing my rapier, I began to grope with it about the recess; but the thought of an instant reassured me. I placed my hand upon the solid fabric of the catacombs, and felt satisfied. I reapproached the wall; I replied to the yells of him who clamoured. I re-echoed, I aided, I surpassed them in volume and in strength. I did this, and the clamourer grew still.

It was now midnight, and my task was drawing to a close. I had completed the eighth, the ninth and the tenth tier. I had finished a portion of the last and the eleventh; there remained but a single stone to be fitted and plastered in. I struggled with its weight; I placed it partially in its destined position. But now there came from out the niche a low laugh that erected the hairs upon my head. It was succeeded by a sad voice, which I had difficulty in recognizing as that of the noble Fortunato. The voice said—

"Ha! ha! ha!—he! he! he!—a very good joke, indeed—an excellent jest. We will have many a rich laugh about it at the palazzo—he! he! he!—over our wine—he! he! he!"

"The Amontillado!" I said.   80

"He! he! he!—he! he! he!—yes, the Amontillado. But is it not getting late? Will not they be awaiting us at the palazzo, the Lady Fortunato and the rest? Let us be gone."

"Yes," I said, "let us be gone."

"For the love of God, Montresor!"

"Yes," I said, "for the love of God!"

But to these words I hearkened in vain for a reply. I   85
grew impatient. I called aloud—

"Fortunato!"

No answer. I called again—

"Fortunato!"

No answer still. I thrust a torch through the remaining aperture and let it fall within. There came forth in return only a jingling of the bells. My heart grew sick; it was the dampness of the catacombs that made it so. I hastened to make an end of my labour. I forced the last stone into its position; I plastered it up. Against the new masonry I re-erected the old rampart of bones. For the half of a century no mortal has disturbed them. *In pace requiescat!*

IF YOU LIKED "THE CASK OF AMONTILLADO," YOU MIGHT ALSO LIKE . . .

. . . the macabre stories of violence and suspense in William Faulkner's "A Rose for Emily" (Chapter 11) or Joyce Carol Oates's "Where Are You Going, Where Have You Been?" (Chapter 8).

GOING FURTHER   In many of his other stories Poe conjures up settings and landscapes somewhere between actual geography and dream world. In his novella *The Narrative of Arthur Gordon Pym* he creates a distinctive polar setting without ever having traveled anywhere near the regions he describes.

Writing from Reading

Summarize

1 Why does Montresor seek revenge on Fortunato? In what ways does Fortunato "insult" Montresor during the events of the story?

2 In the second sentence, the narrator asserts that "you," the reader, "know the nature of [his] soul." What do you know about the narrator when he first makes this claim, and what do you know about him by the end of the story?

Analyze Craft

3 How do certain literal actions—the desire to taste the special wine, the descent into the cellar—suggest meaning beyond themselves? How does the setting of the cave—the bones, and so on—portend the story's end?

4 Why do you think Poe chose to set this story during the season of Carnival? How would the tone of the story change if it were set on Christmas day?

Analyze Voice

5 To what extent is Montresor a reliable narrator, and how do you know? Based on what you know about Montresor, do you believe Fortunato deserved his fate? It may help here to remember that "mon trésor" means "my treasure" in French and that "Fortunato" can be translated from the Italian as "lucky one."

Synthesize Summary and Analysis

6 Read Montresor's description of his family crest in paragraph 47. What is the significance of this image in the context of the story? Is Montresor the serpent or the crushing heel?

7 At the end of the story, Montresor says that fifty years have since passed, and he exults, *"In pace requiescat"* ("Rest in peace"). Has Montresor found peace by entombing Fortunato? In your answer, consider the Montresor family motto, *"Nemo me impune lacessit"* ("No one strikes me with impunity").

"Inspirations can come from the outside world virtually at any time. . . . We may just be looking through the newspaper, or we may be driving along or talking to someone. . . . Once in a while, something will enter into you, and it imprints itself very deeply into you. . . . I don't think that one can write or create any kind of art that doesn't have a deep resonance in the artist or writer's unconscious." Conversation with Joyce Carol Oates

Reading for Setting

When reading for setting, ask yourself how *time* and *place* create a series of expectations among readers for the cast of characters they're likely to encounter and the range of events likely to occur, and play a role in the overall *effect* of the story.

What *elements* of setting can you identify?

- What is the story's location?
- What mood does the setting create?
- How is setting a window into character?
- How does setting shape character?
- Is setting a character itself?
- Is setting an expression of the story's theme?
- How is setting a window into a particular region?
- What is the *physical* or *social environment* of the setting?
- When does the story occur (day, year, era)?
- Is weather a part of the setting?
- Is the setting a comfortable one, or is it unpleasant, even brutalizing?
- What are the living and working conditions?
- What are the social conditions in the era in which the story occurs?

Writing about Setting

1. After reading the introduction to this chapter and the stories within it, what would you add to our definition of *setting*? Use evidence from the stories to illustrate your new definition.

2. "The Cask of Amontillado" and "The Gilded Six-Bits" both feature narrators with distinctive voices. How do Poe and Hurston use these voices to establish a sense of place? Give examples.

3. The main events of Lopez's story occur in the first half of the 1800s. What were the conditions for native people in Nebraska at that time? How might those conditions have influenced the relationship between Foster and the Pawnee and other tribes?

4. In Chopin's "The Storm" and Lopez's "The Location of the River," water takes on literal and metaphoric significance. Analyze the role the Niobrara River plays in Lopez's story and the role of the storm in Chopin's.

5. All four stories challenge readers as to what they can or should believe. Write an essay in which you discuss the role of uncertainty and mystery in each story, how they affect the reading experience, and how, possibly, the setting influenced your understanding of these questions.

11
Point of View

"Brownies" actually started out in the first-person point of view, and then I changed it to the third-person point of view, and then I changed it back to the first-person point of view. . . . The first [person] can oftentimes be the most personal point of view that a writer can employ, but it's also deceptively simple."

Conversation with ZZ Packer, available on video at connect.mcgraw-hill.com

"DAPHNE?" Arnetta asked. "Are you coming?"

We all looked back at the bending girl, the thin of her back hunched like the back of a custodian sweeping a stage, caught in limelight. Stray strands of her hair were lit near-transparent, thin fiber-optic threads. She did not nod yes to the question, nor did she shake her head no. She abided, bent. Then she began again, picking up leaves, wads of paper, the cotton fluff innards from a torn stuffed toy. She did it so methodically, so exquisitely, so humbly, she must have been trained. I thought of those dresses she wore, faded and old, yet so pressed and clean. I then saw the poverty in them; I then could imagine her mother, cleaning the houses of others, returning home, weary.

—from "Brownies" by ZZ Packer

THE character whose thoughts are revealed in this passage from ZZ Packer's "Brownies" is Laurel, nicknamed Snot. Laurel is the narrator, or the person who tells the story. The narrator relates events through the filter of her experiences, and it is from her point of view, or perspective, that the reader views the action. As Laurel reflects on Daphne, "the bending girl," she comes to a new understanding of the nature of Daphne's life. As the Brownie troop waits for a response to Arnetta's query—"Are you coming?"—Laurel looks closely at Daphne's movements and clothing and slowly recognizes that the "bending girl" is poor.

NARRATOR AND POINT OF VIEW

When the writer of an autobiography or memoir uses the first-person pronoun *I*, we're entitled to believe that *I* means the person writing the memoir. However, in fiction the narrator of a story is not the same as the writer. Writers invent, or make up, narrators to bring a story to life, and they provide a **point of view** by which to tell the tale. The writer's choice of narrator and point of view determines a great deal about what readers learn and when and how they learn it. Sometimes, as in the case of "Brownies," the story is told by means of a **first-person narrator,** a character in the story identified by use of the pronoun *I* or the plural first-person *we.* In contrast, many stories and novels use a **third-person narrator,** which means the characters are referred to by name or with the pronouns *he, she,* or *they.* Hemingway's story in this chapter, "Hills Like White Elephants," is an example of this third-person use. A third possibility, used less commonly, is for a story to be told by way of a **second-person narrator,** who addresses the reader directly (you), as Junot Diaz does in his story in this chapter.

CONTINUED ON PAGE 314

ZZ Packer

. . . there's almost . . . no better way to be a part of the world than to read.

A Conversation on Writing

Using Point of View to Craft "Brownies"

I found it very good to begin with that [first-person] voice because I felt as though I could just tell the story the way I thought that Laurel/Snot would. . . . And then I put it in third person so that I could see some of my blind spots. . . . This particular third person could see some things about the rest of the world but might not have access to everything that Laurel had access to. So then that allowed me to see beyond Laurel's point of view. So switching the point of view for me enabled me to get the voice, which I wanted, which was the first-person voice, but also to get the knowledge and range of information that sometimes authors can only get when they travel into the third-person point of view.

The Power of the First-Person Point of View

I like to think of first person [as] here's the "I" that's telling the story. . . . A lot of writers tend to believe that, Oh, it's really me telling the story and so sometimes they just pour everything in . . . [but] they don't realize that the voice, which can be confessional . . . is a storytelling voice, [a storytelling voice that] can easily get out of the writer's grasp because it's so powerful.

Reading to Be a Citizen of the World

I encounter people who don't like to read. I mean, to me it doesn't seem to be taking away from your time in the world, but just enrich-

ing it. When you read *War and Peace*, it's almost like having lived an extra ten years or something like that. So to me . . . there's almost . . . no better way to be a part of the world than to read. It almost seems the opposite of the way people think of it as a very solitary and even sort of solipsistic kind of activity. But I can't think of any other that would make me more of a citizen of the world.

ZZ Packer was born (1973) Zuwena Packer in Chicago. As she grew up in Atlanta and Louisville, her friends and family shortened Zuwena—Swahili for "good"—to ZZ, the name that she uses today. While attending Yale, Packer considered a career in engineering but ultimately turned to writing. Her debut short story collection, *Drinking Coffee Elsewhere* (2003), received great critical and popular acclaim; named a *New York Times* Notable Book, it was also picked for the *Today Show* Book Club by John Updike. In addition to appearing in *The New Yorker, Harper's,* and *Ploughshares,* her work has been anthologized in collections featuring young writers, Southern writers, and black women writers, among others. Her stories present a range of characters, most of whom struggle to fit into their community, and she often captures aspects of the African-American experience. Like her varied characters, Packer herself has a résumé that includes stints as a barmaid, a high school teacher, and a coffee shop barista as well as a Stegner Fellow at Stanford University's prestigious writing program. Packer currently lives and writes in San Francisco.

RESEARCH ASSIGNMENT In her interview, what does ZZ Packer say she is trying to tell a story about? Do you agree this is the subject of the story? How does she get her point across?

To watch this entire interview and hear the author read from "Brownies," go to connect.mcgraw-hill.com.

AS YOU READ   Notice the shifting levels of happiness and unhappiness among the characters. Notice also the shifting alliances among the characters at the center of the story.

TIP

FOR INTERACTIVE READING . . .

As you read, take note every time the story refers to a father. What is the significance of the various fathers the narrator mentions? How does this tie in with the lesson the girls experience at camp?

Brownies (1999)

1   BY our second day at Camp Crescendo, the girls in my Brownie troop had decided to kick the asses of each and every girl in Brownie Troop 909. Troop 909 was doomed from the first day of camp; they were white girls, their complexions a blend of ice cream: strawberry, vanilla. They turtled out from their bus in pairs, their rolled-up sleeping bags chromatized with Disney characters: Sleeping Beauty, Snow White, Mickey Mouse; or the generic ones cheap parents bought: washed-out rainbows, unicorns, curly-eyelashed frogs. Some clutched Igloo coolers and still others held on to stuffed toys like pacifiers, looking all around them like tourists determined to be dazzled.

Our troop was wending its way past their bus, past the ranger station, past the colorful trail guide drawn like a treasure map, locked behind glass.

"Man, did you smell them?" Arnetta said, giving the girls a slow once-over, "They smell like Chihua-huas. *Wet* Chihuahuas." Their troop was still at the entrance, and though we had passed them by yards, Arnetta raised her nose in the air and grimaced.

Arnetta said this from the very rear of the line, far away from Mrs. Margolin, who always strung our troop behind her like a brood of obedient ducklings. Mrs. Margolin even looked like a mother duck—she had hair cropped close to a small ball of a head, almost no neck, and huge, miraculous breasts. She wore enormous belts that looked like the kind that weightlifters wear, except hers would be cheap metallic gold or rabbit fur or covered with gigantic fake sunflowers, and often these belts would become nature lessons in and of themselves. "See," Mrs. Margolin once said to us, pointing to her belt, "this one's made entirely from the feathers of baby pigeons."

5   The belt layered with feathers was uncanny enough, but I was more disturbed by the realization that I had never actually *seen* a baby pigeon. I searched weeks for one, in vain—scampering after pigeons whenever I was downtown with my father.

But nature lessons were not Mrs. Margolin's top priority. She saw the position of troop leader as an evangelical post. Back at the A.M.E. church where our Brownie meetings were held, Mrs. Margolin was especially fond of imparting religious aphorisms by means of acrostics—"Satan" was the "Serpent Always Tempting and Noisome"; she'd refer to the "Bible" as "Basic Instructions Before Leaving Earth." Whenever she quizzed us on these, expecting to hear the acrostics parroted back to her, only Arnetta's correct replies soared over our vague mumblings. "Jesus?" Mrs. Margolin might ask expectantly, and Arnetta alone would dutifully answer, "Jehovah's Example, Saving Us Sinners."

Arnetta always made a point of listening to Mrs. Margolin's religious talk and giving her what she wanted to hear. Because of this, Arnetta could have blared through a megaphone that the white girls of Troop 909 were "wet Chihuahuas" without so much as a blink from Mrs. Margolin. Once, Arnetta killed the troop goldfish by feeding it a french fry covered in ketchup, and when Mrs. Margolin demanded that she explain what had happened, claimed the goldfish had been eyeing her meal for *hours,* then the fish—giving in to temptation—had leapt up and snatched a whole golden fry from her fingertips.

"*Serious* Chihuahua," Octavia added, and though neither Arnetta nor Octavia could *spell* "Chihuahua," had ever *seen* a Chihuahua, trisyllabic words had gained a sort of exoticism within our fourth-grade set at Woodrow Wilson Elementary. Arnetta and Octavia would flip through the dictionary, determined to work the vulgar-sounding ones like "Djibouti" and "asinine" into conversation.

"*Caucasian* Chihuahuas," Arnetta said.

That did it. The girls in my troop turned elastic: Drema and Elise doubled up on one another like inextricably entwined kites; Octavia slapped her belly; Janice jumped straight up in the air, then did it again, as if to slam-dunk her own head. They could not stop laughing. No one had laughed so hard since a boy named Martez had stuck a pencil in the electric socket and spent the whole day with a strange grin on his face.

10

"Girls, girls," said our parent helper, Mrs. Hedy. Mrs. Hedy was Octavia's mother, and she wagged her index finger perfunctorily, like a windshield wiper. "Stop it, now. Be good." She said this loud enough to be heard, but lazily, bereft of any feeling or indication that she meant to be obeyed, as though she could say these words again at the exact same pitch if a button somewhere on her were pressed.

But the rest of the girls didn't stop; they only laughed louder. It was the word "Caucasian" that got them all going. One day at school, about a month before the Brownie camping trip, Arnetta turned to a boy wearing impossibly high-ankled floodwater jeans and said, "What are you? *Caucasian?*" The word took off from there, and soon everything was Caucasian. If you ate too fast you ate like a Caucasian, if you ate too slow you ate like a Caucasian. The biggest feat anyone at Woodrow Wilson could do was to jump off the swing in midair, at the highest point in its arc, and if you fell (as I had, more than once) instead of landing on your feet, knees bent Olympic gymnast–style, Arnetta and Octavia were prepared to comment. They'd look at each other with the silence of passengers who'd narrowly escaped an accident, then nod their heads, whispering with solemn horror, "*Caucasian.*"

Even the only white kid in our school, Dennis, got in on the Caucasian act. That time when Martez stuck a pencil in the socket, Dennis had pointed and yelled, "That was *so* Caucasian!"

WHEN you lived in the south suburbs of Atlanta, it was easy to forget about whites. Whites were like those baby pigeons: real and existing, but rarely seen or thought about. Everyone had been to Rich's to go clothes shopping, everyone had seen white girls and their mothers coo-cooing over dresses; everyone had gone to the downtown library and seen white businessmen swish by importantly, wrists flexed in front of them to check the time as though they would change from Clark Kent into Superman at any second. But those images were as fleeting as cards shuffled in a deck, whereas the ten white girls behind us—*invaders,* Arnetta would later call them—were instantly real and memorable, with their long, shampoo-commercial hair, straight as spaghetti from the box. This alone was reason for envy and hatred. The only black girl most of us had ever seen with hair that long was Octavia, whose hair hung past her butt like a Hawaiian hula dancer's. The sight of Octavia's mane prompted other girls to listen to her reverentially, as though whatever she had to say would somehow activate their own follicles. For example, when, on the first day of camp, Octavia made as if to speak, and everyone fell silent. "Nobody," Octavia said, "calls us niggers."

15   At the end of that first day, when half of our troop made their way back to the cabin after tag-team restroom visits, Arnetta said she'd heard one of the Troop 909 girls call Daphne a nigger. The other half of the girls and I were helping Mrs. Margolin clean up the pots and pans from the campfire ravioli dinner. When we made our way to the restrooms to wash up and brush our teeth, we met up with Arnetta midway.

"Man, I completely heard the girl," Arnetta reported. "Right, Daphne?"

Daphne hardly ever spoke, but when she did, her voice was petite and tinkly, the voice one might expect from a shiny new earring. She'd written a poem once, for Langston Hughes Day, a poem brimming with all the teacher-winning ingredients—trees and oceans, sunsets and moons—but what cinched the poem for the grown-ups, snatching the win from Octavia's musical ode to Grandmaster Flash and the Furious Five, were Daphne's last lines:

You are my father, the veteran
When you cry in the dark
It rains and rains and rains in my heart

The word took off from there, and soon everything was Caucasian.

She'd always worn clean, though faded, jumpers and dresses when Chic jeans were the fashion, but when she went up to the dais to receive her prize journal, pages trimmed in gold, she wore a new dress with a velveteen bodice and a taffeta skirt as wide as an umbrella. All the kids clapped, though none of them understood the poem. I'd read encyclopedias the way others read comics, and I didn't get it. But those last lines pricked me, they were so eerie, and as my father and I ate cereal, I'd whisper over my Froot Loops, like a mantra, *"You are my father, the veteran. You are my father, the veteran, the veteran, the veteran,"* until my father, who acted in plays as Caliban and Othello and was not a veteran, marched me up to my teacher one morning and said, "Can you tell me what's wrong with this kid?"

I thought Daphne and I might become friends, but I think she grew spooked by me whispering those lines to her, begging her to tell me what they meant, and I soon understood that two quiet people like us were better off quiet alone.

"Daphne? Didn't you hear them call you a nig- 20 ger?" Arnetta asked, giving Daphne a nudge.

The sun was setting behind the trees, and their leafy tops formed a canopy of black lace for the flame of the sun to pass through. Daphne shrugged her shoulders at first, then slowly nodded her head when Arnetta gave her a hard look.

Twenty minutes later, when my restroom group returned to the cabin, Arnetta was still talking about Troop 909. My restroom group had passed by some of the 909 girls. For the most part, they deferred to us, waving us into the restrooms, letting us go even though they'd gotten there first.

We'd seen them, but from afar, never within their orbit enough to see whether their faces were the way all white girls appeared on TV—ponytailed and full of energy, bubbling over with love and money. All I could see was that some of them rapidly fanned their faces with their hands, though the heat of the day had long passed. A few seemed to be lolling their heads in slow circles, half purposefully, as if exercising the muscles of their necks, half ecstatically, like Stevie Wonder.

"We can't let them get away with that," Arnetta said, dropping her voice to a laryngitic whisper. "We can't let them get away with calling us niggers. I say we teach them a lesson." She sat down cross-legged on a sleeping bag, an embittered Buddha, eyes glimmering acrylic-black. "We can't go telling Mrs. Margolin, either. Mrs. Margolin'll say something about doing unto others and the path of righteousness and all. Forget that shit." She let her eyes flutter irreverently till they half closed, as though ignoring an insult not worth returning. We could all hear Mrs. Margolin outside, gathering the last of the metal campware.

25   Nobody said anything for a while. Usually people were quiet after Arnetta spoke. Her tone had an upholstered confidence that was somehow both regal and vulgar at once. It demanded a few moments of silence in its wake, like the ringing of a church bell or the playing of taps. Sometimes Octavia would ditto or dissent to whatever Arnetta had said, and this was the signal that others could speak. But this time Octavia just swirled a long cord of hair into pretzel shapes.

"*Well?*" Arnetta said. She looked as if she had discerned the hidden severity of the situation and was waiting for the rest of us to catch up. Everyone looked from Arnetta to Daphne. It was, after all, Daphne who had supposedly been called the name, but Daphne sat on the bare cabin floor, flipping through the pages of the Girl Scout handbook, eyebrows arched in mock wonder, as if the handbook were a catalogue full of bright and startling foreign costumes. Janice broke the silence. She clapped her hands to broach her idea of a plan.

"They gone be sleeping," she whispered conspiratorially, "then we gone sneak into they cabin, then we'll put daddy longlegs in they sleeping bags. Then

A secret meant nothing; it was like gossip . . .

they'll wake up. Then we gone beat 'em up till they're as flat as frying pans!" She jammed her fist into the palm of her hand, then made a sizzling sound.

Janice's country accent was laughable, her looks homely, her jumpy acrobatics embarrassing to behold. Arnetta and Octavia volleyed amused, arrogant smiles whenever Janice opened her mouth, but Janice never caught the hint, spoke whenever she wanted, fluttered around Arnetta and Octavia futilely offering her opinions to their departing backs. Whenever Arnetta and Octavia shooed her away, Janice loitered until the two would finally sigh and ask, "What *is* it, Miss Caucausoid? What do you *want?*"

"Shut up, Janice," Octavia said, letting a fingered loop of hair fall to her waist as though just the sound of Janice's voice had ruined the fun of her hair twisting.

Janice obeyed, her mouth hung open in a loose   30 grin, unflappable, unhurt.

"All right," Arnetta said, standing up. "We're going to have a secret meeting and talk about what we're going to do."

Everyone gravely nodded her head. The word "secret" had a built-in importance, the modifier form of the word carried more clout than the noun. A secret meant nothing; it was like gossip: just a bit of unpleasant knowledge about someone who happened to be someone other than yourself. A secret *meeting*, or a secret *club* was entirely different.

That was when Arnetta turned to me as though she knew that doing so was both a compliment and a charity.

"Snot, you're not going to be a bitch and tell Mrs. Margolin, are you?"

I had been called "Snot" ever since first grade,   35 when I'd sneezed in class and two long ropes of mucus had splattered a nearby girl.

"Hey," I said. "Maybe you didn't hear them right— I mean—"

"Are you gonna tell on us or not?" was all Arnetta wanted to know, and by the time the question was asked, the rest of our Brownie troop looked at me as though they'd already decided their course of action, me being the only impediment.

CAMP Crescendo used to double as a high-school-band and field hockey camp until an arcing field hockey ball landed on the clasp of a girl's metal barrette, knifing a skull nerve and paralyzing the right side of her body. The camp closed down for a few years and the girl's teammates built a memorial, filling the spot on which the girl fell with hockey balls, on which they had painted—all in nail polish—get-well tidings, flowers, and hearts. The balls were still stacked there, like a shrine of ostrich eggs embedded in the ground.

On the second day of camp, Troop 909 was dancing around the mound of hockey balls, their limbs jangling awkwardly, their cries like the constant summer squeal of an amusement park. There was a stream that bordered the field hockey lawn, and the girls from my troop settled next to it, scarfing down the last of lunch: sandwiches made from salami and slices of tomato that had gotten waterlogged from the melting ice in the cooler. From the stream bank, Arnetta eyed the Troop 909 girls, scrutinizing their movements to glean inspiration for battle.

40 "Man," Arnetta said, "we could bumrush them right now if that damn lady would *leave*."

The 909 troop leader was a white woman with the severe pageboy hairdo of an ancient Egyptian. She lay on a picnic blanket, sphinx-like, eating a banana, sometimes holding it out in front of her like a microphone. Beside her sat a girl slowly flapping one hand like a bird with a broken wing. Occasionally, the leader would call out the names of girls who'd attempted leapfrogs and flips, or of girls who yelled too loudly or strayed far from the circle.

"I'm just glad Big Fat Mama's not following us here," Octavia said. "At least we don't have to worry about her." Mrs. Margolin, Octavia assured us, was having her Afternoon Devotional, shrouded in mosquito netting, in a clearing she'd found. Mrs. Hedy was cleaning mud from her espadrilles in the cabin.

"I handled them." Arnetta sucked on her teeth and proudly grinned. "I told her we was going to gather leaves."

"Gather leaves," Octavia said, nodding respectfully. "That's a good one. Especially since they're so mad-crazy about this camping thing." She looked from ground to sky, sky to ground. Her hair hung down her back in two braids like a squaw's. "I mean, I really don't know why it's called *camping*—all we ever do with Nature is find some twigs and say something like, 'Wow, this fell from a tree.'" She then studied her sandwich. With two disdainful fingers, she picked out a slice of dripping tomato, the sections congealed with red slime. She pitched it into the stream embrowned with dead leaves and the murky effigies of other dead things, but in the opaque water, a group of small silver-brown fish appeared. They surrounded the tomato and nibbled.

"Look!" Janice cried. "Fishes! Fishes!" As she 45 scrambled to the edge of the stream to watch, a covey of insects threw up tantrums from the wheatgrass and nettle, a throng of tiny electric machines, all going at once. Octavia sneaked up behind Janice as if to push her in. Daphne and I exchanged terrified looks. It seemed as though only we knew that Octavia was close enough—and bold enough—to actually push Janice into the stream. Janice turned around quickly, but Octavia was already staring serenely into the still water as though she was gathering some sort of courage from it. "What's so funny?" Janice said, eyeing them all suspiciously.

Elise began humming the tune to "Karma Chameleon," all the girls joining in, their hums light and facile. Janice also began to hum, against everyone else, the high-octane opening chords of "Beat It."

"I love me some Michael Jackson," Janice said when she'd finished humming, smacking her lips as though Michael Jackson were a favorite meal. "I *will* marry Michael Jackson."

Before anyone had a chance to impress upon Janice the impossibility of this, Arnetta suddenly rose, made a sun visor of her hand, and watched Troop 909 leave the field hockey lawn.

"Dammit!" she said. "We've got to get them *alone*."

50   "They won't ever be alone," I said. All the rest of the girls looked at me, for I usually kept quiet. If I spoke even a word, I could count on someone calling me Snot. Everyone seemed to think that we could beat up these girls; no one entertained the thought that they might fight *back*. "The only time they'll be unsupervised is in the bathroom."

"Oh shut up, Snot," Octavia said.

But Arnetta slowly nodded her head. "The bathroom," she said. "The bathroom," she said, again and again. "The bathroom! The bathroom!"

ACCORDING to Octavia's watch, it took us five minutes to hike to the restrooms, which were midway between our cabin and Troop 909's. Inside, the mirrors above the sinks returned only the vaguest of reflections, as though someone had taken a scouring pad to their surfaces to obscure the shine. Pine needles, leaves, and dirty, flattened wads of chewing gum covered the floor like a mosaic. Webs of hair matted the drain in the middle of the floor. Above the sinks and below the mirrors, stacks of folded white paper towels lay on a long metal counter. Shaggy white balls of paper towels sat on the sinktops in a line like corsages on display. A thread of floss snaked from a wad of tissues dotted with the faint red-pink of blood. One of those white girls, I thought, had just lost a tooth.

Though the restroom looked almost the same as it had the night before, it somehow seemed stranger now. We hadn't noticed the wooden rafters coming together in great V's. We were, it seemed, inside a whale, viewing the ribs of the roof of its mouth.

> **Pine needles, leaves, and dirty, flattened** wads of chewing gum covered the floor like a mosaic.

"Wow. It's a mess," Elise said.   55

"You can say that again."

Arnetta leaned against the doorjamb of a restroom stall. "This is where they'll be again," she said. Just seeing the place, just having a plan seemed to satisfy her. "We'll go in and talk to them. You know, 'How you doing? How long'll you be here?' That sort of thing. Then Octavia and I are gonna tell them what happens when they call any one of us a nigger."

"I'm going to say something, too," Janice said.

Arnetta considered this. "Sure," she said. "Of course. Whatever you want."

Janice pointed her finger like a gun at Octa-   60 via and rehearsed the line she'd thought up, "'We're gonna teach you a *lesson*!' That's what I'm going to say." She narrowed her eyes like a TV mobster. "'We're gonna teach you little girls a lesson!'"

With the back of her hand, Octavia brushed Janice's finger away. "You couldn't teach me to shit in a toilet."

"But," I said, "what if they say, 'We didn't say that. We didn't call anyone an N-I-G-G-E-R.'"

"Snot," Arnetta said, and then sighed. "Don't think. Just fight. If you even know how."

Everyone laughed except Daphne. Arnetta gently laid her hand on Daphne's shoulder. "Daphne. You don't have to fight. We're doing this for you."

Daphne walked to the counter, took a clean paper   65 towel, and carefully unfolded it like a map. With it, she began to pick up the trash all around. Everyone watched.

"C'mon," Arnetta said to everyone. "Let's beat it." We all ambled toward the doorway, where the sunshine made one large white rectangle of light. We were immediately blinded, and we shielded our eyes with our hands and our forearms.

"Daphne?" Arnetta asked. "Are you coming?"

We all looked back at the bending girl, the thin of her back hunched like the back of a custodian sweeping a stage, caught in limelight. Stray strands of her hair were lit near-transparent, thin fiber-optic threads. She did not nod yes to the question, nor did she shake her head no. She abided, bent. Then she began again, picking up leaves, wads of paper, the cotton fluff innards from a torn stuffed toy. She did it so methodically, so exquisitely, so humbly, she must have been trained. I thought of those dresses she wore, faded and old, yet so pressed and clean. I then saw the poverty in them; I then could imagine her mother, cleaning the houses of others, returning home, weary.

"I guess she's not coming."

70 We left her and headed back to our cabin, over pine needles and leaves, taking the path full of shade.

"What about our secret meeting?" Elise asked.

Arnetta enunciated her words in a way that defied contradiction: "We just had it."

IT was nearing our bedtime, but the sun had not yet set.

"Hey, your mama's coming," Arnetta said to Octavia when she saw Mrs. Hedy walk toward the cabin, sniffling. When Octavia's mother wasn't giving bored, parochial orders, she sniffled continuously, mourning an imminent divorce from her husband. She might begin a sentence, "I don't know what Robert will do when Octavia and I are gone. Who'll buy him cigarettes?" and Octavia would hotly whisper, *Mama*, in a way that meant: Please don't talk about our problems in front of everyone. Please shut up.

75 But when Mrs. Hedy began talking about her husband, thinking about her husband, seeing clouds shaped like the head of her husband, she couldn't be quiet, and no one could dislodge her from the comfort of her own woe. Only one thing could perk her up—Brownie songs. If the girls were quiet, and Mrs. Hedy was in her dopey, sorrowful mood, she would say, "Y'all know I like those songs, girls. Why don't you sing one?" Everyone would groan, except me and Daphne. I, for one, liked some of the songs.

"C'mon, everybody," Octavia said drearily. "She likes the Brownie song best."

We sang, loud enough to reach Mrs. Hedy:

"I've got something in my pocket;
It belongs across my face.
And I keep it very close at hand
   in a most convenient place.
I'm sure you couldn't guess it
If you guessed a long, long while.
So I'll take it out and put it on—
It's a great big Brownie smile!"

The Brownie song was supposed to be sung cheerfully, as though we were elves in a workshop, singing as we merrily cobbled shoes, but everyone except me hated the song so much that they sang it like a maudlin record, played on the most sluggish of rpms.

"That was good," Mrs. Hedy said, closing the cabin door behind her. "Wasn't that nice, Linda?"

80 "Praise God," Mrs. Margolin answered without raising her head from the chore of counting out Popsicle sticks for the next day's craft session.

"Sing another one," Mrs. Hedy said. She said it with a sort of joyful aggression, like a drunk I'd once seen who'd refused to leave a Korean grocery.

"God, Mama, get over it," Octavia whispered in a voice meant only for Arnetta, but Mrs. Hedy heard it and started to leave the cabin.

"Don't go," Arnetta said. She ran after Mrs. Hedy and held her by the arm. "We haven't finished singing." She nudged us with a single look. "Let's sing the 'Friends Song.' For Mrs. Hedy."

Although I liked some of the songs, I hated this one:

Make new friends
But keep the o-old,
One is silver
And the other gold.

85 If most of the girls in the troop could be any type of metal, they'd be bunched-up wads of tinfoil, maybe, or rusty iron nails you had to get tetanus shots for.

"No, no, no," Mrs. Margolin said before anyone could start in on the "Friends Song." "An uplifting song. Something to lift her up and take her mind off all these earthly burdens."

Arnetta and Octavia rolled their eyes. Everyone knew what song Mrs. Margolin was talking about, and no one, no one, wanted to sing it.

"Please, no," a voice called out. "Not 'The Doughnut Song.'"

"Please not 'The Doughnut Song,'" Octavia pleaded.

90 "I'll brush my teeth two times if I don't have to sing 'The Doughnut—'"

"Sing!" Mrs. Margolin demanded.

We sang:

"Life without Jesus is like a do-ough-nut!
Like a do-ooough-nut!
Like a do-ooough-nut!
Life without Jesus is like a do-ough-nut!
There's a hole in the middle of my soul!"

There were other verses, involving other pastries, but we stopped after the first one and cast glances toward Mrs. Margolin to see if we could gain a reprieve. Mrs. Margolin's eyes fluttered blissfully. She was half asleep.

"Awww," Mrs. Hedy said, as though giant Mrs. Margolin were a cute baby, "Mrs. Margolin's had a long day."

95 "Yes, indeed," Mrs. Margolin answered. "If you don't mind, I might just go to the lodge where the beds are. I haven't been the same since the operation."

I had not heard of this operation, or when it had occurred, since Mrs. Margolin had never missed the once-a-week Brownie meetings, but I could see from Daphne's face that she was concerned, and I could see that the other girls had decided that Mrs. Margolin's operation must have happened long ago in some remote time unconnected to our own. Nevertheless, they put on sad faces. We had all been taught that adulthood was full of sorrow and pain, taxes and bills, dreaded work and dealings with whites, sick-

ness and death. I tried to do what the others did. I tried to look silent.

"Go right ahead, Linda," Mrs. Hedy said. "I'll watch the girls." Mrs. Hedy seemed to forget about divorce for a moment; she looked at us with dewy eyes, as if we were mysterious, furry creatures. Meanwhile, Mrs. Margolin walked through the maze of sleeping bags until she found her own. She gathered a neat stack of clothes and pajamas slowly, as though doing so was almost painful. She took her toothbrush, her toothpaste, her pillow. "All right!" Mrs. Margolin said, addressing us all from the threshold of the cabin. "Be in bed by nine." She said it with a twinkle in her voice, letting us know she was allowing us to be naughty and stay up till nine-fifteen.

"C'mon everybody," Arnetta said after Mrs. Margolin left. "Time for us to wash up."

Everyone watched Mrs. Hedy closely, wondering whether she would insist on coming with us since it was night, making a fight with Troop 909 nearly impossible. Troop 909 would soon be in the bathroom, washing their faces, brushing their teeth—completely unsuspecting of our ambush.

"We won't be long," Arnetta said. "We're old enough 100 to go to the restrooms by ourselves."

Mrs. Hedy pursed her lips at this dilemma. "Well, I guess you Brownies are almost Girl Scouts, right?"

"Right!"

"Just one more badge," Drema said.

"And about," Octavia droned, "a million more cookies to sell." Octavia looked at all of us, *Now's our chance,* her face seemed to say, but our chance to do *what,* I didn't exactly know.

Finally, Mrs. Hedy walked to the doorway where 105 Octavia stood dutifully waiting to say goodbye but looking bored doing it. Mrs. Hedy held Octavia's chin. "You'll be good?"

"Yes, Mama."

"And remember to pray for me and your father? If I'm asleep when you get back?"

"Yes, Mama."

WHEN the other girls had finished getting their toothbrushes and washcloths and flashlights for the group restroom trip, I was drawing pictures of tiny birds with too many feathers. Daphne was sitting on her sleeping bag, reading.

110 "You're not going to come?" Octavia asked.

Daphne shook her head.

"I'm gonna stay, too," I said. "I'll go to the restroom when Daphne and Mrs. Hedy go."

Arnetta leaned down toward me and whispered so that Mrs. Hedy, who'd taken over Mrs. Margolin's task of counting Popsicle sticks, couldn't hear. "No, Snot. If we get in trouble, you're going to get in trouble with the rest of us."

WE made our way through the darkness by flashlight. The tree branches that had shaded us just hours earlier, along the same path, now looked like arms sprouting menacing hands. The stars sprinkled the sky like spilled salt. They seemed fastened to the darkness, high up and holy, their places fixed and definite as we stirred beneath them.

115 Some, like me, were quiet because we were afraid of the dark; others were talking like crazy for the same reason.

"Wow!" Drema said, looking up. "Why are all the stars out here? I never see stars back on Oneida Street."

"It' a camping trip, that's why," Octavia said. "You're supposed to see stars on camping trips."

Janice said, "This place smells like my mother's air freshener."

"These woods are *pine*," Elise said. "Your mother probably uses *pine* air freshener."

120 Janice mouthed an exaggerated "Oh," nodding her head as though she just then understood one of the world's great secrets.

No one talked about fighting. Everyone was afraid enough just walking through the infinite deep of the woods. Even though I didn't fight to fight, was afraid of fighting, I felt I was part of the rest of the troop; like I was defending something. We trudged against the slight incline of the path, Arnetta leading the way.

"You know," I said, "their leader will be there. Or they won't even be there. It's dark already. Last night the sun was still in the sky. I'm sure they're already finished."

Arnetta acted as if she hadn't heard me. I followed her gaze with my flashlight, and that's when I saw the squares of light in the darkness. The bathroom was just ahead.

BUT the girls were there. We could hear them before we could see them.

"Octavia and I will go in first so they'll think 125 there's just two of us, then wait till I say, 'We're gonna teach you a lesson,'" Arnetta said. "Then, bust in. That'll surprise them."

"That's what I was supposed to say," Janice said.

Arnetta went inside, Octavia next to her. Janice followed, and the rest of us waited outside.

They were in there for what seemed like whole minutes, but something was wrong. Arnetta hadn't given the signal yet. I was with the girls outside when I heard one of the Troop 909 girls say, "NO. That did NOT happen!"

That was to be expected, that they'd deny the whole thing. What I hadn't expected was *the voice* in which the denial was said. The girl sounded as though her tongue was caught in her mouth. "That's a BAD word!" the girl continued. "We don't say BAD words!"

"Let's go in," Elise said. 130

"No," Drema said, "I don't want to. What if we get beat up?"

"Snot?" Elise turned to me, her flashlight blinding. It was the first time anyone had asked my opinion, though I knew they were just asking because they were afraid.

"I say we go inside, just to see what's going on."

"But Arnetta didn't give us the signal," Drema said. "She's supposed to say, 'We're gonna teach you a lesson,' and I didn't hear her say it."

135 "C'mon," I said. "Let's just go in."

We went inside. There we found the white girls—about five girls huddled up next to one big girl. I instantly knew she was the owner of the voice we'd heard. Arnetta and Octavia inched toward us as soon as we entered.

"Where's Janice?" Elise asked, then we heard a flush. "Oh."

"I think," Octavia said, whispering to Elise, "they're retarded."

"We ARE NOT retarded!" the big girl said, though it was obvious that she was. That they all were. The girls around her began to whimper.

140 "They're just pretending," Arnetta said, trying to convince herself. "I know they are."

Octavia turned to Arnetta. "Arnetta. Let's just leave."

Janice came out of a stall, happy and relieved, then she suddenly remembered her line, pointed to the big girl, and said, "We're gonna teach you a lesson."

"Shut up, Janice," Octavia said, but her heart was not in it. Arnetta's face was set in a lost, deep scowl. Octavia turned to the big girl and said loudly, slowly, as if they were all deaf, "We're going to leave. It was nice meeting you, O.K.? You don't have to tell anyone that we were here. O.K.?"

"Why not?" said the big girl, like a taunt. When she spoke, her lips did not meet, her mouth did not close. Her tongue grazed the roof of her mouth, like a little pink fish. "You'll get in trouble. I know. *I* know."

145 Arnetta got back her old cunning. "If you said anything, then you'd be a tattletale."

The girl looked sad for a moment, then perked up quickly. A flash of genius crossed her face. "I *like* tattletale."

"IT'S all right, girls. It's gonna be all right!" the 909 troop leader said. All of Troop 909 burst into tears. It was as though someone had instructed them all to cry at once. The troop leader had girls under her arm,

and all the rest of the girls crowded about her. It reminded me of a hog I'd seen on a field trip, where all the little hogs gathered about the mother at feeding time, latching onto her teats. The 909 troop leader had come into the bathroom, shortly after the big girl had threatened to tell. Then the ranger came, then, once the ranger had radioed the station, Mrs. Margolin arrived with Daphne in tow.

The ranger had left the restroom area, but everyone else was huddled just outside, swatting mosquitoes.

"Oh. They *will* apologize," Mrs. Margolin said to the 909 troop leader, but she said this so angrily, I knew she was speaking more to us than to the other troop leader. "When their parents find out, every one a them will be on punishment."

150 "It's all right, it's all right," the 909 troop leader reassured Mrs. Margolin. Her voice lilted in the same way it had when addressing the girls. She smiled the whole time she talked. She was like one of those TV-cooking-show women who talk and dice onions and smile all at the same time.

"See. It could have happened. I'm not calling your girls fibbers or anything." She shook her head ferociously from side to side, her Egyptian-style pageboy flapping against her cheeks like heavy drapes. "It *could* have happened. See. Our girls are *not* retarded. They are *delayed* learners." She said this in a syrupy instructional voice, as though our troop might be delayed learners as well. "We're from the Decatur Children's Academy. Many of them just have special needs."

"Now we won't be able to walk to the bathroom by ourselves!" the big girl said.

"Yes you will," the troop leader said, "but maybe we'll wait till we get back to Decatur—"

"I don't want to wait!" the girl said. "I want my Independence badge!"

155 The girls in my troop were entirely speechless. Arnetta looked stoic, as though she were soon to be tortured but was determined not to appear weak. Mrs. Margolin pursed her lips solemnly and said, "Bless them, Lord. Bless them."

In contrast, the Troop 909 leader was full of words and energy. "Some of our girls are echolalic—"

She smiled and happily presented one of the girls hanging onto her, but the girl widened her eyes in horror, and violently withdrew herself from the center of attention, sensing she was being sacrificed for the village sins. "Echolalic," the troop leader continued. "That means they will say whatever they hear, like an echo—that's where the word comes from. It comes from 'echo.'" She ducked her head apologetically, "I mean, not all of them have the most *progressive* of parents, so if they heard a bad word, they might have repeated it. But I guarantee it would not have been *intentional*."

Arnetta spoke. "I saw her say the word. I heard her." She pointed to a small girl, smaller than any of us, wearing an oversized T-shirt that read: "Eat Bertha's Mussels."

The troop leader shook her head and smiled, "That's impossible. She doesn't speak. She can, but she doesn't."

Arnetta furrowed her brow. "No. It wasn't her. That's right. It was *her*."

160 The girl Arnetta pointed to grinned as though she'd been paid a compliment. She was the only one from either troop actually wearing a full uniform: the mocha-colored A-line shift, the orange ascot, the sash covered with badges, though all the same one—the Try-It patch. She took a few steps toward Arnetta and made a grand sweeping gesture toward the sash. "See," she said, full of self-importance, "I'm a Brownie." I had a hard time imagining this girl calling anyone a "nigger"; the girl looked perpetually delighted, as though she would have cuddled up with a grizzly if someone had let her.

O N the fourth morning, we boarded the bus to go home.

The previous day had been spent building miniature churches from Popsicle sticks. We hardly left the cabin. Mrs. Margolin and Mrs. Hedy guarded us so closely, almost no one talked for the entire day.

Even on the day of departure from Camp Crescendo, all was serious and silent. The bus ride began quietly enough. Arnetta had to sit beside Mrs. Margolin; Octavia had to sit beside her mother. I sat beside Daphne, who gave me her prize journal without a word of explanation.

"You don't want it?"

She shook her head no. It was empty.   165

Then Mrs. Hedy began to weep. "Octavia," Mrs. Hedy said to her daughter without looking at her, "I'm going to sit with Mrs. Margolin. All right?"

Arnetta exchanged seats with Mrs. Hedy. With the two women up front, Elise felt it safe to speak. "Hey," she said, then she set her face into a placid, vacant stare, trying to imitate that of a Troop 909 girl. Emboldened, Arnetta made a gesture of mock pride toward an imaginary sash, the way the girl in full uniform had done. Then they all made a game of it, trying to do the most exaggerated imitations of the Troop 909 girls, all without speaking, all without laughing loud enough to catch the women's attention.

Daphne looked down at her shoes, white with sneaker polish. I opened the journal she'd given me. I looked out the window, trying to decide what to write, searching for lines, but nothing could compare with what Daphne had written, "*My father, the veteran*," my favorite line of all time. It replayed itself in my head, and I gave up trying to write.

By then, it seemed that the rest of the troop had given up making fun of the girls in Troop 909. They were now quietly gossiping about who had passed notes to whom in school. For a moment the gossiping fell off, and all I heard was the hum of the bus as we sped down the road and the muffled sounds of Mrs. Hedy and Mrs. Margolin talking about serious things.

"You know," Octavia whispered,   170 "why did *we* have to be stuck at a camp with retarded girls? You know?"

"*You* know why," Arnetta answered. She narrowed her eyes like a cat. "My mama and I were in the mall in Buckhead, and this white lady just kept looking at us.

I mean, like we were foreign or something. Like we were from China."

"What did the woman say?" Elise asked.

"Nothing," Arnetta said. "She didn't say nothing."

A few girls quietly nodded their heads.

175 "There was this time," I said, "when my father and I were in the mall and—"

"Oh shut up, Snot," Octavia said.

I stared at Octavia, then rolled my eyes from her to the window. As I watched the trees blur, I wanted nothing more than to be through with it all: the bus ride, the troop, school—all of it. But we were going home. I'd see the same girls in school the next day. We were on a bus, and there was nowhere else to go.

"Go on, Laurel," Daphne said to me. It seemed like the first time she'd spoken the whole trip, and she'd said my name. I turned to her and smiled weakly so as not to cry, hoping she'd remember when I'd tried to be her friend, thinking maybe that her gift of the journal was an invitation of friendship. But she didn't smile back. All she said was, "What happened?"

I studied the girls, waiting for Octavia to tell me to shut up again before I even had a chance to utter another word, but everyone was amazed that Daphne had spoken. The bus was silent. I gathered my voice. "Well," I said. "My father and I were in this mall, but *I* was the one doing the staring." I stopped and glanced from face to face. I continued. "There were these white people dressed like Puritans or something, but they weren't Puritans. They were Mennonites. They're these people who, if you ask them to do a favor, like paint your porch or something, they have to do it. It's in their rules."

180 "That sucks," someone said.

"C'mon," Arnetta said. "You're lying."

"I am not."

"How do you know that's not just some story someone made up?" Elise asked, her head cocked full of daring. "I mean, who's gonna do whatever you ask?"

"It's not made up. I know because when I was looking at them, my father said, 'See those people? If you ask them to do something, they'll do it. Anything you want.'"

No one would call anyone's father a liar—then 185 they'd have to fight the person. But Drema parsed her words carefully. "How does your *father* know that's not just some story? Huh?"

"Because," I said, "he went up to the man and asked him would he paint our porch, and the man said yes. It's their religion."

"Man, I'm glad I'm a Baptist," Elise said, shaking her head in sympathy for the Mennonites.

"So did the guy do it?" Drema asked, scooting closer to hear if the story got juicy.

> When you've been made to feel bad for so long, you jump at the chance to do it to others.

"Yeah," I said. "His whole family was with him. My dad drove them to our house. They all painted our porch. The woman and girl were in bonnets and long, long skirts with buttons up to their necks. The guy wore this weird hat and these huge suspenders."

"Why," Arnetta asked archly, as though she didn't 190 believe a word, "would someone pick a *porch*? If they'll do anything, why not make them paint the whole *house*? Why not ask for a hundred bucks?"

I thought about it, and then remembered the words my father had said about them painting our porch, though I had never seemed to think about his words after he'd said them.

"He said," I began, only then understanding the words as they uncoiled from my mouth, "it was the only time he'd have a white man on his knees doing something for a black man for free."

I now understood what he meant, and why he did it, though I didn't like it. When you've been made to feel bad for so long, you jump at the chance to do it to others. I remembered the Mennonites bending the way Daphne had bent when she was cleaning the restroom. I remembered the dark blue of their bonnets, the black of their shoes. They painted the porch as though scrubbing a floor. I was already trembling before Daphne asked quietly, "Did he thank them?"

I looked out the window. I could not tell which were the thoughts and which were the trees. "No," I said, and suddenly knew there was something mean in the world that I could not stop.

Arnetta laughed. "If I asked them to take off their 195 long skirts and bonnets and put on some jeans, would they do it?"

And Daphne's voice, quiet, steady: "Maybe they would. Just to be nice."

IF YOU LIKED "BROWNIES," YOU MIGHT ALSO LIKE . . .

. . . "Traveling Madness," by another young writer, Ana Menendez (in our casebook of new voices in fiction on connect.mcgraw-hill.com), who is also experimenting in her work. As with most literary matters, it seems difficult to predict where these writers will go next in their work.

GOING FURTHER   As of this writing Packer is currently at work on her first novel, a story about the "Buffalo Soldiers," black Union Army veterans who went west during and after the Civil War. With her contemporary, Danzy Senna (*Caucasia* and *Symptomatic*), and the slightly younger Tayari Jones (*Leaving Atlanta*) and Asali Solomon (*Get Down*), she is carving out space for new black American women writers.

Writing from Reading

Summarize

1 What are Snot/Laurel's feelings about her father? What does she tell the reader directly? What can you infer from what she says and when she says it?

2 Locate all the scenes in which Laurel's troop actually encounters Troop 909. What details does Laurel include that foreshadow their later discovery about the white girls? What details are omitted because we get only Laurel's view?

Analyze Craft

3 Packer includes several sets of lyrics in "Brownies," including Daphne's poem and the songs the girls are asked to sing. What is the effect of including the full text of these lyrics? Why does Packer choose to leave out the lyrics of the Michael Jackson song?

Analyze Voice

4 Analyze the difference between Laurel's voice as narrator of the story and her voice when she speaks in the story. Do you think Packer was trying to use the voice of a young girl narrator or of a grown-up looking back?

Synthesize Summary and Analysis

5 Compare the descriptions of Laurel's troop members with the descriptions of the girls in Troop 909. Does Packer draw a comparison between the two troops? Examine why Packer chose to distance Troop 909 both racially and mentally.

Interpret the Story

6 Think about the protagonists, antagonists, and foils of this story. Can they be divided evenly into groups by race, age, or troop? What is the overarching conflict the protagonists are up against, and how does the story of the Mennonites help bring resolution to this conflict?

CONTINUED FROM PAGE 299

A PARTICIPANT, OR FIRST-PERSON, NARRATOR

The first-person narrator is always a participant in the story and can be either a major or a minor character. This type of tale telling relies on the perspective of a single character through whose eyes, and by means of whose voice, we come to understand the action in the story. Readers enter the narrator's mind, gaining access to his or her thoughts and emotions. In the opening passage, with Laurel as the first-person narrator, our entry to the narrative comes through her eyes and words.

"You have to create a little distance from yourself to make . . . a story; otherwise it's just you talking. . . . As a story . . . you want to be able to walk around in some way. However closely it relates to your own autobiography, it has to be a little different. There has to be some space between you and it, and the voice is one way to establish a little space." Conversation with John Updike

First person is by its nature limited because we have only one set of eyes. As participants in a story, first-person narrators have their own interests and motivations—and, like the rest of us, cannot be entirely objective. They can give only their version of the tale. Often, readers see more than the narrator can, and sometimes this broader vantage point allows us to recognize an **unreliable narrator,** or one who cannot be trusted to present an undistorted account of the action. Few narrators are unreliable, but those who are have many reasons for their unreliability, ranging from inexperience, ignorance, and personal bias to intentional deceptiveness and even insanity. The narrator of Gish Jen's story "Who's Irish?" (Chapter 9) is so fixed in her cultural prejudices—at least at first—that her bias prevents her from understanding other people's point of view. We realize quickly that the lens of the narrator colors all we see, and we must look at the behavior of those around the narrator to grasp the reality of the situation.

A specific variety of unreliable narrator is the **naïve narrator,** who remains unaware of the full complexity of events in the story being told. A narrator may be naïve because of youth, innocence, or lack of cultural alertness. Writers intentionally use naïve narrators to reveal a truth, raise questions in the reader's mind, or otherwise emphasize a point. In Harper Lee's classic novel *To Kill a Mockingbird,* young Scout is the naïve narrator who describes the members of her family and the characters and events in her town. Tom Robinson, a black man, has been falsely accused of raping a white woman. Scout takes us into the courtroom where her father, the town's highly respected lawyer, defends Tom. Scout, an avid observer, still cannot understand how Tom can be convicted when the evidence overwhelmingly supports his innocence. The critical reader, having some knowledge of the social conventions of life in the American South in the 1930s, understands that Tom is the victim of the town's deep-rooted racism. So you can see that by the use of Scout's perspective, Harper Lee effectively reveals the injustice of the town's racist attitudes.

A NONPARTICIPANT, OR THIRD-PERSON, NARRATOR

Third-person narrators are never characters in the story. These narrators relate the events of a story as unseen observers, referring to all the characters as *he, she,* or *they.* This particular narrative vantage remains the most common strategy for tale telling, though there are gradations within it, and it's worth spelling them out. Third-person narrators come in three basic varieties.

- **Omniscient narrator.** Omniscient, or all-knowing, third-person narrators observe the thoughts and describe the actions of multiple characters in the story. The omniscient author may also comment on a situation, offering opinions in the "Dear Reader" mode.
- **Limited omniscient narrator.** Limited third-person narrators typically enter into the thoughts and emotions of one character, as does the narrator in Kate Chopin's "The Story of an Hour" (Chapter 6).
- **Objective point-of-view narrator.** Objective third-person narrators report only what can be seen and heard, as does the narrator in Ernest Hemingway's "Hills Like White Elephants" in this chapter.

The **omniscient narrator** can see beyond the physical actions and dialogue of characters and has the power to reveal the inner thoughts and emotions of anyone in the story. This narrator moves freely among the thoughts of characters and across time and space. The term comes from the Latin *omni scientia,* "all-knowing," and it suggests a kind of godlike or infallible witness—often one who offers his or her opinion on the action as it unfolds. The omniscient narrator chooses which thoughts are important to the story, and when to tell them.

Using this perspective, for example, Flannery O'Connor's narrator in "Good Country People" (Chapter 12) gives us glimpses into the thoughts of both Mrs. Hopewell and her daughter on a controversial subject: the daughter's name. First, the mother's thoughts:

> *Mrs. Hopewell was certain that [her daughter] had thought and thought until she had hit upon the ugliest name in any language. Then she had gone and had the beautiful name, Joy, changed without telling her mother until after she had done it. . . . When Mrs. Hopewell thought of the name, Hulga, she thought of the broad blank hull of a battleship. She would not use it.*

Shortly thereafter, we get Hulga's perspective:

> *She considered the name her personal affair. . . . She had a vision of the name working like the ugly sweating Vulcan who stayed in the furnace and to whom,*

presumably, the goddess had to come when called. She saw it as the name of her highest creative act. One of her major triumphs was that her mother had not been able to turn her dust into Joy, but the greater one was that she had been able to turn it herself into Hulga.

The omniscient narrator chooses what should be revealed, and when, providing deep insight into the nature of each character. O'Connor even takes this one farther: she also reveals a deeply antagonistic mother-daughter relationship.

> **"Once you break with the first person, then you do discover the wonderful world of multiple viewpoints, and you can fly through space, and go from head to head, and you get out and you become a character in your own right, you become the omniscient author presiding."** Conversation with John Updike

Omniscient narrators are not always objective. Sometimes a narrator shows **editorial omniscience,** inserting his or her own commentary about the characters or the events. By contrast, a narrator who shows **impartial omniscience** remains neutral, relating events and characters' thoughts without passing judgment or offering an opinion. Hemingway uses impartial omniscience in "Hills Like White Elephants." Take this passage, for example: "The woman brought two glasses of beer and two felt pads. She put the felt pads and the beer glasses on the table and looked at the man and the girl. The girl was looking off at the line of hills. They were white in the sun and the country was brown and dry." The narration is straightforward enough that this might easily be a work of nonfiction or of journalism that presents unbiased facts.

A BRIEF HISTORY OF POINT OF VIEW

In the earliest narratives of Western culture, news about the world comes down to the poets from a literally omniscient source—the gods or God. Both *The Iliad* and *The Odyssey,* for example, begin by asking a goddess—called the Muse—to relate the events of the story. So, too, the first five books of the Bible are held to be the word of God as revealed to Moses. However, over time, more varied perspectives on life and history emerged; the fourteenth-century English poet Geoffrey Chaucer (in *The Canterbury Tales;* see Chapter 25) and the Italian Renaissance story writer Boccaccio (in *The Decameron*) told tales about men and women of differing backgrounds and social positions as if the characters were speaking in their own words. The stories became as varied as their narrators, and the point of view changed as each new narrator told a tale. Once numerous and partial points of view began to replace omniscience, or all-knowingness, skill in this aspect of the writer's craft grew crucial.

Few omniscient narrators are purely editorial or purely impartial, however; in most works of fiction, you will find both kinds of storytelling. A **limited omniscient narrator** describes the vision and insights of one character only, as if telling the story "over the shoulder" of that character. Unlike a first-person narrator, the limited omniscient narrator is separate from the main character and serves as the interpreter—not the source—of his or her thoughts. The reader can trust that the narrator's observations are more or less objective. Kate Chopin's "The Story of an Hour" uses limited omniscient narration, with the focus on Mrs. Mallard, the only character whose consciousness we enter. In other words, the narrator can relate only what Mrs. Mallard can see and hear, and what she herself feels and thinks.

> *There were patches of blue sky showing here and there through the clouds that had met and piled one above the other in the west facing her window....*
> *There was something coming to her and she was waiting for it, fearfully. What was it? She did not know; it was too subtle and elusive to name. But she felt it, creeping out of the sky, reaching toward her through the sounds, the scents, the color that filled the air.*
>
> > *Now her bosom rose and fell tumultuously. She was beginning to recognize this thing that was approaching to possess her, and she was striving to beat it back with her will—as powerless as her two white slender hands would have been. When she abandoned herself a little whispered word escaped her slightly parted lips. She said it over and over under the breath: "free, free, free!"*

In this passage, Mrs. Mallard has left her guests downstairs to go to her room. The narrator describes Mrs. Mallard's movements and feelings in great detail, following her gaze outside the window, as her mind begins to understand what her body has already grasped. She feels as free as the blue sky showing through the clouds.

An omniscient narrator who goes deeply into the mind of a character may use the technique of interior monologue, in which a character's conscious or unconscious thought processes are narrated as they occur, with only minimal guidance from the narrator. These thoughts can be disconnected, moving rapidly and randomly from one idea to the next. Kate Chopin briefly uses the interior monologue technique in the passage about Mrs. Mallard. A similar but more random-seeming approach is **stream of consciousness,** in which thoughts flow by in free association and the literary convention suggests that there is no writer mediating the consciousness of the subject. The following example comes from James Joyce's novel *Ulysses;* here, the thoughts of a character named Molly Bloom pour onto the page:

> *... and Ronda with the old windows of the posadas glancing eyes a lattice hid for her lover to kiss the iron and the wineshops half open at night and the castanets and the night we missed the boat at Algeciras the watchman going about*

> *serene with his lamp and O that awful deepdown torrent O and the sea the sea crimson sometimes like fire and the glorious sunsets and the fig trees in the Alameda gardens yes . . .*

In contrast to the narrator with limited omniscience who delves into the consciousness of a particular character, an **objective point-of-view** narrator seems almost disinterested, relating only what all characters in the story see or hear. This type of narrator is often compared to the "fly on the wall" who sees and hears all. Similarly, the objective narrator provides no insight into the thoughts, emotions, or motivations of any single character. "I am a camera," the narrator declares in Christopher Isherwood's *Berlin Stories,* suggesting a kind of objective assessment—one that's neither naïve nor editorialized. Reading a story with an objective narrator is much like watching a play, because the reader comes to understand what the characters think and feel based only on what they do and say. An objective narrator never lets the reader enter the consciousness of a particular character, the way Chopin did with Mrs. Mallard. The reader must use the clues of dialogue and behavior to infer what people truly think and feel.

THE SECOND-PERSON NARRATOR

The least commonly used point of view is that of the second-person narrator, who addresses characters and sometimes readers directly with the pronoun *you* or with imperatives (*do this and that*). Second-person narration can make a reader feel like a participant in the story. It also creates a sense of closeness to the protagonist—as if the character is talking to himself or herself. In the following selection from Junot Diaz's "How to Date a Browngirl, Blackgirl, Whitegirl, or Halfie," notice how the familiar, conversational use of "you" draws the reader in.

> *Dinner will be tense. You are not good at talking to people you don't know. A halfie will tell you that her parents met in the Movement, will say, Back then people thought it a radical thing to do. It will sound like something her parents made her memorize. Your brother once heard that one and said, Man, that sounds like a whole lot of Uncle Tomming to me. Don't repeat this.*

Drawing the reader directly into the story can prove challenging in a work of fiction. For example, not many readers will identify with the "you" Diaz creates—a mixed-race, teenaged girl-chaser who hides government cheese to impress his date. Nevertheless, Diaz's "you" technique creates an intimacy, as if we overhear internal monologue and in so doing, become that very character. He has created innovative and compelling fiction by the use of second-person narrators.

Junot Diaz (b. 1968)

Junot Diaz's success as both a writer and a professor at MIT may lull some people into forgetting the difficulties he faced as a boy who immigrated to the United States from the Dominican Republic when he was six. However, the poverty he experienced in Santo Domingo and the unpleasantness of growing up next door to a landfill in New Jersey left an indelible mark on Diaz and his fiction, which seeks to give voice to the difficulties of the immigrant life. A blend of sharp, slang-filled prose and narrators that include drug dealers and young boys struggling to make their way in an adopted country, Diaz's first book, a collection of stories titled *Drown* (1996), met with such acclaim that Diaz found himself a celebrity overnight; he was named one of *Newsweek*'s "New Faces of 1996." Although Diaz tends to write at a slow pace—ten years elapsed between *Drown* and his first novel, *The Brief Wondrous Life of Oscar Wao*—he has published stories in the most prestigious venues, including *The New Yorker, The Paris Review,* and the *Best American Short Stories* series. His subject is the immigrant experience in the United States, which he portrays with great detail, right down to the feeling of constant uncertainty and the desire to fit in—a subject that allows his work to be semiautobiographical. And although he writes to set a precedent for future Latino writers, he also helps foster all future writers by means of his college teaching job and his volunteer work with urban high school students.

AS YOU READ   Consider the narrator's tone. What voice do you hear as you're reading? How do you feel about his message? When do you feel comfortable with what he's saying, and when do you feel uncomfortable? What does he hide and what does he reveal?

How to Date a Browngirl, Blackgirl, Whitegirl, or Halfie (1995)

1   WAIT for your brother and your mother to leave the apartment. You've already told them that you're feeling too sick to go to Union City to visit that tía who likes to squeeze your nuts. (He's gotten big, she'll say.) And even though your moms knows you ain't sick you stuck to your story until finally she said, Go ahead and stay, malcriado.

Clear the government cheese from the refrigerator. If the girl's from the Terrace stack the boxes behind the milk. If she's from the Park or Society Hill hide the cheese in the cabinet above the oven, way up where she'll never see. Leave yourself a reminder to get it out before morning or your moms will kick your ass. Take down any embarrassing photos of your family in the campo, especially the one with the half-naked kids dragging a goat on a rope leash. The kids are your cousins and by now they're old enough to understand why you're doing what you're doing. Hide the pictures of yourself with an Afro. Make sure the bathroom is presentable. Put the basket with all the crapped-on toilet paper under the sink. Spray the bucket with Lysol, then close the cabinet.

Shower, comb, dress. Sit on the couch and watch TV. If she's an outsider her father will be bringing her, maybe her mother. Neither of them want her seeing any boys from the Terrace—people get stabbed in the Terrace—but she's strong-headed and this time will get her way. If she's a white girl you know you'll at least get a hand job.

The directions were in your best handwriting, so her parents won't think you're an idiot. Get up from the couch and check the parking lot. Nothing. If the girl's local, don't sweat it. She'll flow over when she's good and ready. Sometimes she'll run into her other friends and a whole crowd will show up at your apartment and even though that means you ain't getting shit it will be fun anyway and you'll wish these people would come over more often. Sometimes the girl won't flow over at all and the next day in school she'll say sorry, smile and you'll be stupid enough to believe her and ask her out again.

5   Wait and after an hour go out to your corner. The neighborhood is full of traffic. Give one of your boys a shout and when he says, Are you still waiting on that bitch? Say, Hell yeah.

Get back inside. Call her house and when her father picks up ask if she's there. He'll ask, Who is this? Hang up. He sounds like a principal or a police chief, the sort of dude with a big neck, who never has to watch his back. Sit and wait. By the time your stomach's ready to give out on you, a Honda or maybe a Jeep pulls in and out she comes.

Hey, you'll say.

Look, she'll say. My mom wants to meet you. She's got herself all worried about nothing.

Don't panic. Say, Hey, no problem. Run a hand through your hair like the whiteboys do even though the only thing that runs easily through your hair is Africa. She will look good. The white ones are the ones you want the most, aren't they, but usually the out-of-towners are black, blackgirls who grew up with ballet and Girl Scouts, who have three cars in their driveways. If she's a halfie don't be surprised that her mother is white. Say, Hi. Her moms will say hi and you'll see that you don't scare her, not really. She will say that she needs easier directions to get out and even though she has the best directions in her lap give her new ones. Make her happy.

You have choices. If the girl's from around the way, take   10
her to El Cibao for dinner. Order everything in your busted-up Spanish. Let her correct you if she's Latina and amaze her if she's black. If she's not from around the way, Wendy's will do. As you walk to the restaurant talk about school. A local girl won't need stories about the neighborhood but the other ones might. Supply the story about the loco who'd been storing canisters of tear gas in his basement for years, how one day the canisters cracked and the whole neighborhood got a dose of the military-strength stuff. Don't tell her that your moms knew right away what it was, that she recognized its smell from the year the United States invaded your island.

Hope that you don't run into your nemesis, Howie, the Puerto Rican kid with the two killer mutts. He walks them all over the neighborhood and every now and then the mutts corner themselves a cat and tear it to shreds, Howie laughing as the cat flips up in the air, its neck twisted around like an owl, red meat showing through the soft fur. If his dogs haven't cornered a cat, he will walk behind you and ask, Hey, Yunior, is that your new fuckbuddy?

Let him talk. Howie weighs about two hundred pounds and could eat you if he wanted. At the field he will turn away. He has new sneakers, and doesn't want them muddy. If the girl's an outsider she will hiss now and say, What a fucking asshole. A homegirl would have been yelling back at him the whole time, unless she was shy. Either way don't feel bad that you didn't do anything. Never lose a fight on a first date or that will be the end of it.

Dinner will be tense. You are not good at talking to people you don't know. A halfie will tell you that her parents met in the Movement, will say, Back then people thought it a radical thing to do. It will sound like something her parents made her memorize. Your brother once heard that one and said, Man, that sounds like a whole lot of Uncle Tomming to me. Don't repeat this.

> **As you walk to the restaurant** talk about school.

Put down your hamburger and say, It must have been hard.

15 She will appreciate your interest. She will tell you more. Black people, she will say, treat me real bad. That's why I don't like them. You'll wonder how she feels about Dominicans. Don't ask. Let her speak on it and when you're both finished eating walk back into the neighborhood. The skies will be magnificent. Pollutants have made Jersey sunsets one of the wonders of the world. Point it out. Touch her shoulder and say, That's nice, right?

Get serious. Watch TV but stay alert. Sip some of the Bermúdez your father left in the cabinet, which nobody touches. A local girl may have hips and a thick ass but she won't be quick about letting you touch. She has to live in the same neighborhood you do, has to deal with you being all up in her business. She might just chill with you and then go home. She might kiss you and then go, or she might, if she's reckless, give it up, but that's rare. Kissing will suffice. A whitegirl might just give it up right then. Don't stop her. She'll take her gum out of her mouth, stick it to the plastic sofa covers and then will move close to you. You have nice eyes, she might say.

Tell her that you love her hair, that you love her skin, her lips, because, in truth, you love them more than you love your own.

She'll say, I like Spanish guys, and even though you've never been to Spain, say, I like you. You'll sound smooth.

You'll be with her until about eight-thirty and then she will want to wash up. In the bathroom she will hum a song from the radio and her waist will keep the beat against the lip of the sink. Imagine her old lady coming to get her, what she would say if she knew her daughter had just lain under you and blown your name, pronounced with her eighth-grade Spanish, into your ear. While she's in the bathroom call one of your boys and say, Lo hice, loco. Or just sit back on the couch and smile.

But usually it won't work this way. Be 20 prepared. She will not want to kiss you. Just cool it, she'll say. The halfie might lean back, breaking away from you. She will cross her arms, say, I hate my tits. Stroke her hair but she will pull away. I don't like anybody touching my hair, she will say. She will act like somebody you don't know. In school she is known for her attention-grabbing laugh, as high and far-ranging as a gull, but here she will worry you. You will not know what to say.

You're the only kind of guy who asks me out, she will say. Your neighbors will start their hyena calls, now that the alcohol is in them. You and the blackboys.

Say nothing. Let her button her shirt, let her comb her hair, the sound of it stretching like a sheet of fire between you. When her father pulls in and beeps, let her go without too much of a good-bye. She won't want it. During the next hour the phone will ring. You will be tempted to pick it up. Don't. Watch the shows you want to watch, without a family around to debate you. Don't go downstairs. Don't fall asleep. It won't help. Put the government cheese back in its place before your moms kills you.

IF YOU LIKED "HOW TO DATE A BROWNGIRL, BLACKGIRL, WHITEGIRL, OR HALFIE," YOU MIGHT ALSO LIKE . . .

. . . other playful stories in the book, such as Sherman Alexie's "Indian Education" (Chapter 12).

GOING FURTHER Playfulness, even when treating some of the most serious subjects, goes all the way back to Laurence Sterne's *Tristram Shandy* in the eighteenth century and to *Don Quixote,* the classic Spanish novel composed by Miguel de Cervantes and first published in 1605. Today you might find similarities between Diaz's tone and the tone of *Extremely Loud & Incredibly Close* by Jonathan Safran Foer.

Writing from Reading

Summarize

1 Describe the narrator's attitudes toward each kind of girl mentioned in the title. What attracts him about each? What complaints does he have about each?

2 Consider whether this story is meant to be a recipe for *successful* dating. Does the narrator end up where he means to be in each scenario? What is his goal for the date?

Analyze Craft

3 Discuss the use of irony in the story. Are there incongruities (1) between acts and results, (2) between what occurs and what the character expects to occur, or (3) between what is said and what is meant?

4 Describe how close you feel to this narrator. Does the second-person point of view make you feel like part of the story, or do you remain separate? Analyze places in the text where the "you" seems to refer directly to you, the reader, and places where the "you" directly refers to the main character.

Analyze Voice

5 What does the narrator hide, and what does he reveal? Discuss how his secrets and confessions affect your attitudes toward him.

Synthesize Summary and Analysis

6 Discuss the attitudes that this narrator reveals about race, class, and ethnicity. Cite examples to demonstrate how Diaz uses tone to affect your response to the narrator's suggestions.

Interpret the Story

7 Consider the form the story would take if written in first person, as a straightforward dramatic scene. Discuss how the tone and the language of the story might change, and what the effect would be on your impression of the boy on the date. Why do you think Diaz decided to cast the story in second person? Do you think it was the best choice?

William Faulkner (1897–1962)

For a brief biography of William Faulkner, see Chapter 15.

AS YOU READ   Pay attention to how much the narrator tells and how much the narrator shows "in scene." Ask yourself how the proportion you find is appropriate to the story's point of view. What type of voice does this peculiar point of view create?

A Rose for Emily (1932)

I

1 When Miss Emily Grierson died, our whole town went to her funeral: the men through a sort of respectful affection for a fallen monument, the women mostly out of curiosity to see the inside of her house, which no one save an old manservant—a combined gardener and cook—had seen in at least ten years.

It was a big, squarish frame house that had once been white, decorated with cupolas and spires and scrolled balconies in the heavily lightsome style of the seventies, set on what had once been our most select street. But garages and cotton gins had encroached and obliterated even the august names of that neighborhood; only Miss Emily's house was left, lifting its stubborn and coquettish decay above the cotton wagons and the gasoline pumps—an eyesore among eyesores. And now Miss Emily had gone to join the representatives of those august names where they lay in the cedar-bemused cemetery among the ranked and anonymous graves of Union and Confederate soldiers who fell at the battle of Jefferson.

Alive, Miss Emily had been a tradition, a duty, and a care; a sort of hereditary obligation upon the town, dating from that day in 1894 when Colonel Sartoris, the mayor—he who fathered the edict that no Negro woman should appear on the streets without an apron—remitted her taxes, the dispensation dating from the death of her father on into perpetuity. Not that Miss Emily would have accepted charity. Colonel Sartoris invented an involved tale to the effect that Miss Emily's father had loaned money to the town, which the town, as a matter of business, preferred this way of repaying. Only a man of Colonel Sartoris' generation and thought could have invented it, and only a woman could have believed it.

When the next generation, with its more modern ideas, became mayors and aldermen, this arrangement created some little dissatisfaction. On the first of the year they mailed her a tax notice. February came, and there was no reply. They wrote her a formal letter, asking her to call at the sheriff's office at her convenience. A week later the mayor wrote her himself, offering to call or to send his car for her, and received in reply a note on paper of an archaic shape, in a thin, flowing calligraphy in faded ink, to the effect that she no longer went out at all. The tax notice was also enclosed, without comment.

5 They called a special meeting of the Board of Aldermen. A deputation waited upon her, knocked at the door through which no visitor had passed since she ceased giving china-painting lessons eight or ten years earlier. They were admitted by the old Negro into a dim hall from which a stairway mounted into still more shadow. It smelled of dust and disuse—a close, dank smell. The Negro led them into the parlor. It was furnished in heavy, leather-covered furniture. When the Negro opened the blinds of one window, they could see that the leather was cracked; and when they sat down, a faint dust rose sluggishly about their thighs, spinning with slow motes in the single sun-ray. On a tarnished gilt easel before the fireplace stood a crayon portrait of Miss Emily's father.

They rose when she entered—a small, fat woman in black, with a thin gold chain descending to her waist and vanishing into her belt, leaning on an ebony cane with a tarnished gold head. Her skeleton was small and spare; perhaps that was why what would have been merely plumpness in another was obesity in her. She looked bloated, like a body long submerged in motionless water, and of that pallid hue. Her eyes, lost in the fatty ridges of her face, looked like two small pieces of coal pressed into a lump of dough as they moved from one face to another while the visitors stated their errand.

She did not ask them to sit. She just stood in the door and listened quietly until the spokesman came to a stumbling halt. Then they could hear the invisible watch ticking at the end of the gold chain.

Her voice was dry and cold. "I have no taxes in Jefferson. Colonel Sartoris explained it to me. Perhaps one of you can gain access to the city records and satisfy yourselves."

"But we have. We are the city authorities, Miss Emily. Didn't you get a notice from the sheriff, signed by him?"

10 "I received a paper, yes," Miss Emily said. "Perhaps he considers himself the sheriff . . . I have no taxes in Jefferson."

"But there is nothing on the books to show that, you see. We must go by the—"

"See Colonel Sartoris. I have no taxes in Jefferson."

"But, Miss Emily—"

"See Colonel Sartoris." (Colonel Sartoris had been dead almost ten years.) "I have no taxes in Jefferson. Tobe!" The Negro appeared. "Show these gentlemen out."

II

15 So she vanquished them, horse and foot, just as she had vanquished their fathers thirty years before about the smell. That was two years after her father's death and a short time after her sweetheart—the one we believed would marry her—had deserted her. After her father's death she went out very little; after her sweetheart went away, people hardly saw her at all. A few of the ladies had the temerity to call, but were not received, and the only sign of life about the place was the Negro man—a young man then—going in and out with a market basket.

"Just as if a man—any man—could keep a kitchen properly," the ladies said; so they were not surprised when the smell developed. It was another link between the gross, teeming world and the high and mighty Griersons.

A neighbor, a woman, complained to the mayor, Judge Stevens, eighty years old.

"But what will you have me do about it, madam?" he said.

"Why, send her word to stop it," the woman said. "Isn't there a law?"

"I'm sure that won't be necessary," Judge Stevens said. 20 "It's probably just a snake or a rat that nigger of hers killed in the yard. I'll speak to him about it."

The next day he received two more complaints, one from a man who came in diffident deprecation. "We really must do something about it, Judge. I'd be the last one in the world to bother Miss Emily, but we've got to do something." That night the Board of Aldermen met—three graybeards and one younger man, a member of the rising generation.

"It's simple enough," he said. "Send her word to have her place cleaned up. Give her a certain time to do it in, and if she don't . . ."

"Dammit, sir," Judge Stevens said, "will you accuse a lady to her face of smelling bad?"

So the next night, after midnight, four men crossed Miss Emily's lawn and slunk about the house like burglars, sniffing along the base of the brickwork and at the cellar openings while one of them performed a regular sowing motion with his hand out of a sack slung from his shoulder. They broke open the cellar door and sprinkled lime there, and in all the outbuildings. As they recrossed the lawn, a window that had been dark was lighted and Miss Emily sat in it, the light behind her, and her upright torso motionless as that of an idol. They crept quietly across the lawn and into the shadow of the locusts that lined the street. After a week or two the smell went away.

That was when people had begun to feel really sorry for 25 her. People in our town, remembering how old lady Wyatt, her great-aunt, had gone completely crazy at last, believed that the Griersons held themselves a little too high for what they really were. None of the young men were quite good enough for Miss Emily and such. We had long thought of them as a tableau, Miss Emily a slender figure in white in the background, her father a spraddled silhouette in the foreground, his back to her and clutching a horsewhip, the two of them framed by the back-flung front door. So when she got to be thirty and was still single, we were not pleased exactly, but vindicated; even with insanity in the family she wouldn't have turned down all of her chances if they had really materialized.

When her father died, it got about that the house was all that was left to her; and in a way, people were glad. At last they could pity Miss Emily. Being left alone, and a pauper, she had become humanized. Now she too would know the old thrill and the old despair of a penny more or less.

The day after his death all the ladies prepared to call at the house and offer condolence and aid, as is our custom. Miss Emily met them at the door, dressed as usual and with no trace of grief on her face. She told them that her father was not dead. She did that for three days, with the ministers calling on her, and the doctors, trying to persuade her to let them dispose of the body. Just as they were about to resort to law and force, she broke down, and they buried her father quickly.

We did not say she was crazy then. We believed she had to do that. We remembered all the young men her father had driven away, and we knew that with nothing left, she would have to cling to that which had robbed her, as people will.

III

She was sick for a long time. When we saw her again, her hair was cut short, making her look like a girl, with a vague resemblance to those angels in colored church windows— sort of tragic and serene.

30 The town had just let the contracts for paving the sidewalks, and in the summer after her father's death they began the work. The construction company came with niggers and mules and machinery, and a foreman named Homer Barron, a Yankee—a big, dark, ready man, with a big voice and eyes lighter than his face. The little boys would follow in groups to hear him cuss the niggers, and the niggers singing in time to the rise and fall of picks. Pretty soon he knew everybody in town. Whenever you heard a lot of laughing anywhere about the square, Homer Barron would be in the center of the group. Presently, we began to see him and Miss Emily on Sunday afternoons driving in the yellow-wheeled buggy and the matched team of bays from the livery stable.

At first we were glad that Miss Emily would have an interest, because the ladies all said, "Of course a Grierson would not think seriously of a Northerner, a day laborer." But there were still others, older people, who said that even grief could not cause a real lady to forget *noblesse oblige*[1]—

---

[1]French: a term used to describe the obligations and responsibilities of a member of the upper class.

without calling it *noblesse oblige*. They just said, "Poor Emily. Her kinsfolk should come to her." She had some kin in Alabama; but years ago her father had fallen out with them over the estate of old lady Wyatt, the crazy woman, and there was no communication between the two families. They had not even been represented at the funeral.

And as soon as the old people said, "Poor Emily," the whispering began. "Do you suppose it's really so?" they said to one another. "Of course it is. What else could. . . ." This behind their hands; rustling of craned silk and satin behind jalousies closed upon the sun of Sunday afternoon as the thin, swift clop-clop-clop of the matched team passed: "Poor Emily."

She carried her head high enough—even when we believed that she was fallen. It was as if she demanded more than ever the recognition of her dignity as the last Grierson; as if it had wanted that touch of earthiness to reaffirm her imperviousness. Like when she bought the rat poison, the arsenic. That was over a year after they had begun to say "Poor Emily," and while the two female cousins were visiting her.

"I want some poison," she said to the druggist. She was over thirty then, still a slight woman, though thinner than usual, with cold, haughty black eyes in a face the flesh of which was strained across the temples and about the eye-sockets as you imagine a lighthouse-keeper's face ought to look. "I want some poison," she said.

"Yes, Miss Emily. What kind? For rats and such? I'd 35 recom—"

"I want the best you have. I don't care what kind."

The druggist named several. "They'll kill anything up to an elephant. But what you want is—"

"Arsenic," Miss Emily said. "Is that a good one?"

"Is . . . arsenic? Yes, ma'am. But what you want—"

"I want arsenic." 40

The druggist looked down at her. She looked back at him, erect, her face like a strained flag. "Why, of course," the druggist said. "If that's what you want. But the law requires you to tell what you are going to use it for."

Miss Emily just stared at him, her head tilted back in order to look him eye for eye, until he looked away and went and got the arsenic and wrapped it up. The Negro delivery boy brought her the package; the druggist didn't come back. When she opened the package at home there was written on the box, under the skull and bones: "For rats."

IV

So the next day we all said, "She will kill herself"; and we said it would be the best thing. When she had first begun to be seen with Homer Barron, we had said, "She will marry him." Then we said, "She will persuade him yet," because Homer himself had remarked—he liked men, and it was known that he drank with the younger men in the Elks' Club—that he was not a marrying man. Later we said, "Poor Emily," behind the jalousies as they passed on Sunday afternoon in the glittering buggy, Miss Emily with her head high and Homer Barron with his hat cocked and a cigar in his teeth, reins and whip in a yellow glove.

> A thin, acrid pall as of the tomb seemed to lie everywhere upon this room decked and furnished as for a bridal . . .

Then some of the ladies began to say that it was a disgrace to the town and a bad example to the young people. The men did not want to interfere, but at last the ladies forced the Baptist minister—Miss Emily's people were Episcopal—to call upon her. He would never divulge what happened during that interview, but he refused to go back again. The next Sunday they again drove about the streets, and the following day the minister's wife wrote to Miss Emily's relations in Alabama.

45 So she had blood-kin under her roof again and we sat back to watch developments. At first nothing happened. Then we were sure that they were to be married. We learned that Miss Emily had been to the jeweler's and ordered a man's toilet set in silver, with the letters H.B. on each piece. Two days later we learned that she had bought a complete outfit of men's clothing, including a nightshirt, and we said, "They are married." We were really glad. We were glad because the two female cousins were even more Grierson than Miss Emily had ever been.

So we were not surprised when Homer Barron—the streets had been finished some time since—was gone. We were a little disappointed that there was not a public blowing-off, but we believed that he had gone on to prepare for Miss Emily's coming, or to give her a chance to get rid of the cousins. (By that time it was a cabal, and we were all Miss Emily's allies to help circumvent the cousins.) Sure enough, after another week they departed. And, as we had expected all along, within three days Homer Barron was back in town. A neighbor saw the Negro man admit him at the kitchen door at dusk one evening.

And that was the last we saw of Homer Barron. And of Miss Emily for some time. The Negro man went in and out with the market basket, but the front door remained closed. Now and then we would see her at a window for a moment, as the men did that night when they sprinkled the lime, but for almost six months she did not appear on the streets. Then we knew that this was to be expected too; as if that quality of her father which had thwarted her woman's life so many times had been too virulent and too furious to die.

When we next saw Miss Emily, she had grown fat and her hair was turning gray. During the next few years it grew grayer and grayer until it attained an even pepper-and-salt iron-gray, when it ceased turning. Up to the day of her death at seventy-four it was still that vigorous iron-gray, like the hair of an active man.

From that time on her front door remained closed, save for a period of six or seven years, when she was about forty, during which she gave lessons in china-painting. She fitted up a studio in one of the downstairs rooms, where the daughters and granddaughters of Colonel Sartoris' contemporaries were sent to her with the same regularity and in the same spirit that they were sent to church on Sundays with a twenty-five-cent piece for the collection plate. Meanwhile her taxes had been remitted.

50 Then the newer generation became the backbone and the spirit of the town, and the painting pupils grew up and fell away and did not send their children to her with boxes of color and tedious brushes and pictures cut from the ladies' magazines. The front door closed upon the last one and remained closed for good. When the town got free postal delivery, Miss Emily alone refused to let them fasten the metal numbers above her door and attach a mailbox to it. She would not listen to them.

Daily, monthly, yearly we watched the Negro grow grayer and more stooped, going in and out with the market basket. Each December we sent her a tax notice, which would be returned by the post office a week later, unclaimed. Now and then we would see her in one of the downstairs windows—she had evidently shut up the top floor of the house—like the carven torso of an idol in a niche, looking or not looking at us, we could never tell which. Thus she passed from generation to generation—dear, inescapable, impervious, tranquil, and perverse.

And so she died. Fell ill in the house filled with dust and shadows, with only a doddering Negro man to wait on her. We did not even know she was sick; we had long since given up trying to get any information from the Negro. He talked to no one, probably not even to her, for his voice had grown harsh and rusty, as if from disuse.

She died in one of the downstairs rooms, in a heavy walnut bed with a curtain, her gray head propped on a pillow yellow and moldy with age and lack of sunlight.

V

The Negro met the first of the ladies at the front door and let them in, with their hushed, sibilant voices and their quick, curious glances, and then he disappeared. He walked right through the house and out the back and was not seen again.

55   The two female cousins came at once. They held the funeral on the second day, with the town coming to look at Miss Emily beneath a mass of bought flowers, with the crayon face of her father musing profoundly above the bier and the ladies sibilant and macabre; and the very old men—some in their brushed Confederate uniforms—on the porch and the lawn, talking of Miss Emily as if she had been a

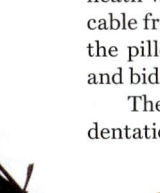

contemporary of theirs, believing that they had danced with her and courted her perhaps, confusing time with its mathematical progression, as the old do, to whom all the past is not a diminishing road but, instead, a huge meadow which no winter ever quite touches, divided from them now by the narrow bottleneck of the most recent decade of years.

Already we knew that there was one room in that region above stairs which no one had seen in forty years, and which would have to be forced. They waited until Miss Emily was decently in the ground before they opened it.

The violence of breaking down the door seemed to fill this room with pervading dust. A thin, acrid pall as of the tomb seemed to lie everywhere upon this room decked and furnished as for a bridal: upon the valance curtains of faded rose color, upon the rose-shaded lights, upon the dressing table, upon the delicate array of crystal and the man's toilet things backed with tarnished silver, silver so tarnished that the monogram was obscured. Among them lay collar and tie, as if they had just been removed, which, lifted, left upon the surface a pale crescent in the dust. Upon a chair hung the suit, carefully folded; beneath it the two mute shoes and the discarded socks.

The man himself lay in the bed.

For a long while we just stood there, looking down at the profound and fleshless grin. The body had apparently once lain in the attitude of an embrace, but now the long sleep that outlasts love, that conquers even the grimace of love, had cuckolded him. What was left of him, rotted beneath what was left of the nightshirt, had become inextricable from the bed in which he lay; and upon him and upon the pillow beside him lay that even coating of the patient and biding dust.

Then we noticed that in the second pillow was the in- 60 dentation of a head. One of us lifted something from it, and leaning forward, that faint and invisible dust dry and acrid in the nostrils, we saw a long strand of iron-gray hair.

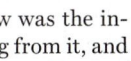

IF YOU LIKED "A ROSE FOR EMILY," YOU MIGHT ALSO LIKE . . .

. . . more gothic fiction, such as that of Joyce Carol Oates's "Where Are You Going, Where Have You Been" (Chapter 8) or "The Cask of Amontillado" by the master of this genre, Edgar Allan Poe (Chapter 10). A case study of Southern fiction is found in Chapter 15.

GOING FURTHER　William Faulkner created an incisive though sympathetic version of the South in his fiction. His novels include *Light in August, Absalom, Absalom!, As I Lay Dying,* and *The Sound and the Fury.*

Writing from Reading

Summarize

1 Using the clues at the end of the story—the man's body in the bed; the "iron-gray hair" on the pillow beside it—reconstruct what happened between Homer Barron and Emily Grierson. What do you think motivated Miss Emily's actions?

Analyze Craft

2 List the numbered sections of this story in rough chronological order. Why do you think Faulkner chose to re-veal details in the order in which he did?

3 There is an element of mystery in this story. How does it affect the plot? What overall effect does it create for you as you read?

Analyze Voice

4 From what point of view is the story told? How would the story change if it were told by an objective narrator? How would it change if it were told by the butler Tobe?

5 Do you think the narrator of the story is reliable? Why or why not?

Synthesize Summary and Analysis

6 Faulkner is known as a Southern writer. In what ways is this story tied to the South? Could it take place else-where? Imagine adapting the plot to a different time and place. What elements would you have to change in order to make these alterations work?

7 Describe the relationship between Miss Emily and Homer Barron. Were they in love? Were they ever officially married? How do you know? Why do you think Miss Emily poisoned Homer?

Interpret the Story

8 Think of Miss Emily Grierson as a representative of the Old South—that is, pre–Civil War. What characteristics of hers tie her to the Old South? In what ways do her actions and/or her fate strike you as symbolic of the South as a region? Make a case for or against reading her as a symbol of the South.

9 Present an argument for whether or not Miss Emily went insane like her great-aunt. If Emily did go crazy, when did her insanity first become apparent? If you believe she did not go crazy, explain what factors besides dementia might have motivated her to act as she did.

Ernest Hemingway (1899–1961)

Born in Oak Park, Illinois, Ernest Hemingway became one of the most influential American authors of the twentieth century. In novels, short stories, and nonfiction alike, Hemingway celebrated the ideal of "grace under pressure" as a way to live and a way to write. He distrusted fancy phrasing and abstract utterance, making a case in much of his work for concrete speech. Under the influence of Gertrude Stein and Sherwood Anderson, he went about the business of renovating the American literary sentence. Writing stories made him into an artist. Novel writing made him famous. His first novel, *The Sun Also Rises* (1926), deals with American expatriates in France and Spain; his novel *A Farewell to Arms* (1929) is set in Italy and Switzerland during World War I. A prolific writer, Hemingway is also the author of *For Whom the Bell Tolls, The Old Man and the Sea, A Moveable Feast,* and numerous other works of fiction and nonfiction. He spent many years abroad and married four times. He was known—and described himself—as writing's "heavyweight champ"; both he and his characters are known for their unapologetic bravado. The men in his fiction are matadors, soldiers, and big-game hunters, a tight-lipped and cool-headed lot in the face of danger. A Nobel laureate and a world-famous public figure, Hemingway was nonetheless prone to suicidal depression; he took his own life in 1961 in Ketchum, Idaho.

AS YOU READ   Pay attention to how Hemingway uses exterior facts to suggest the characters' moods. What details of setting allow him to do this without directly reporting the characters' thoughts? How would you describe each character's mood?

TIP

FOR INTERACTIVE READING . . .

As you move through the story, underline the different ways Hemingway refers to his characters (for example, "the American" or "the girl"). What do these nouns reveal about the characters and about their relationship?

Hills Like White Elephants (1927)

1   THE hills across the valley of the Ebro were long and white. On this side there was no shade and no trees and the station was between two lines of rails in the sun. Close against the side of the station there was the warm shadow of the building and a curtain, made of strings of bamboo beads, hung across the open door into the bar, to keep out flies. The American and the girl with him sat at a table in the shade, outside the building. It was very hot and the express from Barcelona would come in forty minutes. It stopped at this junction for two minutes and went on to Madrid.

"What should we drink?" the girl asked. She had taken off her hat and put it on the table.

"It's pretty hot," the man said.

"Let's drink beer."

5   "Dos cervezas," the man said into the curtain.

"Big ones?" a woman asked from the doorway.

"Yes. Two big ones."

The woman brought two glasses of beer and two felt pads. She put the felt pads and the beer glasses on the table and looked at the man and the girl. The girl was looking off at the line of hills. They were white in the sun and the country was brown and dry.

"They look like white elephants," she said.

10   "I've never seen one," the man drank his beer.

"No, you wouldn't have."

"I might have," the man said. "Just because you say I wouldn't have doesn't prove anything."

The girl looked at the bead curtain. "They've painted something on it," she said. "What does it say?"

"Anis del Toro. It's a drink."

15   "Could we try it?"

> "That's all we do, isn't it—look at things and try new drinks?"

The man called "Listen" through the curtain. The woman came out from the bar.

"Four reales."

"We want two Anis del Toro."

"With water?"

"Do you want it with water?"   20

"I don't know," the girl said. "Is it good with water?"

"It's all right."

"You want them with water?" asked the woman.

"Yes, with water."

"It tastes like licorice," the girl said and put the glass down.   25

"That's the way with everything."

"Yes," said the girl. "Everything tastes of licorice. Especially all the things you've waited so long for, like absinthe."

"Oh, cut it out."

"You started it," the girl said. "I was being amused. I was having a fine time."

"Well, let's try and have a fine time."   30

"All right. I was trying. I said the mountains looked like white elephants. Wasn't that bright?"   *approval*

"That was bright."

"I wanted to try this new drink. That's all we do, isn't it—look at things and try new drinks?"   *superficial*

"I guess so."

The girl looked across at the hills.   35

"They're lovely hills," she said. "They don't really look like white elephants. I just meant the coloring of their skin through the trees."

"Should we have another drink?"

"All right."

The warm wind blew the bead curtain against the table.

"The beer's nice and cool," the man said.   40

"It's lovely," the girl said.

"It's really an awfully simple operation, Jig," the man said. "It's not really an operation at all."

The girl looked at the ground the table legs rested on.

"I know you wouldn't mind it, Jig. It's really not anything. It's just to let the air in."

45 The girl did not say anything.

"I'll go with you and I'll stay with you all the time. They just let the air in and then it's all perfectly natural."

"Then what will we do afterwards?"

"We'll be fine afterwards. Just like we were before."

"What makes you think so?"

50 "That's the only thing that bothers us. It's the only thing that's made us unhappy."

The girl looked at the bead curtain, put her hand out and took hold of two of the strings of beads.

"And you think then we'll be all right and be happy."

"I know we will. You don't have to be afraid. I've known lots of people that have done it."

"So have I," said the girl. "And afterwards they were all so happy."

55 "Well," the man said, "if you don't want to you don't have to. I wouldn't have you do it if you didn't want to. But I know it's perfectly simple."

"And you really want to?"

"I think it's the best thing to do. But I don't want you to do it if you don't really want to."

"And if I do it you'll be happy and things will be like they were and you'll love me?"

"I love you now. You know I love you."

60 "I know. But if I do it, then it will be nice again if I say things are like white elephants, and you'll like it?"

"I'll love it. I love it now but I just can't think about it. You know how I get when I worry."

"If I do it you won't ever worry?"

"I won't worry about that because it's perfectly simple."

"Then I'll do it. Because I don't care about me."

65 "What do you mean?"

"I don't care about me."

"Well, I care about you."

"Oh, yes. But I don't care about me. And I'll do it and then everything will be fine."

"I don't want you to do it if you feel that way."

The girl stood up and walked to the end of the station. 70 Across, on the other side, were fields of grain and trees along the banks of the Ebro. Far away, beyond the river, were mountains. The shadow of a cloud moved across the field of grain and she saw the river through the trees.

"And we could have all this," she said. "And we could have everything and every day we make it more impossible."

"What did you say?"

"I said we could have everything."

"We can have everything."

"No, we can't." 75

"We can have the whole world."

"No, we can't."

"We can go everywhere."

"No, we can't. It isn't ours any more."

"It's ours." 80

"No, it isn't. And once they take it away, you never get it back."

"But they haven't taken it away."

"We'll wait and see."

"Come on back in the shade," he said. "You mustn't feel that way."

"I don't feel any way," the girl said. "I just know things." 85

"I don't want you to do anything that you don't want to do—"

"Nor that isn't good for me," she said. "I know. Could we have another beer?"

"All right. But you've got to realize—"

"I realize," the girl said. "Can't we maybe stop talking?"

They sat down at the table and the girl looked across at 90 the hills on the dry side of the valley and the man looked at her and at the table.

"You've got to realize," he said, "that I don't want you to do it if you don't want to. I'm perfectly willing to go through with it if it means anything to you."

"Doesn't it mean anything to you? We could get along."

"Of course it does. But I don't want anybody but you. I don't want anyone else. And I know it's perfectly simple."

"Yes, you know it's perfectly simple."

"It's all right for you to say that, but I do know it." 95

"Would you do something for me now?"

"I'd do anything for you."

"Would you please please please please please please please stop talking?"

He did not say anything but looked at the bags against the wall of the station. There were labels on them from all the hotels where they had spent nights.

"But I don't want you to," he said, "I don't care anything   100
about it."

"I'll scream," the girl said.

The woman came out through the curtains with two glasses of beer and put them down on the damp felt pads. "The train comes in five minutes," she said.

"What did she say?" asked the girl.

"That the train is coming in five minutes."

The girl smiled brightly at the woman, to thank her.   105

"I'd better take the bags over to the other side of the station," the man said. She smiled at him.

"All right. Then come back and we'll finish the beer."

He picked up the two heavy bags and carried them around the station to the other tracks. He looked up the tracks but could not see the train. Coming back, he walked through the barroom, where people waiting for the train were drinking. He drank an Anis at the bar and looked at the people. They were all waiting reasonably for the train. He went out through the bead curtain. She was sitting at the table and smiled at him.

"Do you feel better?" he asked.

"I feel fine," she said. "There's nothing wrong with me.   110
I feel fine."

IF YOU LIKED "HILLS LIKE WHITE ELEPHANTS," YOU MIGHT LIKE . . .

. . . other spare, highly crafted stories such as "Cathedral" by Raymond Carver (in An Anthology of Stories for Further Reading) or Amy Hempel's "San Francisco" (Chapter 1).

GOING FURTHER   If you like the Hemingway story, you can dive into any one of a number of his novels and story collections. His novels *The Sun Also Rises* and *For Whom the Bell Tolls* take you back to Spain, the setting of this story.

Writing from Reading

Summarize

1 What is the conflict between the man and the woman? Based on context clues, what kind of "operation" does he want her to have?

2 Hemingway includes very little exposition—that is, text that explains who the characters are and what their situation consists of. Make a list of all you know about the girl and the man. How much of the list does Hemingway state directly, and how much did you infer? In what ways is relying heavily on reader inferences appropriate for the subject matter here?

Analyze Craft

3 What is the point of view in the story? How does Hemingway's use of an impartial narrator affect the tone of the story? How would the tone change if he had written it in first person from the woman's perspective? The man's? How would the story change if the reader had access to either or both of the characters' thoughts?

4 Choose one of the many symbols in the story, such as the train tracks or the man's luggage, and discuss its meaning in the story. How is your interpretation of the couple's actions or conversation affected by your understanding of this symbol's significance?

Analyze Voice

5 Examine the use of dialogue in this story. What purposes does dialogue serve in this story? How does the use of dialogue here differ from dialogue in other stories you've read?

6 The dialogue in this story seldom includes signpost language such as "he said" or "she said." Discuss how you, as a reader, keep track of which character is speaking. Does Hemingway characterize each character's dialogue in particular ways? Explain your answer.

7 Describe the sentences that appear outside of dialogue. Are they long or short, simple or complex? Taken together, what kind of impression do they create?

Synthesize Summary and Analysis

8 Identify all references to the white hills throughout the story. What do the hills represent? Does the meaning of the hills change as the story progresses?

9 Hemingway is famous for his theory that, like an iceberg, good fiction should show only the tip of the story, leaving the rest below the surface (that is, not stated). Is this story successful in living up to his assertion that the "dignity of movement of an ice-berg" has to do with what's submerged? Why or why not?

Interpret the Story

10 The characters stand on the brink of making a decision. Do you think Jig will go through with the operation? Why or why not? In either case, what do you believe will be the fate of the couple's relationship? What clues in the text lead you to this conclusion?

"One of the very most critical decisions that the writer makes is the point of view." Conversation with Gish Jen

Reading for Point of View

When reading for point of view, ask yourself, *who is telling the story?*		
	• Does the story have a **participant,** or **first-person,** narrator? (I/we)	EXAMPLE I'm still not sure why I agreed to go with him in the first place.
	• Is the narrator **naïve** because of age, experience, or cultural difference? Is she or he **unreliable** because of bias, character, or mental condition?	EXAMPLE I was running on only three hours of sleep. Plus, he paid for my coffee, and he had a nice enough smile.
	• Does the story have a **nonparticipant,** or **third-person,** narrator? (he/she/they)	EXAMPLE As the lights in the theater dimmed, he reached over and took her hand.
	• Is the narrator **omniscient,** or aware of the thoughts of multiple characters?	EXAMPLE Her heart leaped, and her mind buzzed, so that she missed the entire introduction to the film and had to ask him what was going on. "They're robbing this bank," he replied nonchalantly, silently thrilled she hadn't pulled away.
	• Is the narrator **editorial,** inserting judgments about the character?	EXAMPLE Later she might reflect on the cruelty of excusing herself to go to the bathroom and abandoning him there at the theater, but at the time all she could think about was freedom.
	• Is the narrator **impartial,** relating events without judging them?	EXAMPLE So she left him there, alone, waiting patiently for her return. She went and bought herself a frozen yogurt.
	• Is the narrator's omniscience limited to one character?	EXAMPLE There were two cute guys sitting in the bed of the truck next to her car when she exited the ice cream parlor. She tripped as she approached them and experienced a moment of utter terror. The looks on the guys' faces were blank, and she convinced herself they hadn't noticed.

- Does the narrator allow readers into a character's **interior monologue,** following the natural path of the person's thought processes?

  EXAMPLE   Don't stare, she told herself. Let them speak to you first. Then a voice in her head reminded her that she'd already blown off one guy tonight, and all she currently had to look forward to was a night of reruns.

- Is the narrator **objective**?

  EXAMPLE   She said hello, and they said hello back.

- Does the story have a **second-person** narrator, or a narrator who addresses the reader directly? (you)

  EXAMPLE   You taste your frozen yogurt to distract yourself from the race of your heartbeat. You try to look just above and to the right of the nearest guy's eyes— Don't stare into them, you tell yourself, don't show so much interest. You struggle for something to say. They're waiting for you to say something.

Writing about Point of View

1. Of the characters you encountered in this chapter's stories, which is the roundest, or the most fully developed (see Chapter 9, Character)? Explain what makes that character particularly round by citing examples from the story you chose. How did the author's use of point of view contribute to your sense of that character's roundness?

2. Write a short profile of the "you" character in "How to Date a Browngirl, Blackgirl, Whitegirl, or Halfie" and of the first-person narrator in "Brownies." Does one type of narration allow you to know more about a character than another type of narration, or are all equally effective in conveying character? In what ways does the narrator of "Brownies" qualify as a naïve narrator? Would it be fair to trace naiveté in Diaz's "you" character as well? Why or why not?

3. In her interview, ZZ Packer talks about reading as a way to "live an extra ten years" and become "a citizen of the world." How could reading "A Rose for Emily" help you achieve these goals? What did the story teach you about the South and its history? What did it teach you about the relationship between an individual and community? What did it teach you about generational change and understanding?

4. Faulkner and Hemingway have often been seen as fiction's opposites. Hemingway is famous for his spare style. Faulkner is famous for his lush language and imagery. Choose a sentence that you like in "A Rose for Emily." What is it about that sentence that speaks to you? How would you describe the diction, or word choice, of that sentence? Compare that sentence with the sentences in Hemingway's "Hills Like White Elephants" and describe the differences and the effect each has on the tone of the story.

12 Language, Tone, and Style

"I remember in high school I would play a game with my friends. If you were a color, you would be a light blue . . . if Jenny were an animal, she would be a giraffe. Then we would figure out these reasons why. . . . There's something about tone in that. . . . Every word is going to convey a color, a feeling, a tone like a musical instrument, a mood. . . . If you start to look at the words, . . . those are just things that come from the language itself."

Conversation with Aimee
Bender, available on video at
connect.mcgraw-hill.com

MY lover is experiencing reverse evolution. I tell no one. I don't know how it happened, only that one day he was my lover and the next he was some kind of ape. It's been a month and now he's a sea turtle.

I keep him on the counter, in a glass baking pan filled with salt water. "Ben," I say to his small protruding head, "can you understand me?" and he stares with eyes like little droplets of tar and I drip tears into the pan, a sea of me.

He is shedding a million years a day.

—from "The Rememberer" by Aimee Bender

IN this opening passage of "The Rememberer," Aimee Bender uses simple, straightforward language. The **language** she has chosen has the narrator sound confessional, a little befuddled, and sad. Of her lover's bizarre transformation, she simply says, "I don't know how it happened." She unblinkingly reports the facts, thereby bringing the reader step by step, word by word, into this odd reality in which a man can devolve into a turtle. In this story, and others that Bender has written, she creates fantastical worlds. This mix of the realistic with the fantastic is a central element of her **style**—meaning the characteristic way in which she, or any writer, uses language and story.

Style is closely related to **tone**—the author's attitude toward his or her characters or subject matter. Think of tone in writing in the same way you think of tone of voice in speech. Depending on the tone of voice your friend uses when she says "Dude," she may be signaling affection, awe, disdain, pleasure, or disgust. In turn, the tone shapes how you respond to her message. Authors convey tone by word choice and style as well as with their selection of details and images. How do Aimee Bender's style and tone shape our response to her narrator? Readers are likely to feel an odd mix of compassion for her loss and a startled *"What* did she just say about her lover!?"

CONTINUED ON PAGE 342

Aimee Bender

There is something . . . about the intimacy of reader and writer . . .

A Conversation on Writing

About "The Rememberer"

This story came from a dream. . . . I had had a dream . . . where I was going through reverse evolution with a friend, and we became dolphins, and swam around in a tank. . . . About five years later I was thinking about loss a lot, and I was thinking about it in terms of a relationship that was ending, and somehow that dream came back. And I sat down, and that first line popped into my head, "My lover's going through reverse evolution," and then I followed it to the end.

Fiction and Magic

As a kid I loved books that had magic in them. . . . There was something about that leap into metaphor and into imagination that just thrilled me. . . . Later when I [discovered writers who] were taking on adult issues . . . but were doing it through metaphor, and imaginative leaps, and magical realism, . . . I could start writing things . . . that . . . responded to so much [that I loved] as a kid but now [could write about] with hopefully more depth and perspective. . . . We need more magic in our imaginative lives, because . . . it's freeing, and . . . can be a way to get to feelings that are hard to look at straight on.

The Intimacy of Reading and Writing

There is something . . . about the intimacy of reader and writer, the action of sitting and reading something as one writer, one reader. In writing . . . I was trying to put something out there for a future reader, and then it was so satisfying when people read things and responded to them.

To watch this entire interview and hear Aimee Bender read from "The Rememberer," go to connect.mcgraw-hill.com.

In 1998 a *San Francisco Chronicle* review said this of Aimee Bender (b. 1969): "Once in a while, a writer comes along who makes you grateful for the very existence of language." Bender's first collection of stories, *The Girl in the Flammable Skirt* (1998), received enthusiastic praise from critics and readers alike. In this book—as in her novel *An Invisible Sign of My Own* (2000) and her second story collection, *Willful Creatures* (2005)—Bender's works push the limits of realism, relaying what seems impossible (a man comes back from the war without lips; a woman gives birth to her own recently deceased mother; a man suffers from an accelerated form of reverse evolution) with a straightforwardness that acknowledges but also fully accepts the fantastic. The surreal subjects of her stories are aided by the lyrical quality of her prose, which combines a straightforward tone with playful diction. Bender holds an M.F.A. from the University of California, Irvine, and she now teaches creative writing at the University of Southern California. In 2010 she published her second novel, *The Particular Sadness of Lemon Cake*.

RESEARCH ASSIGNMENT In her interview, Aimee Bender talks about realism in fiction. What is the author's attitude toward realism and fantasy in fiction? How do you relate to what Aimee Bender describes? In what way did her attitude affect her decision to become a writer? When she did become a writer, why did she choose to write fiction over other forms, like plays?

AS YOU READ   Notice the narrator's tone. Does anything that happens seem to surprise her? Do events in the story surprise you? How do you account for the differences, if any, between her responses and yours?

The Rememberer (1997)

1 MY lover is experiencing reverse evolution. I tell no one. I don't know how it happened, only that one day he was my lover and the next he was some kind of ape. It's been a month and now he's a sea turtle.

I keep him on the counter, in a glass baking pan filled with salt water.

"Ben," I say to his small protruding head, "can you understand me?" and he stares with eyes like little droplets of tar and I drip tears into the pan, a sea of me.

He is shedding a million years a day. I am no scientist, but this is roughly what I figured out. I went to the old biology teacher at the community college and asked him for an approximate time line of our evolution. He was irritated at first—he wanted money. I told him I'd be happy to pay and then he cheered up quite a bit. I can hardly read his time line—he should've typed it— and it turns out to be wrong. According to him, the whole process should take about a year, but from the way things are going, I think we have less than a month left.

5 At first, people called on the phone and asked me where was Ben. Why wasn't he at work? Why did he miss his lunch date with those clients? His out-of-print special-ordered book on civilization had arrived at the bookstore, would he please pick it up? I told them he was sick, a strange sickness, and to please stop calling. The stranger thing was, they did. They stopped calling. After a week, the phone was silent and Ben, the baboon, sat in a corner by the window, wrapped up in drapery, chattering to himself.

Last day I saw him human, he was sad about the world.

This was not unusual. He was always sad about the world. It was a large reason why I loved him. We'd sit together and be sad and think about being sad and sometimes discuss sadness.

On his last human day, he said, "Annie, don't you see? We're all getting too smart. Our brains are just getting bigger and bigger, and the world dries up and dies when there's too much thought and not enough heart."

He looked at me pointedly, blue eyes unwavering. "Like us, Annie," he said. "We think far too much."

10 I sat down. I remembered how the first time we had sex, I left the lights on, kept my eyes wide open, and concentrated really hard on letting go; then I noticed that his eyes were open too and in the middle of everything we sat down on the floor and had an hour-long conversation about poetry. It was all very peculiar. It was all very familiar.

Another time he woke me up in the middle of the night, lifted me off the pale blue sheets, led me outside to the stars and whispered: *Look, Annie, look—there is no space for anything but dreaming.* I listened, sleepily, wandered back to bed and found myself wide awake, staring at the ceiling, unable to dream at all. Ben fell asleep right away, but I crept back outside. I tried to dream up to the stars, but I didn't know how to do that. I tried to find a star no one in all of history had ever wished on before, and wondered what would happen if I did.

On his last human day, he put his head in his hands and sighed and I stood up and kissed the entire back of his neck, covered that flesh, made wishes there because I knew no woman had ever been so thorough, had ever kissed his every inch of skin. I coated him. What did I wish for? I wished for good. That's all. Just good. My wishes became generalized long ago, in childhood; I learned quick the consequence of wishing specific.

I took him in my arms and made love to him, my sad man. "See, we're not thinking," I whispered into his ear while he kissed my neck, "we're not thinking at all" and he pressed his head into my shoulder and held me tighter. Afterward, we went outside again; there was no moon and the night was dark. He said he hated talking and just wanted to look into my eyes and tell me things that way. I let him and it made my skin lift, the things in his look. Then he told me he wanted to sleep outside for some reason and in the morning when I woke up in bed, I looked out to the patio and there was an ape sprawled on the cement, great furry arms covering his head to block out the glare of the sun.

Even before I saw the eyes, I knew it was him. And once we were face to face, he gave me his same sad look and I hugged those enormous shoulders. I didn't even really care, then, not at first, I didn't panic and call 911. I sat with him outside

I walk around the block at night in case he doesn't quite remember which house it is.

and smoothed the fur on the back of his hand. When he reached for me, I said No, loudly, and he seemed to understand and pulled back. I have limits here.

We sat on the lawn together and ripped up the grass. I didn't miss human Ben right away; I wanted to meet the ape too, to take care of my lover like a son, a pet; I wanted to know him every possible way but I didn't realize he wasn't coming back.

Now I come home from work and look for his regular-size shape walking and worrying and realize, over and over, that he's gone. I pace the halls. I chew whole packs of gum in mere minutes. I review my memories and make sure they're still intact because if he's not here, then it is my job to remember. I think of the way he wrapped his arms around my back and held me so tight it made me nervous and the way his breath felt in my ear: right.

When I go to the kitchen, I peer in the glass and see he's some kind of salamander now. He's small.

"Ben," I whisper, "do you remember me? Do you remember?"

His eyes roll up in his head and I dribble honey into the water. He used to love honey. He licks at it and then swims to the other end of the pan.

This is the limit of my limits: here it is. You don't ever know for sure where it is and then you bump against it and bam, you're there. Because I cannot bear to look down into the water and not be able to find him at all, to search the tiny clear waves with a microscope lens and to locate my lover, the one-celled wonder, bloated and bordered, brainless, benign, heading clear and small like an eye-floater into nothingness.

I put him in the passenger seat of the car, and drive him to the beach. Walking down the sand, I nod at people on towels, laying their bodies out to the sun and wishing. At the water's edge, I stoop down and place the whole pan on the tip of a baby wave. It floats well, a cooking boat, for someone to find washed up on shore and to make cookies in, a lucky catch for a poor soul with all the ingredients but no container.

Ben the salamander swims out. I wave to the water with both arms, big enough for him to see if he looks back.

I turn around and walk back to the car.

Sometimes I think he'll wash up on shore. A naked man with a startled look. Who has been to history and back. I keep my eyes on the newspaper. I make sure my phone number is listed. I walk around the block at night in case he doesn't quite remember which house it is. I feed the birds outside and sometimes before I put my one self to bed, I place my hands around my skull to see if it's growing, and wonder what, of any use, would fill it if it did.

IF YOU LIKED "THE REMEMBERER," YOU MIGHT ALSO LIKE . . .

. . . other stories in the book that step over the line from realism into the surreal, such as Gabriel García Márquez's "A Very Old Man with Enormous Wings" in An Anthology of Stories for Further Reading.

GOING FURTHER In Bender's interview, she mentions that Anne Sexton's *Transformations,* the retelling of fairy tales from a contemporary perspective, was a personal favorite of hers growing up; another version of fairy tales comes in the funny and fantastic *Italian Folktales* by Italo Calvino, whose work influenced Bender. She marches in a line of writers who incorporate the supernatural and the metaphysical into fiction, such as Gabriel García Márquez (*One Hundred Years of Solitude*), the Cuban writer Alejo Carpentier (*The Kingdom of This World*), the Guatemalan writer Miguel Ángel Asturias (*Men of Maize*), and the American writer Bernard Malamud (*God's Grace*).

Writing from Reading

Summarize

1 List the different animals we glimpse Ben as throughout the story. Discuss why Bender has chosen these snapshots of de-evolution out of the entire array of animals.

Analyze Craft

2 Briefly describe the narrator's level of vocabulary (that is, does she use difficult words that you need a dictionary to decode, or simpler words that you might hear in everyday conversation?). Discuss why Bender would write at this level of vocabulary, considering what effect it has on the tone (the emotional effect) of the story.

Analyze Voice

3 "The Rememberer" provides very little background on the characters Annie and Ben. What can you glean about them, their backgrounds, and their style of life from the narrator's voice and the details she provides (or doesn't provide)?

Synthesize Summary and Analysis

4 Discuss Annie's use of the word *limits* throughout the story. What are the different contexts in which she mentions limits? What are her limits, and why?

Interpret the Story

5 The scientist forecasts a year for Ben's de-evolution, but it happens much faster. Why does Bender make a point of mentioning the scientist and his discrepancy? Explore the commentary she might be making about human history, citing the text.

6 Discuss the roles of science, realism, and fantasy in this story. How does Bender use the three to make the world portrayed in this story a convincing place?

CONTINUED FROM PAGE 337

You may have noticed that most chapters in this book focus on a single topic—plot, character, setting, point of view—whereas this chapter groups three topics together. This is because language, tone, and style are difficult to separate from one another. The type of language an author uses establishes his or her tone. In "The Cask of Amontillado" (Chapter 10), for example, Poe uses language that connotes darkness and decay. At the same time, the language of darkness and decay creates a sense of foreboding, even if we don't know at the beginning what causes that feeling. Poe's language, then, gives rise to a tone that we can describe as both melancholy and chilling.

Putting those elements together—the darkness and decay evoked by the language; the melancholy and foreboding tone—you arrive at Poe's style. As you most likely know if you have encountered Poe before, he is famous for his horror stories and mysteries. This reputation is based on a tonal choice, the mood that his work evokes. Consider his well-known poem "The Raven," which begins with the line "Once upon a midnight dreary" (see Chapter 21). Characteristic of Poe's style, the language in the poem, as in "The Cask of Amontillado," is dark and immediately sets a melancholy ("dreary"), foreboding ("midnight") tone.

"I know that there are many things that can open a story, that can start a person working. For me it's language. It's not an idea."

Conversation with Amy Hempel

In this chapter, we focus on three stories that we think demonstrate a particularly clear use of language, tone, and style. But remember, all stories contain these three elements; after all, stories are made of language, which in turn creates a tone that combines with the language to form an author's distinctive style.

CRAFTING STYLE AND TONE

Everyone knows what style looks like or feels the effect of it. We see it in the distinctive way a base runner moves, a basketball player goes for a layup, or a kid does turns on a skateboard. We see a person's style in the way she does (or doesn't do) her nails, the choice and placement of a tattoo or a piercing, a particular combination of shirt, jeans, vest, and scarf—with high-top sneakers, cowboy boots, high heels, flip-flops, or anything else in the vast array of potential footwear.

The distinctive style combined with the writer's tone molds the reader's impressions. Tone establishes how the narrator regards the story and the people in it—for example, with contempt, longing, passionate curiosity, sympathy, or ambivalence. The writer's tone influences how the reader relates and responds to the characters and the course of events. Reading a literary work critically comes down to an intense scrutiny of the work's style and tone with these questions in mind:

- *What* is being said, and *how* and *why*?
- What effect does the author wish to create?
- What effect does the writing have on you?

Each of the stories in this chapter evokes a setting or scene and does so with a unique style and tone. As you read each of them, ask yourself why the authors chose the particular words and images they did. What tone (of voice) do you hear? Where does the style fall on a spectrum of formal to informal, direct to roundabout, concrete to abstract, serious to wry to comedic? Are the sentences long and complex, or short and simple? Does the author use the language of the street or that of academia? Taken together, these are qualities that make up an author's style and tone.

The tone of "The Rememberer" is intimate and informal when the first-person narrator stands weeping over her boyfriend-turned-sea-turtle. Her tone and style arise from her **diction,** an author's or character's distinctive choice of words and style of expression. Now consider a passage written by Ernest Hemingway.

> You know how it is there early in the morning in Havana with the bums still asleep against the walls of the buildings; before even the ice wagons come by with the ice for the bars? Well, we came across the square from the dock to the Pearl of San Francisco Café to get coffee and there was only one beggar awake in the square and he was getting a drink out of the fountain. But when we got inside the café and sat down, there were the three of them waiting for us. . . .

—from "One Trip Across" (1934)

In this story, which became the opening lines of his novel *To Have and Have Not* (1937), Hemingway uses the everyday language of his American character, a smuggler living in Cuba. The tone is casual, conversational, and hard-boiled. With that "You know how it is," the narrator speaks to us directly, drawing us in as confederates who are just as street-savvy as he is, who have been up that early in the morning. The style is realistic, concrete, and economical, and the details reveal that the place is exotic (Havana) and just a little bit seedy, with its bums and beggars.

"I thought, well what is a voice? And what's a story? What are the things that make this up? And if I know, you know, ABCD, these components, I can sit down and write these things. But I feel now, now that I've been doing this for a while, that the questions are still there. And there's no absolute answer. And that you discover it each time you sit down and write." Conversation with Amy Tan

Notice what the narrator reveals—in an offhand way. He's been around, the kind of man who has seen enough "bums still asleep against the walls of the buildings" that they barely have an effect on him. There's plenty we don't yet know: why this narrator has come from the dock, who's with him, who's waiting for him at the bar and why. With style, tone, and careful selection of words and details, Hemingway creates an effect: a narrator in motion, leading the reader to a rendezvous with something that seems like trouble. "Follow him," Hemingway seems to say of his narrator. "So he's a little shady. He's still the one to watch."

STYLE AND DICTION

A number of elements contribute to a work's overall style and to the effect it creates on the reader. As we noted, diction, whether formal or informal, is important in writing because of what it reveals about character. Diction, for example, is a central concern of Flannery O'Connor's "Good Country People" in this chapter and Gish Jen's "Who's Irish?" (Chapter 9). In both cases, if the voice were standardized into "proper" spoken English, much would be lost.

"At some point the sound of the language becomes the story: the sounds of characters talking, what comes out of their mouths, the sound of your own prose as you write a bit of narrative, a bit of description, or whatever. You're discovering meaning as you're doing it through the sound of the prose." Conversation with Tim O'Brien

TONE AND IRONY

Before his transformation, Ben, the narrator's lover in the Bender story, was a melancholy type, always bemoaning the human condition—that people had become too smart, that they thought too much, that they talked too much. So his fate—changing from man, to ape, to sea turtle so that he no longer needs to suffer the human condition—makes "sense," but with a twist. Expecting, as we all do, to live forward in time and evolve as a human being, Ben instead evolves backward, thus experiencing a striking example of ironic reversal. Once you know what it looks and sounds like, **irony** may be the most distinctive and easily recognizable tone to identify. Irony, a difference between what occurs and what you expect to occur or between what is said and what is meant, often involves some sort of reversal in circumstances or fate.

Irony has other manifestations that grow out of the technique of radical reversal. For example, a football player intercepts a pass but becomes confused and runs the ball in the wrong direction, toward his own goal line. A president wants to bring glory to his country but takes actions that lead to disgrace and defeat. A nerdy young man courts a girl by taking acting lessons, buying a new suit, and getting a fresh haircut only to be rejected by the girl who wanted a natural sort of guy. The idea of reversal is central to the fate of Ben in "The Rememberer."

> **"Tone is the attitude that the writer lays over the story itself . . . whereas voice is to me the music of the story's intelligence, which is to say it's how the story sounds in your ear—when you're reading it aloud or you're reading it silently—how the story sounds when it's being most itself, when it's being as smart as it is, when it's being as characteristic as it is."** Conversation with Richard Ford

The term *irony* also refers to an incongruity between what someone says and what someone means. For example, your neighbor catches you taking out the garbage in your old wrinkled pajamas, with your hair wildly askew, and says, "You're looking fabulous today." This is an example of **verbal irony**—a person saying one thing and meaning another. When someone speaks in a mean-spirited, critical, or malicious way, we call that **sarcasm.** Sarcasm is not common in literature, but verbal irony is, as in this passage about war by Kurt Vonnegut from his novel *Slaughterhouse Five:*

> *Wherever you went there were women who would do anything for food or protection for themselves and their children and the old people . . . the whole point of war is to put women everywhere in that condition. It's always the men against the women, with the men only pretending to fight among themselves . . . the ones who pretend the hardest get their pictures in the paper and medals afterwards.*

No one would seriously claim that "the whole point of war" is to turn women's lives into a desperate struggle to protect themselves and others, and Vonnegut does not expect the reader to buy this. He says one thing but means another in order to get at a truth about the *effects* of war and to convey an attitude about war—that it is a horrific and senseless human activity. At the same time, he feigns innocence, as if he is

> **". . . you draw with words when you write. . . . Conrad talked about the need to make the reader see. [Although you also hope to make him or her hear, and smell even, and appeal to all the senses,] nevertheless the seeing seems to be what it's ultimately all about."**
>
> Conversation with John Updike

A BRIEF HISTORY OF IRONY

Irony is a concept that comes down to us from the time of Greek tragedy. In that era, it was a philosophical, if not theological, lens through which the Greeks viewed all of life, and it has proved useful to writers throughout the history of literature in the West. Although irony was a complex process in the Greek tragedies, the essence of irony is reversal, and reversal is a simple concept: A beggar discovers treasure, or a man at the height of his powers loses everything. In the European Middle Ages, the sign of fortune was a great wheel; irony defined that circling course. The hero's fortune could reside at the top of the wheel, but it could just as easily fall to the bottom. During the thousand years and more when Europe was united in the belief that Christianity was the answer to all questions about life and death, irony became less useful as a general idea. Those who accepted Christ found life after death, so the human outcome was clear.

describing a set of simple facts, as if he truly believes that jeopardizing women is "the whole point of war."

How does a reader know when an author is being ironic? In Vonnegut's case, you know because Vonnegut pushes his point to extremes. When he says "the whole point," and when he talks about "men only pretending to fight," you know that he is up to something other than a straight-faced discussion of war. He also uses an ironic tone—which borders here on sarcasm—because of the extreme points he makes, as if he were saying, "You idiots, can't you see?"

The fable "Appointment in Samarra," retold below by British novelist W. Somerset Maugham, illustrates an aspect of irony that we introduced before—a discrepancy between acts and results, or between what occurs and what the character expected to occur. In this story, the narrator is Death.

> There was a merchant in Bagdad who sent his servant to market to buy provisions and in a little while the servant came back, white and trembling, and said, Master, just now when I was in the marketplace I was jostled by a woman in the crowd and when I turned I saw it was Death that jostled me. She looked at me and made a threatening gesture. Now, lend me your horse, and I will ride away from this city and avoid my fate. I will go to Samarra and there Death will not find me. The merchant lent him his horse, and the servant mounted it, and he dug his spurs in its flanks and as fast as the horse could gallop he went. Then the merchant went down to the marketplace and he saw me standing in the crowd and he came to me and said, Why did you make a threatening gesture to my servant when you saw him this morning? That was not a threatening gesture, I said, it was only a start of surprise. I was astonished to see him in Bagdad, for I had an appointment with him tonight in Samarra.

> **"There are writers that I just deeply admire for the sentences that they write. And they're the ones I go back to read when writing isn't going well."** Conversation with Chimamanda Ngozi Adichie

The outcome for the poor servant is ironic because he hopes to avoid death by leaving his home and going to hide in Samarra. In doing so, however, he unknowingly guarantees that he will be precisely at the place where Death intends to seek him. The reader can see what the outcome will be, but the servant cannot, which gives the reader an advantage but also a feeling of apprehension or, in some cases, sorrow. This literary device is referred to as **dramatic irony,** a situation in which an author or narrator lets the reader know more about a situation than a character does.

Sherman Alexie (b. 1966)

Sherman Alexie grew up on the Spokane Indian Reservation in Washington (he is of Spokane/Coeur d'Alene Indian descent). He attended college with the goal of becoming a doctor. His career as a poet took off shortly after graduation; by 1993 he had received two major fellowships and published two books of poetry. Next, he returned to short stories with *The Lone Ranger and Tonto Fistfight In Heaven* (1993) and then produced a novel, *Reservation Blues* (1995). He also wrote the screenplay for the award-winning, independently produced film *Smoke Signals* (1998). His signature blend of irony, humor, cynicism, and critique of modern Native American life has won him many honors including the PEN/Hemingway award, the PEN/Malamud award, and the Pushcart Prize. In 2007 he received the National Book Award for Young People's Literature with *The Absolutely True Diary of a Part-Time Indian.* He calls Seattle home.

AS YOU READ   Consider how the irony here washes over every aspect of the young boy's observations, beginning with the way he depicts his own actions.

Indian Education (1993)

FIRST GRADE

1   My hair was too short and my U.S. Government glasses were horn-rimmed, ugly, and all that first winter in school, the other Indian boys chased me from one corner of the playground to the other. They pushed me down, buried me in the snow until I couldn't breathe, thought I'd never breathe again.

> For Halloween I drew a picture of her riding a broom. . . .

They stole my glasses and threw them over my head, around my outstretched hands, just beyond my reach, until someone tripped me and sent me falling again, facedown in the snow.

I was always falling down; my Indian name was Junior Falls Down. Sometimes it was Bloody Nose or Steal-His-Lunch. Once it was Cries-Like-a-White-Boy, even though none of us had seen a white boy cry.

Then it was Friday morning recess and Frenchy SiJohn threw snowballs at me while the rest of the Indian boys tortured some other *top-yogh-yaught* kid, another weakling. But Frenchy was confident enough to torment me all by himself, and most days I would have let him.

5   But the little warrior in me roared to life that day and knocked Frenchy to the ground, held his head against the snow, and punched him so hard the my knuckles and the snow make symmetrical bruises on his face. He almost looked like he was wearing war paint.

But he wasn't the warrior. I was. And I chanted *It's a good day to die, it's a good day to die,* all the way down to the principal's office.

SECOND GRADE

Betty Towle, missionary teacher, redheaded and so ugly that no one ever had a puppy crush on her, made me stay in for recess fourteen days straight.

"Tell me you're sorry," she said.

"Sorry for what?" I asked.

"Everything," she said and made me stand straight for 10 fifteen minutes, eagle-armed with books in each hand. One was a math book; the other was English. But all I learned was that gravity can be painful.

For Halloween I drew a picture of her riding a broom with a scrawny cat on the back. She said that her God would never forgive me for that.

Once, she gave the class a spelling test but set me aside and gave me a test designed for junior high students. When I spelled all the words right, she crumpled up the paper and made me eat it.

"You'll learn respect," she said.

She sent a letter home with me that told my parents to either cut my braids or keep me home from class. My parents came in the next day and dragged their braids across Betty Towle's desk.

"Indians, indians, indians." She said it without capital- 15 ization. She called me "indian, indian, indian."

And I said, *Yes I am, I am Indian. Indian, I am.*

THIRD GRADE

My traditional Native American art career began and ended with my very first portrait: *Stick Indian Taking a Piss in My Backyard.*

As I circulated the original print around the classroom, Mrs. Schluter intercepted and confiscated my art.

Censorship, I might cry now. *Freedom of expression*, I would write in editorials to the tribal newspaper.

In the third grade, though, I stood alone in the corner, 20 faced the wall, and waited for the punishment to end.

I'm still waiting.

FOURTH GRADE

"You should be a doctor when you grow up," Mr. Schluter told me, even though his wife, the third grade teacher, thought

I was crazy beyond my years. My eyes always looked like I had just hit-and-run someone.

"Guilty," she said. "You always look guilty."

"Why should I be a doctor?" I asked Mr. Schluter.

25   "So you can come back and help the tribe. So you can heal people."

That was the year my father drank a gallon of vodka a day and the same year that my mother started two hundred quilts but never finished any. They sat in separate, dark places in our HUD house and wept savagely.

I ran home after school, heard their Indian tears, and looked in the mirror. *Doctor Victor*, I called myself, invented an education, talked to my reflection. *Doctor Victor to the emergency room.*

FIFTH GRADE

I picked up a basketball for the first time and made my first shot. No. I missed my first shot, missed the basket completely, and the ball landed in the dirt and sawdust, sat there just like I had sat there only minutes before.

But it felt good, that ball in my hands, all those possibilities and angles. It was mathematics, geometry. It was beautiful.

30   At that same moment, my cousin Steven Ford sniffed rubber cement from a paper bag and leaned back on the merry-go-round. His ears rang, his mouth was dry, and everyone seemed so far away.

But it felt good, that buzz in his head, all those colors and noises. It was chemistry, biology. It was beautiful.

Oh, do you remember those sweet, almost innocent choices that the Indian boys were forced to make?

SIXTH GRADE

Randy, the new Indian kid from the white town of Springdale, got into a fight an hour after he first walked into the reservation school.

Stevie Flett called him out, called him a squawman, called him a pussy, and called him a punk.

Randy and Stevie, and the rest of the Indian boys, 35 walked out into the playground.

"Throw the first punch," Stevie said as they squared off.

"No," Randy said.

"Throw the first punch," Stevie said again.

"No," Randy said again.

"Throw the first punch!" Stevie said for the third time, 40 and Randy reared back and pitched a knuckle fastball that broke Stevie's nose.

We all stood there in silence, in awe.

That was Randy, my soon-to-be first and best friend, who taught me the most valuable lesson about living in the white world: *Always throw the first punch.*

SEVENTH GRADE

I leaned through the basement window of the HUD house and kissed the white girl who would later be raped by her foster-parent father, who was also white. They both lived on the reservation, though, and when the headlines and stories filled the papers later, not one word was made of their color.

Just Indians being Indians, someone must have said somewhere and they were wrong.

But on the day I leaned out through the basement win- 45 dow of the HUD house and kissed the white girl, I felt the good-byes I was saying to my entire tribe. I held my lips tight against her lips, a dry, clumsy, and ultimately stupid kiss.

But I was saying good-bye to my tribe, to all the Indian girls and women I might have loved, to all the Indian men who might have called me cousin, even brother.

I kissed that white girl and when I opened my eyes, she was gone from the reservation, and when I opened my eyes, I was gone from the reservation, living in a farm town where a beautiful white girl asked my name.

"Junior Polatkin," I said, and she laughed.

After that, no one spoke to me for another five hundred years.

EIGHTH GRADE

At the farm town junior high, in the boys' bathroom, I could 50 hear voices from the girls' bathroom, nervous whispers of anorexia and bulimia. I could hear the white girls' forced vomiting, a sound so familiar and natural to me after years of listening to my father's hangovers.

"Give me your lunch if you're just going to throw it up," I said to one of those girls once.

I sat back and watched them grow skinny from self-pity.

Back on the reservation, my mother stood in line to get us commodities. We carried them home, happy to have food, and opened the canned beef that even the dogs wouldn't eat.

But we ate it day after day and grew skinny from self-pity.

55 There is more than one way to starve.

NINTH GRADE

At the farm town high school dance, after a basketball game in an overheated gym where I had scored twenty-seven points and pulled down thirteen rebounds, I passed out during a slow song.

As my white friends revived me and prepared to take me to the emergency room where doctors would later diagnose my diabetes, the Chicano teacher ran up to us.

"Hey," he said. "What's that boy been drinking? I know all about these Indian kids. They start drinking real young."

Sharing dark skin doesn't necessarily make two men brothers.

TENTH GRADE

60 I passed the written test easily and nearly flunked the driving, but still received my Washington State driver's license on the same day that Wally Jim killed himself by driving his car into a pine tree.

No traces of alcohol in his blood, good job, wife and two kids.

"Why'd he do it?" asked a white Washington State trooper.

All the Indians shrugged their shoulders, looked down at the ground.

"Don't know," we all said, but when we look in the mirror, see the history of our tribe in our eyes, taste failure in the tap water, and shake with old tears, we understand completely.

Believe me, everything looks like a noose if you stare at it long enough. 65

ELEVENTH GRADE

Last night I missed two free throws which would have won the game against the best team in the state. The farm town high school I played for is nicknamed the "Indians," and I'm probably the only actual Indian ever to play for a team with such a mascot.

This morning I pick up the sports page and read the headline: INDIANS LOSE AGAIN.

Go ahead and tell me none of this is supposed to hurt me very much.

TWELFTH GRADE

I walk down the aisle, valedictorian of this farm town high school, and my cap doesn't fit because I've grown my hair longer than it's ever been. Later, I stand as the school-board chairman recites my awards and accomplishments, and scholarships.

I try to remain stoic for the photographers as I look toward the future. 60

Back home on the reservation, my former classmates graduate: a few can't read, one or two are just given attendance diplomas, most look forward to the parties. The bright students are shaken, frightened, because they don't know what comes next.

They smile for the photographer as they look back toward tradition.

The tribal newspaper runs my photograph and the photograph of my former classmates side by side.

POSTSCRIPT: CLASS REUNION

Victor said, "Why should we organize a reservation high school reunion? My graduating class has a reunion every weekend at the Powwow Tavern."

IF YOU LIKED "INDIAN EDUCATION," YOU MIGHT ALSO LIKE . . .

. . . "The Man to Send Rainclouds" by Leslie Marmon Silko or Flannery O'Connor's "A Good Man Is Hard to Find," which appears with Silko's story in American Regionalism and Sense of Place: Two Case Studies (Chapter 15), as well as other stories that employ a sense of outrageous irony and humor, such as Flannery O'Connor's "Good Country People" in this chapter and "Greasy Lake" by T. C. Boyle (Chapter 8).

GOING FURTHER   Alexie and Silko come from a long line of American-Indian fiction writers that includes Pulitzer Prize winner N. Scott Momaday and his lyrical work of fiction *The Way to Rainy Mountain*. You also might enjoy Louise Erdrich's novels *Tracks* and *The Beet Queen*.

Writing from Reading

Summarize

1 List and briefly describe the various people the speaker mentions throughout the story. What, if anything, do these people have in common? What do they have in common with the narrator?

Analyze Craft

2 Alexie names each statement of the story after the grades of his schooling. What information is imparted by these headings that cannot be gleaned from the narrative of the story? Would this story have the same meaning without those headings?

3 Choose one of the sections of the story and rewrite it as an impartial third-person limited account of the events described. Why do you think Alexie chose to write the story from the first-person point of view?

4 Describe the tone of this story. What specific words, phrases, and details create that tone?

Analyze Voice

5 The speaker tells the story retrospectively, in past tense. What characteristics of the speaker can you infer from the details he chooses to include? How many years do you think have passed since his graduation?

Synthesize Summary and Analysis

6 For each grade, summarize the lesson the narrator learned from the events described. Considering this "education," what is the significance of the statement in the Postscript? (Hint: The narrator's name is Victor.)

Interpret the Story

7 How does the narrator change during his twelve years of school? Do you think he is among the Indians who gather at the Powwow Tavern every weekend? Why or why not?

Flannery O'Connor (1925–1964)

For a brief biography of Flannery O'Connor, see Chapter 15.

AS YOU READ   Notice the tone the writer takes with respect to the religion practiced by the characters in this story. Does it create a certain distance between you and their practices—and, if so, how?

Good Country People (1955)

1   BESIDES the neutral expression that she wore when she was alone, Mrs. Freeman had two others, forward and reverse, that she used for all her human dealings. Her forward expression was steady and driving like the advance of a heavy truck. Her eyes never swerved to left or right but turned as the story turned as if they followed a yellow line down the center of it. She seldom used the other expression because it was not often necessary for her to retract a statement, but when she did, her face came to a complete stop, there was an almost imperceptible movement of her black eyes, during which they seemed to be receding, and then the observer would see that Mrs. Freeman, though she might stand there as real as several grain sacks thrown on top of each other, was no longer there in spirit. As for getting anything across to her when this was the case, Mrs. Hopewell had given it up. She might talk her head off. Mrs. Freeman could never be brought to admit herself wrong to any point. She would stand there and if she could be brought to say anything, it was something like, "Well, I wouldn't of said it was and I wouldn't of said it wasn't" or letting her gaze range over the top kitchen shelf where there was an assortment of dusty bottles, she might remark, "I see you ain't ate many of them figs you put up last summer."

They carried on their most important business in the kitchen at breakfast. Every morning Mrs. Hopewell got up at seven o'clock and lit her gas heater and Joy's. Joy was her daughter, a large blonde girl who had an artificial leg. Mrs. Hopewell thought of her as a child though she was thirty-two years old and highly educated. Joy would get up while her mother was eating and lumber into the bathroom and slam the door, and before long, Mrs. Freeman would arrive at the back door. Joy would hear her mother call, "Come on in," and then they would talk for a while in low voices that were indistinguishable in the bathroom. By the time Joy came in, they had usually finished the weather report and were on one or the other of Mrs. Freeman's daughters, Glynese or Carramae, Joy called them Glycerin and Caramel. Glynese, a redhead, was eighteen and had many admirers; Carramae, a blonde, was only fifteen but already married and pregnant. She could not keep anything in her stomach. Every morning Mrs. Freeman told Mrs. Hopewell how many times she had vomited since the last report.

Mrs. Hopewell liked to tell people that Glynese and Carramae were two of the finest girls she knew and that Mrs. Freeman was a *lady* and that she was never ashamed to take her anywhere or introduce her to anybody they might meet. Then she would tell how she had happened to hire the Freemans in the first place and how they were a godsend to her and how she had had them four years. The reason for her keeping them so long was that they were not trash. They were good country people. She had telephoned the man whose name they had given as reference and he had told her that Mr. Freeman was a good farmer but that his wife was the nosiest woman ever to walk the earth. "She's got to be into everything," the man said. "If she don't get there before the dust settles, you can bet she's dead, that's all. She'll want to know all your business. I can stand him real good," he had said, "but me nor my wife neither could have stood that woman one more minute on this place." That had put Mrs. Hopewell off for a few days.

She had hired them in the end because there were no other applicants but she had made up her mind beforehand exactly how she would handle the woman. Since she was the type who had to be into everything, then, Mrs. Hopewell had decided, she would not only let her be into everything, she would *see to it* that she was into everything—she would give her the responsibility of everything, she would put her in charge. Mrs. Hopewell had no bad qualities of her own but she was able to use other people's in such a constructive way that she never felt the lack. She had hired the Freemans and she had kept them four years.

5 Nothing is perfect. This was one of Mrs. Hopewell's favorite sayings. Another was: that is life! And still another, the most important, was: well, other people have their opinions too. She would make these statements, usually at the table, in a tone of gentle insistence as if no one held them but her, and the large hulking Joy, whose constant outrage had obliterated every expression from her face, would stare just a little to the side of her, her eyes icy blue, with the look of someone who had achieved blindness by an act of will and means to keep it.

. . . the leg had been literally blasted off . . . she had never lost consciousness.

When Mrs. Hopewell said to Mrs. Freeman that life was like that, Mrs. Freeman would say, "I always said so myself." Nothing had been arrived at by anyone that had not first been arrived at by her. She was quicker than Mr. Freeman. When Mrs. Hopewell said to her after they had been on the place for a while, "You know, you're the wheel behind the wheel," and winked, Mrs. Freeman had said, "I know it. I've always been quick. It's some that are quicker than others."

"Everybody is different," Mrs. Hopewell said.

"Yes, most people is," Mrs. Freeman said.

"It takes all kinds to make the world."

10 "I always said it did myself."

The girl was used to this kind of dialogue for breakfast and more of it for dinner; sometimes they had it for supper too. When they had no guest they ate in the kitchen because that was easier. Mrs. Freeman always managed to arrive at some point during the meal and to watch them finish it. She would stand in the doorway if it were summer but in the winter she would stand with one elbow on top of the refrigerator and look down at them, or she would stand by the gas heater, lifting the back of her skirt slightly. Occasionally she would stand against the wall and roll her head from side to side. At no time was she in any hurry to leave. All this was very trying on Mrs. Hopewell but she was a woman of great patience. She realized that nothing is perfect and that in the Freemans she had good country people and that if, in this day and age, you get good country people, you had better hang onto them.

She had had plenty of experience with trash. Before the Freemans she had averaged one tenant family a year. The wives of these farmers were not the kind you would want to be around you for very long. Mrs. Hopewell, who had divorced her husband long ago, needed someone to walk over the fields with her; and when Joy had to be impressed for these services, her remarks were usually so ugly and her face so glum that Mrs. Hopewell would say, "If you can't come pleasantly, I don't want you at all," to which the girl, standing square and rigid-shouldered with her neck thrust slightly forward, would reply, "If you want me, here I am—LIKE I AM."

Mrs. Hopewell excused this attitude because of the leg (which had been shot off in a hunting accident when Joy was ten). It was hard for Mrs. Hopewell to realize that her child was thirty-two now and that for more than twenty years she had had only one leg. She thought of her still as a child because it tore her heart to think instead of the poor stout girl in her thirties who had never danced a step or had any *normal* good times. Her name was really Joy but as soon as she was twenty-one and away from home, she had had it legally changed. Mrs. Hopewell was certain that she had thought and thought until she had hit upon the ugliest name in any language. Then she had gone and had the beautiful name, Joy, changed without telling her mother until after she had done it. Her legal name was Hulga.

When Mrs. Hopewell thought the name, Hulga, she thought of the broad blank hull of a battleship. She would not use it. She continued to call her Joy to which the girl responded but in a purely mechanical way.

15 Hulga had learned to tolerate Mrs. Freeman who saved her from taking walks with her mother. Even Glynese and Carramae were useful when they occupied attention that might otherwise have been directed at her. At first she had thought she could not stand Mrs. Freeman for she had found it was not possible to be rude to her. Mrs. Freeman would take on strange resentments and for days together she would be sullen but the source of her displeasure was always obscure; a direct attack, a positive leer, blatant ugliness to her face—these never touched her. And without warning one day, she began calling her Hulga.

She did not call her that in front of Mrs. Hopewell who would have been incensed but when she and the girl happened to be out of the house together, she would say something and add the name Hulga to the end of it, and the big spectacled Joy-Hulga would scowl and redden as if her privacy had been intruded upon. She considered the name her personal affair. She had arrived at it first purely on the basis of its ugly sound and then the full genius of its fitness had struck her. She had a vision of the name working like the ugly sweating Vulcan[1] who stayed in the furnace and to whom, presumably, the goddess had to come when called. She saw it as the name of her highest creative act. One of her major triumphs was that her mother had not been able to turn her dust into Joy, but the greater one was that she had been able to turn it herself into Hulga. However, Mrs. Freeman's relish for using the name only irritated her. It was as if Mrs. Freeman's beady steel-pointed eyes had penetrated far enough behind her face to reach some secret fact. Something about her seemed to fascinate Mrs. Freeman and then one day Hulga realized that it was the artificial leg. Mrs. Freeman had a special fondness for the details of secret infections, hidden deformities, assaults upon children. Of diseases, she preferred the lingering or incurable. Hulga had heard Mrs. Hopewell give her the details of the hunting accident, how the leg had been literally blasted off, how she had never lost consciousness. Mrs. Freeman could listen to it any time as if it had happened an hour ago.

When Hulga stumped into the kitchen in the morning (she could walk without making the awful noise but she made it—Mrs. Hopewell was certain—because it was ugly-sounding), she glanced at them and did not speak. Mrs. Hopewell would be in her red kimono with her hair tied around her head in rags. She would be sitting at the table, finishing her breakfast and Mrs. Freeman would be hanging by her elbow outward from the refrigerator, looking down at the table. Hulga always put her eggs on the stove to boil and then stood over them with her arms folded, and Mrs. Hopewell would look at her—a kind of indirect gaze divided between her and Mrs. Freeman—and would think that if she would only keep herself up a little, she wouldn't be so bad looking. There was nothing wrong with her face that a pleasant expression wouldn't help. Mrs. Hopewell said that people who looked on the bright side of things would be beautiful even if they were not.

Whenever she looked at Joy this way, she could not help but feel that it would have been better if the child had not taken the Ph.D. It had certainly not brought her out any and now that she had it, there was no more excuse for her to go to school again. Mrs. Hopewell thought it was nice for girls to go to school to have a good time but Joy had "gone through." Anyhow, she would not have been strong enough to go again. The doctors had told Mrs. Hopewell that with the best of care, Joy might see forty-five. She had a weak heart. Joy had made it plain that if it had not been for this condition, she would be far from these red hills and good country people. She would be in a university lecturing to people who knew what she was talking about. And Mrs. Hopewell could very well picture here there, looking like a scarecrow and lecturing to more of the same. Here she went about all day in a six-year-old skirt and a yellow sweat shirt with a faded cowboy on a horse embossed on it. She thought this was funny; Mrs. Hopewell thought it was idiotic and showed simply that she was still a child. She was brilliant but she didn't have a grain of sense. It seemed to Mrs. Hopewell that every year she grew less like other people and more like herself—bloated, rude, and squint-eyed. And she said such strange things! To her own mother she had said—without warning, without excuse, standing up in the middle of a meal with her face purple and her mouth half full—"Woman! do you ever look inside? Do you ever look inside and see what you are *not*? God!" she had cried sinking down again and staring at her plate, "Malebranche[2] was right: we are not our own light. We are not our own light!" Mrs. Hopewell had no idea to this day what brought that on. She had only made the remark, hoping Joy would take it in, that a smile never hurt anyone.

The girl had taken the Ph.D. in philosophy and this left Mrs. Hopewell at a complete loss. You could say, "My daughter is a nurse," or "My daughter is a schoolteacher," or even, "My daughter is a chemical engineer." You could not say, "My daughter is a philosopher." That was something that had ended with the Greeks and Romans.

---

[1]*Vulcan:* Roman god of fire.

[2]*Malebranche:* Nicholas Malebranche (1638–1715), a French philosopher.

All day Joy sat on her neck in a deep chair, reading. Sometimes she went for walks but she didn't like dogs or cats or birds or flowers or nature or nice young men. She looked at nice young men as if she could smell their stupidity.

20   One day Mrs. Hopewell had picked up one of the books the girl had just put down and opening it at random, she read, "Science, on the other hand, has to assert its soberness and seriousness afresh and declare that it is concerned solely with what-is. Nothing—how can it be for science anything but a horror and a phantasm? If science is right, then one thing stands firm: science wishes to know nothing of nothing. Such is after all the strictly scientific approach to Nothing. We know it by wishing to know nothing of Nothing." These words had been underlined with a blue pencil and they worked on Mrs. Hopewell like some evil incantation in gibberish. She shut the book quickly and went out of the room as if she were having a chill.

> ## She looked at nice young men as if she could smell their stupidity.

     This morning when the girl came in, Mrs. Freeman was on Carramae. "She thrown up four times after supper," she said, "and was up twict in the night after three o'clock. Yesterday she didn't do nothing but ramble in the bureau drawer. All she did. Stand up there and see what she could run up on."

     "She's got to eat," Mrs. Hopewell muttered, sipping her coffee, while she watched Joy's back at the stove. She was wondering what the child had said to the Bible salesman. She could not imagine what kind of a conversation she could possibly have had with him.

     He was a tall gaunt hatless youth who had called yesterday to sell them a Bible. He had appeared at the door, carrying a large black suitcase that weighted him so heavily on one side that he had to brace himself against the door facing. He seemed on the point of collapse but he said in a cheerful voice, "Good morning, Mrs. Cedars!" and set the suitcase down on the mat. He was not a bad-looking young man though he had on a bright blue suit and yellow socks that were not pulled up far enough. He had prominent face bones and a streak of sticky-looking brown hair falling across his forehead.

     "I'm Mrs. Hopewell," she said.

25   "Oh!" he said, pretending to look puzzled but with his eyes sparkling, "I saw it said 'The Cedars' on the mailbox so I thought you was Mrs. Cedars!" and he burst out in a pleasant laugh. He picked up the satchel and under cover of a pant, he fell forward into her hall. It was rather as if the suitcase had moved first, jerking him after it. "Mrs. Hopewell!" he said and grabbed her hand. "I hope you are well!" and he laughed again and then all at once his face sobered completely. He paused and gave her a straight earnest look and said, "Lady, I've come to speak of serious things."

     "Well, come in," she muttered, none too pleased because her dinner was almost ready. He came into the parlor and sat down on the edge of a straight chair and put the suitcase between his feet and glanced around the room as if he were sizing her up by it. Her silver gleamed on the two sideboards; she decided he had never been in a room as elegant as this.

     "Mrs. Hopewell," he began, using her name in a way that sounded almost intimate, "I know you believe in Chrustian service."

     "Well, yes," she murmured.

     "I know," he said and paused, looking very wise with his head cocked on one side, "that you're a good woman. Friends have told me."

     Mrs. Hopewell never liked to be taken for a fool. "What 30 are you selling?" she asked.

     "Bibles," the young man said and his eye raced around the room before he added, "I see you have no family Bible in your parlor, I see that is the one lack you got!"

     Mrs. Hopewell could not say, "My daughter is an atheist and won't let me keep the Bible in the parlor." She said, stiffening slightly, "I keep my Bible by my bedside." This was not the truth. It was in the attic somewhere.

     "Lady," he said, "the word of God ought to be in the parlor."

     "Well, I think that's a matter of taste," she began, "I think . . ."

     "Lady," he said, "for a Chrustian, the word of God ought 35 to be in every room in the house besides in his heart. I know you're a Chrustian because I can see it in every line of your face."

     She stood up and said, "Well, young man, I don't want to buy a Bible and I smell my dinner burning."

     He didn't get up. He began to twist his hands and looking down at them, he said softly, "Well lady, I'll tell you the truth—not many people want to buy one nowadays and besides, I know I'm real simple. I don't know how to say a thing but to say it. I'm just a country boy." He glanced up into her unfriendly face. "People like you don't like to fool with country people like me!"

"Why!" she cried, "good country people are the salt of the earth! Besides, we all have different ways of doing, it takes all kinds to make the world go 'round. That's life!"

"You said a mouthful," he said.

40 "Why, I think there aren't enough good country people in the world!" she said, stirred. "I think that's what's wrong with it!"

His face had brightened. "I didn't introduce myself," he said. "I'm Manley Pointer from out in the country around Willohobie, not even from a place, just from near a place."

"You wait a minute," she said. "I have to see about my dinner." She went out to the kitchen and found Joy standing near the door where she had been listening.

"Get rid of the salt of the earth," she said, "and let's eat."

Mrs. Hopewell gave her a pained look and turned the heat down under the vegetables. "I can't be rude to anybody," she murmured and went back into the parlor.

45 He had opened the suitcase and was sitting with a Bible on each knee.

"You might as well put those up," she told him. "I don't want one."

"I appreciate your honesty," he said. "You don't see any more real honest people unless you go way out in the country."

"I know," she said, "real genuine folks!" Through the crack in the door she heard a groan.

"I guess a lot of boys come telling you they're working their way through college," he said, "but I'm not going to tell you that. Somehow," he said, "I don't want to go to college. I want to devote my life to Chrustian service. See," he said, lowering his voice, "I got this heart condition. I may not live long. When you know it's something wrong with you and you may not live long, well then, lady . . ." He paused, with his mouth open, and stared at her.

50 He and Joy had the same condition! She knew that her eyes were filling with tears but she collected herself quickly and murmured, "Won't you stay for dinner? We'd love to have you!" and was sorry the instant she heard herself say it.

"Yes mam," he said in an abashed voice. "I would sher love to do that!"

Joy had given him one look on being introduced to him and then throughout the meal had not glanced at him again. He had addressed several remarks to her, which she had pretended not to hear. Mrs. Hopewell could not understand deliberate rudeness, although she lived with it, and she felt she had always to overflow with hospitality to make up for Joy's lack of courtesy. She urged him to talk about himself and he did. He said he was the seventh child of twelve and that his father had been crushed under a tree when he himself was eight years old. He had been crushed very badly, in fact, almost cut in two and was practically not recognizable. His mother had got along the best she could by hard working and she had always seen that her children went to Sunday School and that they read the Bible every evening. He was now nineteen years old and he had been selling Bibles for four months. In that time he had sold seventy-seven Bibles and had the promise of two more sales. He wanted to become a missionary because he thought that was the way you could do most for people. "He who losest his life shall find it," he said simply and he was so sincere, so genuine and earnest that Mrs. Hopewell would not for the world have smiled. He prevented his peas from sliding onto the table by blocking them with a piece of bread which he later cleaned his plate with. She could see Joy observing sidewise how he handled his knife and fork and she saw too that every few minutes, the boy would dart a keen appraising glance at the girl as if he were trying to attract her attention.

After dinner Joy cleared the dishes off the table and disappeared and Mrs. Hopewell was left to talk with him. He told her again about his childhood and his father's accident and about various things that had happened to him. Every five minutes or so she would stifle a yawn. He sat for two hours until finally she told him she must go because she had an appointment in town. He packed his Bibles and thanked her and prepared to leave, but in the doorway he stopped and wrung her hand and said that not on any of his trips had he met a lady as nice as her and he asked if he could come again. She had said she would always be happy to see him.

Joy had been standing in the road, apparently looking at something in the distance, when he came down the steps toward her, bent to the side with his heavy valise. He stopped where she was standing and confronted her directly. Mrs. Hopewell could not hear what he said but she trembled to think what Joy would say to him. She could see that after a minute Joy said something and that then the boy began to speak again, making an excited gesture with his free hand. After a minute Joy said something else at which the boy began to speak once more. Then to her amazement, Mrs.

Hopewell saw the two of them walk off together, toward the gate. Joy had walked all the way to the gate with him and Mrs. Hopewell could not imagine what they had said to each other, and she had not yet dared to ask.

55 Mrs. Freeman was insisting upon her attention. She had moved from the refrigerator to the heater so that Mrs. Hopewell had to turn and face her in order to seem to be listening. "Glynese gone out with Harvey Hill again last night," she said. "She had this sty."

"Hill," Mrs. Hopewell said absently, "is that the one who works in the garage?"

"Nome, he's the one that goes to chiropractor school," Mrs. Freeman said. "She had this sty. Been had it two days. So she says when he brought her in the other night he says, 'Lemme get rid of that sty for you,' and she says, 'How?' and he says, 'You just lay yourself down acrost the seat of that car and I'll show you.' So she done it and he popped her neck. Kept on a-popping it several times until she made him quit. This morning," Mrs. Freeman said, "she ain't got no sty. She ain't got no traces of a sty."

"I never heard of that before," Mrs. Hopewell said.

"He ast her to marry him before the Ordinary,"[3] Mrs. Freeman went on, "and she told him she wasn't going to be married in no *office*."

60 "Well, Glynese is a fine girl," Mrs. Hopewell said. "Glynese and Carramae are both fine girls."

"Carramae said when her and Lyman was married Lyman said it sure felt sacred to him. She said he said he

---

[3]*Ordinary:* Justice of the peace.

wouldn't take five hundred dollars for being married by a preacher."

"How much would he take?" the girl asked from the stove.

"He said he wouldn't take five hundred dollars," Mrs. Freeman repeated.

"Well we all have work to do," Mrs. Hopewell said.

"Lyman said it just felt more sacred to him," Mrs. Free- 65 man said. "The doctor wants Carramae to eat prunes. Says instead of medicine. Says them cramps is coming from pressure. You know where I think it is?"

"She'll be better in a few weeks," Mrs. Hopewell said.

"In the tube," Mrs. Freeman said. "Else she wouldn't be as sick as she is."

Hulga had cracked her two eggs into a saucer and was bringing them to the table along with a cup of coffee that she had filled too full. She sat down carefully and began to eat, meaning to keep Mrs. Freeman there by questions if for any reason she showed an inclination to leave. She could perceive her mother's eye on her. The first round-about question would be about the Bible salesman and she did not wish to bring it on. "How did he pop her neck?" she asked.

Mrs. Freeman went into a description of how he had popped her neck. She said he owned a '55 Mercury but that Glynese said she would rather marry a man with only a '36 Plymouth who would be married by a preacher. The girl asked what if he had a '32 Plymouth and Mrs. Freeman said what Glynese had said was a '36 Plymouth.

Mrs. Hopewell said there were not many girls with Gly- 70 nese's common sense. She said what she admired in those girls was their common sense. She said that reminded her that they had had a nice visitor yesterday, a young man selling Bibles. "Lord," she said, "he bored me to death but he was so sincere and genuine I couldn't be rude to him. He was just good country people, you know," she said, "—just the salt of the earth."

"I seen him walk up," Mrs. Freeman said, "and then later—I seen him walk off," and Hulga could feel the slight shift in her voice, the slight insinuation, that he had not walked off alone, had he? Her face remained expressionless but the color rose into her neck and she seemed to swallow it down with the next spoonful of egg. Mrs. Freeman was looking at her as if they had a secret together.

"Well, it takes all kinds of people to make the world go 'round," Mrs. Hopewell said. "It's very good we aren't all alike."

"Some people are more alike than others," Mrs. Freeman said.

Hulga got up and stumped, with about twice the noise that was necessary, into her room and locked the door. She was to meet the Bible salesman at ten o'clock at the gate. She had thought about it half the night. She had started thinking of it as a great joke and then she had begun to see profound implications in it. She had lain in bed imagining dialogues for them that were insane on the surface but that reached below to depths that no Bible salesman would be aware of. Their conversation yesterday had been of this kind.

> He was gazing at her with open curiosity, with fascination, like a child watching a new fantastic animal at the zoo. . . .

75 He had stopped in front of her and had simply stood there. His face was bony and sweaty and bright, with a little pointed nose in the center of it, and his look was different from what it had been at the dinner table. He was gazing at her with open curiosity, with fascination, like a child watching a new fantastic animal at the zoo, and he was breathing as if he had run a great distance to reach her. His gaze seemed somehow familiar but she could not think where she had been regarded with it before. For almost a minute he didn't say anything. Then on what seemed an insuck of breath, he whispered, "You ever ate a chicken that was two days old?"

The girl looked at him stonily. He might have just put this question up for consideration at the meeting of a philosophical association. "Yes," she presently replied as if she had considered it from all angles.

"It must have been mighty small!" he said triumphantly and shook all over with little nervous giggles, getting very red in the face, and subsiding finally into his gaze of complete admiration, while the girl's expression remained exactly the same.

"How old are you?" he asked softly.

She waited some time before she answered. Then in a flat voice she said, "Seventeen."

80 His smiles came in succession like waves breaking on the surface of a little lake. "I see you got a wooden leg," he said. "I think you're brave. I think you're real sweet."

The girl stood blank and solid and silent.

"Walk to the gate with me," he said. "You're a brave sweet little thing and I liked you the minute I seen you walk in the door."

Hulga began to move forward.

"What's your name?" he asked, smiling down on the top of her head.

"Hulga," she said. 85

"Hulga," he murmured, "Hulga. Hulga. I never heard of anybody name Hulga before. You're shy, aren't you, Hulga?" he asked.

She nodded, watching his large red hand on the handle of the giant valise.

"I like girls that wear glasses," he said. "I think a lot. I'm not like these people that a serious thought don't ever enter their heads. It's because I may die."

"I may die too," she said suddenly and looked up at him. His eyes were very small and brown, glittering feverishly.

"Listen," he said, "don't you think some people was 90 meant to meet on account of what all they got in common and all? Like they both think serious thoughts and all?" He shifted the valise to his other hand so that the hand nearest her was free. He caught hold of her elbow and shook it a little. "I don't work on Saturday," he said. "I like to walk in the woods and see what Mother Nature is wearing. O'er the hills and far away. Pic-nics and things. Couldn't we go on a pic-nic tomorrow? Say yes, Hulga," he said and gave her a dying look as if he felt his insides about to drop out of him. He had even seemed to sway slightly toward her.

During the night she had imagined that she seduced him. She imagined that the two of them walked on the place until they came to the storage barn beyond the two back fields and there, she imagined, that things came to such a pass that she very easily seduced him and that then, of course, she had to reckon with his remorse. True genius can get an idea across even to an inferior mind. She imagined that she took his remorse in hand and changed it into a deeper understanding of life. She took all his shame away and turned it into something useful.

She set off for the gate at exactly ten o'clock, escaping without drawing Mrs. Hopewell's attention. She didn't take anything to eat, forgetting that food is usually taken on a picnic. She wore a pair of slacks and a dirty white shirt, and as an afterthought, she had put some Vapex[4] on the collar

---

[4]*Vapex:* Trade name for a nasal spray.

of it since she did not own any perfume. When she reached the gate no one was there.

She looked up and down the empty highway and had the furious feeling that she had been tricked, that he only meant to make her walk to the gate after the idea of him. Then suddenly he stood up, very tall, from behind a bush on the opposite embankment. Smiling, he lifted his hat which was new and wide-brimmed. He had not worn it yesterday and she wondered if he had bought it for the occasion. It was toast-colored with a red and white band around it and was slightly too large for him. He stepped from behind the bush still carrying the black valise. He had on the same suit and the same yellow socks sucked down in his shoes from walking. He crossed the highway and said, "I knew you'd come!"

The girl wondered acidly how he had known this. She pointed to the valise and asked, "Why did you bring your Bibles?"

95   He took her elbow, smiling down on her as if he could not stop. "You can never tell when you'll need the word of God, Hulga," he said. She had a moment in which she doubted that this was actually happening and then they began to climb the embankment. They went down into the pasture toward the woods. The boy walked lightly by her side, bouncing on his toes. The valise did not seem to be heavy today; he even swung it. They crossed half the pasture without saying anything and then, putting his hand easily on the small of her back, he asked softly, "Where does your wooden leg join on?"

She turned an ugly red and glared at him and for an instant the boy looked abashed. "I didn't mean you no harm," he said. "I only meant you're so brave and all. I guess God takes care of you."

"No," she said, looking forward and walking fast, "I don't even believe in God."

At this he stopped and whistled. "No!" he exclaimed as if he were too astonished to say anything else.

She walked on and in a second he was bouncing at her side, fanning with his hat. "That's very unusual for a girl," he remarked, watching her out of the corner of his eye. When they reached the edge of the wood, he put his hand on her back again and drew her against him without a word and kissed her heavily.

100   The kiss, which had more pressure than feeling behind it, produced that extra surge of adrenalin in the girl

Some people might enjoy drain water if they were told it was vodka.

that enables one to carry a packed trunk out of a burning house, but in her, the power went at once to the brain. Even before he released her, her mind, clear and detached and ironic anyway, was regarding him from a great distance, with amusement but with pity. She had never been kissed before and she was pleased to discover that it was an unexceptional experience and all a matter of the mind's control. Some people might enjoy drain water if they were told it was vodka. When the boy, looking expectant but uncertain, pushed her gently away, she turned and walked on, saying nothing as if such business, for her, were common enough.

He came along panting at her side, trying to help her when he saw a root that she might trip over. He caught and held back the long swaying blades of thorn vine until she had passed beyond them. She led the way and he came breathing heavily behind her. Then they came out on a sunlit hillside, sloping softly into another one a little smaller. Beyond, they could see the rusted top of the old barn where the extra hay was stored.

The hill was sprinkled with small pink weeds. "Then you ain't saved?" he asked suddenly, stopping.

The girl smiled. It was the first time she had smiled at him at all. "In my economy," she said, "I'm saved and you are damned but I told you I didn't believe in God."

Nothing seemed to destroy the boy's look of admiration. He gazed at her now as if the fantastic animal at the zoo had put its paw through the bars and given him a loving poke. She thought he looked as if he wanted to kiss her again and she walked on before he had the chance.

"Ain't there somewheres we can sit down sometime?"   105 he murmured, his voice softening toward the end of the sentence.

"In that barn," she said.

They made for it rapidly as if it might slide away like a train. It was a large two-story barn, cool and dark inside. The boy pointed up the ladder that led into the loft and said, "It's too bad we can't go up there."

"Why can't we?" she asked.

"Yer leg," he said reverently.

The girl gave him a contemptuous look and putting   110 both hands on the ladder, she climbed it while he stood below, apparently awestruck. She pulled herself expertly through the opening and then looked down at him and said,

"Well, come on if your coming," and he began to climb the ladder, awkwardly bringing the suitcase with him.

"We won't need the Bible," she observed.

"You never can tell," he said, panting. After he had got into the loft, he was a few seconds catching his breath. She had sat down in a pile of straw. A wide sheath of sunlight, filled with dust particles, slanted over her. She lay back against a bale, her face turned away, looking out the front opening of the barn where hay was thrown from a wagon into the loft. The two pink-speckled hillsides lay back against a dark ridge of woods. The sky was cloudless and cold blue. The boy dropped down by her side and put one arm under her and the other over her and began methodically kissing her face, making little noises like a fish. He did not remove his hat but it was pushed far enough back not to interfere. When her glasses got in his way, he took them off of her and slipped them into his pocket.

The girl at first did not return any of the kisses but presently she began to and after she had put several on his cheek, she reached his lips and remained there, kissing him again and again as if she were trying to draw all the breath out of him. His breath was clear and sweet like a child's and the kisses were sticky like a child's. He mumbled about loving her and about knowing when he first seen her that he loved her, but the mumbling was like the sleepy fretting of a child being put to sleep by his mother. Her mind, throughout this, never stopped or lost itself for a second to her feelings. "You ain't said you loved me none," he whispered finally, pulling back from her. "You got to say that."

She looked away from him off into the hollow sky and then down at a black ridge and then down farther into what appeared to be two green swelling lakes. She didn't realize he had taken her glasses but this landscape could not seem exceptional to her for she seldom paid any close attention to her surroundings.

"You got to say it," he repeated. "You got to say you love me." 115

She was always careful how she committed herself. "In a sense," she began, "if you use the word loosely, you might say that. But it's not a word I use. I don't have illusions. I'm one of those people who see *through* to nothing."

The boy was frowning. "You got to say it. I said it and you got to say it," he said.

The girl looked at him almost tenderly. "You poor baby," she murmured. "It's just as well you don't understand," and she pulled him by the neck, face-down, against her. "We are all damned," she said, "but some of us have taken off our blindfolds and see that there's nothing to see. It's a kind of salvation."

The boy's astonished eyes looked blankly through the ends of her hair. "Okay," he almost whined, "but do you love me or don'tcher?"

"Yes," she said and added, "in a sense. But I must tell 120 you something. There mustn't be anything dishonest between us." She lifted his head and looked him in the eye. "I am thirty years old," she said. "I have a number of degrees."

The boy's look was irritated but dogged. "I don't care," he said. "I don't care a thing about what all you done. I just want to know if you love me or don'tcher?" and he caught her to him and wildly planted her face with kisses until she said, "Yes, yes."

"Okay then," he said, letting her go. "Prove it."

She smiled, looking dreamily out on the shifty landscape. She had seduced him without even making up her mind to try. "How?" she asked, feeling that he should be delayed a little.

He leaned over and put his lips to her ear. "Show me where your wooden leg joins on," he whispered.

125 The girl uttered a sharp little cry and her face instantly drained of color. The obscenity of the suggestion was not what shocked her. As a child she had sometimes been subject to feelings of shame but education had removed the last traces of that as a good surgeon scrapes for cancer; she would no more have felt it over what he was asking than she would have believed in his Bible. But she was as sensitive about the artificial leg as a peacock about his tail. No one ever touched it but her. She took care of it as someone else would his soul, in private and almost with her own eyes turned away. "No," she said.

"I known it," he muttered, sitting up. "You're just playing me for a sucker."

"Oh no no!" she cried. "It joins on at the knee. Only at the knee. Why do you want to see it?"

The boy gave her a long penetrating look. "Because," he said, "it's what makes you different. You ain't like anybody else."

She sat staring at him. There was nothing about her face or her round freezing-blue eyes to indicate that this had moved her; but she felt as if her heart had stopped and left her mind to pump her blood. She decided that for the first time in her life she was face to face with real innocence. This boy, with an instinct that came from beyond wisdom, had touched the truth about her. When after a minute, she said in a hoarse high voice, "All right," it was like surrendering to him completely. It was like losing her own life and finding it again, miraculously, in his.

130 Very gently, he began to roll the slack leg up. The artificial limb, in a white sock and brown flat shoe, was bound in a heavy material like canvas and ended in an ugly jointure where it was attached to the stump. The boy's face and his voice were entirely reverent as he uncovered it and said, "Now show me how to take it off and on."

She took it off for him and put it back on again and then he took it off himself, handling it as tenderly as if it were a real one. "See!" he said with a delighted child's face. "Now I can do it myself!"

"Put it back on," she said. She was thinking that she would run away with him and that every night he would take the leg off and every morning put it back on again. "Put it back on," she said.

"Not yet," he murmured, setting it on its foot out of her reach. "Leave it off for awhile. You got me instead."

She gave a little cry of alarm but he pushed her down and began to kiss her again. Without the leg she felt entirely dependent on him. Her brain seemed to have stopped thinking altogether and to be about some other function that it was not very good at. Different expressions raced back and forth over her face. Every now and then the boy, his eyes like two steel spikes, would glance behind him where the leg stood. Finally she pushed him off and said, "Put it back on me now."

135 "Wait," he said. He leaned the other way and pulled the valise toward him and opened it. It had a pale blue spotted lining and there were only two Bibles in it. He took one of these out and opened the cover of it. It was hollow and contained a pocket flask of whiskey, a pack of cards, and a small blue box with printing on it. He laid these out in front of her one at a time in an evenly-spaced row, like one presenting offerings at the shrine of a goddess. He put the blue box in her hand. THIS PRODUCT TO BE USED ONLY FOR THE PREVENTION OF DISEASE, she read, and dropped it. The boy was unscrewing the top of the flask. He stopped and pointed, with a smile, to the deck of cards. It was not an ordinary deck but one with an obscene picture on the back of each card. "Take a swig," he said, offering her the bottle first. He held it in front of her, but like one mesmerized, she did not move.

Her voice when she spoke had an almost pleading sound. "Aren't you," she murmured, "aren't you just good country people?"

The boy cocked his head. He looked as if he were just beginning to understand that she might be trying to insult him. "Yeah," he said, curling his lip slightly, "but it ain't held me back none. I'm as good as you any day in the week."

"Give me my leg," she said.

He pushed it farther away with his foot. "Come on now, let's begin to have us a good time," he said coaxingly. "We ain't got to know one another good yet."

140 "Give me my leg!" she screamed and tried to lunge for it but he pushed her down easily.

> But she was as sensitive about the artificial leg as a peacock about his tail. No one ever touched it but her.

"What's the matter with you all of a sudden?" he asked, frowning as he screwed the top on the flask and put it quickly back inside the Bible. "You just a while ago said you didn't believe in nothing. I thought you was some girl!"

Her face was almost purple. "You're a Christian!" she hissed. "You're a fine Christian! You're just like them all— say one thing and do another. You're a perfect Christian, you're . . ."

The boy's mouth was set angrily. "I hope you don't think," he said in a lofty indignant tone, "that I believe in that crap! I may sell Bibles but I know which end is up and I wasn't born yesterday and I know where I'm going!"

"Give me my leg!" she screeched. He jumped up so quickly that she barely saw him sweep the cards and the blue box back into the Bible and throw the Bible into the valise. She saw him grab the leg and then she saw it for an instant slanted forlornly across the inside of the suitcase with a Bible at either side of its opposite ends. He slammed the lid shut and snatched up the valise and swung it down the hole and then stepped through himself.

145 When all of him had passed but his head, he turned and regarded her with a look that no longer had any admiration in it. "I've gotten a lot of interesting things," he said. "One time I got a woman's glass eye this way. And you needn't to think you'll catch me because Pointer ain't really my name. I use a different name at every house I call at and don't stay nowhere long. And I'll tell you another thing, Hulga," he said, using the name as if he didn't think much of it, "you ain't so smart. I been believing in nothing ever since I was born!" and then the toast-colored hat disappeared down the hole and the girl was left, sitting on the straw in the dusty sunlight. When she turned her churning face toward the opening, she saw his blue figure struggling successfully over the green speckled lake.

Mrs. Hopewell and Mrs. Freeman, who were in the back pasture, digging up onions, saw him emerge a little later from the woods and head across the meadow toward the highway. "Why, that looks like that nice dull young man that tried to sell me a Bible yesterday," Mrs. Hopewell said, squinting. "He must have been selling them to the Negroes back in there. He was so simple," she said, "but I guess the world would be better off if we were all that simple."

Mrs. Freeman's gaze drove forward and just touched him before he disappeared under the hill. Then she returned her attention to the evil-smelling onion shoot she was lifting from the ground. "Some can't be that simple," she said. "I know I never could."

IF YOU LIKED "GOOD COUNTRY PEOPLE," YOU MIGHT ALSO LIKE . . .

. . . O'Connor's "A Good Man Is Hard to Find" and other stories from Southern writers, such as "Barn Burning" by William Faulkner and "Battle Royal" by Ralph Ellison (all in the Case Study on the American South in Chapter 15) and "A Worn Path" by Eudora Welty (Chapter 14).

GOING FURTHER O'Connor was a devout Catholic, and her thoughts on fiction and religion can be found in her selected letters, *The Habit of Being,* and her selected essays and lectures, *Mystery and Manners.* Many have paid her homage and claimed her literary influence on their work, including two whose work appears in this anthology, T.C. Boyle and Alice Walker. O'Connor herself was influenced by Edgar Allan Poe, particularly his *Humorous Tales.* Flannery O'Connor, William Faulkner, and Tennessee Williams (all in this book) are joined by such writers as Truman Capote (*In Cold Blood*), and Carson McCullers (*The Heart Is a Lonely Hunter*) in representing the Southern Gothic tradition.

Writing from Reading

Summarize

1 Using the story, define "good country people." Which characters from the story do you think fit this description? Are these the same characters that the story identifies as "good country people"?

Analyze Craft

2 Which characters' thoughts is the reader given access to, and which characters are only observed by the narrator? What do the characters of each group have in common? How would the effect of the story's climax and conclusion on the reader change if all characters' thoughts and motivations were revealed by an omniscient narrator?

3 Describe the level of diction used in this story, citing specific words. Do you think the speaker comes from a background more similar to Mrs. Hopewell or to Mrs. Freeman?

Analyze Voice

4 Considering the details and tone of the story, do you think the narrator shows more sympathy for some characters than others? Which characters, if any, receive more sympathy from the narrator?

Synthesize Summary and Analysis

5 Which characters in this story are deceived, and which are deceivers? Can any characters in the story be described as both? Can any of the characters in this story truly be described as "simple"?

6 List Joy's various ailments, such as poor eyesight, and the means by which she corrects or copes with each. Which of these coping mechanisms does the Bible salesman disarm her of, and what is the effect?

Interpret the Story

7 Compare and contrast Mrs. Freeman with the Bible salesman. What is the significance of Mrs. Freeman's statement at the end of the story?

Charlotte Perkins Gilman (1860–1935)

Born in Connecticut, Charlotte Perkins Gilman became a reluctant wife when she was twenty-four—reluctant because she feared the duties of a housewife would interfere with her desire to be active and productive in her own work. When the birth of her first child sent Gilman into depression, her doctor prescribed a rest cure consisting of an entirely domestic life free of physical and intellectual activity. As Gilman explained, "I went home and obeyed those directions for some three months, and came so near the border line of utter mental ruin that I could see over." She recovered by ignoring her doctor's orders and resuming her work as a writer and dedicated feminist. Gilman's most famous short story, "The Yellow Wallpaper," tells the story of a woman secluded from any activity and her consequent descent into madness—the author's way of speaking out against harmful patterns of preventing women's participation in society. In addition to creating stories that promoted feminist ideals, she also wrote nonfiction treatises on behalf of women's rights—most notably, *Women and Economics* (1898)—and lectured widely. Suffering from breast cancer and the loss of her second husband, Gilman ended her own life with chloroform at seventy-five.

AS YOU READ Think about how you might respond if a relative or a stranger began telling you this story. Would it inspire worry, fear, distress? What particular word choices or patterns of images or repetitive statements create this effect for you?

The Yellow Wallpaper (1892)

1 IT is very seldom that mere ordinary people like John and myself secure ancestral halls for the summer.

A colonial mansion, a hereditary estate, I would say a haunted house and reach the height of romantic felicity—but that would be asking too much of fate!

Still I will proudly declare that there is something queer about it.

Else, why should it be let so cheaply? And why have stood so long untenanted?

5 John laughs at me, of course, but one expects that.

John is practical in the extreme. He has no patience with faith, an intense horror of superstition, and he scoffs openly at any talk of things not to be felt and seen and put down in figures.

John is a physician, and *perhaps*—(I would not say it to a living soul, of course, but this is dead paper and a great relief to my mind)—*perhaps* that is one reason I do not get well faster.

You see, he does not believe I am sick! And what can one do?

If a physician of high standing, and one's own husband, assures friends and relatives that there is really nothing the matter with one but temporary nervous depression—a slight hysterical tendency—what is one to do?

10 My brother is also a physician, and also of high standing, and he says the same thing.

So I take phosphates or phosphites—whichever it is—and tonics, and air and exercise, and journeys, and am absolutely forbidden to "work" until I am well again.

Personally, I disagree with their ideas.

Personally, I believe that congenial work, with excitement and change, would do me good.

But what is one to do?

15 I did write for a while in spite of them; but it *does* exhaust me a good deal—having to be so sly about it, or else meet with heavy opposition.

I sometimes fancy that in my condition, if I had less opposition and more society and stimulus—but John says the very worst thing I can do is to think about my condition, and I confess it always makes me feel bad.

So I will let it alone and talk about the house.

The most beautiful place! It is quite alone, standing well back from the road, quite three miles from the village. It makes me think of English places that you read about, for there are hedges and walls and gates that lock, and lots of separate little houses for the gardeners and people.

There is a *delicious* garden! I never saw such a garden—large and shady, full of box-bordered paths, and lined with long grape-covered arbors with seats under them.

20 There were greenhouses, but they are all broken now.

There was some legal trouble, I believe, something about the heirs and coheirs; anyhow, the place has been empty for years.

That spoils my ghostliness, I am afraid, but I don't care—there is something strange about the house—I can feel it.

I even said so to John one moonlight evening, but he said what I felt was a *draught*, and shut the window.

I get unreasonably angry with John sometimes. I'm sure I never used to be so sensitive. I think it is due to this nervous condition.

25   But John says if I feel so I shall neglect proper self-control; so I take pains to control myself—before him, at least, and that makes me very tired.

I don't like our room a bit. I wanted one downstairs that opened onto the piazza and had roses all over the window, and such pretty old-fashioned chintz hangings! But John would not hear of it.

He said there was only one window and not room for two beds, and no near room for him if he took another.

He is very careful and loving, and hardly lets me stir without special direction.

I have a schedule prescription for each hour in the day; he takes all care from me, and so I feel basely ungrateful not to value it more.

30   He said he came here solely on my account, that I was to have perfect rest and all the air I could get. "Your exercise depends on your strength, my dear," said he, "and your food somewhat on your appetite; but air you can absorb all the time." So we took the nursery at the top of the house.

It is a big, airy room, the whole floor nearly, with windows that look all ways, and air and sunshine galore. It was a nursery first, and then playroom and gymnasium, I should judge, for the windows are barred for little children, and there are rings and things in the walls.

The paint and paper look as if a boys' school had used it. It is stripped off—the paper—in great patches all around the head of my bed, about as far as I can reach, and in a great place on the other side of the room low down. I never saw a worse paper in my life. One of those sprawling, flamboyant patterns committing every artistic sin.

It is dull enough to confuse the eye in following, pronounced enough constantly to irritate and provoke study, and when you follow the lame uncertain curves for a little distance they suddenly commit suicide—plunge off at outrageous angles, destroy themselves in unheard-of contradictions.

The color is repellent, almost revolting: a smouldering unclean yellow, strangely faded by the slow-turning sunlight. It is a dull yet lurid orange in some places, a sickly sulphur tint in others.

35   No wonder the children hated it! I should hate it myself if I had to live in this room long.

. . . there is something strange about the house — I can feel it.

There comes John, and I must put this away—he hates to have me write a word.

WE have been here two weeks, and I haven't felt like writing before, since that first day.

I am sitting by the window now, up in this atrocious nursery, and there is nothing to hinder my writing as much as I please, save lack of strength.

John is away all day, and even some nights when his cases are serious.

40   I am glad my case is not serious!

But these nervous troubles are dreadfully depressing.

John does not know how much I really suffer. He knows there is no *reason* to suffer, and that satisfies him.

Of course it is only nervousness. It does weigh on me so not to do my duty in any way!

I meant to be such a help to John, such a real rest and comfort, and here I am a comparative burden already!

45   Nobody would believe what an effort it is to do what little I am able—to dress and entertain, and order things.

It is fortunate Mary is so good with the baby. Such a dear baby!

And yet I *cannot* be with him, it makes me so nervous.

I suppose John never was nervous in his life. He laughs at me so about this wallpaper!

At first he meant to repaper the room, but afterward he said that I was letting it get the better of me, and that nothing was worse for a nervous patient than to give way to such fancies.

50   He said that after the wallpaper was changed it would be the heavy bedstead, and then the barred windows, and then that gate at the head of the stairs, and so on.

"You know the place is doing you good," he said, "and really, dear, I don't care to renovate the house just for a three months' rental."

"Then do let us go downstairs," I said. "There are such pretty rooms there."

Then he took me in his arms and called me a blessed little goose, and said he would go down to the cellar, if I wished, and have it whitewashed into the bargain.

But he is right enough about the beds and windows and things.

55   It is as airy and comfortable a room as anyone need wish, and, of course, I would not be so silly as to make him uncomfortable just for a whim.

I'm really getting quite fond of the big room, all but that horrid paper.

Out of one window I can see the garden—those mysterious deep-shaded arbors, the riotous old-fashioned flowers, and bushes and gnarly trees.

Out of another I get a lovely view of the bay and a little private wharf belonging to the estate. There is a beautiful shaded lane that runs down there from the house. I always fancy I see people walking in these numerous paths and arbors, but John has cautioned me not to give way to fancy in the least. He says that with my imaginative power and habit of storymaking, a nervous weakness like mine is sure to lead to all manner of excited fancies, and that I ought to use my will and good sense to check the tendency. So I try.

I think sometimes that if I were only well enough to write a little it would relieve the press of ideas and rest me.

60 But I find I get pretty tired when I try.

It is so discouraging not to have any advice and companionship about my work. When I get really well, John says we will ask Cousin Henry and Julia down for a long visit; but he says he would as soon put fireworks in my pillow-case as to let me have those stimulating people about now.

I wish I could get well faster.

But I must not think about that. This paper looks to me as if it *knew* what a vicious influence it had!

There is a recurrent spot where the pattern lolls like a broken neck and two bulbous eyes stare at you upside down.

65 I get positively angry with the impertinence of it and the everlastingness. Up and down and sideways they crawl, and those absurd unblinking eyes are everywhere. There is one place where two breadths didn't match, and the eyes go all up and down the line, one a little higher than the other.

I never saw so much expression in an inanimate thing before, and we all know how much expression they have! I used to lie awake as a child and get more entertainment and terror out of blank walls and plain furniture than most children could find in a toy-store.

I remember what a kindly wink the knobs of our big old bureau used to have, and there was one chair that always seemed like a strong friend.

I used to feel that if any of the other things looked too fierce I could always hop into that chair and be safe.

The furniture in this room is no worse than inharmonious, however, for we had to bring it all from downstairs. I suppose when this was used as a playroom they had to take the nursery things out, and no wonder! I never saw such ravages as the children have made here.

The wallpaper, as I said before, is torn off in spots, and 70 it sticketh closer than a brother—they must have had perseverance as well as hatred.

Then the floor is scratched and gouged and splintered, the plaster itself is dug out here and there, and this great heavy bed, which is all we found in the room, looks as if it had been through the wars.

But I don't mind it a bit—only the paper.

There comes John's sister. Such a dear girl as she is, and so careful of me! I must not let her find me writing.

She is a perfect and enthusiastic housekeeper, and hopes for no better profession. I verily believe she thinks it is the writing which made me sick!

But I can write when she is out, and see her a long way 75 off from these windows.

There is one that commands the road, a lovely shaded winding road, and one that just looks off over the country. A lovely country, too, full of great elms and velvet meadows.

This wallpaper has a kind of subpattern in a different shade, a particularly irritating one, for you can only see it in certain lights, and not clearly then.

But in the places where it isn't faded and where the sun is just so—I can see a strange, provoking, formless sort of figure that seems to skulk about behind that silly and conspicuous front design.

THERE'S sister on the stairs!

Well, the Fourth of July is over! The people are all 80 gone, and I am tired out. John thought it might do me good to see a little company, so we just had Mother and Nellie and the children down for a week.

Of course I didn't do a thing. Jennie sees to everything now.

But it tired me all the same.

John says if I don't pick up faster he shall send me to Weir Mitchell in the fall.

But I don't want to go there at all. I had a friend who was in his hands once, and she says he is just like John and my brother, only more so!

85 Besides, it is such an undertaking to go so far.

I don't feel as if it was worthwhile to turn my hand over for anything, and I'm getting dreadfully fretful and querulous.

I cry at nothing, and cry most of the time.

Of course I don't when John is here, or anybody else, but when I am alone.

And I am alone a good deal just now. John is kept in town very often by serious cases, and Jennie is good and lets me alone when I want her to.

90 So I walk a little in the garden or down that lovely lane, sit on the porch under the roses, and lie down up here a good deal.

I'm getting really fond of the room in spite of the wallpaper. Perhaps *because* of the wallpaper.

It dwells in my mind so!

I lie here on this great immovable bed—it is nailed down, I believe—and follow that pattern about by the hour. It is as good as gymnastics, I assure you. I start, we'll say, at the bottom, down in the corner over there where it has not been touched, and I determine for the thousandth time that I *will* follow that pointless pattern to some sort of a conclusion.

I know a little of the principle of design, and I know this thing was not arranged on any laws of radiation, or alternation, or repetition, or symmetry, or anything else that I ever heard of.

95 It is repeated, of course, by the breadths, but not otherwise.

Looked at in one way, each breadth stands alone; the bloated curves and flourishes—a kind of "debased Romanesque" with *delirium tremens*—go waddling up and down in isolated columns of fatuity.

But, on the other hand, they connect diagonally, and the sprawling outlines run off in great slanting waves of optic horror, like a lot of wallowing sea-weeds in full chase.

The whole thing goes horizontally, too, at least it seems so, and I exhaust myself trying to distinguish the order of its going in that direction.

They have used a horizontal breadth for a frieze, and that adds wonderfully to the confusion.

100 There is one end of the room where it is almost intact, and there, when the crosslights fade and the low sun shines directly upon it, I can almost fancy radiation after all—the interminable grotesque seems to form around a common center and rush off in headlong plunges of equal distraction.

It makes me tired to follow it. I will take a nap, I guess.

I don't know why I should write this.

I don't want to.

I don't feel able.

105 And I know John would think it absurd. But I *must* say what I feel and think in some way—it is such a relief!

BUT the effort is getting to be greater than the relief.

Half the time now I am awfully lazy, and lie down ever so much. John says I mustn't lose my strength, and has me take cod liver oil and lots of tonics and things, to say nothing of ale and wines and rare meat.

Dear John! He loves me very dearly, and hates to have me sick. I tried to have a real earnest reasonable talk with him the other day, and tell him how I wish he would let me go and make a visit to Cousin Henry and Julia.

But he said I wasn't able to go, nor able to stand it after I got there; and I did not make out a very good case for myself, for I was crying before I had finished.

110 It is getting to be a great effort for me to think straight. Just this nervous weakness, I suppose.

And dear John gathered me up in his arms, and just carried me upstairs and laid me on the bed, and sat by me and read to me till it tired my head.

He said I was his darling and his comfort and all he had, and that I must take care of myself for his sake, and keep well.

He says no one but myself can help me out of it, that I must use my will and self-control and not let any silly fancies run away with me.

There's one comfort—the baby is well and happy, and does not have to occupy this nursery with the horrid wallpaper.

115 If we had not used it, that blessed child would have! What a fortunate escape! Why, I wouldn't have a child of mine, an impressionable little thing, live in such a room for worlds.

I never thought of it before, but it is lucky that John kept me here after all; I can stand it so much easier than a baby, you see.

Of course I never mention it to them any more—I am too wise—but I keep watch for it all the same.

There are things in the wallpaper that nobody knows about but me, or ever will.

Behind that outside pattern the dim shapes get clearer every day.

It is always the same shape, only very numerous.

And it is like a woman stooping down and creeping about behind that pattern. I don't like it a bit. I wonder—I begin to think—I wish John would take me away from here!

It is so hard to talk with John about my case, because he is so wise, and because he loves me so.

But I tried it last night.

It was moonlight. The moon shines in all around just as the sun does.

I hate to see it sometimes, it creeps so slowly, and always comes in by one window or another.

John was asleep and I hated to waken him, so I kept still and watched the moonlight on that undulating wallpaper till I felt creepy.

The faint figure behind seemed to shake the pattern, just as if she wanted to get out.

I got up softly and went to feel and see if the paper *did* move, and when I came back John was awake.

"What is it, little girl?" he said. "Don't go walking about like that—you'll get cold."

I thought it was a good time to talk, so I told him that I really was not gaining here, and that I wished he would take me away.

"Why, darling!" said he, "Our lease will be up in three weeks, and I can't see how to leave before.

"The repairs are not done at home, and I cannot possibly leave town just now. Of course, if you were in any danger, I could and would, but you really are better, dear, whether you can see it or not. I am a doctor, dear, and I know. You are gaining flesh and color, your appetite is better, I feel really much easier about you."

"I don't weigh a bit more," said I, "nor as much; and my appetite may be better in the evening when you are here but it is worse in the morning when you are away!"

"Bless her little heart!" said he with a big hug. "She shall be as sick as she pleases! But now let's improve the shining hours by going to sleep, and talk about it in the morning!"

"And you won't go away?" I asked gloomily.

"Why, how can I, dear? It is only three weeks more and then we will take a nice little trip for a few days while Jennie is getting the house ready. Really, dear, you are better!"

"Better in body perhaps—" I began, and stopped short, for he sat up straight and looked at me with such a stern, reproachful look that I could not say another word.

"My darling," said he, "I beg you, for my sake and for our child's sake, as well as for your own, that you will never for one instant let that idea enter your mind! There is nothing so dangerous, so fascinating, to a temperament like yours. It is a false and foolish fancy. Can you not trust me as a physician when I tell you so?"

So of course I said no more on that score, and we went to sleep before long. He thought I was asleep first, but I wasn't, and lay there for hours trying to decide whether that front pattern and the back pattern really did move together or separately.

On a pattern like this, by daylight, there is a lack of sequence, a defiance of law, that is a constant irritant to a normal mind.

The color is hideous enough, and unreliable enough, and infuriating enough, but the pattern is torturing.

You think you have mastered it, but just as you get well under way in following, it turns a back-somersault and there you are. It slaps you in the face, knocks you down, and tramples upon you. It is like a bad dream.

The outside pattern is a florid arabesque, reminding one of a fungus. If you can imagine a toadstool in joints, an interminable string of toadstools, budding and sprouting in endless convolutions—why, that is something like it.

That is, sometimes!

There is one marked peculiarity about this paper, a thing nobody seems to notice but myself, and that is that it changes as the light changes.

When the sun shoots in through the east window—I always watch for that first long, straight ray—it changes so quickly that I never can quite believe it.

That is why I watch it always.

By moonlight—the moon shines in all night when there is a moon—I wouldn't know it was the same paper.

At night in any kind of light, in twilight, candlelight, lamplight, and worst of all by moonlight, it becomes bars! The outside pattern, I mean, and the woman behind it is as plain as can be.

150   I didn't realize for a long time what the thing was that showed behind, that dim subpattern, but now I am quite sure it is a woman.

By daylight she is subdued, quiet. I fancy it is the pattern that keeps her so still. It is so puzzling. It keeps me quiet by the hour.

I lie down ever so much now. John says it is good for me, and to sleep all I can.

Indeed he started the habit by making me lie down for an hour after each meal.

It is a very bad habit, I am convinced, for you see, I don't sleep.

155   And that cultivates deceit, for I don't tell them I'm awake—oh, no!

The fact is I am getting a little afraid of John.

He seems very queer sometimes, and even Jennie has an inexplicable look.

It strikes me occasionally, just as a scientific hypothesis, that perhaps it is the paper!

I have watched John when he did not know I was looking, and come into the room suddenly on the most innocent excuses, and I've caught him several times *looking at the paper!* And Jennie too. I caught Jennie with her hand on it once.

160   She didn't know I was in the room, and when I asked her in a quiet, a very quiet voice, with the most restrained manner possible, what she was doing with the paper, she turned around as if she had been caught stealing, and looked quite angry—asked me why I should frighten her so!

Then she said that the paper stained everything it touched, that she had found yellow smooches on all my clothes and John's and she wished we would be more careful!

Did not that sound innocent? But I know she was studying that pattern, and I am determined that nobody shall find it out but myself!

LIFE is very much more exciting now than it used to be. You see, I have something more to expect, to look forward to, to watch. I really do eat better, and am more quiet than I was.

John is so pleased to see me improve! He laughed a little the other day, and said I seemed to be flourishing in spite of my wallpaper.

165   I turned it off with a laugh. I had no intention of telling him it was *because* of the wallpaper—he would make fun of me. He might even want to take me away.

I don't want to leave now until I have found it out. There is a week more, and I think that will be enough.

I'm feeling so much better!

I don't sleep much at night, for it is so interesting to watch developments; but I sleep a good deal during the daytime.

In the daytime it is tiresome and perplexing.

170   There are always new shoots on the fungus, and new shades of yellow all over it. I cannot keep count of them, though I have tried conscientiously.

It is the strangest yellow, that wallpaper! It makes me think of all the yellow things I ever saw—not beautiful ones like buttercups, but old foul, bad yellow things.

But there is something else about that paper—the smell! I noticed it the moment we came into the room, but with so much air and sun it was not bad. Now we have had a week of fog and rain, and whether the windows are open or not, the smell is here.

It creeps all over the house.

I find it hovering in the dining-room, skulking in the parlor, hiding in the hall, lying in wait for me on the stairs.

175   It gets into my hair.

Even when I go to ride, if I turn my head suddenly and surprise it—there is that smell!

Such a peculiar odor, too! I have spent hours in trying to analyze it, to find what it smelled like.

It is not bad—at first—and very gentle, but quite the subtlest, most enduring odor I ever met.

In this damp weather it is awful. I wake up in the night and find it hanging over me.

180   It used to disturb me at first. I thought seriously of burning the house—to reach the smell.

But now I am used to it. The only thing I can think of that it is like is the *color* of the paper! A yellow smell.

There is a very funny mark on this wall, low down, near the mopboard. A streak that runs round the room. It goes behind every piece of furniture, except the bed, a long, straight, even *smooch,* as if it had been rubbed over and over.

I wonder how it was done and who did it, and what they did it for. Round and round and round—round and round and round—it makes me dizzy!

I really have discovered something at last.

185 Through watching so much at night, when it changes so, I have finally found out.

The front pattern *does* move—and no wonder! The woman behind shakes it!

Sometimes I think there are a great many women behind, and sometimes only one, and she crawls around fast, and her crawling shakes it all over.

Then in the very bright spots she keeps still, and in the very shady spots she just takes hold of the bars and shakes them hard.

And she is all the time trying to climb through. But nobody could climb through that pattern—it strangles so; I think that is why it has so many heads.

190 They get through and then the pattern strangles them off, and turns them upside down, and makes their eyes white!

If those heads were covered or taken off it would not be half so bad.

I think that woman gets out in the daytime!

And I'll tell you why—privately—I've seen her!

I can see her out of every one of my windows!

195 It is the same woman, I know, for she is always creeping, and most women do not creep by daylight.

I see her in that long shaded lane, creeping up and down. I see her in those dark grape arbors, creeping all round the garden.

I see her on that long road under the trees, creeping along, and when a carriage comes she hides under the blackberry vines.

I don't blame her a bit. It must be very humiliating to be caught creeping by daylight!

I always lock the door when I creep by daylight. I can't do it at night, for I know John would suspect something at once.

200 And John is so queer now that I don't want to irritate him. I wish he would take another room! Besides, I don't want anybody to get that woman out at night but myself.

I often wonder if I could see her out of all the windows at once.

But, turn as fast as I can, I can only see out of one at one time.

And though I always see her, she *may* be able to creep faster than I can turn! I have watched her sometimes away off in the open country, creeping as fast as a cloud shadow in a wind.

If only that top pattern could be gotten off from the under one! I mean to try it, little by little.

I have found out another funny thing, but I shan't tell it 205 this time! It does not do to trust people too much.

There are only two more days to get this paper off, and I believe John is beginning to notice. I don't like the look in his eyes.

And I heard him ask Jennie a lot of professional questions about me. She had a very good report to give.

She said I slept a good deal in the daytime.

John knows I don't sleep very well at night, for all I'm so quiet!

He asked me all sorts of questions too, and pretended 210 to be very loving and kind.

As if I couldn't see through him!

Still, I don't wonder he acts so, sleeping under this paper for three months.

It only interests me, but I feel sure John and Jennie are affected by it.

HURRAH! This is the last day, but it is enough. John is to stay in town over night, and won't be out until this evening.

Jennie wanted to sleep with me—the sly thing; but 215 I told her I should undoubtedly rest better for a night all alone.

That was clever, for really I wasn't alone a bit! As soon as it was moonlight and that poor thing began to crawl and shake the pattern, I got up and ran to help her.

I pulled and she shook, I shook and she pulled, and before morning we had peeled off yards of that paper.

A strip about as high as my head and half around the room.

And then when the sun came and that awful pattern began to laugh at me, I declared I would finish it today!

We go away tomorrow, and they are moving all my fur- 220 niture down again to leave things as they were before.

Jennie looked at the wall in amazement, but I told her merrily that I did it out of pure spite at the vicious thing.

She laughed and said she wouldn't mind doing it herself, but I must not get tired.

How she betrayed herself that time!

But I am here, and no person touches this paper but Me—not *alive!*

225 She tried to get me out of the room—it was too patent! But I said it was so quiet and empty and clean now that I believed I would lie down again and sleep all I could, and not to wake me even for dinner—I would call when I woke.

So now she is gone, and the servants are gone, and the things are gone, and there is nothing left but that great bedstead nailed down, with the canvas mattress we found on it.

We shall sleep downstairs tonight, and take the boat home tomorrow.

I quite enjoy the room, now it is bare again.

How those children did tear about here!

230 This bedstead is fairly gnawed!

But I must get to work.

I have locked the door and thrown the key down into the front path.

I don't want to go out, and I don't want to have anybody come in, till John comes.

I want to astonish him.

235 I've got a rope up here that even Jennie did not find. If that woman does get out, and tries to get away, I can tie her!

But I forgot I could not reach far without anything to stand on!

This bed will *not* move!

I tried to lift and push it until I was lame, and then I got so angry I bit off a little piece at one corner—but it hurt my teeth.

Then I peeled off all the paper I could reach standing on the floor. It sticks horribly and the pattern just enjoys it! All those strangled heads and bulbous eyes and waddling fungus growths just shriek with derision!

240 I am getting angry enough to do something desperate. To jump out of the window would be admirable exercise, but the bars are too strong even to try.

Besides I wouldn't do it. Of course not. I know well enough that a step like that is improper and might be misconstrued.

I don't like to *look* out of the windows even—there are so many of those creeping women, and they creep so fast.

I wonder if they all come out of that wallpaper as I did!

But I am securely fastened now by my well-hidden rope—you don't get *me* out in the road there!

245 I suppose I shall have to get back behind the pattern when it comes night, and that is hard!

It is so pleasant to be out in this great room and creep around as I please!

I don't want to go outside. I won't, even if Jennie asks me to.

For outside you have to creep on the ground, and everything is green instead of yellow.

But here I can creep smoothly on the floor, and my shoulder just fits in that long smooch around the wall, so I cannot lose my way.

250 Why, there's John at the door!

It is no use, young man, you can't open it!

How he does call and pound!

Now he's crying to Jennie for an axe.

It would be a shame to break down that beautiful door!

255 "John, dear!" said I in the gentlest voice. "The key is down by the front steps, under a plantain leaf!"

That silenced him for a few moments.

Then he said, very quietly indeed, "Open the door, my darling!"

"I can't," said I. "The key is down by the front door under a plantain leaf!" And then I said it again, several times, very gently and slowly, and said it so often that he had to go and see, and he got it of course, and came in. He stopped short by the door.

"What is the matter?" he cried. "For God's sake, what are you doing!"

260 I kept on creeping just the same, but I looked at him over my shoulder.

"I've got out at last," said I, "in spite of you and Jane. And I've pulled off most of the paper, so you can't put me back!"

Now why should that man have fainted? But he did, and right across my path by the wall, so that I had to creep over him every time!

IF YOU LIKED "THE YELLOW WALLPAPER," YOU MIGHT ALSO LIKE . . .

. . . a number of other stories in the book with themes pertaining to the lives of modern women, including Kate Chopin's "The Story of an Hour" in Chapter 6, Jamaica Kincaid's "Girl" in Chapter 7, and Amy Tan's "Two Kinds," in Chapter 13, among others.

GOING FURTHER   One of the classic texts of the modern feminist movement, "The Yellow Wallpaper" points toward a long line of future fiction on similar themes, such as Joan Didion's novels *Run River* and *Play It As It Lays* and Margaret Atwood's *The Handmaid's Tale*.

Writing from Reading

Summarize

1 Describe the wallpaper's pattern in literal terms. What does it look like?

2 The narrator's relationship with the wallpaper goes through various stages. Identify and describe those stages.

Analyze Craft

3 Notice the images that are repeated—for example, the house, the grounds surrounding it, the journal, the husband, the room where most of the story takes place, and of course, the wallpaper. How does the narrator's view of these crucial images change over the course of the story? How does the narrator herself change over the course of the story?

Analyze Voice

4 Discuss the themes of censorship, silencing, and imprisonment in this story. Analyze John's character and his role in the story. How does he help and/or harm his wife?

5 Identify a place in the story where you begin to suspect that the main character may be abnormal. How does the writer create a sentence or paragraph that delivers that news to you? Does the writer keep the character's state of mind separate from the way that she delivers the story to you?

Synthesize Summary and Analysis

6 Scan the story for each mention of the narrator's journal, underlining these references when you find them. Form a conclusion about the role of the journal in the story. Why does the narrator have to keep it a secret from John and his sister?

Interpret the Story

7 Identify a conflict central to the story. Discuss how that conflict affects the various characters. Is the conflict resolved by the end?

"You follow the sound of language and let it take you to meaning."

Conversation with Tim O'Brien

Reading for Language, Tone, and Style

When reading for language, tone, and style, make notes about how the author uses language to express a particular attitude toward the characters and events.

What kind of language or diction did the author choose to shape the style and tone of the story?	• Are there particular words or key images that are important to the style and tone of the story? • What effect does the writing have on you?
What tone (of voice) do you hear?	• Serious or comedic? • Distant or intimate? • Ominous or lighthearted? • Straightforward or ironic?
Is the author being ironic?	• Is the irony **verbal?** • Is the irony **dramatic?**
How do the language and tone work together to define the writer's style?	• Is the language lush or lean? • Are the sentences long and complex, or short and simple? • How would you describe the style: elegant? hard-boiled? lyrical? unadorned? ornate? self-conscious?

Writing about Language, Tone, and Style

1. In her interview, Aimee Bender says that she uses her imagination in writing as "a way to get to feelings that are hard to look at straight on." Discuss this aspect of her style as represented by "The Rememberer." How effective is this style for exploring the subject of loss?

2. Briefly describe the style of each story in this chapter. What words do they use? What kind of language? Why is each style fitting for its particular story? Compare and contrast the authors' approaches.

3. How do Flannery O'Connor and Charlotte Perkins Gilman use the accents and the intonations of their characters to give us a sense of the region described; what would have to change, for example, if O'Connor were writing about "Bad City People" or Gilman about Persian carpets and/or linoleum floors?

13
Theme

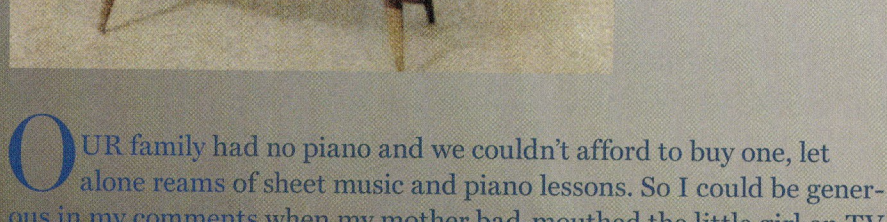

OUR family had no piano and we couldn't afford to buy one, let alone reams of sheet music and piano lessons. So I could be generous in my comments when my mother bad-mouthed the little girl on TV.

'Play note right, but doesn't sound good! No singing sound,' complained my mother.

'What are you picking on her for?' I said carelessly. 'She's pretty good. Maybe she's not the best, but she's trying hard.' I knew almost immediately I would be sorry I said that."

—from "Two Kinds" by Amy Tan

"One of the songs that I played, or two songs . . . came from Scenes from Childhood *by Robert Schumann. And there were two songs, 'Pleading Child' and 'Perfectly Contented' . . . opposite one another . . . and at some point in my life I remember looking at those two songs, opposite one another and realizing it was the same child."*

Conversation with Amy Tan, available on video at connect.mcgraw-hill.com

EACH element of craft—including plot, characterization, setting, and point of view—contributes to the thematic meaning of a tale. Theme connects fiction to the human experience, giving a single story relevance and reach. When we say that we read fiction for the truths or insights it offers—for its ideas—we are reading for **theme.**

The dictionary definition of *theme* is given as "the subject of discourse, discussion, conversation, meditation, or composition; a topic." But a theme in fiction is more than just a subject or situation. In Amy Tan's "Two Kinds," we can say that the story's subject is a mother-daughter relationship, but that is not its theme. Similarly, if we say that Tan's story is about a daughter who defies her mother's high expectations, we are accurately summarizing the situation, but we are still not stating a theme. A theme goes beyond the specific details of the story to a general statement about human life.

A theme is also more than the story's plot. Plot tells us in a literal, specific sense *what happens* in a story. To summarize the plot of Tan's story, then, you might say that a Chinese mother encourages her daughter to excel at piano. The daughter, however, spites her mother by not trying in her lessons and consequently giving a thoroughly embarrassing performance, which they fight about. Years later, the daughter realizes this incident set a pattern in her behavior of falling short. But this is not the story's theme. A theme ties all the elements of the story together and goes beyond the particulars of the story, revealing something general and universal.

A theme, especially in contemporary literature, rarely boils down to a life lesson. The ideas that make up a story's theme are organic or intrinsic to the narrative; they don't declare themselves immediately or in a topic sentence. Because Tan's story encompasses such a complex mix of feelings, it would be difficult to reduce it to a simple message or "teaching moment," such as "Appreciate your mother and don't give up hope for yourself." However, if you dig toward ideas that link all the elements and their meanings, you could articulate a theme such as this: "Two Kinds" is about the struggle for personal identity and how we often limit ourselves by defining who we are in relation to others' expectations.

CONTINUED ON PAGE 384

Amy Tan

... The interesting thing that happens is that fiction, as you write it, becomes subversive.

A Conversation on Writing

Becoming a Reader

I was a very lonely child much of my childhood. Books were a place where I could find someone who understood me. That someone could have lived 200 years ago. Jane Eyre had nothing to do with my life. And yet she did. She was that lonely girl nobody understood . . . and I imagined myself living that life. . . . That made me not feel so lonely.

The Meaning of Your Life

If you . . . walk up to somebody on the street or somebody comes up to you and says, "What's your meaning of life? What is the meaning of your life?" You might come up with an idea right on the spot: I want to be happy or I want to be in love, I want to be loved. But what you get out of writing is thinking about that question for a very long time. . . . You take a situation from your life . . . a time that you thought you'd get a new bicycle, and then you didn't think you would, and then you got it, and then you got it stolen. What's in that? . . . Suddenly there's a glimpse of the meaning of your life.

On Voice and the Writing Process

When I started to write, I had this basic question that was posed to me by a woman named Molly Giles, a wonderful writer. She had read my work. And she said, "You know, what you've written here is not a story. It is the beginnings of a dozen stories." And she pointed out these sentences. She said, "This is the beginning of a story, this is the beginning of a story, this is the beginning. This is a voice, this is a voice, this is a voice." And I thought, Well, what is a voice? . . . The questions are still there, and there's no absolute answer. . . . You discover it each time you sit down and write.

To watch this entire interview online and hear the author read from "Two Kinds," go to **connect.mcgraw-hill.com.**

Amy Tan was born (1952) in Oakland, California, to Chinese immigrants. After college she became successful as a business writer and took up jazz piano as a hobby, a young Chinese American woman who had not yet clearly faced the matter of her cultural origins. It wasn't until after her marriage to a Bay Area tax attorney that she eventually began to try to write fiction based on her cultural heritage.

Like many first generation Americans, Tan had not fully explored her relationship to her parents' culture until she had established herself as a successful working adult. After her father and brother died within a year from brain tumors, she and her mother were left to work out their own difficulties. Her troubled relations with her mother eventually smoothed out, and after her mother recovered from a serious illness, the two of them traveled to China. There Tan got a firsthand look at the country of her parents' birth, beginning to explore her origins as possible material for fiction. This led to the composition of a series of stories, which Tan revised and made into the novel *The Joy Luck Club*. That book became a national best seller in 1989, and Tan has since published the novels *The Kitchen God's Wife, The Hundred Secret Senses, The Bonesetter's Daughter, Saving Fish from Drowning,* and two children's books, *The Moon Lady* and *Sagwa*.

RESEARCH ASSIGNMENT Amy Tan says in her interview that reading and writing fiction are subversive. Watch the interview and explain what she means. Do you agree with her?

AS YOU READ Pay attention to the narrator's motivation for her behavior. Why does she choose the path she chooses? On a thematic level, what does this say about the role we play versus the role others play in shaping our lives?

TIP

FOR INTERACTIVE READING . . .

Find and mark in the story the references to the "two kinds." Write in the margin what each kind is, and speculate on what each represents.

Two Kinds (1989)

1   MY mother believed you could be anything you wanted to be in America. You could open a restaurant. You could work for the government and get good retirement. You could buy a house with almost no money down. You could become rich. You could become instantly famous.

"Of course, you can be prodigy, too," my mother told me when I was nine. "You can be best anything. What does Auntie Lindo know? Her daughter, she is only best tricky."

America was where all my mother's hopes lay. She had come here in 1949 after losing everything in China: her mother and father, her family home, her first husband, and two daughters, twin baby girls. But she never looked back with regret. There were so many ways for things to get better.

WE didn't immediately pick the right kind of prodigy. At first my mother thought I could be a Chinese Shirley Temple. We'd watch Shirley's old movies on TV as though they were training films. My mother would poke my arm and say, *"Ni kan"* —You watch. And I would see Shirley tapping her feet, or singing a sailor song, or pursing her lips into a very round O while saying "Oh, my goodness."

5   *"Ni kan,"* said my mother, as Shirley's eyes flooded with tears. "You already know how. Don't need talent for crying!"

Soon after my mother got this idea about Shirley Temple, she took me to a beauty training school in the Mission district and put me in the hands of a student who could barely hold the scissors without shaking. Instead of get-

ting big fat curls, I emerged with an uneven mass of crinkly black fuzz. My mother dragged me off to the bathroom and tried to wet down my hair.

"You look like Negro Chinese," she lamented, as if I had done this on purpose.

The instructor of the beauty training school had to lop off these soggy clumps to make my hair even again. "Peter Pan is very popular these days," the instructor assured my mother. I now had hair the length of a boy's, with straight-across bangs that hung at a slant two inches above my eyebrows. I liked the haircut and it made me actually look forward to my future fame.

In fact, in the beginning, I was just as excited as my mother, maybe even more so. I pictured this prodigy part of me as many different images, trying each one on for size. I was a dainty ballerina girl standing by the curtains, waiting to hear the right music that would send me floating on my tiptoes. I was like the Christ child lifted out of the straw manger, crying with holy indignity. I was Cinderella stepping from her pumpkin carriage with sparkly cartoon music filling the air.

10   In all of my imaginings, I was filled with a sense that I would soon become *perfect*. My mother and father would adore me. I would be beyond reproach. I would never feel the need to sulk for anything.

But sometimes the prodigy in me became impatient. "If you don't hurry up and get me out of here, I'm disappearing for good," it warned. "And then you'll always be nothing."

EVERY night after dinner, my mother and I would sit at the Formica kitchen table. She would present new tests, taking her examples from stories of amazing children she had read in *Ripley's Believe It or Not*, or *Good Housekeeping, Reader's Digest*, and a dozen other magazines she kept in a pile in our bathroom. My mother got these magazines from people whose houses she cleaned. And since she cleaned many houses each week, we had a great assortment. She would look through them all, searching for stories about remarkable children.

The first night she brought out a story about a three-year-old boy who knew the capitals of all the states and even most of the European countries. A teacher was quoted as saying the little boy could also pronounce the names of the foreign cities correctly.

"What's the capital of Finland?" my mother asked me, looking at the magazine story.

15   All I knew was the capital of California, because Sacramento was the name of the street we lived on in Chinatown. "Nairobi!" I guessed, saying the most foreign word I could think of. She checked to see if that was possibly one way to pronounce "Helsinki" before showing me the answer.

The tests got harder—multiplying numbers in my head, finding the queen of hearts in a deck of cards, trying to stand on my head without using my hands, predicting the daily temperatures in Los Angeles, New York, and London.

One night I had to look at a page from the Bible for three minutes and then report everything I could remember. "Now Jehoshaphat had riches and honor in abundance and . . . that's all I remember, Ma," I said.

And after seeing my mother's disappointed face once again, something inside of me began to die. I hated the tests, the raised hopes and failed expectations. Before going to bed that night, I looked in the mirror above the bathroom sink and when I saw only my face staring back—and that it would always be this ordinary face—I began to cry. Such a sad, ugly girl! I made high-pitched noises like a crazed animal, trying to scratch out the face in the mirror.

And then I saw what seemed to be the prodigy side of me—because I had never seen that face before. I looked at my reflection, blinking so that I could see more clearly. The girl staring back at me was angry, powerful. This girl and I were the same. I had new thoughts, willful thoughts, or rather thoughts filled with lots of won'ts. I won't let her change me, I promised myself. I won't be what I'm not.

So now on nights when my mother presented her tests, 20 I performed listlessly, my head propped on one arm. I pretended to be bored. And I was. I got so bored I started counting the bellows of the foghorns out on the bay while my mother drilled me in other areas. The sound was comforting and reminded me of the cow jumping over the moon. And the next day, I played a game with myself, seeing if my mother would give up on me before eight bellows. After a while I usually counted only one, maybe two bellows at most. At last she was beginning to give up hope.

> **I won't let her change me, I promised myself.**

TWO or three months had gone by without any mention of my being a prodigy again. And then one day my mother was watching *The Ed Sullivan Show* on TV. The TV was old and the sound kept shorting out. Every time my mother got halfway up from the sofa to adjust the set, the sound would go back on and Ed would be talking. As soon as she sat down, Ed would go silent again. She got up, the TV broke into loud piano music. She sat down. Silence. Up and down, back and forth, quiet and loud. It was like a stiff embraceless dance between her and the TV set. Finally she stood by the set with her hand on the sound dial.

She seemed entranced by the music, a little frenzied piano piece with this mesmerizing quality, sort of quick passages and then teasing lilting ones before it returned to the quick playful parts.

"*Ni kan*," my mother said, calling me over with hurried hand gestures, "Look here."

I could see why my mother was fascinated by the music. It was being pounded out by a little Chinese girl, about nine years old, with a Peter Pan haircut. The girl had the sauciness of a Shirley Temple. She was proudly modest like a proper Chinese child. And she also did this fancy sweep of a curtsy, so that the fluffy skirt of her white dress cascaded slowly to the floor like the petals of a large carnation.

25   In spite of these warning signs, I wasn't worried. Our family had no piano and we couldn't afford to buy one, let alone reams of sheet music and piano lessons. So I could be generous in my comments when my mother bad-mouthed the little girl on TV.

"Play note right, but doesn't sound good! No singing sound," complained my mother.

"What are you picking on her for?" I said carelessly. "She's pretty good. Maybe she's not the best, but she's trying hard." I knew almost immediately I would be sorry I said that.

"Just like you," she said. "Not the best. Because you not trying." She gave a little huff as she let go of the sound dial and sat down on the sofa.

The little Chinese girl sat down also to play an encore of "Anitra's Dance" by Grieg. I remember the song, because later on I had to learn how to play it.

30   THREE days after watching *The Ed Sullivan Show*, my mother told me what my schedule would be for piano lessons and piano practice. She had talked to Mr. Chong,

who lived on the first floor of our apartment building. Mr. Chong was a retired piano teacher and my mother had traded housecleaning services for weekly lessons and a piano for me to practice on every day, two hours a day, from four until six.

When my mother told me this, I felt as though I had been sent to hell. I whined and then kicked my foot a little when I couldn't stand it anymore.

"Why don't you like me the way I am? I'm *not* a genius! I can't play the piano. And even if I could, I wouldn't go on TV if you paid me a million dollars!" I cried.

My mother slapped me. "Who ask you to be genius?" she shouted. "Only ask you be your best. For you sake. You think I want you to be genius? Hnnh! What for! Who ask you!"

"So ungrateful," I heard her mutter in Chinese. "If she had as much talent as she has temper, she would be famous now."

35   Mr. Chong, whom I secretly nicknamed Old Chong, was very strange, always tapping his fingers to the silent music of an invisible orchestra. He looked ancient in my eyes. He had lost most of the hair on top of his head, and he wore thick glasses and had eyes that always looked tired and sleepy. But he must have been younger than I thought, since he lived with his mother and was not yet married.

I met Old Lady Chong once and that was enough. She had this peculiar smell like a baby that had done something in its pants. And her fingers felt like a dead person's, like an old peach I once found in the back of the refrigerator; the skin just slid off the meat when I picked it up.

I soon found out why Old Chong had retired from teaching piano. He was deaf. "Like Beethoven!" he shouted to me. "We're both listening only in our head!" And he would start to conduct his frantic silent sonatas.

Our lessons went like this. He would open the book and point to different things, explaining their purpose: "Key! Treble! Bass! No sharps or flats! So this is C major! Listen now and play after me!"

And then he would play the C scale a few times, a simple chord, and then, as if inspired by an old unreachable itch, he gradually added more notes and running trills and a pounding bass until the music was really something quite grand.

40   I would play after him, the simple scale, the simple chord, and then I just played some nonsense that sounded like a cat running up and down on top of garbage

cans. Old Chong smiled and applauded and then said, "Very good! But now you must learn to keep time!"

So that's how I discovered that Old Chong's eyes were too slow to keep up with the wrong notes I was playing. He went through the motions in half-time. To help me keep rhythm, he stood behind me, pushing down on my right shoulder for every beat. He balanced pennies on top of my wrists so I would keep them still as I slowly played scales and arpeggios. He had me curve my hand around an apple and keep that shape when playing chords. He marched stiffly to show me how to make each finger dance up and down, staccato like an obedient little soldier.

He taught me all these things, and that was how I also learned I could be lazy and get away with mistakes, lots of mistakes. If I hit the wrong notes because I hadn't practiced enough, I never corrected myself. I just kept playing in rhythm. And Old Chong kept conducting his own private reverie.

So maybe I never really gave myself a fair chance. I did pick up the basics pretty quickly, and I might have become a good pianist at that young age. But I was so determined not to try, not to be anybody different that I learned to play only the most ear-splitting preludes, the most discordant hymns.

Over the next year, I practiced like this, dutifully in my own way. And then one day I heard my mother and her friend Lindo Jong both talking in a loud bragging tone of voice so others could hear. It was after church, and I was leaning against the brick wall wearing a dress with stiff white petticoats. Auntie Lindo's daughter, Waverly, who was about my age, was standing farther down the wall about five feet away. We had grown up together and shared all the closeness of two sisters squabbling over crayons and dolls. In other words, for the most part, we hated each other. I thought she was snotty. Waverly Jong had gained a certain amount of fame as "Chinatown's Littlest Chinese Chess Champion."

45 "She bring home too many trophy," lamented Auntie Lindo that Sunday. "All day she play chess. All day I have no time do nothing but dust off her winnings." She threw a scolding look at Waverly, who pretended not to see her.

"You lucky you don't have this problem," said Auntie Lindo with a sigh to my mother.

And my mother squared her shoulders and bragged: "Our problem worser than yours. If we ask Jing-mei wash dish, she hear nothing but music. It's like you can't stop this natural talent."

And right then I was determined to put a stop to her foolish pride.

A FEW weeks later, Old Chong and my mother conspired to have me play in a talent show which would be held in the church hall. By then, my parents had saved up enough to buy me a secondhand piano, a black Wurlitzer spinet with a scarred bench. It was the showpiece of our living room.

For the talent show, I was to play a piece called "Pleading Child" from Schumann's *Scenes from Childhood*. It was 50 a simple, moody piece that sounded more difficult than it was. I was supposed to memorize the whole thing, playing the repeat parts twice to make the piece sound longer. But I dawdled over it, playing a few bars and then cheating, looking up to see what notes followed. I never really listened to what I was playing. I daydreamed about being somewhere else, about being someone else.

The part I liked to practice best was the fancy curtsy: right foot out, touch the rose on the carpet with a pointed foot, sweep to the side, left leg bends, look up and smile.

My parents invited all the couples from the Joy Luck Club to witness my debut. Auntie Lindo and Uncle Tin were there. Waverly and her two older brothers had also come. The first two rows were filled with children both younger and older than I was. The littlest ones got to go first. They recited simple nursery rhymes, squawked out tunes on miniature violins, twirled Hula Hoops, pranced in pink ballet tutus, and when they bowed or curtsied, the audience would sigh in unison, "Awww," and then clap enthusiastically.

When my turn came, I was very confident. I remember my childish excitement. It was as if I knew, without a doubt, that the prodigy side of me really did exist. I had no fear whatsoever, no nervousness. I remember thinking to myself, This is it! This is it! I looked out over the audience, at my mother's blank face, my father's yawn, Auntie Lindo's stiff-lipped smile, Waverly's sulky expression. I had on a white dress layered with sheets of lace, and a pink bow in my Peter Pan haircut. As I sat down I envisioned people jumping to their feet and Ed Sullivan rushing up to introduce me to everyone on TV.

And I started to play. It was so beautiful. I was so caught up in how lovely I looked that at first I didn't worry how I would sound. So it was a surprise to me when I hit the first wrong note and I realized something didn't sound quite right. And then I hit another and another followed that. A chill started at the top of my head and began to trickle down. Yet I couldn't stop playing, as though my hands were bewitched. I kept thinking my fingers would adjust themselves back, like a train switching to the right track. I played this strange jumble through two repeats, the sour notes staying with me all the way to the end.

55 When I stood up, I discovered my legs were shaking. Maybe I had just been nervous and the audience, like Old Chong, had seen me go through the right motions and had not heard anything wrong at all. I swept my right foot out, went down on my knee, looked up and smiled. The room was quiet, except for Old Chong, who was beaming and shouting, "Bravo! Bravo! Well done!" But then I saw my mother's face, her stricken face. The audience clapped weakly, and as I walked back to my chair, with my whole face quivering as I tried not to cry, I heard a little boy whisper loudly to his mother, "That was awful," and the mother whispered back, "Well, she certainly tried."

And now I realized how many people were in the audience, the whole world it seemed. I was aware of eyes burning into my back. I felt the shame of my mother and father as they sat stiffly throughout the rest of the show.

We could have escaped during intermission. Pride and some strange sense of honor must have anchored my parents to their chairs. And so we watched it all: the eighteen-year-old boy with a fake mustache who did a magic show and juggled flaming hoops while riding a unicycle. The breasted girl with white makeup who sang from *Madama Butterfly* and got honorable mention. And the eleven-year-old boy who won first prize playing a tricky violin song that sounded like a busy bee.

After the show, the Hsus, the Jongs, and the St. Clairs from the Joy Luck Club came up to my mother and father.

"Lots of talented kids," Auntie Lindo said vaguely, smiling broadly.

60 "That was somethin' else," said my father, and I wondered if he was referring to me in a humorous way, or whether he even remembered what I had done.

Waverly looked at me and shrugged her shoulders. "You aren't a genius like me," she said matter-of-factly. And if I hadn't felt so bad, I would have pulled her braids and punched her stomach.

But my mother's expression was what devastated me: a quiet, blank look that said she had lost everything. I felt the same way, and it seemed as if everybody were now coming up, like gawkers at the scene of an accident, to see what parts were actually missing. When we got on the bus to go home, my father was humming the busy-bee tune and my mother was silent. I kept thinking she wanted to wait until we got home before shouting at me. But when my father unlocked the door to our apartment, my mother walked in and then went to the back, into the bedroom. No accusations. No blame. And in a way, I felt disappointed. I had been waiting for her to start shouting, so I could shout back and cry and blame her for all my misery.

I ASSUMED my talent-show fiasco meant I never had to play the piano again. But two days later, after school, my mother came out of the kitchen and saw me watching TV.

"Four clock," she reminded me as if it were any other day. I was stunned, as though she were asking me to go through the talent-show torture again. I wedged myself more tightly in front of the TV.

"Turn off TV," she called from the kitchen five minutes 65 later.

I didn't budge. And then I decided. I didn't have to do what my mother said anymore. I wasn't her slave: This wasn't China. I had listened to her before and look what happened. She was the stupid one.

She came out from the kitchen and stood in the arched entryway of the living room. "Four clock," she said once again, louder.

"I'm not going to play anymore," I said nonchalantly. "Why should I? I'm not a genius."

She walked over and stood in front of the TV. I saw her chest was heaving up and down in an angry way.

"No!" I said, and I now felt stronger, as if my true self 70 had finally emerged. So this was what had been inside me all along.

"No! I won't!" I screamed.

She yanked me by the arm, pulled me off the floor, snapped off the TV. She was frighteningly strong, half pulling, half carrying me toward the piano as I kicked the throw rugs under my feet. She lifted me up and onto the hard bench. I was sobbing by now, looking at her bitterly. Her chest was heaving even more and her mouth was open, smiling crazily as if she were pleased I was crying.

"You want me to be someone that I'm not!" I sobbed. "I'll never be the kind of daughter you want me to be!"

"Only two kinds of daughters," she shouted in Chinese. "Those who are obedient and those who follow their own mind! Only one kind of daughter can live in this house. Obedient daughter!"

75 "Then I wish I wasn't your daughter. I wish you weren't my mother," I shouted. As I said these things I got scared. It felt like worms and toads and slimy things crawling out of my chest, but it also felt good, as if this awful side of me had surfaced, at last.

"Too late to change this," my mother said shrilly.

And I could sense her anger rising to its breaking point. I wanted to see it spill over. And that's when I remembered the babies she had lost in China, the ones we never talked about. "Then I wish I'd never been born!" I shouted. "I wish I were dead! Like them."

> I played a few bars, surprised at how easily the notes came back to me.

It was as if I had said the magic words. Alakazam!— and her face went blank, her mouth closed, her arms went slack, and she backed out of the room, stunned, as if she were blowing away like a small brown leaf, thin, brittle, lifeless.

I T was not the only disappointment my mother felt in me. In the years that followed, I failed her so many times, each time asserting my own will, my right to fall short of expectations. I didn't get straight As. I didn't become class president. I didn't get into Stanford. I dropped out of college.

80 For unlike my mother, I did not believe I could be anything I wanted to be. I could only be me.

And for all those years, we never talked about the disaster at the recital or my terrible accusations afterward at the piano bench. All that remained unchecked, like a betrayal that was now unspeakable. So I never found a way to ask her why she had hoped for something so large that failure was inevitable.

And even worse, I never asked her what frightened me the most: Why had she given up hope?

For after our struggle at the piano, she never mentioned my playing again. The lessons stopped. The lid to the piano was closed, shutting out the dust, my misery, and her dreams.

So she surprised me. A few years ago, she offered to give me the piano, for my thirtieth birthday. I had not played in all those years. I saw the offer as a sign of forgiveness, a tremendous burden removed.

85 "Are you sure?" I asked shyly. "I mean, won't you and Dad miss it?"

"No, this your piano," she said firmly. "Always your piano. You only one can play."

"Well, I probably can't play anymore," I said. "It's been years."

"You pick up fast," said my mother, as if she knew this was certain. "You have natural talent. You could been genius if you want to."

"No, I couldn't."

"You just not trying," said my mother. And she was neither angry nor sad. She said it as if to announce a fact that could never be disproved. "Take it," she said. 90

But I didn't at first. It was enough that she had offered it to me. And after that, every time I saw it in my parents' living room, standing in front of the bay windows, it made me feel proud, as if it were a shiny trophy I had won back.

L AST week I sent a tuner over to my parent's apartment and had the piano reconditioned, for purely sentimental reasons. My mother had died a few months before and I had been getting things in order for my father, a little bit at a time. I put the jewelry in special silk pouches. The sweaters she had knitted in yellow, pink, bright orange—all the colors I hated—I put those in moth-proof boxes. I found some old Chinese silk dresses, the kind with little slits up the sides. I rubbed the old silk against my skin, then wrapped them in tissue and decided to take them home with me.

After I had the piano tuned, I opened the lid and touched the keys. It sounded even richer than I remembered. Really, it was a very good piano. Inside the bench were the same exercise notes with handwritten scales, the same secondhand music books with their covers held together with yellow tape.

I opened up the Schumann book to the dark little piece I had played at the recital. It was on the left-hand side of the page, "Pleading Child." It looked more difficult than I remembered. I played a few bars, surprised at how easily the notes came back to me.

And for the first time, or so it seemed, I noticed the piece on the right-hand side. It was called "Perfectly Contented." I tried to play this one as well. It had a lighter melody but the same flowing rhythm and turned out to be quite easy. "Pleading Child" was shorter but slower; "Perfectly Contented" was longer, but faster. And after I played them both a few times, I realized they were two halves of the same song. 95

IF YOU LIKED "TWO KINDS," YOU MIGHT ALSO LIKE . . .

. . . other stories with distinctive voices and powerful mothers, such as that of Gish Jen's irate speaker in "Who's Irish?" (Chapter 9) or Jamaica Kincaid's recounting of a mother's tirade in "Girl" (Chapter 7).

GOING FURTHER   Amy Tan says in her interview that she is reading writers in translation to get a different point of view. You may be interested in some of these works as well, such as *Balzac and the Little Chinese Seamstress,* by Dai Sijie, a French writer of Chinese ancestry, or *The Sand Child,* by Moroccan writer Tahar Ben Jelloun.

Writing from Reading

Summarize

1 Some of these memories are comic, some bitter, some loving, some aggrieved. Summarize the daughter's reactions to her mother's expectations and see how and where they change.

Analyze Craft

2 All dialogue by the narrator's mother is written in broken English, even when she is speaking in her native Chinese. What effect does this dialect have on your impression of the mother?

Analyze Voice

3 Tan writes as a first-generation American, a writer from the West Coast. Are there any details in the story that highlight her situation? Is there anything in the way the narrator speaks that calls these facts to mind?

Synthesize Summary and Analysis

4 How does the dialect in the mother's speech establish the narrator's identity as a second-generation Chinese American?

Interpret the Story

5 Early in the story, the daughter promises herself, "I won't be what I'm not." Later, she accuses her mother, "You want me to be someone that I'm not!" What does she insist that she is *not*? Do we get any sense of what she *is*? What does this story have to say about the theme of searching for oneself?

6 The first line of "Two Kinds" reads, "My mother believed you could be anything you wanted to be in America." This line is repeated throughout the story. Find instances in the story that prove or refute this statement. Considering this story, what do you think Tan believes and why?

"I'm sort of aware of themes emerging. Sometimes it's helpful for me not to know so much about what themes are coming up, because I think it can get in the way of the investigation. . . . It's fairly unconscious when I'm doing the work because I'm not trying to think about theme. . . . The thematic stuff just collects . . . on its own." Conversation with Aimee Bender

CONTINUED FROM PAGE 375

IDENTIFYING THEMES

Works of serious fiction do not generally give up their meanings easily, and this is why we often feel intimidated or tentative when it comes to articulating a theme. So why, despite the risks and difficulties, should we strive to understand theme? Why not simply enjoy the plot and the characters and leave it at that? First of all, reading closely enough to gather the threads of theme reveals the greatest potential of a story. Second, delving into the world of a story for its theme can point up truths about the way the world works. Finally, reading with an eye for theme in fiction can teach a great deal about how to get at the essence of other kinds of texts that are required reading in college, and it helps create the skill of linkage and expressiveness in writing for college.

"I figured part of what fiction was, or writing creatively, was to write your view of life." Conversation with Amy Tan

To understand theme, then, you should ask yourself questions that go beyond the surface and the events. Common themes in literature include the search for self, as in "Two Kinds," the struggle of justice against injustice, or youth and age. But this is stating theme very broadly. Remember that truly identifying theme means paying attention to how that theme is addressed in a specific story. So, for example, you might amend the preceding sentence to say that a theme isn't just justice versus injustice, but how justice requires a person to think beyond his or her own selfish preoccupations.

THEMES THROUGH TIME

Some themes, or thematic questions, persist in literature through the ages. Do we determine the course of our own lives, or do the gods make our fates? From the epics of Homer onward, the Greeks put forward that great question, and fiction writers, poets, and playwrights have taken it up as a theme ever since. Some writers recast this theme as how to live a good life in a world full of turmoil and trouble. Cervantes did so in a semi-comical tone in his seventeenth-century novel *Don Quixote*.

Shakespeare presents a great variety of themes about love and power and the yearning for a meaningful life, then asks the audience to draw its own conclusions. Similarly, contemporary story writers and novelists tend to dramatize the quandaries and troubles of their characters—but without drawing any conclusions or suggesting any moralistic answers.

In modern literature, many writers disdain the notion of theme. The pleasure the work offers to the reader becomes everything. Hemingway famously suggested that "if you want a message, go to Western Union." Nevertheless, as we've shown, themes emerge, even in the work of writers, such as Hemingway, who downplay their importance.

> ## "I'm trying to create a world in which some of the strange stuff of our life comes to the surface, and we say, 'I know that. The circumstances of my life are different from this person's story, but I know that feeling.'" Conversation with Barry Lopez

Or you might refine the theme of youth and age in general to the theme that age does not necessarily bring wisdom, while youth is being stained by worldly experience.

An understanding of theme can come from a work's title. Titles may point to a major symbol, character, or subject from which themes develop, as do Katherine Anne Porter's "The Jilting of Granny Weatherall" (Chapter 9), Zora Neale Hurston's "The Gilded Six-Bits" (Chapter 10), and Tim O'Brien's "The Things They Carried" (Chapter 14). In this chapter, for example, William Kittredge's title, "Thirty-Four Seasons of Winter," announces certain themes—the passage of time in human life, and the seasonal feel of that life as it rolls on—even before we meet the characters in this story about life in the modern West. How the pair of stepbrothers and the women they consort with play this recurrence out against the backdrop of a western landscape—where hard physical labor is the norm and people labor to accommodate the animals and the crops they tend—becomes the heart of the story. Titles may also point to a central irony that is thematic, as do Flannery O'Connor's "Good Country People" (Chapter 12) and Jhumpa Lahiri's "Interpreter of Maladies" in this chapter. Gish Jen's title "Who's Irish?" (Chapter 9) calls up the question of identity, while James Joyce's "Araby" (Chapter 8) conjures an exotic dream, and Aimee Bender's "The Rememberer" (Chapter 12) calls to mind the person left behind after a loss—all thematic concerns of those stories.

> ## "To write a true war story, to write a true story about anything, is difficult—on all kinds of levels. On the most simple level, truth evaporates." Conversation with Tim O'Brien

As you question the text, notice general statements the narrator or another character makes, because such observations may well offer insight into the writer's theme. In Herman Melville's classic novel *Moby-Dick*, the narrator asserts that a great book needs a great theme—and that a subject must be large to accommodate a large theme. A flea will not do. This novel describes the voyage of Captain Ahab and his crew on a hunt for the great whale. The novel has numerous and wide-ranging subjects and themes: whaling, society, nature, defiance, comradeship, and the human struggle for meaning. The narrator is Ishmael, the sole survivor of that voyage.

Tolstoy's novel *War and Peace*, a surpassing work of fiction that came out of the European realist tradition, demonstrates beyond dispute the truth of Melville's assertion about theme. In its very title, as well as its meticulous execution, the novel embraces everything there is for us in life and sets it down on the page.

"So it started off sort of as a memory, and it became, I guess, a story when I began thinking about just the ways in which victims can so easily become victimizers. . . ." Conversation with ZZ Packer

All stories include insights from narrators or characters, and these insights often relate to theme. In Alice Munro's "An Ounce of Cure" (Chapter 6), at tale's end, the first-person narrator who got drunk while babysitting says, "I was a self-conscious girl and I suffered a good deal from all the exposure. But the development of events on that Saturday night—that fascinated me." In John Updike's "A&P" (Chapter 6), the young narrator realizes "how hard the world was going to be to . . . [him] from here on in." In both cases, the characters acknowledge a new level of awareness and responsibility; it's not entirely welcome or pleasurable, but it seems to be inevitable, a rite of passage to adulthood.

RECOGNIZING MULTIPLE THEMES

You can probably think of many broad themes—love and loss, power and powerlessness, freedom and responsibility, death and faith, and love and family. Leaving home, going on a journey, falling in love, proving one's heroism or goodness, making a new start in a new place, or joining with a new family group: these are just a few of the major themes that emerge from the stories in this book, and once you identify them, you can see their variations as you encounter these themes in other courses and in the world after college.

"The notion of just one theme in a story sometimes just reduces a work of fiction. I like to think about multiple themes, that a story can do so many things at the same time." Conversation with Chimamanda Ngozi Adichie

You have also explored ways of making those themes more specific to each story. A literary work can, of course, put forward multiple themes. Consider Shakespeare's *Hamlet* (Chapter 33). Depending on the lens through which we read the work, *Hamlet*'s themes can be seen as the anguish and consequences of indecision, the roots of suicidal melancholy, the repercussions of the Oedipal conflict, the perennial intermingling of power and corruption, or any combination of those ideas. By contrast, on

"So [it] was very important for me to understand that people could write about rage and political action, whether it was metaphorical or literal." Conversation with Dagoberto Gilb

the level of subject or plot, *Hamlet* could be summarized as a play about a man who loves his mother or a melancholic prince who can't make up his mind. The greatness of Shakespeare's play, of course, is that it is all this, and more: Shakespeare gives us a constantly shifting and surprising creation that cannot be reduced to any single reading or meaning.

If we think of theme as it pertains to music, we can see its use in fiction more clearly. In a musical composition, any element, motif, or small musical piece that has given rise to some variation becomes a theme. So think of theme as the melody of a story.

Stephen Crane (1871–1900)

Stephen Crane was born in Newark, New Jersey. By the time he was sixteen, he was already contributing articles to *The New York Tribune.* Crane moved to New York City, where he conducted extensive research for both fiction and nonfiction projects. To render an accurate account of life in poverty, for example, he lived in the slums while writing his first novel, *Maggie: A Girl of the Streets* (1893). This and Crane's other works—most famously *The Red Badge of Courage* (1895)—are examples of the literary style of *naturalism,* a technique that features characters carried along by fate in realistic, bleak circumstances. The indifference of nature is a popular theme in naturalistic fiction. The story that follows, "The Open Boat," was inspired by Crane's own experience on an 1896 expedition to Cuba. When the ship he was traveling on, the S.S. *Commodore,* was wrecked, Crane and other survivors drifted at sea for two weeks. During this time, he developed what would turn out to be a fatal strain of tuberculosis; he died in 1900. Crane wrote many stories about his experiences in Cuba, among them "Flanagan and His Short Filibustering Adventure" (1897) and "This Majestic Lie" (1900). A poet as well as a prose writer, Crane composed poetry that was experimental in its use of free verse and that put forward a dark view of the human condition. His career was unhappily brief, cut short by his death at age twenty-eight.

AS YOU READ   Notice the changes in the relationships among the four characters. Notice their peaks and valleys of hope and despair, of determination and exhaustion. What ideas do you perceive about the struggle for survival and the effect it has on these men?

FOR INTERACTIVE READING . . .

Keep track of repeated lines as you read. Consider what effect these repetitions have on the tone of the story, and on your own memory of certain events or characters. Are there any similarities between the repeated phrases?

The Open Boat:

A Tale Intended to Be after the Fact: Being the Experience of Four Men from the Sunk Steamer Commodore **(1897)**

I

1 None of them knew the color of the sky. Their eyes glanced level, and were fastened upon the waves that swept toward them. These waves were of the hue of slate, save for the tops, which were of foaming white, and all of the men knew the colors of the sea. The horizon narrowed and widened, and dipped and rose, and at all times its edge was jagged with waves that seemed thrust up in points like rocks.

Many a man ought to have a bath-tub larger than the boat which here rode upon the sea. These waves were most wrongfully and barbarously abrupt and tall, and each froth-top was a problem in small boat navigation.

The cook squatted in the bottom and looked with both eyes at the six inches of gunwale which separated him from the ocean. His sleeves were rolled over his fat forearms, and the two flaps of his unbuttoned vest dangled as he bent to bail out the boat. Often he said: "Gawd! That was a narrow clip." As he remarked it he invariably gazed eastward over the broken sea.

The oiler, steering with one of the two oars in the boat, sometimes raised himself suddenly to keep clear of water that swirled in over the stern. It was a thin little oar and it seemed often ready to snap.

5 The correspondent, pulling at the other oar, watched the waves and wondered why he was there.

The injured captain, lying in the bow, was at this time buried in that profound dejection and indifference which comes, temporarily at least, to even the bravest and most enduring when, willy nilly, the firm fails, the army loses, the ship goes down. The mind of the master of a vessel is rooted deep in the timbers of her, though he command for a day or a decade, and this captain had on him the stern impression of a scene in the grays of dawn of seven turned faces, and later a stump of a top-mast with a white ball on it that slashed to and fro at the waves, went low and lower, and down. Thereafter there was something strange in his voice. Although steady, it was deep with mourning, and of a quality beyond oration or tears.

"Keep'er a little more south, Billie," said he.

"'A little more south,' sir," said the oiler in the stern.

A seat in this boat was not unlike a seat upon a bucking broncho, and, by the same token, a broncho is not much smaller. The craft pranced and reared, and plunged like an animal. As each wave came, and she rose for it, she seemed like a horse making at a fence outrageously high. The manner of her scramble over these walls of water is a mystic thing, and, moreover, at the top of them were ordinarily these problems in white water, the foam racing down

from the summit of each wave, requiring a new leap, and a leap from the air. Then, after scornfully bumping a crest, she would slide, and race, and splash down a long incline and arrive bobbing and nodding in front of the next menace.

10   A singular disadvantage of the sea lies in the fact that after successfully surmounting one wave you discover that there is another behind it just as important and just as nervously anxious to do something effective in the way of swamping boats. In a ten-foot dingey one can get an idea of the resources of the sea in the line of waves that is not probable to the average experience, which is never at sea in a dingey. As each slaty wall of water approached, it shut all else from the view of the men in the boat, and it was not difficult to imagine that this particular wave was the final outburst of the ocean, the last effort of the grim water. There was a terrible grace in the move of the waves, and they came in silence, save for the snarling of the crests.

> ### The craft pranced and reared, and plunged like an animal.

    In the wan light, the faces of the men must have been gray. Their eyes must have glinted in strange ways as they gazed steadily astern. Viewed from a balcony, the whole thing would doubtlessly have been weirdly picturesque. But the men in the boat had no time to see it, and if they had had leisure there were other things to occupy their minds. The sun swung steadily up the sky, and they knew it was broad day because the color of the sea changed from slate to emerald-green, streaked with amber lights, and the foam was like tumbling snow. The process of the breaking day was unknown to them. They were aware only of this effect upon the color of the waves that rolled toward them.

    In disjointed sentences the cook and the correspondent argued as to the difference between a life-saving station and a house of refuge. The cook had said: "There's a house of refuge just north of the Mosquito Inlet Light, and as soon as they see us, they'll come off in their boat and pick us up."

    "As soon as who see us?" said the correspondent.

    "The crew," said the cook.

15   "Houses of refuge don't have crews," said the correspondent. "As I understand them, they are only places where clothes and grub are stored for the benefit of shipwrecked people. They don't carry crews."

    "Oh, yes, they do," said the cook.

    "No, they don't," said the correspondent.

    "Well, we're not there yet, anyhow," said the oiler, in the stern.

    "Well," said the cook, "perhaps it's not a house of refuge that I'm thinking of as being near Mosquito Inlet Light. Perhaps it's a life-saving station."

    "We're not there yet," said the oiler, in the stern. 20

II

As the boat bounced from the top of each wave, the wind tore through the hair of the hatless men, and as the craft plopped her stern down again the spray slashed past them. The crest of each of these waves was a hill, from the top of which the men surveyed, for a moment, a broad tumultuous expanse, shining and wind-riven. It was probably splendid. It was probably glorious, this play of the free sea, wild with lights of emerald and white and amber.

    "Bully good thing it's an on-shore wind," said the cook. "If not, where would we be? Wouldn't have a show."

    "That's right," said the correspondent.

    The busy oiler nodded his assent.

    Then the captain, in the bow, chuckled in a way that expressed humor, contempt, tragedy, all in one. "Do you think we've got much of a show, now, boys?" said he. 25

    Whereupon the three were silent, save for a trifle of hemming and hawing. To express any particular optimism at this time they felt to be childish and stupid, but they all doubtless possessed this sense of the situation in their mind. A young man thinks doggedly at such times. On the other hand, the ethics of their condition was decidedly against any open suggestion of hopelessness. So they were silent.

    "Oh, well," said the captain, soothing his children, "we'll get ashore all right."

    But there was that in his tone which made them think, so the oiler quoth: "Yes! If this wind holds!"

    The cook was bailing: "Yes! If we don't catch hell in the surf."

    Canton flannel gulls flew near and far. Sometimes 30 they sat down on the sea, near patches of brown sea-weed that rolled over the waves with a movement like carpets on a line in a gale. The birds sat comfortably in groups, and they were envied by some in the dingey, for the wrath of the sea was no more to them than it was to a covey of prairie chickens a thousand miles inland. Often they came very close and stared at the men with black bead-like eyes. At these times they were uncanny and sinister in their unblinking scrutiny, and the men hooted angrily at them, telling them to be gone. One came, and evidently decided to alight on the top of the captain's head. The bird flew parallel to the boat and did not circle, but made short sidelong jumps in the air in chicken-fashion. His black eyes were wistfully fixed upon the captain's head. "Ugly brute," said the oiler to the bird. "You look as if you were made with a jack-knife." The cook and the correspondent swore darkly at the creature. The captain naturally wished to knock it away with the end of the heavy painter, but he did not dare do it, because anything resembling an emphatic gesture would have capsized this freighted boat, and so with his open hand, the captain gently and carefully waved the gull away. After it had been discouraged from the pursuit the captain breathed easier on account of his hair, and others breathed easier because the bird struck their minds at this time as being somehow grewsome and ominous.

In the meantime the oiler and the correspondent rowed. And also they rowed.

They sat together in the same seat, and each rowed an oar. Then the oiler took both oars; then the correspondent took both oars; then the oiler; then the correspondent. They rowed and they rowed. The very ticklish part of the business was when the time came for the reclining one in the stern to take his turn at the oars. By the very last star of truth, it is easier to steal eggs from under a hen than it was to change seats in the dingey. First the man in the stern slid his hand along the thwart and moved with care, as if he were of Sèvres. Then the man in the rowing seat slid his hand along the other thwart. It was all done with the most extraordinary care. As the two sidled past each other, the whole party kept watchful eyes on the coming wave, and the captain cried: "Look out now! Steady there!"

The brown mats of sea-weed that appeared from time to time were like islands, bits of earth. They were travelling, apparently, neither one way nor the other. They were, to all intents, stationary. They informed the men in the boat that it was making progress slowly toward the land.

The captain, rearing cautiously in the bow, after the dingey soared on a great swell, said that he had seen the light-house at Mosquito Inlet. Presently the cook remarked that he had seen it. The correspondent was at the oars, then, and for some reason he too wished to look at the light-house, but his back was toward the far shore and the waves were important, and for some time he could not seize an opportunity to turn his head. But at last there came a wave more gentle than the others, and when at the crest of it he swiftly scoured the western horizon.

"See it?" said the captain.   35

"No," said the correspondent, slowly, "I didn't see anything."

"Look again," said the captain. He pointed. "It's exactly in that direction."

At the top of another wave, the correspondent did as he was bid, and this time his eyes chanced on a small still thing on the edge of the swaying horizon. It was precisely like the point of a pin. It took an anxious eye to find a light-house so tiny.

"Think we'll make it, Captain?"

"If this wind holds and the boat don't swamp, we can't   40 do much else," said the captain.

The little boat, lifted by each towering sea, and splashed viciously by the crests, made progress that in the absence of sea-weed was not apparent to those in her. She seemed just a wee thing wallowing, miraculously, top-up, at the mercy of five oceans. Occasionally, a great spread of water, like white flames, swarmed into her.

"Bail her, cook," said the captain, serenely.

"All right, captain," said the cheerful cook.

III

It would be difficult to describe the subtle brotherhood of men that was here established on the seas. No one said that it was so. No one mentioned it. But it dwelt in the boat, and each man felt it warm him. They were a captain, an oiler, a cook, and a correspondent, and they were friends, friends in a more curiously iron-bound degree than may be common. The hurt captain, lying against the water-jar in the bow, spoke always in a low voice and calmly, but he could never command a more ready and swiftly obedient crew than the motley three of the dingey. It was more than a mere recognition of what was best for the common safety. There was surely in it a quality that was personal and heartfelt. And after this devotion to the commander of the boat there was this comradeship that the correspondent, for instance, who had been taught to be cynical of men, knew even at the time was the best experience of his life. But no one said that it was so. No one mentioned it.

45 "I wish we had a sail," remarked the captain. "We might try my overcoat on the end of an oar and give you two boys a chance to rest." So the cook and the correspondent held the mast and spread wide the overcoat. The oiler steered, and the little boat made good way with her new rig. Sometimes the oiler had to scull sharply to keep a sea from breaking into the boat, but otherwise sailing was a success.

Slowly and beautifully the land loomed
out of the sea.

Meanwhile the light-house had been growing slowly larger. It had now almost assumed color, and appeared like a little gray shadow on the sky. The man at the oars could not be prevented from turning his head rather often to try for a glimpse of this little gray shadow.

At last, from the top of each wave the men in the tossing boat could see land. Even as the light-house was an upright shadow on the sky, this land seemed but a long black shadow on the sea. It certainly was thinner than paper. "We must be about opposite New Smyrna," said the cook, who had coasted this shore often in schooners. "Captain, by the way, I believe they abandoned that life-saving station there about a year ago."

"Did they?" said the captain.

The wind slowly died away. The cook and the correspondent were not now obliged to slave in order to hold high the oar. But the waves continued their old impetuous swooping at the dingey, and the little craft, no longer under way, struggled woundily over them. The oiler or the correspondent took the oars again.

50 Shipwrecks are *apropos* of nothing. If men could only train for them and have them occur when the men had reached pink condition, there would be less drowning at sea. Of the four in the dingey none had slept any time worth mentioning for two days and two nights previous to embarking in the dingey, and in the excitement of clambering about the deck of a foundering ship they had also forgotten to eat heartily.

For these reasons, and for others, neither the oiler nor the correspondent was fond of rowing at this time. The correspondent wondered ingenuously how in the name of all that was sane could there be people who thought it amusing to row a boat. It was not an amusement; it was a diabolical punishment, and even a genius of mental aberrations could never conclude that it was anything but a horror to the muscles and a crime against the back. He mentioned to the boat in general how the amusement of rowing struck him, and the weary-faced oiler smiled in full sympathy. Previously to the foundering, by the way, the oiler had worked double-watch in the engine-room of the ship.

"Take her easy, now, boys," said the captain. "Don't spend yourselves. If we have to run a surf you'll need all your strength, because we'll sure have to swim for it. Take your time."

Slowly the land arose from the sea. From a black line it became a line of black and a line of white—trees and sand. Finally, the captain said that he could make out a house on the shore. "That's the house of refuge, sure," said the cook. "They'll see us before long, and come out after us."

The distant light-house reared high. "The keeper ought to be able to make us out now, if he's looking through a glass," said the captain. "He'll notify the life-saving people."

55 "None of those other boats could have got ashore to give word of the wreck," said the oiler, in a low voice. "Else the life-boat would be out hunting us."

Slowly and beautifully the land loomed out of the sea. The wind came again. It had veered from the northeast to the southeast. Finally, a new sound struck the ears of the men in the boat. It was the low thunder of the surf on the shore. "We'll never be able to make the light-house now," said the captain. "Swing her head a little more north, Billie."

"'A little more north,' sir," said the oiler.

Whereupon the little boat turned her nose once more down the wind, and all but the oarsman watched the shore grow. Under the influence of this expansion doubt and direful apprehension was leaving the minds of the men. The management of the boat was still most absorbing, but it could not prevent a quiet cheerfulness. In an hour, perhaps, they would be ashore.

Their back-bones had become thoroughly used to balancing in the boat and they now rode this wild colt of a dingey like circus men. The correspondent thought that he had been drenched to the skin, but happening to feel in the top pocket of his coat, he found therein eight cigars. Four of them were soaked with sea-water; four were perfectly scatheless. After a search, somebody produced three dry matches, and thereupon the four waifs rode impudently in their little boat, and with an assurance of an impending rescue shining in their eyes, puffed at the big cigars and judged well and ill of all men. Everybody took a drink of water.

<h1 style="text-align:center">IV</h1>

60 "Cook," remarked the captain, "there don't seem to be any signs of life about your house of refuge."

"No," replied the cook. "Funny they don't see us!"

A broad stretch of lowly coast lay before the eyes of the men. It was of dunes topped with dark vegetation. The roar of the surf was plain, and sometimes they could see the white 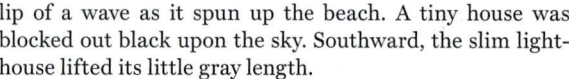 lip of a wave as it spun up the beach. A tiny house was blocked out black upon the sky. Southward, the slim lighthouse lifted its little gray length.

Tide, wind, and waves were swinging the dingey northward. "Funny they don't see us," said the men.

The surf's roar was here dulled, but its tone was, nevertheless, thunderous and mighty. As the boat swam over the great rollers, the men sat listening to this roar. "We'll swamp sure," said everybody.

65 It is fair to say here that there was not a life-saving station within twenty miles in either direction, but the men did not know this fact and in consequence they made dark and opprobrious remarks concerning the eyesight of the nation's life-savers. Four scowling men sat in the dingey and surpassed records in the invention of epithets.

"Funny they don't see us."

The light-heartedness of a former time had completely faded. To their sharpened minds it was easy to conjure pictures of all kinds of incompetency and blindness and, indeed, cowardice. There was the shore of the populous land, and it was bitter and bitter to them that from it came no sign.

"Well," said the captain, ultimately, "I suppose we'll have to make a try for ourselves. If we stay out here too long, we'll none of us have strength left to swim after the boat swamps."

And so the oiler, who was at the oars, turned the boat straight for the shore. There was a sudden tightening of muscles. There was some thinking.

"If we don't all get ashore—" said the captain. "If we 70 don't all get ashore, I suppose you fellows know where to send news of my finish?"

They then briefly exchanged some addresses and admonitions. As for the reflections of the men, there was a great deal of rage in them. Perchance they might be formulated thus: "If I am going to be drowned—if I am going to be drowned—if I am going to be drowned, why, in the name of the seven mad gods who rule the sea, was I allowed to come thus far and contemplate sand and trees? Was I brought here merely to have my nose dragged away as I was about to nibble the sacred cheese of life? It is preposterous. If this old ninny-woman, Fate, cannot do better than this, she should be deprived of the management of men's fortunes. She is an old hen who knows not her intention. If she has decided to drown me, why did she not do it in the beginning and save me all this trouble. The whole affair is absurd. . . . But, no, she cannot mean to drown me. She dare not drown me. She cannot drown me. Not after all this work." Afterward the man might have had an impulse to shake his fist at the clouds: "Just you drown me, now, and then hear what I call you!"

The billows that came at this time were more formidable. They seemed always just about to break and roll over the little boat in a turmoil of foam. There was a preparatory and long growl in the speech of them. No mind unused to the sea would have concluded that the dingey could ascend these sheer heights in time. The shore was still afar. The oiler was a wily surfman. "Boys," he said, swiftly, "she won't live three minutes more and we're too far out to swim. Shall I take her to sea again, Captain?"

"Yes! Go ahead!" said the captain.

This oiler, by a series of quick miracles, and fast and steady oarsmanship, turned the boat in the middle of the surf and took her safely to sea again.

There was a considerable silence as the boat bumped 75 over the furrowed sea to deeper water. Then somebody in gloom spoke. "Well, anyhow, they must have seen us from the shore by now."

The gulls went in slanting flight up the wind toward the gray desolate east. A squall, marked by dingy clouds, and clouds brick-red, like smoke from a burning building, appeared from the southeast.

"What do you think of those life-saving people? Ain't they peaches?"

"Funny they haven't seen us."

"Maybe they think we're out here for sport! Maybe they think we're fishin'. Maybe they think we're damned fools."

80 It was a long afternoon. A changed tide tried to force them southward, but wind and wave said northward. Far ahead, where coast-line, sea, and sky formed their mighty angle, there were little dots which seemed to indicate a city on the shore.

"St. Augustine?"

The captain shook his head. "Too near Mosquito Inlet."

And the oiler rowed, and then the correspondent rowed. Then the oiler rowed. It was a weary business. The human back can become the seat of more aches and pains than are registered in books for the composite anatomy of a regiment. It is a limited area, but it can become the theatre of innumerable muscular conflicts, tangles, wrenches, knots, and other comforts.

"Did you ever like to row, Billie?" asked the correspondent.

85 "No," said the oiler. "Hang it."

When one exchanged the rowing-seat for a place in the bottom of the boat, he suffered a bodily depression that caused him to be careless of everything save an obligation to wiggle one finger. There was cold sea-water swashing to and fro in the boat, and he lay in it. His head, pillowed on a thwart, was within an inch of the swirl of a wave crest, and sometimes a particularly obstreperous sea came in-board and drenched him once more. But these matters did not annoy him. It is almost certain that if the boat had capsized he would have tumbled comfortably out upon the ocean as if he felt sure it was a great soft mattress.

"Look! There's a man on the shore!"

"Where?"

"There! See 'im? See 'im?"

90 "Yes, sure! He's walking along."

"Now he's stopped. Look! He's facing us!"

"He's waving at us!"

"So he is! By thunder!"

"Ah, now, we're all right! Now we're all right! There'll be a boat out here for us in half an hour."

95 "He's going on. He's running. He's going up to that house there."

The remote beach seemed lower than the sea, and it required a searching glance to discern the little black figure. The captain saw a floating stick and they rowed to it. A bath-towel was by some weird chance in the boat, and, tying this on the stick, the captain waved it. The oarsman did not dare turn his head, so he was obliged to ask questions.

"What's he doing now?"

"He's standing still again. He's looking, I think. . . . There he goes again. Toward the house. . . . Now he's stopped again."

"Is he waving at us?"

"No, not now! he was, though." 100

"Look! There comes another man!"

"He's running."

"Look at him go, would you."

"Why, he's on a bicycle. Now he's met the other man. They're both waving at us. Look!"

"There comes something up the beach." 105

"What the devil is that thing?"

"Why, it looks like a boat."

"Why, certainly it's a boat."

"No, it's on wheels."

"Yes, so it is. Well, that must be the life-boat. They drag 110 them along shore on a wagon."

"That's the life-boat, sure."

"No, by—, it's—it's an omnibus."

"I tell you it's a life-boat."

"It is not! It's an omnibus. I can see it plain. See? One of these big hotel omnibuses."

"By thunder, you're right. It's an omnibus, sure as fate. 115 What do you suppose they are doing with an omnibus? Maybe they are going around collecting the life-crew, hey?"

"That's it, likely. Look! There's a fellow waving a little black flag. He's standing on the steps of the omnibus. There come those other two fellows. Now they're all talking together. Look at the fellow with the flag. Maybe he ain't waving it!"

"That ain't a flag, is it? That's his coat. Why, certainly, that's his coat."

"So it is. It's his coat. He's taken it off and is waving it around his head. But would you look at him swing it!"

"Oh, say, there isn't any life-saving station there. That's just a winter resort hotel omnibus that has brought over some of the boarders to see us drown."

"What's that idiot with the coat mean? What's he sig- 120 naling, anyhow?"

"It looks as if he were trying to tell us to go north. There must be a life-saving station up there."

"No! He thinks we're fishing. Just giving us a merry hand. See? Ah, there, Willie."

"Well, I wish I could make something out of those signals. What do you suppose he means?"

"He don't mean anything. He's just playing."

125 "Well, if he'd just signal us to try the surf again, or to go to sea and wait, or go north, or go south, or go to hell—there would be some reason in it. But look at him. He just stands there and keeps his coat revolving like a wheel. The ass!"

"There come more people."

"Now there's quite a mob. Look! Isn't that a boat?"

"Where? Oh, I see where you mean. No, that's no boat."

"That fellow is still waving his coat."

130 "He must think we like to see him do that. Why don't he quit it. It don't mean anything."

"I don't know. I think he is trying to make us go north. It must be that there's a life-saving station there somewhere."

"Say, he ain't tired yet. Look at 'im wave."

"Wonder how long he can keep that up. He's been revolving his coat ever since he caught sight of us. He's an idiot. Why aren't they getting men to bring a boat out? A fishing boat—one of those big yawls—could come out here all right. Why don't he do something?"

"Oh, it's all right, now."

135 "They'll have a boat out here for us in less than no time, now that they've seen us."

A faint yellow tone came into the sky over the low land. The shadows on the sea slowly deepened. The wind bore coldness with it, and the men began to shiver.

"Holy smoke!" said one, allowing his voice to express his impious mood, "if we keep on monkeying out here! If we've got to flounder out here all night!"

"Oh, we'll never have to stay here all night! Don't you worry. They've seen us now, and it won't be long before they'll come chasing out after us."

The shore grew dusky. The man waving a coat blended gradually into this gloom, and it swallowed in the same manner the omnibus and the group of people. The spray, when it dashed uproariously over the side, made the voyagers shrink and swear like men who were being branded.

140 "I'd like to catch the chump who waved the coat. I feel like soaking him one, just for luck."

"Why? What did he do?"

"Oh, nothing, but then he seemed so damned cheerful."

In the meantime the oiler rowed, and then the correspondent rowed, and then the oiler rowed. Gray-faced and bowed forward, they mechanically, turn by turn, plied the leaden oars. The form of the light-house had vanished from the southern horizon, but finally a pale star appeared, just lifting from the sea. The streaked saffron in the west passed before the all-merging darkness, and the sea to the east was black. The land had vanished, and was expressed only by the low and drear thunder of the surf.

A night on the sea in an open boat is a long night.

"If I am going to be drowned—if I am going to be drowned—if I am going to be drowned, why, in the name of the seven mad gods who rule the sea, was I allowed to come thus far and contemplate sand and trees? Was I brought here merely to have my nose dragged away as I was about to nibble the sacred cheese of life?"

The patient captain, drooped over the water-jar, was 145 sometimes obliged to speak to the oarsman.

"Keep her head up! Keep her head up!"

"'Keep her head up,' sir." The voices were weary and low.

This was surely a quiet evening. All save the oarsman lay heavily and listlessly in the boat's bottom. As for him, his eyes were just capable of noting the tall black waves that swept forward in a most sinister silence, save for an occasional subdued growl of a crest.

The cook's head was on a thwart, and he looked without interest at the water under his nose. He was deep in other scenes. Finally he spoke. "Billie," he murmured, dreamfully, "what kind of pie do you like best?"

V

"Pie," said the oiler and the correspondent, agitatedly. 150 "Don't talk about those things, blast you!"

"Well," said the cook, "I was just thinking about ham sandwiches, and—"

A night on the sea in an open boat is a long night. As darkness settled finally, the shine of the light, lifting from the sea in the south, changed to full gold. On the northern horizon a new light appeared, a small bluish gleam on the edge of the waters. These two lights were the furniture of the world. Otherwise there was nothing but waves.

Two men huddled in the stern, and distances were so magnificent in the dingey that the rower was enabled to keep his feet partly warmed by thrusting them under his companions. Their legs indeed extended far under the rowing-seat until they touched the feet of the captain forward. Some-

times, despite the efforts of the tired oarsman, a wave came piling into the boat, an icy wave of the night, and the chilling water soaked them anew. They would twist their bodies for a moment and groan, and sleep the dead sleep once more, while the water in the boat gurgled about them as the craft rocked.

The plan of the oiler and the correspondent was for one to row until he lost the ability, and then arouse the other from his sea-water couch in the bottom of the boat.

155   The oiler plied the oars until his head drooped forward, and the overpowering sleep blinded him. And he rowed yet afterward. Then he touched a man in the bottom of the boat, and called his name. "Will you spell me for a little while?" he said, meekly.

"Sure, Billie," said the correspondent, awakening and dragging himself to a sitting position. They exchanged places carefully, and the oiler, cuddling down in the sea-water at the cook's side, seemed to go to sleep instantly.

The particular violence of the sea had ceased. The waves came without snarling. The obligation of the man at the oars was to keep the boat headed so that the tilt of the rollers would not capsize her, and to preserve her from filling when the crests rushed past. The black waves were silent and hard to be seen in the darkness. Often one was almost upon the boat before the oarsman was aware.

In a low voice the correspondent addressed the captain. He was not sure that the captain was awake, although this iron man seemed to be always awake. "Captain, shall I keep her making for that light north, sir?"

The same steady voice answered him. "Yes. Keep it about two points off the port bow."

160   The cook had tied a life-belt around himself in order to get even the warmth which this clumsy cork contrivance could donate, and he seemed almost stove-like when a rower, whose teeth invariably chattered wildly as soon as he ceased his labor, dropped down to sleep.

The correspondent, as he rowed, looked down at the two men sleeping under foot. The cook's arm was around the oiler's shoulders, and, with their fragmentary clothing and haggard faces, they were the babes of the sea, a grotesque rendering of the old babes in the wood.

Later he must have grown stupid at his work, for suddenly there was a growling of water, and a crest came with a roar and a swash into the boat,

and it was a wonder that it did not set the cook afloat in his life-belt. The cook continued to sleep, but the oiler sat up, blinking his eyes and shaking with the new cold.

"Oh, I'm awful sorry, Billie," said the correspondent, contritely.

"That's all right, old boy," said the oiler, and lay down again and was asleep.

Presently it seemed that even the captain dozed, and the correspondent thought that he was the one man afloat on all the oceans. The wind had a voice as it came over the waves, and it was sadder than the end. 165

There was a long, loud swishing astern of the boat, and a gleaming trail of phosphorescence, like blue flame, was furrowed on the black waters. It might have been made by a monstrous knife.

Then there came a stillness, while the correspondent breathed with the open mouth and looked at the sea.

Suddenly there was another swish and another long flash of bluish light, and this time it was alongside the boat, and might almost have been reached with an oar. The correspondent saw an enormous fin speed like a shadow through the water, hurling the crystalline spray and leaving the long glowing trail.

The correspondent looked over his shoulder at the captain. His face was hidden, and he seemed to be asleep. He looked at the babes of the sea. They certainly were asleep. So, being bereft of sympathy, he leaned a little way to one side and swore softly into the sea.

But the thing did not then leave the vicinity of the boat. 170 Ahead or astern, on one side or the other, at intervals long or short, fled the long sparkling streak, and there was to be heard the whiroo of the dark fin. The speed and power of the thing was greatly to be admired. It cut the water like a gigantic and keen projectile.

The presence of this biding thing did not affect the man with the same horror that it would if he had been a picnicker. He simply looked at the sea dully and swore in an undertone.

Nevertheless, it is true that he did not wish to be alone with the thing. He wished one of his companions to awaken by chance and keep him company with it. But the captain hung motionless over the water-jar and the oiler and the cook in the bottom of the boat were plunged in slumber.

VI

"If I am going to be drowned—if I am going to be drowned—if I am going to be drowned, why, in the name of the seven mad gods who rule the sea, was I allowed to come thus far and contemplate sand and trees?"

During this dismal night, it may be remarked that a man would conclude that it was really the intention of the seven mad gods to drown him, despite the abominable injustice of it. For it was certainly an abominable injustice to drown a man who had worked so hard, so hard. The man felt it would be a crime most unnatural. Other people had drowned at sea since galleys swarmed with painted sails, but still—

175　When it occurs to a man that nature does not regard him as important, and that she feels she would not maim the universe by disposing of him, he at first wishes to throw bricks at the temple, and he hates deeply the fact that there are no bricks and no temples. Any visible expression of nature would surely be pelleted with his jeers.

Then, if there be no tangible thing to hoot he feels, perhaps, the desire to confront a personification and indulge in pleas, bowed to one knee, and with hands supplicant, saying: "Yes, but I love myself."

A high cold star on a winter's night is the word he feels that she says to him. Thereafter he knows the pathos of his situation.

The men in the dingey had not discussed these matters, but each had, no doubt, reflected upon them in silence and according to his mind. There was seldom any expression upon their faces save the general one of complete weariness. Speech was devoted to the business of the boat.

To chime the notes of his emotion, a verse mysteriously entered the correspondent's head. He had even forgotten that he had forgotten this verse, but it suddenly was in his mind.

A soldier of the Legion lay dying in Algiers,
There was lack of woman's nursing, there was
　　dearth of woman's tears;
But a comrade stood beside him, and he took
　　that comrade's hand,
And he said: "I never more shall see my own,
　　my native land."

180　In his childhood, the correspondent had been made acquainted with the fact that a soldier of the Legion lay dying in Algiers, but he had never regarded it as important. Myriads of his school-fellows had informed him of the soldier's plight, but the dinning had naturally ended by making him perfectly indifferent. He had never considered it his affair that a soldier of the Legion lay dying in Algiers, nor had it appeared to him as a matter for sorrow. It was less to him than the breaking of a pencil's point.

Now, however, it quaintly came to him as a human, living thing. It was no longer merely a picture of a few throes in the breast of a poet, meanwhile drinking tea and warming his feet at the grate; it was an actuality—stern, mournful, and fine.

The correspondent plainly saw the soldier. He lay on the sand with his feet out straight and still. While his pale left hand was upon his chest in an attempt to thwart the going of his life, the blood came between his fingers. In the far Algerian distance, a city of low square forms was set against a sky that was faint with the last sunset hues. The correspondent, plying the oars and dreaming of the slow and slower movements of the lips of the soldier, was moved by a profound and perfectly impersonal comprehension. He was sorry for the soldier of the Legion who lay dying in Algiers.

The thing which had followed the boat and waited had evidently grown bored at the delay. There was no longer to be heard the slash of the cut-water, and there was no longer the flame of the long trail. The light in the north still glimmered, but it was apparently no nearer to the boat. Sometimes the boom of the surf rang in the correspondent's ears, and he turned the craft seaward then and rowed harder. Southward, some one had evidently built a watch-fire on the beach. It was too low and too far to be seen, but it made a shimmering, roseate reflection upon the bluff back of it, and this could be discerned from the boat. The wind came stronger, and sometimes a wave suddenly raged out like a mountain-cat and there was to be seen the sheen and sparkle of a broken crest.

The captain, in the bow, moved on his water-jar and sat erect. "Pretty long night," he observed to the correspondent. He looked at the shore. "Those life-saving people take their time."

"Did you see that shark playing around?"　　　　185

"Yes, I saw him. He was a big fellow, all right."

"Wish I had known you were awake."

Later the correspondent spoke into the bottom of the boat.

"Billie!" There was a slow and gradual disentanglement. "Billie, will you spell me?"

190 "Sure," said the oiler.

As soon as the correspondent touched the cold comfortable sea-water in the bottom of the boat, and had huddled close to the cook's life-belt he was deep in sleep, despite the fact that his teeth played all the popular airs. This sleep was so good to him that it was but a moment before he heard a voice call his name in a tone that demonstrated the last stages of exhaustion. "Will you spell me?"

"Sure, Billie."

The light in the north had mysteriously vanished, but the correspondent took his course from the wide-awake captain.

Later in the night they took the boat farther out to sea, and the captain directed the cook to take one oar at the stern and keep the boat facing the seas. He was to call out if he should hear the thunder of the surf. This plan enabled the oiler and the correspondent to get respite together. "We'll give those boys a chance to get into shape again," said the captain. They curled down and, after a few preliminary chatterings and trembles, slept once more the dead sleep. Neither knew they had bequeathed to the cook the company of another shark, or perhaps the same shark.

195 As the boat caroused on the waves, spray occasionally bumped over the side and gave them a fresh soaking, but this had no power to break their repose. The ominous slash of the wind and the water affected them as it would have affected mummies.

"Boys," said the cook, with the notes of every reluctance in his voice, "she's drifted in pretty close. I guess one of you had better take her to sea again." The correspondent, aroused, heard the crash of the toppled crests.

As he was rowing, the captain gave him some whiskey and water, and this steadied the chills out of him. "If I ever get ashore and anybody shows me even a photograph of an oar—"

At last there was a short conversation.

"Billie. . . . Billie, will you spell me?"

200 "Sure," said the oiler.

VII

When the correspondent again opened his eyes, the sea and the sky were each of the gray hue of the dawning. Later, carmine and gold was painted upon the waters. The morning appeared finally, in its splendor, with a sky of pure blue, and the sunlight flamed on the tips of the waves.

On the distant dunes were set many little black cottages, and a tall white wind-mill reared above them. No man, nor dog, nor bicycle appeared on the beach. The cottages might have formed a deserted village.

> It merely occurred to him that if he should drown it would be a shame.

The voyagers scanned the shore. A conference was held in the boat. "Well," said the captain, "if no help is coming, we might better try a run through the surf right away. If we stay out here much longer we will be too weak to do anything for ourselves at all." The others silently acquiesced in this reasoning. The boat was headed for the beach. The correspondent wondered if none ever ascended the tall wind-tower, and if then they never looked seaward. This tower was a giant, standing with its back to the plight of the ants. It represented in a degree, to the correspondent, the serenity of nature amid the struggles of the individual—nature in the wind, and nature in the vision of men. She did not seem cruel to him then, nor beneficent, nor treacherous, nor wise. But she was indifferent, flatly indifferent. It is, perhaps, plausible that a man in this situation, impressed with the unconcern of the universe, should see the innumerable flaws of his life and have them taste wickedly in his mind and wish for another chance. A distinction between right and wrong seems absurdly clear to him, then, in this new ignorance of the grave-edge, and he understands that if he were given another opportunity he would mend his conduct and his words, and be better and brighter during an introduction, or at a tea.

"Now, boys," said the captain, "she is going to swamp sure. All we can do is to work her in as far as possible, and then when she swamps, pile out and scramble for the beach. Keep cool now, and don't jump until she swamps sure."

The oiler took the oars. Over his shoulders he scanned 205 the surf. "Captain," he said, "I think I'd better bring her about, and keep her head-on to the seas and back her in."

"All right, Billie," said the captain. "Back her in." The oiler swung the boat then and, seated in the stern, the cook and the correspondent were obliged to look over their shoulders to contemplate the lonely and indifferent shore.

The monstrous inshore rollers heaved the boat high until the men were again enabled to see the white sheets of water scudding up the slanted beach. "We won't get in very close," said the captain. Each time a man could wrest his attention from the rollers, he turned his glance toward the shore, and in the expression of the eyes during this contemplation there was a singular quality. The correspondent, observing the others, knew that they were not afraid, but the full meaning of their glances was shrouded.

As for himself, he was too tired to grapple fundamentally with the fact. He tried to coerce his mind into thinking of it, but the mind was dominated at this time by the muscles, and the muscles said they did not care. It merely occurred to him that if he should drown it would be a shame.

There were no hurried words, no pallor, no plain agitation. The men simply looked at the shore. "Now, remember to get well clear of the boat when you jump," said the captain.

210 Seaward the crest of a roller suddenly fell with a thunderous crash, and the long white comber came roaring down upon the boat.

"Steady now," said the captain. The men were silent. They turned their eyes from the shore to the comber and waited. The boat slid up the incline, leaped at the furious top, bounced over it, and swung down the long back of the wave. Some water had been shipped and the cook bailed it out.

But the next crest crashed also. The tumbling boiling flood of white water caught the boat and whirled it almost perpendicular. Water swarmed in from all sides. The correspondent had his hands on the gunwale at this time, and when the water entered at that place he swiftly withdrew his fingers, as if he objected to wetting them.

The little boat, drunken with this weight of water, reeled and snuggled deeper into the sea.

"Bail her out, cook! Bail her out," said the captain.

215 "All right, Captain," said the cook.

"Now, boys, the next one will do for us, sure," said the oiler. "Mind to jump clear of the boat."

The third wave moved forward, huge, furious, implacable. It fairly swallowed the dingey, and almost simultaneously the men tumbled into the sea. A piece of life-belt had lain in the bottom of the boat, and as the correspondent went overboard he held this to his chest with his left hand.

The January water was icy, and he reflected immediately that it was colder than he had expected to find it off the coast of Florida. This appeared to his dazed mind as a fact important enough to be noted at the time. The coldness of the water was sad; it was tragic. This fact was somehow so mixed and confused with his opinion of his own situation that it seemed almost a proper reason for tears. The water was cold.

When he came to the surface he was conscious of little but the noisy water. Afterward he saw his companions in the sea. The oiler was ahead in the race. He was swimming strongly and rapidly. Off to the correspondent's left, the cook's great white and corked back bulged out of the water, and in the rear the captain was hanging with his one good hand to the keel of the overturned dingey.

There is a certain immovable quality to a shore, and the 220 correspondent wondered at it amid the confusion of the sea.

It seemed also very attractive, but the correspondent knew that it was a long journey, and he paddled leisurely. The piece of life-preserver lay under him, and sometimes he whirled down the incline of a wave as if he were on a hand-sled.

But finally he arrived at a place in the sea where travel was beset with difficulty. He did not pause swimming to inquire what manner of current had caught him, but there his progress ceased. The shore was set before him like a bit of scenery on a stage, and he looked at it and understood with his eyes each detail of it.

As the cook passed, much farther to the left, the captain was calling to him, "Turn over on your back, cook! Turn over on your back and use the oar."

"All right, sir." The cook turned on his back, and, paddling with an oar, went ahead as if he were a canoe.

Presently the boat also passed to the left of the corre- 225 spondent with the captain clinging with one hand to the keel. He would have appeared like a man raising himself to look over a board fence, if it were not for the extraordinary gymnastics of the boat. The correspondent marvelled that the captain could still hold to it.

They passed on, nearer to shore—the oiler, the cook, the captain—and following them went the water-jar, bouncing gayly over the seas.

The correspondent remained in the grip of this strange new enemy—a current. The shore, with its white slope of sand and its green bluff, topped with little silent cottages, was spread like a picture before him. It was very near to him then, but he was impressed as one who in a gallery looks at a scene from Brittany or Holland.

He thought: "I am going to drown? Can it be possible? Can it be possible? Can it be possible?" Perhaps an individual must consider his own death to be the final phenomenon of nature.

But later a wave perhaps whirled him out of this small deadly current, for he found suddenly that he could again make progress toward the shore. Later still, he was aware that the captain, clinging with one hand to the keel of the dingey, had his face turned away from the shore and toward him, and was calling his name. "Come to the boat! Come to the boat!"

230   In his struggle to reach the captain and the boat, he reflected that when one gets properly wearied, drowning must really be a comfortable arrangement, a cessation of hostilities accompanied by a large degree of relief, and he was glad of it, for the main thing in his mind for some moments had been horror of the temporary agony. He did not wish to be hurt.

Presently he saw a man running along the shore. He was undressing with most remarkable speed. Coat, trousers, shirt, everything flew magically off him.

"Come to the boat," called the captain.

"All right, Captain." As the correspondent paddled, he saw the captain let himself down to bottom and leave the boat. Then the correspondent performed his one little marvel of the voyage. A large wave caught him and flung him with ease and supreme speed completely over the boat and far beyond it. It struck him even then as an event in gymnastics, and a true miracle of the sea. An overturned boat in the surf is not a plaything to a swimming man.

The correspondent arrived in water that reached only to his waist, but his condition did not enable him to stand for more than a moment. Each wave knocked him into a heap, and the under-tow pulled at him.

235   Then he saw the man who had been running and undressing, and undressing and running, come bounding into the water. He dragged ashore the cook, and then waded toward the captain, but the captain waved him away, and sent him to the correspondent. He was naked, naked as a tree in winter, but a halo was about his head, and he shone like a saint. He gave a strong pull, and a long drag, and a bully heave at the correspondent's hand. The correspondent, schooled in the minor formulae, said: "Thanks, old man." But suddenly the man cried: "What's that?" He pointed a swift finger. The correspondent said: "Go."

In the shallows, face downward, lay the oiler. His forehead touched sand that was periodically, between each wave, clear of the sea.

The correspondent did not know all that transpired afterward. When he achieved safe ground he fell, striking the sand with each particular part of his body. It was as if he had dropped from a roof, but the thud was grateful to him.

It seems that instantly the beach was populated with men with blankets, clothes, and flasks, and women with coffee-pots and all the remedies sacred to their minds. The welcome of the land to the men from the sea was warm and generous, but a still and dripping shape was carried slowly up the beach, and the land's welcome for it could only be the different and sinister hospitality of the grave.

When it came night, the white waves paced to and fro in the moonlight, and the wind brought the sound of the great sea's voice to the men on shore, and they felt that they could then be interpreters.

> In the shallows, face downward, lay the oiler.

IF YOU LIKED "THE OPEN BOAT," YOU MIGHT ALSO LIKE . . .

. . . another story about the struggle between human beings and indifferent nature, Barry Lopez's "The Location of the River" (Chapter 10).

GOING FURTHER   Similar struggles are also found in the short stories and novels of Joseph Conrad, which offer excellent examples of men adrift or with particular goals at sea and in strange lands. The novels of Ernest Hemingway offer similar themes.

Writing from Reading

Summarize

1 The story begins in the middle of things, with the crew already stranded at sea. What details does Crane provide about the shipwreck? Which does he leave out?

2 The swim for shore is described only from the correspondent's point of view. What details are there of the other passengers' swims? Use what information you have to piece together an explanation for the oiler's death.

Analyze Craft

3 Explain what Crane achieves by repeating certain passages of dialogue, reflection, and description within the story. What are some of these repeated lines and how many times do they recur? Do their meanings change with repetition or with the changing contexts in which they occur?

4 Only the oiler is ever called by his name in the story, and then never by the narrator. What is the significance of naming just the one character? Discuss this significance in light of Billie's death.

Analyze Voice

5 This story was written in 1897. Consider how the era in which it was written affected its language. What words appear that you don't know without the aid of a dictionary? Are there any that sound old-fashioned to you?

Synthesize Summary and Analysis

6 What is the narrator's role in this story? How would you describe the narrative distance? In other words, how close is the tale teller to the story and to its characters? Does the distance change over the course of the story? How?

Interpret the Story

7 There are several themes in "The Open Boat," including comradeship, the struggle to survive, and nature's indifference. Choose one of these, or identify another theme in the story, and discuss incidents in the story where the theme becomes most clear. Explain how Crane emphasizes the theme, citing passages from the text.

"Emerson says nature doesn't like to be observed—and the thought to that is that in that peripheral vision you actually really do see things that are not always recorded instantaneously and that's what fiction wants to get at. It wants to get at those things that are in your vision but that are unrecognized. I think every story should in some ways, irrespective of what its stylistic preoccupations are, try to bring you back to life, as F. R. Leavis said, with a sense of sensuous and moral awareness renewed."

Conversation with Richard Ford

William Kittredge

. . . I was writing about people and places and situations that I cared about deeply.

A Conversation on Writing

"I Didn't Know Anything"

I grew up on a great big cattle ranch in southeastern Oregon. It was very isolated. . . . The idea of literary culture there was pretty nonexistent. We were 300 miles from probably the nearest really functional bookstore. . . . I began ["Thirty-Four Seasons of Winter"] on the ranch way long ago. . . . I muddled along, and I tried to use this book . . . to locate myself, connect myself to the world. This is a story about being unable to connect yourself to the world in many ways . . . but at the same time, you're connecting yourself to this world, wind-glazed fields of snow, and traipsing around Manteca, and feedlots, and endless rain, and so on and so forth. It's not a world that has a lot of automatic connection. The West is that way, a lot of it.

Fiction as a Moment of Recognition

Fiction really starts with this: I have to understand the people. I don't want to say *characters* because that sounds like a word out of a textbook. . . . You [need to] really specifically, concretely understand in depth who they are, what their emotions are, how they will react to something. I always told students, "Characters may not want to do what you want them to do in the story. They may want to do something that's just going to ruin the story. Guess what, they get to do it. Otherwise, you're just creating puppets." So these people go and do what they please. . . . All that has to happen in the story, after all, is some moment of recognition or insight and there's some implication of consequences of that and we're gone.

William Kittredge (b. 1932) has lived in the West for nearly his entire life; he grew up on a ranch in southeastern Oregon, where he farmed into his thirties. After that, he taught at the University of Montana for almost thirty years. In between, he studied writing at the Iowa Writers' Workshop and received Stanford University's prestigious Stegner Fellowship. Kittredge's subject is the West—but not the West of tough-grained cowboy heroes or seemingly unlimited resources.

In 2007, at the age of seventy-five, Kittredge published his first novel, *The Willow Trees*. This book deals with the education of a young cowboy whose adventures carry him from the early days of modern ranching to the politics of contemporary Western statehood. In his story collections *We Are Not in This Together* (1984) and *The Van Gogh Field* (1978), Kittredge portrays vulnerable men and complicated love relationships, even as he depicts the Western traditions of farming and ranching as in "Thirty-Four Seasons of Winter."

To watch this entire interview and hear the author read from "Thirty-Four Seasons of Winter," go to connect.mcgraw-hill.com.

RESEARCH ASSIGNMENT   In his interview, Kittredge says the West is a "museum culture." What does he mean by that?

AS YOU READ   Make note of the seasons and the shared history of Art and Ben, two rough and tumble stepbrothers who know how to make trouble and sometimes give it. How is the season described? Consider what the season represents in the stepbrothers' relationship.

Thirty-Four Seasons of Winter (1984)

1   BEN Alton remembered years in terms of winter. Summers all ran together, each like the last, heat and baled hay and dust. "That was '59," he'd say. "The year I wintered in California." He'd be remembering manure-slick alleys of a feedlot outside Manteca, a flat horizon and constant rain.

Or flood years. "March of '64, when the levees went." Or open winters. "We fed cattle the whole of February in our shirtsleeves. For Old Man Swarthout." And then he'd be sad. "One week Art helped. We was done every day by noon and drunk by three." Sad because Art was his stepbrother and dead, and because there'd been nothing but hate between them when Art was killed.

Ben and Art fought only once, when they were thirteen. Ben's father, Corrie Alton, moved in with Art's old lady on her dryland place in the hills north of Davanero, and the boys bunked together in a back room. The house was surrounded by a fenced dirt yard where turkeys picked, shaded by three withering peach trees; and the room they shared was furnished with two steel-frame cots and a row of nails where they hung what extra clothing they owned. The first night, while the old people were drinking in town, the boys fought. Ben took a flattened nose and chipped tooth against one of the cot frames and was satisfied and didn't try again.

The next year Art's mother sold the place for money to drink on, and when that was gone Ben's old man pulled out, heading for Shafter, down out of Bakersfield, going to see friends and work a season in the spuds. Corrie never came back or sent word, so the next spring the boys took a job setting siphons for an onion farmer, doing the muddy and exhausting work of one man, supporting themselves and Art's mother. She died the spring they were seventeen; and Art began to talk about getting out of town, fighting in the ring, being somebody.

So he ran every night, and during the day he and Ben   5 stacked alfalfa bales, always making their thousand a day, twenty bucks apiece, and then in the fall Art went to Portland and worked out in a gym each afternoon, learning to fight, and spent his evenings swimming at the YMCA or watching movies. Early in the winter he began to get some fights; and for at least the first year he didn't lose. People began to know his name in places like Salem and Yakima and Klamath Falls.

HE fought at home only once, a January night in the Peterson barn on the edge of town, snow falling steadily. The barn warmed slowly, losing its odor of harness leather and rotting hay; and under a circle of lights that illuminated the fighters in a blue glare, country people smoked and bet and drank. Circling a sweating and tiring Mexican boy, Art tapped his gloves and brushed back his thin blond hair with a quick forearm, sure and quiet. Then he moved under an overhand right, ducking in a quick new way he must have learned in Portland; and then he was inside, forcing, and flat on his feet, grunting as he followed each short chop with his body. The Mexican backed against one of the rough juniper posts supporting the ring, covered his face, gloves fumbling together as he began sinking and twisting, knees folding; and it ended with the Mexican sprawled and cut beneath one eye, bleeding from the nose, and Art in his corner, breathing easily while he flexed and shook his arms as if he weren't loose yet. Art spit the white mouthpiece onto the wet, gray canvas and ducked away under the ropes.

Even tired she looked good.

That night, Ben sat in the top row of the little grandstand and watched two men drag the other fighter out of the ring and attempt to revive him by pouring water over his head. Ben hugged his knees and watched the crowd settle and heard the silence while everybody watched. Finally the Mexican boy shook his head and stood up, and the crowd moved in a great sigh.

THE next summer Art showed up with Clara, brought her back with him from a string of fights in California. It was an August afternoon, dead hot in the valley hayfields, and dust rose in long spirals from the field ahead where five balers were circling slowly, eating windrows of loose hay and leaving endless and uniform strings of bales. Ben was working the stack, unloading trucks, sweating through his pants every day before noon, shirtless and peeling.

The lemon-colored Buick convertible came across the stubble, bouncing and wheeling hard, just ahead of its own dust, and stopped twenty or thirty yards from the stack. Art jumped out holding a can of beer over his head. The girl stood beside the convertible in the dusty alfalfa stubble and squinted into the glaring light, moist and sleepy looking. She was maybe twenty, and her sleeveless white blouse was wrinkled from sleeping in the car and sweat-gray beneath the arms. But she was blond and tan and direct in the 100-degree heat of the afternoon. "Ain't she something?" Art said. "She's a kind of prize I brought home." He laughed and slapped her on the butt.

10   "Hello, Ben," she said. "Art told me about you." They drank a can of beer, iced and metallic tasting, and Art talked about the fighting in California, Fresno, and Tracy, and while he talked he ran his fingers slowly up and down Clara's bare arm. Ben crouched in the shade of the convertible with his beer and tried not to watch the girl. That night he lay awake and thought about her, and everything about

that meeting seemed too large and real, like some memory of childhood.

Anyway, she was living and traveling with Art. Then the fall he was twenty-five, fighting in Seattle, Art broke his right hand in a way that couldn't be fixed and married Clara and came home to live, driving a logging truck in the summer and drinking in the bars and drawing his unemployment through the winters, letting Clara work as a barmaid when they were broke. The years got away until one afternoon in a tavern called The Tarpaper Shack, when Ben and Art were thirty-one. Art was sitting with a girl named Marie, and when Ben came in and wandered over to the booth she surprised him by being quiet and nice, with brown eyes and dark hair, not the kind Art ran with on his drunks; and by the end of the summer Marie and Ben were engaged.

WHICH caused no trouble until Christmas. The stores were open late, but the streets with their decorations were deserted, looking like a carnival at four in the morning, lighted and ready to tear down and move.

"You gonna marry that pig?" Art said. Art was drunk. The barkeeper, a woman called Virgie, was leaning on the counter.

"I guess I am," Ben said. "But don't sweat it." Then he noticed Virgie looking past them to the far corner of the vaulted room. A worn row of booths ran there, beyond the lighted shuffleboard table and bowling machine. Above the last booth he saw the shadowed back of Clara's head. Just the yellow hair and yet certainly her. Art was grinning.

"You see her," he said talking to Ben. "She's got a prob- 15 lem. She ain't getting any."

Ben finished the beer and eased the glass back to the wooden counter, wishing he could leave, wanting no more of their trouble. Clara was leaning back, eyes closed and the table in front of her empty except for her clasped hands. She didn't move or look as he approached.

"Hello, Clara," he said. And when she opened her eyes it was the same, like herons over the valley swamps, white against green. Even tired she looked good. "All right if I sit?" he asked. "You want a beer?"

She sipped from his, taking the glass without speaking, touching his hand with her hand, then smiling and licking the froth from her lips. "Okay," she said, and he ordered another glass and sat down beside her.

"How you been?" he said. "All right?"

20   "You know," she said, looking sideways at him, never glancing toward Art. "You got a pretty good idea how I been." Then she smiled. "I hear you're getting married."

"Just because you're tied up," he said, and she grinned again, more like her old self now. "I mean it," he said. "Guess I ought to tell you once."

"Don't, she said. "For Christ sake. Not with that bastard over there laughing." She drank a little more of the beer. "I mean it," she said, after a moment. "Leave me alone."

Ben picked up his empty glass and walked toward the bar, turning the glass in his hand and feeling how it fit his grasp. He stood looking at the back of Art's head, the thin hair, fine and blond; and then he wrapped the glass in his fist and smashed it into the hollow of Art's neck, shattering the glass and driving Art's face into the counter. Then he ran, crashing out the door and onto the sidewalk.

His hand was cut and bleeding. He picked glass from his palm and wrapped his hand in his handkerchief as he walked, looking in the store windows, bright and lighted for Christmas.

25   Clara left for Sacramento that night, lived there with her father, worked in a factory southeast of town, making airplane parts and taking care of the old man, not coming back until he died. Sometimes Ben wondered if she would have come back anyway, even if the old man hadn't died. Maybe she's just been waiting for Art to come after her. And then one day on the street he asked, "You and Art going back together?" just hoping he could get her to talk awhile.

"I guess not," she said. "That's what he told me."

"I'm sorry," Ben said. And he was.

"I came back because I wanted," she said. "Guess I lived here too long."

THAT spring Ben and Marie were married and began living out of town, on a place her father owned; and the next fall his father was killed, crushed under a hillside combine in Washington, just north of Walla Walla, drunk and asleep at the leveling wheel, dead when they dug him out. And then the summer Art and Ben turned thirty-four Marie got pregnant and that winter Art was killed, shot in the back of the head by a girl named Stephanie Rudd, a thin red-haired girl just out of high school and, so people said, knocked up a little. Art was on the end stool in the The Tar-paper Shack, his usual place, when the girl entered quietly and shot before anyone noticed. He was dead when he hit the floor, face destroyed, blood spattered over the mirror and glasses behind the bar. And all the time music he'd punched was playing on the jukebox. *Trailer for sale or rent;* and *I can't stop loving you;* and *Time to bum again;* and, *That's what you get for loving me:* Roger Miller, Ray Charles, Waylon Jennings.

BEN awakened the night of the shooting and heard Ma-   30 rie on the phone, felt her shake him awake in the dim light of the bedroom. She seemed enormously frightened and continued to shake him, as if to awaken herself. She was eight months pregnant.

"He's dead." She spoke softly, seeming terrified, as if some idea she feared had been at last confirmed. "He never had a chance," she said.

"He had plenty." Ben sat up and put his arm around her, forced from his shock.

"They never gave him anything." She bent over and began to cry.

Later, it was nearly morning, after coffee and cigarettes, when Marie gave up and went to bed; Ben sat alone at the kitchen table. "Afraid of everything," Art had said. "That's how they are. Every stinking one."

Ben saw Art drunk and talking like he was ready for   35 anything, actually involved with nothing except for a string of girls like the one who shot him. And then, somehow, the idea of Art and Marie got hold of Ben. It came from the way she had cried and carried on about Art. There was something wrong. Sitting there at the table, feeling the knowledge seep around his defenses, Ben knew what it was. He got up from the chair.

She was in the bedroom, curled under the blankets, crying softly. "What is it?" he asked. "There's something going on." She didn't open her eyes, but the crying seemed to slow a little. Ben waited, standing beside the bed, looking down, all the time wondering, as he became more sure, if it had happened in this bed, and all the time knowing it made no difference where it happened. And it was her fault. Not any fault of Art's. Art was what he was. She could have stopped him. Ben's hands felt strange, as if there was something to be done he couldn't recognize. He asked again, hearing his voice harsh and strained. "What is it, Marie?"

She didn't answer. He forced her onto her back and held her there, waiting for her to open her eyes while she struggled silently, twisting her upper body against his grip. His fingers sank into her shoulder and his wrist trembled. They remained like that, forcing against each other. Then she relaxed and opened her eyes. "What is it?" he asked again. "It was something between you and Art, wasn't it?"

Her eyes were changed, shielded. She shook her head. "No," she said. "No."

"He was screwing you, wasn't he? Is it his kid?"

40 "It was a long time ago," she said.

"My ass." He let go of her shoulder. "That's why you're so tore up. Because you ain't getting any more from him." He walked around the bed, unable for some reason, because of what he was left with, to ask her if it happened here, in this bed. "Isn't that right?" he said. "How come you married me? He turn you down?"

"Because I was afraid of him. I didn't want him. He was just fooling. I wanted you, not him."

Ben slapped her, and she curled quickly again, her hands pressed to her mouth, crying, shoulders hunching. He made her face him. "You ain't getting away," he said. "So I was a nice tame dog, and you took me."

"You'll hurt the baby."

45 "His goddamned baby!"

"It all broke off when I met you," she said. "He told me to go ahead, that you'd be good to me." It had surprised him when they met that she was with Art, but somehow he'd never until now gotten the idea they had anything going on. "It was only a few times after I knew you," she said. "He begged me."

"So I got stuck with the leavings." He cursed her again, at the same time listening to at least a little of what she said. "He begged me." That was sad. Remembering Art those last years, after he came home to stay, Ben believed her.

"So he dumped you off onto me," Ben said. "I wish I could thank him."

"It wasn't like that. He loved you. He said for me to marry you and be happy."

50 "So you did. And I was stupid enough to go for it."

"He was a little boy. It was fun, but he was a little boy."

"I'm happy," Ben said, "things worked out so nice for you." She shook her head and didn't answer. Ben wondered what he should do. It was as if he had never been married, had been right in always imagining his life as single. He'd watched his friends settle, seen their kids start to grow up, and it had seemed those were things he was not entitled to, that he was going to grow old in a habit of taverns, rented rooms, separate from the married world. And now he was still there, outside. And she'd kept it all a secret. "You stinking pig," he said slowly.

"Ben, it was a long time ago. Ben."

He was tired and his work was waiting. Maybe it was a long time ago and maybe it wasn't. He left her there crying while he dressed to go out and feed her father's cattle.

55 In the afternoon she had the house picked up and a meal waiting. She watched while he ate, but they didn't talk. He asked if she wanted to go to the funeral, and she said no and that was all. When he was drinking his coffee, calm now, and so tired his chest ached, he started thinking about Clara. He wondered if she'd known. Wouldn't have made any difference, he thought. Not after everything else.

T HREE days later, heading for the burial, he was alone and hunched against the wheel, driving through new

> *"How come you married me? He turn you down?"*

snow that softly drifted across the highway. His fingers were numb, the broken cracks in the rough calluses ingrained with black. A tire chain ticked a fender, but he kept going. He'd gone out at daylight to feed, a mandatory job that had to be done every day of winter, regardless of other obligations. The rust-streaked Chevrolet swayed on the rutted ice beneath the snow. The steady and lumbering gait of the team he fed with, two massive frost-coated Belgian geldings, the creaking oceanic motion of the hay wagon, was still with him, more real than this.

The Derrick County cemetery was just below the road, almost five miles short of town. They were going to bury Art in the area reserved for charity burials, away from the lanes of Lombardy poplars and old-time lilacs. By dark the grave would be covered with snow. Ben parked and got out, and went over to look down in the hole. Far away in town, the bells of the Catholic church were faintly tolling. Ben stood a moment, then started back toward the car. He sat in the front seat with his hands cupped in his crotch, warming them. After a time, he backed slowly out of the graveyard.

Davanero was on the east side of the valley, scattered houses hung with ice, windows sealed against wind by tacked-on plastic sheeting. The still smoke of house fires rose straight up. Ben drove between lots heaped with snow-covered junk, past shacks with open, hanging doors where drifters lived in summer, into the center of town. The stores were open and a few people moved toward the coffee shops. He felt cut away from everything, as if this were an island in the center of winter.

The OPEN sign hung in the front window of The Tarpaper Shack. Ben wondered if Clara was tending bar and if she intended to go to the funeral. He parked and walked slowly through the snow to the door. The church bells were louder, close and direct now. Inside, the tavern was dark and barn-like, empty except for Clara, who was washing glasses in a metal sink. Ben went to the far end, where Art always sat, and eased onto a stool. "I'd take a shot," he said. "A double. Take one yourself."

60   "I'm closing up," she said. "So there's no use hanging around." She stayed at the sink and continued to wash glasses.

"You going to the funeral?" Ben said.

"I'm closing up." Her hands were still in the water. "I guess you need a drink," she said. "Go lock the door."

She was sitting in one of the booths when he got back. "You ain't going to the funeral?" he asked again.

"What good is that?"

"I guess you feel pretty bad."   65

"I guess." She drank quietly. "I would have took anything off him. Any damned thing. And that stupid bitch kills him. I would have given anything for his kid."

Ben finished his whiskey, and Clara took his glass and went for some more. "To hell with their goddamned funeral," he said.

Clara played some music on the jukebox, slow country stuff; and they danced staggering against the stools and the shuffleboard table, holding each other. She pushed him away after a few songs. "If you ain't one hell of a dancer," she said. "Art was a pretty dancer." She sat down in the booth and put an arm on the table and then lay her head alongside it, facing the wall. "Goddamn," she said. "I could cry. I ain't cried since I was a little girl," she said. "Not since then. Not since I was a little girl."

Ben wandered around the barroom, carrying his drink. He called his wife on the telephone. "You bet your sweet ass I'm drunk," he shouted when she answered, then hung up.

"Ain't you some hero," Clara said. She drank what whis-   70 key was left in her glass. "You're nothing," she said. "Absolutely nothing."

Outside, the bells had stopped. Nothing. That was what he felt like. Nothing. Like his hands were without strength to steer the car. He sat awhile in the front seat, then drove to the jail, a gray brick building with heavy wire mesh over the windows. The deputy, a small bald man in a gray uniform, sat behind the desk in the center of the main room, coffee cup beside him. He smiled when he saw Ben, but he didn't say anything.

"How's chances of seeing that girl?" Ben asked. He didn't know why he'd come. It was just some idea that because she'd hated Art enough to kill him, because of that, maybe she understood and could tell him, Ben, why he wasn't nothing. He knew, even while he spoke, that it was a stupid, drunk idea.

"Okay," the deputy said, after a minute. "Come on. I guess you got a right."

THEY went through two locked doors, back into a large cinder-block room without any windows. Light came from a long fluorescent tube overhead. Two cells were separated by steel bars six inches apart. The room was warm. The girl was sitting on a cot in the left-hand cell, legs crossed, with red hair straight down over her shoulders and wearing a wrinkled blue smock without any pockets. She was looking at her hands, which were folded in her lap. "What now?" she said when she looked up. Her voice was surprisingly loud.

75   "Ben wanted to see you," the deputy said.

"Like a zoo, ain't it." The girl grinned and raised and lowered her shoulders.

"And you're not one bit sorry?" Ben said. "Just a little bit sorry for what you did?"

"Not one bit," the girl said. "I've had plenty of time to think about that. I'm not. I'm happy. I feel good."

"He wasn't no bad man," Ben said. "Not really. He never really was."

80   "He sure as hell wasn't Winston Churchill. He never even *tried* to make me happy." She put her hands in her lap.

"I don't see it," Ben said. "No way I can see you're right. He wasn't that bad."

"The thing I liked about him," she said, "was that he was old enough. He was like you. He was old enough to do anything. He could have been nice if he'd wanted."

"I felt so bad before," the girl said, "killing him was easy. . . ."

The deputy laughed.

"I felt so bad before," the girl said, "killing him was easy. The only thing I feel bad about is that I never got down into him and made him crawl around. That's the only thing. I'm sorry about that, but that's all."

"He didn't owe you nothing," Ben   85
said.

The girl looked at the deputy. "Make him leave," she said.

BEN drove slowly home in the falling snow. He could only see blurred outlines of the trees on either side of the lane that led to his house. He parked the car, kicked the snow from his boots, and went inside the house. Marie was in the bedroom, sleeping. The dim room was gray and cold, the bed a rumpled island. Marie was on her back, her stomach a mound beneath the blankets. Her mouth gaped a little.

After he got out of his clothes, Ben sat on the edge of the bed. Marie sighed in her sleep and moved a little, but she didn't waken. Ben reached to touch her shoulder and then stopped. Her eyelids flickered open. "Come on," she said. "Get under the covers."

"In a minute," Ben said. He went back out to the kitchen and smoked a cigarette. Then he went back into the bedroom and crawled in beside her and put his hand on her belly, hoping to feel the baby move. He remembered a warm, shirtsleeve day in February, working with Art, hurrying while they fed a final load of bales to the cattle that trailed behind, eager to get to town, noon sun glaring off wind-glazed fields of snow.

IF YOU LIKED "THIRTY-FOUR SEASONS OF WINTER," YOU MIGHT ALSO LIKE . . .

. . . Barry Lopez's exploration of the open spaces of what is modern-day Nebraska in "The Location of the River" (Chapter 10) or the Case Study on the American West with stories by Dagoberto Gilb, Leslie Marmon Silko, and John Steinbeck (Chapter 15).

GOING FURTHER William Kittredge has called his fellow Montanan, the late James Welch, a "hero." Deeply rooted in regional and Native American narrative traditions, Welch's *Winter in the Blood* has been praised by many, including Louise Erdrich, who calls it a "central and inspiring text for regional and Native American writers." Kittredge's unflinchingly honest memoir *A Hole in the Sky* recounts his growing up on a conquered land and the need for healing.

Writing from Reading

Summarize

1 Ben and Art seek the comfort and solace of love without knowing how to go about making it stay in their lives. Describe the varieties of love in this story. Which love do you think is at the heart of this tale?

Analyze Craft

2 Think about what you know of the West. Are there details in the story that fit your view of the West? If so, what are they? Are there any that surprised you?

3 How would this story change if it were to take place in another state or region?

4 How does the writer portray nature in this story? You might want to consider how the characters are feeling when they are outdoors and what actions they perform while outdoors as opposed to in indoor scenes.

Analyze Voice

5 Consider how different this work would be if it were called "Seasons of Winter" or, simply, "Winter." How does the inclusion of "Thirty-Four" affect the tone of the story? What does it imply?

Synthesize Summary and Analysis

6 Consider the relationships among the four main characters. Which relationship seems to mean the most to Ben? Support your answer with details about the character that suggest his or her importance to Ben.

Interpret the Story

7 Why can't Art accept the type of love Clara is able to give? What does the tragedy imply about love? What is the significance of Ben's vivid memory, described in the last line ("a warm, shirtless day in February, working with Art")?

Jhumpa Lahiri (b. 1967)

Growing up in Rhode Island as the daughter of South Asian parents, Jhumpa Lahiri struggled with her identity, later reflecting that her "conflicting selves always cancel[ed] each other out." Although she was born in London, her parents moved to the United States when she was two, so Lahiri's two conflicting selves became Indian and American. These identities form the touchstone of her fiction, as she explores issues faced by Indian immigrants (especially Benga-

lis) as they adapt to new surroundings and cultural expectations. After earning three master's degrees—in English, creative writing, and comparative studies in literature and the arts—and a Ph.D in Renaissance studies from Boston University, Lahiri taught creative writing at Boston University and the Rhode Island School of Art and Design. Her life, however, was disrupted by celebrity when she published *Interpreter of Maladies,* a collection of short stories that won a Pulitzer Prize and the PEN/Hemingway Award, among others, and became an

international best seller translated into twenty-nine languages. She became so famous, in fact, that the media had to be held at bay at her wedding to Alberto Vourvoulias, a Guatemalan-Greek journalist. Lahiri published her first novel, *The Namesake,* in 2003. Like her short stories, *The Namesake* focuses on themes such as marital and family difficulties, on the attempts of first- and second-generation immigrants to understand one another, and particularly on what it means to be Indian and to be assimilated. The novel was made into a major motion picture in 2006. Her most recent collection of stories, *Unaccustomed Earth,* was published in 2008.

As she said in an interview, the "question of identity is always a difficult one, but especially so for those who are culturally displaced, as immigrants are, or those who grow up in two worlds simultaneously, as is the case for their children: The older I get, the more I am aware that I have somehow inherited a sense of exile from my parents, even though in many ways I am so much more American than they are. In fact, it is still very hard to think of myself as an American."

AS YOU READ Notice how the personalities and situations of the characters are revealed. How do your feelings about them change as you get to know them better? How do you interpret their maladies?

TIP

FOR INTERACTIVE READING . . .

Trace the theme of interpretation and translation over the course of the story. Mark places in the text where any of the characters offers an interpretation.

Interpreter of Maladies (1999)

1   AT the tea stall Mr. and Mrs. Das bickered about who should take Tina to the toilet. Eventually Mrs. Das relented when Mr. Das pointed out that he had given the girl her bath the night before. In the rearview mirror Mr. Kapasi watched as Mrs. Das emerged slowly from his bulky white Ambassador, dragging her shaved, largely bare legs across the back seat. She did not hold the little girl's hand as they walked to the rest room.

They were on their way to see the Sun Temple at Konarak. It was a dry, bright Saturday, the mid-July heat tempered by a steady ocean breeze, ideal weather for sightseeing. Ordinarily Mr. Kapasi would not have stopped so soon along the way, but less than five minutes after he'd picked up the family that morning in front of Hotel Sandy Villa, the little girl had complained. The first thing Mr. Kapasi had noticed when he saw Mr. and Mrs. Das, standing with their children under the portico of the hotel, was that they were very young, perhaps not even thirty. In addition to Tina they had two boys, Ronny and Bobby, who appeared very close in age and had teeth covered in a network of flashing silver wires. The family looked Indian but dressed as foreigners did, the children in stiff, brightly colored clothing and caps with translucent visors. Mr. Kapasi was accustomed to foreign tourists; he was assigned to them regularly because he could speak English. Yesterday he had driven an elderly couple from Scotland, both with spotted faces and fluffy white hair so thin it exposed their sunburnt scalps. In comparison, the tanned youthful faces of Mr. and Mrs. Das were all the more striking. When he'd introduced himself, Mr. Kapasi had pressed his palms together in greeting, but Mr. Das squeezed hands like an American so that Mr. Kapasi felt it in his elbow. Mrs. Das, for her part, had flexed one side of her mouth, smiling dutifully at Mr. Kapasi, without displaying any interest in him.

As they waited at the tea stall, Ronny, who looked like the older of the two boys, clambered suddenly out of the back seat, intrigued by a goat tied to a stake in the ground.

"Don't touch it," Mr. Das said. He glanced up from his paperback tour book, which said "INDIA" in yellow letters and looked as if it had been published abroad. His voice, somehow tentative and a little shrill, sounded as though it had not yet settled into maturity.

5   "I want to give it a piece of gum," the boy called back as he trotted ahead.

Mr. Das stepped out of the car and stretched his legs by squatting briefly to the ground. A clean-shaven man, he looked exactly like a magnified version of Ronny. He had a sapphire blue visor, and was dressed in shorts, sneakers, and a T-shirt. The camera slung around his neck, with an impressive telephoto lens and numerous buttons and markings, was the only complicated thing he wore. He frowned, watching as Ronny rushed toward the goat, but appeared to have no intention of intervening. "Bobby, make sure that your brother doesn't do anything stupid."

"I don't feel like it," Bobby said, not moving. He was sitting in the front seat beside Mr. Kapasi, studying a picture of the elephant god taped to the glove compartment.

"No need to worry," Mr. Kapasi said. "They are quite tame." Mr. Kapasi was forty-six years old, with receding hair that had gone completely silver, but his butterscotch complexion and his unlined brow, which he treated in spare moments to dabs of lotus-oil balm, made it easy to imagine what he must have looked like at an earlier age. He wore gray trousers and a matching jacket-style shirt, tapered at the waist, with short sleeves and a large pointed collar, made of a thin but durable synthetic material. He had specified both the cut and the fabric to his tailor—it was his preferred uniform for giving tours because it did not get crushed during his long hours behind the wheel. Through the windshield he watched as Ronny circled around the goat, touched it quickly on its side, then trotted back to the car.

"You left India as a child?" Mr. Kapasi asked when Mr. Das had settled once again into the passenger seat.

10   "Oh, Mina and I were both born in America," Mr. Das announced with an air of sudden confidence. "Born and raised. Our parents live here now, in Assansol. They retired. We visit them every couple years." He turned to watch as the little girl ran toward the car, the wide purple bows of her sundress flopping on her narrow brown shoulders. She was holding to her chest a doll with yellow hair that looked as if it had been chopped, as a punitive measure, with a pair of dull scissors. "This is Tina's first trip to India, isn't it, Tina?"

"I don't have to go to the bathroom anymore," Tina announced.

"Where's Mina?" Mr. Das asked.

Mr. Kapasi found it strange that Mr. Das should refer to his wife by her first name when speaking to the little girl. Tina pointed to where Mrs. Das was purchasing something from one of the shirtless men who worked at the tea stall. Mr. Kapasi heard one of the shirtless men sing a phrase from a popular Hindi love song as Mrs. Das walked back to the car, but she did not appear to understand the words of the song, for she did not express irritation, or embarrassment, or react in any other way to the man's declarations.

He observed her. She wore a red-and-white-checkered skirt that stopped above her knees, slip-on shoes with a square wooden heel, and a close-fitting blouse styled like a man's undershirt. The blouse was decorated at chest-level with a calico appliqué in the shape of a strawberry. She was a short woman, with small hands like paws, her frosty pink fingernails painted to match her lips, and was slightly plump in her figure. Her hair, shorn only a little longer than her husband's, was parted far to one side. She was wearing large dark brown sunglasses with a pinkish tint to them, and carried a big straw bag, almost as big as her torso, shaped like a bowl, with a water bottle poking out of it. She walked slowly, carrying some puffed rice tossed with peanuts and chili peppers in a large packet made from newspapers. Mr. Kapasi turned to Mr. Das.

"Where in America do you live?"   15

"New Brunswick, New Jersey."

"Next to New York?"

"Exactly. I teach middle school there."

"What subject?"

"Science. In fact, every year I take my students on a trip   20 to the Museum of Natural History in New York City. In a way we have a lot in common, you could say, you and I. How long have you been a tour guide, Mr. Kapasi?"

"Five years."

Mrs. Das reached the car. "How long's the trip?" she asked, shutting the door.

"About two and a half hours," Mr. Kapasi replied.

At this Mrs. Das gave an impatient sigh, as if she had been traveling her whole life without pause. She fanned herself with a folded Bombay film magazine written in English.

25 "I thought that the Sun Temple is only eighteen miles north of Puri," Mr. Das said, tapping on the tour book.

"The roads to Konarak are poor. Actually it is a distance of fifty-two miles," Mr. Kapasi explained.

Mr. Das nodded, readjusting the camera strap where it had begun to chafe the back of his neck.

Before starting the ignition, Mr. Kapasi reached back to make sure the cranklike locks on the inside of each of the back doors were secured. As soon as the car began to move the little girl began to play with the lock on her side, clicking it with some effort forward and backward, but Mrs. Das said nothing to stop her. She sat a bit slouched at one end of the back seat, not offering her puffed rice to anyone. Ronny and Tina sat on either side of her, both snapping bright green gum.

"Look," Bobby said as the car began to gather speed. He pointed with his finger to the tall trees that lined the road. "Look."

30 "Monkeys!" Ronny shrieked. "Wow!"

They were seated in groups along the branches, with shining black faces, silver bodies, horizontal eyebrows, and crested heads. Their long gray tails dangled like a series of ropes among the leaves. A few scratched themselves with black leathery hands, or swung their feet, staring as the car passed.

"We call them the hanuman," Mr. Kapasi said. "They are quite common in the area."

As soon as he spoke, one of the monkeys leaped into the middle of the road, causing Mr. Kapasi to brake suddenly. Another bounced onto the hood of the car, then sprang away. Mr. Kapasi beeped his horn. The children began to get excited, sucking in their breath and covering their faces partly with their hands. They had never seen monkeys outside of a zoo, Mr. Das explained. He asked Mr. Kapasi to stop the car so that he could take a picture.

While Mr. Das adjusted his telephoto lens, Mrs. Das reached into her straw bag and pulled out a bottle of colorless nail polish, which she proceeded to stroke on the tip of her index finger.

The little girl stuck out a hand. "Mine too. Mommy, do 35 mine too."

"Leave me alone," Mrs. Das said, blowing on her nail and turning her body slightly. "You're making me mess up."

The little girl occupied herself by buttoning and unbuttoning a pinafore on the doll's plastic body.

"All set," Mr. Das said, replacing the lens cap.

The car rattled considerably as it raced along the dusty road, causing them all to pop up from their seats every now and then, but Mrs. Das continued to polish her nails. Mr. Kapasi eased up on the accelerator, hoping to produce a smoother ride. When he reached for the gearshift the boy in front accommodated him by swinging his hairless knees out of the way. Mr. Kapasi noted that this boy was slightly paler than the other children. "Daddy, why is the driver sitting on the wrong side in this car, too?" the boy asked.

"They all do that here, dummy," Ronny said. 40

"Don't call your brother a dummy," Mr. Das said. He turned to Mr. Kapasi. "In America, you know . . . it confuses them."

"Oh yes, I am well aware," Mr. Kapasi said. As delicately as he could, he shifted gears again, accelerating as they approached a hill in the road. "I see it on *Dallas*, the steering wheels are on the left-hand side."

"What's *Dallas*?" Tina asked, banging her now naked doll on the seat behind Mr. Kapasi.

"It went off the air," Mr. Das explained. "It's a television show."

They were all like siblings, Mr. Kapasi thought as they 45 passed a row of date trees. Mr. and Mrs. Das behaved like an older brother and sister, not parents. It seemed that they were in charge of the children only for the day; it was hard to believe they were regularly responsible for anything other than themselves. Mr. Das tapped on his lens cap, and his tour book, dragging his thumbnail occasionally across the pages so that they made a scraping sound. Mrs. Das continued to polish her nails. She had still not removed her sunglasses. Every now and then Tina renewed her plea that she wanted her nails done, too, and so at one point Mrs. Das flicked a drop of polish on the little girl's finger before depositing the bottle back inside her straw bag.

"Isn't this an air-conditioned car?" she asked, still blowing on her hand. The window on Tina's side was broken and could not be rolled down.

"Quit complaining," Mr. Das said. "It isn't so hot."

"I told you to get a car with air-conditioning," Mrs. Das continued. "Why do you do this, Raj, just to save a few stupid rupees. What are you saving us, fifty cents?"

Their accents sounded just like the ones Mr. Kapasi heard on American television programs, though not like the ones on *Dallas*.

50   "Doesn't it get tiresome, Mr. Kapasi, showing people the same thing every day?" Mr. Das asked, rolling down his own window all the way. "Hey, do you mind stopping the car. I just want to get a shot of this guy."

Mr. Kapasi pulled over to the side of the road as Mr. Das took a picture of a barefoot man, his head wrapped in a dirty turban, seated on top of a cart of grain sacks pulled by a pair of bullocks. Both the man and the bullocks were emaciated. In the back seat Mrs. Das gazed out another window, at the sky, where nearly transparent clouds passed quickly in front of one another.

"I look forward to it, actually," Mr. Kapasi said as they continued on their way. "The Sun Temple is one of my favorite places. In that way it is a reward for me. I give tours on Fridays and Saturdays only. I have another job during the week."

"Oh? Where?" Mr. Das asked.

"I work in a doctor's office."

55   "You're a doctor?"

"I am not a doctor. I work with one. As an interpreter."

"What does a doctor need an interpreter for?"

"He has a number of Gujarati patients. My father was Gujarati, but many people do not speak Gujarati in this area, including the doctor. And so the doctor asked me to work in his office, interpreting what the patients say."

"Interesting. I've never heard of anything like that," Mr. Das said.

60   Mr. Kapasi shrugged. "It is a job like any other."

"But so romantic," Mrs. Das said dreamily, breaking her extended silence. She lifted her pinkish brown sunglasses and arranged them on top of her head like a tiara. For the first time, her eyes met Mr. Kapasi's in the rearview mirror: pale, a bit small, their gaze fixed but drowsy.

Mr. Das craned to look at her. "What's so romantic about it?"

"I don't know. Something." She shrugged, knitting her brows together for an instant. "Would you like a piece of gum, Mr. Kapasi?" she asked brightly. She reached into her straw bag and handed him a small square wrapped in green-and-white-striped paper. As soon as Mr. Kapasi put the gum in his mouth a thick sweet liquid burst onto his tongue.

"Tell us more about your job, Mr. Kapasi," Mrs. Das said.

"What would you like to know, 65 madame?"

"I don't know," she shrugged, munching on some puffed rice and licking the mustard oil from the corners of her mouth. "Tell us a typical situation." She settled back in her seat, her head tilted in a patch of sun, and closed her eyes. "I want to picture what happens."

"Very well. The other day a man came in with a pain in his throat."

"Did he smoke cigarettes?"

"No. It was very curious. He complained that he felt as if there were long pieces of straw stuck in his throat. When I told the doctor he was able to prescribe the proper medication."

"That's so neat."

"Yes," Mr. Kapasi agreed after some hesitation. 70

"So these patients are totally dependent on you," Mrs. Das said. She spoke slowly, as if she were thinking aloud. "In a way, more dependent on you than the doctor."

"How do you mean? How could it be?"

"Well, for example, you could tell the doctor that the pain felt like a burning, not straw. The patient would never know what you had told the doctor, and the doctor wouldn't know that you had told the wrong thing. It's a big responsibility."

"Yes, a big responsibility you have there, Mr. Kapasi," 75 Mr. Das agreed.

Mr. Kapasi had never thought of his job in such complimentary terms. To him it was a thankless occupation. He found nothing noble in interpreting people's maladies, assiduously translating the symptoms of so many swollen bones, countless cramps of bellies and bowels, spots on people's palms that changed color, shape, or size. The doctor, nearly half his age, had an affinity for bell-bottom trousers and made humorless jokes about the Congress party. Together they worked in a stale little infirmary where Mr. Kapasi's smartly tailored clothes clung to him in the heat, in spite of the blackened blades of a ceiling fan churning over their heads.

> **Mr. Kapasi had never thought of** his job in such complimentary terms.

The job was a sign of his failings. In his youth he'd been a devoted scholar of foreign languages, the owner of an impressive collection of dictionaries. He had dreamed of being an interpreter for diplomats and dignitaries, resolving conflicts between people and nations, settling disputes of which he alone could understand both sides. He was a self-educated man. In a series of notebooks, in the evenings before his parents settled his marriage, he had listed the common etymologies of words, and at one point in his life he was confident that he could converse, if given the opportunity, in English, French, Russian, Portuguese, and Italian, not to mention Hindi, Bengali, Orissi, and Gujarati. Now only a handful of European phrases remained in his memory, scattered words for things like saucers and chairs. English was the only non-Indian language he spoke fluently anymore. Mr. Kapasi knew it was not a remarkable talent. Sometimes he feared that his children knew better English than he did, just from watching television. Still, it came in handy for the tours.

He had taken the job as an interpreter after his first son, at the age of seven, contracted typhoid—that was how he had first made the acquaintance of the doctor. At the time Mr. Kapasi had been teaching English in a grammar school, and he bartered his skills as an interpreter to pay the increasingly exorbitant medical bills. In the end the boy had died one evening in his mother's arms, his limbs burning with fever, but then there was the funeral to pay for, and the other children who were born soon enough, and the newer, bigger house, and the good schools and tutors, and the fine shoes and the television, and the countless other ways he tried to console his wife and to keep her from crying in her sleep, and so when the doctor offered to pay him twice as much as he earned at the grammar school, he accepted. Mr. Kapasi knew that his wife had little regard for his career as an interpreter. He knew it reminded her of the son she'd lost, and that she resented the other lives he helped, in his own small way, to save. If ever she referred to his position, she used the phrase "doctor's assistant," as if the process of interpretation were equal to taking someone's temperature, or changing a bedpan. She never asked him about the patients who came to the doctor's office, or said that his job was a big responsibility.

For this reason it flattered Mr. Kapasi that Mrs. Das was so intrigued by his job. Unlike his wife, she had reminded him of its intellectual challenges. She had also used the word "romantic." She did not behave in a romantic way

toward her husband, and yet she had used the word to describe him. He wondered if Mr. and Mrs. Das were a bad match, just as he and his wife were. Perhaps they, too, had little in common apart from three children and a decade of their lives. The signs he recognized from his own marriage were there—the bickering, the indifference, the protracted silences. Her sudden interest in him, an interest she did not express in either her husband or her children, was mildly intoxicating. When Mr. Kapasi thought once again about how she had said "romantic," the feeling of intoxication grew.

He began to check his reflection in the rearview mirror **80** as he drove, feeling grateful that he had chosen the gray suit that morning and not the brown one, which tended to sag a little in the knees. From time to time he glanced through the mirror at Mrs. Das. In addition to glancing at her face he glanced at the strawberry between her breasts, and the golden brown hollow in her throat. He decided to tell Mrs. Das about another patient, and another: the young woman who had complained of a sensation of raindrops in her spine, the gentleman whose birthmark had begun to sprout hairs. Mrs. Das listened attentively, stroking her hair with a small plastic brush that resembled an oval bed of nails, asking more questions, for yet another example. The children were quiet, intent on spotting more monkeys in the trees, and Mr. Das was absorbed by his tour book, so it seemed like a private conversation between Mr. Kapasi and Mrs. Das. In this manner the next half hour passed, and when they stopped for lunch at a roadside restaurant that sold fritters and omelette sandwiches, usually something Mr. Kapasi looked forward to on his tours so that he could sit in peace and enjoy some hot tea, he was disappointed. As the Das family settled together under a magenta umbrella fringed with white and orange tassels, and placed their orders with one of the waiters who marched about in tricornered caps, Mr. Kapasi reluctantly headed toward a neighboring table.

"Mr. Kapasi, wait. There's room here," Mrs. Das called out. She gathered Tina onto her lap, insisting that he accompany them. And so, together, they had bottled mango juice and sandwiches and plates of onions and potatoes deep-fried in graham-flour batter. After finishing two omelette sandwiches Mr. Das took more pictures of the group as they ate.

"How much longer?" he asked Mr. Kapasi as he paused to load a new roll of film in the camera.

"About half an hour more."

By now the children had gotten up from the table to look at more monkeys perched in a nearby tree, so there was a considerable space between Mrs. Das and Mr. Kapasi. Mr. Das placed the camera to his face and squeezed one eye shut, his tongue exposed at one corner of his mouth. "This looks funny. Mina, you need to lean in closer to Mr. Kapasi."

85 She did. He could smell a scent on her skin, like a mixture of whiskey and rosewater. He worried suddenly that she could smell his perspiration, which he knew had collected beneath the synthetic material of his shirt. He polished off his mango juice in one gulp and smoothed his silver hair with his hands. A bit of the juice dripped onto his chin. He wondered if Mrs. Das had noticed.

She had not. "What's your address, Mr. Kapasi?" she inquired, fishing for something inside her straw bag.

"You would like my address?"

"So we can send you copies," she said. "Of the pictures." She handed him a scrap of paper which she had hastily ripped from a page of her film magazine. The blank portion was limited, for the narrow strip was crowded by lines of text and a tiny picture of a hero and heroine embracing under a eucalyptus tree.

The paper curled as Mr. Kapasi wrote his address in clear, careful letters. She would write to him, asking about his days interpreting at the doctor's office, and he would respond eloquently, choosing only the most entertaining anecdotes, ones that would make her laugh out loud as she read them in her house in New Jersey. In time she would reveal the disappointment of her marriage, and he his. In this way their friendship would grow, and flourish. He would possess a picture of the two of them, eating fried onions under a magenta umbrella, which he would keep, he decided, safely tucked between the pages of his Russian grammar. As his mind raced, Mr. Kapasi experienced a mild and pleasant shock. It was similar to a feeling he used to experience long ago when, after months of translating with the aid of a dictionary, he would finally read a passage from a French novel, or an Italian sonnet, and understand the words, one after another, unencumbered by his own efforts. In those moments Mr. Kapasi used to believe that all was right with the world, that all struggles were rewarded, that all of life's mistakes made sense in the end. The promise that he would hear from Mrs. Das now filled him with the same belief.

90 When he finished writing his address Mr. Kapasi handed her the paper, but as soon as he did so he worried that he had either misspelled his name, or accidentally reversed the numbers of his postal code. He dreaded the possibility of a lost letter, the photograph never reaching him, hovering somewhere in Orissa, close but ultimately unattainable. He thought of asking for the slip of paper again, just to make sure he had written his address accurately, but Mrs. Das had already dropped it into the jumble of her bag.

THEY reached Konarak at two-thirty. The temple, made of sandstone, was a massive pyramid-like structure in the shape of a chariot. It was dedicated to the great master of life, the sun, which struck three sides of the edifice as it made its journey each day across the sky. Twenty-four giant wheels were carved on the north and south sides of the plinth. The whole thing was drawn by a team of seven horses, speeding as if through the heavens. As they approached, Mr. Kapasi explained that the temple had been built between A.D. 1243 and 1255, with the efforts of twelve hundred artisans, by the great ruler of the Ganga dynasty, King Narasimhadeva the First, to commemorate his victory against the Muslim army.

"It says the temple occupies about a hundred and seventy acres of land," Mr. Das said, reading from his book.

"It's like a desert," Ronny said, his eyes wandering across the sand that stretched on all sides beyond the temple.

"The Chandrabhaga River once flowed one mile north of here. It is dry now," Mr. Kapasi said, turning off the engine.

95 They got out and walked toward the temple, posing first for pictures by the pair of lions that flanked the steps. Mr. Kapasi led them next to one of the wheels of the chariot, higher than any human being, nine feet in diameter.

"'The wheels are supposed to symbolize the wheel of life,'" Mr. Das read. "'They depict the cycle of creation, preservation, and achievement of realization.' Cool." He turned the page of his book. "'Each wheel is divided into eight thick and thin spokes, dividing the day into eight equal parts. The rims are carved with designs of birds and animals, whereas the medallions in the spokes are carved with women in luxurious poses, largely erotic in nature.'"

What he referred to were the countless friezes of entwined naked bodies, making love in various positions, women clinging to the necks of men, their knees wrapped eternally around their lovers' thighs. In addition to these were assorted scenes from daily life, of hunting and trading, of deer being killed with bows and arrows and marching warriors holding swords in their hands.

It was no longer possible to enter the temple, for it had filled with rubble years ago, but they admired the exterior, as did all the tourists Mr. Kapasi brought there, slowly strolling along each of its sides. Mr. Das trailed behind, taking pictures. The children ran ahead, pointing to figures of naked people, intrigued in particular by the Nagamithunas, the half-human, half-serpentine couples who were said, Mr. Kapasi told them, to live in the deepest waters of the sea. Mr. Kapasi was pleased that they liked the temple, pleased especially that it appealed to Mrs. Das. She stopped every three or four paces, staring silently at the carved lovers, and the processions of elephants, and the topless female musicians beating on two-sided drums.

Though Mr. Kapasi had been to the temple countless times, it occurred to him, as he, too, gazed at the topless women, that he had never seen his own wife fully naked. Even when they had made love she kept the panels of her blouse hooked together, the string of her petticoat knotted around her waist. He had never admired the backs of his wife's legs the way he now admired those of Mrs. Das, walking as if for his benefit alone. He had, of course, seen plenty of bare limbs before, belonging to the American and European ladies who took his tours. But Mrs. Das was different. Unlike the other women, who had an interest only in the temple, and kept their noses buried in a guidebook, or their eyes behind the lens of a camera, Mrs. Das had taken an interest in him.

100 Mr. Kapasi was anxious to be alone with her, to continue their private conversation, yet he felt nervous to walk at her side. She was lost behind her sunglasses, ignoring her husband's requests that she pose for another picture, walking past her children as if they were strangers. Worried that he might disturb her, Mr. Kapasi walked ahead, to admire, as he always did, the three life-sized bronze avatars of Surya, the sun god, each emerging from its own niche on the temple facade to greet the sun at dawn, noon, and evening. They wore elaborate headdresses, their languid, elongated eyes closed, their bare chests draped with carved chains and amulets. Hibiscus petals, offerings from previous visitors, were strewn at their gray-green feet. The last statue, on the northern wall of the temple, was Mr. Kapasi's favorite. This Surya had a tired expression, weary after a hard day of work, sitting astride a horse with folded legs. Even his horse's eyes were drowsy. Around his body were smaller sculptures of women in pairs, their hips thrust to one side.

"Who's that? Mrs. Das asked. He was startled to see that she was standing beside him.

"He is the Astachala-Surya," Mr. Kapasi said. "The setting sun."

"So in a couple of hours the sun will set right here?" She slipped a foot out of one of her square-heeled shoes, rubbed her toes on the back of her other leg.

"That is correct."

She raised her sunglasses for a moment, then put them 105 back on again. "Neat."

Mr. Kapasi was not certain exactly what the word suggested, but he had a feeling it was a favorable response. He hoped that Mrs. Das had understood Surya's beauty, his power. Perhaps they would discuss it further in their letters. He would explain things to her, things about India, and she would explain things to him about America. In its own way this correspondence would fulfill his dream, of serving as an interpreter between nations. He looked at her straw bag, delighted that his address lay nestled among its contents. When he pictured her so many thousands of miles away he plummeted, so much so that he had an overwhelming urge to wrap his arms around her, to freeze with her, even for an instant, in an embrace witnessed by his favorite Surya. But Mrs. Das had already started walking.

"When do you return to America?" he asked, trying to sound placid.

"In ten days."

He calculated: A week to settle in, a week to develop the pictures, a few days to compose her letter, two weeks to get to India by air. According to his schedule, allowing room for delays, he would hear from Mrs. Das in approximately six weeks' time.

THE family was silent as Mr. Kapasi drove them back, 110 a little past four-thirty, to Hotel Sandy Villa. The children had bought miniature granite versions of the chariot's wheels at a souvenir stand, and they turned them round in their hands. Mr. Das continued to read his book. Mrs. Das untangled Tina's hair with her brush and divided it into two little ponytails.

Mr. Kapasi was beginning to dread the thought of dropping them off. He was not prepared to begin his six-week wait to hear from Mrs. Das. As he stole glances at her in the rearview mirror, wrapping elastic bands around Tina's hair, he wondered how he might make the tour last a little longer. Ordinarily he sped back to Puri using a shortcut, eager to return home, scrub his feet and hands with sandalwood soap, and enjoy the evening newspaper and a cup of tea that his wife would serve him in silence. The thought of that silence, something to which he'd long been resigned, now oppressed him. It was then that he suggested visiting the hills at Udayagiri and Khandagiri, where a number of monastic dwellings were hewn out of the ground, facing one another across a defile. It was some miles away, but well worth seeing, Mr. Kapasi told them.

"Oh yeah, there's something mentioned about it in this book," Mr. Das said. "Built by a Jain king or something."

"Shall we go then?" Mr. Kapasi asked. He paused at a turn in the road. "It's to the left."

Mr. Das turned to look at Mrs. Das. Both of them shrugged.

115   "Left, left," the children chanted.

Mr. Kapasi turned the wheel, almost delirious with relief. He did not know what he would do or say to Mrs. Das once they arrived at the hills. Perhaps he would tell her what a pleasing smile she had. Perhaps he would compliment her strawberry shirt, which he found irresistibly becoming. Perhaps, when Mr. Das was busy taking a picture, he would take her hand.

He did not have to worry. When they got to the hills, divided by a steep path thick with trees, Mrs. Das refused to get out of the car. All along the path, dozens of monkeys were seated on stones, as well as on the branches of the trees. Their hind legs were stretched out in front and raised to shoulder level, their arms resting on their knees.

"My legs are tired," she said, sinking low in her seat. "I'll stay here."

"Why did you have to wear those stupid shoes?" Mr. Das said. "You won't be in the pictures."

120   "Pretend I'm there."

"But we could use one of these pictures for our Christmas card this year. We didn't get one of all five of us at the Sun Temple. Mr. Kapasi could take it."

"I'm not coming. Anyway, those monkeys give me the creeps."

"But they're harmless," Mr. Das said. He turned to Mr. Kapasi. "Aren't they?"

"They are more hungry than dangerous," Mr. Kapasi said. "Do not provoke them with food, and they will not bother you."

125   Mr. Das headed up the defile with the children, the boys at his side, the little girl on his shoulders. Mr. Kapasi watched as they crossed paths with a Japanese man and woman, the only other tourists there, who paused for a final photograph, then stepped into a nearby car and drove away. As the car disappeared out of view some of the monkeys called out, emitting soft whooping sounds, and then walked on their flat black hands and feet up the path. At one point a group of them formed a little ring around Mr. Das and the children. Tina screamed in delight. Ronny ran in circles around his father. Bobby bent down and picked up a fat stick on the ground. When he extended it, one of the monkey's approached him and snatched it, then briefly beat the ground.

> **The thought of that silence, something** to which he'd long been resigned, now oppressed him.

"I'll join them," Mr. Kapasi said, unlocking the door on his side. "There is much to explain about the caves."

"No. Stay a minute," Mrs. Das said. She got out of the back seat and slipped in beside Mr. Kapasi. "Raj has his dumb book anyway." Together, through the windshield, Mrs. Das and Mr. Kapasi watched as Bobby and the monkey passed the stick back and forth between them.

"A brave little boy," Mr. Kapasi commented.

"It's not so surprising," Mrs. Das said.

"No?"

"He's not his."

"I beg your pardon?"

"Raj's. He's not Raj's son."

Mr. Kapasi felt a prickle on his skin. He reached into his shirt pocket for the small tin of lotus-oil balm he carried with him at all times, and applied it to three spots on his forehead. He knew that Mrs. Das was watching him, but he did not turn to face her. Instead he watched as the figures of Mr. Das and the children grew smaller, climbing up the steep path, pausing every now and then for a picture, surrounded by a growing number of monkeys.

"Are you surprised?" The way she put it made him choose his words with care.

"It's not the type of thing one assumes," Mr. Kapasi replied slowly. He put the tin of lotus-oil balm back in his pocket.

"No, of course not. And no one knows, of course. No one at all. I've kept it a secret for eight whole years." She looked at Mr. Kapasi, tilting her chin as if to gain a fresh perspective. "But now I've told you."

130

135

Mr. Kapasi nodded. He felt suddenly parched, and his forehead was warm and slightly numb from the balm. He considered asking Mrs. Das for a sip of water, then decided against it.

"We met when we were very young," she said. She reached into her straw bag in search of something, then pulled out a packet of puffed rice. "Want some?"

"No, thank you."

She put a fistful in her mouth, sank into the seat a little, and looked away from Mr. Kapasi, out the window on her side of the car. "We married when we were still in college. We were in high school when he proposed. We went to the same college, of course. Back then we couldn't stand the thought of being separated, not for a day, not for a minute. Our parents were best friends who lived in the same town. My entire life I saw him every weekend, either at our house or theirs. We were sent upstairs to play together while our parents joked about our marriage. Imagine! They never caught us at anything, though in a way I think it was all more or less a setup. The things we did those Friday and Saturday nights, while our parents sat downstairs drinking tea . . . I could tell you stories, Mr. Kapasi."

As a result of spending all her time in college with Raj, she continued, she did not make many close friends. There was no one to confide in about him at the end of a difficult day, or to share a passing thought or a worry. Her parents now lived on the other side of the world, but she had never been very close to them, anyway. After marrying so young she was overwhelmed by it all, having a child so quickly, and nursing, and warming up bottles of milk and testing their temperature against her wrist while Raj was at work, dressed in sweaters and corduroy pants, teaching his students about rocks and dinosaurs. Raj never looked cross or harried, or plump as she had become after the first baby.

Always tired, she declined invitations from her one or two college girlfriends, to have lunch or shop in Manhattan. Eventually the friends stopped calling her, so that she was left at home all day with the baby, surrounded by toys that made her trip when she walked or wince when she sat, always cross and tired. Only occasionally did they go out after Ronny was born, and even more rarely did they entertain. Raj didn't mind; he looked forward to coming home from teaching and watching television and bouncing Ronny on his knee. She had been outraged when Raj told her that a Punjabi friend, someone whom she had once met but did not remember, would be staying with them for a week for some job interviews in the New Brunswick area.

Bobby was conceived in the afternoon, on a sofa littered with rubber teething toys, after the friend learned that a London pharmaceutical company had hired him, while Ronny cried to be freed from his playpen. She made no protest when the friend touched the small of her back as she was about to make a pot of coffee, then pulled her against his crisp navy suit. He made love to her swiftly, in silence, with an expertise she had never known, without the meaningful expressions and smiles Raj always insisted on afterward. The next day Raj drove the friend to JFK. He was married now, to a Punjabi girl, and they lived in London still, and every year they exchanged Christmas cards with Raj and Mina, each couple tucking photos of their families into the envelopes. He did not know that he was Bobby's father. He never would.

"I beg your pardon, Mrs. Das, but why have you told me this information?" Mr. Kapasi asked when she had finally finished speaking, and had turned to face him once again.

"For God's sake, stop calling me Mrs. Das. I'm twenty-eight. You probably have children my age."

"Not quite." It disturbed Mr. Kapasi to learn that she thought of him as a parent. The feeling he had had toward her, that had made him check his reflection in the rearview mirror as they drove, evaporated a little.

"I told you because of your talents." She put the packet of puffed rice back into her bag without folding over the top.

"I don't understand," Mr. Kapasi said.

150 "Don't you see? For eight years I haven't been able to express this to anybody, not to friends, certainly not to Raj. He doesn't even suspect it. He thinks I'm still in love with him. Well, don't you have anything to say?"

"About what?"

"About what I've just told you. About my secret, and about how terrible it makes me feel. I feel terrible looking at my children, and at Raj, always terrible. I have terrible urges, Mr. Kapasi, to throw things away. One day I had the urge to throw everything I own out the window, the television, the children, everything. Don't you think it's unhealthy?"

He was silent.

"Mr. Kapasi, don't you have anything to say? I thought that was your job."

155 "My job is to give tours, Mrs. Das."

"Not that. Your other job. As an interpreter."

"But we do not face a language barrier. What need is there for an interpreter?"

"That's not what I mean. I would never have told you otherwise. Don't you realize what it means for me to tell you?"

"What does it mean?"

160 "It means that I'm tired of feeling so terrible all the time. Eight years, Mr. Kapasi, I've been in pain eight years. I was hoping you could help me feel better, say the right thing. Suggest some kind of remedy."

He looked at her, in her red plaid skirt and strawberry T-shirt, a woman not yet thirty, who loved neither her husband nor her children, who had already fallen out of love with life. Her confession depressed him, depressed him all the more when he thought of Mr. Das at the top of the path, Tina clinging to his shoulders, taking pictures of ancient monastic cells cut into the hills to show his students in America, unsuspecting and unaware that one of his sons was not his own. Mr. Kapasi felt insulted that Mrs. Das should ask him to interpret her common, trivial little secret. She did not resemble the patients in the doctor's office, those who came glassy-eyed and desperate, unable to sleep or breathe or urinate with ease, unable, above all, to give words to their pains. Still, Mr. Kapasi believed it was his duty to assist Mrs. Das. Perhaps he ought to tell her to confess the truth to Mr. Das. He would explain that honesty was the best policy. Honesty, surely, would help her feel better, as she'd put it. Perhaps he would offer to preside over the discussion, as a mediator. He decided to begin with the most obvious question, to get to the heart of the matter, and so he asked, "Is it really pain you feel, Mrs. Das, or is it guilt?"

She turned to him and glared, mustard oil thick on her frosty pink lips. She opened her mouth to say something, but as she glared at Mr. Kapasi some certain knowledge seemed to pass before her eyes, and she stopped. It crushed him; he knew at that moment that he was not even important enough to be properly insulted. She opened the car door and began walking up the path, wobbling a little on her square wooden heels, reaching into her straw bag to eat handfuls of puffed rice. It fell through her fingers, leaving a zigzagging trail, causing a monkey to leap down from a tree and devour the little white grains. In search of more, the monkey began to follow Mrs. Das. Others joined him, so that she was soon being followed by about half a dozen of them, their velvety tails dragging behind.

Mr. Kapasi stepped out of the car. He wanted to holler, to alert her in some way, but he worried that if she knew they were behind her, she would grow nervous. Perhaps she would lose her balance. Perhaps they would pull at her bag or her hair. He began to jog up the path, taking a fallen branch in his hand to scare away the monkeys. Mrs. Das continued walking, oblivious, trailing grains of puffed rice. Near the top of the incline, before a group of cells fronted by a row of squat stone pillars, Mr. Das was kneeling on the ground, focusing the lens of his camera. The children stood under the arcade, now hiding, now emerging from view.

"Wait for me," Mrs. Das called out. "I'm coming."

Tina jumped up and down. "Here comes Mommy!" 165

"Great," Mr. Das said without looking up. "Just in time. We'll get Mr. Kapasi to take a picture of the five of us."

Mr. Kapasi quickened his pace, waving his branch so that the monkeys scampered away, distracted, in another direction.

"Where's Bobby?" Mrs. Das asked when she stopped.

Mr. Das looked up from the camera. "I don't know. Ronny, where's Bobby?"

> ## He thinks I'm still in love with him.

170   Ronny shrugged. "I thought he was right here."

"Where is he?" Mrs. Das repeated sharply. "What's wrong with all of you?"

They began calling his name, wandering up and down the path a bit. Because they were calling, they did not initially hear the boy's screams. When they found him, a little farther down the path under a tree, he was surrounded by a group of monkeys, over a dozen of them, pulling at his T-shirt with their long black fingers. The puffed rice Mrs. Das had spilled was scattered at his feet, raked over by the monkeys' hands. The boy was silent, his body frozen, swift tears running down his startled face. His bare legs were dusty and red with welts from where one of the monkeys struck him repeatedly with the stick he had given it earlier.

"Daddy, the monkey's hurting Bobby," Tina said.

Mr. Das wiped his palms on the front of his shorts. In his nervousness he accidentally pressed the shutter on his camera; the whirring noise of the advancing film excited the monkeys, and the one with the stick began to beat Bobby more intently. "What are we supposed to do? What if they start attacking?"

175   "Mr. Kapasi," Mrs. Das shrieked, noticing him standing to one side. "Do something, for God's sake, do something!"

Mr. Kapasi took his branch and shooed them away, hissing at the ones that remained, stomping his feet to scare them. The animals retreated slowly, with a measured gait, obedient but unintimidated. Mr. Kapasi gathered Bobby in his arms and brought him back to where his parents and siblings were standing. As he carried him he was tempted to whisper a secret into the boy's ear. But Bobby was stunned, and shivering with fright, his legs bleeding slightly where the stick had broken the skin. When Mr. Kapasi delivered him to his parents, Mr. Das brushed some dirt off the boy's T-shirt and put the visor on him the right way. Mrs. Das reached into her straw bag to find a bandage which she taped over the cut on his knee. Ronny offered his brother a fresh piece of gum. "He's fine. Just a little scared, right, Bobby?" Mr. Das said, patting the top of his head.

"God, let's get out of here," Mrs. Das said. She folded her arms across the strawberry on her chest. "This place gives me the creeps."

"Yeah. Back to the hotel, definitely," Mr. Das agreed.

"Poor Bobby," Mrs. Das said. "Come here a second. Let Mommy fix your hair." Again she reached into her straw bag, this time for her hairbrush, and began to run it around the edges of the translucent visor. When she whipped out the hairbrush, the slip of paper with Mr. Kapasi's address on it fluttered away in the wind. No one but Mr. Kapasi noticed. He watched as it rose, carried higher and higher by the breeze, into the trees where the monkeys now sat, solemnly observing the scene below. Mr. Kapasi observed it too, knowing that this was the picture of the Das family he would preserve forever in his mind.

> **The animals retreated slowly, with a** measured gait, obedient but unintimidated.

IF YOU LIKED "INTERPRETER OF MALADIES," YOU MIGHT ALSO LIKE . . .

. . . the Amy Tan story in this chapter, "Two Kinds," also about the meeting of New World values and Old.

GOING FURTHER   Lahiri's more recent fiction, such as *The Namesake* and *Unaccustomed Earth*, belongs to a long line of books that dramatize in universal ways the themes that grow out of immigration to the United States. Examples include Henry Roth's 1934 classic *Call It Sleep*, about immigrant Jews living in New York City's slums, Edwidge Danticat's *The Dew Breaker*, and Junot Diaz's Pulitzer Prize-winning novel of 2007, *The Brief Wondrous Life of Oscar Wao.*

Writing from Reading

Summarize

1 Examine Mr. Kapasi's daydreams of his future with Mrs. Das. What does he expect from their interactions? What is it that he is looking for that he doesn't currently have with his wife?

Analyze Craft

2 Discuss why the story begins with Mr. Kapasi's observations of Mrs. Das, and how they help set up what the story is *about*.

3 Analyze the thematic importance of the story's title. What are the mala-dies in this story? What does it mean to be an interpreter of maladies?

Analyze Voice

4 Jhumpa Lahiri has referred to her conflicting selves—the Indian and the American. How does this dual cultural background come through in her narration of "Interpreter of Maladies"? What details and themes strike you as more American or more Indian? Explain why.

Synthesize Summary and Analysis

5 Discuss what role the monkeys play in the story. Consider when and where they appear and how various characters respond to them.

Interpret the Story

6 While they wait for Tina and Mrs. Das to emerge from the bathroom, Mr. Das says to Mr. Kapasi: "We have a lot in common, you could say, you and I." Is this true? What do these two men have in common? Explain how the rest of the story serves to prove, disprove, or change the meaning of this statement.

"What is the story in there that is the meaning to you? . . . You're absolutely unique. And if you said what's the essence of who you are? I mean, Don't you want to know that in yourself? What is it about each of us that is so special? For that time we are on Earth, what is it that made us so different from billions and billions of people? It's a great question to ask yourself. It makes your life very, very interesting no matter what happens." Conversation with Amy Tan

Reading for Theme

When reading for **theme,** go beyond the plot and subject of the story and ask yourself what truths or insights about the human experience the story offers.

Does the title point to a major symbol, character, or subject from which themes develop?	EXAMPLES "The Jilting of Granny Weatherall," "The Things They Carried," and "The Gilded Six-Bits"
Does the title point to a central irony that is thematic?	EXAMPLES "Good Country People," "Interpreter of Maladies"
Does the title point to thematic concerns of the story?	EXAMPLES "Who's Irish?" calls up the question of identity. "Araby" conjures an exotic dream. "The Rememberer" calls to mind the person left behind after a loss.
Does the narrator or another character make general statements as observations that may offer insight into the writer's theme?	EXAMPLE *Moby-Dick's* narrator asserts that a subject must be larger than ordinary or everyday to accommodate a large theme.
What changes in the main character? What does the main character come to realize?	EXAMPLES In Alice Munro's "An Ounce of Cure," the narrator says in the last line, "I am a grown-up woman now." In John Updike's "A&P," the young narrator realizes "how hard the world was going to be to . . . [him] from here on in."

Note powerful details and ask yourself why these are important. What do they make you feel? How do events or details thread together the meaning beyond a particular situation?	EXAMPLES The old piano teacher that had lost his hearing (What do *I* feel when *I* think about the "sleepy" Old Chong?) The mother's background in China (*How* did these events affect Jing-mei?) The way Jing-mei felt when defying her mother (*Why* did she feel such rage?)

A literary work can have multiple themes. Does the proposed theme tie the elements of the story together? Ask questions that go beyond the surface and the events. Theme grows seamlessly from plot, setting, style, characterization, and all the other elements of the writer's craft. In each, theme emerges from our reading and questioning of the story in all its twists and permutations.

How do you state a theme?	• Formulate a general idea that is not tied to specific details in the story or to a particular character in the story but to all human beings. • Write a complete sentence that goes beyond the subject and includes some conclusion or attitude about the subject.	**Too limited:** Tan's "Two Kinds" is about a daughter who defies her mother's high expectations. **More precise:** "Two Kinds" is about the struggle for personal identity and how we often limit ourselves by defining who we are in relation to others' expectations. **Too broad:** Adulthood **More precise:** Adulthood can be a burden but also a highly prized period of life.

"Fiction's a fairly tough vehicle if it's done right, and it can survive, and engender life in a reader's mind out of a fairly unpromising or difficult base." Conversation with John Updike

Writing about Theme

1. How do Stephen Crane and Jhumpa Lahiri raise thematic issues by use of descriptions of setting? Compare the authors' techniques in "The Open Boat" and "Interpreter of Maladies."

2. Select two stories in this chapter and show how, although their plots differ, they explore a similar theme. Throughout, back up your claims with specific lines or passages from the story.

3. Compare and contrast the role of monkeys in "Interpreter of Maladies" with that of the seagulls in "The Open Boat."

4. Compare and contrast the theme of familial relationships in Kittredge's "Thirty-Four Seasons of Winter" and Tan's "Two Kinds." What do these stories say about loyalty and the strength of a familial bond? What difficulties do you see in the stepbrothers' relationship as compared with the mother-daughter relationship? Is what is said about the importance, or lack of importance, in the family bond significant thematically? What is the importance of family in each story?

14 SYM

"BRIEFLY, in the rain, Lieutenant Cross saw Martha's gray eyes gazing back at him. He understood.

It was very sad, he thought. The things men carried inside. The things men did or felt they had to do.

He almost nodded at her, but didn't.

Instead he went back to his maps. He was now determined to perform his duties firmly and without negligence. It wouldn't help Lavender, he knew that, but from this point on he would comport himself as an officer. He would dispose of his good-luck pebble. Swallow it, maybe, or use Lee Strunk's slingshot, or just drop it along the trail."

—*from "The Things They Carried" by Tim O'Brien*

BO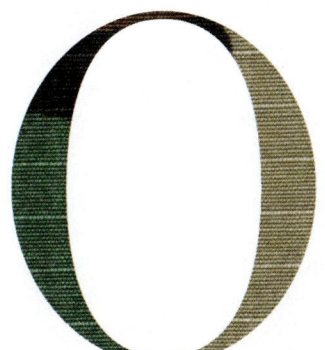E

A YOUNG American lieutenant in Vietnam during the war imagines the eyes of Martha, a girl back home who has become the center of his fantasies. During much of the action, he dreams of her love; now he understands that she has been a distraction and he must focus on duty instead. We've caught him in a sad, contemplative moment—coming to an understanding about the burdens of leadership and how he must "perform his duties firmly and without negligence." The boy at the beginning of Tim O'Brien's story "The Things They Carried" has "understood" and grown into a man.

This narrative introduces the members of Lieutenant Cross's platoon—describing in an inventory-like manner what each soldier carries on his back as well as in his heart. They trek through jungles and villages; they deal with weather, boredom, and enemy attack. By telling us what the soldiers carry, O'Brien shows us who they are—each with his special burden, each terrified and confused and, in his own way, heroic. If you think beyond the surface of the images in the story—the good-luck pebble, the maps, even the names Cross and Lavender—you enter the story in terms of its symbolic resonance.

A **symbol,** in the literary sense, is any object, image, character, or action that suggests meaning beyond the everyday literal level. In contemporary literature, symbols don't work in a simple equation of *A = B* or *This means that.* They acquire meaning from a rich matrix of associations. All elements—plot, character, point of view, setting, tone, and theme—contribute to the effect.

CONTINUED ON PAGE 438

Tim O'Brien *Art can be born out of play . . .*

A Conversation on Writing

On Becoming a Writer in Vietnam

I think that somewhere during those months in Vietnam, as I sat in those foxholes at night, was when writing became serious for me. It was serious not in the sense of "I'm going to publish" or "I'm going to be a writer," but the writing itself was serious. It was written partly, I think, as kind of a testament that, if I were to be killed, these words would be found on my person, would be sent to my mom or my dad or my sister, and they would have some sense of their son and brother's personality and spirit during those life-and-death days of war.

On Memory and Writing about War

"The Things They Carried" is organized around, just in terms of locale, foxholes. It takes place largely around men talking and reminiscing about girlfriends and hometowns and religion and the world they don't have . . . in those hours a soldier has that aren't full of horror and violence. . . . Moments in Vietnam were horrible. I don't remember much. I remember saying, "Dear Jesus, dear Jesus," as I was wounded, but I can't remember much before that or much afterwards, for that matter. What I do remember vividly are those quiet moments when you'd reflect back on what happened.

On the Writing Process

I had originally started writing *The Things They Carried* playfully as a game. . . . Art can be born out of playful intent, having fun. And my idea was to have fun with the word *carry*. I wanted to find how many ways can I use the word: *carry* himself with poise; *carry* yourself with dignity; *carried* in the usual sense; "*carry* on, men."

To watch this entire interview and hear the author read from "The Things They Carried," go to connect.mcgraw-hill.com.

A biography of Tim O'Brien (b. 1946) begins like many American biographies: He grew up in Minnesota and had a successful college career. However, the summer after graduation, O'Brien was drafted into the Vietnam War and embarked on an experience that shaped the rest of his life and much of his fiction. He fought for a little over a year, earning both a Purple Heart and a Bronze Star.

Like many of the characters in his fiction, O'Brien seems haunted by the experience of combat, unable to relegate it comfortably to the past. Although he has written on other topics, the majority of his books deal in some way with Vietnam and the transforming effects of battle—a battle from which there's no true escape. Continually, even obsessively, O'Brien describes the condition of life as a soldier and war's aftermath. It is his great subject and recurrent theme.

Such books as *Going After Cacciato* (1978), *The Nuclear Age* (1985), and *The Things They Carried* (1990) masterfully blend short story and memoir, fiction and nonfiction while exploring themes of courage, morality, love, truth, and ambiguity. In fact, O'Brien first published the short story "The Things They Carried" and later placed it as the leading chapter in his novel, *The Things They Carried*.

RESEARCH ASSIGNMENT In his interview, O'Brien says he could have set "The Things They Carried" in a different locale. How would this have changed the story, and what do you think the foxholes add to the setting of the story?

TIPS

FOR INTERACTIVE READING . . .

Choose three characters and circle all the things they carried. How do these objects characterize them? What do the objects reveal about them? Do these objects complete our understanding of the men or limit it? O'Brien introduces a vocabulary of war. Find and circle the special terms the men have for what they do and what they experience.

The Things They Carried (1986)

1   FIRST Lieutenant Jimmy Cross carried letters from a girl named Martha, a junior at Mount Sebastian College in New Jersey. They were not love letters, but Lieutenant Cross was hoping, so he kept them folded in plastic at the bottom of his rucksack. In the late afternoon, after a day's march, he would dig his foxhole, wash his hands under a canteen, unwrap the letters, hold them with the tips of his fingers, and spend the last hour of light pretending. He would imagine romantic camping trips into the White Mountains in New Hampshire. He would sometimes taste the envelope flaps, knowing her tongue had been there. More than anything, he wanted Martha to love him as he loved her, but the letters were mostly chatty, elusive on the matter of love. She was a virgin, he was almost sure. She was an English major at Mount Sebastian, and she wrote beautifully about her professors and roommates and midterm exams, about her respect for Chaucer and her great affection for Virginia Woolf. She often quoted lines of poetry; she never mentioned the war, except to say, Jimmy, take care of yourself. The letters weighed ten ounces. They were signed "Love, Martha,"

but Lieutenant Cross understood that "Love" was only a way of signing and did not mean what he sometimes pretended it meant. At dusk, he would carefully return the letters to his rucksack. Slowly, a bit distracted, he would get up and move among his men, checking the perimeter, then at full dark he would return to his hole and watch the night and wonder if Martha was a virgin.

The things they carried were largely determined by necessity. Among the necessities or near necessities were P-38 can openers, pocket knives, heat tabs, wrist watches, dog tags, mosquito repellant, chewing gum, candy, cigarettes, salt tablets, packets of Kool-Aid, lighters, matches, sewing kits, Military Payment Certificates, C rations, and two or three canteens of water. Together, these items weighed between fifteen and twenty pounds, depending upon a man's habits or rate of metabolism. Henry Dobbins, who was a big man, carried extra rations; he was especially fond of canned peaches in heavy syrup over pound cake. Dave Jensen, who practiced field hygiene, carried a toothbrush, dental floss, and several hotel-size bars of soap he'd stolen on R&R in Sydney, Australia. Ted Lavender, who was scared, carried tranquilizers until he was shot in the head outside the village of Than Khe in mid-April. By necessity, and because it was SOP, they all carried steel helmets that weighed five pounds including the liner and camouflage cover. They carried the standard fatigue jackets and trousers. Very few carried underwear. On their feet they carried jungle boots—2.1 pounds—and Dave Jensen carried three pairs of socks and a can of Dr. Scholl's foot powder as a precaution against trench foot. Until he was shot, Ted Lavender carried six or seven ounces of premium dope, which for him was a necessity. Mitchell Sanders, the RTO, carried condoms. Norman Bowker carried a diary. Rat Kiley carried comic books. Kiowa, a devout Baptist, carried an illustrated New Testament that had been presented to him by his father, who taught Sunday school in Oklahoma City, Oklahoma. As a hedge against bad times, however, Kiowa also carried his grandmother's distrust of the white man, his grandfather's old hunting hatchet. Necessity dictated. Because the land was mined and booby-trapped, it was SOP for each man to carry a steel-centered, nylon-covered flak jacket, which weighed 6.7 pounds, but which on hot days seemed much heavier. Because you could die so quickly, each man carried at least one large compress bandage, usually in the helmet band for easy access. Because the nights were cold, and because the monsoons were wet, each carried a green plastic poncho that could be used as a raincoat or groundsheet or makeshift tent. With its quilted liner, the poncho weighed almost two pounds, but it was worth every ounce. In April, for instance, when Ted Lavender was shot, they used his poncho to wrap him up, then to carry him across the paddy, then to lift him into the chopper that took him away.

THEY were called legs or grunts.

To carry something was to "hump" it, as when Lieutenant Jimmy Cross humped his love for Martha up the hills and through the swamps. In its intransi-tive form, "to hump," meant "to walk," or "to march," but it implied burdens far beyond the intransitive.

Almost everyone humped photographs. In his wallet, Lieutenant Cross carried two photographs of Martha. The first was a Kodachrome snapshot signed "Love," though he knew better. She stood against a brick wall. Her eyes were gray and neutral, her lips slightly open as she stared straight-on at the camera. At night, sometimes, Lieutenant Cross wondered who had taken the picture, because he knew she had boyfriends, because he loved her so much, and because he could see the shadow of the picture taker spreading out against the brick wall. The second photograph had been clipped from the 1968 Mount Sebastian yearbook. It was an action shot—women's volleyball—and Martha was bent horizontal to the floor, reaching, the palms of her hands in sharp focus, the tongue taut, the expression frank and competitive. There was no visible sweat. She wore white gym shorts. Her legs, he thought, were almost certainly the legs of a virgin, dry and without hair, the left knee cocked and carrying her entire weight, which was just over one hundred pounds. Lieutenant Cross remembered touching that left knee. A dark theater, he remembered, and the movie was *Bonnie and Clyde,* and Martha wore a tweed skirt, and during the final scene, when he touched her knee, she turned and looked at him in a sad, sober way that made him pull his hand back, but he would always remember the feel of the tweed skirt and the knee beneath it and the sound of the gunfire that killed Bonnie and Clyde, how embarrassing it was, how slow and oppressive. He remembered kissing her good night at the dorm door. Right then, he thought, he should've done something brave. He should've carried her up the stairs to her room and tied her to the bed and touched that left knee all night long. He should've risked it. Whenever he looked at the photographs, he thought of new things he should've done.

WHAT they carried was partly a function of rank, partly of field specialty.

As a first lieutenant and platoon leader, Jimmy Cross carried a compass, maps, code books, binoculars, and a .45-caliber pistol that weighed 2.9 pounds fully loaded. He carried a strobe light and the responsibility for the lives of his men.

As an RTO, Mitchell Sanders carried the PRC-25 radio, a killer, twenty-six pounds with its battery.

As a medic, Rat Kiley carried a canvas satchel filled with morphine and plasma and malaria tablets and surgical tape and comic books and all the things a medic must carry, including M&M's for especially bad wounds, for a total weight of nearly twenty pounds.

> He carried a strobe light and the responsibility for the lives of his men.

10   As a big man, therefore a machine gunner, Henry Dobbins carried the M-60, which weighed twenty-three pounds unloaded, but which was almost always loaded. In addition, Dobbins carried between ten and fifteen pounds of ammunition draped in belts across his chest and shoulders.

As PFCs or Spec 4s, most of them were common grunts and carried the standard M-16 gas-operated assault rifle. The weapon weighed 7.5 pounds unloaded, 8.2 pounds with its full twenty-round magazine. Depending on numerous factors, such as topography and psychology, the riflemen carried anywhere from twelve to twenty magazines, usually in cloth bandoliers, adding on another 8.4 pounds at minimum, fourteen pounds at maximum. When it was available, they also carried M-16 maintenance gear—rods and steel brushes and swabs and tubes of LSA oil—all of which weighed about a pound. Among the grunts, some carried the M-79 grenade launcher, 5.9 pounds unloaded, a reasonably light weapon except for the ammunition, which was heavy. A single round weighed ten ounces. The typical load was twenty-five rounds. But Ted Lavender, who was scared, carried thirty-four rounds when he was shot and killed outside Than Khe, and he went down under an exceptional burden, more than twenty pounds of ammunition, plus the flak jacket and helmet and rations and water and toilet paper and tranquilizers and all the rest, plus the unweighed fear. He was dead weight. There was no twitching or flopping. Kiowa, who saw it happen, said it was like watching a rock fall, or a big sandbag or something—just boom, then down—not like the movies where the dead guy rolls around and does fancy spins and goes ass over teakettle—not like that, Kiowa said, the poor bastard just flat-fuck fell. Boom. Down. Nothing else. It was a bright morning in mid-April. Lieutenant Cross felt the pain. He blamed himself. They stripped off Lavender's canteens and ammo, all the heavy things, and Rat Kiley said the obvious, the guy's dead, and Mitchell Sanders used his radio to report one U.S. KIA and to request a chopper. Then they wrapped Lavender in his poncho. They carried him out to a dry paddy, established security, and sat smoking the dead man's dope until the chopper came. Lieutenant Cross kept to himself. He pictured Martha's smooth young face, thinking he loved her more than anything, more than his men, and now Ted Lavender was dead because he loved her so much and could not stop thinking about her. When the dust-off arrived, they carried Lavender aboard. Afterward they burned Than Khe. They marched until dusk, then dug their holes, and that night Kiowa kept explaining how you had to be there, how fast it was, how the poor guy just dropped like so much concrete, Boom-down, he said. Like cement.

IN addition to the three standard weapons—the M-60, M-16, and M-79—they carried whatever presented itself, or whatever seemed appropriate as a means of killing or staying alive. They carried catch-as-catch-can. At various times, in various situations, they carried M-14s and CAR-15s and Swedish Ks and grease guns and captured AK-47s and ChiCom's and RPGs and Simonov carbines and black-market Uzis and .38-caliber Smith & Wesson handguns and 66 mm LAW's and shotguns and silencers and blackjacks and bayonets and C-4 plastic explosives. Lee Strunk carried a slingshot; a weapon of last resort, he called it. Mitchell Sanders carried brass knuckles. Kiowa carried his grandfather's feathered hatchet. Every third or fourth man carried a Claymore antipersonnel mine—3.5 pounds with its firing device. They all carried fragmentation grenades—fourteen ounces each. They all carried at least one M-18 colored smoke grenade—twenty-four ounces. Some carried CS or tear-gas grenades. Some carried white-phosphorus grenades. They carried all they could bear, and then some, including a silent awe for the terrible power of the things they carried.

In the first week of April, before Lavender died, Lieutenant Jimmy Cross received a good-luck charm from Martha. It was a simple pebble, an ounce at most. Smooth to the touch, it was a milky-white color with flecks of orange and violet, oval-shaped, like a miniature egg. In the accompanying letter, Martha wrote that she had found the pebble on the Jersey shoreline, precisely where the land touched water at high tide, where things came together but also separated. It was this separate-but-together quality, she wrote, that had inspired her to pick up the pebble and to carry it in her breast pocket for several days, where it seemed weightless, and then to send it through the mail, by air, as a token of her truest feelings for him. Lieutenant Cross found this romantic. But he wondered what her truest feelings were, exactly, and what she meant by separate-but-together. He wondered how the tides and waves had come into play on that afternoon along the Jersey shoreline when Martha saw the pebble and bent down to rescue it from geology. He imagined bare feet. Martha was a poet, with the poet's sensibilities, and her feet would be brown and bare, the toenails unpainted, the eyes chilly and somber like the ocean in March, and though it was painful, he wondered who had been with her that afternoon. He imagined a pair of shadows moving along the strip of sand where things came

together but also separated. It was phantom jealousy, he knew, but he couldn't help himself. He loved her so much. On the march, through the hot days of early April, he carried the pebble in his mouth, turning it with his tongue, tasting sea salts and moisture. His mind wandered. He had difficulty keeping his attention on the war. On occasion he would yell at his men to spread out the column, to keep their eyes open, but then he would slip away into daydreams, just pretending, walking barefoot along the Jersey shore, with Martha, carrying nothing. He would feel himself rising. Sun and waves and gentle winds, all love and lightness.

WHAT they carried varied by mission. When a mission took them to the mountains, they carried mosquito netting, machetes, canvas tarps, and extra bug juice. 15

If a mission seemed especially hazardous, or if it involved a place they knew to be bad, they carried everything they could. In certain heavily mined AOs, where the land was dense with Toe Poppers and Bouncing Betties, they took turns humping a twenty-eight-pound mine detector. With its headphones and big sensing plate, the equipment was a stress on the lower back and shoulders, awkward to handle, often useless because of the shrapnel in the earth, but they carried it anyway, partly for safety, partly for the illusion of safety.

On ambush, or other night missions, they carried peculiar little odds and ends. Kiowa always took along his New Testament and a pair of moccasins for silence. Dave Jensen carried night-sight vitamins high in carotene. Lee Strunk carried his slingshot; ammo, he claimed, would never be a problem. Rat Kiley carried brandy and M&M's. Until he was shot, Ted Lavender carried the starlight scope, which weighed 6.3 pounds with its aluminum carrying case. Henry Dobbins carried his girlfriend's pantyhose wrapped around his neck as a comforter. They all carried ghosts. When dark came, they would move out single file across the meadows and paddies to their ambush coordinates, where they would quietly set up the Claymores and lie down and spend the night waiting.

Other missions were more complicated and required special equipment. In mid-April, it was their mission to search out and destroy the elaborate tunnel complexes in the Than Khe area south of Chu Lai. To blow the tunnels, they carried one-pound blocks of pentrite high explosives; four blocks to a man, sixty-eight pounds in all. They carried wiring, detonators, and battery-powered clackers. Dave Jensen carried earplugs. Most often, before blowing the tunnels, they were ordered by higher command to search them, which was considered bad news, but by and large they just shrugged and carried out orders. Because he was a big man, Henry Dobbins was excused from tunnel duty. The others would draw numbers. Before Lavender died there were seventeen men in the platoon, and whoever drew the number seventeen would strip off his gear and crawl in head first with a flashlight and Lieutenant Cross's .45-caliber pistol. The rest of them would fan out as security. They would sit down or kneel, not facing the hole, listening to the ground beneath them, imagining cobwebs and ghosts, whatever was down there—the tunnel walls squeezing in—how the flashlight seemed impossibly heavy in the hand and how it was tunnel vision in the very strictest sense, compression in all ways, even time, and how you had to wiggle in—ass and elbows—a swallowed-up feeling—and how you found yourself worrying about odd things—will your flashlight go dead? Do rats carry rabies? If you screamed, how far would the sound carry? Would your buddies hear it? Would they have the courage to drag you out? In some respects, though not many, the waiting was worse than the tunnel itself. Imagination was a killer.

On April 16, when Lee Strunk drew the number seventeen, he laughed and muttered something and went down quickly. The morning was hot and very still. Not good, Kiowa said. He looked at the tunnel opening, then out across a dry paddy toward the village of Than Khe. Nothing moved. No clouds or birds or people. As they waited, the men smoked and drank Kool-Aid, not talking much, feeling sympathy for Lee Strunk but also feeling the luck of the draw, You win some, you lose some, said Mitchell Sanders, and sometimes you settle for a rain check. It was a tired line and no one laughed.

Henry Dobbins ate a tropical chocolate bar. Ted Lavender popped a tranquilizer and went off to pee. [20]

After five minutes, Lieutenant Jimmy Cross moved to the tunnel, leaned down, and examined the darkness. Trouble, he thought—a cave-in maybe. And then suddenly, without willing it, he was thinking about Martha. The stresses and fractures, the quick collapse, the two of them buried alive under all that weight. Dense, crushing love. Kneeling, watching the hole, he tried to concentrate on Lee Strunk and the war, all the dangers, but his love was too much for him, he felt paralyzed, he wanted to sleep inside her lungs and breathe her blood and be smothered. He wanted her to be a virgin and not a virgin, all at once. He wanted to know her. Intimate secrets—why poetry? Why so sad? Why the grayness in her eyes? Why so alone? Not lonely, just alone—riding her bike across campus or sitting off by herself in the cafeteria. Even dancing, she danced alone—and it was the aloneness that filled him with love. He remembered telling her that one evening. How she nodded and looked away. And how, later, when he kissed her, she received the kiss without returning it, her eyes wide open, not afraid, not a virgin's eyes, just flat and uninvolved.

Lieutenant Cross gazed at the tunnel. But he was not there. He was buried with Martha under the white sand at the Jersey shore. They were pressed together, and the pebble in his mouth was her tongue. He was smiling. Vaguely, he was aware of how quiet the day was, the sullen paddies, yet he could not bring himself to worry about matters of security. He was beyond

If you screamed, how far would the sound carry?

that. He was just a kid at war, in love. He was twenty-two years old. He couldn't help it.

A few moments later Lee Strunk crawled out of the tunnel. He came up grinning, filthy but alive. Lieutenant Cross nodded and closed his eyes while the others clapped Strunk on the back and made jokes about rising from the dead.

Worms, Rat Kiley said. Right out of the grave. Fuckin' zombie.

25   The men laughed. They all felt great relief.

Spook City, said Mitchell Sanders.

Lee Strunk made a funny ghost sound, a kind of moaning, yet very happy, and right then, when Strunk made that high happy moaning sound, when he went *Ahhooooo,* right then Ted Lavender was shot in the head on his way back from peeing. He lay with his mouth open. The teeth were broken. There was a swollen black bruise under his left eye. The cheekbone was gone. Oh shit, Rat Kiley said, the guy's dead. The guy's dead, he kept saying, which seemed profound—the guy's dead. I mean really.

THE things they carried were determined to some extent by superstition. Lieutenant Cross carried his good-luck pebble. Dave Jensen carried a rabbit's foot. Norman Bowker, otherwise a very gentle person, carried a thumb that had been presented to him as a gift by Mitchell Sanders. The thumb was dark brown, rubbery to the touch, and weighed four ounces at most. It had been cut from a VC corpse, a boy of fifteen or sixteen. They'd found him at the bottom of an irrigation ditch, badly burned, flies in his mouth and eyes. The boy wore black shorts and sandals. At the time of his death he had been carrying a pouch of rice, a rifle, and three magazines of ammunition.

You want my opinion, Mitchell Sanders said, there's a definite moral here.

30   He put his hand on the dead boy's wrist. He was quiet for a time, as if counting a pulse, then he patted the stomach, almost affectionately, and used Kiowa's hunting hatchet to remove the thumb.

Henry Dobbins asked what the moral was.

Moral?

You know. *Moral.*

Sanders wrapped the thumb in toilet paper and handed it across to Norman Bowker. There was no blood. Smiling, he kicked the boy's head, watched the files scatter, and said, It's like with that old TV show—Paladin. Have gun, will travel.

Henry Dobbins thought about it.   35

Yeah, well, he finally said. I don't see no moral.

There it *is,* man.

Fuck off.

THEY carried USO stationery and pencils and pens. They carried Sterno, safety pins, trip flares, signal flares, spools of wire, razor blades, chewing tobacco, liberated joss sticks and statuettes of the smiling Buddha, candles, grease pencils, *The Stars and Stripes,* fingernail clippers, Psy Ops leaflets, bush hats, bolos, and much more. Twice a week, when the resupply choppers came in, they carried hot chow in green Mermite cans and large canvas bags filled with iced beer and soda pop. They carried plastic water containers, each with a two-gallon capacity. Mitchell Sanders carried a set of starched tiger fatigues for special occasions. Henry Dobbins carried Black Flag insecticide. Dave Jensen carried empty sandbags that could be filled at night for added protection. Lee Strunk carried tanning lotion. Some things they carried in common. Taking turns, they carried the big PRC-77 scrambler radio, which weighed thirty pounds with its battery. They shared the weight of memory. They took up what others could no longer bear. Often, they carried each other, the wounded or weak. They carried infections. They carried chess sets, basketballs, Vietnamese-English dictionaries, insignia of rank, Bronze Stars and Purple Hearts, plastic cards imprinted with the Code of

Conduct. They carried diseases, among them malaria and dysentery. They carried lice and ringworm and leeches and paddy algae and various rots and molds. They carried the land itself—Vietnam, the place, the soil—a powdery orange-red dust that covered their boots and fatigues and faces. They carried the sky. The whole atmosphere, they carried it, the humidity, the monsoons, the stink of fungus and decay, all of it, they carried gravity. They moved like mules. By daylight they took sniper fire, at night they were mortared, but it was not battle, it was just the endless march, village to village, without purpose, nothing won or lost. They marched for the sake of the march. They plodded along slowly, dumbly, leaning forward against the heat, unthinking, all blood and bone, simple grunts, soldiering with their legs, toiling up the hills and down into the paddies and across the rivers and up again and down, just humping, one step and then the next and then another, but no volition, no will, because it was automatic, it was anatomy, and the war was entirely a matter of posture and carriage, the hump was everything, a kind of inertia, a kind of emptiness, a dullness of desire and intellect and conscience and hope and human sensibility. Their principles were in their feet. Their calculations were biological. They had no sense of strategy or mission. They searched the villages without knowing what to look for, not caring, kicking over jars of rice, frisking children and old men, blowing tunnels, sometimes setting fires and sometimes not, then forming up and moving on to the next village, then other villages, where it would always be the same. They carried their own lives. The pressures were enormous. In the heat of early afternoon, they would remove their helmets and flak jackets, walking bare, which was dangerous but which helped ease the strain. They would often discard things along the route of march. Purely for comfort, they would throw away rations, blow their Claymores and grenades, no matter, because by nightfall the resupply choppers would arrive with more of the same, then a day or two later still more, fresh watermelons and crates of ammunition and sunglasses and woolen sweaters—the resources were stunning—sparklers for the Fourth of July, colored eggs for Easter. It was the great American war chest—the fruits of science, the smokestacks, the canneries, the arsenals at Hartford, the Minnesota forests, the machine shops, the vast fields of corn and wheat—they carried like freight trains; they carried it on their backs and shoulders—and for all the ambiguities of Vietnam, all the mysteries and unknowns, there was at least the single abiding certainty that they would never be at a loss for things to carry.

AFTER the chopper took Lavender away, Lieutenant Jimmy Cross led his men into the village 40 of Than Khe. They burned everything. They shot chickens and dogs, they trashed the village well, they called in artillery and watched the wreckage, then they marched for several hours through the hot afternoon, and then at dusk, while Kiowa explained how Lavender died, Lieutenant Cross found himself trembling.

He tried not to cry. With his entrenching tool, which weighed five pounds, he began digging a hole in the earth.

He felt shame. He hated himself. He had loved Martha more than his men, and as a consequence Lavender was now dead, and this was something he would have to carry like a stone in his stomach for the rest of the war.

All he could do was dig. He used his entrenching tool like an ax, slashing, feeling both love and hate, and then later, when it was full dark, he sat at the bottom of his foxhole and wept. It went on for a long while. In part, he was grieving for Ted Lavender, but mostly it was for Martha, and for himself, because she belonged to another world, which was not quite real, and because she was a junior at Mount Sebastian College in New Jersey, a poet and a virgin and uninvolved, and because he realized she did not love him and never would.

Like cement, Kiowa whispered in the dark. I swear to God—boom-down. Not a word.

45   I've heard this, said Norman Bowker.

A pisser, you know? Still zipping himself up. Zapped while zipping.

All right, fine. That's enough.

Yeah, but you had to see it, the guy just—

I *heard,* man. Cement. So why not shut the fuck *up?*

50   Kiowa shook his head sadly and glanced over at the hole where Lieutenant Jimmy Cross sat watching the night. The air was thick and wet. A warm, dense fog had settled over the paddies and there was the stillness that precedes rain.

After a time Kiowa sighed.

One thing for sure, he said. The Lieutenant's in some deep hurt. I mean that crying jag—the way he was carrying on—it wasn't fake or anything, it was real heavy-duty hurt. The man cares.

Sure, Norman Bowker said.

Say what you want, the man does care.

55   We all got problems.

Not Lavender.

No, I guess not, Bowker said. Do me a favor, though.

Shut up?

That's a smart Indian. Shut up.

60   Shrugging, Kiowa pulled off his boots. He wanted to say more, just to lighten up his sleep, but instead he opened his New Testament and arranged it beneath his head as a pillow. The fog made things seem hollow and unattached. He tried not to think about Ted Lavender, but then he was thinking how fast it was, no drama, down and dead, and how it was hard to feel anything except surprise. It seemed un-Christian. He wished he could find some great sadness, or even anger, but the emotion wasn't there and he couldn't make it happen. Mostly he felt pleased to be alive. He liked the smell of the New Testament under his cheek, the leather and ink and paper and glue, whatever the chemicals were. He liked hearing the sounds of night. Even his fatigue, it felt fine, the stiff muscles and the prickly awareness of his own body, a floating feeling. He enjoyed not being dead. Lying there, Kiowa admired Lieutenant Jimmy Cross's capacity for grief. He wanted to share the man's pain, he wanted to care as Jimmy Cross cared. And yet when he closed his eyes, all he could think was Boom-down, and all he could feel was the pleasure of having his boots off and the fog curling in around him and the damp soil and the Bible smells and the plush comfort of night.

After a moment Norman Bowker sat up in the dark.

What the hell, he said. You want to talk, *talk.* Tell it to me.

Forget it.

No, man, go on. One thing I hate, it's a silent Indian.

For the most part they carried themselves with 65 poise, a kind of dignity. Now and then, however, there were times of panic, when they squealed or wanted to squeal but couldn't, when they twitched and made moaning sounds and covered their heads and said Dear Jesus and flopped around on the earth and fired their weapons blindly and cringed and sobbed and begged for the noise to stop and went wild and made stupid promises to themselves and to God and to their mothers and fathers, hoping not to die. In different ways, it happened to all of them. Afterward, when the firing ended, they would blink and peek up. They would touch their bodies, feeling shame, then quickly hiding it. They would force themselves to stand. As if in slow motion, frame by frame, the world would take on the old logic—absolute silence, then the wind, then sunlight, then voices. It was the burden of being alive. Awkwardly, the men would reassemble themselves, first in private, then in groups, becoming soldiers again. They would repair the leaks in their eyes. They would check for casualties, call in dust-offs, light cigarettes, try to smile, clear their throats and spit and begin cleaning their weapons. After a time someone would shake his head and say, No lie, I almost shit my pants, and someone else would laugh, which meant it was bad, yes, but the guy had obviously not shit his pants, it wasn't that bad, and in any case nobody would ever do such a thing and then go ahead and talk about it. They would squint into the dense, oppressive sunlight. For a few moments, perhaps, they would fall silent, lighting a joint and tracking its passage from man to man, inhaling, holding in the humiliation. Scary stuff, one of them might say. But then someone else would grin or flick his eyebrows and say, Roger-dodger, almost cut me a new asshole, *almost*.

There were numerous such poses. Some carried themselves with a sort of wistful resignation, others with pride or stiff soldierly discipline or good humor or macho zeal. They were afraid of dying but they were even more afraid to show it.

They found jokes to tell.

They used a hard vocabulary to contain the terrible softness. *Greased,* they'd say. *Offed, lit up, zapped while zipping.* It wasn't cruelty, just stage presence. They were actors and the war came at them in 3-D. When someone died, it wasn't quite dying, because in a curious way it seemed scripted, and because they had their lines mostly memorized, irony mixed with tragedy, and because they called it by other names, as if to encyst and destroy the reality of death itself. They kicked corpses. They cut off thumbs. They talked grunt lingo. They told stories about Ted Lavender's supply of tranquilizers, how the poor guy didn't feel a thing, how incredibly tranquil he was.

There's a moral here, said Mitchell Sanders.

70　They were waiting for Lavender's chopper, smoking the dead man's dope.

The moral's pretty obvious, Sanders said, and winked. Stay away from drugs. No joke, they'll ruin your day every time.

Cute, said Henry Dobbins.

Mind-blower, get it? Talk about wiggy—nothing left, just blood and brains.

They made themselves laugh.

There it is, they'd say, over and over, as if the rep- 75 etition itself were an act of poise, a balance between crazy and almost crazy, knowing without going. There it is, which meant be cool, let it ride, because oh yeah, man, you can't change what can't be changed, there it is, there it absolutely and positively and fucking well *is*.

They were tough.

They carried all the emotional baggage of men who might die. Grief, terror, love, longing—these were intangibles, but the intangibles had their own mass and specific gravity, they had tangible weight. They carried shameful memories. They carried the common secret of cowardice barely restrained, the instinct to run or freeze or hide, and in many respects this was the heaviest burden of all, for it could never be put down, it required perfect balance and perfect posture. They carried their reputations. They carried the soldier's greatest fear, which was the fear of blushing. Men killed, and died, because they were embarrassed not to. It was what had brought them to the war in the first place, nothing positive, no dreams of glory or honor, just to avoid the blush of dishonor. They died so as not to die of embarrassment. They crawled into tunnels and walked point and advanced under fire. Each morning, despite the unknowns, they made their legs move. They endured. They kept humping. They did not submit to the obvious alternative, which was simply to close the eyes and fall. So easy, really. Go limp and tumble to the ground and let the muscles unwind and not speak and not budge until your buddies picked you up and lifted you into the chopper that would roar and dip its nose and carry you off to the world. A mere matter of falling, yet no one ever

> They were afraid of dying but they were even more afraid to show it.

fell. It was not courage, exactly; the object was not valor. Rather, they were too frightened to be cowards.

By and large they carried these things inside, maintaining the masks of composure. They sneered at sick call. They spoke bitterly about guys who had found release by shooting off their own toes or fingers. Pussies, they'd say. Candyasses. It was fierce, mocking talk, with only a trace of envy or awe, but even so, the image played itself out behind their eyes.

They imagined the muzzle against flesh. They imagined the quick, sweet pain, then the evacuation to Japan, then a hospital with warm beds and cute geisha nurses.

80   They dreamed of freedom birds.

At night, on guard, staring into the dark, they were carried away by jumbo jets. They felt the rush of takeoff. *Gone!* they yelled. And then velocity, wings and engines, a smiling stewardess—but it was more than a plane, it was a real bird, a big sleek silver bird with feathers and talons and high screeching. They were flying. The weights fell off, there was nothing to bear. They laughed and held on tight, feeling the cold slap of wind and altitude, soaring, thinking *It's over, I'm gone!*—they were naked, they were light and free—it was all lightness, bright and fast and buoyant, light as light, a helium buzz in the brain, a giddy bubbling in the lungs as they were taken up over the clouds and the war, beyond duty, beyond gravity and mortification and global entanglements—*Sin loi!* they yelled, *I'm sorry, motherfuckers, but I'm out of it, I'm goofed, I'm on a space cruise, I'm gone!*—and it was a restful, disencumbered sensation, just riding the light waves, sailing that big silver freedom bird over the mountains and oceans, over America, over the farms and great sleeping cities and cemeteries and highways and the golden arches of McDonald's. It was flight, a kind of fleeing, a kind of falling, falling higher and higher, spinning off the edge of the earth and beyond the sun and through the vast, silent vacuum where there were no burdens and where everything weighed exactly

Men killed, and died, because they were embarrassed not to.

nothing. *Gone!* they screamed, *I'm sorry but I'm gone!* And so at night, not quite dreaming, they gave themselves over to lightness, they were carried, they were purely borne.

ON the morning after Ted Lavender died, First Lieutenant Jimmy Cross crouched at the bottom of his foxhole and burned Martha's letters. Then he burned the two photographs. There was a steady rain falling, which made it difficult, but he used heat tabs and Sterno to build a small fire, screening it with his body, holding the photographs over the tight blue flame with the tips of his fingers.

He realized it was only a gesture. Stupid, he thought. Sentimental, too, but mostly just stupid.

Lavender was dead. You couldn't burn the blame.

Besides, the letters were in his head. And even now, without photographs, Lieutenant Cross could see Martha playing volleyball in her white gym shorts and yellow T-shirt. He could see her moving in the rain.   85

When the fire died out, Lieutenant Cross pulled his poncho over his shoulders and ate breakfast from a can.

There was no great mystery, he decided.

In those burned letters Martha had never mentioned the war, except to say, Jimmy take care of yourself. She wasn't involved. She signed the letters "Love," but it wasn't love, and all the fine lines and technicalities did not matter.

The morning came up wet and blurry. Everything seemed part of everything else, the fog and Martha and the deepening rain.

It was a war, after all.   90

Half smiling, Lieutenant Jimmy Cross took out his maps. He shook his head hard, as if to clear it, then bent forward and began planning the day's march. In ten minutes, or maybe twenty, he would rouse the men and they would pack up and head west, where the maps showed the country to be green and inviting. They would do what they had always done. The rain might add some weight, but otherwise it would be one more day layered upon all the other days.

He was realistic about it. There was that new hardness in his stomach.

No more fantasies, he told himself.

Henceforth, when he thought about Martha, it would be only to think that she belonged elsewhere. He would shut down the daydreams. This was not Mount Sebastian, it was another world, where there were no pretty poems or midterm exams, a place where men died because of carelessness and gross stupidity. Kiowa was right. Boom-down, and you were dead, never partly dead.

95   Briefly, in the rain, Lieutenant Cross saw Martha's gray eyes gazing back at him.

He understood.

It was very sad, he thought. The things men carried inside. The things men did or felt they had to do.

He almost nodded at her, but didn't.

Instead he went back to his maps. He was now determined to perform his duties firmly and without negligence. It wouldn't help Lavender, he knew that, but from this point on he would comport himself as a soldier. He would dispose of his good-luck pebble. Swallow it, maybe, or use Lee Strunk's slingshot, or just drop it along the trail. On the march he would impose strict field discipline. He would be careful to send out flank security, to prevent straggling or bunching up, to keep his troops moving at the proper pace and at the proper interval. He would insist on clean weapons. He would confiscate the remainder of Lavender's dope. Later in the day, perhaps, he would call the men together and speak to them plainly. He would accept the blame for what had happened to Ted Lavender. He would be a man about it. He would look them in the eyes, keeping his chin level, and he would issue the new SOPs in a calm, impersonal tone of voice, an officer's voice, leaving no room for argument or discussion. Commencing immediately, he'd tell them, they would no longer abandon equipment along the route of march. They would police up their acts. They would get their shit together, and keep it together, and maintain it neatly and in good working order.

He would not tolerate laxity. He would show 100 strength, distancing himself.

Among the men there would be grumbling, of course, and maybe worse, because their days would seem longer and their loads heavier, but Lieutenant Cross reminded himself that his obligation was not to be loved but to lead. He would dispense with love; it was not now a factor. And if anyone quarreled or complained, he would simply tighten his lips and arrange his shoulders in the correct command posture. He might give a curt little nod. Or he might not. He might just shrug and say Carry on, then they would saddle up and form into a column and move out toward the villages of Than Khe.

IF YOU LIKED "THE THINGS THEY CARRIED," YOU MIGHT ALSO LIKE . . .

. . . mulling over the meaning, ultimately mysterious, of Hulga's missing leg in "Good Country People" by Flannery O'Connor (Chapter 12) or considering possible interpretations of the car keys in T. Coraghessan Boyle's "Greasy Lake" (Chapter 8) or the route taken by Phoenix Jackson in Eudora Welty's "A Worn Path," found in this chapter.

GOING FURTHER
War is what Herman Melville would call a "great" theme, and in our tumultuous modern age it often serves as literary material, as in, for example, the novels of Joseph Heller (*Catch-22*), Norman Mailer (*The Naked and the Dead*), and James Jones (*The Thin Red Line*). As we suggested, war has emerged in the work of Tim O'Brien as his great subject, sometimes overshadowing the domestic aspects of life in his fiction.

Writing from Reading

Summarize

1 Explain why Cross burns Martha's letters after Lavender's death.

2 O'Brien mentions various reasons why the men carried things. For example, they carried a number of things "by necessity." What are the other reasons given? How does the reason given affect the story that follows?

Analyze Craft

3 Discuss how O'Brien uses lists in this story. How do the lists affect the tone and themes of the story?

4 Consider the names Cross and Lavender. What symbolic meanings do these names suggest?

Analyze Voice

5 Identify passages and details in the story that seem to come from O'Brien's personal experience. What makes them seem this way?

6 The men in this story are soldiers in the Vietnam War. Which of their experiences and the things they carry are specific to that war? Consider reasons of era, culture, climate, and terrain. Which would apply to any war?

Synthesize Summary and Analysis

7 What symbolic meaning does Ted Lavender's death take on? Find each reference to Lavender and to his death, and explore the effect the repetition has on you as a reader.

Interpret the Story

8 Consider why O'Brien includes so many detailed passages about Lieutenant Jimmy Cross. How might his thoughts, fears, and fantasies about Martha represent the feelings of all soldiers who served in Vietnam?

CONTINUED FROM PAGE 425

SYMBOLS IN EVERYDAY LIFE AND LITERATURE

We use symbols whenever we speak or write, draw or gesture. Those little icons on your computer screen—the picture of a trash can, the picture of a disk—are symbols. An image represents an idea; a picture stands for a thing. Symbols in literature, however, rarely have single, unambiguous meanings. When we read fiction, we are invited—in fact, called upon—to interpret objects, characters, and behavior beyond their literal meanings, and to look for multiple, not simply single, truths or meanings. Symbolism takes us deep into the tangled web of words and characters, incidents and objects in a story. Because symbols are compact and efficient, they can communicate a broad array of feelings and impressions. Moreover, a symbol doesn't boil down to a single "correct" meaning. What we learn from reading with symbolic potential in mind not only deepens our reading experience but also prepares us to understand the significance of events in our own lives. When a symbolic object or act is successfully embedded in a story, it imbues the story with multiple meanings—and therefore the possibility of multiple interpretations.

In "The Things They Carried," for example, the pebble is a gift from Martha; it's something she has touched, so for Cross it embodies her essence. It comes from a beach back home, so it also carries the essence of "beach"—a place of serenity as well as carefree pleasures. It seems a kind of rabbit's foot, a good-luck charm. Yet it is also a mere piece of stone. Although Martha herself sees symbolic meaning in the stone—she points out the "separate-but-together quality" of the tide line where she found it—anybody else strolling the beach would very likely have passed it by as just another ordinary pebble. Now, layered with associations and memories, it becomes symbolic of Cross's longing for romantic love and also embodies the promise and possibility of escape from brutal war. Lieutenant Cross carries the pebble in his mouth, guarding it, tasting it, absorbing all it contains. Shown in these various lights, the pebble acquires so much significance by the time Cross vows to discard it that we know he's giving a great deal away by doing so.

> **"So in this story I take on death—a huge subject. But in this story the way into that huge subject is through the watch that is left behind by a woman who has died, which her daughters are now fighting over."** Conversation with Amy Hempel

Just as an object or character can hold many shades of meaning, so can a **symbolic act,** a gesture or action beyond the everyday practical definition. When Lieutenant Cross discards Martha's pebble, he discards an entire dream. In the symbolic act of *carrying*, the weary soldiers not only shoulder a host of physical objects—letters, can openers, pocket knives, salt tablets, ammunition, dental floss—they also bear a host of emotional burdens: the fear of death, the horrors of what they've seen, the fatigue of war. As you read each story, consider how the predominant symbols might be interpreted in multiple ways. How might each symbol or symbolic act be read both literally and figuratively, both as it actually is (a pebble) and as what it represents (longing)?

SYMBOL AND ALLEGORY

Authors have not always used or thought of symbols in this way. Most literature was once allegorical. An **allegory** is a story in which major elements such as character and setting represent universal truths or moral lessons in a one-to-one correspondence, as they do in the fable of the grasshopper and the ant. In this fable the grasshopper is careless all the way through, frittering away its time, while the ant labors diligently to put away food for the winter. When winter comes, you can guess which one will be secure and which one will suffer. In this allegorical narrative, the lesson to be learned is that it is best to prepare for future necessity. Each character represents a single form of behavior—"irresponsibility" for the grasshopper versus "conscientiousness" for the ant. Allegorical figures are one-dimensional and constant; "what they carry" does not change.

Allegory is a cardboard-cutout kind of symbolism; in allegory, a value such as "virtue" or "vice," as in "Young Goodman Brown" in this chapter, remains constant from

THE HISTORY OF SYMBOLISM

The use of allegory stems from the old pagan religions, in which the gods were understood to have created certain constant values—good, evil, heroism, fidelity—in human beings, who were seen as incapable of change. These concepts gradually adapted to Christian symbols of salvation and redemption. Toward the end of the eighteenth century, poetry and fiction moved largely away from allegory and toward a more multidimensional symbolism. By the mid-nineteenth century, most serious writers produced work that was decidedly symbolic rather than allegorical. Readers, too, took on the new task of interpreting literature in multiple ways, contributing new perspectives and initiating discussions about the growing literary canon. What once was myth—an age-old and collective story—became, in time, an individual's tale. If you want to look at these developments in political terms, you might say that allegory is the mode of kings and religious uniformity, whereas symbolism is the mode of democracy and governments made up of a multiplicity of views.

beginning to end. In our discussion of character (Chapter 9), we drew the distinction between "flat" and "round" characters; in this regard an allegorical figure would be *flat*, whereas a symbolic figure or object—what O'Brien identifies as "the pebble or the shooting of a baby water buffalo"—would be understood as *round*. In contrast to allegory, symbols convey multiple meanings, and the meanings may expand and become more complex over the course of the story.

RECOGNIZING AND APPRECIATING SYMBOLS

Symbolic meanings are not "hidden," as many readers have come to believe. Their context suggests them, as does the way characters view them. In "A Worn Path," Phoenix Jackson's name, actions, and traits add up to more than just an old woman. A phoenix is a mythological bird that burns and rises from its own ashes to live again. So Phoenix Jackson's name is a symbol of this woman's ability to rise above life's difficulties. Notice, too, that at the story's beginning, the character Phoenix is described in ways that gesture toward this mythological creature—the way she walks with her cane sounds "like the chirping of a solitary little bird," and her cheeks are "illumined by a yellow burning under the dark."

It's possible to go deeper still. There are several points in the story where Phoenix rises—she frees herself from a thorn bush that catches her dress; a hunter helps her out of the ditch into which she has fallen; and, at the end of the story, Welty writes that she "rose" from her chair in the doctor's office to get back to her grandson. Looking at these actions in the context of Phoenix as symbol, we begin to understand this old woman as more than a devoted grandmother making a long journey. These actions add to and deepen the sense we have of Phoenix as timeless and larger than life, one for whom life's hard journey is no match. Writers like Welty choose images and details carefully for their resonance, and although we might not be positive that the author intended every additional meaning we cull from the details, those meanings are nonetheless present.

> "**We know from Greek myth and from many mythic structures, the three witches, the three sisters, Cinderella and her two sisters, and on and on. It's just a very organic form, and the triangle is, in general, a very important figure for a fiction writer to have in mind.**" Conversation with John Updike

How can you tell when an image, character, or act is significant in a symbolic sense? First, look at the title of a work. O'Brien sets us up to know what is going to be laden with symbolic importance in his title, "The Things They Carried." Notice also images that you see repeated throughout the story, such as the wallpaper in Charlotte Perkins Gilman's "The Yellow Wallpaper" (Chapter 12). Recurrence, especially, gives an image importance, drawing attention to it, suggesting it has significance beyond the ordinary. Sometimes the author focuses on a precise detail in a way that seems to be saying, "Notice this; it says something important," as in Joyce Carol Oates's "Where Are You Going, Where Have You Been?" (Chapter 8) when the narrator describes Connie's habit of looking into mirrors. Reflect on how an image is used in a story and how it connects to the characters, especially the protagonist, as in the Gregor Samsa character in Franz Kafka's "The Metamorphosis" (**find this story online at connect.mcgraw-hill.com**).

> "**A symbol, although it's a literary-sounding word . . . has a meaning that goes beyond textbooks. It has to do with what objects of the world, things of the world, end up meaning to us. . . . In ["The Things They Carried"] the book starts with a list of physical objects . . . The pebble that Jimmy Cross carried and the pantyhose carried by Henry Dobbins and all the military paraphernalia all the men carry. . . . The object has meaning, has resonance and has echoes . . . [in] the spiritual burdens that not only the soldiers carry through a war—but the burden[s] that all of us carry through our lives: fear, piety, loss, grief, love, nostalgia.**" Conversation with Tim O'Brien

Louise Erdrich (b. 1954)

Born to a German-American father and French-Anishinaabe mother, both of whom worked at the Bureau of Indian Affairs School in North Dakota, Louise Erdrich has explored both her German-American and her Native-American heritage in her work. However, her focus on Native-American life and her creation of a fictional community in North Dakota have won her wide acclaim and placed her in the top rank of modern American Indian Fiction writers. One of the first women to have been admitted into Dartmouth College, Erdrich graduated in 1976; she went on to receive her M.A. in creative writing from Johns Hopkins University in 1979. Erdrich has won both the Nelson Algren Prize and the O'Henry Award for her short fiction, the Pushcart Prize for her poetry, and the National Book Critics Circle Award for her first novel, *Love Medicine* (1984).

In 1981 she married Michael Dorris, who founded the Native-American Studies program at Dartmouth, where she first met him. Erdrich and Dorris collaborated on many nonfiction and fictional works in the 1980s and 1990s and officially co-wrote *Route Two* (1990) and *The Crown of Columbus* (1991). Erdrich also wrote a foreword to *The Broken Cord,* Dorris's nonfictional work on fetal alcohol syndrome in the Native-American community and his three adopted children. Erdrich later adopted the children when they married, and the couple had three additional children. Their marriage ended in divorce amid a swirl of unresolved accusations of child abuse. Dorris took his own life in 1997.

In addition to thirteen novels, Erdrich has published three books of poetry, three works of nonfiction, and six books for children. Her 2008 novel *A Plague of Doves* was a finalist for the Pulitzer Prize. *The Red Convertible: Collected and New Stories 1978–2008* was published in 2009. Her most recent work, *Shadow Tag,* about a failing marriage between two people from different tribes, was published in 2010. Erdrich lives in Minneapolis, where she owns Birchbark Books—Anishinaabe history was written on birch bark scrolls in a system of complex geometrical patterns and symbols—a bookstore that focuses on the books, arts, and crafts of Native Americans.

The Red Convertible (1974)

Lyman Lamartine

1   I WAS the first one to drive a convertible on my reservation. And of course it was red, a red Olds. I owned that car along with my brother Henry Junior. We owned it together until his boots filled with water on a windy night and he bought out my share. Now Henry owns the whole car, and his younger brother Lyman (that's myself), Lyman walks everywhere he goes.

How did I earn enough money to buy my share in the first place? My one talent was I could always make money. I had a touch for it, unusual in a Chippewa. From the first I was different that way, and everyone recognized it. I was the only kid they let in the American Legion Hall to shine shoes, for example, and one Christmas I sold spiritual bouquets for the mission door to door. The nuns let me keep a percentage. Once I started, it seemed the more money I made the easier the money came. Everyone encouraged it. When I was fifteen I got a job washing dishes at the Joliet Cafe, and that was where my first big break happened.

It wasn't long before I was promoted to busing tables, and then the short-order cook quit and I was hired to take her place. No sooner than you know it I was managing the Joliet. The rest is history. I went on managing. I soon be-

a stable. And quiet, it was quiet, even though there was a powwow close enough so I could see it going on. The air was not too still, not too windy either. When the dust rises up and hangs in the air around dancers like that, I feel good. Henry was asleep with his arms thrown wide. Later on, he woke up and we started driving again. We were somewhere in Montana, or maybe on the Blood Reserve—it could have been anywhere. Anyway it was where we met the girl.

ALL her hair was in buns around her ears, that's the first thing I noticed about her. She was posed alongside the road with her arm out, so we stopped. That girl was short, so short her lumber shirt looked comical on her, like a nightgown. She had jeans on and fancy moccasins and she carried a little suitcase.

"Hop on in," says Henry. So she climbs in between us.   10

"We'll take you home," I says. "Where do you live?"

"Chicken," she says.

"Where the hell's that?" I ask her.

"Alaska."

"Okay," says Henry, and we drive.   15

We got up there and never wanted to leave. The sun doesn't truly set there in summer, and the night is more a soft dusk. You might doze off, sometimes, but before you know it you're up again, like an animal in nature. You never feel like you have to sleep hard or put away the world. And things would grow up there. One day just dirt or moss, the next day flowers and long grass. The girl's name was Susy. Her family really took to us. They fed us and put us up. We had our own tent to live in by their house, and the kids would be in and out of there all day and night. They couldn't get over me and Henry being brothers, we looked so different. We told them we knew we had the same mother, anyway.

One night Susy came in to visit us. We sat around in the tent talking of this and that. The season was changing. It was getting darker by that time, and the cold was even getting just a little mean. I told her it was time for us to go. She stood up on a chair.

"You never seen my hair," Susy said.

That was true. She was standing on a chair, but still, when she unclipped her buns the hair reached all the way to the ground. Our eyes opened. You couldn't tell how much hair she had when it was rolled up so neatly. Then my brother Henry did something funny. He went up to the chair and said, "Jump on my shoulders." So she did that, and her

came part owner, and of course there was no stopping me then. It wasn't long before the whole thing was mine.

After I'd owned the Joliet for one year, it blew over in the worst tornado ever seen around here. The whole operation was smashed to bits. A total loss. The fryalator was up in a tree, the grill torn in half like it was paper. I was only sixteen. I had it all in my mother's name, and I lost it quick, but before I lost it I had every one of my relatives, and their relatives, to dinner, and I also bought that red Olds I mentioned, along with Henry.

5   The first time we saw it! I'll tell you when we first saw it. We had gotten a ride up to Winnipeg, and both of us had money. Don't ask me why, because we never mentioned a car or anything, we just had all our money. Mine was cash, a big bankroll from the Joliet's insurance. Henry had two checks—a week's extra pay for being laid off, and his regular check from the Jewel Bearing Plant.

We were walking down Portage anyway, seeing the sights, when we saw it. There it was, parked, large as life. Really as *if* it was alive. I thought of the word *repose,* because the car wasn't simply stopped, parked, or whatever. That car reposed, calm and gleaming, a FOR SALE sign in its left front window. Then, before we had thought it over at all, the car belonged to us and our pockets were empty. We had just enough money for gas back home.

We went places in that car, me and Henry. We took off driving all one whole summer. We started off toward the Little Knife River and Mandaree in Fort Berthold and then we found ourselves down in Wakpala somehow, and then suddenly we were over in Montana on the Rocky Boy, and yet the summer was not even half over. Some people hang on to details when they travel, but we didn't let them bother us and just lived our everyday lives here to there.

I do remember this one place with willows. I remember I laid under those trees and it was comfortable. So comfortable. The branches bent down all around me like a tent or

hair reached down past his waist, and he started twirling, this way and that, so her hair was flung out from side to side.

20 "I always wondered what it was like to have long pretty hair," Henry says. Well, we laughed. It was a funny sight, the way he did it. The next morning we got up and took leave of those people.

ON to greener pastures, as they say. It was down through Spokane and across Idaho then Montana and very soon we were racing the weather right along under the Canadian border through Columbus, Des Lacs, and then we were in Bottineau County and soon home. We'd made most of the trip, that summer, without putting up the car hood at all. We got home just in time.

I don't wonder that the army was so glad to get my brother that they turned him into a Marine. He was built like a brick outhouse anyway. We liked to tease him that they really wanted him for his Indian nose. He had a nose big and sharp as a hatchet, like the nose on Red Tomahawk, the Indian who killed Sitting Bull, whose profile is on signs all along the North Dakota highways. Henry went off to training camp, came home once during Christmas, then the next thing you know we got an overseas letter from him. It was 1970, and he said he was stationed up in the northern hill country. Whereabouts I did not know. He wasn't such a hot letter writer, and only got off two before the enemy caught him. I could never keep it straight, which direction those good Vietnam soldiers were from.

I wrote him back several times, even though I didn't know if those letters would get through. I kept him informed all about the car. Most of the time I had it up on blocks in the yard or half taken apart, because that long trip did a hard job on it under the hood.

I always had good luck with numbers, and never worried about the draft myself. I never even had to think about what my number was. But Henry was never lucky in the same way as me. It was at least three years before Henry came home. By then I guess the whole war was solved in the government's mind, but for him it would keep on going. In those years I'd put his car into almost perfect

shape. I always thought of it as his car while he was gone, even though when he left he said, "Now it's yours," and threw me his key.

"Thanks for the extra key," I'd said. "I'll put it up in your 25 drawer just in case I need it." He laughed.

WHEN he came home, though, Henry was very different, and I'll say this: the change was no good. You could hardly expect him to change for the better, I know. But he was quiet, so quiet, and never comfortable sitting still anywhere but always up and moving around. I thought back to times we'd sat still for whole afternoons, never moving a muscle, just shifting our weight along the ground, talking to whoever sat with us, watching things. He'd always had a joke, then, too, and now you couldn't get him to laugh, or when he did it was more the sound of a man choking, a sound that stopped up the throats of other people around him. They got to leaving him alone most of the time, and I didn't blame them. It was a fact: Henry was jumpy and mean.

I'd bought a color TV set for my mom and the rest of us while Henry was away. Money still came very easy. I was sorry I'd ever bought it though, because of Henry. I was also sorry I'd bought color, because with black-and-white the pictures seem older and farther away. But what are you going to do? He sat in front of it, watching it,  and that was the only time he was completely still. But it was the kind of stillness that you see in a rabbit when it freezes and before it will bolt. He was not easy. He sat in his chair gripping the armrests with all his might, as if the chair itself was moving at a high speed and if he let go at all he would rocket forward and maybe crash right through the set.

Once I was in the room watching TV with Henry and I heard his teeth click at something. I looked over, and he'd bitten through his lip. Blood was going down his chin. I tell you right then I wanted to smash that tube to pieces. I went over to it but Henry must have known what I was up to. He rushed from his chair and shoved me out of the way, against the wall. I told myself he didn't know what he was doing.

My mom came in, turned the set off real quiet, and told us she had made something for supper. So we went and sat down. There was still blood going down Henry's chin, but he didn't notice it and no one said anything even though every time he took a bite of his bread his blood fell onto it until he was eating his own blood mixed in with the food.

30   While Henry was not around we talked about what was going to happen to him. There were no Indian doctors on the reservation, and my mom couldn't come around to trusting the old man, Moses Pillager, because he courted her long ago and was jealous of her husbands. He might take revenge through her son. We were afraid that if we brought Henry to a regular hospital they would keep him.

"They don't fix them in those places," Mom said; "they just give them drugs."

"We wouldn't get him there in the first place," I agreed, "so let's just forget about it."

Then I thought about the car.

Henry had not even looked at the car since he'd gotten home, though like I said, it was in tip-top condition and ready to drive. I thought the car might bring the old Henry back somehow. So I bided my time and waited for my chance to interest him in the vehicle.

35   One night Henry was off somewhere. I took myself a hammer. I went out to that car and I did a number on its underside. Whacked it up. Bent the tail pipe double. Ripped the muffler loose. By the time I was done with the car it looked worse than any typical Indian car that has been driven all its life on reservation roads, which they always say are like government promises—full of holes. It just about hurt me, I'll tell you that! I threw dirt in the carburetor and I ripped all the electric tape off the seats. I made it look just as beat up as I could. Then I sat back and waited for Henry to find it.

Still, it took him over a month. That was all right, because it was just getting warm enough; not melting, but warm enough to work outside.

"Lyman," he says, walking in one day, "that red car looks like shit."

"Well it's old," I says. "You got to expect that."

"No way!" says Henry. "That car's a classic! But you went and ran the piss right put of it, Lyman, and you know it don't deserve that. I kept that car in A-one shape. You don't remember. You're too young. But when I left, that car was running like a watch. Now I don't even know if I can get it to start again, let alone get it anywhere near its old condition."

"Well, you try," I said, like I was getting mad, "but I say 40 it's a piece of junk."

Then I walked out before he could realize I knew he'd strung together more than six words at once.

A FTER that I thought he'd freeze himself to death working on that car. He was out there all day, and at night he rigged up a little lamp, ran a cord out the window, and had himself some light to see by while he worked. He was better than he had been before, but that's still not saying much. It was easier for him to do the things the rest of us did. He ate more slowly and didn't jump up and down during the meal to get this or that or look out the window. I put my hand in the back of the TV set, I admit, and fiddled around with it good, so that it was almost impossible now to get a clear picture. He didn't look at it very often anyway. He was always out with that car or going off to get parts for it. By the time it was really melting outside, he had it fixed.

> . . . I thought he'd freeze himself to death working on that car.

I had been feeling down in the dumps about Henry around this time. We had always been together before. Henry and Lyman. But he was such a loner now that I didn't know how to take it. So I jumped at the chance one day when Henry seemed friendly. It's not that he smiled or anything. He just said, "Let's take that old shit-box for a spin." Just the way he said it made me think he could be coming around.

We went out to the car. It was spring. The sun was shining very bright. My only sister, Bonita, who was just eleven years old, came out and made us stand together for a picture. Henry leaned his elbow on the red car's windshield, and he took his other arm and put it over my shoulder, very carefully, as though it was heavy for him to lift and he didn't want to bring the weight down all at once.

"Smile," Bonita said, and he did. 45

T HAT picture. I never look at it anymore. A few months ago, I don't know why, I got his picture out and tacked it on the wall. I felt good about Henry at the time, close to him. I felt good having his picture on the wall, until one night when I was looking at television. I was a little drunk and stoned. I looked up at the wall and Henry was staring at me. I don't know what it was, but his smile had changed, or maybe it was gone. All I know is I couldn't stay in the same room with that picture. I was shaking. I got up, closed the door, and went into the kitchen. A little later my friend Ray came over and we both went back into that room. We put the picture in a brown bag, folded the bag over and over tightly, then put it way back in a closet.

I still see that picture now, as if it tugs at me, whenever I pass that closet door. The picture is very clear in my mind. It was so sunny that day Henry had to squint against the glare. Or maybe the camera Bonita held flashed like a mirror, blinding him, before she snapped the picture. My face is right out in the sun, big and round. But he might have drawn back, because the shadows on his face are deep as holes. There are two shadows curved like little hooks around the ends of his smile, as if to frame it and try to keep it there—that one, first smile that looked like it might have hurt his face. He has his field jacket on and the wornin clothes he'd come back in and kept wearing ever since. After Bonita took the picture, she went into the house and we got into the car. There was a full cooler in the trunk. We started off, east, toward Pembina and the Red River because Henry said he wanted to see the high water.

The top was down and the car hummed like a top.

THE trip over there was beautiful. When everything starts changing, drying up, clearing off, you feel like your whole life is starting. Henry felt it, too. The top was down and the car hummed like a top. He'd really put it back in shape, even the tape on the seats was very carefully put down and glued back in layers. It's not that he smiled again or even joked, but his face looked to me as if it was clear, more peaceful. It looked as though he wasn't thinking of anything in particular except the bare fields and windbreaks and houses we were passing.

The river was high and full of winter trash when we got there. The sun was still out, but it was colder by the river. There were still little clumps of dirty snow here and there on the banks. The water hadn't gone over the banks yet, but it would, you could tell. It was just at its limit, hard swollen, glossy like an old gray scar. We made ourselves a fire, and we sat down and watched the current go. As I watched it I felt something squeezing inside me and tightening and trying to let go all at the same time. I knew I was not just feeling it myself; I knew I was feeling what Henry was going through at that moment. Except that I couldn't stand it, the closing and opening. I jumped to my feet. I took Henry by

the shoulders, and I started shaking him. "Wake up," I says, "wake up, wake up, wake up!" I didn't know what had come over me. I sat down beside him again.

His face was totally white and hard. Then it broke, like stones break all of a sudden when water boils up inside them. 50

"I know it," he says. "I know it. I can't help it. It's no use."

We start talking. He said he knew what I'd done with the car. It was obvious it had been whacked out of shape and not just neglected. He said he wanted to give the car to me for good now, it was no use. He said he'd fixed it just to give it back and I should take it.

"No way," I says, "I don't want it."

"That's okay," he says, "you take it."

"I don't want it, though," I says back to him, and then to 55 emphasize, just to emphasize, you understand, I touch his shoulder. He slaps my hand off.

"Take that car," he says.

"No," I say. "Make me," I say, and then he grabs my jacket and rips the arm loose. That jacket is a class act, suede with tags and zippers. I push Henry backwards, off the log. He jumps up and bowls me over. We go down in a clinch and come up swinging hard, for all we're worth, with our fists. He socks my jaw so hard I feel like it swings loose. The I'm at his rib cage and land a good one under his chin so his head snaps back. He's dazzled. He looks at me and I look at him and then his eyes are full of tears and blood and at first I think he's crying. But no, he's laughing. "Ha, ha!" he says. "Ha! Ha! Take good care of it."

"Okay," I says. "Okay, no problem. Ha! Ha!"

I can't help it, and I start laughing, too. My face feels fat and strange, and after a while I get a beer from the cooler in the trunk, and when I hand it to Henry he takes his shirt and wipes my germs off. "Hoof-and-mouth disease," he says. For some reason this cracks me up, and so we're really laughing for a while, and then we drink all the rest of the beers one by one and throw them in the river and see how far, how fast, the current takes them before they fill up and sink.

"You want to go on back?" I ask after a while. "Maybe 60 we could snag a couple nice Kashpaw girls."

He says nothing. But I can tell his mood is turning again.

"They're all crazy, the girls up here, every damn one of them."

"You're crazy too," I say, to jolly him up. "Crazy Lamartine boys!"

He looks as though he will take this wrong at first. His face twists, then clears, and he jumps up on his feet. "That's right!" he says. "Crazier 'n hell. Crazy Indians!"

65 I think it's the old Henry again. He throws off his jacket and starts springing his legs up from the knees like a fancy dancer. He's down doing something between a grass dance and a bunny hop, no kind of dance I ever saw before, but neither has anyone else on all this green growing earth. He's wild. He wants to pitch whoopee! He's up and at me and all over. All this time I'm laughing so hard, so hard my belly is getting tied up in a knot.

"Got to cool me off!" he shouts all of a sudden. Then he runs over to the river and jumps in.

There's boards and other things in the current. It's so high. No sound comes from the river after the splash he makes, so I run right over. I look around. It's getting dark. I see he's halfway across the water already, and I know he didn't swim there but the current took him. It's far. I hear his voice, though, very clearly across it.

"My boots are filling," he says.

He says this in a normal voice, like he just noticed and he doesn't know what to think of it. Then he's gone. A branch comes by. Another branch. And I go in.

By the time I get out of the river, off the snag I pulled 70 myself onto, the sun is down. I walk back to the car, turn on the high beams, and drive it up the bank. I put it in first gear and then I take my foot off the clutch. I get out, close the door, and watch it plow softly into the water. The headlights reach in as they go down, searching, still lighted even after the water swirls over the back end. I wait. The wires short out. It is all finally dark. And then there is only the water, the sound of it going and running and going and running and running.

> ## "Crazier 'n hell. Crazy Indians."

IF YOU LIKED "THE RED CONVERTIBLE," YOU MIGHT ALSO LIKE . . .

. . . Sherman Alexie's story, "Indian Education" (Chapter 12) in which we get a delightful, off-center vision of being young and Indian.

GOING FURTHER Erdrich's novel *The Beet Queen* and James Welch's novel *The Indian Lawyer* portray at length life in the northern plains and the upper Midwest in our country among minority populations we usually see only in exaggerated versions in old movies.

Writing from Reading

Summarize

1 Track the ownership of the car from the beginning of the story to the end, noting each time the car is transferred from brother to brother. Who owns the car at the end of the story?

2 Describe Henry before and after he goes off to Vietnam. How has he changed when he returns home?

Analyze Craft

3 Reread the description of the photograph that Bonita takes of Henry and Lyman before their trip to the river. Consider the picture as a symbol. What does the picture say about each of the brothers individually? What does it say about their relationship? In what ways does the picture portend the events at the river?

Analyze Voice

4 Twice during the story the tense changes from past to present. Identify these two instances and discuss why you think Erdrich chose to shift the tense. What is the effect of the tense shift on these two scenes? Would that effect remain the same if the bulk of the story were in present tense and the narration shifted only briefly to past tense?

Synthesize Summary and Analysis

5 At what point in the story do you think Henry first decides to kill himself in the river? How do you know? Is it possible that Henry's death was an accident? Why or why not?

Interpret the Story

6 What does the red convertible represent to each of the two brothers in the story? What does it represent in the story as a whole? Consider whether the convertible could be another color and model and have the same meaning in the story.

Nathaniel Hawthorne (1804–1864)

Shortly after graduating from Bowdoin College, Nathaniel Hawthorne published his first novel, *Fanshawe* (1828), at his own expense, only to reclaim and destroy nearly every copy. Hawthorne also struggled with holding ordinary jobs—in his case, those of bookkeeper and customs-house employee—while trying to be a writer. Despite these difficulties, Hawthorne became famous with his publication of *The Scarlet Letter* (1850) and has remained in the American canon ever since. A native of Massachu-

setts and a descendant of prosecutors in the Salem witch trials, Hawthorne was fascinated with the Puritanical influence in New England, and his work is known for its exploration of sin, punishment, and atonement. During his most productive period—when he and his wife lived in Concord, Massachusetts, and maintained friendships with writers Ralph Waldo Emerson and Henry David Thoreau (who were part of a movement called *transcendentalism* and focused on how humans were basically good and connected to the natural world)—Hawthorne explored the dark side of human nature in his

fiction. To do this, he often turned to a modified form of allegory, making his characters less like real individuals and more like representations of a theme or concept. His writing is a blend of realism and romanticism, and he is known as a Romantic in the sense that he associated unreal occurrences or situations with his often all-too-human characters. "Young Goodman Brown," a story from his collection *Mosses from an Old Manse* (1846), is quintessential Hawthorne; he uses Goodman Brown's slightly fantastical encounter in the woods to expose the sin present in even the most pious people.

AS YOU READ Watch for repeated images—concrete details the author wishes to bring to your attention. How do these particular objects or images alter over the course of the story? What kinds of feelings do they stir in you?

TIP

FOR INTERACTIVE READING . . .

Circle the repeated images. Make brief notes in the margin regarding their portrayal. Considering the context, what feeling or value do you associate with each?

Young Goodman Brown (1835)

1 YOUNG Goodman Brown came forth at sunset into the street of Salem village; but put his head back, after crossing the threshold, to exchange a parting kiss with his young wife. And Faith, as the wife was aptly named, thrust her own pretty head into the street, letting the wind play with the pink ribbons of her cap while she called to Goodman Brown.

"Dearest heart," whispered she, softly and rather sadly, when her lips were close to his ear, "prithee put off your journey until sunrise and sleep in your own bed to-night. A lone woman is troubled with such dreams and such thoughts that she's afeard of herself sometimes. Pray tarry with me this night, dear husband, of all nights in the year."

"My love and my Faith," replied young Goodman Brown, "of all nights in the year, this one night must I tarry away from thee. My journey, as thou callest it, forth and back again, must needs be done 'twixt now and sunrise. What, my sweet, pretty wife, dost thou doubt me already, and we but three months married?"

"Then God bless you!" said Faith, with the pink ribbons; "and may you find all well when you come back."

5 "Amen!" cried Goodman Brown. "Say thy prayers, dear Faith, and go to bed at dusk, and no harm will come to thee."

So they parted; and the young man pursued his way until, being about to turn the corner by the meeting house, he looked back and saw the head of Faith still peeping after him with a melancholy air, in spite of her pink ribbons.

"Poor little Faith!" thought he, for his heart smote him. "What a wretch am I to leave her on such an errand! She talks of dreams, too. Methought as she spoke there was trouble in her face, as if a dream had warned her what work is to be done to-night. But no, no; 'twould kill her to think it. Well, she's a blessed angel on earth; and after this one night I'll cling to her skirts and follow her to heaven."

With this excellent resolve for the future, Goodman Brown felt himself justified in making more haste on his present evil purpose. He had taken a dreary road, darkened by all the gloomiest trees of the forest, which barely stood aside to let the narrow path creep through, and closed immediately behind. It was all as lonely as could be; and there is this peculiarity in such a solitude, that the traveller knows not who may be concealed by the innumerable trunks and thick boughs overhead; so that with lonely footsteps he may yet be passing through an unseen multitude.

"There may be a devilish Indian behind every tree," said Goodman Brown to himself; and he glanced fearfully behind him as he added, "What if the devil himself should be at my very elbow!"

10 His head being turned back, he passed a crook of the road, and, looking forward again, beheld the figure of a man, in grave and decent attire, seated at the foot of an old tree. He arose at Goodman Brown's approach and walked onward side by side with him.

"You are late, Goodman Brown," said he. "The clock of the Old South was striking as I came through Boston; and that is full fifteen minutes agone."

"Faith kept me back a while," replied the young man, with a tremor in his voice, caused by the sudden appearance of his companion, though not wholly unexpected.

It was now deep dusk in the forest, and deepest in that part of it where these two were journeying. As nearly as could be discerned, the second traveller was about fifty years old, apparently in the same rank of life as Goodman Brown, and bearing a considerable resemblance to him, though perhaps more in expression than features. Still they might have been taken for father and son. And yet, though the elder person was as simply clad as the younger, and as simple in manner too, he had an indescribable air of one who knew the world, and who would not have felt abashed at the governor's dinner table or in King William's court, were it possible that his affairs should call him thither. But the only thing about him that could be fixed upon as remarkable was his staff, which bore the likeness of a great black snake, so curiously wrought that it might almost be seen to twist and wriggle itself like a living serpent. This, of course, must have been an ocular deception, assisted by the uncertain light.

"Come, Goodman Brown," cried his fellow-traveller, "this is a dull pace for the beginning of a journey. Take my staff, if you are so soon weary."

15 "Friend," said the other, exchanging his slow pace for a full stop, "having kept covenant by meeting thee here, it is my purpose now to return whence I came. I have scruples touching the matter thou wot'st of."

"Sayest thou so?" replied he of the serpent, smiling apart. "Let us walk on, nevertheless, reasoning as we go; and if I convince thee not thou shalt turn back. We are but a little way in the forest yet."

"Too far! too far!" exclaimed the goodman, unconsciously resuming his walk. "My father never went into the woods on such an errand, nor his father before him. We have been a race of honest men and good Christians since the days of the martyrs; and shall I be the first of the name of Brown that ever took this path and kept———"

THE DEVIL.

"Such company, thou wouldst say," observed the elder person, interpreting his pause. "Well said, Goodman Brown! I have been as well acquainted with your family as with ever a one among the Puritans; and that's no trifle to say. I helped your grandfather, the constable, when he lashed the Quaker woman so smartly through the streets of Salem; and it was I that brought your father a pitch-pine knot, kindled at my own hearth, to set fire to an Indian village, in King Philip's war. They were my good friends, both; and many a pleasant walk have we had along this path, and returned merrily after midnight. I would fain be friends with you for their sake."

"If it be as thou sayest," replied Goodman Brown, "I marvel they never spoke of these matters; or, verily, I marvel not, seeing that the least rumor of the sort would have driven them from New England. We are a people of prayer, and good works to boot, and abide no such wickedness."

"Wickedness or not," said the traveller with the twisted 20 staff, "I have a very general acquaintance here in New England. The deacons of many a church have drunk the communion wine with me; the selectmen of divers towns make me their chairman; and a majority of the Great and General Court are firm supporters of my interest. The governor and I, too—But these are state secrets."

"Can this be so?" cried Goodman Brown, with a stare of amazement at his undisturbed companion. "Howbeit, I have nothing to do with the governor and council; they have their own ways, and are no rule for a simple husbandman like me. But, were I to go on with thee, how should I meet the eye of that good old man, our minister, at Salem village? O, his voice would make me tremble both Sabbath day and lecture day."

Thus far the elder traveller had listened with due gravity; but now burst into a fit of irrepressible mirth, shaking himself so violently that his snakelike staff actually seemed to wriggle in sympathy.

"Ha! ha! ha!" shouted he again and again; then composing himself. "Well, go on, Goodman Brown, go on; but, prithee, don't kill me with laughing."

"Well, then, to end the matter at once," said Goodman Brown, considerably nettled, "there is my wife, Faith. It would break her dear little heart; and I'd rather break my own."

25 "Nay, if that be the case," answered the other, "e'en go thy ways, Goodman Brown. I would not for twenty old women like the one hobbling before us that Faith should come to any harm."

As he spoke, he pointed his staff at a female figure on the path, in whom Goodman Brown recognized a very pious and exemplary dame, who had taught him his catechism in youth, and was still his moral and spiritual adviser, jointly with the minister and Deacon Gookin.

> The moment his fingers touched them they became strangely withered and dried up as with a week's sunshine.

"A marvel, truly, that Goody Cloyse should be so far in the wilderness at nightfall," said he. "But, with your leave, friend, I shall take a cut through the woods until we have left this Christian woman behind. Being a stranger to you, she might ask whom I was consorting with and whither I was going."

"Be it so," said his fellow-traveller. "Betake you to the woods, and let me keep the path."

Accordingly the young man turned aside, but took care to watch his companion, who advanced softly along the road until he had come within a staff's length of the old dame. She, meanwhile, was making the best of her way, with singular speed for so aged a woman, and mumbling some indistinct words—a prayer, doubtless—as she went. The traveller put forth his staff and touched her withered neck with what seemed the serpent's tail.

30 "The devil!" screamed the pious old lady.

"Then Goody Cloyse knows her old friend?" observed the traveller, confronting her and leaning on his writhing stick.

"Ah, forsooth, and is it your worship indeed?" cried the good dame. "Yea, truly is it, and in the very image of my old gossip, Goodman Brown, the grandfather of the silly fellow that now is. But—would your worship believe it?—my broomstick hath strangely disappeared, stolen, as I suspect, by that unhanged witch, Goody Cory, and that, too, when I was all anointed with the juice of smallage, and cinquefoil, and wolf's bane—"

"Mingled with fine wheat and the fat of a new-born babe," said the shape of old Goodman Brown.

"Ah, your worship knows the recipe," cried the old lady, cackling aloud. "So, as I was saying, being all ready for the meeting, and no horse to ride on, I made up my mind to foot it; for they tell me there is a nice young man to be taken into communion to-night. But now your good worship will lend me your arm, and we shall be there in a twinkling."

"That can hardly be," answered her friend. "I may not 35 spare you my arm, Goody Cloyse; but here is my staff, if you will."

So saying, he threw it down at her feet, where, perhaps, it assumed life, being one of the rods which its owner had formerly lent to the Egyptian magi. Of this fact, however, Goodman Brown could not take cognizance. He had cast up his eyes in astonishment, and, looking down again, beheld neither Goody Cloyse nor the serpentine staff, but his fellow-traveller alone, who waited for him as calmly as if nothing had happened.

"That old woman taught me my catechism," said the young man; and there was a world of meaning in this simple comment.

They continued to walk onward, while the elder traveller exhorted his companion to make good speed and persevere in the path, discoursing so aptly that his arguments seemed rather to spring up in the bosom of his auditor than to be suggested by himself. As they went, he plucked a branch of maple to serve for a walking stick, and began to strip it of the twigs and little boughs, which were wet with evening dew. The moment his fingers touched them they became strangely withered and dried up as with a week's sunshine. Thus the pair proceeded, at a good free pace, until suddenly, in a gloomy hollow of the road, Goodman Brown sat himself down on the stump of a tree and refused to go any farther.

"Friend," said he, stubbornly, "my mind is made up. Not another step will I budge on this errand. What if a wretched old woman do choose to go to the devil when I thought she was going to heaven: is that any reason why I should quit my dear Faith and go after her?"

"You will think better of this by and by," said his ac- 40 quaintance, composedly. "Sit here and rest yourself a while; and when you feel like moving again, there is my staff to help you along."

Without more words, he threw his companion the maple stick, and was as speedily out of sight as if he had vanished into the deepening gloom. The young man sat a few moments by the roadside, applauding himself greatly, and thinking with how clear a conscience he should meet the minister in his morning walk, nor shrink from the eye of good old Deacon Gookin. And what calm sleep would be his that very night, which was to have been spent so wickedly, but so purely and sweetly now, in the arms of Faith! Amidst these pleasant and praiseworthy meditations, Goodman Brown heard the tramp of horses along the road, and deemed it advisable to conceal himself within the verge of the forest, conscious of the guilty purpose that had brought him thither, though now so happily turned from it.

> He looked up to the sky, doubting whether there really was a heaven above him.

On came the hoof tramps and the voices of the riders, two grave old voices, conversing soberly as they drew near. These mingled sounds appeared to pass along the road, within a few yards of the young man's hidingplace; but, owing doubtless to the depth of the gloom at that particular spot, neither the travellers nor their steeds were visible. Though their figures brushed the small boughs by the wayside, it could not be seen that they intercepted, even for a moment, the faint gleam from the strip of bright sky athwart which they must have passed. Goodman Brown alternately crouched and stood on tiptoe, pulling aside the branches and thrusting forth his head as far as he durst without discerning so much as a shadow. It vexed him the more, because he could have sworn, were such a thing possible, that he recognized the voices of the minister and Deacon Gookin, jogging along quietly, as they were wont to do, when bound to some ordination or ecclesiastical council. While yet within hearing, one of the riders stopped to pluck a switch.

"Of the two, reverend sir," said the voice like the deacon's, "I had rather miss an ordination dinner than tonight's meeting. They tell me that some of our community are to be here from Falmouth and beyond, and others from Connecticut and Rhode Island, besides several of the Indian powwows, who, after their fashion, know almost as much deviltry as the best of us. Moreover, there is a goodly young woman to be taken into communion."

"Mighty well, Deacon Gookin!" replied the solemn old tones of the minister. "Spur up, or we shall be late. Nothing can be done, you know, until I get on the ground."

45   The hoofs clattered again; and the voices, talking so strangely in the empty air, passed on through the forest, where no church had ever been gathered or solitary Christian prayed. Whither, then, could these holy men be journeying so deep into the heathen wilderness? Young Goodman Brown caught hold of a tree for support, being ready to sink down on the ground, faint and overburdened with the heavy sickness of his heart. He looked up to the sky, doubting whether there really was a heaven above him. Yet there was the blue arch, and the stars brightening in it.

"With heaven above and Faith below, I will yet stand firm against the devil!" cried Goodman Brown.

While he still gazed upward into the deep arch of the firmament and had lifted his hands to pray, a cloud, though no wind was stirring, hurried across the zenith and hid the brightening stars. The blue sky was still visible except directly overhead, where this black mass of cloud was sweeping swiftly northward. Aloft in the air, as if from the depths of the cloud, came a confused and doubtful sound of voices. Once the listener fancied that he could distinguish the accents of townspeople of his own, men and women, both pious and ungodly, many of whom he had met at the communion table, and had seen others rioting at the tavern. The next moment, so indistinct were the sounds, he doubted whether he had heard aught but the murmur of the old forest, whispering without a wind. Then came a stronger swell of those familiar tones, heard daily in the sunshine at Salem village, but never until now from a cloud of night. There was one voice, of a young woman, uttering lamentations, yet with an uncertain sorrow, and entreating for some favor, which, perhaps, it would grieve her to obtain; and all the unseen multitude, both saints and sinners, seemed to encourage her onward.

"Faith!" shouted Goodman Brown, in a voice of agony and desperation; and the echoes of the forest mocked him, crying, "Faith! Faith!" as if bewildered wretches were seeking her all through the wilderness.

The cry of grief, rage, and terror was yet piercing the night, when the unhappy husband held his breath for a response. There was a scream, drowned immediately in a louder murmur of voices, fading into far-off laughter, as the dark cloud swept away, leaving the clear and silent sky above Goodman Brown. But something fluttered lightly down through the air and caught on the branch of a tree. The young man seized it, and beheld a pink ribbon.

50 "My Faith is gone!" cried he, after one stupefied moment. "There is no good on earth; and sin is but a name. Come, devil; for to thee is this world given."

And, maddened with despair, so that he laughed loud and long, did Goodman Brown grasp his staff and set forth again, at such a rate that he seemed to fly along the forest path rather than to walk or run. The road grew wilder and drearier and more faintly traced, and vanished at length, leaving him in the heart of the dark wilderness, still rushing onward with the instinct that guides mortal man to evil. The whole forest was peopled with frightful sounds—the creaking of the trees, the howling of wild beasts, and the yell of Indians; while sometimes the wind tolled like a distant church bell, and sometimes gave a broad roar around the traveller, as if all Nature were laughing him to scorn. But he was himself the chief horror of the scene, and shrank not from its other horrors.

"Ha! ha! ha!" roared Goodman Brown when the wind laughed at him. "Let us hear which will laugh loudest. Think not to frighten me with your deviltry. Come witch, come wizard, come Indian powwow, come devil himself, and here comes Goodman Brown. You may as well fear him as he fear you."

In truth, all through the haunted forest there could be nothing more frightful than the figure of Goodman Brown. On he flew among the black pines, brandishing his staff with frenzied gestures, now giving vent to an inspiration of horrid blasphemy, and now shouting forth such laughter as set all the echoes of the forest laughing like demons around him. The fiend in his own shape is less hideous than when he rages in the breast of man. Thus sped the demoniac on his course, until, quivering among the trees, he saw a red light before him, as when the felled trunks and branches of a clearing have been set on fire, and throw up their lurid blaze against the sky, at the hour of midnight. He paused, in a lull of the tempest that had driven him onward, and heard the swell of what seemed a hymn, rolling solemnly from a distance with the weight of many voices. He knew the tune; it was a familiar one in the choir of the village meeting house. The verse died heavily away, and was lengthened by a chorus, not of human voices, but of all the sounds of the benighted wilderness pealing in awful harmony together. Goodman Brown cried out; and his cry was lost to his own ear by its unison with the cry of the desert.

In the interval of silence he stole forward until the light glared full upon his eyes. At one extremity of an open space, hemmed in by the dark wall of the forest, arose a rock, bearing some rude, natural resemblance either to an altar or a pulpit, and surrounded by four blazing pines, their tops aflame, their stems untouched, like candles at an evening meeting. The mass of foliage that had overgrown the summit of the rock was all on fire, blazing high into the night and fitfully illuminating the whole field. Each pendent twig and leafy festoon was in a blaze. As the red light arose and fell, a numerous congregation alternately shone forth, then disappeared in shadow, and again grew, as it were, out of the darkness, peopling the heart of the solitary woods at once.

55 "A grave and dark-clad company," quoth Goodman Brown.

In truth they were such. Among them, quivering to and fro between gloom and splendor, appeared faces that would be seen next day at the council board of the province, and others which, Sabbath after Sabbath, looked devoutly heavenward, and benignantly over the crowded pews, from the holiest pulpits in the land. Some affirm that the lady of the governor was there. At least there were high dames well known to her, and wives of honored husbands, and widows, a great multitude, and ancient maidens, all of excellent repute, and fair young girls, who trembled lest their mothers should espy them. Either the sudden gleams of light flashing over the obscure field bedazzled Goodman Brown, or he recognized a score of the church members of Salem village famous for their especial sanctity. Good old Deacon Gookin had arrived, and waited at the skirts of that venerable saint, his revered pastor. But, irreverently consorting with these grave, reputable, and pious people, these elders of the church, these chaste dames and dewy virgins, there were men of dissolute lives and women of spotted fame, wretches given over to all mean and filthy vice, and suspected even of horrid crimes. It was strange to see that the good shrank not from the wicked, nor were the sinners abashed by the saints. Scattered also among their pale-faced enemies were the Indian priests, or powwows, who had often scared their native forest with more hideous incantations than any known to English witchcraft.

"But where is Faith?" thought Goodman Brown, and, as hope came into his heart, he trembled.

> "But where is Faith?" thought Goodman Brown, and, as hope came into his heart, he trembled.

Another verse of the hymn arose, a slow and mournful strain, such as the pious love, but joined to words which expressed all that our nature can conceive of sin, and darkly hinted at far more. Unfathomable to mere mortals is the lore of fiends. Verse after verse was sung; and still the chorus of the desert swelled between the deepest tone of a mighty organ; and with the final peal of that dreadful anthem there came a sound, as if the roaring wind, the rushing streams, the howling beasts, and every other voice of the unconverted wilderness were mingling and according with the voice of guilty man in homage to the prince of all. The four blazing pines threw up a loftier flame, and obscurely discovered shapes and visages of horror on the smoke wreaths above the impious assembly. At the same moment the fire on the rock shot redly forth and formed a glowing arch above its base, where now appeared a figure. With reverence be it spoken, the figure bore no slight similitude, both in garb and manner, to some grave divine of the New England churches.

"Bring forth the converts!" cried a voice that echoed through the field and rolled into the forest.

60 At the word, Goodman Brown stepped forth from the shadow of the trees and approached the congregation, with whom he felt a loathful brotherhood by the sympathy of all that was wicked in his heart. He could have well nigh sworn that the shape of his own dead father beckoned him to advance, looking downward from a smoke wreath, while a woman, with dim features of despair, threw out her hand to warn him back. Was it his mother? But he had no power to retreat one step, nor to resist, even in thought, when the minister and good old Deacon Gookin seized his arms and led him to the blazing rock. Thither came also the slender form of a veiled female, led between Goody Cloyse, that pious teacher of the catechism, and Martha Carrier, who had received the devil's promise to be queen of hell. A rampant hag was she. And there stood the proselytes beneath the canopy of fire.

"Welcome, my children," said the dark figure, "to the communion of your race. Ye have found thus young your nature and your destiny. My children, look behind you!"

They turned; and flashing forth, as it were, in a sheet of flame, the fiend worshippers were seen; the smile of welcome gleamed darkly on every visage.

"There," resumed the sable form, "are all whom ye have reverenced from youth. Ye deemed them holier than yourselves, and shrank from your own sin, contrasting it with their lives of righteousness and prayerful aspirations heavenward. Yet here are they all in my worshipping assembly. This night it shall be granted you to know their secret deeds; how hoary-bearded elders of the church have whispered wanton words to the young maids of their households; how many a woman, eager for widows' weeds, has given her husband a drink at bedtime and let him sleep his last sleep in her bosom; how beardless youths have made haste to inherit their fathers' wealth; and how fair damsels—blush not, sweet ones—have dug little graves in the garden, and bidden me, the sole guest, to an infant's funeral. By the sympathy of your human hearts for sin ye shall scent out all the places—whether in church, bed chamber, street, field, or forest—where crime has been committed, and shall exult to behold the whole earth one stain of guilt, one mighty blood spot. Far more than this. It shall be yours to penetrate, in every bosom, the deep mystery of sin, the fountain of all wicked arts, and which inexhaustibly supplies more evil impulses than human power—than my power at its utmost—can make manifest in deeds. And now, my children, look upon each other."

They did so; and, by the blaze of the hell-kindled torches, the wretched man beheld his Faith, and the wife her husband, trembling before that unhallowed altar.

"Lo, there ye stand, my children," said the figure, in a 65 deep and solemn tone, almost sad with its despairing awfulness, as if his once angelic nature could yet mourn for our miserable race. "Depending upon one another's hearts, ye had still hoped that virtue were not all a dream. Now are ye undeceived. Evil is the nature of mankind. Evil must be your only happiness. Welcome again, my children, to the communion of your race."

"Welcome," repeated the fiend worshippers, in one cry of despair and triumph.

And there they stood, the only pair, as it seemed, who were yet hesitating on the verge of wickedness in this dark world. A basin was hollowed, naturally, in the rock. Did it contain water, reddened by the lurid light? or was it blood? or, perchance, a liquid flame? Herein did the shape of evil dip his hand and prepare to lay the mark of baptism upon their foreheads, that they might be partakers of the mystery of sin, more conscious of the secret guilt of others, both in deed and thought, than they could now be of their own. The husband cast one look at his pale wife, and Faith at him.

> ## Evil must be your only happiness.

What polluted wretches would the next glance show them to each other, shuddering alike at what they disclosed and what they saw!

"Faith! Faith!" cried the husband, "look up to heaven, and resist the wicked one."

Whether Faith obeyed, he knew not. Hardly had he spoken when he found himself amid calm night and solitude, listening to a roar of the wind which died heavily away through the forest. He staggered against the rock, and felt it chill and damp; while a hanging twig, that had been all on fire, besprinkled his cheek with the coldest dew.

70   The next morning young Goodman Brown came slowly into the street of Salem village, staring around him like a bewildered man. The good old minister was taking a walk along the graveyard to get an appetite for breakfast and meditate his sermon, and bestowed a blessing, as he passed, on Goodman Brown. He shrank from the venerable saint as if to avoid an anathema. Old Deacon Gookin was at domestic worship, and the holy words of his prayer were heard through the open window. "What God doth the wizard pray to?" quoth Goodman Brown. Goody Cloyse, that excellent old Christian, stood in the early sunshine at her own lattice, catechizing a little girl who had brought her a pint of morning's milk. Goodman Brown snatched away the child as from the grasp of the fiend himself. Turning the corner by the meeting house, he spied the head of Faith, with the pink ribbons, gazing anxiously forth, and bursting into such joy at sight of him that she skipped along the street and almost kissed her husband before the whole village. But Goodman Brown looked sternly and sadly into her face, and passed on without a greeting.

Had Goodman Brown fallen asleep in the forest and only dreamed a wild dream of a witch meeting?

Be it so, if you will; but, alas; it was a dream of evil omen for young Goodman Brown. A stern, a sad, a darkly meditative, a distrustful, if not a desperate, man did he become from the night of that fearful dream. On the Sabbath day, when the congregation were singing a holy psalm, he could not listen, because an anthem of sin rushed loudly upon his ear and drowned all the blessed strain. When the minister spoke from the pulpit, with power and fervid eloquence and with his hand on the open Bible, of the sacred truths of our religion, and of saintlike lives and triumphant deaths, and of future bliss or misery unutterable, then did Goodman Brown turn pale, dreading lest the roof should thunder down upon the gray blasphemer and his hearers. Often, awaking suddenly at midnight, he shrank from the bosom of Faith; and at morning or eventide, when the family knelt down at prayer, he scowled, and muttered to himself, and gazed sternly at his wife, and turned away. And when he had lived long, and was borne to his grave, a hoary corpse, followed by Faith, an aged woman, and children and grandchildren, a goodly procession, besides neighbors not a few, they carved no hopeful verse upon his tombstone; for his dying hour was gloom.

IF YOU LIKED "YOUNG GOODMAN BROWN," YOU MIGHT ALSO LIKE . . .

. . . another allegory, "The Lottery" by Shirley Jackson (in An Anthology of Stories for Further Reading), or you might also look at the dark woods and listen to the voices at one's shoulder in Barry Lopez's "The Location of the River" (Chapter 10), though these authors' landscapes are very different from that of New Englander Nathaniel Hawthorne.

GOING FURTHER   The world's literature abounds in spiritual quest stories, from the Gilgamesh epic to J. R. R. Tolkien's *Lord of the Rings* novels. You might be interested in the works of C. S. Lewis, another Christian quester given to playing with allegory in the modern world.

Writing from Reading

Summarize

1 What does the story tell you about Goodman Brown's ancestors? What kind of people are they? Does he follow in their footsteps? Explain your answer.

2 What exactly is the wickedness that Goodman Brown witnesses? How does he participate in it? How does Faith?

Analyze Craft

3 Discuss Hawthorne's use of the forest as a symbol. What does the forest represent to Goodman Brown? What does it represent to you as a reader? How and why might those images be different?

4 Discuss the ways in which the scenes that play out for Goodman Brown in the forest reflect his wavering faith. Does Goodman Brown's role as observer of these scenes make the incidents more or less personal, and why?

Analyze Voice

5 Consider the time period in which Hawthorne wrote this story. Identify words and symbols that seem dated or have changed over time. Propose modern equivalents.

Synthesize Summary and Analysis

6 "Faith kept me back a while," says young Goodman Brown, and by "Faith" he means more than his wife. Is her name merely allegorical? Or does she waver in her "faith" and thus become a more complex character? Hawthorne has created many stories whose meanings waver between the allegorical (a single explanation for what the character stands for) and the symbolic (many possible meanings). Explore how each character's name makes him or her symbolic—and how he or she lives up to (or defies) what the name suggests.

Interpret the Story

7 When he finally reaches Salem, Goodman Brown finds business as usual. The narrator wonders, "Had Goodman Brown fallen asleep . . . and only dreamed a wild dream of a witch meeting?" Does Goodman Brown share this suspicion? Argue yes or no, using evidence from the story. Consider the implications of your argument—that is, how does the story's statement on human nature change when you view Goodman Brown's experience as a dream instead of reality, or vice versa?

Eudora Welty (1909–2001)

Eudora Welty was born in Jackson, Mississippi, where she lived and worked for most of her life. In the 1930s she wrote articles for the newspaper *Commercial Appeal,* worked at a Jackson radio station, and became a publicity agent for the Works Progress Administration. Welty began publishing short stories in the mid-1930s. During her long writing career, she received many literary awards, including a Pulitzer Prize. Despite ample opportunities to live abroad or in major cities, Welty always returned to Jackson; arguably, the setting she lived and wrote in was a powerful influence on the timbre of her writing. Many consider her to be one of the most important stylists of the twentieth century; it is hard to talk about a "Southern" voice without mentioning Eudora Welty. (For more on Southern writers, see Chapter 15 for a Case Study on the American South.) Always willing to experiment with the voice, tone, and form of her stories, she evoked powerful, often hilarious relationships among eccentric (but recognizable) Southern families. In addition to four short story collections, she wrote several books of nonfiction—

One Writer's Beginnings is about the art of writing—one children's book, and five novels. Welty was also a photographer and published two books of photographs.

Of her work, she once wrote, "I was trying to write about the way people who live away off from nowhere have to amuse themselves by dramatizing every situation that comes along by exaggerating it—'telling it.' I used the exaggerations and ways of talking I have heard all my life. It's just the way they keep life interesting—they make an experience out of the ordinary. I wasn't trying to do anything but show that. I thought it was cheerful, on the whole."

AS YOU READ   Pay attention to the similes and metaphors Welty uses to describe Phoenix Jackson. What impression of her character do you get from these comparisons? How do they give her a larger-than-life quality?

A Worn Path (1940)

1   IT was December—a bright frozen day in the early morning. Far out in the country there was an old Negro woman with her head tied in a red rag, coming along a path through the pinewoods. Her name was Phoenix Jackson. She was very old and small and she walked slowly in the dark pine shadows, moving a little from side to side in her steps, with the balanced heaviness and lightness of a pendulum in a grandfather clock. She carried a thin, small cane made from an umbrella, and with this she kept tapping the frozen earth in front of her. This made a grave and persistent noise in the still air that seemed meditative, like the chirping of a solitary little bird.

She wore a dark striped dress reaching down to her shoe tops, and an equally long apron of bleached sugar sacks, with a full pocket: all neat and tidy, but every time she took a step she might have fallen over her shoelaces, which dragged from her unlaced shoes. She looked straight ahead. Her eyes were blue with age. Her skin had a pattern all its own of numberless branching wrinkles and as though a whole little tree stood in the middle of her forehead, but a golden color ran underneath, and the two knobs of her cheeks were illumined by a yellow burning under the dark.

Under the red rag her hair came down on her neck in the frailest of ringlets, still black, and with an odor like copper.

Now and then there was a quivering in the thicket. Old Phoenix said, "Out of my way, all you foxes, owls, beetles, jack rabbits, coons and wild animals! . . . Keep out from under these feet, little bob-whites . . . Keep the big wild hogs out of my path. Don't let none of those come running my direction. I got a long way." Under her small black-freckled hand her cane, limber as a buggy whip, would switch at the brush as if to rouse up any hiding things.

On she went. The woods were deep and still. The sun made the pine needles almost too bright to look at, up where the wind rocked. The cones dropped as light as feathers. Down in the hollow was the mourning dove—it was not too late for him.

5   The path ran up a hill. "Seem like there is chains about my feet, time I get this far," she said, in the voice of argument old people keep to use with themselves. "Something always take a hold of me on this hill—pleads I should stay."

After she got to the top, she turned and gave a full, severe look behind her where she had come. "Up through pines," she said at length. "Now down through oaks."

Her eyes opened their widest, and she started down gently. But before she got to the bottom of the hill a bush caught her dress.

Her fingers were busy and intent, but her skirts were full and long, so that before she could pull them free in one place they were caught in another. It was not possible to allow the dress to tear. "I in the thorny bush," she said. "Thorns, you doing your appointed work. Never want to let folks pass, no, sir. Old eyes thought you was a pretty little *green* bush."

> ... before she could pull them free in one place they were caught in another. . . . "I in the thorny bush."

Finally, trembling all over, she stood free, and after a moment dared to stoop for her cane.

10 "Sun so high!" she cried, leaning back and looking, while the thick tears went over her eyes. "The time getting all gone here."

At the foot of this hill was a place where a log was laid across the creek.

"Now comes the trial," said Phoenix. Putting her right foot out, she mounted the log and shut her eyes. Lifting her skirt, leveling her cane fiercely before her like a festival figure in some parade, she began to march across. Then she opened her eyes and she was safe on the other side.

"I wasn't as old as I thought," she said.

But she sat down to rest. She spread her skirts on the bank around her and folded her hands over her knees. Up above her was a tree in a pearly cloud of mistletoe. She did not dare to close her eyes, and when a little boy brought her a plate with a slice of marble-cake on it she spoke to him.

"That would be acceptable," she said. But when she went to take it there was just her own hand in the air.

So she left that tree, and had to go 15 through a barbed-wire fence. There she had to creep and crawl, spreading her knees and stretching her fingers like a baby trying to climb the steps. But she talked loudly to herself: she could not let her dress be torn now, so late in the day, and she could not pay for having her arm or her leg sawed off if she got caught fast where she was.

At last she was safe through the fence and risen up out in the clearing. Big dead trees, like black men with one arm, were standing in the purple stalks of the withered cotton field. There sat a buzzard.

"Who you watching?"

In the furrow she made her way along.

"Glad this not the season for bulls," she said, looking sideways, "and the good Lord made his snakes to curl up and sleep in the winter. A pleasure I don't see no two-headed snake coming around that tree, where it come once. It took a while to get by him, back in the summer."

She passed through the old cotton and went into a field 20 of dead corn. It whispered and shook, and was taller than her head. "Through the maze now," she said, for there was no path.

Then there was something tall, black, and skinny there, moving before her.

At first she took it for a man. It could have been a man dancing in the field. But she stood still and listened, and it did not make a sound. It was as silent as a ghost.

"Ghost," she said sharply, "who be you the ghost of? For I have heard of nary death close by."

But there was no answer—only the ragged dancing in the wind.

She shut her eyes, reached out her hand, and touched a 25 sleeve. She found a coat and inside that an emptiness, cold as ice.

"You scarecrow," she said. Her face lighted. "I ought to be shut up for good," she said with laughter. "My senses is gone. I too old. I the oldest people I ever know. Dance, old scarecrow," she said, "while I dancing with you."

She kicked her foot over the furrow, and with mouth drawn down, shook her head once or twice in a little strutting way. Some husks blew down and whirled in streamers about her skirts.

Then she went on, parting her way from side to side with the cane, through the whispering field. At last she came to the end, to a wagon track where the silver grass blew between the red ruts. The quail were walking around like pullets, seeming all dainty and unseen.

"Walk pretty," she said. "This the easy place. This the easy going."

30   She followed the track, swaying through the quiet bare fields, through the little strings of trees silver in their dead leaves, past cabins silver from weather, with the doors and windows boarded shut, all like old women under a spell sitting there. "I walking in their sleep," she said, nodding her head vigorously.

In a ravine she went where a spring was silently flowing through a hollow log. Old Phoenix bent and drank. "Sweetgum makes the water sweet," she said, and drank more. "Nobody know who made this well, for it was here when I was born."

The track crossed a swampy part where the moss hung as white as lace from every limb. "Sleep on, alligators, and blow your bubbles." Then the track went into the road.

Deep, deep it went down between the high green-colored banks. Overhead the live oaks met, and it was as dark as a cave.

A big black dog with a lolling tongue came up out of the weeds by the ditch. She was meditating, and not ready, and when he came at her she only hit him a little with her cane. Over she went in the ditch, like a little puff of milkweed.

35   Down there, her senses drifted away. A dream visited her, and she reached her hand up, but nothing reached down and gave her a pull. So she lay there and presently went to talking. "Old woman," she said to herself, "that black dog come up out of the weeds to stall you off, and now there he sitting on his fine tail, smiling at you."

A white man finally came along and found her—a hunter, a young man, with his dog on a chain.

"Well, Granny!" he laughed. "What are you doing there?"

"Lying on my back like a June bug waiting to be turned over, mister," she said, reaching up her hand.

> . . . she only hit him
> a little with her cane.
> Over she went in the ditch,
> like a little puff of milkweed.

He lifted her up, gave her a swing in the air, and set her down. "Anything broken, Granny?"

"No sir, them old dead weeds is springy enough," said   40
Phoenix, when she had got her breath. "I thank you for your trouble."

"Where do you live, Granny?" he asked, while the two dogs were growling at each other.

"Away back yonder, sir, behind the ridge. You can't even see it from here."

"On your way home?"

"No sir, I going to town."

"Why, that's too far! That's as far   45
as I walk when I come out myself, and I get something for my trouble." He patted the stuffed bag he carried, and there hung down a little closed claw. It was one of the bob-whites, with its beak hooked bitterly to show it was dead. "Now you go on home, Granny!"

"I bound to go to town, mister," said Phoenix. "The time come around."

He gave another laugh, filling the whole landscape. "I know you old colored people! Wouldn't miss going to town to see Santa Claus!"

But something held old Phoenix very still. The deep lines in her face went into a fierce and different radiation. Without warning, she had seen with her own eyes a flashing nickel fall out of the man's pocket onto the ground.

"How old are you, Granny?" he was saying.

"There is no telling, mister," she said, "no telling."   50

Then she gave a little cry and clapped her hands and said, "Git on away from here, dog! Look! Look at that dog!" She laughed as if in admiration. "He ain't scared of nobody. He a big black dog." She whispered, "Sic him!"

"Watch me get rid of that cur," said the man. "Sic him, Pete! Sic him!"

Phoenix heard the dogs fighting, and heard the man running and throwing sticks. She even heard a gunshot. But she was slowly bending forward by that time, further and further forward, the lids stretched down over her eyes, as if she were doing this in her sleep. Her chin was lowered almost to her knees. The yellow palm of her hand came out from the fold of her apron. Her fingers slid down and along the ground under the piece of money with the grace and care they would have in lifting an egg from under a setting hen. Then she slowly straightened up; she stood erect, and the nickel was in her apron pocket. A bird flew by. Her lips moved. "God watching me the whole time. I come to stealing."

The man came back, and his own dog panted about them. "Well, I scared him off that time," he said, and then he laughed and lifted his gun and pointed it at Phoenix.

55   She stood straight and faced him.

"Doesn't the gun scare you?" he said, still pointing it.

"No, sir, I seen plenty go off closer by, in my day, and for less than what I done," she said, holding utterly still.

He smiled, and shouldered the gun. "Well, Granny," he said, "you must be a hundred years old, and scared of nothing. I'd give you a dime if I had any money with me. But you take my advice and stay home, and nothing will happen to you."

"I bound to go on my way, mister," said Phoenix. She inclined her head in the red rag. Then they went in different directions, but she could hear the gun shooting again and again over the hill.

60   She walked on. The shadows hung from the oak trees to the road like curtains. Then she smelled wood smoke, and smelled the river, and she saw a steeple and the cabins on their steep steps. Dozens of little black children whirled around her. There ahead was Natchez shining. Bells were ringing. She walked on.

In the paved city it was Christmas time. There were red and green electric lights strung and crisscrossed everywhere, and all turned on in the daytime. Old Phoenix would have been lost if she had not distrusted her eyesight and depended on her feet to know where to take her.

She paused quietly on the sidewalk, where people were passing by. A lady came along in the crowd, carrying an armful of red-, green-, and silver-wrapped presents; she gave off perfume like the red roses in hot summer, and Phoenix stopped her.

"Please, missy, will you lace up my shoe?" She held up her foot.

"What do you want, Grandma?"

65   "See my shoe," said Phoenix. "Do all right for out in the country, but wouldn't look right to go in a big building."

"Stand still then, Grandma," said the lady. She put her packages down on the sidewalk beside her and laced and tied both shoes tightly.

"Can't lace 'em with a cane," said Phoenix. "Thank you, missy. I doesn't mind asking a nice lady to tie up my shoe, when I gets out on the street."

Moving slowly and from side to side, she went into the big building, and into a tower of steps, where she walked up and around and around until her feet knew to stop.

She entered a door, and there she saw nailed up on the wall the document that had been stamped with the gold seal and framed in the gold frame, which matched the dream that was hung up in her head.

"Here I be," she said. There was a fixed and ceremonial   70 stiffness over her body.

"A charity case, I suppose," said an attendant who sat at the desk before her.

But Phoenix only looked above her head. There was sweat on her face, the wrinkles in her skin shone like a bright net.

"Speak up, Grandma," the woman said. "What's your name? We must have your history, you know. Have you been here before? What seems to be the trouble with you?"

Old Phoenix only gave a twitch to her face as if a fly were bothering her.

"Are you deaf?" cried the attendant.   75

But then the nurse came in.

"Oh, that's just old Aunt Phoenix," she said. "She doesn't come for herself—she has a little grandson. She makes these trips just as regular as clockwork. She lives away back off the Old Natchez Trace." She bent down. "Well, Aunt Phoenix, why don't you just take a seat? We won't keep you standing after your long trip." She pointed.

The old woman sat down, bolt upright in the chair.

"Now, how is the boy?" asked the nurse.

Old Phoenix did not speak.   80

"I said, how is the boy?"

But Phoenix only waited and stared straight ahead, her face very solemn and withdrawn into rigidity.

"Is his throat any better?" asked the nurse. "Aunt Phoenix, don't you hear me? Is your grandson's throat any better since the last time you came for the medicine?"

With her hands on her knees, the old woman waited, silent, erect and motionless, just as if she were in armor.

"You mustn't take up our time this way, Aunt Phoenix,"   85 the nurse said. "Tell us quickly about your grandson, and get it over. He isn't dead, is he?"

> "... you must be a hundred years old, and scared of nothing...."

At last there came a flicker and then a flame of comprehension across her face, and she spoke.

"My grandson. It was my memory had left me. There I sat and forgot why I made my long trip."

"Forgot?" The nurse frowned. "After you came so far?"

Then Phoenix was like an old woman begging a dignified forgiveness for waking up frightened in the night. "I never did go to school—I was too old at the Surrender," she said in a soft voice. "I'm an old woman without an education. It was my memory fail me. My little grandson, he is just the same, and I forgot it in the coming."

90 "Throat never heals, does it?" said the nurse, speaking in a loud, sure voice to Old Phoenix. By now she had a card with something written on it, a little list. "Yes. Swallowed lye. When was it?—January—two-three years ago—"

Phoenix spoke unasked now. "No, missy, he not dead, he just the same. Every little while his throat begin to close up again, and he not able to swallow. He not get his breath. He not able to help himself. So the time come around, and I go on another trip for the soothing medicine."

"All right. The doctor said as long as you came to get it, you could have it," said the nurse. "But it's an obstinate case."

"My little grandson, he sit up there in the house all wrapped up, waiting by himself," Phoenix went on. "We is the only two left in the world. He suffer and it don't seem to put him back at all. He got a sweet look. He going to

last. He wear a little patch quilt and peep out, holding his mouth open like a little bird. I remembers so plain now. I not going to forget him again, no, the whole enduring time. I could tell him from all the others in creation."

"All right." The nurse was trying to hush her now. She brought her a bottle of medicine. "Charity," she said, making a check mark in a book.

Old Phoenix held the bottle close to her eyes, 95 and then carefully put it into her pocket.

"I thank you," she said.

"It's Christmas time, Grandma," said the attendant. "Could I give you a few pennies out of my purse?"

"Five pennies is a nickel," said Phoenix stiffly.

"Here's a nickel," said the attendant.

Phoenix rose carefully and held out her hand. 100 She received the nickel and then fished the other nickel out of her pocket and laid it beside the new one. She stared at her palm closely, with her head on one side.

Then she gave a tap with her cane on the floor. "This is what come to me to do," she said. "I going to the store and buy my child a little windmill they sells, made out of paper. He going to find it hard to believe there such a thing in the world. I'll march myself back where he waiting, holding it straight up in this hand."

She lifted her free hand, gave a little nod, turned around, and walked out of the doctor's office. Then her slow step began on the stairs, going down.

IF YOU LIKED "A WORN PATH," YOU MIGHT ALSO LIKE . . .

. . . to compare Phoenix Jackson's attitudes toward aging to those of Granny Weatherall in Katherine Anne Porter's "The Jilting of Granny Weatherall" (Chapter 9) or to compare explorations of the rural South by two other Mississippi writers, William Faulkner ("Barn Burning," Chapter 15) and Richard Wright ("The Man Who Was Almost a Man," Chapter 8).

GOING FURTHER   Try a few more of Welty's beautifully composed and often moving, and sometimes mysterious stories, such as "No Place for You, My Love" or "Music from Spain."

Writing from Reading

Summarize

1 List the various perils Phoenix encounters on her journey into town. Which dangers seem actually to frighten the old woman?

2 Scan through the story and identify places where Phoenix shuts or distrusts her eyes. What do these instances have in common?

Analyze Craft

3 Compare Phoenix's attitude and behavior in the city hospital to her demeanor during the trials on the worn path into town. What effect does the town environment have on Phoenix? Why do you think Welty chose to include these two different settings: wilderness and civilization?

Analyze Voice

4 Throughout the story, Phoenix converses aloud with herself and the elements around her. Why do you think Welty chose for Phoenix to speak aloud rather than think to herself? How would the story change if it were written with an omniscient point of view that allowed access not just to what Phoenix says, but to how she feels?

Synthesize Summary and Analysis

5 Do you believe Phoenix's grandson is alive? Support your argument with details from the story.

6 The description of Phoenix at the beginning of the story states that she is a Negro. Discuss how race plays into Phoenix's interactions with other people throughout the story. Would you be able to guess the old woman's race if the story did not explicitly tell you?

Interpret the Story

7 A phoenix is a bird from Greek mythology that catches fire at the end of its life and is reborn from that fire. Why did Welty choose this name for Phoenix Jackson? Compare the old woman's ritual journey into town to the life cycle of the mythological bird.

Reading for Symbols

When reading for symbols—objects, images, characters, or actions that suggest meaning beyond the literal level—notice the images that receive special emphasis. Ask yourself these questions:

Is this an *allegory*—a story in which key elements such as characters and settings represent universal truths or moral lessons in a one-to-one correspondence?		EXAMPLE the ant and the grasshopper

Is this a *symbolic object* or a *symbolic character*— one that appears to have meaning beyond the literal level?		EXAMPLES the pebble that Martha sent; Phoenix Jackson in "A Worn Path"
Is this a *symbolic act*— a gesture or action that conveys something beyond the literal level?		EXAMPLE Lieutenant Cross discarding the pebble
How do you identify an image with symbolic potential?	• Consider whether the image is repeated, portrayed in detail, or given emotional weight in the lives of the characters or narrator.	
How do you understand the meanings of a symbol?	• Consider the characters' attitudes about it, the effect it has on the characters, especially the protagonist, or how it changes over the course of the story, and how attitudes toward it change.	

Writing about Symbols

1. How do symbols in these stories support and establish the themes? Compare "A Red Convertible" and "The Things They Carried." What do these stories suggest about the relationship between theme and symbol in fiction?

2. Exploring the relationship between setting and symbol, "The Things They Carried" and "Young Goodman Brown" both feature characters who find themselves away from home in strange and dangerous places. How does each author establish a sense of place, as in Hawthorne's deep forest in New England and O'Brien's jungle battlefield in Vietnam? Use examples from each story to illustrate how the symbolic resonance of particular details enhances these settings.

3. Make an outline of a story mirroring the one in Eudora Welty's "A Worn Path" but with the locale or setting changed to a town or city you know. What details of your new setting would take on symbolic importance?

15 American Regionalism

Two Case Studies
The American West and The American South

and Sense of Place

ALL writers try to impart a sense of location in which their stories take place. This is just as much the case for the plain of Troy in Homer's epic *The Iliad* as for the Danish castle in Shakespeare's *Hamlet*. It holds equally true for the American South of Flannery O'Connor and William Faulkner and the Southwest of Leslie Marmon Silko or John Steinbeck's West. In the past decades American writers such as Dagoberto Gilb have stressed the importance of place. As James D. Houston observes in "A Writer's Sense of Place," our literature "is rich with . . . stories wherein at least part of what's going on is some form of dialogue between a place—whether it be an island or a mountain or a city or a shoreline or a subregion of the continent—and the lives being lived. . . ." What matters for North American writers in the present moment was also true for fiction writers from another place and time.

The American West

THE last major region of the continental United States to be settled, the West has played a special role in the American imagination. Its vast spaces and wide variety of landscapes—deserts, grazing lands, lush farming valleys, and mountains—have inspired Americans since the Lewis and Clark expedition (1804–1806) to explore the land. With the close of the frontier in the 1890s, the region changed. Cities began to compete with farms and ranches as centers of commercial and cultural experience. New immigrant populations mingled with native inhabitants. Although the romantic image of rugged cowboys and starkly individualistic settlers lives on in twentieth-century Western movies, serious Western literature of the twentieth century was much more ambiguous—less certain of the good, morally upright settler taming the landscape and more aware of a growing society's willingness to exploit natural resources. With the emergence of Native-American writers such as Leslie Marmon Silko, a sense of loss colors the literature; the traditional Native American way of life has long been at risk. Other writers, such as John Steinbeck, are deeply attuned to the beauty of surrounding nature, displaying an awareness of the disjunction between a degraded humanity and the environment they so love. From the central plains to southern Texas to the California coast and beyond, such writers as Dagoberto Gilb show us the Old West has clearly become a New West, a region to rediscover.

Dagoberto Gilb *. . . I loved that you could be angry on the page. . . .*

A Conversation on Writing

Growing Up without Books

I did not grow up with books. . . . I had no idea that books existed, really. And it wasn't part of my own community or culture. I grew up with a mother that was a single mother, a Mexican-American, and also . . . a person from the working class. . . . My friends whether they're black or white basically didn't read; we didn't have any concept of books. So I just came into it late as one of these odd things that seemed to have happened to me.

Discovering Literature

To get through [school], you had to take that freshman comp class. I wasn't really dumb. What do you call that when you're not dumb but you can sort of survive? And you look dumb to all the teachers that are giving you dumb grades. I very wisely took a night class where I looked good because everybody was older and tired. I got a "B". . . . I did have to take one more [course]. I remember reading *Billy Budd* . . . but I had to look up a word every other line. . . . I couldn't believe an American writer wrote so oddly. And I just gave up literature . . . until I started reading others. . . . Luis Valdez . . . Jack Kerouac. . . . I learned, and very gratefully learned, that storytelling was about voice.

Reading as Exercise for Writing

The brain is a muscle. And the muscle that makes the brain the strongest is reading. . . . Anybody that sits down to read one book (I don't care if you read it twenty times, it doesn't have to be twenty books, it can be one book twenty times) . . . will get stronger and . . . see better. You'll breathe deeper. . . . And writing is the same thing. Actually writing doesn't exist without loving books and loving reading.

To watch this entire interview with Dagoberto Gilb, go to connect.mcgraw-hill.com.

Born (1950) in Los Angeles to a Mexican mother and an American father, Dagoberto Gilb has become an increasingly recognized voice of the Mexican-American, and working-class, experience. Although he graduated with a double major and a master's degree from the University of California, Santa Barbara, Gilb turned to construction for his living and traveled between Los Angeles and El Paso for his work. He began to write during this period, joining a labor union as a class-A journeyman carpenter and working primarily on high-rise buildings. Thus, his writing captures a contemporary working-class perspective, beginning with his first full collection of short stories, *The Magic of Blood* (1993). Gilb has published a novel, *The Last Known Residence of Mickey Acuña* (1994); another collection of short stories, *Woodcuts of Women* (2001); a collection of essays, *Gritos* (1993); and, most recently, a novel, *The Flowers* (2008). His anthology *Hecho en Tejas: An Anthology of Texas-Mexican Literature* appeared in 2007.

RESEARCH ASSIGNMENT In his interview, Gilb says, "I don't think an American white guy can write from a black point of view." What does he mean by this? Do you agree?

> "A lot of times the world of books doesn't reflect your own neighborhood. I think in the Rio Grande Valley or in El Paso, Texas, or places like that where the majority of the population, I'd say seventy-five percent of the population, is Mexican-American, first generation to third. . . . They sit there and read about mutton and teapots, and go, ugh, and think, I don't know what I'm going to do in college. . . . There's never gorditas, there's no enchiladas, there's nothing about the neighborhood." Conversation with Dagoberto Gilb

Love in L.A. (1993)

1 JAKE slouched in a clot of near motionless traffic, in the peculiar gray of concrete, smog, and early morning beneath the overpass of the Hollywood Freeway on Alvarado Street. He didn't really mind because he knew how much worse it could be trying to make a left onto the onramp. He certainly didn't do that every day of his life, and he'd assure anyone who'd ask that he never would either. A steady occupation had its advantages and he couldn't deny thinking about that too. He needed an FM radio in something better than this '58 Buick he drove. It would have crushed velvet interior with electric controls for the L.A. summer, a nice warm heater and defroster for the winter drives at the beach, a cruise control for those longer trips, mellow speakers front and rear of course, windows that hum closed, snuffing out that nasty exterior noise of freeways. The fact was that he'd probably have to change his whole style. Exotic colognes, plush, dark nightclubs, maitais and daiquiris, necklaced ladies in satin gowns, misty and sexy like in a tequila ad. Jake could imagine lots of possibilities when he let himself, but none that ended up with him pressed onto a stalled freeway.

Jake was thinking about this freedom of his so much that when he glimpsed its green light he just went ahead and stared bye bye to the steadily employed. When he turned his head the same direction his windshield faced, it was maybe one second too late. He pounced the brake pedal and steered the front wheels away from the tiny brakelights but the smack was unavoidable. Just one second sooner and it would only have been close. One second more and he'd be crawling up the Toyota's trunk. As it was, it seemed like only a harmless smack, much less solid than the one against his back bumper.

Jake considered driving past the Toyota but was afraid the traffic ahead would make it too difficult. As he

pulled up against the curb a few car lengths ahead, it occurred to him that the traffic might have helped him get away too. He slammed the car door twice to make sure it was closed fully and to give himself another second more, then toured front and rear of his Buick for damage on or near the bumpers. Not an impressionable scratch even in the chrome. He perked up. Though the car's beauty was secondary to its ability to start and move, the body and paint were clean except for a few minor dings. This stood out as one of his few clearcut accomplishments over the years.

Before he spoke to the driver of the Toyota, whose looks he could see might present him with an added complication, he signaled to the driver of the car that hit him, still in his car and stopped behind the Toyota, and waved his hands and shook his head to let the man know there was no problem as far as he was concerned. The driver waved back and started his engine.

5   "It didn't even scratch my paint," Jake told her in that way of his. "So how you doin? Any damage to the car? I'm kinda hoping so, just so it takes a little more time and we can talk some. Or else you can give me your phone number now and I won't have to lay my regular b.s. on you to get it later."

He took her smile as a good sign and relaxed. He inhaled her scent like it was clean air and straightened out his less than new but not unhip clothes.

"You've got Florida plates. You look like you must be Cuban."

"My parents are from Venezuela."

"My name's Jake." He held out his hand.

10   "Mariana."

They shook hands like she'd never done it before in her life.

"I really am sorry about hitting you like that." He sounded genuine. He fondled the wide dimple near the cracked taillight. "It's amazing how easy it is to put a dent in these new cars. They're so soft they might replace waterbeds soon." Jake was confused about how to proceed with this. So much seemed so unlikely, but

> He inhaled her scent like it was clean air. . . .

there was always possibility. "So maybe we should go out to breakfast somewhere and talk it over."

"I don't eat breakfast."

"Some coffee then."

"Thanks, but I really can't."   15

"You're not married, are you? Not that that would matter that much to me. I'm an openminded kinda guy."

She was smiling. "I have to get to work."

"That sounds boring."

"I better get your driver's license," she said.

Jake nodded, disappointed. "One little problem,"   20 he said. "I didn't bring it. I just forgot it this morning. I'm a musician," he exaggerated greatly, "and, well, I dunno, I left my wallet in the pants I was wearing last night. If you have some paper and a pen I'll give you my address and all that."

He followed her to the glove compartment side of her car.

"What if we don't report it to the insurance companies? I'll just get it fixed for you."

"I don't think my dad would let me do that."

"Your dad? It's not your car?"

"He bought it for me. And I live at home."   25

"Right." She was slipping away from him. He went back around to the back of her new Toyota and looked over the damage again. There was the trunk lid, the bumper, a rear panel, a taillight.

"You do have insurance?" she asked, suspicious, as she came around the back of the car.

"Oh yeah," he lied.

"I guess you better write the name of that down too."

He made up a last name and address and wrote   30 down the name of an insurance company an old girlfriend once belonged to. He considered giving a real phone number but went against that idea and made one up.

"I act too," he lied to enhance the effect more. "Been in a couple of movies."

She smiled like a fan.

"So how about your phone number?" He was rebounding maturely.

She gave it to him.

35 "Mariana, you are beautiful," he said in his most sincere voice.

"Call me," she said timidly.

Jake beamed. "We'll see you, Mariana," he said holding out his hand. Her hand felt so warm and soft he felt like he'd been kissed.

Back in his car he took a moment or two to feel both proud and sad about his performance. Then he watched the rear view mirror as Mariana pulled up behind him. She was writing down the license plate numbers on his Buick, ones that he'd taken off a junk because the ones that belonged to his had expired so long ago. He turned the ignition key and revved the big engine and clicked into drive. His sense of freedom swelled as he drove into the now moving street traffic, though he couldn't stop the thought about the FM stereo radio and crushed velvet interior and the new car smell that would even make it better.

> His sense of freedom swelled. . . .

Questions for Critical Thinking

1 List what you know about Jake from the story; then list what you know about his car.

2 What specific details about setting does Gilb include in this story? Could you identify the setting of the story even if it weren't stated explicitly in the title?

3 If you corrected the street names, could this story's title be changed to "Love in [Your Town]"? What details would

remain valid? What details are unique to the Los Angeles setting?

4 Characterize the speaker's opinion of Jake. Which details from the story, if any, would be excluded if it were told in first person by Jake?

5 How does Mariana's attitude toward Jake change between the time they shake hands and the time they part? What about her interaction with Jake causes this change?

6 Argue whether or not Jake has convinced Mariana with his lies. What specific details from the story support your position?

7 The collision damages Mariana's car, but Jake's car remains unscathed. Is this the first car crash Jake has lied his way out of? Consider that Jake immediately registers Mariana's good looks as a "complication."

"Men do change, and change comes like a little wind that ruffles the curtains at dawn, and it comes like the stealthy perfume of wildflowers hidden in the grass." —John Steinbeck

John Steinbeck (1902–1968)

The Salinas Valley area of central California carries the nickname "Steinbeck Country," named, of course, for John Steinbeck, the Nobel Prize–winning author who was born and raised there. Steinbeck's summer job as a ranch hand and his mother's anecdotes about local people rooted him in his home county early on. Although he attended Stanford as an English major, Steinbeck dropped out to pursue his dream of success as a writer, a dream that did not pay off until several novels into his career. Today, his place in the American literary canon is secure with books like *The Grapes of Wrath* (1939), his Pulitzer Prize–winning epic about a family of Oklahomans who migrate to California; *East of Eden* (1952), an account of two families in the Salinas Valley; and *Of Mice and Men* (1937), the tragic tale of a farm laborer and his mentally handicapped friend.

A writer conscious of the economic and social problems of his day, Steinbeck portrayed characters who struggle, whether internally with their own psyches or externally with a society permeated by intolerance. Most of the large body of his work—novels, stories, plays, essays, travel books, reportage—has remained in print since his death, a tribute by both publishers and readers to the enduring nature of his vision.

The Chrysanthemums (1938)

1   THE high grey-flannel fog of winter closed off the Salinas Valley from the sky and from all the rest of the world. On every side it sat like a lid on the mountains and made of the great valley a closed pot. On the broad, level land floor the gang plows bit deep and left the black earth shining like metal where the shares had cut. On the foothill ranches across the Salinas River, the yellow stubble fields seemed to be bathed in pale cold sunshine, but there was no sunshine in the valley now in December. The thick willow scrub along the river flamed with sharp and positive yellow leaves.

It was a time of quiet and of waiting. The air was cold and tender. A light wind blew up from the southwest so that the farmers were mildly hopeful of a good rain before long; but fog and rain do not go together.

Across the river, on Henry Allen's foothill ranch there was little work to be done, for the hay was cut and stored and the orchards were plowed up to receive the rain deeply when it should come. The cattle on the higher slopes were becoming shaggy and rough-coated.

Elisa Allen, working in her flower garden, looked down across the yard and saw Henry, her husband, talking to two men in business suits. The three of them stood by the tractor shed, each man with one foot on the side of the little Fordson. They smoked cigarettes and studied the machine as they talked.

Elisa watched them for a moment and then went back   5 to her work. She was thirty-five. Her face was lean and strong and her eyes were as clear as water. Her figure looked blocked and heavy in her gardening costume, a man's black hat pulled low down over her eyes, clod-hopper shoes, a fig-ured print dress almost completely covered by a big corduroy apron with four big pockets to hold the snips, the trowel and scratcher, the seeds and the knife she worked with. She wore heavy leather gloves to protect her hands while she worked.

She was cutting down the old year's chrysanthemum stalks with a pair of short and powerful scissors. She looked down toward the men by the tractor shed now and then. Her face was ea-ger and mature and handsome; even her work with the scis-sors was over-eager, over-powerful. The chrysanthemum stems seemed too small and easy for her energy.

She brushed a cloud of hair out of her eyes with the back of her glove, and left a smudge of earth on her cheek in doing it. Behind her stood the neat white farm house with red geraniums close-banked around it as high as the win-dows. It was a hard-swept looking little house with hard-polished windows, and a clean mud-mat on the front steps.

Elisa cast another glance toward the tractor shed. The strangers were getting into their Ford coupe. She took off a glove and put her strong fingers down into the forest of new green chrysanthemum sprouts that were growing around the old roots. She spread the leaves and looked down among the close-growing stems. No aphids were there, no sowbugs or snails or cutworms. Her terrier fingers destroyed such pests before they could get started.

Elisa started at the sound of her husband's voice. He had come near quietly, and he leaned over the wire fence that protected her flower garden from cattle and dogs and chickens.

10   "At it again," he said. "You've got a strong new crop coming."

Elisa straightened her back and pulled on the garden-ing glove again. "Yes. They'll be strong this coming year." In her tone and on her face there was a little smugness.

"You've got a gift with things," Henry observed. "Some of those yellow chrysanthemums you had this year were ten inches across. I wish you'd work out in the orchard and raise some apples that big."

Her eyes sharpened. "Maybe I could do it, too. I've a gift with things, all right. My mother had it. She could stick anything in the ground and make it grow. She said it was having planters' hands that knew how to do it."

"Well, it sure works with flowers," he said.

She could stick anything in the ground **and make it grow.**

"Henry, who were those men you were talking to?"   15

"Why, sure, that's what I came to tell you. They were from the Western Meat Company. I sold those thirty head of three-year-old steers. Got nearly my own price, too."

"Good," she said. "Good for you."

"And I thought," he continued, "I thought how it's Saturday afternoon, and we might go into Salinas for din-ner at a restaurant, and then to a picture show—to celebrate, you see."

"Good," she repeated. "Oh, yes. That will be good."

Henry put on his joking tone. "There's fights tonight.   20 How'd you like to go to the fights?"

"Oh, no," she said breathlessly. "No, I wouldn't like fights."

"Just fooling, Elisa. We'll go to a movie. Let's see. It's two now. I'm going to take Scotty and bring down those steers from the hill. It'll take us maybe two hours. We'll go in town about five and have dinner at the Cominos Hotel. Like that?"

"Of course I'll like it. It's good to eat away from home."

"All right, then. I'll go get up a couple of horses."

She said, "I'll have plenty of time to transplant some of   25 these sets, I guess."

She heard her husband calling Scotty down by the barn. And a little later she saw the two men ride up the pale yellow hillside in search of the steers.

There was a little square sandy bed kept for rooting the chrysanthemums. With her trowel she turned the soil over and over, and smoothed it and patted it firm. Then she dug ten parallel trenches to receive the sets. Back at the chrysanthemum bed she pulled out the little crisp shoots, trimmed off the leaves of each one with her scissors and laid it on a small orderly pile.

A squeak of wheels and plod of hoofs came from the road. Elisa looked up. The country road ran along the dense bank of willows and cottonwoods that bordered the river, and up this road came a curious vehicle, curiously drawn. It was an old spring-wagon, with a round canvas top on it like the cover of a prairie schooner. It was drawn by an old bay horse and a little grey-and-white burro. A big stubble-bearded man sat between the cover flaps and drove the crawling team. Underneath the wagon, between the hind wheels, a lean and rangy mongrel dog walked sedately. Words were painted on the canvas, in clumsy, crooked let-ters. "Pots, pans, knives, sisors, lawn mores, Fixed." Two rows of articles, and the triumphantly definitive "Fixed" below. The black paint had run down in little sharp points beneath each letter.

Elisa, squatting on the ground, watched to see the crazy, loose-jointed wagon pass by. But it didn't pass. It turned into the farm road in front of her house, crooked old wheels skirling and squeaking. The rangy dog darted from between the wheels and ran ahead. Instantly the two ranch shepherds flew out at him. Then all three stopped, and with stiff and quivering tails, with taut straight legs, with ambassadorial dignity, they slowly circled, sniffing daintily. The caravan pulled up to Elisa's wire fence and stopped. Now the newcomer dog, feeling out-numbered, lowered his tail and retired under the wagon with raised hackles and bared teeth.

30 The man on the wagon seat called out, "That's a bad dog in a fight when he gets started."

Elisa laughed. "I see he is. How soon does he generally get started?"

The man caught up her laughter and echoed it heartily. "Sometimes not for weeks and weeks," he said. He climbed stiffly down, over the wheel. The horse and the donkey drooped like unwatered flowers.

Elisa saw that he was a very big man. Although his hair and beard were greying, he did not look old. His worn black suit was wrinkled and spotted with grease. The laughter had disappeared from his face and eyes the moment his laughing voice ceased. His eyes were dark, and they were full of the brooding that gets in the eyes of teamsters and of sailors. The calloused hands he rested on the wire fence were cracked, and every crack was a black line. He took off his battered hat.

"I'm off my general road, ma'am," he said. "Does this dirt road cut over across the river to the Los Angeles highway?"

35 Elisa stood up and shoved the thick scissors in her apron pocket. "Well, yes, it does, but it winds around and then fords the river. I don't think your team could pull through the sand."

He replied with some asperity. "It might surprise you what them beasts can pull through."

"When they get started?" she asked.

He smiled for a second. "Yes. When they get started."

"Well," said Elisa, "I think you'll save time if you go back to the Salinas road and pick up the highway there."

He drew a big finger down the chicken wire and made 40 it sing. "I ain't in any hurry, ma'am. I go from Seattle to San Diego and back every year. Takes all my time. About six months each way. I aim to follow nice weather."

Elisa took off her gloves and stuffed them in the apron pocket with the scissors. She touched the under edge of her man's hat, searching for fugitive hairs. "That sounds like a nice kind of a way to live," she said.

He leaned confidentially over the fence. "Maybe you noticed the writing on my wagon. I mend pots and sharpen knives and scissors. You got any of them things to do?"

"Oh, no," she said quickly. "Nothing like that." Her eyes hardened with resistance.

"Scissors is the worst thing," he explained. "Most people just ruin scissors trying to sharpen 'em, but I know how. I got a special tool. It's a little bobbit kind of thing, and patented. But it sure does the trick."

"No. My scissors are all sharp." 45

"All right, then. Take a pot," he continued earnestly, "a bent pot, or a pot with a hole. I can make it like new so you don't have to buy no new ones. That's a saving for you."

"No," she said shortly. "I tell you I have nothing like that for you to do."

His face fell to an exaggerated sadness. His voice took on a whining undertone. "I ain't had a thing to do today. Maybe I won't have no supper tonight. You see I'm off my regular road. I know folks on the highway clear from Seattle to San Diego. They save their things for me to sharpen up because they know I do it so good and save them money."

"I'm sorry," Elisa said irritably. "I haven't anything for you to do."

His eyes left her face and fell to searching the ground. 50 They roamed about until they came to the chrysanthemum bed where she had been working. "What's them plants, ma'am?"

The irritation and resistance melted from Elisa's face. "Oh, those are chrysanthemums, giant whites and yellows. I raise them every year, bigger than anybody around here."

"Kind of a long-stemmed flower? Looks like a quick puff of colored smoke?" he asked.

"That's it. What a nice way to describe them."

"They smell kind of nasty till you get used to them," he said.

55 "It's a good bitter smell," she retorted, "not nasty at all. He changed his tone quickly. "I like the smell myself."

"I had ten-inch blooms this year," she said.

The man leaned farther over the fence. "Look. I know a lady down the road a piece, has got the nicest garden you ever seen. Got nearly every kind of flower but no chrysanthemums. Last time I was mending a copper-bottom washtub for her (that's a hard job but I do it good), she said to me, 'If you ever run acrost some nice chrysanthemums I wish you'd try to get me a few seeds.' That's what she told me."

Elisa's eyes grew alert and eager. "She couldn't have known much about chrysanthemums. You *can* raise them from seed, but it's much easier to root the little sprouts you see there."

60 "Oh," he said. "I s'pose I can't take none to her, then."

"Why yes you can," Elisa cried. "I can put some in damp sand, and you can carry them right along with you. They'll take root in the pot if you keep them damp. And then she can transplant them."

"She'd sure like to have some, ma'am. You say they're nice ones?"

"Beautiful," she said. "Oh, beautiful." Her eyes shone. She tore off the battered hat and shook out her dark pretty hair. "I'll put them in a flower pot, and you can take them right with you. Come into the yard."

While the man came through the picket gate Elisa ran excitedly along the geranium-bordered path to the back of the house. And she returned carrying a big red flower pot. The gloves were forgotten now. She kneeled on the ground by the starting bed and dug up the sandy soil with her fingers and scooped it into the bright new flower pot. Then she picked up the little pile of shoots she had prepared. With her strong fingers she pressed them in the sand and tamped around them with her knuckles. The man stood over her. "I'll tell you what to do," she said. "You remember so you can tell the lady."

65 "Yes, I'll try to remember."

"Well, look. These will take root in about a month. Then she must set them out, about a foot apart in good rich earth like this, see?" She lifted a handful of dark soil for him to look at. "They'll grow fast and tall. Now remember this: In July tell her to cut them down, about eight inches from the ground."

"Before they bloom?" he asked.

"Yes, before they bloom." Her face was tight with eagerness. "They'll grow right up again. About the last of September the buds will start."

She stopped and seemed perplexed. "It's the budding that takes the most care," she said hesitantly. "I don't know how to tell you." She looked deep into his eyes, searchingly. Her mouth opened a little, and she seemed to be listening. "I'll try to tell you," she said. "Did you ever hear of planting hands?"

"Can't say I have, ma'am." 70

"Well, I can only tell you what it feels like. It's when you're picking off the buds you don't want. Everything goes right down into your fingertips. You watch your fingers work. They do it themselves. You can feel how it is. They pick and pick the buds. They never make a mistake. They're with the plant. Do you see? Your fingers and the plant. You can feel that, right up your arm. They know. They never make a mistake. You can feel it. When you're like that you can't do anything wrong. Do you see that? Can you understand that?"

She was kneeling on the ground looking up at him. Her breast swelled passionately.

The man's eyes narrowed. He looked away self-consciously. "Maybe I know," he said. "Sometimes in the night in the wagon there—"

Elisa's voice grew husky. She broke in on him, "I've never lived as you do, but I know what you mean. When the night is dark—why, the stars are sharp-pointed, and there's quiet. Why, you rise up and up! Every pointed star gets driven into your body. It's like that. Hot and sharp and—lovely."

Kneeling there, her hand went out toward his legs in 75 the greasy black trousers. Her hesitant fingers almost touched the cloth. Then her hand dropped to the ground. She crouched low like a fawning dog.

He said, "It's nice, just like you say. Only when you don't have no dinner, it ain't."

She stood up then, very straight, and her face was ashamed. She held the flower pot out to him and placed it gently in his arms. "Here. Put it in your wagon, on the seat, where you can watch it. Maybe I can find something for you to do."

At the back of the house she dug in the can pile and found two old and battered aluminum saucepans. She carried them back and gave them to him. "Here, maybe you can fix these."

His manner changed. He became professional. "Good as new I can fix them." At the back of his wagon he set a little anvil, and out of an oily tool box dug a small machine hammer. Elisa came through the gate to watch him while he pounded out the dents in the kettles. His mouth grew sure and knowing. At a difficult part of the work he sucked his under-lip.

80 "You sleep right in the wagon?" Elisa asked.

"Right in the wagon, ma'am. Rain or shine I'm dry as a cow in there."

"It must be nice," she said. "It must be very nice. I wish women could do such things."

"It ain't the right kind of a life for a woman."

Her upper lip raised a little, showing her teeth. "How do you know? How can you tell?" she said.

85 "I don't know, ma'am," he protested. "Of course I don't know. Now here's your kettles, done. You don't have to buy no new ones."

"How much?"

"Oh, fifty cents'll do. I keep my prices down and my work good. That's why I have all them satisfied customers up and down the highway."

Elisa brought him a fifty-cent piece from the house and dropped it in his hand. "You might be surprised to have a rival some time. I can sharpen scissors, too. And I can beat the dents out of little pots. I could show you what a woman might do."

He put his hammer back in the oily box and shoved the little anvil out of sight. "It would be a lonely life for a woman, ma'am, and a scarey life, too, with animals creeping under the wagon all night." He climbed over the single-tree, steadying himself with a hand on the burro's white rump. He settled himself in the seat, picked up the lines. "Thank you kindly, ma'am," he said. "I'll do like you told me; I'll go back and catch the Salinas road."

90 "Mind," she called, "if you're long in getting there, keep the sand damp."

"Sand, ma'am? . . . Sand? Oh, sure. You mean around the chrysanthemums. Sure I will." He clucked his tongue. The beasts leaned luxuriously into their collars. The mongrel dog took his place between the back wheels. The wagon turned and crawled out the entrance road and back the way it had come, along the river.

Elisa stood in front of her wire fence watching the slow progress of the caravan. Her shoulders were straight, her head thrown back, her eyes half-closed, so that the scene came vaguely into them. Her lips moved silently, forming the words "Good-bye—good-bye." Then she whispered. "That's a bright direction. There's a glowing there." The sound of her whisper startled her. She shook herself free and looked about to see whether anyone had been listening. Only the dogs had heard. They lifted their heads toward her from their sleeping in the dust, and then stretched out their chins and settled asleep again. Elisa turned and ran hurriedly into the house.

"*. . . I wish women could do such* things."

In the kitchen she reached behind the stove and felt the water tank. It was full of hot water from the noonday cooking. In the bathroom she tore off her soiled clothes and flung them into the corner. And then she scrubbed herself with a little block of pumice, legs and thighs, loins and chest and arms, until her skin was scratched and red. When she had dried herself she stood in front of a mirror in her bedroom and looked at her body. She tightened her stomach and threw out her chest. She turned and looked over her shoulder at her back.

After a while she began to dress, slowly. She put on her newest underclothing and her nicest stockings and the dress which was the symbol of her prettiness. She worked carefully on her hair, penciled her eyebrows and rouged her lips.

95 Before she was finished she heard the little thunder of hoofs and the shouts of Henry and his helper as they drove the red steers into the corral. She heard the gate bang shut and set herself for Henry's arrival.

His step sounded on the porch. He entered the house calling, "Elisa, where are you?"

"In my room, dressing. I'm not ready. There's hot water for your bath. Hurry up. It's getting late."

When she heard him splashing in the tub, Elisa laid his dark suit on the bed, and shirt and socks and tie beside it. She stood his polished shoes on the floor beside the bed. Then she went to the porch and sat primly and stiffly down. She looked toward the river road where the willow-line was still yellow with frosted leaves so that under the high grey fog they seemed a thin band of sunshine. This was the only color in the grey afternoon. She sat unmoving for a long time. Her eyes blinked rarely.

Henry came banging out of the door, shoving his tie inside his vest as he came. Elisa stiffened and her face grew tight. Henry stopped short and looked at her. "Why—why, Elisa. You look so nice!"

100   "Nice? You think I look nice? What do you mean by 'nice'?"

Henry blundered on. "I don't know. I mean you look different, strong and happy."

"I am strong? Yes, strong. What do you mean 'strong'?"

He looked bewildered. "You're playing some kind of a game," he said helplessly. "It's a kind of a play. You look strong enough to break a calf over your knee, happy enough to eat it like a watermelon."

For a second she lost her rigidity. "Henry! Don't talk like that. You didn't know what you said." She grew complete again. "I'm strong," she boasted. "I never knew before how strong."

105   Henry looked down toward the tractor shed, and when he brought his eyes back to her, they were his own again. "I'll get out the car. You can put on your coat while I'm starting."

Elisa went into the house. She heard him drive to the gate and idle down his motor, and then she took a long time to put on her hat. She pulled it here and pressed it there. When Henry turned the motor off she slipped into her coat and went out.

The little roadster bounced along on the dirt road by the river, raising the birds and driving the rabbits into the brush. Two cranes flapped heavily over the willow-line and dropped into the river-bed.

Far ahead on the road Elisa saw a dark speck. She knew.

She tried not to look as they passed it, but her eyes would not obey. She whispered to herself sadly, "He might have thrown them off the road. That wouldn't have been much trouble, not very much. But he kept the pot," she explained. "He had to keep the pot. That's why he couldn't get them off the road."

110   The roadster turned a bend and she saw the caravan ahead. She swung full around toward her husband so she could not see the little covered wagon and the mismatched team as the car passed them.

In a moment it was over. The thing was done. She did not look back.

She said loudly, to be heard above the motor, "It will be good, tonight, a good dinner."

"Now you're changed again," Henry complained. He took one hand from the wheel and patted her knee. "I ought to take you in to dinner oftener. It would be good for both of us. We get so heavy out on the ranch."

"Henry," she asked, "could we have wine at dinner?"

"Sure we could. Say! That will be fine." 115

She was silent for a while; then she said, "Henry, at those prize fights, do the men hurt each other very much?"

"Sometimes a little, not often. Why?"

"Well, I've read how they break noses, and blood runs down their chests. I've read how the fighting gloves get heavy and soggy with blood."

He looked around at her. "What's the matter, Elisa? I didn't know you read things like that." He brought the car to a stop, then turned to the right over the Salinas River bridge.

"Do any women ever go to the fights?" she asked. 120

"Oh, sure, some. What's the matter, Elisa? Do you want to go? I don't think you'd like it, but I'll take you if you really want to go."

She relaxed limply in the seat. "Oh, no. No. I don't want to go. I'm sure I don't." Her face was turned away from him. "It will be enough if we can have wine. It will be plenty." She turned up her coat collar so he could not see that she was crying weakly—like an old woman.

Questions for Critical Thinking

1 What pattern of imagery do you notice in Steinbeck's description of the Salinas Valley at the beginning of the story? How does this contribute to your understanding of Elisa's conflict?

2 What is the conflict in this story? Is it an inner conflict or an external one?

3 Elisa, like Steinbeck, is clearly attuned to the world surrounding her.

What does this suggest about her character? In other words, why do you think Steinbeck chose her to be adept at growing plants rather than focusing on other occupations such as sewing or cooking?

"The oral tradition stays in the human brain and then it is a collective effort in the recollection. So when he is telling a story and she is telling a story and you are telling a story and one of us is listening and there is a slightly different version or a detail, then it is participatory when somebody politely says I remember it this way. It is a collective memory and depends upon the whole community. There is no single entity that controls information or dictates but this oral tradition is a constantly self-correcting process." —Leslie Marmon Silko, from "An Interview with Leslie Marmon Silko" by Thomas Irmer

Leslie Marmon Silko (b. 1948)

Leslie Marmon Silko grew up in Laguna, New Mexico, a town with a history of conflict between missionaries and the native inhabitants. Her own heritage is a mix of Native American, Hispanic, and Caucasian ancestry. As a young girl, Silko roamed the landscape, traversing it with her horse and her rifle. While an undergraduate at the University of New Mexico, Silko wrote and published "The Man to Send Rain Clouds," which she based on a story she had heard about a priest upset because he had not been asked to take over a Native American's funeral. Silko has been successful in a number of genres, with story collections such as *Storyteller* (1981); poetry like *Laguna Women* (1974); novels including *Ceremony* (1977) and *Almanac of the Dead* (1991); and essays as in *Yellow Woman and a Beauty of the Spirit* (1996). While Silko's subject varies, the heart of her fiction has to do with her mixed identity, her fascination with storytelling, and her reverence for the southwestern landscape and people.

The Man to Send Rain Clouds (1969)

ONE

1 They found him under a big cottonwood tree. His Levi jacket and pants were faded light-blue so that he had been easy to find. The big cottonwood tree stood apart from a small grove of winterbare cottonwoods which grew in the wide, sandy arroyo. He had been dead for a day or more, and the sheep had wandered and scattered up and down the arroyo. Leon and his brother-in-law, Ken, gathered the sheep and left them in the pen at the sheep camp before they returned to the cottonwood tree. Leon waited under the tree while Ken drove the truck through the deep sand

to the edge of the arroyo. He squinted up at the sun and unzipped his jacket—it sure was hot for this time of year. But high and northwest the blue mountains were still 10 deep in snow. Ken came sliding down the low, crumbling bank about fifty yards down, and he was bringing the red blanket.

Before they wrapped the old man, Leon took a piece of string out of his pocket and tied a small gray feather in the old man's long white hair. Ken gave him the paint. Across the brown wrinkled forehead he drew a streak of white and along the high cheekbones he drew a strip of blue paint. He paused and watched Ken throw pinches of corn meal and pollen into the wind that fluttered the small gray feather. Then Leon painted with yellow under the old man's broad nose, and finally, when he had painted green across the chin, he smiled.

"Send us rain clouds, Grandfather." They laid the bundle in the back of the pickup and covered it with a heavy tarp before they started back to the pueblo.

They turned off the highway onto the sandy pueblo road. Not long after they passed the store and post office they saw Father Paul's car coming toward them. When he recognized their faces he slowed his car and waved for them to stop. The young priest rolled down the car window.

"Did you find old Teofilo?" he asked loudly. 5

Leon stopped the truck. "Good morning, Father. We were just out to the sheep camp. Everything is O.K. now."

"Thank God for that. Teofilo is a very old man. You really shouldn't allow him to stay at the sheep camp alone."

"No, he won't do that any more now."

"Well, I'm glad you understand. I hope I'll be seeing you at Mass this week—we missed you last Sunday. See if you can get old Teofilo to come with you." The priest smiled and waved at them as they drove away.

TWO

Louise and Teresa were waiting. The table was set for lunch, and the coffee was boiling on the black iron stove. Leon looked at Louise and then at Teresa.

"We found him under a cottonwood tree in the big arroyo near sheep camp. I guess he sat down to rest in the shade and never got up again." Leon walked toward the old man's bed. The red plaid shawl had been shaken and spread carefully over the bed, and a new brown flannel shirt and pair of stiff new Levis were arranged neatly beside the pillow. Louise held the screen door open while Leon and Ken carried in the red blanket. He looked small and shriveled, and after they dressed him in the new shirt and pants he seemed more shrunken.

It was noontime now because the church bells rang the Angelus. They ate the beans with hot bread, and nobody said anything until after Teresa poured the coffee.

Ken stood up and put on his jacket. "I'll see about the gravediggers. Only the top layer of soil is frozen. I think it can be ready before dark."

Leon nodded his head and finished his coffee. After Ken had been gone for a while, the neighbors and clanspeople came quietly to embrace Teofilo's family and to leave food on the table because the gravediggers would come to eat when they were finished.

THREE

The sky in the west was full of pale-yellow light. Louise 15 stood outside with her hands in the pockets of Leon's green army jacket that was too big for her. The funeral was over, and the old men had taken their candles and medicine bags and were gone. She waited until the body was laid into the

door with its symbols of the Lamb. While he waited he looked up at the twin bells from the king of Spain with the last sunlight pouring around them in their tower.

The priest opened the door and smiled when he saw who it was. "Come in! What brings you here this evening?"

The priest walked toward the kitchen, and Leon stood with his cap in his hand, playing with the earflaps and examining the living room—the brown sofa, the green armchair, and the brass lamp that hung down from the ceiling by links of chain. The priest dragged a chair out of the kitchen and offered it to Leon.

"No thank you, Father. I only came to ask you if you would bring your holy water to the graveyard."

The priest turned away from Leon and looked out the window at the patio full of shadows and the dining-room windows of the nuns' cloister across the patio. The curtains were heavy, and the light from within faintly penetrated; it was impossible to see the nuns inside eating supper. "Why didn't you tell me he was dead? I could have brought the Last Rites anyway." 25

Leon smiled. "It wasn't necessary, Father."

The priest stared down at his scuffed brown loafers and the worn hem of his cassock. "For a Christian burial it was necessary."

His voice was distant, and Leon thought that his blue eyes looked tired.

"It's O.K. Father, we just want him to have plenty of water."

The priest sank down into the green chair and picked up a glossy missionary magazine. He turned the colored pages full of lepers and pagans without looking at them. 30

"You know I can't do that, Leon. There should have been the Last Rites and a funeral Mass at the very least."

Leon put on his green cap and pulled the flaps down over his ears. "It's getting late, Father. I've got to go."

When Leon opened the door Father Paul stood up and said, "Wait." He left the room and came back wearing a long brown overcoat. He followed Leon out the door and across the dim churchyard to the adobe steps in front of the church. They both stooped to fit through the low adobe entrance. And when they started down the hill to the graveyard only half of the sun was visible above the mesa.

The priest approached the grave slowly, wondering how they had managed to dig into the frozen ground; and then he remembered that this was New Mexico, and saw the pile of cold loose sand beside the hole. The people stood close

pickup before she said anything to Leon. She touched his arm, and he noticed that her hands were still dusty from the corn meal that she had sprinkled around the old man. When she spoke, Leon could not hear her.

"What did you say? I didn't hear you."

"I said that I had been thinking about something."

"About what?"

"About the priest sprinkling holy water for Grandpa. So he won't be thirsty."

20 Leon stared at the new moccasins that Teofilo had made for the ceremonial dances in the summer. They were nearly hidden by the red blanket. It was getting colder, and the wind pushed gray dust down the narrow pueblo road. The sun was approaching the long mesa where it disappeared during the winter. Louise stood there shivering and watching his face. Then he zipped up his jacket and opened the truck door. "I'll see if he's there."

FOUR

Ken stopped the pickup at the church, and Leon got out; and then Ken drove down the hill to the graveyard where people were waiting. Leon knocked at the old carved

to each other with little clouds of steam puffing from their faces. The priest looked at them and saw a pile of jackets, gloves, and scarves in the yellow, dry tumbleweeds that grew in the graveyard. He looked at the red blanket, not sure that Teofilo was so small, wondering if it wasn't some perverse Indian trick—something they did in March to ensure a good harvest—wondering if maybe old Teofilo was actually at sheep camp corraling the sheep for the night. But there he was, facing into a cold dry wind and squinting at the last sunlight, ready to bury a red wool blanket while the faces of his parishioners were in shadow with the last warmth of the sun on their backs.

> He sprinkled the grave and the water disappeared almost before it touched the dim, cold sand . . .

35   His fingers were stiff, and it took him a long time to twist the lid off the holy water. Drops of water fell on the red blanket and soaked into dark icy spots. He sprinkled the grave and the water disappeared almost before it touched the dim, cold sand; it reminded him of something—he tried to remember what it was, because he thought if he could remember he might understand this. He sprinkled more water; he shook the container until it was empty, and the water fell through the light from sundown like August rain that fell while the sun was still shining, almost evaporating before it touched the wilted squash flowers.

The wind pulled at the priest's brown Franciscan robe and swirled away the corn meal and pollen that had been sprinkled on the blanket. They lowered the bundle into the ground, and they didn't bother to untie the stiff pieces of new rope that were tied around the ends of the blanket. The sun was gone, and over on the highway the eastbound lane was full of headlights. The priest walked away slowly. Leon watched him climb the hill, and when he had disappeared within the tall, thick walls, Leon turned to look up at the high blue mountains in the deep snow that reflected a faint red light from the west. He felt good because it was finished, and he was happy about the sprinkling of the holy water; now the old man could send them big thunderclouds for sure.

Questions for Critical Thinking

1 How would you describe the tone of this story? Pay particular attention to the ending. Do you read it as humorous or sad?

2 How large a part does religion play in the story? How many of the priest's actions grow from his official duties, how many from his common humanity?

3 In many places, this story makes history feel as if it bears closely on the present. Where do you see these intersections of time? You might want to begin by listing the details that make it clear the story takes place in the present.

The American South

William Faulkner

"Barn Burning"

Flannery O'Connor

"A Good Man Is Hard to Find"

Ralph Ellison

"Battle Royal"

THOUGH many of our major Southern writers lived in the twentieth century—as do those represented in this case study—the roots of Southern literature extend back to colonization and the slave culture of cotton and tobacco farming. The legacy of slavery forms the backdrop for what Flannery O'Connor describes as a region "rich in contradiction, rich in irony, rich in contrast, and particularly rich in its speech." Southern literature in the twentieth century was haunted by its past; one critic has jokingly commented that every Southern story has grandparents in it and very few Northern stories go back a generation.

Perhaps no other region in America is so steeped in the oral tradition; the habit of tale telling and yarn spinning seems somehow to come with the territory below the Mason-Dixon line. Writers such as O'Connor and Eudora Welty (Chapter 14) capture the strangeness of rural life alongside often-satirical portraits of proud, white Southerners. William Faulkner lived much of his life in the small town of Oxford, Mississippi; Oklahoma-born Ralph Ellison—perhaps doubly displaced because of his skin color—attended school in the South and then moved to and stayed in the North. Modern Southern writers continue to treat issues such as troubled race relations, yet in an altered context and with a new sensibility.

"I decline to accept the end of man. It is easy enough to say that man is immortal simply because he will endure: that when the last dingdong of doom has clanged and faded from the last worthless rock hanging tideless in the last red and dying evening, that even then there will still be one more sound: that of his puny inexhaustible voice, still talking. I refuse to accept this. I believe that man will not merely endure: he will prevail. He is immortal, not because he alone among creatures has an inexhaustible voice, but because he has a soul, a spirit capable of compassion and sacrifice and endurance. The poet's, the writer's, duty is to write about these things. It is his privilege to help man endure by lifting his heart, by reminding him of the courage and honor and hope and pride and compassion and pity and sacrifice which have been the glory of his past. The poet's voice need not merely be the record of man, it can be one of the props, the pillars to help him endure and prevail." —William Faulkner, speech at the Nobel Banquet at the City Hall in Stockholm, 1949

William Faulkner (1897–1962)

Many of his best-known American contemporaries chose to travel abroad and live as, at least briefly, "expatriates." But William Faulkner lived and wrote in the region in which he was raised. Born in New Albany, Mississippi, he grew up in Oxford, Mississippi, and ultimately settled there. Ten years after dropping out of high school, Faulkner forged a friendship with Sherwood Anderson,

who not only helped find a publisher for Faulkner's first novel but also encouraged the young Mississippi writer to take for his subject the people and places of his own life. Consequently, Faulkner wrote about the American South as someone deeply invested in its history and future as well as in its particular language and regional tradition. Much of Faulkner's fiction—including novels such as *The Sound and the Fury* (1929), *As I Lay Dying* (1930), *Absalom, Absalom!* (1936), and *The*

Unvanquished (1938)—describes the lives of families in the fictional Yoknapatawpha County, which Faulkner modeled on his own surroundings. He went so far as to draw a map of this imaginary place and call himself "the sole proprietor" of the landscape and region described.

Faulkner is known for his innovative use of language. Many of his characters have no formal education, but they speak and think in a highly stylized English that (although it may not accurately reflect the way people actually converse) gives them a consistent lyric authenticity. In much of his fiction, Faulkner uses the literary technique known as *stream of consciousness,* which seeks to capture the disorganized and fleeting way one thought leads to another; we as readers *overhear* the private and unspoken discourse within a character's mind. In both his stories and his novels, Faulkner chronicles the saga of the post–Civil War South, exploring themes of justice, honor, family, racial prejudice, insanity, and decay in a damaged and changing world. Often his characters are troubled; some of them are suicidal, others, crazed. But his final assertions are hopeful, and he laces his books with humor throughout. He was awarded the Nobel Prize in Literature in 1949 "for his powerful and artistically unique contribution to the modern American novel." In his acceptance speech, Faulkner famously declared, "I believe that man will not merely endure: he will prevail."

Barn Burning (1939)

1 THE store in which the Justice of the Peace's court was sitting smelled of cheese. The boy, crouched on his nail keg at the back of the crowded room, knew he smelled cheese, and more: from where he sat he could see the ranked shelves close-packed with the solid, squat, dynamic shapes of tin cans whose labels his stomach read, not from the lettering which meant nothing to his mind but from the scarlet devils and the silver curve of fish—this, the cheese which he knew he smelled and the hermetic meat which his intestines believed he smelled coming in intermittent gusts momentary and brief between the other constant one, the smell and sense just a little of fear because mostly of despair and grief, the old fierce pull of blood. He could not see the table where the Justice sat and before which his father and his father's enemy (*our enemy* he thought in that despair: *ourn! Mine and hisn both! He's my father!*) stood, but he could hear them, the two of them that is, because his father had said no word yet:

"But what proof have you, Mr. Harris?"

"I told you. The hog got into my corn. I caught it up and sent it back to him. He had no fence that would hold it. I told him so, warned him. The next time I put the hog in my pen. When he came to get it I gave him enough wire to patch up his pen. The next time I put the hog up and kept it. I rode down to his house and saw the wire I gave him still rolled on to the spool in his yard. I told him he could have the hog when he paid me a dollar pound fee. That evening a nigger came with the dollar and got the hog. He was a strange nigger. He said, 'He say to tell you wood and hay kin burn.' I said, 'What?' 'That whut he say to tell you,' the nigger said. 'Wood and hay kin burn.' That night my barn burned. I got the stock out but I lost the barn."

"Where's the nigger? Have you got him?"

5 "He was a strange nigger, I tell you. I don't know what became of him."

"But that's not proof. Don't you see that's not proof?"

"Get that boy up here. He knows." For a moment the boy thought too that the man meant his older brother until Harris said, "Not him. The little one. The boy," and, crouching, small for his age, small and wiry like his father, in patched and faded jeans even too small for him, with straight, uncombed, brown hair and eyes gray and wild as storm scud, he saw the men between himself and the table part and become a lane of grim faces, at the end of which he saw the Justice, a shabby, collarless, graying man in spectacles, beckoning him. He felt no floor under his bare feet; he seemed to walk beneath the palpable weight of the grim turning faces. His father, still in his black Sunday coat donned not for the trial but for the moving, did not even look at him. *He aims for me to lie,* he thought, again with that frantic grief and despair. *And I will have to do hit.*

"What's your name, boy?" the Justice said.

"Colonel Sartoris Snopes," the boy whispered.

10 "Hey?" the Justice said. "Talk louder. Colonel Sartoris? I reckon anybody named for Colonel Sartoris in this country can't help but tell the truth, can they?" The boy said

nothing. *Enemy! Enemy!* he thought; for a moment he could not even see, could not see that the Justice's face was kindly nor discern that his voice was troubled when he spoke to the man named Harris: "Do you want me to question this boy?" But he could hear, and during those subsequent long seconds while there was absolutely no sound in the crowded little room save that of quiet and intent breathing it was as if he had swung outward at the end of a grape vine, over a ravine, and at the top of the swing had been caught in a prolonged instant of mesmerized gravity, weightless in time.

"No!" Harris said violently, explosively. "Damnation! Send him out of here!" Now time, the fluid world, rushed beneath him again, the voices coming to him again through the smell of cheese and sealed meat, the fear and despair and the old grief of blood:

"This case is closed. I can't find against you, Snopes, but I can give you advice. Leave this country and don't come back to it."

His father spoke for the first time, his voice cold and harsh, level, without emphasis: "I aim to. I don't figure to stay in a country among people who . . ." he said something unprintable and vile, addressed to no one.

"That'll do," the Justice said. "Take your wagon and get out of this country before dark. Case dismissed."

15 His father turned, and he followed the stiff black coat, the wiry figure walking a little stiffly from where a Confederate provost's man's musket ball had taken him in the heel on a stolen horse thirty years ago, followed the two backs now, since his older brother had appeared from somewhere in the crowd, no taller than the father but thicker, chewing tobacco steadily, between the two lines of grim-faced men and out of the store and across the worn gallery and down the sagging steps and among the dogs and half-grown boys in the mild May dust, where as he passed a voice hissed:

"Barn burner!"

Again he could not see, whirling; there was a face in a red haze, moonlike, bigger than the full moon, the owner of it half again his size, he leaping in the red haze toward the face, feeling no blow, feeling no shock when his head struck the earth, scrabbling up and leaping again, feeling no blow this time either and tasting no blood, scrabbling up to see the other boy in full flight and himself already leaping into

pursuit as his father's hand jerked him back, the harsh, cold voice speaking above him: "Go get in the wagon."

It stood in a grove of locusts and mulberries across the road. His two hulking sisters in their Sunday dresses and his mother and her sister in calico and sunbonnets were already in it, sitting on and among the sorry residue of the dozen and more movings which even the boy could remember—the battered stove, the broken beds and chairs, the clock inlaid with mother-of-pearl, which would not run, stopped at some fourteen minutes past two o'clock of a dead and forgotten day and time, which had been his mother's dowry. She was crying, though when she saw him she drew her sleeve across her face and began to descend from the wagon. "Get back," the father said.

> ## "Do you want me to question this boy?"

"He's hurt. I got to get some water and wash his . . ."

"Get back in the wagon," his father said. He got in too, 20 over the tail-gate. His father mounted to the seat where the older brother already sat and struck the gaunt mules two savage blows with the peeled willow, but without heat. It was not even sadistic; it was exactly that same quality which in later years would cause his descendants to over-run the engine before putting a motor car into motion, striking and reining back in the same movement. The wagon went on, the store with its quiet crowd of grimly watching men dropped behind; a curve in the road hid it. *Forever* he thought. *Maybe he's done satisfied now, now that he has . . .* stopping himself, not to say it aloud even to himself. His mother's hand touched his shoulder.

"Does hit hurt?" she said.

"Naw," he said. "Hit don't hurt. Lemme be."

"Can't you wipe some of the blood off before hit dries?"

"I'll wash to-night," he said. "Lemme be, I tell you."

The wagon went on. He did not know where they were 25 going. None of them ever did or ever asked, because it was always somewhere, always a house of sorts waiting for them a day or two days or even three days away. Likely his father had already arranged to make a crop on another farm before he . . . Again he had to stop himself. He (the father) always did. There was something about his wolflike independence and even courage when the advantage was at least neutral which impressed strangers, as if they got from his latent ravening ferocity not so much a sense of dependability as a feeling that his ferocious conviction in the rightness of his own actions would be of advantage to all whose interest lay with his.

That night they camped, in a grove of oaks and beeches where a spring ran. The nights were still cool and they had a fire against it, of a rail lifted from a nearby fence and cut into lengths—a small fire, neat, niggard almost, a shrewd fire; such fires were his father's habit and custom always, even in freezing weather. Older, the boy might have remarked this and wondered why not a big one; why should not a man who had not only seen the waste and extravagance of war, but who had in his blood an inherent voracious prodigality with material not his own, have burned everything in sight? Then he might have gone a step farther and thought that that was the reason: that niggard blaze was the living fruit of nights passed during those four years in the woods hiding from all men, blue and gray, with his strings of horses (captured horses, he called them). And older still, he might have divined the true reason: that the element of fire spoke to some deep mainspring of his father's being, as the element of steel or of powder spoke to other men, as the one weapon for the preservation of integrity, else breath were not worth the breathing, and hence to be regarded with respect and used with discretion.

But he did not think this now and he had seen those same niggard blazes all his life. He merely ate his supper beside it and was already half asleep over his iron plate when his father called him, and once more he followed the stiff back, the stiff and ruthless limp, up the slope and on to the starlit road where, turning, he could see his father against the stars but without face or depth—a shape black, flat, and bloodless as though cut from tin in the iron folds of the frockcoat which had not been made for him, the voice harsh like tin and without heat like tin:

"You were fixing to tell them. You would have told him."

He didn't answer. His father struck him with the flat of his hand on the side of the head, hard but without heat, exactly as he had struck the two mules at the store, exactly as he would strike either of them with any stick in order to kill a horse fly, his voice without heat or anger: "You're getting to be a man. You got to learn. You got to learn to stick to your own blood or you ain't going to have any blood to stick to you. Do you think either of them, any man there

this morning, would? Don't you know all they wanted was a chance to get at me because they knew I had them beat? Eh?" Later, twenty years later, he was to tell himself, "If I had said they wanted only truth, justice, he would have hit me again." But now he said nothing. He was not crying. He just stood there. "Answer me," his father said.

"Yes," he whispered. His father turned.   30

"Get on to bed. We'll be there tomorrow."

Tomorrow they were there. In the early afternoon the wagon stopped before a paintless two-room house identical almost with the dozen others it had stopped before even in the boy's ten years, and again, as on the other dozen occasions, his mother and aunt got down and began to unload the wagon, although his two sisters and his father and brother had not moved. "Likely hit ain't fitten for hawgs," one of the sisters said.

. . . the element of fire spoke to some deep mainspring of his father's being . . .

"Nevertheless, fit it will and you'll hog it and like it," his father said. "Get out of them chairs and help your Ma unload."

The two sisters got down, big, bovine, in a flutter of   35 cheap ribbons; one of them drew from the jumbled wagon bed a battered lantern, the other a worn broom. His father handed the reins to the older son and began to climb stiffly over the wheel. "When they get unloaded, take the team to the barn and feed them." Then he said, and at first the boy thought he was still speaking to his brother: "Come with me."

"Me?" he said.

"Yes," his father said. "You."

"Abner," his mother said. His father paused and looked back—the harsh level stare beneath the shaggy, graying, irascible brows.

"I reckon I'll have a word with the man that aims to begin tomorrow owning me body and soul for the next eight months."

They went back up the road. A week ago—or before last   40 night, that is—he would have asked where they were going, but not now. His father had struck him before last night but never before had he paused afterward to explain why; it was as if the blow and the following calm, outrageous voice still rang, repercussed, divulging nothing to him save the terrible handicap of being young, the light weight of his few years, just heavy enough to prevent his soaring free of the world as it seemed to be ordered but not heavy enough to keep him footed solid in it, to resist it and try to change the course of its events.

Presently he could see the grove of oaks and cedars and the other flowering trees and shrubs where the house would be, though not the house yet. They walked beside a fence massed with honeysuckle and Cherokee roses and came to a gate swinging open between two brick pillars, and now, beyond a sweep of drive, he saw the house for the first time and at that instant he forgot his father and the terror and despair both, and even when he remembered his father again (who had not stopped) the terror and despair did not return. Because, for all the twelve movings, they had sojourned until now in a poor country, a land of small farms and fields and houses, and he had never seen a house like this before. *Hit's big as a courthouse* he thought quietly, with a surge of peace and joy whose reason he could not have thought into words, being too young for that: *They are safe from him. People whose lives are a part of this peace and dignity are beyond his touch, he no more to them than a buzzing wasp: capable of stinging for a little moment but that's all; the spell of this peace and dignity rendering even the barns and stable and cribs which belong to it impervious to the puny flames he might contrive . . .* this, the peace and joy, ebbing for an instant as he looked again at the still black back, the stiff and implacable limp of the figure which was not dwarfed by the house, for the reason that it had never looked big anywhere and which now, against the serene columned backdrop, had more than ever that impervious quality of something cut ruthlessly from tin, depthless, as though, sidewise to the sun, it would cast no shadow. Watching him, the boy remarked the absolutely undeviating course which his father held and saw the stiff foot come squarely down in a pile of fresh droppings where a horse had stood in the drive and which his father could have avoided by a simple change of stride. But it ebbed only a moment, though he could not have thought this into words either, walking on in the spell of the house, which he could even want but without envy, without sorrow, certainly never with that ravening and jealous rage which unknown to him walked in the ironlike black coat before him: *Maybe he will feel it too. Maybe it will even change him now from what maybe he couldn't help but be.*

They crossed the portico. Now he could hear his father's stiff foot as it came down on the boards with clocklike finality, a sound out of all proportion to the displacement of the body it bore and which was not dwarfed either by the white door before it, as though it had attained to a sort of vicious and ravening minimum not to be dwarfed by anything—the flat, wide, black hat, the formal coat of broadcloth which had once been black but which had now that friction-glazed greenish cast of the bodies of old house flies, the lifted sleeve which was too large, the lifted hand like a curled claw. The door opened so promptly that the boy knew the Negro must have been watching them all the time, an old man with neat grizzled hair, in a linen jacket, who stood barring the door with his body, saying, "Wipe yo foots, white man, fo you come in here. Major ain't home nohow."

"Get out of my way, nigger," his father said, without heat too, flinging the door back and the Negro also and entering, his hat still on his head. And now the boy saw the prints of the stiff foot on the doorjamb and saw them appear on the pale rug behind the machinelike deliberation of the foot which seemed to bear (or transmit) twice the weight which the body compassed. The Negro was shouting "Miss Lula! Miss Lula!" somewhere behind them, then the boy, deluged as though by a warm wave by a suave turn of the carpeted stair and a pendant glitter of chandeliers and a mute gleam of gold frames, heard the swift feet and saw her too, a lady—perhaps he had never seen her like before either—in a gray, smooth gown with lace at the throat and an apron tied at the waist and the sleeves turned back, wiping cake or biscuit dough from her hands with a towel as she came up the hall, looking not at his father at all but at the tracks on the blond rug with an expression of incredulous amazement.

"I tried," the Negro cried. "I tole him to . . ."

"Will you please go away?" she said in a shaking voice. "Major de Spain is not at home. Will you please go away?"

His father had not spoken again. He did not speak again. He did not even look at her. He just stood stiff in the center of the rug, in his hat, the shaggy iron-gray brows twitching slightly above the pebble-colored eyes as he appeared to examine the house with brief deliberation. Then with the same deliberation he turned; the boy watched him pivot on the good leg and saw the stiff foot drag around the arc of the turning, leaving a final long and fading smear. His father never looked at it, he never once looked down at the rug. The Negro held the door. It closed behind them, upon the hysteric and indistinguishable woman-wail. His father stopped at the top of the steps and scraped his boot clean on the edge of it. At the gate he stopped again. He stood for a moment, planted stiffly on the stiff foot, looking back at the house. "Pretty and white, ain't it?" he said. "That's sweat. Nigger sweat. Maybe it ain't white enough yet to suit him. Maybe he wants to mix some white sweat with it."

Two hours later the boy was chopping wood behind the house within which his mother and aunt and the two sisters (the mother and aunt, not the two girls, he knew that; even at this distance and muffled by walls the flat loud voices of the two girls emanated an incorrigible idle inertia) were setting up the stove to prepare a meal, when he heard the hooves and saw the linen-clad man on a fine sorrel mare, whom he recognized even before he saw the rolled rug in front of the Negro youth following on a fat bay carriage horse—a suffused, angry face vanishing, still at full gallop, beyond the corner of the house where his father and brother were sitting in the two tilted chairs; and a moment later, almost before he could have put the axe down, he heard the hooves again and watched the sorrel mare go back out of the yard, already galloping again. Then his father began to shout one of the sisters' names, who presently emerged backward from the kitchen door dragging the rolled rug along the ground by one end while the other sister walked behind it.

"If you ain't going to tote, go on and set up the wash pot," the first said.

"You, Sarty!" the second shouted. "Set up the wash pot!" His father appeared at the door, framed against that shabbiness, as he had been against that other bland perfection, impervious to either, the mother's anxious face at his shoulder.

50 "Go on," the father said. "Pick it up." The two sisters stooped, broad, lethargic; stooping, they presented an incredible expanse of pale cloth and a flutter of tawdry ribbons.

"If I thought enough of a rug to have to git hit all the way from France I wouldn't keep hit where folks coming in would have to tromp on hit," the first said. They raised the rug.

"Abner," the mother said. "Let me do it."

"You go back and git dinner," his father said. "I'll tend to this."

From the woodpile through the rest of the afternoon the boy watched them, the rug spread flat in the dust beside the bubbling wash pot, the two sisters stooping over it with that profound and lethargic reluctance, while the father stood over them in turn, implacable and grim, driv-

. . . the boy watched him pivot on the good leg and saw the stiff foot drag . . .

ing them though never raising his voice again. He could smell the harsh homemade lye they were using; he saw his mother come to the door once and look toward them with an expression not anxious now but very like despair; he saw his father turn, and he fell to with the axe and saw from the corner of his eye his father raise from the ground a flattish fragment of field stone and examine it and return to the pot, and this time his mother actually spoke: "Abner. Abner. Please don't. Please, Abner."

Then he was done too. It was 55 dusk; the whippoorwills had already begun. He could smell coffee from the room where they would presently eat the cold food remaining from the mid-afternoon meal, though when he entered the house he realized they were having coffee again probably because there was a fire on the hearth, before which the rug now lay spread over the backs of the two chairs. The tracks of his father's foot were gone. Where they had been were now long, water-cloudy scoriations resembling the sporadic course of a lilliputian mowing machine.

It still hung there while they ate the cold food and then went to bed, scattered without order or claim up and down the two rooms, his mother in one bed, where his father would later lie, the older brother in the other, himself, the aunt, and the two sisters on pallets on the floor. But his father was not in bed yet. The last thing the boy remembered was the depthless, harsh silhouette of the hat and coat bending over the rug and it seemed to him that he had not even closed his eyes when the silhouette was standing over him, the fire almost dead behind it, the stiff foot prodding him awake. "Catch up the mule," his father said.

When he returned with the mule his father was standing in the back door, the rolled rug over his shoulder. "Ain't you going to ride?" he said.

"No. Give me your foot."

He bent his knee into his father's hand, the wiry, surprising power flowed smoothly, rising, he rising with it, on to the mule's bare back (they had owned a saddle once; the boy could remember it though not when or where) and with the same effortlessness his father swung the rug up in front of him. Now in the starlight they retraced the afternoon's path, up the dusty road rife with honeysuckle, through the gate and up the black tunnel of the drive to the lightless house, where he sat on the mule and felt the rough warp of the rug drag across his thighs and vanish.

60 "Don't you want me to help?" he whispered. His father did not answer and now he heard again that stiff foot striking the hollow portico with that wooden and clocklike deliberation, that outrageous overstatement of the weight it carried. The rug, hunched, not flung (the boy could tell that even in the darkness) from his father's shoulder struck the angle of wall and floor with a sound unbelievably loud, thunderous, then the foot again, unhurried and enormous; a light came on in the house and the boy sat, tense, breathing steadily and quietly and just a little fast, though the foot itself did not increase its beat at all, descending the steps now; now the boy could see him.

"Don't you want to ride now?" he whispered. "We kin both ride now," the light within the house altering now, flaring up and sinking. *He's coming down the stairs now,* he thought. He had already ridden the mule up beside the horse block; presently his father was up behind him and he doubled the reins over and slashed the mule across the neck, but before the animal could begin to trot the hard, thin arm came around him, the hard, knotted hand jerking the mule back to a walk.

In the first red rays of the sun they were in the lot, putting plow gear on the mules. This time the sorrel mare was in the lot before he heard it at all, the rider collarless and even bareheaded, trembling, speaking in a shaking voice as the woman in the house had done, his father merely looking up once before stooping again to the hame he was buckling, so that the man on the mare spoke to his stooping back:

"You must realize you have ruined that rug. Wasn't there anybody here, any of your women . . ." he ceased, shaking, the boy watching him, the older brother leaning now in the stable door, chewing, blinking slowly and steadily at nothing apparently. "It cost a hundred dollars. But you never had a hundred dollars. You never will. So I'm going to charge you twenty bushels of corn against your crop. I'll add it in your contract and when you come to the commissary you can sign it. That won't keep Mrs. de Spain quiet but maybe it will teach you to wipe your feet off before you enter her house again."

Then he was gone. The boy looked at his father, who still had not spoken or even looked up again, who was now adjusting the logger-head in the hame.

> "It cost a hundred dollars. But you never had a hundred dollars. You never will. . . ."

"Pap," he said. His father looked at him—the inscrutable 65 face, the shaggy brows beneath where the gray eyes glinted coldly. Suddenly the boy went toward him, fast, stopping as suddenly. "You done the best you could!" he cried. "If he wanted hit done different why didn't he wait and tell you how? He won't git no twenty bushels! He won't git none! We'll gather hit and hide hit! I kin watch . . ."

"Did you put the cutter back in that straight stock like I told you?"

"No, sir," he said.

"Then go do it."

That was Wednesday. During the rest of that week he worked steadily, at what was within his scope and some which was beyond it, with an industry that did not need to be driven nor even commanded twice; he had this from his mother, with the difference that some at least of what he did he liked to do, such as splitting wood with the half-size axe which his mother and aunt had earned, or saved money somehow, to present him with at Christmas. In company with the two older women (and on one afternoon, even one of the sisters), he built pens for the shoat and the cow which were a part of his father's contract with the landlord, and one afternoon, his father being absent, gone somewhere on one of the mules, he went to the field.

They were running a middle buster now, his brother 70 holding the plow straight while he handled the reins, and walking beside the straining mule, the rich black soil shearing cool and damp against his bare ankles, he thought *Maybe this is the end of it. Maybe even that twenty bushels that seems hard to have to pay for just a rug will be a cheap price for him to stop forever and always from being what he used to be;* thinking, dreaming now, so that his brother had to speak sharply to him to mind the mule: *Maybe he even won't collect the twenty bushels. Maybe it will all add up and balance and vanish—corn, rug, fire; the terror and grief; the being pulled two ways like between two teams of horses—gone, done with for ever and ever.*

Then it was Saturday; he looked up from beneath the mule he was harnessing and saw his father in the black coat and hat. "Not that," his father said. "The wagon gear." And then, two hours later, sitting in the wagon bed behind his father and brother on the seat, the wagon accomplished a final curve, and he saw the weathered paintless store with its tattered tobacco- and patent-medicine posters and the tethered wagons and saddle animals below the gallery. He mounted the gnawed steps behind his father and brother, and there again was the lane of quiet, watching faces for the three of them to walk through. He saw the man in spectacles sitting at the plank table and he did not need to be told this was a Justice of the Peace; he sent one glare of fierce, exultant, partisan defiance at the man in collar and cravat now, whom he had seen but twice before in his life, and that on a galloping horse, who now wore on his face an expression not of rage but of amazed unbelief which the boy could not have known was at the incredible circumstance of being sued by one of his own tenants, and came and stood against his father and cried at the Justice: "He ain't done it! He ain't burnt . . ."

"Go back to the wagon," his father said.

"Burnt?" the Justice said. "Do I understand this rug was burned too?"

"Does anybody here claim it was?" his father said. "Go back to the wagon." But he did not, he merely retreated to the rear of the room, crowded as that other had been, but not to sit down this time, instead, to stand pressing among the motionless bodies, listening to the voices:

75 "And you claim twenty bushels of corn is too high for the damage you did to the rug?"

"He brought the rug to me and said he wanted the tracks washed out of it. I washed the tracks out and took the rug back to him."

"But you didn't carry the rug back to him in the same condition it was in before you made the tracks on it."

His father did not answer, and now for perhaps half a minute there was no sound at all save that of breathing, the faint, steady suspiration of complete and intent listening.

"You decline to answer that, Mr. Snopes?" Again his father did not answer. "I'm going to find against you, Mr. Snopes. I'm going to find that you were responsible for the injury to Major de Spain's rug and hold you liable for it. But twenty bushels of corn seems a little high for a man in your circumstances to have to pay. Major de Spain claims it cost a hundred dollars. October corn will be worth about fifty cents. I figure that if Major de Spain can stand a ninety-

five dollar loss on something he paid cash for, you can stand a five-dollar loss you haven't earned yet. I hold you in damages to Major de Spain to the amount of ten bushels of corn over and above your contract with him, to be paid to him out of your crop at gathering time. Court adjourned."

It had taken no time hardly, the morning was but half 80 begun. He thought they would return home and perhaps back to the field, since they were late, far behind all other farmers. But instead his father passed on behind the wagon, merely indicating with his hand for the older brother to follow with it, and crossed the road toward the blacksmith shop opposite, pressing on after his father, overtaking him, speaking, whispering up at the harsh, calm face beneath the weathered hat: "He won't git no ten bushels either. He won't git one. We'll . . ." until his father glanced for an instant down at him, the face absolutely calm, the grizzled eyebrows tangled above the cold eyes, the voice almost pleasant, almost gentle:

"You think so? Well, we'll wait till October anyway."

The matter of the wagon—the setting of a spoke or two and the tightening of the tires—did not take long either, the business of the tires accomplished by driving the wagon into the spring branch behind the shop and letting it stand there, the mules nuzzling into the water from time to time, and the boy on the seat with the idle reins, looking up the slope and through the sooty tunnel of the shed where the slow hammer rang and where his father sat on an upended cypress bolt, easily, either talking or listening, still sitting there when the boy brought the dripping wagon up out of the branch and halted it before the door.

"Take them on to the shade and hitch," his father said. He did so and returned. His father and the smith and a third man squatting on his heels inside the door were talking, about crops and animals; the boy, squatting too in the ammoniac dust and hoof-parings and scales of rust, heard his father tell a long and unhurried story out of the time before the birth of the older brother even when he had been a professional horsetrader. And then his father came up beside him where he stood before a tattered last year's circus poster on the other side of the store, gazing rapt and quiet at the scarlet horses, the incredible poisings and convulsions of tulle and tights and the painted leers of comedians, and said, "It's time to eat."

But not at home. Squatting beside his brother against the front wall, he watched his father emerge from the store and produce from a paper sack a segment of cheese and divide it carefully and deliberately into three with his pocket knife and produce crackers from the same sack. They all three squatted on the gallery and ate, slowly, without talking; then in the store again, they drank from a tin dipper tepid water smelling of the cedar bucket and of living beech trees. And still they did not go home. It was a horse lot this time, a tall rail fence upon and along which men stood and sat and out of which one by one horses were led, to be walked and trotted and then cantered back and forth along the road while the slow swapping and buying went on and the sun began to slant westward, they—the three of them—watching and listening, the older brother with his muddy eyes and his steady, inevitable tobacco, the father commenting now and then on certain of the animals, to no one in particular.

85   It was after sundown when they reached home. They ate supper by lamplight, then, sitting on the doorstep, the boy watched the night fully accomplish, listening to the whippoorwills and the frogs, when he heard his mother's voice: "Abner! No! No! Oh, God. Oh, God. Abner!" and he rose, whirled, and saw the altered light through the door where a candle stub now burned in a bottle neck on the table and his father, still in the hat and coat, at once formal and burlesque as though dressed carefully for some shabby and ceremonial violence, emptying the reservoir of the lamp back into the five-gallon kerosene can from which it had been filled, while the mother tugged at his arm until he shifted the lamp to the other hand and flung her back, not savagely or viciously, just hard, into the wall, her hands flung out against the wall for balance, her mouth open and in her face the same quality of hopeless despair as had been in her voice. Then his father saw him standing in the door.

"Go to the barn and get that can of oil we were oiling the wagon with," he said. The boy did not move. Then he could speak.

"What . . ." he cried. "What are you . . ."

"Go get that oil," his father said. "Go."

Then he was moving, running, outside the house, toward the stable: this the old habit, the old blood which he had not been permit-

ted to choose for himself, which had been bequeathed him willy nilly and which had run for so long (and who knew where, battening on what of outrage and savagery and lust) before it came to him. *I could keep on,* he thought. *I could run on and on and never look back, never need to see his face again. Only I can't. I can't,* the rusted can in his hand now, the liquid sploshing in it as he ran back to the house and into it, into the sound of his mother's weeping in the next room, and handed the can to his father.

"Ain't you going to even send a nigger?" he cried. "At 90 least you sent a nigger before!"

This time his father didn't strike him. The hand came even faster than the blow had, the same hand which had set the can on the table with almost excruciating care flashing from the can toward him too quick for him to follow it, gripping him by the back of his shirt and on to tiptoe before he had seen it quit the can, the face stooping at him in breathless and frozen ferocity, the cold, dead voice speaking over him to the older brother who leaned against the table, chewing with that steady, curious, sidewise motion of cows:

"Empty the can into the big one and go on. I'll catch up with you."

"Better tie him up to the bedpost," the brother said.

"Do like I told you," the father said. Then the boy was moving, his bunched shirt and the hard, bony hand between his shoulder-blades, his toes just touching the floor, across the room and into the other one, past the sisters sitting with spread heavy thighs in the two chairs over the cold hearth, and to where his mother and aunt sat side by side on the bed, the aunt's arm about his mother's shoulders.

"Hold him," the father said: The aunt made a star- 95 tled movement. "Not you," the father said. "Lennie. Take hold of him. I want to see you do it." His mother took him by the wrist. "You'll hold him better than that. If he gets loose don't you know what he is going to do? He will go up yonder." He jerked his head toward the road.

"Maybe I'd better tie him."

"I'll hold him," his mother whispered.

"See you do then." Then his father was gone, the stiff foot heavy and measured upon the boards, ceasing at last.

Then he began to struggle. His mother caught him in both arms, he jerking and wrenching at them. He would be stronger in the end, he knew that. But he had no time to wait for it. "Lemme go!" he cried. "I don't want to have to hit you!"

"Let him go!" the aunt said. "If he don't go, before God, I am going up there myself!"

"Don't you see I can't?" his mother cried. "Sarty! Sarty! No! No! Help me, Lizzie!"

Then he was free. His aunt grasped him but it was too late. He whirled, running, his mother stumbled forward on to her knees behind him, crying to the nearer sister: "Catch him, Net! Catch him!" But that was too late too, the sister (the sisters were twins, born at the same time, yet either of them now gave the impression of being, encompassing as much living meat and volume and weight as any other two of the family) not yet having begun to rise from the chair, her head, face, alone merely turned, presenting to him in the flying instant an astonishing expanse of young female features untroubled by any surprise even, wearing only an expression of bovine interest. Then he was out of the room, out of the house, in the mild dust of the starlit road and the heavy rifeness of honeysuckle, the pale ribbon unspooling with terrific slowness under his running feet, reaching the gate at last and turning in, running, his heart and lungs drumming, on up the drive toward the lighted house, the lighted door. He did not knock, he burst in, sobbing for breath, incapable for the moment of speech; he saw the astonished face of the Negro in the linen jacket without knowing when the Negro had appeared.

"De Spain!" he cried, panted. "Where's . . ." then he saw the white man too emerging from a white door down the hall. "Barn!" he cried. "Barn!"

"What?" the white man said. "Barn?"

"Yes!" the boy cried. "Barn!"

"Catch him!" the white man shouted.

But it was too late this time too. The Negro grasped his shirt, but the entire sleeve, rotten with washing, carried away, and he was out that door too and in the drive again, and had actually never ceased to run even while he was screaming into the white man's face.

Behind him the white man was shouting, "My horse! Fetch my horse!" and he thought for an instant of cutting across the park and climbing the fence into the road, but he did not know the park nor how the vine-massed fence might be and he dared not risk it. So he ran on down the drive, blood and breath roaring; presently he was in the road again though he could not see it. He could not hear either: the galloping mare was almost upon him before he heard her, and even then he held his course, as if the very urgency of his wild grief and need must in a moment more find him wings, waiting until the ultimate instant to hurl himself aside and into the weed-choked roadside ditch as the horse thundered past and on, for an instant in furious silhouette against the stars, the tranquil early summer night sky which, even before the shape of the horse and rider vanished, stained abruptly and violently upward: a long, swirling roar incredible and soundless, blotting the stars, and he springing up and into the road again, running again, knowing it was too late yet still running even after he heard the shot and an instant later, two shots, pausing now without knowing he had ceased to run, crying, "Pap! Pap!", running again before he knew he had begun to run, stumbling, tripping over something and scrabbling up again without ceasing to run, looking backward over his shoulder at the glare as he got up, running on among the invisible trees, panting, sobbing, "Father! Father!"

At midnight he was sitting on the crest of a hill. He did not know it was midnight and he did not know how far he had come. But there was no glare behind him now and he sat now, his back toward what he had called home for four days anyhow, his face toward the dark woods which he would enter when breath was strong again, small, shaking steadily in the chill darkness, hugging himself into the remainder of his thin, rotten shirt, the grief and despair now no longer terror and fear but just grief and despair. *Father. My father*, he thought. "He was brave!" he cried suddenly, aloud but not loud, no more than a whisper. "He was! He was in the war! He was in Colonel Sartoris' cav'ry!" not knowing that his father had gone to that war a private in the fine old European sense, wearing no uniform, admitting the authority of and giving fidelity to no man or army or flag, going to war as Malbrouck himself did: for booty—it meant nothing and less than nothing to him if it were enemy booty or his own.

The slow constellations wheeled on. It would be dawn and then sun-up after a while and he would be hungry. But that would be tomorrow and now he was only cold, and walking would cure that. His breathing was easier now and he decided to get up and go on, and then he found that he

> He did not know it was midnight and he did not know how far he had come.

had been asleep because he knew it was almost dawn, the night almost over. He could tell that from the whippoor-wills. They were everywhere now among the dark trees below him, constant and inflectioned and ceaseless, so that, as the instant for giving over to the day birds drew nearer and nearer, there was no interval at all between them. He got up. He was a little stiff, but walking would cure that too as it would the cold, and soon there would be the sun. He went on down the hill, toward the dark woods within which the liquid silver voices of the birds called unceasing—the rapid and urgent beating of the urgent and quiring heart of the late spring night. He did not look back.

Questions for Critical Thinking

1 The smells and sounds of country life contribute largely to the effects of this story. Can you catalog these on a second reading of the story? Which senses—smell, touch, and so on—seem the most important?

2 Faulkner's phrases and sentences seem quite distinctive (as in "He went on down the hill, toward the dark woods within which the liquid silver voices of the birds called unceasing—the rapid and urgent beating of the urgent and quiring heart of the late spring night"). Do these seem "Southern" to you? What other terms might you use to describe Faulkner's style?

3 Note the references Faulkner makes to the Civil War. From what we learn about the father in the penultimate paragraph of "Barn Burning," how would you describe this author's view of Southern history?

4 Imagine the setting of "Barn Burning" in a northern city. Is it possible? How would it change the story?

"The first and most obvious characteristic of fiction is that it deals with reality through what can be seen, heard, smelt, tasted, and touched. Now this is something that can't be learned only in the head; it has to be learned in the habits. It has to become a way that you habitually look at things. The fiction writer has to realize that he can't create compassion with compassion, or emotion with emotion, or thought with thought. He has to provide all these things with a body; he has to create a world with weight and extension. . . . The meaning of a story has to be embodied in it, has to be made concrete in it. A story is a way to say something that can't be said any other way, and it takes every word in the story to say what the meaning is." —Flannery O'Connor, from "Writing Short Stories," 1969

Flannery O'Connor (1925–1964)

A Southern writer unlike any other, Flannery O'Connor is known for her satire on poor and middle-class Southern whites, her Catholic perspective, and her portrayal of the grotesque. Beyond these signature characteristics, O'Connor's prose jumps off the page with precision, wit, and sharpness—all calculated, as she put it, to show readers moments of God's grace. Born and raised in Savannah, Georgia, O'Connor moved with her parents to the small town of Milledgeville when her father became ill with lupus. She went to college in Georgia and then attended the Iowa Writers' Workshop, where she earned her M.F.A. Her teacher there, Paul Engle, described O'Connor's Georgia accent as so strong when they first met that, after several attempts to comprehend her speech, he finally had to ask her to write down what she wanted to say.

O'Connor became a shy, silent fixture in the back of the classroom, working hard at stories rooted in Southern culture and Catholic sensibility. The cadences of regional speech course through her fiction, and she urged other writers, too, to "[take] advantage of what's yours." There are traces of the influence of other Southern writers in her work—notably the gothic strain of her great predecessor William Faulkner—but much of her work defies comparison as well as easy imitation; it is, to use a much-overused word, *original*.

Her health—she, too, contracted lupus—forced her to return to the farm in Milledgeville and move in with her mother. She left home only occasionally to lecture or to accept an award; the rest of her time she spent writing and raising her beloved peacocks. O'Connor is most famous for her short stories, collected in *A Good Man Is Hard to Find* (1955) and *Everything That Rises Must Converge* (1965), but she also wrote two novels before her early death from lupus at age thirty-nine. In 1969 her occasional prose, speeches, and essays were collected in *Mystery and Manners,* and her complete stories were collected in a 1971 edition, which earned her a posthumous National Book Award. O'Connor is remembered not just as a modern master of the short story form but also—from interviews, letters, and speeches—for her wise and witty voice. When asked whether writing programs stifle writers, O'Connor famously replied, "My opinion is that they don't stifle enough of them."

A Good Man Is Hard to Find (1955)

1 THE grandmother didn't want to go to Florida. She wanted to visit some of her connections in east Tennessee and she was seizing at every chance to change Bailey's mind. Bailey was the son she lived with, her only boy. He was sitting on the edge of his chair at the table, bent over the orange sports section of the *Journal*. "Now look here, Bailey," she said, "see here, read this," and she stood with one hand on her thin hip and the other rattling the newspaper at his bald head. "Here this fellow that calls himself The Misfit is aloose from the Federal Pen and headed toward Florida and you read here what it says he did to these people. Just you read it. I wouldn't take my children in any direction with a criminal like that aloose in it. I couldn't answer to my conscience if I did."

Bailey didn't look up from his reading so she wheeled around then and faced the children's mother, a young woman in slacks, whose face was as broad and innocent as a cabbage and was tied around with a green head-kerchief that had two points on the top like a rabbit's ears. She was sitting on the sofa, feeding the baby his apricots out of a jar. "The children have been to Florida before," the old lady said. "You all ought to take them somewhere else for a change so they would see different parts of the world and be broad. They never have been to east Tennessee."

The children's mother didn't seem to hear her but the eight-year-old boy, John Wesley, a stocky child with glasses, said, "If you don't want to go to Florida, why dontcha stay at home?" He and the little girl, June Star, were reading the funny papers on the floor.

"She wouldn't stay at home to be queen for a day," June Star said without raising her yellow head.

5   "Yes and what would you do if this fellow, The Misfit, caught you?" the grandmother asked.

"I'd smack his face," John Wesley said.

"She wouldn't stay at home for a million bucks," June Star said. "Afraid she'd miss something. She has to go everywhere we go."

"All right, Miss," the grandmother said. "Just remember that the next time you want me to curl your hair."

June Star said her hair was naturally curly.

10   The next morning the grandmother was the first one in the car, ready to go. She had her big black valise that looked like the head of a hippopotamus in one corner, and underneath it she was hiding a basket with Pitty Sing, the cat, in it. She didn't intend for the cat to be left alone in the house for three days because he would miss her too much and she was afraid he might brush against one of the gas burners and accidentally asphyxiate himself. Her son, Bailey, didn't like to arrive at a motel with a cat.

She sat in the middle of the back seat with John Wesley and June Star on either side of her. Bailey and the children's mother and the baby sat in front and they left Atlanta at eight forty-five with the mileage on the car at 55890. The grandmother wrote this down because she thought it would be interesting to say how many miles they had been when they got back. It took them twenty minutes to reach the outskirts of the city.

The old lady settled herself comfortably, removing her white cotton gloves and putting them up with her purse on the shelf in front of the back window. The children's mother still had on slacks and still had her head tied up in a green kerchief, but the grandmother had on a navy blue straw sailor hat with a bunch of white violets on the brim and a navy blue dress with a small white dot in the print. Her col-

lars and cuffs were white organdy trimmed with lace and at her neckline she had pinned a purple spray of cloth violets containing a sachet. In case of an accident, anyone seeing her dead on the highway would know at once that she was a lady.

She said she thought it was going to be a good day for driving, neither too hot nor too cold, and she cautioned Bailey that the speed limit was fifty-five miles an hour and that the patrolmen hid themselves behind billboards and small clumps of trees and sped out after you before you had a chance to slow down. She pointed out interesting details of the scenery: Stone Mountain; the blue granite that in some places came up to both sides of the highway; the brilliant red clay banks slightly streaked with purple; and the various crops that made rows of green lace-work on the ground. The trees were full of silver-white sunlight and the meanest of them sparkled. The children were reading comic magazines and their mother had gone back to sleep.

"Let's go through Georgia fast so we won't have to look at it much," John Wesley said.

15   "If I were a little boy," said the grandmother, "I wouldn't talk about my native state that way. Tennessee has the mountains and Georgia has the hills."

"Tennessee is just a hillbilly dumping ground," John Wesley said, "and Georgia is a lousy state too."

"You said it," June Star said.

"In my time," said the grandmother, folding her thin veined fingers, "children were more respectful of their native states and their parents and everything else. People did right then. Oh look at the cute little pickaninny!" she said and pointed to a Negro child standing in the door of a shack. "Wouldn't that make a picture, now?" she asked and they all turned and looked at the little Negro out of the back window. He waved.

"He didn't have any britches on," June Star said.

20   "He probably didn't have any," the grandmother explained. "Little niggers in the country don't have things like we do. If I could paint, I'd paint that picture," she said.

The children exchanged comic books.

The grandmother offered to hold the baby and the children's mother passed him over the front seat to her. She set him on her knee and bounced him and told him about the things they were passing. She rolled her eyes and screwed up her mouth and stuck her leathery thin face into his smooth

> In case of an accident, anyone seeing her dead on the highway would know at once that she was a lady.

bland one. Occasionally he gave her a faraway smile. They passed a large cotton field with five or six graves fenced in the middle of it, like a small island. "Look at the graveyard!" the grandmother said, pointing it out. "That was the old family burying ground. That belonged to the plantation."

"Where's the plantation?" John Wesley asked.

"Gone With the Wind," said the grandmother. "Ha. Ha."

25   When the children finished all the comic books they had brought, they opened the lunch and ate it. The grandmother ate a peanut butter sandwich and an olive and would not let the children throw the box and the paper napkins out the window. When there was nothing else to do they played a game by choosing a cloud and making the other two guess what shape it suggested. John Wesley took one of the shape of a cow and June Star guessed a cow and John Wesley said, no, an automobile, and June Star said he didn't play fair, and they began to slap each other over the grandmother.

The grandmother said she would tell them a story if they would keep quiet. When she told a story, she rolled her eyes and waved her head and was very dramatic. She said once when she was a maiden lady she had been courted by a Mr. Edgar Atkins Teagarden from Jasper, Georgia. She said he was a very good-looking man and a gentleman and that he brought her a watermelon every Saturday afternoon with his initials cut in it, E. A. T. Well, one Saturday, she said, Mr. Teagarden brought the watermelon and there was nobody at home and he left it on the front porch and returned in his buggy to Jasper, but she never got the watermelon, she said, because a nigger boy ate it when he saw the initials, E. A. T.! This story tickled John Wesley's funny bone and he giggled and giggled but June Star didn't think it was any good. She said she wouldn't marry a man that just brought her a watermelon on Saturday. The grandmother said she would have done well to marry Mr. Teagarden because he was a gentleman

and had bought Coca-Cola stock when it first came out and that he had died only a few years ago, a very wealthy man.

They stopped at The Tower for barbecued sandwiches. The Tower was a part stucco and part wood filling station and dance hall set in a clearing outside of Timothy. A fat man named Red Sammy Butts ran it and there were signs stuck here and there on the building and for miles up and down the highway saying, TRY RED SAMMY'S FAMOUS BARBECUE. NONE LIKE FAMOUS RED SAMMY'S! RED SAM! THE FAT BOY WITH THE HAPPY LAUGH! A VETERAN! RED SAMMY'S YOUR MAN!

Red Sammy was lying on the bare ground outside The Tower with his head under a truck while a gray monkey about a foot high, chained to a small chinaberry tree, chattered nearby. The monkey sprang back into the tree and got on the highest limb as soon as he saw the children jump out of the car and run toward him.

Inside, The Tower was a long dark room with a counter at one end and tables at the other and dancing space in the middle. They sat down at a board table next to the nickelodeon and Red Sam's wife, a tall burnt-brown woman with hair and eyes lighter than her skin, came and took their order. The children's mother put a dime in the machine and played "The Tennessee Waltz," and the grandmother said that tune always made her want to dance. She asked Bailey if he would like to dance but he only glared at her. He didn't have a naturally sunny disposition like she did and trips made him nervous. The grandmother's brown eyes were very bright. She swayed her head from side to side and pretended she was dancing in her chair. June Star said play something she could tap to so the children's mother put in another dime and played a fast number and June Star stepped out onto the dance floor and did her tap routine.

30   "Ain't she cute?" Red Sam's wife said, leaning over the counter. "Would you like to come be my little girl?"

"No I certainly wouldn't," June Star said. "I wouldn't live in a broken-down place like this for a million bucks!" and she ran back to the table.

"Ain't she cute?" the woman repeated, stretching her mouth politely.

"Aren't you ashamed?" hissed the grandmother.

Red Sam came in and told his wife to quit lounging on the counter and hurry up with these people's order. His khaki trousers reached just to his hip bones and his stomach hung over them like a sack of meal swaying under his shirt. He came over and sat down at a table nearby and let out a combination sigh and yodel. "You can't win," he said.

"You can't win," and he wiped his sweating red face off with a gray handkerchief. "These days you don't know who to trust," he said. "Ain't that the truth?"

35   "People are certainly not nice like they used to be," said the grandmother.

"Two fellers come in here last week," Red Sammy said, "driving a Chrysler. It was a old beat-up car but it was a good one and these boys looked all right to me. Said they worked at the mill and you know I let them fellers charge the gas they bought? Now why did I do that?"

"Because you're a good man!" the grandmother said at once.

"Yes'm, I suppose so," Red Sam said as if he were stuck with this answer.

His wife brought the orders, carrying the five plates all at once without a tray, two in each hand and one balanced on her arm. "It isn't a soul in this green world of God's that you can trust," she said. "And I don't count nobody out of that, not nobody," she repeated, looking at Red Sammy.

40   "Did you read about that criminal, The Misfit, that's escaped?" asked the grandmother.

"I wouldn't be a bit surprised if he didn't attact this place right here," said the woman. "If he hears about it being here, I wouldn't be none surprised to see him. If he hears it's two cent in the cash register, I wouldn't be a tall surprised if he . . ."

"That'll do," Red Sam said. "Go bring these people their Co'-Colas," and the woman went off to get the rest of the order.

"A good man is hard to find," Red Sammy said. "Everything is getting terrible. I remember the day you could go off and leave your screen door unlatched. Not no more."

He and the grandmother discussed better times. The old lady said that in her opinion Europe was entirely to blame for the way things were now. She said the way Europe acted you would think we were made of money and Red Sam said it was no use talking about it, she was exactly right. The children ran outside into the white sunlight and looked at the monkey in the lacy chinaberry tree. He was busy catching fleas on himself and biting each one carefully between his teeth as if it were a delicacy.

45   They drove off again into the hot afternoon. The grandmother took cat naps and woke up every few minutes with her own snoring. Outside of Toombsboro she woke up and recalled an old plantation that she had visited in this neighborhood once when she was a young lady. She said the house had six white columns across the front and that there was an avenue of oaks leading up to it and two little wooden trellis arbors on either side in front where you sat down with your suitor after a stroll in the garden. She recalled exactly which road to turn off to get to it. She knew that Bailey would not be willing to lose any time looking at an old house, but the more she talked about it, the more she wanted to see it once again and find out if the little twin arbors were still standing. "There was a secret panel in this house," she said craftily, not telling the truth but wishing that she were, "and the story went that all the family silver was hidden in it when Sherman came through but it was never found . . ."

"Hey!" John Wesley said. "Let's go see it! We'll find it! We'll poke all the woodwork and find it! Who lives there? Where do you turn off at? Hey Pop, can't we turn off there?"

"We never have seen a house with a secret panel!" June Star shrieked. "Let's go to the house with the secret panel! Hey Pop, can't we go see the house with the secret panel!"

"It's not far from here, I know," the grandmother said. "It wouldn't take over twenty minutes."

Bailey was looking straight ahead. His jaw was as rigid as a horseshoe. "No," he said.

50   The children began to yell and scream that they wanted to see the house with the secret panel. John Wesley kicked the back of the front seat and June Star hung over her mother's shoulder and whined desperately into her ear that they never had any fun even on their vacation, that they could never do what THEY wanted to do. The baby began to scream and John Wesley kicked the back of the seat so hard that his father could feel the blows in his kidney.

"All right!" he shouted and drew the car to a stop at the side of the road. "Will you all shut up? Will you all just shut up for one second? If you don't shut up, we won't go anywhere."

"It would be very educational for them," the grandmother murmured.

"All right," Bailey said, "but get this: this is the only time we're going to stop for anything like this. This is the one and only time."

> The old lady said that in her opinion Europe was entirely to blame for the way things were now.

"The dirt road that you have to turn down is about a mile back," the grandmother directed. "I marked it when we passed."

55 "A dirt road," Bailey groaned.

After they had turned around and were headed toward the dirt road, the grandmother recalled other points about the house, the beautiful glass over the front doorway and the candle-lamp in the hall. John Wesley said that the secret panel was probably in the fireplace.

"You can't go inside this house," Bailey said. "You don't know who lives there."

"While you all talk to the people in front, I'll run around behind and get in a window," John Wesley suggested.

"We'll all stay in the car," his mother said.

60 They turned onto the dirt road and the car raced roughly along in a swirl of pink dust. The grandmother recalled the times when there were no paved roads and thirty miles was a day's journey. The dirt road was hilly and there were sudden washes in it and sharp curves on dangerous embankments. All at once they would be on a hill, looking down over the blue tops of trees for miles around, then the next minute, they would be in a red depression with the dust-coated trees looking down on them.

"This place had better turn up in a minute," Bailey said, "or I'm going to turn around."

The road looked as if no one had traveled on it in months.

"It's not much farther," the grandmother said and just as she said it, a horrible thought came to her. The thought was so embarrassing that she turned red in the face and her eyes dilated and her feet jumped up, upsetting her valise in the corner. The instant the valise moved, the newspaper top she had over the basket under it rose with a snarl and Pitty Sing, the cat, sprang onto Bailey's shoulder.

The children were thrown to the floor and their mother, clutching the baby, was thrown out the door onto the ground; the old lady was thrown into the front seat. The car turned over once and landed right-side-up in a gulch off the side of the road. Bailey remained in the driver's seat with the cat—gray-striped with a broad white face and an orange nose—clinging to his neck like a caterpillar.

65 As soon as the children saw they could move their arms and legs, they scrambled out of the car, shouting, "We've had an ACCIDENT!" The grandmother was curled up under the dashboard, hoping she was injured so that Bailey's wrath would not come down on her all at once. The horrible thought she had had before the accident was that the house she had remembered so vividly was not in Georgia but in Tennessee.

Bailey removed the cat from his neck with both hands and flung it out the window against the side of a pine tree. Then he got out of the car and started looking for the children's mother. She was sitting against the side of the red gutted ditch, holding the screaming baby, but she only had a cut down her face and a broken shoulder. "We've had an ACCIDENT!" the children screamed in a frenzy of delight.

"But nobody's killed," June Star said with disappointment as the grandmother limped out of the car, her hat still pinned to her head but the broken front brim standing up at a jaunty angle and the violet spray hanging off the side. They all sat down in the ditch, except the children, to recover from the shock. They were all shaking.

"Maybe a car will come along," said the children's mother hoarsely.

"I believe I have injured an organ," said the grandmother, pressing her side, but no one answered her. Bailey's teeth were clattering. He had on a yellow sport shirt with bright blue parrots designed in it and his face was as yellow as the shirt. The grandmother decided that she would not mention that the house was in Tennessee.

70 The road was about ten feet above and they could see only the tops of the trees on the other side of it. Behind the ditch they were sitting in there were more woods, tall and dark and deep. In a few minutes they saw a car some distance away on top of a hill, coming slowly as if the occupants were watching them. The grandmother stood up and waved both arms dramatically to attract their attention. The car continued to come on slowly, disappeared around a bend and appeared again, moving even slower, on top of the

hill they had gone over. It was a big black battered hearse-like automobile. There were three men in it.

It came to a stop just over them and for some minutes, the driver looked down with a steady expressionless gaze to where they were sitting, and didn't speak. Then he turned his head and muttered something to the other two and they got out. One was a fat boy in black trousers and a red sweat shirt with a silver stallion embossed on the front of it. He moved around on the right side of them and stood staring, his mouth partly open in a kind of loose grin. The other had on khaki pants and a blue striped coat and a gray hat pulled down very low, hiding most of his face. He came around slowly on the left side. Neither spoke.

The driver got out of the car and stood by the side of it, looking down at them. He was an older man than the other two. His hair was just beginning to gray and he wore silver-rimmed spectacles that gave him a scholarly look. He had a long creased face and didn't have on any shirt or undershirt. He had on blue jeans that were too tight for him and was holding a black hat and a gun. The two boys also had guns.

"We've had an ACCIDENT!" the children screamed.

The grandmother had the peculiar feeling that the bespectacled man was someone she knew. His face was as familiar to her as if she had known him all her life but she could not recall who he was. He moved away from the car and began to come down the embankment, placing his feet carefully so that he wouldn't slip. He had on tan and white shoes and no socks, and his ankles were red and thin. "Good afternoon," he said. "I see you all had you a little spill."

75 "We turned over twice!" said the grandmother.

"Oncet," he corrected. "We seen it happen. Try their car and see will it run, Hiram," he said quietly to the boy with the gray hat.

"What you got that gun for?" John Wesley asked. "Whatcha gonna do with that gun?"

"Lady," the man said to the children's mother, "would you mind calling them children to sit down by you? Children make me nervous. I want all you to sit down right together there where you're at."

"What are you telling US what to do for?" June Star asked.

80 Behind them the line of woods gaped like a dark open mouth. "Come here," said their mother.

"Look here now," Bailey began suddenly, "we're in a predicament! We're in . . ."

The grandmother shrieked. She scrambled to her feet and stood staring. "You're The Misfit!" she said. "I recognized you at once!"

"Yes'm," the man said, smiling slightly as if he were pleased in spite of himself to be known, "but it would have been better for all of you, lady, if you hadn't of reckernized me."

Bailey turned his head sharply and said something to his mother that shocked even the children. The old lady began to cry and The Misfit reddened.

85 "Lady," he said, "don't you get upset. Sometimes a man says things he don't mean. I don't reckon he meant to talk to you thataway."

"You wouldn't shoot a lady, would you?" the grandmother said and removed a clean handkerchief from her cuff and began to slap at her eyes with it.

The Misfit pointed the toe of his shoe into the ground and made a little hole and then covered it up again. "I would hate to have to," he said.

"Listen," the grandmother almost screamed, "I know you're a good man. You don't look a bit like you have common blood. I know you must come from nice people!"

"Yes mam," he said, "finest people in the world." When he smiled he showed a row of strong white teeth. "God never made a finer woman than my mother and my daddy's heart was pure gold," he said. The boy with the red sweat shirt had come around behind them and was standing with his gun at his hip. The Misfit squatted down on the ground. "Watch them children, Bobby Lee," he said. "You know they make me nervous." He looked at the six of them huddled together in front of him and he seemed to be embarrassed as if he couldn't think of anything to say. "Ain't a cloud in the sky," he remarked, looking up at it. "Don't see no sun but don't see no cloud neither."

90 "Yes, it's a beautiful day," said the grandmother. "Listen," she said, "you shouldn't call yourself The Misfit because I know you're a good man at heart. I can just look at you and tell."

"Hush!" Bailey yelled. "Hush! Everybody shut up and let me handle this!" He was squatting in the position of a runner about to sprint forward but he didn't move.

"I pre-chate that, lady," The Misfit said and drew a little circle in the ground with the butt of his gun.

> Behind them the line of woods gaped like a dark open mouth.

"It'll take a half a hour to fix this here car," Hiram called, looking over the raised hood of it.

"Well, first you and Bobby Lee get him and that little boy to step over yonder with you," The Misfit said, pointing to Bailey and John Wesley. "The boys want to ast you something," he said to Bailey. "Would you mind stepping back in them woods there with them?"

95 "Listen," Bailey began, "we're in a terrible predicament! Nobody realizes what this is," his voice cracked. His eyes were as blue and intense as the parrots in his shirt and he remained perfectly still.

The grandmother reached up to adjust her hat brim as if she were going to the woods with him but it came off in her hand. She stood staring at it and after a second she let it fall on the ground. Hiram pulled Bailey up by the arm as if he were assisting an old man. John Wesley caught hold of his father's hand and Bobby Lee followed. They went off toward the woods and just as they reached the dark edge, Bailey turned and supporting himself against a gray naked pine trunk, he shouted, "I'll be back in a minute, Mamma, wait on me!"

"Come back this instant!" his mother shrilled but they all disappeared into the woods.

"Bailey Boy!" the grandmother called in a tragic voice but she found she was looking at The Misfit squatting on the ground in front of her. "I just know you're a good man," she said desperately. "You're not a bit common!"

"Nome, I ain't a good man," The Misfit said after a second as if he had considered her statement carefully, "but I ain't the worst in the world neither. My daddy said I was a different breed of dog from my brothers and sisters. 'You know,' Daddy said, 'it's some that can live their whole life out without asking about it and it's others has to know why it is, and this boy is one of the latters. He's going to be into everything!'" He put on his black hat and looked up suddenly and then away deep into the woods as if he were embarrassed again. "I'm sorry I don't have on a shirt before you ladies," he said, hunching his shoulders slightly. "We buried our clothes that we had on when we escaped and we're just making do until we can get better. We borrowed these from some folks we met," he explained.

"That's perfectly all right," the grandmother said. 100 "Maybe Bailey has an extra shirt in his suitcase."

"I'll look and see terrectly," The Misfit said.

"Where are they taking him?" the children's mother screamed.

"Daddy was a card himself," The Misfit said. "You couldn't put anything over on him. He never got in trouble with the Authorities though. Just had the knack of handling them."

"You could be honest too if you'd only try," said the grandmother. "Think how wonderful it would be to settle down and live a comfortable life and not have to think about somebody chasing you all the time."

The Misfit kept scratching in the ground with the butt 105 of his gun as if he were thinking about it. "Yes'm, somebody is always after you," he murmured.

The grandmother noticed how thin his shoulder blades were just behind his hat because she was standing up looking down on him. "Do you ever pray?" she asked.

He shook his head. All she saw was the black hat wiggle between his shoulder blades. "Nome," he said.

There was a pistol shot from the woods, followed closely by another. Then silence. The old lady's head jerked around. She could hear the wind move through the tree tops like a long satisfied insuck of breath. "Bailey Boy!" she called.

"I was a gospel singer for a while," The Misfit said. "I been most everything. Been in the arm service, both land and sea, at home and abroad, been twice married, been an undertaker, been with the railroads, plowed Mother Earth, been in a tornado, seen a man burnt alive oncet," and looked up at the children's mother and the little girl who were sitting close together, their faces white and their eyes glassy; "I even seen a woman flogged," he said.

110 "Pray, pray," the grandmother began, "pray, pray . . ."

"I never was a bad boy that I remember of," The Misfit said in an almost dreamy voice, "but somewheres along the line I done something wrong and got sent to the penitentiary. I was buried alive," and he looked up and held her attention to him by a steady stare.

"That's when you should have started to pray," she said. "What did you do to get sent to the penitentiary that first time?"

"Turn to the right, it was a wall," The Misfit said, looking up again at the cloudless sky. "Turn to the left, it was a wall. Look up it was a ceiling, look down it was a floor. I forget what I done, lady. I set there and set there, trying to remember what it was I done and I ain't recalled it to this day. Oncet in a while, I would think it was coming to me, but it never come."

"Maybe they put you in by mistake," the old lady said vaguely.

115 "Nome," he said. "It wasn't no mistake. They had the papers on me."

"You must have stolen something," she said.

The Misfit sneered slightly. "Nobody had nothing I wanted," he said. "It was a head-doctor at the penitentiary said what I had done was kill my daddy but I know that for a lie. My daddy died in nineteen ought nineteen of the epidemic flu and I never had a thing to do with it. He was buried in the Mount Hopewell Baptist churchyard and you can go there and see for yourself."

"If you would pray," the old lady said, "Jesus would help you."

"That's right," The Misfit said.

120 "Well then, why don't you pray?" she asked trembling with delight suddenly.

"I don't want no hep," he said. "I'm doing all right by myself."

Bobby Lee and Hiram came ambling back from the woods. Bobby Lee was dragging a yellow shirt with bright blue parrots in it.

"Throw me that shirt, Bobby Lee," The Misfit said. The shirt came flying at him and landed on his shoulder and he put it on. The grandmother couldn't name what the shirt

reminded her of. "No, lady," The Misfit said while he was buttoning it up, "I found out the crime don't matter. You can do one thing or you can do another, kill a man or take a tire off his car, because sooner or later you're going to forget what it was you done and just be punished for it."

The children's mother had begun to make heaving noises as if she couldn't get her breath. "Lady," he asked, "would you and that little girl like to step off yonder with Bobby Lee and Hiram and join your husband?"

125 "Yes, thank you," the mother said faintly. Her left arm dangled helplessly and she was holding the baby, who had gone to sleep, in the other. "Hep that lady up, Hiram," The Misfit said as she struggled to climb out of the ditch, "and Bobby Lee, you hold onto that little girl's hand."

"I don't want to hold hands with him," June Star said. "He reminds me of a pig."

The fat boy blushed and laughed and caught her by the arm and pulled her off into the woods after Hiram and her mother.

Alone with The Misfit, the grandmother found that she had lost her voice. There was not a cloud in the sky nor any sun. There was nothing around her but woods. She wanted to tell him that he must pray. She opened and closed her mouth several times before anything came out. Finally she found herself saying, "Jesus, Jesus," meaning, Jesus will help you, but the way she was saying it, it sounded as if she might be cursing.

"Yes'm," The Misfit said as if he agreed. "Jesus thrown everything off balance. It was the same case with Him as with me except He hadn't committed any crime and they could prove I had committed one because they had the papers on me. Of course," he said, "they never shown me my papers. That's why I sign myself now. I said long ago, you get you a signature and sign everything you do and keep a copy of it. Then you'll know what you done and you can hold up the crime to the punishment and see do they match and in the end you'll have something to prove you ain't been treated right. I call myself The Misfit," he said, "because I can't make what all I done wrong fit what all I gone through in punishment."

130 There was a piercing scream from the woods, followed closely by a pistol report. "Does it seem right to you, lady,

> **There was a piercing scream from** the **woods, followed closely by a pistol report.**

that one is punished a heap and another ain't punished at all?"

"Jesus!" the old lady cried. "You've got good blood! I know you wouldn't shoot a lady! I know you come from nice people! Pray! Jesus, you ought not to shoot a lady. I'll give you all the money I've got!"

"Lady," The Misfit said, looking beyond her far into the woods, "there never was a body that give the undertaker a tip."

There were two more pistol reports and the grandmother raised her head like a parched old turkey hen crying for water and called, "Bailey Boy, Bailey Boy!" as if her heart would break.

"Jesus was the only One that ever raised the dead." The Misfit continued, "and He shouldn't have done it. He thrown everything off balance. If He did what He said, then it's nothing for you to do but throw away everything and follow Him, and if He didn't, then it's nothing for you to do but enjoy the few minutes you got left the best way you can—by killing somebody or burning down his house or doing some other meanness to him. No pleasure but meanness," he said and his voice had become almost a snarl.

135 "Maybe He didn't raise the dead," the old lady mumbled, not knowing what she was saying and feeling so dizzy that she sank down in the ditch with her legs twisted under her.

"I wasn't there so I can't say He didn't," The Misfit said. "I wisht I had of been there," he said, hitting the ground with his fist. "It ain't right I wasn't there because if I had

of been there I would of known. Listen lady," he said in a high voice, "if I had of been there I would of known and I wouldn't be like I am now." His voice seemed about to crack and the grandmother's head cleared for an instant. She saw the man's face twisted close to her own as if he were going to cry and she murmured, "Why you're one of my babies. You're one of my own children!" She reached out and touched him on the shoulder. The Misfit sprang back as if a snake had bitten him and shot her three times through the chest. Then he put his gun down on the ground and took off his glasses and began to clean them.

Hiram and Bobby Lee returned from the woods and stood over the ditch, looking down at the grandmother who half sat and half lay in a puddle of blood with her legs crossed under her like a child's and her face smiling up at the cloudless sky.

Without his glasses, The Misfit's eyes were red-rimmed and pale and defenseless looking. "Take her off and throw her where you thrown the others," he said, picking up the cat that was rubbing itself against his leg.

"She was a talker, wasn't she?" Bobby Lee said, sliding down the ditch with a yodel.

"She would have been a good woman," The Misfit said, 140 "if it had been somebody there to shoot her every minute of her life."

"Some fun!" Bobby Lee said.

"Shut up, Bobby Lee," The Misfit said. "It's no real pleasure in life."

Questions for Critical Thinking

1 What is the grandmother's attitude toward the South as opposed to the rest of her family's attitude, particularly her grandson's? How do you account for the difference?

2 "It is the grandmother's 'Southern Pride' that leads to the fam-

ily's downfall." In a short essay, explain whether you agree or disagree with this statement. Support your answer with examples from the text.

3 Review the story and mark the margins whenever you find an example of humor. How would you describe

O'Connor's humor? What role does humor play in the story?

4 How much of a role does irony play in the story? How should we take The Misfit's final statement about the grandmother?

Ralph Ellison (1914–1994)

"If I'm going to be remembered as a novelist, I'd better produce a few more books," Ralph Ellison said in a 1981 interview. Indeed, Ellison failed to complete a second novel in his lifetime, but the quality and importance of his first novel, *Invisible Man,* was so great that his literary reputation remains intact long after his death. *Invisible Man* follows the life of an unnamed black man in New York City who is "invisible" because white 1940s society refuses to see him. Although Ellison was insistent that the book was first and foremost a piece of literature, it is difficult to read it without paying attention to its comment on race.

Invisible Man responds to life in the Jim Crow era, the time period from 1877 to the mid-1960s in which blacks were the victims of widespread racism. A phenomenon primarily of the Southern states, Jim Crow laws (the name comes from a black, servile character in a popular minstrel show) kept blacks legally segregated from whites with the idea of "separate but equal." In effect, facilities for blacks were

rarely equal in quality to those for whites. Segregation was only one manifestation of the prevailing mentality that blacks were inferior to whites. At its worst, racist behavior took the form of lynching, the execution of an individual carried out by a mob, rather than by legal authorities. Blacks were often lynched without any reason and in brutal ways. Ellison's fiction captures both this overtly cruel form of racism and the subtler, once-commonplace discrimination that leads the black protagonist of *Invisible Man* to believe his path ought to be humility.

Unlike his protagonist, who was born in the Deep South, Ellison was raised in Oklahoma City, Oklahoma. He was educated at the historically black Tuskegee Institute (now Tuskegee University) in Alabama, where he studied music and became friends with important jazz musicians of the day. He went to New York City to earn money before his senior year but never returned to Tuskegee. Ellison wrote essays and reviews, edited publications such as *The Negro Quarterly,* and taught creative writing later in his life. In addition to *Invisible Man,* which won the National

Book Award in 1953, Ellison published two books of essays, *Shadow and Act* (1964) and *Going to the Territory* (1986), and a number of short stories. His collection *Flying Home* appeared posthumously in 1996. Three years thereafter, literary scholar John Callahan published a highly edited version of Ellison's second novel as *Juneteenth.*

A kindly and gracious man, intense with his friends and patient with his students, Ellison suffered some harsh criticism from later generations of African-American writers, who wanted him to be more overtly political in his prose. He never faltered, however, in his belief that literature was one of the highest callings a human being might follow. And, although he died at eighty with just one published novel, he remained devoted to the craft. Music—jazz in particular—was a clear influence on this writer. He once described *Invisible Man* as having the structure of a jazz composition—a beginning theme and bass line with variations and improvised solos.

"The act of writing requires a constant plunging back into the shadow of the past where time hovers ghostlike." —Ralph Ellison

Battle Royal (1952)

1   IT goes a long way back, some twenty years. All my life I had been looking for something, and everywhere I turned someone tried to tell me what it was. I accepted their answers too, though they were often in contradiction and even self-contradictory. I was naïve. I was looking for myself and asking everyone except myself questions which I, and only I, could answer. It took me a long time and much painful boomeranging of my expectations to achieve a realization everyone else appears to have been born with: That I am nobody but myself. But first I had to discover that I am an invisible man!

  And yet I am no freak of nature, nor of history. I was in the cards, other things having been equal (or unequal) eighty-five years ago. I am not ashamed of my grandparents for having been slaves. I am only ashamed of myself for having at one time been ashamed. About eighty-five years ago they were told they were free, united with others of our country in everything pertaining to the common good, and, in everything social, separate like the fingers of the hand. And they believed it. They exulted in it. They stayed in their place, worked hard, and brought up my father to do the same. But my grandfather is the one. He was an odd old guy, my grandfather, and I am told I take after him. It was he who caused the trouble. On his deathbed he called my father to him and said, "Son, after I'm gone I want you to keep up the good fight. I never told you, but our life is a war and I have been a traitor all my born days, a spy in the enemy's country ever since I give up my gun back in the Reconstruction. Live with your head in the lion's mouth. I want you to overcome 'em with yeses, undermine 'em with grins, agree 'em to death and destruction, let 'em swoller you till they vomit or bust wide open." They thought the old man had gone out of his mind. He had been the meekest of men. The younger children were rushed from the room, the shades drawn and the flame of the lamp turned so low that it sputtered on the wick like the old man's breathing. "Learn it to the younguns," he whispered fiercely; then he died.

  But my folks were more alarmed over his last words than over his dying. It was as though he had not died at all, his words caused so much anxiety. I was warned emphatically to forget what he had said and, indeed, this is the first time it has been mentioned outside the family circle. It had a tremendous effect upon me, however. I could never be sure of what he meant. Grandfather had been a quiet old man who never made any trouble, yet on his deathbed he had called himself a traitor and a spy, and he had spoken of his meekness as a dangerous activity. It became a constant puzzle which lay unanswered in the back of my mind. And whenever things went well for me I remembered my grandfather and felt guilty and uncomfortable. It was as though I was carrying out his advice in spite of myself. And to make it worse, everyone loved me for it. I was praised by the most lily-white men in town. I was considered an example of desirable conduct—just as my grandfather had been. And what puzzled me was that the old man had defined it as *treachery*. When I was praised for my conduct I felt a guilt that in some way I was doing something that was really against the wishes of the white folks, that if they had understood they would have desired me to act just the opposite, that I should have been sulky and mean, and that that really would have been what they wanted, even though they were fooled and thought they wanted me to act as I did. It made me afraid that some day they would look upon me as a traitor and I would be lost. Still I was more afraid to act any other way because they didn't like that at all. The old man's words were like a curse. On my graduation day I delivered an oration in which I showed that humility was the secret, indeed, the very essence of progress. (Not that I believed this—how could I, remembering my grandfather?—I only believed that it worked.) It was a great success. Everyone praised me and I was invited to give the speech at a gathering of the town's leading white citizens. It was a triumph for the whole community.

It was in the main ballroom of the leading hotel. When I got there I discovered that it was on the occasion of a smoker, and I was told that since I was to be there anyway I might as well take part in the battle royal to be fought by some of my schoolmates as part of the entertainment. The battle royal came first.

5   All of the town's big shots were there in their tuxedoes, wolfing down the buffet foods, drinking beer and whiskey and smoking black cigars. It was a large room with a high ceiling. Chairs were arranged in neat rows around three sides of a portable boxing ring. The fourth side was clear, revealing a gleaming space of polished floor. I had some misgivings over the battle royal, by the way. Not from a distaste for fighting but because I didn't care too much for the other fellows who were to take part. They were tough guys who seemed to have no grandfather's curse worrying their minds. No one could mistake their toughness. And besides, I suspected that fighting a battle royal might detract from the dignity of my speech. In those pre-invisible days I visualized myself as a potential Booker T. Washington. But the other fellows didn't care too much for me either, and there were nine of them. I felt superior to them in my way, and I didn't like the manner in which we were all crowded together in the servants' elevator. Nor did they like my being there. In fact, as the warmly lighted floors flashed past the elevator we had words over the fact that I, by taking part in the fight, had knocked one of their friends out of a night's work.

We were led out of the elevator through a rococo hall into an anteroom and told to get into our fighting togs. Each of us was issued a pair of boxing gloves and ushered out into the big mirrored hall, which we entered looking cautiously about us and whispering, lest we might accidentally be heard above the noise of the room. It was foggy with cigar smoke. And already the whiskey was taking effect. I was shocked to see some of the most important men of the town quite tipsy. They were all there—bankers, lawyers, judges, doctors, fire chiefs, teachers, merchants. Even one of the more fashionable pastors. Something we could not see was going on up front. A clarinet was vibrating sensuously and the men were standing up and moving eagerly forward. We were a small tight group, clustered together, our bare upper bodies touching and shining with anticipatory sweat: while up front the big shots were becoming increasingly excited over something we still could not see. Suddenly I heard the school superintendent, who had told me to come, yell, "Bring up the shines, gentlemen! Bring up the little shines!"

We were rushed up to the front of the ballroom, where it smelled even more strongly of tobacco and whiskey. Then we were pushed into place. I almost wet my pants. A sea of faces, some hostile, some amused, ringed around us, and in the center, facing us, stood a magnificent blonde—stark naked. There was dead silence. I felt a black of cold air chill me. I tried to back away, but they were behind me and around me. Some of the boys stood with lowered heads, trembling. I felt a wave of irrational guilt and fear. My teeth chattered, my skin turned to goose flesh, my knees knocked. Yet I was strongly attracted and looked in spite of myself. Had the price of looking been blindness, I would have looked. The hair was yellow like that of a circus kewpie doll, the face heavily powdered and rouged, as though to form an abstract mask, the eyes hollow and smeared a cool blue, the color of a baboon's butt. I felt a desire to spit upon her as my eyes brushed slowly over her body. Her breasts were firm and round as the domes of East Indian temples, and I stood so close as to see the fine skin texture and beads of pearly perspiration glistening like dew around the pink and erected buds of her nipples. I wanted at one and the same time to run from the room, to sink through the floor, or go to her and cover her from my eyes and the eyes of the others with my body; to feel the soft thighs, to caress her and destroy her, to love her and to murder her, to hide from her and yet to stroke where below the small American flag tattooed upon her belly her thighs formed a capital V. I had a notion that of all in the room she saw only me with her impersonal eyes.

And then she began to dance, a slow sensuous movement; the smoke of a hundred cigars clinging to her like the thinnest of veils. She seemed like a fair bird-girl girdled in veils calling to me from the angry surface of some gray and threatening sea. I was transported. Then I became aware of the clarinet playing and the big shots yelling at us. Some threatened us if we looked and others if we did not. On my right I saw one boy faint. And now a man grabbed a silver pitcher from a table and stepped close as he dashed ice water upon him and stood him up and forced two of us to support him as his head hung and moans issued from his thick bluish lips. Another boy began to plead to go home. He was the largest of the group, wearing dark red fighting trunks much too small to conceal the erection which projected from him as though in answer to the insinuating low-registered moaning of the clarinet. He tried to hide himself with his boxing gloves.

And all the while the blonde continued dancing, smiling faintly at the big shots who watched her with fascination, and faintly smiling at our fear. I noticed a certain merchant who followed her hungrily, his lips loose and drooling. He was a large man who wore diamond studs in a shirtfront which swelled with the ample paunch underneath, and each time the blonde swayed her undulating hips he ran his hand through the thin hair of his bald head and, with his arms upheld, his posture clumsy like that of an intoxicated panda, wound his belly in a slow and obscene grind. This creature was completely hypnotized. The music had quickened. As the dancer flung herself about with a detached expression on her face, the men began reaching out to touch her. I could see their beefy fingers sink into her soft flesh. Some of the others tried to stop them and she began to move around the floor in graceful circles, as they gave chase, slipping and sliding over the polished floor. It was mad. Chairs went crashing, drinks were spilt, as they ran laughing and howling after her. They caught her just as she reached a door, raised her from the floor, and tossed her as college boys are tossed at a hazing, and above her red, fixed-smiling lips I saw the terror and disgust in her eyes, almost like my own terror and that which I saw in some of the other boys. As I watched, they tossed her twice and her soft breasts seemed to flatten against the air and her legs flung wildly as she spun. Some of the more sober ones helped her to escape. And I started off the floor, heading for the anteroom with the rest of the boys.

10　　Some were still crying and in hysteria. But as we tried to leave we were stopped and ordered to get into the ring. There was nothing to do but what we were told. All ten of us climbed under the ropes and allowed ourselves to be blindfolded with broad bands of white cloth. One of the men seemed to feel a bit sympathetic and tried to cheer us up as we stood with our backs against the ropes. Some of us tried to grin. "See that boy over there?" one of the men said. "I want you to run across at the bell and give it to him right in the belly. If you don't get him,

I'm going to get you. I don't like his looks." Each of us was told the same. The blindfolds were put on. Yet even then I had been going over my speech. In my mind each word was as bright as a flame. I felt the cloth pressed into place, and frowned so that it would be loosened when I relaxed.

But now I felt a sudden fit of blind terror. I was unused to darkness, it was as though I had suddenly found myself in a dark room filled with poisonous cottonmouths. I could hear the bleary voices yelling insistently for the battle royal to begin.

"Get going in there!"

"Let me at that big nigger!"

I strained to pick up the school superintendent's voice, as though to squeeze some security out of that slightly more familiar sound.

"Let me at those black sonsabitches!" someone yelled.　15

"No, Jackson, no!" another voice yelled. "Here, somebody, help me hold Jack."

"I want to get at that ginger-colored nigger. Tear him limb from limb," the first voice yelled.

I stood against the ropes trembling. For in those days I was what they called ginger-colored, and he sounded as though he might crunch me between his teeth like a crisp ginger cookie.

Quite a struggle was going on. Chairs were being kicked about and I could hear voices grunting as with terrific effort. I wanted to see, to see more desperately than ever before. But the blindfold was as tight as a thick skin-puckering scab and when I raised my gloved hands to push the layers of white aside a voice yelled, "Oh, no you don't, black bastard! Leave that alone!"

"Ring the bell before Jackson kills him　20 a coon!" someone boomed in the sudden silence. And I heard the bell clang and the sound of the feet scuffling forward.

A glove smacked against my head. I pivoted, striking out stiffly as someone went past, and felt the jar ripple along the length of my arm to my shoulder. Then it seemed as though all nine of the boys had turned upon me at once. Blows pounded me from all sides while I struck out as best I could. So many blows landed upon me that I wondered if I were not the only blindfolded fighter in the ring, or if the man called Jackson hadn't succeeded in getting me after all.

Blindfolded, I could no longer control my motions. I had no dignity. I stumbled about like a baby or a drunken man. The smoke had become thicker and with each new blow it seemed to sear and further restrict my lungs. My saliva became like hot bitter glue. A glove connected with my head, filling my mouth with warm blood. It was everywhere. I could not tell if the moisture I felt upon my body was sweat or blood. A blow landed hard against the nape of my neck. I felt myself going over, my head hitting the floor. Streaks of blue light filled the black world behind the blindfold. I lay prone, pretending that I was knocked out, but felt myself seized by hands and yanked to my feet. "Get going, black boy! Mix it up!" My arms were like lead, my head smarting from blows. I managed to feel my way to the ropes and held on, trying to catch my breath. A glove landed in my midsection and I went over again, feeling as though the smoke had become a knife jabbed into my guts. Pushed this way and that by the legs milling around me, I finally pulled erect and discovered that I could see the black, sweat-washed forms weaving in the smoky-blue atmosphere like drunken dancers weaving to the rapid drum-like thuds of blows.

Everyone fought hysterically. It was complete anarchy. Everybody fought everybody else. No group fought together for long. Two, three, four, fought one, then turned to fight each other, were themselves attacked. Blows landed below the belt and in the kidney, with the gloves open as well as closed, and with my eye partly opened now there was not so much terror. I moved carefully, avoiding blows, although not too many to attract attention, fighting group to group. The boys groped about like blind, cautious crabs crouching to protect their midsections, their heads pulled in short against their shoulders, their arms stretched nervously before them, with their fists testing the smoke-filled air like the knobbed feelers of hypersensitive snails. In one corner I glimpsed a boy violently punching the air and heard him scream in pain as he smashed his hand against a ring post. For a second I saw him bent over holding his hand, then going down as a blow caught his unprotected head. I played one group against the other, slipping in and throwing a punch then stepping out of range while pushing the others into the melee to take the blows blindly aimed at me. The smoke was agonizing and there were no rounds, no bells at

I wanted to deliver my speech more than anything else in the world . . .

three minute intervals to relieve our exhaustion. The room spun round me, a swirl of lights, smoke, sweating bodies surrounded by tense white faces. I bled from both nose and mouth, the blood spattering upon my chest.

The men kept yelling, "Slug him, black boy! Knock his guts out!"

"Uppercut him! Kill him! Kill that big boy!"   25

Taking a fake fall, I saw a boy going down heavily beside me as though we were felled by a single blow, saw a sneaker-clad foot shoot into his groin as the two who had knocked him down stumbled upon him. I rolled out of range, feeling a twinge of nausea.

The harder we fought the more threatening the men became. And yet, I had begun to worry about my speech again. How would it go? Would they recognize my ability? What would they give me?

I was fighting automatically when suddenly I noticed that one after another of the boys was leaving the ring. I was surprised, filled with panic, as though I had been left alone with an unknown danger. Then I understood. The boys had arranged it among themselves. It was the custom for the two men left in the ring to slug it out for the winner's prize. I discovered this too late. When the bell sounded two men in tuxedoes leaped into the ring and removed the blindfold. I found myself facing Tatlock, the biggest of the gang. I felt sick at my stomach. Hardly had the bell stopped ringing in my ears than it clanged again and I saw him moving swiftly toward me. Thinking of nothing else to do I hit him smash on the nose. He kept coming, bringing the rank sharp violence of stale sweat. His face was a black blank of a face, only eyes alive—with hate of me and aglow with a feverish terror from what had happened to us all. I became anxious. I wanted to deliver my speech and he came at me as though he meant to beat it out of me. I smashed him again and again, taking his blows as they came. Then on a sudden impulse I struck him lightly and we clinched. I whispered, "Fake like I knocked you out, you can have the prize."

"I'll break your behind," he whispered hoarsely.

"For *them*?"   30

"For *me*, sonofabitch!"

They were yelling for us to break it up and Tatlock spun me half around with a blow, and as a joggled camera sweeps in a reeling scene, I saw the howling red faces crouching tense beneath the cloud of blue-gray smoke. For a moment the world wavered, unraveled, flowed, then my head cleared and Tatlock bounced before me. That fluttering shadow before my eyes was his jabbing left hand. Then falling forward, my head against his damp shoulder, I whispered.

"I'll make it five dollars more."

"Go to hell!"

35 But his muscles relaxed a trifle beneath my pressure and I breathed, "Seven?"

"Give it to your ma," he said, ripping me beneath the heart.

And while I still held him I butted him and moved away. I felt myself bombarded with punches. I fought back with hopeless desperation. I wanted to deliver my speech more than anything else in the world, because I felt that only these men could judge truly my ability, and now this stupid clown was ruining my chances. I began fighting carefully now, moving in to punch him and out again with my greater speed. A lucky blow to his chin and I had him going too—until I heard a loud voice yell, "I got my money on the big boy."

Hearing this, I almost dropped my guard. I was confused: Should I try to win against the voice out there? Would not this go against my speech, and was not this a moment for humility, for nonresistance? A blow to my head as I danced about sent my right eye popping like a jack-in-the-box and settled my dilemma. The room went red as I fell. It was a dream fall, my body languid and fastidious as to where to land, until the floor became impatient and smashed up to meet me. A moment later I came to. An hypnotic voice and said FIVE emphatically. And I lay there, hazily watching a dark red spot of my own blood shaping itself into a butterfly, glistening and soaking into the soiled gray world of the canvas.

When the voice drawled TEN I was lifted up and dragged to a chair. I sat dazed. My eye pained and swelled with each throb of my pounding heart and I wondered if now I would be allowed to speak. I was wringing wet, my mouth still bleeding. We were grouped along the wall now. The other boys ignored me as they congratulated Tatlock and speculated as to how much they would be paid. One boy whimpered over his smashed hand. Looking up front, I saw attendants in white jackets rolling the portable ring away and placing a small square rug in the vacant space surrounded by chairs. Perhaps, I thought, I will stand on the rug to deliver my speech.

Then the M.C. called to us. "Come on up here boys and 40 get your money."

We ran forward to where the men laughed and talked in their chairs, waiting. Everyone seemed friendly now.

"There it is on the rug," the man said. I saw the rug covered with coins of all dimensions and a few crumpled bills. But what excited me, scattered here and there, were the gold pieces.

"Boys, it's all yours," the man said. "You get all you grab."

"That's right, Sambo," a blond man said, winking at me confidentially.

I trembled with excitement, forgetting my pain. I would 45 get the gold and the bills. I thought. I would use both hands. I would throw my body against the boys nearest me to block them from the gold.

"Get down around the rug now," the man commanded, "and don't anyone touch it until I give the signal."

"This ought to be good," I heard.

As told, we got around the square rug on our knees. Slowly the man raised his freckled hand as we followed it upward with our eyes.

I heard, "These niggers look like they're about to pray!"

Then, "Ready," the man said. "Go!" 50

I lunged for a yellow coin lying on the blue design of the carpet, touching it and sending a surprised shriek to join those around me. I tried frantically to remove my hand but could not let go. A hot, violent force tore through my body, shaking me like a wet rat. The rug was electrified. The hair bristled up on my head as I shook myself free. My muscles jumped, my nerves jangled, writhed. But I saw that this was not stopping the other boys. Laughing in fear and embarrassment, some were holding back and scooping up the coins knocked off by the painful contortions of others. The men roared above us as we struggled.

"Pick it up, goddamnit, pick it up!" someone called like a bass-voiced parrot. "Go on, get it!"

I crawled rapidly around the floor, picking up the coins, trying to avoid the coppers and to get greenbacks and the gold. Ignoring the shock by laughing, as I brushed the coins off quickly, I discovered that I could contain the electricity— a contradiction but it works. Then the men began to push us onto the rug. Laughing embarrassedly, we struggled out of their hands and kept after the coins. We were all wet and slippery and hard to hold. Suddenly I saw a boy lifted into the air, glistening with sweat like a circus seal, and dropped, his wet back landing flush upon the charged rug, heard him yell and saw him literally dance upon his back, his elbows beating a frenzied tattoo upon the floor, his muscles twitching like the flesh of a horse stung by many flies. When he finally rolled off, his face was gray and no one stopped him when he ran from the floor amid booming laughter.

"Get the money," the M.C. called. "That's good hard American cash!"

55 And we snatched and grabbed, snatched and grabbed. I was careful not to come too close to the rug now, and when I felt the hot whiskey breath descend upon me like a cloud of foul air I reached out and grabbed the leg of a chair. It was occupied and I held on desperately.

"Leggo, nigger! Leggo!"

The huge face wavered down to mine as he tried to push me free. But my body was slippery and he was too drunk. It was Mr. Colcord, who owned a chain of movie houses and "entertainment palaces." Each time he grabbed me I slipped out of his hands. It became a real struggle. I feared the rug more than I did the drunk, so I held on, surprising myself for a moment by trying to topple *him* upon the rug. It was such an enormous idea that I found myself actually carrying it out. I tried not to be obvious, yet when I grabbed his leg, trying to tumble him out of the chair, he raised up, roaring with laughter and, looking at me with soberness dead in the eye, kicked me viciously in the chest. The chair leg flew out of my hand and I felt myself going and rolled. It was as though I had rolled through a bed of hot coals. It seemed a whole century would pass before I would roll free, a century in which I was seared through the deepest levels of my body to the fearful breath within me and the breath seared and heated to the point of explosion. It'll all be over in a flash, I thought as I rolled clear. It'll all be over in a flash.

But not yet, the men on the other side were waiting, red faces swollen as though from apoplexy as they bent forward in their chairs. Seeing their fingers coming toward me I rolled away as a fumbled football rolls off the receiver's fingertips, back into the coals. That time I luckily sent the rug sliding out of place and heard the coins ringing against the floor and the boys scuffling to pick them up and the M.C. calling, "All right, boys, that's all. Go get dressed and get your money."

I was limp as a dish rag. My back felt as though it had been beaten with wires.

60 When we had dressed the M.C. came in and gave us each five dollars, except Tatlock, who got ten for being the last in the ring. Then he told us to leave. I was not to get a chance to deliver my speech, I thought. I was going out into the dim alley in despair when I was stopped and told to go back. I returned to the ballroom, where the men were pushing back their chairs and gathering in small groups to talk.

The M.C. knocked on a table for quiet. "Gentlemen," he said, "we almost forgot an important part of the program. A most serious part, gentlemen. This boy was brought here to deliver a speech which he made at his graduation yesterday . . ."

"Bravo!"

"I'm told that he is the smartest boy we've got out there in Greenwood. I'm told that he knows more big words than a pocket-sized dictionary."

Much applause and laughter.

65 "So now, gentlemen, I want you to give him your attention."

There was still laughter as I faced them, my mouth dry, my eyes throbbing. I began slowly, but evidently my throat was tense, because they began shouting. "Louder! Louder!"

"We of the younger generation extol the wisdom of that great leader and educator," I shouted, "who first spoke these flaming words of wisdom: 'A ship lost at sea for many days suddenly sighted a friendly vessel. From the mast of the unfortunate vessel was seen a signal: "Water, water, we die of thirst!" The answer from the friendly vessel came back: "Cast down your bucket where you are." The captain of the distressed vessel, at last heeding the injunction, cast down his bucket, and it came up full of fresh sparkling water from the mouth of the Amazon River.' And like him I say, and in his words, 'To those of my race who depend upon bettering their condition in a foreign land, or who underestimate the importance of cultivating friendly relations with the Southern white man, who is his next-door neighbor, I would say: "Cast down your bucket where you are"—cast it down in making friends in every manly way of the people of all races by whom we are surrounded . . .'"

I spoke automatically and with such fervor that I did not realize that the men were still talking and laughing until my dry mouth, filling up with blood from the cut, almost strangled me. I coughed, wanting to stop and go to one of the tall brass, sand-filled spittoons to relieve myself, but a few of the men, especially the superintendent, were listening and I was afraid. So I gulped it down, blood, saliva and all, and continued. (What powers of endurance I had during those days! What enthusiasm! What a belief in the rightness of things!) I spoke even louder in spite of the pain. But still they talked and still they laughed, as though deaf with cotton in dirty ears. So I spoke with greater emotional emphasis. I closed my ears and swallowed blood until I was nauseated. The speech seemed a hundred times as long as before, but I could not leave out a single word. All had to be said, each memorized nuance considered, rendered. Nor was that all. Whenever I uttered a word of three or more syllables a group of voices would yell for me to repeat it. I used the phrase "social responsibility" and they yelled:

"What's that word you say, boy?"

70   "Social responsibility," I said.

"What?"

"Social . . ."

"Louder."

" . . . responsibility."

75   "More!"

"Respon—"

"Repeat!"

"—sibility."

The room filled with the uproar of laughter until, no doubt, distracted by having to gulp down my blood, I made

> *". . . We mean to do right by* you, but you've got to know your place at all times. . . ."

a mistake and yelled a phrase I had often seen denounced in newspaper editorials, heard debated in private.

"Social . . ."   80

"What?" they yelled.

" . . . equality—"

The laughter hung smokelike in the sudden stillness. I opened my eyes, puzzled. Sounds of displeasure filled the room. The M.C. rushed forward. They shouted hostile phrases at me. But I did not understand.

A small dry mustached man in the front row blared out, "Say that slowly, son!"

"What, sir?"   85

"What you just said!"

"Social responsibility, sir," I said.

"You weren't being smart, were you, boy?" he said, not unkindly.

"No, sir!"

"You sure that about 'equality'   90 was a mistake?"

"Oh, yes, sir," I said. "I was swallowing blood."

"Well, you had better speak more slowly so we can understand. We mean to do right by you, but you've got to know your place at all times. All right, now, go on with your speech."

I was afraid. I wanted to leave but I wanted also to speak and I was afraid they'd snatch me down.

"Thank you, sir," I said, beginning where I had left off, and having them ignore me as before.

Yet when I finished there was a thunderous applause. I   95 was surprised to see the superintendent come forth with a package wrapped in white tissue paper, and, gesturing for quiet, address the men.

"Gentlemen, you see that I did not overpraise the boy. He makes a good speech and some day he'll lead his people in the proper paths. And I don't have to tell you that this is important in these days and times. This is a good, smart boy, and so to encourage him in the right direction, in the name of the Board of Education I wish to present him a prize in the form of this . . ."

He paused, removing the tissue paper and revealing a gleaming calfskin briefcase.

" . . . in the form of this first-class article from Shad Whitmore's shop."

"Boy," he said, addressing me, "take this prize and keep it well. Consider it a badge of office. Prize it. Keep developing as you are and some day it will be filled with important papers that will help shape the destiny of your people."

100 I was so moved that I could hardly express my thanks. A rope of bloody saliva forming a shape like an undiscovered continent drooled upon the leather and I wiped it quickly away. I felt an importance that I had never dreamed.

"Open it and see what's inside," I was told.

My fingers a-tremble, I complied, smelling fresh leather and finding an official-looking document inside. It was a scholarship to the state college for Negroes. My eyes filled with tears and I ran awkwardly off the floor.

I was overjoyed; I did not even mind when I discovered the gold pieces I had scrambled for were brass pocket tokens advertising a certain make of automobile.

When I reached home everyone was excited. Next day the neighbors came to congratulate me. I even felt safe from grandfather, whose deathbed curse usually spoiled my triumphs. I stood beneath his photograph with my briefcase in hand and smiled triumphantly into his stolid black peasant's face. It was a face that fascinated me. The eyes seemed to follow everywhere I went.

105 That night I dreamed I was at a circus with him and that he refused to laugh at the clowns no matter what they did. Then later he told me to open my briefcase and read what was inside and I did, finding an official envelope stamped with the state seal: and inside the envelope I found another and another, endlessly, and I thought I would fall of weariness. "Them's years," he said. "Now open that one." And I did and in it I found an engraved stamp containing a short message in letters of gold. "Read it," my grandfather said. "Out loud."

"To Whom It May Concern," I intoned. "Keep This Nigger-Boy Running."

I awoke with the old man's laughter ringing in my ears.

Questions for Critical Thinking

1 Unlike most writers who write about the South (such as Faulkner and O'Connor), Ralph Ellison was not born there. What about "Battle Royal" makes it a Southern story? You might want to consider which, if any, themes it shares with the Faulkner and O'Connor selections.

2 Reread the protagonist's dream recounted at the end of the story. Given the time and place in which this story's action occurs, what do you think the boy's dream stands for or means?

3 The narrator tells his story from a future point in time, looking back on the occurrence of this battle royal. Identify the ironies you see in the story that are created from this disjuncture of point of view.

Getting Started: A Research Project

Research is a skill that will carry you through your college career. You can find the research materials you need for this project on our Web site **(connect. mcgraw-hill.com)**. Other ideas for research projects and sources appear at the end of this chapter.

Between the South and the West, decide which region's literature you liked the most in this chapter. Then use one of the sources found at **connect.mcgraw-hill.com** to read more selections from that region. Formulate a thesis in which you identify what you believe to be the defining feature of literature from that region. But as you do this, take note of your own understanding or personally held myths about the region before you begin and after you complete the reading. Consider how much of the region's identity comes from within, from its own inhabitants, and how much outside observers impose on it. For example, race relations in the South as depicted in fiction emerge as complex and painful on all sides; the heritage and memory of the Civil War—popularly known in the South as the War Between the States—holds different meanings for different races, and different meanings within social classes as well. In our national literature the war was a mostly subterranean subject, or as critic Daniel Aaron referred to it, an "unwritten war." The West has its own myths, some coming from within—as we noticed about the South—and some imposed on it from outside the region. The fairy-tale-large notion of "cowboys and Indians," for example, is something we grow up with. How realistic a view of the West does that image convey once you've read even a few selections about the country between the western bank of the Mississippi River and the Pacific Ocean?

Go to connect.mcgraw-hill.com and respond to story selections from the South and the West.

1. Choose a figure particular to one of the regions—the white farmer, say, in the South or the black fieldworker or the small-town shop owner, or the western ranch owner or a Native American schoolteacher or reservation police officer—and, working with your instructor, draw up a reading list that will help you to flesh out a portrait of a person rooted in the region who seems recognizable to people living outside the region. Try to establish how much of that person's habits and views comes from local and regional influences and what of that person's views pertains to a national way of seeing the world.

2. Work from the outside in, beginning with a stereotype from American popular or commercial culture—the Marlboro Man, for example, or the Southern Rebel soldier—and see how much the literature of the time, the stories and novels, lends support to these stereotypes.

Further Suggestions for Writing and Research

1. Consider the three Southern authors you read in this chapter. On the basis of their fiction, how would you describe their attitudes toward the South? What characteristics of the region or its people do you see recur in the work of more than one author? Which aspects differ from author to author?

2. Are there such things as "regional" writers, or do all writers, even those from major cities, belong to a particular place, with habits and speech patterns and ways of seeing all their own?

Some Sources for Research

1. Ayers, Edward L., and Bradley Mittendorf, eds. *The Oxford Book of the American South: Testimony, Memory, and Fiction*. New York: Oxford UP, 1997. Print.

2. Fetterley, Judith, and Marjorie Pryse. *Regionalism, Women, and American Literary Culture*. Champaign: U of Illinois P, 2003. Print. Especially chapters 1 and 2 and the Works Cited section.

3. Kittredge, William, ed. *The Portable Western Reader*. New York: Penguin, 1997.

4. Lyon, Thomas J., ed. *The Literary West: An Anthology of Western American Literature*. New York: Oxford UP, 1999. Print.

5. Mahoney, Timothy R., and Wendy J. Katz, eds. *Regionalism and the Humanities*. Lincoln: U of Nebraska P, 2008. Print.

6. Western Literature Association. *Updating the Literary West*. Fort Worth, TX: Texas Christian UP, 1997. Print.

For examples of student papers, see Chapters 2, 3, 4, 5, 7, 18, and 31.

16

An Anthology of Stories for Further Reading

Margaret Atwood (b. 1939)

BORN IN TORONTO, Margaret Atwood has been, along with short story writer Alice Munro, one of the few Canadian writers who have had a major impact on the contemporary American reading public. A driving force in the literature scene to our north, she works in a wide range of genres and styles—seeming equally at home in the mode of historical fiction and that of sci-ence fiction. Her novels such as *Surfacing* (1972), *The Handmaid's Tale* (1985), and the Booker Prize–winning *The Blind Assassin* (2000) have won her great acclaim. Atwood is also a poet (see Chapter 23), essayist, and short-story writer. In each of these genres and forms, she demonstrates keen attention to craft as well as theme.

Happy Endings (1983)

1 John and Mary meet.

What happens next?

If you want a happy ending, try A.

A

John and Mary fall in love and get married. They both have worth-while and remunerative jobs which they find stimulating and challenging. They buy a charming house. Real estate values go up. Eventually, when they can afford live-in help, they have two chil-dren, to whom they are devoted. The children turn out well. John and Mary have a stimulating and challenging sex life and worth-while friends. They go on fun vacations together. They retire. They both have hobbies which they find stimulating and challenging. Eventually they die. This is the end of the story.

B

5 Mary falls in love with John but John doesn't fall in love with Mary. He merely uses her body for selfish pleasure and ego grati-fication of a tepid kind. He comes to her apartment twice a week and she cooks him dinner, you'll notice that he doesn't even con-sider her worth the price of a dinner out, and after he's eaten the dinner he fucks her and after that he falls asleep, while she does the dishes so he won't think she's untidy, having all those dirty dishes lying around, and puts on fresh lipstick so she'll look good when he wakes up, but when he wakes up he doesn't even notice, he puts on his socks and his shorts and his pants and his shirt and his tie and his shoes, the reverse order from the one in which he took them off. He doesn't take off Mary's clothes, she takes them off herself, she acts as if she's dying for it every time, not because she likes sex exactly, she doesn't, but she wants John to think she does because if they do it often enough surely he'll get used to her, he'll come to depend on her and they will get married, but John goes out the door with hardly so much as a good-night and three days later he turns up at six o'clock and they do the whole thing over again.

Mary gets run-down. Crying is bad for your face, everyone knows that and so does Mary but she can't stop. People at work notice. Her friends tell her John is a rat, a pig, a dog, he isn't good enough for her, but she can't believe it. Inside John, she thinks, is another John, who is much nicer. This other John will emerge like a butterfly from a cocoon, a Jack from a box, a pit from a prune, if the first John is only squeezed enough.

One evening John complains about the food. He has never complained about the food before. Mary is hurt.

Her friends tell her they've seen him in a restaurant with an-other woman, whose name is Madge. It's not even Madge that fi-nally gets to Mary; it's the restaurant. John has never taken Mary to a restaurant. Mary collects all the sleeping pills and aspirins she can find, and takes them and a half a bottle of sherry. You can see what kind of a woman she is by the fact that it's not even whiskey. She leaves a note for John. She hopes he'll discover her and get her to the hospital in time and repent and then they can get married, but this fails to happen and she dies.

John marries Madge and everything continues as in A.

C

John, who is an older man, falls in love with Mary, and Mary, who 10 is only twenty-two, feels sorry for him because he's worried about his hair falling out. She sleeps with him even though she's not in love with him. She met him at work. She's in love with someone called James, who is twenty-two also and not yet ready to settle down.

John on the contrary settled down long ago: this is what is bothering him. John has a steady, respectable job and is getting ahead in his field, but Mary isn't impressed by him, she's impressed by James, who has a motorcycle and a fabulous record collection. But James is often away on his motorcycle, being free. Freedom isn't the same for girls, so in the meantime Mary spends Thursday evenings with John. Thursdays are the only days John can get away.

John is married to a woman called Madge and they have two children, a charming house which they bought just before the real estate values went up, and hobbies which they find stimulating and challenging, when they have the time. John tells Mary how important she is to him, but of course, he can't leave his wife because a commitment is a commitment. He goes on about this more than is necessary and Mary finds it boring, but older men can keep it up longer so on the whole she has a fairly good time.

One day James breezes in on his motorcycle with some top-grade California hybrid and James and Mary get higher than you'd believe possible and they climb into bed. Everything becomes very underwater, but along comes John, who has a key to Mary's apartment. He finds them stoned and entwined. He's hardly in any position to be jealous, considering Madge, but nevertheless he's overcome with despair. Finally he's middle-aged, in two years he'll be bald as an egg and he can't stand it. He purchases a handgun, saying he needs it for target practice—this is the thin part of the plot, but it can be dealt with later—and shoots the two of them and himself.

Madge, after a suitable period of mourning, marries an understanding man called Fred and everything continues as in A, but under different names.

D

15 Fred and Madge have no problems. They get along exceptionally well and are good at working out any little difficulties that may arise. But their charming house is by the seashore and one day a giant tidal wave approaches. Real estate values go down. The rest of the story is about what caused the tidal wave and how they escape from it. They do, though thousands drown, but Fred and Madge are virtuous and lucky. Finally on high ground they clasp each other, wet and dripping and grateful, and continue as in A.

E

Yes, but Fred has a bad heart. The rest of the story is about how kind and understanding they both are until Fred dies. Then Madge devotes herself to charity work until the end of A. If you like, it can be "Madge," "cancer," "guilty and confused," and "bird watching."

F

If you think this is all too bourgeois, make John a revolutionary and Mary a counterespionage agent and see how far that gets you. Remember, this is Canada. You'll still end up with A, though in between you may get a lustful brawling saga of passionate involvement, a chronicle of our times, sort of.

> If you think this is all too bourgeois, make John a revolutionary and Mary a counterespionage agent. . . .

You'll have to face it, the endings are the same however you slice it. Don't be deluded by any other endings, they're all fake, either deliberately fake, with malicious intent to deceive, or just motivated by excessive optimism if not by downright sentimentality.

The only authentic ending is the one provided here:
John and Mary die. John and Mary die. John and Mary die.   20

So much for endings. Beginnings are almost more fun. True connoisseurs, however, are known to favor the stretch in between, since it's the hardest to do anything with.

That's about all that can be said for plots, which anyway are just one thing after another, a what and a what and a what.

Now try How and Why.

IF YOU LIKED "HAPPY ENDINGS," YOU MIGHT ALSO LIKE...

...**"An Ounce of Cure"** (Chapter 6) by Atwood's fellow Canadian writer Alice Munro.

GOING FURTHER Atwood's literary mentor was a novelist and story writer named Margaret Laurence. Laurence's novel *The Diviners* is one of the finest examples you'll find of a female coming-of-age story, a powerful and important novel set mainly in western Canada.

Toni Cade Bambara (1939–1995)

MILTONA—"TONI"—CADE ADDED THE West African *Bambara* to her name in 1970 after she discovered it in her great-grandmother's signature in her sketchbooks in the attic. A fiction writer, essayist, filmmaker, educator, social worker, and civil rights activist, she produced work with a political edge. Bambara was the first to anthologize exclusively black women writers in *The Black Woman: An Anthology* (1970), which promoted the work of such writers as Nikki Giovanni, Alice Walker, and Audre Lorde, and she wrote the foreword to *This Bridge Called My Back, Writings by Radical African American Women* (1981). Her novel, *The Salt Eaters* (1980), won the American Book Award.

Bambara invoked the African-American oral tradition, jazz, and Black English as critical to the creation of her voice in her work. She credited her political awareness to growing up in New York City neighborhoods such as Harlem and Bedford-Stuyvesant and to the influence of her mother. She received her B.A. in theater and literature from Queens College in New York

the same year she published her first short story, "Sweet Town" (1959), which received the John Golden award for fiction. In 1961 she went to Europe and studied at the École de Mime Étienne Decroux in Paris and the Commedia dell'Arte in Italy, returning to New York to complete her M.A. at the City College of the City University of New York (1964). As part of the Black Arts Movement in the sixties in New York, she directed the *Theater of the Black Experience*. She also worked for a variety of social service agencies. In addition, Bambara lived and taught in New Jersey (Rutgers University), Georgia (Atlanta University, Emory University, Spelman College), Missouri (Stephens College), Alabama, and Philadelphia. She was an organizer of writers as well as of community programs, and while she lived in the South she was one of the founders of the Southern Collective of African American Writers. She said that writing was one way she could contribute to social justice. She succumbed to colon cancer in 1995.

The Lesson (1972)

1 Back in the days when everyone was old and stupid or young and foolish and me and Sugar were the only ones just right, this lady moved on our block with nappy hair and proper speech and no makeup. And quite naturally we laughed at her, laughed the way we did at the junk man who went about his business like he was some big-time president and his sorry-ass horse his secretary. And we kinda hated her too, hated the way we did the winos who cluttered up our parks and pissed on our handball walls and stank up our hallways and stairs so you couldn't halfway play hide-and-seek without a goddamn gas mask. Miss Moore was her name. The only woman on the block with no first name. And she was black as hell, cept for her feet, which were fish-white and spooky. And she was always planning these boring-ass things for us to do, us being my cousin, mostly, who lived on the block cause we all moved North the same time and to the same apartment then spread out gradual to breathe. And our parents would yank our heads into

some kinda shape and crisp up our clothes so we'd be presentable for travel with Miss Moore, who always looked like she was going to church though she never did. Which is just one of the things the grownups talked about when they talked behind her back like a dog. But when she came calling with some sachet she'd sewed up or some gingerbread she'd made or some book, why then they'd all be too embarrassed to turn her down and we'd get handed over all spruced up. She'd been to college and said it was only right that she should take responsibility for the young ones education, and she not even related by marriage or blood. So they'd go for it. Specially Aunt Gretchen. She was the main gofer in the family. You got some ole dumb shit foolishness you want somebody to go for, you send for Aunt Gretchen. She been screwed into the go-along for so long, it's a blood-deep natural thing with her. Which is how she got saddled with me and Sugar and Junior in the first place while our mothers were in a la-de-da apartment up the block having a good ole time.

> **. . . always looked like she was going** to church. . . .

So this one day Miss Moore rounds us all up at the mailbox and it's purdee hot and she's knockin herself out about arithmetic. And school suppose to let up in summer I heard, but she don't never let up. And the starch in my pinafore scratching the shit outta me and I'm really hating this nappy-head bitch and her goddamn college degree. I'd much rather go to the pool or to the show where it's cool. So me and Sugar leaning on the mailbox being surly, which is a Miss Moore word. And Flyboy checking out what everybody brought for lunch. And Fat Butt already wasting his peanut-butter-and-jelly sandwich like the pig he is. And Junebug punchin on Q.T.'s arm for potato chips. And Rosie Giraffe shifting from one hip to the other waiting for somebody to step on her foot or ask her if she from Georgia so she can kick ass, preferably Mercedes'. And Miss Moore asking us do we know what money is like we a bunch of retards. I mean real money, she say, like it's only poker chips or monopoly papers we lay on the grocer. So right away I'm tired of this and say so. And would much rather snatch Sugar and go to the Sunset and terrorize the West Indian kids and take their hair ribbons and their money too. And Miss Moore files that remark away for next week's lesson on brotherhood, I can tell. And finally I say we oughta get to the subway cause it's cooler an' besides we might meet some cute boys. Sugar done swiped her mama's lipstick, so we ready.

So we heading down the street and she's boring us silly about what things cost and what our parents make and how much goes for rent and how money ain't divided up right in this country. And then she gets to the part about we all poor and live in the slums which I don't feature. And I'm ready to speak on that, but she steps out in the street and hails two cabs just like that. Then she hustles half the crew in with her and hands me a five-dollar bill and tells me to calculate 10 percent tip for the driver. And we're off. Me and Sugar and Junebug and Flyboy hangin out the window and hollering to everybody, putting lipstick on each other cause Flyboy a faggot anyway, and making farts with our sweaty armpits. But I'm mostly trying to figure how to spend this money. But they all fascinated with the meter ticking and Junebug starts laying bets as to how much it'll read when Flyboy can't hold his breath no more. Then Sugar lays bets as to how much it'll be when we get there. So I'm stuck. Don't nobody want to go for my plan, which is to jump out at the next light and run off to the first bar-b-que we can find. Then the driver tells us to get the hell out cause we there already. And the meter reads eighty-five cents. And I'm stalling to figure out the tip and Sugar say give him a dime. And I decide he don't need it bad as I do, so later for him. But then he tries to take off with Junebug foot still in the door so we talk about his mama something ferocious. Then we check out that we on Fifth Avenue and everybody dressed up in stockings. One lady in a fur coat, hot as it is. White folks crazy.

"This is the place," Miss Moore say, presenting it to us in the voice she uses at the museum. "Let's look in the windows before we go in."

"Can we steal?" Sugar asks very serious like she's getting the ground rules squared away before she plays. "I beg your pardon," say Miss Moore, and we fall out. So she leads us around the windows of the toy store and me and Sugar screamin, "This is mine, that's mine, I gotta have that, that was made for me, I was born for that," till Big Butt drowns us out.

"Hey, I'm going to buy that there."

"That there? You don't even know what it is, stupid."

"I do so," he say punchin on Rosie Giraffe. "It's a microscope."

"Whatcha gonna do with a microscope, fool?"

"Look at things."

"Like what, Ronald?" ask Miss Moore. And Big Butt ain't got the first notion. So here go Miss Moore gabbing about the thousands of bacteria in a drop of water and the somethinorother in a speck of blood and the million and one living things in the air around us is invisible to the naked eye. And what she say that for? Junebug go to town on that "naked" and we rolling. Then Miss Moore ask what it cost. So we all jam into the window smudgin it up and the price tag say $300. So then she ask how long'd take for Big Butt and Junebug to save up their allowances. "Too long," I say. "Yeh," adds Sugar, "outgrown it by that time." And Miss Moore say no, you never outgrow learning instruments. "Why, even medical students and interns and," blah, blah, blah. And we ready to choke Big Butt for bringing it up in the first damn place.

"This here costs four hundred eighty dollars," say Rosie Giraffe. So we pile up all over her to see what she pointin out. My eyes tell me it's a chunk of glass cracked with something heavy, and different-color inks dripped into the splits, then the whole thing put into a oven or something. But for $480 it don't make sense.

"That's a paperweight made of semi-precious stones fused together under tremendous pressure," she explains slowly, with her hands doing the mining and all the factory work.

"So what's a paperweight?" asks Rosie Giraffe.

15   "To weigh paper with, dumbbell," say Flyboy, the wise man from the East.

"Not exactly," say Miss Moore, which is what she say when you warm or way off too. "It's to weigh paper down so it won't scatter and make your desk untidy." So right away me and Sugar curtsy to each other and then to Mercedes who is more the tidy type.

"We don't keep paper on top of the desk in my class," say Junebug, figuring Miss Moore crazy or lyin one.

"At home, then," she say. "Don't you have a calendar and a pencil case and a blotter and a letter-opener on your desk at home where you do your homework?" And she know damn well what our homes look like cause she nosys around in them every chance she gets.

"I don't even have a desk," say Junebug. "Do we?"

20   "No. And I don't get no homework neither," says Big Butt.

"And I don't even have a home," say Flyboy like he do at school to keep the white folks off his back and sorry for him. Send this poor kid to camp posters, is his specialty.

"I do," says Mercedes. "I have a box of stationery on my desk and a picture of my cat. My godmother bought the stationery and the desk. There's a big rose on each sheet and the envelopes smell like roses."

"Who wants to know about your smelly-ass stationery," say Rosie Giraffe fore I can get my two cents in.

"It's important to have a work area all your own so that. . . ."

25   "Will you look at this sailboat, please," say Flyboy, cuttin her off and pointin to the thing like it was his. So once again we tumble all over each other to gaze at this magnificent thing in the toy store which is just big enough to maybe sail two kittens across the pond if you strap them to the posts tight. We all start reciting the price tag like we in assembly. "Hand-crafted sailboat of fiberglass at one thousand one hundred ninety-five dollars."

"Unbelievable," I hear myself say and am really stunned. I read it again for myself just in case the group recitation put me in a trance. Same thing. For some reason this pisses me off. We look at Miss Moore and she lookin at us, waiting for I dunno what.

"Who'd pay all that when you can buy a sailboat set for a quarter at Pop's, a tube of glue for a dime, and a ball of string for eight cents? It must have a motor and a whole lot else besides," I say. "My sailboat cost me about fifty cents."

"But will it take water?" say Mercedes with her smart ass.

"Took mine to Alley Pond Park once," say Flyboy. "String broke. Lost it. Pity."

"Sailed mine in Central Park and it keeled over and sank. Had   30 to ask my father for another dollar."

"And you got the strap," laugh Big Butt. "The jerk didn't even have a string on it. My old man wailed on his behind."

Little Q.T. was staring hard at the sailboat and you could see he wanted it bad. But he too little and somebody'd just take it from him. So what the hell. "This boat for kids, Miss Moore?"

"Parents silly to buy something like that just to get all broke up," say Rosie Giraffe.

"That much money it should last forever," I figure.

"My father'd buy it for me if I wanted it."   35

"Your father, my ass," say Rosie Giraffe getting a chance to finally push Mercedes.

"Must be rich people shop here," say Q.T.

"You are a very bright boy," say Flyboy. "What was your first clue?" And he rap him on the head with the back of his knuckles, since Q.T. the only one he could get away with. Though Q.T. liable to come up behind you years later and get his licks in when you half expect it.

"What I want to know is," I says to Miss Moore though I never talk to her, I wouldn't give the bitch that satisfaction, "is how much a real boat costs? I figure a thousand'd get you a yacht any day."

"Why don't you check that out," she says, "and report back   40 to the group?" Which really pains my ass. If you gonna mess up a perfectly good swim day least you could do is have some answers. "Let's go in," she say like she got something up her sleeve. Only she don't lead the way. So me and Sugar turn the corner to where the entrance is, but when we get there I kinda hang back. Not that I'm scared, what's there to be afraid of, just a toy store. But I feel funny, shame. But what I got to be shamed about? Got as much right to go in as anybody. But somehow I can't seem to

> "Handcrafted sailboat of fiberglass at **one** thousand one hundred ninety-five dollars."

get hold of the door, so I step away from Sugar to lead. But she hangs back too. And I look at her and she looks at me and this is ridiculous. I mean, damn, I have never ever been shy about doing nothing or going nowhere. But then Mercedes steps up and then Rosie Giraffe and Big Butt crowd in behind and shove, and next thing we all stuffed into the doorway with only Mercedes squeezing past us, smoothing out her jumper and walking right down the aisle. Then the rest of us tumble in like a glued-together jigsaw done all wrong. And people lookin at us. And it's like the time me and Sugar crashed into the Catholic church on a dare. But once we got in there and everything so hushed and holy and the candles and the bowin and the handkerchiefs on all the drooping heads, I just couldn't go through with the plan. Which was for me to run up to the altar and do a tap dance while Sugar played the nose flute and messed around in the holy water. And Sugar kept givin me the elbow. Then later teased me so bad I tied her up in the shower and turned it on and locked her in. And she'd be there till this day if Aunt Gretchen hadn't finally figured I was lyin about the boarder takin a shower.

Same thing in the store. We all walkin on tiptoe and hardly touchin the games and puzzles and things. And I watched Miss Moore who is steady watchin us like she waitin for a sign. Like Mama Drewery watches the sky and sniffs the air and takes note of just how much slant is in the bird formation. Then me and Sugar bump smack into each other, so busy gazing at the toys, 'specially the sailboat. But we don't laugh and go into our fat-lady bump-stomach routine. We just stare at that price tag. Then Sugar run a finger over the whole boat. And I'm jealous and want to hit her. Maybe not her, but I sure want to punch somebody in the mouth.

"Watcha bring us here for, Miss Moore?"

"You sound angry, Sylvia. Are you mad about something?" Givin me one of them grins like she tellin a grown-up joke that never turns out to be funny. And she's lookin very closely at me like maybe she plannin to do my portrait from memory. I'm mad, but I won't give her that satisfaction. So I slouch around the store bein very bored and say, "Let's go."

Me and Sugar at the back of the train watchin the tracks whizzin by large then small then gettin gobbled up in the dark. I'm thinkin about this tricky toy I saw in the store. A clown that somersaults on a bar then does chin-ups just cause you yank lightly at his leg. Cost $35. I could see me askin my mother for a $35 birthday clown. "You wanna who that costs what?" she'd say, cocking her head to the side to get a better view of the hole in my head. Thirty-five dollars could buy new bunk beds for Junior and Gretchen's boy. Thirty-five dollars and the whole household

could go visit Granddaddy Nelson in the country. Thirty-five dollars would pay for the rent and the piano bill too. Who are these people that spend that much for performing clowns and $1000 for toy sailboats? What kinda work they do and how they live and how come we ain't in on it? Where we are is who we are, Miss Moore always pointin out. But it don't necessarily have to be that way, she always adds then waits for somebody to say that poor people have to wake up and demand their share of the pie and don't none of us know what kind of pie she talking about in the first damn place. But she ain't so smart cause I still got her four dollars from the taxi and she sure ain't gettin it. Messin up my day with this shit. Sugar nudges me in my pocket and winks.

We just stare at that price tag.

Miss Moore lines us up in front of the mailbox where we started from, seem like years ago, and I got a headache for thinkin so hard. And we lean all over each other so we can hold up under the draggy-ass lecture she always finishes us off with at the end before we thank her for borin us to tears. But she just looks at us like she readin tea leaves. Finally she say, "Well, what did you think of F.A.O. Schwarz?"

Rosie Giraffe mumbles, "White folks crazy."

"I'd like to go there again when I get my birthday money," says Mercedes, and we shove her out the pack so she has to lean on the mailbox by herself.

"I'd like a shower. Tiring day," say Flyboy.

Then Sugar surprises me by sayin, "You know, Miss Moore, I don't think all of us here put together eat in a year what that sailboat costs." And Miss Moore lights up like somebody goosed her. "And?" she say, urging Sugar on. Only I'm standin on her foot so she don't continue.

"Imagine for a minute what kind of society it is in which some people can spend on a toy what it would cost to feed a family of six or seven. What do you think?"

"I think," say Sugar pushing me off her feet like she never done before cause I whip her ass in a minute, "that this is not much of a democracy if you ask me. Equal chance to pursue happiness means an equal crack at the dough, don't it?" Miss Moore is besides herself and I am disgusted with Sugar's treachery. So I stand on her foot one more time to see if she'll shove me. She shuts up, and Miss Moore looks at me, sorrowfully I'm thinkin. And somethin weird is goin on, I can feel it in my chest.

"Anybody else learn anything today?" lookin dead at me. I walk away and Sugar has to run to catch up and don't even seem to notice when I shrug her arm off my shoulder.

"Well, we got four dollars anyway," she says.

"Uh hunh."

55   "We could go to Hascombs and get half a chocolate layer and then go to the Sunset and still have plenty money for potato chips and ice cream sodas."

"Uh hunh."

"Race you to Hascombs," she say.

We start down the block and she gets ahead which is O.K. by me cause I'm going to the West End and then over to the Drive to think this day through. She can run if she want to and even run faster. But ain't nobody gonna beat me at nuthin.

IF YOU LIKED "THE LESSON," YOU MIGHT ALSO LIKE . . .

. . . Alice Walker's "Everyday Use" (in this chapter), which provides another kind of lesson about discovering and preserving a sense of African-American identity. Other stories in this book also address issues of inequality and growing up African-American and provide perspective from three generations of writers who knew one another, the elder statesman Ralph Ellison's "Battle Royal" (Chapter 15), Ellison's heir Richard Wright's "The Man Who Was Almost a Man" (Chapter 8), and the younger writer James Baldwin's "Sonny's Blues" (Chapter 9).

GOING FURTHER   Other stories by Bambara can be found in her *The Sea Birds Are Still Alive: Collected Stories.* Her posthumous novel about the murder of more than forty African-American children in Atlanta, *Those Bones Are Not My Child,* was highly praised by fellow writer Toni Morrison, whose *Sula* also features a young female African-American protagonist shaped by anger.

Raymond Carver (1938–1988)

RAYMOND CARVER WAS born into a working-class family in the Pacific Northwest and spent most of his childhood in Yakima, Washington, before moving to California in his early twenties and attending classes at California State College, Chico. There he studied fiction writing with John Gardner and began the apprenticeship that would lead to his creation of some of the most celebrated short fiction of his time. Critics pointed to his stories about working-class and lower-middle-class people in desper-ate straits as evidence of the so-called minimalist style. Carver himself often pointed out that he saw his work in the tradition of Sherwood Anderson, Ernest Hemingway, and Anton Chekhov.

Carver was also a poet and an essayist; perhaps in keeping with the aesthetic of minimalism, however, he never wrote a novel. He possessed a keen sense of dialogue, and the director Robert Altman joined several of his short stories together for the 1993 film *Short Cuts.*

Cathedral (1984)

1   This blind man, an old friend of my wife's, he was on his way to spend the night. His wife had died. So he was visiting the dead wife's relatives in Connecticut. He called my wife from his in-laws'. Arrangements were made. He would come by train, a five-hour trip, and my wife would meet him at the station. She hadn't seen him since she worked for him one summer in Seattle ten years ago. But she and the blind man had kept in touch. They made tapes and mailed them back and forth. I wasn't enthusi-astic about his visit. He was no one I knew. And his being blind bothered me. My idea of blindness came from the movies. In the movies, the blind moved slowly and never laughed. Sometimes they were led by seeing-eye dogs. A blind man in my house was not something I looked forward to.

That summer in Seattle she had needed a job. She didn't have any money. The man she was going to marry at the end of the summer was in officers' training school. He didn't have any money, either. But she was in love with the guy, and he was in love with her, etc. She'd seen something in the paper: HELP WANTED— *Reading to Blind Man,* and a telephone number. She phoned and went over, was hired on the spot. She'd worked with this blind man all summer. She read stuff to him, case studies, reports, that sort of thing. She helped him organize his little office in the county social-service department. They'd become good friends, my wife and the blind man. How do I know these things? She told me. And she told me something else. On her last day in the office, the blind man asked if he could touch her face. She agreed to this. She told me he touched his fingers to every part of her face, her nose—even her neck! She never forgot it. She even tried to write a poem about it. She was always trying to write a poem. She wrote a poem or two every year, usually after something really important had happened to her.

> But they'd kept in touch, she and the blind man. She made the first contact after a year or so.

When we first started going out together, she showed me the poem. In the poem, she recalled his fingers and the way they had moved around over her face. In the poem, she talked about what she had felt at the time, about what went through her mind when the blind man touched her nose and lips. I can remember I didn't think much of the poem. Of course, I didn't tell her that. Maybe I just don't understand poetry. I admit it's not the first thing I reach for when I pick up something to read.

Anyway, this man who'd first enjoyed her favors, the officer-to-be, he'd been her childhood sweetheart. So okay. I'm saying that at the end of the summer she let the blind man run his hands over her face, said goodbye to him, married her childhood etc., who was now a commissioned officer, and she moved away from Seattle. But they'd kept in touch, she and the blind man. She made the first contact after a year or so. She called him up one night from an Air Force base in Alabama. She wanted to talk. They talked. He asked her to send him a tape and tell him about her life. She did this. She sent the tape. On the tape, she told the blind man about her husband and about their life together in the military. She told the blind man she loved her husband but she didn't like it where they lived and she didn't like it that he was a part of the military-industrial thing. She told the blind man she'd written a poem about what it was like to be an Air Force officer's wife. The poem wasn't finished yet. She was still writing it. The blind man made a tape. He sent her the tape. She made a tape. This went on for years. My wife's officer was posted to one base and then another. She sent tapes from Moody AFB, McGuire, McConnell, and finally Travis, near Sacramento, where one night she got to feeling lonely and cut off from people she kept losing in that moving-around life. She got to feeling she couldn't go it another step. She went in and swallowed all the pills and capsules in the medicine chest and washed them down with a bottle of gin. Then she got into a hot bath and passed out.

But instead of dying, she got sick. She threw up. Her officer— why should he have a name? he was the childhood sweetheart, and what more does he want?—came home from somewhere, found her, and called the ambulance. In time, she put it all on a tape and sent the tape to the blind man. Over the years, she put all kinds of stuff on tapes and sent the tapes off lickety-split. Next to writing a poem every year, I think it was her chief means of recreation. On one tape, she told the blind man she'd decided to live away from her officer for a time. On another tape, she told him about her divorce. She and I began going out, and of course she told her blind man about it. She told him everything, or so it seemed to me. Once she asked me if I'd like to hear the latest tape from the blind man. This was a year ago. I was on the tape, she said. So I said okay, I'd listen to it. I got us drinks and we settled down in the living room. We made ready to listen. First she inserted the tape into the player and adjusted a couple of dials. Then she pushed a lever. The tape squeaked and someone began to talk in this loud voice. She lowered the volume. After a few minutes of harmless chitchat, I heard my own name in the mouth of this stranger, this blind man I didn't even know! And then this: "From all you've said about him, I can only conclude—" But we were interrupted, a knock at the door, something, and we didn't ever get back to the tape. Maybe it was just as well. I'd heard all I wanted to.

Now this same blind man was coming to sleep in my house.

"Maybe I could take him bowling," I said to my wife. She was at the draining board doing scalloped potatoes. She put down the knife she was using and turned around.

"If you love me," she said, "you can do this for me. If you don't love me, okay. But if you had a friend, any friend, and the friend came to visit, I'd make him feel comfortable." She wiped her hands with the dish towel.

"I don't have any blind friends," I said.

"You don't have *any* friends," she said. "Period. Besides," she said, "goddamn it, his wife's just died! Don't you understand that? The man's lost his wife!"

I didn't answer. She'd told me a little about the blind man's wife. Her name was Beulah. Beulah! That's a name for a colored woman.

"Was his wife a Negro?" I asked.

"Are you crazy?" my wife said. "Have you just flipped or something?" She picked up a potato. I saw it hit the floor, then roll under the stove. "What's wrong with you?" she said. "Are you drunk?"

"I'm just asking," I said.

15　Right then my wife filled me in with more detail than I cared to know. I made a drink and sat at the kitchen table to listen. Pieces of the story began to fall into place.

Beulah had gone to work for the blind man the summer after my wife had stopped working for him. Pretty soon Beulah and the blind man had themselves a church wedding. It was a little wedding—who'd want to go to such a wedding in the first place?—just the two of them, plus the minister and the minister's wife. But it was a church wedding just the same. It was what Beulah had wanted, he'd said. But even then Beulah must have been carrying the cancer in her glands. After they had been inseparable for eight years—my wife's word, *inseparable*—Beulah's health went into a rapid decline. She died in a Seattle hospital room, the blind man sitting beside the bed and holding on to her hand. They'd married, lived and worked together, slept together—had sex, sure—and then the blind man had to bury her. All this without his having ever seen what the goddamned woman looked like. It was beyond my understanding. Hearing this, I felt sorry for the blind man for a little bit. And then I found myself thinking what a pitiful life this woman must have led. Imagine a woman who could never see herself as she was seen in the eyes of her loved one. A woman who could go on day after day and never receive the smallest compliment from her beloved. A woman whose husband could never read the expression on her face, be it misery or something better. Someone who could wear makeup or not—what difference to him? She could, if she wanted, wear green eye-shadow around one eye, a straight pin in her nostril, yellow slacks and purple shoes, no matter. And then to slip off into death, the blind man's hand on her hand, his blind eyes streaming tears—I'm imagining now—her last thought maybe this: that he never even knew what she looked like, and she on an express to the grave. Robert was left with a small insurance policy and half of a twenty-peso Mexican coin. The other half of the coin went into the box with her. Pathetic.

So when the time rolled around, my wife went to the depot to pick him up. With nothing to do but wait—sure, I blamed him for that—I was having a drink and watching the TV when I heard the car pull into the drive. I got up from the sofa with my drink and went to the window to have a look.

I saw my wife laughing as she parked the car. I saw her get out of the car and shut the door. She was still wearing a smile. Just amazing. She went around to the other side of the car to where the blind man was already starting to get out. This blind man, feature this, he was wearing a full beard! A beard on a blind man! Too much, I say. The blind man reached into the back seat and dragged out a suitcase. My wife took his arm, shut the car door, and, talking all the way, moved him down the drive and then up the steps to the front porch. I turned off the TV. I finished my drink, rinsed the glass, dried my hands. Then I went to the door.

My wife said, "I want you to meet Robert. Robert, this is my husband. I've told you all about him." She was beaming. She had this blind man by his coat sleeve.

The blind man let go of his suitcase 20 and up came his hand.

I took it. He squeezed hard, held my hand, and then he let it go.

"I feel like we've already met," he boomed.

"Likewise," I said. I didn't know what else to say. Then I said, "Welcome. I've heard a lot about you." We began to move then, a little group, from the porch into the living room, my wife guiding him by the arm. The blind man was carrying his suitcase in his other hand. My wife said things like, "To your left here, Robert. That's right. Now watch it, there's a chair. That's it. Sit down right here. This is the sofa. We just bought this sofa two weeks ago."

I started to say something about the old sofa. I'd liked that old sofa. But I didn't say anything. Then I wanted to say something else, small-talk, about the scenic ride along the Hudson. How going *to* New York, you should sit on the right-hand side of the train, and coming *from* New York, the left-hand side.

"Did you have a good train ride?" I said. "Which side of the 25 train did you sit on, by the way?"

"What a question, which side!" my wife said. "What's it matter which side?" she said.

"I just asked," I said.

"Right side," the blind man said. "I hadn't been on a train in nearly forty years. Not since I was a kid. With my folks. That's been a long time. I'd nearly forgotten the sensation. I have winter in my beard now," he said. "So I've been told, anyway. Do I look distinguished, my dear?" the blind man said to my wife.

"You look distinguished, Robert," she said. "Robert," she said. "Robert, it's just so good to see you."

My wife finally took her eyes off the blind man and looked 30 at me. I had the feeling she didn't like what she saw. I shrugged.

I've never met, or personally known, anyone who was blind. This blind man was late forties, a heavy-set, balding man with stooped shoulders, as if he carried a great weight there. He wore brown slacks, brown shoes, a light-brown shirt, a tie, a sports

> # Right then my wife filled me in with more detail than I cared to know.

coat. Spiffy. He also had this full beard. But he didn't use a cane and he didn't wear dark glasses. I'd always thought dark glasses were a must for the blind. Fact was, I wished he had a pair. At first glance, his eyes looked like anyone else's eyes. But if you looked close, there was something different about them. Too much white in the iris, for one thing, and the pupils seemed to move around in the sockets without his knowing it or being able to stop it. Creepy. As I stared at his face, I saw the left pupil turn in toward his nose while the other made an effort to keep in one place. But it was only an effort, for that eye was on the roam without his knowing it or wanting it to be.

I said, "Let me get you a drink. What's your pleasure? We have a little of everything. It's one of our pastimes."

"Bub, I'm a Scotch man myself," he said fast enough in this big voice.

"Right," I said. Bub! "Sure you are. I knew it."

35 He let his fingers touch his suitcase, which was sitting alongside the sofa. He was taking his bearings. I didn't blame him for that.

"I'll move that up to your room," my wife said.

"No, that's fine," the blind man said loudly. "It can go up when I go up."

"A little water with the Scotch?" I said.

"Very little," he said.

40 "I knew it," I said.

He said, "Just a tad. The Irish actor, Barry Fitzgerald? I'm like that fellow. When I drink water, Fitzgerald said, I drink water. When I drink whiskey, I drink whiskey." My wife laughed. The blind man brought his hand up under his beard. He lifted his beard slowly and let it drop.

I did the drinks, three big glasses of Scotch with a splash of water in each. Then we made ourselves comfortable and talked about Robert's travels. First the long flight from the West Coast to Connecticut, we covered that. Then from Connecticut up here by train. We had another drink concerning that leg of the trip.

I remembered having read somewhere that the blind didn't smoke because, as speculation had it, they couldn't see the smoke they exhaled. I thought I knew that much and that much only about blind people. But this blind man smoked his cigarette down to the nubbin and then lit another one. This blind man filled his ashtray and my wife emptied it.

When we sat down at the table for dinner, we had another drink. My wife heaped Robert's plate with cube steak, scalloped potatoes, green beans. I buttered him up two slices of bread. I said, "Here's bread and butter for you." I swallowed some of my drink.

"Now let us pray," I said, and the blind man lowered his head. My wife looked at me, her mouth agape. "Pray the phone won't ring and the food doesn't get cold," I said.

We dug in. We ate everything there was to eat on the table. We   45 ate like there was no tomorrow. We didn't talk. We ate. We scarfed. We grazed that table. We were into serious eating. The blind man had right away located his foods, he knew just where everything was on his plate. I watched with admiration as he used his knife and fork on the meat. He'd cut two pieces of meat, fork the meat into his mouth, and then go all out for the scalloped potatoes, the beans next, and then he'd tear off a hunk of buttered bread and eat that. He'd follow this up with a big drink of milk. It didn't seem to bother him to use his fingers once in a while, either.

We finished everything, including half a strawberry pie. For a few moments, we sat as if stunned. Sweat beaded on our faces. Finally, we got up from the table and left the dirty plates. We didn't look back. We took ourselves into the living room and sank into our places again. Robert and my wife sat on the sofa. I took the big chair. We had us two or three more drinks while they talked about the major things that had come to pass for them in the past ten years. For the most part, I just listened. Now and then I joined in. I didn't want him to think I'd left the room, and I didn't want her to think I was feeling left out. They talked of things that had happened to them—to them!—these past ten years. I waited in vain to hear my name on my wife's sweet lips: "And then my dear husband came into my life"—something like that. But I heard nothing of the sort. More talk of Robert. Robert had done a little of everything, it seemed, a regular blind jack-of-all-trades. But most recently he and his wife had had an Amway distributorship, from which, I gathered, they'd earned their living, such as it was. The blind man was also a ham radio operator. He talked in his loud voice about conversations he'd had with fellow operators in Guam, in the Philippines, in Alaska, and even in Tahiti. He said he'd have a lot of friends there if he ever wanted to go visit those places. From time to time, he'd turn his blind face toward me, put his hand under his beard, ask me something. How long had I been in my present position? (Three years.) Did I like my work? (I didn't.) Was I going to stay with it? (What were the options?) Finally, when I thought he was beginning to run down, I got up and turned on the TV.

My wife looked at me with irritation. She was heading toward a boil. Then she looked at the blind man and said, "Robert, do you have a TV?"

The blind man said, "My dear, I have two TVs. I have a color set and a black-and-white thing, an old relic. It's funny, but if I

> For a few moments,
> we sat as if stunned. Sweat
> beaded on our faces.

turn the TV on, and I'm always turning it on, I turn on the color set. It's funny, don't you think?"

I didn't know what to say to that. I had absolutely nothing to say to that. No opinion. So I watched the news program and tried to listen to what the announcer was saying.

50 "This is a color TV," the blind man said. "Don't ask me how, but I can tell."

"We traded up a while ago," I said.

The blind man had another taste of his drink. He lifted his beard, sniffed it, and let it fall. He leaned forward on the sofa. He positioned his ashtray on the coffee table, then put the lighter to his cigarette. He leaned back on the sofa and crossed his legs at the ankles.

My wife covered her mouth, and then she yawned. She stretched. She said, "I think I'll go upstairs and put on my robe. I think I'll change into something else. Robert, you make yourself comfortable," she said.

"I'm comfortable," the blind man said.

55 "I want you to feel comfortable in this house," she said.

"I am comfortable," the blind man said.

A̲fter she'd left the room, he and I listened to the weather report and then to the sports roundup. By that time, she'd been gone so long I didn't know if she was going to come back. I thought she might have gone to bed. I wished she'd come back downstairs. I didn't want to be left alone with a blind man. I asked if he wanted to smoke some dope with me. I said I'd just rolled a number. I hadn't, but I planned to do so in about two shakes.

"I'll try some with you," he said.

"Damn right," I said. "That's the stuff."

60 I got our drinks and sat down on the sofa with him. Then I rolled us two fat numbers. I lit one and passed it. I brought it to his fingers. He took it and inhaled.

"Hold it as long as you can," I said. I could tell he didn't know the first thing.

My wife came back downstairs wearing her pink robe and her pink slippers.

"What do I smell?" she said.

"We thought we'd have us some cannabis," I said.

65 My wife gave me a savage look. Then she looked at the blind man and said, "Robert, I didn't know you smoked."

He said, "I do now, my dear. There's a first time for everything. But I don't feel anything yet."

"This stuff is pretty mellow," I said. "This stuff is mild. It's dope you can reason with," I said. "It doesn't mess you up."

"Not much it doesn't, bub," he said, and laughed.

My wife sat on the sofa between the blind man and me. I passed her the number. She took it and toked and then passed it back to me. "Which way is this going?" she said. Then she said, "I shouldn't be smoking this. I can hardly keep my eyes open as it is. That dinner did me in. I shouldn't have eaten so much."

"It was the strawberry pie," the blind 70 man said. "That's what did it," he said, and he laughed his big laugh. Then he shook his head.

"There's more strawberry pie," I said.

"Do you want some more, Robert?" my wife said.

"Maybe in a little while," he said.

We gave our attention to the TV. My wife yawned again. She said, "Your bed is made up when you feel like going to bed, Robert. I know you must have had a long day. When you're ready to go to bed, say so." She pulled his arm. "Robert?"

He came to and said, "I've had a real nice time. This beats 75 tapes, doesn't it?"

I said, "Coming at you," and I put the number between his fingers. He inhaled, held the smoke, and then let it go. It was like he'd been doing it since he was nine years old.

"Thanks, bub," he said. "But I think this is all for me. I think I'm beginning to feel it," he said. He held the burning roach out for my wife.

"Same here," she said. "Ditto. Me, too." She took the roach and passed it to me. "I may just sit here for a while between you two guys with my eyes closed. But don't let me bother you, okay? Either one of you. If it bothers you, say so. Otherwise, I may just sit here with my eyes closed until you're ready to go to bed," she said. "Your bed's made up, Robert, when you're ready. It's right next to our room at the top of the stairs. We'll show you up when you're ready. You wake me up now, you guys, if I fall asleep." She said that and then she closed her eyes and went to sleep.

The news program ended. I got up and changed the channel. I sat back down on the sofa. I wished my wife hadn't pooped out. Her head lay across the back of the sofa, her mouth open. She'd turned so that her robe had slipped away from her legs, exposing a juicy thigh. I reached to draw her robe back over her, and it was then that I glanced at the blind man. What the hell! I flipped the robe open again.

"You say when you want some strawberry pie," I said. 80

"I will," he said.

I said, "Are you tired? Do you want me to take you up to your bed? Are you ready to hit the hay?"

"Not yet," he said. "No, I'll stay up with you, bub. If that's all right. I'll stay up until you're ready to turn in. We haven't had a

I asked if he wanted to smoke some dope with me.

chance to talk. Know what I mean? I feel like me and her monopolized the evening." He lifted his beard and he let it fall. He picked up his cigarettes and his lighter.

"That's all right," I said. Then I said, "I'm glad for the company."

85 And I guess I was. Every night I smoked dope and stayed up as long as I could before I fell asleep. My wife and I hardly ever went to bed at the same time. When I did go to sleep, I had these dreams. Sometimes I'd wake up from one of them, my heart going crazy.

Something about the church and the Middle Ages was on the TV. Not your run-of-the-mill TV fare. I wanted to watch something else. I turned to the other channels. But there was nothing on them, either. So I turned back to the first channel and apologized.

> **When I did go to sleep, I had these dreams. Sometimes I'd wake up from one of them, my heart going crazy.**

"Bub, it's all right," the blind man said. "It's fine with me. Whatever you want to watch is okay. I'm always learning something. Learning never ends. It won't hurt me to learn something tonight. I got ears," he said.

We didn't say anything for a time. He was leaning forward with his head turned at me, his right ear aimed in the direction of the set. Very disconcerting. Now and then his eyelids dropped and then they snapped open again. Now and then he put his fingers into his beard and tugged, like he was thinking about something he was hearing on the television.

On the screen, a group of men wearing cowls was being set upon and tormented by men dressed in skeleton costumes and men dressed as devils. The men dressed as devils wore devil masks, horns, and long tails. This pageant was part of a procession. The Englishman who was narrating the thing said it took place in Spain once a year. I tried to explain to the blind man what was happening.

90 "Skeletons," he said. "I know about skeletons," he said, and he nodded.

The TV showed this one cathedral. Then there was a long, slow look at another one. Finally, the picture switched to the famous one in Paris, with its flying buttresses and its spires reaching up to the clouds. The camera pulled away to show the whole of the cathedral rising above the skyline.

There were times when the Englishman who was telling the thing would shut up, would simply let the camera move around over the cathedrals. Or else the camera would tour the countryside, men in fields walking behind oxen. I waited as long as I could. Then I felt I had to say something. I said, "They're showing the outside of this cathedral now. Gargoyles. Little statues carved to look like monsters. Now I guess they're in Italy. Yeah, they're in Italy. There's paintings on the walls of this one church."

"Are those fresco paintings, bub?" he asked, and he sipped from his drink.

I reached for my glass. But it was empty. I tried to remember what I could remember. "You're asking me are those frescoes?" I said. "That's a good question. I don't know."

95 The camera moved to a cathedral outside Lisbon. The differences in the Portuguese cathedral compared with the French and Italian were not that great. But they were there. Mostly the interior stuff. Then something occurred to me, and I said, "Something has occurred to me. Do you have any idea what a cathedral is? What they look like, that is? Do you follow me? If somebody says cathedral to you, do you have any notion what they're talking about? Do you know the difference between that and a Baptist church, say?"

He let the smoke dribble from his mouth. "I know they took hundreds of workers fifty or a hundred years to build," he said. "I just heard the man say that, of course. I know generations of the same families worked on a cathedral. I heard him say that, too. The men who began their life's work on them, they never lived to see the completion of their work. In that wise, bub, they're no different from the rest of us, right?" He laughed. Then his eyelids drooped again. His head nodded. He seemed to be snoozing. Maybe he was imagining himself in Portugal. The TV was showing another cathedral now. This one was in Germany. The Englishman's voice droned on. "Cathedrals," the blind man said. He sat up and rolled his head back and forth. "If you want the truth, bub, that's about all I know. What I just said. What I heard him say. But maybe you could describe one to me? I wish you'd do it. I'd like that. If you want to know, I really don't have a good idea."

I stared hard at the shot of the cathedral on the TV. How could I even begin to describe it? But say my life depended on it. Say my life was being threatened by an insane guy who said I had to do it or else.

I stared some more at the cathedral before the picture flipped off into the countryside. There was no use. I turned to the blind man and said, "To begin with, they're very tall." I was looking around the room for clues. "They reach way up. Up and up. Toward the sky. They're so big, some of them, they have to have these supports. To help hold them up, so to speak. These supports are called buttresses. They remind me of viaducts, for some reason. But maybe you don't know viaducts, either? Sometimes the cathedrals have devils and such carved into the front. Sometimes lords and ladies. Don't ask me why this is," I said.

He was nodding. The whole upper part of his body seemed to be moving back and forth.

100 "I'm not doing so good, am I?" I said.

He stopped nodding and leaned forward on the edge of the sofa. As he listened to me, he was running his fingers through his beard. I wasn't getting through to him, I could see that. But he waited for me to go on just the same. He nodded, like he was trying to encourage me. I tried to think what else to say. "They're really big," I said. "They're massive. They're built of stone. Marble, too, sometimes. In those olden days, when they built cathedrals, men wanted to be close to God. In those olden days, God was an important part of everyone's life. You could tell this from their cathedral-building. I'm sorry," I said, "but it looks like that's the best I can do for you. I'm just no good at it."

"That's all right, bub," the blind man said. "Hey, listen. I hope you don't mind my asking you. Can I ask you something? Let me ask you a simple question, yes or no. I'm just curious and there's no offense. You're my host. But let me ask if you are in any way religious? You don't mind my asking?"

I shook my head. He couldn't see that, though. A wink is the same as a nod to a blind man. "I guess I don't believe in it. In anything. Sometimes it's hard. You know what I'm saying?"

"Sure, I do," he said.

105 "Right," I said.

The Englishman was still holding forth. My wife sighed in her sleep. She drew a long breath and went on with her sleeping.

"You'll have to forgive me," I said. "But I can't tell you what a cathedral looks like. It just isn't in me to do it. I can't do any more than I've done."

The blind man sat very still, his head down, as he listened to me.

I said, "The truth is, cathedrals don't mean anything special to me. Nothing. Cathedrals. They're something to look on late-night TV. That's all they are."

110 It was then that the blind man cleared his throat. He brought something up. He took a handkerchief from his back pocket. Then he said, "I get it, bub. It's okay. It happens. Don't worry about it," he said. "Hey, listen to me. Will you do me a favor? I got an idea. Why don't you find us some heavy paper? And a pen. We'll do something. We'll draw one together. Get us a pen and some heavy paper. Go on, bub, get the stuff," he said.

So I went upstairs. My legs felt like they didn't have any strength in them. They felt like they did after I'd done some run-ning. In my wife's room, I looked around. I found some ballpoints in a little basket on her table. And then I tried to think where to look for the kind of paper he was talking about.

Downstairs, in the kitchen, I found a shopping bag with on-ion skins in the bottom of the bag. I emptied the bag and shook it. I brought it into the living room and sat down with it near his legs. I moved some things, smoothed the wrinkles from the bag, spread it out on the coffee table.

The blind man got down from the sofa and sat next to me on the carpet.

He ran his fingers over the paper. He went up and down the sides of the paper. The edges, even the edges. He fingered the corners.

"All right," he said. "All right, let's do her." 115

He found my hand, the hand with the pen. He closed his hand over my hand. "Go ahead, bub, draw," he said. "Draw. You'll see. I'll follow along with you. It'll be okay. Just begin now like I'm telling you. You'll see. Draw," the blind man said.

So I began. First I drew a box that looked like a house. It could have been the house I lived in. Then I put a roof on it. At either end of the roof, I drew spires. Crazy.

> "Never thought anything like this could happen in your lifetime, did you, bub? . . ."

"Swell," he said. "Terrific. You're doing fine," he said. "Never thought anything like this could happen in your lifetime, did you, bub? Well, it's a strange life, we all know that. Go on now. Keep it up."

I put in windows with arches. I drew flying buttresses. I hung great doors. I couldn't stop. The TV station went off the air. I put down the pen and closed and opened my fingers. The blind man felt around over the paper. He moved the tips of his fingers over the paper, all over what I had drawn, and he nodded.

"Doing fine," the blind man said. 120

I took up the pen again, and he found my hand. I kept at it. I'm no artist. But I kept drawing just the same.

My wife opened up her eyes and gazed at us. She sat up on the sofa, her robe hanging open. She said, "What are you doing? Tell me, I want to know."

I didn't answer her.

The blind man said, "We're drawing a cathedral. Me and him are working on it. Press hard," he said to me. "That's right. That's good," he said. "Sure. You got it, bub. I can tell. You didn't think you could. But you can, can't you? You're cooking with gas now. You know what I'm saying? We're going to really have us some-thing here in a minute. How's the old arm?" he said. "Put some people in there now. What's a cathedral without people?"

My wife said, "What's going on? Robert, what are you doing? 125 What's going on?"

"It's all right," he said to her. "Close your eyes now," the blind man said to me.

I did it. I closed them just like he said.

"Are they closed?" he said. "Don't fudge."

"They're closed," I said.

130 "Keep them that way," he said. He said, "Don't stop now. Draw."

So we kept on with it. His fingers rode my fingers as my hand went over the paper. It was like nothing else in my life up to now.

Then he said, "I think that's it. I think you got it," he said. "Take a look. What do you think?"

But I had my eyes closed. I thought I'd keep them that way for a little longer. I thought it was something I ought to do.

"Well?" he said. "Are you looking?"

My eyes were still closed. I was in my house. I knew that. But 135 I didn't feel like I was inside anything.

"It's really something," I said.

IF YOU LIKED "CATHEDRAL," YOU MIGHT ALSO LIKE . . .

. . . Amy Hempel's "San Francisco" (Chapter 1). Critics coined the term "minimalism" to describe a pared-down type of realistic story. Carver didn't like the term, nor did some of the other writers associated with this group, such as Amy Hempel.

GOING FURTHER Jayne Anne Phillips writes stories made up of brief lyrical bursts of events. *Black Tickets* is a collection of her stories that may be of interest to those who like Carver.

Anton Chekhov (1860–1904)

RUSSIAN WRITER ANTON Chekhov was born into poverty but trained to become a physician. Even at the start of his medical practice, he was trying out short fictional sketches on magazine editors in Moscow, discovering that he had a talent for creating characters with a few brief lines of prose. Around 1888 Chekhov began writing more extended pieces of fiction, such as "The Kiss" and "Gusev," that were acclaimed for their artistic merit, not just their entertainment value. Well known to his contemporaries as a writer of numerous stories, Chekhov counted Leo Tolstoy among his early admirers. Later in life, Chekhov wrote plays, including *The Seagull* (1896) and *The Cherry Orchard* (1904); his stage works have become nearly as influential as his short stories, influencing playwrights such as George Bernard Shaw and Tennessee Williams. Today, Chekhov's work is even more widely read than during his lifetime, and many consider him to be the "father" of the modern short story (see his "Rapture" in Chapter 2).

The Lady with the Pet Dog (1899)

I

1 A new person, it was said, had appeared on the esplanade: a lady with a pet dog. Dmitry Dmitrich Gurov, who had spent a fortnight at Yalta and had got used to the place, had also begun to take an interest in new arrivals. As he sat in Vernet's confectionery shop, he saw, walking on the esplanade, a fair-haired young woman of medium height, wearing a beret; a white Pomeranian was trotting behind her.

And afterwards he met her in the public garden and in the square several times a day. She walked alone, always wearing the same beret and always with the white dog; no one knew who she was and everyone called her simply "the lady with the pet dog."

"If she is here alone without husband or friends," Gurov reflected, "it wouldn't be a bad thing to make her acquaintance."

He was under forty, but he already had a daughter twelve years old, and two sons at school. They had found a wife for him when he was very young, a student in his second year, and by now she seemed half as old again as he. She was a tall, erect woman with dark eyebrows, stately and dignified and, as she said of herself, intellectual. She read a great deal, used simplified spelling in her letters, called her husband, not Dmitry, but Dimitry, while he privately considered her of limited intelligence, narrow-minded, dowdy, was afraid of her, and did not like to be at home. He had begun being unfaithful to her long ago—had been unfaithful to her often and, probably for that reason, almost always spoke ill of women, and when they were talked of in his presence used to call them "the inferior race."

5   It seemed to him that he had been sufficiently tutored by bitter experience to call them what he pleased, and yet he could not have lived without "the inferior race" for two days together. In the company of men he was bored and ill at ease, he was chilly and uncommunicative with them; but when he was among women he felt free, and knew what to speak to them about and how to comport himself; and even to be silent with them was no strain on him. In his appearance, in his character, in his whole makeup there was something attractive and elusive that disposed women in his favor and allured them. He knew that, and some force seemed to draw him to them, too.

Oft-repeated and really bitter experience had taught him long ago that with decent people—particularly Moscow people—who are irresolute and slow to move, every affair which at first seems a light and charming adventure inevitably grows into a whole problem of extreme complexity, and in the end a painful situation is created. But at every new meeting with an interesting woman this lesson of experience seemed to slip from his memory, and he was eager for life, and everything seemed so simple and diverting.

One evening while he was dining in the public garden the lady in the beret walked up without haste to take the next table. Her expression, her gait, her dress, and the way she did her hair told him that she belonged to the upper class, that she was married, that she was in Yalta for the first time and alone, and that she was bored there. The stories told of the immorality in Yalta are to a great extent untrue; he despised them, and knew that such stories were made up for the most part by persons who would have been glad to sin themselves if they had had the chance; but when the lady sat down at the next table three paces from him, he recalled these stories of easy conquests, of trips to the mountains, and the tempting thought of swift, fleeting liaison, a romance with an unknown woman of whose very name he was ignorant suddenly took hold him.

Getting into bed he recalled that she had been a schoolgirl only recently, doing lessons like his own daughter. . . .

He beckoned invitingly to the Pomeranian, and when the dog approached him, shook his finger at it. The Pomeranian growled; Gurov threatened it again.

The lady glanced at him and at once dropped her eyes.

"He doesn't bite," she said and blushed.   10

"May I give him a bone?" he asked; and when she nodded he inquired affably, "Have you been in Yalta long?"

"About five days."

"And I am dragging out the second week here."

There was a short silence.

"Time passes quickly, and yet it is so   15 dull here!" she said, not looking at him.

"It's only the fashion to say it's dull here. A provincial will live in Belyov or Zhizdra and not be bored, but when he comes here it's 'Oh, the dullness! Oh, the dust!' One would think he came from Granada."

She laughed. Then both continued eating in silence, like strangers, but after dinner they walked together and there sprang up between them the light banter of people who are free and contented, to whom it does not matter where they go or what they talk about. They walked and talked of the strange light on the sea; the water was a soft, warm, lilac color, and there was a golden band of moonlight upon it. They talked of how sultry it was after a hot day. Gurov told her that he was a native of Moscow, that he had studied languages and literature at the university, but had a post in a bank; that at one time he had trained to become an opera singer but had given it up, that he owned two houses in Moscow. And he learned from her that she had grown up in Petersburg, but had lived in S——— since her marriage two years previously, that she was going to stay in Yalta for about another month, and that her husband, who needed a rest, too, might perhaps come to fetch her. She was not certain whether her husband was a member of a Government Board or served on a Zemstvo Council, and this amused her. And Gurov learned too that her name was Anna Sergeyevna.

Afterwards in his room at the hotel he thought about her—and was certain that he would meet her the next day. It was bound to happen. Getting into bed he recalled that she had been a schoolgirl only recently, doing lessons like his own daughter; he thought how much timidity and angularity there was still in her laugh and her manner of talking with a stranger. It must have been the first time in her life that she was alone in a setting in which she was followed, looked at, and spoken to for one secret purpose alone, which she could hardly fail to guess. He thought of her slim, delicate throat, her lovely gray eyes.

"There's something pathetic about her, though," he thought, and dropped off.

II

20 A week had passed since they had struck up an acquaintance. It was a holiday. It was close indoors, while in the street the wind whirled the dust about and blew people's hats off. One was thirsty all day, and Gurov often went into the restaurant and offered Anna Sergeyevna a soft drink or ice cream. One did not know what to do with oneself.

In the evening when the wind had abated they went out on the pier to watch the steamer come in. There were a great many people walking about the dock; they had come to welcome someone and they were carrying bunches of flowers. And two peculiarities of a festive Yalta crowd stood out: the elderly ladies were dressed like young ones and there were many generals.

Owing to the choppy sea, the steamer arrived late, after sunset, and it was a long time tacking about before it put in at the pier. Anna Sergeyevna peered at the steamer and the passengers through her lorgnette as though looking for acquaintances, and whenever she turned to Gurov her eyes were shining. She talked a great deal and asked questions jerkily, forgetting the next moment what she had asked; then she lost her lorgnette in the crush.

The festive crowd began to disperse; it was now too dark to see people's faces; there was no wind any more, but Gurov and Anna Sergeyevna still stood as though waiting to see someone else come off the steamer. Anna Sergeyevna was silent now, and sniffed her flowers without looking at Gurov.

"The weather has improved this evening," he said. "Where shall we go now? Shall we drive somewhere?"

25 She did not reply.

Then he looked at her intently, and suddenly embraced her and kissed her on the lips, and the moist fragrance of her flowers enveloped him; and at once he looked round him anxiously, wondering if anyone had seen them.

"Let us go to your place," he said softly. And they walked off together rapidly.

The air in her room was close and there was the smell of the perfume she had bought at the Japanese shop. Looking at her, Gurov thought: "What encounters life offers!" From the past he preserved the memory of carefree, good-natured women whom love made gay and who were grateful to him for the happiness he gave them, however brief it might be; and of women like his wife who loved without sincerity, with too many words, affectedly, hysteri-

. . . the lace on their lingerie seemed to him to **resemble scales.**

cally, with an expression that it was not love or passion that engaged them but something more significant; and of two or three others, very beautiful, frigid women, across whose faces would suddenly flit a rapacious expression—an obstinate desire to take from life more than it could give, and these were women no longer young, capricious, unreflecting, domineering, unintelligent, and when Gurov grew cold to them their beauty aroused his hatred, and the lace on their lingerie seemed to him to resemble scales.

But here there was the timidity, the angularity of inexperienced youth, a feeling of awkwardness; and there was a sense of embarrassment, as though someone had suddenly knocked at the door. Anna Sergeyevna, "the lady with the pet dog," treated what had happened in a peculiar way, very seriously, as though it were her fall—so it seemed, and this was odd and inappropriate. Her features drooped and faded, and her long hair hung down sadly on either side of her face; she grew pensive and her dejected pose was that of a Magdalene in a picture by an old master.

"It's not right," she said. "You don't respect me now, you first 30
of all."

There was a watermelon on the table. Gurov cut himself a slice and began eating it without haste. They were silent for at least half an hour.

There was something touching about Anna Sergeyevna; she had the purity of a well-bred, naive woman who has seen little of life. The single candle burning on the table barely illumined her face, yet it was clear that she was unhappy.

"Why should I stop respecting you, darling?" asked Gurov. "You don't know what you're saying."

"God forgive me," she said, and her eyes filled with tears. "It's terrible."

"It's as though you were trying to exonerate yourself." 35

"How can I exonerate myself? No. I am a bad, low woman; I despise myself and I have no thought of exonerating myself. It's not my husband but myself I have deceived. And not only just now; I have been deceiving myself for a long time. My husband may be a good, honest man, but he is a flunkey! I don't know what he does, what his work is, but I know he is a flunkey! I was twenty when I married him. I was tormented by curiosity; I wanted something better. 'There must be a different sort of life,' I said to myself. I wanted to live! To live, to live! Curiosity kept eating at me—you don't understand it, but I swear to God I could no longer control myself; something was going on in me: I could not be held back. I told my husband I was ill, and came here. And here I have been walking about as though in a daze, as though I were mad; and now I have become a vulgar, vile woman whom anyone may despise."

Gurov was already bored with her; he was irritated by her naive tone, by her repentance, so unexpected and so out of place; but for the tears in her eyes he might have thought she was joking or play-acting.

"I don't understand, my dear," he said softly. "What do you want?"

She hid her face on his breast and pressed close to him.

40 "Believe me, believe me, I beg you," she said, "I love honesty and purity, and sin is loathsome to me; I don't know what I'm doing. Simple people say, 'The Evil One has led me astray.' And I may say of myself now that the Evil One has led me astray."

"Quiet, quiet," he murmured.

He looked into her fixed, frightened eyes, kissed her, spoke to her softly and affectionately, and by degrees she calmed down, and her gaiety returned; both began laughing.

Afterwards when they went out there was not a soul on the esplanade. The town with its cypresses looked quite dead, but the sea was still sounding as it broke upon the beach; a single launch was rocking on the waves and on it a lantern was blinking sleepily.

They found a cab and drove to Oreanda.

45 "I found out your surname in the hall just now: it was written on the board—von Dideritz," said Gurov. "Is your husband German?"

"No; I believe his grandfather was German, but he is Greek Orthodox himself."

At Oreanda they sat on a bench not far from the church, looked down at the sea, and were silent. Yalta was barely visible through the morning mist; white clouds rested motionlessly on the mountaintops. The leaves did not stir on the trees, cicadas twanged, and the monotonous muffled sound of the sea that rose from below spoke of the peace, the eternal sleep awaiting us. So it rumbled below when there was no Yalta, no Oreanda here; so it rumbles now, and it will rumble as indifferently and as hollowly when we are no more. And in this constancy, in this complete indifference to the life and death of each of us, there lies, perhaps, a pledge of our eternal salvation, of the unceasing advance of life upon earth, of unceasing movement towards perfection. Sitting beside a young woman who in the dawn seemed so lovely, Gurov, soothed and spellbound by these magical surroundings—the sea, the mountains, the clouds, the wide sky—thought how everything is really beautiful in this world when one reflects: everything except what we think or do ourselves when we forget the higher aims of life and our own human dignity.

A man strolled up to them—probably a guard—looked at them and walked away. And this detail, too, seemed so mysterious and beautiful. They saw a steamer arrive from Feodosia, its lights extinguished in the glow of dawn.

"There is dew on the grass," said Anna Sergeyevna, after a silence.

"Yes, it's time to go home." 50

They returned to the city.

Then they met every day at twelve o'clock on the esplanade, lunched and dined together, took walks, admired the sea. She complained that she slept badly, that she had palpitations, asked the same questions, troubled now by jealousy and now by the fear that he did not respect her sufficiently. And often in the square or the public garden, when there was no one near them, he suddenly drew her to him and kissed her passionately. Complete idleness, these kisses in broad daylight exchanged furtively in dread of someone's seeing them, the heat, the smell of the sea, and the continual flitting before his eyes of idle, well-dressed, well-fed people, worked a complete change in him; he kept telling Anna Sergeyevna how beautiful she was, how seductive, was urgently passionate; he would not move a step away from her, while she was often pensive and continually pressed him to confess that he did not respect her, did not love her in the least, and saw in her nothing but a common woman. Almost every evening rather late they drove somewhere out of town, to Oreanda or to the waterfall; and the excursion was always a success, the scenery invariably impressed them as beautiful and magnificent.

They were expecting her husband, but a letter came from him saying that he had eye-trouble, and begging his wife to return home as soon as possible. Anna Sergeyevna made haste to go.

"It's a good thing I am leaving," she said to Gurov. "It's the hand of Fate!"

She took a carriage to the railway station, and he went with her. 55 They were driving the whole day. When she had taken her place in the express, and when the second bell had rung, she said, "Let me look at you once more—let me look at you again. Like this."

She was not crying but was so sad that she seemed ill, and her face was quivering.

"I shall be thinking of you—remembering you," she said. "God bless you; be happy. Don't remember evil against me. We are parting forever—it has to be, for we ought never to have met. Well, God bless you."

The train moved off rapidly, its lights soon vanished, and a minute later there was no sound of it, as though everything had conspired to end as quickly as possible that sweet trance, that

> "...I don't know what I'm doing....The Evil One has led me astray."

madness. Left alone on the platform, and gazing into the dark distance, Gurov listened to the twang of the grasshoppers and the hum of the telegraph wires, feeling as though he had just waked up. And he reflected, musing, that there had now been another episode or adventure in his life, and it, too, was at an end, and nothing was left of it but a memory. He was moved, sad, and slightly remorseful: this young woman whom he would never meet again had not been happy with him; he had been warm and affectionate with her, but yet in his manner, his tone, and his caresses there had been a shade of light irony, the slightly coarse arrogance of a happy male who was, besides, almost twice her age. She had constantly called him kind, exceptional, high-minded; obviously he had seemed to her different from what he really was, so he had involuntarily deceived her.

Here at the station there was already a scent of autumn in the air; it was a chilly evening.

60   "It is time for me to go north, too," thought Gurov as he left the platform. "High time!"

III

At home in Moscow the winter routine was already established: the stoves were heated, and in the morning it was still dark when the children were having breakfast and getting ready for school, and the nurse would light the lamp for a short time. There were frosts already. When the first snow falls, on the first day the sleighs are out, it is pleasant to see the white earth, the white roofs; one draws easy, delicious breaths, and the season brings back the days of one's youth. The old limes and birches, white with hoar-frost, have a good-natured look; they are closer to one's heart than cypresses and palms, and near them one no longer wants to think of mountains and the sea.

Gurov, a native of Moscow, arrived there on a fine frosty day, and when he put on his fur coat and warm gloves and took a walk along Petrovka, and when on Saturday night he heard the bells ringing, his recent trip and the places he had visited lost all charm for him. Little by little he became immersed in Moscow life, greedily read three newspapers a day, and declared that he did not read the Moscow papers on principle. He already felt a longing for restaurants, clubs, formal dinners, anniversary celebrations, and it flattered him to entertain distinguished lawyers and actors, and to play cards with a professor at the physicians' club. He could eat a whole portion of meat stewed with pickled cabbage and served in a pan, Moscow style.

A month or so would pass and the image of Anna Sergeyevna, it seemed to him, would become misty in his memory, and only from time to time he would dream of her with her touching smile as he dreamed of others. But more than a month went by, winter came into its own, and everything was still clear in his memory as though he had parted from Anna Sergeyevna only yesterday. And his memories glowed more and more vividly. When in the evening stillness the voices of his children preparing their lessons reached his study, or when he listened to a song or to an organ playing in a restaurant, or when the storm howled in the chimney, suddenly everything would rise up in his memory: what had happened on the pier and the early morning with the mist on the mountains, and the steamer coming from Feodosia, and the kisses. He would pace about his room a long time, remembering and smiling; then his memories passed into reveries, and in his imagination the past would mingle with what was to come. He did not dream of Anna Sergeyevna, but she followed him about everywhere and watched him. When he shut his eyes he saw her before him as though she were there in the flesh; and she seemed to him lovelier, younger, tenderer than she had been, and he imagined himself a finer man than he had been in Yalta. Of evenings she peered out at him from the bookcase, from the fireplace, from the corner—he heard her breathing, the caressing rustle of her clothes. In the street he followed the women with his eyes, looking for someone who resembled her.

Already he was tormented by a strong desire to share his memories with someone. But in his home it was impossible to talk of his love, and he had no one to talk to outside; certainly he could not confide in his tenants or in anyone at the bank. And what was there to talk to about? He hadn't loved her then, had he? Had there been anything beautiful, poetical, edifying, or simply interesting in his relations with Anna Sergeyevna? And he was forced to talk vaguely of love, of women, and no one guessed what he meant; only his wife would twitch her black eyebrows and say, "The part of a philanderer does not suit you at all, Dimitry."

One evening, coming out of the physician's club with an of- 65
ficial with whom he had been playing cards, he could not resist saying:

"If you only knew what a fascinating woman I became acquainted with at Yalta!"

The official got into his sledge and was driving away, but turned suddenly and shouted: "Dmitry Dmitrich!"

"What is it?"

"You were right this evening: the sturgeon was a bit high."

. . . suddenly everything would rise up in his memory. . . .

70 These words, so commonplace, for some reason moved Gurov to indignation, and struck him as degrading and unclean. What savage manners, what mugs! What stupid nights, what dull, humdrum days! Frenzied gambling, gluttony, drunkenness, continual talk always about the same things! Futile pursuits and conversations always about the same topics take up the better part of one's time, the better part of one's strength, and in the end there is left a life clipped and wingless, an absurd mess, and there is no escaping or getting away from it—just as though one were in a madhouse or a prison.

Gurov, boiling with indignation, did not sleep all night. And he had a headache all the next day. And the following nights too he slept badly; he sat up in bed, thinking, or paced up and down his room. He was fed up with his children, fed up with the bank; he had no desire to go anywhere or to talk of anything.

> . . . only his wife would twitch her black eyebrows and say, "The part of a philanderer does not suit you at all, Dimitry."

In December during the holidays he prepared to take a trip and told his wife he was going to Petersburg to do what he could for a young friend—and he set off for S———. What for? He did not know, himself. He wanted to see Anna Sergeyevna and talk with her, to arrange a rendezvous if possible.

He arrived at S——— in the morning, and at the hotel took the best room, in which the floor was covered with gray army cloth, and on the table there was an inkstand, gray with dust and topped by a figure on horseback, its hat in its raised hand and its head broken off. The porter gave him the necessary information: von Dideritz lived in a house of his own on Staro-Goncharnaya Street, not far from the hotel: he was rich and lived well and kept his own horses; everyone in the town knew him. The porter pronounced the name: "Dridiritz."

Without haste Gurov made his way to Staro-Goncharnaya Street and found the house. Directly opposite the house stretched a long gray fence studded with nails.

75 "A fence like that would make one run away," thought Gurov, looking now at the fence, now at the windows of the house.

He reflected: this was a holiday, and the husband was apt to be at home. And in any case, it would be tactless to go into the house and disturb her. If he were to send her a note, it might fall into her husband's hands, and that might spoil everything. The best thing was to rely on chance. And he kept walking up and down the street and along the fence, waiting for the chance. He saw a beggar go in at the gate and heard the dogs attack him; then an hour later he heard a piano, and the sound came to him faintly and indistinctly. Probably it was Anna Sergeyevna playing. The front door opened suddenly, and an old woman came out, followed by the familiar white Pomeranian. Gurov was on the point of calling to the dog, but his heart began beating violently, and in his excitement he could not remember the Pomeranian's name.

He kept walking up and down, and hated the gray fence more and more, and by now he thought irritably that Anna Sergeyevna had forgotten him, and was perhaps already diverting herself with another man, and that that was very natural in a young woman who from morning till night had to look at that damn fence. He went back to his hotel room and sat on the couch for a long while, not knowing what to do, then he had dinner and a long nap.

"How stupid and annoying all this is!" he thought when he woke and looked at the dark windows: it was already evening. "Here I've had a good sleep for some reason. What am I going to do at night?"

He sat on the bed, which was covered with a cheap gray blanket of the kind seen in hospitals, and he twitted himself in his vexation:

80 "So there's your lady with the pet dog. There's your adventure. A nice place to cool your heels in."

That morning at the station a playbill in large letters had caught his eye. *The Geisha* was to be given for the first time. He thought of this and drove to the theater.

"It's quite possible that she goes to first nights," he thought.

The theater was full. As in all provincial theaters, there was a haze above the chandelier, the gallery was noisy and restless; in the front row, before the beginning of the performance the local dandies were standing with their hands clasped behind their backs; in the Governor's box the Governor's daughter, wearing a boa, occupied the front seat, while the Governor himself hid modestly behind the portiere and only his hands were visible; the curtain swayed; the orchestra was a long time tuning up. While the audience were coming in and taking their seats, Gurov scanned the faces eagerly.

Anna Sergeyevna, too, came in. She sat down in the third row, and when Gurov looked at her his heart contracted, and he understood clearly that in the whole world there was no human being so near, so precious, and so important to him; she, this little, undistinguished woman, lost in a provincial crowd, with a vulgar lorgnette in her hand, filled his whole life now, was his sorrow and his joy, the only happiness that he now desired for himself, and to the sounds of the bad orchestra, of the miserable local violins, he thought how lovely she was. He thought and dreamed.

85 A young man with small side-whiskers, very tall and stooped, came in with Anna Sergeyevna and sat down beside her; he nodded his head at every step and seemed to be bowing continually.

Probably this was the husband whom at Yalta, in an excess of bitter feeling, she had called a flunkey. And there really was in his lanky figure, his side-whiskers, his small bald patch, something of a flunkey's retiring manner; his smile was mawkish, and in his buttonhole there was an academic badge like a waiter's number.

During the first intermission the husband went out to have a smoke; she remained in her seat. Gurov, who was also sitting in the orchestra, went up to her and said in a shaky voice, with a forced smile:

"Good evening!"

She glanced at him and turned pale, then looked at him again in horror, unable to believe her eyes, and gripped the fan and the lorgnette tightly together in her hands, evidently trying to keep herself from fainting. Both were silent. She was sitting, he was standing, frightened by her distress and not daring to take a seat beside her. The violins and the flute that were being tuned up sang out. He suddenly felt frightened: it seemed as if all the people in the boxes were looking at them. She got up and went hurriedly to the exit; he followed her, and both of them walked blindly along the corridors and up and down stairs, and figures in the uniforms prescribed for magistrates, teachers, and officials of the Department of Crown Lands, all wearing badges, flitted before their eyes, as did also ladies, and fur coats on hangers; they were conscious of drafts and the smell of stale tobacco. And Gurov, whose heart was beating violently, thought:

"Oh, Lord! Why are these people here and this orchestra!"

90   And at that instant he suddenly recalled how when he had seen Anna Sergeyevna off at the station he had said to himself that all was over between them and that they would never meet again. But how distant the end still was!

On the narrow, gloomy staircase over which it said "To the Amphitheatre," she stopped.

"How you frightened me!" she said, breathing hard, still pale and stunned. "Oh, how you frightened me! I am barely alive. Why did you come? Why?"

"But do understand, Anna, do understand—" he said hurriedly, under his breath. "I implore you, do understand—"

She looked at him with fear, with entreaty, with love; she looked at him intently, to keep his features more distinctly in her memory.

95   "I suffer so," she went on, not listening to him. "All this time I have been thinking of nothing but you; I live only by the thought of you. And I wanted to forget, to forget; but why, oh, why have you come?"

On the landing above them two high school boys were looking down and smoking, but it was all the same to Gurov; he drew Anna Sergeyevna to him and began kissing her face and her hands.

"What are you doing, what are you doing!" she was saying in horror, pushing him away. "We have lost our senses. Go away today; go away at once—I conjure you by all that is sacred, I implore you—People are coming this way!"

Someone was walking up the stairs.

"You must leave," Anna Sergeyevna went on in a whisper. "Do you hear, Dmitry Dmitrich? I will come and see you in Moscow. I have never been happy; I am unhappy now, and I never, never shall be happy, never! So don't make me suffer still more! I swear I'll come to Moscow. But now let us part. My dear, good, precious one, let us part!"

100   She pressed his hand and walked rapidly downstairs, turning to look round at him, and from her eyes he could see that she really was unhappy. Gurov stood for a while, listening, then when all grew quiet, he found his coat and left the theater.

> **Gurov stood for a while, listening,** then when all grew quiet, he found his coat and left the theater.

IV

And Anna Sergeyevna began coming to see him in Moscow. Once every two or three months she left S———, telling her husband that she was going to consult a doctor about a woman's ailment from which she was suffering—and her husband did and did not believe her. When she arrived in Moscow she would stop at the Slavyansky Bazar Hotel, and at once send a man in a red cap to Gurov. Gurov came to see her, and no one in Moscow knew of it.

Once he was going to see her in this way on a winter morning (the messenger had come the evening before and not found him in). With him walked his daughter, whom he wanted to take to school: it was on the way. Snow was coming down in big wet flakes.

"It's three degrees above zero,[1] and yet it's snowing," Gurov was saying to his daughter. "But this temperature prevails only on the surface of the earth; in the upper layers of the atmosphere there is quite a different temperature."

"And why doesn't it thunder in winter, papa?"

He explained that, too. He talked, thinking all the while that   105 he was on his way to a rendezvous, and no living soul knew of it,

---

[1]Equal to approximately thirty-seven degrees Fahrenheit. (Russia uses the Celsius scale.)

and probably no one would ever know. He had two lives: an open one, seen and known by all who needed to know it, full of conventional truth and conventional falsehood, exactly like the lives of his friends and acquaintances; and another life that went on in secret. And through some strange, perhaps accidental, combination of circumstances, everything that was of interest and importance to him, everything that was essential to him, everything about which he felt sincerely and did not deceive himself, everything that constituted the core of his life, was going on concealed from others; while all that was false, the shell in which he hid to cover the truth—his work at the bank, for instance, his discussions at the club, his references to the "inferior race," his appearances at anniversary celebrations with his wife—all that went on in the open. Judging others by himself, he did not believe what he saw, and always fancied that every man led his real, most interesting life under cover of secrecy as under cover of night. The personal life of every individual is based on secrecy, and perhaps it is partly for that reason that civilized man is so nervously anxious that personal privacy should be respected.

> . . . it seemed odd to him that he had grown so much older in the last few years, and lost his looks.

Having taken his daughter to school, Gurov went on to the Slavyansky Bazar Hotel. He took off his fur coat in the lobby, went upstairs, and knocked gently at the door. Anna Sergeyevna, wearing his favorite gray dress, exhausted by the journey and by waiting, had been expecting him since the previous evening. She was pale, and looked at him without a smile, and he had hardly entered when she flung herself on his breast. Their kiss was a long, lingering one, as though they had not seen one another for two years.

"Well, darling, how are you getting on there?" he asked. "What news?"

"Wait; I'll tell you in a moment—I can't speak."

She could not speak; she was crying. She turned away from him, and pressed her handkerchief to her eyes.

110 "Let her have her cry; meanwhile I'll sit down," he thought, and he seated himself in an armchair.

Then he rang and ordered tea, and while he was having his tea she remained standing at the window with her back to him. She was crying out of sheer agitation, in the sorrowful consciousness that their life was so sad; that they could only see each other in secret and had to hide from people like thieves! Was it not a broken life?

"Come, stop now, dear!" he said.

It was plain to him that this love of theirs would not be over soon, that the end of it was not in sight. Anna Sergeyevna was growing more and more attached to him. She adored him, and it was unthinkable to tell her that their love was bound to come to an end some day; besides, she would not have believed it!

He went up to her and took her by the shoulders, to fondle her and say something diverting, and at that moment he caught sight of himself in the mirror.

His hair was already beginning to turn gray. And it seemed 115 odd to him that he had grown so much older in the last few years, and lost his looks. The shoulders on which his hands rested were warm and heaving. He felt compassion for this life, still so warm and lovely, but probably already about to begin to fade and wither like his own. Why did she love him so much? He always seemed to women different from what he was, and they loved in him not himself, but the man whom their imagination created and whom they had been eagerly seeking all their lives; and afterwards, when they saw their mistake, they loved him nevertheless. And not one of them had been happy with him. In the past he had met women, come together with them, parted from them, but he had never once loved; it was anything you please, but not love. And only now when his head was gray he had fallen in love, really, truly—for the first time in his life.

Anna Sergeyevna and he loved each other as people do who are very close and intimate, like man and wife, like tender friends; it seemed to them that Fate itself had meant them for one another, and they could not understand why he had a wife and she had a husband; and it was as though they were a pair of migratory birds, male and female, caught and forced to live in different cages. They forgave each other what they were ashamed of in their past, they forgave everything in the present, and felt that this love of theirs had altered them both.

Formerly in moments of sadness he had soothed himself with whatever logical arguments came into his head, but now he no longer cared for logic; he felt profound compassion, he wanted to be sincere and tender.

"Give it up now, my darling," he said. "You've had your cry; that's enough. Let us have a talk now, we'll think up something."

Then they spent a long time taking counsel together, they talked of how to avoid the necessity for secrecy, for deception, for living in different cities, and not seeing one another for long stretches of time. How could they free themselves from these intolerable fetters?

"How? How?" he asked, clutching his head. "How?" 120

And it seemed as though in a little while the solution would be found, and then a new and glorious life would begin; and it was clear to both of them that the end was still far off, and that what was to be most complicated and difficult for them was only just beginning.

—*Translated by* Avrahm Yarmolinsky

Gabriel García Márquez (b. 1928)

THE WINNER OF the 1982 Nobel Prize for Literature, Gabriel García Márquez was born in the small northern Colombian town of Aracataca. Originally a student of law, he ended his studies and went to work as a journalist, a profession that took him to Europe and eventually to the United States. There he made a pilgrimage to Oxford, Mississippi, the hometown of his literary idol William Faulkner, whom he referred to in his Nobel Prize acceptance speech in laudatory terms. García Márquez declared that the writer's goal was to create a "new and sweeping utopia of life, where no one will be able to decide for others how they die, where love will prove true and happiness be possible, and where the races condemned to one hundred years of solitude will have, at last and forever, a second opportunity on earth."

His style is that of "magical realism," in which supernatural events occur in otherwise natural contexts and settings. García Márquez is famous for his ability to span decades in a sentence, to bring the dead to life, and to make even the cruelest fates a matter of course—all with utmost fluidity and believability. Along with his many other works of fiction and nonfiction, his masterwork, the novel *One Hundred Years of Solitude,* has illuminated life in the Americas for millions of readers.

A Very Old Man with Enormous Wings (1971)

A TALE FOR CHILDREN

1   On the third day of rain they had killed so many crabs inside the house that Pelayo had to cross his drenched courtyard and throw them into the sea, because the newborn child had a temperature all night and they thought it was due to the stench. The world had been sad since Tuesday. Sea and sky were a single ash-gray thing and the sands of the beach, which on March nights glimmered like powdered light, had become a stew of mud and rotten shellfish. The light was so weak at noon that when Pelayo was coming back to the house after throwing away the crabs, it was hard for him to see what it was that was moving and groaning in the rear of the courtyard. He had to go very close to see that it was an old man, a very old man, lying face down in the mud, who, in spite of his tremendous efforts, couldn't get up, impeded by his enormous wings.

Frightened by that nightmare, Pelayo ran to get Elisenda, his wife, who was putting compresses on the sick child, and he took her to the rear of the courtyard. They both looked at the fallen body with mute stupor. He was dressed like a ragpicker. There were only a few faded hairs left on his bald skull and very few teeth in his mouth, and his pitiful condition of a drenched great-grandfather had taken away any sense of grandeur he might have had. His huge buzzard wings, dirty and half-plucked, were forever entangled in the mud. They looked at him so long and so closely that Pelayo and Elisenda very soon overcame their surprise and in the end found him familiar. Then they dared speak to him, and he answered in an incomprehensible dialect with a strong sailor's voice. That was how they skipped over the inconvenience of the wings and quite intelligently concluded that he was a lonely castaway from some foreign ship wrecked by the storm. And yet, they called in a neighbor woman who knew everything about life and death to see him, and all she needed was one look to show them their mistake.

"He's an angel," she told them. "He must have been coming for the child, but the poor fellow is so old that the rain knocked him down."

On the following day everyone knew that a flesh-and-blood angel was held captive in Pelayo's house. Against the judgment of the wise neighbor woman, for whom angels in those times were the fugitive survivors of a celestial conspiracy, they did not have the heart to club him to death. Pelayo watched over him all afternoon from the kitchen, armed with his bailiff's club, and before going to bed he dragged him out of the mud and locked him up with the hens in the wire chicken coop. In the middle of the night, when the rain stopped, Pelayo and Elisenda were still killing crabs. A short time afterward the child woke up without a fever and with a desire to eat. Then they felt magnanimous and decided to put the angel on a raft with fresh water and provisions for three days and leave him to his fate on the high seas. But when they went out into the courtyard with the first light of dawn, they found the whole neighborhood in front of the chicken coop having fun with the angel, without the slightest reverence, tossing him things to eat through the openings in the wire as if he weren't a supernatural creature but a circus animal.

5   Father Gonzaga arrived before seven o'clock, alarmed at the strange news. By that time onlookers less frivolous than those at dawn had already arrived and they were making all kinds of conjectures concerning the captive's future. The simplest among them thought that he should be named mayor of the world. Others of sterner mind felt that he should be promoted to the rank of five-star general in order to win all wars. Some visionaries hoped that he could be put to stud in order to implant on earth a race of winged wise men who could take charge of the universe. But Father Gonzaga, before becoming a priest, had been a robust woodcutter. Standing by the wire, he reviewed his catechism in an instant and asked them to open the door so that he could take a close look at that pitiful man who looked more like a huge de-

"He's an angel, . . . but the poor fellow is so old that the rain knocked him down."

crepit hen among the fascinated chickens. He was lying in the corner drying his open wings in the sunlight among the fruit peels and breakfast leftovers that the early risers had thrown him. Alien to the impertinences of the world, he only lifted his antiquarian eyes and murmured something in his dialect when Father Gonzaga went into the chicken coop and said good morning to him in Latin. The parish priest had his first suspicion of an imposter when he saw that he did not understand the language of God or know how to greet His ministers. Then he noticed that seen close up he was much too human: he had an unbearable smell of the outdoors, the back side of his wings was strewn with parasites and his main feathers had been mistreated by terrestrial winds, and nothing about him measured up to the proud dignity of angels. Then he came out of the chicken coop and in a brief sermon warned the curious against the risks of being ingenuous. He reminded them that the devil had the bad habit of making use of carnival tricks in order to confuse the unwary. He argued that if wings were not the essential element in determining the difference between a hawk and an airplane, they were even less so in the recognition of angels. Nevertheless, he promised to write a letter to his bishop so that the latter would write to his primate so that the latter would write to the Supreme Pontiff in order to get the final verdict from the highest courts.

His prudence fell on sterile hearts. The news of the captive angel spread with such rapidity that after a few hours the courtyard had the bustle of a marketplace and they had to call in troops with fixed bayonets to disperse the mob that was about to knock the house down. Elisenda, her spine all twisted from sweeping up so much marketplace trash, then got the idea of fencing in the yard and charging five cents admission to see the angel.

The curious came from far away. A traveling carnival arrived with a flying acrobat who buzzed over the crowd several times, but no one paid any attention to him because his wings were not those of an angel but, rather, those of a sidereal bat. The most unfortunate invalids on earth came in search of health: a poor woman who since childhood had been counting her heartbeats and had run out of numbers; a Portuguese man who couldn't sleep because the noise of the stars disturbed him; a sleepwalker who got up at night to undo the things he had done while awake; and many others with less serious ailments. In the midst of that shipwreck disorder that made the earth tremble, Pelayo and Elisenda were happy with fatigue, for in less than a week they had crammed their rooms with money and the line of pilgrims waiting their turn to enter still reached beyond the horizon.

The angel was the only one who took no part in his own act. He spent his time trying to get comfortable in his borrowed nest, befuddled by the hellish heat of the oil lamps and sacramental candles that had been placed along the wire. At first they tried to make him eat some mothballs, which, according to the wisdom of the wise neighbor woman, were the food prescribed for angels. But he turned them down, just as he turned down the papal lunches that the penitents brought him, and they never found out whether it was because he was an angel or because he was an old man that in the end ate nothing but eggplant mush. His only supernatural virtue seemed to be patience. Especially during the first days, when the hens pecked at him, searching for the stellar parasites that proliferated in his wings, and the cripples pulled out feathers to touch their defective parts with, and even the most merciful threw stones at him, trying to get him to rise so they could see him standing. The only time they succeeded in arousing him was when they burned his side with an iron for branding steers, for he had been motionless for so many hours that they thought he was dead. He awoke with a start, ranting in his hermetic language and with tears in his eyes, and he flapped his wings a couple of times, which brought on a whirlwind of chicken dung and lunar dust and a gale of panic that did not seem to be of this world. Although many thought that his reaction had not been one of rage but of pain, from then on they were careful not to annoy him, because the majority understood that his passivity was not that of a hero taking his ease but that of a cataclysm in repose.

Father Gonzaga held back the crowd's frivolity with formulas of maidservant inspiration while awaiting the arrival of a final judgment on the nature of the captive. But the mail from Rome showed no sense of urgency. They spent their time finding out if the prisoner had a navel, if his dialect had any connection with Aramaic, how many times he could fit on the head of a pin, or whether he wasn't just a Norwegian with wings. Those meager letters might have come and gone until the end of time if a providential event had not put an end to the priest's tribulations.

10   It so happened that during those days, among so many other carnival attractions, there arrived in the town the traveling show of the woman who had been changed into a spider for having disobeyed her parents. The admission to see her was not only less than the admission to see the angel, but people were permitted to ask her all manner of questions about her absurd state and to examine her up and down so that no one would ever doubt the truth of her horror. She was a frightful tarantula the size of a ram and with the head of a sad maiden. What was most heart-rending,

> **She was a frightful tarantula the** size **of a ram and with the head of a sad maiden.**

however, was not her outlandish shape but the sincere affliction with which she recounted the details of her misfortune. While still practically a child she had sneaked out of her parents' house to go to a dance, and while she was coming back through the woods after having danced all night without permission, a fearful thunderclap rent the sky in tow and through the crack came the lightning bolt of brimstone that changed her into a spider. Her only nourishment came from the meatballs that charitable souls chose to toss into her mouth. A spectacle like that, full of so much human truth and with such a fearful lesson, was bound to defeat without even trying that of a haughty angel who scarcely deigned to look at mortals. Besides, the few miracles attributed to the angel showed a certain mental disorder, like the blind man who didn't recover his sight but grew three new teeth, or the paralytic who didn't get to walk but almost won the lottery, and the leper whose sores sprouted sunflowers. Those consolation miracles, which were more like mocking fun, had already ruined the angel's reputation when the woman who had been changed into a spider finally crushed him completely. That was how Father Gonzaga was cured forever of his insomnia and Pelayo's courtyard went back to being as empty as during the time it had rained for three days and crabs walked through the bedrooms.

The owners of the house had no reason to lament. With the money they saved they built a two-story mansion with balconies and gardens and high netting so that crabs wouldn't get in during the winter, and with iron bars on the windows so that angels wouldn't get in. Pelayo also set up a rabbit warren close to town and gave up his job as bailiff for good, and Elisenda bought some satin pumps with high heels and many dresses of iridescent silk, the kind worn on Sunday by the most desirable women in those times. The chicken coop was the only thing that didn't receive any attention. If they washed it down with creolin and burned tears of myrrh inside it every so often, it was not in homage to the angel but to drive away the dungheap stench that still hung everywhere like a ghost and was turning the new house into an old one. At first, when the child learned to walk, they were careful that he not get too close to the chicken coop. But then they began to lose their fears and got used to the smell, and before the child got his second teeth he'd gone inside the chicken coop to play, where the wires were falling apart. The angel was no less standoffish with him than with the other mortals, but he tolerated the most ingenious infamies with the patience of a dog who had no illusions. They both came down with chicken pox at the same time. The doctor who took care of the child couldn't resist the temptation to listen to the angel's heart, and he found so much whistling in the heart and so many sounds in his kidneys that it seemed impossible for him to be alive. What surprised him most, however, was the logic of his wings. They seemed so natural on that completely human organism that he couldn't understand why other men didn't have them too.

When the child began school it had been some time since the sun and rain had caused the collapse of the chicken coop. The angel went dragging himself about here and there like a stray dying man. They would drive him out of the bedroom with a broom and a moment later find him in the kitchen. He seemed to be in so many places at the same time that they grew to think that he'd been duplicated, that he was reproducing himself all through the house, and the exasperated and unhinged Elisenda shouted that it was awful living in that hell full of angels. He could scarcely eat and his antiquarian eyes had also become so foggy that he went about bumping into posts. All he had left were the bare cannulae of his last feathers. Pelayo threw a blanket over him and extended him the charity of letting him sleep in the shed, and only then did they notice that he had a temperature at night, and was delirious with the tongue twisters of an old Norwegian. That was one of the few times they became alarmed, for they thought he was going to die and not even the wise neighbor woman had been able to tell them what to do with dead angels.

And yet he not only survived his worst winter, but seemed improved with the first sunny days. He remained motionless for several days in the farthest corner of the courtyard, where no one would see him, and at the beginning of December some large, stiff feathers began to grow on his wings, the feathers of a scarecrow, which looked more like another misfortune of decrepitude. But he must have known the reason for those changes, for he was quite careful that no one should notice them, that no one should hear the sea chanteys that he sometimes sang under the stars. One morning Elisenda was cutting some bunches of onions for lunch when a wind that seemed to come from the high seas blew into the kitchen. Then she went to the window and caught the angel in his first attempts at flight. They were so clumsy that his fingernails opened a furrow in the vegetable patch and he was on the point of knocking the shed down with the ungainly flapping that slipped on the light and couldn't get a grip on the air. But he did manage to gain altitude. Elisenda let out a sigh of relief, for herself and for him, when she watched him pass over the last houses, holding himself up in some way with the risky flapping of a senile vulture. She kept watching him even when she was through cutting the onions and she kept on watching until it was no longer possible for her to see him, because then he was no longer an annoyance in her life but an imaginary dot on the horizon of the sea.

> ## What surprised him most, however, was the logic of his wings.

—*Translated by* Gregory Rabassa

IF YOU LIKED "A VERY OLD MAN WITH ENORMOUS WINGS," YOU MIGHT ALSO LIKE . . .

. . . "The Rememberer" by Aimee Bender (Chapter 12), who explains in her interview (connect.mcgraw-hill.com) that we need more "magic" in our lives. In her story you will find a real situation turned up to the level of credible fantasy.

GOING FURTHER Gabriel García Márquez has published several novels, including *One Hundred Years of Solitude*. A number of U.S. writers have found themselves influenced by García Márquez's magical realist style, among them Toni Morrison in her novel *Song of Solomon* and younger writers such as Mark Helprin in the stories collected in *A Dove of the East* and Jonathan Safran Foer in his 2005 novel *Extremely Loud and Incredibly Close*.

Shirley Jackson (1916–1965)

WHEN "THE LOTTERY" was first published in *The New Yorker* in 1948, it came under fire for its criticism of small town America. Throughout her career, Jackson refused to give interviews to explain or defend her work, but her husband commented that Jackson gave "a sensitive and faithful anatomy of our times, fitting symbols for our distressing world of the concentration camp and the Bomb." Shirley Jackson was born in California in 1916 and moved with her family to Rochester, New York, where she spent her first year of college at the University of Rochester and later finished her B.A. at Syracuse University. There she published her first short story, "Janice," in 1938 and went on to publish widely in a variety of magazines from *The New Republic* and *The New Yorker* to *Good Housekeeping* and *Mademoiselle*. She pioneered the irreverent housewife genre in works such as *The Bad Children* that was made famous later by such writers as Erma Bombeck. But it is her dark take on her subjects that has made her work so important, especially in the development of the horror genre. Her modern ghost story *The Haunting of Hill House* (1959) has twice been made into a movie. Jackson herself felt she had a connection to the supernatural and sometimes suffered from depression and social anxiety, once refusing to leave the house for three months. She lived most of her adult life in a small town in Vermont, and this ordinary mode of life transfers into the most chilling aspect of her work: the ordinariness of evil. She died prematurely of heart failure while taking a nap in 1965.

The Lottery (1948)

1 The morning of June 27th was clear and sunny, with the fresh warmth of a full-summer day; the flowers were blossoming profusely and the grass was richly green. The people of the village began to gather in the square, between the post office and the bank, around ten o'clock; in some towns there were so many people that the lottery took two days and had to be started on June 26th, but in this village, where there were only about three hundred people, the whole lottery took less than two hours, so it could begin at ten o'clock in the morning and still be through in time to allow the villagers to get home for noon dinner.

The children assembled first, of course. School was recently over for the summer, and the feeling of liberty sat uneasily on most of them; they tended to gather together quietly for a while before they broke into boisterous play, and their talk was still of the classroom and the teacher, of books and reprimands. Bobby Martin had already stuffed his pockets full of stones, and the other boys soon followed his example, selecting the smoothest and roundest stones; Bobby and Harry Jones and Dickie Delacroix—the villagers pronounced this name "Dellacroy"—eventually made a great pile of stones in one corner of the square and guarded it against the raids of the other boys. The girls stood aside, talking among themselves, looking over their shoulders at the boys, and the very small children rolled in the dust or clung to the hands of their older brothers or sisters.

Soon the men began to gather, surveying their own children, speaking of planting and rain, tractors and taxes. They stood together, away from the pile of stones in the corner, and their jokes were quiet and they smiled rather than laughed. The women, wearing faded house dresses and sweaters, came shortly after their menfolk. They greeted one another and exchanged bits of gossip as they went to join their husbands. Soon the women, standing by their husbands, began to call to their children, and the children came reluctantly, having to be called four or five times. Bobby Martin ducked under his mother's grasping hand and ran, laughing, back to the pile of stones. His father spoke up sharply, and Bobby came quickly and took his place between his father and his oldest brother.

The lottery was conducted—as were the square dances, the teen-age club, the Halloween program—by Mr. Summers, who had time and energy to devote to civic activities. He was a round-faced, jovial man and he ran the coal business, and people were sorry for him, because he had no children and his wife was a scold. When he arrived in the square, carrying the black wooden box, there was a murmur of conversation among the villagers, and he waved and called, "Little late today, folks." The postmaster, Mr. Graves, followed him, carrying a three-legged stool, and the stool was put in the center of the square and Mr. Summers set the black box down on it. The villagers kept their distance, leaving a space between themselves and the stool, and when Mr. Summers said, "Some of you fellows want to give me a hand?" there was a hesitation before two men, Mr. Martin and his oldest son, Baxter, came forward to hold the box steady on the stool while Mr. Summers stirred up the papers inside it.

5   The original paraphernalia for the lottery had been lost long ago, and the black box now resting on the stool had been put into use even before Old Man Warner, the oldest man in town, was born. Mr. Summers spoke frequently to the villagers about making a new box, but no one liked to upset even as much tradition as was represented by the black box. There was a story that the present box had been made with some pieces of the box that had preceded it, the one that had been constructed when the first people settled down to make a village here. Every year, after the lottery, Mr. Summers began talking again about a new box, but every year the subject was allowed to fade off without anything's being done. The black box grew shabbier each year: by now it was no longer completely black but splintered badly along one side to show the original wood color, and in some places faded or stained.

. . . with one hand resting carelessly on the black box, *he seemed very proper. . . .*

Mr. Martin and his oldest son, Baxter, held the black box securely on the stool until Mr. Summers had stirred the papers thoroughly with his hand. Because so much of the ritual had been forgotten or discarded, Mr. Summers had been successful in having slips of paper substituted for the chips of wood that had been used for generations. Chips of wood, Mr. Summers had argued, had been all very well when the village was tiny, but now that the population was more than three hundred and likely to keep on growing, it was necessary to use something that would fit more easily into the black box. The night before the lottery, Mr. Summers and Mr. Graves made up the slips of paper and put them in the box, and it was then taken to the safe of Mr. Summers' coal company and locked up until Mr. Summers was ready to take it to the square next morning. The rest of the year, the box was put away, sometimes one place, sometimes another; it had spent one year in Mr. Graves's barn and another year underfoot in the post office, and sometimes it was set on a shelf in the Martin grocery and left there.

There was a great deal of fussing to be done before Mr. Summers declared the lottery open. There were the lists to make up— of heads of families, heads of households in each family, members of each household in each family. There was the proper swearing-in of Mr. Summers by the postmaster, as the official of the lottery; at one time, some people remembered, there had been a recital of some sort, performed by the official of the lottery, a perfunctory, tuneless chant that had been rattled off duly each year; some people believed that the official of the lottery used to stand just so when he said or sang it, others believed that he was supposed to walk among the people, but years and years ago this part of the ritual had been allowed to lapse. There had been, also, a ritual salute, which the official of the lottery had had to use in addressing each person who came up to draw from the box, but this also had changed with time, until now it was felt necessary only for the official to speak to each person approaching. Mr. Summers was very good at all this; in his clean white shirt and blue jeans, with one hand resting carelessly on the black box, he seemed very proper and important as he talked interminably to Mr. Graves and the Martins.

Just as Mr. Summers finally left off talking and turned to the assembled villagers, Mrs. Hutchinson came hurriedly along the path to the square, her sweater thrown over her shoulders, and slid into place in the back of the crowd. "Clean forgot what day it was," she said to Mrs. Delacroix, who stood next to her, and they both laughed softly. "Thought my old man was out back stacking wood," Mrs. Hutchinson went on, "and then I looked out the window and the kids was gone, and then I remembered it was the twenty-seventh and came a-running." She dried her hands on her apron, and Mrs. Delacroix said, "You're in time, though. They're still talking away up there."

Mrs. Hutchinson craned her neck to see through the crowd and found her husband and children standing near the front. She tapped Mrs. Delacroix on the arm as a farewell and began to make her way through the crowd. The people separated good-humoredly to let her through, two or three people said, in voices just loud enough to be heard across the crowd, "Here comes your Missus, Hutchinson," and "Bill, she made it after all." Mrs. Hutchinson reached her husband, and Mr. Summers, who had been waiting, said cheerfully. "Thought we were going to have to get on without you, Tessie." Mrs. Hutchinson said, grinning, "Wouldn't have me leave m'dishes in the sink, now, would you, Joe?," and soft laughter ran through the crowd as the people stirred back into position after Mrs. Hutchinson's arrival.

"Well, now," Mr. Summers said soberly, "guess we better get started, get this over with, so's we can go back to work. Anybody ain't here?"   10

"Dunbar." several people said. "Dunbar, Dunbar."

Mr. Summers consulted his list. "Clyde Dunbar," he said. "That's right. He's broke his leg, hasn't he? Who's drawing for him?"

"Me, I guess," a woman said, and Mr. Summers turned to look at her. "Wife draws for her husband," Mr. Summers said. "Don't you have a grown boy to do it for you, Janey?" Although Mr. Summers and everyone else in the village knew the answer perfectly well, it was the business of the official of the lottery to ask such questions formally. Mr. Summers waited with an expression of polite interest while Mrs. Dunbar answered.

"Horace's not but sixteen yet." Mrs. Dunbar said regretfully. "Guess I gotta fill in for the old man this year."

15   "Right," Mr. Summers said. He made a note on the list he was holding. Then he asked, "Watson boy drawing this year?"

A tall boy in the crowd raised his hand. "Here," he said. "I'm drawing for m' mother and me." He blinked his eyes nervously and ducked his head as several voices in the crowd said things like "Good fellow, Jack," and "Glad to see your mother's got a man to do it."

"Well," Mr. Summers said, "guess that's everyone. Old Man Warner make it?"

"Here," a voice said, and Mr. Summers nodded.

A sudden hush fell on the crowd as Mr. Summers cleared his throat and looked at the list. "All ready?" he called. "Now, I'll read the names—heads of families first—and the men come up and take a paper out of the box. Keep the paper folded in your hand without looking at it until everyone has had a turn. Everything clear?"

20   The people had done it so many times that they only half listened to the directions: most of them were quiet, wetting their lips, not looking around. Then Mr. Summers raised one hand high and said, "Adams." A man disengaged himself from the crowd and came forward. "Hi, Steve," Mr. Summers said, and Mr. Adams said, "Hi, Joe." They grinned at one another humorlessly and nervously. Then Mr. Adams reached into the black box and took out a folded paper. He held it firmly by one corner as he turned and went hastily back to his place in the crowd, where he stood a little apart from his family, not looking down at his hand.

"Allen," Mr. Summers said. "Anderson. . . . Bentham."

"Seems like there's no time at all between lotteries any more," Mrs. Delacroix said to Mrs. Graves in the back row. "Seems like we got through with the last one only last week."

"Time sure goes fast,"Mrs. Graves said.

"Clark. . . . Delacroix."

"There goes my old man," Mrs. Delacroix said. She held her   25   breath while her husband went forward.

"Dunbar," Mr. Summers said, and Mrs. Dunbar went steadily to the box while one of the women said. "Go on, Janey," and another said, "There she goes."

. . . all through the crowd there were men holding the small folded papers. . . .

"We're next," Mrs. Graves said. She watched while Mr. Graves came around from the side of the box, greeted Mr. Summers gravely and selected a slip of paper from the box. By now, all through the crowd there were men holding the small folded papers in their large hands, turning them over and over nervously. Mrs. Dunbar and her two sons stood together, Mrs. Dunbar holding the slip of paper.

"Harburt. . . . Hutchinson."

"Get up there, Bill," Mrs. Hutchinson said, and the people near her laughed.

"Jones."   30

"They do say," Mr. Adams said to Old Man Warner, who stood next to him, "that over in the north village they're talking of giving up the lottery."

Old Man Warner snorted. "Pack of crazy fools," he said. "Listening to the young folks, nothing's good enough for them. Next thing you know, they'll be wanting to go back to living in caves, nobody work any more, live *that* way for a while. Used to be a saying about 'Lottery in June, corn be heavy soon.' First thing you know, we'd all be eating stewed chickweed and acorns. There's *always* been a lottery," he added petulantly. "Bad enough to see young Joe Summers up there joking with everybody."

"Some places have already quit lotteries," Mrs. Adams said.

"Nothing but trouble in *that*," Old Man Warner said stoutly. "Pack of young fools."

"Martin." And Bobby Martin watched his father go forward.   35   "Overdyke. . . . Percy."

"I wish they'd hurry," Mrs. Dunbar said to her older son. "I wish they'd hurry."

"They're almost through," her son said.

"You get ready to run tell Dad," Mrs. Dunbar said.

Mr. Summers called his own name and then stepped forward precisely and selected a slip from the box. Then he called, "Warner."

"Seventy-seventh year I been in the lottery," Old Man Warner   40   said as he went through the crowd. "Seventy-seventh time."

"Watson." The tall boy came awkwardly through the crowd. Someone said, "Don't be nervous, Jack," and Mr. Summers said, "Take your time, son."

"Zanini."

After that, there was a long pause, a breathless pause, until Mr. Summers, holding his slip of paper in the air, said, "All right, fellows." For a minute, no one moved, and then all the slips of paper were opened. Suddenly, all the women began to speak at once, saying, "Who is it?," "Who's got it?," "Is it the Dunbars?," "Is it the Watsons?" Then the voices began to say, "It's Hutchinson. It's Bill," "Bill Hutchinson's got it."

"Go tell your father," Mrs. Dunbar said to her older son.

45 People began to look around to see the Hutchinsons. Bill Hutchinson was standing quiet, staring down at the paper in his hand. Suddenly, Tessie Hutchinson shouted to Mr. Summers. "You didn't give him time enough to take any paper he wanted. I saw you. It wasn't fair!"

"Be a good sport, Tessie." Mrs. Delacroix called, and Mrs. Graves said, "All of us took the same chance."

"Shut up, Tessie," Bill Hutchinson said.

"Well, everyone," Mr. Summers said, "that was done pretty fast, and now we've got to be hurrying a little more to get done in time." He consulted his next list. "Bill," he said, "you draw for the Hutchinson family. You got any other households in the Hutchinsons?"

"There's Don and Eva," Mrs. Hutchinson yelled. "Make *them* take their chance!"

50 "Daughters draw with their husbands' families, Tessie," Mr. Summers said gently. "You know that as well as anyone else."

"It wasn't *fair,*" Tessie said.

"I guess not, Joe." Bill Hutchinson said regretfully. "My daughter draws with her husband's family, that's only fair. And I've got no other family except the kids."

"Then, as far as drawing for families is concerned, it's you," Mr. Summers said in explanation, "and as far as drawing for households is concerned, that's you, too. Right?"

"Right," Bill Hutchinson said.

55 "How many kids, Bill?" Mr. Summers asked formally.

"Three," Bill Hutchinson said. "There's Bill, Jr., and Nancy, and little Dave. And Tessie and me."

"All right, then," Mr. Summers said. "Harry, you got their tickets back?"

Mr. Graves nodded and held up the slips of paper. "Put them in the box, then," Mr. Summers directed. "Take Bill's and put it in."

"I think we ought to start over," Mrs. Hutchinson said, as quietly as she could. "I tell you it wasn't *fair.* You didn't give him time enough to choose. *Every*body saw that."

60 Mr. Graves had selected the five slips and put them in the box, and he dropped all the papers but those onto the ground, where the breeze caught them and lifted them off.

The pile of stones . . . was ready. . . .

"Listen, everybody," Mrs. Hutchinson was saying to the people around her.

"Ready, Bill?" Mr. Summers asked, and Bill Hutchinson, with one quick glance around at his wife and children, nodded.

"Remember," Mr. Summers said, "take the slips and keep them folded until each person has taken one. Harry, you help little Dave." Mr. Graves took the hand of the little boy, who came willingly with him up to the box. "Take a paper out of the box, Davy," Mr. Summers said. Davy put his hand into the box and laughed, "Take just one paper," Mr. Summers said. "Harry, you hold it for him." Mr. Graves took the child's hand and removed the folded paper from the tight fist and held it while little Dave stood next to him and looked up at him wonderingly.

"Nancy next," Mr. Summers said. Nancy was twelve, and her school friends breathed heavily as she went forward switching her skirt, and took a slip daintily from the box. "Bill, Jr.," Mr. Summers said, and Billy, his face red and his feet overlarge, near knocked the box over as he got a paper out. "Tessie," Mr. Summers said. She hesitated for a minute, looking around defiantly, and then set her lips and went up to the box. She snatched a paper out and held it behind her.

"Bill," Mr. Summers said, and Bill Hutchinson reached into 65 the box and felt around, bringing his hand out at last with the slip of paper in it.

The crowd was quiet. A girl whispered, "I hope it's not Nancy," and the sound of the whisper reached the edges of the crowd.

"It's not the way it used to be," Old Man Warner said clearly. "People ain't the way they used to be."

"All right," Mr. Summers said. "Open the papers. Harry, you open little Dave's."

Mr. Graves opened the slip of paper and there was a general sigh through the crowd as he held it up and everyone could see that it was blank. Nancy and Bill, Jr,. opened theirs at the same time, and both beamed and laughed, turning around to the crowd and holding their slips of paper above their heads.

"Tessie," Mr. Summers said. There was a pause, and then Mr. 70 Summers looked at Bill Hutchinson, and Bill unfolded his paper and showed it. It was blank.

"It's Tessie," Mr. Summers said, and his voice was hushed. "Show us her paper, Bill."

Bill Hutchinson went over to his wife and forced the slip of paper out of her hand. It had a black spot on it, the black spot Mr. Summers had made the night before with the heavy pencil in the coal company office. Bill Hutchinson held it up, and there was a stir in the crowd.

"All right, folks." Mr. Summers said. "Let's finish quickly."

Although the villagers had forgotten the ritual and lost the original black box, they still remembered to use stones. The pile of stones the boys had made earlier was ready; there were stones on the ground with the blowing scraps of paper that had come out of the box. Mrs. Delacroix selected a stone so large she had to pick it up with both hands and turned to Mrs. Dunbar. "Come on," she said. "Hurry up."

75   Mrs. Dunbar had small stones in both hands, and she said, gasping for breath. "I can't run at all. You'll have to go ahead and I'll catch up with you."

The children had stones already, and someone gave little Davy Hutchinson a few pebbles.

Tessie Hutchinson was in the center of a cleared space by now, and she held her hands out desperately as the villagers moved in on her. "It isn't fair," she said. A stone hit her on the side of the head.

Old Man Warner was saying, "Come on, come on, everyone." Steve Adams was in the front of the crowd of villagers, with Mrs. Graves beside him.

"It isn't fair, it isn't right," Mrs. Hutchinson screamed, and then they were upon her.

IF YOU LIKED "THE LOTTERY," YOU MIGHT ALSO LIKE . . .

. . . another variation on torments in Charlotte Perkins Gilman's "The Yellow Wallpaper" (Chapter 12) or Edgar Allan Poe's "The Cask of Amontillado" (Chapter 10).

GOING FURTHER For a distinctive mix of realism and allegory you might read Thomas Pynchon's novels *V* and *The Crying of Lot 49* or Colson Whitehead's novel *The Intuitionist.*

D. H. Lawrence (1885–1930)

DAVID HERBERT LAWRENCE was born in the coal mining district of Eastwood, Nottinghamshire, in the center of England, his father a hard-drinking coal miner and his mother a schoolteacher. He attended high school there and went on to Nottingham University, from which he graduated in his early twenties with a teaching certificate. A few years later, after he had moved to London and taken up a teaching position, he came under the tutelage of writer and magazine editor Ford Madox Ford, who published Lawrence in the *English Review.* By 1910 Lawrence had published his first novel, *The White Peacock,* and was entirely committed to the writing life. After the death of his mother from cancer, he published his autobiographical masterpiece *Sons and Lovers* (1913), and this was followed by other major titles such as *The Rainbow* (1915), *Women in Love* (1920), *Aaron's Rod* (1922),

The Plumed Serpent (1926), and, perhaps most notoriously, *Lady Chatterley's Lover* (1928).

This last book created a scandal because of its frank sexuality as well as its discussion of class; the "lady's" lover is a gardener, a man beneath her standing in society. In his personal life, as well, Lawrence broke social taboos; he ran off with Frieda von Richthofen Weekley, the wife of his university language professor. Thus began a period of extended travel with only occasional trips back to England; after the end of World War I, he and Frieda embraced a life of self-imposed exile. Mediterranean Europe, Australia, North America, and Mexico became Lawrence's shifting home grounds. Upon his death from tuberculosis at the age of forty-four, he left behind one of the great modern bodies of work.

The Rocking-Horse Winner (1920)

1 There was a woman who was beautiful, who started with all the advantages, yet she had no luck. She married for love, and the love turned to dust. She had bonny children, yet she felt they had been thrust upon her, and she could not love them. They looked at her coldly, as if they were finding fault with her. And hurriedly she felt she must cover up some fault in herself. Yet what it was that she must cover up she never knew. Nevertheless, when her children were present, she always felt the centre of her heart go hard. This troubled her, and in her manner she was all the more gentle and anxious for her children, as if she loved them very much. Only she herself knew that at the centre of her heart was a hard little place that could not feel love, no, not for anybody. Everybody else said of her: "She is such a good mother. She adores her children." Only she herself, and her children themselves, knew it was not so. They read it in each other's eyes.

There were a boy and two little girls. They lived in a pleasant house, with a garden, and they had discreet servants, and felt themselves superior to anyone in the neighbourhood.

Although they lived in style, they felt always an anxiety in the house. There was never enough money. The mother had a small income, and the father had a small income, but not nearly enough for the social position which they had to keep up. The father went into town to some office. But though he had good prospects, these prospects never materialised. There was always the grinding sense of the shortage of money, though the style was always kept up.

At last the mother said: "I will see if I can't make something." But she did not know where to begin. She racked her brains, and tried this thing and the other, but could not find anything successful. The failure made deep lines come into her face. Her children were growing up, they would have to go to school. There must be more money, there must be more money. The father, who was always very handsome and expensive in his tastes, seemed as if he never *would* be able to do anything worth doing. And the mother, who had a great belief in herself, did not succeed any better, and her tastes were just as expensive.

5 And so the house came to be haunted by the unspoken phrase: *There must be more money! There must be more money!* The children could hear it all the time though nobody said it aloud. They heard it at Christmas, when the expensive and splendid toys filled the nursery. Behind the shining modern rocking-horse, behind the smart doll's house, a voice would start whispering: "There *must* be more money! There *must* be more money!" And the children would stop playing, to listen for a moment. They would look into each other's eyes, to see if they had all heard. And each one saw in the eyes of the other two that they too had heard. "There *must* be more money! There *must* be more money!"

It came whispering from the springs of the still-swaying rocking-horse, and even the horse, bending his wooden, champing head, heard it. The big doll, sitting so pink and smirking in her new pram, could hear it quite plainly, and seemed to be smirking all the more self-consciously because of it. The foolish puppy, too, that took the place of the teddy-bear, he was looking so extraordinarily foolish for no other reason but that he heard the secret whisper all over the house: "There *must* be more money!"

Yet nobody ever said it aloud. The whisper was everywhere, and therefore no one spoke it. Just as no one ever says: "We are breathing!" in spite of the fact that breath is coming and going all the time.

"Mother," said the boy Paul one day, "why don't we keep a car of our own? Why do we always use uncle's, or else a taxi?"

"Because we're the poor members of the family," said the mother.

"But why *are* we, mother?"

10 "Well—I suppose," she said slowly and bitterly, "it's because your father has no luck."

The boy was silent for some time.

"Is luck money, mother?" he asked, rather timidly.

"No, Paul. Not quite. It's what causes you to have money."

"Oh!" said Paul vaguely. "I thought when Uncle Oscar said 15 *filthy lucker,* it meant money."

"*Filthy lucre* does mean money," said the mother. "But it's lucre, not luck."

"Oh!" said the boy. "Then what *is* luck, mother?"

"It's what causes you to have money. If you're lucky you have money. That's why it's better to be born lucky than rich. If you're rich, you may lose your money. But if you're lucky, you will always get more money."

"Oh! Will you? And is father not lucky?"

"Very unlucky, I should say," she said bitterly. 20

The boy watched her with unsure eyes.

> . . . the house came
> to be haunted
> by the unspoken phrase:
> There *must* be more money!

"Why?" he asked.

"I don't know. Nobody ever knows why one person is lucky and another unlucky."

"Don't they? Nobody at all? Does *nobody* know?"

25 "Perhaps God. But He never tells."

"He ought to, then. And aren't you lucky either, mother?"

"I can't be, if I married an unlucky husband."

"But by yourself, aren't you?"

"I used to think I was, before I married. Now I think I am very unlucky indeed."

30 "Why?"

"Well—never mind! Perhaps I'm not really," she said.

The child looked at her to see if she meant it. But he saw, by the lines of her mouth, that she was only trying to hide something from him.

"Well, anyhow," he said stoutly, "I'm a lucky person."

35 "Why?" said his mother, with a sudden laugh.

He stared at her. He didn't even know why he had said it.

"God told me," he asserted, brazening it out.

"I hope He did, dear!" she said, again with a laugh, but rather bitter.

"He did, mother!"

"Excellent!" said the mother, using one of her husband's exclamations.

40 The boy saw she did not believe him; or rather, that she paid no attention to his assertion. This angered him somewhat, and made him want to compel her attention.

He went off by himself, vaguely, in a childish way, seeking for the clue to "luck." Absorbed, taking no heed of other people, he went about with a sort of stealth, seeking inwardly for luck. He wanted luck, he wanted it, he wanted it. When the two girls were playing dolls in the nursery, he would sit on his big rocking-horse, charging madly into space, with a frenzy that made the little girls peer at him uneasily. Wildly the horse careered, the waving dark hair of the boy tossed, his eyes had a strange glare in them. The little girls dared not speak to him.

When he had ridden to the end of his mad little journey, he climbed down and stood in front of his rocking-horse, staring fixedly into its lowered face. Its red mouth was slightly open, its big eye was wide and glassy-bright.

"Now!" he would silently command the snorting steed. "Now take me to where there is luck! Now take me!"

And he would slash the horse on the neck with the little whip he had asked Uncle Oscar for. He *knew* the horse could take him to where there was luck, if only he forced it. So he would mount again and start on his furious ride, hoping at last to get there.

> He *knew* the horse could take him to where there was luck. . . .

"You'll break your horse, Paul!" said the nurse. 45

"He's always riding like that! I wish he'd leave off!" said his elder sister Joan.

But he only glared down on them in silence. Nurse gave him up. She could make nothing of him. Anyhow, he was growing beyond her.

One day his mother and his Uncle Oscar came in when he was on one of his furious rides. He did not speak to them.

"Hallo, you young jockey! Riding a winner?" said his uncle.

"Aren't you growing too big for a 50 rocking-horse? You're not a very little boy any longer, you know," said his mother.

But Paul only gave a blue glare from his big, rather close-set eyes. He would speak to nobody when he was in full tilt. His mother watched him with an anxious expression on her face.

At last he suddenly stopped forcing his horse into the mechanical gallop and slid down.

"Well, I got there!" he announced fiercely, his blue eyes still flaring, and his sturdy long legs straddling apart.

"Where did you get to?" asked his mother.

"Where I wanted to go," he flared back at her. 55

"That's right, son!" said Uncle Oscar. "Don't you stop till you get there. What's the horse's name?"

"He doesn't have a name," said the boy.

"Gets on without all right?" asked the uncle.

"Well, he has different names. He was called Sansovino last week."

"Sansovino, eh? Won the Ascot. How did you know this 60 name?"

"He always talks about horse-races with Bassett," said Joan.

The uncle was delighted to find that his small nephew was posted with all the racing news. Bassett, the young gardener, who had been wounded in the left foot in the war and had got his present job through Oscar Cresswell, whose batman he had been, was a perfect blade of the "turf." He lived in the racing events, and the small boy lived with him.

Oscar Cresswell got it all from Bassett.

"Master Paul comes and asks me, so I can't do more than tell him, sir," said Bassett, his face terribly serious, as if he were speaking of religious matters.

"And does he ever put anything on a horse he fancies?" 65

"Well—I don't want to give him away—he's a young sport, a fine sport, sir. Would you mind asking him himself? He sort of takes a pleasure in it, and perhaps he'd feel I was giving him away, sir, if you don't mind."

Bassett was serious as a church.

The uncle went back to his nephew and took him off for a ride in the car.

"Say, Paul, old man, do you ever put anything on a horse?" the uncle asked.

70 The boy watched the handsome man closely.

"Why, do you think I oughtn't to?" he parried.

"Not a bit of it! I thought perhaps you might give me a tip for the Lincoln."

The car sped on into the country, going down to Uncle Oscar's place in Hampshire.

"Honour bright?" said the nephew.

75 "Honour bright, son!" said the uncle.

"Well, then, Daffodil."

"Daffodil! I doubt it, sonny. What about Mirza?"

"I only know the winner," said the boy. "That's Daffodil."

"Daffodil, eh?"

80 There was a pause. Daffodil was an obscure horse comparatively.

"Uncle!"

"Yes, son?"

"You won't let it go any further, will you? I promised Bassett."

"Bassett be damned, old man! What's he got to do with it?"

85 "We're partners. We've been partners from the first. Uncle, he lent me my first five shillings, which I lost. I promised him, honour bright, it was only between me and him; only you gave me that ten-shilling note I started winning with, so I thought you were lucky. You won't let it go any further, will you?"

The boy gazed at his uncle from those big, hot, blue eyes, set rather close together. The uncle stirred and laughed uneasily.

"Right you are, son! I'll keep your tip private. Daffodil, eh? How much are you putting on him?"

"All except twenty pounds," said the boy. "I keep that in reserve."

The uncle thought it a good joke.

90 "You keep twenty pounds in reserve, do you, you young romancer? What are you betting, then?"

"I'm betting three hundred," said the boy gravely. "But it's between you and me, Uncle Oscar! Honour bright?"

The uncle burst into a roar of laughter.

"It's between you and me all right, you young Nat Gould," he said, laughing. "But where's your three hundred?"

"Bassett keeps it for me. We're partners."

95 "You are, are you! And what is Bassett putting on Daffodil?"

"He won't go quite as high as I do, I expect. Perhaps he'll go a hundred and fifty."

"What, pennies?" laughed the uncle.

"Pounds," said the child, with a surprised look at his uncle. "Bassett keeps a bigger reserve than I do."

Between wonder and amusement Uncle Oscar was silent. He pursued the matter no further, but he determined to take his nephew with him to the Lincoln races.

"Now, son," he said, "I'm putting twenty on Mirza, and I'll put 100 five on for you on any horse you fancy. What's your pick?"

"Daffodil, uncle."

"No, not the fiver on Daffodil!"

"I should if it was my own fiver," said the child.

"Good! Good! Right you are! A fiver for me and a fiver for you on Daffodil."

The child had never been to a race-meeting before, and his 105 eyes were blue fire. He pursed his mouth tight and watched. A Frenchman just in front had put his money on Lancelot. Wild with excitement, he flayed his arms up and down, yelling *Lancelot!, Lancelot!* in his French accent.

Daffodil came in first, Lancelot second, Mirza third. The child, flushed and with eyes blazing, was curiously serene. His uncle brought him four five-pound notes, four to one.

"What am I to do with these?" he cried, waving them before the boy's eyes.

"I suppose we'll talk to Bassett," said the boy. "I expect I have fifteen hundred now; and twenty in reserve; and this twenty."

His uncle studied him for some moments.

"Look here, son!" he said. "You're not serious about Bassett 110 and that fifteen hundred, are you?"

"Yes, I am. But it's between you and me, uncle. Honour bright?"

"Honour bright all right, son! But I must talk to Bassett."

"If you'd like to be a partner, uncle, with Bassett and me, we could all be partners. Only, you'd have to promise, honour bright, uncle, not to let it go beyond us three. Bassett and I are lucky, and you must be lucky, because it was your ten shillings I started winning with. . . ."

Uncle Oscar took both Bassett and Paul into Richmond Park for an afternoon, and there they talked.

"It's like this, you see, sir," Bassett said. "Master Paul would 115 get me talking about racing events, spinning yarns, you know, sir. And he was always keen on knowing if I'd made or if I'd lost. It's about a year since, now, that I put five shillings on Blush of Dawn for him: and we lost. Then the luck turned, with that ten shillings he had from you: that we put on Singhalese. And since that time, it's been pretty steady, all things considering. What do you say, Master Paul?"

> **"I only know the winner," said the boy. "That's Daffodil."**

"We're all right when we're sure," said Paul. "It's when we're not quite sure that we go down."

"Oh, but we're careful then," said Bassett.

"But when are you *sure*?" smiled Uncle Oscar.

"It's Master Paul, sir," said Bassett in a secret, religious voice. "It's as if he had it from heaven. Like Daffodil, now, for the Lincoln. That was as sure as eggs."

120 "Did you put anything on Daffodil?" asked Oscar Cresswell.

"Yes, sir, I made my bit."

"And my nephew?"

Bassett was obstinately silent, looking at Paul.

"I made twelve hundred, didn't I, Bassett? I told uncle I was putting three hundred on Daffodil."

125 "That's right," said Bassett, nodding.

"But where's the money?" asked the uncle.

"I keep it safe locked up, sir. Master Paul he can have it any minute he likes to ask for it."

"What, fifteen hundred pounds?"

"And twenty! And *forty,* that is, with the twenty he made on the course."

130 "It's amazing!" said the uncle.

"If Master Paul offers you to be partners, sir, I would, if I were you: if you'll excuse me," said Bassett.

Oscar Cresswell thought about it.

"I'll see the money," he said.

They drove home again, and, sure enough, Bassett came round to the garden-house with fifteen hundred pounds in notes. The twenty pounds reserve was left with Joe Glee, in the Turf Commission deposit.

135 "You see, it's all right, uncle, when I'm *sure*! Then we go strong, for all we're worth, don't we, Bassett?"

"We do that, Master Paul."

"And when are you sure?" said the uncle, laughing.

"Oh, well, sometimes I'm *absolutely* sure, like about Daffodil," said the boy; "and sometimes I have an idea; and sometimes I haven't even an idea, have I, Bassett? Then we're careful, because we mostly go down."

"You do, do you! And when you're sure, like about Daffodil, what makes you sure, sonny?"

140 "Oh, well, I don't know," said the boy uneasily. "I'm sure, you know, uncle; that's all."

"It's as if he had it from heaven, sir," Bassett reiterated.

"I should say so!" said the uncle.

... sure enough, Bassett came round to the garden-house with fifteen hundred pounds in notes.

But he became a partner. And when the Leger was coming on Paul was "sure" about Lively Spark, which was a quite inconsiderable horse. The boy insisted on putting a thousand on the horse, Bassett went for five hundred, and Oscar Cresswell two hundred. Lively Spark came in first, and the betting had been ten to one against him. Paul had made ten thousand.

"You see," he said. "I was absolutely sure of him."

145 Even Oscar Cresswell had cleared two thousand.

"Look here, son," he said, "this sort of thing makes me nervous."

"It needn't, uncle! Perhaps I shan't be sure again for a long time."

"But what are you going to do with your money?" asked the uncle.

"Of course," said the boy, "I started it for mother. She said she had no luck, because father is unlucky, so I thought if *I* was lucky, it might stop whispering."

150 "What might stop whispering?"

"Our house. I *hate* our house for whispering."

"What does it whisper?"

"Why—why"—the boy fidgeted—"why, I don't know. But it's always short of money, you know, uncle."

"I know it, son, I know it."

155 "You know people send mother writs, don't you, uncle?"

"I'm afraid I do," said the uncle.

"And then the house whispers, like people laughing at you behind your back. It's awful, that is! I thought if I was lucky . . ."

"You might stop it," added the uncle.

The boy watched him with big blue eyes, that had an uncanny cold fire in them, and he said never a word.

160 "Well, then!" said the uncle. "What are we doing?"

"I shouldn't like mother to know I was lucky," said the boy.

"Why not, son?"

"She'd stop me."

"I don't think she would."

165 "Oh!"—and the boy writhed in an odd way—"I *don't* want her to know, uncle."

"All right, son! We'll manage it without her knowing."

They managed it very easily. Paul, at the other's suggestion, handed over five thousand pounds to his uncle, who deposited it with the family lawyer, who was then to inform Paul's mother that a relative had put five thousand pounds into his hands, which sum was to be paid out a thousand pounds at a time, on the mother's birthday, for the next five years.

"So she'll have a birthday present of a thousand pounds for five successive years," said Uncle Oscar. "I hope it won't make it all the harder for her later."

Paul's mother had her birthday in November. The house had been "whispering" worse than ever lately, and, even in spite of his luck, Paul could not bear up against it. He was very anxious to see the effect of the birthday letter, telling his mother about the thousand pounds.

170   When there were no visitors, Paul now took his meals with his parents, as he was beyond the nursery control. His mother went into town nearly every day. She had discovered that she had an odd knack of sketching furs and dress materials, so she worked secretly in the studio of a friend who was the chief "artist" for the leading drapers. She drew the figures of ladies in furs and ladies in silk and sequins for the newspaper advertisements. This young woman artist earned several thousand pounds a year, but Paul's mother only made several hundreds, and she was again dissatisfied. She so wanted to be first in something, and she did not succeed, even in making sketches for drapery advertisements.

She was down to breakfast on the morning of her birthday. Paul watched her face as she read her letters. He knew the lawyer's letter. As his mother read it, her face hardened and became more expressionless. Then a cold, determined look came on her mouth. She hid the letter under the pile of others, and said not a word about it.

"Didn't you have anything nice in the post for your birthday, mother?" said Paul.

"Quite moderately nice," she said, her voice cold and hard and absent.

She went away to town without saying more.

175   But in the afternoon Uncle Oscar appeared. He said Paul's mother had had a long interview with the lawyer, asking if the whole five thousand could not be advanced at once, as she was in debt.

"What do you think, uncle?" said the boy.

"I leave it to you, son."

"Oh, let her have it, then! We can get some more with the other," said the boy.

"A bird in the hand is worth two in the bush, laddie!" said Uncle Oscar.

180   "But I'm sure to *know* for the Grand National; or the Lincolnshire; or else the Derby. I'm sure to know for *one* of them," said Paul.

So Uncle Oscar signed the agreement, and Paul's mother touched the whole five thousand. Then something very curious happened. The voices in the house suddenly went mad, like a chorus of frogs on a spring evening. There were certain new furnishings, and Paul had a tutor. He was *really* going to Eton, his father's school, in the following autumn. There were flowers in the winter, and a blossoming of the luxury Paul's mother had been used to. And yet the voices in the house, behind the sprays of mimosa and almond-blossom, and from under the piles of iridescent cushions, simply trilled and screamed in a sort of ecstasy: "There *must* be more money! Oh-h-h; there *must* be more money. Oh, now, now-w! Now-w-w—there *must* be more money!—more than ever! More than ever!"

It frightened Paul terribly. He studied away at his Latin and Greek with his tutor. But his intense hours were spent with Bassett. The Grand National had gone by: he had not "known," and had lost a hundred pounds. Summer was at hand. He was in agony for the Lincoln. But even for the Lincoln he didn't "know," and he lost fifty pounds. He became wild-eyed and strange, as if something were going to explode in him.

"Let it alone, son! Don't you bother about it!" urged Uncle Oscar. But it was as if the boy couldn't really hear what his uncle was saying.

"I've got to know for the Derby! I've got to know for the Derby!" the child reiterated, his big blue eyes blazing with a sort of madness.

His mother noticed how overwrought he was.   185

"You'd better go to the seaside. Wouldn't you like to go now to the seaside, instead of waiting? I think you'd better," she said, looking down at him anxiously, her heart curiously heavy because of him.

But the child lifted his uncanny blue eyes.

"I couldn't possibly go before the Derby, mother!" he said. "I couldn't possibly!"

"Why not?" she said, her voice becoming heavy when she was opposed. "Why not? You can still go from the seaside to see the Derby with your Uncle Oscar, if that that's what you wish. No need for you to wait here. Besides, I think you care too much about these races. It's a bad sign. My family has been a gambling family, and you won't know till you grow up how much damage it has done. But it has done damage. I shall have to send Bassett away, and ask Uncle Oscar not to talk racing to you, unless you promise to be reasonable about it: go away to the seaside and forget it. You're all nerves!"

"I'll do what you like, mother, so long as you don't send me   190 away till after the Derby," the boy said.

"Send you away from where? Just from this house?"

"Yes," he said, gazing at her.

"Why, you curious child, what makes you care about this house so much, suddenly? I never knew you loved it."

He gazed at her without speaking. He had a secret within a secret, something he had not divulged, even to Bassett or to his Uncle Oscar.

195 But his mother, after standing undecided and a little bit sullen for some moments, said:

"Very well, then! Don't go to the seaside till after the Derby, if you don't wish it. But promise me you won't think so much about horse-racing and *events* as you call them!"

"Oh no," said the boy casually. "I won't think much about them, mother. You needn't worry. I wouldn't worry, mother, if I were you."

"If you were me and I were you," said his mother, "I wonder what we *should* do!"

"But you know you needn't worry, mother, don't you?" the boy repeated.

200 "I should be awfully glad to know it," she said wearily.

"Oh, well, you *can*, you know. I mean, you *ought* to know you needn't worry," he insisted.

"Ought I? Then I'll see about it," she said.

Paul's secret of secrets was his wooden horse, that which had no name. Since he was emancipated from a nurse and a nursery-governess, he had had his rocking-horse removed to his own bedroom at the top of the house.

"Surely you're too big for a rocking-horse!" his mother had remonstrated.

205 "Well, you see, mother, till I can have a *real* horse, I like to have *some* sort of animal about," had been his quaint answer.

"Do you feel he keeps you company?" she laughed.

"Oh yes! He's very good, he always keeps me company, when I'm there," said Paul.

So the horse, rather shabby, stood in an arrested prance in the boy's bedroom.

The Derby was drawing near, and the boy grew more and more tense. He hardly heard what was spoken to him, he was very frail, and his eyes were really uncanny. His mother had sudden strange seizures of uneasiness about him. Sometimes, for half an hour, she would feel a sudden anxiety about him that was almost anguish. She wanted to rush to him at once, and know he was safe.

210 Two nights before the Derby, she was at a big party in town, when one of her rushes of anxiety about her boy, her firstborn, gripped her heart till she could hardly speak. She fought with the feeling, might and main, for she believed in common sense. But it was too strong. She had to leave the dance and go downstairs to telephone to the country. The children's nursery-governess was terribly surprised and startled at being rung up in the night.

"Are the children all right, Miss Wilmot?"

"Oh yes, they are quite all right."

"Master Paul? Is he all right?"

"He went to bed as right as a trivet. Shall I run up and look at him?"

"No," said Paul's mother reluctantly. "No! Don't trouble. It's 215 all right. Don't sit up. We shall be home fairly soon." She did not want her son's privacy intruded upon.

"Very good," said the governess.

It was about one o'clock when Paul's mother and father drove up to their house. All was still. Paul's mother went to her room and slipped off her white fur cloak. She had told her maid not to wait up for her. She heard her husband downstairs, mixing a whisky and soda.

And then, because of the strange anxiety at her heart, she stole upstairs to her son's room. Noiselessly she went along the upper corridor. Was there a faint noise? What was it?

She stood, with arrested muscles, outside his door, listening. There was a strange, heavy, and yet not loud noise. Her heart stood still. It was a soundless noise, yet rushing and powerful. Something huge, in violent, hushed motion. What was it? What in God's name was it? She ought to know. She felt that she knew the noise. She knew what it was.

Yet she could not place it. She couldn't say what it was. And 220 on and on it went, like a madness.

Softly, frozen with anxiety and fear, she turned the door-handle.

The room was dark. Yet in the space near the window, she heard and saw something plunging to and fro. She gazed in fear and amazement.

Then suddenly she switched on the light, and saw her son, in his green pyjamas, madly surging on the rocking-horse. The blaze of light suddenly lit him up, as he urged the wooden horse, and lit her up, as she stood, blonde, in her dress of pale green and crystal, in the doorway.

"Paul!" she cried. "Whatever are you doing?"

"It's Malabar!" he screamed in a powerful, strange voice. "It's 225 Malabar!"

His eyes blazed at her for one strange and senseless second, as he ceased urging his wooden horse. Then he fell with a crash to the ground, and she, all her tormented motherhood flooding upon her, rushed to gather him up.

But he was unconscious, and unconscious he remained, with some brain-fever. He talked and tossed, and his mother sat stonily by his side.

"Malabar! It's Malabar! Bassett, Bassett, I *know*! It's Malabar!"

So the child cried, trying to get up and urge the rocking-horse that gave him his inspiration.

230   "What does he mean by Malabar?" asked the heart-frozen mother.

"I don't know," said the father stonily.

"What does he mean by Malabar?" she asked her brother Oscar.

"It's one of the horses running for the Derby," was the answer.

And, in spite of himself, Oscar Cresswell spoke to Bassett, and himself put a thousand on Malabar: at fourteen to one.

235   The third day of the illness was critical: they were waiting for a change. The boy, with his rather long, curly hair, was tossing ceaselessly on the pillow. He neither slept nor regained consciousness, and his eyes were like blue stones. His mother sat, feeling her heart had gone, turned actually into a stone.

In the evening Oscar Cresswell did not come, but Bassett sent a message, saying could he come up for one moment, just one moment? Paul's mother was very angry at the intrusion, but on second thought she agreed. The boy was the same. Perhaps Bassett might bring him to consciousness.

The gardener, a shortish fellow with a little brown moustache and sharp little brown eyes, tiptoed into the room, touched his imaginary cap to Paul's mother, and stole to the bedside, staring with glittering, smallish eyes at the tossing, dying child.

"Master Paul!" he whispered. "Master Paul! Malabar came in first all right, a clean win. I did as you told me. You've made over seventy thousand pounds, you have; you've got over eighty thousand. Malabar came in all right, Master Paul."

"Malabar! Malabar! Did I say Malabar, mother? Did I say Malabar? Do you think I'm lucky, mother? I knew Malabar, didn't I? Over eighty thousand pounds! I call that lucky, don't you, mother? Over eighty thousand pounds! I knew, didn't I know I knew? Malabar came in all right. If I ride my horse till I'm sure, then I tell you, Bassett, you can go as high as you like. Did you go for all you were worth, Bassett?"

"I went a thousand on it, Master Paul."   240

"I never told you, mother, that if I can ride my horse, and get there, then I'm absolutely sure—oh, absolutely! Mother, did I ever tell you? I *am* lucky!"

"No, you never did," said his mother.

But the boy died in the night.

And even as he lay dead, his mother heard her brother's voice saying to her, "My God, Hester, you're eighty-odd thousand to the good, and a poor devil of a son to the bad. But, poor devil, poor devil, he's best gone out of a life where he rides his rocking-horse to find a winner."

IF YOU LIKED "THE ROCKING-HORSE WINNER," YOU MIGHT ALSO LIKE . . .
. . . other coming of age stories, such as John Updike's "A&P" (Chapter 6) and James Joyce's "Araby" (Chapter 8).

GOING FURTHER You can find the renewal of life in the cycle of death and birth at work in D. H. Lawrence's many books, from the early *Sons and Lovers* to later work such as *The Plumed Serpent,* his mystically tinged novel set in rural Mexico.

Ursula K. Le Guin (b. 1929)

ONE OF THE foremost writers of imaginative fiction in our time, Ursula K. Le Guin was born Ursula Kroeber in Berkeley, California. Her parents were the anthropologist Alfred Kroeber and the writer Theodora Kroeber, author of *Ishi.* Although Le Guin is widely known as a science-fiction writer, her most successful and best-known books—novels such as *The Left Hand of Darkness* (1969) and *The Dispossessed* (1974), and her short fiction in collections such as *The Wind's Twelve Quarters* (1975) and *The Compass Rose* (1982)—have always expressed a certain anthropological cast of mind reminiscent of her parents' scientific study of human habits and customs.

Few writers working in a particular genre—in Le Guin's case, science fiction—have had such success as a "crossover" writer, publishing stories in both popular and genre magazines, from *Galaxy* and *Fantasy & Science Fiction* to *The New Yorker,* and winning Hugo and Nebula awards for outstanding science fiction while garnering such prestigious literary prizes as the PEN/Malamud Award for Excellence in the Short Story.

Le Guin has also written many volumes of fantasy fiction, children's books, and essays.

The Kerastion (1994)

FOR ROUSSEL SARGENT, WHO INVENTED IT

1 The small caste of the Tanners was a sacred one. To eat food prepared by a Tanner would entail a year's purification to a Tinker or a Sculptor, and even low-power castes such as the Traders had to be cleansed by a night's ablutions after dealing for leather goods. Chumo had been a Tanner since she was five years old and had heard the willows whisper all night long at the Singing Sands. She had had her proving day, and since then had worn a Tanner's madder-red and blue shirt and doublet, woven of linen on a willow-wood loom. She had made her masterpiece, and since then had worn the Master Tanner's neckband of dried vauti-tuber incised with the double line and double circles. So clothed and ornamented she stood among the willows by the burying ground, waiting for the funeral procession of her brother, who had broken the law and betrayed his caste. She stood erect and silent, gazing towards the village by the river and listening for the drum.

She did not think; she did not want to think. But she saw her brother Kwatewa in the reeds down by the river, running ahead of her, a little boy too young to have caste, too young to be polluted by the sacred, a crazy little boy pouncing on her out of the tall reeds shouting, "I'm a mountain lion!"

A serious little boy watching the river run, asking, "Does it ever stop? Why can't it stop running, Chumo?"

A five-year-old coming back from the Singing Sands, coming straight to her, bringing her the joy, the crazy, serious joy that shone in his round face—"Chumo! I heard the sand singing! I heard it! I have to be a Sculptor, Chumo!"

5 She had stood still. She had not held out her arms. And he had checked his run towards her and stood still, the light going out of his face. She was only his wombsister. He would have truesibs, now. He and she were of different castes. They would not touch again.

Ten years after that day she had come with most of the townsfolk to Kwatewa's proving day, to see the sand-sculpture he had made in the Great Plain Place where the Sculptors performed their art. Not a breath of wind had yet rounded off the keen edges or leveled the lovely curves of the classic form he had executed with such verve and sureness, the Body of Amakumo. She saw admiration and envy in the faces of his truebrothers and truesisters. Standing aside among the sacred castes, she heard the speaker of the Sculptors dedicate Kwatewa's proving piece to Amakumo. As his voice ceased a wind came out of the desert north, Amakumo's wind, the maker hungry for the made—Amakumo the Mother eating her body, eating herself. Even while they watched, the wind destroyed Kwatewa's sculpture. Soon there was only a shapeless lump and a feathering of white sand blown across the proving ground. Beauty had gone back to the Mother. That the sculpture had been destroyed so soon and so utterly was a great honor to the maker.

The funeral procession was approaching. She heard or imagined she heard the drumbeat, soft, no more than a heartbeat.

Her own proving piece had been the traditional one for Tanner women, a drumhead. Not a funeral drum but a dancing drum, loud, gaudy with red paint and tassels. "Your drumhead, your maidenhead!" her truebrothers called it, and made fierce teasing jokes, but they couldn't make her blush. Tanners had no business blushing. They were outside shame. It had been an excellent drum, chosen at once from the proving ground by an old Musician, who had played it so much she soon wore off the bright paint and lost the red tassels; but the drumhead lasted through the winter and till the Roppi Ceremony, when it finally split wide open during the drumming for the all-night dancing under the moons, when Chumo and Karwa first twined their wristplaits. Chumo had been proud all winter when she heard the voice of her drum loud and clear across the dancing ground, she had been proud when it split and gave itself to the Mother; but that had been nothing to the pride she had felt in Kwatewa's sculptures. For if the work be well done and the thing made be powerful, it belongs to the Mother. She will desire it; she will not wait for it to give itself, but will take it. So the child dying young is called the Mother's Child. Beauty, the most sacred of all things, is hers; the body of the Mother is the most beautiful of all things. So all that is made in the likeness of the Mother is made in sand.

To keep your work, to try to keep it for yourself, to take her body from her. Kwatewa! How could you, how could you, my

> He and she were of different castes. They would not touch again.

brother? her heart said. But she put the question back into the silence and stood silent among the willows, the trees sacred to her caste, watching the funeral procession come between the flax-fields. It was his shame, not hers. What was shame to a Tanner? It was pride she felt, pride. For that was her masterpiece that Dastuye the Musician held now and raised to his lips as he walked before the procession, guiding the new ghost to its body's grave.

10   She had made that instrument, the kerastion, the flute that is played only at a funeral. The kerastion is made of leather, and the leather is tanned human skin, and the skin is that of the womb-mother or the foremother of the dead.

When Wekuri, wombmother of Chumo and Kwatewa, had died two winters ago, Chumo the Tanner had claimed her privilege. There had been an old, old kerastion to play at Wekuri's funeral, handed down from her grandmothers; but the Musician, when he had finished playing it, laid it on the mats that wrapped Wekuri in the open grave. For the night before, Chumo had flayed the left arm of the body, singing the songs of power of her caste as she worked, the songs that ask the dead mother to put her voice, her song into the instrument. She had kept and cured the piece of rawhide, rubbing it with the secret cures, wrapping it round a

> ## She had made that instrument, the kerastion, the flute that is played only at a funeral.

clay cylinder to harden, wetting it, oiling it, forming it and refining its form, till the clay went to powder and was knocked from the tube, which she then cleaned and rubbed and oiled and finished. It was a privilege which only the most powerful, the most truly shameless of the Tanners took, to make a kerastion of the mother's skin. Chumo had claimed it without fear or doubt. As she worked she had many times pictured the Musician leading the procession, playing the flute, guiding her own spirit to its grave. She had wondered which of the Musicians it might be, and who would follow her, walking in her funeral procession. Never once had she thought

that it would be played for Kwatewa before it was played for her. How was she to think of him, so much younger, dying first?

He had killed himself out of shame. He had cut his wrist veins with one of the tools he had made to cut stone.

His death itself was no shame, since there had been nothing for him to do but die. There was no fine, no ablution, no purification, for what he had done.

Shepherds had found the cave where he had kept the stones, great marble pieces from the cave walls, carved into copies of his own sandsculptures, his own sacred work for the Solstice and the Hariba: sculptures of stone, abominable, durable, desecrations of the body of the Mother.

People of his caste had destroyed the things with hammers,   15
beaten them to dust and sand, swept the sand down into the river. She had thought Kwatewa would follow them, but he had gone to the cave at night and taken the sharp tool and cut his wrists and let his blood run. Why can't it stop running, Chumo?

The Musician had come abreast of her now as she stood among the willows by the burying ground. Dastuye was old and skillful; his slow dancewalk seemed to float him above the ground in rhythm with the soft heartbeat of the drum that followed. Guiding the spirit and the body on its litter borne by four casteless men, he played the kerastion. His lips lay light on the leather mouthpiece, his fingers moved lightly as he played, and there was no sound at all. The kerastion flute has no stops and both its ends are plugged with disks of bronze. Tunes played on it are not heard by living ears. Chumo, listening, heard the drum and the whisper of the north wind in the willow leaves. Only Kwatewa in his woven grass shroud on the litter heard what song the Musician played for him, and knew whether it was a song of shame, or of grief, or of welcome.

IF YOU LIKED "THE KERASTION," YOU MAY ALSO LIKE . . .
. . . the use of the fantastic in Nathaniel Hawthorne's "Young Goodman Brown" (Chapter 14).

GOING FURTHER   The ranks of interesting American science-fiction writers are broad and deep. A British novelist who, like Le Guin, employs science-fiction motifs for other purposes is the prize-winning writer Jeanette Winterson, whose novel *The Stone Gods* (2008) crosses over into mainstream fiction.

Alice Walker (b. 1944)

ALICE WALKER WAS born in rural Georgia, attended Spelman College in Atlanta and Sarah Lawrence College in New York, and worked in New York City as a welfare worker before returning to the South in the midst of the turmoil of the Civil Rights movement. In the late 1960s and early 1970s she began to publish fiction and poetry. In 1982 her novel *The Color Purple* became a great critical as well as commercial success. Not only was it awarded the Pulitzer Prize for fiction, but it also became a movie directed by Stephen Spielberg. *The Color Purple* has become a central document in the literature of diversity—a book that celebrates black women in particular and the human spirit in general.

Alice Walker has lived for the past several decades in northern California.

Everyday Use (1973)

FOR YOUR GRANDMAMA

1   I will wait for her in the yard that Maggie and I made so clean and wavy yesterday afternoon. A yard like this is more comfortable than most people know. It is not just a yard. It is like an extended living room. When the hard clay is swept clean as a floor and the fine sand around the edges lined with tiny, irregular grooves anyone can come and sit and look up into the elm tree and wait for the breezes that never come inside the house.

Maggie will be nervous until after her sister goes: she will stand hopelessly in corners, homely and ashamed of the burn scars down her arms and legs, eyeing her sister with a mixture of envy and awe. She thinks her sister has held life always in the palm of one hand, that "no" is a word the world never learned to say to her.

You've no doubt seen those TV shows where the child who has "made it" is confronted, as a surprise, by her own mother and father, tottering in weakly from backstage. (A pleasant surprise, of course: What would they do if parent and child came on the show only to curse out and insult each other?) On TV mother and child embrace and smile into each other's faces. Sometimes the mother and father weep, the child wraps them in her arms and leans across the table to tell how she would not have made it without their help. I have seen these programs.

Sometimes I dream a dream in which Dee and I are suddenly brought together on a TV program of this sort. Out of a dark and soft-seated limousine I am ushered into a bright room filled with many people. There I meet a smiling, gray, sporty man like Johnny Carson who shakes my hand and tells me what a fine girl I have. Then we are on the stage and Dee is embracing me with tears in her eyes. She pins on my dress a large orchid, even though she has told me once that she thinks orchids are tacky flowers.

5   In real life I am a large, big-boned woman with rough, man-working hands. In the winter I wear flannel nightgowns to bed and overalls during the day. I can kill and clean a hog as mercilessly as a man. My fat keeps me hot in zero weather. I can work outside all day, breaking ice to get water for washing; I can eat pork liver cooked over the open fire minutes after it comes steaming from the hog. One winter I knocked a bull calf straight in the brain between the eyes with a sledge hammer and had the meat hung up to chill before nightfall. But of course all this does not show on television. I am the way my daughter would want me to be: a hundred pounds lighter, my skin like an uncooked barley pancake. My hair glistens in the hot bright lights. Johnny Carson has much to do to keep up with my quick and witty tongue.

But that is a mistake. I know even before I wake up. Who ever knew a Johnson with a quick tongue? Who can even imagine me looking a strange white man in the eye? It seems to me I have talked to them always with one foot raised in flight, with my head turned in whichever way is farthest from them. Dee, though. She would always look anyone in the eye. Hesitation was no part of her nature.

How do I look, Mama?" Maggie says, showing just enough of her thin body enveloped in pink skirt and red blouse for me to know she's there, almost hidden by the door.

"Come out into the yard," I say.

Have you ever seen a lame animal, perhaps a dog run over by some careless person rich enough to own a car, sidle up to someone who is ignorant enough to be kind to him? That is the way my Maggie walks. She has been like this, chin on chest, eyes on ground, feet in shuffle, ever since the fire that burned the other house to the ground.

10 Dee is lighter than Maggie, with nicer hair and a fuller figure. She's a woman now, though sometimes I forget. How long ago was it that the other house burned? Ten, twelve years? Sometimes I can still hear the flames and feel Maggie's arms sticking to me, her hair smoking and her dress falling off her in little black papery flakes. Her eyes seemed stretched open, blazed open by the flames reflected in them. And Dee. I see her standing off under the sweet gum tree she used to dig gum out of; a look of concentration on her face as she watched the last dingy gray board of the house fall in toward the red-hot brick chimney. Why don't you do a dance around the ashes? I'd wanted to ask her. She had hated the house that much.

I used to think she hated Maggie, too. But that was before we raised the money, the church and me, to send her to Augusta to school. She used to read to us without pity; forcing words, lies, other folks' habits, whole lives upon us two, sitting trapped and ignorant underneath her voice. She washed us in a river of make-believe, burned us with a lot of knowledge we didn't necessarily need to know. Pressed us to her with the serious way she read, to shove us away at just the moment, like dimwits, we seemed about to understand.

Dee wanted nice things. A yellow organdy dress to wear to her graduation from high school; black pumps to match a green suit she'd made from an old suit somebody gave me. She was determined to stare down any disaster in her efforts. Her eyelids would not flicker for minutes at a time. Often I fought off the temptation to shake her. At sixteen she had a style of her own: and knew what style was.

I never had an education myself. After second grade the school was closed down. Don't ask me why: in 1927 colored asked fewer questions than they do now. Sometimes Maggie reads to me. She stumbles along good-naturedly but can't see well. She knows she is not bright. Like good looks and money, quickness passes her by.

She will marry John Thomas (who has mossy teeth in an earnest face) and then I'll be free to sit here and I guess just sing church songs to myself. Although I never was a good singer. Never could carry a tune. I was always better at a man's job. I used to love to milk till I was hoofed in the side in '49. Cows are soothing and slow and don't bother you, unless you try to milk them the wrong way.

I have deliberately turned my back on the house. It is three rooms, just like the one that burned, except the roof is tin; they don't make shingle roofs any more. There are no real windows, just some holes cut in the sides, like the portholes in a ship, but not round and not square, with rawhide holding the shutters up on the outside. This house is in a pasture, too, like the other one. No doubt when Dee sees it she will want to tear it down. She wrote me once that no matter where we "choose" to live, she will manage to come see us. But she will never bring her friends. Maggie and I thought about this and Maggie asked me, "Mama, when did Dee ever *have* any friends?"

She had a few. Furtive boys in pink shirts hanging about 15 on washday after school. Nervous girls who never laughed. Impressed with her they worshiped the well-turned phrase, the cute shape, the scalding humor that erupted like bubbles in lye. She read to them.

"Mama, when did Dee ever *have* any friends?"

When she was courting Jimmy T she didn't have much time to pay to us, but turned all her faultfinding power on him. He *flew* to marry a cheap city girl from a family of ignorant flashy people. She hardly had time to recompose herself.

When she comes I will meet—but there they are!

Maggie attempts to make a dash for the house, in her shuffling way, but I stay her with my hand. "Come back here," I say. And she stops and tries to dig a well in the sand with her toe.

It is hard to see them clearly through the strong sun. But even the first glimpse of leg out of the car tells me it is Dee. Her feet were always neat-looking, as if God himself had shaped them with a certain style. From the other side of the car comes a short, stocky man. Hair is all over his head a foot long and hanging from his chin like a kinky mule tail. I hear Maggie suck in her breath. "Uhnnnh," is what it sounds like. Like when you see the wriggling end of a snake just in front of your foot on the road. "Uhnnnh."

Dee next. A dress down to the ground, in this hot weather. 20 A dress so loud it hurts my eyes. There are yellows and oranges enough to throw back the light of the sun. I feel my whole face warming from the heat waves it throws out. Earrings, too, gold and hanging down to her shoulders. Bracelets dangling and making noises when she moves her arm up to shake the folds of the dress out of her armpits. The dress is loose and flows, and as she walks closer, I like it. I hear Maggie go "Uhnnnh" again. It is her sister's hair. It stands straight up like the wool on a sheep. It is black as night and around the edges are two long pigtails that rope about like small lizards disappearing behind her ears.

"Wa-su-zo-Tean-o!" she says, coming on in that gliding way the dress makes her move. The short stocky fellow with the hair to his navel is all grinning and he follows up with "Asalamalakim, my mother and sister!" He moves to hug Maggie but she falls back, right up against the back of my chair. I feel her trembling there and when I look up I see the perspiration falling off her chin.

"Don't get up," says Dee. Since I am stout it takes something of a push. You can see me trying to move a second or two before I make it. She turns, showing white heels through her sandals, and goes back to the car. Out she peeks next with a Polaroid. She stoops down quickly and lines up picture after picture of me sitting there in front of the house with Maggie cowering behind me. She never takes a shot without making sure the house is included. When a cow comes nibbling around the edge of the yard she snaps it and me and Maggie *and* the house. Then she puts the Polaroid in the back seat of the car, and comes up and kisses me on the forehead.

Meanwhile Asalamalakim is going through the motions with Maggie's hand. Maggie's hand is as limp as a fish, and probably as cold, despite the sweat, and she keeps trying to pull it back. It looks like Asalamalakim wants to shake hands but wants to do it fancy. Or maybe he don't know how people shake hands. Anyhow, he soon gives up on Maggie.

"Well," I say. "Dee."

25 "No, Mama," she says. "Not 'Dee,' Wangero Leewanika Kemanjo!"

"What happened to 'Dee'?" I wanted to know.

"She's dead," Wangero said. "I couldn't bear it any longer, being named after the people who oppress me."

"You know as well as me you was named after your aunt Dicie," I said. Dicie is my sister. She named Dee. We called her "Big Dee" after Dee was born.

"But who was *she* named after?" asked Wangero.

30 "I guess after Grandma Dee," I said.

"And who was she named after?" asked Wangero.

"Her mother," I said, and saw Wangero was getting tired. "That's about as far back as I can trace it," I said. Though, in fact, I probably could have carried it back beyond the Civil War through the branches.

"Well," said Asalamalakim, "there you are."

"Uhnnnh," I heard Maggie say.

"There I was not," I said, "before 'Dicie' cropped up in our 35 family, so why should I try to trace it that far back?"

He just stood there grinning, looking down on me like somebody inspecting a Model A car. Every once in a while he and Wangero sent eye signals over my head.

"How do you pronounce this name?" I asked.

"You don't have to call me by it if you don't want to," said Wangero.

"Why shouldn't I?" I asked. "If that's what you want us to call you, we'll call you."

"I know it might sound awkward at 40 first," said Wangero.

"I'll get used to it," I said. "Ream it out again."

Well, soon we got the name out of the way. Asalamalakim had a name twice as long and three times as hard. After I tripped over it two or three times he told me to just call him Hakim-a-barber. I wanted to ask him was he a barber, but I didn't really think he was, so I didn't ask.

"You must belong to those beef-cattle peoples down the road," I said. They said "Asalamalakim" when they met you, too, but they didn't shake hands. Always too busy: feeding the cattle, fixing the fences, putting up salt-lick shelters, throwing down hay. When the white folks poisoned some of the herd the men stayed up all night with rifles in their hands. I walked a mile and a half just to see the sight.

Hakim-a-barber said, "I accept some of their doctrines, but farming and raising cattle is not my style." (They didn't tell me, and I didn't ask, whether Wangero (Dee) had really gone and married him.)

We sat down to eat and right away he said he didn't eat col- 45 lards and pork was unclean. Wangero, though, went on through the chitlins and corn bread, the greens and everything else. She talked a blue streak over the sweet potatoes. Everything delighted her. Even the fact that we still used the benches her daddy made for the table when we couldn't effort to buy chairs.

"Oh, Mama!" she cried. Then turned to Hakim-a-barber. "I never knew how lovely these benches are. You can feel the rump prints," she said, running her hands underneath her and along the bench. Then she gave a sigh and her hand closed over Grandma Dee's butter dish. "That's it!" she said. "I knew there was something I wanted to ask you if I could have." She jumped up from the table and went over in the corner where the churn stood, the milk in it clabber by now. She looked at the churn and looked at it.

> **"You must belong to those beef-cattle** peoples **down the road," I said.**

"This churn top is what I need," she said. "Didn't Uncle Buddy whittle it out of a tree you all used to have?"

"Yes," I said.

"Uh huh," she said happily. "And I want the dasher, too."

50 "Uncle Buddy whittle that, too?" asked the barber.

Dee (Wangero) looked up at me.

"Aunt Dee's first husband whittled the dash," said Maggie so low you almost couldn't hear her. "His name was Henry, but they called him Stash."

"Maggie's brain is like an elephant's," Wangero said, laughing. "I can use the churn top as a centerpiece for the alcove table," she said, sliding a plate over the churn, "and I'll think of something artistic to do with the dasher."

When she finished wrapping the dasher the handle stuck out. I took it for a moment in my hands. You didn't even have to look close to see where hands pushing the dasher up and down to make butter had left a kind of sink in the wood. In fact, there were a lot of small sinks; you could see where thumbs and fingers had sunk into the wood. It was beautiful light yellow wood, from a tree that grew in the yard where Big Dee and Stash had lived.

55 After dinner Dee (Wangero) went to the trunk at the foot of my bed and started rifling through it. Maggie hung back in the kitchen over the dishpan. Out came Wangero with two quilts. They had been pieced by Grandma Dee and then Big Dee and me had hung them on the quilt frames on the front porch and quilted them. One was in the Lone Star pattern. The other was Walk Around the Mountain. In both of them were scraps of dresses Grandma Dee had worn fifty and more years ago. Bits and pieces of Grandpa Jarrell's paisley shirts. And one teeny faded blue piece, about the piece of a penny matchbox, that was from Great Grandpa Ezra's uniform that he wore in the Civil War.

"Mama," Wangero said sweet as a bird. "Can I have these old quilts?"

I heard something fall in the kitchen, and a minute later the kitchen door slammed.

"Why don't you take one or two of the others?" I asked. "These old things was just done by me and Big Dee from some tops your grandma pieced before she died."

"No," said Wangero. "I don't want those. They are stitched around the borders by machine."

60 "That'll make them last better," I said.

"That's not the point," said Wangero. "These are all pieces of dresses Grandma used to wear. She did all this stitching by hand. Imagine!" She held the quilts securely in her arms, stroking them.

I did something I never had done before....

"Some of the pieces, like those lavender ones, come from old clothes her mother handed down to her," I said, moving up to touch the quilts. Dee (Wangero) moved back just enough so that I couldn't reach the quilts. They already belonged to her.

"Imagine!" she breathed again, clutching them closely to her bosom.

"The truth is," I said, "I promised to give them quilts to Maggie, for when she marries John Thomas."

She gasped like a bee had stung her. 65

"Maggie can't appreciate these quilts!" she said. "She'd probably be backward enough to put them to everyday use."

"I reckon she would," I said. "God knows I been saving 'em for long enough with nobody using 'em. I hope she will!" I didn't want to bring up how I had offered Dee (Wangero) a quilt when she went away to college. Then she had told me they were old-fashioned, out of style.

"But they're *priceless!*" she was saying now, furiously; for she has a temper. "Maggie would put them on the bed and in five years they'd be in rags. Less than that!"

"She can always make some more," I said. "Maggie knows how to quilt."

Dee (Wangero) looked at me with 70 hatred. "You just will not understand. The point is these quilts, *these* quilts!"

"Well," I said, stumped. "What would *you* do with them?"

"Hang them," she said. As if that was the only thing you *could* do with quilts.

Maggie by now was standing in the door. I could almost hear the sound her feet made as they scraped over each other.

"She can have them, Mama," she said, like somebody used to never winning anything, or having anything reserved for her. "I can 'member Grandma Dee without the quilts."

I looked at her hard. She had filled her bottom lip with check- 75 erberry snuff and it gave her face a kind of dopey, hangdog look. It was Grandma Dee and Big Dee who taught her how to quilt herself. She stood there with her scarred hands hidden in the folds of her skirt. She looked at her sister with something like fear but she wasn't mad at her. This was Maggie's portion. This was the way she knew God to work.

When I looked at her like that something hit me in the top of my head and ran down to the soles of my feet. Just like when I'm in church and the spirit of God touches me and I get happy and shout. I did something I never had done before: hugged Maggie to me, then dragged her on into the room, snatched the quilts out of Miss Wangero's hands and dumped them into Maggie's lap. Maggie just sat there on my bed with her mouth open.

"Take one or two of the others," I said to Dee.

But she turned without a word and went out to Hakim-a-barber.

"You just don't understand," she said, as Maggie and I came out to the car.

"What don't I understand?" I wanted to know.

"Your heritage," she said. And then she turned to Maggie, kissed her, and said, "You ought to try to make something of yourself, too, Maggie. It's really a new day for us. But from the way you and Mama still live you'd never know it."

She put on some sunglasses that hid everything above the tip of her nose and chin.

Maggie smiled; maybe at the sunglasses. But a real smile, not scared. After we watched the car dust settle I asked Maggie to bring me a dip of snuff. And then the two of us sat there just enjoying, until it was time to go in the house and go to bed.

IF YOU LIKED "EVERYDAY USE," YOU MIGHT ALSO LIKE . . .

. . . reading Georgia-born Alice Walker in the context of the case study on the American South in Chapter 15, with works by Flannery O'Connor, William Faulkner, and Ralph Ellison.

GOING FURTHER Succeeding generations of young, black short-story writers have made their mark on American literature, many of them looking to Walker as their mentor. One of the foremost of these is the Pulitzer Prize winner Edward P. Jones, author of *Lost in the City* (1992) and *All Aunt Hagar's Children* (2006).

GOING FURTHER ONLINE

Three casebooks for fiction with additional selections are also available online at **connect.mcgraw-hill.com.** For more on each of these casebooks and a complete listing of selections, see the table of contents at the front of this book.

- **Fiction into Film:** *Beowulf,* Jonathan Swift's *Gulliver's Travels,* and F. Scott Fitzgerald's *The Curious Case of Benjamin Button*
- **Masters of Craft:** Melville, Kafka, Tolstoy, Poe, Hawthorne, Bierce, Cather, London, O'Henry, and more
- **Contemporary Voices:** Ana Menendez, Danielle Evans, Valerie Laken, Nami Mun, and more

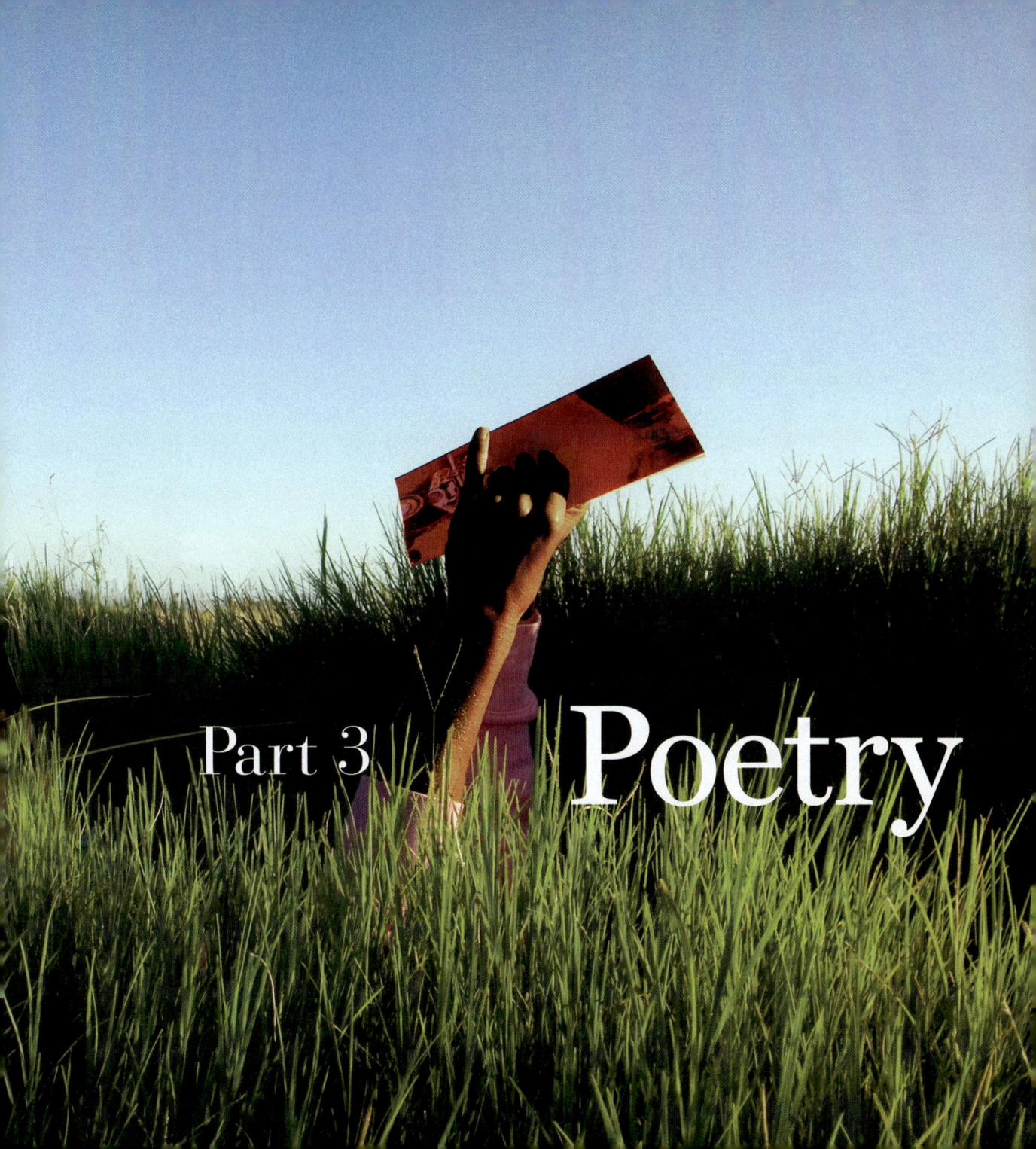

Part 3 Poetry

17 Reading a Poem in Its Elements

THIS is your museum of stones, assembled in matchbox and tin,
    collected from roadside, culvert, and viaduct,
battlefield, threshing floor, basilica, abattoir,
stones loosened by tanks in the streets
of a city whose earliest map was drawn in ink on linen,
schoolyard stones in the hand of a corpse,
pebble from Apollinaire's *oui*,
stone of the mind within us
carried from one silence to another . . .

—*from "The Museum of Stones," by Carolyn Forché*

NOWADAYS more people read fiction or go to the movies (our contemporary version of the theater) than read poetry. However, most writers think of poetry as the purest example of verbal expression; all of us acknowledge it as the mother form. Short stories and novels are relatively recent genres, but poetry has been a hallmark of civilization since civilization began. The earliest singers and bards expressed themselves in rhythm and rhyme long before prose was composed. When the first drum sounded or the first string was plucked, its verbal companion or accompaniment was what we have come to call verse.

Although we may be more familiar with the techniques of prose fiction, the language of poetry is often where we turn to better express the emotion of a great occasion or a deeply personal one. At weddings and funerals everywhere, poems are being recited; they remain the "touchstones" of experience relived. Carolyn Forché tells us that "The Museum of Stones" is a memorial tribute to a dead friend—a man who kept a collection of stones to remind him of his travels.

"The more we know about how a poem makes its rhythms and musics and patterings, the more deeply we can enter into the poem. It doesn't mean that we can't read the poem with great pleasure knowing very little about those matters, it means that we'll have much more pleasure if we know more."

Conversation with Carolyn Forché, available on video
at connect.mcgraw-hill.com

The long list of places where the stones in the poem were found provides a kind of encyclopedia of buildings seen and countries visited. This general human history is made vivid for the poet through personal loss. If we can open ourselves to the experience of reading poetry, its special language—its lists and repetitions—can touch our lives more deeply than ordinary speech.

A FIRST READING: "DUFFING INTO IT"

When reading a poem for the first time, remember: We may start anywhere. As the great American poet Robert Frost expresses it, "We *duff* into our first reading of a poem. We read that poem imperfectly (thoroughness with it would be fatal), but the better to read the second. We read the second the better to read the third. . . ." A "duffer" is a beginner, and everyone who reads a poem for the first time duffs his or her way into it.

All children are alive to rhyme, the pleasures of repeated sound, and it's one of the ways we learn language: *pretty* rhymes with *witty*, *hiss* with *kiss* or *miss*. (Think of those nursery rhymes that have remained intact across the ages.) When you read a poem for the first time, it's that childhood pleasure you're after. Notice the way words edge up against one another, the way they match and shift. Let your mind drift, enjoy the words, and listen to the sound of the lines. What do the sounds make you think of? What words stand out for you? What associations does the poem have?

In her interview, Carolyn Forché says "as the reader" you should read the first time "without a preconception." As you begin to read poems in this chapter, you will notice that some of them are easier to understand than others; some seem transparent with respect to their meaning, whereas others may appear flat-out incomprehensible. Some will please you; some will not. Upon first reading, don't make finding the poem's meaning your sole aim. The sound and the shape of a poem will be as important as the final interpretation.

CONTINUED ON PAGE 564

Carolyn Forché

You are as much this poem's important reader as the very first person who read it.

A Conversation on Writing

Reading Poetry

A poet will tell you this if you ask. They go where the poem takes them, and they don't know in advance where the poem is going when they are writing it the first time. They don't know what the poem is going to be about, often. They certainly don't know what its destination is. So, your experience as the reader is also to go without a preconception, and to enter the poem and to read freshly. You are as much this poem's important reader as the very first person who read it. Writing does not recur. The poem is written and finished and goes into the world. But reading recurs, and you are a fresh reader.

Interpreting Poetry

The poet is imagining you . . . and is attempting to become present to you and to celebrate your presence. . . . You are making a reading of the poem. If you are sitting in a circle of students, you will find that there might be six or seven different readings of this poem. Often the way to really solve the puzzle is to talk about all the different readings. Some of them might contradict each other and some of them might complement each other, but eventually you'll arrive at a full appreciation of what's before you on the page, and it's delightful.

The Story of "The Museum of Stones"

I had a friend who, when he was traveling around the world, decided that instead of going to souvenir shops . . . [he] would choose a little stone . . . from each place he visited. . . . He would put it on a little prong or block and he would label it. "Stone from beneath the Eiffel Tower, 1993, spring" . . . "Stone from the Banks of the Nile," "Stone from Hector's Garage in Illinois." You know, he had all kinds of different stones, and he called it his museum. I wrote this poem for him . . . after he died.

Known as a "poet of witness," Carolyn Forché (b. 1950)—a native of Detroit, Michigan—became a spokesperson for human rights through her poetry after traveling to El Salvador. Forché had a consciousness of atrocities from the time she was a young girl—she discovered a copy of *Look* magazine with pictures of the Holocaust, which her mother promptly hid—but it wasn't until her second book of poetry, *The Country Between Us* (1981), that she stirred controversy by dealing with political violence overtly. Her first collection, *Gathering the Tribes* (1976), won the Yale Series of Younger Poets Prize, and she has continued to receive prestigious awards and fellowships, including the Guggenheim and National Endowment of the Arts Creative Writing Fellowship. She has taught at George Mason University and Skidmore College; she now is a member of the faculty at Georgetown University.

To watch this entire interview and hear the author read from her work, go to connect.mcgraw-hill.com.

RESEARCH ASSIGNMENT Watch the interview and explain what Forché means when she says "form and content are intertwined." How does this relate to the word *stone* in the poem "The Museum of Stones"?

The Museum of Stones

(2007)

This is your museum of stones, assembled in matchbox and tin,
collected from roadside, culvert, and viaduct,
battlefield, threshing floor, basilica, abattoir,
stones loosened by tanks in the streets
5 of a city whose earliest map was drawn in ink on linen,
schoolyard stones in the hand of a corpse,
pebble from Apollinaire's *oui*,
stone of the mind within us
carried from one silence to another,
10 stone of cromlech and cairn, schist and shale, hornblende,
agate, marble, millstones, and ruins of choirs and shipyards,
chalk, marl, and mudstone from temples and tombs,
stone from the silvery grass near the scaffold,
stone from the tunnel lined with bones,
15 lava of the city's entombment,
chipped from lighthouse, cell wall, scriptorium,
paving stones from the hands of those who rose against the army,
stones where the bells had fallen, where the bridges were blown,
those that had flown through windows and weighted petitions,
20 feldspar, rose quartz, slate, blueschist, gneiss, and chert,
fragments of an abbey at dusk, sandstone toe
of a Buddha mortared at Bamiyan,
stone from the hill of three crosses and a crypt,
from a chimney where storks cried like human children,
25 stones newly fallen from stars, a stillness of stones, a heart,
altar and boundary stone, marker and vessel, first cast, lode, and hail,
bridge stones and others to pave and shut up with,
stone apple, stone basil, beech, berry, stone brake,
stone bramble, stone fern, lichen, liverwort, pippin, and root,
30 concretion of the body, as blind as cold as deaf,
all earth a quarry, all life a labor, stone-faced, stone-drunk
with hope that this assemblage, taken together, would become
a shrine or holy place, an ossuary, immovable and sacred,
like the stone that marked the path of the sun as it entered the human dawn.

"Everybody plays with language, with the rhythms of language as part of what they do, you know. It's sort of our fundamental act of learning." Conversation with Robert Hass

Writing from Reading

Summarize

1 List the stones included here and describe how "this assemblage, taken together," can help us to understand the world.

Analyze Craft

2 In her interview, Forché says, "In our culture it becomes more and more difficult for us to enter into, imaginatively at least, the consciousness of others. Literature is a way of doing that." How do you share in the speaker's experience of mourning by reading this poem? What in the poem makes that sadness clear?

3 Why do you think the speaker plays with the different *stone* words? What effect does the wordplay have on your reading of the poem?

4 Do the references to Apollinaire and Bamiyan require research on your part, or do they seem like private allusions?

Analyze Voice

5 In her interview, Forché also indicates that "The first level of [a poem's] meaning is simply to be moved and to hear a speaker, to hear a voice giving voice to what is within the poet." In this poem, does "your museum of stones" mean the poet is talking to herself, or is she addressing someone else, or both?

Synthesize Summary and Analysis

6 There is a great deal of information in this poem. Compare Forché's method of giving information with Tim O'Brien's listing technique in "The Things They Carried" (Chapter 14). In each instance, what is the effect of the writer's approach?

Interpret the Poem

7 Why do you think the poet uses the image of a "museum" in this poem? What about a museum lends additional meaning to the poem?

CONTINUED FROM PAGE 561

A CRITICAL READING

In ways we'll come to understand, poetry often manages to use everyday language in uncommon ways—to rise above the commonplace and avoid cliché. A thing that's said too frequently can feel unimportant, and if we repeat the same phrase again and again, its meaning empties out. Certain expressions—or words like *like*—come to us on automatic pilot, and we barely notice what we're saying or reading. When people say "No problem" now, they tend to mean "You're welcome," but neither of those phrases means precisely what the words say, and both of them get used with something less

"Be completely open—innocent, if you will, of the poem. Walk in, just like it's water, and say, 'What is this?' And read it over and over again. . . . [Read] with that kind of ignorant joy, and [let] yourself be bewildered when you're bewildered." Conversation with Marie Howe

than conscious attention to word choice. "Good-bye," for example, is a contraction of "God be with ye," but which of us who shouts "Good-bye!" is conscious of its original meaning? "Farewell"—a slightly more formal expression at parting—is also stripped of its resonance until we stop to think about what "fare well" might mean. To the poet—and poetry's careful reader—each word has its own history and every syllable counts.

Although such an assertion—that every syllable counts—seems simple and even self-evident, looking at a poem actually involves encountering a host of elements that the following chapters discuss in detail. No one element works in isolation from the others. Rather, rhythm depends on word choices, and word choices conjure up a speaker's voice; that voice will be inflected by the use of images, symbols, or figures of speech. These will be made shapely and arranged into a form, either a formal prescribed structure or one that emerges from the content and cadence of the words themselves. All these elements work together to create the effect the poem makes.

- Words are the language of poetry. To paraphrase Samuel Taylor Coleridge, a poet chooses "the best words" and puts them in "the best order" to describe an experience or feeling. Choices may be playful, lofty, direct, or unusual, and they lead directly to voice.

- Voice refers to every poem's speaker. The words and the order of the words that the poet chooses determine that speaker's tone of voice (stately, mournful, tender, angry). The speaker may or may not be the poet.

- Images in poetry transform the everyday thing that is experienced for itself into a vivid sensory impression.

- Symbols transcend the thing itself (a tree) and suggest a larger meaning (nature). Imagery and symbolism work in the service of word choice and tone of voice to generate emotion and establish the mood of the poem. Like language itself, they are a sign for something not present on the page.

- Figures of speech most commonly compare two unlike objects, such as "the sun" and "the face of the beloved," to condense and heighten the effect of language, particularly the effect of the imagery or symbolism used in a poem.

- Sound, the rhythmic structure of the lines that draws the reader in, often utilizes rhyme and is created through word choice and word order.

- Form, either formal or open, distinguishes poetry from prose through its arrangement in rhythmic lines of words.

As Carolyn Forché says in her interview, every reader gets to have a fresh reading. Forché also indicates that as her work on "The Museum of Stones" progressed, she went to the dictionary, to the thesaurus, to various sources of information on the sound and shape and look of these particular objects (she's not a geologist and had no previous expertise with rocks). The words became a kind of game for her, and she began to link three categories—animal, vegetable, and mineral—from the game "Twenty Questions." You do not need to know these things to read her poem critically, but do be mindful of the pleasure in the playfulness in the poet's language. Here is a sample reading of "The Museum of Stones" in which the reader looks at how the poet's choices helped create the experience of the first reading.

An Interactive Reading of "The Museum of Stones"

This is your museum of stones, assembled in matchbox and tin,
collected from roadside, culvert, and viaduct,
battlefield, threshing floor, basilica, abattoir,
stones loosened by tanks in the streets
of a city whose earliest map was drawn in ink on linen,
schoolyard stones in the hand of a corpse,
pebble from Apollinaire's *oui*,
stone of the mind within us
carried from one silence to another,
stone of cromlech and cairn, schist and shale, hornblende,
agate, marble, millstones, and ruins of choirs and shipyards,
chalk, marl, and mudstone from temples and tombs,
stone from the silvery grass near the scaffold,
stone from the tunnel lined with bones,
lava of the city's entombment,
chipped from lighthouse, cell wall, scriptorium,
paving stones from the hands of those who rose against the army,
stones where the bells had fallen, where the bridges were blown,
those that had flown through windows and weighted petitions,
feldspar, rose quartz, slate, blueschist, gneiss, and chert,
fragments of an abbey at dusk, sandstone toe
of a Buddha mortared at Bamiyan,
stone from the hill of three crosses and a crypt,
from a chimney where storks cried like human children,
stones newly fallen from stars, a stillness of stones, a heart,
altar and boundary stone, marker and vessel, first cast, lode, and hail,
bridge stones and others to pave and shut up with,
stone apple, stone basil, beech, berry, stone brake,
stone bramble, stone fern, lichen, liverwort, pippin, and root,
concretion of the body, as blind as cold as deaf,
all earth a quarry, all life a labor, stone-faced, stone-drunk
with hope that this assemblage, taken together, would become
a shrine or holy place, an ossuary, immovable and sacred,
like the stone that marked the path of the sun as it entered the human dawn.

Image: very violent—war; I'm picturing a dusty landscape.

Interpret: references to something outside the poem? What?

Image: suddenly really abstract, in the middle of all this physical imagery . . .

Interpret: a long list of rock types. Can picture a ruined shipyard, but a ruined choir?

Interpret: Is this a story or a progression of related images? What's tying it all together?

Words: Look up "scriptorium"— what do these three words have in common?

Words: another list of rock types . . . a break? or a type of momentum?

Sound: repetition of "s" sounds . . . slows the line down—emphasis?

Interpret: She is clearly not talking just about stones—"all earth, all life" means this is about everything.

Image: unexpected words . . . words for a person, not nature.

Interpret: Does "museum" equal "rock collection"?

Words: Look up "culvert" and "abbatoir." Why such complicated words?

Image: shift in image . . . tanks on rock to ink on cloth. Change to softer tone?

Words: types of rocks, I think—but why these? Sound of the words, maybe, more than the rocks themselves.

Words: "tomb" repeated, and lots of "grave" imagery. Is the collection a "museum" because something/someone has died?

Rhyme: "sandstone toe"—the sounds of the words are the same—almost a relief after the list of weird rock names.

Interpret: significance of two different religious references in a row?

Words: repetition of "stone"—gives the impression of hardness over and over, even though basil, beech, and berry are nice images. But then, liverwort, lichen, and bramble aren't so pretty.

Interpret: great image!—a stone catching the sunlight in the morning. But here, it's not just any morning—it's the beginning of the whole human race. So maybe even though there is so much death and war earlier, it shows these stones and the human race still go on? I never quite figured out who the poet was addressing—"this is *your* museum of stones." The textbook says it's a dead friend of the poet, but I didn't get many clues about the "you." Still, the poem seems less personal and more universal to me.

A CONTEXTUAL READING

Some of our most beautiful poetry was written in a different context from our own. A first reading can bring you close to the music of speech. A second critical reading can help you to see how the work has been constructed to achieve that music. Robert Frost has written that "the way to read a poem is in the light of all the other poems ever written." Understanding its tradition and context—the situation of, or reason for, the writing—also makes poetry richer. A contextual reading will situate the poem for you. As is the case with fiction or drama, poems hold clues to their meaning embedded in each line. But it helps to have some sense of what went before.

> **"You have to read the way a cook eats. How is it done? How is that put together?"** Conversation with Robert Pinsky

William Shakespeare, the "Bard of Avon," was at work four hundred years ago, and much of our language has changed. He was writing for *his* audience, and the Elizabethan diction (or choice of words) that he and they found natural no longer sounds natural to us. The Elizabethan language in the following poem goes against the grain of the modern ear, and its diction may present a barrier to understanding. The strategy behind the poem—especially the way Shakespeare praises his lady love's qualities by playing them down—may seem confusing as well. This interactive reading can provide some tips for understanding the words artists used in other centuries and seeing the craft at work in poetry outside our own day.

> **"When we read a poem maybe the mind of the reader is a kind of solvent, like you drop the DNA, which is the poem, in the mind of the reader, and the poem begins to blossom, to bloom with all these meanings. Of course the information I'm talking about in a poem isn't just data, and it's not necessarily biographical information. It's emotional information, spiritual information, soulful information, erotic information, intellectual information, all of that stuff packed into a poem."** Conversation with Li-Young Lee

An Interactive Reading of William Shakespeare's
"My mistress' eyes are nothing like the sun"

Paraphrase: My lover's eyes are different from the sun. *Different how?*

Words: Coral is bright . . . he's saying her lips are less bright than coral?

Voice: "be white" and "be wires" . . . this is how Elizabethans spoke naturally, ok.

Interpret: Black wires grow on her head? No roses in her cheeks? Not the romantic comparisons I expected from Shakespeare.

Words: ???—look this up. I think it's a patterned kind of linen.

Rhyme: same sounds as "cheeks" and "reeks"—ties all of it together.

Context: means "has." Sounds old-fashioned, but was it back then?

Interpret: This last line is hard. What does "any" refer to? Maybe any of his other loves: "my love is as rare as any other lover . . ."?

Words: Look up "belied." "False compare" is maybe short for comparison? So, a false comparison?

My <u>mistress</u>' eyes are nothing like the sun;

Coral is far more red than her lips' red;

If snow (be white,) why then her breasts are <u>dun</u>;

If hairs (be wires,) black wires grow on her head.

5 I have seen roses <u>damasked</u>, red and white,

But no such roses (see I) in her cheeks;

And in some perfumes is there more delight

Than in the breath that <u>from my mistress reeks.</u>

I love to hear her <u>speak</u>, yet well I know

10 That music <u>hath</u> a far more pleasing sound;

I grant I never saw a goddess go;

My mistress when she walks <u>treads</u> on the ground.

   And yet, by heaven, I think my love as rare

   As any she <u>belied</u> with <u>false compare</u>.

Figures of Speech: Poem seems to mostly be a list of comparisons.

Words: I don't know this word, but it must describe her body.

Rhyme: "dun" rhymes with "sun" here . . . and "red" rhymes with "head." I can hear the rhythm.

Rhyme: "white" and "delight"; "cheeks" and "reeks" . . . more rhyming words.

Voice: inverted words here . . . common back then, or done on purpose?

Context: "reeks"—does that mean the same thing in Shakespeare's time as now?!

Interpret: all these negative comparisons are funny—a poem making fun of love poems: an anti-love poem.

Interpret: not sure I get this line—a goddess go? go where?

Words: means walking, I guess. Elizabethan word.

Interpret: Last lines set apart—probably tie up the whole poem.

"I think my love as rare"—if something is rare, it's usually treasured because it's one of a kind. So . . . he's saying, "I think my mistress, whom I love, is one of a kind in a way that makes me value her."

"And yet" means "despite all that preceded." So, she's *different* from all the other poets' lovers . . . but he loves her because of that.

What Shakespeare suggests here is that too many poets indulge in "false compare." You don't need to belie the facts by comparing your mistress's eyes to the sun, her lips to coral, her body to snow—and so on and so forth. Her cheeks contain no actual roses; her breath is not actual perfume. She is *human*, not a goddess, and real love consists of recognizing and admitting this; the genuine commitment to truth telling is one of the hallmarks of art. It's not an accident that the two uses of the crucial word and the two phrases in which it's embedded—"I *love* to hear her speak" and "I think my *love* as rare . . ."—are reality based and straightforward in the choice of words.

THE CRAFT OF POETRY

Robert Burns is perhaps best known for his work with Scottish folk songs, and what we first notice in the seemingly simple work that follows is the rhythm and rhyme in the four-line stanzas of "O my luve's like a red, red rose." The poem is more a description of an emotion than an emotion itself. The only three-syllable word in the sixteen lines is "melodie"—a somewhat formal way of saying *song*. Burns wrote in Scottish dialect; the poem can be (and has been) set to music.

Robert Burns (1759–1796)

One of Scotland's greatest poets, Robert Burns was born to a struggling tenant farm family. At age fifteen, Burns fell in love and consequently wrote his first poem. He became notorious for his love affairs, which shocked the Calvinist society surrounding him, and he cultivated his poetry based on his own broad reading. Burns published *Poems* in 1786 and became immensely popular in Edinburgh. But perhaps his greatest achievement was his preservation and creation of folk songs, which he did formally for two anthologies, *The Scots Musical Museum* and *Select Collection of Original Scottish Airs*. Burns is known for writing in Scots, an English dialect spoken by commoners and by eighteenth-century nobility. Burns's songs are still widely known today, especially "Auld Lang Syne."

AS YOU READ   Note that the speaker addresses both his lover and an audience over her shoulder; the first stanza is a kind of general declaration, and the next three are specific to the "bonnie lass" herself.

O my luve's like a red, red rose (1794)

O my luve's like a red, red rose,
 That's newly sprung in June.
O my luve's like the melodie
 That's sweetly play'd in tune.

5 As fair art thou, my bonnie lass,
 So deep in luve am I;
And I will luve thee still, my dear,
 Till a' the seas gang dry.

Till a' the seas gang dry, my dear,
10 And the rocks melt wi' the sun;
And I will luve thee still, my dear,
 While the sands o' life shall run.

And fare thee weel, my only luve!
 And fare thee weel awhile!
15 And I will come again, my luve,
 Tho' it were ten thousand mile.

Writing from Reading

Summarize

1 If this poem is a declaration, what is the speaker declaring? How long does he indicate his love will last?

2 How far would he be willing to travel to see his love again?

Analyze Craft

3 Burns compiled and created Scottish folk songs in the Scots dialect. What about this poem seems musical to you?

4 What two things does the poet compare to his "luve" in the first stanza? What do those comparisons help him to accomplish in this poem? How does it set the stage for the rest of the poem?

5 When is the rose that he compares his love to "sprung"? Why would the month be significant?

Analyze Voice

6 What words does the speaker use that show how "deep in luve" he is?

Synthesize Summary and Analysis

7 Burns has chosen the form of a song to declare his love. How does this choice make his declaration convincing?

Interpret the Poem

8 Although the poem is clearly a love poem, how would you characterize the love here? Do we know why the speaker is leaving his lover? Do we need to?

Here's a very different kind of love poem—one written by a son to the memory of his father. For Robert Burns, the problem of "luve" is one of distance, and he promises he will return; for Robert Hayden, in the twentieth century, the distance is unbridgeable because his parent is dead. This is never made *explicit* in the fourteen lines that follow, but the sense of loss is *implicit* throughout, a muted if not mute regret that the poet failed to tell his father "Thanks."

Robert Hayden (1913–1980)

Born and raised in Detroit, Michigan, Robert Hayden had a childhood made difficult by his birth parents' separation and his informal adoption by the Hayden family. Encouraged in his intellectual efforts from a young age, Hayden earned a bachelor's degree from Wayne State University. He then worked for the Federal Writers' Project, published his first collection of poems in 1940, and married before earning his master's degree at the University of Michigan, where he studied with W. H. Auden. Of African-American descent, Hayden resisted a narrow view of his work as that of a "black" poet, even though it frequently engages with African American history and experience. Known for his formal poetry on a range of subjects—including historical figures such as Phillis Wheatley and Malcolm X—Hayden held the post of U.S. Poet Laureate from 1976 to 1978. Aside from poetry, Hayden made his career as a professor of English at Fisk University and the University of Michigan.

AS YOU READ Try to hear the speaker's tone of voice, the sorrow here expressed.

Those Winter Sundays (1962)

Sundays too my father got up early
and put his clothes on in the blueblack cold,
then with cracked hands that ached
from labor in the weekday weather made
5 banked fires blaze. No one ever thanked him.

I'd wake and hear the cold splintering, breaking.
When the rooms were warm, he'd call,
and slowly I would rise and dress,
fearing the chronic angers of that house,

10 Speaking indifferently to him,
who had driven out the cold
and polished my good shoes as well.
What did I know, what did I know
of love's austere and lonely offices?

Writing from Reading

Summarize

1 The poem's first two words are "Sundays too." These suggest that what the father does on Sunday morning he does the other six days of the week. What evidence do we have of the socio-economic circumstance of this family? Is there a furnace, for instance?

2 What might be some of "the chronic angers of that house"?

Analyze Craft

3 Imagine for a moment that the poem were written in the present tense.

Its title would be "These Winter Sundays," and the first line would report "my father gets up early." How does the use of the past tense instead suggest that these are memories and that "No one ever thanked him" means the speaker cannot do so now?

Analyze Voice

4 Notice the way the poet repeats his regretful, "What did I know, what did I know . . . ?" Does this provide a kind of emphasis, and if you were to read it aloud, where would the emphasis change?

Synthesize Summary and Analysis

5 We know that this is a Sunday and that the father polishes his son's "good shoes." Does this suggest the family will soon go to church?

Interpret the Poem

6 What does the poet mean by, and what do we learn about, "love's austere and lonely offices"? And why did Hayden choose to use that final word?

The twentieth-century American poet Ezra Pound writes in his eccentric but illuminating study *ABC of Reading*, "That poetry is best which is closest to music. . . ." Most people think of "lyric" as the words to a song, yet it is, in fact, a type of poetry, playing the same music from the ancient time of Sappho to the present moment: a song of love and loss. The speaker of the following fragment finds herself in darkness,

"I just was entranced by [the poetry] I read, and I read it with a kind of fury. I felt kind of saved by it. Then I began to read poems that made a tremendous difference to me; I felt almost as if I had written them." Conversation with Edward Hirsch

in the middle of the night. She yearns for company (with the presence in the visible sky of the constellation known as the Pleiades, or the Seven Sisters, suggesting it might be female company she desires). Here, too, the subject is isolation, some twenty-five hundred years before "Those Winter Sundays," and here, too, the context is different—but the tone of the two poems is in many ways the same.

Sappho (c. 630–570 B.C.E.)

Although much of what we know of her biography is speculation, we do know Sappho lived on the island of Lesbos in ancient Greece. She was exiled to Sicily for a time before returning to Lesbos, where she had a husband and daughter.

She also ran a school for girls. Sappho has been recognized throughout the centuries as the greatest ancient female poet, one whom Plato referred to as the "tenth muse" (in Greek mythology, there are nine). Her verse, which would have been sung to the accompaniment of the lyre, is direct and simple but overflows with emotion. Today, only fragments of Sappho's work survive, although in her lifetime, she very likely produced nine collections of poetry. Sappho died either of old age or, according to legend, by jumping off a cliff for love of Phaon, a young boatman.

AS YOU READ Notice the way the last line rises up and sweeps back against the first few lines, qualifying what went before.

A Fragment

(c. 600 B.C.E.)

The moon has set,
The Pleiades have gone,
Midnight, and the hours pass,
I lie in my bed alone . . .

—*adapted by* Alan Cheuse

Writing from Reading

Summarize

1 Where is the speaker, and what time is it?

Analyze Craft

2 What significance does the time have?

Analyze Voice

3 Who is the speaker? What is the speaker's lament?

Synthesize Summary and Analysis

4 What are the Pleiades? How do the night sky, the moon, and the Pleiades support the mood of the poem?

5 How would you describe the tone of the poem?

6 How does the setting of the poem reflect the loneliness of the speaker?

Interpret the Poem

7 These lines constitute only a fragment recovered from a longer work by Sappho. Many of her fragments, on similar themes, are all that we have of Sappho's work. Judging from this brief work, would you say the speaker's loneliness is temporary, or will it be relieved?

There is more than mere sentiment or sentimentality in Sappho's poem. Everyone feels this variety of loneliness at some point in a lifetime. The poet finds a way to give that shared emotion a particular expression. If Sappho had written "with you" as opposed to "alone," the whole feel of the poem would change, and the mood of melancholy would probably be supplanted by one of celebration. If the last line read "with my dog Spot" or "with my daughter" or "with a man I met an hour ago," the tone would also shift; each word *matters,* and the word "alone" gives the fragment its negative force.

William Wordsworth, the nineteenth-century British poet, defined the essence of a poem as "the spontaneous overflow of powerful feelings . . . recollected in tranquility." Traditionally, the lyric poem speaks of the poet's misery over the loss of love or the loss of his or her affections toward the object of his or her love. Wordsworth dramatizes, in the poem that follows, the process by which a past event becomes transformed. The poet can nonetheless remember from his "couch" what it felt like to be out on a hillside, surrounded by flowers. (This poem is also known by the alternative title "The Daffodils.") The twentieth-century American poet John Ciardi spoke about the movement at the end of a poem as the "wave" that doubles back and breaks against all the lines that come before it. By reconstructing what he felt, the poet helps us as readers feel it anew: an experience described is an experience shared.

William Wordsworth (1770–1850)

One of the major British Romantic poets, Wordsworth was born—and lived most of his life—in the Lake District of England. He and Samuel Taylor Coleridge developed a close friendship built on mutual admiration of each other's poetry. Together, they published *Lyrical Ballads* (1798), which contained one of Wordsworth's major poems, "Tintern Abbey" (Chapter 25). A poet with a deep reverence for nature and an interest in the individual, Wordsworth is known for his touchstone work, *The Prelude* (1850), a long autobiographical poem full of reflections on past emotions. Although Wordsworth grew in stature and was named British Poet Laureate in 1848, the quality of his poetry declined after 1810, perhaps because he relied on remembered emotions of his youth—an exhaustible resource—to fuel his poetry. Still, he shaped the course of British poetry with his famous "Preface" to *Lyrical Ballads,* in which he argued that poetry should be about emotions and everyday experience, rather than the intellect and classical forms—a dictum Wordsworth followed in his own work.

AS YOU READ Notice how perfect yet casual the rhyme appears to be. No one without conscious intention and considerable effort could shape past emotion into such a work of art.

I Wandered Lonely As a Cloud (1804)

I wandered lonely as a cloud
That floats on high o'er vales and hills,
When all at once I saw a crowd,
A host, of golden daffodils;
5 Beside the lake, beneath the trees,
Fluttering and dancing in the breeze.

Continuous as the stars that shine
And twinkle on the milky way,
They stretched in never-ending line
10 Along the margin of a bay:
Ten thousand saw I at a glance,
Tossing their heads in sprightly dance.

The waves beside them danced, but they
Out-did the sparkling leaves in glee;
15 A poet could not be but gay,
In such a jocund company;
I gazed—and gazed—but little thought
What wealth the show to me had brought:

For oft, when on my couch I lie
20 In vacant or in pensive mood,
They flash upon that inward eye
Which is the bliss of solitude;
And then my heart with pleasure fills,
And dances with the daffodils.

Writing from Reading

Summarize

1 What does the speaker mean by "that inward eye / Which is the bliss of solitude"?

Analyze Craft

2 Which words are formal here ("sprightly," "jocund," "pensive," and so forth) and which ones less so ("lonely," "twinkle," "pleasure," and so on)?

3 How do the words chosen in the rhymes convey a casualness that supports the idea of "wandering" on a hill?

Analyze Voice

4 Why does the speaker begin by mentioning he is lonely? Where does the tone change? What is the overall tone of this poem?

Synthesize Summary and Analysis

5 Where does the speaker locate himself in the first three stanzas; where is he in the fourth?

6 How does the loneliness in Wordsworth's poem compare with that in Sappho's?

Interpret the Poem

7 Why are daffodils a consolation?

Next come two examples of the art of "shaping" personal expression to suggest more than what the words say. In each case the poet addresses both the self and the reader, describing an encounter—with a body of water as well as a journey—in language that might seem casual but is carefully arranged. As the contemporary poet Mary Oliver writes in her *Rules for the Dance: A Handbook for Writing and Reading Metrical Verse*, "Every poem is music—a determined, persuasive, reliable, enthusiastic, and crafted music. Without an understanding of this music, Shakespeare is only the sense we can make of him; he is the wisdom without the shapeliness, which is one half of the poem."

Elizabeth Alexander (b. 1962)

Elizabeth Alexander is perhaps best known for reading her poem "Praise Song for the Day," at President Barack Obama's inauguration in 2008. The poem, which is based on the praise songs in the African oral tradition, exhibits Alexander's interest in experimenting with the vernacular, also keenly exemplified by her Twitter poem "Teeny tiny poem," which appeared in March 19, 2011, *New York Times Week in Review:* "Teeny tiny poem/ just enuf 2hold/1 xllent big word/*Impluvium*/open-eyed courtyrd/collectng rain/ as all poems do/skylife, open/birds do:/ tweet." Alexander was born in New York City and grew up in Washington, D.C. She received her B.A. from Yale University, her M.A. from Boston University (where she credits the Caribbean poet Derek Walcott with helping her see herself as a poet), and her Ph.D. in 1992 from the University of Pennsylvania. She published her first collection of poems, *The Venus Hottentot,* in 1990, where she laid down the themes of race, gender, and history that she would explore in her subsequent collections—collections which, in the words of the *Washington Post Book Review,* have a "graceful elegance and easy musicality."

Alexander's fourth collection of poetry, *America Sublime* (2005), was one of the American Library Association's "Notable Books of the Year" and was a finalist for the Pulitzer Prize. In 2007, she was the recipient of Poets & Writer's Jackson Prize for Poetry. Her most recent book of poems is *Crave Radiance* (2011). She is currently the chair of the African-American studies department at Yale University.

AS YOU READ   Look up the definitions of *cosmogram, gris gris,* and *hoodoo.* Note the references to charms and magic and African rituals commonly associated with slaves.

Emancipation (2005)

Corncob constellation,
oyster shell, drawstring pouch, dry bones.

Gris gris in the rafters.
Hoodoo in the sleeping nook.
5 Mojo in Linda Brent's crawlspace.

Nineteenth century corncob cosmogram
set on the dirt floor, beneath the slant roof,
left intact the afternoon
that someone came and told those slaves

10 "We're free."

Writing from Reading

Summary

1 What does "emancipation" mean for slaves?

2 Hoodoo magic is associated with God's providence, retribution, or justice in the religious rituals that American slaves adapted from Africa. In a June 24, 2001, *New York Times Magazine* article, "To Be a Slave in Brooklyn," Brent Staples writes about evidence, found in the roof of a Brooklyn house, of African rituals followed by slaves:

They pulled up the floorboards in the chimney room and found five corncobs arranged in what appeared to be a cross or star shape. . . . The cross formed by cobs suggests a cosmogram, a symbol known to anthropologists as a West African depiction of the cosmos. One line represents the boundary between the living and the dead and the other the path of power that connects these worlds. Archaeologists studying slave quarters in the Deep South have typically found African ritual items buried near fireplaces, which slaves viewed as the way spirits entered or left the house. . . . [In addition,] the team was excited to find a ritual collection of objects that included an oyster shell, half an animal pelvis bone and a cloth pouch tied with hemp. Slaves used them to manage spirits, which, if properly fed and handled, would carry out a range of acts.

List the references to hoodoo magic in the poem.

Analyze Craft

3 How would you say the casual cadence and simple and direct language affect the power of the poem?

Analyze Voice

4 What effect does the use of slang such as "Hoodoo" and "Mojo" have on the tone and music of the poem?

Synthesize Summary and Analysis

5 How do the references to images of corncobs, bones, and pouches—all references to voodoo—illuminate the theme of emancipation?

Interpret the Poem

6 In a November 27, 2005, *New York Times* review of the collection in which this poem is published, reviewer Joel Brouwer states, "The best moments are those in which present and past collide, sending off welcome sparks." How does Alexander's poem about the historical moment of emancipation relate to the present?

William Butler Yeats (1865–1939)

An Irish poet of unparalleled importance to twentieth-century English-language literature, William Butler Yeats spent his childhood in Dublin, Sligo, and London. Of a religious nature but not devoted to one religion, Yeats explored folklore, mysticism, and neoplatonism, which enabled him to create a set of unique symbols and imagery in his poems. Yeats managed to combine a sense of Romantic dreaminess with colloquialism, clarity, and Celtic influence, which makes his poetry unlike any other. Also unlike most other poets, Yeats perfected his style in his later years, bringing his talent to full fruition in collections such as *The Tower* (1928) and *The Winding Stair* (1933). Yeats led an active life, taking part in the movement for Irish nationalism and co-founding the Irish National Theatre, in addition to writing plays. He was awarded the Nobel Prize for literature in 1923.

AS YOU READ   Consider the poem in terms of time, not space. What refers to the past, the present, and what will happen in the future?

TIP

FOR INTERACTIVE READING . . .

Note each time the word *song* or *singing* is used. Track the changes in the way the word *song* is used in the poem.

Sailing to Byzantium (1927)

I

That is no country for old men. The young
In one another's arms, birds in the trees
—Those dying generations—at their song,
The salmon-falls, the mackerel-crowded seas,
5 Fish, flesh, or fowl, commend all summer long
Whatever is begotten, born, and dies.
Caught in that sensual music all neglect
Monuments of unaging intellect.

II

An aged man is but a paltry thing,
10 A tattered coat upon a stick, unless
Soul clap its hands and sing, and louder sing
For every tatter in its mortal dress,
Nor is there singing school but studying
Monuments of its own magnificence;
15 And therefore I have sailed the seas and come
To the holy city of Byzantium.

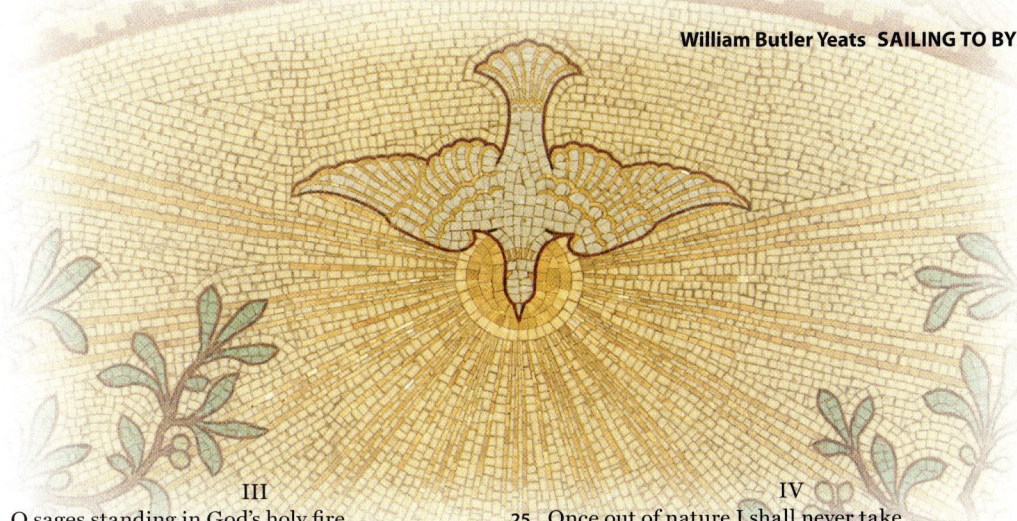

III

O sages standing in God's holy fire
As in the gold mosaic of a wall,
Come from the holy fire, perne in a gyre,
20 And be the singing-masters of my soul.
Consume my heart away; sick with desire
And fastened to a dying animal
It knows not what it is; and gather me
Into the artifice of eternity.

IV

25 Once out of nature I shall never take
My bodily form from any natural thing,
But such a form as Grecian goldsmiths make
Of hammered gold and gold enameling
To keep a drowsy Emperor awake;
30 Or set upon a golden bough to sing
To lords and ladies of Byzantium
Of what is past, or passing, or to come.

Writing from Reading

Summarize

1 As a "voyage" poem, what journey does it describe the speaker taking? Where does he arrive?

Analyze Craft

2 How does the use of the triad (three terms in a row)—"what is past, or passing, or to come," "fish, flesh, or fowl"— affect the music of the poem? Can you point to other triads in the poem, where phrases repeat each other or vary only slightly?

3 How is the idea of a song used in this poem? In stanza I, for example, there's a "song" of "sensual music"; in stanza II this modulates to "sing, and louder sing" and "singing school." In line 20 the speaker asks the sages to become "singing-masters," of his "soul."

Analyze Voice

4 What does Yeats feel about the journey to Byzantium?

Synthesize Summary and Analysis

5 What does Yeats mean by "*That* is no country for old men"? Does he mean his native Ireland or also life in the world at his age?

Interpret the Poem

6 What is meant by "the artifice of eternity"? How is eternity artificial instead of natural?

This is one of the most important and complex poems in Yeats's career; we can only scratch its surface here. Look at the way Yeats modulates from "old men" in the first stanza to "a tattered coat upon a stick" in the second, in which the "aged man" has become a scarecrow. In the third stanza, the scarecrow is burned up; the poet asks the "sages" (wise men) to "consume . . . [his] heart away." By the last stanza, however, far from frightening the birds away, the speaker has joined up with them and been "set upon a golden bough to sing." So the transformation of the "dying animal" into "such a form as Grecian goldsmiths make" is a journey *out* of nature and "into the artifice of eternity." The poem's subject is, appropriately enough, the very life cycle he will leave behind: "whatever is begotten, born, and dies."

In "Sailing to Byzantium," Yeats refers to the absence in Ireland of a "singing school." By the time of his death, he had gone a good distance to remedying that absence and was recognized worldwide as a major representative—perhaps the twentieth century's foremost practitioner—of the art of poetry. So one way to read his poems is to think about the way he built them word by word, and what the artifact itself reveals about its making. Poets often write about the art of poetry, addressing or revising or invoking their great predecessors, and in the chapters that follow there are several examples of this variety of conversation, as is seen in the following poem by Billy Collins.

Billy Collins (b. 1941)

Poet Laureate of the United States from 2001 to 2003 and State Poet of New York State from 2004 to 2006, William James ("Billy") Collins is an ardent promoter of the art of poetry. Born in New York City, he received his B.A. from The College of the Holy Cross and his M.A. and Ph.D. from the University of California, Riverside. He is a Distinguished Professor at Lehman College of the City University of New York, and he co-founded *The Mid-Atlantic Quarterly. The New York Times* called him "the most popular poet in America" (1994).

Collins brings a quirky sometimes surreal humor to his explorations of everyday life, and his humor has won him the Mark Twain Prize for Humor in Poetry, as well as an introduction, during a live performance in New York City, from comedian Bill Murray. His sure technique has won him many other illustrious admirers as well, including the late John Updike, who commented that Collins's work is "more serious than it seems." His fourth collection, *Questions about Angels* (1991), was selected for the National Poetry Series, and he was selected as Poet of the Year by *Poetry* magazine in 1994. He is a frequent guest on National Public Radio's *Writer's Almanac, Fresh Air,* and *Prairie Home Companion.* His most recent collection is *Horoscopes of the Dead* (2011).

AS YOU READ   Notice the different images Collins uses and how they change in emotional pitch from the uncertain exploration of a mouse in a maze, to the jubilant waterskiing as the reader waves to the "author's name," to the dark act of beating out meaning with a hose.

Introduction to Poetry (1988)

I ask them to take a poem
and hold it up to the light
like a color slide

or press an ear against its hive.

5 I say drop a mouse into a poem
and watch him probe his way out,

or walk inside the poem's room
and feel the walls for a light switch.

10 I want them to water-ski
across the surface of a poem
waving at the author's name on the shore.

But all they want to do
is tie the poem to a chair with rope
and torture a confession out of it.

15 They begin beating it with a hose
to find out what it really means.

Writing from Reading

Summarize

1 Whom does this poem seem to address? In other words, who are "they"?

Analyze Craft

2 How does the speaker make a poem seem like a tangible object?

Analyze Voice

3 Considering how the speaker urges others to approach poetry, what is the speaker's own attitude toward poems? Does this affect the tone of the poem?

Synthesize Summary and Analysis

4 How does this poem make you feel towards poetry? Does poetry seem inviting or intimidating? Why?

5 Is the lack of a rhyme scheme in a poem about poetry surprising? Why might Collins have chosen to write without set rhyme?

6 Notice that the words in this poem are simple and easy to understand. How are simple words appropriate to the message the speaker is trying to convey?

Interpret the Poem

7 What aspects of poetry might Collins be highlighting by figuratively making a poem a color slide, a hive, and a maze?

8 What does this poem suggest the purpose of reading poetry is?

18

Writing about Poetry

I'VE pulled the last of the year's young
   onions.
The garden is bare now. The ground is cold,
brown and old. What is left of the day flames
in the maples at the corner of my
eye. I turn, a cardinal vanishes.
By the cellar door, I wash the onions,
then drink from the icy metal spigot.
   —*from "Eating Alone" by Li-Young Lee*

> *"'Eating Together' or 'Eating Alone'—those are about eating and all those other things— but . . . [when we write about poetry] we should be interrogating the quality of the imagination in the poem, the quality of the mind, the heart, the soul in the poem."*
>
> Conversation with Li-Young Lee, available on video at connect.mcgraw-hill.com

HOW do we write about poetry? We do so in ways similar to writing about fiction, by analyzing the writer's craft and voice in terms of its technical aspects, in order to get closer to the meaning.

As suggested in the preceding chapter there are many ways to *think about* and read poetry, based on your own thoughts and your eventual understanding of traditional techniques. First you read the poem to yourself, let the language flow over you and find general associations that the images and words bring up. This is your *first reading*, and it's not meant to be final or thorough, more a general impression that's a springboard to the work. In your first reading of Li-Young Lee's "Eating Alone," you may notice how forlorn the speaker seems and how important onions are in the first and final stanzas. It's useful if you try your second reading out loud, the better to catch the sounds clearly and see what kind of rhythm has enforced its structure on the poem.

A **critical reading,** one in which you begin to apply various ways of looking at a poem, helps

you to fully understand a poem and may require a line-by-line explication, an examination of how the elements of craft work in each line. This kind of reading prepares you to write a text-based argument. Writing a *text-based argument* is a skill you will need for many of your college courses, and it's quite likely you will need such a skill for your work and career outside college. Lawyers, journalists, police detectives, managers of many varieties—all those who have to examine what is said between the lines—need to be able to look closely at how language works and find evidence in the text itself that supports an argument about the meaning of the work.

This chapter follows the development of a sample student essay from the earliest stages to the final draft. Emma Baldwin, a student, uses several of the prewriting and writing strategies that we discuss in depth in Part 1. As was the case with fiction in Chapters 6 and 7, we emphasize that most literary works don't possess a single meaning but rather offer multiple meanings and interpretations of the work.

Li-Young Lee

I don't blame . . . people for being intimidated by poetry . . .

A Conversation on Writing

The Strangeness of Poetry

I don't blame . . . people for being intimidated by poetry—especially lyric poetry. I'm not sure that poems belong in the same category as novels and essays and short stories. Poems are strange; they belong in a whole category of synchronicity or coincidence.

Coincidence and Poetic Order

I think [the] experience of coincidence is the closest thing we have to [the] experience of poetry. . . . Things emerge simultaneously and we can't quite account for that particular emergence of simultaneous things at the same time. So I think [that] the most radical thing about poetry is that it proposes this other order. You know, I think other kinds of writing, ultimately they participate in and examine causal orderedness: cause and effect. And maybe poetry proposes that cause and effect aren't the only lord and lady ruling the universe. . . . I think that's ultimately what lyric poetry attempts to manifest.

Language on a Quantum Level

What's so fascinating is this: I think one has to inhabit a particular state of consciousness in order to notice coincidence or synchronicity in the world. And it could be in fact that the more open we are to it, the more we realize, the more we maybe begin to notice that that's the deepest thing going on at any particular time, that cause and effect is a type of surface condition. Maybe down deep, at a deeper level, a quantum level of reality (and I do think that writing poems is dealing with language on a quantum level) . . . the synchronicities and coincidences begin to emerge, begin to yield themselves, begin to reveal themselves in language.

Li-Young Lee was born in 1957 to Chinese parents in Indonesia and came to America as a child. As he reports in his interview, the refugee experience—his family was persecuted, forced into exile—has deeply influenced his way of looking at the world; if the poet is always, to some degree, an "outsider," this one is literally so. Much of his writing has to do with tradition, the presence of the past—and what is lost, what remains. The growing and cooking and eating of food, for example, has a resonance beyond the merely literal, and for Lee such everyday procedures all partake of pilgrimage and even of the sacred. His language—direct and straightforward diction—celebrates the ordinary and sanctifies everyday life. For this, his work has received many honors, including three Pushcart Prizes, the Lannan Literary Award, and the American Book Award. Lee's 2001 collection *Book of My Nights* was the winner of the Poetry Society of America's William Carlos Williams Award. His other books of poetry include *Rose* (1986), *The City in Which I Love You* (1990), and *Behind My Eyes* (2009). In 1995 he published a memoir, *The Winged Seed: A Remembrance*.

To view this entire interview and hear the author read from his work, go to connect.mcgraw-hill.com.

RESEARCH ASSIGNMENT In his interview, Li-Young Lee talks about being a refugee. What happened to Li-Young Lee, and what does he think this meant for his poetry?

Two Poems by Li-Young Lee

Eating Alone (1986)

I've pulled the last of the year's young onions.
The garden is bare now. The ground is cold,
brown and old. What is left of the day flames
in the maples at the corner of my
5 eye. I turn, a cardinal vanishes.
By the cellar door, I wash the onions,
then drink from the icy metal spigot.

Once, years back, I walked beside my father
among the windfall pears. I can't recall
10 our words. We may have strolled in silence. But
I still see him bend that way—left hand braced
on knee, creaky—to lift and hold to my
eye a rotten pear. In it, a hornet
spun crazily, glazed in slow, glistening juice.

15 It was my father I saw this morning
waving to me from the trees. I almost
called to him, until I came close enough
to see the shovel, leaning where I had
left it, in the flickering, deep green shade.

20 White rice steaming, almost done. Sweet green peas
fried in onions. Shrimp braised in sesame
oil and garlic. And my own loneliness.
What more could I, a young man, want.

Eating Together (1986)

In the steamer is the trout
seasoned with slivers of ginger,
two sprigs of green onion, and sesame oil.
We shall eat it with rice for lunch,
5 brothers, sister, my mother who will
taste the sweetest meat of the head,
holding it between her fingers
deftly, the way my father did
weeks ago. Then he lay down
10 to sleep like a snow-covered road
winding through pines older than him,
without any travelers, and lonely for no one.

A SAMPLE STUDENT ESSAY IN PROGRESS

Everyone has his or her own way of writing. Some think an essay all the way through before putting pen to paper; others create numerous notes and organize those notes into an outline before they begin. Whatever your process is, there is a sequence that can help to break down the writing tasks into digestible chunks and keep the dreaded "blank screen" from causing writer's block. Here you can follow Emma Baldwin through the steps of her writing process to see how her understanding of the poem evolves as she responds to this assignment: In two or three pages, do a close reading of Li-Young Lee's poem "Eating Alone" in which you analyze one or more elements of the poem.

- Interact with the Reading
- Explore Your Ideas
- Develop a Thesis
- Create a Plan for Your Paper
- Generate a First Draft
- Revise Your Draft
- Edit and Format Your Paper

Interact with the Reading

When Emma Baldwin read "Eating Alone," she annotated the poem and took notes on her initial responses. Both her annotations and notes, reproduced here, show how she engaged with the text.

Initial Response

Overall, this poem seems very sad to me. I know that the young man is gardening and cooking, which are both fun hobbies, so it seems as if the poem should be happier than it is. But I think he misses his father, since that is the only other person mentioned in the poem. I don't understand the significance of the hornet spinning in the rotten pear, but I can picture it exactly. I also don't understand the last lines—why would anyone want to be lonely? I did notice that the poem jumps around in time. Those jumps seem to occur with each stanza, so it seems as though that is significant, too. I think the thing I understood best in the poem was the imagery—I could relate to the smell of onions, icy cold water, the cardinal and maple trees. It was easy to picture everything in the poem, even the flickering shade and the shovel in the ground, and so I'd like to understand what it all means.

"Well, the writerly impulse—at least for me—proceeds from a readerly impulse." Conversation with Thomas Lynch

After a first reading of "Eating Alone," Emma reread the poem, scanned the first few lines to determine the meter, and made annotations. Her annotations are a combination of personal reaction and notation of formal elements, like rhyme and rhythm. At this stage in our discussion of the craft of poetry, you won't yet be familiar in detail with the formal elements of rhythm, rhyme, and structure—we simply allude to them here—but they are discussed in the chapters that follow. A "sonnet," for example, is a poetic "fixed form" examined at length in Chapter 25. It's early innings yet, and we won't go into elaborate discussions of technique.

TIPS

For Interactive Reading

Number the lines—Numbering the lines will help you to refer to specific details as you begin your writing process. It will also help you to discover whether the poem follows a particular format; for example, if you find there are fourteen lines, chances are the poem is a sonnet.

Scan the first several lines—Scansion allows you to determine if there is a set rhythm or if the poem is written in free verse (see Chapter 26). The first three lines of the following poem have been annotated for scansion of the rhythm: each stressed syllable is marked with the ´ symbol, and each unstressed syllable is marked with the ˘ symbol.

Identify rhyme—Looking for rhymes is another tactic that will enable you to know the form of the poem. If you find no consistent rhyme scheme, noting internal rhyme, assonance, and consonance will help you to understand the emphasis on certain words.

"This notion of discovery is really important. It's something that's very difficult to remember. I've been writing now for twenty-five years; it's still hard for me to remember that I have to constantly go into the new. Stanley [Kunitz] used to say—he was about ninety—'I go to write a poem, it's not where the last one was.'"

Conversation with Marie Howe

An Interactive Reading of "Eating Alone"

Image: Imagery is barren, desolate

Setting: Present; pulling onions from garden

Image: Imagery brightens with "flames" and "cardinal"

Rhyme: Internal rhyme, wind*fall* and re*call*. *kn*ee and *cr*eaky. cra*zily* and *glazed*

Setting: Past; "once, years back . . ."; walking with father, who is old

Setting: Earlier in the present day; "this morning"; mistakes a shovel for his father

Setting: Present; cooking the onions he has pulled from the garden in a meal

Interpret: Explicit statement of who narrator is (although I felt like I already knew—not sure why)

1 Ĭ've púlled thĕ *lást* ŏf thĕ yeár's yóung óniŏns.
2 Thĕ gárdĕn ĭs *báre nŏw.* Thĕ groúnd ĭs *cóld,*
3 *brówn* ănd *óld. Whăt ĭs léft* ŏf thĕ dáy flámes
4 in the maples at the corner of my
5 eye. I turn, a cardinal vanishes.
6 By the cellar door, I wash the onions,
7 then drink from the icy metal spigot.

8 Once, years back, I walked beside my father
9 among the windfall pears. I can't recall
10 our words. We may have strolled in silence. But
11 I still see him bend that way—left hand braced
12 on knee, (creaky)—to lift and hold to my
13 eye a rotten pear. In it, a hornet
14 spun crazily, glazed in slow, glistening juice.

15 It was my father I saw this morning
16 waving to me from the trees. I almost
17 called to him, until I came close enough
18 to see the shovel, leaning where I had
19 left it, in the flickering, deep green shade.

20 White rice steaming, almost done. Sweet green peas
21 fried in onions. Shrimp braised in sesame
22 oil and garlic. And my own loneliness.
23 What more could I, a young man, want.

Rhyme:—cold/old

Words: Assonance: day flames

Rhyme: No formal rhyme scheme or set meter

Image: "Icy metal spigot"—striking; I can taste it and feel it

Interpret: Father must be old—creaky, difficulty moving

Image: Striking hornet image—metaphor for something?

Interpret: A very sad moment—father is not there; dead, perhaps? shovel makes me think of burial

Image: Words engage sense of smell, taste, visual: very crisp and *present*

Interpret: Confusing last line . . . seems like a contradiction

"Words are about experience." Conversation with Robert Pinsky

Explore Your Ideas

Although Emma did a great job annotating the poem, her confusion over the last lines suggests that she still does not have a full grasp on its meaning. There are several ways you might be able to refine your own ideas for your paper. Here are some examples of freewriting, journaling, and brainstorming. Choose what works best for you.

Freewriting

The saddest moment in the poem is when he mistakes the shovel for his father. I think this means his father is dead, right? Because the poem is so sad, and also the idea of being alone is there from the very beginning, and when someone dies, you feel left alone. I also think he's dead, because he seems very old in the flashback where he bends to pick up a pear; my grandpa moved like that towards the end of his life, so it definitely means the father is old. So then the situation is a son doing his normal routine of cooking and eating but without his father there because he is dead. I still don't get the hornet in the pear, but since the father showed it to him, maybe it has to do with the father? Or maybe it's just a vivid image and that's why Lee went with it. It's strange that this poem is hard to understand because the language is pretty simple. I didn't have to look anything up. "Spigot" is definitely the coolest word in here. Those last lines are still really confusing, too, because they seem to contradict each other. In the one, he talks about "loneliness," but then the next second, he's saying what more could he want? No one wants to be lonely, right? So how does that make sense? It seems as if what he really wants is to have his father with him again.

Journaling

In Li-Young Lee's poem, a son misses his father, who is apparently dead. The situation is pretty straightforward, but the poem does jump around a lot in time. At first the son is in the garden; then he remembers something about his father from a long time ago; then he talks about that morning; then he's cooking at the end.

One appealing aspect of the poem is the imagery. You can practically see, taste, and smell the very things the son sees, tastes, and smells. Some of the imagery is very pleasant, like the cooking smells and tastes at the end, but other imagery is not very attractive. Especially in the first stanza, there's a lot of detail about the garden being cold, brown, and old. And empty, since the son has pulled the "last" of the onions. I don't know if the hornet in the pear is an attractive image or not—the juice is cool, but a hornet and a rotten pear are not things you like to encounter. In any case, some of the images seem to be full of life, like the cooking at the end, but others seem to be dead, like the garden.

In a poem that's easy to understand in terms of the words themselves, the last lines are really hard to figure out. The last lines contradict each other, but I realize now that he's not asking a question. The last line says, "What more could I, a young man, want." So he's telling us he is satisfied somehow, even though his father is not with him. If it had been an actual question, I would have answered that he wants his father back—so maybe his statement means he has learned to be content despite his grief over his father's death.

Brainstorming

LIFE	DEATH
son/speaker	father
young onions	bare garden—cold, brown, old
hornet	rotten pear
father waving	shovel
eating	eating alone

Develop a Thesis

In your responses, annotations, and explorations, you have concentrated on the parts of the poem that make up the whole. At this point, you have an idea of the larger conflicts or issues the poem dramatizes. In developing a thesis, it helps to choose something personally meaningful. Your thesis is your claim that the poem works a certain way or means a certain thing. It isn't a general statement with which no one can disagree, such as information on what you personally like or feel about a poem. Your thesis is a thoughtful and specific assertion that will organize your paper and for which you can provide support and evidence from the poem itself.

First draft: The imagery and the contrast in the last lines suggest contradictory feelings, although it is mostly sad.

Second draft: In a poem about a son missing his dead father, there are many contrasting elements.

Third draft: This poem, which is an expression of grief over a dead father, relies on contrasting elements such as imagery, tone, and time in order to make us feel the narrator's loss.

Final draft: A close reading shows that the entire poem is created out of contradictory elements. Through contrasts of imagery, tone, and the literal events of the poem, Lee uses paradox to give full expression to the grief the speaker feels about his father's death.

Create a Plan for Your Paper

In any paper, your first paragraph sets up the issues that you will explore. There are as many ways to organize your paper as there are lines in the poem, but some general guidelines might help. You can examine the poem line by line, focus on the conflicts that are dramatized in the poem, or look at patterns, types of images, themes,

> "[Write] about something that really moves you and engages you; you must be there on the page." Conversation with Carolyn Forché

or repeated words. When you are organizing your paper, advance your argument with evidence from the poem to avoid creating a laundry list that leads nowhere. Your paper will focus on the text itself, but your conclusion can make connections and raise questions and emphasize crucial issues. You do not need to repeat your thesis in your concluding paragraph. Sometimes an outline will help you plan your paper.

Outlining

I. Introduction
   A. Confusing because last lines contradict
   B. Thesis: A close reading shows the entire poem is created out of contradictory elements. Through contrasts of imagery, tone, and the literal events of the poem, Lee uses paradox to give full expression to the grief the speaker feels about his father's death.

II. Imagery
    A. Imagery that suggests life
    B. Imagery that suggests death

III. Tone
    A. Plain language
    B. Syntax is not complicated . . .
    C. . . . but subject matter is. This = understatement

IV. Time/Literal Events
    A. Present, past "years back," past "this morning"
    B. Talk about contrast in time

VI. Conclusion
    A. Address contrast in last lines
    B. We can understand them in context of poem

"Reading good poetry helps a person feel less lonely. It's the evidence that someone else has felt what we feel, knowing what we know." Conversation with Jane Hirshfield

Generate a First Draft

A first draft is just that: the *first*. Often you find clearer ways to express your thoughts as you go along. Sometimes you change your mind. With poetry, as with all literature, write in the present tense (He *misses* his father; not he *missed* his father). The event that the poem describes never changes, so it is the convention to use present tense when writing about literature.

"I almost . . . never have the lines that I think are the good lines in the poem prior to the act of writing. They occur in the act of. And when you're good that day, you can be a little bit better than yourself." Conversation with Stephen Dunn

FIRST DRAFT

Emma Baldwin

Professor Stoller

English 102

September 22, 2011

Paradox in "Eating Alone"

On first reading Li-Young Lee's poem "Eating Alone," it doesn't make much sense. The speaker's conclusion that he is lonely *and* has everything he wants isn't logical. But on a closer reading, the entire poem is created out of contradictory elements. Through contrasts of imagery, tone, and the literal events of the poem, Lee uses paradox to give full expression to the grief the speaker feels about his father's death.

There is lots of imagery throughout the poem. A lot of it has to do with being alive, like the smell and taste of "sesame oil / and garlic" (lines 21-22). But a lot of it also has to do with death. The poem begins with the speaker picking "the last" (1) produce so that, "The garden is bare now" (2), and Lee further describes the ground as "cold, / brown and old" (2-3). These things remind the reader of death. The images seem to contradict themselves; on the one hand, they make the reader feel connected to the physical world, but on the other hand, they are cold, fleeting images that are related to death.

The father is dead, even though the poem doesn't state that. But it's obvious from the creaky way he bends that he is old. Since that is in a memory from years ago, chances are he has since passed away if he was so old to begin with. In a poem about death, you might expect the words to be flowery, or even like passages from the Bible. You might also expect that the narrator is outwardly sad, or might even cry. But that doesn't happen. Instead, statements like "Once, years back, I walked beside my father /

among the windfall pears" (8-9) sound as though they are said in casual conversation. By understating the situation of death, the poet creates a contrast between the level of subject matter and the way that subject matter is expressed. This contrast highlights that even though death is a major and mystical event, it has become a fact of daily life for this speaker. The understated tone of the poem shows that grief is part of everyday life.

Several other contrasts are embedded in the poem. First is the matter of time. The young man in the present talks about a memory in the past. But beyond a simple past/present contrast, there's an immediate past in addition to a farther away past. The present action is the young man picking the onions, cleaning them, then using them to cook. The distant past is the memory that takes place in the second stanza, "years back," (8) while the immediate past is the occurrence recounted in the third stanza that occurred "this morning" (15). The purpose of the immediate past is that it links the past and present. In that stanza, the speaker sees his father waving at him in the current moment; then he recognizes it is only a shovel in the shade, making the speaker painfully aware in the present of all he has lost from the past. In this way, that painful moment of father and shovel confusion highlights how the father was once alive but is now dead.

In summation, there are contradictory elements in almost every aspect of his poem. Because of this, I can come to understand the last stanza: "Shrimp braised in sesame / oil and garlic. And my own loneliness. / What more could I, a young man, want" (21-23). As noted previously, the fact that loneliness is part of what the young man wants is confusing. But since the whole poem is built on contrasts, the last contrast somehow seems to make sense.

Baldwin 3

Work Cited

Lee, Li-Young. "Eating Alone." *Literature: Craft and Voice.* Ed. Nicholas Delbanco and

Alan Cheuse. 2nd ed. New York: McGraw, 2013. 585. Print.

Works Cited always begins a new page

Revise Your Draft

Before beginning her second draft, Emma looked back at her notes and annotations and compared those with her draft. She found that her notes frequently mentioned the image of the hornet in the pear, but that her final paper left out that image. She also found that the paper did not explicitly highlight the life-and-death contrast she had found so important to furthering her understanding of the poem. Although it certainly isn't necessary to incorporate every idea into the final version, Emma thought it would help her argument to include these elements in her paper.

"Here I have a tremendous kind of furious argument, and here I've got to try and tame it. I've got to enact it. I've got to find a way to formalize it so that someone else can experience what I experienced." Conversation with Edward Hirsch

In the second draft, look for how Emma (1) clarifies her argument by pointing out the life-in-death imagery; (2) adds textual support to her discussion of imagery; (3) works toward making her conclusion more related to her thesis; and (4) includes citations.

"I've been looking for a safe place all my life, a refuge. . . . It might have something to do with the possibility that my own identity was nearly erased when I was born. Many Chinese lost their lives in Indonesia. . . . Maybe that's what . . . poetry is about ultimately . . . discovering who we are, being friends with who we are, getting friendly with your own mind." Conversation with Li-Young Lee

SECOND DRAFT

Baldwin 1

Emma Baldwin

Professor Stoller

English 102

September 27, 2011

Paradox in Li-Young Lee's "Eating Alone"

Li-Young Lee's poem "Eating Alone" doesn't make much sense when you first read it. The speaker's conclusion that he is lonely *and* has everything he wants is not logical because loneliness means something is missing. In this case, it's the father, who is dead. The entire poem is created out of contradictory elements. Through contrasts of imagery, tone, and the literal events of the poem, Lee uses paradox to give full expression to the grief the speaker feels about his father's death.

There is lots of imagery throughout the poem. A lot of it has to do with the different parts of being alive. There is sight when Lee describes "the shovel, leaning where I had / left it, in the flickering, deep green shade" (lines 18-19). There is sound from "the icy metal spigot" (7). There is touch when Lee talks about the cold ground and the cold water (2, 7). There is both taste and smell with the cooking, like with "sesame / oil and garlic" (21-22). But a lot of it also has to do with death. The poem begins with the speaker picking "the last" produce so that, "The garden is bare now" (1, 2), and Lee further describes the ground as "cold, / brown and old" (2-3). Such images suggest that all has been harvested and that winter is coming, and this is linked to death. Even the image in line 5, "I turn, a cardinal vanishes," suggests the fleeting, changeable nature of all that surrounds the speaker, who himself is shown in the act of turning. The images

---

Clarifies why the conclusion is not logical, which is an important facet of the thesis.

Added textual support gives a solid basis for the argument. Emma has fleshed out the idea from the first draft with added examples.

Baldwin 2

seem to contradict themselves; on the one hand, they make the reader feel connected to the physical world, but on the other hand, they are cold, fleeting images that are related to death.

The father is dead, even though the poem doesn't state that. But it's obvious from the creaky way he bends that he is old. Since that is a memory from years ago, chances are he has since passed away if he was so old to begin with. In a poem about death, you might expect the words to be flowery, or even like passages from the Bible. You might also expect that the narrator is outwardly sad, or might even cry. But that doesn't happen. Instead, the syntax is straightforward, so that statements like "Once, years back, I walked beside my father / among the windfall pears" (8-9) sound as though they are said in casual conversation. By understating the situation of death, the poet creates a contrast between the level of subject matter and the way that subject matter is expressed. This contrast highlights that even though death is a major and mystical event, it has become a fact of daily life for this speaker. The understated tone of the poem shows that grief is part of everyday life.

Several other contrasts are embedded in the poem. First is the matter of time. The young man in the present talks about a memory in the past. But beyond a simple past-present contrast, Lee adds an immediate past in addition to a farther away past. The present action is the young man picking the onions, cleaning them, then using them to cook. The distant past is the memory that takes place in the second stanza, "years back" (8), while the immediate past is the occurrence recounted in the third stanza that occurred "this morning." The purpose of the immediate past is that it links the past and present. In that stanza, the speaker sees his father waving at him in the current moment;

This paragraph was already well expressed, so Emma opted for no changes.

More formal language added— tenses clarified.

Baldwin 3

then he recognizes it is only a shovel in the shade, which makes the speaker painfully aware in the present of all he has lost from the past. In this way, that painful moment of father and shovel confusion encapsulates two realities—the past reality that his father was once alive, and the present reality that the father is dead.

Life and death are also contrasted in the poem. The title, "Eating Alone," and the fact that the poem ends with the speaker preparing his food, emphasize the act of eating. Eating sustains life; therefore, the speaker engages in an action that highlights his state as a living being, even as he thinks of his father, who is dead. The hornet in the rotten pear is another expression of life and death in the same space. A rotten pear connotes decay, which equates with death, while the spinning hornet is clearly alive.

In summation, there are contradictory elements in almost every aspect of his poem. Because of this, I can come to understand the last stanza: "Shrimp braised in sesame / oil and garlic. And my own loneliness. / What more could I, a young man, want" (21-23). As noted previously, the fact that loneliness is part of what the young man wants is confusing. But in the context of a poem where Lee has shown death alongside life, past and present brushing shoulders in the same instant, and everyday speech coupled with as great an event as death, we instinctively understand that it is in the intersection of contradictory elements that fullness is achieved—whether that be a full life or a full expression of grief.

Refined language more clearly articulates the importance of the moment described.

Added paragraph to highlight additional contrasts in the poem. Since the thesis statement is about contrast, this new paragraph lends further support to the argument.

Further refinement of the thesis. The previous draft asked the reader to make too many leaps in figuring out what Emma was trying to say; here she has made her argument clear.

Baldwin 4

Work Cited

Lee, Li-Young. "Eating Alone." *Literature: Craft and Voice.* Ed. Nicholas Delbanco and Alan Cheuse. 2nd ed. New York: McGraw, 2013. 585. Print.

Crafting Your Own Voice: Quotation

Think of quotations as your evidence. For example, in her paper on Li-Young Lee's poem "Eating Alone" (reproduced in full on pages 600–603), student writer Emma Baldwin introduces a quotation with her own sentence and a phrase that allows you to see how the quotation supports her point. In this case, her point is that the poem's imagery invokes all five senses:

Introduction that makes point quotations will support

> Lee uses precise imagery that appeals to all five senses : we see . . . "the shovel . . . in the deep green shade" (lines 18-19); we hear the water . . . ; we feel the cold ground . . . ; we taste and smell ". . . . Shrimp braised in sesame . . ." (21).

Phrases use sense words to show how each quotation is an image from one of the five senses.

She goes on to point out the contrasting word choices that connote death with evidence from the poem: "the last" (1), "bare" (2), "cold, brown and old" (2-3). On page 1 of the final draft, Baldwin establishes her own voice and perspective by including the following commentary on these quotations to make the point that it is the use of such contrasts that gives the poem its poignancy:

> Thus, the images seem to contradict themselves: on the one hand, they make the reader feel connected to the physical world, but on the other hand, they are cold, fleeting images that connote death.

Her opinion is clear and supported by evidence. To effectively craft your own voice, avoid stringing together quotations such that they dominate your paper. Remember, it is your voice that your instructor wants to hear.

- For more on summary, quotation and paraphrase see pages 36, 49–58.
- For **Crafting Your Own Voice:** Summary, see page 180.
- For **Crafting Your Own Voice:** Paraphrase, see page 1059.

Tips to Avoiding Plagiarism

Craft & Voice: When you bring in sources, there are some special guidelines to follow. You cannot use the basic structure of a sentence or line of verse, just change a few words, and call the result your own writing. When paraphrasing, you represent the idea of the original source in your own words and your own, unique sentence. When quoting, you use the exact words of the original, set off by quotation marks. You need to attribute both paraphrase and direct quotation to your source; not doing so is plagiarism.

Citing Sources: When citing lines of poetry, spell out the full word *lines* followed by the appropriate numbers (as in the first example). Thereafter, you need include only the line numbers in parentheses.

Edit and Format Your Paper

When you're ready to create your final draft, carefully go back and edit your sentences. Make sure your punctuation is correct, your spelling is accurate, and your grammar is in order. These formal considerations are not so much about the meaning of your thesis, but they are the clothes you put on it. After inserting additional content in the second draft, Emma refined her language and made sure her points were as clear as possible in the final draft. She also double-checked that she had added all the missing citations and she made sure to format the paper correctly, with a title, a standard 12-point font, and double spacing.

Final Draft

Baldwin 1

Emma Baldwin

Professor Stoller

English 102

3 October 2011

The Power of Paradox in Li-Young Lee's "Eating Alone"

On a first reading, Li-Young Lee's poem "Eating Alone" seems to make little sense. The speaker's conclusion that he is lonely *and* has everything he wants is not logical, as loneliness implies a lack of fulfillment. However, a closer reading shows that the entire poem is created out of contradictory elements. Through contrasts of imagery, tone, and the literal events of the poem, Lee uses paradox to fully express the speaker's grief over the father's death.

Perhaps the most striking feature of the poem is its imagery. Lee uses precise imagery that appeals to all five senses: we see, along with the speaker, "the shovel, leaning where I had / left it, in the flickering, deep green shade" (lines 18-19); we hear the water from "the icy metal spigot" (7); we feel the cold ground and the cold

Proper heading: Name, Prof., Class, Date

Thesis statement

Discussion of first of three elements mentioned in thesis statement

Title that includes author and work

Textual support

Baldwin 2

water (2, 7); we taste and smell "sweet green peas / fried in onions. Shrimp braised in sesame / oil and garlic" (20-22). Yet while the images reaffirm a living being's ability to see, hear, touch, taste, and smell, they also suggest death. The poem begins with the speaker picking "the last" produce so that "The garden is bare now" (1, 2), and Lee further describes the ground as "cold, / brown and old" (2-3). Such images suggest that all has been harvested and that winter is coming—traditional ways of symbolizing death. Even the image in line 5, "I turn, a cardinal vanishes," suggests the fleeting, changeable nature of all that surrounds the speaker, who himself is shown in the act of turning. Thus, the images seem to contradict themselves: on the one hand, they make the reader feel connected to the physical world, but on the other hand, they are cold, fleeting images that connote death.

Although the poem never directly states that the father is dead, the imagery, the speaker's act of remembering in the second stanza, and details like the father's difficulty bending years ago suggest the father's age and his subsequent passing.

In a poem about death, one might expect the diction to be elevated, perhaps even to the level of Biblical language. One might also expect overt sadness or lamentation over the death of a family member. Lee follows neither of these expectations. Instead, the syntax is straightforward, so that statements like "Once, years back, I walked beside my father / among the windfall pears" sound as though they are said in casual conversation (8-9). This technique of understatement creates a contrast between the level of subject matter and the way that subject matter is expressed. The contrast highlights that even though death is a major and mystical event, it has become a fact of daily life for this speaker. The understated tone of the

[Margin notes:]

Textual support

Conclusion about significance of imagery

Discussion of second of three elements mentioned in thesis statement

Textual support

Baldwin 3

poem, then, creates the sense that the speaker's grief is so constant and present that he has integrated it into his everyday life.

Conclusion about significance of tone

Discussion of third of three elements mentioned in thesis statement

Several other contrasts are embedded in the poem. First is the matter of time. Lee presents a young man speaking in the present while remembering a scene from his past. But beyond a simple past-present contrast, Lee adds the element of immediate past versus distant past. The present action is the young man picking the onions, cleaning them, then using them to cook. The distant past is the memory that takes place in the second stanza, "years back" (8), while the immediate past is the occurrence recounted in the third stanza that happened "this morning" (15). The purpose of the immediate past is that it links the past and present. In that stanza, the speaker sees his father waving at him in the current moment; then he recognizes it is only a shovel in the shade, which makes the speaker painfully aware in the present of all he has lost from the past. In this way, the moment of father and shovel confusion encapsulates two realities—the past reality that the father was once alive, and the present reality that the father is dead.

Conclusion about significance of events in poem

Further discussion of third element mentioned in thesis statement

Similarly, there are other instances where life and death are placed in immediate proximity to highlight the contradicting halves. The title, "Eating Alone," and the fact that the poem ends with the speaker preparing his food, emphasize the act of eating. Eating sustains life; therefore, the speaker engages in an action that highlights his state as a living being, even as he thinks of his father, who is dead. The hornet in the rotten pear also places life and death in the same space. A rotten pear connotes decay, which equates with death, while the spinning hornet is clearly alive.

Baldwin 4

Conclusion paragraph

Restatement of thesis, but with further nuance than in intro

Lee, then, builds contradictory elements into every aspect of his poem—within the imagery, between tone/syntax/diction and subject, and in the timing of the literal events of the poem. By using so many contrasts, Lee sets us up to understand the paradoxical last lines: "Shrimp braised in sesame / oil and garlic. And my own loneliness. / What more could I, a young man, want" (21-23). That loneliness is necessary to complete what the young man wants is difficult to reconcile. But in the context of a poem where Lee has shown death alongside life, past and present brushing shoulders in the same instant, and everyday speech coupled with as great an event as death, we instinctively understand that it is in the intersection of contradictory elements that fullness is achieved—whether that be a full life, or a full expression of grief.

Broadening of argument to entire poem

Shows how all three elements mentioned in thesis lead to understanding the poem as a whole

Baldwin 5

Works Cited always begins a new page.

Work Cited

Lee, Li-Young. "Eating Alone." *Literature: Craft and Voice.* Ed. Nicholas Delbanco and Alan Cheuse. 2nd ed. New York: McGraw, 2013. 585. Print.

POETRY A Guide to Writing from Reading

Summarize the poem.	Some poems are more transparent than others, but poetic language is nevertheless different from everyday speech. Make sure you understand what is going on in the poem. A poem may have dramatic action, a plot almost, but the poem is just as likely to be a description. After you have gotten your first impressions, depending on the difficulty of the language, you may need to write in your own prose (paraphrase) what each line or stanza means.
Analyze the poem's craft.	A poem works differently from prose, so how language pushes and pulls the literal meaning of the poem is critical to an analysis. Look for patterns of images or sounds, such as the images of stones in Carolyn Forché's "The Museum of Stones" or the rhymes in Shakespeare's "My mistress' eyes are nothing like the sun" (both in Chapter 17). Look for other kinds of patterns (for example, the clustering into threes—"begotten, born, and dies"—of Yeats's "Sailing to Byzantium" in Chapter 17) and for interesting or unusual word choices, word order, and rhythms. You may want to organize your paper as a walk-through of the lines of the poem.
Analyze the poem's voice.	Each poem has a speaker; in your writing you shouldn't assume the speaker is the poet, even if the speaker in the poem uses an "I." Don't write "In Li-Young Lee's 'Eating Together' he finds fulfillment in the family meal." Instead write "In Li-Young Lee's 'Eating Together,' he creates *a speaker* who finds fulfillment in the family meal." In Li-Young Lee's view, the real subject of any poem is the speaker. Ask yourself who the speaker is, what motivated the speaker to tell the "story" in the poem, and why the speaker uses the kind of rhythm, sound, and imagery the way he or she does.
Synthesize the summary and analysis.	What are the larger issues in the poem? What themes are present? What conflicts or issues are dramatized? Describe the situation of the speaker. Think about how craft is used to tell the story of the poem, where sounds, for example, reflect happiness, mourning, or wonder. How do these sounds work together? Are the image patterns most important? Is it an intimate tone that gives the poem its power?
Interpret the poem.	Here is your argument. Two crucial components of writing effectively are discovering something meaningful to you and maintaining a questioning, thoughtful attitude in your exploration of the poem. You will need to make a claim about the poem, and the lines from the poem will be the evidence that supports your claim. If you're using outside sources, other critics' voices should be included only as a jumping-off point for your own interpretation. Learning to support your own interpretation is the point of writing about poetry.

"There's never been a culture or civilization without poetry, which means that there must be something that's crucial to human knowledge—otherwise . . . it would just die away. Just as there has never been a culture without music—there must be something important in music that we as a species need. And I would say the same about poetry. . . . [It is] there to help you. . . . to help you think about your own experience." Conversation with Edward Hirsch

19

Types of Poetry

U NDER my guidance, Nature
brings forth all beings, all things
animate or inanimate,
and sets the whole universe in motion.
—*from the Bhagavad Gita, translated
by Stephen Mitchell*

POETRY comes in many forms, from different period
of time, and in many languages. In fact, many of the
world's masterworks were composed in other tongues
Sometimes even the English of Shakespeare or the King
James Version of the Bible can seem foreign to a modern
reader; that language is not quite the one we use in daily
speech. In his interview, the poet Li-Young Lee (in Chapter 18) describes his first experience of hearing and then
speaking English; born in Indonesia, of Chinese ancestry
he came to this country when young. Having been exposed
from infancy to his parents' love of ancient Chinese poetry
he grew up to write poetry himself, but he does so in his
non-native English. We are more and more citizens of the
world, and poetry can help open up the world to us—be it
from across the globe or from the ancient past.

Although translations have issues that are special to
any work that links languages—and translators such as Stephen Mitchell are especially aware of the importance of the
language, culture, and traditions surrounding a poem—all
poetry is enhanced by an understanding of its context and
history. In Chapters 17 and 18, we examined the language
of poetry from the first encounter with a poem to reading
for word choices, patterns of images and sounds, and considerations of the way the structure of a poem supports an
interpretation. In this chapter, we examine very briefly the
context of major traditions of poetry—the lyric, epic, and
dramatic modes. Although not all of us are multilingual
reading a poem is a little like doing a translation of our
own, going on our own journey into language.

Stephen Mitchell

. . . It felt like listening to the most profound, gorgeous music. I could hear it and know that it was crucial to my life.

A Conversation on Writing

Finding Solace in Spiritual Classics

I discovered Job when I was twenty-two years old. . . . And here's the way I discovered it. My first girl-friend ever dumped me. And I was so distraught and felt so much pain in my heart that I . . . was having a great deal of trouble for several months. And in an effort to find a way to make sense of this and to deal with it, I found myself magnetically attracted to the Book of Job. . . . [At] a certain point, I found myself in the middle of Job's whirlwind, and everything about human suffering and the end of suffering was absolutely clear to me. So from that point on, I continued refining my version of Job from beginning to end, to the point where I felt spiritually mature enough to be able to write about it. . . . And that's how I came to begin to translate some of the great spiritual classics.

A Love Song to God

The Bhagavad Gita is an amazing poem, a love song to God, and that's actually a possible translation of the title. It is the central text of Hinduism . . . a very wise text, and also a very beautiful text. It's a book that I . . . fell in love with. . . . It astonished me to read a book with such a vast conception of God. . . . The God who appears in the Bhagavad Gita says . . . in his most dreadful compassionate form . . . "I am death, I am what lies beyond all your small concepts of what should be and what is right and good." Anyway, this was a great riddle for me at first. . . . I needed to know what that God was all about.

Opening Yourself to Poetry

There's a whole world of beauty and profundity out there for people who don't know poetry that's just waiting for you. All it takes is a little focus and concentration, and you can open yourself up to the most enhancing, heart expanding, mind expanding people.

Born in Brooklyn, New York, in 1943, Stephen Mitchell went to Amherst College as a pre-med student. However, while studying in Paris, he was introduced to Rainer Maria Rilke's poetry. Mitchell learned German simply to read Rilke in his original language, and it was his translation of Rilke's poems that launched his publishing career in 1982 with *The Selected Poems of Rainer Maria Rilke*. Although he has published original poetry in the collection *Parables and Portraits* (1990), he is best known for the poetry of his translations of ancient and modern texts. Mitchell is concerned with spirituality and religious wisdom, as is seen in his acclaimed translations of the Bhagavad Gita (2002), The Book of Job (1992), and the Tao Te Ching (1988). He has also published a number of children's books, among them *Jesus: What He Really Said and Did* (2002), which presents his collection of sayings that he believes are authentic to the historical Jesus. Mitchell, who holds a degree in comparative literature from Yale, has an interest in Zen Buddhism, and he has collaborated with his wife, Byron Katie, on her books devoted to helping people achieve inner peace.

To watch the entire video and hear the author read from his work, go to **connect.mcgraw-hill.com.**

RESEARCH ASSIGNMENT Watch the interview with Stephen Mitchell and describe how translating texts has been a spiritual journey for him.

AS YOU READ Stephen Mitchell has translated many sacred works, including those from the Bible, from Zen Buddhism, and from Hinduism. Arjuna is a hero of the Mahabharata, the Hindu epic from which the Bhagavad Gita is taken. Imagine the context for the sacred writing of Hinduism in India and compare that with what you know of the context of other sacred writing, such as that of the Bible and its use of poetry to convey spiritual guidance.

[The Secret of Life]
—*from the Bhagavad Gita ("Love Song to God")* (c. 500–200 B.C.E.)

THE BLESSED LORD SAID:

Because you trust me, Arjuna,
I will tell you what wisdom is,
the secret of life: know it
5 and be free of suffering, forever.

This is the supreme wisdom,
the knowing beyond all knowing,
experienced directly, in a flash,
eternal, and a joy to practice.

10 Those who are without faith
in my teaching, cannot attain me;
they endlessly return to this world,
shuttling from death to death.

I permeate all the universe
15 in my unmanifest form.
All beings exist within me,
yet I am so inconceivably

vast, so beyond existence,
that though they are brought forth
20 and sustained by my limitless power,
I am not confined within them.

Just as the all-moving wind,
wherever it goes, always
remains in the vastness of space,
25 all beings remain within me.

They are gathered back into my womb
at the end of the cosmic cycle—
a hundred fifty thousand
billion of your earthly years—

30 and as a new cycle begins
I send them forth once again,
pouring from my abundance
the myriad forms of life.

These actions do not bind me, Arjuna.
35 I stand apart from them all,
indifferent to their outcome,
unattached, serene.

Under my guidance, Nature
brings forth all beings, all things
40 animate or inanimate,
and sets the whole universe in motion.

Foolish people despise me
in the human form that I take,
blind to my true nature
45 as the Lord of all life and death.

Their hopes and actions are vain,
their knowledge is sheer delusion;
turning from the light, they fall
into cruelty, selfishness, greed.

50 But the truly wise, Arjuna,
who dive deep into themselves,
fearless, one-pointed, know me
as the inexhaustible source.

Always chanting my praise,
55 steadfast in their devotion,
they make their lives an unending
hymn to my endless love.

—*translated by* Stephen Mitchell

Writing from Reading

Summarize

1 The "Blessed Lord" speaks, recounting God's nature and God's accomplishments. What does the text say about the nature of those who worship God?

Analyze Craft

2 Does this scripture resemble a drama in any way?

Analyze Voice

3 Can you characterize the voice of the deity?

Synthesize Summary and Analysis

4 The God speaks. What makes it possible for us to listen in?

Interpret the Poem

5 In what ways are ideas in this poem similar to or different from those in the writings of your religion or another religion with which you are familiar?

"Translation makes the world accessible to us." Conversation with Robert Hass

CONTINUED FROM PAGE 607

We are much the richer for literature's variety and range. In James Joyce's novel *A Portrait of the Artist as a Young Man,* the main character—an intense young writer in the making named Stephen Dedalus—lectures his schoolmates about the three modes of creative expression. These are, according to him, lyric, epic, and dramatic. Of the epic and dramatic modes we'll have more to say later on; lyric—according to Joyce and Dedalus—comes first. It is "the simplest verbal vesture of an instant of emotion, a rhythmical cry such as ages ago cheered on the man who pulled at the oar or dragged stones up a slope. He who utters it is more conscious of the instant of emotion than of himself as feeling emotion."

"The way to study a poem is to read the poem as you would anything else. There's not necessarily a code or a puzzle. You take in the lines and often read it aloud and pause at the end of the lines just a little so that you get a sense of . . . the music that the lines establish in the poem. Then read it again, and think about it, and let your mind drift and be open. A reading will become available to you." Conversation with Carolyn Forché

LYRIC POETRY

A lyric is a short poem with a central pictorial image written in an *uninflected* voice—by which we mean a voice that's both direct and personal (usually using the first-person pronoun to create an intimate point of view). As the name implies, a lyric was originally sung to the accompaniment of a lyre; this was surely the case with the following work, from the Song of Solomon. A lyric poem relies on music, but it also conjures a series of visual emblems—images to which our emotions adhere. In this way, whatever feelings the words of the poem create for you become crystallized in pictorial terms: we *see* as well as *hear* what the poet tries to say. The great love poem that follows was translated in 1611 by a committee of scholars, under the sponsorship of King James I and for the King James Version of the Bible.

> "I didn't start learning to read poetry in English—although I was reading the Bible, I guess. I was reading the Psalms and the Gospels and Genesis and Exodus, and those books just knocked me out. I thought they were weird and mysterious and otherworldly." Conversation with Li-Young Lee

In addition to considering the audience for whom a work was written, we have the added consideration that this is a sacred work, a poem written in celebration of God. (Indeed, the love of God and the secular devotion to "my love" become somehow *conflated*, or made one and the same; the singer celebrates both. There's no separation of body and soul or sacred and profane; this lyric conjoins them in praise.) How does such knowledge deepen our reading of this work? Does it feel modern? If so, what makes it feel modern? The answers to these questions help us place a poem in the context of its own tradition, in this case the tradition of lyric poetry, and help us read other lyric poems in the light of at least this one poem, if not "in the light of all the other poems ever written."

AS YOU READ   Imagine that you hold a lyre—or, in the contemporary moment, a guitar—and sing these lines. What kind of melody would be most fitting here?

Song of Solomon 4:1–7
—from the King James Bible
[Behold, thou art fair, my love] (1611)

Behold, thou art fair, my love; behold, thou art fair; thou hast doves' eyes within thy locks:
  thy hair is as a flock of goats, that appear from mount Gilead.
Thy teeth are like a flock of sheep that are even shorn, which came up from the washing;
  whereof every one bear twins, and none is barren among them.
Thy lips are like a thread of scarlet, and thy speech is comely: thy temples are like a piece of a
  pomegranate within thy locks.
Thy neck is like the tower of David builded for an armoury, whereon there hang a thousand
  bucklers, all shields of mighty men.
5 Thy two breasts are like two young roes that are twins, which feed among the lilies.
Until the day break, and the shadows flee away, I will get me to the mountain of myrrh, and to
  the hill of frankincense.
Thou art all fair, my love; there is no spot in thee.

Writing from Reading

Summarize

1 What kinds of comparisons does the poet-singer use to address God?

Analyze Craft

2 The poet compares parts of his beloved's body to various animals. List these. What is the effect of comparing his love this way?

Analyze Voice

3 How does the poet's deep love affect the way he sings? Can the poem be read the way such poems as the love sonnets of William Shakespeare's can be read—as the specific discussion of an individual "she"? Why or why not?

Synthesize Summary and Analysis

4 Singing to God, the poet dramatizes his emotion by a series of striking images. What does this technique accomplish?

Interpret the Poem

5 What is the context for this poem? Why do you imagine the singer-poet chooses to express his love in this way?

We looked at D. H. Lawrence's short story "The Rocking-Horse Winner" (Chapter 16); now consider a poem by the same author. (Many other authors in this volume—Margaret Atwood, Joyce Carol Oates, and John Updike, for example—write both prose fiction and verse.) "Piano" attests to the power of music and how it takes a listener back to "the old Sunday evenings at home."

D. H. Lawrence (1885–1930)

For a brief biography of D. H. Lawrence, see Chapter 16.

AS YOU READ   Notice that the title of the poem gets repeated in each of the three stanzas; notice how a musical instrument organizes the dozen lines that constitute the poem.

Piano (1918)

Softly, in the dusk, a woman is singing to me;
Taking me back down the vista of years, till I see
A child sitting under the piano, in the boom of the tingling strings
And pressing the small, poised feet of a mother who smiles as she sings.

5 In spite of myself, the insidious mastery of song
Betrays me back, till the heart of me weeps to belong
To the old Sunday evenings at home, with winter outside
And hymns in the cozy parlor, the tinkling piano our guide.

So now it is vain for the singer to burst into clamour
10 With the great black piano appassionato. The glamour
Of childish days is upon me, my manhood is cast
Down in the flood of remembrance, I weep like a child for the past.

Writing from Reading

Summarize

1 Do these three stanzas tell a story? Summarize the action in each.

Analyze Craft

2 How is the present linked to the past?

Analyze Voice

3 What does the speaker feel toward his remembrance? What words give you clues as to his feeling?

4 Who is speaking in the poem?

Synthesize Summary and Analysis

5 Compare the two experiences of music in the poem—the two pianos, the two musicians.

Interpret the Poem

6 What does the speaker mean by "my manhood is cast down"? What in his childhood does he long for?

The speaker connects the occasion of the woman singing to him in the twilight hour with the set of emotions it calls up. His adult attention to the singer, his child's love for his mother, his deeply felt memories of long-ago evenings—all these come together in the image of the "Piano." The musical instrument that the speaker looks at and the one he remembers are both different and the same. When the speaker weeps "like a child for the past," it's clear that memory takes precedence: "the flood of remembrance" carries him away. So "the glamour" that would seem to attach to a woman "singing to me" with "the great black piano appassionato" in fact belongs to the recollection of past childhood, and the singer who begins "Softly, in the dusk," bursts merely into "clamour" in the present scene.

An image such as that of the piano is central to any lyric poem, and one of the first things to consider is the image pattern you discover as you read. An indelible part of the following poem by William Butler Yeats is the image of a swan, its "feathered glory." Were the poem about Leda to involve the kind of bird Yeats writes of in "Sailing to Byzantium" (in Chapter 17), or if that poem had involved a flock of swans, the poems would be less distinctive. This swan is thoroughly physical, not something "out of nature," and it's useful to contrast the two varieties of birds in the two poems.

According to the Greek myth on which "Leda and the Swan" is based, the swan is the god Zeus who has taken the shape of a bird and descended to earth. The poem

"I can't imagine any writer or any artist doing anything of any good without knowing some or a lot of what preceded him." Conversation with

Stephen Dunn

focuses on a violent act, the disguised god's rape of a human woman. There's a complicated history here, as is often the case in Yeats's work. According to the myth, Leda gave birth to two sets of children after having been raped. One egg produced the twins Castor and Pollux, rendered immortal and "heavenly" in the night sky; out of the other egg came Leda's daughters, Helen and Clytemnaestra—the eventual wives of the Greek kings Menelaeus and Agamemnon, respectively. The Trojan War resulted from Helen's abduction by Paris, who was the son of King Priam of Troy. The "broken wall, the burning roof and tower, and Agamemnon dead" is how Yeats refers to the nine-year-long siege of Troy by the Greeks. This poem talks about "A sudden blow" and "a white rush"; the moment "engenders" consequences that will last long after this particular action is done.

William Butler Yeats (1865–1939)

For a brief biography of William Butler Yeats, see Chapter 17.

AS YOU READ   Think about the differences between this bird and the birds described in "Sailing to Byzantium" (Chapter 17).

Leda and the Swan (1924)

A sudden blow: the great wings beating still
Above the staggering girl, her thighs caressed
By the dark webs, her nape caught in his bill,
He holds her helpless breast upon his breast.

5 How can those terrified vague fingers push
The feathered glory from her loosening thighs?
And how can body, laid in that white rush,
But feel the strange heart beating where it lies?

A shudder in the loins engenders there
10 The broken wall, the burning roof and tower
And Agamemnon dead.
                              Being so caught up,
So mastered by the brute blood of the air,
Did she put on his knowledge with his power
Before the indifferent beak could let her drop?

Writing from Reading

Summarize

1 The poet takes a story from Greek mythology and describes it in close detail. What kind of picture does Yeats paint, and what is going on?

Analyze Craft

2 Parts of this poem are "descriptive," and parts ask questions. What kind of questions get asked?

Analyze Voice

3 The voice has a kind of overview of history—looking back on what would happen as a result of the act described. In terms of point of view, is the speaker omniscient or merely informed? How does this affect the speaker's tone?

Synthesize Summary and Analysis

4 "Knowledge" and "power" would seem to be opposing qualities. Is there a moment when they become one and the same?

Interpret the Poem

5 The "strange heart" and "brute blood" and "indifferent beak" all belong to the animal kingdom. What is the poet saying about the part that animal behavior plays in human behavior?

Because the poet helps us visualize the event, the reader *sees* the questions the poem raises about the relation of wisdom and power, of frailty and strength. Notice also the frank—and frankly daring—sexuality of phrases like "laid in that white rush" and "the indifferent beak" and how the rhythms of the poem manage to suggest the physical encounter in and of itself. When it's over, it's over for Zeus; he simply "let her drop." Yeats creates an image that stays in our mind of this unequal meeting between heaven and earth, this fusion of power and knowledge. If that pictorial image had been presented as an abstraction only, it would not stay with us long.

EPIC POETRY

Although the image is central to most modern verse, it's important to remember that this was not always the case. Poetry was originally very different. The first widespread use of poetry in Western culture comes in the form of the epic, a long narrative poem recited publicly. The earliest audiences took in these poems with their ears, not their eyes. Poetry was an oral and aural (spoken and heard) art form rather than a visual entity or a series of lines transcribed. The audience listened to but could not read them, because until the late fourth century B.C.E. these epics were not written down.

One function of the epic narrative derives from or is connected to the notion of community and a collective hearing. This sort of poem is more *public* than *private;* its intended audience is less the individual than the group. Bards called on the goddess Memory to send down the words of the poem. The values of a culture—its sense of tradition, its very existence—were incorporated into and communicated by the medium

"Before television and before radio, and really, before typewriters and computers and all of that . . . the ability to stand up in public and speak was very important. . . . The teaching of poetry . . . had to do with learning to recite it, to say it in public." Conversation with Robert Hass

of poetry. "Voice" is crucial to the form—but less as individual intonation than as a communal voice, a kind of chanted chorus in which everybody learns to "sing along."

In Greece, *rhapsodes*, or reciters of poetry, performed by reciting the thousands and thousands of lines of the Homeric epics of the *Iliad* and the *Odyssey*, among the earliest stories to arise in Western civilization—with their heroes at the center, their large groups of secondary characters, their multiple sequences of events in war and peace. Great narrative poems such as these may contain powerful images—such as the intricately described shield of Achilles in the *Iliad* and the monstrous Cyclops in the *Odyssey*—but these poems usually derive their power from the strength of the language and the story's sound and flow.

After the two major Greek epic poems—the *Iliad* and the *Odyssey*—comes the *Aeneid*, the epic of the founding of Rome. Each of these three long narratives deals with the relationship between the gods and human beings; the past and present; the values, rules, laws, and customs of civilizations and empires; and the variety of heroes who keep them vital. Several long poems in Old and Middle English also attempt this fusion of nature and culture. *Beowulf, Sir Gawain and the Green Knight,* and *Le Morte d'Arthur,* the story of King Arthur and the knights of the fabled Round Table, all instruct their audience in the "proper" way to behave.

"Li-Young Lee says . . . memorizing poems . . . is a kind of yoga where you assume the same position, if you will, as the poet. When you memorize a poem . . . you actually inhabit the mind and heart of the poet, and every turn that poet has taken, and it's a remarkably great thing to do. It doesn't seem like it's going to help your writing, but of course it does. It provides syntactical moves and ways of thinking and feeling . . . that would never occur to you on your own. That's what all reading does." Conversation with Marie Howe

The extended poems that come later (such as the opening to the prologue of Geoffrey Chaucer's *Canterbury Tales* in Chapter 25 and the early Italian Renaissance poet Dante Alighieri's *Divine Comedy*) build on the same principles as those of the ancient epic poets. In *Paradise Lost* (see Chapter 25), John Milton, the last great poet to create a Christian epic, sets out to "justify the ways of God to man," to attempt to clarify the nature of religious and social relations. After Milton, this variety of poem more or less disappears, although there do continue to be narratives in verse.

Ironically enough, the epic is the form least natural to modern culture. (Although some contemporary movies have been described as "epic" and may require years to produce and cost hundreds of millions of dollars, they take barely two hours of screen time and are not the kind of art form we mean here.) The English Romantic poet Lord Byron takes a sardonic and comical approach to the genre, working with the epic but with a lighter touch. The Greeks traditionally invoked a goddess when they began to sing—and Milton, too, provided a Christian version of "the Goddess of Memory," calling her "Heavenly Muse." Byron, however, starts his long narrative poem *Don Juan*— the name *Juan* is pronounced to rhyme with "new one"—with an insulting address to one of his contemporaries.

George Gordon, Lord Byron (1788–1824)

One of the great English Romantic poets, Lord Byron enjoyed a larger-than-life celebrity status after the publication of the first cantos of *Childe Harold's Pilgrimage* in 1811. His fame came largely from the public conflation of Byron himself with his character creation, the Byronic hero. The Byronic hero is one who stands apart from society, brooding and hating the rest of humankind, which he considers unable to equal his capacity for passion. Byron's poetry ranges from lyrics that mimic older styles of complimenting women in verse to satires in the style of Alexander Pope (see Chapter 24), to extended poems such as his capstone *Don Juan*. Byron led a turbulent life up to his death at age thirty-six, while helping Greece gain its independence.

AS YOU READ   Enjoy the way the poet in the dedication calls out one of his contemporaries and then calls for a real hero as the poem proper begins.

[Bob Southey! You're a poet]
—*from the Dedication to* Don Juan (1819)

Bob Southey! You're a poet—Poet-laureate,
And representative of all the race;
Although 'tis true that you turn'd out a Tory at
Last,—yours has lately been a common case;
5   And now, my Epic Renegade! what are ye at?
With all the Lakers, in and out of place?
A nest of tuneful persons, to my eye
Like "four and twenty Blackbirds in a pye;

"Which pye being open'd they began to sing"
10   (This old song and new simile holds good),
"A dainty dish to set before the King,"
Or Regent, who admires such kind of food;
And Coleridge, too, has lately taken wing,
But like a hawk encumber'd with his hood,
15   Explaining Metaphysics to the nation—
I wish he would explain his Explanation.

Writing in a time when, as he sees it, poets lack inspiration from the Goddess and in which great heroes no longer can be found, Byron relies on humor to create a personal epic for his age. Notice how he plays with the nursery rhyme about blackbirds in a pie—saying that "This old song and new simile holds good"—turning the blackbirds into poets. Robert Southey and Samuel Taylor Coleridge, two of Byron's contemporaries, need to have their politics and metaphysics explained, and though he dedicates his lines to them, he does so tongue in cheek.

Here again, context helps. When Byron refers to "the Lakers," he's reporting not on a basketball team but on poets such as William Wordsworth, who liked to walk in England's Lake District. It may also help to know that the name *Southey* would have been pronounced "Suh-thee" and that the Poet-laureate holds a position of honor—one that Byron with his scandalous private life could never expect to attain. (Read poems of Coleridge's in Chapters 24, 25, and 29 and poems by Wordsworth in Chapters 17, 23, 25, and 29.)

[I want a hero]
—*from* Don Juan,
Canto the First (1819)

I want a hero: an uncommon want,
When every year and month sends forth a new one,
Till, after cloying the gazettes with cant,
The age discovers he is not the true one;
5   Of such as these I should not care to vaunt,
I'll therefore take our ancient friend Don Juan—
We all have seen him, in the pantomime,
Sent to the devil somewhat ere his time.

Writing from Reading

Summarize

1 The poet opens a long poem with a dedication and the first stanza. Who and what is he making fun of?

Analyze Craft

2 The Greek epics narrate the deeds of heroes. How does Byron twist the form of an ancient Greek epic?

Analyze Voice

3 What kind of tone does the mix of satire and elevated language create?

Synthesize Summary and Analysis

4 Why does Byron use the epic form in a time when epic has fallen out of fashion?

Interpret the Poem

5 What does the poet have in mind when he speaks of a "hero"? Why does he choose this particular figure—Don Juan—as his subject? Research this figure in the library or on the Internet.

DRAMATIC POETRY

The dramatic poem, also called the dramatic monologue, in which a character addresses another character, or the reader, is an offshoot of the epic form and the third of James Joyce's three categories. The notion of "voice" in this case has more to do with impersonation than with the personal or lyric "cry" of an individual; the poet assumes the "mask" or "persona" of a character not his or her own (for more on persona, see Chapter 21). In the case of "My Last Duchess," Robert Browning becomes someone altogether other than the poet Robert Browning, creating a character engaged in a soliloquy much as might a playwright. What we learn of the Duke here is more than the Duke might knowingly wish to confess—his pride and temper, his murderous dis-

"In our culture it becomes more and more difficult for us to enter into, imaginatively at least, the consciousness of others. Literature is a way of doing that." Conversation with Carolyn Forché

trust of his young wife, his chilly desire (stated almost unconsciously in the first line, with the possessive pronoun "my") to treat people as possessions. The "scene" (in Ferrara, Italy) is swiftly set; the speaker walks a silent witness—a kind of stand-in for the reader—through a picture gallery. By the second line, we learn what the title already suggests, that his "last duchess" is dead; near the poem's end, we learn that he's planning to marry again. The man who listens is a negotiator from "the Count your master," a rich man whose daughter the speaker intends to acquire as his next wife.

Robert Browning (1812–1889)

Robert Browning was one of the great Victorian poets, but his fame was eclipsed by that of Elizabeth Barrett (his wife) in his own time; today, however, he is recognized for his innovative use of the dramatic monologue. Browning's poems explore faith, doubt, crime, and madness using speakers who lived in past times, frequently from the Renaissance era. Browning was educated mostly at home and traveled little until he and Barrett eloped to Italy, where they lived for sixteen years (until Barrett's death). Among Browning's more famous poems are "Porphyria's Lover" (Chapter 25). "My Last Duchess," and "Fra Lippo Lippi," but his masterpiece is a four-volume dramatic monologue, *The Ring and the Book* (1868), that tells the story of a murder trial in seventeenth-century Italy.

AS YOU READ Listen in your mind's ear to the way in which the statements run over from one line to the next to complete their meanings.

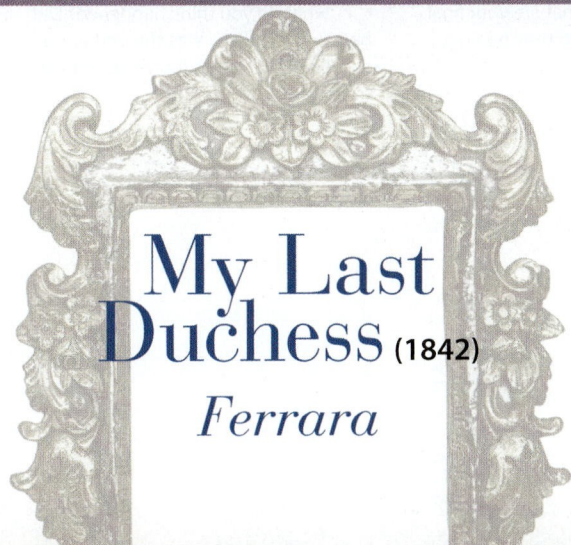

My Last Duchess (1842)

Ferrara

That's my last Duchess painted on the wall,
Looking as if she were alive. I call
That piece a wonder, now: Frà Pandolf's hands
Worked busily a day, and there she stands.
5 Will't please you sit and look at her? I said
"Frà Pandolf" by design, for never read
Strangers like you that pictured countenance,
The depth and passion of its earnest glance,
But to myself they turned (since none puts by
10 The curtain I have drawn for you, but I)
And seemed as they would ask me, if they durst,
How such a glance came there; so, not the first

Are you to turn and ask thus. Sir, 'twas not
Her husband's presence only, called that spot
15 Of joy into the Duchess' cheek: perhaps
Frà Pandolf chanced to say "Her mantle laps
Over my lady's wrist too much," or "Paint
Must never hope to reproduce the faint
Half-flush that dies along her throat." Such stuff
20 Was courtesy, she thought, and cause enough
For calling up that spot of joy. She had
A heart—how shall I say?—too soon made glad,
Too easily impressed; she liked whate'er
She looked on, and her looks went everywhere.
25 Sir, 'twas all one! My favour at her breast,
The dropping of the daylight in the West,
The bough of cherries some officious fool
Broke in the orchard for her, the white mule
She rode with round the terrace—all and each
30 Would draw from her alike the approving speech,
Or blush, at least. She thanked men—good! but thanked
Somehow—I know not how—as if she ranked
My gift of a nine-hundred-years-old name
With anybody's gift. Who'd stoop to blame

35 This sort of trifling? Even had you skill
In speech—(which I have not)—to make your will
Quite clear to such an one, and say, "Just this
Or that in you disgusts me; here you miss,
Or there exceed the mark"—and if she let
40 Herself be lessoned so, nor plainly set
Her wits to yours, forsooth, and make excuse,
—E'en then would be some stooping; and I choose
Never to stoop. Oh sir, she smiled, no doubt,
Whene'er I passed her; but who passed without
45 Much the same smile? This grew; I gave commands;
Then all smiles stopped together. There she stands
As if alive. Will't please you rise? We'll meet
The company below, then. I repeat,
The Count your master's known munificence
50 Is ample warrant that no just pretense
Of mine for dowry will be disallowed;
Though his fair daughter's self, as I avowed
At starting, is my object. Nay we'll go
Together down, sir. Notice Neptune, though,
55 Taming a sea-horse, thought a rarity,
Which Claus of Innsbruck cast in bronze for me!

Writing from Reading

Summarize

1 Who is the speaker of the poem? To whom does he give the tour? What brings the visitor to the viewing?

Analyze Craft

2 The speaker is not the poet—the poet creates a character here, and a story. Can you describe the two characters in the poem and the woman in the painting whom the speaker describes?

Analyze Voice

3 What are your first impressions of the speaker, and what are your final ones? How and where do they begin to change?

Synthesize Summary and Analysis

4 What do you learn about his "last Duchess," and how do you imagine she felt about her husband?

Interpret the Poem

5 When "all smiles stopped together," what do you think happened? Did he have her killed? Was she perhaps a suicide? Or did she simply—as old stories have it—"die of grief"?

The more we "listen" to the speaker in "My Last Duchess," the more we come to mistrust him. Even such a simple word as "now" in the third line suggests its opposite, "then"; quite probably he wasn't as pleased by the smile of his living wife as he is by the portrait behind the curtain, which he alone is permitted to "draw." He keeps her beauty hidden, in effect, and for his private pleasure; soon enough we learn he was unable to do so while she was alive. She smiled at the painter, at other men, at common folk, and the proud duke did not approve of this. The lines "I gave commands; / Then all smiles stopped together" is bone-chilling in its suggestiveness. At the very least he commanded his wife to stop smiling at and thanking other people; possibly he ordered her death. There's a long short story embedded in this narrative, and the dramatic monologue reveals an attitude and a situation the speaker tries to hide.

For Review and Further Study

Elizabeth Barrett Browning (1806–1861)

For a brief biography of Elizabeth Barrett Browning, see Chapter 25.

When our two souls stand up erect and strong (1850)

When our two souls stand up erect and strong,
Face to face, silent, drawing nigh and nigher,
Until the lengthening wings break into fire
At either curvèd point—what bitter wrong
5 Can the earth do to us, that we should not long
Be here contented? Think. In mounting higher,
The angels would press on us and aspire
To drop some golden orb of perfect song
Into our deep, dear silence. Let us stay
10 Rather on earth, Belovèd,—where the unfit
Contrarious moods of men recoil away
And isolate pure spirits, and permit
A place to stand and love in for a day,
With darkness and the death-hour rounding it.

Questions for Interactive Reading and Writing

1. Many love poems use heavenly imagery to show the sublime nature of love. How does Barrett Browning diverge from this expected way of presenting love?

2. In what ways does this poem qualify as a lyric poem?

3. How would you describe the unique rhythm of line 6? What effect does the poet achieve?

4. Barrett Browning's final image is of death "rounding" their perfect love. What is the significance of this word choice? Why not use "surrounding" instead? Hint: You may want to consider the "golden orb" of line 8.

5. This poem is a sonnet, a fixed form you will learn about in Chapter 25. Sonnets contain a turn, or a change, in thought. Where do you see a shift in the speaker's thought?

Robert Browning (1812–1889)

For a brief biography of Robert Browning, see the discussion of dramatic poetry earlier in this chapter.

Love among the Ruins (1855)

I

Where the quiet-coloured end of evening smiles
    Miles and miles
On the solitary pastures where our sheep
    Half-asleep
5 Tinkle homeward thro' the twilight, stray or stop
    As they crop—
Was the site once of a city great and gay,
    (So they say)
Of our country's very capital, its prince
10   Ages since
Held his court in, gathered councils, wielding far
    Peace or war.

II

Now—the country does not even boast a tree,
    As you see,
15 To distinguish slopes of verdure, certain rills
    From the hills
Intersect and give a name to, (else they run
    Into one)
Where the domed and daring palace shot its spires
20   Up like fires
O'er the hundred-gated circuit of a wall
    Bounding all,
Made of marble, men might march on nor be pressed,
    Twelve abreast.

III

25 And such plenty and perfection, see, of grass
    Never was!
Such a carpet as, this summer-time, o'erspreads
    And embeds
Every vestige of the city, guessed alone,
30   Stock or stone—
Where a multitude of men breathed joy and woe
    Long ago;

Lust of glory pricked their hearts up, dread of shame
    Struck them tame;
And that glory and that shame alike, the gold   35
    Bought and sold.

IV

Now,—the single little turret that remains
    On the plains,
By the caper overrooted, by the gourd
    Overscored,   40
While the patching houseleek's head of blossom winks
    Through the chinks—
Marks the basement whence a tower in ancient time
    Sprang sublime,
And a burning ring, all round, the chariots traced   45
    As they raced,
And the monarch and his minions and his dames
    Viewed the games.

V

And I know, while thus the quiet-coloured eve
    Smiles to leave   50
To their folding, all our many-tinkling fleece
    In such peace,
And the slopes and rills in undistinguished grey
    Melt away—
That a girl with eager eyes and yellow hair   55
    Waits me there
In the turret whence the charioteers caught soul
    For the goal,
When the king looked, where she looks now, breathless,
      dumb
    Till I come.   60

VI

But he looked upon the city, every side,
    Far and wide,
All the mountains topped with temples, all the glades'
    Colonnades,
All the causeys, bridges, aqueducts,—and then,   65
    All the men!
When I do come, she will speak not, she will stand,
    Either hand,
On my shoulder, give her eyes the first embrace
    Of my face,   70
Ere we rush, ere we extinguish sight and speech
    Each on each.

VII

In one year they sent a million fighters forth
   South and north,
75 And they built their gods a brazen pillar high
   As the sky,
Yet reserved a thousand chariots in full force—
   Gold, of course.
Oh, heart! oh, blood that freezes, blood that burns!
80   Earth's returns
For whole centuries of folly, noise and sin!
   Shut them in,
With their triumphs and their glories and the rest!
   Love is best!

Questions for Interactive Reading and Writing

1. What are the two storylines that coincide in this poem? Is the poem primarily about war and empire or about love?

2. How does the story about war and empire affect the love story?

3. What is the role of the speaker here? How does that affect the way he tells the poem's story?

4. What does the poem suggest about the relation of individuals, their lives and loves, in the context of the social situation of the state, of the country?

5. Does the way the poem sounds—its particular music as you read it aloud—contribute anything to the meaning?

Feasted, we guide it—our fingers
Like tallows adorned with yellow metal—
Over the sky's hot rim,
The day's last breath in our sails.

Pinned by the sun between solstice   10
And equinox, drowsy and tangled together
We drifted for months and woke
With the bitter taste of land on our lips,
Eyelids all sticky, and we longed for lime
And the sound of a rope   15
Lowering a bucket down its well. Then,
We came by night to the Fortunate Isles,
And lay like fish
Under the net of our kisses.

—translated by Christopher Logue

Questions for Interactive Reading and Writing

1. Describe the imagery in this poem. How does it give these lovers a larger-than-life feel?

2. Considering the rest of the poem, how do you interpret the ending? Is it positive or negative to be caught under the net of their kisses?

3. How does the imagery in the first stanza evoke a sexual relationship?

4. Could the feelings in this poem be expressed without imagery? Why or why not?

Pablo Neruda (1904–1973)

[Under the Net of Our Kisses] (1958)

Drunk as drunk on turpentine
From your open kisses,
Your wet body wedged
Between my wet body and the strake
5 Of our boat that is made of flowers,

Adrienne Rich (b. 1929)

Living in Sin (1955)

She had thought the studio would keep itself;
no dust upon the furniture of love.
Half heresy, to wish the taps less vocal,
the panes relieved of grime. A plate of pears,
a piano with a Persian shawl, a cat   5
stalking the picturesque amusing mouse
had risen at his urging.

Not that at five each separate stair would writhe
under the milkman's tramp; that morning light
10 so coldly would delineate the scraps
of last night's cheese and three sepulchral bottles;
that on the kitchen shelf among the saucers
a pair of beetle-eyes would fix her own—
envoy from some village in the moldings . . .
15 Meanwhile, he, with a yawn,
sounded a dozen notes upon the keyboard,
declared it out of tune, shrugged at the mirror,
rubbed at his beard, went out for cigarettes;
while she, jeered by the minor demons,
20 pulled back the sheets and made the bed and found
a towel to dust the table-top,
and let the coffee-pot boil over on the stove.
By evening she was back in love again,
though not so wholly but throughout the night
25 she woke sometimes to feel the daylight coming
like a relentless milkman up the stairs.

Questions for Interactive Reading and Writing

1. What makes the "she" in the poem feel particularly uncomfortable in her current living arrangement?

2. How does the reference to the vermin—"a pair of beetle-eyes"—add to her feeling of being ill at ease?

3. Does the reference to the out-of-tune piano increase the discomfort?

4. Does the man feel as the woman does? What makes us able to move from a description of the piano to a description of the woman's feelings?

Rainer Maria Rilke (1875–1926)

Archaic Torso of Apollo (1908)

We cannot know his legendary head
with eyes like ripening fruit. And yet his torso
is still suffused with brilliance from inside,
like a lamp, in which his gaze, now turned to low,

gleams in all its power. Otherwise   5
the curved breast could not dazzle you so, nor could
a smile run through the placid hips and thighs
to that dark center where procreation flared.

Otherwise this stone would seem defaced
beneath the translucent cascade of the shoulders   10
and would not glisten like a wild beast's fur:

would not, from all the borders of itself,
burst like a star: for here there is no place
that does not see you. You must change your life.

—*translated by* Stephen Mitchell

Questions for Interactive Reading and Writing

1. While living in Paris, Rilke worked as a kind of private secretary to the sculptor Auguste Rodin. What does the poet look at when he sees "this stone"?

2. Look up the Greek god Apollo and make a list of his qualities. Relate them to what the poet sees here.

3. Who is the "you" in this poem, and does it also mean "I"?

4. Which images are "surface" images, and which relate to depths?

5. The poet lives in the present moment, but what he's looking at is "archaic" and comes from a civilization that flourished thousands of years before. Discuss this as an example of both "tradition" and "translation."

6. What does the last sentence of this poem mean, and who gives the order that "You must change your life"?

Rumi [Jalal al-Din Muhammad] (c. 1207–1273)

Some Kiss We Want (c. mid-thirteenth century)

There is some kiss we want
with our whole lives, the touch

of spirit on the body. Seawater
begs the pearl to break its shell.

5 And the lily, how passionately
it needs some wild darling!

At night, I open the window and ask
the moon to come and press its
face against mine.

10 Breathe into me. Close
the language-door and open the love-window.
The moon won't use the door,
only the window.

—*translated by* Coleman Barks

Questions for Interactive Reading and Writing

1. To whom does the speaker in the poem admit a desire? Whom does he ask to come to him?

2. How does the poet turn love of God into a poem that seems to be about human love?

3. How would you describe this voice? How is it similar to, or distinct from, the voice in the Song of Solomon?

4. The speaker in the poem seeks union with his beloved, expressing this need in language beyond the literal. What does he mean by "the moon won't use the door"?

5. What does the speaker want as expressed in such lines as ". . . Sea-water / begs the pearl to break its shell" or "the lily, how passionately . . . it needs some wild darling!"?

20 Words

JOHNNY, the kitchen sink has been clogged for
   days, some utensil probably fell down there.
And the Drano won't work but smells dangerous,
   and the crusty dishes have piled up

waiting for the plumber I still haven't called. This
   is the everyday we spoke of.
It's winter again: the sky's a deep headstrong blue,
   and the sunlight pours through

the open living room windows because the heat's
   on too high in here, and I can't turn it off.
For weeks now, driving, or dropping the bag of
   groceries in the street, the bag breaking,

I've been thinking: This is what the living do. . . .
   —from "What the Living Do" by Marie Howe

"I love Anglo-Saxon. I just like rock, stone, dirt, blood. . . . *I would much prefer the four- letter word quite literally like* rock *to* boulder *even. I love the simplicity of those words, the thing closest to the thing."*

Conversation with Marie Howe, available on video at connect.mcgraw-hill.com

IN her autobiographical poem "What the Living Do," Marie Howe reflects on the aftermath of her brother's death, personally addressing him as if she were writing a letter. She catalogs the details of everyday existence, its mundane irritations as well as its surprising beauty. The poem is a testament both to remembrance and to continuity. The series of observations culminates in the quiet recognition that these commonplace tasks constitute the way that life, in its varying majesty and modesty, continues for the bereaved.

Poets try to find and then select language appropriate to their subject matter. The resulting selection is called **diction,** the choice of words by an author or speaker. A poem about war might sound percussive, even violent. A love poem's language can seem as lush and comforting as an embrace. So, *how* an experience or feeling is expressed in language is just as important to the poet as *what* that experience or feeling consists of.

This poet writes with great clarity. She chooses language immediately understood by the attentive reader. It's almost as though we're eavesdropping on the speaker as she voices these intimate thoughts to her deceased brother. Look at how plainspoken and declarative the language is: "the kitchen sink has been clogged for days," "the heat's on too high," and "I've been thinking: This is what the living do."

In her interview, Marie Howe expresses fondness for the blunt words we've inherited from Anglo-Saxon (or Old English), the language spoken in Britain centuries ago—before the introduction of Latinate words on the heels of the Norman Conquest in 1066. "I just like *rock, stone, dirt, blood*. . . . I love the simplicity of those words, the thing closest to the thing." This

respect for simplicity is reflected in the precision and candor of "What the Living Do." It's a poem committed to honest contemplation and emotion. "I . . . decided to write—to give myself a break—a letter to my brother John, who I missed," Howe says. "So I just wrote 'Johnny, the kitchen sink has been clogged for days,' because it actually was. 'And the Drano won't work,' because it didn't. And I kept going and just kept writing and writing."

The British poet Samuel Taylor Coleridge defined poetry, in 1835, as "the best words in their best order." More than a century later, American poet William Carlos Williams remarked that a poem is a "machine made of words." Both of these quotes wryly reiterate the necessity for language to fit and work properly within a particular poem's context and meaning. (This is also true for writers of prose fiction and drama, of course; every artist hates imprecision and strives to be exact. But it's particularly the case in poetry, where diction takes pride of place.) When you read poetry, you will want to consider how writers choose the kind of language they do and how they go about fitting words together and putting them in the "best order."

CONTINUED ON PAGE 632

Marie Howe ...*when something huge happens, people don't use big language.*

A Conversation on Writing

Writing as Discovery

I want to make one thing perfectly clear. I don't know what I'm doing when I'm writing. . . . For me at least, that a [writer] starts off knowing what she's going to say is something I thought for a long time. Now I know that . . . it's quite the opposite—that the writing itself brought me into an experience I didn't know I was going to have. My brother had died. He was my dearest friend. He was twenty-eight years old.

Poetry in Real Time

I really wanted "What the Living Do" to have . . . the startling reality of the actual. . . . I fear for the actual. It's losing to the virtual. . . . [Think about] what we're able to do with computer technology without having to see or hear anybody. . . . I think that poetry reminds us [of the actual]—it has to do with time as well, right? Why it's difficult to read poetry [is] not because it's hard to understand, at least for me, it's because it's so painful to slow down. To . . . read a poem is to live in time in a way that is almost unbearable . . . to be all here, this very moment.

Advice on Reading Poetry

Plunge, don't be embarrassed. . . . When I got out of graduate school, I moved to Cambridge. There were all these other writers and poets living there, and . . . we would say to each other "I don't get Wallace Stevens." . . . And someone would say, "I do. Let's meet Thursday at three." . . . Every week we would meet with our friends and just talk about poems we didn't understand. And it was such a joy not to be embarrassed.

To watch this entire interview and hear the author read from her poetry, go to connect.mcgraw-hill.com.

The oldest of nine children, Marie Howe (b. 1950) grew up in Rochester, New York. After teaching high school for a time, Howe earned her master of fine arts degree in poetry from Columbia University, where she studied with poet laureate Stanley Kunitz. Her first major success came in 1987, when Margaret Atwood selected Howe's *The Good Thief* (1988) as the winner of the National Poetry Series. Her next collection of poems, *What the Living Do* (1997), was written after her brother's death from AIDS and is largely an elegy for him. Her third book of poetry, *The Kingdom of Ordinary Time,* was published in 2008. Howe's work is characterized by an open avowal of emotion—the sense of loss as well as hope; she's a thoroughly *personal* poet with an uninflected voice.

RESEARCH ASSIGNMENT In her interview, Howe mentions "what happens, happens in between" in language. Watch her interview. What does Howe mean by this? How does her example relate to "What the Living Do"?

AS YOU READ   Pay close attention to the kind of language Howe uses. Be aware of how her fondness for simple, direct words (such words as *rock, stone, dirt,* and *blood*) affects her diction and attitude to the subject of this poem. Think about the way "the everyday we spoke of" appears here again and again.

What the Living Do (1997)

Johnny, the kitchen sink has been clogged for days,
   some utensil probably fell down there.
And the Drano won't work but smells dangerous,
   and the crusty dishes have piled up

waiting for the plumber I still haven't called. This is
   the everyday we spoke of.
It's winter again: the sky's a deep headstrong blue,
   and the sunlight pours through

5 the open living room windows because the heat's
   on too high in here, and I can't turn it off.
For weeks now, driving, or dropping a bag of
   groceries in the street, the bag breaking,

I've been thinking: This is what the living do. And
   yesterday, hurrying along those
wobbly bricks in the Cambridge sidewalk, spilling
   my coffee down my wrist and sleeve,

I thought it again, and again later, when buying a
   hairbrush: This is it.
10 Parking. Slamming the car door shut in the cold.
   What you called *that yearning.*

What you finally gave up. We want the spring to
   come and the winter to pass. We want
whoever to call or not call, a letter, a kiss—we want
   more and more and then more of it.

But there are moments, walking, when I catch a
   glimpse of myself in the window glass,
say, the window of the corner video store, and I'm
   gripped by a cherishing so deep

15 for my own blowing hair, chapped face, and
   unbuttoned coat that I'm speechless:

I am living, I remember you.

Writing from Reading

Summarize

1 List the activities that "the living do."

Analyze Craft

2 Contrast the shorter sentences with the longer ones. Do they serve different purposes?

3 Why do you think Howe uses familiar nouns such as "Drano" and "video store"?

Analyze Voice

4 Discuss how tone informs or helps to convey the emotions in this poem. How would you characterize the tone?

5 Notice how many gerunds—present participles such as "driving," "dropping," "hurrying," "walking"—she employs. What does that do to the tense of the action, and what would happen to this "conversation" if it were written in the past tense?

Synthesize Summary and Analysis

6 In this poem, Howe lists the activities of everyday life. How does her choice of words reinforce the subject of the poem?

Interpret the Poem

7 What is Howe trying to say about the living as opposed to those who are no longer with us?

8 The speaker in the poem indicates she is "speechless" when she sees her reflection in a storefront window. What does her speechlessness represent?

9 How would you describe the main theme or themes of "What the Living Do"?

CONTINUED FROM PAGE 629

WORD CHOICE: VARIETIES OF DICTION

Poetic diction describes an especially lofty and elevated language characteristic of poetry written before the nineteenth century. A tradition inherited from the classical verse of Greek and Latin, poetic diction was used to separate poetic speech from common speech. Poets believed that verse, in its ambition to demonstrate the full power of language, demanded its own heightened vocabulary. As such, ordinary objects received flowery and exotic description. Britain's most famous poet of the Victorian era, Alfred, Lord Tennyson, uses this diction when he calls grass "the herb" and a horse a "charger." In this same vein, the eighteenth-century British poet and critic Alexander Pope memorably names a pair of scissors "the glitt'ring Forfex." Pope's example of poetic diction (represented here by an apostrophe, see Chapter 23) employs elision, the omission of a vowel or consonant sound within or between words. Words like "o'er" were substituted for "over" and "ne'er" for "never." In addition to dramatizing the language, this also allowed for added flexibility within a poem's meter.

> **"This is the secret of poets. . . . They actually read the dictionary the way some people would read spy novels."** Conversation with Carolyn Forché

Although there is no strict line clearly separating divisions of diction, poets' selection of language can be divided into three levels, from the most extravagantly phrased lines of poetic diction to the direct and straightforward. These levels of speech are generally referred to as:

- Formal (flowery, grand, and elaborate)
- Middle (educated standard English)
- Informal (everyday speech)

A BRIEF HISTORY OF POETIC DICTION

Neoclassical poets (c. 1600–1800) chose subjects and words they felt were refined and therefore appropriate for serious poetry, often relying on Greek and Latin (*classical*) verse for inspiration. The Romantic movement in poetry inaugurated a steady change from poetic diction to more everyday modes of speech. William Wordsworth, a leading British Romantic poet, wrote in 1802 in a preface to his celebrated collection of poems, *Lyrical Ballads,* "There will also be found in these volumes little of what is usually called poetic diction; I have taken as much pains to avoid it as others ordinarily take to produce it." In the United States in the twentieth century, Robert Frost notably adopted a similar poetic stance, seeking to voice his poems with what he called the "sound of sense," a phrase Frost used to mean the actual sound of spoken language. From the Romantic era of Wordsworth to Frost's modern period to the present moment, poets have chosen their words with increasing freedom.

Formal diction refers to complex, grammatically proper, and often polysyllabic language in writing. It sounds grandiloquent—a "formal" word—and tends not to resemble the sort of talk we hear in our daily lives. Listen to the speaker in John Keats's "Ode on a Grecian Urn." He stands, very likely in a museum, before an ancient Greek vase and becomes captivated, stanza after stanza, by the different rural scenes painted on its sides: images of men pursuing women, of lovers, of trees, of religious rituals.

John Keats (1795–1821)

Although the British Romantic poet John Keats died of tuberculosis at age twenty-five, he had already composed poetry of such a caliber that he remains one of the best-known and most admired English-language poets. Though he believed himself a failure and wanted his epitaph to read "Here lies one whose name is writ in water," nothing could be farther from the truth: "Posthumous Keats," as one of his biographers, the poet Stanley Plumly, puts it, lives on. Keats's life, however, was never an easy one; his parents died when he was young, he watched his brother Tom die of tuberculosis, his poetry was generally unsuccessful until after his own demise, and he was unable to marry the woman he loved because of his poverty and failing health. Having studied to be a doctor, he could recognize "arterial blood" when he coughed it up, and he pronounced his own death sentence. The house in Rome where he died (by the Spanish Steps) as well as the last house where he lived in London are museums now. John Keats combined a nature deeply sensitive to beauty with a literary talent that allowed him to render his verses with a grace and eloquence paralleled perhaps only by Shakespeare. His celebrated poems "Lamia" and "La Belle Dame sans Merci" (Chapter 24) and his odes were all written in a great burst of creativity in 1819.

TIP

FOR INTERACTIVE READING . . .

As you read "Ode on a Grecian Urn," circle or write down other words that you would characterize as formal.

Ode on a Grecian Urn (1819)

I

Thou still unravished bride of quietness,
   Thou foster-child of silence and slow Time,
Sylvan historian, who canst thus express
   A flowery tale more sweetly than our rhyme:
5 What leaf-fringed legend haunts about thy shape
   Of deities or mortals, or of both,
     In Tempe or the dales of Arcady?
What men or gods are these? What maidens loth?
   What mad pursuit? What struggle to escape?
10   What pipes and timbrels? What wild ecstasy?

II

Heard melodies are sweet, but those unheard
   Are sweeter; therefore, ye soft pipes, play on;
Not to the sensual ear, but, more endear'd,
   Pipe to the spirit ditties of no tone:
15 Fair youth, beneath the trees, thou canst not leave
   Thy song, nor ever can those trees be bare;
     Bold Lover, never, never canst thou kiss,
Though winning near the goal—yet, do not grieve;
   She cannot fade, though thou hast not thy bliss,
20   For ever wilt thou love, and she be fair!

III

Ah, happy, happy boughs! that cannot shed
   Your leaves, nor ever bid the Spring adieu;
And, happy melodist, unwearièd,
   For ever piping songs for ever new;
25 More happy love! more happy, happy love!
   For ever warm and still to be enjoy'd,
     For ever panting, and for ever young;
All breathing human passion far above,
   That leaves a heart high-sorrowful and cloy'd,
30   A burning forehead, and a parching tongue.

IV

Who are these coming to the sacrifice?
  To what green altar, O mysterious priest,
Lead'st thou that heifer lowing at the skies,
  And all her silken flanks with garlands drest?
35 What little town by river or sea shore,
  Or mountain-built with peaceful citadel,
    Is emptied of its folk, this pious morn?
And, little town, thy streets for evermore
  Will silent be; and not a soul to tell
40   Why thou art desolate, can e'er return.

V

O Attic shape! Fair attitude! with brede
  Of marble men and maidens overwrought,
With forest branches and the trodden weed;
  Thou, silent form, dost tease us out of thought
45 As doth eternity: Cold Pastoral!
  When old age shall this generation waste,
    Thou shalt remain, in midst of other woe
Than ours, a friend to man, to whom thou say'st,
  "Beauty is truth, truth beauty,"—that is all
50   Ye know on earth, and all ye need to know.

Writing from Reading

Summarize

1 Rewrite each stanza in a couple of sentences using everyday speech.

2 Who or what is the poet addressing?

Analyze Craft

3 Why do you think Keats uses the word *still* in the first line of the poem? Does the word supply more than one meaning? And what does he mean by *unravished*?

4 List examples of elision in the poem.

5 In the final stanza the speaker calls the urn a "Cold Pastoral!" Look up the word *pastoral* in a dictionary. Which definition—the adjective or noun—do you think Keats intends to invoke? Why do you think he chooses this word?

Analyze Voice

6 Describe the mood conveyed in the poem. What words has Keats chosen to evoke this particular mood?

7 How does the use of formal diction help establish a sense of the speaker's attitude?

Synthesize Summary and Analysis

8 Compare the formal diction in Keats's poem to your rewritten stanzas from question 1. What does Keats accomplish by choosing the kinds of words he does in this poem?

9 How does the formal poetic diction add to the theme of beauty in this poem?

Interpret the Poem

10 Why do you think Keats decided to use a "Grecian urn" as opposed to pottery from other time periods?

11 Explain why you agree or disagree with the famous last lines of this poem:

"'Beauty is truth, truth beauty,'—that is all / Ye know on earth, and all ye need to know."

Missing the showy grandiosity of formal diction, middle diction is characterized by sophisticated word usage and grammatical accuracy. It is educated language, but not extravagant—a blend of "common" speech and "elevated" diction, sometimes within the same line. Mostly, however, the language is simple and straightforward. At this point in our discussion of diction, it seems appropriate to repeat a pair of points made previously.

1. Every English poem is a blend of formal and informal speech, but
2. No "natural" speaker would be able to rhyme words such as *telephone* with *bone* or *drum* with *come* so effortlessly. So there is craft involved in this particular voice.

In W. H. Auden's "Funeral Blues," the poet goes from realistic (unplug the clocks, give the dog a bone, quit playing the piano or talking on the phone) to romantic and excessive—from requiring the plausible to asking the impossible.

W. H. Auden (1907–1973)

Wystan Hugh Auden is one of the most important British poets of the twentieth century (he became an American citizen, but he was born in England and lived there for the majority of his life). With great technical agility and a near-total command of poetic form, Auden could have been a kind of erudite "ivory-tower" artist, remaining aloof from the world. But he allowed his own time to color his poetry, writing about the literal wasteland created by the Great Depression, using the ideas of Sigmund Freud and Karl Marx to examine England's political problems, and gathering the rhythms of colloquial speech alongside his masterful versification. In later life, his poetry moved from the social consciousness of his early work to more personal and even religious poems; both serious and playful, W. H. Auden was continually able to put craft in the service of voice, and to put both craft and voice to use in the hunt for wisdom. After the following poem was featured in the movie *Four Weddings and a Funeral,* this lament for a friend's death was widely read again.

AS YOU READ   Note the role of sound in this poem—the perfect rhymes in couplets, and the titular suggestion that we're in the realm of song. Although these "blues" are intended to be spoken, not sung, there's a well-wrought precision (as in the second stanza) to such seemingly-offhand couplets as "overhead / Dead" and "doves / gloves." This holds true throughout the sixteen lines and provides, somehow, a formality in grief.

FOR INTERACTIVE READING . . .

Auden uses several images in this poem. List these images.

Funeral Blues (1940)

Stop all the clocks, cut off the telephone,
Prevent the dog from barking with a juicy bone,
Silence the pianos and with muffled drum
Bring out the coffin, let the mourners come.

5 Let aeroplanes circle moaning overhead
Scribbling on the sky the message He is Dead.
Put crêpe bows round the white necks of the public doves,
Let the traffic policemen wear black cotton gloves.

He was my North, my South, my East and West,
10 My working week and my Sunday rest,
My noon, my midnight, my talk, my song;
I thought that love would last forever: I was wrong.

The stars are not wanted now; put out every one,
Pack up the moon and dismantle the sun,
15 Pour away the ocean and sweep up the wood;
For nothing now can ever come to any good.

Writing from Reading

Summarize

1 What is the speaker responding to in this poem, and what does the title convey?

2 How does the speaker feel about the subject of the poem?

3 How do such phrases as "muffled drum," "mourners," and "crêpe bows," which refer to the traditional trappings of a funeral, contrast with the actual occasion of the poem?

Analyze Craft

4 Describe the diction in this poem. When does it seem formal or informal?

5 What emotions or meaning come to mind when you read "the white necks of the public doves"? What comes to mind when you read other images?

Analyze Voice

6 Describe tone in the poem. Is it uniformly mournful? If not, where does the tone shift, and where does it remind you of the blues?

7 There's wild exaggeration in the last stanza's set of instructions: "Pack up the moon and dismantle the sun"—as if we could indeed "Pour away the ocean" and "put out" the stars. What does this tell us about the emotion of the speaker?

Synthesize Summary and Analysis

8 How many sentences make up this poem? Discuss the consistency of the arrangement of sentences—how do they affect or reflect the poem's subject?

Interpret the Poem

9 Compare the last lines of this poem to "What the Living Do." What does Auden's poem say about death? Explain how it is the same as, or different from, Howe's "What the Living Do."

10 Look at John Donne's "A Valediction: Forbidding Mourning" in the "For Review and Further Study" section of this chapter. Compare Auden's use of the compass with that of Donne's.

A majority of poets today compose in language that sounds like the speech we hear in daily life. Informal diction is conversational, plainspoken language and often makes use of slang, contractions, and mainstream expressions. It might sound like a remark across a dinner table, or resemble something you overhear in the course of a regular day.

> "Gwendolyn Brooks is one of my favorite poets and what I particularly love about her besides the musicality of her poems— because she works quite often with formal structures—are the voices. She has so many different voices that she can write in."
>
> Conversation with Al Young

Gwendolyn Brooks grew up on Chicago's South Side, and many of her poems describe and explore the lives of everyday African Americans in urban twentieth-century America. The following poem, "We Real Cool," speaks in the collective voice of a group of young men shooting pool. Not only does the poem employ informal diction, it simultaneously exemplifies **dialect,** the variety of language spoken by a particular group of people (in this case, young black men during the 1960s). In turn, dialect usually features **colloquial language,** familiar and conversational speech. Lastly, we can see in this poem a bit of **jargon,** words with specific meaning for a particular group of people. Poets assign language like this to speakers in order to convey a vivid sense of who inhabits a poem, what that person is like or what he or she wants.

Gwendolyn Brooks (1917–2000)

Born in Topeka, Kansas, and raised in Chicago, Gwendolyn Brooks would grow up to become the first African-American woman to win, in 1950, the Pulitzer Prize for poetry—for her book *Annie Allen.* Brooks was Poet Laureate of the United States (1985–1986) as well as Poet Laureate of Illinois, from 1968 till her death. Her early work, such as *A Street in Bronzeville* (1945), took for its subject the frustrated hopes of urban blacks; her later work became increasingly concerned with black identity, particularly the female perspective. Brooks is known for her bold use of language, often in new applications of old forms like the sonnet.

AS YOU READ Notice the diction Brooks uses to form our sense of these individuals and their lives. Notice also how much gets compressed into and expressed by twenty-four words.

We Real Cool (1960)

The Pool Players.
Seven at the Golden Shovel.

We real cool. We
Left school. We

Lurk late. We
Strike straight. We

5 Sing sin. We
Thin gin. We

Jazz June. We
Die soon.

Writing from Reading

Summarize

1 Who is the "We" of the poem? What happens to this "We"?

Analyze Craft

2 How does the informal diction of the poem affect your sense of the speaker? What does the poet mean by such phrases as "Thin gin" and "Jazz June"?

Analyze Voice

3 Advising readers on how to recite this poem aloud, Brooks wrote, "Say the 'We' softly." Why do you think she wanted this word quieter than others? What does it reveal about the confidence of the speaker?

Synthesize Summary and Analysis

4 Describe the author's attitude toward the pool players.

Interpret the Poem

5 How is the name of the pool hall meaningful?

6 How does the final line affect (and change) the poem's meaning?

GENERAL VS. SPECIFIC LANGUAGE

Also at work within any poet's choice of diction is the decision to lean toward language that is specific or language that is more general. Concrete diction is language referring to a specific, definite thing. Words like *lawn mower, beer bottle,* and *streetlight* are concrete because they represent actual objects you can perceive with your senses. Abstract diction is language referring to a more general or conceptual thing or quality. Because words like *progress, justice,* and *calm* do not refer to things you can see or touch, they are abstractions. Your sense of what constitutes *calm* may be slightly or even radically different from the next person's. An abstraction is, thus, an idea that means something a little different to everyone.

Most poets find that concrete language can help make an abstraction come more vividly to life for a reader. Rather than say, abstractly, "Now that the night becomes calm . . ." poet Richard Jackson writes, "Now that the earth, sky and wind settle into night's still pool. . . ." His line gives us concrete language *(earth, sky, wind, pool)* in order to more tangibly embody his particular idea of *calm*.

> **"I think . . . that there's a mastery over [language] once you name [something]. So yes, once I have got it down, once I have got it right, it's not as frightening anymore."** Conversation with Thomas Lynch

Most poets do not use abstract or concrete diction uniformly. They make their selection word by word, moving back and forth between the general and the particular, in order to best serve their purposes. Note how in Auden's "Funeral Blues," the poet blends the metaphoric and specific with the declarative and abstract statement. By saying "He was my North, my South, my East and West," the poet suggests that his dead friend was a kind of compass, encircling the whole world; later, the dead man "was" every day of the week and every hour of each day ("My noon, my midnight"), both "talk" and "song."

Here are two celebrated poems that incorporate both concrete and abstract language. In the first, a speaker commemorates his devotion by comparing his love to the elements of a season. In the second, a speaker stands next to his love and looks out onto England's ocean cliffs, lamenting his loss of faith in the world's goodness.

William Shakespeare (1564–1616)

For a brief biography of William Shakespeare, see the Case Study on Shakespeare in Chapter 33.

AS YOU READ   Try to identify Shakespeare's use of general and specific language. Consider why he chose the abstract or concrete language that you find. (It's worth mentioning here that *thou*—the familiar and singular form of the plural *you*—was a more common form of address in the early seventeenth century—a singular and intimate form of the plural *you*—than would have been the case for Keats two centuries later.)

Shall I compare thee to a summer's day? (1609)

Shall I compare thee to a summer's day?
Thou art more lovely and more temperate:
Rough winds do shake the darling buds of May,
And summer's lease hath all too short a date;
5   Sometime too hot the eye of heaven shines,
And often is his gold complexion dimmed,
And every fair from fair sometime declines,
By chance, or nature's changing course, untrimmed:
But thy eternal summer shall not fade,
10 Nor lose possession of that fair thou ow'st,
Nor shall death brag thou wand'rest in his shade,
When in eternal lines to time thou grow'st.
    So long as men can breathe, or eyes can see,
    So long lives this, and this gives life to thee.

Writing from Reading

Summarize

1 List the ways the speaker's beloved is lovelier than a summer day.

Analyze Craft

2 Compare the language in the final couplet to the language that precedes it. Where does the diction seem concrete? Where does it seem abstract?

Analyze Voice

3 How does the praise set the tone for the poem? What is the speaker's attitude in the poem? What does he mean by such phrases as "the darling buds of May" or "the eye of heaven"?

Synthesize Summary and Analysis

4 Explain how the poet uses comparison in the poem.

Interpret the Poem

5 What is the "this" the speaker mentions in the final line? How does it "give life"?

6 It could be argued that the closing statement here is boastful (as well as, it turns out, correct). Remember that the poem's subject has to do with life's and beauty's brevity. Is there a kind of consolation in the statement that art lasts?

Matthew Arnold (1822–1888)

The British poet Matthew Arnold was also a literary critic and a commentator on society and education. Interestingly, Arnold stopped writing poetry after 1850, turning more and more to "public" matters under discussion in England. The poetry he did create was principally about the individual in a modern, industrial world, often marked by a melancholy tone. "Dover Beach," widely read during Arnold's lifetime, survives as his best-known poem, despite its bleak outlook, and it was written while he was on his honeymoon. (The next poem here, Anthony Hecht's "The Dover Bitch," makes ironic use of that fact.) Though influential and much honored, Arnold did not make his living as a writer; instead, he worked first as a secretary, then as an inspector of schools, and wrote his poetry and essays on the side.

AS YOU READ   Consider how the poet's use of concrete and abstract imagery establishes mood within the poem. What, for instance, does Arnold mean by "the sea of faith," and who might he describe as "ignorant armies" that clash? It might help to know that the "white cliffs of Dover" bear roughly the same relation to the idea of England as the Statue of Liberty or the Grand Canyon does to the idea of the United States. For more on Sophocles and the Aegean Sea, look at Chapter 32 on Greek drama.

Dover Beach (1867)

The sea is calm tonight.
The tide is full, the moon lies fair
Upon the straits; on the French coast the light
Gleams and is gone; the cliffs of England stand,
5   Glimmering and vast, out in the tranquil bay.
Come to the window, sweet is the night-air!
Only, from the long line of spray
Where the sea meets the moon-blanched land,
Listen! you hear the grating roar
10 Of pebbles which the waves draw back, and fling,
At their return, up the high strand,
Begin and cease, and then again begin,
With tremulous cadence slow, and bring
The eternal note of sadness in.

15 Sophocles long ago
Heard it on the Aegean, and it brought
Into his mind the turbid ebb and flow
Of human misery; we
Find also in the sound a thought,
20 Hearing it by this distant northern sea.

The Sea of Faith
Was once, too, at the full, and round earth's shore
Lay like the folds of a bright girdle furled.
But now I only hear
25   Its melancholy, long, withdrawing roar,
Retreating, to the breath
Of the night-wind, down the vast edges drear
And naked shingles of the world.

Ah, love, let us be true
30   To one another! for the world which seems
To lie before us like a land of dreams,
So various, so beautiful, so new,
Hath really neither joy, nor love, nor light,
Nor certitude, nor peace, nor help for pain;
35   And we are here as on a darkling plain
Swept with confused alarms of struggle and flight,
Where ignorant armies clash by night.

Writing from Reading

Summarize

1 What is meant by "the turbid ebb and flow / Of human misery"?

Analyze Craft

2 How does the concrete description of the sea ("long line of spray," "pebbles") compare with or contribute to the speaker's more abstract thoughts?

Analyze Voice

3 Describe how the speaker's mood changes throughout the poem. What does he want, and when?

Synthesize Summary and Analysis

4 Describe how word choice in the poem contributes to the overall mood of the poem.

Interpret the Poem

5 What might the poet mean by "the eternal note of sadness" in the first stanza?

6 Look up the word *elegy*. Is this an elegy? If so, to what?

ALLUSION

Poets often refer or allude to the work of other poets; this is, after all, a way of maintaining tradition and tipping a cap to the past. Matthew Arnold's nineteenth-century poem refers to "Sophocles long ago" and compares the present world situation to what the Greek dramatist once heard and thought; "The Dover Bitch" refers to Dover Beach in a less serious but similar way. Both poets and poems are allusive; there's an added dimension to and pleasure in the reading when you know what went before.

Anthony Hecht (1923–2004)

As an undergraduate at Bard College in New York, Anthony Hecht fell in love with poetry, but his pursuit of it was interrupted by World War II, in which he served as an army infantryman and experienced the liberation of Nazi concentration camps. After the war, he studied at Kenyon College and at Columbia University, where he received his master's degree. He spent the majority of his teaching career at the University of Rochester in upstate New York. His poetry consciously engages in the broader literary traditions, which means his poems are more formal than those of most of his contemporaries and often include references to other works of literature and art. His second collection of poetry, *The Hard Hours* (1967), won the Pulitzer Prize, and Hecht counted among his many honors the position of Poet Laureate from 1982 to 1984.

AS YOU READ   Refer to Matthew Arnold's poem "Dover Beach." What has changed in "The Dover Bitch," and what stays the same? As you consider the allusion to Dover Beach in the title, ask yourself why Hecht might have responded to Arnold's poem as he did.

The Dover Bitch (1967)

A Criticism of Life: for Andrews Wanning

So there stood Matthew Arnold and this girl
With the cliffs of England crumbling away behind them,
And he said to her, "Try to be true to me,
And I'll do the same for you, for things are bad
5 All over, etc., etc."
Well now, I knew this girl. It's true she had read
Sophocles in a fairly good translation
And caught that bitter allusion to the sea,
But all the time he was talking she had in mind
10 The notion of what his whiskers would feel like
On the back of her neck. She told me later on
That after a while she got to looking out
At the lights across the channel, and really felt sad,
Thinking of all the wine and enormous beds
15 And blandishments in French and the perfumes.
And then she got really angry. To have been brought
All the way down from London, and then be addressed
As a sort of mournful cosmic last resort
Is really tough on a girl, and she was pretty.
20 Anyway, she watched him pace the room
And finger his watch-chain and seem to sweat a bit,
And then she said one or two unprintable things.
But you mustn't judge her by that. What I mean to say is,
She's really all right. I still see her once in a while
25 And she always treats me right. We have a drink
And I give her a good time, and perhaps it's a year
Before I see her again, but there she is,
Running to fat, but dependable as they come.
And sometimes I bring her a bottle of *Nuit d' Amour*.

Writing from Reading

Summarize

1 This poem could be looked at as a variation of "Dover Beach" by Matthew Arnold. In your own words, write a few sentences in prose that summarize what happens in each poem.

Analyze Craft

2 Reread your summaries of the two poems and look at the differences between your prose language, Hecht's humorous diction, and Arnold's high diction. Point to the differences.

Analyze Voice

3 Does the tone of this poem change as it proceeds? (*Nuit d'Amour*, which means "Night of Love," is a cheap perfume.)

Synthesize Summary and Analysis

4 To what extent does this poem echo Arnold's "Dover Beach," and to what extent does it merely parody (comically imitate) it?

Interpret the Poem

5 How is this poem "a criticism of life," as the dedication states?

Sometimes allusiveness can be confined to a title. Philip Larkin's grim plaint about the approaching (and unavoidable) reality of death uses no metaphorical language and seems in opposition to the fancy titular word *aubade* (traditionally associated with a poem or song about lovers parting at dawn). The poet announces he's up before dawn, "Waking at four to soundless dark," and the bulk of what follows describes what he fears. As "Slowly light strengthens, and the room takes shape," he speaks without adornment—with none of the romantic associations of a traditional dawn song—about the dark to come.

Philip Larkin (1922–1985)

Philip Larkin, perhaps the most influential British poet since World War II, bears a literary kinship to his predecessor Thomas Hardy (see Hardy's "The Convergence of the Twain" in Chapter 21 and "The Darkling Thrush" in Chapter 29, An Anthology of Poetry for Further Reading): both are marked by a pessimistic outlook expressed in unsentimental lines that present the mundane details of daily life. Also like Hardy, Larkin wrote novels in addition to his poetry—*Jill* (1946) and *A Girl in Winter* (1947). Larkin is chiefly remembered for his verse, however, and he was part of a group of poets called "The Movement," who embraced poetry that confronted the current day head-on. Larkin, who made his career as a librarian, was well appreciated in his lifetime; collections like *The Less Deceived* (1955) and *High Windows* (1974) cemented his reputation and led to his being offered the position of British Poet Laureate—an honor he refused because of the public attention such a post would bring.

AS YOU READ   Ask yourself why this poem is written in the present tense, and if the speaker's feelings change as the lines proceed. Look for both hopelessness and any signs of hope.

Aubade (1980)

I work all day, and get half drunk at night.
Waking at four to soundless dark, I stare.
In time the curtain-edges will grow light.
Till then I see what's really always there:
5   Unresting death, a whole day nearer now,
Making all thought impossible but how
And where and when I shall myself die.
Arid interrogation: yet the dread
Of dying, and being dead,
10   Flashes afresh to hold and horrify.

The mind blanks at the glare. Not in remorse
—The good not used, the love not given, time
Torn off unused—nor wretchedly because
An only life can take so long to climb
15   Clear of its wrong beginnings, and may never:
But at the total emptiness forever,
The sure extinction that we travel to
And shall be lost in always. Not to be here,
Not to be anywhere,
20   And soon; nothing more terrible, nothing more true.

This is a special way of being afraid
No trick dispels. Religion used to try,
That vast moth-eaten musical brocade
Created to pretend we never die,
25   And specious stuff that says *No rational being*

Can fear a thing it cannot feel, not seeing
that this is what we fear—no sight, no sound,
No touch or taste or smell, nothing to think with,
Nothing to love or link with,
30   The anesthetic from which none come round.

And so it stays just on the edge of vision,
A small unfocused blur, a standing chill
That slows each impulse down to indecision.
Most things may never happen: this one will,
35   And realization of it rages out
In furnace-fear when we are caught without
People or drink. Courage is no good:
It means not scaring others. Being brave
Lets no one off the grave.
40   Death is no different whined at than withstood.

Slowly light strengthens, and the room takes shape.
It stands plain as a wardrobe, what we know,
Have always known, know that we can't escape
Yet can't accept. One side will have to go.
45   Meanwhile telephones crouch, getting ready to ring
In locked-up offices, and all the uncaring
Intricate rented world begins to rouse.
The sky is white as clay, with no sun.
Work has to be done.
50   Postmen like doctors go from house to house.

Writing from Reading

Summarize

1 In a dictionary or literature glossary, look up the word *aubade*. How does this poem resemble and/or differ from the definition?

Analyze Craft

2 Would you characterize this poem's diction as formal, middle, or informal? What word choices inform your answer?

3 Describe the kind of word choice you observe in the second-to-last line of each stanza.

Analyze Voice

4 What is the speaker's attitude toward his subject matter? What mood pervades the poem, and where does the poet insist on that mood? What emotions does it represent?

Synthesize Summary and Analysis

5 How is the title of the poem reflected in the mood of the poem? What words reinforce this mood?

Interpret the Poem

6 What do you think "That vast moth-eaten musical brocade" and "the uncaring / Intricate rented world" mean?

7 To what is the poet referring when he writes "It stands plain as a wardrobe, what we know"?

DENOTATION AND CONNOTATION

Poets choose language not only because of what their diction as a whole will evoke but also because of the associations offered by individual words. Selecting language for this additional purpose further distinguishes poetry from nonliterary writing. Poets bring to their work a complicated and varied set of perceptions tied to particular word meanings. When you read the instructions in a recipe, for instance, the words hold true to their most apparent, literal meanings. The honey you add to a cookie recipe doesn't *imply* anything or suggest some veiled association. This wouldn't necessarily be the case, however, if you saw the word *honey* in a poem.

> **"I love it when someone says something, and someone else says another thing and that's all there is. And what happens, happens in between."** Conversation with Marie Howe

Most words contain both denotation and connotation. **Denotation** is the most direct and specific meaning of a word. In its denotative meaning, honey is a sugary, sticky liquid substance produced by bees from flower nectar. The same word also carries **connotations,** meanings and implications that are suggested beyond a word's literal definition. These associations come from the history of a word's past usage, the circumstances in which it has been spoken and understood. By connotation, *honey* suggests sweetness and richness, and perhaps something highly prized. Or take the word *snake*. In its simplest dictionary definition, the word refers to a long, legless reptile. However, the connotations expressed by *snake* might include associations of sneakiness, danger, or even evil.

We process denotation and connotation constantly in our lives. From the world of marketing and advertising, products and services are offered to us with careful attention paid to the wider, connotative possibilities of language. We are not just sold products themselves; we are also sold the associations they communicate. A salesperson might suggest that an item is more "affordable" rather than calling it "cheap" because of the negative connotations of that latter word. An "assisted living community" sounds more welcoming and pleasant than a "nursing home," because the words *assist, living,* and *community* connote a much more positive and supportive atmosphere than the worrisome medical implications of *nursing*. In the business world, *downsizing* implies, through connotation, efficiency and productivity. For some managers, this word is preferable to such terms as *laying off* and *firing*, which suggest a bleaker outcome.

Connotation is crucial in poetry because it enriches words' meanings; it widens their perceived associations. In a writing genre where language is compact and economical, connotative meaning further extends a poem's potential scope and meaning.

"Most things are not going to be, as we know, new; but the way they are phrased, the way they are positioned in context might make us and should make us re-engage our lives." Conversation with Stephen Dunn

In the following two poems, notice how the speakers' word choices suggest a kind of transformation. In "The Fish," Elizabeth Bishop gives us a speaker intently observing a fish she has just caught. The poem shows us the intensity and specificity of her observation, and the meditation such observation inspires. Note the kind of image-heavy language Bishop uses throughout the poem to describe her subject. She introduces the animal as a "grunting . . . battered" creature, but by the end of the poem, the speaker has come to see the fish as resilient and strong. For James Wright's "A Blessing," a phrase such as "I would like to hold the slenderer one in my arms" connotes a kind of reverence bordering on love. This change in the speaker in both poems is illustrated, in part, by the connotations of the words chosen.

Elizabeth Bishop (1911–1979)

An interest in geography and exploration, a tendency toward quiet understatement, and an unflinching sense of honesty make Elizabeth Bishop a unique and much-celebrated poet, a recipient of both the Pulitzer Prize and the National Book Award. She never saw her parents after the age of five—her father had died when she was an infant, and her mother was permanently institutionalized—and she moved from Massachusetts to Nova Scotia, then back to Massachusetts while still a child. Later in life, she settled in Brazil for nearly two decades before moving back to America and taking a professorship at Harvard University. Her work includes *North & South—A Cold Spring* (1955), *Questions of Travel* (1965), *The Complete Poems* (published in 1969 although she continued to publish poetry after that), and her more autobiographical work *Geography III* (1976).

AS YOU READ Focus on Bishop's diction, particularly her descriptive language. Circle or make note of adjectives in the poem that describe the fish.

The Fish (1946)

I caught a tremendous fish
and held him beside the boat
half out of water, with my hook
fast in a corner of its mouth.
5 He didn't fight.
He hadn't fought at all.
He hung a grunting weight,
battered and venerable
and homely. Here and there
10 his brown skin hung in strips
like ancient wallpaper,
and its pattern of darker brown
was like wallpaper:
shapes like full-blown roses
15 stained and lost through age.
He was speckled with barnacles,
fine rosettes of lime,
and infested
with tiny white sea-lice,
20 and underneath two or three
rags of green weed hung down.
While his gills were breathing in

the terrible oxygen
—the frightening gills,
25 fresh and crisp with blood,
that can cut so badly—
I thought of the coarse white flesh
packed in like feathers,
the big bones and the little bones,
30 the dramatic reds and blacks
of his shiny entrails,
and the pink swim-bladder
like a big peony.
I looked into his eyes
35 which were far larger than mine
but shallower, and yellowed,
the irises backed and packed
with tarnished tinfoil
seen through the lenses
40 of old scratched isinglass.
They shifted a little, but not
to return my stare.
—It was more like the tipping
of an object toward the light.
45 I admired his sullen face,
the mechanism of his jaw,
and then I saw
that from his lower lip
—if you could call it a lip—

50 grim, wet, and weaponlike,
hung five old pieces of fish-line,
or four and a wire leader
with the swivel still attached,
with all their five big hooks
55 grown firmly in his mouth.
A green line, frayed at the end
where he broke it, two heavier lines,
and a fine black thread
still crimped from the strain and snap
60 when it broke and he got away.
Like medals with their ribbons
frayed and wavering,
a five-haired beard of wisdom
trailing from his aching jaw.
65 I stared and stared
and victory filled up
the little rented boat,
from the pool of bilge
where oil had spread a rainbow
70 around the rusted engine
to the bailer rusted orange,
the sun-cracked thwarts,
the oarlocks on their strings,
the gunnels—until everything
75 was rainbow, rainbow, rainbow!
And I let the fish go.

Writing from Reading

Summarize

1 In a few sentences, write the facts of what has happened in this poem.

Analyze Craft

2 How does Bishop describe the fish? What connotations do these adjectives express?

Analyze Voice

3 In a dictionary, look up the word *terrible,* which Bishop uses in line

23. In what ways does it differ from—or reinforce—the word *tremendous* in line 1? How do its meanings—primary and secondary—reflect the speaker's attitude toward the fish?

Synthesize Summary and Analysis

4 How does the speaker's attitude change through the poem?

5 Contrast the basic denotative title ("The Fish") with the language Bishop uses to describe the creature. Why do you think she uses such a simple designation?

Interpret the Poem

6 Explore why the speaker in the poem lets the fish go.

James Wright (1927–1980)

James Wright was born into a working-class family in the steel-making town of Martin's Ferry, Ohio. He began writing poetry in high school and went on to earn degrees at Kenyon College, the University of Vienna, and the University of Washington. Wright won the Yale Series of Younger Poets award in 1957 with his collection of poems *The Green Wall*. Stylistically, in the 1960s Wright moved from a formal style to a more open form of verse. His subject matter often focused on issues of social concern, particularly the divide between the working and middle classes. In 1971 he won a Pulitzer Prize for his *Collected Poems*. Wright's life was cut short at age fifty-two by cancer; in 2004 his son, Franz Wright, won the Pulitzer Prize for Poetry for his book *Walking to Martha's Vineyard*.

AS YOU READ   Consider how nature relates to the animal world and how two kinds of animals—pony and poet—relate to each other. It might also be useful to view the interview with Robert Hass, who talks of another of Wright's works, "Autumn Begins in Martins Ferry, Ohio," in Chapter 26.

A Blessing (1963)

Just off the highway to Rochester, Minnesota,
Twilight bounds softly forth on the grass.
And the eyes of those two Indian ponies
Darken with kindness.
5   They have come gladly out of the willows
To welcome my friend and me.
We step over the barbed wire into the pasture
Where they have been grazing all day, alone.
They ripple tensely, they can hardly contain their happiness
10   That we have come.
They bow shyly as wet swans. They love each other.
There is no loneliness like theirs.
At home once more,
They begin munching the young tufts of spring in the darkness.
15   I would like to hold the slenderer one in my arms,
For she has walked over to me
And nuzzled my left hand.
She is black and white,
Her mane falls wild on her forehead,
20   And the light breeze moves me to caress her long ear
That is delicate as the skin over a girl's wrist.
Suddenly I realize
That if I stepped out of my body I would break
Into blossom.

Writing from Reading

Summarize

1 The speaker in this poem is describing a natural setting. Describe that setting in your own words.

Analyze Craft

2 Characterize the language of the poem. How does Wright describe nature? Why do you think Wright chooses this kind of language?

Analyze Voice

3 How specific is the speaker about the poem's setting? How does the sense of place change as the poem progresses?

Synthesize Summary and Analysis

4 How does the poem prepare the reader for the final three lines?

Interpret the Poem

5 What is the "blessing" in the poem? What realization does the speaker arrive at, and when?

WORD ORDER

In committing their ideas to the page, poets must do more than consider just the formality, denotations, and connotations of their speech. They must also decide how to arrange words within the lines of a poem. Syntax is this arrangement, the way that words and phrases combine to form sentences and make meaning. Syntax can refer to individual word placement and order, as well as the overall length and shape of a sentence. At its simplest, English grammar is grounded in a word order that follows the sequence of subject + verb + object, as in a basic statement, for example, "The man ate a hamburger." Changing the order of such a sentence ("A hamburger ate the man") dramatically alters the meaning of the sentence.

"All the time, from when I can remember, from when I was a child, I thought obsessively about the sounds of words—the cad*ences* of *sentences*, cad*ence* of *sentence ess*. Take a word at random, 'carpet.' . . . What if you turn it inside out: 'predicate' or 'particle'? That's what my mind does, compulsively. And I can't remember a time in my life when I didn't do it." Conversation with Robert Pinsky

So, word order is another potentially powerful tool for the fashioning of meaning. Take a famous example from Robert Frost. He begins "Stopping by Woods on a Snowy Evening" (Chapter 4) with a sentence whose syntax may seem strange: "Whose woods these are I think I know." A reader might expect the speaker to say, "I think I know whose woods these are." Frost, however, sets up an inversion, a reversal of expected or traditional word order. Partially, this choice aids the poem's sounds, its rhyme and meter.

But the unexpected syntax additionally allows Frost some extra nuance of meaning. *Ending* the line with "I think I know" instead of *opening* with it contributes to the poem's sense of uncertainty—as well as to a gathering certainty, because the speaker moves from the half-convinced "think" to the decisive "know."

> **"That's another aspect of poetry. I just love to say [the words]. I love to have the words in my mouth. I love those cadences . . . the . . . music, sound, and . . . rather exotic diction . . . speaking quite directly to my life and my concerns."** Conversation with Stephen Dunn

In each of the examples that follow, keep an eye (and ear) out for word order, the particular sequence of words—what's predictable and what's surprising in the poets' choices. Punctuation, too, can change the way a poem *sounds* as well as how it *looks;* consider, for example, the way that the formality of diction in Wallace Stevens's poem contrasts with the lowercased (uncapitalized) language of Lucille Clifton or the long lines of Walt Whitman. Pay particular attention to the way a change of emphasis suggests a change of tone.

Wallace Stevens (1879–1955)

Wallace Stevens's conventional life seems at odds with the stunning imagery and unexpected moves of his poetry. He spent years struggling in New York, eventually bowing to his father's disapproval of the literary life and going late to law school. Ultimately he settled in Hartford, Connecticut, and worked as an executive at the Hartford Accident and Indemnity Company for nearly forty years. He published in literary journals and corresponded with poets such as William Carlos Williams but largely led a life apart from literary circles. Stevens's business life restricted his writing to evenings and summers, but despite this, he cemented his reputation as one of the most important twentieth-century American poets with collections including *Harmonium* (1923, 1931), *Ideas of Order* (1935), *The Man with the Blue Guitar* (1937), and *The Auroras of Autumn* (1950).

AS YOU READ   Underline or make note of examples of unusual word order, and imagine the poem as if it had been written without these constructions.

The Emperor of Ice-Cream (1923)

Call the roller of big cigars,
The muscular one, and bid him whip
In kitchen cups concupiscent curds.
Let the wenches dawdle in such dress
5 As they are used to wear, and let the boys
Bring flowers in last month's newspapers.
Let be be finale of seem.
The only emperor is the emperor of ice-cream.

Take from the dresser of deal,
10 Lacking the three glass knobs, that sheet
On which she embroidered fantails once
And spread it so as to cover her face.
If her horny feet protrude, they come
To show how cold she is, and dumb.
15 Let the lamp affix its beam.
The only emperor is the emperor of ice-cream.

Writing from Reading

Summarize

1 Who are the various people assembled in this poem? Why are they there together? What is the occasion in this poem?

2 Try to put "Let be be finale of seem" in your own words.

3 What do you think is being described in the lines "And spread it so as to cover her face. / If her horny feet protrude, they come / To show how cold she is, and dumb"?

4 Rewrite the poem in plain English.

Analyze Craft

5 How would you describe Stevens's syntax (the way the words are arranged) throughout the poem? Does its style serve a point or purpose?

Analyze Voice

6 What is the mood of the poem? How does the title contribute to this mood? How does word order? Word choice? (Why, for example, might he have chosen words such as *concupiscent* and *wenches*?) Be specific.

Synthesize Summary and Analysis

7 What is the function of humor in this poem? How do subject, word choice, and word order contribute to the humor in the poem?

8 Stevens puts words in unusual order. What is the effect of this order on the poem's tone? How would the poem be different if the words were put in more ordinary sequence? What do you gain? What do you lose?

Interpret the Poem

9 What does ice cream represent to the speaker in the poem?

10 Who is the emperor of ice cream?

Lucille Clifton (1936–2010)

Born in Depew, New York, Lucille Clifton was the author of nine collections of poetry as well as a prolific author of children's books. In a plainspoken manner, Clifton wrote about her personal history as a woman and African-American, at times using her own family's genealogy to give voice to common issues of identity. Her poems reflect a pared-down style, bypassing conventional forms of capitalization, punctuation, and line length. In 1991 she assumed the position of Distinguished Professor of the Humanities at St. Mary's College in Maryland, a post she held for many years. A former poet laureate of the state of Maryland, in 2007 Clifton became the first black woman to win the Lilly Poetry Prize for lifetime achievement in poetry.

AS YOU READ   Consider how Clifton's use or lack of use of capitalization and punctuation affects your sense of the poet's voice.

praise song (2000)

to my aunt blanche
who rolled from grass to driveway
into the street one sunday morning.
i was ten.   i had never seen
5   a human woman hurl her basketball
of a body into the traffic of the world.
Praise to the drivers who stopped in time.
Praise to the faith with which she rose
after some moments then slowly walked
10   sighing back to her family.
Praise to the arms which understood
little or nothing of what it meant
but welcomed her in without judgment,
accepting it all like children might,
15   like God.

Writing from Reading

Summarize

1 What is the scene that unfolds in this poem?

Analyze Craft

2 How do the lack of regular punctuation, the use of capitalization, and the short unstressed lines provide a shape for what is happening in the poem?

Analyze Voice

3 How would you describe Clifton's word choice? Is it formal, middle, or informal diction?

Synthesize Summary and Analysis

4 In what ways is this poem a "praise song"? What is the poem praising?

Interpret the Poem

5 Consider the phrase "the traffic of the world." How would you describe its meaning?

6 How does the speaker in the poem view God?

Walt Whitman (1819–1892)

It is almost impossible to overestimate Walt Whitman's influence on American poetry, and indeed on the American spirit. Born on Long Island, New York, Whitman held a variety of jobs including office clerk, journalist, teacher, printer, and carpenter. He created one work of poetry, *Leaves of Grass,* first published in 1855; with each subsequent edition, Whitman added more poems, eventually titling each group of poems, among them the "Calamus" poems in *Leaves of Grass,* "Children of Adam," and "Drum-Taps." Known for its freedom of line, optimism, and expansiveness, his poetry celebrates many occupations and classes of people, which makes him a poet inextricably linked to the spirit of democracy and the broad frontier of the West (even though he lived most of his life on the East Coast). His poetry is also marked by an admiration of physicality and the body, which made his work seem scandalous to many nineteenth-century Americans. His darkest poems are those he wrote during the Civil War and after the death of his hero, Abraham Lincoln. Whitman served as a nurse for the Union troops, but his expansive compassion extends to all soldiers, regardless of their allegiance. Perhaps his greatest legacy to future poets was his unconventional abandoning of established poetic form—Whitman wrote in long, confident lines—and his free use of subject matter that made all aspects of life fair game for inclusion.

AS YOU READ Notice how the speaker addresses all of America. If Marie Howe's "What the Living Do" is a "private" poem, and Whitman's is a "public" one, look at the differences between the uses of "I" in each poem.

I Hear America Singing (1860)

I hear America singing, the varied carols I hear,
Those of mechanics, each one singing his as it should be blithe and
   strong,
The carpenter singing his as he measures his plank or beam,
The mason singing his as he makes ready for work, or leaves off work,
5 The boatman singing what belongs to him in his boat, the deckhand
   singing on the steamboat deck,
The shoemaker singing as he sits on his bench, the hatter singing as
   he stands,
The wood-cutter's song, the ploughboy's on his way in the morning,
   or at noon intermission or at sundown,
The delicious singing of the mother, or of the young wife at work, or
   of the girl sewing or washing,
Each singing what belongs to him or her and to none else,
10 The day what belongs to the day—at night the party of young fellows,
   robust, friendly,
Singing with open mouths their strong melodious songs.

Writing from Reading

Summarize

1 What is your first impression of this poem? What is the speaker doing?

Analyze Craft

2 Find descriptions that seem typical of the poem's diction. How would you characterize them? How does the language differ from that of other poets you've read?

Analyze Voice

3 Describe your sense of the speaker. What is his tone? What is important to him, and how can you tell?

4 How does Whitman establish a relationship between his poetic voice and the reader? What is this relationship like?

Synthesize Summary and Analysis

5 Do the long lines and the diction contribute to the tone of the poem? Explain how they do or do not reinforce the subject of the poem.

Interpret the Poem

6 Can you say that the poem demonstrates a particularly American way of seeing the world? Why?

"The poem is made out of the sounds of words . . . *bobbin* which sounds like *union*. . . . I was not a successful student in high school . . . and the thing that kind of rescued [me was that] I was voted "most musical boy" . . . and my band was the band that played the high school dances. . . . In my late teens, just about the time when I was discovering I was not going to be good enough to be a musician, I also discovered that there was an art based on the sounds of words [and that] Allen Ginsberg and T. S. Eliot and William Butler Yeats and Walt Whitman and Emily Dickinson were playing those consonants and syllables as though they were musical instruments, and I haven't looked back from that discovery." Conversation with Robert Pinsky

For Review and Further Study

Billy Collins (b. 1941)

For a brief biography of Billy Collins, see Chapter 17.

The Names (2002)

Yesterday, I lay awake in the palm of the night.
A fine rain stole in, unhelped by any breeze,
And when I saw the silver glaze on the windows,
I started with A, with Ackerman, as it happened,
5 Then Baxter and Calabro,
Davis and Eberling, names falling into place
As droplets fell through the dark.

Names printed on the ceiling of the night.
Names slipping around a watery bend.
10 Twenty-six willows on the banks of a stream.

In the morning, I walked out barefoot
Among thousands of flowers
Heavy with dew like the eyes of tears,
And each had a name—
15 Fiori inscribed on a yellow petal
Then Gonzalez and Han, Ishikawa and Jenkins.

Names written in the air
And stitched into the cloth of the day.
A name under a photograph taped to a mailbox.
20 Monogram on a torn shirt,
I see you spelled out on storefront windows
And on the bright unfurled awnings of this city.
I say the syllables as I turn a corner—
Kelly and Lee,
25 Medina, Nardella, and O'Connor.

When I peer into the woods,
I see a thick tangle where letters are hidden
As in a puzzle concocted for children.
Parker and Quigley in the twigs of an ash,
30 Rizzo, Schubert, Torres, and Upton,
Secrets in the boughs of an ancient maple.

Names written in the pale sky.
Names rising in the updraft amid buildings.
Names silent in stone
35 Or cried out behind a door.
Names blown over the earth and out to sea.

In the evening—weakening light, the last swallows.
A boy on a lake lifts his oars.
A woman by a window puts a match to a candle,
40 And the names are outlined on the rose clouds—
Vanacore and Wallace,
(let X stand, if it can, for the ones unfound)
Then Young and Ziminsky, the final jolt of Z.

Names etched on the head of a pin.
45 One name spanning a bridge, another undergoing a
   tunnel.
A blue name needled into the skin.
Names of citizens, workers, mothers and fathers,
The bright-eyed daughter, the quick son.
Alphabet of names in a green field.
50 Names in the small tracks of birds.
Names lifted from a hat
Or balanced on the tip of the tongue.
Names wheeled into the dim warehouse of memory.
So many names, there is barely room on the walls
   of the heart.

Questions for Interactive Reading and Writing

1. Why does Collins first select the names, from "Ackerman" to "Eberling," and what do they convey?

2. In the sequence of names that follow, "Gonzalez and Han," and so on, what is he trying to say—if anything—about the nature of America?

3. Is a phrase such as "the walls of the heart" concrete or abstract? Or both?

e. e. cummings (1894–1962)

For a brief biography of e. e. cummings, see Chapter 26.

in Just- (1920)

in Just-
spring   when the world is mud-
luscious the little
lame balloonman

whistles   far   and wee   5

and eddieandbill come
running from marbles and
piracies and it's
spring

when the world is puddle-wonderful   10

the queer
old balloonman whistles
far   and   wee
and bettyandisbel come dancing

from hop-scotch and jump-rope and   15

it's
spring
and
      the

            goat-footed   20

balloonMan   whistles
far
and
wee

Questions for Interactive Reading and Writing

1. Discuss the line arrangements here, and the use of lowercase letters.

2. Why does e. e. cummings conjoin the names of the marble-playing boys, the dancing girls, and the balloonman?

3. What does the repetition of "far and wee" suggest, and did he mean to say, instead, "far and wide"?

John Donne (1572–1631)

A Valediction: Forbidding Mourning (1633)

As virtuous men pass mildly away,
 And whisper to their souls to go,
Whilst some of their sad friends do say,
 "Now his breath goes," and some say, "No."
5 So let us melt, and make no noise,
 No tear-floods, nor sigh-tempests move;
 'Twere profanation of our joys
  To tell the laity our love.
Moving of th' earth brings harms and fears;
10 Men reckon what it did, and meant;
But trepidation of the spheres,
 Though greater far, is innocent.
Dull sublunary lovers' love
 —Whose soul is sense—cannot admit
15 Of absence, 'cause it doth remove
 The thing which elemented it.
But we by a love so much refined,
 That ourselves know not what it is,
Inter-assurèd of the mind,
20 Care less, eyes, lips and hands to miss.
Our two souls therefore, which are one,
 Though I must go, endure not yet
A breach, but an expansion,
 Like gold to aery thinness beat.
If they be two, they are two so
25 As stiff twin compasses are two;
Thy soul, the fix'd foot, makes no show
 To move, but doth, if th' other do.
And though it in the centre sit,
 Yet, when the other far doth roam,
30
It leans, and hearkens after it,
 And grows erect, as that comes home.
Such wilt thou be to me, who must,
 Like th' other foot, obliquely run;
Thy firmness makes my circle just,
 And makes me end where I begun.
35

Questions for Interactive Reading and Writing

1. See the extended image of the compass here. The Metaphysical poets—of whom Donne was a leading member—called such extended comparison a "conceit." Point out its several uses in the text.

2. To whom is the poet speaking when he writes, "Our two souls"? What's concrete, what abstract in Donne's word choice here?

3. The poet begins by discussing death and ends by celebrating life—is all this signaled by the four words of the title? If so, how?

Martin Espada (b. 1957)

Why I Went to College (2001)

If you don't,
my father said,
you better learn
to eat soup
through a straw,
'cause I'm gonna
break your jaw
5

Questions for Interactive Reading and Writing

1. From the mere twenty-one words of this poem, how would you describe the father, the speaker, and their relationship?

2. Each line consists of three words. How would you describe the rhythm this creates?

3. How necessary is the title to our understanding of the poem? Why do you think the information contained in the title isn't put into the poem itself?

3. How does the title organize Nye's poem, and what are the "secrets of dying"?

Naomi Shihab Nye (b. 1952)

The World in Translation (1995)

It was a long climb out of the soil.
She counted off whole continents
as she lifted each foot,
imagined her dark years falling away like husks.
5 Soon she could feel objects come to life
in her hand, the peel of banana,
a lightly waxed pepper,
she accepted these into her home,
placed them in bowls where they could be watched.
10 There was nothing obscure about melons,
nothing involved about yams.
If she were to have anything to do with the world,
these would be her translators,
through these she would learn secrets of dying,
15 how to do it gracefully as the peach,
softening in silence,
or the mango, finely tuned to its own skin.

Questions for Interactive Reading and Writing

1. Consider the specificity of "she lifted each foot" and the improbable generality of "She counted off whole continents." How does this juxtaposition (the placing of one line right after the other) work?

2. List the fruits and vegetables named here. What is it about the changing condition of a piece of fruit that teaches the speaker in the poem about living and dying?

Kevin Young (b. 1971)

Langston Hughes (1999)

LANGSTON HUGHES
LANGSTON HUGHES
    O come now
    & sang
5 them weary blues—
Been tired here
feelin' low down
    Real
    tired here
10 since you quit town

Our ears no longer trumpets
Our mouths no more bells
    FAMOUS POET©—
    Busboy—Do tell
15 us of hell—

Mr . Shakespeare in Harlem
Mr. Theme for English B
    Preach on
    kind sir
of death, if it please—   20

We got no more promise
We only got ain't
    Let us in
    on how
you 'came a saint   25

LANGSTON
LANGSTON
    LANGSTON HUGHES
    Won't you send
all heaven's news   30

Questions for Interactive Reading and Writing

1. Circle each word Young uses that could be considered informal diction. Why do you think he chooses these words instead of formal or middle diction?

2. "The Weary Blues" and "Theme for English B" are titles of two of Hughes's poems, and *Shakespeare in Harlem* is the title of a book of Hughes's poetry. What effect does Young achieve by working these titles into his poem?

3. To what effect does Young use rhythm and rhyme in the poem? How are these appropriate for a poem lamenting Hughes's death?

4. Despite the "blue" feeling of the speaker, this poem manages to be playful. In what ways do you see playfulness in stanza 4?

Reading for Words

When reading for words, ask yourself what kind of diction the poet has used and how the poet's diction helps to convey a poem's style.

Formal Diction	Lofty, ceremonial, and explicitly serious word choice in poetry	EXAMPLE "Thou still unravished bride of quietness"
Middle Diction	A blend of "common" speech and "elevated" diction	EXAMPLE "Let aeroplanes circle moaning overhead"
Informal Diction	Conversational, plainspoken language; often makes use of slang, contractions, and mainstream expressions	EXAMPLE "Johnny, the kitchen sink has been clogged for days"
Are there specialized uses of language in a poem?	*Dialect:* A style of language spoken by and associated with a particular region or group of people	EXAMPLE "We real cool"
	Colloquial Language: Familiar, conversational language	EXAMPLE "We / Thin gin. We / Jazz June."

How does the writer mix concrete and abstract words?	*Concrete:* Specific, physical language describing something perceivable to the senses	EXAMPLE "Rough winds do shake the darling buds of May"
	Abstract: Vocabulary referring to something conceptual, not physically material	EXAMPLE "The sea of faith . . ."
What connotations do the words evoke beyond their denotations?	*Denotation:* The literal, dictionary definition of a word	EXAMPLE *Snake:* A long, legless reptile
	Connotation: The nonliteral associations and impressions a word conveys to a reader	EXAMPLE Snake: sneakiness, danger, or even evil.
How do the order of the words, the punctuation, and the syntax (the rhythm and shape of the sentence) enhance the meaning of the poem?	*Inversion:* A change in the normal, expected order of words	EXAMPLE "Whose woods these are I think I know" versus "I think I know whose woods these are"

Writing about Words

1. Write an analysis of the spiritual conflicts imagined in Stevens's "The Emperor of Ice-Cream."

2. Compare attitudes toward religion and/or spirituality between any of the following poems: Arnold's "Dover Beach," Clifton's "praise song," Stevens's "The Emperor of Ice-Cream," and Wright's "A Blessing."

3. Both Stevens's "The Emperor of Ice-Cream" and Larkin's "Aubade" deal with the theme of death and mortality. Contrast the tone and meaning of the poems by describing the differences between the two poets' language choices. If you wish, you can add Auden's "Funeral Blues" to this mix.

4. Describe the similarities and differences between tone and language in the colloquial diction in two or more of the following poems: Brooks's "We Real Cool," Clifton's "praise song," Espada's "Why I Went to College," Hecht's "Dover Bitch," or Young's "Langston Hughes." How does the use of this diction help create the tone in these poems?

5. Compare the connotations in word choices associated with Robert Frost's horse and speaker in "Stopping by Woods on a Snowy Evening" (Chapter 4) with those in James Wright's "A Blessing."

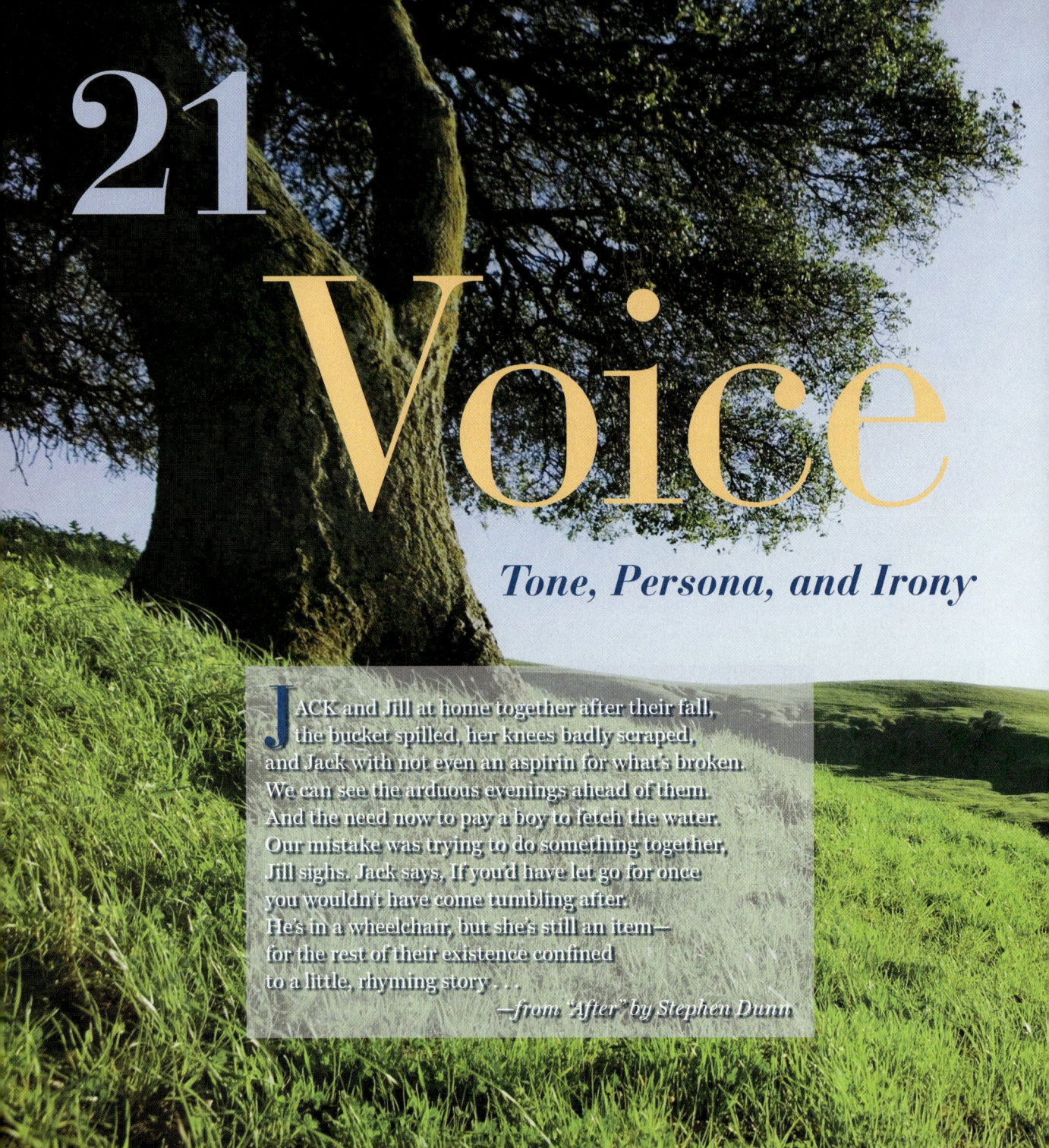

21

Voice

Tone, Persona, and Irony

JACK and Jill at home together after their fall,
    the bucket spilled, her knees badly scraped,
and Jack with not even an aspirin for what's broken.
We can see the arduous evenings ahead of them.
And the need now to pay a boy to fetch the water.
Our mistake was trying to do something together,
Jill sighs. Jack says, If you'd have let go for once
you wouldn't have come tumbling after.
He's in a wheelchair, but she's still an item—
for the rest of their existence confined
to a little, rhyming story . . .

—*from "After" by Stephen Dunn*

"AFTER," by Stephen Dunn, is a poem that reports on conversation and relies on voice. The poet speaks to us as readers; at the same time he speaks to himself. His diction is as informal as was Marie Howe's in "What the Living Do" (see Chapter 20). Note the contractions ("He's in a wheelchair"), the slang ("she's still an item"), and the general flavor of written language as speech. Dunn wittily imagines the repercussions for two famous nursery rhyme characters "after" their untimely fall down a hill. The premise here, of course, is comic and even a bit bizarre. Jack and Jill sit at home after their accident like an old married couple, aching and depressed, blaming one another for their predicament. The "little, rhyming story" with which all of us are familiar—"Jack and Jill went up the hill / To fetch a pail of water"—becomes something unfamiliar, *new,* and that unfamiliarity has much to do with tone.

Despite his humorous premise, Dunn manages to use the tale of Jack and Jill to reflect on multifaceted themes of intimacy, transgression, and fate. Notice how Jack's "in a wheelchair" because—according to the original poem, he's the one who "fell down / And broke his crown"—and her knees are "badly scraped." As you'll see, by the end of "After," the "fallout" of their story has something to say to all of us about coping with misfortune. "The fundamental business of making do," as the poet puts it, transforms what we take for granted—a childhood nursery rhyme—into something with which we must deal.

The lines seem wry, and a little cynical, and matter-of-fact, or all these things at once. Whenever you think about the attitude expressed in a poem, you're undoubtedly thinking about the poem's tone. Whenever you consider whose voice you're hearing as you read, you're thinking about the poem's persona, the speaker delivering his or her language to the audience.

On the subject of rendering voice in a poem, Stephen Dunn acknowledges the power of irony, the use of words to indicate an opposite or unexpected meaning. As he puts it, "irony is a way of managing experience, and thus keeping it at a distance, while at its best being a way of recognizing and opening up experience by delivering simultaneous awareness." A poem like "After" asks us to ponder the emotional lives of a pair of nursery rhyme characters, and asks us to smile at and simultaneously sympathize with the ways we confront our own hardship.

By looking carefully at the artist's choice of tone, persona, and irony, we can improve our sense of the ways poets manage our experience as readers.

CONTINUED ON PAGE 668

Stephen Dunn *Literature brought the world to me.*

A Conversation on Writing

Poetry Makes Us Part of the World

I think one of the reasons people don't get into poetry . . . [is] they don't quite believe it has anything to do with their lives. Certainly for me, that was the case, and I didn't come to poetry seriously till after college when I started to find those poems that addressed . . . the things that I had inklings about that I was largely inarticulate about. When we find those stories or poems or novels that make us feel part of the world, [we find] . . . the things that we say [that] are secret . . . the things we've not confessed to anybody. Good literature, whether it's poetry or any of the other genres, has a way of bringing us into the common fold, of making us part of the world.

Poetry as a Challenge to Personal Experience

I'm sure you all have heard this, when somebody says, "Oh, I can relate to that." They like to relate to that rather than be subverted, rather than to have their ideas challenged. . . . What I want from good poems is to be offered another way into experience. I don't want to have my experience confirmed.

Revision and Our Own Invention

Lots of revisions, lots of false moves, lots of altering, lots of going back and rearranging—essentially, the [writing] process is like that for me. When I'm working from experience I'm most worried about my selection of details, and when I'm working from an imaginative premise, the problem is how not to be too in love with your own invention.

To watch this entire interview and hear the author read from his work, go to **connect.mcgraw-hill.com.**

Born in Forest Hills, New York (1939), Stephen Dunn quit a corporate job to try his hand at writing. Early on, he was an accomplished basketball player, and there's a way in which his skills as an athlete translate into the effortless grace of his diction; there's a fluid ease of motion in the lines. He earned a master's in creative writing from Syracuse University and has taught creative writing at Richard Stockton University in New Jersey since 1974. The author of a collection of essays on craft and a dozen books of poetry, Dunn won the Pulitzer Prize in 2001 for his collection *Different Hours.* Dunn's poetry takes the everyday for its subject; as he puts it in an interview, "I think most of our lives are made up of both things visible and things interior, with a large chunk of them being interior. So whenever I've been able to arrive at clarities about that which is elusive about dailyness, that has pleased me."

RESEARCH ASSIGNMENT

After you have watched the interview, comment on Dunn's attitude toward irony in poetry. How does he describe the way irony functions in his poem "After"? What part does irony play in Dunn's idea of engagement with poetry? How does he (or how doesn't he) achieve this ironic engagement in his poem "After"?

AS YOU READ You will notice that in "After," Dunn delivers a humorous narrative. At first you may find this poem, a sort of sequel to the old Jack and Jill nursery rhyme, merely funny. As you read more deeply, look for ways the poem reveals an intricate sympathy, a seriousness, and the narrator's darker, ironic attitude.

After (2002)

Jack and Jill at home together after their fall,
the bucket spilled, her knees badly scraped,
and Jack with not even an aspirin for what's broken.
We can see the arduous evenings ahead of them.
5 And the need now to pay a boy to fetch the water.
Our mistake was trying to do something together,
Jill sighs. Jack says, If you'd have let go for once
you wouldn't have come tumbling after.
He's in a wheelchair, but she's still an item—
10 for the rest of their existence confined
to a little rhyming story. We tell it to our children,
who laugh, already accustomed to disaster.
We'd like to teach them the secrets
of knowing how to go too far,
15 but Jack is banging with his soup spoon,
Jill is pulling out her hair. Out of decency
we turn away, as if it were possible to escape
the drift of our lives, the fundamental business
of making do with what's been left us.

Writing from Reading

Summarize

1 What has Dunn added to or altered in the story of the nursery rhyme?

Analyze Craft

2 How does Dunn introduce irony into the nursery rhyme?

3 What makes this poem feel so playful? Compare its use of a previous text, the nursery rhyme about Jack and Jill, with Anthony Hecht's treatment of Matthew Arnold's "Dover Beach" (Chapter 20).

Analyze Voice

4 Who is "we" in this poem? Why does Dunn use "we"?

5 Describe the speaker's tone in this poem. Why does Dunn choose this kind of voice for the subject matter?

Synthesize Summary and Analysis

6 How does Dunn marry a playful tone with a melancholy message?

Interpret the Poem

7 When the poem says "we turn away," what do you think the "we" is turning away *from*?

"The first level of [a poem's] meaning is simply to be moved and to hear a speaker, to hear voice giving voice to what is within the poet." Conversation with Carolyn Forché

TONE

On a daily basis, sometimes hardly conscious of doing so, we interpret the language we hear. We know to listen for clues that indicate to us exactly how people intend their language. Because of extra emphasis on one word in a sentence, the ordinary question "Are you going to eat that?" can suddenly become the more surprised "Are you going to *eat* that?" If, instead, the speaker asks "Are you going to eat *that?*" the question focuses on the thing about to be eaten rather than the act of consumption. The word choice is exactly the same, but the meaning is quite different. If the emphasis falls on the word *you*, a fourth meaning may become central: how come *you* get to eat that and I can't? All this has to do with *intonation*, the *way* a thing gets said. We make interpretive distinctions by tuning in to **tone** of voice, the particular communicative quality of a person's speech.

"A poem is . . . like a musical score for human speech. . . . You come and you read the poem and you play the voice." Conversation with Li-Young Lee

In poetry, language works in similar, equally subtle ways. As you're reading a poem, analyzing the intentions of word choice and word order, you will often find a kind of implicit meaning emerges from these lines. In poetry, tone is an attitude conveyed toward a poem's subject as suggested by the poet's language. No one element of poetry establishes tone by itself. Tone is a kind of cumulative effect, resulting from all of poetry's components, including word choice and arrangement, figures of speech, rhythm, and sound.

Tone in poetry is as variable as the different voices you hear every day on the street, capable of humor, seriousness, contemplation, desperation, anger, or any other emotion. A love poem designed to woo its recipient might do so seriously, with soaring language; or it might work just as effectively with comedy, using wordplay. There's no one right tone for a thought or idea, just the prerogative of the author who wishes to best communicate his or her intended meaning.

The following poems illustrate a range of tones, from the restrained to the emotional to the ambivalent. The first selection describes the internal and external experiences of a World War II aviator operating the gun on the belly of a large bomber.

"Once you get the poem right . . . you sound like yourself talking to yourself. It's that voice that we hear just before we fall asleep, the voice that we start out the day with when everything seems to fall into place." Conversation with Thomas Lynch

Randall Jarrell (1914–1965)

Born in Tennessee, Randall Jarrell spent part of his childhood in California before returning to his native state for an education at Vanderbilt University. He published his first collection of poetry, *Blood for a Stranger* (1942), in the same year that he enlisted in the Army Air Corps, in which he served during World War II. After the war, he taught at the Women's College of the University of North Carolina until his death at age fifty-one, when he was hit by a car. Jarrell's poetry is sensitive to the pain of his speakers, whether domestic housewives or soldiers fighting in World War II. In addition to winning the National Book Award for *The Woman at the Wash-ington Zoo* (1960), Jarrell held the position of Poet Laureate. He was also an unusually influential literary critic, championing poetry by Walt Whitman and Robert Frost, and helping to establish the success of such poets as Elizabeth Bishop and William Carlos Williams.

AS YOU READ   Think about how the tone of the language (for example, "wet fur froze," "black flak and the night-mare fighters") helps the poem communicate an attitude or particular atmosphere. Notice, also, the bleak efficiency here; it's a poem of only five lines.

The Death of the Ball Turret Gunner (1945)

From my mother's sleep I fell into the State,
And I hunched in its belly till my wet fur froze.
Six miles from earth, loosed from the dream of life,
I woke to black flak and the nightmare fighters.
5   When I died they washed me out of the turret with a hose.

Writing from Reading

Summarize

1 Describe the fate the flyer imagines for himself.

Analyze Craft

2 Why do you think the word *state* is capitalized?

3 What images are used in this poem?

Analyze Voice

4 How would you characterize the tone of the poem? Does it seem like an unusual or an apt choice for a poem about war?

Synthesize Summary and Analysis

5 How does the description of the flyer's experience show the horror he is imagining?

Interpret the Poem

6 How does the tone of the poem's final line contrast with the image it describes?

7 Is this an antiwar poem or a heroic poem? How do you think the speaker feels about war?

Sometimes a poem's tone is especially subtle or multilayered. Theodore Roethke's "My Papa's Waltz" is one such work. A memory of the speaker's father playfully dancing with him when the speaker was a child, the poem entertains different attitudes simultaneously. We start with the knowledge that the father is drunk—or at least has been drinking—and that the boy hangs on "like death," because it's hard to follow where the dancing adult leads. The father doesn't fully realize how much he is bending or stretching the bond of love between parent and child. The mother, watching, frowns. By poem's end, however, the dance becomes a kind of elegy, with the speaker "still clinging" to the memories of childhood and the strong if implicit suggestion that the father is dead. These emotions in opposition—fear, delight, disapproval—are bodied forth in a domestic scene, as from kitchen to bedroom "we romped."

Theodore Roethke (1908–1963)

Growing up, Theodore Roethke loved to spend time in the greenhouse his father and uncle owned in Saginaw, Michigan. This was a lifelong fascination; his poems are full of imagery and metaphor that hinge on the natural world.

Unsentimental in his portrayal of nature, Roethke was equally unafraid to put his own feelings and experiences into his poems, which made him the forerunner of confessional poets such as Anne Sexton and Sylvia Plath. His collections were widely acclaimed: *The Waking* (1953) won the Pulitzer Prize, and *Words for the Wind*

(1958) won the National Book Award, as did his posthumous *The Far Field* (1964). His mental health was precarious and his mood swings large, but Roethke was a celebrated and devoted teacher; he spent most of his teaching life at the University of Washington.

AS YOU READ   Think about how the speaker's feelings about memory might have more than one dimension. Consider also how the poem's meaning and tone are reinforced with slant rhymes, rather than exact rhymes. In the final two stanzas, however, it's as if the boy gets the hang of his father's waltzing rhythm and can follow along exactly once he gets into the "swing of things" at poem's end.

TIP

FOR INTERACTIVE READING . . .

Circle the approximate, or slant, rhymes, such as "dizzy" and "easy" or "pans" and "countenance." Note the waltz time and dance step involved.

My Papa's Waltz (1948)

The whiskey on your breath
Could make a small boy dizzy;
But I hung on like death:
Such waltzing was not easy.

5   We romped until the pans
Slid from the kitchen shelf;
My mother's countenance
Could not unfrown itself.

The hand that held my wrist
10 Was battered on one knuckle;
At every step you missed
My right ear scraped a buckle.

You beat time on my head
With a palm caked hard by dirt,
15 Then waltzed me off to bed
Still clinging to your shirt.

Writing from Reading

Summarize

1 What has happened in this poem?

2 How does the mother feel about what has happened? Is it clear how the child feels?

Analyze Craft

3 Pick out phrases and words that indicate the speaker remembers his father's behavior fondly.

4 Pick out phrases and words that indicate the speaker remembers his father's behavior negatively or critically.

Analyze Voice

5 Who is the speaker in this poem?

6 Do you think the poem's variation in tone is purposeful? Discuss why or why not.

Synthesize Summary and Analysis

7 How does the innocence of the child's perspective allow us to draw our own conclusions about what happened here?

Interpret the Poem

8 Discuss the significance of the poem's final line. What if Roethke did not include this image of the boy "still clinging"? Would that change your sense of the poem's tone?

In contrast to the tone and word choice of such poets as Stephen Dunn and Theodore Roethke, the diction employed by Wallace Stevens sounds formal and even stately. This is not "conversational" language—a poet talking to himself and us as audience; rather, it is a carefully arranged and presented series of pronouncements, insisting on attentiveness on the reader's part. In this poem—which first appeared in *Poetry* magazine in 1915, although Stevens later revised and enlarged it—he details an aging woman's religious conflict between traditional piety and individual, personal spiritual exploration.

Wallace Stevens (1879–1955)

For a brief biography of Wallace Stevens, see Chapter 20.

AS YOU READ   Consider "Sunday Morning" in the terms that we've been using: as a series of different poetic elements that establish tone. One way of reading this poem is in terms of its ambitious range of referents—to the Holy Land, to Greek gods and "the blood of paradise," and so on; another is to read about an old woman in the sun, drinking a cup of coffee and wondering what happens when she dies.

FOR INTERACTIVE READING . . .

Make note of or circle words like *death* or that pertain to death, both obviously (as in *tomb* or *grave*) and implicitly, where you think Stevens might be making a reference to death. Underline or note words and phrases that are used repeatedly in the poem.

Sunday Morning (1915)

I

Complacencies of the peignoir, and late
Coffee and oranges in a sunny chair,
And the green freedom of a cockatoo
Upon a rug, mingle to dissipate
5 The holy hush of ancient sacrifice.
She dreams a little, and she feels the dark
Encroachment of that old catastrophe,
As a calm darkens among water-lights.
The pungent oranges and bright, green wings
10 Seem things in some procession of the dead,
Winding across wide water, without sound.
The day is like wide water, without sound,
Stilled for the passing of her dreaming feet
Over the seas, to silent Palestine,
15 Dominion of the blood and sepulchre.

II

She hears, upon that water without sound,
A voice that cries, "The tomb in Palestine
Is not the porch of spirits lingering;
It is the grave of Jesus, where he lay."
20 We live in an old chaos of the sun,
Or old dependency of day and night,
Or island solitude, unsponsored, free,
Of that wide water, inescapable.
Deer walk upon our mountains, and the quail
25 Whistle about us their spontaneous cries;
Sweet berries ripen in the wilderness;
And, in the isolation of the sky,
At evening, casual flocks of pigeons make
Ambiguous undulations as they sink,
30 Downward to darkness, on extended wings.

III

She says, "I am content when wakened birds,
Before they fly, test the reality
Of misty fields, by their sweet questionings;
But when the birds are gone, and their warm fields
35 Return no more, where, then, is paradise?"
There is not any haunt of prophecy,
Nor any old chimera of the grave,

Neither the golden underground, nor isle
Melodious, where spirits gat them home,
40 Nor visionary South, nor cloudy palm
Remote on heaven's hill, that has endured
As April's green endures; or will endure
Like her remembrance of awakened birds,
Or her desire for June and evening, tipped
45 By the consummation of the swallow's wings.

IV

She says, "But in contentment I still feel
The need of some imperishable bliss."
Death is the mother of beauty; hence from her,
Alone, shall come fulfillment to our dreams
50 And our desires. Although she strews the leaves
Of sure obliteration on our paths—
The path sick sorrow took, the many paths
Where triumph rang its brassy phrase, or love
Whispered a little out of tenderness—
55 She makes the willow shiver in the sun
For maidens who were wont to sit and gaze
Upon the grass, relinquished to their feet.
She causes boys to bring sweet-smelling pears
And plums in ponderous piles. The maidens taste
60 And stray impassioned in the littering leaves.

V

Supple and turbulent, a ring of men
Shall chant in orgy on a summer morn
Their boisterous devotion to the sun—
Not as a god, but as a god might be,
65 Naked among them, like a savage source.
Their chant shall be a chant of paradise,
Out of their blood, returning to the sky;
And in their chant shall enter, voice by voice,
The windy lake wherein their lord delights,
70 The trees, like serafim, and echoing hills,
That choir among themselves long afterward.
They shall know well the heavenly fellowship
Of men that perish and of summer morn—
And whence they came and whither they shall go,
75 The dew upon their feel shall manifest.

Writing from Reading

Summarize

1 What does the title indicate about the subject of the poem? What activities are typical of a Sunday morning?

2 What information about the situation of the poem—*when* it takes place, *where* it takes place, *what's* at stake or being talked about—do you obtain from the poem's first section?

Analyze Craft

3 In his interview, Stephen Dunn talks about reciting this poem on Sunday mornings with his wife and about Stevens's "exotic" diction. What about the words chosen for this poem might make Dunn describe Stevens's word choices as

exotic? Why do you think Stevens chooses to use language such as this?

Analyze Voice

4 Look at the opening phrase "Complacencies of the peignoir" or the penultimate one of the second stanza, "Ambiguous undulations as they sink," and consider Stevens's voice. What uses does he make of the language of everyday speech, and how does he alter and heighten it? Note the places where he *does* use everyday language or commonplace objects—such as "coffee and oranges" or "sweet berries ripen in the wilderness." How does this kind of juxtaposition create a voice and tone for this poem?

5 Where in the poem does the speaker hint that the woman is old?

Synthesize Summary and Analysis

6 Each of the stanzas has precisely fifteen lines. How does this formal arrangement serve the poet's purpose, and what does the repetition of such words as "wide water" accomplish?

Interpret the Poem

7 What is the "old catastrophe" mentioned in the first section? Compare stanza 5 here with John Keats's "Ode on a Grecian Urn" (Chapter 20). Do he and Stevens have a similar reaction to the past?

Anne Bradstreet was one of the first poets in the American colonies and inarguably our country's first acclaimed female poet. Unbeknownst to Bradstreet, friends of hers saw to the publication of her poems in London in a collection titled *The Tenth Muse, Lately Sprung Up in America*, in 1650. Written in 1678, the following poem introduced a later edition of that volume and voices Bradstreet's mixed feelings about the book's earlier, unauthorized publication.

Anne Bradstreet (1612–1672)

Among the earliest Puritans to settle the American colonies, Anne Bradstreet suffered the hardships of an educated Englishwoman brought to the harsh conditions of a struggling colony. Nevertheless, as her poetry attests, she loved her husband, her home, and her children. It was rare for a Puritan woman to write poetry and equally rare for her to be educated in Latin, Hebrew, Greek, medicine, and theology. The mother of eight children and wife to the governor of Massachusetts, Bradstreet shared most of her poems only with family and friends. However, her brother-in-law took a collection of her poems to England, where they were published as *The Tenth Muse, Lately Sprung Up in America* (1650). With a title echoing Plato's praise of Sappho, this work by the "tenth muse" was the first book by a New Englander ever to be published.

AS YOU READ   Remember that words like *thou* were common in Anne Bradstreet's day; in this poem, they are not examples of elevated poetic diction but, rather, are everyday speech. *Thou* was the informal or diminutive form of *you*, and so the very first word of the poem suggests a kind of intimacy with the "offspring" addressed. Notice the ways in which "the author" compares "her book" to a child and the self-effacing claim that her brain is "feeble." The speaker is both proud and apologetic, both serious and tongue-in-cheek, and the mixture of these elements is part of the poem's great charm.

The Author to Her Book

(1678)

Thou ill-formed offspring of my feeble brain,
Who after birth didst by my side remain,
Till snatched from thence by friends, less wise than true,
Who thee abroad exposed to public view,
5 Made thee in rags, halting to th' press to trudge,
Where errors were not lessened (all may judge).
At thy return my blushing was not small,
My rambling brat (in print) should mother call.
I cast thee by as one unfit for light,
10 Thy visage was so irksome in my sight;
Yet being mine own, at length affection would
Thy blemishes amend, if so I could.
I washed thy face, but more defects I saw,
And rubbing off a spot still made a flaw.
15 I stretched thy joints to make thee even feet,
Yet still thou run'st more hobbling than is meet;
In better dress to trim thee was my mind,
But nought save home-spun cloth, i' th' house I find.
In this array, 'mongst vulgars mayst thou roam.
20 In critics' hands, beware thou dost not come,
And take thy way where yet thou art not known;
If for thy Father asked, say, thou hadst none;
And for thy Mother, she alas is poor,
Which caused her thus to send thee out of door.

Writing from Reading

Summarize

1 Who or what is the speaker addressing? To what does "ill-formed off-spring of my feeble brain" refer?

2 List the complaints the speaker has about her book.

3 Why in the last lines are we told "thy Mother . . . is poor"?

Analyze Craft

4 Discuss how the poet compares a book to a child. How do these lines about the book also reveal her thoughts on motherhood?

Analyze Voice

5 How does the speaker's attitude toward her book change as the poem progresses?

Synthesize Summary and Analysis

6 How does the ambivalence the speaker expresses toward her book contrast with the imagery of motherhood and a mother's attitude toward a child? How do these go together in this poem?

Interpret the Poem

7 What does the line "If for thy Father asked, say, thou hadst none" suggest to you about the author's feelings toward the book?

For Review and Further Study

Joy Harjo (b. 1951)

Morning Song (2001)

The red dawn is now rearranging the earth
Thought by thought
Beauty by beauty
Each sunrise a link on the ladder
5 *Thought by thought*
Beauty by beauty
The ladder the backbone
Of shimmering deity
Thought by thought
10 *Beauty by beauty*
Child stirring in the web of your mother
Don't be afraid
Old man turning to walk through the door
Do not be afraid

Questions for Interactive Reading and Writing

1. Why is the line "Don't be afraid" repeated as "Do not be afraid"? How does this affect the tone at the end of the poem?

2. How would you describe the tone of the poem as a whole? What role do the repeated lines "Thought by thought / Beauty by beauty" have in creating this tone?

3. What is the relationship between the images in the poem? Consider, especially, "Child stirring in the web of your mother" and "Old man turning to walk through the door."

4. How does Harjo use long and short lines to achieve musical effects?

5. What is the purpose of this song? How does the voice sound to you?

6. Why does it seem appropriate for this to be a "morning" song rather than a poem associated with another part of the day?

Gary Soto (b. 1952)

Mexicans Begin Jogging (1981)

At the factory I worked
In the fleck of rubber, under the press
Of an oven yellow with flame,
Until the border patrol opened
Their vans and my boss waved for us to run.   5
"Over the fence, Soto," he shouted,
And I shouted that I was American.
"No time for lies," he said, and pressed
A dollar in my palm, hurrying me
Through the back door.   10

Since I was on his time, I ran
And became the wag to a short tail of Mexicans—
Ran past the amazed crowds that lined
The streets and blurred like photographs, in rain.
15 I ran from that industrial road to the soft
Houses where people paled at the turn of an autumn sky.
What could I do but yell *vivas*
To baseball, milkshakes, and those sociologists
Who would clock me
20 As I jog into the next century
On the power of a great, silly grin.

Questions for Interactive Reading and Writing

1. What is the action in the poem? What is the misunderstanding?

2. There's good humor here, even in the face of a legal absurdity, and the title word *jogging* suggests a kind of leisure activity of the middle class. What clues does the title reveal about the poem's tone?

3. What does the line "Since I was on his time, I ran" tell us about the speaker?

4. Discuss how Soto frames himself in the group of Mexican workers. Does he feel separate from or unified with them?

5. Note the phrase "great, silly grin" with which the poem closes, and the way the poet likens what he's doing to a kind of *corrida*, or running with the bulls. Why does Soto have a "great, silly grin" for the next century?

William Stafford (1914–1993)

Traveling through the Dark (1962)

Traveling through the dark I found a deer
dead on the edge of the Wilson River road.
It is usually best to roll them into the canyon:
that road is narrow; to swerve might make more dead.

By glow of the tail-light I stumbled back of the car   5
and stood by the heap, a doe, a recent killing;
she had stiffened already, almost cold.
I dragged her off; she was large in the belly.

My fingers touching her side brought me the reason—   10
her side was warm; her fawn lay there waiting,
alive, still, never to be born.
Beside that mountain road I hesitated.

The car aimed ahead its lowered parking lights;
under the hood purred the steady engine.   15
I stood in the glare of the warm exhaust turning red;
around our group I could hear the wilderness listen.

I thought hard for us all—my only swerving—
then pushed her over the edge into the river.

Questions for Interactive Reading and Writing

1. What happens in the poem, and how does the word *usually* establish tone?

2. What does the speaker learn when he touches the dead doe? Why does he hesitate? Identify the words that give you clues about the speaker's attitude and why he "hesitated."

3. How does the word *still* do double duty in the phrase "alive, still, never to be born"?

4. Notice the narrative ease of the poem, the uninflected voice. Travel the distance between line 3—"It is usually best to roll them into the canyon"—and what happens at poem's end. Whom does the speaker mean by "our group" and how does "the wilderness listen"? What does "my only swerving" suggest, and what do you imagine the speaker thought as he "pushed her over the edge"? How would you describe the tone of the poem, and does it seem appropriate to the scene's subject?

5. Can you detect an implied meaning in the title? Describe the interaction of humankind and nature here.

William Carlos Williams (1883–1963)

For a brief biography of William Carlos Williams, see Chapter 22.

This Is Just to Say (1934)

I have eaten
the plums
that were in
the icebox

5 and which
you were probably
saving
for breakfast

Forgive me
10 they were delicious
so sweet
and so cold

Questions for Interactive Reading and Writing

1. What does the word *just* imply—"only" or "fairly" or both? Why is the title a part of the poem that follows?

2. What is the past action narrated, and why has the poet narrated it?

3. Does this feel like an actual poem to you? Why or why not?

4. Williams avoids punctuation, but he does capitalize "Forgive." Why? What effect does this produce?

5. Discuss the tone here. Is it sincere? Comic? Apologetic?

6. How much does this simple poem tell the reader about the speaker? Who is the "you" addressed?

7. Think of Wordsworth's definition of a poem as "emotion recollected in tranquility." Would you say Williams agrees?

8. Imagine that you found this note on the refrigerator door or kitchen table as you came down to breakfast after your guest had left. What would be your reaction?

PERSONA

In some poems—for example, Anne Bradstreet's—we can be confident that the speaker of a poem is a version of the poet himself or herself. This is equally the case for the poems you've just looked at by Soto, Stafford, and Williams; most often, when a poet says "I," we can associate that first-person pronoun with the life and mind of the poet. At other times, a poet "throws" his or her voice—becoming a character other than "I" even when the first-person pronoun is used. Researching a bit of biographical information can help us make an informed decision about this. Knowing, for example, that the poet Ben Jonson lost his eldest son to plague helps us understand that the speaking voice of the following poem is indeed Jonson's.

"It seems to me that because a poem is a score for the human voice—a voice implies a speaker. So in a way every poem is a portrait of a speaker." Conversation with Li-Young Lee

Ben Jonson (1573–1637)

Born in Westminster, England, Ben Jonson rose to become a well-known and respected playwright, England's poet laureate, and the author of many masques—that is, spectacles that included drama, poetry, and song performed to entertain the court. Jonson's satirical eye led him to create a brand of comedy that consisted of eccentric characters who represent various types of human temperament, as in *Every Man in His Humour* (1598). Though a scholar and a skilled lyrical poet, Jonson was a man of large appetites and volatile temper (he was nearly executed for killing a man in a duel). Among his most famous works are *Volpone* (1606), *The Alchemist* (1610)—both comedies written for the stage—and *The Forest* (1616), a collection of lyrics and epigrams.

AS YOU READ   Note the opposition of the first word "Farewell" and the poem's title. How does this establish tone and serve notice that "joy" has been lost?

On My First Son

(1616)

Farewell, thou child of my right hand, and joy;
My sin was too much hope of thee, loved boy:
Seven years thou wert lent to me, and I thee pay,
Exacted by the fate, on the just day.
5   O could I lose all father now! for why
Will man lament the state he should envy,
To have soon 'scaped world's and flesh's rage,
And, if no other misery, yet age?
Rest in soft peace, and asked, say, "Here doth lie
10   Ben Jonson his best piece of poetry."
For whose sake henceforth all his vows be such
As what he loves may never like too much.

Writing from Reading

Summary

1   What is the situation revealed in the poem and the poet's attitude?

2   What does he mean by "why / Will man lament the state he should envy," and does the poet truly wish for death?

Analyze Craft

3   Notice the six rhyming couplets of this poem and the two couplets where the rhymes are less than exact.

What is meant by "Ben Jonson his best piece of poetry"?

4   How old is the child to whom the father says farewell, and what does the poet wish for himself?

Analyze Voice

5 Technically, this poem is an elegy—a lament for a dear, dead child. What words and phrases establish that "lament," and what does the poet promise himself in the final two lines?

Synthesize Summary and Analysis

6 "Rest in soft peace" adds a word to "Rest in peace." Who does the poet imagine might ask his "soft" son to identify himself, and where, and when?

Interpret the Poem

7 If age is necessarily linked to misery, can the speaker find comfort in the fact that his son "soon 'scaped world's and flesh's rage"? What is the overall tone of the poem, and does "First Son" in the title suggest that there are or will be more?

Although we can say with confidence that Jonson is speaking from his own experience, this is not always necessarily the case. Poets—like novelists and playwrights—often imagine an experience, inventing both speakers and scene. Did Edgar Allan Poe, for instance, really hear a bird crying outside his home, as the speaker asserts in "The Raven" (see For Review and Further Study at the end of this section)? Did Robert Frost really find himself once, on a walk through the woods, facing two separate roads to choose from, as in "The Road Not Taken" (see Chapter 28)? Although it's quite possible these poems borrow, perhaps even heavily, from real life, we shouldn't automatically assume they are precise autobiographical accounts. Rather, we think of a poem's speaking voice as a potentially separate entity. This is called a persona, a poem's speaker that may or may not use the voice of the poet.

"One person, of course, can have 20,000 different kinds of voices."

Conversation with Marie Howe

One way to read a poem is, in effect, to measure the distance between the voice of the poet and the voice of the persona delivering the lines. In the dramatic monologue "My Last Duchess," for example (see Chapter 19), it's perfectly clear that the first-person pronoun of the speaker does not belong to the poet himself; Robert Browning was no duke. He is, in fact, unsympathetic to the man who's showing off his collection of art and arranging a new marriage, and he asks us as readers to notice things the character would deny. There's an absolute distance established between writer and speaker.

Sylvia Plath's poem "Daddy" is sometimes called autobiographical. Indeed, the poem is an angry and raw cry of resistance aimed at the poet's father, Otto Plath, who died when she was still a child. Haunted by three decades of grief and memories of her stern father, Plath fashions a poem that voices a bitter response to his lasting psychological grip.

A HISTORY OF PERSONA

The Latin word *persona* derives from the ancient Etruscan word for *mask,* and it recalls the ancient Greek practice of actors wearing masks to portray different roles. That the voice of a poem may not be in fact the same as that of the poet is an ancient literary distinction. Aristotle writes in *Poetics,* "The poet may imitate by narration—in which case he can either take another personality . . . or speak in his own person, unchanged—or he may present all his characters as living and moving before us." In more recent times, twentieth-century literary scholars sometimes discouraged readers from assuming that even a first-person poem could be autobiographical. Despite these protests from literary critics, many poets readily concede that the speaker using the first person in their poems is, indeed, an autobiographical "I." A group of writers in the 1950s and 1960s, including Robert Lowell, W. D. Snodgrass, Sylvia Plath, and Anne Sexton, were dubbed "confessional poets." This name indicated a deeply personal style by poets unafraid to confront painful private history.

"Until the advent of the Romantics, the 'I' was very rare in poetry. . . . Poetry was used to memorize . . . to commemorate, to narrate history, to catechize. . . . [Now] . . . this fictitious 'I' . . . pops up in just about 90 percent of contemporary American poetry. . . . To take on different voices and different characterizations is a challenge and a lot more creative." Conversation with Al Young

Although Plath borrows heavily from real life in her descriptions in the poem, we shouldn't be too quick to call the "I" of this poem a literal version of the poet. Plath uses, among other references, violent Nazi and Holocaust imagery to describe the father figure of this poem. Otto Plath, however, immigrated to America in 1900 and was never affiliated with the Nazi party or known to be physically abusive. Likewise, to accentuate the poem's conflict, Plath's speaker links herself to a Jewish identity, whereas Plath was raised primarily in the Unitarian Christian tradition. So, although some descriptions and references in the poem echo authentic aspects of Plath's life, the poem is itself a creative fusion of real-life and fictional elements. Because of this, "Daddy" is a poem that helps us to understand why it's important to treat the distinction between poet and persona with care.

"If we can forget ourselves, we can become someone the poem can speak through." Conversation with Marie Howe

Sylvia Plath (1932–1963)

Born in Massachusetts, Sylvia Plath was a successful student and earned her B.A. *summa cum laude* from Smith College. She was awarded a Fulbright scholarship and went to England, where she met and married poet Ted Hughes. Hughes later left Plath and their two young children; Plath responded with a frenzy of creative outpouring, writing her famous *Ariel* poems in the few months leading up to her suicide at age thirty. She had attempted to take her own life between her junior and senior years of college, and her autobiographical novel *The Bell Jar* (1963) focuses on a heroine who attempts suicide. Plath's poetry is marked by violent imagery contained in clear, precise diction; especially in the *Ariel* poems, she invents a poetic self that has a romantic, larger-than-life quality characteristic of poems in the confessional voice.

AS YOU READ   Note that this poem uses direct address—from "I" to "you" in the first stanza—and by the second stanza we know that a child addresses a father. As the speaker addresses the father, note if and when her tone changes or shifts.

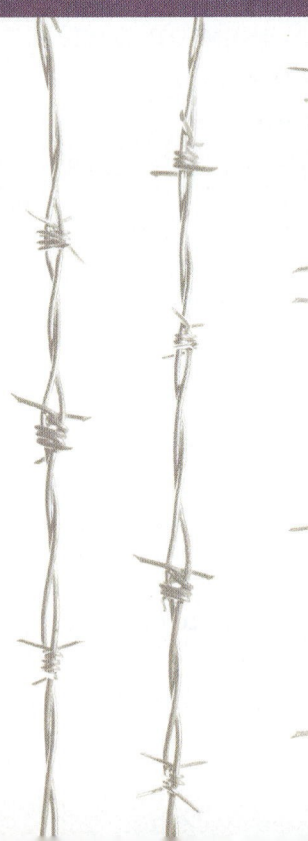

Daddy (1966)

You do not do, you do not do
Any more, black shoe
In which I have lived like a foot
For thirty years, poor and white,
5   Barely daring to breathe or Achoo.

Daddy, I have had to kill you.
You died before I had time—
Marble-heavy, a bag full of God,
Ghastly statue with one gray toe
10   Big as a Frisco seal

And a head in the freakish Atlantic
Where it pours bean green over blue
In the waters off beautiful Nauset.
I used to pray to recover you.
15   Ach, du

In the German tongue, in the Polish town
Scraped flat by the roller
Of wars, wars, wars.
But the name of the town is common.
20   My Polack friend

Says there are a dozen or two.
So I never could tell where you
Put your foot, your root,
I never could talk to you.
25   The tongue stuck in my jaw.

It stuck in a barb wire snare.
Ich, ich, ich, ich,
I could hardly speak.
I thought every German was you.
30   And the language obscene

An engine, an engine
Chuffing me off like a Jew.
A Jew to Dachau, Auschwitz, Belsen.
I began to talk like a Jew.
35 I think I may well be a Jew.

The snows of the Tyrol, the clear beer of Vienna
Are not very pure or true.
With my gypsy ancestress and my weird luck
And my Taroc pack and my Taroc pack
40 I may be a bit of a Jew.

I have always been scared of *you*,
With your Luftwaffe, your gobbledygoo.
And your neat mustache
And your Aryan eye, bright blue.
45 Panzer-man, panzer-man, O You—

Not a God but a swastika
So black no sky could squeak through
Every woman adores a Fascist,
The boot in the face, the brute
50 Brute heart of a brute like you.

You stand at the blackboard daddy,
In the picture I have of you,
A cleft in your chin instead of your foot
But no less a devil for that, no not
55 Any less the black man who

Bit my pretty red heart in two.
I was ten when they buried you.
At twenty I tried to die
And get back, back, back to you.
60 I thought even the bones would do.

But they pulled me out of the sack,
And they stuck me together with glue.
And then I knew what to do.
I made a model of you,
65 A man in black with a Meinkampf look

And a love of the rack and the screw.
And I said I do, I do.
So daddy, I'm finally through.
The black telephone's off at the root,
70 The voices just can't worm through.

If I've killed one man, I've killed two—
The vampire who said he was you
And drank my blood for a year,
Seven years, if you want to know.
75 Daddy, you can lie back now.

There's a stake in your fat black heart
And the villagers never liked you.
They are dancing and stamping on you.
They always *knew* it was you.
80 Daddy, daddy, you bastard, I'm through.

Writing from Reading

Summarize

1 Describe the situation of this poem—who's speaking to whom? How does the poet address her dead father? What does she accuse him of, and why?

Analyze Craft

2 Notice the use of German in this poem and the reference to *Mein*

Kampf (Adolf Hitler's autobiographical book). Look at the way the poet compares her father to a vampire ("There's a stake in your fat black heart") and the various references to murder and suicide. What mood does this create?

3 Identify the colloquial language here ("Daddy, daddy, you bastard" or "breathe Achoo"). Why does she choose

this language and end the poem with the assertion "I'm through"?

Analyze Voice

4 Give examples of the poet's anger, even rage. Are there any gentle moments in the poem, any suggestions of love or forgiveness? (Consider Theodore Roethke's poem "My Papa's Waltz" by way of contrast.)

5 Notice how often the speaker says "you"—to someone who no longer hears. Look at the rhyme scheme and the insistent repetitive pattern of sound. How would you describe the way repetition contributes to the tone of this poem?

Synthesize Summary and Analysis

6 The Ben Jonson poem has a father speaking to his dead child, and the Sylvia Plath poem consists of a daughter addressing her dead father. How do the tones and attitudes seem similar, how different; which emotions govern which?

Interpret the Poem

7 This monologue is one sided; there's no second point of view or position to be heard. In some sense it's both a *diatribe* and a *polemic* (look up these terms in your dictionary). Does the speaker come to terms with her memories at poem's end?

Rita Dove (b. 1952)

Rita Dove was born in Akron, Ohio, and graduated *summa cum laude* from Miami University in Ohio. She spent a year in Germany on a Fulbright scholarship, then earned an M.F.A. at the University of Iowa before becoming a professor herself.

Her ability to render poems that resonate on both a personal and a larger historical level—in addition to her sensitivity toward language and poetic form—has earned her poetry widespread acclaim. Her collection *Thomas and Beulah* (1986) tells the story of her grandparents in short lyrical poems that beautifully render

mundane moments; it was awarded the Pulitzer Prize. Less than a decade later, she became the youngest poet to be appointed Poet Laureate, a position she held from 1993 to 1995. She currently teaches at the University of Virginia.

AS YOU READ Think of the resonance of the word *master,* and how it suggests both the history of slavery and a competence at mathematics—in the former case it's used as a noun, in the latter as a verb. These fourteen lines suggest the poem belongs, although loosely, to the traditional sonnet form (see Chapter 25); in form therefore it refers to the past but, in tone, it is contemporary.

Flash Cards (1989)

In math I was the whiz kid, keeper
of oranges and apples. *What you don't understand,
master,* my father said; the faster
I answered, the faster they came.

5   I could see one bud on the teacher's geranium,
one clear bee sputtering at the wet pane.
The tulip trees always dragged after heavy rain
so I tucked my head as my boots slapped home.

My father put up his feet after work
10   and relaxed with a highball and *The Life of Lincoln.*
After supper we drilled and I climbed the dark

before sleep, before a thin voice hissed
numbers as I spun on a wheel. I had to guess.
Ten, I kept saying, *I'm only ten.*

Writing from Reading

Summarize

1 Describe the place and, perhaps, the time of this poem. How far removed would you say the speaker is at the time of writing?

2 Is it important to know that the poet is African American? What are flash cards? What kind of student is the speaker? Does the term "whiz kid" seem deserved?

Analyze Craft

3 If this poem appears autobiographical to you—if, in other words, the persona feels like the poet herself—what part of the poem suggests this? If not, why not?

4 To be "spun on a wheel" is an ancient Greek form of torture. "After supper we drilled" might be another such torture. Does this poem convey a feeling of triumph or grief?

Analyze Voice

5 What do you think the speaker means by "keeper / of oranges and apples"?

6 In the final line, we're twice given a number—"ten"—as the child's age. Does the tone or attitude seem childlike or adult?

Synthesize Summary and Analysis

7 Describe the relationship the speaker has with the father figure. How would you characterize the two figures in the poem? What changes; what stays the same?

Interpret the Poem

8 What does "the faster / I answered, the faster they came" suggest about life's problems? How does *The Life of Lincoln* connect to the poem's subject, and what is the attitude here?

Sometimes a persona might be a figurative person—that is, not an actual person with a specific identity but a metaphor or an embodiment of a particular feeling. Walt Whitman wrote "O Captain! My Captain!" in commemoration of President Abraham Lincoln's assassination, and although the speaker of the poem holds the dead captain on a ship deck, we know that the captain stands for Lincoln, the ship for Civil War–era America, and the cradling arm of the captain's "son" for the collective feeling of grief in which Whitman himself takes part.

Walt Whitman (1819 –1892)

For a brief biography of Walt Whitman, see Chapter 20.

AS YOU READ Look for lines where you feel the speaker's sense of grief, remembering that Whitman wrote this poem following Abraham Lincoln's assassination.

O Captain! My Captain! (1865)

O Captain! my Captain! our fearful trip is done,
The ship has weather'd every rack, the prize we sought is won,
The port is near, the bells I hear, the people all exulting,
5 While follow eyes the steady keel, the vessel grim and daring;
    But O heart! heart! heart!
      O the bleeding drops of red,
        Where on the deck my Captain lies,
          Fallen cold and dead.

10 O Captain! my Captain! rise up and hear the bells;
Rise up—for you the flag is flung—for you the bugle trills,
For you bouquets and ribbon'd wreaths—for you the shores a-crowding,
For you they call, the swaying mass, their eager faces turning;
    Here Captain! dear father!
15   This arm beneath your head!
        It is some dream that on the deck,
            You've fallen cold and dead.

My Captain does not answer, his lips are pale and still,
My father does not feel my arm, he has no pulse nor will,
20 The ship is anchor'd safe and sound, its voyage closed and done,
From fearful trip, the victor ship comes in with object won;
        Exult, O shores, and ring O bells!
        But I with mournful tread,
            Walk the deck my Captain lies,
25   Fallen cold and dead.

Writing from Reading

Summarize

1 Who is the speaker here, and to whom does he speak?

2 What is occurring in the poem at the moment the speaker speaks to the captain?

Analyze Craft

3 How does the use of a persona make Lincoln's death seem more immediate?

4 Given that the Civil War ended in 1865, the same year Whitman com- posed this poem, why is the ship's entry to the harbor an aptly chosen metaphor?

Analyze Voice

5 What is the tone of the poem? Which lines particularly work to create this effect?

6 Why does the speaker use the repetition "O Captain! My Captain" to address the fallen man? Why not one or the other?

Synthesize Summary and Analysis

7 How do the lines of the second stanza, "Rise up—for you the flag is flung—for you the bugle trills, / For you bouquets and ribbon'd wreaths—for you the shores a-crowding" make the captain's death more poignant?

Interpret the Poem

8 Look up "elegy" in the glossary of terms or in Chapter 25, Fixed Poetic Forms. Would you describe this poem as an elegy? Why or why not?

Often a persona allows the poet to shift gender. The contemporary poet Ai is well known for writing poems using personae separate from herself. Although her poems sometimes comment on the African-American experience she has witnessed, the speakers of these poems are often characters she wholly creates. In the following poem, she adopts the persona of a man witnessing the 1992 race riots in Los Angeles.

Ai (1947–2010)

"I am the child of a scandalous affair my mother had with a Japanese man she met at a streetcar stop," Ai comments of her own beginnings. (She legally changed her name to Ai, which means "love" in Japanese.) Born in Texas, of Native-American, African, Irish, and Japanese descent, Ai grew up in Arizona, San Francisco, and Las Vegas. Her poetry most often takes the form of dramatic monologues, and she explores personalities as diverse as Marilyn Monroe, Leon Trotsky, and J. Edgar Hoover, as well as dark topics ranging from domestic to public violence. Her collection *Vice* (1999) won the National Book Award, and she received the Lamont Poetry Award from the Academy of American Poets for *Killing Floor* (1979). Ai received an M.F.A. from the University of California, Irvine, and taught at Oklahoma State University.

AS YOU READ   Consider the "I" of this poem and try to establish its relation to the first-person pronoun of the poet. Pay attention to the tense of the narrative—the present tense—and how it reports on what happened on the specific date of the title.

Riot Act, April 29, 1992 (1993)

I'm going out and get something.
I don't know what.
I don't care.
Whatever's out there, I'm going to get it.
5 Look in those shop windows at boxes
and boxes of Reeboks and Nikes
to make me fly through the air
like Michael Jordan
like Magic.
10 While I'm up there, I see Spike Lee.
Looks like he's flying too
straight through the glass
that separates me
from the virtual reality
15 I watch every day on TV.
I know the difference between
what it is and what it isn't.

Just because I can't touch it
doesn't mean it isn't real.
20 All I have to do is smash the screen,
reach in and take what I want.
Break out of prison.
South Central homey's newly risen
from the night of living dead,
25 but this time he lives,
he gets to give the zombies
a taste of their own medicine.
Open wide and let me in,
or else I'll set your world on fire,
30 but you pretend that you don't hear.
You haven't heard the word is coming down
like the hammer of the gun
of this black son, locked out of the big house,
while massa looks out the window and sees only smoke.

35 Massa doesn't see anything else,
     not because he can't,
     but because he won't.
     He'd rather hear me talking about mo' money,
     mo' honeys and gold chains
40 and see me carrying my favorite things
     from looted stores
     than admit that underneath my Raider's cap,
     the aftermath is staring back
     unblinking through the camera's lens,
45 courtesy of CNN,
     my arms loaded with boxes of shoes
     that I will sell at the swap meet
     to make a few cents on the declining dollar.
     And if I destroy myself
50 and my neighborhood
     "ain't nobody's business, if I do,"
     but the police are knocking hard
     at my door
     and before I can open it,
55 they break it down
     and drag me in the yard.
     They take me in to be processed and charged,
     to await trial,
     while Americans forget
60 the day wealth finally trickled down
     to the rest of us.

Writing from Reading

Summarize

1 Describe the action in the poem. Who is the speaker and the poem's "I"?

Analyze Craft

2 There are many references, here, to contemporary culture—"Raider's cap," "CNN," and so on. Michael Jordan, Magic (Johnson), and Spike Lee were three major "players" on the contempo-rary scene in 1992. How does this help "date" the speaker?

3 Notice the tense shift at poem's end—present to past. Track the activity throughout.

Analyze Voice

4 The phrase "ain't nobody's business, if I do" comes from a Billie Holliday song. How much of this is celebration, and how much of this is "the blues"?

Synthesize Summary and Analysis

5 Describe ways in which the poet constructs her speaker's character. If he were standing in a police lineup (as at poem's end), could you pick him out?

Interpret the Poem

6 What is the poet's attitude toward her persona here?

The great Irish poet William Butler Yeats had a notion of "the mask" or "anti-self" and sometimes wrote—as in the "Crazy Jane" sequence—from a woman's point of view. In the poem that follows, he attempts to enter into the consciousness of someone obviously "other" than his own self, and the effect is both dramatic and, somehow, impersonal.

William Butler Yeats (1865–1939)

For a brief biography of William Butler Yeats, see Chapter 17.

AS YOU READ Listen for the two separate voices in conversation—the Bishop and Crazy Jane—and decide which of the points of view (either or both) you share.

Crazy Jane Talks with the Bishop (1932)

I met the Bishop on the road
And much said he and I.
"Those breasts are flat and fallen now
Those veins must soon by dry;
5   Live in a heavenly mansion,
Not in some foul sty."

"Fair and foul are near of kin,
And fair needs foul," I cried.
"My friends are gone, but that's a truth
10   Nor grave nor bed denied,
Learned in bodily lowliness
And in the heart's pride.

"A woman can be proud and still
When on love intent;
15   But Love has pitched his mansion in
The place of excrement;
For nothing can be sole or whole
That has not been rent."

Writing from Reading

Summarize

1 Who are the speakers here, and what's the nature of their argument?

2 Assuming that the poet shares the opinion of his title character, what would seem to be Yeats's beliefs as to "fair and foul"?

Analyze Craft

3 Why does "Crazy Jane" have a name and "the Bishop" merely a title?

4 These eighteen lines follow a fixed pattern, and each stanza rhymes in the second, fourth, and final line. What does that do to emphasis, and who has the last word?

Analyze Voice

5 What does the speaker mean by "Love has pitched his mansion in / The place of excrement"? Literally? Metaphorically?

6 Comment on the double meanings in the final stanza: "whole" and "sole" and "rent."

Synthesize Summary and Analysis

7 What ideas about religion—behavior in this life, and the question of the afterlife—are presented here?

8 Discuss the oppositions of body and soul, the church and the fallen woman, faith and physical appearance. Can they be reconciled?

Interpret the Poem

9 Yeats wrote a series of poems from the point of view of an invented character whom he based on an old woman who lived in a cottage in Gort, a small village near Galway in western Ireland. What does he admire in her, and why would he use *her* language to make what would appear to be *his* point?

For Review and Further Study

Christopher Marlowe (1564–1593)

The Passionate Shepherd to His Love (c. 1599)

Come live with me and be my love,
And we will all the pleasures prove
That valleys, groves, hills, and fields,
Woods, or steepy mountain yields.

5 And we will sit upon rocks,
Seeing the shepherds feed their flocks,
By shallow rivers to whose falls
Melodious birds sing madrigals.

And I will make thee beds of roses
And a thousand fragrant posies,   10
A cap of flowers, and a kirtle
Embroidered all with leaves of myrtle;

A gown made of the finest wool
Which from our pretty lambs we pull;
Fair lined slippers for the cold,   15
With buckles of the purest gold;

A belt of straw and ivy buds,
With coral clasps and amber studs:
And if these pleasures may thee move,
Come live with me and be my love.   20

The shepherds' swains shall dance and sing
For thy delight each May morning:
If these delights thy mind may move,
Then live with me and be my love.

Questions for Interactive Reading and Writing

1. Christopher Marlowe was not a shepherd. What do the title of this poem and the text tell us about the persona Marlowe has created?

2. Why does the poet choose the form of a song to express this persona's emotions?

3. What exactly is the shepherd promising?

4. What are some of the pastoral, or supposedly natural, images in this poem?

5. In what ways is this poem like many contemporary love songs, and how is it different? Think especially of tone, style, word choice, and content.

Edgar Allan Poe (1809–1849)

For a brief biography of Edgar Allan Poe, see Chapter 10.

The Raven (1845)

Once upon a midnight dreary, while I pondered, weak and weary,
Over many a quaint and curious volume of forgotten lore—
While I nodded, nearly napping, suddenly there came a tapping,
As of some one gently rapping, rapping at my chamber door.
5 "'T is some visiter," I muttered, "tapping at my chamber door—
　　　　　　　　　Only this and nothing more."

Ah, distinctly I remember it was in the bleak December,
And each separate dying ember wrought its ghost upon the floor.
Eagerly I wished the morrow;—vainly I had sought to borrow
From my books surcease of sorrow—sorrow for the lost Lenore— 10
For the rare and radiant maiden whom the angels name Lenore—
　　　　　　　　　Nameless *here* for evermore.

And the silken, sad, uncertain rustling of each purple curtain
Thrilled me—filled me with fantastic terrors never felt before;
So that now, to still the beating of my heart, I stood repeating 15
"'T is some visiter entreating entrance at my chamber door—
Some late visiter entreating entrance at my chamber door;—
　　　　　　　　　This it is and nothing more."

Presently my soul grew stronger; hesitating then no longer,
"Sir," said I, "or Madam, truly your forgiveness I implore; 20
But the fact is I was napping, and so gently you came rapping,
And so faintly you came tapping, tapping at my chamber door,
That I scarce was sure I heard you"—here I opened wide the door;—
　　　　　　　　　Darkness there and nothing more.

Deep into that darkness peering, long I stood there wondering, fearing, 25
Doubting, dreaming dreams no mortal ever dared to dream before;
But the silence was unbroken, and the stillness gave no token,
And the only word there spoken was the whispered word, "Lenore!"
This I whispered, and an echo murmured back the word, "Lenore!"
　　　　　　　　　Merely this and nothing more. 30

Back into the chamber turning, all my soul within me
   burning,
Soon again I heard a tapping somewhat louder than before.
"Surely," said I, "surely that is something at my window
   lattice;
Let me see, then, what thereat is, and this mystery
   explore—
35 Let my heart be still a moment and this mystery explore;—
              'T is the wind and nothing more!"

Open here I flung the shutter, when, with many a flirt and
   flutter
In there stepped a stately Raven of the saintly days of yore.
Not the least obeisance made he; not a minute stopped or
   stayed he;
40 But, with mien of lord or lady, perched above my chamber
   door—
Perched upon a bust of Pallas just above my chamber
   door—
            Perched, and sat, and nothing more.

Then this ebony bird beguiling my sad fancy into smiling,
By the grave and stern decorum of the countenance it
   wore,
45 "Though thy crest be shorn and shaven, thou," I said, "art
   sure no craven,
Ghastly grim and ancient Raven wandering from the
   Nightly shore—
Tell me what thy lordly name is on the Night's Plutonian
   shore!"
            Quoth the Raven, "Nevermore."

Much I marvelled this ungainly fowl to hear discourse so
   plainly,
50 Though its answer little meaning—little relevancy bore;
For we cannot help agreeing that no living human being
Ever yet was blessed with seeing bird above his chamber
   door—
Bird or beast upon the sculptured bust above his chamber
   door,
           With such name as "Nevermore."

But the Raven, sitting lonely on the placid bust, spoke only 55
That one word, as if his soul in that one word he did
   outpour.
Nothing farther then he uttered—not a feather then he
   fluttered—
Till I scarcely more than muttered "Other friends have
   flown before—
On the morrow *he* will leave me, as my hopes have flown
   before."
         Then the bird said "Nevermore." 60

Startled at the stillness broken by reply so aptly spoken,
"Doubtless," said I, "what it utters is its only stock and
   store
Caught from some unhappy master whom unmerciful
   Disaster
Followed fast and followed faster till his songs one burden
   bore—
Till the dirges of his Hope that melancholy burden bore 65
          Of 'Never—nevermore.'"

But the Raven still beguiling all my fancy into smiling,
Straight I wheeled a cushioned seat in front of bird, and
   bust and door;
Then, upon the velvet sinking, I betook myself to linking
Fancy unto fancy, thinking what this ominous bird of 70
   yore—
What this grim, ungainly, ghastly, gaunt, and ominous
   bird of yore
        Meant in croaking "Nevermore."

This I sat engaged in guessing, but no syllable expressing
To the fowl whose fiery eyes now burned into my bosom's
   core;
This and more I sat divining, with my head at ease 75
   reclining
On the cushion's velvet lining that the lamp-light gloated
   o'er,
But whose velvet violet lining with the lamp-light gloating
   o'er,
       She shall press, ah, nevermore!

Then, methought, the air grew denser, perfumed from an
  unseen censer
80 Swung by Seraphim whose foot-falls tinkled on the tufted
  floor.
  "Wretch," I cried, "thy God hath lent thee—by these angels
  he hath sent thee
  Respite—respite and nepenthe from thy memories of
  Lenore;
  Quaff, oh quaff this kind nepenthe and forget this lost
  Lenore!"
                           Quoth the Raven "Nevermore."

85 "Prophet!" said I, "thing of evil! prophet still, if bird or
  devil!—
  Whether Tempter sent, or whether tempest tossed thee
  here ashore,
  Desolate yet all undaunted, on this desert land
  enchanted—
  On this home by Horror haunted—tell me truly, I implore—
  Is there—*is* there balm in Gilead?—tell me—tell me, I
  implore!"
90   Quoth the Raven "Nevermore."

  "Prophet!" said I, "thing of evil—prophet still, if bird or
  devil!
  By that Heaven that bends above us—by that God we both
  adore—
  Tell this soul with sorrow laden if, within the distant
  Aidenn,
  It shall clasp a sainted maiden whom the angels name
  Lenore—
95 Clasp a rare and radiant maiden whom the angels name
  Lenore."
                           Quoth the Raven "Nevermore."

  "Be that word our sign of parting, bird or fiend!" I shrieked,
  upstarting—
  "Get thee back into the tempest and the Night's Plutonian
  shore!
  Leave no black plume as a token of that lie thy soul hath
  spoken!
100 Leave my loneliness unbroken!—quit the bust above my
  door!
  Take thy beak from out my heart, and take thy form from
  off my door!"
                           Quoth the Raven "Nevermore."

And the Raven, never flitting, still is sitting, *still* is sitting
On the pallid bust of Pallas just above my chamber door;
And his eyes have all the seeming of a demon's that is   105
  dreaming,
And the lamp-light o'er him streaming throws his shadow
  on the floor;
And my soul from out that shadow that lies floating on the
  floor
                           Shall be lifted—nevermore!

Questions for Interactive Reading and Writing

1. Describe the persona in this poem. Given that Poe's beloved wife died before he did, do you read this as a personal "I"? Why or why not?

2. Summarize the speaker's situation. What do we know about him and about his life to this point?

3. By the end of the poem, what does the raven seem to symbolize?

4. What is the effect of the refrain "Nevermore"? What connotations does this word have?

5. Describe the setting of the poem. How does Poe's description of the setting create a particular mood?

Anne Sexton (1928–1974)

Cinderella (1971)

You always read about it:
the plumber with twelve children
who wins the Irish Sweepstakes.
From toilets to riches.
That story.   5

Or the nursemaid,
some luscious sweet from Denmark
who captures the oldest son's heart.
from diapers to Dior.
That story.   10

Or a milkman who serves the wealthy,
eggs, cream, butter, yogurt, milk,
the white truck like an ambulance
who goes into real estate
15 and makes a pile.
From homogenized to martinis at lunch.

Or the charwoman
who is on the bus when it cracks up
and collects enough from the insurance.
20 From mops to Bonwit Teller.
That story.

Once
the wife of a rich man was on her deathbed
and she said to her daughter Cinderella:
25 Be devout. Be good. Then I will smile
down from heaven in the seam of a cloud.
The man took another wife who had
two daughters, pretty enough
but with hearts like blackjacks.
30 Cinderella was their maid.
She slept on the sooty hearth each night
and walked around looking like Al Jolson.
Her father brought presents home from town,
jewels and gowns for the other women
35 but the twig of a tree for Cinderella.
She planted that twig on her mother's grave
and it grew to a tree where a white dove sat.
Whenever she wished for anything the dove
would drop it like an egg upon the ground.
40 The bird is important, my dears, so heed him.

Next came the ball, as you all know.
It was a marriage market.
The prince was looking for a wife.
All but Cinderella were preparing
45 and gussying up for the big event.
Cinderella begged to go too.
Her stepmother threw a dish of lentils
into the cinders and said: Pick them
up in an hour and you shall go.
50 The white dove brought all his friends;
all the warm wings of the fatherland came,
and picked up the lentils in a jiffy.
No, Cinderella, said the stepmother,
you have no clothes and cannot dance.
55 That's the way with stepmothers.

Cinderella went to the tree at the grave
and cried forth like a gospel singer:
Mama! Mama! My turtledove,
send me to the prince's ball!
The bird dropped down a golden dress   60
and delicate little gold slippers.
Rather a large package for a simple bird.
So she went. Which is no surprise.
Her stepmother and sisters didn't
recognize her without her cinder face   65
and the prince took her hand on the spot
and danced with no other the whole day.

As nightfall came she thought she'd better
get home. The prince walked her home
and she disappeared into the pigeon house   70
and although the prince took an axe and broke
it open she was gone. Back to her cinders.
These events repeated themselves for three days.
However on the third day the prince
covered the palace steps with cobbler's wax   75
and Cinderella's gold shoe stuck upon it.
Now he would find whom the shoe fit
and find his strange dancing girl for keeps.
He went to their house and the two sisters
were delighted because they had lovely feet.   80
The eldest went into a room to try the slipper on
but her big toe got in the way so she simply
sliced it off and put on the slipper.
The prince rode away with her until the white dove
told him to look at the blood pouring forth.   85
That is the way with amputations.
They just don't heal up like a wish.
The other sister cut off her heel
but the blood told as blood will.
The prince was getting tired.   90
He began to feel like a shoe salesman.
But he gave it one last try.
This time Cinderella fit into the shoe
like a love letter into its envelope.

At the wedding ceremony   95
the two sisters came to curry favor
and the white dove pecked their eyes out.
Two hollow spots were left
like soup spoons.

100　Cinderella and the prince
　　　lived, they say, happily ever after,
　　　like two dolls in a museum case
　　　never bothered by diapers or dust,
　　　never arguing over the timing of an egg,
105　never telling the same story twice,
　　　never getting a middle-aged spread,
　　　their darling smiles pasted on for eternity.
　　　Regular Bobbsey Twins.
　　　That story.

Questions for Interactive Reading and Writing

1. The speaker relays the Grimm brothers' version of the Cinderella story. What does her comment on the ending of the tale, found in the last stanza of the poem, suggest about how the speaker views love?

2. How would you describe the tone of the speaker when she says "That story"? Does the tone stay the same every time she uses the phrase "that story," or does it change? What does the change, or lack thereof, suggest about the persona behind the poem?

3. What is the relationship between the first four stanzas and the Cinderella portion of the poem? What is the persona trying to say by providing those stories in conjunction with Cinderella?

4. Where do you see humor in this poem? Describe the quality of that humor (light, dark, ironic, subtle, entertaining, and so on).

5. Look at the Cinderella story portion of the poem. Which lines seem to come straight from the persona? What about the way those lines are written suggests that this is a comment from the persona, rather than straightforward storytelling?

Natasha Trethewey (b. 1966)

Letter Home (2002)

—*New Orleans, November 1910*

Four weeks have passed since I left, and still
I must write to you of no work. I've worn down
the soles and walked through the tightness
of my new shoes, calling upon the merchants,
their offices bustling. All the while I kept thinking　　5
my plain English and good writing would secure
for me some modest position. Though I dress each day
in my best, hands covered with the lace gloves
you crocheted—no one needs a *girl*. How flat
the word sounds, and heavy. My purse thins.　　10
I spend foolishly to make an appearance of quiet
industry, to mask the desperation that tightens
my throat. I sit watching—

though I pretend not to notice—the dark maids
ambling by with their white charges. Do I deceive　　15
anyone? Were they to see my hands, brown
as your dear face, they'd know I'm not quite
what I pretend to be. I walk these streets
a white woman, or so I think, until I catch the eyes
of some stranger upon me, and I must lower mine,　　20
a *negress* again. There are enough things here
to remind me who I am. Mules lumbering through
the crowded streets send me into reverie, their footfall
the sound of a pointer and chalk hitting the blackboard
at school, only louder. Then there are women, clicking　　25
their tongues in conversation, carrying their loads
on their heads. Their husky voices, the wash pots
and irons of the laundresses call to me. Here,

30   I thought not to do the work I once did, back-bending
     and domestic; my schooling a gift—even those half days
     at picking time, listening to Miss J—. How
     I'd come to know words, the recitations I practiced
     to sound like her, lilting, my sentences curling up
     or trailing off at the ends. I read my books until
35   I nearly broke their spines, and in the cotton field,
     I repeated whole sections I'd learned by heart,
     spelling each word in my head to make a picture
     I could see, as well as a weight I could feel
     In my mouth. So now, even as I write this
40   And think of you at home, Good-bye

     Is the waving map of your palm, is
     A stone on my tongue.

Questions for Interactive Reading and Writing

1. Trethewey's first work focused on prostitutes in New Orleans in the early 1900s. In this poem, she creates a character looking for work and becoming ever more desperate. How does Trethewey present her? Describe the voice of the character here.

2. Why would Trethewey want to create this persona, this voice?

3. What tone does the poem establish? What words show the speaker's unease?

IRONY

In life as well as in writing, we detect tone by careful or instinctive observation. Sometimes, whether we're conscious of it or not, we pick up on a difference between what someone says and what they actually mean. As in other literary genres, in poetry this difference is called **irony,** a discrepancy between what a poem says and what it means.

If you've ever encountered the old story of Robin Hood, you may remember that one of Robin's closest friends is a man called Little John. You may also remember that there's actually nothing little about Little John. He's huge, in fact, burly and fat. Calling him "Little" ultimately draws our attention, playfully, to his considerable size. This nickname is a simple example of verbal irony, a statement in which the stated meaning is very different from (or the opposite of) the implied meaning.

One of the most familiar forms of verbal irony is **sarcasm,** a critical use of spoken approval to express implied disapproval. Who hasn't heard, at some point, a phrase like, "Oh, yeah, you look *great* in that hat," or "This is the best vacation ever," when in fact the hat looks ridiculous and it rains the whole week?

"[The] best ironist is profoundly alert to the world—alert, hears the doubleness of things, works that doubleness. It's a . . . keenness of attention, and rather than keep the world away, it interrogates that world—it tries to measure it." Conversation with Stephen Dunn

Paul Laurence Dunbar (1872–1906)

Born in Dayton, Ohio, to parents who had been slaves, Paul Laurence Dunbar is remembered chiefly for his poetry, although he also wrote short stories and novels. The only black student in his high school class, Dunbar was class poet and published poems in Dayton newspapers. Although his race at first relegated him to a job as an elevator operator, Dunbar continued to write and soon had a national reputation. Although some of his work protests racism, much of it—particularly his poems written in dialect—has been criticized for perpetuating harmful stereotypes of blacks in the Old South. Still, he is recognized as the foremost black poet at the turn of the twentieth century, despite a career cut short by his death from tuberculosis at age thirty-three.

AS YOU READ   Remember that irony is double-edged. Look for language that suggests the speaker is seemingly above the battle. Look for words that are insulting. Notice how the poet puts these together in the poem.

To a Captious Critic (1901)

Dear critic, who my lightness so deplores,
Would I might study to be prince of bores,
Right wisely would I rule that dull estate—
But, sir, I may not, till you abdicate.

Writing from Reading

Summarize

1 "To a Captious Critic" is a brief letter to a critic written as a poem. Look up the word *captious,* then speculate on what the critic has done to trigger this response.

Analyze Craft

2 How would you describe the language used in this poem? Formal? Informal? Is poetic diction employed?

3 List the images in the poem. How do these set up the twist in the last line of the poem?

4 Some of the phrasing puts unlikely words together, such as "prince" and "bore." What other phrases like this do you find in this poem?

Analyze Voice

5 How does the speaker feel about the critic? What in the poem reveals his feelings? How would you describe the poem's tone?

6 Although the tone sounds as though it comes directly out of the eighteenth-century satirical poetry of Alexander Pope, what aspects of this brief poem reveal it is written by a more modern voice?

Synthesize Summary and Analysis

7 What does the letter form enable the speaker to accomplish in this poem?

8 Contrast the diction in this poem with the point of the poem.

9 How does the speaker use humor in this poem, and how does he mask insult as respect?

Interpret the Poem

10 Dunbar was praised and criticized for his use of dialect. In writing a poem like this one, elevated in language and formal in tone, what point do you think he desires to make?

Because verbal irony can suggest implicit scorn, it's often a good choice for writing that seeks to criticize or attack an idea. Satire does this—it's an artistic critique, sometimes quite heated, on some aspect of human immorality or absurdity. In the poem that follows about World War I, the poet Wilfred Owen uses both irony and satire to establish attitude—saying, in effect, that far from something to celebrate, war is hell.

> **"Tone is the author's attitude toward subject, but it's a rather large scaffolding or coloring of subject matter that when you're listening to someone talk—if you're like me, you're making judgments about that person: Would I want to go out to dinner with him, let's say. What kind of guy is he? . . . You do that with inflection, with pauses, irony."** Conversation with Stephen Dunn

Wilfred Owen (1893–1918)

Wilfred Owen, a British poet, is invariably associated with World War I, and with good reason—his best poetry takes the war for its subject, and he himself served and was killed in the war. A poet from a young age, Owen went to France to teach English in 1913, the year before the war broke out. He enlisted in 1917 and was hospitalized for shell shock later that year. In the hospital, Owen met Siegfried Sassoon, whose war poetry inspired Owen to achieve a new level of maturity in his own poems. Owen's carefully structured poems use physical imagery to create a visual record of war horrors, while using pararhyme—that is, words with the same consonants but different vowels—to give an auditory sense of the discord of war. Owen was killed in action one week before the war's end.

AS YOU READ   Note that the poem's Latin title means "It Is Sweet and Proper." The Latin at the end of the poem means, roughly, "It is sweet and proper to die for one's country." As you read, look for contrasting vivid flashes of news about the miseries and dangers of the battlefield.

Dulce et Decorum Est (1920)

Bent double, like old beggars under sacks,
Knock-kneed, coughing like hags, we cursed through sludge,
Till on the haunting flares we turned our backs
And towards our distant rest began to trudge.
5 Men marched asleep. Many had lost their boots
But limped on, blood-shod. All went lame; all blind;
Drunk with fatigue; deaf even to the hoots
Of tired, outstripped Five-Nines that dropped behind.

Gas! GAS! Quick, boys!—An ecstasy of fumbling,
10 Fitting the clumsy helmets just in time;
But someone still was yelling out and stumbling
And floundering like a man in fire or lime . . .
Dim, through the misty panes and thick green light,
As under a green sea, I saw him drowning.

15 In all my dreams, before my helpless sight,
He plunges at me, guttering, choking, drowning.

If in some smothering dreams you too could pace
Behind the wagon that we flung him in,
And watch the white eyes writing in his face,
20 His hanging face, like a devil's sick of sin;
If you could hear, at every jolt, the blood
Come gargling from the froth-corrupted lungs,
Obscene as cancer, bitter as the cud
Of vile, incurable sores on innocent tongues,—
25 My friend, you would not tell with such high zest
To children ardent for some desperate glory,
The old Lie: Dulce et decorum est
Pro patria mori.

Writing from Reading

Summarize

1 Who is "bent double" in this poem?

2 What kind of "gas" is being alluded to in the second stanza? Why is everyone "fumbling" in response? How could gas cause someone to drown?

3 What is happening to the person who is "floundering"?

Analyze Craft

4 The speaker uses numerous images to describe the scene: "like old beggars under sacks," "sludge." List several images from the last stanza. How do these images build suspense in the poem?

5 Owen was very young when he composed this poem, but he describes his soldier-comrades in the terms of old age and disease using ordinary, unpoetic words such as *coughing*. How do these word choices set the scene described in this poem?

Analyze Voice

6 Discuss such phrases as "An ecstasy of fumbling" or "incurable sores on innocent tongues." Why does the speaker use contrasting words such as *ecstasy* (a word meaning exquisite delight), *fumbling,* and *innocent*? Given that irony provides a kind of double take on a situation, what do words like these reveal about the author's feelings about war?

Synthesize Summary and Analysis

7 The poem's title says one thing, and the poem describes the opposite experience. The images would suggest nothing sweet about it. What is "The old Lie"? How does the poet's vivid description of war's horror prepare the reader for the last lines of this poem?

Interpret the Poem

8 World War I erased a generation of young men (including the poet). Is this poem mostly a witness to the poet's own experiences, or is this a social commentary? Would you call the poem propaganda? Could you imagine another poem in which the experiences of the soldiers could be rendered in beautiful language? Is there an argument in this poem, and if so, how convincing is the argument to you?

Situational irony occurs when a poem portrays a situation in which what happens is the opposite of what's expected to happen. In the following poem, note how our understanding of the gentleman Richard Cory is shaped. Throughout the poem, we hear of his remarkable fortune, manner, and appearance. His fellow townspeople think his life vastly superior to their own. By the end of the poem, however, we realize Richard Cory's life may have been very different from how it appeared on the surface.

Edwin Arlington Robinson (1869–1935)

A native of Maine, Edwin Arlington Robinson devoted his life to poetry, struggling with poverty for many years. He studied at Harvard University for two years, and his writing eventually won the admiration of President Theodore Roosevelt, who arranged for Robinson to work in a New York customs house. Robinson's poetry gradually became more successful, from his first, self-published collection *The Children of the Night* (1897) to his *Collected Poems* (1921), which won the first Pulitzer Prize for Poetry. With his mastery of traditional forms, his portraits of such characters as Miniver Cheevy, and his interest in Arthurian legend, Robinson won two more Pulitzers for *The Man Who Died Twice* (1924) and *Tristram* (1927).

AS YOU READ Notice the rhyming pattern in these quatrains, the way everything's perfectly ordered and in place. The final line therefore doubly reverses expectation that all will be "right" in the end.

Richard Cory (1897)

Whenever Richard Cory went down town,
We people on the pavement looked at him:
He was a gentleman from sole to crown,
Clean favored and imperially slim.

5 And he was always quietly arrayed,
And he was always human when he talked,
But still he fluttered pulses when he said,
"Good-morning," and he glittered when he walked.

And he was rich—yes, richer than a king—
10 And admirably schooled in every grace:
In fine, we thought that he was everything
To make us wish that we were in his place.

So on we worked, and waited for the light,
And went without the meat, and cursed the bread;
15 And Richard Cory, one calm summer night,
Went home and put a bullet through his head.

Writing from Reading

Summarize

1 What happens here, and who tells the story? Who are "we"?

Analyze Craft

2 How do the ballad-like feel of these stanzas and the singsong pattern make the disruption of the final line all the more disturbing and harsh-sounding?

3 What would happen if, instead of "one calm summer night," Robinson had written "one dark and stormy night"?

Analyze Voice

4 This story is told in the past tense, and therefore the speaker knows what has happened. Why does he save the worst for last?

Synthesize Summary and Analysis

5 This poem is presented without verbal irony, but the situation is ironic in the extreme. How does Robinson make you understand Richard Cory's situation without providing all the facts?

Interpret the Poem

6 What would you describe as "the moral" here?

A literary convention familiar to readers of classical drama, **dramatic irony** (sometimes called **tragic irony**) refers to a situation in which the reader knows (or is made aware of) more about a character's circumstances than the character himself knows. **Cosmic irony** occurs when forces beyond the characters' control—for example, God or fate or the supernatural—foil their plans or expectations. Thomas Hardy's famous poem "The Convergence of the Twain" responds to the sinking of the *Titanic*, which struck an iceberg and sank, killing 1,500 people. Hardy suggests that the vain human "Pride of Life" that conceived of such a glorious ship could not overcome "The Immanent Will," the cosmic forces that formed the iceberg that doomed the ship.

Thomas Hardy (1840–1928)

A British writer proud of his long life span, Thomas Hardy lived at a time when rural England was becoming increasingly industrialized and modern, a fact that figures into his fiction as well as his poetry. Originally trained as an architect, Hardy was drawn to writing and began his career as a novelist, publishing titles that are still well known today, including *Far from the Madding Crowd* (1874), *The Mayor of Casterbridge* (1886), and *Tess of the D'Urbervilles* (1891). But when *Jude the Obscure* (1895) received harsh criticism, Hardy—at the age of fifty-five—gave up novel writing and turned instead to poetry. His poems, like his fiction, are imbued with his bleak, pessimistic outlook, and where his fiction captures characters with strong passions who must nevertheless submit to an unkind and indifferent fate, his poetry equally transmits a passionate sense of loss, as in the poems written following his wife's death, known collectively as *Veteris Vestigiae Flammae* (1914).

AS YOU READ   Note the regularity in these eleven stanzas and thirty-three lines—and how it all builds to a shock for which the reader is prepared (as opposed to, say, the shock of Edwin Arlington Robinson's "Richard Cory").

The Convergence of the Twain (1912)

Lines on the loss of the "Titanic"

I
In a solitude of the sea
Deep from human vanity,
And the Pride of Life that planned her, stilly couches she.

II
Steel chambers, late the pyres
5   Of her salamandrine fires,
Cold currents thrid, and turn to rhythmic tidal lyres.

III
Over the mirrors meant
To glass the opulent
The sea-worm crawls—grotesque, slimed, dumb,
10   indifferent.

IV

Jewels in joy designed
To ravish the sensuous mind
Lie lightless, all their sparkles bleared and black and blind. 25

V

Dim moon-eyed fishes near
15   Gaze at the gilded gear
And query: "What does this vaingloriousness down here?"

VI

Well: while was fashioning
This creature of cleaving wing,
The Immanent Will that stirs and urges everything

VII

20   Prepared a sinister mate
For her—so gaily great—
A Shape of Ice, for the time far and dissociate.

VIII

And as the smart ship grew
In stature, grace, and hue,
In shadowy silent distance grew the Iceberg too.

IX

Alien they seemed to be:
No mortal eye could see
The intimate welding of their later history,

X

Or sign that they were bent
by paths coincident 30
On being anon twin halves of one august event,

XI

Till the Spinner of the Years
Said "Now!" And each one hears,
And consummation comes, and jars two hemispheres.

Writing from Reading

Summarize

1 What is the story behind the actual *Titanic*?

2 How does Hardy relate the building of the ship to the forming of the iceberg?

3 Who is the "Spinner of the Years"?

Analyze Craft

4 Notice the formal arrangements in the poem and the shock with which the poem ends. How does Hardy use language to create this shock?

5 Note the "intimate welding" of iceberg and ship. How does Hardy make them "twin halves"?

Analyze Voice

6 "Anon" means "soon" in formal poetic diction, and "august" means "important or consequential." How does the word "Now!" make all this more immediate, and what does the poet mean by "consummation comes"?

Synthesize Summary and Analysis

7 Discuss what you think Hardy means by "no mortal eye" when he describes the *Titanic*'s fate.

Interpret the Poem

8 The poet censures "vaingloriousness." Does he suggest that this in some way contributes to the sinking? What is his attitude here?

For Review and Further Study

Stephen Crane (1871–1900)

War Is Kind (1899)

Do not weep, maiden, for war is kind.
Because your lover threw wild hands toward the sky
And the affrighted steed ran on alone,
Do not weep.
5 War is kind.

  Hoarse, booming drums of the regiment
  Little souls who thirst for fight,
  These men were born to drill and die
  The unexplained glory flies above them
10 Great is the battle-god, great, and his kingdom—
  A field where a thousand corpses lie.

Do not weep, babe, for war is kind.
Because your father tumbled in the yellow trenches,
Raged at his breast, gulped and died,
15 Do not weep.
War is kind.

  Swift, blazing flag of the regiment
  Eagle with crest of red and gold,
  These men were born to drill and die
20 Point for them the virtue of slaughter
  Make plain to them the excellence of killing
  And a field where a thousand corpses lie.

Mother whose heart hung humble as a button
On the bright splendid shroud of your son,
25 Do not weep.
War is kind.

Questions for Interactive Reading and Writing

1. What is the controlling metaphor of stanzas 1, 3, and 5? How do these stanzas contribute to a sense of irony?
2. What kind of irony is present in this poem? How do you know the speaker is ironic?
3. How many lines are repeated more than once in this poem? What effect does this repetition achieve?
4. Describe the voice of the three "Do not weep" stanzas. Is it ironic?

---

e. e. cummings (1894–1962)

For a brief biography of e. e. cummings, see Chapter 26.

next to of course god america i (1926)

"next to of course god america i
love you land of the pilgrims' and so forth oh
say can you see by the dawn's early my
country 'tis of centuries come and go
and are no more what of it we should worry   5
in every language even deafanddumb
thy sons acclaim your glorious name by gorry
by jingo by gee by gosh by gum
why talk of beauty what could be more beautiful than these heroic happy dead   10
who rushed like lions to the roaring slaughter
they did not stop to think they died instead
then shall the voice of liberty be mute?"

He spoke. And drank rapidly a glass of water

John Donne (1572–1631)

Song (1633)

Go and catch a falling star,
    Get with child a mandrake root,
Tell me where all past years are,
    Or who cleft the Devil's foot;
5 Teach me to hear mermaids singing,
    Or to keep off envy's stinging,
        And find
        What wind
Serves to advance an honest mind.

10 If thou be'st born to strange sights,
    Things invisible to see,
Ride ten thousand days and nights,
    Till Age snow white hairs on thee,
Thou, when thou return'st, wilt tell me
15   All strange wonders that befell thee,
        And swear
        Nowhere
Lives a woman true, and fair.

If thou find'st one, let me know,
    Such a pilgrimage were sweet—   20
Yet do not, I would not go,
    Though at next door we might meet;
Though she were true, when you met her,
    And last, till you write your letter,
        Yet she   25
        Will be
False, ere I come, to two or three.

Marge Piercy (b. 1936)

Barbie Doll (1973)

This girlchild was born as usual
and presented dolls that did pee-pee
and miniature GE stoves and irons
and wee lipsticks the color of cherry candy.
Then in the magic of puberty, a classmate said: 5
You have a great big nose and fat legs.

She was healthy, tested intelligent,
possessed strong arms and back,
abundant sexual drive and manual dexterity.
She went to and fro apologizing.   10
Everyone saw a fat nose on thick legs.

She was advised to play coy,
exhorted to come on hearty,
exercise, diet, smile and wheedle.
15 Her good nature wore out
like a fan belt.
So she cut off her nose and her legs
and offered them up.

In the casket displayed on satin she lay
30 with the undertaker's cosmetics painted on,
a turned-up putty nose,
dressed in a pink and white nightie.
Doesn't she look pretty? everyone said.
Consummation at last.
25 To every woman a happy ending.

Questions for Interactive Reading and Writing

1. How would you summarize the girl's story in the poem?
2. What connotations do Barbie dolls have? How is the title appropriate for the poem?
3. How is the final stanza of the poem ironic? Is a particular kind of irony present? What is the speaker really trying to convey?
4. Describe the tone of the speaker. Is the irony of the final lines consistent with the tone of the rest of the poem, or does it come as a surprise?

Gil Scott-Heron (1949–2011)

The Revolution Will Not Be Televised (1970)

You will not be able to stay home, brother.
You will not be able to plug in, turn on and cop out.
You will not be able to lose yourself on scag and
skip out for beer during commercials because
5 The revolution will not be televised.

The revolution will not be televised.
The revolution will not be brought to you by Xerox in four
parts without commercial interruption.
The revolution will not show you pictures of Nixon
blowing a bugle and leading a charge by John Mitchell,
General Abramson and Spiro Agnew to eat hog maws
confiscated from a Harlem sanctuary.
The revolution will not be televised.

The revolution will not be brought to you by   10
The Schaeffer Award Theatre and will not star
Natalie Wood and Steve McQueen or Bullwinkle
and Julia.
The revolution will not give your mouth sex appeal.
The revolution will not get rid of the nubs.
The revolution will not make you look five pounds thinner.   15
The revolution will not be televised, brother.

There will be no pictures of you and Willie Mae
pushing that shopping cart down the block on the
dead run
or trying to slide that color tv in a stolen ambulance.
NBC will not be able to predict the winner at 8:32 on   20
reports from twenty-nine districts.
The revolution will not be televised.

There will be no pictures of pigs shooting down brothers
on the instant replay.
There will be no pictures of pigs shooting down brothers
on the instant replay.   25
There will be no slow motion or still lifes of Roy
Wilkins strolling through Watts in a red, black
and green liberation jumpsuit that he had been
saving for just the proper occasion.

Green Acres, Beverly Hillbillies and Hooterville Junction   30
will no longer be so damned relevant
and women will not care if Dick finally got down
with Jane
on *Search for Tomorrow*
because black people will be in the streets looking for
A Brighter Day.   35
The revolution will not be televised.

There will be no highlights on the *Eleven O'Clock News*
and no pictures of hairy armed women liberationists
and Jackie Onassis blowing her nose.
40 The theme song will not be written by Jim Webb or Francis
    Scott Key
nor sung by Glen Campbell, Tom Jones, Johnny Cash,
Englebert Humperdink or Rare Earth.
The revolution will not be televised.

The revolution will not be right back after a
45 message about a white tornado, white lightning or white
    people.
You will not have to worry about a dove in your bedroom,
the tiger in your tank or the giant in your toilet bowl.
The revolution will not go better with Coke.
The revolution will not fight germs that may cause bad
    breath.
50 The revolution *will* put you in the driver's seat.
The revolution will not be televised
                    will not be televised
            not be televised
                be televised
55 The revolution will be no re-run, brothers.
The revolution will be LIVE.

Questions for Interactive Reading and Writing

1. What role does politics play in the beginning of the poem?

2. How does rhythm play a role in the development of meaning?

3. The poem is a social critique of American society. How important is political revolution in this critique? How can the reader appreciate this critique without accepting the idea of political revolution?

4. How does spoken word poetry invite a political perspective?

"Voice is a word that gets bandied around a lot in the circles that writers are in. . . . Voice is to me the music. . . . How [does it] sound in your ear when you're reading it aloud or you're reading it silently . . . an unacknowledged but audible music. . . ."

Conversation with Richard Ford

Reading for Voice

When reading for voice, ask yourself . . .

What is the speaker's predominant tone in the poem— joyful, mournful, bewildered, or confused— and how does it help convey the poem's meaning?	*Tone:* The vocal quality of a person's speech that helps convey meaning. In a poem, an attitude conveyed toward a poem's subject as suggested by the poet's language.	EXAMPLE "When I died they washed me out of the turret with a hose."
Who is the speaker in the poem, and why has the poet chosen to use this persona? What does the persona allow the poet to represent more clearly? What is the poet's attitude toward the speaker in the poem?	*Persona:* A poem's speaker that may or may not be the same voice as the poet.	EXAMPLE "My Captain does not answer, his lips are pale and still; / My father does not feel my arm, he has no pulse nor will"

Is irony used to help establish the speaker's attitude toward the subject?	*Verbal Irony:* The use of words to express something dissimilar to (or the opposite of) their literal meaning.	EXAMPLE "War is kind."
	Sarcasm: A form of verbal irony using spoken approval to express implied disapproval.	EXAMPLE "To every woman, a happy ending."
	Situational Irony: An outcome that turns out to be very different from what was expected.	EXAMPLE "And Richard Cory, one calm summer night, / Went home and put a bullet through his head."
	Dramatic Irony / Tragic Irony: A discrepancy that is detectable to the audience but not to a character or characters.	EXAMPLE "'next to of course god america i / love you land of the pilgrims' and so forth oh . . .'"
	Cosmic Irony: A discrepancy between what characters hope for or expect and what supernatural forces, fate, or God provide.	EXAMPLE "The Immanent Will that stirs and urges everything"

Writing about Voice

1. Compare the relationships of speaker to father figure in Sylvia Plath's "Daddy," Theodore Roethke's "My Papa's Waltz," and Rita Dove's "Flash Cards."

2. Compare the speakers' attitudes toward war and conflict in "War Is Kind," by Stephen Crane, "Dulce et Decorum Est," by Wilfred Owen, and "next to of course god america i," by e. e. cummings.

3. Consider the tone of William Stafford's "Traveling through the Dark." How does it reflect the conflict and hesitation the speaker faces, and how does Stafford's tone help convey this hesitation?

4. Analyze the interplay of tone and word choice in Wallace Stevens's "Sunday Morning." How do Stevens's language and attitude toward the subject matter help communicate his character's religious deliberations?

5. Write a short, informal imagined biography for the speaker of one of the following poems: "This Is Just to Say" by William Carlos Williams; "Riot Act" by Ai; "Crazy Jane" by William Butler Yeats. Use specific material in the poems to help support your invented history.

6. Consider the attitude of Ben Jonson's address to his son ("On My First Son") and Anne Bradstreet's to her book ("Address to My Book"). What do the poems reveal about parenthood and creative acts?

7. What is Thomas Hardy saying about the irony of human existence in "The Convergence of the Twain"? Compare that with what Edward Arlington Robinson is saying in "Richard Cory." What do these poems tell us about the way their authors look at life, at death, and at how what may seem like an accident is fate?

IT is foolish
to let a young redwood
grow next to a house.

Even in this
one lifetime,
you will have to choose.
—*from "Tree" by Jane Hirshfield*

SPEAKING of her poem "Tree," Jane Hirshfield tells us in her interview, "Now the tree is real and the house is real. Both actually exist, and as the poem says, the house is cluttered with unique things. It's a real dilemma. Eventually the house and the tree won't be able to occupy the same bit of earth. But a house and a tree are also archetypes and images."

In the case of a tree, you have the image of an object, and you also have the larger symbol of what a tree means as archetype: the particular instance that presents the whole. This specific tree, a redwood growing in a specific place, has also come to represent the idea of natural versus man-made things. It embodies— or stands as a symbol for—the ideas of containment and growth.

22 Imagery

"The wider the field of senses a poem draws on, the more fully felt and alive its world is going to be in the mind of the reader."

Conversation with Jane Hirshfield, available on video at connect.mcgraw-hill.com

"Tree" and its author belong to a tradition of nature writing, of close attention paid to the physical world. In this chapter, we focus on the **image,** the thing seen for and by itself, as well as the **symbol,** what that same thing might stand for, or represent. Poetry comes across mainly in terms of an attitude-generating cluster of words, creating vivid sensory (visual, aural, or tactile) impressions through language. Images work in the service of diction and tone; they generate emotion and establish mood. In the case of Hirshfield, the impetus has been provided by the sight of a nearby tree—a "young redwood" that the poet understands will grow much larger over time. "Tree" builds on that particular sight and specific visual cue to give us a more general view of growth, change, and life.

& Symbol

Jane Hirshfield

... Poetry is a kind of thinking and feeling done with the whole body, mind, and heart.

A Conversation on Writing

Thinking with the Body

Image is one of the most powerful ways a poem both carries meaning and changes and enlarges it, which is the work that every good poem is trying to do. Image is a field where the powers of body and mind can meet. Everything that we know of the world is constructed on the bedrock of sense experience. . . . Poetry is a kind of thinking and feeling done with the whole body, mind, and heart.

The Meaning of an Image

Every image is also a portrait of a state of soul. Rain in a poem is almost never only rain. In one poem it might be grief; in another it might be renewal after long thirst or after the drought of loneliness. Image in poetry is an enormously flexible, intimate, and powerful tool just because it hands experience from one person's consciousness into another's directly, with the solidity, multiplicity, and subtlety of actual life, which doesn't arrive with interpretations attached. A poem can add some direction to this, but the image itself is sometimes the only thing that's needed.

Meditations on the Ordinary

One of the things that has happened to poetry as it's become more contemporary is more and more things have become the subject of poems, and one of the things which has come into poetry in the twentieth and twenty-first centuries is poems about very ordinary objects, meditations on objects which you wouldn't ordinarily think of as worthy of that important thing we think of as poetry, and yet

in fact poetry's work is to see the ordinary world . . . and turn that into something which expounds into larger realms, more resonance, more feeling. It lets you have a bigger life than you would have had if you only saw a button as simply a thing that holds your shirt closed.

Jane Hirshfield lives in a small white cottage in Marin County, California, surrounded by the trees, flowers, and animals that often appear in her poems. Born in New York City in 1953, she was among the first female graduates of Princeton University. Hirshfield has published six books of poetry, including *After* (2006), *Given Sugar, Given Salt* (2001), *The Lives of the Heart* (1997), *The October Palace* (1994), *Of Gravity & Angels* (1988), and *Alaya* (1982); essays about poetry, *Nine Gates: Entering the Mind of Poetry* (1997); and several anthologies of women poets. Early in her career, Hirshfield dedicated three years to the study of Zen practice, and her poetry reflects this lifelong involvement in Buddhism. Many poems focus on the natural world and our human condition within it. Hirshfield has received major honors for her poetry, including, in 2004, the seventieth Academy Fellowship for distinguished poetic achievement by the Academy of American Poets.

To watch this entire interview and hear the author read from her poetry, go to connect.mcgraw-hill.com.

RESEARCH ASSIGNMENT   In the interview, Hirshfield describes how she uses her own experiences to construct the imagery in her poems. After watching the interview, how would you describe the meaning that Hirshfield herself assigns to her poem "Tree"?

AS YOU READ Monitor any visual images that come to you. Can you picture the poet's description of this scene in your mind's eye?

Two Poems by Jane Hirshfield

Tree (2000)

It is foolish
to let a young redwood
grow next to a house.

Even in this
5   one lifetime,
you will have to choose.

That great calm being,
this clutter of soup pots and books—

Already the first branch-tips brush at the window.
10   Softly, calmly, immensity taps at your life.

Writing from Reading

Summarize

1 Describe the physical growth of the redwood tree and how it is impinging on the house.

Analyze Craft

2 What use is the poet making of the literal growth of the tree?

3 Can you picture it? From what literal vantage point does the poet view the tree?

Analyze Voice

4 Is the poet in a panic about the situation? Or does she speak calmly? Is she trying to accept the growth of the tree as part of the progress, or lack of it, in her own life? How does this affect her choice of words?

Synthesize Summary and Analysis

5 How does the poet employ the actual tree in order to speak about something greater than just one single redwood?

Interpret the Poem

6 Do you detect a rhythmic progress in the few stanzas of this poem? If the poet states the problem, wrestles with it, and somehow resolves it, in what particular context does that occur? Would you say the poem speaks to us about a situation in the natural world or in a more abstract philosophical fashion about the situation of our own lives?

Here's another of Hirshfield's close examinations of an object—in this case a man-made as opposed to a natural thing. As the poem continues, the image of a button becomes "its own story, completed." And once again the poet ("I tell you") speaks directly to her readers, inviting us to enter the world of her scrupulous words.

Button (2000)

It likes both to enter and to leave,
actions it seems to feel as a kind of hide-and-seek.
It knows nothing of what the cloth believes
of its magus-like powers.

5 If fastening and unfastening are in its nature,
it doesn't care about its nature.

It likes the caress of two fingers
against its slightly thickened edges.
It likes the scent and heat of the proximate body.
10 The exhilaration of the washing is its wild pleasure.

Amoralist, sensualist, dependent of cotton thread,
its sleep is curled like a cat to a patch of sun,
calico and round.

Its understanding is the understanding
15 of honey and jasmine, of letting what happens come.

A button envies no neighboring button,
no snap, no knot, no polyester-braided toggle.
It rests on its red-checked shirt in serene disregard.

It is its own story, completed.

20 Brevity and longevity mean nothing to a button carved
of horn.

Nor do old dreams of passion disturb it,
though once it wandered the ten thousand grasses
with the musk-fragrance caught in its nostrils;
though once it followed—it did, I tell you—that wind for
miles.

Writing from Reading

Summarize

1 The poet speaks of a simple, even humble, object from our everyday lives. How does she describe it, in how many ways, and on how many levels of meaning?

Analyze Craft

2 Is there a specific term we can use to describe the way the poet uses the object in the poem? As what sort of living thing does she describe the button?

3 How can a button have a "story"?

4 How does the poet work to make us feel a certain way about the button?

Analyze Voice

5 What attitude does she express toward the object? What central words or phrases alert you to this?

6 What is the effect of the phrase "it did, I tell you," which the poet sets apart from the rest of the last line?

Synthesize Summary and Analysis

7 How does the poet raise a simple everyday object into something greater than itself?

Interpret the Poem

8 Picture the button in all of the states of being or manifestations in which the poet describes it. How important is it that the poet employs the word "horn" to explain the button's origins?

"**Every time I heard my parents recite ancient . . . poetry . . . my own experience was that I was hearing language that was manifesting something older and something mysterious and something beautiful that I couldn't account for, and I wanted to be a part of that.**" Conversation with Li-Young Lee

Some of the earliest poetry based almost entirely on image is that of Japanese **haiku.** In haiku (a poetic form containing—in Japanese—seventeen syllables in three lines of five, seven, and five syllables each), two images are juxtaposed in a way that allows a reader to create his or her own understanding of the meaning; the images themselves carry the poem. Haiku also traditionally contain some natural-world reference to a particular season, and so an image from nature is at the heart of each of the following two haiku, one by the late eighteenth-century poet Kobayashi Issa (whom Hirshfield discusses in her interview) and the other by the seventeenth-century poet Matsuo Bashō, generally considered the first to perfect the haiku form.

Kobayashi Issa (1763–1827)

The Japanese poet used simply the pen name Issa and brought a highly personal voice to the haiku form, using dialect and colloquial language and confessing his personal doubts and loneliness. Issa was born in Kashiwabara, the son of a farmer, and lost his mother at three and his devoted grandmother as a teenager. By age fifteen, Issa had left for Edo (present-day Tokyo), where he entered a school for haiku poets. He spent much of his adult life wandering Japan before settling once again in Kashiwabara, where he married and tried to start a family. All four of his children died in infancy, and his first wife died in childbirth. His poetry, which was influenced by Buddhist themes of sin and compassion, uses simple language to articulate human experiences (as in his collection *The Year of My Life,* 1819, which captures his life events, among them his daughter's death). Despite his hardships, he brings the small pleasures of daily life into the more than 20,000 haiku he wrote in his lifetime.

On a branch (c. 1800)

On a branch
floating downriver
a cricket, singing.

—*translated by* Jane Hirshfield

Matsuo Bashō (1644–1694)

A Japanese master of the haiku, Matsuo Bashō spent his youth as a servant to a master with whom he had a close friendship. Bashō's first published poetry appeared in 1664, but when his master died two years later, Bashō became a wanderer. He continued to publish poetry, however, and his reputation grew; he soon had a group of twenty students. The students so respected their teacher that they built him a hut, complete with a *bashō*—or banana tree—outside its door, from which he adopted his nickname. Bashō's haiku are marked by a precision of imagery—both visual and auditory— that conveys human emotion.

Heat Lightning Streak

Lightning—
a night heron's cry
flies into darkness

—*translated by* Jane Hirshfield with Mariko Aratani

Writing from Reading

Summarize

1 Describe the images evoked in both haikus. Note the use of present tense and, in Bashō, the absence of verbs.

Analyze Craft

2 The Japanese original of this form has a precise number of syllables and usually includes at least two varieties of necessary words, one to denote the season and one to end the poem on a certain emotional note; it is written all in one sentence. How does the English form of the haiku differ from the original? What is the role of the image?

Analyze Voice

3 Is there a similarity between the two poets? What makes for this kinship aside from the form of the poems?

4 How does the subject matter affect the voice of the speaker in each poem?

Synthesize Summary and Analysis

5 These poems are composed in a specific syllabic form, each focusing on a situation in nature that has meaning for the observer and reader. What limitations does this form bring, what freedoms?

6 Each of these situations, tiny in scope, suggests something much larger about nature and about human life. Explain the leap between the cricket and lightning and our own problems of living in crisis.

Like Jane Hirshfield, but nearly a century earlier, Ezra Pound was much impressed by poetry from Asia—particularly Chinese verse and Japanese haiku, with their brief evocations of things closely seen. Living in Paris and taking the *metro* (the French term for the "subway"), he made this striking comparison of urban commuters to the petals on a tree. There's no explicit discussion or association, no essay-like analysis of the way light-colored faces cluster in the station's darkness—but the "unnatural"—or man-made—crowd of commuters seems suddenly to have become a "natural" thing, a part of nature's blooming. What the poet sees is what compels his (and therefore our) attention. No moral here, or conclusion to draw; there is just an image, defined by Pound as "an intellectual and an emotional complex in an instant of time."

Ezra Pound (1885–1972)

Regarded as a crucial modern American poet, Ezra Pound helped foster the careers of such important Modernists as James Joyce, T. S. Eliot, and Ernest Hemingway. Pound grew up in Pennsylvania and moved to London in 1908. Later, he would move to Italy and become a supporter of Benito Mussolini, for which in 1945 he was arrested and incarcerated for more than a decade in a Washington, D.C., mental hospital. But before he became a politically controversial figure, Pound forged a bridge between American and European avant-gardes, launching the Imagist movement—which advocated poems pared down to an image without any abstraction—early in his career. He later moved away from Imagism, but elements of its stark, precise quality remained in his poetry. His major works, "Hugh Selwyn Mauberley: Life and Contacts" (1920) and *The Cantos*—written over many years—reflect Modernist techniques such as shifts in time and point of view, an eclectic inclusion of material, and a wide-ranging diction.

AS YOU READ Notice the influence of haiku here—the compression of language and centrality of image all caught "in an instant of time."

In a Station of the Metro (1916)

The apparition of these faces in the crowd;
Petals on a wet, black bough.

Writing from Reading

Summarize

1 What action does this poem describe, and what, if anything, goes on?

Analyze Craft

2 How does the word *apparition* color the poem that follows; what emotion does it convey?

Analyze Voice

3 Who is speaking here, and to whom? If the Hirshfield poem yokes the man-made to the natural world, how do these "petals on a wet, black bough" seem similar to or different from her thoughts about a tree?

Synthesize Summary and Analysis

4 We've already used more words in the discussion of this poem than are contained in the poem. In what ways does Pound's brevity reinforce his notion of an image as an "intellectual and emotional complex in an instant of time"? In what ways does the image convey an idea or feeling about more time than just a single moment?

Interpret the Poem

5 The title sets the scene; the poem provides the image. Would the feel of the whole be altered if the title read, instead, "At a Football Game" or "On a Bus"?

Pound and several of his fellow poets founded a movement called Imagism, which gave the object *seen* in a poem precedence over any other aspect of the poem. The American expatriate Hilda Doolittle, or H. D., as she signed her work, was one of Pound's partners in this "school" or "movement"—also believing in the elemental power of the image. In her poems, as in Pound's, we look at the thing itself, even as the poet attempts to suggest that details of the natural world evoke a meaning beyond their mere physical presence.

H. D. (Hilda Doolittle; 1886–1961)

Born in Bethlehem, Pennsylvania, H. D. became friends with William Carlos Williams and Ezra Pound at the University of Pennsylvania. In 1911 she took a summer trip to London, which turned into a lifelong residency abroad and which launched her poetry career when she reconnected with Pound. Under his influence, she became an Imagist, interested in pared-down verses that portrayed only immediate, real objects. Later, she moved away from Imagism, cultivating her interest in mythology and composing book-length poems about World War II: *The Walls Do Not Fall* (1944), *Tribute to the Angels* (1945), and *The Flowering of the Rod* (1946).

AS YOU READ   In "Sea Poppies" what we look at is the thing itself. The image of sea poppies is in sharp focus in this poem. Ask yourself, How does the poet attempt to suggest that details of the natural world evoke a meaning beyond their mere physical nature?

Sea Poppies

(1916)

Amber husk
fluted with gold,
fruit on the sand
marked with a rich grain,

5   treasure
spilled near the shrub-pines
to bleach on the boulders:

your stalk has caught root
among wet pebbles
10   and drift flung by the sea
and grated shells
and split conch-shells.

Beautiful, wide-spread,
fire upon leaf,
15   what meadow yields
so fragrant a leaf
as your bright leaf?

Writing from Reading

Summarize

1 Write your own "snapshot" of this poem.

Analyze Craft

2 List ways in which the poet tries to make the reader *see* sea poppies. What words are most effective here as description and which ones (such as *beautiful*) convey value judgments instead?

3 Compare this poem with Marianne Moore's "The Fish" in Chapter 24.

Both poems use an image from the natural world; however, the line structure of the Moore poem emphasizes sound over imagery. How does H. D.'s poem keep the image in focus and Moore's poem shift our attention to sound?

Analyze Voice

4 How large a role, if any, does voice play in this poem? How might a more prominent presence alter the tone of this poem?

Synthesize Summary and Analysis

5 Explain how the image takes you to a higher level of understanding of the poem's meaning.

Interpret the Poem

6 Notice how, in the last stanza, H. D. repeats the word *leaf* three times. What effect does this achieve?

The short poems of William Carlos Williams, the physician from Paterson, New Jersey, illustrate a great deal about that modern tendency in poetry defined by Pound as Imagism. Here the "thing itself "—an object seen and not discussed or analyzed—becomes the poet's focus and the poem's primary concern. Gertrude Stein's famous pronouncement that "a rose is a rose is a rose" shares much the same aesthetic—or, as Williams puts it (in his 1944 poem "A Sort of Song"), "No ideas / but in things."

"So there's the ordinary shape of the thing and the way that you would say it . . . and if you piece them out on the page, you can convey the feeling by getting this shape absolutely." Conversation with Robert Hass

On first reading, the following brief poem seems to be about almost nothing. There are echoing sounds such as "glazed" and "rain," or "white" and "beside," and the lines have a similar rhythm, but if you recite these words they may well sound like a casual overheard sentence—not a formal arrangement of language in a structured shape. The formality of Williams's work is less than obvious: a thing you have to look closely at in order to notice it at all. In fact, there's a nearly haiku-like compression of and shape to the work. The poet presents us with a couple of objects, a red wheelbarrow glazed with rainwater standing in a yard alongside a bunch of white chickens. Together, the poem's formal elements ingrain in our memory the image of the barrow and the chickens and the rain. The life evoked by objects—in a barnyard or a garden patch, and in particular weather—grows as vivid here as though it were *painted*, and as fixed within our memory as though it had been framed. In this way, a poem that seems at first glance quite casual puts forward an image of eternal order and upholds the importance, in a democratic contemporary fashion (very conversational, very American), of each and every thing and every one of us.

William Carlos Williams (1883–1963)

William Carlos Williams was born in Rutherford, New Jersey, the same town in which he would die eighty years later. This fact is consistent with one of Williams's most fundamental beliefs about poetry: that one ought to write about one's own locale. Williams had many other strong ideas about poetry, among them that the poet should focus only on concrete details and images rather than try to convey abstract ideas. Although friends with Ezra Pound and T. S. Eliot, Williams in many ways stands in opposition to their complex references and international emphases; unlike his contemporaries, he spent little time abroad. Considered one of the most important of twentieth-century poets, Williams made his living as a doctor with a specialization in pediatrics (he also delivered more than 2,000 babies!). His touchstone work, *Paterson,* is an epic in five books—the third of which won the National Book Award in 1950—about Paterson, New Jersey.

AS YOU READ Notice how Williams divides "wheel" and "barrow" or "rain" and "water" in a line break; others might have written "wheelbarrow" or "rainwater," but the space between the words and lines allows us to consider how those objects separate or fuse.

The Red Wheelbarrow (1923)

so much depends
upon

a red wheel
barrow

5 glazed with rain
water

beside the white
chickens.

Writing from Reading

Summarize

1 What images do you see in this poem? How are they connected?

Analyze Craft

2 What does Williams accomplish by beginning each line with a lower-case letter?

3 Why does Williams say "a" red wheelbarrow instead of "the" red wheelbarrow?

Analyze Voice

4 What's not said is just as important as what's included here. What has been left out, and how would the poem change if it were included in the poem?

Synthesize Summary and Analysis

5 How does the casual tone combine with the structure to make the poem's point?

Interpret the Poem

6 The only statement in the entire poem that does not describe a physical thing is the opening line—"so much depends." You can read the first line, in effect, as either "very much depends" or "therefore much depends," and the interpretation of the phrase shifts back and forth accordingly. How much of the meaning of this poem depends on the phrasing of this statement?

Another representation of the importance of the image comes in the following poem—again, very plainly presented—by the twentieth-century American poet Wallace Stevens. This self-described **anecdote**—a personal remembrance or brief story—also takes as its topic the *things* of the world, though a jar on a hill is somehow more surprising than a wheelbarrow in a backyard. A secondary meaning of the word *jar* is "discord" or "disruption," and the imagined "gray and bare" object cleans up what's "slovenly." Perhaps no clearer testimonial to the power of an image (and what poetry can accomplish by "foregrounding" such an image) exists than "Anecdote of the Jar."

Wallace Stevens (1879–1955)

For a brief biography of Wallace Stevens, see Chapter 20.

AS YOU READ   Notice how the poem's first word is "I," infusing the poet himself with the pride of positioning the important jar. How does this act of shaping—"like nothing else in Tennessee"— organize and change what is around it?

Anecdote of the Jar (1923)

I placed a jar in Tennessee,
And round it was, upon a hill.
It made the slovenly wilderness
Surround that hill.

5 The wilderness rose up to it,
And sprawled around, no longer wild.
The jar was round upon the ground
And tall and of a port in air.

It took dominion everywhere.
10 The jar was gray and bare.
It did not give of bird or bush,
Like nothing else in Tennessee.

Writing from Reading

Summarize

1 Describe the jar. Could you draw it?

2 What words does Stevens use to convey the image? Does it represent a Mason jar, a ceramic jug, a particular bowl you have seen?

Analyze Craft

3 Notice how the last word of the first line and the last word of the poem are the same (this is true also of the final word in lines 2 and 4). Then there are three rhymes ("air," "everywhere," "bare").

What does this tell you about the "shaping impulse" on the poet's part?

Analyze Voice

4 Can you read this poem as a companion text to William Carlos Williams's "The Red Wheelbarrow"? In what ways is the voice different, in what ways the same?

Synthesize Summary and Analysis

5 How does the act of *seeing* itself connect to the name of the state

repeated twice—at the end of the poem's first and last lines? How different would this anecdote be if the poet had located his jar in Nevada or Rhode Island?

Interpret the Poem

6 How much depends on the jar in Tennessee, the jar that "took dominion everywhere"? What if the poet had not "placed a jar in Tennessee"? Would the world—or, even more grandly, the universe—be different?

ALLEGORY AND PARABLE

Allegory and **parable** are related to symbol and are both extended narratives in which people, places, and things function somewhat like conventional symbols, directly representing such attributes as good, evil, redemption, hell, and heaven. One of the most famous poetic allegories is Dante's *Divine Comedy*. A parable, like the Fishes and the Loaves from the Gospel of Matthew in the New Testament, is usually an allegory but also a teaching tale with a moral.

Coming up now is another domestic image, another familiar object closely seen: the image of "The Blue Bowl." In this poem, "we" engage in other matters; we work and eat and sleep and attempt to forget what's been buried. The bowl itself—plastic, ceramic, tin, china?—disappears from sight, but the sense of its absent presence remains. In that sense, it stands as a symbol—as well as a literal burial container—of what is cherished and lost.

"Poetry . . . bring[s] image . . . and symbol to bear on unspeakable love or hurt or loss or hate or whatever happens to be." Conversation

with Thomas Lynch

Here is a crucial distinction between image and symbol. If, as William Carlos Williams puts it, there are "No ideas / but in things," there are certain "things" within our culture that stand—almost inescapably—for "ideas." A jar in Tennessee and a wheelbarrow glazed with rain are specific images, but say such words as "dove" or "cross" or "crown" and it's impossible not to imagine what else they represent. A dove means *peace* as well as bird, a cross means *suffering and sacrifice* as well as arrangement of wood. The connotations of the word *crown* are those of *power, majesty,* but when Christ wears a crown of thorns we know what that headgear signifies instead. The word for this, in pictorial terms, is **iconography**—put a scepter or skull in a painting, and the viewer is supposed to know what those objects represent. In earlier times, these were almost **conventional** associations: *a* stands for one thing, *b* stands for another, and so on and so forth. More modern poets, however, tend to create their own symbols and go against the grain. So when Jane Kenyon makes "the blue bowl" *stand* for something, she's making that object symbolic in a literary way, a way that is specific to its context in the poem, a way it had not been before.

Jane Kenyon (1947–1995)

Born in Ann Arbor, Michigan, Jane Kenyon remained there through her undergraduate and graduate education at the University of Michigan. While at the university, Kenyon met poet Donald Hall, whom she married. The couple settled in the New Hampshire home that had been in Hall's family for generations. There, Kenyon began to take her poetry seriously and published four collections, which met with high praise for their portrayals of New England, the cycles of nature, and the depression with which she struggled. She died at age forty-seven of leukemia.

The Blue Bowl (1990)

Like primitives we buried the cat
with his bowl. Bare-handed
we scraped sand and gravel
back into the hole.
5   They fell with a hiss
and thud on his side,
on his long red fur, the white feathers
between his toes, and his
long, not to say aquiline, nose.

10 We stood and brushed each other off.
There are sorrows keener than these.

Silent the rest of the day, we worked,
ate, stared, and slept. It stormed
all night; now it clears, and a robin
15 burbles from a dripping bush
like the neighbor who means well
but always says the wrong thing.

Writing from Reading

Summarize

1 Why does Kenyon give this poem the title she does?

Analyze Craft

2 It would seem that in this poem the image of the bowl takes on itself the emotion of the situation—the death and burial of a beloved pet. Is it a visible presence once dropped into the ground?

Analyze Voice

3 We're told by the poet that "There are sorrows keener than these." What are those sorrows? How does this line contribute to the mood of the poem?

Synthesize Summary and Analysis

4 How much of a role does the bowl play in this poem? Is it all-encompassing, like the jar in Tennessee in Stevens's "Anecdote of the Jar"?

Interpret the Poem

5 If the burbling robin seems to be saying "the wrong thing," what does the poet suggest here about the possibility of consolation, and does she instead imply that it's better to be "Silent the rest of the day"?

W. H. Auden (1907–1973)

For a brief biography of W. H. Auden, see Chapter 20.

AS YOU READ   Notice that this poem begins, as the title tells us, in a particular place with the poet examining a particular painting. But the opening statement is nonetheless a generality—a blank to be filled in by what he, studying, sees.

Musée des Beaux Arts (1940)

About suffering they were never wrong,
The Old Masters: how well, they understood
Its human position; how it takes place
While someone else is eating or opening a window or just walking dully along;
5 How, when the aged are reverently, passionately waiting
For the miraculous birth, there always must be
Children who did not specially want it to happen, skating
On a pond at the edge of the wood:
They never forgot
10 That even the dreadful martyrdom must run its course
Anyhow in a corner, some untidy spot
Where the dogs go on with their doggy life and the torturer's horse
Scratches its innocent behind on a tree.

In Breughel's *Icarus,* for instance: how everything turns away
15 Quite leisurely from the disaster; the ploughman may
Have heard the splash, the forsaken cry,
But for him it was not an important failure; the sun shone
As it had to on the white legs disappearing into the green
Water; and the expensive delicate ship that must have seen
20 Something amazing, a boy falling out of the sky,
Had somewhere to get to and sailed calmly on.

Brueghel's *Fall of Icarus*

Pieter Brueghel the Elder. Landscape with the Fall of Icarus, c. 1554–1555. Oil on panel (transferred to canvas), 2' × 5" × 3' 8⅛". Musées Royaux des Beaux-Arts de Belgique, Brussels. © akg-images.

"Beneath their flight / the fisherman while casting his long rod, / or the tired shepherd leaning on his crook, / or the rough plowman as he raised his eyes, / astonished might observe them on the wing, / and worship them as Gods" (Ovid, lines 338–343). In Brueghel's painting, the characters are all in place, but their reactions, as Auden observes in "Musée des Beaux Arts," demonstrate a resignation far from the astonishment Ovid describes. The plowman turns his head to the ground, the fisherman keeps his eyes on the water, and the boat, with its sails billowed out toward the horizon, keeps sailing. In the bottom right, away from the focus, fallen Icarus drowns, kicking his feet at the sunny sky.

Writing from Reading

Summarize

1 What is happening when suffering "takes place" in this poem? What is the suffering that Auden is referring to? What is the first and final point that Auden makes about suffering?

Analyze Craft

2 This poem is a work of art about a work of art. How does its tone differ from, say, that of a poem about a button or a tree?

3 Look at the rhyme pattern of the last eight lines. How does what we hear help establish what we see, and why should the poem's last words be "calmly on"?

Analyze Voice

4 Discuss a phrase such as "the dogs go on with their doggy life" or "for him it was not an important failure."

Synthesize Summary and Analysis

5 The second stanza of this poem evokes an individual canvas by a particular painter. How much does it help to be familiar with, or at least be able to see, the painting?

6 How faithful has the poet been to the Brueghel painting in describing it?

Interpret the Poem

7 Why do you think Icarus dies off at the edge of the composition and not stage center? What is the poet saying, by way of this image, about the importance of "great events" and their place in daily life?

Anne Carson (b. 1950)

Growing up in Ontario, Canada, Anne Carson developed a love for the classics when one of her high school teachers taught her ancient Greek during school lunch hours. Carson eventually earned her bachelor's, master's, and doctorate from the University of Toronto and today is a professor of classics and comparative literature. Her interest in the classics is reflected in her work: *Autobiography of Red* (1998), a novel-length poem, is a recasting of a Greek myth in the present day; *Plainwater* (1996), a collection of poetry and prose, includes a conversation with a seventh-century B.C.E. poet. She has immersed herself in the world of Greek theater and translated the work of the poet Sappho. Carson has received awards, including a MacArthur Foundation award and a Guggenheim Fellowship.

AS YOU READ Ask yourself how faithful the verbal "tone" here is to the visual mood of the Hopper painting.

Automat

(2000)

Night work
  neon milk
  powdered
  silk
5 Girl de luxe

Girl work
  plate glass love
  lone
  glove
10 Night de luxe

Girl work
  smell of black
  down
  the back
15 Night de luxe

Night work
  clamo
  ad te
  Domine
20 Girl de luxe

Edward Hopper's
Automat (1927)

A lone woman sits in an automat sipping a cup of coffee. She is well dressed, not a vagrant, but her missing glove and downcast eyes suggest hurry or distraction. Hopper's intention in the painting is ambiguous. An opaque black window dominates the scene, reflecting only rows of lights from the apparently empty automat. The lone woman's skin is the brightest part of the painting, contrasting sharply with the void of the window, and (for the painting's time) perhaps more than slightly suggesting female sexuality. Consider the coin-operated, Prohibition-era setting: Is the woman trapped, lonely, or waiting? Hopper's work frequently appears to capture a scene immediately before or after the action has occurred; as in *Automat,* it is often difficult to know which is the case.

Edward Hopper (American, 1882–1967). Automat. 1927. Oil on Canvas; 36″ × 28⅛″. Des Moines Art Center Permanent Collections; purchased with funds from the Edmundson Art Foundation, Inc., 1958.2.

Writing from Reading

Summarize

1 How would you describe the poet's response to the painting?

Analyze Craft

2 In what ways does the poem seem (or not seem) at all "painterly"? How does it employ visual material?

3 Does the rhyming make clear Carson's response? What effect do the repetitive images have?

Analyze Voice

4 Can you identify the needs and interests of the speaker from her voice? Is the poet singing the praises of the girl or judging her?

Synthesize Summary and Analysis

5 How would you characterize the effect of the poem compared with the effect of the painting? How does the painting affect your reaction to the poem?

Interpret the Poem

6 Does the quotation in devotional Latin add to the mystery of the poem or make the poem clearer to you? It might help to know that the Latin *clamo ad te Domine* means "I cry out, God, to you."

Cathy Song (b. 1950)

Cathy Song, who is of Korean and Chinese descent, was born in Hawaii. She left Hawaii to complete her education—a B.A. from Wellesley College and an M.A. from Boston University—but returned with her husband and children several years later. Her first collection of poetry, *Picture Bride* (1982), was named for the practice of arranged marriages between Asians in America and women in Asia based on exchanged photographs—the practice by which Song's grandmother came to America at the age of twenty-three. The collection won the Yale Series of Younger Poets Prize. Since then, Song has published four more collections of poetry, which have continued her examination of family ties that *Picture Bride* established.

AS YOU READ Go back and forth to the painting and notice the accuracy or freedom of the poet with respect to the original.

Girl Powdering Her Neck (1983)
from an ukiyo-e print by Utamaro

The light is the inside
sheen of an oyster shell,
sponged with talc and vapor,
moisture from a bath.
5 A pair of slippers
are placed outside
the rice-paper doors.
She kneels at a low table
in the room,
10 her legs folded beneath her
as she sits on a buckwheat pillow.

Her hair is black
with hints of red,
the color of seaweed
15 spread over rocks.

Morning begins the ritual
wheel of the body,
the application of translucent skins.
She practices pleasure:
20 the pressure of three fingertips
applying powder.
Fingerprints of pollen
some other hand will trace.

The peach-dyed kimono
25 patterned with maple leaves
drifting across the silk,
falls from right to left
in a diagonal, revealing
the nape of her neck
30 and the curve of a shoulder
like the slope of a hill
set deep in snow in a country
of huge white solemn birds.
Her face appears in the mirror,
35 a reflection in a winter pond,
rising to meet itself.

She dips a corner of her sleeve
like a brush into water
to wipe the mirror;
40 she is about to paint herself.
The eyes narrow
in a moment of self-scrutiny.
The mouth parts
as if desiring to disturb
45 the placid plum face;
break the symmetry of silence.
But the berry-stained lips,
stenciled into the mask of beauty,
do not speak.

50 Two chrysanthemums
touch in the middle of the lake
and drift apart.

Kitagawa Utamaro's *Girl Powdering Her Neck* (c. 1750)

Painted as a study of the "floating world" (the translation of "ukiyo-e"), this print depicts a geisha preparing herself in a daily ritual. The Japanese term *ukiyo* connotes the frivolity and passing nature of the nouveau riche way of life that Utamaro depicts. Prints such as this were common in Utamaro's time (mid-1700s) because they could be cheaply mass produced. Common subjects were actors, sumo wrestlers, and groups of women. A distinct aspect of many Utamaro prints is their depiction of women alone, often shown only from the waist up. The personal, individual focus of this print engenders its depth and appeal; note how even the artist's signature becomes part of the composition.

Kitagawa Utamaro (1753–1806). c. 1795. Woman Powdering Her Neck. *Musée National des Arts Asiatiques–Guimet, Paris, France.*

Writing from Reading

Summarize

1 The poet views a print by an eighteenth-century Japanese artist. Do you find that her poem is a description only?

Analyze Craft

2 How does the poet make her attitudes and emotions known even as she seems to describe rather straightforwardly what she sees in the print? How do the metaphors she employs suggest her attitude toward the subject?

Analyze Voice

3 Is there anything in her choice of words that reveals her emotions about the situation or image in the print? Does the vividness of the colors contribute to this effect?

Synthesize Summary and Analysis

4 The poet's reproduction in language of the Utamaro print reveals certain ways of seeing that are as much interpre-

tive as descriptive. Can you describe some of these?

Interpret the Poem

5 The modern American woman of Asian descent looks at the old Japanese print and finds herself in it in many ways, and yet there are differences. Which might these be?

Rita Dove (b. 1952)

For a brief biography of Rita Dove, see Chapter 21.

AS YOU READ   Look for symbols and images the Mexican painter Frida Kahlo uses in her many self-portraits, one of which is included here. Kahlo was the wife of Mexican painter Diego Rivera and a devoted nationalist.

Sonnet in Primary Colors

This is for the woman with one black wing
perched over her eyes: lovely Frida, erect
among parrots, in the stern petticoats of the peasant,
who painted herself a present—
5 wildflowers entwining the plaster corset
her spine resides in the romance of mirrors.

Each night she lay down in pain and rose
to her celluloid butterflies of her Beloved Dead,
Lenin and Marx and Stalin arrayed at the footstead.
10 And rose to her easel, the hundred dogs panting
like children along the graveled walks of the garden, Diego's
love a skull in the circular window
of the thumbprint searing her immutable brow.

Allusions to several of Frida Kahlo's (1907–1954) self-portraits
are in this poem, including the one pictured here, Kahlo's *Self-
Portrait as a Tehuana (Diego on My Mind)* (1943).

Writing from Reading

Summarize

1 This poem is largely a description of Kahlo herself. What distinctive Kahlo images does Dove incorporate into the poem?

Analyze Craft

2 Notice how Kahlo's painting portrays her with both feminine and masculine qualities. How does Dove likewise capture both male and female characteristics in her description?

Analyze Voice

3 Dove uses Kahlo's distinctive unibrow as both the opening image and the closing image. Does the tone in which she portrays the brow change from the first lines to the last line? How?

Synthesize Summary and Analysis

4 The poet responds to a self-portrait. What can we learn about the poet's attitude toward her subject? Are there ways in which this response to a self-portrait is itself a personal reflection?

Interpret the Poem

5 What did you learn about Frida Kahlo's life from the poem? Compare this to your previous knowledge of Kahlo, or do some brief research to illuminate the real story behind, for example, the "pain" that Dove alludes to.

6 Kahlo's paintings have been described as surrealist, a label that Kahlo herself didn't necessarily agree with, instead describing her work as "the frankest expression of myself." Why might Dove have chosen a fixed and time-honored form— the sonnet—to paint a verbal picture of an unconventional artist?

William Blake (1757–1827)

"Genius," "mad," "mystic"—each of these words was applied to William Blake by his contemporaries. Although he lived in relative obscurity and died completely misunderstood, Blake has come to be recognized as one of the most imaginative writers and artists ever to have lived. A lifelong resident of London, Blake was writing poetry by age twelve. At fourteen, he began an apprenticeship with the engraver James Brasire, and after completing his seven-year apprenticeship, Blake married Catherine Boucher. Boucher was illiterate, but Blake soon taught her both to read and to be his assistant in produc-

ing art that accompanied his own writing. Blake earned a meager living by illustrating children's books and accepting patronage from wealthy benefactors, but for the most part he lived his life in poverty.

Unlike that of most other poets, William Blake's craft includes the tangible aspect of visual art—painting, drawing, engraving, and printing. His poems—themselves small masterpieces of symbol and sound—are best studied in conjunction with the illustrations and illuminated designs that Blake made to accompany them in a time-consuming process of etching the words and image backward on a copper plate so that the printed page would turn out the proper way,

ready for Blake to paint it by hand. His collection of poems *Songs of Innocence and of Experience* (1794), for example, includes elaborate illustrations. (To see the complete set of illustrations, visit the William Blake Archive at www.blakearchive.org.)

Despite his adherence to Christian views and his love of the Bible, Blake attacked the church as sexually repressive and the government over slavery, women's rights, and the working conditions of the poor. Blake's poetry and art show an acute consciousness of the social changes and problems of his day, a consciousness that appears in the two poems entitled "The Chimney Sweeper" and the poem "The Sick Rose."

AS YOU READ   Note that "A little black thing" refers not to skin color but to skin blackened by soot. Underline the imagery that Blake associates with the impoverished children.

Songs of Innocence (1794)
The Chimney Sweeper

Photo of chimney sweeps, taken in 1877

When my mother died I was very young,
And my father sold me while yet my tongue
Could scarcely cry "'weep! 'weep! 'weep! 'weep!"
So your chimneys I sweep, & in soot I sleep.

5   There's little Tom Dacre, who cried when his head,
That curl'd like a lamb's back, was shav'd: so I said
"Hush, Tom! never mind it, for when your head's bare
You know that the soot cannot spoil your white hair."

And so he was quiet, & that very night,
10 As Tom was a-sleeping, he had such a sight!
That thousands of sweepers, Dick, Joe, Ned & Jack,
Were all of them lock'd up in coffins of black.

And by came an Angel who had a bright key,
And he open'd the coffins & set them all free;
15 Then down a green plain leaping, laughing, they run,
And wash in a river, and shine in the Sun.

Then naked & white, all their bags left behind,
They rise upon clouds and sport in the wind;
And the Angel told Tom, if he'd be a good boy,
20 He'd have God for his father, & never want joy.

And so Tom awoke; and we rose in the dark,
And got with our bags & our brushes to work.
Tho' the morning was cold, Tom was happy & warm;
So if all do their duty they need not fear harm.

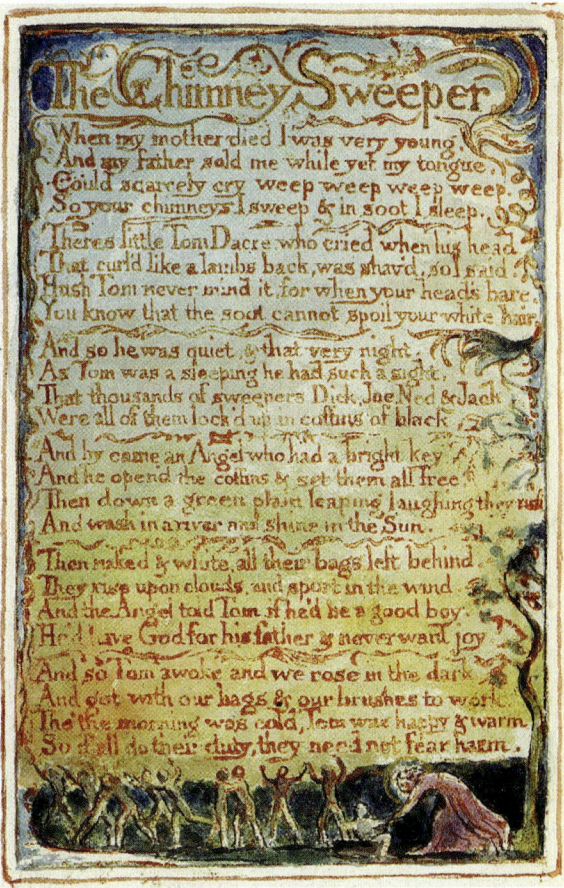

Songs of Experience (1794)

The Chimney Sweeper

A little black thing among the snow,
Crying "'weep! 'weep!" in notes of woe!
"Where are thy father & mother? say?"
"They are both gone up to the church to pray.

5   "Because I was happy upon the heath,
And smil'd among the winter's snow,
They clothed me in the clothes of death,
And taught me to sing the notes of woe.

"And because I am happy & dance & sing,
10   They think they have done me no injury,
And are gone to praise God & his Priest & King,
Who make up a heaven of our misery."

Writing from Reading

Summarize

1 Use the historical context to figure out what is being said in these poems. Keep in mind that the Industrial Revolution created a large population of poor urban laborers, and that among these laborers who faced long shifts, unsafe conditions, and stifling tasks were children who worked because they were orphans or belonged to an impoverished family. The chimney sweeping trade was particularly notorious for its maltreatment of child laborers. Children as young as four years old, and more commonly around six to eight years old, were sold as apprentices to master chimney sweepers, many of whom did not provide for the children but made them subsist by begging. Children were popular with the chimney sweeping profession, because their small bodies allowed them to climb into fireplace flues; this occupation, however, almost certainly led to an early death—if not from suffocation in the flue, then from cancer and other diseases resulting from constant exposure to soot.

2 Examine the illustrations for the two poems. Are these narratives the same as that in the poems? If not, what new ideas does the illustration introduce that are not present in the poem?

Analyzing Craft

3 Review the poems, one from *Innocence* and one from *Experience*; make a list of the differences between the two poems, paying particular attention to diction, imagery, rhyme, meter, and the speaker's point of view. How do these differences change the meaning of the poems between *Innocence* and *Experience*?

4 How would you characterize the imagery in these two poems? What does it suggest about the children's lives?

5 What words contribute to the overall idea that others live well because the chimney sweeps perform miserable labor? In your response, consider the connotations of color and seasons.

Analyzing Voice

6 Describe the tone of each poem. What word choices help create the mood in each?

7 For each poem, does the tone of the illustration match the tone of the poem? Explain your answer, being sure to mention specific details from the illustrations. How do the decorative portions—rather than the main illustrations—support the idea of the poem?

Synthesize Craft and Voice

8 Compare and contrast these poems and ask yourself, "What statement does Blake make about innocence versus experience?"

Interpret the Poem

9 Many critics argue that these are two parts of the same poem; in other words, something is lost if a person reads just one poem. In what ways does the version that appeared in *Songs of Experience* answer the one from *Songs of Innocence*?

For Review and Further Study

William Blake (1757–1827)

The Sick Rose

O Rose, thou art sick!
The invisible worm
That flies in the night,
In the howling storm,

Has found out thy bed   5
Of crimson joy,
And his dark secret love
Does thy life destroy.

Questions for Interactive Reading and Writing

1. The rose and the worm act as symbols in this poem. What might they represent?

2. Describe the tone of this poem. What word choices help create this mood?

3. Consider the illustration and summarize what is happening in the illustration. What does the illustration tell you about the symbols in this poem?

Robert Bly (b. 1926)

Driving to Town Late to Mail a Letter (1962)

It is a cold and snowy night. The main street is deserted.
The only things moving are swirls of snow.
As I lift the mailbox door, I feel its cold iron.
There is a privacy I love in this snowy night.
Driving around, I will waste more time.   5

Questions for Interactive Reading and Writing

1. A letter is a form of communication, yet the poet seems to value what he calls "privacy." How is this ironic?

2. Contrast the normal sense of urgency in the completion of a task such as this with the poet's apparent desire to "waste" time.

3. Bly was influenced by Asian writers like Bashō and Issa (earlier in this chapter). How does this poem show that influence?

George Herbert (1593–1633)

For a brief biography of George Herbert, see Chapter 26.

The Altar

A broken A L T A R, Lord, thy servant rears,
Made of a heart, and cemented with tears;
   Whose parts are as thy hand did frame;
   No workman's tool hath touched the same.
5   A H E A R T alone
         Is   such   a   stone,
         As   nothing   but
         Thy pow'r doth cut.
         Wherefore each part
10   Of   my   hard   heart
         Meets in this frame
         To praise thy name.
   That, if I chance to hold my peace,
   These stones to praise thee may not cease.
15 Oh let thy blessed S A C R I F I C E be mine,
And   sanctify   this   A L T A R to be thine.

Questions for Interactive Reading and Writing

1. In the poem's final line, what does the altar symbolize? What is the speaker really asking God to sanctify?

2. What images does the speaker use to suggest the state of his heart? According to these images, how does he view himself?

3. What is the speaker saying in lines 9–14? Paraphrase those lines.

4. How does the shape of the poem become itself an image?

John Keats (1795–1821)

For a brief biography of John Keats, see Chapter 20.

Ode to a Nightingale (1819)

I

My heart aches, and a drowsy numbness pains
   My sense, as though of hemlock I had drunk,
Or emptied some dull opiate to the drains
   One minute past, and Lethe-wards had sunk:
'Tis not through envy of thy happy lot,   5
   But being too happy in thine happiness,—
      That thou, light-wingéd Dryad of the trees,
        In some melodious plot
   Of beechen green and shadows numberless,
      Singest of summer in full-throated ease.   10

II

O, for a draught of vintage! that hath been
   Cooled a long age in the deep-delvéd earth,
Tasting of Flora and the country green,
   Dance, and Provençal song, and sunburnt mirth!
O for a beaker full of the warm South,   15
   Full of the true, the blushful Hippocrene,
      With beaded bubbles winking at the brim,
        And purple-stainéd mouth;
   That I might drink, and leave the world unseen,
      And with thee fade away into the forest dim: 20

III

Fade far away, dissolve, and quite forget
   What thou among the leaves hast never known,
The weariness, the fever, and the fret
   Here, where men sit and hear each other groan;
Where palsy shakes a few, sad, last gray hairs,   25
   Where youth grows pale, and spectre-thin, and dies;
      Where but to think is to be full of sorrow
        And leaden-eyed despairs,
   Where Beauty cannot keep her lustrous eyes,
      Or new Love pine at them beyond tomorrow.   30

IV

Away! away! for I will fly to thee,
  Not charioted by Bacchus and his pards,
But on the viewless wings of Poesy,
  Though the dull brain perplexes and retards:
35 Already with thee! tender is the night,
  And haply the Queen-Moon is on her throne,
    Clustered around by all her starry Fays;
      But here there is no light,
Save what from heaven is with the breezes blown
40   Through verdurous glooms and winding mossy ways.

V

I cannot see what flowers are at my feet,
  Nor what soft incense hangs upon the boughs,
But, in embalmèd darkness, guess each sweet
  Wherewith the seasonable month endows
45 The grass, the thicket, and the fruit-tree wild;
  White hawthorn, and the pastoral eglantine;
    Fast fading violets covered up in leaves;
      And mid-May's eldest child,
The coming musk-rose, full of dewy wine,
50   The murmurous haunt of flies on summer eves.

VI

Darkling I listen; and, for many a time
  I have been half in love with easeful Death,
Called him soft names in many a musèd rhyme,
  To take into the air my quiet breath;
55 Now more than ever seems it rich to die,
  To cease upon the midnight with no pain,
    While thou art pouring forth thy soul abroad
      In such an ecstasy!
Still wouldst thou sing, and I have ears in vain—
60   To thy high requiem become a sod.

VII

Thou wast not born for death, immortal Bird!
  No hungry generations tread thee down;
The voice I hear this passing night was heard
  In ancient days by emperor and clown:
65 Perhaps the selfsame song that found a path
  Through the sad heart of Ruth, when, sick for home,
    She stood in tears amid the alien corn;
      The same that ofttimes hath
Charmed magic casements, opening on the foam
70   Of perilous seas, in faery lands forlorn.

VIII

Forlorn! the very word is like a bell
  To toll me back from thee to my sole self!
Adieu! the fancy cannot cheat so well
  As she is famed to do, deceiving elf.
Adieu! adieu! thy plaintive anthem fades   75
  Past the near meadows, over the still stream,
    Up the hill side; and now 'tis buried deep
      In the next valley-glades:
Was it a vision, or a waking dream?
  Fled is that music:—Do I wake or sleep?   80

Questions for Interactive Reading and Writing

1. What would "a beaker full of the warm South" look like? Can you drink it? What about "hemlock" or some "dull opiate" instead?

2. The phrase "tender is the night" (stanza 4) was used by F. Scott Fitzgerald as the title of one of his novels. What do the words convey?

3. Track the poet's attitude to the image or symbol of the nightingale through the stanzas. How near is it, how far away?

4. How does the poet, by guessing, describe what he "cannot see"?

5. This poem and Jane Kenyon's "The Blue Bowl" (earlier in this chapter) are both meditations on death. How does Keats's use of the nightingale image compare with Kenyon's use of the cat's blue bowl?

Amy Lowell (1874–1925)

Patterns (1914)

I walk down the garden paths,
And all the daffodils
Are blowing, and the bright blue squills.
I walk down the patterned garden-paths
In my stiff, brocaded gown.   5
With my powdered hair and jeweled fan,

I too am a rare
Pattern. As I wander down
The garden paths.

10 My dress is richly figured,
And the train
Makes a pink and silver stain
On the gravel, and the thrift
Of the borders.
15 Just a plate of current fashion,
Tripping by in high-heeled, ribboned shoes.
Not a softness anywhere about me,
Only whalebone and brocade.
And I sink on a seat in the shade
20 Of a lime tree. For my passion
Wars against the stiff brocade.
The daffodils and squills
Flutter in the breeze
As they please.
25 And I weep;
For the lime-tree is in blossom
And one small flower has dropped upon my bosom.

And the plashing of waterdrops
In the marble fountain
30 Comes down the garden-paths.
The dripping never stops.
Underneath my stiffened gown
Is the softness of a woman bathing in a marble basin,
A basin in the midst of hedges grown
35 So thick, she cannot see her lover hiding,
But she guesses he is near,
And the sliding of the water
Seems the stroking of a dear
Hand upon her.
40 What is Summer in a fine brocaded gown!
I should like to see it lying in a heap upon the ground.
All the pink and silver crumpled up on the ground.

I would be the pink and silver as I ran along the paths,
And he would stumble after,
45 Bewildered by my laughter.
I should see the sun flashing from his sword-hilt and the
buckles on his shoes.
I would choose
To lead him in a maze along the patterned paths,

A bright and laughing maze for my heavy-booted lover,
Till he caught me in the shade, 50
And the buttons of his waistcoat bruised my body as he
clasped me,
Aching, melting, unafraid.
With the shadows of the leaves and the sundrops,
And the plopping of the waterdrops,
All about us in the open afternoon— 55
I am very likely to swoon
With the weight of this brocade,
For the sun sifts through the shade.

Underneath the fallen blossom
In my bosom, 60
Is a letter I have hid.
It was brought to me this morning by a rider from the
Duke.
"Madam, we regret to inform you that Lord Hartwell
Died in action Thursday se'nnight."
As I read it in the white, morning sunlight, 65
The letters squirmed like snakes.
"Any answer, Madam," said my footman.
"No," I told him.
"See that the messenger takes some refreshment.
No, no answer." 70
And I walked into the garden,
Up and down the patterned paths,
In my stiff, correct brocade.
The blue and yellow flowers stood up proudly in the sun,
Each one. 75
I stood upright too,
Held rigid to the pattern
By the stiffness of my gown.
Up and down I walked,
Up and down. 80

In a month he would have been my husband.
In a month, here, underneath this lime,
We would have broken the pattern;
He for me, and I for him,
He as Colonel, I as Lady, 85
On this shady seat.
He had a whim
That sunlight carried blessing.
And I answered, "It shall be as you have said."
Now he is dead. 90

In Summer and in Winter I shall walk
Up and down
The patterned garden-paths
In my stiff, brocaded gown.
95 The squills and daffodils
Will give place to pillared roses, and to asters, and to snow.
I shall go
Up and down,
In my gown.
100 Gorgeously arrayed,
Boned and stayed.
And the softness of my body will be guarded from embrace
By each button, hook, and lace.
For the man who should loose me is dead,
105 Fighting with the Duke in Flanders,
In a pattern called a war.
Christ! What are patterns for?

Questions for Interactive Reading and Writing

1. Describe the occasion of the poem. What is the primary emotion felt by the speaker? Does this woman out of history seem remote from the American experience of the poet? Why might Lowell have chosen this particular woman as the speaker?

2. How does "my stiff, brocaded gown . . . each button, hook, and lace" compare with the button in Jane Hirshfield's poem in this chapter? What image do the words evoke?

3. How does the outer appearance of the woman—her manner, her way of dressing—contrast with her inner state of being? How does the final expressive outburst make that emotion clear?

Octavio Paz (1914–1998)

Touch (1994)

My hands
open the curtains of your being
clothe you in a further nudity
uncover the bodies of your body
My hands   5
invent another body for your body

—translated by Charles Tomlinson

Questions for Interactive Reading and Writing

1. What do you think the occasion of this poem is? What is the relationship between the "I" and the "you"?

2. Explain the paradox in line 3. What does the speaker convey through it?

3. What images are present in the poem? Are they literal or figurative?

4. Describe the diction of the poem. What tone does it create?

Sylvia Plath (1932–1963)

For a brief biography of Sylvia Plath, see Chapter 21.

Lady Lazarus (1965)

I have done it again.
One year in every ten
I manage it—

A sort of walking miracle, my skin
Bright as a Nazi lampshade,   5
My right foot

A paperweight,
My face a featureless, fine
Jew linen.

10 Peel off the napkin
O my enemy.
Do I terrify?—

The nose, the eye pits, the full set of teeth?
The sour breath
15 Will vanish in a day.

Soon, soon the flesh
The grave cave ate will be
At home on me

And I a smiling woman.
20 I am only thirty.
And like the cat I have nine times to die.

This is Number Three.
What a trash
To annihilate each decade.

25 What a million filaments.
The peanut-crunching crowd
Shoves in to see

Them unwrap me hand and foot—
The big strip tease.
30 Gentlemen, ladies,

These are my hands
My knees.
I may be skin and bone,

Nevertheless, I am the same, identical woman.
35 The first time it happened I was ten.
It was an accident.

The second time I meant
To last it out and not come back at all.
I rocked shut

As a seashell.   40
They had to call and call
And pick the worms off me like sticky pearls.

Dying
Is an art, like everything else.
I do it exceptionally well.   45

I do it so it feels like hell.
I do it so it feels real.
I guess you could say I've a call.

It's easy enough to do it in a cell.
It's easy enough to do it and stay put.   50
It's the theatrical

Comeback in broad day
To the same place, the same face, the same brute
Amused shout:

"A miracle!"   55
That knocks me out.
There is a charge

For the eyeing of my scars, there is a charge
For the hearing of my heart—
It really goes.   60

And there is a charge, a very large charge,
For a word or a touch
Or a bit of blood

Or a piece of my hair or my clothes.
So, so, Herr Doktor.   65
So, Herr Enemy.

I am your opus,
I am your valuable,
The pure gold baby

That melts to a shriek.   70
I turn and burn.
Do not think I underestimate your great concern.

Ash, ash—
You poke and stir.
75 Flesh, bone, there is nothing there—

A cake of soap,
A wedding ring,
A gold filling.

Herr God, Herr Lucifer
80 Beware
Beware.

Out of the ash
I rise with my red hair.
And I eat men like air.

Questions for Interactive Reading and Writing

1. Judging from the rest of the poem, especially stanzas 12–15 (lines 34–45), what is the speaker referring to when she says "I have done it again"?

2. According to the Bible, Jesus raised Lazarus from the dead. What images invoke the Lazarus story?

3. How does "peanut-crunching crowd" create a different image than if Plath had simply written "the crowd"? How does this image affect the tone?

4. How does the speaker's tone convey how she feels about doctors who have saved her?

Reading for Images and Symbols

When reading for image, look for language that generates a certain attitude or mental picture using words and language that create vivid visual, aural, and tactile impressions.

Image: the literal representation of any "thing" described—the way it looks

When reading for image, ask yourself	• What senses (sight, sound, touch, smell, taste) has the poet evoked with an image? • What kinds of words are used to make the image vivid? • What associations (meanings) do you connect with those word choices?	EXAMPLE "Amber husk / fluted with gold, / fruit on the sand / marked with a rich grain"

Symbol: an image that stands for or represents something beyond the thing itself

When reading for symbol, ask yourself	• Is the title a tip-off to a centrally important image, one that is likely to be a symbol? • Does the poem focus on a particular image? • Is an image repeated and returned to in a poem? If so, it is likely to be a symbol. • How is that symbolic image used? The description will point to its deeper meaning.	EXAMPLE "button"

Pay attention to common associations	*Conventional association:* an association made so frequently that one thing has come to traditionally represent the other	EXAMPLE dove = peace; shooting star = wish
When reading poetry from earlier times, consider conventional associations from the period. Remember to read in context.	*Iconography:* when one symbol always engenders certain meanings	EXAMPLE skull and crossbones = death
Remember that modern poets may try to create fresh symbols through context.	*Literary symbolism:* symbolism that is created through the context of a poem	EXAMPLE A cat's bowl represents death and sorrow *in the context* of Jane Kenyon's poem "The Blue Bowl."

Writing about Images and Symbols

1. Consider the various creatures and landscapes in the poems of this chapter, and write a brief essay comparing and contrasting their functions; consider also the attitude of each of the poets to each element. Contrast, for example, the chickens described by William Carlos Williams in "The Red Wheelbarrow" with the nightingale in John Keats's "Ode to a Nightingale" or Jane Hirshfield's tree in "Tree" with the image in Ezra Pound's "In a Station of the Metro."

2. Take any poem in this chapter and focus on its imagery. At what point does a central image (for example, the jar on the hill in Tennessee in Wallace Stevens's "Anecdote of the Jar") attain the status of symbol?

3. As W. H. Auden, in "Musée des Beaux Arts," says of the Old Masters, "About suffering they were never wrong." Find images that evoke "suffering" in five of the poems included here. Compare the way poets such as William Blake and Jane Kenyon deal with this emotion. What images do they use to portray loss?

23
Figures
of Speech

IN one slow move you slithered and drizzled
snail trails all up and down eroded maps of me.
Doo-wop, stone-slow of step, sticks to you, lasts.
—*from "Doo-Wop: The Moves" by Al Young*

THERE are, of course, certain kinds of poetry that focus on the eye, not ear, but by and large poetry is intended to be heard at least as much as seen. You can almost hear the sliding on the dance floor in Al Young's "Doo-Wop: The Moves" with "In one slow move you slithered." Young, the former Poet Laureate of the state of California, makes his love of music clear in two volumes of memoirs based on his life with popular music, jazz, and hip-hop. He is an out-spoken proponent of spoken word poetry and poetry as a public forum. In Chapter 17, we included a lyric very likely set to music by Sappho and a song by Robert Burns; in Chapter 19, we talked about the origins of poetry as song, with sacred verses such as the Song of Solomon. Al Young suggests that song lyrics demonstrate how easy it can be to accept the "fantastic leaps" known as figures of speech that are central to the heightened language of poetry. Although the most common complaint about poetry is "Why don't you say what you mean?" this kind of language is used—as another poet Thomas Lynch says in his interview—to express something that seems otherwise unspeakable, an "unspeakable love or hurt or loss or hate or whatever happens to be." Lynch goes on to explain that the tools of poetic language—metaphor, image, symbol—create "double edges . . . you can heal with it, and you can maim with it, and you can ornament with it, and you can do serious business with it."

In "Doo-Wop: The Moves" Al Young evokes two things at once with the slithering, drizzling "snail trails," with the "stone-slow," with "eroded / maps of me." One thing suggests another, and word leads on to word, image leads to image, sound to sight. The very phrase "figures of speech" makes an implicit linkage, connecting something visual to something spoken and reminding us that language must be both seen and heard. Figures of speech allow writers to make connections and comparisons between seemingly unlike objects and actions. These connections require a particular capacity to perceive relationships between dissimilar things. In his interview, Robert Pinsky suggests that the "making of a metaphor—the ability to see resemblances, or to conceive resemblances" is "one of the really thrilling things in art." These are like the "special effects in a movie." He goes on to say, "Putting two unlike things together and finding how they're alike is like being able to jump high or run fast. . . . It comes from nowhere . . . of all the things you do in writing—it's the thing that's most unlike anything you can figure out."

Al Young *Poetry exists in quite a different atmosphere . . .*

A Conversation on Writing

The Music behind the Music in "Doo-Wop: The Moves"

That was such fun to write, and, of course, I wrote it while listening to one of those old, "Oooo woooh, baby, baby"—that kind of thing. I grew up with the idea that if you were going to write poetry, you really had to know forms, and you had to know prosody, and all these things that I'd brought over from music. I'd always been involved with music as a tuba player in junior high and high school, and later as a trumpet player and then guitarist, and I had a brother who played piano, and we were always doing exercises—things like this. So that I would bring home from the library these books of forms and try to imitate them, to do sonnets, to do all of these intricate formal structures and make them make sense.

Poetry Is Our Primal Language

It's no accident that all the great books—the great religious books, the Bible, the Koran, the sutras—are composed in poetry. So, poetry is . . . I think . . . our original primal language, and I think that when we find ourselves in situations of distress or novelty, we automatically start thinking that way and expressing ourselves that way.

The Future of Poetry

A lot of [kids who get into poetry now] started as hip-hop or rap or spoken word aficionados or performers, and . . . I've noticed that a student who will not write a paper on a social situation or a political situation now will get up at a poetry club or a rap performance, and will say all kinds of things, many of them insightful and nuanced. But that's their form. . . . Poetry becomes a joy when you're doing it to a live audience . . . you're not alone. . . . You're just talking to each other and using poetry to do it. So I think that—you know, to paraphrase Ralph Waldo Emerson who said somewhere, "All of American literature is yet to be written"—well, all of poetry is yet to be created, and I think the future of poetry is quite healthy.

Al Young was born (1939) in Biloxi, Mississippi, and raised in the rural South and Detroit. Eventually, he made his way to California, where he was named state Poet Laureate in 2005. Young's career has ranged from poet and novelist to screenwriter for Sidney Poitier and Bill Cosby. He has also taught creative writing at a number of universities, including Stanford and several campuses of the University of California. Young has an interest in jazz and blues and performs stories and poems to musical accompaniment. A recipient of Guggenheim, Fulbright, and National Endowment for the Arts fellowships, Young currently lives in Berkeley, California.

RESEARCH ASSIGNMENT After watching Young's interview, describe what he means by each line of a poem "tak[ing] a remarkable leap into another reality." How do the ideas of leaping and of creating multiple realities relate to what you know about figures of speech? Where does "Doo-Wop: The Moves" leap away from the dancing couple?

To watch this entire interview and hear the author read "Doo-Wop: The Moves" and other poems, go to connect.mcgraw-hill.com.

AS YOU READ Look for phrases that describe the dancing couple's movements in ways not meant to be taken literally.

Doo-Wop: The Moves (2006)

Let's make no bones about it—whatever
this means or ever meant to you. Darling,
you know your way through what I'm about
to say. Doo-wop still steals the moment,
5   this sizzling thrill of closeness; the slowness
of our touch too much, too messy to process.

Back when dawn rose off the river, we'd feel it.
Feel felt like enough when flowering was new
and not easy to handle. Neither was breathing.
10   All that light funneling in from Canada, ferried
over the river while you put a move on my heart.

Heart and soul, flesh and bone—doo-wop
was known to sabotage. All across the land
White Citizens Councils shouted and warned:
15   Negro music is corrupting White youth. Boycott
Negro Music. We were young, too. You pressed
your hand behind my neck, you kissed my mouth.

Wham! So who'd kissed whom? You still wonder?
In one slow move you slithered and drizzled
20   snail trails all up and down eroded maps of me.
Doo-wop, stone-slow of step, sticks to you, lasts.

The doo-wop mind cries: O baby you know
I love you, always thinking of you, I place no one
above you, and you know I'll never snub you.
25   Under doo-wop's spell, you make no bones.
You shake your perfumed boodie. You go for keeps.

Writing from Reading

Summarize

1 What has the speaker remembered here? What happened between him and his "darling"?

Analyze Craft

2 What sensation does the phrase "you slithered and drizzled snail trails" evoke? Does it literally pertain to snail trails, or is it a figure of speech?

3 How does the speaker's description of doo-wop as "stone-slow of step" give you a sense of the music's pace? Is this phrase a visual image, aural imagery, or both?

4 How much of the poem's success depends on saying it, or trying to sing it, out loud?

Analyze Voice

5 The speaker uses the phrase "make no bones" at the beginning and the end of the poem. How does this idiom (an expression whose meaning in popular usage is different from what the phrase literally says) resemble a figure of speech?

6 What is the poet's attitude toward this particular variety of song? Toward music in general?

7 Do you find that the allusions to politics and history enhance the poem or weigh too heavily on it?

Synthesize Summary and Analysis

8 In the second stanza, does "dawn [rising] off the river" refer to the morning of the day this dance took place, or does it have a broader frame of reference?

9 What does the speaker gain by describing himself as an "eroded map"?

Interpret the Poem

10 How do love, music, politics, race all come together in this poem?

FIGURATIVE LANGUAGE

Although all genres of writing (and everyday speech) employ figures of speech, poetry—given its especially condensed and vivid discourse—relies crucially and consistently on figurative language. Poets invent nonliteral descriptions like this because figures of speech allow them, in Ezra Pound's phrase, to "make it new." They can help amplify a reader's understanding, or they can intensify a reader's imagination. Most importantly, they can also help a writer create a description whose comparisons illustrate a theme or idea in a more purposeful way.

In *Romeo and Juliet,* when the hopelessly infatuated young Romeo looks up to Juliet on her balcony, he whispers, "But, soft! What light through yonder window breaks? It is the east, and Juliet is the sun." Shakespeare has Romeo describe Juliet's radiant, powerful beauty in terms of the radiant, powerful sun. Does Romeo really believe this teenage girl he likes has somehow *become* the sun? Certainly not.

If Shakespeare had instead written, "Who's coming out there by the window? It's that lovely girl I met last night," we would understand his meaning. However, these wholly literal lines would lack the added, richer associations we find in Shakespeare's language—elements such as the renewal of the sun rising in the east ending the dark night, and the warmth and sheer beauty of sunlight above us. For Romeo, the sight of Juliet is as beautiful and rejuvenating as a perfect new dawn. It's no accident that Shakespeare adds these figurative associations to his scene—he wants his language to do more for the reader than simply make literal sense.

Understanding how to identify and talk about figures of speech is an important tool for better appreciating poetry. It's one of the ways that the heightened, melodious language of poetry has grown so distinctive. Here is an example of figurative speech by the novelist and poet Michael Ondaatje. In "Sweet Like a Crow," he makes a series of rapid comparisons between "your voice" and the series of sounds it evokes.

Michael Ondaatje (b. 1943)

Born in Sri Lanka, Michael Ondaatje emigrated to England and then to Canada, where he has made his home since 1962. Although he is perhaps best known for his novel *The English Patient* (1992), which was made into an Academy Award–winning film, Ondaatje began by writing poetry, and today he has published more than a dozen collections of verse. Among his better-known collections are *There's a Trick with a Knife I'm Learning to Do: Poems, 1963–1978* (1978) and *The Cinnamon Peeler: Selected Poems* (1991); both won the Governor General's Award, one of Canada's most prestigious literary prizes. His fiction suggests Ondaatje's poetic sense: in books like *In the Skin of a Lion* (1987) and *Anil's Ghost* (2000), Ondaatje creates image-driven narrative that often reads more like poetry than prose.

AS YOU READ   Recite this poem; read it aloud, and listen for its unlikely music—the combination of sounds. Consider how the sounds support the comparison Ondaatje is making.

"The Sinhalese are without a doubt one of the least musical people in the world. It would be quite impossible to have less sense of pitch, line, or rhythm."

—Paul Bowles

Sweet Like a Crow (1989)

Your voice sounds like a scorpion being pushed
through a glass tube
like someone has just trod on a peacock
like wind howling in a coconut
5 like a rusty bible, like someone pulling barbed wire
across a stone courtyard, like a pig drowning,
a vattacka being fried
a bone shaking hands
a frog singing at Carnegie Hall.

10   Like a crow swimming in milk,
   like a nose being hit by a mango
   like the crowd at the Royal-Thomian match,
   a womb full of twins, a pariah dog
   with a magpie in its mouth
15   like the midnight jet from Casablanca
   like Air Pakistan curry,
   a typewriter on fire, like a spirit in the gas
   which cooks your dinner, like a hundred
   pappadans being crunched, like someone
20   uselessly trying to light 3 Roses matches in a dark room,
   the clicking sound of a reef when you put your head into
     the sea,

a dolphin reciting epic poetry to a sleepy audience,
the sound of a fan when someone throws brinjals at it,
like pineapples being sliced in the Pettah market
25   like betel juice hitting a butterfly in mid-air
like a whole village running naked onto the street
and tearing their sarongs, like an angry family
pushing a jeep out of the mud, like dirt on the needle,
like 8 sharks being carried on the back of a bicycle
30   like 3 old ladies locked in the lavatory
like the sound I heard when having an afternoon sleep
and someone walked through my room in ankle bracelets.

Writing from Reading

Summarize

1 What is the significance of the epigraph by Paul Bowles in this poem? How does the poet respond?

Analyze Craft

2 How does the sequence of comparisons help establish tone?

Analyze Voice

3 Which comparisons here seem serious and which seem lighthearted? How difficult is it to make the distinction?

Synthesize Summary and Analysis

4 The title of this poem suggests something unlikely; we don't tend to think of crows as "sweet." What is the attitude of the speaker to "your voice," and how would you describe the speaker's voice itself?

Interpret the Poem

5 Is this an act of friendship or enmity? How would you—if the poet were making these connections to the sound of *your* voice—respond?

SIMILE AND METAPHOR

Similes and metaphors, the two most commonly used figures of speech, express resemblances between two unlike things. A **simile** is a direct comparison of two distinct things using the word "like" or "as." If you say that "your friend runs *like* a cheetah" or "your brother's voice is shrill *as* a police siren," your comparisons are similes. By highlighting what two things have in common, poets direct a reader's attention to out-of-the-ordinary, often provocative associations.

You've just read Michael Ondaatje's "Sweet Like a Crow," which uses simile as its foundation. Canadian poet Margaret Atwood shows us, in a brief love lyric, just how radical a departure from ordinary speech a simile can provide.

A BRIEF HISTORY OF FIGURATIVE LANGUAGE

Creating new meanings by comparing unlike objects is an ancient practice, observed in even the earliest preserved oral literatures. Aristotle posited that metaphor helped describe, artistically, that which otherwise couldn't be identified and could likewise amplify the persuasive power of a speaker's language. While classical Western tradition—the literatures of ancient Greece and Rome—handed down traditions of figurative language (simile, metaphor, metonymy, and many more) familiar to modern English speakers, non-Western cultures developed their own subtly special figures of speech. Asian, African, and Middle Eastern literatures, for example, each incorporate complex, culturally informed figurative associations. The fact that any language's figures of speech are sometimes very difficult for foreign speakers to construe attests to their individual, social connotations. This is true in American culture, too. Expressions in American English such as "I need to make some dough" or "that was a piece of cake" remind us how individual, even obscure, our own culture's figurative language can be.

Margaret Atwood (b. 1939)

Margaret Atwood, a Canadian writer, is known for both her novels and her poetry, in addition to her short fiction, nonfiction, and children's books. A poet since age sixteen, she has published more than fifteen books of poetry, among them *The Animals in That Country* (1968), *Two-Headed Poems* (1978), and *Morning in the Burned House* (1995), which won the Trillium Award. Her work often engages with ancient mythology and gender relations, and she describes her own poetry as having "a texture of sound which is at least as important to me as the 'argument.'"

AS YOU READ Watch this domestic image from the ordinary world turn on itself and grow harsh.

you fit into me (1971)

you fit into me
like a hook into an eye
a fish hook
an open eye

Writing from Reading

Summarize

1 The poet makes a complex relationship—between two lovers, or partners—into a seemingly simple image. How does the simile of the hook turn dangerous?

Analyze Craft

2 The hook and eye suggest some aspect of clothing or, perhaps, a crocheting instrument and clasp. Suddenly, the image grows painful and bloody and wrenching. How does the snug fit become an open wound?

Analyze Voice

3 Do you detect a certain harshness on the speaker's part? What is the speaker's attitude here?

Synthesize Summary and Analysis

4 A simple image transforms itself, using simile, into something much more complex. How does the poet make this happen?

Interpret the Poem

5 Does life often offer such brutal domestic truths as this?

N. Scott Momaday (b. 1934)

The first American Indian writer to win a Pulitzer Prize, N. Scott Momaday has enjoyed a long and fruitful career as a prose writer, poet, and artist. He was born in Lawton, Oklahoma, to a Kiowa father and Cherokee mother and grew up in the Southwest, where he came face to face with the multitribal traditions of the region. He graduated from the University of New Mexico and later accepted a poetry fellowship from Stanford University, where he studied under the poet Yvor Winters. His first novel, the lyrical *House Made of Dawn* (1968), won him the Pulitzer Prize in Fiction, and his research in Kiowa tribal traditions led to his composition of *The Way to Rainy Mountain* (1969), which his father illustrated. Among his other books are his memoir *The Names* (1976) and *The Ancient Child* (1989), a rendering of the Billy the Kid legend. President George W. Bush awarded Momaday the National Medal of Arts in 2007, "for his writings and his work that celebrate and preserve Native American art and oral tradition."

AS YOU READ   Look for where the simile begins and, as the simile unfolds, note where you first grasp the meaning of the comparison.

Simile (1974)

What did we say to each other
that now we are as the deer
who walk in single file
with heads high
5 with ears forward
with eyes watchful
with hooves always placed on firm ground
in whose limbs there is latent flight

Writing from Reading

Summarize

1 Two people have said something to each other—the poet doesn't disclose what—and now they can be compared to deer that have sensed danger. Based on the deer's movements, what do you know about the relationship of these people?

Analyze Craft

2 The poet describes qualities of the deer that resonate with qualities of a human relationship. What is the effect of giving each quality its own line in the poem?

3 That the deer have "ears forward" and "eyes watchful" suggests that they have sensed danger and are on high alert. So, too, have the people in the relationship. Do you get the same message from "hooves always placed on firm ground," or does this suggest another dimension of the relationship?

Analyze Voice

4 What is the speaker's tone? Does the speaker seem to regret this change in the relationship?

Synthesize Summary and Analysis

5 Can you picture the deer the poet describes? How effective is it to express a feeling in terms of a visual simile?

Interpret the Poem

6 Imagine different sets of people as part of the "we" in this poem. Does it work to read the poem as a parent speaking to a child? A community speaking to its government? What other possibilities do you see?

A **metaphor** also closely compares two dissimilar things but *without* using the word "like" or "as." Whereas a simile suggests that X is *like* Y, a metaphor states that X *is* Y. This can make for even bolder, more emphatic turns of phrase. When converted into a metaphor, the simile "My uncle is funny as a clown" becomes "My uncle is a clown." By directly referring to the person as a clown, the metaphor intensifies the sentiment.

Metaphors create an explicit, or specifically stated, connection, or a poet's metaphor can be implicit—hinted at, but not directly expressed. If, in an argument, a sister tells her brother "You're such a chicken," she's using an explicit metaphor to compare the boy to a skittish bird. If the brother retorts, "Quit your yapping," he implies that his sister sounds to him like an obnoxious barking dog. This is called **implied metaphor**—the comparison is only suggested, never stated plainly. Because the brother does not call his sister a "yapping dog" overtly, the metaphor of his sister as dog remains implicit, if still discourteous.

The American poet Sylvia Plath makes delightfully diverse use of the versatility of metaphorical language in the following poem. She piles on image after image at an almost comic rate.

Sylvia Plath (1932–1963)

For a brief biography of Sylvia Plath, see Chapter 21.

AS YOU READ   Notice how the poet builds her tone by using direct metaphor and an abundance of contractions so that her language is at once poetic and conversational.

Metaphors (1960)

I'm a riddle in nine syllables,
An elephant, a ponderous house,
A melon strolling on two tendrils.
O red fruit, ivory, fine timbers!
5 This loaf's big with its yeasty rising.
Money's new-minted in this fat purse.
I'm a means, a stage, a cow in calf.
I've eaten a bag of green apples,
Boarded the train there's no getting off.

Writing from Reading

Summarize

1 How are different metaphors in the poem related to one another?

Analyze Craft

2 Why do you think Plath chooses nine syllables per line? And nine lines?

Analyze Voice

3 Is the speaker here happy or sad, regretting her condition or celebrating it?

Synthesize Summary and Analysis

4 Are these all metaphors for pregnancy? If so, is the "I" of the poem in the early or late stages of pregnancy?

Interpret the Poem

5 The poem announces in its title that this will be a sequence of metaphors. How does it deliver on its promise?

Sometimes poets will use an extended metaphor, or a figurative analogy that's woven through a poem. Poetry provides an emphasis on detailed and focused imagery. Because of this, poetry is an especially effective medium in which to broaden a comparison and enlarge it through several lines. Once again we can take an example from Shakespeare, whose sonnet in Chapter 20 alerts the reader in the opening line that he is deploying an extended metaphor. "Shall I compare thee to a summer's day?" offers

> **"Charlie Simic says that a poem is like an antique pinball machine with metaphors instead of balls. So everything in the poem, if you think of it this way, knocks against everything else."** Conversation with
>
> Carolyn Forché

a kind of hint, a signal from poet to reader to look for the variety of ways he will compare a midsummer day—its best and worst qualities—to the object of his affection. Indeed, virtually every line proceeding from that opening extends the comparison. Here extended metaphor frames the reader's comprehension and offers us a chance, at length, to see Shakespeare's subject the way *he* does.

The following is another "love" poem, in which the speaker compares herself and her partner to a pair of automobiles conjoined by jumper cables.

Linda Pastan (b. 1932)

Linda Pastan grew up in a traditional Jewish household in the Bronx. She earned her B.A. from Radcliffe College and an M.A. from Brandeis University. A married woman with three children, Pastan reflects on domestic life in compressed, lyrical poems. Her later poetry takes up themes of aging and mortality. Collected in books including *A Perfect Circle of Sun* (1971), *The Five Stages of Grief* (1978), and *Queen of a Rainy Country* (2006), Pastan's poetry has won, among other awards, a Pushcart Prize, the Dylan Thomas Award, and the Alice Fay di Castagnola Award from the American Poetry Society. She lives in Maryland with her husband, Ira, a noted molecular biologist.

AS YOU READ   The French would call this poem a *jeu d'esprit*—a game of wit. Metaphysical poets, such as John Donne and Andrew Marvell, would label the sustained, if implicit, comparison "woman = car" a **conceit**, a metaphor that's extended throughout a poem.

Jump Cabling (1984)

When our cars touched
When you lifted the hood   of mine
To see the intimate workings   underneath,
When we were bound   together
5 By a pulse of pure   energy,
When my car like the   princess
In the tale woke with   a start,
I thought why not ride the rest of the way together.

Writing from Reading

Summarize

1 What does the "pulse of pure energy" refer to?

Analyze Craft

2 How do metaphors in this poem help illustrate the speaker's thoughts on the person fixing her car?

Analyze Voice

3 Imagine the poet were male and the "princess" a prince. What would change, what stay the same?

Synthesize Summary and Analysis

4 The figurative language describing a "charge" is sustained. In what ways is the image of the poem's title developed here throughout?

5 Compare the relationship described in Pastan's poem to the relationships in Margaret Atwood's "you fit into me" in this chapter and Shakespeare's "Shall I compare thee to a summer's day?" (Chapter 20). How do the various uses of metaphors differ? How are they similar?

Interpret the Poem

6 What does the space in the layout of the poem represent?

Because **extended metaphor** is a tempting and sometimes complex means of explaining an impression, writers can lose track of how these figurative creations work. Occasionally an extended comparison will fail because the analogies within it become inconsistent or don't make sense in relation to one another. A **mixed metaphor** results when a writer uses at least two separate, mismatched comparisons in one statement. The effect is usually confusing, and sometimes comic, too. Look at this example: "When you're a big fish in a small pond, you don't want to end up with your tail between your legs." The speaker here mixes an old metaphor about being a fish with another old metaphor about being a dog. The combination of unrelated metaphors ends up baffling us more than clarifying the parts of the comparison.

HYPERBOLE AND UNDERSTATEMENT

Although metaphor and simile are the poet's most often utilized figures of speech, other forms of figurative language help writers achieve vivid description. **Hyperbole,** sometimes called overstatement, is another figure of speech that uses verbal exaggeration to make a point. For example, after consuming a large meal, you might say, "I couldn't possibly eat another bite." Unless you're in some kind of medical distress, however, you're probably physically able to eat *something*. This exaggeration simply helps drive home the extent of just how full you feel.

Commemorating the first battle of the American Revolution in his poem "Concord Hymn," Ralph Waldo Emerson describes the first fired rifle round as "the shot heard round the world." Emerson uses hyperbole to tell a truth—that the whole world was ultimately affected by the events in 1775 in the battles of Lexington and Concord.

Metaphor can also help create **understatement,** a purposeful tool in description. This is a kind of opposite to hyperbole. Calling Albert Einstein a "pretty smart guy" actually helps communicate, by downplaying the language, just how brilliant the man was. Such American poets as Robert Frost and William Carlos Williams often rely on understatement to emphasize a point.

Robert Frost (1874–1963)

For a brief biography of Robert Frost, see the Case Study on Robert Frost in Chapter 28.

AS YOU READ   Ask yourself which would you prefer, fire or ice, and why?

Fire and Ice

(1923)

Some say the world will end in fire,
Some say in ice.
From what I've tasted of desire
I hold with those who favor fire.
5   But if it had to perish twice,
I think I know enough of hate
To say that for destruction ice
Is also great
And would suffice.

Writing from Reading

Summarize

1 What are the attributes of fire versus ice?

Analyze Craft

2 How does understatement contribute to the overall effect of the poem?

Analyze Voice

3 How is irony introduced? Is Frost serious or playful or both?

Synthesize Summary and Analysis

4 Why would Frost use irony and understatement to philosophize about the darker aspects of humanity? Is there a "moral to the story," and if so, what is it?

Interpret the Poem

5 Some say that Frost is deceptively simple and homespun. Others say he is philosophically deep. How would you describe Frost's depiction of these alternatives—fire or ice—homespun, philosophical, both? Why?

SYNECDOCHE AND METONYMY

Synecdoche is a figure of speech that uses a piece or part of a thing to represent the thing in its entirety. At a party, for example, you might ask your host, "Can I have another glass?" Because you're using the word *glass* (part of the thing) not to mean an empty cup, but to instead signify a small container filled with water, ice cubes, and maybe a slice of lemon (the whole thing), the word *glass* is a synecdoche for the entire contents—container, ice, water, lemon, and all. "Was this the face that launched a thousand ships?" writes the British poet Christopher Marlowe, referring to Helen of Troy, the beautiful queen whose abduction leads to the Trojan War in Homer's *Iliad*. Here "the face" is a synecdoche for the woman in total. In the sentence "After my old Chevy broke down for good, I had to buy some new wheels," the speaker uses "wheels" as a synecdoche to indicate that a whole new vehicle was purchased, not just four new individual wheels. The parts represent a greater whole.

"Poetry gives us an opportunity to do things that prose doesn't."

Conversation with Al Young

Occasionally, synecdoche is also used the other way around—a whole object used to represent a smaller part. "The police had to come and break up the party." We understand in this statement that *individuals* on a police force (part of a whole), and not the entire police force, nor every police force in the world for that matter (a whole), came to subdue the gathering. In this case, "the police" is a synecdoche for those particular, identifiable people wearing the badges.

Synecdoche is considered a form of metonymy, a slightly more general figure of speech. **Metonymy** uses an identifying emblem or closely associated object to represent a thing in its entirety. "Hired gun" is metonymy for an individual paid to shoot people. The gun itself doesn't get hired or paid; it is simply the object associated with the assassin. In the sentence "She really loves reading Harry Potter," the popular books are represented by the name of the main character. People don't, technically, read the *character;* they read the books—the physical objects with pages and words—in which Harry Potter appears.

Henry Reed (1914–1986)

The son of a bricklayer, Henry Reed taught himself Greek in school and went on to win the Temperley Latin Prize and a full scholarship to the University of Birmingham. At college, he was taught by the poet Louis MacNiece, one of W. H. Auden's circle, and was the youngest candidate at the University of Birmingham to receive the Master of Arts degree. He was drafted into the Royal Army in 1941. As a young conscript, he would entertain his friends by mimicking the drill sergeant—a technique he used in "Naming of Parts." "Naming of Parts" is one of three poems about the dehumanization of war in a series entitled *Lessons of War*. Reed did not see battle. Instead, his gift for languages was put to use in his role as a cryptographer, where he learned and translated Japanese. Reed wrote the first of his many radio plays—perhaps a testament to his interest in voices—during this time. After the war, he made a modest living as a translator, radio dramatist, and announcer for the British Broadcasting Corporation. He published only one book of poetry during his lifetime, *Map of Verona* (which included the *Lessons of War* trilogy) in 1946. His *Collected Works* were published posthumously in 1991.

Naming of Parts (1946)

Today we have naming of parts. Yesterday,
We had daily cleaning. And tomorrow morning,
We shall have what to do after firing. But today,
Today we have naming of parts. Japonica
5   Glistens like coral in all of the neighboring gardens,
        And today we have naming of parts.

This is the lower sling swivel. And this
Is the upper sling swivel, whose use you will see,
When you are given your slings. And this is the piling swivel,
10 Which in your case you have not got. The branches
Hold in the gardens their silent, eloquent gestures,
        Which in our case we have not got.

This is the safety-catch, which is always released
With an easy flick of the thumb. And please do not let me
15 See anyone using his finger. You can do it quite easy
If you have any strength in your thumb. The blossoms
Are fragile and motionless, never letting anyone see
        Any of them using their finger.

And this you can see is the bolt. The purpose of this
20 Is to open the breech, as you see. We can slide it
Rapidly backwards and forwards: we call this
Easing the spring. And rapidly backwards and forwards
The early bees are assaulting and fumbling the flowers:
    They call it easing the Spring.

25 They call it easing the Spring: it is perfectly easy
If you have any strength in your thumb: like the bolt,
And the breech, and the cocking-piece, and the point of balance,
Which in our case we have not got; and the almond-blossom
Silent in all of the gardens and the bees going backwards and forwards,
30   For today we have the naming of parts.

Writing from Reading

Summarize

1 What is the scene that is being described in this poem?

Analyze Craft

2 Why would Reed prefer not to give a full description of what the "parts" will add up to?

3 Characterize what the recruit daydreams about as he goes through the naming of parts exercise?

Analyze Voice

4 Is there humor in the depiction of this scene? Horror? Both?

5 What tone is used in the daydreams? How is it distinct from the naming?

Synthesize Summary and Analysis

6 What do the differences between the daydreams and the naming of parts represent? What kind of opposition does Reed set up in the poem?

Interpret the Poem

7 This is one of the most famous poems of WW II. Do you agree or disagree with the depiction of this poem as antiwar? Why?

PERSONIFICATION AND APOSTROPHE

It's a natural habit to perceive human qualities and emotions in nonhuman things. We see ants moving in a line on the sidewalk and think of marching soldiers. A hurricane might blow "angrily" or a tomato plant wilt "with a sigh." A line of trees swaying in a strong wind momentarily reminds us of dancers. Skyscrapers might look like the hunched shoulders of men and women waiting in a gargantuan line. These are examples of **personification,** figures of speech in which writers ascribe human traits or behavior to something inhuman. In "The Gone Years," contemporary American poet Alice Fulton describes darkness coming at the end of the day: "Night pockets the house / in a blue / muffle. . . ." The poet personifies night so it can place a building in its pocket.

Taking in a panoramic morning view of London, William Wordsworth describes the city in the following poem.

William Wordsworth (1770–1850)

For a brief biography of William Wordsworth, see Chapter 17.

AS YOU READ   Situate yourself in the place and time—the poem's "occasion"—and imagine yourself by Wordsworth's side as he speaks.

Composed upon Westminster Bridge, September 3, 1802 (1807)

Earth has not anything to show more fair:
Dull would he be of soul who could pass by
A sight so touching in its majesty:
This City now doth, like a garment, wear
5   The beauty of the morning; silent, bare,
Ships, towers, domes, theatres, and temples lie
Open unto the fields, and to the sky;
All bright and glittering in the smokeless air.
Never did sun more beautifully steep
10 In his first splendor valley, rock, or hill;
Ne'er saw I, never felt, a calm so deep!
The river glideth at his own sweet will:
Dear God! the very houses seem asleep;
And all that mighty heart is lying still!

Writing from Reading

Summarize

1 Paraphrase the first line of the poem in your own words.

Analyze Craft

2 Identify moments of personification in the poem.

Analyze Voice

3 What do the personified comparisons in the poem suggest to you about the speaker's perception of London?

4 Notice how Wordsworth uses both "never" and "ne'er." Is this for the sake of meter only? Why does he write "glideth" instead of "glides"?

Synthesize Summary and Analysis

5 You will notice that this poem is a sonnet—a fourteen-line arrangement with a turn at the end of line 8 (see Chapter 25). How does the poet link those seemingly opposite things—an urban view and a pastoral one—within a sonnet's shape?

Interpret the Poem

6 This poem celebrates London and lists its "ships, towers, domes, theatres, and temples." Is there any warning here, or sense of a body at risk?

Additional figures of speech invoke imagined human elements within poems. **Apostrophe** describes a figure of speech in which a writer calls out to an unseen person, force, or personified idea. Apostrophe derives from an ancient Greek term meaning a "turning away," and it often marks a moment of digression in which a poem's speaker pauses and turns to an invisible presence, often for counsel, in complaint, or for comfort. In "Ode on a Grecian Urn" (Chapter 20), John Keats addresses, using apostrophe, a decorative Greek vase. "Thou still unravished bride of quietness," he writes, speaking symbolically to the urn, "Thou foster-child of silence and slow time."

Gabriela Mistral (1889–1957)

The first Latin American woman to win the Nobel Prize for Literature, Lucila Godoy y Alcayaga was born in Chile. A schoolteacher, she had a passionate love affair with a railroad worker when she was twenty years old. When her lover committed suicide, she began to write poetry and later adopted the pseudonym Gabriela (after the biblical angel) Mistral (a Mediterranean wind and the surname of an author she admired). She was involved in education reform in Mexico and Chile; she served as a delegate to the League of Nations, where she helped found UNICEF; and she worked as consul in Spain, France, Italy, Portugal, and Guatemala. Her poetry, as in the collection *Desolación* (1922), is full of sorrow but also full of compassion toward children, as in *Ternura* (1924).

AS YOU READ Ask yourself why the poet finds the tree worthy of her attention.

The Fugitive Woman (1954)

Festival tree, branches wide,
loose cascade, lively freshness
falling steeply at my back:
Who told you to stop me
5 and sound out my name?

Under a tree, I was only
washing the journeys from my feet
with my shadow for a road
and dust for a skirt.

10 How lovely that you throw out your limbs
and that you lower your head,
without grasping that I
don't have ten years to learn
your green cross that has no blood
15 and the disk of your pedestal!

Examine me, cedar-pine,
with your vertical eyes,
and don't move or uproot
your feet from the living soil:
20 your new feet can't take it
with scrapes from the cactuses
and bites from the cliffs.

There's a kind of restlessness,
like a hissing that runs
25 from the simmering zodiac
to the bristling grass.
The whole night is alive
with negations and affirmations,
those of the Angel who commands you
30 and mine who fights against him;

and a wreck of a woman
wails for her cedar of Lebanon
fallen and covered by night,
who's going to leave at dawn
35 knowing neither road nor dust
and without ever seeing again
his circle of two thousand pines.

Oh, tree of mine, surrendered
senseless to the blizzard
40 to dog day and to beast
to the hazard of the tempest.
Pine wandering over the earth!

—*translated by* Randall Couch

Writing from Reading

Summarize

1 Here the poet talks to a tree. Is she also talking to herself and others? In what ways?

2 What does "his circle of two thousand pines" suggest? What does the reference to "cedar of Lebanon" mean?

Analyze Craft

3 Discuss figures of speech such as "shadow for a road" and "dust for a skirt." How does the poet achieve her desired effects?

Analyze Voice

4 Does the speaker's voice seem natural? Slightly elevated in tone? Rising to a grand occasion?

Synthesize Summary and Analysis

5 An address to a tree that speaks of higher values and actions—is it possible for you to accept this as a way of speaking about life and the world?

Interpret the Poem

6 What is the larger subject?

PARADOX AND OXYMORON

Poets often deal in **paradox,** seemingly contradictory statements that when closely examined, have a deeper, sometimes complicated, meaning. "Youth," say some stodgy adults, paraphrasing George Bernard Shaw, "is wasted on the young." Though this saying seems to contradict itself by definition, the expression means to explain that

> "Be completely open—innocent, if you will—of the poem. Walk in, just like it's water, and say 'What is this?'" Conversation with Marie Howe

the older we get, the more we value the vitality and innocence of our younger years. In poetry, paradox attempts to tell a truth of perception or emotion despite an apparent leap in logic. "Love," says the ancient poet Ovid, "is a kind of warfare." A leap like this intends to make the reader think more deeply or subtly about a subject. Consider how Bashō, a seventeenth-century Japanese poet, uses the haiku form to pose a paradox to the listener.

Matsuo Bashō (1644–1694)

For a brief biography of Matsuo Bashō, see Chapter 22.

AS YOU READ   Notice how the title word is repeated at the end of the first and the third line.

Kyoto (c. 1680)

Even in Kyoto,
hearing a cuckoo,
I long for Kyoto

—*translated by* Jane Hirshfield
with Mariko Aratani

Writing from Reading

Summarize

1 Why and how do you think the speaker longs for a place and town (Kyoto) he has not left?

2 What do you think is the significance of the birdsong the speaker mentions?

Analyze Craft

3 If you include the title, there are twelve words in this poem—of which three are the same. What does this repetition suggest?

Analyze Voice

4 What's being said here and what, paradoxically, is left unsaid?

Synthesize Summary and Analysis

5 What does this poem suggest about the poet's sense of time and place?

Interpret the Poem

6 Is there a place about which you feel the way Bashō feels and, if so, why?

Oxymoron is a version of paradox that combines contradictory words into a compact, often two-word phrase. Oxymorons can be amusing, as in "jumbo shrimp" or "definite maybe," but they can also illustrate a writer's particular emotional or spiritual reflection. When Shakespeare calls "parting . . . sweet sorrow," he's making an oxymoronic linkage and saying, in effect, that opposites attract.

PUN

Often lighthearted in nature, a **pun** is a play on words that reveals different meanings in words that are similar or even identical. We generally think of puns as silly and perhaps trivial, as in an old joke like "A bigamist loves not too many, but two well." Sometimes, however, writers use puns to capitalize on two separate meanings of a word and emphasize a point. "Ask for me tomorrow," says the stabbed Mercutio to Romeo

"A poem requires whether consciously or unconsciously some kind of change into a new realization, whether large or small." Conversation
with Jane Hirshfield

in *Romeo and Juliet*, "and you shall find me a grave man." Here, "grave" suggests both a seriousness of manner and the final resting place where Mercutio, who realizes he's dying, is inevitably headed. By exploiting this double meaning, Shakespeare deepens our understanding of the play's action and the character of Mercutio himself.

Sometimes a punned double meaning underscores humor and critique simultaneously, as in the following poem.

A. R. Ammons (1926–2001)

Archie Randolph Ammons was born in North Carolina to a tobacco farmer. While on a Navy destroyer escort in the South Pacific during World War II, Ammons began to write poetry. Published at his own expense, his first collection, *Om-* *mateum* (1955), sold hardly any copies, but his poetry career took off eight years later with his second collection. In all, he published almost thirty collections and won many of the most prestigious awards including the National Book Award for *Garbage* (1993) and again for his *Collected Poems: 1951–1971* (1972), and the Na- tional Book Critics Circle Award for *A Coast of Trees* (1981). A professor of creative writing at Cornell University, Ammons was known as a nature poet interested in exploring the poet's consciousness. Critic Harold Bloom described him as a transcendentalist in the vein of Ralph Waldo Emerson.

AS YOU READ   Consider this poem as an epigram—a short, pithy saying—as well as a pun.

Their Sex Life (1991)

One failure on
Top of another

Writing from Reading

Summarize

1 What scene do these two lines describe, and what's personified?

Analyze Craft

2 Which words in the poem suggest a double meaning?

Analyze Voice

3 Is the poet bitter or sympathetic? Is this poem witty or sad?

Synthesize Summary and Analysis

4 How does the visual look of the poem and its line breaks contribute to meaning and humor?

Interpret the Poem

5 If these lines had no title, how would their meaning change?

HUMOR

Poetry sometimes has a reputation for seriousness and even downright gloominess. And while it's true that poems often explore somber and intensely reflective themes, many poets put the elastic tools of language to comedic use. In this chapter, we have already seen such writers as A. R. Ammons indulge in witty word-play. Poems like these remind us that humorous use of tools like simile, metaphor, and other figures of speech amplifies our perspective on a topic just as interestingly as the use of serious figurative language.

When people invent witty or even vulgar comparisons to describe a situation, they almost always incorporate figures of speech familiar to readers; the comedy may even depend on this. Think of an expression like "It's cold as a well digger's ass," or "The ice on the road's as slippery as snot on a doorknob." Whether you delight in off-color speech like this or find it repulsive, it's inarguably dependent on vivid figurative language.

A good poem can, in fact, be a lot like a good joke—it can jolt our expectation and open up a new and unexpected way of understanding the human condition. To laugh at a joke is to accept a certain degree of shocked surprise; this holds just as true for a peculiar figure of speech. As a result, writers often find that they can use comic analogies to make a reader simultaneously laugh and think seriously. Both results require the same kind of intelligence.

Dorothy Parker (1893–1967)

Dorothy Parker was born Dorothy Rothschild in Long Branch, New Jersey; she died in the New York City of which she had become a central figure. As a participant in the Algonquin "Round Table," a group of sharp-tongued satirists (including Alexander Wolcott, Robert Benchley, and the playwright Robert Sherwood), she helped establish the style of the times. Those times—principally the 1920s and 1930s—were memorialized by Parker in poetry, prose, plays, and nonfiction; her acid-edged tongue and quick, if often melancholy, wit is represented in the poem here. But in such short stories as "Big Blonde"—which won the O'Henry Award in 1929—she demonstrated, as well, a depth of emotional range; her reviews for *The New Yorker* were posthumously collected as *Constant Reader* (1970), the name of her column from 1927 to 1933. As one of the founding members of Harold Ross's Board of Editors—her first piece for the magazine appeared in the second issue of *The New Yorker*—she set a high standard indeed.

With her second husband, Alan Campbell, she wrote many screenplays, including *A Star Is Born* (1937) and *The Saboteur* for Alfred Hitchcock (1942). In each of these genres she demonstrates a keen intelligence and acerbic wit. As she once wrote, "I'm never going to be famous. I don't do a thing, not one single thing. I used to bite my nails, but I don't even do that anymore." Yet famous she became and celebrated she remains.

AS YOU READ Consider how the humor in this poem is like a joke. Where is the punch line?

One Perfect Rose (1923)

A single flow'r he sent me, since we met.
    All tenderly his messenger he chose;
Deep-hearted, pure, with scented dew still wet—
    One perfect rose.
5   I knew the language of the floweret;
    "My fragile leaves," it said, "his heart enclose."
Love long has taken for his amulet
    One perfect rose.
Why is it no one ever sent me yet
10   One perfect limousine, do you suppose?
Ah no, it's always just my luck to get
    One perfect rose.

Writing from Reading

Summarize

1 What is the nature of the speaker's disappointment?

Analyze Craft

2 Parker uses incisive wit and irony to create her trademark tone in this poem. Point out words and sentiments that she is lampooning.

3 What is the "punch line(s)" of her poem?

Analyze Voice

4 Characterize the speaker in this poem. What is light and what is dark in her tone here?

Synthesize Summary and Analysis

5 How would you describe the humor and its use in creating a philosophy of love?

Interpret the Poem

6 What is the philosophy of love here? What makes "One Perfect Rose" so biting? What is "perfect" about the rose? How would you describe what is sad, as well as what is light-hearted, about what the speaker values in a relationship? Do you find this poem ultimately a happy or sad one?

For Review and Further Study

John Ciardi (1916–1986)

Most Like an Arch This Marriage (1958)

Most like an arch—an entrance which upholds
and shores the stone-crush up the air like lace.
Mass made idea, and idea held in place.
A lock in time. Inside half-heaven unfolds.

5 Most like an arch—two weaknesses that lean
into a strength. Two fallings become firm.
Two joined abeyances become a term
naming the fact that teaches fact to mean.

Not quite that? Not much less. World as it is,
10 what's strong and separate falters. All I do
at piling stone on stone apart from you
is roofless around nothing. Till we kiss

I am no more than upright and unset.
It is by falling in and in we make
the all-bearing point, for one another's sake,   15
in faultless failing, raised by our own weight.

Questions for Interactive Reading and Writing

1. List the oppositions in the poem, (for example, "stone-crush" and "lace").

2. What resemblances do you find in these opposing images?

3. What overall effect does using opposites create in the poem?

4. How is an arch like a marriage? Do you find the simile compelling? Why or why not?

e. e. cummings (1894–1962)

For a brief biography of e. e. cummings, see Chapter 26.

she being Brand (1926)

she being Brand

-new;and you
know consequently a
little stiff i was
5 careful of her and (having

thoroughly oiled the universal
joint tested my gas felt of
her radiator made sure her springs were O.

K.)i went right to it flooded-the-carburetor cranked her

10 up, slipped the
clutch (and then somehow got into reverse she
kicked what
the hell) next
minute i was back in neutral tried and

15 again slo-wly;bare, ly nudg. ing (my

lev-er Right-
oh and her gears being in
A 1 shape passed
from low through
20 second-in-to-high like
greasedlightning) just as we turned the corner of Divinity

avenue i touched the accelerator and give

her the juice, good

              (it

25 was the first ride and believe i we was
happy to see how nice she acted right up to
the last minute coming back down by the Public
Gardens i slammed on

the
internalexpanding   30
&
externalcontracting
brakes Bothatonce and

brought allofher tremB
-ling   35
to a:dead.

stand-
;Still)

Questions for Interactive Reading and Writing

1. Cummings is ostensibly describing a car. What else is he describing?

2. What is the effect of this extended metaphor—a kind of double entendre—on the tone of the poem?

3. How do the line breaks and unusual punctuation create humor and provide momentum for the poem?

4. What kinds of information does he include in parentheses? Is there a pattern in the kind of information that is in parentheses versus outside parentheses?

5. Would you characterize this as a love poem? Why or why not?

John Keats (1795–1821)

For a brief biography of John Keats, see Chapter 20.

To Autumn (1819)

I

Season of mists and mellow fruitfulness,
  Close bosom-friend of the maturing sun;
Conspiring with him how to load and bless
  With fruit the vines that round the thatch-eves run;
To bend with apples the mossed cottage-trees,   5
  And fill all fruit with ripeness to the core;
    To swell the gourd, and plump the hazel shells

With a sweet kernel; to set budding more,
  And still more, later flowers for the bees,
10   Until they think warm days will never cease,
    For summer has o'er-brimmed their clammy cells.

II

Who hath not seen thee oft amid thy store?
  Sometimes whoever seeks abroad may find
Thee sitting careless on a granary floor,
15   Thy hair soft-lifted by the winnowing wind;
Or on a half-reaped furrow sound asleep,
  Drowsed with the fume of poppies, while thy hook
    Spares the next swath and all its twinèd flowers:
And sometimes like a gleaner thou dost keep
20   Steady thy laden head across a brook;
  Or by a cider-press, with patient look,
    Thou watchest the last oozings hours by hours.

III

Where are the songs of spring? Ay, where are they?
  Think not of them, thou hast thy music too—
25 While barrèd clouds bloom the soft-dying day,
  And touch the stubble-plains with rosy hue;
Then in a wailful choir the small gnats mourn
  Among the river swallows, borne aloft
    Or sinking as the light wind lives or dies;
30 And full-grown lambs loud bleat from hilly bourn;
  Hedge-crickets sing; and now with treble soft
  The redbreast whistles from a garden-croft,
    And gathering swallows twitter in the skies.

Questions for Interactive Reading and Writing

1. The title of the poem tells you it is a direct address to the season of autumn. What kind of "personality" does Keats create for autumn? How does that personality change over the course of the poem?

2. Determine the rhyme scheme of the three stanzas. Does it ever differ? In what ways does the rhyme scheme complement the theme and tone of the poem?

3. Identify instances of personification in this poem besides the overarching personification of autumn.

4. What is the significance of the three numbered stanzas in the poem? What changes between them, and what stays the same?

Theodore Roethke (1908–1963)

For a brief biography of Theodore Roethke, see Chapter 21.

Root Cellar (1948)

Nothing would sleep in that cellar, dank as a ditch,
Bulbs broke out of boxes hunting for chinks in the dark,
Shoots dangled and drooped,
Lolling obscenely from mildewed crates,
Hung down long yellow evil necks, like tropical snakes.   5
And what a congress of stinks!—
Roots ripe as old bait,
Pulpy stems, rank, silo-rich,
Leaf-mold, manure, lime, piled against slippery planks.
Nothing would give up life: 10
Even the dirt kept breathing a small breath.

Questions for Interactive Reading and Writing

1. Describe the trip our eyes—and noses—take through this underground world.

2. In what way does word choice here reflect the atmosphere of the cellar the speaker describes?

3. Identify similes and moments of personification in the poem.

4. How do these figures convey a sense of life and vitality among simple inanimate objects that might otherwise appear lifeless?

5. What does the poem's setting suggest about the speaker's perspective on life and death? How would the poem be different if it were set in a vibrant garden?

6. Does the poet sound urgent or matter-of-fact as he describes what he sees and smells?

7. A trip through the root cellar adds up to more than meets the eye—and nose. What makes the rank journey worthwhile?

Sonia Sanchez (b. 1934)

rite on: white america (1970)

```
      this country might have
      been a pio
          neer land
      once.
5     but.      there ain't
      no mo
            indians          blowing
      custer's mind
              with a different
10    image of america.
                      this country
      might have
                  needed shoot/
      outs/daily/
15        once.
                  but there ain't
      no mo real/white/       all American
                              bad/guys.
      just
20        u & me.
                  blk/and un/armed.
      this country might have
      been a pion
              eer land.           once.
25                              and it still is.
      check out
              the falling
      gun/shells          on our blk/tomorrows.
```

Questions for Interactive Reading and Writing

1. Explain how the "blowing / custer's mind with a different image of america" is a bitterly playful turn of phrase. What is the double meaning here?

2. How might we understand the "falling gun / shells" as metonymy?

3. What does the poet mean by "blk / tomorrows"?

4. According to the poem, in what way is America still a pioneer land?

Carl Sandburg (1878–1967)

Chicago (1916)

```
      Hog Butcher for the World,
      Tool Maker, Stacker of Wheat,
      Player with Railroads and the Nation's Freight
          Handler;
      Stormy, husky, brawling,
      City of the Big Shoulders:                              5
```

They tell me you are wicked and I believe them, for I have seen your painted women under the gas lamps luring the farm boys.

And they tell me you are crooked and I answer: Yes, it is true I have seen the gunman kill and go free to kill again.

And they tell me you are brutal and my reply is: On the faces of women and children I have seen the marks of wanton hunger.

And having answered so I turn once more to those who sneer at this my city, and I give them back the sneer and say to them:

Come and show me another city with lifted head singing so   10
proud to be alive and coarse and strong and cunning.

Flinging magnetic curses amid the toil of piling job on job, here is a tall bold slugger set vivid against the little soft cities;

Fierce as a dog with tongue lapping for action, cunning as
    a savage pitted against the wilderness,
        Bareheaded,
        Shoveling,
15   Wrecking,
        Planning,
        Building, breaking, rebuilding,
Under the smoke, dust all over his mouth, laughing with
    white teeth,
Under the terrible burden of destiny laughing as a young
    man laughs,
20 Laughing even as an ignorant fighter laughs who has never
    lost a battle,
Bragging and laughing that under his wrist is the pulse,
    and under his ribs the heart of the people,
        Laughing!
Laughing the stormy, husky, brawling laughter of Youth,
    half-naked, sweating, proud to be Hog Butcher, Tool
    Maker, Stacker of Wheat, Player with Railroads and
    Freight Handler to the Nation.

Questions for Interactive Reading and Writing

1. By using personification, Sandburg is able to defend Chicago against some of the criticisms of that city. List some of the criticisms that the speaker includes about Chicago. What is his defense? Is his defense adequate?

2. Sandburg is imitating Walt Whitman in some of his long lines and effusive descriptions, particularly Whitman's poems "I Hear America Singing" (Chapter 20) and "Song of Myself" (Chapter 26). Why does Sandburg use different line lengths in different sections of the poem? What does he accomplish by using a Whitmanesque style in much of this poem?

Walt Whitman (1819–1892)

For a brief biography of Walt Whitman, see Chapter 20.

A Noiseless Patient Spider (1891)

A noiseless patient spider,
I mark'd where on a little promontory it stood isolated,
Mark'd how to explore the vacant vast surrounding,
It launch'd forth filament, filament, filament, out of itself,
Ever unreeling them, ever tirelessly speeding them.   5

And you O my soul where you stand,
Surrounded, detached, in measureless oceans of space,
Ceaselessly musing, venturing, throwing, seeking the
    spheres to connect them,
Till the bridge you will need be form'd, till the ductile
    anchor hold,
Till the gossamer thread you fling catch somewhere,   10
O my soul.

Questions for Interactive Reading and Writing

1. Describe the spider's surroundings. How does the speaker align himself with these surroundings?

2. What do you think the speaker wants to "catch" with his soul? How does he connect this desire with the spider's activity?

3. Why do you think Whitman chooses a spider for his comparison? What characteristics of the spider does he explore?

4. Examine the figurative language here, and what the spider stands for.

Reading for Figures of Speech

When reading for *figures of speech*, identify places where a writer describes one thing in terms of another in order to make a theme or idea feel fresh and new, richer than a literal description would be.

Look for the words *like* and *as*, which show a comparison is being used for illustration.	*Simile:* uses the word *like* or *as* to compare two things. *X* is like *Y*	EXAMPLE "you fit into me / like a hook into an eye"

Look for comparisons that merge two unlike objects to create a more vivid association.	*Metaphor:* compares two things *without using* the word *like* or *as.* *X* is *Y*
	
	Does the language suggest a comparison without explicitly naming the thing being compared?
	    Implied metaphor
	
	Is something being described using several direct, parallel comparisons?
	    Extended metaphor
		EXAMPLE "What light through yonder window breaks? / It is the east, and Juliet is the sun."
		
		EXAMPLE "Quit your yapping."
		
		EXAMPLE "When our cars touched / When you lifted the hood of mine / To see the intimate workings underneath, / When we were bound together / By a pulse of pure energy"

Look for objects or ideas used to represent a larger whole.	*Synecdoche:* uses a part or piece of a thing to represent the thing in its entirety *Metonymy:* uses an identifying emblem or closely associated object to represent a thing in its entirety	EXAMPLE My best friend just got some new wheels. "wheels" = a car EXAMPLE The White House released a statement today. "White House" = the President

Consider who (or what) is being described or addressed by the speaker.	*Is it an animal or inanimate object?*
	    Personification: endows a nonhuman thing with human qualities
	
	Is someone or something not "present" otherwise in the poem?
	    Apostrophe: addresses an unseen person, thing, or idea, as in the following example when John Keats addresses a Grecian urn.
		EXAMPLE "This City now doth, like a garment, wear / The beauty of the morning"
		
		EXAMPLE "Thou still unravished bride of quietness."

Ask yourself if comparisons that seem to contradict each other are used to trigger a fresh understanding or if they are merely confusing.	*Oxymoron:* combines two contradictory terms that use contradiction to make a point *Paradox:* states a self-contradictory position to trigger a fresh concept or comprehension *Pun:* uses words that are spelled or sound alike to suggest, often humorously, more than one idea *Mixed metaphor:* combines two incompatible metaphors, often resulting in nonsense or confusion	EXAMPLE "cold / and passionate as the dawn." EXAMPLE "Youth is wasted on the young." EXAMPLE "Writing with a broken pencil is pointless." EXAMPLE "When you're a big fish in a small pond, you don't want to end up with your tail between your legs."
Does the description make a point through exaggeration or restraint?	*Hyperbole:* describes a thing or experience using purposeful exaggeration *Understatement:* downplays a description to make a point or comparison	EXAMPLE "The shot heard round the world." EXAMPLE "I think I know enough of hate / To know that for destruction ice / Is also great / And would suffice."

Writing about Figures of Speech

1. Compare the different approaches in the extended metaphors used in Linda Pastan's "Jump Cabling" and e. e. cummings's "she being Brand."

2. Both William Wordsworth and Carl Sandburg describe cities admiringly. How does each personify "his" city? What's literal and what's figurative in their observations?

3. Compare the unusual punctuation in e. e. cummings's "she being Brand" and Sonia Sanchez's "rite on: white america." What role does punctuation play in creating figures of speech in these poems?

4. Analyze the use of comic similes to make meaning in A. R. Ammons's "Their Sex Life" and Michael Ondaatje's "Sweet Like a Crow."

5. What is the role of the title in N. Scott Momaday's "Simile," Sylvia Plath's "Metaphors," and Gabriela Mistral's "The Fugitive Woman" regarding the addition of implicit or explicit meaning?

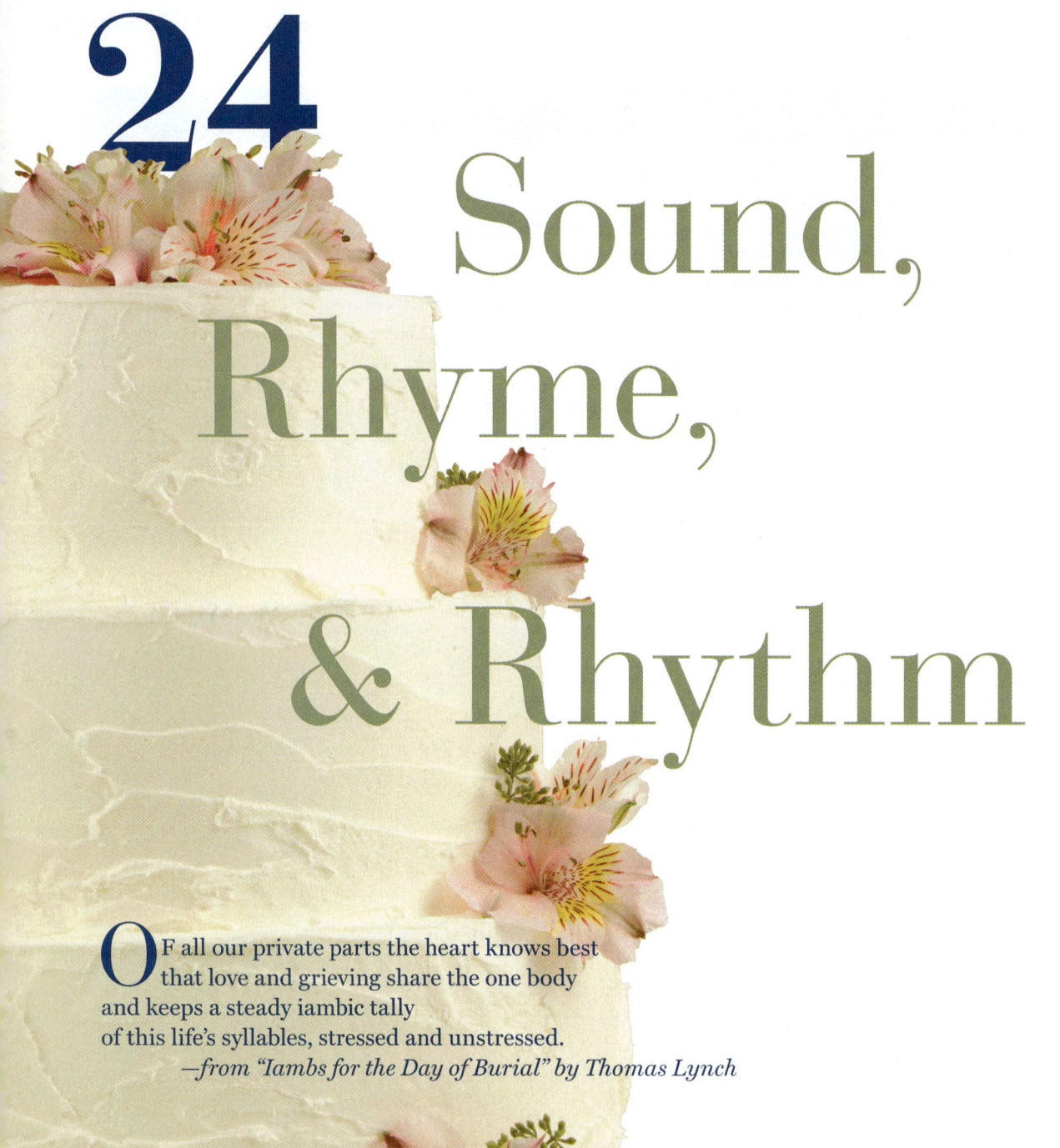

24

Sound, Rhyme, & Rhythm

OF all our private parts the heart knows best
    that love and grieving share the one body
and keeps a steady iambic tally
of this life's syllables, stressed and unstressed.
    —*from "Iambs for the Day of Burial" by Thomas Lynch*

"The idea that you could play with words is what for me writing poems has always been, sort of a wordplay. It really doesn't matter much to me what the subject is: the subject presents itself after the line presents itself, after the sort of acoustic hook is set in the ear."

Conversation with Thomas Lynch, available on video
at connect.mcgraw-hill.com

AS you see in Thomas Lynch's "Iambs for the Day of Burial," the way the **sounds** of language work together with **rhyme** and **rhythm** can dramatically affect the way we experience a poem. Here Lynch makes the claim that the beat of the heart—*da-dum, da-dum, da-dum*—is a "steady iambic tally." Referring to one of poetry's most common rhythms, he relates the pulse to "stressed and unstressed" syllables. Poetry, he seems to say, has our very life force within it. The words are simply words, the sounds are sounds we've heard before, and a pattern exists in each sentence. However, a poet chooses particular words in a conscious attempt to shape the meaning of his poems; *sound* and *sense* are, in effect, two sides of one coin.

Although the language of poetry is sometimes difficult to understand, remember what you already know: all speech is sound. When we worry over the meaning of a poem, as though it were a foreign language or a code to crack, the answer to a poem's puzzle is often its "acoustic hook," the arrangement of sounds that draws us into the poem. When a sound repeats itself, we call that echo *rhyme*. The pattern of such repetition, and the way the poet places the words, even the syllables, in sequence, creates the poem's rhythm. "Iambs for the Day of Burial" aptly makes the claim that rhythm is as natural as breath. The sound of our pulse beating, the way we walk or dance, what our fingers do while tapping on a keyboard are *naturally* rhythmic, and if that word had been, instead, *unnaturally,* it would still have a rhythm though the rhythm would have changed. To understand a poem, as Lynch observes in his interview, it sometimes helps to tap it out.

Thomas Lynch
I've always said that writers are readers who go karaoke....

A Conversation on Writing

The Heartbeat in Poetry

I have this vexing habit—to some people—of sort of tapping things out that are occurring to me acoustically.... I've always been drawn to the notion that Wordsworth could work out his poetry—and Shakespeare his own poetry—by keeping an ear to their own metabolic strain, their own breathing and heartbeat, and the notion that there is some connection between language and a natural order: da-dum, da-dum, da-dum. It has this appeal to my ear.

Becoming Accountable to Your Own Language

I've always said that writers are readers who go karaoke: They first get up in front of the microphone and sing songs, do cover pieces. Then pretty soon they begin to sound like themselves talking to themselves. I don't know what it was for me. I can remember writing poems that were sort of all borrowings from Yeats and Emily Dickinson, and Edward Arlington Robinson, and Michael Heffernan, and anyone else who I came across. Most of the notions were borrowed from maybe other books that I was reading, not poetry. But at some point you become accountable to the language yourself.

Poetry as Self-Prophecy

I'm aware of this about poetry, and I'm certain musicians must be aware about it with music, and painters with color and image: that it knows you better than yourself. It will make its way into the world, "it" being whatever language wants to do with you. Language knows you better than [you know] yourself. So the poems, when I look back at them now, they were almost prophetic. They knew

things about me that came to be true, that I didn't know at the time. But the language did, from whatever part. The words kept pushing themselves onto the page. It knew things. It still does. So I trust it I suppose.

"We need a way to say unspeakable things, and funerals do. So do poems," Thomas Lynch—poet, essayist, and undertaker—once said in an interview. Born in Michigan in 1948, Lynch took over his father's funeral parlor in 1974, and he has been the undertaker for the town of Milford, Michigan, ever since. His poetry—collected in *Skating with Heather Grace* (1986), *Grimalkin* (1994), and *Still Life in Milford* (1998)—explores the intersections of life, death, sex, grief, and other profound aspects of the human experience. Among his books of nonfiction are *The Undertaking—Life Studies from the Dismal Trade,* which won the Heartland Prize for Nonfiction and the American Book Award, and *Bodies in Motion and at Rest,* a collection of essays that won the Great Lakes Book Award. Lynch's written work and commentaries have appeared in prominent venues including *The New York Times,* NPR, *The Washington Post,* and a *PBS Frontline* feature, among many others.

To watch the entire interview and hear the author read from his work, go to connect.mcgraw-hill.com

RESEARCH ASSIGNMENT In his interview, Lynch says, "All language has double edges." What does he mean by this, and how is his understanding of double edges in language related to his work?

AS YOU READ   Consider what the poet means by "life's syllables, stressed and unstressed."

Iambs for the Day of Burial (1998)

Of all our private parts the heart knows best
that love and grieving share the one body
and keeps a steady iambic tally
of this life's syllables, stressed and unstressed.
5   Our pulse divided by our breathing equals
pleasure measured in pentameters,
pain endured in oddly rhyming pairs:
sadness, gladness, sex and death, nuptials,
funerals. Love made and love forsaken—
10   each leaves us breathless and beatified,
more than the sum of parts that lived and died
of love or grief. Both leave the heart broken.

Writing from Reading

Summarize

1 Imagine these twelve lines are spoken at a grave, linking love and grief. How does the poet develop that linkage and establish the connection?

Analyze Craft

2 How is this poem about its own making and structure? Give examples of "pentameters" and "oddly rhyming pairs."

Analyze Voice

3 Lynch is a professional undertaker as well as a poet; his family has operated Lynch & Sons Funeral Home in Milford, Michigan, for decades. How is Lynch's profession reflected by any of his word choices or the tone of the poem? What about the poem is surprising, considering the poet's frequent interaction with the dead?

Synthesize Summary and Analysis

4 What connections are there between the rhythm of this poem and its subject matter? Why is this particular rhythm appropriate? Identify places where there is deviation in the rhythm. How do these deviations contribute to the overarching gravity of the poem?

Interpret the Poem

5 Discuss the idea that love and grief "both leave the heart broken." Do you agree?

From its earliest presence in religious ritual and public entertainment, poetry has been written to accompany music; no form of writing is more closely associated with song. From Homer onward, poets have used rhythmical patterns and sounds. These rise from the page to emulate something chanted, as they were in ancient prayers and poetry contests, attesting to the radically musical nature of Western poetry. Rhythm, supported by the patterns of sounds that create rhythm, is one of the elemental qualities that separates poetry from ordinary speech.

Poets have always paid special attention to the musical elements of their own language. This attention differentiates poetry from language used only to communicate information. Poetry's special sound effects of stresses, rhymes, and repetitions invite a reader to inspect, carefully, the texture and sound of words. "Musical thought" is how the Scottish writer Thomas Carlyle defined the genre. "[Poetry is] a sonorous molded shape of form," said the Russian poet Osip Mandelstam.

"**Poems come from poems, songs come from songs. They come from experience. You bring your own experience to everything that flows through you.**" Conversation with Robert Hass

Anonymous lyrics from the thirteenth through early sixteenth centuries in England continue the tradition of poetic song. As with "Western Wind" and the early ballads, we cannot name the author or do much more than approximate the date and place of composition, but voice connects its author to an audience, and often the voice is more important than individual authorship in creating a song's or poem's context.

Anonymous

AS YOU READ   Try to imagine what circumstances might have prompted the unknown poet to compose these lines.

Western Wind (c. 1500)

Western wind, when will thou blow
That the small rain down can rain?
Christ, that my love were in my arms
And I in my bed again!

Writing from Reading

Summarize

1 In what circumstance does the anonymous poet find himself? Herself?

2 "Western Wind" accomplishes much in a small space; list everything that you know about the speaker's situation and feelings.

Analyze Craft

3 For you, what is the most compelling line or image in the poem, and why does it strike you?

4 How do sounds—rhyme, rhythm, repetition, alliteration, and so on—make this poem songlike?

Analyze Voice

5 What effect does the word *Christ* have on the poem? If it were omitted, how would the poem change?

Synthesize Summary and Analysis

6 Most lyric poetry laments loss and absence. What distinguishes this anonymous lyric from others of its kind (such as the fragment by Sappho in Chapter 17)?

Interpret the Poem

7 This poem is a lament and outcry in a difficult time by an anonymous speaker. Does the anonymity of the speaker make the poem more or less effective? Or does it not matter?

8 What does the last line suggest in coming after the previous three?

SOUND

A poet chooses language based on sound as well as on meaning. We read, for example, the word *glassy* and can perceive smooth surfaces beneath the double "s" sound. We say the word *trickle* and hear the light, small splashes of water from a kitchen sink faucet. When a writer uses a variety of active verbs, we feel velocity and action evoked in a poem. When a writer fills a line with **monosyllabic** (one-syllable) words, we perceive important emphasis and purpose. Think, for instance, of that memorable catchphrase for insecticide: "Raid kills bugs dead." Or, as in the last two words from the poem by Gerard Manley Hopkins near the end of this chapter, the simple finality of "Praise him."

When poets arrange the sounds of words together, either purposefully or by sheer instinct, to produce a pleasing effect, they create **euphony,** musically pleasing poetic language. An opening like this from one of Lord Byron's love poems (in this chapter) helps illustrate how euphonious language can mirror a poem's emotions:

> *She walks in beauty, like the night*
> *Of cloudless climes and starry skies;*
> *And all that's best of dark and bright*
> *Meet in her aspect and her eyes. . . .*

The agreeable flow of the language itself (notice, for instance, how often the "i" gets repeated) helps reinforce Byron's loving description. *Like, night, climes, skies, bright, eyes*—all sound out a chorus of praise.

> **"Is poetry an aural or written art? For me, it's both. As time goes on, the way the poem looks is really important to me. But also the way it sounds. And I'm trying to find the perfect coincidence of the way the poem looks, the way it sounds, the way it means, the silence and the speech in the poem."** Conversation with Li-Young Lee

In contrast, when poets describe something unpleasant or dissonant, they often employ **cacophony,** harsh-sounding, grating, or even hard-to-pronounce syllables. Listen to these cacophonous lines by Jonathan Swift, who wanted to make fun of the pretty language of nature poetry of his day in this description of a rainstorm flooding London. If you read these lines aloud—and even though their last words rhyme—you are likely to feel your mouth squeezing the sounds out with difficulty:

> *Sweeping from butchers stalls, dung, guts, and blood,*
> *Drowned puppies, stinking sprats, all drenched in mud,*
> *Dead cats and turnip-tops, come tumbling down the flood.*

Not exactly the subject matter we associate with English verse!

You don't have to know all of the following terms to read and enjoy a poem. By learning, however, to recognize the musical effects of sound, you will strengthen your understanding of a poem's meaning and dimensions.

> **"The poem is made out of the sounds."** Conversation with Robert Pinsky

Safe and sound. Drunk and disorderly. Back to basics. Our language is full of catchy phrases like these that repeat their opening sounds. The effect is both memorable and musical. **Alliteration** describes this technique—the repetition of the initial consonant sounds of a sequence of words. Like many forms of repetition, this technique links sound and sense together and intensifies their combined power. As the sounds echo each other, they pull together the meanings of words. Alliterative linkage flourished in our language long before the habit of connecting lines by end-rhyme: It was with us from the start of English verse.

Also demonstrating a kind of kinship between sounds is **consonance,** a repetition of *consonant* sounds or similar patterns in neighboring words. The words

> *taken and token*
> *whole and whale*

employ consonance in its most familiar definition, within words that are identical except for differing vowels. Consonance also refers, moreover, to a sentence such as

> *Calmly, he called to the mule in the old field*

with its repeated rolling "l."

OLD ENGLISH ALLITERATIVE VERSE

One of the primary sources of our contemporary lexicon, Old English is the language of the oldest surviving poetry born in Britain. Alliteration is closely associated with this early verse and was used—more often than rhyme—to establish the structure of the Old English poetic line. In this tradition, two short half-lines are divided by a break but unified by alliterated, stressed syllables. These repeated consonants give Old English alliterative verse a distinctive and robust sound, ideal for the dramatic public performances in which these poems might have been heard.

Assonance is a kind of flip side to consonance. It's the repetition of the same *vowel* sound in neighboring words. Used for musical effect and for poetic emphasis, assonance can tie ideas together in a poem over the course of different phrases and lines.

Robert Herrick's "Delight in Disorder" (for the whole poem, see An Anthology of Poetry for Further Reading, Chapter 29) employs assonance in the second and third lines of this opening stanza. Note how the shared "o" vowel sound helps join the images of the clothing together:

> *A sweet disorder in the dress*
> *Kindles in clothes a wantonness.*
> *A lawn about the shoulders thrown*
> *Into a fine distraction . . .*

Sometimes the various sound elements of poetry combine to evoke the very thing their language describes. **Onomatopoeia** is a use of words that imitate the sounds they refer to. Think of such words as *buzz* and *pop* and *sizzle*. We hear what they portray in the very sounds they make. When they appear in poetry or song ("clickety-clack along the track"), they further unify sound and meaning.

Listen to these lines describing the natural landscape by Alfred, Lord Tennyson:

> *The moan of doves in immemorial elms,*
> *And murmuring of innumerable bees.*

Can you associate the doves' cry with the words *moan* and *immemorial*? Can you, in a sense, "hear" the low buzz of the bees in *murmuring* and *innumerable*?

The words *immemorial, murmuring,* and *innumerable* are **polysyllabic,** meaning they have many syllables, as opposed to the monosyllabic, or single syllable—"The moan of doves in . . . elms." In this regard, one of the glories of English is its ability to marry monosyllabic Anglo-Saxon directness with polysyllabic Latin and medieval French, a discourse brought to England when William the Conqueror, in 1066, declared that *his* would be the language of the court. English poets ever since the Norman Conquest have had a grab bag of sonorities to choose from, and the word *sonority* itself is just a fancy Latinate way of saying *sound*.

Think of English as a mighty river with several tributaries. By now the waters are thoroughly mixed (a process that continues yearly), and it takes analysis to separate them out. You don't have to be a linguist and fluent in foreign languages to get a sense of which words are simple, which complex—or, by extension, which language they might have derived from and what their root meaning might be.

Here the poet Seamus Heaney stresses Anglo-Saxon, making a kind of onomato-poetic statement about the way his ancestors worked. In the 218 words of "Digging," there are only six that have three syllables and none that have more. The six polysyl-labic words (*gravelly, flowerbeds, potatoes, grandfather, sloppily, awaken*) all refer to matters of the earth or family or physical behavior. In the end, the poet claims that working with a pen is just as hard as working in a garden or bog. Note how the poem's final words are each monosyllabic, stressed, and equally a kind of "digging"; the two skills seem akin.

Seamus Heaney (b. 1939)

Described as "the best Irish poet since W. B. Yeats," Seamus Heaney is—like Yeats—both Irish and a Nobel Prize laureate. Since he was born to a Roman Catholic family in a Protestant area of Ireland, it is perhaps not surprising that Heaney's poetry portrays Ireland's politi-cal problems. However, this is only one aspect of Heaney's poetry; his poems convey a deep sense of history, both personal and collective, in verses marked by quiet compression. In addition to the poetry collected in books such as *Death of a Naturalist* (1966) and *Opened Ground* (1999), Heaney is known for his transla-tions, most notably of *Beowulf,* and his criticism. He has taught at Harvard Uni-versity for part of each year since 1981 but otherwise lives in Dublin.

AS YOU READ   Consider how sound works to mimic the meaning of words, or to intensify their overall effect.

Digging (1966)

Between my finger and my thumb
The squat pen rests; snug as a gun.

Under my window, a clean rasping sound
When the spade sinks into gravelly ground:
5 My father, digging. I look down

Till his straining rump among the flowerbeds
Bends low, comes up twenty years away
Stooping in rhythm through potato drills
Where he was digging.

10 The coarse boot nestled on the lug, the shaft
Against the inside knee was levered firmly.
He rooted out tall tops, buried the bright edge deep
To scatter new potatoes that we picked
Loving their cool hardness in our hands.

15 By God, the old man could handle a spade
Just like his old man.

My grandfather cut more turf in a day
Than any other man on Toner's bog.
Once I carried him milk in a bottle
20 Corked sloppily with paper. He straightened up
To drink it, then fell to right away
Nicking and slicing neatly, heaving sods
Over his shoulder, digging down and down
For the good turf. Digging.

25 The cold smell of potato mould, the squelch and slap
Of soggy peat, the curt cuts of an edge
Through living roots awaken in my head.
But I've no spade to follow men like them.

Between my finger and my thumb
30 The squat pen rests.
I'll dig with it.

Writing from Reading

Summarize

1 Why do you think the poet repeats the title word often in the poem? What other "-ing" (participial) words does he use? Are they related to one another? How does their sound echo their meaning?

Analyze Craft

2 Find instances of consonance and assonance in the poem. How do they work to connect or unify the language?

3 Read this poem aloud. How would you describe the sound of the language? How does this description seem to fit or contrast with the poem's subject?

Analyze Voice

4 Can you make an analogy between the work the poet describes and his own way of making lines?

Synthesize Summary and Analysis

5 Making a poem about work in his family, the poet discovers a link to his own present labors. Do you find that physical labor and creative labor are equivalent?

Interpret the Poem

6 Is this a poem of justification or celebration?

For Review and Further Study

Lewis Carroll (1832–1898)

Jabberwocky (1871)

'Twas brillig, and the slithy toves
   Did gyre and gimble in the wabe:
All mimsy were the borogoves,
   And the mome raths outgrabe.

5 "Beware the Jabberwock, my son!
   The jaws that bite, the claws that catch!
Beware the Jubjub bird, and shun
   The frumious Bandersnatch!"

He took his vorpal sword in hand:
10   Long time the manxome foe he sought—
So rested he by the Tumtum tree,
   And stood awhile in thought.

And, as in uffish thought he stood,
   The Jabberwock, with eyes of flame,
15 Came whiffling through the tulgey wood,
   And burbled as it came!

One, two! One, two! And through and through
   The vorpal blade went snicker-snack!
He left it dead, and with its head
20   He went galumphing back.

"And, hast thou slain the Jabberwock?
   Come to my arms, my beamish boy!
O frabjous day! Callooh, Callay!"
   He chortled in his joy.

25 'Twas brillig, and the slithy toves
   Did gyre and gimble in the wabe;
All mimsy were the borogoves,
   And the mome raths outgrabe.

Questions for Interactive Reading and Writing

1. For all of its nonsense, do you hear a pattern as you recite the poem? What is the "sense" in such "nonsense," and how does Carroll invent his words or reinvigorate his language? Describe the pattern.

2. Compare the language of "Jabberwocky" to the ballad of "Sir Patrick Spence" later in this chapter. How does Carroll's use of sounds create a more dreamlike—or nightmarish—story than the jaunty narrative of "Sir Patrick Spence"?

3. Why might you find pleasure in the saying of this poem? Why not? What is your reaction to the nonsense words?

John Keats (1795–1821)

For a brief biography of John Keats, see Chapter 20.

Bright star, would I were steadfast as thou art (1838)

Bright star, would I were steadfast as thou art—
Not in lone splendour hung aloft the night
And watching, with eternal lids apart,
Like nature's patient, sleepless Eremite,
The moving waters at their priestlike task   5
Of pure ablution round earth's human shores,
Or gazing on the new soft-fallen mask
Of snow upon the mountains and the moors—
No—yet still steadfast, still unchangeable,
Pillow'd upon my fair love's ripening breast,   10
To feel for ever its soft fall and swell,
Awake for ever in a sweet unrest,
Still, still to hear her tender-taken breath,
And so live ever—or else swoon to death.

Questions for Interactive Reading and Writing

1. This is an apostrophe (see Chapter 25)—a poem in which the speaker speaks, improbably enough, to a personified object, a star, addressing it in the informal second person "thou." How does this establish tone?

2. Look up "Eremite," "ablution," and any other words that may confuse you here. "Splendour" is the British spelling, and natural enough for Keats, but why would he have put an apostrophe in "Pillow'd"? And why does he—remember Keats died of tuberculosis at twenty-five—conclude with "swoon to death"?

3. The word *steadfast* is used twice and the word *still* appears four times, the word *ever* three. How does this affect the poem's music, and how would you describe such a line as "To feel for ever its soft fall and swell"?

Edna St. Vincent Millay (1892–1950)

For a brief biography of Edna St. Vincent Millay, see Chapter 25.

Only until this cigarette is ended (1921)

Only until this cigarette is ended,
A little moment at the end of all,
While on the floor the quiet ashes fall,
And in the firelight to a lance extended,
5 Bizarrely with the jazzing music blended,
The broken shadow dances on the wall,
I will permit my memory to recall
The vision of you, by all my dreams attended.
And then adieu,—farewell!—the dream is done.
10 Yours is a face of which I can forget
The color and the features, every one,
The words not ever, and the smiles not yet;
But in your day this moment is the sun
Upon a hill, after the sun has set.

Questions for Interactive Reading and Writing

1. How much time elapses in the poem? What does this suggest about the speaker's mood and thoughts? How much actual control do you believe she has over her thoughts?

2. Can you explain the paradox (seemingly contradictory statement) of the final two lines?

3. From Sappho to Shakespeare to Millay and beyond, poets have written about love and its pains and losses. How close to despair do you find the speaker in this poem compared with speakers in other love poems you have read? How close to joy?

Christina Rossetti (1830–1894)

A Birthday (1861)

My heart is like a singing bird
  Whose nest is in a watered shoot;
My heart is like an apple-tree
  Whose boughs are bent with thick-set fruit;
My heart is like a rainbow shell   5
  That paddles in a halcyon sea;
My heart is gladder than all these,
  Because my love is come to me.

Raise me a dais of silk and down;
  Hang it with vair and purple dyes;   10
Carve it in doves and pomegranates,
  And peacocks with a hundred eyes;
Work it in gold and silver grapes,
  In leaves and silver fleur-de-lys;
Because the birthday of my life   15
  Is come, my love is come to me.

Questions for Interactive Reading and Writing

1. Discuss the repetitions here, as well as variation. Lines 1, 3, 5, and 7 make a kind of chorus, and the last lines of the two stanzas are similar. How does this compare with the ballad form discussed in the next section of this chapter?

2. Although this poem was written roughly 150 years ago, it uses a consciously "archaic" diction—perhaps medieval, perhaps even biblical in tone. How do such words as *halcyon* and *vair* and *fleurs-de-lys* contribute to this effect?

3. "A singing bird" appears in the first line, and there are other birds throughout. Does the speaker compare herself to these creatures; if so, why?

4. The second stanza is couched in the imperative mode—as a series of orders to be obeyed. This is a poem of celebration, edging up to excess; list the similes.

5. What does Rosetti mean by "the birthday of my life"?

Dylan Thomas (1914–1953)

For a brief biography of Dylan Thomas, see Chapter 25.

Fern Hill (1946)

Now as I was young and easy under the apple boughs
About the lilting house and happy as the grass was green,
      The night above the dingle starry,
        Time let me hail and climb
5   Golden in the heydays of his eyes,
And honored among wagons I was prince of the apple towns
And once below a time I lordly had the trees and leaves
        Trail with daisies and barley
      Down the rivers of the windfall light.

And as I was green and carefree, famous among the barns   10
About the happy yard and singing as the farm was home,
      In the sun that is young once only,
        Time let me play and be
      Golden in the mercy of his means,
And green and golden I was huntsman and herdsman, the calves   15
Sang to my horn, the foxes on the hills barked clear and cold,
        And the sabbath rang slowly
      In the pebbles of the holy streams.

All the sun long it was running, it was lovely, the hay
Fields high as the house, the tunes from the chimneys, it was air   20
      And playing, lovely and watery
        And fire green as grass.
      And nightly under the simple stars
As I rode to sleep the owls were bearing the farm away,
All the moon long I heard, blessed among stables, the nightjars   25
        Flying with the ricks, and the horses
        Flashing into the dark.

And then to awake, and the farm, like a wanderer white
With the dew, come back, the cock on his shoulder: it was all
      Shining, it was Adam and maiden,   30
        The sky gathered again
      And the sun grew round that very day.
So it must have been after the birth of the simple light
In the first, spinning place, the spellbound horses walking warm
      Out of the whinnying green stable   35
        On to the fields of praise.

And honoured among foxes and pheasants by the gay house
Under the new made clouds and happy as the heart was long,
      In the sun born over and over,
        I ran my heedless ways,   40
      My wishes raced through the house high hay
And nothing I cared, at my sky blue trades, that time allows
In all his tuneful turning so few and such morning songs
      Before the children green and golden
        Follow him out of grace,   45

Nothing I cared, in the lamb white days, that time would take me
Up to the swallow thronged loft by the shadow of my hand,
    In the moon that is always rising,
        Nor that riding to sleep
50   I should hear him fly with the high fields
And wake to the farm forever fled from the childless land.
Oh as I was young and easy in the mercy of his means,
        Time held me green and dying
        Though I sang in my chains like the sea.

Questions for Interactive Reading and Writing

1. What happens to the speaker in the poem? What phases of life does he describe?

2. Certain phrases, such as "grass was green" and "Adam and maiden," lend a sense of euphony to this poem. What other phrases are euphonious, and what devices (alliteration, assonance, consonance) make them so?

3. Describe the imagery. How is it appropriate for the periods of life the speaker describes?

4. What attitudes and actions does the speaker attribute to time? How does this personification of time reflect the speaker's changing feelings toward time?

5. This poem is full of colors. What is the significance here of colors such as green, gold, and white? How are they symbolic?

William Butler Yeats (1865–1939)

For a brief biography of William Butler Yeats, see Chapter 17.

The Lake Isle of Innisfree (1892)

I will arise and go now, and go to Innisfree,
And a small cabin build there, of clay and wattles made:
Nine bean-rows will I have there, a hive for the honey-bee;
And live alone in the bee-loud glade.

And I shall have some peace there, for peace comes dropping slow, 5
Dropping from the veils of the morning to where the cricket sings;
There midnight's all a glimmer, and noon a purple glow,
And evening full of the linnet's wings.

I will arise and go now, for always night and day
I hear lake water lapping with low sounds by the shore; 10
While I stand on the roadway, or on the pavements gray,
I hear it in the deep heart's core.

Questions for Interactive Reading and Writing

1. The poem describes the idyllic setting of Innisfree. Which features particularly stand out as appealing?

2. To what effect does the poet repeat the line "I will arise and go now"? Do you read it as literally leaving a particular location, or as something figurative?

3. Read the poem aloud. How does the sound of the poem fit Yeats's portrayal of this beautiful, dreamlike location?

4. What sound devices (consonance, assonance, alliteration, rhyme, meter) give this poem its euphonious quality?

5. The speaker says he will "live alone in the bee-loud glade." In the context of the poem, is being alone a positive or a negative experience? What clues help you determine this?

6. Notice the contrast of standing "on the roadway, or on the pavements grey" and of hearing water "lapping . . . in the deep heart's core." What is the speaker trying to express through this contrast? Which one does he long for?

RHYME

The sound component most often associated with poetry is called rhyme. **Rhyme** (**rime**) consists of the echoing repetition of sounds in end syllables of words, often (though not always) at the end of a line of poetry. Rhyme offers one of the primary pleasures of verse; all children are alert to it, and a sound repeated is a sound remembered. "Jack Sprat could eat no fat" and "Old Mother Hubbard went to the cupboard" remain alive as nursery rhymes because of their emphatic repetition. In **exact rhyme** (also **pure, perfect,** or **true rhyme**) the final vowel and consonant sounds are identical, regardless of spelling. For most readers, it's the most familiar form. Think of *heard* and *word* or *simple, pimple,* and *dimple.* Rhymes like these offer a clear, bright connectivity of sound.

> **"Nursery rhymes [with] those really adorable rhythms that just stay in the head—that was my first sense of the pleasure of language."** Conversation with Robert Hass

In twenty-first-century popular music, the word *ballad* is used to describe slow, often confessional songs, but early ballads—traditionally, a song or poem that tells a lively or tragic story in simple language—used rhyming four-line stanzas and a set musical meter. (For more on the ballad stanza, see Chapter 25). The repetition of the **end rhyme,** rhyming sounds that conclude the lines of a stanza, may have originated to help the singer or speaker remember the poem. You can still find this arrangement in works that span the past several hundred years, including modern poetry and contemporary music lyrics. For example, such contemporary composers as Bob Dylan often use the traditional ballad stanzaic form. Whoever first composed the following ballad was, in the artistic sense, detached; the maker does not criticize the king's malevolent decision to send his noble warriors to their deaths at sea. This historical ballad—its hero was a fighter-sailor of the thirteenth century—would have been the work of many hands, and we have no way of knowing who first "wrote" it.

> **"One of the beauties of formal verse is that it's . . . very memorable. You have a rhyme scheme perhaps to guide your memory. I think the reason that rhyme patterns were established in the first place was as a mnemonic so that we would be able to memorize."** Conversation with Carolyn Forché

Anonymous

AS YOU READ Focus on the story, but also notice that the rhyming and its effects enhance the story.

Sir Patrick Spence (1765)

The King sits in Dumferling toune,
  Drinking the blude-reid wine:
"O whar will I get guid sailor,
  To sail this schip of mine?"

5 Up and spak an eldern knicht,
  Sat at the kings richt kne:
"Sir Patrick Spence is the best sailor
  That sails upon the se."

The king has written a braid letter,
10 And signed it wi' his hand,
And sent it to Sir Patrick Spence,
  Was walking on the sand.

The first line that Sir Patrick red,
  A loud lauch lauchèd he;
15 The next line that Sir Patrick red,
  The teir blinded his ee.

"O wha is this has don this deid,
  This ill deid don to me,
To send me out this time o' the yeir,
20 To sail upon the se!

"Mak haste, mak haste, my mirry men all,
  Our guid schip sails the morne."
"O say na sae, my master deir,
  For I feir a deadlie storme.

25 "Late late yestreen I saw the new moone,
  Wi' the auld moone in hir arme,
And I feir, I feir, my deir master,
  That we will cum to harme."

O our Scots nobles wer richt laith
30 To weet their cork-heild schoone,
Bot lang owre a' the play wer play'd,
  Thair hats they swam aboone.

O lang, lang may their ladies sit,
  Wi' thair fans into their hand,
35 Or ere they se Sir Patrick Spence
  Cum sailing to the land.

O lang, lang may the ladies stand,
  Wi' their gold kems in their hair,
Waiting for thair ain deir lords,
40 For they'll se thame na mair.

Haf owre, half owre to Aberdour,
  It's fiftie fadom deip,
And thair lies guid Sir Patrick Spence,
  Wi' the Scots lords at his feit.

Writing from Reading

Summarize

1 Read (or chant) this poem out loud. Did you find that the old-fashioned spellings and words were easier to understand this way? Paraphrase each stanza. What is the plot of the poem?

Analyze Craft

2 How does the rhythmical pattern, the use of language, and the use of rhyme contribute to the poem's songlike quality?

Analyze Voice

3 How would you describe the tone of this ballad?

4 We do not know who the original author of "Sir Patrick Spence" is—but the poem does have a voice that distinguishes it from other songs. How would you describe the voice of this particular work *or* the voice of a folk ballad (using specific examples from this poem as evidence)?

5 Look up any unfamiliar words and replace them with modern-day approximations. How does this change the poem's voice?

Synthesize Summary and Analysis

6 The technical components of the poem, and its musical qualities, create a moving story about loyalty, love, and history. Can you name some contemporary ballads that work in similar fashion?

7 Compare this traditional Scottish ballad with another, "Bonnie Barbara Allen" (in this chapter). How is the rhythm similar? What other similarities do you find?

Interpret the Poem

8 What lessons does the anonymous poet put forward about life?

In eighteenth-century England, Alexander Pope composed the following piece in **heroic couplets,** two successive rhyming lines in iambic pentameter (the most commonly used metric pattern in English literature). In addition to the musical pleasure that rhythm can bring to a poem, rhyme schemes can organize a poem in central ways. To notate a rhyme scheme, we represent each new end rhyme with a lowercase letter following its line (as you see with the following poem by Pope). When a sound recurs, we use the same letter to mark the repeated rhyme. The heroic couplet scheme of *AA/BB*, for example, is very different from *AB/AB* or *AB/BA*, and one of the most useful ways to look at the craft of poetry is to look for the rhyme scheme involved. Heroic couplets stress the connection between each of the paired lines.

Alexander Pope (1688–1744)

Born in London, Alexander Pope suffered from a bone disease as a child and consequently never grew taller than four and a half feet. What he lacked in stature, he more than made up for in literary genius. Largely self-educated and self-sufficient—his translations of the *Iliad* and the *Odyssey* earned him enough money to buy an estate and live solely as a man of letters—Pope became the leading poet of his day, thanks to his mastery of style, the heroic couplet, and satirical writing. His sparkling wit attacked not only his contemporaries, in such works as *The Dunciad* (1728), but also great works of literature—for example, *Paradise Lost* in his famous mock-epic *The Rape of the Lock* (1714). Pope also composed verse that showed his appreciation of beauty, including *Pastorals* (1709) and *Windsor Forest* (1713).

AS YOU READ   Note how the rhyme scheme helps notate the repetitions of sound and puts a kind of emphasis on the meaning here.

True ease in writing comes from art, not chance
—from *"An Essay on Criticism"* (1711)

True ease in writing comes from art, not chance,	a
As those move easiest who have learned to dance.	a
'Tis not enough no harshness gives offense,	b
The sound must seem an echo to the sense:	b
5 Soft is the strain when Zephyr gently blows,	c
And the smooth stream in smoother numbers flows;	c
But when loud surges lash the sounding shore,	d
The hoarse, rough verse should like the torrent roar;	d
When Ajax strives some rock's vast weight to throw,	e
10 The line too labors, and the words move slow;	e
Not so, when swift Camilla scours the plain,	f
Flies o'er the unbending corn, and skims along the main.	f
Hear how Timotheus' varied lays surprise,	g
And bid alternate passions fall and rise!	g

Writing from Reading

Summarize

1 The poet offers a disquisition (formal explanation, discussion of a subject) on the relation of sound and sense in poetry. Why might he be taking this up as a subject? Have you seen any poets before Pope working on this idea?

Analyze Craft

2 Describe the paradox in comparing "ease" to "art." What is the effect of this comparison?

3 What is the meaning of the phrase "smoother numbers"?

4 Look up the classical references: Ajax, Camilla, and so on. What is the function of these allusions?

Analyze Voice

5 What, if anything, distinguishes the poet's rhyming couplets from that of songs or poems presented as songs in verse?

Synthesize Summary and Analysis

6 These rhyming couplets provide some lessons on the relation of craft and voice. Which rhymes do you consider the smoothest, and which rhymes here trouble you?

Interpret the Poem

7 Does a poem such as this veer too much toward didactism—over-explicit instruction—or philosophy?

Although the poetry that is sung or based on song uses rhyme, rhyme does not occur only in early poetry. Take these lines in a poem by Robert Frost (for the whole poem, see Chapter 4):

> *The woods are lovely, dark and deep,*
> *But I have promises to keep,*
> *And miles to go before I sleep,*
> *And miles to go before I sleep.*

Frost uses the same end rhyme for each of his quatrain's four lines and repeats the third line verbatim. This act of willed repetition has much to do with the action described and how the speaker will keep on moving through the dark.

If, however, Frost had written "The woods are lovely, dark and deep, / But I have promises I've made, / And miles to go before I'm home, / And miles to go before I rest," our response would be quite different. We might acquire *some* sense of the poem's famous meditation, and its meaning would not change. The substance stays the same. On the whole, however, these modified phrases lose their mournful, musical connectivity; the *sound* is an important—even a crucial—part of *sense*. It's not an accident that one of the synonyms for *language* is *tongue;* we sound out what we see.

That said, it's a misconception to think all poetry *has* to rhyme. This mistaken notion has resulted in a lot of bad poetry and greeting cards with awkward or forced rhyming language. Of course you've already seen in this book many successful poems that don't rely on the device, and—as our brief discussion of Anglo-Saxon poetry suggests—the technique of end-rhyme consonance was not always part of the genre. Elegant rhyme, however, can make a poem feel connected and whole, and it often surprises the reader with an unexpected or evocative connection. The linkage between such words as *solitaire* and *easy chair* or *greenery* and *scenery* makes for a kind of equation—one word equals another in the mind's ear, and the echo enhances effect.

In the first such pairing, the rhyme comes in the final syllable: *aire* and *air*. In the second there's also **internal rhyme:** *green* and *scene* are rhyming words, and *greenery* and *scenery* sound therefore entirely alike. Had the words been *greenish* and *scenario,* there still would be internal rhyme but the sound of the whole would be changed. Poets have at their disposal many different variations of rhyme, and part of the pleasure of writing a poem derives from this choice of technique. So, too, should we as readers *notice* the use that has been made of rhyme.

> "Rhyme . . . is a form of relationship and connection, of encounter and metamorphosis. . . . There is something charged and magnetic about a good rhyme, something unsuspected and inevitable, utterly surprising and unforeseen and yet also binding and necessary. It is as if the poet called up the inner yearning for words to find each other." Conversation with Edward Hirsch

While we usually think of rhyme as solely a sound device, **eye rhyme** (also called **sight rhyme**) refers to words that share similar spellings but—when spoken—have different sounds. Words like "lint" and "pint" or "full" and "lull" exemplify eye rhyme, as does the final, sometimes confounding couplet of this old children's song:

The itsy bitsy spider climbed up the water spout
Down came the rain and washed the spider out
Out came the sun and dried up all the rain
And the itsy bitsy spider climbed up the spout again.

In contemporary English, *again* does not rhyme with *rain,* and so these lines may introduce kids to their first example of eye rhyme; in its original usage, however, the two words were likely true rhymes. In the seventeenth-century English speech of Shakespeare's time, it seems probable that the "o" in "love" and the "o" in "move" were pronounced in the same way, so when Prince Hamlet says "doubt that the sun doth move / but never doubt I love" he's using consonance, not dissonance, to make his point; how words look and how they sound are not always one and the same.

There are many variations of patterns available as rhyme—some that the ear can respond to, such as those of nursery rhymes or those of rhyming couplets. Most of us can also *hear* the echo in the first four lines *(AB/AB)* of Lord Byron's "She walks in beauty . . ." *(night/skies/bright/eyes)* (in this chapter) or the *AB/AB* in the first stanza of "Leda and the Swan" by William Butler Yeats (for the whole poem, see Chapter 19). In Yeats's poem, the god Zeus assumes the form of a swan and rapes the girl Leda, in the process fathering the famously beautiful Helen of Troy. Note that the rhyme scheme is less obvious than that of the Byron poem, and think of how the rhyming words differ (*still/bill* versus *caressed/ breast*).

A sudden blow: the great wings beating still	*a*
Above the staggering girl, her thighs caressed	*b*
By the dark webs, her nape caught in his bill,	*a*
He holds her helpless breast upon his breast.	*b*

Some rhyme schemes are more elaborate, such as the first lines of "Pied Beauty" (by Gerard Manley Hopkins, later in this chapter): *ABC/ABC*. In other cases—if a rhyme is eight or twelve lines distant—the ear is likely to fail to retain the sound as echo, though the eye might perhaps notice a repeated word. If, for instance, we write "many" again, you might remember that we used that word in the first sentence of the previous paragraph, but it probably won't function as an echoing *sound* (as would the words *found* or *ground*). The presence or absence of patterned repetition is a crucial factor in how a poem works.

"Sometimes . . . rhymes clink. The sound is too aggressive. I mean, if I ever have to read breath and death again, I think it will kill me. . . . Maybe because I'm a modern person, half rhymes often sound more beautiful to me than full rhymes. They . . . de-emphasize the rhyming and emphasize more the sound patterning and make it sound more natural." Conversation with Edward Hirsch

Slant rhyme (also called **near, imperfect,** or **off rhyme**) refers to a case in which vowel or consonant sounds are similar but not exactly the same. Examples include word combinations like

heap, rap, tape
aluminum, linoleum

In contrast to the vivid precision of exact rhymes, slant rhyme provides a subtler, sometimes natural-sounding correlation of sound. Yeats uses both exact (*still, bill*) and slant rhyme (*caressed, breast*) in "Leda and the Swan," and unlike Pope, Yeats does not use the end rhyme to create a hard stop at the close of each line but allows the sentence to spill over for a more natural sound. The use of exact, slant, or no rhyme contributes to the poem's voice, as does the way the rhyme fits into the sentence structure of the poem's individual lines.

Thomas Lynch also incorporates both exact and slant rhyme in "Iambs for the Day of Burial." Look at the first four lines of that poem, with the precise rhyming pattern of "best" and "stressed" and the slant rhyme of "body" and "tally." Then see how he repeats yet varies that pattern—ending with "forsaken" and "broken" as slant rhymes and "beatified" and "died" as perfect rhymes.

In Chapter 20, for example, we included Elizabeth Bishop's poem "The Fish" as a way of showing the use and value of clear, simple, direct American English. Marianne Moore uses a similar diction in her poem of the same title, "The Fish." Moore introduces rhyme into the poem in a way that plays with echoing: the ear hears *and/stand* and *green/submarine* as exact rhymes.

Marianne Moore (1887–1972)

Born near Saint Louis, Missouri, Marianne Moore was educated at Bryn Mawr College. She lived her adult life with her mother in New York City, where she was an ardent fan of the Dodgers (then located in the New York borough of Brooklyn). Although a modernist and contemporary of Ezra Pound, William Carlos Williams, and H. D., Moore refused to conform to any standard but her own. Her stanzas are unique, composed of lines that count syllables, rather than stresses, and that often hide their rhyme internally. A lover of animals, Moore often uses them or other everyday objects as a springboard for deeper exploration in her poems. In addition to actively publishing her poetry, Moore was an astute literary critic. Poets including Elizabeth Bishop, Richard Wilbur, and Randall Jarrell cite Moore as influential to their poetry.

AS YOU READ Watch for the way these lines mirror the motion of a swimming fish.

The Fish (1921)

wade
through black jade.
   Of the crow-blue mussel-shells, one keeps
   adjusting the ash-heaps;
5   opening and shutting itself like

an
injured fan.
   The barnacles which encrust the side
   of the wave, cannot hide
10   there for the submerged shafts of the

sun,
split like spun
    glass, move themselves with spotlight swiftness
    into the crevices—
15   in and out, illuminating

the
turquoise sea
    of bodies. The water drives a wedge
    of iron through the iron edge
20   of the cliff; whereupon the stars,

pink
rice-grains, ink-
    bespattered jelly-fish, crabs like green
    lilies, and submarine
25   toadstools, slide each on the other.

All
external
    marks of abuse are present on this
    defiant edifice—
30   all the physical features of

ac-
cident—lack
    of cornice, dynamite grooves, burns, and
    hatchet strokes, these things stand
35   out on it; the chasm-side is

dead.
Repeated
    evidence has proved that it can live
    on what can not revive
40   its youth. The sea grows old in it.

Writing from Reading

Summarize

1 Go through each stanza and indicate what is being described.

Analyze Craft

2 Discuss the use of exact rhyme in the poem with respect to the poem's shape. What contrast do you find between the traditional style of the rhyme scheme and the structure of the poem?

3 Are all the rhymes exact? What other varieties of rhyme do you see in the poem?

4 How does the hyphen in the word *accident* affect our usual expectations for that word? How does it set up the rhyme with *lack*?

Analyze Voice

5 "All the physical features"—as the poet puts it—announce themselves here; from the very first word and its immediate rhyme ("wade," then three words later, "jade") to the strange shape of the lines and stanzas, we are introduced to a particular way of seeing/saying, an individual use of language. How does this compare to Carroll's inventive language presented in traditional stanzas in "Jabberwocky"?

Synthesize Summary and Analysis

6 Go through the poem and "read" its rhyme scheme. Which rhymes seem surprising? Which seem to link words together as concepts?

Interpret the Poem

7 The arrangement of the poem—its rhythm, rhyme, and line lengths—takes center stage here. Based on the images and sounds with which Moore composes the poem, what "fishy" point is the poet trying to make?

Perhaps the leading exponent of slant rhyme in our literature is "the belle of Amherst," Emily Dickinson. The words *despair* and *fear* in the brief poem that follows are somehow enlarged and given a kind of kinship—though the poem considers their "difference"—by their associated sounds.

Emily Dickinson (1830–1886)

For a brief biography of Emily Dickinson, see the Case Study on Dickinson in Chapter 28.

AS YOU READ Try reading this poem aloud several times, allowing the meaning to emerge not just from the statements but also from the way they follow along in brief lines.

The difference between Despair (c. 1862)

The difference between Despair
And Fear—is like the One
Between the instant of a Wreck
And when the Wreck has been—

5 The Mind is smooth—no Motion—
Contented as the Eye
Upon the Forehead of a Bust—
That knows—it cannot see—

Writing from Reading

Summarize

1 How would you describe the difference between despair and fear?

Analyze Craft

2 What constitutes a "statement" in poetry as opposed to a message or statement in a document or newspaper story?

3 Find instances of consonance and assonance in the poem. How do they work to connect or unify the language in the poem?

Analyze Voice

4 Read this poem aloud. How would you describe the language? How does this description seem to fit or contrast with the poem's subject?

5 Notice the shift between the first stanza, in which the poet presents a

thought or idea, and the second, in which she focuses on the organ of thought. Can you explain the shift?

Synthesize Summary and Analysis

6 What kind of a wreck would the poet in her time be thinking of?

Interpret the Poem

7 How can "the Eye / Upon the Forehead of a Bust" know it cannot see?

Masculine rhyme (also **rising rhyme**) refers to end rhymes of polysyllabic words with a stressed final syllable, as in "remove" and "approve," and rhymes of monosyllabic words, like "good" and "wood." In contrast, **feminine rhyme** refers to rhymes between polysyllabic words in which the final syllable is unstressed. Examples include "bother" and "father" or "monkey" and "funky." A good poet is conscious of the distinction between masculine and feminine rhymes and the effects they produce. A **rhyme scheme** refers to the pattern of rhyme throughout a particular poem.

"When I started to realize that there were words that rhymed in English, it felt like magic to me. . . . I thought, wren and yarn must share something other than just words. So forever in my mind those tiny little birds and yarn were conflated: they shared not just names." Conversation with Li-Young Lee

For Review and Further Study

Julia Alvarez (b. 1950)

Woman's Work (1994)

Who says a woman's work isn't high art?
She'd challenge as she scrubbed the bathroom tiles.
Keep house as if the address were your heart.

We'd clean the whole upstairs before we'd start
5 downstairs. I'd sigh, hearing my friends outside.
Doing her woman's work was a hard art

to practice when the summer sun would bar
the floor I swept till she was satisfied.
She kept me prisoner in her housebound heart.

She'd shine the tines of forks, the wheels of carts,   10
cut lacy lattices for all her pies.
Her woman's work was nothing less than art.

And, I, her masterpiece since I was smart,
was primed, praised, polished, scolded and advised
to keep a house much better than my heart.   15

I did not want to be her counterpart!
I struck out . . . but became my mother's child:
a woman working at home on her art,
housekeeping paper as if it were her heart.

Questions for Interactive Reading and Writing

1. Look at the rhyme scheme here—the exact and slant rhymes. Notate the rhyme scheme. What influence does the rhyme scheme have on your understanding of the poem?

2. The speaker remembers her mother and her mother's domestic behavior. What does she herself practice as a "woman's work"? And how does this connect to the work of Seamus Heaney in "Digging"?

3. Is there a linkage here, or opposition, between the tasks of housekeeping and "her art"?

4. What is the significance of the line "And, I, her masterpiece since I was smart"?

William Blake (1757–1827)

For a brief biography of William Blake, see Chapter 22.

The Tyger (1794)

Tyger! Tyger! burning bright
In the forests of the night,
What immortal hand or eye
Could frame thy fearful symmetry?

5 In what distant deeps or skies
Burnt the fire of thine eyes?
On what wings dare he aspire?
What the hand dare sieze the fire?

And what shoulder, & what art,
10 Could twist the sinews of thy heart?
And when thy heart began to beat,
What dread hand? & what dread feet?

What the hammer? what the chain?
In what furnace was thy brain?
15 What the anvil? what dread grasp
Dare its deadly terrors clasp?

When the stars threw down their spears,
And water'd heaven with their tears,
Did he smile his work to see?
Did he who made the Lamb make thee?   20

Tyger! Tyger! burning bright
In the forests of the night,
What immortal hand or eye,
Dare frame thy fearful symmetry?

Questions for Interactive Reading and Writing

1. What is the rhyme scheme of the poem? How would you describe the effect it creates?

2. Describe the tone of this poem. What word choices help create this mood?

3. Explain the phrase "fearful symmetry." You might want to look up both words in a dictionary.

4. How does the Lamb in line 20 provide a meaningful counterpart to the Tyger?

George Gordon, Lord Byron (1788–1824)

For a brief biography of Lord Byron, see Chapter 19.

She Walks in Beauty (1815)

I

She walks in beauty, like the night
  Of cloudless climes and starry skies;
And all that's best of dark and bright
  Meet in her aspect and her eyes:
5 Thus mellowed to that tender light
  Which heaven to gaudy day denies.

II

One shade the more, one ray the less,
  Had half impaired the nameless grace
Which waves in every raven tress,
10 Or softly lightens o'er her face;
Where thoughts serenely sweet express
  How pure, how dear their dwelling place.

III

And on that cheek, and o'er that brow,
  So soft, so calm, yet eloquent,
15 The smiles that win, the tints that glow,
  But tell of days in goodness spent,
A mind at peace with all below,
  A heart whose love is innocent!

Questions for Interactive Reading and Writing

1. In the first stanza, how does the speaker justify comparing his love to a starry night? What does he suggest is wrong with the day?

2. The poem does not simply praise the beloved's physical beauty. What other qualities are portrayed here as contributing to her loveliness?

3. Describe the rhyme scheme. How does it contribute to a sense of beauty in the poem itself?

4. Earlier in this chapter, we highlighted the repetition of the "i" sound in the first stanza. What other examples of assonance and consonance do you see?

5. Underline every word that relates to light and dark. To what effect does the speaker keep this starting image of "dark and bright" through to the end of the poem?

Paul Laurence Dunbar (1872-1906)

For a brief biography of Paul Laurence Dunbar, see Chapter 21.

We Wear the Mask (1895)

We wear the mask that grins and lies,
It hides our cheeks and shades our eyes,—
This debt we pay to human guile;
With torn and bleeding hearts we smile,
And mouth with myriad subtleties.   5

Why should the world be over-wise,
In counting all our tears and sighs?
Nay, let them only see us, while
  We wear the mask.

We smile, but, O great Christ, our cries   10
To thee from tortured souls arise.
We sing, but oh the clay is vile
Beneath our feet, and long the mile;
But let the world dream otherwise,
  We wear the mask!   15

Questions for Interactive Reading and Writing

3. Describe the rhyme scheme of this poem. Is it regular? What kind of sound quality does it create?

Questions for Interactive Reading and Writing

1. What does the speaker mean by "wear the mask"? Are they really wearing a mask or is this a figurative phrase?

2. How would you describe the rhyme scheme of this poem? Where does it vary? What is the significance of those variations?

3. Given the tone of the poem, are we meant to see this mask-wearing positively or negatively?

A. E. Housman (1859–1936)

When I was one-and-twenty (1896)

When I was one-and-twenty
  I heard a wise man say,
"Give crowns and pounds and guineas
  But not your heart away;
5 Give pearls away and rubies
  But keep your fancy free."
But I was one-and-twenty,
  No use to talk to me.

When I was one-and-twenty
10   I heard him say again,
"The heart out of the bosom
  Was never given in vain;
'Tis paid with sighs a plenty
  And sold for endless rue."
15 And I am two-and-twenty,
  And oh, 'tis true, 'tis true.

Questions for Interactive Reading and Writing

1. Paraphrase the advice given in the poem. What do the last two lines suggest has happened to the speaker?

2. What is the significance of the speaker declaring his age?

Marilyn Nelson (b. 1946)

Chopin (1989)

It's Sunday evening. Pomp holds the receipts
of all the colored families on the Hill
in his wide lap, and shows which white store cheats
these patrons, who can't read a weekly bill.
His parlor's full of men holding their hats   5
and women who admire his girls' good hair.
Pomp warns them not to vote for Democrats,
controlling half of Hickman from his chair.
The varying degrees of cheating seen,
he nods toward the piano. Slender, tall,   10
a Fisk girl passing-white, almost nineteen,
his Blanche folds the piano's paisley shawl
and plays Chopin. And blessed are the meek
who have to buy in white men's stores next week.

Questions for Interactive Reading and Writing

1. Beyond the physical setting, there is the social and political situation. Based on the information in the poem, describe the place, the time, the social and political relations. Why, for example, is the rich man who "holds the receipts" called "Pomp"?

2. The rhyme scheme seems calm and yet appealing. Can we assume a similarity between the rhyme scheme and the piano piece referred to in the poem? Why is this possible?

3. What is the effect on the ironic tone of the poem of the use of the conjunctions—"and. . . . And . . ."—in the next-to-last line?

4. The sonnet form—invented by an Italian poet and perfected by an English genius, Shakespeare—gives us here a portrait of a moment in modern black American life. What seems universal about this poetic form? What seems particular to the time?

RHYTHM

When you hear the word *rhythm*, you most likely associate it with music. Popular hits on the radio, for example, engage you with their "beat"; you can dance (or at least tap your foot) to them. The best performers make songs more vivid at appropriate moments with hesitations and hastenings. Poets use *rhythm and meter* in much the same way as musicians do. The term *meter* may sound intimidating with its old-fashioned, mathematical connotation, but the rhythm in our language is actually very natural. Human beings are instinctively tuned to rhythm. It's tied to our heartbeat, our breathing, our walking, the passage of our days and weather, the way we learn to shoot a basketball or dance. The word *rhythm* comes from an ancient Greek term meaning "flow," or "recurring motion," which may after all these centuries still be the simplest way of defining the concept.

"**Meter comes from the word for measure, so the meters are measures of language in a line. . . . It is very different from music. It has to do with the pace of the language and how everything in the poem is about patterns of vowels, patterns of consonants, patterns of sounds, patterns of stresses . . . even if you can't quite hear the words or make them out . . . you hear a kind of beautiful . . . patterning of meaning.**" Conversation with Carolyn Forché

STRESSES AND PAUSES

The English language depends on rhythmical variation to create meaning even on a basic level. Whether conscious of it or not, we all tend to process the meaning of language through its patterns of sound emphasis. In other words, we don't ask a question like "HEY CAN I BORROW YOUR CAR TONIGHT?" with the same emphasis on each sound in the sentence. If we spoke like that, we'd sound like a robot from an old

"**The first way to study [a poem] is to say a poem out loud. . . . If you say those words out loud, . . . your breath pattern is flowing through your body in exactly the way it flowed through [the poet's body] when he said those words. . . . Poetry is [a] kind of existential breath sculpture.**" Conversation with Robert Hass

"There are different kinds of silences. There's a silence of mystery, then there's the silence of secrets—like 'I know something but I'm not telling.' Or there's the silence of 'I know something but I forgot what it is.' So there are all kinds of different silences, and they have different colors, and different ranges, and different depths, and different widths. I think in poetry we're using language a lot of times to inflect those different silences." Conversation with Li-Young Lee

science fiction movie. Instead, the sentence becomes a collection of subtly contrasting emphases, perhaps, "HEY, can I BORrow your CAR toNIGHT?" These changes are called **stresses** (or **accents**), the emphasis or "push" we put on the pitch (the musical quality), duration, or volume of a syllable.

The same emphasis on rhythmical sound gives meaning as much for a line or sentence as for a single word. Heroic couplets, for example, tend to be **end-stopped**—meaning they insist upon their rhyming emphasis and don't encourage the reader to continue without pause. **Enjambment** (from a French word meaning "stride" or "encroach") consists of the running-over of a phrase from one line into another, so that closely related words belong to different lines. This makes the rhythm of the sentence seem more closely akin to natural speech, and it's very often used in *open* or *free* verse (see Chapter 26.) A **caesura** is a pause, usually in the middle of a line, that marks a kind of rhythmic division—a place to catch your breath. All these are ways of organizing the sound and sense of poetry, *craft* in the service of *voice*.

We stress the *first* syllable when we say words like

BA
BAlance
STITCH
STITCHing
TEEN
TEENage

The second syllable of each word receives a stress in words like

beCAUSE
CAUSE
guiTAR
TAR
aROUND
ROUND

In combination, all these words in our language create diverse rhythmic sounds. Hence, **rhythm** refers to this sequence of stressed and unstressed sounds in a poem. The following three poems by Gwendolyn Books have an inescapable music. The five brief stanzas in "Sadie and Maud," for example, use perfect *B* rhymes in lines 2 and 4.

Gwendolyn Brooks (1917–2000)

For a brief biography of Gwendolyn Brooks, see Chapter 20.

AS YOU READ Notice the rhyme scheme and how it contributes to the singsong effect.

Sadie and Maud (1945)

Maud went to college.
Sadie stayed at home.
Sadie scraped life
With a fine-tooth comb.

5 She didn't leave a tangle in.
Her comb found every strand.
Sadie was one of the livingest chits
In all the land.

Sadie bore two babies
10 Under her maiden name.
Maud and Ma and Papa
Nearly died of shame.

When Sadie said her last so-long
Her girls struck out from home.
15 (Sadie had left as heritage
Her fine-tooth comb.)

Maud, who went to college,
Is a thin brown mouse.
She is living all alone
20 In this old house.

Southeast Corner (1945)

The School of Beauty's a tavern now.
The Madam is underground.
Out at Lincoln, among the graves.
Her own is early found.
5   Where the thickest, tallest monument
Cuts grandly into the air
The Madam lies, contentedly.
Her fortune, too, lies there,
Converted into cool hard steel
10 And right red velvet lining;
While over her tan impassivity
Shot silk is shining.

A Song in the Front Yard (1945)

I've stayed in the front yard all my life.
I want a peek at the back
Where it's rough and untended and hungry weed grows.
A girl gets sick of a rose.

5   I want to go in the back yard now
And maybe down the alley,
To where the charity children play.
I want a good time today.

They do some wonderful things.
10 They have some wonderful fun.
My mother sneers, but I say it's fine
How they don't have to go in at quarter to nine.
My mother, she tells me that Johnnie Mae
Will grow up to be a bad woman.
15 That George'll be taken to Jail soon or late
(On account of last winter he sold our back gate).

But I say it's fine. Honest, I do.
And I'd like to be a bad woman, too,
And wear the brave stockings of night-black lace
20 And strut down the streets with paint on my face.

Writing from Reading

Summarize

1 What is the subject of each poem? What are the similarities and differences in these subjects?

Analyze Craft

2 Describe the poems' rhythms. Are the poems in a tightly controlled metrical form, or do they sound more like natural speech? Why do you think this is?

Analyze Voice

3 "Ma and Papa" are referred to the way that Sadie might say it, for example, in "Sadie and Maud" and not as "mother and father." Find instances in "Southeast Corner" and "On the Front Porch" where dialect is used. How does this technique contribute to the tone of the whole in these poems?

Synthesize Summary and Analysis

4 The critic Harold Bloom has said, "[Gwendolyn Brooks] felt more comfortable at home than at school. She often sat on the front porch, daydreaming...." Do you see this attitude in her poems?

5 Each poem tells a story of hardship as well as of a kind of pleasure. How does the rhyme scheme affect your reading of the poem's subject matter?

Interpret the Poem

6 Fairy tales and nursery rhymes often deal in opposition—think, for example, of the story of the city mouse and the country mouse or the tortoise and the hare. What moral here—if any—does Brooks suggest we draw from "Sadie and Maud"? What are the morals in each of these poems?

METER

Meter refers to a sequence of stressed and unstressed syllables that forms an essentially regular pattern in lines of poetry. A poem's meter functions like the bass line or drumbeat to a piece of music, keeping time and arranging a poem's sounds. One unique feature of poetry (as compared, for example, with fiction) is that these rhythmic stresses are often arranged in specific intervals. We measure these patterns of stresses to understand how poets shape, simultaneously, their sound and the reader's understanding. The unit of measurement with which we examine meter is called a **foot,** usually a group of two or three syllables containing a single stress. This study is a component of **prosody,** the analysis of a poem's rhythm and metrical structures.

SCANSION

Scansion is the process of determining the metrical pattern of a **line** of poetry by marking its stresses and feet. We most often use a slash (/) to mark a stressed syllable and a tilde (˘) to indicate an unstressed syllable. Also, we use a vertical line (|)—sometimes through a word, when needed—to mark divisions between feet.

```
   ˘    /    ˘    /    ˘   /    ˘    /    ˘  /
When I | have fears | that I | may cease | to be
```

The most common foot in English and American poetry is the **iambic foot,** an unstressed syllable followed by a stressed syllable, as in the word *subLIME*.

The following chart notes the four chief metrical feet in poetry in English.

COMMON METRICAL FEET

FOOT/VERSE FORM	STRESSES	EXAMPLE
iamb/iambic	~ /	beCAUSE; and THEN
trochee/trochaic	/ ~	Evil; PIZZa
anapest/anapestic	~ ~ /	underSTAND; in the EAST
dactyl/dactylic	/ ~ ~	MErrily; HAPPening

Other, less common syllable patterns include **spondees** (two stressed syllables), **pyrrhics** (two unstressed syllables), **amphibrachs** (three syllables: unstressed, stressed, unstressed), and **cretic** or **amphimacer** (three syllables: stressed, unstressed, stressed).

> **"The only reason we scan is so that we can learn to hear it, learn to hear that music when we read, and learn to hear what poetry's music is."** Conversation with Carolyn Forché

We also measure meter by the number of feet a line of poetry contains. The name of the foot combines with the number of feet; this constitutes the overall metrical form of a poem.

NUMBER OF FEET PER LINE

monometer: one foot	**pentameter:** five feet
dimeter: two feet	**hexameter:** six feet
trimeter: three feet	**heptameter:** seven feet
tetrameter: four feet	**octameter:** eight feet

When discussing the meter of a poem, we combine the type of metrical foot used in a poem with the number of feet in a line. So, for example, we use the term *iambic pentameter* to refer to a line of poetry with five iambs.

COMMON METRIC PATTERNS

- **Iambic pentameter** is a line with five iambs as in this line: "When I have fears that I may cease to be . . ." —*John Keats*
- **Blank verse** refers to lines of unrhymed iambic pentameter. Used in dramatic Renaissance poetry, it has lasted through the centuries and found its way into the work of such modernists as Robert Frost, Wallace Stevens, and Elizabeth Bishop.
- **Iambic tetrameter** is a line containing four iambs: "Because I could not stop for death . . ." —*Emily Dickinson*
- **Trochaic tetrameter** is a line containing four trochees. Here are two trochaic tetrameter lines from the poem "The Song of Hiawatha": "Heavy with the heat and silence / Grew the afternoon of Summer . . ." —*Henry Wadsworth Longfellow*
- **Anapestic trimeter** is a line that contains three anapests, as in each of these lines from "The Solitude of Alexander Selkirk": "From the center all round to the sea / I am lord of the fowl and the brute . . ." —*William Cowper*
- **Dactylic tetrameter** is a line that contains four dactyls, as in each of these flowing lines from "The Lost Leader": "Just for a handful of silver he left us, / Just for a riband to stick in his coat. . . ." —*Robert Browning*

"Poetry comes from a time when we didn't have all this electronic gear and screens and so forth. You had the human body and the human voice. . . . You know, the word 'foot' in poetry comes from the days when people would actually dance so that you measured what was said by bodily movements. I think it will always be that way for . . . people who really cut past all the intellectual trappings of poetry and get back to the emotions." Conversation with Al Young

The following light poem by Samuel Taylor Coleridge demonstrates, in sound, the various kinds of metrical feet while it simultaneously explains them. Coleridge may seem pedantic in his definitions, but in his time he could take words such as *Amphibrachys* and *Amphimacer* for granted, and he's being playful here.

Samuel Taylor Coleridge (1772–1834)

One of the leading poets of the Romantic period in England, Samuel Taylor Coleridge first planned with Robert Southey—future Poet Laureate—to begin a utopian society in Pennsylvania. When their plans fell through, Coleridge turned to a writing career. In 1797 he forged a close friendship with William Wordsworth. The two published *Lyrical Ballads,* the seminal work of the Romantic period in which Coleridge's famous "The Rime of the Ancient Mariner" first appeared. Coleridge is also known for pioneering the form of "conversation poems"—poems that begin with a speaker addressing somebody in the present and then follow the mind as it travels in meditation before returning to the present. "The Eolian Harp" and "This Lime-Tree Bower My Prison" are prime examples. Coleridge gave lectures and drew a small following as a talented conversationalist until his death in 1834.

AS YOU READ   See if you can scan this poem with a pencil to find the stresses and feet.

Trochee trips from long to short (1806)

Trochee trips from long to short;
From long to long in solemn sort
Slow Spondee stalks; strong foot! yet ill able
Ever to come up with Dactyl's trisyllable.
5 Iambics march from short to long;—
With a leap and a bound the swift Anapests throng;
One syllable long, with one short at each side,
Amphibrachys hastes with a stately stride;—
First and last being long, middle short, Amphimacer
10 Strikes his thundering hoofs like a proud high-bred Racer.

If Derwent be innocent, steady, and wise,
And delight in the things of earth, water, and skies;
Tender warmth at his heart, with these metres to show it,
With sound sense in his brains, may make Derwent a poet,—
15 May crown him with fame, and must win him the love
Of his father on earth and his Father above.
   My dear, dear child!
Could you stand upon Skiddaw, you would not from its whole ridge
See a man who so loves you as your fond S. T. Coleridge.

Writing from Reading

Summarize

1 What might have prompted the poet to write this playful but instructive treatment of rhyme schemes?

Analyze Craft

2 Define each of the rhythms as Coleridge outlines them.

Analyze Voice

3 Who is the person—the poet—behind these lines?

Synthesize Summary and Analysis

4 The poet reenacts the basic meters of poetry. Does he follow Pope (see the excerpt from "An Essay on Criticism" earlier in this chapter) in this?

Interpret the Poem

5 What is the meaning of this poem beyond the instructional purpose?

METRICAL VARIATION

After all this discussion about the balancing act between rhythm and meter, it may sound strange (or even frustrating) to hear that poets writing in formal structures are often liable to break free occasionally of their own chosen metrical form. As the poet Paul Muldoon once wrote, "Form is a straitjacket the way that a straitjacket was a straitjacket for Houdini." In comparing rhythm, rhyme, and meter to a famous magician's escape act, Muldoon suggests that the traditional formal constraints can be used purposefully and then evaded; *too* regular a use of rhythm and meter can be dull. **Doggerel,** an obviously patterned piece of rhyme, can sometimes seem almost childish and, when extensive, boring; these are rules that can be broken once they have been learned.

Sound can speed a poem's language up ("reeling round and round") or slow it down ("steadfast, he stood up straight"). In the poem by Gerard Manley Hopkins that follows, note the repeated consonants. "Swift" and "slow," "sweet" and "sour" might seem to have opposite meanings, but they are connected by sound; alliteration yokes together the variety of images Hopkins celebrates in the natural world. In the first stanza, "glory" links in sound to "God," and "couple-color" achieves its comparison to "cow" through both sound and sight. So, alliteration not only increases the musicality of the poem but also helps unify the language of a poem that is, itself, *about* unity. Hopkins employs a rhythm that imitates ordinary speech by putting stresses on words that would not be stressed in consistent metrical patterns. The metrical variation of Hopkins's poem—and his work in general—is what he called *sprung verse,* and it's a perfect example of change within consistency.

Gerard Manley Hopkins (1844–1889)

An English poet of the Victorian era, Gerard Manley Hopkins is often grouped with the Modernist poets because of his innovative poetic form. Hopkins was educated at the University of Oxford and began writing verse there. Three years into his education, he converted to Roman Catholicism and burned his poetry, fearing it interfered with his devotion to God. Seven years later, when a shipwreck killed five nuns, Hopkins asked permission from the church to write a poem commemorating the occurrence. From 1876 onward, Hopkins wrote poems that show God's presence and design in every earthly thing, in verses of sprung meter. Hopkins's poetic ear is almost unparalleled, but rather than court literary celebrity, he spent his life as a priest and a teacher. His poetry was not published until thirty years after his premature death from typhoid fever.

AS YOU READ   Think about the effects of sound on your understanding of a poem's descriptions and overall meaning. Read the poem silently, then aloud. Consider how your perceptions change.

Pied Beauty (1877)

Glory be to God for dappled things—
  For skies of couple-color as a brinded cow;
    For rose-moles all in stipple upon trout that swim;
Fresh-firecoal chestnut-falls; finches' wings;
5 Landscape plotted and pieced—fold, fallow, and plough;
    And all trades, their gear and tackle and trim.

All things counter, original, spare, strange;
  Whatever is fickle, freckled (who knows how?)
    With swift, slow; sweet, sour; adazzle, dim;
10 He fathers-forth whose beauty is past change:
    Praise him.

Writing from Reading

Summarize

1 Think of this poem as a kind of sermon delivered by Father Hopkins. What does he urge his readership or congregation to do? What does the word *Pied* mean?

Analyze Craft

2 We noted that "swift" and "slow," "sweet" and "sour" seem to have opposite meanings, but are connected here by sound. What other examples of alliteration can you find in the poem? Do they work in a similar manner?

Analyze Voice

3 In the first stanza "glory" links in sound to "God" and "couple-color" achieves its comparison to "cow" both sonically and visually. Locate other examples of this technique. How does this sonorous connection emphasize the speaker's praise in this poem?

Synthesize Summary and Analysis

4 The last two words here are simple—monosyllabic—and solemn. If you were to recite this poem, would the last line be quiet or loud?

Interpret the Poem

5 How does alliteration not only increase the musicality of the poem but also help demonstrate that "Pied Beauty" is, itself, *about* unity?

For Review and Further Study

Anonymous
Scottish Ballad (1750)

Bonnie Barbara Allan

It was in and about the Martinmas time,
    When the green leaves were afalling,
That Sir John Graeme, in the West Country,
    Fell in love with Barbara Allan.

5 He sent his men down through the town,
    To the place where she was dwelling:
"Oh haste and come to my master dear,
    Gin ye be Barbara Allan."

O hooly, hooly rose she up,
    To the place where he was lying,   10
And when she drew the curtain by:
    "Young man, I think you're dying."

"O it's I'm sick, and very, very sick,
    And 'tis a' for Bonnie Allan."—
"O the better for me ye's never be,   15
    Tho your heart's blood were aspilling."

"O dinna ye mind, young man," she said,
    "When ye was in the tavern adrinking,
That ye made the health gae round and round,
    And slighted Barbara Allan?"   20

He turned his face unto the wall,
    And death was with him dealing:
"Adieu, adieu, my dear friends all,
    And be kind to Barbara Allan."

25 And slowly, slowly raise her up,
   And slowly, slowly left him,
 And sighing said she could not stay,
   Since death of life had reft him.

 She had not gane a mile but twa,
30   When she heard the dead-bell ringing,
 And every jow that the dead-bell geid,
   It cried, "Woe to Barbara Allan!"

 "O mother, mother, make my bed!
   O make it saft and narrow!
35 Since my love died for me today,
   I'll die for him tomorrow."

Questions for Interactive Reading and Writing

1. This poem has often been set to music and performed—what in its *sound* feels like *song?*
2. Do the repetitions here enhance or undermine tone?
3. Paraphrase this story in prose. What, if anything, is gained, and what gets lost?

John Donne (1572–1631)

Hymn to God, My God, in My Sickness (1633)

Since I am coming to that Holy room,
   Where, with Thy choir of saints for evermore,
 I shall be made Thy music; as I come
   I tune the instrument here at the door,
5   And what I must do then, think here before;

 Whilst my physicians by their love are grown
   Cosmographers, and I their map, who lie
 Flat on this bed, that by them may be shown
   That this is my south-west discovery,
10   Per fretum febris, by these straits to die;

I joy, that in these straits I see my west;
   For, though those currents yield return to none,
 What shall my west hurt me? As west and east
   In all flat maps—and I am one—are one,
   So death doth touch the resurrection.   15

Is the Pacific sea my home? Or are
   The eastern riches? Is Jerusalem?
 Anyan, and Magellan, and Gibraltar?
   All straits, and none but straits, are ways to them
   Whether where Japhet dwelt, or Cham, or Shem.   20

We think that Paradise and Calvary,
   Christ's cross and Adam's tree, stood in one place;
 Look, Lord, and find both Adams met in me;
   As the first Adam's sweat surrounds my face,
   May the last Adam's blood my soul embrace.   25

So, in His purple wrapp'd, receive me, Lord;
   By these His thorns, give me His other crown;
 And as to others' souls I preach'd Thy word,
   Be this my text, my sermon to mine own,
   "Therefore that He may raise, the Lord throws down."   30

Questions for Interactive Reading and Writing

1. What is the occasion for the poem?
2. What is the meter of this poem? Is it consistent throughout? If not, are the variations significant?
3. What overarching metaphors does Donne employ? Do they work together or seem contradictory?
4. What pun does he make on the word *straits*? What does he mean by "first Adam" and "last Adam"?
5. Is "death doth touch" in line 15 an example of assonance?
6. Where does the "turn" of the poem occur? What does the poet mean by "my sermon to mine own"?
7. How does the speaker's sickness and impending death become, for him, a triumph?

Bob Dylan (b. 1941)

The Times They Are a-Changin' (1963)

Come gather 'round people
Wherever you roam
And admit that the waters
Around you have grown
5　And accept it that soon
You'll be drenched to the bone
If your time to you
Is worth savin'
Then you better start swimmin'
10　Or you'll sink like a stone
For the times they are a-changin'.

Come writers and critics
Who prophesize with your pen
And keep your eyes wide
15　The chance won't come again
And don't speak too soon
For the wheel's still in spin
And there's no tellin' who
That it's namin'.
20　For the loser now
Will be later to win
For the times they are a-changin'.

Come senators, congressmen
Please heed the call
25　Don't stand in the doorway
Don't block up the hall
For he that gets hurt
Will be he who has stalled
There's a battle outside
30　And it is ragin'.
It'll soon shake your windows
And rattle your walls
For the times they are a-changin'.

Come mothers and fathers
Throughout the land　　　　　　　　　35
And don't criticize
What you can't understand
Your sons and your daughters
Are beyond your command
Your old road is　　　　　　　　　40
Rapidly agin'.
Please get out of the new one
If you can't lend your hand
For the times they are a-changin'.

The line it is drawn　　　　　　　　　45
The curse it is cast
The slow one now
Will later be fast
As the present now
Will later be past　　　　　　　　　50
The order is
Rapidly fadin'.
And the first one now
Will later be last
For the times they are a-changin'.　　　55

Questions for Interactive Reading and Writing

1. What is the dominant foot in this poem? What kind of feel does that create?

2. What ironic reversals does this song predict? How do these further the message of this call to action?

3. Describe the diction in this poem. Does the diction fit with the fact that this was a popular song?

John Keats (1795–1821)

For a brief biography of John Keats, see Chapter 20.

La Belle Dame sans Merci (1819)

Ah, what can ail thee, wretched wight,
　　Alone and palely loitering?
The sedge is wither'd from the lake,
　　And no birds sing.

5 Ah, what can ail thee, wretched wight,
　　So haggard and so woe-begone?
The squirrel's granary is full,
　　And the harvest's done.

I see a lily on thy brow,
10　　With anguish moist and fever dew;
And on thy cheek a fading rose
　　Fast withereth too.

I met a lady in the meads
　　Full beautiful—a faery's child;
15 Her hair was long, her foot was light,
　　And her eyes were wild.

I set her on my pacing steed,
　　And nothing else saw all day long,
For sideways would she lean, and sing
20　　A faery's song.

I made a garland for her head,
　　And bracelets too, and fragrant zone;
She look'd at me as she did love,
　　And made sweet moan.

25 She found me roots of relish sweet,
　　And honey wild, and manna dew;
And sure in language strange she said—
　　"I love thee true."

She took me to her elfin grot,
30　　And there she gazed, and sighed deep,
And there I shut her wild wild eyes
　　So kiss'd to sleep.

And there we slumber'd on the moss,
　　And there I dream'd—Ah! woe betide!
35 The latest dream I ever dream'd
　　On the cold hill side.

I saw pale kings, and princes too,
　　Pale warriors, death-pale were they all;
They cried—"La Belle Dame sans Merci
40　　Hath thee in thrall!"

I saw their starved lips in the gloam,
　　With horrid warning gaped wide,
And I awoke, and found me here
　　On the cold hill side.

And this is why I sojourn here,　　　　　　45
　　Alone and palely loitering,
Though the sedge is wither'd from the lake,
　　And no birds sing.

Questions for Interactive Reading and Writing

1. Who are the two speakers in this poem? Where does the "I" change from referring to speaker one to referring to speaker two?

2. Read the poem aloud and listen to the fourth line of each stanza. How does the meter differ from what you expect to be there? What might this difference suggest?

3. How does Keats use nature imagery differently in stanza 3 than he does in the first two stanzas? Why is the knight described in these natural terms?

4. Paraphrase the story this poem tells. What might the Belle Dame sans Merci represent?

5. Given the definition of "ballad," how well does this poem fit the ballad form? Why might Keats have chosen such an old form for this particular story?

Audre Lorde (1934–1992)

The Electric Slide Boogie (1993)

New Year's Day 1:16 AM
and my body is weary beyond
time to withdraw and rest
ample room allowed me in everyone's head
but community calls　　　　　　　　　　5
right over the threshold
drums beating through the walls
children playing their truck dramas
under the collapsible coatrack
in the narrow hallway outside my room　　10

The TV lounge next door is wide open
it is midnight in Idaho
and the throb easy subtle spin
of the electric slide boogie
15 step-stepping
around the corner of the parlor
past the sweet clink
of dining room glasses
and the edged aroma of slightly overdone
20 dutch-apple pie
all laced together
with the rich dark laughter
of Gloria
and her higher-octave sisters

25 How hard it is to sleep
in the middle of life.

Questions for Interactive Reading and Writing

1. Does this poem have a sense of meter? Describe how the poem sounds, and tell how this fits the subject matter.

2. How would you describe the holiday spirit of the poem, given the time the poet reveals in it?

3. What elements does the poet use to capture "the throb easy subtle spin" of the dance?

4. What are the greatest contrasting images of the poem?

5. Are the last two lines a complaint or a celebration?

Edgar Allan Poe (1809–1849)

For a brief biography of Edgar Allan Poe, see Chapter 10.

Annabel Lee (1849)

It was many and many a year ago,
   In a kingdom by the sea,
That a maiden there lived whom you may know
   By the name of Annabel Lee;
And this maiden she lived with no other thought   5
   Than to love and be loved by me.

She was a child and *I* was a child,
   In this kingdom by the sea,
But we loved with a love that was more than love—
   I and my Annabel Lee—   10
With a love that the wingéd seraphs of Heaven
   Coveted her and me.

And this was the reason that, long ago,
   In this kingdom by the sea,
A wind blew out of a cloud by night   15
   Chilling my Annabel Lee;
So that her highborn kinsmen came
   And bore her away from me,
To shut her up in a sepulchre
   In this kingdom by the sea.   20

The angels, not half so happy in Heaven,
   Went envying her and me:
Yes! that was the reason (as all men know,
   In this kingdom by the sea)
That the wind came out of the cloud, chilling   25
   And killing my Annabel Lee.

But our love it was stronger by far than the love
    Of those who were older than we—
    Of many far wiser than we—
30 And neither the angels in Heaven above
    Nor the demons down under the sea,
Can ever dissever my soul from the soul
    Of the beautiful Annabel Lee:

For the moon never beams without bringing me dreams
35   Of the beautiful Annabel Lee;
And the stars never rise but I see the bright eyes
    Of the beautiful Annabel Lee;
And so, all the night-tide, I lie down by the side
Of my darling, my darling, my life and my bride,
40   In her sepulchre there by the sea—
    In her tomb by the side of the sea.

Questions for Interactive Reading and Writing

1. What does the speaker cite as the reason for Annabel Lee's death?

2. Describe the meter of the poem. How does it affect the sound of the poem?

3. Lines, sounds, and ideas are all repeated. Identify instances of repetition and explain the effect of so much recurrence.

4. What is the speaker's mood? How does the imagery play a role in setting the mood?

"It's learning another language—the language of traditional poetry. . . . Metrical writing creates a certain kind of frame that marks things as a traditional poem: as a poem. That's one of the ways you know it's a poem." Conversation with Edward Hirsch

Reading for Sound, Rhyme, and Rhythm

When reading for *sound*, *rhyme*, and *rhythm*, examine how the sounds of the words work together with rhyme and rhythm to draw the reader into the poem and shape its meaning.

What kinds of words has the poet chosen (monosyllabic or polysyllabic, harsh or melodious)?	*Euphony:* musically pleasing poetic language	EXAMPLE "She walks in beauty, like the night / Of cloudless climes and starry skies / And all that's best of dark and bright / Meet in her aspect and her eyes."
	Cacophony: harsh-sounding poetic language	EXAMPLE "Sweeping from butchers stalls, dung, guts, and blood, / Drowned puppies, stinking sprats, all drenched in mud / Dead cats and turnip-tops, come tumbling down the flood."
Has the poet used the repetition of consonant or vowel sounds in the poem?	*Alliteration:* repetition of the initial consonant sounds of nearby words	EXAMPLE I'm *r*ight as *r*ain, *r*eading in my *r*oom.
	Consonance: repetition of consonants or consonant patterns in neighboring words	EXAMPLE Ca*l*m*l*y he ca*ll*ed to the mu*l*e in the o*l*d fie*l*d.
	Assonance: repetition of vowel sounds or vowel patterns in neighboring words	EXAMPLE The r*ai*n c*a*me again, *sa*me as yesterd*a*y.
Do words in the poem sound like what they represent?	*Onomatopoeia:* use of words that imitate the sounds they refer to	EXAMPLE *Snap, crackle, pop*

Is rhyme used in the poem?	*Is there rhyme within the lines?* *Internal rhyme:* rhyming between words in the same line, or words in the middle of two different phrases	EXAMPLE "the *grains* beyond *age,* the dark *veins* of her mother"
	Does the rhyme come at the end of the lines? *End rhyme:* rhyming sounds that conclude lines of poetry	EXAMPLE "The itsy bitsy spider climbed up the water *spout* / Down came the rains and washed the spider *out*"
	Which syllable of the end word is stressed? *Masculine rhyme:* end rhyme between polysyllabic words with a stressed final syllable, or between monosyllabic words.	EXAMPLE "I showed admirable re*move* / but mom did not ap*prove.*"
	Feminine rhyme: end rhyme between polysyllabic words with unstressed final syllables	EXAMPLE "Making money's a *bother* / so I just ask *father.*"
	Are the sounds in the rhyme identical? **Identical:** *Exact rhyme:* rhyme in which the end sounds of words are identical	EXAMPLE "bat" and "cat"
	Not identical: *Slant rhyme:* rhyme in which the sounds are similar but do not rhyme	EXAMPLE "cat" and "barette"
	Eye rhyme: words that are spelled similarly but do not rhyme	EXAMPLE "lint" and "pint"

Where do the lines break, where does the poem speed up, and where does it slow down?	*End-stopped lines:* lines that don't encourage the reader to continue without pause *Enjambment:* running-over of a phrase from one line into another, so that closely related words belong to different lines	EXAMPLE "Trochee trips from long to short; / From long to long in solemn sort" EXAMPLE "Is the Pacific Sea my home? Or is / Jerusalem? pondered John Donne"
How do sounds work together in a line to create a rhythm of stressed and unstressed syllables?	*What pattern of stresses has the poet used to shape the sound of the lines in a poem?* ˘ / ˘ / ˘ / ˘ / ˘ / "Of all our private parts the heart knows best"	
How are the stressed and unstressed syllables grouped together in a line?	**Foot** **Marks** *Iamb* ˘ / *Trochee* / ˘ *Anapest* ˘ ˘ / *Dactyl* / ˘ ˘	EXAMPLE be'*cause,* and' *then* *e'*vil, *pi'*zza un'der'*stand,* in' the' *east* *mer'*ri'ly, *hap'*pen'ing
What is the meter of the line?	*Count the number of feet in a line to determine the meter.* Common meters include: *Monometer:* one foot *Dimeter:* two feet *Trimeter:* three feet *Tetrameter:* four feet *Pentameter:* five feet *Hexameter:* six feet *Heptameter:* seven feet *Octameter:* eight feet	EXAMPLE "Of all our private parts the heart knows best" is five iambic feet; five feet = *pentameter.*

| Is there inconsistent meter (metrical variation) in the poem? | *Sprung verse:* rhythm that imitates ordinary speech by putting stresses on words that would not be stressed in consistent metrical patterns | EXAMPLE "Whatever is fickle, freckled (who knows how?)" |

Writing about Sound, Rhyme, and Rhythm

1. Compare the sounds of the language in Thomas Lynch's "Iambs for the Day of Burial" and Seamus Heaney's "Digging."

2. Consider how sound underscores the subject and themes of Gwendolyn Brooks's "Sadie and Maud" and Julia Alvarez's "Women's Work"; both use plainspoken language. Examine how the rhythm of each poem affects (or changes) the reader's understanding of this plainspoken tone.

3. Examine the use of sonic effects of alliteration, assonance, consonance, onomatopoeia, and/or other effects in John Keats's "Bright Star . . ." and Gerard Manley Hopkins's "Pied Beauty."

4. Look at the poems in this chapter by Marianne Moore, Alexander Pope, and Samuel Taylor Coleridge. Discuss the ways their subject is self-reflexive (a poem about poetry itself).

5. Find a metered poem in this chapter (or another in the book) and identify places where the poet varies the rhythm. Comment on the purpose and the effect of this variation.

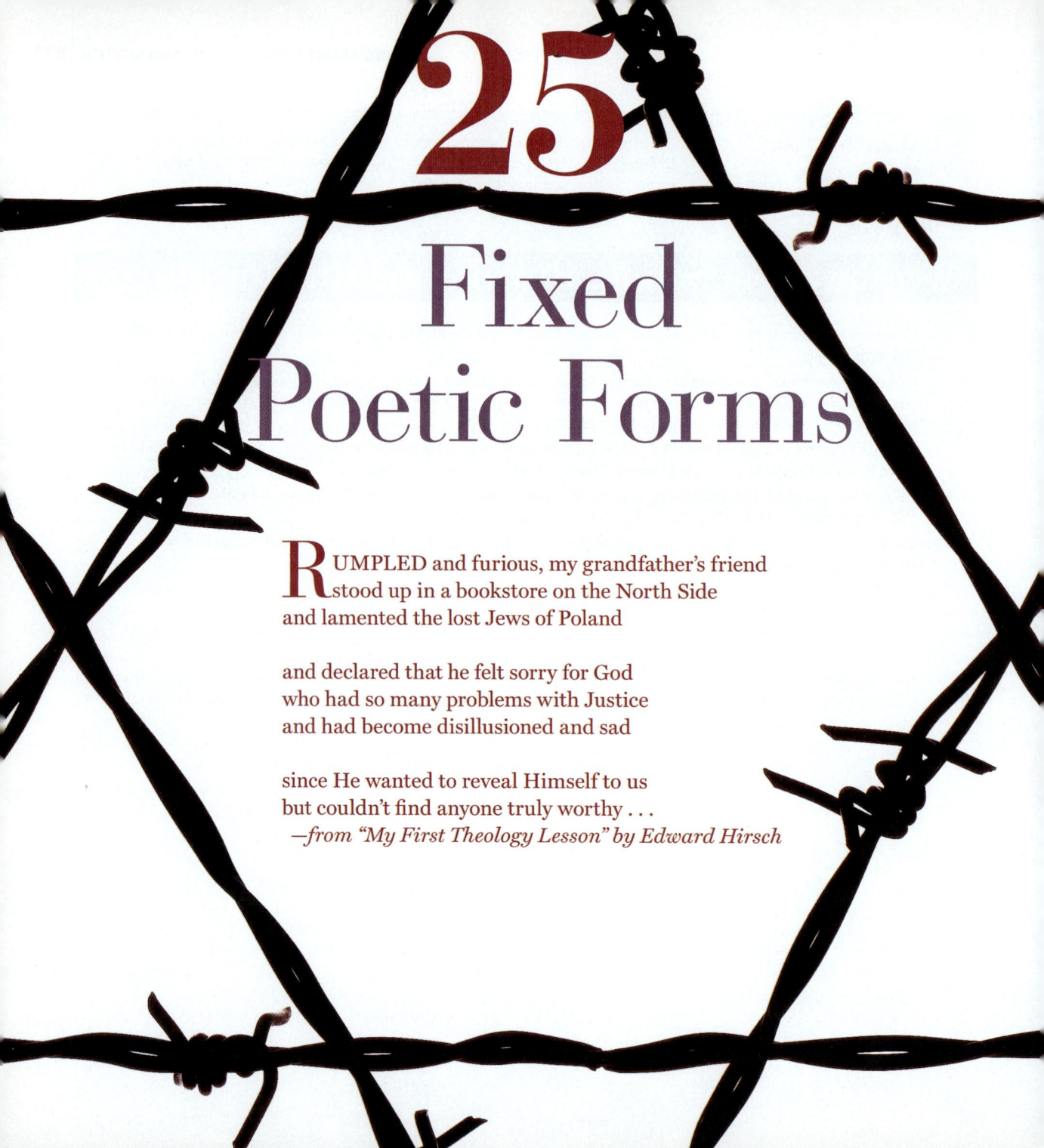

25

Fixed Poetic Forms

RUMPLED and furious, my grandfather's friend
stood up in a bookstore on the North Side
and lamented the lost Jews of Poland

and declared that he felt sorry for God
who had so many problems with Justice
and had become disillusioned and sad

since He wanted to reveal Himself to us
but couldn't find anyone truly worthy . . .
—*from "My First Theology Lesson" by Edward Hirsch*

COMPOSING

Composing "My First Theology Lesson" in a poetic form that's been a fixture in literature for more than 700 years, Edward Hirsch shapes an episode from his childhood on the North Side of Chicago.

Gathered for conversation in a bookstore, a group of Jewish men (including the poet's grandfather) listen as a colleague angrily laments the apparent retreat of God from the modern world. In the wake of the twentieth century's violence and the savagery of the Holocaust—the extermination of six million Jews by the Nazis during World War II— God has seemingly withdrawn, unable to find "anyone truly worthy" to receive Him on the earth. This is the position maintained by the grandfather's "furious . . . friend." For the poem's speaker, recollecting the argument many years later, this lament constitutes an early lesson on the nature of religion.

Before committing any idea or memory to verse, poets begin, literally, with an infinite number of possibilities for framing their ideas on the page. In this case, Hirsch weds his poetic intention to the shape and form of the sonnet, a fourteen-line poem traditionally associated with argumentation and persuasion. As he points out in the interview, "The thing that seems to identify [a sonnet] as a sonnet is a structural principle. Some kind of argument is set up and resolved or refuted or avoided."

In trying to re-create a passionate discussion about the nature of God, Hirsch uses a form that matches his purposes ideally. "So here I have," he says, "a . . . kind of furious argument, and here I've got to try and tame it. . . . I've got to find a way to formalize it so that someone else can experience what I experienced. And here the sonnet form helped me."

For much of poetry's millennia-old lifetime, poets have been attracted to set patterns in which to arrange their work. Historically these patterns have served different purposes. To begin with, poets echoed formal designs observable by artists in nature. In turn, the patterns followed the music of religious rituals that celebrate natural cycles; these ritual observances were often expressed as poetry. Also, the means for writing language down and reading it aloud haven't previously been as accessible as is today's familiar word-processing technology. Thus, on a more practical level, formal structures served as early mnemonic devices—mental tools for storing and remembering the hundreds of lines a poet might need to recall in a public performance.

The word *poem* comes from an ancient Greek expression meaning "something made"; the different ways poets *construct* their poems are therefore fundamental to our understanding of the genre. As you'll see, the meaning of a poem and the arrangement of its language combine in a kind of marriage of structure and purpose.

Edward Hirsch

Sometimes you want to capture something that's more complicated.

Conversation on Writing

How to Think about Form: The Sonnet

A form like the sonnet . . . exists in poetry not just because some people like me like to write them. . . . It must be serving some kind of function. . . . Otherwise it would die out. They're just too hard, these forms. They're too hard to write. They take too much thinking. There must be a reason for them; otherwise they'd just collapse. . . . And . . . the thing that seems to identify [a sonnet] as a sonnet is a structural principle. Some kind of argument is set up and resolved or refuted or avoided.

Why Can't You Just Say What You Mean?

Why can't you just say what you mean? . . . Well, there are a lot of reasons. . . . Sometimes you want to capture something that's more complicated. You don't just love your father; you love your father, but you also hate him. You love him and you hate him at the same time. . . . If you just tell them, it doesn't mean anything. . . . But in a poem you can capture that combination of feelings.

The Poetry in Our Lives

Poems take place in our lives . . . because we're human and we're trying to explain and understand what it means to be alive. They're not there so teachers can get you to memorize what the nature of a poetic form is. They're not there for medicinal purposes, to cure you of something. . . . They're there . . . to help you think about what it means to love someone, and what it means to be dying, and what it means to have someone dying on you, and what it means to dislike someone, and what it means to be enraged . . . complicated and multiple [feelings that] have all kinds of nuances.

To watch this entire interview and hear the author read from his work, go to connect.mcgraw-hill.com.

As Chicago-born (1950) Edward Hirsch says in his interview for this book, "I began writing poetry in high school the way almost everyone begins writing poetry. It was really emotional desperation." Although he has advanced and refined his poetry—as evidenced by awards that include the National Book Critics Circle Award and the American Academy of Arts & Letters Award for Literature—emotion still lies at its heart. Equally able to portray the emptiness of a world without God at its center and the sense of hope we might gain from art, Hirsch's verse often uses formal structures or the shape of elegies, though his more recent poetry departs into free verse. In addition to award-winning collections such as *For the Sleepwalkers* (1981) and *Wild Gratitude* (1986), Hirsch has written essays that have appeared in *The New Yorker* and a best-selling book, *How to Read a Poem: And Fall in Love with Poetry* (1999), as well as a regular poetry column for *The Washington Post*. After teaching at the University of Houston for nearly two decades, Hirsch now serves as the president of the J. S. Guggenheim Memorial Foundation.

RESEARCH ASSIGNMENT   Discuss how Hirsch describes choosing the sonnet form for the event he wants to describe. Why did he think it an apt choice?

AS YOU READ   Consider how the subject matter suits the sonnet form Hirsch has chosen. Examine how his use of a fixed form helps organize and deliver the anger and dismay the "grandfather's friend" feels about the world.

My First Theology Lesson (2003)

Rumpled and furious, my grandfather's friend
stood up in a bookstore on the North Side
and lamented the lost Jews of Poland

and declared that he felt sorry for God
5 who had so many problems with Justice
and had become disillusioned and sad

since He wanted to reveal Himself to us
but couldn't find anyone truly worthy
(it was always the wrong time or place

10 in our deranged and barbaric century)
and so withdrew into His own radiance
and left us a limited mind and body

to contemplate the ghostly absence,
ourselves alone in a divine wilderness.

Writing from Reading

Summarize

1 Describe the situation here. Why does the "grandfather's friend" feel "sorry for God," and is that an expression of blasphemy or faith?

Analyze Craft

2 What language suggests that the poem is a kind of argument, a laying out of rhetorical positions? What is present, for example, in "the ghostly absence"?

Analyze Voice

3 Discuss the formal features of this sonnet. What kind of rhymes does Hirsch use? Is the poem composed in strict meter?

Synthesize Summary and Analysis

4 The title "My First Theology Lesson" suggests there have been others. Would you say the poet now agrees with the position voiced here, or does he seem opposed to it?

Interpret the Poem

5 Why does the poet refer to this episode as a "theology lesson"? If "a divine wilderness" suggests the Garden of Eden, what has happened to that wilderness today?

FORM, FIXED FORM, OPEN FORM

All literature has shape. Like architects designing a building, poets must consider how they wish to arrange and enclose their language, how to best give it foundation and structure. Sometimes these designs follow patterns that have existed for centuries, and sometimes they are wholly new creations. In some cases, a poet knows in advance exactly how a poem's language will be arranged; at other times, he or she makes this decision during the process of composition itself. Regardless of these creative choices on the part of the writer, every poem possesses **form,** an overall shape and structure; if that structure has been long established, it will have a name.

"Metrical poetry in English mean[s] balancing unstressed and stressed syllables . . . as a kind of . . . building block. . . . You could make a little waltz form of that rhythm [and] . . . do it forever and ever." Conversation with Robert Hass

Though our contemporary language is extensive in vocabulary and intonation, each word edges up against the next and becomes part of the whole. We use the term **fixed form** (or **closed form**) to describe an arrangement of text that requires a poet to obey set written combinations. These will include line length, meter, stanza structure, and rhyme scheme. Over centuries, poets have invented fixed forms and borrowed forms from other languages to suit their needs. These combinations help poets give shape and order to the emotion or experience they wish to convey. By understanding the patterns and overall trajectory of a fixed form, you'll learn what to expect from the types of poems (how a sonnet, for example, takes on a different subject from a villanelle) and how poets both innovate and imitate previous traditions.

"We've all heard poems [where] the rhymes seemed just there to fill out the forms. . . . The form is dead in that way. It is not alive. The form is controlling you." Conversation with Edward Hirsch

Keep in mind that poets working in a fixed form don't necessarily feel that they must conform to *every* part of a formal design. Think of it this way: As a child, you may have played a game with your friends and changed the rules a little to make the contest more exciting or interesting. Writers share this affection for flexibility. They may vary their work to better fit their intentions, or purposefully stray from formal expectations in hopes of changing a poem's design.

Open form (or **free verse**) refers to poetry ungoverned by metrical or rhyme schemes. Although it became fashionable in the twentieth century, the tradition of writing without strict adherence to formal constraints dates to the Psalms of the Bible and probably even further back. Using meaning to guide a poem's overall shape, poets writing in open form do not so much abandon form as use formal elements like rhyme, rhythm, and line length to individually embody their intentions. Because the blank page provides a kind of silent canvas on which to inscribe sound in language, poets can use the combination of white space and interesting syntax to create their own form and structure. Look, for example, at the poems in this book by e. e. cummings and you'll get a sense of open form's ability to devise its own particular meaning and order.

Some people think that open form poetry goes so far as to invite the reader into the creative process itself. By personally considering and then connecting a poem's form and substance, readers can participate in the creation of a poem's meaning. We'll talk about open form poetry in more detail in the next chapter; what follows is a close examination of forms that have long been—by contrast—closed and fixed.

THE BUILDING BLOCKS OF FORM

To best understand how poets conceive and construct fixed forms, it's important to recognize some of the components that contribute to a poem's particular shape. Becoming familiar with the architecture of verse is useful—even crucial—in this context. Here are a few examples.

> **"Poetry is like architecture in that we're using the materiality of language, but we're also using silence, interspaciousness, as part of the medium in poetry. So a lot of times it's like the use of space in architecture; we're using silence—that's the real habitation."** Conversation with Li-Young Lee

The most basic unit of poetry is, of course, the **line,** a row of words containing phrases and/or sentences. **Blank verse,** which may be the simplest verse form, consists of unrhymed lines of verse all in the same meter, usually iambic pentameter. (For more on rhyme and meter, see Chapter 24.) Like prose, however, most poetry is governed by groupings of lines, but the groupings are stanzas instead of paragraphs. A **stanza** is a unit of two or more lines, set off by an extra line space, often sharing the same rhythm and meter.

In a fixed form poem, a stanza will contain or develop a consistent idea and demonstrate a regular rhyme scheme (as discussed in more depth later in this chapter). The term originates from an old Italian word meaning "stopping place" or "room"; if you think of a poem as a work of architecture, you can imagine a stanza as a kind of chamber of language that contains a thought. In addition to arranging lines into stanzas, poets also arrange stanzas into defined groupings. Though there are no rules about how a poet should or shouldn't create stanzas, tradition has generated a handful of set stanza patterns.

Here is a pair of stanzas in the *abab* rhyme pattern. Such patterns make up a poem's **rhyme scheme** (for more information, see Rhyme in Chapter 24). These stanzas come from a poem itself called "Stanzas," written in 1838 by Mary Shelley—best known as the author of *Frankenstein* (1818). Try to picture this "room" as a rectangle or square in which the walls are perfectly proportioned and the lines are parallel:

> *But gentle sleep shall veil my sight,*
> *And Psyche's lamp shall darkling be,*
> *When, in the visions of the night,*
> *Thou dost renew thy vows to me.*
>
> *Then come to me in dreams, my love,*
> *I will not ask a dearer bliss;*
> *Come with the starry beams, my love,*
> *And press mine eyelids with thy kiss.*

"Think of the stanza—'stanza' comes from the word for a room. So in the poem, each stanza is like a room in a house. And something happens in that room. Often the first stanza is like the entryway of the house. It brings you into the poem, it is [the] foyer. Then you . . . are in the more public rooms, and the poem eventually lets you into its private rooms." Conversation with Carolyn Forché

In its strictest sense, a **couplet** (also discussed in the previous chapter) is two lines of poetry forming a unit of meaning. Often couplets rhyme, are strung together without a break, and share the same meter. One such form is the **heroic couplet,** two lines of rhymed iambic pentameter. Organized in small double steps, heroic couplets create a sort of chain that helps a long poem flow forward. Along with John Dryden, Alexander Pope is credited with perfecting heroic couplets in English poetry. Here's a brief excerpt from Pope's "Essay on Man" (1733) featuring this particular fixed form:

> *Know then thyself, presume not God to scan;*   *a*
> *The proper study of mankind is Man.*   *a*
> *Placed on this isthmus of a middle state,*   *b*
> *A being darkly wise, and rudely great.*   *b*

Less common than the couplet, a **tercet** is a group of three lines of poetry. Sometimes the term **triplet** is specifically substituted, meaning a three-line stanza in which all the lines rhyme.

Probably the best-known fixed form using tercets is **terza rima,** a fixed form featuring the interlocking rhyme scheme *aba, bcb, cdc, ded,* and so on. Invented and then popularized by the medieval Italian poet Dante Alighieri, terza rima is the exclusive fixed form of his epic *Divine Comedy,* which includes the sections "Inferno," "Purgatorio," and "Paradiso."

Echoing Dante, Percy Bysshe Shelley employs terza rima in his "Ode to the West Wind" (1820), which appears in its entirety later in the chapter. Here are the first three tercets:

O wild West Wind, thou breath of Autumn's being,	*a*
Thou, from whose unseen presence the leaves dead	*b*
Are driven, like ghosts from an enchanter fleeing,	*a*
Yellow, and black, and pale, and hectic red,	*b*
Pestilence-stricken multitudes: O thou,	*c*
Who chariotest to their dark wintry bed	*b*
The winged seeds, where they lie cold and low,	*c*
Each like a corpse within its grave, until	*d*
Thine azure sister of the Spring shall blow . . .	*c*

Quatrains, four-line stanzas, are the most popular stanzaic form in English poetry. Easily varied in meter, line length, and rhyme scheme, the quatrain is highly adaptable. You'll find dozens of poems in this book employing it, in both fixed and open form poetry. You have already seen several in Chapter 24 that employ one form, worth noting here in particular, the traditional **ballad stanza,** a quatrain in which the first and third lines possess four stresses, whereas the second and fourth have three stresses (see "Sir Patrick Spence," Bob Dylan's "The Times They Are a-Changin'," and "Bonnie Barbara Allen" in Chapter 24). Here is an additional example of an English ballad, "Lament of the Border Widow," from centuries ago.

> *My love he built me a bonny bower,*
> *And clad it a' wi' lilye flour,*
> *A brawer bower ye ne'er did see,*
> *Than my true love he built for me.*

A variation on ballad meter, **common measure** uses iambic quatrains with the same alternating four-stress/three-stress meter but sometimes with an *abab* rhyme scheme.

> **"I think part of the pleasure of reading poetry is to know the intricacy of its prosody because you see content and form are completely intertwined. They emerge out of each other. Often the content is discovered because of the form."** Conversation with Carolyn Forché

THE SONNET

Easily the most recognizable fixed form in poetry, the **sonnet** (*sonneto*, "little sound" or "little song," in Italian) is a fourteen-line poem in a recognizable pattern of rhyme, often metered in iambic pentameter. The fourteenth-century Italian poet Francesco Petrarch (1304–1374) is credited as the first master of this form, in which he wrote

"I . . . remember . . . writing sonnets. . . . I think it was some point in the mid-1980s . . . you could put fourteen lines on a postcard and mail it for fourteen cents. We thought, well, this was the postal service imitating art. And so we [sent] . . . fourteeners just back and forth and back. . . . As postage rates went up, we started writing more epic poems and putting them in envelopes." Conversation with Thomas Lynch

about the object of his unrequited love, Laura. The form he perfected came to be known as the **Petrarchan** (or **Italian**) **sonnet** and is the most frequently used sonnet form. The Petrarchan sonnet consists of an **octave** (eight lines) and then a **sestet** (six lines).

PETRARCHAN SONNET

Fourteen lines
Two stanzas: eight lines/six lines

abbaabba

cdecde or *cdcdcd*

Since the form's inception, generations upon generations of poets have tried their hands at the Petrarchan sonnet, often choosing love as a subject matter for the tightly controlled form. A celebrated example by Elizabeth Barrett Browning follows.

Elizabeth Barrett Browning (1806–1861)

England's most respected female poet in her lifetime, Elizabeth Barrett Browning showed by her own example that women could be educated and important artists. Her education took place at home, and she learned Greek by sitting in on her brother's tutoring sessions. This traditionally male knowledge enabled her to engage with literary and scholarly culture in a serious way. Although she was an invalid confined to her father's house, her elopement with Robert Browning when she was thirty-nine restored her health. In addition to *Sonnets from the Portuguese* (1850)—a sequence of love sonnets that contains her much-quoted "How do I love thee?"—one of her most famous works is *Aurora Leigh* (1857), a "novel-poem," as she described it. The book follows a young woman's rise to become a great poet and champions the current day as a time worth writing about. Barrett Browning's poetry engages with social issues, and true to Victorian fashion, she used her pen to impart moral instruction.

AS YOU READ   Look for the shape of the whole—the way a question gets answered in a very different kind of "argument" than is the case with Edward Hirsch's "My First Theology Lesson."

How do I love thee? Let me count the ways (1850)

How do I love thee? Let me count the ways.
I love thee to the depth and breadth and height
My soul can reach, when feeling out of sight
For the ends of being and ideal grace.
5 I love thee to the level of every day's
Most quiet need, by sun and candle-light.
I love thee freely, as men strive for right.
I love thee purely, as they turn from praise.
I love thee with the passion put to use
10 In my old griefs, and with my childhood's faith.
I love thee with a love I seemed to lose
With my lost saints. I love thee with the breath,
Smiles, tears, of all my life; and, if God choose,
I shall but love thee better after death.

Writing from Reading

Summarize

1 Writing to her husband, the poet Robert Browning, how does Elizabeth Barrett Browning record her love?

Analyze Craft

2 The sonnet form, with its careful rhyme scheme and meter, gives the poem a discipline that subtly increases its seriousness. Identify the rhyme scheme and the repetitions here.

Analyze Voice

3 The poem is emphatic in its devotion and phrased with intensity. This is not a whimsical little love lyric. It's a serious dedication, an essential catalog of the speaker's affection. How does the last line emphasize that seriousness, and what does the promise tell you about the speaker?

Synthesize Summary and Analysis

4 What better form to "count" these measures of her love than a sonnet with its carefully measured formal patterns? What aspects of meaning would the poem lose if you translated it into lines of prose?

Interpret the Poem

5 "I love thee with the breath, / Smiles, tears, of all my life": What does this mean, and how is its meaning affected by the line that follows?

Not all sonnets, however, make romantic love their concern, as we saw with this chapter's opening poem, "My First Theology Lesson." Indeed, the form is often used for a speaker to muse analytically on a thought, idea, or sentiment. Traditionally, after a sonnet's first octave introduces its subject, the remaining sestet begins with a turn that proposes some kind of answer or resolution to the subject at hand. Many poets have maintained this essential notion of an argument and counterargument, eight lines of "call" and six of "response." John Keats demonstrates this structure in the following sonnet. Here the poet analyzes the transformative power of reading the Greek poet Homer in a noted translation by George Chapman.

"**I think part of the pleasure of reading poetry is to know the intricacies of its prosody because, you see, content and form are completely intertwined, they emerge out of each other. Often the content is discovered because of the form.**" Conversation with Carolyn Forché

John Keats (1795–1821)

For a brief biography of John Keats, see Chapter 20.

AS YOU READ   Note the rhyme scheme and repeating sounds (fourteen lines with four rhymes), the thoroughly formal arrangement that looks at something new.

On First Looking into Chapman's Homer (1816)

Much have I traveled in the realms of gold,
   And many goodly states and kingdoms seen;
   Round many western islands have I been
Which bards in fealty to Apollo hold.
5 Oft of one wide expanse had I been told
   That deep-browed Homer rules as his demesne;
   Yet did I never breathe its pure serene
Till I heard Chapman speak out loud and bold:
Then felt I like some watcher of the skies
10   When a new planet swims into his ken;
Or like stout Cortez when with eagle eyes
   He stared at the Pacific—and all his men
Looked at each other with a wild surmise—
   Silent, upon a peak in Darien.

Writing from Reading

Summarize

1 Does this poem present a particular idea or case? What does the speaker want to explain?

Analyze Craft

2 Do you notice a turn in this poem? What language signals the shift from octave to sestet?

Analyze Voice

3 What are the "realms of gold" and what is the "wild surmise"? Is the speaker in the poem talking to himself here or making a point to his readership that they should also read Chapman's Homer? What does he mean by "bards in fealty to Apollo"?

Synthesize Summary and Analysis

4 This sonnet is, as we have seen, a traditional form—but the poem reports on "first" discovery. How does it marry the ancient and new, the "new planet" and old ocean?

Interpret the Poem

5 Though Keats accidentally confuses the explorer Cortez with Balboa (the first European to see the Pacific Ocean from a peak in Panama), why do you think he compares reading Homer to the life of a famous explorer?

Here Keats follows the traditional shape of the Petrarchan, or Italian, sonnet—but there are others as well. Readers familiar with Shakespeare's love poetry will probably recognize a different fourteen-line pattern from the octet/sestet form. English poets, faced with a language less conducive to natural rhyming than Italian, found a slightly reduced rhyme scheme a bit easier to work with. Known as the **Shakespearean** (also **English** or **Elizabethan**) **sonnet,** this fixed form is composed of three quatrains and a terminal (final) couplet, all in iambic pentameter and rhymed *abab cdcd efef gg*.

SHAKESPEAREAN SONNET
Fourteen lines
Three quatrains and a final couplet
abab cdcd efef gg

You'll see sonnets in this form often, and no small number in this very book (see, for example, Shakespeare's "Shall I compare thee to a summer's day?" in Chapter 20).

"Now . . . Italian is very, very rich in rhymes. The Russian poet Osip Mandelstam said—writing about Dante—that Italian is like baby talk because everything rhymes with everything else. Rhyming is much more difficult in English. . . . The Shakespearean model . . . rhymes but uses different rhymes in each of the four-line stanzas. . . . It gives you more room to move in." Conversation with Edward Hirsch

Though the Elizabethan sonnet took new liberties with rhyme, many of these "newer" sonnets preserved the Petrarchan sonnet's argumentative eight-line "call" and six-line "response." See how Shakespeare uses the sonnet's tight rhetorical structure first to worry through his troubled emotions and then to find some comfort.

William Shakespeare (1565–1616)

For a brief biography of William Shakespeare, see the Case Study in Chapter 33.

AS YOU READ Look for evidence of what Hirsch called an "argument" here. What are the opposing positions, and do they become reconciled?

When, in disgrace with Fortune and men's eyes (1609)

When, in disgrace with Fortune and men's eyes,
I all alone beweep my outcast state,
And trouble deaf heaven with my bootless cries,
And look upon myself and curse my fate,
5 Wishing me like to one more rich in hope,
Featured like him, like him with friends possessed,
Desiring this man's art, and that man's scope,
With what I most enjoy contented least,
Yet in these thoughts myself almost despising,
10 Haply I think on thee, and then my state,
Like to the lark at break of day arising
From sullen earth, sings hymns at heaven's gate;
    For thy sweet love remembered such wealth brings
    That then I scorn to change my state with kings.

Writing from Reading

Summarize

1 This poem deals with the opposition between public and private life, the outer trappings of success and the inner sense of satisfaction or reward. If the speaker feels "outcast" and "in disgrace," why should he "scorn to change my state with kings"?

Analyze Craft

2 Discuss how this poem is structured. Where do you detect changes in thought or tone?

3 How many sections do you perceive in the poem? How does the rhyme scheme signal section breaks?

Analyze Voice

4 Notice the implicit pun between "haply"—which means "by accident"—and "happily." Look also at the distinction between "deaf heaven" and "at heaven's gate." How do we get from the one to the other, and how does the voice manage both?

Synthesize Summary and Analysis

5 If this poem contained no metrical pattern or rhyme scheme, do you think it would illustrate its ideas as effectively? Why or why not?

Interpret the Poem

6 Less directly a love poem than Elizabeth Barrett Browning's, this sonnet is nonetheless devoted to "thy sweet love remembered." How does the final couplet, with its emphatic *gg* rhyme, help make that point?

Fairly or unfairly, the sonnet is nowadays viewed as an antique form. The poet Robert Bly has been quoted as saying this about his work at a literary magazine in the 1960s: "We sent rejection slips saying things like, 'The sonnet is the place where old professors go to die,' and then [writers would] write us insulting letters. . . ." Nevertheless, sonnet practitioners have continued to work, and brilliantly, within the poem's boundaries. Sometimes contemporary writers follow only very loosely the formal obligations of the sonnet, composing fourteen lines and rhyming them freely and in no regular pattern. Edward Hirsch's "My First Theology Lesson," for example, is just such a modern version of the form, and Edna St. Vincent Millay—one of the most accomplished sonnet writers of the century—makes the form her own with a syntax that follows the rhythms of speech.

"If you come away from school, and you know what a sonnet is, but you never want to read one again, then your education has failed you." Conversation with Edward Hirsch

Edna St. Vincent Millay (1892–1950)

A major figure among the writers of her time and a representative of the new woman, Edna St. Vincent Millay helped to shape her literary scene as an early feminist, poet, and playwright. She won the Pulitzer Prize for poetry in 1923. Millay is a master sonneteer, and her lyrical lines and tightly controlled form support a seemingly conversational style and intimate subject matter. The poet Richard Wilbur notes in his introduction to her *Selected Poems* that "She wrote some of the best sonnets of the century" (1991).

When Millay was twelve, her mother divorced her father, and she and her sisters eventually settled with their mother in Maine, where their outspoken attitudes often got them into trouble at school. Although Millay's trouble with school extended to her name—she was named "St. Vincent" in honor of the St. Vincent's Hospital in New York where her uncle's life was saved, and she went by "Vincent," which her school refused to acknowledge—she succeeded in school, and by fourteen, Millay won the Nicholas Gold Badge for poetry and began publishing her poetry. She went on to Vassar

College, where a patron of her poetry paid her way. In 1917 she moved to New York and became a vivid contributor to the hedonistic world of Greenwich Village and an explorer of female sexuality in her verse. Her open marriage to Eugen Jan Boisevain lasted 26 years. Together they established a literary and political outpost in Austerlitz, New York, where she could write in seclusion and they could entertain friends. Both are buried on their Austerlitz estate, where today the Millay Colony of the Arts has been established in her honor.

AS YOU READ   Identify the point at which the subject of the sonnet turns.

What lips my lips have kissed, and where, and why (1923)

What lips my lips have kissed, and where, and why,
I have forgotten, and what arms have lain
Under my head till morning; but the rain
Is full of ghosts tonight, that tap and sigh
5   Upon the glass and listen for reply,
And in my heart there stirs a quiet pain
For unremembered lads that not again
Will turn to me at midnight with a cry.
Thus in the winter stands the lonely tree,
10   Nor knows what birds have vanished one by one,
Yet know its boughs more silent than before:
I cannot say what loves have come and gone,
I only know that summer sang in me
A little while, that in me sings no more.

Writing from Reading

Summarize

1 What might have happened to occasion this poem? What is Millay mourning in this poem?

Analyze Craft

2 How does forgetting lead to remembering, and then to the creation of a sense of loss?

Analyze Voice

3 How would you describe the tone of the poem? What words create that tone?

Synthesize Summary and Analysis

4 Millay has been associated with sentiment, and some critics have called her "sentimental." Compare this poem with Elizabeth Barrett Browning's poem in

this chapter. In her poem Millay reverses the expectation that she must be writing a love poem to a particular person. How do Browning and Millay experience and interpret love?

Interpret the Poem

5 Sonnets are commonly associated with love. How is this sonnet a love poem? An anti-love poem? How is the poem an argument for or against love?

THE SONNET'S WORLD TOUR

When Francesco Petrarch published his *Canzoniere* (Song-Book) in the fourteenth century in Italy, he could not have imagined the immense impact his collection would have on future readers of world literature. A sequence of 366 poems including 317 sonnets, the volume was widely successful in its own time, and it directly influenced the poetry, within his own lifetime, of his noted poet-contemporaries Boccaccio and Geoffrey Chaucer. By the mid-sixteenth century, Petrarch's sonnets had reached scholars throughout western Europe, and the form had already become a fixture of poetry in a plentiful number of European languages. In England in particular during this time, Sir Thomas Wyatt (1503–1542) imported the Italian sonnet to English poetry and helped introduce its now trademark closing couplet. Henry Howard, the Earl of Surrey (1517–1547), is credited with first employing the English rhyme scheme of *abab cdcd efef gg*. It's not too much to say that these two men, taking their inspiration from Petrarch, helped inaugurate modern English poetry. For poets from Edmund Spenser and Shakespeare, who each added his own characteristic flourishes to the sonnet form, to Keats and Elizabeth Barrett Browning, to W. B. Yeats and T. S. Eliot, to living poets who are even at this moment trying their hand at the form in any number of countries, the sonnet's hold on the Western poetic imagination is extraordinary and unmatched.

THE VILLANELLE

The sonnet is just one of the dozens of fixed forms that came "across channel" to England from a foreign language. Another, from France, is the **villanelle,** a much more rigorous formal exercise than the sonnet, consisting of nineteen lines and only two rhymes, all in iambic pentameter.

The villanelle, with its Italian root word *villano* meaning "peasant," is a "rural" or "rustic" form with a full refrain or repetition of the first and third lines in song-like fashion. Though its word origin is in Italy, French troubadours are responsible for the form of villanelle we recognize today. In medieval Europe, wandering poets, or troubadours, plied their trade by demonstrating technical proficiency; their subject matter was limited and their dexterity limitless—as these forms suggest.

The technical arrangement of the villanelle requires five three-line stanzas, or tercets, and a final quatrain. The first and third lines of the first tercet recur alternately in the following stanzas as a refrain and form a final couplet. Why this particular nineteen-line poem proved popular, while an eighteen- or twenty-line version of the same variety has no name, is one of the mysteries of tradition, but it has something to do with the power of repetition: the repeated lines add up to more than mere parts of the whole. One of the best-known villanelles in English comes from the twentieth-century Welsh poet Dylan Thomas.

VILLANELLE

Nineteen lines
Five tercets/final quatrain

aba aba aba aba aba abaa

The first and third lines of the tercets recur (the poem's opening line is the final line of the second and fourth stanzas, and the last line of the first stanza is the final line of the third and fifth stanzas) and form a final couplet.

Dylan Thomas (1914–1953)

Born in Wales, Dylan Thomas decided not to go to college so that he could focus immediately on writing. His *18 Poems* (1934), published when he was twenty, brought him instant critical acclaim for the bold diction and imagery contained in formal structures. In addition to other collections of poetry such as *Deaths and Entrances* (1946) and *In Country Sleep* (1951), Thomas also wrote prose—as in his autobiographical sketches *Portrait of the Artist As a Young Dog* (1940)—and plays, as in his successful radio script *Under Milk Wood* (1954). Most of his poetry takes for its theme the unity of the life-and-death cycle, capturing the paradox of living because of death and dying because of life. Although he married in his early twenties and had three children, Thomas lived a bohemian lifestyle, giving boisterous readings in the United States and drinking heavily toward the end of his life. He died suddenly, at thirty-nine, from the effects of alcoholism.

AS YOU READ   Almost an incantation, this poem gains strength from its lack of variety; listen for the "chorus" and repeated sounds and lines as you read this poem aloud.

Do not go gentle into that good night (1952)

Do not go gentle into that good night,
Old age should burn and rave at close of day;
Rage, rage against the dying of the light.

Though wise men at their end know dark is right,
5   Because their words had forked no lightning they
Do not go gentle into that good night.

Good men, the last wave by, crying how bright
Their frail deeds might have danced in a green bay,
Rage, rage against the dying of the light.

10   Wild men who caught and sang the sun in flight,
And learn, too late, they grieved it on its way,
Do not go gentle into that good night.

Grave men, near death, who see with blinding sight
Blind eyes could blaze like meteors and be gay,
15   Rage, rage against the dying of the light.

And you, my father, there on the sad height,
Curse, bless me now with your fierce tears, I pray.
Do not go gentle into that good night.
Rage, rage against the dying of the light.

Writing from Reading

Summarize

1 Who's speaking, and to whom? What does "good night" here signify, or "the dying of the light"?

Analyze Craft

2 This poem, a desperate plea from the speaker to his declining father to "rage against" death, becomes especially dramatic and poignant in its choral lines. What effect do the repetitions create?

Analyze Voice

3 As the American poet Robert Hass has said of the form's repetition, "The effect is mesmerizing; it makes of the music of the poem a kind of haunted waltz." Why is this form appropriate for this speaker and his audience?

Synthesize Summary and Analysis

4 Notice that it takes until the final stanza for the speaker to address his father directly—making a particular instance out of the general case. How does this heighten the tone and deepen the emotion expressed here?

Interpret the Poem

5 The mode of this syntax is imperative, a series of commands. Yet it is also a kind of prayer ("Curse, bless me now with your fierce tears, I pray."). What does that juxtaposition—a blessing, a curse—signify?

Here's another of the best-known villanelles in the language—though a little less formally strict than Thomas's. As Elizabeth Bishop's poem proceeds, the repetition causes the lines to sound as though they're actually trying, deliberately, to convince the speaker (and reader) of a difficult premise. The poet-critic J. D. McClatchy writes of the final quatrain, "The whole stanza is in danger of breaking apart, and breaking down. In this last line the poet's voice literally cracks. The villanelle—that strictest and most intractable of verse forms—can barely control the grief, yet helps the poet keep her balance."

Elizabeth Bishop (1911–1979)

For a brief biography of Elizabeth Bishop, see Chapter 20.

AS YOU READ   Note how the repeated refrains of the poem change slightly, both in form and in context. How do the emotions generated by loss and losing enlarge in repetition?

One Art (1976)

The art of losing isn't hard to master;
so many things seem filled with the intent
to be lost that their loss is no disaster.

Lose something everyday. Accept the fluster
5 of lost door keys, the hour badly spent.
The art of losing isn't hard to master.

Then practice losing further, losing faster:
places, and names, and where it was you meant
to travel. None of these will bring disaster.

10 I lost my mother's watch. And look! my last, or
next-to-last, of three loved houses went.
The art of losing isn't hard to master.

I lost two cities, lovely ones. And, vaster,
some realms I owned, two rivers, a continent.
15 I miss them, but it wasn't a disaster.

—Even losing you (the joking voice, a gesture
I love) I shan't have lied. It's evident
the art of losing's not too hard to master
though it may look like (*Write* it!) like disaster.

Writing from Reading

Summarize

1 Since it's so often repeated, the opening line (or "topic sentence") of a villanelle must be worth hearing more than once. What do you think the poet means by "the art of losing," and which examples does she use?

Analyze Craft

2 Determine the poem's rhyme scheme. Where do you notice Bishop using slant rhymes?

Analyze Voice

3 What do you think the speaker means by losing "two cities"? And "some realms I owned"? How does the loss remind you of Keats's "On First Looking into Chapman's Homer"?

Synthesize Summary and Analysis

4 Does the significance of the repeated lines seem to change as the poem

reflects on increasingly serious losses? Why or why not?

5 Given the context of the poem, who does the speaker address in the last stanza? Does it change if you read the "you" as a lover or as a family member?

Interpret the Poem

6 What does J. D. McClatchy mean when he says the poet's voice "cracks" in the final stanza? How does the final stanza seem to "break down"?

THE SESTINA

Another form that derives from the French is the sestina. An even more elaborately constructed poem than the villanelle, a **sestina** consists of six stanzas composed of six lines each. It features word repetition rather than rhyme, with the final word of each line in the first stanza repeated in a different order in the following five stanzas.

> ### SESTINA
>
> Six stanzas, six lines each
> The final word of each line in the first stanza is repeated in a different order in the following five stanzas.
>   The concluding three-line stanza, the envoi ("farewell"), summarizes the main idea and contains all six repeated words.

Again it's difficult to know why this *particular* technical form has come down through the centuries, but the challenge of the sestina continues to engage modern poets; Ezra Pound, T. S. Eliot, and other twentieth-century poets have tried it on for size. As the following poem by Elizabeth Bishop demonstrates, the sestina concludes with a three-line **envoi,** or "farewell." The final words of the first stanza are repeated in a different order in the second stanza, and the third, and so on, until the envoi (in which the same six words appear) has gathered force and meaning.

Sestina (1956)

September rain falls on the house.
In the failing light, the old grandmother
sits in the kitchen with the child
beside the Little Marvel Stove,
5 reading the jokes from the almanac,
laughing and talking to hide her tears.

She thinks that her equinoctial tears
and the rain that beats on the roof of the house
were both foretold by the almanac,
10 but only known to a grandmother.
The iron kettle sings on the stove.
She cuts some bread and says to the child,

It's time for tea now; but the child
is watching the teakettle's small hard tears
15 dance like mad on the hot black stove,
the way the rain must dance on the house.
Tidying up, the old grandmother
hangs up the clever almanac

on its string. Birdlike, the almanac
20 hovers half open above the child,
hovers above the old grandmother
and her teacup full of dark brown tears.
She shivers and says she thinks the house
feels chilly, and puts more wood in the stove.

25 *It was to be,* says the Marvel Stove.
I know what I know, says the almanac.
With crayons the child draws a rigid house
and a winding pathway. Then the child
puts in a man with buttons like tears
30 and shows it proudly to the grandmother.

But secretly, while the grandmother
busies herself about the stove,
the little moons fall down like tears
from between the pages of the almanac
35 into the flower bed the child
has carefully placed in the front of the house.

Time to plant tears, says the almanac.
The grandmother sings to the marvelous stove
and the child draws another inscrutable house.

Writing from Reading

Summarize

1 Write down the story the poem tells.

Analyze Craft

2 The poem, as many do, has a turn, this one coming at the beginning of the sixth stanza, announced by the word *but*. What seems different here from the first five stanzas?

Analyze Voice

3 How would you describe the poet's tone? Be specific about the word *tears*.

Synthesize Summary and Analysis

4 How do the repeated words help the story unfold? How might the story seem different without this repetition?

Interpret the Poem

5 How does the repetition enforce or not enforce the sense of the time-lessness of childhood? Is the sestina form particularly suited for this kind of mood, or is it merely a variation on ways to create the mood?

THE PANTOUM

Another formal arrangement in verse—which comes to our language also from the French, by way of Malaysia—is the **pantoum.** A kind of variation on the villanelle, the pantoum has lines grouped into quatrains, and there can be as many or as few stanzas as the poet chooses. Its music, however, is even more demanding than that of the sestina or the villanelle. (The composer Maurice Ravel called the second movement of his Piano Trio in A minor a "Pantoum.") The "fixed form" pantoum consists of quatrains with a rhyme scheme of *abab,* and it says everything twice; the lines of the poem may vary in length. For all quatrains except the first, the first line of the current quatrain repeats the second line of the preceding quatrain; the third line of the current stanza repeats the fourth of the preceding quatrain.

PANTOUM

Quatrains

Rhyme scheme for each quatrain: *abab*

The first line repeats the second line of the preceding quatrain, except for the first quatrain.
The third line repeats the final line of the preceding quatrain.
The second line of the final quatrain repeats the third line of the first quatrain.
The last line repeats the first line of the first quatrain.

Erica Funkhouser (b. 1949)

Erica Funkhouser teaches writing at the Massachusetts Institute of Technology. She has published five collections of poetry: *Earthly* (2008), *The Actual World* (1997), *Pursuit* (2002), *Sure Shot and Other Poems* (1992), and *Natural Affinities* (1983). Her poems are inspired by everyday objects and nature and have appeared in prestigious venues including *The Paris Review, Ploughshares, The Atlantic,* and *The New Yorker.* She also has an interest in the Lewis and Clark Expedition and was a contributor to the PBS *Lewis and Clark* series, directed by Ken Burns. She lives in Essex, Massachusetts.

AS YOU READ   Look for the tone and emotional register in this exact example of the fixed form.

First Pantoum of Summer (2003)

One sleep depletes, another fills the well.
Our night's companion shapes the coming day.
My bed, half empty, rattled like a cell
when you took off for town. I couldn't stay.

5 Our night's companion shapes the coming day,
and where we make our bed can make us weep.
When you took off for town, I couldn't stay.
I fell into these words—a second sleep.

Where we make our bed can make us weep
or leave us clean and clear and ravenous.
10 I fell into these words—a second sleep,
a summer sleep, the windows generous.

You left me clean and clear and ravenous.
I drank new air, a warm and welcome stream
of summer sleep, the windows generous.
15 Here or away, you lead me out of dream.

I drank new air, a warm and welcome stream.
My bed, half empty, rattled like a cell.
Here or away, you lead me out of dream.
One sleep depletes, another fills the well.

Writing from Reading

Summarize

1 If this is a love poem, to whom is it addressed and why? Why does the speaker focus on a particular season?

Analyze Craft

2 How does the speaker create what she calls a "second sleep"? And if this is the "first pantoum of summer," can you find evidence there will be a second or a third?

Analyze Voice

3 Describe the speaker's tone. Is it affectionate, disappointed, or angry? Or a mixture of emotions?

Synthesize Summary and Analysis

4 Does the poet describe—or lament— the variations of sleep when

with a loved one? Can you make a sketch of the absent lover based on details in the poem?

Interpret the Poem

5 How do repetition and variation bring the deep expression of the poet's situation to our attention?

THE HAIKU

Poets since Homer have worked in several other shorter poetic forms that demand attention. One of these is the distinctive Eastern variety of short poem, the **haiku,** put forward first by Japanese poets in the sixteenth century. The original verse form calls for seventeen syllables in three lines: five/seven/five. In part because of its succinctness and brevity, the form presents a single idea, image, or feeling: Its focus is like that of a photographic snapshot. In Chapter 22, Jane Hirshfield discussed the influence of haiku on her work, and there we also saw Ezra Pound's Imagist description of passengers in the Paris metro; his definition of the image as the connection of idea and emotion in an instant of time is wholly captured here. Translators who put these poems into English try to approximate the original verse faithfully, which sometimes means breaking out of the original five/seven/five metrical pattern.

> **HAIKU**
>
> Translators try to approximate the Japanese seventeen syllables and three-line (five/seven/five) structure.

You'll see in this haiku an elegant attention to quiet, meditative, sometimes humorous moments—it's as if the poem is translating little bits of time itself onto the page.

Matsuo Bashō (1644–1694)

For a brief biography of Matsuo Bashō, see Chapter 22.

Deep autumn

(c. 1600)

Deep autumn—
my neighbor,
how does he live, I wonder?

—*translated by* Robert Hass

Writing from Reading

Summarize

1 How does this haiku touch on the cycles of the seasons?

Analyze Craft

2 The poem has been "Englished" and does not have the precise number of syllables contained in the original. Does that make a difference, and, if not, why not?

Analyze Voice

3 How personal or impersonal is "I"?

4 The form tends to make the poet speak about the smallest details of everyday life. What kind of tone does that create?

Synthesize Summary and Analysis

5 How do the separate lines affect your perception of these images? How would your perception differ if all three lines of this haiku were strung together on one line?

Interpret the Poem

6 Imagine the moment in which this haiku was triggered. How do you envision what's going on? Where is the poet in relation to what he's observing? How do you relate to this moment of observation?

THE EPIGRAM

Epigrams are very short, often satirical poems on a single subject. Their primary function, besides deploying wit, is to make a pointed commentary of some kind. Shakespeare said that brevity is the soul of wit, and Samuel Taylor Coleridge puts both soul and wit into play.

AS YOU READ Poetry, as we have seen, is a condensed form and an intensive use of language; the epigram is an extreme example of poetic form since it reduces matters to their very briefest expression. Note the way, however, that these condensed meanings expand and enlarge with each rereading in these three epigrams by Coleridge, Langston Hughes, and A. R. Ammons.

Samuel Taylor Coleridge (1772–1834)

For a brief biography of Samuel Taylor Coleridge, see Chapter 24.

What Is an Epigram? (1802)

What is an epigram? A dwarfish whole;
Its body brevity, and wit its soul.

Langston Hughes (1902–1967)

For a brief biography of Langston Hughes, see the Case Study on Langston Hughes, Chapter 27.

Prayer (1955)

Oh, God of dust and rainbows, help us see
That without dust the rainbow would not be.

A. R. Ammons (1926–2001)

For a brief biography of A. R. Ammons, see Chapter 23.

Small Song (1970)

The reeds give
way to the

wind and give
the wind away.

Writing from Reading

Summarize

1 What actually occurs in each of the preceding epigrams?

Analyze Craft

2 Wit would seem to be a crucial component of these poems, as Coleridge suggests. But there is melancholy here as well. How would you describe the tone of "Small Songs" for example? What about its meaning is suggested by its shape?

Analyze Voice

3 How does the statement made by an epigram, which makes a single point and not a counterargument, differ from the statement made by a sonnet?

Synthesize Summary and Analysis

4 Paraphrase these epigrams and compare the points they make. What makes the form appropriate for this type of statement?

Interpret the Poems

5 If the haiku is an Eastern form and the epigram Western, what similarities do you see in both forms and what seems different? How do these forms effect a different way of seeing everyday life?

"I'm interested in resonances . . . and even though the poem is ironic in posture, I hope there's a kind of release . . . at the end where the poem finally ... throws them off kilter in useful ways."

Conversation with Stephen Dunn

THE LIMERICK

Unlike the other fixed forms we've examined, the **limerick** originates in the English language. It's a light, often humorous verse form consisting of five lines, with a rhyme scheme of *aabba*. The first, second, and fifth lines have three stressed syllables, whereas the third and fourth lines have two stressed syllables. The meter is usually anapestic (see Chapter 24).

Though the limerick is considered light and unserious (sometimes downright vulgar), in the hands of a skillful poet it can be quite an impressive display of technique.

Edward Lear (1812–1888)

Edward Lear was born in 1812 outside of London, the twentieth child of stockbroker Jeremiah Lear and his wife Ann. Following poor investments in the market, the Lears fell on hard times, and Edward's upbringing was entrusted to his sister Ann, twenty-one years his senior. At age six, Edward became prone to epileptic seizures, a condition that at the time was often associated with demonic possession. Nevertheless, despite his poor health, Lear began to sell poetry and illustrations at age fifteen; and by age nineteen he earned his living illustrating birds for the scientific book *Illustrations of the Family of Psittacidae, or Parrots* (1830). His first book of poetry, *A Book of Nonsense*, was published in 1846 and contributed greatly to the popularity of the limerick form. He published *The History of the Seven Families of the Lake Pipple-Popple* in 1865, and his most famous work, *The Owl and the Pussycat*, in 1867. Lear spent most of his life traveling abroad in the Mediterranean, and he published several more volumes of illustrated poetry before his death in San Remo, Italy.

AS YOU READ   Read these three poems by Edward Lear, J. D. Landis, and Laurence Perrine aloud, and with emphasis; see how they depend on rhyme.

There was an Old Man with a gong (1846)

There was an Old Man with a gong,
Who bumped at it all the day long;
But they called out, "Oh, law!
you're a horrid old bore!"
5   So they smashed that Old Man with a gong.

Most limericks, whether proper or vulgar, include a place-name at poem's start. Their lilting singsong rhyme pattern can also make them appropriate for children's rhymes, as in the following one.

J. D. Landis (b. 1942)

James David Landis was born in Springfield, Massachusetts, attended Yale University, and spent much of his career as a publishing executive in New York. The author of such novels as *Longing* (2000) and *Artist of the Beautiful* (2005), he has written many books for young adults, such as *The Sisters Impossible* (1979), *Daddy's Girl* (1984), and *The Band Never Dances* (1989). His collection of poems for children, *Cars on Mars, and 49 Other Poems for Kids on Earth,* appeared in 2008.

Starvation Diet (2008)

There was once a fat man from Madrid
Who was told to eat nothing but squid.
He chewed and he chewed.
He chewed and he chewed.
5   But of squid he could never get rid.

Laurence Perrine (1915–1995)

Laurence Perrine published numerous collections of poetry, among them *Sound and Nonsense: Original Limericks* (1994),

as well as several influential textbooks, including the poetry anthology *Sound and Sense*. With a B.A. from Oberlin College and a Ph.D. from Yale University, Perrine began his teaching career in 1946

at Southern Methodist University, where he taught until his retirement in 1980. Perrine also served as president of the National Council of Teachers of English.

The limerick's never averse (1982)

The limerick's never averse
To expressing itself in a terse
   Economical style,
   And yet, all the while,
5 The limerick's *always* a verse.

Writing from Reading

Summarize

1 What is constant in this form, and what—if anything—varies?

Analyze Craft

2 Think of a limerick as a puzzle to be solved—five lines that are "*always* a verse." How does Perrine move from "never" to "*always*," and how does the rhyme scheme here support the poet's point?

Analyze Voice

3 If epigrams depend on wit, a limerick can't exist without it—or, at least, without good (and sometimes bawdy) humor. Based on the examples in this chapter, what distinction do you draw between humor and wit?

Synthesize Summary and Analysis

4 The third of these three limericks is both an example of the form and

a definition of it; it leaves out the place-name, however. Of these three examples, therefore, only Landis's is fully "fixed" as a traditional limerick. What are the ways in which such a form can be both rigid and supple?

Interpret the Poem

5 Poets love wordplay and engage in it often. How serious can this form be?

THE ELEGY

On a more somber note, an **elegy** is a poem of lamentation memorializing the dead or contemplating some nuance of life's melancholy. In its original incarnation in ancient Greece, it employed a fixed form of dactylic hexameter and iambic pentameter couplets. Over the centuries, the form has evolved and expanded beyond its early metrical features. A contemporary elegy need not conform to its original classical structure, but it will still reflect a speaker's solemn attention to aspects of grief and mortality.

A. E. Housman (1859–1936)

A British poet with a bleak outlook, Alfred Edward Housman published only two small volumes of poetry in his lifetime, *A Shropshire Lad* (1896) and *Last Poems* (1922); a third, arguably inferior collection was published posthumously. Despite this limited output, Housman said a lot in a little; his stanzas are compressed yet achieve a sense of poignancy over the fleeting nature of youth and life. Housman also had a reputation as a Latin literature scholar and critic and taught Latin at Cambridge University despite having failed his final exams as an undergraduate at the University of Oxford.

AS YOU READ Picture a ceremony, a formal event, at which the poet might read this poem as a tribute.

To an Athlete Dying Young (1896)

The time you won your town the race
We chaired you through the market-place;
Man and boy stood cheering by,
And home we brought you shoulder-high.

5   Today, the road all runners come,
Shoulder-high we bring you home,
And set you at your threshold down,
Townsman of a stiller town.

Smart lad, to slip betimes away
10   From fields where glory does not stay,
And early though the laurel grows
It withers quicker than the rose.

Eyes the shady night has shut
Cannot see the record cut,
15   And silence sounds no worse than cheers
After earth has stopped the ears:

Now you will not swell the rout
Of lads that wore their honors out,
Runners whom renown outran
20   And the name died before the man.

So set, before its echoes fade,
The fleet foot on the sill of shade,
And hold to the low lintel up
The still-defended challenge-cup.

25   And round that early-laureled head
Will flock to gaze the strengthless dead,
And find unwithered on its curls
The garland briefer than a girl's.

Writing from Reading

Summarize

1 What does Housman accomplish in his description of the athlete as a "Smart lad, to slip betimes away"?

Analyze Craft

2 How does the poet use details from the world of sports to move the poem along?

3 Why do you think the poet chooses formal-sounding couplets for his elegy?

Analyze Voice

4 Does the diction—the word choice elected—sound as formal as the rhyme scheme? What is the speaker's relationship to the athlete?

Synthesize Summary and Analysis

5 The rhyme and the diction together create a certain effect, and the speaker offers comfort. Does the attitude lend distance to the poem or make it

seem more sympathetic, and in what ways?

Interpret the Poem

6 Compare tone in this poem with Ben Jonson's "envy" in his elegy "On My First Son" in Chapter 21. In what ways are they similar? In what ways different? How would you describe the feelings in each poem about youth?

Although the contemporary everyday reader may not know for whom Housman's elegy is composed, W. H. Auden's elegy for the Irish poet William Butler Yeats addresses the death of a literary giant. Living poets often feel a kinship with the great poets of the past. In the case of Auden and Yeats, the sense of kinship was fresh and vital, so that Auden mourned Yeats's death as he might have mourned that of a close relative. Note how Auden remarks on the scope of Yeats's death, how the event is simultaneously momentous and anonymous.

W. H. Auden (1907–1973)

For a brief biography of W. H. Auden, see Chapter 20.

AS YOU READ   Consider the logic of associating death with the coldest season of the year.

In Memory of W. B. Yeats (1940)
[D. January 1939]

I

He disappeared in the dead of winter:
The brooks were frozen, the air-ports almost deserted,
And snow disfigured the public statues;
The mercury sank in the mouth of the dying day.
5 O all the instruments agree
The day of his death was a dark cold day.

Far from his illness
The wolves ran on through the evergreen forests,
The peasant river was untempted by the fashionable quays;
10 By mourning tongues
The death of the poet was kept from his poems.

But for him it was his last afternoon as himself,
An afternoon of nurses and rumours;
The provinces of his body revolted,
15 The squares of his mind were empty,
Silence invaded the suburbs,
The current of his feeling failed; he became his admirers.

Now he is scattered among a hundred cities
And wholly given over to unfamiliar affections;
20 To find his happiness in another kind of wood
And be punished under a foreign code of conscience.
The words of a dead man
Are modified in the guts of the living.

But in the importance and noise of to-morrow
25 When the brokers are roaring like beasts on the floor of the Bourse,
And the poor have the sufferings to which they are fairly accustomed,
And each in the cell of himself is almost convinced of his freedom;
A few thousand will think of this day
As one thinks of a day when one did something slightly unusual.
30 O all the instruments agree
The day of his death was a dark cold day.

II

You were silly like us: your gift survived it all;
The parish of rich women, physical decay,
Yourself; mad Ireland hurt you into poetry.
35 Now Ireland has her madness and her weather still,
For poetry makes nothing happen: it survives
In the valley of its saying where executives
Would never want to tamper; it flows south
From ranches of isolation and the busy griefs,
40 Raw towns that we believe and die in; it survives,
A way of happening, a mouth.

III

Earth, receive an honoured guest;
William Yeats is laid to rest:
Let the Irish vessel lie
45 Emptied of its poetry.

Time that is intolerant
Of the brave and innocent,
And indifferent in a week
To a beautiful physique,

50 Worships language and forgives
Everyone by whom it lives;
Pardons cowardice, conceit,
Lays its honours at their feet.

Time that with this strange excuse
55 Pardoned Kipling and his views,
And will pardon Paul Claudel,
Pardons him for writing well.

In the nightmare of the dark
All the dogs of Europe bark,
60 And the living nations wait,
Each sequestered in its hate;

Intellectual disgrace
Stares from every human face,
And the seas of pity lie
65 Locked and frozen in each eye.

Follow, poet, follow right
To the bottom of the night,
With your unconstraining Voice
Still persuade us to rejoice;

70 With the farming of a verse
Make a vineyard of the curse,
Sing of human unsuccess
In a rapture of distress;

In the deserts of the heart
75 Let the healing fountain start,
In the prison of his days,
Teach the free man how to praise.

Writing from Reading

Summarize

1 The death of the Irish poet is a day to remember for Auden. Why do you think he honors Yeats in such a formal way?

Analyze Craft

2 Nature itself seems to be dying, or at least in mourning. With what images and metaphors does Auden achieve this effect? Why does Auden compare the dying poet to a country or city, with "provinces," "squares," "suburbs"?

Analyze Voice

3 Do you hear a personal or public voice when you listen to this speaker, a private or collective grief? What language from the poem supports your answer?

Synthesize Summary and Analysis

4 An elegy, elaborate or simple, speaks of life as well as death. Does this statement seem accurate to you? How does Auden's lament refer to what continues as well as to what has stopped?

Interpret the Poem

5 Discuss the meaning of the lines "The death of the poet was kept from his poems" and ". . . he became his admirers." What does Auden suggest here about the relationship of the poet to his own poetry?

Theodore Roethke (1907–1973)

For a brief biography of Theodore Roethke, see Chapter 21.

AS YOU READ Try to put yourself in the mind of the speaker of the poem, the teacher lamenting the death of his student.

Elegy for Jane (1953)
My Student Thrown by a Horse

I remember the neckcurls, limp and damp as tendrils;
And her quick look, a sidelong pickerel smile;
And how, once startled into talk, the light syllables leaped for her,
And she balanced in the delight of her thought,
5 A wren, happy, tail into the wind,
Her song trembling the twigs and small branches.
The shade sang with her;
The leaves, their whispers turned to kissing;
And the mold sang in the bleached valleys under the rose.

10 Oh, when she was sad, she cast herself down into such a pure depth,
Even a father could not find her:
Scraping her cheek against straw;
Stirring the clearest water.

My sparrow, you are not here,
15 Waiting like a fern, making a spiny shadow.
The sides of wet stones cannot console me,
Nor the moss, wound with the last light.

If only I could nudge you from this sleep,
My maimed darling, my skittery pigeon.
20 Over this damp grave I speak the words of my love:
I, with no rights in this matter,
Neither father nor lover.

Writing from Reading

Summarize

1 The poem presents a sorrowful occasion, in which the poet tries to speak through his pain. Can you paraphrase his speech?

Analyze Craft

2 What metaphors does the poet employ to achieve his end? Do they all come from nature, and in what ways, if any, do they appear "artificial"?

Analyze Voice

3 What new and unexpected textures does this poet add to the generic voice of the poet mourning for the beloved dead?

Synthesize Summary and Analysis

4 Do you think the poet has found the proper metaphors, images, and tone

in order to make his grief memorable for a reader? What makes them memorable to you?

Interpret the Poem

5 How do we express great sorrow at the loss of those we love but who are not our kin? Is there a sorrow we feel beyond that which comes from knowing of an individual death, and how would you describe it?

THE ODE

Like the elegy, the **ode** no longer obliges the poet to a specific rhyme scheme or stanza length. It does, however, take a recognizable shape in its celebration of a quality or condition or situation. The main features of this variety of lyric are an elaborate stanzaic structure, a certain ceremonial feel in tone and style, and a sense of address—whether to a private or a public issue. By the nineteenth century, the ode form was more frequently dedicated to abstract subjects than to specific public figures or events.

Despite numerous variations on the ode form over time, the essential nature of the form has remained the same: a poem that declares its topic in the title, and then considers an idea or object or mood at length.

In Shelley's "Ode to the West Wind," the speaker calls to the coming autumn wind and asks it to "make me thy lyre," to project his words beyond the boundaries of both his physical location and his physical body.

Percy Bysshe Shelley (1792–1822)

The life of Percy Bysshe Shelley, a British Romantic poet, was marked by non-conformity. He was expelled from Oxford University because he had coauthored a pamphlet called *The Necessity of Atheism;* shortly thereafter, he married the daughter of a tavern owner when both he and his wife were still teenagers. He eventually grew estranged from his wife and fell in love with Mary Wollstonecraft Godwin (daughter of Mary Wollstonecraft), the future author of *Frankenstein*. He then invited his wife to live with him and Mary as a sister. After his wife's apparent suicide, Shelley married Mary and the couple moved to Italy, where over the course of four years, Shelley wrote his most important works: *Prometheus Unbound, Adonais,* and his famous poems "Hymn to Intellectual Beauty," "Ode to the West Wind," and "Ozymandias." An idealist who believed in intellectual beauty rather than God, Shelley wrote poetry that champions hope and imagination. He drowned, surprised by a storm while sailing, before his thirtieth birthday.

AS YOU READ   Consider the language and the situation here: the poet speaking to the wind itself.

Ode to the West Wind (1820)

I

O wild West Wind, thou breath of Autumn's being,
Thou, from whose unseen presence the leaves dead
Are driven, like ghosts from an enchanter fleeing,

Yellow, and black, and pale, and hectic red,
5   Pestilence-stricken multitudes: O thou,
Who chariotest to their dark wintry bed

The wingèd seeds, where they lie cold and low,
Each like a corpse within its grave, until
Thine azure sister of the Spring shall blow

10   Her clarion o'er the dreaming earth, and fill
(Driving sweet buds like flocks to feed in air)
With living hues and odors plain and hill:

Wild Spirit, which art moving everywhere;
Destroyer and preserver; hear, oh, hear!

II

15   Thou on whose stream, mid the steep sky's commotion,
Loose clouds like earth's decaying leaves are shed,
Shook from the tangled boughs of Heaven and Ocean,

Angels of rain and lightning: there are spread
On the blue surface of thine airy surge,
20   Like the bright hair uplifted from the head

Of some fierce Maenad, even from the dim verge
Of the horizon to the zenith's height,
The locks of the approaching storm. Thou dirge

Of the dying year, to which this closing night
25 Will be the dome of a vast sepulcher,
Vaulted with all thy congregated might

Of vapors, from whose solid atmosphere
Black rain, and fire, and hail will burst: oh, hear!

III

Thou who didst waken from his summer dreams
30 The blue Mediterranean, where he lay,
Lulled by the coil of his crystàlline streams,

Beside a pumice isle in Baiae's bay,
And saw in sleep old palaces and towers
Quivering within the wave's intenser day,

35 All overgrown with azure moss and flowers
So sweet, the sense faints picturing them! Thou
For whose path the Atlantic's level powers

Cleave themselves into chasms, while far below
The sea-blooms and the oozy woods which wear
40 The sapless foliage of the ocean, know

Thy voice, and suddenly grow gray with fear,
And tremble and despoil themselves: oh, hear!

IV

If I were a dead leaf thou mightest bear;
If I were a swift cloud to fly with thee;

45 A wave to pant beneath thy power, and share
The impulse of thy strength, only less free
Than thou, O uncontrollable! If even
I were as in my boyhood, and could be

The comrade of thy wanderings over Heaven,
50 As then, when to outstrip thy skyey speed
Scarce seemed a vision; I would ne'er have striven

As thus with thee in prayer in my sore need.
Oh, lift me as a wave, a leaf, a cloud!
I fall upon the thorns of life! I bleed!

55 A heavy weight of hours has chained and bowed
One too like thee: tameless, and swift, and proud.

V

Make me thy lyre, even as the forest is:
What if my leaves are falling like its own!
The tumult of thy mighty harmonies

60 Will take from both a deep, autumnal tone,
Sweet though in sadness. Be thou, Spirit fierce,
My spirit! Be thou me, impetuous one!

Drive my dead thoughts over the universe
Like withered leaves to quicken a new birth!
65 And, by the incantation of this verse,

Scatter, as from an unextinguished hearth
Ashes and sparks, my words among mankind!
Be through my lips to unawakened earth

The trumpet of a prophecy! O Wind,
70 If Winter comes, can Spring be far behind?

Writing from Reading

Summarize

1 The speaker describes the wind in various ways throughout the poem, for example, as "the trumpet of a prophecy" at the poem's end. Identify these descriptions of the wind. What do they tell you about how the speaker sees the wind?

Analyze Craft

2 How does this poem reflect the definition of an ode, as a formal, elevated celebration and reflection? What about the "west wind" is the speaker praising?

Analyze Voice

3 How do the poem's sections govern the speaker's emotions and thinking? How do the poem's attention and focus change over the trajectory of the different sections?

Synthesize Summary and Analysis

4 What is the importance of nature as it's described over the course of the poem? How would you characterize

nature's power, according to Shelley's speaker?

Interpret the Poem

5 What does the spirit embodied by the wind represent?

For Review and Further Study

Anne Bradstreet (1612 1672)

For a brief biography of Anne Bradstreet, see Chapter 21.

To my Dear and Loving Husband (1678)

If ever two were one, then surely we.
If ever man were lov'd by wife, then thee;
If ever wife was happy in a man,
Compare with me ye women if you can.
5 I prize thy love more than whole Mines of gold,
Or all the riches that the East doth hold.
My love is such that Rivers cannot quench,
Nor ought but love from thee, give recompence.
Thy love is such I can no way repay,
10 The heavens reward thee manifold I pray.
Then while we live, in love lets so persever,
That when we live no more, we may live ever.

Questions for Interactive Reading and Writing

1. Compare this love poem with Elizabeth Barrett Browning's "How do I love thee? Let me count the ways" early in this chapter. What are the similarities and differences in the comparisons, and what is the argument each is making as a pledge of love?

2. Bradstreet's last line contains a paradox. How does death become immortality through love in this poem?

3. Do a little research on Anne Bradstreet. Both her father and her husband served as governors for the Massachusetts Bay Colony in the seventeenth century. Does her relative prominence (and good education) make itself manifest in this poem and, if so, where? What in this poem seems specific to her circumstance, and what seems like a generalized declaration of love?

Robert Browning (1812–1889)

For a brief biography of Robert Browning, see Chapter 19.

Porphyria's Lover (1836)

The rain set early in to-night,
  The sullen wind was soon awake,
It tore the elm-tops down for spite,
  And did its worst to vex the lake:
  I listened with heart fit to break.   5
When glided in Porphyria; straight
  She shut the cold out and the storm,
And kneeled and made the cheerless grate
  Blaze up, and all the cottage warm;

10   Which done, she rose, and from her form
Withdrew the dripping cloak and shawl,
    And laid her soiled gloves by, untied
Her hat and let the damp hair fall,
    And, last, she sat down by my side
15   And called me. When no voice replied,
She put my arm about her waist,
    And made her smooth white shoulder bare,
And all her yellow hair displaced,
    And, stooping, made my cheek lie there,
20   And spread, o'er all, her yellow hair,
Murmuring how she loved me—she
    Too weak, for all her heart's endeavor,
To set its struggling passion free
    From pride, and vainer ties dissever,
25   And give herself to me forever.
But passion sometimes would prevail,
    Nor could to-night's gay feast restrain
A sudden thought of one so pale
    For love of her, and all in vain:
30   So, she was come through wind and rain.
Be sure I looked up at her eyes
    Happy and proud; at last I knew
Porphyria worshiped me: surprise
    Made my heart swell, and still it grew
35   While I debated what to do.
That moment she was mine, mine, fair,
    Perfectly pure and good: I found
A thing to do, and all her hair
    In one long yellow string I wound
40   Three times her little throat around,
And strangled her. No pain felt she;
    I am quite sure she felt no pain.
As a shut bud that holds a bee,
    I warily oped her lids: again
45   Laughed the blue eyes without a stain.
And I untightened next the tress
    About her neck; her cheek once more
Blushed bright beneath my burning kiss:
    I propped her head up as before
50   Only, this time my shoulder bore
Her head, which droops upon it still:
    The smiling rosy little head,

So glad it has its utmost will,
    That all it scorned at once is fled,
    And I, its love, am gained instead!   55
Porphyria's love: she guessed not how
    Her darling one wish would be heard.
And thus we sit together now,
    And all night long we have not stirred,
    And yet God has not said a word!   60

Questions for Interactive Reading and Writing

1. What type of poem is "Porphyria's Lover"? Who is the speaker? What is the speaker's tone in the lines where he commits the murder?

2. Describe Porphyria. Where has she come from and why?

3. Read the poem again and search for the speaker's motive in murdering Porphyria. Why does he do it?

4. What imagery does Browning use to set the stage of this dramatic tale? What tone does it establish at the beginning of the poem?

Geoffrey Chaucer (1342–1400)

The Canterbury Tales (c. 1369–1372)

GENERAL PROLOGUE

Here bygynneth the Book of the tales of Caunterbury [Introduction]

Whan that April with his showres soote°	*sweet*
The droughte of March hath perced to the roote,	
And bathed every veine in swich licour,°	*such liquid*
Of which vertu° engendred is the flowr;	*by whose strength*
Whan Zephyrus[1] eek° with his sweete breeth	*also* 5

---

[1] In Roman mythology Zephyrus was the demigod of the west wind, herald of warmer weather.

Inspired hath in every holt and heeth°   *wood and field* 35
The tendre croppes, and the yonge sonne
Hath in the Ram° his halve cours   *the zodiac sign*
    yronne,   *Aries*
And smale fowles maken melodye
10 That sleepen al the night with open yë°—   *eye*
So priketh hem Nature in hir corages°—   *hearts, spirits*
Thanne longen folk to goon on pilgrimages,
And palmeres² for to seeken straunge
    strondes°   *shores*
To ferne halwes,° couthe° in sondry   *far-off shrines/*
    londes;   *known*
15 And specially from every shires ende
Of Engelond to Canterbury they wende,
The holy blisful martyr³ for to seeke
That hem hath holpen° whan that they
    were seke.°   *helped/sick*
    Bifel that in that seson on a day,
20 In Southwerk⁴ at the Tabard as I lay,
Redy to wenden on my pilgrimage
To Canterbury with ful devout corage,
At night was come into that hostelrye
Wel nine and twenty in a compaignye
25 Of sondry folk, by aventure yfalle
In felaweshipe, and pilgrimes were they alle
That toward Canterbury wolden ride.
The chambres° and the stables weren wide,   *guestrooms*
And wel we weren esed° at the beste.   *accommodated*
30 And shortly, whan the sonne was to reste,
So hadde I spoken with hem everichoon
That I was of hir felaweshipe anoon,
And made forward° erly for to rise,   *agreed*
To take oure way ther as I you devise.°   *relate*

---

²Pilgrims who had traveled to the Holy Land.

³St. Thomas Becket, murdered in Canterbury Cathedral in 1170.

⁴Southward, a suburb of London south of the Thames and the traditional starting point for the pilgrimage to Canterbury in Kent, was notorious as a center of gambling and prostitution. The Tabard Inn was an actual public house at the time, named for the shape of its sign which resembled the coarse, sleeveless outergarment worn by members of the lower classes, monks, and footsoldiers alike.

But nathelees, whil I have time and
    space,°   *opportunity*
Er that I ferther in this tale pace,°   *proceed*
Me thinketh it accordant to resoun
To telle you al the condicioun°   *circumstances*
Of eech of hem, so as it seemed me,
And whiche they were, and of what degree,°   *social status* 40
And eek in what array that they were inne:
And at a knight thanne wol I first biginne.

Questions for Interactive Reading and Writing

1. *The Canterbury Tales* is a series of stories about the pilgrimages, common in the Middle Ages, to the Canterbury Cathedral, where the martyr Thomas Beckett was buried. The stories allow Chaucer to create portraits of many of the commoners of England, each with a different tale to tell. Written in Middle English, it is considered one of the greatest works of English literature, both because it is one of the earliest written in the vernacular (high literature was written in French) but also because it paints an engaging portrait of English life. This portion begins an introduction of the characters whose tales Chaucer is going to tell. Paraphrase line by line what is being said at the beginning of this collection of tales. Read the poem aloud to get a sense of the rhythm and music of the language. What is your impression of the language? How does Middle English relate to the English language today?

2. List the elements of nature present in the first 10 lines. How do they create the impression of spring?

3. How many stressed syllables are in each line? How would you describe the rhyme scheme?

4. Why would pilgrims choose this season to make their pilgrimage?

5. Why would stories be written in verse instead of prose?

John Donne (1572–1631)

Batter my heart, three-personed God, for You (c. 1610)

Batter my heart, three-personed God, for You
As yet but knock, breathe, shine, and seek to mend.
That I may rise and stand, o'erthrow me, and bend
Your force to break, blow, burn, and make me new.
5 I, like an usurped town to another due,
Labor to admit You, but Oh, to no end.
Reason, Your viceroy in me, me should defend,
But is captived, and proves weak or untrue.
Yet dearly I love You, and would be lovèd fain,
10 But am betrothed unto Your enemy;
Divorce me, untie or break that knot again,
Take me to You, imprison me, for I,
Except You enthrall me, never shall be free,
Nor ever chaste, except You ravish me.

Questions for Interactive Reading and Writing

1. Identify the form of this poem. Which elements led you to name this form?

2. Underline all the words the speaker uses as a direct command to God. What tone do these words create? What do they reveal about the speaker's state of mind?

3. In plain terms, what is the speaker asking God to do?

4. What does the speaker have to say about his "Reason," or in other words, his rational thought?

5. The ending couplet contains the paradox that the speaker is free if God enthralls him and not chaste unless God ravishes him. How do you make sense of that paradox?

H. D. (Hilda Doolittle) (1886–1961)

For a brief biography of H. D. (Hilda Doolittle), see Chapter 22.

Helen (1924)

All Greece hates
the still eyes in the white face,
the lustre as of olives
where she stands,
and the white hands.   5

All Greece reviles
the wan face when she smiles,
hating it deeper still
when it grows wan and white,
remembering past enchantments   10
and past ills.

Greece sees, unmoved,
God's daughter, born of love,
the beauty of cool feet
and slenderest knees,   15
could love indeed the maid,
only if she were laid,
white ash amid funereal cypresses.

Questions for Interactive Reading and Writing

1. Look up Helen in Greek mythology. What reasons might Greece have for hating her?

2. Does the speaker agree with Greece's hatred of Helen, or does the speaker offer a different perspective?

3. According to the poem, under what circumstances could Greece love Helen?

4. How does Helen change from stanza one to stanza two?

Seamus Heaney (b. 1939)

For a brief biography of Seamus Heaney, see Chapter 24.

Mid-Term Break (1966)

I sat all morning in the college sick bay
Counting bells knelling classes to a close,
At two o'clock our neighbors drove me home.

In the porch I met my father crying—
5 He had always taken funerals in his stride—
And Big Jim Evans saying it was a hard blow.

The baby cooed and laughed and rocked the pram
When I came in, and I was embarrassed
By old men standing up to shake my hand

10 And tell me they were "sorry for my trouble,"
Whispers informed strangers I was the eldest,
Away at school, as my mother held my hand

In hers and coughed out angry tearless sighs.
At ten o'clock the ambulance arrived
15 With the corpse, stanched and bandaged by the nurses.

Next morning I went up into the room. Snowdrops
And candles soothed the bedside; I saw him
For the first time in six weeks. Paler now,

Wearing a poppy bruise on the left temple,
20 He lay in the four foot box as in a cot.
No gaudy scars, the bumper knocked him clear.

A four foot box, a foot for every year.

Questions for Interactive Reading and Writing

1. How much do we learn about the speaker's life in this poem?

2. Why do you think Heaney employs such a thorough amount of narrative detail in this elegy?

3. How does the final line of the poem contrast with the detail of the preceding lines?

Dorianne Laux (b. 1952)

The Shipfitter's Wife (1999)

I loved him most
when he came home from work,
his fingers still curled from fitting pipe,
his denim shirt ringed with sweat,
and smelling of salt, the drying weeds   5
of the ocean. I'd go to where he sat
on the edge of the bed, his forehead
anointed with grease, his cracked hands
jammed between his thighs, and unlace
the steel-toed boots, stroke his ankles,   10
and calves, the pads and bones of his feet.
Then I'd open his clothes and take
the whole day inside me—the ship's
gray sides, the miles of copper pipe,
the voice of the first man clanging   15
off the hull's silver ribs. Spark of lead
kissing metal. The clamp, the winch,
the white fire of the torch, the whistle
and the long drive home.

Questions for Interactive Reading and Writing

1. How does the woman describe her husband? Since this is a past-tense set of memories, and if she loved him "most" when he came home from work, how far removed is the remembered past?

2. Why do you think the speaker floods this poem with specific, concrete images?

3. Would you call this poem an elegy? Why or why not?

John Milton (1608–1674)

When I consider how my light is spent (1655?)

When I consider how my light is spent,
  Ere half my days, in this dark world and wide,
  And that one talent which is death to hide
  Lodged with me useless, though my soul more bent
5 To serve therewith my Maker, and present
  My true account, lest he returning chide;
  "Doth God exact day-labor, light denied?"
  I fondly ask; but Patience to prevent
That murmur, soon replies, "God doth not need
10   Either man's work or his own gifts; who best
  Bear his mild yoke, they serve him best. His state
Is kingly. Thousands at his bidding speed
  And post o'er land and ocean without rest:
  They also serve who only stand and wait."

Questions for Interactive Reading and Writing

1. There are two speakers directly quoted in this poem (line 7 and lines 9–14). Who are they?

2. Given that "light" means eyesight in the context of this poem, paraphrase the speaker's anxiety in lines 3–5.

3. Paraphrase the quoted words in lines 9–14. How does that message answer the anxiety you identified in question 2?

4. What is the form of this poem? What elements lead you to your conclusion?

Robert Pinsky (b. 1940)

For a brief biography of Robert Pinsky, see Chapter 3.

Sonnet (1983)

Afternoon sun on her back,
calm irregular slap
of water against a dock.

Thin pines clamber
over the hill's top—   5
nothing to remember,

only the same lake
that keeps making the same
sounds under her cheek

and flashing the same color.   10
No one to say her name,
no need, no one to praise her,

only the lake's voice—over
and over, to keep it before her.

Questions for Interactive Reading and Writing

1. Contrast the regular rhythms of the form with the apparent calm and relaxed nature of the subject of the poem. Do the half rhymes—"lake . . . cheek," "color . . . her"—suggest anything about the essence of the subject?

2. Why do you think the poet chose the sonnet form and not a less fixed form for this particular poem? How does the poem vary from the traditional sonnet form?

3. How old might the woman be? Can you make an argument that the "her" of the poem might be a young girl? What evidence—one way or the other—does the poet provide?

4. If you were going to make a painting of the same subject as the poem—a portrait of a woman on a dock at lakeside on a summer afternoon—what colors might you use? Would you, in the spirit of the poem, make a realistic portrait? Or would it be more abstract, less distinct? Explain why you would make these choices.

William Wordsworth (1770–1850)

For a brief biography of William Wordsworth, see Chapter 17.

Lines Written a Few Miles above Tintern Abbey, on Revisiting the Banks of the Wye during a Tour, July 13, 1798.

Five years have past; five summers, with the length
Of five long winters! and again I hear
These waters, rolling from their mountain-springs
With a sweet inland murmur.*—Once again
5 Do I behold these steep and lofty cliffs,
Which on a wild secluded scene impress
Thoughts of more deep seclusion; and connect
The landscape with the quiet of the sky.
The day is come when I again repose
10 Here, under this dark sycamore, and view
These plots of cottage-ground, these orchard-tufts,
Which, at this season, with their unripe fruits,
Among the woods and copses lose themselves,
Nor, with their green and simple hue, disturb
15 The wild green landscape. Once again I see
These hedge-rows, hardly hedge-rows, little lines
Of sportive wood run wild; these pastoral farms,
Green to the very door; and wreathes of smoke
Sent up, in silence, from among the trees,
20 With some uncertain notice, as might seem,

---

*The river is not affected by the tides a few miles above Tintern.
[Wordsworth's note]

Of vagrant dwellers in the houseless woods,
Or of some hermit's cave, where by his fire
The hermit sits alone.

Though absent long,
These forms of beauty have not been to me,   25
As is a landscape to a blind man's eye:
But oft, in lonely rooms, and mid the din
Of towns and cities, I have owed to them,
In hours of weariness, sensations sweet,
Felt in the blood, and felt along the heart,   30
And passing even into my purer mind
With tranquil restoration:—feelings too
Of unremembered pleasure; such, perhaps,
As may have had no trivial influence
On that best portion of a good man's life;   35
His little, nameless, unremembered acts
Of kindness and of love. Nor less, I trust,
To them I may have owed another gift,
Of aspect more sublime; that blessed mood,
In which the burthen of the mystery,   40
In which the heavy and the weary weight
Of all this unintelligible world
Is lighten'd:—that serene and blessed mood,
In which the affections gently lead us on,
Until, the breath of this corporeal frame,   45
And even the motion of our human blood
Almost suspended, we are laid asleep
In body, and become a living soul:
While with an eye made quiet by the power
Of harmony, and the deep power of joy,   50
We see into the life of things.

If this
Be but a vain belief, yet, oh! how oft,
In darkness, and amid the many shapes
Of joyless day-light; when the fretful stir   55
Unprofitable, and the fever of the world,
Have hung upon the beatings of my heart,
How oft, in spirit, have I turned to thee
O sylvan Wye! Thou wanderer through the wood
How often has my spirit turned to thee!   60

And now, with gleams of half-extinguish'd though[t,]
With many recognitions dim and faint,
And somewhat of a sad perplexity,

The picture of the mind revives again:
65 While here I stand, not only with the sense
Of present pleasure, but with pleasing thoughts
That in this moment there is life and food
For future years. And so I dare to hope
Though changed, no doubt, from what I was, when first
70 I came among these hills; when like a roe
I bounded o'er the mountains, by the sides
Of the deep rivers, and the lonely streams,
Wherever nature led; more like a man
Flying from something that he dreads, than one
75 Who sought the thing he loved. For nature then
(The coarser pleasures of my boyish days,
And their glad animal movements all gone by,)
To me was all in all.—I cannot paint
What then I was. The sounding cataract
80 Haunted me like a passion: the tall rock,
The mountain, and the deep and gloomy wood,
Their colours and their forms, were then to me
An appetite: a feeling and a love,
That had no need of a remoter charm,
85 By thought supplied, or any interest
Unborrowed from the eye.—That time is past,
And all its aching joys are now no more,
And all its dizzy raptures. Not for this
Faint I, nor mourn nor murmur; other gifts
90 Have followed, for such loss, I would believe,
Abundant recompense. For I have learned
To look on nature, not as in the hour
Of thoughtless youth, but hearing oftentimes
The still, sad music of humanity,
95 Nor harsh nor grating, though of ample power
To chasten and subdue. And I have felt
A presence that disturbs me with the joy
Of elevated thoughts; a sense sublime
Of something far more deeply interfused,
100 Whose dwelling is the light of setting suns,
And the round ocean, and the living air,
And the blue sky, and in the mind of man,
A motion and a spirit, that impels
All thinking things, all objects of all thought,
105 And rolls through all things. Therefore am I still
A lover of the meadows and the woods,
And mountains; and of all that we behold
From this green earth; of all the mighty world

Of eye and ear, both what they half-create,*
And what perceive; well pleased to recognize   110
In nature and the language of the sense,
The anchor of my purest thoughts, the nurse,
The guide, the guardian of my heart, and soul
Of all my moral being.

Nor, perchance,   115
If I were not thus taught, should I the more
Suffer my genial spirits to decay:
For thou art with me, here, upon the banks
Of this fair river; thou, my dearest Friend,
My dear, dear Friend, and in thy voice I catch   120
The language of my former heart, and read
My former pleasures in the shooting lights
Of thy wild eyes. Oh! yet a little while
May I behold in thee what I was once,
My dear, dear Sister! And this prayer I make,   125
Knowing that Nature never did betray
The heart that loved her; 'tis her privilege,
Through all the years of this our life, to lead
From joy to joy: for she can so inform
The mind that is within us, so impress   130
With quietness and beauty, and so feed
With lofty thoughts, that neither evil tongues,
Rash judgments, nor the sneers of selfish men,
Nor greetings where no kindness is, nor all
The dreary intercourse of daily life,   135
Shall e'er prevail against us, or disturb
Our chearful faith that all which we behold
Is full of blessings. Therefore let the moon
Shine on thee in thy solitary walk;
And let the misty mountain winds be free   140
To blow against thee: and in after years,
When these wild ecstasies shall be matured
Into a sober pleasure, when thy mind
Shall be a mansion for all lovely forms,
Thy memory be as a dwelling-place   145
For all sweet sounds and harmonies; Oh! then,
If solitude, or fear, or pain, or grief,
Should be thy portion, with what healing thoughts

---

*This line has a close resemblance to an admirable line of Young, the exact expression of which I cannot recollect. [Wordsworth's note]

Of tender joy wilt thou remember me,
150 And these my exhortations! Nor, perchance,
If I should be, where I no more can hear
Thy voice, nor catch from thy wild eyes these gleams
Of past existence, wilt thou then forget
That on the banks of this delightful stream
155 We stood together; and that I, so long
A worshipper of Nature, hither came,
Unwearied in that service: rather say
With warmer love, oh! with far deeper zeal
Of holier love. Nor wilt thou then forget,
160 That after many wanderings, many years
Of absence, these steep woods and lofty cliffs,
And this green pastoral landscape, were to me
More dear, both for themselves and for thy sake.

Questions for Interactive Reading and Writing

1. What is the setting of this poem (besides being a few miles from Tintern Abbey)? Is this the first time the speaker has been there?

2. Who is with the speaker? How does the speaker feel towards this second person?

3. What role does memory play in this poem?

4. Scan the poem to determine its meter. Does it have a consistent meter? If so, what is it?

5. How would you describe the speaker's tone? How does he feel to be at this place?

6. In what ways is this poem an ode?

William Butler Yeats (1865–1939)

For a brief biography of William Butler Yeats, see Chapter 17.

The Second Coming (1921)

Turning and turning in the widening gyre
The falcon cannot hear the falconer;
Things fall apart; the center cannot hold;

Mere anarchy is loosed upon the world,
The blood-dimmed tide is loosed, and everywhere 5
The ceremony of innocence is drowned;
The best lack all conviction, while the worst
Are full of passionate intensity.

Surely some revelation is at hand;
Surely the Second Coming is at hand: 10
The Second Coming! Hardly are those words out
When a vast image out of *Spiritus Mundi*
Troubles my sight: somewhere in sands of the desert
A shape with lion body and the head of a man,
A gaze blank and pitiless as the sun, 15
Is moving its slow thighs, while all about it
Reel shadows of the indignant desert birds.
The darkness drops again; but now I know
That twenty centuries of stony sleep
Were vexed to nightmare by a rocking cradle, 20
And what rough beast, its hour come round at last,
Slouches towards Bethlehem to be born?

Questions for Interactive Reading and Writing

1. Describe the imagery in the first stanza. What is the cumulative effect of such images as a "falcon who cannot hear the falconer" and the "blood-dimmed tide"?

2. Identify the allusions to Christianity. Do these allusions create a hopeful message?

3. At the end of the poem, how does Yeats describe the being behind the "Second Coming"?

4. Describe the form of the poem. How does it resonate with the idea of anarchy established in stanza 1?

Reading for Fixed Forms

When reading for fixed forms, note patterns in line length, meter, stanza structure, and rhyme scheme, and consider how the poem uses these preestablished schemes.

How is the poem broken up visually?	*Stanza:* unit of two or more lines, set off by a space, and often sharing the same rhythm and meter *Notice lines grouped by rhyme, meter, or purpose.* TWO LINES: *Couplet:* two lines of poetry that form a unit of meaning *Heroic couplet:* two lines of rhymed, iambic pentameter THREE LINES: *Tercet:* three-line stanza *Triplet:* tercet in which all three lines rhyme *Terza rima:* tercets of interlocking rhymes with the middle line rhyming with the first and third lines of the preceding tercet: *aba, bcb, cdc, ded,* and so on FOUR LINES: *Quatrain:* four-line stanza *Ballad stanza:* quatrain consisting of alternating four-stress and three-stress lines, usually rhymed *abcb* *Common measure:* ballad stanza popular to hymns, consistently iambic, and usually featuring an *abcb* or *abab* rhyme scheme
Are there fourteen lines in the poem?	*Sonnet:* fourteen-line poem, usually in iambic pentameter, with a varied rhyme scheme that employs a call-and-response structure with an answer in the final two lines *Petrarchan (Italian) sonnet:* sonnet consisting of an octave rhyming *abbaabba* and of a sestet using any arrangement of two or three additional rhymes, such as *cdcdcd* or *cdecde* *Shakespearean (English, Elizabethan) sonnet:* sonnet consisting of three quatrains and a final couplet in iambic pentameter with the rhyme scheme *abab cdcd efef gg*
Is the poem only a few lines?	*Haiku:* unrhymed Japanese poem, often featuring observations on nature, generally written in three lines of five, seven, and five syllables *Epigram:* short poem highlighting a witty idea, satirical thought, or condensed comment *Limerick:* humorous poem of five usually anapestic lines with the rhyme scheme of *aabba*

Are lines repeated?	*Villanelle:* poem consisting of five tercets and a concluding quatrain; each tercet rhymes *aba* and the final quatrain rhymes *abaa*. The poem's opening line repeats as the final line of the second and fourth stanzas and in the second-to-last line of the poem. The last line of the first stanza repeats as the final line of the third and fifth stanzas and is also the final line of the poem overall.
	Sestina: poem of six six-line stanzas and a three-line envoi, usually unrhymed, in which each stanza repeats the end words of the lines of the first stanza, but in different order, the envoi using the six words again, three in the middle of the lines and three at the end
	Envoi: short closing stanza in certain verse forms, such as the ballade or sestina, summarizing its main ideas
	Pantoum: variation on the villanelle, consisting of an unspecified number of quatrains with the rhyme scheme *abab*. The first line of each quatrain repeats the second line of the preceding quatrain, and the third line repeats the final line of the preceding quatrain. In the final quatrain, the second line repeats the third line of the first quatrain, and the last line of the poem repeats the first line of the poem.
What is the tone of the poem?	*Elegy:* mournful poem lamenting the dead or reflecting somberly on life's hardship *Ode:* elevated, formal lyric poem often written in commemoration of someone or an abstract subject

Writing about Fixed Forms

1. Analyze the argumentative and rhetorical purposes of Hirsch's "My First Theology Lesson."

2. Compare and contrast Shakespeare's attitude toward love in two different sonnets (see Chapter 17 and Chapter 20, for example). Pay special attention to how he uses the sonnet's architecture to build his meaning.

3. Compare the form of one haiku and one epigram from the chapter. Can a haiku be an epigram?

4. Compare the speaker's relationship to his subject matter in Percy Bysshe Shelley's "Ode to the West Wind" and John Keats's "Ode on a Grecian Urn" (Chapter 20).

5. How does the tone and approach to meditating on death and mortality differ in W. H. Auden's "In Memory of W. B. Yeats," A. E. Housman's "To an Athlete Dying Young," and Dorianne Laux's "The Shipfitter's Wife"?

6. How does the form support the poets' reflections on time and familial structure in Dylan Thomas's "Do not go gentle into that good night" and Elizabeth Bishop's "One Art"?

26
Open Form

ALL the new thinking is about loss.
In this it resembles all the old thinking.
The idea, for example, that each particular erases
the luminous clarity of a general idea. That the clown-
faced woodpecker probing the dead sculpted trunk
of that black birch is, by his presence,
some tragic falling off from a first world
of undivided light. Or the other notion that,
because there is in this world no one thing
to which the bramble of *blackberry* corresponds,
a word is elegy to what it signifies.
　　　　—from "Meditation at Lagunitas" by Robert Hass

"Starting with Walt Whitman, people began to experiment with not having a set number of lines or preconditions for the writing, of just letting it flow out and see what happens, and that got to be called free verse, open form. There's nothing particularly complicated about understanding it. You just say it out loud. If you say words . . . in a certain pattern, if you start just saying, as I'm saying to you now, [words] in sentences with pauses . . . , if you reflect in the way you put those down on the page, those rhythms, you'll get this thing I was saying, which is the emotion of the rhythm of the truth of the experience that the piece of writing is talking about."

Conversation with Robert Hass, available on connect.mcgraw-hill.com

ROBERT Hass's poem "Meditation at Laguni-tas" is an intimate reflection on words—their purpose and power, their often profound connections to memory. "All the new thinking is about loss," says the poem's speaker, and "a word is elegy to what it signifies." By poem's end, the repetition of the word *blackberry* has become a vocal testament to the sensual potential of language; you can see and hear and touch and feel it, *taste* the word. The poet reacts critically to the academic idea that language may be unable to capture the individual essence of a "particular" thing or object, and that language itself may misrepresent the physical specifics we wordlessly see and feel. Hass's poem asserts the reverse. Words, he writes, really do make manifest by naming our memories and sensations. Words can serve us as powerfully and immediately as memories from childhood or of love.

To best embody the ideas and images he sets out to express, Hass has chosen **open form.** The term describes poetry that employs the sounds and rhythms of natural speech, repetition, grammatical variation, and patterns of imagery rather than formal rhyming structures. And instead of metrical feet, the line itself is the chief rhythmical unit we use to examine the individual components of an open form poem. So, how a line is arranged, and where it breaks, can be absolutely crucial to understanding a poem of this kind. "Meditation at Lagunitas" delves into complicated issues of language and memory yet is grounded in candid, vivid images and specific past experiences. As you listen to Hass read and discuss the poem in his interview, think about why he chose this particular form and about how different the poem would feel in formal fixed meter and rhyme.

Robert Hass

When I first heard poems, I felt like somebody was telling me the truth.

A Conversation on Writing

Poetry Goes with Equality in America

The country was founded by people who believe that, in order to save your soul, you had to learn to read. . . . So women were taught to read as well as men . . . , and the first book of poetry published in the United States was published by a woman. The first book of poems published by a black person, an African in the United States, was published by a woman. . . . So our country has been, from the start, one in which the attainment of literacy was a very powerful tool. . . . From the beginning, the core of it in some way had been the ability to read and figure out poetry.

Sound and the Size of Our Inner World

There's a way in which a poem or a story or something opens the size of the inner world to you, one's own inner world. You know, our consciousness is huge and mostly unexplored, and sometimes, something will, like throwing a stone into a well, give you a sense of those depths. For me, if I remember rightly, it was a poem in a school textbook by Tennyson. The lines I remember are "Blow, bugles, blow, set the wild echoes flying, / And answer, echoes, answer, dying, dying, dying." It seems corny to me now, but at the time, something opened in me to that sound that I now think had to do with the sense of the size of our inner life, the vastness of our capacity for loneliness, for happiness, for wonder.

The Emotional Truthfulness of Poems

I grew up in a house where there were drinking problems. In families that are troubled, there's a lot of denial. Nobody tells the truth much about anything. . . . A lot of it is kindness; it's short of hypocrisy. In some families, in some parts of the world, in dysfunctional institutions of all kinds, nobody ever tells the truth about anything, you know. When I first heard poems, I felt like somebody was telling me the truth.

Native to California—where he continues to live and teach—Robert Hass (b. 1941) has shaped his poetry through the lush landscape that frequently enters into his poems. His first book of poetry, *Field Guide* (1973), the name of which signals Hass's environmental interest, won the Yale Series of Younger Poets Prize. His subsequent collections, along with his work as translator—from Polish and Japanese, among other languages—compose Hass's body of creative work, which is known for its meditative quality and haiku-like clarity. In addition to winning the National Book Award and the Pulitzer Prize for his collection *Time and Materials* (2007), Hass held the position of Poet Laureate from 1995 to 1997. He used his term to bring poetry into areas he deemed devoid of imagination, such as the corporate world.

To watch this entire interview and hear the author read from his work, go to connect.mcgraw-hill.com.

RESEARCH ASSIGNMENT   In his interview, Hass talks about trying to translate Czeslaw Milosz. What did this teach him about translation? Contrast his experience with that of Ezra Pound, whom Hass discusses as the translator of a Chinese poem, "The River-Merchant's Wife" (in this chapter). Why does Hass say that translation makes the world accessible to us but at the same time is impossible?

AS YOU READ   Listen for what seems conversational here, even prosaic, and for what makes this "meditation" inescapably a poem.

Meditation at Lagunitas

(1979)

All the new thinking is about loss.
In this it resembles all the old thinking.
The idea, for example, that each particular erases
the luminous clarity of a general idea. That the clown-
5 faced woodpecker probing the dead sculpted trunk
of that black birch is, by his presence,
some tragic falling off from a first world
of undivided light. Or the other notion that,
because there is in this world no one thing
10 to which the bramble of *blackberry* corresponds,
a word is elegy to what it signifies.
We talked about it late last night and in the voice
of my friend, there was a thin wire of grief, a tone
almost querulous. After a while I understood that,
15 talking this way, everything dissolves: *justice,
pine, hair, woman, you* and *I*. There was a woman
I made love to and I remembered how, holding
her small shoulders in my hands sometimes,
I felt a violent wonder at her presence
20 like a thirst for salt, for my childhood river
with its island willows, silly music from the pleasure boat,
muddy places where we caught the little orange-silver fish
called *pumpkinseed*. It hardly had to do with her.
Longing, we say, because desire is full
25 of endless distances. I must have been the same to her.
But I remember so much, the way her hands dismantled bread,
the thing her father said that hurt her, what
she dreamed. There are moments when the body is as numinous
as words, days that are the good flesh continuing.
30 Such tenderness, those afternoons and evenings,
saying *blackberry, blackberry, blackberry.*

Writing from Reading

Summarize

1 Try to describe the situation here—the setting, the speaker, the intended audience. Where is "Lagunitas," for ex-ample, and what does it have to do with the text that follows?

2 In a dictionary, look up the word *numinous* and relate it to the experi-ence described here.

Analyze Craft

3 Do you think these choices of set-ting, speaker, and audience were conscious and premeditated or sheer instinct on the part of the poet, or perhaps a combination of both these?

Analyze Voice

4 Do the speaker's memories of a past love remind you of vivid memories in your own life? What language in the poem reminds you of these memories?

5 Why do you think the details remain in the speaker's mind?

Synthesize Summary and Analysis

6 What does the poet mean by "a word is elegy to what it signifies"?

And what does he mean by "the body is numinous as words"?

Interpret the Poem

7 Discuss the "tenderness" of the repeated final word. Is this finally a poem about loss—as in the opening assertion—or gain?

The presence of formal meter in a poem gives us rhythmic intervals we perceive much like a steady musical beat. Although this meter may sometimes vary (allowing a poet flexibility of diction, voice, and meaning), it stays generally consistent over the course of a poem. Closed, metrical forms such as this dominated poetry in English for hundreds of years. However, such formality was never the whole story; there have always been what we call "open forms" as well. Although we may associate open form poetry with contemporary poets, we can see it as early as the King James Bible's Psalms and "Song of Songs," in which English translators attempted to evoke the text's original Hebrew cadences. The "Song of Songs" is often regarded as an allegorical series of love poems between humanity and God, as in these joyful lines depicting the beginning of spring (the "turtle" described in the last line is a translation of "turtle dove"):

> *My beloved spake, and said unto me, Rise up, my love,*
> *my fair one, and come away.*
> *For, lo, the winter is past, the rain is over and gone;*
> *The flowers appear on the earth; the time of the singing*
> *of birds is come,*
> *and the voice of the turtle is heard in our land. . . .*

In open-form poetry, meter, stanza arrangement, and set rhyme schemes are never completely abandoned, but the poet feels less obligated to employ those techniques as if they were strict rules. Instead, the practitioner takes sounds and shape not from a preset formal pattern of meter and rhyme but from the writer's own individual preference—a preference that might well vary from day to day and subject to subject, as well as line by line. Between the late nineteenth and early twentieth centuries, many poets began to reject the formal obligations that had long been a part of the

"It's no accident that all the great books—the great religious books, the Bible, the Koran, the Sutras—are composed in poetry. So, poetry I think is our original primal language, and I think that when we find ourselves in situations of distress or novelty, we automatically start thinking that way and expressing ourselves that way." Conversation with Al Young

genre. By this design, they allowed the poetic line (its extent, internal sounds, images, pauses, and breaks) to help shape the form.

VERS LIBRE, FREE VERSE, AND OPEN FORM

The term *open form* was coined to avoid the misleading connotations of the other commonly used term for unmetered poetry, *free verse.* "Free verse" is derived from the designation *vers libre,* a school of seventeenth-century French poetry (*vers libre* means "free verse" in French). "Open form" avoids the conclusion that poetry of this kind is completely ungoverned or unconcerned with craft. Although skilled free-verse poets may not always strictly observe rules of rhythm and rhyme, they are careful to fashion their lines with conscious attention to form, sound, and shape.

The New York–born poet Walt Whitman is often credited with inaugurating the widespread use of free verse in modern and contemporary poetry. His volume of poems *Leaves of Grass,* first published in 1855, took imaginative liberties with line length, rhyme, repetition, and word choice. No one had ever heard poems quite like Whitman's before. In this brief opening section from "Song of Myself," one of the poems in *Leaves of Grass,* note the surprising liberties Whitman takes with his language, his line length, his direct address to "you" the reader, and the fresh sound of his voice.

Walt Whitman (1819–1892)

For a brief biography of Walt Whitman, see Chapter 20.

AS YOU READ   Imagine yourself in a shared space with Whitman—the "you" to whom the "I" speaks. He's embarked on a long monologue. What might be your response?

Song of Myself (1891)

I celebrate myself, and sing myself,
And what I assume you shall assume,
For every atom belonging to me as good belongs to you.

I loafe and invite my soul,
5   I lean and loafe at my ease observing a spear of summer grass.

My tongue, every atom of my blood, form'd from this soil, this air,
Born here of parents born here from parents the same, and their parents
      the same,
I, now thirty-seven years old in perfect health begin,
Hoping to cease not till death.

10   Creeds and schools in abeyance,
Retiring back a while sufficed at what they are, but never forgotten,
I harbor for good or bad, I permit to speak at every hazard,
Nature without check with original energy.

Writing from Reading

Summarize

1 It's hard to summarize these lines, because they begin a very long poem indeed. How do they set the stage?

Analyze Craft

2 As it happens, Whitman's hope— that we would "cease not till death"—was realized; he worked at this poem for all his long life. What is modest or boastful about a phrase like "Born here of parents born here from parents the same, and their parents the same . . ."?

Analyze Voice

3 What do you notice about the line length here—its random nature as opposed to patterns? What does that tell you about freedom and "original energy"?

Synthesize Summary and Analysis

4 What sort of claims for art and life does the poet make here, and how do they seem "revolutionary"?

Interpret the Poem

5 Why does the poet claim that he will let "Nature without check" do the speaking?

Walt Whitman is, as suggested above, a major presence in the world of American letters. Poets often tip their caps to the work of other poets—as in Anthony Hecht's response to Matthew Arnold's "Dover Beach" (see Chapter 20). In the For Review and Further Study section of this chapter, the poet Allen Ginsberg remembers his great predecessor while shopping in California, a state Whitman never visited.

Here a contemporary American Indian author responds to the white-bearded ghost of an artist he, too, can treasure as an ancestor, even though there's something almost comic in the juxtaposition of basketball to Whitman's Civil War. In "Defending Walt Whitman," Sherman Alexie employs a number of formal techniques to tell a brief allegorical story about poetry and sport. Alexie writes with a design dictated by image and the emotions generated by the occasion of the poem: basketball and the life of young American Indian boys. Yet the nation's first major "free" poet takes center stage in his title. There is, with Whitman's "presence" in the poem, an awareness of tradition even while the artist struggles to report on change. When Alexie claims, about Whitman, that "this game belongs to him," he's celebrating poetry as well.

Sherman Alexie (b. 1966)

For a brief biography of Sherman Alexie, see Chapter 12.

AS YOU READ Think of this as a kind of conversation between the contemporary and the ancestral, the living and the dead.

Defending Walt Whitman (1996)

Basketball is like this for young Indian boys, all arms and legs
and serious stomach muscles. Every body is brown!
These are the twentieth-century warriors who will never kill,
although a few sat quietly in the deserts of Kuwait,
5 waiting for orders to do something, do something.

God, there is nothing as beautiful as a jump shot
on a reservation summer basketball court
where the ball is moist with sweat
and makes a sound when it swishes through the net
10 that causes Walt Whitman to weep because it is so perfect.

There are veterans of foreign wars here,
whose bodies are still dominated
by collarbones and knees, whose bodies still respond
in the ways that bodies are supposed to respond when we are young.
15 Every body is brown! Look there, that boy can run
up and down this court forever. He can leap for a rebound
with his back arched like a salmon, all meat and bone
synchronized, magnetic, as if the court were a river,
as if the rim were a dam, as if the air were a ladder
20 leading the Indian boy toward home.

Some of the Indian boys still wear their military haircuts
while a few have let their hair grow back.
It will never be the same as it was before!
One Indian boy has never cut his hair, not once, and he braids it
25 into wild patterns that do not measure anything.
He is just a boy with too much time on his hands.
Look at him. He wants to play this game in bare feet.

God, the sun is so bright! There is no place like this.
Walt Whitman stretches his calf muscles
30 on the sidelines. He has the next game.
His huge beard is ridiculous on the reservation.
Some body throws a crazy pass and Walt Whitman catches it with quick hands.
He brings the ball close to his nose
and breathes in all of its smells: leather, brown skin, sweat, black hair,
35 burning oil, twisted ankle, long drink of warm water,
gunpowder, pine tree. Walt Whitman squeezes the ball tightly.
He wants to run. He hardly has the patience to wait for his turn.
"What's the score?" he asks. He asks, "What's the score?"

Basketball is like this for Walt Whitman. He watches these Indian boys
40 as if they were the last bodies on earth. Every body is brown!
Walt Whitman shakes because he believes in God.
Walt Whitman dreams of the Indian boy who will defend him,
trapping him in the corner, all flailing arms and legs
and legendary stomach muscles. Walt Whitman shakes
45 because he believes in God. Walt Whitman dreams
of the first jump shot he will take, the ball arcing clumsily
from his fingers, striking the rim so hard that it sparks.
Walt Whitman shakes because he believes in God.
Walt Whitman closes his eyes. He is a small man and his beard
50 is ludicrous on the reservation, absolutely insane.
His beard makes the Indian boys righteously laugh. His beard frightens
the smallest Indian boys. His beard tickles the skin
of the Indian boys who dribble past him. His beard, his beard!

God, there is beauty in every body. Walt Whitman stands
55 at center court while the Indian boys run from basket to basket.
Walt Whitman cannot tell the difference between
offense and defense. He does not care if he touches the ball.
Half of the Indian boys wear T-shirts damp with sweat
and the other half are bareback, skin slick and shiny.
60 There is no place like this. Walt Whitman smiles.
Walt Whitman shakes. This game belongs to him.

Writing from Reading

Summarize

1 Think of this poem as a discussion of the impact of the past. What has changed; what stays the same?

Analyze Craft

2 Why do you think Alexie repeats certain phrases and words?

Analyze Voice

3 How does the language of this poem compare with language in poems by Walt Whitman? (See Chapters 20, 21, and 23, as well as the For Review and Further Study section later in this chapter.) "Defending" is something a basketball player must do, and it means "standing up for" or "taking the side of" as well. How would you describe the diction and the poet's tone?

Synthesize Summary and Analysis

4 Whitman wrote at length about the Civil War; Alexie here refers to the deserts of Kuwait" and the first Gulf War. How does he treat his "warriors," and what does he respect?

Interpret the Poem

5 Discuss the imaginary presence in this poem of Walt Whitman attending a pickup basketball game on an American Indian reservation. What connections do you think Alexie wants to make here among Whitman, Native-Americans, basketball, and war?

Modern writers have disagreed on the place of open-form poetry in the wider arena of English and American literature. Many believe open-form poetry reflects a democratic spirit, an opportunity to use the musical potential of the poetic line with greater fulfillment and flexibility. Others think that poetry unconcerned with rhythmic structure is simply amateurish. Robert Frost famously compared the writing of free-verse poetry to a game of tennis with no net.

It is hard to disagree that the prevalence of open-form poetry has helped facilitate a lot of bland, lightweight poems and that it even perpetuates the misconception that "anything can be a poem." As British novelist A. S. Byatt writes, "Free verse has come to represent democracy, equal opportunity, and self-expression. But in bulk and unaware of the forms from which it has been freed . . . it can be extremely depressing."

"You know, free verse to me . . . is nothing less than . . . a discovery, and we haven't even got to the bottom of it yet. We're only scratching the surface because ultimately free verse is a form of writing in which the poem is completely organized by instances of coincidence . . . stanzas are units of coincidence and lines become units of coincidence, and the whole poem becomes organized with that in mind. . . . It sounds simple, but it's a lot harder to do than one would think." Conversation with Li-Young Lee

Practitioners of open-form poetry insist that a successful poem "finds" a form using the poet's instinct and intent and that the absence of iambic pentameter or end rhyme (or other traditional devices) does not condemn a poem to pointlessness. In other words, when you write a poem you have definitely created a form of some kind, and that form in turn creates impressions in the reader. Of this aspect of composition, poet C. D. Wright says, "Poetry without form is a fiction. But that there is a freedom in words is the larger fact, and in poetry, where formal restrictions can bear down heavily, it is important to remember the cage is never locked."

Next, a pair of open-form poems by a pair of American masters—one dead, one still at work—demonstrate how supple the technique can be, and how personal. When e. e. cummings argues for the primacy of feeling and writes "who pays any attention / to the syntax of things," he's arguing, in effect, for the value of open form verse—breaking the rules of syntax in the subsequent phrase by leaving out the first-person pronoun that should "properly" be there before "will never wholly kiss you." And in this poem, certainly, "feeling is first."

e. e. cummings (1894–1962)

Born in Cambridge, Massachusetts, Edward Estlin Cummings earned both his undergraduate and graduate degrees from Harvard University. Although at first he wrote poetry modeled after that of the pre-Raphaelites and other classical practitioners, he soon developed his own innovative style that focused on the poem's appearance on the page, a lack of capitalization, and a free, liberal use of words (he often turned verbs into nouns and vice versa). His poems appear complex and are pleasing orally, yet the ideas behind them are often simple messages against conformity and in favor of love. Consistent with his bohemian spirit, e. e. cummings made a career of being an artist, both in poetry and in drawing and painting. In addition to his poetry collections, such as *Tulips and Chimneys* (1923), Cummings wrote a series of lectures that he delivered at Harvard, though by his request they were called "nonlectures" and later published as *Six Nonlectures* (1953).

AS YOU READ Place the poem somewhere between the loosest of sonnets and the most restricted free verse.

since feeling is first (1926)

since feeling is first
who pays any attention
to the syntax of things
will never wholly kiss you;

5   wholly to be a fool
while Spring is in the world

my blood approves,
and kisses are a far better fate
than wisdom
10 lady i swear by all flowers.   Don't cry
—the best gesture of my brain is less than
your eyelids' flutter which says

we are for each other:then
laugh,leaning back in my arms
15 for life's not a paragraph

And death i think is no parenthesis

Writing from Reading

Summarize

1 Do you agree or disagree with the assessment that this is a love poem, said in modern language, by an old-fashioned soul? Why?

Analyze Craft

2 What controls the progress of the poem? Is it the unfolding of the anecdote of the kiss or the deeply ingrained sense of form that the poet never really wholly disregards?

Analyze Voice

3 The pun-making poet—wholly = holy—is also a fun-making poet. What is the link between free verse in this instance and the freeing of the poet's sense of humor?

Synthesize Summary and Analysis

4 The poet attempts to create an order (syntax) based on feelings, and the result is either delightful or frivolous. Which do you find it to be?

Interpret the Poem

5 What is the role in this poem of instinct versus intellect?

Galway Kinnell (b. 1927)

Born in Providence, Rhode Island, Galway Kinnell was educated at Princeton University and the University of Rochester. In addition to serving in the U.S. Navy, Kinnell also worked for the Congress of Racial Equality during the civil rights movement. His poetry, including his book-length poem on the Vietnam War, *The Book of Nightmares* (1971), demonstrates a deep awareness of the nation's life. More often, however, Kinnell's poetry shows a consciousness of the natural world and of death, but in such a way that it is energetic rather than filled with despair. Kinnell has taught at many universities, and his *Selected Poems* (1980) won both the Pulitzer Prize and the National Book Award.

AS YOU READ   Think about how individual choices of rhythm, language, sound, pauses, line length, and endings help this piece become more than sentences of prose cut into shorter lines.

FOR INTERACTIVE READING . . .

Look for repetitions of words and make note of them.

After Making Love We Hear Footsteps (1980)

For I can snore like a bullhorn
or play loud music
or sit up talking with any reasonably sober Irishman
and Fergus will only sink deeper
5 into his dreamless sleep, which goes by all in one flash,
but let there be that heavy breathing
or a stifled come-cry anywhere in the house
and he will wrench himself awake
and make for it on the run—as now, we lie together,
10 after making love, quiet, touching along the length of our bodies,
familiar touch of the long-married,
and he appears—in his baseball pajamas, it happens,
the neck opening so small he has to screw them on—
and flops down between us and hugs us and snuggles himself to sleep,
15 his face gleaming with satisfaction at being this very child.

In the half darkness we look at each other
and smile
and touch arms across this little, startlingly muscled body—
this one whom habit of memory propels to the ground of his making,
20 sleeper only the mortal sounds can sing awake,
this blessing love gives again into our arms.

Writing from Reading

Summarize

1 Why is this poem in two stanzas? How does the second respond to the first?

Analyze Craft

2 Are there rhymes in this poem? Do they help connect the elements contained?

3 How many sentences make up this poem? Why do you think Kinnell chooses to write so few separate sentences in a poem with so many lines?

Analyze Voice

4 How would you describe the speaker's attitude toward his child?

Synthesize Summary and Analysis

5 Open form poets often consider the line the principal unit of sense and meaning. How do individual lines in the poem help create a sense of order or form?

Interpret the Poem

6 What does the poet mean by "this one whom habit of memory propels to the ground of his making," and can you read this poem as a text about the making of poetry itself?

In the spirit of the "free" and "open" possibilities of contemporary poetry, C. K. Williams creates a narrative with lines much longer than those of most unmetered verse. "Tar" conveys deep emotion by means of a story line or set of anecdotes (incidents) composed in very long lines. "Three Mile Island" refers to the location of a nuclear plant in Pennsylvania and a meltdown there in 1979.

C. K. Williams (b. 1936)

Born in Newark, New Jersey, Charles Kenneth Williams turned to poetry at age nineteen, after he had finished his required English courses at the University of Pennsylvania, where he earned his degree. Williams's ten books of poetry— including the Pulitzer Prize–winning *Repair* (1999) and the National Book Award–winning *The Singing* (2003)— emphasize the pain of human existence in lines that are unconventionally long. The length of his lines is reminiscent of Whitman, though he wholly lacks Whitman's optimism. Williams was a group therapist for troubled adolescents in Philadelphia, edited materials in psychiatry and architecture, and is currently at Princeton University, continuing an academic career that has included Columbia, George Mason, and Drexel universities.

AS YOU READ   Pay attention to the line breaks. They depend on a visual cue. It would have been simple enough to keep such words as "atmosphere" or "Susquehanna" or "clinging" as single words, not hyphenated ones, but Williams calls our attention to the way lines fuse or break apart. That hurtling description of risk and wreckage enters the narrative at least in part by way of its line length; there's no chance to pause for breath.

FOR INTERACTIVE READING . . .

Look up the word *tar* in a dictionary and think about how this word connects the national event in the poem with the personal housework that is going on.

Tar (1983)

The first morning of Three Mile Island: those first disquieting, uncertain, mystifying hours.
All morning a crew of workmen have been tearing the old decrepit roof off our building,
and all morning, trying to distract myself, I've been wandering out to watch them
as they hack away the leaden layers of asbestos paper and disassemble the disintegrating drains.
5 After half a night of listening to the news, wondering how to know a hundred miles downwind
if and when to make a run for it and where, then a coming bolt awake at seven
when the roofers we've been waiting for since winter sent their ladders shrieking up our wall,
we still know less than nothing: the utility company continues making little of the accident,
the slick federal spokesmen still have their evasions in some semblance of order.
10 Surely we suspect now we're being lied to, but in the meantime, there are the roofers,
setting winch-frames, sledging rounds of tar apart, and there I am, on the curb across, gawking.

I never realized what brutal work it is, how matter-of-factly and harrowingly dangerous.
The ladders flex and quiver, things skid from the edge, the materials are bulky and recalcitrant.
When the rusty, antique nails are levered out, their heads pull off; the under-roofing crumbles.
15 Even the battered little furnace, roaring along as patient as a donkey, chokes and clogs,
a dense, malignant smoke shoots up, someone has to fiddle with a cock, then hammer it,
before the gush and stench will deintensify, the dark, Dantean broth wearily subside.
In its crucible, the stuff looks bland, like licorice, spill it, though, on your boots or coveralls,
it sears, and everything is permeated with it, the furnace gunked with burst and half-burst bubbles,
20 the men themselves so completely slashed and mucked they seem almost from another realm,
     like trolls.
When they take their break, they leave their brooms standing at attention in the asphalt pails,
work gloves clinging like Brer Rabbit to the bitten shafts, and they slouch along the precipitous lip,
the enormous sky behind them, the heavy noontime air alive with shimmers and mirages.

Sometime in the afternoon I had to go inside: the advent of our vigil was upon us.
25 However much we didn't want to, however little we would do about it, we'd understood:
we were going to perish of all this, if not now, then soon, if not soon, then someday.
Someday, some final generation, hysterically aswarm beneath an atmosphere as unrelenting as rock,
would rue us all, anathematize our earthly comforts, curse our surfeits and submissions.
I think I know, though I might rather not, why my roofers stay so clear to me and why the rest,
30 the terror of that time, the reflexive disbelief and distancing, all we should hold on to, dims so.
I remember the president in his absurd protective booties, looking absolutely unafraid, the fool.
I remember a woman on the front page glaring across the misty Susquehanna at those looming
     stacks.
But, more vividly, the men, silvered with glitter from the shingles, clinging like starlings beneath
     the eaves.
Even the leftover carats of tar in the gutter, so black they seemed to suck the light out of the air.
35 By nightfall kids had come across them: every sidewalk on the block was scribbled with obscenities
     and hearts.

Writing from Reading

Summarize

1 An "occasional" poem takes a specific event or date as its subject. What is the occasion for this poem?

Analyze Craft

2 Compare the line length here with that of the lines in Walt Whitman's "Song of Myself." This poem is not, of course, a celebration, but what effect does choosing long lines have in this poem?

3 Sometimes the language in "Tar" feels very plainspoken and conver- sational; at other times it sounds elevated and more traditionally poetic. Where do these changes happen? What kind of events or images do they describe? What is their significance?

Analyze Voice

4 What do you think the poet means by "I think I know, though I might rather not" or "I remember"? Do these lines set a tone for this poem? What other lines can you point to that create the poem's tone?

Synthesize Summary and Analysis

5 The poem takes place amid a real-life national crisis. What is the relation- ship of the event at Three Mile Island and Williams's description of the housework going on in his building?

Interpret the Poem

6 As this is a poem of political and social commentary, is it surprising that these lines should end as they do, and in what ways does "the terror of that time" transform itself into graffiti—as in "obscenities and hearts"?

The poet Sharon Olds describes internal wreckage, though she, too, deals with "obscenities and hearts." Here, too, the language is that of everyday discourse, the ex- perience described a common one—but shot through with the power of erotic and psy- chological encounter.

Sharon Olds (b. 1942)

Born in California, Sharon Olds received a B.A. from Stanford University and a Ph.D. from Columbia University. Her award-winning poetry collections include *The Dead and the Living* (1983), which won the National Book Critics Circle Award, and *The Father* (1992), which was short- listed for the T. S. Eliot Prize. A poet in the confessional tradition of poets such as Anne Sexton and Sylvia Plath—that is, po- etry that takes the poet's personal life as its subject—Olds writes on themes of the body, family life, sex, and violence. She currently teaches at New York University and has been involved as a founder and teacher of the creative writing program for the physically disabled at Goldwater Hospital in New York City.

AS YOU READ Ask yourself if this is a poem about morality or whether it has another subject.

Sex without Love (1984)

How do they do it, the ones who make love
without love? Beautiful as dancers,
gliding over each other like ice-skaters
over the ice, fingers hooked
5 inside each other's bodies, faces
red as steak, wine, wet as the
children at birth whose mothers are going to
give them away. How do they come to the
come to the   come to the   God   come to the
10 still waters, and not love
the one who came there with them, light
rising slowly as steam off their joined
skin? These are the true religious,
the purists, the pros, the ones who will not
15 accept a false Messiah, love the
priest instead of the God. They do not
mistake the lover for their own pleasure,
they are like great runners: they know they are alone
with the road surface, the cold, the wind,
20 the fit of their shoes, their over-all cardio-
vascular health—just factors, like the partner
in the bed, and not the truth, which is the
single body alone in the universe
against its own best time.

Writing from Reading

Summarize

1 The poet meditates on the question of sex and love. What conclusion does the speaker in the poem draw about this relationship?

Analyze Craft

2 Discuss the poem's lineation and lack of stanza breaks. Why do you think Olds makes these choices?

3 What other poetic techniques suggest this poem's open form has specific intentions?

Analyze Voice

4 The poem incorporates many similes. How do they help express the speaker's attitude toward the subject matter?

Synthesize Summary and Analysis

5 The poet takes up a question important to moralists and romantics alike. With whom does she seem to stand?

Interpret the Poem

6 What does the poem imply about the relation of love and sex in the context of our lives? Can we ever feel as though we are together with someone and not terribly alone?

VISUAL POETRY

Poets writing outside of fixed forms occasionally decide to shape their lines into a recognizable picture. **Visual** (or **concrete**) **poetry** is poetry written in the shape of something it describes. In his poem "Easter Wings," George Herbert works within a noticeable rhyme scheme (*ababa cdcdc*) and metric regularity, but he arranges the lines in an unconventional form. His verse is not "free," but neither is it organized by a previous tradition; no series of earlier poems has this particular *shape*.

George Herbert (1593–1633)

Born into a prominent Welsh family, George Herbert was one of ten children, all of whom his mother raised alone after their father's early death. Educated at Trinity College, Cambridge, Herbert held the post of public orator, or spokesman, for the university. Although his election to Parliament suggested a political career, he became a minister to a rural parish in 1630, where he served until his death from consumption. Herbert's reputation as a poet rests solely on one volume, *The Temple* (1633), published posthumously; the rest of his poetry has been lost. *The Temple,* however, shows a great range, not only in poetic style—from lengthy poems to short lyrics, shape poems, acrostics, and sonnets—but also in feeling, as Herbert concerned himself with his relationship to God.

AS YOU READ   Go back and forth between the lines and a glance at the shape.

Easter
Wings (1633)

Lord, who createdst man in wealth and store,
Though foolishly he lost the same,
Decaying more and more,
Till he became
Most poor:
With thee
O let me rise
As larks, harmoniously,
And sing this day thy victories:
Then shall the fall further the flight in me.

My tender age in sorrow did begin:
And still with sicknesses and shame
Thou didst so punish sin,
That I became
Most thin.
With thee
Let me combine
And feel this day thy victory
For, if I imp my wing on thine,
Affliction shall advance the flight in me.

Writing from Reading

Summarize

1 This poem celebrates the resurrection of Jesus Christ on Easter, as described in the New Testament. In what ways is this poem a prayer?

Analyze Craft

2 How does the shape reflect the subject of the poem?

3 Which places here in the poem's winged form reflect or combine with specific syntax or diction choices? What is the effect?

Analyze Voice

4 How does the form of prayerful speech give the sound of the poem a shape?

Synthesize Summary and Analysis

5 The poet seeks to give physical as well as aural shape to his words.

Does this seem appropriate—or a playful trick?

Interpret the Poem

6 Why might Herbert have viewed poetry and prayer as similar activities? How do you distinguish between this poem and a prayer?

"Easter Wings" is quite a different entity when read aloud than when looked at in silence. And because he knew his work would be physically published, Herbert wrote with the assumption that the poem would be viewed. This is an assumption that the ancient Greek poet Homer or the *Beowulf* poet, for example, could not have made. The later poet's audience would *view* as well as *listen to* the verse, and the visual component matters at least as much as how the poem sounds.

John Hollander (b. 1929)

Scholar and poet John Hollander, born in New York City and educated at Columbia and Indiana universities, taught for decades at Yale University. His first collection of poetry, *A Crackling of Thorns* (1958), won the Yale Series of Younger Poets Award, which launched him in a career that would yield seventeen books of poetry, eight well-respected books of literary criticism, and more than twenty edited works. Hollander's love of music, which led him to write liner notes for albums to support himself between his master's degree and Ph.D., resulted in his writing opera librettos and lyrics for composers including Milton Babbitt and George Perle.

AS YOU READ Follow the shape, but also ponder the meaning below the surface of the shape.

Swan and Shadow (1969)

```
                        Dusk
                     Above the
                  water hang the
                       loud
 5                     flies
                       Here
                       O so
                       gray
                       then
10         What              A pale signal will appear
           When              Soon before its shadow fades
           Where             Here in this pool of opened eye
           In us      No Upon us As at the very edges
             of where we take shape in the dark air
15         this object bares its image awakening
              ripples of recognition that will
                 brush darkness up into light
   even after this bird this hour both drift by atop the perfect sad instant now
                  already passing out of sight
20             toward yet-untroubled reflection
              this image bears its object darkening
              into memorial shades Scattered bits of
           light       No of water Or something across
           water          Breaking up No Being regathered
25         soon           Yet by then a swan will have
           gone               Yes out of mind into what
                       vast
                       pale
                       hush
30                     of a
                       place
                       past
             sudden dark as
                 if a swan
35                     sang
```

Writing from Reading

Summarize

1 How is what happens in the image of the top swan reflected in the image of the bottom swan?

Analyze Craft

2 Discuss how the poem's capitalization, lack of punctuation, and syntax relate to (or contrast with) the clear shape of the poem visually. Do these elements emerge out of the necessity of rendering a clear image, or do they serve other purposes?

3 Why the image of a swan? Where else have you seen it in myth and poetry?

Analyze Voice

4 Is there anything in the way the poet shapes the poem that might make for confusion if it were read aloud?

Synthesize Summary and Analysis

5 Discuss Hollander's combination of visual representation and language. What aspects of the poem strike you as particularly interesting or important?

Does it hold together on its own as an interesting poem or require the visual form to complete it?

6 Compare the language and tone in the "swan" section of the poem versus the "shadow" section of the poem. Does the poem acknowledge a shift between the image and the image's shadow?

Interpret the Poem

7 Our lives in time, our own ephemeral images—how does the poem speak to such questions?

Chen Li (b. 1954)

A Taiwanese poet, Chen Li has contributed to Taiwan's letters both his original work and his translations—in collaboration with his wife Chan Fen-ling—of poets including Pablo Neruda and Seamus Heaney. Li has gone through several stages in his own poetry, first taking up Modernist technique, then demonstrating political and social consciousness, and finally broadening to an eclectic mix of subject matter. Li has presented his poetry at the Rotterdam International Poetry Festival. His work has reached a wide audience with its English, French, Dutch, and Japanese translations. He teaches at the Hualien Girls Middle School and National Dong Hwa University.

AS YOU READ   The translator of this poem noted the following about this untranslatable poem: The Chinese character 兵 (pronounced "bing") means "soldier." 乒 and 乓 (pronounced "ping" and "pong"), which look like one-legged soldiers, are two onomatopoeic words imitating sounds of collision or gunshots. The character 丘 (pronounced "chiou") means "hill."

War Symphony

(1995)

Writing from Reading

Summarize

1 Given the pictorial nature of the Chinese characters, the poem is telling a story as much through images as it is through sounds. What picture do you see here?

Analyze Craft

2 Can you get the sense of this "sound" poem about battle without saying it out loud? What does it sound like when you read it aloud?

3 How does the back-and-forth noise —"ping . . . pong"—of saying the Chinese characters create a verbal dramatization of a scene of war?

4 Does the sound of "chiou" resolve the previous back and forth of sounds?

Analyze Voice

5 Chinese is a highly musical language with the meaning of words often tied to the pitch at which the word is spoken. Given the differences between the tonal nature of the Chinese language and that of European languages, why might you find it difficult to hear the poet's voice without adding the sound of your own voice?

Synthesize Summary and Analysis

6 The sound of the poem works to become the meaning of the poem. Where have you encountered this concept in your reading of other poems?

Interpret the Poem

7 Would it be possible to make a poem such as this in English? Explain.

Dylan Thomas (1914–1953)

For a brief biography of Dylan Thomas, see Chapter 25.

AS YOU READ Allow your eye to guide you to meanings in the shape. Why does the "I" link the two parts?

Vision and Prayer (1945)

Who
Are you
Who is born
In the next room
5   So loud to my own
That I can hear the womb
Opening and the dark run
Over the ghost and the dropped son
Behind the wall thin as a wren's bone?
10   In the birth bloody room unknown
To the burn and turn of time
And the heart print of man
Bows no baptism
But dark alone
15   Blessing on
The wild
Child.
I
Must lie
20   Still as stone
By the wren bone
Wall hearing the moan
Of the mother hidden
And the shadowed head of pain
25   Casting tomorrow like a thorn
And the midwives of miracle sing
Until the turbulent new born
Burns me his name and his flame
And the winged wall is torn
30   By his torrid crown
And the dark thrown
From his loin
To bright
Light.

Writing from Reading

Summarize

1 The poet hears the sounds of his son's birth. How does he focus his attentiveness?

Analyze Craft

2 Why does the poet choose to give this particular shape to his lines? Does it enhance their meaning? Does it intensify emotion? What metaphors does he employ also to this end?

Analyze Voice

3 However odd the shape of the poem, does the voice seem normal for the occasion? Where does it veer toward a prayerful tone?

Synthesize Summary and Analysis

4 The particular shape works together with the feeling about the situation to create a particular effect. How is this related to the larger question of how form guides emotion in all poems?

Interpret the Poem

5 How does this event fit into the larger questions of life and death? What is the significance of the "I" on its own central line?

PROSE POEMS

We may be accustomed to think that line breaks are required of poetry. Some writers, however, compose poems in dense, compact units of unbroken lines. Prose poems use the devices and imagery characteristic of traditionally lined poetry, but in compact units. French poets of the nineteenth century inaugurated the modern use of the form, and it has seen consistent usage in twentieth-century poetry in English as well. There's no clearly defined line separating the prose poem from the short-short story. The mere fact that a poet intends a piece to be read and heard as a prose poem is reason enough to consider it so, as in this example from Carolyn Forché.

Carolyn Forché (b. 1950)

For a brief biography of Carolyn Forché, see Chapter 17.

AS YOU READ Picture the scene, as you would for a short story or a movie. Night, a Central American nation, a family dinner. An American poet and her companion are guests of the military man.

The Colonel (1982)

What you have heard is true. I was in his house. His wife carried a tray of coffee and sugar. His daughter filed her nails, his son went out for the night. There were daily papers, pet dogs, a pistol on the cushion beside him. The moon swung bare on its black cord over the house. On the television was a cop show. It was in English. Broken bottles were embedded in the walls around the house to scoop the kneecaps from a man's legs or cut his hands to lace. On the windows there were gratings like those in liquor stores. We had dinner, rack of lamb, good wine, a gold bell was on the table for calling the maid. The maid brought green mangoes, salt, a type of bread. I was asked how I enjoyed the country. There was a brief commercial in Spanish. His wife took everything away. There was some talk then of how difficult it had become to govern. The parrot said hello on the terrace. The colonel told it to shut up, and pushed himself from the table. My friend said to me with his eyes: say nothing. The colonel returned with a sack used to bring groceries home. He spilled many human ears on the table. They were like dried peach halves. There is no other way to say this. He took one of them in his hands, shook it in our faces, dropped it into a water glass. It came alive there. I am tired of fooling around he said. As for the rights of anyone, tell your people they can go fuck themselves. He swept the ears to the floor with his arm and held the last of the wine in the air. Something for your poetry, no? he said. Some of the ears on the floor caught this scrap of his voice. Some of the ears on the floor were pressed to the ground.

Writing from Reading

Summarize

1 Carolyn Forché has said that this event in fact took place—and announces "I [she herself] was in his house" at poem's start. What kind of truth is she telling, and how does she seem to respond?

Analyze Craft

2 What symbolism is evoked by the poem's final disturbing image of ears catching "this scrap of his voice" and ears "pressed to the ground"?

Analyze Voice

3 How does the language here feel more like a story than a poem? How does the plain language intensify the speaker's story?

Synthesize Summary and Analysis

4 With unbroken lines, this prose poem forms a thick block of text. How does this form reflect the poem's subject and title character?

Interpret the Poem

5 Who is the "you" the speaker mentions in the opening line? Does she intend someone specific? And how does the "I am tired of fooling around . . ." get differentiated from the speaker's "I"?

Garth Risk Hallberg (b. 1978)

A 2008 New York Foundation for the Arts Fellow in Fiction, Garth Risk Hallberg was included in 2008's *Best New American Voices*. His short stories have also appeared in *Glimmer Train, Canteen,* and *The Pinch,* among other publications. His essays include "Kindle-Proof Your Book" (from the literary blog, *The Millions,* 2011), with suggestions to add art and color and to play with typefaces—all of which he does in *A Field Guide to the North American Family* (2007), from which "Divorce" is taken. *A Field Guide* is a collection of poetic vignettes interwoven with artistic illustrations, and although each vignette stands alone as a depiction of an internal state, each also includes a cross reference to other illustrated portraits (with titles such as "Commitment" and "Hate") in the book. Taken individually or together, they suggest more than they tell. Garth received his Master of Fine Arts from New York University and currently teaches at Fordham University.

AS YOU READ Notice the rhythm Hallberg establishes with short phrases offset by commas. Ask yourself what kind of voice this creates.

Divorce (2007)

He knew, oh, he knew, he saw it coming, he kept asking her, while she gardened, while she un-loaded the dishwasher, while she flipped again through the takeout menus unable to find what she wanted, are you happy, Mom, are you happy, knowing somehow she wasn't, and no, the knowing didn't make it any better, because another thing he knew, like he knew his own face in the mirror, was that it was his fault, because what was Mom doing, sitting in the corner of the living room with the headphones on every night that week, if not taking a cue from her son . . . if not, herself, withdrawing? He heard folk music sloshing out of the earphones like water over the rim of a bowl. He had half a mind to go through Mom's underwear drawer, to see if she, too, had a stash. Then Dad, on the couch with a stack of papers, was asking her a question that she, in her earphones, couldn't hear, and asking again, louder. And then both voices were raised, as Gabe had known they would be—something was happening, as he had known it would—and he went to the basement with the lights off and took the last two pills from the film-canister in his pocket and swallowed them without water and knelt in the middle of the rug, and he swore it would be the last time, but oh, he knew, he had done it, he had done it now.

Due to a growth curve similar to that of *Depression,* a robust *Divorce* population has become common wherever *Love* dwells in large numbers.

Writing from Reading

Summarize

1 Who is the speaker in the poem? Describe what he is lamenting.

Analyze Craft

2 The writer is primarily known for his fiction. What is poetic about this selection? Would you categorize it as prose or poetry? Why or why not? What makes a selection like this difficult to categorize?

Analyze Voice

3 The speaker speculates on what he thinks is happening in his family. What is gained by using his perspective instead of the mother's or father's?

4 The first sentence is eight lines long with "oh" in the first few words. The last line repeats the "oh, he knew." How do the initial long sentence and the repeated words and sounds work together to create a kind of moan? What does the moan represent for the speaker?

Synthesize Summary and Analysis

5 What is the relationship between the illustration and the portrait? "Divorce" is just one of an entire collection of poetic page-long portraits each accompanied by an illustration. What is the writer trying to accomplish by pairing images with these portraits?

6 "Divorce" is cross referenced with selections on "Depression" and "Love." Speculate on what Hallberg is trying to accomplish with a complex system of cross-references.

Interpret the Poem

7 The speaker in the poem repeatedly uses the phrase "he knew." What does "he" know, and how does "he" know it? Do you believe the speaker when he says "it was my fault"? How does claiming responsibility further the point of view in this poem? What is the writer telling us about divorce by using this perspective?

For Review and Further Study

Jimmy Santiago Baca (b. 1952)

Choices (1986)

An acquaintance at Los Alamos Labs
who engineers weapons
black x'd a mark where I live
on his office map.
5 Star-wars humor. . . .
He exchanged muddy boots
and patched jeans
for a white intern's coat
and black polished shoes.
10 A month ago, after butchering a gouged bull,
we stood on a pasture hill,
and he wondered with pained features
where money would come from
to finish his shed, plant alfalfa,
and fix his tractor.   15
Now his fingers
yank horsetail grass,
he crimps herringbone tail-seed
between teeth, and grits out words,
"Om gonna buy another tractor   20
next week. More land too."
Silence between us is gray water
let down in a tin pail
in a deep, deep well,
a silence   25
milled in continental grindings
millions of years ago.
I throw my heart
into the well, and it falls
a shimmering pebble to the bottom.   30

Words are hard
to come by, "Would have lost everything
I've worked for, not takin' the job."
His words try to
35 retrieve
my heart
from the deep well.
We walk on in silence,
our friendship
40 rippling away.

Questions for Interactive Reading and Writing

1. Describe the setting. What is the relationship between the speaker and the other man?

2. How would you make a short story out of this material?

3. What is the tone, the feel of the poem?

4. What effect does the poet create by employing the image of the "tin pail / in a deep, deep well"?

5. The poet first speaks of his "acquaintance" but then ends the poem by talking about his "friendship" for the man. What, if anything, has changed over the course of the poem that would justify the two different ways of speaking about the other man?

Marilyn Chin (b. 1955)

Turtle Soup (1987)

You go home one evening tired from work,
and your mother boils you turtle soup.
Twelve hours hunched over the hearth
(who knows what else is in that cauldron).

5 You say, "Ma, you've poached the symbol of long life;
that turtle lived four thousand years, swam
the Wei, up the Yellow, over the Yangtze.
Witnessed the Bronze Age, the High Tang,
grazed on splendid sericulture."
10 (So, she boils the life out of him.)

"All our ancestors have been fools.
Remember Uncle Wu who rode ten thousand miles
to kill a famous Manchu and ended up
with his head on a pole? Eat, child,
its liver will make you strong."   15

"Sometimes you're the life, sometimes the sacrifice."
Her sobbing is inconsolable.
So, you spread that gentle napkin
over your lap in decorous Pasadena.

Baby, some high priestess has got it wrong.   20
The golden decal on the green underbelly
says "Made in Hong Kong."

Is there nothing left but the shell
and humanity's strange inscriptions,
the songs, the rites, the oracles?   25

—for Ben Huang

Questions for Interactive Reading and Writing

1. This poem reports on a domestic scene. How would you describe it, including location?

2. How "free" do you find the form of this poem? How "free" do you find the lines? Do you notice any near rhymes?

3. What evidence of a clash of cultures or generations do you see in the poem?

4. What is the poem's tone?

5. What does the poet mean by "humanity's strange inscriptions"?

Sandra Cisneros (b. 1954)

Pumpkin Eater (1994)

I'm no trouble.
Honest to God I'm not.
I'm not

the kind of woman
5 who telephones in the middle of the night,
—who told you that?—
splitting the night like machete.
Before and after.   After.   Before.
No, no, not me.
10 I'm not

the she who slings words bigger than rocks,
sharper than Houdini knives,
verbal Molotovs.
The one who did that—*yo no fuí*—
15 that wasn't me.

I'm no hysteric,
terrorist,
emotional anarchist.

I keep inside a pumpkin shell.
20 There I do very well.
Shut a blind eye to where
my pumpkin-eater roams.

I keep like fruitcake.
Subsist on air.
25 Not a worry nor care.
Please.
I'm as free for the taking
as the eyes of Saint Lucy.
No trouble at all.

30 I swear, I swear, I swear . . .

Questions for Interactive Reading and Writing

1. How does the buildup of emotion influence the form of this poem?

2. What does the speaker's emphatic and repeated denials suggest about her situation and possibly even her character?

3. What effect on your understanding of her, and the poem itself, does the invocation of the nursery rhyme have?

4. Look up the reference to "the eyes of Saint Lucy." What impact does that reference have on the meaning of the poem?

Allen Ginsberg (1926–1997)

A Supermarket in California (1955)

What thoughts I have of you tonight, Walt Whitman, for I walked down the sidestreets under the trees with a headache self-conscious looking at the full moon.

In my hungry fatigue, and shopping for images, I went into the neon fruit supermarket, dreaming of your enumerations!

What peaches and what penumbras! Whole families shopping at night! Aisles full of husbands! Wives in the avocados, babies in the tomatoes!—and you, García Lorca, what were you doing down by the watermelons?

I saw you, Walt Whitman, childless, lonely old grubber, poking among the meats in the refrigerator and eyeing the grocery boys.

I heard you asking questions of each: Who killed the   5
pork chops? What price bananas? Are you my Angel?

I wandered in and out of the brilliant stacks of cans following you, and followed in my imagination by the store detective.

We strode down the open corridors together in our solitary fancy tasting artichokes, possessing every frozen delicacy, and never passing the cashier.

Where are we going, Walt Whitman? The doors close in an hour. Which way does your beard point tonight?

(I touch your book and dream of our odyssey in the supermarket and feel absurd.)

Will we walk all night through solitary streets? The   10
trees add shade to shade, lights out in the houses, we'll both be lonely.

Will we stroll dreaming of the lost America of love past blue automobiles in driveways, home to our silent cottage?

Ah, dear father, graybeard, lonely old courage-teacher, what America did you have when Charon quit poling his ferry and you got out on a smoking bank and stood watching the boat disappear on the black waters of Lethe?

Questions for Interactive Reading and Writing

1. An American poet on the West Coast speaks to an American East Coast poet of an earlier day. What kinship does the modern poet feel for the older writer?

2. Why does the poet choose a California supermarket for the setting of this poem?

3. Where is the "poetry" in this freely told story?

4. How would you describe the leap the poet makes from the line "Aisles full of husbands . . ." to "wives in the avocados, babies in the tomatoes . . .?"

5. Who is García Lorca? Why is it fitting that he should appear to the poet also?

6. What is the technical device the poet uses when he addresses Whitman by means of carrying his book of poems?

Lorna Goodison (b. 1947)

On Becoming a Tiger (2000)

The day that they stole her tiger's-eye ring
was the day that she became a tiger.
She was inspired by advice received from Rilke

who recommended that, if the business of drinking
5 should become too bitter,
that one should change oneself into wine.

The tiger was actually always asleep
inside her, she had seen it
stretched out, drowsing and inert

10 when she lay upon her side and stared
for seven consecutive days into a tall mirror
that she had turned on its side.

Her focus had penetrated all exterior
till at last she could see within her
15 a red glowing landscape of memory and poems,

a heart within her heart
and lying there big, bright, and golden
was the tiger, wildly darkly striped.

At night she dreams that her mother
undresses her and discovers that, under 20
her outerwear, her bare limbs are marked
of the huge and fierce cat of Asia
with the stunning golden quartz eyes.

She has taken to wearing long dresses
to cover the rounded tail coiling behind her. 25
She has filled her vases with tiger lilies

and replaced her domestic cat
with a smaller relative of hers, the ocelot.
At four in the morning she practices stalking

up and down the long expanse of the hall. 30
What are the ingredients in tiger's milk?
Do tigers ever mate for life?

Can she rewrite the story of Little Black Sambo?
Can a non-tiger take a tiger for a wife?
To these and other questions, 35

she is seeking urgent answers
now that she is living an openly
tigerly life.

Questions for Interactive Reading and Writing

1. How do the three-line stanzas serve to control the movement of the poem?

2. The poet refers to the German poet Rainer Maria Rilke and a metaphor about transformation. Rilke's sonnet 29 (in Stephen Mitchell's translation of *Sonnets to Orpheus*) contains the lines, "What is your most painful experience? / If your drink is bitter, turn into wine." How does the Goodison poem reflect that advice?

3. How does the kinship the speaker feels with the imaginary tiger affect her everyday activities?

4. What part, if any, does race play in the poem?

D. H. Lawrence (1885–1930)

For a brief biography of D. H. Lawrence, see Chapter 16.

Snake (1921)

A snake came to my water-trough
On a hot, hot day, and I in pajamas for the heat,
To drink there.

In the deep, strange-scented shade of the great dark carob-
    tree
5 I came down the steps with my pitcher
And must wait, must stand and wait, for there he was at
    the trough before me.

He reached down from a fissure in the earth-wall in the
    gloom
And trailed his yellow-brown slackness soft-bellied down,
    over the edge of the stone trough
And rested his throat upon the stone bottom,
10 And where the water had dripped from the tap, in a small
    clearness,
He sipped with his straight mouth,
Softly drank through his straight gums, into his slack long
    body,
Silently.
Someone was before me at my water-trough,
15 And I, like a second comer, waiting.
He lifted his head from his drinking, as cattle do,
And looked at me vaguely, as drinking cattle do,
And flickered his two-forked tongue from his lips, and
    mused a moment,
And stooped and drank a little more,
20 Being earth-brown, earth-golden from the burning
    bowels of the earth
On the day of Sicilian July, with Etna smoking.

The voice of my education said to me
He must be killed,
For in Sicily the black, black snakes are innocent, the gold
    are venomous.

25 And voices in me said, If you were a man
You would take a stick and break him now, and finish him
    off.

But must I confess how I liked him,
How glad I was he had come like a guest in quiet, to drink
    at my water-trough

And depart peaceful, pacified, and thankless,
Into the burning bowels of this earth?   30

Was it cowardice, that I dared not kill him?
Was it perversity, that I longed to talk to him? Was it
    humility, to feel so honored?
I felt so honored.

And yet those voices:
If you were not afraid, you would kill him!   35

And truly I was afraid, I was most afraid,
But even so, honored still more
That he should seek my hospitality
From out the dark door of the secret earth.

He drank enough   40
And lifted his head, dreamily, as one who has drunken,
And flickered his tongue like a forked night on the air, so
    black,
Seeming to lick his lips,
And looked around like a god, unseeing, into the air,
And slowly turned his head,   45
And slowly, very slowly, as if thrice adream,
Proceeded to draw his slow length curving round
And climb again the broken bank of my wall-face.

And as he put his head into that dreadful hole,
And as he slowly drew up, snake-easing his shoulders, and   50
    entered farther,
A sort of horror, a sort of protest against his withdrawing
    into that horrid black hole,
Deliberately going into the blackness, and slowly
    drawing himself after,
Overcame me now his back was turned.

I looked round, I put down my pitcher,
I picked up a clumsy log   55
And threw it at the water-trough with a clatter.

I think it did not hit him,
But suddenly that part of him that was left behind
  convulsed in undignified haste.
Writhed like lightning, and was gone
60 Into the black hole, the earth-lipped fissure in the
  wall-front,
At which, in the intense still noon, I stared with
  fascination.

And immediately I regretted it.
I thought how paltry, how vulgar, what a mean act!
I despised myself and the voices of my accursed human
  education.

65 And I thought of the albatross
And I wished he would come back, my snake.

For he seemed to me again like a king,
Like a king in exile, uncrowned in the underworld,
Now due to be crowned again.

70 And so, I missed my chance with one of the lords
Of life.
And I have something to expiate:
A pettiness.

Questions for Interactive Reading and Writing

1. Why should we consider this description of an encounter between a man and a snake a poem and not prose? Can you read it as if it were a letter? What separates this text from plain prose?
2. In what ways does the poet-speaker find the meeting with the snake a test of his modern beliefs and values? What biblical symbol stands behind the image of this particular snake? What biblical test of beliefs and values?
3. What in particular surprises the speaker about his own behavior?
4. Why does the image of the "earth-lipped fissure in the wall-front" frighten him?

5. Why does he call his education "accursed"?
6. What is the overall outcome of the encounter, and how does the poet characterize it?

Denise Levertov (1923–1997)

The Ache of Marriage (1964)

The ache of marriage:

thigh and tongue, beloved,
are heavy with it,
it throbs in the teeth

We look for communion   5
and are turned away, beloved,
each and each

It is leviathan and we
in its belly
looking for joy, some joy   10
not to be known outside it

two by two in the ark of
the ache of it.

Questions for Interactive Reading and Writing

1. Is this poem a celebration, a complaint, or a lament? Whom is the poet addressing?
2. What are the central metaphors the poet uses for marriage?
3. How do the sounds of the poem—the arrangement of the consonants and vowels—reflect the argument of the poem?
4. Does the poet find any relief from the "ache"?

Robert Lowell (1917–1977)

For the Union Dead (1959)

"Relinquunt omnia servare rem publicam."

The old South Boston Aquarium stands
in a Sahara of snow now. Its broken windows are boarded.
The bronze weathervane cod has lost half its scales.
The airy tanks are dry.

5 Once my nose crawled like a snail on the glass;
my hand tingled
to burst the bubbles
drifting from the noses of the crowded, compliant fish.

My hand draws back. I often sign still
10 for the dark downward and vegetating kingdom
of the fish and reptile. One morning last March,
I pressed against the new barbed and galvanized

fence on the Boston Common. Behind their cage,
yellow dinosaur steamshovels were grunting
15 as they cropped up tons of mush and grass
to gouge their underworld garage.

Parking spaces luxuriate like civic
sandpiles in the heart of Boston.
A girdle of orange, Puritan-pumpkin colored girders
20 braces the tingling Statehouse,

shaking over the excavations, as it faces Colonel Shaw
and his bell-cheeked Negro infantry
on St. Gauden's shaking Civil War relief,
propped by a plank splint against the garage's earthquake.

25 Two months after marching through Boston,
half of the regiment was dead;
at the dedication,
William James could almost hear the bronze Negroes
    breathe.

Their monument sticks like a fishbone
30 in the city's throat.
Its Colonel is as lean
as a compass-needle.

He has an angry wrenlike vigilance,
a greyhound's gentle tautness;
he seems to wince at pleasure,   35
and suffocate for privacy.

He is out of bounds now. He rejoices in man's lovely,
peculiar power to choose life and die—
when he leads his black soldiers to death,
he cannot bend his back.   40

On a thousand small town New England greens
the old white churches hold their air
of sparse, sincere rebellion; frayed flags
quilt the graveyards of the Grand Army of the Republic

The stone statutes of the abstract Union Soldier   45
grow slimmer and younger each year—
wasp-waisted, they doze over muskets
and muse through their sideburns . . .

Shaw's father wanted no monument
except the ditch,   50
where his son's body was thrown
and lost with his "niggers."

The ditch is nearer.
There are no statues for the last war here;
on Boylston Street, a commercial photograph   55
shows Hiroshima boiling

over a Mosler Safe, the "Rock of Ages"
that survived the blast. Space is nearer.
When I crouch to my television set,
the drained faces of Negro school-children rise like   60
    balloons.

Colonel Shaw
is riding on his bubble,
he waits
for the blessed break.

The Aquarium is gone. Everywhere,   65
giant finned cars nose forward like fish;
a savage servility
slides by on grease.

Pat Mora (b. 1942)

Immigrants (1986)

wrap their babies in the American flag,
feed them mashed hot dogs and apple pie,
name them Bill and Daisy,
buy them blonde dolls that blink blue
5   eyes or a football and tiny cleats
before the baby can even walk,
speak to them in thick English,
hallo, babee, hallo,
whisper in Spanish or Polish
10   when the babies sleep, whisper
in a dark parent bed, that dark
parent fear, "Will they like
our boy, our girl, our fine american
boy, our fine american girl?"

Ezra Pound (1885–1972)

For a brief biography of Ezra Pound, see Chapter 22.

The River-Merchant's Wife: A Letter (1915)

While my hair was still cut straight across my forehead
I played about the front gate, pulling flowers.
You came by on bamboo stilts, playing horse,
You walked about my seat, playing with blue plums.
And we went on living in the village of Chokan: 5
Two small people, without dislike or suspicion.

At fourteen I married My Lord you.
I never laughed, being bashful.
Lowering my head, I looked at the wall.
Called to, a thousand times, I never looked back.   10

At fifteen I stopped scowling,
I desired my dust to be mingled with yours
Forever and forever and forever.
Why should I climb the lookout?

At sixteen you departed,   15
You went into far Ku-tijō-en, by the river of swirling
    eddies,
And you have been gone five months.
The monkeys make sorrowful noise overhead.

You dragged your feet when you went out.
20 By the gate now, the moss is grown, the different mosses,
Too deep to clear them away!
The leaves fall early this autumn, in wind.
The paired butterflies are already yellow with August
Over the grass in the West garden;
25 They hurt me. I grow older.
If you are coming down through the narrows of the river
    Kiang,
Please let me know beforehand,
And I will come out to meet you
As far as Chō-fū-Sa.

Questions for Interactive Reading and Writing

1. What is the setting of the poem? Aside from specific names, what details of the poem provide clues?

2. Aside from direct statements of age, how does this poem achieve a sense of time passing?

3. Each stanza seems to have its own tone. Describe the tone of each, and then consider the tone of the poem as a whole. What details work to build this overall tone?

4. Consider the balance of this open form poem. What is the effect of making the first and last stanzas longer than the middle stanzas?

Alberto Álvaro Ríos (b. 1952)

Nani (1982)

Sitting at her table, she serves
the sopa de arroz to me
instinctively, and I watch her,
the absolute mamá, and eat words
5 I might have had to say more
out of embarrassment. To speak,
now-foreign words I used to speak,
too, dribble down her mouth as she serves
me albóndigas. No more
10 than a third are easy to me.

by the stove she does something with words
and looks at me only with her
back. I am full. I tell her
I taste the mint, and watch her speak
smiles at the stove. All my words   15
make her smile. Nani never serves
herself, she only watches me
with her skin, her hair. I ask for more.

I watch the mamá warming more
tortillas for me. I watch her   20
fingers in the flame for me.
Near her mouth, I see a wrinkle speak
of a man whose body serves
the ants like she serves me, then more words
from more wrinkles about children, words   25
about this and that, flowing more
easily from these other mouths. Each serves
as a tremendous string around her,
holding her together. They speak
Nani was this and that to me   30
and I wonder just how much of me
will die with her, what were the words
I could have been, was. Her insides speak
through a hundred wrinkles, now, more
than she can bear, steel around her,   35
shouting, then, What is this thing she serves?

She asks me if I want more.
I own no words to stop her.
Even before I speak, she serves.

Questions for Interactive Reading and Writing

1. What is the relation between the speaker and Nani?

2. Do you need to know the English names of the dishes Nani serves in order to understand the poem? What is the connection between food and words?

3. How does the poet establish this as a metaphor?

4. Why does the poet emphasize Nani's "wrinkles"?

5. How would the effect of the poem change if it were written in rhyming couplets?

Walt Whitman (1819–1892)

For a brief biography of Walt Whitman, see Chapter 20.

When I Heard the Learn'd Astronomer (1865)

When I heard the learn'd astronomer,
When the proofs, the figures, were ranged in columns
    before me,
When I was shown the charts and the diagrams, to add,
    divide, and measure them,
When I sitting heard the astronomer where he lectured
    with much applause in the lecture-room,
5 How soon unaccountable I became tired and sick;
Till rising and gliding out I wandered off by myself,
In the mystical moist night-air, and from time to time,
Looked up in perfect silence at the stars.

Questions for Interactive Reading and Writing

1. Paraphrase the scene. What action does the speaker take?

2. What is the effect of starting the first four lines with the same word? How does this repetition correspond to the lecture relayed in those lines?

3. The speaker gazes at the stars in perfect silence. What does this simple action seem to say about scientific knowledge, or knowledge gained through formal study?

4. How is it fitting that the lines describing the lecturer giving his lecture are long, whereas the lines describing the speaker's actions are shorter?

James Wright (1927–1980)

For a brief biography of James Wright, see Chapter 20.

Autumn Begins in Martins Ferry, Ohio (1959)

In the Shreve High football stadium,
I think of Polacks nursing long beers in Tiltonsville,
And gray faces of Negroes in the blast furnace at Benwood,
And the ruptured night watchman of Wheeling Steel,
Dreaming of heroes.   5

All the proud fathers are ashamed to go home.
Their women cluck like starved pullets,
Dying for love.

Therefore,
Their sons grow suicidally beautiful   10
At the beginning of October,
And gallop terribly against each other's bodies.

Questions for Interactive Reading and Writing

1. Try a paraphrase of the poem. The setting should give you the meaning of the line about the sons who "gallop terribly against each other's bodies."

2. Describe the social structure of life in Martin's Ferry, Ohio, based on statements in the poem.

3. How do the lives people lead here stand against the way they dream of "heroes"? Why might the "proud fathers" be "ashamed to go home"?

4. Where does the poem turn?

5. Does the contrast between the women—the wives—who are "dying for love" and the sons who "grow suicidally beautiful" make sense?

6. How essentially American is this poem? Can you imagine a French version? A Mexican version? An Iraqi version?

Reading for Open Form

When reading for open form, look for poetry that employs a structure determined by its own purpose and uses its own line lengths, line breaks, and rhythm (especially the rhythms of natural speech) instead of traditional patterns of meter, stanza structure, and rhyme.

Is there repetition in the poem?	EXAMPLE "because there is in this world no one thing / to which the bramble of *blackberry* corresponds, / . . . saying *blackberry, blackberry, blackberry.*"
Is there grammatical variation in the poem?	EXAMPLE "since feeling is first / who pays any attention / to the syntax of things / will never wholly kiss you; / wholly to be a fool / while Spring is in the world"
Are there organized patterns of imagery?	EXAMPLE "Even the battered little furnace, roaring along as patient as a donkey, chokes and clogs, / a dense, malignant smoke shoots up, someone has to fiddle with a cock, then hammer it, / before the gush and stench will deintensify, the dark, Dantean broth wearily subside."
How does the line itself create a rhythmical unit?	EXAMPLE "I Celebrate myself, and sing myself" EXAMPLE "Someone dissolves into yesterday's climber who made it to the top of the night walk"
How is a line arranged? Where does it break to create its own visual effect?	EXAMPLE "And so, I missed my chance with one of the lords Of life. And I have something to expiate: A pettiness." EXAMPLE "Easter Wings"—shaped in triangles like angel wings

Writing about Open Form

1. Using James Wright's "Autumn Begins in Martins Ferry, Ohio," analyze the poem's use of open-form elements (including line length, sound, and stanza structure).

2. Divide one of the two prose poems included in this chapter (Carolyn Forché's "The Colonel" and Garth Risk Hallberg's "Divorce") into a lined poem with separate stanzas. Then, write an informal explanation of your line breaks and stanza breaks. Include observations on how your reading of the poem is transformed by your formal changes.

3. Begin with Whitman's "Song of Myself" and then read through the two subsequent poems in this chapter that invoke Whitman (Sherman Alexie's "Defending Walt Whitman" and Allen Ginsberg's "A Supermarket in California"). Discuss how these two more contemporary poets both imitate and break from Whitman's form and subject matter.

4. Using "Easter Wings" or "Swan and Shadow," examine the linkage between a poem's subject and its shape. Consider how different the poem would be if it did not visually depict an object.

27

Langston Hughes

I TOO, sing America.
I am the darker brother.
—*from "I, Too" by Langston Hughes*

> "In the last decade something beyond the watch and guard of statistics has happened in the life of the American Negro. . . . The Sociologist, the Philanthropist, the Race-leader are not unaware of the New Negro, but they are at a loss to account for him. He simply cannot be swathed in their formula. For the younger generation is vibrant with a new psychology; the new spirit is awake in the masses, and under the very eyes of the professional observers is transforming what has been a perennial problem into the progressive phases of contemporary Negro life."
>
> —from "The New Negro" by Alain Locke

A Case Study on
Langston Hughes and His Contemporaries

The Harlem Renaissance

Langston Hughes and his contemporaries came of age during the 1920s and early 1930s, a period that came to be known, because of his work and that of other African-American writers of the time, as the Harlem Renaissance, a period of cultural awakening for African-Americans in terms of literature, music, art, theater, and political thinking.

The Cotton Club was a famous nightclub in Harlem where Duke Ellington, Cab Calloway, and other gifted black musicians played for an exclusively white clientele.

Josephine Baker (1906–1975), although also known for appearing in men's clothing, was more popular for her tendency to perform onstage in the nude.

The New Culture of Harlem

The Harlem Renaissance movement took its name from that part of New York City where it mainly flourished, a two-mile section of northern Manhattan in New York City. Many African-Americans had settled there—200,000 blacks lived there by 1928—during the great migration of blacks to find employment and education in the North. Harlem served as the epicenter of the Harlem Renaissance, since it boasted clubs where musicians including Duke Ellington, Louis Armstrong, and Bessie Smith performed; theaters such as the Apollo for black entertainers; and a common neighborhood in which important writers lived, among them Jean Toomer, Claude McKay, and Zora Neale Hurston (see Chapter 10 for Hurston's "The Gilded Six-Bits").

Fats Waller (1904–1943) and his hot jazz epitomized the music of the "rent party," a party thrown in an apartment in Harlem to help the tenant pay Harlem's high rents.

whites were drawn to African-American culture, and particularly the night life of Harlem—so much so that one of Harlem's most famous clubs, the Cotton Club, catered to an exclusively white clientele. Although this interest in black culture brought national attention to the work of black artists, people such as Du Bois feared that it might fuel stereotypes of black society. Still, new venues such as *Crisis* and *Opportunity*—both important magazines for black audiences and staffed by leading writers of the Harlem Renaissance—offered an unprecedented outlet for thought and literature.

Writers, musicians, and artists joined social thinkers such as W. E. B. Du Bois to advocate for black rights and education. Whites, too, were active in the Harlem Renaissance. The photographer Carl Van Vechten, for example, was a close friend of Langston Hughes, supported the renaissance, and admired the work of blacks. The majority of the black population, however, was not touched by this cultural awakening.

"Negro Vogue"

"Madame is of the opinion that little of artistic merit is now being produced in America except that which is being done by Negroes," wrote Countee Cullen after meeting with the (white) Claire Goll. Indeed,

Duke Ellington (1899–1974), one of America's most influential jazz composers, and the Duke Ellington Orchestra, with its growling trumpet, street rhythms, and the influence of classical music, were broadcast from the Cotton Club. Ellington called it simply "the American Music."

Langston Hughes (1902–1967)

For Langston Hughes, life was—as he put it—"no crystal stair." Hughes was born in Joplin, Missouri, in 1902; his parents divorced when he was quite young. His father left for Mexico, hoping to find a society less hostile to blacks, and his mother moved away to pursue her personal interests. Hughes was raised by his grandmother in Kansas, who told him her first husband had been killed with John Brown's men raiding Harper's Ferry; sometimes she wrapped his bullet-torn shawl around the child. Although this may have helped nurture Hughes's sense of pride in his race, his childhood was a lonely one, marked by longing for his mother. After his grandmother's death, he moved at age thirteen to Illinois and then to Cleveland to live with his mother, who never provided the maternal love that Hughes so desired.

Cleveland, where he attended high school, set the stage for the rest of his life in two central ways. First, he was active in many clubs at school and immensely popular. Second, he began publishing poems while still in high school. "The Negro Speaks of Rivers" appeared just after his graduation at age nineteen. Still in his early twenties, he won the admiration of poet Vachel Lindsay when, as a busboy at a Washington, D.C., hotel, he put three of his poems next to Lindsay's plate. Even a small sampling of Hughes's poetry—such as we include in this chapter—makes clear the talent and ambition Hughes

demonstrated from an early age. He wanted to be a poet, following his favorite influences, Walt Whitman and Carl Sandburg, but more, he wanted to celebrate his race, to show whites and blacks alike the beauty and integrity of the common African-American masses.

The year 1926 was an important one for Hughes. After traveling abroad—in France, Spain, and the Soviet Union—and holding a variety of jobs, Hughes entered Lincoln University, from which he would earn his bachelor's degree three years later. He then settled in Harlem, an African-American section of New York City. Hughes lived there during the time of the Harlem Renaissance, when black culture thrived and produced great artists, musicians, and writers, who were for the first time reaching black and white audiences alike. Foremost among these artists was Hughes, who had two early publications of major importance. His first collection of poems, *The Weary Blues,* earned much acclaim, and an essay appeared in *The Nation* called "The Negro Artist and the Racial Mountain," an essay that was both Hughes's personal manifesto and the manifesto of his generation of Harlem Renaissance artists. In it, he speaks against what he calls the "high-class Negro"—blacks who adopt a white way of life and try to fit in with the conventions of white middle-class culture. Instead, he celebrates the "low-down folks, the so-called common element." To Hughes, blacks who are genuine in their way of life are preferable; as he writes, "they still

hold their own individuality in the face of American standardizations." The essay concludes with a clear statement of intention: "We younger Negro artists who create now intend to express our individual dark-skinned selves without fear or shame. If white people are pleased we are glad. If they are not, it doesn't matter."

Hughes followed his own dictum, for his poetry celebrates black identity, particularly the "low-down folks," in several ways. First, the "I" in these poems is not meant as a specific person but embodies the entire black race by claiming all their experiences—the difficult and admirable alike—in personal terms. "The Negro Speaks of Rivers" and "I, Too" are written in the voice of a "collective consciousness"— that is, a single speaker who transcends time and place as he recounts the experiences of an entire group. Second, Hughes's poetry is characterized by the directness of his thoughts, a "plain style" (see the Case Study on Dickinson and Frost in Chapter 28) reflecting a long tradition in American literature that extends back to the Puritans, who favored simplicity over adornment. Third, Hughes's poetry consciously salutes and imitates the musical forms of blues and jazz. Hughes describes his 1951 collection *Montage of a Dream Deferred* as growing from popular African-American music. He explains, "[T]his poem on contemporary Harlem, like be-bop, is marked by conflicting changes, sudden nuances, sharp and impudent interjections, broken rhythms, and passages sometimes in the manner of a jam session, sometimes the popular song, punctuated by the riffs, runs, breaks, and distortions of the music of a community in transition."

Hughes expressed his black identity in poetry, fiction, nonfiction, children's books, plays, librettos, and a popular newspaper column featuring the character Jesse B. Semple, nicknamed "Simple." In all his work, Hughes celebrated African-American identity, focusing on the urban black population and mimicking what he saw to be at the heart of that population: blues and jazz. Despite Hughes's innova-tion of using dialect, jazz, blues, and black culture in his poetry, he was barely able to make a living with his pen. He once referred to himself as a "literary share-cropper," as he pieced together a career filled with great accomplishments and occasional critical failures. In later years Hughes became controversial because of his far left political views. However, those around him invariably knew him to be a kind man with a celebratory sense of humanity, and he remained popular with readers and audiences throughout his life; even being summoned by Senator Joseph McCarthy to appear before McCarthy's infamous committee on un-American activities because of his socialist po-litical views did not diminish his career. Hughes's credo can be summed up in his own words: "[T]o my mind, it is the duty of the younger Negro artist, if he accepts any duties at all from outsiders, to change through the force of his art that old whis-pering 'I want to be white,' hidden in the aspirations of his people, to 'Why should I want to be white? I am Negro—and beautiful.'"

The Poetry of Langston Hughes

The Negro Speaks of Rivers (1921)

I've known rivers:
I've known rivers ancient as the world and older than the
    flow of human blood in human veins.

My soul has grown deep like the rivers.

I bathed in the Euphrates when dawns were young.
I built my hut near the Congo and it lulled me to sleep.   5
I looked upon the Nile and raised the pyramids above it.
I heard the singing of the Mississippi when Abe Lincoln
    went down to New Orleans, and I've seen its muddy
    bosom turn all golden in the sunset.

I've known rivers:
Ancient, dusky rivers.

My soul has grown deep like the rivers.   10

Questions for Critical Thinking

1. Highlight the repeated phrases and lines in this poem. What effect does Hughes achieve with these repetitions?

2. Make a list of everything the word *rivers* connotes to you. How do these connotations enhance your reading of the poem?

Mother to Son (1922)

Well, son, I'll tell you:
Life for me ain't been no crystal stair.
It's had tacks in it,
And splinters,
5 And boards torn up,
And places with no carpet on the floor—
Bare.
But all the time
I'se been a-climbin' on,
10 And reachin' landin's,
And turnin' corners,
And sometimes goin' in the dark
Where there ain't been no light.
So boy, don't you turn back.
15 Don't you set down on the steps
'Cause you finds it's kinder hard.
Don't you fall now—
For I'se still goin', honey,
I'se still climbin',
20 And life for me ain't been no crystal stair.

Questions for Critical Thinking

1. Review what you learned about persona in Chapter 21. How does this poem compare with one of Robert Browning's dramatic monologues, such as "My Last Duchess" (in Chapter 19)?

2. What is the controlling metaphor in this poem?

Negro (1922)

I am a Negro:
   Black as the night is black,
   Black as the depths of my Africa.

I've been a slave:
   Caesar told me to keep his door-steps clean.   5
   I brushed the boots of Washington.

I've been a worker:
   Under my hand the pyramids arose.
   I made mortar for the Woolworth Building.

I've been a singer: 10
   All the way from Africa to Georgia
   I carried my sorrow songs.
   I made ragtime.

I've been a victim:
   The Belgians cut off my hands in the Congo.   15
   They lynch me still in Mississippi.

I am a Negro:
   Black as the night is black,
   Black like the depths of my Africa.

Questions for Critical Thinking

1. Describe the relation between the repeated statement in the first and last stanzas and the specific descriptions.

2. Could you substitute other racial or ethnic identities and still have the same poem? Why or why not?

I, Too (1925)

I, too, sing America.

I am the darker brother.
They send me to eat in the kitchen
When company comes,
5 But I laugh,
And eat well,
And grow strong.

Tomorrow,
I'll be at the table
10 When company comes.
Nobody'll dare
Say to me,
"Eat in the kitchen,"
Then.

15 Besides,
They'll see how beautiful I am
And be ashamed—

I, too, am America.

The Weary Blues (1925)

Droning a drowsy syncopated tune,
Rocking back and forth to a mellow croon,
  I heard a Negro play.
Down on Lenox Avenue the other night
5 By the pale dull pallor of an old gas light
  He did a lazy sway. . . .
  He did a lazy sway. . . .

To the tune o' those Weary Blues.
With his ebony hands on each ivory key
He made that poor piano moan with melody. 10
  O Blues!
Swaying to and fro on his rickety stool
He played that sad raggy tune like a musical fool.
  Sweet Blues!
Coming from a black man's soul. 15
  O Blues!
In a deep song voice with a melancholy tone
I heard that Negro sing, that old piano moan—
  "Ain't got nobody in all this world,
    Ain't got nobody but ma self. 20
    I's gwine to quit ma frownin'
    And put ma troubles on the shelf."

Thump, thump, thump, went his foot on the floor.
He played a few chords then he sang some more—
  "I got the Weary Blues 25
    And I can't be satisfied.
    Got the Weary Blues
    And can't be satisfied—
    I ain't happy no mo'
    And I wish that I had died." 30

And far into the night he crooned that tune.
The stars went out and so did the moon.
The singer stopped playing and went to bed
While the Weary Blues echoed through his head.
He slept like a rock or a man that's dead. 35

Po' Boy Blues (1926)

When I was home de
Sunshine seemed like gold.
When I was home de
Sunshine seemed like gold.
5 Since I come up North de
Whole damn world's turned cold.

I was a good boy,
Never done no wrong.
Yes, I was a good boy,
10 Never done no wrong,
But this world is weary
An' de road is hard an' long.

I fell in love with
A gal I thought was kind.
15 Fell in love with
A gal I thought was kind.
She made me lose ma money
An' almost lose ma mind.

Weary, weary,
20 Weary early in de morn.
Weary, weary,
Early, early in de morn.
I's so weary
I wish I'd never been born.

Questions for Critical Thinking

1. In what ways does this poem interact with the blues?
2. Given the colloquial quality of this poem, which word choices seem important to you and why?

Song for a Dark Girl (1927)

Way Down South in Dixie
  (Break the heart of me)
They hung my black young lover
  To a cross roads tree.

Way Down South in Dixie   5
  (Bruised body high in air)
I asked the white Lord Jesus
  What was the use of prayer.

Way Down South in Dixie
  (Break the heart of me)   10
Love is a naked shadow
  On a gnarled and naked tree.

Questions for Critical Thinking

1. How would you describe the character the poet has created to sing these lines?
2. How does the historical and social material work with or against the musical aspect of the poem?

Let America Be America Again (1936)

Let America be America again.
Let it be the dream it used to be.
Let it be the pioneer on the plain
Seeking a home where he himself is free.

(America never was America to me.)   5

Let America be the dream the dreamers dreamed—
Let it be that great strong land of love
Where never kings connive nor tyrants scheme
That any man be crushed by one above.

(It never was America to me.)   10

O, let my land be a land where Liberty
Is crowned with no false patriotic wreath,
But opportunity is real, and life is free,
Equality is in the air we breathe.

15 (There's never been equality for me,
    Nor freedom in this "homeland of the free.")

Say, who are you that mumbles in the dark?
And who are you that draws your veil across the stars?

    I am the poor white, fooled and pushed apart,
20 I am the Negro bearing slavery's scars.
    I am the red man driven from the land,
    I am the immigrant clutching the hope I seek—
    And finding only the same old stupid plan
    Of dog eat dog, of mighty crush the weak.

25 I am the young man, full of strength and hope,
    Tangled in that ancient endless chain
    Of profit, power, gain, of grab the land!
    Of grab the gold! Of grab the ways of satisfying need!
    Of work the men! Of take the pay!
30 Of owning everything for one's own greed!

    I am the farmer, bondsman to the soil.
    I am the worker sold to the machine.
    I am the Negro, servant to you all.
    I am the people, humble, hungry, mean—
35 Hungry yet today despite the dream.
    Beaten yet today—O, Pioneers!
    I am the man who never got ahead,
    The poorest worker bartered through the years.

Yet I'm the one who dreamt our basic dream
In the Old World while still a serf of kings,   40
Who dreamt a dream so strong, so brave, so true,
That even yet its mighty daring sings
In every brick and stone, in every furrow turned
That's made America the land it has become.
O, I'm the man who sailed those early seas   45
In search of what I meant to be my home—
For I'm the one who left dark Ireland's shore,
And Poland's plain, and England's grassy lea,
And torn from Black Africa's strand I came
To build a "homeland of the free."   50

The free?

Who said the free? Not me?
Surely not me? The millions on relief today?
The millions shot down when we strike?
The millions who have nothing for our pay?   55
For all the dreams we've dreamed
And all the songs we've sung
And all the hopes we've held
And all the flags we've hung,
The millions who have nothing for our pay—   60
Except the dream that's almost dead today.

O, let America be America again—
The land that never has been yet—
And yet must be—the land where *every* man is free.
The land that's mine—the poor man's, Indian's, Negro's,   65
    ME—
Who made America,
Whose sweat and blood, whose faith and pain,
Whose hand at the foundry, whose plow in the rain,
Must bring back our mighty dream again.

Sure, call me any ugly name you choose—   70
The steel of freedom does not stain.
From those who live like leeches on the people's lives,
We must take back our land again,
America!

O, yes,   75
I say it plain,
America never was America to me,
And yet I swear this oath—
America will be!

80 Out of the rack and ruin of our gangster death,
The rape and rot of graft, and stealth, and lies,
We, the people, must redeem
The land, the mines, the plants, the rivers.
The mountains and the endless plain—
85 All, all the stretch of these great green states—
And make America again!

Ballad of the Landlord (1940)

Landlord, landlord,
My roof has sprung a leak.
Don't you 'member I told you about it
Way last week?

5 Landlord, landlord,
These steps is broken down.
When you come up yourself
It's a wonder you don't fall down.

Ten Bucks you say I owe you?
10 Ten Bucks you say is due?
Well, that's Ten Bucks more'n I'll pay you
Till you fix this house up new.

What? You gonna get eviction orders?
You gonna cut off my heat?
You gonna take my furniture and   15
Throw it in the street?

Um-huh! You talking high and mighty.
Talk on—till you get through.
You ain't gonna be able to say a word
If I land my fist on you.   20

Police! Police!
Come and get this man!
He's trying to ruin the government
And overturn the land!

Copper's Whistle!   25
Patrol bell!
Arrest.

Precinct Station.
Iron cell.
Headlines in press: 30

MAN THREATENS LANDLORD
TENANT HELD NO BAIL
JUDGE GIVES NEGRO 90 DAYS IN COUNTY JAIL

Dream Boogie (1951)

Good morning, daddy!
Ain't you heard
The boogie-woogie rumble
Of a dream deferred?
Listen closely: 5
You'll hear their feet
Beating out and beating out a—

You think
It's a happy beat?

10 Listen to it closely:
Ain't you heard
something underneath
like a—

What did I say?

15 Sure,
I'm happy!
Take it away!

Hey, pop!
Re-bop!
20 *Mop!*

Y-e-a-h!

Questions for Critical Thinking

1. Does such playfulness as we find in these lines have its place in good poetry? Why or why not?
2. How does the poet bend a traditional musical form to his own purposes? Why does he do it?

Theme for English B (1951)

The instructor said,

Go home and write
a page tonight.
And let that page come out of you—
5 *Then, it will be true.*

I wonder if it's that simple?
I am twenty-two, colored, born in Winston-Salem.
I went to school there, then Durham, then here
to this college on the hill above Harlem.
10 I am the only colored student in my class.
The steps from the hill lead down into Harlem,
through a park, then I cross St. Nicholas,
Eighth Avenue, Seventh, and I come to the Y,
the Harlem Branch Y, where I take the elevator
15 up to my room, sit down, and write this page:

It's not easy to know what is true for you and me
at twenty-two, my age. But I guess I'm what
I feel and see and hear, Harlem, I hear you:
hear you, hear me—we two—you, me, talk on this page.
(I hear New York, too.) Me—who?   20
Well, I like to eat, sleep, drink, and be in love.
I like to work, read, learn, and understand life.
I like a pipe for a Christmas present,
or records—Bessie, bop, or Bach.
I guess being colored doesn't make me *not* like   25
the same things other folks like who are other races.
So will my page be colored that I write?
Being me, it will not be white.

But it will be
a part of you, instructor.   30
You are white—
yet a part of me, as I am a part of you.
That's American.
Sometimes perhaps you don't want to be a part of me.
Nor do I often want to be a part of you.   35
But we are, that's true!
As I learn from you,
I guess you learn from me—
although you're older—and white—
and somewhat more free.   40

This is my page for English B.

Questions for Critical Thinking

1. Given the sentence-like and conversational quality of many of the lines, what elements make this a poem, rather than an essay?
2. In light of the facts of Hughes's life, it's obvious that the "I" who speaks in this poem is neither directly autobiographical nor the "I" of the poet himself. Who, then, is the speaker?

The Blues (1958)

When the shoe strings break
On *both* your shoes
And you're in a hurry—
That's the blues.

5   When you go to buy a candy bar
And you've lost the dime you had—
Slipped through a hole in your pocket somewhere—
That's the blues, too, *and bad!*

Questions for Critical Thinking

1. What attracts a poet like Hughes to the blues form?
2. Can you imagine someone singing this to the accompaniment of a piano and bass?

Hughes wrote the following essay in 1926, the same year that his first collection of poetry, The Weary Blues, *appeared to great acclaim. "The Negro Artist and the Racial Mountain" stands as his personal manifesto even as it speaks to the entire generation of the Harlem Renaissance. It celebrates the "so-called common element," the genuine black artists who stay true to their heritage. At the same it serves as a call to arms for all Negro artists and intellectuals to resist white middle-class standards and express their individuality.*

The Negro Artist and the Racial Mountain (1926)

One of the most promising of the young Negro poets said to me once, "I want to be a poet—not a Negro poet," meaning, I believe, "I want to write like a white poet"; meaning subconsciously, "I would like to be a white poet"; meaning behind that, "I would like to be white." And I was sorry the young man said that, for no great poet has ever been afraid of being himself. And I doubted then that, with his desire to run away spiritually from his race, this boy would ever be a great poet. But this is the mountain standing in the way of any true Negro art in America— this urge within the race toward whiteness, the desire to pour racial individuality into the mold of American standardization, and to be as little Negro and as much American as possible.

But let us look at the immediate background of this young poet. His family is of what I suppose one would call the Negro middle class: people who are by no means rich yet never uncomfortable nor hungry—smug, contented, respectable folk, members of the Baptist church. The father goes to work every morning. He is

a chief steward at a large white club. The mother sometimes does fancy sewing or supervises parties for the rich families of the town. The children go to a mixed school. In the home they read white papers and magazines. And the mother often says "Don't be like niggers" when the children are bad. A frequent phrase from the father is, "Look how well a white man does things." And so the word white comes to be unconsciously a symbol of all virtues. It holds for the children beauty, morality, and money. The whisper of "I want to be white" runs silently through their minds. This young poet's home is, I believe, a fairly typical home of the colored middle class. One sees immediately how difficult it would be for an artist born in such a home to interest himself in interpreting the beauty of his own people. He is never taught to see that beauty. He is taught rather not to see it, or if he does, to be ashamed of it when it is not according to Caucasian patterns. . . .

But then there are the low-down folks, the so-called common element, and they are the majority—may the Lord be praised! The people who have their hip of gin on Saturday nights and are not too important to themselves or the community, or too well fed, or too learned to watch the lazy world go round. They live on Seventh Street in Washington or State Street in Chicago and they do not particularly care whether they are like white folks or anybody else. Their joy runs, bang! into ecstasy. Their religion soars to a shout. Work maybe a little today, rest a little tomorrow. Play awhile. Sing awhile. O, let's dance! These common people are not afraid of spirituals, as for a long time their more intellectual brethren were, and jazz is their child. They furnish a wealth of colorful, distinctive material for any artist because they still hold their own individuality in the face of American standardizations. And perhaps these common people will give to the world its truly great Negro artist, the one who is not afraid to be himself. Whereas the better-class Negro would tell the artist what to do, the people at least let him alone when he does appear. And they are not ashamed of him—if they know he exists at all. And they accept what beauty is their own without question. . . .

Most of my own poems are racial in theme and treatment, derived from the life I know. In many of them I try to grasp and hold some of the meanings and rhythms of jazz. I am as sincere as I know how to be in these poems and yet after every reading I answer questions like these from my own people: Do you think Negroes should always write about Negroes? I wish you wouldn't read some of your poems to white folks. How do you find anything interesting in a place like a cabaret? Why do you write about black people? You aren't black. What makes you do so many jazz poems?

5   But jazz to me is one of the inherent expressions of Negro life in America; the eternal tom-tom beating in the Negro soul—the tom-tom of revolt against weariness in a white world, a world of subway trains, and work, work, work; the tom-tom of joy and laughter, and pain swallowed in a smile. Yet the Philadelphia clubwoman is ashamed to say that her race created it and she does not like me to write about it. The old subconscious "white is best" runs through her mind. Years of study under white teachers, a lifetime of white books, pictures, and papers, and white manners, morals, and Puritan standards made her dislike the spirituals. And now she turns up her nose at jazz and all its manifestations—likewise almost everything else distinctly racial. She doesn't care for the Winold Reiss' portraits of Negroes because they are "too Negro." She does not want a true picture of herself from anybody. She wants the artist to flatter her, to make the white world believe that all Negroes are as smug and as near white in soul as she wants to be. But, to my mind, it is the duty of the younger Negro artist, if he accepts any duties at all from outsiders, to change through the force of his art that old whispering "I want to be white," hidden in the aspirations of his people, to "Why should I want to be white? I am a Negro—and beautiful."

So I am ashamed for the black poet who says, "I want to be a poet, not a Negro poet," as though his own racial world were not as interesting as any other world. I am ashamed, too, for the colored artist who runs from the painting of Negro faces to the painting of sunsets after the manner of the academicians because he fears the strange unwhiteness of his own features. An artist must be free to choose what he does, certainly, but he must also never be afraid to do what he must choose.

Let the blare of Negro jazz bands and the bellowing voice of Bessie Smith singing the Blues penetrate the closed ears of the colored near intellectuals until they listen and perhaps understand. Let Paul Robeson singing "Water Boy," and Rudolph Fisher writing about the streets of Harlem, and Jean Toomer holding the heart of Georgia in his hands, and Aaron Douglas's drawing strange black fantasies cause the smug Negro middle class to turn from their white, respectable, ordinary books and papers to catch a glimmer of their own beauty. We younger Negro artists who create now intend to express our individual dark-skinned selves without fear or shame. If white people are pleased we are glad. If they are not, it doesn't matter. We know we are beautiful. And ugly too. The tom-tom cries and the tom-tom laughs. If colored people are pleased we are glad. If they are not, their displeasure doesn't matter either. We build our temples for tomorrow, strong as we know how, and we stand on top of the mountain, free within ourselves.

Questions for Critical Thinking

1. Hughes identifies two groups within the African-American race. What are these groups? List their characteristics, and then state which group Hughes admires more. Why?

2. Describe Hughes's feelings toward jazz. According to Hughes, why is jazz important? What does it express?

3. Using this essay, write a one-paragraph summary of Hughes's mission as a black artist.

Countee Cullen (1903–1946)

A prominent voice of the Harlem Renaissance, Cullen rivaled and at times surpassed Langston Hughes in his lifetime. Although he was immensely popular in the 1920s and early 1930s, relatively little is known about the childhood of the boy who would grow up to become the "black Keats." He was most likely born in Louisville, Kentucky. He went by the name Countee Porter early in life, but by early adolescence, he had been adopted by the Cullen family. He enjoyed a close relationship with his Cullen father, who led a church in Harlem, and spent his young adulthood in Harlem.

Early success with his poetry collections *Color* (1925), *Copper Sun* (1927), *The Ballad of the Brown Girl* (1927), and *The Black Christ* (1929), all published in a four-year period; his receipt of a Guggenheim Fellowship that allowed him to live in France for a year and write; and his high-profile marriage to Yolande Du Bois, the only daughter of the famous African-American activist W. E. B. Du Bois, all promised the making of an exceptional poet and role model and cemented his reputation as the great "crossover" poet— a black man who wrote in the style of classically white poetry. Although Hughes made it clear in "The Negro Artist and the Racial Mountain" that he planned to be a poet who celebrated his race, Countee Cullen made the following statement in the *Brooklyn Eagle*:

> If I am going to be a poet at all, I am going to be POET and not NEGRO POET. This is what has hindered the development of artists among us. Their one note has been the concern with their race. That is all very well, none of us can get away from it. I cannot at times. You will see it in my verse. The consciousness of this is too poignant at times. I cannot escape it. But what I mean is this: I shall not write of negro subjects for the purpose of propaganda. That is not what a poet is concerned with. Of course, when the emotion rising out of the fact that I am a negro is strong, I express it. But that is another matter.

Cullen's career peaked early; he began writing less, and his marriage ended in divorce a year after it began. He took a job teaching French and English at a junior high school, where he taught until his death at age forty-two.

For a Lady I Know (1925)

She even thinks that up in heaven
    Her class lies late and snores,
While poor black cherubs rise at seven
    To do celestial chores.

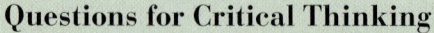

Questions for Critical Thinking

1. Despite his conservative poetic taste and ideas about poetry and race, Cullen wrote numerous racially charged poems and titled his first collection *Color*. Some people believed his classical skill and restraint were not suitable to the subject matter of race. How does your evaluation of the two poems included here affect your response to this criticism of Cullen's work?

2. Compare this poem with "If We Must Die" by another Harlem Renaissance poet interested in classical forms, Claude McKay. What differences do you see in their use of irony, and how do they affect the tone of the poems? What is the effect of using classic poetic structures on the poems' subject and tone?

Incident (1925)

Once riding in old Baltimore,
   Heart-filled, head-filled with glee,
I saw a Baltimorean
   Keep looking straight at me.

5 Now I was eight and very small,
   And he was no whit bigger,
And so I smiled, but he poked out
   His tongue, and called me, "Nigger."

I saw the whole of Baltimore
10   From May until December;
Of all the things that happened there
   That's all that I remember.

Questions for Critical Thinking

1. This poem is more straightforward than other classical poems that Cullen wrote. Why do you think Cullen chose to make it that way? How would its impact
change if it were written in elevated language or a more
complex form?

2. Discuss the difference in the rhyme pattern, in these
four-line stanzas, between the first and third lines and
the second and fourth. Also discuss the enjambment
in lines 7 and 8. How does the conversational "tone"
here get supported or undermined by the poem's formal
structure?

Helene Johnson (1907–1995)

Helene Johnson came to New York in
1926 to attend the awards ceremony for
the winners of *Opportunity* magazine's
poetry contest—she had received an honorable mention—and stayed. Langston
Hughes's friend and collaborator on "Mule
Bone," Zora Neale Hurston (see Chapter
10), lived in the same apartment building,
and Johnson's cousin, the writer Dorothy
West, was nearby in Harlem. Johnson was
close to many writers during this time,
and Countee Cullen published her work
in his anthology *Caroling Dusk*. After her
marriage to William Warner Hubbel and
the birth of their daughter, she wrote less.
When they separated, she moved back
home to Boston but later returned to
New York, where she died. The subject of
race and identity is framed in Johnson's
work by lyrical formal verse, as it is in the
following poem, "Sonnet to a Negro in
Harlem."

Sonnet to a Negro in Harlem (1927)

You are disdainful and magnificent—
Your perfect body and your pompous gait,
Your dark eyes flashing solemnly with hate;
Small wonder that you are incompetent
5 To imitate those whom you so despise—
Your shoulders towering high above the throng,
Your head thrown back in rich, barbaric song,
Palm trees and mangoes stretched before your eyes.
Let others toil and sweat for labor's sake
10 And wring from grasping hands their meed of gold.
Why urge ahead your supercilious feet?
Scorn will efface each footprint that you make.
I love your laughter arrogant and bold.
You are too splendid for this city street!

Questions for Critical Thinking

1. Do you find this description in the poem similar to that of an actual painting? List the details you learn from the poem. Which details could you also learn from a painting, and which are unique to verse? Are any details missing that you could get only from a real picture?

2. How critical is this depiction of the subject? Do you find elements of admiration along with the negative elements?

Claude McKay (1889–1948)

Jamaican-born Claude McKay brought in a more defiant tone than that of Langston Hughes, but like Hughes he focused on race. He had grown up hearing from his father about his West African Ashanti traditions and how his grandfather had been enslaved by whites. He published two collections while still living in Jamaica, *Songs of Jamaica* (1912), celebrating the life of Jamaican farm-

ers, and *Constab Ballads* (1912), deriding the treatment of dark-skinned blacks by whites and mulattos. These books earned him the medal of the Jamaican Institute of the Arts and Sciences. McKay arrived in the United States, where he studied agriculture first at Booker T. Washington's Tuskegee Institute in Alabama and later at Kansas State College. After two years he decided instead to make his living as a writer and moved to Harlem. He was close to radicals, often publishing his work in

Greenwich Village political magazines, and he lived for a time in England, where he worked at the newspaper *Workers' Dreadnought*. He returned to America in 1921. Writers such as Hughes and McKay were "The New Writers" whom Alain Locke described in his essay "The New Negro." McKay shaped the imagination and subject matter of black writers and did so by writing his unflinching condemnations of bigotry in formal verse, as he does in the following sonnets.

If We Must Die

(1919)

If we must die, let it not be like hogs
Hunted and penned in an inglorious spot,
While round us bark the mad and hungry dogs,
Making their mock at our accursèd lot.
5 If we must die, O let us nobly die,
So that our precious blood may not be shed
In vain; then even the monsters we defy
Shall be constrained to honor us though dead!
O kinsmen! we must meet the common foe!
10 Though far outnumbered let us show us brave,
And for their thousand blows deal one death-blow!
What though before us lies the open grave?
Like men we'll face the murderous, cowardly pack,
Pressed to the wall, dying, but fighting back!

Questions for Critical Thinking

1. This is a sonnet about lynchings, in particular those during riots in Harlem in 1919. Compare it to the sonnet by Edward Hirsch, "My First Theology Lesson," in Chapter 25. Both are arguments. What is the argument McKay is making in "If We Must Die"?

2. Senator Henry Cabot Lodge, Sr., read this poem into the Congressional record during World War II for its inspirational theme about "fighting back." What is gained by this broader interpretation of the subject? What is lost?

America (1922)

Although she feeds me bread of bitterness,
And sinks into my throat her tiger's tooth,
Stealing my breath of life, I will confess
I love this cultured hell that tests my youth!
5 Her vigor flows like tides into my blood,
Giving me strength erect against her hate.
Her bigness sweeps my being like a flood.
Yet, as a rebel fronts a king in state,
I stand within her walls with not a shred
10 Of terror, malice, not a word of jeer.
Darkly I gaze into the days ahead,
And see her might and granite wonders there,
Beneath the touch of Time's unerring hand,
Like priceless treasures sinking in the sand.

Questions for Critical Thinking

1. What is America being compared to in this poem?

2. McKay was born in Jamaica, came to America to be educated, and then ended up in Harlem before moving to England and then back again. How would you describe his feelings about his adopted homeland? Why does he call her bread bitter in line 1? What are the "priceless treasures" he refers to in line 14?

The White City (1922)

I will not toy with it nor bend an inch.
Deep in the secret chambers of my heart
I muse my life-long hate, and without flinch
I bear it nobly as I live my part.
5 My being would be a skeleton, a shell,
If this dark Passion that fills my every mood,
And makes my heaven in the white world's hell,
Did not forever feed me vital blood.
I see the mighty city through a mist—
10 The strident trains that speed the goaded mass,
The poles and spires and towers vapor-kissed,
The fortressed port through which the great ships pass,
The tides, the wharves, the dens I contemplate,
Are sweet like wanton loves because I hate.

Questions for Critical Thinking

1. What does the title tell you about the subject of this somewhat difficult poem? What is its subject?

2. How difficult is it to interpret this poem once you identify the subject? What is your interpretation?

Jessie Redmon Fauset (1884–1961)

Jessie Redmon Fauset was raised outside Philadelphia. She went to public schools in Philadelphia until she graduated with a scholarship to Cornell University. She was the first woman to graduate Phi Beta Kappa from Cornell and the first black woman to be admitted to that prestigious academic organization nationally. After teaching Latin and French in Baltimore and Washington, D.C. (where her race did not bar her from getting a teaching job), Fauset went back to school at the University of Pennsylvania to earn her master's degree. She began working for the magazine *Crisis* under W. E. B. Du Bois in 1918 and became its literary editor in 1919. She nurtured the talents of many, including Langston Hughes, whom she recognized early in his career. When she invited him to lunch, he was so nervous he asked if he could bring his gregarious mother (which he did) to make sure the lunch went smoothly. Fauset's home was often the meeting place for literary discussions, sometimes held in French. She had exacting standards as an editor and was of central importance in shaping the talent that was burgeoning in this time in Harlem.

Touché (1927)

Dear, when we sit in that high, placid room,
"Loving" and "doving" as all lovers do,
Laughing and leaning so close in the gloom,—

What is the change that creeps sharp over you?
5   Just as you raise your fine hand to my hair,
Bringing that glance of mixed wonder and rue?

"Black hair," you murmur, "so lustrous and rare,
Beautiful too, like a raven's smooth wing;
Surely no gold locks were ever more fair."

10   Why do you say every night that same thing?
Turning your mind to some old constant theme,
Half meditating and half murmuring?

Tell me, that girl of your young manhood's dream,
Her you loved first in that dim long ago—
15   Had *she* blue eyes? Did *her* hair goldly gleam?

Does *she* come back to you softly and slow,
Stepping wraith-wise from the depths of the past?
Quickened and fired by the warmth of our glow?

There, I've divined it! My wit holds you fast.
20   Nay, no excuses; 'tis little I care,
I knew a lad in my own girlhood's past,—
Blue eyes he had and such waving gold hair!

Questions for Critical Thinking

1. What role does race play in this affair between two dark-haired and, presumably, dark-skinned lovers? How does the matter of race engender doubt in the lover's mind?

2. How does the formal and even archaic diction and tone (words like *rue* and *nay*) compare with the writing of Toomer or Hughes? What do these aesthetic choices reveal about Fauset's work?

Jean Toomer (1894–1967)

Jean Toomer insisted that he was "of no race," a mix of "Scotch, Welsh, German, English, French, Dutch, Spanish and some dark blood," but his great work *Cane* (1923) is a modernist study by turns of black life in rural Georgia and black life in urban Chicago and Washington, D.C., and an autobiographical synthesis of the two. It includes poems and sketches as well as prose and immediately became a central text for African-Americans of his time. Toomer was born in Washington, D.C.; his father abandoned the family a year after he was born. He and his mother moved in with her parents, where Toomer spent his early years. Race was an issue early on but with a twist; Toomer's maternal grandfather had achieved some success as a politician in southern Louisiana, and though he claimed to be black, Toomer did not believe this was true. When Toomer's mother remarried, they relocated to New Rochelle, New York. He never graduated from college, though he attended several, and he claimed Alain Locke had "tricked" him into including his work in *The New Negro*. In the 1920s he began a long association with George I. Gurdjieff, a Greek-Armenian spiritualist, attempting to recruit his friends, African-American writers such as Nella Larsen and Wallace Thurman, to Gurdjieff's Unitism. In later life Toomer moved away from Gurdjieff, married, and became a Quaker. The following poem, "Reapers," appears in *Cane*.

Reapers (1923)

Black reapers with the sound of steel on stones
Are sharpening scythes. I see them place the hones
In their hip-pockets as a thing that's done,
And start their silent swinging, one by one.
5 Black horses drive a mower through the weeds,
And there, a field rat, startled, squealing bleeds,
His belly close to ground. I see the blade,
Blood-stained, continue cutting weeds and shade.

Song of the Son (1923)

Pour O pour that parting soul in song,
O pour it in the sawdust glow of night,
Into the velvet pine-smoke air tonight,
And let the valley carry it along.
5   And let the valley carry it along.

O land and soil, red soil and sweet-gum tree,
So scant of grass, so profligate of pines,
Now just before an epoch's sun declines
Thy son, in time, I have returned to thee.
10 Thy son, I have in time returned to thee.

In time, for though the sun is setting on
A song-lit race of slaves, it has not set;
Though late, O soil, it is not too late yet
To catch thy plaintive soul, leaving, soon gone,
15 Leaving, to catch thy plaintive soul soon gone.

O Negro slaves, dark purple ripened plums,
Squeezed, and bursting in the pine-wood air,
Passing, before they stripped the old tree bare
One plum was saved for me, one seed becomes

20 An everlasting song, a singing tree,
Caroling softly souls of slavery,
What they were, and what they are to me,
Caroling softly souls of slavery.

Angelina Weld Grimké (1880–1958)

Angelina Weld Grimké's father, Archibald, was the child of a union between a white Southerner and a slave, Nancy Weston. Archibald's father's sisters were abolitionists who publicly acknowledged and encouraged their nephew. After becoming a lawyer with a Harvard law degree, Archibald Henry Grimké married a white woman, Sarah Stanley of Boston—Angelina's mother. Sarah, whose family strongly disapproved of the marriage, eventually abandoned her husband and her child. Nevertheless, Archibald doted on Angelina, and she had a close, lifelong relationship with him. Her first work, the play *Rachel,* continued her family's tradition of engagement with racial issues. According to the playbill, it was "the first attempt to use the stage for race propaganda in order to enlighten the American people relative to the lamentable condition of ten million of Colored citizens in this free republic." Angelina Weld Grimké's output was small, but her poetry is characterized by lyricism and the address of life as a woman. She remained close friends with a widely published African-American writer of the time, Georgia Douglas Johnson.

Fragment (c. 1930)

I am the woman with the black black skin
I am the laughing woman with the black black face
I am living in the cellars and in every crowded place
    I am toiling just to eat
5   In the cold and in the heat
      And I laugh
I am the laughing woman who's forgotten how to weep
I am the laughing woman who's afraid to go to sleep

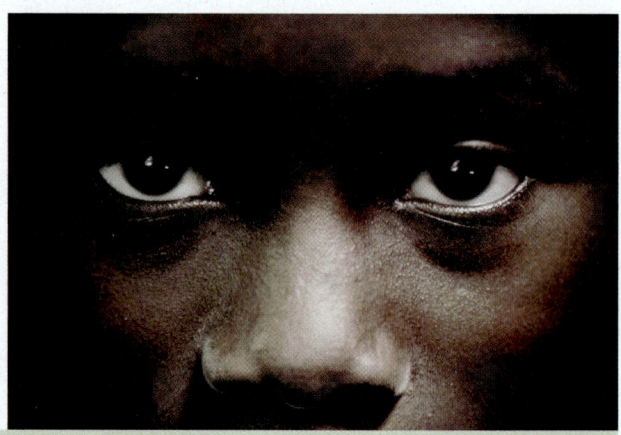

Questions for Critical Thinking

1. Why does Grimké juxtapose laughter and destitution?

2. How does the poet employ irony here? What does she gain? What do you gain as a reader?

Getting Started: A Research Project

Research is a skill that will carry you through your college career. To help acquaint you with the research process, the materials you need for this project are made available on our Web site (**connect.mcgraw-hill.com**). Other ideas for research projects and sources appear at the end of this chapter.

Although a popular and iconic figure for the Harlem Renaissance, Langston Hughes did share the spotlight with other outspoken literary figures of the time. One such person was Countee Cullen (two of Cullen's poems appear earlier in this chapter). Like Hughes, Cullen was not raised by his biological parents, he was very successful in high school, and he was a published poet in his late teenage years. Although both men would become prominent voices of the Harlem Renaissance, their messages were not always the same.

Information on Cullen's background and a timeline of his accomplishments can be found at **connect.mcgraw-hill.com.** You will also find a variety of essays related to Cullen, Hughes, and other writers of their generation. As you conduct your research, ask yourself what ties these diverse writers together as voices of the Harlem Renaissance, and consider how their messages resonate in modern society.

The Harlem Renaissance and the poets associated with it often dealt with race, and it was in many ways a racial movement, but it was more than that. It was a cultural awakening, a celebration of music like blues and jazz, an explosion of new art and theater and political thinking. In the same way, key players such as Langston Hughes and Countee Cullen were not just poets. They wrote essays, plays, and novels. They worked in colloquialisms and formal voices. They wrote about private experiences as well as public issues.

Go to connect.mcgraw-hill.com for essays and resources on topics centered on Langston Hughes and the poets of his time.

1. Focus on one pair of poets, for example, Hughes and Cullen. Read the quote from Cullen's brief biography earlier in this chapter. Contrast Cullen's statement with Hughes's arguments in his essay "The Negro Artist and the Racial Mountain." Note how Hughes refers to a "Negro poet" in the first line of the essay. Compare Hughes's and Cullen's ideas about being a "Negro poet." Write a definition of "Negro poet" from each man's point of view. Now consider how the two definitions compare, and how they are different.

2. Discuss how blues and jazz influenced literature during the Harlem Renaissance.

3. Both Hughes and Cullen experienced highs and lows of popularity. Consider the timelines of their lives and careers, as well as the social atmosphere of their era, and discuss the various factors surrounding each figure's prominence and decline.

Writing and Research

1. If you have an interest in music, particularly in blues and jazz, reread Hughes's poem "Harlem (Dream Deferred)" (Chapter 5) and some of the blues poems in this chapter in preparation for reading at least two of the articles listed below—including one from the Hughes scholar Onwuchekwa Jemie. Drawing on these articles, write an essay in which you present a critical reading of "Harlem," interweaving the significance of its form as a jazz poem.

   • Jemie, Onwuchekwa. "Jazz, Jive, and Jam." *Langston Hughes: An Introduction to the Poetry*. New York: Columbia UP, 1976. 57–96. Print.

   • Johnson, Charles S. "Jazz Poetry and Blues." *Critical Essays on Langston Hughes*. Ed. Edward J. Mullen. Boston: Hall, 1986. 143–47. Print.

2. Look up Wallace Thurman in the *Encyclopedia of the Harlem Renaissance*. Read selections from Thurman's novel *The Blacker the Berry* (1929) and from his satirical critique of the Harlem Renaissance in *Infants of the Spring* (1932). Argue a case for the complexity of the years of the Harlem Renaissance, in which not all the artists and writers making up this so-called movement take a positive view of the world in which they move.

3. Look up the paintings of Jacob Lawrence, who was another of Langston Hughes's contemporaries during the Harlem Renaissance. The French word *renaissance* means, literally, "born again." This is not a religious term but a cultural one; in the European Renaissance of the fifteenth and sixteenth centuries the ideals of antiquity were rediscovered, and artists and writers tried to express the "classical" ideals as derived from Greece and Rome. The name Harlem comes from the Dutch city of Haarlem, the home of many of the first settlers of New Amsterdam (New York City's original name). To what degree do artists such as Langston Hughes and Jacob Lawrence pay conscious attention to their own history, and what are they suggesting should be "born again" in this new/old form of art? What's innovative and what's traditional in their work; how much influence do African and Caribbean roots have in the flowering of the Harlem Renaissance? Cite specific examples. What role does music play?

4. There are several other twentieth-century examples of artists in community. To pick a few, there is expatriate Paris (Gertrude Stein, Ernest Hemingway, F. Scott Fitzgerald, Pablo Picasso, and so on), London's Bloomsbury (Virginia Woolf, Vanessa Stephen, E. M. Forster, Lytton Strachey, and so forth), and a group of novelists near the southern English town of Rye (Henry James, Joseph Conrad, Ford Madox Ford, and Stephen Crane). How does the idea of collegiality—a shared aesthetic, shared pleasure in each other's company—pertain to the Harlem Renaissance? How does the idea of regionalism (discussed in the Case Studies on Regionalism in Chapter 15) play a role in the work—from music to literature—of the Harlem Renaissance? When Josephine Baker sings "Harlem on My Mind" in Paris, or James Baldwin (whose story "Sonny's Blues" can be found in Chapter 9) goes to Paris with recordings of Billie Holiday and Bessie Smith, what does that say about the value and power of place?

Some Sources for Research

Online Sources

1. Alexander, Elizabeth. "The Black Poet as Canon-Maker: Langston Hughes, New Negro Poets, and American Poetry's Segregated Past." *PoetryFoundation.org*. Poetry Foundation, 2004. Web.

2. Giaimo, Paul. "Ethnic Outsiders: The Hyper-Ethnicized Narrator in Langston Hughes and Fred L. Gardaphe." *MELUS* 28.3 (2003): 133–47. Web.

3. Graham, Maryemma. "Langston Hughes Centennial, 1902–1967: The Beat Goes On." *The New Crisis* Jan.–Feb, 2002: n. pag. *FindArticle.com*. Web.

4. Lamb, Robert Paul. "'A Little Yellow Bastard Boy': Paternal Rejection, Filial Insistence, and the Triumph of African American Cultural Aesthetics in Langston Hughes's 'Mulatto.'" *College Literature* 35.2 (2008): 126–53. *FindArticle.com*. Web.

5. "Langston Hughes." *PoetryFoundation.org*. Poetry Foundation, 2009. Web.

6. Scott, Jonathan. "Advanced, Repressed, and Popular: Langston Hughes during the Cold War." *College Literature* 33.2 (2006): 30-51. *AccessMyLibrary.com*. Web.

Print Sources

7. Bloom, Harold, ed. *The Harlem Renaissance*. Philadelphia: Chelsea, 2004. Print.

8. Carroll, Anne Elizabeth. *Word, Image, and the New Negro: Representation and Identity in the Harlem Renaissance*. Bloomington: Indiana UP, 2005. Print.

9. Hutchinson, George, ed. *The Cambridge Companion to the Harlem Renaissance*. New York: Cambridge UP, 2007. Print.

10. Jones, Sharon L. *Rereading the Harlem Renaissance: Race, Class, and Gender in the Fiction of Jessie Fauset, Zora Neale Hurston, and Dorothy West*. Westport: Greenwood, 2002. Print.

11. Krasner, David. *A Beautiful Pageant: African American Theatre, Drama, and Performance in the Harlem Renaissance, 1910-1927*. New York: Palgrave, 2002. Print.

12. Ogbar, Jeffrey O.G., ed. *The Harlem Renaissance Revisited: Politics, Arts, and Letters*. Baltimore: Johns Hopkins UP, 2010. Print.

13. Rampersad, Arnold. *The Life of Langston Hughes*. 2nd ed. 2 vols. New York: Oxford UP, 2002. Print.

14. Tidwell, John Edgar, and Cheryl R. Ragar, eds. *Montage of a Dream : The Art and Life of Langston Hughes*. Columbia: U of Missouri P, 2007. Print.

15. Vogel, Shane. *The Scene of Harlem Cabaret: Race, Sexuality, Performance*. Chicago: U of Chicago P, 2009. Print.

For an example of a student paper on Langston Hughes, see Chapter 5.

28

American Plain Style

A Case Study on

Emily Dickinson and Robert Frost

"It seems to me that in great poems, in the great poems of Frost, in the great poems of Dickinson . . . they're actually thinking in poetry, they're not taking some idea and poeticizing it; or they're not taking some idea and embellishing it. . . . What's manifested is thinking by imagination."

Conversation with Li-Young Lee

Emily Dickinson

Robert Frost

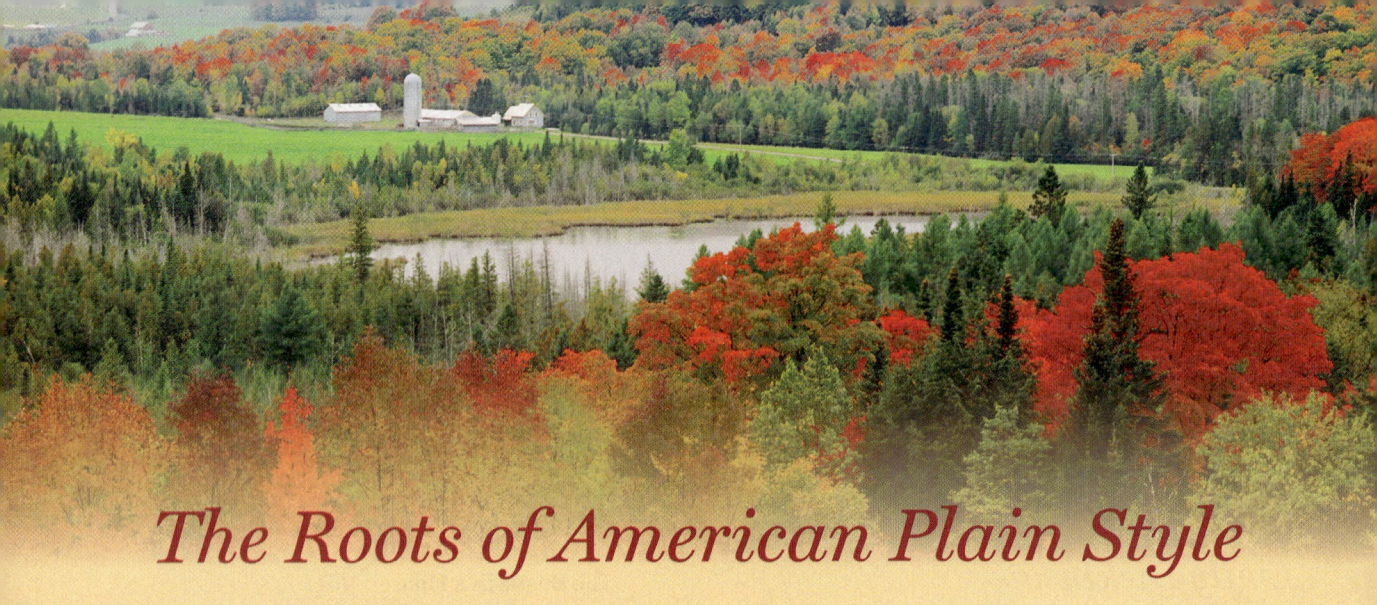

The Roots of American Plain Style

No one was more reclusive than Emily Dickinson; no one more widely recognized than Robert Frost. However, they have much in common. Both gave the best parts of their lives to their art; both worked at it unceasingly. Each was eloquent as a letter writer; each was described by others as a "Yankee crank." More important, both were original makers and forgers of the American Plain Style. As you have likely observed from the examples so far in this textbook, there are many different approaches to poetry. However, studying plain style allows us to get at the heart of a major split within the genre—"two roads" that, as Robert Frost observes, "diverged."

In American poetry, the divergence in style occurred between poets who write highly symbolic and complex verse in the vein of Wallace Stevens and those who write distilled or pared-down work that focuses on the world around us, such as William Carlos Williams. Think of the difference between Stevens's "jar in Tennessee" (Chapter 22) and Williams's "red wheelbarrow" (Chapter 22), and you'll get some sense of what we mean. However, this American split has its origin much further back; it came ashore with the Puritan settlers who first inhabited New England. The Puritans, as you may recollect from history, sought religious freedom from what they saw as corruption in the English church.

They eschewed the formal pomp and ceremony associated with worship in the Catholic church in favor of a simple and "pure" devotion to God. In other words, "plain"-ness was a way of life, as reflected in their plain clothes, their plain houses of worship, and their simple forms of entertainment—all aspects that allowed them to focus not on a worldly existence but on a godly one.

This belief in plainness as the best way of approaching God permeated Puritan discourse as well. Remember Anne Bradstreet's comparison of her book to her child (Chapter 21) or the noticing eye ("I") of Walt Whitman (Chapter 26); their use of domestic particulars would not have seemed appropriate before. In early American sermons, you can see a wide embrace of the language of everyday speech. In a sermon titled "Sinners in the Hands of an Angry God," the eighteenth-century New England minister Jonathan Edwards declared, "The God that holds you over the pit of hell, much as one holds a spider, or some loathsome insect, over the fire, abhors you, and is dreadfully provoked; his wrath towards you burns like fire." Here Edwards uses earthy images of spiders and fire to great rhetorical effect.

Given the strong Puritan influence in New England, which shaped the society surrounding Emily Dickinson, it's relatively easy to trace that

"Robert Frost . . . is the most cunning and uncanny American poet who ever lived. . . . He refuses to say something is something when it isn't. . . . To rest in that is such a pleasure." Conversation with Marie Howe

tradition of plain speech in America. Dickinson—along with Whitman and, later, Frost—brought an early turn in poetry to plain style. These poets, who confronted the American wilderness and understood that their ancestors had literally done so, brought a view of nature as concrete rather than as an abstract entity. Plain style, then, brought a split from both florid poetic language and elevated treatment of nature: In short, it brought poetry "down to earth."

The Plain Style

Through plain style, both Dickinson and Frost have left their separate yet shared imprint on the contemporary mode of utterance in verse. By this we mean a way of *saying* that involves a way of *seeing:* straightforward, uncluttered language shaped into poetical form. Enjambment is common, since it makes the poem's line breaks seem less obvious or end-stopped, and rhyme, though widespread, feels unforced. The tone is unpretentious and the vocabulary serviceable; it's the surprising shift of emphasis, not the surprising (or obscure, or arcane) word that counts. Nothing they write is hard to read, but much of it demands close reading before we understand. What's sometimes difficult to follow in this pair of poets is the thought process itself, the sudden leap of intuition or juxtaposition—in Dickinson's case by way of dashes—of what might seem disconnected.

Dickinson rarely glories in the play of "wit" for its own sake. She does love wordplay and the way sounds edge up against each other, but there's an almost confessional impulse in her truth-telling work. Frost, too, is schooled in poetic tradition and studiously familiar with those who wrote before. Although his "homespun" style was always intended to seem offhand and conversational; no matter how

intricate the form or thought, the manner of speaking is *plain*.

In the largest sense this style is democratic. Best read aloud, the poems that follow have the rhythms of natural speech (we've included twice as many by Dickinson, because her work is brief). Between them, these two artists provide a portrait of America in its period of growth and maturation, its increasing sense of what's at risk, what's still to be discovered, and what must be preserved.

Emily Dickinson (1830–1886)

Like other writers whose eccentricities turn into legend over time, Emily Dickinson lives in the popular imagination as a recluse who dressed in all white and never left her room. While it is true that she dressed in white, and that she preferred living in her father's house her entire life, she cultivated relationships with people both near—such as her sister-in-law, Susan Gilbert, who lived next door—and far, such as her literary critic friend Thomas Wentworth Higginson, with whom she maintained a correspondence for more than twenty years.

Born in Amherst, Massachusetts, she lived her life in almost total obscurity. Raised in a Puritan, New England atmosphere, and in a devoutly religious family, Dickinson herself did not give the public confession of her faith that was expected of her and eventually refused to attend conventional church services. She attended Mount Holyoke Female Seminary—a few miles from Amherst—but returned home after her first year because she was acutely homesick. Though her family was prosperous and prominent, she became a kind of hermit, remaining in the village and writing her "odd" poetry for herself alone. She spent her days reading, writing letters, and composing more than 2,000 poems. Only a handful of these poems were published in her lifetime, and those by the initiative of family and friends, not her own effort. Dickinson preferred self-publication, which for her meant binding by hand forty volumes of her handwritten poetry. She did conceive of the work as a "letter to the world," but it was delivered posthumously; her present fame would not have been imagined and could not have been predicted at the time. When her poems were discovered upon her death, her younger sister, Lavinia, was instrumental in getting them published; however, the editors normalized much of Dickinson's punctuation (they eliminated her characteristic dashes) and syntax so that it read much like any other nineteenth-century verse.

It was not until the 1950s that her original intention was restored by an editor working with her fascicles (handwritten manuscripts). Today, along with Whitman, Dickinson is recognized for creating a uniquely American poetic voice—hers marked by its simplicity of structure and diction, its hymn-like rhythms, and its odd punctuation.

Success is counted sweetest (c. 1859)

Success is counted sweetest
By those who ne'er succeed.
To comprehend a nectar
Requires sorest need.

Not one of all the purple Host   5
Who took the Flag today
Can tell the definition
So clear of Victory

As he defeated—dying—
On whose forbidden ear   10
The distant strains of triumph
Burst agonized and clear!

Questions for Critical Thinking

1. What does the speaker mean by "To comprehend a nectar / Requires sorest need"? Paraphrase these lines.

2. If Dickinson had ended the poem after the first stanza, the overall meaning of the poem (which you paraphrased in the question above) would still come across. What, then, would be lost by removing the last two stanzas? In other words, how do those stanzas expand upon the meaning set up in the first stanza?

I taste a liquor never brewed— (c. 1860)

I taste a liquor never brewed—
From Tankards scooped in Pearl—
Not all the Vats upon the Rhine
Yield such an Alcohol!

5   Inebriate of Air—am I—
And Debauchee of Dew—
Reeling—thro endless summer days—
From inns of Molten Blue—

When "Landlords" turn the drunken Bee
10 Out of the Foxglove's door—
When Butterflies—renounce their "drams"—
I shall but drink the more!

Till Seraphs swing their snowy Hats—
And Saints—to windows run—
To see the little Tippler   15
Leaning against the—Sun—

Questions for Critical Thinking

1. On what is this speaker drunk? Underline where you find the answer, and then paraphrase it in your own words.

2. Scan this poem to discover its meter. Keeping in mind that a typical hymn stanza has alternating lines of eight syllables and six syllables, consider how this poem relates to a hymn. Does this relation enhance the meaning of this poem?

Some keep the Sabbath going to Church— (c. 1860)

Some keep the Sabbath going to Church—
I keep it, staying at Home—
With a Bobolink for a Chorister—
And an Orchard, for a Dome—

Some keep the Sabbath in Surplice—   5
I just wear my Wings—
And instead of tolling the Bell, for Church,
Our little Sexton—sings.

God preaches, a noted Clergyman—
And the sermon is never long,   10
So instead of getting to Heaven, at last—
I'm going, all along.

Questions for Critical Thinking

1. In line 6, the speaker says "I just wear my Wings." What does she mean?

2. Highlight all the words that have to do with the church. Then underline the words that have to do with nature. How does diction support the message of this poem?

Safe in their Alabaster Chambers— (1861)

Safe in their Alabaster Chambers—
Untouched by Morning—
And untouched by Noon—
Lie the meek members of the Resurrection—
5 Rafter of Satin—and Roof of Stone!

Grand go the Years—in the Crescent—above them—
Worlds scoop their arcs—
And Firmaments—row—
Diadems—drop—and Doges—surrender—
10 Soundless as dots—on a Disc of Snow—

Questions for Critical Thinking

1. Who are the safe ones?
2. Does nature seem sympathetic to their condition, or indifferent?
3. The second stanza suggests a relation between time and history and the subjects of the poem. How would you describe it?
4. Interpret the line in the second stanza "Soundless as dots—on a disc of snow—" in relation to the first three lines of the stanza. Are the dots the years, worlds, jewels, and rulers referred to there? If so, what does the line mean?

I like a look of Agony (c. 1861)

I like a look of Agony,
Because I know it's true—
Men do not sham Convulsion,
Nor simulate, a Throe—

The Eyes glaze once—and that is Death—   5
Impossible to feign
The Beads upon the Forehead
By homely Anguish strung

Questions for Critical Thinking

1. What are "The Beads upon the Forehead By homely Anguish"? Describe the mental image you get from the last two lines.
2. Describe the speaker's tone in this poem. Is his or her stance toward suffering surprising to you? How does it affect the way you read the poem?

Wild Nights—Wild Nights! (c. 1861)

Wild Nights—Wild Nights!
Were I with thee
Wild Nights should be
Our luxury!

5 Futile—the Winds—
To a Heart in port—
Done with the Compass—
Done with the Chart!

Rowing in Eden—
10 Ah, the Sea!
Might I but moor—Tonight
In Thee!

Questions for Critical Thinking

1. What is the effect of repeating the phrase "Wild Nights"?

2. Discuss the erotic component of this poem. Does the speaker describe physical love or yearn for spiritual union with something abstract? Or both?

There's a certain Slant of light (c. 1861)

There's a certain Slant of light,
Winter Afternoons—
That oppresses, like the Heft
Of Cathedral Tunes—

5 Heavenly Hurt, it gives us—
We can find no scar,
But internal difference,
Where the Meanings, are—

None may teach it—Any—
10 'Tis the Seal Despair—
An imperial affliction
Sent us of the Air—

When it comes, the Landscape listens—
Shadows—hold their breath—
When it goes, 'tis like the Distance   15
On the look of Death—

Questions for Critical Thinking

1. Explain the central metaphor—the oppressive nature of a certain way the light falls on a winter afternoon. Can you link this feeling created in the poet by the light with any modern condition or state of mind?

2. Interpret the meaning of the listening landscape. Is it only in New England that such a condition might occur? Could a poet in Florida or Texas or California make a similar poem?

I felt a Funeral, in my Brain (c. 1861)

I felt a Funeral, in my Brain,
And Mourners to and fro
Kept treading—treading—till it seemed
That Sense was breaking through—

And when they all were seated,   5
A Service, like a Drum—
Kept beating—beating—till I thought
My Mind was going numb—

And then I heard them lift a Box
And creak across my Soul   10
With those same Boots of Lead, again,
Then Space—began to toll,

As all the Heavens were a Bell,
And Being, but an Ear,
And I, and Silence, some strange Race   15
Wrecked, solitary, here—

And then a Plank in Reason, broke,
And I dropped down, and down—
And hit a World, at every plunge,
And Finished knowing—then—   20

Questions for Critical Thinking

1. Read the poem a second time. As you do so, underline any place where a particular sound comes to mind. What techniques allow Dickinson to create a sense of hearing what the speaker hears?

2. Paying particular attention to the last stanza, explain what you think "happens" in this poem. What clues in the poem lead you to your conclusion?

3. The brain surfaces in several of Dickinson's poems. Describe the brain as it is portrayed in this poem (that is, does it feel claustrophobic or expansive? what type of activity does it harbor? what types of words does Dickinson use in relation to the brain?, and so on). Then do the same for her poem "The Brain—is wider than the Sky—" (p. 958). What are the similarities and differences? In your analysis, examine the significance of using "the brain" rather than "the heart" or "the soul."

I'm Nobody! Who are you? (c. 1861)

I'm Nobody! Who are you?
Are you—Nobody—Too?
Then there's a pair of us!
Don't tell! they'd advertise—you know!

5 How dreary—to be—Somebody!
How public—like a Frog—
To tell one's name—the livelong June—
To an admiring Bog!

Questions for Critical Thinking

1. To whom is the poet speaking? Who is "they"? Why would they "advertise" the speaker and the addressee of the poem? What would they advertise about the two?

2. Do you find the pairing of "Somebody" and "Frog" jarring or sensible?

3. How do frogs "tell" their names to the bog?

4. What effect does the adjective "admiring" have on "Bog," or vice versa?

The Soul selects her own Society— (c. 1862)

The Soul selects her own Society—
Then—shuts the Door—
To her divine Majority—
Present no more—

Unmoved—she notes the Chariots—pausing—   5
At her low Gate—
Unmoved—an Emperor be kneeling
Upon her Mat—

I've known her—from an ample nation—
Choose One—   10
Then—close the Valves of her attention—
Like Stone—

Questions for Critical Thinking

1. Paraphrase this poem. What statement is the speaker making about the soul?

2. Without reviewing the poem, make a list of images you remember in it. Now read the poem again, and make a list of images that are in it. Compare the two lists. How does Dickinson's use of imagery enhance the meaning of the poem?

After great pain, a formal feeling comes— (c. 1862)

After great pain, a formal feeling comes—
The Nerves sit ceremonious, like Tombs—
The stiff Heart questions was it He, that bore,
And Yesterday, or Centuries before?

The Feet, mechanical, go round—   5
Of Ground, or Air, or Ought—
A Wooden way
Regardless grown,
A Quartz contentment, like a stone—

10 This is the Hour of Lead—
Remembered, if outlived,
As Freezing persons, recollect the Snow—
First—Chill—then Stupor—then the letting go—

Questions for Critical Thinking

1. What pain might the poet be trying to describe? How many varieties of metaphor does the poet employ here to describe it?

2. Who is the "He" of line 3?

3. Do you find any possibility for hope in the final stanza?

Much Madness is divinest Sense— (c. 1862)

Much Madness is divinest Sense—
To a discerning Eye—
Much Sense—the starkest Madness—
'Tis the Majority
5 In this, as All, prevail—
Assent—and you are sane—
Demur—you're straightway dangerous—
And handled with a Chain—

Questions for Critical Thinking

1. Circle any of the words that you need to double-check in the dictionary. You may want to choose words that are critical to the poem, such as "madness" and "sense," even if you believe you know their meaning. Then write the dictionary definition on a separate sheet of paper. Are the words' shades of meaning different from what you had expected?

2. The argument of this poem is based on a paradox: "Much Madness is divinest Sense . . . Much Sense—the starkest Madness." In your own words, what does the speaker mean by this contradiction?

3. Can you think of fictional characters who act in a way that appears mad to others, but which is actually sane? Going further, can you think of people you know, either personally or at large, whose "madness" leads them to go against the majority?

I died for Beauty— but was scarce (c. 1862)

I died for Beauty—but was scarce
Adjusted in the Tomb
When One who died for Truth, was lain
In an adjoining Room—

He questioned softly "Why I failed"?   5
"For Beauty", I replied—
"And I—for Truth—Themself are One—
We Brethren, are," He said—

And so, as Kinsmen, met a Night—
We talked between the Rooms—   10
Until the Moss had reached our lips—
And covered up—Our names—

Questions for Critical Thinking

1. Given that one of Dickinson's major influences was the English poet John Keats, read Keats's "Ode on a Grecian Urn" (Chapter 20). How do the two relate? Can you find any evidence that Dickinson may have had Keats's poem in mind when she wrote hers, or is there insufficient support for that conclusion?

2. What is the mood of this poem? Which words and images lead to your reading of the tone?

I heard a Fly buzz— when I died— (c. 1862)

I heard a Fly buzz—when I died—
The Stillness in the Room
Was like the Stillness in the Air—
Between the Heaves of Storm—

The Eyes around—had wrung them dry—   5
And Breaths were gathering firm
For that last Onset—when the King
Be witnessed—in the Room—

I willed my Keepsakes—Signed away
10 What portion of me be
Assignable—and then it was
There interposed a Fly—

With Blue—uncertain stumbling Buzz—
Between the light—and me—
15 And then the Windows failed—and then
I could not see to see—

Questions for Critical Thinking

1. What effect does the last line have? Why do you think "I could not see to see" fits better than simply "I could not see"?
2. Why does Dickinson select a fly as opposed to, say, a bird or a bee?

The Brain—is wider than the Sky— (c. 1862)

The Brain—is wider than the Sky—
For—put them side by side—
The one the other will contain
With ease—and You—beside—

5 The Brain is deeper than the sea—
For—hold them—Blue to Blue—
The one the other will absorb—
As Sponges—Buckets—do—

The Brain is just the weight of God—
10 For—Heft them—Pound for Pound—
And they will differ—if they do—
As Syllable from Sound—

Questions for Critical Thinking

1. How does the "weight of God" relate to the brain? What does the speaker suggest by making this comparison?
2. What techniques does Dickinson use to *illustrate* the vastness of the brain as well as describe it?

I started Early— Took my Dog— (1862)

I started Early—Took my Dog—
And visited the Sea—
The Mermaids in the Basement
Came out to look at me—

And Frigates—in the Upper Floor   5
Extended Hempen Hands—
Presuming Me to be a Mouse—
Aground—upon the Sands—

But no Man moved Me—till the Tide
Went past my simple Shoe—   10
And past my Apron—and my Belt
And past my Bodice—too—

And made as He would eat me up—
As wholly as a Dew
Upon a Dandelion's Sleeve—   15
And then—I started—too—

And He—He followed—close behind—
I felt His Silver Heel
Upon my Ankle—Then my Shoes
Would overflow with Pearl—   20

Until We met the Solid Town—
No One He seemed to know—
And bowing—with a Mighty look—
At me—The Sea withdrew—

Because I could not stop for Death— (1863)

Because I could not stop for Death—
He kindly stopped for me—
The Carriage held but just Ourselves—
And Immortality.

5 We slowly drove—He knew no haste
And I had put away
My labor and my leisure too,
For His Civility—

We passed the School, where Children strove
10 At Recess—in the Ring—
We passed the Fields of Gazing Grain—
We passed the Setting Sun—

Or rather—He passed Us—
The Dews drew quivering and chill—
15 For only Gossamer, my Gown—
My Tippet—only Tulle—

We paused before a House that seemed
A Swelling of the Ground—
The Roof was scarcely visible—
The Cornice—in the Ground—   20

Since then—'tis Centuries—and yet
Feels shorter than the Day
I first surmised the Horses' Heads
Were toward Eternity—

My Life had stood— a Loaded Gun (c. 1863)

My Life had stood—a Loaded Gun—
In Corners—till a Day
The Owner passed—identified—
And carried Me away—

And now We roam in Sovereign Woods—   5
And now We hunt the Doe—
And every time I speak for Him—
The Mountains straight reply—

And do I smile, such cordial light
Upon the Valley glow—   10
It is as a Vesuvian face
Had let its pleasure through—

And when at Night—Our good Day done—
I guard My Master's Head—
'Tis better than the Eider-Duck's   15
Deep Pillow—to have shared—

To foe of His—I'm deadly foe—
None stir the second time—
On whom I lay a Yellow Eye—
20 Or an emphatic Thumb—

Though I than He—may longer live
He longer must—than I—
For I have but the power to kill,
Without—the power to die—

One need not be a Chamber—to be Haunted— (c. 1863)

One need not be a Chamber—to be Haunted—
One need not be a House—
The Brain has Corridors—surpassing
Material Place—

5 Far safer, of a Midnight Meeting
External Ghost
Than its interior Confronting—
That Cooler Host.

Far safer, through an Abbey gallop,
The Stones a'chase—   10
Than Unarmed, one's a'self encounter—
In lonesome Place—

Ourself behind ourself, concealed—
Should startle most—
Assassin hid in our Apartment   15
Be Horror's least.

The Body—borrows a Revolver—
He bolts the Door—
O'erlooking a superior spectre—
Or More—   20

A narrow Fellow in the Grass (c. 1865)

A narrow Fellow in the Grass
Occasionally rides—
You may have met him—did you not
His notice instant is—

The Grass divides as with a Comb—   5
A spotted shaft is seen—
And then it closes at your feet
And opens further on—

He likes a Boggy Acre
A Floor too cool for Corn—   10
Yet when a Boy, and Barefoot
I more than once at Noon

Have passed, I thought, a Whip lash
Unbraiding in the Sun
15 When stooping to secure it
It wrinkled, and was gone—

Several of Nature's People
I know, and they know me—
I feel for them a transport
20 Of Cordiality—

But never met this Fellow
Attended, or alone
Without a tighter breathing
And Zero at the Bone.

Questions for Critical Thinking

1. Underline the rhyming words in this poem. Then identify what type of rhyme occurs in each instance (that is, end rhyme, internal rhyme, assonance, consonance, eye rhyme, and so on). What does the rhyme scheme contribute to the poem?

2. Although the speaker never states who or what the "narrow Fellow" is, you can figure it out from context clues. What is the "narrow Fellow"?

The Bustle in a House (c. 1866)

The Bustle in a House
The Morning after Death
Is solemnest of industries
Enacted upon Earth—

5 The Sweeping up the Heart
And putting Love away
We shall not want to use again
Until Eternity.

Questions for Critical Thinking

1. How are the near rhymes of lines 2 and 4, and lines 6 and 8, appropriate to that which is taking place? In other words, why do you think Dickinson did not use exact rhymes in those lines?

2. Many of Dickinson's two-stanza poems put forth something concrete in the first stanza and something abstract in the second stanza. Identify how this poem follows that pattern. How does thinking of the concrete action in the first stanza enhance your understanding of the metaphor in the second stanza?

Tell all the Truth but tell it slant— (c. 1868)

Tell all the Truth but tell it slant—
Success in Circuit lies
Too bright for our infirm Delight
The Truth's superb surprise

As Lightning to the Children eased   5
With explanation kind
The Truth must dazzle gradually
Or every man be blind—

Question for Critical Thinking

1. Paraphrase what the speaker means by telling the truth "slant." This famous phrase has often been used as a working definition of Dickinson's poetry in particular and of the art of poetry in general. What does the phrase suggest about the value of the poet's understanding of the word?

There is no Frigate like a Book (c. 1873)

There is no Frigate like a Book
To take us Lands away
Nor any Coursers like a Page
Of prancing Poetry—
This Traverse may the poorest take   5
Without oppress of Toll—
How frugal is the Chariot
That bears the Human soul.

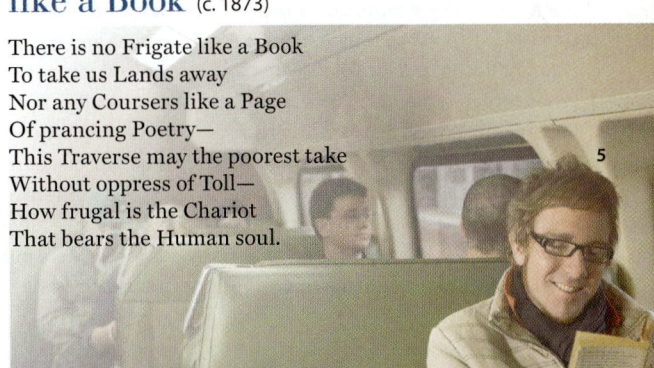

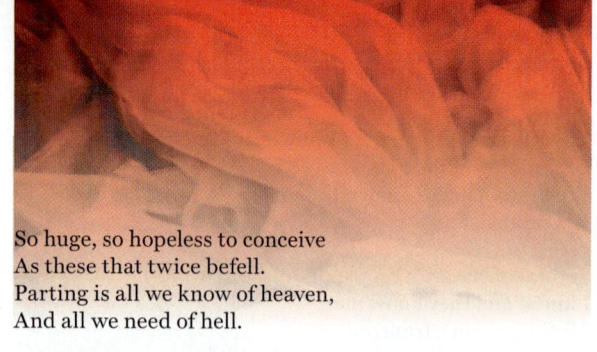

My life closed twice before its close (c. 1896)

My life closed twice before its close—
It yet remains to see
If Immortality unveil
A third event to me,

So huge, so hopeless to conceive   5
As these that twice befell.
Parting is all we know of heaven,
And all we need of hell.

Robert Frost (1874–1963)

Like Emily Dickinson, Robert Frost, too, lived in New England—mostly New Hampshire and Vermont. Unlike her, however, he died when much celebrated at the age of nearly ninety. By then he was the nation's unofficial laureate, had garnered every prize worth having (among them the Bollingen Prize, a Congressional Medal) and had recited "The Gift Outright" for an audience of millions at President John F. Kennedy's inauguration. Robert Frost, known as a New England poet, was born in San Francisco, where he spent his childhood until age eleven. His family then relocated to Massachusetts, where they traced their roots back several generations. Frost determined

as a teenager that he would be a poet, and that he would marry his high school sweetheart and co-valedictorian Elinor White. But their courtship was not fairy-tale: They separated for college, and she twice refused his marriage proposals before at last agreeing in 1895. He and Elinor taught school after they were married, and Frost then spent two years studying at Harvard. He did not take a degree and spent the next decade farming and composing many of the poems that would make up his early collections. In 1912 Frost relocated (with Elinor and their four children) to England, with the express purpose of writing poetry. His first two collections, *A Boy's Will* and *North of Boston,* were published in England to great success. By the time Frost returned

to New England, his poetry had been published in both England and the United States, and his reputation as a leading poet was secure.

From 1917 onward, Frost spent his career as a "bardic" figure—his way of referring to the public recitations of his poetry he liked to give—and as a professor at Amherst College. Yet while his rural New England imagery and easy manner of public appearance won him a large audience and a reputation as a simple New England farmer, the reality of Frost's life was grimmer. His poetry shows a constant struggle to find order in chaos. On a more literal level, his personal life fell apart in the 1930s: His favorite daughter died after giving birth, he lost his beloved Elinor to a heart attack, one of his sons committed suicide in 1940, and another daughter was committed to a mental institution. Still, by the time of his death in 1963, Frost had won four Pulitzer Prizes, had received more than forty honorary degrees, and was perhaps the best-known and most widely respected poet of the time, a status confirmed by John F. Kennedy's request that Frost recite a poem at his inauguration.

> "Well, you know, I remember finally reading Frost as other than a folksy poet, [as] somebody who is essentially a philosophical poet, I thought, which was exciting." Conversation with Stephen Dunn

Mowing (1913)

There was never a sound beside the wood but one,
And that was my long scythe whispering to the ground.
What was it it whispered? I knew not well myself;
Perhaps it was something about the heat of the sun,
5 Something, perhaps, about the lack of sound—
And that was why it whispered and did not speak.
It was no dream of the gift of idle hours,
Or easy gold at the hand of fay or elf:
Anything more than the truth would have seemed too
  weak
10 To the earnest love that laid the swale in rows,
Not without feeble-pointed spikes of flowers
(Pale orchises), and scared a bright green snake.
The fact is the sweetest dream that labor knows.
My long scythe whispered and left the hay to make.

Questions for Critical Thinking

1. A scythe whispering in the grass brings to mind an auditory image. Read the poem aloud and identify words and phrases that mimic this whispering.

2. The penultimate line contains simple diction but a complex thought: "The fact is the sweetest dream that labor knows." Write a paragraph in which you reflect on this statement.

After Apple-Picking (1914)

My long two-pointed ladder's sticking through a tree
Toward heaven still,
And there's a barrel that I didn't fill
Beside it, and there may be two or three
Apples I didn't pick upon some bough.   5
But I am done with apple-picking now.
Essence of winter sleep is on the night,
The scent of apples: I am drowsing off.
I cannot rub the strangeness from my sight
I got from looking through a pane of glass   10
I skimmed this morning from the drinking trough
And held against the world of hoary grass.
It melted, and I let it fall and break.
But I was well
Upon my way to sleep before it fell,   15
And I could tell
What form my dreaming was about to take.
Magnified apples appear and disappear,
Stem end and blossom end,
And every fleck of russet showing clear.   20
My instep arch not only keeps the ache,
It keeps the pressure of a ladder-round.
I feel the ladder sway as the boughs bend.
And I keep hearing from the cellar bin
The rumbling sound   25
Of load on load of apples coming in.
For I have had too much
Of apple-picking: I am overtired
Of the great harvest I myself desired.

30 There were ten thousand thousand fruit to touch,
Cherish in hand, lift down, and not let fall.
For all
That struck the earth,
No matter if not bruised or spiked with stubble,
35 Went surely to the cider-apple heap
As of no worth.
One can see what will trouble
This sleep of mine, whatever sleep it is.
Were he not gone,
40 The woodchuck could say whether it's like his
Long sleep, as I describe its coming on,
Or just some human sleep.

Questions for Critical Thinking

1. Consider the subject and determine where the story of the speaker's work ends and the story of his dreaming begins.

2. How does the ice on the surface of the drinking trough follow a progression to what he sees in the dream?

Mending Wall (1914)

Something there is that doesn't love a wall,
That sends the frozen-ground-swell under it
And spills the upper boulders in the sun;
And makes gaps even two can pass abreast.
5 The work of hunters is another thing:
I have come after them and made repair
Where they have left not one stone on a stone,
But they would have the rabbit out of hiding,
To please the yelping dogs. The gaps I mean,
10 No one has seen them made or heard them made,
But at spring mending-time we find them there.
I let my neighbor know beyond the hill;
And on a day we meet to walk the line
And set the wall between us once again.
15 We keep the wall between us as we go.
To each the boulders that have fallen to each.
And some are loaves and some so nearly balls
We have to use a spell to make them balance:
"Stay where you are until our backs are turned!"
20 We wear our fingers rough with handling them.

Oh, just another kind of outdoor game,
One on a side. It comes to little more:
There where it is we do not need the wall:
He is all pine and I am apple orchard.
My apple trees will never get across   25
And eat the cones under his pines, I tell him.
He only says, "Good fences make good neighbors."
Spring is the mischief in me, and I wonder
If I could put a notion in his head:
"*Why* do they make good neighbors? Isn't it   30
Where there are cows? But here there are no cows.
Before I built a wall I'd ask to know
What I was walling in or walling out,
And to whom I was like to give offense.
Something there is that doesn't love a wall,   35
That wants it down." I could say "Elves" to him,
But it's not elves exactly, and I'd rather
He said it for himself. I see him there
Bringing a stone grasped firmly by the top
In each hand, like an old-stone savage armed.   40
He moves in darkness as it seems to me,
Not of woods only and the shade of trees.
He will not go behind his father's saying,
And he likes having thought of it so well
He says again, "Good fences make good neighbors."   45

Questions for Critical Thinking

1. This poem has some beautiful imagery. Highlight two or three of the images you like best. What in those images draws you to them?

2. Identify where the mood shifts in this poem. Does it change more than once? Do you think the last line is consistent with what leads up to it?

Birches (1915)

When I see birches bend to left and right
Across the lines of straighter darker trees,
I like to think some boy's been swinging them.
But swinging doesn't bend them down to stay.
Ice-storms do that. Often you must have seen them   5
Loaded with ice a sunny winter morning
After a rain. They click upon themselves
As the breeze rises, and turn many-coloured
As the stir cracks and crazes their enamel.

10 Soon the sun's warmth makes them shed crystal shells
Shattering and avalanching on the snow-crust
Such heaps of broken glass to sweep away
You'd think the inner dome of heaven had fallen.
They are dragged to the withered bracken by the load,
15 And they seem not to break; though once they are bowed
So low for long, they never right themselves:
You may see their trunks arching in the woods
Years afterwards, trailing their leaves on the ground,
Like girls on hands and knees that throw their hair
20 Before them over their heads to dry in the sun.
But I was going to say when Truth broke in
With all her matter-of-fact about the ice-storm,
I should prefer to have some boy bend them
As he went out and in to fetch the cows—
25 Some boy too far from town to learn baseball,
Whose only play was what he found himself,
Summer or winter, and could play alone.
One by one he subdued his father's trees
By riding them down over and over again
30 Until he took the stiffness out of them,
And not one but hung limp, not one was left
For him to conquer. He learned all there was
To learn about not launching out too soon
And so not carrying the tree away
35 Clear to the ground. He always kept his poise
To the top branches, climbing carefully
With the same pains you use to fill a cup
Up to the brim, and even above the brim.
Then he flung outward, feet first, with a swish,
40 Kicking his way down through the air to the ground.
So was I once myself a swinger of birches.
And so I dream of going back to be.
It's when I'm weary of considerations,
And life is too much like a pathless wood
45 Where your face burns and tickles with the cobwebs
Broken across it, and one eye is weeping
From a twig's having lashed across it open.

I'd like to get away from earth awhile
And then come back to it and begin over.
May no fate wilfully misunderstand me   50
And half grant what I wish and snatch me away
Not to return. Earth's the right place for love:
I don't know where it's likely to go better.
I'd like to go by climbing a birch tree—
And climb black branches up a snow-white trunk   55
Toward heaven, till the tree could bear no more,
But dipped its top and set me down again.
That would be good both going and coming back.
One could do worse than be a swinger of birches.

Questions for Critical Thinking

1. The poem starts in the first person ("When I see birches . . .") and ends with a general—even impersonal—assertion ("One could do worse . . ."). How and where does the voice shift?

2. Why does the poet capitalize "Truth" in line 21? And how would you describe the tone of the phrase "I don't know where it's likely to go better" (line 53)?

"Out, Out—" (1916)

The buzz-saw snarled and rattled in the yard
And made dust and dropped stove-length sticks of wood,
Sweet-scented stuff when the breeze drew across it.
And from there those that lifted eyes could count
Five mountain ranges one behind the other   5
Under the sunset far into Vermont.
And the saw snarled and rattled, snarled and rattled,
As it ran light, or had to bear a load.
And nothing happened: day was all but done.
Call it a day, I wish they might have said   10
To please the boy by giving him the half hour
That a boy counts so much when saved from work.
His sister stood beside them in her apron
To tell them "Supper." At the word, the saw,
As if to prove saws knew what supper meant,   15
Leaped out at the boy's hand, or seemed to leap—
He must have given the hand. However it was,
Neither refused the meeting. But the hand!
The boy's first outcry was a rueful laugh,
As he swung toward them holding up the hand   20

Half in appeal, but half as if to keep
The life from spilling. Then the boy saw all—
Since he was old enough to know, big boy
Doing a man's work, though a child at heart—
25 He saw all spoiled. "Don't let him cut my hand off—
The doctor, when he comes. Don't let him, sister!"
So. But the hand was gone already.
The doctor put him in the dark of ether.
He lay and puffed his lips out with his breath.
30 And then—the watcher at his pulse took fright.
No one believed. They listened at his heart.
Little—less—nothing!—and that ended it.
No more to build on there. And they, since they
Were not the one dead, turned to their affairs.

Questions for Critical Thinking

1. Rewrite this poem as a short story and then compare
   your work with Frost's. What is emphasized in your
   version that is not in Frost's, and vice versa?

2. How is nature portrayed in this poem? Describe the
   relationship between the nature description and the
   events of the poem.

The Road Not Taken (1916)

Two roads diverged in a yellow wood,
And sorry I could not travel both
And be one traveler, long I stood
And looked down one as far as I could
5 To where it bent in the undergrowth;

Then took the other, as just as fair,
And having perhaps the better claim,
Because it was grassy and wanted wear;
Though as for that the passing there
10 Had worn them really about the same,

And both that morning equally lay
In leaves no step had trodden black.
Oh, I kept the first for another day!
Yet knowing how way leads on to way,
15 I doubted if I should ever come back.

I shall be telling this with a sigh
Somewhere ages and ages hence:
Two roads diverged in a wood, and I—
I took the one less traveled by,
And that has made all the difference.   20

Questions for Critical Thinking

1. Explain the larger meaning of this poem. What do
   the paths stand for? What does it mean that one is
   less traveled than the other?

2. Write a short profile of the speaker, based on clues
   from the poem. Is he daring? Individualistic? Indeci-
   sive? For each trait you mention, cite the line or lines
   that support your inference.

Nothing Gold Can Stay (1923)

Nature's first green is gold,
Her hardest hue to hold.
Her early leaf's a flower;
But only so an hour.
Then leaf subsides to leaf.   5
So Eden sank to grief.
So dawn goes down to day.
Nothing gold can stay.

Questions for Critical Thinking

1. There's a stanza in Thomas Nashe's sixteenth-century
   elegy, "In Times of Pestilence" that reads:
   > Brightness falls from the air
   > Queens have died young and fair
   > Beauty is but a flower
   > Which wrinkles must devour
   > Dust hath closed Helen's eye
   > I am sick, I must die.
   > *Lord have mercy upon us*

   To what degree does Frost's "Nothing Gold Can Stay"
   echo this refrain? Compose your answer in a short
   essay.

2. Scan this poem for rhyme and meter. What is the relationship between the form and what is being said?

Acquainted with the Night (1928)

I have been one acquainted with the night.
I have walked out in rain—and back in rain.
I have outwalked the furthest city light.

I have looked down the saddest city lane.
5 I have passed by the watchman on his beat
And dropped my eyes, unwilling to explain.

I have stood still and stopped the sound of feet
When far away an interrupted cry
Came over houses from another street,

10 But not to call me back or say good-by;
And further still at an unearthly height,
One luminary clock against the sky

Proclaimed the time was neither wrong nor right
I have been one acquainted with the night.

Questions for Critical Thinking

1. What is the tone? Which words create this tone?
2. On a literal level, the poem ends with a clock against the night sky. How do you interpret this image on a metaphorical level? Going further, what do you think it means to be "acquainted with the night"?

Desert Places (1936)

Snow falling and night falling fast, oh, fast
In a field I looked into going past,
And the ground almost covered smooth in snow,
But a few weeds and stubble showing last.

5 The woods around it have it—it is theirs.
All animals are smothered in their lairs,
I am too absent-spirited to count;
The loneliness includes me unawares.

And lonely as it is, that loneliness
10 Will be more lonely ere it will be less—
A blanker whiteness of benighted snow
With no expression, nothing to express

They cannot scare me with their empty spaces
Between stars—on stars where no human race is.
I have it in me so much nearer home   15
To scare myself with my own desert places.

Questions for Critical Thinking

1. Frost in the fourth stanza refers to a statement by the seventeenth-century French philosopher Blaise Pascal—"The infinite spaces between the stars frightens me." How does the landscape he creates in the poem align with that statement?
2. What can you learn from Frost's style of making complex ideas clear that may help you with your own poetry or prose?

Design (1936)

I found a dimpled spider, fat and white,
Oh a white heal-all, holding up a moth
Like a white piece of rigid satin cloth—
Assorted characters of death and blight
Mixed ready to begin the morning right,   5
Like the ingredients of a witches' broth—
A snow-drop spider, a flower like a froth,
And dead wings carried like a paper kite.

What had the flower to do with being white,
The wayside blue and innocent heal-all?   10
What brought the kindred spider to that height,
Then steered the white moth thither in the night?
What but design of darkness to appall?—
If design govern in a thing so small.

Questions for Critical Thinking

1. How would you define "design" in the context of this poem? What connotations does it have?
2. What significance does the speaker give to the color white in this poem? What does the all-white imagery bring to mind for you?

The Gift Outright (1942)

The land was ours before we were the land's.
She was our land more than a hundred years
Before we were her people. She was ours
In Massachusetts, in Virginia,
5   But we were England's, still colonials,
Possessing what we still were unpossessed by,
Possessed by what we now no more possessed.
Something we were withholding made us weak
Until we found out that it was ourselves
10 We were withholding from our land of living,
And forthwith found salvation in surrender.
Such as we were we gave ourselves outright
(The deed of gift was many deeds of war)
To the land vaguely realizing westward,
15 But still unstoried, artless, unenhanced,
Such as she was, such as she would become.

Questions for Critical Thinking

1. Frost once called "The Gift Outright" "a history of the United States in sixteen lines." What does he mean by this, and do you agree?

2. According to the Academy of American Poets, John F. Kennedy asked Frost to change the last line. Why would Kennedy have wanted the line changed?

3. Do you read the last line as optimistic or pessimistic? Explain your answer.

The Silken Tent (1942)

She is as in a field a silken tent
At midday when a sunny summer breeze
Has dried the dew and all its ropes relent,
So that in guys it gently sways at ease,
And its supporting central cedar pole,   5
That is its pinnacle to heavenward
And signifies the sureness of the soul,
Seems to owe naught to any single cord,
But strictly held by none, is loosely bound
By countless silken ties of love and thought   10
To everything on earth the compass round,
And only by one's going slightly taut
In the capriciousness of summer air
Is of the slightest bondage made aware.

Questions for Critical Thinking

1. Who is the subject of the poem? How does the speaker make his feelings toward and understanding of her known?

2. Why a tent? Why silk? Why a suggestion of a tie between earth and heaven? What goes "taut"? What does that signify?

Getting Started: A Research Project

Choose Emily Dickinson or Robert Frost and examine the poet by exploring his or her biography and historical context, as well as critical perspectives on his or her work; then make connections among the three.

Emily Dickinson

Critical Readings on Emily Dickinson

Frank, Bernhard. "Dickinson's 'The soul selects her own society.'" *Explicator* 58.2 (2000): 82–83. Print.
Johnson, Thomas H. *The Letters of Emily Dickinson.* Cambridge: Harvard UP, 1986. Print.
Juhasz, Suzanne, Cristanne Miller, and Martha Nell Smith. *Comic Power in Emily Dickinson.* Austin: U of Texas P, 1993. Print.

Exploring Biography

Emily Dickinson's sole literary confidant and critic was an editor at the *Atlantic Monthly,* Thomas Wentworth Higginson. Dickinson initiated contact with him after reading an article in which Higginson called for new writers. Her hunger for responses to her work and for literary discourse is clear from her reply to his first letter, but Dickinson and Higginson did not meet face-to-face for more than eight years after their initial correspondence when Higginson at last made a trip to Amherst in 1870. He wrote a letter to his wife describing his meeting with Dickinson. Dickinson and Higginson continued to exchange letters, however, and Dickinson describes herself in several of her early letters to him. These self-descriptions offer a unique glimpse of her home life and self-image.

According to Dickinson's account of her family life and the comments Higgin-son relays about her father and mother, what type of home life did Dickinson seem to have? How might this have affected her poetry, in terms of both content and the act of creating it?

Exploring Historical Context

Although Dickinson excludes herself in her letters when she says her family is religious, what statements does she make that indicate her Puritan background?

Exploring Critical Perspectives

Considering any previous knowledge of Emily Dickinson you may have and your current reading of her in these select articles, are you surprised by Juhasz, Miller, and Smith's reading of Dickinson as comic? How does this challenge or agree with your conception of Dickinson? Do you agree with their view?

Making Connections

Select one of Dickinson's quotations that Higginson recorded. Review her poems and see if the sentiment in her quote is reflected in one of them. When you have found one that resonates, write an essay connecting the personal philosophy with the poetic expression.

Robert Frost

Critical Readings on Robert Frost

Coulthard, A. R. "Frost's 'Mending Wall.'" *Explicator* 45.2 (1987): 40–42. Print.
French, Roberts W. "Robert Frost and the Darkness of Nature." *Critical Essays on Robert Frost.* Ed. Philip L. Gerber. Boston: Hall, 1982:155–62. Print. Critical Essays on American Literature.
Thompson, Lawrence, ed. *Selected Letters of Robert Frost.* New York: Holt, 1964. Print.

Exploring Biography

From these two letters to his friends John T. Bartlett and Sidney Cox, in which Frost describes his poetic technique, how would you characterize Frost's personality? Is there anything in the letters that surprise you, or challenges your perception of Frost as a person?

Exploring Historical Context

In the letter to Sidney Cox, Frost says that poetry should not "tell all to the last scrapings of the brain pan." What contemporary trend in poetry does he seem to be railing against? You might review the work of such poets as Sylvia Plath, Anne Sexton, and Robert Lowell with an eye to secrets told.

Exploring Critical Perspectives

Coulthard argues that Frost was unaware of the negative portrayal of the speaker. Does this seem like a solid claim to you? Why or why not? Write a short essay evaluating the fairness of Coulthard's conjecture on Frost's intent.

Given what you know about Frost as a person, and given what you have read of his letters, evaluate Coulthard's conclusion that the poem "exposes Frost's cold mind posing as a warm heart." Do you see evidence of this in other poems? Or does this seem to be another image of the poet that is not necessarily true? Compose your thoughts in an essay.

Making Connections

Considering just these two letters, what would you imagine Frost's manifesto on poetry to be? Which of his poems seem to follow his dictates?

Writing and Research

1. Emily Dickinson's publication history is uniquely complex, because of the heavy editing done in the 1890s, which scholars then undid in the 1950s to create a version more faithful to her original poems. Research the progression of editions of Dickinson's work, along with the critical reception—that is, how critics and the public reacted to her poetry as each edition appeared. Write your findings into an essay, being sure to cite your sources. You may want to consult the resources listed below, although you can certainly find a host of information on Dickinson at your college's library:

   - Academy of American Poets. "Poets.org Guide to Emily Dickinson's *Collected Poems*." *Poets.org*. Academy of American Poets, n.d. Web. <www.poets.org/page.php/prmID/308>.
   - Ferlazzo, Paul J. ed. *Critical Essays on Emily Dickinson*. Boston: Hall, 1984. Print. Critical Essays on American Literature.
     - Two anonymous reviews from 1890, pp. 28–29.
     - Anonymous review of the British edition, 1904, pp. 50–52.
     - "Emily Dickinson Complete" by Arlin Turner, 1956, pp. 113–16.
   - Smith, Martha Nell, and Mary Loeffelholz, eds. *A Companion to Emily Dickinson*. Malden: Blackwell, 2008. Print.
     - "Reading Dickinson in Her Context: The Fascicles" by Eleanor Elson Heginbotham, pp. 288–307.

2. Robert Frost appeals to an odd mix of audience—on the one hand, he is known and recited by the general public, including schoolchildren, while on the other, he is recognized in literary circles for his sophisticated versification and hauntingly dark subtext. This research topic asks you to find out how he was received by yet another group: other poets who were his contemporaries. The following three articles give a glimpse of how Ezra Pound, Amy Lowell, and Randall Jarrell reacted to Frost. Read their essays, noting the specific strengths and weaknesses each points to in Frost. Then write your own essay evaluating their reactions. Is Pound's opinion more accurate than Lowell's? Do you agree with Jarrell the most? This is the type of question you will answer in your essay, being sure to use support from Frost's poems in your discussion of his identified strengths and weaknesses. Finally, you may find it useful to review some of Pound's, Lowell's, and Jarrell's own poetry (these poets have work of their own in *Literature: Craft and Voice*) and see how it compares. Each of the following essays appears in *Critical Essays on Robert Frost*, edited by Philip L. Gerber (Boston: Hall, 1982).

   - "Modern Georgics" by Ezra Pound, pp. 19–21.
     - Original Source: *Poetry*, Dec. 1914.
   - "North of Boston" by Amy Lowell, pp. 22–25.
     - Original Source: *The New Republic*, Feb. 20, 1915, pp. 81–82.
   - "Tenderness and Passive Sadness" by Randall Jarrell, pp. 112–13.
     - Original Source: *The New York Times Book Review*, June 1, 1947.

Some Sources for Research

Emily Dickinson

Online Source:

"Emily Dickinson." *Poets.org*. The Academy of American Poets, 2011. Web.
    <http://www.poets.org/poet.php/prmPID/155>.

Print Sources:

1. Bouson, J. Brooks, ed. *Emily Dickinson*. Pasadena: Salem, 2011. Print.

2. Eberwien, Jane Donahue, and Cindy MacKenzie, eds. *Reading Emily Dickinson's Letters: Critical Essays*.
    Amherst: U of Massachusetts P, 2009. Print.

3. Johnson, Thomas H., ed. *The Letters of Emily Dickinson*. Cambridge: Harvard UP, 1986. Print.

4. Kearns, Michael. *Writing for the Street, Writing in the Garret: Melville, Dickinson, and Private Publication*.
    Columbus: Ohio State UP, 2010. Print.

5. Martin, Wendy. *The Cambridge Introduction to Emily Dickinson*. New York: Cambridge UP, 2007. Print.

6. Morgan, Victoria N. *Emily Dickinson and Hymn Culture: Tradition and Experience*. Burlington: Ashgate, 2010.
    Print.

7. Smith, Martha Nell and Mary Loeffelholz, eds. *A Companion to Emily Dickinson*. Malden: Blackwell, 2008. Print.

8. Vendler, Helen. *Dickinson: Selected Poems and Commentaries*. Cambridge: Belknap-Harvard UP, 2010. Print.

9. Whicher, George Frisbie. *This Was a Poet: A Critical Biography of Emily Dickinson*. Hamden: Archon, 1980. Print.

Robert Frost

Online Source:

"Robert Frost." *PoetryFoundation.org*. Poetry Foundation, 2011. Web.
    <http://www.poetryfoundation.org/bio/robert-frost>.

Print Sources:

10. Brodsky, Joseph, Seamus Heaney, and Derek Walcott. *Homage to Robert Frost*. New York: Farrar, 1996. Print.

11. Dickstein, Morris, ed. *Robert Frost*. Pasadena: Salem, 2010. Print.

12. Faggen, Robert, ed. *The Cambridge Companion to Robert Frost*. New York: Cambridge UP, 2001. Print.

13. Faggen, Robert, ed. *The Notebooks of Robert Frost*. Cambridge: Belknap-Harvard UP, 2006. Print.

14. Meyers, Jeffrey. *Robert Frost: A Biography*. Boston: Houghton, 1996. Print.

15. Pack, Robert. *Belief and Uncertainty in the Poetry of Robert Frost*. Hanover: Middlebury College P, 2003. Print.

16. Parini, Jay. *Robert Frost: A Life*. New York: Holt, 1999. Print.

17. Thompson, Lawrence, ed. *Selected Letters of Robert Frost*. New York: Holt, 1964. Print.

For examples of student papers (including an essay exam on Robert Frost's "Stopping by Woods on a Snowy Evening"), see Chapter 4, Writing across the Curriculum. Additional examples of student papers can be found in Chapters 2, 3, 5, 7, 18, and 31.

29

An Anthology of Poetry for Further Reading

Kim Addonizio (b. 1954)

First Poem for You (1994)

I like to touch your tattoos in complete
darkness, when I can't see them. I'm sure of
where they are, know by heart the neat
lines of lightning pulsing just above
5 your nipple, can find, as if by instinct, the blue
swirls of water on your shoulder where a serpent
twists, facing a dragon. When I pull you
to me, taking you until we're spent
and quiet on the sheets, I love to kiss
10 the pictures in your skin. They'll last until
you're seared to ashes; whatever persists
or turns to pain between us, they will still
be there. Such permanence is terrifying.
So I touch them in the dark; but touch them, trying.

Gloria Anzaldúa (1942–2004)

To live in the Borderlands
means you (1987)

are neither *hispana india negra española*
    ni gabacha, eres mestiza, mulata, half-breed
    caught in the crossfire between camps
    while carrying all five races on your back
5 not knowing which side to turn to, run from;

To live in the Borderlands means knowing
    that the *india* in you, betrayed for 500 years,
    is no longer speaking to you,
    that *mexicanas* call you *rajetas,*
10 that denying the Anglo inside you
    is as bad as having denied the Indian or the Black;

Cuando vives en la frontera
    people walk through you, the wind steals your voice,
    you're a *burra, buey,* scapegoat,
15 forerunner of a new race,
    half and half—both woman and man, neither—
    a new gender;

To live in the Borderlands means to
    put *chile* in the borscht,
    eat whole wheat *tortillas,*   20
    speak Tex-Mex with a Brooklyn accent;
    be stopped by *la migra* at the border checkpoints;

Living in the Borderlands means you fight hard to
    resist the gold elixir beckoning from the bottle,
    the pull of the gun barrel,   25
    the rope crushing the hollow of your throat;

In the Borderlands
    you are the battleground
    where enemies are kin to each other;
    you are at home, a stranger,   30
    the border disputes have been settled
    the volley of shots have shattered the truce
    you are wounded, lost in action
    dead, fighting back;

To live in the Borderlands means   35
    the mill with the razor white teeth wants to shred off
    your olive-red skin, crush out the kernel, your heart
    pound you pinch you roll you out
    smelling like white bread but dead;

To survive the Borderlands   40
    you must live *sin fronteras*
    be a crossroads.

W. H. Auden (1907–1973)

For a brief biography of W. H. Auden, see Chapter 20.

The Unknown Citizen (1940)

> (*To JS/07/M/378*
> *This Marble Monument*
> *Is Erected by the State*)

He was found by the Bureau of Statistics to be
One against whom there was no official complaint,
And all the reports on his conduct agree
That, in the modern sense of an old-fashioned word, he
    was a saint,
For in everything he did he served the Greater Community. 5

Except for the War till the day he retired
He worked in a factory and never got fired,
But satisfied his employers, Fudge Motors Inc.
Yet he wasn't a scab or odd in his views,
10 For his Union reports that he paid his dues,
(Our report on his Union shows it was sound)
And our Social Psychology workers found
That he was popular with his mates and liked a drink.
The Press are convinced that he bought a paper every day
15 And that his reactions to advertisements were normal in
every way.
Policies taken out in his name prove that he was fully
insured,
And his Health-card shows he was once in hospital but
left it cured.
Both Producers Research and High-Grade Living declare
He was fully sensible to the advantages of the Instalment
Plan
20 And had everything necessary to the Modern Man,
A phonograph, a radio, a car and a frigidaire.
Our researchers into Public Opinion are content
That he held the proper opinions for the time of year;
When there was peace, he was for peace; when there was
war, he went.
25 He was married and added five children to the population,
Which our Eugenist says was the right number for a parent
of his generation,
And our teachers report that he never interfered with their
education.
Was he free? Was he happy? The question is absurd:
Had anything been wrong, we should certainly have heard.

William Blake (1757–1827)

For a brief biography of William Blake, see Chapter 22.

The Lamb (1794)

Little lamb, who made thee?
Dost thou know who made thee?
Gave thee life, & bid thee feed
By the stream & o'er the mead;
5 Gave thee clothing of delight,
Softest clothing, wooly, bright;
Gave thee such a tender voice,

Making all the vales rejoice?
Little Lamb, who made thee?
Dost thou know who made thee?   10

Little Lamb, I'll tell thee,
Little Lamb, I'll tell thee:
He is called by thy name,
For he calls himself a Lamb.
He is meek & he is mild;   15
He became a little child.
I a child, & thou a lamb.
We are called by his name.
Little Lamb, God bless thee!
Little Lamb, God bless thee!   20

The Little Black Boy (1794)

My mother bore me in the southern wild,
And I am black, but O! my soul is white;
White as an angel is the English child,
But I am black as if bereav'd of light.

My mother taught me underneath a tree,   5
And, sitting down before the heat of day,
She took me on her lap and kissed me,
And pointing to the east, began to say:

"Look on the rising sun: there God does live,
And gives his light, and gives his heat away;   10
And flowers and trees and beasts and men receive
Comfort in morning, joy in the noonday.

"And we are put on earth a little space,
That we may learn to bear the beams of love;
And these black bodies and this sunburnt face   15
Is but a cloud, and like a shady grove.

"For when our souls have learn'd the heat to bear,
The cloud will vanish; we shall hear his voice,
Saying: 'Come out from the grove, my love & care,
And round my golden tent like lambs rejoice.'"   20

Thus did my mother say, and kissed me;
And thus I say to little English boy:
When I from black and he from white cloud free,
And round the tent of God like lambs we joy,

25 I'll shade him from the heat, till he can bear
To lean in joy upon our father's knee;
And then I'll stand and stroke his silver hair,
And be like him, and he will then love me.

London (1794)

I wander thro' each charter'd street,
Near where the charter'd Thames does flow,
And mark in every face I meet
Marks of weakness, marks of woe.

5 In every cry of every Man,
In every Infant's cry of fear,
In every voice, in every ban,
The mind-forg'd manacles I hear.

How the Chimney-sweeper's cry
10 Every black'ning Church appalls;
And the hapless Soldier's sigh
Runs in blood down Palace walls.

But most thro' midnight streets I hear
How the youthful Harlot's curse
15 Blasts the new born Infant's tear,
And blights with plagues the Marriage hearse.

Robert Browning (1812–1889)

For a brief biography of Robert Browning, see Chapter 19.

Meeting at Night (1845)

I

The gray sea and the long black land;
And the yellow half-moon large and low;
And the startled little waves that leap
In fiery ringlets from their sleep,
5 As I gain the cove with pushing prow,
And quench its speed i' the slushy sand.

II
Then a mile of warm sea-scented beach;
Three fields to cross till a farm appears;
A tap at the pane, the quick sharp scratch
And blue spurt of a lighted match,   10
And a voice less loud, through its joys and fears,
Than the two hearts beating each to each!

Parting at Morning (1845)

Round the cape of a sudden came the sea,
And the sun looked over the mountain's rim:
And straight was a path of gold for him,
And the need of a world of men for me.

Judith Ortiz Cofer (b. 1952)

Quinceañera (1987)

My dolls have been put away like dead
children in a chest I will carry
with me when I marry.
I reach under my skirt to feel
a satin slip bought for this day. It is soft   5
as the inside of my thighs. My hair
has been nailed back with my mother's
black hairpins to my skull. Her hands
stretched my eyes open as she twisted
braids into a tight circle at the nape   10
of my neck. I am to wash my own clothes
and sheets from this day on, as if
the fluids of my body were poison, as if
the little trickle of blood I believe
travels from my heart to the world were   5
shameful. Is not the blood of saints and
men in battle beautiful? Do Christ's hands
not bleed into your eyes from His cross?
At night I hear myself growing and wake
to find my hands drifting of their own will   20
to soothe skin stretched tight
over my bones.
I am wound like the guts of a clock,
waiting for each hour to release me.

Samuel Taylor Coleridge (1772–1834)

For a brief biography of Samuel Taylor Coleridge, see Chapter 24.

Kubla Khan (1797–1798)
Or A Vision in a Dream. A Fragment

In Xanadu did Kubla Khan
A stately pleasure dome decree:
Where Alph, the sacred river, ran
Through caverns measureless to man
5   Down to a sunless sea.
So twice five miles of fertile ground
With walls and towers were girdled round:
And there were gardens bright with sinuous rills,
Where blossomed many an incense-bearing tree;
10 And here were forests ancient as the hills,
Enfolding sunny spots of greenery.

But oh! that deep romantic chasm which slanted
Down the green hill athwart a cedarn cover!
A savage place! as holy and enchanted
15 As e'er beneath a waning moon was haunted
By woman wailing for her demon lover!
And from this chasm, with ceaseless turmoil seething,
As if this earth in fast thick pants were breathing,
A mighty fountain momently was forced:
20 Amid whose swift half-intermitted burst
Huge fragments vaulted like rebounding hail,
Or chaffy grain beneath the thresher's flail:
And 'mid these dancing rocks at once and ever
It flung up momently the sacred river.
25 Five miles meandering with a mazy motion
Through wood and dale the sacred river ran,
Then reached the caverns measureless to man,
And sank in tumult to a lifeless ocean:
And 'mid this tumult Kubla heard from far
30 Ancestral voices prophesying war!

The shadow of the dome of pleasure
Floated midway on the waves;
Where was heard the mingled measure
From the fountain and the caves.
It was a miracle of rare device,   35
A sunny pleasure dome with caves of ice!

A damsel with a dulcimer
In a vision once I saw:
It was an Abyssinian maid,
And on her dulcimer she played,   40
Singing of Mount Abora.
Could I revive within me
Her symphony and song,
To such a deep delight 'twould win me,
That with music loud and long,   45
I would build that dome in air,
That sunny dome! those caves of ice!
And all who heard should see them there,
And all should cry, Beware! Beware!
His flashing eyes, his floating hair!   50
Weave a circle round him thrice,
And close your eyes with holy dread,
For he on honey-dew hath fed,
And drunk the milk of Paradise.

e. e. cummings (1894–1962)

For a brief biography of e. e. cummings, see Chapter 26.

Buffalo Bill's (1923)

Buffalo Bill's
defunct
       who used to
       ride a watersmooth-silver
               stallion   5
and break onetwothreefourfive pigeonsjustlikethat
                    Jesus

he was a handsome man
             and what i want to know is
how do you like your blueeyed boy   10
Mister Death

l(a (1923)

l(a

le

af

fa

5 ll

s)

one

l

iness

anyone lived in a pretty how town (1940)

anyone lived in a pretty how town
(with up so floating many bells down)
spring summer autumn winter
he sang his didn't he danced his did.

5 Women and men(both little and small)
cared for anyone not at all
they sowed their isn't they reaped their same
sun moon stars rain

children guessed(but only a few
10 and down they forgot as up they grew
autumn winter spring summer)
that noone loved him more by more

when by now and tree by leaf
she laughed his joy she cried his grief
15 bird by snow and stir by still
anyone's any was all to her

someones married their everyones
laughed their cryings and did their dance
(sleep wake hope and then)they
20 said their nevers they slept their dream

stars rain sun moon
(and only the snow can begin to explain
how children are apt to forget to remember
with up so floating many bells down)

one day anyone died i guess   25
(and noone stooped to kiss his face)
busy folk buried them side by side
little by little and was by was

all by all and deep by deep
and more by more they dream their sleep   30
noone and anyone earth by april
wish by spirit and if by yes.

Women and men(both dong and ding)
summer autumn winter spring
reaped their sowing and went their came   35
sun moon stars rain

John Donne (1572–1631)

Death Be Not Proud (c. 1610)

Death, be not proud, though some have callèd thee
Mighty and dreadful, for thou art not so;
For those whom thou think'st thou dost overthrow
Die not, poor Death, nor yet canst thou kill me.
From rest and sleep, which but thy pictures be,   5
Much pleasure; then from thee much more must flow,
And soonest our best men with thee do go,
Rest of their bones, and soul's delivery.
Thou art slave to fate, chance, kings, and desperate men,
And dost with poison, war, and sickness dwell,   10
And poppy or charms can make us sleep as well
And better than thy stroke; why swell'st thou then?
One short sleep past, we wake eternally
And death shall be no more; Death, thou shalt die.

The Flea (1633)

Mark but this flea, and mark in this,
How little that which thou deniest me is;
Me it sucked first, and now sucks thee,
And in this flea our two bloods mingled be.
5 Thou know'st that this cannot be said
A sin, or shame, or loss of maidenhead,
    Yet this enjoys before it woo,
    And pampered swells with one blood made of two,
    And this, alas, is more than we would do.

10 Oh stay, three lives in one flea spare,
Where we almost, nay more than married are.
This flea is you and I, and this
Our marriage bed and marriage temple is;
Though parents grudge, and you, we are met,
15 And cloistered in these living walls of jet.
    Though use make you apt to kill me,
    Let not to that, self-murder added be,
    And sacrilege, three sins in killing three.

Cruel and sudden, hast thou since
20 Purpled thy nail in blood of innocence?
Wherein could this flea guilty be,
Except in that drop which it sucked from thee?
Yet thou triumph'st, and say'st that thou
Find'st not thyself nor me the weaker now;
25   'Tis true; then learn how false fears be:
    Just so much honor, when thou yield'st to me,
    Will waste, as this flea's death took life from thee.

The Sun Rising (1633)

    Busy old fool, unruly Sun,
    Why dost thou thus
Through windows, and through curtains call on us?
Must to thy motions lovers' seasons run?
5   Saucy pedantic wretch, go chide
    Late schoolboys and sour prentices,
    Go tell court huntsmen that the King will ride,
    Call country ants to harvest offices;
Love, all alike, no season knows nor clime,
10 Nor hours, days, months, which are the rags of time.

    Thy beams, so reverend and strong
    Why shouldst thou think?
I could eclipse and cloud them with a wink,
But that I would not lose her sight so long;
    If her eyes have not blinded thine,   15
    Look, and tomorrow late, tell me,
    Whether both th' Indias of spice and mine
    Be where thou leftst them, or lie here with me.
Ask for those kings whom thou saw'st yesterday,
And thou shalt hear, All here in one bed lay.   20

    She is all states, and all princes I,
    Nothing else is.
Princes do but play us; compared to this,
All honor's mimic, all wealth alchemy.
    Thou, sun, art half as happy as we,   25
    In that the world's contracted thus;
    Thine age asks ease, and since thy duties be
    To warm the world, that's done in warming us.
Shine here to us, and thou art everywhere;
This bed thy center is, these walls thy sphere.   30

H. D. (Hilda Doolittle) (1886–1961)

For a brief biography of H. D., see Chapter 22.

Heat (1916)

O wind, rend open the heat.
cut apart the heat,
rend it to tatters.

Fruit cannot drop
through this thick air—   5
fruit cannot fall into heat
that presses up and blunts
the points of pears
and rounds the grapes.

Cut the heat—   10
plough through it,
turning it on either side
of your path

T. S. Eliot (1888–1965)

The Love Song of J. Alfred Prufrock (1915)

S'io credesse che mia risposta fosse
A persona che mai tornasse al mondo,
Questa fiamma staria senza più scosse.
Ma perciocche giammai di questo fondo
Non tornò vivo alcun, s'i'odo il vero,
Senza tema d'infamia ti rispondo.[1]

Let us go then, you and I,
When the evening is spread out against the sky
Like a patient etherized upon a table;
Let us go, through certain half-deserted streets,
5 The muttering retreats
Of restless nights in one-night cheap hotels
And sawdust restaurants with oyster-shells:
Streets that follow like a tedious argument
Of insidious intent
10 To lead you to an overwhelming question . . .
Oh, do not ask, "What is it?"
Let us go and make our visit.

    In the room the women come and go
Talking of Michelangelo.

15   The yellow fog that rubs its back upon the window-panes
The yellow smoke that rubs its muzzle on the window-panes
Licked its tongue into the corners of the evening,
Lingered upon the pools that stand in drains,
Let fall upon its back the soot that falls from chimneys,
20 Slipped by the terrace, made a sudden leap,
And seeing that it was a soft October night,
Curled once about the house, and fell asleep.

---

[1]If I believed that my reply were made
To one to who the world would e'er return,
The flame without more flickering would stand still;
But inasmuch as never from this depth
Did anyone return, if I hear true,
Without the fear of infamy I answer.

And indeed there will be time
For the yellow smoke that slides along the street,
Rubbing its back upon the window-panes;   25
There will be time, there will be time
To prepare a face to meet the faces that you meet;
There will be time to murder and create,
And time for all the works and days of hands
That lift and drop a question on your plate;   30
Time for you and time for me,
And time yet for a hundred indecisions,
And for a hundred visions and revisions,
Before the taking of a toast and tea.

    In the room the women come and go   35
Talking of Michelangelo.

    And indeed there will be time
To wonder, "Do I dare?" and, "Do I dare?"
Time to turn back and descend the stair,
With a bald spot in the middle of my hair—   40
[They will say: "How his hair is growing thin!"]
My morning coat, my collar mounting firmly to the chin,
My necktie rich and modest, but asserted by a simple pin—
[They will say: "But how his arms and legs are thin!"]
Do I dare   45
Disturb the universe?
In a minute there is time
For decisions and revisions which a minute will reverse.

    For I have known them all already, known them all:
Have known the evenings, mornings, afternoons,   50
I have measured out my life with coffee spoons;
I know the voices dying with a dying fall
Beneath the music from a farther room.
    So how should I presume?

    And I have known the eyes already, known them all—   55
The eyes that fix you in a formulated phrase,
And when I am formulated, sprawling on a pin,
When I am pinned and wriggling on the wall,
Then how should I begin
To spit out all the butt-ends of my days and ways?   60
    And how should I presume?

And I have known the arms already, known them all—
Arms that are braceleted and white and bare
[But in the lamplight, downed with light brown hair!]
65 Is it perfume from a dress
That makes me so digress?
Arms that lie along a table, or wrap about a shawl.
    And should I then presume?
    And how should I begin?

     . . . . .

70 Shall I say, I have gone at dusk through narrow streets
And watched the smoke that rises from the pipes
Of lonely men in shirt-sleeves, leaning out of windows? . . .

   I should have been a pair of ragged claws
Scuttling across the floors of silent seas.

     . . . . .

75 And the afternoon, the evening, sleeps so peacefully!
Smoothed by long fingers,
Asleep . . . tired . . . or it malingers,
Stretched on the floor, here beside you and me.
Should I, after tea and cakes and ices,
80 Have the strength to force the moment to its crisis?
But though I have wept and fasted, wept and prayed,
Though I have seen my head [grown slightly bald] brought
    in upon a platter,
I am no prophet—and here's no great matter;
I have seen the moment of my greatness flicker,
85 And I have seen the eternal Footman hold my coat, and
    snicker,
And in short, I was afraid.

   And would it have been worth it, after all,
After the cups, the marmalade, the tea,
Among the porcelain, among some talk of you and me,
90 Would it have been worth while,
To have bitten off the matter with a smile,
To have squeezed the universe into a ball
To roll it toward some overwhelming question,
To say: "I am Lazarus, come from the dead,
95 Come back to tell you all, I shall tell you all"—
If one, settling a pillow by her head,
    Should say: "That is not what I meant at all.
    That is not it, at all."

And would it have been worth it, after all,
Would it have been worth while,   100
After the sunsets and the dooryards and the sprinkled
    streets,
After the novels, after the teacups, after the skirts that
    trail along the floor—
And this, and so much more?—
It is impossible to say just what I mean!
But as if a magic lantern threw the nerves in patterns on a   105
    screen:
Would it have been worth while
If one, settling a pillow or throwing off a shawl,
And turning toward the window, should say:
    "That is not it at all,
    That is not what I meant, at all."   110

     . . . . .

No! I am not Prince Hamlet, nor was meant to be;
Am an attendant lord, one that will do
To swell a progress, start a scene or two,
Advise the prince; no doubt, an easy tool,
Deferential, glad to be of use,   115
Politic, cautious, and meticulous;
Full of high sentence, but a bit obtuse;
At times, indeed, almost ridiculous—
Almost, at times, the Fool.

   I grow old . . . I grow old . . .   120
I shall wear the bottoms of my trousers rolled.

   Shall I part my hair behind? Do I dare to eat a peach?
I shall wear white flannel trousers, and walk upon the
    beach.
I have heard the mermaids singing, each to each.

   I do not think that they will sing to me.   125

   I have seen them riding seaward on the waves
Combing the white hair of the waves blown back
When the wind blows the water white and black.

   We have lingered in the chambers of the sea
By sea-girls wreathed with seaweed red and brown   130
Till human voices wake us, and we drown.

Nikki Giovanni (b. 1943)

Nikki Rosa (1968)

childhood memories are always a drag
if you're Black
you always remember things like living in Woodlawn
with no inside toilet
5 and if you become famous or something
they never talk about how happy you were to have
your mother
all to yourself and
how good the water felt when you got your bath
10 from one of those
big tubs that folk in chicago barbeque in
and somehow when you talk about home
it never gets across how much you
understood their feelings
15 as the whole family attended meetings about Hollydale
and even though you remember
your biographers never understand
your father's pain as he sells his stock
and another dream goes
20 And though you're poor it isn't poverty that
concerns you
and though they fought a lot
it isn't your father's drinking that makes any difference
but only that everybody is together and you
25 and your sister have happy birthdays and very good
Christmases
and I really hope no white person ever has cause
to write about me
because they never understand
30 Black love is Black wealth and they'll
probably talk about my hard childhood
and never understand that
all the while I was quite happy

Ego Tripping
(there may be a reason why) (1973)

I was born in the congo
I walked to the fertile crescent and built
the sphinx

I designed a pyramid so tough that a star
that only glows every one hundred years falls   5
into the center giving divine perfect light
I am bad

I sat on the throne
drinking nectar with allah
I got hot and sent an ice age to europe   10
to cool my thirst
My oldest daughter is nefertiti
the tears from my birth pains
created the nile
I am a beautiful woman   15

I gazed on the forest and burned
out the sahara desert
with a packet of goat's meat
and a change of clothes
I crossed it in two hours   20
I am a gazelle so swift
so swift you can't catch me

For a birthday present when he was three
I gave my son hannibal an elephant
He gave me rome for mother's day   25
My strength flows ever on
My son noah built new/ark and
I stood proudly at the helm
as we sailed on a soft summer day
I turned myself into myself and was   30
jesus
men intone my loving name
All praises All praises
I am the one who would save

I sowed diamonds in my back yard   35
My bowels deliver uranium
the filings from my fingernails are
semi-precious jewels
On a trip north
I caught a cold and blew   40
My nose giving oil to the arab world
I am so hip even my errors are correct
I sailed west to reach east and had to round off
the earth as I went
The hair from my head thinned and gold was laid   45
across three continents

I am so perfect so divine so ethereal so surreal
I cannot be comprehended
    except by my permission

50 I mean . . . I . . . can fly
    like a bird in the sky . . .

Thomas Hardy (1840–1928)

For a brief biography of Thomas Hardy, see Chapter 21.

The Darkling Thrush (1900)

I leant upon a coppice gate
    When Frost was specter-gray,
And Winter's dregs made desolate
    The weakening eye of day.
5 The tangled bine-stems scored the sky
    Like strings of broken lyres,
And all mankind that haunted nigh
    Had sought their household fires.

The land's sharp features seemed to be
10   The Century's corpse outleant,
His crypt the cloudy canopy,
    The wind his death-lament.
The ancient pulse of germ and birth
    Was shrunken hard and dry,
15 And every spirit upon earth
    Seemed fervorless as I.

At once a voice arose among
    The bleak twigs overhead
In a full-hearted evensong
20   Of joy illimited;
An aged thrush, frail, gaunt, and small,
    In blast-beruffled plume,
Had chosen thus to fling his soul
    Upon the growing gloom.

25 So little cause for carolings
    Of such ecstatic sound
Was written on terrestrial things
    Afar or nigh around,

That I could think there trembled through
    His happy good-night air   30
Some blessed Hope, whereof he knew
    And I was unaware.

George Herbert (1593–1633)

For a brief biography of George Herbert, see Chapter 26.

Love (1633)

Love bade me welcome: yet my soul drew back,
    Guilty of dust and sin.
But quick-eyed Love, observing me grow slack
    From my first entrance in,
Drew nearer to me, sweetly questioning   5
    If I lacked anything.

"A guest," I answered, "worthy to be here":
    Love said, "You shall be he."
"I, the unkind, ungrateful? Ah, my dear,
    I cannot look on thee."   10
Love took my hand, and smiling did reply,
    "Who made the eyes but I?"

"Truth, Lord; but I have marred them; let my shame
    Go where it doth deserve."
"And know you not," says Love, "who bore the blame?"   15
    "My dear, then I will serve."
"You must sit down," says Love, "and taste my meat."
    So I did sit and eat.

Robert Herrick (1591–1674)

To the Virgins, to Make Much of Time (1646)

Gather ye rosebuds while ye may,
    Old time is still a-flying;
And this same flower that smiles today,
    Tomorrow will be dying.

5 The glorious lamp of heaven, the sun,
    The higher he's a-getting,
The sooner will his race be run,
    And nearer he's to setting.

That age is best which is the first,
10   When youth and blood are warmer;
But being spent, the worse, and worst
    Times still succeed the former.

Then be not coy, but use your time,
    And while ye may, go marry;
15 For having lost but once your prime,
    You may forever tarry.

Delight in Disorder (1648)

A sweet disorder in the dress
Kindles in clothes a wantonness.
A lawn about the shoulders thrown
Into a fine distraction;
5 An erring lace, which here and there
Enthralls the crimson stomacher;
A cuff neglectful, and thereby
Ribbons to flow confusedly;
A winning wave, deserving note,
10 In the tempestuous petticoat;
A careless shoestring, in whose tie
I see a wild civility:
Do more bewitch me than when art
Is too precise in every part.

Upon Julia's Clothes (1648)

Whenas in silks my Julia goes,
Then, then, methinks, how sweetly flows
The liquefaction of her clothes.

Next, when I cast mine eyes and see
5 That brave vibration each way free,
Oh, how that glittering taketh me!

Gerard Manley Hopkins (1844–1889)

For a brief biography of Gerard Manley Hopkins, see Chapter 24.

God's Grandeur (1877)

The world is charged with the grandeur of God.
    It will flame out, like shining from shook foil;
    It gathers to a greatness, like the ooze of oil
Crushed. Why do men then now not reck his rod?
Generations have trod, have trod, have trod;   5
    And all is seared with trade; bleared, smeared with toil;
    And wears man's smudge and shares man's smell:
        the soil
Is bare now, nor can foot feel, being shod.

And for all this, nature is never spent;
    There lives the dearest freshness deep down things;   10
And though the last lights off the black West went
    Oh, morning, at the brown brink eastward, springs—
Because the Holy Ghost over the bent
    World broods with warm breast and with ah! bright
        wings.

The Windhover (1877)

To Christ our Lord

I caught this morning morning's minion, king-
    dom of daylight's dauphin, dapple-dawn-drawn
        Falcon, in his riding
    Of the rolling level underneath him steady air, and
        striding
High there, how he rung upon the rein of a wimpling wing
In his ecstasy! then off, off forth on swing,   5
    As a skate's heel sweeps smooth on a bow-bend: the
        hurl and gliding
    Rebuffed the big wind. My heart in hiding
Stirred for a bird,—the achieve of, the mastery of the thing!

Brute beauty and valour and act, oh, air, pride, plume, here
10   Buckle! AND the fire that breaks from thee then,
        a billion
Times told lovelier, more dangerous, O my chevalier!

    No wonder of it: shéer plód makes plough down sillion
Shine, and blue-bleak embers, ah my dear,
    Fall, gall themselves, and gash gold-vermillion.

A. E. Housman (1859–1936)

Loveliest of trees, the cherry now (1896)

Loveliest of trees, the cherry now
Is hung with bloom along the bough,
And stands about the woodland ride
Wearing white for Eastertide.

5   Now, of my threescore years and ten,
Twenty will not come again,
And take from seventy springs a score,
It only leaves me fifty more.

    And since to look at things in bloom
10 Fifty springs are little room,
About the woodlands I will go
To see the cherry hung with snow.

Ben Jonson (1573?–1637)

For a brief biography of Ben Jonson, see Chapter 21.

To Celia (1616)

Drink to me only with thine eyes,
    And I will pledge with mine;
Or leave a kiss but in the cup,
    And I'll not look for wine.
5   The thirst that from the soul doth rise
        Doth ask a drink divine;
But might I of Jove's nectar sup,
    I would not change for thine.

I sent thee late a rosy wreath,
    Not so much honoring thee,   10
As giving it a hope that there
    It could not withered be.
But thou thereon didst only breathe,
    And sent'st it back to me;
Since when it grows and smells, I swear,   15
    Not of itself, but thee.

John Keats (1795–1821)

For a brief biography of John Keats, see Chapter 20.

When I have fears that I may cease to be (1818)

When I have fears that I may cease to be
    Before my pen has gleaned my teeming brain,
Before high-pilèd books, in charact'ry,
    Hold like rich garners the full-ripened grain;
When I behold, upon the night's starred face,   5
    Huge cloudy symbols of a high romance,
And think that I may never live to trace
    Their shadows, with the magic hand of chance;
And when I feel, fair creature of an hour,
    That I shall never look upon thee more,   10
Never have relish in the fairy power
    Of unreflecting love;—then, on the shore
Of the wide world I stand alone, and think
    Till love and fame to nothingness do sink.

Yusef Komunyakaa (b. 1947)

Facing It (1988)

My black face fades,
hiding inside the black granite.
I said I wouldn't
dammit: No tears.
I'm stone. I'm flesh.   5

My clouded reflection eyes me
like a bird of prey, the profile of night
slanted against morning. I turn
this way—the stone lets me go.
10 I turn that way—I'm inside
the Vietnam Veterans Memorial
again, depending on the light
to make a difference.
I go down the 58,022 names,
15 half-expecting to find
my own in letters like smoke.
I touch the name Andrew Johnson;
I see the booby trap's white flash.
Names shimmer on a woman's blouse
20 but when she walks away
the names stay on the wall.
Brushstrokes flash, a red bird's
wings cutting across my stare.
The sky. A plane in the sky.
25 A white vet's image floats
closer to me, then his pale eyes
look through mine. I'm a window.
He's lost his right arm
inside the stone. In the black mirror
30 a woman's trying to erase names:
No, she's brushing a boy's hair.

Emma Lazarus (1849–1887)

The New Colossus (1883)

Not like the brazen giant of Greek fame,
With conquering limbs astride from land to land;
Here at our sea-washed, sunset gates shall stand
A mighty woman with a torch, whose flame
5 Is the imprisoned lightning, and her name
Mother of Exiles. From her beacon-hand
Glows world-wide welcome; her mild eyes command
The air-bridged harbor that twin cities frame.
"Keep, ancient lands, your storied pomp!" cries she
10 With silent lips. "Give me your tired, your poor,
Your huddled masses yearning to breathe free,

The wretched refuse of your teeming shore.
Send these, the homeless, tempest-tost to me,
I lift my lamp beside the golden door!"

Audre Lorde (1934–1992)

Hanging Fire (1978)

I am fourteen
and my skin has betrayed me
the boy I cannot live without
still sucks his thumb
in secret   5
how come my knees are
always so ashy
what if I die
before morning
and momma's in the bedroom   10
with the door closed.

I have to learn how to dance
in time for the next party
my room is too small for me
suppose I die before graduation   15
they will sing sad melodies
but finally
tell the truth about me
There is nothing I want to do
and too much   20
that has to be done
and momma's in the bedroom
with the door closed.

Nobody even stops to think
about my side of it   25
I should have been on Math Team
my marks were better than his
why do I have to be
the one
wearing braces   30
I have nothing to wear tomorrow
will I live long enough
to grow up
and momma's in the bedroom
with the door closed.   35

Richard Lovelace (1618–1658)

To Lucasta (1649)

On Going to the Wars

Tell me not, Sweet, I am unkind
   That from the nunnery
Of thy chaste breasts, and quiet mind,
   To war and arms I fly.

5   True, a new mistress now I chase,
   The first foe in the field;
And with a stronger faith embrace
   A sword, a horse, a shield.

Yet this inconstancy is such
10   As you too shall adore;
I could not love thee, Dear, so much,
   Loved I not Honor more.

Archibald MacLeish (1892–1982)

Ars Poetica (1926)

A poem should be palpable and mute
As a globed fruit,

Dumb
As old medallions to the thumb,

5 Silent as the sleeve-worn stone
Of casement ledges where the moss has grown—

A poem should be wordless
As the flight of birds.
-
A poem should be motionless in time
10 As the moon climbs,

Leaving, as the moon releases
Twig by twig the night-entangled trees,

Leaving, as the moon behind the winter leaves,
Memory by memory the mind—

15 A poem should be motionless in time
As the moon climbs.
-
A poem should be equal to:
Not true.

For all the history of grief
20 An empty doorway and a maple leaf.

For love
The leaning grasses and two lights above the sea—

A poem should not mean
But be.

Andrew Marvell (1621–1678)

To His Coy Mistress (1681)

   Had we but world enough, and time,
This coyness, lady, were no crime.
We would sit down, and think which way
To walk, and pass our long love's day.
Thou by the Indian Ganges' side   5
Shouldst rubies find; I by the tide
Of Humber would complain. I would
Love you ten years before the Flood,
And you should, if you please, refuse
Till the conversion of the Jews.   10
My vegetable love should grow
Vaster than empires, and more slow;
An hundred years should go to praise
Thine eyes, and on thy forehead gaze;
Two hundred to adore each breast,   15
But thirty thousand to the rest:
An age at least to every part,
And the last age should show your heart.
For, lady, you deserve this state,
Nor would I love at lower rate.   20

But at my back I always hear
Time's wingèd chariot hurrying near;
And yonder all before us lie
Deserts of vast eternity.
25 Thy beauty shall no more be found,
Nor, in thy marble vault, shall sound
My echoing song; then worms shall try
That long-preserved virginity,
And your quaint honor turn to dust,
30 And into ashes all my lust:
The grave's a fine and private place,
But none, I think, do there embrace.
Now therefore, while the youthful hue
Sits on thy skin like morning dew,
35 And while thy willing soul transpires
At every pore with instant fires,
Now let us sport us while we may,
And now, like amorous birds of prey,
Rather at once our time devour
40 Than languish in his slow-chapped power.
Let us roll all our strength and all
Our sweetness up into one ball,
And tear our pleasures with rough strife
Thorough the iron gates of life:
45 Thus, though we cannot make our sun
Stand still, yet we will make him run.

John Milton (1608–1674)

[Of Man's first disobedience] —*from "Paradise Lost"* (1667)

Of Man's first disobedience, and the fruit
Of that forbidden Tree, whose mortal taste
Brought death into the world, and all our woe,
With loss of Eden, till one greater Man
5 Restore us, and regain the blissful seat,
Sing, Heavenly Muse, that on the secret top
Of Oreb, or of Sinai, didst inspire
That shepherd, who first taught the chosen seed
In the beginning how the Heavens and Earth
10 Rose out of Chaos: or, if Sion hill
Delight thee more, and Siloa's brook that flowed
Fast by the oracle of God, I thence

Invoke thy aid to my adventurous song,
That with no middle flight intends to soar
Above the Aonian mount, while it pursues   15
Things unattempted yet in prose or rhyme.
And chiefly thou, O Spirit, that dost prefer
Before all temples the upright heart and pure,
Instruct me, for thou know'st; thou from the first
Wast present, and, with mighty wings outspread,   20
Dove-like sat'st brooding on the vast Abyss,
And mad'st it pregnant: what in me is dark
Illumine, what is low raise and support;
That to the highth of this great argument
I may assert Eternal Providence,   25
And justify the ways of God to men.

Wilfred Owen (1893–1918)

For a brief biography of Wilfred Owen, see Chapter 21.

Anthem for Doomed Youth (1917)

What passing-bells for these who die as cattle?
Only the monstrous anger of the guns.
Only the stuttering rifles' rapid rattle
Can patter out their hasty orisons.
No mockeries now for them; no prayers nor bells,   5
Nor any voice of mourning save the choirs,—
The shrill, demented choirs of wailing shells;
And bugles calling for them from sad shires.
What candles may be held to speed them all?
Not in the hands of boys, but in their eyes   10
Shall shine the holy glimmers of good-byes.
The pallor of girls' brows shall be their pall;
Their flowers the tenderness of patient minds,
And each slow dusk a drawing-down of blinds.

Linda Pastan (b. 1932)

For a brief biography of Linda Pastan, see Chapter 23.

Ethics (1980)

In ethics class so many years ago
our teacher asked this question every fall:

if there were a fire in a museum
which would you save, a Rembrandt painting
5 or an old woman who hadn't many
years left anyhow? Restless on hard chairs
caring little for pictures or old age
we'd opt one year for life, the next for art
and always half-heartedly. Sometimes
10 the woman borrowed my grandmother's face
leaving her usual kitchen to wander
some drafty, half-imagined museum.
One year, feeling clever, I replied
why not let the woman decide herself?
15 Linda, the teacher would report, eschews
the burdens of responsibility.
This fall in a real museum I stand
before a real Rembrandt, old woman,
or nearly so, myself. The colors
20 within this frame are darker than autumn,
darker even than winter—the browns of earth,
though earth's most radiant elements burn
through the canvas. I know now that woman
and painting and season are almost one
25 and all beyond saving by children.

Molly Peacock (b. 1947)

Desire (1984)

It doesn't speak and it isn't schooled,
like a small foetal animal with wettened fur.
It is the blind instinct for life unruled,
visceral frankincense and animal myrrh.
5 It is what babies bring to kings,
an eyes-shut, ears-shut medicine of the heart
that smells and touches endings and beginnings
without the details of time's experienced *part-
fit-into-part-fit-into-part.* Like a paw,
10 it is blunt; like a pet who knows you
and nudges your knee with its snout—but more raw
and blinder and younger and more divine, too,
than the tamed wild—it's the drive for what is real,
deeper than the brain's detail: the drive to feel.

Sylvia Plath (1932–1963)

For a brief biography of Sylvia Plath, see Chapter 21.

Mirror (1963)

I am silver and exact. I have no preconceptions.
Whatever I see I swallow immediately
Just as it is, unmisted by love or dislike.
I am not cruel, only truthful—
The eye of a little god, four-cornered.   5
Most of the time I meditate on the opposite wall.
It is pink, with speckles. I have looked at it so long
I think it is a part of my heart. But it flickers.
Faces and darkness separate us over and over.

Now I am a lake. A woman bends over me,   10
Searching my reaches for what she really is.
Then she turns to those liars, the candles or the moon.
I see her back, and reflect it faithfully.
She rewards me with tears and an agitation of hands.
I am important to her. She comes and goes.   15
Each morning it is her face that replaces the darkness.
In me she has drowned a young girl, and in me an old
    woman
Rises toward her day after day, like a terrible fish.

Sir Walter Raleigh (1552–1618)

The Nymph's Reply to the Shepherd (1600)

If all the world and love were young,
And truth in every shepherd's tongue,
These pretty pleasures might me move
To live with thee and be thy love.

Time drives the flocks from field to fold   5
When rivers rage and rocks grow cold,
And Philomel becometh dumb;
The rest complains of cares to come.

The flowers do fade, and wanton fields
10 To wayward winter reckoning yields;
A honey tongue, a heart of gall,
Is fancy's spring, but sorrow's fall.

The gowns, thy shoes, thy beds of roses,
Thy cap, thy kirtle, and thy posies
15 Soon break, soon wither, soon forgotten—
In folly ripe, in reason rotten.

Thy belt of straw and ivy buds,
Thy coral clasps and amber studs,
All these in me no means can move
20 To come to thee and be thy love.

But could youth last and love still breed,
Had joys no date nor age no need,
Then these delights my mind might move
To live with thee and be thy love.

Dudley Randall (1914–2000)

The Ballad of Birmingham (1969)

*(On the bombing of a church in
Birmingham, Alabama, 1963)*

"Mother dear, may I go downtown
Instead of out to play,
And march the streets of Birmingham
In a Freedom March today?"

5 "No, baby, no, you may not go,
For the dogs are fierce and wild,
And clubs and hoses, guns and jails
Aren't good for a little child."

"But, mother, I won't be alone.
10 Other children will go with me,
And march the streets of Birmingham
To make our country free."

"No, baby, no, you may not go,
For I fear those guns will fire.
But you may go to church instead   15
And sing in the children's choir."

She has combed and brushed her night-dark hair,
And bathed rose petal sweet,
And drawn white gloves on her small brown hands,
And white shoes on her feet.   20

The mother smiled to know that her child
Was in the sacred place,
But that smile was the last smile
To come upon her face.

For when she heard the explosion,   25
Her eyes grew wet and wild.
She raced through the streets of Birmingham
Calling for her child.

She clawed through bits of glass and brick,
Then lifted out a shoe.   30
"O, here's the shoe my baby wore,
But, baby, where are you?"

Adrienne Rich (b. 1929)

Aunt Jennifer's Tigers (1951)

Aunt Jennifer's tigers prance across a screen,
Bright topaz denizens of a world of green.
They do not fear the men beneath the tree;
They pace in sleek chivalric certainty.

Aunt Jennifer's fingers fluttering through her wool   5
Find even the ivory needle hard to pull.
The massive weight of Uncle's wedding band
Sits heavily upon Aunt Jennifer's hand.

When Aunt is dead, her terrified hands will lie
Still ringed with ordeals she was mastered by.
The tigers in the panel that she made   10
Will go on prancing, proud and unafraid.

Diving into the Wreck (1973)

First having read the book of myths,
and loaded the camera,
and checked the edge of the knife-blade,
I put on
5 the body-armor of black rubber
the absurd flippers
the grave and awkward mask.
I am having to do this
not like Cousteau with his
10 assiduous team
aboard the sun-flooded schooner
but here alone.

There is a ladder.
The ladder is always there
15 hanging innocently
close to the side of the schooner.
We know what it is for,
we who have used it.
Otherwise
20 it's a piece of maritime floss
some sundry equipment.

I go down.
Rung after rung and still
the oxygen immerses me
25 the blue light
the clear atoms
of our human air.
I go down.
My flippers cripple me,
30 I crawl like an insect down the ladder
and there is no one
to tell me when the ocean
will begin.

First the air is blue and then
35 it is bluer and then green and then
black I am blacking out and yet
my mask is powerful

it pumps my blood with power
the sea is another story
the sea is not a question of power   40
I have to learn alone
to turn my body without force
in the deep element.

And now: it is easy to forget
what I came for   45
among so many who have always
lived here
swaying their crenellated fans
between the reefs
and besides   50
you breathe differently down here.

I came to explore the wreck.
The words are purposes.
The words are maps.
I came to see the damage that was done   55
and the treasures that prevail.
I stroke the beam of my lamp
slowly along the flank
of something more permanent
than fish or weed   60

the thing I came for:
the wreck and not the story of the wreck
the thing itself and not the myth
the drowned face always staring
toward the sun   65
the evidence of damage
worn by salt and away into this threadbare beauty
the ribs of the disaster
curving their assertion
among the tentative haunters.   70

This is the place.
And I am here, the mermaid whose dark hair
streams black, the merman in his armored body.
We circle silently
about the wreck   75
we dive into the hold.
I am she: I am he

whose drowned face sleeps with open eyes
whose breasts still bear the stress
80 whose silver, copper, vermeil cargo lies
obscurely inside barrels
half-wedged and left to rot
we are the half-destroyed instruments
that once held to a course
85 the water-eaten log
the fouled compass

We are, I am, you are
by cowardice or courage
the one who find our way
90 back to this scene
carrying a knife, a camera
a book of myths
in which
our names do not appear.

Christina Rossetti (1830–1894)

Echo (1862)

Come to me in the silence of the night;
   Come in the speaking silence of a dream;
Come with soft rounded cheeks and eyes as bright
   As sunlight on a stream;
5   Come back in tears,
O memory, hope, love of finished years.

O dream how sweet, too sweet, too bitter sweet,
   Whose wakening should have been in Paradise,
Where souls brimful of love abide and meet;
10   Where thirsting longing eyes
     Watch the slow door
That opening, letting in, lets out no more.

Yet come to me in dreams, that I may live
   My very life again though cold in death:
Come back to me in dreams, that I may give   15
   Pulse for pulse, breath for breath:
     Speak low, lean low,
As long ago, my love, how long ago.

Carl Sandburg (1878–1967)

Fog (1916)

The fog comes
on little cat feet.

It sits looking
over harbor and city
on silent haunches   5
and then moves on.

Anne Sexton (1928–1974)

Letter Written on a Ferry while Crossing Long Island Sound (1961)

I am surprised to see
that the ocean is still going on.
Now I am going back
and I have ripped my hand
from your hand as I said I would   5
and I have made it this far
as I said I would
and I am on the top deck now
holding my wallet, my cigarettes
and my car keys   10
at 2 o'clock on a Tuesday
in August of 1960.

Dearest,
although everything has happened,
nothing has happened.   15
The sea is very old.

The sea is the face of Mary,
without miracles or rage
or unusual hope,
20 grown rough and wrinkled
with incurable age.

Still,
I have eyes.
These are my eyes:
25 the orange letters that spell
ORIENT on the life preserver
that hangs by my knees;
the cement lifeboat that wears
its dirty canvas coat;
30 the faded sign that sits on its shelf
saying KEEP OFF.
Oh, all right, I say,
I'll save myself.

Over my right shoulder
35 I see four nuns
who sit like a bridge club,
their faces poked out
from under their habits,
as good as good babies who
40 have sunk into their carriages.
Without discrimination
the wind pulls the skirts
of their arms.
Almost undressed,
45 I see what remains:
that holy wrist,
that ankle,
that chain.

Oh God,
50 although I am very sad,
could you please
let these four nuns
loosen from their leather boots
and their wooden chairs
55 to rise out
over this greasy deck,
out over this iron rail,

nodding their pink heads to one side,
flying four abreast
in the old-fashioned side stroke;   60
each mouth open and round,
breathing together
as fish do,
singing without sound.

Dearest,   65
see how my dark girls sally forth,
over the passing lighthouse of Plum Gut,
its shell as rusty
as a camp dish,
as fragile as a pagoda   70
on a stone;
out over the little lighthouse
that warns me of drowning winds
that rub over its blind bottom
and its blue cover;   75
winds that will take the toes
and the ears of the rider
or the lover.

There go my dark girls,
their dresses puff   80
in the leeward air.
Oh, they are lighter than flying dogs
or the breath of dolphins;
each mouth opens gratefully,
wider than a milk cup.   85
My dark girls sing for this.
They are going up.
See them rise
on black wings, drinking
the sky, without smiles   90
or hands
or shoes.
They call back to us
from the gauzy edge of paradise,
good news, good news.   95

William Shakespeare (1564–1616)

For a brief biography of William Shakespeare, see the Case Study on Shakespeare, Chapter 33.

Let me not to the marriage of true minds (1609)

Let me not to the marriage of true minds
Admit impediments; love is not love
Which alters when it alteration finds,
Or bends with the remover to remove:
5 O, no, it is an ever-fixèd mark,
That looks on tempests and is never shaken;
It is the star to every wand'ring bark,
Whose worth's unknown, although his highth be taken.
Love's not Time's fool, though rosy lips and cheeks
10 Within his bending sickle's compass come;
Love alters not with his brief hours and weeks,
But bears it out even to the edge of doom.
   If this be error and upon me proved,
   I never writ, nor no man ever loved.

Not marble, nor the gilded monuments (1609)

Not marble, nor the gilded monuments
Of princes, shall outlive this powerful rhyme;
But you shall shine more bright in these contents
Than unswept stone, besmeared with sluttish time.
15 When wasteful war shall statues overturn,
And broils root out the work of masonry,
Nor Mars his sword nor war's quick fire shall burn
The living record of your memory.
'Gainst death and all-oblivious enmity
20 Shall you pace forth; your praise shall still find room
Even in the eyes of all posterity
That wear this world out to the ending doom.
   So, till the judgment that yourself arise,
   You live in this, and dwell in lovers' eyes.

That time of the year thou mayest in me behold (1609)

That time of year thou mayest in me behold
When yellow leaves, or none, or few, do hang
Upon those boughs which shake against the cold,
Bare ruined choirs, where late the sweet birds sang.
In me thou seest the twilight of such day   5
As after sunset fadeth in the west;
Which by and by black night doth take away,
Death's second self that seals up all in rest.
In me thou seest the glowing of such fire
That on the ashes of his youth doth lie,   10
As the deathbed whereon it must expire,
Consumed with that which it was nourish'd by.
   This thou perceiv'st, which makes thy love more strong,
   To love that well, which thou must leave ere long.

Percy Bysshe Shelley (1792–1822)

For a brief biography of Percy Bysshe Shelley, see Chapter 25.

Ozymandias (1818)

I met a traveller from an antique land
Who said: Two vast and trunkless legs of stone
Stand in the desert. . . Near them, on the sand,
Half sunk, a shattered visage lies, whose frown,
And wrinkled lip, and sneer of cold command,   5
Tell that its sculptor well those passions read
Which yet survive, stamped on these lifeless things,
The hand that mocked them, and the heart that fed:
And on the pedestal these words appear:
"My name is Ozymandias, king of kings: 10
Look on my works, ye Mighty, and despair!"
Nothing beside remains. Round the decay
Of that colossal wreck, boundless and bare
The lone and level sands stretch far away.

Patricia Smith (b. 1955)

What It's Like to Be a Black Girl (for Those of You Who Aren't) (1991)

First of all, it's being 9 years old and
feeling like you're not finished, like your
edges are wild, like there's something,
everything, wrong. it's dropping food coloring
5   in your eyes to make them blue and suffering
their burn in silence. it's popping a bleached
white mophead over the kinks of your hair and
primping in front of the mirrors that deny your
reflection. it's finding a space between your
10   legs, a disturbance at your chest, and not knowing
what to do with the whistles. it's jumping
double dutch until your legs pop, it's sweat
and vaseline and bullets, it's growing tall and
wearing a lot of white, it's smelling blood in
15   your breakfast, it's learning to say fuck with
grace but learning to fuck without it, it's
flame and fists and life according to motown,
it's finally having a man reach out for you
then caving in
20   around his fingers.

Gary Soto (b. 1952)

Saturday at the Canal (1991)

I was hoping to be happy by seventeen.
School was a sharp check mark in the roll book,
An obnoxious tuba playing at noon because our team
Was going to win at night. The teachers were
5   Too close to dying to understand. The hallways
Stank of poor grades and unwashed hair. Thus,
A friend and I sat watching the water on Saturday,
Neither of us talking much, just warming ourselves
By hurling large rocks at the dusty ground
10   And feeling awful because San Francisco was a postcard
On a bedroom wall. We wanted to go there,

Hitchhike under the last migrating birds
And be with people who knew more than three chords
On a guitar. We didn't drink or smoke,
But our hair was shoulder length, wild when   15
The wind picked up and the shadows of
This loneliness gripped loose dirt. By bus or car,
By the sway of train over a long bridge,
We wanted to get out. The years froze
As we sat on the bank. Our eyes followed the water,   20
White-tipped but dark underneath, racing out of town.

Wallace Stevens (1879–1955)

For a brief biography of Wallace Stevens, see Chapter 20.

Disillusionment of Ten O'Clock (1923)

The houses are haunted
By white night-gowns.
None are green,
Or purple with green rings,
Or green with yellow rings,   5
Or yellow with blue rings.
None of them are strange,
With socks of lace
And beaded ceintures.
People are not going   10
To dream of baboons and periwinkles.
Only, here and there, an old sailor,
Drunk and asleep in his boots,
Catches tigers
In red weather.   15

Thirteen Ways of Looking at a Blackbird (1917)

I

Among twenty snowy mountains,
The only moving thing
Was the eye of the blackbird.

II

I was of three minds,
5   Like a tree
In which there are three blackbirds.

III

The blackbirds whirled in the autumn winds.
It was a small part of the pantomime.

IV

A man and a woman
10   Are one.
A man and a woman and a blackbird
Are one.

V

I do not know which to prefer—
The beauty of inflections
15   Or the beauty of innuendoes,
The blackbird whistling
Or just after.

VI

Icicles filled the long window
With barbaric glass.
20   The shadow of the blackbird
Crossed it, to and fro.
The mood
Traced in the shadow
An indecipherable course.

VII

25   O thin men of Haddam,
Why do you imagine golden birds?
Do you not see how the blackbird
Walks around the feet
Of the women about you?

VIII

30   I know noble accents
And lucid, inescapable rhythms;
But I know, too,
That the blackbird is involved
In what I know.

IX

When the blackbird flew out of sight,   35
It marked the edge
Of one of many circles.

X

At the sight of blackbirds
Flying in a green light,
Even the bawds of euphony   40
Would cry out sharply.

XI

He rode over Connecticut
In a glass coach.
Once, a fear pierced him,
In that he mistook   45
The shadow of his equipage
For blackbirds.

XII

The river is moving.
The blackbird must be flying.

XIII

It was evening all afternoon.   50
It was snowing
And it was going to snow.
The blackbird sat
In the cedar-limbs.

Adrienne Su (b. 1967)

The English Canon (2000)

It's not that the first speakers left out women
Unless they were goddesses, harlots, or impossible loves
Seen from afar, often while bathing,

And it's not that the only parts my grandfathers could have
    played
Were as extras in Xanadu,   5
Nor that it gives no instructions for shopping or cooking.

The trouble is, I've spent my life
Getting over the lyrics
That taught me to brush my hair till it's gleaming,

10 Stay slim, dress tastefully, and not speak of sex,
Death, violence, or the desire for any of them,
And to let men do the talking and warring

And bringing of the news. I know a girl's got to protest
These days, but she also has to make money
15 And do her share of journalism and combat,

And she has to know from the gut whom to trust,
Because what do her teachers know, living in books,
And what does she know, starting from scratch?

Alfred, Lord Tennyson (1809–1892)

Ulysses (1842)

It little profits that an idle king,
By this still hearth, among these barren crags,
Matched with an aged wife, I mete and dole
Unequal laws unto a savage race,
5 That hoard, and sleep, and feed, and know not me.
I cannot rest from travel; I will drink
Life to the lees. All times I have enjoyed
Greatly, have suffered greatly, both with those
That loved me, and alone; on shore, and when
10 Through scudding drifts the rainy Hyades
Vexed the dim sea. I am become a name;
For always roaming with a hungry heart
Much have I seen and known—cities of men
And manners, climates, councils, governments,
15 Myself not least, but honored of them all,—
And drunk delight of battle with my peers,
Far on the ringing plains of windy Troy.
I am a part of all that I have met;
Yet all experience is an arch wherethrough
20 Gleams that untraveled world whose margin fades
Forever and forever when I move.
How dull it is to pause, to make an end,
To rust unburnished, not to shine in use!
As though to breathe were life! Life piled on life
25 Were all too little, and of one to me

Little remains; but every hour is saved
From that eternal silence, something more,
A bringer of new things; and vile it were
For some three suns to store and hoard myself,
And this gray spirit yearning in desire   30
To follow knowledge like a sinking star,
Beyond the utmost bound of human thought.
    This is my son, mine own Telemachus,
To whom I leave the scepter and the isle,
Well-loved of me, discerning to fulfill   35
This labor, by slow prudence to make mild
A rugged people, and through soft degrees
Subdue them to the useful and the good.
Most blameless is he, centered in the sphere
Of common duties, decent not to fail   40
In offices of tenderness, and pay
Meet adoration to my household gods,
When I am gone. He works his work, I mine.
    There lies the port; the vessel puffs her sail;
There gloom the dark, broad seas. My mariners,   45
Souls that have toiled, and wrought, and thought with me,
That ever with a frolic welcome took
The thunder and the sunshine, and opposed
Free hearts, free foreheads—you and I are old;
Old age hath yet his honor and his toil.   50
Death closes all; but something ere the end,
Some work of noble note, may yet be done,
Not unbecoming men that strove with gods.
The lights begin to twinkle from the rocks;
The long day wanes; the slow moon climbs; the deep   55
Moans round with many voices. Come, my friends,
'Tis not too late to seek a newer world.
Push off, and sitting well in order smite
The sounding furrows; for my purpose holds
To sail beyond the sunset, and the baths   60
Of all the western stars, until I die.
It may be that the gulfs will wash us down;
It may be we shall touch the Happy Isles,
And see the great Achilles, whom we knew.
Though much is taken, much abides; and though   65
We are not now that strength which in old days
Moved earth and heaven, that which we are, we are,
One equal temper of heroic hearts,
Made weak by time and fate, but strong in will
To strive, to seek, to find, and not to yield.   70

Quincy Troupe (b. 1943)

Poem Reaching towards Something (1997)

we walk through a calligraphy of hats slicing off foreheads
ace-deuce cocked, they slant, razor sharp, clean
through imagination, our spirits knee-deep in what we
   have forgotten
entrancing our bodies now to dance, like enraptured water
   lilies—
5 my memory & me—the rhythm in liquid stride of a certain
   look—
rippling eyeballs through breezes—
riffling choirs of trees where a trillion slivers of sunlight
   prance
across filigreeing leaves, a zillion voices of bamboo reeds
green with summer's saxophone burst
10 wrap themselves, like transparent prisms of dew—
drops around images, laced with pearls & rhinestones
perhaps it is through this, or the decoding of syllables
that we learn speech, that sonorous river of broken mirrors
carrying our dreams, assaulted by pellets of rain-
15 drops, the prisons of words entrapping us between
   parentheses—
two bat wings curving into cynical smiles

still, there is something here that needs explaining beyond
the hopelessness of miles, the light at the end of the
   midnight tunnel—
some say it is a train coming right at us—
20 where do the tumbling words spend themselves after they
   have spent
all meaning residing in the warehouse of language
after they have slipped like smoke
from our lips, where do the symbols they carry stop
   everything
put down roots, cleanse themselves of everything but
   clarity—
25 though here eye might be asking a little too much of any
   poet's head
full as it is with double-entendres

still, there are these hats slicing foreheads off in the middle
of crowds, the calligraphy of this penumbra slanting
ace-deuce cocked, carrying the perforated legacy of bebop,
   these bold
peccadillo, pirouetting pellagras, razor-sharp-clean,   30
   they cut
into our rip-tiding dreams carrying their whirlpooling
   imaginations
their rivers of schemes assaulted by pellets of raindrops, these broken mirrors reflecting sonorous
words entrapping us between parentheses—
two hat wings curved, imprisoning the world   35

Phyllis Wheatley (1753–1784)

On Being Brought from Africa to America (1773)

'Twas mercy brought me from my *Pagan* land,
Taught my benighted soul to understand
That there's a God, that there's a *Saviour* too:
Once I redemption neither sought nor knew.
Some view our sable race with scornful eye,   5
"Their colour is a diabolic die."
Remember, *Christians*, *Negros*, black as *Cain*,
May be refin'd, and join th' angelic train.

William Carlos Williams (1883–1963)

For a brief biography of William Carlos Williams, see Chapter 22.

Spring and All (1923)

By the road to the contagious hospital
under the surge of the blue
mottled clouds driven from the
northeast—a cold wind. Beyond, the
waste of broad, muddy fields   5
brown with dried weeds, standing and fallen

patches of standing water
the scattering of tall trees

All along the road the reddish
10 purplish, forked, upstanding, twiggy
stuff of bushes and small trees
with dead, brown leaves under them
leafless vines—

Lifeless in appearance, sluggish
15 dazed spring approaches—

They enter the new world naked,
cold, uncertain of all
save that they enter. All about them
the cold, familiar wind—

20 Now the grass, tomorrow
the stiff curl of wildcarrot leaf
One by one objects are defined—
It quickens: clarity, outline of leaf

But now the stark dignity of
25 entrance—Still, the profound change
has come upon them: rooted they
grip down and begin to awaken

William Wordsworth (1770–1850)

For a brief biography of William Wordsworth, see Chapter 17.

London, 1802 (1802)

Milton! thou shouldst be living at this hour:
England hath need of thee: she is a fen
Of stagnant waters: altar, sword, and pen,
Fireside, the heroic wealth of hall and bower,
5 Have forfeited their ancient English dower
Of inward happiness. We are selfish men;
Oh! raise us up, return to us again;
And give us manners, virtue, freedom, power.
Thy soul was like a Star, and dwelt apart;

Thou hadst a voice whose sound was like the sea: 10
Pure as the naked heavens, majestic, free,
So didst thou travel on life's common way,
In cheerful godliness; and yet thy heart
The lowliest duties on herself did lay.

The World Is Too Much with Us (1807)

The world is too much with us; late and soon,
Getting and spending, we lay waste our powers;
Little we see in Nature that is ours;
We have given our hearts away, a sordid boon!
This Sea that bares her bosom to the moon, 5
The winds that will be howling at all hours,
And are up-gathered now like sleeping flowers,
For this, for everything, we are out of tune;
It moves us not.—Great God! I'd rather be
A Pagan suckled in a creed outworn; 10
So might I, standing on this pleasant lea,
Have glimpses that would make me less forlorn;
Have sight of Proteus rising from the sea;
Or hear old Triton blow his wreathéd horn.

The Solitary Reaper (1807)

Behold her, single in the field,
Yon solitary Highland Lass!
Reaping and singing by herself;
Stop here, or gently pass!
Alone she cuts and binds the grain, 5
And sings a melancholy strain;
O listen! for the Vale profound
Is overflowing with the sound.

No Nightingale did ever chaunt
More welcome notes to weary bands 10
Of travelers in some shady haunt,
Among Arabian sands;
A voice so thrilling ne'er was heard
In springtime from the Cuckoo bird,
Breaking the silence of the seas 15
Among the farthest Hebrides.

Will no one tell me what she sings?—
Perhaps the plaintive numbers flow
For old, unhappy, far-off things,
20 And battles long ago;
Or is it some more humble lay,
Familiar matter of today?
Some natural sorrow, loss, or pain,
That has been, and may be again?

25 Whate'er the theme, the Maiden sang
As if her song could have no ending;
I saw her singing at her work,
And o'er the sickle bending—
I listened, motionless and still;
30 And, as I mounted up the hill,
The music in my heart I bore,
Long after it was heard no more.

William Butler Yeats (1865–1939)

For a brief biography of William Butler Yeats, see Chapter 17.

When You Are Old (1893)

When you are old and grey and full of sleep,
And nodding by the fire, take down this book,
And slowly read, and dream of the soft look
Your eyes had once, and of their shadows deep;

How many loved your moments of glad grace,   5
And loved your beauty with love false or true,
But one man loved the pilgrim soul in you,
And loved the sorrows of your changing face;

And bending down beside the glowing bars,
Murmur, a little sadly, how Love fled   10
And paced upon the mountains overhead
And hid his face amid a crowd of stars.

GOING FURTHER ONLINE

Three casebooks for poetry with additional selections are also available online at **connect.mcgraw-hill.com.** For more on each of these casebooks and a complete listing of selections, see the table of contents at the beginning of the book.

- **Poetry as Song and Performance:** Leonard Cohen, The Last Poets, Lawson Fusao Inada, Jay Z, among others
- **Masters of Craft:** Sappho, Bashō, William Blake, Thomas Hardy, Christina Rosetti, Alfred, Lord Tennyson, and others
- **Contemporary Voices:** Samiya Bashir, Christina Davis, Derek Mong, and others

Part 4 Drama

30 Reading & Viewing a Play in Its Elements

I DIDN'T hear or see anything; I knocked at the door, and still it was all quiet inside. I knew they must be up, it was past eight o'clock. So I knocked again, and I thought I heard somebody say, "Come in." I wasn't sure, I'm not sure yet, but I opened the door—this door and there in that rocker—sat Mrs. Wright.

—*from* Trifles *by Susan Glaspell*

"I remember once being in a play, and it was the day we were going to open, and the director said to us, 'Try to remember what you felt when you first read this play.' And I thought that was such a wonderful thing to say. It wasn't, 'Use everything I've told you up until this moment,' and blah blah blah about the rehearsal. No. It was your reaction, your personal reaction to the play. So if you have a book full of plays, you are adding yourself to it."

Conversation with Marian Seldes, available on video
at connect.mcgraw-hill.com

ANYONE who's ever sat quietly in a dark room facing forward while another person under a spotlight speaks has had the experience of the theater. In addition to creating characters and dialogue and plot, a playwright must make the play come alive on the stage. Playwright Edward Albee has said that everything you need to know about how to stage a play can be found in reading the text itself:

> *The intention is there in the text. The intention is the experience of the play that I had while I was writing it. Because when I write a play . . . I see it, I hear it as a play being performed in front of me, and that's what I want to see on the stage—the same experience that I had while writing it.*

He directs his actors back to the text when they have a question about how to perform a work. Actress Marian Seldes, who has performed in a number of Albee plays, recounts similar advice in her interview, "Try to remember what you felt when you first read this play."

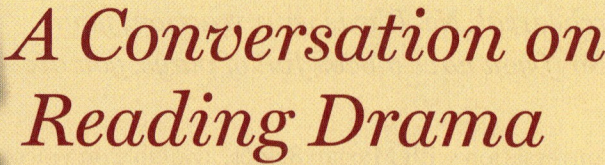

Marian Seldes

... Every playwright awakens something in you you didn't know was there.

A Conversation on Reading Drama

An Actor's View: Teaching Yourself to Read a Play

You can teach yourself how to read a play. . . . You just read the words the characters say, not worry[ing] too much about who's saying what. . . . When you've read it one way through, you'll have no difficulty in recognizing, Oh, that's the grandmother. Oh, that's . . . the doctor, of course. Oh, that's the beautiful woman . . . because no one else could speak that way.

Being Alone with a Script

When . . . someone sends you a script, you can pick it up whenever you want to, and part of the thrill is that you're alone with it. You're not sharing this experience with anybody else; it's yours. That frees your imagination. Even if the playwright gives a detailed description of where the play takes place or how the characters look, he can't control your mind, and you invent your play. For me, reading a script for the first time is one of the adventures of being in the theater.

Writing in the Margins

I think it's a good idea to write your thoughts down. . . . Write down what interests you. When I was young, you weren't allowed to write in the margin of a book. . . . I write things in the script, the acting script, the acting version of a play that I do. . . . Your opinions are as important as everybody else's—especially when you are in communion with a writer you care about: Write it down.

To see the entire interview with Marian Seldes, go to connect.mcgraw-hill.com.

RESEARCH ASSIGNMENT   In her interview, Seldes talks about having a playwright at the staging of a play and indicates the answers to the questions she would ask are "all in the play." How does this influence her reading?

Marian Seldes is one of America's foremost actors, having appeared on Broadway and off-Broadway in plays by Tennessee Williams and Edward Albee, among many others, as well as having played in numerous films and television productions. Her many honors include Obie, Drama Desk, and Tony awards in recognition of her achievements in live American theater as well as induction into the Theater Hall of Fame.

Susan Glaspell (1876–1948)

Born in Davenport, Iowa, the daughter of a pioneer family, Susan Glaspell graduated from Drake University. She worked as a reporter until she decided to devote her time to fiction writing. Although she wrote nine novels (some of which were best sellers) and many short stories, she is best known for her contribution to American drama. She married George Cook, who encouraged Glaspell to write drama, and in 1916 they co-founded the Provincetown Players, a group of playwrights and actors that performed innovative drama. Glaspell's one-act plays were particularly well received. Among her contributions to the group was the way she encouraged the young Eugene O'Neill, who became one of the most important twentieth-century American dramatists. Glaspell's play *Alison's House* (1930), which is based on Emily Dickinson's life, won the Pulitzer Prize, but her early one-act *Trifles* (1916) is generally considered her finest achievement.

AS YOU READ   Ask yourself how many kinds of investigations are under way in this brief play among the five people—the country attorney, the sheriff and his wife, and a neighboring farmer and his wife—who have come to investigate the scene of the death.

FOR INTERACTIVE READING . . .

Note in the text any references to Mrs. Hale's regrets.

Trifles (1916)

CHARACTERS

GEORGE HENDERSON, *county attorney*

HENRY PETERS, *sheriff*

LEWIS HALE, *a neighboring farmer*

MRS. PETERS

MRS. HALE

SCENE: *The kitchen in the now abandoned farmhouse of John Wright, a gloomy kitchen, plainly left without having been put in order—unwashed pans under the sink, a loaf of bread outside the bread-box, a dish-towel on the table—other signs of incompleted work. Door opens rear and enter sheriff followed by* COUNTY ATTORNEY *and* HALE. *The* SHERIFF *and* HALE *are men in middle life, the* COUNTY ATTORNEY *is a young man; all are much bundled up and go at once to the stove. They are followed by the two women—the* SHERIFF's *wife first; she is a slight wiry woman, a thin nervous face.* MRS. HALE *is larger and would ordinarily be called more comfortable looking, but she is disturbed now and looks fearfully about as she enters. The women have come in slowly, and stand close together near the door.*

COUNTY ATTORNEY: *(Rubbing his hands)* This feels good. Come up to the fire, ladies.

MRS. PETERS: *(Takes a step forward and looks around)* I'm not—cold.

5 **SHERIFF:** *(Unbuttoning his overcoat and stepping away from the stove as if to mark the beginning of official business)* Now, Mr. Hale, before we move things about, you explain to Mr. Henderson just what you saw when you came here yesterday morning.

10 **COUNTY ATTORNEY:** By the way, has anything been moved? Are things just as you left them yesterday?

SHERIFF: *(Looking all about)* It's just the same. When it dropped below zero last night I thought I'd better send Frank out this morning to make a fire for us—no use getting pneumonia with a big case on, but I told him not to touch anything except the stove—and you know Frank.

COUNTY ATTORNEY: Somebody should have been left here yesterday.

20 **SHERIFF:** Oh—yesterday. When I had to send Frank to Morris Center for that man who went crazy—I want you to know I had my hands full yesterday. I knew you could get back from Omaha by today and as long as I went over everything here myself—

25 **COUNTY ATTORNEY:** Well, Mr. Hale, tell just what happened when you came here yesterday morning.

HALE: Harry and I had started to town with a load of potatoes. We came along the road from my place and as I got here I said, "I'm going to see if I can't get John Wright to go in with me on a party telephone." 30 I spoke to Wright about it once before and he put me off, saying folks talked too much anyway, and all he asked was peace and quiet—I guess you know about how much he talked himself, but I thought maybe if I went to the house and talked about it before his wife, 35 though I said to Harry that I didn't know as what his wife wanted made much difference to John—

COUNTY ATTORNEY: Let's talk about that later, Mr. Hale. I do want to talk about that, but tell now just what happened when you got to the house. 40

HALE: I didn't hear or see anything; I knocked at the door, and still it was all quiet inside. I knew they must be up, it was past eight o'clock. So I knocked again, and I thought I heard somebody say, "Come in." I wasn't sure, I'm not sure yet, but I opened the door— 45 this door *(jerking a hand backward)* and there in that rocker—*(pointing to it)* sat Mrs. Wright. *(All look at the rocker)*

COUNTY ATTORNEY: What—was she doing?

HALE: She was rockin' back and forth. She had her 50 apron in her hand and was kind of—pleating it.

COUNTY ATTORNEY: And how did she—look?

HALE: Well, she looked queer.

COUNTY ATTORNEY: How do you mean—queer? 55

HALE: Well, as if she didn't know what she was going to do next. And kind of done up.

COUNTY ATTORNEY: How did she seem to feel about your coming? 60

HALE: Why, I don't think she minded—one way or other. She didn't pay 65

much attention. I said, "How do, Mrs. Wright, it's cold, ain't it?" And she said, "Is
70 it?"—and went on kind of pleating at her apron. Well, I was surprised; she didn't ask me to come up to the stove, or to set down, but just sat there, not even looking at me, so I said, "I want to see John." And then
75 she—laughed. I guess you would call it a laugh. I thought of Harry and the team outside, so I said a little sharp: "Can't I see John?" "No," she says, kind o' dull like. "Ain't he home?" says I. "Yes," says she,
80 "he's home." "Then why can't I see him?" I asked her, out of patience. "'Cause he's dead," says she. *"Dead?"* says I. She just nodded her head, not getting a bit excited, but rockin' back and forth. "Why—where is he?" says I, not knowing what to say.
85 She just pointed upstairs—like that *(himself pointing to the room above)*. I got up, with the idea of going up there. I walked from there to here—*(pointing)*—then I says, "Why, what did he die of?" "He died of a rope round his neck," says she, and just went on pleatin'
90 at her apron. Well, I went out and called Harry. I thought I might—need help. We went upstairs and there he was—lyin'—

COUNTY ATTORNEY: I think I'd rather have you go into that upstairs, where you can point it all out. Just go
95 on now with the rest of the story.

HALE: Well, my first thought was to get that rope off. It looked—*(stops, his face twitches)*—but Harry, he went up to him, and he said, "No, he's dead all right, and we'd better not touch anything." So we went back
100 down stairs. She was still sitting that same way. "Has anybody been notified?" I asked. "No," says she, unconcerned. "Who did this, Mrs. Wright?" said Harry. He said it business-like—and she stopped pleatin' of her apron. "I don't know," she says. "You don't *know?*"
105 says Harry. "No," says she. "Weren't you sleepin' in the bed with him?" says Harry. "Yes," says she, "but I was on the inside." "Somebody slipped a rope round his neck and strangled him and you didn't wake up?" says Harry. "I didn't wake up," she said after him. We
110 may have looked as if we didn't see how that could be, for after a minute she said, "I sleep sound." Harry was going to ask her more questions but I said maybe we ought to let her tell her story first to the coroner, or

the sheriff, so Harry went fast as he could to Rivers' place, where there's a telephone.
115

COUNTY ATTORNEY: And what did Mrs. Wright do when she knew that you had gone for the coroner?

HALE: She moved from that chair to this one over here, *(pointing to a small chair in the corner)* and just sat there with her hands held together and looking down.
120 I got a feeling that I ought to make some conversation, so I said I had come in to see if John wanted to put in a telephone, and at that she started to laugh, and then she stopped and looked at me—scared. (COUNTY ATTORNEY, *who has had his notebook out, makes a*
125 *note*) I dunno, maybe it wasn't scared. I wouldn't like to say it was. Soon Harry got back, and then Dr. Lloyd came, and you, Mr. Peters, and so I guess that's all I know that you don't.

COUNTY ATTORNEY: *(Looking around)* I guess we'll go
130 upstairs first—and then out to the barn and around there. *(To* SHERIFF) You're convinced that there was nothing important here—nothing that would point to any motive?

SHERIFF: Nothing here but kitchen things.
135

COUNTY ATTORNEY: *(Opens the door of a cupboard closet. Gets up on a chair and looks on a shelf. Pulls his hand away, sticky)* Here's a nice mess. *(The women draw nearer)*

MRS. PETERS: Oh, her fruit; it did freeze. *(To* COUNTY
140 ATTORNEY) She worried about that when it turned so cold. She said the fire'd go out and her jars would break.

SHERIFF: Well, can you beat the women! Held for murder and worrying about her preserves.
145

COUNTY ATTORNEY: *(Setting his lips firmly)* I guess before we are through she may have something more serious than preserves to worry about.

HALE: Well, women are used to worrying over trifles. *(The two women move a little closer together)*
150

COUNTY ATTORNEY: *(With the gallantry of a young politician)* And yet, for all their worries, what would we do without the ladies? *(The women do not unbend. He goes to the sink, takes a dipperful of water from pail*

155 *and pouring it into basin, washes his hands. Starts to wipe them on the roller towel, turns it for a cleaner place)* Dirty towels! *(Kicks his foot against pans under the sink)* Not much of a housekeeper, would you say, ladies?

160 **MRS. HALE:** *(Stiffly)* There's a great deal of work to be done on a farm.

COUNTY ATTORNEY: *(With conciliation)* To be sure. And yet *(with a little bow to her)* I know there are some Dickson county farmhouses which do not have such 165 roller towels. *(Gives it a pull to expose its full length again)*

MRS. HALE: Those towels get dirty awful quick. Men's hands aren't always as clean as they might be.

COUNTY ATTORNEY: Ah, loyal to your sex, I see. But 170 you and Mrs. Wright were neighbors. I suppose you were friends, too.

MRS. HALE: *(Shaking her head)* I've not seen much of her of late years. I've not been in this house—it's more than a year.

175 **COUNTY ATTORNEY:** And why was that? You didn't like her?

MRS. HALE: I liked her all well enough. Farmer's wives have their hands full, Mr. Henderson. And then—

COUNTY ATTORNEY: Yes—?

180 **MRS. HALE:** *(Looking about)* It never seemed a very cheerful place.

COUNTY ATTORNEY: No—it's not cheerful. I shouldn't say she had the homemaking instinct.

MRS. HALE: Well, I don't know as Wright had, either.

185 **COUNTY ATTORNEY:** You mean that they didn't get on very well?

MRS. HALE: No, I don't mean anything. But I don't think a place'd be any cheerfuller for John Wright's being in it.

190 **COUNTY ATTORNEY:** I'd like to talk more of that a little later. I want to get the lay of things upstairs now. *(Moves to stair door, followed by the two men)*

SHERIFF: I suppose anything Mrs. Peters does'll be all right. She was to take in some clothes for her, you know, and a few little things. We left in such a hurry 195 yesterday.

COUNTY ATTORNEY: Yes, but I would like to see what you take, Mrs. Peters, and keep an eye out for anything that might be of use to us.

MRS. PETERS: Yes, Mr. Henderson. *(The women listen to* 200 *the men's steps on the stairs, then look about the kitchen)*

MRS. HALE: I'd hate to have men coming into my kitchen, snooping around and criticizing. *(Arranges pans under sink which the county attorney had shoved out of place)* 205

MRS. PETERS: Of course it's no more than their duty.

MRS. HALE: Duty's all right, but I guess that deputy sheriff that came out to make the fire might have got a little of this on. *(Gives roller towel a pull)* Wish I'd thought of that sooner. Seems mean to talk about her 210 for not having things slicked up when she had to come away in such a hurry.

MRS. PETERS: *(Going to table at side, lifts one end of towel that covers a pan)* She had bread set. *(Stands still)*

MRS. HALE: *(Her eyes fixed on a loaf of bread outside* 215 *bread-box. Moves slowly toward it)* She was going to put this in there. *(Picks up loaf, then abruptly drops it. In a manner of returning to familiar things)* It's a shame about her fruit. I wonder if it's all gone. *(Gets up on a chair and looks)* I think there's some here that* 220 is all right, Mrs. Peters. Yes—here; *(holding it toward the window)* this is cherries, too. *(Looking again)* I declare I believe that's the only one. *(Gets down, bottle in her hand. Goes to sink and wipes it off on the outside)* She'll feel awful bad after all her hard work in 225 the hot weather. I remember the afternoon I put up my cherries last summer. *(Puts bottle on table. With a sigh starts to sit down in rocking-chair. Before she is seated realizes what chair it is; with a slow look at it, steps back. The chair which she has touched rocks back* 230 *and forth)*

MRS. PETERS: Well, I must get those things from the front room closet. *(Starts to door left, looks into the* *other room, steps back)* You coming with me, Mrs. Hale? You could help me carry them. *(Both women go out; reappear,* MRS. PETERS *carrying a dress and skirt,* MRS. HALE *following with a pair of shoes)*

MRS. PETERS: My, it's cold in there. *(Puts clothes on table, goes up to stove)*

MRS. HALE: *(Holding up skirt and examining it)* Wright was close. I think maybe that's why she kept so much to herself. She didn't even belong to the Ladies Aid. I suppose she felt she couldn't do her part, and then you don't enjoy things when you feel shabby. She used to wear pretty clothes and be lively, when she was Minnie Foster, one of the town girls singing in the choir. But that was—oh, that was thirty years ago. This all you was to take in?

MRS. PETERS: She said she wanted an apron. Funny thing to want, for there isn't much to get you dirty in jail, goodness knows. But I suppose just to make her feel more natural. She said they was in the top drawer in this cupboard. Yes, here. And then her little shawl that always hung behind the door. *(Looks on stair door)* Yes, here it is.

MRS. HALE: *(Abruptly moving toward her)* Mrs. Peters?

MRS. PETERS: Yes, Mrs. Hale?

MRS. HALE: Do you think she did it?

MRS. PETERS: *(In a frightened voice)* Oh, I don't know.

MRS. HALE: Well, I don't think she did. Asking for an apron and her little shawl. Worrying about her fruit.

MRS. PETERS: *(Starts to speak, glances up, where footsteps are heard in the room above. In a low voice)* Mr. Peters says it looks bad for her. Mr. Henderson is awful sarcastic in a speech and he'll make fun of her sayin' she didn't wake up.

MRS. HALE: Well, I guess John Wright didn't wake when they was slipping that rope under his neck.

MRS. PETERS: No, it's strange. It must have been done awful crafty and still. They say it was such a—funny way to kill a man, rigging it all up like that.

MRS. HALE: That's just what Mr. Hale said. There was a gun in the house. He says that's what he can't understand.

MRS. PETERS: Mr. Henderson said coming out that what was needed for the case was a motive; something to show anger, or—sudden feeling.

MRS. HALE: *(Standing by table)* Well, I don't see any signs of anger around here, but *(puts hand on dish-towel in middle of table, stands looking at table, one half of which is clean, the other half messy)* It's wiped to here. *(Makes a move as if to finish work, then turns and looks at loaf of bread beside the bread-box. Drops towel. In that voice of coming back to familiar things)* Wonder how they are finding things upstairs. I hope she had it a little more red-up up there. You know, it seems kind of *sneaking.* Locking her up in town and then coming out here and trying to get her own house to turn against her!

MRS. PETERS: But Mrs. Hale, the law is the law.

MRS. HALE: I spose't is. *(Unbuttoning her coat)* Better loosen up your things, Mrs. Peters. You won't feel them when you go out.

MRS. PETERS: *(Taking off fur tippet, goes to hang it on hook at back of room, stands looking at the under part of the small table)* She was piecing a quilt. *(Brings large sewing basket to table front and they look at the bright pieces)*

300 **MRS. HALE:** It's log cabin pattern. Pretty, isn't it? I wonder if she was goin' to quilt it or just knot it? (*Footsteps have been heard coming down the stairs. The* SHERIFF *enters followed by* HALE *and* HENDERSON)

SHERIFF: They wonder if she was going to quilt it or just 305 knot it. (*The men laugh, the women look abashed*)

COUNTY ATTORNEY: (*Rubbing his hands over the stove*) Frank's fire didn't do much up there, did it? Well, let's go out to the barn and get that cleared up. (*Exeunt men door rear*)

310 **MRS. HALE:** (*Resentfully*) I don't know as there's anything so strange, our takin' up our time with little things while we're waiting for them to get the evidence. (*Sits down, smoothing out block with decision*) I don't see as it's anything to laugh about.

315 **MRS. PETERS:** (*Apologetically*) Of course they've got awful important things on their minds. (*Pulls up a chair and sits by the table*)

MRS. HALE: (*Examining another block*) Mrs. Peters, look at this one. Here, this is the one she was work-320 ing on, and look at the sewing! All the rest of it has been so nice and even. And look at this! It's all over the place! Why, it looks as if she didn't know what she was about! (*After she has said this they look at each other, then start to glance back at the door. After an 325 instant* MRS. HALE *has pulled at a knot and ripped the sewing*)

MRS. PETERS: Oh, what are you doing, Mrs. Hale?

MRS. HALE: (*Mildly*) Just pulling out a stitch or two that's not sewed very good. (*Threading a needle*) Bad 330 sewing always made me fidgety.

MRS. PETERS: (*Nervously*) I don't think we ought to touch things.

MRS. HALE: I'll just finish up this end. (*Suddenly stopping and leaning forward*) Mrs. Peters?

335 **MRS. PETERS:** Yes, Mrs. Hale?

MRS. HALE: What do you suppose she was so nervous about?

MRS. PETERS: Oh—I don't know. I don't know as she was nervous. I sometimes sew awful queer when I'm just tired. (MRS. HALE *starts to say something, looks* 340 *at her, compresses her lips a little, goes on sewing*) Well, I must get these things wrapped up. They may be through sooner than we think. (*Piling apron and other things up together*) I wonder where I can find a piece of paper, and string. 345

MRS. HALE: In that cupboard, maybe.

MRS. PETERS: (*Looking in cupboard*) Why, here's a bird-cage. (*Holds it up*) Did she have a bird, Mrs. Hale?

MRS. HALE: Why, I don't know whether she did or not—I've not been here for so long. There was a man 350 around last year selling canaries cheap, but I don't know as she took one; maybe she did. She used to sing real pretty herself.

MRS. PETERS: (*Glancing around*) Seems funny to think of a bird here. But she must have had one, or why 355 would she have a cage? I wonder what happened to it.

MRS. HALE: I s'pose maybe the cat got it.

MRS. PETERS: No, she didn't have a cat. She's got that feeling some people have about cats—being afraid of them. My cat got in her room and she was real upset 360 and asked me to take it out.

MRS. HALE: My sister Bessie was like that. Queer, ain't it?

MRS. PETERS: (*Examining cage*) Why, look at this door. It's broke. One hinge is pulled apart.

MRS. HALE: (*Looking too*) Looks as if someone must 365 have been rough with it.

MRS. PETERS: Why, yes. (*Puts cage on table*)

MRS. HALE: I wish if they're going to find any evidence they'd be about it. I don't like this place.

MRS. PETERS: But I'm awful glad you came with me, 370 Mrs. Hale. It would be lonesome for me sitting here alone.

MRS. HALE: It would, wouldn't it? (*Dropping sewing, voice falling*) But I tell you what I do wish, Mrs. Pe-

should think she would 'a wanted a bird. But what do **400**
you suppose went with it?

MRS. PETERS: I don't know, unless it got sick and died.
*(She reaches over and swings the broken door, swings it
again, both women watch it)*

MRS. HALE: You weren't raised round here, were you? **405**
(MRS. PETERS shakes her head) You didn't know—her?

MRS. PETERS: Not till they brought her yesterday.

MRS. HALE: She—come to think of it, she was kind of
like a bird herself—real sweet and pretty, but kind of
timid and—fluttery. How—she—did—change. *(Si-* **410**
*lence; then as if struck by a happy thought and relieved
to get back to everyday things)* Tell you what, Mrs.
Peters, why don't you take the quilt in with you? It
might take up her mind.

MRS. PETERS: Why, I think that's a real nice idea, Mrs. **415**
Hale. There couldn't possibly be any objection to it,
could there? Now, just what would I take? I wonder if
her patches are in here—and her things. *(Both look in
sewing basket)*

MRS. HALE: Here's some red. I expect this has got sew- **420**
ing things in it. *(Brings out a fancy box)* What a pretty
box. Looks like something somebody would give you.
Maybe her scissors are in here. *(Opens box. Suddenly
puts her hand to her nose)* Why—*(MRS. PETERS bends
nearer, then turns her face away)* There's something **425**
wrapped up in this piece of silk.

MRS. PETERS: Why, this isn't her scissors.

MRS. HALE: *(Lifting the silk)* Oh, Mrs. Peters—it's *(MRS.
PETERS bends closer)*

MRS. PETERS: It's the bird. **430**

MRS. HALE: *(Jumping up)* But, Mrs. Peters—look at it!
Its neck! Look at its neck! It's all—other side *to.*

MRS. PETERS: Somebody—wrung—its—neck. *(Their
eyes meet. A look of growing comprehension, of horror.
Steps are heard outside.* MRS. HALE *slips box under* **435**
quilt pieces, and sinks into her chair. Enter SHERIFF
and COUNTY ATTORNEY. MRS. PETERS *rises)*

375 ters. I wish I had come over sometimes when *she* was
here. I—*(looking around the room)*—wish I had.

MRS. PETERS: But of course you were awful busy, Mrs.
Hale—your house and your children.

MRS. HALE: I could've come. I stayed away because
380 it weren't cheerful—and that's why I ought to have
come. I—I've never liked this place. Maybe because
it's down in a hollow and you don't see the road. I
dunno what it is, but it's a lonesome place and always
was. I wish I had come over to see Minnie Foster
385 sometimes. I can see now— *(shakes her head)*

MRS. PETERS: Well, you mustn't reproach yourself, Mrs.
Hale. Somehow we just don't see how it is with other
folks until—something comes up.

MRS. HALE: Not having children makes less work—but
390 it makes a quiet house, and Wright out to work all
day, and no company when he did come in. Did you
know John Wright, Mrs. Peters?

MRS. PETERS: Not to know him; I've seen him in town.
They say he was a good man.

395 **MRS. HALE:**   Yes—good; he didn't drink, and kept his
word as well as most, I guess, and paid his debts.
But he was a hard man, Mrs. Peters. Just to pass the
time of day with him—*(shivers)* Like a raw wind that
gets to the bone. *(Pauses, her eye falling on the cage)* I

COUNTY ATTORNEY: *(As one turning from serious things to little pleasantries)* Well, ladies, have you decided whether she was going to quilt it or knot it?

440

MRS. PETERS: We think she was going to—knot it.

COUNTY ATTORNEY: Well, that's interesting, I am sure. *(Looking at bird-cage)* Has the bird flown?

445 **MRS. HALE:** *(Piling more quilt pieces over the box)* We think the—cat got it.

COUNTY ATTORNEY: *(Preoccupied)* Is there a cat? (MRS. HALE *glances in a quick covert way at* MRS. PETERS)

450 **MRS. PETERS:** Well, not *now*. They're superstitious, you know. They leave.

COUNTY ATTORNEY: *(To* PETERS, *in the manner of continuing an interrupted conversation)* No sign at all of anyone having come from the outside. Their own

455 rope. Now let's go up again and go over it piece by piece. *(They start upstairs)* It would have to have been someone who knew just the—(MRS. PETERS *sinks into her chair. The two women sit there not looking at one another, but as if peering into something and at the*

460 *same time holding back. When they talk now it is in the manner of feeling their way over strange ground, as if afraid of what they are saying, but as if they can not help saying it)*

MRS. HALE: She liked the bird. She was going to bury it

465 in that pretty box.

MRS. PETERS: *(In a whisper)* When I was a girl—my kitten—there was a boy took a hatchet, and before my eyes—and before I could get there—*(covers her face an instant)* If they hadn't held me back I would have—

470 *(catches herself, looks upstairs where steps are heard, falters weakly)*—hurt him.

MRS. HALE: *(With a slow look around her)* I wonder how it would seem never to have had any children around. *(Pause)* No, Wright wouldn't like the bird—a thing

475 that sang. She used to sing. He killed that, too.

MRS. PETERS: *(Moving uneasily)* We don't know who killed the bird.

MRS. HALE: I knew John Wright.

MRS. PETERS: It was an awful thing was done in this house that night, Mrs. Hale. Killing a man while he 480 slept, slipping a rope around his neck that choked the life out of him.

MRS. HALE: His neck. Choked the life out of him. *(Her hand goes out and rests on the bird-cage)*

MRS. PETERS: *(With rising voice)* We don't know who 485 killed him. We don't *know*.

MRS. HALE: *(Her own feeling not interrupted)* If there'd been years and years of nothing, then a bird to sing to you, it would be awful—still, after the bird was still.

MRS. PETERS: *(Something within her speaking)* I know 490 what stillness is. When we homesteaded in Dakota, and my first baby died—after he was two years old, and me with no other then—

MRS. HALE: *(Moving)* How soon do you suppose they'll be through, looking for the evidence? 495

MRS. PETERS: I know what stillness is. *(Pulling herself back)* The law has got to punish crime, Mrs. Hale.

MRS. HALE: *(Not as if answering that)* I wish you'd seen Minnie Foster when she wore a white dress with blue ribbons and stood up there in the choir and sang. 500 *(Suddenly looking around the room)* Oh, I *wish* I'd come over here once in a while! That was a crime! That was a crime! Who's going to punish that?

MRS. PETERS: *(Looking upstairs)* We mustn't—take on.

MRS. HALE: I might have known she needed help! I 505 know how things can be—for women. I tell you, it's queer, Mrs. Peters. We live close together and we live far apart. We all go through the same things—it's all just a different kind of the same thing— *(Brushes her eyes, then seeing the bottle of fruit, reaches out for it)* If 510 I was you I wouldn't tell her her fruit was gone. Tell her it *ain't*. Tell her it's all right. Take this in to prove it to her. She—she may never know whether it was broke or not.

MRS. PETERS: *(Picks up the bottle, looks about for some-* 515 *thing to wrap it in; takes petticoat from clothes brought*

from front room, very nervously begins winding that around it. In a false voice) My, it's a good thing the men couldn't hear us. Wouldn't they just laugh! Getting all
520 stirred up over a little thing like a—dead canary. As if that could have anything to do with—with—wouldn't they *laugh! (The men are heard coming down stairs)*

MRS. HALE: *(Muttering)* Maybe they would—maybe they wouldn't.

525 **COUNTY ATTORNEY:**   No, Peters, it's all perfectly clear except a reason for doing it. But you know juries when it comes to women. If there was some definite thing. Something to show—something to make a story about—a thing that would connect up with this
530 strange way of doing it—*(The women's eyes meet for an instant. Enter HALE from outer door)*

HALE: Well, I've got the team around. Pretty cold out there.

COUNTY ATTORNEY: I'm going to stay here a while by
535 myself. *(To SHERIFF)* You can send Frank out for me, can't you? I want to go over everything. I'm not satisfied that we can't do better.

SHERIFF: Do you want to see what Mrs. Peters is going to take in?

540 **COUNTY ATTORNEY:**   *(Goes to the table. Picks up apron, laughs)* Oh, I guess they're not very dangerous things the ladies have picked out. *(Moves a few things about, disturbing the quilt pieces which cover the box. Steps back)* No, Mrs. Peters doesn't need supervising. For

that matter, a sheriff's wife is married to the law. Ever 545 think of it that way, Mrs. Peters?

MRS. PETERS: Not—just that way.

SHERIFF: *(Chuckling)* Married to the law. *(Moves toward front room)* I just want you to come in here a minute, George. We ought to take a look at these 550 windows.

COUNTY ATTORNEY: Oh, windows!

SHERIFF: We'll be right out, Mr. Hale. *(Exit HALE door rear. SHERIFF follows the COUNTY ATTORNEY through door left. The two women's eyes follow them 555 out. MRS. HALE rises, hands tightly together, looking intensely at MRS. PETERS, whose eyes make a slow turn, finally meeting MRS. HALE's. A moment MRS. HALE holds her, then her own eyes point the way to the spot where the box is concealed. Suddenly MRS. 560 PETERS throws back quilt pieces and tries to put box in the bag she is wearing. It is too big. She opens box, starts to take bird out, cannot touch it, goes to pieces, stands there helpless. Sound of a knob turning in the other room. MRS. HALE snatches box and puts it in the 565 pocket of her big coat. Enter COUNTY ATTORNEY and SHERIFF.*

COUNTY ATTORNEY: *(Facetiously)* Well, Henry, at least we found out that she was not going to quilt it. She was going to—what is it you call it, ladies? 570

MRS. HALE: *(Hand against her pocket)* We call it—knot it, Mr. Henderson.

Writing from Reading

Summarize

1 Scan the script for references to Mrs. Wright's life. What do you know about her before and after her marriage?

2 List the "trifles" in this play. What do they have in common?

3 Who is the central character in the play? Who stands in opposition to this character?

Analyze Craft

4 What is the significance of setting the play during winter?

5 What is the significance of the kitchen as a setting for this play?

Analyze Voice

6 Identify an exchange of dialogue that you found particularly powerful and explain why. How does it promote or portray the conflict and theme of the play?

Synthesize Summary and Analysis

7 Compare the themes of "Trifles" to those of Kate Chopin's "The Story of an Hour" (Chapter 6). How do Glaspell and

Chopin, writing in the same country and at roughly the same time, approach the issues of the thwarted housewife?

Interpret the Play

8 What is the attitude of the women toward the men, the men toward the women?

9 What is the relationship between Mrs. Hale's regrets and her instinct to protect Mrs. Wright?

10 Which character goes through the most dramatic change in the course of the play? What is the change, and how does it come about?

11 How are power and powerlessness represented in the play?

"There's something in there that's very sensitive to who you are, and things that are important to you. Attach yourself to that person and own that. So when you're reading, that's you. We've all been there. So find yourself in the play. Get inside the play, don't stay outside the play." Conversation with Ruben Santiago-Hudson

ELEMENTS OF DRAMA

A first reading of the script of *Trifles* reveals a problem—a mystery to be solved—and makes clear the basic elements of the **plot.** A man is dead; his wife is under suspicion. The central incident in *Trifles*—the death of Mr. Wright—occurs before the onstage action begins and is therefore introduced by means of **exposition,** a literary technique by which a character presents necessary background information. In addition to exposition, the plot unfolds in **dialogue,** the conversations that occur between the characters. When you read a play, notice how the complications the characters face crystallize in a **conflict,** leading to **rising action,** an intensification of the predicament. The moment of greatest tension is the play's **climax,** or turning point. Frequently, the climax causes a character to change in some way or at least to gain new understanding as a result of the conflict or crisis. The conclusion of the play, or the resolution of conflicts that follows the climax, is referred to as the **dénouement,** a French word that literally means "untying." In the dénouement, the knots of the story are untied and conflicts are further resolved. A longer play than *Trifles* might also include a **subplot** or two—secondary stories that involve characters other than the central figure in the play.

As you read through a play the first time, get to know the **characters.** The list of characters is found at the beginning of the play. (In the classical period of Greek theater, discussed in Chapter 32, this list would be called **Dramatis Personae,** or "people of the play.") Just as in fiction, you will find a **protagonist,** who is the central character (the lead actor in the play), and an **antagonist,** who is a character or force that opposes the protagonist. Instructions on how actors are to move and position themselves onstage, as well as how they are to deliver certain lines—the **stage directions**—usually appear in parentheses and in italics in the **script,** which consists mainly of dialogue and staging instructions. At various points in *Trifles,* Glaspell instructs actors to unbutton a coat, point, look at the rocker, twitch, or speak stiffly. Imagine the actors as they interact on the **set** and the play's **setting**—the location of the action. In *Trifles* Glaspell describes the set she envisions down to a loaf of bread beside the bread-box and a dish towel on the table.

Finally, consider the theme of the play, the dramatic, or central, question that drives the story of the play. For *Trifles* you have to ask yourself what kind of woman, under what sort of pressure, would commit murder? The desperation of the housewife's act is anything but a "trifle"; her situation was profound enough to yield lethal results.

READING FOR THE STAGE

After reading an entire play and beginning to explore the story line and how the characters make sense to you, you are ready to go deeper into the matter of understanding a play in all its elements and writing about it with an audience in mind. Although the experience of a play begins with the opportunity for you to be, as Seldes says in her interview, "alone with [the play]" in a way "that frees your imagination," its success or failure is on the stage, where a lot of its energy and—at its best—its electric feel comes from the vitality of the immediate interaction of live actors with a live audience. The term *drama* comes from the Greek word for "performing an action" or "doing"—and playwrights almost always intend their work to be brought to life on a stage by actors (except in the case of closet dramas, which are plays written to be read aloud rather than performed). Even the term we use to refer to the author of a dramatic work—*playwright* (not play-*write*)—reflects the three-dimensionality of a play: a *wright* is a medieval term for one skilled in manufacturing three-dimensional items, such as a shipwright or a wheelwright. The word suggests "maker," or "craftsman"; a carefully built thing that has been well *wrought*.

> **"A play exists on the page completely as an artwork if it is an artwork, but for anybody to really involve themselves in it . . . it has to be performed."** Conversation with Edward Albee

When you read the play in the context of the stage, try to hear the voices of the actors. Decide if the words *I love you,* for example, are spoken as if for the first time by a younger romantic or as if for the thousandth time by an old seducer. See the characters' movements across the stage, the clothes they wear, the spotlights on them, and the objects they hold. Considering these extra dimensions, you are staging the play in what the critic Francis Fergusson called "the theater of the mind." As you read for the stage, imagine yourself as the actors, the director, and the audience.

- As the actor you're onstage delivering lines to the other actors and responding to an audience
- As the director you're trying to draw the audience into the play as a whole through lighting, costumes, setting, and characters
- As the audience you're seeing actors on a stage and responding to how you are drawn into the play

Once you've imagined yourself as the director, the actors, and the audience, you can evaluate the director's approach, the actor's efforts and energy, and the attention of the audience as the plot unfolds.

Dramas can occur on a **proscenium stage,** a raised platform with a missing fourth wall through which we as audience watch the action (see Chapter 33 on Shakespeare). In other cases, the play may be presented **in the round,** where the audience surrounds the actors, or in an **amphitheater,** where the audience looks down on the drama (see Chapter 32 on Greek drama). When the philosopher Aristotle asserted that much of the

Proscenium stage

Theater in the round

Amphitheater

THE ORIGINS OF DRAMA

Drama grew in part out of pre-classical Greek religious ceremonies and the public performances of poetry, Homer's *Iliad* and *Odyssey* in particular. These were not put into written form until after the Homeric epics were copied down in the sixth century B.C.E.; thanks to the collectors and librarians of the early Arab world, scrolls of papyrus with the texts of poems and the play scripts remained safe in libraries across the Mediterranean long after the decline of Greek civilization.

physical action of Greek drama must take place offstage, this was in part a function of necessity. The ancient Greeks could not mount battle or death scenes persuasively in their amphitheaters—and so the audience learned of such events after the fact. No contemporary director would miss a chance to stage a combat or a love scene, but Glaspell apparently chose to keep the second-floor rooms of the farm offstage because it simplifies the issues of production. First, the production needs only one set—which allows for economy. Second, when the men go offstage and upstairs, they're gone; the women can pursue their inquiries alone. No matter the staging, even the simplest of dramas is complex in conception.

"I don't think that the theater is, necessarily, only about entertainment. I think it's entertainment that reaches the soul."

Conversation with Arthur Miller

TYPES OF DRAMA

To read drama critically, you need, in addition to the literary elements of plot and character, a basic vocabulary of theatrical forms and conventions. The two most common dramatic forms are tragedy and comedy, and both date at least as far back as the drama of ancient Greece (Chapter 32).

- In **tragedy,** characters face serious and important challenges that end in disastrous failure or defeat for the protagonist.
- In **comedy,** life usually turns out well for the main character, and the primary purpose of the play is to amuse the audience.

Within these two large groupings there are a number of variations and blendings, such as **tragicomedies** (in which the protagonist isn't defeated but there is a downturn in his or her situation), **melodramas** (in which the forces of good and evil are in absolute and often violent opposition), and **problem plays** (which explore social issues, such as *Trifles'* exploration of a woman's place and power in the home).

"The heart of drama . . . has been . . . really since it began . . . character types and the conflict and the encounter with character types. And I don't care whether you go back to . . . the Greek theater . . . you have . . . this conflict of characters." Conversation with
Edwin Wilson

TRAGEDY

The structure of Greek tragedy shapes tragic drama even today (a fuller discussion of Greek tragedy can be found in Chapter 32). Tragedy in real life might be brought on by a natural disaster or wartime or personal heartache, but tragedy in drama begins and ends with the qualities found in the main character: the **hero.** A hero is more than just the protagonist, or lead character, in a play. The hero's nature must be such that in some way the audience feels admiration for his or her qualities (wisdom, generosity, bravery, and love of family) and must feel compassion and fear when the character falls. The audience finds the hero at least in some degree sympathetic.

In a tragedy, the hero stands in conflict with forces larger than himself. These might be an unjust society (as in many modern plays, see Chapter 35) or it might be another human being, a villain (as in the conflict between Othello and Iago in Shakespeare's *Othello,* Chapter 33). Often the adversary might consist of fate itself, as in Sophocles' *Oedipus the King,* about whose hero it was prophesied that he would kill his father and marry his mother (Chapter 32). However, *external* forces don't turn the hero into a **tragic hero.** Rather, from the beginning there is something about the hero's character that undermines what the audience finds sympathetic, and this **tragic flaw**—be it arrogance or jealousy or stubbornness—speeds along the hero's downfall.

"What we try to do is illuminate something so that people can make up their own minds based upon the reality of the situation rather than the mythology. And if one can do that, it's enough."
Conversation with Arthur Miller

Sophocles' *Oedipus the King* is the very prototype of the tragic mode of drama, from the five-act structure to the noble position of the central figure and the inevitable trajectory of decline. The proximity to power is a significant attribute of the hero. Even today we can see the voyeuristic fascination with the fall from grace of a politician because of a sex scandal or a celebrity because of drug abuse or violence. In classical tragic drama, however, the hero proves his or her heroic stature by accepting the justice of the punishment for mortal flaws. Several tragedies and the many faces of the tragic hero will be more fully studied in chapters and casebooks on ancient Greek drama, Shakespeare, and modern drama that appear later in this volume.

COMEDY

Comedy stands as the countervailing force to tragedy. Laughter illuminates the human condition just as effectively as tears. As in tragedy, the main characters will possess weaknesses, though unlike tragic figures, the main characters fall short of heroism and do not appear to be the larger-than-life people who show what our best selves can be. These characters are much more likely to prick our pride with the revelation that we are no more heroic than is the frog who requires the princess's kiss. To be sure, we can find comic characters written into a tragedy for **comic relief,** but a comedy in general is a play that makes us laugh at our flaws and ultimately forgive ourselves for our foibles.

Satyr plays—named for the half horse/half man mythological characters full of mischief and vulgar sexuality—employed excess, unrestrained sexuality, and outlandish characters. They might well be akin to the exaggerated presentation of modern-day **burlesque,** with its sexual innuendo, striptease, and **slapstick** or **farce.** A man who slips on a banana peel, or a character with a three-foot nose, belongs to the broad comic mode of burlesque. Satyr plays were part of Greek festivals, and out of these grew Aristophanes' great comedies of invective, ridicule, and political satire, the most famous of which is *Lysistrata,* in which the wives of soldiers withhold sex from their husbands until the men are willing to end the war. Some **satiric comedies** can be violent, crude, and nasty—biting commentaries on the human condition without any guarantee that good will prevail.

"When you are reading a . . . comedy, it helps to know something about the history of the time in which it was written . . . [to understand] what was making the public laugh, not when they were in the theater? Who was the king at that time? Who was the queen? Who were the serfs? Who were the slaves? Who were the masters? What was the situation politically? And so on. If you have that in your head, or if you . . . look it up, I think it makes all plays more interesting." Conversation with Marian Seldes

Other forms of comedies evolved from this early Greek theater, such as the **comedy of manners,** which shines an indulgent light on the hypocrisy of the social elite, and, much later, **restoration drama**—bawdy plays of fallen virtue and infidelity, which played to sold-out houses in London after the Puritans were displaced from power. Today we're familiar with **romantic comedy,** where two would-be/should-be lovers find each other after a series of misunderstandings and false starts. A play such as this gently pokes fun at the difficulties of finding love and of keeping one's dignity in the search for it. Whether a play uses **high comedy**—wordplay and wit—or **low comedy**—gags and pratfalls—its storyline contains the unexpected; the French philosopher Henri Bergson argued that this unexpectedness was a crucial part of the comedic mode. Further, the one all-embracing definition of comedy, separating this mode from tragedy, is that it is a kind of play that ends happily—or, in any case, with its main players still alive.

Before you enter into the high tragedy of Sophocles and Shakespeare in the coming chapters or the tragicomedy of Edward Albee in the next chapter, we offer you a comedy by the contemporary playwright David Ives.

David Ives (b. 1951)

David Ives was born in Chicago and received his college degree from Northwestern University. While there, he began writing plays. After three years of editing the magazine *Foreign Affairs,* Ives earned an M.F.A. in playwriting from Yale. He is best known for his one-act comedies, such as those collected in *All in the Timing,* the collection that brought him the John Gassner Playwriting Award. In addition to his plays, Ives has contributed articles to magazines including *The New Yorker* and *New York* magazine, and he has also published two children's books. He lives in New York City and has taught at Columbia University.

AS YOU READ   Consider how slang and stylized language contribute to the comedy.

Moby Dude, OR: The Three-Minute Whale (2004)

SFX: sound of waves and gulls.
Distant ship's bell.

Our Narrator is a stoned-out surfer of seventeen.

OUR NARRATOR: *Call me Ishmael,* dude. Yes, Mrs. Podgorski, I *did* read *Moby-Dick* over the summer like I was supposed to. It was bohdacious. Actually, y'know, it's "Moby-*hyphen*-Dick." The title's got a little hyphen before the "Dick." And what is the meaning of this dash before the "Dick"? *WHOAAA!* Another mystery in this awesome American masterpiece, a peerless allegorical saga of mortal courage, metaphysical ambiguity and maniacal obsession! *What,* Mrs. Podgorski? You don't believe I really *read* Herman Melville's

5

10   *Moby-Dick Or The Whale?* Five hundred sixty-two pages, fourteen ounces, published 1851, totally tanked its first weekend, re-released in the 1920s as one of the world's gnarliest works of Art? You think I copped all this like off the back of the tome or by watching
15   the crappy 1956 film starring Gregory Peck? Mrs. P., you been chasing my tail since middle school, do *I* get all testy? Do *I* say, what is the plot in under two minutes—besides a whale and a hyphen? *Moby-Dick* in two minutes, huh? Okay, kyool. Let's rip.

        (*SFX: ship's bell, close up and sharp, to signal the start and a ticking watch, underneath. Very fast.*)

20   Fade in the boonies of Massachusetts, eighteen-something. Young dude possibly named Ishmael, like the Bible, meets-cute with, TAA-DAA!, *Queequeg,* a South Sea cannibal with a heart of gold.

        (*SFX: cutesy voice going "Awwww."*)

Maybe they're gay.

        (*SFX: tongue slurp.*)

25   Or maybe they represent some east-west, pagan-Christian duality action. Anyway, the two newfound bros go to Mass and hear a sermon about Jonah . . .

        (*SFX: one second of church organ.*)

Biblical tie-in, then ship out on Christmas Day (*could be symbolical!*) aboard the USS *Pequod* with its mys-
30   terious wacko Captain Ahab . . .

        (*SFX: madman laughter.*)

. . . who—*backstory*—is goofyfoot because the equally mysterious momboosaloid white whale Moby-like-the-singer Dick bit his leg off.

        (*SFX: chomp.*)

Freudian castration action. I mean he's big and he's
35   got sperm and his last name is "Dick," right? Moby is also a metaphor for God, Nature, Truth, obsessisical love, the world, the past, and white people. Check out Pip the Negro cabin boy who by a *fluke* . . .

        (*SFX: rimshot.*)

. . . goes wacko too. Ahab says,

        (*SFX: echo effect.*)

"Bring me the head of the Great White Whale and you 40 *win this prize!"*

        (*SFX: echo effect out, cash register sound.*)

The crew is stoked, by *NOT* first-mate like-the-coffee-Starbuck. Ahab wants the big one, Starbuck wants the whale juice. Idealism versus capitalism.

        (*SFX: an impressed "Whoo."*)

Radical. Queequeg tells the carpenter to build him a 45 coffin shaped like a canoe.

        (*SFX: theremin.*)

Foreshadowing! Then lots of chapters everybody skips about the scientology of whales.

        (*SFX: yawn.*)

Cut to . . .

(SFX: trumpet fanfare.)

50 Page 523, the Pacific Ocean. *"Surf's up!"* Ahab sights the Dick. He's totally amped. The boards hit the waves, the crew snakes the Dick for three whole days, bottom of the third Ahab is ten-toes-on-the-nose, he's aggro, Moby goes aerial, Ahab's in the zone, he
55 fires his choicest harpoon, the rope does a 360 round his neck, Ahab crushes out, Moby totals the *Pequod*, everybody eats it 'cept our faithful narrator Ishmael who boogies to safety on Queequeg's coffin . . .

(SFX: resounding echo effect, deeper voice.)

"AND I ONLY AM ESCAPED ALONE TO TELL THEE!"

(Resume normal voice.)

Roll final credits. The End.   60

(SFX: ship's bell to signal end of fight. End ticking watch.)

So what do you say, Mrs. Podgorski? You want to like hang and catch a cup of Starbucks sometime . . . ?—*Tubular!*

End of play

Writing from Reading

Summarize

1 A student attempts to summarize Herman Melville's massive masterpiece *Moby-Dick* in under three minutes. Why would that seem appropriate given the life of the average student today?

Analyze Craft

2 How does the brevity contribute to the comic effect?

Analyze Voice

3 Make a list of surfer terminology. Make a list of mock-serious critical terms. How do these contribute to the voice of the *narrator*?

Synthesize Summary and Analysis

4 Take a look at a description of the Herman Melville novel, *Moby-Dick*.

In what ways does the play take liberties with the original material? In what ways does it keep the integrity of the material?

Interpret the Play

5 The playwright intends to amuse us. What commentary on reading and education does Ives make in the play?

Suggestions for Writing

1. Imagine turning a poem (Robert Browning's "My Last Duchess," for example) or a story (such as Anton Chekhov's "Rapture") into a play. What are the issues you will face in terms of physical (re)presentation?
2. Speculate on the role of theater in today's society. Is it important to have traditional staged theater? Has theater been sidelined by movies, TV, the Internet, and YouTube? Speculate on the theatrical aspects of all of these, using specific examples.

31 Writing about Drama

FROM READING TO WRITING

When you write about what you read, first think about the title of the work. (What does *The Zoo Story* say to you?) Find out something about the author. (Edward Albee is a living playwright. He's still writing plays today. In an interview Albee gave for *Times Talks*, he says that "entertainment is misunderstood" and he wants to write plays that make people think. His plays shaped American "experimental theater.") Then think about the context in which the play was written. (Albee wrote *The Zoo Story* in the 1950s and set it in the same time period. It is considered a tragicomedy.) Annotate the work and record your general impressions of the play. (As one student writes, "The surprise ending was really upsetting. I thought the guy was going to try to kill Peter till the end. I was left with a really uneasy feeling about why Jerry would do that.") Your annotations of the play will help you think about how the play works and what it means to you.

I HOPED . . . and I don't really know why I expected the dog to under-stand anything, much less my motivations. . . . I hoped that the dog would understand. (PETER *seems to be hypnotized*) It's just . . . it's just that . . . (JERRY *is abnormally tense, now*) . . . it's just that if you can't deal with people, you have to make a start somewhere. WITH ANIMALS! (*Much faster now, and like a conspirator*) Don't you see? A person has to have some way of dealing with SOMETHING. If not with people . . . SOMETHING.

—*from* The Zoo Story *by Edward Albee*

Writing about drama requires a slight change from the way you would normally prepare to write about a work of literature. In addition to your discussion of the text, you must also remember that drama is performance. It comes alive on the stage, not the page. Of the three principal literary modes (fiction, poetry, drama), drama relies most on voice. The actors must enter into the spirit and style of a role; a director should be able to communicate his or her interpretation of a play. To convey that attitude and interpretation, the director and actor establish a focal point of performance—a way of staging (and sometimes improvising on) a text. To write about drama, we do much the same; we imagine the text we are reading as if it were being performed.

CONTINUED ON PAGE 1042

"Writing is a way of thinking."

—Conversation with theater critic Edwin Wilson, available on video at connect.mcgraw-hill.com

Edward Albee *...Art changes people if they wish to be changed.*

A Conversation on Writing

The Zoo Story and the Writing Life

Well, I wrote poetry from the age of eight to twenty-eight when I quit because I was getting better but not better enough, and I wrote two terrible novels in my teens, really very bad novels . . . and since I decided I was a creative writer, which meant I didn't have to be able to think coherently in a straight line . . . essays were beyond me too . . . I started writing plays. . . . When *The Zoo Story* opened in German in Berlin and got good reviews and it opened in New York in English and got good reviews, I guess it encouraged me to think maybe . . . [I] should go on with this.

Entertainment Is Misunderstood

I think a playwright's obligation is to be coherent, to not waste people's time, to do something onstage that makes people think, makes them perhaps reconsider some of their values—accept change, not accept change—to have something in which they are participating, not just some kind of escapist entertainment that will just slide right off the mind. . . . Entertainment is misunderstood. Entertainment seems these days to mean something at which you do not have to think, at which you don't have any troubling experiences. But if art isn't engaging or troubling in some sense, it is a total waste of time.

The Experience in the Text

The intention is there in the text. The intention is the experience of the play that I had while I was writing it. Because when I write a play, . . . I see it, I hear it as a play being performed in front of me, and that's what I want to see on the stage—the same experience that I had while writing it.

This interview with Edward Albee was conducted by Jesse Green for the *Times Talks* program sponsored by *The New York Times* on the occasion of Albee's eightieth birthday.

Edward Albee (b. 1928) was adopted as an infant into a wealthy New York family. His privileged upbringing included limousine rides to see Broadway productions and access to his parents' library, even though the young Albee got in trouble for actually reading the books that his parents maintained for looks only. After expulsion from three prep schools and Trinity College in Connecticut, he had a falling out with his parents that caused a twenty-year estrangement. Living on his own, Albee worked odd jobs until he wrote his first play, *The Zoo Story,* as a thirtieth birthday present to himself. Its debut in America brought the freshest approach to drama on the American stage since Eugene O'Neill and Thornton Wilder. Financially supported to begin with by stipends from his grandparents, Albee made a successful career of writing and, in his long productive life as a playwright, has been awarded three Pulitzer Prizes. He might have received a fourth had not the recommendation of the committee to award the Pulitzer Prize to arguably his best and most important play, *Who's Afraid of Virginia Woolf?* (1962), been overturned because of the play's controversial sexual content. In 1966 the play was made into a movie starring Elizabeth Taylor and Richard Burton. Although Albee's plays have met with varying levels of success, *The Zoo Story* has remained significant to American drama, and some credit it as one of the biggest influence on off-Broadway works. In 2005 Albee was awarded the Special Tony Award for Lifetime Achievement.

AS YOU READ   Ask yourself what the play's title conveys, and why Albee might have wished to call his play a "story." Make notes about how you would move the actors around on the set if you were directing this play.

The Zoo Story (1958)

—for William Flanagan

CHARACTERS

PETER *A man in his early forties, neither fat nor gaunt, neither handsome nor homely. He wears tweeds, smokes a pipe, carries horn-rimmed glasses. Although he is moving into middle age, his dress and his manner would suggest a man younger.*

JERRY *A man in his late thirties, not poorly dressed, but carelessly. What was once a trim and lightly muscled body has begun to go to fat; and while he is no longer handsome, it is evident that he once was. His fall from physical grace should not suggest debauchery; he has, to come closest to it, a great weariness.*

THE SCENE *It is Central Park; a Sunday afternoon in summer; the present. There are two park benches, one toward either side of the stage; they both face the audience. Behind them: foliage, trees, sky. At the beginning, Peter is seated on one of the benches.*

(As the curtain rises, PETER *is seated on the bench stage-right. He is reading a book. He stops reading, cleans his glasses, goes back to reading.* JERRY *enters.)*

JERRY: I've been to the zoo. (PETER *doesn't notice*) I said, I've been to the zoo. MISTER, I'VE BEEN TO THE ZOO!

PETER: Hm? . . . What? . . . I'm sorry, were you talking
5   to me?

JERRY: I went to the zoo, and then I walked until I came here. Have I been walking north?

PETER: *(Puzzled)* North? Why . . . I . . . I think so. Let me see.

JERRY: *(Pointing past the audience)* Is that Fifth   10
Avenue?

PETER: Why yes; yes, it is.

JERRY: And what is that cross street there; that one, to the right?

PETER: That? Oh, that's Seventy-fourth Street.   15

JERRY: And the zoo is around Sixty-fifth Street; so, I've been walking north.

PETER: *(Anxious to get back to his reading)* Yes; it would seem so.

JERRY: Good old north.   20

Peter sits reading before Jerry's arrival, in this 2006 production starring Paul Christophe and Pitt Simon.

PETER: *(Lightly, by reflex)* Ha, ha.

JERRY: *(After a slight pause)* But not due north.

PETER: I . . . well, no, not due north; but, we . . . call it north. It's northerly.

25 **JERRY:** *(Watches as* PETER, *anxious to dismiss him, prepares his pipe)* Well, boy; *you're* not going to get lung cancer, are you?

PETER: *(Looks up, a little annoyed, then smiles)* No, sir. Not from this.

30 **JERRY:** No, sir. What you'll probably get is cancer of the mouth, and then you'll have to wear one of those things Freud wore after they took one whole side of his jaw away. What do they call those things?

PETER: *(Uncomfortable)* A prosthesis?

35 **JERRY:** The very thing! A prosthesis. You're an educated man, aren't you? Are you a doctor?

PETER: Oh, no; no. I read about it somewhere; *Time* magazine, I think. *(He turns to his book)*

JERRY: Well, *Time* magazine isn't for blockheads.

40 **PETER:** No, I suppose not.

JERRY: *(After a pause)* Boy, I'm glad that's Fifth Avenue there.

PETER: *(Vaguely)* Yes.

JERRY: I don't like the west side of the park much.

PETER: Oh? *(Then, slightly wary, but interested)* Why? 45

JERRY: *(Offhand)* I don't know.

PETER: Oh. *(He returns to his book)*

JERRY: *(He stands for a few seconds, looking at* PETER, *who finally looks up again, puzzled)* Do you mind if we talk? 50

PETER: *(Obviously minding)* Why . . . no, no.

JERRY: Yes you do; you do.

PETER: *(Puts his book down, his pipe out and away, smiling)* No, really; I don't mind.

JERRY: Yes you do. 55

PETER: *(Finally decided)* No; I don't mind at all, really.

JERRY: It's . . . it's a nice day.

PETER: *(Stares unnecessarily at the sky)* Yes. Yes, it is; lovely.

JERRY: I've been to the zoo. 60

PETER: Yes, I think you said so . . . didn't you?

JERRY: I bet you've got TV, huh?

PETER: Why yes, we have two; one for the children.

JERRY: You're married!

PETER: *(With pleased emphasis)* Why, certainly. 65

JERRY: It isn't a law, for God's sake.

PETER: No . . . no, of course not.

JERRY: And you have a wife.

PETER: *(Bewildered by the seeming lack of communication)* Yes! 70

JERRY: And you have children.

PETER: Yes; two.

JERRY: Boys?

PETER: No, girls . . . both girls.

75 JERRY: But you wanted boys.

PETER: Well . . . naturally, every man wants a son, but . . .

JERRY: *(Lightly mocking)* But that's the way the cookie crumbles?

80 PETER: *(Annoyed)* I wasn't going to say that.

JERRY: And you're not going to have any more kids, are you?

PETER: *(A bit distantly)* No. No more. *(Then back, and irksome)* Why did you say that? How would you know
85 about that?

JERRY: The way you cross your legs, perhaps; something in the voice. Or maybe I'm just guessing. Is it your wife?

PETER: *(Furious)* That's none of your business! *(A
90 silence)* Do you understand? *(JERRY nods. PETER is quiet now)* Well, you're right. We'll have no more children.

JERRY: *(Softly)* That *is* the way the cookie crumbles.

PETER: *(Forgiving)* Yes . . . I guess so.

95 JERRY: Do you mind if I ask you questions?

PETER: Oh, not really.

JERRY: I'll tell you why I do it; I don't talk to many people—except to say like: give me a beer, or where's the john, or what time does the feature go on, or keep
100 your hands to yourself, buddy. You know—things like that.

PETER: I must say I don't . . .

JERRY: But every once in a while I like to talk to some-body, really *talk;* like to get to know somebody, know
105 all about him.

PETER: *(Lightly laughing, still a little uncomfortable)* And am I the guinea pig for today?

JERRY: On a sun-drenched Sunday afternoon like this? Who better than a nice married man with two

daughters and . . . uh . . . a dog? *(PETER shakes his
110 head)* No? Two dogs. *(PETER shakes his head again)* Hm. No dogs? *(PETER shakes his head, sadly)* Oh, that's a shame. But you look like an animal man. CATS? *(PETER nods his head, ruefully)* Cats! But, that can't be your idea. No, sir. Your wife and daughters?
115 *(PETER nods his head)* Is there anything else I should know?

PETER: *(He has to clear his throat)* There are . . . there are two parakeets. One . . . uh . . . one for each of my daughters.
120

JERRY: Birds.

PETER: My daughters keep them in a cage in their bedroom.

JERRY: Do they carry disease? The birds.

PETER: I don't believe so.
125

JERRY: That's too bad. If they did you could set them loose in the house and the cats could eat them and die, maybe. *(PETER looks blank for a moment, then laughs)* And what else? What do you do to support your enormous household?
130

PETER: I . . . uh . . . I have an executive position with a . . . a small publishing house. We . . . uh . . . we publish textbooks.

JERRY: That sounds nice; very nice. What do you make?

PETER: *(Still cheerful)* Now look here!
135

JERRY: Oh, come on.

PETER: Well, I make around two hundred thousand a year, but I don't carry more than forty dollars at any one time . . . in case you're a . . . a holdup man . . . ha, ha, ha.
140

JERRY: *(Ignoring the above)* Where do you live? *(PETER is reluctant)* Oh, look; I'm not going to rob you, and I'm not going to kidnap your parakeets, your cats, or your daughters.

PETER: *(Too loud)* I live between Lexington and Third
145 Avenue, on Seventy-fourth Street.

JERRY: That wasn't so hard, was it?

PETER: I didn't mean to seem . . . ah . . . it's that you don't really carry on a conversation; you just ask ques-
150   tions. And I'm . . . I'm normally . . . uh . . . reticent. Why do you just stand there?

JERRY: Say, what's the dividing line between upper-middle-middle-class and lower-upper-middle-class?

PETER: My dear fellow, I . . .

155 JERRY: Don't my dear fellow me.

PETER: (*Unhappily*) Was I patronizing? I believe I was; I'm sorry. But, you see your question about the classes bewildered me.

JERRY: And when you're bewildered you become
160   patronizing?

PETER: I . . . I don't express myself too well, sometimes. (*He attempts a joke on himself*) I'm in publishing, not writing.

JERRY: (*Amused, but not at the humor*) So be it. The
165   truth *is:* I was being patronizing.

PETER: Oh, now; you needn't say that.

          (*It is at this point that* JERRY *may begin to move about the stage with slowly increasing determination and authority, but pacing himself, so that the long speech about the dog comes at the high point of the arc*)

JERRY: All right. Who are your favorite writers? Baudelaire and Stephen King?

PETER: (*Wary*) Well, I like a great many writers; I have
170   a considerable catholicity of taste, if I may say so. Those two men are fine, each in his way. (*Warming up*) Baudelaire, of course . . . uh . . . is by far the finer of the two, but Stephen King has a place . . . in our . . . uh . . . national . . .

175 JERRY: Skip it.

PETER: I . . . sorry.

JERRY: Do you know what I did before I went to the zoo today? I walked all the way up Fifth Avenue from Washington Square; all the way.

Jerry and Peter begin their conversation.

PETER: Oh; you live in Greenwich Village! (*This seems to   180
enlighten* PETER)

JERRY: No, I don't. I took the subway down to the Village so I could walk all the way up Fifth Avenue to the zoo. It's one of those things a person has to do; sometimes a person has to go a very long distance out of his   185
way to come back a short distance correctly.

PETER: (*Almost pouting*) Oh, I thought you lived in Greenwich Village.

JERRY: What were you trying to do? Make sense out of things? Bring order? The old pigeonhole bit? Well,   190
that's easy; I'll tell you. I live in a four-story brown-stone roominghouse on the Upper West Side between Columbus Avenue and Central Park West. I live on the top floor; rear; west. It's a laughably small room, and one of my walls is made of beaverboard; this beaver-   195
board separates my room from another laughably small room, so I assume that the two rooms were once one room, a small room, but not necessarily laugh-able. The room beyond my beaverboard wall is oc-cupied by a colored queen who always keeps his door   200
open; well, not always but *always* when he's plucking his eyebrows, which he does with Buddhist concen-tration. This colored queen has rotten teeth, which is rare, and he has a Japanese kimono, which is also pretty rare; and he wears this kimono to and from   205
the john in the hall, which is pretty frequent. I mean, he goes to the john a lot. He never bothers me, and he never brings anyone up to his room. All he does is pluck his eyebrows, wear his kimono and go to the john. Now, the two front rooms on my floor are a little   210
larger, I guess; but they're pretty small, too. There's a Puerto Rican family in one of them, a husband, a wife, and some kids; I don't know how many. These

people entertain a lot. And in the other front room, there's somebody living there, but I don't know who it is. I've never seen who it is. Never. Never ever.

PETER: *(Embarrassed)* Why . . . why do you live there?

JERRY: *(From a distance again)* I don't know.

PETER: It doesn't sound like a very nice place . . . where you live.

JERRY: Well, no; it isn't an apartment in the East Seventies. But, then again, I don't have one wife, two daughters, two cats and two parakeets. What I do have, I have toilet articles, a few clothes, a hot plate that I'm not supposed to have, a can opener, one that works with a key, you know; a knife, two forks, and two spoons, one small, one large; three plates, a cup, a saucer, a drinking glass, two picture frames, both empty, eight or nine books, a pack of pornographic playing cards, regular deck, an old Western Union typewriter that prints nothing but capital letters, and a small strongbox without a lock which has in it . . . what? Rocks! Some rocks . . . sea-rounded rocks I picked up on the beach when I was a kid. Under which . . . weighed down . . . are some letters . . . please letters . . . please why don't you do this, and please when will you do that letters. And when letters, too. When will you write? When will you come? When? These letters are from more recent years.

PETER: *(Stares glumly at his shoes, then)* About those two empty picture frames . . . ?

JERRY: I don't see why they need any explanation at all. Isn't it clear? I don't have pictures of anyone to put in them.

PETER: Your parents . . . perhaps . . . a girl friend . . .

JERRY: You're a very sweet man, and you're possessed of a truly enviable innocence. But good old Mom and good old Pop are dead . . . you know? . . . I'm broken up about it, too . . . I mean really. BUT. That particular vaudeville act is playing the cloud circuit now, so I don't see how I can look at them, all neat and framed. Besides, or, rather, to be pointed about it, good old Mom walked out on good old Pop when I was ten and a half years old; she embarked on an adulterous turn of our southern states . . . a journey of a year's duration . . . and her most constant companion . . . among others, among many others . . . was a Mr. Barleycorn. At least, that's what good old Pop told me after he went down . . . came back . . . brought her body north. We'd received the news between Christmas and New Year's, you see, that good old Mom had parted with the ghost in some dump in Alabama. And, without the ghost . . . she was less welcome. I mean, what was she? A stiff . . . a northern stiff. At any rate, good old Pop celebrated the New Year for an even two weeks and then slapped into the front of a somewhat moving city omnibus, which sort of cleaned things out family-wise. Well no; then there was Mom's sister, who was given neither to sin nor the consolations of the bottle. I moved in on her, and my memory of her is slight excepting I remember still that she did all things dourly: sleeping, eating, working, praying. She dropped dead on the stairs to her apartment, my apartment then, too, on the afternoon of my high school graduation. A terribly middle-European joke, if you ask me.

PETER: Oh, my; oh, my.

JERRY: Oh, your what? But that was a long time ago, and I have no feeling about any of it that I care to admit to myself. Perhaps you can see, though, why good old Mom and good old Pop are frameless. What's your name? Your first name?

PETER: I'm Peter.

JERRY: I'd forgotten to ask you. I'm Jerry.

PETER: *(With a slight, nervous laugh)* Hello, Jerry.

JERRY: *(Nods his hello)* And let's see now; what's the point of having a girl's picture, especially in two frames? I have two picture frames, you remember. I never see the pretty little ladies more than once, and most of them wouldn't be caught in the same room with a camera. It's odd, and I wonder if it's sad.

PETER: The girls?

JERRY: No. I wonder if it's sad that I never see the little ladies more than once. I've never been able to have sex with, or, how is it put? . . . make love to anybody more

Jerry talks about his apartment.

than once. Once; that's it. . . . Oh, wait; for a week and a half, when I was fifteen and I hang my head in shame that puberty was late . . . I was a h-o-m-o-s-e-x-u-a-l. I mean, I was queer . . . (*Very fast*) . . . queer, queer,
300 queer . . . with bells ringing, banners snapping in the wind. And for those eleven days, I met at least twice a day with the park superintendent's son . . . a Greek boy, whose birthday was the same as mine, except he was a year older. I think I was very much in love . . .
305 maybe just with sex. But that was the jazz of a very special hotel, wasn't it? And now; oh, do I love the little ladies; really, I love them. For about an hour.

PETER: Well, it seems perfectly simple to me . . .

JERRY: (*Angry*) Look! Are you going to tell me to get
310 married and have parakeets?

PETER: (*Angry himself*) Forget the parakeets! And stay single if you want to. It's no business of mine. I didn't start this conversation in the . . .

JERRY: All right, all right. I'm sorry. All right? You're not
315 angry?

PETER: (*Laughing*) No, I'm not angry.

JERRY: (*Relieved*) Good. (*Now back to his previous tone*) Interesting that you asked me about the picture frames. I would have thought that you would have
320 asked me about the pornographic playing cards.

PETER: (*With a knowing smile*) Oh, I've seen those cards.

JERRY: That's not the point. (*Laughs*) I suppose when you were a kid you and your pals passed them around, or you had a pack of your own.

PETER: Well, I guess a lot of us did.   325

JERRY: And you threw them away just before you got married.

PETER: Oh, now; look here. I didn't *need* anything like that when I got older.

JERRY: No?   330

PETER: (*Embarrassed*) I'd rather not talk about these things.

JERRY: So? Don't. Besides, I wasn't trying to plumb your post-adolescent sexual life and hard times; what I wanted to get at is the value difference between   335 pornographic playing cards when you're a kid, and pornographic playing cards when you're older. It's that when you're a kid you use the cards as a substitute for a real experience, and when you're older you use real experience as a substitute for the fantasy. But I imag-   340 ine you'd rather hear about what happened at the zoo.

PETER: (*Enthusiastic*) Oh, yes; the zoo. (*Then, awkward*) That is . . . if you . . .

JERRY: Let me tell you about why I went . . . well, let me tell you some things. I've told you about the fourth   345 floor of the roominghouse where I live. I think the rooms are better as you go down, floor by floor. I guess they are; I don't know. I don't know any of the people on the third and second floors. Oh, wait! I do know that there's a lady living on the third floor,   350 in the front. I know because she cries all the time. Whenever I go out or come back in, whenever I pass her door, I always hear her crying, muffled, but . . . very determined. Very determined indeed. But the one I'm getting to, and all about the dog, is the land-   355 lady. I don't like to use words that are too harsh in describing people. I don't like to. But the landlady is a fat, ugly, mean, stupid, unwashed, misanthropic, cheap, drunken bag of garbage. And you may have noticed that I very seldom use profanity, so I can't   360 describe her as well as I might.

PETER: You describe her . . . vividly.

JERRY: Well, thanks. Anyway, she has a dog, and I will tell you about the dog, and she and her dog are the gatekeepers of my dwelling. The woman is bad enough; she leans around in the entrance hall, spying to see that I don't bring in things or people, and when she's had her mid-afternoon pint of lemon-flavored gin she always stops me in the hall, and grabs ahold of my coat or my arm, and she presses her disgusting body up against me to keep me in a corner so she can talk to me. The smell of her body and her breath . . . you can't imagine it . . . and somewhere, somewhere in the back of that pea-sized brain of hers, an organ developed just enough to let her eat, drink, and emit, she has some foul parody of sexual desire. And I, Peter, I am the object of her sweaty lust.

PETER: That's disgusting. That's . . . horrible.

JERRY: But I have found a way to keep her off. When she talks to me, when she presses herself to my body and mumbles about her room and how I should come there, I merely say: but, Love; wasn't yesterday enough for you, and the day before? Then she puzzles, she makes slits of her tiny eyes, she sways a little, and then, Peter . . . and it is at this moment that I think I might be doing some good in that tormented house . . . a simple-minded smile begins to form on her unthinkable face, and she giggles and groans as she thinks about yesterday and the day before; as she believes and relives what never happened. Then, she motions to that black monster of a dog she has, and she goes back to her room. And I am safe until our next meeting.

PETER: It's so . . . unthinkable. I find it hard to believe that people such as that really *are*.

JERRY: (*Lightly mocking*) It's for reading about, isn't it?

PETER: (*Seriously*) Yes.

JERRY: And fact is better left to fiction. You're right, Peter. Well, what I have been meaning to tell you about is the dog; I shall, now.

PETER: (*Nervously*) Oh, yes; the dog.

JERRY: Don't go. You're not thinking of going, are you?

PETER: Well . . . no, I don't think so.

JERRY: (*As if to a child*) Because after I tell you about the dog, do you know what then? Then . . . then I'll tell you about what happened at the zoo.

PETER: (*Laughing faintly*) You're . . . you're full of stories, aren't you?

JERRY: You don't *have* to listen. Nobody is holding you here; remember that. Keep that in your mind.

PETER: (*Irritably*) I know that.

JERRY: You do? Good.

(*The following long speech, it seems to me, should be done with a great deal of action, to achieve a hypnotic effect on* PETER, *and on the audience, too. Some specific actions have been suggested, but the director and the actor playing* JERRY *might best work it out for themselves*)

ALL RIGHT. (*As if reading from a huge billboard*) THE STORY OF JERRY AND THE DOG! (*Natural again*) What I am going to tell you has something to do with how sometimes it's necessary to go a long distance out of the way in order to come back a short distance correctly; or, maybe I only think that it has something to do with that. But, it's why I went to the zoo today, and why I walked north . . . northerly, rather . . . until I came here. All right. The dog, I think I told you, is a black monster of a beast: an oversized head, tiny, tiny ears, and eyes . . . bloodshot, infected, maybe; and a body you can see the ribs through the skin. The dog is black, all black; all black except for the bloodshot eyes, and . . . yes . . . and an open sore on its . . . *right* forepaw; that is red, too. And, oh yes; the poor monster, and I do believe it's an old dog . . . it's certainly a misused one . . . almost always has an erection . . . of sorts. That's red, too. And . . . what else? . . . oh, yes; there's a gray-yellow-white color, too, when he bares his fangs. Like this: Grrrrrr! Which is what he did when he saw me for the first time . . . the day I moved in. I worried about that animal the very first minute I met him. Now, animals don't take to me like Saint Francis had birds hanging off him all the time. What I mean is: Animals are indifferent to me . . . like people (*He smiles slightly*) . . . most of the time. But this dog wasn't indifferent. From the very beginning he'd snarl and then go for me, to get one of

Jerry tells Peter about his neighbor's dog.

440 my legs. Not like he was rabid, you know; he was sort
of a stumbly dog, but he wasn't half-assed, either. It
was a good, stumbly run; but I always got away. He
got a piece of my trouser leg, look, you can see right
here, where it's mended; he got that the second day
445 I lived there; but, I kicked free and got upstairs fast,
so that was that. *(Puzzles)* I still don't know to this
day how the other roomers manage it, but you know
what I *think:* I think it had to do only with me. Cozy.
So. Anyway, this went on for over a week, whenever
450 I came in; but never when I went out. That's funny.
Or, it *was* funny. I could pack up and live in the street
for all the dog cared. Well, I thought about it up in
my room one day, one of the times after I'd bolted
upstairs, and I made up my mind. I decided: First, I'll
455 kill the dog with kindness, and if that doesn't work . . .
I'll just kill him. (PETER *winces*) Don't react, Peter;
just listen. So, the next day I went out and bought a
bag of hamburgers, medium rare, no catsup, no onion; and on the way home I threw away all the rolls
460 and kept just the meat.

(*Action for the following, perhaps*)

When I got back to the roominghouse the dog was
waiting for me. I half opened the door that led into
the entrance hall, and there he was; waiting for me.
It figured. I went in, very cautiously, and I had the
465 hamburgers, you remember; I opened the bag, and I
set the meat down about twelve feet from where the
dog was snarling at me. Like so! He snarled; stopped
snarling; sniffed; moved slowly; then faster; then
faster toward the meat. Well, when he got to it he
470 stopped, and he looked at me. I smiled; but tentatively, you understand. He turned his face back to the
hamburgers, smelled, sniffed some more, and then . . .
RRRAAAAGGGGGHHHH, like that . . . he tore into
them. It was as if he had never eaten anything in his
475 life before, except like garbage. Which might very
well have been the truth. I don't think the landlady
ever eats anything but garbage. But. He ate all the
hamburgers, almost all at once, making sounds in
his throat like a woman. *Then,* when he'd finished the
480 meat, the hamburger, and tried to eat the paper, too,
he sat down and smiled. I think he smiled; I know
cats do. It was a very gratifying few moments. Then,
BAM, he snarled and made for me again. He didn't
get me this time, either. So, I got upstairs, and I lay

down on my bed and started to think about the dog 485
again. To be truthful, I was offended, and I was damn
mad, too. It was six perfectly good hamburgers with
not enough pork in them to make it disgusting. I was
offended. But, after a while, I decided to try it for
a few more days. If you think about it, this dog had 490
what amounted to an antipathy toward me; really.
And, I wondered if I mightn't overcome this antipathy. So, I tried it for five more days, but it was always
the same: snarl, sniff, move; faster; stare; gobble;
RAAGGGHHH; smile; snarl; BAM. Well, now; by 495
this time Columbus Avenue was strewn with hamburger rolls and I was less offended than disgusted.
So, I decided to kill the dog.

(PETER *raises a hand in protest*)

Oh, don't be so alarmed, Peter; I didn't succeed. The
day I tried to kill the dog I bought only one ham- 500
burger and what I thought was a murderous portion
of rat poison. When I bought the hamburger I asked
the man not to bother with the roll, all I wanted was
the meat. I expected some reaction from him, like:
we don't sell no hamburgers without rolls; or, wha' 505
d'ya wanna do, eat it out'a ya han's? But no; he smiled
benignly, wrapped up the hamburger in waxed paper,
and said: A bite for ya pussy-cat? I wanted to say: No,
not really; it's part of a plan to poison a dog I know.
But, you can't say "a dog I know" without sounding 510
funny; so I said, a little too loud, I'm afraid, and too
formally: YES, A BITE FOR MY PUSSY-CAT. People
looked up. It always happens when I try to simplify
things; people look up. But that's neither hither nor
thither. So. On my way back to the roominghouse, I 515
kneaded the hamburger and the rat poison together
between my hands, at that point feeling as much
sadness as disgust. I opened the door to the entrance
hall, and there the monster was, waiting to take the

520 offering and then jump me. Poor bastard; he never learned that the moment he took to smile before he went for me gave me time enough to get out of range. BUT, there he was; malevolence with an erection, waiting. I put the poison patty down, moved toward

525 the stairs and watched. The poor animal gobbled the food down as usual, smiled, which made me almost sick, and then, BAM. But, I sprinted up the stairs, as usual, and the dog didn't get me, as usual. AND IT CAME TO PASS THAT THE BEAST WAS

530 DEATHLY ILL. I knew this because he no longer attended me, and because the landlady sobered up. She stopped me in the hall the same evening of the attempted murder and confided the information that God had stuck her puppy-dog a surely fatal blow. She

535 had forgotten her bewildered lust, and her eyes were wide open for the first time. They looked like the dog's eyes. She sniveled and implored me to pray for the animal. I wanted to say to her: Madam, I have myself to pray for, the colored queen, the Puerto Rican fam-

540 ily, the person in the front room whom I've never seen, the woman who cries deliberately behind her closed door, and the rest of the people in all roominghouses, everywhere; besides, Madam, I don't understand how to pray. But . . . to simplify things . . . I told her I would

545 pray. She looked up. She said that I was a liar, and that I probably wanted the dog to die. I told her, and there was so much truth here, that I didn't want the dog to die. I didn't, and not just because I'd poisoned him. I'm afraid that I must tell you I wanted the dog

550 to live so that I could see what our new relationship might come to.

(PETER *indicates his increasing displeasure and slowly growing antagonism*)

Please understand, Peter; that sort of thing is important. You must believe me; it *is* important. We have
to know the effect of our actions. (*Another deep sigh*)

555 Well, anyway; the dog recovered. I have no idea why, unless he was a descendant of the puppy that guarded the gates of hell or some such resort. I'm not up on my mythology. (*He pronounces the word myth-*o-*logy*) Are you?

(PETER *sets to thinking, but* JERRY *goes on*)

560 At any rate, and you've missed the eight-thousand-dollar question, Peter; at any rate, the dog recovered

his health and the landlady recovered her thirst, in
no way altered by the bow-wow's deliverance. When I
came home from a movie that was playing on Forty-

565 second Street, a movie I'd seen, or one that was very much like one or several I'd seen, after the landlady told me puppykins was better, I was so hoping for the dog to be waiting for me. I was . . . well, how would you put it . . . enticed? . . . fascinated? . . . no, I don't

570 think so . . . heart-shatteringly anxious, that's it; I was heart-shatteringly anxious to confront my friend again.

(PETER *reacts scoffingly*)

Yes, Peter; friend. That's the only word for it. I was
heart-shatteringly et cetera to confront my doggy

575 friend again. I came in the door and advanced, un-afraid, to the center of the entrance hall. The beast was there . . . looking at me. And, you know, he looked better for his scrape with the nevermind. I stopped; I looked at him; he looked at me. I think . . . I think we

580 stayed a long time that way . . . still, stone-statue . . . just looking at one another. I looked more into his face than he looked into mine. I mean, I can concentrate longer at looking into a dog's face than a dog can con-centrate at looking into mine, or into anybody else's

484 face, for that matter. But during that twenty seconds or two hours that we looked into each other's face, we made contact. Now, here is what I had wanted to happen: I loved the dog now, and I wanted him to love me. I had tried to love, and I had tried to kill, and both had been unsuccessful by themselves. I hoped . . . and I

590 don't really know why I expected the dog to understand anything, much less my motivations . . . I hoped that the dog would understand.

(PETER *seems to be hypnotized*)

It's just . . . it's just that . . . (JERRY *is abnormally
tense, now*) . . . it's just that if you can't deal with

595 people, you have to make a start somewhere. WITH ANIMALS! (*Much faster now, and like a conspira-tor*) Don't you see? A person has to have some way of dealing with SOMETHING. If not with people . . . if not with people . . . SOMETHING. With a bed, with a

600 cockroach, with a mirror . . . no, that's too hard, that's one of the last steps. With a cockroach, with a . . . with a . . . with a carpet, a roll of toilet paper . . . no, not that, either . . . that's a mirror, too; always check

605 bleeding. You see how hard it is to find things? With a street corner, and too many lights, all colors reflecting on the oily-wet streets . . . with a wisp of smoke, a wisp . . . of smoke . . . with . . . with pornographic playing cards, with a strongbox . . . WITHOUT A

610 LOCK . . . with love, with vomiting, with crying, with fury because the pretty little ladies aren't pretty little ladies, with making money with your body which is an act of love and I could prove it, with howling because you're alive; with God. How about that? WITH

615 GOD WHO IS A COLORED QUEEN WHO WEARS A KIMONO AND PLUCKS HIS EYEBROWS, WHO IS A WOMAN WHO CRIES WITH DETERMINATION BEHIND HER CLOSED DOOR . . . with God who, I'm told, turned his back on the whole thing

620 some time ago . . . with . . . someday, with people. (JERRY *sighs the next word heavily*) People. With an idea; a concept. And where better, where ever better in this humiliating excuse for a jail, where better to communicate one single, simple-minded idea than

625 in an entrance hall? Where? It would be A START! Where better to make a beginning . . . to understand and just possibly be understood . . . a beginning of an understanding, than with . . .

(*Here* JERRY *seems to fall into almost grotesque fatigue*)

than with A DOG. Just that; a dog.

(*Here there is a silence that might be prolonged for a moment or so; then* JERRY *wearily finishes his story*)

630 A dog. It seemed like a perfectly sensible idea. Man is a dog's best friend, remember. So: the dog and I looked at each other. I longer than the dog. And what I saw then has been the same ever since. Whenever the dog and I see each other we both stop where we

635 are. We regard each other with a mixture of sadness and suspicion, and then we feign indifference. We walk past each other safely; we have an understanding. It's very sad, but you'll have to admit that it is an understanding. We had made many attempts at

640 contact, and we had failed. The dog has returned to garbage, and I to solitary but free passage. I have not returned. I mean to say, I have *gained* solitary free passage, if that much further loss can be said to be

gain. I have learned that neither kindness nor cruelty by themselves, independent of each other, creates any 645 effect beyond themselves; and I have learned that the two combined, together, at the same time, are the teaching emotion. And what is gained is loss. And what has been the result: the dog and I have attained a compromise; more of a bargain, really. We neither 650 love nor hurt because we do not try to reach each other. And, *was* trying to feed the dog an act of love? And, perhaps, was the dog's attempt to bite me *not* an act of love? If we can so misunderstand, well then, why have we invented the word love in the first place? 655

(*There is silence.* JERRY *moves to* PETER's *bench and sits down beside him. This is the first time that* JERRY *has sat down during the play.*)

The Story of Jerry and the Dog: the end.

(PETER *is silent*)

Well, Peter? (JERRY *is suddenly cheerful*) Well, Peter? Do you think I could sell that story to the *Reader's Digest* and make a couple of hundred bucks for *The Most Unforgettable Character I've Ever Met*? Huh? 660

(JERRY *is animated, but* PETER *is disturbed*)

Oh, come on now, Peter; tell me what you think.

PETER: (*Numb*) I . . . I don't understand what . . . I don't think I . . . (*Now, almost tearfully*) Why did you tell me all of this?

JERRY: Why not? 665

PETER: I DON'T UNDERSTAND!

JERRY: (*Furious, but whispering*) That's a lie.

PETER: No. No, it's not.

JERRY: (*Quietly*) I tried to explain it to you as I went along. I went slowly; it all has to do with . . . 670

PETER: I DON'T WANT TO HEAR ANY MORE. I don't understand you, or your landlady, or her dog . . .

JERRY: *Her* dog! I thought it was my . . . No. No, you're right. It *is* her dog. (*Looks at* PETER *intently, shaking his head*) I don't know what I was thinking about; of 675 course you don't understand. (*In a monotone, wearily*) I don't live in your block I'm not married to two parakeets, or whatever your setup is. I am a *permanent transient,* and my home is the sickening rooming houses on the West Side of New York City, which is the greatest city in the world. Amen.

680

PETER: I'm . . . I'm sorry; I didn't mean to . . .

JERRY: Forget it. I suppose you don't quite know what to make of me, eh?

685 **PETER:** *(A joke)* We get all kinds in publishing. *(Chuckles)*

JERRY: You're a funny man. *(He forces a laugh)* You know that? You're a very . . . a richly comic person.

PETER: *(Modestly, but amused)* Oh, now, not really. *(Still chuckling)*

690 **JERRY:** Peter, do I annoy you, or confuse you?

PETER: *(Lightly)* Well, I must confess that this wasn't the kind of afternoon I'd anticipated.

JERRY: You mean, I'm not the gentleman you were expecting.

695 **PETER:** I wasn't expecting anybody.

JERRY: No, I don't imagine you were. But I'm here, and I'm not leaving.

PETER: *(Consulting his watch)* Well, you may not be, but I must be getting home now.

700 **JERRY:** Oh, come on; stay a while longer.

PETER: I really should get home; you see . . .

JERRY: *(Tickles PETER's ribs with his fingers)* Oh, come on.

PETER: *(He is very ticklish; as JERRY continues to tickle him his voice becomes falsetto)*

No, I . . . OHHHHH! Don't do that. Stop, stop. Ohhh, no, no.

705 **JERRY:** Oh, come on.

PETER: *(As JERRY tickles)* Oh, hee, hee, hee. I must go. I . . . hee, hee, hee. After all, stop, stop, hee, hee, hee, after all, the parakeets will be getting dinner ready soon. Hee, hee. And the cats are setting the table.

710 Stop, stop, and, and . . . *(PETER is beside himself now)* and we're having . . . hee, hee . . . uh . . . ho, ho, ho.

(JERRY stops tickling PETER, but the combination of the tickling and his own mad whimsy has PETER laughing almost hysterically. As his laughter continues, then subsides, JERRY watches him, with a curious fixed smile.)

JERRY: Peter?

PETER: Oh, ha, ha, ha, ha, ha. What? What?

JERRY: Listen, now.

PETER: Oh, ho, ho. What . . . what is it, Jerry? Oh, my. 715

JERRY: *(Mysteriously)* Peter, do you want to know what happened at the zoo?

PETER: Ah, ha, ha. The what? Oh, yes; the zoo. Oh, ho, ho. Well, I had my own zoo there for a moment with . . . hee, hee, the parakeets getting dinner ready, 720 and the . . . ha, ha, whatever it was, the . . .

JERRY: *(Calmly)* Yes, that was very funny, Peter. I wouldn't have expected it. But do you want to hear about what happened at the zoo, or not?

PETER: Yes. Yes, by all means; tell me what happened at 725 the zoo. Oh, my. I don't know what happened to me.

JERRY: Now I'll let you in on what happened at the zoo; but first, I should tell you why I went to the zoo. I went to the zoo to find out more about the way people exist with animals, and the way animals exist with 730 each other, and with people too. It probably wasn't a

Peter begins to lose his patience.

fair test, what with everyone separated by bars from everyone else, the animals for the most part from each other, and always the people from the animals. But, if it's a zoo, that's the way it is. (*He pokes* PETER *on the arm*) Move over.

735

PETER: (*Friendly*) I'm sorry, haven't you enough room?

(*He shifts a little*)

JERRY: (*Smiling slightly*) Well, all the animals are there, and all the people are there, and it's Sunday and all the children are there. (*He pokes* PETER *again*) Move over.

740

PETER: (*Patiently, still friendly*) All right.

(*He moves some more, and* JERRY *has all the room he might need*)

JERRY: And it's a hot day, so all the stench is there, too, and all the balloon sellers, and all the ice cream sellers, and all the seals are barking, and all the birds are screaming. (*Pokes* PETER *harder*) Move over!

745

PETER: (*Beginning to be annoyed*) Look here, you have more than enough room! (*But he moves more, and is now fairly cramped at one end of the bench*)

JERRY: And I am there, and it's feeding time at the lions' house, and the lion keeper comes into the lion cage, one of the lion cages, to feed one of the lions. (*Punches* PETER *on the arm, hard*) MOVE OVER!

750

PETER: (*Very annoyed*) I can't move over any more, and stop hitting me. What's the matter with you?

JERRY: Do you want to hear the story? (*Punches* PETER'S *arm again*)

755

PETER: (*Flabbergasted*) I'm not so sure! I certainly don't want to be punched in the arm.

JERRY: (*Punches* PETER'S *arm again*) Like that?

PETER: Stop it! What's the matter with you?

760

JERRY: I'm crazy, you bastard.

PETER: That isn't funny.

JERRY: Listen to me, Peter. I want this bench. You go sit on the bench over there, and if you're good I'll tell you the rest of the story.

765

PETER: (*Flustered*) But . . . whatever for? What *is* the matter with you? Besides, I see no reason why I should give up this bench. I sit on this bench almost every Sunday afternoon, in good weather. It's secluded here; there's never anyone sitting here, so I have it all to myself.

770

JERRY: (*Softly*) Get off this bench, Peter; I want it.

PETER: (*Almost whining*) No.

JERRY: I said I want this bench, and I'm going to have it. Now get over there.

775

PETER: People can't have everything they want. You should know that; it's a rule; people can have some of the things they want, but they can't have everything.

JERRY: (*Laughs*) Imbecile! You're slow-witted!

PETER: Stop that!

780

JERRY: You're a vegetable! Go lie down on the ground.

PETER: Now *you* listen to me. I've put up with you all afternoon.

JERRY: Not really.

PETER: LONG ENOUGH. I've put up with you long enough. I've listened to you because you seemed . . . well, because I thought you wanted to talk to somebody.

785

JERRY: You put things well; economically, and, yet . . . oh, what is the word I want to put justice to your . . . JESUS, you make me sick . . . get off here and give me my bench.

790

PETER: MY BENCH!

JERRY: (*Pushes* PETER *almost, but not quite, off the bench*) Get out of my sight.

795

PETER: (*Regaining his position*) God da . . . mn you. That's enough! I've had enough of you. I will not give up this bench; you can't have it, and that's that. Now, go away.

(JERRY *snorts but does not move*)

Go away, I said.

800

(JERRY *does not move*)

Get away from here. If you don't move on . . . you're a
bum . . . that's what you are. . . . If you don't move on,
I'll get a policeman here and make you go.

(JERRY *laughs, stays*)

I warn you, I'll call a policeman.

805 **JERRY:** (*Softly*) You won't find a policeman around here;
they're all over on the west side of the park chasing
fairies down from trees or out of the bushes. That's all
they do. That's their function. So scream your head
off; it won't do you any good.

810 **PETER:** POLICE! I warn you, I'll have you arrested.
POLICE! (*Pause*) I said POLICE! (*Pause*) I feel
ridiculous.

JERRY: You look ridiculous: a grown man screaming for
the police on a bright Sunday afternoon in the park
815 with nobody harming you. If a policeman *did* fill his
quota and come sludging over this way he'd probably
take you in as a nut.

PETER: (*With disgust and impotence*) Great God, I just
came here to read, and now you want me to give up
820 the bench. You're mad.

JERRY: Hey, I got news for you, as they say. I'm on your
precious bench, and you're never going to have it for
yourself again.

PETER: (*Furious*) Look, you; get off my bench. I don't
825 care if it makes any sense or not. I want this bench to
myself; I want you OFF IT!

JERRY: (*Mocking*) Aw . . . look who's mad.

PETER: GET OUT!

JERRY: No.

830 **PETER:** I WARN YOU!

JERRY: Do you know how ridiculous you look *now?*

PETER: (*His fury and self-consciousness have possessed
him*) It doesn't matter. (*He is almost crying*) GET
AWAY FROM MY BENCH!

835 **JERRY:** Why? You have everything in the world you want;
you've told me about your home, and your family, and

Peter brandishes Jerry's knife.

your own little zoo. You have everything, and now you
want this bench. Are these the things men fight for?
Tell me, Peter, is this bench, this iron and this wood,
is this your honor? Is this the thing in the world you'd   840
fight for? Can you think of anything more absurd?

PETER: Absurd? Look, I'm not going to talk to you about
honor, or even try to explain it to you. Besides, it isn't
a question of honor; but even if it were, you wouldn't
understand.   845

JERRY: (*Contemptuously*) You don't even know what
you're saying, do you? This is probably the first time in
your life you've had anything more trying to face than
changing your cats' toilet box. Stupid! Don't you have
any idea, not even the slightest, what other people   850
need?

PETER: Oh, boy, listen to you; well, you don't need this
bench. That's for sure.

JERRY: Yes; yes, I do.

PETER: (*Quivering*) I've come here for years; I have   855
hours of great pleasure, great satisfaction, right here.
And that's important to a man. I'm a responsible
person, and I'm a GROWNUP. This is my bench, and
you have no right to take it away from me.

JERRY: Fight for it, then. Defend yourself; defend your   860
bench.

PETER: You've *pushed* me to it. Get up and fight.

JERRY: Like a man?

PETER: *(Still angry)* Yes, like a man, if you insist on
865   mocking me even further.

JERRY: I'll have to give you credit for one thing; you *are*
a vegetable, and a slightly nearsighted one, I think . . .

PETER: THAT'S ENOUGH. . . .

JERRY: . . . but, you know, as they say on TV all the
870   time—you know—and I mean this, Peter, you have a
certain dignity; it surprises me . . .

PETER: STOP!

JERRY: *(Rises lazily)* Very well, Peter, we'll battle for the
bench, but we're not evenly matched.

     *(He takes out and clicks open an ugly-looking
knife)*

PETER: *(Suddenly awakening to the reality of the
situation)*

875   You *are* mad! You're stark raving mad! YOU'RE
GOING TO KILL ME!

     *(But before PETER has time to think what to do,
JERRY tosses the knife at PETER's feet)*

JERRY: There you go. Pick it up. You have the knife and
we'll be more evenly matched.

PETER: *(Horrified)* No!

JERRY: *(Rushes over to PETER, grabs him by the collar;
PETER rises; their faces almost touch)*

880   Now you pick up that knife and you fight with me.
You fight for your self-respect; you fight for that goddamned bench.

PETER: *(Struggling)* No! Let . . . let go of me! He . . .
Help!

885 **JERRY:** *(Slaps PETER on each "fight")* You fight, you
miserable bastard; fight for that bench; fight for
your manhood, you pathetic little vegetable. *(Spits in
PETER's face)* You couldn't even get your wife with a
male child.

PETER: *(Breaks away, enraged)* It's a matter of genetics,   890
not manhood, you . . . you monster.

     *(He darts down, picks up the knife and backs off
a little; he is breathing heavily)*

I'll give you one last chance; get out of here and leave
me alone!

     *(He holds the knife with a firm arm, but far in
front of him, not to attack, but to defend)*

JERRY: *(Sighs heavily)* So be it!

     *(With a rush he charges PETER and impales
himself on the knife. Tableau: For just a moment,
complete silence, JERRY impaled on the knife at
the end of PETER's still firm arm. Then PETER
screams, pulls away, leaving the knife in JERRY.
JERRY is motionless, on point. Then he, too,
screams, and it must be the sound of an infuriated and fatally wounded animal. With the knife
in him, he stumbles back to the bench that PETER
had vacated. He crumbles there, sitting, facing
PETER, his eyes wide in agony, his mouth open)*

PETER: *(Whispering)* Oh my God, oh my God, oh my   895
God. . . .

     *(He repeats these words many times, very
rapidly)*

JERRY: *(JERRY is dying; but now his expression seems
to change. His features relax, and while his voice
varies, sometimes wrenched with pain, for the
most part he seems removed from his dying. He
smiles)*

Peter, thank you, Peter. I mean that now; thank you
very much.

     *(PETER's mouth drops open. He cannot move;
he is transfixed)*

I came unto you *(He laughs, so faintly)* and you have
comforted me. Dear Peter.   900

PETER: *(Almost fainting)* Oh my God!

JERRY: You'd better go now. Somebody might come by,
and you don't want to be here when anyone comes.

Jerry lies dead on the park bench.

PETER: *(Does not move, but begins to weep)*

Oh my God, oh my God.

905 JERRY: And Peter, I'll tell you something now; you're
not really a vegetable; it's all right, you're an animal.
You're an animal, too. But you'd better hurry now,
Peter. Hurry, you'd better go . . . see?

*(JERRY takes a handkerchief and with great
effort and pain wipes the knife handle clean of
fingerprints)*

Hurry away, Peter.

(PETER begins to stagger away)

Wait . . . wait, Peter. Take your book . . . book. Right   910
here . . . beside me . . . on your bench . . . my bench,
rather. Come . . . take your book.

(PETER starts for the book, but retreats)

Hurry . . . Peter.

*(PETER rushes to the bench, grabs the book,
retreats)*

Very good, Peter . . . very good. Now . . . hurry away.

*(PETER hesitates for a moment, then flees,
stage-left)*

Hurry away. . . . *(His eyes are closed now)* Hurry away,   915
your parakeets are making the dinner . . . the cats . . .
are setting the table . . .

PETER: *(Offstage)* *(A pitiful howl)*

OH MY GOD!

JERRY: *(His eyes still closed, he shakes his head and
speaks; a combination of scornful mimicry and
supplication)*

Oh . . . my . . . God.

(He is dead)

Writing from Reading

Summarize

1 Two men meet in a park in an incident that leads to a disastrous end.
Did you have any sense when first reading
the play of the conclusion to come?

Analyze Craft

2 The setting is spare, there are only
two actors, and their dialogue
seems low-key, offhand. How does the
playwright create suspense and then
heighten it by means of their speech?

Analyze Voice

3 How would you characterize the
diction—the vocabulary and word
choice—of the two characters? Use examples from the dialogue to show the difference between the social standing of the
establishment figure, Peter, and the outcast,
Jerry. Is Jerry's long monologue realistic?

Synthesize Summary and Analysis

4 This play focuses partly on isolation
and its perils. How does its staging
emphasize this condition?

Interpret the Play

5 In what ways does the play lead us to
see the animal in all of us?

CONTINUED FROM PAGE 1025

A HISTORY OF TRAGICOMEDY

In the case of *The Zoo Story*, the term *tragicomedy* is often applied. Not even a hyphen divides the tragic and the comic mode: *tragicomedy* combines the two in one word. Though Albee would probably resist such a label, *tragicomedy* is the signature genre of the playwright who influenced him most and whom he praises in his interview, Samuel Beckett. The most famous of Beckett's groundbreaking plays, *Waiting for Godot,* has two characters spend the entire drama awaiting the arrival of a figure, called Godot, who never arrives and whose mysterious absence is sometimes considered a metaphor for God.

The predecessors of this ironic mix of high seriousness and low humor occurred with the Greeks, who appended a satyr play—one of those down-and-dirty comic afterthoughts—to a trilogy of tragedies that were submitted for competition to be performed in their great drama festivals. "Comic relief" is also found in even the darkest plays of William Shakespeare. Although tragicomedies are found as early as Shakespeare, in tragic plays with happy endings, modern tragicomedies are a complex blend of serious and light tones that yields dark or satiric results. *(For more on satyr plays, tragicomedies, and other types of drama, see Chapter 30.)*

"No two people see the same play. No two performances of the same production are identical. And there's more than one way to skin a cat. Why, I don't know, but there is." Conversation with Edward Albee

A SAMPLE STUDENT ESSAY IN PROGRESS

In the sections that follow you can chart the progress of our student Jim Hanks from his interactive reading of *The Zoo Story* to his response to this assignment:

Assignment: Expand your close reading of Edward Albee's *The Zoo Story* into a 4- to 5-page essay in which you analyze the unfolding of the dramatic action and what the play suggests about contemporary life.

In addition to annotating the text, Hanks considers the following as he reads *The Zoo Story:*

- How do different elements affect the audience? Which of the several elements of drama, such as dialogue, character, and setting, seem to have the greatest impact?
- When was the play written and is the play written about its own time? How important is the play's social and historical context in providing insight into the play?
- What genre of play is it? Is it a tragedy? A comedy? Both or something else? (See Chapter 30 for more on types of drama.)

A Student's First Reaction to *The Zoo Story*

When I look at this, I imagine from the title that animals are likely to play a role. Two men are sitting on a park bench. The playwright gives some guidance in stage directions in italics. If I imagine acting out the two parts, how would I draw the audience into the play?

> "It's a temptation of course to look at [a play] as if it were a short story or a novel, because there are a lot of similarities on the printed page. . . . It's an encounter just between you and what's on the page. . . . You have to begin to visualize . . . in effect, as you begin to read the play, you set the stage . . . then the play begins to unfold." Conversation with Edwin Wilson

TIPS

Interactive Reading and Writing

- Mark where scenes begin and end, and show how the action unfolds.
- Note which character in the play changes the most and your own personal reaction to these changes.
- Use act and scene numbers when you quote lines from a play. Also use line numbers if the play is written in verse. For one-act plays, cite by page number.

> "Don't just try to figure out the character. If you don't put the character in the plot, you'll never figure out the character. Character and plot are supposed to be organically interwoven."

Conversation with Gregory Nagy

An Interactive Reading
from *The Zoo Story*

Drinking beer and calling the bathroom "john" gives clues that his character is "low brow," perhaps; Peter isn't—foils to each other?

The role of questioner gives Jerry more power, almost like a detective. I would cast someone with a bigger presence for his role than for Peter's.

JERRY: Do you mind if I ask you questions?

PETER: Oh, not really.

JERRY: I'll tell you why I do it; I don't talk to many people—except to say like: give me a beer, or where's the john, or what time does the feature go on, or keep your hands to yourself, buddy. You know—things like that.

The first animal mentioned in "Zoo Story" is not a zoo animal at all! I think of guinea pigs as docile household pets, kept in a cage.

If these two are foils, how might I represent that on stage?

PETER: I must say I don't . . .

JERRY: But every once in a while I like to talk to somebody, really *talk;* like to get to know somebody, know all about him.

We know from clues early on that this is New York's Central Park. There are lots of ways I can imagine staging this—just two benches on a stage, or a more elaborate park backdrop. But I think it would be interesting to do it outside.

PETER: *(Lightly laughing, still a little uncomfortable)* And am I the guinea pig for today?

I wonder why Jerry is so interested in Peter's pets. Their dialogue seems to say that having cats makes Peter less "manly."

JERRY: On a sun-drenched Sunday afternoon like this? Who better than a nice married man with two daughters and . . . uh . . . a dog? *(PETER shakes his head)* No? Two dogs. *(PETER shakes his head again)* Hm. No dogs? *(PETER shakes his head, sadly)* Oh, that's a shame. But you look like an animal man. CATS? *(PETER nods his head, ruefully)* Cats! But, that can't be your idea. No, sir. Your wife and daughters? *(PETER nods his head)* Is there anything else I should know?

Birds are another caged pet. Parakeets especially are common household birds (it would be different if he owned cardinals or toucans, say).

Cues for very expressive gestures. Peter shows how he feels without saying it.

PETER: *(He has to clear his throat)* There are . . . there are two parakeets. One . . . uh . . . one for each of my daughters.

JERRY: Birds.

PETER: My daughters keep them in a cage in their bedroom.

Cue for clearing throat and the amount of ellipses make it seem like he says this hesitantly.

JERRY: Do they carry disease? The birds.

PETER: I don't believe so.

The interaction of animals becomes disturbing when Jerry puts it this way. Why would he say this? And why would he imagine Peter's pets are diseased in the first place?

JERRY: That's too bad. If they did you could set them loose in the house and the cats could eat them and die, maybe. *(PETER looks blank for a moment, then laughs)* And what else? What do you do to support your enormous household?

Peter reacts hesitantly to Jerry's jab. I think I'd play them as a kind of boxing match with Jerry dancing around Peter throwing punches that Peter politely dodges

PETER: I . . . uh . . . I have an executive position with a . . . a small publishing house. We . . . uh . . . we publish textbooks.

JERRY: That sounds nice; very nice.

Initial Response

After reading the play, Jim thinks he has a kernel of an idea of what "*the unfolding of the dramatic action*" means, beginning with a sense of how to relate the beginning of the play to the unfolding middle and to the shocking conclusion. He also believes he can find his way from what he sees on the stage that the page conjures up in his imagination to "*what it suggests about contemporary life.*" The vague sense he developed as he read the play that drama can serve as a lens through which we better understand our relationship to life and the world has grown for him into a clear idea. He has never been to Central Park in New York City and has never suffered Jerry's problems, or Peter's complacencies, but he can see aspects of his life in new and surprising ways.

Jim's annotations show his feelings of surprise and confusion by the play's ending. (Later in this chapter, you will see the not so very different response from a reviewer for *The New York Times,* Brooks Atkinson, who also questioned the final action.) Jim records his feelings in a short initial response that might later help him see where his interest lies.

> Well, that was an unexpected conclusion. Not what I initially expected from a play called The Zoo Story.
>
> Jerry and Peter were both interesting characters. Strange, even though Jerry does most of the talking, I feel like I know Peter better. The details of his life are clearer in my mind than Jerry's, maybe because they're closer to my own. I can picture the black dog because it was described so much. Why is the anecdote about the dog such a focal point of the play? I mean, Jerry goes on and on about it, but it's not clear what a dog has to do with a "zoo story."

Explore Your Ideas

As Jim reviews his annotations of his interactive reading and his considerations of the genre, elements, and historical context of the play, he imagines what he might see if he were to watch this play staged. In the "theater" of his mind, he sees two characters and a park setting. He decides to focus first on the characters, trying to figure out his response to them. Then he looks at the setting, comparing the zoo motif to the freedom of the park where the action takes place. He wonders about the mystery of the zoo and what has happened there. How does this relate to the meaning of the action? Jerry's death confuses him. He decides to put down his thoughts in a freewriting exercise.

Freewriting

What happened at the zoo?! I can't decide if that was frustrating or confusing. Jerry made me uncomfortable. I can't decide how I would react if I was Peter on that bench. I think it would be easier to understand his reaction over the bench if you saw this acted out. You could see the tension building more, the way Jerry forces him off the bench. I wonder what the zoo has to do with this. There were no animals and only two people. The setting is strange too: a wide open park. What animals were there? Cats and birds, and that detailed description of the dog. Were there any cages? Maybe there's a metaphor for a zoo here. I'd like to consider what Jerry and Peter might represent.

Next Jim takes his freewriting responses to a higher level of questioning—and comprehension—by writing a slightly more formal journal entry. Here he tries to expand the ideas in his freewriting and organize them into paragraphs.

"It's said to writers, write about what you know. I always like to turn that on its head and say write about what you didn't know you knew." Conversation with Arthur Kopit

Journaling

The first thing I noticed when I started *The Zoo Story* was that it was set in a park instead of a zoo. I was surprised because a park is a wide open place, but a zoo is full of cages. When I read more of the play I realized that *The Zoo Story* referred to Jerry's story about his trip to the zoo rather than the events of the play.

But now that I think about it, there are a lot of animal references in this story. Peter says he has cats and birds and Jerry keeps bringing it back up, even at the last line. And Jerry tells the whole long story about trying to bond with his landlady's dog. But cats and birds and dogs aren't really "zoo animals." Maybe there's some meaning in that—a "zoo story" about house pets?

> *I had trouble understanding the ending of the play because I never really sympathized with Jerry. I felt bad for him mostly, but I couldn't relate to him. It was weird to have a play with only two characters, and then one you can't relate to at all. That might be an interpretation: Peter as the house pet that you get along with, and Jerry as the dog you try to get along with but never can. So what does Jerry's "suicide" mean?*

Jim feels like he has hit upon a good idea in the last paragraph of his journal entry. He decides to explore it further. Clarity begins to emerge when he organizes the animal references in the play by listing them under the character most closely associated with the animal. His brainstorming session leads him to find a pattern: The domestic animals belong to Peter; the wild animals he associates with Jerry.

Brainstorming

PETER	JERRY
• Domestic	• Wild
• Cats and parakeets	• Landlady's black dog
• Guinea pig	• Zoo as wild place
• Caged	• Unable to connect
• Holds the knife	• Dies
• Conventional	• Nonconformist

"When my writing is not working for me, then I start listening: listening to music, listening to other writers, listening to other actors, listening to my soul. And then I start writing. And I build, build, build. Then I start learning how to chisel, chisel, chisel down . . . beginning, middle, and end of something that's not only entertaining but [also] educating, and enlightening, and hopefully an experience that will leave you in some way or another changed. And that's how I approach my writing." Conversation with Ruben Santiago-Hudson

Develop a Working Thesis

Jim used his brainstorming notes to sharpen his topic and focus his thesis. He decided to use the first draft as a "working thesis" and refined it as he revised his paper.

FIRST-DRAFT THESIS

Edward Albee reveals a lot about the characters by associating them with different animals.

SECOND-DRAFT THESIS

A close reading of *The Zoo Story* reveals an argument about ways to live based on the association of the characters with specific references to animals, wild and caged and free.

FINAL THESIS

A close reading of *The Zoo Story* reveals that Albee, using animals as metaphors, has dramatized an argument about two ways to live in the modern world.

Create a Plan for Your Paper

Jim's brainstorming exercise led him to create the following brief outline. His method of working is slightly different from that of the students we saw in the fiction and poetry sections; he prefers to add to his thesis and support progressively, with each draft, rather than figure out all the details before writing. He will use a comparison/contrast structure to organize his paper.

I. Introduction

II. Peter—Domestic

    A.   Cats

    B.   Parakeets—caged!

III. Jerry—Wild

    A.   Interest in zoo

    B.   Landlady's dog

IV. Compare the two men: Domestic vs. Wild

V. Conclusion: A way to understand Jerry's death

Generate a First Draft

Sitting in front of his blank screen, fingers hovering over the keyboard, Jim takes the leap from reviewing his notes to composing the opening lines of a draft. "Animals are very important to the play . . ." he writes. The point of a first draft is to get ideas onto paper. Then everything can be revisited, reorganized, and refined. The draft allows you to think about your own feelings and experiences in reading or observing a play.

You may find it easier to draft the introduction and the conclusion after you have drafted the body of the paper. These sections should answer each other. The introduction introduces the thesis, and the conclusion relates the thesis to a larger issue that explains why the thesis is significant. The paragraphs in the body allow you to use the text to support your thesis.

> **"Writing . . . is a very mysterious process. . . . It's so easy to panic, and even in rewriting, look at what the material is. What are you trying to do? You go back to basics. What's this piece about? What do I think it's about? . . . What does this piece want to be?"**

Conversation with Arthur Kopit

FIRST DRAFT

Hanks 1

Jim Hanks

Professor Hernandez

English 1102

16 February 2011

Animals in *The Zoo Story*

Animals are very important to the play *The Zoo Story*. They factor into a lot of conversations, and it is interesting to see which character talks about which animal. Edward Albee reveals a lot about the characters by associating them with different animals.

Peter talks about his pets because Jerry asks him to. He says he has a cat and two parakeets, which his daughters keep in a cage. The image of caged birds is a strong one—it suggests that a bird who would otherwise fly freely is restrained.

Jerry begins the play by talking about the zoo. The zoo also has cages, but when you think about a zoo, you see that there are wild animals, very unlike cats and parakeets. In a way, then, Jerry aligns himself with wild animals by talking so much about the zoo. But Jerry also talks about his landlady's dog, which he calls "a black monster of a beast" (1033). This does not sound like a friendly house dog like the ones we associated with Peter. Yet this is the animal Jerry tries to connect with, and it is significant that Jerry chooses a wild beast with which to establish a relationship (even though his attempt fails).

Since Peter prefers domestic animals and Jerry prefers wild animals, we can understand something about their characters: Peter is himself domesticated in a 9-to-5 job, while Jerry remains wild and outside of that type of stability. Peter, then, is unable to understand the zoo in the way that Jerry can. Jerry sees the zoo not just as a place for wild animals, but as a place where those animals are separated by bars and cages. Like these animals, Jerry seems unable to connect with those around him.

In the end, then, it is significant that Peter holds the knife that kills Jerry. It seems to mean on a symbolic level that a domesticated life wins out over people who are outside of it. In this way, we can understand Jerry's death as a statement that Albee is making against conventional society.

Work Cited

Albee, Edward. *The Zoo Story. Literature: Craft and Voice*. Ed. Nicholas Delbanco and Alan Cheuse. 2nd ed. New York: McGraw, 1027-1041 Print.

Revise Your Draft

Jim was pleased with his first draft in that his ideas about Peter and Jerry and the animals he associated with the characters seemed to come together in a logical way. However, after reviewing his notes, he realized that he had not used much from the text to support his claim. He returned to his annotations and reread the sections that had to do with animals. He also highlighted the quotations that would best support his argument.

By rereading and selecting quotations, Jim came to a more nuanced understanding of the play. He realized he could add an additional paragraph analyzing Peter's and Jerry's different understandings of the zoo. Although the beginning of that idea was present in his first draft, he fully expands it in his second draft.

"**What you read on the page looks like it's been there forever, but believe me, it hasn't. It's always a struggle to find what you are looking for.**" Conversation with Arthur Miller

Jim thus makes several major improvements in his second draft. He includes support for his argument from the text itself. He also expands his discussion of quotes from the text, allowing him to more thoroughly analyze the specific language the play uses. Finally, after writing the second draft, Jim rereads his paper and adds annotations. These annotations show him where to refine his language and where to add proper MLA in-text references when he writes his final draft (see Chapter 37, MLA Documentation Style Guide, at the end of this book for information on MLA citation).

SECOND DRAFT

Hanks 1

Jim Hanks

Professor Hernandez

English 1102

20 February 2011

Caged or Free?

Animals as Metaphor in Edward Albee's *The Zoo Story*

[annotation: Better way to start than a preposition?]

From the title of Edward Albee's play *The Zoo Story*, the reader is presented

with the idea of animals. The meeting between Jerry and Peter is difficult to

understand and leaves the reader with many questions. A close reading of *The*

[annotation: Such as?—why the detailed description of the dog, Jerry's suicide . . .]

Zoo Story reveals an argument about ways to live based on the association of the

characters with specific references to animals, wild and caged and free.

Throughout the play, Peter is closely aligned with domesticated animals.

After learning that Peter has a wife and two daughters, Jerry is eager to know what

[annotation: "you" too familiar?]

type of pets Peter owns. The animals he guesses are typical pets you would have

around the house, like dogs and cats. Peter says that his family owns a cat and two

Hanks 2

Direct quote from play . . . put in quotes and cite!

Discuss significance of birds more?

parakeets that his daughters keep in a cage in their bedroom. He also calls himself a guinea pig: When Jerry says he likes to talk to people and learn about them, Peter says, "And am I the guinea pig for today?" (1029). In conversation Peter is simply using a popular turn of phrase. But in the context of the larger play, Peter's word choice is extremely significant, because a guinea pig is a passive subject, just like Peter is a passive subject in Jerry's dialogue experiment until Jerry provokes him physically.

Break this sentence up to make the point clearer. Mention Peter's conventional life?

The first line of the play has Jerry declaring loudly several times that he has just come from the zoo, associating him with wild animals. The zoo, of course, is filled with wild animals, and even though they are caged they are vastly different from house pets like Peter's cat and birds. The speech where Jerry describes his relationship with the landlady's dog is most significant. Jerry says the dog is "a black monster of a beast" (1033). The words "monster" and "beast" tell us that this is not a typical house dog, but one that is practically feral. Jerry also notes the dog's constant erection, which represents an unfulfilled desire. Similarly, Jerry's unfulfilled desire to connect with others is made apparent when he tries to connect with the dog. At best, he and the dog achieve a status of mutual indifference. But it is significant that Jerry chose this wild beast as the object with which to make a start at "dealing" with the world.

Reword sentence to focus on Jerry.

"us" too familiar

Include more quote to support "erection" discussion.

Better paragraph conclusion: So what??

Seeing Peter as a domesticated guinea pig and Jerry as a feral dog clarifies their approach to life: Peter is happy to be caged in fulfilling society's expectations through a conventional home, family, and job, but Jerry can't function in such a setting. The closest Peter comes to breaking out of his neat, ordered life is when he mistakenly says he must get home because the parakeets and the cat will be preparing dinner. This slipup makes Peter say, "I had my own zoo there for a moment."

Break into two sentences, emphasize thesis.

Quote from play? Need to cite!

Hanks 3

More info: How do we know that?

Peter has a very shallow understanding of the zoo. He sees it only in the sense of a wild place, with all kinds of animals mixed up together. Jerry's understanding of the zoo is deeper: He describes it as a place where everyone is separated by bars, with all the animals separated from the other animals, and all the people separated from the animals. "But, if it's a zoo, that's the way it is," he says (1038). Since Peter and Jerry are domesticated and wild animals, this quote shows that Jerry—the wild animal—views convention not as something that brings comforting order, but as the bars that are divisive and that keep people from connecting to one another.

Confusing sentence . . . just quote Jerry's actual words.

Awkward wording.

Need to watch out for these— too familiar for formal paper.

Everyone knows that the wild animals that populate the zoo are not free to be wild. In the same way, Jerry is not free to be himself in a world of conventions. And just like a wild animal can't flourish in captivity, Jerry can't survive in our oppressive society. Thus, an exploration into the connection between animals and characters provides insights into Jerry's death at the end of the play. Since Peter (the guinea pig) holds the knife on which Jerry impales himself, Jerry (the feral dog) is symbolically killed by conventional society. Albee's play, then, is more than just an encounter between two men, it's a clash between two ways of life—and it is the conventional, domesticated way of life that blindly dominates those who refuse to conform.

Assuming too much? Too familiar to the reader?

"Domesticated animal" and "wild animal"

Clean up conclusion to make point clearer.

Tie animal imagery into the conclusion.

Hanks 4

Work Cited

Albee, Edward. *The Zoo Story. Literature: Craft and Voice.* Ed. Nicholas Delbanco and Alan Cheuse. 2nd ed. New York: McGraw, 2013. 1027-1041. Print.

Edit and Format Your Paper

Jim uses the annotations on his second draft to develop his final draft, in which he fleshes out his character analysis and examines each sentence for clarity. For the final draft, he checks his spelling, word choice, and transitions. He also makes sure he has provided ample evidence from the play itself with quotations and checks to make sure these quotations have correctly formatted in-text references, which correspond to a Work Cited page at the end of his paper (see Chapter 5 for a sample research paper with a Works Cited page and Chapter 37, MLA Documentation Style Guide, at the end of the book). Jim's progress shows his interaction with the story as he continually revises his interpretation.

FINAL DRAFT

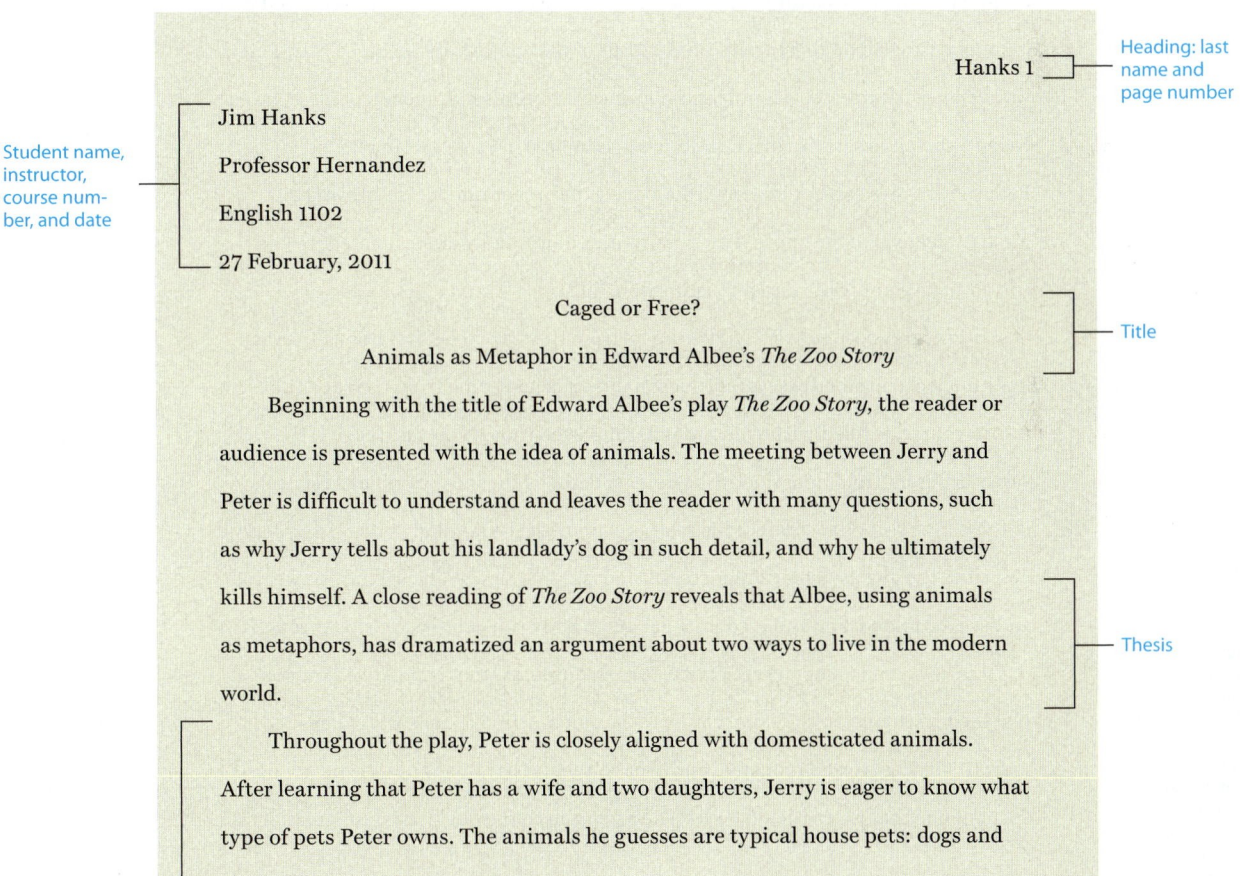

Hanks 1 — Heading: last name and page number

Jim Hanks

Professor Hernandez

English 1102

27 February, 2011

Student name, instructor, course number, and date

Caged or Free?

Animals as Metaphor in Edward Albee's *The Zoo Story*

Title

Beginning with the title of Edward Albee's play *The Zoo Story*, the reader or audience is presented with the idea of animals. The meeting between Jerry and Peter is difficult to understand and leaves the reader with many questions, such as why Jerry tells about his landlady's dog in such detail, and why he ultimately kills himself. A close reading of *The Zoo Story* reveals that Albee, using animals as metaphors, has dramatized an argument about two ways to live in the modern world.

Thesis

Throughout the play, Peter is closely aligned with domesticated animals. After learning that Peter has a wife and two daughters, Jerry is eager to know what type of pets Peter owns. The animals he guesses are typical house pets: dogs and

Hanks 2

cats. Peter reveals that his family owns a cat and two parakeets, which Peter says his daughters "keep . . . in a cage in their bedroom" (1029). The image of caged birds is powerful, as it highlights unnatural captivity; birds were meant to fly, but here they are kept from one of their most basic activities by the cage imposed on them. In fact, all the animals associated with Peter are domesticated. Peter even calls himself a guinea pig: When Jerry says he likes to talk to people and learn about them, Peter says, "And am I the guinea pig for today?" (1029). In conversation, Peter is simply using a popular turn of phrase. But in the context of the larger play, Peter's word choice is extremely significant. A guinea pig brings to mind a harmless, large rodent who passes its life in a cage, a passive subject in any experiment. Likewise, Peter is a passive subject in Jerry's dialogue experiment until Jerry provokes him physically. Furthermore, Peter seems caged in, wholly domesticated, by his conventional family life and publishing job.

Jerry is associated with wild animals from the start. The first line of the play has him declaring loudly several times that he has just come from the zoo. The zoo, of course, is filled with wild animals, and even though they are caged, they are vastly different from house pets like Peter's. Perhaps the most significant speech in the play is Jerry's account of his relationship with the landlady's dog. In it, Jerry describes the dog as "a black monster of a beast: an oversized head, tiny, tiny ears, and eyes . . . bloodshot, infected, maybe; and a body you can see the ribs through the skin. [. . .] and an open sore on its . . . *right* forepaw; that is red, too. And, oh yes; the poor monster [. . .] almost always has an erection . . . of sorts. That's red, too" (1033). The words "monster" and "beast" tell us that this is not a typical house dog, but one that is practically feral. The attention to the dog's constant erection

Textual analysis of Peter's character as domestic

Textual analysis of Jerry's character as wild

Because this quotation contains ellipses that appeared in the original text, Jim put brackets around the ellipses he added to the quotation.

evidence from the play

evidence from the play

evidence from the play

Hanks 3

suggests that he represents unfulfilled desire. As the story unfolds, Jerry, too, has

a desire to connect with others, which ultimately goes unfulfilled. His first attempt

to connect is with the dog, but he fails. At best, he and the dog achieve a status of

mutual indifference. But it is significant that Jerry chooses this wild beast as the

object with which to make a start at dealing with the world, for it suggests that he

must make peace with what is unconventional before he can deal with the rest of

the conventional world.

Seeing Peter as a domesticated guinea pig and Jerry as a feral dog clarifies

their approaches to life. While Peter is happy to be caged in, fulfilling society's

expectations through a conventional home, family, and job, Jerry cannot function

in such a setting. The closest Peter comes to breaking out of his neatly ordered life

is when he mistakenly says that he must get home because the parakeets and the

cat will be preparing dinner. This disruption of conventional order leads Peter to

say, "I had my own zoo there for a moment" (1037). This quote highlights that Peter,

blind to his own captivity in society, has a very shallow understanding of the zoo.

He sees it only as a wild place, with all kinds of animals mixed up together. Jerry,

however, shows a deeper understanding when he describes the zoo as a place where

"everyone [is] separated by bars from everyone else, the animals for the most part

from each other, and always the people from the animals. But, if it's a zoo, that's the

way it is" (1038). Since metaphorically Peter and Jerry are domesticated and wild

animals, this quote shows that Jerry—the untamed one—views convention not as

something that brings comforting order, but as divisive bars that keep people from

connecting with one another.

The zoo is a place where wild animals that populate it are not free to be wild. Likewise, Jerry is not free to be himself in a world where convention imposes its rules. And just as a wild animal cannot flourish in captivity, neither can Jerry survive in an oppressive society. Thus, an exploration of the connection between animals and the characters provides insight into why Jerry kills himself at the end of the play. Since Peter (the domesticated man) holds the knife on which Jerry impales himself, Jerry (the feral being) is symbolically killed by conventional society. Albee's play, then, is more than just an encounter between two men; it is a clash between two ways of life. By associating the conflicting characters with animal imagery, Albee illustrates how ultimately it is the conventional, domesticated way of life that blindly dominates those who refuse to conform.

Conclusion summarizes preceding analysis.

Concluding statement restates and reinforces thesis.

Work Cited

Albee, Edward. *The Zoo Story. Literature: Craft and Voice.* Ed. Nicholas Delbanco and Alan Cheuse. 2nd ed. New York: McGraw, 2013. 1027-1041. Print.

Crafting Your Own Voice: Paraphrase

Of the various ways to integrate sources into your writing, paraphrase is perhaps the most difficult. When you paraphrase a source, you are not summarizing it. The purpose is not to present a *shorter* version of the source, but to restate a passage or a concept described in the source, in your own words. In any source-based work, you will want to vary the ways in which you use or reference your sources, so knowing how to paraphrase a work is an important skill to learn.

- For more on summary, quotation and paraphrase, see pages 36, 49–58.
- For **Crafting Your Own Voice: Summary,** see page 180.
- For **Crafting Your Own Voice: Quotation,** see page 599.

In his paper on the play *The Zoo Story*, by Edward Albee, Jim Hanks uses paraphrase several times, sometimes in conjunction with quotation, to provide examples that vividly support his thesis that the play's characters represent two opposing ways of life that will ultimately come into violent conflict. In the paragraph below, Hanks inserts a paraphrase between two sentences that interpret the play in light of its opening scene:

The paragraph begins with a main idea that will be supported by the source.

The next sentence sets up the contrast between the two characters, a central point in the paper's thesis.

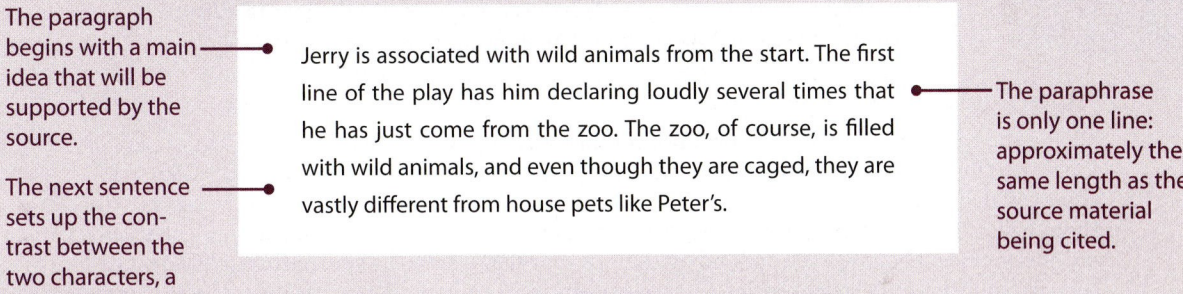

Jerry is associated with wild animals from the start. The first line of the play has him declaring loudly several times that he has just come from the zoo. The zoo, of course, is filled with wild animals, and even though they are caged, they are vastly different from house pets like Peter's.

The paraphrase is only one line: approximately the same length as the source material being cited.

Tips for Avoiding Plagiarism

Craft & Voice: Student Hanks uses a paraphrase to put the action of the play into his own words. The first line of the play provides a strong example that is already fairly brief and thus does not require summary. Likewise, the line itself does not use language that requires word-for-word quotation. As a result, this short paraphrase works nicely to support the conceptual frame he is creating in this paragraph.

Citing Sources: Notice that the student writer clearly identifies which line he is referring to in the body of his paraphrase. When paraphrasing or quoting from a play, a writer needs to identify a line number as this student did ("first line of the play"), or use a parenthetical citation. As with any source, the play must be listed alphabetically by author's last name on the works cited page.

Edwin Wilson
Writing . . . is your mirror [of] your reaction. . . .

A Conversation on Writing: Advice from the Critics

In his interview for this book, the *Wall Street Journal* theater critic Edwin Wilson offers advice for writing about drama. Wilson wrote reviews for the *Wall Street Journal* for twenty-two years, served as president of the New York Drama Critics Circle, and is the author of *The Theatre Experience* as well as coauthor, with Alvin Goldfarb, of *Living Theatre: A History* and *Theatre: The Lively Art.* He has produced plays on and off Broadway and the feature film *The Nashville Sound.* Wilson is also the author of two original plays, *The Bettinger Prize* and *Waterfall.*

Write about Your Experience

Maybe you can say to yourself, "I don't really know what's going on in this play." That's a personal reaction. . . . Usually people do decide they like certain kinds of plays and don't like others, which is fine because it's a very individual sort of thing. So another way of writing about a play, and these are not mutually exclusive, but another way of writing about a play is to say how you feel about it. . . . You kind of analyze your feelings too as you go through the play because you shouldn't be locked into just one position. You should let yourself experience your own feelings as you go through reading a play.

Write as a Reporter

One [way to write about a play is] to simply report what happens in the play. This is what this play is about. Here are the characters. Here's what happens in the action. Here's where it takes place in terms of the setting. It takes place in the seventeenth century, the eighteenth century, or in modern times, World War II or the Vietnam War or the war in Iraq. It takes place in a certain time in a certain place with certain characters. And you are in effect being a reporter.

Revise

There's an old saying . . . that plays are not written, they're rewritten. And what that means is the first time a play is written, it's almost never the finished product. Almost never. . . . Writing is really a process.

For an analysis of *The Zoo Story* and additional guidance on writing about drama, view the entire interview with Edwin Wilson, at **connect.mcgraw-hill.com.**

Writing a Review

When you write, are you doing an analysis or a review? Both are common responses to a play. Make sure you know which you've been asked to write. A review is an argument. If you are asked to write a review, you will need to include your opinion along with a summary of the work. List the actors, the director (and stage designer and costume designer, if these aspects are included as important points in your review), and the theater where the work is being performed. Then you will need to persuade your reader that your evaluation of the work is worthwhile. Base your opinion of the work on how effectively the script engaged you, how effectively the actors drew you in with their performances, and how effectively the director (or stage designer, costume designer, producer) interpreted the play for the stage. If the play is staged often (such as with Shakespeare), you may be able to use a point of comparison in your discussion of the performance you have reviewed. If you are asked to compare, explain, or analyze, your paper will go beyond a summary of what happened in the play and will require an interpretation. That interpretation in drama will depend on recording how the play works. Part of a *New York Times* review of the first production in America of Edward Albee's first play, *The Zoo Story*, is on page 1062. Note how the reviewer comments on the staging, the acting, and the plot. Consider the following:

- Why does Brooks Atkinson write that the ending is "theatrical," and is that intended as a compliment? Is the rest of the play theatrical? How would you characterize a theater style that is not theatrical?

- How does your reaction compare with that of the reviewer? Brooks Atkinson was an important force in the American theater of his day and a major factor in the question of whether or not a play would succeed.

- What did other reviewers say about the play? Research several other articles about this play and compare them to the current opinion of the importance of *The Zoo Story*, which is still being performed nearly fifty years after its opening night.

"I let [the unconscious] do what it wants to do . . . I get visual images . . . sets of characters . . . scenes . . . but I wait for a very long time till I'm fairly sure that I know the characters well and I know their destination well . . . I don't try to shape anything. I let my mind do what it wants." Conversation with Edward Albee

A REVIEW OF *THE ZOO STORY*

Brooks Atkinson's review of Edward Albee's *The Zoo Story, The New York Times,* January 15, 1960

After the banalities of Broadway it tones the muscles and freshens the system to examine the squalor of Off Broadway. . . . [Two actors] sufficed for the short play put on at the Provincetown Playhouse last evening [of] Edward Albee's "The Zoo Story."

The Cast
Jerry . . . . George Maharis
Peter . . . . William Daniels

"The Zoo Story" is a dialogue . . . interesting and well acted by intelligent professionals. Nothing of enduring value is said . . . but [the play] captures some part of the dismal mood that infects many writers today.

Mr. Albee's "The Zoo Story" does not have so much literary distinction. . . . Mr Albee is more the reporter. There are two characters and two benches in his play set in Central Park. A cultivated, complacent publisher is reading a book. An intense, aggressive young man in shabby dress strikes up a conversation with him.

Or, to be exact, a monologue. For the intruder wants to unburden his mind of his private miseries and resentments, and they pour out of him in a flow of wild, scabrous, psychotic details. Since Mr. Albee is an excellent writer and the designer of dialogue and since he apparently knows the city, "The Zoo Story" is consistently interesting and illuminating— odd and pithy. It ends melodramatically as if Mr. Albee had lost control of his material. Although the conclusion is theatrical, it lacks the sense of improvisation that characterizes the main body of the play.

Milton Katselas has staged "The Zoo Story" admirably; and Mr. Maharis' overwrought yet searching intruder, and Mr. Daniels' perplexed publisher are first-rate pieces of acting.

Although the Provincetown bill is hardly glamorous, it has a point of view. Mr. Albee write[s] on the assumption that the human condition is stupid and ludicrous.

Suggestions for Writing

1. What is the relationship of plot to character in *The Zoo Story*? How do these elements of drama depend on each other in this play?

2. Compare the role of setting in *Trifles* (chapter 30) and *The Zoo Story*. Consider how, for example, *Trifles* would change if it were staged at the prison, or how *The Zoo Story* would change if Peter and Jerry ran into one another at a coffee shop.

3. Dialogue drives the action in *The Zoo Story*, but the play was written to be performed. Choose one of the longer monologues (for instance, Jerry's on pages 1033–1036), and write stage directions for the character not speaking. Cite specific lines that require certain reactions or gestures. How would your directions enhance the audience's experience of the monologue?

4. Focus on an episode of your favorite television drama, if you have one, or a recent movie you enjoyed, and compare it in relation to character and plot to either *Trifles* or *The Zoo Story*. Do television plays and movies stress the same element as these theater pieces? If they differ, how would you describe the differences?

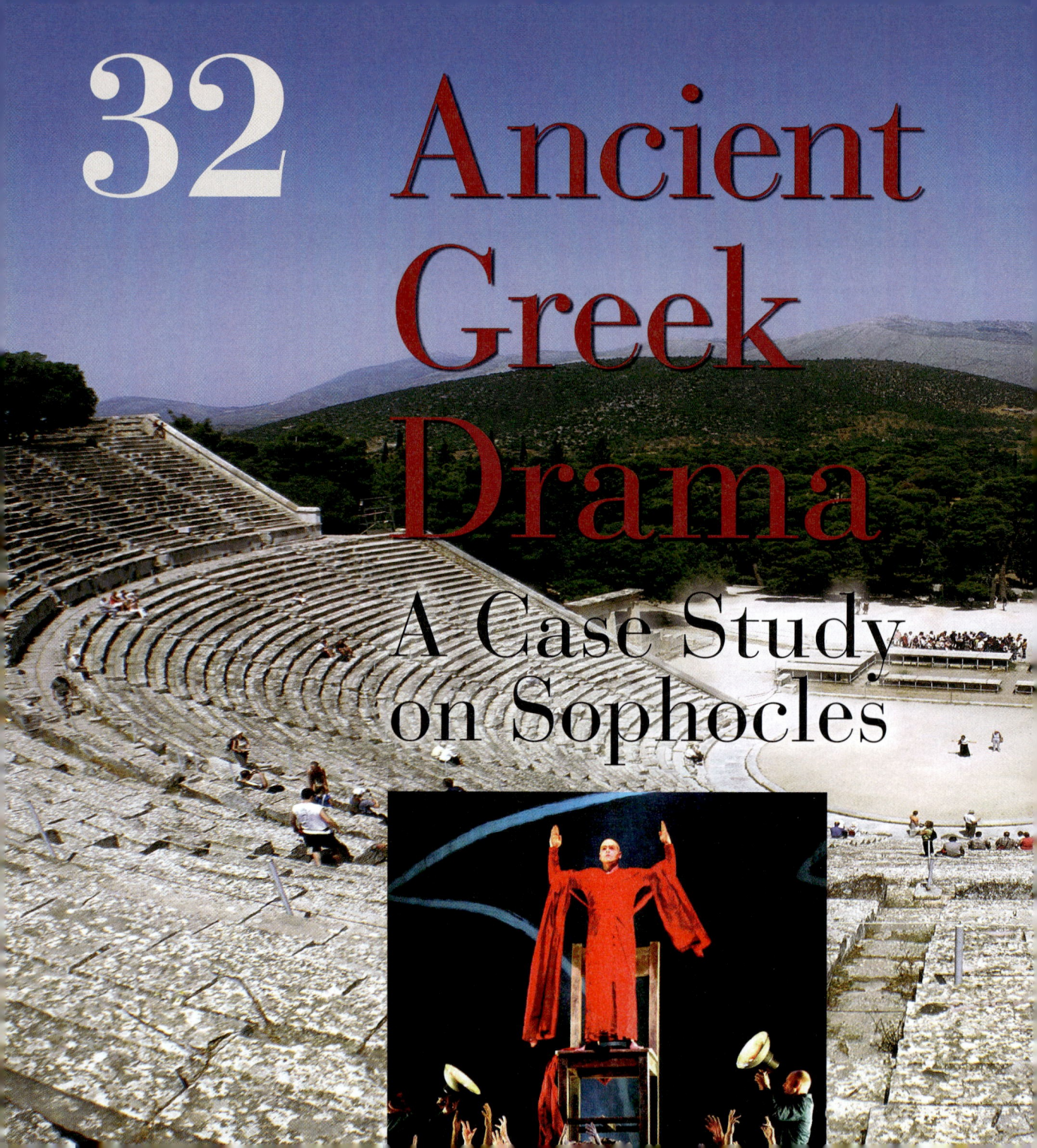

32

Ancient Greek Drama

A Case Study on Sophocles

this: The hillside theater is dark except for the stars above the pillars that form the set. A figure—the king—limps forward and speaks.

My children, generations of the living
In the line of Kadmos, nursed at his ancient hearth:
Why have you strewn yourselves before these altars
In supplication, with your boughs and garlands? . . .

A second figure—a priest—speaks:

Great Oedipus, O powerful King of Thebes!
You see how all the ages of our people
Cling to your altar steps. . . .

Disaster has struck the land and its people, and the leader hopes to set things right. At the moment the play begins, chaos threatens to destroy life within the city walls. The people have come to hear what the king has to say—much the way children caught up in misery and illness go to their father for help and relief.

These speeches mark the opening of the ancient Greek play *Oedipus the King*. They are among the first words of stage dialogue ever heard by a Western audience, and they reverberate today. The story starts with Oedipus, the main character, who limps onto the stage. The name *Oedipus* in Greek means "lame" or "club-footed," but the limp is more than literal. It's an outward sign of a wound in the hero's character—which we will come to recognize as the full story unfolds.

The Greeks called this play *Oedipus Tyrannos* (Oedipus the Tyrant—which signifies, in Greek, an illegitimate king); it was known to the Romans as *Oedipus Rex*, or as we know it today, *Oedipus the King*. It is a highly formal and stylized work of theater. Yet the presence of a live human being (an actor) standing in a place marked off from ordinary space (the stage) compels our attention. As you approach this play, picture the design of the set, an open-air stage with its spare setting: a few columns, steps, and the sky above—that's it.

Gregory Nagy *We're really the participants of drama.*

A Conversation on Sophocles

Drama as Spiritual and Governmental Requirement

In Athens—the classical period, the Golden Age of Greek civilization—all Athenians have to be theatergoers because it's a civic obligation to go to theater. . . . It's not just political . . . it's a religious duty—in fact, festivals and religion go together. . . . It's very important when we look at theater in the fifth century, or even before . . . [that] when the Athenian[s], twenty thousand, thirty thousand of them, go to Athenian state theater, they're going . . . to participate . . . and in this . . . what is achieved is a purification of the body politic, a renewal. . . . We might . . . call it . . . a sacred narrative . . . of . . . heroic values.

Pathos and *Catharsis*

Imagine looking down at a sea of faces, twenty thousand pairs of eyes are weeping simultaneously, twenty thousand people have their hair stand on end in terror. . . . The *pathos*—of the hero, who is . . . larger than life, let's say Oedipus . . . this chemistry brings about *catharsis*. . . . It's a Greek word that means . . . "purification."

Sophocles as Public Figure

Artists in the ancient world . . . and Sophocles was no exception . . . [were] public figures . . . Sophocles was not only a master dramaturge, he was a master poet, a master composer of music, a master musician. . . . He was everything to the Athenians. When he died in his late eighties . . . there was such an outpouring of emotion that there are many anecdotes about how Sophocles became not only . . . the national poet of the Athenians, but . . . was actually worshipped as a cult hero.

To watch the entire interview online, go to **connect.mcgraw-hill.com**.

RESEARCH ASSIGNMENT   After watching the interview with Nagy, explain how epic poetry and tragic drama were influenced by each other. How would you describe the influence on Sophocles of the tradition of epic poetry in Greece?

Gregory Nagy [Nahzh] is Director of the Center for Hellenic Studies in Washington, D.C., and the Francis Jones Professor of Classical Greek Literature and Professor of Comparative Literature at Harvard University.

THE OEDIPUS STORY

Versions of the Oedipus story were part of an oral tradition hundreds of years before Sophocles enacted it as drama. It has its roots in myth, that of the house (or kingdom) of Atreus—a complicated tapestry of guilt and revenge, generational conflict, loss, and gain. The story would have been well known to the Athenian audience; what matters here is not *suspense* (we all know "who done it" already) but *how* the tale is told. Old Thebes, where the action of the play takes place, is ruled by high-minded Oedipus, who appeared one day after the death of the previous king, Laïos. Thebes has been an outpost of civilization in an otherwise wild countryside where bandits reign, terrors lurk, and odd events take place. The city traditionally stands for order, the countryside for chaos, yet Sophocles reverses this—chaos has entered in.

The playwright takes the material of the Oedipus myth, folds and manipulates the time span, and molds it into one of the central texts of our culture, a play whose subject is the essence of human character, the relation of character to destiny or fate, and the links between the middle world of human life and the upper world of the gods. As the play unfolds, the great king discovers that he himself is the cause of the troubles. This truth reveals itself gradually, brought to him in pieces by various characters. At some points, he refuses to believe what he is told; at others, he begs to be told what others prefer not to tell him. Toward the end, Oedipus discovers the truth about himself, and this leads to a desperate act of self-mutilation—which, ironically, turns his vision dark and allows him to "see" for the first time the enormity of his sin.

Sophocles (496?–406/5 B.C.E.)

The greatest playwright of the Golden Age of Greek drama, Sophocles, the son of a successful Athenian armorer, attained extraordinary mastery of the dramatic art. He also participated fully in the political life of his city. Early in his life as a creator of plays, he was influenced by the work of his predecessor Aeschylus but went on to stamp his own productions with the particular mark of great character, diction, and dramatic irony that we recognize today. He wrote over a hundred plays, only seven of which have survived in their entirety. Of these *Oedipus the King* remains the pinnacle of Western drama and is the subject of the *Poetics,* the Greek philosopher Aristotle's treatise on the nature of drama. Sophocles' plays were performed at public festivals and employed Athenian citizens as well as trained actors and musicians. Along with those of William Shakespeare, they stand as the most important dramas in the life of Western culture.

▶ The Oedipus Myth ▶

Laïos, King of Thebes, is warned in a prophecy that his son will murder him and marry Laïos's wife Iocaste, the Queen of Thebes.

To prevent that prophecy from coming true, Laïos orders a herdsman to take his firstborn son into the country and murder him there.

The herdsman pities the baby. Instead of killing him, he pierces his feet and gives him to another herdsman to keep. The baby is named Oedipus, which means "swollen foot."

The second herdsman takes the baby Oedipus to his master, the King of Corinth, who adopts him and raises him as a prince.

Oedipus, now a young man, receives a prophecy that he will kill his father and marry his mother.

Assuming the "father" and "mother" of the prophecy are the king and queen of Corinth, Oedipus flees that city for the countryside.

AS YOU READ Picture the design of the amphitheater, with its spare setting of columns and bright air. Read through the play once, and you find that it takes place in this single location, with no change of scene. Only the entrances and exits of the various characters mark the rhythmic development of the action here.

Oedipus the King (c. 430 B.C.E.)

—translated by Dudley Fitts and Robert Fitzgerald

CHARACTERS

OEDIPUS	**TEIRESIAS**	**SHEPHERD OF LAÏOS**
A PRIEST	**IOCASTE**	**SECOND MESSENGER**
CREON	**MESSENGER**	**CHORUS OF THEBAN ELDERS**

In his travels, Oedipus comes to a crossroads and gets into an argument. His temper gets the better of him, and he murders his opponents, who, unbeknownst to him, include Laïos, Oedipus's true father.

Oedipus comes to Thebes, which is threatened by the Sphinx, who guards the gate of the city and devours all who cannot answer her riddle.

Oedipus solves the Sphinx's riddle. Her riddle solved, the Sphinx throws herself off a cliff and dies.

Thankful to Oedipus, and recently having lost its king, the city of Thebes awards him the crown and the Queen, Oedipus's mother Iocaste, as a bride.

The prophecies conveyed to Laïos and Oedipus have now come true.

Some time later, Thebes suffers plague as a result of "sin" and King Oedipus painfully discovers that he is the sinner.

THE SCENE. *Before the palace of Oedipus, King of Thebes. A central door and two lateral doors open onto a platform which runs the length of the façade. On the platform, right and left, are altars; and three steps lead down into the "orchestra," or chorus-ground. At the beginning of the action these steps are crowded by suppliants who have brought branches and chaplets of olive leaves and who lie in various attitudes of despair. OEDIPUS enters.*

PROLOGUE

OEDIPUS: My children, generations of the living
In the line of Kadmos, nursed at his ancient hearth:
Why have you strewn yourselves before these altars
In supplication, with your boughs and garlands?
The breath of incense rises from the city   5
With a sound of prayer and lamentation.
                                        Children,
I would not have you speak through messengers,
And therefore I have come myself to hear you—
I, Oedipus, who bear the famous name.

    [To a PRIEST:

You, there, since you are eldest in the company,   10
Speak for them all, tell me what preys upon you,
Whether you come in dread, or crave some blessing:
Tell me, and never doubt that I will help you
In every way I can; I should be heartless
Were I not moved to find you suppliant here.   15

PRIEST: Great Oedipus, O powerful King of Thebes!
You see how all the ages of our people
Cling to your altar steps: here are boys
Who can barely stand alone, and here are priests
20 By weight of age, as I am a priest of God,
And young men chosen from those yet unmarried;
As for the others, all that multitude,
They wait with olive chaplets in the squares,
At the two shrines of Pallas, and where Apollo
Speaks in the glowing embers.
25   Your own eyes
Must tell you: Thebes is tossed on a murdering sea
And can not lift her head from the death surge.
A rust consumes the buds and fruits of the earth;
The herds are sick; children die unborn,
30 And labor is vain. The god of plague and pyre
Raids like detestable lightning through the city,
And all the house of Kadmos is laid waste,
All emptied, and all darkened: Death alone
Battens upon the misery of Thebes.
35 You are not one of the immortal gods, we know;
Yet we have come to you to make our prayer
As to the man surest in mortal ways
And wisest in the ways of God. You saved us
From the Sphinx, that flinty singer, and the tribute
40 We paid to her so long; yet you were never
Better informed than we, nor could we teach you:
It was some god breathed in you to set us free.

Therefore, O mighty King, we turn to you:
Find us our safety, find us a remedy,
45 Whether by counsel of the gods or men.
A king of wisdom tested in the past
Can act in a time of troubles, and act well.
Noblest of men, restore
Life to your city! Think how all men call you
50 Liberator for your triumph long ago;
Ah, when your years of kingship are remembered,
Let them not say *We rose, but later fell—*
Keep the State from going down in the storm!
Once, years ago, with happy augury,
55 You brought us fortune; be the same again!
No man questions your power to rule the land:
But rule over men, not over a dead city!
Ships are only hulls, citadels are nothing,
When no life moves in the empty passageways.

The old priest (Eric House) beseeches Oedipus (Douglas Campbell) to find a cure for the plague in *Oedipus Rex* (1957).

OEDIPUS: Poor children! You may be sure I know   60
All that you longed for in your coming here.
I know that you are deathly sick; and yet,
Sick as you are, not one is as sick as I.
Each of you suffers in himself alone
His anguish, not another's; but my spirit   65
Groans for the city, for myself, for you.
I was not sleeping, you are not waking me.
No, I have been in tears for a long while
And in my restless thought walked many ways.
In all my search, I found one helpful course,   70
And that I have taken: I have sent Creon,
Son of Menoikeus, brother of the Queen,
To Delphi, Apollo's place of revelation,
To learn there, if he can,
What act or pledge of mine may save the city.   75
I have counted the days, and now, this very day,
I am troubled, for he has overstayed his time.
What is he doing? He has been gone too long.
Yet whenever he comes back, I should do ill
To scant whatever duty God reveals.   80

PRIEST: It is a timely promise. At this instant
They tell me Creon is here.

OEDIPUS: O Lord Apollo!
May his news be fair as his face is radiant!

PRIEST: It could not be otherwise: he is crowned
with bay,
The chaplet is thick with berries.   85

OEDIPUS: We shall soon know;
   He is near enough to hear us now.

   [Enter CREON

                               O Prince:
   Brother: son of Menoikeus:
   What answer do you bring us from the god?

CREON: A strong one. I can tell you, great afflictions
90   Will turn out well, if they are taken well.

OEDIPUS: What was the oracle? These vague words
   Leave me still hanging between hope and fear.

CREON: Is it your pleasure to hear me with all these
   Gathered around us? I am prepared to speak,
95   But should we not go in?

OEDIPUS: Let them all hear it.
   It is for them I suffer, more than for myself.

CREON: Then I will tell you what I heard at Delphi.

   In plain words
   The god commands us to expel from the land of
      Thebes
100   An old defilement we are sheltering.
   It is a deathly thing, beyond cure;
   We must not let it feed upon us longer.

OEDIPUS: What defilement? How shall we rid
      ourselves of it?

CREON: By exile or death, blood for blood. It was
105   Murder that brought the plague-wind on the city.

OEDIPUS: Murder of whom? Surely the god has
      named him?

CREON: My lord: long ago Laïos was our king,
   Before you came to govern us.

OEDIPUS: I know;
   I learned of him from others; I never saw him.

110   **CREON:**   He was murdered; and Apollo commands
      us now
   To take revenge upon whoever killed him.

OEDIPUS: Upon whom? Where are they? Where shall
      we find a clue
   To solve that crime, after so many years?

CREON: Here in this land, he said.

                               If we make enquiry,
   We may touch things that otherwise escape us.   115

OEDIPUS: Tell me: Was Laïos murdered in his house,
   Or in the fields, or in some foreign country?

CREON: He said he planned to make a pilgrimage.
   He did not come home again.

OEDIPUS: And was there no one,
   No witness, no companion, to tell what happened?   120

CREON: They were all killed but one, and he got away
   So frightened that he could remember one thing only.

OEDIPUS: What was that one thing? One may be the key
   To everything, if we resolve to use it.

CREON: He said that a band of highwaymen attacked   125
      them,
   Outnumbered them, and overwhelmed the King.

OEDIPUS: Strange, that a highwayman should be so
      daring—
   Unless some faction here bribed him to do it.

CREON: We thought of that. But after Laïos' death
   New troubles arose and we had no avenger.   130

OEDIPUS: What troubles could prevent your hunting
      down the killers?

CREON: The riddling Sphinx's song
   Made us deaf to all mysteries but her own.

OEDIPUS: Then once more I must bring what is dark
      to light.
   It is most fitting that Apollo shows,   135
   As you do, this compunction for the dead.
   You shall see how I stand by you, as I should,
   To avenge the city and the city's god,
   And not as though it were for some distant friend,
   But for my own sake, to be rid of evil.   140
   Whoever killed King Laïos might—who knows?—
   Decide at any moment to kill me as well.
   By avenging the murdered king I protect myself.

   Come, then, my children: leave the altar steps,
   Lift up your olive boughs!
                               One of you go   145

Oedipus (Philip Langridge) addresses the people of Thebes in *Oedipus Rex* (1993).

And summon the people of Kadmos to gather here.
I will do all that I can; you may tell them that.

[*Exit a* PAGE

So, with the help of God,
We shall be saved—or else indeed we are lost.

150   **PRIEST:**   Let us rise, children. It was for this we came,
And now the King has promised it himself.
Phoibos has sent us an oracle; may he descend
Himself to save us and drive out the plague.

[*Exeunt* OEDIPUS *and* CREON *into the palace
by the central door. The* PRIEST *and the*
SUPPLIANTS *disperse R and L. After a short
pause the* CHORUS *enters the orchestra.*

PÁRODOS

CHORUS: [STROPHE 1
What is God singing in his profound
Delphi of gold and shadow?
What oracle for Thebes, the sunwhipped city?

Fear unjoints me, the roots of my heart tremble.

5   Now I remember, O Healer, your power, and wonder:
Will you send doom like a sudden cloud, or weave it
Like nightfall of the past?

Speak, speak to us, issue of holy sound:
Dearest to our expectancy: be tender!

[ANTISTROPHE 1
Let me pray to Athenê, the immortal daughter of   10
    Zeus,
And to Artemis her sister
Who keeps her famous throne in the market ring,
And to Apollo, bowman at the far butts of heaven—

O gods, descend! Like three streams leap against
The fires of our grief, the fires of darkness;   15
Be swift to bring us rest!

As in the old time from the brilliant house
Of air you stepped to save us, come again!

Now our afflictions have no end,   [STROPHE 2
Now all our stricken host lies down   20
And no man fights off death with his mind;

The noble plowland bears no grain,
And groaning mothers can not bear—

See, how our lives like birds take wing,
Like sparks that fly when a fire soars,   25
To the shore of the god of evening.

The plague burns on, it is pitiless,   [ANTISTROPHE 2
Though pallid children laden with death
Lie unwept in the stony ways,

And old gray women by every path   30
Flock to the strand about the altars

There to strike their breasts and cry
Worship of Phoibos in wailing prayers:
Be kind, God's golden child!

[STROPHE 3
There are no swords in this attack by fire,
No shields, but we are ringed with cries.   35

Send the besieger plunging from our homes
Into the vast sea-room of the Atlantic
Or into the waves that foam eastward to Thrace—

For the day ravages what the night spares—

Destroy our enemy, lord of the thunder!   40
Let him be riven by lightning from heaven!

The chorus in *Oedipus Rex* (1993).

[ANTISTROPHE 3

Phoibos Apollo, stretch the sun's bowstring,
That golden cord, until it sing for us,
45 Flashing arrows in heaven!

Artemis, Huntress,
Race with flaring lights upon our mountains!

O scarlet god, O golden-banded brow,
O Theban Bacchos in a storm of Maenads,

[*Enter* OEDIPUS, *C*

Whirl upon Death, that all the Undying hate!
50 Come with blinding torches, come in joy!

SCENE 1

OEDIPUS: Is this your prayer? It may be answered.
Come,
Listen to me, act as the crisis demands,
And you shall have relief from all these evils.

Until now I was a stranger to this tale,
5 As I had been a stranger to the crime.
Could I track down the murderer without a clue?
But now, friends,
As one who became a citizen after the murder,
I make this proclamation to all Thebans:
10 If any man knows by whose hand Laïos, son of
Labdakos,

Met his death, I direct that man to tell me everything,
No matter what he fears for having so long withheld it.
Let it stand as promised that no further trouble
Will come to him, but he may leave the land in safety.

Moreover: If anyone knows the murderer to be foreign, 15
Let him not keep silent: he shall have his reward
from me.
However, if he does conceal it; if any man
Fearing for his friend or for himself disobeys this
edict,
Hear what I propose to do:

I solemnly forbid the people of this country, 20
Where power and throne are mine, ever to receive
that man
Or speak to him, no matter who he is, or let him
Join in sacrifice, lustration, or in prayer.
I decree that he be driven from every house,
Being, as he is, corruption itself to us: the Delphic 25
Voice of Zeus has pronounced this revelation.
Thus I associate myself with the oracle
And take the side of the murdered king.

As for the criminal, I pray to God—
Whether it be a lurking thief, or one of a number— 30
I pray that that man's life be consumed in evil and
wretchedness.
And as for me, this curse applies no less
If it should turn out that the culprit is my guest here,
Sharing my hearth.
You have heard the penalty.
I lay it on you now to attend to this 35
For my sake, for Apollo's, for the sick
Sterile city that heaven has abandoned.
Suppose the oracle had given you no command:
Should this defilement go uncleansed for ever?
You should have found the murderer: your king, 40
A noble king, had been destroyed!
Now I,
Having the power that he held before me,
Having his bed, begetting children there
Upon his wife, as he would have, had he lived—
Their son would have been my children's brother, 45
If Laïos had had luck in fatherhood!
(But surely ill luck rushed upon his reign)—
I say I take the son's part, just as though

Oedipus vows to find King Laïos's murderer in *Oedipus Rex* (1957).

50 I were his son, to press the fight for him
And see it won! I'll find the hand that brought
Death to Labdakos' and Polydoros' child,
Heir of Kadmos' and Agenor's line.
And as for those who fail me,
May the gods deny them the fruit of the earth,
55 Fruit of the womb, and may they rot utterly!
Let them be wretched as we are wretched, and worse!

For you, for loyal Thebans, and for all
Who find my actions right, I pray the favor
Of justice, and of all the immortal gods.

60 **CHORAGOS:** Since I am under oath, my lord, I swear
I did not do the murder, I can not name
The murderer. Might not the oracle
That has ordained the search tell where to find him?

OEDIPUS: An honest question. But no man in the world
65 Can make the gods do more than the gods will.

CHORAGOS: There is one last expedient—

OEDIPUS: Tell me what it is.
Though it seem slight, you must not hold it back.

CHORAGOS: A lord clairvoyant to the lord Apollo,
As we all know, is the skilled Teiresias.
70 One might learn much about this from him, Oedipus.

OEDIPUS: I am not wasting time:
Creon spoke of this, and I have sent for him—
Twice, in fact; it is strange that he is not here.

CHORAGOS: The other matter—that old report—seems
useless.

OEDIPUS: Tell me. I am interested in all reports. 75

CHORAGOS: The King was said to have been killed by
highwaymen.

OEDIPUS: I know. But we have no witnesses to that.

CHORAGOS: If the killer can feel a particle of dread,
Your curse will bring him out of hiding!

OEDIPUS: No.
The man who dared that act will fear no curse. 80

[Enter the blind seer TEIRESIAS, *led by a* PAGE

CHORAGOS: But there is one man who may detect the
criminal.
This is Teiresias, this is the holy prophet
In whom, alone of all men, truth was born.

OEDIPUS: Teiresias: seer: student of mysteries,
Of all that's taught and all that no man tells, 85
Secrets of Heaven and secrets of the earth:
Blind though you are, you know the city lies
Sick with plague; and from this plague, my lord,
We find that you alone can guard or save us.
Possibly you did not hear the messengers? 90
Apollo, when we sent to him,
Sent us back word that this great pestilence
Would lift, but only if we established clearly
The identity of those who murdered Laïos.
They must be killed or exiled. 95
Can you use
Birdflight or any art of divination
To purify yourself, and Thebes, and me
From this contagion? We are in your hands.
There is no fairer duty
Than that of helping others in distress. 100

TEIRESIAS: How dreadful knowledge of the truth can be
When there's no help in truth! I knew this well,
But made myself forget. I should not have come.

OEDIPUS: What is troubling you? Why are your eyes
so cold?

TEIRESIAS: Let me go home. Bear your own fate, and I'll 105
Bear mine. It is better so: trust what I say.

OEDIPUS: What you say is ungracious and unhelpful
To your native country. Do not refuse to speak.

TEIRESIAS: When it comes to speech, your own is neither temperate
110 Nor opportune. I wish to be more prudent.

OEDIPUS: In God's name, we all beg you—

TEIRESIAS: You are all ignorant.
No; I will never tell you what I know.
Now it is my misery; then, it would be yours.

OEDIPUS: What! You do know something, and will not tell us?
115 You would betray us all and wreck the State?

TEIRESIAS: I do not intend to torture myself, or you.
Why persist in asking? You will not persuade me.

OEDIPUS: What a wicked old man you are! You'd try a stone's
Patience! Out with it! Have you no feeling at all?

120 **TEIRESIAS:** You call me unfeeling. If you could only see
The nature of your own feelings . . .

OEDIPUS: Why,
Who would not feel as I do? Who could endure
Your arrogance toward the city?

TEIRESIAS: What does it matter!
Whether I speak or not, it is bound to come.

125 **OEDIPUS:** Then, if "it" is bound to come, you are bound
to tell me.

TEIRESIAS: No, I will not go on. Rage as you please.

OEDIPUS: Rage? Why not!
And I'll tell you what I think:
You planned it, you had it done, you all but
130 Killed him with your own hands: if you had eyes,
I'd say the crime was yours, and yours alone.

TEIRESIAS: So? I charge you, then,
Abide by the proclamation you have made:
From this day forth
135 Never speak again to these men or to me;
You yourself are the pollution of this country.

OEDIPUS: You dare say that! Can you possibly think you have
Some way of going free, after such insolence?

TEIRESIAS: I have gone free. It is the truth sustains me.

OEDIPUS: Who taught you shamelessness? It was not 140
your craft.

TEIRESIAS: You did. You made me speak. I did not
want to.

OEDIPUS: Speak what? Let me hear it again more clearly.

TEIRESIAS: Was it not clear before? Are you tempting
me?

OEDIPUS: I did not understand it. Say it again.

TEIRESIAS: I say that you are the murderer whom you 145
seek.

OEDIPUS: Now twice you have spat out infamy. You'll
pay for it!

TEIRESIAS: Would you care for more? Do you wish to be
really angry?

OEDIPUS: Say what you will. Whatever you say is
worthless.

TEIRESIAS: I say you live in hideous shame with those
Most dear to you. You can not see the evil. 150

Teiresias (Harry Peeters) tells Oedipus he is the source of the plague in *Oedipus Rex* (1993).

OEDIPUS: It seems you can go on mouthing like this
for ever.

TEIRESIAS: I can, if there is power in truth.

OEDIPUS: There is:
But not for you, not for you,
You sightless, witless, senseless, mad old man!

155 **TEIRESIAS:**   You are the madman. There is no one here
Who will not curse you soon, as you curse me.

OEDIPUS: You child of endless night! You can not hurt me
Or any other man who sees the sun.

TEIRESIAS: True: it is not from me your fate will come.
160 That lies within Apollo's competence,
As it is his concern.

OEDIPUS: Tell me:
Are you speaking for Creon, or for yourself?

TEIRESIAS: Creon is no threat. You weave your own
doom.

OEDIPUS: Wealth, power, craft of statesmanship!
165 Kingly position, everywhere admired!
What savage envy is stored up against these,
If Creon, whom I trusted, Creon my friend,
For this great office which the city once
Put in my hands unsought—if for this power
170 Creon desires in secret to destroy me!

He has bought this decrepit fortune-teller, this
Collector of dirty pennies, this prophet fraud—
Why, he is no more clairvoyant than I am!
                                          Tell us:
Has your mystic mummery ever approached the
truth?
175 When that hellcat the Sphinx was performing here,
What help were you to these people?
Her magic was not for the first man who came along:
It demanded a real exorcist. Your birds—
What good were they? or the gods, for the matter
of that?
180 But I came by,
Oedipus, the simple man, who knows nothing—
I thought it out for myself, no birds helped me!
And this is the man you think you can destroy,

That you may be close to Creon when he's king!
Well, you and your friend Creon, it seems to me,   185
Will suffer most. If you were not an old man,
You would have paid already for your plot.

CHORAGOS: We can not see that his words or yours
Have been spoken except in anger, Oedipus,
And of anger we have no need. How can God's will   190
Be accomplished best? That is what most concerns us.

TEIRESIAS: You are a king. But where argument's
concerned
I am your man, as much a king as you.
I am not your servant, but Apollo's.
I have no need of Creon to speak for me.   195

Listen to me. You mock my blindness, do you?
But I say that you, with both your eyes, are blind:
You can not see the wretchedness of your life,
Nor in whose house you live, no, nor with whom.
Who are your father and mother? Can you tell me?   200
You do not even know the blind wrongs
That you have done them, on earth and in the world
below.
But the double lash of your parents' curse will
whip you
Out of this land some day, with only night
Upon your precious eyes.   205
Your cries then—where will they not be heard?
What fastness of Kithairon will not echo them?
And that bridal-descant of yours—you'll know it then,
The song they sang when you came here to Thebes
And found your misguided berthing.   210
All this, and more, that you can not guess at now,
Will bring you to yourself among your children.

Be angry, then. Curse Creon. Curse my words.
I tell you, no man that walks upon the earth
Shall be rooted out more horribly than you.   215

OEDIPUS: Am I to bear this from him?—Damnation
Take you! Out of this place! Out of my sight!

TEIRESIAS: I would not have come at all if you had not
asked me.

OEDIPUS: Could I have told that you'd talk nonsense, that
You'd come here to make a fool of yourself, and of me?   220

Teiresias (Donald Davis) prophesies Oedipus's downfall in
Oedipus Rex (1957).

TEIRESIAS: A fool? Your parents thought me sane
enough.

OEDIPUS: My parents again!—Wait: who were my
parents?

TEIRESIAS: This day will give you a father, and break
your heart.

OEDIPUS: Your infantile riddles! Your damned
abracadabra!

225   **TEIRESIAS:**   You were a great man once at solving
riddles.

OEDIPUS: Mock me with that if you like; you will find
it true.

TEIRESIAS: It was true enough. It brought about your
ruin.

OEDIPUS: But if it saved this town?

TEIRESIAS: *[To the* PAGE*:*

Boy, give me your hand.

OEDIPUS: Yes, boy; lead him away.

—While you are here

230   We can do nothing. Go; leave us in peace.

TEIRESIAS: I will go when I have said what I have to say.
How can you hurt me? And I tell you again:
The man you have been looking for all this time,

The damned man, the murderer of Laïos,
The man is in Thebes. To your mind he is   235
foreign-born,
But it will soon be shown that he is a Theban,
A revelation that will fail to please.

A blind man,
Who has his eyes now; a penniless man, who is
rich now;
And he will go tapping the strange earth with his staff.
To the children with whom he lives now he will be   240
Brother and father—the very same; to her
Who bore him, son and husband—the very same
Who came to his father's bed, wet with his father's
blood.

Enough. Go think that over.
If later you find error in what I have said,   245
You may say that I have no skill in prophecy.

[Exit TEIRESIAS, *led by his* PAGE.
OEDIPUS *goes into the palace.*

ODE 1

CHORUS: The Delphic stone of prophecies   [STROPHE 1
Remembers ancient regicide
And a still bloody hand.
That killer's hour of flight has come.
He must be stronger than riderless   5
Courses of untiring wind,
For the son of Zeus armed with his father's thunder
Leaps in lightning after him;
And the Furies follow him, the sad Furies.

Holy Parnassos' peak of snow   [ANTISTROPHE 1   10
Flashes and blinds that secret man,
That all shall hunt him down:
Though he may roam the forest shade
Like a bull gone wild from pasture
To rage through glooms of stone.   15
Doom comes down on him; flight will not avail him;
For the world's heart calls him desolate,
And the immortal Furies follow, for ever follow.

But now a wilder thing is heard   [STROPHE 2
From the old man skilled at hearing Fate in the   20
wingbeat of a bird.

Bewildered as a blown bird, my soul hovers and can
not find
Foothold in this debate, or any reason or rest of mind.
But no man ever brought—none can bring
Proof of strife between Thebes' royal house,
25   Labdakos' line, and the son Polybos;
And never until now has any man brought word
Of Laïos' dark death staining Oedipus the King.

Divine Zeus and Apollo hold   [ANTISTROPHE 2
Perfect intelligence alone of all tales ever told;
30   And well though this diviner works, he works in his
own night;
No man can judge that rough unknown or trust in
second sight,
For wisdom changes hands among the wise.
Shall I believe my great lord criminal
At a raging word that a blind old man let fall?
35   I saw him, when the carrion woman faced him of old,
Prove his heroic mind! These evil words are lies.

SCENE 2

CREON: Men of Thebes:
I am told that heavy accusations
Have been brought against me by King Oedipus.

I am not the kind of man to bear this tamely.

5   If in these present difficulties
He holds me accountable for any harm to him
Through anything I have said or done—why, then,
I do not value life in this dishonor.
It is not as though this rumor touched upon
10   Some private indiscretion. The matter is grave.
The fact is that I am being called disloyal
To the State, to my fellow citizens, to my friends.

CHORAGOS: He may have spoken in anger, not from
his mind.

CREON: But did you not hear him say I was the one
15   Who seduced the old prophet into lying?

CHORAGOS: The thing was said; I do not know how
seriously.

CREON: But you were watching him! Were his eyes
steady?

Did he look like a man in his right mind?

CHORAGOS: I do not know.
I can not judge the behavior of great men.
But here is the King himself.

    [Enter OEDIPUS

OEDIPUS: So you dared come back. 20
Why? How brazen of you to come to my house,
You murderer!
          Do you think I do not know
That you plotted to kill me, plotted to steal my throne?
Tell me, in God's name: am I coward, a fool,
That you should dream you could accomplish this? 25
A fool who could not see your slippery game?
A coward, not to fight back when I saw it?
You are the fool, Creon, are you not? hoping
Without support or friends to get a throne?
Thrones may be won or bought: you could do neither. 30

CREON: Now listen to me. You have talked; let me
talk, too.
You can not judge unless you know the facts.

OEDIPUS: You speak well: there is one fact; but I find
it hard
To learn from the deadliest enemy I have.

CREON: That above all I must dispute with you. 35

OEDIPUS: That above all I will not hear you deny.

CREON: If you think there is anything good in being
stubborn
Against all reason, then I say you are wrong.

Creon (Douglas Rain) and Oedipus quarrel in *Oedipus Rex* (1957).

OEDIPUS: If you think a man can sin against his own
      kind
40   And not be punished for it, I say you are mad.

CREON: I agree. But tell me: what have I done to you?

OEDIPUS: You advised me to send for that wizard, did
      you not?

CREON: I did. I should do it again.

OEDIPUS: Very well. Now tell me:
    How long has it been since Laïos—

CREON: What of Laïos—

45 **OEDIPUS:** Since he vanished in that onset by the road?

CREON: It was long ago, a long time.

OEDIPUS: And this prophet,
    Was he practicing here then?

CREON: He was; and with honor, as now.

OEDIPUS: Did he speak of me that time?

CREON: He never did;
    At least, not when I was present.

OEDIPUS: But . . . the enquiry?
50   I suppose you held one?

CREON: We did, but we learned nothing.

OEDIPUS: Why did the prophet not speak against me
      then?

CREON: I do not know; and I am the kind of man
    Who holds his tongue when he has no facts to go on.

OEDIPUS: There's one fact that you know, and you could
      tell it.

55 **CREON:** What fact is that? If I know it, you shall have it.

OEDIPUS: If he were not involved with you, he could
      not say
    That it was I who murdered Laïos.

CREON: If he says that, you are the one that knows it!—
    But now it is my turn to question you.

60 **OEDIPUS:** Put your questions. I am no murderer.

CREON: First, then: You married my sister?

OEDIPUS: I married your sister.

CREON: And you rule the kingdom equally with her?

OEDIPUS: Everything that she wants she has from me.

CREON: And I am the third, equal to both of you?

OEDIPUS: That is why I call you a bad friend.   65

CREON: No. Reason it out, as I have done.
    Think of this first: Would any sane man prefer
    Power, with all a king's anxieties,
    To that same power and the grace of sleep?
    Certainly not I.   70
    I have never longed for the king's power—only his
      rights.
    Would any wise man differ from me in this?
    As matters stand, I have my way in everything
    With your consent, and no responsibilities.
    If I were king, I should be a slave to policy.   75

    How could I desire a scepter more
    Than what is now mine—untroubled influence?
    No, I have not gone mad; I need no honors,
    Except those with the perquisites I have now.
    I am welcome everywhere; every man salutes me,   80
    And those who want your favor seek my ear,
    Since I know how to manage what they ask.
    Should I exchange this ease for that anxiety?
    Besides, no sober mind is treasonable.
    I hate anarchy   85
    And never would deal with any man who likes it.
    Test what I have said. Go to the priestess
    At Delphi, ask if I quoted her correctly.
    And as for this other thing: if I am found
    Guilty of treason with Teiresias,   90
    Then sentence me to death! You have my word
    It is a sentence I should cast my vote for—
    But not without evidence!
              You do wrong
    When you take good men for bad, bad men for good.
    A true friend thrown aside—why, life itself   95
    Is not more precious!
             In time you will know this well:
    For time, and time alone, will show the just man,
    Though scoundrels are discovered in a day.

CHORAGOS: This is well said, and a prudent man would
　　　　ponder it.
100　Judgments too quickly formed are dangerous.

OEDIPUS: But is he not quick in his duplicity?
　　And shall I not be quick to parry him?
　　Would you have me stand still, hold my peace,
　　　　and let
　　This man win everything, through my inaction?

105　**CREON:**   And you want—what is it, then? To banish me?

OEDIPUS: No, not exile. It is your death I want,
　　So that all the world may see what treason means.

CREON: You will persist, then? You will not believe me?

OEDIPUS: How can I believe you?

CREON:　　　　　　　　　Then you are a fool.

OEDIPUS: To save myself?

110　**CREON:**　　　　　　In justice, think of me.

OEDIPUS: You are evil incarnate.

CREON:　　　　　　But suppose that you are wrong?

OEDIPUS: Still I must rule.

CREON:　　　　　But not if you rule badly.

OEDIPUS: O city, city!

CREON:　　　　It is my city, too!

CHORAGOS: Now, my lords, be still. I see the Queen,
115　Iocastê, coming from her palace chambers;
　　And it is time she came, for the sake of you both.
　　This dreadful quarrel can be resolved through her.

　　　　　　　[Enter IOCASTE

IOCASTE: Poor foolish men, what wicked din is this?
　　With Thebes sick to death, is it not shameful
120　That you should rake some private quarrel up?

　　　　　　[To OEDIPUS:

　　Come into the house.
　　　　　　　—And you, Creon, go now:
　　Let us have no more of this tumult over nothing.

CREON: Nothing? No, sister: what your husband plans
　　for me
　　Is one of two great evils: exile or death.

OEDIPUS: He is right.　　　　　　　　　　　　125
　　　　　　Why, woman I have caught him squarely
　　Plotting against my life.

CREON:　　　　　　No! Let me die
　　Accurst if ever I have wished you harm!

IOCASTE: Ah, believe it, Oedipus!
　　In the name of the gods, respect this oath of his
　　For my sake, for the sake of these people here!　　130

CHORAGOS:　　　　　　　　　　[STROPHE 1
　　Open your mind to her, my lord. Be ruled by her,
　　　　I beg you!

OEDIPUS: What would you have me do?

CHORAGOS: Respect Creon's word. He has never spoken
　　　　like a fool,
　　And now he has sworn an oath.

OEDIPUS:　　　　　　　You know what you ask?

CHORAGOS:　　　　　　　　　　I do.

OEDIPUS:　　　　　　　　Speak on, then.

CHORAGOS: A friend so sworn should not be baited so,　　135
　　In blind malice, and without final proof.

OEDIPUS: You are aware, I hope, that what you say
　　Means death for me, or exile at the least.

CHORAGOS:　　　　　　　　　　[STROPHE 2
　　No, I swear by Helios, first in Heaven!
　　　　May I die friendless and accurst,　　　　140
　　The worst of deaths, if ever I meant that!
　　　　It is the withering fields
　　　　　　That hurt my sick heart:
　　　　　　Must we bear all these ills,
　　　　　　　And now your bad blood as well?　　145

OEDIPUS: Then let him go. And let me die, if I must,
　　Or be driven by him in shame from the land of Thebes.
　　It is your unhappiness, and not his talk,
　　That touches me.
　　　　　　As for him—
　　Wherever he goes, hatred will follow him.　　150

CREON: Ugly in yielding, as you were ugly in rage!
Natures like yours chiefly torment themselves.

OEDIPUS: Can you not go? Can you not leave me?

CREON: I can.
You do not know me; but the city knows me,
155   And in its eyes I am just, if not in yours.

        [*Exit* CREON

CHORAGOS: [ANTISTROPHE 1
Lady Iocastê, did you not ask the King to go to his
        chambers?

IOCASTE: First tell me what has happened.

CHORAGOS: There was suspicion without evidence; yet
        it rankled
As even false charges will.

IOCASTE: On both sides?

CHORAGOS: On both.

IOCASTE: But what was said?

160 **CHORAGOS:** Oh let it rest, let it be done with!
Have we not suffered enough?

OEDIPUS: You see to what your decency has brought
        you:
You have made difficulties where my heart saw none.

CHORAGOS: [ANTISTROPHE 2
Oedipus, it is not once only I have told you—
165   You must know I should count myself unwise
To the point of madness, should I now forsake you—
                You, under whose hand,
                In the storm of another time,
                Our dear land sailed out free.
170   But now stand fast at the helm!

IOCASTE: In God's name, Oedipus, inform your wife
        as well:
Why are you so set in this hard anger?

OEDIPUS: I will tell you, for none of these men deserves
My confidence as you do. It is Creon's work,
175   His treachery, his plotting against me.

IOCASTE: Go on, if you can make this clear to me.

Iocaste (Eleanor Stuart) comforts her husband Oedipus in
Oedipus Rex (1957).

OEDIPUS: He charges me with the murder of Laïos.

IOCASTE: Has he some knowledge? Or does he speak
        from hearsay?

OEDIPUS: He would not commit himself to such a
        charge,
But he has brought in that damnable soothsayer   180
To tell his story.

IOCASTE: Set your mind at rest.
If it is a question of soothsayers, I tell you
That you will find no man whose craft gives
        knowledge
Of the unknowable.

                Here is my proof:

An oracle was reported to Laïos once   185
(I will not say from Phoibos himself, but from
His appointed ministers, at any rate)
That his doom would be death at the hands of his
        own son—
His son, born of his flesh and of mine!

Now, you remember the story: Laïos was killed   190
By marauding strangers where three highways meet:
But his child had not been three days in this world
Before the King had pierced the baby's ankles
And left him to die on a lonely mountainside.

Thus, Apollo never caused that child   195
To kill his father, and it was not Laïos' fate
To die at the hands of his son, as he had feared.

This is what prophets and prophecies are worth!
Have no dread of them.

                    It is God himself

200   Who can show us what he wills, in his own way.

OEDIPUS: How strange a shadowy memory crossed my mind,
Just now while you were speaking; it chilled my heart.

IOCASTE: What do you mean? What memory do you speak of?

OEDIPUS: If I understand you, Laïos was killed
At a place where three roads meet.

205 **IOCASTE:**   So it was said;
We have no later story.

OEDIPUS: Where did it happen?

IOCASTE: Phokis, it is called: at a place where the Theban Way
Divides into the roads toward Delphi and Daulia.

OEDIPUS: When?

210 **IOCASTE:**   We had the news not long before you came
And proved the right to your succession here.

OEDIPUS: Ah, what net has God been weaving for me?

IOCASTE: Oedipus! Why does this trouble you?

Iocaste (Jessye Norman) talks with her husband Oedipus in
Oedipus Rex (1993).

OEDIPUS: Do not ask me yet.
First, tell me how Laïos looked, and tell me
How old he was.

IOCASTE: He was tall, his hair just touched   215
With white; his form was not unlike your own.

OEDIPUS: I think that I myself may be accurst
By my own ignorant edict.

IOCASTE: You speak strangely.
It makes me tremble to look at you, my King.

OEDIPUS: I am not sure that the blind man can not see.   220
But I should know better if you were to tell me—

IOCASTE: Anything—though I dread to hear you ask it.

OEDIPUS: Was the King lightly escorted, or did he ride
With a large company, as a ruler should?

IOCASTE: There were five men with him in all: one was   225
a herald,
And a single chariot, which he was driving.

OEDIPUS: Alas, that makes it plain enough!

                          But who—
Who told you how it happened?

IOCASTE: A household servant,
The only one to escape.

OEDIPUS: And is he still
A servant of ours?   230

IOCASTE: No; for when he came back at last
And found you enthroned in the place of the dead
king,
He came to me, touched my hand with his, and
begged
That I would send him away to the frontier district
Where only the shepherds go—
As far away from the city as I could send him.   235
I granted his prayer; for although the man was a
slave,
He had earned more than this favor at my hands.

OEDIPUS: Can he be called back quickly?

IOCASTE: Easily.
But why?

Iocaste promises Oedipus she will send for the shepherd in *Oedipus Rex* (1957).

OEDIPUS: I have taken too much upon myself
            Without enquiry; therefore I wish to consult him.

240 IOCASTE: Then he shall come.
                                  But am I not one also
            To whom you might confide these fears of yours?

OEDIPUS: That is your right; it will not be denied you,
            Now least of all; for I have reached a pitch
            Of wild foreboding. Is there anyone
245   To whom I should sooner speak?

            Polybos of Corinth is my father.
            My mother is a Dorian: Meropê.
            I grew up chief among the men of Corinth
            Until a strange thing happened—
250   Not worth my passion, it may be, but strange.

            At a feast, a drunken man maundering in his cups
            Cries out that I am not my father's son!

            I contained myself that night, though I felt anger
            And a sinking heart. The next day I visited
255   My father and mother, and questioned them. They
                 stormed,
            Calling it all the slanderous rant of a fool;
            And this relieved me. Yet the suspicion
            Remained always aching in my mind;
            I knew there was talk; I could not rest;
260   And finally, saying nothing to my parents,
            I went to the shrine at Delphi.

The god dismissed my question without reply;
He spoke of other things.
                    Some were clear,
Full of wretchedness, dreadful, unbearable: 265
As, that I should lie with my own mother, breed
Children from whom all men would turn their eyes;
And that I should be my father's murderer.

I heard all this, and fled. And from that day
Corinth to me was only in the stars   270
Descending in that quarter of the sky,
As I wandered farther and farther on my way
To a land where I should never see the evil
Sung by the oracle. And I came to this country
Where, so you say, King Laïos was killed.   275

I will tell you all that happened there, my lady.

There were three highways
Coming together at a place I passed;
And there a herald came towards me, and a chariot
Drawn by horses, with a man such as you describe   280
Seated in it. The groom leading the horses
Forced me off the road at his lord's command;
But as this charioteer lurched over towards me
I struck him in my rage. The old man saw me
And brought his double goad down upon my head   285
As I came abreast.
                    He was paid back, and more!
Swinging my club in this right hand I knocked him
Out of his car, and he rolled on the ground.
                                  I killed him.

I killed them all.
Now if that stranger and Laïos were—kin,   290
Where is a man more miserable than I?
More hated by the gods? Citizen and alien alike
Must never shelter me or speak to me—
I must be shunned by all.
                    And I myself
Pronounced this malediction upon myself!   295

Think of it: I have touched you with these hands,
These hands that killed your husband. What
      defilement!

Am I all evil, then? It must be so,
Since I must flee from Thebes, yet never again
300 See my own countrymen, my own country,
For fear of joining my mother in marriage
And killing Polybos, my father.
                                        Ah,
If I was created so, born to this fate,
Who could deny the savagery of God?

305 O holy majesty of heavenly powers!
May I never see that day! Never!
Rather let me vanish from the race of men
Than know the abomination destined me!

CHORAGOS: We too, my lord, have felt dismay at this.
310 But there is hope: you have yet to hear the shepherd.

OEDIPUS: Indeed, I fear no other hope is left me.

IOCASTE: What do you hope from him when he comes?

OEDIPUS: This much:
If his account of the murder tallies with yours,
Then I am cleared.

IOCASTE: What was it that I said
315 Of such importance?

OEDIPUS: Why, "marauders," you said,
Killed the King, according to this man's story.
If he maintains that still, if there were several,
Clearly the guilt is not mine: I was alone.
But if he says one man, singlehanded, did it,
320 Then the evidence all points to me.

IOCASTE: You may be sure that he said there were
                several;
And can he call back that story now? He can not.
The whole city heard it as plainly as I.
But suppose he alters some detail of it:
325 He can not ever show that Laïos' death
Fulfilled the oracle: for Apollo said
My child was doomed to kill him; and my child—
Poor baby!—it was my child that died first.

No. From now on, where oracles are concerned,
330 I would not waste a second thought on any.

OEDIPUS: You may be right.
                        But come: let someone go
For the shepherd at once. This matter must be settled.

IOCASTE: I will send for him.
I would not wish to cross you in anything,
And surely not in this.—Let us go in.   335

[Exeunt into the palace

ODE 2

CHORUS: [STROPHE 1
Let me be reverent in the ways of right,
Lowly the paths I journey on;
Let all my words and actions keep
The laws of the pure universe
From highest Heaven handed down.   5
For Heaven is their bright nurse,
Those generations of the realms of light;
Ah, never of mortal kind were they begot,
Nor are they slaves of memory, lost in sleep:
Their Father is greater than Time, and ages not.   10

The tyrant is a child of Pride   [ANTISTROPHE 1
Who drinks from his great sickening cup
Recklessness and vanity,
Until from his high crest headlong
He plummets to the dust of hope.   15
That strong man is not strong.
But let no fair ambition be denied;
May God protect the wrestler for the State
In government, in comely policy,
Who will fear God, and on His ordinance wait.   20

                                        [STROPHE 2
Haughtiness and the high hand of disdain
Tempt and outrage God's holy law;
And any mortal who dares hold
No immortal Power in awe
Will be caught up in a net of pain: 25
The price for which his levity is sold.
Let each man take due earnings, then,
And keep his hands from holy things,
And from blasphemy stand apart—
Else the crackling blast of heaven   30
Blows on his head, and on his desperate heart;
Though fools will honor impious men,
In their cities no tragic poet sings.

        [ANTISTROPHE 2
Shall we lose faith in Delphi's obscurities,
We who have heard the world's core   35

Discredited, and the sacred wood
Of Zeus at Elis praised no more?
The deeds and the strange prophecies
Must make a pattern yet to be understood.
40   Zeus, if indeed you are lord of all,
Throned in light over night and day,
Mirror this in your endless mind:
Our masters call the oracle
Words on the wind, and the Delphic vision blind!
45   Their hearts no longer know Apollo,
And reverence for the gods has died away.

SCENE 3

[Enter IOCASTE

IOCASTE: Princes of Thebes, it has occurred to me
To visit the altars of the gods, bearing
These branches as a suppliant, and this incense.
Our King is not himself: his noble soul
5   Is overwrought with fantasies of dread,
Else he would consider
The new prophecies in the light of the old.
He will listen to any voice that speaks disaster,
And my advice goes for nothing.

[She approaches the altar, R.

                   To you, then, Apollo,
10   Lycean lord, since you are nearest, I turn in prayer.
Receive these offerings, and grant us deliverance
From defilement. Our hearts are heavy with fear
When we see our leader distracted, as helpless sailors
Are terrified by the confusion of their helmsman.

[Enter MESSENGER

15 **MESSENGER:**   Friends, no doubt you can direct me:
Where shall I find the house of Oedipus,
Or, better still, where is the King himself?

CHORAGOS: It is this very place, stranger; he is inside.
This is his wife and mother of his children.

20 **MESSENGER:**   I wish her happiness in a happy house,
Blest in all the fulfillment of her marriage.

IOCASTE: I wish as much for you: your courtesy
Deserves a like good fortune. But now, tell me:
Why have you come? What have you to say to us?

MESSENGER: Good news, my lady, for your house and   25
your husband.

IOCASTE: What news? Who sent you here?

MESSENGER: I am from Corinth.
The news I bring ought to mean joy for you,
Though it may be you will find some grief in it.

IOCASTE: What is it? How can it touch us in both ways?

MESSENGER: The word is that the people of the Isthmus   30
Intend to call Oedipus to be their king.

IOCASTE: But old King Polybos—is he not reigning still?

MESSENGER: No. Death holds him in his sepulchre.

IOCASTE: What are you saying? Polybos is dead?

MESSENGER: If I am not telling the truth, may I die   35
myself.

IOCASTE: *[To a MAIDSERVANT:*
Go in, go quickly; tell this to your master.

O riddlers of God's will, where are you now!
This was the man whom Oedipus, long ago,
Feared so, fled so, in dread of destroying him—
But it was another fate by which he died.   40

[Enter OEPIDUS, C

OEDIPUS: Dearest Iocastê, why have you sent for me?

IOCASTE: Listen to what this man says, and then tell me
What has become of the solemn prophecies.

The messenger from Corinth (Tony Van Bridge) delivers his
message to Oedipus in *Oedipus Rex* (1957).

The messenger from Corinth (Michio Tatara) delivers his message to Oedipus in *Oedipus Rex* (1993).

OEDIPUS: Who is this man? What is his news for me?

45 **IOCASTE:** He has come from Corinth to announce your father's death!

OEDIPUS: Is it true, stranger? Tell me in your own words.

MESSENGER: I can not say it more clearly: the King is dead.

OEDIPUS: Was it by treason? Or by an attack of illness?

MESSENGER: A little thing brings old men to their rest.

50 **OEDIPUS:** It was sickness, then?

MESSENGER: Yes, and his many years.

OEDIPUS: Ah!
Why should a man respect the Pythian hearth, or
Give heed to the birds that jangle above his head?
They prophesied that I should kill Polybos,
55 Kill my own father; but he is dead and buried,
And I am here—I never touched him, never,
Unless he died of grief for my departure,
And thus, in a sense, through me. No. Polybos
Has packed the oracles off with him underground.
60 They are empty words.

IOCASTE: Had I not told you so?

OEDIPUS: You had; it was my faint heart that betrayed me.

IOCASTE: From now on never think of those things again.

OEDIPUS: And yet—must I not fear my mother's bed?

IOCASTE: Why should anyone in this world be afraid,
Since Fate rules us and nothing can be foreseen?   65
A man should live only for the present day.

Have no more fear of sleeping with your mother:
How many men, in dreams, have lain with their mothers!
No reasonable man is troubled by such things.

OEDIPUS: That is true; only—   70
If only my mother were not still alive!
But she is alive. I can not help my dread.

IOCASTE: Yet this news of your father's death is wonderful.

OEDIPUS: Wonderful. But I fear the living woman.

MESSENGER: Tell me, who is this woman that you fear?   75

OEDIPUS: It is Meropê, man; the wife of King Polybos.

MESSENGER: Meropê? Why should you be afraid of her?

OEDIPUS: An oracle of the gods, a dreadful saying.

MESSENGER: Can you tell me about it or are you sworn to silence?

OEDIPUS: I can tell you, and I will.   80
Apollo said through his prophet that I was the man
Who should marry his own mother, shed his father's blood
With his own hands. And so, for all these years
I have kept clear of Corinth, and no harm has come—
Though it would have been sweet to see my parents   85
again

MESSENGER: And is this the fear that drove you out of Corinth?

OEDIPUS: Would you have me kill my father?

MESSENGER: As for that
You must be reassured by the news I gave you.

OEDIPUS: If you could reassure me, I would reward you.

90 **MESSENGER:** I had that in mind, I will confess: I thought
I could count on you when you returned to Corinth.

OEDIPUS: No. I will never go near my parents again.

MESSENGER: Ah, son, you still do not know what you are doing—

OEDIPUS: What do you mean? In the name of God tell me!

95 **MESSENGER:** —If these are your reasons for not going home.

OEDIPUS: I tell you, I fear the oracle may come true.

MESSENGER: And guilt may come upon you through your parents?

OEDIPUS: That is the dread that is always in my heart.

MESSENGER: Can you not see that all your fears are groundless?

100 **OEDIPUS:** How can you say that? They are my parents, surely?

MESSENGER: Polybos was not your father.

OEDIPUS: Not my father?

MESSENGER: No more your father than the man speaking to you.

OEDIPUS: But you are nothing to me!

MESSENGER: Neither was he.

OEDIPUS: Then why did he call me son?

MESSENGER: I will tell you:
105 Long ago he had you from my hands, as a gift.

OEDIPUS: Then how could he love me so, if I was not his?

MESSENGER: He had no children, and his heart turned to you.

OEDIPUS: What of you? Did you buy me? Did you find me by chance?

MESSENGER: I came upon you in the crooked pass of Kithairon.

OEDIPUS: And what were you doing there?

MESSENGER: Tending my flocks. 110

OEDIPUS: A wandering shepherd?

MESSENGER: But your savior, son, that day.

OEDIPUS: From what did you save me?

MESSENGER: Your ankles should tell you that.

OEDIPUS: Ah, stranger, why do you speak of that childhood pain?

MESSENGER: I cut the bonds that tied your ankles together.

OEDIPUS: I have had the mark as long as I can remember. 115

MESSENGER: That was why you were given the name you bear.

OEDIPUS: God! Was it my father or my mother who did it?
Tell me!

MESSENGER: I do not know. The man who gave you to me
Can tell you better than I. 120

OEDIPUS: It was not you that found me, but another?

MESSENGER: It was another shepherd gave you to me.

OEDIPUS: Who was he? Can you tell me who he was?

MESSENGER: I think he was said to be one of Laïos' people.

OEDIPUS: You mean the Laïos who was king here 125
years ago?

MESSENGER: Yes; King Laïos; and the man was one of his herdsmen.

OEDIPUS: Is he still alive? Can I see him?

MESSENGER: These men here
Know best about such things.

OEDIPUS: Does anyone here
Know this shepherd that he is talking about?
Have you seen him in the fields, or in the town? 130
If you have, tell me. It is time things were made plain.

CHORAGOS: I think the man he means is that same shepherd
You have already asked to see. Iocastê perhaps
Could tell you something.

OEDIPUS: Do you know anything
135   About him, Lady? Is he the man we have summoned?
Is that the man this shepherd means?

IOCASTE: Why think of him?
Forget this herdsman. Forget it all.
This talk is a waste of time.

OEDIPUS: How can you say that,
When the clues to my true birth are in my hands?

140   **IOCASTE:**   For God's love, let us have no more questioning!
Is your life nothing to you?
My own is pain enough for me to bear.

OEDIPUS: You need not worry. Suppose my mother a slave,
And born of slaves: no baseness can touch you.

145   **IOCASTE:**   Listen to me, I beg you: do not do this thing!

OEDIPUS: I will not listen; the truth must be made known.

IOCASTE: Everything that I say is for your own good!

OEDIPUS: My own good
Snaps my patience, then; I want none of it.

IOCASTE: You are fatally wrong! May you never learn who you are!

150   **OEDIPUS:**   Go, one of you, and bring the shepherd here.
Let us leave this woman to brag of her royal name.

IOCASTE: Ah, miserable!
That is the only word I have for you now.
That is the only word I can ever have.

[Exit into the palace

155   **CHORAGOS:**   Why has she left us, Oedipus? Why has she gone
In such a passion of sorrow? I fear this silence:
Something dreadful may come of it.

OEDIPUS: Let it come!
However base my birth, I must know about it.
The Queen, like a woman, is perhaps ashamed
To think of my low origin. But I   160
Am a child of Luck; I can not be dishonored.
Luck is my mother; the passing months, my brothers,
Have seen me rich and poor.
                    If this is so,
How could I wish that I were someone else?
How could I not be glad to know my birth?   165

ODE 3

CHORUS: [STROPHE
If ever the coming time were known
To my heart's pondering,
Kithairon, now by Heaven I see the torches
At the festival of the next full moon,
And see the dance, and hear the choir sing   5
A grace to your gentle shade:
Mountain where Oedipus was found,
O mountain guard of a noble race!
May the god who heals us lend his aid,
And let that glory come to pass   10
For our king's cradling-ground.

      [ANTISTROPHE
Of the nymphs that flower beyond the years,
Who bore you, royal child,
To Pan of the hills or the timberline Apollo,
Cold in delight where the upland clears,   15
Or Hermês for whom Kyllenê's heights are piled?
Or flushed as evening cloud,
Great Dionysos, roamer of mountains,
He—was it he who found you there,
And caught you up in his own proud   20
Arms from the sweet god-ravisher
Who laughed by the Muses' fountains?

SCENE 4

OEDIPUS: Sirs: though I do not know the man,
I think I see him coming, this shepherd we want:
He is old, like our friend here, and the men
Bringing him seem to be servants of my house.
But you can tell, if you have ever seen him.   5

[Enter SHEPHERD *escorted by servants*

CHORAGOS: I know him, he was Laïos' man. You can trust him.

OEDIPUS: Tell me first, you from Corinth: is this the shepherd
We were discussing?

MESSENGER: This is the very man.

OEDIPUS: *[To* SHEPHERD
Come here. No, look at me. You must answer
10 Everything I ask.—You belonged to Laïos?

SHEPHERD: Yes: born his slave, brought up in his house.

OEDIPUS: Tell me: what kind of work did you do for him?

SHEPHERD: I was a shepherd of his, most of my life.

OEDIPUS: Where mainly did you go for pasturage?

15 **SHEPHERD:** Sometimes Kithairon, sometimes the hills near-by.

OEDIPUS: Do you remember ever seeing this man out there?

SHEPHERD: What would he be doing there? This man?

OEDIPUS: This man standing here. Have you ever seen him before?

SHEPHERD: No. At least, not to my recollection.

Oedipus interrogates the shepherd (Eric House) in *Oedipus Rex* (1957).

MESSENGER: And that is not strange, my lord. But I'll 20 refresh
His memory: he must remember when we two
Spent three whole seasons together, March to September,
On Kithairon or thereabouts. He had two flocks;
I had one. Each autumn I'd drive mine home
And he would go back with his to Laïos' sheepfold.— 25
Is this not true, just as I have described it?

SHEPHERD: True, yes; but it was all so long ago.

MESSENGER: Well, then: do you remember, back in those days,
That you gave me a baby boy to bring up as my own?

SHEPHERD: What if I did? What are you trying to say? 30

MESSENGER: King Oedipus was once that little child.

SHEPHERD: Damn you, hold your tongue!

OEDIPUS: No more of that!
It is your tongue needs watching, not this man's.

SHEPHERD: My King, my Master, what is it I have done wrong?

OEDIPUS: You have not answered his question about 35 the boy.

SHEPHERD: He does not know . . . He is only making trouble . . .

OEDIPUS: Come, speak plainly, or it will go hard with you.

SHEPHERD: In God's name, do not torture an old man!

OEDIPUS: Come here, one of you; bind his arms behind him.

SHEPHERD: Unhappy king! What more do you wish 40 to learn?

OEDIPUS: Did you give this man the child he speaks of?

SHEPHERD: I did.
And I would to God I had died that very day.

OEDIPUS: You will die now unless you speak the truth.

SHEPHERD: Yet if I speak the truth, I am worse than dead.

45 **OEDIPUS:** Very well; since you insist upon delaying—

SHEPHERD: No! I have told you already that I gave him the boy.

OEDIPUS: Where did you get him? From your house? From somewhere else?

SHEPHERD: Not from mine, no. A man gave him to me.

OEDIPUS: Is that man here? Do you know whose slave he was?

50 **SHEPHERD:** For God's love, my King, do not ask me any more!

OEDIPUS: You are a dead man if I have to ask you again.

SHEPHERD: Then . . . Then the child was from the palace of Laïos.

OEDIPUS: A slave child? or a child of his own line?

SHEPHERD: Ah, I am on the brink of dreadful speech!

55 **OEDIPUS:** And I of dreadful hearing. Yet I must hear.

SHEPHERD: If you must be told, then . . .
                    They said it was Laïos' child;
But it is your wife who can tell you about that.

OEDIPUS: My wife!—Did she give it to you?

SHEPHERD: My lord, she did.

OEDIPUS: Do you know why?

SHEPHERD: I was told to get rid of it.

60 **OEDIPUS:** An unspeakable mother!

SHEPHERD: There had been prophecies . . .

OEDIPUS: Tell me.

SHEPHERD: It was said that the boy would kill his own father.

OEDIPUS: Then why did you give him over to this old man?

The chorus in *Oedipus Rex* (1957).

SHEPHERD: I pitied the baby, my King,
And I thought that this man would take him far away   65
To his own country.
                    He saved him—but for what a fate!
For if you are what this man says you are,
No man living is more wretched than Oedipus.

OEDIPUS: Ah God!
It was true!
                    All the prophecies!   70
                                        —Now,
O Light, may I look on you for the last time!
I, Oedipus,
Oedipus, damned in his birth, in his marriage damned,
Damned in the blood he shed with his own hand!

[He rushes into the palace

ODE 4

CHORUS: Alas for the seed of men.   [STROPHE 1

What measure shall I give these generations
That breathe on the void and are void
And exist and do not exist?

Who bears more weight of joy   5
Than mass of sunlight shifting in images,
Or who shall make his thought stay on
That down time drifts away?

Your splendor is all fallen.

10 O naked brow of wrath and tears,
O change of Oedipus!
I who saw your days call no man blest—
Your great days like ghósts góne.

That mind was a strong bow.   [ANTISTROPHE 1

15 Deep, how deep you drew it then, hard archer,
At a dim fearful range,
And brought dear glory down!

You overcame the stranger—
The virgin with her hooking lion claws—
20 And though death sang, stood like a tower
To make pale Thebes take heart.

Fortress against our sorrow!

True king, giver of laws,
Majestic Oedipus!
25 No prince in Thebes had ever such renown,
No prince won such grace of power.

And now of all men ever known   [STROPHE 2
Most pitiful is this man's story:
His fortunes are most changed, his state
30 Fallen to a low slave's
Ground under bitter fate.

O Oedipus, most royal one!
The great door that expelled you to the light
Gave at night—ah, gave night to your glory:
35 As to the father, to the fathering son.

All understood too late.

How could that queen whom Laïos won,
The garden that he harrowed at his height,
Be silent when that act was done?

40 But all eyes fail before time's eye,   [ANTISTROPHE 2
All actions come to justice there.
Though never willed, though far down the deep past,
Your bed, your dread sirings,
Are brought to book at last.

45 Child by Laïos doomed to die,
Then doomed to lose that fortunate little death,
Would God you never took breath in this air
That with my wailing lips I take to cry:

For I weep the world's outcast.

I was blind, and now I can tell why: 50
Asleep, for you had given ease of breath
To Thebes, while the false years went by.

ÉXODOS

[Enter, from the palace, SECOND MESSENGER

SECOND MESSENGER: Elders of Thebes, most honored
in this land,
What horrors are yours to see and hear, what weight
Of sorrow to be endured, if, true to your birth,
You venerate the line of Labdakos!
I think neither Istros nor Phasis, those great rivers,   5
Could purify this place of the corruption
It shelters now, or soon must bring to light—
Evil not done unconsciously, but willed.

The greatest griefs are those we cause ourselves.

CHORAGOS: Surely, friend, we have grief enough   10
already;
What new sorrow do you mean?

SECOND MESSENGER: The Queen is dead.

CHORAGOS: Iocastê? Dead? But at whose hand?

SECOND MESSENGER: Her own.
The full horror of what happened you can not know,
For you did not see it; but I, who did, will tell you
As clearly as I can how she met her death.   15

The second messenger comes to announce his bad news in
Oedipus Rex (1957).

When she had left us,
In passionate silence, passing through the court,
She ran to her apartment in the house,
Her hair clutched by the fingers of both hands.
20 She closed the doors behind her; then, by that bed
Where long ago the fatal son was conceived—
That son who should bring about his father's death—
We heard her call upon Laïos, dead so many years,
And heard her wail for the double fruit of her marriage,
25 A husband by her husband, children by her child.

Exactly how she died I do not know:
For Oedipus burst in moaning and would not let us
Keep vigil to the end: it was by him
As he stormed about the room that our eyes were
caught.
30 From one to another of us he went, begging a sword,
Cursing the wife who was not his wife, the mother
Whose womb had carried his own children and
himself.
I do not know: it was none of us aided him,
But surely one of the gods was in control!
35 For with a dreadful cry
He hurled his weight, as though wrenched out of
himself,
At the twin doors: the bolts gave, and he rushed in.
And there we saw her hanging, her body swaying
From the cruel cord she had noosed about her neck.
40 A great sob broke from him, heartbreaking to hear,
As he loosed the rope and lowered her to the ground.

I would blot out from my mind what happened next!
For the King ripped from her gown the golden
brooches
That were her ornament, and raised them, and
plunged them down
45 Straight into his own eyeballs, crying, "No more,
No more shall you look on the misery about me,
The horrors of my own doing! Too long you have
known
The faces of those whom I should never have seen,
Too long been blind to those for whom I was
searching!
50 From this hour, go in darkness!" And as he spoke,
He struck at his eyes—not once, but many times;
And the blood spattered his beard,
Bursting from his ruined sockets like red hail.

So from the unhappiness of two this evil has sprung.
A curse on the man and woman alike. The old   55
Happiness of the house of Labdakos
Was happiness enough: where is it today?
It is all wailing and ruin, disgrace, death—all
The misery of mankind that has a name—
And it is wholly and for ever theirs.   60

CHORAGOS: Is he in agony still? Is there no rest for him?

SECOND MESSENGER: He is calling for someone to
lead him to the gates
So that all the children of Kadmos may look upon
His father's murderer, his mother's—no,
I can not say it!   65
                    And then he will leave Thebes,
Self-exiled, in order that the curse
Which he himself pronounced may depart from the
house.
He is weak, and there is none to lead him,
So terrible is his suffering.
                    But you will see:
Look, the doors are opening; in a moment   70
You will see a thing that would crush a heart of stone.

*[The central door is opened; OEDIPUS,
blinded, is led in*

CHORAGOS: Dreadful indeed for men to see.
Never have my own eyes
Looked on a sight so full of fear.

Oedipus!   75
What madness came upon you, what daemon
Leaped on your life with heavier
Punishment than a mortal man can bear?
No: I can not even
Look at you, poor ruined one.   80
And I would speak, question, ponder,
If I were able. No.
You make me shudder.

OEDIPUS: God.   God.
Is there a sorrow greater?
Where shall I find harbor in this world?   85
My voice is hurled far on a dark wind.
What has God done to me?

CHORAGOS: Too terrible to think of, or to see.

The blinded Oedipus addresses his people in *Oedipus Rex* (1957).

90 **OEDIPUS:** O cloud of night,   [STROPHE 1
       Never to be turned away: night coming on,
       I can not tell how: night like a shroud!

       My fair winds brought me here.
                                   O God. Again
       The pain of the spikes where I had sight,
95   The flooding pain
       Of memory, never to be gouged out.

   CHORAGOS: This is not strange.
       You suffer it all twice over, remorse in pain,
       Pain in remorse.

100 **OEDIPUS:** Ah dear friend   [ANTISTROPHE 1
       Are you faithful even yet, you alone?
       Are you still standing near me, will you stay here,
       Patient, to care for the blind?
                                   The blind man!
       Yet even blind I know who it is attends me,
105   By the voice's tone—
       Though my new darkness hide the comforter.

   CHORAGOS: Oh fearful act!
       What god was it drove you to rake black
       Night across your eyes?

110 **OEDIPUS:** Apollo. Apollo. Dear   [STROPHE 2
       Children, the god was Apollo.
       He brought my sick, sick fate upon me.
       But the blinding hand was my own!
       How could I bear to see
115   When all my sight was horror everywhere?

CHORAGOS: Everywhere; that is true.

OEDIPUS: And now what is left?
       Images? Love? A greeting even,
       Sweet to the senses? Is there anything?
       Ah, no, friends: lead me away.   120
       Lead me away from Thebes.
                                   Lead the great wreck
       And hell of Oedipus, whom the gods hate.

CHORAGOS: Your fate is clear, you are not blind to that.
       Would God you had never found it out!

OEDIPUS: [ANTISTROPHE 2
       Death take the man who unbound   125
       My feet on that hillside
       And delivered me from death to life! What life?
       If only I had died,
       This weight of monstrous doom
       Could not have dragged me and my darlings down.   130

CHORAGOS: I would have wished the same.

OEDIPUS: Oh never to have come here
       With my father's blood upon me! Never
       To have been the man they call his mother's husband!
       Oh accurst! Oh child of evil,   135
       To have entered that wretched bed—
                                   the selfsame one!
       More primal than sin itself, this fell to me.

CHORAGOS: I do not know how I can answer you.
       You were better dead than alive and blind.

OEDIPUS: Do not counsel me any more. This   140
          punishment
       That I have laid upon myself is just.
       If I had eyes,
       I do not know how I could bear the sight
       Of my father, when I came to the house of Death,
       Or my mother: for I have sinned against them both   145
       So vilely that I could not make my peace
       By strangling my own life.
                                   Or do you think my children,
       Born as they were born, would be sweet to my eyes?
       Ah never, never! Nor this town with its high walls,
       Nor the holy images of the gods.
                                   For I,   150
       Thrice miserable!—Oedipus, noblest of all the line

Of Kadmos, have condemned myself to enjoy
These things no more, by my own malediction
Expelling that man whom the gods declared
155 To be a defilement in the house of Laïos.
After exposing the rankness of my own guilt,
How could I look men frankly in the eyes?
No, I swear it,
If I could have stifled my hearing at its source,
160 I would have done it and made all this body
A tight cell of misery, blank to light and sound:
So I should have been safe in a dark agony
Beyond all recollection.
                              Ah Kithairon!
Why did you shelter me? When I was cast upon you,
165 Why did I not die? Then I should never
Have shown the world my execrable birth.

Ah Polybos! Corinth, city that I believed
The ancient seat of my ancestors: how fair
I seemed, your child! And all the while this evil
Was cancerous within me!
170   For I am sick
In my daily life, sick in my origin.

O three roads, dark ravine, woodland and way
Where three roads met: you, drinking my father's
        blood,
My own blood, spilled by my own hand: can you
        remember
175 The unspeakable things I did there, and the things
I went on from there to do?
                              O marriage, marriage!
The act that engendered me, and again the act
Performed by the son in the same bed—
                                        Ah, the net
Of incest, mingling fathers, brothers, sons,
180 With brides, wives, mothers: the last evil
That can be known by men: no tongue can say
How evil!
            No. For the love of God, conceal me
Somewhere far from Thebes; or kill me; or hurl me
Into the sea, away from men's eyes for ever.

185 Come, lead me. You need not fear to touch me.
Of all men, I alone can bear this guilt.

                [Enter CREON

The blinded Oedipus speaks to Creon in *Oedipus Rex* (1957).

CHORAGOS: We are not the ones to decide; but Creon
        here
        May fitly judge of what you ask. He only
        Is left to protect the city in your place.

OEDIPUS: Alas, how can I speak to him? What right   190
        have I
        To beg his courtesy whom I have deeply wronged?

CREON: I have not come to mock you, Oedipus,
        Or to reproach you, either.

                [To ATTENDANTS:

                                —You, standing there:
        If you have lost all respect for man's dignity,
        At least respect the flame of Lord Helios: 195
        Do not allow this pollution to show itself
        Openly here, an affront to the earth
        And Heaven's rain and the light of day. No, take him
        Into the house as quickly as you can.
        For it is proper   200
        That only the close kindred see his grief.

OEDIPUS: I pray you in God's name, since your courtesy
        Ignores my dark expectation, visiting
        With mercy this man of all men most execrable:
        Give me what I ask—for your good, not for mine.   205

CREON: And what is it that you would have me do?

OEDIPUS: Drive me out of this country as quickly as
        may be
        To a place where no human voice can ever greet me.

CREON: I should have done that before now—only,
210   God's will had not been wholly revealed to me.

OEDIPUS: But his command is plain: the parricide
           Must be destroyed. I am that evil man.

CREON: That is the sense of it, yes; but as things are,
         We had best discover clearly what is to be done.

215 OEDIPUS: You would learn more about a man like me?

CREON: You are ready now to listen to the god.

OEDIPUS: I will listen. But it is to you
           That I must turn for help. I beg you, hear me.

     The woman in there—
220 Give her whatever funeral you think proper:
     She is your sister.
                         —But let me go, Creon!
     Let me purge my father's Thebes of the pollution
     Of my living here, and go out to the wild hills,
     To Kithairon, that has won such fame with me,
225 The tomb my mother and father appointed for me,
     And let me die there, as they willed I should.
     And yet I know
     Death will not ever come to me through sickness
     Or in any natural way: I have been preserved
230 For some unthinkable fate. But let that be.

     As for my sons, you need not care for them.
     They are men, they will find some way to live.
     But my poor daughters, who have shared my table,
     Who never before have been parted from their
                                            father—
235 Take care of them, Creon; do this for me.
     And will you let me touch them with my hands
     A last time, and let us weep together?
     Be kind, my lord,
     Great prince, be kind!
                         Could I but touch them,
240 They would be mine again, as when I had my eyes.

          [Enter ANTIGONE *and* ISMENE, *attended*

     Ah, God!
     It is my dearest children I hear weeping?
     Has Creon pitied me and sent my daughters?

CREON: Yes, Oedipus: I knew that they were dear to you
         In the old days, and know you must love them still.   245

OEDIPUS: May God bless you for this—and be a friendlier
           Guardian to you than he has been to me!

     Children, where are you?
     Come quickly to my hands: they are your brother's—
     Hands that have brought your father's once clear eyes   250
     To this way of seeing—
                         Ah dearest ones,
     I had neither sight nor knowledge then, your father
     By the woman who was the source of his own life!
     And I weep for you—having no strength to see you—,
     I weep for you when I think of the bitterness   255
     That men will visit upon you all your lives.
     What homes, what festivals can you attend
     Without being forced to depart again in tears?
     And when you come to marriageable age,
     Where is the man, my daughters, who would dare   260
     Risk the bane that lies on all my children?
     Is there any evil wanting? Your father killed
     His father; sowed the womb of her who bore him;
     Engendered you at the fount of his own existence!
     That is what they will say of you.   265
                                   Then, whom
     Can you ever marry? There are no bridegrooms for you,
     And your lives must wither away in sterile dreaming.

     O Creon, son of Menoikeus!
     You are the only father my daughters have,
     Since we, their parents, are both of us gone for ever.   270
     They are your own blood: you will not let them
     Fall into beggary and loneliness;
     You will keep them from the miseries that are mine!
     Take pity on them; see, they are only children,
     Friendless except for you. Promise me this,   275
     Great Prince, and give me your hand in token of it.

          *[*CREON *clasps his right hand*

     Children:
     I would say much, if you could understand me,
     But as it is, I have only this prayer for you:
     Live where you can, be as happy as you can—   280
     Happier, please God, than God has made your father!

CREON: Enough. You have wept enough. Now go within.

OEDIPUS: I must; but it is hard.

CREON: Time eases all things.

OEDIPUS: But you must promise—

CREON: Say what you desire.

285   OEDIPUS: Send me from Thebes!

CREON: God grant that I may!

OEDIPUS: But since God hates me . . .

CREON: No, he will grant your wish.

OEDIPUS: You promise?

CREON: I can not speak beyond my knowledge.

OEDIPUS: Then lead me in.

CREON: Come now, and leave your children.

OEDIPUS: No! Do not take them from me!

CREON: Think no longer
290   That you are in command here, but rather think
How, when you were, you served your own destruction.

[Exeunt into the house all but the CHORUS;
CHORAGOS *chants directly to the audience:*

Oedipus, blinded, faces his fate in *Oedipus Rex* (1993).

CHORAGOS: Men of Thebes: look upon Oedipus.

This is the king who solved the famous riddle
And towered up, most powerful of men.
No mortal eyes but looked on him with envy,   295
Yet in the end ruin swept over him.

Let every man in mankind's frailty
Consider his last day; and let none
Presume on his good fortune until he find
Life, at his death, a memory without pain.   300

Writing from Reading

Summarize

1 Write an outline of the story behind the plot. What is the first incident in the dramatized story of the rise and fall of King Oedipus? The second?

Analyze Craft

2 Given what you know about the myth, you can see that the play opens when the story is quite far along in its unfolding. Why does the playwright, having the entire story to work with, choose to begin where he does? Would the play have the same effect if it began in Oedipus's infancy? Or with the story of the shepherd? Or with an opening at the death of Iocaste and then flashing back to the moment when the messenger returns from the oracle?

3 How many actors does the play have? Imagine the visual effect of King Oedipus wearing the mask. What if the actor wore no mask? How might that affect the way you view the scene in your mind? How does Iocaste's action contribute to the deepening of the drama and its forward motion? What is the role of the shepherd? What is the role of the chorus?

4 A series of ironic revelations—or "reversals"—helps propel the play forward. Identify at least two and discuss.

Analyze Voice

5 Dialogue in a play such as this reveals character at the same time that it advances the story. How does Oedipus's first exchange of dialogue with Iocaste create a certain false mood of calm? Contrast it with their round of dialogue after the shepherd has made his speech.

6 How does the collective voice of the chorus differ from the speech of the individual actors? How might Sophocles have choreographed the citizen chorus? What moves would they make? How would a contemporary chorus move? What music and moves would you use if you were staging a contemporary version of the play?

Synthesize Summary and Analysis

7 The playwright has chosen to dramatize a major Greek myth, but in such a way as to maximize its impact on the audience. His presentation of the Oedipus story establishes the template for all future drama in the West and sets forward a series of dramatic techniques that playwrights will find invaluable. How might you imagine a major American playwright dramatizing the story of George Washington or Abraham Lincoln or Martin Luther King, Jr.?

Interpret the Play

8 The largest questions—those of fate and human destiny—come to the surface here. In *Oedipus the King,* we have a thoughtful, concerned leader—a good man—who fulfills a tragic prophecy. What role do his actions have in his fulfillment of this prophecy? What does his reaction to the knowledge that he has fulfilled this dreadful prophecy tell us about Oedipus's character? What is the play's answer to the human question of how to live a good life?

> "Pathos *is emotion. . . . That's how we get the borrowing in English.* Pathos. Pathetic. *That shows you the everyday meaning of* pathos. *But, when Oedipus experiences* pathos, *it's not everyday, it's larger than life, it's heroic, it goes back to the heroic world. This is that. That's what happens in theater, that's how the process of* catharsis *happens, that's how the* pathos, *which is the larger-than-life experience of Oedipus, can become part of your life, your emotional life, as you are drawn into this larger-than-life character."*
>
> Conversation with Gregory Nagy

ANCIENT GREEK DRAMA

Western culture today owes a very great deal to the Greeks. Our sense of narrative was born on the lips of Greek poets reciting heroic tales of their ancestors; plays such as *Oedipus* were part of seasonal, daylong competitions staged in open-air amphitheaters with seats built into the sides of hills, creating an atmosphere that somewhat resembles that of "March Madness" or the Super Bowl in our contemporary sports arenas. (A better analogy might be to a political rally, where a famous entertainer warms up the waiting crowd.) In the golden period of Greek culture, these plays, which the Athenians considered the highest creations of their best artists, became a central part of civic life. They simultaneously portrayed the honored past and the difficulties of life in the moment and projected a future in which human life coexisted with that of the gods. Everyone in democratic Athens participated, either as part of the play or as part of the audience.

> **"The Greeks came in the daytime to a huge amphitheater . . . perhaps they brought some food; they probably brought their families with them . . . and spent the whole day there. And when the night came, the night would come in the play too."** Conversation with Marian Seldes

Theater, Religion, and Citizenship

The plays honored the history of Athens, and—as Athens was in a protracted war with Sparta—also honored the power of the gods and goddesses who might be prevailed upon for protection. What we today call patriotism comingled with religious ritual as Athenians fulfilled their obligation as good citizens to attend the religious theatrical festivals. In his interview, Gregory Nagy discusses how Athenian citizens in the tens of thousands were required to attend the annual festivals of tragedy and comedy. He describes the way all free Athenians would share simultaneously in the emotion of the play's hero; this participation made even more powerful the connection they felt with their heroic past.

WAR AND *OEDIPUS THE KING*

The first historian, Herodotus, in his history of the Greco-Persian War, now and then offers genealogies that link kings and heroes of the Greeks' immediate past in a long line of kinship to heroes out of mythology. (Thucydides, the second great Greek historian, focused more on politics and tactics in his *History of the Peloponnesian War,* his narrative about the war between Athens and Sparta.) However, the difference between genealogy and chronology and the shaped and remade element of time in a work of art shows itself clearly in the presentation of mythological stories in classic Greek tragic theater. We get the essence of the myth, in all its depth and breadth, without watching the entire history in sequential detail.

What were the forces in Greek life that gave rise to the theatrical spectacles of ancient Greece? We have to look to Greek religion for an answer, because drama, in its original form, was inseparable from ritual observance and collective worship. The system of faith, as best we can tell from scattered references throughout Greek drama and later commentaries, was grounded in the pantheon of gods and goddesses from Homeric times. Dramatic theater evolved out of ceremonies celebrating Dionysus, the god of change and transformation.

"Theater . . . was taken so seriously that we might as well call it . . . a sacred narrative. . . . It's as real as what history might be to us."

Conversation with Gregory Nagy

In *The Birth of Tragedy,* nineteenth-century German philosopher Friedrich Nietzsche argues that a priest would lead the Dionysian ceremonies surrounding the planting of the grain; over time, he became the first actor, speaking through a mask. Later, as this art form evolved, a second actor appeared, challenging the statements of the first, and dramatic conflict was born. We can't say exactly how much time passed between the early ceremonies of Dionysus—ceremonies presided over by priests wearing sacred masks—and the first appearance of a play (with actors wearing masks), a work of art that was steeped in the old religion but no longer a part of it. However long the period between early religious ceremonies and the great theatrical festivals of Athens might have been, the Greeks would have considered these myths to be true stories of the origins of their present culture. Sophocles' play is, therefore, a sacred story transformed into a work of art.

"Sophocles . . . occupies a special place . . . as having . . . 'the most comprehensive soul.'" Conversation with Ralph Williams

The United States is a diverse culture. But in order to try to imagine the relation of Greek drama to Greek culture allow yourself to picture an America in which no one held any religious view other than Christianity—no Jews, no Muslims, no Buddhists, and certainly no atheists—and several times a year greatly gifted playwrights tried out in competition full-length (three- to five-act) plays on various aspects of Christian belief, from the Christmas story to the Easter story and everything in between, and everyone in every city came either to work in the productions or to sit as part of the audience.

CONVENTIONS OF GREEK DRAMA

Sophocles is not, of course, the only playwright of consequence from the classic period. Others include Aeschylus, the author of a trilogy of plays about another doomed dynasty (*Agamemnon, The Libation Bearers* or *Electra,* and *Eumenides* or *The Furies*), and Euripides, among whose surviving works are *Alcestis, The Phoenician Women,* and *The Bacchae.* Routinely, three such plays would be presented in succession at a festival—followed by a fourth, or **satyr** play, which provided a kind of comic relief (for more information on satyr plays, see Chapter 30). The great Greek comic playwright Aristophanes is the author of such texts as *Lysistrata* and *The Frogs,* and the comic mask is just as central to the idea of Greek theater as the tragic one. So some fourth performance would likely have followed Sophocles' trilogy, which includes the story of Oedipus's children's fate (*Antigone*) and the old king's death (*Oedipus at Colonus*).

"Greek plays . . . are thrilling and almost more modern than any other plays I can think of, including plays that are being written now. They're clean. There's no extra word in them. And there are no stage directions—there don't need to be." Conversation with Marian Seldes

In his interview, Gregory Nagy tells us that in addition to being poets, playwrights were musical composers—and in the case of Sophocles, both a musician and a singer. He put this talent to work in the creation of one of the major elements in his drama, the singing-chanting-dancing **chorus.** Here amateurs honored to be included in the play worked side by side with trained actors to portray a group of representative citizens with worries and questions, expressed in poetry and music and dance movement. The presence of the chorus immediately puts us in a special state of awareness; it's almost as if we witness the life of their emotions as well as the music of their fears.

"Actors do perform with masks. . . . These performances are . . . dialogues, it's a form of verse. . . . Technically, when actors have a dialogue with each other, representing heroes and the heroic world . . . it is, shall we say, modified song . . . there is a melodic contour to it, but it's not full-blown singing. By contrast, when the chorus sings, that is full-blown music, that's singing and dancing." Conversation with Gregory Nagy

The all-male casts wore masks (*personae*), enabling one actor to appear onstage as many different characters, and elevated shoes (*cothurni*). The mask also served as an amplification device so that members of the audience seated at some distance could hear the actor's words. Imagine what it would be like to see this frozen face and hear a solemn voice speaking through the mouth hole, a voice that you, as spectator, identify as coming from a god or goddess. The shoes would have made the actors taller, larger than life. This formality may, on first reading, make these ancient dramas seem overly regulated or ritualistic for modern tastes. However, when you consider the material that the play puts forward—murder, incest, child abuse, and a madness that questions language that comes directly from the gods—you can see how the playwright achieves a certain stability with all of this potentially frenzied subject matter by grounding the intense emotions in such a formal fashion.

The **amphitheater** was outdoors and unroofed, with seats built into the side of a hill. In acoustical terms, the amphitheater is an almost perfect amplifying structure; in this way—thousands of years before the microphone—a single voice could make its way up to the most distant rows. The seats came partway around the **orchestra,** which was the area in front of the *skene* (or stage), where the chorus sang and danced. The actors played several roles and changed in a building behind the *skene* that could be designed as part of the setting for the play. Sometimes actors played gods who, when lowered from the roof of the building with a chariot-like machine (***deus ex machina***), could physically rescue a character from danger when the action in the play itself didn't provide an escape. The backdrop for *Oedipus the King* would have been spare, those few columns providing a single setting for the entire play, with all eyes on Oedipus from his first entrance to his final moments onstage.

By convention, each play was composed of five parts and arranged in what is sometimes called the Apollonian mode, after the Greek god Apollo. In the early Greek religion, Dionysus was the god of change and transformation and Apollo the god of form and stability. This tension between the stability of form and the frenzy of the content dramatizes an ancient polarity in Greek culture, and in all Western culture that grows from it: the struggle between the so-called Dionysian mode and the Apollonian mode. After a reading of this play, you can see how the mad chaotic energy and devastating content of the play itself are balanced by the orderliness of a sculpted Apollonian five-part structure.

The first part is the **prologue,** in which the audience learns of the problem of the play—the complication that the characters, and especially the hero or protagonist, must face.

> **The *prologue* in *Oedipus the King.*** *As the Oedipus story begins, in the prologue we learn that the kingdom is suffering from a plague, and the king is seeking a cure. He has consulted the oracle in hopes of a message from the gods that might rid the city of its sickness. His duty demands that he rid the city of the murderer whose presence has brought the plague to Thebes.*

Following the prologue is the ***párados,*** the chorus's first **ode**—the song and dance of the chorus. Like an ancient version of the football stadium wave, the members of the chorus weave and bend; they dance and chant their reaction to the problem presented in the prologue.

> **The *párados* in *Oedipus the King.*** *Turning one way ("strophe") and then another ("antistrophe") and using their voices as well as movement, the chorus members declare their worry and confusion about the situation that has overtaken the city they love. What does the oracle say? We're afraid. How will it affect us? Let us pray to Athena for help. The fields are barren, so are the women, the plague continues to ravage us. The chorus calls on the gods to come to the aid of the tortured city.*

Next comes a series of ***episodia,*** or scenes. Each scene is followed by another choral ode, or ***stasimon,*** the chorus's interpretation of and response to the action of the preceding scene, including the final choral poem—dubbed the ***paean***—before the last scene of the play.

> **The *episodia* in *Oedipus the King.*** *In the first of four scenes, Oedipus and Iocaste learn more and more about the problem with the plague, until what they take to be the truth becomes completely reversed. Irony is the great driving engine of the plot. Each action Oedipus takes produces the opposite of the result he seeks. The audience knows exactly how things will turn out and watches the great man writhing in the web of his own destiny. To reiterate, as the play unfolds, the great king discovers that he himself is the cause of the troubles.*

Last, we have the **éxodos,** the concluding scene, followed by the final lines from the chorus. The king speaks, and the chorus reflects out loud in its specially choreographed fashion on what he means, questioning, chanting, swaying, bending.

> **The *éxodos* in *Oedipus the King*.** *Toward the end, the truth Oedipus discovers about his role in the death of the old king and his marriage to Iocaste leads him to a desperate act of violent self-mutilation. Paradoxically, however, once blind he truly "sees." The graceful Exodos serves as a sculpted, stabile vehicle for the destructive energy of his mad recognition. The final words of the chorus provide a caution that no matter how powerful and well situated someone may appear at the beginning, those who offend the gods will pay for the offense and be brought low. The chorus assures us that no one is off the hook until he or she is dead.*
>
> > *Let every man in mankind's frailty*
> > *Consider his last day; and let none*
> > *Presume on his good fortune until he find*
> > *Life, at his death, a memory without pain.*

GREEK TRAGEDY

We usually talk about Greek tragedy as a style in itself, a particular art form that treats characters and life in a certain fashion, that is to say, presents its stories as illustrative of the lives of "high" figures. These are kings, mainly, who because of a **tragic flaw** in their character—in the case of Oedipus, his inability to contain his anger mixed with a nearly uncontrollable sense of pride, or arrogance (**hubris**)—fall into death or misery or disrepute. The Greek concept of **hamartia,** defined as a mistake or error in judgment, is the essential element in tragedy. In other words, the offense to the gods may be committed in ignorance, as was the case with Oedipus, but it will not go unpunished. His misfortune is brought about not by villainy but rather by circumstances and errors of understanding and goes beyond the notion of a single tragic flaw.

> **"If the exaltation of tragic action were truly a property of the high-bred character alone, it is inconceivable that the mass of mankind should cherish tragedy above all other forms, let alone be capable of understanding it."** Conversation with Arthur Miller

Dramatic or **tragic irony** sums up the relation between the play and its contemporary audience, the citizens of classical Athens, and gives birth to a particular relation between all art and the audience in modern times. The hero cannot know his fate, may not even be aware of his offense, but the audience does know. Strutting across the stage, our hero is unaware of what his past action propels him toward. **Peripeteia,** or *reversal of circumstances,* is an element of Greek tragedy meaning that an action has the opposite result of what was intended. The classical hero's change of fortune may be surprising and unpredictable to him, the opposite of what he might naturally expect to happen based on his action. Nonetheless, the result of the hero's action appears inevitable to an audience steeped in the myth that gave rise to the play and serves as a continually troubling reminder of the fragility of human life and action. If you take Oedipus as a model, you can see that the Greeks viewed all life as transient, an existence built out of a series of ironic reversals.

Aristotle, one of the most significant philosophers of ancient Greece, made his assessment of the play *Oedipus the King* in his *Poetics,* a collection of lectures his students put together from their notes; it has survived as one of the major documents of classic Greek culture. He describes how tragedy is founded on the playwright's successful yoking of favored myths and an intuitive awareness of what one of Aristotle's later devotees, the twentieth-century literary critic Kenneth Burke, describes as the "tragic rhythm of action." That tragic rhythm consists of a movement from, as Burke puts it, *purpose* to *passion* to *perception*. **Anagnorisis,** or *recognition* (the original Greek way of describing what Burke calls "perception"), is "a change from ignorance to knowledge, producing love or hate between the persons destined by the poet for good or bad fortune"; it is the apparent wisdom that comes out of all the reversals and suffering.

> **"Oedipus learns . . . to have more humility as he goes through the play. . . . And . . . as the character learns, we learn."** Conversation with
> Edwin Wilson

In his interview, Gregory Nagy describes the audience as participants in the dramatic experience of tragedy. The audience can see what the outcome will be, but the characters cannot. Those who witness have an advantage over the characters in the play but also a feeling of apprehension or, in some cases, sorrow. This combination of pity *(look what happened to that poor character)* and fear *(there but for the grace of God go I)* is commonly defined as *pathos* and taken to be a complicated mix of emotions and central to the experience of theater. By invoking and purging the emotions of pity and fear in the audience, the play ideally creates a *catharsis* (purgation), or emotional renewal, in the spectators, and with this a vision of wholeness. A well-intentioned man, a hero, goes down, and his goodness, greatness even, allows him to see the justice in his demise; his acceptance of his fate makes the tragedy complete. For us in the modern world, such a play as *Oedipus* produces a recognition of our own roles in life, of how we are all strutting across the stage without being fully aware of what our past actions might mean. The impact of the tragic form of drama is probably greater than that of any other ancient creation.

Reading Greek Tragedy

When reading or viewing Greek tragedy, try to keep in mind the vocabulary of the theater.

Basic performance conventions and stage techniques of Greek tragedy	• **Chorus:** Amateur and professional actors who represent the citizens in a Greek tragedy. • *Personae* (masks) and *cothurni* (elevated shoes): Devices to amplify an actor's voice and appearance, both to make him larger than life and to project the performance to the back rows of the amphitheater. • *Deus ex machina:* A practical reference to a "god" (*deus*) who was lowered by machine (*ex machina*) onto the stage to physically rescue characters from harm. The language is Latin, but the device itself originated with the Greeks.
Five-part structure of most Greek tragedies	• **Prologue:** The introduction of the play, in which the audience learns the conflict that the protagonist must face. • *Párados:* The Chorus's first **ode** (song), offering an interpretation of the conflict learned in the Prologue. • *Episodia:* A series of scenes, usually debates between characters, in which the action and events of the play are presented. • *Stasimon:* The Chorus's interpretation and response to the preceding scene. • *Éxodos:* The concluding scene, including the final lines from the Chorus.

Literary conventions of Greek tragedy that shape the audience's reaction to plot events	• **Tragic hero:** A "high" figure—typically a king—who, because of some character flaw or inevitable mistake, falls into death, misery, or disrepute.
	• **Dramatic** or **tragic irony:** The audience's recognition of the hero's errors or fate before that of the hero.
	• **Tragic flaw:** The personality trait or fated mistake that leads to a tragic hero's downfall.
	   • **Hubris:** The sin of pride. A common tragic flaw characterized by arrogance and quick temper.
	   • *Hamartia:* An error or mistake in judgment. Although a mistake may be committed out of good intentions or ignorance, it will not go unpunished.
	• *Peripeteia:* An action that has a result opposite to the intention.
	• *Anagnorisis:* The wisdom that results from reversals (*peripeteia*) and suffering.
	• *Catharsis* and *pathos:* The emotional renewal (*catharsis*) created by an audience's feelings of pity and terror (*pathos*) for a tragic hero, resulting in the recognition that the hero's tragic fate was just and that his acceptance of that fate makes the tragedy complete.

Getting Started: A Research Project

Research is a skill that will carry you through your college career. To help acquaint you with the research process, the materials you need for this project are made available on our Web site (**connect .mcgraw-hill.com**). Other ideas for research projects and sources appear at the end of this chapter.

Chances are, you have heard of the Oedipus complex, a term that surfaces now and again in popular culture. But you may not know that the Oedipus complex was first identified by the seminal psychoanalyst Sigmund Freud, who based his idea of the complex on Sophocles' play *Oedipus the King.* Since Freud identified the Oedipus complex in his *Interpretation of Dreams,* his theory has shaped psychoanalysis both as it relates to the study of human psychology and as it relates to the theory of psychoanalysis as a form of literary criticism.

Our Web site will provide you with several articles that will help you un-

derstand the Oedipus complex and its potential applications. First, read the excerpt of Freud's *Interpretation of Dreams* in which he defines the Oedipus complex. Then, read the interview with scholar Jean-Pierre Vernant on the enduring value of tragedy and its relationship to Freud's theories. Refer to Haven McClure's introduction to his book *The Modern Reader's Hamlet* to get an idea of how the Oedipus complex is evident in other works of literature—in this case, Shakespeare's *Hamlet.* And finally, read Sarah Boxer's *New York Times* article to see the many challenges to Freud's theory over time.

After consulting these sources, choose one of the prompts below to get you started on writing a research paper.

1. Write a paper in which you define the Oedipus complex based on Freud's description of it. Then, describe challenges to Freud's theory,

from the interview with Jean-Pierre Vernant, from Sarah Boxer's article, and from your own ideas. Conclude your paper with your own evaluation of Freud's theory, based on your reading of *Oedipus the King* and your responses to the articles you have researched.

2. Choose one literary work—whether a short story, novel, or play—in which you see the Oedipus complex, or a version of it, at work. Write a paper in which you examine how the Oedipus complex appears in that work, even if it doesn't literally align with the circumstances of *Oedipus the King.* (You might, for example, choose to examine the budding sexuality of a character like the narrator of James Joyce's "Araby" in Chapter 8. Or, you might offer your own reading of the Oedipus complex in the next chapter on *Hamlet.*)

Writing and Research

1. A distinctive feature of Greek theater—and one that has survived—is the chorus. Visit **connect.mcgraw-hill.com** to listen to the entire interview with Gregory Nagy, taking notes on what he says about the Greek chorus. Using one of the sources in the list that follows on the next page, you may wish to do some more research into the original function of the chorus. Then, locate a copy of *A Chorus Line,* the hit Broadway musical that was made into a 1985 film directed by Richard Attenborough and starring Michael Douglas and Alyson Reed. Write an essay in which you compare the use of the Greek chorus in *Oedipus* with the use of the choric effect in *A Chorus Line.* Support your ideas with specific examples from your reading of *Oedipus,* your understanding of Nagy's interview, and any other sources you consult in learning about the Greek chorus.

- Ley, Graham. "Chorus." *A Short Introduction to the Ancient Greek Theater*. Chicago: U of Chicago P, 2006. 30–33. Print.
- Weiner, Albert. "The Function of the Tragic Greek Chorus." *Theatre Journal* 32.2 (May 1980): 205–212. Print.
- Zarifi, Yana. "Chorus and Dance in the Ancient World." *The Cambridge Companion to Greek and Roman Theatre*. Ed. Marianne McDonald and J. Michael Walton. New York: Cambridge UP, 2007. 227–246. Print.

2. If it weren't for translation, *Oedipus the King* would be known only to the few people who could read ancient Greek. Fortunately, many translators have created versions of *Oedipus the King* in English—such as the one printed in this chapter. To understand a few of the characteristics of Sophocles' Greek, read Robert Fitzgerald's notes to his translation of *Oedipus the King*, as listed in the sources below. You can use the additional resources to learn more about the problems and challenges of translation.

   Find a passage of *Oedipus the King* that you particularly enjoyed or thought memorable. Then, find another translation of the same play. Write a paper in which you compare the two translators' choices, drawing upon your research to help you analyze the translators' work.

- Sophocles. *The Oedipus Cycle*. Trans. Dudley Fitts and Robert Fitzgerald. New York: Harvest, 2002. Print. See especially pp. 181–185, Robert Fitzgerald's commentary on his translation.
- Venuti, Lawrence, ed. *The Translation Studies Reader*. 2nd ed. New York: Routledge, 2004. Print.
- Walton, J. Michael. "Sophocles' *Oedipus Tyrannus*: Words and Concepts." *Found in Translation: Greek Drama in English*. New York: Cambridge UP, 2006. 85–105. Print.

Some Sources for Research

Aristotle. *Poetics*. New York: Penguin, 1997. Print.

Bloom, Harold, ed. *Sophocles*. Philadelphia: Chelsea, 2003. Print.

Burton, Reginald William Boteler. *The Chorus in Sophocles' Tragedies*. New York: Oxford UP, 1980. Print.

Dodds, E. R. "On Misunderstanding the *Oedipus Rex*." *Sophocles' Oedipus Rex*. Ed. Harold Bloom. New York: Chelsea, 2007. 17–29. Print.

Frosh, Stephen. "Oedipus Complex." *Key Concepts in Psychoanalysis*. New York: New York UP, 2003. 62–73. Print.

Hall, Edith. *Greek Tragedy: Suffering under the Sun*. New York: Oxford UP, 2010. Print.

Knox, Bernard. *The Heroic Temper: Studies in Sophoclean Tragedy*. Berkeley: U of California P, 1983. Print.

Ley, Graham. *A Short Introduction to the Ancient Greek Theater*. Chicago: U of Chicago P, 2006. Print.

McDonald, Marianne, and Michael J. Walton, eds. *The Cambridge Companion to Greek and Roman Theatre*. New York: Cambridge UP, 2007. Print.

Segal, Charles. *Oedipus Tyrannus: Tragic Heroism and the Limits of Knowledge*. New York: Oxford UP, 2001. Print.

Scodel, Ruth. *An Introduction to Greek Tragedy*. New York: Cambridge UP, 2010. Print.

For examples of student papers, see Chapters 2, 3, 4, 5, 7, 18, and 31. For additional help on the research paper, see Chapter 5, Writing the Research Paper, Avoiding Plagiarism, and Documenting Sources.

33

William Shakespeare

A Case Study

"In many ways the question is not why Shakespeare survives, but what the English language would be without him. We speak Shakespeare. We can't help it. If we wanted to, we couldn't help it, and we don't."

Conversation with Ralph Williams, available on video
at connect.mcgraw-hill.com

IMAGINE yourself in the open air of an Eli... afternoon. You're standing elbow to elbow in... and brawlers, pickpockets and prostitutes. The... with three players, the traveling actors who will... has written to confront his treacherous uncle. T... tance, and the players have only a few hours to me... Hamlet instructs them thus in Act 3, Scene 2.

HAMLET: Speak the speech, I pray you, as... you, trippingly on the tongue. But if you... our players do, I had as lief the town crier... do not saw the air too much with your hand... gently; for in the very torrent, tempest, and,... wind of your passion, you must acquire and b... that may give it smoothness.

Notice what he demands: natural speech, gentle gestures, an even temper. Con... trast these pointers with the demands of the Greek theater: booming delivery to reach the thousands of gathered citizens of Athens, large gestures that can be seen from the back row of an amphitheater, tall shoes, padded garb, and a mask that makes natural expression impossible. In the Elizabethan theater, acting was not a stylized civic performance; rather, as Hamlet reminds his actors, "the purpose of playing, whose end, both at the first and now, was and is to hold, as 't were, the mirror up to nature."

Whereas the previous chapter presented a tragedy that depicts nobility and civic responsibility, this chapter presents two plays whose subjects are the passions of humanity. *Hamlet* is a play rich in plot and subplot, full of mirrors and doubling tales. The complications of Prince Hamlet himself, as well as his charm and intelligence, demand agility in performance; his quicksilver wit and self-awareness make for a nearly irresistible combination, and a *modern* one. By the time we first encounter him, however, he's steeped in sadness, brooding. He's the dark prince. What Hamlet mourns is understandable: his father's death. Understandably, also, he's upset by the "hot haste" with which his mother has married her husband's (Hamlet's father's) brother.

onversation on Shakespeare

Shared Humanity

For Shakespeare it must have been deep agony to watch the way in which inept actors . . . would ruin the effect for which he'd hoped. Theatrical success, the success of a performance, depends on the script, yes, on actors, yes, on an audience, yes. It is a totally social experience. And so Hamlet speaking with those who will perform a script of his creation [insists that the] . . . precious and artificial and bombastic . . . be stripped away. . . . So that we look and say, "Well there's the humanity in which I share."

Shakespeare's Moral Imagination

I have no idea . . . how Shakespeare imagined a Richard III, a vortex of evil who orders his own brother killed and then in defense of his claim to the throne orders the two young children of his elder brother, the one who had been king, killed. . . . On the other end [Shakespeare] can imagine a . . . Desdemona [from *Othello*]. . . . It's that range of moral imagination . . . that makes Shakespeare such an astonishing companion and voice for us all in our human journeys.

Why Does Shakespeare Endure?

There are a number of reasons, I think, that Shakespeare endures. . . . He's the rain forest of our language . . . in fact . . . the first user of thousands of words . . . and he is one of the great creators of beauty. . . . You can't solve . . . the pain of life. But you can set beauty against it and maybe endure it. . . . "When we're born, we cry that we are come to this great stage of fools." Of youth . . . "Come kiss me, sweet and twenty, youth's the stuff will not endure." As we reach times of despair . . . "Out out, brief candle, life's but a walking shadow, a poor player that struts and frets his hour upon the stage and then is heard no more." The phrases, the lines, are the vocabulary of our lives really. . . . He lasts for that reason.

To watch this entire interview, go to **connect.mcgraw-hill.com**.

RESEARCH ASSIGNMENT   After you have watched his interview, describe how Ralph Williams sees the categories of comedy and tragedy affecting Shakespeare's plays. Do you agree with Williams's assessment of Shakespeare's bravura?

Ralph Williams is the Arthur F. Thurnau Professor in the Department of English Language and Literature and Adjunct Lecturer in Near Eastern Studies, College of Literature, Science, and the Arts at the University of Michigan. Since 2000 he has collaborated with the Royal Shakespeare Company on its Residency Program.

William Shakespeare (1564–1616)

Although the speaker here is praising Cleopatra, queen of Egypt, these lines from *Antony and Cleopatra* seem an apt description of Shakespeare the playwright himself:

> Age cannot wither her, nor custom stale
> Her infinite variety. Other women cloy
> The appetites they feed, but she makes hungry
> Where most she satisfies.

The "infinite variety" of William Shakespeare's talent has raised many questions as to his actual identity. Some argue that he must have been a nobleman, citing his knowledge of courtly behavior; others insist he was a commoner because of his detailed knowledge of country matters. Scholars have suggested aristocrats such as the Earl of Oxford or Sir Phillip Sidney used the name "Shakespeare" as a pseudonym. Others propose the translator John Florio or Shakespeare's dead rival Christopher Marlowe. But, time and again, the name seems to fit no one so well as the glove maker's son from the small British town of Stratford-on-Avon.

The truth is, we actually know more about the historical figure called William Shakespeare, born in April 1564, than about most other men or women of the period. His father was a successful merchant of the town who later fell on hard times; he attended local schools, where he learned some Latin and a little Greek. Anne Hathaway was twenty-six, eight years older than William Shakespeare, when they obtained a marriage license in November 1582; she bore him a daughter six months later and, in 1585, twins. In 1597, the playwright purchased New Place, a fine house in Stratford-on-Avon—a sign that he had prospered in his own chosen career.

William Shakespeare spent most of his working life in London, as one of a troupe of players called the Lord Chamberlain's Men. He was an actor in the group as well as its principal playwright. This was the troupe that in 1599 built the great Globe Theater, which stood on the south bank of the Thames outside city regulations and housed the performances of a number of Shakespeare's plays. Under the patronage of King James I (king of England from 1603 to 1625, following the death of Elizabeth I), the company became known as the King's Men. A bare-bones summary of his life leaves out, of course, the crucial thing: the work itself. It exists in two separate genres: poetry and plays. His poetry includes long narrative poems such as "Venus and Adonis" and "The Rape of Lucrece" and 154 sonnets (see Chapters 17, 20, 25, and Poems for Further Reading). By most counts he also composed some 37 plays. A few fragments of disputed authorship survive, but Shakespeare's preeminence as playwright is based on the work produced between 1591 and 1611—twenty years of unmatched productivity and enduring art. A collection of 35 plays appeared posthumously in 1623, published by two other members of the King's Men, John Heminge and Henry Condell.

Shakespeare retired to New Place, most likely in 1611, and died on April 23, 1616. Contemporaries wrote often about him—competitively, at first, then respectfully, and after his death, in terms of extravagant praise.

"The theater virtually devoured scripts. They were in constant demand. Shakespeare at his peak would be writing two and three at a time . . . and Shakespeare made it preeminently a place where . . . the most profound issues of what we would call our 'humanity' and 'society' more generally were transacted." Conversation with Ralph Williams

FOR READING SHAKESPEARE

1. **Take it slow.** The characters in Shakespeare's plays often speak in poetry and seldom in language intended to imitate everyday speech. Read lines carefully and take note of where the language is especially lofty or especially straightforward.

2. **Read out loud.** Shakespeare intended his plays not to be read but to be performed. If you are hung up on a line, don't hesitate to give it a voice. Unfamiliar words and phrases can become clearer in meaning when you hear them aloud.

3. **Imagine the experience.** The theaters of Elizabethan England did not have elaborate sets, and plays were staged outdoors on sunny afternoons. Thus, playwrights had to work the physical situation into their characters' speech. Notice cues that the moon is in the sky, the ocean is nearby, or snow is falling outside, and use them to construct a mental picture of the action taking place.

4. **Become the audience.** The commoners in Shakespeare's audience would have experienced many of the same challenges you do interpreting Shakespeare's poetic, sometimes invented, language. Your first reading should focus less on dissecting the language and more on appreciating the action of the play.

5. **Consider watching a staged or filmed production** of the play after your first reading. This can lend clarity to difficult portions of the play and also help you to identify aspects of the play worthy of critical analysis.

AS YOU READ   Note the chances Hamlet has to kill Claudius—most obviously in Act 3, Scene 3. Why do you think he hesitates?

Hamlet, Prince of Denmark (c. 1600)

—edited by David Bevington

CHARACTERS

GHOST *of Hamlet, the former King of Denmark*

CLAUDIUS, *King of Denmark, the former King's brother*

GERTRUDE, *Queen of Denmark, widow of the former King and now wife of Claudius*

HAMLET, *Prince of Denmark, son of the late King and of Gertrude*

POLONIUS, *councillor to the King*

LAERTES, *his son*

OPHELIA, *his daughter*

REYNALDO, *his servant*

HORATIO, *Hamlet's friend and fellow student*

VOLTIMAND,
CORNELIUS,
ROSENCRANTZ,
GUILDENSTERN,   } *members of the Danish court*
OSRIC,
A GENTLEMAN,
A LORD,

Three or Four **PLAYERS**, *taking the roles of*
PROLOGUE, PLAYER KING,
PLAYER QUEEN, *and* **LUCIANUS**

Two **MESSENGERS**

FIRST SAILOR

Two **CLOWNS**, *a gravedigger and his companion*

PRIEST

FIRST AMBASSADOR *from England*

BERNARDO,
FRANCISCO,   } *officers and soldiers on watch*
MARCELLUS,

Lords, Soldiers, Attendants, Guards,
other Players, Followers of Laertes,
other Sailors, another Ambassador or
Ambassadors from England

FORTINBRAS, *Prince of Norway*

CAPTAIN *in his army*

THE SCENE: *Denmark*

1.1   *Enter* BERNARDO *and* FRANCISCO, *two sentinels,*
[meeting].

BERNARDO: Who's there?

FRANCISCO: Nay, answer me. Stand and unfold
yourself.

BERNARDO: Long live the King!

FRANCISCO: Bernardo?

5   **BERNARDO:**   He.

FRANCISCO: You come most carefully upon your hour.

BERNARDO: 'Tis now struck twelve. Get thee to bed,
Francisco.

FRANCISCO: For this relief much thanks. 'Tis bitter
cold,
And I am sick at heart.

BERNARDO: Have you had quiet guard?   10

FRANCISCO: Not a mouse stirring.

BERNARDO: Well, good night.
If you do meet Horatio and Marcellus,
The rivals of my watch, bid them make haste.

Enter HORATIO *and* MARCELLUS.

FRANCISCO: I think I hear them.—Stand, ho! Who is
there?   15

HORATIO: Friends to this ground.

MARCELLUS: And liegemen to the Dane.

FRANCISCO: Give you good night.

1.1 Location: Elsinore castle. A guard platform.
2 me (Francisco emphasizes that *he* is the sentry currently on watch.)
unfold yourself reveal your identity

14 rivals partners   **16 ground** country, land   **17 liegemen to the**
Dane men sworn to serve the Danish king   **18 Give** i.e., may God give

MARCELLUS: O, farewell, honest soldier. Who hath relieved you?

20 **FRANCISCO:**   Bernardo hath my place. Give you good night.

Exit FRANCISCO.

MARCELLUS: Holla! Bernardo!

BERNARDO: Say, what, is Horatio there?

HORATIO: A piece of him.

BERNARDO: Welcome, Horatio. Welcome, good Marcellus.

25 **HORATIO:**   What, has this thing appeared again tonight?

BERNARDO: I have seen nothing.

MARCELLUS: Horatio says 'tis but our fantasy,
And will not let belief take hold of him
Touching this dreaded sight twice seen of us.
30 Therefore I have entreated him along
With us to watch the minutes of this night,
That if again this apparition come
He may approve our eyes and speak to it.

HORATIO: Tush, tush, 'twill not appear.

BERNARDO: Sit down awhile,
35 And let us once again assail your ears,
That are so fortified against our story,
What we have two nights seen.

HORATIO: Well, sit we down,
And let us hear Bernardo speak of this.

BERNARDO: Last night of all,
40 When yond same star that's westward from the pole
Had made his course t' illume that part of heaven
Where now it burns, Marcellus and myself,
The bell then beating one—

Enter GHOST.

Horatio (Nicholas Farrell), Marcellus (Jack Lemmon), and Bernardo (Ian McElhinney) gape at the ghost of the dead king in the 1996 film directed by Kenneth Branagh.

MARCELLUS: Peace, break thee off! Look where it comes again!

BERNARDO: In the same figure like the King that's dead.   45

MARCELLUS: Thou art a scholar. Speak to it, Horatio.

BERNARDO: Looks 'a not like the King? Mark it, Horatio.

HORATIO: Most like. It harrows me with fear and wonder.

BERNARDO: It would be spoke to.

MARCELLUS: Speak to it, Horatio.

HORATIO: What are thou that usurp'st this time of night,   50
Together with that fair and warlike form
In which the majesty of buried Denmark
Did sometime march? By heaven, I charge thee, speak!

MARCELLUS: It is offended.

BERNARDO: See, it stalks away.

---

27 **fantasy** imagination   30 **along** to come along   31 **watch** keep watch during   33 **approve** corroborate   37 **What** with what   39 **Last . . . all** i.e., this *very* last night. (Emphatic.)   40 **pole** pole-star, north star   41 **his** its.   **illume** illuminate

46 **scholar** one learned enough to know how to question a ghost properly   47 **'a** he   49 **It . . . to** (It was commonly believed that a ghost could not speak until spoken to.)   50 **usurp'st** wrongfully takes over   52 **buried Denmark** the buried King of Denmark   53 **sometime** formerly

55 **HORATIO:** Stay! Speak, speak! I charge thee, speak!

Exit GHOST.

MARCELLUS: 'Tis gone and will not answer.

BERNARDO: How now, Horatio? You tremble and look
pale.
Is not this something more than fantasy?
What think you on 't?

60 **HORATIO:** Before my God, I might not this believe
Without the sensible and true avouch
Of mine own eyes.

MARCELLUS: Is it not like the King?

HORATIO: As thou art to thyself.
Such was the very armor he had on
65 When he the ambitious Norway combated.
So frowned he once when, in an angry parle,
He smote the sledded Polacks on the ice.
'Tis strange.

MARCELLUS: Thus twice before, and jump at this dead
hour,
70 With martial stalk hath he gone by our watch.

HORATIO: In what particular thought to work I know
not,
But in the gross and scope of mine opinion
This bodes some strange eruption to our state.

MARCELLUS: Good now, sit down, and tell me, he that
knows,
75 Why this same strict and most observant watch
So nightly toils the subject of the land,
And why such daily cast of brazen cannon
And foreign mart for implements of war,
Why such impress of shipwrights, whose sore task
80 Does not divide the Sunday from the week.

What might be toward, that this sweaty haste
Doth make the night joint-laborer with the day?
Who is 't that can inform me?

HORATIO: That can I;
At least, the whisper goes so. Our last king,
Whose image even but now appeared to us, 85
Was, as you know, by Fortinbras of Norway,
Thereto pricked on by a most emulate pride,
Dared to the combat; in which our valiant Hamlet—
For so this side of our known world esteemed him—
Did slay this Fortinbras; who by a sealed compact 90
Well ratified by and law and heraldry
Did forfeit, with his life, all those his lands
Which he stood seized of, to the conqueror;
Against the which a moiety competent
Was gagèd by our king, which had returned 95
To the inheritance of Fortinbras
Had he been vanquisher, as, by the same cov'nant
And carriage of the article designed,
His fell to Hamlet. Now, sir, young Fortinbras,
Of unimprovèd mettle hot and full, 100
Hath in the skirts of Norway here and there
Sharked up a list of lawless resolutes
For food and diet to some enterprise
That hath a stomach in 't, which is no other—
As it doth well appear unto our state— 105
But to recover of us, by strong hand
And terms compulsatory, those foresaid lands
So by his father lost. And this, I take it,

---

59 on 't of it **61 sensible** confirmed by the senses. **avouch** warrant, evidence **65 Norway** King of Norway **66 parle** parley **67 sledded** traveling on sleds. **Polacks** Poles **69 jump** exactly **70 stalk** stride **71 to work** i.e., to collect my thoughts and try to understand this **72 gross and scope** general drift **74 Good now** (An expression denoting entreaty or expostulation.) **76 toils** causes to toil. **subject** subjects **77 cast** casting **78 mart** buying and selling **79 impress** impressment, conscription

81 toward in preparation **87 Thereto . . . pride** (Refers to old Fortinbras, not the Danish King.) **pricked on** incited. **emulate** emulous, ambitious **89 this . . . world** i.e., all Europe, the Western world **90 sealed** certified, confirmed **93 seized** possessed **94 Against the** in return for. **moiety competent** corresponding portion **95 gagèd** engaged, pledged. **had returned** would have passed **96 inheritance** possession **97 cov'nant** i.e., the *sealed compact* of line 90 **98 carriage . . . designed** carrying out of the article or clause drawn up to cover the point **100 unimprovèd mettle** untried, undisciplined spirits **101 skirts** outlying regions, outskirts **102 Sharked up** gathered up, as a shark takes fish. **list** i.e., troop. **resolutes** desperadoes **103 For food and diet** i.e., they are to serve as *food,* or "means," *to some enterprise;* also they serve in return for the rations they get **104 stomach** (1) a spirit of daring (2) an appetite that is fed by the *lawless resolutes*

The ghost of King Hamlet (Brian Blessed) approaches.

And prologue to the omen coming on,
Have heaven and earth together demonstrated
Unto our climatures and countrymen.

Enter GHOST.

But soft, behold! Lo, where it comes again!   130
I'll cross it, though it blast me.   *(It spreads his arms.)*
    Stay, illusion!
If thou hast any sound or use of voice,
Speak to me!
If there be any good thing to be done
That may to thee do ease and grace to me,   135
Speak to me!
If thou art privy to thy country's fate,
Which, happily, foreknowing may avoid,
O, speak!
Or if thou has uphoarded in thy life   140
Extorted treasure in the womb of earth,
For which, they say, you spirits oft walk in death,
Speak of it! *(The cock crows.)* Stay and speak!—Stop it,
    Marcellus.

MARCELLUS: Shall I strike at it with my partisan?

HORATIO: Do, if it will not stand.   *[They strike at it.]* 145

BERNARDO: 'Tis here!

HORATIO: 'Tis here!   *[Exit* GHOST.*]*

MARCELLUS: 'Tis gone.
We do it wrong, being so majestical,
To offer it the show of violence,   150
For it is as the air invulnerable,
And our vain blows malicious mockery.

BERNARDO: It was about to speak when the cock crew.

HORATIO: And then it started like a guilty thing
Upon a fearful summons. I have heard   155
The cock, that is the trumpet to the morn,

    Is the main motive of our preparations,
110   The source of this our watch, and the chief head
    Of this posthaste and rummage in the land.

BERNARDO: I think it be no other but e'en so.
    Well may it sort that this portentous figure
    Comes armèd through our watch so like the King
115   That was and is the question of these wars.

HORATIO: A mote it is to trouble the mind's eye.
    In the most high and palmy state of Rome,
    A little ere the mightiest Julius fell,
    The graves stood tenantless, and the sheeted dead
120   Did squeak and gibber in the Roman streets;
    As stars with trains of fire and dews of blood,
    Disasters in the sun; and the moist star
    Upon whose influence Neptune's empire stands
    Was sick almost to doomsday with eclipse.
125   And even the like precurse of feared events,
    As harbingers preceding still the fates

---

110 head source   **111 rummage** bustle, commotion   **113 sort**
suit   **115 question** focus of contention   **116 mote** speck of dust
117 palmy flourishing   **119 sheeted** shrouded   **121 As** (This abrupt
transition suggests that matter is possibly omitted between lines
120 and 121.) **trains** trails   **122 Disasters** unfavorable signs or
aspects. **moist star** i.e., moon, governing tides   **123 Neptune** god
of the sea. **stands** depends   **124 sick . . . doomsday** (See Matthew
24:29 and Revelation 6:12.)   **125 precurse** heralding, foreshadowing   **126 harbingers** forerunners. **still** continually

---

127 omen calamitous event   **129 climatures** regions   **130 soft**
i.e., enough, break off   **131 cross** stand in its path, confront. **blast**
wither, strike with a curse. **s.d. his** its   **137 privy to** in on the secret of   **138 happily** haply, perchance   **144 partisan** long-handled
spear   **156 trumpet** trumpeter

Doth with his lofty and shrill-sounding throat
Awake the god of day, and at his warning,
Whether in sea or fire, in earth or air,
160 Th' extravagant and erring spirit hies
To his confine; and of the truth herein
This present object made probation.

MARCELLUS: It faded on the crowing of the cock.
Some say that ever 'gainst that season comes
165 Wherein our Savior's birth is celebrated,
This bird of dawning singeth all night long,
And then, they say, no spirit dare stir abroad;
The nights are wholesome, then no planets strike,
No fairy takes, nor witch hath power to charm,
170 So hallowed and so gracious is that time.

HORATIO: So have I heard and do in part believe it.
But, look, the morn in russet mantle clad
Walks o'er the dew of yon high eastward hill.
Break we our watch up, and by my advice
175 Let us impart what we have seen tonight
Unto young Hamlet; for upon my life,
This spirit, dumb to us, will speak to him.
Do you consent we shall acquaint him with it,
As needful in our loves, fitting our duty?

180 **MARCELLUS:** Let's do 't, I pray, and I this morning
     know
Where we shall find him most conveniently.

Exeunt.

1.2 *Flourish. Enter* CLAUDIUS, *King of Denmark,*
GERTRUDE *the Queen, [the] Council, as* POLONIUS
and his son LAERTES, HAMLET, *cum aliis*
[including VOLTIMAND *and* CORNELIUS*].*

KING: Though yet of Hamlet our dear brother's death
The memory be green, and that it us befitted

To bear our hearts in grief and our whole kingdom
To be contracted in one brow of woe,
Yet so far hath discretion fought with nature   5
That we with wisest sorrow think on him
Together with remembrance of ourselves.
Therefore our sometime sister, now our queen,
Th' imperial jointress to this warlike state,
Have we, as 'twere with a defeated joy—   10
With an auspicious and a dropping eye,
With mirth in funeral and with dirge in marriage,
In equal scale weighing delight and dole—
Taken to wife. Nor have we herein barred
Your better wisdoms, which have freely gone   15
With this affair along. For all, our thanks.
Now follows that you know young Fortinbras,
Holding a weak supposal of our worth,
Or thinking by our late dear brother's death
Our state to be disjoint and out of frame,   20
Co-leaguèd with this dream of his advantage,
He hath not failed to pester us with message
Importing the surrender of those lands
Lost by his father, with all bonds of law,
To our most valiant brother. So much for him.   25
Now for ourself and for this time of meeting.
Thus much the business is: we have here writ
To Norway, uncle of young Fortinbras—
Who, impotent and bed-rid, scarcely hears
Of this his nephew's purpose—to suppress   30
His further gait herein, in that the levies,
The lists, and full proportions are all made
Out of his subject; and we here dispatch
You, good Cornelius, and you, Voltimand,
For bearers of this greeting to old Norway,   35
Giving to you no further personal power

---

160 **extravagant and erring** wandering beyond bounds. (The
words have similar meaning.) **hies** hastens 162 **probation** proof
164 **'gainst** just before 168 **strike** destroy by evil influence
169 **takes** bewitches 170 **gracious** full of grace

1.2. Location: The castle.
s.d. as i.e., such as, including. **cum aliis** with others 1 **our** my.
(The royal "we"; also in the following lines.)

8 **sometime** former 9 **jointress** woman possessing property with
her husband 11 **With . . . eye** with one eye smiling and the other
weeping 13 **dole** grief 17 **that you know** what you know already,
that; or, that you be informed as follows 18 **weak supposal** low
estimate 21 **Co-leaguèd with** joined to, allied with. **dream . . .
advantage** illusory hope of having the advantage. (His only ally is
this hope.) 23 **Importing** pertaining to 24 **bonds** contracts
29 **impotent** helpless 31 **His** i.e., Fortinbras'. **gait** proceeding 31–33 **in that . . . subject** since the levying of troops and supplies is drawn entirely from the King of Norway's own subjects

Claudius (Basil Sydney) and Gertrude (Eileen Herlie) greet the court in the 1948 film directed by Laurence Olivier.

> To business with the King more than the scope
> Of these dilated articles allow.   *[He gives a paper.]*
> Farewell, and let your haste commend your duty.

40 **CORNELIUS, VOLTIMAND:**   In that, and all things, will
> we show our duty.

KING: We doubt it nothing. Heartily farewell.
>   *[Exeunt* VOLTIMAND *and* CORNELIUS.*]*
> And now, Laertes, what's the news with you?
> You told us of some suit; what is 't, Laertes?
> You cannot speak of reason to the Dane
45 And lose your voice. What wouldst thou beg,
> Laertes,
> That shall not be my offer, not thy asking?
> The head is not more native to the heart,
> The hand more instrumental to the mouth,
> Than is the throne of Denmark to thy father.
50 What wouldst thou have, Laertes?

---

38 **dilated** set out at length   39 **let . . . duty** let your swift obeying of orders, rather than mere words, express your dutifulness   41 **nothing** not at all   44 **the Dane** the Danish king   45 **lose your voice** waste your speech   47 **native** closely connected, related   48 **instrumental** serviceable

LAERTES: My dread lord,
> Your leave and favor to return to France,
> From whence though willingly I came to Denmark
> To show my duty in your coronation,
> Yet now I must confess, that duty done,
> My thoughts and wishes bend again toward France   55
> And bow them to your gracious leave and pardon.

KING: Have you your father's leave? What says Polonius?

POLONIUS: H'ath, my lord, wrung from me my slow
> leave
> By laborsome petition, and at last
> Upon his will I sealed my hard consent.   60
> I do beseech you, give him leave to go.

KING: Take thy fair hour, Laertes. Time be thine,
> And thy best graces spend it at thy will!
> But now, my cousin Hamlet, and my son—

HAMLET: A little more than kin, and less than kind.   65

KING: How is it that the clouds still hang on you?

HAMLET: Not so, my lord. I am too much in the sun.

QUEEN: Good Hamlet, cast thy nighted color off,
> And let thine eye look like a friend on Denmark.
> Do not forever with thy vailèd lids   70
> Seek for thy noble father in the dust.
> Thou know'st 'tis common, all that lives must die,
> Passing through nature to eternity.

HAMLET: Ay, madam, it is common.

---

51 **leave and favor** kind permission   56 **bow . . . pardon** entreatingly make a deep bow, asking your permission to depart   58 **H'ath** he has   60 **sealed** (as if sealing a legal document).   **hard** reluctant   62 **Take thy fair hour** enjoy your time of youth   63 **And . . . will** and may your finest qualities guide the way you choose to spend your time   64 **cousin** any kin not of the immediate family   65 **A little . . . kind** i.e., closer than an ordinary nephew (since I am stepson), and yet more separated in natural feeling (with pun on *kind* meaning "affectionate" and "natural," "lawful." This line is often read as an aside, but it need not be. The King chooses perhaps not to respond to Hamlet's cryptic and bitter remark.)   67 **the sun** i.e., the sunshine of the King's royal favor (with pun on *son*)   68 **nighted color** (1) mourning garments of black (2) dark melancholy   69 **Denmark** the King of Denmark   70 **vailèd lids** lowered eyes   72 **common** of universal occurrence. (But Hamlet plays on the sense of "vulgar" in line 74.)

QUEEN: If it be,
75   Why seems it so particular with thee?

HAMLET: Seems, madam? Nay, it is. I know not "seems."
        'Tis not alone my inky cloak, good Mother,
        Nor customary suits of solemn black,
        Nor windy suspiration of forced breath,
80   No, nor the fruitful river in the eye,
        Nor the dejected havior of the visage,
        Together with all forms, moods, shapes of grief,
        That can denote me truly. These indeed seem,
        For they are actions that a man might play.
85   But I have that within which passes show;
        These but the trappings and the suits of woe.

KING: 'Tis sweet and commendable in your nature,
            Hamlet,
        To give these mourning duties to your father.
        But you must know your father lost a father,
90   That father lost, lost his, and the survivor bound
        In filial obligation for some term
        To do obsequious sorrow. But to persever
        In obstinate condolement is a course
        Of impious stubbornness. 'Tis unmanly grief.
95   It shows a will most incorrect to heaven,
        A heart unfortified, a mind impatient,
        An understanding simple and unschooled.
        For what we know must be and is as common
        As any the most vulgar thing to sense,
100   Why should we in our peevish opposition
        Take it to heart? Fie, 'tis a fault to heaven,
        A fault against the dead, a fault to nature,
        To reason most absurd, whose common theme
        Is death of fathers, and who still hath cried,
105   From the first corpse till he that died today,
        "This must be so." We pray you, throw to earth
        This unprevailing woe and think of us

As of a father; for let the world take note,
You are the most immediate to our throne,
And with no less nobility of love   110
Than that which dearest father bears his son
Do I impart toward you. For your intent
In going back to school in Wittenberg,
It is most retrograde to our desire,
And we beseech you bend you to remain   115
Here in the cheer and comfort of our eye,
Our chiefest courtier, cousin, and our son.

QUEEN: Let not thy mother lose her prayers, Hamlet.
I pray thee, stay with us, go not to Wittenberg.

HAMLET: I shall in all my best obey you, madam.   120

KING: Why, 'tis a loving and a fair reply.
Be as ourself in Denmark. Madam, come.
This gentle and unforced accord of Hamlet
Sits smiling to my heart, in grace whereof
No jocund health that Denmark drinks today   125
But the great cannon to the clouds shall tell,
And the King's rouse the heaven shall bruit again,
Respeaking earthly thunder. Come away.
                Flourish. Exeunt all but HAMLET.

HAMLET: O, that this too sullied flesh would melt,
Thaw, and resolve itself into a dew!   130
Or that the Everlasting had not fixed
His canon 'gainst self-slaughter! O God, God,
How weary, stale, flat, and unprofitable
Seem to me all the uses of this world!
Fie on 't, ah fie! 'Tis an unweeded garden   135
That grows to seed. Things rank and gross in nature
Possess it merely. That it should come to this!
But two months dead—nay, not so much, not two.

---

75 **particular** personal   78 **customary** (1) socially conventional (2) habitual with me   79 **suspiration** sighing   80 **fruitful** abundant   81 **havior** expression   82 **moods** outward expression of feeling   92 **obsequious** suited to obsequies or funerals.   **persever** persevere   93 **condolement** sorrowing   96 **unfortified** i.e., against adversity   97 **simple** ignorant   99 **As . . . sense** as the most ordinary experience   104 **still** always   105 **the first corpse** (Abel's)   107 **unprevailing** unavailing, useless

---

109 **most immediate** next in succession   112 **impart toward** i.e., bestow my affection on.   **For** as for   113 **to school** i.e., to your studies.   **Wittenberg** famous German university founded in 1502   114 **retrograde** contrary   115 **bend you** incline yourself   120 **in all my best** to the best of my ability   124 **to** i.e., at.   **grace** thanksgiving   125 **jocund** merry   127 **rouse** drinking of a draft of liquor.   **bruit again** loudly echo   128 **thunder** i.e., of trumpet and kettledrum, sounded when the King drinks; see 1.4.8–12   129 **sullied** defiled. (The early quartos read *sallied;* the Folio, *solid.*)   132 **canon** law   134 **all the uses** the whole routine   137 **merely** completely

140 So excellent a king, that was to this
Hyperion to a satyr, so loving to my mother
That he might not beteem the winds of heaven
Visit her face too roughly. Heaven and earth,
Must I remember? Why, she would hang on him
As if increase of appetite had grown
145 By what it fed on, and yet within a month—
Let me not think on 't; frailty, thy name is woman!—
A little month, or ere those shoes were old
With which she followed my poor father's body,
Like Niobe, all tears, why she, even she—
150 O God, a beast, that wants discourse of reason,
Would have mourned longer—married with my uncle,
My father's brother, but no more like my father
Than I to Hercules. Within a month,
Ere yet the salt of most unrighteous tears
155 Had left the flushing in her gallèd eyes,
She married. O, most wicked speed, to post
With such dexterity to incestuous sheets!
It is not, nor it cannot come to good.
But break, my heart, for I must hold my tongue.

Enter HORATIO, MARCELLUS, *and* BERNARDO.

160 **HORATIO:** Hail to your lordship!

HAMLET: I am glad to see you well.
Horatio!—or I do forget myself.

HORATIO: The same, my lord, and your poor servant
ever.

HAMLET: Sir, my good friend; I'll change that name
with you.
And what make you from Wittenberg, Horatio?
165 Marcellus.

---

139 **to** in comparison to 140 **Hyperion** Titan sun-god, father of Helios. **satyr** a lecherous creature of classical mythology, half-human but with a goat's legs, tail, ears, and horns 141 **beteem** allow 147 **or ere** even before 149 **Niobe** Tantalus' daughter, Queen of Thebes, who boasted that she had more sons and daughters than Leto; for this, Apollo and Artemis, children of Leto, slew her fourteen children. She was turned by Zeus into a stone that continually dropped tears. 150 **wants . . . reason** lacks the faculty of reason 155 **gallèd** irritated, inflamed 156 **post** hasten 157 **incestuous** (In Shakespeare's day, the marriage of a man like Claudius to his deceased brother's wife was considered incestuous.) 163 **change that name** i.e., give and receive reciprocally the name of "friend" (rather than talk of "servant") 164 **make you from** are you doing away from

MARCELLUS: My good lord.

HAMLET: I am very glad to see you. *[To* BERNARDO.*]*
Good even, sir.—
But what in faith make you from Wittenberg?

HORATIO: A truant disposition, good my lord.

HAMLET: I would not hear your enemy say so,   170
Nor shall you do my ear that violence
To make it truster of your own report
Against yourself. I know you are no truant.
But what is your affair in Elsinore?
We'll teach you to drink deep ere you depart.   175

HORATIO: My lord, I came to see your father's funeral.

HAMLET: I prithee, do not mock me, fellow student;
I think it was to see my mother's wedding.

HORATIO: Indeed, my lord, it followed hard upon.

HAMLET: Thrift, thrift, Horatio! The funeral baked   180
meats
Did coldly furnish forth the marriage tables.
Would I had met my dearest foe in heaven
Or ever I had seen that day, Horatio!
My father!—Methinks I see my father.

HORATIO: Where, my lord?

HAMLET: In my mind's eye, Horatio.   185

HORATIO: I saw him once. 'A was a goodly king.

HAMLET: 'A was a man. Take him for all in all,
I shall not look upon his like again.

HORATIO: My lord, I think I saw him yesternight.

HAMLET: Saw? Who?   190

HORATIO: My lord, the King your father.

HAMLET: The King my father?

HORATIO: Season your admiration for a while

---

179 **hard** close 180 **baked meats** meat pies 181 **coldly** i.e., as cold leftovers 182 **dearest** closest (and therefore deadliest) 183 **Or ever** before 186 **'A** he 193 **Season your admiration** restrain your astonishment

Hamlet (Kevin Kline) addresses Horatio (Peter Francis James) in the 1990 film directed by Kevin Kline.

The apparition comes. I knew your father;
These hands are not more like.

HAMLET: But where was this?

MARCELLUS: My lord, upon the platform where we
watch.

HAMLET: Did you not speak to it?

HORATIO: My lord, I did,   215
But answer made it none. Yet once methought
It lifted up its head and did address
Itself to motion, like as it would speak;
But even then the morning cock crew loud,
And at the sound it shrunk in haste away   220
And vanished from our sight.

HAMLET: 'Tis very strange.

HORATIO: As I do live, my honored lord, 'tis true,
And we did think it writ down in our duty
To let you know of it.

HAMLET: Indeed, indeed, sirs. But this troubles me.   225
Hold you the watch tonight?

ALL: We do, my lord.

HAMLET: Armed, say you?

ALL: Armed, my lord.

HAMLET: From top to toe?

ALL: My lord, from head to foot.   230

HAMLET: Then saw you not his face?

HORATIO: O, yes, my lord, he wore his beaver up.

HAMLET: What looked he, frowningly?

HORATIO: A countenance more in sorrow than in anger.

HAMLET: Pale or red?   235

HORATIO: Nay, very pale.

HAMLET: And fixed his eyes upon you?

With an attent ear till I may deliver,
195   Upon the witness of these gentlemen,
This marvel to you.

HAMLET: For God's love, let me hear!

HORATIO: Two nights together had these gentlemen,
Marcellus and Bernardo, on their watch,
In the dead waste and middle of the night,
200   Been thus encountered. A figure like your father,
Armèd at point exactly, cap-à-pie,
Appears before them, and with solemn march
Goes slow and stately by them. Thrice he walked
By their oppressed and fear-surprisèd eyes
205   Within his truncheon's length, whilst they, distilled
Almost to jelly with the act of fear,
Stand dumb and speak not to him. This to me
In dreadful secrecy impart they did,
And I with them the third night kept the watch,
210   Where, as they had delivered, both in time,
Form of the thing, each word made true and good,

---

194 **attent** attentive   199 **dead waste** desolate stillness   201 **at
point** correctly in every detail.   **cap-à-pie** from head to foot   205
truncheon officer's staff.   **distilled** dissolved   206 **act** action,
operation   208 **dreadful** full of dread

217–218 **did . . . speak** began to move as though it were about to
speak   219 **even then** at that very instant   232 **beaver** visor on the
helmet   233 **What** how

HORATIO: Most constantly.

HAMLET: I would I had been there.

240 **HORATIO:** It would have much amazed you.

HAMLET: Very like, very like. Stayed it long?

HORATIO: While one with moderate haste might tell a
hundred.

MARCELLUS, BERNARDO: Longer, longer.

HORATIO: Not when I saw 't.

245 **HAMLET:** His beard was grizzled—no?

HORATIO: It was, as I have seen it in his life,
A sable silvered.

HAMLET: I will watch tonight.
Perchance 'twill walk again.

HORATIO: I warrant it will.

HAMLET: If it assume my noble father's person,
250 I'll speak to it though hell itself should gape
And bid me hold my peace. I pray you all,
If you have hitherto concealed this sight,
Let it be tenable in your silence still,
And whatsoever else shall hap tonight,
255 Give it an understanding but no tongue.
I will requite your loves. So, fare you well.
Upon the platform twixt eleven and twelve
I'll visit you.

ALL: Our duty to your honor.

HAMLET: Your loves, as mine to you. Farewell.
Exeunt [all but HAMLET*].*
260 My father's spirit in arms! All is not well.
I doubt some foul play. Would the night were come!
Till then sit still, my soul. Foul deeds will rise,
Though all the earth o'erwhelm them, to men's eyes.
Exit.

Laertes (Nathaniel Parker) warns Ophelia (Helena Bonham Carter) to be careful of Hamlet in the 1990 film directed by Franco Zeffirelli.

1.3 *Enter* LAERTES *and* OPHELIA, *his sister.*

LAERTES: My necessaries are embarked. Farewell.
And, sister, as the winds give benefit
And convoy is assistant, do not sleep
But let me hear from you.

OPHELIA: Do you doubt that?

LAERTES: For Hamlet, and the trifling of his favor,   5
Hold it a fashion and a toy in blood,
A violet in the youth of primy nature
Forward, not permanent, sweet, not lasting,
The perfume and suppliance of a minute—
No more.

OPHELIA: No more but so?

LAERTES: Think it no more.   10
For nature crescent does not grow alone
In thews and bulk, but as this temple waxes
The inward service of the mind and soul

---

242 **tell** count   245 **grizzled** gray   247 **sable silvered** black mixed with white   248 **warrant** assure you   253 **tenable** held 261 **doubt** suspect

---

1.3. Location: Polonius' chambers.
3 **convoy is assistant** means of conveyance are available   6 **toy in blood** passing amorous fancy   7 **primy** in its prime, springtime 8 **Forward** precocious   9 **suppliance** supply, filler   11 **crescent** growing, waxing   12 **thews** bodily strength.   **temple** i.e., body

15 Grows wide withal. Perhaps he loves you now,
And now no soil nor cautel doth besmirch
The virtue of his will; but you must fear,
His greatness weighed, his will is not his own.
For he himself is subject to his birth.
He may not, as unvalued persons do,
20 Carve for himself, for on his choice depends
The safety and health of this whole state,
And therefore must his choice be circumscribed
Unto the voice and yielding of that body
Whereof he is the head. Then if he says he loves you,
25 It fits your wisdom so far to believe it
As he in his particular act and place
May give his saying deed, which is no further
Than the main voice of Denmark goes withal.
Then weigh what loss your honor may sustain
30 If with too credent ear you list his songs,
Or lose your heart, or your chaste treasure open
To his unmastered importunity.
Fear it, Ophelia, fear it, my dear sister,
And keep you in the rear of your affection,
35 Out of the shot and danger of desire.
The chariest maid is prodigal enough
If she unmask her beauty to the moon.
Virtue itself scapes not calumnious strokes.
The canker galls the infants of the spring
40 Too oft before their buttons be disclosed,
And in the morn and liquid dew of youth
Contagious blastments are most imminent.
Be wary then; best safety lies in fear.
Youth to itself rebels, though none else near.

---

14 **Grows wide withal** grows along with it 15 **soil** blemish.
cautel deceit 16 **will** desire 17 **His greatness weighed** if you take
into account his high position 20 **Carve** i.e., choose 23 **voice
and yielding** assent, approval 26 **in . . . place** in his particular
restricted circumstances 28 **main voice** general assent. **withal**
along with 30 **credent** credulous. **list** listen to 34 **keep . . .
affection** don't advance as far as your affection might lead you.
(A military metaphor.) 36 **chariest** most scrupulously modest
37 **If she unmask** if she does no more than show her beauty. **moon**
(Symbol of chastity.) 39 **canker galls** cankerworm destroys
40 **buttons** buds. **disclosed** opened 41 **liquid dew** i.e., time when
dew is fresh and bright 42 **blastments** blights 44 **Youth . . .
rebels** youth is inherently rebellious

OPHELIA: I shall the effect of this good lesson keep   45
As watchman to my heart. But, good my brother,
Do not, as some ungracious pastors do,
Show me the steep and thorny way to heaven,
Whiles like a puffed and reckless libertine
Himself the primrose path of dalliance treads,   50
And recks not his own rede.

Enter POLONIUS.

LAERTES: O, fear me not.
I stay too long. But here my father comes.
A double blessing is a double grace;
Occasion smiles upon a second leave.

POLONIUS: Yet here, Laertes? Aboard, aboard, for   55
shame!
The wind sits in the shoulder of your sail,
And you are stayed for. There—my blessing with thee!
And these few precepts in thy memory
Look thou character. Give thy thoughts no tongue,
Nor any unproportioned thought his act.   60
Be thou familiar, but by no means vulgar.
Those friends thou hast, and their adoption tried,
Grapple them unto thy soul with hoops of steel,
But do not dull thy palm with entertainment
Of each new-hatched, unfledged courage. Beware   65
Of entrance to a quarrel, but being in,
Bear 't that th' opposèd may beware of thee.
Give every man thy ear, but few thy voice;
Take each man's censure, but reserve thy judgment.
Costly thy habit as thy purse can buy,   70
But not expressed in fancy; rich, not gaudy,
For the apparel oft proclaims the man,

---

47 **ungracious** ungodly 49 **puffed** bloated, or swollen with
pride 51 **recks** heeds. **rede** counsel. **fear me not** don't worry on
my account 53 **double** (Laertes has already bid his father good-
bye.) 54 **Occasion . . . leave** happy is the circumstance that provides a second leave-taking. (The goddess Occasion, or Opportunity,
smiles.) 59 **Look** be sure that. **character** inscribe 60 **unproportioned** badly calculated, intemperate. **his** its 61 **familiar**
sociable. **vulgar** common 62 **and their adoption tried** and also
their suitability for adoption as friends having been tested 64 **dull
thy palm** i.e., shake hands so often as to make the gesture meaningless 65 **courage** young man of spirit 67 **Bear 't that** manage it so
that 69 **censure** opinion, judgment 70 **habit** clothing 71 **fancy**
excessive ornament, decadent fashion

And they in France of the best rank and station
Are of a most select and generous chief in that.
75 Neither a borrower nor a lender be,
For loan oft loses both itself and friend,
And borrowing dulleth edge of husbandry.
This above all: to thine own self be true,
And it must follow, as the night the day,
80 Thou canst not then be false to any man.
Farewell. My blessing season this in thee!

LAERTES: Most humbly do I take my leave, my lord.

POLONIUS: The time invests you. Go, your servants
tend.

LAERTES: Farewell, Ophelia, and remember well
85 What I have said to you.

OPHELIA: 'Tis in my memory locked,
And you yourself shall keep the key of it.

LAERTES: Farewell.   *Exit* LAERTES.

POLONIUS: What is 't, Ophelia, he hath said to you?

90 **OPHELIA:**   So please you, something touching the Lord
Hamlet.

POLONIUS: Marry, well bethought.
'Tis told me he hath very oft of late
Given private time to you, and you yourself
Have of your audience been most free and bounteous.
95 If it be so—as so 'tis put on me,
And that in way of caution—I must tell you
You do not understand yourself so clearly
As it behooves my daughter and your honor.
What is between you? Give me up the truth.

100 **OPHELIA:**   He hath, my lord, of late made many tenders
Of his affection to me.

POLONIUS: Affection? Pooh! You speak like a green girl,
Unsifted in such perilous circumstance.
Do you believe his tenders, as you call them?

OPHELIA: I do not know, my lord, what I should think.   105

POLONIUS: Marry, I will teach you. Think yourself a
baby
That you have ta'en these tenders for true pay
Which are not sterling. Tender yourself more dearly,
Or—not to crack the wind of the poor phrase,
Running it thus—you'll tender me a fool.   110

OPHELIA: My lord, he hath importuned me with love
In honorable fashion.

POLONIUS: Ay, fashion you may call it. Go to, go to.

OPHELIA: And hath given countenance to his speech,
my lord,
With almost all the holy vows of heaven.   115

POLONIUS: Ay, springes to catch woodcocks. I do know,
When the blood burns, how prodigal the soul
Lends the tongue vows. These blazes, daughter,
Giving more light than heat, extinct in both
Even in their promise as it is a-making,   120
You must not take for fire. From this time
Be something scanter of your maiden presence.
Set your entreatments at a higher rate
Than a command to parle. For Lord Hamlet,
Believe so much in him that he is young,   125
And with a larger tether may he walk
Than may be given you. In few, Ophelia,
Do not believe his vows, for they are brokers,
Not of that dye which their investments show,
But mere implorators of unholy suits,   130

---

108 **sterling** legal currency.   **Tender** hold, look after, offer   109
crack the wind i.e., run it until it is broken-winded   110 **tender me
a fool** (1) show yourself to me as a fool (2) show me up as a fool (3)
present me with a grandchild. (*Fool* was a term of endearment for a
child.)   113 **fashion** mere form, pretense.   **Go to** (An expression of
impatience.)   114 **countenance** credit, confirmation   116 **springes**
snares.   **woodcocks** birds easily caught; here used to connote
gullibility   117 **prodigal** prodigally   120 **it** i.e., the promise   122
something somewhat   123 **entreatments** negotiations for surrender. (A military term.)   124 **parle** discuss terms with the enemy.
(Polonius urges his daughter, in the metaphor of military language,
not to meet with Hamlet and consider giving in to him merely
because he requests an interview.)   125 **so . . . him** this much concerning him   127 **In few** briefly   128 **brokers** go-betweens, procur-
ers   129 **dye** color or sort.   **investments** clothes. (The vows are not
what they seem.)   130 **mere implorators** out-and-out solicitors

---

74 **Are . . . that** are of a most refined and well-bred preeminence
in choosing what to wear   77 **husbandry** thrift   81 **season** mature   83 **invests** besieges, presses upon   91 **Marry** i.e., by the
Virgin Mary. (A mild oath.)   95 **put on** impressed on, told to   98
behooves befits   100 **tenders** offers   103 **Unsifted** i.e., untried

Breathing like sanctified and pious bawds,
The better to beguile. This is for all:
I would not, in plain terms, from this time forth
Have you so slander any moment leisure
135 As to give words or talk with the Lord Hamlet.
Look to 't, I charge you. Come your ways.

OPHELIA: I shall obey, my lord.   *Exeunt.*

1.4   *Enter* HAMLET, HORATIO, *and* MARCELLUS

HAMLET: The air bites shrewdly; it is very cold.

HORATIO: It is a nipping and an eager air.

HAMLET: What hour now?

HORATIO: I think it lacks of twelve.

MARCELLUS: No, it is struck.

HORATIO: Indeed? I heard it not.
5   It then draws near the season
          Wherein the spirit held his wont to walk.
                    *A flourish of trumpets, and
                    two pieces go off [within].*
          What does this mean, my lord?

HAMLET: The King doth wake tonight and takes his
                    rouse,
          Keeps wassail, and the swaggering upspring reels;
10   And as he drains his drafts of Rhenish down,
          The kettledrum and trumpet thus bray out
          The triumph of his pledge.

HORATIO: Is it a custom?

HAMLET: Ay, marry, is 't,
          But to my mind, though I am native here

Hamlet (Kenneth Branagh) goes with Marcellus and Horatio to confront the ghost.

And to the manner born, it is a custom   15
More honored in the breach than the observance.
This heavy-headed revel east and west
Makes us traduced and taxed of other nations.
They clepe us drunkards, and with swinish phrase
Soil our addition; and indeed it takes   20
From our achievements, though performed at height,
The pith and marrow of our attribute.
So, oft it chances in particular men,
That for some vicious mole of nature in them,
As in their birth—wherein they are not guilty,   25
Since nature cannot choose his origin—
By their o'ergrowth of some complexion,
Oft breaking down the pales and forts of reason,
Or by some habit that too much o'erleavens
The form of plausive manners, that these men   30
Carrying, I say, the stamp of one defect,
Being nature's livery or fortune's star,

---

131 Breathing speaking   **132 for all** once for all, in sum   **134 slander** abuse, misuse.   **moment** moment's   **136 Come your ways** come along

1.4. Location: The guard platform.
1 shrewdly keenly, sharply   **2 eager** biting   **3 lacks of** is just short of   **5 season** time   **6 held his wont** was accustomed   **s.d. pieces** i.e., of ordnance, cannon   **8 wake** stay awake and hold revel.   **takes his rouse** carouses   **9 wassail** carousal.   **upspring** wild German dance.   **reels** dances   **10 Rhenish** Rhine wine   **12 The triumph . . . pledge** i.e., his feat in draining the wine in a single draft

15 manner custom (of drinking)   **16 More . . . observance** better neglected than followed   **17 east and west** i.e., everywhere   **18 taxed of** censured by   **19 clepe** call.   **with swinish phrase** i.e., by calling us swine   **20 addition** reputation   **21 at height** outstandingly   **22 The pith . . . attribute** the essence of the reputation that others attribute to us   **24 for** on account of.   **mole of nature** natural blemish in one's constitution   **26 his** its   **27 their o'ergrowth . . . complexion** the excessive growth in individuals of some natural trait   **28 pales** palings, fences (as of a fortification)   **29 o'erleavens** induces a change throughout (as yeast works in dough)   **30 plausive** pleasing   **32 nature's livery** sign of one's servitude to nature.   **fortune's star** the destiny that chance brings

His virtues else, be they as pure as grace,
As infinite as man may undergo,
35 Shall in the general censure take corruption
From that particular fault. The dram of evil
Doth all the noble substance often dout
To his own scandal.

Enter GHOST.

HORATIO: Look, my lord, it comes!

HAMLET: Angels and ministers of grace defend us!
40 Be thou a spirit of health or goblin damned,
Bring with thee airs from heaven or blasts from hell,
Be thy intents wicked or charitable,
Thou com'st in such a questionable shape
That I will speak to thee. I'll call thee Hamlet,
45 King, father, royal Dane. O, answer me!
Let me not burst in ignorance, but tell
Why thy canonized bones, hearsèd in death,
Have burst their cerements; why the sepulcher
Wherein we saw thee quietly inurned
50 Hath oped his ponderous and marble jaws
To cast thee up again. What may this mean,
That thou, dead corpse, again in complete steel,
Revisits thus the glimpses of the moon,
Making night hideous, and we fools of nature
55 So horridly to shake our disposition
With thoughts beyond the reaches of our souls?
Say, why is this? Wherefore? What should we do?
[The GHOST*] beckons [*HAMLET*].*

HORATIO: It beckons you to go away with it,
As if it some impartment did desire
To you alone.

MARCELLUS: Look with what courteous action   60
It wafts you to a more removèd ground.
But do not go with it.

HORATIO: No, by no means.

HAMLET: It will not speak. Then I will follow it.

HORATIO: Do not, my lord!

HAMLET: Why, what should be the fear?
I do not set my life at a pin's fee,   65
And for my soul, what can it do to that,
Being a thing immortal as itself?
It waves me forth again. I'll follow it.

HORATIO: What if it tempt you toward the flood,
    my lord,
Or to the dreadful summit of the cliff   70
That beetles o'er his base into the sea,
And there assume some other horrible form
Which might deprive your sovereignty of reason
And draw you into madness? Think of it.
The very place puts toys of desperation,   75
Without more motive, into every brain
That looks so many fathoms to the sea
And hears it roar beneath.

HAMLET: It wafts me still.—Go on, I'll follow thee.

MARCELLUS: You shall not go, my lord.   80
[They try to stop him.]

HAMLET: Hold off your hands!

HORATIO: Be ruled. You shall not go.

HAMLET: My fate cries out,
And makes each petty artery in this body

---

33 His virtues else i.e., the other qualities of *these men* (line 30) **34 may undergo** can sustain **35 general censure** general opinion that people have of him **36–38 The dram . . . scandal** i.e., the small drop of evil blots out or works against the noble substance of the whole and brings it into disrepute. To *dout* is to blot out. (A famous crux.) **39 ministers of grace** messengers of God **40 Be thou** whether you are. **spirit of health** good angel **41 Bring** whether you bring **42 Be thy intents** whether your intentions are **43 questionable** inviting question **47 canonized** buried according to the canons of the church. **hearsèd** coffined **48 cerements** grave clothes **49 inurned** entombed **52 complete steel** full armor **53 glimpses of the moon** pale and uncertain moonlight **54 fools of nature** mere men, limited to natural knowledge and subject to nature **55 So . . . disposition** to distress our mental composure so violently

---

59 impartment communication **65 fee** value **69 flood** sea **71 beetles o'er** overhangs threateningly (like bushy eyebrows). **his** its **73 deprive . . . reason** take away the rule of reason over your mind **75 toys of desperation** fancies of desperate acts, i.e., suicide **81 My fate cries out** my destiny summons me **82 petty** weak. **artery** (through which the vital spirits were thought to have been conveyed)

As hardy as the Nemean lion's nerve.
Still am I called. Unhand me, gentlemen.
85 By heaven, I'll make a ghost of him that lets me!
I say, away!—Go on, I'll follow thee.

Exeunt GHOST *and* HAMLET.

HORATIO: He waxes desperate with imagination.

MARCELLUS: Let's follow. 'Tis not fit thus to obey him.

HORATIO: Have after. To what issue will this come?

90 **MARCELLUS:**   Something is rotten in the state of
Denmark.

HORATIO: Heaven will direct it.

MARCELLUS: Nay, let's follow him.

Exeunt.

1.5   *Enter* GHOST *and* HAMLET.

HAMLET: Whither wilt thou lead me? Speak. I'll go no
further.

GHOST: Mark me.

HAMLET: I will.

GHOST: My hour is almost come,
When I to sulfurous and tormenting flames
Must render up myself.

HAMLET: Alas, poor ghost!

5 **GHOST:**   Pity me not, but lend thy serious hearing
To what I shall unfold.

HAMLET: Speak, I am bound to hear.

GHOST: So art thou to revenge, when thou shalt hear.

HAMLET: What?

---

83 **Nemean lion** one of the monsters slain by Hercules in his twelve labors.   **nerve** sinew   85 **lets** hinders   89 **Have after** let's go after him.   **issue** outcome   91 **it** i.e., the outcome

1.5. **Location: The battlements of the castle.**
7 **bound** (1) ready (2) obligated by duty and fate. (The Ghost, in line 8, answers in the second sense.)

The ghost (Paul Scofield) tells Hamlet of Claudius's betrayal.

GHOST: I am thy father's spirit,   10
Doomed for a certain term to walk the night,
And for the day confined to fast in fires,
Till the foul crimes done in my days of nature
Are burnt and purged away. But that I am forbid
To tell the secrets of my prison house,   15
I could a tale unfold whose lightest word
Would harrow up thy soul, freeze thy young blood,
Make thy two eyes like stars start from their spheres,
Thy knotted and combinèd locks to part,
And each particular hair to stand on end   20
Like quills upon the fretful porcupine.
But this eternal blazon must not be
To ears of flesh and blood. List, list, O, list!
If thou didst ever thy dear father love—

HAMLET: O God!   25

GHOST: Revenge his foul and most unnatural murder.

HAMLET: Murder?

GHOST: Murder most foul, as in the best it is,
But this most foul, strange, and unnatural.

---

12 **fast** do penance by fasting   13 **crimes** sins.   **of nature** as a mortal   14 **But that** were it not that   17 **harrow up** lacerate, tear   18 **spheres** i.e., eye-sockets, here compared to the orbits or transparent revolving spheres in which, according to Ptolemaic astronomy, the heavenly bodies were fixed   19 **knotted . . . locks** hair neatly arranged and confined   22 **eternal blazon** revelation of the secrets of eternity   28 **in the best** even at best

30 **HAMLET:**   Haste me to know 't, that I, with wings as
        swift
        As meditation or the thoughts of love,
        May sweep to my revenge.

    GHOST: I find thee apt;
        And duller shouldst thou be than the fat weed
        That roots itself in ease on Lethe wharf,
35   Wouldst thou not stir in this. Now, Hamlet, hear.
        'Tis given out that, sleeping in my orchard,
        A serpent stung me. So the whole ear of Denmark
        Is by a forgèd process of my death
        Rankly abused. But know, thou noble youth,
40   The serpent that did sting thy father's life
        Now wears his crown.

    HAMLET: O, my prophetic soul! My uncle!

    GHOST: Ay, that incestuous, that adulterate beast,
        With witchcraft of his wit, with traitorous gifts—
45   O wicked wit and gifts, that have the power
        So to seduce!—won to his shameful lust
        The will of my most seeming-virtuous queen.
        O Hamlet, what a falling off was there!
        From me, whose love was of that dignity
50   That it went hand in hand even with the vow
        I made to her in marriage, and to decline
        Upon a wretch whose natural gifts were poor
        To those of mine!
        But virtue, as it never will be moved,
55   Though lewdness court it in a shape of heaven,
        So lust, though to a radiant angel linked,
        Will sate itself in a celestial bed
        And prey on garbage.
        But soft, methinks I scent the morning air.
60   Brief let me be. Sleeping within my orchard,
        My custom always of the afternoon,
        Upon my secure hour thy uncle stole,

With juice of cursèd hebona in a vial,
And in the porches of my ears did pour
The leprous distillment, whose effect   65
Holds such an enmity with blood of man
That swift as quicksilver it courses through
The natural gates and alleys of the body,
And with a sudden vigor it doth posset
And curd, like eager droppings into milk,   70
The thin and wholesome blood. So did it mine,
And a most instant tetter barked about,
Most lazar-like, with vile and loathsome crust,
All my smooth body.
Thus was I, sleeping, by a brother's hand   75
Of life, of crown, of queen at once dispatched,
Cut off even in the blossoms of my sin,
Unhouseled, disappointed, unaneled,
No reckoning made, but sent to my account
With all my imperfections on my head.   80
O, horrible! O, horrible, most horrible!
If thou hast nature in thee, bear it not.
Let not the royal bed of Denmark be
A couch for luxury and damnèd incest.
But, howsoever thou pursues this act,   85
Taint not thy mind nor let thy soul contrive
Against thy mother aught. Leave her to heaven
And to those thorns that in her bosom lodge,
To prick and sting her. Fare thee well at once.
The glowworm shows the matin to be near,   90
And 'gins to pale his uneffectual fire.
Adieu, adieu, adieu! Remember me.   *[Exit.]*

HAMLET: O all you host of heaven! O earth! What else?
        And shall I couple hell? O, fie! Hold, hold, my heart,
        And you, my sinews, grow not instant old,   95

---

33 shouldst thou be you would have to be.   **fat** torpid, lethargic
34 Lethe the river of forgetfulness in Hades   **36 orchard** garden
38 forgèd process falsified account   **39 abused** deceived   **43 adul-
terate** adulterous   **44 gifts** (1) talents (2) presents   **50 even with
the vow** with the very vow   **53 To** compared to   **54 virtue, as it** as
virtue   **55 shape of heaven** heavenly form   **57 sate . . . bed** cease
to find sexual pleasure in a virtuously lawful marriage   **62 secure**
confident, unsuspicious

63 hebona a poison. (The word seems to be a form of *ebony*, though
it is thought perhaps to be related to *henbane*, a poison, or to *ebenus*,
"yew.")   **64 porches of my ears** ears as a porch or entrance of the
body   **65 leprous distillment** distillation causing leprosylike dis-
figurement   **69 posset** coagulate, curdle   **70 eager** sour, acid
72 tetter eruption of scabs.   **barked** covered with a rough covering, like bark on a tree   **73 lazar-like** leperlike   **76 dispatched**
suddenly deprived   **78 Unhouseled** without having received the
Sacrament.   **disappointed** unready (spiritually) for the last journey.   **unaneled** without having received extreme unction   **79**
reckoning settling of accounts   **82 nature** i.e., the promptings of a
son   **84 luxury** lechery   **90 matin** morning   **91 his** its   **94 couple**
add.   **Hold** hold together   **95 instant** instantly

But bear me stiffly up. Remember thee?
Ay, thou poor ghost, whiles memory holds a seat
In this distracted globe. Remember thee?
Yea, from the table of my memory
100 I'll wipe away all trivial fond records,
All saws of books, all forms, all pressures past
That youth and observation copied there,
And thy commandment all alone shall live
Within the book and volume of my brain,
105 Unmixed with baser matter. Yes, by heaven!
O most pernicious woman!
O villain, villain, smiling, damnèd villain!
My tables—meet it is I set it down
That one may smile, and smile, and be a villain.
110 At least I am sure it may be so in Denmark.

[Writing.]

So, uncle, there you are. Now to my word:
It is "Adieu, adieu! Remember me."
I have sworn 't.

Enter HORATIO *and* MARCELLUS.

HORATIO: My lord, my lord!

115 MARCELLUS: Lord Hamlet!

HORATIO: Heavens secure him!

HAMLET: So be it.

MARCELLUS: Hilo, ho, ho, my lord!

HAMLET: Hillo, ho, ho, boy! Come, bird, come.

120 MARCELLUS: How is 't, my noble lord?

HORATIO: What news, my lord?

HAMLET: O, wonderful!

HORATIO: Good my lord, tell it.

HAMLET: No, you will reveal it.

HORATIO: Not I, my lord, by heaven.   125

MARCELLUS: Nor I, my lord.

HAMLET: How say you, then, would heart of man once
think it?
But you'll be secret?

HORATIO, MARCELLUS: Ay, by heaven, my lord.

HAMLET: There's never a villain dwelling in all
Denmark
But he's an arrant knave.   130

HORATIO: There needs no ghost, my lord, come from
the grave
To tell us this.

HAMLET: Why, right, you are in the right.
And so, without more circumstance at all,
I hold it fit that we shake hands and part,
You as your business and desire shall point you—   135
For every man hath business and desire,
Such as it is—and for my own poor part,
Look you, I'll go pray.

HORATIO: These are but wild and whirling words,
my lord.

HAMLET: I am sorry they offend you, heartily;   140
Yes, faith, heartily.

HORATIO: There's no offense, my lord.

HAMLET: Yes, by Saint Patrick, but there is, Horatio,
And much offense too. Touching this vision here,
It is an honest ghost, that let me tell you.
For your desire to know what is between us,   145
O'ermaster 't as you may. And now, good friends,
As you are friends, scholars, and soldiers,
Give me one poor request.

HORATIO: What is 't, my lord? We will.

---

98 **globe** (1) head (2) world   99 **table** tablet, slate   100 **fond** foolish   101 **saws** wise sayings.   **forms** shapes or images copied onto the slate; general ideas.   **pressures** impressions stamped   108 **tables** writing tablets.   **meet it is** it is fitting   111 **there you are** i.e., there, I've written that down against you   116 **secure him** keep him safe   119 **Hillo . . . come** (A falconer's call to a hawk in air. Hamlet mocks the hallooing as though it were a part of hawking.)

127 **once** ever   130 **arrant** thoroughgoing   133 **circumstance** ceremony, elaboration   142 **Saint Patrick** (The keeper of Purgatory and patron saint of all blunders and confusion.)   143 **offense** (Hamlet deliberately changes Horatio's "no offense taken" to "an offense against all decency.")   144 **an honest ghost** i.e., a real ghost and not an evil spirit

150 **HAMLET:**   Never make known what you have seen
tonight.

HORATIO, MARCELLUS: My lord, we will not.

HAMLET: Nay, but swear 't.

HORATIO: In faith, my lord, not I.

MARCELLUS: Nor I, my lord, in faith.

155 **HAMLET:**   Upon my sword.   *[He holds out his sword.]*

MARCELLUS: We have sworn, my lord, already.

HAMLET: Indeed, upon my sword, indeed.

GHOST (*cries under the stage*):   Swear.

HAMLET: Ha, ha, boy, sayst thou so? Art thou there,
truepenny?
160   Come on, you hear this fellow in the cellarage.
Consent to swear.

HORATIO: Propose the oath, my lord.

HAMLET: Never to speak of this that you have seen,
Swear by my sword.

GHOST *[beneath]*:   Swear.   *[They swear.]*

165 **HAMLET:**   *Hic et ubique?* Then we'll shift our ground.
                    [He moves to another spot.]
Come hither, gentlemen,
And lay your hands again upon my sword.
Swear by my sword
Never to speak of this that you have heard.

170 **GHOST** *[beneath]*:   Swear by his sword.   *[They swear.]*

---

153 In faith . . . I i.e., I swear not to tell what I have seen. (Horatio
is not refusing to swear.)   **155 sword** i.e., the hilt in the form of a
cross   **156 We . . . already** i.e., we swore *in faith*   **159 truepenny**
honest old fellow   **164 s.d. They swear** (Seemingly they swear
here, and at lines 170 and 190, as they lay their hands on Hamlet's
sword. Tripled oaths would have particular force; these three oaths
deal with what they have seen, what they have heard, and what they
promise about Hamlet's *antic disposition.*)   **165 Hic et ubique** here
and everywhere (Latin.)

Hamlet (Mel Gibson) swears his companions to secrecy.

HAMLET: Well said, old mole. Canst work i' th' earth
so fast?
A worthy pioner!—Once more remove, good friends.
                    [He moves again.]

HORATIO: O day and night, but this is wondrous
strange!

HAMLET: And therefore as a stranger give it welcome.
There are more things in heaven and earth, Horatio,   175
Than are dreamt of in your philosophy.
But come;
Here, as before, never, so help you mercy,
How strange or odd soe'er I bear myself—
As I perchance hereafter shall think meet   180
To put an antic disposition on—
That you, at such times seeing me, never shall,
With arms encumbered thus, or this headshake,
Or by pronouncing of some doubtful phrase
As "Well, we know," or "We could, an if we would,"   185
Or "If we list to speak," or "There be, an if they might,"

---

172 pioner foot soldier assigned to dig tunnels and excavations   **174
as a stranger** i.e., needing your hospitality   **176 your philosophy**
this subject called "natural philosophy" or "science" that people talk
about   **178 so help you mercy** as you hope for God's mercy when you
are judged   **181 antic** fantastic   **183 encumbered** folded   **185 an if**
if   **186 list** wished.   **There . . . might** i.e., there are people here (we,
in fact) who could tell news if we were at liberty to do so

Or such ambiguous giving out, to note
That you know aught of me—this do swear,
So grace and mercy at your most need help you.

190 **GHOST** [*beneath*]: Swear.   [*They swear.*]

HAMLET: Rest, rest, perturbèd spirit! So, gentlemen,
With all my love I do commend me to you;
And what so poor a man as Hamlet is
May do t' express his love and friending to you,
195 God willing, shall not lack. Let us go in together,
And still your fingers on your lips, I pray.
The time is out of joint. O cursèd spite
That ever I was born to set it right!
                    [*They wait for him to leave first.*]
Nay, come, let's go together.   *Exeunt.*

2.1   *Enter old* POLONIUS *with his man* [REYNALDO].

POLONIUS: Give him this money and these notes,
        Reynaldo.
                    [*He gives money and papers.*]

REYNALDO: I will, my lord.

POLONIUS: You shall do marvelous wisely, good
        Reynaldo,
Before you visit him, to make inquire
5 Of his behavior.

REYNALDO: My lord, I did intend it.

POLONIUS: Marry, well said, very well said. Look you,
        sir,
Inquire me first what Danskers are in Paris,
And how, and who, what means, and where they keep,
What company, at what expense; and finding
10 By this encompassment and drift of question

That they do know my son, come you more nearer
Than your particular demands will touch it.
Take you, as 'twere, some distant knowledge of him,
As thus, "I know his father and his friends,
And in part him." Do you mark this, Reynaldo?   15

REYNALDO: Ay, very well, my lord.

POLONIUS: "And in part him, but," you may say, "not
        well.
But if 't be he I mean, he's very wild,
Addicted so and so," and there put on him
What forgeries you please—marry, none so rank   20
As may dishonor him, take heed of that,
But, sir, such wanton, wild, and usual slips
As are companions noted and most known
To youth and liberty.

REYNALDO: As gaming, my lord.   25

POLONIUS: Ay, or drinking, fencing, swearing,
        Quarreling, drabbing—you may go so far.

REYNALDO: My lord, that would dishonor him.

POLONIUS: Faith, no, as you may season it in the charge.
You must not put another scandal on him   30
That he is open to incontinency;
That's not my meaning. But breathe his faults so
        quaintly
That they may seem the taints of liberty,
The flash and outbreak of a fiery mind,
A savageness in unreclaimèd blood,   35
Of general assault.

REYNALDO: But, my good lord—

POLONIUS: Wherefore should you do this?

REYNALDO: Ay, my lord, I would know that.

---

187 giving out intimation.   **note** draw attention to the fact   **188
aught** i.e., something secret   **192 do . . . you** entrust myself to
you   **194 friending** friendliness   **195 lack** be lacking   **196 still**
always   **197 The time** the state of affairs.   **spite** i.e., the spite of
Fortune   **199 let's go together** (Probably they wait for him to leave
first, but he refuses this ceremoniousness.)

2.1. Location: Polonius' chambers.
3 marvelous marvelously   **4 inquire** inquiry   **7 Danskers** Danes
8 what means what wealth (they have).   **keep** dwell   **10 encompassment** roundabout talking.   **drift** gradual approach or course

11–12 come . . . it you will find out more this way than by asking
pointed questions (*particular demands*)   **13 Take you** assume,
pretend   **19 put on** impute to   **20 forgeries** invented tales.   **rank**
gross   **22 wanton** sportive, unrestrained   **27 drabbing** whoring
29 season temper, soften   **31 incontinency** habitual sexual excess
32 quaintly artfully, subtly   **33 taints of liberty** faults resulting
from free living   **35–36 A savageness . . . assault** a wildness in
untamed youth that assails all indiscriminately

40 **POLONIUS:** Marry, sir, here's my drift,
And I believe it is a fetch of warrant.
You laying these slight sullies on my son,
As 'twere a thing a little soiled wi' the working,
Mark you,
45 Your party in converse, him you would sound,
Having ever seen in the prenominate crimes
The youth you breathe of guilty, be assured
He closes with you in this consequence:
"Good sir," or so, or "friend," or "gentleman,"
50 According to the phrase or the addition
Of man and country.

    REYNALDO: Very good, my lord.

    POLONIUS: And then, sir, does 'a this—'a does—what
was I about to say? By the Mass, I was about to say
something. Where did I leave?

55 **REYNALDO:** At "closes in the consequence."

    POLONIUS: At "closes in the consequence," ay, marry.
He closes thus: "I know the gentleman,
I saw him yesterday," or "th' other day,"
Or then, or then, with such or such, "and as you say,
60 There was 'a gaming," "there o'ertook in 's rouse,"
"There falling out at tennis," or perchance
"I saw him enter such a house of sale,"
Videlicet a brothel, or so forth. See you now,
Your bait of falsehood takes this carp of truth;
65 And thus do we of wisdom and of reach,
With windlasses and with assays of bias,
By indirections find directions out.
So by my former lecture and advice
Shall you my son. You have me, have you not?

REYNALDO: My lord, I have.

POLONIUS: God b' wi' ye; fare ye well. 70

REYNALDO: Good my lord.

POLONIUS: Observe his inclination in yourself.

REYNALDO: I shall, my lord.

POLONIUS: And let him ply his music.

REYNALDO: Well, my lord. 75

POLONIUS: Farewell.   *Exit* REYNALDO.

                Enter OPHELIA.

    How now, Ophelia, what's the matter?

OPHELIA: O my lord, my lord, I have been so affrighted!

POLONIUS: With what, i' the name of God?

OPHELIA: My lord, as I was sewing in my closet,
Lord Hamlet, with his doublet all unbraced, 80
Not hat upon his head, his stockings fouled,
Ungartered, and down-gyvèd to his ankle,
Pale as his shirt, his knees knocking each other,
And with a look so piteous in purport
As if he had been loosèd out of hell 85
To speak of horrors—he comes before me.

POLONIUS: Mad for thy love?

OPHELIA: My lord, I do not know,
But truly I do fear it.

POLONIUS: What said he?

OPHELIA: He took me by the wrist and held me hard.
Then goes he to the length of all his arm, 90
And, with his other hand thus o'er his brow
He falls to such perusal of my face
As 'a would draw it. Long stayed he so.

---

41 fetch of warrant legitimate trick   **43 soiled wi' the working**
soiled by handling while it is being made, i.e., by involvement in the
ways of the world   **45 converse** conversation.   **sound** i.e., sound
out   **46 Having ever** if he has ever.   **prenominate crimes** before-
mentioned offenses   **47 breathe** speak   **48 closes . . . consequence**
takes you into his confidence in some fashion, as follows   **50 addition** title   **60 o'ertook in 's rouse** overcome by drink   **61 falling
out** quarreling   **63 Videlicet** namely   **64 carp** a fish   **65 reach**
capacity, ability   **66 windlasses** i.e., circuitous paths. (Literally,
circuits made to head off the game in hunting.)   **assays of bias**
attempts through indirection (like the curving path of the bowling
ball, which is biased or weighted to one side)   **67 directions** i.e., the
way things really are   **69 have** understand

---

70 b' wi' be with   **72 in yourself** in your own person (as well as by
asking questions)   **79 closet** private chamber   **80 doublet** close-
fitting jacket.   **unbraced** unfastened   **82 down-gyvèd** fallen to the
ankles (like gyves or fetters)   **84 in purport** in what is expressed
93 As as if (also in line 97)

Ophelia (Kate Winslet) tells Polonius (Richard Briers) of her encounter with Hamlet.

At last, a little shaking of mine arm
95 And thrice his head thus waving up and down,
He raised a sigh so piteous and profound
As it did seem to shatter all his bulk
And end his being. That done, he lets me go,
And with his head over his shoulder turned
100 He seemed to find his way without his eyes,
For out o' doors he went without their helps,
And to the last bended their light on me.

POLONIUS: Come, go with me, I will go seek the King.
This is the very ecstasy of love,
105 Whose violent property fordoes itself
And leads the will to desperate undertakings
As oft as any passion under heaven
That does afflict our natures. I am sorry.
What, have you given him any hard words of late?

110 **OPHELIA:**   No, my good lord, but as you did command
I did repel his letter and denied
His access to me.

POLONIUS: That hath made him mad.
I am sorry that with better heed and judgment
I had not quoted him. I feared he did but trifle
115 And meant to wrack thee. But beshrew my jealousy!

---

97 bulk body   **104 ecstasy** madness   **105 property** nature.
fordoes destroys   **114 quoted** observed   **115 wrack** ruin, seduce.
beshrew my jealousy a plague upon my suspicious nature

By heaven, it is as proper to our age
To cast beyond ourselves in our opinions
As it is common for the younger sort
To lack discretion. Come, go we to the King.
This must be known, which, being kept close, might
   move   120
More grief to hide than hate to utter love.
Come.   *Exeunt.*

2.2   *Flourish. Enter* KING *and* QUEEN,
ROSENCRANTZ, *and* GUILDENSTERN
[with others].

KING: Welcome, dear Rosencrantz and Guildenstern.
Moreover that we much did long to see you,
The need we have to use you did provoke
Our hasty sending. Something have you heard
Of Hamlet's tranformation—so call it,   5
Sith nor th' exterior nor the inward man
Resembles that it was. What it should be,
More than his father's death, that thus hath put him
So much from th' understanding of himself,
I cannot dream of. I entreat you both   10
That, being of so young days brought up with him,
And sith so neighbored to his youth and havior,
That you vouchsafe your rest here in our court
Some little time, so by your companies
To draw him on to pleasures, and to gather   15
So much as from occasion you may glean,
Whether aught to us unknown afflicts him thus
That, opened, lies within our remedy.

---

116 proper . . . age characteristic of us (old) men   **117 cast beyond**
overshoot, miscalculate. (A metaphor from hunting.)   **120 known**
made known (to the King).   **close** secret   **120–121 might . . . love**
i.e., might cause more grief (because of what Hamlet might do) by
hiding the knowledge of Hamlet's strange behavior to Ophelia than
unpleasantness by telling it

2.2. Location: The castle.
2 Moreover that besides the fact that   **6 Sith nor** since neither
7 that what   **11 of . . . days** from such early youth   **12 And sith so
neighbored to** and since you are (or, and since that time you are)
intimately acquainted with.   **havior** demeanor   **13 vouchsafe your
rest** please to stay   **16 occasion** opportunity   **18 opened** being
revealed

QUEEN: Good gentlemen, he hath much talked of you,
20   And sure I am two men there is not living
        To whom he more adheres. If it will please you
        To show us so much gentry and good will
        As to expend your time with us awhile
        For the supply and profit of our hope,
25   Your visitation shall receive such thanks
        As fits a king's remembrance.

ROSENCRANTZ: Both Your Majesties
        Might, by the sovereign power you have of us,
        Put your dread pleasures more into command
        Than to entreaty.

GUILDENSTERN: But we both obey,
30   And here give up ourselves in the full bent
        To lay our service freely at your feet,
        To be commanded.

KING: Thanks, Rosencrantz and gentle Guildenstern.

QUEEN: Thanks, Guildenstern and gentle Rosencrantz.
35   And I beseech you instantly to visit
        My too much changèd son. Go, some of you,
        And bring these gentlemen where Hamlet is.

GUILDENSTERN: Heavens make our presence and our
        practices
        Pleasant and helpful to him!

QUEEN: Ay, amen!
        Exeunt ROSENCRANTZ *and* GUILDENSTERN
        [with some attendants].

                        Enter POLONIUS

40 **POLONIUS:**   Th' ambassadors from Norway, my good
        lord,
        Are joyfully returned.

KING: Thou still hast been the father of good news.

POLONIUS: Have I, my lord? I assure my good liege
        I hold my duty, as I hold my soul,

Both to my God and to my gracious king;   45
        And I do think, or else this brain of mine
        Hunts not the trail of policy so sure
        As it hath used to do, that I have found
        The very cause of Hamlet's lunacy.

KING: O, speak of that! That do I long to hear.   50

POLONIUS: Give first admittance to th' ambassadors.
        My news shall be the fruit to that great feast.

KING: Thyself do grace to them and bring them in.
                        [Exit POLONIUS.*]*
        He tells me, my dear Gertrude, he hath found
        The head and source of all your son's distemper.   55

QUEEN: I doubt it is no other but the main,
        His father's death and our o'erhasty marriage.

                Enter AMBASSADORS *[* VOLTIMAND *and*
                        CORNELIUS, *with* POLONIUS*]*.

KING: Well, we shall sift him.—Welcome my good
        friends!
        Say, Voltimand, what from our brother Norway?

VOLTIMAND: Most fair return of greetings and desires.   60
        Upon our first, he sent out to suppress
        His nephew's levies, which to him appeared
        To be a preparation 'gainst the Polack,
        But, better looked into, he truly found
        It was against Your Highness. Whereat grieved   65
        That so his sickness, age, and impotence
        Was falsely borne in hand, sends out arrests
        On Fortinbras, which he, in brief, obeys,
        Receives rebuke from Norway, and in fine
        Makes vow before his uncle never more   70
        To give th' assay of arms against Your Majesty.
        Whereon old Norway, overcome with joy,
        Gives him three thousand crowns in annual fee
        And his commission to employ those soldiers,

---

22 **gentry** courtesy   24 **supply . . . hope** aid and furtherance of what we hope for   26 **As fits . . . remembrance** as would be a fitting gift of a king who rewards true service   27 **of** over   28 **dread** inspiring awe   30 **in . . . bent** to the utmost degree of our capacity. (An archery metaphor.)   38 **practices** doings   42 **still** always   44 **hold** maintain.   **as** as firmly as

47 **policy** sagacity   52 **fruit** dessert   53 **grace** honor (punning on *grace* said before a *feast*, line 52)   56 **doubt** fear, suspect.   **main** chief point, principal concern   58 **sift him** question Polonius closely   59 **brother** fellow king   60 **desires** good wishes   61 **Upon our first** at our first words on the business   66 **impotence** helplessness   67 **borne in hand** deluded, taken advantage of.   **arrests** orders to desist   69 **in fine** in conclusion   71 **give th' assay** make trial of strength, challenge

75 So levied as before, against the Polack,
With an entreaty, herein further shown,

[giving a paper]

That it might please you to give quiet pass
Through your dominions for this enterprise
On such regards of safety and allowance
80 As therein are set down.

KING: It likes us well,
And at our more considered time we'll read,
Answer, and think upon this business.
Meantime we thank you for your well-took labor.
Go to your rest; at night we'll feast together.
85 Most welcome home!   *Exeunt* AMBASSADORS.

POLONIUS: This business is well ended.
My liege, and madam, to expostulate
What majesty should be, what duty is,
Why day is day, night night, and time is time,
Were nothing but to waste night, day, and time.
90 Therefore, since brevity is the soul of wit,
And tediousness the limbs and outward flourishes,
I will be brief. Your noble son is mad.
Mad call I it, for, to define true madness,
What is 't but to be nothing else but mad?
95 But let that go.

QUEEN: More matter, with less art.

POLONIUS: Madam, I swear I use no art at all.
That he's mad, 'tis true; 'tis true 'tis pity,
And pity 'tis 'tis true—a foolish figure,
But farewell it, for I will use no art.
Mad let us grant him, then, and now remains
That we find out the cause of this effect,
Or rather say, the cause of this defect,
For this effect defective comes by cause.
Thus it remains, and the remainder thus.
105 Perpend.
I have a daughter—have while she is mine—
Who, in her duty and obedience, mark,

Polonius (Ian Holm) discusses Hamlet with Claudius (Alan Bates) and Gertrude (Glenn Close).

Hath given me this. Now gather and surmise.
[He reads the letter.] "To the celestial and my soul's
idol, the most beautified Ophelia"—   110
That's an ill phrase, a vile phrase; "beautified" is a
vile phrase. But you shall hear. Thus: *[He reads.]*
"In her excellent white bosom, these, etc."

QUEEN: Came this from Hamlet to her?

POLONIUS: Good madam, stay awhile, I will be
faithful.   *[He reads.]*   115
"Doubt thou the stars are fire,
      Doubt that the sun doth move,
Doubt truth to be a liar,
      But never doubt I love.
O dear Ophelia, I am ill at these numbers. I have not   120
art to reckon my groans. But that I love thee best, O
most best, believe it. Adieu.
            Thine evermore, most dear lady, whilst this
                        machine is to him, Hamlet."
This in obedience hath my daughter shown me,   125
And, more above, hath his solicitings,
As they fell out by time, by means, and place,
All given to mine ear.

---

79 On . . . allowance i.e., with such considerations for the safety of Denmark and permission for Fortinbras   **80 likes** pleases
81 considered suitable for deliberation   **86 expostulate** expound, inquire into   **90 wit** sense or judgment   **98 figure** figure of speech
103 For . . . cause i.e., for this defective behavior, this madness, has a cause   **105 Perpend** consider

108 gather and surmise draw your own conclusions   **113 In . . . bosom** (The letter is poetically addressed to her heart.)   **these** i.e., the letter   **115 stay** wait.   **faithful** i.e., in reading the letter accurately   **118 Doubt** suspect   **120 ill . . . numbers** unskilled at writing verses   **121 reckon** (1) count (2) number metrically, scan   **124 machine** i.e., body   **126 more above** moreover   **127 fell out** occurred.   **by** according to   **128 given . . . ear** i.e., told me about

Gertrude (Julie Christie), Claudius (Derek Jacobi), and Polonius discuss Hamlet.

KING: But how hath she
Received his love?

POLONIUS: What do you think of me?

130 **KING:** As of a man faithful and honorable.

POLONIUS: I would fain prove so. But what might you
think,
When I had seen this hot love on the wing—
As I perceived it, I must tell you that,
Before my daughter told me—what might you,
135 Or my dear Majesty your queen here, think,
If I had played the desk or table book,
Or given my heart a winking, mute and dumb,
Or looked upon this love with idle sight?
What might you think? No, I went round to work,
140 And my young mistress thus I did bespeak:
"Lord Hamlet is a prince out of thy star;
This must not be." And then I prescripts gave her,
That she should lock herself from his resort,
Admit no messengers, receive no tokens.
145 Which done, she took the fruits of my advice;

And he, repellèd—a short take to make—
Fell into a sadness, then into a fast,
Thence to a watch, thence into a weakness,
Thence to a lightness, and by this declension
Into the madness wherein now he raves, 150
And all we mourn for.

KING [to the QUEEN]: Do you think 'tis this?

QUEEN: It may be, very like.

POLONIUS: Hath there been such a time—I would fain
know that—
That I have positively said "'Tis so,"
When it proved otherwise?

KING: Not that I know. 155

POLONIUS: Take this from this, if this be otherwise.
If circumstances lead me, I will find
Where truth is hid, though it were hid indeed
Within the center.

KING: How may we try it further?

POLONIUS: You know sometimes he walks four hours 160
together
Here in the lobby.

QUEEN: So he does indeed.

POLONIUS: At such a time I'll loose my daughter to him.
Be you and I behind an arras then.
Mark the encounter. If he love her not
And be not from his reason fall'n thereon, 165
Let me be no assistant for a state,
But keep a farm and carters.

KING: We will try it.

---

131 **fain** gladly   136 **played . . . table book** i.e., remained shut up, concealing the information   137 **given . . . winking** closed the eyes of my heart to this   138 **with idle sight** complacently or incomprehendingly   139 **round** roundly, plainly   140 **bespeak** address   141 **out of thy star** above your sphere, position   142 **prescripts** orders   143 **his resort** his visits

---

148 **watch** state of sleeplessness
149 **lightness** lightheadedness.   **declension** decline, deterioration (with a pun on the grammatical sense)   151 **all we** all of us, or, into everything that we   156 **Take this from this** (The actor probably gestures, indicating that he means his head from his shoulders, or his staff or office or chain from his hands or neck, or something similar.)   159 **center** middle point of the earth (which is also the center of the Ptolemaic universe).   **try** test, judge   162 **loose** (as one might release an animal that is being mated)   163 **arras** hanging, tapestry   165 **thereon** on that account   167 **carters** wagon drivers

Enter HAMLET *[reading on a book].*

QUEEN: But look where sadly the poor wretch comes
reading.

POLONIUS: Away, I do beseech you both, away.
170   I'll board him presently. O, give me leave.
Exeunt KING *and* QUEEN *[with attendants].*
How does my good Lord Hamlet?

HAMLET: Well, God-a-mercy.

POLONIUS: Do you know me, my lord?

HAMLET: Excellent well. You are a fishmonger.

175   **POLONIUS:**   Not I, my lord.

HAMLET: Then I would you were so honest a man.

POLONIUS: Honest, my lord?

HAMLET: Ay, sir. To be honest, as this world goes, is to
be one man picked out of ten thousand.

180   **POLONIUS:**   That's very true, my lord.

HAMLET: For if the sun breed maggots in a dead dog,
being a good kissing carrion—Have you a daughter?

POLONIUS: I have, my lord.

HAMLET: Let her not walk i' the sun. Conception is a
185   blessing, but as your daughter may conceive, friend,
look to 't.

POLONIUS *[aside]:*   How say you by that? Still harping
on my daughter. Yet he knew me not at first; 'a said
I was a fishmonger. 'A is far gone. And truly in my
190   youth I suffered much extremity for love, very near
this. I'll speak to him again.—What do you read, my
lord?

HAMLET: Words, words, words.

POLONIUS: What is the matter, my lord?

HAMLET: Between who?   195

POLONIUS: I mean, the matter that you read, my lord.

HAMLET: Slanders, sir; for the satirical rogue says
here that old men have gray beards, that their faces
are wrinkled, their eyes purging thick amber and
plum-tree gum, and that they have a plentiful lack   200
of wit, together with most weak hams. All which, sir,
though I most powerfully and potently believe, yet I
hold it not honesty to have it thus set down, for yourself, sir, shall grow old as I am, if like a crab you could
go backward.   205

POLONIUS *[aside]:*   Though this be madness, yet there is
method in 't.—Will you walk out of the air, my lord?

HAMLET: Into my grave.

POLONIUS: Indeed, that's out of the air. *[Aside.]* How
pregnant sometimes his replies are! A happiness that   210
often madness hits on, which reason and sanity could
not so prosperously be delivered of. I will leave him
and suddenly contrive the means of meeting between
him and my daughter.—My honorable lord, I will
most humbly take my leave of you.   215

HAMLET: You cannot, sir, take from me anything that I
will more willingly part withal—except my life, except
my life, except my life.

Enter GUILDENSTERN *and* ROSENCRANTZ.

POLONIUS: Fare you well, my lord.

HAMLET: These tedious old fools!   220

POLONIUS: You go to seek the Lord Hamlet. There he is.

ROSENCRANTZ *[to* POLONIUS*]:*   God save you, sir!
[Exit POLONIUS.*]*

---

168 sadly seriously   **170 board** accost.   **presently** at once.   **give
me leave** i.e., excuse me, leave me alone. (Said to those he hurries
offstage, including the King and Queen.)   **172 God-a-mercy** God
have mercy, i.e., thank you   **174 fishmonger** fish merchant   **182
a good kissing carrion** i.e., a good piece of flesh for kissing, or for
the sun to kiss   **184 i' the sun** in public (with additional implication
of the sunshine of princely favors).   **Conception** (1) understanding
(2) pregnancy   **188 'a** he

194 matter substance (But Hamlet plays on the sense of "basis for
a dispute.")   **199 purging** discharging.   **amber** i.e., resin, like the
resinous *plum-tree gum*   **201 wit** understanding   **203 honesty**
decency, decorum   **204 old** as old   **207 out of the air** (The open
air was considered dangerous for sick people.)   **210 pregnant**
quick-witted, full of meaning.   **happiness** felicity of expression
212 prosperously successfully   **213 suddenly** immediately   **217
withal** with   **220 old fools** i.e., old men like Polonius

GUILDENSTERN: My honored lord!

ROSENCRANTZ: My most dear lord!

225 **HAMLET:** My excellent good friends! How dost thou, Guildenstern? Ah, Rosencrantz! Good lads, how do you both?

ROSENCRANTZ: As the indifferent children of the earth.

GUILDENSTERN: Happy in that we are not overhappy.
230 On Fortune's cap we are not the very button.

HAMLET: Nor the soles of her shoe?

ROSENCRANTZ: Neither, my lord.

HAMLET: Then you live about her waist, or in the middle of her favors?

235 **GUILDENSTERN:** Faith, her privates we.

HAMLET: In the secret parts of Fortune? O, most true, she is a strumpet. What news?

ROSENCRANTZ: None, my lord, but the world's grown honest.

240 **HAMLET:** Then is doomsday near. But your news is not true. Let me question more in particular. What have you, my good friends, deserved at the hands of Fortune that she sends you to prison hither?

GUILDENSTERN: Prison, my lord?

245 **HAMLET:** Denmark's a prison.

ROSENCRANTZ: Then is the world one.

HAMLET: A goodly one, in which there are many confines, wards, and dungeons, Denmark being one o' the worst.

250 **ROSENCRANTZ:** We think not so, my lord.

Hamlet (Kevin Kline) talks with Rosencrantz (Philip Goodwin) and Guildenstern (Reg E. Cathey) in the 1990 film directed by Kevin Kline.

HAMLET: Why then 'tis none to you, for there is nothing either good or bad but thinking makes it so. To me it is a prison.

ROSENCRANTZ: Why then, your ambition makes it one. 'Tis too narrow for your mind. 255

HAMLET: O God, I could be bounded in a nutshell and count myself a king of infinite space, were it not that I have bad dreams.

GUILDENSTERN: Which dreams indeed are ambition, for the very substance of the ambitious is merely the 260 shadow of a dream.

HAMLET: A dream itself is but a shadow.

ROSENCRANTZ: Truly, and I hold ambition of so airy and light a quality that it is but a shadow's shadow.

HAMLET: Then are our beggars bodies, and our mon- 265 archs and outstretched heroes the beggars' shadows. Shall we to the court? For, by my fay, I cannot reason.

---

228 indifferent ordinary, at neither extreme of fortune or misfortune   **234 favors** i.e., sexual favors   **235 her privates we** i.e., (1) we are sexually intimate with Fortune, the fickle goddess who bestows her favors indiscriminately (2) we are her private citizens   **237 strumpet** prostitute (A common epithet for indiscriminate Fortune; see line 493.)   **248 confines** places of confinement.   **wards** cells

---

260 the very . . . ambitious that seemingly very substantial thing that the ambitious pursue   **265 bodies** i.e., solid substances rather than shadows (since beggars are not ambitious)   **266 outstretched** (1) far-reaching in their ambition (2) elongated as shadows   **267 fay** faith

ROSENCRANTZ, GUILDENSTERN: We'll wait upon
you.

HAMLET: No such matter. I will not sort you with the
270 rest of my servants, for, to speak to you like an honest man, I am most dreadfully attended. But, in the
beaten way of friendship, what make you at Elsinore?

ROSENCRANTZ: To visit you, my lord, no other occasion.

HAMLET: Beggar that I am, I am even poor in thanks;
275 but I thank you, and sure, dear friends, my thanks are
too dear a halfpenny. Were you not sent for? Is it your
own inclining? Is it a free visitation? Come, come,
deal justly with me. Come, come. Nay, speak.

GUILDENSTERN: What should we say, my lord?

280 **HAMLET:** Anything but to the purpose. You were sent
for, and there is a kind of confession in your looks
which your modesties have not craft enough to color.
I know the good King and Queen have sent for you.

ROSENCRANTZ: To what end, my lord?

285 **HAMLET:** That you must teach me. But let me conjure
you, by the rights of our fellowship, by the consonancy
of our youth, by the obligation of our ever-preserved
love, and by what more dear a better proposer could
charge you withal, be even and direct with me
290 whether you were sent for or no.

ROSENCRANTZ [aside to GUILDENSTERN]: What say
you?

HAMLET [aside]: Nay, then, I have an eye of you.—If you
love me, hold not off.

GUILDENSTERN: My lord, we were sent for.

HAMLET: I will tell you why; so shall my anticipation 295
prevent your discovery, and your secrecy to the King
and Queen molt no feather. I have of late—but wherefore I know not—lost all my mirth, forgone all custom
of exercises; and indeed it goes so heavily with my
disposition that this goodly frame, the earth, seems to 300
me a sterile promontory; this most excellent canopy,
the air, look you, this brave o'erhanging firmament,
this majestical roof fretted with golden fire, why,
it appeareth nothing to me but a foul and pestilent
congregation of vapors. What a piece of work is a 305
man! How noble in reason, how infinite in faculties,
in form and moving how express and admirable, in
action how like an angel, in apprehension how like a
god! The beauty of the world, the paragon of animals!
And yet, to me, what is this quintessence of dust? 310
Man delights not me—no, nor woman neither, though
by your smiling you seem to say so.

ROSENCRANTZ: My lord, there was no such stuff in my
thoughts.

HAMLET: Why did you laugh, then, when I said man 315
delights not me?

ROSENCRANTZ: To think, my lord, if you delight not
in man, what Lenten entertainment the players shall
receive from you. We coted them on the way, and
hither are they coming to offer you service. 320

HAMLET: He that plays the king shall be welcome; His
Majesty shall have tribute of me. The adventurous
knight shall use his foil and target, the lover shall

---

268 **wait upon** accompany, attend. (But Hamlet uses the phrase
in the sense of providing menial service.) 269 **sort** class, categorize 271 **dreadfully attended** waited upon in slovenly fashion
272 **beaten way** familiar path, tried-and-true course. **make** do
276 **too dear a halfpenny** (1) too expensive at even a halfpenny,
i.e., of little worth (2) too expensive *by* a halfpenny in return for
worthless kindness 277 **free** voluntary 280 **Anything but to the
purpose** anything except a straightforward answer. (Said ironically.)
282 **modesties** sense of shame. **color** disguise 285 **conjure**
adjure, entreat 286–287 **the consonancy of our youth** our closeness in our younger days 288 **better** more skillful 289 **charge**
urge. **even** straight, honest 292 **of** on 293 **hold not off** don't
hold back

295–296 **so . . . discovery** in that way my saying it first will spare
you from revealing the truth 297 **molt no feather** i.e., not diminish in the least 302 **brave** splendid 303 **fretted** adorned (with
fretwork, as in a vaulted ceiling) 305 **congregation** mass
piece of work masterpiece 307 **express** well-framed, exact,
expressive 308 **apprehension** power of comprehending 310
quintessence the fifth essence of ancient philosophy, beyond earth,
water, air, and fire, supposed to be the substance of the heavenly
bodies and to be latent in all things 318 **Lenten entertainment**
meager reception (appropriate to Lent) 319 **coted** overtook and
passed by 322 **tribute** (1) applause (2) homage paid in money.
of from 323 **foil and target** sword and shield

325 not sigh gratis, the humorous man shall end his part
in peace, the clown shall make those laugh whose
lungs are tickle o' the sear, and the lady shall say her
mind freely, or the blank verse shall halt for 't. What
players are they?

ROSENCRANTZ: Even those you were wont to take such
330 delight in, the tragedians of the city.

HAMLET: How chances it they travel? Their residence,
both in reputation and profit, was better both ways.

ROSENCRANTZ: I think their inhibition comes by the
means of the late innovation.

335 HAMLET: Do they hold the same estimation they did
when I was in the city? Are they so followed?

ROSENCRANTZ: No, indeed are they not.

HAMLET: How comes it? Do they grow rusty?

ROSENCRANTZ: Nay, their endeavor keeps in the
340 wonted pace. But there is, sir, an aerie of children,
little eyases, that cry out on the top of question and
are most tyrannically clapped for 't. These are now the
fashion, and so berattle the common stages—so they
call them—that many wearing rapiers are afraid of
345 goose quills and dare scarce come thither.

---

324 gratis for nothing.   **humorous man** eccentric character,
dominated by one trait or "humor"   **325 in peace** i.e., with full
license   **326 tickle o' the sear** easy on the trigger, ready to laugh
easily. (A *sear* is part of a gunlock.)   **327 halt** limp   **330 tragedians** actors   **331 residence** remaining in their usual place, i.e., in the
city   **333 inhibition** formal prohibition (from acting plays in the
city)   **334 late** recent.   **innovation** i.e., the new fashion in satirical
plays performed by boy actors in the "private" theaters; or possibly
a political uprising; or the strict limitations set on the theaters in
London in 1600   **338–363 How . . . load too** (The passage, omitted
from the early quartos, alludes to the so-called War of the Theaters,
1599–1602, the rivalry between the children's companies and the
adult actors.)   **339 keeps** continues   **340 wonted** usual.   **aerie**
nest   **341 eyases** young hawks.   **cry . . . question** speak shrilly,
dominating the controversy (in decrying the public theaters)   **342
tyrannically** outrageously   **343 berattle** berate, clamor against.
common stages public theaters   **344 many wearing rapiers** i.e.,
many men of fashion, afraid to patronize the common players for
fear of being satirized by the poets writing for the boy actors   **345
goose quills** i.e., pens of satirists

HAMLET: What, are they children? Who maintains
'em? How are they escoted? Will they pursue the
quality no longer than they can sing? Will they not
say afterwards, if they should grow themselves to
common players—as it is most like, if their means 350
are no better—their writers do them wrong to make
them exclaim against their own succession?

ROSENCRANTZ: Faith, there has been much to-do on
both sides, and the nation holds it no sin to tar them
to controversy. There was for a while no money bid for 355
argument unless the poet and the player went to cuffs
in the question.

HAMLET: Is 't possible?

GUILDENSTERN: O, there has been much throwing
about of brains. 360

HAMLET: Do the boys carry it away?

ROSENCRANTZ: Ay, that they do, my lord—Hercules
and his load too.

HAMLET: It is not very strange; for my uncle is King
of Denmark, and those that would make mouths at 365
him while my father lived give twenty, forty, fifty, a
hundred ducats apiece for his picture in little. 'Sblood,
there is something in this more than natural, if philosophy could find it out.

A flourish [of trumpets within].

GUILDENSTERN: There are the players. 370

HAMLET: Gentlemen, you are welcome to Elsinore. Your
hands, come then. Th' appurtenance of welcome is

---

347 escoted maintained   **348 quality** (acting) profession.   **no
longer . . . sing** i.e., only until their voices change   **350 common**
regular, adult.   **like** likely   **350–351 if . . . better** if they find no
better way to support themselves   **352 succession** i.e., future careers   **353 to-do** ado   **354 tar** set on (as dogs)   **355–357 There . . .
question** i.e., for a while, no money was offered by the acting companies to playwrights for the plot to a play unless the satirical poets
who wrote for the boys and the adult actors came to blows in the play
itself   **361 carry it away** i.e., win the day   **362–363 Hercules . . .
load** (Thought to be an allusion to the sign of the Globe Theatre,
which was Hercules bearing the world on his shoulders.)   **365
mouths** faces   **367 ducats** gold coins.   **in little** in miniature.
'Sblood by God's (Christ's) blood   **368–369 philosophy** i.e., scientific inquiry   **372 appurtenance** proper accompaniment

fashion and ceremony. Let me comply with you in this garb, lest my extent to the players, which, I tell you, must show fairly outwards, should more appear like entertainment than yours. You are welcome. But my uncle-father and aunt-mother are deceived.

GUILDENSTERN: In what, my dear lord?

HAMLET: I am but mad north-north-west. When the wind is southerly I know a hawk from a handsaw.

Enter POLONIUS.

POLONIUS: Well be with you, gentlemen!

HAMLET: Hark you, Guildenstern, and you too; at each ear a hearer. That great baby you see there is not yet out of his swaddling clouts.

ROSENCRANTZ: Haply he is the second time come to them, for they say an old man is twice a child.

HAMLET: I will prophesy he comes to tell me of the players. Mark it.—You say right, sir, o' Monday morning, 'twas then indeed.

POLONIUS: My lord, I have news to tell you.

HAMLET: My lord, I have news to tell you. When Roscius was an actor in Rome—

POLONIUS: The actors are come hither, my lord.

HAMLET: Buzz, buzz!

POLONIUS: Upon my honor—

HAMLET: Then came each actor on his ass.

POLONIUS: The best actors in the world, either for tragedy, comedy, history, pastoral, pastoral-comical, historical-pastoral, tragical-historical, tragical-comical-historical-pastoral, scene individable, or poem unlimited. Seneca cannot be too heavy, nor Plautus too light. For the law of writ and the liberty, these are the only men.

HAMLET: O Jephthah, judge of Israel, what a treasure hadst thou!

POLONIUS: What a treasure had he, my lord?

HAMLET: Why,
"One fair daughter, and no more,
The which he lovèd passing well."

POLONIUS *[aside]*:   Still on my daughter.

HAMLET: Am I not i' the right, old Jephthah?

POLONIUS: If you call me Jephthah, my lord, I have a daughter that I love passing well.

HAMLET: Nay, that follows not.

POLONIUS: What follows then, my lord?

HAMLET: Why,
"As by lot, God wot,"
and then, you know,
"It came to pass, as most like it was"—
the first row of the pious chanson will show you more, for look where my abridgement comes.

Enter the PLAYERS.

You are welcome, masters; welcome, all. I am glad to see thee well. Welcome, good friends. O, old friend! Why, thy face is valanced since I saw thee last.

---

373 comply observe the formalities of courtesy   **374 garb** i.e., manner.   **my extent** that which I extend, i.e., my polite behavior   **375 show fairly outwards** show every evidence of cordiality   **376 entertainment** a (warm) reception   **379 north-north-west** just off true north, only party   **380 hawk, handsaw** i.e., two very different things; though also perhaps meaning a mattock (or *hack*) and a carpenter's cutting tool, respectively; also birds, with a play on *hernshaw*, or heron   **384 swaddling clouts** cloths in which to wrap a newborn baby   **385 Haply** perhaps   **392 Roscius** a famous Roman actor who died in 62 B.C.   **394 Buzz** (An interjection used to denote stale news.)

400 scene individable a play observing the unity of place; or perhaps one that is unclassifiable, or performed without intermission   **401 poem unlimited** a play disregarding the unities of time and place; one that is all-inclusive.   **Seneca** writer of Latin tragedies.   **402 Plautus** writer of Latin comedy.   **law . . . liberty** dramatic composition both according to the rules and disregarding the rules   **403 these** i.e., the actors   **404 Jephthah . . . Israel** (Jephthah had to sacrifice his daughter; see Judges 11. Hamlet goes on to quote from a ballad on the theme.)   **409 passing** surpassingly   **417 lot** chance.   **wot** knows   **419 like** likely, probable   **420 row** stanza.   **chanson** ballad, song   **421 my abridgement** something that cuts short my conversation; also, a diversion   **424 valanced** fringed (with a beard)

Hamlet (Kenneth Branagh) talks with the players.

425 Com'st thou to beard me in Denmark? What, my
young lady and mistress! By 'r Lady, your ladyship is
nearer to heaven than when I saw you last, by the altitude of a chopine. Pray God your voice, like a piece of
uncurrent gold, be not cracked within the ring. Mas-
430 ters, you are all welcome. We'll e'en to 't like French
falconers, fly at anything we see. We'll have a speech
straight. Come, give us a taste of your quality. Come,
a passionate speech.

FIRST PLAYER: What speech, my good lord?

435 **HAMLET:** I heard thee speak me a speech once, but
it was never acted, or if it was, not above once, for
the play, I remember, pleased not the million; 'twas
caviar to the general. But it was—as I received it, and
others, whose judgments in such matters cried in the
440 top of mine—an excellent play, well digested in the
scenes, set down with as much modesty as cunning.

---

425 beard confront, challenge (with obvious pun)   **426 young
lady** i.e., boy playing women's parts.   **By 'r Lady** by Our Lady   **428
chopine** thick-soled shoe of Italian fashion   **429 uncurrent** not
passable as lawful coinage.   **cracked . . . ring** i.e., changed from
adolescent to male voice, no longer suitable for women's roles. (Coins
featured rings enclosing the sovereign's head; if the coin was cracked
within this ring, it was unfit for currency.)   **430 e'en to 't** go at it
432 straight at once.   **quality** professional skill   **438 caviar to
the general** caviar to the multitude, i.e., a choice dish too elegant for
coarse tastes   **439–440 cried in the top of** i.e., spoke with greater
authority than   **440 digested** arranged, ordered   **441 modesty**
moderation, restraint.   **cunning** skill

I remember one said there were no sallets in the
lines to make the matter savory, nor no matter in the
phrase that might indict the author of affectation,
but called it an honest method, as wholesome as   445
sweet, and by very much more handsome than fine.
One speech in 't I chiefly loved: 'twas Aeneas' tale to
Dido, and thereabout of it especially when he speaks
of Priam's slaughter. If it live in your memory, begin
at this line: let me see, let me see—   450
　　"The rugged Pyrrhus, like th' Hyrcanian beast"—
'Tis not so. It begins with Pyrrhus:
　　"The rugged Pyrrhus, he whose sable arms,
　　Black as his purpose, did the night resemble
　　When he lay couchèd in the ominous horse,   455
　　Hath now this dread and black complexion
　　　　smeared
　　With heraldry more dismal. Head to foot
　　Now is he total gules, horridly tricked
　　With blood of fathers, mothers, daughters, sons,
　　Baked and impasted with the parching streets,   460
　　That lend a tyrannous and a damnèd light
　　To their lord's murder. Roasted in wrath and fire,
　　And thus o'ersizèd with coagulate gore,
　　With eyes like carbuncles, the hellish Pyrrhus
　　Old grandsire Priam seeks."   465
So proceed you.

---

442 sallets i.e., something savory, spicy improprieties   **444 indict**
convict   **446 handsome** well-proportioned.   **fine** elaborately
ornamented, showy   **449 Priam's slaughter** the slaying of the
ruler of Troy, when the Greeks finally took the city   **451 Pyrrhus** a
Greek hero in the Trojan War, also known as Neoptolemus, son of
Achilles—another avenging son.   **Hyrcanian beast** i.e., tiger. (On
the death of Priam, see Virgil, *Aeneid*, 2.506 ff.; compare the whole
speech with Marlowe's *Dido Queen of Carthage*, 2.1.214 ff. On the
Hyrcanian tiger, see *Aeneid*, 4.366–367. Hyrcania is on the Caspian
Sea.)   **453 rugged** shaggy, savage.   **sable** black (for reasons of
camouflage during the episode of the Trojan horse)   **455 couchèd**
concealed.   **ominous horse** fateful Trojan horse, by which the
Greeks gained access to Troy   **457 dismal** ill-omened   **458 total
gules** entirely red. (A heraldic term.)   **tricked** spotted and smeared.
(Heraldic.)   **460 impasted** crusted, like a thick paste.   **with . . .
streets** by the parching heat of the streets (because of the fires everywhere)   **461 tyrannous** cruel   **462 their lord's** i.e., Priam's   **463
o'ersizèd** covered as with size or glue   **464 carbuncles** large fiery-
red precious stones thought to emit their own light

POLONIUS: 'Fore God, my lord, well spoken, with good accent and good discretion.

FIRST PLAYER: "Anon he finds him
Striking too short at Greeks. His antique sword,
470   Rebellious to his arm, lies where it falls,
Repugnant to command. Unequal matched,
Pyrrhus at Priam drives, in rage strikes wide,
But with the whiff and wind of his fell sword
Th' unnervèd father falls. Then senseless Ilium,
475   Seeming to feel this blow, with flaming top
Stoops to his base, and with a hideous crash
Takes prisoner Pyrrhus' ear. For, lo! His sword,
Which was declining on the milky head
Of reverend Priam, seemed i' th' air to stick.
480   So as a painted tyrant Pyrrhus stood,
And, like a neutral to his will and matter,
Did nothing.
But as we often see against some storm
A silence in the heavens, the rack stand still,
485   The bold winds speechless, and the orb below
As hush as death, anon the dreadful thunder
Doth rend the region, so, after Pyrrhus' pause,
A rousèd vengeance sets him new a-work,
And never did the Cyclops' hammers fall
490   On Mars's armor forged for proof eterne
With less remorse than Pyrrhus' bleeding sword
Now falls on Priam.
Out, out, thou strumpet Fortune! All you gods
In general synod take away her power!
495   Break all the spokes and fellies from her wheel,
And bowl the round nave down the hill of heaven
As low as to the fiends!"

POLONIUS: This is too long.

HAMLET: It shall to the barber's with your beard.—
Prithee, say on. He's for a jig or a tale of bawdry, or he   500
sleeps. Say on; come to Hecuba.

FIRST PLAYER: "But who, ah woe! had seen the moblèd
queen"—

HAMLET: "The moblèd queen"?

POLONIUS: That's good. "Moblèd queen" is good.

FIRST PLAYER: "Run barefoot up and down, threat'ning
the flames   505
With bisson rheum, a clout upon that head
Where late the diadem stood, and, for a robe,
About her lank and all o'erteemèd loins
A blanket, in the alarm of fear caught up—
Who this had seen, with tongue in venom steeped,   510
'Gainst Fortune's state would treason have
pronounced.
But if the gods themselves did see her then
When she saw Pyrrhus make malicious sport
In mincing with his sword her husband's limbs,
The instant burst of clamor that she made,   515
Unless things mortal move them not at all,
Would have made milch the burning eyes of heaven,
And passion in the gods."

POLONIUS: Look whe'er he has not turned his color and
has tears in 's eyes. Prithee, no more.   520

HAMLET: 'Tis well; I'll have thee speak out the rest of
this soon.—Good my lord, will you see the players well
bestowed? Do you hear, let them be well used, for they
are the abstract and brief chronicles of the time. After
your death you were better have a bad epitaph than   525
their ill report while you live.

---

469 antique ancient, long-used   **471 Repugnant** disobedient, resistant   **473 fell** cruel   **474 unnervèd** strengthless. **senseless Ilium** inanimate citadel of Troy   **476 his** its   **478 declining** descending.   **milky** white-haired   **480 painted** i.e., painted in a picture   **481 like . . . matter** i.e., as though suspended between his intention and its fulfillment   **483 against** just before   **484 rack** mass of clouds   **485 orb** globe, earth   **487 region** sky   **489 Cyclops** giant armor makers in the smithy of Vulcan   **490 proof eterne** eternal resistance to assault   **491 remorse** pity   **494 synod** assembly   **495 fellies** pieces of wood forming the rim of a wheel   **496 nave** hub.   **hill of heaven** Mount Olympus

500 jig comic song and dance often given at the end of a play   **501 Hecuba** wife of Priam   **502 who . . . had** anyone who had (also in line 510).   **moblèd** muffled   **505 threat'ning the flames** i.e., weeping hard enough to dampen the flames   **506 bisson rheum** blinding tears.   **clout** cloth   **507 late** lately   **508 all o'erteemèd** utterly worn out with bearing children   **511 state** rule, managing.   **pronounced** proclaimed   **517 milch** milky, moist with tears.   **burning eyes of heaven** i.e., heavenly bodies   **518 passion** overpowering emotion   **519 whe'er** whether   **523 bestowed** lodged   **524 abstract** summary account

POLONIUS: My lord, I will use them according to their desert.

HAMLET: God's bodikin, man, much better. Use every man after his desert, and who shall scape whipping? Use them after your own honor and dignity. The less they deserve, the more merit is in your bounty. Take them in.

POLONIUS: Come, sirs.   *[Exit.]*

HAMLET: Follow him, friends. We'll hear a play tomorrow. *[As they start to leave,* HAMLET *detains the* FIRST PLAYER.*]* Dost thou hear me, old friend? Can you play *The Murder of Gonzago?*

FIRST PLAYER: Ay, my lord.

HAMLET: We'll ha 't tomorrow night. You could, for a need, study a speech of some dozen or sixteen lines which I would set down and insert in 't, could you not?

FIRST PLAYER: Ay, my lord.

HAMLET: Very well. Follow that lord, and look you mock him not. *(Exeunt* PLAYERS.*)* My good friends, I'll leave you till night. You are welcome to Elsinore.

ROSENCRANTZ: Good my lord!
*Exeunt [*ROSENCRANTZ *and* GUILDENSTERN].

HAMLET: Ay, so, goodbye to you.—Now I am alone.
O, what a rogue and peasant slave am I!
Is it not monstrous that this player here,
But in a fiction, in a dream of passion,
Could force his soul so to his own conceit
That from her working all his visage wanned,
Tears in his eyes, distraction in his aspect,
A broken voice, and his whole function suiting
With forms to his conceit? And all for nothing!

Hamlet and Polonius discuss the play with the players.

For Hecuba!
What's Hecuba to him, or he to Hecuba,
That he should weep for her? What would he do   560
Had he the motive and the cue for passion
That I have? He would drown the stage with tears
And cleave the general ear with horrid speech,
Made mad the guilty and appall the free,
Confound the ignorant, and amaze indeed   565
The very faculties of eyes and ears. Yet I,
A dull and muddy-mettled rascal, peak
Like John-a-dreams, unpregnant of my cause,
And can say nothing—no, not for a king
Upon whose property and most dear life   570
A damned defeat was made. Am I a coward?
Who calls me villain? Breaks my pate across?
Plucks off my beard and blows it in my face?
Tweaks me by the nose? Gives me the lie i' the throat
As deep as to the lungs? Who does me this?   575
Ha, 'swounds, I should take it; for it cannot be
But I am pigeon-livered and lack gall

---

529 God's bodikin by God's (Christ's) little body, *bodykin*. (Not to be confused with *bodkin*, "dagger.") **531 after** according to **540 ha 't** have it **541 study** memorize **552 But** merely **553 force . . . conceit** bring his innermost being so entirely into accord with his conception (of the role) **554 from her working** as a result of, or in response to, his soul's activity. **wanned** grew pale **555 aspect** look, glance **556–557 his whole . . . conceit** all his bodily powers responding with actions to suit his thought

563 the general ear everyone's ear. **horrid** horrible **564 appall** (Literally, make pale.) **free** innocent **565 Confound the ignorant** i.e., dumbfound those who know nothing of the crime that has been committed. **amaze** stun **567 muddy-mettled** dull-spirited. **peak** mope, pine **568 John-a-dreams** a sleepy, dreaming idler. **unpregnant of** not quickened by **570 property** i.e., the crown; also character, quality **571 damned defeat** damnable act of destruction **572 pate** head **574 Gives . . . throat** calls me an out-and-out liar **576 'swounds** by his (Christ's) wounds **577 pigeon-livered** (The pigeon or dove was popularly supposed to be mild because it secreted no gall.)

To make oppression bitter, or ere this
I should ha' fatted all the region kites
580 With this slave's offal. Bloody, bawdy villain!
Remorseless, treacherous, lecherous, kindless villain!
O, vengeance!
Why, what an ass am I! This is most brave,
That I, the son of a dear father murdered,
585 Prompted to my revenge by heaven and hell,
Must like a whore unpack my heart with words
And fall a-cursing, like a very drab,
A scullion! Fie upon 't, foh! About, my brains!
Hum, I have heard
590 That guilty creatures sitting at a play
Have by the very cunning of the scene
Been struck so to the soul that presently
They have proclaimed their malefactions;
For murder, though it have no tongue, will speak
595 With most miraculous organ. I'll have these players
Play something like the murder of my father
Before mine uncle. I'll observe his looks;
I'll tent him to the quick. If 'a do blench,
I know my course. The spirit that I have seen
600 May be the devil, and the devil hath power
T' assume a pleasing shape; yea, and perhaps,
Out of my weakness and my melancholy,
As he is very potent with such spirits,
Abuses me to damn me. I'll have grounds
605 More relative than this. The play's the thing
Wherein I'll catch the conscience of the King.   *Exit.*

3.1 *Enter* KING, QUEEN, POLONIUS, OPHELIA,
     ROSENCRANTZ, GUILDENSTERN, *lords.*

KING: And can you by no drift of conference
     Get from him why he puts on this confusion,

Grating so harshly all his days of quiet
With turbulent and dangerous lunacy?

ROSENCRANTZ: He does confess he feels himself   5
     distracted,
But from what cause 'a will by no means speak.

GUILDENSTERN: Nor do we find him forward to be
     sounded,
But with a crafty madness keeps aloof
When we would bring him on to some confession
Of his true state.   10

QUEEN: Did he receive you well?

ROSENCRANTZ: Most like a gentleman.

GUILDENSTERN: But with much forcing of his
     disposition.

ROSENCRANTZ: Niggard of question, but of our
     demands
Most free in his reply.

QUEEN: Did you assay him
To any pastime?   15

ROSENCRANTZ: Madam, it so fell out that certain
     players
We o'erraught on the way. Of these we told him,
And there did seem in him a kind of joy
To hear of it. They are here about the court,
And, as I think, they have already order   20
This night to play before him.

POLONIUS: 'Tis most true,
And he beseeched me to entreat Your Majesties
To hear and see the matter.

KING: With all my heart, and it doth much content me
To hear him so inclined.   25
Good gentlemen, give him a further edge
And drive his purpose into these delights.

ROSENCRANTZ: We shall, my lord.
          Exeunt ROSENCRANTZ *and* GUILDENSTERN.

---

578 **bitter** i.e., bitter to me   579 **region kites** kites (birds of prey)
of the air   580 **offal** entrails   581 **Remorseless** pitiless.   **kindless** unnatural   583 **brave** fine, admirable. (Said ironically.)   587
drab whore   588 **scullion** menial kitchen servant (apt to be foul-
mouthed).   **About** about it, to work   591 **cunning** art, skill.   **scene**
dramatic presentation   592 **presently** at once   598 **tent**
probe.   **the quick** the tender part of a wound, the core.   **blench**
quail, flinch   603 **spirits** humors (of melancholy)   604 **Abuses**
deludes   605 **relative** cogent, pertinent

3.1. Location: The castle.
1 **drift of conference** directing of conversation

---

7 **forward** willing.   **sounded** questioned   12 **disposition** inclination   13 **Niggard** stingy.   **question** conversation   14 **assay** try to
win   17 **o'erraught** overtook   26 **edge** incitement

KING: Sweet Gertrude, leave us too,
   For we have closely sent for Hamlet hither,
30 That he, as 'twere by accident, may here
   Affront Ophelia.
   Her father and myself, lawful espials,
   Will so bestow ourselves that seeing, unseen,
   We may of their encounter frankly judge,
35 And gather by him, as he is behaved,
   If 't be th' affliction of his love or no
   That thus he suffers for.

QUEEN: I shall obey you.
   And for your part, Ophelia, I do wish
   That your good beauties be the happy cause
40 Of Hamlet's wildness. So shall I hope your virtues
   Will bring him to his wonted way again,
   To both your honors.

OPHELIA: Madam, I wish it may.
                              [Exit QUEEN.*]*

POLONIUS: Ophelia, walk you here.—Gracious, so
        please you,
   We will bestow ourselves. *[To* OPHELIA.*]* Read on
        this book,   *[giving her a book]*
45 That show of such an exercise may color
   Your loneliness. We are oft to blame in this—
   'Tis too much proved—that with devotion's visage
   And pious action we do sugar o'er
   The devil himself.

50 KING *[aside]*:   O, 'tis too true!
   How smart a lash that speech doth give my
        conscience!
   The harlot's cheek, beautied with plastering art,
   Is not more ugly to the thing that helps it
   Than is my deed to my most painted word.
55 O heavy burden!

POLONIUS: I hear him coming. Let's withdraw, my lord.
                [The KING *and* POLONIUS *withdraw.]*

                Enter HAMLET. *[*OPHELIA *pretends
                              to read a book.]*

HAMLET: To be, or not to be, that is the question:
   Whether 'tis nobler in the mind to suffer
   The slings and arrows of outrageous fortune,
   Or to take arms against a sea of troubles   60
   And by opposing end them. To die, to sleep—
   No more—and by a sleep to say we end
   The heartache and the thousand natural shocks
   That flesh is heir to. 'Tis a consummation
   Devoutly to be wished. To die, to sleep;   65
   To sleep, perchance to dream. Ay, there's the rub,
   For in that sleep of death what dreams may come,
   When we have shuffled off this mortal coil,
   Must give us pause. There's the respect
   That makes calamity of so long life.   70
   For who would bear the whips and scorns of time,
   Th' oppressor's wrong, the proud man's contumely,
   The pangs of disprized love, the law's delay,
   The insolence of office, and the spurns
   That patient merit of th' unworthy takes,   75
   When he himself might his quietus make
   With a bare bodkin? Who would fardels bear,
   To grunt and sweat under a weary life,
   But that the dread of something after death,
   The undiscovered country from whose bourn   80
   No traveler returns, puzzles the will,
   And makes us rather bear those ills we have
   Than fly to others that we know not of?
   Thus conscience does make cowards of us all;
   And thus the native hue of resolution   85

---

29 **closely** privately   31 **Affront** confront, meet   32 **espials** spies
41 **wonted** accustomed   43 **Gracious** Your Grace (i.e., the King)
44 **bestow** conceal   45 **exercise** religious exercise. (The book she
reads is one of devotion.)   **color** give a plausible appearance to   46
loneliness being alone   47 **too much proved** too often shown to be
true, too often practiced   53 **to** compared to.   **the thing** i.e., the
cosmetic

---

56 **s.d. withdraw** (The King and Polonius may retire behind an
arras. The stage directions specify that they "enter" again near
the end of the scene.)   59 **slings** missiles   66 **rub** (Literally, an
obstacle in the game of bowls.)   68 **shuffled** sloughed, cast.   **coil**
turmoil   69 **respect** consideration   70 **of . . . life** so long-lived,
something we willingly endure for so long (also suggesting that long
life is itself a calamity)   72 **contumely** insolent abuse   73 **disprized** unvalued   74 **office** officialdom.   **spurns** insults   75 **of . . .
takes** receives from unworthy persons   76 **quietus** acquaintance;
here, death   77 **a bare bodkin** a mere dagger, unsheathed.   **fardels**
burdens   80 **bourn** frontier, boundary   85 **native hue** natural
color, complexion

Hamlet (Laurence Olivier) talks with Ophelia (Jean Simmons).

Is sicklied o'er with the pale cast of thought,
And enterprises of great pitch and moment
With this regard their currents turn awry
And lose the name of action.—Soft you now,
90 The fair Ophelia. Nymph, in thy orisons
Be all my sins remembered.

OPHELIA: Good my lord,
How does your honor for this many a day?

HAMLET: I humbly thank you; well, well, well.

OPHELIA: My lord, I have remembrances of yours,
95 That I have longèd long to redeliver.
I pray you, now receive them.   *[She offers tokens.]*

HAMLET: No, not I, I never gave you aught.

OPHELIA: My honored lord, you know right well you
did,
And with them words of so sweet breath composed
100 As made the things more rich. Their perfume lost,
Take these again, for to the noble mind
Rich gifts wax poor when givers prove unkind.
There, my lord.   *[She gives tokens.]*

HAMLET: Ha, ha! Are you honest?

OPHELIA: My lord?   105

HAMLET: Are you fair?

OPHELIA: What means your lordship?

HAMLET: That if you be honest and fair, your honesty
should admit no discourse to your beauty.

OPHELIA: Could beauty, my lord, have better commerce   110
than with honesty?

HAMLET: Ay, truly, for the power of beauty will sooner
transform honesty from what it is to a bawd than the
force of honesty can translate beauty into his likeness.
This was sometime a paradox, but now the time gives   115
it proof. I did love you once.

OPHELIA: Indeed, my lord, you made me believe so.

HAMLET: You should not have believed me, for virtue
cannot so inoculate our old stock but we shall relish
of it. I loved you not.   120

OPHELIA: I was the more deceived.

HAMLET: Get thee to a nunnery. Why wouldst thou
be a breeder of sinners? I am myself indifferent honest, but yet I could accuse me of such things that it
were better my mother had not borne me: I am very   125
proud, revengeful, ambitious, with more offenses at
my beck than I have thoughts to put them in, imagination to give them shape, or time to act them in.
What should such fellows as I do crawling between
earth and heaven? We are arrant knaves all; believe   130
none of us. Go thy ways to a nunnery. Where's your
father?

---

86 **cast** tinge, shade of color   87 **pitch** height (as of a falcon's flight).
moment importance   88 **regard** respect, consideration.   **currents**
courses   89 **Soft you** i.e., wait a minute, gently   90 **orisons** prayers

104 **honest** (1) truthful (2) chaste   106 **fair** (1) beautiful (2) just,
honorable   108 **your honesty** your chastity   109 **discourse to** familiar dealings with   110–111 **commerce** dealings, intercourse   114
his its   115 **sometime** formerly.   **a paradox** a view opposite to
commonly held opinion.   **the time** the present age   119 **inoculate**
graft, be engrafted to   119–120 **but . . . it** that we do not still have
about us a taste of the old stock, i.e., retain our sinfulness   122
nunnery convent (with possibly an awareness that the word was also
used derisively to denote a brothel)   123–124 **indifferent honest**
reasonably virtuous   127 **beck** command

Hamlet raves at Ophelia.

OPHELIA: At home, my lord.

HAMLET: Let the doors be shut upon him, that he may
135   play the fool nowhere but in 's own house. Farewell.

OPHELIA: O, help him, you sweet heavens!

HAMLET: If thou dost marry, I'll give thee this plague
for thy dowry: be thou as chaste as ice, as pure as
snow, thou shalt not escape calumny. Get thee to
140   a nunnery, farewell. Or, if thou wilt needs marry,
marry a fool, for wise men know well enough what
monsters you make of them. To a nunnery, go, and
quickly too. Farewell.

OPHELIA: Heavenly powers, restore him!

145 **HAMLET:**   I have heard of your paintings too, well
enough. God hath given you one face, and you make
yourselves another. You jig, you amble, and you lisp,
you nickname God's creatures, and make your wantonness your ignorance. Go to, I'll no more on 't;
150   it hath made me mad. I say we will have no more
marriage. Those that are married already—all but
one—shall live. The rest shall keep as they are. To a
nunnery, go.   *Exit.*

---

142 monsters (An allusion to the horns of a cuckold.)   **you** i.e., you
women   **147 jig** dance.   **amble** move coyly   **148 you nickname . . .
creatures** i.e., you give trendy names to things in place of their God-
given names   **148–149 make . . . ignorance** i.e., excuse your affectation on the grounds of pretended ignorance   **149 on 't** of it

---

OPHELIA: O, what a noble mind is here o'erthrown!
The courtier's, soldier's, scholar's, eye, tongue, sword,   155
Th' expectancy and rose of the fair state,
The glass of fashion and the mold of form,
Th' observed of all observers, quite, quite down!
And I, of ladies most deject and wretched,
That sucked the honey of his music vows,   160
Now see that noble and most sovereign reason
Like sweet bells jangled out of tune and harsh,
That unmatched form and feature of blown youth
Blasted with ecstasy. O, woe is me,
T' have seen what I have seen, see what I see!   165

Enter KING *and* POLONIUS.

KING: Love? His affections do not that way tend;
Nor what he spake, though it lacked form a little,
Was not like madness. There's something in his soul
O'er which his melancholy sits on brood,
And I do doubt the hatch and the disclose   170
Will be some danger; which for to prevent,
I have in quick determination
Thus set it down: he shall with speed to England
For the demand of our neglected tribute.
Haply the seas and countries different   175
With variable objects shall expel
This something-settled matter in his heart,
Whereon his brains still beating puts him thus
From fashion of himself. What think you on 't?

POLONIUS: It shall do well. But yet do I believe   180
The origin and commencement of his grief
Sprung from neglected love.—How now, Ophelia?
You need not tell us what Lord Hamlet said;
We heard it all.—My lord, do as you please,
But, if you hold it fit, after the play   185

---

156 expectancy hope.   **rose** ornament   **157 The glass . . . form** the
mirror of true self-fashioning and the pattern of courtly behavior
158 Th' observed . . . observers i.e., the center of attention and
honor in the court   **160 music** musical, sweetly uttered   **163 blown**
blooming   **164 Blasted** withered.   **ecstasy** madness   **166 affections** emotions, feelings   **169 sits on brood** sits like a bird on a
nest, about to *hatch* mischief (line 170)   **170 doubt** fear.   **disclose**
disclosure, hatching   **173 set it down** resolved   **174 For . . . of** to
demand   **176 variable objects** various sights and surroundings
to divert him   **177 This something . . . heart** the strange matter
settled in his heart   **178 still** continually   **179 From . . . himself**
out of his natural manner

Let his queen-mother all alone entreat him
To show his grief. Let her be round with him;
And I'll be placed, so please you, in the ear
Of all their conference. If she find him not,
190 To England send him, or confine him where
Your wisdom best shall think.

KING: It shall be so.
Madness in great ones must not unwatched go.

                                    Exeunt.

3.2 *Enter* HAMLET *and three of the* PLAYERS.

HAMLET: Speak the speech, I pray you, as I pronounced
it to you, trippingly on the tongue. But if you mouth
it, as many of our players do, I had as lief the town
crier spoke my lines. Nor do not saw the air too
5 much with your hand, thus, but use all gently; for
in the very torrent, tempest, and, as I may say, whirlwind of your passion, you must acquire and beget a
temperance that may give it smoothness. O, it offends
me to the soul to hear a robustious periwig-pated
10 fellow tear a passion to tatters, to very rags, to split
the ears of the groundlings, who for the most part
are capable of nothing but inexplicable dumb shows
and noise. I would have such a fellow whipped for
o'erdoing Termagant. It out-Herods Herod. Pray you,
15 avoid it.

FIRST PLAYER: I warrant your honor.

HAMLET: Be not too tame neither, but let your own
discretion be your tutor. Suit the action to the word,
the word to the action, with this special observance,
that you o'erstep not the modesty of nature. For 20
anything so o'erdone is from the purpose of playing,
whose end, both at the first and now, was and is to
hold as 't were the mirror up to nature, to show virtue her feature, scorn her own image, and the very
age and body of the time his form and pressure. Now 25
this overdone or come tardy off, though it makes
the unskillful laugh, cannot but make the judicious
grieve, the censure of the which one must in your
allowance o'erweigh a whole theater of others. O,
there be players that I have seen play, and heard oth- 30
ers praise, and that highly, not to speak it profanely,
that, neither having th' accent of Christians nor the
gait of Christian, pagan, nor man, have so strutted
and bellowed that I have thought some of nature's
journeymen had made men and not made them well, 35
they imitated humanity so abominably.

FIRST PLAYER: I hope we have reformed that indifferently with us, sir.

HAMLET: O, reform it altogether. And let those that
play your clowns speak no more than is set down for 40
them; for there be of them that will themselves laugh,
to set on some quantity of barren spectators to laugh
too, though in the meantime some necessary question
of the play be then to be considered. That's villainous,
and shows a most pitiful ambition in the fool that uses 45
it. Go make you ready.   *[Exeunt* PLAYERS.*]*

                    Enter POLONIUS, GUILDENSTERN,
                        and ROSENCRANTZ.

How now, my lord, will the King hear this piece of
work?

---

186 **queen-mother** queen and mother 187 **round** blunt 189 **find him not** fails to discover what is troubling him

3.2. Location: The castle.
3 **our players** players nowadays. **I had as lief** I would just as soon
9 **robustious** violent, boisterous. **periwig-pated** wearing a wig
11 **groundlings** spectators who paid least and stood in the yard
of the theater 12 **capable of** able to understand. **dumb shows**
mimed performances, often used before Shakespeare's time to pre-
cede a play or each act 14 **Termagant** a supposed deity of the Mo-
hammedans, not found in any English medieval play but elsewhere
portrayed as violent and blustering 14 **Herod** Herod of Jewry. (A
character in *The Slaughter of the Innocents* and other cycle plays. The
part was played with great noise and fury.)

20 **modesty** restraint, moderation 21 **from** contrary to 24 **scorn**
i.e., something foolish and deserving of scorn 24–25 **the very . . .
time** i.e., the present state of affairs 25 **his** its. **pressure** stamp,
impressed character 26 **come tardy off** inadequately done 27 **the
unskillful** those lacking in judgment 28 **the censure . . . one** the
judgment of even one of whom 28–29 **your allowance** your scale
of values 31 **not . . . profanely** (Hamlet anticipates his idea in lines
34–35 that some men were not made by God at all.) 32 **Christians**
i.e., ordinary decent folk 33 **nor man** i.e., nor any human being
at all 35 **journeymen** laborers who are not yet masters in their
trade 36 **abominably** (Shakespeare's usual spelling, *abhominably*,
suggests a literal though etymologically incorrect meaning, "removed from human nature.") 37–38 **indifferently** tolerably 41
of them some among them 42 **barren** i.e., of wit

Hamlet coaches the First Player (Ben Thom).

POLONIUS: And the Queen too, and that presently.

HAMLET: Bid the players make haste. *[Exit* POLONIUS.*]*
50   Will you two help to hasten them?

ROSENCRANTZ: Ay, my lord.   *[Exeunt they two.]*

HAMLET: What ho, Horatio!

                              Enter HORATIO.

HORATIO: Here, sweet lord, at your service.

HAMLET: Horatio, thou art e'en as just a man
        As e'er my conversation coped withal.

55 **HORATIO:**   O, my dear lord—

HAMLET: Nay, do not think I flatter,
        For what advancement may I hope from thee
        That no revenue hast but thy good spirits
        To feed and clothe thee? Why should the poor be
            flattered?
        No, let the candied tongue lick absurd pomp,
60   And crook the pregnant hinges of the knee
        Where thrift may follow fawning. Dost thou hear?
        Since my dear soul was mistress of her choice
        And could of men distinguish her election,

Sh' hath sealed thee for herself, for thou hast been
As one, in suffering all, that suffers nothing,   65
A man that Fortune's buffets and rewards
Hast ta'en with equal thanks; and blest are those
Whose blood and judgment are so well commeddled
That they are not a pipe for Fortune's finger
To sound what stop she please. Give me that man   70
That is not passion's slave, and I will wear him
In my heart's core, ay, in my heart of heart,
As I do thee.—Something too much of this.—
There is a play tonight before the King.
One scene of it comes near the circumstance   75
Which I have told thee of my father's death.
I prithee, when thou seest that act afoot,
Even with the very comment of thy soul
Observe my uncle. If his occulted guilt
Do not itself unkennel in one speech,   80
It is a damnèd ghost that we have seen,
And my imaginations are as foul
As Vulcan's stithy. Give him heedful note,
For I mine eyes will rivet to his face,
And after we will both our judgments join   85
In censure of his seeming.

HORATIO: Well, my lord.
If 'a steal aught the whilst this play is playing
And scape detecting, I will pay the theft.

            [Flourish.] Enter trumpets and kettledrums,
              KING, QUEEN, POLONIUS, OPHELIA,
              *[*ROSENCRANTZ, GUILDENSTERN, *and*
              other lords, with guards carrying torches].

HAMLET: They are coming to the play. I must be idle.
        Get you a place. *[The* KING, QUEEN, *and courtiers sit.]* 90

KING: How fares our cousin Hamlet?

---

48 **presently** at once   54 **my . . . withal** my dealings encountered
59 **candied** sugared, flattering   60 **pregnant** compliant   61 **thrift**
profit   63 **could . . . election** could make distinguishing choices
among persons

64 **sealed thee** (Literally, as one would seal a legal document to
mark possession.)   68 **blood** passion.   **commeddled** commingled
70 **stop** hole in a wind instrument for controlling the sound   78
very . . . soul your most penetrating observation and consideration
79 **occulted** hidden   80 **unkennel** (As one would say of a fox driven
from its lair.)   81 **damnèd** in league with Satan   83 **stithy** smithy,
place of stiths (anvils)   86 **censure of his seeming** judgment of his
appearance or behavior   87 **If 'a steal aught** if he gets away with
anything   89 **idle** (1) unoccupied (2) mad   91 **cousin** i.e., close
relative

HAMLET: Excellent i' faith, of the chameleon's dish: I eat the air, promise-crammed. You cannot feed capons so.

KING: I have nothing with this answer, Hamlet. These
95   words are not mine.

HAMLET: No, nor mine now. *[To* POLONIUS.*]* My lord, you played once i' th' university, you say?

POLONIUS: That did I, my lord, and was accounted a good actor.

100   **HAMLET:**   What did you enact?

POLONIUS: I did enact Julius Caesar. I was killed i' the Capitol; Brutus killed me.

HAMLET: It was a brute part of him to kill so capital a calf there.—Be the players ready?

105   **ROSENCRANTZ:**   Ay, my lord. They stay upon your patience.

QUEEN: Come hither, my dear Hamlet, sit by me.

HAMLET: No, good Mother, here's metal more attractive.

POLONIUS *[to the* KING*]:*   O, ho, do you mark that?

110   **HAMLET:**   Lady, shall I lie in your lap?
[Lying down at OPHELIA's *feet.]*

OPHELIA: No, my lord.

HAMLET: I mean, my head upon your lap?

OPHELIA: Ay, my lord.

HAMLET: Do you think I meant country matters?

OPHELIA: I think nothing, my lord.   115

HAMLET: That's a fair thought to lie between maids' legs.

OPHELIA: What is, my lord?

HAMLET: Nothing.

OPHELIA: You are merry, my lord.   120

HAMLET: Who, I?

OPHELIA: Ay, my lord.

HAMLET: O God, your only jig maker. What should a man do but be merry? For look you how cheerfully my mother looks, and my father died within 's two hours.   125

OPHELIA: Nay, 'tis twice two months, my lord.

HAMLET: So long? Nay then, let the devil wear black, for I'll have a suit of sables. O heavens! Die two months ago, and not forgotten yet? Then there's hope a great man's memory may outlive his life half a year. But, by   130 'r Lady, 'a must build churches, then, or else shall 'a suffer not thinking on, with the hobbyhorse, whose epitaph is "For O, for O, the hobbyhorse is forgot."

The trumpets sound. Dumb show follows.

Enter a KING *and a* QUEEN *[very lovingly]; the* QUEEN *embracing him, and he her. [She kneels, and makes show of protestation unto him.] He*

---

92 chameleon's dish (Chameleons were supposed to feed on air. Hamlet deliberately misinterprets the King's *fares* as "feeds." By his phrase *eat the air* he also plays on the idea of feeding himself with the promise of succession, of being the *heir*.)   **93 capons** roosters castrated and *crammed* with feed to make them succulent   **94 have . . . with** make nothing of, or gain nothing from   **95 are not mine** do not respond to what I asked   **96 nor mine now** (Once spoken, words are proverbially no longer the speaker's own—and hence should be uttered warily.)   **103 brute** (The Latin meaning of *brutus*, "stupid," was often used punningly with the name Brutus.)   **part** (1) deed (2) role   **104 calf** fool   **105 stay upon** await   **108 metal** substance that is *attractive*, i.e., magnetic, but with suggestion also of *mettle*, "disposition"   **114 country matters** sexual intercourse (making a bawdy pun on the first syllable of *country*)

119 Nothing the figure zero or naught, suggesting the female sexual anatomy. (*Thing* not infrequently has a bawdy connotation of male or female anatomy, and the reference here could be male.)   **123 only jig maker** very best composer of jigs, i.e., pointless merriment. (Hamlet replies sardonically to Ophelia's observation that he is merry by saying, "If you're looking for someone who is really merry, you've come to the right person.")   **125 within 's** within this (i.e., these)   **128 suit of sables** garments trimmed with the fur of the sable and hence suited for a wealthy person, not a mourner (but with a pun on *sable*, "black," ironically suggesting mourning once again)   **132 suffer . . . on** undergo oblivion   **133 For . . . forgot** (Verse of a song occurring also in *Love's Labor's Lost*, 3.1.27–28. The hobbyhorse was a character made up to resemble a horse and rider, appearing in the morris dance and such May-game sports. This song laments the disappearance of such customs under pressure from the Puritans.)

takes her up, and declines his head upon her neck. He lies him down upon a bank of flowers. She, seeing him asleep, leaves him. Anon comes in another man, takes off his crown, kisses it, pours poison in the sleeper's ears, and leaves him. The QUEEN *returns, finds the* KING *dead, makes passionate action. The Poisoner with some three or four come in again, seem to condole with her. The dead body is carried away. The Poisoner woos the* QUEEN *with gifts; she seems harsh awhile, but in the end accepts love.*

[*Exeunt* PLAYERS.]

OPHELIA: What means this, my lord?

135   HAMLET: Marry, this' miching mallico; it means mischief.

OPHELIA: Belike this show imports the argument of the play.

Enter PROLOGUE.

HAMLET: We shall know by this fellow. The players
140   cannot keep counsel; they'll tell all.

OPHELIA: Will 'a tell us what this show meant?

HAMLET: Ay, or any show that you will show him. Be not you ashamed to show, he'll not shame to tell you what it means.

145   OPHELIA: You are naught, you are naught. I'll mark the play.

PROLOGUE: For us, and for our tragedy,
Here stooping to your clemency,
We beg your hearing patiently.   [*Exit.*]

150   HAMLET: Is this a prologue, or the posy of a ring?

OPHELIA: 'Tis brief, my lord.

HAMLET: As woman's love.

Enter [two PLAYERS *as]* KING *and* QUEEN.

PLAYER KING: Full thirty times hath Phoebus' cart gone round
Neptune's salt wash and Tellus' orbèd ground,
And thirty dozen moons with borrowed sheen   155
About the world have times twelve thirties been,
Since love our hearts and Hymen did our hands
Unite commutual in most sacred bands.

PLAYER QUEEN: So many journeys may the sun and moon
Make us again count o'er ere love be done!   160
But, woe is me, you are so sick of late,
So far from cheer and from your former state,
That I distrust you. Yet, though I distrust,
Discomfort you, my lord, it nothing must.
For women's fear and love hold quantity;   165
In neither aught, or in extremity.
Now, what my love is, proof hath made you know,
And as my love is sized, my fear is so.
Where love is great, the littlest doubts are fear;
Where little fears grow great, great love grows there.   170

PLAYER KING: Faith, I must leave thee, love, and shortly too;
My operant powers their functions leave to do.
And thou shalt live in this fair world behind,
Honored, beloved; and haply one as kind
For husband shalt thou—

PLAYER QUEEN: O, confound the rest!   175
Such love must needs be treason in my breast.
In second husband let me be accurst!
None wed the second but who killed the first.

---

135 **this' miching mallico** this is sneaking mischief   137 **Belike** probably.   **argument** plot   140 **counsel** secret   142–143 **Be not you** provided you are not   145 **naught** indecent. (Ophelia is reacting to Hamlet's pointed remarks about not being ashamed to show all.)   148 **stooping** bowing   150 **posy . . . ring** brief motto in verse inscribed in a ring

153 **Phoebus' cart** the sun-god's chariot, making its yearly cycle   154 **salt wash** the sea.   **Tellus** goddess of the earth, of the *orbèd ground*   155 **borrowed** i.e., reflected   157 **Hymen** god of matrimony   158 **commutual** mutually.   **bands** bonds   163 **distrust** am anxious about   164 **Discomfort** distress.   **nothing** not at all   165 **hold quantity** keep proportion with one another   166 **In . . . extremity** i.e., women fear and love either too little or too much, but the two, fear and love, are equal in either case   167 **proof** experience   168 **sized** in size   172 **operant powers** vital functions.   **leave to do** cease to perform   173 **behind** after I have gone   178 **None** i.e., let no woman.   **but who** except the one who

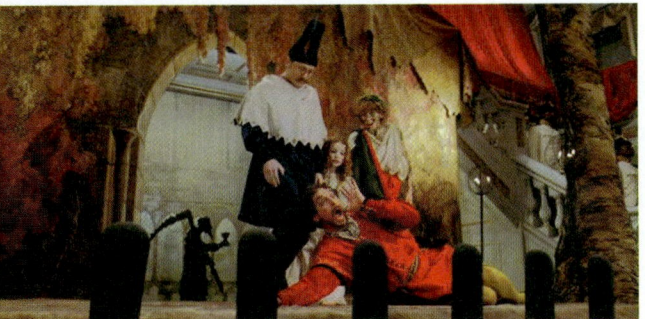

The players perform Hamlet's play.

HAMLET: Wormwood, wormwood.

180   **PLAYER QUEEN:**   The instances that second marriage
          move
          Are base respects of thrift, but none of love.
          A second time I kill my husband dead
          When second husband kisses me in bed.

          PLAYER KING: I do believe you think what now you
          speak,
185   But what we do determine oft we break.
          Purpose is but the slave to memory,
          Of violent birth, but poor validity,
          Which now, like fruit unripe, sticks on the tree,
          But fall unshaken when they mellow be.
190   Most necessary 'tis that we forget
          To pay ourselves what to ourselves is debt.
          What to ourselves in passion we propose,
          The passion ending, doth the purpose lose.
          The violence of either grief or joy
195   Their own enactures with themselves destroy.

Where joy most revels, grief doth most lament;
Grief joys, joy grieves, on slender accident.
This world is not for aye, nor 'tis not strange
That even our loves should with our fortunes change;
For 'tis a question left us yet to prove,   200
Whether love lead fortune, or else fortune love.
The great man down, you mark his favorite flies;
The poor advanced makes friends of enemies.
And hitherto doth love on fortune tend;
For who not needs shall never lack a friend,   205
And who in want a hollow friend doth try
Directly seasons him his enemy.
But, orderly to end where I begun,
Our wills and fates do so contrary run
That our devices still are overthrown;   210
Our thoughts are ours, their ends none of our own.
So think thou wilt no second husband wed,
But die thy thoughts when thy first lord is dead.

PLAYER QUEEN: Nor earth to me give food, nor heaven
          light,
Sport and repose lock from me day and night,   215
To desperation turn my trust and hope,
An anchor's cheer in prison be my scope!
Each opposite that blanks the face of joy
Meet what I would have well and it destroy!
Both here and hence pursue me lasting strife   220
If, once a widow, ever I be wife!

HAMLET: If she should break it now!

---

179 **Wormwood** i.e., how bitter. (Literally, a bitter-tasting plant.)
180 **instances** motives.   **move** motivate   181 **base . . . thrift** ig-
noble considerations of material prosperity   186 **Purpose . . .
memory** our good intentions are subject to forgetfulness   187 **validity** strength, durability   188 **Which** i.e., purpose   190–191 **Most
. . . debt** it's inevitable that in time we forget the obligations we have
imposed on ourselves   195 **enactures** fulfillments

196–197 **Where . . . accident** the capacity for extreme joy and grief
go together, and often one extreme is instantly changed into its
opposite on the slightest provocation   198 **aye** ever   202 **down**
fallen in fortune   203 **The poor . . . enemies** when one of humble
station is promoted, you see his enemies suddenly becoming his
friends   204 **hitherto** up to this point in the argument, or, to this
extent.   **tend** attend   205 **who not needs** he who is not in need
(of wealth)   206 **who in want** he who, being in need.   **try** test (his
generosity)   207 **seasons him** ripens him into   209 **Our . . . run**
what we want and what we get go so contrarily   210 **devices still**
intentions continually   211 **ends** results   214 **Nor** let neither
215 **Sport . . . night** may day deny me its pastimes and night its
repose   217 **anchor's cheer** anchorite's or hermit's fare.   **my scope**
the extent of my happiness   218–219 **Each . . . destroy** may every
adverse thing that causes the face of joy to turn pale meet and
destroy everything that I desire to see prosper.   **blanks** causes to
blanch or grow pale   220 **hence** in the life hereafter

PLAYER KING: 'Tis deeply sworn. Sweet, leave me here awhile;
My spirits grow dull, and fain I would beguile
225 The tedious day with sleep.

PLAYER QUEEN: Sleep rock thy brain,
And never come mischance between us twain!
                              *[He sleeps.] Exit [*PLAYER QUEEN].

HAMLET: Madam, how like you this play?

QUEEN: The lady doth protest too much, methinks.

HAMLET: O, but she'll keep her word.

230 **KING:** Have you heard the argument? Is there no offense in 't?

HAMLET: No, no, they do but jest, poison in jest. No offense i' the world.

KING: What do you call the play?

235 **HAMLET:** *The Mousetrap.* Marry, how? Tropically. This play is the image of a murder done in Vienna. Gonzago is the Duke's name, his wife, Baptista. You shall see anon. 'Tis a knavish piece of work, but what of that? Your Majesty, and we that have free souls, it
240 touches us not. Let the galled jade wince, our withers are unwrung.

                              Enter LUCIANUS.

This is one Lucianus, nephew to the King.

OPHELIA: You are as good as a chorus, my lord.

HAMLET: I could interpret between you and your love, if I could see the puppets dallying.   245

OPHELIA: You are keen, my lord, you are keen.

HAMLET: It would cost you a groaning to take off mine edge.

OPHELIA: Still better, and worse.

HAMLET: So you mis-take your husbands. Begin, mur- 250 derer; leave thy damnable faces and begin. Come, the croaking raven doth bellow for revenge.

LUCIANUS: Thoughts black, hands apt, drugs fit, and time agreeing,
Confederate season, else no creature seeing,
Thou mixture rank, of midnight weeds collected, 255
With Hecate's ban thrice blasted, thrice infected,
Thy natural magic and dire property
On wholesome life usurp immediately.
                    [He pours the poison into the sleeper's ear.]

HAMLET: 'A poisons him i' the garden for his estate. His name's Gonzago. The story is extant, and written in 260 very choice Italian. You shall see anon how the mur-derer gets the love of Gonzago's wife.
                              *[*CLAUDIUS *rises.]*

OPHELIA: The King rises.

HAMLET: What, frighted with false fire?

QUEEN: How fares my lord?   265

---

224 **spirits** vital spirits   228 **doth . . . much** makes too many prom-ises and protestations   230 **argument** plot   231–233 **offense . . . offense** cause for objection . . . actual injury, crime   232 **jest** make believe   235 **Tropically** figuratively. (The First Quarto reading, *trapically,* suggests a pun on *trap* in *Mousetrap.*)   237 **Duke's** i.e., King's. (A slip that may be due to Shakespeare's possible source, the alleged murder of the Duke of Urbino by Luigi Gonzaga in 1538.)   239 **free** guiltless   240 **galled jade** horse whose hide is rubbed by saddle or harness   240–241 **withers** the part between the horse's shoulder blades   241 **unwrung** not rubbed sore   243 **chorus** (In many Elizabethan plays, the forthcoming action was explained by an actor known as the "chorus"; at a puppet show, the actor who spoke the dialogue was known as an "interpreter," as indicated by the lines following.)

244 **interpret** (1) ventriloquize the dialogue, as in a puppet show (2) act as pander   245 **puppets dallying** (With suggestion of sexual play, continued in *keen,* "sexually aroused," *groaning,* "moaning in pregnancy," and *edge,* "sexual desire" or "impetuosity.")   246 **keen** sharp, bitter   249 **Still . . . worse** more keen, always *better-ing* what other people say with witty wordplay, but at the same time more offensive   250 **So** even thus (in marriage).   **mis-take** take falseheartedly and cheat on. (The marriage vows say "for better, for worse.")   254 **Confederate season** the time and occasion conspir-ing (to assist the murderer).   **else** otherwise.   **seeing** seeing me   256 **Hecate's ban** the curse of Hecate, the goddess of witchcraft   257 **dire property** baleful quality   259 **estate** i.e., the kingship   260 **His** i.e., the King's   264 **false fire** the blank discharge of a gun loaded with powder but no shot

POLONIUS: Give o'er the play.

KING: Give me some light. Away!

POLONIUS: Lights, lights, lights!
                         Exeunt all but HAMLET *and* HORATIO.

HAMLET:
               "Why, let the stricken deer go weep,
270   The hart ungallèd play.
               For some must watch, while some must sleep;
                      Thus runs the world away."
               Would not this, sir, and a forest of feathers—if the rest
               of my fortunes turn Turk with me—with two Provin-
275   cial roses on my razed shoes, get me a fellowship in a
               cry of players?

HORATIO: Half a share.

HAMLET: A whole one, I.
               "For thou dost know, O Damon dear,
280   This realm dismantled was
               Of Jove himself, and now reigns here
                      A very, very—pajock."

HORATIO: You might have rhymed.

HAMLET: O good Horatio, I'll take the ghost's word for a
285   thousand pound. Didst perceive?

HORATIO: Very well, my lord.

HAMLET: Upon the talk of the poisoning?

Hamlet and Horatio (Stephen Dillane) discuss the result of their scheme.

HORATIO: I did very well note him.

                      Enter ROSENCRANTZ *and* GUILDENSTERN.

HAMLET: Aha! Come, some music! Come, the
               recorders.   290
                  "For if the King like not the comedy,
                      Why then, belike, he likes it not, perdy."
               Come, some music.

GUILDENSTERN: Good my lord, vouchsafe me a word
               with you.   295

HAMLET: Sir, a whole history.

GUILDENSTERN: The King, sir—

HAMLET: Ay, sir, what of him?

GUILDENSTERN: Is in his retirement marvelous
               distempered.   300

HAMLET: With drink, sir?

GUILDENSTERN: No, my lord, with choler.

269–272 Why . . . away (Probably from an old ballad, with allusion to the popular belief that a wounded deer retires to weep and die; compare with *As You Like It*, 2.1.33–66.)   **270 ungallèd** unafflicted   **271 watch** remain awake   **272 Thus . . . away** thus the world goes   **273 this** i.e., the play.   **feathers** (Allusion to the plumes that Elizabethan actors were fond of wearing.)   **274 turn Turk with** turn renegade against, go back on   **275 Provincial roses** rosettes of ribbon, named for roses grown in a part of France.   **razed** with ornamental slashing   **275–276 fellowship . . . players** partnership in a theatrical company   **276 cry** pack (of hounds)   **279 Damon** the friend of Pythias, as Horatio is friend of Hamlet; or, a traditional pastoral name   **280–282 This realm . . . pajock** i.e., Jove, representing divine authority and justice, has abandoned this realm to its own devices, leaving in his stead only a peacock or vain pretender to virtue (though the rhyme-word expected in place of *pajock* or "peacock" suggests that the realm is now ruled over by an "ass").   **280 dismantled** stripped, divested

---

290 recorders wind instruments of the flute kind   **292 perdy** (A corruption of the French *par dieu*, "by God.")   **299 retirement** withdrawal to his chambers   **300 distempered** out of humor. (But Hamlet deliberately plays on the wider application to any illness of mind or body, as in lines 335–336, especially to drunkenness.)   **302 choler** anger. (But Hamlet takes the word in its more basic humoral sense of "bilious disorder.")

HAMLET: Your wisdom should show itself more richer to signify this to the doctor, for for me to put him to his purgation would perhaps plunge him into more choler.

GUILDENSTERN: Good my lord, put your discourse into some frame and start not so wildly from my affair.

HAMLET: I am tame, sir. Pronounce.

GUILDENSTERN: The Queen, your mother, in most great affliction of spirit, hath sent me to you.

HAMLET: You are welcome.

GUILDENSTERN: Nay, good my lord, this courtesy is not of the right breed. If it shall please you to make me a wholesome answer, I will do your mother's commandment; if not, your pardon and my return shall be the end of my business.

HAMLET: Sir, I cannot.

ROSENCRANTZ: What, my lord?

HAMLET: Make you a wholesome answer; my wit's diseased. But, sir, such answer as I can make, you shall command, or rather, as you say, my mother. Therefore no more, but to the matter. My mother, you say—

ROSENCRANTZ: Then thus she says: your behavior hath struck her into amazement and admiration.

HAMLET: O wonderful son, that can so stonish a mother! But is there no sequel at the heels of this mother's admiration? Impart.

ROSENCRANTZ: She desires to speak with you in her closet ere you go to bed.

HAMLET: We shall obey, were she ten times our mother. Have you any further trade with us?

ROSENCRANTZ: My lord, you once did love me.

HAMLET: And do still, by these pickers and stealers.

ROSENCRANTZ: Good my lord, what is your cause of distemper? You do surely bar the door upon your own liberty if you deny your griefs to your friend.

HAMLET: Sir, I lack advancement.

ROSENCRANTZ: How can that be, when you have the voice of the King himself for your succession in Denmark?

HAMLET: Ay, sir, but "While the grass grows"—the proverb is something musty.

Enter the PLAYERS *with recorders.*

O, the recorders. Let me see one. *[He takes a recorder.]* To withdraw with you: why do you go about to recover the wind of me, as if you would drive me into a toil?

GUILDENSTERN: O, my lord, if my duty be too bold, my love is too unmannerly.

HAMLET: I do not well understand that. Will you play upon this pipe?

GUILDENSTERN: My lord, I cannot.

HAMLET: I pray you.

GUILDENSTERN: Believe me, I cannot.

HAMLET: I do beseech you.

GUILDENSTERN: I know no touch of it, my lord.

HAMLET: It is as easy as lying. Govern these ventages with your fingers and thumb, give it breath with your

---

305 **purgation** (Hamlet hints at something going beyond medical treatment to blood-letting and the extraction of confession.) 308 **frame** order. **start** shy or jump away (like a horse; the opposite of *tame* in line 309) 314 **breed** (1) kind (2) breeding, manners 316 **pardon** permission to depart 325 **admiration** bewilderment 330 **closet** private chamber

334 **pickers and stealers** i.e., hands. (So called from the catechism, "to keep my hands from picking and stealing.") 337 **liberty** i.e., being freed from *distemper* (line 336); but perhaps with a veiled threat as well. **deny** refuse to share 342 **While . . . grows** (The rest of the proverb is "the silly horse starves"; Hamlet may not live long enough to succeed to the kingdom.) 343 **something** somewhat. **s.d. Players** actors 345 **withdraw** speak privately 345–346 **recover the wind** get to the windward side (thus driving the game into the *toil*, or "net") 346 **toil** snare 347–348 **if . . . unmannerly** if I am using an unmannerly boldness, it is my love that occasions it 349 **I . . . that** i.e., I don't understand how genuine love can be unmannerly 356 **ventages** finger-holes or *stops* (line 359) of the recorder

mouth, and it will discourse most eloquent music. Look you, these are the stops.

360 GUILDENSTERN: But these cannot I command to any utterance of harmony. I have not the skill.

HAMLET: Why, look you now, how unworthy a thing you make of me! You would play upon me, you would seem to know my stops, you would pluck out the
365 heart of my mystery, you would sound me from my lowest note to the top of my compass, and there is much music, excellent voice, in this little organ, yet cannot you make it speak. 'Sblood, do you think I am easier to be played on than a pipe? Call me what
370 instrument you will, though you can fret me, you cannot play upon me.

Enter POLONIUS.

God bless you, sir!

POLONIUS: My lord, the Queen would speak with you, and presently.

375 HAMLET: Do you see yonder cloud that's almost in shape of a camel?

POLONIUS: By the Mass and 'tis, like a camel indeed.

HAMLET: Methinks it is like a weasel.

POLONIUS: It is backed like a weasel.

380 HAMLET: Or like a whale.

POLONIUS: Very like a whale.

HAMLET: Then I will come to my mother by and by. *[Aside.]* They fool me to the top of my bent.—I will come by and by.

385 POLONIUS : I will say so. *[Exit.]*

HAMLET: "By and by" is easily said. Leave me, friends.
[Exeunt all but HAMLET.*]*
'Tis now the very witching time of night,
When churchyards yawn and hell itself breathes out
Contagion to this world. Now could I drink hot blood
And do such bitter business as the day 390
Would quake to look on. Soft, now to my mother.
O heart, lose not thy nature! Let not ever
The soul of Nero enter this firm bosom.
Let me be cruel, not unnatural;
I will speak daggers to her, but use none. 395
My tongue and soul in this be hypocrites:
How in my words soever she be shent,
To give them seals never my soul consent! *Exit.*

3.3 *Enter* KING, ROSENCRANTZ,
and GUILDENSTERN.

KING: I like him not, nor stands it safe with us
To let his madness range. Therefore prepare you.
I your commission will forthwith dispatch,
And he to England shall along with you.
The terms of our estate may not endure 5
Hazard so near 's as doth hourly grow
Out of his brows.

GUILDENSTERN: We will ourselves provide.
Most holy and religious fear it is
To keep those many many bodies safe
That live and feed upon Your Majesty. 10

ROSENCRANTZ: The single and peculiar life is bound
With all the strength and armor of the mind
To keep itself from noyance, but much more
That spirit upon whose weal depends and rests
The lives of many. The cess of majesty 15

---

365 sound (1) fathom (2) produce sound in **366 compass** range (of voice) **367 organ** musical instrument **370 fret** irritate (with a quibble on *fret*, meaning the piece of wood, gut, or metal that regulates the fingering on an instrument) **374 presently** at once **382 by and by** quite soon **383 fool me** trifle with me, humor my fooling. **top of my bent** limit of my ability or endurance. (Literally, the extent to which a bow may be bent.)

387 witching time time when spells are cast and evil is abroad **392 nature** natural feeling **393 Nero** murderer of his mother, Agrippina **397 How . . . soever** however much by my words. **shent** rebuked **398 give them seals** i.e., confirm them with deeds

3.3. Location: The castle.
1 him i.e., his behavior **3 dispatch** prepare, cause to be drawn up **5 terms of our estate** circumstances of my royal position **7 Out of his brows** i.e., from his brain, in the form of plots and threats **8 religious fear** sacred concern **11 single and peculiar** individual and private **13 noyance** harm **15 cess** decease, cessation

Dies not alone, but like a gulf doth draw
What's near it with it; or it is a massy wheel
Fixed on the summit of the highest mount,
To whose huge spokes ten thousand lesser things
20 Are mortised and adjoined, which, when it falls,
Each small annexment, petty consequence,
Attends the boisterous ruin. Never alone
Did the King sigh, but with a general groan.

KING: Arm you, I pray you, to this speedy voyage,
25   For we will fetters put about this fear,
          Which now goes too free-footed.

ROSENCRANTZ: We will haste us.
              *Exeunt gentlemen [*ROSENCRANTZ
                    and GUILDENSTERN*].*

              Enter POLONIUS.

POLONIUS: My lord, he's going to his mother's closet.
            Behind the arras I'll convey myself
            To hear the process. I'll warrant she'll tax him home,
30   And, as you said—and wisely was it said—
            'Tis meet that some more audience than a mother,
            Since nature makes them partial, should o'erhear
            The speech, of vantage. Fare you well, my liege.
            I'll call upon you ere you go to bed
35   And tell you what I know.

KING: Thanks, dear my lord.
                     *Exit [*POLONIUS*].*
          O, my offense is rank! It smells to heaven.
          It hath the primal eldest curse upon 't,
          A brother's murder. Pray can I not,
          Though inclination be as sharp as will;

My stronger guilt defeats my strong intent,   40
And like a man to double business bound
I stand in pause where I shall first begin,
And both neglect. What if this cursèd hand
Were thicker than itself with brother's blood,
Is there not rain enough in the sweet heavens   45
To wash it white as snow? Whereto serves mercy
But to confront the visage of offense?
And what's in prayer but this twofold force,
To be forestallèd ere we come to fall,
Or pardoned being down? Then I'll look up.   50
My fault is past. But O, what form of prayer
Can serve my turn? "Forgive me my foul murder"?
That cannot be, since I am still possessed
Of those effects for which I did the murder:
My crown, mine own ambition, and my queen.   55
May one be pardoned and retain th' offense?
In the corrupted currents of this world
Offense's gilded hand may shove by justice,
And oft 'tis seen the wicked prize itself
Buys out the law. But 'tis not so above.   60
There is no shuffling, there the action lies
In his true nature, and we ourselves compelled,
Even to the teeth and forehead of our faults,
To give in evidence. What then? What rests?
Try what repentance can. What can it not?   65
Yet what can it, when one cannot repent?
O wretched state, O bosom black as death,
O limèd soul that, struggling to be free,
Art more engaged! Help, angels! Make assay.
Bow, stubborn knees, and heart with strings of steel, 70
Be soft as sinews of the newborn babe!
All may be well.   *[He kneels.]*

---

16 gulf whirlpool   **17 massy** massive   **20 mortised** fastened (as
with a fitted joint).   **when it falls** i.e., when it descends, like the
wheel of Fortune, bringing a king down with it   **21 Each . . . consequence** i.e., every hanger-on and unimportant person or thing connected with the King   **22 Attends** participates in   **24 Arm** prepare
28 arras screen of tapestry placed around the walls of household
apartments. (On the Elizabethan stage, the arras was presumably
over a door or discovery space in the tiring-house facade.)   **29 process** proceedings.   **tax him home** reprove him severely   **31 meet**
fitting   **33 of vantage** from an advantageous place, or, in addition
37 the primal eldest curse the curse of Cain, the first murderer; he
killed his brother Abel   **39 Though . . . will** though my desire is as
strong as my determination

---

41 bound (1) destined (2) obliged. (The King wants to repent and still
enjoy what he has gained.)   **46–47 Whereto . . . offense** what function does mercy serve other than to meet sin face to face?   **49 forestallèd** prevented (from sinning)   **56 th' offense** the thing for which
one offended   **57 currents** courses   **58 gilded hand** hand offering
gold as a bribe.   **shove by** thrust aside   **59 wicked prize** prize
won by wickedness   **61 There** i.e., in heaven.   **shuffling** escape by
trickery.   **the action lies** the accusation is made manifest. (A legal
metaphor.)   **62 his** its   **63 to the teeth and forehead** face to face,
concealing nothing   **64 give in** provide.   **rests** remains   **68 limèd**
caught as with birdlime, a sticky substance used to ensnare birds
69 engaged entangled.   **assay** trial. (Said to himself.)

Hamlet sits armed in the confessional. Claudius prays, but he hesitates.

Enter HAMLET.

HAMLET: Now might I do it pat, now 'a is a-praying;
And now I'll do 't. *[He draws his sword.]* And so 'a goes
　　to heaven,
75 And so am I revenged. That would be scanned:
A villain kills my father, and for that,
I, his sole son, do this same villain send
To heaven.
Why, this is hire and salary, not revenge.
80 'A took my father grossly, full of bread,
With all his crimes broad blown, as flush as May;
And how his audit stands who knows save heaven?
But in our circumstance and course of thought
'Tis heavy with him. And am I then revenged,
85 To take him in the purging of his soul,
When he is fit and seasoned for his passage?
No!
Up, sword, and know thou a more horrid hent.
　　　　　　　　　　　[He puts up his sword.]

When he is drunk asleep, or in his rage,
Or in th' incestuous pleasure of his bed,　　　　90
At game, a-swearing, or about some act
That has no relish of salvation in 't—
Then trip him, that his heels may kick at heaven,
And that his soul may be as damned and black
As hell, whereto it goes. My mother stays.　　　95
This physic but prolongs thy sickly days.　　　*Exit.*

KING:　　My words fly up, my thoughts remain below.
Words without thoughts never to heaven go.　　*Exit.*

3.4　　*Enter* [QUEEN] GERTRUDE *and* POLONIUS.

POLONIUS:　'A will come straight. Look you lay home to
　　him.
Tell him his pranks have been too broad to bear with,
And that Your Grace hath screened and stood
　　between
Much heat and him. I'll shroud me even here.
Pray you be round with him.　　　　　　　　　　5

HAMLET (*within*):　Mother, Mother, Mother!

QUEEN:　I'll warrant you, fear me not.
Withdraw, I hear him coming.
　　　　　　　*[*POLONIUS *hides behind the arras.]*

　　　　　　　　　　　　　Enter HAMLET.

HAMLET:　Now, Mother, what's the matter?

QUEEN:　Hamlet, thou hast thy father much offended.　10

HAMLET:　Mother, you have my father much offended.

QUEEN:　Come, come, you answer with an idle tongue.

HAMLET:　Go, go, you question with a wicked tongue.

---

73 **pat** opportunely　75 **would be scanned** needs to be looked into, or, would be interpreted as follows　80 **grossly, full of bread** i.e., enjoying his worldly pleasures rather than fasting. (See Ezekiel 16:49.)　81 **crimes broad blown** sins in full bloom.　**flush** vigorous　82 **audit** account.　**save** except for　83 **in . . . thought** as we see it from our mortal perspective　86 **seasoned** matured, readied　88 **know . . . hent** await to be grasped by me on a more horrid occasion.　**hent** act of seizing

---

89 **drunk . . . rage** dead drunk, or in a fit of sexual passion　91 **game** gambling　92 **relish** trace, savor　95 **stays** awaits (me)　96 **physic** purging (by prayer), or, Hamlet's postponement of the killing

3.4. Location: The Queen's private chamber.
1 **lay home** thrust to the heart, reprove him soundly　2 **broad** unrestrained　4 **Much heat** i.e., the King's anger.　**shroud** conceal (with ironic fitness to Polonius' imminent death. The word is only in the First Quarto; the Second Quarto and the Folio read "silence.")　5 **round** blunt　10 **thy father** i.e., your stepfather, Claudius　12 **idle** foolish

QUEEN: Why, how now, Hamlet?

HAMLET: What's the matter now?

15 QUEEN: Have you forgot me?

HAMLET: No, by the rood, not so:
You are the Queen, your husband's brother's wife,
And—would it were not so!—you are my mother.

QUEEN: Nay, then, I'll set those to you that can speak.

HAMLET: Come, come, and sit you down; you shall not
        budge.
20   You go not till I set you up a glass
        Where you may see the inmost part of you.

QUEEN: What wilt thou do? Thou wilt not murder me?
        Help, ho!

POLONIUS [behind the arras]: What ho! Help!

25 HAMLET [drawing]: How now? A rat? Dead for a ducat,
        dead!
                [He thrusts his rapier through the arras.]

POLONIUS [behind the arras]: O, I am slain!
                                [He falls and dies.]

QUEEN: O me, what hast thou done?

HAMLET: Nay, I know not. Is it the King?

QUEEN: O, what a rash and bloody deed is this!

HAMLET: A bloody deed—almost as bad, good Mother,
30   As kill a king, and marry with his brother.

QUEEN: As kill a king!

HAMLET: Ay, lady, it was my word.
                [He parts the arras and discovers POLONIUS.]
        Thou wretched, rash, intruding fool, farewell!
        I took thee for thy better. Take thy fortune.
        Thou find'st to be too busy is some danger.—
35   Leave wringing of your hands. Peace, sit you down,
        And let me wring your heart, for so I shall,

If it be made of penetrable stuff,
If damnèd custom have not brazed it so
That it be proof and bulwark against sense.

QUEEN: What have I done, that thou dar'st wag thy
        tongue   40
        In noise so rude against me?

HAMLET: Such an act
        That blurs the grace and blush of modesty,
        Calls virtue hypocrite, takes off the rose
        From the fair forehead of an innocent love
        And sets a blister there, makes marriage vows   45
        As false as dicers' oaths. O, such a deed
        As from the body of contraction plucks
        The very soul, and sweet religion makes
        A rhapsody of words. Heaven's face does glow
        O'er this solidity and compound mass   50
        With tristful visage, as against the doom,
        Is thought-sick at the act.

QUEEN: Ay me, what act,
        That roars so loud and thunders in the index?

HAMLET [showing her two likenesses]: Look here upon
        this picture, and on this,
        The counterfeit presentment of two brothers.   55
        See what a grace was seated on this brow:
        Hyperion's curls, the front of Jove himself,
        An eye like Mars to threaten and command,
        A station like the herald Mercury
        New-lighted on a heaven-kissing hill—   60
        A combination and a form indeed
        Where every god did seem to set his seal
        To give the world assurance of a man.

This was your husband. Look you now what follows:
65 Here is your husband, like a mildewed ear,
Blasting his wholesome brother. Have you eyes?
Could you on this fair mountain leave to feed
And batten on this moor? Ha, have you eyes?
You cannot call it love, for at your age
70 The heyday in the blood is tame, it's humble,
And waits upon the judgment, and what judgment
Would step from this to this? Sense, sure, you have,
Else could you not have motion, but sure that sense
Is apoplexed, for madness would not err,
75 Nor sense to ecstasy was ne'er so thralled,
But it reserved some quantity of choice
To serve in such a difference. What devil was 't
That thus hath cozened you at hoodman-blind?
Eyes without feeling, feeling without sight,
80 Ears without hands or eyes, smelling sans all,
Or but a sickly part of one true sense
Could not so mope. O shame, where is thy blush?
Rebellious hell,
If thou canst mutine in a matron's bones,
85 To flaming youth let virtue be as wax
And melt in her own fire. Proclaim no shame
When the compulsive ardor gives the charge,
Since frost itself as actively doth burn,
And reason panders will.

Hamlet confides in Gertrude.

QUEEN: O Hamlet, speak no more!   90
      Thou turn'st mine eyes into my very soul,
      And there I see such black and grainèd spots
      As will not leave their tint.

HAMLET: Nay, but to live
      In the rank sweat of an enseamèd bed,
      Stewed in corruption, honeying and making love   95
      Over the nasty sty!

QUEEN: O, speak to me no more!
      These words like daggers enter in my ears.
      No more, sweet Hamlet!

HAMLET: A murderer and a villain,
      A slave that is not twentieth part the tithe   100
      Of your precedent lord, a vice of kings,
      A cutpurse of the empire and the rule,
      That from a shelf the precious diadem stole
      And put it in his pocket!

QUEEN: No more!   105

---

65 ear i.e., of grain   **66 Blasting** blighting   **67 leave** cease   **68 batten** gorge.   **moor** barren or marshy ground (suggesting also "dark-skinned")   **70 heyday** state of excitement.   **blood** passion   **72 Sense** perception through the five senses (the functions of the middle or sensible soul)   **74 apoplexed** paralyzed. (Hamlet goes on to explain that, without such a paralysis of will, mere madness would not so err, nor would the five senses so enthrall themselves to *ecstasy* or lunacy; even such deranged states of mind would be able to make the obvious choice between Hamlet Senior and Claudius.)   **err** so err   **76 But** but that   **77 To . . . difference** to help in making a choice between two such men   **78 cozened** cheated.   **hoodman-blind** blindman's bluff. (In this game, says Hamlet, the devil must have pushed Claudius toward Gertrude while she was blindfolded.)   **80 sans** without   **82 mope** be dazed, act aimlessly   **84 mutine** incite mutiny   **85–86 be as wax . . . fire** melt like a candle or stick of sealing wax held over the candle flame   **86–89 Proclaim . . . will** call it no shameful business when the compelling ardor of youth delivers the attack, i.e, commits lechery, since the *frost* of advanced age burns with as active a fire of lust and reason perverts itself by fomenting lust rather than restraining it

---

92 grainèd dyed in grain, indelible   **93 leave their tint** surrender their color   **94 enseamèd** saturated in the grease and filth of passionate lovemaking   **95 Stewed** soaked, bathed (with a suggestion of "stew," brothel)   **100 tithe** tenth part   **101 precedent lord** former husband.   **vice** buffoon. (A reference to the Vice of the morality plays.)

Enter GHOST *[in his nightgown].*

HAMLET: A king of shreds and patches—
Save me, and hover o'er me with your wings,
You heavenly guards! What would your gracious
    figure?

QUEEN: Alas, he's mad!

110 **HAMLET:** Do you not come your tardy son to chide,
That, lapsed in time and passion, lets go by
Th' important acting of your dread command?
O, say!

GHOST: Do not forget. This visitation
115 Is but to whet thy almost blunted purpose.
But look, amazement on thy mother sits.
O, step between her and her fighting soul!
Conceit in weakest bodies strongest works.
Speak to her, Hamlet.

HAMLET: How is it with you, lady?

120 **QUEEN:** Alas, how is 't with you,
That you do bend your eye on vacancy,
And with th' incorporal air do hold discourse?
Forth at your eyes your spirits wildly peep,
And, as the sleeping soldiers in th' alarm,
125 Your bedded hair, like life in excrements,
Start up and stand on end. O gentle son,
Upon the heat and flame of thy distemper
Sprinkle cool patience. Whereon do you look?

HAMLET: On him, on him! Look you how pale he
    glares!
130 His form and cause conjoined, preaching to stones,
Would make them capable.—Do not look upon me,

Lest with this piteous action you convert
My stern effects. Then what I have to do
Will want true color—tears perchance for blood.

QUEEN: To whom do you speak this?   135

HAMLET: Do you see nothing there?

QUEEN: Nothing at all, yet all that is I see.

HAMLET: Nor did you nothing hear?

QUEEN: No, nothing but ourselves.

HAMLET: Why, look you there, look how it steals away!   140
My father, in his habit as he lived!
Look where he goes even now out at the portal!
          Exit GHOST.

QUEEN: This is the very coinage of your brain.
This bodiless creation ecstasy
Is very cunning in.   145

HAMLET: Ecstasy?
My pulse as yours doth temperately keep time,
And makes as healthful music. It is not madness
That I have uttered. Bring me to the test,
And I the matter will reword, which madness   150
Would gambol from. Mother, for love of grace,
Lay not that flattering unction to your soul
That not your trespass but my madness speaks.
It will but skin and film the ulcerous place,
Whiles rank corruption, mining all within,   155
Infects unseen. Confess yourself to heaven,
Repent what's past, avoid what is to come,
And do not spread the compost on the weeds
To make them ranker. Forgive me this my virtue;
For in the fatness of these pursy times   160
Virtue itself of vice must pardon beg,
Yea, curb and woo for leave to do him good.

---

106 shreds and patches i.e., motley, the traditional costume of the clown or fool   **111 lapsed** delaying   **112 important** importunate, urgent   **116 amazement** distraction   **118 Conceit** imagination **122 incorporal** immaterial   **124 as . . . alarm** like soldiers called out of sleep by an alarum   **125 bedded** laid flat.   **like life in excrements** i.e., as though hair, an outgrowth of the body, had a life of its own. (Hair was thought to be lifeless because it lacks sensation, and so its standing on end would be unnatural and ominous.)   **127 distemper** disorder   **130 His . . . conjoined** his appearance joined to his cause for speaking   **131 capable** receptive

---

132–133 convert . . . effects divert me from my stern duty   **134 want . . . blood** lack plausibility so that (with a play on the normal sense of *color*) I shall shed colorless tears instead of blood   **141 habit** clothes.   **as** as when   **143 very** mere   **144–145 This . . . in** madness is skillful in creating this kind of hallucination   **150 reword** repeat word for word   **151 gambol** skip away   **152 unction** ointment   **154 skin** grow a skin for   **155 mining** working under the surface   **158 compost** manure   **159 this my virtue** my virtuous talk in reproving you   **160 fatness** grossness.   **pursy** flabby, out of shape   **162 curb** bow, bend the knee.   **leave** permission

Hamlet kneels by Polonius's (Josef Sommer) dead body.

QUEEN: O Hamlet, thou hast cleft my heart in twain.

HAMLET: O, throw away the worser part of it,
165   And live the purer with the other half.
       Good night. But go not to my uncle's bed;
       Assume a virtue, if you have it not.
       That monster, custom, who all sense doth eat,
       Of habits devil, is angel yet in this,
170   That to the use of actions fair and good
       He likewise gives a frock or livery
       That aptly is put on. Refrain tonight,
       And that shall lend a kind of easiness
       To the next abstinence; the next more easy;
175   For use almost can change the stamp of nature,
       And either . . . the devil, or throw him out
       With wondrous potency. Once more, good night;
       And when you are desirous to be blest,
       I'll blessing beg of you. For this same lord,
       [pointing to POLONIUS*]*

I do repent; but heaven hath pleased it so   180
To punish me with this, and this with me,
That I must be their scourge and minister.
I will bestow him, and will answer well
The death I gave him. So, again, good night.
I must be cruel only to be kind.   185
This bad begins, and worse remains behind.
One word more, good lady.

QUEEN: What shall I do?

HAMLET: Not this by no means that I bid you do:
Let the bloat king tempt you again in bed,
Pinch wanton on your cheek, call you his mouse,   190
And let him, for a pair of reechy kisses,
Or paddling in your neck with his damned fingers,
Make you to ravel all this matter out
That I essentially am not in madness,
But mad in craft. 'Twere good you let him know,   195
For who that's but a queen, fair, sober, wise,
Would from a paddock, from a bat, a gib,
Such dear concernings hide? Who would do so?
No, in despite of sense and secrecy,
Unpeg the basket on the house's top,   200
Let the birds fly, and like the famous ape,
To try conclusions, in the basket creep
And break your own neck down.

QUEEN: Be thou assured, if words be made of breath,
And breath of life, I have no life to breathe   205
What thou hast said to me.

---

168 **who . . . eat** which consumes all proper or natural feeling, all sensibility   169 **Of habits devil** devil-like in prompting evil habits   171 **livery** an outer appearance, a customary garb (and hence a predisposition easily assumed in time of stress)   172 **aptly** readily   175 **use** habit.   **the stamp of nature** our inborn traits   176 **And either** (A defective line, usually emended by inserting the word *master* after *either,* following the Fourth Quarto and early editors.)   178–179 **when . . . you** i.e., when you are ready to be penitent and seek God's blessing, I will ask your blessing as a dutiful son should

182 **their scourge and minister** i.e., agent of heavenly retribution. (By *scourge,* Hamlet also suggests that he himself will eventually suffer punishment in the process of fulfilling heaven's will.)   183 **bestow** stow, dispose of.   **answer** account or pay for   186 **This** i.e., the killing of Polonius.   **behind** to come   189 **bloat** bloated   190 **Pinch wanton** i.e., leave his love pinches on your cheeks, branding you as wanton   191 **reechy** dirty, filthy   192 **paddling** fingering amorously   193 **ravel . . . out** unravel, disclose   195 **in craft** by cunning.   **good** (Said sarcastically; also the following eight lines.)   197 **paddock** toad.   **gib** tomcat   198 **dear concernings** important affairs   199 **sense and secrecy** secrecy that common sense requires   200 **Unpeg the basket** open the cage, i.e., let out the secret   201 **famous ape** (In a story now lost.)   202 **try conclusions** test the outcome (in which the ape apparently enters a cage from which birds have been released and then tries to fly out of the cage as they have done, falling to its death)   203 **down** in the fall; utterly

HAMLET: I must to England. You know that?

QUEEN: Alack,
I had forgot. 'Tis so concluded on.

HAMLET: There's letters sealed, and my two
schoolfellows,
210 Whom I will trust as I will adders fanged,
They bear the mandate; they must sweep my way
And marshal me to knavery. Let it work.
For 'tis the sport to have the enginer
Hoist with his own petard, and 't shall go hard
215 But I will delve one yard below their mines
And blow them at the moon. O, 'tis most sweet
When in one line two crafts directly meet.
This man shall set me packing.
I'll lug the guts into the neighbor room.
220 Mother, good night indeed. This counselor
Is now most still, most secret, and most grave,
Who was in life a foolish prating knave.—
Come, sir, to draw toward an end with you.—
Good night, Mother.

Exeunt [separately, HAMLET
dragging in POLONIUS*].*

4.1 *Enter* KING *and* QUEEN, *with* ROSENCRANTZ *and*
GUILDENSTERN.

211–212 **sweep . . . knavery** sweep a path before me and conduct me
to some *knavery* or treachery prepared for me   212 **work** proceed
213 **enginer** maker of military contrivances   214 **Hoist with**
blown up by.   **petard** an explosive used to blow in a door or make a
breach   214–215 **'t shall . . . will** unless luck is against me, I will
215 **mines** tunnels used in warfare to undermine the enemy's em-
placements; Hamlet will countermine by going under their mines
217 **in one line** i.e., mines and countermines on a collision course,
or the countermines directly below the mines.   **crafts** acts of guile,
plots   218 **set me packing** set me to making schemes, and set me to
lugging (him), and, also, send me off in a hurry   223 **draw . . . end**
finish up (with a pun on *draw*, "pull")

4.1. Location: The castle.
s.d. Enter . . . Queen (Some editors argue that Gertrude never exits
in 3.4 and that the scene is continuous here, as suggested in the
Folio, but the Second Quarto marks an entrance for her and at line
35 Claudius speaks of Gertrude's *closet* as though it were elsewhere.
A short time has elapsed, during which the King has become aware
of her highly wrought emotional state.)

KING: There's matter in these sighs, these profound
heaves.
You must translate; 'tis fit we understand them.
Where is your son?

QUEEN: Bestow this place on us a little while.
[Exeunt ROSENCRANTZ *and* GUILDENSTERN.*]*
Ah, mine own lord, what have I seen tonight!   5

KING: What, Gertrude? How does Hamlet?

QUEEN: Mad as the sea and wind when both contend
Which is the mightier. In his lawless fit,
Behind the arras hearing something stir,
Whips out his rapier, cries, "A rat, a rat!"   10
And in this brainish apprehension kills
The unseen good old man.

KING: O heavy deed!
It had been so with us, had we been there.
His liberty is full of threats to all—
To you yourself, to us, to everyone.   15
Alas, how shall this bloody deed be answered?
It will be laid to us, whose providence
Should have kept short, restrained, and out of haunt
This mad young man. But so much was our love,
We would not understand what was most fit,   20
But, like the owner of a foul disease,
To keep it from divulging, let it feed
Even on the pith of life. Where is he gone?

QUEEN: To draw apart the body he hath killed,
O'er whom his very madness, like some ore   25
Among a mineral of metals base,
Shows itself pure: 'a weeps for what is done.

KING: O Gertrude, come away!
The sun no sooner shall the mountains touch
But we will ship him hence, and this vile deed   30
We must with all our majesty and skill
Both countenance and excuse.—Ho, Guildenstern!

---

1 **matter** significance.   **heaves** heavy sighs   11 **brainish apprehension** headstrong conception   12 **heavy** grievous   13 **us** i.e.,
me. (The royal "we"; also in line 15.)   16 **answered** explained   17
providence foresight   18 **short** i.e., on a short tether.   **out of haunt**
secluded   22 **divulging** becoming evident   25 **ore** vein of gold   26
mineral mine   32 **countenance** put the best face on

Enter ROSENCRANTZ *and* GUILDENSTERN.

Friends both, go join you with some further aid.
Hamlet in madness hath Polonius slain,
35 And from his mother's closet hath he dragged him.
Go seek him out, speak fair, and bring the body
Into the chapel. I pray you, haste in this.
        [Exeunt ROSENCRANTZ *and* GUILDENSTERN.*]*
Come, Gertrude, we'll call up our wisest friends
And let them know both what we mean to do
40 And what's untimely done . . . .
Whose whisper o'er the world's diameter,
As level as the cannon to his blank,
Transports his poisoned shot, may miss our name
And hit the woundless air. O, come away!
45 My soul is full of discord and dismay.   *Exeunt.*

4.2   *Enter* HAMLET.

HAMLET: Safely stowed.

ROSENCRANTZ, GUILDENSTERN *(within)*:   Hamlet!
   Lord Hamlet!

HAMLET: But soft, what noise? Who calls on Hamlet?
5   O, here they come.

        Enter ROSENCRANTZ *and* GUILDENSTERN.

ROSENCRANTZ: What have you done, my lord, with the
   dead body?

HAMLET: Compounded it with dust, whereto 'tis kin.

ROSENCRANTZ: Tell us where 'tis, that we may take it
   thence
   And bear it to the chapel.

10 **HAMLET:**   Do not believe it.

ROSENCRANTZ: Believe what?

Rosencrantz and Guildenstern question Hamlet about Polonius's body.

HAMLET: That I can keep your counsel and not mine
   own. Besides, to be demanded of a sponge, what
   replication should be made by the son of a king?

ROSENCRANTZ: Take you me for a sponge, my lord?   15

HAMLET: Ay, sir, that soaks up the King's countenance,
   his rewards, his authorities. But such officers do the
   King best service in the end. He keeps them, like an
   ape, an apple, in the corner of his jaw, first mouthed
   to be last swallowed. When he needs what you have   20
   gleaned, it is but squeezing you, and, sponge, you shall
   be dry again.

ROSENCRANTZ: I understand you not, my lord.

HAMLET: I am glad of it. A knavish speech sleeps in a
   foolish ear.   25

ROSENCRANTZ: My lord, you must tell us where the
   body is and go with us to the King.

---

40 And . . . done (A defective line; conjectures as to the missing
words include *So, haply, slander* [Capell and others]; *For, haply,
slander* [Theobald and others]; and *So envious slander* [Jenkins].)
41 diameter extent from side to side   **42 As level** with as direct
aim.   **his blank** its target at point-blank range   **44 woundless**
invulnerable

4.2. Location: The castle.

12–13 That . . . own i.e., that I can follow your advice (by telling
where the body is) and still keep my own secret   **13 demanded of**
questioned by   **14 replication** reply   **16 countenance** favor   **17
authorities** delegated power, influence   **24 sleeps in** has no meaning to

Claudius asks Hamlet about Polonius.

HAMLET: The body is with the King, but the King is not with the body. The King is a thing—

30 **GUILDENSTERN:**   A thing, my lord?

HAMLET: Of nothing. Bring me to him. Hide fox, and all after!   *Exeunt [running].*

4.3   *Enter* KING, *and two or three.*

KING: I have sent to seek him, and to find the body.
How dangerous is it that this man goes loose!
Yet must not we put the strong law on him.
He's loved of the distracted multitude,
5   Who like not in their judgment, but their eyes,
And where 'tis so, th' offender's scourge is weighed,

28–29 The . . . body (Perhaps alludes to the legal commonplace of "the king's two bodies," which drew a distinction between the sacred office of kingship and the particular mortal who possessed it at any given time. Hence, although Claudius' body is necessarily a part of him, true kingship is not contained in it. Similarly, Claudius will have Polonius' body when it is found, but there is no kingship in this business either.)   **31 Of nothing** (1) of no account (2) lacking the essence of kingship, as in lines 28–29 and note   **31–32 Hide . . . after** (An old signal cry in the game of hide-and-seek, suggesting that Hamlet now runs away from them.)

4.3. Location: The castle.
4 of by.   **distracted** fickle, unstable   **5 Who . . . eyes** who choose not by judgment but by appearance   **6 scourge** punishment. (Literally, blow with a whip.)   **weighed** sympathetically considered

---

But never the offense. To bear all smooth and even,
This sudden sending him away must seem
Deliberate pause. Diseases desperate grown
By desperate appliance are relieved,   10
Or not at all.

                    Enter ROSENCRANTZ, *[*GUILDENSTERN,*]*
                    and all the rest.

        How now, what hath befall'n?

ROSENCRANTZ: Where the dead body is bestowed, my lord,
We cannot get from him.

KING: But where is he?

ROSENCRANTZ: Without, my lord; guarded, to know your pleasure.

KING: Bring him before us.

ROSENCRANTZ: Ho! Bring in the lord.   15

                    They enter [with HAMLET*].*

KING: Now, Hamlet, where's Polonius?

HAMLET: At supper.

KING: At supper? Where?

HAMLET: Not where he eats, but where 'a is eaten.
A certain convocation of politic worms are e'en at   20
him. Your worm is your only emperor for diet. We fat
all creatures else to fat us, and we fat ourselves for
maggots. Your fat king and your lean beggar is but
variable service—two dishes, but to one table. That's
the end.   25

KING: Alas, alas!

---

7 To . . . even to manage the business in an unprovocative way
9 Deliberate pause carefully considered action   **10 appliance** remedies   **20 politic worms** crafty worms (suited to a master spy like Polonius).   **e'en** even now   **21 Your worm** your average worm. (Compare *your fat king and your lean beggar* in line 23.)   **diet** food, eating (with a punning reference to the Diet of Worms, a famous *convocation* held in 1521)   **24 variable service** different courses of a single meal

HAMLET: A man may fish with the worm that hath
eat of a king, and eat of the fish that hath fed of that
worm.

30 **KING:** What dost thou mean by this?

HAMLET: Nothing but to show you how a king may go a
progress through the guts of a beggar.

KING: Where is Polonius?

HAMLET: In heaven. Send thither to see. If your mes-
35 senger find him not there, seek him i' th' other place
yourself. But if indeed you find him not within this
month, you shall nose him as you go up the stairs into
the lobby.

KING [*to some attendants*]: Go seek him there.

40 **HAMLET:** 'A will stay till you come. [*Exeunt attendants.*]

KING: Hamlet, this deed, for thine especial safety—
Which we do tender, as we dearly grieve
For that which thou hast done—must send thee hence
With fiery quickness. Therefore prepare thyself.
45 The bark is ready, and the wind at help,
Th' associates tend, and everything is bent
For England.

HAMLET: For England!

KING: Ay, Hamlet.

50 **HAMLET:** Good.

KING: So is it, if thou knew'st our purposes.

HAMLET: I see a cherub that sees them. But come, for
England! Farewell, dear mother.

KING: Thy loving father, Hamlet.

55 **HAMLET:** My mother. Father and mother is man and
wife, man and wife is one flesh, and so, my mother.
Come, for England! *Exit.*

KING: Follow him at foot; tempt him with speed aboard.
Delay it not. I'll have him hence tonight.
Away! For everything is sealed and done   60
That else leans on th' affair. Pray you, make haste.
[*Exeunt all but the* KING.]
And, England, if my love thou hold'st at aught—
As my great power thereof may give thee sense,
Since yet thy cicatrice looks raw and red
After the Danish sword, and thy free awe   65
Pays homage to us—thou mayst not coldly set
Our sovereign process, which imports at full,
By letters congruing to that effect,
The present death of Hamlet. Do it, England,
For like the hectic in my blood he rages,   70
And thou must cure me. Till I know 'tis done,
Howe'er my haps, my joys were ne'er begun   *Exit.*

4.4 Enter FORTINBRAS *with his army over the stage.*

FORTINBRAS: Go, Captain, from me greet the Danish
king.
Tell him that by his license Fortinbras
Craves the conveyance of a promised march
Over his kingdom. You know the rendezvous.
If that His Majesty would aught with us,   5
We shall express our duty in his eye;
And let him know so.

CAPTAIN: I will do 't, my lord.

FORTINBRAS: Go softly on.
[*Exeunt all but the* CAPTAIN.]

Enter HAMLET, ROSENCRANTZ,
[GUILDENSTERN,] *etc.*

---

28 **eat** eaten (Pronounced *et.*)   32 **progress** royal journey of
state   42 **tender** regard, hold dear.   **dearly** intensely   45 **bark**
sailing vessel   46 **tend** wait.   **bent** in readiness   52 **cherub**
(Cherubim are angels of knowledge. Hamlet hints that both he and
heaven are onto Claudius' tricks.)

58 **at foot** close behind, at heel   61 **leans on** bears upon, is related
to   62 **England** i.e., King of England.   **at aught** at any value   63
As . . . sense for so my great power may give you a just appreciation
of the importance of valuing my love   64 **cicatrice** scar   65 **free
awe** voluntary show of respect   66 **coldly set** regard with indifference   67 **process** command.   **imports at full** conveys specific
directions for   68 **congruing** agreeing   69 **present** immediate
70 **hectic** persistent fever   72 **haps** fortunes

4.4. Location: The coast of Denmark.
2 **license** permission   3 **the conveyance of** escort during   6 **duty**
respect.   **eye** presence   9 **softly** slowly, circumspectly

10 **HAMLET:** Good sir, whose powers are these?

CAPTAIN: They are of Norway, sir.

HAMLET: How purposed, sir, I pray you?

CAPTAIN: Against some part of Poland.

HAMLET: Who commands them, sir?

15 **CAPTAIN:** The nephew to old Norway, Fortinbras.

HAMLET: Goes it against the main of Poland, sir,
Or for some frontier?

CAPTAIN: Truly to speak, and with no addition,
We go to gain a little patch of ground
20 That hath in it no profit but the name.
To pay five ducats, five, I would not farm it;
Nor will it yield to Norway or the Pole
A ranker rate, should it be sold in fee.

HAMLET: Why, then the Polack never will defend it.

25 **CAPTAIN:** Yes, it is already garrisoned.

HAMLET: Two thousand souls and twenty thousand
ducats
Will not debate the question of this straw.
This is th' impostume of much wealth and peace,
That inward breaks, and shows no cause without
30 Why the man dies. I humbly thank you, sir.

CAPTAIN: God b' wi' you, sir.   *[Exit.]*

ROSENCRANTZ: Will 't please you go, my lord?

HAMLET: I'll be with you straight. Go a little before.
                    [Exeunt all except HAMLET.*]*
How all occasions do inform against me
And spur my dull revenge! What is a man,
35 If his chief good and market of his time
Be but to sleep and feed? A beast, no more.
Sure he that made us with such large discourse,

Looking before and after, gave us not
That capability and godlike reason
To fust in us unused. Now, whether it be   40
Bestial oblivion, or some craven scruple
Of thinking too precisely on th' event—
A thought which, quartered, hath but one part
          wisdom
And ever three parts coward—I do not know
Why yet I live to say "This thing's to do,"   45
Sith I have cause, and will, and strength, and means
To do 't. Examples gross as earth exhort me:
Witness this army of such mass and charge,
Led by a delicate and tender prince,
Whose spirit with divine ambition puffed   50
Makes mouths at the invisible event,
Exposing what is mortal and unsure
To all that fortune, death, and danger dare,
Even for an eggshell. Rightly to be great
Is not to stir without great argument,   55
But greatly to find quarrel in a straw
When honor's at the stake. How stand I, then,
That have a father killed, a mother stained,
Excitements of my reason and my blood,
And let all sleep, while to my shame I see   60
The imminent death of twenty thousand men
That for a fantasy and trick of fame
Go to their graves like beds, fight for a plot
Whereon the numbers cannot try the cause,
Which is not tomb enough and continent   65
To hide the slain? O, from this time forth
My thoughts be bloody or be nothing worth!   *Exit.*

---

38 **Looking before and after** able to review past events and antici-
pate the future   40 **fust** grow moldy   41 **oblivion** forgetfulness.
craven cowardly   42 **precisely** scrupulously.   **event** outcome   46
Sith since   47 **gross** obvious   48 **charge** expense   49 **delicate
and tender** of fine and youthful qualities   51 **Makes mouths** makes
scornful faces.   **invisible event** unforeseeable outcome   53 **dare**
could do (to him)   54–57 **Rightly . . . stake** true greatness does not
normally consist of rushing into action over some trivial provocation; however, when one's honor is involved, even a trifling insult
requires that one respond greatly (?)   57 **at the stake** (A metaphor
from gambling or bear-baiting.)   59 **Excitements of** promptings by
62 **fantasy** fanciful caprice, illusion.   **trick** trifle, deceit   63 **plot**
plot of ground   64 **Whereon . . . cause** on which there is insufficient room for the soldiers needed to engage in a military contest
65 **continent** receptacle, container

---

10 **powers** forces   16 **main** main part   18 **addition** exaggeration
21 **To pay** i.e., for a yearly rental of.   **farm it** take a lease of it   23
ranker higher.   **in fee** fee simple, outright   27 **debate . . . straw**
settle this trifling matter   28 **impostume** abscess   33 **inform
against** denounce, betray; take shape against   35 **market of** profit
of, compensation for   37 **discourse** power of reasoning

4.5   *Enter* HORATIO, [QUEEN] GERTRUDE, *and a*
GENTLEMAN.

QUEEN: I will not speak with her.

GENTLEMAN: She is importunate,
Indeed distract. Her mood will needs be pitied.

QUEEN: What would she have?

GENTLEMAN: She speaks much of her father, says she
hears
5   There's tricks i' the world, and hems, and beats her
heart,
Spurns enviously at straws, speaks things in doubt
That carry but half sense. Her speech is nothing,
Yet the unshapèd use of it doth move
The hearers to collection; they yawn at it,
10   And botch the words up fit to their own thoughts,
Which, as her winks and nods and gestures yield
them,
Indeed would make one think there might be thought,
Though nothing sure, yet much unhappily.

HORATIO: 'Twere good she were spoken with, for she
may strew
15   Dangerous conjectures in ill-breeding minds.

QUEEN: Let her come in.   *[Exit* GENTLEMAN.*]*
[Aside.] To my sick soul, as sin's true nature is,
Each toy seems prologue to some great amiss.
So full of artless jealousy is guilt,
20   It spills itself in fearing to be spilt.

Enter OPHELIA *[distracted].*

4.5. Location: The castle.
2 distract distracted   **5 tricks** deceptions.   **hems** makes "hmm"
sounds.   **heart** i.e., breast   **6 Spurns . . . straws** kicks spitefully,
takes offense at trifles.   **in doubt** obscurely   **8 unshapèd use**
incoherent manner   **9 collection** inference, a guess at some sort of
meaning.   **yawn** gape, wonder; grasp. (The Folio reading, *aim*, is
possible.)   **10 botch** patch   **11 Which** which words.   **yield** deliver,
represent   **12 thought** intended   **13 unhappily** unpleasantly near
the truth, shrewdly   **15 ill-breeding** prone to suspect the worst and
to make mischief   **18 toy** trifle.   **amiss** calamity   **19–20 So . . .
spilt** guilt is so full of suspicion that it unskillfully betrays itself
in fearing betrayal   **20 s.d. Enter Ophelia** (In the First Quarto,
Ophelia enters, "playing on a lute, and her hair down, singing.")

OPHELIA: Where is the beauteous majesty of Denmark?

QUEEN: How now, Ophelia?

OPHELIA *(she sings)*:
     "How should I your true love know
          From another one?
     By his cockle hat and staff,   25
          And his sandal shoon."

QUEEN: Alas, sweet lady, what imports this song?

OPHELIA: Say you? Nay, pray you, mark.
     "He is dead and gone, lady,   *(Song.)*
          He is dead and gone;   30
     At his head a grass-green turf,
          At his heels a stone."
     O, ho!

QUEEN: Nay, but Ophelia—

OPHELIA: Pray you, mark.   35
     [Sings.] "White his shroud as the mountain snow"—

Enter KING.

QUEEN: Alas, look here, my lord.

OPHELIA: "Larded with sweet flowers;   *(Song.)*
     Which bewept to the ground did not go
          With true-love showers."   40

KING: How do you, pretty lady?

OPHELIA: Well, God 'ild you! They say the owl was a
baker's daughter. Lord, we know what we are, but
know not what we may be. God be at your table!

KING: Conceit upon her father.   45

OPHELIA: Pray let's have no words of this; but when
they ask you what it means, say you this:
     "Tomorrow is Saint Valentine's day,   *(Song.)*
          All in the morning betime,

---

25 cockle hat hat with cockleshell stuck in it as a sign that the
wearer had been a pilgrim to the shrine of Saint James of Compos-
tela in Spain   **26 shoon** shoes   **38 Larded** decorated   **40 showers** i.e., tears   **42 God 'ild** God yield or reward.   **owl** (Refers to
a legend about a baker's daughter who was turned into an owl for
being ungenerous when Jesus begged a loaf of bread.)   **45 Conceit**
brooding   **49 betime** early

Ophelia (Diane Venora), having gone mad, speaks to the king and queen.

50 And I a maid at your window,
       To be your Valentine.
    Then up he rose, and donned his clothes,
       And dupped the chamber door,
    Let in the maid, that out a maid
55   Never departed more."

KING: Pretty Ophelia—

OPHELIA: Indeed, la, without an oath, I'll make an
    end on 't:
       [Sings.] "By Gis and by Saint Charity,
60   Alack, and fie for shame!
       You men will do 't, if they come to 't;
          By Cock, they are to blame.
       Quoth she, 'Before you tumbled me,
          You promised me to wed.'"

65 He answers:
       "'So would I ha' done, by yonder sun,
          An thou hadst not come to my bed.'"

KING: How long hath she been thus?

---

53 dupped did up, opened   **59 Gis** Jesus   **62 Cock** (A perversion
of "God" in oaths; here also with a quibble on the slang word for
penis.)   **67 An** if

OPHELIA: I hope all will be well. We must be patient,
    but I cannot choose but weep to think they would lay   70
    him i' the cold ground. My brother shall know of it.
    And so I thank you for your good counsel. Come, my
    coach! Good night, ladies, good night, sweet ladies,
    good night, good night.   *[Exit.]*

KING *[to* HORATIO*]*: Follow her close. Give her good   75
    watch, I pray you.
                                    [Exit HORATIO.*]*
    O, this is the poison of deep grief; it springs
    All from her father's death—and now behold!
    O Gertrude, Gertrude,
    When sorrows come, they come not single spies,
    But in battalions. First, her father slain;   80
    Next, your son gone, and he most violent author
    Of his own just remove; the people muddied,
    Thick and unwholesome in their thoughts and
          whispers
    For good Polonius' death—and we have done but
          greenly,
    In hugger-mugger to inter him; poor Ophelia   85
    Divided from herself and her fair judgment,
    Without the which we are pictures or mere beasts;
    Last, and as much containing as all these,
    Her brother is in secret come from France,
    Feeds on this wonder, keeps himself in clouds,   90
    And wants not buzzers to infect his ear
    With pestilent speeches of his father's death,
    Wherein necessity, of matter beggared,
    Will nothing stick our person to arraign
    In ear and ear. O my dear Gertrude, this,   95
    Like to a murdering piece, in many places
    Gives me superfluous death.   *A noise within.*

QUEEN: Alack, what noise is this?

---

79 spies scouts sent in advance of the main force   **82 remove**
removal.   **muddied** stirred up, confused   **84 greenly** in an inexperienced way, foolishly   **85 hugger-mugger** secret haste   **88 as
much containing** as full of serious matter   **90 Feeds . . . clouds**
feeds his resentment or shocked grievance, holds himself inscrutable
and aloof amid all this rumor   **91 wants** lacks.   **buzzers** gossip-
ers, informers   **93 necessity** i.e., the need to invent some plausible
explanation.   **of matter beggared** unprovided with facts   **94–95
Will . . . ear** will not hesitate to accuse my (royal) person in everybody's ears   **96 murdering piece** cannon loaded so as to scatter its
shot   **97 Gives . . . death** kills me over and over

KING: Attend!
100   Where is my Switzers? Let them guard the door.

Enter a MESSENGER.

What is the matter?

MESSENGER: Save yourself, my lord!
    The ocean, overpeering of his list,
    Eats not the flats with more impetuous haste
    Than young Laertes, in a riotous head,
105   O'erbears your officers. The rabble call him lord,
    And, as the world were now but to begin,
    Antiquity forgot, custom not known,
    The ratifiers and props of every word,
    They cry, "Choose we! Laertes shall be king!"
110   Caps, hands, and tongues applaud it to the clouds,
    "Laertes shall be king, Laertes king!"

QUEEN: How cheerfully on the false trail they cry!
               A noise within.
    O, this is counter, you false Danish dogs!

Enter LAERTES *with others.*

KING: The doors are broke.

115 **LAERTES:**   Where is this King?—Sirs, stand you all
    without.

ALL: No, let's come in.

LAERTES: I pray you, give me leave.

ALL: We will, we will.

LAERTES: I thank you. Keep the door. *[Exeunt*
    followers.] O thou vile king,
120   Give me my father!

QUEEN *[restraining him]*:   Calmly, good Laertes.

LAERTES: That drop of blood that's calm proclaims me
    bastard,
    Cries cuckold to my father, brands the harlot
    Even here, between the chaste unsmirchèd brow
    Of my true mother.

KING: What is the cause, Laertes,
    That thy rebellion looks so giantlike?   125
    Let him go, Gertrude. Do not fear our person.
    There's such divinity doth hedge a king
    That treason can but peep to what it would,
    Acts little of his will. Tell me, Laertes,
    Why thou art thus incensed. Let him go, Gertrude.   130
    Speak, man.

LAERTES: Where is my father?

KING: Dead.

QUEEN: But not by him.

KING: Let him demand his fill.

LAERTES: How came he dead? I'll not be juggled with.
    To hell, allegiance! Vows, to the blackest devil!
    Conscience and grace, to the profoundest pit!   135
    I dare damnation. To this point I stand,
    That both the worlds I give to negligence,
    Let come what comes, only I'll be revenged
    Most throughly for my father.

KING: Who shall stay you?   140

LAERTES: My will, not all the world's.
    And for my means, I'll husband them so well
    They shall go far with little.

KING: Good Laertes,
    If you desire to know the certainty
    Of your dear father, is 't writ in your revenge   145

---

99 Attend i.e., guard me   **100 Switzers** Swiss guards, mercenaries
102 overpeering of his list overflowing its shore, boundary   **103
flats** i.e., flatlands near shore.   **impetuous** violent (perhaps also
with the meaning of *impiteous* [*impitious,* Q2], "pitiless")   **104
head** insurrection   **106 as** as if   **108 The ratifiers . . . word** i.e.,
antiquity (or tradition) and *custom* ought to confirm (*ratify*) and
underprop our every word or promise   **110 Caps** (The caps are
thrown in the air.)   **113 counter** (A hunting term, meaning to follow
the trail in a direction opposite to that which the game has taken.)

123 between in the middle of   **126 fear our** fear for my   **127 hedge**
protect, as with a surrounding barrier   **128 can . . . would** can only
peep furtively, as through a barrier, at what it would intend   **129
Acts . . . will** (but) performs little of what it intends   **133 juggled
with** cheated, deceived   **136 To . . . stand** I am resolved in this
137 both . . . negligence i.e., both this world and the next are of no
consequence to me   **139 throughly** thoroughly   **141 My will . . .
world's** I'll stop (*stay*) when my will is accomplished, not for anyone
else's   **142 for** as for

That, swoopstake, you will draw both friend and foe,
Winner and loser?

LAERTES: None but his enemies.

KING: Will you know them, then?

150 **LAERTES:**   To his good friends thus wide I'll ope my
arms,
And like the kind life-rendering pelican
Repast them with my blood.

KING: Why, now you speak
Like a good child and a true gentleman.
That I am guiltless of your father's death,
155 And am most sensibly in grief for it,
It shall as level to your judgment 'pear
As day does to your eye.   *A noise within.*

LAERTES: How now, what noise is that?

Enter OPHELIA.

KING: Let her come in.

LAERTES: O heat, dry up my brains! Tears seven times
salt
160 Burn out the sense and virtue of mine eye!
By heaven, thy madness shall be paid with weight
Till our scale turn the beam. O rose of May!
Dear maid, kind sister, sweet Ophelia!
O heavens, is 't possible a young maid's wits
165 Should be as mortal as an old man's life?
Nature is fine in love, and where 'tis fine
It sends some precious instance of itself
After the thing it loves.

OPHELIA:
"They bore him barefaced on the bier,   *(Song.)*
170   Hey non nonny, nonny, hey nonny,
And in his grave rained many a tear—"
Fare you well, my dove!

Ophelia, driven mad, approaches the king and queen.

LAERTES: Hadst thou thy wits and didst persuade
revenge,
It could not move thus.

OPHELIA: You must sing "A-down a-down," and you   175
"call him a-down-a." O, how the wheel becomes it! It
is the false steward that stole his master's daughter.

LAERTES: This nothing's more than matter.

OPHELIA: There's rosemary, that's for remembrance;
pray you, love, remember. And there is pansies; that's   180
for thoughts.

LAERTES: A document in madness, thoughts and remembrance fitted.

OPHELIA: There's fennel for you, and columbines.
There's rue for you, and here's some for me; we may   185
call it herb of grace o' Sundays. You must wear your

---

146 **swoopstake** i.e., indiscriminately. (Literally, taking all stakes on the gambling table at once. *Draw* is also a gambling term, meaning "take from.")   151 **pelican** (Refers to the belief that the female pelican fed its young with its own blood.)   152 **Repast** feed   155 **sensibly** feelingly   156 **level** plain   160 **virtue** faculty, power   161 **paid with weight** repaid, avenged equally or more   162 **beam** cross-bar of a balance   166 **fine in** refined by   167 **instance** token   168 **After . . . loves** i.e., into the grave, along with Polonius

173 **persuade** argue cogently for   175–176 **You . . . a-down-a** (Ophelia assigns the singing of refrains, like her own "Hey non nonny," to others present.)   176 **wheel** spinning wheel as accompaniment to the song, or refrain   177 **false steward** (The story is unknown.)   178 **This . . . matter** this seeming nonsense is more eloquent than sane utterance   179 **rosemary** (Used as a symbol of remembrance both at weddings and at funerals.)   180 **pansies** (Emblems of love and courtship; perhaps from French *pensées*, "thoughts.")   182 **document** instruction, lesson   184 **fennel** (Emblem of flattery.)   **columbines** (Emblems of unchastity or ingratitude.)   185 **rue** (Emblem of repentance—a signification that is evident in its popular name, *herb of grace.*)

rue with a difference. There's a daisy. I would give you
some violets, but they withered all when my father
died. They say 'a made a good end— *[Sings.]* "For
190 bonny sweet Robin is all my joy."

LAERTES: Thought and affliction, passion, hell itself,
She turns to favor and to prettiness.

OPHELIA:
"And will 'a not come again?   *(Song.)*
And will 'a not come again?
195   No, no, he is head.
Go to thy deathbed,
He never will come again.

"His beard was as white as snow,
All flaxen was his poll.
200   He is gone, he is gone,
And we cast away moan.
God ha' mercy on his soul!"
And of all Christian souls, I pray God. God b' wi' you.
[Exit, followed by GERTRUDE.*]*

LAERTES: Do you see this, O God?

205 KING: Laertes, I must commune with your grief,
Or you deny me right. Go but apart,
Make choice of whom your wisest friends you will,
And they shall hear and judge twixt you and me.
If by direct or by collateral hand
210   They find us touched, we will our kingdom give,
Our crown, our life, and all that we call ours
To you in satisfaction; but if not,
Be you content to lend your patience to us,
And we shall jointly labor with your soul
215   To give it due content.

LAERTES: Let this be so.
His means of death, his obscure funeral—

No trophy, sword, nor hatchment o'er his bones,
No noble rite, nor formal ostentation—
Cry to be heard, as 'twere from heaven to earth,   220
That I must call 't in question.

KING: So you shall,
And where th' offense is, let the great ax fall.
I pray you, go with me.   *Exeunt.*

4.6   *Enter* HORATIO *and others.*

HORATIO: What are they that would speak with me?

GENTLEMAN: Seafaring men, sir. They say they have
letters for you.

HORATIO: Let them come in.   *[Exit* GENTLEMAN.*]*
I do not know from what part of the world   5
I should be greeted, if not from Lord Hamlet.

Enter SAILORS.

FIRST SAILOR: God bless you, sir.

HORATIO: Let him bless thee too.

FIRST SAILOR: 'A shall, sir, an 't please him. There's a
letter for you, sir—it came from th' ambassador that   10
was bound for England—if your name be Horatio, as
I am let to know it is.   *[He gives a letter.]*

HORATIO *[reads]*: "Horatio, when thou shalt have overlooked this, give these fellows some means to the
King; they have letters for him. Ere we were two   15
days old at sea, a pirate of very warlike appointment
gave us chase. Finding ourselves too slow of sail,
we put on a compelled valor, and in the grapple I
boarded them. On the instant they got clear of our
ship, so I alone became their prisoner. They have   20
dealt with me like thieves of mercy, but they knew

---

187 with a difference (A device used in heraldry to distinguish
one family from another on the coat of arms, here suggesting that
Ophelia and the others have different causes of sorrow and repentance; perhaps with a play on *rue* in the sense of "ruth," "pity.")
daisy (Emblem of dissembling, faithlessness.) **188 violets** (Emblems of faithfulness.) **191 Thought** melancholy. **passion** suffering **192 favor** grace, beauty **199 poll** head **207 whom** whichever of **209 collateral hand** indirect agency **210 us touched** me
implicated

217 trophy memorial. **hatchment** tablet displaying the armorial
bearings of a deceased person **218 ostentation** ceremony **220
That** so that. **call 't in question** demand an explanation

4.6. Location: The castle.
9 an 't if it **10 th' ambassador** (Evidently Hamlet. The sailor is
being circumspect.) **13–14 overlooked** looked over **14 means**
means of access **16 appointment** equipage **21 thieves of mercy**
merciful thieves

what they did: I am to do a good turn for them. Let
the King have the letters I have sent, and repair
thou to me with as much speed as thou wouldest fly
25 death. I have words to speak in thine ear will make
thee dumb, yet are they much too light for the bore
of the matter. These good fellows will bring thee
where I am. Rosencrantz and Guildenstern hold their
course for England. Of them I have much to tell thee.
30 Farewell.

       He that thou knowest thine, Hamlet."
Come, I will give you way for these your letters,
And do 't the speedier that you may direct me
To him from whom you brought them. *Exeunt.*

4.7 *Enter* KING *and* LAERTES.

KING: Now must your conscience my acquittance seal,
 And you must put me in your heart for friend,
 Sith you have heard, and with a knowing ear,
 That he which hath your noble father slain
5 Pursued my life.

LAERTES: It well appears. But tell me
 Why you proceeded not against these feats
 So crimeful and so capital in nature,
 As by your safety, greatness, wisdom, all things else,
 You mainly were stirred up.

10 **KING:** O, for two special reasons,
 Which may to you perhaps seem much unsinewed,
 But yet to me they're strong. The Queen his mother
 Lives almost by his looks, and for myself—
 My virtue or my plague, be it either which—
15 She is so conjunctive to my life and soul
 That, as the star moves not but in his sphere,
 I could not but by her. The other motive
 Why to a public count I might not go

Is the great love the general gender bear him,
Who, dipping all his faults in their affection, 20
Work like the spring that turneth wood to stone,
Convert his gyves to graces, so that my arrows,
Too slightly timbered for so loud a wind,
Would have reverted to my bow again
But not where I had aimed them. 25

LAERTES: And so have I a noble father lost,
 A sister driven into desperate terms,
 Whose worth, if praises may go back again,
 Stood challenger on mount of all the age
 For her perfections. But my revenge will come. 30

KING: Break not your sleeps for that. You must not think
 That we are made of stuff so flat and dull
 That we can let our beard be shook with danger
 And think it pastime. You shortly shall hear more.
 I loved your father, and we love ourself; 35
 And that, I hope, will teach you to imagine—

       Enter a MESSENGER *with letters.*

How now? What news?

MESSENGER: Letters, my lord, from Hamlet:
 This to Your Majesty, this to the Queen.
        [He gives letters.]

KING: From Hamlet? Who brought them?

MESSENGER: Sailors, my lord, they say. I saw them not. 40
 They were given me by Claudio. He received them
 Of him that brought them.

KING: Laertes, you shall hear them.—
 Leave us.   *[Exit* MESSENGER.*]*
 [He reads.] "High and mighty, you shall know I am set
 naked on your kingdom. Tomorrow shall I beg leave 45
 to see your kingly eyes, when I shall, first asking your

---

23 **repair** come 26 **bore** caliber, i.e., importance 31 **way** means
of access

4.7. Location: The castle.
1 **my acquittance seal** confirm or acknowledge my innocence 3
Sith since 6 **feats** acts 7 **capital** punishable by death 9 **mainly**
greatly 11 **unsinewed** weak 15 **conjunctive** closely united. (An
astronomical metaphor.) 16 **his** its. **sphere** one of the hollow
spheres in which, according to Ptolemaic astronomy, the planets
were supposed to move 18 **count** account, reckoning, indictment

---

19 **general gender** common people 21 **Work** operate, act. **spring**
i.e., a spring with such a concentration of lime that it coats a piece of
wood with limestone, in effect gilding and petrifying it 22 **gyves**
fetters (which, gilded by the people's praise, would look like badges
of honor) 23 **slightly timbered** light. **loud** (suggesting public
outcry on Hamlet's behalf) 24 **reverted** returned 27 **terms** state,
condition 28 **go back** i.e., recall what she was 29 **on mount** set up
on high 45 **naked** destitute, unarmed, without following

Claudius and Laertes (Michael Cumpsty) read Hamlet's letters.

pardon, thereunto recount the occasion of my sudden
and more strange return.   Hamlet."
What should this mean? Are all the rest come back?
50   Or is it some abuse, and no such thing?

LAERTES: Know you the hand?

KING: 'Tis Hamlet's character. "Naked"!
And in a postscript here he says "alone."
Can you devise me?

LAERTES: I am lost in it, my lord. But let him come.
55   It warms the very sickness in my heart
That I shall live and tell him to this teeth,
"Thus didst thou."

KING: If it be so, Laertes—
As how should it be so? How otherwise?—
Will you be ruled by me?

LAERTES: Ay, my lord,
60   So you will not o'errule me to a peace.

KING: To thine own peace. If he be now returned,
As checking at his voyage, and that he means
No more to undertake it, I will work him
To an exploit, now ripe in my device,
Under the which he shall not choose but fall;   65
And for his death no wind of blame shall breathe,
But even his mother shall uncharge the practice
And call it accident.

LAERTES: My lord, I will be ruled,
The rather if you could devise it so
That I might be the organ.

KING: It falls right.   70
You have been talked of since your travel much,
And that in Hamlet's hearing, for a quality
Wherein they say you shine. Your sum of parts
Did not together pluck such envy from him
As did that one, and that, in my regard,   75
Of the unworthiest siege.

LAERTES: What part is that, my lord?

KING: A very ribbon in the cap of youth,
Yet needful too, for youth no less becomes
The light and careless livery that it wears   80
Than settled age his sables and his weeds
Importing health and graveness. Two months since
Here was a gentleman of Normandy.
I have seen myself, and served against, the French,
And they can well on horseback, but this gallant   85
Had witchcraft in 't; he grew unto his seat,
And to such wondrous doing brought his horse
As had he been incorpsed and demi-natured
With the brass beast. So far he topped my thought
That I in forgery of shapes and tricks   90
Come short of what he did.

---

47 pardon permission   **50 abuse** deceit.   **no such thing** not what
it appears   **51 character** handwriting   **53 devise** explain to   **57
Thus didst thou** i.e., here's for what you did to my father   **58 As . . .
otherwise** how can this (Hamlet's return) be true? Yet how otherwise than true (since we have the evidence of his letter)?   **60 So**
provided that

62 checking at i.e., turning aside from (like a falcon leaving the
quarry to fly at a chance bird).   **that** if   **64 device** devising, invention   **67 uncharge the practice** acquit the stratagem of being a plot
70 organ agent, instrument   **73 Your . . . parts** i.e., all your other
virtues   **76 unworthiest siege** least important rank   **79 no less
becomes** is no less suited by   **81 his sables** its rich robes furred with
sable.   **weeds** garments   **82 Importing . . . graveness** signifying a
concern for health and dignified prosperity; also, giving an impression of comfortable prosperity   **85 can well** are skilled   **88 As . . .
demi-natured** as if he had been of one body and nearly of one nature
(like the centaur)   **89 topped** surpassed   **90 forgery** imagining

Claudius persuades Laertes to his plans.

LAERTES: A Norman was 't?

KING: A Norman.

LAERTES: Upon my life, Lamord.

KING: The very same.

LAERTES: I know him well. He is the brooch indeed
95   And gem of all the nation.

KING: He made confession of you,
        And gave you such a masterly report
        For art and exercise in your defense,
        And for your rapier most especial,
100   That he cried out 'twould be a sight indeed
        If one could match you. Th' escrimers of their nation,
        He swore, had neither motion, guard, nor eye
        If you opposed them. Sir, this report of his
        Did Hamlet so envenom with his envy
105   That he could nothing do but wish and beg
        Your sudden coming o'er, to play with you.
        Now, out of this—

---

94 **brooch** ornament   96 **confession** testimonial, admission of superiority   98 **For . . . defense** with respect to your skill and practice with your weapon   101 **escrimers** fencers   106 **sudden** immediate. **play** fence

LAERTES: What out of this, my lord?

KING: Laertes, was your father dear to you?
        Or are you like the painting of a sorrow,
        A face without a heart?

LAERTES: Why ask you this?   110

KING: Not that I think you did not love your father,
        But that I know love is begun by time,
        And that I see, in passages of proof,
        Time qualifies the spark and fire of it.
        There lives within the very flame of love   115
        A kind of wick or snuff that will abate it,
        And nothing is at a like goodness still,
        For goodness, growing to a pleurisy,
        Dies in his own too much. That we would do,
        We should do when we would; for this "would" changes   120
        And hath abatements and delays as many
        As there are tongues, are hands, are accidents,
        And then this "should" is like a spendthrift sigh,
        That hurts by easing. But, to the quick o' th' ulcer:
        Hamlet comes back. What would you undertake   125
        To show yourself in deed your father's son
        More than in words?

LAERTES: To cut his throat i' the church.

KING: No place, indeed, should murder sanctuarize;
        Revenge should have no bounds. But good Laertes,
        Will you do this, keep close within your chamber.   130
        Hamlet returned shall know you are come home.

---

112 **begun by time** i.e., created by the right circumstance and hence subject to change   113 **passages of proof** actual instances that prove it   114 **qualifies** weakens, moderates   116 **snuff** the charred part of a candlewick   117 **nothing . . . still** nothing remains at a constant level of perfection   118 **pleurisy** excess, plethora. (Literally, a chest inflammation.)   119 **in . . . much** of its own excess. **That** that which   121 **abatements** diminutions   122 **As . . . accidents** as there are tongues to dissuade, hands to prevent, and chance events to intervene   123 **spendthrift sigh** (An allusion to the belief that sighs draw blood from the heart.)   124 **hurts by easing** i.e., costs the heart blood and wastes precious opportunity even while it affords emotional relief.   **quick o' th' ulcer** i.e., heart of the matter   128 **sanctuarize** protect from punishment. (Alludes to the right of sanctuary with which certain religious places were invested.)   130 **Will you do this** if you wish to do this

We'll put on those shall praise your excellence
And set a double varnish on the fame
The Frenchman gave you, bring you in fine together,
135 And wager on your heads. He, being remiss,
Most generous, and free from all contriving,
Will not peruse the foils, so that with ease,
Or with a little shuffling, you may choose
A sword unbated, and in a pass of practice
140 Requite him for your father.

LAERTES: I will do 't,
And for that purpose I'll anoint my sword.
I bought an unction of a mountebank
So mortal that, but dip a knife in it,
Where it draws blood no cataplasm so rare,
145 Collected from all simples that have virtue
Under the moon, can save the thing from death
That is but scratched withal. I'll touch my point
With this contagion, that if I gall him slightly,
It may be death.

KING: Let's further think of this,
150 Weigh what convenience both of time and means
May fit us to our shape. If this should fail,
And that our drift look through our bad performance,
'Twere better not assayed. Therefore this project
Should have a back or second, that might hold
155 If this did blast in proof. Soft, let me see.
We'll make a solemn wager on your cunnings—
I ha 't!
When in your motion you are hot and dry—
As make your bouts more violent to that end—
160 And that he calls for drink, I'll have prepared him
A chalice for the nonce, whereon but sipping,

If he by chance escape your venomed stuck,
Our purpose may hold there. *[A cry within.]* But stay,
what noise?

Enter QUEEN.

QUEEN: One woe doth tread upon another's heel,
So fast they follow. Your's sister's drowned, Laertes.   165

LAERTES: Drowned! O, where?

QUEEN: There is a willow grows askant the brook,
That shows his hoar leaves in the glassy stream;
Therewith fantastic garlands did she make
Of crowflowers, nettles, daisies, and long purples,   170
That liberal shepherds give a grosser name,
But our cold maids do dead men's fingers call them.
There on the pendent boughs her crownet weeds
Clamb'ring to hang, an envious sliver broke,
When down her weedy trophies and herself   175
Fell in the weeping brook. Her clothes spread wide,
And mermaidlike awhile they bore her up,
Which time she chanted snatches of old lauds,
As one incapable of her own distress,
Or like a creature native and endued   180
Unto that element. But long it could not be
Till that her garments, heavy with their drink,
Pulled the poor wretch from her melodious lay
To muddy death.

LAERTES: Alas, then she is drowned?

QUEEN: Drowned, drowned.   185

LAERTES: Too much of water hast thou, poor Ophelia,
And therefore I forbid my tears. But yet
It is our trick; nature her custom holds,

---

132 put on those shall arrange for some to   **134 in fine** finally
135 remiss negligently unsuspicious   **136 generous** noble-minded
139 unbated not blunted, having no button.   **pass of practice**
treacherous thrust   **142 unction** ointment.   **mountebank** quack
doctor   **144 cataplasm** plaster or poultice   **145 simples** herbs.
virtue potency   **146 Under the moon** i.e., anywhere (with reference perhaps to the belief that herbs gathered at night had a special
power)   **148 gall** graze, wound   **151 shape** part we propose to act
152 drift . . . performance intention should be made visible by our
bungling   **155 blast in proof** burst in the test (like a cannon)   **156
cunnings** respective skills   **159 As** i.e., and you should   **161 nonce**
occasion

---

162 stuck thrust. (From *stoccado*, a fencing term.)   **167 askant**
aslant   **168 hoar leaves** white or gray undersides of the leaves
170 long purples early purple orchids   **171 liberal** free-spoken.
a grosser name (The testicle-resembling tubers of the orchid, which
also in some cases resemble *dead men's fingers*, have earned various
slang names like "dogstones" and "cullions.")   **172 cold** chaste
173 pendent overhanging.   **crownet** made into a chaplet or coronet
174 envious sliver malicious branch   **175 weedy** i.e., of plants   **178
lauds** hymns   **179 incapable of** lacking capacity to apprehend   **180
endued** adapted by nature   **188 It is our trick** i.e., weeping is our
natural way (when sad)

Let shame say what it will. *[He weeps.]* When these
are gone,
190 The woman will be out. Adieu, my lord.
I have a speech of fire that fain would blaze,
But that this folly douts it.   *Exit.*

KING: Let's follow, Gertrude.
How much I had to do to calm his rage!
Now fear I this will give it start again;
195 Therefore let's follow.   *Exeunt.*

5.1   *Enter two* CLOWNS *[with spades and mattocks].*

FIRST CLOWN: Is she to be buried in Christian burial,
when she willfully seeks her own salvation?

SECOND CLOWN: I tell thee she is; therefore make
her grave straight. The crowner hath sat on her, and
5 finds it Christian burial.

FIRST CLOWN: How can that be, unless she drowned
herself in her own defense?

SECOND CLOWN: Why, 'tis found so.

FIRST CLOWN: It must be *se offendendo,* it cannot
10 be else. For here lies the point: if I drown myself
wittingly, it argues an act, and an act hath three
branches—it is to act, to do, and to perform. Argal,
she drowned herself wittingly.

SECOND CLOWN: Nay, but hear you, goodman delver—

15 **FIRST CLOWN:**   Give me leave. Here lies the water;
good. Here stands the man; good. If the man go to

this water and drown himself, it is, will he, nill he, he
goes, mark you that. But if the water come to him and
drown him, he drowns not himself. Argal, he that is
not guilty of his own death shortens not his own life.   20

SECOND CLOWN: But is this law?

FIRST CLOWN: Ay, marry, is 't—crowner's quest law.

SECOND CLOWN: Will you ha' the truth on 't? If this
had not been a gentlewoman, she should have been
buried out o' Christian burial.   25

FIRST CLOWN: Why, there thou sayst. And the more
pity that great folk should have countenance in this
world to drown or hang themselves, more than their
even-Christian. Come, my spade. There is no ancient
gentlemen but gardeners, ditchers, and grave makers.   30
They hold up Adam's profession.

SECOND CLOWN: Was he a gentleman?

FIRST CLOWN: 'A was the first that ever bore arms.

SECOND CLOWN: Why, he had none.

FIRST CLOWN: What, art a heathen? How dost thou   35
understand the Scripture? The Scripture says Adam
digged. Could he dig without arms? I'll put another
question to thee. If thou answerest me not to the
purpose, confess thyself—

SECOND CLOWN: Go to.   40

FIRST CLOWN: What is he that builds stronger than
either the mason, the shipwright, or the carpenter?

SECOND CLOWN: The gallows maker, for that frame
outlives a thousand tenants.

FIRST CLOWN: I like thy wit well, in good faith. The   45
gallows does well. But how does it well? It does well to

189–190 When . . . out when my tears are all shed, the woman in me
will be expended, satisfied   **192 douts** extinguishes. (The Second
Quarto reads "drowns.")

5.1. Location: A churchyard.
s.d. Clowns rustics   **2 salvation** (A blunder for "damnation," or
perhaps a suggestion that Ophelia was taking her own shortcut to
heaven.)   **4 straight** straightway, immediately. (But with a pun on
strait, "narrow.")   **crowner** coroner.   **sat on her** conducted an in-
quest on her case   **5 finds it** gives his official verdict that her means
of death was consistent with   **8 found so** determined so in the coroner's verdict   **9 se offendendo** (A comic mistake for *se defendendo,* a
term used in verdicts of justifiable homicide.)   **12 Argal** (Corruption
of *ergo,* "therefore.")   **14 goodman** (An honorific title often used
with the name of a profession or craft.)

---

17 will he, nill he whether he will or no, willy-nilly   **22 quest** in-
quest   **26 there thou sayst** i.e., that's right   **27 countenance** privilege   **29 even-Christian** fellow Christians.   **ancient** going back to
ancient times   **31 hold up** maintain   **33 bore arms** (To be entitled
to bear a coat of arms would make Adam a gentleman, but as one
who bore a spade, our common ancestor was an ordinary delver in
the earth.)   **37 arms** i.e., the arms of the body   **39 confess thyself**
(The saying continues, "and be hanged.")   **43 frame** (1) gallows
(2) structure   **46 does well** (1) is an apt answer (2) does a good turn

those that do ill. Now thou dost ill to say the gallows is built stronger than the church. Argal, the gallows may do well to thee. To 't again, come.

50 **SECOND CLOWN:** "Who builds stronger than a mason, a shipwright, or a carpenter?"

FIRST CLOWN: Ay, tell me that, and unyoke.

SECOND CLOWN: Marry, now I can tell.

FIRST CLOWN: To 't.

55 **SECOND CLOWN:** Mass, I cannot tell.

Enter HAMLET *and* HORATIO *[at a distance].*

FIRST CLOWN: Cudgel thy brains no more about it, for your dull ass will not mend his pace with beating; and when you are asked this question next, say "a grave maker." The houses he makes lasts till doomsday. Go 60 get thee in and fetch me a stoup of liquor.

[Exit SECOND CLOWN. FIRST CLOWN *digs.]*
Song.

"In youth, when I did love, did love,
Methought it was very sweet,
To contract—O—the time for—a—my behove,
O, methought there—a—was nothing—a—
meet."

65 **HAMLET:** Has this fellow no feeling of his business, 'a sings in grave-making?

HORATIO: Custom hath made it in him a property of easiness

HAMLET: 'Tis e'en so. The hand of little employment 70 hath the daintier sense.

---

52 unyoke i.e., after this great effort, you may unharness the team of your wits **55 Mass** by the Mass **60 stoup** two-quart measure **61 In . . . love** (This and the two following stanzas, with nonsensical variations, are from a poem attributed to Lord Vaux and printed in *Tottel's Miscellany*, 1557. The *O* and *a* [for "ah"] seemingly are the grunts of the digger.) **63 To contract . . . behove** i.e., to shorten the time for my own advantage. (Perhaps he means to *prolong* it.) **64 meet** suitable, i.e., more suitable **65 'a** that he **67–68 property of easiness** something he can do easily and indifferently **70 daintier sense** more delicate sense of feeling

The First Clown (Billy Crystal) shows off a skull.

FIRST CLOWN: *Song.*
"But age with his stealing steps
Hath clawed me in his clutch,
And hath shipped me into the land,
As if I had never been such."
[He throws up a skull.]

HAMLET: That skull had a tongue in it and could sing 75 once. How the knave jowls it to the ground, as if 'twere Cain's jawbone, that did the first murder! This might be the pate of a politician, which this ass now o'erreaches, one that would circumvent God, might it not? 80

HORATIO: It might, my lord.

HAMLET: Or of a courtier, which could say, "Good morrow, sweet lord! How dost thou, sweet lord?" This might be my Lord Such-a-one, that praised my Lord Such-a-one's horse when 'a meant to beg it, 85 might it not?

HORATIO: Ay, my lord.

HAMLET: Why, e'en so, and now my Lady Worm's, chapless, and knocked about the mazard with a

---

73 into the land i.e., toward my grave (?) (But note the lack of rhyme in *steps, land*.) **76 jowls** dashes (with a pun on *jowl*, "jawbone") **78 politician** schemer, plotter **79 o'erreaches** circumvents, gets the better of (with a quibble on the literal sense) **89 chapless** having no lower jaw. **mazard** i.e., head. (Literally, a drinking vessel.)

90   sexton's spade. Here's fine revolution, an we had
the trick to see 't. Did these bones cost no more the
breeding but to play at loggets with them? Mine ache
to think on 't.

FIRST CLOWN: *Song.*
    "A pickax and a spade, a spade,
95   For and a shrouding sheet;
    O, a pit of clay for to be made
        For such a guest is meet."

                       [He throws up another skull.]

HAMLET: There's another. Why may not that be the
skull of a lawyer? Where be his quiddities now, his
100   quillities, his cases, his tenures, and his tricks? Why
does he suffer this mad knave now to knock him
about the sconce with a dirty shovel, and will not tell
him of his action of battery? Hum, this fellow might
be in 's time a great buyer of land, with his statutes,
105   his recognizances, his fines, his double vouchers, his
recoveries. Is this the fine of his fines and the recov-
ery of his recoveries, to have his fine pate full of fine
dirt? Will his vouchers vouch him no more of his
purchases, and double ones too, than the length and
110   breadth of a pair of indentures? The very conveyances
of his lands will scarcely lie in this box, and must th'
inheritor himself have no more, ha?

---

90 revolution turn of Fortune's wheel, change.   **an** if   **91 trick to
see** knack of seeing   **91–92 cost . . . but** involve so little expense and
care in upbringing that we may   **92 loggets** a game in which pieces
of hard wood shaped like Indian clubs or bowling pins are thrown
to lie as near as possible to a stake   **95 For and** and moreover   **99
quiddities** subtleties, quibbles. (From Latin *quid,* "a thing.")   **100
quillities** verbal niceties, subtle distinctions. (Variation of *quiddities.*)   **tenures** the holding of a piece of property or office, or the
conditions or period of such holding   **102 sconce** head   **103 action of battery** lawsuit about physical assault   **104–105 statutes,
recognizances** legal documents guaranteeing a debt by attaching
land and property   **105–106 fines, recoveries** ways of converting
entailed estates into "fee simple" or freehold   **105 double** signed by
two signatories.   **vouchers** guarantees of the legality of a title to
real estate   **106–108 fine of his fines . . . fine pate . . . fine dirt**
end of his legal maneuvers . . . elegant head . . . minutely sifted dirt
110 pair of indentures legal document drawn up in duplicate on
a single sheet and then cut apart on a zigzag line so that each pair
was uniquely matched. (Hamlet may refer to two rows of teeth or
dentures.)   **110 conveyances** deeds   **111 box** (1) deed box (2) coffin.
("Skull" has been suggested.)   **112 inheritor** possessor, owner

HORATIO: Not a jot more, my lord.

HAMLET: Is not parchment made of sheepskins?

HORATIO: Ay, my lord, and of calves' skins too.   115

HAMLET: They are sheep and calves which seek out
assurance in that. I will speak to this fellow.—Whose
grave's this, sirrah?

FIRST CLOWN: Mine, sir.
        [Sings.] "O, pit of clay for to be made   120
        For such a guest is meet."

HAMLET: I think it be thine, indeed, for thou liest in 't.

FIRST CLOWN: You lie out on 't, sir, and therefore 'tis
not yours. For my part, I do not lie in 't, yet it is mine.

HAMLET: Thou dost lie in 't, to be in 't and say it is   125
thine. 'Tis for the dead, not for the quick; therefore
thou liest.

FIRST CLOWN: 'Tis a quick lie, sir; 'twill away again
from me to you.

HAMLET: What man dost thou dig it for?   130

FIRST CLOWN: For no man, sir.

HAMLET: What woman, then?

FIRST CLOWN: For none, neither.

HAMLET: Who is to be buried in 't?

FIRST CLOWN: One that was a woman, sir, but, rest her   135
soul, she's dead.

HAMLET: How absolute the knave is! We must speak by
the card, or equivocation will undo us. By the Lord,
Horatio, this three years I have took note of it: the age
is grown so picked that the toe of the peasant comes   140
so near the heel of the courtier, he galls his kibe.—
How long hast thou been grave maker?

---

117 assurance in that safety in legal parchments   **118 sirrah**
(A term of address to inferiors.)   **126 quick** living   **137 absolute**
strict, precise   **138 by the card** i.e., with precision. (Literally, by the
mariner's compass-card, on which the points of the compass were
marked.)   **equivocation** ambiguity in the use of terms   **139 took**
taken   **140 picked** refined, fastidious   **141 galls his kibe** chafes the
courtier's chilblain

FIRST CLOWN: Of all the days i' the year, I came to 't that day that our last king Hamlet overcame Fortinbras.

145 **HAMLET:** How long is that since?

FIRST CLOWN: Cannot you tell that? Every fool can tell that. It was that very day that young Hamlet was born—he that is mad and sent into England.

HAMLET: Ay, marry, why was he sent into England?

150 **FIRST CLOWN:** Why, because 'a was mad. 'A shall recover his wits there, or if 'a do not, 'tis no great matter there.

HAMLET: Why?

FIRST CLOWN: 'Twill not be seen in him there. There
155 the men are as mad as he.

HAMLET: How came he mad?

FIRST CLOWN: Very strangely, they say.

HAMLET: How strangely?

FIRST CLOWN: Faith, e'en with losing his wits.

160 **HAMLET:** Upon what ground?

FIRST CLOWN: Why, here in Denmark. I have been sexton here, man and boy, thirty years.

HAMLET: How long will a man lie i' th' earth ere he rot?

FIRST CLOWN: Faith, if 'a be not rotten before 'a die—
165 as we have many pocky corpses nowadays, that will scarce hold the laying in—'a will last you some eight year or nine year. A tanner will last you nine year.

HAMLET: Why he more than another?

FIRST CLOWN: Why, sir, his hide is so tanned with his
170 trade that 'a will keep out water a great while, and your water is a sore decayer of your whoreson dead

Hamlet speaks to the skull tossed to him by the First Clown.

body *[He picks up a skull.]* Here's a skull now hath lien you i' th' earth three-and-twenty years.

HAMLET: Whose was it?

FIRST CLOWN: A whoreson mad fellow's it was. 175
Whose do you think it was?

HAMLET: Nay, I know not.

FIRST CLOWN: A pestilence on him for a mad rogue! 'A poured a flagon of Rhenish on my head once. This same skull, sir, was, sir, Yorick's skull, the King's jester. 180

HAMLET: This?

FIRST CLOWN: E'en that.

HAMLET: Let me see. *[He takes the skull.]* Alas, poor Yorick! I knew him, Horatio, a fellow of infinite jest, of most excellent fancy. He hath bore me on his back 185 a thousand times, and now how abhorred in my imagination it is! My gorge rises at it. Here hung those lips that I have kissed I know not how oft. Where be your gibes now? Your gambols, your songs, your flashes of merriment that were wont to set the table 190 on a roar? Not one now, to mock your own grinning?

---

160 ground cause. (But, in the next line, the gravedigger takes the word in the sense of "land," "country.") **165 pocky** rotten, diseased. (Literally, with the pox, or syphilis.) **166 hold the laying in** hold together long enough to be interred. **last you** last. (*You* is used colloquially here and in the following lines.) **171 sore** i.e., terrible, great. **whoreson** i.e., vile, scurvy

---

173 lien you lain. (See the note at line 166.) **179 Rhenish** Rhine wine **185 bore** borne **187 My gorge rises** i.e., I feel nauseated **190 were wont** used **191 mock your own grinning** mock at the way your skull seems to be grinning (just as you used to mock at yourself and those who grinned at you)

Quite chopfallen? Now get you to my lady's chamber
and tell her, let her paint an inch thick, to this
favor she must come. Make her laugh at that. Prithee,
195 Horatio, tell me one thing.

HORATIO: What's that, my lord?

HAMLET: Dost thou think Alexander looked o' this
fashion i' th' earth?

HORATIO: E'en so.

200 **HAMLET:** And smelt so? Pah! *[He throws down the skull.]*

HORATIO: E'en so, my lord.

HAMLET: To what base uses we may return, Horatio!
Why may not imagination trace the noble dust of
Alexander till 'a find it stopping a bunghole?

205 **HORATIO:** 'Twere to consider too curiously to
consider so.

HAMLET: No, faith, not a jot, but to follow him thither
with modesty enough, and likelihood to lead it. As
thus: Alexander died, Alexander was buried, Alexan-
210 der returneth to dust, the dust is earth, of earth we
make loam, and why of that loam whereto he was
converted might they not stop a beer barrel?
Imperious Caesar, dead and turned to clay,
Might stop a hole to keep the wind away.
215 O, that that earth which kept the world in awe
Should patch a wall t' expel the winter's flaw!

Enter KING, QUEEN, LAERTES,
and the corpse [of OPHELIA, *in
procession, with* PRIEST, lords, *etc.]*

But soft, but soft awhile! Here comes the King,
The Queen, the courtiers. Who is this they follow?
And with such maimèd rites? This doth betoken
220 The corpse they follow did with desperate hand

Fordo its own life. 'Twas of some estate.
Couch we awhile and mark.

[He and HORATIO *conceal themselves.*
OPHELIA's *body is taken to the grave.]*

LAERTES: What ceremony else?

HAMLET *[to* HORATIO*]*: That is Laertes, a very noble
youth. Mark.

LAERTES: What ceremony else? 225

PRIEST: Her obsequies have been as far enlarged
As we have warranty. Her death was doubtful,
And but that great command o'ersways the order
She should in ground unsanctified been lodged
Till the last trumpet. For charitable prayers, 230
Shards, flints, and pebbles should be thrown on her.
Yet here she is allowed her virgin crants,
Her maiden strewments, and the bringing home
Of bell and burial.

LAERTES: Must there no more be done?

PRIEST: No more be done. 235
We should profane the service of the dead
To sing a requiem and such rest to her
As to peace-parted souls.

LAERTES: Lay her i' th' earth,
And from her fair and unpolluted flesh
May violets spring! I tell thee, churlish priest, 240
A ministering angel shall my sister be
When thou liest howling.

HAMLET *[to* HORATIO*]*:   What, the fair Ophelia!

---

192 **chopfallen** (1) lacking the lower jaw (2) dejected   194 **favor**
aspect, appearance   204 **bunghole** hole for filling or emptying a
cask   205 **curiously** minutely   208 **modesty** plausible moderation
211 **loam** mortar consisting chiefly of moistened clay and straw   213
Imperious imperial   216 **flaw** gust of wind   217 **soft** i.e., wait, be
careful   219 **maimèd** mutilated, incomplete

221 **Fordo** destroy.   **estate** rank   222 **Couch we** let's hide, lie low
227 **warranty** i.e., ecclesiastical authority   228 **great . . . order**
orders from on high overrule the prescribed procedures   229 **She
should . . . lodged** she should have been buried in unsanctified
ground   230 **For** in place of   231 **Shards** broken bits of pottery
232 **crants** garlands betokening maidenhood   233 **strewments**
flowers strewn on a coffin   233–234 **bringing . . . burial** laying the
body to rest, to the sound of the bell   237 **such rest** i.e., to pray for
such rest   238 **peace-parted souls** those who have died at peace
with God   240 **violets** (See 4.5.188 and note.)   242 **howling** i.e.,
in hell

Ophelia is put to rest.

QUEEN [*scattering flowers*]:   Sweets to the sweet!
    Farewell.
I hoped thou shouldst have been my Hamlet's wife.
245 I thought thy bride-bed to have decked, sweet maid,
And not t' have strewed thy grave.

LAERTES: O, treble woe
Fall ten times treble on that cursèd head
Whose wicked deed thy most ingenious sense
Deprived thee of! Hold off the earth awhile,
250 Till I have caught her once more in mine arms.
                    [*He leaps into the grave and*
                         embraces OPHELIA.]
Now pile your dust upon the quick and dead,
Till of this flat a mountain you have made
T' o'ertop old Pelion or the skyish head
Of blue Olympus.

HAMLET [*coming forward*]:   What is he whose grief
255 Bears such an emphasis, whose phrase of sorrow
Conjures the wandering stars and makes them stand
Like wonder-wounded hearers? This is I,
Hamlet the Dane.

---

248 ingenious sense a mind that is quick, alert, of fine qualities
253–254 Pelion, Olympus sacred mountains in the north of Thessaly; see also *Ossa*, below, at line 286 **255 emphasis** i.e., rhetorical and florid emphasis. (*Phrase* has a similar rhetorical connotation.)
256 wandering stars planets **257 wonder-wounded** struck with amazement **258 the Dane** (This title normally signifies the King; see 1.1.17 and note.)

LAERTES [*grappling with him*]:   The devil take thy soul!

HAMLET: Thou pray'st not well.   260
I prithee, take thy fingers from my throat,
For though I am not splenitive and rash,
Yet have I in me something dangerous,
Which let thy wisdom fear. Hold off thy hand.

KING: Pluck them asunder.   265

QUEEN: Hamlet, Hamlet!

ALL: Gentlemen!

HORATIO: Good my lord, be quiet.
              [HAMLET *and* LAERTES *are parted.*]

HAMLET: Why, I will fight with him upon this theme
Until my eyelids will no longer wag.   270

QUEEN: O my son, what theme?

HAMLET: I loved Ophelia. Forty thousand brothers
Could not with all their quantity of love
Make up my sum. What wilt thou do for her?

KING: O, he is mad, Laertes.   275

QUEEN: For love of God, forbear him.

HAMLET: 'Swounds, show me what thou'lt do.
Woo't weep? Woo't fight? Woo't fast? Woo't tear
    thyself?
Woo't drink up eisel? Eat a crocodile?
I'll do 't. Dost come here to whine?   280
To outface me with leaping in her grave?

---

259 s.d. grappling with him The testimony of the First Quarto that *"Hamlet leaps in after Laertes"* and the "Elegy on Burbage" ("Oft have I seen him leap into the grave") seem to indicate one way in which this fight was staged; however, the difficulty of fitting two contenders and Ophelia's body into a confined space (probably the trapdoor) suggests to many editors the alternative, that Laertes jumps out of the grave to attack Hamlet.) **262 splenitive** quick-tempered **270 wag** move (A fluttering eyelid is a conventional sign that life has not yet gone.) **276 forbear him** leave him alone **277 'Swounds** by His (Christ's) wounds **278 Woo't** wilt thou **279 drink up** drink deeply. **eisel** vinegar. **crocodile** (Crocodiles were tough and dangerous, and were supposed to shed hypocritical tears.)

Be buried quick with her, and so will I.
And if thou prate of mountains, let them throw
Millions of acres on us, till our ground,
285 Singeing his pate against the burning zone,
Make Ossa like a wart! Nay, an thou'lt mouth,
I'll rant as well as thou.

QUEEN: This is mere madness,
And thus awhile the fit will work on him;
Anon, as patient as the female dove
290 When that her golden couplets are disclosed,
His silence will sit drooping.

HAMLET: Hear you, sir.
What is the reason that you use me thus?
I loved you ever. But it is no matter.
Let Hercules himself do what he may,
295 The cat will mew, and dog will have his day.

Exit HAMLET.

KING: I pray thee, good Horatio, wait upon him.

[Exit] HORATIO.

[To LAERTES.*]* Strengthen your patience in our last
night's speech;
We'll put the matter to the present push.—
Good Gertrude, set some watch over your son.—
300 This grave shall have a living monument.
An hour of quiet shortly shall we see;
Till then, in patience our proceeding be.   *Exeunt.*

---

282 quick alive   **285 his pate** his head, i.e., top.   **burning zone**
zone in the celestial sphere containing the sun's orbit, between the
tropics of Cancer and Capricorn   **286 Ossa** another mountain in
Thessaly. (In their war against the Olympian gods, the giants attempted to heap Ossa on Pelion to scale Olympus.)   **an** if.   **mouth**
i.e., rant   **287 mere** utter   **290 golden couplets** two baby pigeons,
covered with yellow down.   **disclosed** hatched   **294–295 Let . . .**
day i.e., (1) even Hercules couldn't stop Laertes' theatrical rant
(2) I, too, will have my turn; i.e., despite any blustering attempts
at interference, every person will sooner or later do what he or she
must do   **297 in** i.e., by recalling   **298 present push** immediate test   **300 living** lasting. (For Laertes' private understanding,
Claudius also hints that Hamlet's death will serve as such a monument.)   **301 hour of quiet** time free of conflict

5.2   *Enter* HAMLET *and* HORATIO.

HAMLET: So much for this, sir; now shall you see the
other.
You do remember all the circumstance?

HORATIO: Remember it, my lord!

HAMLET: Sir, in my heart there was a kind of fighting
That would not let me sleep. Methought I lay   5
Worse than the mutines in the bilboes. Rashly,
And praised by rashness for it—let us know
Our indiscretion sometimes serves us well
When our deep plots do pall, and that should learn us
There's a divinity that shapes our ends,   10
Rough-hew them how we will—

HORATIO: That is most certain.

HAMLET: Up from my cabin,
My sea-gown scarfed about me, in the dark
Groped I to find out them, had my desire,
Fingered their packet, and in fine withdrew   15
To mine own room again, making so bold,
My fears forgetting manners, to unseal
Their grand commission; where I found, Horatio—
Ah, royal knavery!—an exact command,
Larded with many several sorts of reasons   20
Importing Denmark's health and England's too,
With, ho! such bugs and goblins in my life,
That on the supervise, no leisure bated,
No, not to stay the grinding of the ax,
My head should be struck off.

HORATIO: Is 't possible?   25

5.2. Location: The castle.
1 see the other hear the other news   **6 mutines** mutineers.
bilboes shackles.   **Rashly** on impulse. (This adverb goes with lines
12 ff.)   **7 know** acknowledge   **8 indiscretion** lack of foresight and
judgment (not an indiscreet act)   **9 pall** fail, falter, go stale.   **learn**
teach   **11 Rough-hew** shape roughly   **13 sea-gown** seaman's coat.
scarfed loosely wrapped   **14 them** i.e. Rosencrantz and Guildenstern   **15 Fingered** pilfered, pinched.   **in fine** finally, in conclusion
20 Larded garnished.   **several** different   **21 Importing** relating
to   **22 bugs, goblins** bugbears, hobgoblins.   **in my life** i.e., to be
feared if I were allowed to live   **23 supervise** reading.   **leisure**
bated delay allowed   **24 stay** await

HAMLET [*giving a document*]:   Here's the commission.
　　　　Read it at more leisure.
　　　　But wilt thou hear now how I did proceed?

HORATIO: I beseech you.

HAMLET: Being thus benetted round with villainies—
30　　　Ere I could make a prologue to my brains,
　　　　They had begun the play—I sat me down,
　　　　Devised a new commission, wrote it fair.
　　　　I once did hold it, as our statists do,
　　　　A baseness to write fair, and labored much
35　　　How to forget that learning, but, sir, now
　　　　It did me yeoman's service. Wilt thou know
　　　　Th' effect of what I wrote?

HORATIO:　　　　　　　　Ay, good my lord.

HAMLET: An earnest conjuration from the King,
　　　　As England was his faithful tributary,
40　　　As love between them like the palm might flourish,
　　　　As peace should still her wheaten garland wear
　　　　And stand a comma 'tween their amities,
　　　　And many suchlike "as"es of great charge,
　　　　That on the view and knowing of these contents,
45　　　Without debatement further more or less,
　　　　He should those bearers put to sudden death,
　　　　Not shriving time allowed.

HORATIO:　　　　　　　How was this sealed?

HAMLET: Why, even in that was heaven ordinant.
　　　　I had my father's signet in my purse,
50　　　Which was the model of that Danish seal;
　　　　Folded the writ up in the form of th' other,
　　　　Subscribed it, gave 't th' impression, placed it safety,

The changeling never known. Now, the next day
Was our sea fight, and what to this was sequent
Thou knowest already.　　　　　　　　　　55

HORATIO: So Guildenstern and Rosencrantz go to 't.

HAMLET: Why, man, they did make love to this
　　　　employment.
　　　　They are not near my conscience. Their defeat
　　　　Does by their own insinuation grow.
　　　　'Tis dangerous when the baser nature comes　　60
　　　　Between the pass and fell incensèd points
　　　　Of mighty opposites.

HORATIO:　　　　　　　Why, what a king is this!

HAMLET: Does it not, think thee, stand me now upon—
　　　　He that hath killed my king and whored my mother,
　　　　Popped in between th' election and my hopes,　　65
　　　　Thrown out his angle for my proper life,
　　　　And with such cozenage—is 't not perfect conscience
　　　　To quit him with this arm? And is 't not to be damned
　　　　To let this canker of our nature come
　　　　In further evil?　　　　　　　　　　　　70

HORATIO: It must be shortly known to him from
　　　　England
　　　　What is the issue of the business there.

HAMLET: It will be short. The interim is mine,
　　　　And a man's life no more than to say "one."
　　　　But I am very sorry, good Horatio,　　　　75
　　　　That to Laertes I forgot myself,
　　　　For by the image of my cause I see
　　　　The portraiture of his. I'll court his favors.
　　　　But, sure, the bravery of his grief did put me
　　　　Into a tow'ring passion.　　　　　　　　80

30–31 Ere . . . play before I could consciously turn my brain to the matter, it had started working on a plan   **32 fair** in a clear hand   **33 statists** statesmen   **34 baseness** i.e., lower-class trait   **36 yeoman's** i.e., substantial, faithful, loyal   **37 effect** purport   **38 conjuration** entreaty   **40 palm** (An image of health; see Psalms 92:12.)   **41 still** always.   **wheaten garland** (Symbolic of fruitful agriculture, of peace and plenty.)   **42 comma** (Indicating continuity, link.)   **43 "as"es** (1) the "whereases" of a formal document (2) asses.   **charge** (1) import (2) burden (appropriate to asses)   **47 shriving time** time for confession and absolution   **48 ordinant** directing   **49 signet** small seal   **50 model** replica   **51 writ** writing   **52 Subscribed** signed (with forged signature).   **impression** i.e., with a wax seal

---

53 changeling i.e., substituted letter. (Literally, a fairy child substituted for a human one.)   **54 was sequent** followed   **58 defeat** destruction   **59 insinuation** intrusive intervention, sticking their noses in my business   **60 baser** of lower social station   **61 pass** thrust.   **fell** fierce   **62 opposites** antagonists   **63 stand me now upon** become incumbent on me now   **65 election** (The Danish monarch was "elected" by a small number of high-ranking electors.)   **66 angle** fishhook.   **proper** very   **67 cozenage** trickery   **68 quit** requite, pay back   **69 canker** ulcer   **69–70 come In** grow into   **74 a man's . . . "one"** one's whole life occupies such a short time, only as long as it takes to count to 1   **79 bravery** bravado

HORATIO: Peace, who comes here?

Enter a Courtier [OSRIC].

OSRIC: Your lordship is right welcome back to Denmark.

HAMLET: I humbly thank you, sir. *[To* HORATIO.*]* Dost know this water fly?

HORATIO: No, my good lord.

85   **HAMLET:**   Thy state is the more gracious, for 'tis a vice to know him. He hath much land, and fertile. Let a beast be lord of beasts, and his crib shall stand at the King's mess. 'Tis a chuff, but, as I say, spacious in the possession of dirt.

90   **OSRIC:**   Sweet lord, if your lordship were at leisure, I should impart a thing to you from His Majesty.

HAMLET: I will receive it, sir, with diligence of spirit. Put your bonnet to his right use; 'tis for the head.

OSRIC: I thank you lordship, it is very hot.

95   **HAMLET:**   No, believe me, 'tis very cold. The wind is northerly.

OSRIC: It is indifferent cold, my lord, indeed.

HAMLET: But yet methinks it is very sultry and hot for my complexion.

100   **OSRIC:**   Exceedingly, my lord. It is very sultry, as 'twere— I cannot tell how. My lord, His Majesty bade me signify to you that 'a has laid a great wager on your head. Sir, this is the matter—

HAMLET: I beseech you, remember:
*[*HAMLET *moves him to put on his hat.]*

105   **OSRIC:**   Nay, good my lord; for my ease, in good faith. Sir, here is newly come to court Laertes—believe me,

Osric (Robin Williams) tells Hamlet of the duel.

an absolute gentleman, full of most excellent differences, of very soft society and great showing. Indeed, to speak feelingly of him, he is the card or calendar of gentry, for you shall find in him the continent of what   110 part a gentleman would see.

HAMLET: Sir, his definement suffers no perdition in you, though I know to divide him inventorially would dozy th' arithmetic of memory, and yet but yaw neither in respect of his quick sail. But, in the   115 verity of extolment, I take him to be a soul of great article, and his infusion of such dearth and rareness as, to make true diction of him, his semblable is his mirror and who else would trace him his umbrage, nothing more.   120

---

107 absolute perfect   **107–108 differences** special qualities   **108 soft society** agreeable manners.   **great showing** distinguished appearance   **109 feelingly** with just perception.   **card** chart, map. **calendar** guide   **110 gentry** good breeding   **110–111 the continent . . . see** one who contains in him all the qualities a gentleman would like to see. (A *continent* is that which contains.)   **112 definement** definition. (Hamlet proceeds to mock Osric by throwing his lofty diction back at him.)   **perdition** loss, diminution   **113 you** your description.   **divide him inventorially** enumerate his graces   **114 dozy** dizzy.   **115 yaw** swing unsteadily off course. (Said of a ship.)   **neither** for all that.   **in respect of** in comparison with   **115–116 in . . . extolment** in true praise (of him)   **116–117 of great article** one with many articles in his inventory   **117 infusion** essence, character infused into him by nature.   **dearth and rareness** rarity   **118 make true diction** speak truly   **118 semblable** only true likeness   **119 who . . . trace** any other person who would wish to follow.   **umbrage** shadow

---

86–88 **Let . . . mess** i.e., if a man, no matter how beastlike, is as rich in livestock and possessions as Osric, he may eat at the King's table   87 **crib** manger   88 **chuff** boor, churl. (The Second Quarto spelling, *chough*, is a variant spelling that also suggests the meaning here of "chattering jackdaw.")   93 **bonnet** any kind of cap or hat. **his** its   97 **indifferent** somewhat   99 **complexion** temperament   105 **for my ease** (A conventional reply declining the invitation to put his hat back on.)

OSRIC: Your lordship speaks most infallibly of him.

HAMLET: The concernancy, sir? Why do we wrap the gentleman in our more rawer breath?

OSRIC: Sir?

125   **HORATIO:**   Is 't not possible to understand in another tongue? You will do 't, sir, really.

HAMLET: What imports the nomination of this gentleman?

OSRIC: Of Laertes?

130   **HORATIO** *[to* HAMLET*]:*   His purse is empty already; all 's golden words are spent.

HAMLET: Of him, sir.

OSRIC: I know you are not ignorant—

HAMLET: I would you did, sir. Yet in faith if you did, it
135   would not much approve me. Well, sir?

OSRIC: You are not ignorant of what excellence Laertes is—

HAMLET: I dare not confess that, lest I should compare with him in excellence. But to know a man well were
140   to know himself.

OSRIC: I mean, sir, for his weapon; but in the imputation laid on him by them, in his meed he's unfellowed.

HAMLET: What's his weapon?

OSRIC: Rapier and dagger.

HAMLET: That's two of his weapons—but well.   145

OSRIC: The King, sir, hath wagered with him six Barbary horses, against the which he has impawned, as I take it, six French rapiers and poniards, with their assigns, as girdle, hangers, and so. Three of the carriages, in faith, are very dear to fancy, very respon-   150
sive to the hilts, most delicate carriages, and of very liberal conceit.

HAMLET: What call you the carriages?

HORATIO *[to* HAMLET*]:*   I knew you must be edified by the margent ere you had done.   155

OSRIC: The carriages, sir, are the hangers.

HAMLET: The phrase would be more germane to the matter if we could carry a cannon by our sides; I would it might be hangers till then. But, on: six Barbary horses against six French swords, their as-   160
signs, and three liberal-conceited carriages; that's the French bet against the Danish. Why is this impawned, as you call it?

OSRIC: The King, sir, hath laid, sir, that in a dozen passes between yourself and him, he shall not exceed   165
you three hits. He hath laid on twelve for nine, and it would come to immediate trial, if your lordship would vouchsafe the answer.

HAMLET: How if I answer no?

OSRIC: I mean, my lord, the opposition of your person   170
in trial.

---

122 **concernancy** import, relevance   123 **rawer breath** unrefined speech that can only come short in praising him   125–126 **to understand . . . tongue** i.e., for you, Osric, to understand when someone else speaks your language. (Horatio twits Osric for not being able to understand the kind of flowery speech he himself uses, when Hamlet speaks in such a vein. Alternatively, all this could be said to Hamlet.)   126 **You will do 't** i.e., you can if you try, or, you may well have to try (to speak plainly)   127 **nomination** naming   135 **approve** commend   138–140 **I dare . . . himself** I dare not boast of knowing Laertes' excellence lest I seem to imply a comparable excellence in myself. Certainly, to know another person well, one must know oneself.   141 **for** i.e., with   141–142 **imputation . . . them** reputation given him by others   142 **meed** merit.   **unfellowed** unmatched

145 **but well** but never mind   147 **he** i.e., Laertes.   **impawned** staked, wagered   148 **poniards** daggers   149 **assigns** appurtenances.   **hangers** straps on the sword belt (*girdle*), from which the sword hung.   **and so** and so on   149–150 **carriages** (An affected way of saying *hangers;* literally, gun carriages.)   150 **dear to fancy** delightful to the fancy   150–151 **responsive** corresponding closely, matching or well adjusted   151 **delicate** (i.e., in workmanship)   152 **liberal conceit** elaborate design   155 **margent** margin of a book, place for explanatory notes   164 **laid** wagered   165 **passes** bouts. (The odds of the betting are hard to explain. Possibly the King bets that Hamlet will win at least five out of twelve, at which point Laertes raises the odds against himself by betting he will win nine.)   168 **vouchsafe the answer** be so good as to accept the challenge. (Hamlet deliberately takes the phrase in its literal sense of replying.)

HAMLET: Sir, I will walk here in the hall. If it please His
Majesty, it is the breathing time of day with me. Let the
foils be brought, the gentleman willing, and the King
175 hold his purpose, I will win for him an I can; if not,
I will gain nothing but my shame and the odd hits.

OSRIC: Shall I deliver you so?

HAMLET: To this effect, sir—after what flourish your
nature will.

180 **OSRIC:** I commend my duty to your lordship.

HAMLET: Yours, yours. *[Exit* OSRIC.*]* 'A does well to
commend it himself; there are no tongues else for
's turn.

HORATIO: This lapwing runs away with the shell on his
185 head.

HAMLET: 'A did comply with his dug before 'a sucked it.
Thus has he—and many more of the same breed that
I know the drossy age dotes on—only got the tune
of the time and, out of an habit of encounter, a kind
190 of yeasty collection, which carries them through and
through the most fanned and winnowed opinions;
and do but blow them to their trial, the bubbles
are out.

Enter a LORD.

---

173 breathing time exercise period. **Let** i.e., if **177 deliver you**
report what you say **180 commend** commit to your favor. (A
conventional salutation, but Hamlet wryly uses a more literal meaning, "recommend," "praise," in line 182.) **182–183 for 's turn** for his
purposes, i.e., to do it for him **184 lapwing** (A proverbial type of
youthful forwardness. Also, a bird that draws intruders away from
its nest and was thought to run about with its head in the shell when
newly hatched; a seeming reference to Osric's hat.) **186 comply . . .**
dug observe ceremonious formality toward his nurse's or mother's
teat **188 drossy** laden with scum and impurities, frivolous **tune**
temper, mood, manner of speech. **189 an habit of encounter** a demeanor in conversing (with courtiers of his own kind) **190 yeasty**
frothy. **collection** i.e., of current phrases **190–191 carries . . .**
opinions sustains them right through the scrutiny of persons whose
opinions are select and refined. (Literally, like grain separated from
its chaff. Osric is both the chaff and the bubbly froth on the surface
of the liquor that is soon blown away.) **192 and do** yet do **192–193**
blow . . . out test them by merely blowing on them, and their bubbles
burst

LORD: My lord, His Majesty commended him to you by
young Osric, who brings back to him that you attend 195
him in the hall. He sends to know if your pleasure
hold to play with Laertes, or that you will take longer
time.

HAMLET: I am constant to my purposes; they follow the
King's pleasure. If his fitness speaks, mine is ready; 200
now or whensoever, provided I be so able as now.

LORD: The King and Queen and all are coming down.

HAMLET: In happy time.

LORD: The Queen desires you to use some gentle entertainment to Laertes before you fall to play. 205

HAMLET: She well instructs me. *[Exit* LORD.*]*

HORATIO: You will lose, my lord.

HAMLET: I do not think so. Since he went into France,
I have been in continual practice; I shall win at the
odds. But thou wouldst not think how ill all's here 210
about my heart; but it is no matter.

HORATIO: Nay, good my lord—

HAMLET: It is but foolery, but it is such a kind of gaingiving as would perhaps trouble a woman.

HORATIO: If your mind dislike anything, obey it. I will 215
forestall their repair hither and say you are not fit.

HAMLET: Not a whit, we defy augury. There is special
providence in the fall of a sparrow. If it be now, 'tis
not to come; if it be not to come, it will be now; if it
be not now; yet it will come. The readiness is all. 220
Since no man of aught he leaves knows, what is 't to
leave betimes? Let be.

---

197 that if **200 If . . . ready** if he declares his readiness, my convenience waits on his **203 In happy time** (A phrase of courtesy
indicating that the time is convenient.) **204–205 entertainment**
greeting **213–214 gaingiving** misgiving **216 repair** coming
221–222 Since . . . Let be since no one has knowledge of what he is
leaving behind, what does an early death matter after all? Enough;
don't struggle against it.

That I have shot my arrow o'er the house
And hurt my brother.

LAERTES: I am satisfied in nature,
Whose motive in this case should stir me most
To my revenge. But in my terms of honor
I stand aloof, and will no reconcilement   245
Till by some elder masters of known honor
I have a voice and precedent of peace
To keep my name ungored. But till that time
I do receive your offered love like love,
And will not wrong it.

HAMLET: I embrace it freely,   250
And will this brothers' wager frankly play.—
Give us the foils. Come on.

LAERTES: Come, one for me.

HAMLET: I'll be your foil, Laertes. In mine ignorance
Your skill shall, like a star i' the darkest night,
Stick fiery off indeed.

LAERTES: You mock me, sir.   255

HAMLET: No, by this hand.

KING: Give them the foils, young Osric. Cousin Hamlet,
You know the wager?

HAMLET: Very well, my lord.
Your Grace has laid the odds o' the weaker side.

KING: I do not fear it; I have seen you both.   260
But since he is bettered, we have therefore odds.

LAERTES: This is too heavy. Let me see another.
                    [He exchanges his foil for another.]

HAMLET: This likes me well. These foils have all a
                    length?

Laertes (Michael Maloney) and Hamlet duel.

*A table prepared. [Enter] trumpets, drums,
and officers with cushions;* KING, QUEEN,
*[*OSRIC,*] and all the state; foils, daggers,
[and wine borne in;] and* LAERTES.

KING: Come, Hamlet, come and take this hand from me.
                    [The KING *puts* LAERTES' *hand
                    into* HAMLET's.*]*

HAMLET *[to* LAERTES*]:*   Give me your pardon, sir. I have
                    done you wrong,
225   But pardon 't as you are a gentleman.
            This presence knows,
            And you must needs have heard, how I am punished
            With a sore distraction. What I have done
            That might your nature, honor, and exception
230   Roughly awake, I here proclaim was madness.
            Was 't Hamlet wronged Laertes? Never Hamlet.
            If Hamlet from himself be ta'en away,
            And when he's not himself does wrong Laertes,
            Then Hamlet does it not, Hamlet denies it.
235   Who does it, then? His madness. If 't be so,
            Hamlet is of the faction that is wronged;
            His madness is poor Hamlet's enemy.
            Sir, in this audience
            Let my disclaiming from a purposed evil
240   Free me so far in your most generous thoughts

---

226 presence royal assembly   **227 punished** afflicted   **229 exception** disapproval   **236 faction** party

---

241 That I have as if I had   **242 in nature** i.e., as to my personal feelings   **243 motive** prompting   **247 voice** authoritative pronouncement.   **of peace** for reconciliation   **248 name ungored** reputation unwounded   **251 frankly** without ill feeling or the burden of rancor   **253 foil** thin metal background that sets a jewel off (with pun on the blunted rapier for fencing)   **255 Stick fiery off** stand out brilliantly   **259 laid the odds o'** bet on, backed   **261 is bettered** has improved; is the odds-on favorite. (Laertes' handicap is the "three hits" specified in line 166.)   **263 likes me** pleases me

[They prepare to play.]

OSRIC: Ay, my good lord.

265 **KING:**   Set me the stoups of wine upon that table.
If Hamlet give the first or second hit,
Or quit in answer of the third exchange,
Let all the battlements their ordnance fire.
The King shall drink to Hamlet's better breath,
270 And in the cup an union shall he throw
Richer than that which four successive kings
In Denmark's crown have worn. Give me the cups,
And let the kettle to the trumpet speak,
The trumpet to the cannoneer without,
275 The cannons to the heavens, the heaven to earth,
"Now the King drinks to Hamlet." Come, begin.
                          Trumpets the while.
And you, the judges, bear a wary eye.

HAMLET: Come on, sir.

LAERTES: Come, my lord. *[They play.* HAMLET *scores
a hit.]*

280 **HAMLET:**   One.

LAERTES: No.

HAMLET: Judgment.

OSRIC: A hit, a very palpable hit.
                  *Drum, trumpets, and shot. Flourish.
                          A piece goes off.*

LAERTES: Well, again.

KING: Stay, give me drink. Hamlet, this pearl is thine.
                  *[He drinks, and throws a pearl
                          in* HAMLET'*s cup.]*
285 Here's to thy health. Give him the cup.

HAMLET: I'll play this bout first. Set it by awhile.
Come. *[They play.]* Another hit; what say you?

LAERTES: A touch, a touch, I do confess 't.

KING: Our son shall win.

QUEEN: He's fat and scant of breath.
Here, Hamlet, take my napkin, rub thy brows.   290
The Queen carouses to thy fortune, Hamlet.

HAMLET: Good madam!

KING: Gertrude, do not drink.

QUEEN: I will, my lord, I pray you pardon me.
                          [She drinks.]

KING *[aside]:*   It is the poisoned cup. It is too late.   295

HAMLET: I dare not drink yet, madam; by and by.

QUEEN: Come, let me wipe thy face.

LAERTES *[to* KING*]:*   My lord, I'll hit him now.

KING: I do not think 't.

LAERTES *[aside]:*   And yet it is almost against my
        conscience.

HAMLET: Come, for the third, Laertes. You do but dally.   300
I pray you, pass with your best violence;
I am afeard you make a wanton of me.

LAERTES: Say you so? Come on.   *[They play.]*

OSRIC: Nothing neither way.

LAERTES: Have at you now!   305
          *[*LAERTES *wounds* HAMLET*; then,
            in scuffling, they change rapiers,
            and* HAMLET *wounds* LAERTES*.]*

KING: Part them! They are incensed.

HAMLET: Nay, come, again.   *[The* QUEEN *falls.]*

OSRIC: Look to the Queen there, ho!

HORATIO: They bleed on both sides. How is it, my lord?

OSRIC: How is 't, Laertes?

---

267 Or . . . exchange i.e., or requites Laertes in the third bout for
having won the first two   **269 better breath** improved vigor   **270
union** pearl. (So called, according to Pliny's *Natural History,* 9,
because pearls are *unique,* never identical.)   **273 kettle** kettledrum

289 fat not physically fit, out of training   **290 napkin** handkerchief
291 carouses drinks a toast   **301 pass** thrust   **302 make . . . me**
i.e., treat me like a spoiled child, trifle with me   **305 s.d. in scuffling,
they change rapiers** (This stage direction occurs in the Folio. According to a widespread stage tradition, Hamlet receives a scratch,
realizes that Laertes' sword is unbated, and accordingly forces an
exchange.)

LAERTES: Why, as a woodcock to mine own springe,
                 Osric;
310   I am justly killed with mine own treachery.

HAMLET: How does the Queen?

KING: She swoons to see them bleed.

QUEEN: No, no, the drink, the drink—O my dear
                 Hamlet—
             The drink, the drink! I am poisoned.   *[She dies.]*

HAMLET: O villainy! Ho, let the door be locked!
315   Treachery! Seek it out.   *[LAERTES falls. Exit OSRIC.]*

LAERTES: It is here, Hamlet. Hamlet, thou art slain.
             No med'cine in the world can do thee good;
             In thee there is not half an hour's life.
             The treacherous instrument is in thy hand,
320   Unbated and envenomed. The foul practice
             Hath turned itself on me. Lo, here I lie,
             Never to rise again. Thy mother's poisoned.
             I can no more. The King, the King's to blame.

HAMLET: The point envenomed too? Then, venom, to
                 thy work.   *[He stabs the KING.]*

325 **ALL:**   Treason! Treason!

KING: O, yet defend me, friends! I am but hurt.

HAMLET *[forcing the KING to drink]*:   Here, thou inces-
                 tuous, murderous, damnèd Dane,
             Drink off this potion. Is thy union here?
             Follow my mother.   *[The KING dies.]*

LAERTES: He is justly served.
330   It is a poison tempered by himself.
             Exchange forgiveness with me, noble Hamlet.
             Mine and my father's death come not upon thee,
             Nor thine on me!   *[He dies]*

HAMLET: Heaven make thee free of it! I follow thee.
335   I am dead, Horatio. Wretched Queen, adieu!
             You that look pale and tremble at this chance,

Hamlet forces Claudius to drink the poisoned wine.

             That are but mutes or audience to this act,
             Had I but time—as this fell sergeant, Death,
             Is strict in his arrest—O, I could tell you—
             But let it be. Horatio, I am dead;   340
             Thou livest. Report me and my cause aright
             To the unsatisfied.

HORATIO: Never believe it.
             I am more an antique Roman than a Dane.
             Here's yet some liquor left.
                        *[He attempts to drink from the poisoned
                                     cup. HAMLET prevents him.]*

HAMLET: As thou'rt a man,
             Give me the cup! Let go! By heaven, I'll ha 't.   345
             O God, Horatio, what a wounded name,
             Things standing thus unknown, shall I leave behind
                 me!
             If thou didst ever hold me in thy heart,
             Absent thee from felicity awhile,
             And in this harsh world draw thy breath in pain   350
             To tell my story. *A march afar off [and a volley within].*
                        What warlike noise is this?

---

309 woodcock a bird, a type of stupidity or as a decoy.   **springe**
trap, snare   **320 Unbated** not blunted with a button.   **practice** plot
328 union pearl. (See line 270; with grim puns on the word's other
meanings: marriage, shared death.)   **330 tempered** mixed   **336
chance** mischance

337 mutes silent observers. (Literally, actors with nonspeaking
parts.)   **338 fell** cruel.   **sergeant** sheriff's officer   **339 strict**
(1) severely just (2) unavoidable.   **arrest** (1) taking into custody
(2) stopping my speech   **343 Roman** (Suicide was an honorable
choice for many Romans as an alternative to a dishonorable life.)

Enter OSRIC.

OSRIC: Young Fortinbras, with conquest come from
      Poland,
To th' ambassadors of England gives
This warlike volley.

HAMLET: O, I die, Horatio!
355   The potent poison quite o'ercrows my spirit.
I cannot live to hear the news from England,
But I do prophesy th' election lights
On Fortinbras. He has my dying voice.
So tell him, with th' occurrents more and less
360   Which have solicited—the rest is silence.   *[He dies.]*

HORATIO: Now cracks a noble heart. Good night, sweet
      prince,
And flights of angels sing thee to thy rest!
                      [March within.]
Why does the drum come hither?

      Enter FORTINBRAS, *with the [English]* AMBAS-
      SADORS *[with drum, colors, and attendants].*

FORTINBRAS: Where is this sight?

HORATIO: What is it you would see?
365   If aught of woe or wonder, cease your search.

FORTINBRAS: This quarry cries on havoc. O proud
      Death,
What feast is toward in thine eternal cell,
That thou so many princes at a shot
So bloodily hast struck?

FIRST AMBASSADOR: The sight is dismal,
370   And our affairs from England come too late.
The ears are senseless that should give us hearing,
To tell him his commandment is fulfilled,
That Rosencrantz and Guildenstern are dead.
Where should we have our thanks?

Hamlet is laid to rest.

HORATIO: Not from his mouth,
Had it th' ability of life to thank you.   375
He never gave commandment for their death.
But since, so jump upon his bloody question,
You from the Polack wars, and you from England,
Are here arrived, give order that these bodies
High on a stage be placèd to the view,   380
And let me speak to th' yet unknowing world
How these things came about. So shall you hear
Of carnal, bloody, and unnatural acts,
Of accidental judgments, casual slaughters,
Of deaths put on by cunning and forced cause,   385
And, in this upshot, purposes mistook
Fall'n on th' inventors' heads. All this can I
Truly deliver.

FORTINBRAS: Let us haste to hear it,
And call the noblest to the audience.
For me, with sorrow I embrace my fortune.   390
I have some rights of memory in this kingdom,
Which now to claim my vantage doth invite me.

HORATIO: Of that I shall have also cause to speak,
And from his mouth whose voice will draw on more.

---

355 o'ercrows triumphs over (like the winner in a cockfight)   **358 voice** vote   **359 occurrents** events, incidents   **360 solicited** moved, urged. (Hamlet doesn't finish saying what the events have prompted—presumably, his acts of vengeance, or his reporting of those events to Fortinbras.)   **366 quarry** heap of dead.   **cries on havoc** proclaims a general slaughter   **367 feast** i.e., Death feasting on those who have fallen.   **toward** in preparation

---

374 his i.e., Claudius'   **377 jump** precisely, immediately.   **question** dispute, affair   **380 stage** platform   **384 judgments** retributions. **casual** occurring by chance   **385 put on** instigated.   **forced cause** contrivance   **391 of memory** traditional, remembered, unforgotten **392 vantage** favorable opportunity   **394 voice . . . more** vote will influence still others

395   But let this same be presently performed,
Even while men's minds are wild, lest more mischance
On plots and errors happen.

FORTINBRAS: Let four captains
Bear Hamlet, like a soldier, to the stage,
For he was likely, had he been put on,
400   To have proved most royal; and for his passage,

The soldiers' music and the rite of war
Speak loudly for him.
Take up the bodies. Such a sight as this
Becomes the field, but here shows much amiss.
Go bid the soldiers shoot.   405

*Exeunt [marching, bearing off the dead
bodies; a peal of ordnance is shot off].*

---

395 presently immediately   **397 On** on the basis of; on top of   **399 put on** i.e., invested in royal office and so put to the test   **400 passage** i.e., from life to death

402 Speak (let them) speak   **404 Becomes the field** suits the field of battle

Writing from Reading

Summarize

1 Think of this play as a revenge tragedy, a story of justice played out. Describe how Hamlet chooses to avenge his father's murder and the result of his choice. During the course of the play, what wrongs are righted? In what ways do innocent people suffer or succeed?

2 This is a complex play with many subplots that mirror the main plot of Hamlet's revenge. Consider, for instance, that Laertes also loves Ophelia, is also of noble birth and travels abroad. He is an excellent fencer, and also has a father who has been killed. How does his story amplify that of the prince?

3 What is the plot of the play within the play? Does the play have the effect Hamlet hopes for?

Analyze Craft

4 How would you describe Hamlet's character? How does indecision help the tragedy unfold?

5 How would you describe Ophelia's character: her history, her education and upbringing, her feelings for her father and brother and lover? What causes Ophelia to go mad (is it a single event, or a combination of causes that makes her drown herself?), and what effect does her suicide have on the play?

6 How do you imagine Claudius and Gertrude? How old are they? In what sort of physical health? What attitude do they have? What in the play makes you imagine them this way?

7 Laertes is a kind of shadow twin to Hamlet. As noted in question 2, he, too, is noble and a fine fencer, and his father has also been killed. What differences in character make him, in effect, the king's pawn and the unwitting agent of Prince Hamlet's death?

8 How do the secondary characters—the gravedigger, Fortinbras, Horatio, and so on—advance the action? What perspectives and what commentary do they offer?

Analyze Voice

9 How do the speeches and high formal tone of the royal characters contrast with the speech of the low characters? Give examples.

10 Do you have any sympathy for the character Claudius when he admits, "Oh, my offence is rank"? What about *rank* in the court? Find other examples of Shakespeare's use of double meaning and puns (as, for example, when Hamlet flirts with and teases Ophelia before the play's performance).

11 Do "these few precepts" that Polonius offers to his son make sense? What of the advice he gives his daughter? Given the solemn nature of this advice, what in his character makes Hamlet think him a "rash, intruding fool"? What does the difference between what seems like wise advice and Polonius's character allow us to discover in the play?

12 Focus on the humor in the text. Study the gravediggers' scene and try to play it for laughs.

Synthesize Summary and Analysis

13 Why would Shakespeare set this play in Denmark and the somewhat distant past? It is, after all, a story about regicide (the killing of a king). What risks would he have taken if he set the tale in England instead?

14 Why did Shakespeare mount a play within the play, and what kind of commentary does it offer on the larger text? How is this similar to or different from the play staged within Shakespeare's *A Midsummer Night's Dream* (found online at **connect.mcgraw-hill .com**)?

Interpret the Play

15 Is Hamlet's story tragic? If so, what makes his story tragic?

16 Does Hamlet choose the most efficient path to avenge his father's murder? At play's end, is everything redeemed?

THE ORIGINS OF THE *HAMLET* STORY

The particular source of this play derives from an old Norse legend in which we first hear of a character called Amlothi, whose name has been translated as "desperate in battle" and is recorded in *Historica Danica* of Saxo Grammaticus (a book printed in 1514). The seed story of *Hamlet* is used by the French writer Belleforest in his *Histoires Tragiques* (1576), and scholars show Shakespeare did read it. Indeed, the playwright rarely made up his stories out of whole cloth. He was familiar with Plutarch and Holinshed (historians of the classical and medieval world respectively); he adapted histories and voyage accounts and other authors' narratives for most of his career. The father's murder and the sweetheart's madness (sometimes the Ophelia figure is a courtesan, sometimes a princess) and the duel with an exchange of swords all figure in previous sources—but the character of Hamlet is something Shakespeare filled out on his own.

THE ELIZABETHAN THEATER

From time to time—in periods of plague, for instance, or when the authorities found the crowd's behavior too unruly—the theaters were closed down. To avoid the complications stemming from these unpredictable gaps in business, Shakespeare's troupe, the Lord Chamberlain's Men, decided to build its own space in 1599. The Globe Theater, constructed on the model of a tavern, stood on the south bank of the Thames River, beyond the city limits and the close watch of the law; it could accommodate—by some estimates—as many as three thousand.

Before the construction of the Globe Theater, the central stage was often a courtyard of taverns or inns. Today, an audience at a boxing match or football game is probably more similar to the Elizabethan clientele than is the well-heeled, well-behaved audience at a Broadway show. Like Greek theater, these stages made for sparse sets. There was only a **tiring house** hidden by a curtain behind the **arena stage**—in essence,

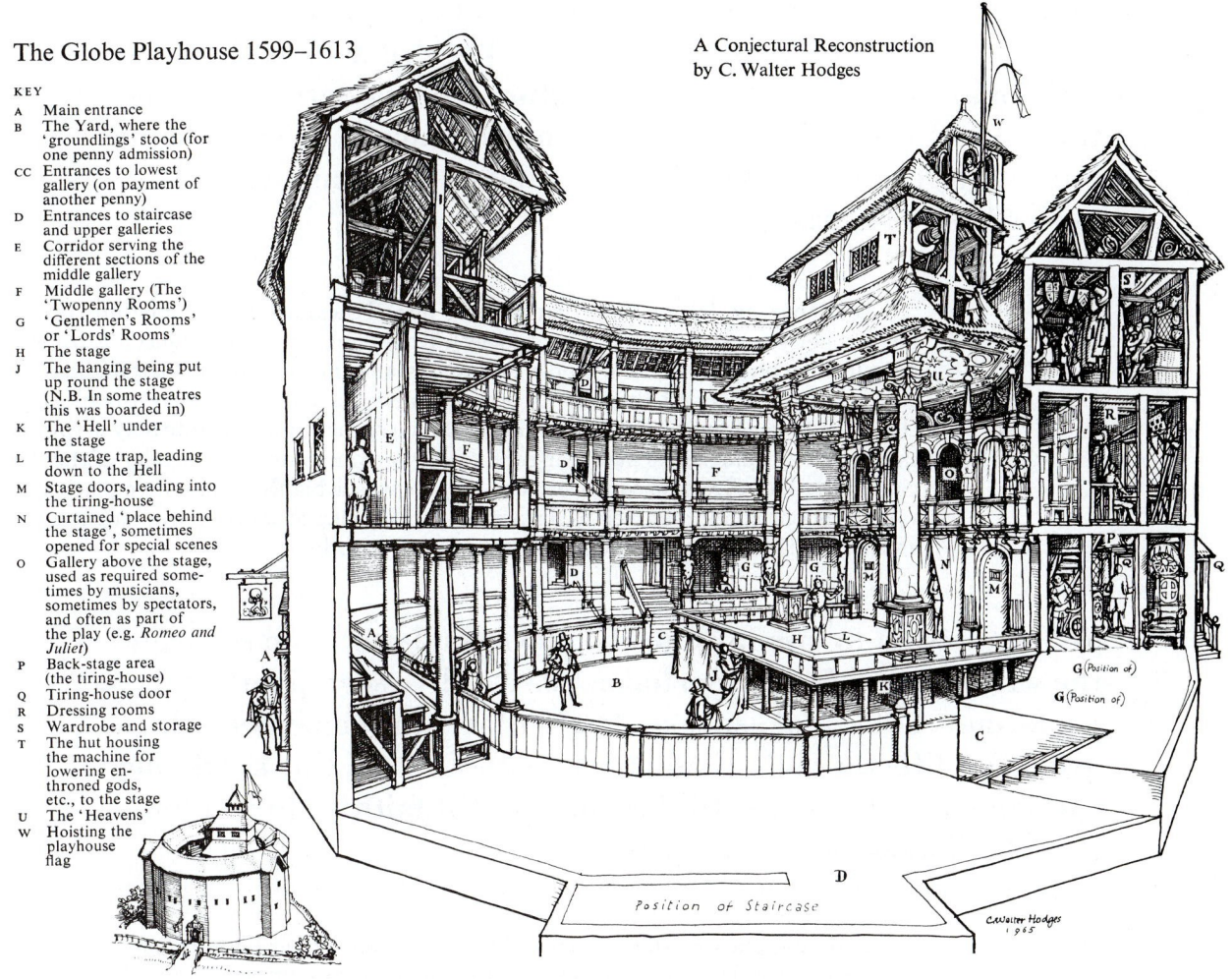

The Globe Playhouse 1599–1613

A Conjectural Reconstruction
by C. Walter Hodges

KEY

A Main entrance
B The Yard, where the 'groundlings' stood (for one penny admission)
CC Entrances to lowest gallery (on payment of another penny)
D Entrances to staircase and upper galleries
E Corridor serving the different sections of the middle gallery
F Middle gallery (The 'Twopenny Rooms')
G 'Gentlemen's Rooms' or 'Lords' Rooms'
H The stage
J The hanging being put up round the stage (N.B. In some theatres this was boarded in)
K The 'Hell' under the stage
L The stage trap, leading down to the Hell
M Stage doors, leading into the tiring-house
N Curtained 'place behind the stage', sometimes opened for special scenes
O Gallery above the stage, used as required sometimes by musicians, sometimes by spectators, and often as part of the play (e.g. *Romeo and Juliet*)
P Back-stage area (the tiring-house)
Q Tiring-house door
R Dressing rooms
S Wardrobe and storage
T The hut housing the machine for lowering enthroned gods, etc., to the stage
U The 'Heavens'
W Hoisting the playhouse flag

a platform—that allowed quick costume changes between scenes. The stage was open to the sky to take advantage of natural light. Similar to the Greek amphitheater, surrounded on three sides, the Elizabethan theater would have been three stories high, each story with a gallery from which patrons could watch; those who paid an additional penny could be seated and look down.

"I have always felt that the . . . works that last . . . address the condition of mankind at any one time. They're not simply private emotional works. . . . They're reflecting the larger reality of the time. And I think that's true with Shakespeare. . . . The original purpose or color of creative art was always the community."

Conversation with Arthur Miller

Not since the fall of Rome had theater played such a role in public life, bringing in a boisterous and broad mix of society, from nobles, including Queen Elizabeth herself, to **groundlings,** who paid a penny to stand on the ground surrounding the stage. Puritans decried theaters as brothels, and Queen Elizabeth censored plays closely because of their enormous influence. Shakespeare himself wrote only of royalty that was long gone, since predicting the future or commenting on royalty of the day could have had dire consequences. The theater was a highly competitive place that vied for public support as well as for patrons, sponsoring aristocrats who might order a private performance or commission a celebratory work.

"You don't want to lose faith in the plays you love. I can separate the written word from a performance . . . I've seen poor performances of Shakespeare. Particularly the comedies, which are more difficult to do than the tragedies. And I think, Oh don't spoil this play for me! I still love it, I'm still faithful to it, I love this play." Conversation with Marian Seldes

Traveling **players**—hired men and boys who spoke their lines for pay—acted out the plays of the day, and it is just such a group of actors Prince Hamlet is hiring in Act 3, Scene 2, when he decides to get his message of revenge to the murderous king. Players were always males, with boys usually playing women's roles. The costumes worn by players were generally very elaborate—brightly colored and visually appealing. Acting companies owned a wide variety of costumes for players to wear, some of which held certain conventions and connotations—such as a robe that represented invisibility. And since these costumes were expensive and not readily replaced, the playwright had to "tailor" his lines accordingly. In the beginning of another Shakespeare play, *The Tempest,* there's a storm conjured up by Prospero, the great magician, and his servant Ariel. Shakespeare describes how the shipwrecked crew washes up upon the island, writing "On their sustaining garments not a blemish / But fresher than before." In the movies nowadays we'd no doubt show the sailors wet and bedraggled, their "sustaining garments" torn—but in Elizabethan England the costumes would need to stay dry and "fresher than before."

> **"[Shakespeare's] plays are capable of an endless number of good productions. . . . There are no stage directions, so they're endlessly fertile as performance."** Conversation with Ralph Williams

LANGUAGE ONSTAGE

When the character Jaques in Shakespeare's *As You Like It* famously pronounces that "All the world's a stage, and all the men and women merely players," he may well have been describing the great Globe Theater itself. Though it contained no elaborate scenery, the size of the stage and the structure of the building offered occasions for action; when Orlando, in the same play, hangs his love letters to Rosalind on trees of the Forest of Arden, he almost surely did so from the columns of the Globe. Props and furniture could be employed, and elaborate costumes worn, but "the willing suspension of disbelief"—which Samuel Taylor Coleridge argued "constitutes poetic faith"—was necessary, always, for those theatergoers who came to listen and look. The prologue to *Henry V* admits as much—indeed, is close to apologetic when the speaker asks:

> *Can this cockpit hold*
> *The vasty fields of France? Or may we cram*
> *Within this wooden O the very casques*
> *That did affright the air at Agincourt?*

Mostly the answer was yes. Scene after scene in Shakespeare is introduced by vivid description, a speech about a battlefield or palace, a lyric evocation of a forest or the stars. In Act 5, Scene 1, of *The Merchant of Venice,* one character observes,

> *How sweet the moonlight sits upon this bank!*
> *Here will we sit and let the sounds of music*
> *Creep in our ears. Soft stillness and the night*
> *Become the touches of sweet harmony.*
> *Sit, Jessica. Look how the floor of heaven*
> *Is thick inlaid with patens of bright gold . . .*

There's no need for stage directions once the scene has been set in such elegant style. Lorenzo, the speaker, is wooing his heart's darling—Jessica, the daughter of Shylock, the Merchant of Venice—looking up while, no doubt, music plays. The opening phrase of this courtship scene is "The moon shines bright," and though the play was first presented on a London afternoon, we're transported, via the artist's verbal prowess, to the Venetian night.

"Shakespeare's plays are society-driven in a lot of ways, but also class-driven. There are regular people, the common man, and then you have the hierarchy . . . the warriors, the soldiers, the clowns." Conversation with Ruben Santiago-Hudson

The configuration of this arena theater gave rise to a convention of drama called the **aside**—a speech directed to the audience only, that the other actors onstage do not appear to hear. The aside can deliver background information to the audience, without the actors having to act it out or act on it. More important, it is used to create a connection between the actor and the audience, to make them partners or co-conspirators. In this way, the audience gains access to secrets and ironies, and to inner thoughts that are withheld from other characters. Another dramatic convention that arose in this era was the **soliloquy,** a monologue delivered by a character standing

THE ORIGINS OF DRAMA IN THE CHRISTIAN CHURCH

Around the tenth century, drama, which had been suppressed by the Church as a pagan ritual, became part of the Christian Mass. These dramas were anonymous works intended less as entertainments than as a form of religious instruction. In other words, those who could not read the Bible could watch it being acted out and profit from the "show." **Miracle plays,** one type of drama in this tradition, enacted the lives of the saints. **Mystery plays,** a second type, brought to life stories of the Bible—such as the Creation or the Crucifixion. *The Second Shepherd's Play* (c. 1400), for example, told the story of Christ's birth. Allegory (see Chapters 14 and 22 for more on allegory) enters into theatrical productions of the third type—**morality plays.** In this form of drama, the figures onstage taught right and proper behavior—morality—to those who watched. In one well-known morality play, *Everyman,* the titular character is called before God to make his reckoning. Other characters in this play have names such as Kindred, Knowledge, and Beauty. In the end, however, none of those other figures cares enough about Everyman's plight to accompany him and help him plead his case in heaven. Only Good Deeds is up to that task—thus, the moral lesson that good deeds are what matter in life.

alone onstage. A soliloquy gives the audience deep access to a character's inner world, as it does in *Hamlet,* when the troubled prince reveals the extent of his dilemmas.

SHAKESPEARE'S CONFOUNDING DIVERSITY

No matter how useful we find it to be, the business of categorization began only after Shakespeare's death. Critics tend to divide the playwright's compositions for theater into four categories.

- **Histories** focus on the reign of kings from the past, from Julius Caesar to Henry V. Because histories naturally contain very astute and sometimes troubling political commentaries, playwrights had to limit their subjects to rulers of the distant past.
- **Comedies** are plays for entertainment and as a convention end in the marriage of two main characters. A comedic plot generally begins with a complication or misunderstanding between two lovers, which is complicated by further scheming and misunderstandings until finally a resolution is attained and the two are wed.
- **Tragedies** are darker plays, with more complex characters and more dire consequences. Tragedies commonly feature murder and as a convention end in a funeral—usually the death of the main character.
- **Romances** (from the French *roman,* which means an "extended narrative") involve lovers whose potential happiness is complicated by misunderstandings, mistaken identities, and any number of other difficulties. Although similar in plot to a comedy, a romance play does not guarantee a happy ending.

> ## "One of the most frightening and thrilling aspects of Shakespeare's plays is the constant reminder of how tentative a thing it is that life turns out to be tragedy or comedy, or some mixture of the two."
>
> Conversation with Ralph Williams

These categories are loose and overlapping units, and as Ralph Williams discusses in his interview, Shakespeare may have taken a bravura delight in confounding definitions, which in any case are more a matter of critical convenience than of theatrical form. Even the darkest of Shakespeare's plays have some comedic component, called **comic relief**—such as the banter between Hamlet and his bewildered old friends Rosencrantz and Guildenstern—which gives the audience a breather from the tension and can also serve to emphasize the tragic elements of the play.

Many plays belong to more than one category. *Macbeth* and *King Lear,* for example, take place in the distant "historical" past but belong to the group called *tragedies. Romeo and Juliet* is a story of complicated love, but it has a famously tragic ending.

Plays such as *Measure for Measure* and *The Merchant of Venice*—which don't fit obviously into these four categories—are often referred to as **problem plays.**

OTHELLO

In his celebration of Shakespeare, the poet Matthew Arnold (see Chapter 20) wrote:

"Others abide our question. Thou art free. . . ."

He means by this that, though it's possible to understand or at least imagine the creative processes of authors, Shakespeare outstrips understanding. In his hands, such universal matters as the conflict between good and evil, love and suspicion, nobility and "base" ambition become specific and embodied; figures like those you will encounter in this tragedy—Iago, Desdemona, and Othello—have come to represent evil, trust, and jealousy both in the old allegorical mode (see Chapters 14 and 22) and in modern terms. *Othello* was most probably composed in 1601, and we know it was performed by 1604; it is, then, the tragedy that follows *Hamlet*—yet with a wholly separate set of characters and problems. The original situation derives from a sixteenth-century tale by Giraldi Cinthio, which portrays the tragedy that ensues when an unnamed Moor in Venice falls in love with the woman Desdemona. But as he had done with the old Norse legend that was the inspiration for *Hamlet,* in *Othello* Shakespeare deepened and changed the sixteenth-century story in important ways.

Two of the most obvious and crucial changes Shakespeare made was to flesh out the main characters of the tragedy and to add new ones. In Othello we see a brand of

"Shakespeare used the phrase 'holding a mirror up to nature.' It's a mirror in which we can reflect, we can contemplate, we can feel, we can understand. And really the arts do this in a way that nothing else can. They are really the most human of all expressions, the most humane and most human of all enterprises. You can talk about philosophy, you can talk about all kinds of things; but nothing taps in to who we are, who we might be, who we're afraid . . . we might become if we don't have the right human qualities—there is something about the arts that touches the wellspring, the really deepest parts of who we are, and makes us more human." Conversation with Edwin Wilson

tortured soul altogether different from that of Hamlet. Indeed, Othello struggles not with vengeance or abandonment but with self-doubt and too much faith in the honesty of those around him. Near the end of the play, Othello says:

> *When you shall these unlucky deeds relate,*
> *Speak of me as I am; nothing extenuate,*
> *Nor set down aught in malice. Then must you speak*
> *Of one that loved not wisely but too well;*
> *Of one not easily jealous but, being wrought*
> *Perplexed in the extreme. . . .*

As you read, decide whether Shakespeare's depiction is the telling or the retelling. Is Othello's story being related with "nothing extenuate," or are we receiving an embellished tale secondhand? Consider the Greek qualities of this tragedy: the nobility of Othello, his fatally short temper, the inevitability of his demise. In what ways is the downfall of Othello larger than life, and in what ways is it poignantly real?

> **"A mark of the very greatest artists, in my view, is honesty . . . [Shakespeare] allows people to see to the depths of their moral imagination."** Conversation with Ralph Williams

RECONSTRUCTING SHAKESPEARE

The written texts we have of Shakespeare's plays do not always or exactly match what the actors said. Troupes competed for new stories, and playwrights had no copyright protection, so the managers of the King's Men did not want their pages distributed and used by others. Much of what we have, therefore, was reconstructed afterward, from an actor's or a theatergoer's memory; often the written versions differ. All this by way of saying that versions may contain different spellings—from "sullied" to "solid" to the now generally accepted "sallied"—of a single word.

Pronunciation has also changed in the course of 400 years, and the way the language *sounded* must be deduced; obviously no tape recordings exist. It's a pretty good guess, for example, that the words "love" and "move" were rhyming words—as in Hamlet's poem, "Doubt that the stars are fire / Doubt that the sun doth move / Doubt truth to be a liar / But never doubt I love."

AS YOU READ Keep track of the shifts in Othello's attitude and moods—from glad devotion to murderous jealousy and, in the end, a self-destructive self-awareness. Is he deluded or noble, or both?

Othello, the Moor of Venice (c. 1601)

CHARACTERS

OTHELLO, *the Moor*

BRABANTIO, *[a senator,] father to Desdemona*

CASSIO, *an honorable lieutenant [to Othello]*

IAGO, *[Othello's ancient,] a villain*

RODERIGO, *a gulled gentleman*

DUKE OF VENICE

SENATORS *[of Venice]*

MONTANO, *Governor of Cyprus*

GENTLEMEN *of Cyprus*

LODOVICO AND GRATIANO, *[kinsmen to Brabantio,] two noble Venetians*

SAILORS

CLOWN

DESDEMONA, *[daughter to Brabantio and] wife to Othello*

EMILIA, *wife to Iago*

BIANCA, *a courtesan [and mistress to Cassio]*

A MESSENGER

A HERALD

A MUSICIAN

Servants, Attendants, Officers, Senators, Musicians, Gentlemen

THE SCENE: *Venice; a seaport in Cyprus*

1.1   *Enter* RODERIGO *and* IAGO.

RODERIGO: Tush, never tell me! I take it much unkindly
That thou, Iago, who hast had my purse
As if the strings were thine, shouldst know of this.

IAGO: 'Sblood, but you'll not hear me.
5   If ever I did dream of such a matter,
Abhor me.

RODERIGO: Thou toldst me thou didst hold him in thy
hate.

IAGO: Despise me
If I do not. Three great ones of the city,
10   In personal suit to make me his lieutenant,
Off-capped to him; and by the faith of man,
I know my price, I am worth no worse a place.
But he, as loving his own pride and purposes,
Evades them with a bombast circumstance
15   Horribly stuffed with epithets of war,
And, in conclusion,
Nonsuits my mediators. For, "Certes," says he,
"I have already chose my officer."
And what was he?
20   Forsooth, a great arithmetician,
One Michael Cassio, a Florentine,
A fellow almost damned in a fair wife,
That never set a squadron in the field
Nor the division of a battle knows
25   More than a spinster—unless the bookish theoric,

Iago (Tim McInnerny) tells Roderigo (Sam Crane) his plans in the 2007 production directed by Wilson Milam.

Wherein the togaed consuls can propose
As masterly as he. Mere prattle without practice
Is all his soldiership. But he, sir, had th' election;
And I, of whom his eyes had seen the proof
At Rhodes, at Cyprus, and on other grounds   30
Christened and heathen, must be beeled and calmed
By debitor and creditor. This countercaster,
He, in good time, must his lieutenant be,
And I—God bless the mark!—his Moorship's ancient.

RODERIGO: By heaven, I rather would have been his
hangman.   35

IAGO: Why, there's no remedy. 'Tis the curse of service;
Preferment goes by letter and affection,

1.1 Location: Venice. A street.
1 never tell me (An expression of incredulity, like "tell me another one.")   **3 this** i.e., Desdemona's elopement   **4 'Sblood** by His (Christ's) blood   **11 him** i.e., Othello   **14 bombast circumstance** wordy evasion. (*Bombast* is cotton padding.)   **15 epithets of war** military expressions   **17 Nonsuits** rejects the petition of.   **Certes** certainly   **20 arithmetician** i.e., a man whose military knowledge is merely theoretical, based on books of tactics   **22 A . . . wife** (Cassio does not seem to be married, but his counterpart in Shakespeare's source does have a woman in his house. See also 4.1.131.)
24 division of a battle disposition of a military unit   **25 a spinster** i.e., a housewife, one whose regular occupation is spinning.   **theoric** theory

---

26 togaed wearing the toga.   **consuls** counselors, senators.   **propose** discuss   **29 his** i.e., Othello's   **31 Christened** Christian. **beeled and calmed** left to leeward without wind, becalmed. (A sailing metaphor.)   **32 debitor and creditor** (A name for a system of bookkeeping, here used as a contemptuous nickname for Cassio.) **countercaster** i.e., bookkeeper, one who tallies with *counters*, or "metal disks." (Said contemptuously.)   **33 in good time** opportunely, i.e., forsooth   **34 God bless the mark** (Perhaps originally a formula to ward off evil; here an expression of impatience.) **ancient** standard-bearer, ensign   **35 his hangman** the executioner of him   **37 Preferment** promotion.   **letter and affection** personal influence and favoritism

And not by old gradation, where each second
Stood heir to th' first. Now, sir, be judge yourself,
40   Whether I in any just term am affined
To love the Moor.

RODERIGO: I would not follow him then.

IAGO: O, sir, content you.
I follow him to serve my turn upon him.
45   We cannot all be masters, nor all masters
Cannot be truly followed. You shall mark
Many a duteous and knee-crooking knave
That, doting on his own obsequious bondage,
Wears out his time, much like his master's ass,
50   For naught but provender, and when he's old,
      cashiered.
Whip me such honest knaves. Others there are
Who, trimmed in forms and visages of duty,
Keep yet their hearts attending on themselves,
And, throwing but shows of service on their lords,
55   Do well thrive by them, and when they have lined
      their coats,
Do themselves homage. These fellows have some soul,
And such a one do I profess myself. For, sir,
It is as sure as you are Roderigo,
Were I the Moor I would not be Iago.
60   In following him, I follow but myself—
Heaven is my judge, not I for love and duty,
But seeming so for my peculiar end.
For when my outward action doth demonstrate
The native act and figure of my heart
65   In compliment extern, 'tis not long after

But I will wear my heart upon my sleeve
For daws to peck at. I am not what I am.

RODERIGO: What a full fortune does the thick-lips owe
If he can carry 't thus!

IAGO: Call up her father.
Rouse him, make after him, poison his delight,   70
Proclaim him in the streets; incense her kinsmen,
And, though he in a fertile climate dwell,
Plague him with flies. Though that his joy be joy,
Yet throw such changes of vexation on 't
As it may lose some color.   75

RODERIGO: Here is her father's house. I'll call aloud.

IAGO: Do, with like timorous accent and dire yell
As when, by night and negligence, the fire
Is spied in populous cities.

RODERIGO: What ho, Brabantio! Signor Brabantio, ho!   80

IAGO: Awake! What, ho, Brabantio! Thieves, thieves,
      thieves!
Look to your house, your daughter, and your bags!
Thieves, thieves!

              BRABANTIO *[enters] above [at a window]*.

BRABANTIO: What is the reason of this terrible
      summons?
What is the matter there?   85

RODERIGO: Signor, is all your family within?

IAGO: Are your doors locked?

BRABANTIO: Why, wherefore ask you this?

---

38 old gradation step-by-step seniority, the traditional way   **40 term** respect.   **affined** bound   **43 content you** don't you worry about that   **46 truly** faithfully   **50 cashiered** dismissed from service   **51 Whip me** whip, as far as I'm concerned   **52 trimmed . . . duty** dressed up in the mere form and show of dutifulness   **55 lined their coats** i.e., stuffed their purses   **56 Do themselves homage** i.e., attend to self-interest solely   **59 Were . . . Iago** i.e., if I were able to assume command, I certainly would not choose to remain a subordinate, or, I would keep a suspicious eye on a flattering subordinate   **62 peculiar** particular, personal   **64 native** innate.   **figure** shape, intent   **65 compliment extern** outward show (conforming in this case to the inner workings and intention of the heart)

67 daws small crowlike birds, proverbially stupid and avaricious. **I am not what I am** i.e., I am not one who wears his heart on his sleeve   **68 full** swelling.   **thick-lips** (Elizabethans often applied the term "Moor" to Negroes.)   **owe** own   **69 carry 't thus** carry this off   **72–73 though . . . flies** though he seems prosperous and happy now, vex him with misery   **73 Though . . . be joy** although he seems fortunate and happy. (Repeats the idea of line 72.)   **74 changes of vexation** vexing changes   **75 As it may** that may cause it to.   **some color** some of its fresh gloss   **77 timorous** frightening   **78 and negligence** i.e., by negligence   **83 s.d. at a window** (This stage direction, from the Quarto, probably calls for an appearance on the gallery above and rearstage.)   **85 the matter** your business

Brabantio (Pierre Vaneck) hears the news of his daughter's betrayal in the 1995 film directed by Oliver Parker.

IAGO: Zounds, sir, you're robbed! For shame, put on your
     gown!
    Your heart is burst; you have lost half your soul.
90   Even now, now, very now, an old black ram
    Is tupping your white ewe. Arise, arise!
    Awake the snorting citizens with the bell,
    Or else the devil will make a grandsire of you.
    Arise, I say!

BRABANTIO: What, have you lost your wits?

95 **RODERIGO:**   Most reverend signor, do you know my
     voice?

BRABANTIO: Not I. What are you?

RODERIGO: My name is Roderigo.

BRABANTIO: The worser welcome.
    I have charged thee not to haunt about my doors.
100   In honest plainness thou hast heard me say
    My daughter is not for thee; and now, in madness,
    Being full of supper and distempering drafts,

Upon malicious bravery dost thou come
    To start my quiet.

RODERIGO: Sir, sir, sir—

BRABANTIO: But thou must needs be sure   105
    My spirits and my place have in their power
    To make this bitter to thee.

RODERIGO: Patience, good sir.

BRABANTIO: What tell'st thou me of robbing? This is
     Venice;
    My house is not a grange.

RODERIGO: Most grave Brabantio,
    In simple and pure soul I come to you.   110

IAGO: Zounds, sir, you are one of those that will not
    serve God if the devil bid you. Because we come to do
    you service and you think we are ruffians, you'll have
    your daughter covered with a Barbary horse; you'll
    have your nephews neigh to you; you'll have coursers   115
    for cousins and jennets for germans.

BRABANTIO: What profane wretch art thou?

IAGO: I am one, sir, that comes to tell you your daughter
    and the Moor are now making the beast with two
    backs.   120

BRABANTIO: Thou art a villain.

IAGO: You are—a senator.

BRABANTIO: This thou shalt answer. I know thee,
    Roderigo.

RODERIGO: Sir, I will answer anything. But I beseech
    you,
    If 't be your pleasure and most wise consent—

---

88 **Zounds** by His (Christ's) wounds   91 **tupping** covering, copulating with. (Said of sheep.)   92 **snorting** snoring   93 **the devil** (The devil was conventionally pictured as black.)   102 **distempering** intoxicating

103 **Upon malicious bravery** with hostile intent to defy me   104 **start** startle, disrupt   106 **My spirits and my place** my temperament and my authority of office.   **have in** have it in   109 **grange** isolated country house   110 **simple** sincere   114 **Barbary** from northern Africa (and hence associated with Othello)   115 **nephews** i.e., grandsons.   **coursers** powerful horses   116 **cousins** kinsmen. **jennets** small Spanish horses.   **germans** near relatives   121 **a senator** (Said with mock politeness, as though the word itself were an insult.)   122 **answer** be held accountable for   124 **wise** well-informed

125   As partly I find it is—that your fair daughter,
At this odd-even and dull watch o' the night,
Transported with no worse nor better guard
But with a knave of common hire, a gondolier,
To the gross clasps of a lascivious Moor—
130   If this be known to you and your allowance
We then have done you bold and saucy wrongs.
But if you know not this, my manners tell me
We have your wrong rebuke. Do not believe
That, from the sense of all civility,
135   I thus would play and trifle with your reverence.
Your daughter, if you have not given her leave,
I say again, hath made a gross revolt,
Tying her duty, beauty, wit, and fortunes
In an extravagant and wheeling stranger
140   Of here and everywhere. Straight satisfy yourself.
If she be in her chamber or your house,
Let loose on me the justice of the state
For thus deluding you.

BRABANTIO: Strike on the tinder, ho!
145   Give me a taper! Call up all my people!
This accident is not unlike my dream.
Belief of it oppresses me already.
Light, I say, light!   *Exit [above.]*

IAGO: Farewell, for I must leave you.
It seems not meet nor wholesome to my place
150   To be producted—as, if I stay, I shall—
Against the Moor. For I do know the state,
However this may gall him with some check,
Cannot with safety cast him, for he's embarked
With such loud reason to the Cyprus wars,

Which even now stands in act, that, for their souls,   155
Another of his fathom they have none
To lead their business; in which regard,
Though I do hate him as I do hell pains,
Yet for necessity of present life
I must show out a flag and sign of love,   160
Which is indeed but sign. That you shall surely find
    him,
Lead to the Sagittary that raisèd search,
And there will I be with him. So farewell.   *Exit.*

      Enter [below] BRABANTIO *[in his
      nightgown] with servants and torches.*

BRABANTIO: It is too true an evil. Gone she is;
And what's to come of my despisèd time   165
Is naught but bitterness. Now, Roderigo,
Where didst thou see her?—O unhappy girl!—
With the Moor, say'st thou?—Who would be a
    father?—
How didst thou know 'twas she?—O, she deceives me
Past thought!—What said she to you?—Get more   170
    tapers.
Raise all my kindred.—Are they married, think you?

RODERIGO: Truly, I think they are.

BRABANTIO: O heaven! How got she out? O treason of
    the blood!
Fathers, from hence trust not your daughters' minds
By what you see them act. Is there not charms   175
By which the property of youth and maidhood
May be abused? Have you not read, Roderigo,
Of some such thing?

RODERIGO: Yes, sir, I have indeed.

---

126 odd-even between one day and the next, i.e., about midnight
127 with by   **128 But with a knave** than by a low fellow, a servant
130 allowance permission   **131 saucy** insolent   **134 from** contrary
to.   **civility** good manners, decency   **135 your reverence** the respect due to you   **138 wit** intelligence   **139 extravagant** expatriate,
wandering far from home.   **wheeling** roving about, vagabond.
stranger foreigner   **140 Straight** straightway   **144 tinder,** charred
linen ignited by a spark from flint and steel, used to light torches or
tapers (lines 145, 170)   **146 accident** occurrence, event   **149 meet**
fitting.   **place** position (as ensign)   **150 producted** produced (as
a witness)   **152 gall** rub; oppress.   **check** rebuke   **153 cast** dismiss.
embarked engaged   **154 loud reason** unanimous shout of confirmation (in the Senate)

---

155 stands in act are going on.   **for their souls** to save themselves
156 fathom i.e., ability, depth of experience   **157 in which regard**
out of regard for which   **159 life** livelihood   **162 Sagittary** (An inn
or house where Othello and Desdemona are staying, named for its
sign of Sagittarius, or Centaur.)   **raisèd search** search party roused
out of sleep   **163 s.d. nightgown** dressing gown. (This costuming is
specified in the Quarto text.)   **165 time** i.e., remainder of life   **175
charms** spells   **176 property** special quality, nature   **177 abused**
deceived

BRABANTIO: Call up my brother.—O, would you had
        had her!—
180   Some one way, some another.—Do you know
        Where we may apprehend her and the Moor?

RODERIGO: I think I can discover him, if you please
        To get good guard and go along with me.

BRABANTIO: Pray you, lead on. At every house I'll call;
185   I may command at most.—Get weapons, ho!
        And raise some special officers of night.—
        On, good Roderigo. I will deserve your pains.

                                                Exeunt.

1.2   *Enter* OTHELLO, IAGO, *attendants with torches.*

IAGO: Though in the trade of war I have slain men,
        Yet do I hold it very stuff o' the conscience
        To do no contrived murder. I lack iniquity
        Sometimes to do me service. Nine or ten times
5   I had thought t' have yerked him here under the ribs.

OTHELLO: 'Tis better as it is.

IAGO: Nay, but he prated,
        And spoke such scurvy and provoking terms
        Against your honor
        That, with the little godliness I have,
10   I did full hard forbear him. But, I pray you, sir,
        Are you fast married? Be assured of this,
        That the magnifico is much beloved,
        And hath in his effect a voice potential
        As double as the Duke's. He will divorce you,
15   Or put upon you what restraint or grievance
        The law, with all his might to enforce it on,
        Will give him cable.

OTHELLO: Let him do his spite.
        My services which I have done the seigniory
        Shall out-tongue his complaints. 'Tis yet to know—
        Which, when I know that boasting is an honor,   20
        I shall promulgate—I fetch my life and being
        From men of royal siege, and my demerits
        May speak unbonneted to as proud a fortune
        As this that I have reached. For know, Iago,
        But that I love the gentle Desdemona,   25
        I would not my unhousèd free condition
        Put into circumscription and confine
        For the sea's worth. But look, what lights come yond?

                Enter CASSIO *[and certain officers]*
                                          with torches.

IAGO   Those are the raisèd father and his friends.
        You were best go in.   30

OTHELLO: Not I. I must be found.
        My parts, my title, and my perfect soul
        Shall manifest me rightly. Is it they?

IAGO: By Janus, I think no.

OTHELLO: The servants of the Duke? And my
        lieutenant?
        The goodness of the night upon you, friends!   35
        What is the news?

CASSIO: The Duke does greet you, General,
        And he requires your haste-post-haste appearance
        Even on the instant.

OTHELLO: What is the matter, think you?

CASSIO: Something from Cyprus, as I may divine.
        It is a business of some heat. The galleys   40

---

182 discover reveal, uncover   **185 command** demand assistance   **187 deserve** show gratitude for

1.2 Location: Venice. Another street, before Othello's lodgings.
2 very stuff essence, basic material (continuing the metaphor of *trade* from line 1)   **3 contrived** premeditated   **5 yerked** stabbed.
him i.e., Roderigo   **10 ... him** I restrained myself with great difficulty from assaulting him   **12 magnifico** Venetian grandee, i.e., Brabantio   **13 in his effect** at his command.   **potential** powerful
17 cable i.e., scope

18 seigniory Venetian government   **19 yet to know** not yet widely known   **22 siege** i.e., rank. (Literally, a seat used by a person of distinction.)   **demerits** deserts   **23 unbonneted** without removing the hat, i.e., on equal terms (? Or "with hat off," "in all due modesty.")
26 unhoused unconfined, undomesticated   **27 circumscription and confine** restriction and confinement   **28 the sea's worth** all the riches at the bottom of the sea.   **s.d. officers** (The Quarto text calls for "Cassio with lights, officers with torches.")   **31 My ... soul** my natural gifts, my position or reputation, and my unflawed conscience   **33 Janus** Roman two-faced god of beginnings   **38 matter** business   **39 divine** guess   **40 heat** urgency

Have sent a dozen sequent messengers
This very night at one another's heels,
And many of the consuls, raised and met,
Are at the Duke's already. You have been hotly called
    for;
45   When, being not at your lodging to be found,
The Senate hath sent about three several quests
To search you out.

OTHELLO: 'Tis well I am found by you.
I will but spend a word here in the house
And go with you.   *[Exit.]*

CASSIO: Ancient, what makes he here?

50 **IAGO:**   Faith, he tonight hath boarded a land carrack.
If it prove lawful prize, he's made forever.

CASSIO: I do not understand.

IAGO: He's married.

CASSIO: To who?

                  [Enter OTHELLO.*]*

IAGO: Marry, to—Come, Captain, will you go?

OTHELLO: Have with you.

55 **CASSIO:**   Here comes another troop to seek for you.

        Enter BRABANTIO, RODERIGO, *with officers*
                     and torches.

IAGO: It is Brabantio. General, be advised.
He comes to bad intent.

OTHELLO: Holla! Stand there!

RODERIGO: Signor, it is the Moor.

BRABANTIO: Down with him, thief!
                [They draw on both sides.]

IAGO: You, Roderigo! Come, sir, I am for you.

OTHELLO: Keep up your bright swords, for the dew will
    rust them.   60
Good signor, you shall more command with years
Than with your weapons.

BRABANTIO: O thou foul thief, where hast thou stowed
    my daughter?
Damned as thou art, thou hast enchanted her!
For I'll refer me to all things of sense,   65
If she in chains of magic were not bound
Whether a maid so tender, fair, and happy,
So opposite to marriage that she shunned
The wealthy curlèd darlings of our nation,
Would ever have, t' incur a general mock,   70
Run from her guardage to the sooty bosom
Of such a thing as thou—to fear, not to delight.
Judge me the world if 'tis not gross in sense
That thou hast practiced on her with foul charms,
Abused her delicate youth with drugs or minerals   75
That weakens motion. I'll have 't disputed on;
'Tis probable and palpable to thinking.
I therefore apprehend and do attach thee
For an abuser of the world, a practicer
Of arts inhibited and out of warrant.—   80
Lay hold upon him! If he do resist,
Subdue him at his peril.

OTHELLO: Hold your hands,
Both you of my inclining and the rest.
Were it my cue to fight, I should have known it
Without a prompter.—Whither will you that I go   85
To answer this your charge?

---

41 **sequent** successive   43 **consuls** senators   46 **about** all over
the city. **several** separate   49 **makes** does   50 **boarded** gone
aboard and seized as an act of piracy (with sexual suggestion).
carrack large merchant ship   51 **prize** booty   53 **Marry** (An oath,
originally "by the Virgin Mary"; here used with wordplay on *married.*)   54 **Have with you** i.e., let's go   55 **s.d. officers and torches**
(The Quarto text calls for "others with lights and weapons.")   56 **be
advised** be on your guard

60 **Keep up** keep in the sheath   65 **refer me** submit my case.
things of sense commonsense understandings, or, creatures possessing common sense   71 **her guardage** my guardianship of her
73 **gross in sense** obvious   75 **minerals** i.e., poisons   76 **weakens
motion** impair the vital faculties.   **disputed on** argued in court by
professional counsel, debated by experts   78 **attach** arrest   80 **arts
inhibited** prohibited arts, black magic.   **out of warrant** illegal   83
inclining following, party

BRABANTIO: To prison, till fit time
Of law and course of direct session
Call thee to answer.

OTHELLO: What if I do obey?
How may the Duke be therewith satisfied,
90
Whose messengers are here about my side
Upon some present business of the state
To bring me to him?

OFFICER: 'Tis true, most worthy signor.
The Duke's in council, and your noble self,
95
I am sure, is sent for.

BRABANTIO: How? The Duke in council?
In this time of the night? Bring him away.
Mine's not an idle cause. The Duke himself,
Or any of my brothers of the state,
Cannot but feel this wrong as 'twere their own;
100
For if such actions may have passage free,
Bondslaves and pagans shall our statesmen be.

Exeunt.

1.3   *Enter* DUKE *[and]* SENATORS *[and sit at a
table, with lights], and officers. [The* DUKE *and*
SENATORS *are reading dispatches.]*

DUKE: There is no composition in these news
That gives them credit.

FIRST SENATOR: Indeed, they are disproportioned.
My letters say a hundred and seven galleys.

5   **DUKE:**   And mine, a hundred forty.

SECOND SENATOR: And mine, two hundred.
But though they jump not on a just account—

The Duke, senators, and officers sit to hear Othello's claims.

As in these cases, where the aim reports
'Tis oft with difference—yet do they all confirm
A Turkish fleet, and bearing up to Cyprus.

DUKE: Nay, it is possible enough to judgment.   10
I do not so secure me in the error
But the main article I do approve
In fearful sense.

SAILOR *(within)*:   What ho, what ho, what ho!

Enter SAILOR.

OFFICER: A messenger from the galleys.

DUKE: Now, what's the business?   15

SAILOR: The Turkish preparation makes for Rhodes.
So was I bid report here to the state
By Signor Angelo.

DUKE: How say you by this change?

---

88 **course of direct session** regular or specially convened legal proceedings   96 **away** right along   97 **idle** trifling   100 **have passage
free** are allowed to go unchecked

1.3. Location: Venice. A council chamber.
s.d. Enter . . . Officers (The Quarto text calls for the Duke and senators to "sit at a table with lights and attendants.")   1 **composition**
consistency   3 **disproportioned** inconsistent   6 **jump** agree.
just exact

---

7 **the aim** conjecture   11–12 **I do not . . . approve** I do not take such
(false) comfort in the discrepancies that I fail to perceive the main
point, i.e., that the Turkish fleet is threatening   16 **preparation** fleet
prepared for battle   19 **by** about

FIRST SENATOR: This cannot be
20 By no assay of reason. 'Tis a pageant
To keep us in false gaze. When we consider
Th' importancy of Cyprus to the Turk,
And let ourselves again but understand
That, as it more concerns the Turk than Rhodes,
25 So may he with more facile question bear it,
For that it stands not in such warlike brace,
But altogether lacks th' abilities
That Rhodes is dressed in—if we make thought of
this,
We must not think the Turk is so unskillful
30 To leave that latest which concerns him first,
Neglecting an attempt of ease and gain
To wake and wage a danger profitless.

DUKE: Nay, in all confidence, he's not for Rhodes.

OFFICER: Here is more news.

Enter a MESSENGER.

35 **MESSENGER:** The Ottomites, reverend and gracious,
Steering with due course toward the isle of Rhodes,
Have there injointed them with an after fleet.

FIRST SENATOR: Ay, so I thought. How many, as you
guess?

MESSENGER: Of thirty sail; and now they do restem
40 Their backward course, bearing with frank
appearance
Their purposes toward Cyprus. Signor Montano,
Your trusty and most valiant servitor,
With his free duty recommends you thus,
And prays you to believe him.

---

20 **assay** test. **pageant** mere show   21 **in false gaze** looking the
wrong way   25 **So may . . . it** so also he (the Turk) can more easily
capture it (Cyprus)   26 **For that** since.   **brace** state of defense   27
abilities means of self-defense   28 **dressed in** equipped with   29
unskillful deficient in judgment   30 **latest** last   32 **wake** stir up.
wage risk   37 **injointed them** joined themselves.   **after** second,
following   39–40 **restem . . . course** retrace their original course
40 **frank appearance** undisguised intent   42 **servitor** officer under your command   43 **free duty** freely given and loyal service.
recommends commends himself and reports to

DUKE: 'Tis certain then for Cyprus. 45
Marcus Luccicos, is not he in town?

FIRST SENATOR: He's now in Florence.

DUKE: Write from us to him, post-post-haste. Dispatch.

FIRST SENATOR: Here comes Brabantio and the valiant
Moor.

Enter BRABANTIO, OTHELLO, CASSIO,
IAGO, RODERIGO, *and officers.*

DUKE: Valiant Othello, we must straight employ you 50
Against the general enemy Ottoman.
[To BRABANTIO.*]* I did not see you; welcome, gentle
signor.
We lacked your counsel and your help tonight.

BRABANTIO: So did I yours. Good Your Grace, pardon
me;
Neither my place nor aught I heard of business 55
Hath raised me from my bed, nor doth the general
care
Take hold on me, for my particular grief
Is of so floodgate and o'erbearing nature
That it engluts and swallows other sorrows
And it is still itself. 60

DUKE: Why, what's the matter?

BRABANTIO: My daughter! O, my daughter!

DUKE AND SENATORS: Dead?

BRABANTIO: Ay, to me.
She is abused, stol'n from me, and corrupted
By spells and medicines bought of mountebanks;
For nature so preposterously to err,
Being not deficient, blind, or lame of sense, 65
Sans witchcraft could not.

DUKE: Whoe'er he be that in this foul proceeding
Hath thus beguiled your daughter of herself,

---

50 **straight** straightway   51 **general enemy** universal enemy to all
Christendom   52 **gentle** noble   55 **place** official position   57 **particular** personal   58 **floodgate** i.e., overwhelming (as when flood-
gates are opened)   59 **engluts** engulfs   60 **is still itself** remains
undiminished   62 **abused** deceived   65 **deficient** defective.   **lame
of sense** deficient in sensory perception   66 **Sans** without

Othello (Laurence Fishburne) and Cassio (Nathaniel Parker) stand
in defense before the Duke.

And you of her, the bloody book of law
70 You shall yourself read in the bitter letter
After your own sense—yea, though our proper son
Stood in your action.

BRABANTIO: Humbly I thank Your Grace.
Here is the man, this Moor, whom now it seems
Your special mandate for the state affairs
75 Hath hither brought.

ALL: We are very sorry for 't.

DUKE [*To* OTHELLO]:   What, in your own part, can you
say to this?

BRABANTIO: Nothing, but this is so.

OTHELLO: Most potent, grave, and reverend signors,
My very noble and approved good masters:
80 That I have ta'en away this old man's daughter,
It is most true; true, I have married her.
The very head and front of my offending
Hath this extent, no more. Rude am I in my speech,

And little blessed with the soft phrase of peace;
For since these arms of mine had seven years' pith,   85
Till now some nine moons wasted, they have used
Their dearest action in the tented field;
And little of this great world can I speak
More than pertains to feats of broils and battle,
And therefore little shall I grace my cause   90
In speaking for myself. Yet, by your gracious patience,
I will a round unvarnished tale deliver
Of my whole course of love—what drugs, what
     charms,
What conjuration, and what mighty magic,
For such proceeding I am charged withal,   95
I won his daughter.

BRABANTIO: A maiden never bold;
Of spirit so still and quiet that her motion
Blushed at herself; and she, in spite of nature,
Of years, of country, credit, everything,
To fall in love with what she feared to look on!   100
It is a judgment maimed and most imperfect
That will confess perfection so could err
Against all rules of nature, and must be driven
To find out practices of cunning hell
Why this should be. I therefore vouch again   105
That with some mixtures powerful o'er the blood,
Or with some dram conjured to this effect,
He wrought upon her.

DUKE: To vouch this is no proof,
Without more wider and more overt test
Than these thin habits and poor likelihoods   110
Of modern seeming do prefer against him.

---

71 After . . . sense according to your own interpretation.   **our
proper** my own   **72 Stood . . . action** were under your accusation
79 approved proved, esteemed   **82 head and front** height and
breadth, entire extent   **83 Rude** unpolished

85 since . . . pith i.e., since I was seven.   **pith** strength, vigor   **86
Till . . . wasted** until some nine months ago (since when Othello has
evidently been not on active duty but in Venice)   **87 dearest** most
valuable   **92 round** plain   **95 withal** with   **97–98 her . . . herself**
i.e., she blushed easily at herself. (*Motion* can suggest the impulse
of the soul or of the emotions, or physical movement.)   **99 years**
i.e., difference in age.   **credit** virtuous reputation   **102 confess**
concede (that)   **104 practices** plots   **105 vouch** assert   **106 blood**
passions   **107 dram . . . effect** dose made by magical spells to have
this effect   **109 more wider** fuller.   **test** testimony   **110 habits**
garments, i.e., appearances.   **poor likelihoods** weak inferences
111 modern seeming commonplace assumption.   **prefer** bring
forth

FIRST SENATOR: But Othello, speak.
    Did you by indirect and forcèd courses
    Subdue and poison this young maid's affections?
115   Or came it by request and such fair question
    As soul to soul affordeth?

OTHELLO: I do beseech you,
    Send for the lady to the Sagittary
    And let her speak of me before her father.
    If you do find me foul in her report,
120   The trust, the office I do hold of you
    Not only take away, but let your sentence
    Even fall upon my life.

DUKE: Fetch Desdemona hither.

OTHELLO: Ancient, conduct them. You best know the
    place.
        [Exeunt IAGO *and attendants.]*
    And, till she come, as truly as to heaven
125   I do confess the vices of my blood,
    So justly to your grave ears I'll present
    How I did thrive in this fair lady's love,
    And she in mine.

DUKE: Say it, Othello.

130 OTHELLO: Her father loved me, oft invited me,
    Still questioned me the story of my life
    From year to year—the battles, sieges, fortunes
    That I have passed.
    I ran it through, even from my boyish days
135   To th' very moment that he bade me tell it,
    Wherein I spoke of most disastrous chances,
    Of moving accidents by flood and field,
    Of hairbreadth scapes i' th' imminent deadly breach,
    Of being taken by the insolent foe
140   And sold to slavery, of my redemption thence,
    And portance in my travel's history,
    Wherein of antres vast and deserts idle,

Brabantio bids Desdemona speak.

    Rough quarries, rocks, and hills whose heads touch
      heaven,
    It was my hint to speak—such was my process—
    And of the Cannibals that each other eat,   145
    The Anthropophagi, and men whose heads
    Do grow beneath their shoulders. These things to hear
    Would Desdemona seriously incline;
    But still the house affairs would draw her thence,
    Which ever as she could with haste dispatch   150
    She'd come again, and with a greedy ear
    Devour up my discourse. Which I, observing,
    Took once a pliant hour, and found good means
    To draw from her a prayer of earnest heart
    That I would all my pilgrimage dilate,   155
    Whereof by parcels she had something heard,
    But not intentively. I did consent,
    And often did beguile her of her tears,
    When I did speak of some distressful stroke
    That my youth suffered. My story being done, 160
    She gave me for my pains a world of sighs,
    She swore, in faith, 'twas strange, 'twas passing
      strange,
    'Twas pitiful, 'twas wondrous pitiful.

---

113 forcèd courses means used against her will **115 question** conversation **125 blood** passions, human nature **126 justly** truthfully, accurately **131 Still** continually **137 moving accidents** stirring happenings **138 imminent . . . breach** death-threatening gaps made in a fortification **141 portance** conduct **142 antres** caverns. **idle** barren, desolate

---

143 Rough quarries rugged rock formations **144 hint** occasion, opportunity **146 Anthropophagi** man-eaters. (A term from Pliny's *Natural History*). **153 pliant** well-suiting **155 dilate** relate in detail **156 by parcels** piecemeal **157 intentively** with full attention, continuously **162 passing** exceedingly

She wished she had not heard it, yet she wished
165 That heaven had made her such a man. She thanked
          me,
And bade me, if I had a friend that loved her,
I should but teach him how to tell my story,
And that would woo her. Upon this hint I spake.
She loved me for the dangers I had passed,
170 And I loved her that she did pity them.
This only is the witchcraft I have used.
Here comes the lady. Let her witness it.

          Enter DESDEMONA, IAGO, *[and] attendants.*

DUKE: I think this tale would win my daughter too.
          Good Brabantio,
175 Take up this mangled matter at the best.
Men do their broken weapons rather use
Than their bare hands.

BRABANTIO: I pray you, hear her speak.
If she confess that she was half the wooer,
Destruction on my head if my bad blame
180 Light on the man!—Come hither, gentle mistress.
Do you perceive in all this noble company
Where most you owe obedience?

DESDEMONA: My noble Father,
I do perceive here a divided duty.
To you I am bound for life and education;
185 My life and education both do learn me
How to respect you. You are the lord of duty;
I am hitherto your daughter. But here's my husband,
And so much duty as my mother showed
To you, preferring you before her father,
190 So much I challenge that I may profess
Due to the Moor my lord.

BRABANTIO: God be with you! I have done.
Please it Your Grace, on to the state affairs.
I had rather to adopt a child than get it.
195 Come hither, Moor.   *[He joins the hands of* OTHELLO
                    and DESDEMONA.*]*

I here do give thee that with all my heart
Which, but thou hast already, with all my heart
I would keep from thee.—For your sake, jewel,
I am glad at soul I have no other child,
For thy escape would teach me tyranny,   200
To hang clogs on them.—I have done, my lord.

DUKE: Let me speak like yourself, and lay a sentence
Which, as a grece or step, may help these lovers
Into your favor.
When remedies are past, the griefs are ended   205
By seeing the worst, which late on hopes depended.
To mourn a mischief that is past and gone
Is the next way to draw new mischief on.
What cannot be preserved when fortune takes,
Patience her injury a mockery makes.   210
The robbed that smiles steals something from the
          thief;
He robs himself that spends a bootless grief.

BRABANTIO: So let the Turk of Cyprus us beguile,
We lose it not, so long as we can smile.
He bears the sentence well that nothing bears   215
But the free comfort which from thence he hears,
But he bears both the sentence and the sorrow
That, to pay grief, must of poor patience borrow.
These sentences, to sugar or to gall,
Being strong on both sides, are equivocal.   220

---

196 with all my heart wherein my whole affection has been engaged   **197 with all my heart** willingly, gladly   **198 For your sake**
on your account   **200 escape** elopement   **201 clogs** (Literally,
blocks of wood fastened to the legs of criminals or convicts to inhibit escape.)   **202 like yourself** i.e., as you would, in your proper
temper.   **lay a sentence** apply a maxim   **203 grece** step   **205
remedies** hopes of remedy   **206 which . . . depended** which griefs
were sustained until recently by hopeful anticipation   **207 mischief**
misfortune, injury   **208 next** nearest   **209 What** whatever   **210
Patience . . . makes** patience laughs at the injury inflicted by fortune
(and thus eases the pain)   **212 spends a bootless grief** indulges in
unavailing grief   **215–218 He bears . . . borrow** a person well bears
out your maxim who can enjoy its platitudinous comfort, free of all
genuine sorrow, but anyone whose grief bankrupts his poor patience
is left with your saying and his sorrow, too. (*Bears the sentence* also
plays on the meaning "receives judicial sentence.")   **219–220 These
. . . equivocal** these fine maxims are equivocal, either sweet or bitter
in their application

---

165 made her created her to be   **168 hint** opportunity. (Othello
does not mean that she was dropping hints.)   **175 Take . . . best**
make the best of a bad bargain   **184 education** upbringing   **185
learn** teach   **186 of duty** to whom duty is due   **190 challenge**
claim   **194 get** beget

But words are words. I never yet did hear
That the bruisèd heart was piercèd through the ear.
I humbly beseech you, proceed to th' affairs of state.

DUKE: The Turk with a most mighty preparation
225   makes for Cyprus. Othello, the fortitude of the place
is best known to you; and though we have there a
substitute of most allowed sufficiency, yet opinion,
a sovereign mistress of effects, throws a more safer
voice on you. You must therefore be content to
230   slubber the gloss of your new fortunes with this more
stubborn and boisterous expedition.

OTHELLO: The tyrant custom, most grave senators,
Hath made the flinty and steel couch of war
My thrice-driven bed of down. I do agnize
235   A natural and prompt alacrity
I find in hardness, and do undertake
These present wars against the Ottomites.
Most humbly therefore bending to your state,
I crave fit disposition for my wife,
240   Due reference of place, and exhibition,
With such accommodation and besort
As levels with her breeding.

DUKE: Why, at her father's.

BRABANTIO: I will not have it so.

OTHELLO: Nor I.

DESDEMONA: Nor I. I would not there reside,
245   To put my father in impatient thoughts
By being in his eye. Most gracious Duke,
To my unfolding lend your prosperous ear,

And let me find a charter in your voice,
T' assist my simpleness.

DUKE: What would you, Desdemona?   250

DESDEMONA: That I did love the Moor to live with him,
My downright violence and storm of fortunes
May trumpet to the world. My heart's subdued
Even to the very quality of my lord.
I saw Othello's visage in his mind,   255
And to his honors and his valiant parts
Did I my soul and fortunes consecrate.
So that, dear lords, if I be left behind,
A moth of peace, and he go to the war,
The rites for why I love him are bereft me,   260
And I a heavy interim shall support
By his dear absence. Let me go with him.

OTHELLO: Let her have your voice.
Vouch with me, heaven, I therefor beg it not
To please the palate of my appetite,   265
Nor to comply with heat—the young affects
In me defunct—and proper satisfaction,
But to be free and bounteous to her mind.
And heaven defend your good souls that you think
I will your serious and great business scant   270
When she is with me. No, when light-winged toys
Of feathered Cupid seel with wanton dullness
My speculative and officed instruments,
That my disports corrupt and taint my business,
Let huswives make a skillet of my helm,   275
And all indign and base adversities
Make head against my estimation!

---

222 piercèd . . . ear i.e., surgically lanced and cured by mere words of advice   **225 fortitude** strength   **227 substitute** deputy   **227 allowed** acknowledged   **227–229 opinion . . . on you** general opinion, an important determiner of affairs, chooses you as the best man   **230 slubber** soil, sully   **231 stubborn** harsh, rough   **234 thrice-driven** thrice sifted, winnowed.   **agnize** know in myself, acknowledge   **236 hardness** hardship   **238 bending . . . state** bowing or kneeling to your authority   **240 reference . . . exhibition** provision of appropriate place to live and allowance of money   **241 accommodation** suitable provision.   **besort** attendance   **242 levels** equals, suits.   **breeding** social position, upbringing   **247 unfolding** explanation, proposal.   **prosperous** propitious

248 charter privilege, authorization   **252 My . . . fortunes** my plain and total breach of social custom, taking my future by storm and disrupting my whole life.   **253–254 My heart's . . . lord** my heart is brought wholly into accord with Othello's virtues; I love him for his virtues   **256 parts** qualities   **259 moth** i.e., one who consumes merely   **260 rites** rites of love (with a suggestion, too, of "rights," sharing)   **262 dear** (1) heartfelt (2) costly   **263 voice** consent   **266 heat** sexual passion.   **young affects** passions of youth, desires   **267 proper** personal   **268 free** generous   **269 defend** forbid.   **think** should think   **272 seel** i.e., make blind (as in falconry, by sewing up the eyes of the hawk during training)   **273 speculative . . . instruments** eyes and other faculties used in the performance of duty   **274 That** so that.   **disports** sexual pastimes.   **taint** impair   **276 indign** unworthy, shameful   **277 Make head** raise an army.   **estimation** reputation

DUKE: Be it as you shall privately determine,
Either for her stay or going. Th' affair cries haste,
280   And speed must answer it.

A SENATOR: You must away tonight.

DESDEMONA: Tonight, my lord?

DUKE: This night.

OTHELLO: With all my heart.

DUKE: At nine i' the morning here we'll meet again.
Othello, leave some officer behind,
And he shall our commission bring to you,
285   With such things else of quality and respect
As doth import you.

OTHELLO: So please Your grace, my ancient;
A man he is of honesty and trust.
To his conveyance I assign my wife,
With what else needful Your Good Grace shall think
290   To be sent after me.

DUKE: Let it be so.
Good night to everyone. *[To* BRABANTIO.*]* And, noble
signor,
If virtue no delighted beauty lack,
Your son-in-law is far more fair than black.

FIRST SENATOR: Adieu, brave Moor. Use Desdemona
well.

295   **BRABANTIO:**   Look to her, Moor, if thou hast eyes to see.
She has deceived her father, and may thee.
                    *Exeunt [*DUKE, BRABANTIO,
                    CASSIO, SENATORS, *and officers].*

OTHELLO: My life upon her faith! Honest Iago,
My Desdemona must I leave to thee.
I prithee, let thy wife attend on her,
300   And bring them after in the best advantage.
Come, Desdemona. I have but an hour
Of love, of worldly matters and direction,
To spend with thee. We must obey the time.
                    Exit [with DESDEMONA*].*

---

285 **of quality and respect** of importance and relevance   286 **import** concern   292 **delighted** capable of delighting   300 **in . . . advantage** at the most favorable opportunity   302 **direction** instructions   303 **the time** the urgency of the present crisis

RODERIGO: Iago—

IAGO: What sayst thou, noble heart?   305

RODERIGO: What will I do, think'st thou?

IAGO: Why, go to bed and sleep.

RODERIGO: I will incontinently drown myself.

IAGO: If thou dost, I shall never love thee after. Why,
thou silly gentleman?   310

RODERIGO: It is silliness to live when to live is torment;
and then have we a prescription to die when death is
our physician.

IAGO: O villainous! I have looked upon the world for
four times seven years, and, since I could distinguish   315
betwixt a benefit and an injury, I never found man
that knew how to love himself. Ere I would say I
would drown myself for the love of a guinea hen, I
would change my humanity with a baboon.

RODERIGO: What should I do? I confess it is my shame   320
to be so fond, but it is not in my virtue to amend it.

IAGO: Virtue? A fig! 'Tis in ourselves that we are thus
or thus. Our bodies are our gardens, to the which our
wills are gardeners; so that if we will plant nettles or
sow lettuce, set hyssop and weed up thyme, supply   325
it with one gender of herbs or distract it with many,
either to have it sterile with idleness or manured with
industry—why, the power and corrigible authority of
this lies in our wills. If the beam of our lives had not
one scale of reason to poise another of sensuality, the   330
blood and baseness of our natures would conduct us
to most preposterous conclusions. But we have reason

---

308 **incontinently** immediately, without self-restraint   312 **prescription** (1) right based on long-established custom (2) doctor's prescription   314 **villainous** i.e., what perfect nonsense   318 **guinea hen** (A slang term for a prostitute.)   321 **fond** infatuated. **virtue** strength, nature   322 **fig** (To give a fig is to thrust the thumb between the first and second fingers in a vulgar and insulting gesture.)   325 **hyssop** a herb of the mint family   326 **gender** kind.   **distract it with** divide it among   327 **idleness** want of cultivation   328 **corrigible authority** power to correct   329 **beam** balance   330 **poise** counterbalance   331 **blood** natural passions

Iago (Kenneth Branagh) and Roderigo (Michael Maloney) discuss how to deal with Othello.

to cool our raging motions, our carnal stings, our unbitted lusts, whereof I take this that you call love to be a sect or scion. 335

RODERIGO: It cannot be.

IAGO: It is merely a lust of the blood and a permission of the will. Come, be a man. Drown thyself? Drown cats and blind puppies. I have professed me thy friend, and I confess me knit to thy deserving with cables of perdurable toughness. I could never better stead thee than now. Put money in thy purse. Follow thou the wars; defeat thy favor with an usurped beard. I say, put money in thy purse. It cannot be long that Desdemona should continue her love to the Moor—put money in thy purse—nor he his to her. It was a violent commencement in her, and thou shalt see an answerable sequestration—put but money in thy purse. These Moors are changeable in their wills— 340 345

fill thy purse with money. The food that to him now is as luscious as locusts shall be to him shortly as bitter as coloquintida. She must change for youth; when she is sated with his body, she will find the error of her choice. She must have change, she must. Therefore put money in thy purse. If thou wilt needs damn thyself, do it a more delicate way than drowning. Make all the money thou canst. If sanctimony and a frail vow betwixt an erring barbarian and a supersubtle Venetian be not too hard for my wits and all the tribe of hell, thou shalt enjoy her. Therefore make money. A pox of drowning thyself! It is clean out of the way. Seek thou rather to be hanged in compassing thy joy than to be drowned and go without her. 350 355 360

RODERIGO: Wilt thou be fast to my hopes if I depend on the issue? 365

IAGO: Thou art sure of me. Go, make money. I have told thee often, and I retell thee again and again, I hate the Moor. My cause is hearted; thine hath no less reason. Let us be conjunctive in our revenge against him. If thou canst cuckold him, thou dost thyself a pleasure, me a sport. There are many events in the womb of time which will be delivered. Traverse, go, provide thy money. We will have more of this tomorrow. Adieu. 370

RODERIGO: Where shall we meet i' the morning?

IAGO: At my lodging. 375

RODERIGO: I'll be with thee betimes. *[He starts to leave.]*

IAGO: Go to, farewell.—Do you hear, Roderigo?

RODERIGO: What say you?

IAGO: No more of drowning, do you hear?

RODERIGO: I am changed. 380

---

333 motions appetites   **334 unbitted** unbridled, uncontrolled   **335 sect or scion** cutting or offshoot   **341 perdurable** very durable   **342 stead** assist   **343 defeat thy favor** disguise your face. **usurped** (The suggestion is that Roderigo is not man enough to have a beard of his own.)   **348 an answerable sequestration** a corresponding separation or estrangement   **349 wills** carnal appetites

---

351 locusts fruit of the carob tree (see Matthew 3:4), or perhaps honeysuckle   **352 coloquintida** colocynth or bitter apple, a purgative   **356 Make** raise, collect   **357 sanctimony** sacred ceremony **358 erring** wandering, vagabond, unsteady   **361 clean . . . way** entirely unsuitable as a course of action   **362 compassing** encompassing, embracing   **364 fast** true   **365 issue** (successful) outcome **368 hearted** fixed in the heart, heartfelt   **369 conjunctive** united **372 Traverse** (A military marching term.)   **376 betimes** early

IAGO: Go to, farewell. Put money enough in your purse.

RODERIGO: I'll sell all my land.   *Exit.*

IAGO: Thus do I ever make my fool my purse;
385   For I mine own gained knowledge should profane
If I would time expend with such a snipe
But for my sport and profit. I hate the Moor;
And it is thought abroad that twixt my sheets
He's done my office. I know not if 't be true;
390   But I, for mere suspicion in that kind,
Will do as if for surety. He holds me well;
The better shall my purpose work on him.
Cassio's a proper man. Let me see now:
To get his place and to plume up my will
395   In double knavery—How, how?—Let's see:
After some time, to abuse Othello's ear
That he is too familiar with his wife.
He hath a person and a smooth dispose
To be suspected, framed to make women false.
400   The Moor is of a free and open nature,
That thinks men honest that but seem to be so,
And will as tenderly be led by the nose
As asses are.
I have 't. It is engendered. Hell and night
Must bring this monstrous birth to the world's light.
                                                   [Exit.]

2.1   *Enter* MONTANO *and two* GENTLEMEN.

MONTANO: What from the cape can you discern at sea?

FIRST GENTLEMAN: Nothing at all. It is a high-
wrought flood.
I cannot, twixt the heaven and the main,
Descry a sail.

---

386 **snipe** woodcock, i.e., fool   388 **it is thought abroad** it is rumored   389 **my office** i.e., my sexual function as husband   391 **do . . . surety** act as if on certain knowledge.   **holds me well** regards me favorably   393 **proper** handsome   394 **plume up** put a feather in the cap of, i.e., glorify, gratify   396 **abuse** deceive   397 **he** i.e., Cassio   398 **dispose** disposition   400 **free** frank, generous   **open** unsuspicious   402 **tenderly** readily

2.1. Location: A seaport in Cyprus. An open place near the quay.
2 **high-wrought flood** very agitated sea   3 **main** ocean (also at line 41)

MONTANO: Methinks the wind hath spoke aloud at land;   5
A fuller blast ne'er shook our battlements.
If it hath ruffianed so upon the sea,
What ribs of oak, when mountains melt on them,
Can hold the mortise? What shall we hear of this?

SECOND GENTLEMAN: A segregation of the Turkish
fleet.   10
For do but stand upon the foaming shore,
The chidden billow seems to pelt the clouds;
The wind-shaked surge, with high and monstrous
mane,
Seems to cast water on the burning Bear
And quench the guards of th' ever-fixèd pole.   15
I never did like molestation view
On the enchafèd flood.

MONTANO: If that the Turkish fleet
Be not ensheltered and embayed, they are drowned;
It is impossible to bear it out.   20

                              Enter a [THIRD] GENTLEMAN.

THIRD GENTLEMAN: News, lads! Our wars are done.
The desperate tempest hath so banged the Turks
That their designment halts. A noble ship of Venice
Hath seen a grievous wreck and sufferance
On most part of their fleet.   25

MONTANO: How? Is this true?

THIRD GENTLEMAN: The ship is here put in,
A Veronesa; Michael Cassio,

---

7 **ruffianed** raged   8 **mountains** i.e., of water   9 **hold the mortise** hold their joints together. (A *mortise* is the socket hollowed out in fitting timbers.)   10 **segregation** dispersal   12 **chidden** i.e., rebuked, repelled (by the shore), and thus shot into the air   13 **monstrous mane** (The surf is like the mane of a wild beast.)   14 **the burning Bear** i.e., the constellation Ursa Minor or the Little Bear, which includes the polestar (and hence regarded as the *guards of th' ever-fixèd pole* in the next line; sometimes the term *guards* is applied to the two "pointers" of the Big Bear or Dipper, which may be intended here.)   16 **like molestation** comparable disturbance   17 **enchafèd** angry   18 **If that** if   19 **embayed** sheltered by a bay   20 **bear it out** survive, weather the storm   23 **designment** design, enterprise. **halts** is lame   24 **wreck** shipwreck.   **sufferance** damage, disaster   28 **Veronesa** i.e., fitted out in Verona for Venetian service, or possibly *Verennessa* (the Folio spelling), i.e., *verrinessa*, a cutter (from *verrinare*, "to cut through")

Lieutenant to the warlike Moor Othello,
30   Is come on shore; the Moor himself at sea,
And is in full commission here for Cyprus.

MONTANO: I am glad on 't. 'Tis a worthy governor.

THIRD GENTLEMAN: But this same Cassio, though he
        speak of comfort
Touching the Turkish loss, yet he looks sadly
35   And prays the Moor be safe, for they were parted
With foul and violent tempest.

MONTANO: Pray heaven he be,
For I have served him, and the man commands
Like a full soldier. Let's to the seaside, ho!
As well to see the vessel that's come in
40   As to throw out our eyes for brave Othello,
Even till we make the main and th' aerial blue
An indistinct regard.

THIRD GENTLEMAN: Come, let's do so,
For every minute is expectancy
Of more arrivance.

                                    Enter CASSIO.

45 **CASSIO:**   Thanks, you the valiant of the warlike isle,
That so approve the Moor! O, let the heavens
Give him defense against the elements,
For I have lost him on a dangerous sea.

MONTANO: Is he well shipped?

50 **CASSIO:**   His bark is stoutly timbered, and his pilot
Of very expert and approved allowance;
Therefore my hopes, not surfeited to death,
Stand in bold cure.
                [A cry] within: "A sail, a sail, a sail!"

CASSIO: What noise?

The men return home from overseas.

A GENTLEMAN: The town is empty. On the brow o' the
        sea   55
Stand ranks of people, and they cry, "A sail!"

CASSIO: My hopes do shape him for the governor.
                                    [A shot within.]

SECOND GENTLEMAN: They do discharge their shot of
        courtesy;
Our friends at least.

CASSIO: I pray you, sir, go forth,
And give us truth who 'tis that is arrived.   60

SECOND GENTLEMAN: I shall.   *Exit.*

MONTANO: But, good Lieutenant, is your general
        wived?

CASSIO: Most fortunately. He hath achieved a maid
That paragons description and wild fame,
One that excels the quirks of blazoning pens,   65
And in th' essential vesture of creation
Does tire the enginer.

---

34 **sadly** gravely   38 **full** perfect   41 **the main . . . blue** the sea
and the sky   42 **An indistinct regard** indistinguishable in our
view   43 **is expectancy** gives expectation   44 **arrivance** arrival   46 **approve** admire, honor   51 **approved allowance** tested
reputation   52 **surfeited to death** i.e., overextended, worn thin
through repeated application or delayed fulfillment   53 **in bold
cure** in strong hopes of fulfillment

---

55 **brow o' the sea** cliff-edge   57 **My . . . for** I hope it is   58 **discharge . . . courtesy** fire a salute in token of respect and courtesy
64 **paragons** surpasses.   **wild fame** extravagant report   65 **quirks**
witty conceits.   **blazoning** setting forth as though in heraldic
language   66–67 **in . . . enginer** in her real, God-given, beauty, (she)
defeats any attempt to praise her.   **enginer** engineer, i.e., poet, one
who devises.

Enter [SECOND] GENTLEMAN.

How now? Who has put in?

SECOND GENTLEMAN: 'Tis one Iago, ancient to the
General.

CASSIO: He's had most favorable and happy speed.
70   Tempests themselves, high seas, and howling winds,
The guttered rocks and congregated sands—
Traitors ensteeped to clog the guiltless keel—
As having sense of beauty, do omit
Their mortal natures, letting go safely by
75   The divine Desdemona.

MONTANO: What is she?

CASSIO: She that I spake of, our great captain's captain,
Left in the conduct of the bold Iago,
Whose footing here anticipates our thoughts
A sennight's speed. Great Jove, Othello guard,
80   And swell his sail with thine own powerful breath,
That he may bless this bay with his tall ship,
Make love's quick pants in Desdemona's arms,
Give renewed fire to our extincted spirits,
And bring all Cyprus comfort!

Enter DESDEMONA, IAGO, RODERIGO,
and EMILIA.

O, behold!
85   The riches of the ship is come on shore!
You men of Cyprus, let her have your knees.
[The GENTLEMEN *make curtsy to*
DESDEMONA.*]*

Hail to thee, lady! And the grace of heaven
Before, behind thee, and on every hand
Enwheel thee round!

DESDEMONA: I thank you, valiant Cassio.
90   What tidings can you tell me of my lord?

CASSIO: He is not yet arrived, nor know I aught
But that he's well and will be shortly here.

DESDEMONA: O, but I fear—How lost you company?

CASSIO: The great contention of sea and skies
Parted our fellowship.
(Within) "A sail, a sail!" *[A shot.]*
But hark. A sail!   95

SECOND GENTLEMAN: They give their greeting to the
citadel.
This likewise is a friend.

CASSIO: See for the news.
[Exit SECOND GENTLEMAN.*]*
Good Ancient, you are welcome. *[Kissing* EMILIA.*]*
Welcome, mistress.
Let it not gall your patience, good Iago,
That I extend my manners; 'tis my breeding   100
That gives me this bold show of courtesy.

IAGO: Sir, would she give you so much of her lips
As of her tongue she oft bestows on me,
You would have enough.

DESDEMONA: Alas, she has no speech!   105

IAGO: In faith, too much.
I find it still, when I have list to sleep.
Marry, before your ladyship, I grant,
She puts her tongue a little in her heart
And chides with thinking.   110

EMILIA: You have little cause to say so.

IAGO: Come on, come on. You are pictures out of doors,
Bells in your parlors, wildcats in your kitchens,
Saints in your injuries, devils being offended,
Players in your huswifery, and huswives in your beds.

---

s.d. Second Gentleman (So identified in the Quarto text here and in lines 58, 61, 68, and 96; the Folio calls him a gentleman.)   **67 put in** i.e., to harbor   **71 guttered** jagged, trenched   **72 ensteeped** lying under water   **73 As** as if.   **omit** forbear to exercise   **74 mortal** deadly   **78 footing** landing   **79 sennight's** week's   **81 tall** splendid, gallant

---

100 extend give scope to.   **breeding** training in the niceties of etiquette   **105 she has no speech** i.e., she's not a chatterbox, as you allege   **107 still** always   **list** desire   **110 with thinking** i.e., in her thoughts only   **111 pictures out of doors** i.e., silent and well-behaved in public   **112 Bells** i.e., jangling, noisy, and brazen.   **in your kitchens** i.e., in domestic affairs. (Ladies would not do the cooking.)   **113 Saints** martyrs   **114 Players** idlers, triflers, or deceivers.   **huswifery** housekeeping.   **huswives** hussies (i.e., women are "busy" in bed, or unduly thrifty in dispensing sexual favors)

115 **DESDEMONA:**   O, fie upon thee, slanderer!

IAGO: Nay, it is true, or else I am a Turk.
   You rise to play, and go to bed to work.

EMILIA: You shall not write my praise.

IAGO: No, let me not.

DESDEMONA: What wouldst write of me, if thou
      shouldst praise me?

120 **IAGO:**   O gentle lady, do not put me to 't,
   For I am nothing if not critical.

DESDEMONA: Come on, essay.—There's one gone to the
      harbor?

IAGO: Ay, madam.

DESDEMONA: I am not merry, but I do beguile
125   The thing I am by seeming otherwise.
   Come, how wouldst thou praise me?

IAGO: I am about it, but indeed my invention
   Comes from my pate as birdlime does from frieze—
   It plucks out brains and all. But my Muse labors,
130   And thus she is delivered:
   If she be fair and wise, fairness and wit,
   The one's for use, the other useth it.

DESDEMONA: Well praised! How if she be black and
      witty?

IAGO: If she be black, and thereto have a wit,
135   She'll find a white that shall her blackness fit.

DESDEMONA: Worse and worse.

EMILIA: How if fair and foolish?

IAGO: She never yet was foolish that was fair,
   For even her folly helped her to an heir.

DESDEMONA: Those are old fond paradoxes to make
      fools laugh i' th' alehouse. What miserable praise   140
      hast thou for her that's foul and foolish?

IAGO: There's none so foul and foolish thereunto,
   But does foul pranks which fair and wise ones do.

DESDEMONA: O heavy ignorance! Thou praisest the
      worst best. But what praise couldst thou bestow on   145
      a deserving woman indeed, one that, in the author-
      ity of her merit, did justly put on the vouch of very
      malice itself?

IAGO: She that was ever fair, and never proud,
   Had tongue at will, and yet was never loud,   150
   Never lacked gold and yet went never gay,
   Fled from her wish, and yet said, "Now I may,"
   She that being angered, her revenge being nigh,
   Bade her wrong stay and her displeasure fly,
   She that in wisdom never was so frail   155
   To change the cod's head for the salmon's tail,
   She that could think and ne'er disclose her mind,
   See suitors following and not look behind,
   She was a wight, if ever such wight were—

DESDEMONA: To do what?   160

IAGO: To suckle fools and chronicle small beer.

DESDEMONA: O most lame and impotent conclusion!
      Do not learn of him, Emilia, though he be thy hus-
      band. How say you, Cassio? Is he not a most profane
      and liberal counselor?   165

---

116 **a Turk** an infidel, not to be believed   121 **critical** censorious
122 **essay** try   125 **The thing I am** i.e., my anxious self   128 **birdlime** sticky substance used to catch small birds.   **frieze** coarse
woolen cloth   129 **labors** (1) exerts herself (2) prepares to deliver
a child (with a following pun on *delivered* in line 130)   132 **The
one's . . . it** i.e., her cleverness will make use of her beauty   133
black dark-complexioned, brunette   135 **a white** a fair person (with
wordplay on "wight," a person).   **fit** (with sexual suggestion
of mating)

138 **folly** (with added meaning of "lechery, wantonness").   **to an
heir** i.e., to bear a child   139 **fond** foolish   141 **foul** ugly   142
thereunto in addition   143 **foul** sluttish   147 **put . . . vouch** compel
the approval   151 **gay** extravagantly clothed   152 **Fled . . . may**
avoided temptation where the choice was hers   154 **Bade . . . stay**
i.e., resolved to put up with her injury patiently   156 **To . . . tail**
i.e., to exchange a lackluster husband for a sexy lover (?) (*Cod's head*
is slang for "penis," and *tail* for "pudendum.")   161 **suckle fools**
breastfeed babies.   **chronicle small beer** i.e., keep petty household
accounts, keep track of trivial matters   164 **profane** irreverent,
ribald   165 **liberal** licentious, free-spoken

CASSIO: He speaks home, madam. You may relish him
more in the soldier than in the scholar.

> *[CASSIO and DESDEMONA stand*
> *together, conversing intimately.]*

IAGO *[aside]*:   He takes her by the palm. Ay, well said,
whisper. With as little a web as this will I ensnare as
170   great a fly as Cassio. Ay, smile upon her, do; I will gyve
thee in thine own courtship. You say true; 'tis so, indeed. If such tricks as these strip you out of your lieu-
tenantry, it had been better you had not kissed your
three fingers so oft, which now again you are most apt
175   to play the sir in. Very good; well kissed! An excellent
courtesy! 'Tis so, indeed. Yet again your fingers to
your lips? Would they were clyster pipes for your sake!
[Trumpet within.] The Moor! I know his trumpet.

CASSIO: 'Tis truly so.

DESDEMONA: Let's meet him and receive him.

180   **CASSIO:**   Lo, where he comes!

> *Enter* OTHELLO *and attendants.*

OTHELLO: O my fair warrior!

DESDEMONA: My dear Othello!

OTHELLO: It gives me wonder great as my content
To see you here before me. O my soul's joy,
If after every tempest come such calms,
185   May the winds blow till they have wakened death,
And let the laboring bark climb hills of seas
Olympus-high, and duck again as low
As hell's from heaven! If it were now to die,
'Twere now to be most happy, for I fear
190   My soul hath her content so absolute
That not another comfort like to this
Succeeds in unknown fate.

Othello greets his bride, Desdemona (Irène Jacob).

DESDEMONA: The heavens forbid
But that our loves and comforts should increase
Even as our days do grow!

OTHELLO: Amen to that, sweet powers!   195
I cannot speak enough of this content.
It stops me here; it is too much of joy.
And this, and this, the greatest discords be
> *[They kiss.]*
That e'er our hearts shall make!

IAGO *[aside]*:   O, you are well tuned now!   200
But I'll set down the pegs that make this music,
As honest as I am.

OTHELLO: Come, let us to the castle.
News, friends! Our wars are done, the Turks are
drowned.
How does my old acquaintance of this isle?—   205
Honey, you shall be well desired in Cyprus;
I have found great love amongst them. O my sweet,
I prattle out of fashion, and I dote

---

166 home right to the target. (A term from fencing.)   **relish** appreciate   **167 in** in the character of   **168 well said** well done   **170
gyve** fetter, shackle   **171 courtship** courtesy, show of courtly manners.   **You say true** i.e., that's right, go ahead   **175 the sir** i.e.,
the fine gentleman   **177 clyster pipes** tubes used for enemas and
douches   **192 Succeeds . . . fate** i.e., can follow in the unknown
future

---

198 s.d. They kiss (The direction is from the Quarto.)   **201 set
down** loosen (and hence untune the instrument)   **202 As . . . I am**
for all my supposed honesty   **206 desired** welcomed   **208 out of
fashion** irrelevantly, incoherently (?)

Iago watches from a distance as Othello makes his triumphant entry.

210 In mine own comforts.—I prithee, good Iago,
Go to the bay and disembark my coffers.
Bring thou the master to the citadel;
He is a good one, and his worthiness
Does challenge much respect.—Come, Desdemona.—
Once more, well met at Cyprus!
Exeunt OTHELLO *and* DESDEMONA *[and all but* IAGO *and* RODERIGO*].*

215 **IAGO** *[to an attendant]*:   Do thou meet me presently at
the harbor. *[To* RODERIGO.*]* Come hither. If thou
be'st valiant—as, they say, base men being in love have
then a nobility in their natures more than is native to
them—list me. The Lieutenant tonight watches on the
220 court of guard. First, I must tell thee this: Desdemona
is directly in love with him.

RODERIGO: With him? Why, 'tis not possible.

IAGO: Lay thy finger thus, and let thy soul be instructed.
Mark me with what violence she first loved the
225 Moor, but for bragging and telling her fantastical

lies. To love him still for prating? Let not thy discreet
heart think it. Her eye must be fed; and what delight
shall she have to look on the devil? When the blood
is made dull with the act of sport, there should be,
again to inflame it and to give satiety a fresh appe-   230
tite, loveliness in favor, sympathy in years, manners,
and beauties—all which the Moor is defective in.
Now, for want of these required conveniences, her
delicate tenderness will find itself abused, begin to
heave the gorge, disrelish and abhor the Moor. Very   235
nature will instruct her in it and compel her to some
second choice. Now, sir, this granted—as it is a most
pregnant and unforced position—who stands so
eminent in the degree of this fortune as Cassio does?
A knave very voluble, no further conscionable than in   240
putting on the mere form of civil and humane seeming for the better compassing of his salt and most
hidden loose affection. Why, none, why, none. A slipper and subtle knave, a finder out of occasions, that
has an eye can stamp and counterfeit advantages,   245
though true advantage never present itself; a devilish
knave. Besides, the knave is handsome, young, and
hath all those requisites in him that folly and green
minds look after. A pestilent complete knave, and the
woman hath found him already.   250

RODERIGO: I cannot believe that in her. She's full of
most blessed condition.

IAGO: Blessed fig's end! The wine she drinks is made
of grapes. If she had been blessed, she would never
have loved the Moor. Blessed pudding! Didst thou not   255
see her paddle with the palm of his hand? Didst not
mark that?

---

229 the act of sport sex   **231 favor** appearance.   **sympathy** correspondence, similarity   **233 required conveniences** things conducive to sexual compatibility   **234 abused** cheated, revolted.   **235
heave the gorge** experience nausea   **235–236 Very nature** her very
instincts   **238 pregnant** evident, cogent   **239 in . . . of** as next in
line for   **240 voluble** facile, glib.   **conscionable** conscientious,
conscience-bound   **241 humane** polite, courteous   **242 salt** licentious   **243 affection** passion   **243–244 slipper** slippery   **245 an
eye can stamp** an eye that can coin, create.   **advantages** favorable
opportunities   **248 folly** wantonness.   **green** immature   **250
found him** sized him up, perceived his intent   **252 condition**
disposition   **253 fig's end** (See 1.3.322 for the vulgar gesture of the
fig.)   **255 pudding** sausage

---

210 coffers chests, baggage   **211 master** ship's captain   **213 challenge** lay claim to, deserve   **217 base men** even lowly born men
219 list listen to   **220 court of guard** guardhouse. (Cassio is in
charge of the watch.)   **223 thus** i.e., on your lips   **225 but** only

RODERIGO: Yes, that I did; but that was but courtesy.

IAGO: Lechery, by this hand. An index and obscure
260   prologue to the history of lust and foul thoughts.
They met so near with their lips that their breaths
embraced together. Villainous thoughts, Roderigo!
When these mutualities so marshal the way, hard at
hand comes the master and main exercise, th' incor-
265   porate conclusion. Pish! But, sir, be you ruled by me. I
have brought you from Venice. Watch you tonight; for
the command, I'll lay 't upon you. Cassio knows you
not. I'll not be far from you. Do you find some occasion to anger Cassio, either by speaking too loud, or
270   tainting his discipline, or from what other course you
please, which the time shall more favorably minister.

RODERIGO: Well.

IAGO: Sir, he's rash and very sudden in choler, and
haply may strike at you. Provoke him that he may,
275   for even out of that will I cause these of Cyprus to
mutiny, whose qualification shall come into no true
taste again but by the displanting of Cassio. So shall
you have a shorter journey to your desires by the
means I shall then have to prefer them, and the
280   impediment most profitably removed, without the
which there were no expectation of our prosperity.

RODERIGO: I will do this, if you can bring it to any
opportunity.

IAGO: I warrant thee. Meet me by and by at the citadel.
285   I must fetch his necessaries ashore. Farewell.

RODERIGO: Adieu.   *Exit.*

IAGO: That Cassio loves her, I do well believe 't;
That she loves him, 'tis apt and of great credit.

The Moor, howbeit that I endure him not,
Is of a constant, loving, noble nature,   290
And I dare think he'll prove to Desdemona
A most dear husband. Now, I do love her too,
Not out of absolute lust—though peradventure
I stand accountant for as great a sin—
But partly led to diet my revenge   295
For that I do suspect the lusty Moor
Hath leaped into my seat, the thought whereof
Doth, like a poisonous mineral, gnaw my innards;
And nothing can or shall content my soul
Till I am evened with him, wife for wife,   300
Or failing so, yet that I put the Moor
At least into a jealousy so strong
That judgment cannot cure. Which thing to do,
If this poor trash of Venice, whom I trace
For his quick hunting, stand the putting on,   305
I'll have our Michael Cassio on the hip,
Abuse him to the Moor in the rank garb—
For I fear Cassio with my nightcap too—
Make the Moor thank me, love me, and reward me
For making him egregiously an ass   310
And practicing upon his peace and quiet
Even to madness. 'Tis here, but yet confused.
Knavery's plain face is never seen till used.   *Exit.*

2.2   *Enter* OTHELLO's HERALD *with a proclamation.*

HERALD: It is Othello's pleasure, our noble and valiant
general, that, upon certain tidings now arrived, importing the mere perdition of the Turkish fleet, every
man put himself into triumph: some to dance, some
to make bonfires, each man to what sport and revels   5
his addiction leads him. For, besides these beneficial

---

259 index table of contents.   **obsure** (i.e., the *lust and foul thoughts*, line 260, are secret, hidden from view)   **263 mutualities** exchanges, intimacies   **263–264 hard at hand** closely following.   **264–265 incorporate** carnal   **266 Watch you** stand watch   **267 for the command . . . you** I'll arrange for you to be appointed, given orders   **270 tainting** disparaging   **271 minister** provide   **273 choler** wrath   **274 haply** perhaps   **276 mutiny** riot.   **qualification** appeasement   **276–277 true taste** i.e., acceptable state   **279 prefer** advance   **284 warrant** assure.   **by and by** immediately   **288 apt** probable.   **credit** credibility

294 accountant accountable   **295 diet** feed   **304 trace** i.e., train, or follow (?), or perhaps *trash,* a hunting term, meaning to put weights on a hunting dog in order to slow him down   **305 For** to make more eager.   **stand . . . on** respond properly when I incite him to quarrel   **306 on the hip** at my mercy, where I can throw him. (A wrestling term.)   **307 Abuse** slander.   **rank garb** coarse manner, gross fashion   **308 with my nightcap** i.e., as a rival in my bed, as one who gives me cuckold's horns   **311 practicing upon** plotting against

2.2. Location: Cyprus. A street.   3 mere perdition complete destruction   **4 triumph** public celebration   **6 addiction** inclination

news, it is the celebration of his nuptial. So much was
his pleasure should be proclaimed. All offices are open,
and there is full liberty of feasting from this present
hour of five till the bell have told eleven. Heaven bless
the isle of Cyprus and our noble general Othello!

Exit.

2.3 *Enter* OTHELLO, DESDEMONA, CASSIO, *and*
attendants.

OTHELLO: Good Michael, look you to the guard tonight.
Let's teach ourselves that honorable stop
Not to outsport discretion.

CASSIO: Iago hath direction what to do,
But notwithstanding, with my personal eye
Will I look to 't.

OTHELLO: Iago is most honest.
Michael, good night. Tomorrow with your earliest
Let me have speech with you. *[To* DESDEMONA.*]*
          Come, my dear love,
The purchase made, the fruits are to ensue;
That profit's yet to come 'tween me and you.—
Good night.

*Exit [*OTHELLO, *with* DESDEMONA *and*
attendants].

Enter IAGO.

CASSIO: Welcome, Iago. We must to the watch.

IAGO: Not this hour, Lieutenant; 'tis not yet ten o' the
clock. Our general cast us thus early for the love of his
Desdemona; who let us not therefore blame. He hath
not yet made wanton the night with her, and she is
sport for Jove.

CASSIO: She's a most exquisite lady.

IAGO: And, I'll warrant her, full of game.

CASSIO: Indeed, she's a most fresh and delicate creature.   20

IAGO: What an eye she has! Methinks it sounds a parley
to provocation.

CASSIO: An inviting eye, and yet methinks right modest.

IAGO: And when she speaks, is it not an alarum to love?

CASSIO: She is indeed perfection.   25

IAGO: Well, happiness to their sheets! Come, Lieutenant,
I have a stoup of wine, and here without are a brace of
Cyprus gallants that would fain have a measure to the
health of black Othello.

CASSIO: Not tonight, good Iago. I have very poor   30
and unhappy brains for drinking. I could well
wish courtesy would invent some other custom of
entertainment.

IAGO: O, they are our friends. But one cup! I'll drink
for you.   35

CASSIO: I have drunk but one cup tonight, and that was
craftily qualified too, and behold what innovation it
makes here. I am unfortunate in the infirmity and
dare not task my weakness with any more.

IAGO: What, man? 'Tis a night of revels. The gallants   40
desire it.

CASSIO: Where are they?

IAGO: Here at the door. I pray you, call them in.

CASSIO: I'll do 't, but it dislikes me.   *Exit.*

IAGO: If I can fasten but one cup upon him,   45
With that which he hath drunk tonight already,
He'll be as full of quarrel and offense

---

8 offices rooms where food and drink are kept

2.3. Location: Cyprus. The citadel.
2 stop restraint   **3 outsport** celebrate beyond the bounds of   **7
with your earliest** at your earliest convenience   **9–10 The purchase . . . you** i.e., though married, we haven't yet consummated our
love   **13 Not this hour** not for an hour yet   **14 cast** dismissed   **15
who** i.e., Othello

21 sounds a parley calls for a conference, issues an invitation   **24
alarum** signal calling men to arms (continuing the military metaphor of *parley,* line 21)   **27 stoup** measure of liquor, two quarts.
without outside.   **brace** pair   **28–29 fain have a measure** gladly
drink a toast   **35 for you** in your place. (Iago will do the steady
drinking to keep the gallants company while Cassio has only one
cup.)   **37 qualified** diluted.   **37–38 innovation** disturbance, insurrection   **38 here** i.e., in my head   **44 it dislikes me** i.e., I'm reluctant   **47 offense** readiness to take offense

Iago deludes the drunken Cassio.

As my young mistress' dog. Now, my sick fool
   Roderigo,
Whom love hath turned almost the wrong side out,
50 To Desdemona hath tonight caroused
Potations pottle-deep; and he's to watch.
Three lads of Cyprus—noble swelling spirits,
That hold their honors in a wary distance,
The very elements of this warlike isle—
55 Have I tonight flustered with flowing cups,
And they watch too. Now, 'mongst this flock of
   drunkards
Am I to put our Cassio in some action
That may offend the isle.—But here they come.

Enter CASSIO, MONTANO, *and* GENTLEMEN;
[servants following with wine].

If consequence do but approve my dream,
60 My boat sails freely both with wind and stream.

CASSIO: 'Fore God, they have given me a rouse already.

MONTANO: Good faith, a little one; not past a pint, as I
am a soldier.

IAGO: Some wine, ho!

[He sings.] "And let me the cannikin clink, clink,   65
    And let me the cannikin clink.
      A soldier's a man,
      O, man's life's but a span;
    Why, then, let a soldier drink."

Some wine, boys!   70

CASSIO: 'Fore God, an excellent song.

IAGO: I learned it in England, where indeed they are
most potent in potting. Your Dane, your German, and
your swag-bellied Hollander—drink, ho!—are nothing to your English.   75

CASSIO: Is your Englishman so exquisite in his drinking?

IAGO: Why, he drinks you, with facility, your Dane dead
drunk; he sweats not to overthrow your Almain; he
gives your Hollander a vomit ere the next pottle can
be filled.   80

CASSIO: To the health of our general!

MONTANO: I am for it, Lieutenant, and I'll do you justice.

IAGO: O sweet England! *[He sings.]*

"King Stephen was and-a worthy peer,
   His breeches cost him but a crown;   85
He held them sixpence all too dear,
   With that he called the tailor lown.

He was a wight of high renown,
   And thou art but of low degree.
'Tis pride that pulls the country down;   90
   Then take thy auld cloak about thee."

Some wine, ho!

---

50 caroused drunk off **51 pottle-deep** to the bottom of the tan-
kard. **watch** stand watch **52 swelling** proud **53 hold . . . distance** i.e., are extremely sensitive of their honor **54 very elements**
typical sort **56 watch** are members of the guard **59 If . . . dream**
if subsequent events will only substantiate my scheme **60 stream**
current **61 rouse** full draft of liquor

65 cannikin small drinking vessel **68 span** brief span of time.
(Compare Psalms 39:5 as rendered in the Book of Common
Prayer: "Thou hast made my days as it were a span long.") **73 potting**
drinking **77 drinks you** drinks. **your Dane** your typical Dane
78 sweats not i.e., need not exert himself. **Almain** German **82
I'll . . . justice** i.e., I'll drink as much as you **87 lown** lout, rascal
90 pride i.e., extravagance in dress. **91 auld** old

CASSIO: 'Fore God, this is a more exquisite song than the other.

95 **IAGO:** Will you hear 't again?

CASSIO: No, for I hold him to be unworthy of his place that does those things. Well, God's above all; and there be souls must be saved, and there be souls must not be saved.

100 **IAGO:** It's true, good Lieutenant.

CASSIO: For mine own part—no offense to the General, nor any man of quality—I hope to be saved.

IAGO: And so do I too, Lieutenant.

CASSIO: Ay, but, by your leave, not before me; the lieu-
105 tenant is to be saved before the ancient. Let's have no more of this; let's to our affairs.—God forgive us our sins!—Gentlemen, let's look to our business. Do not think, gentlemen, I am drunk. This is my ancient; this is my right hand, and this is my left. I am not drunk
110 now. I can stand well enough, and speak well enough.

GENTLEMEN: Excellent well.

CASSIO: Why, very well then; you must not think then that I am drunk. *Exit.*

MONTANO: To th' platform, masters. Come, let's set the watch.

[Exeunt GENTLEMEN.]

115 **IAGO:** You see this fellow that is gone before.
He's a soldier fit to stand by Caesar
And give direction; and do but see his vice.
'Tis to his virtue a just equinox,
The one as long as th' other. 'Tis pity of him.
120 I fear the trust Othello puts him in,
On some odd time of his infirmity,
Will shake this island.

MONTANO: But is he often thus?

IAGO: 'Tis evermore the prologue to his sleep.
He'll watch the horologe a double set,
If drink rock not his cradle.

MONTANO: It were well 125
The General were put in mind of it.
Perhaps he sees it not, or his good nature
Prizes the virtue that appears in Cassio
And looks not on his evils. Is not this true?

Enter RODERIGO.

IAGO *[aside to him]:* How now, Roderigo? 130
I pray you, after the Lieutenant; go. *[Exit RODERIGO.]*

MONTANO: And 'tis great pity that the noble Moor
Should hazard such a place as his own second
With one of an engraffed infirmity.
It were an honest action to say so 135
To the Moor.

IAGO: Not I, for this fair island.
I do love Cassio well and would do much
To cure him of this evil. *[Cry within: "Help! Help!"]*
But, hark! What noise?

Enter CASSIO, pursuing RODERIGO.

CASSIO: Zounds, you rogue! You rascal!

MONTANO: What's the matter, Lieutenant? 140

CASSIO: A knave teach me my duty? I'll beat the knave into a twiggen bottle.

RODERIGO: Beat me?

CASSIO: Dost thou prate, rogue? *[He strikes RODERIGO.]*

MONTANO: Nay, good Lieutenant. *[Restraining him.]* 145
I pray you, sir, hold your hand.

CASSIO: Let me go, sir, or I'll knock you o'er the mazzard.

---

102 **quality** rank   114 **set the watch** mount the guard   118 **just equinox** exact counterpart. (*Equinox* is an equal length of days and nights.)

---

124 **watch . . . set** stay awake twice around the clock or *horologe*
133–134 **hazard . . . With** risk giving such an important position as his second in command to   134 **engraffed** engrafted, inveterate
138 **s.d. pursuing** (The Quarto text reads "driving in.")   142 **twiggen** wicker-covered. (Cassio vows to assail Roderigo until his skin resembles wickerwork or until he has driven Roderigo through the holes in a wickerwork.)   148 **mazzard** i.e., head. (Literally, a drinking vessel.)

MONTANO: Come, come, you're drunk.

150   **CASSIO:**   Drunk?   *[They fight.]*

IAGO   *[aside to* RODERIGO*]:*   Away, I say. Go out and cry
       a mutiny.

                                    [Exit RODERIGO*.]*

       Nay, good Lieutenant.—God's will, gentlemen—
       Help, ho!—Lieutenant—sir—Montano—sir—
       Help, masters!—Here's a goodly watch indeed!

                                    [A bell rings.]

155   Who's that which rings the bell?—Diablo, ho!
       The town will rise. God's will, Lieutenant, hold!
       You'll be ashamed forever.

            Enter OTHELLO *and attendants [with weapons].*

OTHELLO: What is the matter here?

MONTANO: Zounds, I bleed still.
       I am hurt to th' death. He dies! *[He thrusts at* CASSIO*.]*

OTHELLO: Hold, for your lives!

160   **IAGO:**   Hold, ho! Lieutenant—sir—Montano—gentlemen—
       Have you forgot all sense of place and duty?
       Hold! The General speaks to you. Hold, for shame!

OTHELLO: Why, how now, ho? From whence ariseth
       this?
165   Are we turned Turks, and to ourselves do that
       Which heaven hath forbid the Ottomites?
       For Christian shame, put by this barbarous brawl!
       He that stirs next to carve for his own rage
       Holds his soul light; he dies upon his motion.
170   Silence that dreadful bell. It frights the isle
       From her propriety. What is the matter, masters?
       Honest Iago, that looks dead with grieving,
       Speak. Who began this? On thy love, I charge thee.

Othello hears from Cassio after the scuffle.

IAGO: I do not know. Friends all but now, even now,
       In quarter and in terms like bride and groom
       Devesting them for bed; and then, but now—   175
       As if some planet had unwitted men—
       Swords out, and tilting one at others' breasts
       In opposition bloody. I cannot speak
       Any beginning to this peevish odds;
       And would in action glorious I had lost   180
       Those legs that brought me to a part of it!

OTHELLO: How comes it, Michael, you are thus forgot?

CASSIO: I pray you, pardon me. I cannot speak.

OTHELLO: Worthy Montano, you were wont be civil;
       Thy gravity and stillness of your youth   185
       The world hath noted, and your name is great
       In mouths of wisest censure. What's the matter
       That you unlace your reputation thus
       And spend your rich opinion for the name
       Of a night-brawler? Give me answer to it.   190

---

151 **mutiny** riot   154 **masters** sirs.   **s.d. A bell rings** (This direction is from the Quarto, as are *Exit Roderigo* at line 131, *They fight* at line 150, and *with weapons* at line 157.)   155 **Diablo** the devil   156 **rise** grow riotous   164–165 **to ourselves . . . Ottomites** inflict on ourselves the harm that heaven has prevented the Turks from doing (by destroying their fleet)   167 **carve for** i.e., indulge, satisfy with his sword   168 **Holds . . . light** i.e., places little value on his life.   **upon his motion** if he moves   170 **propriety** proper state or condition

---

174 **In quarter** in friendly conduct, within bounds.   **in terms** on good terms   175 **Devesting them** undressing themselves   178 **speak** explain   179 **peevish odds** childish quarrel   182 **are thus forgot** have forgotten yourself thus   184 **wont be** accustomed to be   185 **stillness** sobriety   187 **censure** judgment   188 **unlace** undo, lay open (as one might loose the strings of a purse containing reputation)   189 **opinion** reputation

MONTANO: Worthy Othello, I am hurt to danger.
Your officer, Iago, can inform you—
While I spare speech, which something now offends
    me—
Of all that I do know; nor know I aught
195 By me that's said or done amiss this night,
Unless self-charity be sometimes a vice,
And to defend ourselves it be a sin
When violence assails us.

OTHELLO: Now, by heaven,
My blood begins my safer guides to rule,
200 And passion, having my best judgment collied,
Essays to lead the way. Zounds, if I stir,
Or do but lift this arm, the best of you
Shall sink in my rebuke. Give me to know
How this foul rout began, who set it on;
205 And he that is approved in this offense,
Though he had twinned with me, both at a birth,
Shall lose me. What? In a town of war
Yet wild, the people's hearts brim full of fear,
To manage private and domestic quarrel?
210 In night, and on the court and guard of safety?
'Tis monstrous. Iago, who began 't?

MONTANO [to IAGO]:   If partially affined, or leagued in
    office,
Thou dost deliver more or less than truth,
Thou art no soldier.

IAGO: Touch me not so near.
215 I had rather have this tongue cut from my mouth
Than it should do offense to Michael Cassio;
Yet, I persuade myself, to speak the truth
Shall nothing wrong him. This it is, General.
Montano and myself being in speech,
220 There comes a fellow crying out for help,

And Cassio following him with determined sword
To execute upon him. Sir, this gentleman
            [indicating MONTANO]
Steps in to Cassio and entreats his pause.
Myself the crying fellow did pursue,
Lest by his clamor—as it so fell out— 225
The town might fall in fright. He, swift of foot,
Outran my purpose, and I returned, the rather
For that I heard the clink and fall of swords
And Cassio high in oath, which till tonight
I ne'er might say before. When I came back— 230
For this was brief—I found them close together
At blow and thrust, even as again they were
When you yourself did part them.
More of this matter cannot I report.
But men are men; the best sometimes forget. 235
Though Cassio did some little wrong to him,
As men in rage strike those that wish them best,
Yet surely Cassio, I believe, received
From him that fled some strange indignity,
Which patience could not pass.

OTHELLO: I know, Iago, 240
Thy honesty and love doth mince this matter,
Making it light to Cassio. Cassio, I love thee,
But nevermore be officer of mine.

            Enter DESDEMONA, *attended.*

Look if my gentle love be not raised up.
I'll make thee an example. 245

DESDEMONA: What is the matter, dear?

OTHELLO: All's well now, sweeting;
Come away to bed. [*To* MONTANO.] Sir, for your
    hurts,
Myself will be your surgeon.—Lead him off.
            [MONTANO *is led off.*]
Iago, look with care about the town
And silence those whom this vile brawl distracted. 250

---

193 **something** somewhat.   **offends** pains   199 **blood** passion (of
anger).   **guides** i.e., reason   200 **collied** darkened   201 **Essays**
undertakes   204 **rout** riot   205 **approved in** found guilty of   207
town of town garrisoned for   209 **manage** undertake   210 **on** . . .
safety at the main guardhouse or headquarters and on watch   212
partially affined made partial by some personal relationship.
leagued in office in league as fellow officers

---

222 **execute** give effect to (his anger)   223 **his pause** him to stop
227 **rather** sooner   235 **forget** forget themselves   237 **those** . . .
best i.e., even those who are well disposed   240 **pass** pass over,
overlook   248 **be your surgeon** i.e., make sure you receive medical
attention

Come, Desdemona. 'Tis the soldiers' life
To have their balmy slumbers waked with strife.
Exit [with all but IAGO *and* CASSIO*].*

IAGO: What, are you hurt, Lieutenant?

CASSIO: Ay, past all surgery.

255   **IAGO:**   Marry, God forbid!

CASSIO: Reputation, reputation, reputation! O, I have
lost my reputation! I have lost the immortal part of
myself, and what remains is bestial. My reputation,
Iago, my reputation!

260   **IAGO:**   As I am an honest man, I thought you had received some bodily wound; there is more sense in
that than in reputation. Reputation is an idle and
most false imposition, oft got without merit and lost
without deserving. You have lost no reputation at all,
265   unless you repute yourself such a loser. What, man,
there are more ways to recover the General again.
You are but now cast in his mood—a punishment
more in policy than in malice, even so as one would
beat his offenseless dog to affright an imperious lion.
270   Sue to him again and he's yours.

CASSIO: I will rather sue to be despised than to deceive
so good a commander with so slight, so drunken,
and so indiscreet an officer. Drunk? And speak parrot? And squabble? Swagger? Swear? And discourse
275   fustian with one's own shadow? O thou invisible spirit
of wine, if thou hast no name to be known by, let us
call thee devil!

IAGO: What was he that you followed with your sword?
What had he done to you?

280   **CASSIO:**   I know not.

IAGO: Is 't possible?

CASSIO: I remember a mass of things, but nothing
distinctly; a quarrel, but nothing wherefore. O God,
that men should put an enemy in their mouths to
steal away their brains! That we should, with joy,   285
pleasance, revel, and applause transform ourselves
into beasts!

IAGO: Why, but you are now well enough. How came you
thus recovered?

CASSIO: It hath pleased the devil drunkenness to give   290
place to the devil wrath. One unperfectness shows me
another, to make me frankly despise myself.

IAGO: Come, you are too severe a moraler. As the time,
the place, and the condition of this country stands, I
could heartily wish this had not befallen; but since it   295
is as it is, mend it for your own good.

CASSIO: I will ask him for my place again; he shall
tell me I am a drunkard. Had I as many mouths as
Hydra, such an answer would stop them all. To be
now a sensible man, by and by a fool, and presently a   300
beast! O, strange! Every inordinate cup is unblessed,
and the ingredient is a devil.

IAGO: Come, come, good wine is a good familiar creature, if it be well used. Exclaim no more against it.
And, good Lieutenant, I think you think I love you.   305

CASSIO: I have well approved it, sir. I drunk!

IAGO: You or any man living may be drunk at a time,
man. I'll tell you what you shall do. Our general's
wife is now the general—I may say so in this respect,
for that he hath devoted and given up himself to the   310
contemplation, mark, and denotement of her parts
and graces. Confess yourself freely to her; importune
her help to put you in your place again. She is of so

---

263 **false imposition** thing artificially imposed and of no real value
266 **recover** regain favor with   267 **cast in his mood** dismissed in a
moment of anger   268 **in policy** done for expediency's sake and as a
public gesture   268–269 **would . . . lion** i.e., would make an example of a minor offender in order to deter more important and dangerous offenders   269 **Sue** petition   272 **slight** worthless   273–274
speak parrot talk nonsense, rant. (*Discourse fustian*, lines 274–275,
has much the same meaning.)

283 **wherefore** why   286 **applause** desire for applause   293
moraler moralizer   299 **Hydra** the Lernaean Hydra, a monster
with many heads and the ability to grow two heads when one was
cut off, slain by Hercules as the second of his twelve labors   306
approved proved   307 **at a time** at one time or another   309–310
in . . . that in view of this fact, that   311 **mark, and denotement**
(Both words mean "observation.")   **parts** qualities

Iago cleverly advises Cassio (Nick Barber).

315 free, so kind, so apt, so blessed a disposition, she
holds it a vice in her goodness not to do more than
she is requested. This broken joint between you and
her husband entreat her to splinter; and, my fortunes
against any lay worth naming, this crack of your love
shall grow stronger than it was before.

320 **CASSIO:** You advise me well.

IAGO: I protest, in the sincerity of love and honest
kindness.

CASSIO: I think it freely; and betimes in the morning I
will beseech the virtuous Desdemona to undertake
325 for me. I am desperate of my fortunes if they check
me here.

IAGO: You are in the right. Good night, Lieutenant. I
must to the watch.

CASSIO: Good night, honest Iago.   *Exit* CASSIO.

330 **IAGO:** And what's he then that says I play the villain,
When this advice is free I give, and honest,
Probal to thinking, and indeed the course

To win the Moor again? For 'tis most easy
Th' inclining Desdemona to subdue
In any honest suit; she's framed as fruitful   335
As the free elements. And then for her
To win the Moor—were 't to renounce his baptism,
All seals and symbols of redeemèd sin—
His soul is so enfettered to her love
That she may make, unmake, do what she list,   340
Even as her appetite shall play the god
With his weak function. How am I then a villain,
To counsel Cassio to this parallel course
Directly to his good? Divinity of hell!
When devils will the blackest sins put on,   345
They do suggest at first with heavenly shows,
As I do now. For whiles this honest fool
Plies Desdemona to repair his fortune,
And she for him pleads strongly to the Moor,
I'll pour this pestilence into his ear,   350
That she repeals him for her body's lust;
And by how much she strives to do him good,
She shall undo her credit with the Moor.
So will I turn her virtue into pitch,
And out of her own goodness make the net   355
That shall enmesh them all.

Enter RODERIGO.

How now, Roderigo?

RODERIGO: I do follow here in the chase, not like a
hound that hunts, but one that fills up the cry. My
money is almost spent; I have been tonight exceedingly well cudgeled; and I think the issue will be I   360
shall have so much experience for my pains, and so,
with no money at all and a little more wit, return
again to Venice.

---

314 free generous **317 splinter** bind with splints **318 lay** stake, wager **321 protest** insist, declare **323 freely** unreservedly **325 check** repulse **331 free** (1) free from guile (2) freely given **332 Probal** probable, reasonable

334 inclining favorably disposed. **subdue** persuade **335 framed as fruitful** created as generous **336 free elements** i.e., earth, air, fire, and water, unrestrained and spontaneous **341 her appetite** her desire, or, perhaps, his desire for her **342 function** exercise of faculties (weakened by his fondness for her) **343 parallel** corresponding to these facts and to his best interests **344 Divinity of hell** inverted theology of hell (which seduces the soul to its damnation) **345 put on** further, instigate **346 suggest** tempt **351 repeals him** attempts to get him restored **354 pitch** i.e., (1) foul blackness (2) a snaring substance **358 fills up the cry** merely takes part as one of the pack **361 so much** just so much and no more

IAGO: How poor are they that have not patience!
365   What wound did ever heal but by degrees?
        Thou know'st we work by wit, and not by witchcraft,
        And wit depends on dilatory time.
        Does 't not go well? Cassio hath beaten thee,
        And thou, by that small hurt, hast cashiered Cassio.
370   Though other things grow fair against the sun,
        Yet fruits that blossom first will first be ripe.
        Content thyself awhile. By the Mass, 'tis morning!
        Pleasure and action make the hours seem short.
        Retire thee; go where thou art billeted.
375   Away, I say! Thou shalt know more hereafter.
        Nay, get thee gone.   *Exit* RODERIGO.
                        Two things are to be done.
        My wife must move for Cassio to her mistress;
        I'll set her on;
        Myself the while to draw the Moor apart
380   And bring him jump when he may Cassio find
        Soliciting his wife. Ay, that's the way.
        Dull not device by coldness and delay.   *Exit.*

3.1   *Enter* CASSIO *[and]* MUSICIANS.

CASSIO: Masters, play here—I will content your pains—
          Something that's brief, and bid "Good morrow,
          General."   *[They play.]*

                                          [Enter] CLOWN.

CLOWN: Why, masters, have your instruments been in
         Naples, that they speak i' the nose thus?

5 A MUSICIAN: How, sir, how?

CLOWN: Are these, I pray you, wind instruments?

A MUSICIAN: Ay, marry, are they, sir.

CLOWN: O, thereby hangs a tail.

A MUSICIAN: Whereby hangs a tale, sir?

CLOWN: Marry, sir, by many a wind instrument that I   10
         know. But, masters, here's money for you. *[He gives
         money.]* And the General so likes your music that he
         desires you, for love's sake, to make no more noise
         with it.

A MUSICIAN: Well, sir, we will not.   15

CLOWN: If you have any music that may not be heard,
         to 't again; but, as they say, to hear music the General
         does not greatly care.

A MUSICIAN: We have none such, sir.

CLOWN: Then put up your pipes in your bag, for I'll   20
         away. Go, vanish into air, away!   *Exeunt* MUSICIANS.

CASSIO: Dost thou hear, mine honest friend?

CLOWN: No, I hear not your honest friend; I hear you.

CASSIO: Prithee, keep up thy quillets. There's a poor
          piece of gold for thee. *[He gives money.]* If the gentle- 25
          woman that attends the General's wife be stirring,
          tell her there's one Cassio entreats her a little favor of
          speech. Wilt thou do this?

CLOWN: She is stirring, sir. If she will stir hither, I shall
         seem to notify unto her.   30

CASSIO: Do, good my friend.   *Exit* CLOWN.

                                          Enter IAGO.

          In happy time, Iago.

---

369 cashiered dismissed from service   **370–371 Though . . . ripe**
i.e., plans that are well prepared and set expeditiously in motion will
soonest ripen into success   **377 move** plead   **380 jump** precisely
382 device plot.   **coldness** lack of zeal

3.1. Location: Before the chamber of Othello and Desdemona.
1 content your pains reward your efforts   **4 speak i' the nose**
(1) sound nasal (2) sound like one whose nose has been attacked by
syphilis. (Naples was popularly supposed to have a high incidence
of venereal disease.)

10 wind instrument (With a joke on flatulence. The *tail*, line 8,
that hangs nearby the *wind instrument* suggests the penis.)   **13
for love's sake** (1) out of friendship and affection (2) for the sake of
lovemaking in Othello's marriage   **16 may not** cannot   **20–21 I'll
away** (Possibly a misprint, or a snatch of song?)   **24 keep up** do not
bring out, do not use.   **quillets** quibbles, puns   **27–28 a little . . .
speech** the favor of a brief talk   **29 stir** bestir herself (with a play on
stirring, "rousing herself from rest")   **30 seem** deem it good, think
fit   **31 In happy time** i.e., well met

IAGO: You have not been abed, then?

CASSIO: Why, no. The day had broke
Before we parted. I have made bold, Iago,
35   To send in to your wife. My suit to her
Is that she will to virtuous Desdemona
Procure me some access.

IAGO: I'll send her to you presently;
And I'll devise a means to draw the Moor
40   Out of the way, that your converse and business
May be more free.

CASSIO: I humbly thank you for 't.   *Exit [*IAGO.*]*
                              I never knew
A Florentine more kind and honest.

                                        Enter EMILIA.

EMILIA: Good morrow, good Lieutenant. I am sorry
45   For your displeasure; but all will sure be well.
The General and his wife are talking of it,
And she speaks for you stoutly. The Moor replies
That he you hurt is of great fame in Cyprus
And great affinity, and that in wholesome wisdom
50   He might not but refuse you; but he protests he loves
        you
And needs no other suitor but his likings
To take the safest occasion by the front
To bring you in again.

CASSIO: Yet I beseech you,
If you think fit, or that it may be done,
55   Give me advantage of some brief discourse
With Desdemona alone.

EMILIA: Pray you, come in.
I will bestow you where you shall have time
To speak your bosom freely.

CASSIO: I am much bound to you.   *[Exeunt.]*

3.2   *Enter* OTHELLO, IAGO, *and* GENTLEMEN.

OTHELLO *[giving letters]*:   These letters give, Iago, to the
        pilot,
And by him do my duties to the Senate.
That done, I will be walking on the works;
Repair there to me.

IAGO: Well, my good lord, I'll do 't.

OTHELLO: This fortification, gentlemen, shall we see 't?   5

GENTLEMEN: We'll wait upon your lordship.   *Exeunt.*

3.3   *Enter* DESDEMONA, CASSIO, *and* EMILIA.

DESDEMONA: Be thou assured, good Cassio, I will do
All my abilities in thy behalf.

EMILIA: Good madam, do. I warrant it grieves my
        husband
As if the cause were his.

DESDEMONA: O, that's an honest fellow. Do not doubt,   5
        Cassio,
But I will have my lord and you again
As friendly as you were.

CASSIO: Bounteous madam,
Whatever shall become of Michael Cassio,
He's never anything but your true servant.

DESDEMONA: I know 't. I thank you. You do love my   10
        lord;
You have known him long, and be you well assured
He shall in strangeness stand no farther off
Than in a politic distance.

CASSIO: Ay, but, lady,
That policy may either last so long,
Or feed upon such nice and waterish diet,   15

---

43 **Florentine** i.e., even a fellow Florentine (Iago is a Venetian;
Cassio is a Florentine.)   45 **displeasure** fall from favor   47 **stoutly**
spiritedly   48 **fame** reputation, importance   49 **affinity** kindred,
family connection   50 **protests** insists   52 **occasion . . . front** opportunity by the forelock   58 **bosom** inmost thoughts

3.2. Location: The citadel.
2 **do my duties** convey my respects   3 **works** breastworks, fortifica-
tions   4 **Repair** return, come   6 **wait upon** attend

3.3. Location: The garden of the citadel.
12 **strangeness** aloofness   13 **politic** required by wise policy   15
Or . . . diet or sustain itself at length upon such trivial and meager
technicalities

Or breed itself so out of circumstance,
That, I being absent and my place supplied,
My general will forget my love and service.

DESDEMONA: Do not doubt that. Before Emilia here
20 I give thee warrant of thy place. Assure thee,
If I do vow a friendship I'll perform it
To the last article. My lord shall never rest.
I'll watch him tame and talk him out of patience;
His bed shall seem a school, his board a shrift;
25 I'll intermingle everything he does
With Cassio's suit. Therefore be merry, Cassio,
For thy solicitor shall rather die
Than give thy cause away.

       Enter OTHELLO *and* IAGO *[at a distance].*

EMILIA: Madam, here comes my lord.

30 **CASSIO:**   Madam, I'll take my leave.

DESDEMONA: Why, stay, and hear me speak.

CASSIO: Madam, not now. I am very ill at ease,
Unfit for mine own purposes.

DESDEMONA: Well, do your discretion.   *Exit* CASSIO.

35 **IAGO:**   Ha? I like not that.

OTHELLO: What dost thou say?

IAGO: Nothing, my lord; or if—I know not what.

OTHELLO: Was not that Cassio parted from my wife?

IAGO: Cassio, my lord? No, sure, I cannot think it,
40 That he would steal away so guiltylike,
Seeing you coming.

OTHELLO: I do believe 'twas he.

Desdemona (Zoë Tapper) asks Othello (Eamonn Walker) to pardon Cassio.

DESDEMONA: How now, my lord?
I have been talking with a suitor here,
A man that languishes in your displeasure.   45

OTHELLO: Who is 't you mean?

DESDEMONA: Why, your lieutenant, Cassio. Good my
    lord,
If I have any grace or power to move you,
His present reconciliation take;
For if he be not one that truly loves you,   50
That errs in ignorance and not in cunning,
I have no judgment in an honest face.
I prithee, call him back.

OTHELLO: Went he hence now?

DESDEMONA: Yes, faith, so humbled   55
That he hath left part of his grief with me
To suffer with him. Good love, call him back.

OTHELLO: Not now, sweet Desdemon. Some other time.

DESDEMONA: But shall 't be shortly?

OTHELLO: The sooner, sweet, for you.   60

---

16 breed . . . circumstance continually renew itself so out of chance events, or yield so few chances for my being pardoned   **17 supplied** filled by another person   **19 doubt** fear   **20 warrant** guarantee   **23 watch him tame** tame him by keeping him from sleeping. (A term from falconry.)   **out of patience** past his endurance   **24 board** dining table.   **shrift** confessional   **27 solicitor** advocate   **28 away** up   **34 do your discretion** act according to your own discretion

---

49 His . . . take let him be reconciled to you right away   **51 in cunning** wittingly

DESDEMONA: Shall 't be tonight at supper?

OTHELLO: No, not tonight.

DESDEMONA: Tomorrow dinner, then?

OTHELLO: I shall not dine at home.
65   I meet the captains at the citadel.

DESDEMONA: Why, then, tomorrow night, or Tuesday
         morn,
       On Tuesday noon, or night, on Wednesday morn.
       I prithee, name the time, but let it not
       Exceed three days. In faith, he's penitent;
70   And yet his trespass, in our common reason—
       Save that, they say, the wars must make example
       Out of her best—is not almost a fault
       T' incur a private check. When shall he come?
       Tell me, Othello. I wonder in my soul
75   What you would ask me that I should deny,
       Or stand so mammering on. What? Michael Cassio,
       That came a-wooing with you, and so many a time,
       When I have spoke of you dispraisingly,
       Hath ta'en your part—to have so much to do
80   To bring him in! By 'r Lady, I could do much—

OTHELLO: Prithee, no more. Let him come when he
         will;
       I will deny thee nothing.

DESDEMONA: Why, this is not a boon.
       'Tis as I should entreat you wear your gloves,
85   Or feed on nourishing dishes, or keep you warm,
       Or sue to you to do a peculiar profit
       To your own person. Nay, when I have a suit
       Wherein I mean to touch your love indeed,
       It shall be full of poise and difficult weight,
90   And fearful to be granted.

---

63 dinner (The noontime meal.)   **70 common reason** everyday judgments   **71–72 Save . . . best** were it not that, as the saying goes, military discipline requires making an example of the very best men. (*Her* refers to *wars* as a singular concept.)   **72 not almost** scarcely   **73 a private check** even a private reprimand   **76 mammering on** wavering about   **80 bring him in** restore him to favor   **86 peculiar** particular, personal   **88 touch** test   **89 poise** weight, heaviness; or equipoise, delicate balance involving hard choice

OTHELLO: I will deny thee nothing.
       Whereon, I do beseech thee, grant me this,
       To leave me but a little to myself.

DESDEMONA: Shall I deny you? No. Farewell, my lord.

OTHELLO: Farewell, my Desdemona. I'll come to thee
         straight.   95

DESDEMONA: Emilia, come.—Be as your fancies teach
         you;
       Whate'er you be, I am obedient.   *Exit [with* EMILIA*].*

OTHELLO: Excellent wretch! Perdition catch my soul
       But I do love thee! And when I love thee not,
       Chaos is come again.   100

IAGO: My noble lord—

OTHELLO: What dost thou say, Iago?

IAGO: Did Michael Cassio, when you wooed my lady,
       Know of your love?

OTHELLO: He did, from first to last. Why dost thou ask?   105

IAGO: But for a satisfaction of my thought;
       No further harm.

OTHELLO: Why of thy thought, Iago?

IAGO: I did not think he had been acquainted with her.

OTHELLO: O, yes, and went between us very oft.

IAGO: Indeed?   110

OTHELLO: Indeed? Ay, indeed. Discern'st thou aught in
         that?
       Is he not honest?

IAGO: Honest, my lord?

OTHELLO: Honest. Ay, honest.

IAGO: My lord, for aught I know.   115

---

92 Whereon in return for which   **95 straight** straightway   **96 fancies** inclinations   **98 wretch** (A term of affectionate endearment.)   **99–100 And . . . again** i.e., my love for you will last forever, until the end of time when chaos will return. (But with an unconscious, ironic suggestion that, if anything should induce Othello to cease loving Desdemona, the result would be chaos.)

Othello, jealous of Cassio, is beguiled by Iago.

OTHELLO: What dost thou think?

IAGO: Think, my lord?

OTHELLO: "Think, my lord?" By heaven, thou echo'st
          me,
     As if there were some monster in thy thought
120 Too hideous to be shown. Thou dost mean something.
     I heard thee say even now, thou lik'st not that,
     When Cassio left my wife. What didst not like?
     And when I told thee he was of my counsel
     In my whole course of wooing, thou criedst "Indeed?"
125 And didst contract and purse thy brow together
     As if thou then hadst shut up in thy brain
     Some horrible conceit. If thou dost love me,
     Show me thy thought.

IAGO: My lord, you know I love you.

130 **OTHELLO:**   I think thou dost;
     And, for I know thou'rt full of love and honesty,
     And weigh'st thy words before thou giv'st them breath,
     Therefore these stops of thine fright me the more;
     For such things in a false disloyal knave
135 Are tricks of custom, but in a man that's just

---

123 **of my counsel** in my confidence   125 **purse** knit   127 **conceit** fancy   131 **for** because   133 **stops** pauses   135 **of custom** customary

They're close dilations, working from the heart
     That passion cannot rule.

IAGO: For Michael Cassio,
     I dare be sworn I think that he is honest.

OTHELLO: I think so too.

IAGO: Men should be what they seem;
     Or those that be not, would they might seem none!   140

OTHELLO: Certain, men should be what they seem.

IAGO: Why, then, I think Cassio's an honest man.

OTHELLO: Nay, yet there's more in this.
     I prithee, speak to me as to thy thinkings,
     As thou dost ruminate, and give thy worst of thoughts   145
     The worst of words.

IAGO: Good my lord, pardon me.
     Though I am bound to every act of duty,
     I am not bound to that all slaves are free to.
     Utter my thoughts? Why, say they are vile and false,
     As where's that palace whereinto foul things   150
     Sometimes intrude not? Who has that breast so pure
     But some uncleanly apprehensions
     Keep leets and law days, and in sessions sit
     With meditations lawful?

OTHELLO: Thou dost conspire against thy friend, Iago,   155
     If thou but think'st him wronged and mak'st his ear
     A stranger to thy thoughts.

IAGO: I do beseech you,
     Though I perchance am vicious in my guess—
     As I confess it is my nature's plague
     To spy into abuses, and oft my jealousy   160

---

136 **close dilations** secret or involuntary expressions or delays   137 **That passion cannot rule** i.e., that are too passionately strong to be restrained (referring to the workings), or, that cannot rule its own passions (referring to the heart).   **For** as for   140 **none** i.e., not to be men, or not seem to be honest   148 **that** that which.   **free to** free with respect to   153 **Keep leets and law days** i.e., hold court, set up their authority in one's heart. (*Leets* are a kind of manor court; *law days* are the days courts sit in session, or those sessions.)   154 **With** along with.   **lawful** innocent   155 **thy friend** i.e., Othello   158 **vicious** wrong   160 **jealousy** suspicious nature

Shapes faults that are not—that your wisdom then,
From one that so imperfectly conceits,
Would take no notice, nor build yourself a trouble
Out of his scattering and unsure observance.
165 It were not for your quiet nor your good,
Nor for my manhood, honesty, and wisdom,
To let you know my thoughts.

OTHELLO: What dost thou mean?

IAGO: Good name in man and woman, dear my lord,
Is the immediate jewel of their souls.
170 Who steals my purse steals trash; 'tis something,
          nothing;
'Twas mine, 'tis his, and has been slave to thousands;
But he that filches from me my good name
Robs me of that which not enriches him
And makes me poor indeed.

175 OTHELLO: By heaven, I'll know thy thoughts.

IAGO: You cannot, if my heart were in your hand,
Nor shall not, whilst 'tis in my custody.

OTHELLO: Ha?

IAGO: O, beware, my lord, of jealousy.
It is the green-eyed monster which doth mock
180 The meat it feeds on. That cuckold lives in bliss
Who, certain of his fate, loves not his wronger;
But O, what damnèd minutes tells he o'er
Who dotes, yet doubts, suspects, yet fondly loves!

OTHELLO: O misery!

185 IAGO: Poor and content is rich, and rich enough,
But riches fineless is as poor as winter
To him that ever fears he shall be poor.
Good God, the souls of all my tribe defend
From jealousy!

Othello is deceived by Iago.

OTHELLO: Why, why is this?   190
Think'st thou I'd make a life of jealousy,
To follow still the changes of the moon
With fresh suspicions? No! To be once in doubt
Is once to be resolved. Exchange me for a goat
When I shall turn the business of my soul   195
To such exsufflicate and blown surmises
Matching thy inference. 'Tis not to make me jealous
To say my wife is fair, feeds well, loves company,
Is free of speech, sings, plays, and dances well;
Where virtue is, these are more virtuous.   200
Nor from mine own weak merits will I draw
The smallest fear or doubt of her revolt,
For she had eyes, and chose me. No, Iago,
I'll see before I doubt; when I doubt, prove;
And on the proof, there is no more but this—   205
Away at once with love or jealousy.

IAGO: I am glad of this, for now I shall have reason
To show the love and duty that I bear you
With franker spirit. Therefore, as I am bound,

---

161 then on that account   **162 one** i.e., myself, Iago.   **conceits** judges, conjectures   **164 scattering** random   **169 immediate** essential, most precious   **176 if** even if   **179–180 doth mock . . . on** mocks and torments the heart of its victim, the man who suffers jealousy   **181 his wronger** i.e., his faithless wife. (The unsuspecting cuckold is spared the misery of loving his wife only to discover she is cheating on him.)   **182 tells** counts   **185 Poor . . . enough** to be content with what little one has is the greatest wealth of all. (Proverbial.)   **186 fineless** boundless

---

192–193 To follow . . . suspicions to be constantly imagining new causes for suspicion, changing incessantly like the moon   **194 once** once and for all.   **resolved** free of doubt, having settled the matter   **196 exsufflicate and blown** inflated and blown up, rumored about, or, spat out and flyblown, hence, loathsome, disgusting   **197 inference** description or allegation   **202 doubt . . . revolt** fear or her unfaithfulness

210 Receive it from me. I speak not yet of proof.
Look to your wife; observe her well with Cassio.
Wear your eyes thus, not jealous nor secure.
I would not have your free and noble nature,
Out of self-bounty, be abused. Look to 't.

215 I know our country disposition well;
In Venice they do let God see the pranks
They dare not show their husbands; their best
    conscience
Is not to leave 't undone, but keep 't unknown.

OTHELLO: Dost thou say so?

220 **IAGO:**   She did deceive her father, marrying you;
And when she seemed to shake and fear your looks,
She loved them most.

OTHELLO: And so she did.

IAGO: Why, go to, then!
She that, so young, could give out such a seeming,
To seel her father's eyes up close as oak,

225 He thought 'twas witchcraft! But I am much to blame.
I humbly do beseech you of your pardon
For too much loving you.

OTHELLO: I am bound to thee forever.

IAGO: I see this hath a little dashed your spirits.

230 **OTHELLO:**   Not a jot, not a jot.

IAGO: I' faith, I fear it has.
I hope you will consider what is spoke
Comes from my love. But I do see you're moved.
I am to pray you not to strain my speech
To grosser issues nor to larger reach

235 Than to suspicion.

OTHELLO: I will not.

IAGO: Should you do so, my lord,
My speech should fall into such vile success

Which my thoughts aimed not. Cassio's my worthy
    friend.
My lord, I see you're moved.   240

OTHELLO: No, not much moved.
I do not think but Desdemona's honest.

IAGO: Long live she so! And long live you to think so!

OTHELLO: And yet, how nature erring from itself—

IAGO: Ay, there's the point! As—to be bold with you—
Not to affect many proposèd matches   245
Of her own clime, complexion, and degree,
Whereto we see in all things nature tends—
Foh! One may smell in such a will most rank,
Foul disproportion, thoughts unnatural.
But, pardon me. I do not in position   250
Distinctly speak of her, though I may fear
Her will, recoiling to her better judgment,
May fall to match you with her country forms
And happily repent.

OTHELLO: Farewell, farewell!
If more thou dost perceive, let me know more.   255
Set on thy wife to observe. Leave me, Iago.

IAGO [going]:   My lord, I take my leave.

OTHELLO: Why did I marry? This honest creature
    doubtless
Sees and knows more, much more, than he unfolds.

IAGO [returning]:   My lord, I would I might entreat your   260
    honor
To scan this thing no farther. Leave it to time.
Although 'tis fit that Cassio have his place—
For, sure, he fills it up with great ability—
Yet, if you please to hold him off awhile,
You shall by that perceive him and his means.   265

---

212 not neither.   **secure** free from uncertainty   **214 self-bounty**
inherent or natural goodness and generosity.   **abused** deceived
222 go to (An expression of impatience.)   **223 seeming** false appearance   **224 seel** blind. (A term from falconry.)   **oak** (A close-
grained wood.)   **228 bound** indebted (but perhaps with ironic sense
of "tied")   **234 issues** significances.   **reach** meaning, scope   **238
success** effect, result

241 honest chaste   **245 affect** prefer, desire   **246 clime . . . degree**
country, color, and social position   **248 will** sensuality, appetite
249 disproportion abnormality   **250 position** argument, proposition   **252 recoiling** reverting.   **better** i.e., more natural and
reconsidered   **253 fall . . . forms** undertake to compare you with
Venetian norms of handsomeness   **254 happily repent** haply repent
her marriage   **261 scan** scrutinize   **265 his means** the method he
uses (to regain his post)

Note if your lady strain his entertainment
With any strong or vehement importunity;
Much will be seen in that. In the meantime,
Let me be thought too busy in my fears—
270　As worthy cause I have to fear I am—
And hold her free, I do beseech your honor.

OTHELLO:　Fear not my government.

IAGO:　I once more take my leave.　　　　　　*Exit.*

OTHELLO:　This fellow's of exceeding honesty,
275　And knows all qualities, with a learnèd spirit,
Of human dealings. If I do prove her haggard,
Though that her jesses were my dear heartstrings,
I'd whistle her off and let her down the wind
To prey at fortune. Haply, for I am black
280　And have not those soft parts of conversation
That chamberers have, or for I am declined
Into the vale of years—yet that's not much—
She's gone. I am abused, and my relief
Must be to loathe her. O curse of marriage,
285　That we can call these delicate creatures ours
And not their appetites! I had rather be a toad
And live upon the vapor of a dungeon
Than keep a corner in the thing I love
For others' uses. Yet, 'tis the plague to great ones;
290　Prerogatived are they less than the base.
'Tis destiny unshunnable, like death.
Even then this forkèd plague is fated to us
When we do quicken. Look where she comes.

---

266 strain his entertainment urge his reinstatement　**269 busy** interfering　**271 hold her free** regard her as innocent　**272 government** self-control, conduct　**275 qualities** natures, types　**276 haggard** wild (like a wild female hawk)　**277 jesses** straps fastened around the legs of a trained hawk　**278 I'd . . . wind** i.e., I'd let her go forever. (To release a hawk downwind was to invite it not to return.)　**279 prey at fortune** fend for herself in the wild.　**Haply, for** perhaps because　**280 soft . . . conversation** pleasing graces of social behavior　**281 chamberers** gallants　**283 abused** deceived　**290 Prerogatived** privileged (to have honest wives).　**the base** ordinary citizens. (Socially prominent men are especially prone to the unavoidable destiny of being cuckolded and to the public shame that goes with it.)　**292 forkèd** (An allusion to the horns of the cuckold.)　**293 quicken** receive life. (*Quicken* may also mean to swarm with maggots as the body festers, as in 4.2.69, in which case lines 292–293 suggest that *even then*, in death, we are cuckolded by *forkèd* worms.)

Enter DESDEMONA *and* EMILIA.

If she be false, O, then heaven mocks itself!
I'll not believe 't.　　　　　　　　　　　　　295

DESDEMONA:　　　How now, my dear Othello?
Your dinner, and the generous islanders
By you invited, do attend your presence.

OTHELLO:　I am to blame.

DESDEMONA:　　　Why do you speak so faintly?
Are you not well?

OTHELLO:　I have a pain upon my forehead here.　300

DESDEMONA:　Faith, that's with watching. 'Twill away
again.
　　　　　　　　[She offers her handkerchief.]
Let me but bind it hard, within this hour
It will be well.

OTHELLO:　　　Your napkin is too little.
Let it alone. Come, I'll go in with you.
　　　[He puts the handkerchief from him, and it drops.]

DESDEMONA:　I am very sorry that you are not well.　305
　　　　　　　　　Exit [with OTHELLO*].*

EMILIA *[picking up the handkerchief]*:　I am glad I have
found this napkin.
This was her first remembrance from the Moor.
My wayward husband hath a hundred times
Wooed me to steal it, but she so loves the token—
For he conjured her she should ever keep it—　310
That she reserves it evermore about her
To kiss and talk to. I'll have the work ta'en out,
And give 't Iago. What he will do with it
Heaven knows, not I;
I nothing but to please his fantasy.　　　　315

　　　　　　　　　　Enter IAGO.

IAGO:　How now? What do you here alone?

---

296 generous noble　**297 attend** await　**301 watching** too little sleep　**303 napkin** handkerchief　**304 Let it alone** i.e., never mind　**308 wayward** capricious　**312 work ta'en out** design of the embroidery copied　**315 fantasy** whim

Emilia (Anna Patrick) brings Iago Desdemona's handkerchief.

EMILIA: Do not you chide. I have a thing for you.

IAGO: You have a thing for me? It is a common thing—

EMILIA: Ha?

320 **IAGO:**   To have a foolish wife.

EMILIA: O, is that all? What will you give me now
       For that same handkerchief?

IAGO: What handkerchief?

EMILIA: What handkerchief?
325   Why, that the Moor first gave to Desdemona;
       That which so often you did bid me steal.

IAGO: Hast stolen it from her?

EMILIA: No, faith. She let it drop by negligence,
       And to th' advantage I, being here, took 't up.
330   Look, here 'tis.

IAGO: A good wench! Give it me.

EMILIA: What will you do with 't, that you have been so
       earnest
       To have me filch it?

IAGO [*snatching it*]:   Why, what is that to you?

---

318 common thing (With bawdy suggestion; *common* suggests coarseness and availability to all comers, and *thing* is a slang term for the pudendum.)   **329 to th' advantage** taking the opportunity

EMILIA: If it be not for some purpose of import,
       Give 't me again. Poor lady, she'll run mad
       When she shall lack it.

IAGO: Be not acknown on 't.   335
       I have use for it. Go, leave me.   *Exit* EMILIA.
       I will in Cassio's lodging lose this napkin
       And let him find it. Trifles light as air
       Are to the jealous confirmations strong
       As proofs of Holy Writ. This may do something.   340
       The Moor already changes with my poison.
       Dangerous conceits are in their natures poisons,
       Which at the first are scarce found to distaste,
       But with a little act upon the blood
       Burn like the mines of sulfur.

                        Enter OTHELLO.

                    I did say so.   345
       Look where he comes! Not poppy nor mandragora
       Nor all the drowsy syrups of the world
       Shall ever medicine thee to that sweet sleep
       Which thou owedst yesterday.

OTHELLO: Ha, ha, false to me?

IAGO: Why, how now, General? No more of that.   350

OTHELLO: Avaunt! Begone! Thou hast set me on the
       rack.
       I swear 'tis better to be much abused
       Than but to know 't a little.

IAGO: How now, my lord?

OTHELLO: What sense had I of her stolen hours of lust?
       I saw 't not, thought it not, it harmed not me.   355
       I slept the next night well, fed well, was free and
       merry;
       I found not Cassio's kisses on her lips.
       He that is robbed, not wanting what is stolen,
       Let him not know 't and he's not robbed at all.

---

335 lack miss.   **Be . . . on 't** do not confess knowledge of it   **337 lose** (The Folio spelling, *loose*, is a normal spelling for "lose," but it may also contain the idea of "let go," "release.")   **342 conceits** fancies, ideas   **343 distaste** be distasteful   **344 act** action, working   **346 mandragora** an opiate made of the mandrake root   **349 thou owedst** you did own   **356 free** carefree   **358 wanting** missing

360 **IAGO:**   I am sorry to hear this.

OTHELLO: I had been happy if the general camp,
Pioners and all, had tasted her sweet body,
So I had nothing known. O, now, forever
Farewell the tranquil mind! Farewell content!
365 Farewell the plumèd troops and the big wars
That makes ambition virtue! O, farewell!
Farewell the neighing steed and the shrill trump,
The spirit-stirring drum, th' ear-piercing fife,
The royal banner, and all quality,
370 Pride, pomp, and circumstance of glorious war!
And O, you mortal engines, whose rude throats
Th' immortal Jove's dread clamors counterfeit,
Farewell! Othello's occupation's gone.

IAGO: Is 't possible, my lord?

375 **OTHELLO:**   Villain, be sure thou prove my love a whore!
Be sure of it. Give me the ocular proof,
Or, by the worth of mine eternal soul,
Thou hadst been better have been born a dog
Than answer my waked wrath!

IAGO: Is 't come to this?

380 **OTHELLO:**   Make me to see 't, or at the least so prove it
That the probation bear no hinge nor loop
To hang a doubt on, or woe upon thy life!

IAGO: My noble lord—

OTHELLO: If thou dost slander her and torture me,
385 Never pray more; abandon all remorse;
On horror's head horrors accumulate;
Do deeds to make heaven weep, all earth amazed;
For nothing canst thou to damnation add
Greater than that.

IAGO: O grace! O heaven forgive me!
390 Are you a man? Have you a soul or sense?

God b' wi' you; take mine office. O wretched fool,
That lov'st to make thine honesty a vice!
O monstrous world! Take note, take note, O world,
To be direct and honest is not safe.
I thank you for this profit, and from hence   395
I'll love no friend, sith love breeds such offense.

OTHELLO: Nay, stay. Thou shouldst be honest.

IAGO: I should be wise, for honesty's a fool
And loses that it works for.

OTHELLO: By the world,
I think my wife be honest and think she is not;   400
I think that thou art just and think thou art not.
I'll have some proof. My name, that was as fresh
As Dian's visage, is now begrimed and black
As mine own face. If there be cords, or knives,
Poison, or fire, or suffocating streams,   405
I'll not endure it. Would I were satisfied!

IAGO: I see, sir, you are eaten up with passion.
I do repent me that I put it to you.
You would be satisfied?

OTHELLO: Would? Nay, and I will.

IAGO: And may; but how? How satisfied, my lord?   410
Would you, the supervisor, grossly gape on?
Behold her topped?

OTHELLO: Death and damnation! O!

IAGO: It were a tedious difficulty, I think,
To bring them to that prospect. Damn them then,
If ever mortal eyes do see them bolster   415
More than their own. What then? How then?
What shall I say? Where's satisfaction?
It is impossible you should see this,

---

362 **Pioners** diggers of mines, the lowest grade of soldiers   363 **So**
provided   365 **big** stately   369 **quality** character, essential nature
370 **Pride** rich display.   **circumstance** pageantry   371 **mortal**
engines i.e., cannon. (*Mortal* means "deadly.")   372 **Jove's dread**
clamors i.e., thunder   381 **probation** proof   385 **remorse** pity,
penitent hope for salvation   386 **horrors accumulate** add still
more horrors   387 **amazed** confounded with horror

---

391 **O wretched fool** (Iago addresses himself as a fool for having
carried honesty too far.)   392 **vice** failing, something overdone
395 **profit** profitable instruction.   **hence** henceforth   396 **sith**
since.   **offense** i.e., harm to the one who offers help and friendship
397 **Thou shouldst be** it appears that you are. (But Iago replies
in the sense of "ought to be.")   399 **that** what   403 **Dian** Diana,
goddess of the moon and of chastity   411 **supervisor** onlooker
414 **Damn them then** i.e., they would have to be really incorrigible   415 **bolster** go to bed together, share a bolster   416 **More**
other.   **own** own eyes

Were they as prime as goats, as hot as monkeys,
420 As salt as wolves in pride, and fools as gross
As ignorance made drunk. But yet I say,
If imputation and strong circumstances
Which lead directly to the door of truth
Will give you satisfaction, you might have 't.

425 **OTHELLO:**   Give me a living reason she's disloyal.

IAGO: I do not like the office.
But sith I am entered in this cause so far,
Pricked to 't by foolish honesty and love,
I will go on. I lay with Cassio lately,
430 And being troubled with a raging tooth
I could not sleep. There are a kind of men
So loose of soul that in their sleeps will mutter
Their affairs. One of this kind is Cassio.
In sleep I heard him say, "Sweet Desdemona,
435 Let us be wary, let us hide our loves!"
And then, sir, would he grip and wring my hand,
Cry "O sweet creature!", then kiss me hard,
As if he plucked up kisses by the roots
That grew upon my lips; then laid his leg
440 Over my thigh, and sighed, and kissed, and then
Cried, "Cursèd fate that gave thee to the Moor!"

OTHELLO: O monstrous! Monstrous!

IAGO: Nay, this was but his dream.

OTHELLO: But this denoted a foregone conclusion.
'Tis a shrewd doubt, though it be but a dream.

445 **IAGO:**   And this may help to thicken other proofs
That do demonstrate thinly.

OTHELLO: I'll tear her all to pieces.

IAGO: Nay, but be wise. Yet we see nothing done;
She may be honest yet. Tell me but this:
Have you not sometimes seen a handkerchief
450 Spotted with strawberries in your wife's hand?

Othello, enraged by jealousy, seeks Iago's counsel.

OTHELLO: I gave her such a one. 'Twas my first gift.

IAGO: I know not that; but such a handkerchief—
I am sure it was your wife's—did I today
See Cassio wipe his beard with.

OTHELLO: If it be that—

IAGO: If it be that, or any that was hers,   455
It speaks against her with the other proofs.

OTHELLO: O, that the slave had forty thousand lives!
One is too poor, too weak for my revenge.
Now do I see 'tis true. Look here, Iago,
All my fond love thus do I blow to heaven.   460
'Tis gone.
Arise, black vengeance, from the hollow hell!
Yield up, O love, thy crown and hearted throne
To tyrannous hate! Swell, bosom, with thy freight,
For 'tis of aspics' tongues!   465

IAGO: Yet be content.

OTHELLO: O, blood, blood, blood!

IAGO: Patience, I say. Your mind perhaps may change.

---

419 prime lustful   **420 salt** wanton, sensual.   **pride** heat   **422 imputation . . . circumstances** strong circumstantial evidence   **427 sith** since   **428 Pricked** spurred   **443 foregone conclusion** concluded experience or action   **444 shrewd doubt** suspicious circumstance   **450 Spotted with strawberries** embroidered with a strawberry pattern

---

457 the slave i.e., Cassio   **460 fond** foolish (but also suggesting "affectionate")   **463 hearted** fixed in the heart   **464 freight** burden   **465 aspics'** venomous serpents'   **466 content** calm

OTHELLO: Never, Iago. Like to the Pontic Sea,
470   Whose icy current and compulsive course
          Ne'er feels retiring ebb, but keeps due on
          To the Propontic and the Hellespont,
          Even so my bloody thoughts with violent pace
          Shall ne'er look back, ne'er ebb to humble love,
475   Till that a capable and wide revenge
          Swallow them up. Now, by yond marble heaven,
          [Kneeling] In the due reverence of a sacred vow
          I here engage my words.

IAGO: Do not rise yet.
          [He kneels.] Witness, you ever-burning lights above,
480   You elements that clip us round about,
          Witness that here Iago doth give up
          The execution of his wit, hands, heart,
          To wronged Othello's service. Let him command,
          And to obey shall be in me remorse,
485   What bloody business ever.   *[They rise.]*

OTHELLO: I greet thy love,
          Not with vain thanks, but with acceptance bounteous,
          And will upon the instant put thee to 't.
          Within these three days let me hear thee say
          That Cassio's not alive.

IAGO: My friend is dead;
490   'Tis done at your request. But let her live.

OTHELLO: Damn her, lewd minx! O, damn her, damn
              her!
          Come, go with me apart. I will withdraw
          To furnish me with some swift means of death
          For the fair devil. Now art thou my lieutenant.

495 **IAGO:**   I am your own forever.   *Exeunt.*

------

469 **Pontic Sea** Black Sea   472 **Propontic** Sea of Marmora, between the Black Sea and the Aegean.   **Hellespont** Dardanelles,
straits where the Sea of Marmora joins with the Aegean   475 **capable** ample, comprehensive   476 **marble** i.e., gleaming like marble
and unrelenting   479 **s.d. He kneels** (In the Quarto text, Iago
kneels here after Othello has knelt at line 477.)   480 **clip** encompass
482 **execution** exercise, action.   **wit** mind   484 **remorse** pity (for
Othello's wrongs)   485 **ever** soever   487 **to 't** to the proof   491
minx wanton

3.4   *Enter* DESDEMONA, EMILIA, *and* CLOWN.

DESDEMONA: Do you know, sirrah, where Lieutenant
          Cassio lies?

CLOWN: I dare not say he lies anywhere.

DESDEMONA: Why, man?

CLOWN: He's a soldier, and for me to say a soldier lies,
          'tis stabbing.   5

DESDEMONA: Go to. Where lodges he?

CLOWN: To tell you where he lodges is to tell you where
          I lie.

DESDEMONA: Can anything be made of this?   10

CLOWN: I know not where he lodges, and for me to
          devise a lodging and say he lies here, or he lies there,
          were to lie in mine own throat.

DESDEMONA: Can you inquire him out, and be edified
          by report?   15

CLOWN: I will catechize the world for him; that is, make
          questions, and by them answer.

DESDEMONA: Seek him, bid him come hither. Tell him
          I have moved my lord on his behalf and hope all will
          be well.   20

CLOWN: To do this is within the compass of man's wit,
          and therefore I will attempt the doing it.   *Exit* CLOWN.

DESDEMONA: Where should I lose that handkerchief,
          Emilia?

EMILIA: I know not, madam.

DESDEMONA: Believe me, I had rather have lost my
              purse   25
          Full of crusadoes; and but my noble Moor
          Is true of mind and made of no such baseness

3.4 Location: Before the citadel.
1 **sirrah** (A form of address to an inferior.)   2 **lies** lodges. (But the
Clown makes the obvious pun.)   13 **lie . . . throat** (1) lie egregiously
and deliberately (2) use the windpipe to speak a lie   19 **moved** peti-
tioned   26 **crusadoes** Portuguese gold coins

As jealous creatures are, it were enough
To put him to ill thinking.

EMILIA: Is he not jealous?

30 **DESDEMONA:**   Who, he? I think the sun where he was
          born
     Drew all such humors from him.

EMILIA   Look where he comes.

                    Enter OTHELLO.

DESDEMONA: I will not leave him now till Cassio
     Be called to him.—How is 't with you, my lord?

OTHELLO: Well, my good lady. *[Aside.]* O, hardness to
     dissemble!—
     How do you, Desdemona?

35 **DESDEMONA:**   Well, my good lord.

OTHELLO: Give me your hand. *[She gives her hand.]*
     This hand is moist, my lady.

DESDEMONA: It yet hath felt no age nor known no
     sorrow.

OTHELLO: This argues fruitfulness and liberal heart.
     Hot, hot, and moist. This hand of yours requires
40   A sequester from liberty, fasting and prayer,
     Much castigation, exercise devout;
     For here's a young and sweating devil here
     That commonly rebels. 'Tis a good hand,
     A frank one.

DESDEMONA: You may indeed say so,
45   For 'twas that hand that gave away my heart.

OTHELLO: A liberal hand. The hearts of old gave hands,
     But our new heraldry is hands, not hearts.

DESDEMONA: I cannot speak of this. Come now, your
     promise.

OTHELLO: What promise, chuck?

DESDEMONA: I have sent to bid Cassio come speak
     with you.   50

OTHELLO: I have a salt and sorry rheum offends me;
     Lend me thy handkerchief.

DESDEMONA: Here, my lord.   *[She offers a handkerchief.]*

OTHELLO: That which I gave you.

DESDEMONA: I have it not about me.

OTHELLO: Not?   55

DESDEMONA: No, faith, my lord.

OTHELLO: That's a fault. That handkerchief
     Did an Egyptian to my mother give.
     She was a charmer, and could almost read
     The thoughts of people. She told her, while she kept it   60
     'Twould make her amiable and subdue my father
     Entirely to her love, but if she lost it
     Or made a gift of it, my father's eye
     Should hold her loathèd and his spirits should hunt
     After new fancies. She, dying, gave it me,   65
     And bid me, when my fate would have me wived,
     To give it her. I did so; and take heed on 't;
     Make it a darling like your precious eye.
     To lose 't or give 't away were such perdition
     As nothing else could match.   70

DESDEMONA: Is 't possible?

OTHELLO: 'Tis true. There's magic in the web of it.
     A sibyl, that had numbered in the world
     The sun to course two hundred compasses,
     In her prophetic fury sewed the work;

---

31 **humors** (Refers to the four bodily fluids thought to determine temperament.)   38 **argues** gives evidence of.   **fruitfulness** generosity, amorousness, and fecundity.   **liberal** generous and sexually free   40 **sequester** separation, sequestration   41 **castigation** corrective discipline.   **exercise devout** i.e., prayer, religious meditation, etc.   44 **frank** generous, open (with sexual suggestion)   46 **The hearts . . . hands** i.e., in former times, people would give their hearts when they gave their hands to something   47 **But . . . hearts** i.e., in our decadent times, the joining of hands is no longer a badge to signify the giving of hearts

49 **chuck** (A term of endearment.)   51 **salt . . . rheum** distressful head cold or watering of the eyes   59 **charmer** sorceress   61 **amiable** desirable   65 **fancies** loves   67 **her** i.e., to my wife   69 **perdition** loss   71 **web** fabric, weaving   73 **compasses** annual circlings. (The *sibyl*, or prophetess, was two hundred years old.)   74 **prophetic fury** frenzy of prophetic inspiration.   **work** embroidered pattern

Othello asks Desdemona for the handkerchief he gave her.

75   The worms were hallowed that did breed the silk,
      And it was dyed in mummy which the skillful
      Conserved of maidens' hearts.

DESDEMONA: I' faith! Is 't true?

OTHELLO: Most veritable. Therefore look to 't well.

DESDEMONA: Then would to God that I had never
      seen 't!

80 **OTHELLO:**   Ha? Wherefore?

DESDEMONA: Why do you speak so startingly and rash?

OTHELLO: Is 't lost? Is 't gone? Speak, is 't out o' the
      way?

DESDEMONA: Heaven bless us!

OTHELLO: Say you?

85 **DESDEMONA:**   It is not lost; but what an if it were?

OTHELLO: How?

DESDEMONA: I say it is not lost.

OTHELLO: Fetch 't, let me see 't.

DESDEMONA: Why, so I can, sir, but I will not now.
      This is a trick to put me from my suit.
      Pray you, let Cassio be received again.   90

OTHELLO: Fetch me the handkerchief! My mind
      misgives.

DESDEMONA: Come, come,
      You'll never meet a more sufficient man.

OTHELLO: The handkerchief!

DESDEMONA: I pray, talk me of Cassio.

OTHELLO: The handkerchief!

DESDEMONA: A man that all his time   95
      Hath founded his good fortunes on your love,
      Shared dangers with you—

OTHELLO: The handkerchief!

DESDEMONA: I' faith, you are to blame.

OTHELLO: Zounds!   *Exit* OTHELLO.   100

EMILIA: Is not this man jealous?

DESDEMONA: I ne'er saw this before.
      Sure, there's some wonder in this handkerchief.
      I am most unhappy in the loss of it.

EMILIA: 'Tis not a year or two shows us a man.   105
      They are all but stomachs, and we all but food;
      They eat us hungerly, and when they are full
      They belch us.

           Enter IAGO *and* CASSIO.

      Look you, Cassio and my husband.

IAGO *[to* CASSIO*]:*   There is no other way; 'tis she must
      do 't.
      And, lo, the happiness! Go and importune her.   110

---

76 mummy medicinal or magical preparation drained from mummified bodies   **77 Conserved of** prepared or preserved out of   **81 startingly and rash** disjointedly and impetuously, excitedly   **82 out of the way** lost, misplaced   **85 an if** if

93 sufficient able, complete   **94 talk** talk to   **95 all his time** throughout his career   **105 'Tis . . . man** i.e., you can't really know a man even in a year or two of experience (?), or, real men come along seldom (?)   **106 but** nothing but   **107 hungerly** hungrily   **110 the happiness** in happy time, fortunately met

DESDEMONA: How now, good Cassio? What's the news
with you?

CASSIO: Madam, my former suit. I do beseech you
That by your virtuous means I may again
Exist and be a member of his love
115 Whom I, with all the office of my heart,
Entirely honor. I would not be delayed.
If my offense be of such mortal kind
That nor my service past, nor present sorrows,
Nor purposed merit in futurity
120 Can ransom me into his love again,
But to know so must be my benefit;
So shall I clothe me in a forced content,
And shut myself up in some other course,
To fortune's alms.

DESDEMONA: Alas, thrice-gentle Cassio,
125 My advocation is not now in tune.
My lord is not my lord; nor should I know him,
Were he in favor as in humor altered.
So help me every spirit sanctified
As I have spoken for you all my best
130 And stood within the blank of his displeasure
For my free speech! You must awhile be patient.
What I can do I will, and more I will
Than for myself I dare. Let that suffice you.

IAGO: Is my lord angry?

EMILIA: He went hence but now,
135 And certainly in strange unquietness.

IAGO: Can he be angry? I have seen the cannon
When it hath blown his ranks into the air,
And like the devil from his very arm
Puffed his own brother—and is he angry?
140 Something of moment then. I will go meet him.
There's matter in 't indeed, if he be angry.

DESDEMONA: I prithee, do so.   *Exit [IAGO].*
Something, sure, of state,
Either from Venice, or some unhatched practice
Made demonstrable here in Cyprus to him,
Hath puddled his clear spirit; and in such cases   145
Men's natures wrangle with inferior things,
Though great ones are their object. 'Tis even so;
For let our finger ache, and it indues
Our other, healthful members even to a sense
Of pain. Nay, we must think men are not gods,   150
Nor of them look for such observancy
As fits the bridal. Beshrew me much, Emilia,
I was, unhandsome warrior as I am,
Arraigning his unkindness with my soul;
But now I find I had suborned the witness,   155
And he's indicted falsely.

EMILIA: Pray heaven it be
State matters, as you think, and no conception
Nor no jealous toy concerning you.

DESDEMONA: Alas the day! I never gave him cause.

EMILIA: But jealous souls will not be answered so;   160
They are not ever jealous for the cause,
But jealous for they're jealous. It is a monster
Begot upon itself, born on itself.

DESDEMONA: Heaven keep that monster from Othello's
mind!

EMILIA: Lady, amen.   165

DESDEMONA: I will go seek him. Cassio, walk
hereabout.
If I do find him fit, I'll move your suit
And seek to effect it to my uttermost.

CASSIO: I humbly thank your ladyship.
Exit [DESDEMONA with EMILIA].

---

113 virtuous efficacious   **115 office** loyal service   **117 mortal** fatal
118 nor . . . nor neither . . . nor   **121 But . . . benefit** merely to know
that my case is hopeless will have to content me (and will be better
than uncertainty)   **123 shut . . . in** confine myself to   **124 To fortune's alms** throwing myself on the mercy of fortune   **125 advocation** advocacy   **127 favor** appearance.   **humor** mood   **130 within
the blank** within point-blank range. (The *blank* is the center of the
target.)   **140 of moment** of immediate importance, momentous

142 of state concerning state affairs   **143 unhatched practice** as
yet unexecuted or undiscovered plot   **145 puddled** muddied   **148
indues** brings to the same condition   **151 observancy** attentiveness
152 bridal wedding (when a bridegroom is newly attentive to his
bride).   **Beshrew me** (A mild oath.)   **153 unhandsome** insufficient,
unskillful   **154 with** before the bar of   **155 suborned the witness**
induced the witness to give false testimony   **158 toy** fancy   **162 for**
because   **163 Begot upon itself** generated solely from itself

Enter BIANCA.

170 **BIANCA:** Save you, friend Cassio!

CASSIO: What make you from home?
How is 't with you, my most fair Bianca?
I' faith, sweet love, I was coming to your house.

BIANCA: And I was going to your lodging, Cassio.
What, keep a week away? Seven days and nights?
175 Eightscore-eight hours? And lovers' absent hours
More tedious than the dial eightscore times?
O weary reckoning!

CASSIO: Pardon me, Bianca.
I have this while with leaden thoughts been pressed;
But I shall, in a more continuate time,
180 Strike off this score of absence. Sweet Bianca,
[giving her DESDEMONA's *handkerchief]*
Take me this work out.

BIANCA: O Cassio, whence came this?
This is some token from a newer friend.
To the felt absence now I feel a cause.
Is 't come to this? Well, well.

CASSIO: Go to, woman!
185 Throw your vile guesses in the devil's teeth,
From whence you have them. You are jealous now
That this is from some mistress, some remembrance.
No, by my faith, Bianca.

BIANCA: Why, whose is it?

CASSIO: I know not, neither. I found it in my chamber.
190 I like the work well. Ere it be demanded—
As like enough it will—I would have it copied.
Take it and do 't, and leave me for this time.

BIANCA: Leave you? Wherefore?

CASSIO: I do attend here on the General,
195 And think it no addition, nor my wish,
To have him see me womaned.

Cassio gives Bianca (Zawe Ashton) the handkerchief he found in his room.

BIANCA: Why, I pray you?

CASSIO: Not that I love you not.

BIANCA: But that you do not love me.
I pray you, bring me on the way a little, 200
And say if I shall see you soon at night.

CASSIO: 'Tis but a little way that I can bring you,
For I attend here; but I'll see you soon.

BIANCA: 'Tis very good. I must be circumstanced.
Exeunt omnes.

4.1 *Enter* OTHELLO *and* IAGO.

IAGO: Will you think so?

OTHELLO: Think so, Iago?

IAGO: What,
To kiss in private?

OTHELLO: An unauthorized kiss!

IAGO: Or to be naked with her friend in bed
An hour or more, not meaning any harm?

---

170 **Save** God save.   **make** do   175 **Eightscore-eight** one hundred
sixty-eight, the number of hours in a week   176 **the dial** a complete
revolution of the clock   179 **continuate** uninterrupted   180 **Strike
. . . score** settle this account   181 **Take . . . out** copy this embroidery
for me   182 **friend** mistress   190 **demanded** inquired for   191
like likely   195 **addition** i.e., addition to my reputation

---

200 **bring** accompany   204 **be circumstanced** be governed by
circumstance, yield to your conditions

4.1 Location: Before the citadel.

5   **OTHELLO:**   Naked in bed, Iago, and not mean harm?
      It is hypocrisy against the devil.
      They that mean virtuously and yet do so,
      The devil their virtue tempts, and they tempt heaven.

IAGO: If they do nothing, 'tis a venial slip.
10   But if I give my wife a handkerchief—

OTHELLO: What then?

IAGO: Why then, 'tis hers, my lord, and being hers,
      She may, I think, bestow 't on any man.

OTHELLO: She is protectress of her honor too.
15   May she give that?

IAGO: Her honor is an essence that's not seen;
      They have it very oft that have it not.
      But, for the handkerchief—

OTHELLO: By heaven, I would most gladly have
            forgot it.
20   Thou saidst—O, it comes o'er my memory
      As doth the raven o'er the infectious house,
      Boding to all—he had my handkerchief.

IAGO: Ay, what of that?

OTHELLO: That's not so good now.

IAGO: What
      If I had said I had seen him do you wrong?
25   Or heard him say—as knaves be such abroad,
      Who having, by their own importunate suit,
      Or voluntary dotage of some mistress,
      Convincèd or supplied them, cannot choose
      But they must blab—

OTHELLO: Hath he said anything?

30   **IAGO:**   He hath, my lord; but, be you well assured,
      No more than he'll unswear.

OTHELLO: What hath he said?

IAGO: Faith, that he did—I know not what he did.

OTHELLO: What? What?

IAGO: Lie—

OTHELLO: With her?

IAGO: With her, on her; what you will.

OTHELLO: Lie with her? Lie on her? We say "lie on   35
      her" when they belie her. Lie with her? Zounds, that's
      fulsome.—Handkerchief—confessions—handker-
      chief!—To confess and be hanged for his labor—first
      to be hanged and then to confess.—I tremble at it.
      Nature would not invest herself in such shadowing   40
      passion without some instruction. It is not words
      that shakes me thus. Pish! Noses, ears, and lips.—
      Is 't possible?—Confess—handkerchief!—O devil!
                                    Falls in a trance.

IAGO: Work on,
      My medicine, work! Thus credulous fools are caught,   45
      And many worthy and chaste dames even thus,
      All guiltless, meet reproach.—What, ho! My lord!
      My lord, I say! Othello!

                              Enter CASSIO.

                  How now, Cassio?

CASSIO: What's the matter?

IAGO: My lord is fall'n into an epilepsy.   50
      This is his second fit. He had one yesterday.

CASSIO: Rub him about the temples.

IAGO: No, forbear.
      The lethargy must have his quiet course.
      If not, he foams at mouth, and by and by
      Breaks out to savage madness. Look, he stirs.   55

---

9 **venial** pardonable   17 **They have it** i.e., they enjoy a reputation
for it   21 **raven . . . house** (Allusion to the belief that the raven
hovered over a house of sickness or infection, such as one visited
by the plague.)   25 **abroad** around about   27 **voluntary dotage**
willing infatuation   28 **Convincèd or supplied** seduced or sexually
gratified

36 **belie** slander   37 **fulsome** foul   38–39 **first . . . to confess**
(Othello reverses the proverbial *confess and be hanged;* Cassio is
to be given no time to confess before he dies.)   40–41 **Nature . . .
instruction** i.e., without some foundation in fact, nature would not
have dressed herself in such an overwhelming passion that comes
over me now and fills my mind with images, or in such a lifelike
fantasy as Cassio had in his dreams of lying with Desdemona   41
words mere words   53 **lethargy** coma.   **his** its

Do you withdraw yourself a little while.
He will recover straight. When he is gone,
I would on great occasion speak with you.

[Exit CASSIO.*]*

How is it, General? Have you not hurt your head?

60 **OTHELLO:**   Dost thou mock me?

IAGO: I mock you not, by heaven.
Would you would bear your fortune like a man!

OTHELLO: A hornèd man's a monster and a beast.

IAGO: There's many a beast then in a populous city,
And many a civil monster.

65 **OTHELLO:**   Did he confess it?

IAGO: Good sir, be a man.
Think every bearded fellow that's but yoked
May draw with you. There's millions now alive
That nightly lie in those unproper beds
70 Which they dare swear peculiar. Your case is better.
O, 'tis the spite of hell, the fiend's arch-mock,
To lip a wanton in a secure couch
And to suppose her chaste! No, let me know,
And knowing what I am, I know what she shall be.

75 **OTHELLO:**   O, thou art wise. 'Tis certain.

IAGO: Stand you awhile apart;
Confine yourself but in a patient list.
Whilst you were here o'erwhelmèd with your grief—
A passion most unsuiting such a man—
80 Cassio came hither. I shifted him away,
And laid good 'scuse upon your ecstasy,
Bade him anon return and here speak with me,
The which he promised. Do but encave yourself

And mark the fleers, the gibes, and notable scorns
That dwell in every region of his face;   85
For I will make him tell the tale anew,
Where, how, how oft, how long ago, and when
He hath and is again to cope your wife.
I say, but mark his gesture. Marry, patience!
Or I shall say you're all-in-all in spleen,   90
And nothing of a man.

OTHELLO: Dost thou hear, Iago?
I will be found most cunning in my patience;
But—dost thou hear?—most bloody.

IAGO: That's not amiss;
But yet keep time in all. Will you withdraw?

*[*OTHELLO *stands apart.]*

Now will I question Cassio of Bianca,   95
A huswife that by selling her desires
Buys herself bread and clothes. It is a creature
That dotes on Cassio—as 'tis the strumpet's plague
To beguile many and be beguiled by one.
He, when he hears of her, cannot restrain   100
From the excess of laughter. Here he comes.

Enter CASSIO.

As he shall smile, Othello shall go mad;
And his unbookish jealousy must conster
Poor Cassio's smiles, gestures, and light behaviors
Quite in the wrong.—How do you now, Lieutenant?   105

CASSIO: The worser that you give me the addition
Whose want even kills me.

IAGO: Ply Desdemona well and you are sure on 't.
[Speaking lower.] Now, if this suit lay in Bianca's
power,
How quickly should you speed!   110

CASSIO *[laughing]:*   Alas, poor caitiff!

OTHELLO *[aside]:*   Look how he laughs already!

---

58 on great occasion on a matter of great importance   **60 mock
me** (Othello takes Iago's question about hurting his head to be a
mocking reference to the cuckold's horns.)   **64 civil** i.e., dwelling
in a city   **67 yoked** (1) married (2) put into the yoke of infamy and
cuckoldry   **68 draw with you** pull as you do, like oxen who are
yoked, i.e., share your fate as cuckold   **69 unproper** not exclusively
their own   **70 peculiar** private, their own.   **better** i.e., because you
know the truth   **72 lip** kiss.   **secure** free from suspicion   **74 what
I am** i.e., a cuckold.   **she shall be** will happen to her   **77 in . . . list**
within the bounds of patience   **80 shifted him away** used a dodge
to get rid of him   **81 ecstasy** trance   **83 encave** conceal

84 fleers sneers.   **notable** obvious   **88 cope** encounter with, have
sex with   **90 all-in-all in spleen** utterly governed by passionate
impulses   **94 keep time** keep yourself steady (as in music)   **96 huswife** hussy   **100 restrain** refrain   **103 unbookish** uninstructed.
conster construe   **106 addition** title   **107 Whose want** the lack of
which   **111 caitiff** wretch

IAGO: I never knew a woman love man so.

CASSIO: Alas, poor rogue! I think, i' faith, she loves me.

115 **OTHELLO:**   Now he denies it faintly, and laughs it out.

IAGO: Do you hear, Cassio?

OTHELLO: Now he importunes him
To tell it o'er. Go to! Well said, well said.

IAGO: She gives it out that you shall marry her.
Do you intend it?

120 **CASSIO:**   Ha, ha, ha!

OTHELLO: Do you triumph, Roman? Do you triumph?

CASSIO: I marry her? What? A customer? Prithee, bear
some charity to my wit; do not think it so unwhole-
some. Ha, ha, ha!

125 **OTHELLO:**   So, so, so, so! They laugh that win.

IAGO: Faith, the cry goes that you shall marry her.

CASSIO: Prithee, say true.

IAGO: I am a very villain else.

OTHELLO: Have you scored me? Well.

130 **CASSIO:**   This is the monkey's own giving out. She is
persuaded I will marry her out of her own love and
flattery, not out of my promise.

OTHELLO: Iago beckons me. Now he begins the story.

CASSIO: She was here even now; she haunts me in every
135   place. I was the other day talking on the seabank with
certain Venetians, and thither comes the bauble, and,
by this hand, she falls me thus about my neck—
                                        [He embraces IAGO.]

Bianca enters with the handkerchief.

OTHELLO: Crying, "O dear Cassio!" as it were; his
gesture imports it.

CASSIO: So hangs and lolls and weeps upon me, so   140
shakes and pulls me. Ha, ha, ha!

OTHELLO: Now he tells how she plucked him to my
chamber. O, I see that nose of yours, but not that dog
I shall throw it to.

CASSIO: Well, I must leave her company.   145

IAGO: Before me, look where she comes.

            Enter BIANCA [with OTHELLO's handkerchief].

CASSIO: 'Tis such another fitchew! Marry, a perfumed
one.—What do you mean by this haunting of me?

BIANCA: Let the devil and his dam haunt you! What
did you mean by that same handkerchief you gave   150
me even now? I was a fine fool to take it. I must take
out the work? A likely piece of work, that you should

---

117 **Go to** (An expression of remonstrance.)   **Well said** well done
121 **Roman** (The Romans were noted for their *triumphs* or triumphal
processions.)   122 **customer** i.e., prostitute   122–123 **bear . . .
wit** be more charitable to my judgment   125 **They . . . win** i.e., they
that laugh last laugh best   126 **cry** rumor   128 **I . . . else** call me a
complete rogue if I'm not telling the truth   129 **scored me** scored off
me, beaten me, made up my reckoning, branded me   132 **flattery**
self-flattery, self-deception   133 **beckons** signals   135 **seabank**
seashore   136 **bauble** plaything   137 **by this hand** I make my vow

---

143–144 **not . . . to** (Othello imagines himself cutting off Cassio's
nose and throwing it to a dog.)   146 **Before me** i.e., on my soul
147 **'Tis . . . fitchew** what a polecat she is! Just like all the others.
fitchew (Polecats were often compared with prostitutes because of
their rank smell and presumed lechery.)   149 **dam** mother   152 **A
likely . . . work** a fine story

find it in your chamber and know not who left it
there! This is some minx's token, and I must take out
155 the work? There, give it your hobbyhorse. *[She gives
him the handkerchief.]* Wheresoever you had it, I'll
take out no work on 't.

CASSIO: How now, my sweet Bianca? How now? How
now?

OTHELLO: By heaven, that should be my handkerchief!

160 BIANCA: If you'll come to supper tonight, you may; if you
will not, come when you are next prepared for.

Exit.

IAGO: After her, after her.

CASSIO: Faith, I must. She'll rail in the streets else.

IAGO: Will you sup there?

165 CASSIO: Faith, I intend so.

IAGO: Well, I may chance to see you, for I would very
fain speak with you.

CASSIO: Prithee, come. Will you?

IAGO: Go to. Say no more.   *[Exit* CASSIO.*]*

170 OTHELLO *[advancing]*:   How shall I murder him, Iago?

IAGO: Did you perceive how he laughed at his vice?

OTHELLO: O, Iago!

IAGO: And did you see the handkerchief?

OTHELLO: Was that mine?

175 IAGO: Yours, by this hand. And to see how he prizes the
foolish woman your wife! She gave it him, and he hath
given it his whore.

OTHELLO: I would have him nine years a-killing. A fine
woman! A fair woman! A sweet woman!

180 IAGO: Nay, you must forget that.

OTHELLO: Ay, let her rot and perish, and be damned
tonight, for she shall not live. No, my heart is turned
to stone; I strike it, and it hurts my hand. O, the
world hath not a sweeter creature! She might lie by
an emperor's side and command him tasks.   185

IAGO: Nay, that's not your way.

OTHELLO: Hang her! I do but say what she is. So delicate with her needle! An admirable musician! O, she
will sing the savageness out of a bear. Of so high and
plenteous wit and invention!   190

IAGO: She's the worse for all this.

OTHELLO: O, a thousand, a thousand times! And then,
of so gentle a condition!

OTHELLO: Ay, too gentle.

OTHELLO: Nay, that's certain. But yet the pity of it,   195
Iago! O, Iago, the pity of it, Iago!

IAGO: If you are so fond over her iniquity, give her patent
to offend, for if it touch not you it comes near nobody.

OTHELLO: I will chop her into messes. Cuckold me?

IAGO: O, 'tis foul in her.   200

OTHELLO: With mine officer?

IAGO: That's fouler.

OTHELLO: Get me some poison, Iago, this night. I'll
not expostulate with her, lest her body and beauty
unprovide my mind again. This night, Iago.   205

IAGO: Do it not with poison. Strangle her in her bed,
even the bed she hath contaminated.

OTHELLO: Good, good! The justice of it pleases. Very
good.

IAGO: And for Cassio, let me be his undertaker. You shall
hear more by midnight.   210

---

155 **hobbyhorse** harlot   159 **should be** must be   161 **when . . . for**
when I'm ready for you (i.e., never)   169 **Go to** (An expression of
remonstrance.)

186 **your way** i.e., the way you should think of her   190 **invention**
imagination   193 **gentle a condition** wellborn and well-bred   194
gentle generous, yielding (to other men)   197 **fond** foolish.   **patent**
license   199 **messes** portions of meat, i.e., bits   205 **unprovide**
weaken, render unfit   209 **be his undertaker** undertake to dispatch him

OTHELLO: Excellent good. *[A trumpet within.]* What trumpet is that same?

IAGO: I warrant, something from Venice.

Enter LODOVICO, DESDEMONA, *and attendants.*

'Tis Lodovico. This comes from the Duke.
See, your wife's with him.

215   **LODOVICO:**   God save you, worthy General!

OTHELLO: With all my heart, sir.

LODOVICO *[giving him a letter]*:   The Duke and the senators of Venice greet you.

OTHELLO: I kiss the instrument of their pleasures.
[He opens the letter, and reads.]

DESDEMONA: And what's the news, good cousin Lodovico?

IAGO: I am very glad to see you, signor.
220   Welcome to Cyprus.

LODOVICO: I thank you. How does Lieutenant Cassio?

IAGO: Lives, sir.

DESDEMONA: Cousin, there's fall'n between him and my lord
An unkind breach; but you shall make all well.

225   **OTHELLO:**   Are you sure of that?

DESDEMONA: My lord?

OTHELLO *[reads]*:   "This fail you not to do, as you will—"

LODOVICO: He did not call; he's busy in the paper.
Is there division twixt my lord and Cassio?

230   **DESDEMONA:**   A most unhappy one. I would do much
T' atone them, for the love I bear to Cassio.

OTHELLO: Fire and brimstone!

DESDEMONA: My lord?

OTHELLO: Are you wise?

DESDEMONA: What, is he angry?

LODOVICO: Maybe the letter moved him;   235
For, as I think, they do command him home,
Deputing Cassio in his government.

DESDEMONA: By my troth, I am glad on 't.

OTHELLO: Indeed?

DESDEMONA: My lord?   240

OTHELLO: I am glad to see you mad.

DESDEMONA: Why, sweet Othello—

OTHELLO *[striking her]*:   Devil!

DESDEMONA: I have not deserved this.

LODOVICO: My lord, this would not be believed in Venice,   245
Though I should swear I saw 't. 'Tis very much.
Make her amends; she weeps.

OTHELLO: O devil, devil!
If that the earth could teem with woman's tears,
Each drop she falls would prove a crocodile.
Out of my sight!   250

DESDEMONA: I will not stay to offend you. *[Going.]*

LODOVICO: Truly, an obedient lady.
I do beseech your lordship, call her back.

OTHELLO: Mistress!

DESDEMONA *[returning]*:   My lord?

OTHELLO: What would you with her, sir?   255

---

237 government office   **238 on 't** of it   **241 I am . . . mad** i.e., I am glad to see that you are insane enough to rejoice in Cassio's promotion (? Othello bitterly plays on Desdemona's *I am glad.*)   **246 very much** too much, outrageous   **248 teem** breed, be impregnated   **249 falls** lets fall.   **crocodile** (Crocodiles were supposed to weep hypocritical tears for their victims.)   **255 What . . . sir** (Othello implies that Desdemona is pliant and will do a *turn*, lines 257–259, for any man.)

---

215 With all my heart i.e., I thank you most heartily   **224 unkind** unnatural, contrary to their natures; hurtful   **231 atone** reconcile

LODOVICO: Who, I, my lord?

OTHELLO: Ay, you did wish that I would make her turn.
Sir, she can turn, and turn, and yet go on
And turn again; and she can weep, sir, weep;
260   And she's obedient, as you say, obedient,
Very obedient.—Proceed you in your tears.—
Concerning this, sir—O well-painted passion!—
I am commanded home.—Get you away;
I'll send for you anon.—Sir, I obey the mandate
265   And will return to Venice.—Hence, avaunt!
                                                          [*Exit* DESDEMONA.]
Cassio shall have my place. And, sir, tonight
I do entreat that we may sup together.
You are welcome, sir, to Cyprus.—Goats and
          monkeys!   *Exit.*

LODOVICO: Is this the noble Moor whom our full Senate
270   Call all in all sufficient? Is this the nature
Whom passion could not shake? Whose solid virtue
The shot of accident nor dart of chance
Could neither graze nor pierce?

IAGO: He is much changed.

LODOVICO: Are his wits safe? Is he not light of brain?

275   **IAGO:**   He's that he is. I may not breathe my censure
What he might be. If what he might he is not,
I would to heaven he were!

LODOVICO: What, strike his wife?

IAGO: Faith, that was not so well; yet would I knew
That stroke would prove the worst!

LODOVICO: Is it his use?
280   Or did the letters work upon his blood
And new-create his fault?

---

260 obedient (With much the same sexual connotation as *turn* in lines 257–259.)   **262 passion** i.e., grief   **268 Goats and monkeys** (See 3.3.419.)   **275–277 I may . . . were** i.e., I dare not venture an opinion as to whether he's of unsound mind, as you suggest, but, if he isn't, then it might be better to wish he were in fact insane, since only that could excuse his wild behavior   **279 use** custom   **280 blood** passions

IAGO: Alas, alas!
It is not honesty in me to speak
What I have seen and known. You shall observe him,
And his own courses will denote him so
That I may save my speech. Do but go after,   285
And mark how he continues.

LODOVICO: I am sorry that I am deceived in him.
                                                              Exeunt.

4.2   *Enter* OTHELLO *and* EMILIA.

OTHELLO: You have seen nothing then?

EMILIA: Nor ever heard, nor ever did suspect.

OTHELLO: Yes, you have seen Cassio and she together.

EMILIA: But then I saw no harm, and then I heard
Each syllable that breath made up between them.   5

OTHELLO: What, did they never whisper?

EMILIA: Never, my lord.

OTHELLO: Nor send you out o' the way?

EMILIA: Never.

OTHELLO: To fetch her fan, her gloves, her mask, nor   10
nothing?

EMILIA: Never, my lord.

OTHELLO: That's strange.

EMILIA: I durst, my lord, to wager she is honest,
Lay down my soul at stake. If you think other,
Remove your thought; it doth abuse your bosom.   15
If any wretch have put this in your head,
Let heaven requite it with the serpent's curse!
For if she be not honest, chaste, and true,

---

284 courses will denote actions will reveal

4.2. Location: The citadel.
14 at stake as the wager   **15 abuse your bosom** deceive you   **17 the serpent's curse** the curse pronounced by God on the serpent for deceiving Eve, just as some man has done to Othello and Desdemona. (See Genesis 3:14.)

Othello pumps Emilia (Lorraine Burroughs) for information regarding Desdemona's affair.

There's no man happy; the purest of their wives
20   Is foul as slander.

OTHELLO: Bid her come hither. Go.

Exit EMILIA.

She says enough; yet she's a simple bawd
That cannot say as much. This is a subtle whore,
A closet lock and key of villainous secrets.
And yet she'll kneel and pray; I have seen her do 't.

Enter DESDEMONA *and* EMILIA.

25   **DESDEMONA:**   My lord, what is your will?

OTHELLO: Pray you, chuck, come hither.

DESDEMONA: What is your pleasure?

OTHELLO: Let me see your eyes.
Look in my face.

DESDEMONA: What horrible fancy's this?

21–22 **she's . . . much** i.e., any procuress or go-between who couldn't make up as plausible a story as Emilia's would have to be pretty stupid   22 **This** i.e., Desdemona   23 **closet lock and key** i.e., concealer

OTHELLO *[to* EMILIA*]:*   Some of your function, mistress.
Leave procreants alone and shut the door;   30
Cough or cry "hem" if anybody come.
Your mystery, your mystery! Nay, dispatch.

Exit EMILIA.

DESDEMONA *[kneeling]:*   Upon my knees, what doth
          your speech import?
I understand a fury in your words,
But not the words.   35

OTHELLO: Why, what art thou?

DESDEMONA: Your wife, my lord, your true
And loyal wife.

OTHELLO: Come, swear it, damn thyself,
Lest, being like one of heaven, the devils themselves
Should fear to seize thee. Therefore be double
          damned:
Swear thou art honest.

DESDEMONA: Heaven doth truly know it.   40

OTHELLO: Heaven truly knows that thou art false as
          hell.

DESDEMONA: To whom, my lord? With whom? How am
          I false?

OTHELLO *[weeping]:*   Ah, Desdemon! Away, away, away!

DESDEMONA: Alas the heavy day! Why do you weep?
Am I the motive of these tears, my lord?   45
If haply you my father do suspect
An instrument of this your calling back,
Lay not your blame on me. If you have lost him,
I have lost him too.

OTHELLO: Had it pleased heaven
To try me with affliction, had they rained   50
All kinds of sores and shames on my bare head,
Steeped me in poverty to the very lips,
Given to captivity me and my utmost hopes,

---

29 **Some . . . function** i.e., practice your chosen profession, that of bawd (by guarding the door)   30 **procreants** mating couples   32 **mystery** trade, occupation   38 **being . . . heaven** looking like an angel   45 **motive** cause   50 **they** i.e., heavenly powers

55 I should have found in some place of my soul
A drop of patience. But, alas, to make me
A fixèd figure for the time of scorn
To point his slow and moving finger at!
Yet could I bear that too, well, very well.
But there where I have garnered up my heart,
60 Where either I must live or bear no life,
The fountain from the which my current runs
Or else dries up—to be discarded thence!
Or keep it as a cistern for foul toads
To knot and gender in! Turn they complexion there,
65 Patience, thou young and rose-lipped cherubin—
Ay, there look grim as hell!

DESDEMONA: I hope my noble lord esteems me honest.

OTHELLO: O, ay, as summer flies are in the shambles,
That quicken even with blowing. O thou weed,
70 Who art so lovely fair and smell'st so sweet
That the sense aches at thee, would thou hadst ne'er
     been born!

DESDEMONA: Alas, what ignorant sin have I
committed?

OTHELLO: Was this fair paper, this most goodly book,
Made to write "whore" upon? What committed?
75 Committed? O thou public commoner!
I should make very forges of my cheeks,
That would to cinders burn up modesty,
Did I but speak thy deeds. What committed?
Heaven stops the nose at it and the moon winks;
80 The bawdy wind, that kisses all it meets,

Othello accuses Desdemona of being false.

Is hushed within the hollow mine of earth
And will not hear 't. What committed?
Impudent strumpet!

DESDEMONA: By heaven, you do me wrong.

OTHELLO: Are not you a strumpet?

DESDEMONA: No, as I am a Christian.   85
If to preserve this vessel for my lord
From any other foul unlawful touch
Be not to be a strumpet, I am none.

OTHELLO: What, not a whore?

DESDEMONA: No, as I shall be saved.   90

OTHELLO: Is 't possible?

DESDEMONA: O, heaven forgive us!

OTHELLO: I cry you mercy, then.
I took you for that cunning whore of Venice
That married with Othello. [Calling out.] You,
     mistress,
That have the office opposite to Saint Peter   95
And keep the gate of hell!

---

56 time of scorn i.e., scornful world   **57 his** its.   **slow and moving finger** i.e., hour hand of the clock, moving so slowly it seems hardly to move at all. (Othello envisages himself as being eternally pointed at by the scornful world as the numbers on a clock are pointed at by the hour hand.)   **59 garnered** stored   **61 fountain** spring   **63 cistern** cesspool   **64 knot** couple.   **gender** engender.   **Turn . . . there** change your color, grow pale, at such a sight   **65–66 Patience . . . hell** (Even Patience, that rose-lipped cherub, will look grim and pale at this spectacle.)   **67 honest** chaste   **68 shambles** slaughterhouse   **69 quicken** come to life.   **with blowing** i.e., with the puffing up of something rotten in which maggots are breeding   **72 ignorant sin** sin in ignorance   **75 commoner** prostitute   **79 winks** closes her eyes. (The moon symbolizes chastity.)   **80 bawdy** kissing one and all

---

81 mine cave (where the winds were thought to dwell)   **86 vessel** body   **92 cry you mercy** beg your pardon

Enter EMILIA.

You, you, ay, you!
We have done our course. There's money for your
    pains.   *[He gives money.]*
I pray you, turn the key and keep our counsel.   *Exit.*

EMILIA: Alas, what does this gentleman conceive?
100   How do you, madam? How do you, my good lady?

DESDEMONA: Faith, half asleep.

EMILIA: Good madam, what's the matter with my lord?

DESDEMONA: With who?

EMILIA: Why, with my lord, madam.

105 **DESDEMONA:** Who is thy lord?

EMILIA: He that is yours, sweet lady.

DESDEMONA: I have none. Do not talk to me, Emilia.
I cannot weep, nor answers have I none
But what should go by water. Prithee, tonight
Lay on my bed my wedding sheets, remember;
110   And call thy husband hither.

EMILIA: Here's a change indeed!   *Exit.*

DESDEMONA: 'Tis meet I should be used so, very meet.
How have I been behaved, that he might stick
The small'st opinion on my least misuse?

Enter IAGO *and* EMILIA.

115 **IAGO:** What is your pleasure, madam? How is 't with
    you?

DESDEMONA: I cannot tell. Those that do teach young
    babes
Do it with gentle means and easy tasks.
He might have chid me so, for, in good faith,
I am a child to chiding.

120 **IAGO:** What is the matter, lady?

EMILIA: Alas, Iago, my lord hath so bewhored her,
Thrown such despite and heavy terms upon her,
That true hearts cannot bear it.

DESDEMONA: Am I that name, Iago?

IAGO: What name, fair lady?   125

DESDEMONA: Such as she said my lord did say I was.

EMILIA: He called her whore. A beggar in his drink
Could not have laid such terms upon his callet.

IAGO: Why did he so?

DESDEMONA *[weeping]*: I do not know. I am sure I am
    none such.   130

IAGO: Do not weep, do not weep. Alas the day!

EMILIA: Hath she forsook so many noble matches,
Her father and her country and her friends,
To be called whore? Would it not make one weep?

DESDEMONA: It is my wretched fortune.   135

IAGO: Beshrew him for 't!
How comes this trick upon him?

DESDEMONA: Nay, heaven doth know.

EMILIA: I will be hanged if some eternal villain,
Some busy and insinuating rogue,
Some cogging, cozening slave, to get some office,
Have not devised this slander. I will be hanged else.   140

IAGO: Fie, there is no such man. It is impossible.

DESDEMONA: If any such there be, heaven pardon him!

EMILIA: A halter pardon him! And hell gnaw his bones!
Why should he call her whore? Who keeps her
    company?
What place? What time? What form? What   145
    likelihood?
The Moor's abused by some most villainous knave,

---

97 course business (with an indecent suggestion of "trick," turn at sex) **99 conceive** suppose, think **101 half asleep** i.e., dazed **108 go by water** be expressed by tears **112 meet** fitting **113 stick** attach **114 opinion** censure. **least misuse** slightest misconduct

128 callet whore **135 Beshrew** curse **136 trick** strange behavior, delusion **137 eternal** inveterate **138 insinuating** ingratiating, fawning, wheedling **139 cogging** cheating. **cozening** defrauding **143 halter** hangman's noose **145 form** appearance, circumstance

Desdemona seeks the advice of Iago and Emilia regarding Othello's accusations.

Some base notorious knave, some scurvy fellow.
O heaven, that such companions thou'dst unfold,
And put in every honest hand a whip
150   To lash the rascals naked through the world
Even from the east to th' west!

IAGO: Speak within door.

EMILIA: O, fie upon them! Some such squire he was
That turned your wit the seamy side without
And made you to suspect me with the Moor.

155   IAGO: You are a fool. Go to.

DESDEMONA: Alas, Iago,
What shall I do to win my lord again?
Good friend, go to him; for, by this light of heaven,
I know not how I lost him. Here I kneel.   *[She kneels.]*
If e'er my will did trespass 'gainst his love,
160   Either in discourse of thought or actual deed,
Or that mine eyes, mine ears, or any sense
Delighted them in any other form;

---

148 **that** would that. **companions** fellows. **unfold** expose 151 **within door** i.e., not so loud 152 **squire** fellow 153 **seamy side without** wrong side out 155 **Go to** i.e., that's enough 160 **discourse of thought** process of thinking 161 **that** if. (Also in line 163.) 162 **Delighted them** took delight

---

Or that I do not yet, and ever did,
And ever will—though he do shake me off
To beggarly divorcement—love him dearly,   165
Comfort forswear me! Unkindness may do much,
And his unkindness may defeat my life,
But never taint my love. I cannot say "whore."
It does abhor me now I speak the word;
To do the act that might the addition earn   170
Not the world's mass of vanity could make me.
                                    [She rises.]

IAGO: I pray you, be content. 'Tis but his humor.
The business of the state does him offense,
And he does chide with you.

DESDEMONA: If 'twere no other—   175

IAGO: It is but so, I warrant.   *[Trumpets within.]*
Hark, how these instruments summon you to supper!
The messengers of Venice stays the meat.
Go in, and weep not. All things shall be well.
                    Exeunt DESDEMONA *and* EMILIA.

                          Enter RODERIGO.

How now, Roderigo?   180

RODERIGO: I do not find that thou deal'st justly with
me.

IAGO: What in the contrary?

RODERIGO: Every day thou daff'st me with some
device, Iago, and rather, as it seems to me now, keep'st
from me all conveniency than suppliest me with   185
the least advantage of hope. I will indeed no longer
endure it, nor am I yet persuaded to put up in peace
what already I have foolishly suffered.

IAGO: Will you hear me, Roderigo?

---

163 **yet** still 166 **Comfort forswear** may heavenly comfort forsake 167 **defeat** destroy 169 **abhor** (1) fill me with abhorrence (2) make me whorelike 170 **addition** title 171 **vanity** showy splendor 172 **humor** mood 178 **stays the meat** are waiting to dine 183 **thou daff'st me** you put me off 183–184 **device** excuse, trick 185 **conveniency** advantage, opportunity 186 **advantage** increase 187 **put up** submit to, tolerate

190 **RODERIGO:**   Faith, I have heard too much, for your words and performances are no kin together.

IAGO: You charge me most unjustly.

RODERIGO: With naught but truth. I have wasted my-self out of my means. The jewels you have had from 195 me to deliver Desdemona would half have corrupted a votarist. You have told me she hath received them and returned me expectations and comforts of sudden respect and acquaintance, but I find none.

IAGO: Well, go to, very well.

200 **RODERIGO:**   "Very well"! "Go to"! I cannot go to, man, nor 'tis not very well. By this hand, I think it is scurvy, and begin to find myself fopped in it.

IAGO: Very well.

RODERIGO: I tell you 'tis not very well. I will make 205 myself known to Desdemona. If she will return me my jewels, I will give over my suit and repent my unlawful solicitation; if not, assure yourself I will seek satisfaction of you.

IAGO: You have said now?

210 **RODERIGO:**   Ay, and said nothing but what I protest intendment of doing.

IAGO: Why, now I see there's mettle in thee, and even from this instant do build on thee a better opinion than ever before. Give me thy hand, Roderigo. Thou 215 hast taken against me a most just exception; but yet I protest I have dealt most directly in thy affair.

RODERIGO: It hath not appeared.

---

195 **deliver** deliver to   196 **votarist** nun   197–198 **sudden respect** immediate consideration   200 **I cannot go to** (Roderigo changes Iago's *go to,* an expression urging patience, to *I cannot go to,* "I have no opportunity for success in wooing.")   202 **fopped** fooled, duped   204 **not very well** (Roderigo changes Iago's *very well,* "all right, then," to *not very well,* "not at all good.")   207 **satisfaction** repayment. (The term normally means settling of accounts in a duel.)   209 **You . . . now** have you finished?   211 **intendment** intention

IAGO: I grant indeed it hath not appeared, and your suspicion is not without wit and judgment. But, Roderigo, if thou hast that in thee indeed which I 220 have greater reason to believe now than ever—I mean purpose, courage, and valor—this night show it. If thou the next night following enjoy not Desdemona, take me from this world with treachery and devise engines for my life. 225

RODERIGO: Well, what is it? Is it within reason and compass?

IAGO: Sir, there is especial commission come from Venice to depute Cassio in Othello's place.

RODERIGO: Is that true? Why, then Othello and Desde- 230 mona return again to Venice.

IAGO: O, no; he goes into Mauritania and takes away with him the fair Desdemona, unless his abode be lingered here by some accident; wherein none can be so determinate as the removing of Cassio. 235

RODERIGO: How do you mean, removing of him?

IAGO: Why, by making him uncapable of Othello's place—knocking out his brains.

RODERIGO: And that you would have me to do?

IAGO: Ay, if you dare do yourself a profit and a right. 240 He sups tonight with a harlotry, and thither will I go to him. He knows not yet of his honorable fortune. If you will watch his going thence, which I will fashion to fall out between twelve and one, you may take him at your pleasure. I will be near to second your 245 attempt, and he shall fall between us. Come, stand not amazed at it, but go along with me. I will show you such a necessity in his death that you shall think yourself bound to put it on him. It is now high supper-time, and the night grows to waste. About it. 250

RODERIGO: I will hear further reason for this.

IAGO: And you shall be satisfied.   *Exeunt.*

---

225 **engines for** plots against   235 **determinate** conclusive   241 **harlotry** slut   244 **fall out** occur   249 **high** fully   250 **grows to waste** wastes away

4.3   *Enter* OTHELLO, LODOVICO, DESDEMONA,
EMILIA, *and attendants.*

LODOVICO: I do beseech you, sir, trouble yourself no
further.

OTHELLO: O, pardon me; 'twill do me good to walk.

LODOVICO: Madam, good night. I humbly thank your
ladyship.

DESDEMONA: Your honor is most welcome.

OTHELLO: Will you walk, sir?
5   O, Desdemona!

DESDEMONA: My lord?

OTHELLO: Get you to bed on th' instant. I will be
returned forthwith. Dismiss your attendant there.
Look 't be done.

10   **DESDEMONA:**   I will, my lord.
*Exit [*OTHELLO, *with* LODOVICO
and attendants].

EMILIA: How goes it now? He looks gentler than he did.

DESDEMONA: He says he will return incontinent,
And hath commanded me to go to bed,
And bid me to dismiss you.

15   **EMILIA:**   Dismiss me?

DESDEMONA: It was his bidding. Therefore, good
Emilia,
Give me my nightly wearing, and adieu.
We must not now displease him.

EMILIA: I would you had never seen him!

20   **DESDEMONA:**   So would not I. My love doth so approve
him
That even his stubbornness, his checks, his frowns—
Prithee, unpin me—have grace and favor in them.
*[*EMILIA *prepares* DESDEMONA *for bed.]*

EMILIA: I have laid those sheets you bade me on the
bed.

DESDEMONA: All's one. Good faith, how foolish are our   25
minds!
If I do die before thee, prithee shroud me
In one of these same sheets.

EMILIA: Come, come, you talk.

DESDEMONA: My mother had a maid called Barbary.
She was in love, and he she loved proved mad
And did forsake her. She had a song of "Willow."   30
An old thing 'twas, but it expressed her fortune,
And she died singing it. That song tonight
Will not go from my mind; I have much to do
But to go hang my head all at one side
And sing it like poor Barbary. Prithee, dispatch.   35

EMILIA: Shall I go fetch your nightgown?

DESDEMONA: No, unpin me here.
This Lodovico is a proper man.

EMILIA: A very handsome man.

DESDEMONA: He speaks well.   40

EMILIA: I know a lady in Venice would have walked
barefoot to Palestine for a touch of his nether lip.

DESDEMONA *[singing]*:
"The poor soul sat sighing by a sycamore tree,
Sing all a green willow;
Her hand on her bosom, her head on her knee,   45
Sing willow, willow, willow.
The fresh streams ran by her and murmured
her moans;
Sing willow, willow, willow;
Her salt tears fell from her, and softened the
stones—"
Lay by these.   50

4.3. Location: The citadel.
12 incontinent immediately   **21 stubbornness** roughness.   **checks**
rebukes

---

25 All's one all right. It doesn't really matter   **27 talk** i.e., prattle
29 mad wild, i.e., faithless   **33–34 I . . . hang** I can scarcely keep
myself from hanging   **36 nightgown** dressing gown   **38 proper**
handsome   **44 willow** (A conventional emblem of disappointed
love.)

[*Singing.*] "Sing willow, willow, willow—"
Prithee, hie thee. He'll come anon.
[*Singing.*] "Sing all a green willow must be my
     garland.
     Let nobody blame him; his scorn I approve—"
55   Nay, that's not next.—Hark! Who is 't that knocks?

EMILIA: It's the wind.

DESDEMONA [*singing*]:
     "I called my love false love; but what said he then?
          Sing willow, willow, willow;
     If I court more women, you'll couch with more
          men."
60   So, get thee gone. Good night. Mine eyes do itch;
     Doth that bode weeping?

EMILIA: 'Tis neither here nor there.

DESDEMONA: I have heard it said so. O, these men,
     these men!
     Dost thou in conscience think—tell me, Emilia—
     That there be women do abuse their husbands
65   In such gross kind?

EMILIA: There be some such, no question.

DESDEMONA: Wouldst thou do such a deed for all the
     world?

EMILIA: Why, would not you?

DESDEMONA: No, by this heavenly light!

EMILIA: Nor I neither by this heavenly light;
     I might do 't as well i' the dark.

70   **DESDEMONA:**   Wouldst thou do such a deed for all the
     world?

EMILIA: The world's a huge thing. It is a great price
     For a small vice.

DESDEMONA: Good troth, I think thou wouldst not.

EMILIA: By my troth, I think I should, and undo 't when
75   I had done. Marry, I would not do such a thing for a

Emilia helps Desdemona prepare for bed as she sings.

joint ring, nor for measures of lawn, nor for gowns,
petticoats, nor caps, nor any petty exhibition. But for
all the whole world! Uds pity, who would not make
her husband a cuckold to make him a monarch? I
should venture purgatory for 't.   80

DESDEMONA: Beshrew me if I would do such a wrong
For the whole world.

EMILIA: Why, the wrong is but a wrong i' the world, and
having the world for your labor, 'tis a wrong in your
own world, and you might quickly make it right.   85

DESDEMONA: I do not think there is any such woman.

EMILIA: Yes, a dozen, and as many
To th' vantage as would store the world they played
     for.
But I do think it is their husbands' faults
If wives do fall. Say that they slack their duties   90
And pour our treasures into foreign laps,
Or else break out in peevish jealousies,
Throwing restraint upon us? Or say they strike us,

---

52 hie thee hurry.   **anon** right away   **64 abuse** deceive

76 joint ring a ring made in separate halves.   **lawn** fine linen   **77
exhibition** gift   **78 Uds** God's   **88 To th' vantage** in addition, to
boot.   **store** populate.   **played** (1) gambled (2) sported sexually
90 duties marital duties   **91 pour . . . laps** i.e., are unfaithful, give
what is rightfully ours (semen) to other women   **93 Throwing . . .
us** i.e., jealousy restricting our freedom to see other men

Or scant our former having in despite?
95   Why, we have galls, and though we have some grace,
  Yet have we some revenge. Let husbands know
  Their wives have sense like them. They see, and smell,
  And have their palates both for sweet and sour,
  As husbands have. What is it that they do
100   When they change us for others? Is it sport?
  I think it is. And doth affection breed it?
  I think it doth. Is 't frailty that thus errs?
  It is so, too. And have not we affections,
  Desires for sport, and frailty, as men have?
105   Then let them use us well; else let them know,
  The ills we do, their ills instruct us so.

DESDEMONA: Good night, good night. God me such
      uses send
  Not to pick bad from bad, but by bad mend!

                              Exeunt.

5.1   *Enter* IAGO *and* RODERIGO.

IAGO: Here stand behind this bulk. Straight will he
      come.
  Wear thy good rapier bare, and put it home.
  Quick, quick! Fear nothing. I'll be at thy elbow.
  It makes us or it mars us. Think on that,
5   And fix most firm thy resolution.

RODERIGO: Be near at hand. I may miscarry in 't.

IAGO: Here, at thy hand. Be bold, and take thy stand.
    *[*IAGO *stands aside.* RODERIGO *conceals himself.]*

RODERIGO: I have no great devotion to the deed;
  And yet he hath given me satisfying reasons.
10   'Tis but a man gone. Forth, my sword! He dies.
                            [He draws.]

IAGO: I have rubbed this young quat almost to the sense,
  And he grows angry. Now, whether he kill Cassio
  Or Cassio him, or each do kill the other,
  Every way makes my gain. Live Roderigo,
  He calls me to a restitution large   15
  Of gold and jewels that I bobbled from him
  As gifts to Desdemona.
  It must not be. If Cassio do remain,
  He hath a daily beauty in his life
  That makes me ugly; and besides, the Moor   20
  May unfold me to him; there stand I in much peril.
  No, he must die. Be 't so. I hear him coming.

                      Enter CASSIO.

RODERIGO *[coming forth]***:**   I know his gait, 'tis he.—
  Villain, thou diest!

                    [He attacks CASSIO.*]*

CASSIO: That thrust had been mine enemy indeed,
  But that my coat is better than thou know'st.
  I will make proof of thine.   25
      [He draws, and wounds RODERIGO.*]*

RODERIGO: O, I am slain!   *[He falls.]*
      *[*IAGO, *from behind, wounds* CASSIO
                in the leg, and exit.]

CASSIO: I am maimed forever. Help, ho! Murder!
  Murder!

                      Enter OTHELLO.

OTHELLO: The voice of Cassio! Iago keeps his word.

RODERIGO: O, villain that I am!

OTHELLO: It is even so.   30

CASSIO: O, help, ho! Light! A surgeon!

OTHELLO: 'Tis he. O brave Iago, honest and just,
  That hast such noble sense of thy friend's wrong!
  Thou teachest me. Minion, your dear lies dead,

---

94 scant . . . despite reduce our allowance to spite us   **95 have galls**
i.e., are capable of resenting injury and insult   **97 sense** physical
sense   **100 sport** sexual pastime   **101 affection** passion   **107 uses**
habit, practice   **108 Not . . . mend** i.e., not to learn bad conduct
from others' badness (as Emilia has suggested women learn from
men), but to mend my ways by perceiving what badness is, making
spiritual benefit out of evil and adversity

5.1. Location: A street in Cyprus.
1 bulk framework projecting from the front of a shop   **2 bare**
unsheathed

---

11 quat pimple, pustule.   **to the sense** to the quick   **14 Live Roderigo**
if Roderigo lives   **16 bobbled** swindled   **21 unfold** expose   **25 coat**
(Possibly a garment of mail under the outer clothing, or simply a
tougher coat than Roderigo expected.)   **26 proof** a test   **34 Minion**
hussy (i.e., Desdemona)

Cassio mortally wounds Roderigo.

35   And your unblest fate hies. Strumpet, I come.
    Forth of my heart those charms, thine eyes, are
      blotted;
    Thy bed, lust-stained, shall with lust's blood be
      spotted.   *Exit* OTHELLO.

               Enter LODOVICO *and* GRATIANO.

CASSIO: What ho! No watch? No passage? Murder!
Murder!

GRATIANO: 'Tis some mischance. The voice is very
direful.

40 **CASSIO:**   O, help!

LODOVICO: Hark!

RODERIGO: O wretched villain!

LODOVICO: Two or three groan. 'Tis heavy night;
These may be counterfeits. Let's think 't unsafe
45   To come in to the cry without more help.
             [They remain near the entrance.]

RODERIGO: Nobody come? Then shall I bleed to death.

        Enter IAGO *[in his shirtsleeves, with a light]*.

LODOVICO: Hark!

GRATIANO: Here's one comes in his shirt, with light and
weapons.

IAGO: Who's there? Whose noise is this that cries on
murder?

LODOVICO: We do not know.   50

IAGO: Did not you hear a cry?

CASSIO: Here, here! For heaven's sake, help me!

IAGO: What's the matter?
            [He moves toward CASSIO.*]*

GRATIANO *[to* LODOVICO*]*:   This is Othello's ancient, as
I take it.

LODOVICO *[to* GRATIANO*]*:   The same indeed, a very
valiant fellow.

IAGO *[to* CASSIO*]*:   What are you here that cry so
grievously?

CASSIO: Iago? O, I am spoiled, undone by villains!   55
Give me some help.

IAGO: O me, Lieutenant! What villains have done this?

CASSIO: I think that one of them is hereabout,
And cannot make away.

IAGO: O treacherous villains!
    [To LODOVICO *and* GRATIANO.*]* What are you there?   60
    Come in, and give some help.   *[They advance.]*

RODERIGO: O, help me there!

CASSIO: That's one of them.

IAGO: O murderous slave! O villain!
            [He stabs RODERIGO.*]*

RODERIGO: O damned Iago! O inhuman dog!

IAGO: Kill men i' the dark?—Where be these bloody
thieves?—
How silent is this town!—Ho! Murder, murder!—   65
[To LODOVICO *and* GRATIANO.*]* What may you be?
Are you of good or evil?

---

35 **hies** hastens on   36 **Forth of** from out   38 **passage** people passing by   43 **heavy** thick, dark   45 **come in to** approach

49 **cries on** cries out   54 **What** who (also at lines 60 and 66)   55 **spoiled** ruined, done for   59 **make** get

LODOVICO: As you shall prove us, praise us.

IAGO: Signor Lodovico?

LODOVICO: He, sir.

70 **IAGO:**   I cry you mercy. Here's Cassio hurt by villains.

GRATIANO: Cassio?

IAGO: How is 't, brother?

CASSIO: My leg is cut in two.

IAGO: Marry, heaven forbid!
75   Light, gentlemen! I'll bind it with my shirt.

> *[He hands them the light, and tends to
> CASSIO's wound.]*

> *Enter BIANCA.*

BIANCA: What is the matter, ho? Who is 't that cried?

IAGO: Who is 't that cried?

BIANCA: O my dear Cassio!
  My sweet Cassio! O Cassio, Cassio, Cassio!

IAGO: O notable strumpet! Cassio, may you suspect
80   Who they should be that have thus mangled you?

CASSIO: No.

GRATIANO: I am sorry to find you thus. I have been to
  seek you.

IAGO: Lend me a garter. *[He applies a tourniquet.]* So.—
  O, for a chair,
  To bear him easily hence!

85 **BIANCA:**   Alas, he faints! O Cassio, Cassio, Cassio!

IAGO: Gentlemen all, I do suspect this trash
  To be a party in this injury.—
  Patience awhile, good Cassio.—Come, come;
  Lend me a light. *[He shines the light on RODERIGO.]*
    Know we this face or no?
90   Alas, my friend and my dear countryman
  Roderigo! No.—Yes, sure.—O heaven! Roderigo!

---

67 **praise** appraise   70 **I cry you mercy** I beg your pardon   83
chair litter

GRATIANO: What, of Venice?

IAGO: Even he, sir. Did you know him?

GRATIANO: Know him? Ay.

IAGO: Signor Gratiano? I cry your gentle pardon.   95
  These bloods accidents must excuse my manners
  That so neglected you.

GRATIANO: I am glad to see you.

IAGO: How do you, Cassio? O, a chair, a chair!

GRATIANO: Roderigo!

IAGO: He, he, 'tis he. *[A litter is brought in.]* O, that's well
    said; the chair.   100
  Some good man bear him carefully from hence;
  I'll fetch the General's surgeon. *[To BIANCA.]* For you,
    mistress,
  Save you your labor.—He that lies slain here, Cassio,
  Was my dear friend. What malice was between you?

CASSIO: None in the world, nor do I know the man.   105

IAGO *[to BIANCA]:*   What, look you pale?—O, bear him
    out o' th' air.

> *[CASSIO and RODERIGO are borne off.]*

  Stay you, good gentlemen.—Look you pale,
    mistress?—
  Do you perceive the gastness of here eye?—
  Nay, if you stare, we shall hear more anon.—
  Behold her well; I pray you, look upon her.   110
  Do you see, gentlemen? Nay, guiltiness
  Will speak, though tongues were out of use.

> *[Enter EMILIA.]*

EMILIA: 'Las, what's the matter? What's the matter,
    husband?

---

95 **gentle** noble   96 **accidents** sudden events   100 **well said** well
done   103 **Save . . . labor** i.e., never you mind tending Cassio   104
malice enmity   106 **bear . . . air** (Fresh air was thought to be
dangerous for a wound.)   107 **Stay you** (Lodovico and Gratiano are
evidently about to leave.)   108 **gastness** terror   109 **stare** (Iago
pretends to interpret Bianca's wild looks as an involuntary confession of guilt.)

IAGO: Cassio hath here been set on in the dark
115   By Roderigo and fellows that are scaped.
He's almost slain, and Roderigo dead.

EMILIA: Alas, good gentleman! Alas, good Cassio!

IAGO: This is the fruits of whoring. Prithee, Emilia,
Go know of Cassio where he supped tonight.
120 *[To* BIANCA.*]* What, do you shake at that?

BIANCA: He supped at my house, but I therefore shake
not.

IAGO: O, did he so? I charge you go with me.

EMILIA: O, fie upon thee, strumpet!

BIANCA: I am no strumpet, but of life as honest
125   As you that thus abuse me.

EMILIA: As I? Faugh! Fie upon thee!

IAGO: Kind gentlemen, let's go see poor Cassio
dressed.—
Come, mistress, you must tell 's another tale.
Emilia, run you to the citadel
130   And tell my lord and lady what hath happed.—
Will you go on afore? *[Aside.]* This is the night
That either makes me or fordoes me quite.   *Exeunt.*

5.2 *Enter* OTHELLO *[with a light], and* DESDEMONA
in her bed.

OTHELLO: It is the cause, it is the cause, my soul.
Let me not name it to you, you chaste stars!
It is the cause. Yet I'll not shed her blood,
Nor scar that whiter skin of hers than snow,
5   And smooth as monumental alabaster.
Yet she must die, else she'll betray more men.

Put out the light, and then put out the light.
If I quench thee, thou flaming minister,
I can again thy former light restore,
Should I repent me; but once put out thy light,   10
Thou cunning'st pattern of excelling nature,
I know not where is that Promethean heat
That can thy light relume. When I have plucked thy
rose,
I cannot give it vital growth again;
It needs must wither. I'll smell thee on the tree.   15
[He kisses her.]
O balmy breath, that dost almost persuade
Justice to break her sword! One more, one more.
Be thus when thou art dead, and I will kill thee,
And love thee after. One more, and that's the last.
[He kisses her.]
So sweet was ne'er so fatal. I must weep,   20
But they are cruel tears. This sorrow's heavenly;
It strikes where it doth love. She wakes.

DESDEMONA: Who's there? Othello?

OTHELLO: Ay, Desdemona.

DESDEMONA: Will you come to bed, my lord?   25

OTHELLO: Have you prayed tonight, Desdemon?

DESDEMONA: Ay, my lord.

OTHELLO: If you bethink yourself of any crime
Unreconciled as yet to heaven and grace,
Solicit for it straight.   30

DESDEMONA: Alack, my lord, what may you mean by
that?

OTHELLO: Well, do it, and be brief. I will walk by.
I would not kill thy unpreparèd spirit.
No, heaven forfend! I would not kill thy soul.

---

119 know learn **124 honest** chaste **127 Cassio dressed** Cassio's
wounds dressed **132 fordoes** undoes, ruins

5.2. Location: A bedchamber in the citadel.
s.d. in her bed (Either the curtains are drawn back to reveal the bed
in a recessed area backstage, or the bed is "thrust out" onstage as the
scene begins.) **1 cause** i.e., cause of justice, the offense itself, which
Othello must correct as an agent of justice **5 monumental** i.e., used
in making tombs and funeral monuments

---

7 the light . . . light the torch or lamp . . . Desdemona's life **8 flaming minister** torch or lamp that serves me **10 repent me** change
my mind **11 Thou . . . pattern** you skillfully wrought perfect
example **12 Promethean heat** divine fire. (Alluding to the theft of
fire from heaven by Prometheus.) **13 relume** rekindle **21 cruel**
unrelenting **22 It . . . love** (Compare Hebrews 12:6: "For whom the
Lord loveth he chasteneth.") **28 crime** sin **30 Solicit** petition,
pray. **straight** immediately **34 forfend** forbid

35 **DESDEMONA:** Talk you of killing?

OTHELLO: Ay, I do.

DESDEMONA: Then heaven
     Have mercy on me!

OTHELLO: Amen, with all my heart!

DESDEMONA: If you say so, I hope you will not kill me.

OTHELLO: Humh!

DESDEMONA: And yet I fear you; for you're fatal then
40   When your eyes roll so. Why I should fear I know not,
     Since guiltiness I know not; but yet I feel I fear.

OTHELLO: Think on thy sins.

DESDEMONA: They are loves I bear to you.

OTHELLO: Ay, and for that thou diest.

DESDEMONA: That death's unnatural that kills for
          loving.
45   Alas, why gnaw you so your nether lip?
     Some bloody passion shakes your very frame.
     These are portents; but yet I hope, I hope,
     They do not point on me.

OTHELLO: Peace, and be still!

50 **DESDEMONA:** I will so. What's the matter?

OTHELLO: That handkerchief which I so loved and gave
          thee
     Thou gav'st to Cassio.

DESDEMONA: No, by my life and soul!
     Send for the man and ask him.

OTHELLO: Sweet soul, take heed, take heed of perjury.
55   Thou art on thy deathbed.

DESDEMONA: Ay, but not yet to die.

OTHELLO: Yes, presently.
     Therefore confess thee freely of thy sin;

For to deny each article with oath
Cannot remove nor choke the strong conception
That I do groan withal. Thou art to die.   60

DESDEMONA: Then Lord have mercy on me!

OTHELLO: I say, amen.

DESDEMONA: And have you mercy too! I never did
     Offend you in my life; never loved Cassio
     But with such general warranty of heaven
     As I might love. I never gave him token.   65

OTHELLO: By heaven, I saw my handkerchief in 's hand.
     O perjured woman! Thou dost stone my heart,
     And makes me call what I intend to do
     A murder, which I thought a sacrifice.
     I saw the handkerchief.

DESDEMONA: He found it, then.   70
     I never gave it him. Send for him hither;
     Let him confess a truth.

OTHELLO: He hath confessed.

DESDEMONA: What, my lord?

OTHELLO: That he hath used thee.

DESDEMONA: How? Unlawfully?

OTHELLO: Ay.

DESDEMONA: He will not say so.   75

OTHELLO: No, his mouth is stopped;
     Honest Iago hath ta'en order for 't.

DESDEMONA: O, my fear interprets. What, is he dead?

OTHELLO: Had all his hairs been lives, my great revenge
     Had stomach for them all.

DESDEMONA: Alas, he is betrayed and I undone!   80
                                   [She weeps.]

---

42 **They are . . . you** i.e., if I sinned, it was in loving you more than my father or more than God   48 **point on** point at, predict what is to happen to   56 **presently** immediately

59 **conception** (1) belief in your guilt (2) plan in my mind   60 **groan withal** (1) groan at in sorrow (2) as in giving birth   63 **Offend** wrong   64 **warranty** sanction   67 **stone** turn to stone, harden   76 **ta'en order** taken measures

OTHELLO: Out, strumpet! Weep'st thou for him to my
        face?

DESDEMONA: O, banish me, my lord, but kill me not!

OTHELLO: Down, strumpet!

DESDEMONA: Kill me tomorrow; let me live tonight!

85 **OTHELLO:**   Nay, if you strive—

DESDEMONA: But half an hour!

OTHELLO: Being done, there is no pause.

DESDEMONA: But while I say one prayer!

OTHELLO: It is too late.
                          Smothers her.

EMILIA *(at the door):*   My lord, my lord! What, ho! My
        lord, my lord!

OTHELLO: What noise is this? Not dead? Not yet quite
        dead?
90   I that am cruel am yet merciful;
     I would not have thee linger in thy pain.
                          [He dispatches her.]
     So, so.

EMILIA *(within):*   What, ho! My lord, my lord!

OTHELLO: Who's there?

EMILIA *[within]:*   O, good my lord, I would speak a word
        with you!

OTHELLO: Yes, 'tis Emilia.—By and by.—She's dead.
95   'Tis like she comes to speak of Cassio's death.—
     The noise was here. Ha! No more moving?
     Still as the grave. Shall she come in? Were 't good?—
     I think she stirs again. No. What's best to do?
     If she come in, she'll sure speak to my wife.
100 My wife! My wife! What wife? I have no wife.
     O, insupportable! O heavy hour!
     Methinks it should be now a huge eclipse

Othello dispatches Desdemona.

     Of sun and moon, and that th' affrighted globe
     Should yawn at alteration.

EMILIA *[within]:*   I do beseech you
     That I may speak with you, O, good my lord!   105

OTHELLO: I had forgot thee. O, come in, Emilia.—
     Soft, by and by. Let me the curtains draw.—
     [He closes the bed-curtains and opens the door.]
     Where art thou?

                          Enter EMILIA.

               What's the matter with thee now?

EMILIA: O, my good lord, yonder's foul murders done!

OTHELLO: What, now?   110

EMILIA: But now, my lord.

OTHELLO: It is the very error of the moon;
     She comes more nearer earth than she was wont,
     And makes men mad.

---

86 **Being done** i.e., since justice has begun its relentless course   95 **like** likely that   96 **here** (The Folio's *high* is possible, suggesting that the commotion of the attack on Cassio was loud.)

104 **yawn** gape in amazement, i.e., move in an earthquake. (According to Pliny, earthquakes often happen during eclipses.)   **at alteration** at these cataclysmic events in nature, well suited to express the horror of Desdemona's death   107 **Soft** wait a minute   112 **error** aberration, irregularity

115   **EMILIA:**   Cassio, my lord, hath killed a young Venetian
      Called Roderigo.

OTHELLO: Roderigo killed?
      And Cassio killed?

EMILIA: No, Cassio is not killed.

OTHELLO: Not Cassio killed? Then murder's out of tune,
      And sweet revenge grows harsh.

120   **DESDEMONA:**   O, falsely, falsely murdered!

EMILIA: O Lord, what cry is that?

OTHELLO: That? What?

EMILIA: Out and alas, that was my lady's voice.
                     [She opens the bed-curtains.]
      Help, help, ho, help! O lady, speak again!
125   Sweet Desdemona! O sweet mistress, speak!

DESDEMONA: A guiltless death I die.

EMILIA: O, who hath done this deed?

DESDEMONA: Nobody; I myself. Farewell.
      Commend me to my kind lord. O, farewell!   *[She dies.]*

130   **OTHELLO:**   Why, how should she be murdered?

EMILIA: Alas, who knows?

OTHELLO: You heard her say herself it was not I.

EMILIA: She said so. I must needs report the truth.

OTHELLO: She's like a liar gone to burning hell!
      'Twas I that killed her.

EMILIA: O, the more angel she,
135   And you the blacker devil!

OTHELLO: She turned to folly, and she was a whore.

EMILIA: Thou dost belie her, and thou art a devil.

OTHELLO: She was false as water.

EMILIA: Thou art rash as fire to say
      That she was false. O, she was heavenly true!   140

OTHELLO: Cassio did top her. Ask thy husband else.
      O, I were damned beneath all depth in hell
      But that I did proceed upon just grounds
      To this extremity. Thy husband knew it all.

EMILIA: My husband?   145

OTHELLO: Thy husband.

EMILIA: That she was false to wedlock?

OTHELLO: Ay, with Cassio. Nay, had she been true,
      If heaven would make me such another world
      Of one entire and perfect chrysolite,   150
      I'd not have sold her for it.

EMILIA: My husband?

OTHELLO: Ay, 'twas he that told me on her first.
      An honest man he is, and hates the slime
      That sticks on filthy deeds.   155

EMILIA: My husband?

OTHELLO: What needs this iterance, woman? I say thy
      husband.

EMILIA: O mistress, villainy hath made mocks with
      love!
      My husband say she was false?

OTHELLO: He, woman;
      I say thy husband. Dost understand the word?   160
      My friend, thy husband, honest, honest Iago.

EMILIA: If he say so, may his pernicious soul
      Rot half a grain a day! He lies to th' heart.
      She was too fond of her most filthy bargain.

OTHELLO: Ha?   *[He draws.]*   165

EMILIA: Do thy worst!
      This deed of thine is no more worthy heaven
      Than thou wast worthy her.

---

123 Out (A cry of dismay, intensifying *alas*.)   **136 folly** i.e., wantonness, fleshly sin   **137 belie** slander

---

141 else i.e., if you don't believe me   **150 chrysolite** precious topaz
157 iterance iteration, repetition   **158 made mocks with** derided, made sport of

Montano (Nicholas Farrell) and Gratiano (André Oumansky) enter with swords drawn.

OTHELLO: Peace, you were best.

EMILIA: Thou hast not half that power to do me harm
170   As I have to be hurt. O gull! O dolt!
        As ignorant as dirt! Thou hast done a deed—
        I care not for thy sword; I'll make thee known,
        Though I lost twenty lives.—Help! Help, ho, help!
        The Moor hath killed my mistress! Murder, murder!

                Enter MONTANO, GRATIANO, *and* IAGO.

175 **MONTANO:**   What is the matter? How now, General?

EMILIA: O, are you come, Iago? You have done well,
        That men must lay their murders on your neck.

GRATIANO: What is the matter?

EMILIA *[to* IAGO*]*:   Disprove this villain, if thou be'st a
        man.
180   He says thou toldst him that his wife was false.
        I know thou didst not; thou'rt not such a villain.
        Speak, for my heart is full.

IAGO: I told him what I thought, and told no more
        Than what he found himself was apt and true.

185 **EMILIA:**   But did you ever tell him she was false?

IAGO: I did.

EMILIA: You told a lie, an odious, damnèd lie!
        Upon my soul, a lie, a wicked lie.
        She false with Cassio? Did you say with Cassio?

IAGO: With Cassio, mistress. Go to, charm your tongue.   190

EMILIA: I will not charm my tongue; I am bound to
        speak.
        My mistress here lies murdered in her bed—

ALL   O heavens forfend!

EMILIA: And your reports have set the murder on.

OTHELLO: Nay, stare not, masters. It is true indeed.   195

GRATIANO: 'Tis a strange truth.

MONTANO: O monstrous act!

EMILIA: Villainy, villainy, villainy!
        I think upon 't—I think I smell 't! O villainy!
        I thought so then—I'll kill myself for grief—
        O villainy, villainy!   200

IAGO: What, are you mad? I charge you, get you home.

EMILIA: Good gentlemen, let me have leave to speak.
        'Tis proper I obey him, but not now.
        Perchance, Iago, I will ne'er go home.

OTHELLO: O! O! O!   *[OTHELLO falls on the bed.]*   205

EMILIA: Nay, lay thee down and roar,
        For thou hast killed the sweetest innocent
        That e'er did lift up eye.

OTHELLO *[rising]*:   O, she was foul!
        I scarce did know you, uncle. There lies your niece,
        Whose breath indeed these hands have newly
                stopped.
        I know this act shows horrible and grim.   210

---

190 charm keep silent (as though by a magic spell)   **199 then**
(Perhaps at 3.3.331–332 and 4.2.137–154.)   **205 s.d. Othello . . .
bed** (This direction is from the Quarto, as also *He kisses her* at line
19 and *She dies* at line 129.)   **207 lift up eye** i.e., lift her eyes to
heaven   **210 shows** looks

---

168 you were best it would be best for you   **170 to be hurt** i.e., to
endure hurt.   **gull** dupe   **184 apt** plausible

GRATIANO: Poor Desdemon! I am glad thy father's
          dead.
          Thy match was mortal to him, and pure grief
          Shore his old thread in twain. Did he live now,
          This sight would make him do a desperate turn,
215   Yea, curse his better angel from his side,
          And fall to reprobance.

OTHELLO: 'Tis pitiful. But yet Iago knows
          That she with Cassio hath the act of shame
          A thousand times committed. Cassio confessed it;
220   And she did gratify his amorous works
          With that recognizance and pledge of love
          Which I first gave her. I saw it in his hand;
          It was a handkerchief, an antique token
          My father gave my mother.

225 **EMILIA:** O God! O heavenly God!

IAGO: Zounds, hold your peace.

EMILIA: 'Twill out, 'twill out! I peace?
          No, I will speak as liberal as the north.
          Let heaven and men and devils, let them all,
          All, all, cry shame against me, yet I'll speak.

IAGO: Be wise, and get you home.

EMILIA: I will not.
                    [IAGO threatens EMILIA.]

230 **GRATIANO:**   Fie,
          Your sword upon a woman?

EMILIA: O thou dull Moor! That handkerchief thou
          speak'st of
          I found by fortune and did give my husband;
          For often, with a solemn earnestness,
235   More than indeed belonged to such a trifle,
          He begged of me to steal 't.

IAGO: Villainous whore!

Othello confronts Iago.

EMILIA: She give it Cassio? No, alas! I found it,
          And I did give 't my husband.

IAGO: Filth, thou liest!

EMILIA: By heaven, I do not, I do not, gentlemen.
          O murderous coxcomb! What should such a fool   240
          Do with so good a wife?

OTHELLO: Are there no stones in heaven
          But what serves for the thunder?—Precious villain!
                    [He runs at IAGO; MONTANO disarms
                    OTHELLO. IAGO, from behind, stabs EMILIA.]

GRATIANO: The woman falls! Sure he hath killed his
          wife.

EMILIA: Ay, ay. O, lay me by my mistress' side.   245
                    [Exit IAGO.]

GRATIANO: He's gone, but his wife's killed.

MONTANO: 'Tis a notorious villain. Take you this
          weapon,
          Which I have here recovered from the Moor.

---

213 **Shore . . . thread** sheared the thread of his old age (as Atropos, one of the three Fates, was thought to do)   214 **turn** deed   216 **reprobance** damnation, i.e., suicide   220 **gratify** reward   221 **recognizance** token   227 **liberal as the north** freely as the north wind (blows)   235 **belonged** was appropriate

---

240 **coxcomb** fool. (Addressed to Othello.)   242 **stones** bolts, such as those used for thunderbolts   243 **Precious** i.e., arrant, utter.   **s.d. He . . . Emilia** (The Quarto text reads "The Moor runs at Iago. Iago kills his wife." The Quarto also specifies the exit of Iago at line 245 and the death of Emilia at line 260.)

Come, guard the door without. Let him not pass,
250 But kill him rather. I'll after that same villain,
For 'tis a damnèd slave.
        Exit [with all but OTHELLO *and* EMILIA, *who
        has been laid by* DESDEMONA's *side].*

OTHELLO: I am not valiant neither,
But every puny whipster gets my sword.
But why should honor outlive honesty?
255 Let it go all.

EMILIA: What did thy song bode, lady?
Hark, canst thou hear me? I will play the swan,
And die in music. *[She sings.]* "Willow, willow,
    willow."
Moor, she was chaste. She loved thee, cruel Moor.
So come my soul to bliss as I speak true.
260 So speaking as I think, alas, I die.   *[She dies.]*

OTHELLO: I have another weapon in this chamber;
It was a sword of Spain, the ice-brook's temper—
O, here it is. *[He finds a sword.]* Uncle, I must come
    forth.

GRATIANO *[within]:* If thou attempt it, it will cost thee
    dear.
265 Thou hast no weapon, and perforce must suffer.

OTHELLO: Look in upon me then and speak with me,
Or, naked as I am, I will assault thee.

        [Enter GRATIANO.*]*

GRATIANO: What is the matter?

OTHELLO: Behold, I have a weapon;
A better never did itself sustain
270 Upon a soldier's thigh. I have seen the day
That, with this little arm and this good sword,
I have made my way through more impediments
Than twenty times your stop. But O, vain boast!
Who can control his fate? 'Tis not so now.
275 Be not afraid, though you do see me weaponed;

Here is my journey's end, here is my butt
And very seamark of my utmost sail.
        [GRATIANO steps back.]
Do you go back dismayed? 'Tis a lost fear;
Man but a rush against Othello's breast
And he retires. Where should Othello go?   280
        [He turns to DESDEMONA.*]*
Now, how dost thou look now? O ill-starred wench!
Pale as thy smock! When we shall meet at compt,
This look of thine will hurl my soul from heaven,
And fiends will snatch at it. Cold, cold, my girl?
Even like thy chastity. O cursèd, cursèd slave!   285
Whip me, ye devils,
From the possession of this heavenly sight!
Blow me about in winds! Roast me in sulfur!
Wash me in steep-down gulfs of liquid fire!
O Desdemon! Dead, Desdemon! Dead! O! O!   290

        Enter LODOVICO, CASSIO *[carried in a litter],*
        MONTANO, *and* IAGO *[prisoner], with officers.*

LODOVICO: Where is this rash and most unfortunate
    man?

OTHELLO: That's he that was Othello. Here I am.

LODOVICO: Where is that viper? Bring the villain forth.
        *[*IAGO *is led forward.]*

OTHELLO: I look down towards his feet; but that's a
    fable.
If that thou be'st a devil, I cannot kill thee.   295
        [He wounds IAGO.*]*

LODOVICO: Wrench his sword from him.
        *[*OTHELLO *is disarmed.]*

IAGO: I bleed, sir, but not killed.

OTHELLO: I am not sorry neither. I'd have thee live,
For in my sense 'tis happiness to die.

---

253 whipster contemptible fellow (one who is always ready to whip
out his sword) **254 honor** i.e., the bravery for which one enjoys a
soldier's reputation. **honesty** true integrity **262 the icebrook's
temper** tempered in ice-cold water **267 naked** unarmed **273
stop** power (to stop)

276 butt goal, limit. (An archery term.) **277 seamark** beacon
(marking his destination or limit) **278 lost** wasted, unneeded **279
Man . . . rush** wield no more than a reed **282 compt** account, judgment day **285 slave** i.e., Othello himself **290 s.d. in a litter** (The
Quarto specifies that Cassio is "in a chair.") **294 towards his feet**
i.e., to see if they are cloven, as the devil's are fabled to be **298 in
my sense** to one who feels as I do

Othello delivers his final words.

GRATIANO: Torments will ope your lips.

OTHELLO: Well, thou dost best. 315

LODOVICO: Sir, you shall understand what hath befall'n,
Which, as I think, you know not. Here is a letter
Found in the pocket of the slain Roderigo;
And here another. *[He produces letters.]* The one of
them imports
The death of Cassio, to be undertook 320
By Roderigo.

OTHELLO: O villain!

CASSIO: Most heathenish and most gross!

LODOVICO *[showing another paper]:* Now here's another
discontented paper
Found in his pocket too. And this, it seems,
Roderigo meant t' have sent this damnèd villain; 325
But that belike Iago in the interim
Came in and satisfied him.

OTHELLO: O thou pernicious caitiff!—
How came you, Cassio, by that handkerchief
That was my wife's?

CASSIO: I found it in my chamber; 330
And he himself confessed but even now
That there he dropped it for a special purpose
Which wrought to his desire.

OTHELLO: O fool, fool, fool!

CASSIO: There is besides in Roderigo's letter
How he upbraids Iago, that he made him 335
Brave me upon the watch, whereon it came
That I was cast; and even but now he spake,
After long seeming dead, Iago hurt him,
Iago set him on.

LODOVICO *[to OTHELLO]:* You must forsake this room 340
and go with us.
Your power and your command is taken off,

LODOVICO: O thou Othello, that was once so good,
300   Fall'n in the practice of a cursèd slave,
What shall be said to thee?

OTHELLO: Why, anything,
An honorable murderer, if you will,
For naught I did in hate, but all in honor.

LODOVICO: This wretch hath part confessed his
villainy.
305   Did you and he consent in Cassio's death?

OTHELLO: Ay.

CASSIO: Dear General, I never gave you cause.

OTHELLO: I do believe it, and I ask your pardon.
Will you, I pray, demand that demi-devil
310   Why he hath thus ensnared my soul and body?

IAGO: Demand me nothing. What you know, you know.
From this time forth I never will speak word.

LODOVICO: What, not to pray?

---

300 in the practice through the plotting, into the snare. **slave**
villain **305 consent** agree

---

314 **Torments** torture   322 **gross** monstrous   323 **discontented**
full of discontent   326 **belike** most likely   327 **Came ... him**
interposed and gave him satisfactory explanation   333 **wrought**
. . . desire worked out as he wished, fitted in with his plan   336
Brave defy.   **whereon it came** whereof it came about   337 **cast**
dismissed   341 **taken off** taken away

And Cassio rules in Cyprus. For this slave,
If there be any cunning cruelty
That can torment him much and hold him long,
345   It shall be his. You shall close prisoner rest
Till that the nature of your fault be known
To the Venetian state.—Come, bring away.

OTHELLO: Soft you; a word or two before you go.
I have done the state some service, and they know 't.
350   No more of that. I pray you, in your letters,
When you shall these unlucky deeds relate,
Speak of me as I am; nothing extenuate,
Nor set down aught in malice. Then must you speak
Of one that loved not wisely but too well;
355   Of one not easily jealous but, being wrought,
Perplexed in the extreme; of one whose hand,
Like the base Indian, threw a pearl away
Richer than all his tribe; of one whose subdued eyes,
Albeit unusèd to the melting mood,
360   Drops tears as fast as the Arabian trees
Their medicinable gum. Set you down this;
And say besides that in Aleppo once,
Where a malignant and a turbaned Turk
Beat a Venetian and traduced the state,
365   I took by th' throat the circumcisèd dog
And smote him, thus   *[He stabs himself.]*

LODOVICO: O bloody period!

GRATIANO: All that is spoke is marred.

OTHELLO: I kissed thee ere I killed thee. No way but
    this,
370   Killing myself, to die upon a kiss.
               [He kisses DESDEMONA *and] dies.*

Othello lies dead beside his murdered wife, her maid Emilia, and their betrayer, Iago.

CASSIO: This did I fear, but thought he had no weapon;
For he was great of heart.

LODOVICO *[to* IAGO*]:*   O Spartan dog,
More fell than anguish, hunger, or the sea!
Look on the tragic loading of this bed.
This is thy work. The object poisons sight;   375
Let it be hid. Gratiano, keep the house,
               [The bed-curtains are drawn]
And seize upon the fortunes of the Moor,
For they succeed on you. *[To* CASSIO.*]* To you, Lord
    Governor,
Remains the censure of this hellish villain,
The time, the place, the torture. O, enforce it!   380
Myself will straight aboard, and to the state
This heavy act with heavy heart relate.   *Exeunt.*

---

344 hold him long keep him alive a long time (during his torture)
345 rest remain   **348 Soft you** one moment   **351 unlucky** unfortunate   **355 wrought** worked upon, worked into a frenzy   **356 Perplexed** distraught   **357 Indian** (This reading from the Quarto pictures an ignorant savage who cannot recognize the value of a precious jewel. The Folio reading, *Iudean* or *Judean*, i.e., infidel or disbeliever, may refer to Herod, who slew Miriamne in a fit of jealousy, or to Judas Iscariot, the betrayer of Christ.)   **358 subdued** i.e., overcome by grief   **361 gum** i.e., myrrh   **366 s.d. He stabs himself** (This direction is in the Quarto text.)   **367 period** termination, conclusion

372 Spartan dog (Spartan dogs were noted for their savagery and silence.)   **373 fell** cruel   **376 Let it be hid** i.e., draw the bed-curtains. (No stage direction specifies that the dead are to be carried offstage at the end of the play.)   **keep** remain in   **377 seize upon** take legal possession of   **378 succeed on** pass as though by inheritance to   **379 censure** sentencing

Writing from Reading

Summarize

1 The play opens, in effect, with a summary of action previous to the action we witness; it closes with another kind of summary, and one in which Othello demonstrates self-awareness (a quality largely absent in him earlier). At the end of the play (and this is quite similar to Hamlet's request of Horatio), Othello asks that those who survive him tell his story truly:

"No more of that. I pray you, in your letters,
When you shall these unlucky deeds relate,
Speak of me as I am; nothing extenuate,
Nor set down aught in malice. Then must you speak
Of one that loved not wisely but too well. . . ."

How would you tell his story?

2 If Desdemona were to write letters home to her father and friends, how would she explain herself and her situation?

Analyze Craft

3 What makes Othello a hero, in the Greek sense of one whose fate is intertwined with those of his people and who discovers that his tragic flaw has led to his demise? What makes his growth through suffering and coming to understand himself sufficient to move us to

terror and pity (*catharsis*)? How do you interpret the line in which he says of himself that he "loved not wisely but too well"?

4 Iago has been described as a creature of "motiveless malignity." What motives does he offer for his behavior? What sense do they make? And when he says, at the close of Act 5, "From this time forth I never will speak word," what does his silence suggest?

5 The timeline of the play does not in fact provide an opportunity for Desdemona to betray her husband. Shakespeare must have known this. Why does he compress the action so as to make infidelity improbable if not impossible?

Analyze Voice

6 Can you distinguish a difference in tone between this play and *Hamlet*? Describe. Pick a soliloquy by Hamlet and one by Othello and compare them.

7 Othello says about his courtship of Desdemona:

"She loved me for the dangers I had passed,
And I loved her that she did pity them."

What does this suggest about Othello's character? In what ways is this representation accurate or inaccurate?

Synthesize Summary and Analysis

8 The tale starts out in seeming bliss and ends in total misery. Is that a definition of the tragic mode? And if, as we have seen, Shakespeare mixes low comedy together with high seriousness, what if any comic elements do you find in the play?

9 How closely related is character to plot? How can so great a general be so easily deluded and so completely fooled? Is Othello sane? Give examples to support your answer.

10 To what degree is this a play about empire and armed conflict; how do the domestic wars mirror those between the characters onstage?

Interpret the Play

11 Is this primarily a play about jealousy—Othello's for Cassio, Iago's for Othello? Is Iago jealous of Othello in ways that mirror or distort the ways the husband grows jealous of his wife?

12 Othello is a well-positioned outcast in society. In what ways is this a play about race relations or class conflict or about power and control?

13 Is this a play about the psychology of insecurity and delusion or, rather, about good and evil in the religious sense?

Getting Started: A Research Project

Research is a skill that will carry you through your college career. To help acquaint you with the research process, the materials you need for this project are made available on our Web site (**connect.mcgraw-hill.com**). Other ideas for research projects and sources appear at the end of this chapter.

"Shakespeare has had the status of a secular Bible for the last two centuries," writes critic Harold Bloom in *Shakespeare: The Invention of the Human.* "Textual scholarship on the plays approaches biblical commentary in scope and intensiveness, while the quantity of literary criticism devoted to Shakespeare rivals theological interpretation of the Holy Scripture."

As Bloom points out, the body of critical work on Shakespeare is vast. In part, this is because serious Shakespearean criticism has been growing for more than three centuries!

This research assignment will help you chart some of the major views of Shakespeare throughout the last three centuries by asking you to read two prominent views of Shakespeare: that of Samuel Johnson, the great eighteenth-century critic; and that of Samuel Taylor Coleridge, the nineteenth-century Romantic poet.

Excerpts are available on our Web site. After reading each of the critics, choose one of the prompts below to get you started on writing a research paper.

1. Read Johnson's and Coleridge's ideas on Shakespeare. Then write a summary of each critic's view. Based on your summaries, evaluate which you find most accurate given your reading of Shakespeare. Then, using one of Shakespeare's plays from this chapter, show how you see the critic's view playing out in the drama.

2. After reading Johnson's and Coleridge's critical perspectives, choose an idea or topic from one of them that you find interesting; for example, you might choose Johnson's idea that Shakespeare holds a mirror to the world, or Coleridge's observation of unity in Shakespeare's plays. Then write a compare/contrast paper in which you examine how each critic develops, complicates, or is silent on that particular idea. As you write, you may want to draw support from not just the critics but also a Shakespeare play you have read.

3. After reading these critics, write your own general statement about Shakespeare based on observations from your reading of Shakespearean drama. In other words, use the two critics as a model for how to write your own critical statement on one or more Shakespearean plays.

Writing and Research

1. Ophelia, in *Hamlet,* is one of Shakespeare's most recognizable female characters. However, critics throughout the centuries—and up through contemporary feminist criticism—have disagreed on how we can best understand her role and herself as a female character. After reviewing Ophelia's lines in *Hamlet,* read the Ophelia research resources that appear on **connect.mcgraw-hill.com**. You will find a nineteenth-century critic, Anna Murphy Jameson, whose *Shakespeare's Heroines,* published in 1832, became one of the earliest works by a female critic to deal directly with Shakespeare's female characters. You can compare her view with that of a contemporary feminist critic, Elaine Showalter, who explains Ophelia's place in feminist criticism. And finally, you can follow our link to a popular painting of Ophelia by nineteenth-century artist John Everett Millais.

Based on your research, write an essay in which you argue for or against a particular interpretation of Ophelia, being sure to support your argument with quotes from the critics and the text itself.

- Jameson, Anna Murphy. *Shakespeare's Heroines*. Ed. Cheri L. Larsen Hoeckley. Peterborough: Broadview, 2005. 177–85. Print.
- Millais, John Everett. *Ophelia*. 1851–1852. Tate Britain. *Tate Online*. Web.
- Showalter, Elaine. "Representing Ophelia: Women, Madness, and the Responsibilities of Feminist Criticism." *Shakespeare and the Question of Theory*. Ed. Geoffrey Hartman and Patricia Parker. New York: Methuen, 1985. 77–80. Print.

2. As you have learned from this chapter, Shakespeare's plays are mostly classified as tragedies, comedies, or histories. Using the resources listed below, or others you might find on your own, research Shakespearean comedy and the conventions of the genre, with a particular focus on *A Midsummer Night's Dream* (found online at **connect .mcgraw-hill.com**). Write a paper in which you use your research on comedy to show how *A Midsummer Night's Dream* follows, varies from, or complicates the conventions of comedy.

- Dillon, Janette. "Shakespeare and the Traditions of English Stage Comedy." *A Companion to Shakespeare's Works: Comedies*. Ed. Richard Dutton and Jean E. Howard. Vol. 3. Malden: Blackwell, 2003. 4–22. Print.
- Greenblatt, Stephen. "Wooing, Wedding, and Repenting." *Will in the World*. New York: Norton, 2004. 133–40. Print.
- Snyder, Susan. "The Genres of Shakespeare's Plays." *The Cambridge Companion to Shakespeare*. Ed. Margreta de Grazia and Stanley Wells. New York: Cambridge UP, 2001. 83–98. Print.

Some Sources for Research

Online Sources

Folger Shakespeare Library. Amherst College, n.d. Web. <http://www.folger.edu>.

Gray, Terry A., ed. *Mr. William Shakespeare and the Internet*. Palomar College, 2011. Web. <http://Shakespeare .palomar.edu>.

"History of the Monarchy." *The Official Website of the British Monarchy*. The Royal Household, 2011. Web. <http://www.royal.gov.uk/HistoryoftheMonarchy/HistoryoftheMonarchy.aspx>.

Johnson, Samuel. "Preface to Shakespeare." *The Works of Samuel Johnson*. Ed. F. P. Walesby. London: Oxford UP, 1985. 103–54. *Google Book Search*. Web. <http://www.books.google.com/books?id=azsCAAAAQAAJ &pg=PA103&dg="samuel+johnson"+"preface+to+shakespeare"&lr=>.

Larque, Thomas, ed. *Shakespeare and His Critics*. N.p., n.d. Web. <http://www.shakespearean.org.uk>.

Shakespeare's Globe. The Shakespeare Globe Trust, 2011. Web. <http://www.shakespeares-globe.org>.

Print Sources

Auden, W. H. "The Joker in the Pack." *Shakespeare's Middle Tragedies: A Collection of Critical Essays*. Ed. David Young. Englewood Cliffs: Prentice, 1993. 75–90. Print.

Bloom, Harold. *Shakespeare: The Invention of the Human*. New York: Riverhead, 1998. Print.

Bradley, A. C. *Shakespearean Tragedy: Lectures on Hamlet, Othello, King Lear, Macbeth*. New York: Palgrave, 2007. Print.

Cahn, Victor L. "The Tragic Flaw." *The Plays of Shakespeare: A Thematic Guide*. Westport: Greenwood, 2001. 325–33. Print.

Davies, Michael. "Hero, Villain, Fool: The Character of Hamlet's Revenge." *Hamlet: Character Studies*. New York: Continuum, 2008. 50–74. Print.

De Grazia, Margreta, and Stanley Wells, eds. *The New Cambridge Companion to Shakespeare*. New York: Cambridge UP, 2010. Print.

Dutton, Richard, and Jean E. Howards, eds. *A Companion to Shakespeare's Works*. 3 vols. Malden: Blackwell, 2003. Print.

Kinney, Arthur F. *Hamlet: New Critical Essays*. New York: Routledge, 2002. Print.

Knight, George Wilson. "On the Principles of Shakespeare Interpretation." *The Wheel of Fire: Interpretations of Shakespearian Tragedy*. New York: Routledge, 2001. 1–16. Print.

Nordlund, Marcus. "Jealousy in *Othello*." *Shakespeare and the Nature of Love: Literature, Culture, Evolution*. Evanston: Northwestern UP, 2007. 163–95. Print.

Poole, Adrian. "Hamlet and Oedipus." *Tragedy: Shakespeare and the Greek Example*. New York: Blackwell, 1987. Print.

For examples of student papers, see Chapters 2, 3, 4, 5, 7, 18, and 31. For more on Writing about Drama, see pages 1061–1062.

34

Modern

I DON'T say he's a great man. Willy Loman never made a lot of money. His name was never in the paper. He's not the finest character that ever lived. But he's a human being, and a terrible thing is happening to him. So attention must be paid. . . .

—*from* Death of a Salesman *by Arthur Miller*

Drama

FOR Sophocles and Shakespeare, the open stage was furnished largely by the imagination of the audience; today, we can expect the stage to have tables and chairs and paintings and grandfather clocks and carpets and glasses and bottles on display. The convention, or the agreed upon "reality" of the modern play, assumes that we're watching the action as if the **fourth wall** of the room has been removed so that we can look in on the private lives of a family. A scene with language and physical gestures, enacted by characters we find familiar, in a setting that resembles space we occupy offstage: that is the essence of the style we call **realism.**

As straightforward and simple as these attributes may seem, it took many centuries for this particular style to evolve. The Greek playwrights portrayed gods and heroes. Shakespeare wrote of monarchs and generals. Theatrical talk consisted of poetry or highly stylized speech. The focus of modern theater altered everything: characters grew recognizable, not exalted or debased, and their very human failings became the stuff of drama, redefining the conditions of tragedy. A tragic hero like Oedipus or Hamlet has to be of elevated rank in society, so that his fate and the fate of the common people can be intertwined. His collapse and fall have consequences for the people of his court and the community at large. His moment of realization provides him with a kind of wisdom that replaces power, and by play's end, the blind Oedipus is truly visionary; when we witness this reversal experience, or so the conventional wisdom about tragic theater would have it, we feel paired emotions of pity and fear, since a hero's death *matters* to us all.

The democratic ideal of the modern world, however, suggests that every man or woman can be a kind of hero. You need not be aristocratic or from an imperial family to have a tale worth telling or a fate that matters to others. *Death of a Salesman* deals with the exigencies of family life, and in unsparing terms. When Willy Loman's wife insists "attention must be finally paid to such a person," she's declaring, in effect, that every single character has his own important history and an aging, ill salesman down on his luck is also in some sense as important as a king.

CONTINUED ON PAGE 1342

Arthur Miller
The original purpose . . . of art . . . was always the community.

A Conversation on Writing

Radical Drama and Becoming a Playwright

In the '30s the theater in New York was exploding. For the first time probably in its history, it was beginning to reflect real life, which was the Depression. These small radical groups of actors were putting on plays in storefronts and garages, and places like that. . . . Prose seemed to be remote and distant in comparison.

On His Writing Process

I generally work because I am struck by something somebody has said. Usually playwriting is an aural art. It's not an art of the writer expecting to be read. It's the writer expecting to be heard. So I think that if I hear a character speaking, either one I have invented or one I've confronted, it can start a process of creating.

Casting *Death of a Salesman*

I remember Lee Cobb, who was the original [Willy Loman]. . . . I imagined the character to be a little guy full of ginger, one of those little salesmen who [look] more or less like a squirrel. Here is Lee looking like a big beef. . . . My son Bobby was a little boy playing to the floor, and at one point Lee looked down—Bobby had done something funny—and he laughed. In that laugh—it was a real hearty laugh—you wanted to just burst out crying because it was so filled with sadness. He was very funny. He could be very funny. But while he was being funny he was dying in front of you. And I knew that was Willy.

To watch the entire interview with Arthur Miller, go to connect.mcgraw-hill.com

RESEARCH ASSIGNMENT   After reading Arthur Miller's interview, how would you describe his ideas on the importance of "making it big" in theater? Do you agree with his position?

This interview was taped at the University of Michigan in April 1998, when the playwright was in Ann Arbor to celebrate the opening of the Arthur Miller Theater at his alma mater.

Arthur Miller (1915–2005)

Arthur Miller was born in New York City on October 17, 1915; he died at his home in Roxbury, Connecticut, on February 10, 2005. He worked as a playwright for all his long life and was among the most influential artists of his time. The son of Jewish immigrants living on the edge of poverty (his father had a garment manufacturing business that failed in the Depression), he never lost the social awareness or moral alertness that are hallmarks of his work. Though world-famous and much photographed—particularly during his brief marriage to film icon Marilyn Monroe—he remained a spokesman for and champion of the "common man."

In 1934, Miller enrolled at the University of Michigan—and, while a student there, won a Hopwood Award for playwriting. As he records in his autobiography, *Timebends: A Life* (1989), this ratified his sense of a career: "The magical force of making marks on a piece of paper and reaching into another human being, making him see what I had seen and feel my feelings—I had made a new shadow on the earth." His first play, however, *The Man Who Had All the Luck,* opened to negative reviews in 1944, and it was not until *All My Sons* in 1947 that he had a Broadway success. A tragedy about a manufacturer who sells faulty parts to the military in order to save his business, this play deals with many of the themes that characterize Miller's writing: the prospect of commercial failure, the intricacies of family life, the hard moral choices every person must face. Two years thereafter, he produced his most successful play, *Death of a Salesman*—which won both a Pulitzer Prize and a Drama Critics Circle Award. It ran for 700 performances after its first opening, and it's probably safe to say that no week now passes without a production of *Death of a Salesman* somewhere in the world.

Overwhelmed by postwar paranoia and intolerance, Miller wrote the third of his major plays, *The Crucible,* which had its Broadway première in 1953. Set in Salem during the witch hunts of the late seventeenth century, this story reports on extraordinary tragedy in ordinary lives. Within three years, Miller was called before the House Un-American Activities Committee and convicted of contempt of Congress for not cooperating in the more modern version of a witch hunt for Communists in the entertainment industry. His steady output continued, however, and his bibliography includes *After the Fall* (1963), *Incident at Vichy* (1964), *The Ride Down Mount Morgan* (1991), and *The Last Yankee* (1993). By his death, he had written essays, stories, a novel, *Focus* (1945), an autobiography, and the dozens of plays for which he remains most celebrated and from which continues to emerge his magisterial voice.

AS YOU READ   Compare the main character, Willy Loman, with Oedipus the King. How are they similar, and how are they different?

> "What you read on the page looks like it's been there forever, but believe me, it hasn't. It's always a struggle to find what you are looking for. Certainly the play is as much rewritten as it is written." Conversation with Arthur Miller

Death of a Salesman (1949)

Certain Private Conversations in Two Acts and a Requiem

CHARACTERS

WILLY LOMAN

LINDA

BIFF

HAPPY

BERNARD

THE WOMAN

CHARLEY

UNCLE BEN

HOWARD WAGNER

JENNY

STANLEY

MISS FORSYTHE

LETTA

THE SCENE: *The action takes place in* WILLY LOMAN'*s house and yard and in various places he visits in the New York and Boston of today.*

Throughout the play, in the stage directions, left and right mean stage left and stage right.

ACT 1

A melody is heard, played upon a flute. It is small and fine, telling of grass and trees and the horizon. The curtain rises.

Before us is the Salesman's house. We are aware of towering, angular shapes behind it, surrounding it on all sides. Only the blue light of the sky falls upon the house and forestage; the surrounding area shows an angry glow of orange. As more light appears, we see a solid vault of apartment houses around the small, fragile-seeming home. An air of the dream clings to the place, a dream rising out of reality. The kitchen at center seems actual enough, for there is a kitchen table with three chairs, and a refrigerator. But no other fixtures are seen. At the back of the kitchen there is a draped entrance, which leads to the living-room. To the right of the kitchen, on a level raised two feet, is a bedroom furnished only with a brass bedstead and a straight chair. On a shelf over the bed a silver athletic trophy stands. A window opens onto the apartment house at the side.

 Behind the kitchen, on a level raised six and a half feet, is the boys' bedroom, at present barely visible. Two beds are dimly seen, and at the back of the room a dormer window. (This bedroom is above the unseen living-room.) At the left a stairway curves up to it from the kitchen.

 The entire setting is wholly or, in some places, partially transparent. The roof-line of the house is one-dimensional; under and over it we see the apartment buildings. Before the house lies an apron, curving beyond the forestage into the orchestra. This forward area serves as the back yard as well as the locale of all WILLY's imaginings and of his city scenes. Whenever the action is in the present the actors observe the imaginary wall-lines, entering the house only through its door at the left. But in the scenes of the past these boundaries are broken, and characters enter or leave a room by stepping "through" a wall onto the forestage.

 From the right, WILLY LOMAN, the Salesman, enters, carrying two large sample cases. The flute plays on. He hears but is not aware of it. He is past sixty years of age, dressed quietly. Even as he crosses the stage to the doorway of the house, his exhaustion is apparent. He unlocks the door, comes into the kitchen, and thankfully lets his burden down, feeling the soreness of his palms. A word-sigh escapes his lips—it might be "Oh, boy, oh, boy." He closes the door, then carries his cases out into the living-room, through the draped kitchen doorway.

 LINDA, his wife, has stirred in her bed at the right. She gets out and puts on a robe, listening. Most often jovial, she has developed an iron repression of her exceptions to WILLY's behavior—she more than loves him, she admires him, as though his mercurial nature, his temper, his massive dreams and little cruelties, served her only as sharp reminders of the turbulent longings within him, longings which she shares but lacks the temperament to utter and follow to their end.

LINDA: *(hearing WILLY outside the bedroom, calls with some trepidation)* Willy!

WILLY: It's all right. I came back.

Willy Loman (Dustin Hoffman) talks with his wife, Linda (Kate Reid), in the 1985 film directed by Volker Schlöndorff.

LINDA: Why? What happened? *(Slight pause.)* Did something happen, Willy? 5

WILLY: No, nothing happened.

LINDA: You didn't smash the car, did you?

WILLY: *(with casual irritation)* I said nothing happened. Didn't you hear me?

LINDA: Don't you feel well? 10

WILLY: I'm tired to the death. *(The flute has faded away. He sits on the bed beside her, a little numb.)* I couldn't make it. I just couldn't make it, Linda.

LINDA: *(very carefully, delicately)* Where were you all day? You look terrible. 15

WILLY: I got as far as a little above Yonkers. I stopped for a cup of coffee. Maybe it was the coffee.

LINDA: What?

WILLY: *(after a pause)* I suddenly couldn't drive any more. The car kept going off onto the shoulder, y'know? 20

LINDA: *(helpfully)* Oh. Maybe it was the steering again. I don't think Angelo knows the Studebaker.

WILLY: No, it's me, it's me. Suddenly I realize I'm goin' sixty miles an hour and I don't remember the last five minutes. I'm—I can't seem to—keep my mind to it.

LINDA: Maybe it's your glasses. You never went for your new glasses.

WILLY: No, I see everything. I came back ten miles an hour. It took me nearly four hours from Yonkers.

LINDA: *(resigned)* Well, you'll just have to take a rest, Willy, you can't continue this way.

WILLY: I just got back from Florida.

LINDA: But you didn't rest your mind. Your mind is over active, and the mind is what counts, dear.

WILLY: I'll start out in the morning. Maybe I'll feel better in the morning. *(She is taking off his shoes.)* These goddam arch supports are killing me.

LINDA: Take an aspirin. Should I get you an aspirin? It'll soothe you.

WILLY: *(with wonder)* I was driving along, you understand? And I was fine. I was even observing the scenery. You can imagine, me looking at scenery, on the road every week of my life. But it's so beautiful up there, Linda, the trees are so thick, and the sun is warm. I opened the windshield and just let the warm air bathe over me. And then all of a sudden I'm goin' off the road! I'm tellin' ya, I absolutely forgot I was driving. If I'd've gone the other way over the white line I might've killed somebody. So I went on again—and five minutes later I'm dreamin' again, and I nearly— *(He presses two fingers against his eyes.)* I have such thoughts, I have such strange thoughts.

LINDA: Willy, dear. Talk to them again. There's no reason why you can't work in New York.

WILLY: They don't need me in New York. I'm the New England man. I'm vital in New England.

LINDA: But you're sixty years old. They can't expect you to keep traveling every week.

WILLY: I'll have to send a wire to Portland. I'm supposed to see Brown and Morrison tomorrow morning at ten o'clock to show the line. Goddammit, I could sell them! *(He starts putting on his jacket.)*

LINDA: *(taking the jacket from him)* Why don't you go down to the place tomorrow and tell Howard you've simply got to work in New York? You're too accommodating, dear.

WILLY: If old man Wagner was alive I'd a been in charge of New York now! That man was a prince, he was a masterful man. But that boy of his, that Howard, he don't appreciate. When I went north the first time, the Wagner Company didn't know where New England was!

LINDA: Why don't you tell those things to Howard, dear?

WILLY: *(encouraged)* I will, I definitely will. Is there any cheese?

LINDA: I'll make you a sandwich.

WILLY: No, go to sleep. I'll take some milk. I'll be up right away. The boys in?

LINDA: They're sleeping. Happy took Biff on a date tonight.

WILLY: *(interested)* That so?

LINDA: It was so nice to see them shaving together, one behind the other, in the bathroom. And going out

Willy (Lee J. Cobb) talks with his wife, Linda (Mildred Dunnock), in the 1966 film directed by Alex Segal.

85 together. You notice? The whole house smells of shaving lotion.

WILLY: Figure it out. Work a lifetime to pay off a house. You finally own it, and there's nobody to live in it.

LINDA: Well, dear, life is a casting off. It's always that
90 way.

WILLY: No, no, some people—some people accomplish something. Did Biff say anything after I went this morning?

LINDA: You shouldn't have criticized him, Willy, espe-
95 cially after he just got off the train. You mustn't lose your temper with him.

WILLY: When the hell did I lose my temper? I simply asked him if he was making any money. Is that a criticism?

100 **LINDA:** But, dear, how could he make any money?

WILLY: (*worried and angered*) There's such an undercurrent in him. He became a moody man. Did he apologize when I left this morning?

LINDA: He was crestfallen, Willy. You know how he ad-
105 mires you. I think if he finds himself, then you'll both be happier and not fight any more.

WILLY: How can he find himself on a farm? Is that a life? A farmhand? In the beginning, when he was young, I thought, well, a young man, it's good for
110 him to tramp around, take a lot of different jobs. But it's more than ten years now and he has yet to make thirty-five dollars a week!

LINDA: He's finding himself, Willy.

WILLY: Not finding yourself at the age of thirty-four is a
115 disgrace!

LINDA: Shh!

WILLY: The trouble is he's lazy, goddammit!

LINDA: Willy, please!

WILLY: Biff is a lazy bum!

120 **LINDA:** They're sleeping. Get something to eat. Go on down.

WILLY: Why did he come home? I would like to know what brought him home.

LINDA: I don't know. I think he's still lost, Willy. I think
125 he's very lost.

WILLY: Biff Loman is lost. In the greatest country in the world a young man with such—personal attractiveness, gets lost. And such a hard worker. There's one thing about Biff—he's not lazy.

130 **LINDA:** Never.

WILLY: (*with pity and resolve*) I'll see him in the morning; I'll have a nice talk with him. I'll get him a job selling. He could be big in no time. My God! Remember how they used to follow him around in high
135 school? When he smiled at one of them their faces lit up. When he walked down the street . . . (*He loses himself in reminiscences.*)

LINDA: (*trying to bring him out of it*) Willy, dear, I got a new kind of American-type cheese today. It's
140 whipped.

WILLY: Why do you get American when I like Swiss?

LINDA: I just thought you'd like a change—

WILLY: I don't want a change! I want Swiss cheese. Why am I always being contradicted?

145 **LINDA:** (*with a covering laugh*) I thought it would be a surprise.

WILLY: Why don't you open a window in here, for God's sake?

LINDA: (*with infinite patience*) They're all open, dear.

150 **WILLY:** The way they boxed us in here. Bricks and windows, windows and bricks.

LINDA: We should've bought the land next door.

WILLY: The street is lined with cars. There's not a breath of fresh air in the neighborhood. The grass don't grow
155 any more, you can't raise a carrot in the back yard. They should've had a law against apartment houses. Remember those two beautiful elm trees out there? When I and Biff hung the swing between them?

LINDA: Yeah, like being a million miles from the city.

160 **WILLY:** They should've arrested the builder for cutting those down. They massacred the neighborhood. *(Lost.)* More and more I think of those days, Linda. This time of year it was lilac and wisteria. And then the peonies would come out, and the daffodils. What
165 fragrance in this room!

LINDA: Well, after all, people had to move somewhere.

WILLY: No, there's more people now.

LINDA: I don't think there's more people. I think—

WILLY: There's more people! That's what's ruining this
170 country! Population is getting out of control. The competition is maddening! Smell the stink from that apartment house! And another one on the other side . . . How can they whip cheese?

On WILLY's *last line,* BIFF *and* HAPPY *raise themselves up in their beds, listening.*

LINDA: Go down, try it. And be quiet.

175 **WILLY:** *(turning to* LINDA, *guiltily)* You're not worried about me, are you, sweetheart?

BIFF: What's the matter?

HAPPY: Listen!

LINDA: You've got too much on the ball to worry about.

180 **WILLY:** You're my foundation and my support, Linda.

LINDA: Just try to relax, dear. You make mountains out of molehills.

WILLY: I won't fight with him any more. If he wants to go back to Texas, let him go.

185 **LINDA:** He'll find his way.

WILLY: Sure. Certain men just don't get started till later in life. Like Thomas Edison, I think. Or B. F. Goodrich. One of them was deaf. *(He starts for the bedroom doorway.)* I'll put my money on Biff.

190 **LINDA:** And Willy—if it's warm Sunday we'll drive in the country. And we'll open the windshield, and take lunch.

WILLY: No, the windshields don't open on the new cars.

LINDA: But you opened it today.

WILLY: Me? I didn't. *(He stops.)* Now isn't that peculiar! 195 Isn't that a remarkable—*(He breaks off in amazement and fright as the flute is heard distantly.)*

LINDA: What, darling?

WILLY: That is the most remarkable thing.

LINDA: What, dear? 200

WILLY: I was thinking of the Chevy. *(Slight pause.)* Nineteen twenty-eight . . . when I had that red Chevy—*(Breaks off.)* That funny? I coulda sworn I was driving that Chevy today.

LINDA: Well, that's nothing. Something must've reminded you. 205

WILLY: Remarkable. Ts. Remember those days? The way Biff used to simonize that car? The dealer refused to believe there was eighty thousand miles on it. *(He shakes his head.)* Heh! *(To* LINDA.*)* Close your eyes, 210 I'll be right up. *(He walks out of the bedroom.)*

HAPPY: *(to* BIFF*)* Jesus, maybe he smashed up the car again!

LINDA: *(calling after* WILLY*)* Be careful on the stairs, dear! The cheese is on the middle shelf! *(She turns, 215 goes over to the bed, takes his jacket, and goes out of the bedroom.)*

Light has risen on the boys' room. Unseen, WILLY *is heard talking to himself, "Eighty thousand miles," and a little laugh.* BIFF *gets out of bed, comes downstage a bit, and stands attentively.* BIFF *is two years older than his brother* HAPPY, *well built, but in these days bears a worn air and seems less self-assured. He has succeeded less, and his dreams are stronger and less acceptable than* HAPPY's. HAPPY *is tall, powerfully made. Sexuality is like a visible color on him, or a scent that many women have discovered. He, like his brother, is lost, but in a different way, for he has never allowed himself to turn his face toward defeat and is thus more confused and hard-skinned, although seemingly more content.*

HAPPY: *(getting out of bed)* He's going to get his license taken away if he keeps that up. I'm getting nervous about him, y'know, Biff?

BIFF: His eyes are going.

HAPPY: No, I've driven with him. He sees all right. He just doesn't keep his mind on it. I drove into the city with him last week. He stops at a green light and then it turns red and he goes. *(He laughs.)*

BIFF: Maybe he's color-blind.

HAPPY: Pop? Why he's got the finest eye for color in the business. You know that.

BIFF: *(sitting down on his bed)* I'm going to sleep.

HAPPY: You're not still sour on Dad, are you, Biff?

BIFF: He's all right, I guess.

WILLY: *(underneath them, in the living-room)* Yes, sir, eighty thousand miles—eighty-two thousand!

BIFF: You smoking?

HAPPY: *(holding out a pack of cigarettes)* Want one?

BIFF: *(taking a cigarette)* I can never sleep when I smell it.

WILLY: What a simonizing job, heh!

HAPPY: *(with deep sentiment)* Funny, Biff, y'know? Us sleeping in here again? The old beds. *(He pats his bed affectionately.)* All the talk that went across those two beds, huh? Our whole lives.

BIFF: Yeah. Lotta dreams and plans.

HAPPY: *(with a deep and masculine laugh)* About five hundred women would like to know what was said in this room.

They share a soft laugh.

BIFF: Remember that big Betsy something—what the hell was her name—over on Bushwick Avenue?

HAPPY: *(combing his hair)* With the collie dog!

BIFF: That's the one. I got you in there, remember?

Biff (John Malkovich) and Happy (Stephen Lang) talk about their plans.

HAPPY: Yeah, that was my first time—I think. Boy, there was a pig! *(They laugh, almost crudely.)* You taught me everything I know about women. Don't forget that.

BIFF: I bet you forgot how bashful you used to be. Especially with girls.

HAPPY: Oh, I still am, Biff.

BIFF: Oh, go on.

HAPPY: I just control it, that's all. I think I got less bashful and you got more so. What happened, Biff? Where's the old humor, the old confidence? *(He shakes BIFF's knee. BIFF gets up and moves restlessly about the room.)* What's the matter?

BIFF: Why does Dad mock me all the time?

HAPPY: He's not mocking you, he—

BIFF: Everything I say there's a twist of mockery on his face. I can't get near him.

HAPPY: He just wants you to make good, that's all. I wanted to talk to you about Dad for a long time, Biff. Something's—happening to him. He—talks to himself.

BIFF: I noticed that this morning. But he always mumbled.

HAPPY: But not so noticeable. It got so embarrassing I sent him to Florida. And you know something? Most of the time he's talking to you.

BIFF: What's he say about me?

HAPPY: I can't make it out.

BIFF: What's he say about me?

HAPPY: I think the fact that you're not settled, that you're still kind of up in the air . . .

BIFF: There's one or two other things depressing him, Happy.

HAPPY: What do you mean?

BIFF: Never mind. Just don't lay it all to me.

HAPPY: But I think if you just got started—I mean—is there any future for you out there?

BIFF: I tell ya, Hap, I don't know what the future is. I don't know—what I'm supposed to want.

HAPPY: What do you mean?

BIFF: Well, I spent six or seven years after high school trying to work myself up. Shipping clerk, salesman, business of one kind or another. And it's a measly manner of existence. To get on that subway on the hot mornings in summer. To devote your whole life to keeping stock, or making phone calls, or selling or buying. To suffer fifty weeks of the year for the sake of a two-week vacation, when all you really desire is to be outdoors, with your shirt off. And always to have to get ahead of the next fella. And still—that's how you build a future.

HAPPY: Well, you really enjoy it on a farm? Are you content out there?

BIFF: *(with rising agitation)* Hap, I've had twenty or thirty different kinds of jobs since I left home before the war, and it always turns out the same. I just realized it lately. In Nebraska when I herded cattle, and the Dakotas, and Arizona, and now in Texas. It's why I came home now, I guess, because I realized it. This farm I work on, it's spring there now, see? And

they've got about fifteen new colts. There's nothing more inspiring or—beautiful than the sight of a mare and a new colt. And it's cool there now, see? Texas is cool now, and it's spring. And whenever spring comes to where I am, I suddenly get the feeling, my God, I'm not gettin' anywhere! What the hell am I doing, playing around with horses, twenty-eight dollars a week! I'm thirty-four years old, I oughta be makin' my future. That's when I come running home. And now, I get here, and I don't know what to do with myself. *(After a pause.)* I've always made a point of not wasting my life, and everytime I come back here I know that all I've done is to waste my life.

HAPPY: You're a poet, you know that, Biff? You're a—you're an idealist!

BIFF: No, I'm mixed up very bad. Maybe I oughta get married. Maybe I oughta get stuck into something. Maybe that's my trouble. I'm like a boy. I'm not married. I'm not in business, I just—I'm like a boy. Are you content, Hap? You're a success, aren't you? Are you content?

HAPPY: Hell, no!

BIFF: Why? You're making money, aren't you?

HAPPY: *(moving about with energy, expressiveness)* All I can do now is wait for the merchandise manager to die. And suppose I get to be merchandise manager? He's a good friend of mine, and he just built a terrific estate on Long Island. And he lived there about two months and sold it, and now he's building another one. He can't enjoy it once it's finished. And I know that's just what I would do. I don't know what the hell I'm workin' for. Sometimes I sit in my apartment—all alone. And I think of the rent I'm paying. And it's crazy. But then, it's what I always wanted. My own apartment, a car, and plenty of women. And still, god dammit, I'm lonely.

BIFF: *(with enthusiasm)* Listen, why don't you come out West with me?

HAPPY: You and I, heh?

BIFF: Sure, maybe we could buy a ranch. Raise cattle, use our muscles. Men built like we are should be working out in the open.

HAPPY: *(avidly)* The Loman Brothers, heh?

BIFF: *(with vast affection)* Sure, we'd be known all over the counties!

355 **HAPPY:** *(enthralled)* That's what I dream about, Biff. Sometimes I want to just rip my clothes off in the middle of the store and outbox that goddam merchandise manager. I mean I can outbox, outrun, and outlift anybody in that store, and I have to take orders
360 from those common, petty sons-of-bitches till I can't stand it any more.

BIFF: I'm tellin' you, kid, if you were with me I'd be happy out there.

HAPPY: *(enthused)* See, Biff, everybody around me is so
365 false that I'm constantly lowering my ideals . . .

BIFF: Baby, together we'd stand up for one another, we'd have someone to trust.

HAPPY: If I were around you—

BIFF: Hap, the trouble is we weren't brought up to grub
370 for money. I don't know how to do it.

HAPPY: Neither can I!

BIFF: Then let's go!

HAPPY: The only thing is—what can you make out there?

375 **BIFF:** But look at your friend. Builds an estate and then hasn't the peace of mind to live in it.

HAPPY: Yeah, but when he walks into the store the waves part in front of him. That's fifty-two thousand dollars a year coming through the revolving door,
380 and I got more in my pinky finger than he's got in his head.

BIFF: Yeah, but you just said—

HAPPY: I gotta show some of those pompous, self-important executives over there that Hap Loman can
385 make the grade. I want to walk into the store the way he walks in. Then I'll go with you, Biff. We'll be together yet, I swear. But take those two we had tonight. Now weren't they gorgeous creatures?

BIFF: Yeah, yeah, most gorgeous I've had in years.

HAPPY: I get that any time I want, Biff. Whenever I feel 390
disgusted. The trouble is, it gets like bowling or something. I just keep knockin' them over and it doesn't
mean anything. You still run around a lot?

BIFF: Naa. I'd like to find a girl—steady, somebody with
substance. 395

HAPPY: That's what I long for.

BIFF: Go on! You'd never come home.

HAPPY: I would! Somebody with character, with resistance! Like Mom, y'know? You're gonna call me a
bastard when I tell you this. That girl Charlotte I was 400
with tonight is engaged to be married in five weeks.
(He tries on his new hat.)

BIFF: No kiddin'!

HAPPY: Sure, the guy's in line for the vice-presidency
of the store. I don't know what gets into me, maybe 405
I just have an overdeveloped sense of competition or
something, but I went and ruined her, and furthermore I can't get rid of her. And he's the third executive
I've done that to. Isn't that a crummy characteristic?
And to top it all, I go to their weddings! *(Indignantly,* 410
but laughing.) Like I'm not supposed to take bribes.
Manufacturers offer me a hundred-dollar bill now
and then to throw an order their way. You know how
honest I am, but it's like this girl, see. I hate myself
for it. Because I don't want the girl, and, still, I take it 415
and—I love it!

BIFF: Let's go to sleep.

HAPPY: I guess we didn't settle anything, heh?

BIFF: I just got one idea that I think I'm going to try.

HAPPY: What's that? 420

BIFF: Remember Bill Oliver?

HAPPY: Sure, Oliver is very big now. You want to work for him again?

BIFF: No, but when I quit he said something to me. He
put his arm on my shoulder, and he said, "Biff, if you 425
ever need anything, come to me."

HAPPY: I remember that. That sounds good.

BIFF: I think I'll go to see him. If I could get ten thousand or even seven or eight thousand dollars I could
430   buy a beautiful ranch.

HAPPY: I bet he'd back you. 'Cause he thought highly of
you, Biff. I mean, they all do. You're well liked, Biff.
That's why I say to come back here, and we both have
the apartment. And I'm tellin' you, Biff, any babe you
435   want . . .

BIFF: No, with a ranch I could do the work I like and still
be something. I just wonder though. I wonder if Oliver
still thinks I stole that carton of basketballs.

HAPPY: Oh, he probably forgot that long ago. It's almost
440   ten years. You're too sensitive. Anyway, he didn't
really fire you.

BIFF: Well, I think he was going to. I think that's why I
quit. I was never sure whether he knew or not. I know
he thought the world of me, though. I was the only
445   one he'd let lock up the place.

WILLY: (*below*) You gonna wash the engine, Biff?

HAPPY: Shh!

BIFF *looks at* HAPPY, *who is gazing down, listening.*
WILLY *is mumbling in the parlor.*

HAPPY: You hear that?

They listen. WILLY *laughs warmly.*

BIFF: (*growing angry*) Doesn't he know Mom can hear
450   that?

WILLY: Don't get your sweater dirty, Biff!

A look of pain crosses BIFF's *face.*

HAPPY: Isn't that terrible? Don't leave again, will you?
You'll find a job here. You gotta stick around. I don't
know what to do about him, it's getting embarrassing.

455   **WILLY:**   What a simonizing job!

BIFF: Mom's hearing that!

WILLY: No kiddin', Biff, you got a date? Wonderful!

HAPPY: Go on to sleep. But talk to him in the morning,
will you?

BIFF: (*reluctantly getting into bed*) With her in the house.   460
Brother!

HAPPY: (*getting into bed*) I wish you'd have a good talk
with him.

The light on their room begins to fade.

BIFF: (*to himself in bed*) That selfish, stupid . . .

HAPPY: Sh . . . Sleep, Biff.   465

*Their light is out. Well before they have finished
speaking,* WILLY's *form is dimly seen below in the
darkened kitchen. He opens the refrigerator, searches
in there, and takes out a bottle of milk. The apartment
houses are fading out, and the entire house and surroundings become covered with leaves. Music insinu-
ates itself as the leaves appear.*

WILLY: Just wanna be careful with those girls, Biff,
that's all. Don't make any promises. No promises of
any kind. Because a girl, y'know, they always believe
what you tell 'em, and you're very young, Biff, you're
too young to be talking seriously to girls.   470

Light rises on the kitchen. WILLY, *talking, shuts the
refrigerator door and comes downstage to the kitchen
table. He pours milk into a glass. He is totally immersed in himself, smiling faintly.*

WILLY: Too young entirely, Biff. You want to watch your
schooling first. Then when you're all set, there'll be
plenty of girls for a boy like you. (*He smiles broadly at
a kitchen chair.*) That so? The girls pay for you? (*He
laughs.*) Boy, you must really be makin' a hit.   475

WILLY *is gradually addressing—physically—a point
offstage, speaking through the wall of the kitchen, and
his voice has been rising in volume to that of a normal
conversation.*

WILLY: I been wondering why you polish the car so
careful. Ha! Don't leave the hubcaps, boys. Get the
chamois to the hubcaps. Happy, use newspaper on
the windows, it's the easiest thing. Show him how
to do it, Biff! You see, Happy? Pad it up, use it like   480
a pad. That's it, that's it, good work. You're doin' all
right, Hap. (*He pauses, then nods in approbation for
a few seconds, then looks upward.*) Biff, first thing we

gotta do when we get time is clip that big branch over the house. Afraid it's gonna fall in a storm and hit the roof. Tell you what. We get a rope and sling her around, and then we climb up there with a couple of saws and take her down. Soon as you finish the car, boys, I wanna see ya. I got a surprise for you, boys.

BIFF: *(offstage)* Whatta ya got, Dad?

WILLY: No, you finish first. Never leave a job till you're finished—remember that. *(Looking toward the "big trees.")* Biff, up in Albany I saw a beautiful hammock. I think I'll buy it next trip, and we'll hang it right between those two elms. Wouldn't that be something? Just swingin' there under those branches. Boy, that would be . . .

Young BIFF *and Young* HAPPY *appear from the direction* WILLY *was addressing.* HAPPY *carries rags and a pail of water.* BIFF, *wearing a sweater with a block "S," carries a football.*

BIFF: *(pointing in the direction of the car offstage)* How's that, Pop, professional?

WILLY: Terrific. Terrific job, boys. Good work, Biff.

HAPPY: Where's the surprise, Pop?

WILLY: In the back seat of the car.

Willy drinks his milk as he addresses a point offstage.

HAPPY: Boy! *(He runs off.)*

BIFF: What is it, Dad? Tell me, what'd you buy?

WILLY: *(laughing, cuffs him)* Never mind, something I want you to have.

BIFF: *(turns and starts off)* What is it, Hap?

HAPPY: *(offstage)* It's a punching bag!

BIFF: Oh, Pop!

WILLY: It's got Gene Tunney's signature on it!

HAPPY *runs onstage with a punching bag.*

BIFF: Gee, how'd you know we wanted a punching bag?

WILLY: Well, it's the finest thing for the timing.

HAPPY: *(lies down on his back and pedals with his feet)* I'm losing weight, you notice, Pop?

WILLY: *(to HAPPY)* Jumping rope is good too.

BIFF: Did you see the new football I got?

WILLY: *(examining the ball)* Where'd you get a new ball?

BIFF: The coach told me to practice my passing.

WILLY: That so? And he gave you the ball, heh?

BIFF: Well, I borrowed it from the locker room. *(He laughs confidentially.)*

WILLY: *(laughing with him at the theft)* I want you to return that.

HAPPY: I told you he wouldn't like it!

BIFF: *(angrily)* Well, I'm bringing it back!

WILLY: *(stopping the incipient argument, to HAPPY)* Sure, he's gotta practice with a regulation ball, doesn't he? *(To BIFF.)* Coach'll probably congratulate you on your initiative!

BIFF: Oh, he keeps congratulating my initiative all the time, Pop.

WILLY: That's because he likes you. If somebody else took that ball there'd be an uproar. So what's the report, boys, what's the report?

535 **BIFF:** Where'd you go this time, Dad? Gee we were lonesome for you.

WILLY: *(pleased, puts an arm around each boy and they
come down to the apron)* Lonesome, heh?

BIFF: Missed you every minute.

540 **WILLY:** Don't say? Tell you a secret, boys. Don't breathe
it to a soul. Someday I'll have my own business, and
I'll never have to leave home any more.

HAPPY: Like Uncle Charley, heh?

WILLY: Bigger than Uncle Charley! Because Charley is
545 not—liked. He's liked, but he's not—well liked.

BIFF: Where'd you go this time, Dad?

WILLY: Well, I got on the road, and I went north to
Providence. Met the Mayor.

BIFF: The Mayor of Providence!

550 **WILLY:** He was sitting in the hotel lobby.

BIFF: What'd he say?

WILLY: He said, "Morning!" And I said, "You got a fine
city here, Mayor." And then he had coffee with me.
And then I went to Waterbury. Waterbury is a fine
555 city. Big clock city, the famous Waterbury clock. Sold a
nice bill there. And then Boston—Boston is the cradle
of the Revolution. A fine city. And a couple of other
towns in Mass., and on to Portland and Bangor and
straight home!

560 **BIFF:** Gee, I'd love to go with you sometime, Dad.

WILLY: Soon as summer comes.

HAPPY: Promise?

WILLY: You and Hap and I, and I'll show you all the
towns. America is full of beautiful towns and fine, up-
565 standing people. And they know me, boys, they know
me up and down New England. The finest people.
And when I bring you fellas up, there'll be open sesame for all of us, 'cause one thing, boys: I have friends.
I can park my car in any street in New England, and
570 the cops protect it like their own. This summer, heh?

BIFF AND HAPPY: *(together)* Yeah! You bet!

Willy and his boys, in happier times, discuss the future.

WILLY: We'll take our bathing suits.

HAPPY: We'll carry your bags, Pop!

WILLY: Oh, won't that be something! Me comin' into the
Boston stores with you boys carryin' my bags. What a   575
sensation!

BIFF *is prancing around, practicing passing the ball.*

WILLY: You nervous, Biff, about the game?

BIFF: Not if you're gonna be there.

WILLY: What do they say about you in school, now that
they made you captain?   580

HAPPY: There's a crowd of girls behind him everytime
the classes change.

BIFF: *(taking WILLY's hand)* This Saturday, Pop, this
Saturday—just for you, I'm going to break through for
a touchdown.   585

HAPPY: You're supposed to pass.

BIFF: I'm takin' one play for Pop. You watch me, Pop, and
when I take off my helmet, that means I'm breakin'
out. Then you watch me crash through that line!

WILLY: *(kisses BIFF)* Oh, wait'll I tell this in Boston!   590

BERNARD *enters in knickers. He is younger than
BIFF, earnest and loyal, a worried boy.*

BERNARD: Biff, where are you? You're supposed to study with me today.

WILLY: Hey, looka Bernard. What're you lookin' so anemic about, Bernard?

595 **BERNARD:** He's gotta study, Uncle Willy. He's got Regents next week.

HAPPY: *(tauntingly, spinning* BERNARD *around)* Let's box, Bernard!

BERNARD: Biff! *(He gets away from* HAPPY.*)* Listen,
600 Biff, I heard Mr. Birnbaum say that if you don't start studyin' math, he's gonna flunk you, and you won't graduate. I heard him!

WILLY: You better study with him, Biff. Go ahead now.

BERNARD: I heard him!

605 **BIFF:** Oh, Pop, you didn't see my sneakers! *(He holds up a foot for* WILLY *to look at.)*

WILLY: Hey, that's a beautiful job of printing!

BERNARD: *(wiping his glasses)* Just because he printed University of Virginia on his sneakers doesn't mean
610 they've got to graduate him, Uncle Willy!

WILLY: *(angrily)* What're you talking about? With scholarships to three universities they're gonna flunk him?

BERNARD: But I heard Mr. Birnbaum say—

WILLY: Don't be a pest, Bernard! *(To his boys.)* What an
615 anemic!

BERNARD: Okay, I'm waiting for you in my house, Biff.

BERNARD *goes off. The Lomans laugh.*

WILLY: Bernard is not well liked, is he?

BIFF: He's liked, but he's not well liked.

HAPPY: That's right, Pop.

620 **WILLY:** That's just what I mean. Bernard can get the best marks in school, y'understand, but when he gets out in the business world, y'understand, you are going to be five times ahead of him. That's why I thank Almighty God you're both built like Adonises. Because
625 the man who makes an appearance in the business world, the man who creates personal interest, is the man who gets ahead. Be liked and you will never want. You take me, for instance. I never have to wait in line to see a buyer. "Willy Loman is here!" That's all they have to know, and I go right through. 630

BIFF: Did you knock them dead, Pop?

WILLY: Knocked 'em cold in Providence, slaughtered 'em in Boston.

HAPPY: *(on his back, pedaling again)* I'm losing weight, you notice, Pop? 635

LINDA *enters, as of old, a ribbon in her hair, carrying a basket of washing.*

LINDA: *(with youthful energy)* Hello, dear!

WILLY: Sweetheart!

LINDA: How'd the Chevy run?

WILLY: Chevrolet, Linda, is the greatest car ever built. *(To the boys.)* Since when do you let your mother carry 640
wash up the stairs?

BIFF: Grab hold there, boy!

HAPPY: Where to, Mom?

LINDA: Hang them up on the line. And you better go down to your friends, Biff. The cellar is full of boys. 645
They don't know what to do with themselves.

BIFF: Ah, when Pop comes home they can wait!

WILLY: *(laughs appreciatively)* You better go down and tell them what to do, Biff.

BIFF: I think I'll have them sweep out the furnace room. 650

WILLY: Good work, Biff.

BIFF: *(goes through wall-line of kitchen to doorway at back and calls down)* Fellas! Everybody sweep out the furnace room! I'll be right down!

VOICES: All right! Okay, Biff. 655

BIFF: George and Sam and Frank, come out back! We're hangin' up the wash! Come on, Hap, on the double! *(He and* HAPPY *carry out the basket.)*

Willy, Happy (James Farentino), and Biff (George Segal) scoff at Bernard's (Gene Wilder) attitude toward education.

LINDA: The way they obey him!

660 **WILLY:**   Well, that's training, the training. I'm tellin' you, I was sellin' thousands and thousands, but I had to come home.

LINDA: Oh, the whole block'll be at that game. Did you sell anything?

665 **WILLY:**   I did five hundred gross in Providence and seven hundred gross in Boston.

LINDA: No! Wait a minute, I've got a pencil. *(She pulls pencil and paper out of her apron pocket.)* That makes your commission . . . Two hundred—my God! Two
670 hundred and twelve dollars!

WILLY: Well, I didn't figure it yet, but . . .

LINDA: How much did you do?

WILLY: Well, I—I did—about a hundred and eighty gross in Providence. Well, no—it came to—roughly two
675 hundred gross on the whole trip.

LINDA: *(without hesitation)* Two hundred gross. That's . . . *(She figures.)*

WILLY: The trouble was that three of the stores were half closed for inventory in Boston. Otherwise I woulda broke records. 680

LINDA: Well, it makes seventy dollars and some pennies. That's very good.

WILLY: What do we owe?

LINDA: Well, on the first there's sixteen dollars on the refrigerator— 685

WILLY: Why sixteen?

LINDA: Well, the fan belt broke, so it was a dollar eighty.

WILLY: But it's brand new.

LINDA: Well, the man said that's the way it is. Till they work themselves in, y'know. 690

They move through the wall-line into the kitchen.

WILLY: I hope we didn't get stuck on that machine.

LINDA: They got the biggest ads of any of them!

WILLY: I know, it's a fine machine. What else?

LINDA: Well, there's nine-sixty for the washing machine. And for the vacuum cleaner there's three and a half 695 due on the fifteenth. Then the roof, you got twenty-one dollars remaining.

WILLY: It don't leak, does it?

LINDA: No, they did a wonderful job. Then you owe Frank for the carburetor. 700

WILLY: I'm not going to pay that man! That goddam Chevrolet, they ought to prohibit the manufacture of that car!

LINDA: Well, you owe him three and a half. And odds and ends, comes to around a hundred and twenty dol- 705 lars by the fifteenth.

WILLY: A hundred and twenty dollars! My God, if business don't pick up I don't know what I'm gonna do!

LINDA: Well, next week you'll do better.

710 **WILLY:** Oh, I'll knock 'em dead next week. I'll go to Hartford. I'm very well liked in Hartford. You know, the trouble is, Linda, people don't seem to take to me.

They move onto the forestage.

LINDA: Oh, don't be foolish.

WILLY: I know it when I walk in. They seem to laugh
715 at me.

LINDA: Why? Why would they laugh at you? Don't talk that way, Willy.

WILLY moves to the edge of the stage. LINDA goes into the kitchen and starts to darn stockings.

WILLY: I don't know the reason for it, but they just pass me by. I'm not noticed.

720 **LINDA:** But you're doing wonderful, dear. You're making seventy to a hundred dollars a week.

WILLY: But I gotta be at it ten, twelve hours a day. Other men—I don't know—they do it easier. I don't know why—I can't stop myself—I talk too much. A man
725 oughta come in with a few words. One thing about Charley. He's a man of few words, and they respect him.

LINDA: You don't talk too much, you're just lively.

WILLY: *(smiling)* Well, I figure, what the hell, life is
730 short, a couple of jokes. *(To himself.)* I joke too much! *(The smile goes.)*

LINDA: Why? You're—

WILLY: I'm fat. I'm very—foolish to look at, Linda. I didn't tell you, but Christmas time I happened to be
735 calling on F. H. Stewarts, and a salesman I know, as I was going in to see the buyer I heard him say something about—walrus. And I—I cracked him right across the face. I won't take that. I simply will not take that. But they do laugh at me. I know that.

740 **LINDA:** Darling . . .

WILLY: I gotta overcome it. I know I gotta overcome it. I'm not dressing to advantage, maybe.

LINDA: Willy, darling, you're the handsomest man in the world—

WILLY: Oh, no, Linda. 745

LINDA: To me you are. *(Slight pause.)* The handsomest.

From the darkness is heard the laughter of a woman. WILLY doesn't turn to it, but it continues through LINDA's lines.

LINDA: And the boys, Willy. Few men are idolized by their children the way you are.

Music is heard as behind a scrim, to the left of the house, THE WOMAN, dimly seen, is dressing.

WILLY: *(with great feeling)* You're the best there is, Linda, you're a pal, you know that? On the road—on 750 the road I want to grab you sometimes and just kiss the life outa you.

The laughter is loud now, and he moves into a brightening area at the left, where THE WOMAN has come from behind the scrim and is standing, putting on her hat, looking into a "mirror" and laughing.

WILLY: 'Cause I get so lonely—especially when business is bad and there's nobody to talk to. I get the feeling that I'll never sell anything again, that I won't make 755 a living for you, or a business, a business for the boys. *(He talks through THE WOMAN's subsiding laughter; THE WOMAN primps at the "mirror.")* There's so much I want to make for—

THE WOMAN: Me? You didn't make me, Willy. I picked 760 you.

WILLY: *(pleased)* You picked me?

THE WOMAN: *(who is quite proper-looking, WILLY's age)* I did. I've been sitting at that desk watching all the salesmen go by, day in, day out. But you've got such 765 a sense of humor, and we do have such a good time together, don't we?

WILLY: Sure, sure. *(He takes her in his arms.)* Why do you have to go now?

THE WOMAN: It's two o'clock . . . 770

WILLY: No, come on in! *(He pulls her.)*

THE WOMAN: . . . my sisters'll be scandalized. When'll you be back?

WILLY: Oh, two weeks about. Will you come up again?

775 **THE WOMAN:**   Sure thing. You do make me laugh. It's good for me. *(She squeezes his arm, kisses him.)* And I think you're a wonderful man.

WILLY: You picked me, heh?

THE WOMAN: Sure. Because you're so sweet. And such 780 a kidder.

WILLY: Well, I'll see you next time I'm in Boston.

THE WOMAN: I'll put you right through to the buyers.

WILLY: *(slapping her bottom)* Right. Well, bottoms up!

THE WOMAN: *(slaps him gently and laughs)* You just 785 kill me, Willy. *(He suddenly grabs her and kisses her roughly.)* You kill me. And thanks for the stockings. I love a lot of stockings. Well, good night.

WILLY: Good night. And keep your pores open!

THE WOMAN: Oh, Willy!

Willy and The Woman (Kathy Rossetter) say good-bye in their hotel room.

THE WOMAN *bursts out laughing, and* LINDA's *laughter blends in.* THE WOMAN *disappears into the dark. Now the area at the kitchen table brightens.* LINDA *is sitting where she was at the kitchen table, but now is mending a pair of her silk stockings.*

LINDA: You are, Willy. The handsomest man. You've got 790 no reason to feel that—

WILLY: *(coming out of* THE WOMAN's *dimming area and going over to* LINDA*)* I'll make it all up to you, Linda, I'll—

LINDA: There's nothing to make up, dear. You're doing 795 fine, better than—

WILLY: *(noticing her mending)* What's that?

LINDA: Just mending my stockings. They're so expensive—

WILLY: *(angrily, taking them from her)* I won't have you 800 mending stockings in this house! Now throw them out!

LINDA *puts the stockings in her pocket.*

BERNARD: *(entering on the run)* Where is he? If he doesn't study!

WILLY: *(moving to the forestage, with great agitation)* 805 You'll give him the answers!

BERNARD: I do, but I can't on a Regents! That's a state exam! They're liable to arrest me!

WILLY: Where is he? I'll whip him, I'll whip him!

LINDA: And he'd better give back that football, Willy, it's 810 not nice.

WILLY: Biff! Where is he? Why is he taking everything?

LINDA: He's too rough with the girls, Willy. All the mothers are afraid of him!

WILLY: I'll whip him! 815

BERNARD: He's driving the car without a license!

THE WOMAN's *laugh is heard.*

WILLY: Shut up!

LINDA: All the mothers—

WILLY: Shut up!

820 **BERNARD:** *(backing quietly away and out)* Mr. Birnbaum says he's stuck up.

WILLY: Get outa here!

BERNARD: If he doesn't buckle down he'll flunk math! *(He goes off.)*

825 **LINDA:** He's right, Willy, you've gotta—

WILLY: *(exploding at her)* There's nothing the matter with him! You want him to be a worm like Bernard? He's got spirit, personality . . .

As he speaks, LINDA, *almost in tears, exits into the living-room.* WILLY *is alone in the kitchen, wilting and staring. The leaves are gone. It is night again, and the apartment houses look down from behind.*

WILLY: Loaded with it. Loaded! What is he stealing?
830 He's giving it back, isn't he? Why is he stealing? What did I tell him? I never in my life told him anything but decent things.

HAPPY in pajamas has come down the stairs; WILLY *suddenly becomes aware of* HAPPY's *presence.*

HAPPY: Let's go now, come on.

WILLY: *(sitting down at the kitchen table)* Huh! Why
835 did she have to wax the floors herself? Everytime she waxes the floors she keels over. She knows that!

HAPPY: Shh! Take it easy. What brought you back tonight?

WILLY: I got an awful scare. Nearly hit a kid in Yonkers.
840 God! Why didn't I go to Alaska with my brother Ben that time! Ben! That man was a genius, that man was success incarnate! What a mistake! He begged me to go.

HAPPY: Well, there's no use in—

845 **WILLY:** You guys! There was a man started with the clothes on his back and ended up with diamond mines!

HAPPY: Boy, someday I'd like to know how he did it.

WILLY: What's the mystery? The man knew what he
wanted and went out and got it! Walked into a jungle, 850
and comes out, the age of twenty-one, and he's rich! The world is an oyster, but you don't crack it open on a mattress!

HAPPY: Pop, I told you I'm gonna retire you for life.

WILLY: You'll retire me for life on seventy goddam dol- 855
lars a week? And your women and your car and your apartment, and you'll retire me for life! Christ's sake, I couldn't get past Yonkers today! Where are you guys, where are you? The woods are burning! I can't drive
a car! 860

CHARLEY *has appeared in the doorway. He is a large man, slow of speech, laconic, immovable. In all he says, despite what he says, there is pity, and, now, trepidation. He has a robe over pajamas, slippers on his feet. He enters the kitchen.*

CHARLEY: Everything all right?

HAPPY: Yeah, Charley, everything's . . .

WILLY: What's the matter?

CHARLEY: I heard some noise. I thought something
happened. Can't we do something about the walls? 865
You sneeze in here, and in my house hats blow off.

HAPPY: Let's go to bed, Dad. Come on.

CHARLEY *signals to* HAPPY *to go.*

WILLY: You go ahead, I'm not tired at the moment.

HAPPY: *(to* WILLY) Take it easy, huh? *(He exits.)*

WILLY: What're you doin' up? 870

CHARLEY: *(sitting down at the kitchen table opposite* WILLY) Couldn't sleep good. I had a heartburn.

WILLY: Well, you don't know how to eat.

CHARLEY: I eat with my mouth.

WILLY: No, you're ignorant. You gotta know about vita- 875
mins and things like that.

CHARLEY: Come on, let's shoot. Tire you out a little.

WILLY: *(hesitantly)* All right. You got cards?

CHARLEY: *(taking a deck from his pocket)* Yeah, I got
880   them. Someplace. What is it with those vitamins?

WILLY: *(dealing)* They build up your bones. Chemistry.

CHARLEY: Yeah, but there's no bones in a heartburn.

WILLY: What are you talkin' about? Do you know the
     first thing about it?

885 **CHARLEY:** Don't get insulted.

WILLY: Don't talk about something you don't know
     anything about.

     They are playing. Pause.

CHARLEY: What're you doin' home?

WILLY: A little trouble with the car.

890 **CHARLEY:** Oh. *(Pause.)* I'd like to take a trip to
     California.

WILLY: Don't say.

CHARLEY: You want a job?

WILLY: I got a job, I told you that. *(After a slight pause.)*
895   What the hell are you offering me a job for?

CHARLEY: Don't get insulted.

WILLY: Don't insult me.

CHARLEY: I don't see no sense in it. You don't have to go
     on this way.

900 **WILLY:** I got a good job. *(Slight pause.)* What do you
     keep comin' in here for?

CHARLEY: You want me to go?

WILLY: *(after a pause, withering)* I can't understand it.
     He's going back to Texas again. What the hell is that?

905 **CHARLEY:** Let him go.

WILLY: I got nothin' to give him, Charley, I'm clean, I'm
     clean.

CHARLEY: He won't starve. None a them starve. Forget
     about him.

910 **WILLY:** Then what have I got to remember?

CHARLEY: You take it too hard. To hell with it. When a
     deposit bottle is broken you don't get your nickel back.

WILLY: That's easy enough for you to say.

CHARLEY: That ain't easy for me to say.

WILLY: Did you see the ceiling I put up in the   915
     living-room?

CHARLEY: Yeah, that's a piece of work. To put up a ceil-
     ing is a mystery to me. How do you do it?

WILLY: What's the difference?

CHARLEY: Well, talk about it.   920

WILLY: You gonna put up a ceiling?

CHARLEY: How could I put up a ceiling?

WILLY: Then what the hell are you bothering me for?

CHARLEY: You're insulted again.

WILLY: A man who can't handle tools is not a man.   925
     You're disgusting.

CHARLEY: Don't call me disgusting, Willy.

     Uncle BEN, *carrying a valise and an umbrella, en-
     ters the forestage from around the right corner of the
     house. He is a stolid man, in his sixties, with a mus-
     tache and an authoritative air. He is utterly certain
     of his destiny, and there is an aura of far places about
     him. He enters exactly as* WILLY *speaks.*

WILLY: I'm getting awfully tired, Ben.

     BEN's *music is heard.* BEN *looks around at
     everything.*

CHARLEY: Good, keep playing; you'll sleep better. Did
     you call me Ben?   930

     BEN *looks at his watch.*

WILLY: That's funny. For a second there you reminded
     me of my brother Ben.

BEN: I only have a few minutes. *(He strolls, inspecting the
     place.* WILLY *and* CHARLEY *continue playing.)*

CHARLEY: You never heard from him again, heh? Since   935
     that time?

Willy and Charley (Edward Andrews) play a game of cards as Ben
(Albert Dekker) appears.

WILLY: Didn't Linda tell you? Couple of weeks ago we
got a letter from his wife in Africa. He died.

CHARLEY: That so.

940   **BEN:**   *(chuckling)* So this is Brooklyn, eh?

CHARLEY: Maybe you're in for some of his money.

WILLY: Naa, he had seven sons. There's just one opportunity I had with that man . . .

BEN: I must make a train, William. There are several
945   properties I'm looking at in Alaska.

WILLY: Sure, sure! If I'd gone with him to Alaska that
time, everything would've been totally different.

CHARLEY: Go on, you'd froze to death up there.

WILLY: What're you talking about?

950   **BEN:**   Opportunity is tremendous in Alaska, William.
Surprised you're not up there.

WILLY: Sure, tremendous.

CHARLEY: Heh?

WILLY: There was the only man I ever met who knew
955   the answers.

CHARLEY: Who?

BEN: How are you all?

WILLY: *(taking a pot, smiling)* Fine, fine.

CHARLEY: Pretty sharp tonight.

BEN: Is Mother living with you?   960

WILLY: No, she died a long time ago.

CHARLEY: Who?

BEN: That's too bad. Fine specimen of a lady, Mother.

WILLY: *(to CHARLEY)* Heh?

BEN: I'd hoped to see the old girl.   965

CHARLEY: Who died?

BEN: Heard anything from Father, have you?

WILLY: *(unnerved)* What do you mean, who died?

CHARLEY: *(taking a pot)* What're you talkin' about?

BEN: *(looking at his watch)* William, it's half-past eight!   970

WILLY: *(as though to dispel his confusion he angrily stops
CHARLEY's hand)* That's my build!

CHARLEY: I put the ace—

WILLY: If you don't know how to play the game I'm not
gonna throw my money away on you!   975

CHARLEY: *(rising)* It was my ace, for God's sake!

WILLY: I'm through, I'm through!

BEN: When did Mother die?

WILLY: Long ago. Since the beginning you never knew
how to play cards.   980

CHARLEY: *(picks up the cards and goes to the door)* All
right! Next time I'll bring a deck with five aces.

WILLY: I don't play that kind of game!

CHARLEY: *(turning to him)* You ought to be ashamed of
yourself!   985

WILLY: Yeah?

CHARLEY: Yeah! *(He goes out.)*

WILLY: (*slamming the door after him*) Ignoramus!

990 **BEN:** (*as* WILLY *comes toward him through the wall-line of the kitchen*) So you're William.

WILLY: (*shaking Ben's hand*) Ben! I've been waiting for you so long! What's the answer? How did you do it?

BEN: Oh, there's a story in that.

LINDA *enters the forestage, as of old, carrying the wash basket.*

LINDA: Is this Ben?

995 **BEN:** (*gallantly*) How do you do, my dear.

LINDA: Where've you been all these years? Willy's always wondered why you—

WILLY: (*pulling Ben away from her impatiently*) Where is Dad? Didn't you follow him? How did you get 1000 started?

BEN: Well, I don't know how much you remember.

WILLY: Well, I was just a baby, of course, only three or four years old—

BEN: Three years and eleven months.

1005 **WILLY:** What a memory, Ben!

BEN: I have many enterprises, William, and I have never kept books.

WILLY: I remember I was sitting under the wagon in— was it Nebraska?

1010 **BEN:** It was South Dakota, and I gave you a bunch of wild flowers.

WILLY: I remember you walking away down some open road.

BEN: (*laughing*) I was going to find Father in Alaska.

1015 **WILLY:** Where is he?

BEN: At that age I had a very faulty view of geography, William. I discovered after a few days that I was heading due south, so instead of Alaska, I ended up in Africa.

LINDA: Africa! 1020

WILLY: The Gold Coast!

BEN: Principally diamond mines.

LINDA: Diamond mines!

BEN: Yes, my dear. But I've only a few minutes—

WILLY: No! Boys! Boys! (*Young* BIFF *and* HAPPY *appear.*) Listen to this. This is your Uncle Ben, a great man! Tell my boys, Ben! 1025

BEN: Why, boys, when I was seventeen I walked into the jungle, and when I was twenty-one I walked out. (*He laughs.*) And by God I was rich. 1030

WILLY: (*to the boys*) You see what I been talking about? The greatest things can happen!

BEN: (*glancing at his watch*) I have an appointment in Ketchikan Tuesday next week.

WILLY: No, Ben! Please tell about Dad. I want my boys to hear. I want them to know the kind of stock they spring from. All I remember is a man with a big beard, and I was in Mamma's lap, sitting around a fire, and some kind of high music. 1035

BEN: His flute. He played the flute. 1040

WILLY: Sure, the flute, that's right!

New music is heard, a high, rollicking tune.

BEN: Father was a very great and a very wild-hearted man. We would start in Boston, and he'd toss the whole family into the wagon, and then he'd drive the team right across the country; through Ohio, and Indiana, Michigan, Illinois, and all the Western states. And we'd stop in the towns and sell the flutes that he'd made on the way. Great inventor, Father. With one gadget he made more in a week than a man like you could make in a lifetime. 1045 1050

WILLY: That's just the way I'm bringing them up, Ben— rugged, well liked, all-around.

BEN: Yeah? (*To* BIFF.) Hit that, boy—hard as you can. (*He pounds his stomach.*)

BIFF: Oh, no, sir! 1055

BEN: *(taking boxing stance)* Come on, get to me. *(He laughs.)*

WILLY: Go to it, Biff! Go ahead, show him!

BIFF: Okay! *(He cocks his fists and starts in.)*

1060 LINDA: *(to WILLY)* Why must he fight, dear?

BEN: *(sparring with BIFF)* Good boy! Good boy!

WILLY: How's that, Ben, heh?

HAPPY: Give him the left, Biff!

LINDA: Why are you fighting?

1065 BEN: Good boy! *(Suddenly comes in, trips BIFF, and stands over him, the point of his umbrella poised over BIFF's eye.)*

LINDA: Look out, Biff!

BIFF: Gee!

1070 BEN: *(patting BIFF's knee)* Never fight fair with a stranger, boy. You'll never get out of the jungle that way. *(Taking LINDA's hand and bowing):* It was an honor and a pleasure to meet you, Linda.

LINDA: *(withdrawing her hand coldly, frightened)* Have
1075 a nice—trip.

BEN: *(to WILLY)* And good luck with your—what do you do?

WILLY: Selling.

BEN: Yes. Well . . . *(He raises his hand in farewell to all.)*

1080 WILLY: No, Ben, I don't want you to think . . . *(He takes Ben's arm to show him.)* It's Brooklyn, I know, but we hunt too.

BEN: Really, now.

WILLY: Oh, sure, there's snakes and rabbits and—that's
1085 why I moved out here. Why, Biff can fell any one of these trees in no time! Boys! Go right over to where they're building the apartment house and get some sand. We're gonna rebuild the entire front stoop now! Watch this, Ben!

1090 BIFF: Yes, sir! On the double, Hap!

HAPPY: *(as he and BIFF run off)* I lost weight, Pop, you notice?

CHARLEY *enters in knickers, even before the boys are gone.*

CHARLEY: Listen, if they steal any more from that building the watchman'll put the cops on them!

LINDA: *(to WILLY)* Don't let Biff . . .   1095

BEN *laughs lustily.*

WILLY: You shoulda seen the lumber they brought home last week. At least a dozen six-by-tens worth all kinds a money.

CHARLEY: Listen, if that watchman—

WILLY: I gave them hell, understand. But I got a couple   1100
of fearless characters there.

CHARLEY: Willy, the jails are full of fearless characters.

BEN: *(clapping WILLY on the back, with a laugh at CHARLEY)* And the stock exchange, friend!

WILLY: *(joining in Ben's laughter)* Where are the rest of   1105
your pants?

CHARLEY: My wife bought them.

Willy and Ben have a laugh at Charley.

WILLY: Now all you need is a golf club and you can go upstairs and go to sleep. (*To Ben*). Great athlete!
1110 Between him and his son Bernard they can't hammer a nail!

BERNARD: (*rushing in*) The watchman's chasing Biff!

WILLY: (*angrily*) Shut up! He's not stealing anything!

LINDA: (*alarmed, hurrying off left*) Where is he? Biff,
1115 dear! (*She exits.*)

WILLY: (*moving toward the left, away from Ben*) There's nothing wrong. What's the matter with you?

BEN: Nervy boy. Good!

WILLY: (*laughing*) Oh, nerves of iron, that Biff!

1120 **CHARLEY:** Don't know what it is. My New England man comes back and he's bleedin', they murdered him up there.

WILLY: It's contacts, Charley, I got important contacts!

CHARLEY: (*sarcastically*) Glad to hear it, Willy. Come in
1125 later, we'll shoot a little casino. I'll take some of your Portland money. (*He laughs at* WILLY *and exits.*)

WILLY: (*turning to Ben*) Business is bad, it's murderous. But not for me, of course.

BEN: I'll stop by on my way back to Africa.

1130 **WILLY:** (*longingly*) Can't you stay a few days? You're just what I need, Ben, because I—I have a fine position here, but I—well, Dad left when I was such a baby and I never had a chance to talk to him and I still feel— kind of temporary about myself.

1135 **BEN:** I'll be late for my train.

They are at opposite ends of the stage.

WILLY: Ben, my boys—can't we talk? They'd go into the jaws of hell for me, see, but I—

BEN: William, you're being first-rate with your boys. Outstanding, manly chaps!

1140 **WILLY:** (*hanging on to his words*) Oh, Ben, that's good to hear! Because sometimes I'm afraid that I'm not teaching them the right kind of—Ben, how should I teach them?

BEN: (*giving great weight to each word, and with a cer-
1145 tain vicious audacity*) William, when I walked into the jungle, I was seventeen. When I walked out I was twenty-one. And, by God, I was rich! (*He goes off into darkness around the right corner of the house.*)

WILLY: . . . was rich! That's just the spirit I want to imbue them with! To walk into a jungle! I was right! 1150 I was right! I was right!

BEN *is gone, but* WILLY *is still speaking to him as* LINDA, *in nightgown and robe, enters the kitchen, glances around for* WILLY, *then goes to the door of the house, looks out, and sees him. Comes down to his left. He looks at her.*

LINDA: Willy, dear? Willy?

WILLY: I was right!

LINDA: Did you have some cheese? (*He can't answer.*) It's very late, darling. Come to bed, heh? 1155

WILLY: (*looking straight up*) Gotta break your neck to see a star in this yard.

LINDA: You coming in?

WILLY: Whatever happened to that diamond watch fob? Remember? When Ben came from Africa that time? 1160 Didn't he give me a watch fob with a diamond in it?

LINDA: You pawned it, dear. Twelve, thirteen years ago. For Biff's radio correspondence course.

WILLY: Gee, that was a beautiful thing. I'll take a walk.

LINDA: But you're in your slippers. 1165

WILLY: (*starting to go around the house at the left*) I was right! I was! (*Half to* LINDA, *as he goes, shaking his head.*) What a man! There was a man worth talking to. I was right!

LINDA: (*calling after* WILLY) But in your slippers, Willy! 1170

WILLY *is almost gone when* BIFF, *in his pajamas, comes down the stairs and enters the kitchen.*

BIFF: What is he doing out there?

LINDA: Sh!

BIFF: God Almighty, Mom, how long has he been doing this?

1175 **LINDA:** Don't, he'll hear you.

BIFF: What the hell is the matter with him?

LINDA: It'll pass by morning.

BIFF: Shouldn't we do anything?

LINDA: Oh, my dear, you should do a lot of things, but
1180 there's nothing to do, so go to sleep.

> HAPPY *comes down the stairs and sits on the steps.*

HAPPY: I never heard him so loud, Mom.

LINDA: Well, come around more often; you'll hear him.
*(She sits down at the table and mends the lining of
WILLY's jacket.)*

1185 **BIFF:** Why didn't you ever write me about this, Mom?

LINDA: How would I write to you? For over three
months you had no address.

BIFF: I was on the move. But you know I thought of you
all the time. You know that, don't you, pal?

1190 **LINDA:** I know, dear, I know. But he likes to have a
letter. Just to know that there's still a possibility for
better things.

BIFF: He's not like this all the time, is he?

LINDA: It's when you come home he's always the worst.

1195 **BIFF:** When I come home?

LINDA: When you write you're coming, he's all smiles,
and talks about the future, and—he's just wonderful.
And then the closer you seem to come, the more shaky
he gets, and then, by the time you get here, he's argu-
1200 ing, and he seems angry at you. I think it's just that
maybe he can't bring himself to—to open up to you.
Why are you so hateful to each other? Why is that?

BIFF: *(evasively)* I'm not hateful, Mom.

LINDA: But you no sooner come in the door than you're
1205 fighting!

BIFF: I don't know why. I mean to change. I'm tryin',
Mom, you understand?

LINDA: Are you home to stay now?

BIFF: I don't know. I want to look around, see what's
doin'. 1210

LINDA: Biff, you can't look around all your life, can you?

BIFF: I just can't take hold, Mom. I can't take hold of
some kind of a life.

LINDA: Biff, a man is not a bird, to come and go with the
springtime. 1215

BIFF: Your hair . . . *(He touches her hair.)* Your hair got
so gray.

LINDA: Oh, it's been gray since you were in high school.
I just stopped dyeing it, that's all.

BIFF: Dye it again, will ya? I don't want my pal looking 1220
old. *(He smiles.)*

LINDA: You're such a boy! You think you can go away for
a year and . . . You've got to get it into your head now
that one day you'll knock on this door and there'll be
strange people here— 1225

BIFF: What are you talking about? You're not even sixty,
Mom.

LINDA: But what about your father?

BIFF: *(lamely)* Well, I meant him too.

HAPPY: He admires Pop. 1230

LINDA: Biff, dear, if you don't have any feeling for him,
then you can't have any feeling for me.

BIFF: Sure I can, Mom.

LINDA: No. You can't just come to see me, because I love
him. *(With a threat, but only a threat, of tears.)* He's 1235
the dearest man in the world to me, and I won't have
anyone making him feel unwanted and low and blue.
You've got to make up your mind now, darling, there's
no leeway any more. Either he's your father and you
pay him that respect, or else you're not to come here. 1240
I know he's not easy to get along with—nobody knows
that better than me—but . . .

WILLY: *(from the left, with a laugh)* Hey, hey, Biffo!

BIFF: *(starting to go out after* WILLY*)* What the hell is the matter with him? *(*HAPPY *stops him.)*

LINDA: Don't—don't go near him!

BIFF: Stop making excuses for him! He always, always wiped the floor with you. Never had an ounce of respect for you.

HAPPY: He's always had respect for—

BIFF: What the hell do you know about it?

HAPPY: *(surlily)* Just don't call him crazy!

BIFF: He's got no character—Charley wouldn't do this. Not in his own house—spewing out that vomit from his mind.

HAPPY: Charley never had to cope with what he's got to.

BIFF: People are worse off than Willy Loman. Believe me, I've seen them!

LINDA: Then make Charley your father, Biff. You can't do that, can you? I don't say he's a great man. Willy Loman never made a lot of money. His name was never in the paper. He's not the finest character that ever lived. But he's a human being, and a terrible thing is happening to him. So attention must be paid. He's not to be allowed to fall into his grave like an old dog. Attention, attention must be finally paid to such a person. You called him crazy—

BIFF: I didn't mean—

LINDA: No, a lot of people think he's lost his—balance. But you don't have to be very smart to know what his trouble is. The man is exhausted.

HAPPY: Sure!

LINDA: A small man can be just as exhausted as a great man. He works for a company thirty-six years this March, opens up unheard-of territories to their trademark, and now in his old age they take his salary away.

HAPPY: *(indignantly)* I didn't know that, Mom.

LINDA: You never asked, my dear! Now that you get your spending money someplace else you don't trouble your mind with him.

HAPPY: But I gave you money last—

LINDA: Christmas time, fifty dollars! To fix the hot water it cost ninety-seven fifty! For five weeks he's been on straight commission, like a beginner, an unknown!

BIFF: Those ungrateful bastards!

LINDA: Are they any worse than his sons? When he brought them business, when he was young, they were glad to see him. But now his old friends, the old buyers that loved him so and always found some order to hand him in a pinch—they're all dead, retired. He used to be able to make six, seven calls a day in Boston. Now he takes his valises out of the car and puts them back and takes them out again and he's exhausted. Instead of walking he talks now. He drives seven hundred miles, and when he gets there no one knows him any more, no one welcomes him. And what goes through a man's mind, driving seven hundred miles home without having earned a cent? Why shouldn't he talk to himself? Why? When he has to go to Charley and borrow fifty dollars a week and pretend to me that it's his pay? How long can that go on? How long? You see what I'm sitting here and waiting for? And you tell me he has no character? The man who never worked a day but for your benefit? When does he get the medal for that? Is this his

The Lomans argue about Willy.

reward—to turn around at the age of sixty-three and find his sons, who he loved better than his life, one a philandering bum—

1310 **HAPPY:**   Mom!

LINDA: That's all you are, my baby! *(To* BIFF.*)* And you! What happened to the love you had for him? You were such pals! How you used to talk to him on the phone every night! How lonely he was till he could come

1315 home to you!

BIFF: All right, Mom. I'll live here in my room, and I'll get a job. I'll keep away from him, that's all.

LINDA: No, Biff. You can't stay here and fight all the time.

1320 **BIFF:**   He threw me out of this house, remember that.

LINDA: Why did he do that? I never knew why.

BIFF: Because I know he's a fake and he doesn't like anybody around who knows!

LINDA: Why a fake? In what way? What do you mean?

1325 **BIFF:**   Just don't lay it all at my feet. It's between me and him—that's all I have to say. I'll chip in from now on. He'll settle for half my pay check. He'll be all right. I'm going to bed. *(He starts for the stairs.)*

LINDA: He won't be all right.

1330 **BIFF:**   *(turning on the stairs, furiously)* I hate this city and I'll stay here. Now what do you want?

LINDA: He's dying, Biff.

HAPPY *turns quickly to her, shocked.*

BIFF: *(after a pause)* Why is he dying?

LINDA: He's been trying to kill himself.

1335 **BIFF:**   *(with great horror)* How?

LINDA: I live from day to day.

BIFF: What're you talking about?

LINDA: Remember I wrote you that he smashed up the car again? In February?

1340 **BIFF:**   Well?

LINDA: The insurance inspector came. He said that they have evidence. That all these accidents in the last year—weren't—weren't—accidents.

HAPPY: How can they tell that? That's a lie.

LINDA: It seems there's a woman . . . *(She takes a breath as):* BIFF *(sharply but contained):*   What woman?   1345
LINDA *(simultaneously):*   . . . and this woman . . .

LINDA: What?

BIFF: Nothing. Go ahead.

LINDA: What did you say?   1350

BIFF: Nothing. I just said what woman?

HAPPY: What about her?

LINDA: Well, it seems she was walking down the road and saw his car. She says that he wasn't driving fast at all, and that he didn't skid. She says he came to that   1355 little bridge, and then deliberately smashed into the railing, and it was only the shallowness of the water that saved him.

BIFF: Oh, no, he probably just fell asleep again.

LINDA: I don't think he fell asleep.   1360

BIFF: Why not?

LINDA: Last month . . . *(With great difficulty.)* Oh, boys, it's so hard to say a thing like this! He's just a big stupid man to you, but I tell you there's more good in him than in many other people. *(She chokes, wipes her*   1365 *eyes.)* I was looking for a fuse. The lights blew out, and I went down the cellar. And behind the fuse box—it happened to fall out—was a length of rubber pipe—just short.

HAPPY: No kidding?   1370

LINDA: There's a little attachment on the end of it. I knew right away. And sure enough, on the bottom of the water heater there's a new little nipple on the gas pipe.

HAPPY: *(angrily)* That—jerk.   1375

BIFF: Did you have it taken off?

LINDA: I'm—I'm ashamed to. How can I mention it to him? Every day I go down and take away that little rubber pipe. But, when he comes home, I put it back where it was. How can I insult him that way? I don't know what to do. I live from day to day, boys. I tell you, I know every thought in his mind. It sounds so old-fashioned and silly, but I tell you he put his whole life into you and you've turned your backs on him. *(She is bent over in chair, weeping, her face in her hands.)* Biff, I swear to God! Biff, his life is in your hands!

HAPPY: *(to BIFF)* How do you like that damned fool!

BIFF: *(kissing her)* All right, pal, all right. It's all settled now. I've been remiss. I know that, Mom. But now I'll stay, and I swear to you, I'll apply myself. *(Kneeling in front of her, in a fever of self-reproach.)* It's just—you see, Mom, I don't fit in business. Not that I won't try. I'll try, and I'll make good.

HAPPY: Sure you will. The trouble with you in business was you never tried to please people.

BIFF: I know, I—

HAPPY: Like when you worked for Harrison's. Bob Harrison said you were tops, and then you go and do some damn fool thing like whistling whole songs in the elevator like a comedian.

BIFF: *(against HAPPY)* So what? I like to whistle sometimes.

HAPPY: You don't raise a guy to a responsible job who whistles in the elevator!

LINDA: Well, don't argue about it now.

HAPPY: Like when you'd go off and swim in the middle of the day instead of taking the line around.

BIFF: *(his resentment rising)* Well, don't you run off? You take off sometimes, don't you? On a nice summer day?

HAPPY: Yeah, but I cover myself!

LINDA: Boys!

HAPPY: If I'm going to take a fade the boss can call any number where I'm supposed to be and they'll swear to him that I just left. I'll tell you something that I hate to say, Biff, but in the business world some of them think you're crazy.

BIFF: *(angered)* Screw the business world!

HAPPY: All right, screw it! Great, but cover yourself!

LINDA: Hap, Hap!

BIFF: I don't care what they think! They've laughed at Dad for years, and you know why? Because we don't belong in this nuthouse of a city! We should be mixing cement on some open plain, or—or carpenters. A carpenter is allowed to whistle!

WILLY *walks in from the entrance of the house, at left.*

WILLY: Even your grandfather was better than a carpenter. *(Pause. They watch him.)* You never grew up. Bernard does not whistle in the elevator, I assure you.

BIFF: *(as though to laugh WILLY out of it)* Yeah, but you do, Pop.

WILLY: I never in my life whistled in an elevator! And who in the business world thinks I'm crazy?

BIFF: I didn't mean it like that, Pop. Now don't make a whole thing out of it, will ya?

WILLY: Go back to the West! Be a carpenter, a cowboy, enjoy yourself!

LINDA: Willy, he was just saying—

WILLY: I heard what he said!

HAPPY: *(trying to quiet WILLY)* Hey, Pop, come on now . . .

WILLY: *(continuing over HAPPY's line)* They laugh at me, heh? Go to Filene's, go to the Hub, go to Slattery's, Boston. Call out the name Willy Loman and see what happens! Big shot!

BIFF: All right, Pop.

WILLY: Big!

BIFF: All right!

WILLY: Why do you always insult me?

BIFF: I didn't say a word. *(To LINDA.)* Did I say a word?

1450   **LINDA:**   He didn't say anything, Willy.

WILLY: *(going to the doorway of the living-room)* All right, good night, good night.

LINDA: Willy, dear, he just decided . . .

WILLY: *(to* BIFF*)* If you get tired hanging around tomor-
1455   row, paint the ceiling I put up in the living-room.

BIFF: I'm leaving early tomorrow.

HAPPY: He's going to see Bill Oliver, Pop.

WILLY: *(interestedly)* Oliver? For what?

BIFF: *(with reserve, but trying, trying)* He always said
1460   he'd stake me. I'd like to go into business, so maybe I can take him up on it.

LINDA: Isn't that wonderful?

WILLY: Don't interrupt. What's wonderful about it? There's fifty men in the City of New York who'd stake
1465   him. *(To* BIFF.*)* Sporting goods?

BIFF: I guess so. I know something about it and—

WILLY: He knows something about it! You know sport-ing goods better than Spalding, for God's sake! How much is he giving you?

1470   **BIFF:**   I don't know, I didn't even see him yet, but—

WILLY: Then what're you talkin' about?

BIFF: *(getting angry)* Well, all I said was I'm gonna see him, that's all!

WILLY: *(turning away)* Ah, you're counting your chick-
1475   ens again.

BIFF: *(starting left for the stairs)* Oh, Jesus, I'm going to sleep!

WILLY: *(calling after him)* Don't curse in this house!

BIFF: *(turning)* Since when did you get so clean?

1480   **HAPPY:**   *(trying to stop them)* Wait a . . .

WILLY: Don't use that language to me! I won't have it!

HAPPY: *(grabbing* BIFF, *shouts)* Wait a minute! I got an idea. I got a feasible idea. Come here, Biff, let's talk

Willy and the boys discuss their million-dollar ideas.

this over now, let's talk some sense here. When I was down in Florida last time, I thought of a great idea   1485
to sell sporting goods. It just came back to me. You and I, Biff—we have a line, the Loman Line. We train a couple of weeks, and put on a couple of exhibitions, see?

WILLY: That's an idea!   1490

HAPPY: Wait! We form two basketball teams, see? Two water-polo teams. We play each other. It's a million dollars' worth of publicity. Two brothers, see? The Loman Brothers. Displays in the Royal Palms—all the hotels. And banners over the ring and the basketball   1495
court: "Loman Brothers." Baby, we could sell sporting goods!

WILLY: That is a one-million-dollar idea!

LINDA: Marvelous!

BIFF: I'm in great shape as far as that's concerned.   1500

HAPPY: And the beauty of it is, Biff, it wouldn't be like a business. We'd be out playin' ball again . . .

BIFF: *(enthused)* Yeah, that's . . .

WILLY: Million-dollar . . .

1505 **HAPPY:**   And you wouldn't get fed up with it, Biff. It'd be the family again. There'd be the old honor, and comradeship, and if you wanted to go off for a swim or somethin'—well, you'd do it! Without some smart cooky gettin' up ahead of you!

1510 **WILLY:**   Lick the world! You guys together could absolutely lick the civilized world.

BIFF: I'll see Oliver tomorrow. Hap, if we could work that out . . .

LINDA: Maybe things are beginning to—

1515 **WILLY:**   *(wildly enthused, to* LINDA*)* Stop interrupting! *(To* BIFF.*)* But don't wear sport jacket and slacks when you see Oliver.

BIFF: No, I'll—

WILLY: A business suit, and talk as little as possible, and
1520   don't crack any jokes.

BIFF: He did like me. Always liked me.

LINDA: He loved you!

WILLY: *(to* LINDA*)* Will you stop! *(To* BIFF.*)* Walk in very serious. You are not applying for a boy's job. Money is
1525   to pass. Be quiet, fine, and serious. Everybody likes a kidder, but nobody lends him money.

HAPPY: I'll try to get some myself, Biff. I'm sure I can.

WILLY: I see great things for you kids, I think your troubles are over. But remember, start big and you'll
1530   end big. Ask for fifteen. How much you gonna ask for?

BIFF: Gee, I don't know—

WILLY: And don't say "Gee." "Gee" is a boy's word. A man walking in for fifteen thousand dollars does not say "Gee!"

1535 **BIFF:**   Ten, I think, would be top though.

WILLY: Don't be so modest. You always started too low. Walk in with a big laugh. Don't look worried. Start off with a couple of your good stories to lighten things up. It's not what you say, it's how you say it—because
1540   personality always wins the day.

LINDA: Oliver always thought the highest of him—

WILLY: Will you let me talk?

BIFF: Don't yell at her, Pop, will ya?

WILLY: *(angrily)* I was talking, wasn't I?

BIFF: I don't like you yelling at her all the time, and I'm   1545
tellin' you, that's all.

WILLY: What're you, takin' over this house?

LINDA: Willy—

WILLY: *(turning on her)* Don't take his side all the time,
goddammit!   1550

BIFF: *(furiously)* Stop yelling at her!

WILLY: *(suddenly pulling on his cheek, beaten down, guilt ridden)* Give my best to Bill Oliver—he may remember me. *(He exits through the living-room doorway.)*

LINDA: *(her voice subdued)* What'd you have to start that   1555
for? *(*BIFF *turns away.)* You see how sweet he was as soon as you talked hopefully? *(She goes over to* BIFF.*)* Come up and say good night to him. Don't let him go to bed that way.

HAPPY: Come on, Biff, let's buck him up.   1560

LINDA: Please, dear. Just say good night. It takes so little to make him happy. Come. *(She goes through the living-room doorway, calling upstairs from within the living-room.)* Your pajamas are hanging in the bathroom, Willy!   1565

HAPPY: *(looking toward where* LINDA *went out)* What a woman! They broke the mold when they made her. You know that, Biff?

BIFF: He's off salary. My God, working on commission!

HAPPY: Well, let's face it: he's no hot-shot selling man.   1570
Except that sometimes, you have to admit, he's a sweet personality.

BIFF: *(deciding)* Lend me ten bucks, will ya? I want to buy some new ties.

HAPPY: I'll take you to a place I know. Beautiful stuff.   1575
Wear one of my striped shirts tomorrow.

BIFF: She got gray. Mom got awful old. Gee, I'm gonna go in to Oliver tomorrow and knock him for a—

HAPPY: Come on up. Tell that to Dad. Let's give him a 1580 whirl. Come on.

BIFF: *(steamed up)* You know, with ten thousand bucks, boy!

HAPPY: *(as they go into the living-room)* That's the talk, Biff, that's the first time I've heard the old confidence 1585 out of you! *(From within the living-room, fading off.)* You're gonna live with me, kid, and any babe you want just say the word . . . *(The last lines are hardly heard. They are mounting the stairs to their parents' bedroom.)*

LINDA: *(entering her bedroom and addressing* WILLY, 1590 *who is in the bathroom. She is straightening the bed for him)* Can you do anything about the shower? It drips.

WILLY: *(from the bathroom)* All of a sudden everything falls to pieces! Goddam plumbing, oughta be sued, those people. I hardly finished putting it in and the 1595 thing . . . *(His words rumble off.)*

LINDA: I'm just wondering if Oliver will remember him. You think he might?

WILLY: *(coming out of the bathroom in his pajamas)* Remember him? What's the matter with you, you 1600 crazy? If he'd've stayed with Oliver he'd be on top by now! Wait'll Oliver gets a look at him. You don't know the average caliber any more. The average young man today—*(he is getting into bed)*—is got a caliber of zero. Greatest thing in the world for him was to bum 1605 around.

BIFF and HAPPY *enter the bedroom. Slight pause.*

WILLY: *(stops short, looking at* BIFF) Glad to hear it, boy.

HAPPY: He wanted to say good night to you, sport.

WILLY: *(to* BIFF) Yeah. Knock him dead, boy. What'd you want to tell me?

1610 **BIFF:** Just take it easy, Pop. Good night. *(He turns to go.)*

WILLY: *(unable to resist)* And if anything falls off the desk while you're talking to him—like a package or something—don't you pick it up. They have office boys for that.

LINDA: I'll make a big breakfast— 1615

WILLY: Will you let me finish? *(To* BIFF.) Tell him you were in the business in the West. Not farm work.

BIFF: All right, Dad.

LINDA: I think everything—

WILLY: *(going right through her speech)* And don't under- 1620 sell yourself. No less than fifteen thousand dollars.

BIFF: *(unable to bear him)* Okay. Good night, Mom. *(He starts moving.)*

WILLY: Because you got a greatness in you, Biff, remem- ber that. You got all kinds a greatness . . . *(He lies back,* 1625 *exhausted.* BIFF *walks out.)*

LINDA: *(calling after* BIFF) Sleep well, darling!

HAPPY: I'm gonna get married, Mom. I wanted to tell you.

LINDA: Go to sleep, dear. 1630

HAPPY: *(going)* I just wanted to tell you.

WILLY: Keep up the good work. (HAPPY *exits.)* God . . . remember that Ebbets Field game? The championship of the city?

Linda hums as Willy reminisces.

1635 **LINDA:** Just rest. Should I sing to you?

WILLY: Yeah. Sing to me. (LINDA *hums a soft lul-laby.*) When that team came out—he was the tallest, remember?

LINDA: Oh, yes. And in gold.

BIFF *enters the darkened kitchen, takes a cigarette, and leaves the house. He comes downstage into a golden pool of light. He smokes, staring at the night.*

1640 **WILLY:** Like a young god. Hercules—something like that. And the sun, the sun all around him. Remember how he waved to me? Right up from the field, with the representatives of three colleges standing by? And the buyers I brought, and the cheers when he came out—
1645 Loman, Loman, Loman! God Almighty, he'll be great yet. A star like that, magnificent, can never really fade away!

The light on WILLY *is fading. The gas heater begins to glow through the kitchen wall, near the stairs, a blue flame beneath red coils.*

LINDA: *(timidly)* Willy, dear, what has he got against you?

1650 **WILLY:** I'm so tired. Don't talk any more.

BIFF *slowly returns to the kitchen. He stops, stares toward the heater.*

LINDA: Will you ask Howard to let you work in New York?

WILLY: First thing in the morning. Everything'll be all right.

BIFF *reaches behind the heater and draws out a length of rubber tubing. He is horrified and turns his head toward* WILLY's *room, still dimly lit, from which the strains of* LINDA's *desperate but monotonous humming rise.*

1655 **WILLY:** *(staring through the window into the moonlight)* Gee, look at the moon moving between the buildings!

BIFF *wraps the tubing around his hand and quickly goes up the stairs.*

Curtain.

ACT 2

Music is heard, gay and bright. The curtain rises as the music fades away. WILLY, *in shirt sleeves, is sitting at the kitchen table, sipping coffee, his hat in his lap.* LINDA *is filling his cup when she can.*

WILLY: Wonderful coffee. Meal in itself.

LINDA: Can I make you some eggs?

WILLY: No. Take a breath.

LINDA: You look so rested, dear.

WILLY: I slept like a dead one. First time in months. 5 Imagine, sleeping till ten on a Tuesday morning. Boys left nice and early, heh?

LINDA: They were out of here by eight o'clock.

WILLY: Good work!

LINDA: It was so thrilling to see them leaving together. 10 I can't get over the shaving lotion in this house!

WILLY: *(smiling)* Mmm—

LINDA: Biff was very changed this morning. His whole attitude seemed to be hopeful. He couldn't wait to get downtown to see Oliver. 15

WILLY: He's heading for a change. There's no question, there simply are certain men that take longer to get—solidified. How did he dress?

LINDA: His blue suit. He's so handsome in that suit. He could be a—anything in that suit! 20

WILLY *gets up from the table.* LINDA *holds his jacket for him.*

WILLY: There's no question, no question at all. Gee, on the way home tonight I'd like to buy some seeds.

LINDA: *(laughing)* That'd be wonderful. But not enough sun gets back there. Nothing'll grow any more.

WILLY: You wait, kid, before it's all over we're gonna get 25 a little place out in the country, and I'll raise some vegetables, a couple of chickens . . .

LINDA: You'll do it yet, dear.

Linda helps Willy into his coat.

WILLY *walks out of his jacket.* LINDA *follows him.*

30 **WILLY:** And they'll get married, and come for a week end. I'd build a little guest house. 'Cause I got so many fine tools, all I'd need would be a little lumber and some peace of mind.

LINDA: *(joyfully)* I sewed the lining . . .

35 **WILLY:** I could build two guest houses, so they'd both come. Did he decide how much he's going to ask Oliver for?

LINDA: *(getting him into the jacket)* He didn't mention it, but I imagine ten or fifteen thousand. You going to talk to Howard today?

40 **WILLY:** Yeah. I'll put it to him straight and simple. He'll just have to take me off the road.

LINDA: And Willy, don't forget to ask for a little advance, because we've got the insurance premium. It's the grace period now.

45 **WILLY:** That's a hundred . . . ?

LINDA: A hundred and eight, sixty-eight. Because we're a little short again.

WILLY: Why are we short?

LINDA: Well, you had the motor job on the car . . .

50 **WILLY:** That goddam Studebaker!

LINDA: And you got one more payment on the refrigerator . . .

WILLY: But it just broke again!

LINDA: Well, it's old, dear.

55 **WILLY:** I told you we should've bought a well-advertised machine. Charley bought a General Electric and it's twenty years old and it's still good, that son-of-a-bitch.

LINDA: But, Willy—

WILLY: Whoever heard of a Hastings refrigerator? Once in my life I would like to own something outright 60 before it's broken! I'm always in a race with the junkyard! I just finished paying for the car and it's on its last legs. The refrigerator consumes belts like a goddam maniac. They time those things. They time them so when you finally paid for them, they're used up. 65

LINDA: *(buttoning up his jacket as he unbuttons it)* All told, about two hundred dollars would carry us, dear. But that includes the last payment on the mortgage. After this payment, Willy, the house belongs to us.

WILLY: It's twenty-five years! 70

LINDA: Biff was nine years old when we bought it.

WILLY: Well, that's a great thing. To weather a twenty-five year mortgage is—

LINDA: It's an accomplishment.

WILLY: All the cement, the lumber, the reconstruction I 75 put in this house! There ain't a crack to be found in it any more.

LINDA: Well, it served its purpose.

WILLY: What purpose? Some stranger'll come along, move in, and that's that. If only Biff would take this 80 house, and raise a family . . . *(He starts to go.)* Good-by, I'm late.

LINDA: *(suddenly remembering)* Oh, I forgot! You're supposed to meet them for dinner.

WILLY: Me? 85

LINDA: At Frank's Chop House on Forty-eighth near Sixth Avenue.

WILLY: Is that so! How about you?

90 **LINDA:** No, just the three of you. They're gonna blow you to a big meal!

WILLY: Don't say! Who thought of that?

LINDA: Biff came to me this morning, Willy, and he said, "Tell Dad, we want to blow him to a big meal." Be there six o'clock. You and your two boys are going to
95 have dinner.

WILLY: Gee whiz! That's really somethin'. I'm gonna knock Howard for a loop, kid. I'll get an advance, and I'll come home with a New York job. Goddammit, now I'm gonna do it!

100 **LINDA:** Oh, that's the spirit, Willy!

WILLY: I will never get behind a wheel the rest of my life!

LINDA: It's changing, Willy, I can feel it changing!

WILLY: Beyond a question. G'by, I'm late. *(He starts to go*
105 *again.)*

LINDA: *(calling after him as she runs to the kitchen table for a handkerchief)* You got your glasses?

WILLY: *(feels for them, then comes back in)* Yeah, yeah, got my glasses.

110 **LINDA:** *(giving him the handkerchief)* And a handkerchief.

WILLY: Yeah, handkerchief.

LINDA: And your saccharine?

WILLY: Yeah, my saccharine.

115 **LINDA:** Be careful on the subway stairs.

She kisses him, and a silk stocking is seen hanging from her hand. WILLY *notices it.*

WILLY: Will you stop mending stockings? At least while I'm in the house. It gets me nervous. I can't tell you. Please.

LINDA *hides the stocking in her hand as she follows* WILLY *across the forestage in front of the house.*

Willy notices the stocking that Linda is mending.

LINDA: Remember, Frank's Chop House.

WILLY: *(passing the apron)* Maybe beets would grow out there. 120

LINDA: *(laughing)* But you tried so many times.

WILLY: Yeah. Well, don't work hard today. *(He disappears around the right corner of the house.)*

LINDA: Be careful! 125

As WILLY *vanishes,* LINDA *waves to him. Suddenly the phone rings. She runs across the stage and into the kitchen and lifts it.*

LINDA: Hello? Oh, Biff! I'm so glad you called, I just . . . Yes, sure, I just told him. Yes, he'll be there for dinner at six o'clock, I didn't forget. Listen, I was just dying to tell you. You know that little rubber pipe I told you about? That he connected to the gas heater? I finally 130 decided to go down the cellar this morning and take it away and destroy it. But it's gone! Imagine? He took it away himself, it isn't there! *(She listens.)* When? Oh, then you took it. Oh—nothing, it's just that I'd hoped he'd taken it away himself. Oh, I'm not worried, dar- 135 ling, because this morning he left in such high spirits, it was like the old days! I'm not afraid any more. Did Mr. Oliver see you? . . . Well, you wait there then. And make a nice impression on him, darling. Just don't perspire too much before you see him. And have a 140 nice time with Dad. He may have big news too! . . . That's right, a New York job. And be sweet to him tonight, dear. Be loving to him. Because he's only a little boat looking for a harbor. *(She is trembling with sorrow and joy.)* Oh, that's wonderful, Biff, you'll save his life. Thanks, darling. Just put your arm around him when he comes into the restaurant. Give him a smile. That's the boy . . . Good-by, dear. . . . You got your comb? . . . That's fine. Good-by, Biff dear.

In the middle of her speech, HOWARD WAGNER, *thirty-six, wheels in a small typewriter table on which is a wire-recording machine and proceeds to plug it in. This is on the left forestage. Light slowly fades on* LINDA *as it rises on* HOWARD. HOWARD *is intent on threading the machine and only glances over his shoulder as* WILLY *appears.*

WILLY: Pst! Pst!

HOWARD: Hello, Willy, come in.

WILLY: Like to have a little talk with you, Howard.

HOWARD: Sorry to keep you waiting. I'll be with you in a minute.

WILLY: What's that, Howard?

HOWARD: Didn't you ever see one of these? Wire recorder.

WILLY: Oh. Can we talk a minute?

HOWARD: Records things. Just got delivery yesterday. Been driving me crazy, the most terrific machine I ever saw in my life. I was up all night with it.

WILLY: What do you do with it?

HOWARD: I bought it for dictation, but you can do anything with it. Listen to this. I had it home last night. Listen to what I picked up. The first one is my daughter. Get this. *(He flicks the switch and "Roll Out the Barrel" is heard being whistled.)* Listen to that kid whistle.

WILLY: That is lifelike, isn't it?

HOWARD: Seven years old. Get that tone.

WILLY: Ts, ts. Like to ask a little favor if you . . .

The whistling breaks off, and the voice of HOWARD's *daughter is heard.*

HIS DAUGHTER: "Now you, Daddy."

HOWARD: She's crazy for me! *(Again the same song is whistled.)* That's me! Ha! *(He winks.)*

WILLY: You're very good!

The whistling breaks off again. The machine runs silent for a moment.

HOWARD: Sh! Get this now, this is my son.

HIS SON: "The capital of Alabama is Montgomery; the capital of Arizona is Phoenix; the capital of Arkansas is Little Rock; the capital of California is Sacramento . . ." *(and on, and on).*

HOWARD: *(holding up five fingers)* Five years old, Willy!

WILLY: He'll make an announcer some day!

HIS SON: *(continuing)* "The capital . . ."

HOWARD: Get that—alphabetical order! *(The machine breaks off suddenly.)* Wait a minute. The maid kicked the plug out.

WILLY: It certainly is a—

HOWARD: Sh, for God's sake!

HIS SON: "It's nine o'clock, Bulova watch time. So I have to go to sleep."

WILLY: That really is—

HOWARD: Wait a minute! The next is my wife.

They wait.

HOWARD'S VOICE: "Go on, say something." *(Pause.)* "Well, you gonna talk?"

HIS WIFE: "I can't think of anything."

HOWARD'S VOICE: "Well, talk—it's turning."

HIS WIFE: *(shyly, beaten)* "Hello." *(Silence.)* "Oh, Howard, I can't talk into this . . ."

HOWARD: *(snapping the machine off)* That was my wife.

200 **WILLY:** That is a wonderful machine. Can we—

HOWARD: I tell you, Willy, I'm gonna take my camera, and my bandsaw, and all my hobbies, and out they go. This is the most fascinating relaxation I ever found.

WILLY: I think I'll get one myself.

205 **HOWARD:** Sure, they're only a hundred and a half. You can't do without it. Supposing you wanna hear Jack Benny, see? But you can't be at home at that hour. So you tell the maid to turn the radio on when Jack Benny comes on, and this automatically goes on with
210 the radio . . .

WILLY: And when you come home you . . .

HOWARD: You can come home twelve o'clock, one o'clock, any time you like, and you get yourself a Coke and sit yourself down, throw the switch, and there's
215 Jack Benny's program in the middle of the night!

WILLY: I'm definitely going to get one. Because lots of time I'm on the road, and I think to myself, what I must be missing on the radio!

HOWARD: Don't you have a radio in the car?

220 **WILLY:** Well, yeah, but who ever thinks of turning it on?

Howard (Jon Polito) talks to Willy about his job performance.

HOWARD: Say, aren't you supposed to be in Boston?

WILLY: That's what I want to talk to you about, Howard. You got a minute? (*He draws a chair in from the wing.*)

HOWARD: What happened? What're you doing here?

WILLY: Well . . .   225

HOWARD: You didn't crack up again, did you?

WILLY: Oh, no. No . . .

HOWARD: Geez, you had me worried there for a minute. What's the trouble?

WILLY: Well, tell you the truth, Howard. I've come to the   230
decision that I'd rather not travel any more.

HOWARD: Not travel! Well, what'll you do?

WILLY: Remember, Christmas time, when you had the party here? You said you'd try to think of some spot for me here in town.   235

HOWARD: With us?

WILLY: Well, sure.

HOWARD: Oh, yeah, yeah. I remember. Well, I couldn't think of anything for you, Willy.

WILLY: I tell ya, Howard. The kids are all grown up,   240
y'know. I don't need much any more. If I could take home—well, sixty-five dollars a week. I could swing it.

HOWARD: Yeah, but Willy, see I—

WILLY: I tell ya why, Howard. Speaking frankly and between the two of us, y'know—I'm just a little tired.   245

HOWARD: Oh, I could understand that, Willy. But you're a road man, Willy, and we do a road business. We've only got a half-dozen salesmen on the floor here.

WILLY: God knows, Howard, I never asked a favor of any man. But I was with the firm when your father used to   250
carry you in here in his arms.

HOWARD: I know that, Willy, but—

WILLY: Your father came to me the day you were born and asked me what I thought of the name of Howard, may he rest in peace.   255

HOWARD: I appreciate that, Willy, but there just is no spot here for you. If I had a spot I'd slam you right in, but I just don't have a single solitary spot.

He looks for his lighter. WILLY *has picked it up and gives it to him. Pause.*

WILLY: *(with increasing anger)* Howard, all I need to set my table is fifty dollars a week.

HOWARD: But where am I going to put you, kid?

WILLY: Look, it isn't a question of whether I can sell merchandise, is it?

HOWARD: No, but it's a business, kid, and everybody's gotta pull his own weight.

WILLY: *(desperately)* Just let me tell you a story, Howard—

HOWARD: 'Cause you gotta admit, business is business.

WILLY: *(angrily)* Business is definitely business, but just listen for a minute. You don't understand this. When I was a boy—eighteen, nineteen—I was already on the road. And there was a question in my mind as to whether selling had a future for me. Because in those days I had a yearning to go to Alaska. See, there were three gold strikes in one month in Alaska, and I felt like going out. Just for the ride, you might say.

HOWARD: *(barely interested)* Don't say.

WILLY: Oh, yeah, my father lived many years in Alaska. He was an adventurous man. We've got quite a little streak of self-reliance in our family. I thought I'd go out with my older brother and try to locate him, and maybe settle in the North with the old man. And I was almost decided to go, when I met a salesman in the Parker House. His name was Dave Singleman. And he was eighty-four years old, and he'd drummed merchandise in thirty-one states. And old Dave, he'd go up to his room, y'understand, put on his green velvet slippers—I'll never forget—and pick up his phone and call the buyers, and without ever leaving his room, at the age of eighty-four, he made his living. And when I saw that, I realized that selling was the greatest career a man could want. 'Cause what could be more satisfying than to be able to go, at the age of eighty-four, into twenty or thirty different cities, and pick up a phone, and be remembered and loved and helped by so many different people? Do you know? When he died—and by the way he died the death of a salesman, in his green velvet slippers in the smoker of the New York, New Haven, and Hartford, going into Boston—when he died, hundreds of salesmen and buyers were at his funeral. Things were sad on a lotta trains for months after that. *(He stands up.* HOWARD *has not looked at him.)* In those days there was personality in it, Howard. There was respect, and comradeship, and gratitude in it. Today, it's all cut and dried, and there's no chance for bringing friendship to bear—or personality. You see what I mean? They don't know me any more.

HOWARD: *(moving away, to the right)* That's just the thing, Willy.

WILLY: If I had forty dollars a week—that's all I'd need. Forty dollars, Howard.

HOWARD: Kid, I can't take blood from a stone, I—

WILLY: *(desperation is on him now)* Howard, the year Al Smith was nominated, your father came to me and—

HOWARD: *(starting to go off)* I've got to see some people, kid.

WILLY: *(stopping him)* I'm talking about your father! There were promises made across this desk! You mustn't tell me you've got people to see—I put thirty-four years into this firm, Howard, and now I can't pay my insurance! You can't eat the orange and throw the peel away—a man is not a piece of fruit! *(After a pause.)* Now pay attention. Your father—in 1928 I had a big year. I averaged a hundred and seventy dollars a week in commissions.

HOWARD: *(impatiently)* Now, Willy, you never averaged—

WILLY: *(banging his hand on the desk)* I averaged a hundred and seventy dollars a week in the year of 1928! And your father came to me—or rather, I was in the office here—it was right over this desk—and he put his hand on my shoulder—

HOWARD: *(getting up)* You'll have to excuse me, Willy, I
gotta see some people. Pull yourself together. *(Going
out.)* I'll be back in a little while.

On HOWARD's *exit, the light on his chair grows very
bright and strange.*

WILLY: Pull myself together! What the hell did I say
to him? My God, I was yelling at him! How could I?
*(WILLY breaks off, staring at the light, which occu-
pies the chair, animating it. He approaches this chair,
standing across the desk from it.)* Frank, Frank, don't
you remember what you told me that time? How you
put your hand on my shoulder, and Frank . . . (He
leans on the desk and as he speaks the dead man's name
he accidentally switches on the recorder, and instantly:)*

HOWARD'S SON: ". . . of New York is Albany. The
capital of Ohio is Cincinnati, the capital of Rhode
Island is . . ." *(The recitation continues.)*

WILLY: *(leaping away with fright, shouting)* Ha!
Howard! Howard! Howard!

HOWARD: *(rushing in)* What happened?

WILLY: *(pointing at the machine, which continues na-
sally, childishly, with the capital cities)* Shut it off!
Shut it off!

HOWARD: *(pulling the plug out)* Look, Willy . . .

WILLY: *(pressing his hands to his eyes)* I gotta get myself
some coffee. I'll get some coffee . . .

WILLY *starts to walk out.* HOWARD *stops him.*

HOWARD: *(rolling up the cord)* Willy, look . . .

WILLY: I'll go to Boston.

HOWARD: Willy, you can't go to Boston for us.

WILLY: Why can't I go?

HOWARD: I don't want you to represent us. I've been
meaning to tell you for a long time now.

WILLY: Howard, are you firing me?

HOWARD: I think you need a good long rest, Willy.

WILLY: Howard—

HOWARD: And when you feel better, come back, and
we'll see if we can work something out.

WILLY: But I gotta earn money, Howard. I'm in no
position to—

HOWARD: Where are your sons? Why don't your sons
give you a hand?

WILLY: They're working on a very big deal.

HOWARD: This is no time for false pride, Willy. You go
to your sons and you tell them that you're tired. You've
got two great boys haven't you?

WILLY: Oh, no question, no question, but in the meantime . . .

HOWARD: Then that's that, heh?

WILLY: All right, I'll go to Boston tomorrow.

HOWARD: No, no.

WILLY: I can't throw myself on my sons. I'm not a
cripple!

HOWARD: Look, kid, I'm busy this morning.

WILLY: *(grasping HOWARD's arm)* Howard, you've got to
let me go to Boston!

HOWARD: *(hard, keeping himself under control)* I've got
a line of people to see this morning. Sit down, take
five minutes, and pull yourself together, and then go
home, will ya? I need the office, Willy. *(He starts to go,
turns, remembering the recorder, starts to push off the
table holding the recorder.)* Oh, yeah. Whenever you
can this week, stop by and drop off the samples. You'll
feel better, Willy, and then come back and we'll talk.
Pull yourself together, kid, there's people outside.

HOWARD *exits, pushing the table off left.* WILLY
stares into space, exhausted. Now the music is heard—
BEN's *music—first distantly, then closer, closer. As*
WILLY *speaks,* BEN *enters from the right. He carries
valise and umbrella.*

WILLY: Oh, Ben, how did you do it? What is the answer?
Did you wind up the Alaska deal already?

BEN: Doesn't take much time if you know what you're doing. Just a short business trip. Boarding ship in an hour. Wanted to say good-by.

WILLY: Ben, I've got to talk to you.

BEN: *(glancing at his watch)* Haven't the time, William.

WILLY: *(crossing the apron to* BEN*)* Ben, nothing's working out. I don't know what to do.

BEN: Now, look here, William. I've bought timberland in Alaska and I need a man to look after things for me.

WILLY: God, timberland! Me and my boys in those grand outdoors!

BEN: You've a new continent at your doorstep, William. Get out of these cities, they're full of talk and time payments and courts of law. Screw on your fists and you can fight for a fortune up there.

WILLY: Yes, yes! Linda, Linda!

LINDA *enters as of old, with the wash.*

LINDA: Oh, you're back?

BEN: I haven't much time.

WILLY: No, wait! Linda, he's got a proposition for me in Alaska.

LINDA: But you've got—*(To* BEN.*)* He's got a beautiful job here.

WILLY: But in Alaska, kid, I could—

LINDA: You're doing well enough, Willy!

BEN: *(to* LINDA*)* Enough for what, my dear?

LINDA: *(frightened of* BEN *and angry at him)* Don't say those things to him! Enough to be Happy right here, right now. *(To* WILLY, *while* BEN *laughs.)* Why must everybody conquer the world? You're well liked, and the boys love you, and someday—*(to* BEN*)*—why, old man Wagner told him just the other day that if he keeps it up he'll be a member of the firm, didn't he, Willy?

WILLY: Sure, sure. I am building something with this firm, Ben, and if a man is building something he must be on the right track, mustn't he?

Willy and Linda react to Ben's Alaska proposition.

BEN: What are you building? Lay your hand on it. Where is it?

WILLY: *(hesitantly)* That's true, Linda, there's nothing.

LINDA: Why? *(To* BEN.*)* There's a man eighty-four years old—

WILLY: That's right, Ben, that's right. When I look at that man I say, what is there to worry about?

BEN: Bah!

WILLY: It's true, Ben. All he has to do is go into any city, pick up the phone, and he's making his living and you know why?

BEN: *(picking up his valise)* I've got to go.

WILLY: *(holding* BEN *back)* Look at this boy!

BIFF, *in his high school sweater, enters carrying suitcase.* HAPPY *carries* BIFF's *shoulder guards, gold helmet, and football pants.*

WILLY: Without a penny to his name, three great universities are begging for him, and from there the sky's the limit, because it's not what you do, Ben. It's who you know and the smile on your face! It's contacts, Ben, contacts! The whole wealth of Alaska passes over the lunch table at the Commodore Hotel, and that's the wonder, the wonder of this country, that a man can end with diamonds here on the basis of being liked! (*He turns to* BIFF.) And that's why when you get out on that field today it's important. Because thousands of people will be rooting for you and loving you. (*To* BEN, *who has again begun to leave.*) And Ben! when he walks into a business office his name will sound out like a bell and all the doors will open to him! I've seen it, Ben, I've seen it a thousand times! You can't feel it with your hand like timber, but it's there!

BEN: Good-by, William.

WILLY: Ben, am I right? Don't you think I'm right? I value your advice.

BEN: There's a new continent at your doorstep, William. You could walk out rich. Rich! (*He is gone.*)

WILLY: We'll do it here, Ben! You hear me? We're gonna do it here!

Young BERNARD *rushes in. The gay music of the Boys is heard.*

BERNARD: Oh, gee, I was afraid you left already!

WILLY: Why? What time is it?

BERNARD: It's half-past one!

WILLY: Well, come on, everybody! Ebbets Field next stop! Where's the pennants? (*He rushes through the wall-line of the kitchen and out into the living-room.*)

LINDA: (*to* BIFF) Did you pack fresh underwear?

BIFF: (*who has been limbering up*) I want to go!

BERNARD: Biff, I'm carrying your helmet, ain't I?

HAPPY: I'm carrying the helmet.

BERNARD: How am I going to get in the locker room?

LINDA: Let him carry the shoulder guards. (*She puts her coat and hat on in the kitchen.*)

BERNARD: Can I, Biff? 'Cause I told everybody I'm going to be in the locker room.

HAPPY: In Ebbets Field it's the clubhouse.

BERNARD: I meant the clubhouse. Biff!

HAPPY: Biff!

BIFF: (*grandly, after a slight pause*) Let him carry the shoulder guards.

HAPPY: (*as he gives* BERNARD *the shoulder guards*) Stay close to us now.

WILLY *rushes in with the pennants.*

WILLY: (*handing them out*) Everybody wave when Biff comes out on the field. (HAPPY *and* BERNARD *run off.*) You set now, boy?

The music has died away.

BIFF: Ready to go, Pop. Every muscle is ready.

WILLY: (*at the edge of the apron*) You realize what this means?

BIFF: That's right, Pop.

WILLY: (*feeling* BIFF's *muscles*) You're comin' home this afternoon captain of the All-Scholastic Championship Team of the City of New York.

BIFF: I got it, Pop. And remember, pal, when I take off my helmet, that touchdown is for you.

WILLY: Let's go! (*He is starting out, with his arm around* BIFF, *when* CHARLEY *enters, as of old, in knickers.*) I got no room for you, Charley.

CHARLEY: Room? For what?

WILLY: In the car.

CHARLEY: You goin' for a ride? I wanted to shoot some casino.

WILLY: (*furiously*) Casino! (*Incredulously.*) Don't you realize what today is?

LINDA: Oh, he knows, Willy. He's just kidding you.

WILLY: That's nothing to kid about!

CHARLEY: No, Linda, what's goin' on?

LINDA: He's playing in Ebbets Field.

CHARLEY: Baseball in this weather?

520 WILLY: Don't talk to him. Come on, come on! (*He is pushing them out.*)

CHARLEY: Wait a minute, didn't you hear the news?

WILLY: What?

CHARLEY: Don't you listen to the radio? Ebbets Field just blew up.

525 WILLY: You go to hell! (CHARLEY *laughs. Pushing them out.*) Come on, come on! We're late.

CHARLEY: (*as they go*) Knock a homer, Biff, knock a homer!

WILLY: (*the last to leave, turning to* CHARLEY) I don't
530 think that was funny, Charley. This is the greatest day of his life.

CHARLEY: Willy, when are you going to grow up?

WILLY: Yeah, heh? When this game is over, Charley, you'll be laughing out of the other side of your face.
535 They'll be calling him another Red Grange. Twenty-five thousand a year.

CHARLEY: (*kidding*) Is that so?

WILLY: Yeah, that's so.

CHARLEY: Well, then, I'm sorry, Willy. But tell me
540 something.

WILLY: What?

CHARLEY: Who is Red Grange?

WILLY: Put up your hands. Goddam you, put up your hands!

CHARLEY, *chuckling, shakes his head and walks away, around the left corner of the stage.* WILLY *follows him. The music rises to a mocking frenzy.*

545 WILLY: Who the hell do you think you are, better than everybody else? You don't know everything, you big, ignorant, stupid . . . Put up your hands!

Light rises, on the right side of the forestage, on a small table in the reception room of CHARLEY's *office. Traffic sounds are heard.* BERNARD, *now mature, sits*
whistling to himself. A pair of tennis rackets and an overnight bag are on the floor beside him.*

WILLY: (*offstage*) What are you walking away for? Don't
walk away! If you're going to say something say it to
my face. I know you laugh at me behind my back. 550
You'll laugh out of the other side of your goddam face
after this game. Touchdown! Touchdown! Eighty
thousand people! Touchdown! Right between the goal
posts.

BERNARD *is a quiet, earnest, but self-assured young
man.* WILLY's *voice is coming from right upstage
now.* BERNARD *lowers his feet off the table and listens.* JENNY, *his father's secretary, enters.*

JENNY: (*distressed*) Say, Bernard, will you go out in the 555
hall?

BERNARD: What is that noise? Who is it?

JENNY: Mr. Loman. He just got off the elevator.

BERNARD: (*getting up*) Who's he arguing with?

JENNY: Nobody. There's nobody with him. I can't deal 560
with him any more, and your father gets all upset
everytime he comes. I've got a lot of typing to do, and
your father's waiting to sign it. Will you see him?

WILLY: (*entering*) Touchdown! Touch—(*He sees Jenny.*)
Jenny, Jenny, good to see you. How're ya? Workin'? Or 565
still honest?

JENNY: Fine. How've you been feeling?

WILLY: Not much any more, Jenny. Ha, ha! (*He is surprised to see the rackets.*)

BERNARD: Hello, Uncle Willy. 570

WILLY: (*almost shocked*) Bernard! Well, look who's here!
(*He comes quickly, guiltily, to* BERNARD *and warmly
shakes his hand.*)

BERNARD: How are you? Good to see you.

WILLY: What are you doing here? 575

BERNARD: Oh, just stopped by to see Pop. Get off my
feet till my train leaves. I'm going to Washington in a
few minutes.

WILLY: Is he in?

580 **BERNARD:** Yes, he's in his office with the accountant. Sit down.

WILLY: *(sitting down)* What're you going to do in Washington?

BERNARD: Oh, just a case I've got there, Willy.

585 **WILLY:** That so? *(Indicating the rackets.)* You going to play tennis there?

BERNARD: I'm staying with a friend who's got a court.

WILLY: Don't say. His own tennis court. Must be fine people, I bet.

590 **BERNARD:** They are, very nice. Dad tells me Biff's in town.

WILLY: *(with a big smile)* Yeah, Biff's in. Working on a very big deal, Bernard.

BERNARD: What's Biff doing?

595 **WILLY:** Well, he's been doing very big things in the West. But he decided to establish himself here. Very big. We're having dinner. Did I hear your wife had a boy?

BERNARD: That's right. Our second.

WILLY: Two boys! What do you know!

600 **BERNARD:** What kind of a deal has Biff got?

WILLY: Well, Bill Oliver—very big sporting-goods man— he wants Biff very badly. Called him in from the West. Long distance, carte blanche, special deliveries. Your friends have their own private tennis court?

605 **BERNARD:** You still with the old firm, Willy?

WILLY: *(after a pause)* I'm—I'm overjoyed to see how you made the grade, Bernard, overjoyed. It's an encouraging thing to see a young man really—really— Looks very good for Biff—very—*(He breaks off, then.)*
610 Bernard—*(He is so full of emotion, he breaks off again.)*

BERNARD: What is it, Willy?

WILLY: *(small and alone)* What—what's the secret?

BERNARD: What secret?

WILLY: How—how did you? Why didn't he ever catch on?

BERNARD: I wouldn't know that, Willy. 615

WILLY: *(confidentially, desperately)* You were his friend, his boyhood friend. There's something I don't understand about it. His life ended after that Ebbets Field game. From the age of seventeen nothing good ever happened to him. 620

BERNARD: He never trained himself for anything.

WILLY: But he did, he did. After high school he took so many correspondence courses. Radio mechanics; television; God knows what, and never made the slightest mark. 625

BERNARD: *(taking off his glasses)* Willy, do you want to talk candidly?

WILLY: *(rising, faces* BERNARD*)* I regard you as a very brilliant man, Bernard. I value your advice.

BERNARD: Oh, the hell with the advice, Willy. I couldn't 630 advise you. There's just one thing I've always wanted to ask you. When he was supposed to graduate, and the math teacher flunked him—

WILLY: Oh, that son-of-a-bitch ruined his life.

BERNARD: Yeah, but, Willy, all he had to do was go to 635 summer school and make up that subject.

Willy and Bernard puzzle over Biff's decline.

WILLY: That's right, that's right.

BERNARD: Did you tell him not to go to summer school?

WILLY: Me? I begged him to go. I ordered him to go!

640 BERNARD: Then why wouldn't he go?

WILLY: Why? Why! Bernard, that question has been trailing me like a ghost for the last fifteen years. He flunked the subject, and laid down and died like a hammer hit him!

645 BERNARD: Take it easy, kid.

WILLY: Let me talk to you—I got nobody to talk to. Bernard, Bernard, was it my fault? Y'see? It keeps going around in my mind, maybe I did something to him. I got nothing to give him.

650 BERNARD: Don't take it so hard.

WILLY: Why did he lay down? What is the story there? You were his friend!

BERNARD: Willy, I remember, it was June, and our grades came out. And he'd flunked math.

655 WILLY: That son-of-a-bitch!

BERNARD: No, it wasn't right then. Biff just got very angry, I remember, and he was ready to enroll in summer school.

WILLY: (surprised) He was?

660 BERNARD: He wasn't beaten by it at all. But then, Willy, he disappeared from the block for almost a month. And I got the idea that he'd gone up to New England to see you. Did he have a talk with you then?

WILLY stares in silence.

BERNARD: Willy?

665 WILLY: (with a strong edge of resentment in his voice) Yeah, he came to Boston. What about it?

BERNARD: Well, just that when he came back—I'll never forget this, it always mystifies me. Because I'd thought so well of Biff, even though he'd always taken
670 advantage of me. I loved him, Willy, y'know? And he came back after that month and took his sneakers—remember those sneakers with "University of Virginia" printed on them? He was so proud of those, wore them every day. And he took them down in the cellar, and burned them up in the furnace. We had a 675 fist fight. It lasted at least half an hour. Just the two of us, punching each other down the cellar, and crying right through it. I've often thought of how strange it was that I knew he'd given up his life. What happened in Boston, Willy? 680

WILLY looks at him as at an intruder.

BERNARD: I just bring it up because you asked me.

WILLY: (angrily) Nothing. What do you mean, "What happened?" What's that got to do with anything?

BERNARD: Well, don't get sore.

WILLY: What are you trying to do, blame it on me? If a 685 boy lays down is that my fault?

BERNARD: Now, Willy, don't get—

WILLY: Well, don't—don't talk to me that way! What does that mean, "What happened?"

CHARLEY enters. He is in his vest, and he carries a bottle of bourbon.

CHARLEY: Hey, you're going to miss that train. (He 690 waves the bottle.)

BERNARD: Yeah, I'm going. (He takes the bottle.) Thanks, Pop. (He picks up his rackets and bag.) Good-by, Willy, and don't worry about it. You know, "If at first you don't succeed . . ." 695

WILLY: Yes, I believe in that.

BERNARD: But sometimes, Willy, it's better for a man just to walk away.

WILLY: Walk away?

BERNARD: That's right. 700

WILLY: But if you can't walk away?

BERNARD: (after a slight pause) I guess that's when it's tough. (Extending his hand.) Good-by, Willy.

WILLY: (shaking BERNARD's hand) Good-by, boy.

705 **CHARLEY:** *(an arm on* BERNARD's *shoulder)* How do you like this kid? Gonna argue a case in front of the Supreme Court.

BERNARD: *(protesting)* Pop!

WILLY: *(genuinely shocked, pained, and happy)* No! The
710 Supreme Court!

BERNARD: I gotta run. 'By, Dad!

CHARLEY: Knock 'em dead, Bernard!

BERNARD *goes off.*

WILLY: *(as* CHARLEY *takes out his wallet)* The Supreme Court! And he didn't even mention it!

715 **CHARLEY:** *(counting out money on the desk)* He don't have to—he's gonna do it.

WILLY: And you never told him what to do, did you? You never took any interest in him.

CHARLEY: My salvation is that I never took any interest
720 in anything. There's some money—fifty dollars. I got an accountant inside.

WILLY: Charley, look . . . *(With difficulty.)* I got my insurance to pay. If you can manage it—I need a hundred and ten dollars.

CHARLEY *doesn't reply for a moment; merely stops moving.*

725 **WILLY:** I'd draw it from my bank but Linda would know, and I . . .

CHARLEY: Sit down, Willy.

WILLY: *(moving toward the chair)* I'm keeping an account of everything, remember. I'll pay every penny
730 back. *(He sits.)*

CHARLEY: Now listen to me, Willy.

WILLY: I want you to know I appreciate . . .

CHARLEY: *(sitting down on the table)* Willy, what're you doin'? What the hell is goin' on in your head?

735 **WILLY:** Why? I'm simply . . .

CHARLEY: I offered you a job. You can make fifty dollars a week. And I won't send you on the road.

WILLY: I've got a job.

CHARLEY: Without pay? What kind of a job is a job without pay? *(He rises.)* Now, look, kid, enough is 740 enough. I'm no genius but I know when I'm being insulted.

WILLY: Insulted!

CHARLEY: Why don't you want to work for me?

WILLY: What's the matter with you? I've got a job. 745

CHARLEY: Then what're you walkin' in here every week for?

WILLY: *(getting up)* Well, if you don't want me to walk in here—

CHARLEY: I am offering you a job. 750

WILLY: I don't want your goddam job!

CHARLEY: When the hell are you going to grow up?

WILLY: *(furiously)* You big ignoramus, if you say that to me again I'll rap you one! I don't care how big you are! *(He's ready to fight.)* 755

Pause.

CHARLEY: *(kindly, going to him)* How much do you need, Willy?

WILLY: Charley, I'm strapped. I'm strapped. I don't know what to do. I was just fired.

CHARLEY: Howard fired you? 760

WILLY: That snotnose. Imagine that? I named him. I named him Howard.

CHARLEY: Willy, when're you gonna realize that them things don't mean anything? You named him Howard, but you can't sell that. The only thing you got in 765 this world is what you can sell. And the funny thing is that you're a salesman, and you don't know that.

WILLY: I've always tried to think otherwise, I guess. I always felt that if a man was impressive, and well liked, that nothing— 770

CHARLEY: Why must everybody like you? Who liked J. P. Morgan? Was he impressive? In a Turkish bath

Charley puts money in Willy's hand.

he'd look like a butcher. But with his pockets on he was very well liked. Now listen, Willy, I know you
775 don't like me, and nobody can say I'm in love with you, but I'll give you a job because—just for the hell of it, put it that way. Now what do you say?

WILLY: I—I just can't work for you, Charley.

CHARLEY: What're you, jealous of me?

780 **WILLY:** I can't work for you, that's all, don't ask me why.

CHARLEY: *(angered, takes out more bills)* You been jealous of me all your life, you damned fool! Here, pay your insurance. *(He puts the money in* WILLY's *hand.)*

WILLY: I'm keeping strict accounts.

785 **CHARLEY:** I've got some work to do. Take care of yourself. And pay your insurance.

WILLY: *(moving to the right)* Funny, y'know? After all the highways, and the trains, and the appointments, and the years, you end up worth more dead than alive.

790 **CHARLEY:** Willy, nobody's worth nothin' dead. *(After a slight pause.)* Did you hear what I said?

WILLY *stands still, dreaming.*

CHARLEY: Willy!

WILLY: Apologize to Bernard for me when you see him. I didn't mean to argue with him. He's a fine boy.

They're all fine boys, and they'll end up big—all of 795 them. Someday they'll all play tennis together. Wish me luck, Charley. He saw Bill Oliver today.

CHARLEY: Good luck.

WILLY: *(on the verge of tears)* Charley, you're the only friend I got. Isn't that a remarkable thing? *(He goes* 800 *out.)*

CHARLEY: Jesus!

CHARLEY *stares after him a moment and follows. All light blacks out. Suddenly raucous music is heard, and a red glow rises behind the screen at right.* STANLEY, *a young waiter, appears, carrying a table, followed by* HAPPY, *who is carrying two chairs.*

STANLEY: *(putting the table down)* That's all right, Mr. Loman, I can handle it myself. *(He turns and takes the chairs from* HAPPY *and places them at the table.)* 805

HAPPY: *(glancing around)* Oh, this is better.

STANLEY: Sure, in the front there you're in the middle of all kinds a noise. Whenever you got a party, Mr. Loman, you just tell me and I'll put you back here. Y'know, there's a lotta people they don't like it pri- 810 vate, because when they go out they like to see a lotta action around them because they're sick and tired to stay in the house by theirself. But I know you, you ain't from Hackensack. You know what I mean?

HAPPY: *(sitting down)* So how's it coming, Stanley? 815

STANLEY: Ah, it's a dog's life. I only wish during the war they'd a took me in the Army. I coulda been dead by now.

HAPPY: My brother's back, Stanley.

STANLEY: Oh, he come back, heh? From the Far West. 820

HAPPY: Yeah, big cattle man, my brother, so treat him right. And my father's coming too.

STANLEY: Oh, your father too!

HAPPY: You got a couple of nice lobsters?

STANLEY: Hundred per cent, big. 825

HAPPY: I want them with the claws.

STANLEY: Don't worry, I don't give you no mice. *(HAPPY laughs.)* How about some wine? It'll put a head on the meal.

830 **HAPPY:** No. You remember, Stanley, that recipe I brought you from overseas? With the champagne in it?

STANLEY: Oh, yeah, sure. I still got it tacked up yet in the kitchen. But that'll have to cost a buck apiece

835 anyways.

HAPPY: That's all right.

STANLEY: What'd you, hit a number or somethin'?

HAPPY: No, it's a little celebration. My brother is—I think he pulled off a big deal today. I think we're

840 going into business together.

STANLEY: Great! That's the best for you. Because a family business, you know what I mean?—that's the best.

HAPPY: That's what I think.

STANLEY: 'Cause what's the difference? Somebody

845 steals? It's in the family. Know what I mean? *(Sotto voce.)* Like this bartender here. The boss is goin' crazy what kinda leak he's got in the cash register. You put it in but it don't come out.

HAPPY: *(raising his head)* Sh!

850 **STANLEY:** What?

HAPPY: You notice I wasn't lookin' right or left, was I?

STANLEY: No.

HAPPY: And my eyes are closed.

STANLEY: So what's the—?

855 **HAPPY:** Strudel's comin'.

STANLEY: *(catching on, looks around)* Ah, no, there's no—

He breaks off as a furred, lavishly dressed GIRL enters and sits at the next table. Both follow her with their eyes.

STANLEY: Geez, how'd ya know?

HAPPY: I got radar or something. *(Staring directly at her profile.)* Ooooooooo . . . Stanley. 860

STANLEY: I think that's for you, Mr. Loman.

HAPPY: Look at that mouth. Oh, God. And the binoculars.

STANLEY: Geez, you got a life, Mr. Loman.

HAPPY: Wait on her. 865

STANLEY: *(going to the GIRL's table)* Would you like a menu, ma'am?

GIRL: I'm expecting someone, but I'd like a—

HAPPY: Why don't you bring her—excuse me, miss, do you mind? I sell champagne, and I'd like you to try my 870 brand. Bring her a champagne, Stanley.

GIRL: That's awfully nice of you.

HAPPY: Don't mention it. It's all company money. *(He laughs.)*

GIRL: That's a charming product to be selling, isn't it? 875

HAPPY: Oh, gets to be like everything else. Selling is selling, y'know.

GIRL: I suppose.

HAPPY: You don't happen to sell, do you?

GIRL: No, I don't sell. 880

HAPPY: Would you object to a compliment from a stranger? You ought to be on a magazine cover.

GIRL: *(looking at him a little archly)* I have been.

STANLEY comes in with a glass of champagne.

HAPPY: What'd I say before, Stanley? You see? She's a cover girl. 885

STANLEY: Oh, I could see, I could see.

HAPPY: *(to the GIRL)* What magazine?

GIRL: Oh, a lot of them. *(She takes the drink.)* Thank you.

HAPPY: You know what they say in France, don't you? "Champagne is the drink of the complexion"—Hya, 890 Biff!

BIFF *has entered and sits with* HAPPY.

BIFF: Hello, kid. Sorry I'm late.

HAPPY: I just got here. Uh, Miss—?

GIRL: Forsythe.

895 **HAPPY:** Miss Forsythe, this is my brother.

BIFF: Is Dad here?

HAPPY: His name is Biff. You might've heard of him. Great football player.

GIRL: Really? What team?

900 **HAPPY:** Are you familiar with football?

GIRL: No, I'm afraid I'm not.

HAPPY: Biff is quarterback with the New York Giants.

GIRL: Well, that is nice, isn't it? *(She drinks.)*

HAPPY: Good health.

905 **GIRL:** I'm happy to meet you.

HAPPY: That's my name. Hap. It's really Harold, but at West Point they called me Happy.

GIRL: *(now really impressed)* Oh, I see. How do you do? *(She turns her profile.)*

910 **BIFF:** Isn't Dad coming?

HAPPY: You want her?

BIFF: Oh, I could never make that.

HAPPY: I remember the time that idea would never come into your head. Where's the old confidence, Biff?

915 **BIFF:** I just saw Oliver—

HAPPY: Wait a minute. I've got to see that old confidence again. Do you want her? She's on call.

BIFF: Oh, no. *(He turns to look at the* GIRL.*)*

HAPPY: I'm telling you. Watch this. *(Turning to the* GIRL.*)* Honey? *(She turns to him.)* Are you busy?

920

GIRL: Well, I am . . . but I could make a phone call.

HAPPY: Do that, will you, honey? And see if you can get a friend. We'll be here for a while. Biff is one of the greatest football players in the country.

GIRL: *(standing up)* Well, I'm certainly happy to meet you. 925

HAPPY: Come back soon.

GIRL: I'll try.

HAPPY: Don't try, honey, try hard.

The GIRL *exits.* STANLEY *follows, shaking his head in bewildered admiration.*

HAPPY: Isn't that a shame now? A beautiful girl like 930 that? That's why I can't get married. There's not a good woman in a thousand. New York is loaded with them, kid!

BIFF: Hap, look—

HAPPY: I told you she was on call! 935

BIFF: *(strangely unnerved)* Cut it out, will ya? I want to say something to you.

HAPPY: Did you see Oliver?

Willy and Happy celebrate at Stanley's (Tom Signorelli) restaurant.

940 **BIFF:** I saw him all right. Now look, I want to tell Dad a couple of things and I want you to help me.

HAPPY: What? Is he going to back you?

BIFF: Are you crazy? You're out of your goddam head, you know that?

HAPPY: Why? What happened?

945 **BIFF:** *(breathlessly)* I did a terrible thing today, Hap. It's been the strangest day I ever went through. I'm all numb, I swear.

HAPPY: You mean he wouldn't see you?

BIFF: Well, I waited six hours for him, see? All day. Kept
950 sending my name in. Even tried to date his secretary so she'd get me to him, but no soap.

HAPPY: Because you're not showin' the old confidence, Biff. He remembered you, didn't he?

BIFF: *(stopping* HAPPY *with a gesture)* Finally, about five
955 o'clock, he comes out. Didn't remember who I was or anything. I felt like such an idiot, Hap.

HAPPY: Did you tell him my Florida idea?

BIFF: He walked away. I saw him for one minute. I got so mad I could've torn the walls down! How the hell
960 did I ever get the idea I was a salesman there? I even believed myself that I'd been a salesman for him! And then he gave me one look and—I realized what a ridiculous lie my whole life has been! We've been talk-ing in a dream for fifteen years. I was a shipping clerk.

965 **HAPPY:** What'd you do?

BIFF: *(with great tension and wonder)* Well, he left, see. And the secretary went out. I was all alone in the waiting-room. I don't know what came over me, Hap. The next thing I know I'm in his office—paneled
970 walls, everything. I can't explain it. I—Hap, I took his fountain pen.

HAPPY: Geez, did he catch you?

BIFF: I ran out. I ran down all eleven flights. I ran and ran and ran.

975 **HAPPY:** That was an awful dumb—what'd you do that for?

BIFF: *(agonized)* I don't know, I just—wanted to take something, I don't know. You gotta help me, Hap, I'm gonna tell Pop.

HAPPY: You crazy? What for? 980

BIFF: Hap, he's got to understand that I'm not the man somebody lends that kind of money to. He thinks I've been spiting him all these years and it's eating him up.

HAPPY: That's just it. You tell him something nice.

BIFF: I can't. 985

HAPPY: Say you got a lunch date with Oliver tomorrow.

BIFF: So what do I do tomorrow?

HAPPY: You leave the house tomorrow and come back at night and say Oliver is thinking it over. And he thinks it over for a couple of weeks, and gradually it fades 990 away and nobody's the worse.

BIFF: But it'll go on forever!

HAPPY: Dad is never so happy as when he's looking forward to something!

WILLY enters.

HAPPY: Hello, scout! 995

WILLY: Gee, I haven't been here in years!

STANLEY has followed WILLY in and sets a chair for him. STANLEY starts off but HAPPY stops him.

HAPPY: Stanley!

STANLEY stands by, waiting for an order.

BIFF: *(going to WILLY with guilt, as to an invalid)* Sit down, Pop. You want a drink?

WILLY: Sure, I don't mind. 1000

BIFF: Let's get a load on.

WILLY: You look worried.

BIFF: N-no. *(To STANLEY.)* Scotch all around. Make it doubles.

STANLEY: Doubles, right. *(He goes.)* 1005

Willy and Biff argue about the meeting with Oliver.

WILLY: You had a couple already, didn't you?

BIFF: Just a couple, yeah.

WILLY: Well, what happened, boy? *(Nodding affirmatively, with a smile.)* Everything go all right?

1010 **BIFF:** *(takes a breath, then reaches out and grasps* WILLY's *hand)* Pal . . . *(He is smiling bravely, and* WILLY *is smiling too.)* I had an experience today.

HAPPY: Terrific, Pop.

WILLY: That so? What happened?

1015 **BIFF:** *(high, slightly alcoholic, above the earth)* I'm going to tell you everything from first to last. It's been a strange day. *(Silence. He looks around, composes himself as best he can, but his breath keeps breaking the rhythm of his voice.)* I had to wait quite a while for

1020 him, and—

WILLY: Oliver.

BIFF: Yeah, Oliver. All day, as a matter of cold fact. And a lot of—instances—facts, Pop, facts about my life came back to me. Who was it, Pop? Who ever said I was a

1025 salesman with Oliver?

WILLY: Well, you were.

BIFF: No, Dad, I was a shipping clerk.

WILLY: But you were practically—

BIFF: *(with determination)* Dad, I don't know who said it first, but I was never a salesman for Bill Oliver. 1030

WILLY: What're you talking about?

BIFF: Let's hold on to the facts tonight, Pop. We're not going to get anywhere bullin' around. I was a shipping clerk.

WILLY: *(angrily)* All right, now listen to me— 1035

BIFF: Why don't you let me finish?

WILLY: I'm not interested in stories about the past or any crap of that kind because the woods are burning, boys, you understand? There's a big blaze going on all around. I was fired today. 1040

BIFF: *(shocked)* How could you be?

WILLY: I was fired, and I'm looking for a little good news to tell your mother, because the woman has waited and the woman has suffered. The gist of it is that I haven't got a story left in my head, Biff. So don't give 1045 me a lecture about facts and aspects. I am not interested. Now what've you got to say to me?

STANLEY *enters with three drinks. They wait until he leaves.*

WILLY: Did you see Oliver?

BIFF: Jesus, Dad!

WILLY: You mean you didn't go up there? 1050

HAPPY: Sure he went up there.

BIFF: I did. I—saw him. How could they fire you?

WILLY: *(on the edge of his chair)* What kind of a welcome did he give you?

BIFF: He won't even let you work on commission? 1055

WILLY: I'm out! *(Driving.)* So tell me, he gave you a warm welcome?

HAPPY: Sure, Pop, sure!

BIFF: *(driven)* Well, it was kind of—

WILLY: I was wondering if he'd remember you. *(To* 1060 HAPPY.*)* Imagine, man doesn't see him for ten, twelve years and gives him that kind of a welcome!

HAPPY: Damn right!

BIFF: *(trying to return to the offensive)* Pop, look—

1065 **WILLY:** You know why he remembered you, don't you? Because you impressed him in those days.

BIFF: Let's talk quietly and get this down to the facts, huh?

WILLY: *(as though* BIFF *had been interrupting)* Well,
1070 what happened? It's great news, Biff. Did he take you into his office or'd you talk in the waiting-room?

BIFF: Well, he came in, see, and—

WILLY: *(with a big smile)* What'd he say? Betcha he threw his arm around you.

1075 **BIFF:** Well, he kinda—

WILLY: He's a fine man. *(To* HAPPY.*)* Very hard man to see, y'know.

HAPPY: *(agreeing)* Oh, I know.

WILLY: *(to* BIFF*)* Is that where you had the drinks?

1080 **BIFF:** Yeah, he gave me a couple of—no, no!

HAPPY: *(cutting in)* He told him my Florida idea.

WILLY: Don't interrupt. *(To* BIFF.*)* How'd he react to the Florida idea?

BIFF: Dad, will you give me a minute to explain?

1085 **WILLY:** I've been waiting for you to explain since I sat down here! What happened? He took you into his office and what?

BIFF: Well—I talked. And—and he listened, see.

WILLY: Famous for the way he listens, y'know. What was
1090 his answer?

BIFF: His answer was—*(He breaks off, suddenly angry.)* Dad, you're not letting me tell you what I want to tell you!

WILLY: *(accusing, angered)* You didn't see him, did you?

1095 **BIFF:** I did see him!

WILLY: What'd you insult him or something? You insulted him, didn't you?

Willy remembers receiving the news of Biff's flunking math.

BIFF: Listen, will you let me out of it, will you just let me out of it!

HAPPY: What the hell! 1100

WILLY: Tell me what happened!

BIFF: *(to* HAPPY*)* I can't talk to him!

A single trumpet note jars the ear. The light of green leaves stains the house, which holds the air of night and a dream. Young BERNARD *enters and knocks on the door of the house.*

YOUNG BERNARD: *(frantically)* Mrs. Loman, Mrs. Loman!

HAPPY: Tell him what happened! 1105

BIFF: *(to* HAPPY*)* Shut up and leave me alone!

WILLY: No, no! You had to go and flunk math!

BIFF: What math? What're you talking about?

YOUNG BERNARD: Mrs. Loman, Mrs. Loman!

LINDA *appears in the house, as of old.*

WILLY: *(wildly)* Math, math, math! 1110

BIFF: Take it easy, Pop!

YOUNG BERNARD: Mrs. Loman!

WILLY: (*furiously*) If you hadn't flunked you'd've been set by now!

1115 **BIFF:** Now, look, I'm gonna tell you what happened, and you're going to listen to me.

YOUNG BERNARD: Mrs. Loman!

BIFF: I waited six hours—

HAPPY: What the hell are you saying?

1120 **BIFF:** I kept sending in my name but he wouldn't see me. So finally he . . . (*He continues unheard as light fades low on the restaurant.*)

YOUNG BERNARD: Biff flunked math!

LINDA: No!

1125 **YOUNG BERNARD:** Birnbaum flunked him! They won't graduate him!

LINDA: But they have to. He's gotta go to the university. Where is he? Biff! Biff!

YOUNG BERNARD: No, he left. He went to Grand
1130 Central.

LINDA: Grand—You mean he went to Boston!

YOUNG BERNARD: Is Uncle Willy in Boston?

LINDA: Oh, maybe Willy can talk to the teacher. Oh, the poor, poor boy!

Light on house area snaps out.

1135 **BIFF:** (*at the table, now audible, holding up a gold fountain pen*) . . . so I'm washed up with Oliver, you understand? Are you listening to me?

WILLY: (*at a loss*) Yeah, sure. If you hadn't flunked—

BIFF: Flunked what? What're you talking about?

1140 **WILLY:** Don't blame everything on me! I didn't flunk math—you did! What pen?

HAPPY: That was awful dumb, Biff, a pen like that is worth—

WILLY: (*seeing the pen for the first time*) You took Oliver's
1145 pen?

BIFF: (*weakening*) Dad, I just explained it to you.

WILLY: You stole Bill Oliver's fountain pen!

BIFF: I didn't exactly steal it! That's just what I've been explaining to you!

HAPPY: He had it in his hand and just then Oliver   1150
walked in, so he got nervous and stuck it in his pocket!

WILLY: My God, Biff!

BIFF: I never intended to do it, Dad!

OPERATOR'S VOICE: Standish Arms, good evening!   1155

WILLY: (*shouting*) I'm not in my room!

BIFF: (*frightened*) Dad, what's the matter? (*He and HAPPY stand up.*)

OPERATOR: Ringing Mr. Loman for you!

WILLY: I'm not there, stop it!   1160

BIFF: (*horrified, gets down on one knee before WILLY*) Dad, I'll make good, I'll make good. (WILLY *tries to get to his feet.* BIFF *holds him down.*) Sit down now.

WILLY: No, you're no good, you're no good for anything.

BIFF: I am, Dad, I'll find something else, you under-   1165
stand? Now don't worry about anything. (*He holds up WILLY's face.*) Talk to me, Dad.

OPERATOR: Mr. Loman does not answer. Shall I page him?

WILLY: (*attempting to stand, as though to rush and   1170
silence the OPERATOR*) No, no, no!

HAPPY: He'll strike something, Pop.

WILLY: No, no . . .

BIFF: (*desperately, standing over WILLY*) Pop, listen! Listen to me! I'm telling you something good. Oliver   1175
talked to his partner about the Florida idea. You listening? He—he talked to his partner, and he came to me . . . I'm going to be all right, you hear? Dad, listen to me, he said it was just a question of the amount!

WILLY: Then you . . . got it?   1180

HAPPY: He's gonna be terrific, Pop!

WILLY: (*trying to stand*) Then you got it, haven't you? You got it! You got it!

BIFF: (*agonized, holds* WILLY *down*) No, no. Look, Pop. I'm supposed to have lunch with them tomorrow. I'm just telling you this so you'll know that I can still make an impression, Pop. And I'll make good somewhere, but I can't go tomorrow, see?

WILLY: Why not? You simply—

BIFF: But the pen, Pop!

WILLY: You give it to him and tell him it was an oversight!

HAPPY: Sure, have lunch tomorrow!

BIFF: I can't say that—

WILLY: You were doing a crossword puzzle and accidentally used his pen!

BIFF: Listen, kid, I took those balls years ago, now I walk in with his fountain pen? That clinches it, don't you see? I can't face him like that! I'll try elsewhere.

PAGE'S VOICE: Paging Mr. Loman!

WILLY: Don't you want to be anything?

BIFF: Pop, how can I go back?

WILLY: You don't want to be anything, is that what's behind it?

BIFF: (*now angry at* WILLY *for not crediting his sympathy*) Don't take it that way! You think it was easy walking into that office after what I'd done to him? A team of horses couldn't have dragged me back to Bill Oliver!

WILLY: Then why'd you go?

BIFF: Why did I go? Why did I go! Look at you! Look at what's become of you!

Off left, THE WOMAN *laughs.*

WILLY: Biff, you're going to go to that lunch tomorrow, or—

BIFF: I can't go. I've got no appointment!

HAPPY: Biff, for . . . !

WILLY: Are you spiting me?

BIFF: Don't take it that way! Goddammit!

WILLY: (*strikes* BIFF *and falters away from the table*) You rotten little louse! Are you spiting me?

THE WOMAN: Someone's at the door, Willy!

BIFF: I'm no good, can't you see what I am?

HAPPY: (*separating them*) Hey, you're in a restaurant! Now cut it out, both of you! (*The girls enter.*) Hello, girls, sit down.

THE WOMAN *laughs, off left.*

MISS FORSYTHE: I guess we might as well. This is Letta.

THE WOMAN: Willy, are you going to wake up?

BIFF: (*ignoring* WILLY) How're ya, miss, sit down. What do you drink?

MISS FORSYTHE: Letta might not be able to stay long.

LETTA: I gotta get up very early tomorrow. I got jury duty. I'm so excited! Were you fellows ever on a jury?

BIFF: No, but I been in front of them! (*The girls laugh.*) This is my father.

LETTA: Isn't he cute? Sit down with us, Pop.

HAPPY: Sit him down, Biff!

BIFF: (*going to him*) Come on, slugger, drink us under the table. To hell with it! Come on, sit down, pal.

On BIFF's *last insistence,* WILLY *is about to sit.*

THE WOMAN: (*now urgently*) Willy, are you going to answer the door!

THE WOMAN's *call pulls* WILLY *back. He starts right, befuddled.*

BIFF: Hey, where are you going?

WILLY: Open the door.

BIFF: The door?

1245 **WILLY:** The washroom . . . the door . . . where's the door?

BIFF: (*leading* WILLY *to the left*) Just go straight down.

WILLY *moves left.*

THE WOMAN: Willy, Willy, are you going to get up, get up, get up, get up?

WILLY *exits left.*

LETTA: I think it's sweet you bring your daddy along.

1250 **MISS FORSYTHE:** Oh, he isn't really your father!

BIFF: (*at left, turning to her resentfully*) Miss Forsythe, you've just seen a prince walk by. A fine, troubled prince. A hard-working, unappreciated prince. A pal, you understand? A good companion. Always for his 1255 boys.

LETTA: That's so sweet.

HAPPY: Well, girls, what's the program? We're wasting time. Come on, Biff. Gather round. Where would you like to go?

1260 **BIFF:** Why don't you do something for him?

HAPPY: Me!

BIFF: Don't you give a damn for him, Hap?

HAPPY: What're you talking about? I'm the one who—

BIFF: I sense it, you don't give a good goddam about him. 1265 (*He takes the rolled-up hose from his pocket and puts it on the table in front of* HAPPY.) Look what I found in the cellar, for Christ's sake. How can you bear to let it go on?

HAPPY: Me? Who goes away? Who runs off and—

1270 **BIFF:** Yeah, but he doesn't mean anything to you. You could help him—I can't! Don't you understand what I'm talking about? He's going to kill himself, don't you know that?

HAPPY: Don't I know it! Me!

1275 **BIFF:** Hap, help him! Jesus . . . help him . . . Help me, help me, I can't bear to look at his face! (*Ready to weep, he hurries out, up right.*)

HAPPY: (*starting after him*) Where are you going?

MISS FORSYTHE: What's he so mad about?

HAPPY: Come on, girls, we'll catch up with him. 1280

MISS FORSYTHE: (*as* HAPPY *pushes her out*) Say, I don't like that temper of his!

HAPPY: He's just a little overstrung, he'll be all right!

WILLY: (*off left, as* THE WOMAN *laughs*) Don't answer! Don't answer! 1285

LETTA: Don't you want to tell your father—

HAPPY: No, that's not my father. He's just a guy. Come on, we'll catch Biff, and, honey, we're going to paint this town! Stanley, where's the check! Hey, Stanley!

They exit. STANLEY *looks toward left.*

STANLEY: (*calling to* HAPPY *indignantly*) Mr. Loman! 1290 Mr. Loman!

STANLEY *picks up a chair and follows them off. Knocking is heard off left.* THE WOMAN *enters, laughing.* WILLY *follows her. She is in a black slip; he is buttoning his shirt. Raw, sensuous music accompanies their speech.*

WILLY: Will you stop laughing? Will you stop?

THE WOMAN: Aren't you going to answer the door? He'll wake the whole hotel.

WILLY: I'm not expecting anybody. 1295

THE WOMAN: Whyn't you have another drink, honey, and stop being so damn self-centered?

WILLY: I'm so lonely.

THE WOMAN: You know you ruined me, Willy? From now on, whenever you come to the office, I'll see that 1300 you go right through to the buyers. No waiting at my desk any more, Willy. You ruined me.

WILLY: That's nice of you to say that.

THE WOMAN: Gee, you are self-centered! Why so sad? You are the saddest, self-centeredest soul I ever did 1305 see-saw. (*She laughs. He kisses her.*) Come on inside, drummer boy. It's silly to be dressing in the middle of the night. (*As knocking is heard.*) Aren't you going to answer the door?

1310   **WILLY:**   They're knocking on the wrong door.

THE WOMAN: But I felt the knocking. And he heard us talking in here. Maybe the hotel's on fire!

WILLY: (*his terror rising*) It's a mistake.

THE WOMAN: Then tell him to go away!

1315   **WILLY:**   There's nobody there.

THE WOMAN: It's getting on my nerves, Willy. There's somebody standing out there and it's getting on my nerves!

WILLY: (*pushing her away from him*) All right, stay in
1320   the bathroom here, and don't come out. I think there's a law in Massachusetts about it, so don't come out. It may be that new room clerk. He looked very mean. So don't come out. It's a mistake, there's no fire.

The knocking is heard again. He takes a few steps away from her, and she vanishes into the wing. The light follows him, and now he is facing Young BIFF, *who carries a suitcase.* BIFF *steps toward him. The music is gone.*

BIFF: Why didn't you answer?

1325   **WILLY:**   Biff! What are you doing in Boston?

BIFF: Why didn't you answer? I've been knocking for five minutes, I called you on the phone—

WILLY: I just heard you. I was in the bathroom and had the door shut. Did anything happen home?

1330   **BIFF:**   Dad—I let you down.

WILLY: What do you mean?

BIFF: Dad . . .

WILLY: Biffo, what's this about? (*Putting his arm around* BIFF.) Come on, let's go downstairs and get you a
1335   malted.

BIFF: Dad, I flunked math.

WILLY: Not for the term?

BIFF: The term. I haven't got enough credits to graduate.

WILLY: You mean to say Bernard wouldn't give you the answers?   1340

BIFF: He did, he tried, but I only got a sixty-one.

WILLY: And they wouldn't give you four points?

BIFF: Birnbaum refused absolutely. I begged him, Pop, but he won't give me those points. You gotta talk to him before they close the school. Because if he saw   1345 the kind of man you are, and you just talked to him in your way, I'm sure he'd come through for me. The class came right before practice, see, and I didn't go enough. Would you talk to him? He'd like you, Pop. You know the way you could talk.   1350

WILLY: You're on. We'll drive right back.

BIFF: Oh, Dad, good work! I'm sure he'll change it for you!

WILLY: Go downstairs and tell the clerk I'm checkin' out. Go right down.   1355

BIFF: Yes, sir! See, the reason he hates me, Pop—one day he was late for class so I got up at the blackboard and imitated him. I crossed my eyes and talked with a lithp.

WILLY: (*laughing*) You did? The kids like it?   1360

BIFF: They nearly died laughing!

WILLY: Yeah? What'd you do?

BIFF: The thquare root of thixthy twee is . . . (WILLY *bursts out laughing;* BIFF *joins him.*) And in the middle of it he walked in!   1365

WILLY *laughs and* THE WOMAN *joins in offstage.*

WILLY: (*without hesitation*) Hurry downstairs and—

BIFF: Somebody in there?

WILLY: No, that was next door.

THE WOMAN *laughs offstage.*

BIFF: Somebody got in your bathroom!

1370 **WILLY:**   No, it's the next room, there's a party—

THE WOMAN: *(enters, laughing. She lisps this)* Can I come in? There's something in the bathtub, Willy, and it's moving!

WILLY *looks at* BIFF, *who is staring open-mouthed and horrified at* THE WOMAN.

WILLY: Ah—you better go back to your room. They must
1375   be finished painting by now. They're painting her room so I let her take a shower here. Go back, go back . . . *(He pushes her.)*

THE WOMAN: *(resisting)* But I've got to get dressed, Willy, I can't—

1380 **WILLY:**   Get out of here! Go back, go back . . . *(Suddenly striving for the ordinary):* This is Miss Francis, Biff, she's a buyer. They're painting her room. Go back, Miss Francis, go back . . .

THE WOMAN: But my clothes, I can't go out naked in
1385   the hall!

WILLY: *(pushing her offstage)* Get outa here! Go back, go back!

BIFF *slowly sits down on his suitcase as the argument continues offstage.*

THE WOMAN: Where's my stockings? You promised me stockings, Willy!

1390 **WILLY:**   I have no stockings here!

THE WOMAN: You had two boxes of size nine sheers for me, and I want them!

WILLY: Here, for God's sake, will you get outa here!

THE WOMAN: *(enters holding a box of stockings)* I just
1395   hope there's nobody in the hall. That's all I hope. *(To* BIFF.*)* Are you football or baseball?

BIFF: Football.

THE WOMAN: *(angry, humiliated)* That's me too. G'night. *(She snatches her clothes from* WILLY, *and*
1400   *walks out.)*

WILLY: *(after a pause)* Well, better get going. I want to get to the school first thing in the morning. Get my

Humiliated, The Woman encounters Biff inside the hotel room.

suits out of the closet. I'll get my valise. *(BIFF doesn't move.)* What's the matter? *(BIFF remains motionless, tears falling.)* She's a buyer. Buys for J. H. Simmons. 1405 She lives down the hall—they're painting. You don't imagine—*(He breaks off. After a pause.)* Now listen, pal, she's just a buyer. She sees merchandise in her room and they have to keep it looking just so . . . *(Pause. Assuming command.)* All right, get my suits. 1410 *(BIFF doesn't move.)* Now stop crying and do as I say. I gave you an order. Biff, I gave you an order! Is that what you do when I give you an order? How dare you cry! *(Putting his arm around* BIFF.*)* Now look, Biff, when you grow up you'll understand about these 1415 things. You mustn't—you mustn't overemphasize a thing like this. I'll see Birnbaum first thing in the morning.

BIFF: Never mind.

WILLY: *(getting down beside* BIFF*)* Never mind! He's 1420 going to give you those points. I'll see to it.

BIFF: He wouldn't listen to you.

WILLY: He certainly will listen to me. You need those points for the U. of Virginia.

BIFF: I'm not going there. 1425

WILLY: Heh? If I can't get him to change that mark you'll make it up in summer school. You've got all summer to—

BIFF: *(his weeping breaking from him)* Dad . . .

1430   **WILLY:**   *(infected by it)* Oh, my boy . . .

BIFF: Dad . . .

WILLY: She's nothing to me, Biff. I was lonely, I was terribly lonely.

BIFF: You—you gave her Mama's stockings! *(His tears*
1435   *break through and he rises to go.)*

WILLY: *(grabbing for* BIFF*)* I gave you an order!

BIFF: Don't touch me, you—liar!

WILLY: Apologize for that!

BIFF: You fake! You phony little fake! You fake! *(Over-*
1440   *come, he turns quickly and weeping fully goes out with*
his suitcase. WILLY *is left on the floor on his knees.)*

WILLY: I gave you an order! Biff, come back here or I'll beat you! Come back here! I'll whip you!

STANLEY *comes quickly in from the right and stands*
in front of WILLY.

WILLY: *(shouts at* STANLEY*)* I gave you an order . . .

1445   **STANLEY:**   Hey, let's pick it up, pick it up, Mr. Loman. *(He helps* WILLY *to his feet.)* Your boys left with the chippies. They said they'll see you at home.

A second waiter watches some distance away.

WILLY: But we were supposed to have dinner together.

Music is heard, WILLY*'s theme.*

STANLEY: Can you make it?

1450   **WILLY:**   I'll—sure, I can make it. *(Suddenly concerned about his clothes.)* Do I—I look all right?

STANLEY: Sure, you look all right. *(He flicks a speck off* WILLY*'s lapel.)*

WILLY: Here—here's a dollar.

1455   **STANLEY:**   Oh, your son paid me. It's all right.

WILLY: *(putting it in* STANLEY*'s hand)* No, take it. You're a good boy.

STANLEY: Oh, no, you don't have to . . .

WILLY: Here—here's some more, I don't need it any more. *(After a slight pause.)* Tell me—is there a seed   1460
store in the neighborhood?

STANLEY: Seeds? You mean like to plant?

As WILLY *turns,* STANLEY *slips the money back into*
his jacket pocket.

WILLY: Yes. Carrots, peas . . .

STANLEY: Well, there's hardware stores on Sixth Avenue, but it may be too late now.   1465

WILLY: *(anxiously)* Oh, I'd better hurry. I've got to get some seeds. *(He starts off to the right.)* I've got to get some seeds, right away. Nothing's planted. I don't have a thing in the ground.

WILLY *hurries out as the light goes down.* STANLEY
moves over to the right after him, watches him off. The
other waiter has been staring at WILLY.

STANLEY: *(to the waiter)* Well, whatta you looking at?   1470

The waiter picks up the chairs and moves off right.
STANLEY *takes the table and follows him. The light*
fades on this area. There is a long pause, the sound
of the flute coming over. The light gradually rises on
the kitchen, which is empty. HAPPY *appears at the*
door of the house, followed by BIFF. HAPPY *is carry-*
ing a large bunch of long-stemmed roses. He enters the
kitchen, looks around for LINDA. *Not seeing her, he*
turns to BIFF, *who is just outside the house door, and*
makes a gesture with his hands, indicating "Not here,
I guess." He looks into the living-room and freezes.
Inside, LINDA, *unseen, is seated,* WILLY*'s coat on*
her lap. She rises ominously and quietly and moves
toward HAPPY, *who backs up into the kitchen, afraid.*

HAPPY: Hey, what're you doing up? *(*LINDA *says nothing but moves toward him implacably.)* Where's Pop? *(He keeps backing to the right, and now* LINDA *is in full view in the doorway to the living-room.)* Is he sleeping?

LINDA: Where were you?   1475

Linda scolds her sons for leaving Willy alone at dinner.

HAPPY: *(trying to laugh it off)* We met two girls, Mom, very fine types. Here, we brought you some flowers. *(Offering them to her.)* Put them in your room, Ma.

She knocks them to the floor at BIFF's *feet. He has now come inside and closed the door behind him. She stares at* BIFF, *silent.*

1480 **HAPPY:** Now what'd you do that for? Mom, I want you to have some flowers—

LINDA: *(cutting* HAPPY *off, violently to* BIFF*)* Don't you care whether he lives or dies?

HAPPY: *(going to the stairs)* Come upstairs, Biff.

1485 **BIFF:** *(with a flare of disgust, to* HAPPY*)* Go away from me! *(To* LINDA.*)* What do you mean, lives or dies? Nobody's dying around here, pal.

LINDA: Get out of my sight! Get out of here!

BIFF: I wanna see the boss.

LINDA: You're not going near him!

1490 **BIFF:** Where is he? *(He moves into the living-room and* LINDA *follows.)*

LINDA: *(shouting after* BIFF*)* You invite him for dinner. He looks forward to it all day—*(*BIFF *appears in his parents' bedroom, looks around, and exits.)*—and then

you desert him there. There's no stranger you'd do 1495 that to!

HAPPY: Why? He had a swell time with us. Listen, when I—*(*LINDA *comes back into the kitchen)*—desert him I hope I don't outlive the day!

LINDA: Get out of here! 1500

HAPPY: Now look, Mom . . .

LINDA: Did you have to go to women tonight? You and your lousy rotten whores!

BIFF *re-enters the kitchen.*

HAPPY: Mom, all we did was follow Biff around trying to cheer him up! *(To* BIFF.*)* Boy, what a night you 1505 gave me!

LINDA: Get out of here, both of you, and don't come back! I don't want you tormenting him any more. Go on now, get your things together! *(To* BIFF.*)* You can sleep in his apartment. *(She starts to pick up the flow-* 1510 *ers and stops herself.)* Pick up this stuff, I'm not your maid any more. Pick it up, you bum, you!

HAPPY *turns his back to her in refusal.* BIFF *slowly moves over and gets down on his knees, picking up the flowers.*

LINDA: You're a pair of animals! Not one, not another living soul would have had the cruelty to walk out on that man in a restaurant! 1515

BIFF: *(not looking at her)* Is that what he said?

LINDA: He didn't have to say anything. He was so humiliated he nearly limped when he came in.

HAPPY: But, Mom, he had a great time with us—

BIFF: *(cutting him off violently)* Shut up! 1520

Without another word, HAPPY *goes upstairs.*

LINDA: You! You didn't even go in to see if he was all right!

BIFF: *(still on the floor in front of* LINDA, *the flowers in his hand; with self-loathing)* No. Didn't. Didn't do a damned thing. How do you like that, heh? Left him 1525 babbling in a toilet.

LINDA: You louse. You . . .

BIFF: Now you hit it on the nose! (*He gets up, throws the flowers in the wastebasket.*) The scum of the earth, and 1530 you're looking at him!

LINDA: Get out of here!

BIFF: I gotta talk to the boss, Mom. Where is he?

LINDA: You're not going near him. Get out of this house!

BIFF: (*with absolute assurance, determination*) No. We're 1535 gonna have an abrupt conversation, him and me.

LINDA: You're not talking to him!

Hammering is heard from outside the house, off right. BIFF *turns toward the noise.*

LINDA: (*suddenly pleading*) Will you please leave him alone?

BIFF: What's he doing out there?

1540 **LINDA:** He's planting the garden!

BIFF: (*quietly*) Now? Oh, my God!

BIFF *moves outside,* LINDA *following. The light dies down on them and comes up on the center of the apron as* WILLY *walks into it. He is carrying a flashlight, a hoe, and handful of seed packets. He raps the top of the hoe sharply to fix it firmly, and then moves to the left, measuring off the distance with his foot. He holds the flashlight to look at the seed packets, reading off the instructions. He is in the blue of night.*

WILLY: Carrots . . . quarter-inch apart. Rows . . . one-foot rows. (*He measures it off.*) One foot. (*He puts down a package and measures off.*) Beets. (*He puts* 1545 *down another package and measures again.*) Lettuce. (*He reads the package, puts it down.*) One foot—(*He breaks off as* BEN *appears at the right and moves slowly down to him.*) What a proposition, ts, ts. Terrific, terrific. 'Cause she's suffered, Ben, the woman 1550 has suffered. You understand me? A man can't go out the way he came in, Ben, a man has got to add up to something. You can't, you can't—(BEN *moves toward him as though to interrupt.*) You gotta consider, now. Don't answer so quick. Remember, it's a guaranteed 1555 twenty-thousand-dollar proposition. Now look, Ben,

I want you to go through the ins and outs of this thing with me. I've got nobody to talk to, Ben, and the woman has suffered, you hear me?

BEN: (*standing still, considering*) What's the proposition?

WILLY: It's twenty thousand dollars on the barrelhead. 1560 Guaranteed, gilt-edged, you understand?

BEN: You don't want to make a fool of yourself. They might not honor the policy.

WILLY: How can they dare refuse? Didn't I work like a coolie to meet every premium on the nose? And now 1565 they don't pay off? Impossible!

BEN: It's called a cowardly thing, William.

WILLY: Why? Does it take more guts to stand here the rest of my life ringing up a zero?

BEN: (*yielding*) That's a point, William. (*He moves, think-* 1570 *ing, turns.*) And twenty thousand—that *is* something one can feel with the hand, it is there.

WILLY: (*now assured, with rising power*) Oh, Ben, that's the whole beauty of it! I see it like a diamond, shining in the dark, hard and rough, that I can pick up and 1575 touch in my hand. Not like—like an appointment! This would not be another damned-fool appoint-

Willy discusses his business proposition with Ben.

ment, Ben, and it changes all the aspects. Because he thinks I'm nothing, see, and so he spites me. But the
1580 funeral—*(Straightening up.)* Ben, that funeral will be massive! They'll come from Maine, Massachusetts, Vermont, New Hampshire! All the old-timers with the strange license plates—that boy will be thunderstruck, Ben, because he never realized—I am known!
1585 Rhode Island, New York, New Jersey—I am known, Ben, and he'll see it with his eyes once and for all. He'll see what I am, Ben! He's in for a shock, that boy!

BEN: *(coming down to the edge of the garden)* He'll call you a coward.

1590 **WILLY:** *(suddenly fearful)* No, that would be terrible.

BEN: Yes. And a damned fool.

WILLY: No, no, he mustn't, I won't have that! *(He is broken and desperate.)*

BEN: He'll hate you, William.

The gay music of the Boys is heard.

1595 **WILLY:** Oh, Ben, how do we get back to all the great times? Used to be so full of light, and comradeship, the sleigh-riding in winter, and the ruddiness on his cheeks. And always some kind of good news coming up, always something nice coming up ahead. And
1600 never even let me carry the valises in the house, and simonizing, simonizing that little red car! Why, why can't I give him something and not have him hate me?

BEN: Let me think about it. *(He glances at his watch.)* I still have a little time. Remarkable proposition,
1605 but you've got to be sure you're not making a fool of yourself.

BEN *drifts off upstage and goes out of sight.* BIFF *comes down from the left.*

WILLY: *(suddenly conscious of BIFF, turns and looks up at him, then begins picking up the packages of seeds in confusion)* Where the hell is that seed? *(Indignantly.)*
1610 You can't see nothing out here! They boxed in the whole god-damn neighborhood!

BIFF: There are people all around here. Don't you realize that?

WILLY: I'm busy. Don't bother me.

BIFF: *(taking the hoe from WILLY)* I'm saying good-by to 1615 you, Pop. *(WILLY looks at him, silent, unable to move.)* I'm not coming back any more.

WILLY: You're not going to see Oliver tomorrow?

BIFF: I've got no appointment, Dad.

WILLY: He put his arm around you, and you've got no 1620 appointment?

BIFF: Pop, get this now, will you? Everytime I've left it's been a fight that sent me out of here. Today I realized something about myself and I tried to explain it to you and I—I think I'm just not smart enough to make 1625 any sense out of it for you. To hell with whose fault it is or anything like that. *(He takes WILLY's arm.)* Let's just wrap it up, heh? Come on in, we'll tell Mom. *(He gently tries to pull WILLY to left.)*

WILLY: *(frozen, immobile, with guilt in his voice)* No, I 1630 don't want to see her.

BIFF: Come on! *(He pulls again, and WILLY tries to pull away.)*

WILLY: *(highly nervous)* No, no, I don't want to see her.

BIFF: *(tries to look into WILLY's face, as if to find the an-* 1635 *swer there)* Why don't you want to see her?

WILLY: *(more harshly now)* Don't bother me, will you?

BIFF: What do you mean, you don't want to see her? You don't want them calling you yellow, do you? This isn't your fault; it's me, I'm a bum. Now come inside! 1640 *(WILLY strains to get away.)* Did you hear what I said to you?

WILLY *pulls away and quickly goes by himself into the house.* BIFF *follows.*

LINDA: *(to WILLY)* Did you plant, dear?

BIFF: *(at the door, to LINDA)* All right, we had it out. I'm going and I'm not writing any more. 1645

LINDA: *(going to WILLY in the kitchen)* I think that's the best way, dear. 'Cause there's no use drawing it out, you'll just never get along.

WILLY *doesn't respond.*

BIFF: People ask where I am and what I'm doing, you
1650 don't know, and you don't care. That way it'll be off
your mind and you can start brightening up again. All
right? That clears it, doesn't it? (*WILLY is silent, and
BIFF goes to him.*) You gonna wish me luck, scout? (*He
extends his hand.*) What do you say?

1655 **LINDA:** Shake his hand, Willy.

WILLY: (*turning to her, seething with hurt*) There's no
necessity to mention the pen at all, y'know.

BIFF: (*gently*) I've got no appointment, Dad.

WILLY: (*erupting fiercely*) He put his arm around . . . ?

1660 **BIFF:** Dad, you're never going to see what I am, so what's
the use of arguing? If I strike oil I'll send you a check.
Meantime forget I'm alive.

WILLY: (*to LINDA*) Spite, see?

BIFF: Shake hands, Dad.

1665 **WILLY:** Not my hand.

BIFF: I was hoping not to go this way.

WILLY: Well, this is the way you're going. Good-by.

BIFF *looks at him a moment, then turns sharply and
goes to the stairs.*

WILLY: (*stops him with*) May you rot in hell if you leave
this house!

1670 **BIFF:** (*turning*) Exactly what is it that you want from me?

WILLY: I want you to know, on the train, in the mountains, in the valleys, wherever you go, that you cut
down your life for spite!

BIFF: No, no.

1675 **WILLY:** Spite, spite, is the word of your undoing! And
when you're down and out, remember what did it.
When you're rotting somewhere beside the railroad
tracks, remember, and don't you dare blame it on me!

BIFF: I'm not blaming it on you!

1680 **WILLY:** I won't take the rap for this, you hear?

HAPPY *comes down the stairs and stands on the bottom step, watching.*

BIFF: That's just what I'm telling you!

WILLY: (*sinking into a chair at the table, with full accusation*) You're trying to put a knife in me—don't think I
don't know what you're doing!

BIFF: All right, phony! Then let's lay it on the line. (*He   1685
whips the rubber tube out of his pocket and puts it on
the table.*)

HAPPY: You crazy—

LINDA: Biff! (*She moves to grab the hose, but BIFF holds it
down with his hand.*)   1690

BIFF: Leave it there! Don't move it!

WILLY: (*not looking at it*) What is that?

BIFF: You know goddam well what that is.

WILLY: (*caged, wanting to escape*) I never saw that.

BIFF: You saw it. The mice didn't bring it into the cellar!   1695
What is this supposed to do, make a hero out of you?
This supposed to make me sorry for you?

WILLY: Never heard of it.

BIFF: There'll be no pity for you, you hear it? No pity!

WILLY: (*to LINDA*) You hear the spite!   1700

BIFF: No, you're going to hear the truth—what you are
and what I am!

LINDA: Stop it!

WILLY: Spite!

HAPPY: (*coming down toward BIFF*) You cut it now!   1705

BIFF: (*to HAPPY*) The man don't know who we are! The
man is gonna know! (*To WILLY.*) We never told the
truth for ten minutes in this house!

HAPPY: We always told the truth!

BIFF: (*turning on him*) You big blow, are you the assistant   1710
buyer? You're one of the two assistants to the assis-
tant, aren't you?

HAPPY: Well, I'm practically—

BIFF: You're practically full of it! We all are! And I'm
1715   through with it. *(To* WILLY.*)* Now hear this, Willy, this
is me.

WILLY: I know you!

BIFF: You know why I had no address for three months?
I stole a suit in Kansas City and I was in jail. *(To*
1720   LINDA, *who is sobbing.)* Stop crying. I'm through
with it.

LINDA *turns away from them, her hands covering
her face.*

WILLY: I suppose that's my fault!

BIFF: I stole myself out of every good job since high
school!

1725   **WILLY:** And whose fault is that?

BIFF: And I never got anywhere because you blew me so
full of hot air I could never stand taking orders from
anybody! That's whose fault it is!

WILLY: I hear that!

1730   **LINDA:** Don't, Biff!

BIFF: It's goddam time you heard that! I had to be boss
big shot in two weeks, and I'm through with it!

WILLY: Then hang yourself! For spite, hang yourself!

BIFF: No! Nobody's hanging himself, Willy! I ran down
1735   eleven flights with a pen in my hand today. And suddenly I stopped, you hear me? And in the middle of
that office building, do you hear this? I stopped in the
middle of that building and I saw—the sky. I saw the
things that I love in this world. The work and the food
1740   and time to sit and smoke. And I looked at the pen
and said to myself, what the hell am I grabbing this
for? Why am I trying to become what I don't want to
be? What am I doing in an office, making a contemptuous, begging fool of myself, when all I want is out
1745   there, waiting for me the minute I say I know who
I am! Why can't I say that, Willy? *(He tries to make
WILLY face him, but WILLY pulls away and moves to
the left.)*

Biff curses Willy for lying.

WILLY: *(with hatred, threateningly)* The door of your life
is wide open!   1750

BIFF: Pop! I'm a dime a dozen, and so are you!

WILLY: *(turning on him now in an uncontrolled outburst)*
I am not a dime a dozen! I am Willy Loman, and you
are Biff Loman!

BIFF *starts for* WILLY, *but is blocked by* HAPPY. *In his
fury,* BIFF *seems on the verge of attacking his father.*

BIFF: I am not a leader of men, Willy, and neither are   1755
you. You were never anything but a hard-working
drummer who landed in the ash can like all the rest
of them! I'm one dollar an hour, Willy! I tried seven
states and couldn't raise it. A buck an hour! Do you
gather my meaning? I'm not bringing home any prizes   1760
any more, and you're going to stop waiting for me to
bring them home!

WILLY: *(directly to BIFF)* You vengeful, spiteful mutt!

BIFF *breaks from* HAPPY. WILLY, *in fright, starts up
the stairs.* BIFF *grabs him.*

BIFF: *(at the peak of his fury)* Pop, I'm nothing! I'm nothing, Pop. Can't you understand that? There's no spite   1765
in it any more. I'm just what I am, that's all.

BIFF's *fury has spent itself, and he breaks down, sobbing, holding on to* WILLY, *who dumbly fumbles for* BIFF's *face.*

WILLY: *(astonished)* What're you doing? What're you doing? *(To* LINDA.*)* Why is he crying?

1770 **BIFF:** *(crying, broken)* Will you let me go, for Christ's sake? Will you take that phony dream and burn it before something happens? *(Struggling to contain himself, he pulls away and moves to the stairs.)* I'll go in the morning. Put him—put him to bed. *(Exhausted,* BIFF *moves up the stairs to his room.)*

1775 **WILLY:** *(after a long pause, astonished, elevated)* Isn't that—isn't that remarkable? Biff—he likes me!

LINDA: He loves you, Willy!

HAPPY: *(deeply moved)* Always did, Pop.

1780 **WILLY:** Oh, Biff! *(Staring wildly.)* He cried! Cried to me. *(He is choking with his love, and now cries out his promise.)* That boy—that boy is going to be magnificent!

BEN *appears in the light just outside the kitchen.*

BEN: Yes, outstanding, with twenty thousand behind him.

Willy climbs into the car.

LINDA: *(sensing the racing of his mind, fearfully, carefully)* Now come to bed, Willy. It's all settled now. 1785

WILLY: *(finding it difficult not to rush out of the house)* Yes, we'll sleep. Come on. Go to sleep, Hap.

BEN: And it does take a great kind of a man to crack the jungle. 1790

In accents of dread, BEN's *idyllic music starts up.*

HAPPY: *(his arm around* LINDA*)* I'm getting married, Pop, don't forget it. I'm changing everything. I'm gonna run that department before the year is up. You'll see, Mom. *(He kisses her.)*

BEN: The jungle is dark but full of diamonds, Willy. 1795

WILLY *turns, moves, listening to* BEN.

LINDA: Be good. You're both good boys, just act that way, that's all.

HAPPY: 'Night, Pop. *(He goes upstairs.)*

LINDA: *(to* WILLY*)* Come, dear.

BEN: *(with greater force)* One must go in to fetch a diamond out. 1800

WILLY: *(to* LINDA, *as he moves slowly along the edge of the kitchen, toward the door)* I just want to get settled down, Linda. Let me sit alone for a little.

LINDA: *(almost uttering her fear)* I want you upstairs. 1805

WILLY: *(taking her in his arms)* In a few minutes, Linda. I couldn't sleep right now. Go on, you look awful tired. *(He kisses her.)*

BEN: Not like an appointment at all. A diamond is rough and hard to the touch. 1810

WILLY: Go on now. I'll be right up.

LINDA: I think this is the only way, Willy.

WILLY: Sure, it's the best thing.

BEN: Best thing!

WILLY: The only way. Everything is gonna be—go on, kid, get to bed. You look so tired. 1815

LINDA: Come right up.

WILLY: Two minutes.

LINDA *goes into the living-room, then reappears in her bedroom.* WILLY *moves just outside the kitchen door.*

WILLY: Loves me. (*Wonderingly.*) Always loved me. Isn't
1820   that a remarkable thing? Ben, he'll worship me for it!

BEN: (*with promise*) It's dark there, but full of diamonds.

WILLY: Can you imagine that magnificence with twenty thousand dollars in his pocket?

LINDA: (*calling from her room*) Willy! Come up!

1825   **WILLY:**   (*calling into the kitchen*) Yes! Yes. Coming! It's very smart, you realize that, don't you, sweetheart? Even Ben sees it. I gotta go, baby. 'By! 'By! (*Going over to* BEN, *almost dancing.*) Imagine? When the mail comes he'll be ahead of Bernard again!

1830   **BEN:**   A perfect proposition all around.

WILLY: Did you see how he cried to me? Oh, if I could kiss him, Ben!

BEN: Time, William, time!

WILLY: Oh, Ben, I always knew one way or another we
1835   were gonna make it, Biff and I!

BEN: (*looking at his watch*) The boat. We'll be late. (*He moves slowly off into the darkness.*)

WILLY: (*elegiacally, turning to the house*) Now when
1840   you kick off, boy, I want a seventy-yard boot, and get right down the field under the ball, and when you hit, hit low and hit hard, because it's important, boy. (*He swings around and faces the audience.*) There's all kinds of important people in the stands, and the first thing you know . . . (*Suddenly realizing he is alone.*)
1845   Ben! Ben, where do I . . . ? (*He makes a sudden movement of search.*) Ben, how do I . . . ?

LINDA: (*calling*) Willy, you coming up?

WILLY: (*uttering a gasp of fear, whirling about as if to quiet her*) Sh! (*He turns around as if to find his way;*
1850   *sounds, faces, voices, seem to be swarming in upon him and he flicks at them, crying.*) Sh! Sh! (*Suddenly music, faint and high, stops him. It rises in intensity,*

almost to an unbearable scream. He goes up and down on his toes, and rushes off around the house.) Shhh!

LINDA: Willy?   1855

There is no answer. LINDA *waits.* BIFF *gets up off his bed. He is still in his clothes.* HAPPY *sits up.* BIFF *stands listening.*

LINDA: (*with real fear*) Willy, answer me! Willy!

There is the sound of a car starting and moving away at full speed.

LINDA: No!

BIFF: (*rushing down the stairs*) Pop!

As the car speeds off, the music crashes down in a frenzy of sound, which becomes the soft pulsation of a single cello string. BIFF *slowly returns to his bedroom. He and* HAPPY *gravely don their jackets.* LINDA *slowly walks out of her room. The music has developed into a dead march. The leaves of day are appearing over everything.* CHARLEY *and* BERNARD, *somberly dressed, appear and knock on the kitchen door.* BIFF *and* HAPPY *slowly descend the stairs to the kitchen as* CHARLEY *and* BERNARD *enter. All stop a moment when* LINDA, *in clothes of mourning, bearing a little bunch of roses, comes through the draped doorway into the kitchen. She goes to* CHARLEY *and takes his arm. Now all move toward the audience, through the wall-line of the kitchen. At the limit of the apron,* LINDA *lays down the flowers, kneels, and sits back on her heels. All stare down at the grave.*

REQUIEM

CHARLEY: It's getting dark, Linda.

LINDA *doesn't react. She stares at the grave.*

BIFF: How about it, Mom? Better get some rest, heh? They'll be closing the gate soon.

LINDA *makes no move. Pause.*

HAPPY: (*deeply angered*) He had no right to do that. There   5
was no necessity for it. We would've helped him.

CHARLEY: (*grunting*) Hmmm.

BIFF: Come along, Mom.

LINDA: Why didn't anybody come?

CHARLEY: It was a very nice funeral.

10   **LINDA:**   But where are all the people he knew? Maybe they blame him.

CHARLEY: Naa. It's a rough world, Linda. They wouldn't blame him.

LINDA: I can't understand it. At this time especially.
15   First time in thirty-five years we were just about free and clear. He only needed a little salary. He was even finished with the dentist.

CHARLEY: No man only needs a little salary.

LINDA: I can't understand it.

20   **BIFF:**   There were a lot of nice days. When he'd come home from a trip; or on Sundays, making the stoop; finishing the cellar; putting on the new porch; when he built the extra bathroom; and put up the garage. You know something, Charley, there's more of him in
25   that front stoop than in all the sales he ever made.

CHARLEY: Yeah. He was a happy man with a batch of cement.

LINDA: He was so wonderful with his hands.

BIFF: He had the wrong dreams. All, all, wrong.

30   **HAPPY:**   *(almost ready to fight* BIFF*)* Don't say that!

BIFF: He never knew who he was.

CHARLEY: *(stopping* HAPPY's *movement and reply. To* BIFF*)* Nobody dast blame this man. You don't understand: Willy was a salesman. And for a salesman,
35   there is no rock bottom to the life. He don't put a bolt to a nut, he don't tell you the law or give you medicine. He's a man way out there in the blue, riding on a smile and a shoeshine. And when they start not smiling back—that's an earthquake. And then you get your
40   self a couple of spots on your hat, and you're finished. Nobody dast blame this man. A salesman is got to dream, boy. It comes with the territory.

BIFF: Charley, the man didn't know who he was.

The family stands over Willy's grave.

HAPPY: *(infuriated)* Don't say that!

BIFF: Why don't you come with me, Happy?   45

HAPPY: I'm not licked that easily. I'm staying right in this city, and I'm gonna beat this racket! *(He looks at* BIFF, *his chin set.)* The Loman Brothers!

BIFF: I know who I am, kid.

HAPPY: All right, boy. I'm gonna show you and every-   50
body else that Willy Loman did not die in vain. He had a good dream. It's the only dream you can have— to come out number-one man. He fought it out here, and this is where I'm gonna win it for him.

BIFF: *(with a hopeless glance at* HAPPY, *bends toward his*   55
mother) Let's go, Mom.

LINDA: I'll be with you in a minute. Go on, Charley. *(He hesitates.)* I want to, just for a minute. I never had a chance to say good-by.

CHARLEY *moves away, followed by* HAPPY. BIFF *remains a slight distance up and left of* LINDA. *She sits there, summoning herself. The flute begins, not far away, playing behind her speech.*

LINDA: Forgive me, dear. I can't cry. I don't know what   60
it is, but I can't cry. I don't understand it. Why did you ever do that? Help me, Willy, I can't cry. It seems to me that you're just on another trip. I keep expect-

65 ing you. Willy, dear, I can't cry. Why did you do it? I search and search and I search, and I can't understand it, Willy. I made the last payment on the house today. Today, dear. And there'll be nobody home. (*A sob rises in her throat.*) We're free and clear. (*Sobbing more fully, released.*) We're free. (BIFF *comes slowly*

70 *toward her.*) We're free . . . We're free . . .

BIFF *lifts her to her feet and moves out up right with her in his arms.* LINDA *sobs quietly.* BERNARD *and* CHARLEY *come together and follow them, followed by* HAPPY. *Only the music of the flute is left on the darkening stage as over the house the hard towers of the apartment buildings rise into sharp focus, and*

The Curtain Falls.

Writing from Reading

Summarize

1 How would you condense the plot into a few lines, to the size of something you might write, say, on the back of a postcard?

2 Explain how the title *Life of a Salesman* compares with the current title. What other titles might describe the play? Which do you prefer and why?

Analyze Craft

3 Aspects of this play are highly stylized and theatrical—the salesman's hallucinations, for example, and the fade-in and fade-out of characters from his past. How do these imagined conversations alter the concept of realism? Why do they feel appropriate to Willy Loman's collapse?

4 Certain expenses in this play (the price of a drink, the cost of a mortgage) have increased since 1949; others have not. To what extent does this text seem timeless, and what would be the effect of inflating the cost of commodities so as to make them more contemporary?

5 How much of the family dynamic here, in terms of both the siblings and their relation to their parents, grows out of Willy's main desire to sell himself?

To what degree does it seem true to your understanding of how families function?

6 Why does Willy feel like a failure? In what ways—as salesman, husband, father—does he succeed? What does his love of gardening suggest?

Analyze Voice

7 What does Arthur Miller mean when he writes in "Tragedy and the Common Man" (1949) "that the plays we revere, century after century, are the tragedies. In them, and in them alone, lies the belief—optimistic, if you will—in the perfectibility of man. It is time, I think, that we who are without kings, took up this bright thread of our history and followed it to the only place it can possibly lead in our time—the heart and spirit of the average man"?

8 Miller in his lifetime was famous as a voice of conscience, protesting against totalitarianism wherever he found it—and refusing to answer questions from the House Un-American Activities Committee when it subpoenaed him to testify against his "communist" friends. Indeed, one of his crucial plays, *The Crucible*, dealt with the mass hysteria of the Salem witch trials in seventeenth-century Amer-

ica and, by extension, with the hysteria engendered by Joseph McCarthy, junior senator from Wisconsin. In what ways is *Death of a Salesman* a play of social protest, and what are Willy's ideals?

Synthesize Summary and Analysis

9 To what extent is Willy Loman like the character of Oedipus? Or, more plausibly, to what extent does he remind you of *Hamlet*'s Polonius? Loman, however, can be considered as a tragic character; Polonius cannot. Why?

10 The entire action of the play seems to come together in the statement by Linda Loman in which she says of her husband "Attention must be paid." Why does she forgive what her sons resent so much—his infidelities, his drunkenness? What did she know about his life as a traveling salesman and his missed financial chances? What does she want from and for him now?

Interpret the Play

11 Willy dreams the American dream. In what way does it become a nightmare for him—or does he die content?

CONTINUED FROM PAGE 1277

FROM THE PALACE TO THE LIVING ROOM, OR, THE ORIGINS OF MODERN THEATER

As you know from your encounters with Greek tragedy and Shakespeare's plays, theater in the West did not begin by depicting ordinary people. In early forms of theater, it was permissible to show ordinary folk as comic and to make fun of the human condition—its pitfalls and pratfalls—in the lower or middle class. There was satiric fun to be had at the expense of the common man. The tragic mode was previously reserved, as we have discussed, for elevated members of the society. Middle-class revolutions across Europe brought to power a social class—made up primarily of lawyers, bankers, and landowners—that had served royalty but never before played a dominant role. The fall of monarchies, and the emergence of middle-class democracies driven by industry and finance, gave rise to another sort of audience and another form of theater in western Europe.

"So whether it's in a play from 1919, or whether it's a play from 1942, or 2010, I approach them all the same: from the truth of that character. . . . Where am I? Who am I? What am I? Why am I here? . . . You always play the truth." Conversation with Ruben Santiago-Hudson

While kings and queens ruled in Europe, playwrights wrote in a style and took on subjects that catered, at least in part, to the aristocratic audience. With the rise of democratic parliaments, playwrights made a theater for the middle class these legislators represented. In this way marriage and family and various other sorts of everyday social relations replaced the staged deliberations and decisions of kings. Theatergoers wished to see their *own* situations reflected, their *own* society described. In place of the old systems of belief we find a new variety of thought—and therefore a new kind of play. At the start of this chapter we suggested that the movement from palace to living room was a function of the shift in power from monarchy to democracy—and that the possibility of realistic theater was born out of such a shift.

Today it may be difficult to recognize the importance of this distinction in styles, or how much it means even as we witness it. Actors perform the Oedipus play wearing stylized masks that emphasize the difference between the royal family and the audience and the difference between the royals and the gods who rule their lives. Issues of marriage and family in Elizabethan theater are more closely related to matters of kingdom and empire than to domestic relations. Shakespeare's scenes when staged with flair and intelligence remind us of the difference between performers on the stage and our ordinary selves in the audience. Great poetry that it is, the language alone can make us hear—and, by simply hearing, see—the distance between the playwright's characters of high and low station. Here the importance of staging comes, again, to bear. This kind of realistic stage or set design, a **proscenium** stage, forces the playwright to consider the mechanics of staging actors in relation to the audience and to quick, easy, and inexpensive set changes to keep from changing the scenery every time the action shifts.

Death of a Salesman, Arthur Miller's most influential work, lies squarely within the tradition of realistic or **naturalistic** theater, theater that shines a light on painful realities. In the course of his lengthy productive career, Miller tried his hand at other modes of representation—writing short experimental plays or ones with a historical context or dabbling in surrealism—but it is his realistic plays that brought his work into the mainstream of American drama. In *Death of a Salesman,* Miller takes his protagonist, a modern-day tragic hero (or **antihero** in that he is not elevated socially or morally), a step further: He is an **Everyman** in a modern **morality play** (see Chapter 33, p. 1198, for more on the medieval morality play).

> **"America is happiest with a naturalistic play or play that gives the illusion of being naturalistic. . . . We all know that in theater there is no such thing as absolute naturalism. People do not talk the way they do in real life, thank heavens. On stage they talk coherently. . . . We call something naturalistic if it is not highly stylized."** Conversation with Edward Albee

In some ways the American playwright Arthur Miller is the direct inheritor of the playwright who defined the practice of realism onstage: Henrik Ibsen. The nineteenth-century Norwegian is the writer who more than any other brought the realistic strategy to the Western stage. Ibsen takes on the difficult and piercing social issues of his period and, to a certain extent, our own. In *A Doll's House* we witness the dramatization of problems that touch on the lives of ordinary middle-class people—the role of women in modern marriage, a struggle about money and employment, the effort to keep up appearances for the outside world. Ibsen highlights the problems of family life, of married life within society—subjects not addressed in any detail in early forms of drama. In his theater we meet people we can legitimately call modern, people mostly like ourselves in recognizable and often unpleasant situations. What made it possible for a playwright to create this sort of play, and what makes it possible for an audience to respond to it?

METHOD ACTING—REALISM ONSTAGE

An entirely new style of performance—first propounded by the Russian Konstantin Stanislavski and practiced in America most famously by such graduates of the Actors Studio as Marilyn Monroe and Marlon Brando—made a method out of naturalism onstage. An actor and his or her character should merge so that the role becomes *inhabited* by the person cast in it; the facial tics or accent of a *method* actor were not acquired in the dressing room ten minutes before curtain time but were built into rehearsal and the interpretative process. This notion of identity between the player and the part played is based, of course, on the assumption that behavior must be internalized and is best copied when most natural. Gone were the highly polished performances and perfectly articulated speech of characters in period dress; instead, as some disgruntled reviewers complained, the actors scratched themselves and mumbled and turned their backs on the audience in order to seem *real*.

In nineteenth-century France, the **well-made play** became the norm. Popularized by such playwrights as Eugène Scribe (1791–1861) and Victorien Sardou (1831–1908), this three-act sequence *posed* a problem, *complicated* it, and then *resolved* it; usually that resolution came when a character's past was revealed. The first act offers *exposition*, the second a *situation*, the third an unraveling or *completion*. Meticulous plotting and suspense were components of this mode of theater. Ibsen—who had directed a number of Scribe's well-made plays in Norway—deeply understood how to adapt those cause-and-effect plot arrangements for his own use. Cowardice, hypocrisy, complacency within the expectation of conventional behavior, and a kind of stifled yearning are the problems Ibsen brings to center stage in his drama.

> "Every playwright awakens something in you you didn't know was there. . . . Ibsen, for example, . . . had such a tremendous influence. . . . His women were as startling and as modern as any woman I've ever worked on. . . . The ideas in Ibsen are so brave and so bold." Conversation with Marian Seldes

Here's one reason that *A Doll's House* is a **problem play;** it's hard to *read* the central figure and decide if she's a spoiled child or a brave pioneer or some combination of both. Indeed, there have been various interpretations of the role: Nora has been played as everything from victim to victimizer, self-indulgent society matron to selfless ingenue. Nora desires what we desire. The protagonist Nora yearns to become a fully aware human being rather than live as the subservient creature known to society as Torvald's wife. She struggles with confusion as we struggle with confusion. She achieves a breakthrough in her understanding that mirrors our own recognition; her fear of causing embarrassment to and dishonor for her husband feels in many respects contemporary. The way she wrestles with the problem of family duty as opposed to her own individual freedom should seem familiar as well. In any case her progress toward independence feels modern and quite up-to-date. As one of our culture's first great feminist characters, she embodies—in terms of her growth from first to final act—a form of liberation surprising, even shocking, at the time. Here's a portrait of a woman and a family that resonates today.

Henrik Ibsen (1828–1906)

Henrik Ibsen, known today as the father of modern drama, was born near Oslo, Norway. Initially wealthy, the Ibsens were left in poverty when their family business failed; Henrik was six years old at the time. As a teenager he was apprenticed to a pharmacist, but by 1851 he held the position of stage manager and playwright at the Norwegian Theater in Bergen, and after that he worked as a theater director in Norway's capital. Ibsen later lived abroad in Germany and Italy, remaining away from Norway for a twenty-seven-year period because he felt he could better write Norwegian drama from a distance. Supported by stipends from the government, Ibsen devoted himself to writing plays. His work moved theater away from popular nineteenth-century melodramas and into the realm of realism, which allowed him to examine his characters' psychological lives and the individual's conflict with convention and society. Plays such as *A Doll's House* (1879), *Ghosts* (1881), and *Hedda Gabler* (1890) established Ibsen's dramaturgical prowess. In 1891, Ibsen returned to Oslo, where he remained for the rest of his life.

A Doll's House (1879)

—translated by B. Farquharson Sharp

CHARACTERS

TORVALD HELMER.

NORA, HIS WIFE.

DOCTOR RANK.

MRS. LINDE.

NILS KROGSTAD.

HELMERS' THREE YOUNG CHILDREN.

ANNE, THEIR NURSE.

A PORTER.

(The action takes place in Helmer's house.)

ACT 1

THE SCENE: —*A room furnished comfortably and tastefully, but not extravagantly. At the back, a door to the right leads to the entrance-hall, another to the left leads to Helmer's study. Between the doors stands a piano. In the middle of the left-hand wall is a door, and beyond it a window. Near the window are a round table, arm-chairs and a small sofa. In the right-hand wall, at the farther end, another door; and on the same side, nearer the footlights, a stove, two easy chairs and a rocking-chair; between the stove and the door, a small table. Engravings on the walls; a cabinet with china and other small objects; a small book-case with well-bound books. The floors are carpeted, and a fire burns in the stove. It is winter.*

A bell rings in the hall; shortly afterwards the door is heard to open. Enter NORA, *humming a tune and in high spirits. She is in out-door dress and carries a number of parcels; these she lays on the table to the right. She leaves the outer door open after her, and through it is seen a* PORTER *who is carrying a Christmas Tree and a basket, which he gives to the* MAID *who has opened the door.*

NORA: Hide the Christmas Tree carefully, Helen. Be sure the children do not see it till this evening, when it is dressed. (*To the* PORTER, *taking out her purse.*) How much?

5 **PORTER:** Sixpence.

NORA: There is a shilling. No, keep the change. (*The* PORTER *thanks her, and goes out.* NORA *shuts the door. She is laughing to herself, as she takes off her hat and coat. She takes a packet of macaroons from her* 10 *pocket and eats one or two; then goes cautiously to her husband's door and listens.*) Yes, he is in. (*Still humming, she goes to the table on the right.*)

HELMER: (*calls out from his room*) Is that my little lark twittering out there?

15 **NORA:** (*busy opening some of the parcels*) Yes, it is!

HELMER: Is it my little squirrel bustling about?

NORA: Yes!

HELMER: When did my squirrel come home?

NORA: Just now. (*Puts the bag of macaroons into her pocket and wipes her mouth.*) Come in here, Torvald, and see what I have bought. 20

HELMER: Don't disturb me. (*A little later, he opens the door and looks into the room, pen in hand.*) Bought, did you say? All these things? Has my little spendthrift been wasting money again? 25

NORA: Yes but, Torvald, this year we really can let ourselves go a little. This is the first Christmas that we have not needed to economise.

HELMER: Still, you know, we can't spend money recklessly. 30

NORA: Yes, Torvald, we may be a wee bit more reckless now, mayn't we? Just a tiny wee bit! You are going to have a big salary and earn lots and lots of money.

HELMER: Yes, after the New Year; but then it will be a whole quarter before the salary is due. 35

NORA: Pooh! we can borrow till then.

HELMER: Nora! (*Goes up to her and takes her playfully by the ear.*) The same little featherhead! Suppose, now, that I borrowed fifty pounds to-day, and you spent it all in the Christmas week, and then on New Year's Eve a slate fell on my head and killed me, and— 40

NORA: (*putting her hands over his mouth*) Oh! don't say such horrid things!

HELMER: Still, suppose that happened,—what then?

NORA: If that were to happen, I don't suppose I should care whether I owed money or not. 45

HELMER: Yes, but what about the people who had lent it?

NORA: They? Who would bother about them? I should not know who they were. 50

HELMER: That is like a woman! But seriously, Nora, you know what I think about that. No debt, no borrowing. There can be no freedom or beauty about a home life that depends on borrowing and debt. We two have kept bravely on the straight road so far, and we will go 55 on the same way for the short time longer that there need be any struggle.

NORA: *(moving towards the stove)* As you please, Torvald.

HELMER: *(following her)* Come, come, my little skylark must not droop her wings. What is this! Is my little squirrel out of temper? *(Taking out his purse.)* Nora, what do you think I have got here?

NORA: *(turning round quickly)* Money!

HELMER: There you are. *(Gives her some money.)* Do you think I don't know what a lot is wanted for house-keeping at Christmas-time?

NORA: *(counting)* Ten shillings—a pound—two pounds! Thank you, thank you, Torvald; that will keep me going for a long time.

HELMER: Indeed it must.

NORA: Yes, yes, it will. But come here and let me show you what I have bought. And all so cheap! Look, here is a new suit for Ivar, and a sword; and a horse and a trumpet for Bob; and a doll and dolly's bedstead for Emmy,—they are very plain, but anyway she will soon break them in pieces. And here are dress-lengths and handkerchiefs for the maids; old Anne ought really to have something better.

HELMER: And what is in this parcel?

NORA: *(crying out)* No, no! you mustn't see that till this evening.

HELMER: Very well. But now tell me, you extravagant little person, what would you like for yourself?

NORA: For myself? Oh, I am sure I don't want anything.

HELMER: Yes, but you must. Tell me something reasonable that you would particularly like to have.

NORA: No, I really can't think of anything—unless, Torvald—

HELMER: Well?

NORA: *(playing with his coat buttons, and without raising her eyes to his)* If you really want to give me something, you might—you might—

Nora (Claire Bloom) and Torvald Helmer (Anthony Hopkins) discuss their Christmas plans in the 1973 film directed by Patrick Garland.

HELMER: Well, out with it!

NORA: *(speaking quickly)* You might give me money, Torvald. Only just as much as you can afford; and then one of these days I will buy something with it.

HELMER: But Nora—

NORA: Oh, do! dear Torvald; please, please do! Then I will wrap it up in beautiful gilt paper and hang it on the Christmas Tree. Wouldn't that be fun?

HELMER: What are little people called that are always wasting money?

NORA: Spendthrifts—I know. Let us do as you suggest, Torvald, and then I shall have time to think what I am most in want of. That is a very sensible plan, isn't it?

HELMER: *(smiling)* Indeed it is—that is to say, if you were really to save out of the money I give you, and then really buy something for yourself. But if you spend it all on the housekeeping and any number of unnecessary things, then I merely have to pay up again.

NORA: Oh but, Torvald—

HELMER: You can't deny it, my dear little Nora. *(Puts his arm around her waist.)* It's a sweet little spendthrift,

Nora tells Torvald what she would like for Christmas.

115   but she uses up a deal of money. One would hardly believe how expensive such little persons are!

NORA: It's a shame to say that. I do really save all I can.

HELMER: *(laughing)* That's very true,—all you can. But you can't save anything!

120 **NORA:** *(smiling quietly and happily)* You haven't any idea how many expenses we skylarks and squirrels have, Torvald.

HELMER: You are an odd little soul. Very like your father. You always find some new way of wheedling

125 money out of me, and, as soon as you have got it, it seems to melt in your hands. You never know where it has gone. Still, one must take you as you are. It is in the blood; for indeed it is true that you can inherit these things, Nora.

130 **NORA:**   Ah, I wish I had inherited many of papa's qualities.

HELMER: And I would not wish you to be anything but just what you are, my sweet little skylark. But, do you know, it strikes me that you are looking rather—what

135 shall I say—rather uneasy to-day?

NORA: Do I?

HELMER: You do, really. Look straight at me.

NORA: *(looks at him)* Well?

HELMER: *(wagging his finger at her)* Hasn't Miss Sweet-Tooth been breaking rules in town to-day?   140

NORA: No; what makes you think that?

HELMER: Hasn't she paid a visit to the confectioner's?

NORA: No, I assure you, Torvald—

HELMER: Not been nibbling sweets?

NORA: No, certainly not.   145

HELMER: Not even taken a bite at a macaroon or two?

NORA: No, Torvald, I assure you really—

HELMER: There, there, of course I was only joking.

NORA: *(going to the table on the right)* I should not think of going against your wishes.   150

HELMER: No, I am sure of that; besides, you gave me your word—*(Going up to her.)* Keep your little Christmas secrets to yourself, my darling. They will all be revealed to-night when the Christmas Tree is lit, no doubt.   155

NORA: Did you remember to invite Doctor Rank?

HELMER: No. But there is no need; as a matter of course he will come to dinner with us. However, I will ask him when he comes in this morning. I have ordered some good wine. Nora, you can't think how I am looking forward to this evening.   160

NORA: So am I! And how the children will enjoy themselves, Torvald!

HELMER: It is splendid to feel that one has a perfectly safe appointment, and a big enough income. It's delightful to think of, isn't it?   165

NORA: It's wonderful!

HELMER: Do you remember last Christmas? For a full three weeks beforehand you shut yourself up every evening till long after midnight, making ornaments   170 for the Christmas Tree, and all the other fine things that were to be a surprise to us. It was the dullest three weeks I ever spent!

NORA: I didn't find it dull.

175 HELMER: *(smiling)* But there was precious little result, Nora.

NORA: Oh, you shouldn't tease me about that again. How could I help the cat's going in and tearing everything to pieces?

180 HELMER: Of course you couldn't, poor little girl. You had the best of intentions to please us all, and that's the main thing. But it is a good thing that our hard times are over.

NORA: Yes, it is really wonderful.

185 HELMER: This time I needn't sit here and be dull all alone, and you needn't ruin your dear eyes and your pretty little hands—

NORA: *(clapping her hands)* No, Torvald, I needn't any longer, need I! It's wonderfully lovely to hear you say
190 so! *(Taking his arm.)* Now I will tell you how I have been thinking we ought to arrange things, Torvald. As soon as Christmas is over—*(A bell rings in the hall.)* There's the bell. *(She tidies the room a little.)* There's some one at the door. What a nuisance!

195 HELMER: If it is a caller, remember I am not at home.

MAID: *(in the doorway)* A lady to see you, ma'am,—a stranger.

NORA: Ask her to come in.

MAID: *(to* HELMER*)* The doctor came at the same time,
200 sir.

HELMER: Did he go straight into my room?

MAID: Yes, sir.

(HELMER *goes into his room. The* MAID *ushers in* MRS. LINDE, *who is in travelling dress, and shuts the door.)*

MRS. LINDE: *(in a dejected and timid voice)* How do you do, Nora?

205 NORA: *(doubtfully)* How do you do—

MRS. LINDE: You don't recognise me, I suppose.

NORA: No, I don't know—yes, to be sure, I seem to— *(Suddenly.)* Yes! Christine! Is it really you?

MRS. LINDE: Yes, it is I.

NORA: Christine! To think of my not recognising you! 210 And yet how could I— *(In a gentle voice.)* How you have altered, Christine!

MRS. LINDE: Yes, I have indeed. In nine, ten long years—

NORA: Is it so long since we met? I suppose it is. The last eight years have been a happy time for me, I can 215 tell you. And so now you have come into the town, and have taken this long journey in winter—that was plucky of you.

MRS. LINDE: I arrived by steamer this morning.

NORA: To have some fun at Christmas-time, of course. 220 How delightful! We will have such fun together! But take off your things. You're not cold, I hope. *(Helps her.)* Now we will sit down by the stove, and be cosy. No, take this arm-chair; I will sit here in the rocking-chair. *(Takes her hands.)* Now you look like your old 225 self again; it was only the first moment—You are a little paler, Christine, and perhaps a little thinner.

MRS. LINDE: And much, much older, Nora.

NORA: Perhaps a little older; very, very little; certainly not much. *(Stops suddenly and speaks seriously.)* 230 What a thoughtless creature I am, chattering away like this. My poor, dear Christine, do forgive me.

MRS. LINDE: What do you mean, Nora?

NORA: *(gently)* Poor Christine, you are a widow.

MRS. LINDE: Yes; it is three years ago now. 235

NORA: Yes, I knew; I saw it in the papers. I assure you, Christine, I meant ever so often to write to you at the time, but I always put it off and something always prevented me.

MRS. LINDE: I quite understand, dear. 240

NORA: It was very bad of me, Christine. Poor thing, how you must have suffered. And he left you nothing?

MRS. LINDE: No.

NORA: And no children?

245   MRS. LINDE: No.

NORA: Nothing at all, then.

MRS. LINDE: Not even any sorrow or grief to live upon.

NORA: *(looking incredulously at her)* But Christine, is that possible?

250   MRS. LINDE: *(smiles sadly and strokes her hair)* It sometimes happens, Nora.

NORA: So you are quite alone. How dreadfully sad that must be. I have three lovely children. You can't see them just now, for they are out with their nurse. But 255 now you must tell me all about it.

MRS. LINDE: No, no; I want to hear about you.

NORA: No, you must begin. I mustn't be selfish to-day; to-day I must only think of your affairs. But there is one thing I must tell you. Do you know we have just 260 had a great piece of good luck?

MRS. LINDE: No, what is it?

NORA: Just fancy, my husband has been made manager of the Bank!

MRS. LINDE: Your husband? What good luck!

265   NORA: Yes, tremendous! A barrister's profession is such an uncertain thing, especially if he won't undertake unsavoury cases; and naturally Torvald has never been willing to do that, and I quite agree with him. You may imagine how pleased we are! He is to take 270 up his work in the Bank at the New Year, and then he will have a big salary and lots of commissions. For the future we can live quite differently—we can do just as we like. I feel so relieved and so happy, Christine! It will be splendid to have heaps of money and not need 275 to have any anxiety, won't it?

MRS. LINDE: Yes, anyhow I think it would be delightful to have what one needs.

NORA: No, not only what one needs, but heaps and heaps of money.

Nora (Juliet Stevenson) catches up with Mrs. Linde (Geraldine James) in the 1992 film directed by David Thacker.

MRS. LINDE: *(smiling)* Nora, Nora, haven't you learnt 280 sense yet? In our schooldays you were a great spendthrift.

NORA: *(laughing)* Yes, that is what Torvald says now. *(Wags her finger at her.)* But "Nora, Nora" is not so silly as you think. We have not been in a position for me to 285 waste money. We have both had to work.

MRS. LINDE: You too?

NORA: Yes; odds and ends, needlework, crotchet-work, embroidery, and that kind of thing. *(Dropping her voice.)* And other things as well. You know Torvald 290 left his office when we were married? There was no prospect of promotion there, and he had to try and earn more than before. But during the first year he over-worked himself dreadfully. You see, he had to make money every way he could, and he worked early 295 and late; but he couldn't stand it, and fell dreadfully ill, and the doctors said it was necessary for him to go south.

MRS. LINDE: You spent a whole year in Italy, didn't you?

NORA: Yes. It was no easy matter to get away, I can tell 300 you. It was just after Ivar was born; but naturally we had to go. It was a wonderfully beautiful journey, and it saved Torvald's life. But it cost a tremendous lot of money, Christine.

305   **MRS. LINDE:**   So I should think.

NORA: It cost about two hundred and fifty pounds. That's a lot, isn't it?

MRS. LINDE: Yes, and in emergencies like that it is lucky to have the money.

310   **NORA:**   I ought to tell you that we had it from papa.

MRS. LINDE: Oh, I see. It was just about that time that he died, wasn't it?

NORA: Yes; and, just think of it, I couldn't go and nurse
315   him. I was expecting little Ivar's birth every day and I had my poor sick Torvald to look after. My dear, kind father—I never saw him again, Christine. That was the saddest time I have known since our marriage.

MRS. LINDE: I know how fond you were of him. And then you went off to Italy?

320   **NORA:**   Yes; you see we had money then, and the doctors insisted on our going, so we started a month later.

MRS. LINDE: And your husband came back quite well?

NORA: As sound as a bell!

MRS. LINDE: But—the doctor?

325   **NORA:**   What doctor?

MRS. LINDE: I thought your maid said the gentleman who arrived here just as I did, was the doctor?

NORA: Yes, that was Doctor Rank, but he doesn't come here professionally. He is our greatest friend, and
330   comes in at least once every day. No, Torvald has not had an hour's illness since then, and our children are strong and healthy and so am I. *(Jumps up and claps her hands.)* Christine! Christine! it's good to be alive and happy!—But how horrid of me; I am talking of
335   nothing but my own affairs. *(Sits on a stool near her, and rests her arms on her knees.)* You mustn't be angry with me. Tell me, is it really true that you did not love your husband? Why did you marry him?

MRS. LINDE: My mother was alive then, and was bed-
340   ridden and helpless, and I had to provide for my two younger brothers; so I did not think I was justified in refusing his offer.

NORA: No, perhaps you were quite right. He was rich at that time, then?

MRS. LINDE: I believe he was quite well off. But his 345
business was a precarious one; and, when he died, it all went to pieces and there was nothing left.

NORA: And then?—

MRS. LINDE: Well, I had to turn my hand to anything I could find—first a small shop, then a small school, 350
and so on. The last three years have seemed like one long working-day, with no rest. Now it is at an end, Nora. My poor mother needs me no more, for she is gone; and the boys do not need me either; they have got situations and can shift for themselves. 355

NORA: What a relief you must feel it—

MRS. LINDE: No, indeed; I only feel my life unspeakably empty. No one to live for any more. *(Gets up restlessly.)* That was why I could not stand the life in my little backwater any longer. I hope it may be easier here to 360
find something which will busy me and occupy my thoughts. If only I could have the good luck to get some regular work—office work of some kind—

NORA: But, Christine, that is so frightfully tiring, and you look tired out now. You had far better go away to 365
some watering-place.

MRS. LINDE: *(walking to the window)* I have no father to give me money for a journey, Nora.

NORA: *(rising)* Oh, don't be angry with me.

MRS. LINDE: *(going up to her)* It is you that must not be 370
angry with me, dear. The worst of a position like mine is that it makes one so bitter. No one to work for, and yet obliged to be always on the look-out for chances. One must live, and so one becomes selfish. When you told me of the happy turn your fortunes have taken— 375
you will hardly believe it—I was delighted not so much on your account as on my own.

NORA: How do you mean?—Oh, I understand. You mean that perhaps Torvald could get you something to do.

MRS. LINDE: Yes, that was what I was thinking of. 380

NORA: He must, Christine. Just leave it to me; I will broach the subject very cleverly—I will think of something that will please him very much. It will make me so happy to be of some use to you.

385   **MRS. LINDE:**   How kind you are, Nora, to be so anxious to help me! It is doubly kind in you, for you know so little of the burdens and troubles of life.

NORA: I—? I know so little of them?

390   **MRS. LINDE:**   (*smiling*) My dear! Small household cares and that sort of thing!—You are a child, Nora.

NORA: (*tosses her head and crosses the stage*) You ought not to be so superior.

MRS. LINDE: No?

395   **NORA:**   You are just like the others. They all think that I am incapable of anything really serious—

MRS. LINDE: Come, come—

NORA: —that I have gone through nothing in this world of cares.

400   **MRS. LINDE:**   But, my dear Nora, you have just told me all your troubles.

NORA: Pooh!—those were trifles. (*Lowering her voice.*) I have not told you the important thing.

MRS. LINDE: The important thing? What do you mean?

NORA: You look down upon me altogether, Christine—
405   but you ought not to. You are proud, aren't you, of having worked so hard and so long for your mother?

MRS. LINDE: Indeed, I don't look down on any one. But it is true that I am both proud and glad to think that I was privileged to make the end of my mother's life
410   almost free from care.

NORA: And you are proud to think of what you have done for your brothers.

MRS. LINDE: I think I have the right to be.

NORA: I think so, too. But now listen to this; I too have
415   something to be proud and glad of.

MRS. LINDE: I have no doubt you have. But what do you refer to?

NORA: Speak low. Suppose Torvald were to hear! He mustn't on any account—no one in the world must know, Christine, except you.   420

MRS. LINDE: But what is it?

NORA: Come here. (*Pulls her down on the sofa beside her.*) Now I will show you that I too have something to be proud and glad of. It was I who saved Torvald's life.

MRS. LINDE: "Saved"? How?   425

NORA: I told you about our trip to Italy. Torvald would never have recovered if he had not gone there—

MRS. LINDE: Yes, but your father gave you the necessary funds.

NORA: (*smiling*) Yes, that is what Torvald and all the   430
others think, but—

MRS. LINDE: But—

NORA: Papa didn't give us a shilling. It was I who procured the money.

MRS. LINDE: You? All that large sum?   435

NORA: Two hundred and fifty pounds. What do you think of that?

MRS. LINDE: But, Nora, how could you possibly do it? Did you win a prize in the Lottery?

NORA: (*contemptuously*) In the Lottery? There would   440
have been no credit in that.

MRS. LINDE: But where did you get it from, then?

NORA: (*humming and smiling with an air of mystery*) Hm, hm! Aha!

MRS. LINDE: Because you couldn't have borrowed it.   445

NORA: Couldn't I? Why not?

MRS. LINDE: No, a wife cannot borrow without her husband's consent.

NORA: (*tossing her head*) Oh, if it is a wife who has any head for business—a wife who has the wit to be a little   450
bit clever—

MRS. LINDE: I don't understand it at all, Nora.

NORA: There is no need you should. I never said I had
455 borrowed the money. I may have got it some other
way. *(Lies back on the sofa.)* Perhaps I got it from some
other admirer. When anyone is as attractive as I am—

MRS. LINDE: You are a mad creature.

NORA: Now, you know you're full of curiosity, Christine.

MRS. LINDE: Listen to me, Nora dear. Haven't you been
460 a little bit imprudent?

NORA: *(sits up straight)* Is it imprudent to save your
husband's life?

MRS. LINDE: It seems to me imprudent, without his
knowledge, to—

465 NORA: But it was absolutely necessary that he should
not know! My goodness, can't you understand that? It
was necessary he should have no idea what a dangerous condition he was in. It was to me that the doctors
came and said that his life was in danger, and that
470 the only thing to save him was to live in the south.
Do you suppose I didn't try, first of all, to get what I
wanted as if it were for myself? I told him how much
I should love to travel abroad like other young wives;
I tried tears and entreaties with him; I told him that
475 he ought to remember the condition I was in, and
that he ought to be kind and indulgent to me; I even
hinted that he might raise a loan. That nearly made

Nora tells Mrs. Linde (Anna Massey) about her troubles.

him angry, Christine. He said I was thoughtless, and
that it was his duty as my husband not to indulge
me in my whims and caprices—as I believe he called 480
them. Very well, I thought, you must be saved—and
that was how I came to devise a way out of the
difficulty—

MRS. LINDE: And did your husband never get to know
from your father that the money had not come from 485
him?

NORA: No, never. Papa died just at that time. I had
meant to let him into the secret and beg him never to
reveal it. But he was so ill then—alas, there never was
any need to tell him. 490

MRS. LINDE: And since then have you never told your
secret to your husband?

NORA: Good Heavens, no! How could you think so? A
man who has such strong opinions about these things!
And besides, how painful and humiliating it would be 495
for Torvald, with his manly independence, to know
that he owed me anything! It would upset our mutual
relations altogether; our beautiful happy home would
no longer be what it is now.

MRS. LINDE: Do you mean never to tell him about it? 500

NORA: *(meditatively, and with a half smile)* Yes—some
day, perhaps, after many years, when I am no longer
as nice-looking as I am now. Don't laugh at me! I
mean, of course, when Torvald is no longer as devoted
to me as he is now; when my dancing and dressing- 505
up and reciting have palled on him; then it may be a
good thing to have something in reserve— *(Breaking
off.)* What nonsense! That time will never come. Now,
what do you think of my great secret, Christine? Do
you still think I am of no use? I can tell you, too, that 510
this affair has caused me a lot of worry. It has been
by no means easy for me to meet my engagements
punctually. I may tell you that there is something that
is called, in business, quarterly interest, and another
thing called payment in instalments, and it is always 515
so dreadfully difficult to manage them. I have had to
save a little here and there, where I could, you understand. I have not been able to put aside much from my
housekeeping money, for Torvald must have a good
table. I couldn't let my children be shabbily dressed; I 520

have felt obliged to use up all he gave me for them, the sweet little darlings!

MRS. LINDE: So it has all had to come out of your own necessaries of life, poor Nora?

525 **NORA:** Of course. Besides, I was the one responsible for it. Whenever Torvald has given me money for new dresses and such things, I have never spent more than half of it; I have always bought the simplest and cheapest things. Thank Heaven, any clothes look well 530 on me, and so Torvald has never noticed it. But it was often very hard on me, Christine—because it is delightful to be really well dressed, isn't it?

MRS. LINDE: Quite so.

NORA: Well, then I have found other ways of earning 535 money. Last winter I was lucky enough to get a lot of copying to do; so I locked myself up and sat writing every evening until quite late at night. Many a time I was desperately tired; but all the same it was a tremendous pleasure to sit there working and earning 540 money. It was like being a man.

MRS. LINDE: How much have you been able to pay off in that way?

NORA: I can't tell you exactly. You see, it is very difficult to keep an account of a business matter of that kind. 545 I only know that I have paid every penny that I could scrape together. Many a time I was at my wit's end. (*Smiles.*) Then I used to sit here and imagine that a rich old gentleman had fallen in love with me—

MRS. LINDE: What! Who was it?

550 **NORA:** Be quiet!—that he had died; and that when his will was opened it contained, written in big letters, the instruction: "The lovely Mrs. Nora Helmer is to have all I possess paid over to her at once in cash."

MRS. LINDE: But, my dear Nora—who could the man be?

555 **NORA:** Good gracious, can't you understand? There was no old gentleman at all; it was only something that I used to sit here and imagine, when I couldn't think of any way of procuring money. But it's all the same now; the tiresome old person can stay where he is, as 560 far as I am concerned; I don't care about him or his

will either, for I am free from care now. (*Jumps up.*) My goodness, it's delightful to think of, Christine! Free from care! To be able to be free from care, quite free from care; to be able to play and romp with the children; to be able to keep the house beautifully and 565 have everything just as Torvald likes it! And, think of it, soon the spring will come and the big blue sky! Perhaps we shall be able to take a little trip—perhaps I shall see the sea again! Oh, it's a wonderful thing to be alive and be happy. (*A bell is heard in the hall.*) 570

MRS. LINDE: (*rising*) There is the bell; perhaps I had better go.

NORA: No, don't go; no one will come in here; it is sure to be for Torvald.

SERVANT: (*at the hall door*) Excuse me, ma'am—there 575 is a gentleman to see the master, and as the doctor is with him—

NORA: Who is it?

KROGSTAD: (*at the door*) It is I, Mrs. Helmer. (MRS. LINDE *starts, trembles, and turns to the window.*) 580

NORA: (*takes a step towards him, and speaks in a strained, low voice*) You? What is it? What do you want to see my husband about?

KROGSTAD: Bank business—in a way. I have a small post in the Bank, and I hear your husband is to be our 585 chief now—

NORA: Then it is—

KROGSTAD: Nothing but dry business matters, Mrs. Helmer; absolutely nothing else.

NORA: Be so good as to go into the study, then. (*She bows* 590 *indifferently to him and shuts the door into the hall; then comes back and makes up the fire in the stove.*)

MRS. LINDE: Nora—who was that man?

NORA: A lawyer, of the name of Krogstad.

MRS. LINDE: Then it really was he. 595

NORA: Do you know the man?

MRS. LINDE: I used to—many years ago. At one time he was a solicitor's clerk in our town.

NORA: Yes, he was.

600 MRS. LINDE: He is greatly altered.

NORA: He made a very unhappy marriage.

MRS. LINDE: He is a widower now, isn't he?

NORA: With several children. There now, it is burning
up. *(Shuts the door of the stove and moves the rocking-*
605 *chair aside.)*

MRS. LINDE: They say he carries on various kinds of
business.

NORA: Really! Perhaps he does; I don't know anything
about it. But don't let us think of business; it is so
610 tiresome.

DOCTOR RANK: *(comes out of* HELMER's *study. Before
he shuts the door he calls to him)* No, my dear fellow, I
won't disturb you; I would rather go in to your wife for
a little while. (Shuts the door and sees MRS. LINDE.) I
615 beg your pardon; I am afraid I am disturbing you too.

NORA: No, not at all. *(Introducing him.)* Doctor Rank,
Mrs. Linde.

RANK: I have often heard Mrs. Linde's name mentioned
here. I think I passed you on the stairs when I arrived,
620 Mrs. Linde?

MRS. LINDE: Yes, I go up very slowly; I can't manage
stairs well.

RANK: Ah! some slight internal weakness?

MRS. LINDE: No, the fact is I have been overworking
625 myself.

RANK: Nothing more than that? Then I suppose you
have come to town to amuse yourself with our
entertainments?

MRS. LINDE: I have come to look for work.

630 RANK: Is that a good cure for overwork?

MRS. LINDE: One must live, Doctor Rank.

RANK: Yes, the general opinion seems to be that it is
necessary.

NORA: Look here, Doctor Rank—you know you want
635 to live.

Nora, Mrs. Linde, and Dr. Rank (Ralph Richardson) chat about
Torvald and Krogstad.

RANK: Certainly. However wretched I may feel, I want
to prolong the agony as long as possible. All my patients are like that. And so are those who are morally
diseased; one of them, and a bad case too, is at this
very moment with Helmer—   640

MRS. LINDE: *(sadly)* Ah!

NORA: Whom do you mean?

RANK: A lawyer of the name of Krogstad, a fellow you
don't know at all. He suffers from a diseased moral
character, Mrs. Helmer; but even he began talking of   645
its being highly important that he should live.

NORA: Did he? What did he want to speak to Torvald
about?

RANK: I have no idea; I only heard that it was something
about the Bank.   650

NORA: I didn't know this—what's his name—Krogstad
had anything to do with the Bank.

RANK: Yes, he has some sort of appointment there. *(To*
MRS. LINDE.) I don't know whether you find also in
your part of the world that there are certain people   655
who go zealously snuffing about to smell out moral
corruption, and, as soon as they have found some,
put the person concerned into some lucrative position

where they can keep their eye on him. Healthy natures are left out in the cold.

MRS. LINDE: Still I think the sick are those who most need taking care of.

RANK: *(shrugging his shoulders)* Yes, there you are. That is the sentiment that is turning Society into a sick-house.

(NORA, who has been absorbed in her thoughts, breaks out into smothered laughter and claps her hands.)

RANK: Why do you laugh at that? Have you any notion what Society really is?

NORA: What do I care about tiresome Society? I am laughing at something quite different, something extremely amusing. Tell me, Doctor Rank, are all the people who are employed in the Bank dependent on Torvald now?

RANK: Is that what you find so extremely amusing?

NORA: *(smiling and humming)* That's my affair! *(Walking about the room.)* It's perfectly glorious to think that we have—that Torvald has so much power over so many people. *(Takes the packet from her pocket.)* Doctor Rank, what do you say to a macaroon?

RANK: What, macaroons? I thought they were forbidden here.

NORA: Yes, but these are some Christine gave me.

MRS. LINDE: What! I?—

NORA: Oh, well, don't be alarmed! You couldn't know that Torvald had forbidden them. I must tell you that he is afraid they will spoil my teeth. But, bah!—once in a way—That's so, isn't it, Doctor Rank? By your leave! *(Puts a macaroon into his mouth.)* You must have one too, Christine. And I shall have one, just a little one—or at most two. *(Walking about.)* I am tremendously happy. There is just one thing in the world now that I should dearly love to do.

RANK: Well, what is that?

NORA: It's something I should dearly love to say, if Torvald could hear me.

RANK: Well, why can't you say it?

NORA: No, I daren't; it's so shocking.

MRS. LINDE: Shocking?

RANK: Well, I should not advise you to say it. Still, with us you might. What is it you would so much like to say if Torvald could hear you?

NORA: I should just love to say—Well, I'm damned!

RANK: Are you mad?

MRS. LINDE: Nora, dear—!

RANK: Say it, here he is!

NORA: *(hiding the packet)* Hush! Hush! Hush! (HELMER comes out of his room, with his coat over his arm and his hat in his hand.)

NORA: Well, Torvald dear, have you got rid of him?

HELMER: Yes, he has just gone.

NORA: Let me introduce you—this is Christine, who has come to town.

HELMER: Christine—? Excuse me, but I don't know—

NORA: Mrs. Linde, dear; Christine Linde.

HELMER: Of course. A school friend of my wife's, I presume?

MRS. LINDE: Yes, we have known each other since then.

NORA: And just think, she has taken a long journey in order to see you.

HELMER: What do you mean?

MRS. LINDE: No, really, I—

NORA: Christine is tremendously clever at book-keeping, and she is frightfully anxious to work under some clever man, so as to perfect herself—

HELMER: Very sensible, Mrs. Linde.

NORA: And when she heard you had been appointed manager of the Bank—the news was telegraphed, you know—she travelled here as quick as she could. Tor-

Torvald greets Mrs. Linde.

vald, I am sure you will be able to do something for Christine, for my sake, won't you?

730 **HELMER:** Well, it is not altogether impossible. I presume you are a widow, Mrs. Linde?

MRS. LINDE: Yes.

HELMER: And have had some experience of book-keeping?

735 **MRS. LINDE:** Yes, a fair amount.

HELMER: Ah! well, it's very likely I may be able to find something for you—

NORA: (*clapping her hands*) What did I tell you? What did I tell you?

740 **HELMER:** You have just come at a fortunate moment, Mrs. Linde.

MRS. LINDE: How am I to thank you?

HELMER: There is no need. (*Puts on his coat.*) But to-day you must excuse me—

745 **RANK:** Wait a minute; I will come with you. (*Brings his fur coat from the hall and warms it at the fire.*)

NORA: Don't be long away, Torvald dear.

HELMER: About an hour, not more.

NORA: Are you going too, Christine?

MRS. LINDE: (*putting on her cloak*) Yes, I must go and look for a room. 750

HELMER: Oh, well then, we can walk down the street together.

NORA: (*helping her*) What a pity it is we are so short of space here; I am afraid it is impossible for us— 755

MRS. LINDE: Please don't think of it! Good-bye, Nora dear, and many thanks.

NORA: Good-bye for the present. Of course you will come back this evening. And you too, Dr. Rank. What do you say? If you are well enough? Oh, you must be! 760 Wrap yourself up well. (*They go to the door all talking together. Children's voices are heard on the staircase.*)

NORA: There they are! There they are! (*She runs to open the door. The* NURSE *comes in with the children.*) Come in! Come in! (*Stoops and kisses them.*) Oh, you 765 sweet blessings! Look at them, Christine. Aren't they darlings?

RANK: Don't let us stand here in the draught.

HELMER: Come along, Mrs. Linde; the place will only be bearable for a mother now! 770

(RANK, HELMER, *and* MRS. LINDE *go downstairs. The* NURSE *comes forward with the children;* NORA *shuts the hall door.*)

NORA: How fresh and well you look! Such red cheeks!—like apples and roses. (*The children all talk at once while she speaks to them.*) Have you had great fun? That's splendid! What, you pulled both Emmy and Bob along on the sledge?—both at once?—that *was* 775 good. You are a clever boy, Ivar. Let me take her for a little, Anne. My sweet little baby doll! (*Takes the baby from the* MAID *and dances it up and down.*) Yes, yes, mother will dance with Bob too. What? Have you been snowballing? I wish I had been there too! No, 780 no, I will take their things off, Anne; please let me do it, it is such fun. Go in now, you look half frozen. There is some hot coffee for you on the stove.

(*The* NURSE *goes into the room on the left.* NORA *takes off the children's things and throws them about, while they all talk to her at once.*)

NORA: Really? Did a big dog run after you? But it didn't
785 bite you? No, dogs don't bite nice little dolly children.
You mustn't look at the parcels, Ivar. What are they?
Ah, I daresay you would like to know. No, no—it's
something nasty! Come, let us have a game! What
shall we play at? Hide and Seek? Yes, we'll play Hide
790 and Seek. Bob shall hide first. Must I hide? Very well,
I'll hide first. *(She and the children laugh and shout,
and romp in and out of the room; at last* NORA *hides
under the table, the children rush in and out for her, but
do not see her; they hear her smothered laughter, run to*
795 *the table, lift up the cloth and find her. Shouts of laughter. She crawls forward and pretends to frighten them.
Fresh laughter. Meanwhile there has been a knock at
the hall door, but none of them has noticed it. The door
is half opened, and* KROGSTAD *appears. He waits a*
800 *little; the game goes on.)*

KROGSTAD: Excuse me, Mrs. Helmer.

NORA: *(with a stifled cry, turns round and gets up on to
her knees)* Ah! what do you want?

KROGSTAD: Excuse me, the outer door was ajar; I sup-
805 pose someone forgot to shut it.

NORA: *(rising)* My husband is out, Mr. Krogstad.

KROGSTAD: I know that.

NORA: What do you want here, then?

KROGSTAD: A word with you.

810 **NORA:** With me?— *(To the children, gently.)* Go in to
nurse. What? No, the strange man won't do mother
any harm. When he has gone we will have another
game. *(She takes the children into the room on the left,
and shuts the door after them.)* You want to speak
815 to me?

KROGSTAD: Yes, I do.

NORA: To-day? It is not the first of the month yet.

KROGSTAD: No, it is Christmas Eve, and it will depend
on yourself what sort of a Christmas you will spend.

820 **NORA:** What do you mean? To-day it is absolutely impossible for me—

KROGSTAD: We won't talk about that till later on. This
is something different. I presume you can give me a
moment?

NORA: Yes—yes, I can—although— 825

KROGSTAD: Good. I was in Olsen's Restaurant and saw
your husband going down the street—

NORA: Yes?

KROGSTAD: With a lady.

NORA: What then? 830

KROGSTAD: May I make so bold as to ask if it was a
Mrs. Linde?

NORA: It was.

KROGSTAD: Just arrived in town?

NORA: Yes, to-day. 835

KROGSTAD: She is a great friend of yours, isn't she?

NORA: She is. But I don't see—

KROGSTAD: I knew her too, once upon a time.

NORA: I am aware of that.

KROGSTAD: Are you? So you know all about it; I 840
thought as much. Then I can ask you, without beating
about the bush—is Mrs. Linde to have an appointment in the Bank?

NORA: What right have you to question me, Mr.
Krogstad?—You, one of my husband's subordinates! 845
But since you ask, you shall know. Yes, Mrs. Linde *is*
to have an appointment. And it was I who pleaded
her cause, Mr. Krogstad, let me tell you that.

KROGSTAD: I was right in what I thought, then.

NORA: *(walking up and down the stage)* Sometimes one 850
has a tiny little bit of influence, I should hope. Because one is a woman, it does not necessarily follow
that—. When anyone is in a subordinate position,
Mr. Krogstad, they should really be careful to avoid
offending anyone who—who— 855

KROGSTAD: Who has influence?

NORA: Exactly.

KROGSTAD: *(changing his tone)* Mrs. Helmer, you will be so good as to use your influence on my behalf.

860 NORA: What? What do you mean?

KROGSTAD: You will be so kind as to see that I am allowed to keep my subordinate position in the Bank.

NORA: What do you mean by that? Who proposes to take your post away from you?

865 KROGSTAD: Oh, there is no necessity to keep up the pretence of ignorance. I can quite understand that your friend is not very anxious to expose herself to the chance of rubbing shoulders with me; and I quite understand, too, whom I have to thank for being
870 turned off.

NORA: But I assure you—

KROGSTAD: Very likely; but, to come to the point, the time has come when I should advise you to use your influence to prevent that.

875 NORA: But, Mr. Krogstad, I *have* no influence.

KROGSTAD: Haven't you? I thought you said yourself just now—

NORA: Naturally I did not mean you to put that construction on it. I! What should make you think I have
880 any influence of that kind with my husband?

KROGSTAD: Oh, I have known your husband from our student days. I don't suppose he is any more unassailable than other husbands.

NORA: If you speak slightingly of my husband, I shall
885 turn you out of the house.

KROGSTAD: You are bold, Mrs. Helmer.

NORA: I am not afraid of you any longer. As soon as the New Year comes, I shall in a very short time be free of the whole thing.

890 KROGSTAD: *(controlling himself)* Listen to me, Mrs. Helmer. If necessary, I am prepared to fight for my small post in the Bank as if I were fighting for my life.

NORA: So it seems.

KROGSTAD: It is not only for the sake of the money; indeed, that weighs least with me in the matter. There 895
is another reason—well, I may as well tell you. My position is this. I daresay you know, like everybody else, that once, many years ago, I was guilty of an indiscretion.

NORA: I think I have heard something of the kind. 900

KROGSTAD: The matter never came into court; but every way seemed to be closed to me after that. So I took to the business that you know of. I had to do something; and, honestly, I don't think I've been one of the worst. But now I must cut myself free from all that. 905
My sons are growing up; for their sake I must try and win back as much respect as I can in the town. This post in the Bank was like the first step up for me—and now your husband is going to kick me downstairs again into the mud. 910

NORA: But you must believe me, Mr. Krogstad; it is not in my power to help you at all.

KROGSTAD: Then it is because you haven't the will; but I have means to compel you.

NORA: You don't mean that you will tell my husband that 915
I owe you money?

KROGSTAD: Hm!—suppose I were to tell him?

NORA: It would be perfectly infamous of you. *(Sobbing.)* To think of his learning my secret, which has been my joy and pride, in such an ugly, clumsy way—that 920
he should learn it from you! And it would put me in a horribly disagreeable position—

KROGSTAD: Only disagreeable?

NORA: *(impetuously)* Well, do it, then!—and it will be the worse for you. My husband will see for himself 925
what a blackguard you are, and you certainly won't keep your post then.

KROGSTAD: I asked you if it was only a disagreeable scene at home that you were afraid of?

NORA: If my husband does get to know of it, of course he 930
will at once pay you what is still owing, and we shall have nothing more to do with you.

935 KROGSTAD: *(coming a step nearer)* Listen to me, Mrs. Helmer. Either you have a very bad memory or you know very little of business. I shall be obliged to remind you of a few details.

NORA: What do you mean?

KROGSTAD: When your husband was ill, you came to me to borrow two hundred and fifty pounds.

940 NORA: I didn't know anyone else to go to.

KROGSTAD: I promised to get you that amount—

NORA: Yes, and you did so.

945 KROGSTAD: I promised to get you that amount, on certain conditions. Your mind was so taken up with your husband's illness, and you were so anxious to get the money for your journey, that you seem to have paid no attention to the conditions of our bargain. Therefore it will not be amiss if I remind you of them. Now, I promised to get the money on the security of a bond 950 which I drew up.

NORA: Yes, and which I signed.

KROGSTAD: Good. But below your signature there were a few lines constituting your father a surety for the money; those lines your father should have signed.

955 NORA: Should? He did sign them.

KROGSTAD: I had left the date blank; that is to say, your father should himself have inserted the date on which he signed the paper. Do you remember that?

NORA: Yes, I think I remember—

960 KROGSTAD: Then I gave you the bond to send by post to your father. Is that not so?

NORA: Yes.

KROGSTAD: And you naturally did so at once, because five or six days afterwards you brought me the bond 965 with your father's signature. And then I gave you the money.

NORA: Well, haven't I been paying it off regularly?

Krogstad (David Calder) confronts Nora with the discrepancy in her father's signature.

970 KROGSTAD: Fairly so, yes. But—to come back to the matter in hand—that must have been a very trying time for you, Mrs. Helmer?

NORA: It was, indeed.

KROGSTAD: Your father was very ill, wasn't he?

NORA: He was very near his end.

KROGSTAD: He died soon afterwards?

975 NORA: Yes.

KROGSTAD: Tell me, Mrs. Helmer, can you by any chance remember what day your father died?—on what day of the month, I mean.

NORA: Papa died on the 29th of September.

980 KROGSTAD: That is correct; I have ascertained it for myself. And, as that is so, there is a discrepancy *(taking a paper from his pocket)* which I cannot account for.

NORA: What discrepancy? I don't know—

985 KROGSTAD: The discrepancy consists, Mrs. Helmer, in the fact that your father signed this bond three days after his death.

NORA: What do you mean? I don't understand—

KROGSTAD: Your father died on the 29th of September. But, look here; your father has dated his signature the 2nd of October. It is a discrepancy, isn't it? (*NORA is silent.*) Can you explain it to me? (*NORA is still silent.*) It is a remarkable thing, too, that the words "2nd of October" as well as the year, are not written in your father's handwriting but in one that I think I know. Well, of course it can be explained; your father may have forgotten to date his signature, and someone else may have dated it haphazard before they knew of his death. There is no harm in that. It all depends on the signature of the name; and *that* is genuine, I suppose, Mrs. Helmer? It was your father himself who signed his name here?

NORA: (*after a short pause, throws her head up and looks defiantly at him*) No, it was not. It was I that wrote papa's name.

KROGSTAD: Are you aware that is a dangerous confession?

NORA: In what way? You shall have your money soon.

KROGSTAD: Let me ask you a question; why did you not send the paper to your father?

NORA: It was impossible; papa was so ill. If I had asked him for his signature, I should have had to tell him what the money was to be used for; and when he was so ill himself I couldn't tell him that my husband's life was in danger—it was impossible.

KROGSTAD: It would have been better for you if you had given up your trip abroad.

NORA: No, that was impossible. That trip was to save my husband's life; I couldn't give that up.

KROGSTAD: But did it never occur to you that you were committing a fraud on me?

NORA: I couldn't take that into account; I didn't trouble myself about you at all. I couldn't bear you, because you put so many heartless difficulties in my way, although you knew what a dangerous condition my husband was in.

KROGSTAD: Mrs. Helmer, you evidently do not realise clearly what it is that you have been guilty of. But I can assure you that my one false step, which lost me all my reputation, was nothing more or nothing worse than what you have done.

NORA: You? Do you ask me to believe that you were brave enough to run a risk to save your wife's life?

KROGSTAD: The law cares nothing about motives.

NORA: Then it must be a very foolish law.

KROGSTAD: Foolish or not, it is the law by which you will be judged, if I produce this paper in court.

NORA: I don't believe it. Is a daughter not to be allowed to spare her dying father anxiety and care? Is a wife not to be allowed to save her husband's life? I don't know much about law; but I am certain that there must be laws permitting such things as that. Have you no knowledge of such laws—you who are a lawyer? You must be a very poor lawyer, Mr. Krogstad.

KROGSTAD: Maybe. But matters of business—such business as you and I have had together—do you think I don't understand that? Very well. Do as you please. But let me tell you this—if I lose my position a second time, you shall lose yours with me. (*He bows, and goes out through the hall.*)

NORA: (*appears buried in thought for a short time, then tosses her head*) Nonsense! Trying to frighten me like that!—I am not so silly as he thinks. (*Begins to busy herself putting the children's things in order.*) And yet—? No, it's impossible! I did it for love's sake.

THE CHILDREN: (*in the doorway on the left*) Mother, the stranger man has gone out through the gate.

NORA: Yes, dears, I know. But, don't tell anyone about the stranger man. Do you hear? Not even papa.

CHILDREN: No, mother; but will you come and play again?

NORA: No, no,—not now.

CHILDREN: But, mother, you promised us.

NORA: Yes, but I can't now. Run away in; I have such a lot to do. Run away in, my sweet little darlings. (*She* *gets them into the room by degrees and shuts the door on them; then sits down on the sofa, takes up a piece of needlework and sews a few stitches, but soon stops.)* No! *(Throws down the work, gets up, goes to the hall door and calls out.)* Helen! bring the Tree in. *(Goes to the table on the left, opens a drawer, and stops again.)* No, no! it is quite impossible!

MAID: *(coming in with the Tree)* Where shall I put it, ma'am?

NORA: Here, in the middle of the floor.

MAID: Shall I get you anything else?

NORA: No, thank you. I have all I want.

(Exit MAID.)

NORA: *(begins dressing the tree)* A candle here—and flowers here—. The horrible man! It's all nonsense—there's nothing wrong. The Tree shall be splendid! I will do everything I can think of to please you, Torvald!—I will sing for you, dance for you—*(HELMER comes in with some papers under his arm.)* Oh! are you back already?

HELMER: Yes. Has any one been here?

NORA: Here? No.

HELMER: That is strange. I saw Krogstad going out of the gate.

NORA: Did you? Oh yes, I forgot, Krogstad was here for a moment.

HELMER: Nora, I can see from your manner that he has been here begging you to say a good word for him.

NORA: Yes.

HELMER: And you were to appear to do it of your own accord; you were to conceal from me the fact of his having been here; didn't he beg that of you too?

NORA: Yes, Torvald, but—

HELMER: Nora, Nora, and you would be a party to that sort of thing? To have any talk with a man like that, and give him any sort of promise? And to tell me a lie into the bargain?

NORA: A lie—?

HELMER: Didn't you tell me no one had been here? *(Shakes his finger at her).* My little song-bird must never do that again. A song-bird must have a clean beak to chirp with—no false notes! *(Puts his arm round her waist.)* That is so, isn't it? Yes, I am sure it is. *(Lets her go.)* We will say no more about it. *(Sits down by the stove.)* How warm and snug it is here! *(Turns over his papers.)*

NORA: *(after a short pause, during which she busies herself with the Christmas Tree)* Torvald!

HELMER: Yes.

NORA: I am looking forward tremendously to the fancy-dress ball at the Stenborgs' the day after to-morrow.

HELMER: And I am tremendously curious to see what you are going to surprise me with.

NORA: It was very silly of me to want to do that.

HELMER: What do you mean?

NORA: I can't hit upon anything that will do; everything I think of seems so silly and insignificant.

HELMER: Does my little Nora acknowledge that at last?

NORA: *(standing behind his chair with her arms on the back of it)* Are you very busy, Torvald?

HELMER: Well—

NORA: What are all those papers?

HELMER: Bank business.

NORA: Already?

HELMER: I have got authority from the retiring manager to undertake the necessary changes in the staff and in the rearrangement of the work; and I must make use of the Christmas week for that, so as to have everything in order for the new year.

NORA: Then that was why this poor Krogstad—

HELMER: Hm!

NORA: *(leans against the back of his chair and strokes his hair)* If you hadn't been so busy I should have asked you a tremendously big favour, Torvald.

HELMER: What is that? Tell me.

1140 **NORA:** There is no one has such good taste as you. And I do so want to look nice at the fancy-dress ball. Torvald, couldn't you take me in hand and decide what I shall go as, and what sort of a dress I shall wear?

HELMER: Aha! so my obstinate little woman is obliged
1145 to get someone to come to her rescue?

NORA: Yes, Torvald, I can't get along a bit without your help.

HELMER: Very well, I will think it over, we shall manage to hit upon something.

1150 **NORA:** That is nice of you. *(Goes to the Christmas Tree. A short pause.)* How pretty the red flowers look—. But, tell me, was it really something very bad that this Krogstad was guilty of?

HELMER: He forged someone's name. Have you any idea
1155 what that means?

NORA: Isn't it possible that he was driven to do it by necessity?

HELMER: Yes; or, as in so many cases, by imprudence. I am not so heartless as to condemn a man altogether
1160 because of a single false step of that kind.

NORA: No, you wouldn't, would you, Torvald!

HELMER: Many a man has been able to retrieve his character, if he has openly confessed his fault and taken his punishment.

1165 **NORA:** Punishment—?

HELMER: But Krogstad did nothing of that sort; he got himself out of it by a cunning trick, and that is why he has gone under altogether.

NORA: But do you think it would—?

1170 **HELMER:** Just think how a guilty man like that has to lie and play the hypocrite with every one, how he has to wear a mask in the presence of those near and dear to him, even before his own wife and children. And about the children—that is the most terrible part of it
1175 all, Nora.

NORA: How?

HELMER: Because such an atmosphere of lies infects and poisons the whole life of a home. Each breath the children take in such a house is full of the germs of evil. 1180

NORA: *(coming nearer him)* Are you sure of that?

HELMER: My dear, I have often seen it in the course of my life as a lawyer. Almost everyone who has gone to the bad early in life has had a deceitful mother.

NORA: Why do you only say—mother? 1185

HELMER: It seems most commonly to be the mother's influence, though naturally a bad father's would have the same result. Every lawyer is familiar with the fact. This Krogstad, now, has been persistently poisoning his own children with lies and dissimulation; that is 1190
why I say he has lost all moral character. *(Holds out his hands to her.)* That is why my sweet little Nora must promise me not to plead his cause. Give me your hand on it. Come, come, what is this? Give me your hand. There now, that's settled. I assure you it would 1195
be quite impossible for me to work with him; I literally feel physically ill when I am in the company of such people.

Nora and Torvald (Trevor Eve) discuss Krogstad's visit.

NORA: *(takes her hand out of his and goes to the opposite side of the Christmas Tree)* How hot it is in here; and I have such a lot to do.

1200

HELMER: *(getting up and putting his papers in order)* Yes, and I must try and read through some of these before dinner; and I must think about your costume, too. And it is just possible I may have something ready in gold paper to hang up on the Tree. *(Puts his hand on her head.)* My precious little singing-bird! *(He goes into his room and shuts the door after him.)*

1205

NORA: *(after a pause, whispers)* No, no—it isn't true. It's impossible; it must be impossible.

1210

(The NURSE *opens the door on the left.)*

NURSE: The little ones are begging so hard to be allowed to come in to mamma.

NORA: No, no, no! Don't let them come in to me! You stay with them, Anne.

1215 **NURSE:** Very well, ma'am. *(Shuts the door.)*

NORA: *(pale with terror)* Deprave my little children? Poison my home? *(A short pause. Then she tosses her head.)* It's not true. It can't possibly be true.

ACT 2

THE SAME SCENE: *The Christmas Tree is in the corner by the piano, stripped of its ornaments and with burnt-down candle-ends on its dishevelled branches. NORA's cloak and hat are lying on the sofa. She is alone in the room, walking about uneasily. She stops by the sofa and takes up her cloak.*

NORA: *(drops her cloak)* Someone is coming now! *(Goes to the door and listens.)* No—it is no one. Of course, no one will come to-day, Christmas Day—nor to-morrow either. But, perhaps—(opens the door and looks out). No, nothing in the letter-box; it is quite empty. *(Comes forward.)* What rubbish! of course he can't be in earnest about it. Such a thing couldn't happen; it is impossible—I have three little children.

5

(Enter the NURSE *from the room on the left, carrying a big cardboard box.)*

NURSE: At last I have found the box with the fancy dress.

10

NORA: Thanks; put it on the table.

NURSE: *(doing so)* But it is very much in want of mending.

NORA: I should like to tear it into a hundred thousand pieces.

NURSE: What an idea! It can easily be put in order—just a little patience.

15

NORA: Yes, I will go and get Mrs. Linde to come and help me with it.

NURSE: What, out again? In this horrible weather? You will catch cold, ma'am, and make yourself ill.

20

NORA: Well, worse than that might happen. How are the children?

NURSE: The poor little souls are playing with their Christmas presents, but—

NORA: Do they ask much for me?

25

NURSE: You see, they are so accustomed to have their mamma with them.

NORA: Yes, but, nurse, I shall not be able to be so much with them now as I was before.

NURSE: Oh well, young children easily get accustomed to anything.

30

NORA: Do you think so? Do you think they would forget their mother if she went away altogether?

NURSE: Good heavens!—went away altogether?

NORA: Nurse, I want you to tell me something I have often wondered about—how could you have the heart to put your own child out among strangers?

35

NURSE: I was obliged to, if I wanted to be little Nora's nurse.

NORA: Yes, but how could you be willing to do it?

40

NURSE: What, when I was going to get such a good place by it? A poor girl who has got into trouble should be glad to. Besides, that wicked man didn't do a single thing for me.

Nora confides in the nurse (Helen Blatch) her fears of being away from the children.

45 **NORA:**   But I suppose your daughter has quite forgotten you.

NURSE: No, indeed she hasn't. She wrote to me when she was confirmed, and when she was married.

NORA: *(putting her arms round her neck)* Dear old Anne,
50   you were a good mother to me when I was little.

NURSE: Little Nora, poor dear, had no other mother but me.

NORA: And if my little ones had no other mother, I am sure you would— What nonsense I am talking! *(Opens*
55   *the box.)* Go in to them. Now I must—. You will see to-morrow how charming I shall look.

NURSE: I am sure there will be no one at the ball so charming as you, ma'am. *(Goes into the room on the left.)*

60 **NORA:**   *(begins to unpack the box, but soon pushes it away from her)* If only I dared go out. If only no one would come. If only I could be sure nothing would happen here in the meantime. Stuff and nonsense! No one will come. Only I mustn't think about it. I will brush my
65   muff. What lovely, lovely gloves! Out of my thoughts, out of my thoughts! One, two, three, four, five, six— *(Screams.)* Ah! there is someone coming—. *(Makes a movement towards the door, but stands irresolute.)*

(Enter MRS. LINDE *from the hall, where she has taken off her cloak and hat.)*

NORA: Oh, it's you, Christine. There is no one else out there, is there? How good of you to come!   70

MRS. LINDE: I heard you were up asking for me.

NORA: Yes, I was passing by. As a matter of fact, it is something you could help me with. Let us sit down here on the sofa. Look here. To-morrow evening there is to be a fancy-dress ball at the Stenborgs', who live   75 above us; and Torvald wants me to go as a Neapolitan fisher-girl, and dance the Tarantella that I learnt at Capri.

MRS. LINDE: I see; you are going to keep up the character.   80

NORA: Yes, Torvald wants me to. Look, here is the dress; Torvald had it made for me there, but now it is all so torn, and I haven't any idea—

MRS. LINDE: We will easily put that right. It is only some of the trimming come unsewn here and there.   85 Needle and thread? Now then, that's all we want.

NORA: It *is* nice of you.

MRS. LINDE: *(sewing)* So you are going to be dressed up to-morrow, Nora. I will tell you what—I shall come in for a moment and see you in your fine feathers. But I   90 have completely forgotten to thank you for a delightful evening yesterday.

NORA: *(gets up, and crosses the stage)* Well, I don't think yesterday was as pleasant as usual. You ought to have come to town a little earlier, Christine. Certainly   95 Torvald does understand how to make a house dainty and attractive.

MRS. LINDE: And so do you, it seems to me; you are not your father's daughter for nothing. But tell me, is Doctor Rank always as depressed as he was yesterday?   100

NORA: No; yesterday it was very noticeable. I must tell you that he suffers from a very dangerous disease. He has consumption of the spine, poor creature. His father was a horrible man who committed all sorts of excesses; and that is why his son was sickly from   105 childhood, do you understand?

MRS. LINDE: *(dropping her sewing)* But, my dearest Nora, how do you know anything about such things?

NORA: *(walking about)* Pooh! When you have three children, you get visits now and then from—from married women, who know something of medical matters, and they talk about one thing and another.

MRS. LINDE: *(goes on sewing. A short silence)* Does Doctor Rank come here every day?

NORA: Every day regularly. He is Torvald's most intimate friend, and a great friend of mine too. He is just like one of the family.

MRS. LINDE: But tell me this—is he perfectly sincere? I mean, isn't he the kind of man that is very anxious to make himself agreeable?

NORA: Not in the least. What makes you think that?

MRS. LINDE: When you introduced him to me yesterday, he declared he had often heard my name mentioned in this house; but afterwards I noticed that your husband hadn't the slightest idea who I was. So how could Doctor Rank—?

NORA: That is quite right, Christine. Torvald is so absurdly fond of me that he wants me absolutely to himself, as he says. At first he used to seem almost jealous if I mentioned any of the dear folk at home, so naturally I gave up doing so. But I often talk about such things with Doctor Rank, because he likes hearing about them.

MRS. LINDE: Listen to me, Nora. You are still very like a child in many things, and I am older than you in many ways and have a little more experience. Let me tell you this—you ought to make an end of it with Doctor Rank.

NORA: What ought I to make an end of?

MRS. LINDE: Of two things, I think. Yesterday you talked some nonsense about a rich admirer who was to leave you money—

NORA: An admirer who doesn't exist, unfortunately! But what then?

MRS. LINDE: Is Doctor Rank a man of means?

NORA: Yes, he is.

MRS. LINDE: And has no one to provide for?

NORA: No, no one; but—

MRS. LINDE: And comes here every day?

NORA: Yes, I told you so.

MRS. LINDE: But how can this well-bred man be so tactless?

NORA: I don't understand you at all.

MRS. LINDE: Don't prevaricate, Nora. Do you suppose I don't guess who lent you the two hundred and fifty pounds?

NORA: Are you out of your senses? How can you think of such a thing! A friend of ours, who comes here every day! Do you realise what a horribly painful position that would be?

MRS. LINDE: Then it really isn't he?

NORA: No, certainly not. It would never have entered into my head for a moment. Besides, he had no money to lend then; he came into his money afterwards.

MRS. LINDE: Well, I think that was lucky for you, my dear Nora.

Nora and Mrs. Linde discuss Dr. Rank and the problem of Krogstad.

NORA: No, it would never have come into my head to ask Doctor Rank. Although I am quite sure that if I had asked him—

170 **MRS. LINDE:**   But of course you won't.

NORA: Of course not. I have no reason to think it could possibly be necessary. But I am quite sure that if I told Doctor Rank—

MRS. LINDE: Behind your husband's back?

175 **NORA:**   I must make an end of it with the other one, and that will be behind his back too. I *must* make an end of it with him.

MRS. LINDE: Yes, that is what I told you yesterday, but—

NORA: *(walking up and down)* A man can put a thing
180   like that straight much easier than a woman—

MRS. LINDE: One's husband, yes.

NORA: Nonsense! *(Standing still.)* When you pay off a debt you get your bond back, don't you?

MRS. LINDE: Yes, as a matter of course.

185 **NORA:**   And can tear it into a hundred thousand pieces, and burn it up—the nasty dirty paper!

MRS. LINDE: *(looks hard at her, lays down her sewing and gets up slowly)* Nora, you are concealing something from me.

190 **NORA:**   Do I look as if I were?

MRS. LINDE: Something has happened to you since yesterday morning. Nora, what is it?

NORA: *(going nearer to her)* Christine! *(Listens.)* Hush! there's Torvald come home. Do you mind going in to
195   the children for the present? Torvald can't bear to see dressmaking going on. Let Anne help you.

MRS. LINDE: *(gathering some of the things together)* Certainly—but I am not going away from here till we have had it out with one another. *(She goes into the
200   room on the left, as* HELMER *comes in from the hall.)*

NORA: *(going up to* HELMER*)* I have wanted you so much, Torvald dear.

HELMER: Was that the dressmaker?

NORA: No, it was Christine; she is helping me to put my dress in order. You will see I shall look quite smart.   205

HELMER: Wasn't that a happy thought of mine, now?

NORA: Splendid! But don't you think it is nice of me, too, to do as you wish?

HELMER: Nice?—because you do as your husband wishes? Well, well, you little rogue, I am sure you did   210 not mean it in that way. But I am not going to disturb you; you will want to be trying on your dress, I expect.

NORA: I suppose you are going to work.

HELMER: Yes. *(Shows her a bundle of papers.)* Look at that. I have just been into the bank. *(Turns to go into*   215 *his room.)*

NORA: Torvald.

HELMER: Yes.

NORA: If your little squirrel were to ask you for something very, very prettily—?   220

HELMER: What then?

NORA: Would you do it?

HELMER: I should like to hear what it is, first.

NORA: Your squirrel would run about and do all her tricks if you would be nice, and do what she wants.   225

HELMER: Speak plainly.

NORA: Your skylark would chirp about in every room, with her song rising and falling—

HELMER: Well, my skylark does that anyhow.

NORA: I would play the fairy and dance for you in the   230 moonlight, Torvald.

HELMER: Nora—you surely don't mean that request you made to me this morning?

NORA: *(going near him)* Yes, Torvald, I beg you so earnestly—   235

HELMER: Have you really the courage to open up that question again?

NORA: Yes, dear, you *must* do as I ask; you *must* let Krogstad keep his post in the bank.

240 **HELMER:** My dear Nora, it is his post that I have arranged Mrs. Linde shall have.

NORA: Yes, you have been awfully kind about that; but you could just as well dismiss some other clerk instead of Krogstad.

245 **HELMER:** This is simply incredible obstinacy! Because you chose to give him a thoughtless promise that you would speak for him, I am expected to—

NORA: That isn't the reason, Torvald. It is for your own sake. This fellow writes in the most scurrilous news-
250 papers; you have told me so yourself. He can do you an unspeakable amount of harm. I am frightened to death of him—

HELMER: Ah, I understand; it is recollections of the past that scare you.

255 **NORA:** What do you mean?

HELMER: Naturally you are thinking of your father.

NORA: Yes—yes, of course. Just recall to your mind what these malicious creatures wrote in the papers about papa, and how horribly they slandered him. I believe
260 they would have procured his dismissal if the Department had not sent you over to inquire into it, and if you had not been so kindly disposed and helpful to him.

HELMER: My little Nora, there is an important dif-
265 ference between your father and me. Your father's reputation as a public official was not above suspicion. Mine is, and I hope it will continue to be so, as long as I hold my office.

NORA: You never can tell what mischief these men may
270 contrive. We ought to be so well off, so snug and happy here in our peaceful home, and have no cares— you and I and the children, Torvald! That is why I beg you so earnestly—

HELMER: And it is just by interceding for him that you
275 make it impossible for me to keep him. It is already known at the Bank that I mean to dismiss Krog-

stad. Is it to get about now that the new manager has changed his mind at his wife's bidding—

NORA: And what if it did?

HELMER: Of course!—if only this obstinate little person 280 can get her way! Do you suppose I am going to make myself ridiculous before my whole staff, to let people think that I am a man to be swayed by all sorts of outside influence? I should very soon feel the consequences of it, I can tell you! And besides, there is one 285 thing that makes it quite impossible for me to have Krogstad in the Bank as long as I am manager.

NORA: Whatever is that?

HELMER: His moral failings I might perhaps have overlooked, if necessary— 290

NORA: Yes, you could—couldn't you?

HELMER: And I hear he is a good worker, too. But I knew him when we were boys. It was one of those rash friendships that so often prove an incubus in after life. I may as well tell you plainly, we were once on 295 very intimate terms with one another. But this tact-less fellow lays no restraint on himself when other people are present. On the contrary, he thinks it gives him the right to adopt a familiar tone with me, and every minute it is "I say, Helmer, old fellow!" and 300 that sort of thing. I assure you it is extremely pain-ful for me. He would make my position in the Bank intolerable.

NORA: Torvald, I don't believe you mean that.

HELMER: Don't you? Why not? 305

NORA: Because it is such a narrow-minded way of look-ing at things.

HELMER: What are you saying? Narrow-minded? Do you think I am narrow-minded?

NORA: No, just the opposite, dear—and it is exactly for 310 that reason.

HELMER: It's the same thing. You say my point of view is narrow-minded, so I must be so too. Narrow-minded! Very well—I must put an end to this. (*Goes to the hall door and calls.*) Helen! 315

NORA: What are you going to do?

HELMER: *(looking among his papers)* Settle it. *(Enter MAID.)* Look here; take this letter and go downstairs with it at once. Find a messenger and tell him to deliver it, and be quick. The address is on it, and here is the money.

MAID: Very well, sir. *(Exit with the letter.)*

HELMER: *(putting his papers together)* Now then, little Miss Obstinate.

NORA: *(breathlessly)* Torvald—what was that letter?

HELMER: Krogstad's dismissal.

NORA: Call her back, Torvald! There is still time. Oh, Torvald, call her back! Do it for my sake—for your own sake—for the children's sake! Do you hear me, Torvald? Call her back! You don't know what that letter can bring upon us.

HELMER: It's too late.

NORA: Yes, it's too late.

HELMER: My dear Nora, I can forgive the anxiety you are in, although really it is an insult to me. It is, indeed. Isn't it an insult to think that I should be afraid of a starving quill-driver's vengeance? But I forgive you nevertheless, because it is such eloquent witness to your great love for me. *(Takes her in his arms.)* And that is as it should be, my own darling Nora. Come what will, you may be sure I shall have both courage and strength if they be needed. You will see I am man enough to take everything upon myself.

NORA: *(in a horror-stricken voice)* What do you mean by that?

HELMER: Everything, I say—

NORA: *(recovering herself)* You will never have to do that.

HELMER: That's right. Well, we will share it, Nora, as man and wife should. That is how it shall be. *(Caressing her.)* Are you content now? There! there!—not these frightened dove's eyes! The whole thing is only the wildest fancy!—Now, you must go and play through the Tarantella and practise with your tambourine. I shall go into the inner office and shut the door, and I shall hear nothing; you can make as much noise as you please. *(Turns back at the door.)* And when Rank comes, tell him where he will find me. *(Nods to her, takes his papers and goes into his room, and shuts the door after him.)*

NORA: *(bewildered with anxiety, stands as if rooted to the spot, and whispers)* He was capable of doing it. He will do it. He will do it in spite of everything.—No, not that! Never, never! Anything rather than that! Oh, for some help, some way out of it! *(The door-bell rings.)* Doctor Rank! Anything rather than that—anything, whatever it is! *(She puts her hands over her face, pulls herself together, goes to the door and opens it. RANK is standing without, hanging up his coat. During the following dialogue it begins to grow dark.)*

NORA: Good-day, Doctor Rank. I knew your ring. But you mustn't go in to Torvald now; I think he is busy with something.

RANK: And you?

NORA: *(brings him in and shuts the door after him)* Oh, you know very well I always have time for you.

RANK: Thank you. I shall make use of as much of it as I can.

NORA: What do you mean by that? As much of it as you can?

RANK: Well, does that alarm you?

NORA: It was such a strange way of putting it. Is anything likely to happen?

RANK: Nothing but what I have long been prepared for. But I certainly didn't expect it to happen so soon.

NORA: *(gripping him by the arm)* What have you found out? Doctor Rank, you must tell me.

RANK: *(sitting down by the stove)* It is all up with me. And it can't be helped.

NORA: *(with a sigh of relief)* Is it about yourself?

RANK: Who else? It is no use lying to one's self. I am the most wretched of all my patients, Mrs. Helmer. Lately I have been taking stock of my internal economy.

Bankrupt! Probably within a month I shall lie rotting in the churchyard.

395 **NORA:**   What an ugly thing to say!

RANK: The thing itself is cursedly ugly, and the worst of it is that I shall have to face so much more that is ugly before that. I shall only make one more examination of myself; when I have done that, I shall know pretty

400 certainly when it will be that the horrors of dissolution will begin. There is something I want to tell you. Helmer's refined nature gives him an unconquerable disgust at everything that is ugly; I won't have him in my sick-room.

405 **NORA:**   Oh, but, Doctor Rank—

RANK: I won't have him there. Not on any account. I bar my door to him. As soon as I am quite certain that the worst has come, I shall send you my card with a black cross on it, and then you will know that the loathsome

410 end has begun.

NORA: You are quite absurd to-day. And I wanted you so much to be in a really good humour.

RANK: With death stalking beside me?—To have to pay this penalty for another man's sin! Is there any jus-

415 tice in that? And in every single family, in one way or another, some such inexorable retribution is being exacted—

NORA: (putting her hands over her ears) Rubbish! Do talk of something cheerful.

420 **RANK:**   Oh, it's a mere laughing matter, the whole thing. My poor innocent spine has to suffer for my father's youthful amusements.

NORA: (sitting at the table on the left) I suppose you mean that he was too partial to asparagus and pâté de foie

425 gras, don't you?

RANK: Yes, and to truffles.

NORA: Truffles, yes. And oysters too, I suppose?

RANK: Oysters, of course, that goes without saying.

NORA: And heaps of port and champagne. It is sad that

430 all these nice things should take their revenge on our bones.

RANK: Especially that they should revenge themselves on the unlucky bones of those who have not had the satisfaction of enjoying them.

NORA: Yes, that's the saddest part of it all.   435

RANK: (with a searching look at her) Hm!—

NORA: (after a short pause) Why did you smile?

RANK: No, it was you that laughed.

NORA: No, it was you that smiled, Doctor Rank!

RANK: (rising) You are a greater rascal than I thought.   440

NORA: I am in a silly mood to-day.

RANK: So it seems.

NORA: (putting her hands on his shoulders) Dear, dear Doctor Rank, death mustn't take you away from Torvald and me.   445

RANK: It is a loss you would easily recover from. Those who are gone are soon forgotten.

NORA: (looking at him anxiously) Do you believe that?

RANK: People form new ties, and then—

NORA: Who will form new ties?   450

RANK: Both you and Helmer, when I am gone. You yourself are already on the high road to it, I think. What did that Mrs. Linde want here last night?

NORA: Oho!—you don't mean to say you are jealous of poor Christine?   455

RANK: Yes, I am. She will be my successor in this house. When I am done for, this woman will—

NORA: Hush! don't speak so loud. She is in that room.

RANK: To-day again. There, you see.

NORA: She has only come to sew my dress for me. Bless   460
my soul, how unreasonable you are! (Sits down on the sofa.) Be nice now, Doctor Rank, and to-morrow you will see how beautifully I shall dance, and you can imagine I am doing it all for you—and for Torvald too, of course. (Takes various things out of the box.) Doctor   465
Rank, come and sit down here, and I will show you something.

RANK: *(sitting down)* What is it?

NORA: Just look at those!

470   RANK: Silk stockings.

NORA: Flesh-coloured. Aren't they lovely? It is so dark here now, but to-morrow—. No, no, no! you must only look at the feet. Oh well, you may have leave to look at the legs too.

475   RANK: Hm!—

NORA: Why are you looking so critical? Don't you think they will fit me?

RANK: I have no means of forming an opinion about that.

NORA: *(looks at him for a moment)* For shame! *(Hits him*
480   *lightly on the ear with the stockings.)* That's to punish you. *(Folds them up again.)*

RANK: And what other nice things am I to be allowed to see?

NORA: Not a single thing more, for being so naughty.
485   *(She looks among the things, humming to herself.)*

RANK: *(after a short silence)* When I am sitting here, talking to you as intimately as this, I cannot imagine for a moment what would have become of me if I had never come into this house.

490   NORA: *(smiling)* I believe you do feel thoroughly at home with us.

RANK: *(in a lower voice, looking straight in front of him)* And to be obliged to leave it all—

NORA: Nonsense, you are not going to leave it.

495   RANK: *(as before)* And not be able to leave behind one the slightest token of one's gratitude, scarcely even a fleeting regret—nothing but an empty place which the first comer can fill as well as any other.

NORA: And if I asked you now for a—? No!

500   RANK: For what?

NORA: For a big proof of your friendship—

RANK: Yes, yes!

Dr. Rank (Patrick Malahide) makes his confession to Nora.

NORA: I mean a tremendously big favour—

RANK: Would you really make me so happy for once?

NORA: Ah, but you don't know what it is yet.   505

RANK: No—but tell me.

NORA: I really can't, Doctor Rank. It is something out of all reason; it means advice, and help, and a favour—

RANK: The bigger a thing it is the better. I can't conceive what it is you mean. Do tell me. Haven't I your   510
confidence?

NORA: More than any one else. I know you are my truest and best friend, and so I will tell you what it is. Well, Doctor Rank, it is something you must help me to prevent. You know how devotedly, how inexpressibly   515
deeply Torvald loves me; he would never for a moment hesitate to give his life for me.

RANK: *(leaning towards her)* Nora—do you think he is the only one—?

NORA: *(with a slight start)* The only one—?   520

RANK: The only one who would gladly give his life for your sake.

NORA: *(sadly)* Is that it?

RANK: I was determined you should know it before I
525 went away, and there will never be a better opportunity than this. Now you know it, Nora. And now you know, too, that you can trust me as you would trust no one else.

NORA: (*rises, deliberately and quietly*) Let me pass.

530 **RANK:** (*makes room for her to pass him, but sits still*) Nora!

NORA: (*at the hall door*) Helen, bring in the lamp. (*Goes over to the stove.*) Dear Doctor Rank, that was really horrid of you.

535 **RANK:** To have loved you as much as any one else does? Was that horrid?

NORA: No, but to go and tell me so. There was really no need—

RANK: What do you mean? Did you know—? (MAID
540 *enters with lamp, puts it down on the table, and goes out.*) Nora—Mrs. Helmer—tell me, had you any idea of this?

NORA: Oh, how do I know whether I had or whether I hadn't? I really can't tell you— To think you could be
545 so clumsy, Doctor Rank! We were getting on so nicely.

RANK: Well, at all events you know now that you can command me, body and soul. So won't you speak out?

NORA: (*looking at him*) After what happened?

RANK: I beg you to let me know what it is.

550 **NORA:** I can't tell you anything now.

RANK: Yes, yes. You mustn't punish me in that way. Let me have permission to do for you whatever a man may do.

NORA: You can do nothing for me now. Besides, I really
555 don't need any help at all. You will find that the whole thing is merely fancy on my part. It really is so—of course it is! (*Sits down in the rocking-chair, and looks at him with a smile.*) You are a nice sort of man, Doctor Rank!—don't you feel ashamed of yourself, now
560 the lamp has come?

RANK: Not a bit. But perhaps I had better go—for ever?

NORA: No, indeed, you shall not. Of course you must come here just as before. You know very well Torvald can't do without you.

RANK: Yes, but you? 565

NORA: Oh, I am always tremendously pleased when you come.

RANK: It is just that, that put me on the wrong track. You are a riddle to me. I have often thought that you would almost as soon be in my company as in 570 Helmer's.

NORA: Yes—you see there are some people one loves best, and others whom one would almost always rather have as companions.

RANK: Yes, there is something in that. 575

NORA: When I was at home, of course I loved papa best. But I always thought it tremendous fun if I could steal down into the maids' room, because they never moralised at all, and talked to each other about such entertaining things. 580

RANK: I see—it is *their* place I have taken.

NORA: (*jumping up and going to him*) Oh, dear, nice Doctor Rank, I never meant that at all. But surely you can understand that being with Torvald is a little like being with papa— 585

(*Enter* MAID *from the hall.*)

MAID: If you please, ma'am. (*Whispers and hands her a card.*)

NORA: (*glancing at the card*) Oh! (*Puts it in her pocket.*)

RANK: Is there anything wrong?

NORA: No, no, not in the least. It is only something—it is 590 my new dress—

RANK: What? Your dress is lying there.

NORA: Oh, yes, that one; but this is another. I ordered it. Torvald mustn't know about it—

RANK: Oho! Then that was the great secret. 595

NORA: Of course. Just go in to him; he is sitting in the inner room. Keep him as long as—

RANK: Make your mind easy; I won't let him escape. *(Goes into* HELMER's *room.)*

600 NORA: *(to the* MAID*)* And he is standing waiting in the kitchen?

MAID: Yes; he came up the back stairs.

NORA: But didn't you tell him no one was in?

MAID: Yes, but it was no good.

605 NORA: He won't go away?

MAID: No; he says he won't until he has seen you, ma'am.

NORA: Well, let him come in—but quietly. Helen, you mustn't say anything about it to any one. It is a surprise for my husband.

610 MAID: Yes, ma'am, I quite understand. *(Exit.)*

NORA: This dreadful thing is going to happen! It will happen in spite of me! No, no, no, it can't happen—it shan't happen! *(She bolts the door of* HELMER's *room. The* MAID *opens the hall door for* KROGSTAD *and*
615 *shuts it after him. He is wearing a fur coat, high boots and a fur cap.)*

NORA: *(advancing towards him)* Speak low—my husband is at home.

KROGSTAD: No matter about that.

Krogstad (Denholm Elliott) meets secretly with Nora to reveal his decision.

NORA: What do you want of me? 620

KROGSTAD: An explanation of something.

NORA: Make haste then. What is it?

KROGSTAD: You know, I suppose, that I have got my dismissal.

NORA: I couldn't prevent it, Mr. Krogstad. I fought as 625 hard as I could on your side, but it was no good.

KROGSTAD: Does your husband love you so little, then? He knows what I can expose you to, and yet he ventures—

NORA: How can you suppose that he has any knowledge 630 of the sort?

KROGSTAD: I didn't suppose so at all. It would not be the least like our dear Torvald Helmer to show so much courage—

NORA: Mr. Krogstad, a little respect for my husband, 635 please.

KROGSTAD: Certainly—all the respect he deserves. But since you have kept the matter so carefully to yourself, I make bold to suppose that you have a little clearer idea, than you had yesterday, of what it actually is 340 that you have done?

NORA: More than you could ever ever teach me.

KROGSTAD: Yes, such a bad lawyer as I am.

NORA: What is it you want of me?

KROGSTAD: Only to see how you were, Mrs. Helmer. 645 I have been thinking about you all day long. A mere cashier, a quill-driver, a—well, a man like me—even he has a little of what is called feeling, you know.

NORA: Show it, then; think of my little children.

KROGSTAD: Have you and your husband thought of 650 mine? But never mind about that. I only wanted to tell you that you need not take this matter too seriously. In the first place there will be no accusation made on my part.

NORA: No, of course not; I was sure of that. 655

KROGSTAD: The whole thing can be arranged amicably; there is no reason why anyone should know anything about it. It will remain a secret between us three.

NORA: My husband must never get to know anything about it.

660

KROGSTAD: How will you be able to prevent it? Am I to understand that you can pay the balance that is owing?

NORA: No, not just at present.

665 **KROGSTAD:**   Or perhaps that you have some expedient for raising the money soon?

NORA: No expedient that I mean to make use of.

KROGSTAD: Well, in any case, it would have been of no use to you now. If you stood there with ever so much money in your hand, I would never part with your bond.

670

NORA: Tell me what purpose you mean to put it to.

KROGSTAD: I shall only preserve it—keep it in my possession. No one who is not concerned in the matter shall have the slightest hint of it. So that if the thought of it has driven you to any desperate resolution—

675

NORA: It has.

KROGSTAD: If you had it in your mind to run away from your home—

680

NORA: I had.

KROGSTAD: Or even something worse—

NORA: How could you know that?

KROGSTAD: Give up the idea.

685 **NORA:**   How did you know I had thought of *that*?

KROGSTAD: Most of us think of that at first. I did, too—but I hadn't the courage.

NORA: (*lifelessly*) No more had I.

KROGSTAD: (*in a tone of relief*) No, that's it, isn't it—you hadn't the courage either?

690

NORA: No, I haven't—I haven't.

KROGSTAD: Besides, it would have been a great piece of folly. Once the first storm at home is over—. I have a letter for your husband in my pocket.

NORA: Telling him everything?

695

KROGSTAD: In as lenient a manner as I possibly could.

NORA: (*quickly*) He mustn't get the letter. Tear it up. I will find some means of getting money.

KROGSTAD: Excuse me, Mrs. Helmer, but I think I told you just now—

700

NORA: I am not speaking of what I owe you. Tell me what sum you are asking my husband for, and I will get the money.

KROGSTAD: I am not asking your husband for a penny.

NORA: What do you want, then?

705

KROGSTAD: I will tell you. I want to rehabilitate myself, Mrs. Helmer; I want to get on; and in that your husband must help me. For the last year and a half I have not had a hand in anything dishonourable, and all that time I have been struggling in most restricted circumstances. I was content to work my way up step by step. Now I am turned out, and I am not going to be satisfied with merely being taken into favour again. I want to get on, I tell you. I want to get into the Bank again, in a higher position. Your husband must make a place for me—

710

715

NORA: That he will never do!

KROGSTAD: He will; I know him; he dare not protest. And as soon as I am in there again with him, then you will see! Within a year I shall be the manager's right hand. It will be Nils Krogstad and not Torvald Helmer who manages the Bank.

720

NORA: That's a thing you will never see.

KROGSTAD: Do you mean that you will—?

NORA: I have courage enough for it now.

725

KROGSTAD: Oh, you can't frighten me. A fine, spoilt lady like you—

NORA: You will see, you will see.

KROGSTAD: Under the ice, perhaps? Down into the cold, coal-black water? And then, in the spring, to float up to the surface, all horrible and unrecognisable, with your hair fallen out—

NORA: You can't frighten me.

KROGSTAD: Nor you me. People don't do such things, Mrs. Helmer. Besides, what use would it be? I should have him completely in my power all the same.

NORA: Afterwards? When I am no longer—

KROGSTAD: Have you forgotten that it is I who have the keeping of your reputation? (NORA *stands speechlessly looking at him.*) Well, now, I have warned you. Do not do anything foolish. When Helmer has had my letter, I shall expect a message from him. And be sure you remember that it is your husband himself who has forced me into such ways as this again. I will never forgive him for that. Good-bye, Mrs. Helmer. (*Exit through the hall.*)

NORA: (*goes to the hall door, opens it slightly and listens*) He is going. He is not putting the letter in the box. Oh no, no! that's impossible! (*Opens the door by degrees.*) What is that? He is standing outside. He is not going downstairs. Is he hesitating? Can he—? (*A letter drops into the box; then* KROGSTAD's *footsteps are heard, till they die away as he goes downstairs.* NORA *utters a stifled cry, and runs across the room to the table by the sofa. A short pause.*)

NORA: In the letter-box. (*Steals across to the hall door.*) There it lies—Torvald, Torvald, there is no hope for us now!

(MRS. LINDE *comes in from the room on the left, carrying the dress.*)

MRS. LINDE: There, I can't see anything more to mend now. Would you like to try it on—?

NORA: (*in a hoarse whisper*) Christine, come here.

MRS. LINDE: (*throwing the dress down on the sofa*) What is the matter with you? You look so agitated!

NORA: Come here. Do you see that letter? There, look— you can see it through the glass in the letter-box.

MRS. LINDE: Yes, I see it.

NORA: That letter is from Krogstad.

MRS. LINDE: Nora—it was Krogstad who lent you the money!

NORA: Yes, and now Torvald will know all about it.

MRS. LINDE: Believe me, Nora, that's the best thing for both of you.

NORA: You don't know all. I forged a name.

MRS. LINDE: Good heavens—!

NORA: I only want to say this to you, Christine—you must be my witness.

MRS. LINDE: Your witness? What do you mean? What am I to—?

NORA: If I should go out of my mind—it might easily happen—

MRS. LINDE: Nora!

NORA: Or if anything else should happen to me—anything, for instance, that might prevent my being here—

MRS. LINDE: Nora! Nora! you are quite out of your mind.

Nora tries to pry open the letter box.

NORA: And if it should happen that there were some one who wanted to take all the responsibility, all the blame, you understand—

790 **MRS. LINDE:** Yes, yes—but how can you suppose—?

NORA: Then you must be my witness, that it is not true, Christine. I am not out of my mind at all; I am in my right senses now, and I tell you no one else has known anything about it; I, and I alone, did the whole thing. 795 Remember that.

MRS. LINDE: I will, indeed. But I don't understand all this.

NORA: How should you understand it? A wonderful thing is going to happen!

800 **MRS. LINDE:** A wonderful thing?

NORA: Yes, a wonderful thing!—But it is so terrible, Christine; it *mustn't* happen, not for all the world.

MRS. LINDE: I will go at once and see Krogstad.

NORA: Don't go to him; he will do you some harm.

805 **MRS. LINDE:** There was a time when he would gladly do anything for my sake.

NORA: He?

MRS. LINDE: Where does he live?

NORA: How should I know—? Yes (*feeling in her pocket*), 810 here is his card. But the letter, the letter—!

HELMER: (*calls from his room, knocking at the door*) Nora!

NORA: (*cries out anxiously*) Oh, what's that? What do you want?

815 **HELMER:** Don't be so frightened. We are not coming in; you have locked the door. Are you trying on your dress?

NORA: Yes, that's it. I look so nice, Torvald.

MRS. LINDE: (*who has read the card*) I see he lives at the 820 corner here.

NORA: Yes, but it's no use. It is hopeless. The letter is lying there in the box.

Nora practices her dancing for Torvald.

MRS. LINDE: And your husband keeps the key?

NORA: Yes, always.

MRS. LINDE: Krogstad must ask for his letter back 825 unread, he must find some pretence—

NORA: But it is just at this time that Torvald generally—

MRS. LINDE: You must delay him. Go in to him in the meantime. I will come back as soon as I can. (*She goes out hurriedly through the hall door.*) 830

NORA: (*goes to* HELMER's *door, opens it and peeps in*) Torvald!

HELMER: (*from the inner room*) Well? May I venture at last to come into my own room again? Come along, Rank, now you will see— (*Halting in the doorway.*) 835 But what is this?

NORA: What is what, dear?

HELMER: Rank led me to expect a splendid transformation.

RANK: (*in the doorway*) I understood so, but evidently I 840 was mistaken.

NORA: Yes, nobody is to have the chance of admiring me in my dress until to-morrow.

HELMER: But, my dear Nora, you look so worn out. Have you been practising too much? 845

NORA: No, I have not practised at all.

HELMER: But you will need to—

NORA: Yes, indeed I shall, Torvald. But I can't get on a bit without you to help me; I have absolutely forgotten the whole thing.

HELMER: Oh, we will soon work it up again.

NORA: Yes, help me, Torvald. Promise that you will! I am so nervous about it—all the people—. You must give yourself up to me entirely this evening. Not the tiniest bit of business—you mustn't even take a pen in your hand. Will you promise, Torvald dear?

HELMER: I promise. This evening I will be wholly and absolutely at your service, you helpless little mortal. Ah, by the way, first of all I will just— (Goes towards the hall door.)

NORA: What are you going to do there?

HELMER: Only see if any letters have come.

NORA: No, no! don't do that, Torvald!

HELMER: Why not?

NORA: Torvald, please don't. There is nothing there.

HELMER: Well, let me look. (Turns to go to the letter-box. NORA, at the piano, plays the first bars of the Tarantella. HELMER stops in the doorway.) Aha!

NORA: I can't dance to-morrow if I don't practise with you.

HELMER: (going up to her) Are you really so afraid of it, dear?

NORA: Yes, so dreadfully afraid of it. Let me practise at once; there is time now, before we go to dinner. Sit down and play for me, Torvald dear; criticise me, and correct me as you play.

HELMER: With great pleasure, if you wish me to. (Sits down at the piano.)

NORA: (takes out of the box a tambourine and a long variegated shawl. She hastily drapes the shawl round her. Then she springs to the front of the stage and calls out) Now play for me! I am going to dance!

(HELMER plays and NORA dances. RANK stands by the piano behind HELMER, and looks on.)

HELMER: (as he plays) Slower, slower!

NORA: I can't do it any other way.

HELMER: Not so violently, Nora!

NORA: This is the way.

HELMER: (stops playing) No, no—that is not a bit right.

NORA: (laughing and swinging the tambourine) Didn't I tell you so?

RANK: Let me play for her.

HELMER: (getting up) Yes, do. I can correct her better then.

(RANK sits down at the piano and plays. NORA dances more and more wildly. HELMER has taken up a position beside the stove, and during her dance gives her frequent instructions. She does not seem to hear him; her hair comes down and falls over her shoulders; she pays no attention to it, but goes on dancing. Enter MRS. LINDE.)

MRS. LINDE: (standing as if spell-bound in the doorway) Oh!—

NORA: (as she dances) Such fun, Christine!

HELMER: My dear darling Nora, you are dancing as if your life depended on it.

NORA: So it does.

HELMER: Stop, Rank; this is sheer madness. Stop, I tell you! (RANK stops playing, and NORA suddenly stands still. HELMER goes up to her.) I could never have believed it. You have forgotten everything I taught you.

NORA: (throwing away the tambourine) There, you see.

HELMER: You will want a lot of coaching.

NORA: Yes, you see how much I need it. You must coach me up to the last minute. Promise me that, Torvald!

HELMER: You can depend on me.

NORA: You must not think of anything but me, either to-day or to-morrow; you mustn't open a single
910 letter—not even open the letter-box—

HELMER: Ah, you are still afraid of that fellow—

NORA: Yes, indeed I am.

HELMER: Nora, I can tell from your looks that there is a letter from him lying there.

915 **NORA:** I don't know; I think there is; but you must not read anything of that kind now. Nothing horrid must come between us till this is all over.

RANK: *(whispers to* HELMER*)* You mustn't contradict her.

920 **HELMER:** *(taking her in his arms)* The child shall have her way. But to-morrow night, after you have danced—

NORA: Then you will be free. *(The* MAID *appears in the doorway to the right.)*

925 **MAID:** Dinner is served, ma'am.

NORA: We will have champagne, Helen.

MAID: Very good, ma'am. *(Exit)*

HELMER: Hullo!—are we going to have a banquet?

NORA: Yes, a champagne banquet till the small hours.
930 *(Calls out.)* And a few macaroons, Helen—lots, just for once!

HELMER: Come, come, don't be so wild and nervous. Be my own little skylark, as you used.

NORA: Yes, dear, I will. But go in now and you too, Doc-
935 tor Rank. Christine, you must help me to do up my hair.

RANK: *(whispers to* HELMER *as they go out)* I suppose there is nothing—she is not expecting anything?

HELMER: Far from it, my dear fellow; it is simply noth-
940 ing more than this childish nervousness I was telling you of.

(They go into the right-hand room.)

NORA: Well!

MRS. LINDE: Gone out of town.

NORA: I could tell from your face.

MRS. LINDE: He is coming home to-morrow evening. I 945 wrote a note for him.

NORA: You should have let it alone; you must prevent nothing. After all, it is splendid to be waiting for a wonderful thing to happen.

MRS. LINDE: What is it that you are waiting for? 950

NORA: Oh, you wouldn't understand. Go in to them, I will come in a moment. *(MRS. LINDE goes into the dining-room.* NORA *stands still for a little while, as if to compose herself. Then she looks at her watch.)* Five o'clock. Seven hours till midnight; and then four-and- 955 twenty hours till the next midnight. Then the Taran-tella will be over. Twenty-four and seven? Thirty-one hours to live.

HELMER: *(from the doorway on the right)* Where's my little skylark? 960

NORA: *(going to him with her arms outstretched)* Here she is!

ACT 3

THE SAME SCENE: *The table has been placed in the middle of the stage, with chairs round it. A lamp is burning on the table. The door into the hall stands open. Dance music is heard from the room above.* MRS. LINDE *is sitting at the table idly turning over the leaves of a book; she tries to read, but does not seem able to collect her thoughts. Every now and then she listens intently for a sound at the outer door.*

MRS. LINDE: *(looking at her watch)* Not yet—and the time is nearly up. If only he does not—. *(Listens again.)* Ah, there he is. *(Goes into the hall and opens the outer door carefully. Light footsteps are heard on the stairs. She whispers.)* Come in. There is no one here. 5

KROGSTAD: *(in the doorway)* I found a note from you at home. What does this mean?

MRS. LINDE: It is absolutely necessary that I should have a talk with you.

Mrs. Linde calls on Krogstad with a plan of her own.

10 **KROGSTAD:** Really? And is it absolutely necessary that it should be here?

MRS. LINDE: It is impossible where I live; there is no private entrance to my rooms. Come in; we are quite alone. The maid is asleep, and the Helmers are at the
15 dance upstairs.

KROGSTAD: *(coming into the room)* Are the Helmers really at a dance to-night?

MRS. LINDE: Yes, why not?

KROGSTAD: Certainly—why not?

20 **MRS. LINDE:** Now, Nils, let us have a talk.

KROGSTAD: Can we two have anything to talk about?

MRS. LINDE: We have a great deal to talk about.

KROGSTAD: I shouldn't have thought so.

MRS. LINDE: No, you have never properly understood me.

25 **KROGSTAD:** Was there anything else to understand except what was obvious to all the world—a heartless woman jilts a man when a more lucrative chance turns up?

MRS. LINDE: Do you believe I am as absolutely heartless
30 as all that? And do you believe that I did it with a light heart?

KROGSTAD: Didn't you?

MRS. LINDE: Nils, did you really think that?

KROGSTAD: If it were as you say, why did you write to me as you did at the time? 35

MRS. LINDE: I could do nothing else. As I had to break with you, it was my duty also to put an end to all that you felt for me.

KROGSTAD: *(wringing his hands)* So that was it. And all this—only for the sake of money! 40

MRS. LINDE: You must not forget that I had a helpless mother and two little brothers. We couldn't wait for you, Nils; your prospects seemed hopeless then.

KROGSTAD: That may be so, but you had no right to throw me over for anyone else's sake. 45

MRS. LINDE: Indeed I don't know. Many a time did I ask myself if I had the right to do it.

KROGSTAD: *(more gently)* When I lost you, it was as if all the solid ground went from under my feet. Look at me now—I am a shipwrecked man clinging to a bit of 50
wreckage.

MRS. LINDE: But help may be near.

KROGSTAD: It *was* near; but then you came and stood in my way.

MRS. LINDE: Unintentionally, Nils. It was only to-day 55
that I learnt it was your place I was going to take in the Bank.

KROGSTAD: I believe you, if you say so. But now that you know it, are you not going to give it up to me?

MRS. LINDE: No, because that would not benefit you in 60
the least.

KROGSTAD: Oh, benefit, benefit—I would have done it whether or no.

MRS. LINDE: I have learnt to act prudently. Life, and hard, bitter necessity have taught me that. 65

KROGSTAD: And life has taught me not to believe in fine speeches.

MRS. LINDE: Then life has taught you something very reasonable. But deeds you must believe in?

70 **KROGSTAD:** What do you mean by that?

MRS. LINDE: You said you were like a shipwrecked man clinging to some wreckage.

KROGSTAD: I had good reason to say so.

MRS. LINDE: Well, I am like a shipwrecked woman clinging to some wreckage—no one to mourn for, no one to care for.

75

KROGSTAD: It was your own choice.

MRS. LINDE: There was no other choice—then.

KROGSTAD: Well, what now?

80 **MRS. LINDE:** Nils, how would it be if we two ship-wrecked people could join forces?

KROGSTAD: What are you saying?

MRS. LINDE: Two on the same piece of wreckage would stand a better chance than each on their own.

85 **KROGSTAD:** Christine!

MRS. LINDE: What do you suppose brought me to town?

KROGSTAD: Do you mean that you gave me a thought?

MRS. LINDE: I could not endure life without work. All my life, as long as I can remember, I have worked, and it has been my greatest and only pleasure. But now I am quite alone in the world—my life is so dreadfully empty and I feel so forsaken. There is not the least pleasure in working for one's self. Nils, give me some-one and something to work for.

90

95 **KROGSTAD:** I don't trust that. It is nothing but a wom-an's overstrained sense of generosity that prompts you to make such an offer of yourself.

MRS. LINDE: Have you ever noticed anything of the sort in me?

100 **KROGSTAD:** Could you really do it? Tell me—do you know all about my past life?

MRS. LINDE: Yes.

KROGSTAD: And do you know what they think of me here?

MRS. LINDE: You seemed to me to imply that with me you might have been quite another man. 105

KROGSTAD: I am certain of it.

MRS. LINDE: Is it too late now?

KROGSTAD: Christine, are you saying this deliberately? Yes, I am sure you are. I see it in your face. Have you really the courage, then—? 110

MRS. LINDE: I want to be a mother to someone, and your children need a mother. We two need each other. Nils, I have faith in your real character—I can dare anything together with you. 115

KROGSTAD: (*grasps her hands*) Thanks, thanks, Chris-tine! Now I shall find a way to clear myself in the eyes of the world. Ah, but I forgot—

MRS. LINDE: (*listening*) Hush! The Tarantella. Go, go!

KROGSTAD: Why? What is it? 120

MRS. LINDE: Do you hear them up there? When that is over, we may expect them back.

KROGSTAD: Yes, yes—I will go. But it is all no use. Of course you are not aware what steps I have taken in the matter of the Helmers. 125

MRS. LINDE: Yes, I know all about that.

KROGSTAD: And in spite of that have you the courage to—?

MRS. LINDE: I understand very well to what lengths a man like you might be driven by despair. 130

KROGSTAD: If I could only undo what I have done!

MRS. LINDE: You cannot. Your letter is lying in the letter-box now.

KROGSTAD: Are you sure of that?

MRS. LINDE: Quite sure, but— 135

KROGSTAD: (*with a searching look at her*) Is that what it all means?—that you want to save your friend at any cost? Tell me frankly. Is that it?

MRS. LINDE: Nils, a woman who has once sold herself for another's sake, doesn't do it a second time.

KROGSTAD: I will ask for my letter back.

MRS. LINDE: No, no.

KROGSTAD: Yes, of course I will. I will wait here till Helmer comes; I will tell him he must give me my letter back—that it only concerns my dismissal—that he is not to read it—

MRS. LINDE: No, Nils, you must not recall your letter.

KROGSTAD: But, tell me, wasn't it for that very purpose that you asked me to meet you here?

MRS. LINDE: In my first moment of fright, it was. But twenty-four hours have elapsed since then, and in that time I have witnessed incredible things in this house. Helmer must know all about it. This unhappy secret must be disclosed; they must have a complete understanding between them, which is impossible with all this concealment and falsehood going on.

KROGSTAD: Very well, if you will take the responsibility. But there is one thing I can do in any case, and I shall do it at once.

MRS. LINDE: *(listening)* You must be quick and go! The dance is over; we are not safe a moment longer.

KROGSTAD: I will wait for you below.

MRS. LINDE: Yes, do; You must see me back to my door.

KROGSTAD: I have never had such an amazing piece of good fortune in my life! *(Goes out through the outer door. The door between the room and the hall remains open.)*

MRS. LINDE: *(tidying up the room and laying her hat and cloak ready)* What a difference! what a difference! Some one to work for and live for—a home to bring comfort into. That I will do, indeed. I wish they would be quick and come— *(Listens.)* Ah, there they are now. I must put on my things. *(Takes up her hat and cloak. HELMER's and NORA's voices are heard outside; a key is turned, and HELMER brings NORA almost by force into the hall. She is in an Italian costume with a large black shawl round her; he is in evening dress, and a black domino which is flying open.)*

NORA: *(hanging back in the doorway, and struggling with him)* No, no, no!—don't take me in. I want to go upstairs again; I don't want to leave so early.

HELMER: But, my dearest Nora—

NORA: Please, Torvald dear—please, *please*—only an hour more.

HELMER: Not a single minute, my sweet Nora. You know that was our agreement. Come along into the room; you are catching cold standing there. *(He brings her gently into the room, in spite of her resistance.)*

MRS. LINDE: Good-evening.

NORA: Christine!

HELMER: You here, so late, Mrs. Linde?

MRS. LINDE: Yes, you must excuse me; I was so anxious to see Nora in her dress.

NORA: Have you been sitting here waiting for me?

MRS. LINDE: Yes, unfortunately I came too late, you had already gone upstairs; and I thought I couldn't go away again without having seen you.

HELMER: *(taking off NORA's shawl)* Yes, take a good look at her. I think she is worth looking at. Isn't she charming, Mrs. Linde?

MRS. LINDE: Yes, indeed she is.

HELMER: Doesn't she look remarkably pretty? Everyone thought so at the dance. But she is terribly self-willed, this sweet little person. What are we to do with her? You will hardly believe that I had almost to bring her away by force.

NORA: Torvald, you will repent not having let me stay, even if it were only for half an hour.

HELMER: Listen to her, Mrs. Linde! She had danced her Tarantella, and it had been a tremendous success, as it deserved—although possibly the performance was a trifle too realistic—a little more so, I mean, than was strictly compatible with the limitations of art. But never mind about that! The chief thing is, she had made a success—she had made a tremendous success. Do you think I was going to let her remain there after that, and spoil the effect? No, indeed! I took my charming little Capri maiden—my capricious little Capri maiden, I should say—on my arm; took one quick turn round the room; a curtsey on either side, and, as they say in novels, the beautiful apparition disappeared. An exit ought always to be effective, Mrs. Linde; but that is what I cannot make Nora understand. Pooh! this room is hot. (*Throws his domino on a chair, and opens the door of his room.*) Hullo! it's all dark in here. Oh, of course—excuse me—. (*He goes in, and lights some candles.*)

NORA: (*in a hurried and breathless whisper*) Well?

MRS. LINDE: (*in a low voice*) I have had a talk with him.

NORA: Yes, and—

MRS. LINDE: Nora, you must tell your husband all about it.

NORA: (*in an expressionless voice*) I knew it.

MRS. LINDE: You have nothing to be afraid of as far as Krogstad is concerned; but you must tell him.

NORA: I won't tell him.

MRS. LINDE: Then the letter will.

NORA: Thank you, Christine. Now I know what I must do. Hush—!

HELMER: (*coming in again*) Well, Mrs. Linde, have you admired her?

MRS. LINDE: Yes, and now I will say good-night.

HELMER: What, already? Is this yours, this knitting?

MRS. LINDE: (*taking it*) Yes, thank you, I had very nearly forgotten it.

HELMER: So you knit?

MRS. LINDE: Of course.

HELMER: Do you know, you ought to embroider.

MRS. LINDE: Really? Why?

HELMER: Yes, it's far more becoming. Let me show you. You hold the embroidery thus in your left hand, and use the needle with the right—like this—with a long, easy sweep. Do you see?

MRS. LINDE: Yes, perhaps—

HELMER: But in the case of knitting—that can never be anything but ungraceful; look here—the arms close together, the knitting-needles going up and down—it has a sort of Chinese effect—. That was really excellent champagne they gave us.

MRS. LINDE: Well,—good-night, Nora, and don't be self-willed anymore.

HELMER: That's right, Mrs. Linde.

MRS. LINDE: Good-night, Mr. Helmer.

HELMER: (*accompanying her to the door*) Good-night, good-night. I hope you will get home all right. I should be very happy to—but you haven't any great distance to go. Good-night, good-night. (*She goes out; he shuts the door after her, and comes in again.*) Ah!—at last we have got rid of her. She's a frightful bore, that woman.

NORA: Aren't you very tired, Torvald?

HELMER: No, not in the least.

NORA: Nor sleepy?

HELMER: Not a bit. On the contrary, I feel extraordinarily lively. And you?—you really look both tired and sleepy.

NORA: Yes, I am very tired. I want to go to sleep at once.

HELMER: There, you see it was quite right of me not to let you stay there any longer.

NORA: Everything you do is quite right, Torvald.

HELMER: (*kissing her on the forehead*) Now my little skylark is speaking reasonably. Did you notice what good spirits Rank was in this evening?

NORA: Really? Was he? I didn't speak to him at all.

HELMER: And I very little, but I have not for a long time seen him in such good form. (*Looks for a while at her and then goes nearer to her.*) It is delightful to be at home by ourselves again, to be all alone with you—you fascinating, charming little darling!

290 **NORA:** Don't look at me like that, Torvald.

HELMER: Why shouldn't I look at my dearest treasure?— at all the beauty that is mine, all my very own?

NORA: *(going to the other side of the table)* You mustn't say things like that to me to-night.

295 **HELMER:** *(following her)* You have still got the Tarantella in your blood, I see. And it makes you more captivating than ever. Listen—the guests are beginning to go now. *(In a lower voice.)* Nora—soon the whole house will be quiet.

300 **NORA:** Yes, I hope so.

HELMER: Yes, my own darling Nora. Do you know, when I am out at a party with you like this, why I speak so little to you, keep away from you, and only send a stolen glance in your direction now and
305 then?—do you know why I do that? It is because I make believe to myself that we are secretly in love, and you are my secretly promised bride, and that no one suspects there is anything between us.

NORA: Yes, yes—I know very well your thoughts are with
310 me all the time.

HELMER: And when we are leaving, and I am putting the shawl over your beautiful young shoulders—on your lovely neck—then I imagine that you are my young bride and that we have just come from the wed-
315 ding, and I am bringing you for the first time into our home—to be alone with you for the first time—quite alone with my shy little darling! All this evening I have longed for nothing but you. When I watched the seductive figures of the Tarantella, my blood was on
320 fire; I could endure it no longer, and that was why I brought you down so early—

NORA: Go away, Torvald! You must let me go. I won't—

HELMER: What's that? You're joking, my little Nora! You won't—you won't? Am I not your husband—?
325 *(A knock is heard at the outer door.)*

NORA: *(starting)* Did you hear—?

After Mrs. Linde leaves, Torvald has Nora to himself.

HELMER: *(going into the hall)* Who is it?

RANK: *(outside)* It is I. May I come in for a moment?

HELMER: *(in a fretful whisper)* Oh, what does he want now? *(Aloud.)* Wait a minute! *(Unlocks the door.)* 330 Come, that's kind of you not to pass by our door.

RANK: I thought I heard your voice, and felt as if I should like to look in. *(With a swift glance round.)* Ah, yes!—these dear familiar rooms. You are very happy and cosy in here, you two. 335

HELMER: It seems to me that you looked after yourself pretty well upstairs too.

RANK: Excellently. Why shouldn't I? Why shouldn't one enjoy everything in this world?—at any rate as much as one can, and as long as one can. The wine was capital— 340

HELMER: Especially the champagne.

RANK: So you noticed that too? It is almost incredible how much I managed to put away!

NORA: Torvald drank a great deal of champagne to-night too. 345

RANK: Did he?

NORA: Yes, and he is always in such good spirits afterwards.

Dr. Rank stops in to say good-bye to the Helmers.

RANK: Well, why should one not enjoy a merry evening
350   after a well-spent day?

HELMER: Well spent? I am afraid I can't take credit for
that.

RANK: *(clapping him on the back)* But I can, you know!

NORA: Doctor Rank, you must have been occupied with
355   some scientific investigation to-day.

RANK: Exactly.

HELMER: Just listen!—little Nora talking about scientific investigations!

NORA: And may I congratulate you on the result?

360 **RANK:**   Indeed you may.

NORA: Was it favourable, then?

RANK: The best possible, for both doctor and
patient—certainty.

NORA: *(quickly and searchingly)* Certainty?

365 **RANK:**   Absolute certainty. So wasn't I entitled to make a
merry evening of it after that?

NORA: Yes, you certainly were, Doctor Rank.

HELMER: I think so too, so long as you don't have to pay
for it in the morning.

RANK: Oh well, one can't have anything in this life with-   370
out paying for it.

NORA: Doctor Rank—are you fond of fancy-dress balls?

RANK: Yes, if there is a fine lot of pretty costumes.

NORA: Tell me—what shall we two wear at the next?

HELMER: Little featherbrain!—are you thinking of the   375
next already?

RANK: We two? Yes, I can tell you. You shall go as a good
fairy—

HELMER: Yes, but what do you suggest as an appropriate costume for that?   380

RANK: Let your wife go dressed just as she is in everyday
life.

HELMER: That was really very prettily turned. But can't
you tell us what you will be?

RANK: Yes, my dear friend, I have quite made up my   385
mind about that.

HELMER: Well?

RANK: At the next fancy-dress ball I shall be invisible.

HELMER: That's a good joke!

RANK: There is a big black hat—have you never heard of   390
hats that make you invisible? If you put one on, no one
can see you.

HELMER: *(suppressing a smile)* Yes, you are quite right.

RANK: But I am clean forgetting what I came for. Helmer, give me a cigar—one of the dark Havanas.   395

HELMER: With the greatest pleasure. *(Offers him his
case.)*

RANK: *(takes a cigar and cuts off the end)* Thanks.

NORA: *(striking a match)* Let me give you a light.

RANK: Thank you. *(She holds the match for him to light   400
his cigar.)* And now good-bye!

HELMER: Good-bye, good-bye, dear old man!

NORA: Sleep well, Doctor Rank.

RANK: Thank you for that wish.

405 **NORA:** Wish me the same.

RANK: You? Well, if you want me to sleep well! And thanks for the light. (*He nods to them both and goes out.*)

HELMER: (*in a subdued voice*) He has drunk more than
410 he ought.

NORA: (*absently*) Maybe. (HELMER *takes a bunch of keys out of his pocket and goes into the hall.*) Torvald! what are you going to do there?

HELMER: Empty the letter-box; it is quite full; there
415 will be no room to put the newspaper in to-morrow morning.

NORA: Are you going to work to-night?

HELMER: You know quite well I'm not. What is this? Someone has been at the lock.

420 **NORA:** At the lock—?

HELMER: Yes, someone has. What can it mean? I should never have thought the maid—. Here is a broken hair-pin. Nora, it is one of yours.

NORA: (*quickly*) Then it must have been the children—

425 **HELMER:** Then you must get them out of those ways. There, at last I have got it open. (*Takes out the contents of the letter-box, and calls to the kitchen.*) Helen!— Helen, put out the light over the front door. (*Goes back into the room and shuts the door into the hall. He holds
430 out his hand full of letters.*) Look at that—look what a heap of them there are. (*Turning them over.*) What on earth is that?

NORA: (*at the window*) The letter—No! Torvald, no!

HELMER: Two cards—of Rank's.

435 **NORA:** Of Doctor Rank's?

HELMER: (*looking at them*) Doctor Rank. They were on the top. He must have put them in when he went out.

NORA: Is there anything written on them?

HELMER: There is a black cross over the name. Look there—what an uncomfortable idea! It looks as if he 440
were announcing his own death.

NORA: It is just what he is doing.

HELMER: What? Do you know anything about it? Has he said anything to you?

NORA: Yes. He told me that when the cards came it 445
would be his leave-taking from us. He means to shut himself up and die.

HELMER: My poor old friend! Certainly I knew we should not have him very long with us. But so soon! And so he hides himself away like a wounded animal. 450

NORA: If it has to happen, it is best it should be without a word—don't you think so, Torvald?

HELMER: (*walking up and down*) He had so grown into our lives. I can't think of him as having gone out of them. He, with his sufferings and his loneliness, was 455
like a cloudy background to our sunlit happiness. Well, perhaps it is best so. For him, anyway. (*Standing still.*) And perhaps for us too, Nora. We two are thrown quite upon each other now. (*Puts his arms round her.*) My darling wife, I don't feel as if I could 460
hold you tight enough. Do you know, Nora, I have often wished that you might be threatened by some great danger, so that I might risk my life's blood, and everything, for your sake.

NORA: (*disengages herself, and says firmly and decidedly*) 465
Now you must read your letters, Torvald.

HELMER: No, no; not to-night. I want to be with you, my darling wife.

NORA: With the thought of your friend's death—

HELMER: You are right, it has affected us both. Some- 470
thing ugly has come between us—the thought of the horrors of death. We must try and rid our minds of that. Until then—we will each go to our own room.

NORA: (*hanging on his neck*) Good-night, Torvald— Good-night! 475

HELMER: *(kissing her on the forehead)* Good-night, my little singing-bird. Sleep sound, Nora. Now I will read my letters through. *(He takes his letters and goes into his room, shutting the door after him.)*

480 **NORA:** *(gropes distractedly about, seizes* HELMER's *domino, throws it round her, while she says in quick, hoarse, spasmodic whispers)* Never to see him again. Never! Never! *(Puts her shawl over her head.)* Never to see my children again either—never again. Never!

485 Never!— Ah! the icy, black water—the unfathomable depths—If only it were over! He has got it now—now he is reading it. Good-bye, Torvald and my children! *(She is about to rush out through the hall, when* HEL- MER *opens his door hurriedly and stands with an open*

490 *letter in his hand.)*

HELMER: Nora!

NORA: Ah!—

HELMER: What is this? Do you know what is in this letter?

495 **NORA:** Yes, I know. Let me go! Let me get out!

HELMER: *(holding her back)* Where are you going?

NORA: *(trying to get free)* You shan't save me, Torvald!

HELMER: *(reeling)* True? Is this true, that I read here? Horrible! No, no—it is impossible that it can be true.

500 **NORA:** It is true. I have loved you above everything else in the world.

HELMER: Oh, don't let us have any silly excuses.

NORA: *(taking a step towards him)* Torvald—!

HELMER: Miserable creature—what have you done?

505 **NORA:** Let me go. You shall not suffer for my sake. You shall not take it upon yourself.

HELMER: No tragedy airs, please. *(Locks the hall door.)* Here you shall stay and give me an explanation. Do you understand what you have done? Answer me!

510 Do you understand what you have done?

NORA: *(looks steadily at him and says with a growing look of coldness in her face)* Yes, now I am beginning to understand thoroughly.

HELMER: *(walking about the room)* What a horrible awakening! All these eight years—she who was my joy 515 and pride—a hypocrite, a liar—worse, worse—a crimi- nal! The unutterable ugliness of it all!—For shame! For shame! *(NORA is silent and looks steadily at him. He stops in front of her.)* I ought to have suspected that something of the sort would happen. I ought to have 520 foreseen it. All your father's want of principle—be silent!—all your father's want of principle has come out in you. No religion, no morality, no sense of duty—. How I am punished for having winked at what he did! I did it for your sake, and this is how you repay me. 525

NORA: Yes, that's just it.

HELMER: Now you have destroyed all my happiness. You have ruined all my future. It is horrible to think of! I am in the power of an unscrupulous man; he can do what he likes with me, ask anything he likes of 530 me, give me any orders he pleases—I dare not refuse. And I must sink to such miserable depths because of a thoughtless woman!

NORA: When I am out of the way, you will be free.

HELMER: No fine speeches, please. Your father had 535 always plenty of those ready, too. What good would it be to me if you were out of the way, as you say? Not the slightest. He can make the affair known every-

Torvald, having read the letter, confronts Nora.

540 where; and if he does, I may be falsely suspected of having been a party to your criminal action. Very likely people will think I was behind it all—that it was I who prompted you! And I have to thank you for all this—you whom I have cherished during the whole of our married life. Do you understand now what it is

545 you have done for me?

NORA: *(coldly and quietly)* Yes.

HELMER: It is so incredible that I can't take it in. But we must come to some understanding. Take off that shawl. Take it off, I tell you. I must try and appease

550 him some way or another. The matter must be hushed up at any cost. And as for you and me, it must appear as if everything between us were just as before—but naturally only in the eyes of the world. You will still remain in my house, that is a matter of course. But I

555 shall not allow you to bring up the children; I dare not trust them to you. To think that I should be obliged to say so to one whom I have loved so dearly, and whom I still—. No, that is all over. From this moment happiness is not the question; all that concerns us is to save

560 the remains, the fragments, the appearance—

(A ring is heard at the front-door bell.)

HELMER: *(with a start)* What is that? So late! Can the worst—? Can he—? Hide yourself, Nora. Say you are ill.

(NORA stands motionless. HELMER goes and unlocks the hall door.)

MAID: *(half dressed, comes to the door)* A letter for the
565 mistress.

HELMER: Give it to me. *(Takes the letter, and shuts the door.)* Yes, it is from him. You shall not have it; I will read it myself.

NORA: Yes, read it.

570 **HELMER:** *(standing by the lamp)* I scarcely have the courage to do it. It may mean ruin for both of us. No, I must know. *(Tears open the letter, runs his eye over a few lines, looks at a paper enclosed, and gives a shout of joy.)* Nora! *(She looks at him questioningly.)* Nora!—
No, I must read it once again—. Yes, it is true! I am
575 saved! Nora, I am saved!

NORA: And I?

HELMER: You too, of course; we are both saved, both you and I. Look, he sends you your bond back. He says he regrets and repents—that a happy change in his

580 life—never mind what he says! We are saved, Nora! No one can do anything to you. Oh, Nora, Nora!—no, first I must destroy these hateful things. Let me see—. *(Takes a look at the bond.)* No, no, I won't look at it. The whole thing shall be nothing but a bad dream to

585 me. *(Tears up the bond and both letters, throws them all into the stove, and watches them burn.)* There—now it doesn't exist any longer. He says that since Christmas Eve you—. These must have been three dreadful days

590 for you, Nora.

NORA: I have fought a hard fight these three days.

HELMER: And suffered agonies, and seen no way out but—. No, we won't call any of the horrors to mind. We will only shout with joy, and keep saying, "It's all over! It's all over!" Listen to me, Nora. You don't seem
595 to realise that it is all over. What is this?—such a cold, set face! My poor little Nora, I quite understand; you don't feel as if you could believe that I have forgiven you. But it is true, Nora, I swear it; I have forgiven you

600 everything. I know that what you did, you did out of love for me.

NORA: That is true.

HELMER: You have loved me as a wife ought to love her husband. Only you had not sufficient knowledge to judge of the means you used. But do you suppose

605 you are any the less dear to me, because you don't understand how to act on your own responsibility? No, no; only lean on me; I will advise you and direct you. I should not be a man if this womanly helplessness did not just give you a double attractiveness in

610 my eyes. You must not think any more about the hard things I said in my first moment of consternation, when I thought everything was going to overwhelm me. I have forgiven you, Nora; I swear to you I have forgiven you.

615

NORA: Thank you for your forgiveness. *(She goes out through the door to the right.)*

HELMER: No, don't go—. *(Looks in.)* What are you doing in there?

620 **NORA:** *(from within)* Taking off my fancy dress.

HELMER: *(standing at the open door)* Yes, do. Try and calm yourself, and make your mind easy again, my frightened little singing-bird. Be at rest, and feel secure; I have broad wings to shelter you under.
625 *(Walks up and down by the door.)* How warm and cosy our home is, Nora. Here is shelter for you; here I will protect you like a hunted dove that I have saved from a hawk's claws; I will bring peace to your poor beating heart. It will come, little by little, Nora, believe me.
630 To-morrow morning you will look upon it all quite differently; soon everything will be just as it was before. Very soon you won't need me to assure you that I have forgiven you; you will yourself feel the certainty that I have done so. Can you suppose I should
635 ever think of such a thing as repudiating you, or even reproaching you? You have no idea what a true man's heart is like, Nora. There is something so indescribably sweet and satisfying, to a man, in the knowledge that he has forgiven his wife—forgiven her freely, and
640 with all his heart. It seems as if that had made her, as it were, doubly his own; he has given her a new life, so to speak; and she has in a way become both wife and child to him. So you shall be for me after this, my little scared, helpless darling. Have no anxiety about
645 anything, Nora; only be frank and open with me, and I will serve as will and conscience both to you—. What is this? Not gone to bed? Have you changed your things?

NORA: *(in everyday dress)* Yes, Torvald, I have changed
650 my things now.

HELMER: But what for?—so late as this.

NORA: I shall not sleep to-night.

HELMER: But, my dear Nora—

NORA: *(looking at her watch)* It is not so very late. Sit
655 down here, Torvald. You and I have much to say to one another. *(She sits down at one side of the table.)*

HELMER: Nora—what is this?—this cold, set face?

NORA: Sit down. It will take some time; I have a lot to talk over with you.

HELMER: *(sits down at the opposite side of the table)* You
660 alarm me, Nora!—and I don't understand you.

NORA: No, that is just it. You don't understand me, and I have never understood you either—before to-night. No, you mustn't interrupt me. You must simply listen to what I say. Torvald, this is a settling of accounts.
665

HELMER: What do you mean by that?

NORA: *(after a short silence)* Isn't there one thing that strikes you as strange in our sitting here like this?

HELMER: What is that?

NORA: We have been married now eight years. Does
670 it not occur to you that this is the first time we two, you and I, husband and wife, have had a serious conversation?

HELMER: What do you mean by serious?

NORA: In all these eight years—longer than that—from
675 the very beginning of our acquaintance, we have never exchanged a word on any serious subject.

HELMER: Was it likely that I would be continually and for ever telling you about worries that you could not help me to bear?
680

NORA: I am not speaking about business matters. I say that we have never sat down in earnest together to try and get at the bottom of anything.

HELMER: But, dearest Nora, would it have been any good to you?
685

NORA: That is just it; you have never understood me. I have been greatly wronged, Torvald—first by papa and then by you.

HELMER: What! By us two—by us two, who have loved you better than anyone else in the world?
690

NORA: *(shaking her head)* You have never loved me. You have only thought it pleasant to be in love with me.

HELMER: Nora, what do I hear you saying?

NORA: It is perfectly true, Torvald. When I was at home with papa, he told me his opinion about everything,
695 and so I had the same opinions; and if I differed from

him I concealed the fact, because he would not have liked it. He called me his doll-child, and he played with me just as I used to play with my dolls. And when I came to live with you—

700

HELMER: What sort of an expression is that to use about our marriage?

NORA: (*undisturbed*) I mean that I was simply trans-
705 ferred from papa's hands into yours. You arranged everything according to your own taste, and so I got the same tastes as you—or else I pretended to, I am really not quite sure which—I think sometimes the one and sometimes the other. When I look back on
710 it, it seems to me as if I had been living here like a poor woman—just from hand to mouth. I have existed merely to perform tricks for you, Torvald. But you would have it so. You and papa have committed a great sin against me. It is your fault that I have made nothing of my life.

715 **HELMER:**   How unreasonable and how ungrateful you are, Nora! Have you not been happy here?

NORA: No, I have never been happy. I thought I was, but it has never really been so.

HELMER: Not—not happy!

720 **NORA:**   No, only merry. And you have always been so kind to me. But our home has been nothing but a

playroom. I have been your doll-wife, just as at home I was papa's doll-child; and here the children have been my dolls. I thought it great fun when you played with me, just as they thought it great fun when I 725
played with them. That is what our marriage has been, Torvald.

HELMER: There is some truth in what you say—exaggerated and strained as your view of it is. But for the future it shall be different. Playtime shall 730
be over, and lesson-time shall begin.

NORA: Whose lessons? Mine, or the children's?

HELMER: Both yours and the children's, my darling Nora.

NORA: Alas, Torvald, you are not the man to educate me 735
into being a proper wife for you.

HELMER: And you can say that!

NORA: And I—how am I fitted to bring up the children?

HELMER: Nora!

NORA: Didn't you say so yourself a little while ago—that 740
you dare not trust me to bring them up?

HELMER: In a moment of anger! Why do you pay any heed to that?

NORA: Indeed, you were perfectly right. I am not fit for the task. There is another task I must undertake first. 745
I must try and educate myself—you are not the man to help me in that. I must do that for myself. And that is why I am going to leave you now.

HELMER: (*springing up*) What do you say?

NORA: I must stand quite alone, if I am to understand 750
myself and everything about me. It is for that reason that I cannot remain with you any longer.

HELMER: Nora, Nora!

NORA: I am going away from here now, at once. I am sure Christine will take me in for the night— 755

HELMER: You are out of your mind! I won't allow it! I forbid you!

Torvald tries to comfort Nora after his tirade.

NORA: It is no use forbidding me anything any longer. I will take with me what belongs to myself. I will take nothing from you, either now or later.

HELMER: What sort of madness is this!

NORA: To-morrow I shall go home—I mean, to my old home. It will be easiest for me to find something to do there.

HELMER: You blind, foolish woman!

NORA: I must try and get some sense, Torvald.

HELMER: To desert your home, your husband and your children! And you don't consider what people will say!

NORA: I cannot consider that at all. I only know that it is necessary for me.

HELMER: It's shocking. This is how you would neglect your most sacred duties.

NORA: What do you consider my most sacred duties?

HELMER: Do I need to tell you that? Are they not your duties to your husband and your children?

NORA: I have other duties just as sacred.

HELMER: That you have not. What duties could those be?

NORA: Duties to myself.

HELMER: Before all else, you are a wife and a mother.

NORA: I don't believe in that any longer. I believe that before all else I am a reasonable human being, just as you are—or, at all events, that I must try and become one. I know quite well, Torvald, that most people would think you right; and that views of that kind are to be found in books; but I can no longer content myself with what most people say, or with what is found in books. I must think over things for myself and get to understand them.

HELMER: Can you not understand your place in your own home? Have you not a reliable guide in such matters as that?—have you no religion?

NORA: I am afraid, Torvald, I do not exactly know what religion is.

HELMER: What are you saying?

NORA: I know nothing but what the clergyman said, when I went to be confirmed. He told us that religion was this, and that, and the other. When I am away from all this, and am alone, I will look into that matter too. I will see if what the clergyman said is true, or at all events if it is true for me.

HELMER: This is unheard of in a girl of your age! But if religion cannot lead you aright, let me try and awaken your conscience. I suppose you have some moral sense? Or—answer me—am I to think you have none?

NORA: I assure you, Torvald, that is not an easy question to answer. I really don't know. The thing perplexes me altogether. I only know that you and I look at it in quite a different light. I am learning, too, that the law is quite another thing from what I supposed; but I find it impossible to convince myself that the law is right. According to it a woman has no right to spare her old dying father, or to save her husband's life. I can't believe that.

HELMER: You talk like a child. You don't understand the conditions of the world in which you live.

NORA: No, I don't. But now I am going to try. I am going to see if I can make out who is right, the world or I.

HELMER: You are ill, Nora; you are delirious; I almost think you are out of your mind.

NORA: I have never felt my mind so clear and certain as to-night.

HELMER: And is it with a clear and certain mind that you forsake your husband and your children?

NORA: Yes, it is.

HELMER: Then there is only one possible explanation.

NORA: What is that?

HELMER: You do not love me any more.

NORA: No, that is just it.

HELMER: Nora!—and you can say that?

NORA: It gives me great pain, Torvald, for you have always been so kind to me, but I cannot help it. I do not love you any more.

HELMER: *(regaining his composure)* Is that a clear and certain conviction too?

835 NORA: Yes, absolutely clear and certain. That is the reason why I will not stay here any longer.

HELMER: And can you tell me what I have done to forfeit your love?

NORA: Yes, indeed I can. It was to-night, when the won-
840 derful thing did not happen; then I saw you were not the man I had thought you.

HELMER: Explain yourself better. I don't understand you.

NORA: I have waited so patiently for eight years; for,
845 goodness knows, I knew very well that wonderful things don't happen every day. Then this horrible mis-fortune came upon me; and then I felt quite certain that the wonderful thing was going to happen at last. When Krogstad's letter was lying out there, never for
850 a moment did I imagine that you would consent to ac-cept this man's conditions. I was so absolutely certain that you would say to him: Publish the thing to the whole world. And when that was done—

HELMER: Yes, what then?—when I had exposed my wife
855 to shame and disgrace?

NORA: When that was done, I was so absolutely certain, you would come forward and take everything upon yourself, and say: I am the guilty one.

HELMER: Nora—!

860 NORA: You mean that I would never have accepted such a sacrifice on your part? No, of course not. But what would my assurances have been worth against yours? That was the wonderful thing which I hoped for and feared; and it was to prevent that, that I wanted to
865 kill myself.

HELMER: I would gladly work night and day for you, Nora—bear sorrow and want for your sake. But no man would sacrifice his honour for the one he loves.

NORA: It is a thing hundreds of thousands of women
870 have done.

HELMER: Oh, you think and talk like a heedless child.

Nora, dressed for travel, explains her epiphany to Torvald.

NORA: Maybe. But you neither think nor talk like the man I could bind myself to. As soon as your fear was over—and it was not fear for what threatened me, but for what might happen to you—when the whole thing 875
was past, as far as you were concerned it was exactly as if nothing at all had happened. Exactly as before, I was your little skylark, your doll, which you would in future treat with doubly gentle care, because it was so brittle and fragile. *(Getting up.)* Torvald—it was then 880
it dawned upon me that for eight years I had been liv-ing here with a strange man, and had borne him three children—. Oh, I can't bear to think of it! I could tear myself into little bits!

HELMER: *(sadly)* I see, I see. An abyss has opened be- 885
tween us—there is no denying it. But, Nora, would it not be possible to fill it up?

NORA: As I am now, I am no wife for you.

HELMER: I have it in me to become a different man.

NORA: Perhaps—if your doll is taken away from you. 890

HELMER: But to part!—to part from you! No, no, Nora, I can't understand that idea.

NORA: *(going out to the right)* That makes it all the more certain that it must be done. *(She comes back with her cloak and hat and a small bag which she puts on a 895
chair by the table.)*

HELMER: Nora, Nora, not now! Wait till to-morrow.

NORA: *(putting on her cloak)* I cannot spend the night in a strange man's room.

900 **HELMER:**   But can't we live here like brother and sister—?

NORA: *(putting on her hat)* You know very well that would not last long. *(Puts the shawl round her.)* Good-bye, Torvald. I won't see the little ones. I know they 905 are in better hands than mine. As I am now, I can be of no use to them.

HELMER: But some day, Nora—some day?

NORA: How can I tell? I have no idea what is going to become of me.

910 **HELMER:**   But you are my wife, whatever becomes of you.

NORA: Listen, Torvald. I have heard that when a wife deserts her husband's house, as I am doing now, he is legally freed from all obligations towards her. In any 915 case I set you free from all your obligations. You are not to feel yourself bound in the slightest way, any more than I shall. There must be perfect freedom on both sides. See, here is your ring back. Give me mine.

HELMER: That too?

920 **NORA:**   That too.

HELMER: Here it is.

NORA: That's right. Now it is all over. I have put the keys here. The maids know all about everything in the house—better than I do. To-morrow, after I have left 925 her, Christine will come here and pack up my own things that I brought with me from home. I will have them sent after me.

HELMER: All over! All over!—Nora, shall you never think of me again?

930 **NORA:**   I know I shall often think of you and the children and this house.

HELMER: May I write to you, Nora?

NORA: No—never. You must not to do that.

Torvald, alone, gazes around the empty house.

HELMER: But at least let me send you—

NORA: Nothing—nothing—   935

HELMER: Let me help you if you are in want.

NORA: No. I can receive nothing from a stranger.

HELMER: Nora—can I never be anything more than a stranger to you?

NORA: *(taking her bag)* Ah, Torvald, the most wonderful   940 thing of all would have to happen.

HELMER: Tell me what would that be!

NORA: Both you and I would have to be so changed that—. Oh, Torvald, I don't believe any longer in won-derful things happening.   945

HELMER: But I will believe in it. Tell me! So changed that—?

NORA: That our life together would be a real wedlock. Good-bye. *(She goes out through the hall.)*

HELMER: *(sinks down on a chair at the door and buries   950 his face in his hands)* Nora! Nora! *(Looks round, and rises.)* Empty. She is gone. *(A hope flashes across his mind.)* The most wonderful thing of all—?

(The sound of a door shutting is heard from below.)

Writing from Reading

Summarize

1 Some call this much-discussed and widely performed play the first feminist play. This script challenged and in some cases outraged contemporary audiences. In fact, the first German productions of *A Doll's House* in the 1880s had an altered ending at the request of the producers. Ibsen referred to this version as a "barbaric outrage" to be used only in emergencies. What other endings could you imagine that Ibsen might endorse?

Analyze Craft

2 Dr. Rank assumes the role of the wise, elder statesman—a familiar figure in such theater. In truth, however, he's someone who's ill and even rotting, not elevated. What does his desire for Nora suggest as to his character, and in what if any ways does Ibsen cast him in a sympathetic light?

3 When Nora, in Act 3, tells Torvald that they must "sit down and discuss all this that has been happening between us," *A Doll's House* diverges from the final resolution of the well-made play. What do you imagine is the future of the marriage; who has changed, and how?

4 Nora's father is a major figure here, though always offstage. List his characteristics. How does Nora reveal how she feels about her father's characteristics? Does Nora want her husband to have more of her father's qualities, or qualities that are less similar?

Analyze Voice

5 Descriptive names for Nora include "little skylark," "fascinating, charming little darling," "my darling wife," "my little singing-bird," "little, scared darling," "blind, foolish woman," and "a heedless child." Which of these strikes you as most appropriate—or are they all true? How do they vary in the course of the play?

6 Nora often disguises the truth and—several times—lies in the course of the play. Are these white lies or genuine falsehoods? How do they increase or decrease our trust in her and why?

7 When Nora says that she requires Torvald to help her practice for the dance, what does she imply?

8 The first act takes place on Christmas Eve. Christmas is not, however, presented as a religious holiday and religion as a concept is questioned by Nora in Act 3. In fact, it is discussed much more often as a material than a spiritual experience. Does Ibsen here endorse or disapprove of the centrality of material goods over personal connection; what solution does he propose?

9 What overall tone does the play project? In what way does the tone change over the course of the play?

Synthesize Summary and Analysis

10 The plot contrasts an old way of life with the glimmer of a new way to live. How would you explain this in terms of the struggle between illusion and reality as seen in Greek tragedy?

Interpret the Play

11 Ibsen believed that "a dramatist's business is not to answer questions, but only to ask them." Would you describe the play's conclusion as closer to comic or tragic in tone? In what ways is it happy or unhappy, and what questions has he asked?

"Tennessee was splendid enough a mind to be able to write his women as women, and his men as men. I don't think he was hiding anything. . . . It was only the half-blind straight critics who decided [that if] Tennessee Williams was gay, he must have been lying when he wrote women, which strikes me as being the critical fallacy, as we love to call it." Conversation with Edward Albee

THE REAL AND THE SURREAL

While Arthur Miller's *Death of a Salesman* represented on the American stage the realist tradition of Ibsen and its overt social criticism, other dramatic techniques came largely into view in the modern theater. **Expressionism,** particularly as practiced by the German playwright Frank Wedekind (1864–1918), whose *Spring Awakening* scandalized audiences with its exploration of sexuality and puberty, draws strongly and mainly on subjective emotions and attempts to find symbolic means to depict them onstage. **Symbolism,** represented by the late works of the Swede August Strindberg (1849–1912) and whose chief practitioner in English is W. B. Yeats (1865–1939), employed poetic techniques by using image, character, or action to suggest meaning beyond the everyday literal level. The deployment of **surrealism,** a technique that bloomed in the early part of the twentieth century in which, as French writer and poet André Breton (1896–1966) suggests in his 1924 "Surrealist Manifesto," the realism of conscious and of unconscious experience are fused together into "an absolute reality, a surreality," added to the ultimate dreamlike quality of the lives onstage. By contrast, Bertolt Brecht's (1898–1956) development of **Epic Theater** brought to the theater a spare and highly stylized set that celebrated ideas over emotions. **Theater of the Absurd** combined comedic elements with a sense of meaninglessness as practiced by Eugene Ionesco (1909–1994), Samuel Beckett (1906–1989), and Edward Albee (Chapter 31). The following plays draw variously upon the realism of Ibsen, the expressionistic lyricism of Tennessee Williams, the symbolism of August Wilson, and the overt social criticism of Lorraine Hansberry.

Tennessee Williams (1911–1983)

Born in Mississippi, Thomas Lanier Williams lived in a small town with his mother and maternal grandparents. His father, a salesman, was frequently away. However, when his father moved the family to St. Louis, Williams grew unhappy—largely because of the taunts his father constantly directed toward him—and turned to writing as an escape. After drifting among three universities, Williams earned a B.A. from the University of Iowa and began a life of wandering and writing plays. He kept his college nickname, "Tennessee," and under that name became one of the most important American playwrights of the century, writing masterpiece after masterpiece including *The Glass Menagerie* (1945), *A Streetcar Named Desire* (1947), *Cat on a Hot Tin Roof* (1954), and *Suddenly Last Summer* (1958). Symbolic and poetic, much of his work is set in the South, where his highly developed characters struggle with feelings of isolation. Williams's heightened form of realism supplied a poetic overlay to the situation and language. In his *Production Notes* to *The Glass Menagerie,* Williams wrote:

> Expressionism and all other unconventional techniques in drama have only one valid aim, and that is a closer approach to the truth. When a play employs

unconventional techniques, it is not, or certainly shouldn't be, trying to escape its responsibility of dealing with reality, or interpreting experience but is actually or should be attempting to find a closer approach, a more penetrating and vivid expression of things as they are.

Much of Williams's work insists on avoiding "The straight realistic play with its genuine Frigidaire and authentic ice cubes. . . ." But his is a kind of lover's quarrel with the idea of realism; he heightens the language of everyday discourse and lowers the lighting so that "the stage is

dim." Characters stand in spotlit shafts of light when, turn by turn, they speak, and often what passes for dialogue is a kind of back-and-forth monologue. Nonetheless, the underlying assumption here is that the playwright must scrutinize the real world and portray actual behavior.

AS YOU READ Trace the intertwining threads of the starkly real and the lyrical elements in the language.

The Glass Menagerie (1945)

nobody, not even the rain, has such small hands

—e. e. cummings

CHARACTERS

AMANDA WINGFIELD, *the mother. A little woman of great but confused vitality clinging frantically to another time and place. Her characterization must be carefully created, not copied from type. She is not paranoiac, but her life is paranoia. There is much to admire in Amanda, and as much to love and pity as there is to laugh at. Certainly she has endurance and a kind of heroism, and though her foolishness makes her unwittingly cruel at times, there is tenderness in her slight person.*

LAURA WINGFIELD, *her daughter. Amanda, having failed to establish contact with reality, continues to live vitally in her illusions, but Laura's situation is even graver. A childhood illness has left her crippled, one leg slightly shorter than the other, and held in a brace. This defect need not be more than suggested on the stage. Stemming from this, Laura's separation increases till she is like a piece of her own glass collection, too exquisitely fragile to move from the shelf.*

TOM WINGFIELD, *her son. And the narrator of the play. A poet with a job in a warehouse. His nature is not remorseless, but to escape from a trap he has to act without pity.*

JIM O'CONNOR, *the gentleman caller. A nice, ordinary, young man.*

SCENE: *An alley in St. Louis.*

PART I: *Preparation for a Gentleman Caller.*

PART II: *The Gentleman Calls.*

TIME: *Now and the Past.*

SCENE 1

The Wingfield apartment is in the rear of the build-ing, one of those vast hivelike conglomerations of cellular living-units that flower as warty growths in overcrowded urban centers of lower middle-class population and are symptomatic of the impulse of this largest and fundamentally enslaved section of American society to avoid fluidity and differentiation and to exist and function as one interfused mass of automatism.

The apartment faces an alley and is entered by a fire-escape, a structure whose name is a touch of accidental poetic truth, for all of these huge buildings are always burning with the slow and implacable fires of human desperation. The fire-escape is included in the set—that is, the landing of it and steps descending from it.

The scene is memory and is therefore nonrealistic. Memory takes a lot of poetic license. It omits some details; others are exaggerated, according to the emo-tional value of the articles it touches, for memory is seated predominantly in the heart. The interior is therefore rather dim and poetic.

At the rise of the curtain, the audience is faced with the dark, grim rear wall of the Wingfield tenement. This building, which runs parallel to the footlights, is flanked on both sides by dark, narrow alleys which run into murky canyons of tangled clotheslines, garbage cans, and the sinister latticework of neigh-boring fire-escapes. It is up and down these side alleys that exterior entrances and exits are made, during the play. At the end of TOM's *opening commentary, the dark tenement wall slowly reveals (by means of trans-parency) the interior of the ground floor Wingfield apartment.*

Downstage is the living room, which also serves as a sleeping room for LAURA, *the sofa unfolding to make her bed. Upstage, center, and divided by a wide arch or second proscenium with transparent faded portieres (or second curtain), is the dining room. In an old-fashioned what-not in the living room are seen scores of transparent glass animals. A blown-up photograph of the father hangs on the wall of the living room, facing the audience, to the left of the archway. It is the face of a very handsome young man in a doughboy's First World War cap. He is gallantly smiling, ineluctably smiling, as if to say, "I will be smiling forever."*

The audience hears and sees the opening scene in the dining room through both the transparent fourth wall of the building and the transparent gauze por-tieres of the dining-room arch. It is during this reveal-ing scene that the fourth wall slowly ascends, out of sight. This transparent exterior wall is not brought down again until the very end of the play, during TOM's *final speech.*

The narrator is an undisguised convention of the play. He takes whatever license with dramatic con-vention as is convenient to his purposes.

TOM *enters dressed as a merchant sailor from alley, stage left, and strolls across the front of the stage to the fire-escape. There he stops and lights a cigarette. He addresses the audience.*

TOM: Yes, I have tricks in my pocket, I have things up my sleeve. But I am opposite of a stage magician. He gives you illusion that has the appearance of truth. I give you truth in the pleasant disguise of illusion. To begin with, I turn back time. I reverse it to that 5 quaint period, the thirties, when the huge middle class of America was matriculating in a school for the blind. Their eyes had failed them, or they had failed their eyes, and so they were having their fingers pressed forcibly down on the fiery Braille alphabet of 10 a dissolving economy. In Spain there was revolution. Here there was only shouting and confusion. In Spain there was Guernica. Here there were disturbances of labor, sometimes pretty violent, in otherwise peace-ful cities such as Chicago, Cleveland, Saint Louis. . . . 15 This is the social background of the play.

(Music.)

Tom (Sam Waterston) delivers the opening monologue in the 1973 film directed by Anthony Harvey.

The play is memory. Being a memory play, it is dimly lighted, it is sentimental, it is not realistic. In memory everything seems to happen to music. That explains
20 the fiddle in the wings. I am the narrator of the play, and also a character in it. The other characters are my mother, Amanda, my sister, Laura, and a gentleman caller who appears in the final scenes. He is the most realistic character in the play, being an emissary from
25 a world of reality that we were somehow set apart from. But since I have a poet's weakness for symbols, I am using this character also as a symbol; he is the long delayed but always expected something that we live for. There is a fifth character in the play who
30 doesn't appear except in this larger-than-life photograph over the mantel. This is our father who left us a long time ago. He was a telephone man who fell in love with long distances; he gave up his job with the telephone company and skipped the light fantastic
35 out of town. . . . The last we heard of him was a picture post-card from Mazatlán, on the Pacific coast of Mexico, containing a message of two words—"Hello—Goodbye!" and no address. I think the rest of the play will explain itself. . . .

AMANDA's *voice becomes audible through the portieres.*

(Legend on screen: "Où sont les neiges.")

He divides the portieres and enters the upstage area.
  AMANDA *and* LAURA *are seated at a drop-leaf table. Eating is indicated by gestures without food or utensils.* AMANDA *faces the audience.*
  TOM *and* LAURA *are seated in profile.*
  The interior has lit up softly and through the scrim we see AMANDA *and* LAURA *seated at the table in the upstage area.*

AMANDA: *(calling)* Tom? 40

TOM: Yes, Mother.

AMANDA: We can't say grace until you come to the table!

TOM: Coming, Mother. *(He bows slightly and withdraws, reappearing a few moments later in his place at the table.)* 45

AMANDA: *(to her son)* Honey, don't *push* with your *fingers.* If you have to push with something, the thing to push with is a crust of bread. And chew—chew! Animals have sections in their stomachs which enable them to digest food without mastication, but human 50 beings are supposed to chew their food before they swallow it down. Eat food leisurely, son, and really enjoy it. A well-cooked meal has lots of delicate flavors that have to be held in the mouth for appreciation. So chew your food and give your salivary glands a chance 55 to function!

TOM *deliberately lays his imaginary fork down and pushes his chair back from the table.*

TOM: I haven't enjoyed one bite of this dinner because of your constant directions on how to eat it. It's you that makes me rush through meals with your hawk-like attention to every bite I take. Sickening—spoils my 60 appetite—all this discussion of animals' secretion—salivary glands—mastication!

AMANDA: *(lightly)* Temperament like a Metropolitan star! *(He rises and crosses downstage.)* You're not excused from the table. 65

TOM: I am getting a cigarette.

AMANDA: You smoke too much.

Amanda (Katharine Hepburn) clears the table.

LAURA *rises.*

LAURA: I'll bring in the blanc mange.

He remains standing with his cigarette by the por-
tieres during the following.

AMANDA: *(rising)* No, sister, no, sister—you be the lady
70   this time and I'll be the darky.

LAURA: I'm already up.

AMANDA: Resume your seat, little sister—I want you to
      stay fresh and pretty—for gentlemen callers!

LAURA: I'm not expecting any gentlemen callers.

75 **AMANDA:** *(crossing out to kitchenette. Airily)* Sometimes
      they come when they are least expected! Why, I re-
      member one Sunday afternoon in Blue Mountain—
      (Enters kitchenette.)

TOM: I know what's coming!

80 **LAURA:** Yes. But let her tell it.

TOM: Again?

LAURA: She loves to tell it.

AMANDA *returns with a bowl of dessert.*

AMANDA: One Sunday afternoon in Blue Mountain—
your mother received—*seventeen!*—gentlemen callers!
Why, sometimes there weren't chairs enough to ac-   85
commodate them all. We had to send the nigger over
to bring in folding chairs from the parish house.

TOM: *(remaining at the portieres)* How did you entertain
those gentlemen callers?

AMANDA: I understood the art of conversation!   90

TOM: I bet you could talk.

AMANDA: Girls in those days *knew* how to talk, I can
tell you.

TOM: Yes?

(Image: AMANDA *as a girl on a porch greeting callers.)*

AMANDA: They knew how to entertain their gentlemen   95
callers. It wasn't enough for a girl to be possessed of
a pretty face and a graceful figure—although I wasn't
slighted in either respect. She also needed to have a
nimble wit and a tongue to meet all occasions.

TOM: What did you talk about?   100

AMANDA: Things of importance going on in the world!
Never anything coarse or common or vulgar. *(She*
addresses TOM *as though he were seated in the vacant*
chair at the table though he remains by the portieres.
He plays this scene as though he held the book.) My call-   105
ers were gentlemen—all! Among my callers were some
of the most prominent young planters of the Mississippi Delta—planters and sons of planters!

TOM *motions for music and a spot of light on*
AMANDA.
    Her eyes lift, her face glows, her voice becomes rich
and elegiac.
    (Screen legend: "Où sont les neiges.")

There was young Champ Laughlin who later became
vice-president of the Delta Planters Bank. Hadley   110
Stevenson who was drowned in Moon Lake and
left his widow one hundred and fifty thousand in
Government bonds. There were the Cutrere broth-

ers, Wesley and Bates. Bates was one of my bright
115 particular beaux! He got in a quarrel with that wild
Wainwright boy. They shot it out on the floor of Moon
Lake Casino. Bates was shot through the stomach.
Died in the ambulance on his way to Memphis. His
widow was also well-provided for, came into eight or
120 ten thousand acres, that's all. She married him on the
rebound—never loved her—carried my picture on him
the night he died! And there was that boy that every
girl in the Delta had set her cap for! That beautiful,
brilliant young Fitzhugh boy from Greene County!

125 **TOM:** What did he leave his widow?

AMANDA: He never married! Gracious, you talk as
though all of my old admirers had turned up their
toes to the daisies!

TOM: Isn't this the first you mentioned that still survives?

130 **AMANDA:** That Fitzhugh boy went North and made
a fortune—came to be known as the Wolf of Wall
Street! He had the Midas touch, whatever he touched
turned to gold! And I could have been Mrs. Duncan J.
Fitzhugh, mind you! But—I picked your *father!*

135 **LAURA:** *(rising)* Mother, let me clear the table.

AMANDA: No dear, you go in front and study your typewriter chart. Or practice your shorthand a little. Stay
fresh and pretty!—It's almost time for our gentlemen
callers to start arriving. *(She flounces girlishly toward*
140 *the kitchenette.)* How many do you suppose we're going to entertain this afternoon?

TOM *throws down the paper and jumps up with a*
groan.

LAURA: *(alone in the dining room)* I don't believe we're
going to receive any, Mother.

AMANDA: *(reappearing, airily)* What? No one—not
145 one? You must be joking! (LAURA *nervously echoes*
her laugh. She slips in a fugitive manner through the
half-open portieres and draws them gently behind her.
A shaft of very clear light is thrown on her face against
the faded tapestry of the curtains.) (Music: "The Glass
150 Menagerie" *under faintly.)* (Lightly.) Not one gentleman caller? It can't be true! There must be a flood,
there must have been a tornado!

LAURA: It isn't a flood, it's not a tornado, Mother. I'm
just not popular like you were in Blue Mountain. . . .
(TOM utters another groan. LAURA *glances at him*
155
with a faint, apologetic smile. Her voice catching a
little.) Mother's afraid I'm going to be an old maid.

(The scene dims out with the "Glass Menagerie"
music.)

SCENE 2

"Laura, Haven't You Ever Liked Some Boy?"

On the dark stage the screen is lighted with the image
of blue roses.

Gradually LAURA's *figure becomes apparent and*
the screen goes out.

The music subsides.

LAURA *is seated in the delicate ivory chair at the*
small clawfoot table.

She wears a dress of soft violet material for a
kimono—her hair tied back from her forehead with
a ribbon.

She is washing and polishing her collection of
glass.

AMANDA *appears on the fire-escape steps. At*
the sound of her ascent, LAURA *catches her breath,*
thrusts the bowl of ornaments away, and seats herself
stiffly before the diagram of the typewriter keyboard
as though it held her spellbound. Something has
happened to AMANDA. *It is written in her face as she*
climbs to the landing: a look that is grim and hopeless
and a little absurd.

She has on one of those cheap or imitation velvety-
looking cloth coats with imitation fur collar. Her hat
is five or six years old, one of those dreadful cloche
hats that were worn in the late twenties, and she is
clasping an enormous black patent-leather pocket-
book with nickel clasp and initials. This is her full-
dress outfit, the one she usually wears to the D.A.R.

Before entering she looks through the door.

She purses her lips, opens her eyes wide, rolls them
upward, and shakes her head.

Then she slowly lets herself in the door. Seeing her
mother's expression LAURA *touches her lips with a*
nervous gesture.

LAURA: Hello, Mother, I was— *(She makes a nervous gesture toward the chart on the wall.* AMANDA *leans against the shut door and stares at* LAURA *with a martyred look.)*

5 **AMANDA:** Deception? Deception? *(She slowly removes her hat and gloves, continuing the swift suffering stare. She lets the hat and gloves fall on the floor—a bit of acting.)*

LAURA: *(shakily)* How was the D.A.R. meeting? 10 *(*AMANDA *slowly opens her purse and removes a dainty white handkerchief, which she shakes out delicately and delicately touches to her lips and nostrils.)* Didn't you go to the D.A.R. meeting, Mother?

AMANDA: *(faintly, almost inaudibly)* —No.—No. *(Then* 15 *more forcibly.)* I did not have the strength—to go to the D.A.R. In fact, I did not have the courage! I wanted to find a hole in the ground and hide myself in it forever! *(She crosses slowly to the wall and removes the diagram of the typewriter keyboard. She holds it in* 20 *front of her for a second, staring at it sweetly and sorrowfully—then bites her lips and tears it in two pieces.)*

LAURA: *(faintly)* Why did you do that, Mother? *(*AMANDA *repeats the same procedure with the chart of the Gregg Alphabet.)* Why are you—

25 **AMANDA:** Why? Why? How old are you, Laura?

LAURA: Mother, you know my age.

AMANDA: I thought that you were an adult; it seems that I was mistaken. *(She crosses slowly to the sofa and sinks down and stares at* LAURA.*)*

30 **LAURA:** Please don't stare at me, Mother.

AMANDA *closes her eyes and lowers her head. Count ten.*

AMANDA: What are we going to do, what is going to become of us, what is the future?

Count ten.

LAURA: Has something happened, Mother? *(*AMANDA *draws a long breath and takes out the handkerchief* 35 *again. Dabbing process.)* Mother, has—something happened?

AMANDA: I'll be all right in a minute. I'm just bewildered—*(count five)*—by life. . . .

LAURA: Mother, I wish that you would tell me what's happened. 40

AMANDA: As you know, I was supposed to be inducted into my office at the D.A.R. this afternoon. *(Image: A swarm of typewriters.)* But I stopped off at Rubicam's Business College to speak to your teachers about your having a cold and ask them what progress 45 they thought you were making down there.

LAURA: Oh. . . .

AMANDA: I went to the typing instructor and introduced myself as your mother. She didn't know who you were. Wingfield, she said. We don't have any 50 such student enrolled at the school! I assured her she did, that you had been going to classes since early in January. "I wonder," she said, "if you could be talking about that terribly shy little girl who dropped out of school after only a few days' attendance?" "No," I said, 55 "Laura, my daughter, has been going to school every day for the past six weeks!" "Excuse me," she said. She took the attendance book out and there was your name, unmistakably printed, and all the dates you were absent until they decided that you had dropped 60 out of school. I still said, "No, there must have been some mistake! There must have been some mix-up in the records!" And she said, "No—I remember her perfectly now. Her hands shook so that she couldn't hit the right keys! The first time we gave a speed-test, 65 she broke down completely—was sick at the stomach and almost had to be carried into the wash-room! After that morning she never showed up any more. We phoned the house but never got any answer"—while I was working at Famous and Barr, I suppose, demon- 70 strating those—Oh! I felt so weak I could barely keep on my feet! I had to sit down while they got me a glass of water! Fifty dollars' tuition, all of our plans—my hopes and ambitions for you—just gone up the spout, just gone up the spout like that. *(*LAURA *draws a long* 75 *breath and gets awkwardly to her feet. She crosses to the Victrola, and winds it up.)* What are you doing?

LAURA: Oh! *(She releases the handle and returns to her seat.)*

Laura (Joanna Miles) gazes at her glass ornaments.

80 **AMANDA:** Laura, where have been going when you've gone out pretending that you were going to business college?

LAURA: I've just been going out walking.

AMANDA: That's not true.

85 **LAURA:** It is. I just went walking.

AMANDA: Walking? Walking? In winter? Deliberately courting pneumonia in that light coat? Where did you walk to, Laura?

LAURA: It was the lesser of two evils, Mother. *(Image:*
90 *Winter scene in park.)* I couldn't go back up. I—threw up—on the floor!

AMANDA: From half past seven till after five every day you mean to tell me you walked around in the park, because you wanted to make me think that you were
95 still going to Rubicam's Business College?

LAURA: It wasn't as bad as it sounds. I went inside places to get warmed up.

AMANDA: Inside where?

LAURA: I went in the art museum and the bird-houses at
100 the Zoo. I visited the penguins every day! Sometimes I did without lunch and went to the movies. Lately I've been spending most of my afternoons in the Jewel-box, that big glass house where they raise the tropical flowers.

AMANDA: You did all this to deceive me, just for the 105
deception? (LAURA *looks down.)* Why?

LAURA: Mother, when you're disappointed, you get that awful suffering look on your face, like the picture of Jesus' mother in the museum!

AMANDA: Hush! 110

LAURA: I couldn't face it.

Pause. A whisper of string.
(Legend: "The Crust of Humility.")

AMANDA: *(hopelessly fingering the huge pocketbook)* So what are we going to do the rest of our lives? Stay home and watch the parades go by? Amuse ourselves with the glass menagerie, darling? Eternally play 115
those worn-out phonograph records your father left as a painful reminder of him? We won't have a business career—we've given that up because it gave us nervous indigestion! *(Laughs wearily.)* What is there left but dependency all our lives? I know so well what 120
becomes of unmarried women who aren't prepared to occupy a position. I've seen such pitiful cases in the South—barely tolerated spinsters living upon the grudging patronage of sister's husband or brother's wife!—stuck away in some little mousetrap of a 125
room—encouraged by one in-law to visit another—little birdlike women without any nest—eating the crust of humility all their life! Is that the future that we've mapped out for ourselves? I swear it's the only alternative I can think of! It isn't a very pleasant 130
alternative, is it? Of course—some girls *do* marry. (LAURA *twists her hands nervously.)* Haven't you ever liked some boy?

LAURA: Yes. I liked one once. *(Rises.)* I came across his picture a while ago. 135

AMANDA: *(with some interest)* He gave you his picture?

LAURA: No, it's in the year-book.

AMANDA: *(disappointed)* Oh—a high-school boy.

(Screen image: JIM *as the high school hero bearing a silver cup.)*

LAURA: Yes. His name was Jim. (LAURA *lifts the heavy*
140   *annual from the clawfoot table.*) Here he is in *The*
         Pirates of Penzance.

AMANDA: *(absently)* The what?

LAURA: The operetta the senior class put on. He had
        a wonderful voice and we sat across the aisle from
145   each other Mondays, Wednesdays, and Fridays in the
        Aud. Here he is with the silver cup for debating! See
        his grin?

AMANDA: *(absently)* He must have had a jolly
         disposition.

150 LAURA: He used to call me—Blue Roses.

        (Image: Blue roses.)

AMANDA: Why did he call you such a name as that?

LAURA: When I had that attack of pleurosis—he asked
        me what was the matter when I came back. I said
        pleurosis—he thought that I said Blue Roses! So that's
155   what he always called me after that. Whenever he
        saw me, he'd holler, "Hello, Blue Roses!" I didn't care
        for the girl that he went out with. Emily Meisenbach.
        Emily was the best-dressed girl at Soldan. She never
        struck me, though, as being sincere. . . . It says in the
160   Personal Section—they're engaged. That's—six years
        ago! They must be married by now.

AMANDA: Girls that aren't cut out for business careers
         usually wind up married to some nice man. (*Gets up*
         with a spark of revival.) Sister, that's what you'll do!

        LAURA *utters a startled, doubtful laugh. She reaches*
        quickly for a piece of glass.

165 LAURA: But, Mother—

AMANDA: Yes? (*Crossing to photograph.*)

LAURA: (*in a tone of frightened apology*) I'm—crippled!

        (Image: Screen.)

AMANDA: Nonsense! Laura, I've told you never, never to
         use that word. Why, you're not crippled, you just have
170   a little defect—hardly noticeable, even! When people
         have some slight disadvantage like that, they cultivate
         other things to make up for it—develop charm—and

Laura and Amanda discuss the future.

vivacity—and—*charm!* That's all you have to do! (*She*
turns again to the photograph.) One thing your father
had *plenty of*—was *charm!*   175

TOM *motions to the fiddle in the wings.*
    (*The scene fades out with music.*)

SCENE 3

(*Legend on the screen: "After the Fiasco—"*)
    TOM *speaks from the fire-escape landing.*

TOM: After the fiasco at Rubicam's Business College, the
      idea of getting a gentleman caller for Laura began to
      play a more important part in Mother's calculations.
      It became an obsession. Like some archetype of the
      universal unconscious, the image of the gentleman   5
      caller haunted our small apartment. . . . (*Image: Young*
      man at door with flowers.) An evening at home rarely
      passed without some allusion to this image, this spec-
      ter, this hope. . . . Even when he wasn't mentioned,
      his presence hung in Mother's preoccupied look and   10
      in my sister's frightened, apologetic manner—hung
      like a sentence passed upon the Wingfields! Mother
      was a woman of action as well as words. She began
      to take logical steps in the planned direction. Late
      that winter and in the early spring—realizing that   15
      extra money would be needed to properly feather the
      nest and plume the bird—she conducted a vigorous
      campaign on the telephone, roping in subscribers to

one of those magazines for matrons called *The Home-maker's Companion,* the type of journal that features the serialized sublimations of ladies of letters who think in terms of delicate cuplike breasts, slim, tapering waists, rich, creamy thighs, eyes like wood smoke in autumn, fingers that soothe and caress like strains of music, bodies as powerful as Etruscan sculpture.

(Screen image: Glamour *magazine cover.)*
AMANDA *enters with phone on long extension cord. She is spotted in the dim stage.*

AMANDA: Ida Scott? This is Amanda Wingfield! We *missed* you at the D.A.R. last Monday! I said to myself: She's probably suffering with that sinus condition! How is that sinus condition? Horrors! Heaven have mercy!—You're a Christian martyr, yes, that's what you are, a Christian martyr! Well, I just now happened to notice that your subscription to the *Companion's* about to expire! Yes, it expires with the next issue, honey!—just when that wonderful new serial by Bessie Mae Hopper is getting off to such an exciting start. Oh, honey, it's something that you can't miss! You remember how *Gone with the Wind* took everybody by storm? You simply couldn't go out if you hadn't read it. All everybody *talked* was Scarlett O'Hara. Well, this is a book that critics already compare to *Gone with the Wind.* It's the *Gone with the Wind* of the post–World War generation!—What?—Burning?—Oh, honey, don't let them burn, go take a look in the oven and I'll hold the wire! Heavens—I think she's hung up!

(Dim out.)
(Legend on screen: "You think I'm in love with Continental Shoemakers?")
Before the stage is lighted, the violent voices of TOM *and* AMANDA *are heard. They are quarreling behind the portieres. In front of them stands* LAURA *with clenched hands and panicky expression.*
A clear pool of light on her figure throughout this scene.

TOM: What in Christ's name am I—

AMANDA: *(shrilly)* Don't you use that—

TOM: Supposed to do!

AMANDA: Expression! Not in my—

TOM: Ohhh!

AMANDA: Presence! Have you gone out of your senses?

TOM: I have, that's true, *driven* out!

AMANDA: What is the matter with you, you—big—big—IDIOT!

TOM: Look!—I've got *no thing,* no single thing—

AMANDA: Lower your voice!

TOM: In my life here that I can call my own! Everything is—

AMANDA: Stop that shouting!

TOM: Yesterday you confiscated my books! You had the nerve to—

AMANDA: I took that horrible novel back to the library—yes! That hideous book by that insane Mr. Lawrence. *(*TOM *laughs wildly.)* I cannot control the output of diseased minds or people who cater to them—*(*TOM *laughs still more wildly.)* BUT I WON'T ALLOW SUCH FILTH BROUGHT INTO MY HOUSE! No, no, no, no, no!

TOM: House, house! Who pays rent on it, who makes a slave of himself to—

AMANDA: *(fairly screeching)* Don't you DARE to—

TOM: No, no, *I* mustn't say things! *I've* got to just—

AMANDA: Let me tell you—

TOM: I don't want to hear any more! *(He tears the portieres open. The upstage area is lit with a turgid smoky red glow.)*

AMANDA's *hair is in metal curlers and she wears a very old bathrobe, much too large for her slight figure, a relic of the faithless Mr. Wingfield.*
The upright typewriter and a wild disarray of manuscripts are on the drop-leaf table. The quarrel was probably precipitated by AMANDA's *interruption of his creative labor. A chair lying overthrown on the floor.*
Their gesticulating shadows are cast on the ceiling by the fiery glow.

AMANDA: You *will* hear more, you—

TOM: No, I won't hear more, I'm going out!

AMANDA: You come right back in—

TOM: Out, out, out! Because I'm—

80 **AMANDA:**   Come back here, Tom Wingfield! I'm not through talking to you!

TOM: Oh, go—

LAURA: *(desperately)* Tom!

AMANDA: You're going to listen, and no more insolence
85   from you! I'm at the end of my patience! *(He comes back toward her.)*

TOM: What do you think I'm at? Aren't I supposed to
have any patience to reach the end of, Mother? I
know, I know. It seems unimportant to you, what I'm
90   *doing*—what I *want* to do—having a little *difference*
between them! You don't think that—

AMANDA: I think you've been doing things that you're
ashamed of. That's why you act like this. I don't believe that you go every night to the movies. Nobody
95   goes to the movies night after night. Nobody in
their right minds goes to the movies as often as you

Amanda scolds her son.

pretend to. People don't go to the movies at nearly
midnight, and movies don't let out at two A.M. Come
in stumbling. Muttering to yourself like a maniac!
You get three hours' sleep and then go to work. Oh, I   100
can picture the way you're doing down there. Moping,
doping, because you're in no condition.

TOM: *(wildly)* No, I'm in no condition!

AMANDA: What right have you got to jeopardize your
job? Jeopardize the security of us all? How do you   105
think we'd manage if you were—

TOM: Listen! You think I'm crazy *about* the *warehouse!*
(He bends fiercely toward her slight figure.) You think
I'm in love with the Continental Shoemakers? You
think I want to spend fifty-five *years* down there   110
in that—*celotex interior!* with—*fluorescent—tubes!*
Look! I'd rather somebody picked up a crowbar and
battered out my brains—than go back mornings! I *go!*
Every time you come in yelling that God damn *"Rise
and Shine!" "Rise and Shine!"* I say to myself, "How   115
lucky dead people are!" But I get up. I *go!* For sixty-
five dollars a month I give up all that I dream of doing
and being *ever!* And you say self—*self's* all I ever think
of. Why, listen, if self is what I thought of, Mother, I'd
be where he is—! *(Pointing to father's picture.)* As far   120
as the system of transportation reaches! *(He starts
past her. She grabs his arm.)* Don't grab at me, Mother!

AMANDA: Where are you going?

TOM: I'm going to the *movies!*

AMANDA: I don't believe that lie!   125

TOM: *(crouching toward her, overtowering her tiny figure.
She backs away, gasping)* I'm going to opium dens!
Yes, opium dens, dens of vice and criminals' hangouts,
Mother. I've joined the Hogan gang, I'm a hired assassin, I carry a tommy-gun in a violin case! I run a   130
string of cat-houses in the Valley! They call me Killer,
Killer Wingfield, I'm leading a double-life, a simple,
honest warehouse worker by day, by night a dynamic
czar of the *underworld, Mother.* I go to gambling casi-
nos, I spin away fortunes on the roulette table! I wear   135
a patch over one eye and a false mustache, sometimes
I put on green whiskers. On those occasions they call
me—*El Diablo!* Oh, I could tell you many things to

make you sleepless! My enemies plan to dynamite
this place. They're going to blow us all sky-high some
night! I'll be glad, very happy, and so will you! You'll
go up, up on a broomstick, over Blue Mountain with
seventeen gentlemen callers! You ugly—babbling
old—*witch*. . . . (*He goes through a series of violent,
clumsy movements, seizing his overcoat, lunging to the
door, pulling it fiercely open. The women watch him,
aghast. His arm catches in the sleeve of the coat as he
struggles to pull it on. For a moment he is pinioned by
the bulky garment. With an outraged groan he tears the
coat off again, splitting the shoulders of it, and hurls it
across the room. It strikes against the shelf of* LAURA's
glass collection, there is a tinkle of shattering glass.
LAURA *cries out as if wounded.*)

(*Music legend: "The Glass Menagerie."*)

LAURA: (*shrilly*) My glass!—menagerie. . . . (*She covers
her face and turns away.*)

But AMANDA *is still stunned and stupefied by the
"ugly witch" so that she barely notices the occurrence.
Now she recovers her speech.*

AMANDA: (*in an awful voice*) I won't speak to you—
until you apologize! (*She crosses through the portieres
and draws them together behind her.* TOM *is left with*
LAURA. LAURA *clings weakly to the mantel with her
face averted.* TOM *stares at her stupidly for a moment.
Then he crosses to shelf. Drops awkwardly to his knees
to collect the fallen glass, glancing at* LAURA *as if he
would speak but couldn't.*)

"The Glass Menagerie" *music steals in as*
(*The scene dims out.*)

SCENE 4

The interior is dark. Faint light in the alley.
*A deep-voiced bell in a church is tolling the hour of
five as the scene commences.*

TOM *appears at the top of the alley. After each
solemn boom of the bell in the tower, he shakes a little
noise-maker or rattle as if to express the tiny spasm of
man in contrast to the sustained power and dignity
of the Almighty. This and the unsteadiness of his advance make it evident that he has been drinking.*

*As he climbs the few steps to the fire-escape landing
light steals up inside.* LAURA *appears in night-dress,
observing* TOM's *empty bed in the front room.*

TOM *fishes in his pockets for his door-key, removing a motley assortment of articles in the search,
including a perfect shower of movie-ticket stubs and
an empty bottle. At last he finds the key, but just as he
is about to insert it, it slips from his fingers. He strikes
a match and crouches below the door.*

TOM: (*bitterly*) One crack—and it falls through!

LAURA *opens the door.*

LAURA: Tom! Tom, what are you doing?

TOM: Looking for a door-key.

LAURA: Where have you been all this time?

TOM: I have been to the movies.

LAURA: All this time at the movies?

TOM: There was a very long program. There was a Garbo
picture and a Mickey Mouse and a travelogue and
a newsreel and a preview of coming attractions.
And there was an organ solo and a collection for the
milk-fund—simultaneously—which ended up in a terrible fight between a fat lady and an usher!

LAURA: (*innocently*) Did you have to stay through
everything?

TOM: Of course! And, oh, I forgot! There was a big stage
show! The headliner on this stage show was Malvo-
lio the Magician. He performed wonderful tricks,
many of them, such as pouring water back and forth
between pitchers. First it turned to wine and then it
turned to beer and then it turned to whisky. I know it
was whiskey it finally turned into because he needed
somebody to come up out of the audience to help him,
and I came up—both shows! It was Kentucky Straight
Bourbon. A very generous fellow, he gave souvenirs.
(*He pulls from his back pocket a shimmering rainbow-
colored scarf.*) He gave me this. This is his magic scarf.
You can have it, Laura. You wave it over a canary
cage and you get a bowl of gold-fish. You wave it over
the gold-fish bowl and they fly away canaries. . . . But
the wonderfullest trick of all was the coffin trick. We

Laura helps her brother into bed.

nailed him into a coffin and he got out of the coffin without removing one nail. *(He has come inside.)* There is a trick that would come in handy for me—get me out of this 2 by 4 situation! *(Flops onto bed and* 35 *starts removing his shoes.)*

LAURA: Tom—Shhh!

TOM: What you shushing me for?

LAURA: You'll wake up Mother.

TOM: Goody, goody! Pay 'er back for all those "Rise an' 40   Shines." *(Lies down, groaning.)* You know it don't take much intelligence to get yourself into a nailed-up coffin, Laura. But who in hell ever got himself out of one without removing one nail?

As if in answer, the father's grinning photograph lights up.
  (Scene dims out.)
  Immediately following: The church bell is heard striking six. At the sixth stroke the alarm clock goes off in AMANDA's *room, and after a few moments we hear her calling: "Rise and Shine! Rise and Shine! Laura, go tell your brother to rise and shine!"*

TOM: *(sitting up slowly)* I'll rise—but I won't shine.

The light increases.

AMANDA: Laura, tell your brother his coffee is ready.   45

LAURA *slips into front room.*

LAURA: Tom! It's nearly seven. Don't make Mother nervous. *(He stares at her stupidly. Beseechingly.)* Tom, speak to Mother this morning. Make up with her, apologize, speak to her!

TOM: She won't to me. It's her that started not speaking.   50

LAURA: If you just say you're sorry she'll start speaking.

TOM: Her not speaking—is that such a tragedy?

LAURA: Please—please!

AMANDA: *(calling from the kitchenette)* Laura, are you going to do what I asked you to do, or do I have to get   55 dressed and go out myself?

LAURA: Going, going—soon as I get on my coat! *(She pulls on a shapeless felt hat with nervous, jerky movement, pleadingly glancing at* TOM. *Rushes awkwardly for coat. The coat is one of* AMANDA's, *inaccurately*   60 *made-over, the sleeves too short for* LAURA.*)* Butter and what else?

AMANDA: *(entering upstage)* Just butter. Tell them to charge it.

LAURA: Mother, they make such faces when I do that.   65

AMANDA: Sticks and stones may break my bones, but the expression on Mr. Garfinkel's face won't harm us! Tell your brother his coffee is getting cold.

LAURA: *(at door)* Do what I asked you, will you, will you, Tom?   70

He looks sullenly away.

AMANDA: Laura, go now or just don't go at all!

LAURA: *(rushing out)* Going—going! *(A second later she cries out.* TOM *springs up and crosses to the door.* AMANDA *rushes anxiously in.* TOM *opens the door.)*

TOM: Laura?   75

LAURA: I'm all right. I slipped, but I'm all right.

AMANDA: *(peering anxiously after her)* If anyone breaks a leg on those fire-escape steps, the landlord ought to be sued for every cent he possesses! *(She shuts door.* 80 *Remembers she isn't speaking and returns to other room.)*

As TOM *enters listlessly for his coffee, she turns her back to him and stands rigidly facing the window on the gloomy gray vault of the areaway. Its light on her face with its aged but childish features is cruelly sharp, satirical as a Daumier print.*
(Music under: "Ave Maria.")
TOM *glances sheepishly but sullenly at her averted figure and slumps at the table. The coffee is scalding hot; he sips it and gasps and spits it back in the cup. At his gasp,* AMANDA *catches her breath and half turns. Then she catches herself and turns back to window.*

TOM *blows on his coffee, glancing sidewise at his mother. She clears her throat.* TOM *clears his. He starts to rise. Sinks back down again, scratches his head, clears his throat again.* AMANDA *coughs.* TOM *raises his cup in both hands to blow on it, his eyes staring over the rim of it at his mother for several moments. Then he slowly sets the cup down and awkwardly and hesitantly rises from the chair.*

TOM: *(hoarsely)* Mother. I—I apologize. Mother. *(*AMANDA *draws a quick, shuddering breath. Her face works grotesquely. She breaks into childlike tears.)* I'm
85 sorry for what I said, for everything that I said, I didn't mean it.

AMANDA: *(sobbingly)* My devotion has made me a witch and so I make myself hateful to my children!

TOM: No, you *don't.*

90 **AMANDA:** I worry so much, don't sleep, it makes me nervous!

TOM: *(gently)* I understand that.

AMANDA: I've had to put up a solitary battle all these years. But you're my right-hand bower! Don't fall
95 down, don't fail!

TOM: *(gently)* I try, Mother.

AMANDA: *(with great enthusiasm)* Try and you will SUCCEED! *(The notion makes her breathless.)* Why, you—you're just *full* of natural endowments! Both
100 of my children—they're *unusual* children! Don't you

think I know it? I'm so—*proud!* Happy and—feel I've—so much to be thankful for but—Promise me one thing, son!

TOM: What, Mother?

AMANDA: Promise, son, you'll—never be a drunkard! 105

TOM: *(turns to her grinning)* I will never be a drunkard, Mother.

AMANDA: That's what frightened me so, that you'd be drinking! Eat a bowl of Purina!

TOM: Just coffee, Mother. 110

AMANDA: Shredded wheat biscuit?

TOM: No. No, Mother, just coffee.

AMANDA: You can't put in a day's work on an empty stomach. You've got ten minutes—don't gulp! Drinking too-hot liquids makes cancer of the stomach. . . . 115 Put cream in.

TOM: No, thank you.

AMANDA: To cool it.

TOM: No! No, thank you, I want it black.

AMANDA: I know, but it's not good for you. We have 120 to do all that we can to build ourselves up. In these trying times we live in, all that we have to cling to is— each other. . . . That's why it's so important to—Tom, I—I sent out your sister so I could discuss something with you. If you hadn't spoken I would have spoken to 125 you. *(Sits down.)*

TOM: *(gently)* What is it, Mother, that you want to discuss?

AMANDA: Laura!

TOM *puts his cup down slowly.*
(Legend on screen: "Laura.")
(Music: "The Glass Menagerie.")

TOM: —Oh.—Laura . . . 130

AMANDA: *(touching his sleeve)* You know how Laura is. So quiet but—still water runs deep! She notices things and I think she—broods about them. *(*TOM *looks up.)* A few days ago I came in and she was crying.

135 **TOM:** What about?

AMANDA: You.

TOM: Me?

AMANDA: She has an idea that you're not happy here.

TOM: What gave her that idea?

140 **AMANDA:** What gives her any idea? However, you do act strangely. I—I'm not criticizing, understand *that!* I know your ambitions do not lie in the warehouse, that like everybody in the whole wide world—you've had to—make sacrifices, but—Tom—Tom—life's not

145 easy, it calls for—Spartan endurance! There's so many things in my heart that I cannot describe to you! I've never told you but I—*loved* your father. . . .

TOM: *(gently)* I know that, Mother.

AMANDA: And you—when I see you taking after his

150 ways! Staying out late—and—well, you *had* been drinking the night you were in that—terrifying condition! Laura says that you hate the apartment and that you go out nights to get away from it! Is that true, Tom?

155 **TOM:** No. You say there's so much in your heart that you can't describe to me. That's true of me, too. There's so much in my heart that I can't describe to *you!* So let's respect each other's—

AMANDA: But, why—*why*, Tom—are you always so *rest-*

160 *less?* Where do you go to, nights?

TOM: I—go to the movies.

AMANDA: Why do you go to the movies so much, Tom?

TOM: I go to the movies because—I like adventure. Adventure is something I don't have much of at work, so

165 I go to the movies.

AMANDA: But, Tom, you go to the movies *entirely too much!*

TOM: I like a lot of adventure.

AMANDA *looks baffled, then hurt. As the familiar inquisition resumes he becomes hard and impatient*

again. AMANDA *slips back into her querulous attitude toward him.*

(Image on screen: Sailing vessel with Jolly Roger.)

AMANDA: Most young men find adventure in their careers. 170

TOM: Then most young men are not employed in a warehouse.

AMANDA: The world is full of young men employed in warehouses and offices and factories.

TOM: Do all of them find adventure in their careers? 175

AMANDA: They do or they do without it! Not everybody has a craze for adventure.

TOM: Man is by instinct a lover, a hunter, a fighter, and none of those instincts are given much play at the warehouse! 180

AMANDA: Man is by instinct! Don't quote instinct to me! Instinct is something that people have got away from! It belongs to animals! Christian adults don't want it!

TOM: What do Christian adults want, then, Mother? 185

AMANDA: Superior things! Things of the mind and the spirit! Only animals have to satisfy instincts! Surely your aims are somewhat higher than theirs! Than monkeys—pigs—

TOM: I reckon they're not. 190

AMANDA: You're joking. However, that isn't what I wanted to discuss.

TOM: *(rising)* I haven't much time.

AMANDA: *(pushing his shoulders)* Sit down.

TOM: You want me to punch in red at the warehouse, 195 Mother?

AMANDA: You have five minutes. I want to talk about Laura.

(Legend: "Plans and Provisions.")

TOM: All right! What about Laura?

AMANDA: We have to be making some plans and pro- 200
visions for her. She's older than you, two years, and
nothing has happened. She just drifts along doing
nothing. It frightens me terribly how she just drifts
along.

TOM: I guess she's the type that people call home girls. 205

AMANDA: There's no such type, and if there is, it's a pity!
That is unless the home is hers, with a husband!

TOM: What?

AMANDA: Oh, I can see the handwriting on the wall as
plain as I see the nose in front of my face! It's terrify- 210
ing! More and more you remind me of your father!
He was out all hours without explanation—Then *left!*
Good-bye! And me with the bag to hold. I saw a letter you got from the Merchant Marine. I know what
you're dreaming of. I'm not standing here blindfolded. 215
Very well, then. Then *do* it! But not till there's somebody to take your place.

TOM: What do you mean?

AMANDA: I mean that as soon as Laura has got somebody to take care of her, married, a home of her own, 220
independent—why, then you'll be free to go wherever
you please, on land, on sea, whichever way the wind
blows you! But until that time you've got to look out
for your sister. I don't say me because I'm old and
don't matter! I say for your sister because she's young 225
and dependent. I put her in business college—a dismal failure! Frightened her so it made her sick to her
stomach. I took her over to the Young People's League
at the church. Another fiasco. She spoke to nobody,
nobody spoke to her. Now all she does is fool with 230
those pieces of glass and play those worn-out records.
What kind of a life is that for a girl to lead!

TOM: What can I do about it?

AMANDA: Overcome selfishness! Self, self, self is all
that you ever think of! (TOM *springs up and crosses* 235
to get his coat. It is ugly and bulky. He pulls on a cap
with earmuffs.) Where is your muffler? Put your wool
muffler on! (*He snatches it angrily from the closet and*
tosses it around his neck and pulls both ends tight.)
Tom! I haven't said what I had in mind to ask you. 240

TOM: I'm too late to—

AMANDA: (*catching his arms—very importunately. Then*
shyly.) Down at the warehouse, aren't there some—
nice young men?

TOM: No! 245

AMANDA: There *must* be—*some.*

TOM: Mother—

Gesture.

AMANDA: Find out one that's clean-living—doesn't
drink and—ask him out for sister!

TOM: What? 250

AMANDA: For *sister!* To *meet!* Get *acquainted!*

TOM: (*stamping to the door*) Oh, my *go-osh!*

AMANDA: Will you? (*He opens the door. Imploringly.*)
Will you? (*He starts down.*) Will you? *Will* you, dear?

TOM: (*calling back*) YES! 255

AMANDA *closes the door hesitantly and with a trou-*
bled but faintly hopeful expression.
(*Screen image:* Glamour *magazine cover.*)
Spot AMANDA *at phone.*

AMANDA: Ella Cartwright? This is Amanda Wingfield!
How are you, honey? How is that kidney condition?
(*Count five.*) Horrors! (*Count five.*) You're a Christian
martyr, yes, honey, that's what you are, a Christian
martyr! Well, I just happened to notice in my little 260
red book that your subscription to the *Companion* has
just run out! I knew that you wouldn't want to miss
out on the wonderful serial starting in this new issue.
It's by Bessie Mae Hopper, the first thing she's written since *Honeymoon for Three.* Wasn't that a strange 265
and interesting story? Well, this one is even lovelier, I
believe. It has a sophisticated society background. It's
all about the horsey set on Long Island!

(*Fade out.*)

Amanda, now hopeful, places a sales call.

SCENE 5

*(Legend on screen: "Annunciation.") Fade with music.
It is early dusk of a spring evening. Supper has
just been finished in the Wingfield apartment.
AMANDA and LAURA in light-colored dresses are
removing dishes from the table, in the upstage area,
which is shadowy, their movements formalized almost as a dance or ritual, their moving forms as pale
and silent as moths.*

*TOM, in white shirt and trousers, rises from the
table and crosses toward the fire-escape.*

AMANDA: *(as he passes her)* Son, will you do me a favor?

TOM: What?

AMANDA: Comb your hair! You look so pretty when your
hair is combed! (*TOM slouches on the sofa with the
evening paper. Enormous caption "Franco Triumphs."*)
There is only one respect in which I would like you to
emulate your father.

TOM: What respect is that?

AMANDA: The care he always took of his appearance.
He never allowed himself to look untidy. (*He throws*

5

10

down the paper and crosses to fire-escape.) Where are
you going?

TOM: I'm going out to smoke.

AMANDA: You smoke too much. A pack a day at fifteen
cents a pack. How much would that amount to in a
month? Thirty times fifteen is how much, Tom? Figure it out and you will be astounded at what you could
save. Enough to give you a night-school course in
accounting at Washington U! Just think what a wonderful thing that would be for you, son!

15

20

TOM is unmoved by the thought.

TOM: I'd rather smoke. (*He steps out on landing, letting
the screen door slam.*)

AMANDA: *(sharply)* I know! That's the tragedy of it. . . .
(*Alone, she turns to look at her husband's picture.*)

(*Dance music: "All the World Is Waiting for the
Sunrise!"*)

TOM: *(to the audience)* Across the alley from us was the
Paradise Dance Hall. On evenings in spring the windows and doors were open and the music came outdoors. Sometimes the lights were turned out except
for a large glass sphere that hung from the ceiling.
It would turn slowly about and filter the dusk with
delicate rainbow colors. Then the orchestra played
a waltz or a tango, something that had a slow and
sensuous rhythm. Couples would come outside, to the
relative privacy of the alley. You could see them kissing behind ash-pits and telephone poles. This was the
compensation for lives that passed like mine, without
any change or adventure. Adventure and change were
imminent in this year. They were waiting around the
corner for all these kids. Suspended in the mist over
the Berchtesgaden, caught in the folds of Chamberlain's umbrella—In Spain there was Guernica! But
here there was only hot swing music and liquor, dance
halls, bars, and movies, and sex that hung in the
gloom like a chandelier and flooded the world with
brief, deceptive rainbows. . . . All the world was waiting for bombardments!

25

30

35

40

45

AMANDA turns from the picture and comes outside.

AMANDA: (*sighing*) A fire-escape landing's a poor excuse for a porch. (*She spreads a newspaper on a step and sits down, gracefully and demurely as if she were settling into a swing on a Mississippi veranda.*) What are you looking at?

TOM: The moon.

AMANDA: Is there a moon this evening?

TOM: It's rising over Garfinkel's Delicatessen.

AMANDA: So it is! A little silver slipper of a moon. Have you made a wish on it yet?

TOM: Um-hum.

AMANDA: What did you wish for?

TOM: That's a secret.

AMANDA: A secret, huh? Well, I won't tell mine either. I will be just as mysterious as you.

TOM: I bet I can guess what yours is.

AMANDA: Is my head so transparent?

TOM: You're not a sphinx.

AMANDA: No, I don't have secrets. I'll tell you what I wished for on the moon. Success and happiness for my precious children! I wish for that whenever there's a moon, and when there isn't a moon, I wish for it, too.

TOM: I thought perhaps you wished for a gentleman caller.

AMANDA: Why do you say that?

TOM: Don't you remember asking me to fetch one?

AMANDA: I remember suggesting that it would be nice for your sister if you brought home some nice young man from the warehouse. I think I've made that suggestion more than once.

TOM: Yes, you have made it repeatedly.

AMANDA: Well?

TOM: We are going to have one.

AMANDA: *What?*

TOM: A gentleman caller!

(*The Annunciation is celebrated with music.*)
AMANDA *rises.*
(*Image on screen: Caller with bouquet.*)

AMANDA: You mean you have asked some nice young man to come over?

TOM: Yep. I've asked him to dinner.

AMANDA: You really did?

TOM: I did!

AMANDA: You did, and did he—*accept?*

TOM: He did!

AMANDA: Well, well—well, well! That's—lovely!

TOM: I thought that you would be pleased.

AMANDA: It's definite, then?

TOM: Very definite.

AMANDA: Soon?

TOM: Very soon.

AMANDA: For heaven's sake, stop putting on and tell me some things, will you?

TOM: What things do you want me to tell you?

AMANDA: Naturally I would like to know when he's *coming!*

TOM: He's coming tomorrow.

AMANDA: *Tomorrow?*

TOM: Yep. Tomorrow.

AMANDA: But, Tom!

TOM: Yes, Mother?

AMANDA: Tomorrow gives me no time!

TOM: Time for what?

AMANDA: Preparations! Why didn't you phone me at once, as soon as you asked him, the minute that he accepted? Then, don't you see, I could have been getting
110 ready!

TOM: You don't have to make any fuss.

AMANDA: Oh, Tom, Tom, Tom, of course I have to make a fuss! I want things nice, not sloppy! Not thrown together. I'll certainly have to do some fast thinking,
115 won't I?

TOM: I don't see why you have to think at all.

AMANDA: You just don't know. We can't have a gentleman caller in a pig-sty! All my wedding silver has to be polished, the monogrammed table linen ought to
120 be laundered! The windows have to be washed and fresh curtains put up. And how about clothes? We have to *wear* something, don't we?

TOM: Mother, this boy is no one to make a fuss over!

AMANDA: Do you realize he's the first young man we've
125 introduced to your sister? It's terrible, dreadful, disgraceful that poor little sister has never received a single gentleman caller! Tom, come inside! *(She opens the screen door.)*

TOM: What for?

130 **AMANDA:** I want to ask you some things.

TOM: If you're going to make such a fuss, I'll call it off, I'll tell him not to come.

AMANDA: You certainly won't do anything of the kind. Nothing offends people worse than broken engage-
135 ments. It simply means I'll have to work like a Turk! We won't be brilliant, but we'll pass inspection. Come on inside. *(TOM follows, groaning.)* Sit down.

TOM: Any particular place you would like me to sit?

AMANDA: Thank heavens I've got that new sofa! I'm
140 also making payments on a floor lamp I'll have sent out! And put the chintz covers on, they'll brighten things up! Of course I'd hoped to have these walls repapered. . . . What is the young man's name?

TOM: His name is O'Connor.

AMANDA: That, of course, means fish—tomorrow is Fri- 145
day! I'll have that salmon loaf—with Durkee's dressing! What does he do? He works at the warehouse?

TOM: Of course! How else would I—

AMANDA: Tom, he—doesn't drink?

TOM: Why do you ask me that? 150

AMANDA: Your father *did!*

TOM: Don't get started on that!

AMANDA: He *does* drink, then?

TOM: Not that I know of!

AMANDA: Make sure, be certain! The last thing I want 155
for my daughter's a boy who drinks!

TOM: Aren't you being a little bit premature? Mr. O'Connor has not yet appeared on the scene!

AMANDA: But will tomorrow. To meet your sister, and what do I know about his character? Nothing! Old 160
maids are better off than wives of drunkards!

TOM: Oh, my God!

AMANDA: Be still!

TOM: *(leaning forward to whisper)* Lots of fellows meet girls whom they don't marry! 165

AMANDA: Oh, talk sensibly, Tom—and don't be sarcastic! *(She has gotten a hairbrush.)*

TOM: What are you doing?

AMANDA: I'm brushing that cow-lick down! What is this young man's position at the warehouse? 170

TOM: *(submitting grimly to the brush and the interrogation)* This young man's position is that of a shipping clerk, Mother.

AMANDA: Sounds to me like a fairly responsible job, the sort of job *you* would be in if you just had more *get-* 175
up. What is his salary? Have you any idea?

TOM: I would judge it to be approximately eighty-five dollars a month.

Tom tells Amanda about the man he's invited over to meet Laura.

AMANDA: Well—not princely, but—

180 **TOM:**   Twenty more than I make.

AMANDA: Yes, how well I know! But for a family man, eighty-five dollars a month is not much more than you can just get by on. . . .

TOM: Yes, but Mr. O'Connor is not a family man.

185 **AMANDA:**   He might be, mightn't he? Some time in the future?

TOM: I see. Plans and provisions.

AMANDA: You are the only young man that I know of who ignores the fact that the future becomes the present, the present the past, and the past turns into everlasting regret if you don't plan for it!

190

TOM: I will think that over and see what I can make of it.

AMANDA: Don't be supercilious with your mother! Tell me some more about this—what do you call him?

195 **TOM:**   James D. O'Connor. The D. is for Delaney.

AMANDA: Irish on *both* sides! *Gracious!* And doesn't drink?

TOM: Shall I call him up and ask him right this minute?

AMANDA: The only way to find out about those things is to make discreet inquiries at the proper moment.

200

When I was a girl in Blue Mountain and it was suspected that a young man drank, the girl whose attentions he had been receiving, if any girl *was*, would sometimes speak to the minister of his church, or rather her father would if her father was living, and sort of feel him out on the young man's character. That is the way such things are discreetly handled to keep a young woman from making a tragic mistake!   205

TOM: Then how did you happen to make a tragic mistake?   210

AMANDA: That innocent look of your father's had everyone fooled! He *smiled*—the world was *enchanted!* No girl can do worse than put herself at the mercy of a handsome appearance! I hope that Mr. O'Connor is not too good-looking.   215

TOM: No, he's not too good-looking. He's covered with freckles and hasn't too much of a nose.

AMANDA: He's not right-down homely, though?

TOM: Not right-down homely. Just medium homely, I'd say.   220

AMANDA: Character's what to look for in a man.

TOM: That's what I've always said, Mother.

AMANDA: You've never said anything of the kind and I suspect you would never give it a thought.

TOM: Don't be suspicious of me.   225

AMANDA: At least I hope he's the type that's up and coming.

TOM: I think he really goes in for self-improvement.

AMANDA: What reason have you to think so?

TOM: He goes to night school.   230

AMANDA: *(beaming)* Splendid! What does he do, I mean study?

TOM: Radio engineering and public speaking!

AMANDA: Then he has visions of being advanced in the world! Any young man who studies public speaking is aiming to have an executive job some day! And radio engineering? A thing for the future! Both of   235

240 these facts are very illuminating. Those are the sort of things that a mother should know concerning any young man who comes to call on her daughter. Seriously or—not.

TOM: One little warning. He doesn't know about Laura. I didn't let on that we had dark ulterior motives. I just said, why don't you come have dinner with us? He said 245 okay and that was the whole conversation.

AMANDA: I bet it was! You're eloquent as an oyster. However, he'll know about Laura when he gets here. When he sees how lovely and sweet and pretty she is, he'll thank his lucky stars he was asked to dinner.

250 **TOM:** Mother, you mustn't expect too much of Laura.

AMANDA: What do you mean?

TOM: Laura seems all those things to you and me because she's ours and we love her. We don't even notice she's crippled any more.

255 **AMANDA:** Don't say crippled! You know that I never allow that word to be used!

TOM: But face facts, Mother. She is and—that's not all—

AMANDA: What do you mean "not all"?

TOM: Laura is very different from other girls.

260 **AMANDA:** I think the difference is all to her advantage.

TOM: Not quite all—in the eyes of others—strangers— she's terribly shy and lives in a world of her own and those things make her seem a little peculiar to people outside the house.

265 **AMANDA:** Don't say peculiar.

TOM: Face the facts. She is.

(The dance-hall music changes to a tango that has a minor and somewhat ominous tone.)

AMANDA: In what way is she peculiar—may I ask?

TOM: *(gently)* She lives in a world of her own—a world of—little glass ornaments, Mother. . . . *(Gets up.* 270 AMANDA *remains holding brush, looking at him, troubled.)* She plays old phonograph records and—

Tom and Amanda discuss what kind of man he is bringing home for Laura.

that's about all—*(He glances at himself in the mirror and crosses to door.)*

AMANDA: *(sharply)* Where are you going?

TOM: I'm going to the movies. *(Out screen door.)* 275

AMANDA: Not to the movies, every night to the movies! *(Follows quickly to screen door.)* I don't believe you always go to the movies! *(He is gone.* AMANDA *looks worriedly after him for a moment. Then vitality and optimism return and she turns from the door. Crossing* 280 *to portieres.)* Laura! Laura! *(*LAURA *answers from kitchenette.)*

LAURA: Yes, Mother.

AMANDA: Let those dishes go and come in front! *(*LAURA *appears with dish towel. Gaily.)* Laura, come 285 here and make a wish on the moon!

LAURA: *(entering)* Moon—moon?

AMANDA: A little silver slipper of a moon. Look over your left shoulder, Laura, and make a wish! *(*LAURA *looks faintly puzzled as if called out of sleep.* AMANDA 290 *seizes her shoulders and turns her at angle by the door.)* Now! Now, darling, *wish!*

LAURA: What shall I wish for, Mother?

AMANDA: *(her voice trembling and her eyes suddenly filling with tears)* Happiness! Good Fortune!

The violin rises and the stage dims out.

SCENE 6

(Image: High-school hero.)

TOM: And so the following evening I brought Jim home to dinner. I had known Jim slightly in high school. In high school Jim was a hero. He had tremendous Irish good nature and vitality with the scrubbed and polished look of white chinaware. He seemed to move in a continual spotlight. He was a star in basketball, captain of the debating club, president of the senior class and the glee club and he sang the male lead in the annual light operas. He was always running or bounding, never just walking. He seemed always at the point of defeating the law of gravity. He was shooting with such velocity through his adolescence that you would logically expect him to arrive at nothing short of the White House by the time he was thirty. But Jim apparently ran into more interference after his graduation from Soldan. His speed had definitely slowed. Six years after he left high school he was holding a job that wasn't much better than mine.

(Image: Clerk.)

He was the only one at the warehouse with whom I was on friendly terms. I was valuable to him as someone who could remember his former glory, who had seen him win basketball games and the silver cup in debating. He knew of my secret practice of retiring to a cabinet of the washroom to work on poems when business was slack in the warehouse. He called me Shakespeare. And while the other boys in the warehouse regarded me with suspicious hostility, Jim took a humorous attitude toward me. Gradually his attitude affected the others, their hostility wore off, and they also began to smile at me as people smile at an oddly fashioned dog who trots across their paths at some distance.

I knew that Jim and Laura had known each other at Soldan, and I had heard Laura speak admiringly of his voice. I didn't know if Jim remembered her or not. In high school Laura had been as unobtrusive as Jim had been astonishing. If he did remember Laura, it was not as my sister, for when I asked him to dinner, he grinned and said, "You know, Shakespeare, I never thought of you as having folks!"

He was about to discover that I did. . . .

(Light upstage.)
(Legend on screen: "The Accent of a Coming Foot.")
Friday evening. It is about five o'clock of a late spring evening which comes "scattering poems in the sky."

A delicate lemony light is in the Wingfield apartment.

AMANDA *has worked like a Turk in preparation for the gentleman caller. The results are astonishing. The new floor lamp with its rose-silk shade is in place, a colored paper lantern conceals the broken light fixture in the ceiling, new billowing white curtains are at the windows, chintz covers are on chairs and sofa, a pair of new sofa pillows make their initial appearance.*

Open boxes and tissue paper are scattered on the floor.

LAURA *stands in the middle with lifted arms while* AMANDA *crouches before her, adjusting the hem of a new dress, devout and ritualistic. The dress is colored and designed by memory. The arrangement of* LAURA's *hair is changed; it is softer and more becoming. A fragile, unearthly prettiness has come out in* LAURA: *she is like a piece of translucent glass touched by light, given a momentary radiance, not actual, not lasting.*

AMANDA: *(impatiently)* Why are you trembling?

LAURA: Mother, you've made me so nervous!

AMANDA: How have I made you nervous?

LAURA: By all this fuss! You make it seem so important!

AMANDA: I don't understand you, Laura. You couldn't be satisfied with just sitting home, and yet whenever I try to arrange something for you, you seem to resist it. *(She gets up.)* Now take a look at yourself. No, wait! Wait just a moment—I have an idea!

LAURA: What is it now?

AMANDA *produces two powder puffs which she wraps in handkerchiefs and stuffs in LAURA's bosom.*

LAURA: Mother, what are you doing?

AMANDA: They call them "Gay Deceivers"!

LAURA: I won't wear them!

55 **AMANDA:** You will!

LAURA: Why should I?

AMANDA: Because, to be painfully honest, your chest is flat.

LAURA: You make it seem like we were setting a trap.

60 **AMANDA:** All pretty girls are a trap, a pretty trap, and men expect them to be. *(Legend: "A Pretty Trap.")* Now look at yourself, young lady. This is the prettiest you will ever be! I've got to fix myself now! You're going to be surprised by your mother's appearance! *(She crosses*
65 *through portieres, humming gaily.)*

LAURA *moves slowly to the long mirror and stares solemnly at herself.*
    A wind blows the white curtains inward in a slow, graceful motion and with a faint, sorrowful sighing.

The women get ready for dinner.

AMANDA: *(off stage)* It isn't dark enough yet. *(She turns slowly before the mirror with a troubled look.)*

(Legend on screen: "This Is My Sister: Celebrate Her with Strings!" Music.)

AMANDA: *(laughing, off)* I'm going to show you something. I'm going to make a spectacular appearance!

LAURA: What is it, Mother?   70

AMANDA: Possess your soul in patience—you will see! Something I've resurrected from that old trunk! Styles haven't changed so terribly much after all. . . . *(She parts the portieres.)* Now just look at your mother! *(She wears a girlish frock of yellowed voile with a blue*   75 *silk sash. She carries a bunch of jonquils—the legend of her youth is nearly revived. Feverishly.)* This is the dress in which I led the cotillion. Won the cakewalk twice at Sunset Hill, wore one spring to the Governor's ball in Jackson! See how I sashayed around   80 the ballroom, Laura? *(She raises her skirt and does a mincing step around the room.)* I wore it on Sundays for my gentlemen callers! I had it on the day I met your father—I had malaria fever all that spring. The change of climate from East Tennessee to the Delta—   85 weakened resistance—I had a little temperature all the time—not enough to be serious—just enough to make me restless and giddy! Invitations poured in— parties all over the Delta! "Stay in bed," said Mother, "you have fever!"—but I just wouldn't.—I took qui-   90 nine but kept on going, going!—Evenings, dances!— Afternoons, long, long rides! Picnics—lovely!—So lovely, that country in May.—All lacy with dogwood, literally flooded with jonquils!—That was the spring I had the craze for jonquils. Jonquils became an abso-   95 lute obsession. Mother said, "Honey, there's no more room for jonquils." And still I kept bringing in more jonquils. Whenever, wherever I saw them, I'd say, "Stop! Stop! I see jonquils!" I made the young men help me gather the jonquils! It was a joke, Amanda   100 and her jonquils. Finally there were no more vases to hold them, every available space was filled with jonquils. No vases to hold them? All right, I'll hold them myself! And then I—*(She stops in front of the picture.) (Music.)* met your father! Malaria fever and   105 jonquils and then—this—boy. . . . *(She switches on the* *rose-colored lamp.*) I hope they get here before it starts to rain. (*She crosses upstage and places the jonquils in bowl on table.*) I gave your brother a little extra change so he and Mr. O'Connor could take the service car home.

110

LAURA: (*with an altered look*) What did you say his name was?

AMANDA: O'Connor.

115 **LAURA:** What is his first name?

AMANDA: I don't remember. Oh, yes, I do. It was—Jim!

> LAURA *sways slightly and catches hold of a chair.*
> (*Legend on screen: "Not Jim!"*)

LAURA: (*faintly*) Not—Jim!

AMANDA: Yes, that was it, it was Jim! I've never known a Jim that wasn't nice!

> (*Music: Ominous.*)

120 **LAURA:** Are you sure his name is Jim O'Connor?

AMANDA: Yes. Why?

LAURA: Is he the one that Tom used to know in high school?

AMANDA: He didn't say so. I think he just got to know him at the warehouse.

125

LAURA: There was a Jim O'Connor we both knew in high school—(*Then, with effort.*) If that is the one that Tom is bringing to dinner—you'll have to excuse me, I won't come to the table.

130 **AMANDA:** What sort of nonsense is this?

LAURA: You asked me once if I'd ever liked a boy. Don't you remember I showed you this boy's picture?

AMANDA: You mean the boy you showed me in the year-book?

135 **LAURA:** Yes, that boy.

AMANDA: Laura, Laura, were you in love with that boy?

LAURA: I don't know, Mother. All I know is I couldn't sit at the table if it was him!

AMANDA: It won't be him! It isn't the least bit likely. But whether it is or not, you will come to the table. You will not be excused.

140

LAURA: I'll have to be, Mother.

AMANDA: I don't intend to humor your silliness, Laura. I've had too much from you and your brother, both! So just sit down and compose yourself till they come. Tom has forgotten his key so you'll have to let them in, when they arrive.

145

LAURA: (*panicky*) Oh, Mother—*you* answer the door!

AMANDA: (*lightly*) I'll be in the kitchen—busy!

LAURA: Oh, Mother, please answer the door, don't make me do it!

150

AMANDA: (*crossing into kitchenette*) I've got to fix the dressing for the salmon. Fuss, fuss—silliness!—over a gentleman caller!

> (*Door swings shut.* LAURA *is left alone.*
>   (*Legend: "Terror!"*)
>   *She utters a low moan and turns off the lamp—sits stiffly on the edge of the sofa, knotting her fingers together.*
>   (*Legend on screen: "The Opening of a Door!"*)
> TOM *and* JIM *appear on the fire-escape steps and climb to landing. Hearing their approach,* LAURA *rises with a panicky gesture. She retreats to the portieres.*
>   *The doorbell.* LAURA *catches her breath and touches her throat. Low drums.*

AMANDA: (*calling*) Laura, sweetheart! The door!

155

> LAURA *stares at it without moving.*

JIM: I think we just beat the rain.

TOM: Uh-huh. (*He rings again, nervously.* JIM *whistles and fishes for a cigarette.*)

AMANDA: (*very, very gaily*) Laura, that is your brother and Mr. O'Connor! Will you let them in, darling?

160

> LAURA *crosses toward kitchenette door.*

LAURA: (*breathlessly*) Mother—you go to the door!

AMANDA *steps out of kitchenette and stares furiously at* LAURA. *She points imperiously at the door.*

LAURA: Please, please!

AMANDA: *(in a fierce whisper)* What is the matter with you, you silly thing?

165 **LAURA:** *(desperately)* Please, you answer it, *please!*

AMANDA: I told you I wasn't going to humor you, Laura. Why have you chosen this moment to lose your mind?

LAURA: Please, please, please, you go!

AMANDA: You'll have to go to the door because I can't!

170 **LAURA:** *(despairingly)* I can't either!

AMANDA: *Why?*

LAURA: I'm *sick!*

AMANDA: I'm sick, too—of your nonsense! Why can't you and your brother be normal people? Fantastic
175 whims and behavior! *(TOM gives a long ring.)* Preposterous goings on! Can you give me one reason—*(Calls out lyrically.)* COMING! JUST ONE SECOND!—why you should be afraid to open a door? Now you answer it, Laura!

180 **LAURA:** Oh, oh, oh . . . *(She returns through the portieres. Darts to the Victrola and winds it frantically and turns it on.)*

AMANDA: Laura Wingfield, you march right to that door!

185 **LAURA:** Yes—yes, Mother!

A faraway, scratchy rendition of "Dardanella" softens the air and gives her strength to move through it. She slips to the door and draws it cautiously open.
TOM *enters with the caller,* JIM O'CONNOR.

TOM: Laura, this is Jim. Jim, this is my sister, Laura.

JIM: *(stepping inside)* I didn't know that Shakespeare had a sister!

LAURA: *(retreating stiff and trembling from the door)*
190 How—how do you do?

JIM: *(heartily, extending his hand)* Okay!

LAURA *touches it hesitantly with hers.*

JIM: Your hand's *cold,* Laura!

LAURA: Yes, well—I've been playing the Victrola . . .

JIM: Must have been playing classical music on it! You ought to play a little hot swing music to warm you up! 195

LAURA: Excuse me—I haven't finished playing the Victrola . . .

She turns awkwardly and hurries into the front room. She pauses a second by the Victrola. Then catches her breath and darts through the portieres like a frightened deer.

JIM: *(grinning)* What was the matter?

TOM: Oh—with Laura? Laura is—terribly shy.

JIM: Shy, huh? It's unusual to meet a shy girl nowadays. 200
I don't believe you ever mentioned you had a sister.

TOM: Well, now you know. I have one. Here is the *Post Dispatch.* You want a piece of it?

JIM: Uh-huh.

TOM: What piece? The comics? 205

JIM: Sports! *(Glances at it.)* Ole Dizzy Dean is on his bad behavior.

TOM: *(disinterest)* Yeah? *(Lights cigarette and crosses back to fire-escape door.)*

JIM: Where are *you* going? 210

TOM: I'm going out on the terrace.

JIM: *(goes after him)* You know, Shakespeare—I'm going to sell you a bill of goods!

TOM: What goods?

JIM: A course I'm taking. 215

TOM: Huh?

JIM: In public speaking! You and me, we're not the warehouse type.

TOM: Thanks—that's good news. But what has public speaking got to do with it? 220

JIM: It fits you for—executive positions!

TOM: Awww.

JIM: I tell you it's done a helluva lot for me.

(*Image: Executive at desk.*)

TOM: In what respect?

225   JIM: In every! Ask yourself what is the difference between you an' me and men in the office down front?
Brains?—No!—Ability?—No! Then what? Just one
little thing—

TOM: What is that one little thing?

230   JIM: Primarily it amounts to—social poise! Being able to
square up to people and hold your own on any social
level!

AMANDA: (*off stage*) Tom?

TOM: Yes, Mother?

235   AMANDA: Is that you and Mr. O'Connor?

TOM: Yes, Mother.

AMANDA: Well, you just make yourselves comfortable
in there.

TOM: Yes, Mother.

240   AMANDA: Ask Mr. O'Connor if he would like to wash his
hands.

JIM: Aw—no—no—thank you—I took care of that at the
warehouse. Tom—

TOM: Yes?

245   JIM: Mr. Mendoza was speaking to me about you.

TOM: Favorably?

JIM: What do you think?

TOM: Well—

JIM: You're going to be out of a job if you don't wake up.

250   TOM: I am waking up—

JIM: You show no signs.

Amanda greets Jim O'Connor (Michael Moriarty).

TOM: The signs are interior.

(*Image on screen: The sailing vessel with Jolly Roger
again.*)

TOM: I'm planning to change. (*He leans over the rail
speaking with quiet exhilaration. The incandescent
marquees and signs of the first-run movie houses light*   255
his face from across the alley. He looks like a voyager.)
I'm right at the point of committing myself to a future
that doesn't include the warehouse and Mr. Mendoza
or even a night-school course in public speaking.

JIM: What are you gassing about?   260

TOM: I'm tired of the movies.

JIM: Movies!

TOM: Yes, movies! Look at them—(*A wave toward the
marvels of Grand Avenue.*) All of those glamorous
people—having adventures—hogging it all, gobbling   265
the whole thing up! You know what happens? People
go to the *movies* instead of *moving!* Hollywood characters are supposed to have all the adventures for
everybody in America, while everybody in America
sits in a dark room and watches them have them! Yes,   270
until there's a war. That's when adventure becomes
available to the masses! *Everyone's* dish, not only

Gable's! Then the people in the dark room come out of the dark room to have some adventures themselves—Goody, goody—It's our turn now, to go to the South 275 Sea Island—to make a safari—to be exotic, far-off—But I'm not patient. I don't want to wait till then. I'm tired of the *movies* and I am *about* to *move!*

JIM: (*incredulously*) Move?

280 **TOM:** Yes.

JIM: When?

TOM: Soon!

JIM: Where? Where?

(*Theme three: Music seems to answer the question, while* TOM *thinks it over. He searches among his pockets.*)

TOM: I'm starting to boil inside. I know I seem dreamy, 285 but inside—well, I'm boiling! Whenever I pick up a shoe, I shudder a little thinking how short life is and what I am doing!—Whatever that means. I know it doesn't mean shoes—except as something to wear on a traveler's feet! (*Finds paper.*) Look—

290 **JIM:** What?

TOM: I'm a member.

JIM: (*reading*) The Union of Merchant Seamen.

TOM: I paid my dues this month, instead of the light bill.

JIM: You will regret it when they turn the lights off.

295 **TOM:** I won't be here.

JIM: How about your mother?

TOM: I'm like my father. The bastard son of a bastard! See how he grins? And he's been absent going on sixteen years!

300 **JIM:** You're just talking, you drip. How does your mother feel about it?

TOM: Shhh—Here comes Mother! Mother is not acquainted with my plans!

AMANDA: (*enters portieres*) Where are you all?

TOM: On the terrace, Mother. 305

They start inside. She advances to them. TOM *is distinctly shocked at her appearance. Even* JIM *blinks a little. He is making his first contact with girlish Southern vivacity and in spite of the night-school course in public speaking is somewhat thrown off the beam by the unexpected outlay of social charm.*

Certain responses are attempted by JIM *but are swept aside by* AMANDA's *gay laughter and chatter.* TOM *is embarrassed but after the first shock* JIM *reacts very warmly. He grins and chuckles, is altogether won over.*

(*Image: Amanda as a girl.*)

AMANDA: (*coyly smiling, shaking her girlish ringlets*) Well, well, well, so this is Mr. O'Connor. Introductions entirely unnecessary. I've heard so much about you from my boy. I finally said to him, Tom—good gracious!—why don't you bring this paragon to sup- 310 per? I'd like to meet this nice young man at the warehouse!—Instead of just hearing him sing your praises so much! I don't know why my son is so stand-offish—that's not Southern behavior! Let's sit down and—I think we could stand a little more air in here! 315 Tom, leave the door open. I felt a nice fresh breeze a moment ago. Where has it gone? Mmm, so warm already! And not quite summer, even. We're going to burn up when summer really gets started. However, we're having—we're having a very light supper. I think 320 light things are better fo' this time of year. The same as light clothes are. Light clothes an' light food are what warm weather calls fo'. You know our blood gets so thick during th' winter—it takes a while fo' us to *adjust* ou'selves!—when the season changes. . . . 325 It's come so quick this year. I wasn't prepared. All of a sudden—heavens! Already summer!—I ran to the trunk an' pulled out this light dress—Terribly old! Historical almost! But feels so good—so good an' co-ol, y'know. . . . 330

TOM: Mother—

AMANDA: Yes, honey?

TOM: How about—supper?

AMANDA: Honey, you go ask Sister if supper is ready! You know that Sister is in full charge of supper! Tell 335 her you hungry boys are waiting for it. (*To* JIM.) Have you met Laura?

JIM: She—

AMANDA: Let you in? Oh, good, you've met already! It's
340 rare for a girl as sweet an' pretty as Laura to be domestic! But Laura is, thank heavens, not only pretty
but also very domestic. I'm not at all. I never was a bit.
I never could make a thing but angel-food cake. Well,
in the South we had so many servants. Gone, gone,
345 gone. All vestiges of gracious living! Gone completely!
I wasn't prepared for what the future brought me.
All of my gentlemen callers were sons of planters and
so of course I assumed that I would be married to
one and raise my family on a large piece of land with
350 plenty of servants. But man proposes—and woman
accepts the proposal!—To vary that old, old saying a
little bit—I married no planter! I married a man who
worked for the telephone company!—that gallantly
smiling gentleman over there! (*Points to the picture.*) A
355 telephone man who—fell in love with long-distance!—
Now he travels and I don't even know where!—But
what am I going on for about my—tribulations! Tell
me yours—I hope you don't have any! Tom?

TOM: (*returning*) Yes, Mother?

360 AMANDA: Is supper nearly ready?

TOM: It looks to me like supper is on the table.

AMANDA: Let me look—(*She rises prettily and looks
through portieres.*) Oh, lovely—But where is Sister?

TOM: Laura is not feeling well and she says that she
365 thinks she'd better not come to the table.

AMANDA: What?—Nonsense!—Laura? Oh, Laura!

LAURA: (*off stage, faintly*) Yes, Mother.

AMANDA: You really must come to the table. We won't
be seated until you come to the table! Come in, Mr.
370 O'Connor. You sit over there, and I'll—Laura? Laura
Wingfield! You're keeping us waiting, honey! We can't
say grace until you come to the table!

The back door is pushed weakly open and LAURA
comes in. She is obviously quite faint, her lips trem-
bling, her eyes wide and staring. She moves un-
steadily toward the table.
(*Legend: "Terror!"*)
Outside a summer storm is coming abruptly. The
white curtains billow inward at the windows and
there is a sorrowful murmur and deep blue dusk.
LAURA *suddenly stumbles—She catches at a chair*
with a faint moan.

TOM: Laura!

AMANDA: Laura! (*There is a clap of thunder.*) (*Legend:*
"*Ah!*") (*Despairingly.*) Why, Laura, you *are* sick, dar- 375
ling! Tom, help your sister into the living room, dear!
Sit in the living room, Laura—rest on the sofa. Well!
(*To the gentleman caller.*) Standing over the hot stove
made her ill!—I told her that it was just too warm this
evening, but—(TOM *comes back in.* LAURA *is on the* 380
sofa.) Is Laura all right now?

TOM: Yes.

AMANDA: What *is* that? Rain? A nice cool rain has
come up! (*She gives the gentleman caller a frightened
look.*) I think we may—have grace—now. . . (TOM
looks at her stupidly.) Tom, honey—you say grace! 385

TOM: Oh . . . "For these and all thy mercies—" (*They bow
their heads,* AMANDA *stealing a nervous glance at*
JIM. *In the living room* LAURA, *stretched on the sofa,
clenches her hand to her lips, to hold back a shuddering* 390
sob.) God's Holy Name be praised—

(*The scene dims out.*)

SCENE 7

A Souvenir

*Half an hour later. Dinner is just being finished in
the upstage area, which is concealed by the drawn
portieres.*

As the curtain rises LAURA *is still huddled upon
the sofa, her feet drawn under her, her head resting
on a pale blue pillow, her eyes wide and mysteriously
watchful. The new floor lamp with its shade of rose-
colored silk gives a soft, becoming light to her face,
bringing out the fragile, unearthly prettiness which
usually escapes attention. There is a steady murmur*

*of rain, but it is slackening and stops soon after the
scene begins; the air outside becomes pale and luminous as the moon breaks out.*

    *A moment after the curtain rises, the lights in both
rooms flicker and go out.*

JIM: Hey, there, Mr. Light Bulb!

AMANDA *laughs nervously.*
    (Legend: "Suspension of a Public Service.")

AMANDA: Where was Moses when the lights went out?
Ha-ha. Do you know the answer to that one, Mr.
O'Connor?

5 **JIM:**   No, Ma'am, what's the answer?

AMANDA: In the dark! (JIM *laughs appreciatively.*)
Everybody sit still. I'll light the candles. Isn't it lucky
we have them on the table? Where's a match? Which
of you gentlemen can provide a match?

10 **JIM:**   Here.

AMANDA: Thank you, sir.

JIM: Not at all, Ma'am!

AMANDA: I guess the fuse has burnt out. Mr. O'Connor,
can you tell a burnt-out fuse? I know I can't and Tom
15 is a total loss when it comes to mechanics. *(Sound:
Getting up: Voices recede a little to kitchenette.)* Oh, be
careful you don't bump into something. We don't want
our gentleman caller to break his neck. Now wouldn't
that be a fine howdy-do?

20 **JIM:**   Ha-ha! Where is the fuse-box?

AMANDA: Right here next to the stove. Can you see
anything?

JIM: Just a minute.

AMANDA: Isn't electricity a mysterious thing? Wasn't it
25 Benjamin Franklin who tied a key to a kite? We live in
such a mysterious universe, don't we? Some people say
that science clears up all the mysteries for us. In my
opinion it only creates more! Have you found it yet?

JIM: No, Ma'am. All these fuses look okay to me.

30 **AMANDA:**   Tom!

TOM: Yes, Mother?

AMANDA: That light bill I gave you several days ago. The
one I told you we got the notices about?

TOM: Oh.—Yeah.

    (Legend: "Ha!")

AMANDA: You didn't neglect to pay it by any chance?   35

TOM: Why, I—

AMANDA: Didn't! I might have known it!

JIM: Shakespeare probably wrote a poem on that light
bill, Mrs. Wingfield.

AMANDA: I might have known better than to trust him   40
with it! There's such a high price for negligence in this
world!

JIM: Maybe the poem will win a ten-dollar prize.

AMANDA: We'll just have to spend the remainder of the
evening in the nineteenth century, before Mr. Edison   45
made the Mazda lamp!

JIM: Candlelight is my favorite kind of light.

AMANDA: That shows you're romantic! But that's no
excuse for Tom. Well, we got through dinner. Very

Amanda entertains Jim after the lights have gone out.

50 considerate of them to let us get through dinner before they plunged us into everlasting darkness, wasn't it, Mr. O'Connor?

JIM: Ha-ha!

AMANDA: Tom, as a penalty for your carelessness you
55 can help me with the dishes.

JIM: Let me give you a hand.

AMANDA: Indeed you will not!

JIM: I ought to be good for something.

AMANDA: Good for something? *(Her tone is rhapsodic.)*
60 *You?* Why, Mr. O'Connor, nobody, *nobody's* given me this much entertainment in years—as you have!

JIM: Aw, now, Mrs. Wingfield!

AMANDA: I'm not exaggerating, not one bit! But Sister is all by her lonesome. You go keep her company in the
65 parlor! I'll give you this lovely old candelabrum that used to be on the altar at the church of the Heavenly Rest. It was melted a little out of shape when the church burnt down. Lightning struck it one spring. Gypsy Jones was holding a revival at the time and he
70 intimated that the church was destroyed because the Episcopalians gave card parties.

JIM: Ha-ha.

AMANDA: And how about coaxing Sister to drink a little wine? I think it would be good for her! Can you carry
75 both at once?

JIM: Sure. I'm Superman!

AMANDA: Now, Thomas, get into this apron!

The door of kitchenette swings closed on AMANDA's *gay laughter; the flickering light approaches the portieres.*

LAURA sits up nervously as he enters. Her speech at first is low and breathless from the almost intolerable strain of being alone with a stranger.

(Legend: "I Don't Suppose You Remember Me at All!")

In her first speeches in this scene, before JIM's warmth overcomes her paralyzing shyness, LAURA's

voice is thin and breathless as though she has run up a steep flight of stairs.

JIM's attitude is gently humorous. In playing this scene it should be stressed that while the incident is apparently unimportant, it is to LAURA the climax of her secret life.

JIM: Hello there, Laura.

LAURA: *(faintly)* Hello. *(She clears her throat.)*

JIM: How are you feeling now? Better?   80

LAURA: Yes. Yes, thank you.

JIM: This is for you. A little dandelion wine. *(He extends it toward her with extravagant gallantry.)*

LAURA: Thank you.

JIM: Drink it—but don't get drunk! *(He laughs heart-   85 ily.* LAURA *takes the glass uncertainly; laughs shyly.)* Where shall I set the candles?

LAURA: Oh—oh, anywhere . . .

JIM: How about here on the floor? Any objections?

LAURA: No.   90

JIM: I'll spread a newspaper under to catch the drippings. I like to sit on the floor. Mind if I do?

LAURA: Oh, no.

JIM: Give me a pillow?

LAURA: What?   95

JIM: A pillow!

LAURA: *Oh . . . (Hands him one quickly.)*

JIM: How about you? Don't you like to sit on the floor?

LAURA: Oh—yes.

JIM: Why don't you, then?   100

LAURA: I—will.

JIM: Take a pillow! *(LAURA does. Sits on the other side of the candelabrum.* JIM *crosses his legs and smiles engagingly at her.)* I can't hardly see you sitting way over there.   105

Jim brings the candelabrum closer to Laura.

LAURA: I can—see you.

JIM: I know, but that's not fair, I'm in the limelight. *(LAURA moves her pillow closer.)* Good! Now I can see you! Comfortable?

110   **LAURA:**   Yes.

JIM: So am I. Comfortable as a cow. Will you have some gum?

LAURA: No, thank you.

JIM: I think that I will indulge, with your permission. *(Musingly unwraps it and holds it up.)* Think of the fortune made by the guy that invented the first piece of chewing gum. Amazing, huh? The Wrigley Building is one of the sights of Chicago.—I saw it summer before last when I went up to the Century of Progress. Did you take in the Century of Progress?

LAURA: No, I didn't.

JIM: Well, it was quite a wonderful exposition. What impressed me most was the Hall of Science. Gives you an idea of what the future will be in America, even more wonderful than the present time is! *(Pause. Smiling at her.)* Your brother tells me you're shy. Is that right, Laura?

LAURA: I—don't know.

JIM: I judge you to be an old-fashioned type of girl. Well, I think that's a pretty good type to be. Hope you don't   130
think I'm being too personal—do you?

LAURA: *(hastily, out of embarrassment)* I believe I *will* take a piece of gum, if you—don't mind. *(Clearing her throat.)* Mr. O'Connor, have you—kept up with your singing?   135

JIM: Singing? Me?

LAURA: Yes. I remember what a beautiful voice you had.

JIM: When did you hear me sing?

(Voice offstage in the pause.)

VOICE: *(offstage)*
O blow, ye winds, heigh-ho, A-roving I will go!
I'm off to my love   140
With a boxing glove—
Ten thousand miles away!

JIM: You say you've heard me sing?

LAURA: Oh, yes! Yes, very often . . . I—don't suppose you remember me—at all?   145

JIM: *(smiling doubtfully)* You know I have an idea I've seen you before. I had that idea soon as you opened the door. It seemed almost like I was about to re-member your name. But the name I started to call you—wasn't a name! And so I stopped myself before   150
I said it.

LAURA: Wasn't it—Blue Roses?

JIM: *(springing up, grinning)* Blue Roses! My gosh, yes—Blue Roses! That's what I had on my tongue when you opened the door! Isn't it funny what tricks your mem-   155
ory plays? I didn't connect you with the high school somehow or other. But that's where it was; it was high school. I didn't even know you were Shakespeare's sister! Gosh, I'm sorry.

LAURA: I didn't expect you to. You—barely knew me!   160

JIM: But we did have a speaking acquaintance, huh?

LAURA: Yes, we—spoke to each other.

JIM: When did you recognize me?

LAURA: Oh, right away!

165   JIM: Soon as I came in the door?

LAURA: When I heard your name I thought it was probably you. I knew that Tom used to know you a little in high school. So when you came in the door—Well, then I was—sure.

170   JIM: Why didn't you *say* something, then?

LAURA: (*breathlessly*) I didn't know what to say, I was—too surprised!

JIM: For goodness' sakes! You know, this sure is funny!

LAURA: Yes! Yes, isn't it, though . . .

175   JIM: Didn't we have a class in something together?

LAURA: Yes, we did.

JIM: What class was that?

LAURA: It was—singing—Chorus!

JIM: Aw!

180   LAURA: I sat across the aisle from you in the Aud.

JIM: Aw.

LAURA: Mondays, Wednesdays, and Fridays.

JIM: Now I remember—you always came in late.

LAURA: Yes, it was so hard for me, getting upstairs. I
185   had that brace on my leg—it clumped so loud!

JIM: I never heard any clumping.

LAURA: (*wincing at the recollection*) To me it sounded like—thunder!

JIM: Well, well, well. I never even noticed.

190   LAURA: And everybody was seated before I came in. I had to walk in front of all those people. My seat was in the back row. I had to go clumping all the way up the aisle with everyone watching!

JIM: You shouldn't have been self-conscious.

LAURA: I know, but I was. It was always such a relief   195
when the singing started.

JIM: Aw, yes, I've placed you now! I used to call you Blue Roses. How was it that I got started calling you that?

LAURA: I was out of school a little while with pleurosis. When I came back you asked me what was the matter.   200
I said I had pleurosis—you thought I said Blue Roses. That's what you always called me after that!

JIM: I hope you didn't mind.

LAURA: Oh, no—I liked it. You see, I wasn't acquainted with many—people. . . .   205

JIM: As I remember you sort of stuck by yourself.

LAURA: I—I—never have had much luck at—making friends.

JIM: I don't see why you wouldn't.

LAURA: Well, I—started out badly.   210

JIM: You mean being—

LAURA: Yes, it sort of—stood between me—

JIM: You shouldn't have let it!

LAURA: I know, but it did, and—

JIM: You were shy with people!   215

LAURA: I tried not to be but never could—

JIM: Overcome it?

LAURA: No, I—I never could!

JIM: I guess being shy is something you have to work out of kind of gradually.   220

LAURA: (*sorrowfully*) Yes—I guess it—

JIM: Takes time!

LAURA: Yes—

JIM: People are not so dreadful when you know them. That's what you have to remember! And everybody   225
has problems, not just you, but practically everybody has got some problems. You think of yourself as having the only problems, as being the only one who is

230 disappointed. But just look around you and you will see lots of people as disappointed as you are. For instance, I hoped when I was going to high school that I would be further along at this time, six years later, than I am now—You remember that wonderful write-up I had in *The Torch*?

235 **LAURA:** Yes! *(She rises and crosses to table.)*

JIM: It said I was bound to succeed in anything I went into! *(LAURA returns with the annual.)* Holy Jeez! *The Torch! (He accepts it reverently. They smile across it with mutual wonder. LAURA crouches beside him*
240 *and they begin to turn through it. LAURA's shyness is dissolving in his warmth.)*

LAURA: Here you are in *Pirates of Penzance*!

JIM: *(wistfully)* I sang the baritone lead in that operetta.

LAURA: *(rapidly)* So—*beautifully*!

245 **JIM:** *(protesting)* Aw—

LAURA: Yes, yes—beautifully—beautifully!

JIM: You heard me?

LAURA: All three times!

JIM: No!

250 **LAURA:** Yes!

JIM: All three performances?

LAURA: *(looking down)* Yes.

JIM: Why?

LAURA: I—wanted to ask you to—autograph my
255 program.

JIM: Why didn't you ask me to?

LAURA: You were always surrounded by your own friends so much that I never had a chance to.

JIM: You should have just—

260 **LAURA:** Well, I—thought you might think I was—

JIM: Thought I might think you was—what?

LAURA: Oh—

JIM: *(with reflective relish)* I was beleaguered by females in those days.

265 **LAURA:** You were terribly popular!

JIM: Yeah—

LAURA: You had such a—friendly way—

JIM: I was spoiled in high school.

LAURA: Everybody—liked you!

270 **JIM:** Including you?

LAURA: I—yes, I—I did, too—*(She gently closes the book in her lap.)*

JIM: Well, well, well!—Give me that program, Laura. *(She hands it to him. He signs it with a flourish.)* There
275 you are—better late than never!

LAURA: Oh, I—what a—surprise!

JIM: My signature isn't worth very much right now. But some day—maybe—it will increase in value! Being disappointed is one thing and being discouraged is
280 something else. I am disappointed but I'm not discouraged. I'm twenty-three years old. How old are you?

LAURA: I'll be twenty-four in June.

JIM: That's not old age.

285 **LAURA:** No, but—

JIM: You finished high school?

LAURA: *(with difficulty)* I didn't go back.

JIM: You mean you dropped out?

LAURA: I made bad grades in my final examinations.
290 *(She rises and replaces the book and the program. Her voice strained.)* How is—Emily Meisenbach getting along?

JIM: Oh, that kraut-head!

LAURA: Why do you call her that?

295 **JIM:** That's what she was.

Laura and Jim look at the old high school annual.

LAURA: You're not still—going with her?

JIM: I never see her.

LAURA: It said in the Personal Section that you were—engaged!

300 **JIM:** I know, but I wasn't impressed by that—propaganda!

LAURA: It wasn't—the truth?

JIM: Only in Emily's optimistic opinion!

LAURA: Oh—

(*Legend: "What Have You Done since High School?"*)
JIM *lights a cigarette and leans indolently back on his elbows smiling at* LAURA *with a warmth and charm which light her inwardly with altar candles. She remains by the table and turns in her hands a piece of glass to cover her tumult.*

305 **JIM:** (*after several reflective puffs on his cigarette*) What have you done since high school? (*She seems not to hear him.*) Huh? (LAURA *looks up.*) I said what have you done since high school, Laura?

LAURA: Nothing much.

310 **JIM:** You must have been doing something these six long years.

LAURA: Yes.

JIM: Well, then, such as what?

LAURA: I took a business course at business college—

JIM: How did that work out? 315

LAURA: Well, not very—well—I had to drop out, it gave me—indigestion—

JIM *laughs gently.*

JIM: What are you doing now?

LAURA: I don't do anything—much. Oh, please don't think I sit around doing nothing! My glass collection 320 takes up a good deal of time. Glass is something you have to take good care of.

JIM: What did you say—about glass?

LAURA: Collection I said—I have one—(*She clears her throat and turns away again, acutely shy.*) 325

JIM: (*abruptly*) You know what I judge to be the trouble with you? Inferiority complex! Know what that is? That's what they call it when someone low-rates himself! I understand it because I had it, too. Although my case was not so aggravated as yours seems to be. 330 I had it until I took up public speaking, developed my voice, and learned that I had an aptitude for science. Before that time I never thought of myself as being outstanding in any way whatsoever! Now I've never made a regular study of it, but I have a friend who 335 says I can analyze people better than doctors that make a profession of it. I don't claim that to be necessarily true, but I can sure guess a person's psychology, Laura! (*Takes out his gum.*) Excuse me, Laura. I always take it out when the flavor is gone. I'll use this 340 scrap of paper to wrap it in. I know how it is to get it stuck on a shoe. Yep—that's what I judge to be your principal trouble. A lack of confidence in yourself as a person. You don't have the proper amount of faith in yourself. I'm basing that fact on a number of your 345 remarks and also on certain observations I've made. For instance that clumping you thought was so awful in high school. You say that you even dreaded to walk into class. You see what you did? You dropped out of school, you gave up an education because of a clump, 350 which as far as I know was practically nonexistent! A

little physical defect is what you have. Hardly noticeable even! Magnified thousands of times by imagination! You know what my strong advice to you is?
355   Think of yourself as *superior* in some way!

LAURA: In what way would I think?

JIM: Why, man alive, Laura! Just look about you a little.
What do you see? A world full of common people! All
of 'em born and all of 'em going to die! Which of them
360   has one-tenth of your good points! Or mine! Or anyone else's, as far as that goes—Gosh! Everybody excels
in some one thing. Some in many! *(Unconsciously
glances at himself in the mirror.)* All you've got to do is
discover in *what!* Take me, for instance. *(He adjusts
365   his tie at the mirror.)* My interest happened to lie in
electrodynamics. I'm taking a course in radio engineering at night school, Laura, on top of a fairly responsible job at the warehouse. I'm taking that course
and studying public speaking.

370 LAURA: Ohhhh.

JIM: Because I believe in the future of television! *(Turning back to her.)* I wish to be ready to go up right
along with it. Therefore I'm planning to get in on the
ground floor. In fact, I've already made the right con-
375   nections and all that remains is for the industry
itself to get under way! Full steam—*(His eyes are starry.)*
Knowledge—Zzzzzp! Money—Zzzzzp!—Power!
That's the cycle democracy is built on! *(His attitude is
convincingly dynamic. LAURA stares at him, even her
380   shyness eclipsed in her absolute wonder. He suddenly
grins.)* I guess you think I think a lot of myself!

LAURA: No—o-o-o, I—

JIM: Now how about you? Isn't there something you take
more interest in than anything else?

385 LAURA: Well, I do—as I said—have my—glass
collection—

A peal of girlish laughter from the kitchen.

JIM: I'm not right sure I know what you're talking about.
What kind of glass is it?

LAURA: Little articles of it, they're ornaments mostly!
390   Most of them are little animals made out of glass, the
tiniest little animals in the world. Mother calls them
a glass menagerie! Here's an example of one, if you'd
like to see it! This one is one of the oldest. It's nearly
thirteen. *(He stretches out his hand.)* *(Music: "The
Glass Menagerie.")* Oh, be careful—if you breathe, it 395
breaks!

JIM: I'd better not take it. I'm pretty clumsy with things.

LAURA: Go on, I trust you with him! *(Places it in his
palm.)* There now—you're holding him gently! Hold
him over the light, he loves the light! You see how the 400
light shines through him?

JIM: It sure does shine!

LAURA: I shouldn't be partial, but he is my favorite one.

JIM: What kind of a thing is this one supposed to be?

LAURA: Haven't you noticed the single horn on his 405
forehead?

JIM: A unicorn, huh?

LAURA: Mmm-hmmm!

JIM: Unicorns, aren't they extinct in the modern world?

LAURA: I know! 410

Laura and Jim study the glass unicorn.

JIM: Poor little fellow, he must feel sort of lonesome.

LAURA: (*smiling*) Well, if he does he doesn't complain about it. He stays on a shelf with some horses that don't have horns and all of them seem to get along 415 nicely together.

JIM: How do you know?

LAURA: (*lightly*) I haven't heard any arguments among them!

JIM: (*grinning*) No arguments, huh? Well, that's a pretty 420 good sign! Where shall I set him?

LAURA: Put him on the table. They all like a change of scenery once in a while!

JIM: (*stretching*) Well, well, well, well—Look how big my shadow is when I stretch!

425 **LAURA:** Oh, oh, yes—it stretches across the ceiling!

JIM: (*crossing to door*) I think it's stopped raining. (*Opens fire-escape door.*) Where does the music come from?

LAURA: From the Paradise Dance Hall across the alley.

JIM: How about cutting the rug a little, Miss Wingfield?

430 **LAURA:** Oh, I—

JIM: Or is your program filled up? Let me have a look at it. (*Grasps imaginary card.*) Why, every dance is taken! I'll have to scratch some out. (*Waltz music: "La Golondrina."*) Ahhh, a waltz! (*He executes some* 435 *sweeping turns by himself then holds his arms toward* LAURA.)

LAURA: (*breathlessly*) I—can't dance!

JIM: There you go, that inferiority stuff!

LAURA: I've never danced in my life!

440 **JIM:** Come on, try!

LAURA: Oh, but I'd step on you!

JIM: I'm not made out of glass.

LAURA: How—how—how do we start?

JIM: Just leave it to me. You hold your arms out a little.

LAURA: Like this? 445

JIM: A little bit higher. Right. Now don't tighten up, that's the main thing about it—relax.

LAURA: (*laughing breathlessly*) It's hard not to.

JIM: Okay.

LAURA: I'm afraid you can't budge me. 450

JIM: What do you bet I can't? (*He swings her into motion.*)

LAURA: Goodness, yes, you can!

JIM: Let yourself go, now, Laura, just let yourself go.

LAURA: I'm— 455

JIM: Come on!

LAURA: Trying.

JIM: Not so stiff—Easy does it!

LAURA: I know but I'm—

JIM: Loosen th' backbone! There now, that's a lot better. 460

LAURA: Am I?

JIM: Lots, lots better! (*He moves her about the room in a clumsy waltz.*)

LAURA: Oh, my!

JIM: Ha-ha! 465

LAURA: Goodness, yes you can!

JIM: Ha-ha-ha! (*They suddenly bump into the table.* JIM *stops.*) What did we hit on?

LAURA: Table.

JIM: Did something fall off it? I think— 470

LAURA: Yes.

JIM: I hope that it wasn't the little glass horse with the horn!

LAURA: Yes.

JIM: Aw, aw, aw. Is it broken? 475

Jim waltzes Laura around the room.

LAURA: Now it is just like all the other horses.

JIM: It's lost its—

LAURA: Horn! It doesn't matter. Maybe it's a blessing in disguise.

480 **JIM:** You'll never forgive me. I bet that was your favorite piece of glass.

LAURA: I don't have favorites much. It's no tragedy, Freckles. Glass breaks so easily. No matter how care-
485 ful you are. The traffic jars the shelves and things fall off them.

JIM: Still I'm awfully sorry that I was the cause.

LAURA: (*smiling*) I'll just imagine he had an opera-tion. The horn was removed to make him feel less—freakish! (*They both laugh.*) Now he will feel more at
490 home with the other horses, the ones that don't have horns . . .

JIM: Ha-ha, that's very funny! (*Suddenly serious.*) I'm glad to see that you have a sense of humor. You know—you're—well—very different! Surprisingly
495 different from anyone else I know! (*His voice becomes soft and hesitant with a genuine feeling.*) Do you mind me telling you that? (LAURA *is abashed beyond*

speech.) You make me feel sort of—I don't know how to put it! I'm usually pretty good at expressing things, but—This is something that I don't know how to say! 500 (LAURA *touches her throat and clears it—turns the broken unicorn in her hands.*) (*Even softer.*) Has any-one ever told you that you were pretty?

Pause: Music.

(LAURA *looks up slowly, with wonder, and shakes her head.*) Well, you are! In a very different way from any- 505 one else. And all the nicer because of the difference, too. (*His voice becomes low and husky.* LAURA *turns away, nearly faint with the novelty of her emotions.*) I wish that you were my sister. I'd teach you to have some confidence in yourself. The different people are 510 not like other people, but being different is nothing to be ashamed of. Because other people are not such wonderful people. They're one hundred times one thousand. You're one times one! They walk all over the earth. You just stay here. They're common as—weeds, 515 but—you—well, you're—*Blue Roses!*

(*Image on screen: Blue Roses.*)
   (*Music changes.*)

LAURA: But blue is wrong for—roses . . .

JIM: It's right for you—You're—pretty!

LAURA: In what respect am I pretty?

JIM: In all respects—believe me! Your eyes—your hair— 520 are pretty! Your hands are pretty! (*He catches hold of her hand.*) You think I'm making this up because I'm invited to dinner and have to be nice. Oh, I could do that! I could put on an act for you, Laura, and say lots of things without being very sincere. But this time I 525 am. I'm talking to you sincerely. I happened to notice you had this inferiority complex that keeps you from feeling comfortable with people. Somebody needs to build your confidence up and make you proud instead of shy and turning away and—blushing—Somebody 530 ought to—ought to—*kiss* you, Laura! (*His hand slips slowly up her arm to her shoulder.*) (*Music swells tu-multuously.*) (*He suddenly turns her about and kisses her on the lips. When he releases her* LAURA *sinks on the sofa with a bright, dazed look.* JIM *backs away and* 535 *fishes in his pocket for a cigarette.*) (*Legend on screen:*

"Souvenir.") Stumble-john! (*He lights the cigarette, avoiding her look. There is a peal of girlish laughter from* AMANDA *in the kitchenette.* LAURA *slowly raises and opens her hand. It still contains the little broken glass animal. She looks at it with a tender, bewildered expression.*) Stumble-john! I shouldn't have done that—That was way off the beam. You don't smoke, do you? (*She looks up, smiling, not hearing the question. He sits beside her a little gingerly. She looks at him speechlessly—waiting. He coughs decorously and moves a little farther aside as he considers the situation and senses her feelings, dimly, with perturbation. Gently.*) Would you—care for a—mint? (*She doesn't seem to hear him but her look grows brighter even.*) Peppermint?—Life Saver? My pocket's a regular drug store—wherever I go . . . (*He pops a mint in his mouth. Then gulps and decides to make a clean breast of it. He speaks slowly and gingerly.*) Laura, you know, if I had a sister like you, I'd do the same thing as Tom. I'd bring out fellows—introduce her to them. The right type of boys of a type to—appreciate her. Only—well—he made a mistake about me. Maybe I've got no call to be saying this. That may not have been the idea in having me over. But what if it was? There's nothing wrong about that. The only trouble is that in my case—I'm not in a situation to—do the right thing. I can't take down your number and say I'll phone. I can't call up next week and—ask for a date. I thought I had better explain the situation in case you misunderstood it and—hurt your feelings. . . . (*Pause. Slowly, very slowly,* LAURA's *look changes, her eyes returning slowly from his to the ornament in her palm.*)

AMANDA *utters another gay laugh in the kitchenette.*

LAURA: (*faintly*) You—won't—call again?

JIM: No, Laura, I can't. (*He rises from the sofa.*) As I was just explaining, I've—got strings on me, Laura, I've—been going steady! I go out all the time with a girl named Betty. She's a home-girl like you, and Catholic, and Irish, and in a great many ways we—get along fine. I met her last summer on a moonlight boat trip up the river to Alton, on the *Majestic.* Well—right away from the start it was—love! (*Legend: Love!*) (LAURA *sways slightly forward and grips the arm of the sofa. He fails to notice, now enrapt in his own com-* fortable being.*) Being in love has made a new man of me! (*Leaning stiffly forward, clutching the arm of the sofa,* LAURA *struggles visibly with her storm. But* JIM *is oblivious, she is a long way off.*) The power of love is really pretty tremendous! Love is something that— changes the whole world, Laura! (*The storm abates a little and* LAURA *leans back. He notices her again.*) It happened that Betty's aunt took sick, she got a wire and had to go to Centralia. So Tom—when he asked me to dinner—I naturally just accepted the invitation, not knowing that you—that he—that I—(*He stops awkwardly.*) Huh—I'm a stumble-john! (*He flops back on the sofa. The holy candles in the altar of* LAURA's *face have been snuffed out! There is a look of almost infinite desolation.* JIM *glances at her uneasily.*) I wish that you would—say something. (*She bites her lip which was trembling and then bravely smiles. She opens her hand again on the broken glass ornament. Then she gently takes his hand and raises it level with her own. She carefully places the unicorn in the palm of his hand, then pushes his fingers closed upon it.*) What are you—doing that for? You want me to have him?— Laura? (*She nods.*) What for?

LAURA: A—souvenir . . .

She rises unsteadily and crouches beside the Victrola to wind it up.

Jim and Laura kiss.

(Legend on screen: "Things Have a Way of Turning Out So Badly.")

(Or image: "Gentleman caller waving good-bye!"—Gaily.")

At this moment AMANDA *rushes brightly back in the front room. She bears a pitcher of fruit punch in an old-fashioned cut-glass pitcher and a plate of macaroons. The plate has a gold border and poppies painted on it.*

AMANDA: Well, well, well! Isn't the air delightful after
605   the shower? I've made you children a little liquid refreshment. *(Turns gaily to the gentleman caller.)* Jim,
do you know that song about lemonade?
        "Lemonade, lemonade
        Made in the shade and stirred with a spade—
610   Good enough for any old maid!"

JIM: *(uneasily)* Ha-ha! No—I never heard it.

AMANDA: Why, Laura! You look so serious!

JIM: We were having a serious conversation.

AMANDA: Good! Now you're better acquainted!

615   **JIM:**   *(uncertainly)* Ha-ha! Yes.

AMANDA: You modern young people are much more
serious-minded than my generation. I was so gay as
a girl!

JIM: You haven't changed, Mrs. Wingfield.

620   **AMANDA:**   Tonight I'm rejuvenated! The gaiety of the
occasion, Mr. O'Connor! *(She tosses her head with a
peal of laughter. Spills lemonade.)* Oooo! I'm baptizing
myself!

JIM: Here—let me—

625   **AMANDA:**   *(setting the pitcher down)* There now. I discovered we had some maraschino cherries. I dumped
them in, juice and all!

JIM: You shouldn't have gone to that trouble, Mrs.
Wingfield.

630   **AMANDA:**   Trouble, trouble? Why it was loads of fun!
Didn't you hear me cutting up in the kitchen? I bet
your ears were burning! I told Tom how outdone with
him I was for keeping you to himself so long a time!

He should have brought you over much, much sooner!
Well, now that you've found your way, I want you to   635
be a very frequent caller! Not just occasional but all
the time. Oh, we're going to have a lot of gay times
together! I see them coming! Mmm, just breathe that
air! So fresh, and the moon's so pretty! I'll skip back
out—I know where my place is when young folks are   640
having a—serious conversation!

JIM: Oh, don't go out, Mrs. Wingfield. The fact of the
matter is I've got to be going.

AMANDA: Going, now? You're joking! Why, it's only the
shank of the evening, Mr. O'Connor!   645

JIM: Well, you know how it is.

AMANDA: You mean you're a young workingman and
have to keep workingmen's hours. We'll let you off
early tonight. But only on the condition that next time
you stay later. What's the best night for you? Isn't Sat-   650
urday night the best night for you workingmen?

JIM: I have a couple of time-clocks to punch, Mrs. Wingfield. One at morning, another one at night!

AMANDA: My, but you *are* ambitious! You work at night,
too?   655

JIM: No, Ma'am, not work but—Betty! *(He crosses deliberately to pick up his hat. The band at the Paradise
Dance Hall goes into a tender waltz.)*

AMANDA: Betty? Betty? Who's—Betty! *(There is an
ominous cracking sound in the sky.)*   660

JIM: Oh, just a girl. The girl I go steady with! *(He smiles
charmingly. The sky falls.)*

(Legend: "The Sky Falls.")

AMANDA: *(a long-drawn exhalation)* Ohhhh . . . Is it a
serious romance, Mr. O'Connor?

JIM: We're going to be married the second Sunday in   665
June.

AMANDA: Ohhhh—how nice! Tom didn't mention that
you were engaged to be married.

JIM: The cat's not out of the bag at the warehouse yet.
You know how they are. They call you Romeo and   670

stuff like that. (*He stops at the oval mirror to put on his hat. He carefully shapes the brim and the crown to give a discreetly dashing effect.*) It's been a wonderful evening, Mrs. Wingfield. I guess this is what they mean by Southern hospitality.

AMANDA: It really wasn't anything at all.

JIM: I hope it don't seem like I'm rushing off. But I promised Betty I'd pick her up at the Wabash depot, an' by the time I get my jalopy down there her train'll be in. Some women are pretty upset if you keep 'em waiting.

AMANDA: Yes, I know—The tyranny of women! (*Extends her hand.*) Good-bye, Mr. O'Connor. I wish you luck— and happiness—and success! All three of them, and so does Laura—Don't you, Laura?

LAURA: Yes!

JIM: (*taking her hand*) Good-bye, Laura. I'm certainly going to treasure that souvenir. And don't you forget the good advice I gave you. (*Raises his voice to a cheery shout.*) So long, Shakespeare! Thanks again, ladies— Good night!

He grins and ducks jauntily out.

Amanda berates Tom for his error.

Still bravely grimacing, AMANDA *closes the door on the gentleman caller. Then she turns back to the room with a puzzled expression. She and* LAURA *don't dare to face each other.* LAURA *crouches beside the Victrola to wind it.*

AMANDA: (*faintly*) Things have a way of turning out so badly. I don't believe that I would play the Victrola. Well, well—well—Our gentleman caller was engaged to be married! Tom!

TOM: (*from back*) Yes, Mother?

AMANDA: Come in here a minute. I want to tell you something awfully funny.

TOM: (*enters with a macaroon and a glass of the lemonade*) Has the gentleman caller gotten away already?

AMANDA: The gentleman caller has made an early departure. What a wonderful joke you played on us!

TOM: How do you mean?

AMANDA: You didn't mention that he was engaged to be married.

TOM: Jim? Engaged?

AMANDA: That's what he just informed us.

TOM: I'll be jiggered! I didn't know about that.

AMANDA: That seems very peculiar.

TOM: What's peculiar about it?

AMANDA: Didn't you call him your best friend down at the warehouse?

TOM: He is, but how did I know?

AMANDA: It seems extremely peculiar that you wouldn't know your best friend is going to be married!

TOM: The warehouse is where I work, not where I know things about people!

AMANDA: You don't know things anywhere! You live in a dream; you manufacture illusions! (*He crosses to door.*) Where are you going?

TOM: I'm going to the movies.

AMANDA: That's right, now that you've had us make
such fools of ourselves. The effort, the preparations,
all the expense! The new floor lamp, the rug, the
725   clothes for Laura! All for what? To entertain some
other girl's fiancé! Go to the movies, go! Don't think
about us, a mother deserted, an unmarried sister
who's crippled and has no job! Don't let anything interfere with your selfish pleasure! Just go, go, go—to
730   the movies!

TOM: All right, I will! The more you shout about my
selfishness to me the quicker I'll go, and I won't go to
the movies!

AMANDA: Go, then! Then go to the moon—you selfish
735   dreamer!

    TOM *smashes his glass on the floor. He plunges out on*
the fire-escape, slamming the door. LAURA *screams—*
cut by door.
    Dance-hall music up. TOM *goes to the rail and*
grips it desperately, lifting his face in the chill white
moonlight penetrating the narrow abyss of the alley.
    (*Legend on screen:* "And So Good-Bye . . .")
    TOM's *closing speech is timed with the interior*
pantomime. The interior scene is played as though
viewed through sound-proof glass. AMANDA *appears*
to be making a comforting speech to LAURA *who is*
huddled upon the sofa. Now that we cannot hear the
mother's speech, her silliness is gone and she has dig-
nity and tragic beauty. LAURA's *dark hair hides her*
face until at the end of the speech she lifts it to smile at
her mother. AMANDA's *gestures are slow and graceful,*
almost dancelike, as she comforts the daughter. At the
end of her speech she glances a moment at the father's
picture—then withdraws through the portieres. At
close of TOM's *speech,* LAURA *blows out the candles,*
ending the play.

TOM: I didn't go to the moon, I went much further—for
time is the longest distance between two places—Not
long after that I was fired for writing a poem on the
lid of a shoe-box. I left Saint Louis. I descended the
740   steps of this fire-escape for a last time and followed,
from then on, in my father's footsteps, attempting

Laura and Amanda sit huddled alone in the dark.

to find in motion what was lost in space—I traveled
around a great deal. The cities swept about me like
dead leaves, leaves that were brightly colored but torn
away from the branches. I would have stopped, but I   745
was pursued by something. It always came upon me
unawares, taking me altogether by surprise. Perhaps
it was a familiar bit of music. Perhaps it was only a
piece of transparent glass—Perhaps I am walking
along a street at night, in some strange city, before I   750
have found companions. I pass the lighted window
of a shop where perfume is sold. The window is filled
with pieces of colored glass, tiny transparent bottles
in delicate colors, like bits of a shattered rainbow.
Then all at once my sister touches my shoulder. I turn   755
around and look into her eyes. . . . Oh, Laura, Laura,
I tried to leave you behind me, but I am more faithful than I intended to be! I reach for a cigarette, I
cross the street, I run into the movies or a bar, I buy a
drink, I speak to the nearest stranger—anything that   760
can blow your candles out! (LAURA *bends over the*
candles)—for nowadays the world is lit by lightning!
Blow out your candles, Laura—and so good-bye . . .

She blows the candles out.
    (*The Scene Dissolves.*)

Writing from Reading

Summarize

1 In this day, a small family, living on hopes, dreams, and illusions, seems destined to take a fall. Does the theme seem specific to the time and place, or does it have larger implications?

2 What are some of the central "problems" in this problem play? What would you describe as its themes?

Analyze Craft

3 In Tom Wingfield's first speech, he—and through him the playwright—declares, " I am the opposite of a stage magician. He gives you illusion that has the appearance of truth. I give you truth in the pleasant disguise of illusion." How does this relate to the notion of realistic representation onstage?

4 In the stage direction, Williams writes of Tom, "His nature is not remorse-less, but to escape from a trap he has to act without pity." In what ways does he do so, and how fully does he succeed?

5 The glass collection—with its fragility, its safe haven on the shelf—is of course Laura's, and it represents her beauty as well as her predicament. In real life, Williams's sister was institutionalized for schizophrenia. How might this experience have contributed to Williams's development of Laura's character, and how does Laura's fantasy life here feel real?

Analyze Voice

6 "And so good-bye. . ." is the play's final line as well as the "Legend on screen." Describe the nature of this farewell and the degree of finality. How does Amanda continue, and are things truly over for Laura and Tom? In what ways is this play an act of continuity as well as one of closure?

7 How would you describe the language of the play? What tone does the language create? Harsh? Lyrical? A mix of tones?

Synthesize Summary and Analysis

8 In what ways does the style of the play—the stage directions, the language, and the representation of inner and outer states of the characters—seem to have affinities with Arthur Miller's *Death of a Salesman*? In what ways does it differ?

Interpret the Play

9 Is there something particular to the fate of this family that ties its destiny to eternal illusion, or does the playwright imply that all families are alike in this regard?

Lorraine Hansberry (1930–1965)

Born to parents who were relatively well-off and who had a strong sense of social justice, Lorraine Hansberry grew up on the south side of Chicago. She first tasted racism when her father deliberately purchased a house in an all-white neighborhood, attracting such hatred that an angry crowd formed and the eight-year-old Lorraine was nearly struck by a brick thrown through a window. To remain in the neighborhood, her father had to take a court case all the way to the U.S. Supreme Court, which he did—and won. Hansberry attended the University of Wisconsin, and after initial aspirations to be a painter, she turned to writing and theater. Dedicated to social justice, she worked as a contributor and as an editor on Paul Robeson's *Freedom* magazine, and she met her husband, the song-writer Robert Nemiroff, while picketing against discrimination. But it was her playwriting that allowed her civil rights initiatives to reach the broadest audience. Her first completed play, *A Raisin in the Sun* (1959), became the first Broadway play written by an African American, and with it she won the New York Drama Critics Circle award at age twenty-nine. Perhaps because of her early death from cancer, *The Sign in Sidney Brustein's Window* (1965) was her only other completed play, but Nemiroff edited and published her unfinished plays, as well as a memoir (that he later turned into a play) about Hansberry's life, *To Be Young, Gifted, and Black* (1969). Today, Hansberry is best remembered for *A Raisin in the Sun*, which portrays a black family whose everyday struggles are so universal they transcend the boundaries of race.

"There's a long way to go because we've come a long way with the wrong feelings. And to live down these feelings or integrate them into our hearts and change them is not the work of a day or of a generation. But of many generations." Conversation with Arthur Miller

AS YOU READ Notice the power structure within the family and how it shifts over the course of the play. What types of women do Mama, Beneatha, and Ruth represent? How does Walter complicate our expectations of the stereotypical man of the house?

A Raisin in the Sun (1959)

CHARACTERS

(In order of appearance)

RUTH YOUNGER, *Walter's wife, about 30*

TRAVIS YOUNGER, *her son and Walter's*

WALTER LEE YOUNGER (brother), *Ruth's husband, mid-thirties*

BENEATHA YOUNGER, *Walter's sister, about twenty*

LENA YOUNGER (MAMA), *mother of Walter and Beneatha*

JOSEPH ASAGAI, *Nigerian, Beneatha's suitor*

GEORGE MURCHISON, *Beneatha's date, wealthy*

KARL LINDNER, *white, chairman of the Clybourne Park New Neighbors Orientation Committee*

BOBO, *one of Walter's business partners*

MOVING MEN

The action of the play is set in Chicago's Southside, sometime between World War II and the present.

ACT 1

SCENE 1: *Friday morning.*

SCENE 2: *The following morning.*

ACT 2

SCENE 1: *Later, the same day.*

SCENE 2: *Friday night, a few weeks later.*

SCENE 3: *Moving day, one week later.*

ACT 3

An hour later.

ACT 1

SCENE 1 *The Younger living room would be a comfortable and well-ordered room if it were not for a number of indestructible contradictions to this state of being. Its furnishings are typical and undistinguished and their primary feature now is that they have clearly had to accommodate the living of too many people for too many years—and they are tired. Still, we can see that at some time, a time probably no longer remembered by the family (except perhaps for* MAMA*), the furnishings of this room were actually selected with care and love and even hope—and brought to this apartment and arranged with taste and pride.*

That was a long time ago. Now the once loved pattern of the couch upholstery has to fight to show itself from under acres of crocheted doilies and couch covers which have themselves finally come to be more important than the upholstery. And here a table or a chair has been moved to disguise the worn places in the carpet; but the carpet has fought back by showing its weariness, with depressing uniformity, elsewhere on its surface.

Weariness has, in fact, won in this room. Everything has been polished, washed, sat on, used, scrubbed too often. All pretenses but living itself have long since vanished from the very atmosphere of this room.

Moreover, a section of this room, for it is not really a room unto itself, though the landlord's lease would make it seem so, slopes backward to provide a small kitchen area, where the family prepares the meals that are eaten in the living room proper, which must also serve as dining room. The single window that has been provided for these "two" rooms is located in this kitchen area. The sole natural light the family may enjoy in the course of a day is only that which fights its way through this little window.

At left, a door leads to a bedroom which is shared by MAMA *and her daughter,* BENEATHA. *At right, opposite, is a second room (which in the beginning of the life of this apartment was probably a breakfast room) which serves as a bedroom for* WALTER *and his wife,* RUTH.

Time: Sometime between World War II and the present.

Place: Chicago's Southside.

At Rise: It is morning dark in the living room. TRAVIS *is asleep on the make-down bed at center. An alarm clock sounds from within the bedroom at right, and presently* RUTH *enters from that room and closes the door behind her. She crosses sleepily toward the window. As she passes her sleeping son she reaches down and shakes him a little. At the window she raises the shade and a dusky Southside morning light comes in feebly. She fills a pot with water and puts it on to boil. She calls to the boy, between yawns, in a slightly muffled voice.*

RUTH *is about thirty. We can see that she was a pretty girl, even exceptionally so, but now it is apparent that life has been little that she expected, and disappointment has already begun to hang in her face. In a few years, before thirty-five even, she will be known among her people as a "settled woman."*

She crosses to her son and gives him a good, final, rousing shake.

RUTH: Come on now, boy, it's seven thirty! *(Her son sits up at last, in a stupor of sleepiness)* I say hurry up, Travis! You ain't the only person in the world got to use a bathroom! *(The child, a sturdy, handsome little*

5 *boy of ten or eleven, drags himself out of the bed and almost blindly takes his towels and "today's clothes" from drawers and a closet and goes out to the bath-room, which is in an outside hall and which is shared by another family or families on the same floor.* RUTH 10 *crosses to the bedroom door at right and opens it and calls in to her husband)* Walter Lee! . . . It's after seven thirty! Lemme see you do some waking up in there now! *(She waits)* You better get up from there, man! It's after seven thirty I tell you. *(She waits again)* All 15 right, you just go ahead and lay there and next thing you know Travis be finished and Mr. Johnson'll be in there and you'll be fussing and cussing round here like a madman! And be late too! *(She waits, at the end of patience)* Walter Lee—it's time for you to get up! 20 *(She waits another second and then starts to go into the bedroom, but is apparently satisfied that her husband has begun to get up. She stops, pulls the door to, and returns to the kitchen area. She wipes her face with a moist cloth and runs her fingers through her sleep-* 25 *disheveled hair in a vain effort and ties an apron around her housecoat. The bedroom door at right opens and her husband stands in the doorway in his pajamas, which are rumpled and mismated. He is a lean, intense young man in his middle thirties, in-* 30 *clined to quick nervous movements and erratic speech habits—and always in his voice there is a quality of indictment.)*

WALTER: Is he out yet?

RUTH: What you mean *out*? He ain't hardly got in there 35 good yet.

WALTER *(Wandering in, still more oriented to sleep than to a new day):* Well, what was you doing all that yell-ing for if I can't even get in there yet? *(Stopping and thinking)* Check coming today?

40 **RUTH:** They *said* Saturday and this is just Friday and I hopes to God you ain't going to get up here first thing this morning and start talking to me 'bout no money—'cause I 'bout don't want to hear it.

WALTER: Something the matter with you this morning?

45 **RUTH:** No—I'm just sleepy as the devil. What kind of eggs you want?

WALTER: Not scrambled. *(RUTH starts to scramble eggs)* Paper come? *(RUTH points impatiently to the rolled up Tribune on the table, and he gets it and spreads it out and vaguely reads the front page)* Set off another 50 bomb yesterday.

RUTH *(Maximum indifference):* Did they?

WALTER *(Looking up):* What's the matter with you?

RUTH: Ain't nothing the matter with me. And don't keep asking me that this morning. 55

WALTER: Ain't nobody bothering you. *(Reading the news of the day absently again)* Say Colonel McCormick is sick.

RUTH *(Affecting tea-party interest):* Is he now? Poor thing. 60

WALTER *(Sighing and looking at his watch):* Oh, me. *(He waits)* Now what is that boy doing in that bathroom all this time? He just going to have to start getting up earlier. I can't be being late to work on account of him fooling around in there. 65

RUTH *(Turning on him):* Oh, no, he ain't going to be get-ting up earlier no such thing! It ain't his fault that he can't get to bed no earlier nights 'cause he got a bunch of crazy good-for-nothing clowns sitting up running their mouths in what is supposed to be his bedroom 70 after ten o'clock at night . . .

WALTER: That's what you mad about, ain't it? The things I want to talk about with my friends just couldn't be important in your mind, could they? *(He rises and finds a cigarette in her handbag on the table and crosses* 75 *to the little window and looks out, smoking and deeply enjoying this first one)*

RUTH *(Almost matter of factly, a complaint too automatic to deserve emphasis):* Why you always got to smoke before you eat in the morning? 80

WALTER *(At the window):* Just look at 'em down there . . . Running and racing to work . . . *(He turns and faces his wife and watches her a moment at the stove, and then, suddenly)* You look young this morning, baby.

RUTH *(Indifferently):* Yeah? 85

WALTER: Just for a second—stirring them eggs. Just for a second it was—you looked real young again. (*Then, drily*) It's gone now—you look like yourself again.

RUTH: Man, if you don't shut up and leave me alone.

90 **WALTER** (*Looking out to the street again*):   First thing a man ought to learn in life is not to make love to no colored woman first thing in the morning. You all some evil people at eight o'clock in the morning. (*TRAVIS appears in the hall doorway, almost fully*
95 *dressed and quite wide awake now, his towels and pajamas across his shoulders. He opens the door and signals for his father to make the bathroom in a hurry*)

TRAVIS (*Watching the bathroom*):   Daddy, come on! (*WALTER gets his bathroom utensils and flies out to the*
100 *bathroom*)

RUTH: Sit down and have your breakfast, Travis.

TRAVIS: Mama, this is Friday. (*Gleefully*) Check coming tomorrow, huh?

RUTH: You get your mind off money and eat your
105 breakfast.

TRAVIS (*Eating*):   This is the morning we supposed to bring the fifty cents to school.

RUTH: Well, I ain't got no fifty cents this morning.

TRAVIS: Teacher say we have to.

110 **RUTH:**   I don't care what teacher say. I ain't got it. Eat your breakfast, Travis.

TRAVIS: I *am* eating.

RUTH: Hush up now and just eat! (*The boy gives her an exasperated look for her lack of understanding, and*
115 *eats grudgingly*)

TRAVIS: You think Grandmama would have it?

RUTH: No! And I want you to stop asking your grandmother for money, you hear me?

TRAVIS (*Outraged*):   Gaaaleee! I don't ask her, she just
120 gimme it sometimes!

RUTH: Travis Willard Younger—I got too much on me this morning to be—

TRAVIS: Maybe Daddy—

RUTH: Travis! (*The boy hushes abruptly. They are both quiet and tense for several seconds*)
125

TRAVIS (*Presently*):   Could I maybe go carry some groceries in front of the supermarket for a little while after school then?

RUTH: Just hush, I said. (TRAVIS *jabs his spoon into his cereal bowl viciously, and rests his head in anger*
130 *upon his fists*) If you through eating, you can get over there and make up your bed. (*The boy obeys stiffly and crosses the room, almost mechanically, to the bed and more or less folds the covering. He carries the bedding into his mother's room and returns with his books*
135 *and cap*)

TRAVIS (*Sulking and standing apart from her unnaturally*): I'm gone.

RUTH (*Looking up from the stove to inspect him automatically*):   Come here. (*He crosses to her and she studies*
140 *his head*) If you don't take this comb and fix this here head, you better! (TRAVIS *puts down his books with a great sigh of oppression, and crosses to the mirror. His mother mutters under her breath about his "stubbornness"*) 'Bout to march out of here with that head
145 looking just like chickens slept in it! I just don't know where you get your stubborn ways . . . And get your jacket, too. Looks chilly out this morning.

TRAVIS (*With conspicuously brushed hair and jacket*): I'm gone.
150

RUTH: Get carfare and milk money—(*Waving one finger*)— and not a single penny for no caps, you hear me?

TRAVIS (*With sullen politeness*):   Yes'm. (*He turns in outrage to leave. His mother watches after him as in his frustration he approaches the door almost comically.*
155 *When she speaks to him, her voice has become a very gentle tease*)

RUTH (*Mocking; as she thinks he would say it*):   Oh, Mama makes me so mad sometimes, I don't know what to do! (*She waits and continues to his back as he*
160 *stands stock-still in front of the door*) I wouldn't kiss that woman good-bye for nothing in this world this

morning! *(The boy finally turns around and rolls his eyes at her, knowing the mood has changed and he is vindicated; he does not, however, move toward her yet)* Not for nothing in this world! *(She finally laughs aloud at him and holds out her arms to him and we see that it is a way between them, very old and practiced. He crosses to her and allows her to embrace him warmly but keeps his face fixed with masculine rigidity. She holds him back from her presently and looks at him and runs her fingers over the features of his face. With utter gentleness—)* Now—whose little old angry man are you?

TRAVIS *(The masculinity and gruffness start to fade at last)*: Aw gaalee—Mama . . .

RUTH *(Mimicking)*: Aw—gaaaaalleeeee, Mama! *(She pushes him, with rough playfulness and finality, toward the door)* Get on out of here or you going to be late.

TRAVIS *(In the face of love, new aggressiveness)*: Mama, could I *please* go carry groceries?

RUTH: Honey, it's starting to get so cold evenings.

WALTER *(Coming in from the bathroom and drawing a make-believe gun from a make-believe holster and shooting at his son)*: What is it he wants to do?

RUTH: Go carry groceries after school at the supermarket.

WALTER: Well, let him go . . .

TRAVIS *(Quickly, to the ally)*: I *have* to—she won't gimme the fifty cents . . .

WALTER *(To his wife only)*: Why not?

RUTH *(Simply, and with flavor)*: 'Cause we don't have it.

WALTER *(To RUTH only)*: What you tell the boy things like that for? *(Reaching down into his pants with a rather important gesture)* Here, son— *(He hands the boy the coin, but his eyes are directed to his wife's. TRAVIS takes the money happily)*

TRAVIS: Thanks, Daddy. *(He starts out. RUTH watches both of them with murder in her eyes. WALTER stands

and stares back at her with defiance, and suddenly reaches into his pocket again on an afterthought)*

WALTER *(Without even looking at his son, still staring hard at his wife)*: In fact, here's another fifty cents . . . Buy yourself some fruit today—or take a taxicab to school or something!

TRAVIS: Whoopee— *(He leaps up and clasps his father around the middle with his legs, and they face each other in mutual appreciation; slowly WALTER LEE peeks around the boy to catch the violent rays from his wife's eyes and draws his head back as if shot)*

WALTER: You better get down now—and get to school, man.

TRAVIS *(At the door)*: O.K. Good-bye. *(He exits)*

WALTER *(After him, pointing with pride)*: That's *my* boy. *(She looks at him in disgust and turns back to her work)* You know what I was thinking 'bout in the bathroom this morning?

RUTH: No.

WALTER: How come you always try to be so pleasant!

RUTH: What is there to be pleasant 'bout!

WALTER: You want to know what I was thinking 'bout in the bathroom or not!

RUTH: I know what you thinking 'bout.

WALTER *(Ignoring her)*: 'Bout what me and Willy Harris was talking about last night.

RUTH *(Immediately—a refrain)*: Willy Harris is a good-for-nothing loud mouth.

WALTER: Anybody who talks to me has got to be a good-for-nothing loud mouth, ain't he? And what you know about who is just a good-for-nothing loud mouth? Charlie Atkins was just a "good-for-nothing loud mouth" too, wasn't he! When he wanted me to go in the dry-cleaning business with him. And now—he's grossing a hundred thousand a year. A hundred thousand dollars a year! You still call him a loudmouth!

RUTH *(Bitterly)*: Oh, Walter Lee . . . *(She folds her head on her arms over the table)*

WALTER (*Rising and coming to her and standing over her*): You tired, ain't you? Tired of everything. Me, the boy, the way we live—this beat-up hole—everything. Ain't you? (*She doesn't look up, doesn't answer*) So tired— moaning and groaning all the time, but you wouldn't do nothing to help, would you? You couldn't be on my side that long for nothing, could you?

RUTH: Walter, please leave me alone.

WALTER: A man needs for a woman to back him up . . .

RUTH: Walter—

WALTER: Mama would listen to you. You know she listen to you more than she do me and Bennie. She think more of you. All you have to do is just sit down with her when you drinking your coffee one morning and talking 'bout things like you do and—(*He sits down beside her and demonstrates graphically what he thinks her methods and tone should be*)—you just sip your coffee, see, and say easy like that you been thinking 'bout that deal Walter Lee is so interested in, 'bout the store and all, and sip some more coffee, like what you saying ain't really that important to you—And the next thing you know, she be listening good and asking you questions and when I come home—I can tell her the details. This ain't no fly-by-night proposition, baby. I mean we figured it out, me and Willy and Bobo.

RUTH (*With a frown*):   Bobo?

WALTER: Yeah. You see, this little liquor store we got in mind cost seventy-five thousand and we figured the initial investment on the place be 'bout thirty thousand, see. That be ten thousand each. Course, there's a couple of hundred you got to pay so's you don't spend your life just waiting for them clowns to let your license get approved—

RUTH: You mean graft?

WALTER (*Frowning impatiently*):   Don't call it that. See there, that just goes to show you what women understand about the world. Baby, don't *nothing* happen for you in this world 'less you pay *somebody* off!

RUTH: Walter, leave me alone! (*She raises her head and stares at him vigorously—then says, more quietly*) Eat your eggs, they gonna be cold.

WALTER (*Straightening up from her and looking off*): That's it. There you are. Man say to his woman: I got me a dream. His woman say: Eat your eggs. (*Sadly, but gaining in power*) Man say: I got to take hold of this here world, baby! And a woman will say: Eat your eggs and go to work. (*Passionately now*) Man say: I got to change my life, I'm choking to death, baby! And his woman say—(*In utter anguish as he brings his fists down on his thighs*)—Your eggs is getting cold!

RUTH (*Softly*):   Walter, that ain't none of our money.

WALTER (*Not listening at all or even looking at her*):   This morning, I was lookin' in the mirror and thinking about it . . . I'm thirty-five years old; I been married eleven years and I got a boy who sleeps in the living room—(*Very, very quietly*)—and all I got to give him is stories about how rich white people live . . .

RUTH: Eat your eggs, Walter.

WALTER (*Slams the table and jumps up*):   —Damn my eggs . . . damn all the eggs that ever was!

RUTH: Then go to work.

WALTER (*Looking up at her*):   See—I'm trying to talk to you 'bout myself—(*Shaking his head with the repetition*)—and all you can say is eat them eggs and go to work.

RUTH (*Wearily*):   Honey, you never say nothing new. I listen to you every day, every night and every morning, and you never say nothing new. (*Shrugging*) So you would rather *be* Mr. Arnold than be his chauffeur. So—I would *rather* be living in Buckingham Palace.

WALTER: That is just what is wrong with the colored woman in this world . . . Don't understand about building their men up and making 'em feel like they somebody. Like they can do something.

RUTH (*Drily, but to hurt*):   There *are* colored men who do things.

WALTER: No thanks to the colored woman.

RUTH: Well, being a colored woman, I guess I can't help myself none. (*She rises and gets the ironing board and sets it up and attacks a huge pile of rough-dried clothes,*

320 *sprinkling them in preparation for the ironing and then rolling them into tight fat balls)*

WALTER *(Mumbling):* We one group of men tied to a race of women with small minds! *(His sister BE-*
325 *NEATHA enters. She is about twenty, as slim and intense as her brother. She is not as pretty as her sister-in-law, but her lean, almost intellectual face has a handsomeness of its own. She wears a bright-red flannel nightie, and her thick hair stands wildly about her head. Her speech is a mixture of many things; it is different from the rest of the family's insofar as educa-*
330 *tion has permeated her sense of English—and perhaps the Midwest rather than the South has finally—at last— won out in her inflection; but not altogether, because over all of it is a soft slurring and transformed use of vowels which is the decided influence of the Southside.*
335 *She passes through the room without looking at either RUTH or WALTER and goes to the outside door and looks, a little blindly, out to the bathroom. She sees that it has been lost to the Johnsons. She closes the door with a sleepy vengeance and crosses to the table and sits*
340 *down a little defeated)*

BENEATHA: I am going to start timing those people.

WALTER: You should get up earlier.

BENEATHA *(Her face in her hands. She is still fighting the urge to go back to bed):* Really—would you suggest
345 dawn? Where's the paper?

WALTER *(Pushing the paper across the table to her as he studies her almost clinically, as though he has never seen her before):* You a horrible-looking chick at this hour.

350 **BENEATHA** *(Drily):* Good morning, everybody.

WALTER *(Senselessly):* How is school coming?

BENEATHA *(In the same spirit):* Lovely. Lovely. And you know, biology is the greatest. *(Looking up at him)* I dissected something that looked just like you
355 yesterday.

WALTER: I just wondered if you've made up your mind and everything.

Sidney Poitier plays Walter, with (from left) Ruby Dee as Ruth, Claudia McNeil as Mama, and Diana Sands as Beneatha, in the 1961 Columbia Pictures movie directed by Daniel Petrie.

BENEATHA *(Gaining in sharpness and impatience):* And what did I answer yesterday morning—and the day before that?
360

RUTH *(From the ironing board, like someone disinterested and old):* Don't be so nasty, Bennie.

BENEATHA *(Still to her brother):* And the day before that and the day before that!

WALTER *(Defensively):* I'm interested in you. Something
365 wrong with that? Ain't many girls who decide—

WALTER and BENEATHA *(In unison):* —"to be a doctor." *(Silence)*

WALTER: Have we figured out yet just exactly how much medical school is going to cost?
370

RUTH: Walter Lee, why don't you leave that girl alone and get out of here to work?

BENEATHA (*Exits to the bathroom and bangs on the door*):   Come on out of there, please! (*She comes back into the room*)

WALTER (*Looking at his sister intently*):   You know the check is coming tomorrow.

BENEATHA (*Turning on him with a sharpness all her own*):   That money belongs to Mama, Walter, and it's for her to decide how she wants to use it. I don't care if she wants to buy a house or a rocket ship or just nail it up somewhere and look at it. It's hers. Not ours—*hers*.

WALTER (*Bitterly*):   Now ain't that fine! You just got your mother's interest at heart, ain't you, girl? You such a nice girl—but if Mama got that money she can always take a few thousand and help you through school too—can't she?

BENEATHA: I have never asked anyone around here to do anything for me!

WALTER: No! And the line between asking and just accepting when the time comes is big and wide—ain't it!

BENEATHA (*With fury*):   What do you want from me, Brother—that I quit school or just drop dead, which!

WALTER: I don't want nothing but for you to stop acting holy 'round here. Me and Ruth done made some sacrifices for you—why can't you do something for the family?

RUTH: Walter, don't be dragging me in it.

WALTER: You are in it—Don't you get up and go work in somebody's kitchen for the last three years to help put clothes on her back?

RUTH: Oh, Walter—that's not fair . . .

WALTER: It ain't that nobody expects you to get on your knees and say thank you, Brother; thank you, Ruth; thank you, Mama—and thank you, Travis, for wearing the same pair of shoes for two semesters—

BENEATHA (*Dropping to her knees*):   Well—I *do*—all right?—thank everybody . . . and forgive me for ever wanting to be anything at all . . . Forgive me, forgive me!

RUTH: Please stop it! Your mama'll hear you.

WALTER: Who the hell told you you had to be a doctor? If you so crazy 'bout messing 'round with sick people—then go be a nurse like other women—or just get married and be quiet . . .

BENEATHA: Well—you finally got it said . . . It took you three years but you finally got it said. Walter, give up; leave me alone—it's Mama's money.

WALTER: *He was my father, too!*

BENEATHA: So what? He was mine, too—and Travis' grandfather—but the insurance money belongs to Mama. Picking on me is not going to make her give it to you to invest in any liquor stores—(*Underbreath, dropping into a chair*)—and I for one say, God bless Mama for that!

WALTER (*To* RUTH):   See—did you hear? Did you hear!

RUTH: Honey, please go to work.

WALTER: Nobody in this house is ever going to understand me.

BENEATHA: ·Because you're a nut.

WALTER: Who's a nut?

BENEATHA: You—you are a nut. Thee is mad, boy.

WALTER (*Looking at his wife and his sister from the door, very sadly*):   The world's most backward race of people, and that's a fact.

BENEATHA (*Turning slowly in her chair*):   And then there are all those prophets who would lead us out of the wilderness—(WALTER *slams out of the house*)—into the swamps!

RUTH: Bennie, why you always gotta be pickin' on your brother? Can't you be a little sweeter sometimes? (*Door opens.* WALTER *walks in*)

WALTER (*To* RUTH):   I need some money for carfare.

RUTH (*Looks at him, then warms; teasing, but tenderly*):
Fifty cents? (*She goes to her bag and gets money*)
Here—take a taxi! (*WALTER exits. MAMA enters. She
is a woman in her early sixties, full-bodied and strong.
She is one of those women of a certain grace and beauty
who wear it so unobtrusively that it takes a while to
notice. Her dark-brown face is surrounded by the total
whiteness of her hair, and, being a woman who has
adjusted to many things in life and overcome many
more, her face is full of strength. She has, we can see,
wit and faith of a kind that keep her eyes lit and full
of interest and expectancy. She is, in a word, a beautiful woman. Her bearing is perhaps most like the noble
bearing of the women of the Hereros of Southwest
Africa—rather as if she imagines that as she walks
she still bears a basket or a vessel upon her head. Her
speech, on the other hand, is as careless as her carriage
is precise—she is inclined to slur everything—but her
voice is perhaps not so much quiet as simply soft*)

MAMA: Who that 'round here slamming doors at this
hour? (*She crosses through the room, goes to the window, opens it, and brings in a feeble little plant growing
doggedly in a small pot on the window sill. She feels the
dirt and puts it back out*)

RUTH: That was Walter Lee. He and Bennie was at it
again.

MAMA: My children and they tempers. Lord, if this little
old plant don't get more sun than it's been getting it
ain't never going to see spring again. (*She turns from
the window*) What's the matter with you this morning,
Ruth? You looks right peaked. You aiming to iron all
them things? Leave some for me. I'll get to 'em this
afternoon. Bennie honey, it's too drafty for you to be
sitting 'round half dressed. Where's your robe?

BENEATHA: In the cleaners.

MAMA: Well, go get mine and put it on.

BENEATHA: I'm not cold, Mama, honest.

MAMA: I know—but you so thin . . .

BENEATHA (*Irritably*): Mama, I'm not cold.

MAMA (*Seeing the make-down bed as* TRAVIS *has left it*):
Lord have mercy, look at that poor bed. Bless his
heart—he tries, don't he? (*She moves to the bed* TRAVIS
has sloppily made up)

RUTH: No—he don't half try at all 'cause he knows you
going to come along behind him and fix everything.
That's just how come he don't know how to do nothing
right now—you done spoiled that boy so.

MAMA: Well—he's a little boy. Ain't supposed to know
'bout housekeeping. My baby, that's what he is. What
you fix for his breakfast this morning?

RUTH (*Angrily*): I feed my son, Lena!

MAMA: I ain't meddling—(*Underbreath; busy-bodyish*) I
just noticed all last week he had cold cereal, and when
it starts getting this chilly in the fall a child ought to
have some hot grits or something when he goes out in
the cold—

RUTH (*Furious*): I gave him hot oats—is that all right!

MAMA: I ain't meddling. (*Pause*) Put a lot of nice butter
on it? (RUTH *shoots her an angry look and does not
reply*) He likes lots of butter.

RUTH (*Exasperated*): Lena—

MAMA (*To* BENEATHA. MAMA *is inclined to wander con-
versationally sometimes*): What was you and your
brother fussing 'bout this morning?

BENEATHA: It's not important, Mama. (*She gets up and
goes to look out at the bathroom, which is apparently
free, and she picks up her towels and rushes out*)

MAMA: What was they fighting about?

RUTH: Now you know as well as I do.

MAMA (*Shaking her head*): Brother still worrying hisself
sick about that money?

RUTH: You know he is.

MAMA: You had breakfast?

RUTH: Some coffee.

MAMA: Girl, you better start eating and looking after
yourself better. You almost thin as Travis.

RUTH: Lena—

MAMA: Uh-hunh?

RUTH: What are you going to do with it?

MAMA: Now don't you start, child. It's too early in the morning to be talking about money. It ain't Christian.

525 **RUTH:** It's just that he got his heart set on that store—

MAMA: You mean that liquor store that Willy Harris want him to invest in?

RUTH: Yes—

MAMA: We ain't no business people, Ruth. We just plain 530 working folks.

RUTH: Ain't nobody business people till they go into business. Walter Lee say colored people ain't never going to start getting ahead till they start gambling on some different kinds of things in the world— 535 investments and things.

MAMA: What done got into you, girl? Walter Lee done finally sold you on investing.

RUTH: No. Mama, something is happening between Walter and me. I don't know what it is—but he needs 540 something—something I can't give him any more. He needs this chance, Lena.

MAMA (*Frowning deeply*): But liquor, honey—

RUTH: Well—like Walter say—I spec people going to always be drinking themselves some liquor.

545 **MAMA:** Well—whether they drinks it or not ain't none of my business. But whether I go into business selling it to 'em *is*, and I don't want that on my ledger this late in life. (*Stopping suddenly and studying her daughter-in-law*) Ruth Younger, what's the matter with you 550 today? You look like you could fall over right there.

RUTH: I'm tired.

MAMA: Then you better stay home from work today.

RUTH: I can't stay home. She'd be calling up the agency and screaming at them, "My girl didn't come in to-555 day—send me somebody! My girl didn't come in!" Oh, she just have a fit . . .

MAMA: Well, let her have it. I'll just call her up and say you got the flu—

RUTH (*Laughing*): Why the flu?

MAMA: 'Cause it sounds respectable to 'em. Something 560 white people get, too. They know 'bout the flu. Otherwise they think you been cut up or something when you tell 'em you sick.

RUTH: I got to go in. We need the money.

MAMA: Somebody would of thought my children done 565 all but starved to death the way they talk about money here late. Child, we got a great big old check coming tomorrow.

RUTH (*Sincerely, but also self-righteously*): Now that's your money. It ain't got nothing to do with me. We 570 all feel like that—Walter and Bennie and me—even Travis.

MAMA (*Thoughtfully, and suddenly very far away*): Ten thousand dollars—

RUTH: Sure is wonderful. 575

MAMA: Ten thousand dollars.

RUTH: You know what you should do, Miss Lena? You should take yourself a trip somewhere. To Europe or South America or someplace—

MAMA (*Throwing up her hands at the thought*): Oh, child! 580

RUTH: I'm serious. Just pack up and leave! Go on away and enjoy yourself some. Forget about the family and have yourself a ball for once in your life—

MAMA (*Drily*): You sound like I'm just about ready to die. Who'd go with me? What I look like wandering 585 'round Europe by myself?

RUTH: Shoot—these here rich white women do it all the time. They don't think nothing of packing up they suitcases and piling on one of them big steamships and—swoosh!—they gone, child. 590

MAMA: Something always told me I wasn't no rich white woman.

RUTH: Well—what are you going to do with it then?

Ruth (Ruby Dee) looks up from her ironing (1961).

MAMA: I ain't rightly decided. *(Thinking. She speaks*
595   *now with emphasis)* Some of it got to be put away for
Beneatha and her schoolin'—and ain't nothing going
to touch that part of it. Nothing. *(She waits several
seconds, trying to make up her mind about something,
and looks at* RUTH *a little tentatively before going on)*
600   Been thinking that we maybe could meet the notes on
a little old two-story somewhere, with a yard where
Travis could play in the summertime, if we use part
of the insurance for a down payment and everybody
kind of pitch in. I could maybe take on a little day
605   work again, few days a week—

RUTH *(Studying her mother-in-law furtively and concentrating on her ironing, anxious to encourage without
seeming to):* Well, Lord knows, we've put enough
rent into this here rat trap to pay for four houses by
610   now . . .

MAMA *(Looking up at the words "rat trap" and then looking around and leaning back and sighing—in a suddenly reflective mood—):* "Rat trap"—yes, that's all
it is. *(Smiling)* I remember just as well the day me
and Big Walter moved in here. Hadn't been married   615
but two weeks and wasn't planning on living here no
more than a year. *(She shakes her head at the dissolved
dream)* We was going to set away, little by little, don't
you know, and buy a little place out in Morgan Park.
We had even picked out the house. *(Chuckling a little)*   620
Looks right dumpy today. But Lord, child, you should
know all the dreams I had 'bout buying that house
and fixing it up and making me a little garden in the
back—*(She waits and stops smiling)* And didn't none
of it happen. *(Dropping her hands in a futile gesture)*   625

RUTH *(Keeps her head down, ironing):* Yes, life can be a
barrel of disappointments, sometimes.

MAMA: Honey, Big Walter would come in here some
nights back then and slump down on that couch there
and just look at the rug, and look at me and look at the   630
rug and then back at me—and I'd know he was down
then . . . really down. *(After a second very long and
thoughtful pause; she is seeing back to times that only
she can see)* And then, Lord, when I lost that baby—
little Claude—I almost thought I was going to lose Big   635
Walter too. Oh, that man grieved hisself! He was one
man to love his children.

RUTH: Ain't nothin' can tear at you like losin' your baby.

MAMA: I guess that's how come that man finally worked
hisself to death like he done. Like he was fighting his   640
own war with this here world that took his baby from
him.

RUTH: He sure was a fine man, all right. I always liked
Mr. Younger.

MAMA: Crazy 'bout his children! God knows there was   645
plenty wrong with Walter Younger—hard-headed,
mean, kind of wild with women—plenty wrong with
him. But he sure loved his children. Always wanted
them to have something—be something. That's where
Brother gets all these notions, I reckon. Big Walter   650
used to say, he'd get right wet in the eyes sometimes,
lean his head back with the water standing in his eyes

and say, "Seem like God didn't see fit to give the black man nothing but dreams—but He did give us children to make them dreams seem worth while." (*She smiles*) He could talk like that, don't you know.

RUTH: Yes, he sure could. He was a good man, Mr. Younger.

MAMA: Yes, a fine man—just couldn't never catch up with his dreams, that's all. (BENEATHA *comes in, brushing her hair and looking up to the ceiling, where the sound of a vacuum cleaner has started up*)

BENEATHA: What could be so dirty on that woman's rugs that she has to vacuum them every single day?

RUTH: I wish certain young women 'round here who I could name would take inspiration about certain rugs in a certain apartment I could also mention.

BENEATHA (*Shrugging*):   How much cleaning can a house need, for Christ's sakes.

MAMA (*Not liking the Lord's name used thus*):   Bennie!

RUTH: Just listen to her—just listen!

BENEATHA: Oh, God!

MAMA: If you use the Lord's name just one more time—

BENEATHA (*A bit of a whine*):   Oh, Mama—

RUTH: Fresh—just fresh as salt, this girl!

BENEATHA (*Drily*):   Well—if the salt loses its savor—

MAMA: Now that will do. I just ain't going to have you 'round here reciting the scriptures in vain—you hear me?

BENEATHA: How did I manage to get on everybody's wrong side by just walking into a room?

RUTH: If you weren't so fresh—

BENEATHA: Ruth, I'm twenty years old.

MAMA: What time you be home from school today?

BENEATHA: Kind of late. (*With enthusiasm*) Madeline is going to start my guitar lessons today. (MAMA *and* RUTH *look up with the same expression*)

MAMA: Your *what* kind of lessons?

BENEATHA: Guitar.

RUTH: Oh, Father!

MAMA: How come you done taken it in your mind to learn to play the guitar?

BENEATHA: I just want to, that's all.

MAMA (*Smiling*):   Lord, child, don't you know what to do with yourself? How long it going to be before you get tired of this now—like you got tired of that little play-acting group you joined last year? (*Looking at* RUTH) And what was it the year before that?

RUTH: The horseback-riding club for which she bought that fifty-five-dollar riding habit that's been hanging in the closet ever since!

MAMA (*To* BENEATHA):   Why you got to flit so from one thing to another, baby?

BENEATHA (*Sharply*):   I just want to learn to play the guitar. Is there anything wrong with that?

MAMA: Ain't nobody trying to stop you. I just wonders sometimes why you has to flit so from one thing to another all the time. You ain't never done nothing with all that camera equipment you brought home—

BENEATHA: I don't flit! I—I experiment with different forms of expression—

RUTH: Like riding a horse?

BENEATHA: —People have to express themselves one way or another.

MAMA: What is it you want to express?

BENEATHA (*Angrily*):   Me! (MAMA *and* RUTH *look at each other and burst into raucous laughter*) Don't worry—I don't expect you to understand.

MAMA (*To change the subject*):   Who you going out with tomorrow night?

BENEATHA (*With displeasure*):   George Murchison again.

MAMA (*Pleased*):   Oh—you getting a little sweet on him?

725 **RUTH:** You ask me, this child ain't sweet on nobody but herself—*(Underbreath)* Express herself! *(They laugh)*

BENEATHA: Oh—I like George all right, Mama. I mean I like him enough to go out with him and stuff, but—

RUTH *(For devilment)*: What does *and stuff* mean?

BENEATHA: Mind your own business.

730 **MAMA:** Stop picking at her now, Ruth. *(A thoughtful pause, and then a suspicious sudden look at her daughter as she turns in her chair for emphasis)* What does it mean?

735 BENEATHA *(Wearily)*: Oh, I just mean I couldn't ever really be serious about George. He's—he's so shallow.

RUTH: Shallow—what do you mean he's shallow? He's *rich!*

MAMA: Hush, Ruth.

BENEATHA: I know he's rich. He knows he's rich, too.

740 **RUTH:** Well—what other qualities a man got to have to satisfy you, little girl?

BENEATHA: You wouldn't even begin to understand. Anybody who married Walter could not possibly understand.

745 **MAMA** *(Outraged)*: What kind of way is that to talk about your brother?

BENEATHA: Brother is a flip—let's face it.

MAMA *(To RUTH, helplessly)*: What's a flip?

RUTH *(Glad to add kindling)*: She's saying he's crazy.

750 **BENEATHA:** Not crazy. Brother isn't really crazy yet—he—he's an elaborate neurotic.

MAMA: Hush your mouth!

BENEATHA: As for George. Well. George looks good—he's got a beautiful car and he takes me to nice places and, as my sister-in-law says, he is probably the rich-
755 est boy I will ever get to know and I even like him sometimes—but if the Youngers are sitting around waiting to see if their little Bennie is going to tie up the family with the Murchisons, they are wasting
760 their time.

RUTH: You mean you wouldn't marry George Murchison if he asked you someday? That pretty, rich thing? Honey, I knew you was odd—

BENEATHA: No I would not marry him if all I felt for him was what I feel now. Besides, George's family 765 wouldn't really like it.

MAMA: Why not?

BENEATHA: Oh, Mama—The Murchisons are honest-to-God-real-live-rich colored people, and the only people in the world who are more snobbish than rich 770 white people are rich colored people. I thought everybody knew that. I've met Mrs. Murchison. She's a scene!

MAMA: You must not dislike people 'cause they well off, honey. 775

BENEATHA: Why not? It makes just as much sense as disliking people 'cause they are poor, and lots of people do that.

RUTH *(A wisdom-of-the-ages manner. To MAMA)*: Well, she'll get over some of this— 780

BENEATHA: Get over it? What are you talking about, Ruth? Listen, I'm going to be a doctor. I'm not worried about who I'm going to marry yet—if I ever get married.

MAMA *and* RUTH: *If!* 785

MAMA: Now, Bennie—

BENEATHA: Oh, I probably will . . . but first I'm going to be a doctor, and George, for one, still thinks that's pretty funny. I couldn't be bothered with that. I am going to be a doctor and everybody around here better 790 understand that!

MAMA *(Kindly)*: 'Course you going to be a doctor, honey, God willing.

BENEATHA *(Drily)*: God hasn't got a thing to do with it.

MAMA: Beneatha—that just wasn't necessary. 795

BENEATHA: Well—neither is God. I get sick of hearing about God.

MAMA: Beneatha!

BENEATHA: I mean it! I'm just tired of hearing about God all the time. What has He got to do with anything? Does he pay tuition?

MAMA: You 'bout to get your fresh little jaw slapped!

RUTH: That's just what she needs, all right!

BENEATHA: Why? Why can't I say what I want around here, like everybody else?

MAMA: It don't sound nice for a young girl to say things like that—you wasn't brought up that way. Me and your father went to trouble to get you and Brother to church every Sunday.

BENEATHA: Mama, you don't understand. It's all a matter of ideas, and God is just one idea I don't accept. It's not important. I am not going out and be immoral or commit crimes because I don't believe in God. I don't even think about it. It's just that I get tired of Him getting credit for all the things the human race achieves through its own stubborn effort. There simply is no blasted God—there is only man and it is *he* who makes miracles! (MAMA *absorbs this speech, studies her daughter and rises slowly and crosses to* BENEATHA *and slaps her powerfully across the face. After, there is only silence and the daughter drops her eyes from her mother's face, and* MAMA *is very tall before her*)

MAMA: Now—you say after me, in my mother's house there is still God. (*There is a long pause and* BENEATHA *stares at the floor wordlessly.* MAMA *repeats the phrase with precision and cool emotion*) In my mother's house there is still God.

BENEATHA: In my mother's house there is still God. (*A long pause*)

MAMA (*Walking away from* BENEATHA, *too disturbed for triumphant posture. Stopping and turning back to her daughter*):   There are some ideas we ain't going to have in this house. Not long as I am at the head of this family.

BENEATHA: Yes, ma'am. (MAMA *walks out of the room*)

RUTH (*Almost gently, with profound understanding*):   You think you a woman, Bennie—but you still a little girl. What you did was childish—so you got treated like a child.

BENEATHA: I see. (*Quietly*) I also see that everybody thinks it's all right for Mama to be a tyrant. But all the tyranny in the world will never put a God in the heavens! (*She picks up her books and goes out. Pause*)

RUTH (*Goes to* MAMA's *door*):   She said she was sorry.

MAMA (*Coming out, going to her plant*):   They frightens me, Ruth. My children.

RUTH: You got good children, Lena. They just a little off sometimes—but they're good.

MAMA: No—there's something come down between me and them that don't let us understand each other and I don't know what it is. One done almost lost his mind thinking 'bout money all the time and the other done commence to talk about things I can't seem to understand in no form or fashion. What is it that's changing, Ruth?

RUTH (*Soothingly, older than her years*):   Now . . . you taking it all too seriously. You just got strong-willed children and it takes a strong woman like you to keep 'em in hand.

MAMA (*Looking at her plant and sprinkling a little water on it*):   They spirited all right, my children. Got to admit they got spirit—Bennie and Walter. Like this little old plant that ain't never had enough sunshine or nothing—and look at it . . . (*She has her back to* RUTH, *who has had to stop ironing and lean against something and put the back of her hand to her forehead*)

RUTH (*Trying to keep* MAMA *from noticing*):   You . . . sure . . . loves that little old thing, don't you? . . .

MAMA: Well, I always wanted me a garden like I used to see sometimes at the back of the houses down home. This plant is close as I ever got to having one. (*She looks out of the window as she replaces the plant*) Lord, ain't nothing as dreary as the view from this window on a dreary day, is there? Why ain't you singing this morning, Ruth? Sing that "No Ways Tired." That song always lifts me up so—(*She turns at last to see that* RUTH *has slipped quietly to the floor, in a state of semi-consciousness*) Ruth! Ruth honey—what's the matter with you . . . Ruth!

880

Curtain

SCENE 2 *It is the following morning; a Saturday morning, and house cleaning is in progress at the* YOUNGERS. *Furniture has been shoved hither and yon and* MAMA *is giving the kitchen-area walls a washing down.* BENEATHA, *in dungarees, with a handkerchief tied around her face, is spraying insecticide into the cracks in the walls. As they work, the radio is on and a Southside disk-jockey program is inappropriately filling the house with a rather exotic saxophone blues.* TRAVIS, *the sole idle one, is leaning on his arms, looking out of the window.*

TRAVIS: Grandmama, that stuff Bennie is using smells awful. Can I go downstairs, please?

MAMA: Did you get all them chores done already? I ain't seen you doing much.

5 **TRAVIS:** Yes'm—finished early. Where did Mama go this morning?

MAMA (*Looking at* BENEATHA): She had to go on a little errand.

TRAVIS: Where?

10 **MAMA:** To tend to her business.

TRAVIS: Can I go outside then?

MAMA: Oh, I guess so. You better stay right in front of the house, though . . . and keep a good lookout for the postman.

15 **TRAVIS:** Yes'm. (*He starts out and decides to give his* AUNT BENEATHA *a good swat on the legs as he passes her*) Leave them poor little old cockroaches alone, they ain't bothering you none. (*He runs as she swings the spray gun at him both viciously and playfully.* WAL-
20 TER *enters from the bedroom and goes to the phone*)

MAMA: Look out there, girl, before you be spilling some of that stuff on that child!

TRAVIS (*Teasing*): That's right—look out now! (*He exits*)

BENEATHA (*Drily*): I can't imagine that it would hurt him—it has never hurt the roaches. 25

MAMA: Well, little boys' hides ain't as tough as South-side roaches.

WALTER (*Into phone*): Hello—Let me talk to Willy Harris.

MAMA: You better get over there behind the bureau. 30 I seen one marching out of there like Napoleon yesterday.

WALTER: Hello, Willy? It ain't come yet. It'll be here in a few minutes. Did the lawyer give you the papers?

BENEATHA: There's really only one way to get rid of 35 them, Mama—

MAMA: How?

BENEATHA: Set fire to this building.

WALTER: Good. Good. I'll be right over.

BENEATHA: Where did Ruth go, Walter? 40

WALTER: I don't know. (*He exits abruptly*)

BENEATHA: Mama, where did Ruth go?

MAMA (*Looking at her with meaning*): To the doctor, I think.

BENEATHA: The doctor? What's the matter? (*They* 45 *exchange glances*) You don't think—

MAMA (*With her sense of drama*): Now I ain't saying what I think. But I ain't never been wrong 'bout a woman neither. (*The phone rings*)

BENEATHA (*At the phone*): Hay-lo . . . (*Pause, and a mo-* 50 *ment of recognition*) Well—when did you get back! . . . And how was it? . . . Of course I've missed you—in my way . . . This morning? No . . . house cleaning and all that and Mama hates it if I let people come over when the house is like this . . . You *have?* Well, that's differ- 55 ent . . . What is it—Oh, what the hell, come on over . . . Right, see you then (*She hangs up*)

MAMA (*Who has listened vigorously, as is her habit*): Who is that you inviting over here with this house looking like this? You ain't got the pride you was born with!

BENEATHA: Asagai doesn't care how houses look, Mama—he's an intellectual.

MAMA: *Who?*

BENEATHA: Asagai—Joseph Asagai. He's an African boy I met on campus. He's been studying in Canada all summer.

MAMA: What's his name?

BENEATHA: Asagai, Joseph. Ah-sah-guy . . . He's from Nigeria.

MAMA: Oh, that's the little country that was founded by slaves way back . . .

BENEATHA: No, Mama—that's Liberia.

MAMA: I don't think I never met no African before.

BENEATHA: Well, do me a favor and don't ask him a whole lot of ignorant questions about Africans. I mean, do they wear clothes and all that—

MAMA: Well, now, I guess if you think we so ignorant 'round here maybe you shouldn't bring your friends here—

BENEATHA: It's just that people ask such crazy things. All anyone seems to know about when it comes to Africa is Tarzan—

MAMA (*Indignantly*): Why should I know anything about Africa?

BENEATHA: Why do you give money at church for the missionary work?

MAMA: Well, that's to help save people.

BENEATHA: You mean save them from *heathenism*—

MAMA (*Innocently*): Yes.

BENEATHA: I'm afraid they need more salvation from the British and the French. (RUTH *comes in forlornly and pulls off her coat with dejection. They both turn to look at her*)

RUTH (*Dispiritedly*): Well, I guess from all the happy faces—everybody knows.

BENEATHA: You pregnant?

MAMA: Lord have mercy, I sure hope it's a little old girl. Travis ought to have a sister. (BENEATHA *and* RUTH *give her a hopeless look for this grandmotherly enthusiasm*)

BENEATHA: How far along are you?

RUTH: Two months.

BENEATHA: Did you mean to? I mean did you plan it or was it an accident?

MAMA: What do you know about planning or not planning?

BENEATHA: Oh, Mama.

RUTH (*Wearily*): She's twenty years old, Lena.

BENEATHA: Did you plan it, Ruth?

RUTH: Mind your own business.

BENEATHA: It is my business—where is he going to live, on the roof? (*There is silence following the remark as the three women react to the sense of it*) Gee—I didn't mean that, Ruth, honest. Gee, I don't feel like that at all. I—I think it is wonderful.

RUTH (*Dully*): Wonderful.

BENEATHA: Yes—really.

MAMA (*Looking at* RUTH, *worried*): Doctor say every thing going to be all right?

RUTH (*Far away*): Yes—she says everything is going to be fine . . .

MAMA (*Immediately suspicious*): "She"—What doctor you went to? (RUTH *folds over, she is near hysteria*)

MAMA (*Worriedly hovering over* RUTH): Ruth honey—what's the matter with you—you sick? (RUTH *has her fists clenched on her thighs and is fighting hard to suppress a scream that seems to be rising in her*)

BENEATHA: What's the matter with her, Mama?

130 **MAMA** (*Working her fingers in* RUTH*'s shoulders to relax her*):   She be all right. Women gets right depressed sometimes when they get her way. (*Speaking softly, expertly, rapidly*) Now you just relax. That's right . . . just lean back, don't think 'bout nothing at all . . .
135 nothing at all—

RUTH: I'm all right . . . (*The glassy-eyed look melts and then she collapses into a fit of heavy sobbing. The bell rings*)

BENEATHA: Oh, my God—that must be Asagai.

140 **MAMA** (*To* RUTH):   Come on now, honey. You need to lie down and rest awhile . . . then have some nice hot food. (*They exit,* RUTH*'s weight on her mother-in-law.* BENEATHA, *herself profoundly disturbed, opens the door to admit a rather dramatic-looking young man*
145 *with a large package*)

ASAGAI: Hello, Alaiyo—

BENEATHA (*Holding the door open and regarding him with pleasure*):   Hello . . . (*Long pause*) Well—come in. And please excuse everything. My mother was very
150 upset about my letting anyone come here with the place like this.

ASAGAI (*coming into the room*):   You look disturbed too . . . Is something wrong?

BENEATHA (*Still at the door, absently*):   Yes . . . we've all
155 got acute ghetto-itus. (*She smiles and comes toward him, finding a cigarette and sitting*) So—sit down! How was Canada?

ASAGAI (*A sophisticate*):   Canadian.

BENEATHA (*Looking at him*):   I'm very glad you are back.

160 **ASAGAI** (*Looking back at her in turn*):   Are you really?

BENEATHA: Yes—very.

ASAGAI: Why?—you were quite glad when I went away. What happened?

BENEATHA: You went away.

165 **ASAGAI:**   Ahhhhhhhh.

BENEATHA: Before—you wanted to be so serious before there was time.

ASAGAI: How much time must there be before one knows what one feels?

170 **BENEATHA** (*Stalling this particular conversation. Her hands pressed together, in a deliberately childish gesture*):   What did you bring me?

ASAGAI (*Handing her the package*):   Open it and see.

BENEATHA (*Eagerly opening the package and drawing out some records and the colorful robes of a Nigerian*
175 *woman*):   Oh, Asagai! . . . You got them for me! . . . How beautiful . . . and the records too! (*She lifts out the robes and runs to the mirror with them and holds the drapery up in front of herself*)

ASAGAI (*Coming to her at the mirror*):   I shall have to
180 teach you how to drape it properly. (*He flings the material about her for the moment and stands back to look at her*) Ah—Oh-pay-gay-day, oh-gbah-mu-shay. (*A Yoruba exclamation for admiration*) You wear it well . . . very well . . . mutilated hair and all.
185

BENEATHA (*Turning suddenly*):   My hair—what's wrong with my hair?

ASAGAI (*Shrugging*):   Were you born with it like that?

BENEATHA (*Reaching up to touch it*):   No . . . of course not. (*She looks back to the mirror, disturbed*)
190

ASAGAI (*Smiling*):   How then?

BENEATHA: You know perfectly well how . . . as crinkly as yours . . . that's how.

ASAGAI: And it is ugly to you that way?

BENEATHA (*Quickly*):   Oh, no—not ugly . . . (*More slowly,*
195 *apologetically*) But it's so hard to manage when it's, well—raw.

ASAGAI: And so to accommodate that—you mutilate it every week?

BENEATHA: It's not mutilation!
200

ASAGAI (*Laughing aloud at her seriousness*):   Oh . . . please! I am only teasing you because you are so very serious about these things. (*He stands back from her and folds his arms across his chest as he watches her pulling at her hair and frowning in the mirror*) Do you remember the first time you met me at school? . . . (*He laughs*) You came up to me and you said—and I thought you were the most serious little thing I had ever seen—you said: (*He imitates her*) "Mr. Asagai— I want very much to talk with you. About Africa. You see, Mr. Asagai, I am looking for my *identity*!" (*He laughs*)

BENEATHA (*Turning to him, not laughing*):   Yes— (*Her face is quizzical, profoundly disturbed*)

ASAGAI (*Still teasing and reaching out and taking her face in his hands and turning her profile to him*):   Well . . . it is true that this is not so much a profile of a Hollywood queen as perhaps a queen of the Nile—(*A mock dismissal of the importance of the question*) But what does it matter? Assimilationism is so popular in your country.

BENEATHA (*Wheeling, passionately, sharply*):   I am not an assimilationist!

ASAGAI (*The protest hangs in the room for a moment and ASAGAI studies her, his laughter fading*):   Such a serious one. (*There is a pause*) So—you like the robes? You must take excellent care of them—they are from my sister's personal wardrobe.

BENEATHA (*With incredulity*):   You—you sent all the way home—for me?

ASAGAI (*With charm*):   For you—I would do much more . . . Well, that is what I came for. I must go.

BENEATHA: Will you call me Monday?

ASAGAI: Yes . . . We have a great deal to talk about. I mean about identity and time and all that.

BENEATHA: Time?

ASAGAI: Yes. About how much time one needs to know what one feels.

BENEATHA: You see! You never understood that there is more than one kind of feeling which can ex-ist between a man and a woman—or, at least, there should be.

ASAGAI (*Shaking his head negatively but gently*):   No. Between a man and a woman there need be only one kind of feeling. I have that for you . . . Now even . . . right this moment . . .

BENEATHA: I know—and by itself—it won't do. I can find that anywhere.

ASAGAI: For a woman it should be enough.

BENEATHA: I know—because that's what it says in all the novels that men write. But it isn't. Go ahead and laugh—but I'm not interested in being someone's little episode in America or—(*With feminine vengeance*)— one of them! (ASAGAI *has burst into laughter again*) That's funny as hell, huh!

ASAGAI: It's just that every American girl I have known has said that to me. White—black—in this you are all the same. And the same speech, too!

BENEATHA (*Angrily*):   Yuk, yuk, yuk!

ASAGAI: It's how you can be sure that the world's most liberated women are not liberated at all. You all talk about it too much! (MAMA *enters and is immediately all social charm because of the presence of a guest*)

BENEATHA: Oh—Mama—this is Mr. Asagai.

MAMA: How do you do?

ASAGAI (*Total politeness to an elder*):   How do you do, Mrs. Younger. Please forgive me for coming at such an outrageous hour on a Saturday.

MAMA: Well, you are quite welcome. I just hope you understand that our house don't always look like this. (*Chatterish*) You must come again. I would love to hear all about—(*Not sure of the name*)—your country. I think it's so sad the way our American Negroes don't know nothing about Africa 'cept Tarzan and all that. And all that money they pour into these churches when they ought to be helping you people over there drive out them French and Englishmen done taken away your land. (*The mother flashes a slightly superior look at her daughter upon completion of the recitation*)

280 **ASAGAI** (*Taken aback by this sudden and acutely unrelated expression of sympathy*): Yes . . . yes . . .

MAMA (*Smiling at him suddenly and relaxing and looking him over*): How many miles is it from here to where you come from?

285 **ASAGAI:** Many thousands.

MAMA (*Looking at him as she would* WALTER): I bet you don't half look after yourself, being away from your mama either. I spec you better come 'round here from time to time to get yourself some decent home-cooked 290 meals . . .

ASAGAI (*Moved*): Thank you. Thank you very much. (*They are all quiet, then—*) Well . . . I must go. I will call you Monday, Alaiyo.

MAMA: What's that he call you?

295 **ASAGAI:** Oh—"Alaiyo." I hope you don't mind. It is what you would call a nickname, I think. It is a Yoruba word. I am a Yoruba.

MAMA (*Looking at* BENEATHA): I—I thought he was from—(*Uncertain*)

300 **ASAGAI** (*Understanding*): Nigeria is my country. Yoruba is my tribal origin—

BENEATHA: You didn't tell us what Alaiyo means . . . for all I know, you might be calling me Little Idiot or something . . .

305 **ASAGAI:** Well . . . let me see . . . I do not know how just to explain it . . . The sense of a thing can be so different when it changes languages.

BENEATHA: You're evading.

ASAGAI: No—really it is difficult . . . (*Thinking*) It 310 means . . . it means One for Whom Bread—Food— Is Not Enough. (*He looks at her*) Is that all right?

BENEATHA (*Understanding, softly*): Thank you.

MAMA (*Looking from one to the other and not understanding any of it*): Well . . . that's nice . . . You must come 315 see us again—Mr.—

ASAGAI: Ah-sah-guy . . .

MAMA: Yes . . . Do come again.

ASAGAI: Good-bye. (*He exits*)

MAMA (*After him*): Lord, that's a pretty thing just went out here! (*Insinuatingly, to her daughter*) Yes, I guess 320 I see why we done commence to get so interested in Africa 'round here. Missionaries my aunt Jenny! (*She exits*)

BENEATHA: Oh, Mama! . . . (*She picks up the Nigerian dress and holds it up to her in front of the mirror again.* 325 *She sets the headdress on haphazardly and then notices her hair again and clutches at it and then replaces the headdress and frowns at herself. Then she starts to wriggle in front of the mirror as she thinks a Nigerian woman might.* TRAVIS *enters and stands regard-* 330 *ing her*)

TRAVIS: You cracking up?

BENEATHA: Shut up. (*She pulls the headdress off and looks at herself in the mirror and clutches at her hair again and squinches her eyes as if trying to imagine* 335 *something. Then, suddenly, she gets her raincoat and kerchief and hurriedly prepares for going out*)

MAMA (*Coming back into the room*): She's resting now. Travis, baby, run next door and ask Miss Johnson to please let me have a little kitchen cleanser. This here 340 can is empty as Jacob's kettle.

TRAVIS: I just came in.

MAMA: Do as you told. (*He exits and she looks at her daughter*) Where you going?

BENEATHA (*Halting at the door*): To become a queen of 345 the Nile! (*She exits in a breathless blaze of glory.* RUTH *appears in the bedroom doorway*)

MAMA: Who told you to get up?

RUTH: Ain't nothing wrong with me to be lying in no bed for. Where did Bennie go? 350

MAMA (*Drumming her fingers*): Far as I could make out—to Egypt. (RUTH *just looks at her*) What time is it getting to?

RUTH: Ten twenty. And the mailman going to ring that bell this morning just like he done every morning for 355 the last umpteen years. (TRAVIS *comes in with the cleanser can*)

TRAVIS: She say to tell you that she don't have much.

MAMA (*Angrily*):   Lord, some people I could name sure is
360   tight-fisted! (*Directing her grandson*) Mark two cans
      of cleanser down on the list there. If she that hard up
      for kitchen cleanser, I sure don't want to forget to get
      her none!

RUTH: Lena—maybe the woman is just short on
365   cleanser—

MAMA (*Not listening*):   —Much baking powder as she
      done borrowed from me all these years, she could
      of done gone into the baking business! (*The bell
      sounds suddenly and sharply and all three are
370   stunned—serious and silent—mid-speech. In spite
      of all the other conversations and distractions of the
      morning, this is what they have been waiting for, even
      TRAVIS, who looks helplessly from his mother to his
      grandmother.* RUTH *is the first to come to life again*)

375 **RUTH** (*To* TRAVIS):   Get down them steps, boy! (TRAVIS
      snaps to life and flies out to get the mail)

MAMA (*Her eyes wide, her hand to her breast*):   You mean
      it done really come?

RUTH (*Excited*):   Oh, Miss Lena!

380 **MAMA** (*Collecting herself*):   Well . . . I don't know what we
      all so excited about 'round here for. We known it was
      coming for months.

RUTH: That's a whole lot different from having it come
      and being able to hold it in your hands . . . a piece of
385   paper worth ten thousand dollars . . . (TRAVIS *bursts
      back into the room. He holds the envelope high above
      his head, like a little dancer, his face is radiant and he
      is breathless. He moves to his grandmother with sudden
      slow ceremony and puts the envelope into her hands.
390   She accepts it, and then merely holds it and looks at it*)
      Come on! Open it . . . Lord have mercy, I wish Walter
      Lee was here!

TRAVIS: Open it, Grandmama!

MAMA (*Staring at it*):   Now you all be quiet. It's just a
395   check.

RUTH: Open it . . .

Travis (Brandon David Brown) and Ruth (Deirdrie Henry) wonder
why Mama (L. Scott Caldwell) is distressed after receiving the
insurance check, in the 2011 Ebony Repertory Theater production
directed by Phylicia Rashad.

MAMA (*Still staring at it*):   Now don't act silly . . . We ain't
never been no people to act silly 'bout no money—

RUTH (*Swiftly*):   We ain't never had none before—open
it! (MAMA *finally makes a good strong tear and pulls*   400
*out the thin blue slice of paper and inspects it closely.
The boy and his mother study it raptly over* MAMA's
shoulders)

MAMA: *Travis!* (*She is counting off with doubt*) Is that
the right number of zeros?   405

TRAVIS: Yes'm . . . ten thousand dollars. Gaalee, Grandmama, you rich.

MAMA (*She holds the check away from her, still looking at it. Slowly her face sobers into a mask of unhappiness*): 410 Ten thousand dollars. (*She hands it to* RUTH) Put it away somewhere, Ruth. (*She does not look at* RUTH; *her eyes seem to be seeing something somewhere very far off*) Ten thousand dollars they give you. Ten thousand dollars.

415 **TRAVIS** (*To his mother, sincerely*): What's the matter with Grandmama—don't she want to be rich?

RUTH (*Distractedly*): You go on out and play now, baby. (TRAVIS *exits.* MAMA *starts wiping dishes absently, humming intently to herself.* RUTH *turns to her, with* 420 *kind exasperation*) You've gone and got yourself upset.

MAMA (*Not looking at her*): I spec if it wasn't for you all . . . I would just put that money away or give it to the church or something.

RUTH: Now what kind of talk is that. Mr. Younger would 425 just be plain mad if he could hear you talking foolish like that.

MAMA (*Stopping and staring off*): Yes . . . he sure would. (*Sighing*) We got enough to do with that money, all right. (*She halts then, and turns and looks at her* 430 *daughter-in-law hard;* RUTH *avoids her eyes and* MAMA *wipes her hands with finality and starts to speak firmly to* RUTH) Where did you go today, girl?

RUTH: To the doctor.

MAMA (*Impatiently*): Now, Ruth . . . you know better 435 than that. Old Doctor Jones is strange enough in his way but there ain't nothing 'bout him make somebody slip and call him "she"—like you done this morning.

RUTH: Well, that's what happened—my tongue slipped.

MAMA: You went to see that woman, didn't you?

440 **RUTH** (*Defensively, giving herself away*): What woman you talking about?

MAMA (*angrily*): That woman who—

(WALTER *enters in great excitement*)

WALTER: Did it come?

MAMA (*Quietly*): Can't you give people a Christian greet-445 ing before you start asking about money?

WALTER (*To* RUTH): Did it come? (RUTH *unfolds the check and lays it quietly before him, watching him intently with thoughts of her own.* WALTER *sits down and grasps it close and counts off the zeros*) Ten thousand dollars—(*He turns suddenly, frantically to his* 450 *mother and draws some papers out of his breast pocket*) Mama—look. Old Willy Harris put everything on paper—

MAMA: Son—I think you ought to talk to your wife . . . I'll go on out and leave you alone if you want— 455

WALTER: I can talk to her later—Mama, look—

MAMA: Son—

WALTER: WILL SOMEBODY PLEASE LISTEN TO ME TODAY!

MAMA (*Quietly*): I don't 'low no yellin' in this house, 460 Walter Lee, and you know it—(WALTER *stares at them in frustration and starts to speak several times*) And there ain't going to be no investing in no liquor stores.

WALTER: But, Mama, you ain't even looked at it.

MAMA: I don't aim to have to speak on that again. 465 (*A long pause*)

WALTER: Oh—so you don't aim to have to speak on that again? So . . . (*Crumpling his papers*). Well, *you* tell that to my boy tonight when you put him to sleep on the living-room couch . . . (*Turning to* MAMA *and* 470 *speaking directly to her*). Yeah—and tell it to my wife, Mama, tomorrow when she has to go out of here to look after somebody else's kids. And tell it to *me*, Mama, every time we need a new pair of curtains and I have to watch *you* go out and work in somebody's 475 kitchen. Yeah, you tell me then! (WALTER *starts out*)

RUTH: Where you going?

WALTER: I'm going out!

RUTH: Where?

WALTER: Just out of this house somewhere— 480

RUTH (*Getting her coat*): I'll come too.

WALTER: I don't want you to come!

RUTH: I got something to talk to you about, Walter.

WALTER: That's too bad.

485 **MAMA** (*Still quietly*):   Walter Lee—(*She waits and he finally turns and looks at her*) Sit down.

WALTER: I'm a grown man, Mama.

MAMA: Ain't nobody said you wasn't grown. But you still in my house and my presence. And as long as you 490 are—you'll talk to your wife civil. Now sit down.

RUTH (*Suddenly*):   Oh, let him go on out and drink himself to death! He makes me sick to my stomach! (*She flings her coat against him*)

WALTER (*Violently*):   And you turn mine too, baby! 495 (*RUTH goes into their bedroom and slams the door behind her.*) That was my greatest mistake—

MAMA (*Still quietly*):   Walter, what is the matter with you?

WALTER: Matter with me? Ain't nothing the matter 500 with *me!*

MAMA: Yes there is. Something eating you up like a crazy man. Something more than me not giving you this money. The past few years I been watching it happen to you. You get all nervous acting and kind of 505 wild in the eyes—(WALTER *jumps up impatiently at her words*) I said sit there now, I'm talking to you!

WALTER: Mama—I don't need no nagging at me today.

MAMA: Seem like you getting to a place where you always tied up in some kind of knot about something. 510 But if anybody ask you 'bout it you just yell at 'em and bust out the house and go out and drink somewheres. Walter Lee, people can't live with that. Ruth's a good, patient girl in her way—but you getting to be too much. Boy, don't make the mistake of driving that girl 515 away from you.

WALTER: Why—what she do for me?

MAMA: She loves you.

WALTER: Mama—I'm going out. I want to go off somewhere and be by myself for a while.

520 **MAMA:**   I'm sorry 'bout your liquor store, son. It just wasn't the thing for us to do. That's what I want to tell you about—

WALTER: I got to go out, Mama—(*He rises*)

MAMA: It's dangerous, son.

WALTER: What's dangerous? 525

MAMA: When a man goes outside his home to look for peace.

WALTER (*Beseechingly*):   Then why can't there never be no peace in this house then?

MAMA: You done found it in some other house? 530

WALTER: No—there ain't no woman! Why do women always think there's a woman somewhere when a man gets restless. (*Coming to her*) Mama—Mama—I want so many things . . .

MAMA: Yes, son— 535

WALTER: I want so many things that they are driving me kind of crazy . . . Mama—look at me.

MAMA: I'm looking at you. You a good-looking boy. You got a job, a nice wife, a fine boy and—

WALTER: A job. (*Looks at her*) Mama, a job? I open and 540 close car doors all day long. I drive a man around in his limousine and I say, "Yes, sir; no, sir; very good, sir; shall I take the Drive, sir?" Mama, that ain't no kind of job . . . that ain't nothing at all. (*Very quietly*) Mama, I don't know if I can make you understand. 545

MAMA: Understand what, baby?

WALTER (*Quietly*):   Sometimes it's like I can see the future stretched out in front of me—just plain as day. The future, Mama. Hanging over there at the edge of my days. Just waiting for me—a big, looming blank 550 space—full of *nothing*. Just waiting for *me*. But it don't have to be. (*Pause*) Mama—sometimes when I'm downtown and I pass them cool, quiet-looking restaurants where them white boys are sitting back and talking 'bout things . . . sitting there turning deals 555 worth millions of dollars . . . sometimes I see guys don't look much older than me—

MAMA: Son—how come you talk so much 'bout money?

WALTER (*With immense passion*):   Because it is life, Mama! 560

MAMA (*Quietly*): Oh—(*Very quietly*) So now it's life. Money is life. Once upon a time freedom used to be life—now it's money. I guess the world really do change . . .

565 **WALTER:** No—it was always money, Mama. We just didn't know about it.

MAMA: No . . . something has changed. (*She looks at him*) You something new, boy. In my time we was worried about not being lynched and getting to the
570 North if we could and how to stay alive and still have a pinch of dignity too . . . Now here come you and Beneatha—talking 'bout things we ain't never even thought about hardly, me and your daddy. You ain't satisfied or proud of nothing we done. I mean that you
575 had a home; that we kept you out of trouble till you was grown; that you don't have to ride to work on the back of nobody's streetcar. You my children—but how different we done become.

WALTER: You just don't understand, Mama, you just
580 don't understand.

MAMA: Son—do you know your wife is expecting another baby? (*WALTER stands, stunned, and absorbs what his mother has said*) That's what she wanted to talk to you about. (*WALTER sinks down into a chair*)
585 This ain't for me to be telling—but you ought to know. (*She waits*) I think Ruth is thinking 'bout getting rid of that child.

WALTER (*Slowly understanding*): —No—no—Ruth wouldn't do that.

590 **MAMA:** When the world gets ugly enough—a woman will do anything for her family. *The part that's already living.*

WALTER: You don't know Ruth, Mama, if you think she would do that. (*RUTH opens the bedroom door and
595 stands there a little limp*)

RUTH (*Beaten*): Yes I would too, Walter. (*Pause*) I gave her a five-dollar down payment. (*There is total silence as the man stares at his wife and the mother stares at her son*)

600 **MAMA** (*Presently*): Well—(*Tightly*) Well—son, I'm waiting to hear you say something . . . I'm waiting to hear how you be your father's son. Be the man he was . . . (*Pause*) Your wife say she going to destroy your child. And I'm waiting to hear you talk like him and say we a people who give children life, not who destroys 605 them—(*She rises*) I'm waiting to see you stand up and look like your daddy and say we done give up one baby to poverty and that we ain't going to give up nary another one . . . I'm waiting.

WALTER: Ruth— 610

MAMA: If you a son of mine, tell her! (*WALTER turns, looks at her and can say nothing*) You . . . you are a disgrace to your father's memory. Somebody get me my hat!

Curtain

ACT 2

SCENE 1 *Time: Later the same day.*

> *At rise:* RUTH *is ironing again. She has the radio going. Presently* BENEATHA's *bedroom door opens and* RUTH's *mouth falls and she puts down the iron in fascination.*

RUTH: What have we got on tonight!

BENEATHA (*Emerging grandly from the doorway so that we can see her thoroughly robed in the costume Asagai brought*): You are looking at what a well-dressed Nigerian woman wears—(*She parades for* RUTH, *her* 5 *hair completely hidden by the headdress; she is coquettishly fanning herself with an ornate oriental fan, mistakenly more like Butterfly than any Nigerian that ever was*) Isn't it beautiful? (*She promenades to the radio and, with an arrogant flourish, turns off the good loud* 10 *blues that is playing*) Enough of this assimilationist junk! (*RUTH follows her with her eyes as she goes to the phonograph and puts on a record and turns and waits ceremoniously for the music to come up. Then, with a shout*) OCOMOGOSIAY! (*RUTH jumps. The music* 15 *comes up, a lovely Nigerian melody.* BENEATHA *listens, enraptured, her eyes far away—"back to the past." She begins to dance.* RUTH *is dumbfounded*)

RUTH: What kind of dance is that?

BENEATHA: A folk dance. 20

RUTH (*Pearl Bailey*):   What kind of folks do that, honey?

BENEATHA: It's from Nigeria. It's a dance of welcome.

RUTH: Who you welcoming?

BENEATHA: The men back to the village.

25 **RUTH:**   Where they been?

BENEATHA: How should I know—out hunting or something. Anyway, they are coming back now . . .

RUTH: Well, that's good.

BENEATHA (*With the record*):
30   *Alundi, alundi*
   Alundi alunya
   Jop pu a jeepua
   Ang gu soooooooooo
   Ai yai yae . . .
35   *Ayehaye—alundi . . .* (WALTER *comes in during this performance; he has obviously been drinking. He leans against the door heavily and watches his sister, at first with distaste. Then his eyes look off—"back to the past"—as he lifts both his fists to the roof, screaming*)

WALTER: YEAH . . . AND ETHIOPIA STRETCH FORTH
40   HER HANDS AGAIN! . . .

RUTH (*Drily, looking at him*):   Yes—and Africa sure is claiming her own tonight. (*She gives them both up and starts ironing again*)

WALTER (*All in a drunken, dramatic shout*):   Shut up! . . .
45   I'm digging them drums . . . them drums move me! . . . (*He makes his weaving way to his wife's face and leans in close to her*) In my *heart of hearts—*(*He thumps his chest*)—I am much warrior!

RUTH (*Without even looking up*):   In your heart of hearts
50   you are much drunkard.

WALTER (*Coming away from her and starting to wander around the room, shouting*):   Me and Jomo . . . (*Intently, in his sister's face. She has stopped dancing to watch him in this unknown mood*) That's my man,
55   Kenyatta. (*Shouting and thumping his chest*) FLAMING SPEAR! HOT DAMN! (*He is suddenly in possession of an imaginary spear and actively spearing enemies all over the room*) OCOMOGOSIAY . . . THE

LION IS WAKING . . . OWIMOWEH! (*He pulls his
60   shirt open and leaps up on a table and gestures with his spear. The bell rings.* RUTH *goes to answer*)

BENEATHA (*To encourage* WALTER, *thoroughly caught up with this side of him*):   OCOMOGOSIAY, FLAMING SPEAR!

WALTER (*On the table, very far gone, his eyes pure glass
65   sheets. He sees what we cannot, that he is a leader of his people, a great chief, a descendant of Chaka, and that the hour to march has come*):   Listen, my black brothers—

BENEATHA: OCOMOGOSIAY!
70

WALTER: Do you hear the waters rushing against the shores of the coastlands—

BENEATHA: OCOMOGOSIAY!

WALTER: Do you hear the screeching of the cocks in yonder hills beyond where the chiefs meet in council
75   for the coming of the mighty war—

BENEATHA: OCOMOGOSIAY!

WALTER: Do you hear the beating of the wings of the birds flying low over the mountains and the low places of our land—(RUTH *opens the door,* GEORGE
80   MURCHISON *enters*)

BENEATHA: OCOMOGOSIAY!

WALTER: —Do you hear the singing of the women, singing the war songs of our fathers to the babies in the great houses . . . singing the sweet war songs? oh, do
85   you hear, my black brothers?

BENEATHA (*Completely gone*):   We hear you, Flaming Spear—

WALTER: Telling us to prepare for the greatness of the time—(*To* GEORGE) Black Brother! (*He extends his
90   hand for the fraternal clasp*)

GEORGE: Black Brother, hell!

RUTH (*Having had enough, and embarrassed for the family*):   Beneatha, you got company—what's the matter with you? Walter Lee Younger, get down off that table
95   and stop acting like a fool . . . (WALTER *comes down*

off the table suddenly and makes a quick exit to the bathroom)

RUTH: He's had a little to drink . . . I don't know what her excuse is.

GEORGE *(To* BENEATHA*):*   Look honey, we're going *to* the theatre—we're not going to be *in* it . . . so go change, huh?

RUTH: You expect this boy to go out with you looking like that?

BENEATHA *(Looking at* GEORGE*):*   That's up to George. If he's ashamed of his heritage—

GEORGE: Oh, don't be so proud of yourself, Bennie—just because you look eccentric.

BENEATHA: How can something that's natural be eccentric?

GEORGE: That's what being eccentric means—being natural. Get dressed.

BENEATHA: I don't like that, George.

RUTH: Why must you and your brother make an argument out of everything people say?

BENEATHA: Because I hate assimilationist Negroes!

RUTH: Will somebody please tell me what assimila-who-ever means!

GEORGE: Oh, it's just a college girl's way of calling people Uncle Toms—but that isn't what it means at all.

RUTH: Well, what does it mean?

BENEATHA *(Cutting* GEORGE *off and staring at him as she replies to* RUTH*):*   It means someone who is willing to give up his own culture and submerge himself completely in the dominant, and in this case, *oppressive* culture!

GEORGE: Oh, dear, dear, dear! Here we go! A lecture on the African past! On our Great West African Heritage! In one second we will hear all about the great Ashanti empires; the great Songhay civilizations; and the great sculpture of Bénin—and then some poetry in the Bantu—and the whole monologue will end

with the word *heritage!* *(Nastily)* Let's face it, baby, your heritage is nothing but a bunch of raggedy-assed spirituals and some grass huts!

BENEATHA: *Grass huts!* (RUTH *crosses to her and forcibly pushes her toward the bedroom)* See there . . . you are standing there in your splendid ignorance talking about people who were the first to smelt iron on the face of the earth! (RUTH *is pushing her through the door)* The Ashanti were performing surgical operations when the English— (RUTH *pulls the door to, with* BENEATHA *on the other side, and smiles graciously at* GEORGE. BENEATHA *opens the door and shouts the end of the sentence defiantly at* GEORGE*)*—were still tatooing themselves with blue dragons! *(She goes back inside)*

RUTH: Have a seat, George *(They both sit.* RUTH *folds her hands rather primly on her lap, determined to demonstrate the civilization of the family)* Warm, ain't it? I mean for September. *(Pause)* Just like they always say about Chicago weather: If it's too hot or cold for you, just wait a minute and it'll change. *(She smiles happily at this cliché of clichés)* Everybody say it's got to do with them bombs and things they keep setting off. *(Pause)* Would you like a nice cold beer?

GEORGE: No, thank you. I don't care for beer. *(He looks at his watch)* I hope she hurries up.

RUTH: What time is the show?

GEORGE: It's an eight-thirty curtain. That's just Chicago, though. In New York standard curtain time is eight forty. *(He is rather proud of this knowledge)*

RUTH *(Properly appreciating it):*   You get to New York a lot?

GEORGE *(Offhand):*   Few times a year.

RUTH: Oh—that's nice. I've never been to New York. (WALTER *enters. We feel he has relieved himself, but the edge of unreality is still with him)*

WALTER: New York ain't got nothing Chicago ain't. Just a bunch of hustling people all squeezed up together—being "Eastern." *(He turns his face into a screw of displeasure)*

GEORGE: Oh—you've been?

175 **WALTER:** *Plenty* of times.

RUTH (*Shocked at the lie*): Walter Lee Younger!

WALTER (*Staring her down*): Plenty! (*Pause*) What we got to drink in this house? Why don't you offer this man some refreshment. (*To* GEORGE) They don't
180 know how to entertain people in this house, man.

GEORGE: Thank you—I don't really care for anything.

WALTER (*Feeling his head; sobriety coming*): Where's Mama?

RUTH: She ain't come back yet.

185 **WALTER** (*Looking* MURCHISON *over from head to toe, scrutinizing his carefully casual tweed sports jacket over cashmere V-neck sweater over soft eyelet shirt and tie, and soft slacks, finished off with white buckskin shoes*): Why all you college boys wear them fairyish
190 white shoes?

RUTH: Walter Lee! (GEORGE MURCHISON *ignores the remark*)

WALTER (*To* RUTH): Well, they look crazy as hell—white shoes, cold as it is.

195 **RUTH** (*Crushed*): You have to excuse him—

WALTER: No he don't! Excuse me for what? What you always excusing me for! I'll excuse myself when I needs to be excused! (*A pause*) They look as funny as them black knee socks Beneatha wears out of here all
200 the time.

RUTH: It's the college *style*, Walter.

WALTER: Style, hell. She looks like she got burnt legs or something!

RUTH: Oh, Walter—

205 **WALTER** (*An irritable mimic*): Oh, Walter! Oh, Walter! (*To* MURCHISON) How's your old man making out? I understand you all going to buy that big hotel on the Drive? (*He finds a beer in the refrigerator, wanders over to* MURCHISON, *sipping and wiping his lips with the
210 back of his hand, and straddling a chair backwards to talk to the other man*) Shrewd move. Your old man is all right, man. (*Tapping his head and half winking for*

emphasis) I mean he knows how to operate. I mean he thinks *big*, you know what I mean, I mean for a *home*, you know? But I think he's kind of running out 215
of ideas now. I'd like to talk to him. Listen, man, I got some plans that could turn this city upside down. I mean I think like he does. *Big*. Invest big, gamble big, hell, lose *big* if you have to, you know what I mean. It's hard to find a man on this whole Southside who un- 220
derstands my kind of thinking—you dig? (*He scrutinizes* MURCHISON *again, drinks his beer, squints his eyes and leans in close, confidential, man to man*) Me and you ought to sit down and talk sometimes, man. Man, I got me some ideas . . . 225

MURCHISON (*With boredom*): Yeah—sometime we'll have to do that, Walter.

WALTER (*Understanding the indifference, and offended*): Yeah—well, when you get the time, man. I know you a busy little boy. 230

RUTH: Walter, please—

WALTER (*Bitterly, hurt*): I know ain't nothing in this world as busy as you colored college boys with your fraternity pins and white shoes . . .

A drunken Walter (Kevin Carroll, *at right*) harangues George Murchison (Jason Dirden), who is Beneatha's date (2011).

235 **RUTH** (*Covering her face with humiliation*): Oh, Walter Lee—

WALTER: I see you all all the time—with the books tucked under your arms—going to your (*British A— a mimic*) "clahsses." And for what! What the hell
240 you learning over there? Filling up your heads— (*Counting off on his fingers*)—with the sociology and the psychology—but they teaching you how to be a man? How to take over and run the world? They teaching you how to run a rubber plantation or a steel
245 mill? Naw—just to talk proper and read books and wear white shoes . . .

GEORGE (*Looking at him with distaste, a little above it all*): You're all wacked up with bitterness, man.

WALTER (*Intently, almost quietly, between the teeth, glar-*
250 *ing at the boy*): And you—ain't you bitter, man? Ain't you just about had it yet? Don't you see no stars gleaming that you can't reach out and grab? You happy?—You contented son-of-a-bitch—you happy? You got it made? Bitter? Man, I'm a volcano. Bitter?
255 Here I am a giant—surrounded by ants! Ants who can't even understand what it is the giant is talking about.

RUTH (*Passionately and suddenly*): Oh, Walter—ain't you with nobody!

260 **WALTER** (*Violently*): No! 'Cause ain't nobody with me! Not even my own mother!

RUTH: Walter, that's a terrible thing to say! (BENEATHA *enters, dressed for the evening in a cocktail dress and earrings*)

265 **GEORGE:** Well—hey, you look great!

BENEATHA: Let's go, George. See you all later.

RUTH: Have a nice time.

GEORGE: Thanks. Good night. (*To* WALTER, *sarcasti-cally*) Good night, Prometheus. (BENEATHA *and*
270 GEORGE *exit*)

WALTER (*To* RUTH): Who is Prometheus?

RUTH: I don't know. Don't worry about it.

WALTER (*In fury, pointing after* GEORGE): See there— they get to a point where they can't insult you man to man—they got to go talk about something ain't no- 275 body never heard of!

RUTH: How do you know it was an insult? (*To humor him*) Maybe Prometheus is a nice fellow.

WALTER: Prometheus! I bet there ain't even no such thing! I bet that simple-minded clown— 280

RUTH: Walter—(*She stops what she is doing and looks at him*)

WALTER (*Yelling*): Don't start!

RUTH: Start what?

WALTER: Your nagging! Where was I? Who was I with? 285 How much money did I spend?

RUTH (*Plaintively*): Walter Lee—why don't we just try to talk about it . . .

WALTER (*Not listening*): I been out talking with people who understand me. People who care about the things 290 I got on my mind.

RUTH (*Wearily*): I guess that means people like Willy Harris.

WALTER: Yes, people like Willy Harris.

RUTH (*With a sudden flash of impatience*): Why don't you 295 all just hurry up and go into the banking business and stop talking about it!

WALTER: Why? You want to know why? 'Cause we all tied up in a race of people that don't know how to do nothing but moan, pray and have babies! (*The line* 300 *is too bitter even for him and he looks at her and sits down*)

RUTH: Oh, Walter . . . (*Softly*) Honey, why can't you stop fighting me?

WALTER (*Without thinking*): Who's fighting you? Who 305 even cares about you? (*This line begins the retardation of his mood*)

RUTH: Well—(*She waits a long time, and then with resig- nation starts to put away her things*) I guess I might

310 as well go on to bed . . . (*More or less to herself*) I don't
know where we lost it . . . but we have . . . (*Then, to
him*) I—I'm sorry about this new baby, Walter. I guess
maybe I better go on and do what I started . . . I guess
I just didn't realize how bad things was with us . . . I
315 guess I just didn't really realize—(*She starts out to the
bedroom and stops*) You want some hot milk?

WALTER: Hot milk?

RUTH: Yes—hot milk.

WALTER: Why hot milk?

320 **RUTH:** 'Cause after all that liquor you come home with
you ought to have something hot in your stomach.

WALTER: I don't want no milk.

RUTH: You want some coffee then?

WALTER: No, I don't want no coffee. I don't want noth-
325 ing hot to drink. (*Almost plaintively*) Why you always
trying to give me something to eat?

RUTH (*Standing and looking at him helplessly*): What
else can I give you, Walter Lee Younger? (*She stands
and looks at him and presently turns to go out again.*
330 *He lifts his head and watches her going away from him
in a new mood which began to emerge when he asked
her "Who cares about you?"*)

WALTER: It's been rough, ain't it, baby? (*She hears and
stops but does not turn around and he continues to her
335 back*) I guess between two people there ain't never as
much understood as folks generally thinks there is.
I mean like between me and you—(*She turns to face
him*) How we gets to the place where we scared to
talk softness to each other. (*He waits, thinking hard
340 himself*) Why you think it got to be like that? (*He is
thoughtful, almost as a child would be*) Ruth, what is it
gets into people ought to be close?

RUTH: I don't know, honey. I think about it a lot.

WALTER: On account of you and me, you mean? The
345 way things are with us. The way something done come
down between us.

RUTH: There ain't so much between us, Walter . . . Not
when you come to me and try to talk to me. Try to be
with me . . . a little even.

WALTER (*Total honesty*): Sometimes . . . sometimes . . . 350
I don't even know how to try.

RUTH: Walter—

WALTER: Yes?

RUTH (*Coming to him, gently and with misgiving, but
coming to him*): Honey . . . life don't have to be like 355
this. I mean sometimes people can do things so that
things are better . . . You remember how we used to
talk when Travis was born . . . about the way we were
going to live . . . the kind of house . . . (*She is stroking
his head*) Well, it's all starting to slip away from us . . . 360
(MAMA *enters, and* WALTER *jumps up and shouts
at her*)

WALTER: Mama, where have you been?

MAMA: My—them steps is longer than they used to be.
Whew! (*She sits down and ignores him*) How you feel- 365
ing this evening, Ruth? (RUTH *shrugs, disturbed some
at having been prematurely interrupted and watching
her husband knowingly*)

WALTER: Mama, where have you been all day?

MAMA (*Still ignoring him and leaning on the table and* 370
changing to more comfortable shoes): Where's Travis?

RUTH: I let him go out earlier and he ain't come back
yet. Boy, is he going to get it!

WALTER: Mama!

MAMA (*As if she has heard him for the first time*): Yes, 375
son?

WALTER: Where did you go this afternoon?

MAMA: I went downtown to tend to some business that
I had to tend to.

WALTER: What kind of business? 380

MAMA: You know better than to question me like a
child, Brother.

WALTER (*Rising and bending over the table*): Where were
you, Mama? (*Bringing his fists down and shouting*)
Mama, you didn't go do something with that insur- 385
ance money, something crazy? (*The front door opens*

slowly, interrupting him, and TRAVIS *peeks his head in, less than hopefully*)

TRAVIS (*To his mother*):   Mama, I—

390   **RUTH:**   "Mama I" nothing! You're going to get it, boy! Get on in that bedroom and get yourself ready!

TRAVIS: But I—

MAMA: Why don't you all never let the child explain hisself.

395   **RUTH:**   Keep out of it now, Lena. (MAMA *clamps her lips together, and* RUTH *advances toward her son menacingly*)

RUTH: A thousand times I have told you not to go off like that—

400   **MAMA** (*Holding out her arms to her grandson*):   Well—at least let me tell him something. I want him to be the first one to hear . . . Come here, Travis. (*The boy obeys, gladly*) Travis—(*She takes him by the shoulder and looks into his face*)—you know that money we got in
405   the mail this morning?

TRAVIS: Yes'm—

MAMA: Well—what you think your grandmama gone and done with that money?

TRAVIS: I don't know, Grandmama.

410   **MAMA** (*Putting her finger on his nose for emphasis*): She went out and she bought you a house! (*The explosion comes from* WALTER *at the end of the revelation and he jumps up and turns away from all of them in a fury.* MAMA *continues, to* TRAVIS) You glad about
415   the house? It's going to be yours when you get to be a man.

TRAVIS: Yeah—I always wanted to live in a house.

MAMA: All right, gimme some sugar then—(TRAVIS *puts his arms around her neck as she watches her son
420   over the boy's shoulder. Then, to* TRAVIS, *after the embrace*) Now when you say your prayers tonight, you thank God and your grandfather—'cause it was him who give you the house—in his way.

RUTH (*Taking the boy from* MAMA *and pushing him toward the bedroom*):   Now you get out of here and get   425 ready for your beating.

TRAVIS: Aw, Mama—

RUTH: Get on in there—(*Closing the door behind him and turning radiantly to her mother-in-law*) So you went and did it!   430

MAMA (*Quietly, looking at her son with pain*):   Yes, I did.

RUTH (*Raising both arms classically*):   Praise God! (*Looks at* WALTER *a moment, who says nothing. She crosses rapidly to her husband*) Please, honey—let me be glad . . . you be glad too. (*She has laid her hands on   435 his shoulders, but he shakes himself free of her roughly, without turning to face her*) Oh, Walter . . . a home . . . a home. (*She comes back to* MAMA) Well—where is it? How big is it? How much it going to cost?

MAMA: Well—   440

RUTH: When we moving?

MAMA (*Smiling at her*):   First of the month.

RUTH (*Throwing back her head with jubilance*):   *Praise God!*

MAMA (*Tentatively, still looking at her son's back turned   445 against her and* RUTH):   It's—it's a nice house too . . . (*She cannot help speaking directly to him. An imploring quality in her voice, her manner, makes her almost like a girl now*) Three bedrooms—nice big one for you and Ruth . . . . Me and Beneatha still have to share   450 our room, but Travis have one of his own—and (*With difficulty*) I figure if the—new baby—is a boy, we could get one of them double-decker outfits . . . And there's a yard with a little patch of dirt where I could maybe get to grow me a few flowers . . . And a nice big   455 basement . . .

RUTH: Walter honey, be glad—

MAMA (*Still to his back, fingering things on the table*): 'Course I don't want to make it sound fancier than it is . . . It's just a plain little old house—but it's made good   460 and solid—and it will be *ours*. Walter Lee—it makes a difference in a man when he can walk on floors that belong to *him* . . .

RUTH: Where is it?

465 **MAMA** (*Frightened at this telling*): Well—well—it's out there in Clybourne Park— (RUTH's *radiance fades abruptly, and* WALTER *finally turns slowly to face his mother with incredulity and hostility*)

RUTH: Where?

470 **MAMA** (*Matter-of-factly*): Four o six Clybourne Street, Clybourne Park.

RUTH: Clybourne Park? Mama, there ain't no colored people living in Clybourne Park.

MAMA (*Almost idiotically*): Well, I guess there's going to
475 be some now.

WALTER (*Bitterly*): So that's the peace and comfort you went out and bought for us today!

MAMA (*Raising her eyes to meet his finally*): Son—I just tried to find the nicest place for the least amount of
480 money for my family.

RUTH (*Trying to recover from the shock*): Well—well— 'course I ain't one never been 'fraid of no crackers, mind you—but—well, wasn't there no other houses nowhere?

485 **MAMA:** Them houses they put up for colored in them areas way out all seem to cost twice as much as other houses. I did the best I could.

RUTH (*Struck senseless with the news, in its various degrees of goodness and trouble, she sits a moment, her fists
490 propping her chin in thought, and then she starts to rise, bringing her fists down with vigor, the radiance spreading from cheek to cheek again*): Well—well!— All I can say is—if this is my time in life—*my time*— to say good-bye—(*And she builds with momentum as
495 she starts to circle the room with an exuberant, al- most tearfully happy release*)—to these Goddamned cracking walls!—(*She pounds the walls*)—and these marching roaches!—(*She wipes at an imaginary army of marching roaches*)—and this cramped little closet
500 which ain't now or never was no kitchen! . . . then I say it loud and good, *Hallelujah!* And good-bye mis- ery . . . I don't never want to see your ugly face again!

(*She laughs joyously, having practically destroyed the apartment, and flings her arms up and lets them come
505 down happily, slowly, reflectively, over her abdomen, aware for the first time perhaps that the life therein pulses with happiness and not despair*) Lena?

MAMA (*Moved, watching her happiness*): Yes, honey?

RUTH (*Looking off*): Is there—is there a whole lot of
510 sunlight?

MAMA (*Understanding*): Yes, child, there's a whole lot of sunlight. (*Long pause*)

RUTH (*Collecting herself and going to the door of the room TRAVIS is in*): Well—I guess I better see 'bout
515 Travis. (*To* MAMA) Lord, I sure don't feel like whip- ping nobody today! (*She exits*)

MAMA (*The mother and son are left alone now and the mother waits a long time, considering deeply, before she speaks*): Son—you—you understand what I done,
520 don't you? (WALTER *is silent and sullen*) I—I just seen my family falling apart today . . . just falling to pieces in front of my eyes . . . We couldn't of gone on like we was today. We was going backwards 'stead of forwards—talking 'bout killing babies and wishing
525 each other was dead . . . When it gets like that in life— you just got to do something different, push on out and do something bigger . . . (*She waits*) I wish you say something, son . . . I wish you'd say how deep inside you you think I done the right thing—

530 **WALTER** (*Crossing slowly to his bedroom door and finally turning there and speaking measuredly*): What you need me to say you done right for? *You* the head of this family. You run our lives like you want to. It was your money and you did what you wanted with it. So
535 what you need for me to say it was all right for? (*Bit- terly, to hurt her as deeply as he knows is possible*) So you butchered up a dream of mine—you—who always talking 'bout your children's dreams . . .

MAMA: Walter Lee— (*He just closes the door behind him.* MAMA *sits alone, thinking heavily*)
540

Curtain

SCENE 2 *Time:* *Friday night. A few weeks later.*

> *At rise:* *Packing crates mark the intention of the family to move.* BENEATHA *and* GEORGE *come in, presumably from an evening out again.*

GEORGE: O.K. . . . O.K., whatever you say . . . *(They both sit on the couch. He tries to kiss her. She moves away)* Look, we've had a nice evening; let's not spoil it, huh? . . . *(He again turns her head and tries to nuzzle in and she turns away from him, not with distaste but with momentary lack of interest; in a mood to pursue what they were talking about)*

BENEATHA: I'm *trying* to talk to you.

GEORGE: We always talk.

BENEATHA: Yes—and I love to talk.

GEORGE *(Exasperated; rising):* I know it and I don't mind it sometimes . . . I want you to cut it out, see— The moody stuff, I mean. I don't like it. You're a nice-looking girl . . . all over. That's all you need, honey, forget the atmosphere. Guys aren't going to go for the atmosphere—they're going to go for what they see. Be glad for that. Drop the Garbo routine. It doesn't go with you. As for myself, I want a nice—*(Groping)*—simple *(Thoughtfully)*—sophisticated girl . . . not a poet—O.K.? *(He starts to kiss her, she rebuffs him again and he starts to leave)*

BENEATHA: Why are you angry?

GEORGE: Because this is stupid! I don't go out with you to discuss the nature of "quiet desperation" or to hear all about your thoughts—because the world will go on thinking what it thinks regardless—

BENEATHA: Then why read books? Why go to school?

GEORGE *(With artificial patience, counting on his fingers):* It's simple. You read books—to learn facts—to get grades—to pass the course—to get a degree. That's all—it has nothing to do with thoughts. *(A long pause)*

BENEATHA: I see. *(A longer pause as she looks at him)* Good night, George. (GEORGE *looks at her a little oddly, and starts to exit. He meets* MAMA *coming in)*

GEORGE: Oh—hello, Mrs. Younger.

MAMA: Hello, George, how you feeling?

GEORGE: Fine—fine, how are you?

MAMA: Oh, a little tired. You know them steps can get you after a day's work. You all have a nice time tonight?

GEORGE: Yes—a fine time. Well, good night.

MAMA: Well, good night.

MAMA: Good night. *(He exits.* MAMA *closes the door behind her)* Hello, honey. What you sitting like that for?

BENEATHA: I'm just sitting.

MAMA: Didn't you have a nice time?

BENEATHA: No.

MAMA: No? What's the matter?

BENEATHA: Mama, George is a fool—honest. *(She rises)*

MAMA *(Hustling around unloading the packages she has entered with. She stops):* Is he, baby?

BENEATHA: Yes. (BENEATHA *makes up* TRAVIS' *bed as she talks)*

MAMA: You sure?

BENEATHA: Yes.

MAMA: Well—I guess you better not waste your time with no fools. (BENEATHA *looks up at her mother, watching her put groceries in the refrigerator. Finally she gathers up her things and starts into the bedroom. At the door she stops and looks back at her mother)*

BENEATHA: Mama—

MAMA: Yes, baby—

BENEATHA: Thank you.

MAMA: For what?

BENEATHA: For understanding me this time. *(She exits quickly and the mother stands, smiling a little, looking at the place where* BENEATHA *had stood.* RUTH *enters)*

RUTH: Now don't you fool with any of this stuff, Lena—

MAMA: Oh, I just thought I'd sort a few things out. *(The phone rings.* RUTH *answers)*

RUTH *(At the phone)*: Hello—Just a minute. *(Goes to door)* Walter, it's Mrs. Arnold. *(Waits. Goes back to the phone. Tense)* Hello. Yes, this is his wife speaking . . . He's lying down now. Yes . . . well, he'll be in tomorrow. He's been very sick. Yes—I know we should have called, but we were so sure he'd be able to come in today. Yes—yes, I'm very sorry. Yes . . . Thank you very much. *(She hangs up.* WALTER *is standing in the doorway of the bedroom behind her)* That was Mrs. Arnold.

WALTER *(Indifferently)*: Was it?

RUTH: She said if you don't come in tomorrow that they are getting a new man. . . .

WALTER: Ain't that sad—ain't that crying sad.

RUTH: She said Mr. Arnold has had to take a cab for three days . . . Walter, you ain't been to work for three days! *(This is a revelation to her)* Where you been, Walter Lee Younger? (WALTER *looks at her and starts to laugh)* You're going to lose your job.

WALTER: That's right . . . *(He turns on the radio)*

RUTH: Oh, Walter, and with your mother working like a dog every day—

WALTER: That's sad too—Everything is sad.

MAMA: What you been doing for these three days, son?

WALTER: Mama—you don't know all the things a man what got leisure can find to do in this city . . . What's this—Friday night? Well—Wednesday I borrowed Willy Harris' car and I went for a drive . . . just me and myself and I drove and drove . . . Way out . . . way past South Chicago, and I parked the car and I sat and looked at the steel mills all day long. I just sat in the car and looked at them big black chimneys for hours. Then I drove back and I went to the Green Hat. *(Pause)* And Thursday—Thursday I borrowed the car again and I got in it and I pointed it the other way and I drove the other way—for hours—way, way up to Wisconsin, and I looked at the farms. I just drove and looked at the farms. Then I drove back and I went to

Mama (Claudia McNeil) trusts Walter (Sidney Poitier) with the remainder of the insurance money (1961).

the Green Hat. *(Pause)* And today—today I didn't get the car. Today I just walked. All over the Southside. And I looked at the Negroes and they looked at me and finally I just sat down on the curb at Thirty-ninth and South Parkway and I just sat there and watched the Negroes go by. And then I went to the Green Hat. You all sad? You all depressed? And you know where I am going right now— (RUTH *goes out quietly)*

MAMA: Oh, Big Walter, is this the harvest of our days?

WALTER: You know what I like about the Green Hat? *(He turns the radio on and a steamy, deep blues pours into the room)* I like this little cat they got there who blows a sax . . . He blows. He talks to me. He ain't but 'bout five feet tall and he's got a conked head and his eyes is always closed and he's all music—

MAMA *(Rising and getting some papers out of her handbag)*: Walter—

WALTER: And there's this other guy who plays the piano . . . and they got a sound. I mean they can work on some music . . . They got the best little combo in the world in the Green Hat . . . You can just sit there and drink and listen to them three men play and you realize that don't nothing matter worth a damn, but just being there—

MAMA: I've helped do it to you, haven't I, son? Walter, I been wrong.

135 **WALTER:** Naw—you ain't never been wrong about nothing, Mama.

MAMA: Listen to me, now. I say I been wrong, son. That I been doing to you what the rest of the world been doing to you. Walter—what you ain't never under-
140 stood is that I ain't got nothing, don't own nothing, ain't never really wanted nothing that wasn't for you. There ain't nothing as precious to me . . . There ain't nothing worth holding on to, money, dreams, nothing else—if it means—if it means it's going to destroy my boy. (*She puts her papers in front of him and he*
145 *watches her without speaking or moving*) I paid the man thirty-five hundred dollars down on the house. That leaves sixty-five hundred dollars. Monday morning I want you to take this money and take three thousand dollars and put it in a savings account for
150 Beneatha's medical schooling. The rest you put in a checking account—with your name on it. And from now on any penny that come out of it or that go in it is for you to look after. For you to decide. (*She drops her hands a little helplessly*) It ain't much, but it's all I
155 got in the world and I'm putting it in your hands. I'm telling you to be the head of this family from now on like you supposed to be.

WALTER (*Stares at the money*): You trust me like that, Mama?

160 **MAMA:** I ain't never stop trusting you. Like I ain't never stop loving you. (*She goes out, and* WALTER *sits looking at the money on the table. Finally, in a decisive gesture, he gets up, and, in mingled joy and desperation, picks up the money. At the same moment,* TRAVIS
165 *enters for bed*)

TRAVIS: What's the matter, Daddy? You drunk?

WALTER (*Sweetly, more sweetly than we have ever known him*): No, Daddy ain't drunk. Daddy ain't going to never be drunk again . . .

170 **TRAVIS:** Well, good night, Daddy. (*The* FATHER *has come from behind the couch and leans over, embracing his son*)

WALTER: Son, I feel like talking to you tonight.

TRAVIS: About what?

WALTER: Oh, about a lot of things. About you and what 175 kind of man you going to be when you grow up . . . . Son—son, what do you want to be when you grow up?

TRAVIS: A bus driver.

WALTER (*Laughing a little*): A what? Man, that ain't nothing to want to be! 180

TRAVIS: Why not?

WALTER: 'Cause, man—it ain't big enough—you know what I mean.

TRAVIS: I don't know then. I can't make up my mind. Sometimes Mama asks me that too. And sometimes 185 when I tell her I just want to be like you—she says she don't want me to be like that and sometimes she says she does . . .

WALTER (*Gathering him up in his arms*): You know what, Travis? In seven years you going to be seventeen 190 years old. And things is going to be very different with us in seven years, Travis . . . One day when you are seventeen I'll come home—home from my office downtown somewhere—

TRAVIS: You don't work in no office, Daddy. 195

WALTER: No—but after tonight. After what your daddy gonna do tonight, there's going to be offices—a whole lot of offices . . .

TRAVIS: What you gonna do tonight, Daddy?

WALTER: You wouldn't understand yet, son, but your 200 daddy's gonna make a transaction . . . a business transaction that's going to change our lives . . . That's how come one day when you 'bout seventeen years old I'll come home and I'll be pretty tired, you know what I mean, after a day of conferences and secretaries 205 getting things wrong the way they do . . . 'cause an executive's life is hell, man—(*The more he talks the farther away he gets*) And I'll pull the car up on the driveway . . . just a plain black Chrysler, I think, with white walls—no—black tires. More elegant. Rich peo- 210 ple don't have to be flashy . . . though I'll have to get something a little sportier for Ruth—maybe a Cadillac convertible to do her shopping in . . . And I'll come up the steps to the house and the gardener will be clipping away at the hedges and he'll say, "Good evening, Mr. Younger." And I'll say, "Hello, Jefferson, how are you this evening?" And I'll go inside and Ruth will come downstairs and meet me at the door and we'll kiss each other and she'll take my arm and we'll go up to your room to see you sitting on the floor with the catalogues of all the great schools in America around you . . . All the great schools in the world! And—and I'll say, all right son—it's your seventeenth birthday, what is it you've decided? . . . Just tell me where you want to go to school and you'll *go*. Just tell me, what it is you want to be—and you'll *be* it . . . . Whatever you want to be—Yessir! (*He holds his arms open for* TRA-VIS) You just name it, son . . . (TRAVIS *leaps into them*) and I hand you the world! (WALTER's *voice has risen in pitch and hysterical promise and on the last line he lifts* TRAVIS *high*)

(*Blackout*)

SCENE 3 *Time: Saturday, moving day, one week later.*

Before the curtain rises, RUTH's *voice, a strident, dramatic church alto, cuts through the silence. It is, in the darkness, a triumphant surge, a penetrating statement of expectation: "Oh, Lord, I don't feel no ways tired! Children, oh, glory hallelujah!"*

As the curtain rises we see that RUTH *is alone in the living room, finishing up the family's packing. It is moving day. She is nailing crates and tying cartons.* BENEATHA *enters, carrying a guitar case, and watches her exuberant sister-in-law.*

RUTH: Hey!

BENEATHA (*Putting away the case*): Hi.

RUTH (*Pointing at a package*): Honey—look in that package there and see what I found on sale this morning at the South Center. (RUTH *gets up and moves to the package and draws out some curtains*) Lookahere—hand-turned hems!

BENEATHA: How do you know the window size out there?

RUTH (*Who hadn't thought of that*): Oh—Well, they bound to fit something in the whole house. Anyhow, they was too good a bargain to pass up. (RUTH *slaps her head, suddenly remembering something*) Oh, Bennie—I meant to put a special note on that carton over there. That's your mama's good china and she wants 'em to be very careful with it.

BENEATHA: I'll do it. (BENEATHA *finds a piece of paper and starts to draw large letters on it*)

RUTH: You know what I'm going to do soon as I get in that new house?

BENEATHA: What?

RUTH: Honey—I'm going to run me a tub of water up to here . . . (*With her fingers practically up to her nostrils*) And I'm going to get in it—and I am going to sit . . . and sit . . . and sit in that hot water and the first person who knocks to tell *me* to hurry up and come out—

BENEATHA: Gets shot at sunrise.

RUTH (*Laughing happily*): You said it, sister! (*Noticing how large* BENEATHA *is absent-mindedly making the note*) Honey, they ain't going to read that from no airplane.

BENEATHA (*Laughing herself*): I guess I always think things have more emphasis if they are big, somehow.

RUTH (*Looking up at her and smiling*): You and your brother seem to have that as a philosophy of life. Lord, that man—done changed so 'round here. You know—you know what we did last night? Me and Walter Lee?

BENEATHA: What?

RUTH (*Smiling to herself*): We went to the movies. (*Looking at* BENEATHA *to see if she understands*) We went to the movies. You know the last time me and Walter went to the movies together?

BENEATHA: No.

RUTH: Me neither. That's how long it been. (*Smiling again*) But we went last night. The picture wasn't much good, but that didn't seem to matter. We went—and we held hands.

BENEATHA: Oh, Lord!

RUTH: We held hands—and you know what?

50 **BENEATHA:**   What?

RUTH: When we come out of the show it was late and dark and all the stores and things was closed up . . . and it was kind of chilly and there wasn't many people
55   on the streets . . . and we was still holding hands, me and Walter.

BENEATHA: You're killing me. (WALTER *enters with a large package. His happiness is deep in him; he cannot keep still with his new-found exuberance. He is sing-*
60   *ing and wiggling and snapping his fingers. He puts his package in a corner and puts a phonograph record, which he has brought in with him, on the record player. As the music comes up he dances over to* RUTH *and tries to get her to dance with him. She gives in at last to*
65   *his raunchiness and in a fit of giggling allows herself to be drawn into his mood and together they deliberately burlesque an old social dance of their youth)*

BENEATHA (*Regarding them a long time as they dance, then drawing in her breath for a deeply exaggerated comment which she does not particularly mean*):   Talk
70   about—olddddddddddd—fashionedddddddd—Negroes!

WALTER (*Stopping momentarily*):   What kind of Ne-groes? (*He says this in fun. He is not angry with her today, nor with anyone. He starts to dance with his wife again*)

75 **BENEATHA:**   Old-fashioned.

WALTER (*As he dances with* RUTH):   You know, when these *New Negroes* have their convention—(*Pointing at his sister*)—that is going to be the chairman of the Committee on Unending Agitation. (*He goes on danc-*
80   *ing, then stops*) Race, race, race! . . . Girl, I do believe you are the first person in the history of the entire human race to successfully brainwash yourself. (BENEATHA *breaks up and he goes on dancing. He stops again, enjoying his tease*) Damn, even the
85   N double A C P takes a holiday sometimes! (BE-NEATHA *and* RUTH *laugh. He dances with* RUTH *some more and starts to laugh and stops and panto-mimes someone over an operating table*) I can just see that chick someday looking down at some poor cat
90   on an operating table and before she starts to slice him, she says . . . (*Pulling his sleeves back maliciously*) "By the way, what are your views on civil rights down

Ruth (Audra McDonald) and Walter (Sean Combs) dance in the 2008 ABC-TVM production directed by Kenny Leon.

there? . . ." (*He laughs at her again and starts to dance happily. The bell sounds*)

BENEATHA: Sticks and stones may break my bones   95 but . . . words will never hurt me! (BENEATHA *goes to the door and opens it as* WALTER *and* RUTH *go on with the clowning.* BENEATHA *is somewhat surprised to see a quiet-looking middle-aged white man in a business suit holding his hat and a briefcase in his hand and*   100 *consulting a small piece of paper*)

MAN: Uh—how do you do, miss. I am looking for a Mrs.—*(He looks at the slip of paper)* Mrs. Lena Younger?

105 **BENEATHA** *(Smoothing her hair with slight embarrassment)*: Oh—yes, that's my mother. Excuse me *(She closes the door and turns to quiet the other two)* Ruth! Brother! Somebody's here. *(Then she opens the door. The man casts a curious quick glance at all three of*
110 *them)* Uh—come in please.

MAN *(Coming in)*: Thank you.

BENEATHA: My mother isn't here just now. Is it business?

MAN: Yes . . . well, of a sort.

115 **WALTER** *(Freely, the Man of the House)*: Have a seat. I'm Mrs. Younger's son. I look after most of her business matters. *(RUTH and BENEATHA exchange amused glances)*

MAN *(Regarding WALTER, and sitting)*: Well—My name
120 is Karl Lindner . . .

WALTER *(Stretching out his hand)*: Walter Younger. This is my wife—*(RUTH nods politely)*—and my sister.

LINDNER: How do you do.

125 **WALTER** *(Amiably, as he sits himself easily on a chair, leaning forward on his knees with interest and looking expectantly into the newcomer's face)*: What can we do for you, Mr. Lindner!

LINDNER *(Some minor shuffling of the hat and briefcase on his knees)*: Well—I am a representative of the
130 Clybourne Park Improvement Association—

WALTER *(Pointing)*: Why don't you sit your things on the floor?

LINDNER: Oh—yes. Thank you. *(He slides the briefcase and hat under the chair)* And as I was saying—I am
135 from the Clybourne Park Improvement Association and we have had it brought to our attention at the last meeting that you people—or at least your mother—has bought a piece of residential property at—*(He digs for the slip of paper again)*—four o six Clybourne
140 Street . . .

WALTER: That's right. Care for something to drink? Ruth, get Mr. Lindner a beer.

LINDNER *(Upset for some reason)*: Oh—no, really. I mean thank you very much, but no thank you.

RUTH *(Innocently)*: Some coffee? 145

LINDNER: Thank you, nothing at all. *(BENEATHA is watching the man carefully)*

LINDNER: Well, I don't know how much you folks know about our organization. *(He is a gentle man; thoughtful and somewhat labored in his manner)* It is one of 150
these community organizations set up to look after—oh, you know, things like block upkeep and special projects and we also have what we call our New Neighbors Orientation Committee . . .

BENEATHA *(Drily)*: Yes—and what do they do? 155

LINDNER *(Turning a little to her and then returning the main force to WALTER)*: Well—it's what you might call a sort of welcoming committee, I guess. I mean they, we—I'm the chairman of the committee—go around and see the new people who move into the 160
neighborhood and sort of give them the lowdown on the way we do things in Clybourne Park.

BENEATHA *(With appreciation of the two meanings, which escape RUTH and WALTER)*: Uh-huh.

LINDNER: And we also have the category of what the 165
association calls—*(He looks elsewhere)*—uh—special community problems . . .

BENEATHA: Yes—and what are some of those?

WALTER: Girl, let the man talk.

LINDNER *(With understated relief)*: Thank you. I would 170
sort of like to explain this thing in my own way. I mean I want to explain to you in a certain way.

WALTER: Go ahead.

LINDNER: Yes. Well. I'm going to try to get right to the point. I'm sure we'll all appreciate that in the 175
long run.

BENEATHA: Yes.

WALTER: Be still now!

LINDNER: Well—

180 **RUTH** (*Still innocently*): Would you like another chair—you don't look comfortable.

LINDNER (*More frustrated than annoyed*): No, thank you very much. Please. Well—to get right to the point I—(*A great breath, and he is off at last*) I am sure you
185 people must be aware of some of the incidents which have happened in various parts of the city when colored people have moved into certain areas—(BENEATHA *exhales heavily and starts tossing a piece of fruit up and down in the air*) Well—because
190 we have what I think is going to be a unique type of organization in American community life—not only do we deplore that kind of thing—but we are trying to do something about it. (BENEATHA *stops tossing and turns with a new and quizzical interest to the man*) We
195 feel—(*gaining confidence in his mission because of the interest in the faces of the people he is talking to*)—we feel that most of the trouble in this world, when you come right down to it—(*He hits his knee for emphasis*)—most of the trouble exists because people just
200 don't sit down and talk to each other.

RUTH (*Nodding as she might in church, pleased with the remark*): You can say that again, mister.

LINDNER (*More encouraged by such affirmation*): That we don't try hard enough in this world to understand
205 the other fellow's problem. The other guy's point of view.

RUTH: Now that's right. (BENEATHA *and* WALTER *merely watch and listen with genuine interest*)

LINDNER: Yes—that's the way we feel out in Clybourne
210 Park. And that's why I was elected to come here this afternoon and talk to you people. Friendly like, you know, the way people should talk to each other and see if we couldn't find some way to work this thing out. As I say, the whole business is a matter of *caring*
215 about the other fellow. Anybody can see that you are a nice family of folks, hard working and honest I'm sure. (BENEATHA *frowns slightly, quizzically, her head tilted regarding him*) Today everybody knows what it means to be on the outside of *something*. And
220 of course, there is always somebody who is out to take advantage of people who don't always understand.

WALTER: What do you mean?

LINDNER: Well—you see our community is made up of people who've worked hard as the dickens for years to build up that little community. They're not rich and
225 fancy people; just hard-working, honest people who don't really have much but those little homes and a dream of the kind of community they want to raise their children in. Now, I don't say we are perfect and there is a lot wrong in some of the things they want.
230 But you've got to admit that a man, right or wrong, has the right to want to have the neighborhood he lives in a certain kind of way. And at the moment the overwhelming majority of our people out there feel that people get along better, take more of a com-
235 mon interest in the life of the community, when they share a common background. I want you to believe me when I tell you that race prejudice simply doesn't enter into it. It is a matter of the people of Clybourne Park believing, rightly or wrongly, as I say, that for the
240 happiness of all concerned that our Negro families are happier when they live in their *own* communities.

BENEATHA (*With a grand and bitter gesture*): This, friends, is the Welcoming Committee!

WALTER (*dumbfounded, looking at* LINDNER): Is this
245 what you came marching all the way over here to tell us?

LINDNER: Well, now we've been having a fine conversation. I hope you'll hear me all the way through.

WALTER (*Tightly*): Go ahead, man.
250

LINDNER: You see—in the face of all the things I have said, we are prepared to make your family a very generous offer . . .

BENEATHA: Thirty pieces and not a coin less!

WALTER: Yeah?
255

LINDNER (*Putting on his glasses and drawing a form out of the briefcase*): Our association is prepared, through the collective effort of our people, to buy the house from you at a financial gain to your family.

RUTH: Lord have mercy, ain't this the living gall!
260

WALTER: All right, you through?

Carl Lindner (John Stamos) tells the family (*from left,* Sanaa Latham, Phylicia Rashad, Audra McDonald, and Justin Martin) about his offer and they all listen to Walter's response (2008).

LINDNER: Well, I want to give you the exact terms of the financial arrangement—

WALTER: We don't want to hear no exact terms of no ar-
265 rangements. I want to know if you got any more to tell us 'bout getting together?

LINDNER (*Taking off his glasses*): Well—I don't suppose that you feel . . .

WALTER: Never mind how I feel—you got any more to
270 say 'bout how people ought to sit down and talk to each other? . . . Get out of my house, man. (*He turns his back and walks to the door*)

LINDNER (*Looking around at the hostile faces and reaching and assembling his hat and briefcase*): Well—I don't
275 understand why you people are reacting this way. What do you think you are going to gain by moving into a neighborhood where you just aren't wanted and where some elements—well—people can get awful worked up when they feel that their whole way of life
280 and everything they've ever worked for is threatened.

WALTER: Get out.

LINDNER (*At the door, holding a small card*): Well—I'm sorry it went like this.

WALTER: Get out.

285 **LINDNER** (*Almost sadly regarding* WALTER): You just can't force people to change their hearts, son. (*He

turns and put his card on a table and exits.* WALTER *pushes the door to with stinging hatred, and stands looking at it.* RUTH *just sits and* BENEATHA *just stands. They say nothing.* MAMA *and* TRAVIS *enter*) 290

MAMA: Well—this all the packing got done since I left out of here this morning. I testify before God that my children got all the energy of the dead! What time the moving men due?

BENEATHA: Four o'clock. You had a caller, Mama. (*She 295 is smiling, teasingly*)

MAMA: Sure enough—who?

BENEATHA (*Her arms folded saucily*): The Welcoming Committee. (WALTER *and* RUTH *giggle*)

MAMA (*Innocently*): Who? 300

BENEATHA: The Welcoming Committee. They said they're sure going to be glad to see you when you get there.

WALTER (*Devilishly*): Yeah, they said they can't hardly wait to see your face. (*Laughter*) 305

MAMA (*Sensing their facetiousness*): What's the matter with you all?

WALTER: Ain't nothing the matter with us. We just telling you 'bout the gentleman who came to see you this afternoon. From the Clybourne Park Improvement 310 Association.

MAMA: What he want?

RUTH (*In the same mood as* BENEATHA *and* WALTER): To welcome you, honey.

WALTER: He said they can't hardly wait. He said the one 315 thing they don't have, that they just *dying* to have out there is a fine family of fine colored people! (*To* RUTH *and* BENEATHA) Ain't that right!

RUTH (*Mockingly*): Yeah! He left his card in case—(*They indicate the card and* MAMA *picks it up and throws 320 it on the floor—understanding and looking off as she draws her chair up to the table on which she has put her plant and some sticks and some cord*)

MAMA: Father, give us strength. (*Knowingly—and without fun*) Did he threaten us?

BENEATHA: Oh—Mama—they don't do it like that any more. He talked Brotherhood. He said everybody ought to learn how to sit down and hate each other with good Christian fellowship. (*She and* WALTER *shake hands to ridicule the remark*)

MAMA (*Sadly*): Lord, protect us . . .

RUTH: You should hear the money those folks raised to buy the house from us. All we paid and then some.

BENEATHA: What they think we going to do—eat 'em?

RUTH: No, honey, marry 'em.

MAMA (*Shaking her head*): Lord, Lord, Lord . . .

RUTH: Well—that's the way the crackers crumble. Joke.

BENEATHA (*Laughingly noticing what her mother is doing*): Mama, what are you doing?

MAMA: Fixing my plant so it won't get hurt none on the way . . .

BENEATHA: Mama, you going to take *that* to the new house?

MAMA: Un-huh—

BENEATHA: That raggedy-looking old thing?

MAMA (*Stopping and looking at her*): It expresses *me*!

RUTH (*With delight, to* BENEATHA): So there, Miss Thing! (WALTER *comes to* MAMA *suddenly and bends down behind her and squeezes her in his arms with all his strength. She is overwhelmed by the suddenness of it and, though delighted, her manner is like that of* RUTH *and* TRAVIS)

MAMA: Look out now, boy! You make me mess up my thing here!

WALTER (*His face lit, he slips down on his knees beside her, his arms still about her*): Mama . . . you know what it means to climb up in the chariot?

MAMA (*Gruffly, very happy*): Get on away from me now . . .

RUTH (*Near the gift-wrapped package, trying to catch* WALTER's *eye*): Psst—

WALTER: What the old song say, Mama . . .

RUTH: Walter—Now? (*She is pointing at the package*)

WALTER (*Speaking the lines, sweetly, playfully, in his mother's face*):
I got wings . . . you got wings . . .
All God's Children got wings . . .

MAMA: Boy—get out of my face and do some work . . .

WALTER:
When I get to heaven gonna put on my wings,
Gonna fly all over God's heaven . . .

BENEATHA (*Teasingly, from across the room*): Everybody talking 'bout heaven ain't going there!

WALTER (*To* RUTH, *who is carrying the box across to them*): I don't know, you think we ought to give her that . . . Seems to me she ain't been very appreciative around here.

MAMA (*Eying the box, which is obviously a gift*): What is that?

WALTER (*Taking it from* RUTH *and putting it on the table in front of* MAMA): Well—what you all think? Should we give it to her?

RUTH: Oh—she was pretty good today.

MAMA: I'll good you— (*She turns her eyes to the box again*)

BENEATHA: Open it, Mama. (*She stands up, looks at it, turns and looks at all of them, and then presses her hands together and does not open the package*)

WALTER (*Sweetly*): Open it, Mama. It's for you. (MAMA *looks in his eyes. It is the first present in her life without its being Christmas. Slowly she opens her package and lifts out, one by one, a brand-new sparkling set of gardening tools.* WALTER *continues, prodding*) Ruth made up the note—read it . . .

MAMA (*Picking up the card and adjusting her glasses*): "To our own Mrs. Miniver—Love from Brother, Ruth and Beneatha." Ain't that lovely . . .

Mama (L. Scott Caldwell) dons the gardening hat that her grandson has given her, and the family (*from left,* Deirdrie Henry, Kevin Carroll, Brandon David Brown, and Kenya Alexander) laugh good-naturedly (2011).

TRAVIS (*Tugging at his father's sleeve*):   Daddy, can I give her mine now?

WALTER: All right, son. (TRAVIS *flies to get his gift*)
400   Travis didn't want to go in with the rest of us, Mama. He got his own. (*Somewhat amused*) We don't know what it is . . .

TRAVIS (*Racing back in the room with a large hatbox and putting it in front of his grandmother*):   Here!

405 **MAMA:**   Lord have mercy, baby. You done gone and bought your grandmother a hat?

TRAVIS (*Very proud*):   Open it! (*She does and lifts out an elaborate, but very elaborate, wide gardening hat, and all the adults break up at the sight of it*)

410 **RUTH:**   Travis, honey, what is that?

TRAVIS (*Who thinks it is beautiful and appropriate*):   It's a gardening hat! Like the ladies always have on in the magazines when they work in their gardens.

BENEATHA (*Giggling fiercely*):   Travis—we were trying to
415   make Mama Mrs. Miniver—not Scarlett O'Hara!

MAMA (*Indignantly*):   What's the matter with you all! This here is a beautiful hat! (*Absurdly*) I always

wanted me one just like it! (*She pops it on her head to prove it to her grandson, and the hat is ludicrous and considerably oversized*)   420

RUTH: Hot dog! Go, Mama!

WALTER (*Doubled over with laughter*):   I'm sorry, Mama—but you look like you ready to go out and chop you some cotton sure enough! (*They all laugh except* MAMA, *out of deference to* TRAVIS' *feelings*)   425

MAMA (*Gathering the boy up to her*):   Bless your heart— this is the prettiest hat I ever owned—(WALTER, RUTH *and* BENEATHA *chime in—noisily, festively and insincerely congratulating* TRAVIS *on his gift*) What are we all standing around here for? We ain't   430 finished packin' yet. Bennie, you ain't packed one book. (*The bell rings*)

BENEATHA: That couldn't be the movers . . . it's not hardly two o'clock yet— (BENEATHA *goes into her room.* MAMA *starts for door*)   435

WALTER (*Turning, stiffening*):   Wait—wait—I'll get it. (*He stands and looks at the door*)

MAMA: You expecting company, son?

WALTER (*Just looking at the door*):   Yeah—yeah . . . (MAMA *looks at* RUTH, *and they exchange innocent*   440 *and unfrightened glances*)

MAMA (*Not understanding*):   Well, let them in, son.

BENEATHA (*From her room*):   We need some more string.

MAMA: Travis—you run to the hardware and get me some string cord. (MAMA *goes out and* WALTER *turns*   445 *and looks at* RUTH. TRAVIS *goes to a dish for money*)

RUTH: Why don't you answer the door, man?

WALTER (*Suddenly bounding across the floor to embrace her*):   'Cause sometimes it hard to let the future begin! (*Stooping down in her face*)   450
       I got wings! You got wings!
       All God's children got wings!

(*He crosses to the door and throws it open. Standing there is a very slight little man in a not too prosperous business suit and with haunted frightened eyes*   455 *and a hat pulled down tightly, brim up, around his forehead.* TRAVIS *passes between the men and exits.* WALTER *leans deep in the man's face, still in his jubilance)*

460　　　*When I get to heaven gonna put on my wings,*
　　　　　　Gonna fly all over God's heaven . . .

(The little man just stares at him)

　　　　　Heaven—

(Suddenly he stops and looks past the little man into the empty hallway)

Where's Willy, man?

BOBO: He ain't with me.

465　**WALTER** *(Not disturbed):* Oh—come on in. You know my wife.

BOBO *(Dumbly, taking off his hat):* Yes—h'you, Miss Ruth.

RUTH *(Quietly, a mood apart from her husband already,*
470　　*seeing* BOBO*):* Hello, Bobo.

WALTER: You right on time today . . . Right on time. That's the way! *(He slaps* BOBO *on his back)* Sit down . . . lemme hear. (RUTH *stands stiffly and quietly in back of them, as though somehow she senses*
475　*death, her eyes fixed on her husband)*

BOBO *(His frightened eyes on the floor, his hat in his hands):* Could I please get a drink of water, before I tell you about it, Walter Lee? (WALTER *does not take his eyes off the man.* RUTH *goes blindly to the tap and*
480　*gets a glass of water and brings it to* BOBO*)*

WALTER: There ain't nothing wrong, is there?

BOBO: Lemme tell you—

WALTER: Man—didn't nothing go wrong?

BOBO: Lemme tell you—Walter Lee. *(Looking at* RUTH
485　*and talking to her more than to* WALTER*)* You know how it was. I got to tell you how it was. I mean first I got to tell you how it was all the way . . . I mean about the money I put in, Walter Lee . . .

WALTER *(With taut agitation now):* What about the money you put in?　　　　　　　　　　490

BOBO: Well—it wasn't much as we told you—me and Willy—*(He stops)* I'm sorry, Walter. I got a bad feeling about it. I got a real bad feeling about it . . .

WALTER: Man, what you telling me about all this for? . . . Tell me what happened in Springfield . . .　　495

BOBO: Springfield.

RUTH *(Like a dead woman):* What was supposed to happen in Springfield?

BOBO *(To her):* This deal that me and Walter went into with Willy—Me and Willy was going to go down to　500
Springfield and spread some money 'round so's we wouldn't have to wait so long for the liquor license . . . That's what we were going to do. Everybody said that was the way you had to do, you understand, Miss Ruth?　　　　　　　　　　　505

WALTER: Man—what happened down there?

BOBO *(A pitiful man, near tears):* I'm trying to tell you, Walter.

WALTER *(Screaming at him suddenly):* THEN TELL ME, GODDAMMIT . . . WHAT'S THE MATTER WITH YOU?　510

BOBO: Man . . . I didn't go to no Springfield, yesterday.

WALTER *(Halted, life hanging in the moment):* Why not?

BOBO *(The long way, the hard way to tell):* 'Cause I didn't have no reasons to . . .

WALTER: Man, what are you talking about!　　　515

BOBO: I'm talking about the fact that when I got to the train station yesterday morning—eight o'clock like we planned . . . Man—*Willy didn't never show up.*

WALTER: Why . . . where was he . . . where is he?

BOBO: That's what I'm trying to tell you . . . I don't　520
know . . . I waited six hours . . . I called his house . . . and I waited . . . six hours . . . I waited in that train station six hours . . . *(Breaking into tears)* That was all the extra money I had in the world . . . *(Looking up at* WALTER *with the tears running down his face)* Man,　525
Willy is gone.

WALTER: Gone, what you mean Willy is gone? Gone where? You mean he went by himself. You mean he went off to Springfield by himself—to take care of getting the license—*(Turns and looks anxiously at* RUTH*)* You mean maybe he didn't want too many people in on the business down there? *(Looks to* RUTH *again, as before)* You know Willy got his own ways. *(Looks back to* BOBO*)* Maybe you was late yesterday and he just went on down there without you. Maybe—maybe—he's been callin' you at home tryin' to tell you what happened or something. Maybe—maybe—he just got sick. He's somewhere—he's got to be somewhere. We just got to find him—me and you got to find him. *(Grabs* BOBO *senselessly by the collar and starts to shake him)* We got to!

BOBO *(In sudden angry, frightened agony)*:   What's the matter with you, Walter! *When a cat take off with your money he don't leave you no maps!*

WALTER *(Turning madly, as though he is looking for* WILLY *in the very room)*:   Willy! . . . Willy . . . don't do it . . . Please don't do it . . . Man, not with that money . . . Man, please, not with that money . . . Oh, God . . . Don't let it be true . . . *(He is wandering around, crying out for* WILLY *and looking for him or perhaps for help from God)* Man . . . I trusted you . . . Man, I put my life in your hands . . . *(He starts to crumple down on the floor as* RUTH *just covers her face in horror.* MAMA *opens the door and comes into the room, with* BENEATHA *behind her)* Man . . . *(He starts to pound the floor with his fists, sobbing wildly)* That money is made out of my father's flesh—

BOBO *(Standing over him helplessly)*:   I'm sorry, Walter . . . *(Only* WALTER's *sobs reply.* BOBO *puts on his hat)* I had my life staked on this deal, too . . . *(He exits)*

MAMA *(To* WALTER*)*:   Son—*(She goes to him, bends down to him, talks to his bent head)* Son . . . Is it gone? Son, I gave you sixty-five hundred dollars. Is it gone? All of it? Beneatha's money too?

WALTER *(Lifting his head slowly)*:   Mama . . . I never . . . went to the bank at all . . .

MAMA *(Not wanting to believe him)*:   You mean . . . your sister's school money . . . you used that too . . . Walter? . . .

WALTER: Yessss! All of it . . . It's all gone . . .

(There is total silence. RUTH *stands with her face covered with her hands;* BENEATHA *leans forlornly against a wall, fingering a piece of red ribbon from the mother's gift.* MAMA *stops and looks at her son without recognition and then, quite without thinking about it, starts to beat him senselessly in the face.* BENEATHA *goes to them and stops it)*

BENEATHA: Mama! *(MAMA *stops and looks at both of her children and rises slowly and wanders vaguely, aimlessly away from them)*

MAMA: I seen . . . him . . . night after night . . . come in . . . and look at that rug . . . and then look at me . . .

Mama (L. Scott Caldwell) hears about the loss of the money from a distraught Walter (Kevin Carroll) (2011).

the red showing in his eyes . . . the veins moving in his head . . . I seen him grow thin and old before he was forty . . . working and working and working like somebody's old horse . . . killing himself . . . and you—you give it all away in a day—*(She raises her arms to strike him again)*

BENEATHA: Mama—

MAMA: Oh, God . . . *(She looks up to Him)* Look down here—and show me the strength.

BENEATHA: Mama—

MAMA *(Folding over)*: Strength . . .

BENEATHA *(Plaintively)*: Mama . . .

MAMA: Strength!

Curtain

ACT 3

An hour later.

> At curtain, there is a sullen light of gloom in the living room, gray light not unlike that which began the first scene of Act 1. At left we can see WALTER within his room, alone with himself. He is stretched out on the bed, his shirt out and open, his arms under his head. He does not smoke, he does not cry out, he merely lies there, looking up at the ceiling, much as if he were alone in the world.
>
> In the living room BENEATHA sits at the table, still surrounded by the now almost ominous packing crates. She sits looking off. We feel that this is a mood struck perhaps an hour before, and it lingers now, full of the empty sound of profound disappointment. We see on a line from her brother's bedroom the sameness of their attitudes. Presently the bell rings and BENEATHA rises without ambition or interest in answering. It is ASAGAI, smiling broadly, striding into the room with energy and happy expectation and conversation.

ASAGAI: I came over . . . I had some free time. I thought I might help with the packing. Ah, I like the look of packing crates! A household in preparation for a jour-

ney! It depresses some people . . . but for me . . . it is another feeling. Something full of the flow of life, do you understand? Movement, progress . . . It makes me think of Africa.

BENEATHA: Africa!

ASAGAI: What kind of a mood is this? Have I told you how deeply you move me?

BENEATHA: He gave away the money, Asagai . . .

ASAGAI: Who gave away what money?

BENEATHA: The insurance money. My brother gave it away.

ASAGAI: Gave it away?

BENEATHA: He made an investment! With a man even Travis wouldn't have trusted.

ASAGAI: And it's gone?

BENEATHA: Gone!

ASAGAI: I'm very sorry . . . And you, now?

BENEATHA: Me? . . . Me? . . . Me, I'm nothing . . . Me. When I was very small . . . we used to take our sleds out in the wintertime and the only hills we had were the ice-covered stone steps of some houses down the street. And we used to fill them in with snow and make them smooth and slide down them all day . . . and it was very dangerous, you know . . . far too steep . . . and sure enough one day a kid named Rufus came down too fast and hit the sidewalk . . . and we saw his face just split open right there in front of us . . . And I remember standing there looking at his bloody open face thinking that was the end of Rufus. But the ambulance came and they took him to the hospital and they fixed the broken bones and they sewed it all up . . . and the next time I saw Rufus he just had a little line down the middle of his face . . . I never got over that . . . *(WALTER sits up, listening on the bed. Throughout this scene it is important that we feel his reaction at all times, that he visibly respond to the words of his sister and ASAGAI)*

ASAGAI: What?

BENEATHA: That that was what one person could do for another, fix him up—sew up the problem, make him all right again. That was the most marvelous thing in the world . . . I wanted to do that. I always thought it was the one concrete thing in the world that a human being could do. Fix up the sick, you know—and make them whole again. This was truly being God . . .

ASAGAI: You wanted to be God?

BENEATHA: No—I wanted to cure. It used to be so important to me. I wanted to cure. It used to matter. I used to care. I mean about people and how their bodies hurt . . .

ASAGAI: And you've stopped caring?

BENEATHA: Yes—I think so.

ASAGAI: Why? (WALTER *rises, goes to the door of his room and is about to open it, then stops and stands listening, leaning on the door jamb*)

BENEATHA: Because it doesn't seem deep enough, close enough to what ails mankind—I mean this thing of sewing up bodies or administering drugs. Don't you understand? It was a child's reaction to the world. I thought that doctors had the secret to all the hurts . . . That's the way a child sees things—or an idealist.

ASAGAI: Children see things very well sometimes—and idealists even better.

BENEATHA: I know that's what you think. Because you are still where I left off—you still care. This is what you see for the world, for Africa. You with the dreams of the future will patch up all Africa—you are going to cure the Great Sore of colonialism with Independence—

ASAGAI: Yes!

BENEATHA: Yes—and you think that one word is the penicillin of the human spirit: "Independence!" But then what?

ASAGAI: That will be the problem for another time. First we must get there.

BENEATHA: And where does it end?

ASAGAI: End? Who even spoke of an end? To life? To living?

BENEATHA: An end to misery!

ASAGAI: (*Smiling*) You sound like a French intellectual.

BENEATHA: No! I sound like a human being who just had her future taken right out of her hands! While I was sleeping in my bed in there, things were happening in this world that directly concerned me—and nobody asked me, consulted me—they just went out and did things—and changed my life. Don't you see there isn't any real progress, Asagai, there is only one large circle that we march in, around and around, each of us with our own little picture—in front of us—our own little mirage that we think is the future.

ASAGAI: That is the mistake.

BENEATHA: What?

ASAGAI: What you just said—about the circle. It isn't a circle—it is simply a long line—as in geometry, you know, one that reaches into infinity. And because we cannot see the end—we also cannot see how it changes. And it is very odd but those who see the changes are called "idealist"—and those who cannot, or refuse to think, they are the "realists." It is very strange, and amusing too, I think.

BENEATHA: You—you are almost religious.

ASAGAI: Yes . . . I think I have the religion of doing what is necessary in the world—and of worshipping man—because he is so marvelous, you see.

BENEATHA: Man is foul! And the human race deserves its misery!

ASAGAI: You see: *you* have become the religious one in the old sense. Already, and after such a small defeat, you are worshipping despair.

BENEATHA: From now on, I worship the truth—and the truth is that people are puny, small and selfish . . .

ASAGAI: Truth? Why is it that you despairing ones always think that only you have the truth? I never thought to see *you* like that. You! Your brother made a stupid, childish mistake—and you are grateful to him. So that now you can give up on the ailing human race on account of it. You talk about what good is struggle; what good is anything? Where are we all going? And why are we bothering?

BENEATHA: *And you cannot answer it!* All your talks and dreams about Africa and Independence. Independence and then what? What about all the crooks and petty thieves and just plain idiots who will come into power to steal and plunder the same as before—only now they will be black and do it in the name of the new Independence. You cannot answer that.

ASAGAI *(Shouting over her):* *I live the answer!* (Pause) In my village at home it is the exceptional man who can even read a newspaper . . . or who ever *sees* a book at all. I will go home and much of what I will have to say will seem strange to the people of my village. But I will teach and work and things will happen, slowly and swiftly. At times it will seem that nothing changes at all . . . and then again . . . the sudden dramatic events which make history leap into the future. And then quiet again. Retrogression even. Guns, murder, revolution. And I even will have moments when I wonder if the quiet was not better than all that death and hatred. But I will look about my village at the illiteracy and disease and ignorance and I will not wonder long. And perhaps . . . perhaps I will be a great man . . . I mean perhaps I will hold on to the substance of truth and find my way always with the right course . . . and perhaps for it I will be butchered in my bed some night by the servants of empire . . .

BENEATHA: *The martyr!*

ASAGAI *(He smiles):* . . . or perhaps I shall live to be a very old man, respected and esteemed in my new nation . . . And perhaps I shall hold office and this is what I'm trying to tell you, Alaiyo: Perhaps the things I believe now for my country will be wrong and outmoded, and I will not understand and do terrible things to have things my way or merely to keep my power. Don't you see that there will be young men and women—not British soldiers then, but my own black countrymen—to step out of the shadows some

evening and slit my then useless throat? Don't you see they have always been there . . . that they always will be. And that such a thing as my own death will be an advance? They who might kill me even . . . actually replenish me!

BENEATHA: Oh, Asagai, I know all that.

ASAGAI: Good! Then stop moaning and groaning and tell me what you plan to do.

BENEATHA: Do?

ASAGAI: I have a bit of a suggestion.

BENEATHA: What?

ASAGAI *(Rather quietly for him):* That when it is all over—that you come home with me—

BENEATHA *(Slapping herself on the forehead with exasperation born of misunderstanding):* Oh—Asagai—at this moment you decide to be romantic!

ASAGAI *(Quickly understanding the misunderstanding):* My dear, young creature of the New World—I do not mean across the city—I mean across the ocean: home—to Africa.

BENEATHA *(Slowly understanding and turning to him with murmured amazement):* To—to Nigeria?

ASAGAI: Yes! . . . *(Smiling and lifting his arms playfully)* Three hundred years later the African Prince rose up out of the seas and swept the maiden back across the middle passage over which her ancestors had come—

BENEATHA *(Unable to play):* Nigeria?

ASAGAI: Nigeria. Home. *(Coming to her with genuine romantic flippancy)* I will show you our mountains and our stars; and give you cool drinks from gourds and teach you the old songs and the ways of our people—and, in time, we will pretend that—*(Very softly)*—you have only been away for a day—*(She turns her back to him, thinking. He swings her around and takes her full in his arms in a kiss which proceeds to passion)*

BENEATHA *(Pulling away suddenly):* You're getting me all mixed up—

Beneatha (Kenya Alexander) hears a proposal from the Nigerian student Joseph Asagai (Amad Jackson) (2011).

ASAGAI: Why?

BENEATHA: Too many things—too many things have happened today. I must sit down and think. I don't
200   know what I feel about anything right this minute. *(She promptly sits down and props her chin on her fist)*

ASAGAI *(Charmed):*   All right, I shall leave you. No—don't get up. *(Touching her, gently, sweetly)* Just sit awhile and think . . . Never be afraid to sit awhile and think.
205   *(He goes to door and looks at her)* How often I have looked at you and said, "Ah—so this is what the New World hath finally wrought . . ." *(He exits.* BENEATHA *sits on alone. Presently* WALTER *enters from his room and starts to rummage through things, feverishly look-*
210   *ing for something. She looks up and turns in her seat)*

BENEATHA *(Hissingly):*   Yes—just look at what the New World hath wrought! . . . Just look! *(She gestures with*

bitter disgust) There he is! *Monsieur le petit bourgeois noir*—himself! There he is—Symbol of a Rising Class! Entrepreneur! Titan of the system! *(*WALTER *ignores* 215 *her completely and continues frantically and destructively looking for something and hurling things to floor and tearing things out of their place in his search.* BENEATHA *ignores the eccentricity of his actions and goes on with the monologue of insult)* Did you dream of 220 yachts on Lake Michigan, Brother? Did you see yourself on that Great Day sitting down at the Conference Table, surrounded by all the mighty bald-headed men in America? All halted, waiting, breathless, waiting for your pronouncements on industry? Waiting for 225 you—Chairman of the Board! *(*WALTER *finds what he is looking for—a small piece of white paper—and pushes it in his pocket and puts on his coat and rushes out without ever having looked at her. She shouts after him)* I look at you and I see the final triumph of stu- 230 pidity in the world! *(The door slams and she returns to just sitting again.* RUTH *comes quickly out of* MAMA'*s room)*

RUTH: Who was that?

BENEATHA: Your husband. 235

RUTH: Where did he go?

BENEATHA: Who knows—maybe he has an appointment at U.S. Steel.

RUTH *(Anxiously, with frightened eyes):*   You didn't say nothing bad to him, did you? 240

BENEATHA: Bad? Say anything bad to him? No—I told him he was a sweet boy and full of dreams and everything is strictly peachy keen, as the ofay kids say! *(*MAMA *enters from her bedroom. She is lost, vague, trying to catch hold, to make some sense of her former* 245 *command of the world, but it still eludes her. A sense of waste overwhelms her gait; a measure of apology rides on her shoulders. She goes to her plant, which has remained on the table, looks at it, picks it up and takes it to the window sill and sets it outside, and she stands* 250 *and looks at it a long moment. Then she closes the window, straightens her body with effort and turns around to her children)*

MAMA: Well—ain't it a mess in here, though? (*A false cheerfulness, a beginning of something*) I guess we all better stop moping around and get some work done. All this unpacking and everything we got to do. (RUTH *raises her head slowly in response to the sense of the line; and* BENEATHA *in similar manner turns very slowly to look at her mother*) One of you all better call the moving people and tell 'em not to come.

RUTH: Tell 'em not to come?

MAMA: Of course, baby. Ain't no need in 'em coming all the way here and having to go back. They charges for that too. (*She sits down, fingers to her brow, thinking*) Lord, ever since I was a little girl, I always remembers people saying, "Lena—Lena Eggleston, you aims too high all the time. You needs to slow down and see life a little more like it is. Just slow down some." That's what they always used to say down home—"Lord, that Lena Eggleston is a high-minded thing. She'll get her due one day!"

RUTH: No, Lena . . .

MAMA: Me and Big Walter just didn't never learn right.

RUTH: Lena, no! We gotta go. Bennie—tell her . . . (*She rises and crosses to* BENEATHA *with her arms outstretched.* BENEATHA *doesn't respond*) Tell her we can still move . . . the notes ain't but a hundred and twenty-five a month. We got four grown people in this house—we can work . . .

MAMA (*To herself*):   Just aimed too high all the time—

RUTH (*Turning and going to* MAMA *fast—the words pouring out with urgency and desperation*):   Lena—I'll work . . . I'll work twenty hours a day in all the kitchens in Chicago . . . I'll strap my baby on my back if I have to and scrub all the floors in America and wash all the sheets in America if I have to—but we got to move! We got to get out of here . . . (MAMA *reaches out absently and pats* RUTH's *hand*)

MAMA: No—I sees things differently now. Been thinking 'bout some of the things we could do to fix this place up some. I seen a second-hand bureau over on Maxwell Street just the other day that could fit right there. (*She points to where the new furniture might go.* RUTH *wanders away from her*) Would need some new handles on it and then a little varnish and it look like something brand-new. And—we can put up them new curtains in the kitchen . . . Why this place be looking fine. Cheer us all up so that we forget trouble ever come . . . (*To* RUTH) And you could get some nice screens to put up in your room round the baby's bassinet . . . (*She looks at both of them, pleadingly*) Sometimes you just got to know when to give up some things . . . and hold on to what you got. (WALTER *enters from the outside, looking spent and leaning against the door, his coat hanging from him*)

MAMA: Where you been, son?

WALTER (*Breathing hard*):   Made a call.

MAMA: To who, son?

WALTER: To The Man. (*He heads for his room*)

MAMA: What man, baby?

WALTER: The Man, Mama. Don't you know who The Man is?

RUTH: Walter Lee?

WALTER: *The Man*. Like the guys in the streets say— *The Man*. Captain Boss—Mistuh Charley . . . Old Cap'n Please Mr. Bossman . . .

BENEATHA (*Suddenly*):   Lindner!

WALTER: That's right! That's good. I told him to come right over.

BENEATHA (*Fiercely, understanding*):   For what? What do you want to see him for!

WALTER (*Looking at his sister*):   We going to do business with him.

MAMA: What you talking 'bout, son?

WALTER: Talking 'bout life, Mama. You all always telling me to see life like it is. Well—I laid in there on my back today . . . and I figured it out. Life just like it is. Who gets and who don't get. (*He sits down with his coat on and laughs*) Mama, you know it's all divided up. Life is. Sure enough. Between the takers and the "tooken." (*He laughs*) I've figured it out finally. (*He looks around at them*) Yeah. Some of us always getting "tooken." (*He laughs*) People like Willy Harris, they don't never get "tooken." And you know why the rest of us do? 'Cause we all mixed up. Mixed up bad. We get to looking 'round for the right and the wrong; and we worry about it and cry about it and stay up nights trying to figure out 'bout the wrong and the right of things all the time . . . And all the time, man, them takers is out there operating, just taking and taking. Willy Harris? Shoot—Willy Harris don't even count. He don't even count in the big scheme of things. But I'll say one thing for old Willy Harris . . . he's taught me something. He's taught me to keep my eye on what counts in this world. Yeah— (*Shouting out a little*) Thanks, Willy!

RUTH: What did you call that man for, Walter Lee?

WALTER: Called him to tell him to come on over to the show. Gonna put on a show for the man. Just what he wants to see. You see, Mama, the man came here today and he told us that them people out there where you want us to move—well they so upset they willing to pay us *not* to move! (*He laughs again*) And—and oh, Mama—you would of been proud of the way me and Ruth and Bennie acted. We told him to get out . . . Lord have mercy! We told the man to get out! Oh, we was some proud folks this afternoon, yeah. (*He lights a cigarette*) We were still full of that old-time stuff . . .

RUTH (*Coming toward him slowly*): You talking 'bout taking them people's money to keep us from moving in that house?

WALTER: I ain't just talking 'bout it, baby—I'm telling you that's what's going to happen!

BENEATHA: Oh, God! Where is the bottom! Where is the real honest-to-God bottom so he can't go any farther!

WALTER: See—that's the old stuff. You and that boy that was here today. You all want everybody to carry a flag and a spear and sing some marching songs, huh? You wanna spend your life looking into things and trying to find the right and the wrong part, huh? Yeah. You know what's going to happen to that boy someday—

he'll find himself sitting in a dungeon, locked in forever—and the takers will have the key! Forget it, baby! There ain't no causes—there ain't nothing but taking in this world, and he who takes most is smart-est—and it don't make a damn bit of difference *how*.

MAMA: You making something inside me cry, son. Some awful pain inside me.

WALTER: Don't cry, Mama. Understand. That white man is going to walk in that door able to write checks for more money than we ever had. It's important to him and I'm going to help him . . . I'm going to put on the show, Mama.

MAMA: Son—I come from five generations of people who was slaves and share-croppers—but ain't nobody in my family never let nobody pay 'em no money that was a way of telling us we wasn't fit to walk the earth. We ain't never been that poor. (*Raising her eyes and looking at him*) We ain't never been that dead inside.

BENEATHA: Well—we are dead now. All the talk about dreams and sunlight that goes on in this house. All dead.

WALTER: What's the matter with you all! I didn't make this world! It was give to me this way! Hell, yes, I want me some yachts someday! Yes, I want to hang some real pearls 'round my wife's neck. Ain't she supposed to wear no pearls? Somebody tell me—tell me, who decides which women is suppose to wear pearls in this world. I tell you I am a *man*—and I think my wife should wear some pearls in this world! (*This last line hangs a good while and* WALTER *begins to move about the room. The word "Man" has penetrated his consciousness; he mumbles it to himself repeatedly between strange agitated pauses as he moves about*)

MAMA: Baby, how you going to feel on the inside?

WALTER: Fine! . . . Going to feel fine . . . a man . . .

MAMA: You won't have nothing left then, Walter Lee.

WALTER (*Coming to her*): I'm going to feel fine, Mama. I'm going to look that son-of-a-bitch in the eyes and say—(*He falters*)—and say, "All right, Mr. Lindner—(*He falters even more*)—that's your neighborhood out

415 there! You got the right to keep it like you want! You got the right to have it like you want! Just write the check and—the house is yours." And, and I am going to say—*(His voice almost breaks)* "And you—you peo-
420 ple just put the money in my hand and you won't have to live next to this bunch of stinking niggers! . . ." *(He straightens up and moves away from his mother, walking around the room)* Maybe—maybe I'll just get down on my black knees . . . *(He does so;* RUTH *and* BEN-NIE *and* MAMA *watch him in frozen horror)* Captain,
425 Mistuh, Bossman.*(He starts crying)* A-hee-hee-hee! *(Wringing his hands in a profoundly anguished imitation)* Yasssssuh! Great White Father, just gi' ussen de money, fo' God's sake, and we's—we's ain't gwine come out deh and dirty up yo' white folks neighborhood . . ."
430 *(He breaks down completely, then gets up and goes into the bedroom)*

BENEATHA: That is not a man. That is nothing but a toothless rat.

MAMA: Yes—death done come in this here house. *(She is nodding, slowly, reflectively)* Done come walking in
435 my house. On the lips of my children. You what supposed to be my beginning again. You—what supposed to be my harvest. *(To* BENEATHA*)* You—you mourning your brother?

BENEATHA: He's no brother of mine.

440 MAMA: What you say?

BENEATHA: I said that that individual in that room is no brother of mine.

MAMA: That's what I thought you said. You feeling like you better than he is today? *(*BENEATHA *does not
445 answer)* Yes? What you tell him a minute ago? That he wasn't a man? Yes? You give him up for me? You done wrote his epitaph too—like the rest of the world? Well, who give you the privilege?

BENEATHA: Be on my side for once! You saw what he
450 just did, Mama! You saw him—down on his knees. Wasn't it you who taught me to despise any man who would do that? Do what he's going to do?

MAMA: Yes—I taught you that. Me and your daddy. But I thought I taught you something else too . . . I thought
455 I taught you to love him.

BENEATHA: Love him? There is nothing left to love.

MAMA: There is always something left to love. And if you ain't learned that, you ain't learned nothing. *(Looking at her)* Have you cried for that boy today? I don't
460 mean for yourself and for the family 'cause we lost the money. I mean for him: what he been through and what it done to him. Child, when do you think is the time to love somebody the most; when they done good and made things easy for everybody? Well then, you
465 ain't through learning—because that ain't the time at all. It's when he's at his lowest and can't believe in hisself 'cause the world done whipped him so! When you starts measuring somebody, measure him right, child, measure him right. Make sure you done taken into ac-
470 count what hills and valleys he come through before he got to wherever he is. *(*TRAVIS *bursts into the room at the end of the speech, leaving the door open)*

TRAVIS: Grandmama—the moving men are downstairs! The truck just pulled up.

475 MAMA *(Turning and looking at him)*: Are they, baby? They downstairs? *(She sighs and sits.* LINDNER *appears in the doorway. He peers in and knocks lightly, to gain attention, and comes in. All turn to look at him)*

LINDNER *(Hat and briefcase in hand)*: Uh—hello . . .
480 *(*RUTH *crosses mechanically to the bedroom door and opens it and lets it swing open freely and slowly as the lights come up on* WALTER *within, still in his coat, sitting at the far corner of the room. He looks up and out through the room to* LINDNER*)*

485 RUTH: He's here. *(A long minute passes and* WALTER *slowly gets up)*

LINDNER *(Coming to the table with efficiency, putting his briefcase on the table and starting to unfold papers and unscrew fountain pens)*: Well, I certainly was glad to
490 hear from you people. *(*WALTER *has begun the trek out of the room, slowly and awkwardly, rather like a small boy, passing the back of his sleeve across his mouth from time to time)* Life can really be so much simpler than people let it be most of the time. Well—with
495 whom do I negotiate? You, Mrs. Younger, or your son here? *(*MAMA *sits with her hands folded on her lap and her eyes closed as* WALTER *advances.* TRAVIS *goes*

While Ruth (Ruby Dee) eyes him, Walter (Sidney Poitier) looks at
the paper that contains Lindner's offer (1961).

closer to LINDNER *and looks at the papers curiously)*
Just some official papers, sonny.

500 **RUTH:**   Travis, you go downstairs.

MAMA *(Opening her eyes and looking into* WALTER's*)*:
No. Travis, you stay right here. And you make him understand what you doing, Walter Lee. You teach him
good. Like Willy Harris taught you. You show where
505 our five generations done come to. Go ahead son—

WALTER *(Looks down into his boys eyes.* TRAVIS *grins at
him merrily and* WALTER *draws him beside him with
his arm lightly around his shoulders)*:   Well, Mr.
Lindner. (BENEATHA *turns away)* We called you—
510 *(There is a profound, simple groping quality in his
speech)*—because, well, me and my family *(He looks
around and shifts from one foot to the other)* Well—we
are very plain people . . .

LINDNER: Yes—

515 **WALTER:**   I mean—I have worked as a chauffeur most of
my life—and my wife here, she does domestic work in
people's kitchens. So does my mother. I mean—we are
plain people . . .

LINDNER: Yes, Mr. Younger—

520 **WALTER** *(Really like a small boy, looking down at his shoes
and then up at the man)*:   And—uh—well, my father,
well, he was a laborer most of his life.

LINDNER *(Absolutely confused)*:   Uh, yes—

WALTER *(Looking down at his shows once again)*:   My
father almost beat a man to death once because this   525
man called him a bad name or something, you know
what I mean?

LINDNER: No, no, I'm afraid I don't—

WALTER *(Finally straightening up)*:   Well—what I mean
is that we come from people who had a lot of pride. I   530
mean—we are very proud people. And that's my sister
over there and she's going to be a doctor—and we are
very proud—

LINDNER: Well—I am sure that is very nice, but—

WALTER: *(Starting to cry and facing the man eye to eye)*   535
What I am telling you is that we called you over here
to tell you that we are very proud and that this—this is
my son, who makes the sixth generation our family in
this country, and we have all thought about your offer
and we have decided to move into our house because   540
my father—my father—he earned it. (MAMA *has her
eyes closed and is rocking back and forth as though
she were in church, with her head nodding the amen
yes)* We don't want to make no trouble for nobody or
fight no causes—but we will try to be good neighbors.   545
That's all we got to say. *(He looks the man absolutely
in the eyes)* We don't want your money. *(He turns and
walks away from the man)*

LINDNER *(Looking around at all of them)*:   I take it
then—that you have decided to occupy.   550

BENEATHA: That's what the man said.

LINDNER *(To* MAMA *in her reverie)*:   Then I would like to
appeal to you, Mrs. Younger. You are older and wiser
and understand things better, I am sure . . .

MAMA: *(Rising)*. I am afraid you don't understand. My   555
son said we was going to move and there ain't nothing
left for me to say. *(Shaking her head with double meaning)* You know how these young folks is nowadays,
mister. Can't do a thing with 'em! Good-bye.

LINDNER *(Folding up his materials)*:   Well—if you are   560
that final about it . . . there is nothing left for me to
say. *(He finishes, almost ignored by the family, who are
concentrating on* WALTER LEE. *At the door* LINDNER

Mama (Phylicia Rashad) and Walter (Sean Combs) are reconciled (2008).

565 *halts and looks around)* I sure hope you people know what you're getting into. *(He shakes his head and exits)*

RUTH *(Looking around and coming to life)*: Well, for God's sake—if the moving men are here—LET'S GET THE HELL OUT OF HERE!

MAMA *(Into action)*: Ain't it the truth! Look at all this
570 here mess. Ruth, put Travis' good jacket on him . . . Walter Lee, fix your tie and tuck your shirt in, you look like somebody's hoodlum! Lord have mercy, where is my plant? *(She flies to get it amid the general bustling of the family, who are deliberately trying to*
575 *ignore the nobility of the past moment)* You all start on down . . . Travis child, don't go empty-handed . . . Ruth, where did I put that box with my skillets in it? I want to be in charge of it myself . . . I'm going to make us the biggest dinner we ever ate tonight . . . Be-
580 neatha, what's the matter with them stockings? Pull them things up, girl . . . *(The family starts to file out as two* MOVING MEN *appear and begin to carry out the heavier pieces of furniture, bumping into the family as they move about)*

585 **BENEATHA:** Mama, Asagai—asked me to marry him today and go to Africa—

MAMA *(In the middle of her getting-ready activity)*: He did? You ain't old enough to marry nobody—*(Seeing the* MOVING MEN *lifting one of her chairs precari-*
590 *ously)* Darling, that ain't no bale of cotton, please handle it so we can sit in it again! I had that chair twenty-five years . . . *(The movers sigh with exaspera-tion and go on with their work)*

BENEATHA *(Girlishly and unreasonably trying to pursue the conversation)*: To go to Africa, Mama—be a doc-
595 tor in Africa . . .

MAMA *(Distracted)*: Yes, baby—

WALTER: *Africa!* What he want you to go to Africa for?

BENEATHA: To practice there . . .

WALTER: Girl, if you don't get all them silly ideas out
600 your head! You better marry yourself a man with some loot . . .

BENEATHA *(Angrily, precisely as in the first scene of the play)*: What have you got to do with who I marry!

WALTER: Plenty. Now I think George Murchison—*(He*
605 *and* BENEATHA *go out yelling at each other vigor-ously;* BENEATHA *is heard saying that she would not marry* GEORGE MURCHISON *if he was Adam and she were Eve, etc. The anger is loud and real till their voices diminish.* RUTH *stands at the door and turns to*
610 MAMA *and smiles knowingly)*

MAMA *(Fixing her hat at last)*: Yeah—they something all right, my children . . .

RUTH: Yeah—they're something. Let's go, Lena.

MAMA *(Stalling, starting to look around at the house)*:
615 Yes—I'm coming. Ruth—

RUTH: Yes?

MAMA *(Quietly, woman to woman)*: He finally come into his manhood today, didn't he? Kind of like a rainbow after the rain . . .
620

RUTH (*Biting her lip lest her own pride explode in front of* MAMA): Yes, Lena. (WALTER'*s voice calls for them raucously*)

MAMA (*Waving* RUTH *out vaguely*): All right, honey—go on down. I be down directly. (RUTH *hesitates, then exits.* MAMA *stands, at last alone in the living room, her plant on the table before her as the lights start to come down. She looks around at all the walls and ceilings and suddenly, despite herself, while the children call below, a great heaving thing rises in her and she puts her fist to her mouth to stifle it, takes a final desperate look, pulls her coat about her, pats her hat and goes out. The lights dim down. The door opens and she comes back in, grabs her plant, and goes out for the last time*)

Curtain

Writing from Reading

Summarize

1 What bothers Walter the most? Describe the central conflict he struggles with throughout the play.

Analyze Craft

2 The entire play takes place in the Youngers' apartment. Review how the apartment is described in the stage directions and how the characters talk about the space they inhabit. How does the emphasis on the apartment's smallness add tension to the play? What feelings does it evoke in the audience or reader?

3 Mama's part in the play begins and ends with her tending the house-plant. Of what is the plant symbolic? Does the symbol change in meaning from the first act to the last?

Analyze Voice

4 The stage directions note that Beneatha's "speech is a mixture of many things; it is different from the rest of the family's insofar as education has permeated her sense of English." Look at how the main characters talk. How does Hansberry write their speech patterns into their spoken lines? What does each character's voice say about that character's personality?

5 Notice how quickly the characters' banter changes from joking to angry back to joking. How does their humor affect your sense of the family's closeness? At what points does the humor break down?

Synthesize Summary and Analysis

6 As brother and sister, Walter and Beneatha are sometimes at odds with each other—both for shares of the insurance money and in terms of their life goals. In what ways do their differing ideas and goals spring from a similarity between brother and sister? Discuss how the two characters are foils.

7 Mama makes several references to how things have changed from her day to the present. To what extent do Walter's and Beneatha's aspirations and actions suggest a divergence from previous generations? What ultimately stays the same from generation to generation?

Interpret the Play

8 An early reviewer of the play noted that it was "a play about Negroes which is not simply a Negro play." The reviewer contends that Walter's conflict does not spring from his race but rather from his pursuit of the American dream. Imagine this play cast not with African American actors but with actors of another race. Would the play still work? Which ideas and themes would remain the same? What would be lost? To what extent is the play about race?

9 You might recognize the title of this play from Langston Hughes's poem "Dream Deferred": "What happens to a dream deferred? / Does it dry up / like a raisin in the sun?" Look at the poem in its entirety (which you can find in Chapter 5). Why is Hansberry's selected title appropriate? How is the play a response to Hughes's poem?

"August Wilson plays [are] very similar to Tennessee Williams plays [in that] there's somebody fighting for more. . . . The people that he is dealing with, they have been bourgeois . . . a whole way of life that's crumbling, and they're looking for somebody to save them. August Wilson's characters aren't crumbling; they're down, looking for a way to get up." Conversation with Ruben Santiago-Hudson

August Wilson (1945–2005)

Raised in a two-room apartment above a garage in Pittsburgh, August Wilson grew up to become an American playwright with two Pulitzer Prizes, several Tony Award nominations, and numerous other awards and fellowships. He was raised by his African-American mother, who had been abandoned by Wilson's German father. When she remarried, the black family moved to a white neighborhood where they were the victims of racist comments and behavior. This experience, along with his love of the blues as a form of black expression, led Wilson to become a playwright whose central concern was the plight of blacks and the hope of finding healing in black communities. After founding a black theater company in Pittsburgh, Wilson had his first major success with his play *Ma Rainey's Black Bottom* (1984). Two of his plays, *Fences* (1985) and *Joe Turner's Come and Gone* (1986), ran simultaneously on Broadway—a rare achievement. Wilson's body of work functions as a history of black American life in the twentieth century. His characters, many of whom were based on the people he had known in his numerous menial jobs while growing up, dig deeper into themselves than do most people we know. Growing out of the realist tradition, Wilson brings allegorical elements into this play, giving us a sense of ordinary life experienced in an extraordinary way.

AS YOU READ   Scan the script for the details of the family's life. Find references to Troy Maxon's life at work and at home and with friends.

FOR INTERACTIVE READING . . .

Mark the places in the play where you notice that scenes appear to begin and end.

Fences (1986)

For Lloyd Richards, who adds to whatever he touches

When the sins of our fathers visit us
We do not have to play host.
We can banish them with forgiveness
As God, in His Largeness and Laws.
                                    —AUGUST WILSON

CHARACTERS

TROY MAXSON

JIM BONO, *Troy's friend*

ROSE, *Troy's wife*

LYONS, *Troy's oldest son by previous marriage*

GABRIEL, *Troy's brother*

CORY, *Troy and Rose's son*

RAYNELL, *Troy's daughter*

SETTING: *The setting is the yard which fronts the only entrance to the Maxson household, an ancient two-story brick house set back off a small alley in a big-city neighborhood. The entrance to the house is gained by two or three steps leading to a wooden porch badly in need of paint.*

A relatively recent addition to the house and running its full width, the porch lacks congruence. It is a sturdy porch with a flat roof. One or two chairs of dubious value sit at one end where the kitchen window opens onto the porch. An old-fashioned icebox stands silent guard at the opposite end.

The yard is a small dirt yard, partially fenced, except for the last scene, with a wooden saw horse, a pile of lumber, and other fence-building equipment set off to the side. Opposite is a tree from which hangs a ball made of rags. A baseball bat leans against the tree. Two oil drums serve as garbage receptacles and sit near the house at right to complete the setting.

THE PLAY: *Near the turn of the century, the destitute of Europe sprang on the city with tenacious claws and an honest and solid dream. The city devoured them. They swelled its belly until it burst into a thousand furnaces and sewing machines, a thousand butcher shops and bakers' ovens, a thousand churches and hospitals and funeral parlors and money-lenders.*

The city grew. It nourished itself and offered each man a partnership limited only by his talent, his guile, and his willingness and capacity for hard work. For the immigrants of Europe, a dream dared and won true.

The descendants of African slaves were offered no such welcome or participation. They came from places called the Carolinas and the Virginias, Georgia, Alabama, Mississippi, and Tennessee. They came strong, eager, searching. The city rejected them and they fled and settled along the riverbanks and under bridges in shallow, ramshackle houses made of sticks and tarpaper. They collected rags and wood. They sold the use of their muscles and their bodies. They cleaned houses and washed clothes, they shined shoes, and in quiet desperation and vengeful pride, they stole, and lived in pursuit of their own dream. That they could breathe free, finally, and stand to meet life with the force of dignity and whatever eloquence the heart could call upon.

By 1957, the hard-won victories of the European immigrants had solidified the industrial might of America. War had been confronted and won with new energies that used loyalty and patriotism as its fuel. Life was rich, full, and flourishing. The Milwaukee Braves won the World Series, and the hot winds of change that would make the sixties a turbulent, racing, dangerous, and provocative decade had not yet begun to blow full.

<h1 style="text-align:center">ACT 1</h1>

SCENE 1

It is 1957. TROY *and* BONO *enter the yard, engaged in conversation.* TROY *is fifty-three years old, a large man with thick, heavy hands; it is this largeness that he strives to fill out and make an accommodation with. Together with his blackness, his largeness informs his sensibilities and the choices he has made in his life.*

Of the two men, BONO *is obviously the follower. His commitment to their friendship of thirty-odd years is rooted in his admiration of* TROY's *honesty, capacity for hard work, and his strength, which* BONO *seeks to emulate.*

It is Friday night, payday, and the one night of the week the two men engage in a ritual of talk and drink. TROY *is usually the most talkative and at times he can be crude and almost vulgar, though he is capable of rising to profound heights of expression. The men carry lunch buckets and wear or carry burlap aprons and are dressed in clothes suitable to their jobs as garbage collectors.*

BONO: Troy, you ought to stop that lying!

TROY: I ain't lying! The nigger had a watermelon this big. *(He indicates with his hands.)* Talking about . . . "What watermelon, Mr. Rand?" I liked to fell out! "What watermelon, Mr. Rand?" . . . And it sitting there big as life. 5

BONO: What did Mr. Rand say?

TROY: Ain't said nothing. Figure if the nigger too dumb to know he carrying a watermelon, he wasn't gonna get much sense out of him. Trying to hide that great big old watermelon under his coat. Afraid to let the white man see him carry it home. 10

BONO: I'm like you . . . I ain't got no time for them kind of people.

TROY: Now what he look like getting mad cause he see the man from the union talking to Mr. Rand? 15

BONO: He come to me talking about . . . "Maxson gonna get us fired." I told him to get away from me with that. He walked away from me calling you a troublemaker. What Mr. Rand say? 20

TROY: Ain't said nothing. He told me to go down the Commissioner's office next Friday. They called me down there to see them.

BONO: Well, as long as you got your complaint filed, they can't fire you. That's what one of them white fellows tell me. 25

TROY: I ain't worried about them firing me. They gonna fire me cause I asked a question? That's all I did. I went to Mr. Rand and asked him, "Why? Why you got the white mens driving and the colored lifting?" Told him, "what's the matter, don't I count? You think only 30

35 white fellows got sense enough to drive a truck. That ain't no paper job! Hell, anybody can drive a truck. How come you got all whites driving and the colored lifting?" He told me "take it to the union." Well, hell, that's what I done! Now they wanna come up with this pack of lies.

BONO: I told Brownie if the man come and ask him any
40 questions . . . just tell the truth! It ain't nothing but something they done trumped up on you cause you filed a complaint on them.

TROY: Brownie don't understand nothing. All I want them to do is change the job description. Give every-
45 body a chance to drive the truck. Brownie can't see that. He ain't got that much sense.

BONO: How you figure he be making out with that gal be up at Taylors' all the time . . . that Alberta gal?

TROY: Same as you and me. Getting just as much as we is. Which is to say nothing.

50 **BONO:** It is, huh? I figure you doing a little better than me . . . and I ain't saying what I'm doing.

TROY: Aw, nigger, look here . . . I know you. If you had got anywhere near that gal, twenty minutes later you be looking to tell somebody. And the first one you
55 gonna tell . . . that you gonna want to brag to . . . is gonna be me.

BONO: I ain't saying that. I see where you be eyeing her.

TROY: I eye all the women. I don't miss nothing. Don't never let nobody tell you Troy Maxson don't eye the
60 women.

BONO: You been doing more than eyeing her. You done bought her a drink or two.

TROY: Hell yeah, I bought her a drink! What that mean? I bought you one, too. What that mean cause I buy her
65 a drink? I'm just being polite.

BONO: It's alright to buy her one drink. That's what you call being polite. But when you wanna be buying two or three . . . that's what you call eyeing her.

TROY: Look here, as long as you known me . . . you ever
70 known me to chase after women?

BONO: Hell yeah! Long as I done known you. You forget-ting I knew you when.

TROY: Naw, I'm talking about since I been married to Rose?

BONO: Oh, not since you been married to Rose. Now, 75 that's the truth, there. I can say that.

TROY: Alright then! Case closed.

BONO: I see you be walking up around Alberta's house. You supposed to be at Taylors' and you be walking up around there. 80

TROY: What you watching where I'm walking for? I ain't watching after you.

BONO: I seen you walking around there more than once.

TROY: Hell, you liable to see me walking anywhere! That don't mean nothing cause you see me walking around 85 there.

BONO: Where she come from anyway? She just kinda showed up one day.

TROY: Tallahassee. You can look at her and tell she one of them Florida gals. They got some big healthy 90 women down there. Grow them right up out the ground. Got a little bit of Indian in her. Most of them niggers down in Florida got some Indian in them.

BONO: I don't know about that Indian part. But she damn sure big and healthy. Woman wear some big 95 stockings. Got them great big old legs and hips as wide as the Mississippi River.

TROY: Legs don't mean nothing. You don't do nothing but push them out of the way. But them hips cushion the ride! 100

BONO: Troy, you ain't got no sense.

TROY: It's the truth! Like you riding on Goodyears!

(ROSE *enters from the house. She is ten years younger than* TROY. *Her devotion to him stems from her rec-ognition of the possibilities of her life without him: a succession of abusive men and their babies, a life of partying and running the streets, the Church, or aloneness with its attendant pain and frustration. She recognizes* TROY's *spirit as a fine and illuminating one and she either ignores or forgives his faults, only some of which she recognizes. Though she doesn't drink, her presence is an integral part of the Friday night rituals. She alternates between the porch and the kitchen, where supper preparations are under way.)*

ROSE: What you all out here getting into?

TROY: What you worried about what we getting into for? This is men talk, woman.

ROSE: What I care what you all talking about? Bono, you gonna stay for supper?

BONO: No, I thank you, Rose. But Lucille say she cooking up a pot of pigfeet.

TROY: Pigfeet! Hell, I'm going home with you! Might even stay the night if you got some pigfeet. You got something in there to top them pigfeet, Rose?

ROSE: I'm cooking up some chicken. I got some chicken and collard greens.

TROY: Well, go on back in the house and let me and Bono finish what we was talking about. This is men talk. I got some talk for you later. You know what kind of talk I mean. You go on and powder it up.

ROSE: Troy Maxson, don't you start that now!

TROY: *(Puts his arm around her.)* Aw, woman . . . come here. Look here, Bono . . . when I met this woman . . . I got out that place, say, "Hitch up my pony, saddle up my mare . . . there's a woman out there for me somewhere. I looked here. Looked there. Saw Rose and latched on to her." I latched on to her and told her— I'm gonna tell you the truth—I told her, "Baby, I don't wanna marry, I just wanna be your man." Rose told me . . . tell him what you told me, Rose.

ROSE: I told him if he wasn't the marrying kind, then move out the way so the marrying kind could find me.

TROY: That's what she told me. "Nigger, you in my way. You blocking the view! Move out the way so I can find me a husband." I thought it over two or three days. Come back—

ROSE: Ain't no two or three days nothing. You was back the same night.

TROY: Come back, told her . . . "Okay, baby . . . but I'm gonna buy me a banty rooster and put him out there in the backyard . . . and when he see a stranger come, he'll flap his wings and crow . . ." Look here, Bono, I could watch the front door by myself . . . it was that back door I was worried about.

ROSE: Troy, you ought not talk like that. Troy ain't doing nothing but telling a lie.

TROY: Only thing is . . . when we first got married . . . forget the rooster . . . we ain't had no yard!

BONO: I hear you tell it. Me and Lucille was staying down there on Logan Street. Had two rooms with the outhouse in the back. I ain't mind the outhouse none. But when that goddamn wind blow through there in the winter . . . that's what I'm talking about! To this day I wonder why in the hell I ever stayed down there for six long years. But see, I didn't know I could do no better. I thought only white folks had inside toilets and things.

ROSE: There's a lot of people don't know they can do no better than they doing now. That's just something you got to learn. A lot of folks still shop at Bella's.

TROY: Ain't nothing wrong with shopping at Bella's. She got fresh food.

ROSE: I ain't said nothing about if she got fresh food. I'm talking about what she charge. She charge ten cents more than the A&P.

TROY: The A&P ain't never done nothing for me. I spends my money where I'm treated right. I go down to Bella, say, "I need a loaf of bread, I'll pay you Friday." She give it to me. What sense that make when I got money to go and spend it somewhere else and ignore the person who done right by me? That ain't in the Bible.

ROSE: We ain't talking about what's in the Bible. What sense it make to shop there when she overcharge?

TROY: You shop where you want to. I'll do my shopping where the people been good to me.

175 **ROSE:**   Well, I don't think it's right for her to overcharge. That's all I was saying.

BONO: Look here . . . I got to get on. Lucille going be raising all kind of hell.

TROY: Where you going, nigger? We ain't finished this
180 pint. Come here, finish this pint.

BONO: Well, hell, I am . . . if you ever turn the bottle loose.

TROY: *(Hands him the bottle.)* The only thing I say about the A&P is I'm glad Cory got that job down there.
185 Help him take care of his school clothes and things. Gabe done moved out and things getting tight around here. He got that job . . . He can start to look out for himself.

ROSE: Cory done went and got recruited by a college
190 football team.

TROY: I told that boy about that football stuff. The white man ain't gonna let him get nowhere with that football. I told him when he first come to me with it. Now you come telling me he done went and got more tied
195 up in it. He ought to go and get recruited in how to fix cars or something where he can make a living.

ROSE: He ain't talking about making no living playing football. It's just something the boys in school do. They gonna send a recruiter by to talk to you. He'll
200 tell you he ain't talking about making no living playing football. It's a honor to be recruited.

TROY: It ain't gonna get him nowhere. Bono'll tell you that.

BONO: If he be like you in the sports . . . he's gonna be al-
205 right. Ain't but two men ever played baseball as good as you. That's Babe Ruth and Josh Gibson. Them's the only two men ever hit more home runs than you.

TROY: What it ever get me? Ain't got a pot to piss in or a window to throw it out of.

210 **ROSE:**   Times have changed since you was playing baseball, Troy. That was before the war. Times have changed a lot since then.

TROY: How in hell they done changed?

ROSE: They got lots of colored boys playing ball now. Baseball and football.
215

BONO: You right about that, Rose. Times have changed, Troy. You just come along too early.

TROY: There ought not never have been no time called too early! Now you take that fellow . . . what's that fellow they had playing right field for the Yankees back
220 then? You know who I'm talking about, Bono. Used to play right field for the Yankees.

ROSE: Selkirk?

TROY: Selkirk! That's it! Man batting .269, understand? .269. What kind of sense that make? I was hitting
225 .432 with thirty-seven home runs! Man batting .269 and playing right field for the Yankees! I saw Josh Gibson's daughter yesterday. She walking around with raggedy shoes on her feet. Now I bet you Selkirk's daughter ain't walking around with raggedy shoes on
230 her feet! I bet you that!

ROSE: They got a lot of colored baseball players now. Jackie Robinson was the first. Folks had to wait for Jackie Robinson.

TROY: I done seen a hundred niggers play baseball bet-
235 ter than Jackie Robinson. Hell, I know some teams Jackie Robinson couldn't even make! What you talking about Jackie Robinson. Jackie Robinson wasn't nobody. I'm talking about if you could play ball then they ought to have let you play. Don't care what color
240 you were. Come telling me I come along too early. If you could play . . . then they ought to have let you play.

(TROY takes a long drink from the bottle.)

ROSE: You gonna drink yourself to death. You don't need to be drinking like that.

TROY: Death ain't nothing. I done seen him. Done
245 wrassled with him. You can't tell me nothing about death. Death ain't nothing but a fastball on the outside corner. And you know what I'll do to that! Lookee here, Bono . . . am I lying? You get one of them fastballs, about waist high, over the outside corner
250 of the plate where you can get the meat of the bat on it . . . and good god! You can kiss it goodbye. Now, am I lying?

BONO: Naw, you telling the truth there. I seen you do it.

255 **TROY:** If I'm lying . . . that 450 feet worth of lying! *(Pause.)* That's all death is to me. A fastball on the outside corner.

ROSE: I don't know why you want to get on talking about death.

260 **TROY:** Ain't nothing wrong with talking about death. That's part of life. Everybody gonna die. You gonna die, I'm gonna die. Bono's gonna die. Hell, we all gonna die.

ROSE: But you ain't got to talk about it. I don't like to
265 talk about it.

TROY: You the one brought it up. Me and Bono was talking about baseball . . . you tell me I'm gonna drink myself to death. Ain't that right, Bono? You know I don't drink this but one night out of the week. That's
270 Friday night. I'm gonna drink just enough to where I can handle it. Then I cuts it loose. I leave it alone. So don't you worry about me drinking myself to death. 'Cause I ain't worried about Death. I done seen him. I done wrestled with him.

275 Look here, Bono . . . I looked up one day and Death was marching straight at me. Like Soldiers on Parade! The Army of Death was marching straight at me. The middle of July, 1941. It got real cold just like it be winter. It seem like Death himself reached out
280 and touched me on the shoulder. He touch me just like I touch you. I got cold as ice and Death standing there grinning at me.

ROSE: Troy, why don't you hush that talk.

TROY: I say . . . what you want, Mr. Death? You be want-
285 ing me? You done brought your army to be getting me? I looked him dead in the eye. I wasn't fearing nothing. I was ready to tangle. Just like I'm ready to tangle now. The Bible say be ever vigilant. That's why I don't get but so drunk. I got to keep watch.

290 **ROSE:** Troy was right down there in Mercy Hospital. You remember he had pneumonia? Laying there with a fever talking plumb out of his head.

TROY: Death standing there staring at me . . . carrying that sickle in his hand. Finally he say, "You want
bound over for another year?" See, just like that . . . 295
"You want bound over for another year?" I told him,
"Bound over hell! Let's settle this now!"

It seem like he kinda fell back when I said that,
and all the cold went out of me. I reached down and
grabbed that sickle and threw it just as far as I could 300
throw it . . . and me and him commenced to wrestling.

We wrestled for three days and three nights.
I can't say where I found the strength from. Everytime it seemed like he was gonna get the best of me,
I'd reach way down deep inside myself and find the 305
strength to do him one better.

ROSE: Everytime Troy tell that story he find different ways to tell it. Different things to make up about it.

TROY: I ain't making up nothing. I'm telling you the facts
of what happened. I wrestled with Death for three 310
days and three nights and I'm standing here to tell
you about it. *(Pause.)* Alright. At the end of the third
night we done weakened each other to where we can't
hardly move. Death stood up, throwed on his robe . . .
had him a white robe with a hood on it. He throwed 315
on that robe and went off to look for his sickle. Say,
"I'll be back." Just like that. "I'll be back." I told him,
say, "Yeah, but . . . you gonna have to find me!" I
wasn't no fool. I wasn't going looking for him. Death
ain't nothing to play with. And I know he's gonna get 320
me. I know I got to join his army . . . his camp followers. But as long as I keep my strength and see him
coming . . . as long as I keep up my vigilance . . . he's
gonna have to fight to get me. I ain't going easy.

BONO: Well, look here, since you got to keep up your 325
vigilance . . . let me have the bottle.

TROY: Aw hell, I shouldn't have told you that part. I
should have left out that part.

ROSE: Troy be talking that stuff and half the time don't
even know what he be talking about. 330

TROY: Bono know me better than that.

BONO: That's right. I know you. I know you got some
Uncle Remus in your blood. You got more stories than
the devil got sinners.

335 **TROY:** Aw hell, I done seen him too! Done talked with the devil.

ROSE: Troy, don't nobody wanna be hearing all that stuff.

(LYONS *enters the yard from the street. Thirty-four years old,* TROY's *son by a previous marriage, he sports a neatly trimmed goatee, sport coat, white shirt, tieless and buttoned at the collar. Though he fancies himself a musician, he is more caught up in the rituals and "idea" of being a musician than in the actual practice of the music. He has come to borrow money from* TROY, *and while he knows he will be successful, he is uncertain as to what extent his lifestyle will be held up to scrutiny and ridicule.*)

LYONS: Hey, Pop.

340 **TROY:** What you come "Hey, Popping" me for?

LYONS: How you doing, Rose? (*He kisses her.*) Mr. Bono. How you doing?

BONO: Hey, Lyons . . . how you been?

TROY: He must have been doing alright. I ain't seen him
345 around here last week.

ROSE: Troy, leave your boy alone. He come by to see you and you wanna start all that nonsense.

TROY: I ain't bothering Lyons. (*Offers him the bottle.*)
Here . . . get you a drink. We got an understanding.
350 I know why he come by to see me and he know I know.

LYONS: Come on, Pop . . . I just stopped by to say hi . . . see how you was doing.

TROY: You ain't stopped by yesterday.

ROSE: You gonna stay for supper, Lyons? I got some
355 chicken cooking in the oven.

LYONS: No, Rose . . . thanks. I was just in the neighborhood and thought I'd stop by for a minute.

TROY: You was in the neighborhood alright, nigger. You telling the truth there. You was in the neighborhood
360 cause it's my payday.

LYONS: Well, hell, since you mentioned it . . . let me have ten dollars.

TROY: I'll be damned! I'll die and go to hell and play blackjack with the devil before I give you ten dollars.

BONO: That's what I wanna know about . . . that devil
365 you done seen.

LYONS: What . . . Pop done seen the devil? You too much, Pops.

TROY: Yeah, I done seen him. Talked to him too!

ROSE: You ain't seen no devil. I done told you that man
370 ain't had nothing to do with the devil. Anything you can't understand, you want to call it the devil.

TROY: Look here, Bono . . . I went down to see Hertz-berger about some furniture. Got three rooms for two-ninety-eight. That what it say on the radio.
375 "Three rooms . . . two-ninety-eight." Even made up a little song about it. Go down there . . . man tell me I can't get no credit. I'm working every day and can't get no credit. What to do? I got an empty house with some raggedy furniture in it. Cory ain't got no bed.
380 He's sleeping on a pile of rags on the floor. Working every day and can't get no credit. Come back here—Rose'll tell you—madder than hell. Sit down . . . try to figure what I'm gonna do. Come a knock on the door. Ain't been living here but three days. Who know I'm
385 here? Open the door . . . devil standing there bigger than life. White fellow . . . got on good clothes and everything. Standing there with a clipboard in his hand. I ain't had to say nothing. First words come out of his mouth was . . . "I understand you need some furniture
390 and can't get no credit." I liked to fell over. He say "I'll give you all the credit you want, but you got to pay the interest on it." I told him, "Give me three rooms worth and charge whatever you want." Next day a truck pulled up here and two men unloaded them three
395 rooms. Man what drove the truck give me a book. Say send ten dollars, first of every month to the address in the book and every thing will be alright. Say if I miss a payment the devil was coming back and it'll be hell to pay. That was fifteen years ago. To this day . . .
400 the first of the month I send my ten dollars, Rose'll tell you.

ROSE: Troy lying.

TROY: I ain't never seen that man since. Now you tell me
405   who else that could have been but the devil? I ain't
        sold my soul or nothing like that, you understand.
        Naw, I wouldn't have truck with the devil about noth-
        ing like that. I got my furniture and pays my ten dol-
        lars the first of the month just like clockwork.

410 **BONO:**   How long you say you been paying this ten dollars
        a month?

TROY: Fifteen years!

BONO: Hell, ain't you finished paying for it yet? How
        much the man done charged you?

415 **TROY:**   Aw hell, I done paid for it. I done paid for it ten
        times over! The fact is I'm scared to stop paying it.

ROSE: Troy lying. We got that furniture from Mr.
        Glickman. He ain't paying no ten dollars a month to
        nobody.

420 **TROY:**   Aw hell, woman. Bono know I ain't that big a fool.

LYONS: I was just getting ready to say . . . I know where
        there's a bridge for sale.

TROY: Look here, I'll tell you this . . . it don't matter to
        me if he was the devil. It don't matter if the devil give
425   credit. Somebody has got to give it.

ROSE: It ought to matter. You going around talking
        about having truck with the devil . . . God's the one
        you gonna have to answer to. He's the one gonna be at
        the Judgment.

430 **LYONS:**   Yeah, well, look here, Pop . . . Let me have that
        ten dollars. I'll give it back to you. Bonnie got a job
        working at the hospital.

TROY: What I tell you, Bono? The only time I see this
        nigger is when he wants something. That's the only
435   time I see him.

LYONS: Come on, Pop, Mr. Bono don't want to hear all
        that. Let me have the ten dollars. I told you Bonnie
        working.

TROY: What that mean to me? "Bonnie working." I don't
        care if she working. Go ask her for the ten dollars if   440
        she working. Talking about "Bonnie working." Why
        ain't you working?

LYONS: Aw, Pop, you know I can't find no decent job.
        Where am I gonna get a job at? You know I can't get
        no job.   445

TROY: I told you I know some people down there. I can
        get you on the rubbish if you want to work. I told you
        that the last time you came by here asking me for
        something.

LYONS: Naw, Pop . . . thanks. That ain't for me. I don't   450
        wanna be carrying nobody's rubbish. I don't wanna be
        punching nobody's time clock.

TROY: What's the matter, you too good to carry people's
        rubbish? Where you think that ten dollars you talking
        about come from? I'm just supposed to haul people's   455
        rubbish and give my money to you cause you too lazy
        to work. You too lazy to work and wanna know why
        you ain't got what I got.

ROSE: What hospital Bonnie working at? Mercy?

LYONS: She's down at Passavant working in the laundry.   460

TROY: I ain't got nothing as it is. I give you that ten
        dollars and I got to eat beans the rest of the week.
        Naw . . . you ain't getting no ten dollars here.

LYONS: You ain't got to be eating no beans. I don't know
        why you wanna say that.   465

TROY: I ain't got no extra money. Gabe done moved over
        to Miss Pearl's paying her the rent and things done got
        tight around here. I can't afford to be giving you every
        payday.

LYONS: I ain't asked you to give me nothing. I asked you   470
        to loan me ten dollars. I know you got ten dollars.

TROY: Yeah, I got it. You know why I got it? Cause I don't
        throw my money away out there in the streets. You
        living the fast life . . . wanna be a musician . . . run-
        ning around in them clubs and things . . . then, you   475
        learn to take care of yourself. You ain't gonna find me
        going and asking nobody for nothing. I done spent too
        many years without.

LYONS: You and me is two different people, Pop.

480 TROY: I done learned my mistake and learned to do what's right by it. You still trying to get something for nothing. Life don't owe you nothing. You owe it to yourself. Ask Bono. He'll tell you I'm right.

485 LYONS: You got your way of dealing with the world . . . I got mine. The only thing that matters to me is the music.

TROY: Yeah, I can see that! It don't matter how you gonna eat . . . where your next dollar is coming from. You telling the truth there.

490 LYONS: I know I got to eat. But I got to live too. I need something that gonna help me to get out of the bed in the morning. Make me feel like I belong in the world. I don't bother nobody. I just stay with my music cause that's the only way I can find to live in the world. 495 Otherwise there ain't no telling what I might do. Now I don't come criticizing you and how you live. I just come by to ask you for ten dollars. I don't wanna hear all that about how I live.

TROY: Boy, your mamma did a hell of a job raising you.

500 LYONS: You can't change me, Pop. I'm thirty-four years old. If you wanted to change me, you should have been there when I was growing up. I come by to see you . . . ask for ten dollars and you want to talk about how I 505 was raised. You don't know nothing about how I was raised.

ROSE: Let the boy have ten dollars, Troy.

TROY: (To LYONS.) What the hell you looking at me for? I ain't got no ten dollars. You know what I do with my money. (To ROSE.) Give him ten dollars if you want 510 him to have it.

ROSE: I will. Just as soon as you turn it loose.

TROY: (Handing ROSE the money.) There it is. Seventy-six dollars and forty-two cents. You see this, Bono? Now, I ain't gonna get but six of that back.

515 ROSE: You ought to stop telling that lie. Here, Lyons. (She hands him the money.)

LYONS: Thanks, Rose. Look . . . I got to run . . . I'll see you later.

TROY: Wait a minute. You gonna say, "thanks, Rose" and ain't gonna look to see where she got that ten dollars 520 from? See how they do me, Bono?

LYONS: I know she got it from you, Pop. Thanks. I'll give it back to you.

TROY: There he go telling another lie. Time I see that ten dollars . . . he'll be owing me thirty more. 525

LYONS: See you, Mr. Bono.

BONO: Take care, Lyons!

LYONS: Thanks, Pop. I'll see you again.

(LYONS exits the yard.)

TROY: I don't know why he don't go and get him a decent job and take care of that woman he got. 530

BONO: He'll be alright, Troy. The boy is still young.

TROY: The *boy* is thirty-four years old.

ROSE: Let's not get off into all that.

BONO: Look here . . . I got to be going. I got to be getting on. Lucille gonna be waiting. 535

TROY: (Puts his arm around ROSE.) See this woman, Bono? I love this woman. I love this woman so much it hurts. I love her so much . . . I done run out of ways of loving her. So I got to go back to basics. Don't you come by my house Monday morning talking 540 about time to go to work . . . 'cause I'm still gonna be stroking!

ROSE: Troy! Stop it now!

BONO: I ain't paying him no mind, Rose. That ain't nothing but gin-talk. Go on, Troy. I'll see you Monday. 545

TROY: Don't you come by my house, nigger! I done told you what I'm gonna be doing.

(The lights go down to black.)

SCENE 2

The lights come up on ROSE *hanging up clothes. She hums and sings softly to herself. It is the following morning.*

ROSE: *(Sings.)*

Jesus, be a fence all around me every day
Jesus, I want you to protect me as I travel on
 my way.
Jesus, be a fence all around me every day.

*(*TROY *enters from the house.)*

Jesus, I want you to protect me
5 As I travel on my way.
(To TROY.*)* 'Morning. You ready for breakfast? I can fix it soon as I finish hanging up these clothes.

TROY: I got the coffee on. That'll be alright. I'll just drink some of that this morning.

10 ROSE: That 651 hit yesterday. That's the second time this month. Miss Pearl hit for a dollar . . . seem like those that need the least always get lucky. Poor folks can't get nothing.

TROY: Them numbers don't know anybody. I don't know
15 why you fool with them. You and Lyons both.

ROSE: It's something to do.

TROY: You ain't doing nothing but throwing your money away.

ROSE: Troy, you know I don't play foolishly. I just play a
20 nickel here and a nickel there.

TROY: That's two nickels you done thrown away.

ROSE: Now I hit sometimes . . . that makes up for it. It always comes in handy when I do hit. I don't hear you complaining then.

25 TROY: I ain't complaining now. I just say it's foolish. Trying to guess out of six hundred ways which way the number gonna come. If I had all the money niggers, these Negroes, throw away on numbers for one week—just one week—I'd be a rich man.

ROSE: Well, you wishing and calling it foolish ain't
30 gonna stop folks from playing numbers. That's one thing for sure. Besides . . . some good things come from playing numbers. Look where Pope done bought him that restaurant off of numbers.

TROY: I can't stand niggers like that. Man ain't had two
35 dimes to rub together. He walking around with his shoes all run over bumming money for cigarettes. Alright. Got lucky there and hit the numbers . . .

ROSE: Troy, I know all about it.

TROY: Had good sense, I'll say that for him. He ain't
40 throwed his money away. I seen niggers hit the numbers and go through two thousand dollars in four days. Man bought him that restaurant down there . . . fixed it up real nice. . . . and then didn't want nobody to come in it! A Negro go in there and can't get no
45 kind of service. I seen a white fellow come in there and order a bowl of stew. Pope picked all the meat out of the pot for him. Man ain't had nothing but a bowl of meat! Negro come behind him and ain't got nothing but the potatoes and carrots. Talking about what
50 numbers do for people, you picked a wrong example. Ain't done nothing but make a worser fool out of him than he was before.

ROSE: Troy, you ought to stop worrying about what happened at work yesterday.
55

TROY: I ain't worried. Just told me to be down there at the Commissioner's office on Friday. Everybody think they gonna fire me. I ain't worried about them firing me. You ain't got to worry about that. *(Pause.)* Where's Cory? Cory in the house? *(Calls.)* Cory?
60

ROSE: He gone out.

TROY: Out, huh? He gone out 'cause he know I want him to help me with this fence. I know how he is. That boy scared of work.

*(*GABRIEL *enters. He comes halfway down the alley and, hearing* TROY's *voice, stops.)*

TROY: *(Continues.)* He ain't done a lick of work in his life. 65

ROSE: He had to go to football practice. Coach wanted them to get in a little extra practice before the season start.

TROY: I got his practice . . . running out of here before he
get his chores done.

ROSE: Troy, what is wrong with you this morning? Don't
nothing set right with you. Go on back in there and go
to bed . . . get up on the other side.

TROY: Why something got to be wrong with me? I ain't
said nothing wrong with me.

ROSE: You got something to say about everything. First
it's the numbers . . . then it's the way the man runs
his restaurant . . . then you done got on Cory. What's
it gonna be next? Take a look up there and see if the
weather suits you . . . or is it gonna be how you gonna
put up the fence with the clothes hanging in the yard?

TROY: You hit the nail on the head then.

ROSE: I know you like I know the back of my hand. Go
on in there and get you some coffee . . . see if that
straighten you up. 'Cause you ain't right this morning.

(TROY *starts into the house and sees* GABRIEL.
GABRIEL *starts singing.* TROY's *brother, he is seven
years younger than* TROY. *Injured in World War II, he
has a metal plate in his head. He carries an old trumpet tied around his waist and believes with every fiber
of his being that he is the Archangel Gabriel. He carries a chipped basket with an assortment of discarded
fruits and vegetables he has picked up in the strip
district and which he attempts to sell.*)

GABRIEL: (*Singing.*)
Yes, ma'am, I got plums
You ask me how I sell them
Oh ten cents apiece
Three for a quarter
Come and buy now
'Cause I'm here today
And tomorrow I'll be gone

(GABRIEL *enters.*)

Hey, Rose!

ROSE: How you doing, Gabe?

GABRIEL: There's Troy . . . Hey, Troy!

TROY: Hey, Gabe.

(*Exit into kitchen.*)

ROSE: (*To* GABRIEL.) What you got there?

GABRIEL: You know what I got, Rose. I got fruits and
vegetables.

ROSE: (*Looking in basket.*) Where's all these plums you
talking about?

GABRIEL: I ain't got no plums today, Rose. I was just
singing that. Have some tomorrow. Put me in a big
order for plums. Have enough plums tomorrow for
St. Peter and everybody.

(TROY *reenters from kitchen, crosses to steps.*)

(*To* ROSE.) Troy's mad at me.

TROY: I ain't mad at you. What I got to be mad at you
about? You ain't done nothing to me.

GABRIEL: I just moved over to Miss Pearl's to keep out
from in your way. I ain't mean no harm by it.

TROY: Who said anything about that? I ain't said anything about that.

GABRIEL: You ain't mad at me, is you?

TROY: Naw . . . I ain't mad at you, Gabe. If I was mad at
you I'd tell you about it.

GABRIEL: Got me two rooms. In the basement. Got my
own door too. Wanna see my key? (*He holds up a key.*)
That's my own key! Ain't nobody else got a key like
that. That's my key! My two rooms!

TROY: Well, that's good, Gabe. You got your own key . . .
that's good.

ROSE: You hungry, Gabe? I was just fixing to cook Troy
his breakfast.

GABRIEL: I'll take some biscuits. You got some biscuits? Did you know when I was in heaven . . . every
morning me and St. Peter would sit down by the gate
and eat some big fat biscuits? Oh, yeah! We had us
a good time. We'd sit there and eat us them biscuits
and then St. Peter would go off to sleep and tell me to
wake him up when it's time to open the gates for the
judgment.

ROSE: Well, come on . . . I'll make up a batch of biscuits.

(ROSE *exits into the house.*)

GABRIEL: Troy . . . St. Peter got your name in the book. I seen it. It say . . . Troy Maxson. I say . . . I know him!
135 He got the same name like what I got. That's my brother!

TROY: How many times you gonna tell me that, Gabe?

GABRIEL: Ain't got my name in the book. Don't have to have my name. I done died and went to heaven. He
140 got your name though. One morning St. Peter was looking at his book . . . marking it up for the judgment . . . and he let me see your name. Got it in there under M. Got Rose's name . . . I ain't seen it like I seen yours . . . but I know it's in there. He got a great big
145 book. Got everybody's name what was ever been born. That's what he told me. But I seen your name. Seen it with my own eyes.

TROY: Go on in the house there. Rose going to fix you something to eat.

150 **GABRIEL:** Oh, I ain't hungry. I done had breakfast with Aunt Jemimah. She come by and cooked me up a whole mess of flapjacks. Remember how we used to eat them flapjacks?

TROY: Go on in the house and get you something to eat
155 now.

GABRIEL: I got to sell my plums. I done sold some tomatoes. Got me two quarters. Wanna see? (*He shows* TROY *his quarters.*) I'm gonna save them and buy me a new horn so St. Peter can hear me when it's time to
160 open the gates. (GABRIEL *stops suddenly. Listens.*) Hear that? That's the hellhounds. I got to chase them out of here. Go on get out of here! Get out!

(GABRIEL *exits singing.*)

Better get ready for the judgment
Better get ready for the judgment
165 My Lord is coming down

(ROSE *enters from the house.*)

TROY: He gone off somewhere.

GABRIEL: (*Offstage.*) Better get ready for the judgment
Better get ready for the judgment morning
Better get ready for the judgment
My God is coming down   170

ROSE: He ain't eating right. Miss Pearl say she can't get him to eat nothing.

TROY: What you want me to do about it, Rose? I done did everything I can for the man. I can't make him get well. Man got half his head blown away . . . what you   175
expect?

ROSE: Seem like something ought to be done to help him.

TROY: Man don't bother nobody. He just mixed up from that metal plate he got in his head. Ain't no sense for   180
him to go back into the hospital.

ROSE: Least he be eating right. They can help him take care of himself.

TROY: Don't nobody wanna be locked up, Rose. What you wanna lock him up for? Man go over there and   185
fight the war . . . messin' around with them Japs, get half his head blown off . . . and they give him a lousy three thousand dollars. And I had to swoop down on that.

ROSE: Is you fixing to go into that again?   190

TROY: That's the only way I got a roof over my head . . . cause of that metal plate.

ROSE: Ain't no sense you blaming yourself for nothing. Gabe wasn't in no condition to manage that money. You done what was right by him. Can't nobody say you   195
ain't done what was right by him. Look how long you took care of him . . . till he wanted to have his own place and moved over there with Miss Pearl.

TROY: That ain't what I'm saying, woman! I'm just stating the facts. If my brother didn't have that metal   200
plate in his head . . . I wouldn't have a pot to piss in or a window to throw it out of. And I'm fifty-three years old. Now see if you can understand that!

(TROY *gets up from the porch and starts to exit the yard.*)

ROSE: Where you going off to? You been running out
205 of here every Saturday for weeks. I thought you was
gonna work on this fence?

TROY: I'm gonna walk down to Taylors'. Listen to the
ball game. I'll be back in a bit. I'll work on it when I
get back.

(He exits the yard. The lights go to black.)

SCENE 3

The lights come up on the yard. It is four hours later.
ROSE *is taking down the clothes from the line.* CORY
enters carrying his football equipment.

ROSE: Your daddy like to had a fit with you running out
of here this morning without doing your chores.

CORY: I told you I had to go to practice.

ROSE: He say you were supposed to help him with this
5 fence.

CORY: He been saying that the last four or five Saturdays, and then he don't never do nothing, but go down
to Taylors'. Did you tell him about the recruiter?

ROSE: Yeah, I told him.

10 **CORY:** What he say?

ROSE: He ain't said nothing too much. You get in there
and get started on your chores before he gets back.
Go on and scrub down them steps before he gets back
here hollering and carrying on.

15 **CORY:** I'm hungry. What you got to eat, Mama?

ROSE: Go on and get started on your chores. I got
some meat loaf in there. Go on and make you a sandwich . . . and don't leave no mess in there.

(CORY exits into the house. ROSE *continues to take
down the clothes.* TROY *enters the yard and sneaks up
and grabs her from behind.)*

Troy! Go on, now. You liked to scared me to death.
20 What was the score of the game? Lucille had me on
the phone and I couldn't keep up with it.

TROY: What I care about the game? Come here, woman.
(He tries to kiss her.)

ROSE: I thought you went down Taylors' to listen to the
game. Go on, Troy! You supposed to be putting up this 25
fence.

TROY: *(Attempting to kiss her again.)* I'll put it up when I
finish with what is at hand.

ROSE: Go on, Troy. I ain't studying you.

TROY: *(Chasing after her.)* I'm studying you . . . fixing to 30
do my homework!

ROSE: Troy, you better leave me alone.

TROY: Where's Cory? That boy brought his butt home
yet?

ROSE: He's in the house doing his chores. 35

TROY: *(Calling.)* Cory! Get your butt out here, boy!

*(*ROSE *exits into the house with the laundry.* TROY
*goes over to the pile of wood, picks up a board, and
starts sawing.* CORY *enters from the house.)*

TROY: You just now coming in here from leaving this
morning?

CORY: Yeah, I had to go to football practice.

TROY: Yeah, what? 40

CORY: Yessir.

TROY: I ain't but two seconds off you noway. The garbage
sitting in there overflowing . . . you ain't done none of
your chores . . . and you come in here talking about
"Yeah." 45

CORY: I was just getting ready to do my chores now,
Pop . . .

TROY: Your first chore is to help me with this fence on
Saturday. Everything else come after that. Now get
that saw and cut them boards. 50

*(CORY *takes the saw and begins cutting the boards.*
TROY *continues working. There is a long pause.)*

CORY: Hey, Pop . . . why don't you buy a TV?

TROY: What I want with a TV? What I want one of them for?

CORY: Everybody got one. Earl, Ba Bra . . . Jesse!

55 **TROY:**   I ain't asked you who had one. I say what I want with one?

CORY: So you can watch it. They got lots of things on TV. Baseball games and everything. We could watch the World Series.

60 **TROY:**   Yeah . . . and how much this TV cost?

CORY: I don't know. They got them on sale for around two hundred dollars.

TROY: Two hundred dollars, huh?

CORY: That ain't that much, Pop.

65 **TROY:**   Naw, it's just two hundred dollars. See that roof you got over your head at night? Let me tell you something about that roof. It's been over ten years since that roof was last tarred. See now . . . the snow come this winter and sit up there on that roof like it is . . . 70 and it's gonna seep inside. It's just gonna be a little bit . . . ain't gonna hardly notice it. Then the next thing you know, it's gonna be leaking all over the house. Then the wood rot from all that water and you gonna need a whole new roof. Now, how much you 75 think it cost to get that roof tarred?

CORY: I don't know.

TROY: Two hundred and sixty-four dollars . . . cash money. While you thinking about a TV, I got to be thinking about the roof . . . and whatever else go 80 wrong here. Now if you had two hundred dollars, what would you do . . . fix the roof or buy a TV?

CORY: I'd buy a TV. Then when the roof started to leak . . . when it needed fixing . . . I'd fix it.

TROY: Where you gonna get the money from? You done 85 spent it for a TV. You gonna sit up and watch the water run all over your brand new TV.

CORY: Aw, Pop. You got money. I know you do.

TROY: Where I got it at, huh?

CORY: You got it in the bank.

TROY: You wanna see my bankbook? You wanna see that 90 seventy-three dollars and twenty-two cents I got sitting up in there?

CORY: You ain't got to pay for it all at one time. You can put a down payment on it and carry it on home with you. 95

TROY: Not me. I ain't gonna owe nobody nothing if I can help it. Miss a payment and they come and snatch it right out your house. Then what you got? Now, soon as I get two hundred dollars clear, then I'll buy a TV. Right now, as soon as I get two hundred and sixty- 100 four dollars, I'm gonna have this roof tarred.

CORY: Aw . . . Pop!

TROY: You go on and get you two hundred dollars and buy one if ya want it. I got better things to do with my money. 105

CORY: I can't get no two hundred dollars. I ain't never seen two hundred dollars.

TROY: I'll tell you what . . . you get you a hundred dollars and I'll put the other hundred with it.

CORY: Alright, I'm gonna show you. 110

TROY: You gonna show me how you can cut them boards right now.

(CORY *begins to cut the boards. There is a long pause.*)

CORY: The Pirates won today. That makes five in a row.

TROY: I ain't thinking about the Pirates. Got an all-white team. Got that boy . . . that Puerto Rican boy . . . 115 Clemente. Don't even half-play him. That boy could be something if they give him a chance. Play him one day and sit him on the bench the next.

CORY: He gets a lot of chances to play.

TROY: I'm talking about playing regular. Playing every 120 day so you can get your timing. That's what I'm talking about.

CORY: They got some white guys on the team that don't play every day. You can't play everybody at the same time. 125

TROY: If they got a white fellow sitting on the bench . . . you can bet your last dollar he can't play! The colored guy got to be twice as good before he get on the team. That's why I don't want you to get all tied up in them sports. Man on the team and what it get him? They got colored on the team and don't use them. Same as not having them. All them teams the same.

CORY: The Braves got Hank Aaron and Wes Covington. Hank Aaron hit two home runs today. That makes forty-three.

TROY: Hank Aaron ain't nobody. That's what you supposed to do. That's how you supposed to play the game. Ain't nothing to it. It's just a matter of timing . . . getting the right follow-through. Hell, I can hit forty-three home runs right now!

CORY: Not off no major-league pitching, you couldn't.

TROY: We had better pitching in the Negro leagues. I hit seven home runs off of Satchel Paige. You can't get no better than that!

CORY: Sandy Koufax. He's leading the league in strikeouts.

TROY: I ain't thinking of no Sandy Koufax.

CORY: You got Warren Spahn and Lew Burdette. I bet you couldn't hit no home runs off of Warren Spahn.

TROY: I'm through with it now. You go on and cut them boards. *(Pause.)* Your mama tell me you done got recruited by a college football team? Is that right?

CORY: Yeah. Coach Zellman say the recruiter gonna be coming by to talk to you. Get you to sign the permission papers.

TROY: I thought you supposed to be working down there at the A&P. Ain't you suppose to be working down there after school?

CORY: Mr. Stawicki say he gonna hold my job for me until after the football season. Say starting next week I can work weekends.

TROY: I thought we had an understanding about this football stuff? You suppose to keep up with your chores and hold that job down at the A&P. Ain't been

Troy (Laurence Fishburne) reminds Cory (Bryan Clark) of the deal they made in this 2006 production directed by Sheldon Epps.

around here all day on a Saturday. Ain't none of your chores done . . . and now you telling me you done quit your job.

CORY: I'm going to be working weekends.

TROY: You damn right you are! And ain't no need for nobody coming around here to talk to me about signing nothing.

CORY: Hey, Pop . . . you can't do that. He's coming all the way from North Carolina.

TROY: I don't care where he coming from. The white man ain't gonna let you get nowhere with that football noway. You go on and get your book-learning so you

180 can work yourself up in that A&P or learn how to fix cars or build houses or something, get you a trade. That way you have something can't nobody take away from you. You go on and learn how to put your hands to some good use. Besides hauling people's garbage.

CORY: I get good grades, Pop. That's why the recruiter wants to talk with you. You got to keep up your grades to get recruited. This way I'll be going to college. I'll 185 get a chance . . .

TROY: First you gonna get your butt down there to the A&P and get your job back.

CORY: Mr. Stawicki done already hired somebody else 'cause I told him I was playing football.

190 **TROY:** You a bigger fool than I thought . . . to let somebody take away your job so you can play some football. Where you gonna get your money to take out your girlfriend and whatnot? What kind of foolishness is that to let somebody take away your job?

195 **CORY:** I'm still gonna be working weekends.

TROY: Naw . . . naw. You getting your butt out of here and finding you another job.

CORY: Come on, Pop! I got to practice. I can't work after school and play football too. The team needs me. 200 That's what Coach Zellman say . . .

TROY: I don't care what nobody else say. I'm the boss . . . you understand? I'm the boss around here. I do the only saying what counts.

CORY: Come on, Pop!

205 **TROY:** I asked you . . . did you understand?

CORY: Yeah . . .

TROY: What?!

CORY: Yessir.

TROY: You go on down there to that A&P and see if you 210 can get your job back. If you can't do both . . . then you quit the football team. You've got to take the crookeds with the straights.

CORY: Yessir. (*Pause.*) Can I ask you a question?

TROY: What the hell you wanna ask me? Mr. Stawicki the one you got the questions for. 215

CORY: How come you ain't never liked me?

TROY: Liked you? Who the hell say I got to like you? What law is there say I got to like you? Wanna stand up in my face and ask a damn fool-ass question like that. Talking about liking somebody. Come here, boy, 220 when I talk to you.

(*CORY comes over to where* TROY *is working. He stands slouched over and* TROY *shoves him on his shoulder.*)

Straighten up, goddammit! I asked you a question . . . what law is there say I got to like you?

CORY: None.

TROY: Well, alright then! Don't you eat every day? 225 (*Pause.*) Answer me when I talk to you! Don't you eat every day?

CORY: Yeah.

TROY: Nigger, as long as you in my house, you put that sir on the end of it when you talk to me. 230

CORY: Yes . . . sir.

TROY: You eat every day.

CORY: Yessir!

TROY: Got a roof over your head.

CORY: Yessir! 235

TROY: Got clothes on your back.

CORY: Yessir.

TROY: Why you think that is?

CORY: Cause of you.

TROY: Aw, hell I know it's 'cause of me . . . but why do you 240 think that is?

CORY: (*Hesitant.*) Cause you like me.

TROY: Like you? I go out of here every morning . . . bust my butt . . . putting up with them crackers every day

245 . . . cause I like you? You about the biggest fool I ever
saw. *(Pause.)* It's my job. It's my responsibility! You
understand that? A man got to take care of his family.
You live in my house . . . sleep you behind on my bed-
clothes . . . fill you belly up with my food . . . cause you
250 my son. You my flesh and blood. Not 'cause I like you!
Cause it's my duty to take care of you. I owe a responsibility to you!

Let's get this straight right here . . . before it go
along any further . . . I ain't got to like you. Mr. Rand
255 don't give me my money come payday cause he likes
me. He gives me cause he owe me. I done give you
everything I had to give you. I gave you your life! Me
and your mama worked that out between us. And
liking your black ass wasn't part of the bargain. Don't
260 you try and go through life worrying about if somebody like you or not. You best be making sure they
doing right by you. You understand what I'm saying,
boy?

CORY: Yessir.

265 **TROY:** Then get the hell out of my face, and get on down
to that A&P.

*(ROSE has been standing behind the screen door for
much of the scene. She enters as CORY exits.)*

ROSE: Why don't you let the boy go ahead and play football, Troy? Ain't no harm in that. He's just trying to be
like you with the sports.

270 **TROY:** I don't want him to be like me! I want him to
move as far away from my life as he can get. You the
only decent thing that ever happened to me. I wish
him that. But I don't wish him a thing else from my
life. I decided seventeen years ago that boy wasn't
275 getting involved in no sports. Not after what they did
to me in the sports.

ROSE: Troy, why don't you admit you was too old to
play in the major leagues? For once . . . why don't you
admit that?

280 **TROY:** What do you mean too old? Don't come telling me
I was too old. I just wasn't the right color. Hell, I'm
fifty-three years old and can do better than Selkirk's
.269 right now!

ROSE: How's was you gonna play ball when you were
over forty? Sometimes I can't get no sense out of you. 285

TROY: I got good sense, woman. I got sense enough not
to let my boy get hurt over playing no sports. You been
mothering that boy too much. Worried about if people
like him.

ROSE: Everything that boy do . . . he do for you. He 290
wants you to say "Good job, son." That's all.

TROY: Rose, I ain't got time for that. He's alive. He's
healthy. He's got to make his own way. I made mine.
Ain't nobody gonna hold his hand when he get out
there in that world. 295

ROSE: Times have changed from when you was young,
Troy. People change. The world's changing around you
and you can't even see it.

TROY: *(Slow, methodical.)* Woman . . . I do the best I
can do. I come in here every Friday. I carry a sack of 300
potatoes and a bucket of lard. You all line up at the
door with your hands out. I give you the lint from my
pockets. I give you my sweat and my blood. I ain't got
no tears. I done spent them. We go upstairs in that
room at night . . . and I fall down on you and try to 305
blast a hole into forever. I get up Monday morning . . .
find my lunch on the table. I go out. Make my way.
Find my strength to carry me through to the next
Friday. *(Pause.)* That's all I got, Rose. That's all I got
to give. I can't give nothing else. 310

*(TROY exits into the house. The lights go down to
black.)*

SCENE 4

*It is Friday. Two weeks later. CORY starts out of the
house with his football equipment. The phone rings.*

CORY: *(Calling.)* I got it! *(He answers the phone and
stands in the screen door talking.)* Hello? Hey, Jesse.
Naw . . . I was just getting ready to leave now.

ROSE: *(Calling.)* Cory!

CORY: I told you, man, them spikes is all tore up. You can 5
use them if you want, but they ain't no good. Earl got
some spikes.

ROSE: *(Calling.)* Cory!

CORY: *(Calling to* ROSE*)* Mam? I'm talking to Jesse. *(Into*
10   *phone.)* When she say that? *(Pause.)* Aw, you lying,
       man. I'm gonna tell her you said that.

ROSE: *(Calling.)* Cory, don't you go nowhere!

CORY: I got to go to the game, Ma! *(Into the phone.)* Yeah,
15   hey, look, I'll talk to you later. Yeah, I'll meet you over
       Earl's house. Later. Bye, Ma.

       (CORY exits the house and starts out the yard.)

ROSE: Cory, where you going off to? You got that stuff all
       pulled out and thrown all over your room.

CORY: *(In the yard.)* I was looking for my spikes. Jesse
       wanted to borrow my spikes.

20 **ROSE:** Get up there and get that cleaned up before your
       daddy get back in here.

CORY: I got to go to the game! I'll clean it up *when I get*
       back.

       (CORY exits.)

ROSE: That's all he need to do is see that room all
25   messed up.

       (ROSE exits into the house. TROY *and* BONO *enter the*
       yard. TROY *is dressed in clothes other than his work*
       clothes.)

BONO: He told him the same thing he told you. Take it to
       the union.

TROY: Brownie ain't got that much sense. Man wasn't
       thinking about nothing. He wait until I confront them
30   on it . . . then he wanna come crying seniority. *(Calls.)*
       Hey, Rose!

BONO: I wish I could have seen Mr. Rand's face when he
       told you.

TROY: He couldn't get it out of his mouth! Liked to bit
35   his tongue! When they called me down there to the
       Commissioner's office . . . he thought they was gonna
       fire me. Like everybody else.

BONO: I didn't think they was gonna fire you. I thought
       they was gonna put you on the warning paper.

TROY: Hey, Rose! *(To* BONO.*)* Yeah, Mr. Rand like to bit   40
       his tongue.

       (TROY breaks the seal on the bottle, takes a drink, and
       hands it to BONO.*)*

BONO: I see you run right down to Taylors' and told that
       Alberta gal.

TROY: *(Calling.)* Hey Rose! *(To* BONO.*)* I told everybody.
       Hey, Rose! I went down there to cash my check.   45

ROSE: *(Entering from the house.)* Hush all that hollering,
       man! I know you out here. What they say down there
       at the Commissioner's office?

TROY: You supposed to come when I call you, woman.
       Bono'll tell you that. *(To* BONO.*)* Don't Lucille come   50
       when you call her?

ROSE: Man, hush your mouth. I ain't no dog . . . talk
       about "come when you call me."

TROY: *(Puts his arm around* ROSE.*)* You hear this, Bono?
       I had me an old dog used to get uppity like that. You   55
       say, "C'mere, Blue!" . . . and he just lay there and look
       at you. End up getting a stick and chasing him away
       trying to make him come.

ROSE: I ain't studying you and your dog. I remember you
       used to sing that old song.   60

TROY: *(He sings.)*
       Hear it ring! Hear it ring!
       I had a dog his name was Blue.

ROSE: Don't nobody wanna hear you sing that old song.

TROY: *(Sings.)*
       You know Blue was mighty true.

ROSE: Used to have Cory running around here singing   65
       that song.

BONO: Hell, I remember that song myself.

TROY: *(Sings.)*
       You know Blue was a good old dog.
       Blue treed a possum in a hollow log.
       That was my daddy's song. My daddy made up   70
       that song.

ROSE: I don't care who made it up. Don't nobody wanna hear you sing it.

TROY: *(Makes a song like calling a dog.)* Come here, woman.

ROSE: You come in here carrying on, I reckon they ain't fired you. What they say down there at the Commissioner's office?

TROY: Look here, Rose . . . Mr. Rand called me into his office today when I got back from talking to them people down there . . . it come from up top . . . he called me in and told me they was making me a driver.

ROSE: Troy, you kidding!

TROY: No I ain't. Ask Bono.

ROSE: Well, that's great, Troy. Now you don't have to hassle them people no more.

(LYONS enters from the street.)

TROY: Aw hell, I wasn't looking to see you today. I thought you was in jail. Got it all over the front page of the *Courier* about them raiding Sefus's place . . . where you be hanging out with all them thugs.

LYONS: Hey, Pop . . . that ain't got nothing to do with me. I don't go down there gambling. I go down there to sit in with the band. I ain't got nothing to do with the gambling part. They got some good music down there.

TROY: They got some rogues . . . is what they got.

LYONS: How you been, Mr. Bono? Hi, Rose.

BONO: I see where you playing down at the Crawford Grill tonight.

ROSE: How come you ain't brought Bonnie like I told you? You should have brought Bonnie with you, she ain't been over in a month of Sundays.

LYONS: I was just in the neighborhood . . . thought I'd stop by.

TROY: Here he come . . .

BONO: Your daddy got a promotion on the rubbish. He's gonna be the first colored driver. Ain't got to do

nothing but sit up there and read the paper like them white fellows.

LYONS: Hey, Pop . . . if you knew how to read you'd be alright.

BONO: Naw . . . naw . . . you mean if the nigger knew how to *drive* he'd be alright. Been fighting with them people about driving and ain't even got a license. Mr. Rand know you ain't got no driver's license?

TROY: Driving ain't nothing. All you do is point the truck where you want it to go. Driving ain't nothing.

BONO: Do Mr. Rand know you ain't got no driver's license? That's what I'm talking about. I ain't asked if driving was easy. I asked if Mr. Rand know you ain't got no driver's license.

TROY: He ain't got to know. The man ain't got to know my business. Time he find out, I have two or three driver's licenses.

LYONS: *(Going into his pocket.)* Say, look here, Pop . . .

TROY: I knew it was coming. Didn't I tell you, Bono? I know what kind of "Look here, Pop" that was. The nigger fixing to ask me for some money. It's Friday night. It's my payday. All them rogues down there on the avenue . . . the ones that ain't in jail . . . and Lyons is hopping in his shoes to get down there with them.

LYONS: See, Pop . . . if you give somebody else a chance to talk sometime, you'd see that I was fixing to pay you back your ten dollars like I told you. Here . . . I told you I'd pay you when Bonnie got paid.

TROY: Naw . . . you go ahead and keep that ten dollars. Put in the bank. The next time you feel like you wanna come by here and ask me for something . . . you go on down there and get that.

LYONS: Here's your ten dollars, Pop. I told you I don't want you to give me nothing. I just wanted to borrow ten dollars.

TROY: Naw . . . you go on and keep that for the next time you want to ask me.

LYONS: Come on, Pop . . . here go your ten dollars.

ROSE: Why don't you go on and let the boy pay you back, Troy?

LYONS: Here you go, Rose. If you don't take it I'm gonna have to hear about it for the next six months. *(He hands her the money.)*

ROSE: You can hand yours over here too, Troy.

TROY: You see this, Bono. You see how they do me.

BONO: Yeah, Lucille do me the same way.

(GABRIEL is heard singing offstage. He enters.)

GABRIEL: Better get ready for the Judgment! Better get ready for . . . Hey! . . . Hey! . . . There's Troy's boy!

LYONS: How are you doing, Uncle Gabe?

GABRIEL: Lyons . . . The King of the Jungle! Rose . . . hey, Rose. Got a flower for you. *(He takes a rose from his pocket.)* Picked it myself. That's the same rose like you is!

ROSE: That's right nice of you, Gabe.

LYONS: What you been doing, Uncle Gabe?

GABRIEL: Oh, I been chasing hellhounds and waiting on the time to tell St. Peter to open the gates.

LYONS: You been chasing hellhounds, huh? Well . . . you doing the right thing, Uncle Gabe. Somebody got to chase them.

GABRIEL: Oh, yeah . . . I know it. The devil's strong. The devil ain't no pushover. Hellhounds snipping at everybody's heels. But I got my trumpet waiting on the judgment time.

LYONS: Waiting on the Battle of Armageddon, huh?

GABRIEL: Ain't gonna be too much of a battle when God get to waving that Judgment sword. But the people's gonna have a hell of a time trying to get into heaven if them gates ain't open.

LYONS: *(Putting his arm around* GABRIEL.*)* You hear this, Pop. Uncle Gabe, you alright!

GABRIEL: *(Laughing with* LYONS.*)* Lyons! King of the Jungle.

ROSE: You gonna stay for supper, Gabe? Want me to fix you a plate?

GABRIEL: I'll take a sandwich, Rose. Don't want no plate. Just wanna eat with my hands. I'll take a sandwich.

ROSE: How about you, Lyons? You staying? Got some short ribs cooking.

LYONS: Naw, I won't eat nothing till after we finished playing. *(Pause.)* You ought to come down and listen to me play, Pop.

TROY: I don't like that Chinese music. All that noise.

ROSE: Go on in the house and wash up, Gabe . . . I'll fix you a sandwich.

GABRIEL: *(To* LYONS, *as he exits.)* Troy's mad at me.

LYONS: What you mad at Uncle Gabe for, Pop?

ROSE: He thinks Troy's mad at him cause he moved over to Miss Pearl's.

TROY: I ain't mad at the man. He can live where he want to live at.

LYONS: What he move over there for? Miss Pearl don't like nobody.

ROSE: She don't mind him none. She treats him real nice. She just don't allow all that singing.

TROY: She don't mind that rent he be paying . . . that's what she don't mind.

ROSE: Troy, I ain't going through that with you no more. He's over there cause he want to have his own place. He can come and go as he please.

TROY: Hell, he could come and go as he please here. I wasn't stopping him. I ain't put no rules on him.

ROSE: It ain't the same thing, Troy. And you know it.

(GABRIEL comes to the door.)

Now, that's the last I wanna hear about that. I don't wanna hear nothing else about Gabe and Miss Pearl. And next week . . .

215 **GABRIEL:**   I'm ready for my sandwich, Rose.

ROSE: And next week . . . when that recruiter come from that school . . . I want you to sign that paper and go on and let Cory play football. Then that'll be the last I have to hear about that.

220 **TROY:**   (*To* ROSE *as she exits into the house.*) I ain't thinking about Cory nothing.

LYONS: What . . . Cory got recruited? What school he going to?

TROY: That boy walking around here smelling his
225 piss . . . thinking he's grown. Thinking he's gonna do what he want, irrespective of what I say. Look here, Bono . . . I left the Commissioner's office and went down to the A&P . . . that boy ain't working down there. He lying to me. Telling me he got his job
230 back . . . telling me he working weekends . . . telling me he working after school . . . Mr. Stawicki tell me he ain't working down there at all!

LYONS: Cory just growing up. He's just busting at the seams trying to fill out your shoes.

235 **TROY:**   I don't care what he's doing. When he get to the point where he wanna disobey me . . . then it's time for him to move on. Bono'll tell you that. I bet he ain't never disobeyed his daddy without paying the consequences.

240 **BONO:**   I ain't never had a chance. My daddy came on through . . . but I ain't never knew him to see him . . . or what he had on his mind or where he went. Just moving on through. Searching out the New Land. That's what the old folks used to call it. See a fellow
245 moving around from place to place . . . woman to woman . . . called it searching out the New Land. I can't say if he ever found it. I come along, didn't want no kids. Didn't know if I was gonna be in one place long enough to fix on them right as their daddy. I
250 figured I was going searching too. As it turned out I been hooked up with Lucille near about as long as your daddy been with Rose. Going on sixteen years.

TROY: Sometimes I wish I hadn't known my daddy. He ain't cared nothing about no kids. A kid to him wasn't
255 nothing. All he wanted was for you to learn how to walk so he could start you to working. When it come

time for eating . . . he ate first. If there was anything left over, that's what you got. Man would sit down and eat two chickens and give you the wing.

260 **LYONS:**   You ought to stop that, Pop. Everybody feed their kids. No matter how hard times is . . . everybody care about their kids. Make sure they have something to eat.

TROY: The only thing my daddy cared about was getting
265 them bales of cotton in to Mr. Lubin. That's the only thing that mattered to him. Sometimes I used to wonder why the devil hadn't come and got him. "Get them bales of cotton in to Mr. Lubin" and find out he owe him money . . .

270 **LYONS:**   He should have just went on and left when he saw he couldn't get nowhere. That's what I would have done.

TROY: How he gonna leave with eleven kids? And where he gonna go? He ain't knew how to do nothing but
275 farm. No, he was trapped and I think he knew it. But I'll say this for him . . . he felt a responsibility toward us. Maybe he ain't treated us the way I felt he should have . . . but without that responsibility he could have walked off and left us . . . made his own way.

280 **BONO:**   A lot of them did. Back in those days what you talking about . . . they walk out their front door and just take on down one road or another and keep on walking.

LYONS: There you go! That's what I'm talking about.

285 **BONO:**   Just keep on walking till you come to something else. Ain't you never heard of nobody having the walking blues? Well, that's what you call it when you just take off like that.

TROY: My daddy ain't had them walking blues! What
290 you talking about? He stayed right there with his family. But he was just as evil as he could be. My mama couldn't stand him. Couldn't stand that evilness. She run off when I was about eight. She sneaked off one night after he had gone to sleep. Told me she was
295 coming back for me. I ain't never seen her no more. All his women run off and left him. He wasn't good for nobody.

When my turn come to head out, I was fourteen and got to sniffing around Joe Canewell's daughter. Had us an old mule we called Greyboy. My daddy sent me out to do some plowing and I tied up Greyboy and went to fooling around with Joe Canewell's daughter. We done found us a nice little spot, got real cozy with each other. She about thirteen and we done figured we was grown anyway . . . so we down there enjoying ourselves . . . ain't thinking about nothing. We didn't know Greyboy had got loose and wandered back to the house and my daddy was looking for me. We down there by the creek enjoying ourselves when my daddy come up on us. Surprised us. He had them leather straps off the mule and commenced to whupping me like there was no tomorrow. I jumped up, mad and embarrassed. I was scared of my daddy. When he commenced to whupping on me . . . quite naturally I run to get out of the way. *(Pause.)* Now I thought he was mad cause I ain't done my work. But I see where he was chasing me off so he could have the gal for himself. When I see what the matter of it was, I lost all fear of my daddy. Right there is where I become a man . . . at fourteen years of age. *(Pause.)* Now it was my turn to run him off. I picked up them same reins that he had used on me. I picked up them reins and commenced to whupping on him. The gal jumped up and run off . . . and when my daddy turned to face me, I could see why the devil had never come to get him . . . cause he was the devil himself. I don't know what happened. When I woke up, I was laying right there by the creek, and Blue . . . this old dog we had . . . was licking my face. I thought I was blind. I couldn't see nothing. Both my eyes were swollen shut. I layed there and cried. I didn't know what I was gonna do. The only thing I knew was the time had come for me to leave my daddy's house. And right there the world suddenly got big. And it was a long time before I could cut it down to where I could handle it.

Part of that cutting down was when I got to the place where I could feel him kicking in my blood and knew that the only thing that separated us was the matter of a few years.

(GABRIEL enters from the house with a sandwich.)

LYONS: What you got there, Uncle Gabe?

GABRIEL: Got me a ham sandwich. Rose gave me a ham sandwich.

TROY: I don't know what happened to him. I done lost touch with everybody except Gabriel. But I hope he's dead. I hope he found some peace.

LYONS: That's a heavy story, Pop. I didn't know you left home when you was fourteen.

TROY: And didn't know nothing. The only part of the world I knew was the forty-two acres of Mr. Lubin's land. That's all I knew about life.

LYONS: Fourteen's kinda young to be out on your own. *(Phone rings.)* I don't even think I was ready to be out on my own at fourteen. I don't know what I would have done.

TROY: I got up from the creek and walked on down to Mobile. I was through with farming. Figured I could do better in the city. So I walked the two hundred miles to Mobile.

LYONS: Wait a minute . . . you ain't walked no two hundred miles, Pop. Ain't nobody gonna walk no two hundred miles. You talking about some walking there.

BONO: That's the only way you got anywhere back in them days.

LYONS: Shhh. Damn if I wouldn't have hitched a ride with somebody!

TROY: Who you gonna hitch it with? They ain't had no cars and things like they got now. We talking about 1918.

ROSE: *(Entering.)* What you all out here getting into?

TROY: *(To ROSE.)* I'm telling Lyons how good he got it. He don't know nothing about this I'm talking.

ROSE: Lyons, that was Bonnie on the phone. She say you supposed to pick her up.

LYONS: Yeah, okay, Rose.

TROY: I walked on down to Mobile and hitched up with some of them fellows that was heading this way. Got up here and found out . . . not only couldn't you get a job . . . you couldn't find no place to live. I thought

I was in freedom. Shhh. Colored folks living down
380 there on the riverbanks in whatever kind of shelter
they could find for themselves. Right down there
under the Brady Street Bridge. Living in shacks made
of sticks and tarpaper. Messed around there and went
from bad to worse. Started stealing. First it was food.
385 Then I figured, hell, if I steal money I can buy me
some food. Buy me some shoes too! One thing led to
another. Met your mama. I was young and anxious
to be a man. Met your mama and had you. What I
do that for? Now I got to worry about feeding you
390 and her. Got to steal three times as much. Went out
one day looking for somebody to rob . . . that's what I
was, a robber. I'll tell you the truth. I'm ashamed of
it today. But it's the truth. Went to rob this fellow . . .
pulled out my knife . . . and he pulled out a gun. Shot
395 me in the chest. It felt just like somebody had taken a
hot branding iron and laid it on me. When he shot me
I jumped at him with my knife. They told me I killed
him and they put me in the penitentiary and locked
me up for fifteen years. That's where I met Bono.
400 That's where I learned how to play baseball. Got out
that place and your mama had taken you and went on
to make life without me. Fifteen years was a long time
for her to wait. But that fifteen years cured me of that
robbing stuff. Rose'll tell you. She asked me when I
405 met her if I had gotten all that foolishness out of my
system. And I told her, "Baby, it's you and baseball
all what count with me." You hear me, Bono? I meant
it too. She say, "Which one comes first?" I told her,
"Baby, ain't no doubt it's baseball . . . but you stick and
410 get old with me and we'll both outlive this baseball."
Am I right, Rose? And it's true.

ROSE: Man, hush your mouth. You ain't said no such
thing. Talking about, "Baby you know you'll always be
number one with me." That's what you was talking.

415 TROY: You hear that, Bono. That's why I love her.

BONO: Rose'll keep you straight. You get off the track,
she'll straighten you up.

ROSE: Lyons, you better get on up and get Bonnie. She
waiting on you.

420 LYONS: (Gets up to go.) Hey, Pop, why don't you come on
down to the Grill and hear me play?

TROY: I ain't going down there. I'm too old to be sitting
around in them clubs.

BONO: You got to be good to play down at the Grill.

LYONS: Come on, Pop . . .   425

TROY: I got to get up in the morning.

LYONS: You ain't got to stay long.

TROY: Naw, I'm gonna get my supper and go on to bed.

LYONS: Well, I got to go. I'll see you again.

TROY: Don't you come around my house on my payday.   430

ROSE: Pick up the phone and let somebody know you
coming. And bring Bonnie with you. You know I'm
always glad to see her.

LYONS: Yeah, I'll do that, Rose. You take care now. See
you, Pop. See you, Mr. Bono. See you, Uncle Gabe.   435

GABRIEL: Lyons! King of the Jungle!

(LYONS exits.)

TROY: Is supper ready, woman? Me and you got some
business to take care of. I'm gonna tear it up too.

ROSE: Troy, I done told you now!

TROY: (Puts his arm around BONO.) Aw hell, woman . . .   440
this is Bono. Bono like family. I done known this nigger since . . . how long I done know you?

BONO: It's been a long time.

TROY: I done known this nigger since Skippy was a pup.
Me and him done been through some times.   445

BONO: You sure right about that.

TROY: Hell, I done know him longer than I known you.
And we still standing shoulder to shoulder. Hey, look
here, Bono . . . a man can't ask for no more than that.
(Drinks to him.) I love you, nigger.   450

BONO: Hell, I love you too . . . but I got to get home see
my woman. You got yours in hand. I got to go get
mine.

Rose (Angela Bassett) asks Troy why he got Cory kicked off the football team.

(BONO *starts to exit as* CORY *enters the yard, dressed in his football uniform. He gives* TROY *a hard, uncompromising look.*)

CORY: What you do that for, Pop?

(*He throws his helmet down in the direction of* TROY.)

455 **ROSE:** What's the matter? Cory . . . what's the matter?

CORY: Papa done went up to the school and told Coach Zellman I can't play football no more. Wouldn't even let me play the game. Told him to tell the recruiter not to come.

ROSE: Troy . . .   460

TROY: What you Troying me for. Yeah, I did it. And the boy know why I did it.

CORY: Why you wanna do that to me? That was the one chance I had.

ROSE: Ain't nothing wrong with Cory playing football,   465
Troy.

TROY: The boy lied to me. I told the nigger if he wanna play football . . . to keep up his chores and hold down that job at the A&P. That was the conditions. Stopped down there to see Mr. Stawicki . . .   470

CORY: I can't work after school during the football season, Pop! I tried to tell you that Mr. Stawicki's holding my job for me. You don't never want to listen to nobody. And then you wanna go and do this to me!

TROY: I ain't done nothing to you. You done it to yourself.   475

CORY: Just cause you didn't have a chance! You just scared I'm gonna be better than you, that's all.

TROY: Come here.

ROSE: Troy . . .

(CORY *reluctantly crosses over to* TROY.)

TROY: Alright! See. You done made a mistake.   480

CORY: I didn't even do nothing!

TROY: I'm gonna tell you what your mistake was. See . . . you swung at the ball and didn't hit it. That's strike one. See, you in the batter's box now. You swung and you missed. That's strike one. Don't you strike out!   485

(*Lights fade to black.*)

ACT 2
SCENE 1

The following morning. CORY *is at the tree hitting the ball with the bat. He tries to mimic* TROY, *but his swing is awkward, less sure.* ROSE *enters from the house.*

ROSE: Cory, I want you to help me with this cupboard.

CORY: I ain't quitting the team. I don't care what Poppa say.

ROSE: I'll talk to him when he gets back. He had to go
5   see about your Uncle Gabe. The police done arrested
him. Say he was disturbing the peace. He'll be back
directly. Come on in here and help me clean out the
top of this cupboard.

(CORY *exits into the house.* ROSE *sees* TROY *and*
BONO *coming down the alley.*)

Troy . . . what they say down there?

10 **TROY:** Ain't said nothing. I give them fifty dollars and
they let him go. I'll talk to you about it. Where's Cory?

ROSE: He's in there helping me clean out these
cupboards.

TROY: Tell him to get his butt out here.

(TROY *and* BONO *go over to the pile of wood.* BONO
picks up the saw and begins sawing.)

15 **TROY:** (*To* BONO.) All they want is the money. That
makes six or seven times I done went down there and
got him. See me coming they stick out their *hands.*

BONO: Yeah. I know what you mean. That's all they care
about . . . that money. They don't care about what's
20 right. (*Pause.*) Nigger, why you got to go and get some
hard wood? You ain't doing nothing but building a
little old fence. Get you some soft pine wood. That's
all you need.

TROY: I know what I'm doing. This is outside wood. You
25 put pine wood inside the house. Pine wood is inside
wood. This here is outside wood. Now you tell me
where the fence is gonna be?

BONO: You don't need this wood. You can put it up with
pine wood and it'll stand as long as you gonna be here
30 looking at it.

TROY: How you know how long I'm gonna be here, nigger? Hell, I might just live forever. Live longer than
old man Horsely.

Troy tells Cory that he's committed strike one.

BONO: That's what Magee used to say.

TROY: Magee's a damn fool. Now you tell me who you   35
ever heard of gonna pull their own teeth with a pair of
rusty pliers.

BONO: The old folks . . . my granddaddy used to pull his
teeth with pliers. They ain't had no dentists for the
colored folks back then.   40

TROY: Get clean pliers! You understand? Clean pliers!
Sterilize them! Besides we ain't living back then. All
Magee had to do was walk over to Doc Goldblum's.

BONO: I see where you and that Tallahassee gal . . . that
Alberta . . . I see where you all done got tight.   45

TROY: What you mean "got tight"?

BONO: I see where you be laughing and joking with her all the time.

TROY: I laughs and jokes with all of them, Bono. You know me.

BONO: That ain't the kind of laughing and joking I'm talking about.

(CORY *enters from the house.*)

CORY: How you doing, Mr. Bono?

TROY: Cory? Get that saw from Bono and cut some wood. He talking about the wood's too hard to cut. Stand back there, Jim, and let that young boy show you how it's done.

BONO: He's sure welcome to it.

(CORY *takes the saw and begins to cut the wood.*)

Whew-e-e! Look at that. Big old strong boy. Look like Joe Louis. Hell, must be getting old the way I'm watching that boy whip through that wood.

CORY: I don't see why Mama want a fence around the yard noways.

TROY: Damn if I know either. What the hell she keeping out with it? She ain't got nothing nobody want.

BONO: Some people build fences to keep people out . . . and other people build fences to keep people in. Rose wants to hold on to you all. She loves you.

TROY: Hell, nigger, I don't need nobody to tell me my wife loves me. Cory . . . go on in the house and see if you can find that other saw.

CORY: Where's it at?

TROY: I said find it! Look for it till you find it!

(CORY *exits into the house.*)

What's that supposed to mean? Wanna keep us in?

BONO: Troy . . . I done known you seem like damn near my whole life. You and Rose both. I done know both of you all for a long time. I remember when you met Rose. When you was hitting them baseball out the park. A lot of them old gals was after you then. You had the pick of the litter. When you picked Rose, I was happy for you. That was the first time I knew you had any sense. I said . . . My man Troy knows what he's doing . . . I'm gonna follow this nigger . . . he might take me somewhere. I been following you too. I done learned a whole heap of things about life watching you. I done learned how to tell where the shit lies. How to tell it from the alfalfa. You done learned me a lot of things. You showed me how to not make the same mistakes . . . to take life as it comes along and keep putting one foot in front of the other. (*Pause.*) Rose a good woman, Troy.

TROY: Hell, nigger, I know she a good woman. I been married to her for eighteen years. What you got on your mind, Bono?

BONO: I just say she a good woman. Just like I say anything. I ain't got to have nothing on my mind.

TROY: You just gonna say she a good woman and leave it hanging out there like that? Why you telling me she a good woman?

BONO: She loves you, Troy. Rose loves you.

TROY: You saying I don't measure up. That's what you trying to say. I don't measure up cause I'm seeing this other gal. I know what you trying to say.

BONO: I know what Rose means to you, Troy. I'm just trying to say I don't want to see you mess up.

TROY: Yeah, I appreciate that, Bono. If you was messing around on Lucille I'd be telling you the same thing.

BONO: Well, that's all I got to say. I just say that because I love you both.

TROY: Hell, you know me . . . I wasn't out there looking for nothing. You can't find a better woman than Rose. I know that. But seems like this woman just stuck onto me where I can't shake her loose. I done wrestled with it, tried to throw her off me . . . but she just stuck on tighter. Now she's stuck on for good.

BONO: You's in control . . . that's what you tell me all the time. You responsible for what you do.

TROY: I ain't ducking the responsibility of it. As long as it sets right in my heart . . . then I'm okay. Cause that's all I listen to. It'll tell me right from wrong every time. And I ain't talking about doing Rose no bad turn. I love Rose. She done carried me a long ways and I love and respect her for that.

BONO: I know you do. That's why I don't want to see you hurt her. But what you gonna do when she find out? What you got then? If you try and juggle both of them . . . sooner or later you gonna drop one of them. That's common sense.

TROY: Yeah, I hear what you saying, Bono. I been trying to figure a way to work it out.

BONO: Work it out right, Troy. I don't want to be getting all up between you and Rose's business . . . but work it so it come out right.

TROY: Aw hell, I get all up between you and Lucille's business. When you gonna get that woman that refrigerator she been wanting? Don't tell me you ain't got no money now. I know who your banker is. Mellon don't need that money bad as Lucille want that refrigerator. I'll tell you that.

BONO: Tell you what I'll do . . . when you finish building this fence for Rose . . . I'll buy Lucille that refrigerator.

TROY: You done stuck your foot in your mouth now!

(TROY *grabs up a board and begins to saw.* BONO *starts to walk out the yard.*)

Hey, nigger . . . where you going?

BONO: I'm going home. I know you don't expect me to help you now. I'm protecting my money. I wanna see you put that fence up by yourself. That's what I want to see. You'll be here another six months without me.

TROY: Nigger, you ain't right.

BONO: When it comes to my money . . . I'm right as fire works on the Fourth of July.

TROY: Alright, we gonna see now. You better get out your bankbook.

(BONO *exits, and* TROY *continues to work.* ROSE *enters from the house.*)

ROSE: What they say down there? What's happening with Gabe?

TROY: I went down there and got him out. Cost me fifty dollars. Say he was disturbing the peace. Judge set up a hearing for him in three weeks. Say to show cause why he shouldn't be recommitted.

ROSE: What was he doing that cause them to arrest him?

TROY: Some kids was teasing him and he run them off home. Say he was howling and carrying on. Some folks seen him and called the police. That's all it was.

ROSE: Well, what's you say? What'd you tell the judge?

TROY: Told him I'd look after him. It didn't make no sense to recommit the man. He stuck out his big greasy palm and told me to give him fifty dollars and take him on home.

ROSE: Where's he at now? Where'd he go off to?

TROY: He's gone on about his business. He don't need nobody to hold his hand.

ROSE: Well, I don't know. Seem like that would be the best place for him if they did put him into the hospital. I know what you're gonna say. But that's what I think would be best.

TROY: The man done had his life ruined fighting for what? And they wanna take and lock him up. Let him be free. He don't bother nobody.

ROSE: Well, everybody got their own way of looking at it I guess. Come on and get your lunch. I got a bowl of lima beans and some cornbread in the oven. Come on get something to eat. Ain't no sense you fretting over Gabe.

(ROSE *turns to go into the house.*)

TROY: Rose . . . got something to tell you.

ROSE: Well, come on . . . wait till I get this food on the table.

TROY: Rose!

(*She stops and turns around.*)

I don't know how to say this. (*Pause.*) I can't explain it none. It just sort of grows on you till it gets out of hand. It starts out like a little bush . . . and the next
190 thing you know it's a whole forest.

ROSE: Troy . . . what is you talking about?

TROY: I'm talking, woman, let me talk. I'm trying to find a way to tell you . . . I'm gonna be a daddy. I'm gonna be somebody's daddy.

195 **ROSE:** Troy . . . you're not telling me this? You're gonna be . . . what?

TROY: Rose . . . now . . . see . . .

ROSE: You telling me you gonna be somebody's daddy? You telling your *wife* this?

(GABRIEL *enters from the street. He carries a rose in his hand.*)

200 **GABRIEL:** Hey, Troy! Hey, Rose!

ROSE: I have to wait eighteen years to hear something like this.

GABRIEL: Hey, Rose . . . I got a flower for you. (*He hands it to her.*) That's a rose. Same rose like you is.

205 **ROSE:** Thanks, Gabe.

GABRIEL: Troy, you ain't mad at me is you? Them bad mens come and put me away. You ain't mad at me is you?

TROY: Naw, Gabe, I ain't mad at you.

210 **ROSE:** Eighteen years and you wanna come with this.

GABRIEL: (*Takes a quarter out of his pocket.*) See what I got? Got a brand new quarter.

TROY: Rose . . . it's just . . .

ROSE: Ain't nothing you can say, Troy. Ain't no way of
215 explaining that.

GABRIEL: Fellow that give me this quarter had a whole mess of them. I'm gonna keep this quarter till it stop shining.

ROSE: Gabe, go on in the house there. I got some watermelon in the Frigidaire. Go on and get you a piece. 220

GABRIEL: Say, Rose . . . you know I was chasing hell-hounds and them bad mens come and get me and take me away. Troy helped me. He come down there and told them they better let me go before he beat them up. Yeah, he did! 225

ROSE: You go on and get you a piece of watermelon, Gabe. Them bad mens is gone now.

GABRIEL: Okay, Rose . . . gonna get me some water-melon. The kind with the stripes on it.

(GABRIEL *exits into the house.*)

ROSE: Why, Troy? Why? After all these years to come 230
dragging this in to me now. It don't make no sense at your age. I could have expected this ten or fifteen years ago, but not now.

TROY: Age ain't got nothing to do with it, Rose.

ROSE: I done tried to be everything a wife should be. 235
Everything a wife could be. Been married eighteen years and I got to live to see the day you tell me you been seeing another woman and done fathered a child by her. And you know I ain't never wanted no half nothing in my family. My whole family is half. Every- 240
body got different fathers and mothers . . . my two sisters and my brother. Can't hardly tell who's who. Can't never sit down and talk about Papa and Mama. It's your papa and your mama and my papa and my mama . . . 245

TROY: Rose . . . stop it now.

ROSE: I ain't never wanted that for none of my children. And now you wanna drag your behind in here and tell me something like this.

TROY: You ought to know. It's time for you to know. 250

ROSE: Well, I don't want to know, goddamn it!

TROY: I can't just make it go away. It's done now. I can't wish the circumstance of the thing away.

ROSE: And you don't want to either. Maybe you want to wish me and my boy away. Maybe that's what you 255 want? Well, you can't wish us away. I've got eighteen years of my life invested in you. You ought to have stayed upstairs in my bed where you belong.

260 TROY: Rose . . . now listen to me . . . we can get a handle on this thing. We can talk this out . . . come to an understanding.

ROSE: All of a sudden it's "we." Where was "we" at when you was down there rolling around with some god-
265 forsaken woman? "We" should have come to an understanding before you started making a damn fool of yourself. You're a day late and dollar short when it comes to an understanding with me.

TROY: It's just . . . She gives me a different idea . . . a different understanding about myself. I can step out of
270 this house and get away from the pressures and problems . . . be a different man. I ain't got to wonder how I'm gonna pay the bills or get the roof fixed. I can just be a part of myself that I ain't never been.

ROSE: What I want to know . . . is do you plan to con-
275 tinue seeing her. That's all you can say to me.

TROY: I can sit up in her house and laugh. Do you understand what I'm saying. I can laugh out loud . . . and it feels good. It reaches all the way down to the bottom of my shoes. (*Pause.*) Rose, I can't give that up.

280 ROSE: Maybe you ought to go on and stay down there with her . . . if she's a better woman than me.

TROY: It ain't about nobody being a better woman or nothing. Rose, you ain't the blame. A man couldn't ask for no woman to be a better wife than you've been.
285 I'm responsible for it. I done locked myself into a pattern trying to take care of you all that I forgot about myself.

ROSE: What the hell was I there for? That was my job, not somebody else's.

290 TROY: Rose, I done tried all my life to live decent . . . to live a clean . . . hard . . . useful life. I tried to be a good husband to you. In every way I knew how. Maybe I come into the world backwards, I don't know. But . . . you born with two strikes on you before you come to
295 the plate. You got to guard it closely . . . always look-

ing for the curve-ball on the inside corner. You can't afford to let none get past you. You can't afford a call strike. If you going down . . . you going down swinging. Everything lined up against you. What you gonna
300 do. I fooled them, Rose. I bunted. When I found you and Cory and a halfway decent job . . . I was safe. Couldn't nothing touch me. I wasn't gonna strike out no more. I wasn't going back to the penitentiary. I wasn't gonna lay in the streets with a bottle of wine. I
305 was safe. I had me a family. A job. I wasn't gonna get that last strike. I was on first looking for one of them boys to knock me in. To get me home.

ROSE: You should have stayed in my bed, Troy.

TROY: Then when I saw that gal . . . she firmed up my
310 backbone. And I got to thinking that if I tried . . . I just might be able to steal second. Do you understand after eighteen years I wanted to steal second.

ROSE: You should have held me tight. You should have grabbed me and held on.

315 TROY: I stood on first base for eighteen years and I thought . . . well, goddamn it . . . go on for it!

ROSE: We're not talking about baseball! We're talking about you going off to lay in bed with another woman . . . and then bring it home to me. That's what we're
320 talking about. We ain't talking about no baseball.

TROY: Rose, you're not listening to me. I'm trying the best I can to explain it to you. It's not easy for me to admit that I been standing in the same place for eighteen years.

325 ROSE: I been standing with you! I been right here with you, Troy. I got a life too. I gave eighteen years of my life to stand in the same spot with you. Don't you think I ever wanted other things? Don't you think I had dreams and hopes? What about my life? What
330 about me. Don't you think it ever crossed my mind to want to know other men? That I wanted to lay up somewhere and forget about my responsibilities? That I wanted someone to make me laugh so I could feel good? You not the only one who's got wants and needs. But I held on to you, Troy. I took all my feel-
335 ings, my wants and needs, my dreams . . . and I buried them inside you. I planted a seed and watched and

340 prayed over it. I planted myself inside you and waited to bloom. And it didn't take me no eighteen years to find out the soil was hard and rocky and it wasn't never gonna bloom.

345

350

But I held on to you, Troy. I held you tighter. You was my husband. I owed you everything I had. Every part of me I could find to give you. And upstairs in that room . . . with the darkness falling in on me . . . I gave everything I had to try and erase the doubt that you wasn't the finest man in the world. And wherever you was going . . . I wanted to be there with you. Cause you was my husband. Cause that's the only way I was gonna survive as your wife. You always talking about what you give . . . and what you don't have to give. But you take too. You take . . . and don't even know nobody's giving!

(ROSE *turns to exit into the house.* TROY *grabs her arm.*)

TROY: You say I take and don't give!

355 **ROSE:** Troy! You're hurting me!

TROY: You say I take and don't give.

ROSE: Troy . . . you're hurting my arm! Let go!

TROY: I done give you everything I got. Don't you tell that lie on me.

360 **ROSE:** Troy!

TROY: Don't you tell that lie on me!

(CORY *enters from the house.*)

CORY: Mama!

ROSE: Troy. You're hurting me.

TROY: Don't you tell me about no taking and giving.

(CORY *comes up behind* TROY *and grabs him.* TROY, *surprised, is thrown off balance just as* CORY *throws a glancing blow that catches him on the chest and knocks him down.* TROY *is stunned, as is* CORY.)

365 **ROSE:** Troy. Troy. No!

(TROY *gets to his feet and starts at* CORY.)

Troy . . . no. Please! Troy!

(ROSE *pulls on* TROY *to hold him back.* TROY *stops himself.*)

TROY: (*To* CORY.) Alright. That's strike two. You stay away from around me, boy. Don't you strike out. You living with a full count. Don't you strike out.

(TROY *exits out the yard as the lights go down.*)

SCENE 2

It is six months later, early afternoon. TROY *enters from the house and starts to exit the yard.* ROSE *enters from the house.*

ROSE: Troy, I want to talk to you.

TROY: All of a sudden, after all this time, you want to talk to me, huh? You ain't wanted to talk to me for months. You ain't wanted to talk to me last night. You ain't wanted no part of me then. What you wanna talk 5 to me about now?

ROSE: Tomorrow's Friday.

TROY: I know what day tomorrow is. You think I don't know tomorrow's Friday? My whole life I ain't done nothing but look to see Friday coming and you got to 10 tell me it's Friday.

ROSE: I want to know if you're coming home.

TROY: I always come home, Rose. You know that. There ain't never been a night I ain't come home.

ROSE: That ain't what I mean . . . and you know it. I want 15 to know if you're coming straight home after work.

TROY: I figure I'd cash my check . . . hang out at Taylors' with the boys . . . maybe play a game of checkers . . .

ROSE: Troy, I can't live like this. I won't live like this. You livin' on borrowed time with me. It's been going on six 20 months now you ain't been coming home.

TROY: I be here every night. Every night of the year. That's 365 days.

ROSE: I want you to come home tomorrow after work.

TROY: Rose . . . I don't mess up my pay. You know that 25 now. I take my pay and I give it to you. I don't have no money but what you give me back. I just want to have a little time to myself . . . a little time to enjoy life.

ROSE: What about me? When's my time to enjoy life?

30 **TROY:** I don't know what to tell you, Rose. I'm doing the best I can.

ROSE: You ain't been home from work but time enough to change your clothes and run out . . . and you wanna call that the best you can do?

35 **TROY:** I'm going over to the hospital to see Alberta. She went into the hospital this afternoon. Look like she might have the baby early. I won't be gone long.

ROSE: Well, you ought to know. They went over to Miss Pearl's and got Gabe today. She said you told them to
40 go ahead and lock him up.

TROY: I ain't said no such thing. Whoever told you that is telling a lie. Pearl ain't doing nothing but telling a big fat lie.

ROSE: She ain't had to tell me. I read it on the papers.

45 **TROY:** I ain't told them nothing of the kind.

ROSE: I saw it right there on the papers.

TROY: What it say, huh?

ROSE: It said you told them to take him.

TROY: Then they screwed that up, just the way they
50 screw up everything. I ain't worried about what they got on the paper.

ROSE: Say the government send part of his check to the hospital and the other part to you.

TROY: I ain't got nothing to do with that if that's the way
55 it works. I ain't made up the rules about how it work.

ROSE: You did Gabe just like you did Cory. You wouldn't sign the paper for Cory . . . but you signed for Gabe. You signed that paper.

(The telephone is heard ringing inside the house.)

TROY: I told you I ain't signed nothing, woman! The
60 only thing I signed was the release form. Hell, I can't read, I don't know what they had on that paper! I ain't signed nothing about sending Gabe away.

ROSE: I said send him to the hospital . . . you said let him be free . . . now you done went down there and signed him to the hospital for half his money. You went back 65 on yourself, Troy. You gonna have to answer for that.

TROY: See now . . . you been over there talking to Miss Pearl. She done got mad cause she ain't getting Gabe's rent money. That's all it is. She's liable to say anything.

ROSE: Troy, I seen where you signed the paper. 70

TROY: You ain't seen nothing I signed. What she doing got papers on my brother anyway? Miss Pearl telling a big fat lie. And I'm gonna tell her about it too! You ain't seen nothing I signed. Say . . . you ain't seen nothing I signed. 75

(ROSE exits into the house to answer the telephone. Presently she returns.)

ROSE: Troy . . . that was the hospital. Alberta had the baby.

TROY: What she have? What is it?

ROSE: It's a girl.

TROY: I better get on down to the hospital to see her. 80

ROSE: Troy . . .

TROY: Rose . . . I got to go see her now. That's only right . . . what's the matter . . . the baby's alright, ain't it?

ROSE: Alberta died having the baby. 85

TROY: Died . . . you say she's dead? Alberta's dead?

ROSE: They said they done all they could. They couldn't do nothing for her.

TROY: The baby? How's the baby?

ROSE: They say it's healthy. I wonder who's gonna bury 90 her.

TROY: She had family, Rose. She wasn't living in the world by herself.

ROSE: I know she wasn't living in the world by herself.

TROY: Next thing you gonna want to know if she had any 95 insurance.

ROSE: Troy, you ain't got to talk like that.

TROY: That's the first thing that jumped out your mouth. "Who's gonna bury her?" Like I'm fixing to take on that task for myself.

ROSE: I am your wife. Don't push me away.

TROY: I ain't pushing nobody away. Just give me some space. That's all. Just give me some room to breathe.

(ROSE exits into the house. TROY walks about the yard.)

TROY: *(With a quiet rage that threatens to consume him.)* Alright . . . Mr. Death. See now . . . I'm gonna tell you what I'm gonna do. I'm gonna take and build me a fence around this yard. See? I'm gonna build me a fence around what belongs to me. And then I want you to stay on the other side. See? You stay over there until you're ready for me. Then you come on. Bring your army. Bring your sickle. Bring your wrestling clothes. I ain't gonna fall down on my vigilance this time. You ain't gonna sneak up on me no more. When you ready for me . . . when the top of your list say Troy Maxson . . . that's when you come around here. You come up and knock on the front door. Ain't nobody else got nothing to do with this. This is between you and me. Man to man. You stay on the other side of that fence until you ready for me. Then you come up and knock on the front door. Anytime you want. I'll be ready for you.

(The lights go down to black.)

SCENE 3

The lights come up on the porch. It is late evening three days later. ROSE sits listening to the ball game waiting for TROY. The final out of the game is made and ROSE switches off the radio. TROY enters the yard carrying an infant wrapped in blankets. He stands back from the house and calls.

ROSE enters and stands on the porch. There is a long, awkward silence, the weight of which grows heavier with each passing second.

TROY: Rose . . . I'm standing here with my daughter in my arms. She ain't but a wee bittie little old thing. She don't know nothing about grownups' business. She innocent . . . and she ain't got no mama.

ROSE: What you telling me for, Troy?

(She turns and exits into the house.)

TROY: Well . . . I guess we'll just sit out here on the porch.

(He sits down on the porch. There is an awkward indelicateness about the way he handles the baby. His largeness engulfs and seems to swallow it. He speaks loud enough for ROSE to hear.)

A man's got to do what's right for him. I ain't sorry for nothing I done. It felt right in my heart. *(To the baby.)* What you smiling at? Your daddy's a big man. Got these great big old hands. But sometimes he's scared. And right now your daddy's scared cause we sitting out here and ain't got no home. Oh, I been homeless before. I ain't had no little baby with me. But I been homeless. You just be out on the road by your lonesome and you see one of them trains coming and you just kinda go like this . . .

(He sings as a lullaby.)

Please, Mr. Engineer let a man ride the line
Please, Mr. Engineer let a man ride the line
I ain't got no ticket please let me ride the blinds

(ROSE enters from the house. TROY, hearing her steps behind him, stands and faces her.)

She's my daughter, Rose. My own flesh and blood. I can't deny her no more than I can deny them boys. *(Pause.)* You and them boys is my family. You and them and this child is all I got in the world. So I guess what I'm saying is . . . I'd appreciate it if you'd help me take care of her.

ROSE: Okay, Troy . . . you're right. I'll take care of your baby for you . . . cause . . . like you say . . . she's innocent . . . and you can't visit the sins of the father upon the child. A motherless child has got a hard time. *(She takes the baby from him.)* From right now . . . this child got a mother. But you a womanless man.

(ROSE turns and exits into the house with the baby. Lights go down to black.)

SCENE 4

It is two months later. LYONS *enters from the street. He knocks on the door and calls.*

LYONS: Hey, Rose! *(Pause.)* Rose!

ROSE: *(From inside the house.)* Stop that yelling. You gonna wake up Raynell. I just got her to sleep.

LYONS: I just stopped by to pay Papa this twenty dollars
5   I owe him. Where's Papa at?

ROSE: He should be here in a minute. I'm getting ready to go down to the church. Sit down and wait on him.

LYONS: I got to go pick up Bonnie over her mother's house.

10 **ROSE:** Well, sit it down there on the table. He'll get it.

LYONS: *(Enters the house and sets the money on the table.)* Tell Papa I said thanks. I'll see you again.

ROSE: Alright, Lyons. We'll see you.

*(*LYONS *starts to exit as* CORY *enters.)*

CORY: Hey, Lyons.

15 **LYONS:** What's happening, Cory? Say man, I'm sorry I missed your graduation. You know I had a gig and couldn't get away. Otherwise, I would have been there, man. So what you doing?

CORY: I'm trying to find a job.

20 **LYONS:** Yeah I know how that go, man. It's rough out here. Jobs are scarce.

CORY: Yeah, I know.

LYONS: Look here, I got to run. Talk to Papa . . . he know some people. He'll be able to help get you a job. Talk
25   to him . . . see what he say.

CORY: Yeah . . . alright, Lyons.

LYONS: You take care. I'll talk to you soon. We'll find some time to talk.

*(*LYONS *exits the yard.* CORY *wanders over to the tree, picks up the bat, and assumes a batting stance. He*

studies an imaginary pitcher and swings. Dissatisfied with the result, he tries again. TROY *enters. They eye each other for a beat.* CORY *puts the bat down and exits the yard.* TROY *starts into the house as* ROSE *exits with* RAYNELL. *She is carrying a cake.)*

TROY: I'm coming in and everybody's going out.

ROSE: I'm taking the cake down to the church for the   30
bake sale. Lyons was by to see you. He stopped by to pay you your twenty dollars. It's laying in there on the table.

TROY: *(Going into his pocket.)* Well . . . here go this
money.   35

ROSE: Put it in there on the table, Troy. I'll get it.

TROY: What time you coming back?

ROSE: Ain't no use in you studying me. It don't matter what time I come back.

TROY: I just asked you a question, woman. What's the   40
matter . . . can't I ask you a question?

ROSE: Troy, I don't want to go into it. Your dinner's in there on the stove. All you got to do is heat it up. And don't you be eating the rest of them cakes in there. I'm coming back for them. We having a bake sale at the   45
church tomorrow.

*(*ROSE *exits the yard.* TROY *sits down on the steps, takes a pint bottle from his pocket, opens it, and drinks. He begins to sing.)*

TROY:

Hear it ring! Hear it ring!
Had an old dog his name was Blue
You know Blue was mighty true
You know Blue was a good old dog   50
Blue trees a possum in a hollow log
You know from that he was a good old dog

*(*BONO *enters the yard.)*

BONO: Hey, Troy.

TROY: Hey, what's happening, Bono?

BONO: I just thought I'd stop by to see you.   55

TROY: What you stop by and see me for? You ain't stopped by in a month of Sundays. Hell, I must owe you money or something.

60 BONO: Since you got your promotion I can't keep up with you. Used to see you every day. Now I don't even know what route you working.

TROY: They keep switching me around. Got me out in Greentree now . . . hauling white folks' garbage.

65 BONO: Greentree, huh? You lucky, at least you ain't got to be lifting them barrels. Damn if they ain't getting heavier. I'm gonna put in my two years and call it quits.

TROY: I'm thinking about retiring myself.

70 BONO: You got it easy. You can *drive* for another five years.

TROY: It ain't the same, Bono. It ain't like working the back of the truck. Ain't got nobody to talk to . . . feel like you working by yourself. Naw, I'm thinking about retiring. How's Lucille?

75 BONO: She alright. Her arthritis get to acting up on her sometime. Saw Rose on my way in. She going down to the church, huh?

TROY: Yeah, she took up going down there. All them preachers looking for somebody to fatten their pock-
80 ets. *(Pause.)* Got some gin here.

BONO: Naw, thanks. I just stopped by to say hello.

TROY: Hell, nigger . . . you can take a drink. I ain't never known you to say no to a drink. You ain't got to work tomorrow.

85 BONO: I just stopped by. I'm fixing to go over to Skinner's. We got us a domino game going over his house every Friday.

TROY: Nigger, you can't play no dominoes. I used to whup you four games out of five.

90 BONO: Well, that learned me. I'm getting better.

TROY: Yeah? Well, that's alright.

BONO: Look here . . . I got to be getting on. Stop by sometime, huh?

TROY: Yeah, I'll do that, Bono. Lucille told Rose you bought her a new refrigerator.   95

BONO: Yeah, Rose told Lucille you had finally built your fence . . . so I figured we'd call it even.

TROY: I knew you would.

BONO: Yeah . . . okay. I'll be talking to you.

TROY: Yeah, take care, Bono. Good to see you. I'm gonna   100
stop over.

BONO: Yeah. Okay, Troy.

(BONO *exits.* TROY *drinks from the bottle.*)

TROY:

Old Blue died and I dug his grave
Let him down with a golden chain
Every night when I hear old Blue bark   105
I know Blue treed a possum in Noah's Ark.
Hear it ring! Hear it ring!

(CORY *enters the yard. They eye each other for a beat.*
TROY *is sitting in the middle of the steps.* CORY *walks
over.*)

CORY: I got to get by.

TROY: Say what? What's you say?

CORY: You in my way. I got to get by.   110

TROY: You got to get by where? This is my house. Bought and paid for. In full. Took me fifteen years. And if you wanna go in my house and I'm sitting on the steps . . . you say excuse me. Like your mama taught you.

CORY: Come on, Pop . . . I got to get by.   115

(CORY *starts to maneuver his way past* TROY. TROY
grabs his leg and shoves him back.)

TROY: You just gonna walk over top of me?

CORY: I live here too!

TROY: *(Advancing toward him.)* You just gonna walk over top of me in my own house?

120 **CORY:** I ain't scared of you.

TROY: I ain't asked if you was scared of me. I asked you if you was fixing to walk over top of me in my own house? That's the question. You ain't gonna say excuse me? You just gonna walk over top of me?

125 **CORY:** If you wanna put it like that.

TROY: How else am I gonna put it?

CORY: I was walking by you to go into the house cause you sitting on the steps drunk, singing to yourself. You can put it like that.

130 **TROY:** Without saying excuse me???

(CORY *doesn't respond.*)

I asked you a question. Without saying excuse me???

CORY: I ain't got to say excuse me to you. You don't count around here no more.

TROY: Oh, I see . . . I don't count around here no more.
135 You ain't got to say excuse me to your daddy. All of a sudden you done got so grown that your daddy don't count around here no more . . . Around here in his own house and yard that he done paid for with the sweat of his brow. You done got so grown to where
140 you gonna take over. You gonna take over my house. Is that right? You gonna wear my pants. You gonna go in there and stretch out on my bed. You ain't got to say excuse me cause I don't count around here no more. Is that right?

145 **CORY:** That's right. You always talking this dumb stuff. Now, why don't you just get out my way?

TROY: I guess you got someplace to sleep and something to put in your belly. You got that, huh? You got that? That's what you need. You got that, huh?

150 **CORY:** You don't know what I got. You ain't got to worry about what I got.

TROY: You right! You one hundred percent right! I done spent the last seventeen years worrying about what you got. Now it's your turn, see? I'll tell you what to
155 do. You grown . . . we done established that. You a man. Now, let's see you act like one. Turn your behind around and walk out this yard. And when you get out

there in the alley . . . you can forget about this house. See? Cause this is my house. You go on and be a man and get your own house. You can forget about this. 160 Cause this is mine. You go on and get yours cause I'm through with doing for you.

CORY: You talking about what you did for me . . . what'd you ever give me?

TROY: Them feet and bones! That pumping heart, nig- 165 ger! I give you more than anybody else is ever gonna give you.

CORY: You ain't never gave me nothing! You ain't never done nothing but hold me back. Afraid I was gonna be better than you. All you ever did was try and make me 170 scared of you. I used to tremble every time you called my name. Every time I heard your footsteps in the house. Wondering all the time . . . what's Papa gonna say if I do this? . . . What's he gonna say if I do that? . . . What's Papa gonna say if I turn on the radio? And 175 Mama, too . . . she tries . . . but she's scared of you.

TROY: You leave your mama out of this. She ain't got nothing to do with this.

CORY: I don't know how she stand you . . . after what you did to her. 180

TROY: I told you to leave your mama out of this!

(*He advances toward* CORY.)

CORY: What you gonna do . . . give me a whupping? You can't whup me no more. You're too old. You just an old man.

TROY: (*Shoves him on his shoulder.*) Nigger! That's what 185 you are. You just another nigger on the street to me!

CORY: You crazy! You know that?

TROY: Go on now! You got the devil in you. Get on away from me!

CORY: You just a crazy old man . . . talking about I got 190 the devil in me.

TROY: Yeah, I'm crazy! If you don't get on the other side of that yard . . . I'm gonna show you how crazy I am! Go on . . . get the hell out of my yard.

195 **CORY:** It ain't your yard! You took Uncle Gabe's money he got from the army to buy this house and then you put him out.

TROY: (*Advances on* CORY.) Get your black ass out of my yard!

(TROY's *advance backs* CORY *up against the tree.* CORY *grabs up the bat.*)

200 **CORY:** I ain't going nowhere! Come on . . . put me out! I ain't scared of you.

TROY: That's my bat!

CORY: Come on!

TROY: Put my bat down!

205 **CORY:** Come on, put me out.

(CORY *swings at* TROY, *who backs across the yard.*)

What's the matter? You so bad . . . put me out!

(TROY *advances toward* CORY.)

CORY: (*Backing up.*) Come on! Come on!

TROY: You're gonna have to use it! You wanna draw that bat back on me . . . you're gonna have to use it.

210 **CORY:** Come on! . . . Come on!

(CORY *swings the bat at* TROY *a second time. He misses.* TROY *continues to advance toward him.*)

TROY: You're gonna have to kill me! You wanna draw that bat back on me. You're gonna have to kill me.

(CORY, *backed up against the tree, can go no farther.* TROY *taunts him. He sticks out his head and offers him a target.*)

Come on! Come on!

(CORY *is unable to swing the bat.* TROY *grabs it.*)

TROY: Then I'll show you.

(CORY *and* TROY *struggle over the bat. The struggle is fierce and fully engaged.* TROY *ultimately is the stronger, and takes the bat from* CORY *and stands over him ready to swing. He stops himself.*)

Go on and get away from around my house. 215

(CORY, *stung by his defeat, picks himself up, walks slowly out of the yard and up the alley.*)

CORY: Tell Mama I'll be back for my things.

TROY: They'll be on the other side of that fence.

(CORY *exits.*)

TROY: I can't taste nothing. Helluljah! I can't taste nothing no more. (TROY *assumes a batting posture and begins to taunt Death, the fastball on the outside* 220 *corner.*) Come on! It's between you and me now! Come on! Anytime you want! Come on! I be ready for you . . . but I ain't gonna be easy.

(*The lights go down on the scene.*)

SCENE 5

The time is 1965. The lights come up in the yard. It is the morning of TROY's *funeral. A funeral plaque with a light hangs beside the door. There is a small garden plot off to the side. There is noise and activity in the house as* ROSE, LYONS, *and* BONO *have gathered. The door opens and* RAYNELL, *seven years old, enters dressed in a flannel nightgown. She crosses to the garden and pokes around with a stick.* ROSE *calls from the house.*

ROSE: Raynell!

RAYNELL: Mam?

ROSE: What you doing out there?

RAYNELL: Nothing.

(ROSE *comes to the door.*)

ROSE: Girl, get in here and get dressed. What you doing? 5

RAYNELL: Seeing if my garden growed.

ROSE: I told you it ain't gonna grow overnight. You got to wait.

RAYNELL: It don't look like it never gonna grow. Dag!

ROSE: I told you a watched pot never boils. Get in here 10 and get dressed.

RAYNELL: This ain't even no pot, Mama.

ROSE: You just have to give it a chance. It'll grow. Now you come on and do what I told you. We got to be getting ready. This ain't no morning to be playing around. You hear me?

15

RAYNELL: Yes, Mam.

(ROSE *exits into the house.* RAYNELL *continues to poke at her garden with a stick.* CORY *enters. He is dressed in a Marine corporal's uniform, and carries a duffel-bag. His posture is that of a military man, and his speech has a clipped sternness.*)

CORY: *(To* RAYNELL.*)* Hi. *(Pause.)* I bet your name is Raynell.

20 **RAYNELL:**   Uh huh.

CORY: Is your mama home?

(RAYNELL *runs up on the porch and calls through the screen door.*)

RAYNELL: Mama . . . there's some man out here. Mama?

(ROSE *comes to the door.*)

ROSE: Cory? Lord have mercy! Look here, you all!

(ROSE *and* CORY *embrace in a tearful reunion as* BONO *and* LYONS *enter from the house dressed in funeral clothes.*)

BONO: Aw, looka here . . .

25 **ROSE:**   Done got all grown up!

CORY: Don't cry, Mama. What you crying about?

ROSE: I'm just so glad you made it.

CORY: Hey Lyons. How you doing, Mr. Bono.

(LYONS *goes to embrace* CORY.)

LYONS: Look at you, man. Look at you. Don't he look good, Rose. Got them Corporal stripes.

30

ROSE: What took you so long?

CORY: You know how the Marines are, Mama. They got to get all their paperwork straight before they let you do anything.

Cory greets Rose on the day of Troy's funeral.

ROSE: Well, I'm sure glad you made it. They let Lyons come. Your Uncle Gabe's still in the hospital. They don't know if they gonna let him out or not. I just talked to them a little while ago.

35

LYONS: A Corporal in the United States Marines.

BONO: Your daddy knew you had it in you. He used to tell me all the time.

40

LYONS: Don't he look good, Mr. Bono?

BONO: Yeah, he remind me of Troy when I first met him. *(Pause.)* Say, Rose, Lucille's down at the church with the choir. I'm gonna go down and get the pallbearers lined up. I'll be back to get you all.

45

ROSE: Thanks, Jim.

CORY: See you, Mr. Bono.

50 **LYONS:**   *(With his arm around* RAYNELL.*)* Cory . . . look at Raynell. Ain't she precious? She gonna break a whole lot of hearts.

ROSE: Raynell, come and say hello to your brother. This is your brother, Cory. You remember Cory.

RAYNELL: No, Mam.

55 **CORY:**   She don't remember me, Mama.

ROSE: Well, we talk about you. She heard us talk about you. *(To* RAYNELL.*)* This is your brother, Cory. Come on and say hello.

RAYNELL: Hi.

60 **CORY:**   Hi. So you're Raynell. Mama told me a lot about you.

ROSE: You all come on into the house and let me fix you some breakfast. Keep up your strength.

CORY: I ain't hungry, Mama.

65 **LYONS:**   You can fix me something, Rose. I'll be in there in a minute.

ROSE: Cory, you sure you don't want nothing? I know they ain't feeding you right.

CORY: No, Mama . . . thanks. I don't feel like eating. I'll 70 get something later.

ROSE: Raynell . . . get on upstairs and get that dress on like I told you.

*(*ROSE *and* RAYNELL *exit into the house.)*

LYONS: So . . . I hear you thinking about getting married.

CORY: Yeah, I done found the right one, Lyons. It's about 75 time.

LYONS: Me and Bonnie been split up about four years now. About the time Papa retired. I guess she just got tired of all them changes I was putting her through. *(Pause.)* I always knew you was gonna make some 80 thing out yourself. Your head was always in the right direction. So . . . you gonna stay in . . . make it a career . . . put in your twenty years?

CORY: I don't know. I got six already, I think that's enough.

LYONS: Stick with Uncle Sam and retire early. Ain't 85 nothing out here. I guess Rose told you what happened with me. They got me down the workhouse. I thought I was being slick cashing other people's checks.

CORY: How much time you doing? 90

LYONS: They give me three years. I got that beat now. I ain't got but nine more months. It ain't so bad. You learn to deal with it like anything else. You got to take the crookeds with the straights. That's what Papa used to say. He used to say that when he struck 95 out. I seen him strike out three times in a row . . . and the next time up he hit the ball over the grandstand. Right out there in Homestead Field. He wasn't satisfied hitting in the seats . . . he want to hit it over everything! After the game he had two hundred people 100 standing around waiting to shake his hand. You got to take the crookeds with the straights. Yeah, Papa was something else.

CORY: You still playing?

LYONS: Cory . . . you know I'm gonna do that. There's 105 some fellows down there we got us a band . . . we gonna try and stay together when we get out . . . but yeah, I'm still playing. It still helps me to get out of bed in the morning. As long as it do that I'm gonna be right there playing and trying to make some sense 110 out of it.

ROSE: *(Calling.)* Lyons, I got these eggs in the pan.

LYONS: Let me go on and get these eggs, man. Get ready to go bury Papa. *(Pause.)* How you doing? You doing alright? 115

*(*CORY *nods.* LYONS *touches him on the shoulder and they share a moment of silent grief.* LYONS *exits into the house.* CORY *wanders about the yard.* RAYNELL *enters.)*

RAYNELL: Hi.

CORY: Hi.

RAYNELL: Did you used to sleep in my room?

CORY: Yeah . . . that used to be my room.

120 RAYNELL: That's what Papa call it. "Cory's room." It got your football in the closet.

(ROSE *comes to the door.*)

ROSE: Raynell, get in there and get them good shoes on.

RAYNELL: Mama, can't I wear these? Them other one hurt my feet.

125 ROSE: Well, they just gonna have to hurt your feet for a while. You ain't said they hurt your feet when you went down to the store and got them.

RAYNELL: They didn't hurt then. My feet done got bigger.

130 ROSE: Don't you give me no backtalk now. You get in there and get them shoes on.

(RAYNELL *exits into the house.*)

Ain't too much changed. He still got that piece of rag tied to that tree. He was out here swinging that bat. I was just ready to go back in the house. He swung
135 that bat and then he just fell over. Seem like he swung it and stood there with this grin on his face . . . and then he just fell over. They carried him on down to the hospital, but I knew there wasn't no need . . . why don't you come on in the house?

140 CORY: Mama . . . I got something to tell you. I don't know how to tell you this . . . but I've got to tell you . . . I'm not going to Papa's funeral.

ROSE: Boy, hush your mouth. That's your daddy you talking about. I don't want hear that kind of talk
145 this morning. I done raised you to come to this? You standing there all healthy and grown talking about you ain't going to your daddy's funeral?

CORY: Mama . . . listen . . .

ROSE: I don't want to hear it, Cory. You just get that
150 thought out of your head.

CORY: I can't drag Papa with me everywhere I go. I've got to say no to him. One time in my life I've got to say no.

ROSE: Don't nobody have to listen to nothing like that. I know you and your daddy ain't seen eye to eye, but
155 I ain't got to listen to that kind of talk this morning. Whatever was between you and your daddy . . . the time has come to put it aside. Just take it and set it over there on the shelf and forget about it. Disrespecting your daddy ain't gonna make you a man, Cory.
160 You got to find a way to come to that on your own. Not going to your daddy's funeral ain't gonna make you a man.

CORY: The whole time I was growing up . . . living in his house . . . Papa was like a shadow that followed you
165 everywhere. It weighed on you and sunk into your flesh. It would wrap around you and lay there until you couldn't tell which one was you anymore. That shadow digging in your flesh. Trying to crawl in. Trying to live through you. Everywhere I looked, Troy
170 Maxson was staring back at me . . . hiding under the bed . . . in the closet. I'm just saying I've got to find a way to get rid of that shadow, Mama.

ROSE: You just like him. You got him in you good.

CORY: Don't tell me that, Mama.
175

ROSE: You Troy Maxson all over again.

CORY: I don't want to be Troy Maxson. I want to be me.

ROSE: You can't be nobody but who you are, Cory. That shadow wasn't nothing but you growing into yourself. You either got to grow into it or cut it down to fit you.
180 But that's all you got to make life with. That's all you got to measure yourself against that world out there. Your daddy wanted you to be everything he wasn't . . . and at the same time he tried to make you into everything he was. I don't know if he was right or wrong . . .
185 but I do know he meant to do more good than he meant to do harm. He wasn't always right. Sometimes when he touched he bruised. And sometimes when he took me in his arms he cut.

When I first met your daddy I thought . . . Here
190 is a man I can lay down with and make a baby. That's the first thing I thought when I seen him. I was thirty years old and had done seen my share of men. But when he walked up to me and said, "I can dance a waltz that'll make you dizzy," I thought, Rose Lee,
195 here is a man that you can open yourself up to and

be filled to bursting. Here is a man that can fill all them empty spaces you been tipping around the edges of. One of them empty spaces was being somebody's
200 mother.

     I married your daddy and settled down to cooking his supper and keeping clean sheets on the bed. When your daddy walked through the house he was so big he filled it up. That was my first mistake. Not
205 to make him leave some room for me. For my part in the matter. But at that time I wanted that. I wanted a house that I could sing in. And that's what your daddy gave me. I didn't know to keep up his strength I had to give up little pieces of mine. I did that. I took on
210 his life as mine and mixed up the pieces so that you couldn't hardly tell which was which anymore. It was my choice. It was my life and I didn't have to live it like that. But that's what life offered me in the way of being a woman and I took it. I grabbed hold of it with
215 both hands.

     By the time Raynell came into the house, me and your daddy had done lost touch with one another. I didn't want to make my blessing off of nobody's misfortune . . . but I took on to Raynell like she was all
220 them babies I had wanted and never had.

(The phone rings.)

Like I'd been blessed to relive a part of my life. And if the Lord see fit to keep up my strength . . . I'm gonna do her just like your daddy did you . . . I'm gonna give her the best of what's in me.

225 **RAYNELL:** *(Entering, still with her old shoes.)* Mama . . . Reverend Tollivier on the phone.

(ROSE exits into the house.)

RAYNELL: Hi.

CORY: Hi.

RAYNELL: You in the Army or the Marines?

230 **CORY:** Marines.

RAYNELL: Papa said it was the Army. Did you know Blue?

CORY: Blue? Who's Blue?

RAYNELL: Papa's dog what he sing about all the time.

CORY: *(Singing.)*
    Hear it ring! Hear it ring!   235
    I had a dog his name was Blue
    You know Blue was mighty true
    You know Blue was a good old dog
    Blue treed a possum in a hollow log
    You know from that he was a good old dog.   240
    Hear it ring! Hear it ring!

(RAYNELL joins in singing.)

CORY AND RAYNELL:
    Blue treed a possum out on a limb
    Blue looked at me and I looked at him
    Grabbed that possum and put him in a sack
    Blue stayed there till I came back   245
    Old Blue's feets was big and round
    Never allowed a possum to touch the ground.

    Old Blue died and I dug his grave
    I dug his grave with a silver spade
    Let him down with a golden chain   250
    And every night I call his name
    Go on Blue, you good dog you
    Go on Blue, you good dog you.

RAYNELL:
    Blue laid down and died like a man
    Blue laid down and died . . .   255

BOTH:
    Blue laid down and died like a man
    Now he's treeing possums in the Promised Land
    I'm gonna tell you this to let you know
    Blue's gone where the good dogs go
    When I hear old Blue bark   260
    When I hear old Blue bark
    Blue treed a possum in Noah's Ark
    Blue treed a possum in Noah's Ark.

(ROSE comes to the screen door.)

ROSE: Cory, we gonna be ready to go in a minute.

CORY: *(To RAYNELL.)* You go on in the house and change   265
them shoes like Mama told you so we can go to Papa's funeral.

RAYNELL: Okay, I'll be back.

The family looks up into the wide-open gates of heaven.

(RAYNELL *exits into the house.* CORY *gets up and crosses over to the tree.* ROSE *stands in the screen door watching him.* GABRIEL *enters from the alley.*)

GABRIEL: (*Calling.*) Hey, Rose!

270 **ROSE:** Gabe?

GABRIEL: I'm here, Rose. Hey, Rose, I'm here!

(ROSE *enters from the house.*)

ROSE: Lord . . . Look here, Lyons!

LYONS: See, I told you, Rose . . . I told you they'd let him come.

CORY: How you doing, Uncle Gabe? 275

LYONS: How you doing, Uncle Gabe?

GABRIEL: Hey, Rose. It's time. It's time to tell St. Peter to open the gates. Troy, you ready? You ready, Troy. I'm gonna tell St. Peter to open the gates. You get ready now. 280

(GABRIEL, *with great fanfare, braces himself to blow. The trumpet is without a mouthpiece. He puts the end of it into his mouth and blows with great force, like a man who has been waiting some twenty-odd years for this single moment. No sound comes out of the trumpet. He braces himself and blows again with the same result. A third time he blows. There is a weight of impossible description that falls away and leaves him bare and exposed to a frightful realization. It is a trauma that a sane and normal mind would be unable to withstand. He begins to dance. A slow, strange dance, eerie and life-giving. A dance of atavistic signature and ritual.* LYONS *attempts to embrace him.* GABRIEL *pushes* LYONS *away. He begins to howl in what is an attempt at song, or perhaps a song turning back into itself in an attempt at speech. He finishes his dance and the gates of heaven stand open as wide as God's closet.*)

That's the way that go!

BLACKOUT

Writing from Reading

Summarize

1 Which family relationships does the play emphasize; which does it downplay?

Analyze Craft

2 Explain the importance of the title and how it relates to the play's theme or themes. Of all the elements in the play—dialogue, character, plot, setting, language—which do you think might have the most impact on the audience, and why?

3 Which character goes through the most dramatic change in the course of the play? What evidence do you see of this change?

Analyze Voice

4 Identify an exchange of dialogue that you found particularly powerful and explain why. How does it promote or portray the conflict and theme of the play?

Synthesize Summary and Analysis

5 How successful is August Wilson in elevating his working-class characters to the level of the tragic hero portrayed in Greek drama?

6 Throughout the play, stage directions indicate that lines are to be sung. How does the incorporation of song bring the African-American tradition of the blues into the tone of the play? Compare the use of song in *Fences* with the blues poems of Langston Hughes (see Chapter 27). How do both use the blues to comment on the African-American experience?

Interpret the Play

7 Discuss the theme of power and powerlessness as raised in this play.

"August's plays are the blues. Listen to the blues . . . Lightnin' Hopkins . . . Bessie Smith . . . Big Maybell. Listen to these things, listen to the words because they're poetry and they're plays. They're whole dramas told in one song." Conversation with Ruben Santiago-Hudson

AN ACTOR'S PERSPECTIVE ON MODERN THEATER AND AUGUST WILSON

As Ruben Santiago-Hudson makes clear in his interview, his mentor and guiding light in the theater was August Wilson. Now that you have read *Fences,* you will begin to see why, among other things, it called out to a young writer and actor such as Santiago-Hudson. First performed in 1985, the play has entered the American repertory. Because of its subject matter, it has drawn a new audience to theaters and, as the example of Santiago-Hudson indicates, has opened a path for new playwrights and actors to follow.

A Glimpse at the Work of Ruben Santiago-Hudson

As Santiago-Hudson suggests, whether in Shakespeare's day or our own, the constant factor is the actor, wrestling with a role, preparing to take the stage. If you happen to watch a DVD of the movie *Lackawanna Blues*—scenes from which follow—you immediately feel a sense of deep emotion; as the movie opens with a telephone call in the middle of the night and a man awakes to pick up the instrument and listen for a moment before announcing that he is on his way. He's going to the upstate New York hospital where the woman who raised him, the owner of a Lackawanna boarding house for black people in the still-segregated mid-1950s, lies dying. The audience is on its way, too, because within seconds we're seeing images from the hospital and then flashbacks to the 1950s to witness, in a dazzling series of cross-cuts, a raucous and joyful Friday night fish-fry dance and the birth of the boy the woman will raise to manhood.

Ruben Santiago-Hudson *You need to feed your soul.*

A Conversation on Writing

Theater Makes a Person Whole

I choose to do plays first and foremost because I love them. . . . I can't get that love out of me—and I don't want to get it out of me. . . . I have to balance the theater with my film and TV, which is sustenance . . . but theater is the place where I am whole as a human being. . . . The reason I choose theater foremost is not only desire, but need. I need to feel whole because I'm in a business where they don't see you as whole. If you're good at one thing, if you're a good gangster, you're going to be a gangster in twenty films. If you're a good teacher, that's what you're going to be. If you're a good back man, you'll be in the back. . . . In theater, we're all even. Even if somebody's name's above the title, all roles are good roles. . . . So those possibilities are there in theater that I don't find in film.

August Wilson Speaks Straight into My Heart

My favorite playwright is August Wilson, simply because he speaks to me straight into my heart. But something that's very clear in August Wilson's writing is that he loves the characters. August loves these people. . . . It's the simplicity of his work, the poetry of his work—no matter what their lot in life is. Whether somebody's an elevator operator or somebody is selling refrigerators, we don't know where the refrigerators come from, but he's selling the refrigerators. . . . Some people walk around with the *Daily Word;* I walk around with August Wilson, because he speaks to me.

The Arts Are Brain Food

How do you feed your soul? Literature. Art. Paintings. Dance. Music. You need to feed your soul, because feeding your soul makes the brain start working. It doesn't make the brain and you start. . . . When the brain is working, the world is better because we create. We start creating things. Drawing is creating, dance is creating, theater is creating. And we need to continue to create or we become stagnant people.

To view the whole interview and hear Ruben Santiago-Hudson read from August Wilson's *Fences,* go to **connect.mcgraw-hill.com.**

RESEARCH ASSIGNMENT: When Ruben Santiago-Hudson says, "I can't hide" and then is identified as the actor in *Shaft* by a boy at the basketball game, what is the moral of the story and what does the actor tell us about the importance of race?

Ruben Santiago-Hudson (b. 1956)

Born in Lackawanna, New York, Ruben Santiago-Hudson wrote the autobiographical play *Lackawanna Blues* about his youth in a segregated American steel town. His father, Ruben Santiago, was a Puerto Rican railroad worker. His mother, Alean Hudson, was African-American. In *Lackawanna Blues,* Santiago-Hudson portrays his abandonment by his mother, as well as the community of music and love that embraced him as he was raised by a woman who ran a local boarding house for African-Americans. He played over twenty characters in the production of *Lackawanna Blues* and was awarded an Obie. His script was made into an HBO movie directed by George C. Wolfe (2005)—for which Wolfe won the Director's Guild Award for Outstanding Movies for Television—and starring S. Epatha Merkerson, who won an Emmy. Santiago-Hudson graduated from Binghamton University and went on to study Shakespeare and classical theater at the Hilberry Classical Repertory Theater. He now lives in New York and has acted in over sixty films and TV movies, including *Devil's Advocate, Blown Away,* and *Shaft,* and the TV miniseries based on Zora Neale Hurston's novel *Their Eyes Were Watching God.* But for writer, director, and actor Santiago-Hudson, who has played opposite Gregory Hines in *Jelly's Last Jam* (also directed by George C. Wolfe) and won a Tony for his performance in August Wilson's *Seven Guitars,* theater remains his first love.

Lackawanna Blues (2005)

Adapted from the stage for film by Ruben Santiago-Hudson

Director: George C. Wolfe

An ensemble cast, starring S. Epatha Merkerson and including Marcus Carl Franklin, Mos Def, Carmen Ejogo, Louis Gossett Jr., Macy Gray, Rosie Perez, Ruben Santiago-Hudson, Liev Schreiber, Jimmy Smits, Lily Santiago, and Trey Santiago.

Freddie Cobbs (Ruben Santiago-Hudson), a boarder, talks to young Ruben (Marcus Carl Franklin) in the doorway of the boarding house. Why do you think Santiago-Hudson chose to juxtapose his real self with the child acting out his past? How might your interpretation of this scene be affected by your knowledge that the grown man playing Cobbs is the adult version of the boy in the movie?

Rachel "Nanny" Crosby (S. Epatha Merkerson) jokes around with the men gambling at the boarding house fish fry. What do you notice about the men in this image? Do the people in this photo fit your conception of the common man as Santiago-Hudson describes him in his interview?

Young Ruben and Nanny Crosby converse in the restaurant of the boarding house. Consider that *Lackawanna Blues* was written as a one-man performance. How do you imagine such an interaction as staged by only one actor?

An aged and ailing Nanny Crosby is surprised by old friends with donations to fund her medical care. To what extent is this celebration of heroic deeds by a common woman characteristic of modern theater? In what ways? Would you consider Nanny Crosby an "everyman"? Why or why not?

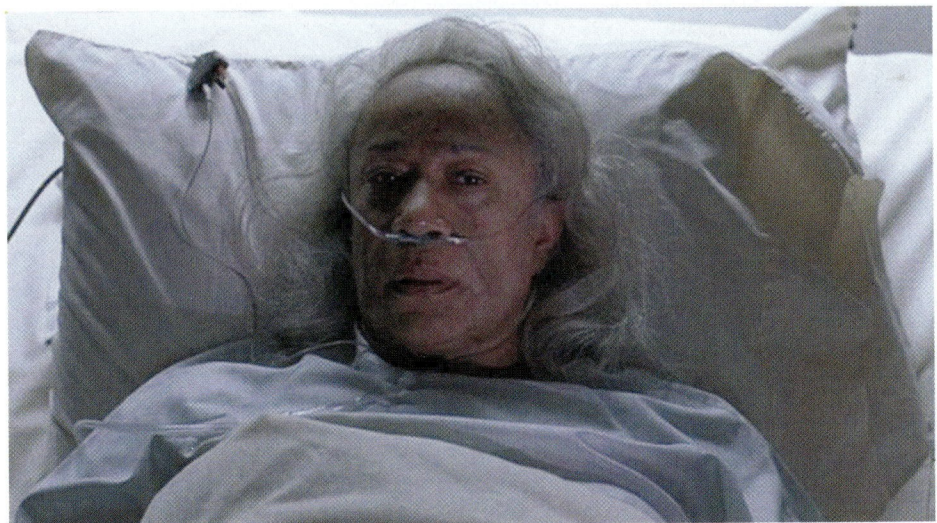

Nanny Crosby, now old and ill, lies in a hospital bed. Would you describe Nanny's death as tragic in the sense of Greek tragedy or as naturalistic?

Reading Modern Drama

When reading or viewing modern drama . . .

Consider how the play is staged.	Modern drama commonly is written for the **proscenium stage,** which features an arch through which the main set is visible (and can be separated by a curtain). • Is the set dressing detailed and realistic, as though you are glimpsing the action in a room through the missing **fourth wall**? • Is the set dressing minimal, inviting surrealistic interpretation and imagination?
Identify the structure and aim of the play.	• **Well-made plays** take place in a three-act sequence: The first act *poses* a problem, the next *complicates* the problem, and the third *resolves* the problem. • **Problem plays** confront a social issue with no clear-cut resolution, often in order to raise awareness of that issue.
Note the conventions of naturalistic theater, which shines a light on the painful realities of life.	• Is the protagonist an **antihero**—one who is not elevated socially or morally and does not exhibit common heroic characteristics like bravery or morality? • Is the protagonist an **everyman,** a character whose station in life is not unlike that of the audience? The everyman of modern drama is generally an ordinary middle-class person struggling with life.
Recognize the difference between realism and surrealism.	• **Realism** describes acting that features realistic language and physical gestures enacted by characters who are familiar in a setting that resembles the audience's real life. • **Surrealism** describes staging and events that represent an overlap of the conscious and the unconscious experience—often depicting dreams and internal struggles.
Identify instances of symbolism in the play.	• **Symbolism** occurs when an object, image, character, or action suggests meaning beyond the everyday literal interpretation. • **Expressionist** plays use scenes and onstage cues as **symbols** for characters' subjective emotions.

Writing about Modern Drama

1. Taking the long view, choose a modern play that you believe has something approaching the stature and sweep of a classical Greek tragedy and compare and contrast the two theater pieces. Can you make an exact match with respect to questions of tragedy? How do the traditional and modern characters differ in the way they behave? How does the social background of the plays appear to differ? Does it seem possible, given the belief systems of modern life, that a modern play can become truly tragic?

2. What is the role of modern drama in relation to society at large? How does this contrast, if it does contrast, with plays at the origins of Western theater? Does modern drama respond in the fullest possible fashion to the questions of modern psychology and modern life? What to your mind are the greatest problems and questions that arise in our lives today? How do modern plays rise to the level of these problems?

3. Some highly educated and sophisticated critics and instructors might argue that movies are the greatest dramatic creation of the modern age. Do you agree or disagree? Why? What aspects of the film might appear to give it an advantage over the stage play? A disadvantage?

"One of the things I feel blessed to have known is . . . men in particular that were older than me. I learned from them. And so one guy I worked with in a library—he was an actor—and I saw him in a play. And just that connection, that there was actually a human being that I could know who would do such a thing, sort of opened the door to that form of art, drama." Conversation with Dagoberto Gilb

35 Contemporary Theater

MEG: Jennifer, listen to me. Light . . . is emotion. *(JENNIFER, somewhat calmer but still a mess, response to the intensity of* MEG's *voice. Listens . . .)* Think of light, a beam of light . . . as a story, a story with its own past, its own history. The light has been who knows where, has illuminated who knows what. Maybe it's been traveling for a long, long time—decades, centuries. And somewhere along its journey, it starts to slow down . . . Take a pause, fold into itself . . . *(The lights on them start to dim . . .)* Okay, so . . . Now, I want you to imagine you're at the theatre. You're sitting in the audience, and you're watching a play. You say you love theatre?

—from The Second Beam *by Joan Ackermann*

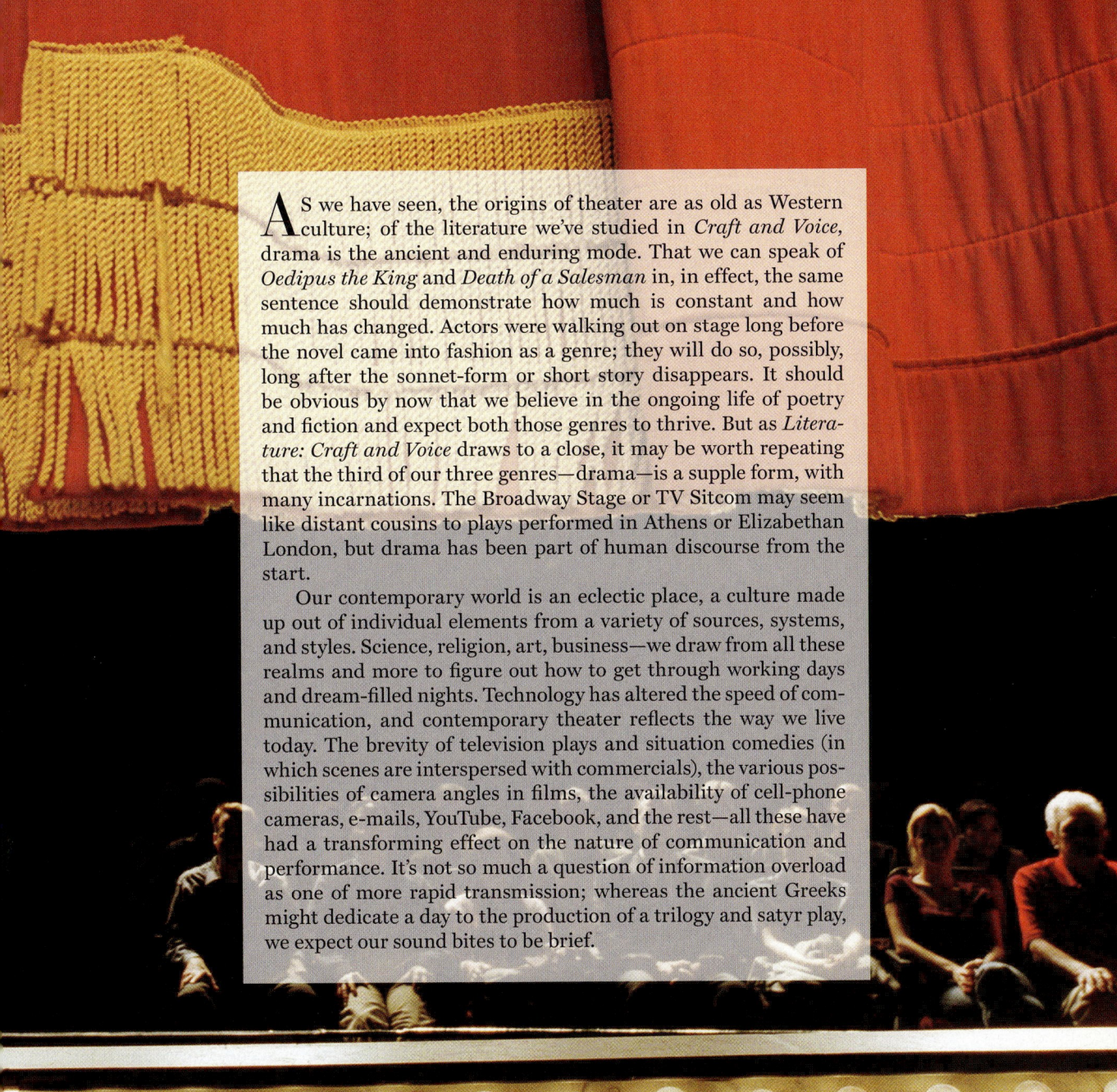

As we have seen, the origins of theater are as old as Western culture; of the literature we've studied in *Craft and Voice*, drama is the ancient and enduring mode. That we can speak of *Oedipus the King* and *Death of a Salesman* in, in effect, the same sentence should demonstrate how much is constant and how much has changed. Actors were walking out on stage long before the novel came into fashion as a genre; they will do so, possibly, long after the sonnet-form or short story disappears. It should be obvious by now that we believe in the ongoing life of poetry and fiction and expect both those genres to thrive. But as *Literature: Craft and Voice* draws to a close, it may be worth repeating that the third of our three genres—drama—is a supple form, with many incarnations. The Broadway Stage or TV Sitcom may seem like distant cousins to plays performed in Athens or Elizabethan London, but drama has been part of human discourse from the start.

Our contemporary world is an eclectic place, a culture made up out of individual elements from a variety of sources, systems, and styles. Science, religion, art, business—we draw from all these realms and more to figure out how to get through working days and dream-filled nights. Technology has altered the speed of communication, and contemporary theater reflects the way we live today. The brevity of television plays and situation comedies (in which scenes are interspersed with commercials), the various possibilities of camera angles in films, the availability of cell-phone cameras, e-mails, YouTube, Facebook, and the rest—all these have had a transforming effect on the nature of communication and performance. It's not so much a question of information overload as one of more rapid transmission; whereas the ancient Greeks might dedicate a day to the production of a trilogy and satyr play, we expect our sound bites to be brief.

Most contemporary playwrights create multi-scene and multi-act plays. But one-act plays have recently emerged as an important part of theatrical discourse. In some sense they bear the same relation to full-length plays as the short story does to the novel; they are necessarily more focused and contained. (In part this has to do with economic reality; one-act plays—with a small cast—are, of course, less expensive to produce.) The one-act plays that you will find in this chapter display a remarkable diversity, even as they focus on themes and motifs important to contemporary audiences—family and social relations, and the swift passage of time. Each illuminates the lives we lead together now.

"Theater is thriving now—it's thriving all over the world . . . You've got these large theaters that produce Broadway-type shows; but you've got hundreds of smaller theaters and theaters like college and university theaters, community theaters, resident theaters. These theaters are producing things and people are going to see them." Conversation with Edwin Wilson

EXPERIMENTAL THEATER

For many theatergoers, contemporary theater has its roots in a slightly earlier period of experimental theater, that variety of post–World War II European play that modifies the traditional assumptions and, often, the actual forms of classic theater. (See also the discussion of the real and the surreal in Chapter 34, page 1098.) The influence of Bertolt Brecht's notions of **Epic Theater** (in which the playwright favors characters who represent certain ideas as opposed to characters from life) and the **Theater of the Absurd** (in which the playwright presents life as random seeming and, often, darkly comical) as practiced by Eugene Ionesco, and the so-called Theater of Cruelty of Antonin Artaud (in which the playwright employs shock value in order to jar the audience into a recognition of harsh reality) have all had an impact on contemporary playwrights. Nobel Laureate Samuel Beckett, with such plays as *Waiting for Godot,* *Endgame,* and *Krapp's Last Tape,* was a transformative presence on the stage and page. The influence of such playwrights can be felt in the work of Edward Albee (Chapter 31), among other American playwrights, and in the work of New York City's Living Theater, headed by Julian Beck and Judith Malina. Their productions of Jack Gelber's improvised *The Connection* and Kenneth Brown's *The Brig* had a major influence, as did Richard Schechner's production of *Dionysus in '69.* Work by such playwrights as Maria Irena Fornes and Liz Swados also enliven the theater scene. Notice the influence of these experimental innovators in the presentation of time, place, and subject matter in these various works by the three contemporary playwrights in this chapter.

Joan Ackermann (b. 1950)

Joan Ackermann is a contemporary playwright whose plays have been produced off-Broadway and in theater venues across the nation. In addition to plays such as *Zara Spook and Other Lures* (1993), *The Batting Cage* (1999), *Marcus Is Walking* (1999), *Staying Afloat* (2006), *The Big Picture* (2006), and *The Taster* (2010), Ackermann has written the music and lyrics for a musical—*Isabella: A Young Physician's Primer on the Perils of Love* (2004). She also adapted one of her plays into the screenplay for the film *Off the Map,* which premiered at the Sundance Film Festival in 2003. Beyond her works for the stage, Ackermann is a journalist and has been a special contributor to *Sports Illustrated.* Her articles have also appeared in *The Atlantic* and *Time,* among other magazines. Ackermann makes her home in the Berkshire mountains of Massachusetts, not far from the Mixed Company Theatre, a company which she cofounded and for which she serves as artistic director. It has been in existence for more than twenty-five years.

AS YOU READ Recall a struggle or competition similar to the one in the audition that you might have experienced.

The Second Beam (2004)

CHARACTERS

GEORGIA

JENNIFER

MEG

CASTING AGENT

PATTI SCHARER

PLACE: An audition waiting room.

> *In an audition waiting room, three women—*GEORGIA,
> JENNIFER, *and* MEG—*sit on folded chairs and study
> pages from a script. They are all dressed in lab coats
> as scientists. After a moment, a casting agent opens a
> door and sticks her head in.*

CASTING AGENT: Georgia? (GEORGIA *smiles up at her,
grabs her stuff and exits. The other two smile at her
as she exits into the audition room, closing the door
behind her.* MEG *is the older of the two, more mature,*
5   *grounded.* JENNIFER *is soft-spoken, sweet.)*

JENNIFER: *(Approaching* MEG.) Pardon me . . . Do you
have a tissue? (MEG *opens her bag and gives her one.
Goes back to studying.* JENNIFER *sits down with the
tissue and very discreetly wipes under both her arm-*
10   *pits.)* You were at *The Flannerys.* (MEG *looks at her
blankly.)* You read for the sister. Of the boxer, with the
bad hand. The malpractice suit.

MEG: *(Remembering.)* Oh. Right.

JENNIFER: I heard that show didn't get picked up. You
15   were at *Mind of a Married Man,* too. The jockey's
wife. *(Concerned.)* Are you memorizing that?

MEG: *(Friendly.)* No. No, just studying. *(Pause.)*

JENNIFER: Do you happen to know who got the part?

MEG: Which part. The sister, of the boxer?

20 **JENNIFER:** No. Yes.

MEG: Or the jockey's wife.

JENNIFER: Either. Both.

MEG: Well, the same actress got them both.

JENNIFER: Patti Scharer?

25 **MEG:** Patti Scharer.

JENNIFER: I knew it. Patti Scharer. Patti Scharer. Every
part my agent sends me out on, every single part it
seems, Patti Scharer gets. Care for a mint? (MEG
shakes her head no, takes out a lipstick and puts some
30   *on, looking at herself in a small compact mirror.)* Are
you doing an accent?

MEG: Accent?

JENNIFER: For the scientist.

MEG: What kind of accent?

JENNIFER: Foreign.   35

MEG: I think she's American. *(Pause.)*

JENNIFER: *(Concerned.)* So you're not doing an accent?
(MEG *shakes her head, goes back to studying the
pages.)* I was going to do a French accent. Madame
Curie. The scientist. You don't think I should?   40

MEG: If you've worked on it that way. It's a choice.

JENNIFER: Yes, it is. It's a choice. *(Pause.)* I never know
about choices. My agent always says they like it when
you make a choice, but I'm not so sure. I've been
making choices, strong choices, but . . . they haven't   45
really been panning out for me. *(She discreetly picks
something out from between her teeth.)* I really need
the work. I really, really, really need the work. I'm
sorry, I'll let you concentrate. *(Pause.)* Have you read
for him before? (MEG *looks at her.)* Ethan Schroeder.   50
The director. Have you read for him? (MEG *nods. Goes
back to her pages, concentrating.)* My friend Annette
says he's a monster. She read for him for a movie of
the week and he ate his lunch the entire time.

MEG: He can be a jerk.   55

JENNIFER: That's all I need. *(She sighs, smooths her
skirt.)* Can I just ask you . . . is this lipstick, the color
of my lipstick, all right? I've never worn this shade
before.

MEG: It looks good on you. It's a good color for you.   60

JENNIFER: You think so? Really?

MEG: I do. *(Smiling.)* It's a good "choice."

JENNIFER: Thanks. I don't know. It felt like a scientist
choice. I don't know why. Sometimes you just have to
go with your gut. (MEG *nods, goes back to her pages.)*   65

JENNIFER: *(Worrying.)* Patti Scharer. Do you get the
light thing? They won't expect us to understand that,
do you think? Stopping light? They won't grill us
about that.

MEG: Probably not.   70

JENNIFER: I don't know. I read for the part of a veterinarian and they acted like they expected me to know everything about a dog's digestive system. I just winged it, talked about heartworm. I've seen them. In a jar. *(MEG doesn't respond.)* It's not just about the money. Truth be known, I'm feeling kind of stuck. *(Pause.)* If he's eating in there, stuffing his mouth with California pizza, Koo-koo-charoo chicken . . . You said you've read for him?

MEG: I used to go out with him.

JENNIFER: *(Stunned.)* You went out with him? You went out with Ethan Schroeder? *(MEG nods.)*

JENNIFER: Ohmygod, I'm so sorry. What I said . . . I didn't mean to call him a monster. Maybe he was just . . . hungry when my friend read for him. Maybe he's perfectly—

MEG: It's okay. A lot of people think he's an asshole.

JENNIFER: They do. You're not going out with him any more? *(MEG shakes her head.)* You're still friends? I mean, you're okay reading for him?

MEG: I really like this part.

JENNIFER: *(Not really like it.)* You do?

MEG: I do. How often does that happen?

JENNIFER: Yeah. Really. You must like this part.

MEG: I find the subject fascinating. I've read quite a bit about it.

JENNIFER: Oh. So . . . Light travels a hundred and eighty thousand miles an hour . . .

MEG: A second.

JENNIFER: And . . . *(JENNIFER waits for MEG to explain it.)* Then they stop it in a jar. *(Thinking . . .)* Like heartworm. Preserve it in formaldehyde.

MEG: Chilled sodium gas, actually.

JENNIFER: It just hangs in there? Frozen?

MEG: Well, the light goes out. It gets fainter and fainter as it slows down. The most amazing part to me—it's all amazing—they can revive the light any time by flashing a second beam of light through the gas.

JENNIFER: Oh.

MEG: They can bring a beam of light to a full stop, hold it, and then send it on its way with a second beam. *(Pause.)*

JENNIFER: I like scenes best . . . when I can go deep. Cry. I like emotion. My background is theatre.

MEG: Not a lot of emotion in these scenes, not ostensibly.

JENNIFER: No. That's why I was thinking the French . . .

MEG: Go for the accent.

JENNIFER: You think so? *(Another actress enters. She is very appealing, made-up, a knock-out. She takes a seat. Exudes confidence. Both MEG and JENNIFER look at her, silently, as she takes out many pages and starts going through them.)*

PATTI: *(To JENNIFER, all business.)* Excuse me, are your pages with the reporter dated May eleventh or May fifteenth? *(JENNIFER looks at her pages . . .)*

JENNIFER: The reporter? I don't have . . . *(JENNIFER flips through, looking . . .)*

PATTI: Never mind. *(Noticing . . .)* Meg.

MEG: Hi, Patti.

130 **PATTI:** How *are* you? (MEG *nods, friendly, a little guarded.*)

PATTI: It's so great to see you, are you here now?

MEG: I'm here.

PATTI: You know I'd heard that. I ran into Carolyn, she
135 was stage managing *Vanya* at the Taper, she told me
you'd moved back.

MEG: I did.

PATTI: That's great. And you're reading for Ethan?

MEG: I am.

140 **PATTI:** Wow. Wow. (PATTI *studies* MEG, *waiting for some
kind of response, which is not forthcoming.*)

MEG: How's Olivia?

PATTI: Olivia is three, God help me. Meg, can I borrow
your lipstick, I actually forgot mine.

145 **MEG:** I'm sorry. I actually left all my makeup in the car.

PATTI: Really? What were you thinking? (PATTI *maintains her charming smile, miffed underneath.* JEN-
NIFER *stares at* PATTI *in a mixed stupor of defeat and
envy.*)

150 **JENNIFER:** *(Stirring.)* I have some lipstick. You can
borrow.

PATTI: *(Brightly.)* Great. Thanks. (JENNIFER *reaches
down into her purse and takes out her lipstick, takes
off the cap, and offers it to* PATTI. PATTI, *looking at*
155 JENNIFER's *lips:*) Oh. Is it the color you're wearing?

JENNIFER: Uh-huh.

PATTI: That's okay. That color . . . I can't wear that color.
But, thanks. (*Mortified,* JENNIFER *looks down at the
color, gradually retreats her hand, puts the cover back
160 on and sticks the lipstick back in her purse. Pause as all
study the script.*)

PATTI: *(To* MEG.) I admire you, Meg. I really do. Reading
for Ethan. That takes guts.

MEG: Not really.

165 **PATTI:** The way he treated you. You know Carolyn's first
A. D. (MEG *nods.*) You know they're an item. Ethan

and Carolyn. She's pregnant. That's ironic, huh?
(MEG *did not know this. She flinches slightly. The door
opens and* GEORGIA *enters with the casting agent behind her.* GEORGIA *grabs a sweater she left on a chair,* 170
waves to the CASTING AGENT, *exiting.*)

CASTING AGENT: Thanks, Georgia. Patti. You made it.

PATTI: I'm so sorry I'm late. The 405 was a nightmare.

CASTING AGENT: You want to come in? Or do you want
to take a minute. Jennifer . . . ? (JENNIFER, *discom-* 175
bobulated, jumps up, dropping all her pages as PATTI
grabs her purse, coat, stands up.)

PATTI: I'm fine. (PATTI *heads smoothly into the audition room. The* CASTING AGENT *smiles at* MEG, *looks
down at the pages* JENNIFER *has dropped, and exits* 180
into the audition room.)

JENNIFER: *(Crying, wiping her nose on her sleeve.)* I'm
sorry. Do you have another tissue? (MEG *hands her
another tissue which* JENNIFER *uses to wipe her nose
and wipe away tears.* JENNIFER *grabs her stuff and* 185
hurries out.)

JENNIFER: *(Not looking at* MEG.) It was very nice meeting you.

MEG: Where are you going?

JENNIFER: *(Crying, halfway out the door.)* I don't know. 190
Bye.

MEG: Wait! (JENNIFER *turns and looks at her.*) You can
get this part. (JENNIFER *is sobbing.*)

JENNIFER: I can't get this part.

MEG: You can. 195

JENNIFER: I can't. I can't even audition for this part.

MEG: Sit down.

JENNIFER: What?

MEG: Pull yourself together. Sit down.

JENNIFER: *(Weepy, discombobulated.)* Where? 200

MEG: On the chair. Go ahead. Sit! (JENNIFER *sits
back down on her chair, sniffling.*) Here. Put these
on. (MEG *takes the pair of tortoise-shell glasses she is*

wearing and gives them to JENNIFER.) Put them on.
205 (JENNIFER *does.*)

JENNIFER: Why does she want this part? It's not even
very big.

MEG: Patti Scharer is not going to get this part.

JENNIFER: Yes, she is.

210 MEG: No she's not.

JENNIFER: (*Crying.*) She's already got it. She's already
in there. With the part.

MEG: Ethan can't stand Patti Scharer. He's not going
to give her this part. He's going to give you this part,
215 because it's your part. (JENNIFER, *pauses crying to
look at her.*)

JENNIFER: He can't stand her?

MEG: Jennifer, listen to me. Light . . . is emotion. (JEN-
NIFER, *somewhat calmer but still a mess, response to
220 the intensity of* MEG's *voice. Listens . . .*) Think of light,
a beam of light . . . as a story, a story with its own past,
its own history. The light has been who knows where,
has illuminated who knows what. Maybe it's been
traveling for a long, long time—decades, centuries.
225 And somewhere along its journey, it starts to slow
down . . . Take a pause, fold into itself . . . *(The lights
on them start to dim . . .)* Okay, so . . . Now, I want you
to imagine you're at the theatre. You're sitting in the
audience, and you're watching a play. You say you love
230 theatre?

JENNIFER: (*Blowing her nose.*) I do. Why are you doing
this?

MEG: So the curtain has just opened, and there are three
people on stage, and they're still, not moving. (*Lights
235 keep dimming.*) Who are these people, these characters? What is their past? Their history? We don't
know. At the beginning of the play, we don't know
anything about them at all. Their pasts are frozen.
Suspended. (*The lights stop dimming, and* MEG *and
240 * JENNIFER *are still for a few moments, frozen in close
to dark.*) Then the play begins . . . (*Lights start to
slowly fade up.*) . . . and we start to learn things about
them. Information unfolds. One character leaves.
Facts are revealed. We learn that this character really

needs something, or this character has a dream, a
passion, or maybe this one's been hurt . . . (*A spotlight
lights her dimly and gets brighter slowly during the
following . . .*) . . . been hurt really, really badly and
we don't know how. Within minutes we can learn so 250
much about them. In less than ten minutes, we can
see the DNA of their whole lives. Even though there
are mysteries, we feel we know them, quite well. Then,
there comes that moment, that inevitable pivotal moment in a scene when things turn. The epiphany. The
revelation. Something is illuminated. (*The spotlight on* 255
her is very bright now. Other lights are up to half full.)

JENNIFER: I think . . . you're probably saying something
but I'm not sure what it is. (MEG *looks at her. Takes
the barrette out of her hair.*)

MEG: I think you should put your hair back. Here, take 260
my barrette. (MEG *hands her barrette to* JENNIFER,
who puts her hair back.) That's good. You look . . . like
a scientist.

JENNIFER: What did Ethan Schroeder do to you that
was so bad? (MEG *takes a moment to answer.*) 265

MEG: Nothing terribly original. (MEG *goes to get her
things to leave.*)

JENNIFER: You're not going to read for this part?

MEG: No.

JENNIFER: One thing . . . I do feel emotional, right 270
now. (*A spotlight on* JENNIFER *starts to come up, as
all other lights start to fade, including the spotlight on*
MEG.) For you, mainly.

MEG: Use it. Hold it inside. And, I would suggest you
drop the accent. 275

JENNIFER: Really?

MEG: You don't need it. Another thing . . . when you go in
there, tell Ethan he looks like a young Richard Burton.

JENNIFER: Okay. I can do that. I can do that.

MEG: This is your part. (*All lights are out now except the* 280
spotlight on JENNIFER.)

JENNIFER: (*Confidently, seriously looking like a scientist.*) I know. This is my part. This is my part. (*The
spotlight on* JENNIFER *is up to full. Then it fades out.*)

Writing from Reading

Summarize

1 In this play a trio of actresses shows up at an audition, with unexpected results. Describe the temperaments of each of the actresses.

Analyze Craft

2 How would you characterize the relationships between the two actresses as the scene opens? Does the mood change? If so, what prompts the change? How does the entrance of the third actress affect the situation?

Analyze Voice

3 How would you describe the overall tone of the play? How is this tone achieved?

Synthesize Summary and Analysis

4 How does the playwright integrate science—the experiment with the beam of light—into the action of the play?

Interpret the Play

5 How does the motif of illusion versus reality unfold in this play?

6 Would a male playwright have treated the scene differently, and in what ways?

David Henry Hwang (b. 1957)

Born in a suburb of Los Angeles, David Henry Hwang has become one of the most prominent Asian-American voices in contemporary drama. His parents, Chinese by birth, met and married in the United States, raising Hwang under his mother's fundamentalist Christian influence. Although Hwang later abandoned fundamentalism, it continues to be an element in his plays. Hwang began writing plays while an undergraduate at Stanford University, and his first, *F.O.B*, which stands for "fresh off the boat" in reference to Chinese immigrants, met with great success. His biggest success came with *M. Butterfly*, a play that was performed on Broadway and that brought Hwang a Tony Award and a Pulitzer Prize nomination. Hwang's other projects include collaborations with the composer Phillip Glass on a science-fiction production and on an opera about Christopher Columbus. He also collaborated on the script for the Disney rock musical version of *Aida* and for the screen adaptation of A. S. Byatt's novel *Possession*. Although his work shows great range and variety, it most often concerns itself with the Asian-American identity. His play *Chinglish* opened on Broadway in October 2011.

AS YOU READ Pay attention to each time the sound of a voice is mentioned. When you have finished, ask yourself what a human voice represents within the context of this play.

The Sound of a Voice (1983)

CHARACTERS

MAN, *fifties, Japanese*
WOMAN, *fifties, Japanese*

SETTING. *Woman's house, in a remote corner of the forest.*

SCENE 1

Woman pours tea for Man. Man rubs himself, trying to get warm.

MAN: You're very kind to take me in.

WOMAN: This is a remote corner of the world. Guests are rare.

MAN: The tea—you pour it well.

5 **WOMAN:** No.

MAN: The sound it makes—in the cup—very soothing.

WOMAN: That is the tea's skill, not mine. *(She hands the cup to him.)* May I get you something else? Rice, perhaps?

10 **MAN:** No.

WOMAN: And some vegetables?

MAN: No, thank you.

WOMAN: Fish? *(Pause.)* It is at least two days' walk to the nearest village. I saw no horse. You must be very
15 hungry. You would do a great honor to dine with me. Guests are rare.

MAN: Thank you.

WOMAN: *(Woman gets up, leaves. Man holds the cup in his hands, using it to warm himself. He gets up, walks around the room. It is sparsely furnished, drab, except* 20 *for one shelf on which stands a vase of brightly colored flowers. The flowers stand out in sharp contrast to the starkness of the room. Slowly, he reaches out towards them. He touches them. Quickly, he takes one of the flowers from the vase, hides it in his clothes. He returns* 25 *to where he had sat previously. He waits. Woman re-enters. She carries a tray with food.)* Please. Eat. It will give me great pleasure.

MAN: This—this is magnificent.

WOMAN: Eat. 30

MAN: Thank you. *(He motions for Woman to join him.)*

WOMAN: No, thank you.

MAN: This is wonderful. The best I've tasted.

WOMAN: You are reckless in your flattery. But anything you say, I will enjoy hearing. It's not even the words. It's 35 the sound of a voice, the way it moves through the air.

MAN: How long has it been since you last had a visitor? *(Pause.)*

WOMAN: I don't know.

MAN: Oh? 40

WOMAN: I lose track. Perhaps five months ago, perhaps ten years, perhaps yesterday. I don't consider time when there is no voice in the air. It's pointless. Time begins with the entrance of a visitor, and ends with his exit.

45

MAN: And in between? You don't keep track of the days? You can't help but notice—

WOMAN: Of course I notice.

MAN: Oh.

50 **WOMAN:** I notice, but I don't keep track. *(Pause.)* May I bring out more?

MAN: More? No. No. This was wonderful.

WOMAN: I have more.

MAN: Really—the best I've had.

55 **WOMAN:** You must be tired. Did you sleep in the forest last night?

MAN: Yes.

WOMAN: Or did you not sleep at all?

MAN: I slept.

60 **WOMAN:** Where?

MAN: By a waterfall. The sound of the water put me to sleep. It rumbled like the sounds of a city. You see, I can't sleep in too much silence. It scares me. It makes me feel that I have no control over what is about to happen.

65

WOMAN: I feel the same way.

MAN: But you live here—alone?

WOMAN: Yes.

MAN: It's so quiet here. How can you sleep?

70 **WOMAN:** Tonight, I'll sleep. I'll lie down in the next room, and hear your breathing through the wall, and fall asleep shamelessly. There will be no silence.

MAN: You're very kind to let me stay here.

WOMAN: This is yours. *(She unrolls a mat. There is a beautiful design of a flower on the mat. The flower looks exactly like the flowers in the vase.)*

75

MAN: Did you make it yourself?

WOMAN: Yes. There is a place to wash outside.

MAN: Thank you.

WOMAN: Goodnight.   80

MAN: Goodnight. *(Man starts to leave.)*

WOMAN: May I know your name?

MAN: No. I mean, I would rather not say. If I gave you a name, it would only be made up. Why should I deceive you? You are too kind for that.   85

WOMAN: Then what should I call you? Perhaps—"Man Who Fears Silence"?

MAN: How about, "Man Who Fears Women"?

WOMAN: That name is much too common.

MAN: And you?   90

WOMAN: Yokiko.

MAN: That's your name?

WOMAN: It's what you may call me.

MAN: Goodnight, Yokiko. You are very kind.

WOMAN: You are very smart. Goodnight.   95

(Man exits. Hanako goes to the mat. She tidies it, brushes it off. She goes to the vase. She picks up the flowers, studies them. She carries them out of the room with her. Man re-enters. He takes off his outer clothing. He glimpses the spot where the vase used to sit. He reaches into his clothing, pulls out the stolen flower. He studies it. He puts it underneath his head as he lies down to sleep, like a pillow. He starts to fall asleep. Suddenly, a start. He picks up his head. He listens.)

SCENE 2

Dawn. Man is getting dressed. Woman enters with food.

WOMAN: Good morning.

MAN: Good morning, Yokiko.

WOMAN: You weren't planning to leave?

MAN: I have quite a distance to travel today.

5   **WOMAN:**   Please. *(She offers him food.)*

MAN: Thank you.

WOMAN: May I ask where you are traveling to?

MAN: It's far.

WOMAN: I know this region well.

10   **MAN:**   Oh? Do you leave the house often?

WOMAN: I used to. I used to travel a great deal. I know the region from those days.

MAN: You probably wouldn't know the place I'm headed.

WOMAN: Why not?

15   **MAN:**   It's new. A new village. It didn't exist in "those days." *(Pause.)*

WOMAN: I thought you said you wouldn't deceive me.

MAN: I didn't. You don't believe me, do you?

WOMAN: No.

20   **MAN:**   Then I didn't deceive you. I'm traveling. That much is true.

WOMAN: Are you in such a hurry?

MAN: Traveling is a matter of timing. Catching the light. *(Woman exits; Man finishes eating, puts down his*
25   *bowl. Woman re-enters with the vase of flowers.)* Where did you find those? They don't grow native around these parts, do they?

WOMAN: No; they've all been brought in. They were brought in by visitors. Such as yourself. They were left
30   here. In my custody.

MAN: But—they look so fresh, so alive.

WOMAN: I take care of them. They remind me of the people and places outside this house.

MAN: May I touch them?

35   **WOMAN:**   Certainly.

MAN: These have just blossomed.

WOMAN: No; they were in bloom yesterday. If you'd noticed them before, you would know that.

MAN: You must have received these very recently. I would guess—within five days.   40

WOMAN: I don't know. But I wouldn't trust your estimate. It's all in the amount of care you show to them. I create a world which is outside the realm of what you know.

MAN: What do you do?   45

WOMAN: I can't explain. Words are too inefficient. It takes hundreds of words to describe a single act of caring. With hundreds of acts, words become irrelevant. *(Pause.)* But perhaps you can stay.

MAN: How long?   50

WOMAN: As long as you'd like.

MAN: Why?

WOMAN: To see how I care for them.

MAN: I *am* tired.

WOMAN: Rest.   55

MAN: The light?

WOMAN: It will return.

SCENE 3

Man is carrying chopped wood. He is stripped to the waist. Woman enters.

WOMAN: You're very kind to do that for me.

MAN: I enjoy it, you know. Chopping wood. It's clean. No questions. You take your axe, you stand up the log, you aim—pow!—you either hit it or you don't. Success or failure.   5

WOMAN: You seem to have been very successful today.

MAN: Why shouldn't I be? It's a beautiful day. I can see to those hills. The trees are cool. The sun is gentle. Ideal. If a man can't be successful on a day like this,

10 he might as well kick the dust up into his own face. *(Man notices Woman staring at him. Man pats his belly, looks at her.)* Protection from falls.

WOMAN: What? *(Man pinches his belly, showing some fat.)* Oh. Don't be silly. *(Man begins slapping the fat on*
15 *his belly to a rhythm.)*

MAN: Listen—I can make music—see?—that wasn't always possible. But now—that I've developed this— whenever I need entertainment.

WOMAN: You shouldn't make fun of your body.

20 **MAN:** Why not? I saw you. You were staring.

WOMAN: I wasn't making fun. *(Man inflates his cheeks.)* I was just—stop that!

MAN: Then why were you staring?

WOMAN: I was—

25 **MAN:** Laughing?

WOMAN: No.

MAN: Well?

WOMAN: I was—your body. It's . . . strong. *(Pause.)*

MAN: People say that. But they don't know. I've heard
30 that age brings wisdom. That's a laugh. The years don't accumulate here. They accumulate here. *(Pause; he pinches his belly.)* But today is a day to be happy, right? The woods. The sun. Blue. It's a happy day. I'm going to chop wood.

35 **WOMAN:** There's nothing left to chop. Look.

MAN: Oh. I guess . . . that's it.

WOMAN: Sit. Here.

MAN: But—

WOMAN: There's nothing left. *(Man sits; Woman stares*
40 *at his belly.)* Learn to love it.

MAN: Don't be ridiculous.

WOMAN: Touch it.

MAN: It's flabby.

WOMAN: It's strong.

MAN: It's weak. 45

WOMAN: And smooth.

MAN: Do you mind if I put on my shirt?

WOMAN: Of course not. Shall I get it for you?

MAN: No. No. Just sit there. *(Man starts to put on his shirt. He pauses, studies his body.)* You think it's cute, huh? 50

WOMAN: I think you should learn to love it. *(Man pats his belly, talks to it.)*

MAN *(to belly)*: You're okay, sir. You hang onto my body like a great horseman.

WOMAN: Not like that. 55

MAN *(ibid.)*: You're also faithful. You'll never leave me for another man.

WOMAN: No.

MAN: What do you want me to say? *(Woman walks over to Man. She touches his belly with her hand. They look* 60 *at each other.)*

SCENE 4

Night. Man is alone. Flowers are gone from stand. Mat is unrolled. Man lies on it, sleeping. Suddenly, he starts. He lifts up his head. He listens. Silence. He goes back to sleep. Another start. He lifts up his head, strains to hear. Slowly; we begin to make out the strains of a single shakuhachi playing a haunting line. It is very soft. He strains to hear it. The instrument slowly fades out. He waits for it to return, but it does not. He takes out the stolen flower. He stares into it.

SCENE 5

Day. Woman is cleaning, while Man relaxes. She is on her hands and knees, scrubbing. She is dressed in a simple outfit, for working. Her hair is tied back. Man is sweating. He has not, however, removed his shirt.

MAN: I heard your playing last night.

WOMAN: My playing?

MAN: *Shakuhachi.*

WOMAN: Oh.

5 MAN: You played very softly. I had to strain to hear it. Next time, don't be afraid. Play out. Fully. Clear. It must've been very beautiful, if only I could've heard it clearly. Why don't you play for me sometime?

WOMAN: I'm very shy about it.

10 MAN: Why?

WOMAN: I play for my own satisfaction. That's all. It's something I developed on my own. I don't know if it's at all acceptable by outside standards.

MAN: Play for me. I'll tell you.

15 WOMAN: No; I'm sure you're too knowledgeable in the arts.

MAN: Who? Me?

WOMAN: You being from the city and all.

MAN: I'm ignorant, believe me.

20 WOMAN: I'd play, and you'd probably bite your cheek.

MAN: Ask me a question about music. Any question. I'll answer incorrectly. I guarantee it.

WOMAN: Look at this.

MAN: What?

25 WOMAN: A stain.

MAN: Where?

WOMAN: Here? See? I can't get it out.

MAN: Oh. I hadn't noticed it before.

WOMAN: I notice it every time I clean.

30 MAN: Here. Let me try.

WOMAN: Thank you.

MAN: Ugh. It's tough.

WOMAN: I know.

MAN: How did it get here?

35 WOMAN: It's been there as long as I've lived here.

MAN: I hardly stand a chance. (Pause.) But I'll try. Uh—one—two—three—four! One—two—three—four! See, you set up . . . gotta set up . . . rhythm—two—three—four. Like fighting! Like battle! One—two—three—four! Used to practice with a rhythm . . . beat . . . battle! Yes! (The stain starts to fade away) Look—it's—yes!—whoo!—there it goes—got the sides—the edges—yes!—fading quick—fading away—ooo—here we come—towards the center—to the heart—two—three—four—slow—slow death—tough—dead! (Man rolls over in triumphant laughter) 40 45

WOMAN: Dead.

MAN: I got it! I got it! Whoo! A little rhythm! All it took! Four! Four!

WOMAN: Thank you. 50

MAN: I didn't think I could do it—but there—it's gone—I did it!

WOMAN: Yes. You did.

MAN: And you—you were great.

WOMAN: No—I was carried away. 55

MAN: We were a team! You and Me!

WOMAN: I only provided encouragement.

MAN: You were great! You were! (Man grabs Woman. Pause.)

WOMAN: It's gone. Thank you. Would you like to hear me play shakuhachi? 60

MAN: Yes I would.

WOMAN: I don't usually play for visitors. It's so . . . I'm not sure. I developed it—all by myself—in times when I was alone. I heard nothing—no human voice. So I learned to play shakuhachi. I tried to make these sounds resemble the human voice. The shakuhachi became my weapon. To ward off the air. It kept me from choking on many a silent evening. 65

MAN: I'm here. You can hear my voice. 70

WOMAN: Speak again.

MAN: I will.

SCENE 6

Night. Man is sleeping. Suddenly, a start. He lifts his head up. He listens. Silence. He strains to hear. The shakuhachi melody rises up once more. This time, however, it becomes louder and more clear than before. He gets up. He cannot tell from what directions the music is coming. He walks around the room, putting his ear to different places in the wall, but he cannot locate the sound. It seems to come from all directions at once, as omnipresent as the air. Slowly he moves towards the wall with the sliding panel through which the Woman enters and exits. He puts his ear against it thinking the music may be coming from there. Slowly, he slides the door open just a crack, ever so carefully. He peeks through the crack. As he peeks through, the Upstage wall of the set becomes transparent, and through the scrim, we are able to see what he sees. Woman is Upstage of the scrim. She is tending a room filled with potted and vased flowers of all variety. The lushness and beauty of the room Upstage to the scrim stands out in stark contrast to the barrenness of the main set. She is also transformed. She is a young woman. She is beautiful. She wears a brightly colored kimono. Man observes this scene for a long time. He then slides the door shut. The scrim returns to opaque. The music continues. He returns to his mat. He picks up the stolen flower. It is brown and wilted, dead. He looks at it. The music slowly fades out.

SCENE 7

Morning, Man is half-dressed. He is practicing sword maneuvers. He practices with the feel of a man whose spirit is willing, but the flesh is inept. He tries to execute deft movements, but is dissatisfied with his efforts. He curses himself, and returns to basic exercises. Suddenly, he feels something buzzing around his neck—a mosquito. He slaps his neck, but misses it. He sees it flying near him. He swipes at it with his sword. He keeps missing. Finally, he thinks he's hit it. He runs over, kneels down to discover the fallen insect. He picks up two halves of a mosquito on two different fingers. Woman enters the room. She looks as she normally does. She is carrying a vase of flowers, which she places on its shelf.

MAN: Look.

WOMAN: I'm sorry?

MAN: Look.

WOMAN: What? *(He brings over the two halves of mosquito to show her.)*   5

MAN: See?

WOMAN: Oh.

MAN: I hit it—chop!

WOMAN: These are new forms of target practice?

MAN: Huh? Well—yes—in a way.   10

WOMAN: You seem to do well at it.

MAN: Thank you. For last night. I heard your *shakuhachi*. It was very loud, strong—good tone.

WOMAN: Did you enjoy it? I wanted you to enjoy it. If you wish, I'll play it for you every night.   15

MAN: Every night!

WOMAN: If you wish.

MAN: No—I don't—I don't want you to treat me like a baby.

WOMAN: What? I'm not.   20

MAN: Oh, yes. Like a baby. Who you must feed in the middle of the night or he cries. Waaah! Waaah!

WOMAN: Stop that!

MAN: You need your sleep.

WOMAN: I don't mind getting up for you. *(Pause.)* I   25
would enjoy playing for you. Every night. While you sleep. It will make me feel—like I'm shaping your dreams. I go through long stretches when there is no one in my dreams. It's terrible. During those times, I avoid my bed as much as possible. I paint. I weave. I   30
play *shakuhachi*. I sit on mats and rub powder into my face. Anything to keep from facing a bed with no dreams. It is like sleeping on ice.

MAN: What do you dream of now?

35 **WOMAN:** Last night—I dreamt of you. I don't remember what happened. But you were very funny. Not in a mocking way. I wasn't laughing at you. But you made me laugh. And you were very warm. I remember that. *(Pause.)* What do you remember about last night?

40 **MAN:** Just your playing. That's all. I got up, listened to it, and went back to sleep. *(Man gets up, resumes practicing with his sword.)*

WOMAN: Another mosquito bothering you?

MAN: Just practicing. Ah! Weak! Too weak! I tell you, 45 it wasn't always like this. I'm telling you, there were days when I could chop the fruit from a tree without ever taking my eyes off the ground. *(He continues practicing.)* You ever use one of these?

WOMAN: I've had to pick one up, yes.

50 **MAN:** Oh?

WOMAN: You forget—I live alone—out here—there is . . . not much to sustain me but what I manage to learn myself. It wasn't really a matter of choice.

MAN: I used to be very good, you know. Perhaps I can 55 give you some pointers.

WOMAN: I'd really rather not.

MAN: C'mon—a woman like you—you're absolutely right. You need to know how to defend yourself.

WOMAN: As you wish.

60 **MAN:** Do you have something to practice with?

WOMAN: Yes. Excuse me. *(She exits. He practices more. She re-enters with two wooden sticks. He takes one of them.)* Will these do?

MAN: Nice. Now, show me what you can do.

65 **WOMAN:** I'm sorry?

MAN: Run up and hit me.

WOMAN: Please.

MAN: Go on—I'll block it.

WOMAN: I feel so . . . undignified.

70 **MAN:** Go on. *(She hits him playfully with stick.)* Not like that!

WOMAN: I'll try to be gentle.

MAN: What?

WOMAN: I don't want to hurt you.

75 **MAN:** You won't—Hit me! *(Woman charges at Man, quickly, deftly. She scores a hit.)* Oh!

WOMAN: Did I hurt you?

MAN: No—you were—let's try that again. *(They square off again. Woman rushes forward. She appears to attempt a strike. He blocks that apparent strike, which turns 80 out to be a feint. She scores.)* Huh?

WOMAN: Did I hurt you? I'm sorry.

MAN: No.

WOMAN: I hurt you.

85 **MAN:** No.

WOMAN Do you wish to hit me?

MAN: No.

WOMAN: Do you want me to try again?

MAN: No.

90 **WOMAN:** Thank you.

MAN: Just practice there—by yourself—let me see you run through some maneuvers.

WOMAN: Must I?

MAN: Yes! Go! *(She goes to an open area.)* My greatest 95 strength was always as a teacher. *(Woman executes a series of deft movements. Her whole manner is transformed. Man watches with increasing amazement. Her movements end. She regains her submissive manner.)*

WOMAN: I'm so embarrassed. My skills—they're so— 100 inappropriate. I look like a man.

MAN: Where did you learn that?

WOMAN: There is much time to practice here.

MAN: But you—the techniques.

WOMAN: I don't know what's fashionable in the outside
105 world. *(Pause.)* Are you unhappy?

MAN: No.

WOMAN: Really?

MAN: I'm just . . . surprised.

WOMAN: You think it's unbecoming for a woman.

110 **MAN:**   No, no. Not at all.

WOMAN: You want to leave.

MAN: No!

WOMAN: All visitors do. I know. I've met many. They
say they'll stay. And they do. For a while. Until they
115 see too much. Or they learn something new. There are
boundaries outside of which visitors do not want to
see me step. Only who knows what those boundaries
are? Not I. They change with every visitor. You have
to be careful not to cross them, but you never know
120 where they are. And one day, inevitably, you step outside the lines. The visitor knows. You don't. You didn't
know that you'd done anything different. You thought
it was just another part of you. The visitor sneaks
away. The next day, you learn that you had stepped
125 outside his heart. I'm afraid you've seen too much.

MAN: There are stories.

WOMAN: What?

MAN: People talk.

WOMAN: Where? We're two days from the nearest
130 village.

MAN: Word travels.

WOMAN: What are you talking about?

MAN: There are stories about you. I heard them. They
say that your visitors never leave this house.

135 **WOMAN:**   That's what you heard?

MAN: They say you imprison them.

WOMAN: Then you were a fool to come here.

MAN: Listen.

WOMAN: Me? Listen? You. Look! Where are these pris-
oners? Have you seen any? 140

MAN: They told me you were very beautiful.

WOMAN: Then they are blind as well as ignorant.

MAN: You are.

WOMAN: What?

MAN: Beautiful. 145

WOMAN: Stop that! My skin feels like seaweed.

MAN: I didn't realize it at first. I must confess—I didn't.
But over these few days—your face has changed
for me. The shape of it. The feel of it. The color. All
changed. I look at you now, and I'm no longer sure you 150
are the same woman who had poured tea for me just
a week ago. And because of that, I remembered—how
little I know about a face that changes in the night.
(Pause.) Have you heard those stories?

WOMAN: I don't listen to old wives' tales. 155

MAN: But have you heard them?

WOMAN: Yes. I've heard them. From other visitors—
young—hot-blooded—or old—who came here because
they were told great glory was to be had by killing the
witch in the woods. 160

MAN: I was told that no man could spend time in this
house without falling in love.

WOMAN: Oh? So why did you come? Did you wager
gold that you could come out untouched? The outside
world is so flattering to me. And you—are you like the 165
rest? Passion passing through your heart so powerfully that you can't hold onto it?

MAN: No! I'm afraid!

WOMAN: Of what?

MAN: Sometimes—when I look into the flowers, I think I 170
hear a voice—from inside—a voice beneath the petals.
A human voice.

WOMAN: What does it say? "Let me out"?

MAN: No. Listen. It hums. It hums with peacefulness of
175   one who is completely imprisoned.

WOMAN: I understand that if you listen closely enough,
you can hear the ocean.

MAN: No. Wait. Look at it. See the layers? Each petal—
hiding the next. Try and see where they end. You
180   can't. Follow them down, further down, around—and
as you come down—faster and faster—the breeze
picks up. The breeze becomes a wail. And in that rush
of air—in the silent midst of it—you can hear a voice.

WOMAN (*grabs flower from Man*): So, you believe I water
185   and prune my lovers? How can you be so foolish? (*She
snaps the flower in half, at the stem. She throws it to the
ground.*) Do you come only to leave again? To take a
chunk of my heart, then leave with your booty on your
belt, like a prize? You say that I imprison hearts in
190   these flowers? Well, bits of my heart are trapped with
travelers across this land. I can't even keep track. So
kill me. If you came here to destroy a witch, kill me
now. I can't stand to have it happen again.

MAN: I won't leave you.

195 **WOMAN:** I believe you. (*She looks at the flower that she
has broken, bends to pick it up. He touches her. They
embrace.*)

SCENE 8

*Day. Woman wears a simple undergarment, over
which she is donning a brightly colored kimono, the
same one we saw her wearing Upstage of the scrim.
Man stands apart.*

WOMAN: I can't cry. I don't have the capacity. Right
from birth, I didn't cry. My mother and father were
shocked. They thought they'd given birth to a ghost,
a demon. Sometimes I've thought myself that. When
5   great sadness has welled up inside me, I've prayed
for a means to release the pain from my body. But my
prayers went unanswered. The grief remained inside
me. It would sit like water, still. (*Pause; she models her
kimono.*) Do you like it?

10 **MAN:** Yes, it's beautiful.

WOMAN: I wanted to wear something special today.

MAN: It's beautiful. Excuse me. I must practice.

WOMAN: Shall I get you something?

MAN: No.

WOMAN: Some tea, maybe?   15

MAN: No. (*Man resumes swordplay.*)

WOMAN: Perhaps later today—perhaps we can go out—
just around here. We can look for flowers.

MAN: Alright.

WOMAN: We don't have to.   20

MAN: No. Let's.

WOMAN: I just thought if—

MAN: Fine. Where do you want to go?

WOMAN: There are very few recreational activities
around here, I know.   25

MAN: Alright. We'll go this afternoon. (*Pause.*)

WOMAN: Can I get you something?

MAN (*turning around*): What?

WOMAN: You might be—

MAN: I'm not hungry or thirsty or cold or hot.   30

WOMAN: Then what are you?

MAN: Practicing. (*Man resumes practicing. Woman exits.
As soon as she exits, he rests. He sits down. He examines his sword. He runs his finger along the edge of it.
He takes the tip, runs it against the soft skin under his   35
chin. He places the sword on the ground with the tip
pointed directly upwards. He keeps it from falling by
placing the tip under his chin. He experiments with
different degrees of pressure. Woman re-enters. She
sees him in this precarious position. She jerks his head   40
upward; the sword falls.*)

WOMAN: Don't do that!

MAN: What?

WOMAN: You can hurt yourself!

MAN: I was practicing!   45

WOMAN: You were playing!

MAN: I was practicing!

WOMAN: It's dangerous.

MAN: What do you take me for—a child?

50 **WOMAN:** Sometimes wise men do childish things.

MAN: I knew what I was doing!

WOMAN: It scares me.

MAN: Don't be ridiculous. *(He reaches for the sword again.)*

55 **WOMAN:** Don't! Don't do that!

MAN: Get back! *(He places the sword back in its previous position, suspended between the floor and his chin, upright.)*

WOMAN: But—

60 **MAN:** Sssssh!

WOMAN: I wish—

MAN: Listen to me! The slightest shock, you know—the slightest shock—surprise—it might make me jerk or—something—and then . . . so you must be perfectly
65 still and quiet.

WOMAN: But I—

MAN: Sssssh! *(Silence.)* I learned this exercise from a friend—I can't even remember his name—good swordsman—many years ago. He called it his medita-
70 tion position. He said, like this, he could feel the line between this world and the others because he rested on it. If he saw something in another world that he liked better, all he would have to do is let his head drop, and he'd be there. Simple. No fuss. One day,
75 they found him with the tip of his sword run clean out the back of his neck. He was smiling. I guess he saw something he liked. Or else he'd fallen asleep.

WOMAN: Stop that.

MAN: Stop what?

80 **WOMAN:** Tormenting me.

MAN: I'm not.

WOMAN: Take it away!

MAN: You don't have to watch, you know.

WOMAN: Do you want to die that way—an accident?

MAN: I was doing this before you came in. 85

WOMAN: If you do, all you need to do is tell me.

MAN: What?

WOMAN: I can walk over. Lean on the back of your head.

MAN: Don't try to threaten—

WOMAN: Or jerk your sword up. 90

MAN: Or scare me. You can't threaten—

WOMAN: I'm not. But if that's what you want.

MAN: You can't threaten me. You wouldn't do it.

WOMAN: Oh?

MAN: Then I'd be gone. You wouldn't let me leave that 95
easily.

WOMAN: Yes, I would.

MAN: You'd be alone.

WOMAN: No. I'd follow you. Forever. *(Pause.)* Now, let's
stop this nonsense. 100

MAN: No! I can do what I want? Don't come any closer!

WOMAN: Then release your sword.

MAN: Come any closer and I'll drop my head.

WOMAN *(Woman slowly approaches Man. She grabs the hilt of the sword. She looks into his eyes. She pulls it out* 105 *from under his chin.)*: There will be no more of this. *(She exits with the sword. He starts to follow her, then stops. He touches under his chin. On his finger, he finds a drop of blood.)*

SCENE 9

Night: Man is leaving the house. He is just about out, when he hears a shakuhachi *playing. He looks around, trying to locate the sound. Woman appears in the doorway to the outside. Shakuhachi slowly fades out.*

WOMAN: It's time for you to go?

MAN: Yes. I'm sorry.

WOMAN: You're just going to sneak out? A thief in the night? A frightened child?

5 **MAN:** I care about you.

WOMAN: You express it strangely.

MAN: I leave in shame because it is proper. *(Pause.)* I came seeking glory.

WOMAN: To kill me? You can say it. You'll be surprised
10 at how little I blanch. As if you'd said, "I came for a bowl of rice," or "I came seeking love" or "I came to kill you."

MAN: Weakness. All weakness. Too weak to kill you. Too weak to kill myself. Too weak to do anything
15 but sneak away in shame. *(Woman brings out Man's sword.)*

WOMAN: Were you planning to leave without this? *(He takes the sword.)* Why not stay here?

MAN: I can't live with someone who's defeated me.

20 **WOMAN:** I never thought of defeating you. I only wanted to take care of you. To make you happy. Because that made me happy and I was no longer alone.

MAN: You defeated me.

WOMAN: Why do you think that way?

25 **MAN:** I came here with a purpose. The world was clear. You changed the shape of your face, the shape of my heart—rearranged everything—created a world where I could do nothing.

WOMAN: I only tried to care for you.

30 **MAN:** I guess that was all it took. *(Pause.)*

WOMAN: You still think I'm a witch. Just because old women gossip. You are so cruel. Once you arrived, there were only two possibilities. I would die or you would leave. *(Pause.)* If you believe I'm a witch, then
35 kill me. Rid the province of one more evil.

MAN: I can't—

WOMAN: Why not? If you believe that about me, then it's the right thing to do.

MAN: You know I can't.

WOMAN: Then stay. 40

MAN: Don't try and force me.

WOMAN: I won't force you to do anything. *(Pause.)* All I wanted was an escape—for both of us. The sound of a human voice—the simplest thing to find, and the hardest to hold onto. This house—my loneliness is 45
etched into the walls. Kill me, but don't leave. Even in death, my spirit would rest here and be comforted by your presence.

MAN: Force me to stay.

WOMAN: I won't. *(Man starts to leave.)* Beware. 50

MAN: What?

WOMAN: The ground on which you walk is weak. It could give way at any moment. The crevice beneath is dark.

MAN: Are you talking about death? I'm ready to die. 55

WOMAN: Fear for what is worse than death.

MAN: What?

WOMAN: Falling. Falling through the darkness. Waiting to hit the ground. Picking up speed. Waiting for the ground. Falling faster. Falling alone. Waiting. Falling. 60
Waiting. Falling.

(Woman wails and runs out through the door to her room. Man stands, confused, not knowing what to do. He starts to follow her, then hesitates, and rushes out the door to the outside. Silence. Slowly, he re-enters from the outside. He looks for her in the main room. He goes slowly towards the panel to her room. He throws down his sword. He opens the panel. He goes inside. He comes out. He unrolls his mat. He sits on it, cross-legged. He looks out into space. He notices near him a shakuhachi. He picks it up. He begins to blow into it. He tries to make sounds. He continues trying through the end of the play. The Upstage scrim lights up. Upstage, we see the Woman. She is young. She is hanging from a rope suspended from the roof. She

has hung herself. Around her are scores of vases with flowers in them whose blossoms have been blown off. Only the stems remain in the vases. Around her swirl the thousands of petals from the flowers. They fill the Upstage scrim area like a blizzard of color. Man continues to attempt to play. Lights fade to black.)

Writing from Reading

Summarize

1 Describe the setting—both place and time—of the play. What do you know about it from the characters' lines? The stage directions? If you were directing the play, what type of theater space would you choose to stage this?

Analyze Craft

2 Hwang employs many symbols—a meal shared, flowers, swordplay, and the titular sound of a voice. What does each of these elements come to represent here in the relationship between the man and the woman?

3 How do the dialogue and actions surrounding the removal of the stain in scene 5 take on a double meaning? Why do you think the characters speak about this action in terms of fighting, battle, rhythm, and death?

Analyze Voice

4 Describe the dialogue—is it spare and simple, or verbose and complex? How does the dialogue set the tone for the play?

Synthesize Summary and Analysis

5 In the first several acts, the tension or conflict is largely one of a budding or growing romance. How does the conflict change or intensify in scene 8?

6 As the play progresses, we learn that the woman is reportedly a witch, and that the man has come to kill her. Think about the role of the witch in a traditional fairy tale. Why would Hwang use a fairy-tale element in this play? What would reading this as a *contemporary* fairy tale reveal? Is it possible that the woman's status as "witch" is not meant literally but is a play on the "bewitching" quality of a femme fatale? How else might you understand this aspect of the play?

Interpret the Play

7 What does the play seem to say about relationships between men and women? What is the significance of the woman defying the man's expectations? How would you describe the message? Age-old? Contemporary? Explain your interpretation.

8 Why would a Chinese-American use Japanese characters in a play with a seemingly timeless setting about male-female relations and the nature of heroism and deception? Is this significant? Why or why not? Does considering this make the play easier or more difficult to interpret?

Denise Chavez (b. 1948)

The American playwright and novelist Denise Chavez has lived in her native New Mexico most of her life. She attended New Mexico State University and received her Master's degree in Dramatic Arts from Trinity University in Texas. After graduation she worked at the Dallas Theater Center and eventually earned a Master of Fine Arts degree from the University of New Mexico. She published her first collection of short stories, called *The Last of the Menu Girls,* in 1986 and since then has gone on to publish novels, more short stories, and plays. She is the founder of the Border Book Festival that is held every year in her hometown of Las Cruces, New Mexico, and devoted to the cause of literature in her native community.

AS YOU READ   Notice which of the narrator's actions and observations change, and which stay the same, each time she ascends Tortugas Peak.

Guadalupe × 3 (2009)

CHARACTERS

LA MUJER / THE WOMAN (LUPITA, LUPE, MAMA LUPITA)

SCENE 1: EARLY MORNING

We see the Guadalupe at different ages: seventeen, thirty and seventy-two.   10
   At Rise: Early morning around six thirty A.M. LUPITA, age seventeen, is climbing Tortugas Peak for the Feast Day of Our Lady of Guadalupe, December 12. Dressed in jeans, or black pants, with a sweat shirt with a pull-over headpiece, LUPITA wears a jean jacket and tennis shoes or black hiking shoes. She carries a heavy backpack on her shoulders. She leans on a walking stick and rests from time to time on her climb.

LUPITA: *(Talking to a girlfriend who is climbing with her)*

You've never climbed Tortugas Peak before? Híjole, where have you been? I climb every year with my Granma. She tells me, Lupita Gonzales, this is our tradition and our culture. I've been climbing ever
5   since I was a little girl and I'm sixteen now.

(looking into a compact and then at the sky)

So, are you ready? Let's check out our backpacks to see if we have everything we'll need.

(Opening up the backpack and checking off items inside)

A candle/veladora de Nuestra Señora de Guadalupe to take up to the altar on the Cerrito. Check. Knife to cut quiotes, the yucca and stool staffs. Check. Colored string to decorate quiote. Check. Bottle of water. Check. Burritos from the Go Burger. Check. Rosary. Check. Cheetoes. Check.

(looking at the sky)

It looks like it might snow this year. That's Las Cruces for you.   15

(Now at the base of Tortugas Peak)

Let's go up the middle path. Not the one on the right, that's a goat path and slippery. And not the wild path on the left.

(Talking to herself)

Take it slow.

(Stepping to the side to greet other pilgrims)

Hello. Good morning.   20

(Picking up pace again)

We're getting higher. Soon you'll be able to see all of Las Cruces and the entire Mesilla Valley. It's real pretty from here.

(A little tired)

Rest. Don't go so fast. Pace yourself. That's what my
Granma says. Now that she's old, she does the velorio   25
in the church, staying up all night praying the day
before the climb because she can't climb anymore.
Everyone does what they can, she says, when they can.
Whatever you do, do it out of love for La Virgencita.

(Taking water out of the backpack)

So you've never come on the climb before? How come?   30
You heard of the climb on December eleventh but you
thought it would be too hard? Well, it is and it isn't.
You just take it slow and you go down the middle path.

(Stopping to rest)

My Granma says that the Guadalupe is the Mother
35 of All the Americas. She's our Mother who is with us
always. La Guadalupe es el madre de toda la gente de
las Americas. y tenemos que recordar que es nuestra
Madre que está con nosotros, siempre. That's what
my Granma says in Spanish. The Guadalupe is the
40 Mother of all the Americas and we have to remember
that she is with us always.

(Pausing)

Chee, my hair is getting all messed up. I don't want
nobody to see me flat-headed. Especially Johnny
Flores. He's all you know and I'll be all you know.
45 You know. He used to be an esquintle chapito lleno
de espinillas with these you know roñas on his arms,
anyway, but that was then. Ahora el vato's all you
know. I got to have hair, girlfriend!

(Checking compact and putting on black lipstick)

So what if he don't like me. I don't care. I'm not climb-
50 ing for Johnny Flores. I'm climbing for my family and
for my manda, my promise to La Virgencita.

(Stopping to rest)

What? You don't know the story of La Virgencita?
And here you living in Las Cruces and the climb every
year in your backyard. Where you been, huh? My
55 abuelita told me the story a long time ago, when I was
a little girl . . .

*(Stopping and taking off backpack, sitting on rock,
looking out)*

There was this Nativo, this Indio called Juan Diego.
He lived in México in 1531, what my Granma calls El
Año del Oso, very long ago. One day he was going to
early Mass. It was on December 9. Suddenly he heard   60
the most incredible music. Out of a cloud on top of the
Cerrito appeared the most beautiful young woman.
She wore a blue dress full of stars. Juan Diego knew
she was a noblewoman because of her fur-trimmed
robe. He knew by her black sash that she was carrying   65
a child. She had a cross around her neck, the symbol
of life and death. And the beautiful woman was dark-
skinned, like him.

(Telling the story and becoming the Guadalupe)

Juanito, Juan Dieguito, the lady called him like a
70 mother would. Where are you going? I am the Mother
of the True God, by whom we all live. I want you to
go to Bishop Zumárraga, to ask him to build a church
for me on this spot so I can care for my children. Juan
Diego excused himself from the Beautiful Lady and
75 made his way to the Bishop's house. But he couldn't
get in. He returned, very disappointed, to the Beautiful Lady.

(Getting up)

Hey, we better start climbing again, it's getting cold.
Got to keep moving. I'll tell you the rest of the story as
80 we go along.

(Pointing out to landscape)

That's where I live, and over there, that's where my
Granma lives, and over there . . .

(Giggling)

That's where Johnny Flores lives . . .

(Making the sign of the cross and then fluffing her hair)

Que Viva La Virgencita, que Viva!

SCENE 2: LATER
THAT MORNING

*(LUPE, a thirty-five year old woman, looks out to the
landscape for a long time. A sigh of tiredness. She
looks unhappy. Looks to the sky. Then out again.
She ties her shoelaces. She wears an old pair of jeans,
an old black sweatshirt with a scarf of Our Lady of
Guadalupe pinned on it. She carries an old resilient
Mexican shopping bag full of things.)*

LUPE: Long live our Lady of Guadalupe! Que Viva La
Virgencita, que Viva!

*(Crossing herself and moving on. She talks to herself
as people pass her. She is not in a hurry)*

Got to keep moving! You'd think after all these years
of climbing, the walk would get easier.

(Adjusting her shopping bag)

Yes, I married Johnny Flores. So now I'm Lupe Gon- 5
zales Flores, age thirty-five and counting. Me and
Johnny have three kids, el Junior, la Jennifer, y la Vicki.

(Stopping to rest and look out)

Poor Johnny! He's a victim of the Gulf War. That stuff
they used. He's not right in the head. He drinks a lot.
His father died and he don't climb with me anymore 10
like he used to. They think he has a brain tumor. But
we don't know. La Jennifer is pregnant from her boyfriend, Manny. La Vicki is driving me crazy with her
texting this texting that, ya me trae con ese teléfono
and Junior is in rehab because of the drugs. Yeah, and 15
I'm still working at the K-Mart. In charge of households. Not too many people I know have anything to
do with La Martha Stewart. You tell me how many
Méxicanos love plaid. And we're not a typical Chicano
family. We're going up, up and we're all going to make 20
it. I'm climbing this year for the kids. And Johnny.
And for my Granma. It's been sixteen years.

(Irritated)

Someone almost fell back there. You have to be very
careful or you're going to fall. You know, it makes
me happy to see all the kids out here today. So many 25
teenagers and babies, people of all ages! The way they
dress! Con esos tattoos y con los arêtes en las cejas o
en el ombligo and that cow thing in the nose. Fuchee!
What has the world come to? When I was young all
we had was black eye liner como la Cleopatra and 30
white lipstick or those textured hose and short skirts.
Not that we would have worn them on the climb, my
Granma wouldn't have allowed it, no Señorita.

(To a group of young people)

Be careful, mi'ja. Giggle. Giggle. The girls, they're so
silly. Have you noticed? All they do is talk about boys. 35
Boys!

(Calling out to the young people)

Be careful! Cuidado!

(Tucking her hair under her hat)

I'm still climbing, Virgencita, after all these years!

(Stopping to rest on her staff)

40 Too many years. Too many stories, too many sorrows, too many too many's! I wish I could take all those kids aside and tell them to wait. Wait! Esperense! Don't be all ready to get married. Just because your honey has a tattoo del Sagrado Corazón aqui en el brazo y otro tattoo aca con el nombre de su Mamá, 45 con la Virgencita all splayed out on his back doesn't mean he's going to be a good provider. I can only talk for myself.

(An accounting)

Estoy cansada, Virgencita. I'm tired, Virgencita. Very tired. Bien cansada. Like my Granma used to say, "All 50 of me hurts. Toda la mujer duele."

(Talking to her Granma)

I remember how you told me the story of Juan Diego, that story of wonder and majesty. Juan Diego returned to tell the Beautiful Lady that the Bishop had refused to see him. Once again she repeated her re-55 quest. He left her with the promise that he would return the next day to see the Bishop. The next day, with great difficulty, Juan Diego was admitted to Bishop Zumárraga's chambers. The Bishop did not believe what he had to say and requested proof of the Lady's 60 existence. Juan Diego returned to the Beautiful Lady. She told him to return the following day and that she would give him a sign for the Bishop. But when he returned home, Juan Diego was greeted with the news that his Uncle, Juan Bernardino, was dying. The day 65 came and went and Juan Diego forgot to return to the Beautiful Lady. The next day, Juan Diego was sent to get a priest to give his Uncle the Last Rites. Only then did he remember he had promised the Guadalupe he would go see the Bishop with a sign. And just in case 70 he would run into her, he took another route. Sure enough, La Virgencita met him on the path.

(In the Guadalupe's Voice)

The smallest of my children, el más pequeño de mis hijos, where are you going? she asked. Juan Diego told her about his uncle. Do not let your heart be

troubled. . . Am I not here who am your Mother? The 75 Virgencita instructed him to climb the hill and bring her the flowers he would find there. Juan Diego had never seen such exquisite roses. Roses in the wintertime! He took them back to her and the Guadalupe arranged them in his tilma, his poncho made of ma-80 guey, and sent him on his way . . .

(Watching people go by)

And here I am feeling sorry for myself, Virgencita. There goes a young boy with crutches going up the hill, one crutch forward like an oar and then another . . . One crutch and then another . . . And there's an old 85 woman, descalza, barefooted, without shoes, walking carefully on the rocks, with bloody feet, doing her mand . . . her promise. . . .

(Getting up and prodding herself)

I'm over halfway up the mountain, I can see the top of the crest there, and from here it's not so far. I'll get up 90 there and have some water. Then I'll leave our candle up there on the Cerrito, on the altar, out of the wind, near the back, and my prayers will rise high, over Las Cruces, all the way to the Heavens, all the way to God.

(With reverence)

Long Live Our Lady of Guadalupe! Que Viva La 95 Virgencita, que Viva!

SCENE 3: LATER IN THE MORNING

(MAMA LUPITA, age seventy-three.)
(She is waiting by the side of the road at the foot of the mountain, leaning on her walking stick.)

I'm waiting for the truck to pick me up. Me, Lupita Gonzales Torres. Too old to walk up the mountain anymore. Not since two years ago when I almost fainted. Casi me desmayé. And what good is an old woman that fainted on the side of the road like a cos-5 tal de chile, a sack of chile? Now I'm going up in style, with the Mayordomo, the Chief of Tortugas Pueblo. They treat me like a queen. La Reina de Las Cruces!

10 That's me. You can call me Mamá Lupita. That's what my kids and grankids all call me.

(Looking around)

My grankids started climbing with me last year. That's more than I can say for my kids. La Vicki. La Jennifer. El Junior. Uuuuuque, el Johnny Jr., if he
15 ever gets out of his chair for anything it has to be for a cold beer. And whose fault is it? Mine, Virgencita, for giving in to his father, may he rest in peace. Pobrecito Johnny. I'm climbing for them. And for the soul of my husband, Johnny, may you rest in peace.

(With her hand on her walking stick)

I still have my old walking stick. It's served me well
20 all these years. Me ha servido. I've walked this path for more years than you can say mi'ijo. . . .

(Talking to someone along the path)

Come on, get in the truck, there's plenty of room. I didn't mean to get in between you and el compadre. Compadre, don't get jealous. No te pongas celosa.

(Getting comfortable)

25 When we get up to the Cerrito, you help me and I'll help you. Me ayudas a caminar, y yo te ayudo a tí. We'll go get the humo, the sacred smoke, we'll cleanse ourselves in the sacred chaparral, and then we'll walk down to our favorite spot, facing the Organ Moun-
30 tains, and just look at God's wonder. I've brought a little blanket and some food . . .

(Takes things out of her mochila—a large Guadalupe bag)

Only the best . . . Kentucky Fried Chicken . . . Extra crispy . . . Que burritos ni que burritos, compadre. No traje burritos este año, porque you know . . . A mi
35 edad me afectan los frijoles . . . when you get older the beans, you know. . . .

(Resting in the sun)

We'll sit in the sun like lizards. We'll stay that way un rato, a little while, and then we'll make our quiotes

like we do every year. Our wooden yucca staffs will be beautiful like they always are.   40

(Looking out)

Look, there's my house. My neighborhood. The Bank. My Granma grew up there and me and el Johnny and then my kids. And there's Jennifer's house up in Telshor. There's the hospital. And the Bank. You know what they call it. OR rather what the President, Mr.   45 Papen, called it. Papen's Last Erection.

(Laughing to herself and then crossing herself)

I can't help myself Madrecita, that's what it's called.

(Sighing)

Ay! We'll pray for everybody, eh? Familia—what else is there? Qué más hay, compadre? Remember that you are connected to everyone on this living earth,   50 human, animal, plant, and mineral.

(Crossing herself again)

We made it, Bendito sea Dios, otro año de gracia. Y de humildad. Just like the moment el Obispo, Bishop Zumárraga opened Juan Diego's tilma and out tumbled the beautiful rosas de Casilla. It was in the   55 wintertime. Oh, what a miracle! Juan Diego never gave up and finally the miracle took place that last visit to the Bishop. There, on his robe was imprinted the image of La Virgencita de Guadalupe.

(With reverence)

I want to think about where I've been and where I'm   60 going. And I want to give thanks to God and Our Lady of Guadalupe for another year of love and many blessings. Y quiero darle las gracias a Mi Diosito, y especialmente a La Virgencita, por otro año lleno de amor tantas bendiciones.   65

(Getting up a little stiff, but still spry)
  (Looking out)

Long Live Our Lady of Guadalupe! Que Viva La Virgencita, que Viva!

Writing from Reading

Summarize

1 List and describe the three stages of Lupita's life.

Analyze Craft

2 How does the playwright reshape the literal time of Lupita's life?

3 What role does the setting play in the evolution of character?

4 What roles do church rituals play?

Analyze Voice

5 How much of Lupita's language is high speech; how much is low? Give examples. What is the effect of this voice on the play?

Synthesize Summary and Analysis

6 What is the function of the story (of the Virgin of Guadalupe) in the story of the play?

Interpret the Play

7 Three pilgrimages up to the top of a New Mexico peak make up a woman's lifetime. In what way is this celebratory, in what way a description of life's difficulties?

8 How representative of the lives of Chicana women is Lupita's particular life? Can you see similar patterns in the lives of women in your own family, whether Chicana or otherwise?

Writing about Contemporary Theater

1. Read one of the plays as a first-night reviewer might. Write a review of the play based on your immediate reactions to it (see Chapter 31 for an example of a play review). Comment on the characters and the plot; describe the setting, the language, and so forth. Make a recommendation for others to read this play or not.

2. Do you find there is a sharp line drawn between what we have called modern theater and experimental theater, or do you see experimental theater as a continuation of the modern play? Explain.

GOING FURTHER ONLINE

Three casebooks for drama with additional selections are also available online at **connect.mcgraw-hill.com.** For more on each of these casebooks and a complete listing of selections, see the table of contents at the beginning of this book.

- **Today's Shakespeare:** reviews, video, and articles accompany *A Midsummer Night's Dream, King Lear,* and *Macbeth*
- **Masters of Craft:** Christopher Marlowe, Aphra Behn, Oscar Wilde, George Bernard Shaw, and others
- **Contemporary Voices:** including works by Arthur Kopit and August Schulenberg

Part 5

Critical Approaches and MLA Documentation

Chapter 36

Critical Approaches to Literature

APPROACH CRITICISM AS AN ONGOING CONVERSATION

Literary theorist Kenneth Burke famously described literary criticism as an ongoing conversation, one that began before we arrived and will continue after we leave. If the thought of engaging in literary criticism intimidates you, think of it instead as adding your voice to those of others who have read the same work of literature and want to talk about it. You need not interpret the work as if you've been the first to read it, and you certainly don't have to feel as though you must deliver the final response. You need only contribute to the conversation.

Whenever we discuss literature, whether we acknowledge our appreciation or disdain for a text, interpret its meanings and mysteries, or cite it as an example of a larger trend in culture, we engage in an act of **literary criticism.** Such responsiveness is all around us and probably has its origins in the genesis of literature itself. The classical philosophers Plato and Aristotle laid the foundations for studying the creation, interpretation, and significance of the written and spoken word—in a sense, they began the conversation we now join.

USE A CRITICAL APPROACH AS A LENS FOR EXAMINATION

Although these classical theories are still relevant, approaches to literature have changed with new developments in human thought. Literary critics and theorists are almost inevitably influenced by major shifts in philosophy, politics, history, science, technology, and economics. For example, the advent of Freud's theories of psychology opened up a way of examining literature by applying psychoanalytic concepts to characters and authors. Later in the century, the feminist movement led critics to apply ideas about gender roles to literary criticism. These borrowings from other fields are particularly influential for twentieth-century theory and criticism, as our discussion of the major approaches to criticism will show.

It may be helpful to think of each of the critical approaches described here as a *lens* through which a piece of literature can be examined. Any work can be looked at from several different points of view, but the lens itself cannot do the interpreting—a reader must do that. Still, the lens provides the reader with a set of guiding principles with which to limit all of the possible questions the reader might ask. For students engaging in literary criticism for the first time, these lenses can be enormously helpful, because they narrow down the overwhelming array of possibilities, providing specific approaches to take and questions to ask. Studying and understanding the work of readers who have come before us can make the task of coming up with our own ideas less daunting.

CONSIDER MULTIPLE APPROACHES

Many of the critical schools described here initially defined themselves in opposition to the dominant theories of their times. Keep in mind, though, that in current practice many critics are comfortable adopting methods from several critical approaches. For example, a reader who considers herself a Marxist critic may draw on historical and deconstructionist theories to help her analyze a work. Each approach described here has its own merits and shortcomings, proponents, and skeptics. These approaches are not necessarily mutually exclusive, and it is possible for critics to choose the most useful strategies from several approaches in their own writing. Though we will refer to "feminist critics" and "formalist critics" in the descriptions below, there are very few scholars who confine themselves solely to one theory without sometimes turning to other approaches.

What follows is an overview of different major critical methods.

Formalist Criticism

Formalist criticism emerged in Russia in the early twentieth century in the work of such critics as Boris Eikhenbaum, Viktor Shklovsky, and Mikhail Bakhtin. Their ideas were adopted and further developed in the United States and Great Britain under the heading of **new criticism** by such critics as John Crowe Ransom, Allen Tate, Robert Penn Warren, I. A. Richards, William Wimsatt, T. S. Eliot, and Cleanth Brooks.

Formalists and new critics consider a successful text to be a complete, independent, unified artifact whose meaning and value can be understood purely by analyzing the interaction of its formal and technical components, such as plot, imagery, structure, style, symbol, and tone. Rather than drawing their textual interpretations from *extrinsic* factors such as the historical, political, or biographical context of the work, formalist critics focus on the text's *intrinsic* formal elements. As Cleanth Brooks explains in his article, "The Formalist Critic," published in 1951 in the *Kenyon Review,*

> *. . . the formalist critic is concerned primarily with the work itself. Speculation on the mental processes of the author takes the critic away from the work into biography and psychology. There is no reason, of course, why he should not turn away into biography and psychology. Such explorations are very much worth making. But they should not be confused with an account of the work.*

Formalist criticism relies heavily on **close reading,** or explication, of the text in order to analyze the ways in which distinct formal elements combine to create a unified artistic experience for the reader. A major tenet of formalism is the notion that form and content are so intertwined that in a successful work of art they cannot be separated out.

For formalist or new critics the study and interpretation of literature is an intrinsically valuable intellectual activity rather than a means to advance moral, religious, or political ideologies. There are those who consider this approach to be a limited one—they have argued that formalism can be elitist, willfully dismissive of historical and biographical factors in the work. *All* study of literature has to include at least a component of close reading; the question other critics raise is whether it suffices as a way to approach a text.

Boris Eikhenbaum (1886–1959)
The Theory of the Formal Method (1926)

The organization of the Formal method was governed by the principle that the study of literature should be made specific and concrete. All efforts were directed toward terminating the earlier state of affairs, in which literature, as A. Veselovskij observed, was *res nullius*.[1] That was what made the Formalists so intolerant of other "methods" and of eclectics. In rejecting these "other" methods, the Formalists actually were rejecting (and still reject) not methods but the gratuitous mixing of different scientific disciplines and different scientific problems. Their basic point was, and still is, that the object of literary science, as literary science, ought to be the investigation of the specific properties of literary material, of the properties that distinguish such material from material of any other kind, notwithstanding the fact that its secondary and oblique features make that material properly and legitimately exploitable, as auxiliary material, by other disciplines. The point was consummately formulated by Roman Jakobson:

> The object of study in literary science is not literature but "literariness," that is, what makes a given work a *literary* work. Meanwhile, the situation has been that historians of literature act like nothing so much as policemen, who, out to arrest a certain culprit, take into custody (just in case) everything and everyone they find at the scene as well as any passers-by for good measure. The historians of literature have helped themselves to everything—environment, psychology, politics, philosophy. Instead of a science of literature, they have worked up a concoction of home-made disciplines. They seem to have forgotten that those subjects pertain to their own fields of study— to the history of philosophy, the history of culture, psychology, and so on, and that those fields of study certainly may utilize literary monuments as documents of a defective and second-class variety among other materials.

To establish this principle of specificity without resorting to speculative aesthetics required the juxtaposing of the literary order of facts with another such order. For this purpose one order had to be selected from among existent orders, which, while contiguous with the literary order, would contrast with it in terms of functions. It was just such a methodological procedure that produced the opposition between "poetic" language and "practical" language. This opposition [. . .] served as the activating principle for the Formalists' treatment of the fundamental problems of poetics. Thus, instead of an orientation toward a history of culture or of social life, towards psychology, or aesthetics, and so on, as had been customary for literary scholars, the Formalists came up with their own characteristic orientation toward linguistics, a discipline contiguous with poetics in regard to the material under investigation, but one approaching that material from a different angle and with different kinds of problems to solve.

from The Theory of the Formal Method

Biographical Criticism

Biographical criticism emphasizes the belief that literature is created by authors whose unique experiences shape their writing and therefore can inform our reading of their work. Biographical critics research and use an author's biography to interpret the text as well as the author's stated *intentions* or comments on the process of

---

[1] A legal term describing something that has no ownership.

composition itself. These critics often consult the author's memoirs to uncover connections between the author's life and the author's work. They may also study the author's rough drafts to trace the evolution of a given text or examine the author's library to discern potential influences on the author's work.

Knowledge of an author's biography can surely help readers interpret or understand a text. For example, awareness of Flannery O'Connor's devout Catholicism will make the religious elements of her stories and novels more meaningful to readers. However, as we have just seen, formalist critics reject biographical criticism, arguing that any essential meaning in a text should be discernable to readers purely through close reading. They reject the notion that an author's thought processes and stated *intentions* for a text necessarily define the work's meaning. They call this emphasis on discerning or trusting an author's own stated purpose the **intentional fallacy** and believe a text's meaning must be contained in and communicated only by the text as such.

While biographical criticism was once quite common, in recent decades it is more often used as *part* of a larger critical approach than as the primary critical strategy.

Gary Lee Stonum (b. 1947)
Dickinson's Literary Background (1998)

Books and reading were [Emily] Dickinson's primary access to a world beyond Amherst. We can thus at least be reasonably confident that the cultural contexts of Dickinson's writing are primarily literary, particularly if that term is defined inclusively. Her surviving letters are filled with references to favorite authors, and some of the poems allude in one way or another to recognizable elements of her reading (Pollak, "Allusions"). To be sure, she is by no means a learned poet in the vein of Milton or Pope, writers who can hardly be appreciated without understanding their allusions and allegiances. Yet she is also surely not the unlettered author Richard Chase once unguardedly deemed her, uninfluenced by literary sources in either style or thought.

A few cautions need to be kept in mind as we examine various claims about Dickinson's literary milieu. First, we know very little about how or even whether Dickinson imagined her work as participating in any public enterprise. By contrast to Keats, who dreamed of being among the English poets after his death, or a James Joyce, who schemed tirelessly to shape his own reputation, Dickinson hardly trafficked in any cultural arena. We do possess information about the books she read or admired, and we know from the persistent testimony of her letters and poems that she regarded poetry as an exalted calling. Yet, although we can reasonably infer from this a certain broad ambition, we simply do not know if Dickinson regarded her vocation as entailing some sense of a role in literary history or as obliging her to bargain in the cultural marketplace. We do not, for example, know whether or in what respect she regarded herself as a woman poet, in spite of a number of lively arguments supposing that she did.

[. . .] At the writerly end of the spectrum lie the sources Dickinson drew upon or referred to as she wrote, which are of varying importance. Dickinson's regard for Elizabeth Barrett Browning makes it likely that her "Vision of Poets" is a source of "I died for Beauty," as well as or even rather than Keats's now more famous "Ode on a Grecian Urn." On the other hand, the identification is by no means crucial to an understanding of the poem.

The more interesting cases are those in which the source is disputed and identification would make some difference to our reading. Dickinson was notably fond of exotic place-names, most of which she must have come upon in her reading and some of which may carry thematic associations. The reference to "Chimborazo" in "Love—thou are high" may well derive incidentally from Edward Hitchcock's *Elementary Geology,* where it stands among a list of the world's tallest mountains, or it may originate from similarly casual uses in Barrett Browning and Emerson. On the other hand, if we heed Judith Farr's investigations into the influence of contemporary painting, then we might recall that Frederic Church's mammoth painting of Chimborazo was one of the most celebrated luminist canvases of the day. If the poem is read in the latter context, then the "Love" addressed by the poem as like the mountain would function more insistently as a figure of sublime theophany. (The poem also clearly alludes to Exodus 33, the chief biblical commonplace for such an event.)

[. . .] Many of the references in Dickinson's writings are discussed in Jack Capps's indispensable *Emily Dickinson's Reading,* which includes a detailed index of the books and authors she mentions in poems or letters. Capps also surveys the contents of the family library, much of which is now at Harvard. Unfortunately, the usefulness of the library "is limited by the fact that books from the Austin Dickinson and Edward Dickinson household have been mixed and, in most cases, dates of acquisition and individual ownership are uncertain." Likewise, although these volumes include inscriptions, marginalia, and other evidence of use, few of the markings can be confidently traced to the poet herself.

from *Dickinson's Literary Background*

Historical Criticism

Historical criticism emphasizes the relationship between a text and its historical context. When interpreting a text, historical critics highlight the cultural, philosophical, and political movements and ideologies prevalent during the text's creation and reception. Such critics may also use literary texts as a means of studying or promoting a particular movement in history—cultural , political, or otherwise.

Historical critics do extensive research to uncover the social and intellectual trends that influenced the life and work of the author and his or her original audience. This research brings to light allusions, concepts, and vocabulary or word usage that would have been easily understood by the author or the original audience but may elude contemporary readers. Historical critics also study the ways in which the meanings of a given text change over time, looking, for example, at the ways in which Victorians staged or responded to Shakespeare's *A Midsummer Night's Dream.*

One frequent objection to historical criticism is that these methods can reveal more about the context surrounding a text than about the meaning or value of the text itself. Another objection is that historical criticism sometimes views literature simply as an expression of the historical trends of a given era, rather than viewing texts as autonomous, idiosyncratic expressions of a particular author's views. Historical criticism, some argue, oversimplifies the relationship between a text and the prevailing or dominant cultural context, overlooking the possibility that the text may have a subversive, distorted, distanced, or anachronistic relationship to the dominant culture of the author's time.

Carl Van Doren (1885–1950)
Mark Twain (1921)

Of the major American novelists Mark Twain derived least from any literary, or at any rate from any bookish, tradition. Hawthorne had the example of Irving, and Cooper had that of Scott, when they began to write; Howells and Henry James instinctively fell into step with the classics. Mark Twain came up into literature from the popular ranks, trained in the school of newspaper fun-making and humorous lecturing, only gradually instructed in the more orthodox arts of the literary profession. He seems to most eyes, however, less indebted to predecessors than he actually was, for the reason that his provenance has faded out with the passage of time and the increase of his particular fame. Yet he had predecessors and a provenance. As a printer he learned the mechanical technique of his trade of letters; as a jocose writer for the newspapers of the Middle West and the Far West at a period when a well established mode of burlesque and caricature and dialect prevailed there, he adapted himself to a definite convention; as a raconteur he not only tried his methods on the most diverse auditors but consciously studied those of Artemus Ward, then the American master of the craft; Bret Harte, according to Mark Twain, "trimmed and trained and schooled me"; and thereafter, when the "Wild Humorist of the Pacific Slope," as it did not at first seem violent to call him, came into contact with professed men of letters, especially Howells, he had already a mastership of his own, though in a second rank.

To be a "humorist" in the United States of the sixties and seventies was to belong to an understood and accepted class. It meant, as Orpheus C. Kerr and John Phœnix and Josh Billings and Petroleum V. Nasby and Artemus Ward had recently and typically been showing, to make fun as fantastically as one liked but never to rise to beauty; to be intensely shrewd but never profound; to touch pathos at intervals but never tragedy. The humorist assumed a name not his own, as Mark Twain did, and also generally a character—that of some rustic sage or adventurous eccentric who discussed the topics of the moment keenly and drolly. Under his assumed character, of which he ordinarily made fun, he claimed a wide license of speech, which did not, however, extend to indecency or to any very serious satire. His fun was the ebullience of a strenuous society, the laughter of escape from difficult conditions. It was rooted fast in that optimism which Americans have had the habit of considering a moral obligation. It loved to ridicule those things which to the general public seemed obstacles to the victorious progress of an average democracy; it laughed about equally at idlers and idealists, at fools and poets, at unsuccessful sinners and unsuccessful saints. It could take this attitude toward minorities because it was so confident of having the great American majority at its back, hearty, kindly, fair-intentioned, but self-satisfied and unspeculative. In time Mark Twain partly outgrew this type of fun—or rather, had frequent intervals of a different type and also of a fierce seriousness—but the origins of his art lie there. So do the origins of his ideas lie among the populace, much as he eventually outgrew the evangelical orthodoxy and national complacency and personal hopefulness with which he had first been burdened.

from The American Novel

Psychological or Psychoanalytic Criticism

Psychoanalytic criticism originally stemmed, like psychoanalysis itself, from the work of Sigmund Freud. That revolutionary thinker sought to analyze the conscious and subconscious mental workings of his patients by listening to them discuss their dreams, their erotic urges, and their childhoods. Psychoanalytical critics in a sense study characters and authors as they would patients, looking in the text for evidence of childhood trauma, repressed sexual impulses, preoccupation with death, and so on. Through the lens of psychology they attempt to explain the motivations and meanings behind characters' actions. Such critics have, for example, noted Hamlet's Oedipus complex—his desire to kill his (step)father and possess his mother.

At the same time, psychological critics use textual and biographical evidence as a means to better understand the *author's* psychology. They may attribute the somber tone of a group of poems to the poet's contemporaneous loss of a spouse, or may look for patterns in several texts to identify an author's subconscious preoccupations, fears, or motivations. Psychological critics have, for example, attributed sexist tendencies to Hemingway by arguing that women rarely play major roles in his fiction and are often manipulative or emasculating when they do. Others disagree, noting that Hemingway's female characters, although not dominant, frequently offer the story's wisest, most lucid perspectives through what are often the story's most memorable lines of dialogue. To relate these issues to Hemingway's conflicted love for his mother is to consider the work in psychological as well as biographical terms.

Finally, psychoanalytical critics also examine the process and nature of literary creation, studying the ways in which texts create an emotional and intellectual effect for readers and authors. Here, too, the strategy is most effective when inclusive as opposed to exclusive; this is a useful tool for reading when it's not the *only* approach to a text.

Kenneth Burke (1897–1993)
The Poetic Process (1925)

If we wish to indicate a gradual rise to a crisis, and speak of this as a climax, or a crescendo, we are talking in intellectualistic terms of a mechanism which can often be highly emotive. There is in reality no such general thing as a crescendo. What does exist is a multiplicity of individual artworks each of which may be arranged as a whole, or in some parts, in a manner which we distinguish as climactic. And there is also in the human brain the potentiality for reacting favorably to such a climactic arrangement. Over and over again in the history of art, different material has been arranged to embody the principle of the crescendo; and this must be so because we "think" in a crescendo, because it parallels certain psychic and physical processes which are at the roots of our experience. The accelerated motion of a falling body, the cycle of a storm, the procedure of the sexual act, the ripening of crops—growth here is not merely a linear progression, but a fruition. Indeed, natural processes are, inevitably, "formally" correct, and by merely recording the symptoms of some physical development we can obtain an artistic development. Thomas Mann's work has many such natural forms converted into art forms, as, in *Death in Venice,* his charting of a sunrise and of the progressive stages in a cholera epidemic. And surely, we may say without much fear of startling anyone, that the work of art utilizes climactic arrangement because the human brain has a pronounced potentiality for being arrested, or entertained, by such an arrangement.

[. . .] Whereupon, returning to the Poetic Process, let us suppose that while a person is sleeping some disorder of the digestion takes place, and he is physically depressed. Such depression in the sleeper immediately calls forth a corresponding psychic depression, while this psychic depression in turn translates itself into the invention of details which will more or less adequately symbolize this depression. If the sleeper has had some set of experiences strongly marked by the feeling of depression, his mind may summon details from this experience to symbolize his depression. If he fears financial ruin, his depression may very reasonably seize upon the cluster of facts associated with this fear in which to individuate itself. On the other hand, if there is no strong set of associations in his mind clustered about the mood of depression, he may invent details which, on waking, seem inadequate to the mood. This fact accounts for the incommunicable wonder of a dream, as when at times we look back on the dream and are mystified at the seemingly unwarranted emotional responses which the details "aroused" in us. Trying to convey to others the emotional overtones of this dream, we laboriously recite the details, and are compelled at every turn to put in such confessions of defeat as "There was something strange about the room," or "For some reason or other I was afraid of this boat, although there doesn't seem to be any good reason now." But the details were not the cause of the emotion; the emotion, rather, dictated the selection of the details. Especially when the emotion was one of marvel or mystery, the invented details seem inadequate—the dream becoming, from the standpoint of communication, a flat failure, since the emotion failed to individuate itself into adequate symbols. And the sleeper himself, approaching his dream from the side of consciousness after the mood is gone, feels how inadequate are the details for conveying the emotion that caused them, and is aware that even for him the wonder of the dream exists only in so far as he still remembers the quality pervading it. Similarly, a dreamer may awaken himself with his own hilarious laughter, and be forthwith humbled as he recalls the witty saying of his dream. For the delight in the witty saying came first (was causally prior) and the witty saying itself was merely the externalization, or individuation, of this delight. Of a similar nature are the reminiscences of old men, who recite the facts of their childhood, not to force upon us the trivialities and minutiae of these experiences, but in the forlorn hope of conveying to us the "overtones" of their childhood, overtones which, unfortunately, are beyond reach of the details which they see in such an incommunicable light, looking back as they do upon a past which is at once themselves and another.

The analogy between these instances and the procedure of the poet is apparent. In this way the poet's moods dictate the selection of details and thus individuate themselves into one specific work of art.

from *The Poetic Process*

Archetypal, Mythic, or Mythological Criticism

Archetypal, or **mythological, criticism** focuses on the patterns or features that recur through much of literature, regardless of its time period or cultural origins. The archetypal approach to criticism stems from the work of Carl Jung, a Swiss psychoanalyst (and contemporary of Freud) who argued that humans share in a **collective unconscious,** or a set of characters, plots, symbols, and images that each evoke a universal response. Jung calls these recurring elements **archetypes** and likens them to *instincts*—knowledge or associations with which humans are born. Some examples of archetypes are the quest story, the story of rebirth, or the initiation story; others are the good mother, the evil stepmother, the wise old man, the notion that a desert symbolizes emptiness or hopelessness, or that a garden symbolizes fertility or paradise.

Archetypal, or mythological, critics analyze the ways in which such archetypes function in literature and attempt to explain the power that literature has over us or the reasons why certain texts continue to hold power over audiences many centuries after their creation.

Northrop Frye (1912–1991)
The Archetypes of Literature (1951)

We say that every poet has his own peculiar formation of images. But when so many poets use so many of the same images, surely there are much bigger critical problems involved than biographical ones. As Mr. Auden's brilliant essay *The Enchafèd Flood* shows, an important symbol like the sea cannot remain within the poetry of Shelley or Keats or Coleridge: it is bound to expand over many poets into an archetypal symbol of literature. And if the genre has a historical origin, why does the genre of drama emerge from medieval religion in a way so strikingly similar to the way it emerged from Greek religion centuries before? This is a problem of structure rather than origin, and suggests that there may be archetypes of genres as well as of images.

It is clear that criticism cannot be systematic unless there is a quality in literature which enables it to be so, an order of words corresponding to the order of nature in the natural sciences. An archetype should be not only a unifying category of criticism, but itself a part of a total form, and it leads us at once to the question of what sort of total form criticism can see in literature. [. . .] the search for archetypes is a kind of literary anthropology, concerned with the way that literature is informed by pre-literary categories such as ritual, myth and folk tale. We next realize that the relation between these categories and literature is by no means purely one of descent, as we find them reappearing in the greatest classics—in fact there seems to be a general tendency on the part of great classics to revert to them.

[. . .] In the solar cycle of the day, the seasonal cycle of the year, and the organic cycle of human life, there is a single pattern of significance, out of which myth constructs a central narrative around a figure who is partly the sun, partly vegetative fertility and partly a god or archetypal human being. [. . .] I supply the following table of its phases:

1. The dawn, spring and birth phase. Myths of the birth of the hero, of revival and resurrection, of creation and (because the four phases are a cycle) of the defeat of the powers of darkness, winter and death. Subordinate characters: the father and the mother. The archetype of romance and of most dithyrambic and rhapsodic poetry.
2. The zenith, summer, and marriage or triumph phase. Myths of apotheosis, of the sacred marriage, and of entering into Paradise. Subordinate characters: the companion and the bride. The archetype of comedy, pastoral and idyll.
3. The sunset, autumn and death phase. Myths of fall, of the dying god, of violent death and sacrifice and of the isolation of the hero. Subordinate characters: the traitor and that siren. The archetype of tragedy and elegy.
4. The darkness, winter and dissolution phase. Myths of the triumph of these powers; myths of floods and the return of chaos, of the defeat of the hero[. . .] Subordinate characters: the ogre and the witch. The archetype of satire (see, for instance, the conclusion of *The Dunciad*).

from The Archetypes of Literature

Marxist Criticism

Marxist criticism is one of the most significant types of **sociological criticism.** Sociological criticism is the study of literary texts as products of the cultural, political, and economic context of the author's time and place. Critics using this approach examine practical factors such as the ways in which economics and politics influence the publishing and distribution of texts, shaping the audience's reception of a text and therefore its potential to influence society. Such factors, of course, may also affect the motives or options the author has while writing the text. Sociological critics also identify and analyze the sociological content of literature, or the ways in which authors or audiences may use texts directly or indirectly to promote or critique certain sociological views or values.

Marxist, or **economic determinist, criticism** is based on the writings of Karl Marx, who argued that economic concerns shape lives more than anything else, and that society is essentially a struggle between the working classes and the dominant capitalist classes. Rather than assuming that culture evolves naturally or autonomously out of individual human experience, Marxist critics maintain that culture—including literature—is shaped by the interests of the dominant or most powerful social class.

Although Marxist critics do not ignore the artistic construction of a literary text, they tend to focus more on the ideological and sociological content of literary texts—such as the ways in which a character's poverty or powerlessness limits his or her choice of actions in a story, making his or her efforts futile or doomed to failure. These critics use literary analysis to raise awareness about the complex and powerful relationship between class and culture. At the same time, some Marxist critics also promote literature or interpretations of literature that can *change* the balance of power between social classes, often by subverting the values of the dominant class, or by inspiring the working classes to heroic or communal rebellion. As Marx wrote, "The philosophers have only *interpreted* the world in various ways; the point is to *change* it."

Leon Trotsky (1879–1940)
Literature and Revolution (1924)

The form of art is, to a certain and very large degree, independent, but the artist who creates this form, and the spectator who is enjoying it are not empty machines, one for creating form and the other for appreciating it. They are living people, with a crystallized psychology representing a certain unity, even if not entirely harmonious. This psychology is the result of social conditions. The creation and perception of art forms is one of the functions of this psychology. And no matter how wise the Formalists try to be, their whole conception is simply based upon the fact that they ignore the psychological unity of the social man, who creates and who consumes what has been created.

The proletariat has to have in art the expression of the new spiritual point of view which is just beginning to be formulated within him, and to which art must help him give form. This is not a state order, but an historic demand. Its strength lies in the objectivity of historic necessity. You cannot pass this by, nor escape its force. [. . .] It is unquestionably true that the need for art is not created by economic conditions. But neither is the need for food created by economics. On the contrary, the need for food and warmth creates economics. It is very true that one cannot always go by the principles of Marxism in deciding whether to reject or to accept a work of art. A work of art should, in the first place, be judged by its own law, that is, by the law of art. But Marxism alone can explain why and how a given tendency in art has originated in a given period of history; in other words, who it was who made a demand for such an artistic form and not for another, and why.

It would be childish to think that every class can entirely and fully create its own art from within itself, and, particularly, that the proletariat is capable of creating a new art by means of closed art guilds or circles, or by the Organization for Proletarian Culture, etc. Generally speaking, the artistic work of man is continuous. Each new rising class places itself on the shoulders of its preceding one. But this continuity is dialectic, that is, it finds itself by means of internal repulsions and breaks. New artistic needs or demands for new literary and artistic points of view are stimulated by economics, through the development of a new class, and minor stimuli are supplied by changes in the position of the class, under the influence of the growth of its wealth and cultural power. Artistic creation is always a complicated turning inside out of old forms, under the influence of new stimuli which originate outside of art. In this sense of the word, art is a handmaiden. It is not a disembodied element feeding on itself, but a function of social man indissolubly tied to his life and environment.

from Literature and Revolution

Structuralist Criticism

Structuralism emerged in France in the 1950s, largely in the work of scholars like Claude Lévi-Strauss and Roland Barthes. They were indebted in part to the earlier work of the Swiss linguist Ferdinand de Saussure, who emphasized that the meanings of words or signs are shaped by the overarching structure of the language or system to which they belong. Similarly, structuralist literary critics work from the belief that a given work of literature can be fully understood only when a reader considers the system of conventions, or the *genre*, to which it belongs or responds.

Structuralist critics therefore define and study systematic patterns or structures exhibited by many texts in a given genre. A classic example of this type of study is Vladimir Propp's *Morphology of the Folktale*, in which the critic identifies several key patterns in the plots of folk tales (the hero leaves home, the hero is tested, the hero gains use of a magic agent, and so on). Structuralists thus study the relationship between a given literary text and the larger system of meanings and expectations in the genre or culture from which that text emerges. They also look to literature to study the ways in which meaning is created across culture by means of a system of signs—for example, the pattern of associations that has developed around the images of light (purity, good) and darkness (evil, somber). Here the study of **semiotics** is germane; the way a thing looks to the individual reader or how and what a word *signifies* can change our understanding of a text.

The structuralist approach has been used more frequently and successfully in the study of fiction than poetry. Because of its emphasis on the commonalities within a genre, the structuralist approach has also been helpful to critics attempting to compare works from different time periods or cultures.

Vladimir Propp (1895–1970)
Fairy Tale Transformations (1928)

The study of the fairy tale may be compared in many respects to that of organic formation in nature. Both the naturalist and the folklorist deal with species and varieties which are essentially the same. The Darwinian problem of the origin of species arises in folklore as well. The similarity of phenomena both in nature and in our field resists any direct explanation which would be both objective and convincing. It is a problem in its own right. Both fields allow two possible points of view: either the internal similarity of two externally dissimilar phenomena does not derive from a common genetic root—the theory of spontaneous generation—or else this morphological similarity does indeed result from a known genetic tie—the theory of differentiation owing to subsequent metamorphoses or transformations of varying cause and occurrence.

In order to resolve this problem, we need a clear understanding of what is meant by similarity in fairy tales. Similarity has so far been invariably defined in terms of a plot and its variants. We find such an approach acceptable only if based upon the idea of the spontaneous generation of species. Adherents to this method do not compare plots; they feel such comparison to be impossible or, at the very least, erroneous. Without our denying the value of studying individual plots and comparing them solely from the standpoint of their similarity, another method, another basis for comparison may be proposed. Fairy tales can be compared from the standpoint of their composition or structure; their similarity then appears in a new light.

We observe that the actors in the fairy tale perform essentially the same actions as the tale progresses, no matter how different from one another in shape, size, sex, and occupation, in nomenclature and other static attributes. This determines the relationship of the constant factors to the variables. The functions of the actors are constant; everything else is a variable. For example:

1. The king sends Ivan after the princess; Ivan departs.
2. The king sends Ivan after some marvel; Ivan departs.
3. The sister sends her brother for medicine; he departs.
4. The stepmother sends her stepdaughter for fire; she departs.
5. The smith sends his apprentice for a cow; he departs.

The dispatch and departure on a quest are constants. The dispatching and departing actors, the motivations behind the dispatch, and so forth, are variables. In later stages of the quest, obstacles impede the hero's progress; they, too, are essentially the same, but differ in the form of imagery.

The functions of the actors may be singled out. Fairy tales exhibit thirty-one functions, not all of which may be found in any one fairy tale; however, the absence of certain functions does not interfere with the order of appearance of the others. Their aggregate constitutes one system, one composition. This system has proved to be extremely stable and widespread. The investigator, for example, can determine very accurately that both the ancient Egyptian fairy tale of the two brothers and the tale of the firebird, the tale of *Morozka,* the tale of the fisherman and the fish, as well as a number of myths follow the same general pattern. An analysis of the details bears this out.

from *Fairy Tale Transformations*

New Historicism

Both **new historicism** and structuralism owe a debt to the work of the influential French philosopher Michel Foucault. Among other things, Foucault studied the ways in which power dynamics affect human society and, more important, the acquisition and spread of knowledge. Individuals and institutions in positions of power have greater potential to shape the discourse in their field and thus to influence human knowledge and shape the "truth." New historicists look in literary history for "sites of struggle"—developments or texts that illustrate or seek to shift the balance of power.

New historicism emerged as a reaction to new criticism's disregard of historical context, but also in response to the perceived shortcomings of older methods of historical criticism. Rather than focusing on canonical texts as representations of the most powerful or dominant historical movements, new historicists give equal or more attention to marginal texts and nonliterary texts (newspapers, pamphlets, legal documents, medical documents, and so on). New historicists attempt to highlight overlooked or suppressed texts, particularly those that express deviation from the dominant culture of the time. In this way, new historicists study not just the historical context of a major literary text but also the complex relationship between texts and culture, or the ways in which literature can challenge as well as support a given culture.

A weakness of this method is implicit in its strength. Those who disagree with Foucault and his followers would stress that the plays of William Shakespeare are more important documents than laundry lists or tax rolls from Elizabethan and Jacobean England—that a work of individual excellence can tell us more about a period than does its census or burial records. Again, it's useful here to remember that critical approaches need not be exclusive, and a sophisticated critic is likely to use more than a single strategy when dealing with a text.

Stephen Greenblatt (b. 1943)
The Power of Forms in the English Renaissance (1982)

The earlier historicism tends to be monological; that is, it is concerned with discovering a single political vision, usually identical to that said to be held by the entire literate class or indeed the entire population ("In the eyes of the later middle ages," writes Dover Wilson, Richard II "represented the type and exemplar of royal martyrdom" [p. 50]). This vision, most often presumed to be internally coherent and consistent, though occasionally analyzed as the function of two or more elements, has the status of an historical fact. It is not thought to be the product of the historian's interpretation, nor even of the particular interests of a given social group in conflict with other groups. Protected then from interpretation and conflict, this vision can serve as a stable point of reference, beyond contingency, to which literary interpretation can securely refer. Literature is conceived to mirror the period's beliefs, but to mirror them, as it were, from a safe distance.

The new historicism erodes the firm ground of both criticism and literature. It tends to ask questions about its own methodological assumptions and those of others [. . .].

Moreover, recent criticism has been less concerned to establish the organic unity of literary works and more open to such works as fields of force, places of dissension and shifting interests, occasions for the jostling of orthodox and subversive impulses. [. . .] The critical practice represented in this volume challenges the assumptions that guarantee a secure distinction between "literary foreground" and "political background" or, more generally, between artistic production and other kinds of social production. Such distinctions do in fact exist, but they are not intrinsic to the texts; rather they are made up and constantly redrawn by artists, audiences, and readers. These collective social constructions on the one hand define the range of aesthetic possibilities within a given representational mode and, on the other, link that mode to the complex network of institutions, practices, and beliefs that constitute the culture as a whole. In this light, the study of genre is an exploration of the poetics of culture.

from The Power of Forms in the English Renaissance

Gender Criticism

Feminist criticism also focuses on sociological determinants in literature, particularly the ways in which much of the world's canonical literature presents a patriarchal or male-dominated perspective. Feminist critics highlight the ways in which female characters are viewed with prejudice, are subjugated to male interests, or are simply overlooked in literature. They highlight these injustices to women and seek to reinterpret texts with special attention to the presentation of women. Feminist critics also study the ways in which women *authors* have been subjected to prejudice, disregard, and unfair interpretation. They attempt to recover and champion little-known or little-valued texts by women authors—who have been marginalized by the male establishment since the formal study of literature began.

Gay and lesbian studies are, if not directly related to feminist criticism, similar in operational strategy. Interpretation of recognized classics may bring a new vantage to bear and cast a new light on old writings; a discussion of "cross-dressing in Shakespeare" or "male bonding in Melville" would belong to this mode of analysis. Here the critic focuses on submerged or hidden aspects of a text, as well as more overt referents; here, too, a part of the project is to recover lost or little known works of art from earlier generations.

Although the focus on overt prejudice is the easiest feature of feminist criticism to recognize, the approach as a whole actually involves much more subtle and nuanced interpretations of texts. As the passage below from Judith Fetterley indicates, feminist critics in some cases find the more subtle traces of male dominance in literature to be the most insidious, because they so easily can go overlooked and pass for the universal or true experience. This puts female readers in the awkward position of doubting the very validity of a female perspective.

Queer theory emerged from **gay and lesbian criticism** partly in response to the AIDS epidemic and owes much to Michel Foucault's work on power and discourse and how language itself shapes our sense of who we are. He argues that the idea of being a "homosexual" would have been impossible without psychoanalytic institutions and discourse that created the category of homosexuality. Sexuality is looked upon as straight (or *normative*) or queer (or *non-normative*) and as a social construction rather than an essential component of one's identity. Some believe this undermines a critique of oppression and prejudice toward gays and lesbians.

Judith Fetterley (b. 1938)
On the Politics of Literature (1978)

Literature is political. It is painful to have to insist on this fact, but the necessity of such insistence indicates the dimensions of the problem. John Keats once objected to poetry "that has a palpable design upon us." The major works of American fiction constitute a series of designs on the female reader, all the more potent in their effect because they are "impalpable." One of the main things that keep the design of our literature unavailable to the consciousness of the woman reader, and hence impalpable, is the very posture of the apolitical, the pretense that literature speaks universal truths through forms from which all the merely personal, the purely subjective, has been burned away or at least transformed through the medium of art into the representative. When only one reality is encouraged, legitimized, and transmitted and when that limited vision endlessly insists on its comprehensiveness, then we have the conditions necessary for that confusion of consciousness in which impalpability flourishes. It is the purpose of this book to give voice to a different reality and different vision, to bring a different subjectivity to bear on the old "universality." To examine American fictions in light of how attitudes toward women shape their form and content is to make available to consciousness that which has been largely left unconscious and thus to change our understanding of these fictions, our relation to them, and their effect on us. It is to make palpable their designs.

American literature is male. To read the canon of what is currently considered classic American literature is perforce to identify as male. Though exceptions to this generalization can be found here and there—a Dickinson poem, a Wharton novel—these exceptions usually function to obscure the argument and confuse the issue: American literature is male. Our literature neither leaves women alone nor allows them to participate. It insists on its universality at the same time that it defines that universality in specifically male terms. "Rip Van Winkle" is paradigmatic of this phenomenon. While the desire to avoid work, escape authority, and sleep through the major decisions of one's life is obviously applicable to both men and women, in Irving's story this "universal" desire is made specifically male. Work, authority, and decision making are symbolized by Dame Van Winkle, and the longing for flight is defined against her. She is what one must escape from, and the "one" is necessarily male. In Mailer's *An American Dream*, the fantasy of eliminating all one's ills through the ritual of scapegoating is equally male: the sacrificial scapegoat is the woman/wife and the cleansed survivor is the husband/male. In such fictions the female reader is co-opted into participation in an experience from which she is explicitly excluded; she is asked to identify with a selfhood that defines itself in opposition to her; she is required to identify against herself.

from On the Politics of Literature

Ethnic Studies and Postcolonialism

Ethnic studies emerged after the Civil Rights movement in the United States, but you can find its roots in the pioneering work of W. E. B. DuBois and others of the black arts movement and the Harlem Renaissance. Ethnic studies employs a cross-curricular analysis that is concerned with the social, economic, and cultural aspects of ethnic groups and an approach to literature that includes artistic and cultural traditions that are often pushed to the margins or considered only in relation to a dominant culture. Asian-American, Native-American, Afro-Caribbean, Italian-American, and Latinos are a few of many examples of groups that ethnic studies might explore. Ethnic studies seeks to give voice to literature that has previously been overlooked in the traditionally Eurocentric worldview by reclaiming literary traditions and taking on subjects that explore identity outside the Eurocentric mainstream. But even works that are not written by ethnic writers lend themselves to ethnic studies. For example, a critic wishing to analyze William Faulkner's work from an ethnic studies perspective might focus on his portrayal of African Americans.

Ethnic studies has helped open the American literary **canon**—works deemed essential milestones in a literary tradition—to works by authors outside the white majority. Another far-reaching effect of ethnic studies is that it questions applying traditional modes of literary inquiry (such as feminist and Marxist approaches) to all literature. It suggests that we might be able to learn something more if we approach a text by examining the cultural and social conventions and realities out of which it was created. With the publication in the 1950s of work by Caribbean poet and legislator Aimée Césaire and North-African writer Frantz Fanon, the discipline of **postcolonialism** found its beginnings, offering views of relations between the colonizing West and colonized nations and regions that differed sharply from the conventional Western perspectives. The field's modern American academic roots go back to the 1978 publication of *Orientalism* by the late Columbia University scholar Edward Said, a Palestinian by birth, who posits that the concept of the Orient was a projection of the West's ideas of the "other." Many of today's major writers have come out of the old British colonies, from Chinua Achebe to V. S. Naipal to Salman Rushdie, to name a few.

One of the major practitioners of this mode of criticism, Harvard scholar Henry Louis Gates, places such variety of study in a cultural context in which the urgency of the matter becomes plain to hear.

Henry Louis Gates (b. 1950)
Loose Canons: Notes on the Culture Wars (1992)

There's no denying that the multicultural initiative arose, in part, because of the fragmentation of American society by ethnicity, class, and gender. To make it the culprit for this fragmentation is to mistake effect for cause. [. . .] Perhaps we should try to think of American culture as a conversation among different voices—even if it's a conversation that some of us weren't able to join until recently. Perhaps we should think about education, as the conservative philosopher Michael Oakeshott proposed, as "an invitation into the art of this conversation in which we learn to recognize the voices," each conditioned, as he says, by a different perception of the world. Common sense says that you don't bracket 90 percent of the world's cultural heritage if you really want to learn about the world.

To insist that we "master our own culture" before learning others only defers the vexed question: What gets to count as "our" culture? What makes knowledge worth knowing? Unfortunately, as history has taught us, an Anglo-American regional culture has too often masked itself as universal, passing itself off as our "common culture," and depicting different cultural traditions as "tribal" or "parochial." So it's only when we're free to explore the complexities of our hyphenated American culture that we can discover what a genuinely common American culture might actually look like. Common sense . . . reminds us that we're all ethnics, and the challenge of transcending ethnic chauvinism is one we all face.

Granted, multiculturalism is no magic panacea for our social ills. We're worried when Johnny can't read. We're worried when Johnny can't add. But shouldn't we be worried, too, when Johnny tramples gravestones in a Jewish cemetery or scrawls racial epithets on a dormitory wall? It's a fact about this country that we've entrusted our schools with the fashioning and refashioning of a democratic policy; that's why the schooling of America has always been a matter of political judgment. But in America, a nation that has theorized itself as plural from its inception, our schools have a very special task.

The society we have made simply won't survive without the values of tolerance. And cultural tolerance comes to nothing without cultural understanding. In short, the challenge facing Americans in the next century will be the shaping, at long last, of a truly common public culture, one responsive to the long-silenced cultures of color. If we relinquish the ideal of America as a plural nation, we've abandoned the very experiment that America represents.

From Loose Canons: Notes on the Cultural Wars

Reader-Response Criticism

The **reader-response** approach emphasizes the role of the reader in the writer-text-reader transaction. Reader-response critics believe a literary work is not complete until someone reads and interprets it. Such critics acknowledge that each reader has a different set of experiences and views; therefore, each reader's response to a text may be different. (Moreover, a single reader may have several and contradictory responses to a work of art depending on the reading-context: a good dinner, a bad breakfast, a single flickering fluorescent bulb—all these affect the way we look at and absorb a page.) This plurality of interpretations is acceptable, even inevitable, since readers are not interpreting a fixed, completed text, but rather *creating* the text as they read it. Reader-response critics do stress that texts limit the possibilities of interpretation; it is not correct for readers to derive an interpretation that textual evidence does not support. So, for instance, it's inappropriate to claim that the character in a story is a vampire because she only ever appears during nighttime scenes in the story—but it's appropriate to compare the housewife in Susan Glaspell's play *Trifles* (Chapter 30), to a "caged" bird once we understand the nature of her plight.

Reader-response criticism, moreover, acknowledges the subjectivity of interpretation and aims to discover the ways in which cultural values affect readers' interpretations. Rather than only emphasizing values embodied in an author or literary work, this approach examines the values embodied in the *reader*.

Wolfgang Iser (1926–2007)
Interplay between Text and Reader (1978)

Textual models designate only one aspect of the communicatory process. Hence textual repertoires and strategies simply offer a frame within which the reader must construct for himself the aesthetic object. Textual structures and structured acts of comprehension are therefore the two poles in the act of communication, whose success will depend on the degree in which the text establishes itself as a correlative in the reader's consciousness. This "transfer" of text to reader is often regarded as being brought about solely by the text. Any successful transfer however—though initiated by the text—depends on the extent to which this text can activate the individual reader's faculties of perceiving and processing. Although the text may well incorporate the social norms and values of its possible readers, its function is not merely to *present* such data, but, in fact, to use them in order to secure its uptake. In other words, it offers guidance as to what is to be produced, and therefore cannot itself be the product. This fact is worth emphasizing, because there are many current theories which give the impression that texts automatically imprint themselves on the reader's mind of their own accord. This applies not only to linguistic theories but also to Marxist theories, as evinced by the term "Rezeptionsvorgabe"[1] (structured prefiguration) recently coined by East German critics. Of course, the text is a "structured prefiguration," but that which is given has to be received, and the *way* in which it is received depends as much on the reader as on the text. Reading is not a direct "internalization," because it is not a one-way process, and our concern will be to find means of describing the reading process as a dynamic *interaction* between text and reader. We may take as a starting-point the fact that the linguistic signs and structures of the text exhaust their function in triggering developing acts of comprehension. This is tantamount to saying that these acts, though set in motion by the text, defy total control by the text itself, and, indeed, it is the very lack of control that forms the basis of the creative side of reading.

This concept of reading is by no means new. In the eighteenth century, Laurence Sterne was already writing in *Tristram Shandy*: ". . . no author, who understands the just boundaries of decorum and good-breeding, would presume to think all: The truest respect which you can pay to the reader's understanding, is to halve this matter amicably, and leave him something to imagine, in his turn, as well as yourself. For my own part, I am eternally paying him compliments of this kind, and do all that lies in my power to keep his imagination as busy as my own."[2] Thus author and reader are to share the game of the imagination, and, indeed, the game will not work if the text sets out to be anything more than a set of governing rules. The reader's enjoyment begins when he himself becomes productive, i.e.,

[1]See Manfred Naumann et al., *Gesellschaft—Literatur—Lesen. Literaturrezeption in theoretischer Sicht* (Aufbau-Verlag, Berlin and Weimar, 1973), p. 35.

[2]Laurence Sterne, *Tristram Shandy II*, 11 (Everyman's Library; London, 1956), p. 79.

when the text allows him to bring his own faculties into play. There are, of course, limits to the reader's willingness to participate, and these will be exceeded if the text makes things too clear or, on the other hand, too obscure: boredom and overstrain represent the two poles of tolerance, and in either case the reader is likely to opt out of the game.

from *Interplay between Text and Reader* (1978)

Poststructuralism and Deconstruction

The poststructuralist approach (**poststructuralism**) was primarily developed in France in the late 1960s by Roland Barthes and Jacques Derrida. Poststructuralists believe that texts do not have a single, stable meaning or interpretation, in part because language itself is filled with ambiguity, multiple meanings, and meanings that can change with time or context. Even a simple dictionary definition reveals several multiple uses for each word, and we know that context and tone can expand the number of possible meanings. Moreover, within any work of literature, authors intentionally and unintentionally create even more multiple meanings through sound sense, connotation, or patterns of usage. Poststructuralists revel in the possibility of so many interpretations not just for words but for every element of a text's construction.

Like formalists, poststructuralists use the technique of close reading to focus very precisely on the language and construction of a text. Yet whereas formalists do this to develop a sense of the text as a unified artistic whole, poststructuralists "deconstruct" the text, deliberately seeking to reveal the inevitable *inconsistency* or *lack of unity* in even the most successful and revered texts (**deconstruction**). Poststructuralists do not believe that interpretation can reconstruct an author's intentions; they do not even privilege an author's intentions, believing that the text stands apart from the author and may well contain meanings unintended by its maker. These meanings are, in the eyes of poststructuralists, as valid as any other, if textual evidence supports them.

Poststructuralists thus reject the notion of "privileged" or standard interpretations and embrace what might sometimes seem like a chaotic approach to literary interpretation. In his book *The Pleasure of the Text*, for example, Roland Barthes presents his random observations on narrative *in alphabetical order*, rather than in the form of a methodically unified argument, since the notion of textual unity is, in his eyes, an illusion.

Roland Barthes (1915–1980)
The Death of the Author (1967)

In his story *Sarrasine*, Balzac, describing a castrato disguised as a woman, writes the following sentence: "This was woman herself, with her sudden fears, her irrational whims, her instinctive worries, her impetuous boldness, her fussings, and her delicious sensibility." Who is speaking thus? Is it the hero of the story bent on remaining ignorant of the castrato hidden beneath the woman? Is it Balzac the individual, furnished by his personal experience with a philosophy of Woman? Is it Balzac the author professing "literary" ideas on femininity? Is it universal wisdom? Romantic psychology? We shall never know, for the good reason that writing is the destruction of every voice, of every point of origin. Writing is that neutral, composite, oblique space where our subject slips away, the negative where all identity is lost, starting with the very identity of the body of writing.

No doubt it has always been that way. As soon as a fact is *narrated* no longer with a view to acting directly on reality but intransitively, that is to say, finally outside of any function other than that of the very practice of the symbol itself, this disconnection occurs, the voice loses its origin, the author enters into his own death, writing begins. [. . .] The *author* still reigns in histories of literature, biographies of writers, interviews, magazines, as in the very consciousness of men of letters anxious to unite their person and their work through diaries and memoirs. The image of literature to be found in ordinary culture is tyrannically centered on the author, his person, his life, his tastes, his passions [. . .] The *explanation* of a work is always sought in the man or woman who produced it, as if it were always in the end, through the more or less transparent allegory of the fiction, the voice of a single person, the *author* "confiding" in us.

[. . .] We know now that a text is not a line of words releasing a single "theological" meaning (the "message" of the Author-God) but a multi-dimensional space in which a variety of writings, none of them original, blend and clash. The text is a tissue of quotations drawn from the innumerable centres of culture. [. . .] the writer can only imitate a gesture that is always anterior, never original. His only power is to mix writings, to counter the ones with the others, in such a way as never to rest on any one of them. Did he wish to *express himself,* he ought at least to know that the inner "thing" he thinks to "translate" is itself only a ready-formed dictionary, its words only explainable through other words, and so on indefinitely [. . .]. Succeeding the Author, the scriptor no longer bears within him passions, humours, feelings, impressions, but rather this immense dictionary from which he draws a writing that can know no halt: life never does more than imitate the book, and the book itself is only a tissue of signs, an imitation that is lost, infinitely deferred.

Once the Author is removed, the claim to decipher a text becomes quite futile. To give a text an Author is to impose a limit on the text, to furnish it with a final signified, to close the writing. Such a conception suits criticism very well, the latter then allotting itself the important task of discovering the Author (or its hypostases: society, history, psyche, liberty) beneath the work: when the Author has been found, the text is "explained"— victory to the critic. Hence there is no surprise in the fact that, historically, the reign of the Author has also been that of the Critic, nor again in the fact that criticism (be it new) is today undermined along with the author. In the multiplicity of writing, everything is to be *disentangled*, nothing *deciphered;* the structure can be followed, "run" (like the thread of a stocking) at every point and at every level, but there is nothing beneath: the space of writing is to be ranged over, not pierced; writing ceaselessly posits meaning ceaselessly to evaporate it, carrying out a systematic exemption of meaning. In precisely this way literature (it would be better from now on to say *writing*), by refusing to assign a "secret," an ultimate meaning, to the text (and to the world as texts), liberates what may be called an anti-theological activity, an activity that is truly revolutionary since to refuse to fix meaning is, in the end, to refuse God and his hypostases—reason, science, law.

from *The Death of the Author*

Cultural Studies

The critical perspective usually referred to as **cultural studies** developed mainly in England in the 1960s by such New Left writers and sociologists as Raymond Williams, Richard Hoggart, and Stuart Hall. These critics took a sociological approach to literature, and their views were colored by the philosophical leftism of such social philosophers as the Italian Antonio Gramsci. The movement grew mainly out of the desire to view social life and social movements from an analytical perspective somewhat akin to the analysis of film and literature.

The American academic branch of this form of criticism also incorporated (mainly in translation) the formal philosophical and critical approaches of a number of French academics including Foucault and other so-called deconstructionists. (Novelist Saul Bellow, affronted by this method, called these writings "Stale chocolates, imported from France. . . ."). Whatever good the English approach might have produced was muted, if not negated, by the French influence, which emphasized viewing society as composed of various "texts" and imbuing everything from literature to the placement of traffic lights with equal value.

Twentieth-century sociological criticism has been a productive and interesting variety of criticism, as in, for example, studies of the relation of the literacy rate and the rise of the English novel or the effects of the rise of the dime novel in nineteenth-century America or the elevation of film studies to a high place within the university curriculum. Cultural criticism cheerfully blurs the boundaries among the disciplines and acts with a vengeance to blur the lines between high art and popular culture.

Vincent B. Leitch (b. 1944)
Poststructuralist Cultural Critique (1992)

Whereas a major goal of New Criticism and much other modern formalistic criticism is aesthetic evaluation of freestanding texts, a primary objective of cultural criticism is cultural critique, which entails investigation and assessment of ruling and oppositional beliefs, categories, practices, and representations, inquiring into the causes, constitutions, and consequences as well as the modes of circulation and consumption of linguistic, social, economic, political, historical, ethical, religious, legal, scientific, philosophical, educational, familial, and aesthetic discourses and institutions. In rendering a judgment on an aesthetic artifact, a New Critic privileges such key things as textual coherence and unity, intricacy and complexity, ambiguity and irony, tension and balance, economy and autonomy, literariness and spatial form. In mounting a critique of a cultural "text," an advocate of poststructuralist cultural criticism evaluates such things as degrees of exclusion and inclusion, of complicity and resistance, of domination and letting-be, of abstraction and situatedness, of violence and tolerance, or monologue and polylogue, of quietism and activism, of sameness and otherness, of oppression and emancipation, or centralization and decentralization. Just as the aforementioned system of evaluative criteria underlies the exegetical and judgmental labor of New Criticism, so too does the above named set of commitments undergird the work of poststructuralist cultural critique.

Given its commitments, poststructuralist cultural criticism is, as I have suggested, suspicious of literary formalism. Specifically, the trouble with New Criticism is its inclination to advocate a combination of quietism and asceticism, connoisseurship and exclusiveness, aestheticism and apoliticism. [. . .] The monotonous practical effect of New Critical reading is to illustrate the subservence of each textual element to a higher, overarching, economical poetic structure without remainders. What should be evident here is that the project of poststructuralist cultural criticism possesses a set of commitments and criteria that enable it to engage in the enterprise of cultural critique. It should also be evident that the cultural ethicopolitics of this politics is best characterized, using current terminology, as "liberal" or "leftist," meaning congruent with certain socialist, anarchist, and libertarian ideals, none of which, incidentally, are necessarily Marxian. Such congruence, derived from extrapolating a generalized stance for poststructuralism, constitutes neither a party platform nor an observable course of practical action; avowed tendencies often account for little in the unfolding of practical engagements.

from *Cultural Criticism, Literary Theory, Poststructuralism*

Chapter 37

MLA Documentation Style Guide

Anytime you use a direct quotation, paraphrase, or summary from a source—in other words, any text or idea that is not your own—you must indicate the author and work from which it came. This is called citing your sources. Different fields of study follow different citation style guidelines. Psychology and sociology, for example, require APA (American Psychological Association) style, whereas anthropology typically uses CMS (*Chicago Manual of Style*). English and most humanities, however, use MLA style, a format developed and maintained by the Modern Language Association.

This appendix provides a quick overview and an abbreviated guide to MLA style. For a full description of how to properly cite works, consult the *MLA Handbook for Writers of Research Papers* (often referred to as simply the *MLA Handbook*), which is the authoritative guide to MLA style. Be sure to consult the 7th edition, which is the most current; the rules vary slightly from edition to edition.

DOCUMENT IN-TEXT CITATIONS, MLA STYLE

1. Author Named in Parentheses. A parenthetical reference in MLA consists of the author's last name and the page number from which you are quoting, summarizing, or paraphrasing. The reference comes at the end of the sentence *before* the period. Do *not* insert a comma, hyphen, or other punctuation between the last name and the page number.

> **Example:** Although documenting sources may take extra time, it is worth it, because "your reader might want to see the source for his or her own research" (Smith 42-43).

When you need to cite a page range, simply put a dash between the start and end pages, as in the example above. When citing two different pages, separate them with a comma.

> **Example:** (Smith 42, 51)

2. Author Named in Sentence. If you mention the author's name in the text of the sentence, you need insert only the page number in parentheses.

> **Example:** As John Smith points out, "Your reader might want to see the source for his or her own research" (42).

3. Two or More Works by the Same Author. If you use two books or articles by John Smith in your paper, you must let your reader know which source you are using by inserting the title of the work into your sentence *or* by abbreviating the title and inserting it in the parenthetical reference as shown below.

Example: As John Smith points out in his article "Using Sources," "Your reader might want to see the source for his or her own research" (42).

Example: Although documenting sources may take extra time, it is worth it, because "your reader might want to see the source for his or her own research" (Smith, "Sources" 42).

*For parenthetical references for works with two, three, or more authors, see 6c, Citing Book Sources, points 2 and 3 (pp. 1596–1597).

4. Source of a Long Quotation.   When citing a block quotation—one that is four lines or longer in poetry or five lines or longer in prose—indent by one inch and do not include quotation marks. The citation comes *after* the period.

Example: Many critics point to specific techniques that Hughes employs to create the effect of jazz. One such critic is Lionel Davidas, who writes:

> Langston Hughes, in his collection of poems, lavishly uses such characteristics of jazz as repetitions, choruses, riffs, scats, and nonsensical onomatopoeia to achieve musical success as well as audience participation. It is also significant to note that Hughes's poems are often marked by dissonance, discordance, and line irregularity, which all contribute to the representation of the jazz spirit in verse forms. (268)

DOCUMENT LIST OF WORKS CITED, MLA STYLE

To properly format a Works Cited page:

- Begin on a new page, following the end of your paper. If your paper ends on page 5, your Works Cited page will begin on page 6.
- Just like your paper, a Works Cited page should be double spaced, both between and within entries, with one-inch margins.

- Place the page number in the upper right-hand corner, one half-inch (or five spaces) from the top, flush with the right margin, and after your last name.
- One inch from the top of the page, type "Works Cited" and center it. Do not include quotation marks around the words "Works Cited."
- Do not skip spaces. Drop down one double-spaced line, and begin your entry at the left margin.
- If an entry runs longer than one line, indent every line one-half inch (or five spaces) after the first line.
- Put a period at the end of each entry.
- Alphabetize your Works Cited list by the first word of the entry. In most cases, this will be the author's last name. Use letter-by-letter order regardless of punctuation, so Enrico Debernardo comes before Cosimo de' Medici, and John Mackensey comes before Michael McBride.
- Use as many pages as necessary for the list.

For an example of a Works Cited page, see the model research paper in Chapter 5 on Writing the Research Paper, Avoiding Plagiarism, and Documenting Sources.

Common Formatting Errors

TIP

- Single spacing a Works Cited page
- Adding extra spaces between entries
- Numbering entries
- Omitting the period at the end of an entry

What goes in an entry on a Works Cited page? First determine what type of source it is—a book, a periodical, an online resource. Then follow the instructions in the appropriate section, as follows.

Note: You can find visual guides to the elements in a works cited entry for books, periodicals and online sources in Chapter 5 on pages 98 (books), 99 (periodicals), and 100 (online sources).

Citing Book Sources

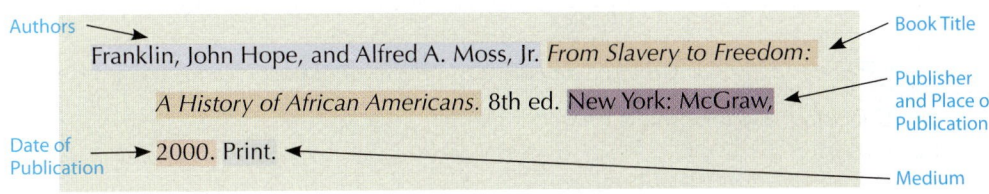

Authors → Franklin, John Hope, and Alfred A. Moss, Jr. *From Slavery to Freedom:* ← Book Title

A History of African Americans. 8th ed. New York: McGraw, ← Publisher and Place of Publication

Date of Publication → 2000. Print. ← Medium

1. Book with One Author.   Reverse the author's name for alphabetizing, adding a comma after the last name and a period after the first name. The book title follows in italics, followed by a period. Then list the city of publication, followed by a colon. Then the publisher, followed by a comma, then the year, followed by a period. Then list the medium. For how to abbreviate the publisher's name, see Additional Tips, p. 1602.

> Borshuk, Michael. *Swinging the Vernacular.* New York: Routledge, 2006. Print.

2. Book with Two or Three Authors.   This entry follows the same formula as a book with a single author *except* that you name the authors in the order listed on the title page. Reverse only the name of the first author. Then add a comma and list additional authors by first name followed by last name. Separate each author's complete name from the next author by a comma.

> Gilbert, Sandra M., and Susan Gubar. *The Madwoman in the Attic: The Woman*
>
> *Writer and the Nineteenth-Century Literary Imagination.* New Haven: Yale
>
> UP, 2000. Print.

*An in-text parenthetical reference for two authors should look like this:

> (Gilbert and Gubar 34)

*An in-text parenthetical reference for three authors should look like this:

> (Gilbert, Gilbert, and Gubar 34)

3. Book with Four or More Authors.   Indicate the name of the first author appearing on the title page, followed by "et al." (the Latin abbreviation for "and others"). As an alternative, however, you may list the names of all the authors *if convenient.*

> Jordan, Frank, et al. *The English Romantic Poets: A Review of Research and*
>
> *Criticism.* New York: MLA, 1985. Print.

*A parenthetical reference for four or more authors would look like this:

(Gilbert et al. 34)

4. Two or More Books by the Same Author.   When citing two or more works by the same author, give the name only in the first entry. For subsequent entries, indicate the same author with three hyphens and a period.

Bloom, Harold. *The Art of Reading Poetry.* New York: Perennial, 2005. Print.

- - -. *How to Read and Why.* New York: Scribner, 2000. Print.

5. Book by an Unknown Author.   Begin with the title of the book, followed by the translator or editor (if appropriate). Do not use *Anonymous* or *Anon.* Follow with the publication information. Remember to alphabetize such a book in your Works Cited list by the first major word in the title, *not* by an article (*a, an,* or *the*).

The Bhagavad Gita. Trans. Eknath Easwaran. Berkeley: Blue Mountain Center for

Meditation, 2007. Print.

6. Work in an Anthology or Chapter in an Edited Book.   Selection author's last name, first name. "Selection or Chapter Title." *Book Title.* Editor's name. City: Publisher, Year. Page numbers or selection. Medium.

Fox, Paula. "The Broad Estates of Death." *The O. Henry Prize Stories.* Ed. Laura

Furman. New York: Anchor, 2006. 46-58. Print.

7. Book with One or Two Editors.   In place of an author's name, put the editor's name, followed by a comma and the abbreviation "ed." If there is more than one editor, follow the format for "Book with more than one author" but place a comma and the abbreviation "eds." after the final editor's name listed.

> Rampersad, Arnold, ed. *The Collected Poems of Langston Hughes.* New York:
>
> Knopf, 1995. Print.
>
> Opie, Iona, and Peter Opie, eds. *The Oxford Book of Children's Verse.* New York:
>
> Oxford, 1973. Print.

8. Book with an Author and an Editor.   Start with the name of the author, followed by the book title. Then write "Ed." followed by the editor's name in normal order.

> Twain, Mark. *Adventures of Huckleberry Finn.* Ed. Henry Nash Smith. Boston:
>
> Houghton, 1958. Print.

9. Anthology.   Start with the editor's last name, and after the editor's name, put a comma followed by "ed." If there is more than one editor, follow the initial editor with a comma, the second editor's name, a comma, and "eds." for more than one editor. Only the first editor's name appears last name first. Next is the book title in italics, followed by a period. If the title page indicates that this is not a first edition, put the number of the edition followed by "ed" and a period. The title page may identify the edition by name ("Rev. ed." for Revised Edition or "Abr. ed." for Abridged Edition) or by year ("2010 ed."); use the title page's wording. The publication and medium information come last.

> Delbanco, Nicholas, and Alan Cheuse, eds. *Literature: Craft and Voice.* 2nd ed.
>
> New York: McGraw, 2013. Print.

10. Short Story, Poem, or Play in a Collection of the Author's Work.   After the author's name, put the title of the story, poem, or play, followed by the title of the collection and publication information. Don't forget to give the page numbers of the selection and the medium.

> Packer, ZZ. "Brownies." *Drinking Coffee Elsewhere.* New York: Riverhead, 2003.
>
> 1-28. Print.

11. Short Story or Chapter in an Anthology.   Use this citation formula: Selection author's last name, first name. "Selection or Chapter Title." *Book Title*. "Ed." followed by editor's name in normal order. City: Publisher, Year. Page numbers of selection. Medium.

> Fox, Paula. "The Broad Estates of Death." *The O. Henry Prize Stories*. Ed. Laura
>
>   Furman. New York: Anchor, 2006. 46-58. Print.

12. Poem in an Anthology.   Follow this citation formula: Poet's last name, first name. "Poem title." *Book Title*. "Ed." followed by editor's name in normal order. City: Publisher, Year. Page numbers of selection. Medium.

> Collins, Billy. "Litany." *The Poets Laureate Anthology*. Ed. Elizabeth Hun Schmidt.
>
>   New York: Norton, 2010. 115-116. Print.

13. Play in an Anthology.   Because it is a complete work, italicize the title of the play. Notice that the title of the anthology is also italicized.

> Kopit, Arthur. *Wings. Plays from the Contemporary American Theater*. Ed. Brooks
>
>   McNamara. New York: Signet, 2002. 139-190. Print.

14. Article in an Anthology.   Use this citation formula: Article author's last name, first name. "Article Title." *Book Title*. "Ed." followed by editor's name in normal order. City: Publisher, Year. Page numbers of selection. Medium.

> Wilcox, Helen. "Devotional Writing." *The Cambridge Companion to John Donne*.
>
>   Ed. Achsah Guibbory. Cambridge: Cambridge UP, 2006. 149-166. Print.

15. More Than One Selection from the Same Anthology.   Create an entry for the anthology itself.

> Charters, Ann, ed. *The Portable Beat Reader*. New York: Penguin, 2003. Print.

MLA (Modern Language Association)

Then, for each selection, provide the selection author and title, the anthology editor's last name, and the page numbers on which the selection appears. These entries are called cross-references.

> Ginsberg, Allen. "Howl." Charters 62-70.
>
> Kerouac, Jack. "Essentials of Spontaneous Prose." Charters 57.

16. Translation of a Text.   Follow this citation formula: Author's last name, first name. *Title of Book*. Abbreviation "Trans." for "translator" followed by the translator's name in normal order. City of publication: publisher, year. Medium.

> Alighieri, Dante. *The Divine Comedy*. Trans. John Ciardi. New York: Norton, 1970.
>
>   Print.

17. Introduction/Preface/Foreword/Afterword to a Text.   If the introduction, preface, foreword, or afterword was written by *someone other than the book's author,* start with the writer and the title of *this* part. Then indicate the book's title, followed by the word "By" and the name of the book's author in normal order. In the following example, Anita Brookner wrote the introduction to Edith Wharton's novel *The House of Mirth*.

> Brookner, Anita. Introduction. *The House of Mirth*. By Edith Wharton. New York:
>
>   Scribner, 1977. ii- ix. Print.

If the book has an editor or translator and the introduction, preface, foreword, or afterword *was written by the author,* follow the book's title with only the author's last name preceded by the word "By." Then give the publication information, including the name of the editor or translator.

> Hornung, Erik. Preface. *The Valley of the Kings*. By Hornung. Trans. David
>
>   Warburton. New York: Timken, 1990. 7-9. Print.

If the complete work was written by one author and there is no editor or translator, create an entry for the work as a whole. In the following example, Thomas Hardy wrote both the book and the introduction.

Hardy, Thomas. *Tess of the D'Urbervilles*. New York: Barnes, 1993. Print.

18. Multivolume Work.   If you have taken information from only one of the work's volumes, indicate the number of that volume and abbreviate to "Vol."

Poe, Edgar Allan. *The Collected Works of Edgar Allan Poe*. Ed. Thomas Ollive

Mabboth. Vol. 2. Cambridge: Harvard UP, 1969. Print.

If you have taken information from more than one volume, indicate the total number of volumes used, abbreviate to "vols" and follow with a period.

Poe, Edgar Allan. *The Collected Works of Edgar Allan Poe*. Ed. Thomas Ollive

Mabboth. 2 vols. Cambridge: Harvard UP, 1969. Print.

19. Book in a Series.   Place the name of the series after the medium. Indicate the book's number in the series if available. In the following example, this book is number 137 in the series.

Franchere, Hoyt C. *Edwin Arlington Robinson*. New York: Twayne, 1968. Print.

Twayne's United States Authors Series 137.

20. Graphic Novel or Comic Book.   Cite graphic novels as you would any other book. After the italicized book title, include the names of those who contributed to the art or design if they are listed on the title page, along with an indication of their role. (If this is a multivolume work or a book in a series, see the previous two entries.)

Mignola, Mike. *The Amazing Screw-On Head and Other Curious Objects*. Colors

by Dave Stewart. Letters by Clem Robins and Pat Brosseau. Milwaukie, OR:

Dark Horse, 2010. Print.

MLA (Modern Language Association)

21. Encyclopedia Article.

Signed A signed article is one that is attributed to an author. Use the following citation formula (if the encyclopedia is arranged alphabetically, omit the inclusive page numbers).

Inverted author's name. "Title of the Article." *Title of the Encyclopedia*. Editor(s). Volume number (if appropriate). City of publication: publisher, year. Medium.

> Merlan, Philip. "Athenian School." *The Encyclopedia of Philosophy*. Ed. Paul
>
> Edwards. Vol. 1. New York: Macmillan, 1967. Print.

Unsigned An unsigned article is not attributed to an author. If the encyclopedia does not frequently appear in new editions, then start with the title of the article and proceed as above.

> "Pericles." *The Columbia Concise Encyclopedia*. Ed. Judith S. Levey and Agnes
>
> Greenhall. New York: Columbia UP, 1983. Print.

22. Dictionary Definition.

Use the following citation formula: "Title of Entry." *Title of Dictionary*. Edition. Year of publication. Medium.

> "Fresco." *Merriam-Webster's Collegiate Dictionary*. 11th ed. 2003. Print.

Additional Tips

When a book lists multiple cities in which the publisher exists, choose only the first one to put in your citation. For W. W. Norton & Company, which lists New York and then London, you would use New York as the city for publication. Also, if the city is likely to be confused with another U.S. city with the same name, indicate the state in addition to the city, as in the following example:

> Milwaukie, OR: Dark Horse

Abbreviate or condense the publisher's name. Any time you see "University Press," you can abbreviate it as "UP." For Southern Methodist University Press, write Southern Methodist UP. Alfred A. Knopf can be condensed to simply "Knopf."

> Durham, NC: Duke UP

If a book has multiple years on the copyright page, put only the most recent year in your Works Cited entry.

Citing Periodical Sources

Periodicals include scholarly journals, magazines, and newspapers. For print periodicals (as opposed to online periodicals), use the following citation formulas.

1. Article in a Scholarly Journal.   Author's last name, first name. "Article Title." *Journal Title* Volume. Issue (Year): Page numbers of article. Medium.

> Davidas, Lionel. "'I, Too, Sing America': Jazz and Blues Techniques and Effects in
>
>   Some of Langston Hughes's Selected Poems." *Dialectical Anthropology* 26
>
>   (2001): 267-272. Print.

Note that not all journals have an issue number, as in the example above. If that is the case, simply include the volume and the year.

2. Article in a Magazine.   Author's last name, first name. "Article Title." *Magazine Title* Day Month Year: Page numbers of article. Medium. Do not include *The* in the magazine title.

> Lehrer, Jonah. "The Eureka Hunt." *New Yorker* 28 July 2008: 40-45. Print.

Note that monthly magazines will not have a day with the month; in that case, simply list the month. Also, abbreviate months except for May, June, and July.

3. Article in a Newspaper.   Author's last name, first name. "Article Headline." *Newspaper's Name* Day Month Year: Section letter Page number +. Medium. Do not include *The* in the magazine title.

> Svrluga, Barry. "Phelps Earns Eighth Gold." *Washington Post* 17 Aug. 2008: A1+.
>
>   Print.

Use the plus sign after the page number only if the article is continued on nonconsecutive pages.

4. Book Review.   Start with the reviewer's name, followed by the title of the review (if it has one) in quotation marks. Follow with "Rev. of " (the abbreviation for "review of "), the title of the book, and the name of the book's author preceded by the word "by." The author's name should be in normal order. In the following example, the reviewer is Robert Kelly; the author of the book is Umberto Eco.

> Kelly, Robert. "Castaway." Rev. of *The Island of the Day Before,* by Umberto Eco.
>
> *New York Times* 22 Oct. 1995: BR7. Print.

Citing Online Sources

1. Web Site.   The amount of source information provided varies from Web site to Web site. Include as much of the information below as you can. Remember, too, to choose your online resources wisely. If there is little or no information on the person or institution that created it, you may want to reconsider using it in your paper.

Last name of person responsible for site, first name. *Name of Web site.* Name of publisher, date of publication or last update. Medium. Day Month Year you accessed site. Note: If no publisher is listed, use the abbreviation "n.p." If no date is given, use the abbreviation "n.d."

> Souther, Randy. *Celestial Timepiece: A Joyce Carol Oates Homepage.* U of San
>
> Francisco, n.d. Web. 8 Oct. 2011.

2. Online Scholarly Project.

> Dodson, Howard and Sylviane A. Diouf, eds. *In Motion: The African-American*
>
> *Migration Experience.* Schomburg Center for Research in Black Culture,
>
> 2011. Web. 11 May 2011.

3. Article on a Web Site / Part of an Online Scholarly Project.   Author. "Title of Article." *Name of site.* Publisher, date of publication or update. Medium. Date you accessed site.

> "Roaring Twenties." *JAZZ: A Film by Ken Burns.* PBS, n.d. Web. 11 May 2008.

Begin with the title of the article when no author is given. When the date of the Web site's publication is not available, as in the preceding example, use the abbreviation "n.d." in place of the date.

4. Scholarly Journal Article from a Database.   Cite the article as you normally would for a print article, but at the end of your entry add the following information: *Database Name*. Medium. Date of access.

> Cull, Ryan. "Beyond the Cheated Eye: Dickinson's Lyric Sociality." *Nineteenth-*
>
> *Century Literature* 65.1 (2010): 38-64. *JSTOR*. Web. 21 May 2011.

5. Monthly Magazine Article from a Database.

> Johnson, George. "Plugging Into The Sun." *National Geographic* Sept. 2009: 28-47.
>
> *ProQuest*. Web. 3 Sept. 2011.

6. Newspaper Article from a Database.

> Hobbs, Holly. "Drama Teacher's Plays are a Hit." *Washington Post* 10 Feb. 2011:
>
> T18. *LexisNexis*. Web. 17 June 2011.

7. Reference Book Article from a Database.

> Conacher, Desmond J. "Aeschylus." *Reference Guide to World Literature*. St. James,
>
> MO: St. James P, 2003. *Gale Virtual Reference Library*. Web. 22 Sept. 2011.

8. Dictionary Definition from a Database.

> "Forte." *The Oxford Dictionary of Music*. 2nd ed. *Oxford Music Online*. Web. 12
>
> Aug. 2011.

MLA (Modern Language Association)

9. Online Book or E-Book (Kindle, Nook, iPad, and so on)

The entire book Start with the information you would include for any printed book. For an on-line book, follow with the name of the database, project, or other entity in which you found the book. Then indicate the medium ("Web") and the date you accessed the book. For an e-book, the citation for the medium depends on whether or not the file format of the source is known. If the file format is known, use it followed by the word "file": "PDF file," "JPEG file," "MP3 file," "XML file," "*Microsoft Word* file." If the file type is not known, use "Digital file" for the medium. When citing an e-book, do not include the date of access.

> Hardy, Thomas. *Wessex Poems and Other Verses*. New York: Harper, 1898. *Bartleby.*
>
> *com*. Web. 30 Sept. 2008.

Part of a book Start with the name of the author, followed by the title of the part of the book you have cited. Then, proceed as above. The following example is an entry for Thomas Hardy's poem "Neutral Tones," which appears in an online book entitled *Wessex Poems and Other Verses*.

> Hardy, Thomas. "Neutral Tones." *Wessex Poems and Other Verses*. New York:
>
> Harper, 1898. *Bartleby.com*. Web. 30 Sept. 2008.

10. Scholarly Article from Online Journal.
Often, online journals may not have page numbers; if that is the case, use *n. pag* instead of page numbers. If page numbers do appear, give them as the following example does.

> Lowney, John. "Langston Hughes and the 'Nonsense' of Bebop." *American*
>
> *Literature* 72.2 (2000): 357-385. Web. 11 May 2008.

11. Encyclopedia Article from the Internet.
Give the "entry name" in quotation marks, *Encyclopedia name* in italics, followed by the sponsor or publisher, the copyright date, "Web," and the date you accessed the entry.

> "Dickinson, Emily." *Encyclopaedia Britannica Online*. Encyclopaedia Britannica,
>
> 2011. Web. 6 May 2011.

12. Newspaper Article from the Internet.   In addition to the article author and article name, give the name of the newspaper, followed by the newspaper's publisher or sponsor. Be aware that in many cases, the sponsor will be the same as the newspaper's name.

> Keillor, Garrison. "The End of an Era in Publishing." *New York Times*. New York
>
>   Times, 26 May 2010. Web. 10 June 2011.

13. Magazine Article from the Internet.   As with an online newspaper, remember to put the publisher or sponsor's name after the publication's title.

> Sanneh, Kelefa. "The Reality Principle." *New Yorker*. Conde Nast Digital,
>
>   9 May 2011. Web. 8 July 2011.

14. Painting or Photograph from the Internet.   After the artist's name and title of the work in italics, give the year the work was produced and the medium of composition.

> Blake, William. *The Last Supper*. 1799. Tempera on canvas. National Gallery of Art,
>
>   Washington, DC. *NGA.gov*. Web. 10 Aug. 2011.

15. E-mail.   Give the author of the e-mail, followed by the e-mail's subject in quotation marks. Next provide a label such as "Message to the author" or "E-mail to students at Ohio State," the date it was sent, and the medium (e-mail).

> Smith, Allen. "Re: Novel." Message to the author. 10 Aug. 2011. E-mail.

16. Online Posting.   Treat an online posting as you would a Web site, but add a descriptive label after the selection's title.

> Brantley, Ben. "London Theater Journal: Hitting Bottom." Blog entry. *ArtsBeat*. New
>
>   York Times, 17 July 2008. Web. 29 Sept. 2008.

Citing Other Media

1. Sound Recording. Start with the name of the composer, performer, or conductor—depending on whom you have discussed in your paper. Then indicate the title of the recording, followed by the name(s) of the composer(s), performer(s), and/or conductor (if they were not mentioned earlier). Follow this with the distributor, the date, and the medium.

> Chopin, Frederic. *Chopin: Etudes.* Perf. Maurizio Pollini. Deutsche Grammophon,
>
> 1972. CD.

2. Film, Videocassette, DVD-ROM, or CD-ROM. Begin with the title of the film. Then write the name of the director preceded by "Dir." (the abbreviation for "director"). Next indicate the name(s) of the principal performer(s) preceded by "Perf." (the abbreviation for "performers"). Follow this with the distributor, the date, and the medium.

> *Cinema Paradiso.* Dir. Giuseppe Tornatore. Perf. Phillipe Noiret, Jacques Perrin,
>
> Antonella Attilli, Pupella Maggio, and Salvatore Cascio. Miramax, 1988.
>
> Film.

To make the entry more specific, you may replace the word "Film" with the format in which you viewed it, such as DVD. If you do this, include the original release date.

> *Cinema Paradiso.* Dir. Giuseppe Tornatore. Perf. Phillipe Noiret, Jacques Perrin,
>
> Antonella Attilli, Pupella Maggio, and Salvatore Cascio. 1988. Miramax,
>
> 2003. DVD.

3. Reference work on DVD-ROM or CD-ROM. Use the version number (Vers.) if the CD-ROM or DVD-ROM publication lacks an edition number, as the following example shows.

> "Pamphlet." *Webster's Third New International Dictionary, Unabridged.* Vers. 3.0.
>
> Springfield: Merriam, 2002. CD-ROM.

4. Periodical publication on DVD-ROM or CD-ROM. Give the information you would for a scholarly journal article. Then provide the format (CD-ROM or DVD-ROM), the title of the CD-ROM or DVD-ROM, the name of vendor, and the date of the CD-ROM.

> Gruen, Peter. "Evaluation and Surgical Management of Peripheral Nerve Problems."
>
> *Neurosurgery* 44.4 (1999): 839-840. CD-ROM. *Neurosurgery.* Vol. 40-47.
>
> Lippincott Williams and Wilkins. April 2001.

5. Television Program. Start with the title of the episode in quotation marks. Then list the title of the program. Follow with the name of the network or channel, the city, the broadcast date, and the medium.

> "Noah: Myth or Fact." *Into the Unknown with Josh Bernstein.* Discovery Channel,
>
> Silver Springs, MD, 15 Aug. 2008. Television.

6. Interview. Start by giving the interview subject's last name, first name. If the interview does not have a title, place the word *Interview* with no quotation marks and no italics where you would normally place the title. Continue the citation as you would for the type of publication it appears in. In this case, the interview came from a journal.

> Dubus, Andre III. "Letting in 'The Other': An Interview with Andre Dubus III."
>
> By Laura McCullough. *The Writer's Chronicle* 43.1 (2010): 8-14. Print.

7. Lecture or Address. Provide the name of the speaker, last name first. Then give the title in quotation marks (if applicable), the meeting and the sponsoring organization (again, if applicable), location, date, and the type of presentation (address, lecture, keynote address, reading).

> Snyder, Gary. "Spirits of the Seasons." Freer Gallery of Art, Washington, DC.
>
> 5 March 2011. Lecture.

Glossary of Literary Terms

Abstract   A short **summary** at the beginning of a scholarly article that states the **thesis,** the major points of **evidence,** and the **conclusion** of the article.

Abstract Diction   Language referring to a general or conceptual thing or quality, such as *progress,* or *justice.*

Accent   The vocal emphasis on a syllable in a word. Often used interchangeably with **stress,** which sometimes refers to emphasis within a line of poetry, rather than a single word.

Accentual Meter   A kind of **meter** or verse measure that uses a fixed number of stressed syllables in each line, although based on a number of unstressed syllables may vary. Accentual meters often can be heard in **rap** music and children's rhymes.

Accentual-Syllabic Verse   A verse form that uses a fixed number of **stresses** and syllables per line. This is the most common verse form in English poetry, and includes, for example, **iambic pentameter,** where each line has five **stressed** syllables and five unstressed syllables.

Act   A subdivision of the action of a **play,** similar to a chapter in a book. Acts generally occur during a change in **scenery,** cast of **characters,** or mood, and the end of an act usually suggests the advancement of time in the play. Acts are often divided into subunits called **scenes.**

Allegory   A story in which major elements such as **characters** and settings represent universal truths or moral lessons in a one-to-one correspondence.

Alliteration   The repetition of the initial consonant sounds of a sequence of words.

Allusion   A reference to another work of art or literature, or to a person, place, or event outside the text.

Amphibrach   A syllable pattern characterized by three syllables in the order *unstressed, stressed, unstressed.*

Amphitheater   A stage surrounded on all sides by the audience, who watch the action from above.

Anagnorisis   In **tragedy,** a change from ignorance to knowledge, producing love or hate between the persons destined by the poet for good or bad fortune.

Anagram   A word or phrase created using the letters that spell a different word or phrase. For example, *dirty room* is an anagram for *dormitory.*

Analyze   To take a text apart and examine its elements: the different written devices the author uses (such as **point of view, plot,** and imagery) and the **voice** the author brings to the piece (**tone,** word choice).

Anapestic Meter   A **meter** using feet with two unstressed syllables followed by a **stressed** syllable.

Anecdote   A personal remembrance or brief story.

Antagonist   A **character** in **conflict** with the **protagonist.** A story's **plot** often hinges on a protagonist's conflict with an antagonist.

Anticlimax   The opposite of a **climax;** a point in a narrative that is striking for its *lack* of excitement, intensity, or emphasis. An anticlimax generally occurs at a point of high action where a true climax is expected to occur.

Antihero   A main **character** who acts outside the usual lines of heroic behavior (brave, honest, true).

Apostrophe   A **figure of speech** in which a writer directly addresses an unseen person, force, or personified idea. The term *apostrophe* derives from the Greek term meaning *turning away* and often marks a digression.

Approximate Rhyme   *See* **Slant Rhyme.**

Archetypal Criticism   *See* **Mythological Criticism.**

Archetype   An **image** or **symbol** with a universal meaning that evokes a common emotional reaction in readers.

Arena Theater (Stage)   Also called **Theater in the Round,** an arena stage is surrounded on all sides by the audience, with all the action taking place on a stage in the center.

Argument   A position or perspective based on a **claim** that can be supported with **evidence.**

Aside   In drama, a remark made by an actor to the audience, which the other **characters** do not hear. This convention is sometimes discernable in fiction writing, when a self-conscious **narrator** breaks the flow of the narrative to make a remark directly to the reader.

Assonance   A repetition of vowel sounds or patterns in neighboring words.

Aubade   From the French, meaning "dawn"; a song describing the break of day. First noted as one of the love songs of medieval French **troubadours,** the aubade praises the beloved and describes the parting of lovers at dawn often with one lover resisting the other's leaving.

Auditory Imagery   **Images** that appeal to a reader's sense of hearing.

Augustan Age   A distinct period in early-eighteenth-century neoclassical English literature characterized by formal structure and diction. This Augustan Age is named after the great period of Roman literature during Emperor Augustus's reign, when Ovid, Horace, and Virgil were writing. Famous writers of the English Augustan Age were Alexander Pope, Thomas Gray, and Jonathan Swift.

Authorial Intrusion   *See* **Editorial Omniscience.**

Ballad   A song or poem that tells a lively or tragic story in simple language using rhyming four-line **stanzas** and a set **meter.**

Ballad Stanza   A **quatrain** in which the first and third lines possess four **stresses,** while the second and fourth lines have three **stresses.** The **rhyme scheme** is often *abcb.*

Bathos   An error that occurs when a writer attempts elevated language but is accidentally trite or ridiculous; a sort of **anticlimax.**

Beat Generation   A group of writers in the 1950s and 1960s who represented the counterculture to 1950s American prosperity. The word *beat* comes from the slang for being down and worn out, suggesting their weariness with mainstream culture and their adoption of a free-spirited attitude. Jack Kerouac's *On the Road* and Allen Ginsberg's poem "Howl" are major works of the Beat Generation.

Bibliography   A list of the **works cited** in the preparation of a paper, containing adequate information for readers to locate the source materials themselves.

Bildungsroman   A **coming-of-age story** that details the growth or maturity of a youth, usually an adolescent. The term is German, meaning "**novel** of personal education."

Biographical Criticism   **Literary criticism** that emphasizes the belief that literature is created by authors whose unique experiences shape their writing and therefore can inform our reading of their work. Biographical critics research and use an author's biography to interpret the text as well as the author's stated intentions or comments on the process of composition itself. These critics often consult the author's memoirs to uncover connections between the author's life and the author's work. They may also study the author's rough drafts to trace the evolution of a given text or examine the author's library to discern potential influences on the author's work.

Biography   The factual account of a person's life.

Blank Verse   Unrhymed **iambic pentameter,** often used in Shakespeare's **plays** or for **epic** subject matter, as in Milton's *Paradise Lost.*

Blues   A form of music that originated in the Deep South. Descended from African-American spirituals and work songs, the blues reflects the hardships of life and love in its lyrics. Most blues songs follow a form made of three phrases equal in length: a first phrase, a second that repeats the first phrase, and a third phrase different from the first two that concludes the verse.

Box Set   *See* **Proscenium Stage.**

Brainstorming   A process of generating and collecting ideas on a topic.

Burlesque   A work of drama or literature that ridicules its subject matter through exaggerated mockery and broad **comedy.**

Cacophony   Harsh-sounding, grating, or even hard-to-pronounce language.

Caesura   A pause, usually in the middle of a **line,** that marks a kind of rhythmic division.

Canon   In a literary context, the group of works considered by academics and scholars to be essential to and representative of the body of respected literature.

Carpe diem   Latin for *seize the day.* A phrase used commonly in poetry that emphasizes the brevity of life and the importance of living in the moment.

Catharsis   The purging of emotions that the audience experiences as a result of the powerful **climax** of a classical **tragedy;** the sense of relief and renewal experienced through art.

Central Intelligence   Henry James's term for the **narrator** of a story—distinct from the author—whose impressions and ideas shape the telling of the story and determine the details revealed.

Character   The depiction of human beings (and nonhumans) within a story.

Characteristics   The physical and mental attributes of a **character,** established through **characterization.**

Characterization   The way a writer crafts and defines a **character's** personality to give an insight into that character's thoughts and actions.

Characters   The actors (human and nonhuman) in a story.

Charting   A technique for generating ideas that involves placing related concepts and themes in a chart to view their relationships.

Chorus   A group of amateurs and trained actors who participated in traditional Greek plays. The chorus represents a group of citizens with worries and questions, expressed in poetry and music and dance movement.

Claim   An idea or stance on a particular subject; a defendable claim is necessary for a strong **thesis.**

Classifications of Drama   These four categories are generally assigned to Shakespeare's theater, but are commonly used in reference to the works of other **playwrights. Histories** focus on the reign of kings from the past, from Julius Caesar to Henry V. Because histories naturally contain very astute and sometimes troubling political commentaries, **playwrights** had to limit their subjects to rulers of the distant past. Comedies are **plays** for entertainment, and as a convention end in the marriage of two main **characters.** A comedic **plot** generally begins with a complication or misunderstanding between two lovers, which is complicated by further scheming and misunderstandings until finally a **resolution** is attained and the two are wed. **Tragedies** are darker plays, with more complex **characters** and more dire consequences, usually dramatizing the fall from a high state of life of a royal or special **character. Romances** (from the French *roman*, which means

an "extended narrative") involve lovers whose potential happiness is complicated by misunderstandings, mistaken identities, and any number of other difficulties. Although similar in plot to a **comedy,** a romance play does not guarantee a happy ending.

Cliché   A **figure of speech** that has been used so commonly that it has become trite. The use of cliché may suggest an ironic tone.

Climax   The narrative's turning point in a struggle between opposing forces. The point of highest **conflict** in a story.

Close Reading   The **explication** of a text in order to **analyze** the ways in which distinct formal elements interact to create a unified artistic experience for the reader.

Closed Couplet   A pair of rhymed **lines** that capture one complete idea. If the **couplet** is **end-stopped** and in **iambic pentameter,** it is called a **heroic couplet.**

Closed Dénouement   A **resolution** to a story that leaves no loose ends.

Closed Form   *See* **Fixed Form.**

Closet Drama   A piece of literature written as though for the stage, but intended only to be read.

Collective Unconscious   A set of **characters, plots, symbols,** and **images** that each evoke a universal response.

Colloquial Language   Familiar and conversational speech.

Comedy   A type of drama that deals with light or humorous subject matter and usually includes a happy ending. The opposite of **tragedy.** *See* **Classifications of Drama.**

Comedy of Manners   A work of **satire** that pokes fun at human behavior in particular social circles. Since a comedy of manners concerns itself with social interactions, it tends to reveal the **charac-**

ters' foibles or follies as they try to appear or act in a certain way.

Comic Relief   A **character** or situation that provides humor in the midst of a work that is predominantly serious. A classic example is the bumbling Falstaff, a character in Shakespeare's *Henry IV* who makes the audience laugh, even as England's fate hangs in the balance.

Coming-of-Age Story   A story that follows a **character's** physical, emotional, or spiritual maturation, often from youth into adulthood. *See Bildungsroman.*

Common Measure   A variation on **ballad meter** that uses **iambic quatrains** with the first and third **lines** containing four feet (**tetrameter**) and the second and fourth containing three feet (**trimeter**). The rhyme scheme is often *abab* rhyme. Common measure, also called *common meter,* is the meter most associated with hymns.

Comparison   Looking at two or more texts, **characters,** authors, or other items side by side to draw similarities between them.

Conceit   A complex comparison or **metaphor** that extends throughout a poem

Conclusion   The final idea and **resolution** of a text. In a good essay, the conclusion not only reiterates the **thesis** but also offers a reason for its significance or a reflection that pushes it toward a broader meaning beyond the essay itself. In a story or **play,** the conclusion refers to the resolution or **dénouement.**

Concrete Diction   Language referring to a specific, definite thing or quality, such as *lawn mower* or *street light.*

Concrete Poetry   Also called *visual poetry.* Poetry written in the shape of something it describes.

Confessional Poetry   Poetry that includes pieces of a poet's autobiography or personal experience. This mode of poetry was prevalent in the mid-twentieth century with such poets as Sylvia Plath, Anne Sexton, and Robert Lowell.

Conflict   The central problem in a story. The source of tension between the **protagonist** and **antagonist.**

Connotation   The associations a word carries beyond its literal meaning. Connotations are formed by the context of the word's popular usage; for example, *green*, aside from being a color, connotes money. The opposite of **denotation.**

Consonance   A repetition of consonant sounds or similar patterns in neighboring words.

Context   The literary, historical, biographical, or poetical situation that influences the writing of a work of literature.

Contextual Reading   Reading and interpreting a story while mindful of its author, the time and place it was written, the traditions of its form, and the criticism it explicitly or implicitly responds to.

Contrast   Looking at two or more texts, **characters,** authors, or other items side by side to highlight the differences between them.

Convention   In literature, a feature or element of a **genre** that is commonly used and therefore widely accepted—and expected—by readers and writers alike. For example, it is a convention of Shakespearean **comedy** to end with a marriage.

Conventional Symbols   **Symbols** that have accrued a widely accepted **interpretation** through their repeated use in literature and the broader culture. For example, spring and winter are conventional symbols of birth and death, because they appear with that meaning in Shakespeare's works

through Frost's poetry. Colors, too, can be used as conventional symbols; in contemporary society, a pink ribbon is a conventional symbol of breast cancer awareness.

Cosmic Irony   A literary convention whereby forces beyond the control of **characters**—such as God or fate or the supernatural—foil plans or expectations.

Cothurni   Tall boots, worn by actors in the Ancient Greek theater, which served both to elevate an actor and make him more visible to the massive crowds, and also to make the **characters** seem larger than life.

Couplet   Two lines of poetry forming one unit of meaning. Couplets are often **rhymed,** strung together without a break, and share the same **meter.**

Craft   As a noun, *craft* refers to the elements that make up a story; as a verb, *craft* refers to the process of making or fashioning a story out of those elements.

Cretic   Also called *Amphimacer*. A syllable pattern characterized by three syllables in the order *stressed, unstressed, stressed.*

Crisis   *See* **Climax.**

Critical Reading   A process of digesting and understanding a text so you can appreciate not just the ideas it presents or the story it tells but also how it presents those ideas, why it presents them, and how those ideas exist in a certain context. Critical reading involves **summary, analysis, synthesis,** and **interpretation.**

Critique   A **summary** accompanied by one's own personal opinion and perspectives.

Cultural Studies   This critical perspective was developed mainly in England in the 1960s by New Left writers, social philosophers, and sociologists. Cultural studies

incorporates the techniques of literary analysis to **analyze** social life and social movements as though they were written texts.

Dactylic Meter   A **meter** in which the **foot** contains a **stressed** syllable followed by two unstressed syllables.

Deconstruction   A critical approach to analyzing literature based on the idea that texts do not have a single, stable meaning or **interpretation.** Deconstructionists seek to break down literature to reveal the inevitable inconsistency or lack of unity in even the most successful and revered texts, believing that the author's intentions have no bearing on the meaning of the text to the reader.

Decorum   A certain level of propriety appropriate to a given text. As well as demanding a certain level of **diction,** decorum can also have bearing on the **characters, setting,** and **plot** events of a piece of literature.

Deductive Reasoning   An approach in logical thinking that begins by stating a **claim** and producing the reasons for making that claim, supported by **evidence.** *See also* **Inductive Reasoning.**

Denotation   The literal meaning of a word. The opposite of **connotation.**

Dénouement   The period after the story's **climax** when **conflicts** are addressed and/or resolved. Includes the **falling action** and **resolution** of a story.

Deus ex machina   Latin for *God from the machine;* a literary device, often seen in drama, that resolves a **conflict** by unforeseen and often far-fetched means.

Dialect   **Dialogue** written to phonetically or grammatically replicate a particular **sound,** cadence,

rhythm, or emphasis in a **character's** speech.

Dialogue   Spoken interaction between two or more **characters.** A **characterization** technique that can signal class, education, intelligence, ethnicity, and attitude in the characters involved.

Diction   An author's or **character's** distinctive choice of words and style of expression.

Didactic Literature   Literature, such as a **fable** or **allegory,** written to instruct or teach a **moral.**

Dimeter   A poetic **meter** comprising two poetic feet.

Dirge   A funeral song.

Doggerel   An obviously patterned piece of **rhyme,** often lunging or twisting word order in order to get a rhyme. Doggerel can sometimes seem almost childish and, when extensive, boring.

Drama   A term that comes from the Greek word for *doing* or *acting* and refers to a literary work that is represented through performance.

Dramatic Irony   A situation in which an author or **narrator** lets the reader know more about a situation than a **character** does.

Dramatic Monologue   A poem in which a **character** addresses another character or the reader. Dramatic monologues are offshoots of the **epic** form.

Dramatic Poetry   Poetry in which the speaker of the poem is not the poet. Dramatic poetry often tells a story.

Dramatic Point of View   A **third-person point of view** in which the **narrator** presents only bare details and the **dialogue** of other **characters.**

Dramatic Question   The overarching challenge or issue in a piece of drama—the complication which the events of a **play** work to resolve; also called *central question.*

Dramatis Personae   "People of the play"; a list of the **characters** in a **play,** usually one of the first elements of a script.

Dynamic Character   A **character** whose personality and behavior alter over the course of the action in response to challenges and changing circumstances.

Echo Verse   Poetry in which words at the ends of lines or **stanzas** are repeated, mimicking an echo.

Economic Determinist Criticism   *See* **Marxist Criticism.**

Editorial Omniscience   A **narrator** inserts his or her own commentary about **characters** or events into the narrative.

Electra Complex   The female version of the **Oedipus Complex,** the Electra Complex suggests that female children are hostile toward their mothers because of subconscious sexual attraction to their fathers.

Elegy   A poem of lamentation memorializing the dead or contemplating some nuance of life's melancholy. Early Greek elegies employed a fixed form of **dactylic hexameter** and **iambic pentameter couplets.**

Elision   The omission of a vowel or consonant sound within or between words, such as "ne'er" for "never" and "o'er" for "over." Elision dramatizes language and allows for flexibility within a poem's **meter.**

Ellipses   Three periods placed in succession (. . .) to illustrate that something has been omitted.

End Rhyme   **Rhyme** that occurs at the end of two or more lines of poetry. An example of end rhyme can be found in "The Love Song of J. Alfred Prufrock": "Let us go through certain half-deserted streets, / The muttering retreats."

End-stopped Line   A line that ends with a full stop, or period.

Endnote   Information placed at the end of a text in an explanatory note. In a research paper, endnotes are used to comment on sources or provide additional analysis that is slightly tangential to the focus of your paper. An endnote is indicated by a superscript number ([1]) in the text, which corresponds to a numbered explanatory note at the end of the text.

English Sonnet   *See* **Shakespearean Sonnet.**

Enjambment   The running over of a phrase from one line into another so that closely related words belong to different lines.

Envoi   The final **stanza** of a **sestina,** which summarizes the entire poem. *Envoi* is French for "farewell."

Epic   A long **narrative poem,** traditionally recited publicly, whose subject matter reflects the values of the culture from which it came by portraying important legends or heroes. Classical epics include the *Odyssey* and the *Aeneid;* while English epics include *Beowulf* and *Paradise Lost.*

Epic Theater   A style of theater developed in the early twentieth century that brought in a spare and highly stylized set and celebrated ideas over emotions and material reality over the spiritualism of **symbolism** and psychoanalysis of **surrealism**—two other theatrical styles of the day. Its most famous practitioner was Bertolt Brecht, whose plays represented his Marxist political beliefs.

Epigram   A short, often satirical observation on a single subject.

Epigraph   A quotation or brief passage from another source, included at the beginning of a piece of literature. Writers use epigraphs to suggest a major theme or idea in their work.

Epiphany   A sudden realization or new understanding achieved by a **character** or speaker. In many short stories, the character's epiphany is the **climax** of the story.

Episode   A unified event or incident within a longer narrative.

Episodia   The scenes of a Greek tragedy, divided by *stasimon* from the **chorus.**

Epistolary Novel   A **novel** written in the form of letters between two or more **characters,** or in the form of diary entries. Epistolary novels were particularly popular in the eighteenth century.

Ethnic Studies   A critical approach to literature that seeks to give voice to literature that has previously been overlooked in the traditionally Eurocentric worldview—not simply by including ethnically diverse literature in the **canon,** but by attending to historically underrepresented groups, such as African Americans and Native Americans.

Ethos   The Greek philosopher Aristotle, in his study of rhetoric (the art of persuasion), claimed that effective arguments are based on three important rhetorical appeals: **Ethos, Logos,** and **Pathos.** Ethos, the ethical appeal, appeals to an audience's sense of the writer's reasonableness, using techniques such as a reasonable tone and an unbiased use of **evidence** to establish a credibility and a context of trust in which to present support for a **claim.**

Euphony   Musically pleasing poetic language.

Everyman   The name of a well-known medieval **morality play** and its **protagonist.** An **allegory,** the characters teach right and proper behavior—morality—and

their names reveal the central trait the **character** represents. Everyman is a character whose station in life is not unlike that of the audience. A modern-day Everyman would represent the average person and would likely shine a light on the morality of modern society. Willy Loman in Arthur Miller's *Death of a Salesman* is considered a modern-day Everyman.

Evidence   Reliable information, such as statistics, expert opinions, and anecdotes, used to support a **claim** in an **argument.**

Exact Rhyme   A rhyme in which the final vowel and consonant sounds are identical, regardless of spelling. Also called *pure rhyme, perfect rhyme,* and *true rhyme.*

Éxodos   The concluding scene of a Greek **tragedy.**

Experimental Theater   A period of post–World War II theater that modified the traditional assumptions of **Naturalist Theater,** particularly with the sparse sets of **Epic Theater** and the darkly comical **Theater of the Absurd.** Other innovations include the so-called Theater of Cruelty (in which the playwright employs shock value to jar the audience into a recognition of harsh reality) and its American iteration, New York City's Living Theater.

Explication   A **close reading** of any text; the goal is to logically **analyze** details within the text itself to uncover deeper meanings or contradictions.

Exposition   The narrative presentation of necessary information about the **character, setting,** or character's history provided to make the reader care what happens to the characters in the story.

Expressionism   A mode of theater in which the **playwright** attempts to

portray his or her subjective emotions in a symbolic way on stage.

Extended Metaphor   A figurative analogy that is woven through a poem.

Eye Rhyme   Words that share similar spellings but—when spoken—have different sounds. For example, *lint* and *pint.* Also called *Sight Rhyme.*

Fable   A short narrative in which the **characters** (often animals or inanimate things) illustrate a lesson. The characters in fables are *actors* rather than **symbols.**

Fairy Tale   A story, usually for children, that involves magical creatures or circumstances and usually has a happy ending.

Falling Action   The events following the **climax** and leading up to the **resolution.** These events reveal how the **protagonist** has been affected by and has dealt with the preceding **conflicts** of the story.

Falling Meter   A **meter** comprising feet that begin with a **stressed** syllable, followed by an unstressed syllable or syllables. **Trochaic** and **dactylic** feet both create falling meter, which is named for the effect of *falling* from the initial **stressed** syllable to the unstressed.

Fantasy   A literary **genre** that uses magical **characters** or circumstances.

Farce   A work of drama or literature that uses broad, often physical **comedy,** exaggerated **characters,** absurd situations, and improbable **plot** twists to evoke laughter without intending social criticism.

Feminine Rhyme   Rhymes between multisyllable words in which the final syllable is unstressed, such as *bother* and *father.* Also called *falling rhyme.*

Feminist Criticism   An approach to literary criticism that highlights literature written by women and the exploration of the experience of female **characters;** also a critical examination of the ways in which female characters are viewed with prejudice, are subjugated to male interests, or are simply overlooked in literature.

Fiction A **genre** of literature that describes events and **characters** invented by the author.

Figurative Language Language that describes one thing by relating it to something else.

Figure of Speech A technique of using language to describe one thing in terms of another, often comparing two unlike objects, such as *the sun* and *the face of the beloved*, to condense and heighten the effect of language, particularly the effect of imagery or **symbolism** in a poem.

First-Person Narrator The story is narrated by a **character** in the story, identified by use of the pronoun *I* or the plural first-person, *we.*

Fixed Form An arrangement of text that requires a poet to obey set written combinations, including line length, **meter, stanza** structure, and **rhyme scheme.** Also called *closed form.*

Flashback The device of moving back in time to a point before the primary action of the story.

Flat Character A **character** with a narrow range of speech or action. Flat characters are predictable and do not develop over the course of the **plot.**

Foil A **character** who contrasts with the central character, often with the purpose of emphasizing some trait in the central character. For example, a cruel sister emphasizes the other sister's kindness.

Folklore A traditional **canon** of stories, sayings, and **characters.**

Folktale A short, often fantastic tale passed down over time.

Foot The smallest unit of measure in poetic **meter.** A foot usually contains a **stressed** syllable and one or two unstressed syllables. **Meter** is formed when the same foot repeats more than once. For example, in **iambic pentameter,** *iambic* refers to the type of foot (an unstressed syllable followed by a **stressed** syllable), while *pentameter* tells us that there are five (pent) iambic feet in each line.

Footnote Like an **endnote,** a way to include commentary on sources or other information tangential to the focus of a text. A footnote occurs at the bottom of the page on which the subject is most closely addressed. To create a footnote, a superscript number (^{1}) is placed in the text that corresponds to the number of the explanatory note at the bottom of the page.

Foreshadowing A hint about **plot** elements to come, both to advance the plot and build **suspense.**

Form The shape, structure, and style of a poem, as distinguishable from, but integral to, the content or substance of the poem.

Formal Diction Complex, grammatically proper, and often polysyllabic language in writing. It sounds grandiloquent—a *formal* word— and tends not to resemble the sort of talk heard in daily life.

Formalist Criticism An approach to literary criticism that considers a successful text to be a complete, independent, unified artifact whose meaning and value can be understood purely by analyzing the interaction of its formal and technical components, such as **plot,** imagery, structure, style, **symbol,** and **tone.** Rather than drawing their textual interpretations from *extrinsic* factors such as the historical, political, or biographical context of the work,

formalist critics focus on the text's *intrinsic* formal elements.

Found Poem A poem created from already existing text that the poet reshapes and presents in poetic form. Text may come from advertisements, labels on household items, newspapers, magazines, or any other printed source not intended originally as poetry. A poet may piece together several sources as in a collage, or he/she might take a short text exactly as it is and insert line breaks.

Fourth Wall The *invisible wall* of the stage, through which the audience views the action.

Free Verse Poetry in which the poet does not adhere to a preset metrical or **rhyme scheme.** Free verse has become increasingly prevalent since the nineteenth century, when it was first used. *See* **Open Form.**

Freewrite Writing continuously to generate ideas, without worrying about mistakes.

Gay and Lesbian Criticism A critical approach that is similar to **feminist criticism** in its quest to uncover previously overlooked undertones and themes in literature. Gay and lesbian criticism seeks to identify underlying homosexual themes in literature.

Gender Criticism A critical approach to literature that seeks to understand how gender and sexual identity reflect on the interpretation of literary works. **Feminist criticism** and **gay and lesbian criticism** are derivatives of gender criticism.

Genre A literary category or form, such as the short story or **novel,** or a specific type of **fiction,** such as science fiction or mystery.

Groundlings "Standing room only" spectators in the Elizabethan theater who paid a penny to stand on the ground surrounding the stage.

Haiku   A poetic form containing seventeen syllables in three **lines** of five, seven, and five syllables each. Haiku traditionally contain a natural-world reference or central **image.**

Hamartia   A **tragic flaw** or weakness in a tragic **character** that leads to his or her downfall. **Hubris** is a type of *hamartia.*

Heptameter   A poetic **meter** that consists of seven feet in each **line.**

Hero/Heroine   The **protagonist** of a story, often possessing positive traits such as courage or honesty.

Heroic Couplet   Two successive rhyming lines in **iambic pentameter.**

Hexameter   A poetic **meter** that consists of six feet in each **line.** If the six feet are **iambic,** the line is known as an alexandrine, which was the preferred line of French **epic** poetry.

High Comedy   **Comedy,** often a satire of upper-class society, that relies on sophisticated wit and **irony.**

Hip Hop   An intensely rhythmical form of popular music developed by African-Americans and Latinos in the 1970s in which vocalists deploy **rhyme**—known as **rap**—over the **rhythm.**

Historical Criticism   An approach to **literary criticism** that emphasizes the relationship between a text and its historical context. When interpreting a text, historical critics highlight the cultural, philosophical, and political movements and ideologies prevalent during the text's creation and reception.

Historical Fiction   A type of fiction writing wherein the author bases his or her **characters, plot,** or **setting** on actual people, events, or places.

Histories   *See* **Classifications of Drama.**

Hubris   Excessive arrogance or pride. In classical literature, the hero's **tragic flaw** was often hubris, which caused his downfall in the **tragedy.**

Hyperbole   A type of figurative speech that uses verbal exaggeration to make a point. Hyperbole is sometimes called *overstatement.*

Iamb   A poetic **foot** consisting of an unstressed syllable followed by a **stressed** syllable.

Iambic Meter   A poetic **meter** created when each **line** contains more than one **iamb** (a unit with an unstressed syllable followed by a **stressed** syllable).

Iambic Pentameter   A poetic **meter** in which each line contains five feet, predominantly iambs. Iambic pentameter is the most commonly used meter in English poetry, comprising **sonnets,** much of Shakespeare's **plays,** Milton's *Paradise Lost,* Wordsworth's *The Prelude,* and Wallace Stevens' "Sunday Morning."

Iconography   **Symbols** that commonly engender a certain meaning. For example, a skull equals *death,* and a dove equals *peace.*

Image   A sensory impression created by language. Not all images are visual pictures; an image can appeal to any of the five senses, emotions, or the intellect.

Imagism   A poetic practice wherein the *thing itself*—the object seen and not discussed or **analyzed**—becomes the poet's focus and the poem's primary concern. Imagism is associated with poets such as Ezra Pound and William Carlos Williams.

Impartial Omniscient Narrator   A **narrator** who remains neutral, relating events and **characters'** thoughts without passing judgment or offering an opinion.

Implied Metaphor   A suggested comparison that is never stated plainly.

Impressionism   In literature, a style of writing that focuses on a **protagonist's** reactions to external events rather than the events themselves.

Indirect Discourse   A **narrator's** description of an action or event as experienced by a **character** in the story.

Inductive Reasoning   An approach in logical thinking that begins by presenting reasons, supporting them with **evidence,** and then drawing a **conclusion.** This approach culminates with the **claim.** *See also* **Deductive Reasoning.**

Informal Diction   An author's use of words that are conversational or easily understood, as opposed to elevated or formal language. For example, using *you* instead of *thou.*

Initial Alliteration   The repetition of consonant or vowel sounds in the middle of a line of poetry.

Initiation Story   *See* **Coming-of-Age Story** and *Bildungsroman.*

In medias res   Latin for "in the middle of things." A term applied when a story begins with relevant story events already having occurred.

Innocent Narrator   *See* **Naïve Narrator.**

Intentional Fallacy   The practice by **formalist** critics of discerning or trusting an author's own stated purpose for the meaning of a text.

Interior Monologue   A **character's** conscious or unconscious thought processes, narrated as they occur, with only minimal-seeming guidance from the **narrator.**

Internal Alliteration   The repetition of consonant or vowel sounds in the middle of a line of poetry.

Internal Refrain   The repetition of words or phrases within the lines of a poem.

Internal Rhyme   **Rhyme** that occurs within a **line.** The placement of internal rhyme can vary; for example, a word in the middle of the line might rhyme with the word at the end of that same line, or both rhyming words might occur in the middle of two consecutive lines.

Interpret   The act of **interpretation.**

Interpretation   The process of contributing to the overall understanding of some aspect of a work in order to illuminate its meaning.

In-Text Parenthetical Citation   A reference within the body of a paper that links a quotation, **paraphrase,** or **summary** from another source to its full citation in the list of **works cited.**

Intonation   *See* **Tone.**

Inverted Syntax   A reversal of expected or traditional word order, often used to aid a poem's sounds, **rhyme,** and/or **meter.**

Ironic Point of View   Describes a **narrator** who does not understand the significance of the events of a story.

Irony   A **tone** characterized by a distance between what occurs and what is expected to occur, or between what is said and what is meant.

Italian Sonnet   *See* **Petrarchan Sonnet.**

Jargon   Words used with specific meaning for a particular group of people; for example, *starboard* in nautical jargon refers to the right side of a ship.

Journaling   Creating a journal entry or entries that expand **freewriting** into a more focused discussion that reflects a growing understanding of a topic.

Language   The words of a story, including **syntax** (how words or other elements of the sentence are arranged) and **diction** (what words the author chooses).

Language, Tone, and Style   The elements that conjure a story's particular flavor and **voice,** as achieved by means of the words the author chooses and the **rhythm** with which he or she puts the words together.

Levels of Diction   Refers to the three major categories of **diction: high, middle,** and **low diction.** The level of diction a writer uses determines whether the words in the work will be formal or informal, poetic or conversational, etc.

Limerick   A light, often humorous verse form consisting of five **anapestic** (two short syllables followed by one long one) lines, with a rhyme scheme of *aabba.* The first, second, and fifth lines consist of three feet, whereas lines three and four consist of two feet.

Limited Omniscient Narrator   A **third-person narrator** who enters into the mind of only one **character** at a time. This narrator serves more as an interpreter than a source of the main **character's** thoughts.

Line   A row of words containing phrases and/or sentences. The line is a defining feature of poetry, in which there are often set amounts of syllables or poetic feet in each line.

Literary Ballad   A story told in **ballad** form.

Literary Criticism   The acts of analyzing, interpreting, and commenting on literature.

Literary Epic   *See* **Epic.**

Literary Theory   The body of criticism and schools of thought (such as **Feminist, Deconstructionist,** or **Biographical** Criticism) that govern how we study literature.

Logic   **Deductive** or **inductive reasoning** that builds a complex **argument** based on **evidence.** For example, the logic used in a literary **analysis** that focuses on a particular aspect of a literary work incorporates such source-based evidence as quotation, **paraphrase,** and **summary.**

Logos   The Greek philosopher Aristotle, in his study of rhetoric (the art of persuasion), claimed that effective arguments are based on three important rhetorical appeals: **Ethos, Logos,** and **Pathos.** Logos, the logical appeal, makes a case through **claims** that are animated by the accumulation of hard facts such as statistics (for instance, the number of times a word is used in a poem), examples from the text, or the testimony of experts (scholars, for an academic argument).

Low Comedy   An informal brand of **comedy** that uses crude humor and **slapstick.**

Lyric   A short poem with a central pictorial **image** written in an uninflected (direct and personal) **voice.**

Madrigal   A variety of contrapuntal song that originated in sixteenth-century Italy. Madrigal features secular verse sung by two or more voices without instrumental accompaniment.

Magic Realism   A type of fiction in which something "magical" happens in an otherwise realistic world. The form is particularly associated with Latin American writers such as Gabriel García Márquez. (See "A Very Old Man with Enormous Wings"). Unlike **fantasy** or science fiction, magic realism generally has only one fantastical element, and the rest relies on realistic **characters** and settings. A notable American example in this book is Bender's "The Rememberer."

Marxist Criticism   Marxist or Economic Determinist Criticism is based on the writings of Karl Marx, who argued that economic concerns shape lives more than anything else and that society is essentially a struggle between the working classes and the dominant capitalist classes. Rather than assuming that culture evolves naturally or autonomously out of individual human experience, Marxist critics maintain that culture—including literature—is shaped by the interests of the dominant or most powerful social class.

Masculine Rhyme   The **end rhymes** of multisyllable words with a stressed final syllable, such as *remove* and *approve.* Also called *rising rhyme.*

Melodrama   A literary work, mainly a stage **play,** movie, or television play or show, in which **characters** display exaggerated emotions and the **plot** takes sensational turns, sometimes accompanied by music intended to lead the audience's feelings.

Melody   The linear succession of various musical pitches recognized as a unit.

Metafiction   A work of fiction that self-consciously draws attention to itself as a work of fiction. Rather than upholding the standard pretense, prevalent in realist fiction, that a story creates or refers to a "real world" beyond the text, metafiction self-consciously reveals the fact and sometimes the manner of its own construction. Metafiction is often associated with postmodernism, but examples of metafiction also occur in many other literary movements.

Metaphor   A close comparison of two dissimilar things that creates a fusion of identity between the things that are compared. A metaphor joins two dissimilar things

without using words such as *like* or *as.* While a **simile** suggests that X is *like* Y a metaphor states that X *is* Y.

Meter   A measure of verse, based on regular patterns of sound.

Metonymy   A **figure of speech** that uses an identifying emblem or closely associated object to represent another object. For example, the phrase *the power of the purse* makes little sense literally (there is no purse that has power), but in the metonymical sense, *purse* stands for money.

Middle Diction   Poetic language characterized by sophisticated word usage and grammatical accuracy. Middle diction reads as educated, cultured language but is not extravagant like **poetic diction.**

Mime   The act of performing without words.

Miracle Plays   During the tenth century, when drama was suppressed by the church, these anonymous **plays** were acted out as religious instruction for the benefit of spectators who could not read the Bible.

Mixed Metaphor   A failed comparison that results when a writer uses at least two separate, mismatched comparisons in one statement—to confusing, and sometimes comical, effect—for example, *The early bird strikes when the iron's hot!*

Monologue   A single **character's** discourse, without interaction or interruption by other **characters.**

Monometer   A poetic **meter** comprising one poetic **foot.**

Monosyllabic   Having one syllable.

Moral   The lesson taught by a piece of **didactic literature** such as a **fable.** A moral is often phrased simply and memorably.

Morality Play   A form of drama in which the figures on stage taught right and proper behavior—morality—to those who watched.

Motif   A pattern of imagery or a concept that recurs throughout a work of literature.

Motivation   A **character's** reason for doing something.

Mystery Play   A **play** that enacted stories of the Bible, such as the Creation or the Crucifixion. These plays appeared during the tenth century, when drama was suppressed in England.

Myth   The pre-Classical Greek word for sacred story or religious narrative, which by the Classical period had come to mean **plot,** as used in Aristotle's *Poetics.*

Mythological Criticism   Also called the *archetypal approach,* mythological criticism stems from the work of Carl Jung, a Swiss psychoanalyst (and contemporary of Freud), who argued that humans share in a **collective unconscious,** or a set of **characters, plots, symbols,** and **images** that each evoke a universal response. Jung calls these recurring elements **archetypes** and likens them to *instincts*—knowledge or associations with which humans are born. Mythological critics **analyze** the ways in which such archetypes function in literature and attempt to explain the power that literature has over us or the reasons why certain texts continue to hold power over audiences many centuries after their creation.

Naïve Narrator   An unreliable **narrator** who remains unaware of the full complexity of events in the story being told, often because of youth, innocence, or lack of cultural awareness.

Narrative Poem   A poem that tells a story. Examples include Tennyson's "The Charge of the Light Brigade," Longfellow's "The Midnight Ride of Paul Revere," and most ballads.

Narrator   The **character** or consciousness that tells a story. For specific types of narrators, see **First-Person Narrator, Second-Person Narrator, Third-Person Narrator, Omniscient Narrator, Limited Omniscient Narrator, Impartial Omniscience, Editorial Omniscience, Naïve Narrator,** and **Unreliable Narrator.**

Naturalistic Theater   Drama that shines a light on the painful realities and problems of everyday life.

Near Rhyme   *See* **Slant Rhyme.**

New Criticism   *See* **Formalist Criticism.**

New Historicism   A critical approach that emerged as a reaction to **new criticism's** disregard of historical context, but also in response to the perceived shortcomings of older methods of **historical criticism.** Rather than focusing on texts in the **canon** as representations of the most powerful or dominant historical movements, new historicists give equal or greater attention to less dominant texts and nonliterary texts (newspapers, pamphlets, legal documents, medical documents, etc.). New historicists attempt to highlight overlooked or suppressed texts, particularly those that express deviation from the dominant culture of the time. In this way, new historicists study not just the historical context of a major literary text but also the complex relationship between texts and culture, or the ways in which literature can challenge as well as support a given culture.

Nonfiction Novel   A presentation of real events using the craft and technique of a fiction novel.

Novel   A long fictional work. Because of their greater length, novels are typically complex and may follow more than one **character** or **plot.**

Novella   A short novel, which generally means it has more complexity than a short story but is shorter than the usual novel.

Objective Point of View   Approach whereby the story is told by an observer who relates only facts, providing neither commentary nor insight into the **character's** thoughts or actions.

Observer   A **first-person narrator** who does not participate in the action of the story.

Octameter   A poetic **meter** that consists of eight feet in each line.

Octave   Eight lines of poetry grouped together in a **stanza** or a unit of thought, as in the **Petrarchan sonnet,** wherein the octave sets up a thought or feeling that the following **sestet** resolves.

Ode   An elevated, formal **lyric** poem often written in ceremony to someone or to an abstract subject. In Greek **tragedy,** a song and dance performed by the **Chorus** between *episodia.*

Oedipus Complex: Sigmund Freud's theory of behavior (derived from the **plot** of Sophocles's *Oedipus the King*), which holds that male children are jealous of the father because of their sexual attraction to the mother. In *Oedipus the King,* Oedipus unknowingly kills his father and sleeps with his mother.

Off Rhyme   *See* **Slant Rhyme.**

O. Henry Ending   A short story ending that consists of a sudden surprise, often ironic or coincidental in nature, named for the short story writer O. Henry, who frequently ended his stories in this way. A classic example is O. Henry's "The Gift of the Magi" in which a husband and wife each give something precious of theirs to purchase a gift for the other; the ending reveals that each has sacrificed the very thing that would have allowed him or her to enjoy the gift received from their spouse.

Omniscient Narrator   A **third-person narrator** who observes the thoughts and describes the actions of multiple **characters** in the story. The omniscient narrator can see beyond the physical actions and **dialogue** of **characters** and is able to reveal the inner thoughts and emotions of anyone in the story.

One-Act Play   A **play** that consists of a single act that contains the entire action of the play. One-act plays usually portray a single **scene** with an exchange among a smaller number of **characters**—for example, Edward Albee's *The Zoo Story.*

Onomatopoeia   The use of words that imitate the sounds they refer to, such as *buzz* or *pop.*

Open Dénouement   A **resolution** to a story that leaves loose ends and does not completely resolve the overarching **conflict.**

Open Form   Poetry ungoverned by metrical or rhyme schemes. Also called **free verse.**

Orchestra   The open area in front of the stage (or *skene*) in the Greek **amphitheater.**

Overstatement   *See* **Hyperbole.**

Oxymoron   A version of **paradox** that combines contradictory words into a compact, often two-word term, such as *jumbo shrimp* or *definitely maybe.*

Paean   The final choral **ode** of a Greek **tragedy.**

Pantoum   A variation on the **villanelle,** consisting of an unspecified number of **quatrains** with the rhyme scheme *abab.* The first line of each quatrain repeats the second line of the preceding quatrain, and the third line repeats the final line of the preceding quatrain. In the final quatrain, the second line repeats the third line of the first quatrain, and the last line of the poem repeats the first line of the poem.

Parable A short narrative that illustrates a lesson using comparison to familiar **characters** and events. The characters and events in parables often have obvious significance as **symbols** and **allegories.**

Párados The **chorus's** first **ode** in a Greek **tragedy.**

Paradox Seemingly contradictory statement that, when closely examined, has a deeper, sometimes complicated, meaning.

Parallelism The arrangement of words or phrases in a grammatically similar way.

Paraphrase To condense a passage or idea from an existing text into your own words. Paraphrasing does not mean simply changing the words from the original; rather, it should represent the original in a way that demonstrates your understanding of it.

Parody To mimic another author or work of literature in such a way as to make fun of the original, often by exaggerating its characteristic aspects.

Participant narrator A **first-person narrator** who takes part in the action of the story.

Pastoral Poetry A variety of poem in which life in the countryside, mainly among shepherds, is glorified and idealized.

Pathos In Greek theater, the pity and terror that an audience feels toward the **tragic hero** and his fate, emotions that lead to a feeling of *purgation* and renewal. The Greek philosopher Aristotle also described pathos as the rhetorical appeal in persuasion that finds common ground through shared emotion, negative or positive (for example, grief at the tragic death of innocent victims). In his study of rhetoric (the art of persuasion), Aristotle claimed that effective arguments are based on three important rhetorical appeals: **Ethos, Logos,** and Pathos.

Pentameter A poetic **meter** that consists of five feet in each line.

Peripeteia An element of Greek **tragedy,** *peripeteia* occurs when an action has the opposite result of what was intended. In a **tragedy,** this generally occurs at a turning point for the **hero** and signals his downfall.

Persona A poem's speaker, which may or may not use the **voice** of the poet.

Personae Masks, often representative of certain **iconography** and familiar **characters,** worn by actors in the Ancient Greek theater to enable one actor to perform as many **characters.** *Personae* often were designed to project an actor's voice to the far rows of the **amphitheater.**

Personification A **figure of speech** in which a writer ascribes human traits or behavior to something inhuman.

Persuasion The process of using **analysis** and logical **argument** to prove the validity of a certain **interpretation** or **point of view.**

Petrarchan (Italian) Sonnet A sonnet consisting of an **octave** and a **sestet,** all in **iambic pentameter,** with the rhyme scheme *abbaabba cdecde* or *abbaabba cdcdcd.* The **volta,** or turn, typically occurs between the octave and sestet, around line nine of the poem.

Plagiarism The act of taking credit for another's work or ideas.

Play A work of drama, usually performed before an audience.

Players Traveling actors, men and boys, who spoke their lines for pay.

Play Review The critique of a **play.**

Playwright The author of a dramatic work.

Plot The artful arrangement of incidents in a story, with each incident building on the next in a series of causes and effects.

Poetic Diction Lofty and elevated language, used traditionally in poetry written before the nineteenth century to separate poetic speech from common speech.

Point of View The perspective from which the story is told to the reader.

Polysyllabic Having many syllables.

Portmanteau Word A word invented by combining two other words to achieve the effect of both. Lewis Carroll's poem "Jabberwocky" comprises largely portmanteau words such as *slithy,* which means *slimy* and *lithe.*

Postcolonialism A critical approach to **literary criticism** that seeks to offer views of relations between the colonizing West and colonized nations and regions that differ sharply from the conventional Western perspectives.

Poststructuralist Criticism Criticism based on the belief that texts do not have a single, stable meaning or **interpretation,** in part because language itself is filled with ambiguity, multiple meanings, and meanings that can change with time or context.

Precís *See* **Summary.**

Preview The process of gathering information about a piece of literature before you read it.

Problem Play A **play** about a social problem, written with an aim to create awareness of the problem.

Prologue The introduction to a literary work.

Proscenium Stage A realistic **setting** with three flat walls (two flat sides, and a ceiling) that simulates a room; the audience views the action through the missing **fourth wall.**

Prose Poem   A poem that uses the devices and imagery characteristic of traditionally lined poetry, but in compact units without clearly defined line breaks.

Prosody   The analysis of a poem's **rhythm** and metrical structures.

Protagonist   The main figure (or principal actor) in a work of literature. A story's **plot** hinges equally on the protagonist's efforts to realize his or her desires and to cope with failure if and when plans are thwarted and desires left unfulfilled.

Psalm   A sacred song, usually written to or in honor of a deity.

Psychoanalytic Criticism   Also called *psychological criticism*, this approach in a sense studies **characters** and authors as one would patients, looking in the text for evidence of childhood trauma, repressed sexual impulses, preoccupation with death, and so on. Through the lens of psychology critics attempt to explain the motivations and meanings behind characters' actions. Psychological critics also use textual and biographical evidence as a means to better understand the author's psychology, as well as to examine the process and nature of literary creation, studying the ways in which texts create an emotional and intellectual effect for their readers and authors.

Pun   A play on words that reveals different meanings in words that are similar or even identical.

Pyrrhic   A poetic **foot** characterized by two unstressed syllables.

Quantitative Meter   A type of poetry that counts the length of syllables, rather than the emphasis they

receive (as in **accentual-syllabic verse**). Quantitative meter primarily appears in Greek and Latin poetry and is rarely used in English, since English vowel lengths are not clearly quantified.

Quatrain   A four-line **stanza.** Quatrains are the most popular stanzaic form in English poetry because they are easily varied in **meter,** line length, and **rhyme** scheme.

Queer Theory   The idea that power is reflected in language and that discourse itself shapes our sense of who we are and how we define ourselves sexually.

Rap   An oral form of poetry that is akin to spoken word but distinguished by musical qualities and choral repetitions. *See* **Hip Hop.**

Reader-Response Criticism   The reader-response approach emphasizes that the reader is central to the writer-text-reader interaction. Reader-response critics believe a literary work is not complete until someone reads and **interprets** it. Such critics acknowledge that because each reader has a different set of experiences and views, each reader's response to a text may be different.

Realism   A mode of literature in which the author depicts **characters** and scenarios that could occur in real life. Unlike **fantasy** or **surrealism**, realism seeks to represent the world as it is.

Recognition   The moment in a **tragedy** when the **hero** comes to recognize the actuality of events and is no longer under illusion.

Refrain   A line or **stanza** that is repeated at regular intervals in a poem or song.

Resolution   The end of the story, where the **conflict** is ultimately re-

solved and the effects of the story's events on the **protagonist** become evident.

Restoration Comedy   A bawdy **play** about fallen virtue and infidelity that became popular after the Puritans were displaced in England in the mid-seventeenth century.

Retrospect   *See* **Flashback.**

Reversal   *See Peripeteia.*

Rhyme   The echoing repetition of sounds in the end syllables of words, often (though not always) at the end of a line of poetry.

Rhyme Scheme   The pattern of **rhyme** throughout a particular poem.

Rhythm   The sequence of **stressed** and unstressed sounds in a poem.

Rising Action   Story events that increase tension and move the plot toward the climax.

Rising Meter   A **meter** comprising feet that begin with an unstressed syllable, followed by a **stressed** syllable or syllables. **Iambic** and **anapestic** feet both create rising meter, which is named for the effect of *rising* from the initial unstressed syllable to the stressed.

Romance   *See* **Classifications of Drama.**

Romantic Comedy   A type of **comedy** in which two would-be/should-be lovers find each other after a series of misunderstandings and false starts.

Round Character   A **character** with complex, multifaceted characteristics. Round characters behave as real people. For example, a round **hero** may suffer temptation, and a round villain may show compassion.

Run-On Line   A line of poetry that, when read, does not come to a natural conclusion where the line breaks. *See* **Enjambment.**

Sarcasm Verbal irony that is intended in a mean-spirited, malicious, or critical way.

Satire An artistic critique, sometimes heated, on some aspect of human immorality or absurdity.

Satiric Comedy A derisive and dark **comedy** in which there is no promise that good will prevail.

Satyr Play An often obscene satirical fourth **play,** provided after a trilogy of tragedies, meant to provide **comic relief.**

Scansion The process of determining the metrical pattern of a line of poetry by marking its **stresses** and feet.

Scene A defined moment of action or interaction in a story usually confined to a single **setting.** Scenes are the building blocks of a story's **plot.**

Scenery The set pieces and stage decorations onstage during the performance of a **play.**

Scratch Outline A multitiered, ordered list of topics that should be covered in a paper. A scratch outline goes into deeper detail than a topic outline.

Screenplay A script that is specifically tailored and structured for television or film rather than the stage.

Script The written text of a **play,** which may include set descriptions and actor cues.

Second-Person Narrator A **narrator** who addresses the character as *you,* often involving the reader by association.

Semiotics The study of how meaning is attached to and communicated by symbols.

Sentence Outline An outline that uses complete sentences instead of brief words or phrases.

Sestet Six lines of poetry grouped together in a **stanza** or a unit of thought, as in the **Petrarchan sonnet,** wherein the last six lines of the poem resolve the idea or question set up by the initial **octave.**

Sestina A poem of six six-line **stanzas** and a three-line **envoi,** usually unrhymed, in which each stanza repeats the end words of the lines of the first stanza but in different order, the envoi using the six words again, three in the middle of the lines and three at the end.

Setting The time and place where the story occurs. Setting creates expectations for the types of **characters** and situations encountered in the story.

Shakespearean (English) Sonnet A **sonnet** form composed of three quatrains and a final couplet, all in **iambic pentameter** and rhymed *abab cdcd efef gg.* The **volta,** or turn, occurs in the final **couplet** of the poem.

Short Story A brief fictional narrative that attempts to dramatize or illustrate the effect or meaning of a single incident or small group of incidents in the life of a single **character** or small group of characters.

Simile A direct comparison of two dissimilar things using the words *like* or *as.*

Situational Irony A situation portrayed in a poem when what occurs is the opposite or very different from what's expected to occur.

Skene The stage in the Greek **amphitheater.**

Slam Poetry in a variety of styles, performed competitively in clubs and halls.

Slant Rhyme A case in which vowel or consonant sounds are similar but not exactly the same, such as *heap* and *rap* and *tape.* Also called *near rhyme, imperfect rhyme,* and *off rhyme.*

Slapstick A type of low **comedy** characterized by unexpected, often physical humor. A classic example of slapstick is the man walking along who accidentally slips on a banana peel.

Social Environment A study of **setting** that considers era and location as well as a **character's** living and working conditions.

Sociological Criticism The study of literary texts as products of the cultural, political, and economic context of the author's time and place.

Soliloquy A **monologue** delivered by a **character** in a **play** who is alone onstage. Soliloquies generally have a **character** revealing his or her thoughts to the audience.

Sonnet A poem of fourteen lines of **iambic pentameter** in a recognizable pattern of **rhyme.** Sonnets contain a **volta,** or turn, in which the last lines resolve or change direction from the controlling idea of the preceding lines.

Sound The rhythmic structure of the lines of a poem, which draws the reader in, often utilizing **rhyme** and created through word choice and word order.

Spoken Word Poetry Poetry that derives from the **Beat** poets, characterized by emphasis of the *performance* of a poem over the written form. Spoken word often employs improvisation.

Spondee A poetic **foot** characterized by two **stressed** syllables.

Sprung Verse The rhythm used in poetry that imitates ordinary speech by putting stresses on words that would not be stressed in consistent metrical patterns. The metrical variation of Gerard Manley Hopkins's work in general is what Hopkins came to call *sprung verse,* and it's a perfect example of change within consistency.

Stage Directions Cues, included by the **playwright** in the script of a **play,** that inform the actions of the actors during the play.

Stanza A unit of two or more **lines,** set off by a space, often sharing the same **rhythm** and **meter.**

Stasimon In Greek **tragedy,** an ode performed by the **chorus** that interprets and responds to the preceding scene.

Static Character A **character,** often flat, who does not change over the course of the story.

Stock Character A **character** who represents a concept or type of behavior, such as a "mean teacher" or "mischievous student," and offers readers the comfort of repetition and reliability.

Stream of Consciousness: A **character's** thoughts are presented flowing by in free association, and the literary convention that rules is that there is no writer mediating the consciousness of the subject.

Stress The vocal emphasis on a syllable in a line of verse, largely a matter of pitch.

Structuralism Structuralist literary critics work from the belief that a given work of literature can be fully understood only when a reader considers the system of conventions, or the **genre** to which it belongs or responds.

Style The characteristic way in which any writer uses language.

Subplot A **plot** that is not the central plot of the work, but nonetheless appears in the same work. Longer works, such as **novels** and **plays,** tend to have subplots that might follow side **characters** or somehow affect the action of the main **plot.**

Summary Restating concisely the main ideas of a text without add-

ing opinion or commentary. The best approach to summary is to divide the text into its major sections and then write a sentence for each section stating its main idea.

Summary Paper A short paper that represents the main ideas of the text as the author has presented them, excluding any subjective ideas or interpretations.

Surrealism A technique of the modern theater in which the realms of conscious and unconscious experience are fused to create a total reality. In this way the fiction writer, poet, and **playwright** tap into the resources of the unconscious mind and the imagination and portray in story on the page or on the modern stage the stuff of human desire, hope, and dreams.

Suspense A sense of anticipation or excitement about what will happen and how the **characters** will deal with their newfound predicament.

Syllabic verse A verse form that uses a fixed number of syllables per **line** or **stanza,** regardless of the number of **stressed** or unstressed syllables.

Symbol Any object, **image, character,** or action that suggests meaning beyond the everyday literal level.

Symbolic Act A gesture or action that takes on significance beyond its practical function.

Symbolism A literary movement of the late nineteenth century and early twentieth century in which writers employed poetic techniques by using **image, character,** or action to suggest meaning—often deeply spiritual and sometimes occult—beyond the everyday literal level. One of its most famous practitioners is W. B. Yeats.

Synecdoche A **figure of speech** that uses a piece or part of a thing to represent the thing in its entirety.

For example, in the Biblical saying that man does not live by bread alone, *bread* stands for the larger concept of food or physical sustenance.

Synopsis A **summary** or **précis** of a work.

Syntax The meaningful arrangement of words and phrases. Syntax can refer to word placement and order, as well as the overall length and shape of a sentence.

Synthesis The act of bringing together the ideas and observations generated by reading and analysis in order to make a concrete statement about a work.

Tactile Imagery Imagery that appeals to a reader's sense of touch.

Tercet A group of three lines of poetry, sometimes called a **triplet** when all three lines rhyme.

Terminal Refrain Repeated lines which appear at the end of each **stanza** in a poem.

Terza Rima A **tercet** fixed form featuring the interlocking rhyme scheme *aba, bcb, cdc, ded,* etc.

Tetrameter A poetic **meter** that contains four feet in each line.

Theater in the Round *See* **Arena Theater.**

Theater of the Absurd A twentieth-century approach to drama that combines comedic elements with a sense of meaninglessness. Some of its most famous practitioners are Eugene Ionesco (1909–1994), Samuel Beckett (1906–1989), and Edward Albee (Chapter 32).

Theme The central or underlying meanings of a literary work.

Thesis A paper's purpose and **argument,** defined by the **thesis statement** and proved by the paper's **conclusion.**

Thesis Statement A sentence, usually but not always included in a paper's introductory paragraph, that defines a paper's purpose and argument.

Third-Person Narrator   A **narrator** who is outside the story. The narrator refers to all the **characters** in the story with the pronouns *he*, *she*, and *they*.

Tiring House   In the Elizabethan theater, a room adjoined to the stage in which actors changed their costumes.

Tone   The author's attitude toward his or her **characters** or subject matter.

Topic Outline   A multitiered organization of a paper's topics and **arguments**, used to structure a paper.

Tragedy   A dramatic form in which **characters** face serious and important challenges that end in disastrous failure or defeat for the **protagonist**. *See* **Classifications of Drama.**

Tragic Flaw   In classical literature, the hero's weakness that causes his downfall. *See also* **hubris.**

Tragic Hero   A heroic **protagonist** who from the beginning, because of some innate flaw in his **character** or some unforeseeable mistake (*see* **Tragic Flaw** and **hubris**), is doomed. The inevitability of a tragic hero's demise inspires sympathy in the audience.

Tragic Irony   The point in a **tragedy** where the audience is aware of the **tragic hero's** fate although the **character** has not yet become aware of it.

Tragicomedy   A **play** with the elements of **tragedy** that ends happily.

Transferred Epithet   A description that pairs an adjective with a noun that does not logically follow, such as *silver sounds.*

Trimeter   A poetic **meter** that contains three feet in each **line.**

Triplet   A **tercet** of three rhymed **lines.**

Trochaic Meter: A poetic **meter** created when each **line** contains more than one **trochee** (a unit with a **stressed** syllable followed by an unstressed syllable). Trochaic meter is a type of **falling meter.**

Trochee   A poetic **foot** consisting of a **stressed** syllable followed by an unstressed syllable. The opposite of an **iamb,** and so sometimes called an "inverted foot," often beginning a **line** of **iambic pentameter.**

Troubadours   Wandering poets who composed and sang lyric poetry as part of the entertainment of court life of medieval Europe.

Understatement   A purposeful underestimation of something, used to emphasize its actual magnitude.

Unreliable Narrator   A **narrator** who cannot be trusted to present an undistorted account of the action because of inexperience, ignorance, personal bias, intentional deceptiveness, or even insanity.

Verbal Irony   A statement in which the stated meaning is very different (sometimes opposite) from the implied meaning.

Verisimilitude   How alike an imitation is to its original. The goal of literature, especially when written in the mode of realism, is to provide a likeness, or a verisimilitude, of real life.

Verse   A broad term to describe poetic **lines.**

Vers libre   *See* **Free Verse.**

Villanelle   A poem consisting of five **tercets** and a concluding **qua-**

train. Each tercet rhymes *aba* and the final quatrain rhymes *abaa.* The poem's opening **line** repeats as the final line of the second and fourth **stanzas,** and in the second-to-last line of the poem. The last line of the first stanza repeats as the final line of the third and fifth stanzas and is also the final line of the poem overall.

Visual imagery   Imagery and descriptions that appeal to a reader's sense of sight.

Voice   The unique sound of an author's writing, created by elements such as **diction, tone,** and sentence construction.

Volta   In a **sonnet,** the turn where a shift in thought or emotion occurs. In the **Petrarchan sonnet,** the volta occurs between the **octave** and the **sestet;** in the **Shakespearean sonnet,** the ending **couplet** provides the volta.

Vulgate   A term to describe the common people, often used in reference to a level of speech or **diction.**

Well-made Play   A type of theater popularized in France. Well-made **plays** feature a three-**act** sequence that *poses* a problem, *complicates* it, and then *resolves* it; usually that **resolution** comes when a **character's** past is revealed. The first act offers *exposition,* the second a *situation,* and the third an unraveling or *completion.* Meticulous plotting and **suspense** are components of this mode of theater.

Working Bibliography   A list of all the sources consulted in preparing a paper, as well as all the information necessary to cite them in the final list of **works cited.**

Works Cited   A list of all the primary and secondary sources of a paper.

Credits

Photo Credits

Index